Engaging Videos explore a variety of business topics related to the theory students are learning in class. **Exercise Quizzes** assess students' comprehension of the concepts in each video.

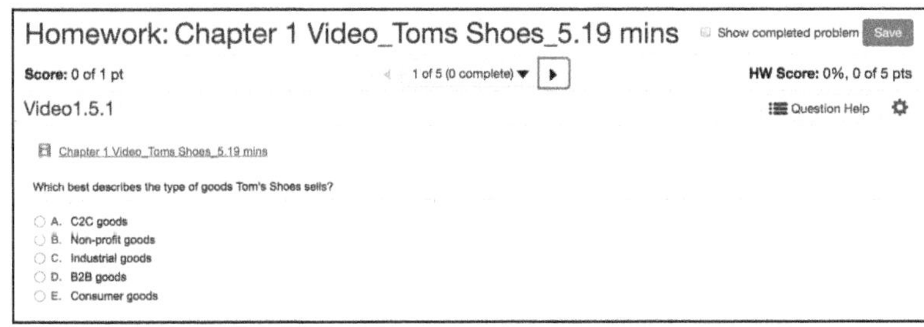

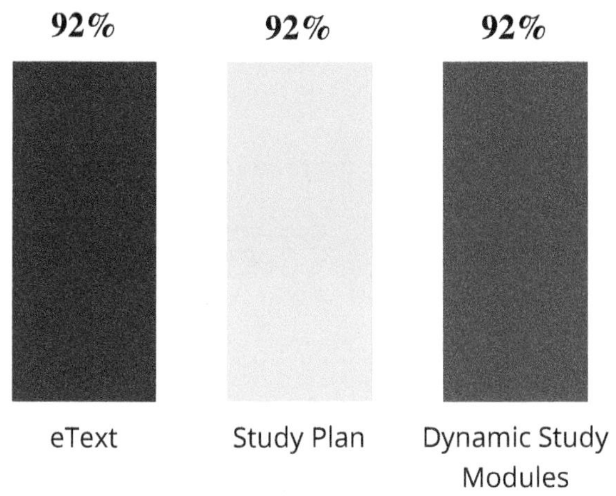

Dynamic Study Modules use the latest developments in cognitive science and help students study chapter topics by adapting to their performance in real time.

% of students who found learning aid helpful

Pearson eText enhances student learning with engaging and interactive lecture and example videos that bring learning to life.

The **Gradebook** offers an easy way for you and your students to see their performance in your course.

of students would tell their instructor to keep using MyLab Marketing

For additional details visit: www.pearson.com/mylab/marketing

Marketing

An Introduction

Fourteenth Edition

GARY ARMSTRONG
University of North Carolina

PHILIP KOTLER
Northwestern University

Vice President, Business, Economics, and UK Courseware: Donna Battista
Director of Portfolio Management: Stephanie Wall
Executive Portfolio Manager: Lynn M. Huddon
Editorial Assistant: Rachel Chou
Vice President, Product Marketing: Roxanne McCarley
Senior Product Marketer: Becky Brown
Product Marketing Assistant: Marianela Silvestri
Manager of Field Marketing, Business Publishing: Adam Goldstein
Field Marketing Manager: Nicole Price
Vice President, Production and Digital Studio, Arts and Business: Etain O'Dea
Director, Production and Digital Studio, Business and Economics: Ashley Santora
Managing Producer, Business: Melissa Feimer
Content Producer: Michelle Zeng
Operations Specialist: Carol Melville
Design Lead: Kathryn Foot
Manager, Learning Tools: Brian Surette
Senior Learning Tools Strategist: Emily Biberger
Managing Producer, Digital Studio and GLP: James Bateman
Managing Producer, Digital Studio: Diane Lombardo
Digital Studio Producer: Monique Lawrence
Digital Studio Producer: Alana Coles
Project Management, Interior Design, and Cover Design: Integra Software Services
Cover Art: David Arts/Shutterstock
Printer/Binder: LSC Communications
Cover Printer: LSC Communications

Library of Congress Cataloging-in-Publication Data

Names: Armstrong, Gary (Gary M.), author. | Kotler, Philip, author.
Title: Marketing: an introduction / Gary Armstrong, Philip Kotler.
Description: 14 Edition. | Hoboken, NJ: Pearson, [2018] | Revised edition of the authors' Marketing, [2017] | Includes bibliographical references and index.
Identifiers: LCCN 2018045243 | ISBN 9780135192122 (main title)
Subjects: LCSH: Marketing.
Classification: LCC HF5415 .K625 2018 | DDC 658.8—dc23
LC record available at https://lccn.loc.gov/2018045243

ISBN 10: 0-13-519212-9
ISBN 13: 978-0-13-519212-2

6 2022

To Kathy, Betty, Mandy, Matt, KC, Keri,
Delaney, Molly, Macy, and Ben; Nancy, Amy, Melissa, and Jessica

Brief Contents

PART 1 DEFINING MARKETING AND THE MARKETING PROCESS 2

1 Marketing: Creating Customer Value and Engagement 2
2 Company and Marketing Strategy: Partnering to Build Customer Engagement, Value, and Relationships 36

PART 2 UNDERSTANDING THE MARKETPLACE AND CONSUMER VALUE 64

3 Analyzing the Marketing Environment 64
4 Managing Marketing Information to Gain Customer Insights 96
5 Understanding Consumer and Business Buyer Behavior 132

PART 3 DESIGNING A CUSTOMER VALUE-DRIVEN STRATEGY AND MIX 170

6 Customer Value-Driven Marketing Strategy: Creating Value for Target Customers 170
7 Products, Services, and Brands: Building Customer Value 202
8 Developing New Products and Managing the Product Life Cycle 238
9 Pricing: Understanding and Capturing Customer Value 264
10 Marketing Channels: Delivering Customer Value 300
11 Retailing and Wholesaling 334
12 Engaging Consumers and Communicating Customer Value: Advertising and Public Relations 368
13 Personal Selling and Sales Promotion 404
14 Direct, Online, Social Media, and Mobile Marketing 434

PART 4 EXTENDING MARKETING 466

15 The Global Marketplace 466
16 Sustainable Marketing: Social Responsibility and Ethics 496

APPENDIX 1 COMPANY CASES 525
APPENDIX 2 MARKETING PLAN 557
APPENDIX 3 MARKETING BY THE NUMBERS 569
APPENDIX 4 CAREERS IN MARKETING 587

Glossary 599
References 607
Index 629

Contents

Preface *xix*
Acknowledgments *xxiv*
About the Authors *xxvi*

PART 1 DEFINING MARKETING AND THE MARKETING PROCESS 2

1 Marketing: Creating Customer Value and Engagement 2

Objectives Outline 2 • Previewing the Concepts 2 • First Stop: Amazon: Obsessed with Creating Customer Value, Engagement, and Relationships 3

What Is Marketing? 4
Marketing Defined 5 • The Marketing Process 5

Understanding the Marketplace and Customer Needs 6
Customer Needs, Wants, and Demands 6 • Market Offerings—Products, Services, and Experiences 7 • Customer Value and Satisfaction 7
Marketing at Work 1.1: Buffalo Wild Wings: Fueling the Sports Fan Experience 8
Exchanges and Relationships 9 • Markets 9

Designing a Customer Value-Driven Marketing Strategy and Plan 10
Customer Value-Driven Marketing Strategy 10 • Preparing an Integrated Marketing Plan and Program 14

Managing Customer Relationships and Capturing Customer Value 15
Engaging Customers and Managing Customer Relationships 15 • Capturing Value from Customers 20

The Changing Marketing Landscape 23
The Digital Age: Online, Mobile, and Social Media Marketing 23
Marketing at Work 1.2: Snickers Hungerithm: Engaging Customers in Real Time 25
The Growth of Not-for-Profit Marketing 27 • Rapid Globalization 28 • Sustainable Marketing—The Call for More Environmental and Social Responsibility 29 • So, What Is Marketing? Pulling It All Together 29 • Developing Skills for Your Career 31

REVIEWING AND EXTENDING THE CONCEPTS 32
CHAPTER REVIEW AND KEY TERMS • Objectives Review 32 • Key Terms 33
DISCUSSION AND CRITICAL THINKING • Discussion Questions 33 • Critical Thinking Exercises 34
MINICASES AND APPLICATIONS • Online, Mobile, and Social Media Marketing 34 • Marketing Ethics 34 • Marketing by the Numbers 35 • Company Cases 35 • Video Case 35

2 Company and Marketing Strategy: Partnering to Build Customer Engagement, Value, and Relationships 36

Objectives Outline 36 • Previewing the Concepts 36 • First Stop: Starbucks's Marketing Strategy: Delivering "The Starbucks Experience" 37

Company-Wide Strategic Planning: Defining Marketing's Role 38
Defining a Market-Oriented Mission 39 • Setting Company Objectives and Goals 40

Designing the Business Portfolio 40
Marketing at Work 2.1: Airbnb's Mission: Belong Anywhere—Don't Stay There. Live There. 41
Analyzing the Current Business Portfolio 43 • The Boston Consulting Group Approach 43 • Developing Strategies for Growth and Downsizing 45

Planning Marketing: Partnering to Build Customer Relationships 46
Partnering with Other Company Departments 47 • Partnering with Others in the Marketing System 48

Marketing Strategy and the Marketing Mix 48
Customer Value-Driven Marketing Strategy 49
Marketing at Work 2.2: Tesla: On a Fast Track from Upstart Nicher to Mass-Market Brand 51
Developing an Integrated Marketing Mix 52

Managing the Marketing Effort and Marketing Return on Investment 54
Managing the Marketing Effort 54 • Measuring and Managing Marketing Return on Investment 58

REVIEWING AND EXTENDING THE CONCEPTS 60
CHAPTER REVIEW AND KEY TERMS • Objectives Review 60 • Key Terms 61
DISCUSSION AND CRITICAL THINKING • Discussion Questions 61 • Critical Thinking Exercises 61
MINICASES AND APPLICATIONS • Online, Mobile, and Social Media Marketing 62 • Marketing Ethics 62 • Marketing by the Numbers 62 • Video Case 63 • Company Cases 63

PART 2 UNDERSTANDING THE MARKETPLACE AND CONSUMER VALUE 64

3 Analyzing the Marketing Environment 64

Objectives Outline 64 • Previewing the Concepts 64 • First Stop: Microsoft: Adapting to the Fast-Changing Marketing Environment 65

The Microenvironment and Macroenvironment 66
The Microenvironment 66 • The Macroenvironment 70

The Demographic and Economic Environments 70
The Demographic Environment 70 • The Economic Environment 78

The Natural and Technological Environments 79
The Natural Environment 79 • The Technological Environment 80
Marketing at Work 3.1: Patagonia's "Conscious Consumption"—Telling Consumers to Buy Less 81

The Political–Social and Cultural Environments 83
The Political and Social Environment 83 • The Cultural Environment 87

Responding to the Marketing Environment 89
Marketing at Work 3.2: In the Social Media Age: When the Dialogue Gets Nasty 90

REVIEWING AND EXTENDING THE CONCEPTS 92
CHAPTER REVIEW AND KEY TERMS • Objectives Review 92 • Key Terms 93
DISCUSSION AND CRITICAL THINKING • Discussion Questions 93 • Critical Thinking Exercises 94
MINICASES AND APPLICATIONS • Online, Mobile, and Social Media Marketing 94 • Marketing Ethics 94 • Marketing by the Numbers 95 • Video Case 95 • Company Cases 95

4 Managing Marketing Information to Gain Customer Insights 96

Objectives Outline 96 • Previewing the Concepts 96 • First Stop: Marketing Research at P&G: Creating Irresistibly Superior Experiences 97

Marketing Information and Customer Insights 98
Marketing Information and Today's "Big Data" 98 • Managing Marketing Information 99

Assessing Information Needs and Developing Data 100
Assessing Marketing Information Needs 100 • Developing Marketing Information 101

Marketing Research 103
Traditional Marketing Research in Transition 103 • Defining the Problem and Research Objectives 104 • Developing the Research Plan 105 • Gathering Secondary Data 106 • Primary Data Collection 106

Marketing at Work 4.1: Behavioral and Social Targeting: Sophisticated Marketing or Just a Little Creepy? 113

Implementing the Research Plan 116 • Interpreting and Reporting the Findings 116

Analyzing and Using Marketing Information 117
Customer Relationship Management (CRM) 117 • Big Data, Marketing Analytics, and Artificial Intelligence 118 • Distributing and Using Marketing Information 119

Marketing at Work 4.2: Artificial Intelligence in Marketing: "A Bigger Deal Than Fire or Electricity" 120

Other Marketing Information Considerations 122
Marketing Research in Small Businesses and Nonprofit Organizations 122 • International Marketing Research 123 • Public Policy and Ethics in Marketing Research 124

REVIEWING AND EXTENDING THE CONCEPTS 126

CHAPTER REVIEW AND KEY TERMS • Objectives Review 126 • Key Terms 128
DISCUSSION AND CRITICAL THINKING • Discussion Questions 128 • Critical Thinking Exercises 128
MINICASES AND APPLICATIONS • Online, Mobile, and Social Media Marketing 129 • Marketing Ethics 129 • Marketing by the Numbers 130 • Video Case 130 • Company Cases 131

5 Understanding Consumer and Business Buyer Behavior 132

Objectives Outline 132 • Previewing the Concepts 132 • First Stop: Shinola: Nobody's Confusing Sh*t with Shinola Anymore 133

Consumer Markets and Consumer Buyer Behavior 134
Model of Consumer Behavior 134 • Characteristics Affecting Consumer Behavior 135

Marketing at Work 5.1: Tapping Social Media Moms as Brand Ambassadors 141

The Buyer Decision Process 148
Need Recognition 148 • Information Search 149 • Evaluation of Alternatives 149 • Purchase Decision 150 • Postpurchase Behavior 150

The Buyer Decision Process for New Products 151
Stages in the Adoption Process 151 • Individual Differences in Innovativeness 151 • Influence of Product Characteristics on Rate of Adoption 152

Business Markets and Business Buyer Behavior 153
Business Markets 153 • Business Buyer Behavior 156 • Major Types of Buying Situations 156 • Participants in the Business Buying Process 157 • Major Influences on Business Buyers 157

The Business Buyer Decision Process 159
Problem Recognition 159 • General Need Description 160 • Product Specification 160 • Supplier Search 160 • Proposal Solicitation 160 • Supplier Selection 160 • Order-Routine Specification 161 • Performance Review 161

Engaging Business Buyers with Digital and Social Marketing 161
E-procurement and Online Purchasing 161 • Business-to-Business Digital and Social Media Marketing 162

Marketing at Work 5.2: GE: A Model for B-to-B Digital and Social Media Marketing 163

REVIEWING AND EXTENDING THE CONCEPTS 165

CHAPTER REVIEW AND KEY TERMS • Objectives Review 165 • Key Terms 166
DISCUSSION AND CRITICAL THINKING • Discussion Questions 167 • Critical Thinking Exercises 167
MINICASES AND APPLICATIONS • Online, Mobile, and Social Media Marketing 167 • Marketing Ethics 168 • Marketing by the Numbers 168 • Video Case 169 • Company Cases 169

PART 3 DESIGNING A CUSTOMER VALUE-DRIVEN STRATEGY AND MIX 170

6 Customer Value-Driven Marketing Strategy: Creating Value for Target Customers 170

Objectives Outline 170 • Previewing the Concepts 170 • First Stop: Dunkin': Targeting the Average Joe 171

Marketing Strategy 172

Market Segmentation 173
Segmenting Consumer Markets 173

Marketing at Work 6.1: Mountain Dew: "Doin' the Dew" with Brand Superfans 179

Segmenting Business Markets 180 • Segmenting International Markets 181 • Requirements for Effective Segmentation 182

Market Targeting 182
Evaluating Market Segments 183 • Selecting Target Market Segments 183

Differentiation and Positioning 189
Positioning Maps 190 • Choosing a Differentiation and Positioning Strategy 190

Marketing at Work 6.2: ALDI's Less-for-Much-Less Value Proposition: You Can't Eat Frills, So Why Pay for Them? 196

Communicating and Delivering the Chosen Position 197

REVIEWING AND EXTENDING THE CONCEPTS 198

CHAPTER REVIEW AND KEY TERMS • Objectives Review 198 • Key Terms 199
DISCUSSION AND CRITICAL THINKING • Discussion Questions 199 • Critical Thinking Exercises 199
MINICASES AND APPLICATIONS • Online, Mobile, and Social Media Marketing 200 • Marketing Ethics 200 • Marketing by the Numbers 200 • Video Case 201 • Company Cases 201

7 Products, Services, and Brands: Building Customer Value 202

Objectives Outline 202 • Previewing the Concepts 202 • First Stop: Nike: More Than Just Innovative Sports Gear—a Total Brand Experience 203

What Is a Product? 204
Products, Services, and Experiences 204 • Levels of Product and Services 205 • Product and Service Classifications 206

Product and Service Decisions 209
Individual Product and Service Decisions 209
Marketing at Work 7.1: Brand Logo Makeovers for the Digital Age 214
Product Line Decisions 216 • Product Mix Decisions 217

Services Marketing 219
The Nature and Characteristics of a Service 219 • Marketing Strategies for Service Firms 220 • The Service Profit Chain 220

Branding Strategy: Building Strong Brands 224
Brand Equity and Brand Value 224 • Building Strong Brands 226
Marketing at Work 7.2: Store Brands: Price Is Important, but It's More about the Customer Experience 229
Managing Brands 233

REVIEWING AND EXTENDING THE CONCEPTS 234
CHAPTER REVIEW AND KEY TERMS • Objectives Review 234 • Key Terms 235
DISCUSSION AND CRITICAL THINKING • Discussion Questions 235 • Critical Thinking Exercises 235
MINICASES AND APPLICATIONS • Online, Mobile, and Social Media Marketing 236 • Marketing Ethics 236 • Marketing by the Numbers 236 • Video Case 237 • Company Cases 237

8 Developing New Products and Managing the Product Life Cycle 238

Objectives Outline 238 • Previewing the Concepts 238 • First Stop: Samsung: Enriching Customers' Lives through New-Product Innovation 239

New Product Development Strategy 240

The New Product Development Process 241
Idea Generation 241 • Idea Screening 243 • Concept Development and Testing 243 • Marketing Strategy Development 244 • Business Analysis 245 • Product Development 246 • Test Marketing 246 • Commercialization 247 • Managing New Product Development 248
Marketing at Work 8.1: Google (. . .er, Alphabet): The New Product Moonshot Factory 250

Product Life-Cycle Strategies 251
Introduction Stage 253
Marketing at Work 8.2: Intuit: Reinvention and the Product Life Cycle 254
Growth Stage 255 • Maturity Stage 255 • Decline Stage 257

Additional Product and Service Considerations 258
Product Decisions and Social Responsibility 258 • International Product and Services Marketing 259

REVIEWING AND EXTENDING THE CONCEPTS 260
CHAPTER REVIEW AND KEY TERMS • Objectives Review 260 • Key Terms 261
DISCUSSION AND CRITICAL THINKING • Discussion Questions 261 • Critical Thinking Exercises 262
MINICASES AND APPLICATIONS • Online, Mobile, and Social Media Marketing 262 • Marketing Ethics 262 • Marketing by the Numbers 263 • Video Case 263 • Company Cases 263

9 Pricing: Understanding and Capturing Customer Value 264

Objectives Outline 264 • Previewing the Concepts 264 • First Stop: Apple: Premium Priced and Worth It 265

Major Pricing Strategies 267
Customer Value–Based Pricing 267
Marketing at Work 9.1: Good Value at Spirit Airlines: Getting Less but Paying Much Less for It 270
Cost-Based Pricing 271 • Competition-Based Pricing 273

Other Internal and External Considerations Affecting Price Decisions 274
Overall Marketing Strategy, Objectives, and Mix 274 • Organizational Considerations 275 • The Market and Demand 276 • The Economy 277 • Other External Factors 278

New Product Pricing Strategies 279
Market-Skimming Pricing 279 • Market-Penetration Pricing 279

Product Mix Pricing Strategies 280
Product Line Pricing 280 • Optional-Product Pricing 280 • Captive-Product Pricing 280 • By-Product Pricing 281 • Product Bundle Pricing 281

Price Adjustment Strategies and Price Changes 282
Discount and Allowance Pricing 282 • Segmented Pricing 282 • Psychological Pricing 283 • Promotional Pricing 284 • Geographical Pricing 285 • Dynamic and Personalized Pricing 286 • International Pricing 288 • Price Changes 289

Public Policy and Pricing 292

Marketing at Work 9.2: Pharmaceutical Pricing: No Easy Answers 293

Pricing within Channel Levels 294 • Pricing across Channel Levels 295

REVIEWING AND EXTENDING THE CONCEPTS 296

CHAPTER REVIEW AND KEY TERMS • Objectives Review 296 • Key Terms 297
DISCUSSION AND CRITICAL THINKING • Discussion Questions 297 • Critical Thinking Exercises 298
MINICASES AND APPLICATIONS • Online, Mobile, and Social Media Marketing 298 • Marketing Ethics 298 • Marketing by the Numbers 299 • Video Case 299 • Company Cases 299

10 Marketing Channels: Delivering Customer Value 300

Objectives Outline 300 • Previewing the Concepts 300 • First Stop: Netflix's Channel Innovation: Finding the Future by Abandoning the Past 301

Supply Chains and the Value Delivery Network 302
The Nature and Importance of Marketing Channels 303 • How Channel Members Add Value 304

Channel Behavior and Organization 306
Channel Behavior 306 • Vertical Marketing Systems 307 • Horizontal Marketing Systems 309 • Multichannel Distribution Systems 310 • Changing Channel Organization 311

Marketing at Work 10.1: Lyft: Disrupting and Disintermediating Urban Transportation Channels 312

Channel Design Decisions 314
Analyzing Consumer Needs 314 • Setting Channel Objectives 315 • Identifying Major Alternatives 315 • Evaluating the Major Alternatives 316 • Designing International Distribution Channels 317

Channel Management Decisions 317
Selecting Channel Members 318 • Managing and Motivating Channel Members 318

Marketing at Work 10.2: Working with Channel Partners to Create Value for Customers 319

Evaluating Channel Members 320 • Public Policy and Distribution Decisions 321

Marketing Logistics and Supply Chain Management 321
Nature and Importance of Marketing Logistics 322 • Sustainable Supply Chains 323 • Goals of the Logistics System 324 • Major Logistics Functions 324 • Integrated Logistics Management 327

REVIEWING AND EXTENDING THE CONCEPTS 329

CHAPTER REVIEW AND KEY TERMS • Objectives Review 329 • Key Terms 330
DISCUSSION AND CRITICAL THINKING • Discussion Questions 330 • Critical Thinking Exercises 331
MINICASES AND APPLICATIONS • Online, Mobile, and Social Media Marketing 331 • Marketing Ethics 331 • Marketing by the Numbers 332 • Video Case 332 • Company Cases 332

11 Retailing and Wholesaling 334

Objectives Outline 334 • Previewing the Concepts 334 • First Stop: Walmart: A Battle between Titans in the New World of Retail 335

Retailing 336

Retailing: Connecting Brands with Consumers 336 • The Shifting Retailing Model 337 • Types of Store Retailers 338

Marketing at Work 11.1: Costco: Merchandising Magic that Competitors Can't Match 342

Omni-Channel Retailing: Blending In-Store, Online, Mobile, and Social Media Channels 345

Retailer Marketing Decisions 346

Segmentation, Targeting, Differentiation, and Positioning Decisions 347 • Product Assortment and Services Decision 348 • Price Decision 349 • Promotion Decision 350 • Place Decision 350

Retailing Trends and Developments 351

Tighter Consumer Spending 352 • New Retail Forms, Shortening Retail Life Cycles, and Retail Convergence 352 • The Rise of Megaretailers 353 • Growing Importance of Retail Technology 354 • Green Retailing 354

Marketing at Work 11.2: AR and VR in Retailing: Extending and Enhancing the Shopping Experience 355

Global Expansion of Major Retailers 357

Wholesaling 357

Types of Wholesalers 359 • Trends in Wholesaling 361

REVIEWING AND EXTENDING THE CONCEPTS 363

CHAPTER REVIEW AND KEY TERMS • Objectives Review 363 • Key Terms 364
DISCUSSION AND CRITICAL THINKING • Discussion Questions 364 • Critical Thinking Exercises 365
MINICASES AND APPLICATIONS • Online, Mobile, and Social Media Marketing 365 • Marketing Ethics 365 • Marketing by the Numbers 366 • Video Case 366 • Company Cases 367

12 Engaging Consumers and Communicating Customer Value: Advertising and Public Relations 368

Objectives Outline 368 • Previewing the Concepts 368 • First Stop: Snickers: "You're Not You When You're Hungry" 369

The Promotion Mix 370

Integrated Marketing Communications 371

The New Marketing Communications Model 371

Marketing at Work 12.1: Just Don't Call It Advertising: It's Content Marketing 373

The Need for *Integrated* Marketing Communications 374 • Shaping the Overall Promotion Mix 376

Advertising and Major Advertising Decisions 379

Setting Advertising Objectives 379

Marketing at Work 12.2: Microsoft's Comparative Advertising: "I Couldn't Do That on My Mac" 381

Setting the Advertising Budget 383 • Developing Advertising Strategy 384 • Evaluating Advertising Effectiveness and the Return on Advertising Investment 394 • Other Advertising Considerations 394

Public Relations 396

The Role and Impact of PR 397 • Major Public Relations Tools 398

REVIEWING AND EXTENDING THE CONCEPTS 399

CHAPTER REVIEW AND KEY TERMS • Objectives Review 399 • Key Terms 400
DISCUSSION AND CRITICAL THINKING • Discussion Questions 400 • Critical Thinking Exercises 400

MINICASES AND APPLICATIONS • Online, Mobile, and Social Media Marketing 401 • Marketing Ethics 401 • Marketing by the Numbers 401 • Video Case 402 • Company Cases 402

13 Personal Selling and Sales Promotion 404

Objectives Outline 404 • Previewing the Concepts 404 • First Stop: Salesforce: You Need a Great Sales Force to Sell Salesforce 405

Personal Selling 406

The Nature of Personal Selling 406 • The Role of the Sales Force 407

Managing the Sales Force 408

Designing the Sales Force Strategy and Structure 409 • Recruiting and Selecting Salespeople 412 • Training Salespeople 413 • Compensating Salespeople 414 • Supervising and Motivating Salespeople 414 • Evaluating Salespeople and Sales Force Performance 415 • Social Selling: Online, Mobile, and Social Media Tools 416

Marketing at Work 13.1: B-to-B Salespeople: In This Digital and Social Media Age, Who Needs Them Anymore? 417

The Personal Selling Process 419

Steps in the Selling Process 420 • Personal Selling and Managing Customer Relationships 422

Sales Promotion 423

The Rapid Growth of Sales Promotion 423 • Sales Promotion Objectives 424 • Major Sales Promotion Tools 424

Marketing at Work 13.2: Red Bull: The Mother of All Event Marketers 427

Developing the Sales Promotion Program 429

REVIEWING AND EXTENDING THE CONCEPTS 430

CHAPTER REVIEW AND KEY TERMS • Objectives Review 430 • Key Terms 431

DISCUSSION AND CRITICAL THINKING • Discussion Questions 431 • Critical Thinking Exercises 431

MINICASES AND APPLICATIONS • Online, Mobile, and Social Media Marketing 432 • Marketing Ethics 432 • Marketing by the Numbers 433 • Video Case 433 • Company Cases 433

14 Direct, Online, Social Media, and Mobile Marketing 434

Objectives Outline 434 • Previewing the Concepts 434 • First Stop: Coca-Cola's Digital Marketing: Making the Brand a Part of the Customer's Story 435

Direct and Digital Marketing 436

The New Direct Marketing Model 436 • Rapid Growth of Direct and Digital Marketing 437 • Benefits of Direct and Digital Marketing to Buyers and Sellers 437

Forms of Direct and Digital Marketing 438

Marketing in the Digital Age 439

Online Marketing 440

Social Media and Mobile Marketing 445

Social Media Marketing 445

Marketing at Work 14.1: Instagram: A Win-Win-Win for the Company, Advertisers, and Instagrammers 446

Mobile Marketing 450

Marketing at Work 14.2: Mobile Marketing: Engaging Consumers in Moments That Matter 451

Traditional Direct Marketing Forms 453

Direct-Mail Marketing 453 • Catalog Marketing 454 • Telemarketing 455 • Direct-Response Television Marketing 456 • Kiosk Marketing 456 • Public Policy Issues in Direct and Digital Marketing 457

REVIEWING AND EXTENDING THE CONCEPTS 460

CHAPTER REVIEW AND KEY TERMS • Objectives Review 460 • Key Terms 462
DISCUSSION AND CRITICAL THINKING • Discussion Questions 462 • Critical Thinking Exercises 462
MINICASES AND APPLICATIONS • Online, Mobile, and Social Media Marketing 463 • Marketing Ethics 463 • Marketing by the Numbers 464 • Video Case 464 • Company Cases 465

PART 4 EXTENDING MARKETING 466

15 The Global Marketplace 466

Objectives Outline 466 • Previewing the Concepts 466 • First Stop: IKEA: Just the Right Balance between Global Standardization and Local Adaptation 467

Global Marketing Today 468

Elements of the Global Marketing Environment 470

Marketing at Work 15.1: International Marketing: Targeting the Bottom of the Economic Pyramid 473

Deciding Whether to Go Global 478
Deciding Which Markets to Enter 478

Deciding How to Enter the Market 480

Exporting 480 • Joint Venturing 481 • Direct Investment 482

Deciding on the Global Marketing Program 483

Product 484

Marketing at Work 15.2: 7-Eleven: Making Life a Little Easier for People around the Globe 485

Promotion 487 • Price 488 • Distribution Channels 489

Deciding on the Global Marketing Organization 490

REVIEWING AND EXTENDING THE CONCEPTS 491

CHAPTER REVIEW AND KEY TERMS • Objectives Review 491 • Key Terms 492
DISCUSSION AND CRITICAL THINKING • Discussion Questions 492 • Critical Thinking Exercises 492
MINICASES AND APPLICATIONS • Online, Mobile, and Social Media Marketing 493 • Marketing Ethics 493 • Marketing by the Numbers 494 • Video Case 494 • Company Cases 495

16 Sustainable Marketing: Social Responsibility and Ethics 496

Objectives Outline 496 • Previewing the Concepts 496 • First Stop: Sustainability at Unilever: Creating a Better Future Every Day 497

Sustainable Marketing 498

Social Criticisms of Marketing 500

Marketing's Impact on Individual Consumers 500

Marketing at Work 16.1: Starbucks: Serving the Underserved—Doing Good *and* Doing Well 504

Marketing's Impact on Society as a Whole 506 • Marketing's Impact on Other Businesses 508

Consumer Actions to Promote Sustainable Marketing 509

Consumerism 509 • Environmentalism 510 • Public Actions to Regulate Marketing 513

Business Actions toward Sustainable Marketing 513

Sustainable Marketing Principles 513

Marketing at Work 16.2: CVS Health: Balancing Purpose with Profit 516

Marketing Ethics and the Sustainable Company 518
Marketing Ethics 518 • The Sustainable Company 520

REVIEWING AND EXTENDING THE CONCEPTS 521
CHAPTER REVIEW AND KEY TERMS • Objectives Review 521 • Key Terms 522
DISCUSSION AND CRITICAL THINKING • Discussion Questions 522 • Critical Thinking Exercises 522
MINICASES AND APPLICATIONS • Online, Mobile, and Social Media Marketing 522 • Marketing Ethics 523 • Marketing by the Numbers 523 • Video Case 524 • Company Cases 524

Appendix 1 Company Cases 525
Appendix 2 Marketing Plan 557
Appendix 3 Marketing by the Numbers 569
Appendix 4 Careers in Marketing 587

Glossary 599
References 607
Index 629

Preface

New to This Edition

All That's New in Marketing

The fourteenth edition of *Marketing: An Introduction* reflects the major trends and shifting forces that impact marketing in this digital age of customer value, engagement, and relationships. Here are just some of the major new and continuing changes you'll find in this edition.

- *Customer engagement framework:* The fourteenth edition continues to build on its *customer engagement* framework—creating direct and continuous customer involvement in shaping brands, brand conversations, brand experiences, and brand community. New coverage and fresh examples throughout the text address the latest customer engagement tools, practices, and developments.

- *Fast-changing marketing trends and topics:* This edition adds fresh coverage of both traditional marketing areas and fast-changing topics such as digital, mobile, and social media marketing; customer engagement marketing; big data, artificial intelligence, and new marketing analytics; the major digital transformation in marketing research; omni-channel marketing and the massive shifts in today's retailing; real-time customer listening and marketing; marketing content creation and native advertising; B-to-B social media and social selling; online and dynamic pricing; sustainability; global marketing; and much more.

- *Online, mobile, social media, and other digital marketing technologies:* Keeping up with digital concepts, technologies, and practices has become a top priority and major challenge for today's marketers. The fourteenth edition of *Marketing: An Introduction* provides thoroughly refreshed, up-to-date coverage of these explosive developments in every chapter—from digital, online, mobile, and social media engagement technologies in Chapters 1, 5, 12, and 14; to "big data," new marketing analytics, and artificial intelligence in Chapters 3 and 4; to the massive shift to omni-channel and digital retailing in Chapter 13; to the increasing use of augmented and virtual reality in Chapters 4 and 13. A Chapter 1 section on The Digital Age: Online, Mobile, and Social Media Marketing introduces the exciting new developments in digital and social media marketing. Then, a Chapter 14 section on Direct, Online, Social Media, and Mobile Marketing digs more deeply into digital marketing tools such as online sites, social media, mobile ads and apps, online video, email, and other digital platforms that engage consumers anywhere, anytime via their computers, smartphones, tablets, and other digital devices.

- *Content marketing and marketing communications:* The fourteenth edition continues to track fast-changing developments in marketing communications and the creation of brand content. Marketers no longer simply create integrated marketing communications programs; they join with customers and media to curate and share marketing content in paid, owned, earned, and shared media. You won't find fresher coverage of these important topics in any other marketing text.

New Real-World Brand Stories, Highlights, Cases, and In-Text Examples

The fourteenth edition of *Marketing: An Introduction* is loaded with new brand stories, highlight features, cases, in-text examples, and end-of-chapter exercises and features that illustrate brand strategies and contemporary marketing issues and let students apply what they've learned.

- *New company cases and end-of-chapter applications and exercises:* The fourteenth edition provides 16 new company cases by which students can apply what they learn to actual company situations. End-of-chapter discussion questions, critical thinking exercises, and other applications features are also new and revised.

- *Chapter-opening stories, Marketing at Work highlights, and in-text examples:* The fourteenth edition brings marketing to life with new or heavily revised chapter-opening vignettes, boxed features that highlight relevant companies and marketing issues, and new in-text examples throughout.

Solving Teaching and Learning Challenges

Today's marketing is all about creating customer value and engagement in a fast-changing, increasingly digital and social marketplace. Marketing starts with understanding consumer needs and wants, determining which target markets the organization can serve best, and developing a compelling value proposition by which the organization can attract and grow valued consumers. Then, more than just making a sale, today's marketers want to engage customers and build deep customer relationships that make their brands a meaningful part of consumers' conversations and lives.

In this digital age, to go along with their tried-and-true traditional marketing methods, marketers have a dazzling set of new online, mobile, and social media tools for engaging customers anytime, anyplace to jointly shape brand conversations, experiences, and community. If marketers do these things well, they will reap the rewards in terms of market share, profits, and customer equity. In the fourteenth edition of *Marketing: An Introduction*, students learn how customer value and customer engagement drive every good marketing strategy.

To improve student results, we recommend pairing the text content with MyLab Marketing, the teaching and learning platform that empowers every student. By combining trusted author content with digital tools and a flexible platform, MyLab personalizes the learning experience and will help students learn and retain key course concepts while developing skills that future employers are seeking in their candidates.

Five Major Customer Value and Engagement Themes

The fourteenth edition of *Marketing: An Introduction* builds on five major customer value and engagement themes:

1. ***Creating value* for *customers in order to capture value* from *customers in return.*** Today's marketers must be good at *creating customer value, engaging customers,* and *managing customer relationships*. In return, they capture value from customers in the form of sales, profits, and customer equity. This innovative *customer value and engagement framework* is introduced at the start of Chapter 1 in a unique five-step marketing process model, which details how marketing *creates* customer value and *captures* value in return. The framework is carefully developed in the first two chapters and then fully integrated throughout the remainder of the text.

2. ***Customer Engagement and Today's Digital and Social Media.*** New digital and social media have taken today's marketing by storm, dramatically changing how companies and brands engage consumers, and how consumers connect and influence each other's brand behaviors. The fourteenth edition thoroughly explores the exciting new digital, mobile, and social media technologies that help brands to engage customers more deeply and interactively. It starts with two major Chapter 1 sections: *Customer Engagement and Today's Digital and Social* Media and *The Digital Age: Online, Mobile, and Social Media.* A refreshed Chapter 14 on *Direct, Online, Social Media, and Mobile Marketing* summarizes the latest developments in digital engagement and relationship-building tools. Everywhere in between, you'll find revised and expanded coverage of the exploding use of digital and social marketing tools.

3. ***Building and managing strong, value-creating brands.*** Well-positioned brands with strong brand equity provide the basis upon which to build customer value and profitable customer relationships. Today's marketers must position their brands powerfully and manage them well to create valued brand experiences. The fourteenth edition provides a deep focus on brands, anchored by a Chapter 8 section on *Branding Strategy: Building Strong Brands.*

4. ***Measuring and managing return on marketing.*** Especially in uneven economic times, marketing managers must ensure that their marketing dollars are being well spent. "Marketing accountability"—measuring and managing marketing return on investment—has now become an important part of strategic marketing decision making. This emphasis on marketing accountability is addressed in Chapter 2, Appendix 3 *Marketing by the Numbers,* and throughout the fourteenth edition.

5. ***Sustainable marketing around the globe.*** As technological developments make the world an increasingly smaller and more fragile place, marketers must be good at marketing their brands globally and in sustainable ways. New material throughout the fourteenth edition emphasizes the concepts of global marketing and sustainable marketing—meeting the present needs of consumers and businesses while also preserving or enhancing the ability of future generations to meet their needs. The fourteenth edition integrates global marketing and sustainability topics throughout the text. It then provides focused coverage on each topic in Chapters 15 and 16, respectively.

In-Text Teaching and Learning Features

Marketing: An Introduction provides a wealth of chapter-opening, within-chapter, and end-of-chapter learning features that help students to learn, link, and apply major concepts.

- ***Integrated chapter-opening preview sections.*** The active and integrative chapter-opening spread in each chapter starts with an *Objectives Outline*, which provides a helpful preview of chapter contents and learning objectives, complete with page numbers. Next comes a *Previewing the Concepts* section that briefly previews chapter concepts, links them with previous chapter concepts, and introduces the chapter-opening story. Finally, a *First Stop* chapter-opening vignette—an engaging, deeply developed, illustrated, and annotated marketing story—introduces the chapter material and sparks student interest.

- ***Author comments and figure annotations.*** Throughout each chapter, author comments ease and enhance student learning by introducing and explaining major chapter sections and figures.

- ***Reviewing and extending the concepts.*** Sections at the end of each chapter summarize key chapter concepts and provide questions and exercises by which students can review and apply what they've learned. The *Chapter Review and Key Terms* section reviews major chapter concepts and links them to chapter objectives. It also provides a helpful listing of chapter key terms by order of appearance with page numbers that facilitate easy reference. A *Discussion and Critical Thinking* section provides discussion questions and critical thinking exercises that help students to keep track of and apply what they've learned in the chapter.

- ***Minicases and Applications.*** Sections at the end of each chapter provide brief *Online, Mobile, and Social Media Marketing; Marketing Ethics*; and *Marketing by the Numbers* applications cases that facilitate discussion of current issues and company situations in areas such as mobile and social marketing, ethics, and financial marketing analysis. A *Video Case* section contains short vignettes to be used with a set of short videos and questions that accompany the fourteenth edition in MyLab Marketing.

Chapter 1: Marketing: Creating Customer Value and Engagement 35

Marketing by the Numbers Gillette Trying to Shave Off Competition

Gillette, Procter & Gamble's powerhouse razor
riencing challenges from consumer trends and
competitors. Gillette and close competitor Schic
on product innovation and higher prices. Indeed
es first contained two blades, then three, and nc
now have swiveling balls that let the blades pi
to vibrate, and Gillette recently applied for a
zor that heats up. And with each addition, prices
accordingly. Even though Gillette produces exc
that garnered $1.5 billion in sales last year, it face
by the continuing consumer trend of "beardedne
"scruff" or "stubble" look that's not likely to
Online upstarts like Dollar Shave Club, Harry's,
com are also eating away at Gillette's sales. And
patent expired on its Mach3 razor, rival Schick
a less expensive compatible refill blade cartri
Gillette still captures more than 50 percent mar

Company Cases 1 Chick-fil-

See Appendix 1 for cases appropriate for this ch
Case 1, Chick-fil-A: Getting Better befor ger. Chick-fil-A has quietly become the largest
by holding tenaciously to the philosophy that th
able way to do business is to provide the best po
experience.

Video Case Eskimo Joe's

Since 1975, Eskimo Joe's has been a popular w
Stillwater, Oklahoma. Through word of mouth
logo spread via T-shirts, it rapidly became a fa
grab a beer for students at Oklahoma State. But
a basic beer joint has grown into something mu
the drinking age changed from 18 to 21 in the

MyLab Marketing

If assigned by your instructor, complete these
in the MyLab.

1-16. Compare and contrast needs, wants, and demands. Which on
influence? (AACSB: Communication; Reflective Thinking)

1-17. Is it fair to single out specific products for restrictions such as
City proposed size cap on soft drinks? Discuss this argument
this issue: government, soft drink marketers, and consumers.
and Oral Communication; Reflective Thinking)

Appendix 3 Marketing by the Numbers

Marketing managers are facing increased accountability for the financial implications of their actions. This appendix provides a basic introduction to measuring marketing financial performance. Such financial analysis guides marketers in making sound marketing decisions and in assessing the outcomes of those decisions.

The appendix is built around a hypothetical manufacturer of home automation products—Wise Domotics ("domotics" refers to information technology in the home). The company is introducing a device that allows users to control all internet-connected smart devices in their homes. Users will be able to control lighting, temperature, multimedia,

Appendix 1 Company Cases

Company Case 1

Chick-fil-A: Getting Better before Getting Bigger

Chick-fil-A is dominating the U.S. fast-food market. Whereas McDonald's, Subway, Burger King, and Taco Bell trudge along at the top of the heap, Chick-fil-A has quietly grown from a Southeast regional favorite into the largest chicken chain and the eighth-largest quick-service food purveyor in the country. The chain sells significantly more food per restaurant than any of its competitors—three times that of Taco Bell or Wendy's and more than four times what the KFC Colonel fries up. And it does this without even opening its doors on Sundays. With annual revenues of $8 billion and annual average growth of 16 percent, the chicken champ from Atlanta shows no signs of slowing down.

How does Chick-fil-A do it? By focusing on customers. Since the first Chick-fil-A restaurant opened for business in the late 1960s, the chain's founders have held tenaciously to the philosophy that the most sustainable way to do business is to provide the best possible customer experience.

Applying Some Pressure

Chick-fil-A founder S. Truett Cathy was no stranger to the restaurant business. Owning and operating restaurants in Georgia in the 1940s, '50s, and '60s, he was led by his experience to investigate a better (and faster) way to cook chicken. He discovered a pressure fryer that could cook a chicken breast in the same amount of time it took to cook a fast-food burger. Developing the chicken sandwich as a burger alternative, he registered the name "Chick-fil-A, Inc." and opened the first Chick-fil-A restaurant in 1967.

company's trademarked slogan—"We didn't invent the chicken, just the chicken sandwich"—has kept the company on track for decades. Although it has carefully and strategically added other items to the menu, it's the iconic chicken sandwich in all its varieties that primarily drives the brand's image and the company's revenues. This focus has helped the company give customers what they want year after year without being tempted to develop a new flavor of the month.

Getting It Right

Also central to Chick-fil-A's mission is to "have a positive influence on all who come in contact with Chick-fil-A." Although seemingly a tall order to fill, this sentiment permeates every aspect of its business. Not long ago, current Chick-fil-A CEO Dan Cathy was deeply affected by a note that his wife taped to their refrigerator. In a recent visit to a local Chick-fil-A store, she had not only received the wrong order, she had been overcharged. She circled the amount on her receipt, wrote "I'll be back when you get it right" next to it, and posted it on the fridge for her husband to see.

That note prompted Dan Cathy to double down on customer service. He initiated a program by which all Chick-fil-A employees were retrained to go the "second mile" in providing service to everyone. That "second mile" meant not only meeting basic standards of cleanliness and politeness but going above and beyond by delivering each order to the customer's table with unexpected touches such as a fresh-cut flower or ground pepper for salads.

The experience of a recent patron illustrates the level of service Chick-fil-A's customers have come to expect as well as the innovative spirit that makes such service possible:

> My daughter and I stopped at Chick-fil-A on our way home. The parking lot was full, the drive-thru was packed...but the love we have for the chicken sandwiches and waffle potato fries! So we

- ***Company Cases.*** *Appendix 1* contains 16 all-new company cases that help students apply major marketing concepts and critical thinking to real company and brand situations. Each end-of-chapter section identifies applicable cases for the chapter.

Developing Employability Skills

Marketing at Work features. Each chapter contains two deeply developed highlight features that provide in-depth looks at real brand marketing strategies and contemporary marketing issues. For example, students learn how retail titans Walmart and Amazon are battling it out for supremacy in the new omni-channel retailing world; how Netflix uses big data and advanced marketing analytics to personalize each customer's experience; why Apple's products fly off the shelves despite their premium prices; how Instagram has made itself a win-win-win for the company, advertisers, and Instagrammers alike; how Coca-Cola, long a master of mass market advertising, has now also mastered digital, mobile, and social media marketing; and how outdoor apparel and gear maker Patagonia urges "conscious consumption," telling customer to buy *less* of its products. They learn that artificial intelligence in marketing is now "a bigger deal than fire and electricity"; how companies are increasingly using augmented and virtual reality to enhance consumer shopping experiences; and how mobile

120 Part 2: Understanding the Marketplace and Consumer Value

MARKETING AT WORK 4.2

Artificial Intelligence in Marketing: "A Bigger Deal Than Fire or Electricity"

[illegible] you feel the urge for that first jolt of caffeine. As you get in your car, you tap the Starbucks app on your phone and ask for "the usual." Your Starbucks virtual barista replies in her familiar, cheerful voice: "One tall caramel latte!" She then politely suggests a breakfast snack—a Vermont maple nut muffin—not your usual, but it sure sounds good. You agree. "Thanks! Your order will be ready for pickup in five to seven minutes minutes at University and 28th," she confirms. "Would you like to pay for that with your credit card on file?" You step inside the store, bypass the long lines, and grab your order—no fuss, no muss. Welcome to the world of artificial intelligence (AI).

This is just one example of how AI has exploded onto the marketing scene. Starbucks has long been into cutting-edge technology—a full 25 percent of its transactions are already placed through its smartphone apps. But My Starbucks Barista is more than just an ordering app. It uses artificial intelligence to create personalized customer experiences and manage real-time customer interactions, based on everything from customers' past transactions and preferences to demographics, store trends and inventories, and local traffic and weather conditions.

>> Artificial Intelligence: The My Starbucks Barista uses artificial intelligence to create personalized customer experiences and manage real-time customer interactions, based on everything from customers' past transactions and preferences to local traffic and weather conditions.

Elias Stein Illustration

Artificial intelligence is sweeping the world. It involves machines that think and learn in a way that looks and feels human but with a lot more analytical capacity. The engine behind the AI's explosive growth is big data. Raw data is flowing in from everywhere: customer transaction and interaction data, web and social media data, news and environmental data, and data from more than 50 billion connected devices—combing through vast amounts of data to unearth customer and market insights that help marketers sharpen their targeting, personalize customer engagements, design new products, and even craft better ads in real time.

Today's machines are smart and eerily human. IBM's Watson "is loquacious; it can tell jokes, answer questions, and write songs," notes one observer. "Google's AI can now read lips

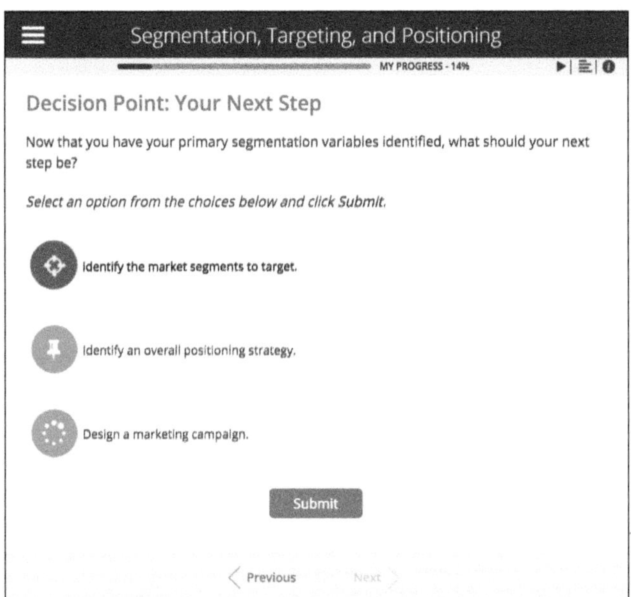

marketing engages consumers in the moments that matter. No other text brings marketing to life like the fourteenth edition of *Marketing: An Introduction*.

Marketing Plan appendix. *Appendix 2* contains a detailed sample marketing plan that helps students to apply important marketing planning concepts.

Marketing by the Numbers appendix. An innovative and freshly revised *Appendix 3* provides students with a comprehensive introduction to the marketing financial analysis that helps guide, assess, and support marketing decisions. A detailed exercise at the end of each chapter lets students apply analytical and financial thinking to that chapter's concepts and links the chapter to the Marketing by the Numbers appendix.

Careers in Marketing. *Appendix 4* helps students to explore marketing career paths and lays out a process for landing a marketing job that best matches their special skills and interests.

Mini Sims in MyLab Marketing give students the opportunity to apply their knowledge to real-world decision making scenarios.

Instructor Teaching Resources

This program comes with the following teaching resources.

Supplements Available to Instructors at www.pearsonhighered.com	Features of the Supplement
Instructor's Manual authored by Tony Henthorne from University of Nevada, Las Vegas	**Chapter-by-chapter summaries** • Examples and activities not in the main book • Teaching outlines • Teaching tips • Solutions to all questions and problems in the book
Test Bank authored by Susan Leshnower from Midland College	**4,000 multiple-choice, true/false, short- answer, and graphing questions with these annotations:** • Difficulty level (1 for straight recall, 2 for some analysis, 3 for complex analysis) • Type (Multiple-choice, true/false, short-answer, essay • Topic (The term or concept the question supports) • Learning objective • AACSB learning standard (Written and Oral Communication; Ethical Understanding and Reasoning; Analytical Thinking; Information Technology; Interpersonal Relations and Teamwork; Diverse and Multicultural Work; Reflective Thinking; Application of Knowledge)
Computerized TestGen	**TestGen allows instructors to:** • Customize, save, and generate classroom tests • Edit, add, or delete questions from the Test Item Files • Analyze test results • Organize a database of tests and student results.
PowerPoints authored by Helen Davis from Jefferson Community College	**Slides include all the graphs, tables, and equations in the textbook.** PowerPoints meet accessibility standards for students with disabilities. Features include, but not limited to: • Keyboard and Screen Reader access • Alternative text for images • High color contrast between background and foreground colors

Acknowledgments

No book is the work only of its authors. We greatly appreciate the valuable contributions of several people who helped make this new edition possible. As always, we owe extra-special thanks to Keri Jean Miksza for her dedicated and valuable contributions to *all* phases of the project and to her husband Pete and daughters Lucy and Mary for all the support they provide Keri during this very absorbing project.

We owe substantial thanks to Andy Norman of Drake University for his skillful help in developing chapter vignettes and highlights, company cases, and the Marketing Plan appendix. This and previous editions have benefited greatly from Andy's assistance. We also thank Laurie Babin of the University of Louisiana at Monroe for her continued efforts in updating the end-of-chapter Marketing by the Numbers assignments and for keeping our Marketing by the Numbers appendix fresh. We thank Colette Wolfson of Ivy Tech Community College for her dedicated work in developing and revising the end-of-chapter features. Additional thanks also go to Jennifer Barr, Tony Henthorne, and Douglas Martin.

Many reviewers at other colleges and universities provided valuable comments and suggestions for this and previous editions. We are indebted to the following colleagues for their thoughtful inputs:

George Bercovitz, *York College*
Pari S. Bhagat, Ph.D., *Indiana University of Pennsylvania*
Sylvia Clark, *St. John's University*
Linda Jane Coleman, *Salem State University*
Mary Conran, *Temple University*
Datha Damron-Martinez, *Truman State University*
Lawrence K. Duke, *Drexel University*
Barbara S. Faries, MBA, *Mission College*
Ivan Filby, *Greenville College*
John Gaskins, *Longwood University*
Karen Halpern, *South Puget Sound Community College*
Jan Hardesty, *University of Arizona*
Hella-Ilona Johnson, *Olympic College*
David Koehler, *University of Illinois at Chicago*
Michelle Kunz, *Morehead State University*
Susan Mann, *University of Northwestern Ohio*
Thomas F. Marshall, M.B.E., *Owens Community College*
Nora Martin, *University of South Carolina*
Erika Matulich, *University of Tampa*
Marc Newman, *Hocking College*
John T. Nolan, *SUNY, Buffalo State*
Nikolai Ostapenko, *University of the District of Columbia*
Vic Piscatello, *University of Arizona*
Bill Rice, *California State University*
David Robinson, *University of California, Berkeley*
William M. Ryan, *University of Connecticut*
Elliot Schreiber, *Drexel University*
Lisa Simon, *Cal Poly, San Luis Obispo*
Robert Simon, *University of Nebraska, Lincoln*
Keith Starcher, *Indiana Wesleyan University*
John Talbott, *Indiana University*
Rhonda Tenenbaum, *Queens College*

Deborah Utter, *Boston University*
Tom Voigt, *Judson University*
Terry Wilson, *East Stroudsburg University*

We also owe a great deal to the people at Pearson Education who helped develop this book. Executive Portfolio Manager Lynn Huddon provided resources and support during the revision. Content Producer Michelle Zeng provided valuable assistance and advice in guiding this complex revision project through development and production. We'd also like to thank Stephanie Wall for her able assistance along the way. We are proud to be associated with the fine professionals at Pearson. We also owe a mighty debt of gratitude to Senior Content Project Manager Allison Campbell and the team at Integra.

Finally, we owe many thanks to our families for all of their support and encouragement—Kathy, Betty, Mandy, Matt, KC, Keri, Delaney, Molly, Macy, and Ben from the Armstrong clan and Nancy, Amy, Melissa, and Jessica from the Kotler family. To them, we dedicate this book.

Gary Armstrong
Philip Kotler

About the Authors

As a team, Gary Armstrong and Philip Kotler provide a blend of skills uniquely suited to writing an introductory marketing text. Professor Armstrong is an award-winning teacher of undergraduate business students. Professor Kotler is one of the world's leading authorities on marketing. Together they make the complex world of marketing practical, approachable, and enjoyable.

GARY ARMSTRONG is Crist W. Blackwell Distinguished Professor Emeritus of Undergraduate Education in the Kenan-Flagler Business School at the University of North Carolina at Chapel Hill. He holds undergraduate and master's degrees in business from Wayne State University in Detroit, and he received his Ph.D. in marketing from Northwestern University. Dr. Armstrong has contributed numerous articles to leading business journals. As a consultant and researcher, he has worked with many companies on marketing research, sales management, and marketing strategy.

But Professor Armstrong's first love has always been teaching. His long-held Blackwell Distinguished Professorship is the only permanent endowed professorship for distinguished undergraduate teaching at the University of North Carolina at Chapel Hill. He has been very active in the teaching and administration of Kenan-Flagler's undergraduate program. His administrative posts have included Chair of Marketing, Associate Director of the Undergraduate Business Program, Director of the Business Honors Program, and many others. Through the years, he has worked closely with business student groups and has received several UNC campuswide and Business School teaching awards. He is the only repeat recipient of the school's highly regarded Award for Excellence in Undergraduate Teaching, which he received three times. Most recently, Professor Armstrong received the UNC Board of Governors Award for Excellence in Teaching, the highest teaching honor bestowed by the 16-campus University of North Carolina system.

PHILIP KOTLER is S. C. Johnson & Son Distinguished Professor of International Marketing at the Kellogg School of Management, Northwestern University. He received his master's degree at the University of Chicago and his Ph.D. at M.I.T., both in economics. Dr. Kotler is author of Marketing Management (Pearson), now in its 15th edition and the most widely used marketing textbook in graduate schools of business worldwide. He has authored more than 60 successful books and more than 150 articles in leading journals. He is the only three-time winner of the coveted Alpha Kappa Psi award for the best annual article in the *Journal of Marketing*.

Professor Kotler was named the first recipient of four major awards: the *Distinguished Marketing Educator of the Year Award* and the *William L. Wilkie "Marketing for a Better World" Award*, both given by the American Marketing Association; the *Philip Kotler Award for Excellence in Health Care Marketing* presented by the Academy for Health Care Services Marketing; and the *Sheth Foundation Medal for Exceptional Contribution to Marketing Scholarship and Practice*. He is a charter member of the Marketing Hall of Fame, was voted the first Leader in Marketing Thought by the American Marketing Association, and was named the Founder of Modern Marketing Management in the *Handbook of Management Thinking*. His numerous other major honors include the Sales and Marketing Executives International *Marketing Educator of the Year Award*; the European Association of Marketing Consultants and Trainers *Marketing Excellence Award*; the *Charles Coolidge Parlin Marketing Research Award*; and the *Paul D. Converse Award*, given by the American Marketing Association to honor "outstanding contributions to science in marketing." A recent *Forbes* survey ranks Professor Kotler in the top 10 of the world's most influential business thinkers. And in a *Financial Times* poll of 1,000 senior executives across the world, Professor Kotler was ranked as the fourth "most influential business writer/guru" of the twenty-first century.

Dr. Kotler has served as chairman of the College of Marketing of the Institute of Management Sciences, a director of the American Marketing Association, and a trustee of the Marketing Science Institute. He has consulted with many major U.S. and international companies in the areas of marketing strategy and planning, marketing organization, and international marketing. He has traveled and lectured extensively throughout Europe, Asia, and South America, advising companies and governments about global marketing practices and opportunities.

Marketing

Creating Customer Value and Engagement

Objectives Outline

- OBJECTIVE 1-1 **Define marketing and outline the steps in the marketing process.** See: What Is Marketing? (pp 4–6)
- OBJECTIVE 1-2 **Explain the importance of understanding the marketplace and customers and identify the five core marketplace concepts.** See: Understanding the Marketplace and Customer Needs (pp 6–10)
- OBJECTIVE 1-3 **Identify the key elements of a customer value-driven marketing strategy and discuss the marketing management orientations that guide marketing strategy.** See: Designing a Customer Value-Driven Marketing Strategy and Plan (pp 10–14)
- OBJECTIVE 1-4 **Discuss customer relationship management and identify strategies for creating value for customers and capturing value from customers in return.** See: Managing Customer Relationships and Capturing Customer Value (pp 15–23)
- OBJECTIVE 1-5 **Describe the major trends and forces that are changing the marketing landscape in this age of relationships.** See: The Changing Marketing Landscape (pp 23–31)

Previewing the Concepts

This first chapter introduces you to the basic concepts of marketing. We start with the question: What is marketing? Simply put, marketing is engaging customers and managing profitable customer relationships. The aim of marketing is to create value for customers in order to capture value from customers in return. Next we discuss the five steps in the marketing process—from understanding customer needs to designing customer value-driven marketing strategies and integrated marketing programs to building customer relationships and capturing value for the firm. Finally, we discuss the major trends and forces affecting marketing in this new age of digital, mobile, and social media. Understanding these basic concepts and forming your own ideas about what they really mean to you will provide a solid foundation for all that follows.

Let's start with a good story about marketing in action at Amazon, by far the nation's leading online marketer. The secret to Amazon's success? It's really no secret at all. Amazon is flat-out customer obsessed. It has a deep-down passion for creating customer value, engagement, and relationships. In return, customers reward Amazon with their buying dollars and loyalty. You'll see this theme of creating customer value in order to capture value in return repeated throughout this chapter and the remainder of the text.

First Stop

Amazon: Obsessed with Creating Customer Value, Engagement, and Relationships

When you think of shopping online—or of shopping anywhere, for that matter—chances are good that you think first of Amazon. The online pioneer first opened its virtual doors in 1995, selling books out of founder Jeff Bezos's garage in suburban Seattle. Amazon still sells books—lots and lots of books. But it now sells just about everything else as well, from electronics, tools, housewares, apparel, and groceries to fashions, loose diamonds, musical instruments, and Maine lobsters. And Amazon is rapidly moving beyond online selling, not just into physical stores but also into video and music streaming, cloud services, and the Internet of Things. If one company represents where the world is now headed, it's probably Amazon.

From the start, Amazon has grown explosively. Its annual sales have rocketed from a modest $150 million in 1997 to $177 billion today. During just the past three years, Amazon's revenues have more than tripled. Last year, the company sold more than 5 billion items to its more than 90 million Amazon Prime members alone—that's an average of 159 items every second. Currently, Amazon is the nation's second-largest retailer, trailing only Walmart. And as unthinkable as it might have seemed only a few years ago, at its current growth rate, Amazon could overtake even mighty Walmart in as little as six years.

What has made Amazon such an amazing success story? Jeff Bezos puts it in three simple words: "Obsess over customers." To its core, the company is relentlessly customer driven. "The thing that drives everything is creating genuine value for customers," says Bezos. Amazon believes that if it does what's good for customers, profits will follow.

Amazon wants to deliver a special experience to every customer. Most Amazon.com regulars feel a surprisingly strong relationship with the company, especially given the almost complete lack of actual human interaction. Amazon obsesses over making each customer's experience uniquely personal. For example, the Amazon.com site greets customers with their very own home pages, complete with personalized site content and recommendations based on their past purchase and browsing histories and the purchasing patterns of customers with similar profiles. If it has 300 million customers, Amazon reasons, it should have 300 million stores.

Visitors to Amazon.com receive a unique blend of benefits: huge selection, good value, low prices, and convenience. But it's the "discovery" factor that makes the buying experience really special. Once on Amazon.com, you're compelled to stay for a while—looking, learning, and discovering. More than just a place to buy things, Amazon.com has become a kind of online community in which customers can browse for products, research purchase alternatives, and share opinions and reviews with other visitors. In this way, Amazon does much more than just sell goods online. It engages customers and creates direct, personalized customer relationships and satisfying experiences.

From the very start, selection, convenience, and value have been the foundation stones of the Amazon experience. Amazon's primary goal is to help customers get whatever they want in the shortest possible time at the right price. To create even greater selection and discovery for customers, Amazon allows competing retailers—from mom-and-pop operations to Marks & Spencer—to sell their products on Amazon.com through the Amazon Marketplace, creating a virtual shopping mall of incredible proportions.

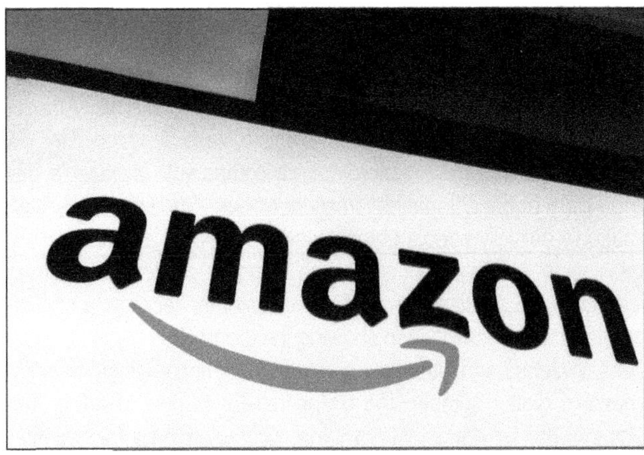

» Amazon does much more than just sell goods online. It engages customers and creates satisfying customer experiences. "The thing that drives everything is creating genuine value for customers," says Amazon founder Jeff Bezos.

Jonathan Weiss/Alamy Stock Photo

Amazon's innovations have made the order and delivery process a breeze. First it was 1-Click ordering that lets customers purchase and ship to preset options with just one click. Then Amazon added Dash Buttons, shortcuts that let customers quickly find and reorder favorite products on Amazon's mobile app. And if there's no smartphone or app handy, customers equipped with an Amazon Echo smart speaker can now voice-shop with a simple command, "Alexa, reorder laundry detergent." Amazon's artificial intelligence–driven digital assistant will place and ship the order for them.

Amazon's deep-down passion for creating customer value, engagement, and relationships has made it the nation's leading online retailer. Amazon has become the model for companies that are obsessively and successfully focused on delivering customer value.

As for delivery, no other seller—online or offline—has been more effective than Amazon in getting the goods to its customers fast. As much as it sells products and convenience, Amazon also sells "speed." When the online giant first introduced Amazon Prime more than a decade ago, free 48-hour shipping was unheard of; now it's standard across the industry. So Amazon introduced Amazon Prime Now, delivery within two *hours* or less. "It's cheap, easy, and insanely fast," says one awestruck customer.

According to the vice president of Amazon Prime Now, her business boils down to two simple questions: "Do you have what I want, and can you get it to me when I need it?" Amazon continues to invest heavily in making the answers to both questions a resounding "yes." To build an even faster and more reliable customer delivery experience, Amazon is rapidly amassing its own fleets of delivery vans, trucks, and Boeing 767 cargo planes that will make it less dependent on third-party shippers such as FedEx, UPS, and the U.S. postal service. It's also actively exploring more futuristic options, such as delivery drones and driverless vehicles.

In its quest to create the perfect customer experience, Amazon pursues endless innovation. For example, take Amazon Key. For as little as $199, the Amazon Key kit comes with Amazon's new Cloud Cam and a compatible smart door lock. Once installed, it lets Amazon's delivery people unlock customers' doors and leave packages inside, safely out of the reach of porch pirates or inclement weather. Once a delivery is made, the customer receives a notification along with a short video showing the drop-off.

As Walmart and other store retailers are increasingly invading Amazon's digital domain, the online retailer is now invading their brick-and-mortar worlds. It knows that a complete customer relationship will require merging online and offline selling into the seamless cross-channel shopping experience that today's consumers expect. For example, Amazon purchased upscale grocery chain Whole Foods Market, which not only accelerates its push into grocery retailing but also provides a physical store platform for the selling and more speedy delivery of other kinds of goods. Amazon is also opening AmazonBooks bookstores and AmazonGo grocery stores, which provide a new twist on convenience by using cameras and sensors to detect what customers take from shelves and let them "just walk out," automatically charging purchases to their accounts.

So what sweeping new customer-pleasing changes can you expect from Amazon in the next 10 years? According to Bezos, that's not the most important question. The more important question is what's *not* going to change? And at Amazon, that's creating real customer value. "We know that customers want low prices," says Bezos, "and I know that's going to be true 10 years from now. They want fast delivery; they want vast selection. And so...we know the energy we put into [those things] today will still be paying off dividends for our customers 10 years from now."

Thus, Amazon has become the poster child for companies that are obsessively and successfully focused on delivering customer value. "Our customers are loyal to us right up until the second somebody offers them a better service," says Bezos. "And I love that. It's super-motivating for us." He concludes, "When things get complicated, we simplify them by asking, 'What's best for the customer?' We believe that if we do that, things will work out in the long term."[1]

Today's successful companies have one thing in common: Like Amazon, they are strongly customer focused and heavily committed to marketing. These companies share a passion for satisfying customer needs in well-defined target markets. They motivate everyone in the organization to help build lasting customer relationships based on creating value.

Customer relationships and value are especially important today. Facing dramatic technological advances and deep economic, social, and environmental challenges, today's customers are reassessing how they engage with brands. New digital, mobile, and social media developments have revolutionized how consumers shop and interact, in turn calling for new marketing strategies and tactics. It's now more important than ever to build strong customer engagement, relationships, and advocacy based on real and enduring customer value.

We'll discuss the exciting new challenges facing both customers and marketers later in the chapter. But first, let's introduce the basics of marketing.

Author Comment
Pause here and think about how you'd answer this question before studying marketing. Then see how your answer changes as you read the chapter.

What Is Marketing?

OBJECTIVE 1-1 Define marketing and outline the steps in the marketing process.

Marketing, more than any other business function, deals with customers. Although we will soon explore more detailed definitions of marketing, perhaps the simplest definition is this one: Marketing is engaging customers and managing profitable customer relationships. The twofold goal of marketing is to attract new customers by promising superior value and to keep and grow current customers by delivering value and satisfaction.

For example, Amazon dominates the online marketplace by creating a world-class online buying experience that helps customers to "find and discover anything they might want to buy online." Facebook has attracted more than 2 billion active web and mobile users worldwide by helping them to "connect and share with the people in their lives." And Starbucks dominates the U.S. out-of-home coffee market by "creating a culture of warmth and belonging, where everyone is welcome."[2]

Sound marketing is critical to the success of every organization. Large for-profit firms such as Google, Target, Coca-Cola, Procter & Gamble, and Microsoft use marketing. But so do not-for-profit organizations, such as colleges, hospitals, museums, symphony orchestras, and even churches.

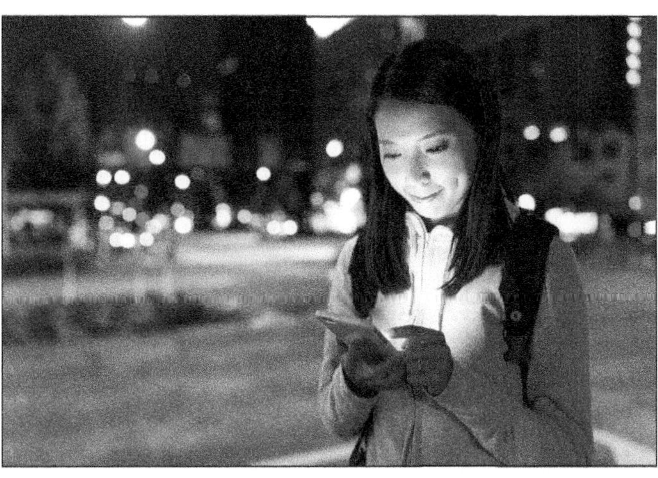

>> **Marketing is all around you, in good old traditional forms and in a host of new forms, from websites and mobile apps to online videos and social media.**

Leung Cho Pan/123 RF

You already know a lot about marketing—it's all around you. Marketing comes to you in the good old traditional forms: You see it in the abundance of products at your nearby shopping mall and the ads that fill your TV screen, spice up your magazines, or stuff your mailbox. >> But in recent years, marketers have assembled a host of new marketing approaches, everything from imaginative websites and smartphone apps to blogs, online videos, and social media. These new approaches do more than just blast out messages to the masses. They reach you directly, personally, and interactively. Today's marketers want to become a part of your life and enrich your experiences with their brands. They want to help you live their brands.

At home, at school, where you work, and where you play, you see marketing in almost everything you do. Yet there is much more to marketing than meets the consumer's casual eye. Behind it all is a massive network of people, technologies, and activities competing for your attention and purchases. This book will give you a complete introduction to the basic concepts and practices of today's marketing. In this chapter, we begin by defining marketing and the marketing process.

Marketing Defined

What *is* marketing? Many people think of marketing as only selling and advertising. We are bombarded every day with TV commercials, catalogs, spiels from salespeople, and online pitches. However, selling and advertising are only the tip of the marketing iceberg.

Today, marketing must be understood not in the old sense of making a sale—"telling and selling"—but in the new sense of satisfying customer needs. If the marketer engages consumers effectively, understands their needs, develops products that provide superior customer value, and prices, distributes, and promotes them well, these products will sell easily. In fact, according to management guru Peter Drucker, "The aim of marketing is to make selling unnecessary."[3] Selling and advertising are only part of a larger marketing mix—a set of marketing tools that work together to engage customers, satisfy customer needs, and build customer relationships.

Broadly defined, marketing is a social and managerial process by which individuals and organizations obtain what they need and want through creating and exchanging value with others. In a narrower business context, marketing involves building profitable, value-laden exchange relationships with customers. Hence, we define **marketing** as the process by which companies engage customers, build strong customer relationships, and create customer value in order to capture value from customers in return.[4]

Marketing
The process by which companies engage customers, build strong customer relationships, and create customer value in order to capture value from customers in return.

The Marketing Process

>> **Figure 1.1** presents a simple, five-step model of the marketing process for creating and capturing customer value. In the first four steps, companies work to understand consumers, create customer value, and build strong customer relationships. In the final step, companies reap the rewards of creating superior customer value. By creating value for consumers, they in turn capture value from consumers in the form of sales, profits, and long-term customer equity.

In this chapter and the next, we examine the steps of this simple model of marketing. In this chapter, we review each step but focus more on the customer relationship steps—understanding customers, engaging and building relationships with customers, and capturing value from customers. In Chapter 2, we look more deeply into the second and third steps—designing value-creating marketing strategies and constructing marketing programs.

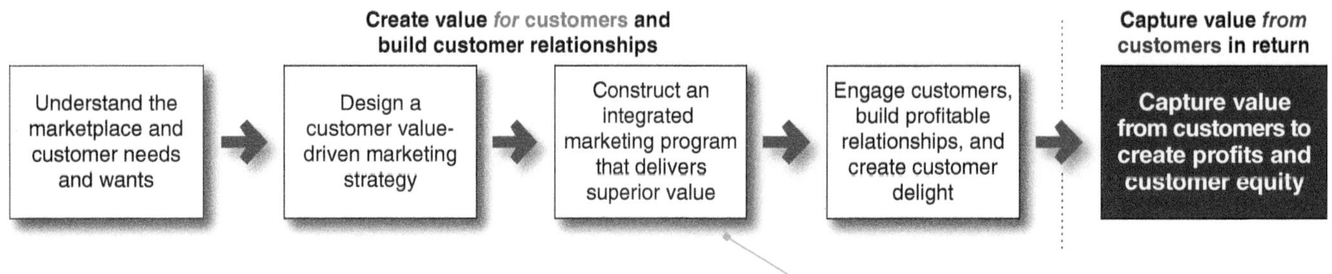
Create value *for* customers and build customer relationships
Capture value *from* customers in return
Understand the marketplace and customer needs and wants
Design a customer value-driven marketing strategy
Construct an integrated marketing program that delivers superior value
Engage customers, build profitable relationships, and create customer delight
Capture value from customers to create profits and customer equity

Figure 1.1 The Marketing Process: Creating and Capturing Customer Value

This important figure shows marketing in a nutshell. By creating value *for* customers, marketers capture value *from* customers in return. This five-step process forms the marketing framework for the rest of the chapter and the remainder of the text.

Author Comment
Marketing is all about creating value for customers. So, as the first step in the marketing process, the company must fully understand customers and the marketplace.

Understanding the Marketplace and Customer Needs

OBJECTIVE 1-2 **Explain the importance of understanding the marketplace and customers and identify the five core marketplace concepts.**

As a first step, marketers need to understand customer needs and wants and the marketplace in which they operate. We examine five core customer and marketplace concepts: (1) needs, wants, and demands; (2) market offerings (products, services, and experiences); (3) value and satisfaction; (4) exchanges and relationships; and (5) markets.

Customer Needs, Wants, and Demands

Needs
States of felt deprivation.

Wants
The form human needs take as they are shaped by culture and individual personality.

Demands
Human wants that are backed by buying power.

The most basic concept underlying marketing is that of human needs. Human **needs** are states of felt deprivation. They include basic physical needs for food, clothing, warmth, and safety; social needs for belonging and affection; and individual needs for knowledge and self-expression. Marketers did not create these needs; they are a basic part of the human makeup.

Wants are the form human needs take as they are shaped by culture and individual personality. An American needs food but wants a Big Mac, fries, and a soft drink. A person in Papua, New Guinea, needs food but wants taro, rice, yams, and pork. Wants are shaped by one's society and are described in terms of objects that will satisfy those needs. When backed by buying power, wants become **demands**. Given their wants and resources, people demand products and services with benefits that add up to the most value and satisfaction.

Companies go to great lengths to learn about and understand customer needs, wants, and demands. They conduct consumer research, analyze mountains of customer data, and observe customers as they shop and interact, offline and online. People at all levels of the company—including top management—stay close to customers:[5]

SHARE
Post
SMILE
POSE & Post

Staying close to customers: Energetic Target CEO Brian Cornell makes regular unannounced visits to Target stores, accompanied by local moms and loyal Target shoppers.

Ackerman + Gruber

> To see up close what their customers experience, Airbnb's CEO Brian Chesky and his co-founder Joe Gebbia regularly stay at the company's host locations. When Airbnb first listed rentals back in 2009, Chesky and Gebbia personally visited all of their New York hosts, staying with them, writing reviews, and making sure they lived up to the company's lofty vision. Such personal visits help the pair to shape new customer solutions based on real user experience. Similarly, Target's energetic CEO, Brian Cornell, makes regular unannounced visits to Target stores, accompanied by local moms and loyal Target shoppers. Cornell likes nosing around stores and getting a real feel for what's going on. It gives him "great, genuine feedback." He and other Target executives even visit customers in their homes, opening closet doors and poking around in cupboards to understand their product choices and buying habits.

Market Offerings—Products, Services, and Experiences

Market offerings
Some combination of products, services, information, or experiences offered to a market to satisfy a need or want.

Consumers' needs and wants are fulfilled through **market offerings**—some combination of products, services, information, or experiences offered to a market to satisfy a need or a want. Market offerings are not limited to physical products. They also include services—activities or benefits offered for sale that are essentially intangible and do not result in the ownership of anything. Examples include banking, airline, hotel, retailing, and home repair services.

More broadly, market offerings also include other entities, such as persons, places, organizations, information, ideas, and causes. For example, to market the cause of suicide prevention, rapper Logic worked with the National Suicide Prevent Lifeline (NSPL) to create a seven-minute online public service video embedded with his song "1-800-273-8255," the NSPL phone number. The results of this lone song and video were staggering. On the day the song and video were released, calls to the Lifeline shot up more than 25 percent, and Google searches for the number doubled. In the following months, visits to the NSPL website increased more than 30 percent.[6]

Marketing myopia
The mistake of paying more attention to the specific products a company offers than to the benefits and experiences produced by these products.

Many sellers make the mistake of paying more attention to the specific products they offer than to the benefits and experiences produced by these products. These sellers suffer from **marketing myopia**. They are so taken with their products that they focus only on existing wants and lose sight of underlying customer needs.[7] They forget that a product is only a tool to solve a consumer problem. A manufacturer of quarter-inch drill bits may think that the customer needs a drill bit. But what the customer *really* needs is a quarter-inch hole. These sellers will have trouble if a new product comes along that serves the customer's need better or less expensively. The customer will have the same *need* but will *want* the new product.

Smart marketers look beyond the attributes of the products and services they sell. By orchestrating several services and products, they create brand experiences for consumers. For example, your local Buffalo Wild Wings restaurant doesn't just serve up wings and beer; it gives customers the ultimate "Wings. Beer. Sports." fan experience (see Marketing at Work 1.1). And the Walt Disney World Resort doesn't just offer amusement park rides, it uses its famed Disney magic to create carefully orchestrated family experiences:[8]

>> Each year, more than 40 million people flock to the Walt Disney World Resort, making it the world's number one tourist attraction. What brings so many people to Disney World? Part of the answer lies in its many attractions. The resort's four major theme parks—Magic Kingdom, Epcot, Disney's Hollywood Studios, and Disney's Animal Kingdom—brim with such attractions as the Expedition Everest, Twilight Zone Tower of Terror, Space Mountain, Soarin', Toy Story Mania, Spaceship Earth, Kilimanjaro Safaris, and Star Tours. But the real "Disney Magic" lies in the company's obsessive dedication to "make people happy" and to "make dreams come true."

Disney goes to extremes to fulfill guests' very high expectations and dreams. Employees are carefully trained in how to do the hard work of helping people have fun. They are taught to be enthusiastic, helpful, and always friendly. They learn that they are in the entertainment business and that they are "cast members" whose job is to be enthusiastic, knowledgeable, and professional in serving Disney's "guests." Each cast member, they learn, plays a vital role in the Disney World "show," whether it's as a "security host" (police), "transportation host" (driver), "custodial host" (street cleaner), or "food and beverage host" (restaurant worker). Thus, you don't just visit Walt Disney World Resort; you immerse yourself in a carefully choreographed experience—a world of wonder where dreams come true and things still work the way they should.

>> Marketing experiences: You don't just visit Walt Disney World Resort; you immerse yourself in a carefully choreographed experience—a world where dreams come true and things still work the way they should.

Sunshine/Alamy Stock Photo

Customer Value and Satisfaction

Consumers usually face a broad array of products and services that might satisfy a given need. How do they choose among these many market offerings? Customers form expectations about the value and satisfaction that various market offerings will deliver and buy accordingly. Satisfied customers buy again and tell others about their good experiences. Dissatisfied customers often switch to competitors and disparage the product to others.

MARKETING AT WORK 1.1

Buffalo Wild Wings: Fueling the Sports Fan Experience

"Wings. Beer. Sports." That's the long-standing motto for the fast-growing Buffalo Wild Wings restaurant chain. "B-Dubs"—as it's known to avid regulars—focuses on food and sports and "everything in between."

There's no doubt about it. Buffalo Wild Wings more than lives up to the "wings" and "beer" parts of the equation. It serves up wings in an abundant variety: boned or boneless, with five dry seasonings and 17 signature sauces ranging on the heat scale from Sweet BBQ (traditional BBQ sauce: satisfyingly sweet with no heat) to Desert Heat (smoky, sweet, and chili pepper seasoning) to Reformulated Blazin' (so good it's scary—made with the unrelenting heat of the ghost pepper). To wash it all down, each B-Dubs restaurant pours as many as 30 different draft beers, with a full selection of domestic, import, and craft beer brands. You won't go hungry or thirsty at B-Dubs.

However, the Buffalo Wild Wings recipe for success goes much deeper than just selling wings and beer for profit. What really packs 'em in and keeps 'em coming back is the B-Dubs customer experience. Customers do gobble up the wings—more than 13.5 million wings chain-wide on last Super Bowl Sunday alone. But even more important, they come to B-Dubs to watch sports, trash talk, cheer on their sports teams, and meet old friends and make new ones—that is, a total eating and social experience. "We realize that we're not just in the business of selling wings," says the company. "We're something much bigger. We're in the business of fueling the sports fan experience. Our mission is to WOW people every day!"

Everything about B-Dubs is designed to deliver the ultimate sports experience, for any fan of any sport. The WOW begins the minute you step into any of Buffalo Wild Wings's 1,230 restaurants. This is not your average dark-and-dank sports bar. Instead, a B-Dubs is like a miniature stadium, with high ceilings, ample natural light, and brightly colored furnishings and wall coverings. The newest Buffalo Wild Wings "Stadia" restaurants are divided into barrier-free zones—including a bar area and a separate dining area. And every B-Dubs has 60 to 70 really big flat-screen TVs lining the walls, over the bar, and about everywhere else, ensuring that every table has the best seat in the house no matter what your team or sport, including live streaming of local college and even high school events. B-Dubs creates an exciting environment that makes it the next best thing to being at the game—or something even better.

There's an experience for everyone at Buffalo Wild Wings. The chain appeals to a wide range of customers, from pub-loving sports nuts to families looking for an affordable evening out. Singles and couples gravitate to the bar area; families stick to the carpeted areas with booths. In addition to streaming sports events of all kinds on the big screens, B-Dubs supplies tableside tablets upon which customers can play poker or trivia games. A social jukebox feature lets guests control the music that plays on the restaurant's sound system.

It seems like there's always something happening in a B-Dubs to engage customers and enhance the experience. Take the chain's infamous Blazin' Wing Challenge—which promises a trophy-style T-shirt and a place on the Wall of Fame to any customer who can down a dozen wings with the chain's hottest signature sauce in no more than six minutes. That's no easy feat considering that the Blazin' sauce is 60 times hotter than typical jalapeño sauce. During the six-minute binge, challengers are not allowed to use napkins or utensils, touch their faces, or eat or drink anything other than the wings (no dipping sauces, please). The menu boasts plenty of warnings, and servers advise most people not to even attempt the challenge. And before taking the plunge, each challenger signs a waiver agreeing that he or she "voluntarily assumes all risk of loss, damage, injury, illness, or death that may be sustained by him or her as a result." As you can imagine, when a challenge is announced over the PA, it usually draws a crowd.

Buffalo Wild Wings never rushes its guests. Whereas many other casual-dining restaurants have a "turn-and-burn" philosophy—cycling as many paying guests as possible through each table—at B-Dubs it's just the opposite. Buffalo Wild Wings encourages people to linger longer, enjoy the food, and soak up the ambiance.

To help make that happen, the chain has created a special staff position at each restaurant. In addition to the usual waitstaff, each table has a "Guest Experience Captain." The captain is like a host at any party, moving from table to table, chatting with guests, personalizing their experiences, and making sure their needs are met. Want a special game on one screen with another game on the screen next to it? Your Guest Experience Captain sees to it. Need help with a tablet? Your captain lends

>> Customer-focused mission: The Buffalo Wild Wings mission is to provide a total eating and social environment that "fuels the sports fan experience" through in-store and online engagement.

a hand. Want to try some new sauces? Your captain will make suggestions and even bring out samples of different sauces with complimentary fries for dipping.

Adding Guest Experience Captains is a major expense, especially when multiplied across shifts in all 1,230 stores. But Buffalo Wild Wings reasons that the captains will more than pay for themselves by enhancing the all-important guest experience, keeping customers around longer, and bringing them back more often. Buffalo Wild Wings restaurants with captains are achieving record levels of customer satisfaction and loyalty compared with those that have not yet brought captains on board.

True to its "ultimate sports experience" mission, Buffalo Wild Wings actively engages its customers digitally and socially outside its restaurants as well as inside. In fact, the company brags that it's the number-one brand in its industry for digital fan engagement. B-Dubs's very active website draws 3 million visitors per month. The brand has more than 12 million Facebook fans, 699,000 Twitter followers, and very active YouTube and Instagram pages. It recently launched GameBreak, an app for fantasy football and other games that can be played inside or outside its restaurants. GameBreak players visit more often, stay longer, and tend to buy maybe one more basket of wings or that second or third beer. In all, Buffalo Wild Wings creates a host of both in-store and online promotions that inspire camaraderie. "It's about giving [customers] tools to not just be spectators but advocates of the brand," says the chain.

Catering to the customer experience has paid big dividends for Buffalo Wild Wings. B-Dubs is now the nation's number-one seller of chicken wings and largest pourer of draft beer. Over the past five years, as other casual-dining restaurants have struggled with fierce competition and slow growth, B-Dubs's sales have jumped 250 percent and profits have tripled. The chain's "hottest wing coating available comes with a warning to B-Dubs' customers: 'keep away from eyes, pets, and children.' The sauce is called 'Blazin',' says one analyst. "That term also happens to be a good description of the [brand's] performance lately."

Sources: "Super Bowl's Annual Buffalo-Wing Binge Eased by Lower Prices," *Advertising Age,* February 2, 2018, http://adage.com/article/special-report-super-bowl/super-bowl-s-annual-buffalo-wing-binge-eased-lower-prices/312209/; Demitrios Kalogeropoulos, "3 Reasons Buffalo Wild Wings Can Keep Soaring in 2015," *The Motley Fool,* January 9, 2015, www.fool.com/investing/general/2015/01/09/3-reasons-why-buffalo-wild-wings-can-keep-soaring.aspx; Bryan Gruley, "The Sloppy Empire: How Buffalo Wild Wings Turned the Sports Bar into a $1.5 Billion Juggernaut," *Bloomberg Businessweek,* April 13–19, 2015, pp. 62–65; Tanya Dua, "The Buffalo Wild Wings Recipe for the 'Ultimate Sports Experience,'" August 4, 2015, https://digiday.com/marketing/buffalo-wild-wings-recipe-ultimate-sports-experience/; and www.22squared.com/work/project/buffalo-wild-wings; http://ir.buffalowildwings.com/financials.cfm, http://worldwidewingsus.com/default.aspx?Page=About, and www.buffalowildwings.com/en/, accessed September 2018.

Marketers must be careful to set the right level of expectations. If they set expectations too low, they may satisfy those who buy but fail to attract enough buyers. If they set expectations too high, buyers will be disappointed. Customer value and customer satisfaction are key building blocks for developing and managing customer relationships. We will revisit these core concepts later in the chapter.

Exchanges and Relationships

Exchange
The act of obtaining a desired object from someone by offering something in return.

Marketing occurs when people decide to satisfy their needs and wants through exchange relationships. **Exchange** is the act of obtaining a desired object from someone by offering something in return. In the broadest sense, the marketer tries to bring about a response to some market offering. The response may be more than simply buying or trading products and services. A political candidate, for instance, wants votes; a church wants membership and participation; an orchestra wants an audience; and a social action group wants idea acceptance.

Marketing consists of actions taken to create, maintain, and grow desirable exchange relationships with target audiences involving a product, service, idea, or other object. Companies want to build strong relationships by consistently delivering superior customer value. We will expand on the important concept of managing customer relationships later in the chapter.

Markets

Market
The set of all actual and potential buyers of a product or service.

The concepts of exchange and relationships lead to the concept of a market. A **market** is the set of actual and potential buyers of a product or service. These buyers share a particular need or want that can be satisfied through exchange relationships.

Marketing means managing markets to bring about profitable customer relationships. However, creating these relationships takes work. Sellers must search for and engage buyers, identify their needs, design good market offerings, set prices for them, promote them, and store and deliver them. Activities such as consumer research, product development, communication, distribution, pricing, and service are core marketing activities.

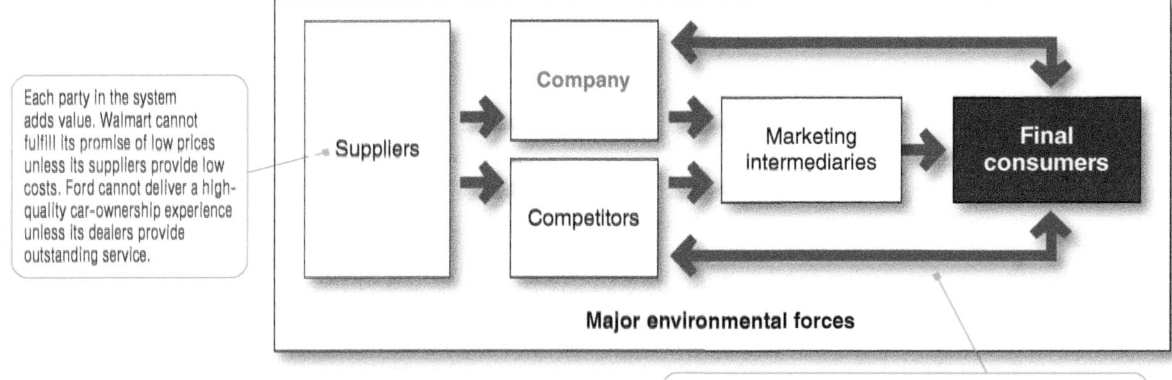
Each party in the system adds value. Walmart cannot fulfill its promise of low prices unless its suppliers provide low costs. Ford cannot deliver a high-quality car-ownership experience unless its dealers provide outstanding service.
Suppliers
Company
Competitors
Marketing intermediaries
Final consumers
Major environmental forces
Arrows represent relationships that must be developed and managed to create customer value and profitable customer relationships.

>> **Figure 1.2 A Modern Marketing System**

Although we normally think of marketing as being carried out by sellers, buyers also carry out marketing. Consumers market when they search for products, interact with companies to obtain information, and make their purchases. In fact, today's digital technologies, from websites and smartphone apps to the explosion of social media, have empowered consumers and made marketing a truly two-way affair. Thus, in addition to customer relationship management, today's marketers must also deal effectively with customer-managed relationships. Marketers are no longer asking only "How can we influence our customers?" but also "How can our customers influence us?" and even "How can our customers influence each other?"

>> **Figure 1.2** shows the main elements in a marketing system. Marketing involves serving a market of final consumers in the face of competitors. The company and competitors research the market and interact with consumers to understand their needs. Then they create and exchange market offerings, messages, and other marketing content with consumers, either directly or through marketing intermediaries. Each party in the system is affected by major environmental forces (demographic, economic, natural, technological, political, and social/cultural).

Each party in the system adds value for the next level. The arrows represent relationships that must be developed and managed. Thus, a company's success at engaging customers and building profitable relationships depends not only on its own actions but also on how well the entire system serves the needs of final consumers. Walmart cannot fulfill its promise of low prices unless its suppliers provide merchandise at low costs. And Ford cannot deliver a high-quality car-ownership experience unless its dealers provide outstanding sales and service.

Author Comment
Once a company fully understands its consumers and the marketplace, it must decide which customers it will serve and how it will bring them value.

Designing a Customer Value-Driven Marketing Strategy and Plan

OBJECTIVE 1-3 **Identify the key elements of a customer value-driven marketing strategy and discuss the marketing management orientations that guide marketing strategy.**

Customer Value-Driven Marketing Strategy

Marketing management
The art and science of choosing target markets and building profitable relationships with them.

Once it fully understands consumers and the marketplace, marketing management can design a customer value-driven marketing strategy. We define **marketing management** as the art and science of choosing target markets and building profitable relationships with them. The marketing manager's aim is to engage, keep, and grow target customers by creating, delivering, and communicating superior customer value.

To design a winning marketing strategy, the marketing manager must answer two important questions: What customers will we serve (what's our target market)? and How can we serve these customers best (what's our value proposition)? We will discuss these marketing strategy concepts briefly here and then look at them in more detail in Chapters 2 and 6.

Selecting Customers to Serve

The company must first decide whom it will serve. It does this by dividing the market into segments of customers (market segmentation) and selecting which segments it will go after (target marketing). Some people think of marketing management as finding as many customers as possible and increasing demand. But marketing managers know that they cannot serve all customers in every way. By trying to serve all customers, they may not serve any customers well. Instead, the company wants to select only customers that it can serve well and profitably. For example, Nordstrom profitably targets affluent professionals; Dollar General profitably targets families with more modest means.

Ultimately, marketing managers must decide which customers they want to target and on the level, timing, and nature of their demand. Simply put, marketing management is customer management and demand management.

Choosing a Value Proposition

Production concept
The idea that consumers will favor products that are available and highly affordable; therefore, the organization should focus on improving production and distribution efficiency.

The company must also decide how it will serve targeted customers—how it will differentiate and position itself in the marketplace. A brand's value proposition is the set of benefits or values it promises to deliver to consumers to satisfy their needs. JetBlue promises to put "You Above All" by bringing "humanity back to travel." By contrast, Spirit Airlines gives you "Bare Fare" pricing: "Less Money. More Go." Homewood Suites by Hilton wants you to "Make yourself at home." Meanwhile, the Hyatt Regency brand declares that sometimes "It's good not to be home." Its ads highlight the joys of traveling and the fun things that people do when they are traveling on business. And Amazon's Echo smart speaker is "Always ready, connected, and fast. Just ask." >> By contrast, the Sonos One with Amazon Alexa is "The smart speaker for music lovers." It gives you all the advantages of Alexa but with high-quality Sonos sound.

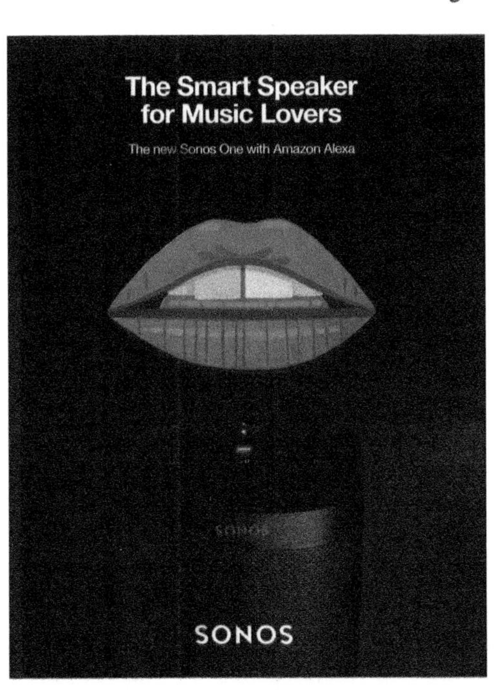

>> Value propositions: Sonos positions its Sonos One with Amazon Alexa as "The smart speaker for music lovers." It gives you all the advantages of Alexa but with high-quality Sonos sound.
The Advertising Archives/Alamy Stock Photo

Such value propositions differentiate one brand from another. They answer the customer's question: "Why should I buy your brand rather than a competitor's?" Companies must design strong value propositions that give them the greatest advantage in their target markets.

Marketing Management Orientations

Marketing management wants to design strategies that will engage target customers and build profitable relationships with them. But what philosophy should guide these marketing strategies? What weight should be given to the interests of customers, the organization, and society? Very often, these interests conflict.

There are five alternative concepts under which organizations design and carry out their marketing strategies: the production, product, selling, marketing, and societal marketing concepts.

The Production Concept. The **production concept** holds that consumers will favor products that are available and highly affordable. Therefore, management should focus on improving production and distribution efficiency. This concept is one of the oldest orientations that guide sellers.

The production concept is still a useful philosophy in some situations. For example, both personal computer maker Lenovo and home appliance maker Haier dominate the highly competitive, price-sensitive Chinese market through low labor costs, high production efficiency, and mass distribution. However, although useful in some situations, the production concept can lead to marketing myopia. Companies adopting this orientation run a major risk of focusing too narrowly on their own operations and losing sight of the real objective—satisfying customer needs and building customer relationships.

Product concept
The idea that consumers will favor products that offer the most quality, performance, and features; therefore, the organization should devote its energy to making continuous product improvements.

The Product Concept. The **product concept** holds that consumers will favor products that offer the most in quality, performance, and innovative features. Under this concept, marketing strategy focuses on making continuous product improvements.

Product quality and improvement are important parts of most marketing strategies. However, focusing only on the company's products can also lead to marketing myopia. For example, some manufacturers believe that if they can "build a better mousetrap, the world will beat a path to their doors." But they are often rudely shocked. Buyers may be looking for a better solution to a mouse problem but not necessarily for a better mousetrap. The better solution might be a chemical spray, an exterminating service, a house cat, or something else that suits their needs even better than a mousetrap. Furthermore, a better mousetrap will not sell unless the manufacturer designs, packages, and prices it attractively; places it in convenient distribution channels; brings it to the attention of people who need it; and convinces buyers that it is a better product.

Selling concept
The idea that consumers will not buy enough of the firm's products unless the firm undertakes a large-scale selling and promotion effort.

The Selling Concept. Many companies follow the **selling concept**, which holds that consumers will not buy enough of the firm's products unless it undertakes a large-scale selling and promotion effort. The selling concept is typically practiced with unsought goods—those that buyers do not normally think of buying, such as life insurance or blood donations. These industries must be good at tracking down prospects and selling them on a product's benefits.

Such aggressive selling, however, carries high risks. It focuses on creating sales transactions rather than on building long-term, profitable customer relationships. The aim often is to sell what the company makes rather than to make what the market wants. It assumes that customers who are coaxed into buying the product will like it. Or, if they don't like it, they will possibly forget their disappointment and buy it again later. These are usually poor assumptions.

Marketing concept
A philosophy in which achieving organizational goals depends on knowing the needs and wants of target markets and delivering the desired satisfactions better than competitors do.

The Marketing Concept. The **marketing concept** holds that achieving organizational goals depends on knowing the needs and wants of target markets and delivering the desired satisfactions better than competitors do. Under the marketing concept, customer focus and value are the paths to sales and profits. Instead of a product-centered make-and-sell philosophy, the marketing concept is a customer-centered sense-and-respond philosophy. The job is not to find the right customers for your product but to find the right products for your customers.

>> **Figure 1.3** contrasts the selling concept and the marketing concept. The selling concept takes an inside-out perspective. It starts with the factory, focuses on the company's existing products, and calls for heavy selling and promotion to obtain profitable sales. It focuses primarily on customer conquest—getting short-term sales with little concern about who buys or why.

In contrast, the marketing concept takes an outside-in perspective. As Herb Kelleher, the colorful founder of Southwest Airlines, once put it, "We don't have a marketing department; we have a customer department." The marketing concept starts with a well-defined market, focuses on customer needs, and integrates all the marketing activities that affect customers. In turn, it yields profits by creating relationships with the right customers based on customer value and satisfaction.

Implementing the marketing concept often means more than simply responding to customers' stated desires and obvious needs. Customer-driven companies research customers deeply to learn about their desires, gather new product ideas, and test product improvements. Such customer-driven marketing usually works well when a clear need exists and when customers know what they want.

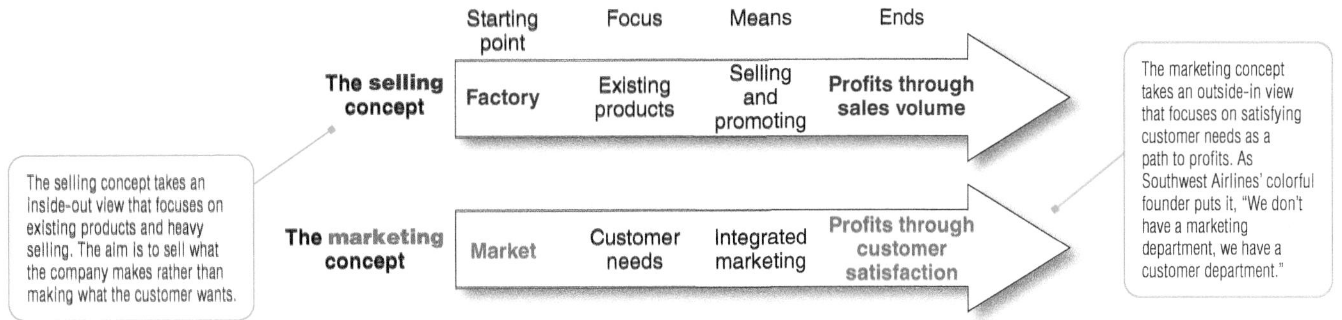
Starting point
Focus
Means
Ends
The selling concept
Factory
Existing products
Selling and promoting
Profits through sales volume
The marketing concept
Market
Customer needs
Integrated marketing
Profits through customer satisfaction
The selling concept takes an inside-out view that focuses on existing products and heavy selling. The aim is to sell what the company makes rather than making what the customer wants.
The marketing concept takes an outside-in view that focuses on satisfying customer needs as a path to profits. As Southwest Airlines' colorful founder puts it, "We don't have a marketing department, we have a customer department."

Figure 1.3 Selling and Marketing Concepts Contrasted

In many cases, however, customers don't know what they want or even what is possible. As Henry Ford once was believed to have remarked, "If I'd asked people what they wanted, they would have said faster horses."[9] For example, even 20 years ago, how many consumers would have thought to ask for now-commonplace products such as tablet computers, smartphones, digital cameras, 24-hour online buying, digital video and music streaming, and GPS systems in their cars and phones? Such situations call for *customer-driving* marketing—understanding customer needs even better than customers themselves do and creating products and services that meet both existing and latent needs, now and in the future. As legendary Apple cofounder Steve Jobs once said, "Our job is to figure out what [consumers are] going to want before they do. ...Our task is to read things that are not yet on the page."[10]

Societal marketing concept
The idea that a company's marketing decisions should consider consumers' wants, the company's requirements, consumers' long-run interests, and society's long-run interests.

The Societal Marketing Concept. The **societal marketing concept** questions whether the pure marketing concept overlooks possible conflicts between consumer short-run wants and consumer long-run welfare. Is a firm that satisfies the immediate needs and wants of target markets always doing what's best for its consumers in the long run? The societal marketing concept holds that marketing strategy should deliver value to customers in a way that maintains or improves both the consumer's and society's well-being. It calls for sustainable marketing, socially and environmentally responsible marketing that meets the present needs of consumers and businesses while also preserving or enhancing the ability of future generations to meet their needs.

Even more broadly, many leading business and marketing thinkers are now preaching the concept of *shared value*, which recognizes that societal needs, not just economic needs, define markets.[11] The concept of shared value focuses on creating economic value in a way that also creates value for society. A growing number of companies known for their hard-nosed approaches to business—such as Google, GE, IBM, Johnson & Johnson, Unilever, and Walmart—are rethinking the interactions between society and corporate performance. They are concerned not just with short-term economic gains but with the well-being of their customers, the depletion of natural resources needed by their businesses, the welfare of key suppliers, and the economic well-being of the communities in which they operate.

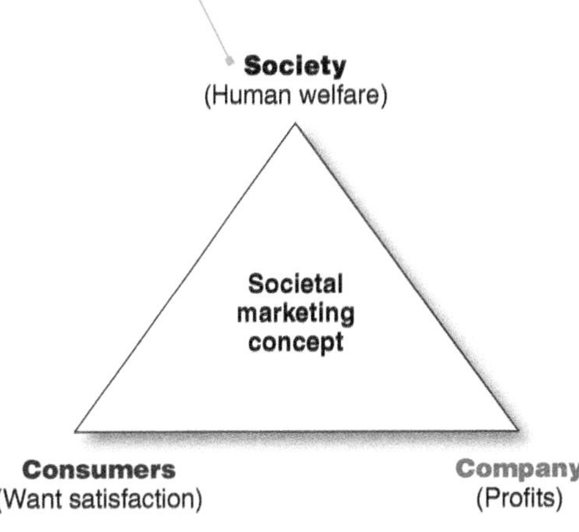
As the text example shows, Jeni's Splendid Ice Creams knows that doing good can benefit both the community and the company. It thrives by "making better ice creams and bringing people together."
Society
(Human welfare)
Societal marketing concept
Consumers
(Want satisfaction)
Company
(Profits)

Figure 1.4 Three Considerations Underlying the Societal Marketing Concept

As **Figure 1.4** shows, companies should balance three considerations in setting their marketing strategies: company profits, consumer wants, and society's interests. Small but fast-growing Jeni's Splendid Ice Creams operates this way:[12]

> Jeni's Splendid Ice Creams makes and sells really good artisan ice cream in its own scoop shops, with exotic flavors such as Goat Cheese with Red Cherries, Wildberry Lavender, and Riesling Poached Pear sorbet. But Jeni's does more than just make and sell ice cream. It also dedicates itself to a deeply felt mission of "making better ice creams and bringing people together. That's what gets us out of bed in the morning and keeps us up late at night." Jeni's follows what it calls

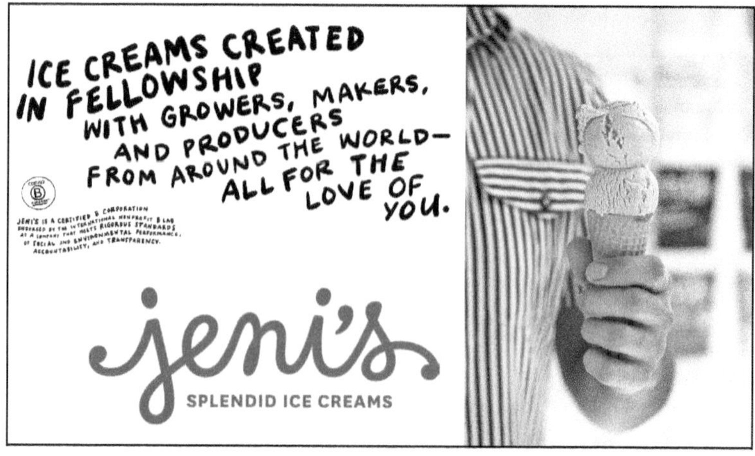

» The societal marketing concept: Jeni's Splendid Ice Cream does more than just make good ice cream. It makes "ice creams created in fellowship with growers, makers, and producers from around the world all for the love of you."

Jeni's Splendid Ice Creams, LLC

a "fellowship model"—making great ice creams for communities, by communities. » Signs in Jeni's shops proudly proclaim: "Ice creams created in fellowship with growers, makers, and producers from around the world all for the love of you."

To achieve this ambitious mission, Jeni's sources its ingredients carefully, using whole fruits and vegetables, milk from local grass-grazed cows, and herbs and wildflower honey from nearby farms, along with fair-trade vanilla and bean-to-bar direct trade chocolate. Jeni's believes in "buying directly and paying fairly for the ingredients, in having minimal impact on the environment, and in building and shaping community." It also works to involve its local communities. "Each time we open a store... we spend time in the neighborhoods; we want residents and visitors to be our partners. We think of our company as a community." Thanks to its societal mission, Jeni's is thriving. In 15 years, the business has grown from a pint-sized local operation to 34 scoop shops in 10 cities, all with devoted followings. You'll also find Jeni's in more 3,000 grocery stores, suggesting that doing good can benefit both the community and the company.

Preparing an Integrated Marketing Plan and Program

The company's marketing strategy outlines which customers it will serve and how it will create value for these customers. Next, the marketer develops an integrated marketing program that will actually deliver the intended value to target customers. The marketing program builds customer relationships by transforming the marketing strategy into action. It consists of the firm's marketing mix, the set of marketing tools the firm uses to implement its marketing strategy.

The major marketing mix tools are classified into four broad groups, called the four Ps of marketing: product, price, place, and promotion. To deliver on its value proposition, the firm must first create a need-satisfying market offering (product). It must then decide how much it will charge for the offering (price) and how it will make the offering available to target consumers (place). Finally, it must engage target consumers, communicate about the offering, and persuade consumers of the offer's merits (promotion). The firm must blend each marketing mix tool into a comprehensive integrated marketing program that communicates and delivers the intended value to chosen customers. We will explore marketing programs and the marketing mix in much more detail in later chapters.

LINKING THE CONCEPTS

Stop here for a moment and stretch your mind. What have you learned so far about marketing? Set aside the more formal definitions we've examined and try to develop your own understanding of marketing.

- In *your own words*, what *is* marketing? Write down *your* definition. Does your definition include such key concepts as customer value, engagement, and relationships?
- What does marketing *mean* to you? How does it affect your daily life?
- What brand of athletic shoes did you purchase last? Describe your relationship with Nike, adidas, New Balance, Asics, Reebok, Puma, Converse, or whatever brand of shoes you purchased.

Author Comment
Doing a good job with the first three steps in the marketing process sets the stage for step four, building and managing customer relationships.

Managing Customer Relationships and Capturing Customer Value

OBJECTIVE 1-4 Discuss customer relationship management and identify strategies for creating value for customers and capturing value from customers in return.

Engaging Customers and Managing Customer Relationships

The first three steps in the marketing process—understanding the marketplace and customer needs, designing a customer value-driven marketing strategy, and constructing a marketing program—all lead up to the fourth and most important step: engaging customers and managing profitable customer relationships. We first discuss the basics of customer relationship management. Then we examine how companies go about engaging customers on a deeper level in this age of digital and social marketing.

Customer Relationship Management

Customer relationship management is perhaps the most important concept of modern marketing. In the broadest sense, **customer relationship management** is the overall process of building and maintaining profitable customer relationships by delivering superior customer value and satisfaction. It deals with all aspects of acquiring, engaging, and growing customers.

Customer relationship management
The overall process of building and maintaining profitable customer relationships by delivering superior customer value and satisfaction.

Relationship Building Blocks: Customer Value and Satisfaction. The key to building lasting customer relationships is to create superior customer value and satisfaction. Satisfied customers are more likely to be loyal customers and give the company a larger share of their business.

Attracting and retaining customers can be a difficult task. Customers often face a bewildering array of products and services from which to choose. A customer buys from the firm that offers the highest **customer-perceived value**—the customer's evaluation of the difference between all the benefits and all the costs of a market offering relative to those of competing offers. Importantly, customers often do not judge values and costs "accurately" or "objectively." They act on *perceived* value.

Customer-perceived value
The customer's evaluation of the difference between all the benefits and all the costs of a marketing offer relative to those of competing offers.

To some consumers, value might mean sensible products at affordable prices. To other consumers, however, value might mean paying more to get more. For example, a Steinway piano—any Steinway piano—costs a lot. But to those who own one, a Steinway is a great value:[13]

>> Perceived value: A Steinway piano—any Steinway piano—costs a lot. But to a Steinway customer, it's a small price to pay for the value of owning one.

A Steinway grand piano typically runs anywhere from about $70,000 to as high as several hundred thousand dollars. The most popular model sells for about $87,000. But ask anyone who owns a Steinway grand piano, and they'll tell you that, when it comes to Steinway, price is nothing; the Steinway experience is everything. Steinway makes very high-quality pianos—handcrafting each Steinway from more than 12,000 individual parts requires up to one full year. But, more importantly, owners get the Steinway mystique. The Steinway name evokes images of classical concert stages and the celebrities and performers who've owned and played Steinway pianos across more than 165 years. But Steinways aren't just for world-class pianists and the wealthy. Ninety-nine percent of all Steinway buyers are amateurs who perform only in their dens.

So is a Steinway piano worth its premium price compared with less expensive pianos? To many consumers, the answer is no. >> But to Steinway customers, whatever a Steinway costs, it's a small price to pay for the value of owning one. As one Steinway user puts it, "A pianist without a Steinway, for me, is the same as a singer without a voice." Says another, "My friendship with the Steinway piano is one of the most important and beautiful things in my life." Who can put a price on such feelings?

Customer satisfaction
The extent to which a product's perceived performance matches a buyer's expectations.

Customer satisfaction depends on the product's perceived performance relative to a buyer's expectations. If the product's performance falls short of expectations, the customer is dissatisfied. If performance matches expectations, the customer is satisfied. If performance exceeds expectations, the customer is highly satisfied or delighted.

Outstanding marketing companies go out of their way to keep important customers satisfied. Most studies show that higher levels of customer satisfaction lead to greater customer loyalty, which in turn results in better company performance. Companies aim to delight customers by promising only what they can deliver and then delivering more than they promise. Delighted customers not only make repeat purchases but also become willing brand advocates and "customer evangelists" who spread the word about their good experiences to others.

For companies interested in delighting customers, exceptional value and service become part of the overall company culture. For example, L.L.Bean—the iconic American outdoor apparel and equipment retailer—was founded on the principle that keeping customers satisfied is the key to building lasting relationships.[14]

> Year after year, L.L.Bean lands in the top 10 of virtually every list of top service companies, including J.D. Power's most recent list of "customer service champions." The customer-service culture runs deep at L.L.Bean. >> More than 100 years ago, Leon Leonwood Bean founded the company on a philosophy of complete customer satisfaction, expressed in the following guarantee: "I do not consider a sale complete until [the] goods are worn out and the customer [is] still satisfied." To this day, customers can return any item, no questions asked, up to a year after purchase.
>
> The company's customer-service philosophy is perhaps best summed up in founder L.L.'s answer to the question "What is a customer?" His answer still forms the backbone of the company's values: "A customer is the most important person ever in this company—in person or by mail. A customer is not dependent on us, we are dependent on him. A customer is not an interruption of our work, he is the purpose of it. We are not doing a favor by serving him, he is doing us a favor by giving us the opportunity to do so. A customer is not someone to argue or match wits with. Nobody ever won an argument with a customer. A customer is a person who brings us his wants. It is our job to handle them profitably to him and to ourselves." Adds former L.L.Bean CEO Leon Gorman: "A lot of people have fancy things to say about customer service, but it's just a day-in, day-out, ongoing, never-ending, persevering, compassionate kind of activity."

NOTICE

I do not consider a sale complete until goods are worn out and customer still satisfied.

We will thank anyone to return goods that are not perfectly satisfactory.

Should the person reading this notice know of anyone who is not satisfied with our goods, I will consider it a favor to be notified.

Above all things we wish to avoid having a dissatisfied customer.

>> Customer satisfaction: Customer service champion L.L.Bean was founded on a philosophy of complete customer satisfaction. As founder Leon Leonwood Bean put it, "I do not consider a sale complete until [the] goods are worn out and the customer [is] still satisfied."
L.L.Bean

Other companies that have become legendary for customer delight and their service heroics include Zappos.com, Amazon.com, Chick-fil-A, Nordstrom department stores, and JetBlue Airways. However, a company doesn't need to have over-the-top service to create customer delight. For example, no-frills grocery chain ALDI has highly satisfied customers, even though they have to bag their own groceries. ALDI's everyday very low pricing on good-quality products delights customers and keeps them coming back. Thus, customer satisfaction comes not just from service heroics but from how well a company delivers on its basic value proposition and helps customers solve their buying problems. "Most customers don't want to be 'wowed,'" says one marketing consultant. "They [just] want an effortless experience."[15]

Although a customer-centered firm seeks to deliver high customer satisfaction relative to competitors, it does not attempt to maximize customer satisfaction. A company can always increase customer satisfaction by lowering its prices or increasing its services. But this may result in lower profits. Thus, the purpose of marketing is to generate customer value profitably. This requires a very delicate balance: The marketer must continue to generate more customer value and satisfaction but not "give away the house."

Customer Relationship Levels and Tools. Companies can build customer relationships at many levels, depending on the nature of the target market. At one extreme, a company with many low-margin customers may seek to develop basic relationships with them. For example, P&G's Tide detergent does not phone or call on all of its consumers to get to know them personally. Instead, Tide creates engagement and relationships through product experiences, brand-building advertising, websites, and social media. At the other extreme, in markets with few customers and high margins, sellers want to create full partnerships with key customers. For example, P&G sales representatives work closely with Walmart, Kroger, and other large retailers that sell Tide. In between these two extremes, other levels of customer relationships are appropriate.

Beyond offering consistently high value and satisfaction, marketers can use specific marketing tools to develop stronger bonds with customers. For example, many companies offer frequency marketing programs that reward customers who buy frequently or in large amounts. Airlines offer frequent-flier programs, hotels give room upgrades to frequent guests, and supermarkets give patronage discounts to "very important customers."

These days almost every brand has a loyalty rewards program. Such programs can enhance and strengthen a customer's brand experience. For example, JetBlue's TrueBlue loyalty program offers the usual frequent-flier points and rewards but adds some nice enhancements such as no blackout dates and family sharing. More important, the TrueBlue program personalizes the customer experience. >> Each TrueBlue member has customized web and mobile pages, complete with a dashboard that shows available points, JetBlue activity history, connections with JetBlue rewards partners, and trip- and flight-planning links. The personalized pages not only make it easy for TrueBlue members to manage their points and rewards, they are also a handy one-stop trip-planning tool, all geared to an individual member's profile. As one member describes it: "Once you're an official TrueBlue member, go hog wild filling out your profile. Upload that stunning selfie with the blue filter as your member picture, pick your favorite JetBlue destinations, even create an ultimate dream itinerary to the Blue Ridge Mountains. . . ." JetBlue's pledge to members: "TrueBlue. For your loyalty, we give you ours."[16]

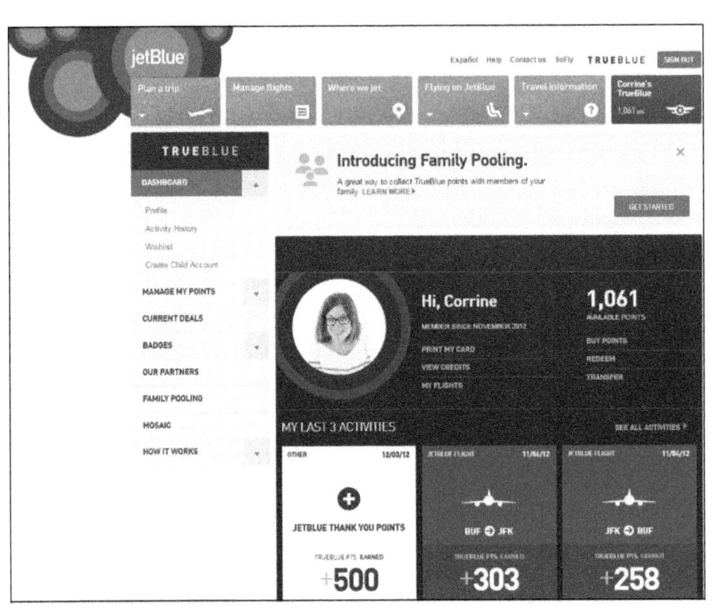

>> Relationship marketing tools: JetBlue's TrueBlue loyalty program personalizes and strengthens the customer's brand experience, including a customized dashboard for managing points, rewards, and trips. JetBlue's pledge to members, "TrueBlue. For your loyalty, we give you ours."

JetBlue and Corrine Spring

Significant changes are occurring in the nature of customer-brand relationships. Today's digital technologies—the internet and the surge in online, mobile, and social media—have profoundly changed the ways that people on the planet relate to one another. In turn, these events have had a huge impact on how companies and brands connect with customers and how customers connect with and influence each other's brand behaviors.

Customer Engagement and Today's Digital, Mobile, and Social Media

The digital age has spawned a dazzling set of new customer relationship-building tools, from websites, online ads and videos, mobile ads and apps, and blogs to online communities and the major social media, such as Facebook, Twitter, YouTube, Snapchat, and Instagram.

Customer-engagement marketing
Making the brand a meaningful part of consumers' conversations and lives by fostering direct and continuous customer involvement in shaping brand conversations, experiences, and community.

Yesterday's companies focused mostly on mass marketing to broad segments of customers at arm's length. By contrast, today's companies are using online, mobile, and social media to refine their targeting and to engage customers more deeply and interactively. The old marketing involved marketing brands to consumers. The new marketing is **customer-engagement marketing**—fostering direct and continuous customer involvement in shaping brand conversations, brand experiences, and brand community.

Customer-engagement marketing goes beyond just selling a brand to consumers. Its goal is to make the brand a meaningful part of consumers' conversations and lives.

The burgeoning internet and social media have given a huge boost to customer-engagement marketing. Today's consumers are better informed, more connected, and more empowered than ever before. Newly empowered consumers have more information about brands, and they have a wealth of digital platforms for airing and sharing their brand views with others. Thus, marketers are now embracing not only customer relationship management but also *customer-managed relationships*, in which customers connect with companies and with each other to help forge and share their own brand experiences. Beyond building brand loyalty and purchasing, marketers want to create *brand advocacy*, by which satisfied customers initiate favorable interactions with others about a brand.

Greater consumer empowerment means that companies can no longer rely on marketing by *intrusion*. Instead, they must practice marketing by *attraction*—creating market offerings and messages that engage consumers rather than interrupt them. Hence, most marketers now combine their mass-media marketing efforts with a rich mix of online, mobile, and social media marketing that promotes brand-consumer engagement, brand conversations, and brand advocacy among customers.

For example, companies post their latest ads and videos on social media sites, hoping they'll go viral. They maintain an extensive presence on Facebook, Instagram, Twitter, Snapchat, YouTube, Google+, and other social media to start conversations with and between customers, address customer service issues, research customer reactions, and drive traffic to relevant articles, web and mobile marketing sites, contests, videos, and other brand activities. They launch their own blogs, mobile apps, brand microsites, and consumer-generated review systems, all with the aim of engaging customers on a more personal, interactive level. Skilled use of social media can get consumers involved with a brand, talking about it, and advocating it to others.

The key to engagement marketing is to find ways to enter targeted consumers' conversations with engaging and relevant brand messages. Simply posting a humorous video, creating a social media page, or hosting a blog isn't enough. Successful engagement marketing means making relevant and genuine contributions to targeted consumers' lives and interactions. Consider Bark, the subscription service that sends subscribers monthly BarkBoxes packed with toys and treats for their dogs:[17]

>> Engaging customers: Rather than using intrusive, hard-sell product pitches, Bark interacts with customers in humorous ways about their favorite mutual topic—"the weird dogs we live with and the funny things they do."

@ChangoTheHandsomePittie

>> Bark sells BarkBox subscriptions to dog lovers. But rather than using intrusive, hard-sell product pitches, Bark interacts with customers in humorous ways about their favorite mutual topic—"the weird dogs we live with and the funny things they do." Bark was founded by dog lovers, so the brand relates easily to its audience of people who are "just like us, total weirdos about their dogs." The brand's marketers use social media to share original comedic videos and relatable stories that entertain dog lovers more than they hawk BarkBox subscriptions. "We start conversations about dogs and form relationships with people around dogs in general," says a Bark content creator. "And 85 percent of our content doesn't even mention BarkBox specifically." Bark strives to make real connections. "Whether we're telling a fart joke or sharing a sentimental story of a pug puppy that looks like a meatball, we have to have an air of authenticity," says Bark's head marketer.

Bark's relational approach has engaged a substantial following, with 500,000 subscribers to its delivery service and more than 4 million fans on Facebook and Instagram. One recent video featuring a viral rap about being a dog mom on Mother's Day drew 42 million views. Customers also help with Bark's marketing, regularly posting photos and videos of their dogs eagerly tearing open their monthly BarkBoxes. And the brand's first major TV spot, aired late last year, was largely inspired by user-produced content posted on social media feeds. "Yes, we're trying to sell you something," says the marketer, "but even if you don't want it, we're making sure the content is still valuable to your time."

Consumer-Generated Marketing

Consumer-generated marketing
Brand exchanges created by consumers themselves—both invited and uninvited—by which consumers are playing an increasing role in shaping their own brand experiences and those of other consumers.

One form of customer-engagement marketing is **consumer-generated marketing**, by which consumers themselves play roles in shaping their own brand experiences and those of others. This might happen through uninvited consumer-to-consumer exchanges in blogs, social media, and other digital forums. But increasingly, companies themselves are inviting consumers to play a more active role in shaping products and brand content.

Some companies ask consumers for new product and service ideas. For example, Oreo recently ran a #MyOreoCreation contest asking fans to come up with new flavor ideas. Three finalist flavors hit the stores for two months before fans voted online for a winner, who received $500,000. As another example, at the My Starbucks Idea site, Starbucks collects ideas from customers on new products, store changes, and just about anything else that might make their Starbucks experience better. "You know better than anyone else what you want from Starbucks," says the company at the website. "So tell us. What's your Starbucks idea? Revolutionary or simple—we want to hear it." The site invites customers to share their ideas, vote on and discuss the ideas of others, and see which ideas Starbucks has implemented.[18]

Other companies invite consumers to play a role in shaping ads and social media content. For example, all-electric carmaker Tesla recently held a fan-made ad contest, with three winning "charmingly low-budget" commercials selected from 10 finalists by public voting (via Twitter likes). Tesla posted the finalist ads online simultaneously with the launch of its Model 3 sedan, drawing millions of views and sparking interactions among dedicated Tesla fans. >> One top-three winner: "Sonja's Super Quick Tesla Fan Video" by YouTuber Sonja Jasansky of Minnesota, a super-quick and ultra-quirky video highlighting Tesla specifications and debunking common misconceptions.[19]

>> Consumer-generated marketing: "Charmingly low-budget" fan-made Tesla ads drew millions of online views and sparked interactions among dedicated Tesla fans.

Sonja Maria

Similarly, Mountain Dew stirred up user-generated content to create buzz around a limited-time reintroduction of its iconic Baja Blast flavor. It began with a discreet Rogue Wave social media campaign in which it posted tantalizing hints on Facebook, Snapchat, Instagram, and Twitter about bringing Baja Blast back. For example, on Snapchat, the brand showed quick clips of bottles. Mountain Dew fans responded with a flood of tweets and other social media chatter. "Some of our fans even created collages of all the images featuring Baja over the last few days to confirm to other members of Dew Nation that Baja was coming back," says Mountain Dew's digital brand manager. Mountain Dew then created ads on social media and men's lifestyle websites incorporating consumers' tweets. The result: Online chatter about Baja Blast shot up 170 percent.[20]

Despite the successes, however, harnessing consumer-generated content can be a time-consuming and costly process, and companies may find it difficult to mine even a little gold from all the content submitted. Moreover, because consumers have so much control over social media content, inviting their input can sometimes backfire. As a classic example, McDonald's famously launched a Twitter campaign using the hashtag #McDStories, hoping that it would inspire heartwarming stories about Happy Meals. Instead, the effort was hijacked by Twitter users, who turned the hashtag into a "bashtag" by posting less-than-appetizing messages about their bad experiences with the fast-food chain. McDonald's pulled the campaign within only two hours, but the hashtag was still churning weeks, even months later.[21]

As consumers become more connected and empowered and as the boom in digital and social media continues, consumer brand engagement—whether invited by marketers or not—will be an increasingly important marketing force. Through a profusion of consumer-generated videos, shared reviews, blogs, mobile apps, and websites, consumers are playing a growing role in shaping their own and other consumers' brand experiences. Brands must embrace this increased consumer empowerment and master the digital and social media relationship tools or risk being left behind.

Partner Relationship Management

When it comes to creating customer value and building strong customer relationships, today's marketers know that they can't go it alone. They must work closely with a variety of marketing partners. In addition to being good at customer relationship management, marketers must also be good at **partner relationship management**—working with others inside and outside the company to jointly engage and bring more value to customers.

Partner relationship management
Working closely with partners in other company departments and outside the company to jointly bring greater value to customers.

Traditionally, marketers have been charged with understanding customers and representing customer needs to different company departments. However, in today's more connected world, every functional area in the organization can interact with customers. The new thinking is that—no matter what your job is in a company—you must understand marketing and be customer focused. Rather than letting each department go its own way, firms must link all departments in the cause of creating customer value.

Marketers must also partner with suppliers, channel partners, and others outside the company. Marketing channels consist of distributors, retailers, and others who connect the company to its buyers. The supply chain describes a longer channel, stretching from raw materials to components to final products that are carried to final buyers. Through supply chain management, companies today are strengthening their connections with partners all along the supply chain. They know that their fortunes rest on how well their entire supply chain performs against competitors' supply chains.

Author Comment
Look back at Figure 1.1. In the first four steps of the marketing process, the company creates value for target customers and builds strong relationships with them. If it does that well, it can capture value from customers in return, in the form of loyal customers who buy and continue to buy the company's brands.

Capturing Value from Customers

The first four steps in the marketing process outlined in Figure 1.1 involve engaging customers and building customer relationships by creating and delivering superior customer value. The final step involves capturing value in return in the form of sales, market share, and profits. By creating superior customer value, the firm creates satisfied customers who stay loyal, buy more, and advocate the brand to others. This, in turn, means greater long-run returns for the firm. Here, we discuss the outcomes of creating customer value: customer loyalty and retention, share of market and share of customer, and customer equity.

Customer lifetime value
The value of the entire stream of purchases a customer makes over a lifetime of patronage.

Creating Customer Loyalty and Retention

Good customer relationship management creates customer satisfaction. In turn, satisfied customers remain loyal and talk favorably to others about the company and its products. Studies show big differences in the loyalty between satisfied and dissatisfied customers. Even slight dissatisfaction can create an enormous drop in loyalty. Thus, the aim of customer relationship management is to create not only customer satisfaction but also customer delight.

Keeping customers loyal makes good economic sense. Loyal customers spend more and stay around longer. Research also shows that it's five times cheaper to keep an old customer than acquire a new one. Conversely, customer defections can be costly. Losing a customer means losing more than a single sale. It means losing the entire stream of purchases that the customer would make over a lifetime of patronage. For example, here is a classic illustration of **customer lifetime value**:[22]

> Stew Leonard, who operates a highly profitable four-store supermarket in Connecticut and New York, once said that he saw $50,000 flying out of his store every time he saw a sulking customer. Why? Because his average customer spent about $100 a week, shopped 50 weeks a year, and remained in the area for about 10 years. If this customer had an unhappy experience and switched to another supermarket, Stew Leonard's lost $50,000 in lifetime revenue. The loss could be much greater if the disappointed customer shared the bad experience with other customers and caused them to defect.

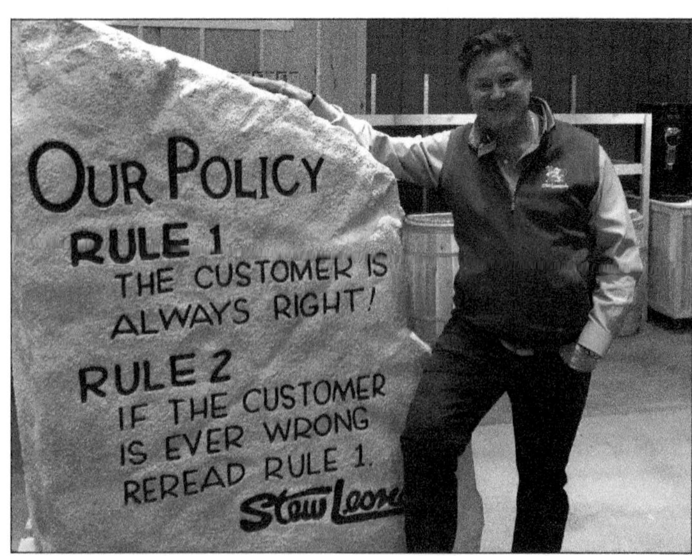

>> Customer lifetime value: To keep customers coming back, Stew Leonard's has created the "Disneyland of dairy stores." Rule #1—The customer is always right. Rule #2—If the customer is ever wrong, reread Rule #1.

Courtesy of Stew Leonard's

> To keep customers coming back, Stew Leonard's has created what has been called the "Disneyland of Dairy Stores," complete with costumed characters, scheduled entertainment, a petting zoo, and animatronics throughout the store. From its humble beginnings as a small dairy store in 1969, Stew Leonard's has grown at an amazing pace. It's built 30 additions onto the original store, which now serves more than 300,000 customers each week. >> This legion of loyal shoppers is largely a result of the store's passionate approach to customer service. "Rule #1: The customer is always right. Rule #2: If the customer is ever wrong, reread Rule #1."

Stew Leonard's is not alone in assessing customer lifetime value. Lexus, for example, estimates that a single satisfied and loyal customer is worth more than $600,000 in lifetime sales, and the estimated lifetime value of a Starbucks customer is more than $14,000.[23] In fact, a company can lose money on a specific transaction but still benefit greatly from a long-term relationship. This means that companies must aim high in building customer relationships. Customer delight creates an emotional relationship with a brand, not just a rational preference. And that relationship keeps customers coming back.

Growing Share of Customer

Share of customer
The portion of the customer's purchasing that a company gets in its product categories.

Beyond simply retaining good customers to capture customer lifetime value, good customer relationship management can help marketers increase their **share of customer**—the share they get of the customer's purchasing in their product categories. Thus, banks want to increase "share of wallet." Supermarkets and restaurants want to get more "share of stomach." Car companies want to increase "share of garage," and airlines want greater "share of travel."

To increase share of customer, firms can offer greater variety to current customers. Or they can create programs to cross-sell and up-sell to market more products and services to existing customers. For example, Amazon is highly skilled at leveraging relationships with its more than 300 million customers worldwide to increase its share of each customer's spending budget:[24]

> Once they log onto Amazon.com, customers often buy more than they intend, and Amazon does all it can to help make that happen. The online giant continues to broaden its merchandise assortment, carrying millions of products and creating an ideal spot for one-stop shopping. And based on each customer's purchase and search history, the company recommends related products that might be of interest. This recommendation system influences some 35 percent of all sales. Amazon's ingenious Amazon Prime and Amazon Prime Now shipping programs have also helped boost its share of customers' wallets. According to one analyst, the ingenious Amazon Prime programs "convert casual shoppers, who gorge on the gratification of having purchases reliably appear two days [or even two hours] after the order, into Amazon addicts." Amazon's Prime membership has doubled over the past two years to 90 million. And, on average, a Prime customer spends 4.6 times more than a non-Prime customer.

Building Customer Equity

We can now see the importance of not only acquiring customers but also keeping and growing them. The value of a company comes from the value of its current and future customers. Customer relationship management takes a long-term view. Companies want to not only create profitable customers but also "own" them for life, earn a greater share of their purchases, and capture their customer lifetime value.

Customer equity
The total combined customer lifetime values of all of the company's customers.

What Is Customer Equity? The ultimate aim of customer relationship management is to produce high customer equity.[25] **Customer equity** is the total combined customer lifetime values of all of the company's current and potential customers. As such, it's a measure of the future value of the company's customer base. Clearly, the more loyal the firm's profitable customers, the higher its customer equity. Customer equity may be a better measure of a firm's performance than current sales or market share. Whereas sales and market share reflect the past, customer equity suggests the future. Consider Cadillac:[26]

In the 1970s and 1980s, Cadillac had some of the most loyal customers in the industry. To an entire generation of car buyers, the name Cadillac defined "The Standard of the World." Cadillac's share of the luxury car market reached a whopping 51 percent in 1976, and based on market share and sales, the brand's future looked rosy. However, measures of customer equity would have painted a bleaker picture. Cadillac customers were getting older (average age 60), and average customer lifetime value was falling. Many Cadillac buyers were on their last cars. Thus, although Cadillac's market share was good, its customer equity was not.

Compare this with BMW. Its more youthful and vigorous image didn't win BMW the early market share war. However, it did win BMW younger customers (average age about 40) with higher customer lifetime values. The result: In the years that followed, BMW's market share and profits soared while Cadillac's fortunes eroded badly. BMW overtook Cadillac in the 1980s. In recent years, Cadillac has struggled to make the Caddy cool again with edgier, high-performance designs that target a younger generation of consumers. More recently, the brand has billed itself as "The New Standard of the World" with marketing pitches based on "power, performance, and design," attributes that position it more effectively against the likes of BMW and Audi. >> Recent ads feature young achievers and invite consumers to "Dare Greatly" and "Drive the world forward." As a result, although it still lags other luxury brands, Cadillac's share of the luxury car market has risen modestly in recent years. The moral: Marketers should care not just about current sales and market share. Customer lifetime value and customer equity are the name of the game.

>> Managing customer equity: To increase customer equity, Cadillac is making the classic car cool again among younger buyers, encouraging consumers to "Dare Greatly."

General Motors

Building the Right Relationships with the Right Customers. Companies should manage customer equity carefully. They should view customers as assets that need to be managed and maximized. But not all customers, not even all loyal customers, are good investments. Surprisingly, some loyal customers can be unprofitable, and some disloyal customers can be profitable. Which customers should the company acquire and retain?

The company can classify customers according to their potential profitability and manage its relationships with them accordingly. >> **Figure 1.5** classifies customers into one of four relationship groups, according to their profitability and projected loyalty.[27] Each group requires a different relationship management strategy. *Strangers* show low potential profitability and little projected loyalty. There is little fit between the company's offerings and their needs. The relationship management strategy for these customers is simple: Don't invest anything in them; make money on every transaction.

Butterflies are potentially profitable but not loyal. There is a good fit between the company's offerings and their needs. However, like real butterflies, we can enjoy them for only a short while and then they're gone. An example is stock market investors who trade shares often and in large amounts but who enjoy hunting out the best deals without building a regular relationship with any single brokerage company. Efforts to convert butterflies into loyal customers are rarely successful. Instead, the company should enjoy the butterflies for the moment. It should create satisfying and profitable transactions with them, capturing as much of their business as possible in the short time during which they buy from the company. Then it should move on and cease investing in them until the next time around.

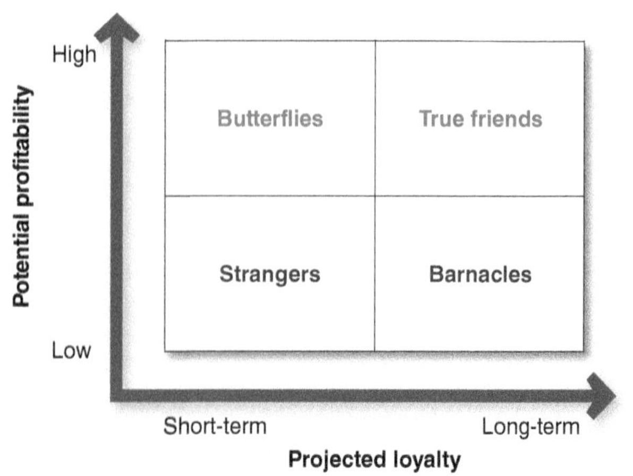

>> Figure 1.5 Customer Relationship Groups

True friends are both profitable and loyal. There is a strong fit between their needs and the company's offerings. The firm wants to make continuous relationship investments to delight these customers and engage, nurture, retain, and grow them. It wants to turn true friends into true believers, who come back regularly and tell others about their good experiences with the company.

Barnacles are highly loyal but not very profitable. There is a limited fit between their needs and the company's offerings. An example is smaller bank customers who bank regularly but do not generate enough returns to cover the costs of maintaining their accounts. Like barnacles on the hull of a ship, they create drag. Barnacles are perhaps the most problematic customers. The company might be able to improve their profitability by selling them more, raising their fees, or reducing service to them. However, if they cannot be made profitable, they should be "fired."

For example, Best Buy offers an attractive returns policy but has found that a small segment of customers abuses this policy. So it uses an outside firm, Retail Equation, to track and score individual customer returns behavior. The system is designed to identify the 1 percent of shoppers whose behavior suggests returns fraud or abuse. A shopper who exceeds a certain score is informed that future returns will be denied, even if it means losing the customer. "You could do things that are inside the posted rules, but if you are violating the intent of the rules, like every item you're purchasing you're using and then returning, then at a certain point you become not a profitable customer for [Best Buy]," says a Retail Equation executive.[28]

The point here is an important one: Different types of customers require different engagement and relationship management strategies. The goal is to build the right relationships with the right customers.

LINKING THE CONCEPTS

We've covered a lot of ground. Again, pause for a moment and develop *your own* thoughts about marketing.

- In *your own words*, what *is* marketing, and what does it seek to accomplish?
- How well does Amazon manage its relationships with customers? What customer relationship management strategy does it use? What relationship management strategy does Walmart use?
- Think of a company for which you are a "true friend." What strategy does this company use to manage its relationship with you?

Author Comment
Marketing doesn't take place in a vacuum. Now that we've discussed the five steps in the marketing process, let's look at how the ever-changing marketplace affects both consumers and the marketers who serve them. We'll look more deeply into these and other marketing environment factors in Chapter 3.

The Changing Marketing Landscape

OBJECTIVE 1-5 Describe the major trends and forces that are changing the marketing landscape in this age of relationships.

Every day, dramatic changes are occurring in the marketplace. Richard Love of HP observed, "The pace of change is so rapid that the ability to change has now become a competitive advantage." Yogi Berra, the legendary New York Yankees catcher and manager, summed it up more simply when he said, "The future ain't what it used to be." As the marketplace changes, so must those who serve it.

In this section, we examine the major trends and forces that are changing the marketing landscape and challenging marketing strategy. We look at four major developments: the digital age, the growth of not-for-profit marketing, rapid globalization, and the call for sustainable marketing practices.

The Digital Age: Online, Mobile, and Social Media Marketing

The explosive growth in digital technology has fundamentally changed the way we live—how we communicate, share information, access entertainment, and shop. Welcome to the age of the *Internet of Things (IoT)*, a global environment where everything and everyone is digitally connected to everything and everyone else. More than 4 billion people—52 percent of the world's population—are now online; more than 80 percent of all American adults own smartphones. These numbers will only grow as digital technology rockets into the future.[29]

Most consumers are totally smitten with all things digital. For example, according to one study, 71 percent of Americans keep their mobile phone next to them when they sleep; 3 percent sleep with phone in hand. Six in 10 young adults in the United States use primarily online streaming services to watch TV, and 85 percent of U.S. adults get their news via mobile devices. Importantly to marketers, U.S. consumers make 9 percent of their purchases online, and it's estimated that more than half of total U.S. retail sales are either transacted directly or influenced by online research.[30]

The consumer love affair with digital and mobile technology makes it fertile ground for marketers trying to engage customers. So it's no surprise that the internet and rapid advances in digital and social media have taken the marketing world by storm. **Digital and social media marketing** involves using digital marketing tools such as websites, social media, mobile ads and apps, online video, email, blogs, and other digital platforms to engage consumers anywhere, anytime via their computers, smartphones, tablets, internet-ready TVs, and other digital devices. These days, almost every company is reaching out to customers with multiple websites, newsy tweets and Facebook pages, Instagram posts and Snapchat stories, viral ads and videos posted on YouTube, rich-media emails, and mobile apps that solve consumer problems and help them shop.

Digital and social media marketing
Using digital marketing tools such as websites, social media, mobile apps and ads, online video, email, and blogs to engage consumers anywhere, at any time, via their digital devices.

>> Online brand communities: At Sony's PlayStation Community, game enthusiasts can follow social media posts, watch the latest videos, discover which games are trending, share content, and interact with other fans—all in real time.

Jens Schlueter/Getty Images

At the most basic level, marketers set up company and brand websites that provide information and promote the company's products. Many companies also set up online brand community sites, where customers can congregate and exchange brand-related interests and information. For example, beauty products retailer Sephora's Beauty Insider Community—"the world's largest beauty forum"—is a thriving online community where customers can ask questions, share ideas and reviews, post photos, and get beauty advice and inspiration from other enthusiasts. >> And Sony's PlayStation Forums site serves as a social hub for PlayStation PS4 game enthusiasts. It's a place where fans can follow social media posts about PS4, watch the latest PS4 videos, discover which PS4 games are trending on social networks, share content, and interact with other fans—all in real time.[31]

Beyond brand websites, most companies are also integrating social and mobile media into their marketing mixes.

Social Media Marketing

It's hard to find a brand website, or even a traditional media ad, that doesn't feature links to the brand's Facebook, Instagram, Twitter, YouTube, Snapchat, Pinterest, LinkedIn, or other social media sites. Social media provide exciting opportunities to extend customer engagement and get people talking about a brand.

Some social media are huge—Facebook has more than 2 *billion* active monthly users, Instagram more than 800 million, Twitter more than 328 million, and Snapchat 255 million. Reddit, the online social news community, has 234 million unique visitors each month from 185 countries. But smaller, more focused social media sites are also thriving, such as CafeMom, an online community of 20 million moms who exchange advice, entertainment, and commiseration at the community's online, Facebook, Twitter, Pinterest, YouTube, Google+, and mobile sites. Even tiny sites can attract active audiences, such as Birdpost.com for avid birdwatchers or Ravelry.com for knitters and crocheters.[32]

Online social media provide a digital home where people can connect and share important information and moments in their lives. As a result, they offer an ideal platform for real-time marketing, by which marketers can engage consumers in the moment by linking brands to important trending topics, real-world events, causes, personal occasions, or other happenings in consumers' lives. Candy maker Mars did this with its award-winning Snickers Hungerithm social media campaign, which monitored the "mood" of the internet and offered real-time price discounts to consumers when the internet was "hungry" (see Marketing at Work 1.2).

MARKETING AT WORK 1.2

Snickers Hungerithm: Engaging Customers in Real Time

Mars is the world's number one candy maker, and its flagship brand—Snickers—is the world's number one candy brand. Snickers has long been positioned on its "Snickers satisfies" promise—on the stomach-filling, energy-packed properties of the popular chocolate-covered bar crammed with nougat, caramel, and peanuts. For the past several years, Mars has extended the Snickers positioning with its award-winning and fun "You're not you when you're hungry" campaign. The campaign features whacky ads and other executions in which people become someone else and behave badly when they are hungry. Once they eat a Snickers, however, they become themselves again.

The "You're not you when you're hungry" campaign taps into a universal appeal: hunger. The positioning is as powerful for women as for men; for older generations as for younger ones; for office workers, factory workers, or students; in the United States or Australia or even Russia (Snickers' second-largest market). And the appeal is immediate—hunger pops up regularly throughout the day, triggered by needs both physical and emotional.

Candy is an impulse category. On any given purchase occasion, consumers are presented with dozens, even hundreds, of options. So if Snickers wants to be the brand people reach for, it needs to be top-of-mind when the mood strikes. With this in mind, Snickers recently launched an innovative marketing campaign in Australia—called "Hungerithm"—that played off both the immediacy of its "You're not you" hunger appeal and the real-time capabilities of social and mobile media.

Building on the notion that people get cranky when they are hungry, Snickers developed an algorithm—or "Hungerithm"—that gauged the public's general irritability real-time by monitoring social media chatter. Built with the help of MIT and Google, Hungerithm analyzed some 14,000 social media posts a day across platforms such as Twitter, Facebook, and YouTube. It looked at 3,000 commonly used words and phrases, even interpreting slang and sarcasm, to take what one analyst called "a virtual fist-shaking temperature of the internet"—ranging from "Annoyed," "On Edge," or "Irritable" to "Losing It" or even "Full Meltdown." Snickers then linked the public mood in real time with the price of Snickers at 7-Eleven stores. The angrier the internet got (suggesting the hungrier people were), the lower the price of Snickers at the local 7-Eleven, with prices dropping by as much as 82 percent.

Mars introduced the Hungerithm campaign with a barrage of TV spots, online videos, and social media posts. "The Internet can be an angry place," said the first Hungerithm promotion. "But what if that's just because we're hungry?" The conclusion: "Angry internet = cheaper Snickers. Now, when the weather's crappy, you'll get cheaper Snickers. Political scandal? Cheaper Snickers. Meteor strike? Definitely cheaper Snickers."

The digital- and mobile-driven Hungerithm campaign targeted people at peak mood-producing moments and places—traffic jams, bad weather, high-profile sports events, or polarizing political shenanigans. It responded in real time with Facebook and Twitter posts addressing breaking political, social, and entertainment news. Mobile-fed coupons let consumers lock in the Snickers price of the moment and directed them to the nearest 7-Eleven.

The real-time design of Hungerithm was for real. The promotion updated every 10 minutes—144 times a day. The Hungerithm website kept a constant posting of the price and mood indicators, and Snickers partnered with two of Australia's top morning TV shows to give regular price and mood updates. Following the Hungerithm "index" became somewhat of a national pastime in Australia, engaging consumers at a high level.

The Hungerithm campaign produced stunning results. Snickers sales jumped 67 percent during the promotion, with a 1,740 percent increase in Facebook traffic and a 120 percent leap in Snickers mentions on Twitter. Hoping to duplicate the campaign's success elsewhere, Mars has now selectively rolled out the Snickers Hungerithm campaign globally.

Price slashing can be risky. But in the case of Hungerithm, Snickers strategically linked its price discounts to the essence of the brand, creating valuable consumer engagement. According

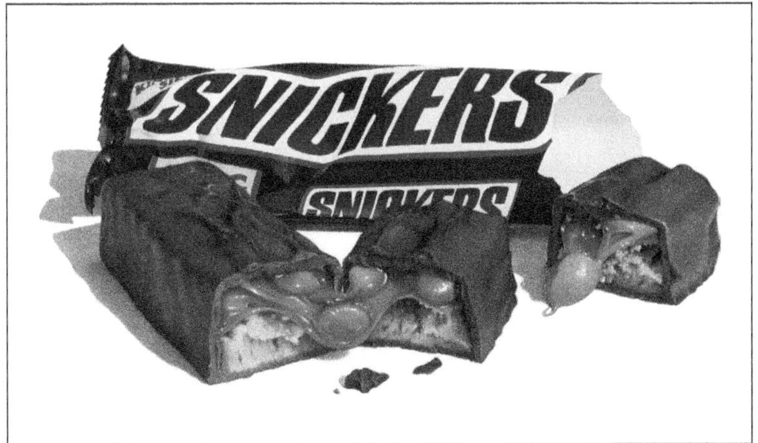

>> Real-time marketing: The Snickers "Hungerithm" campaigned linked the public mood in real time with the price of Snickers. "Angry internet = cheaper Snickers."

Judy Unger/Alamy Stock Photo

to Mars's chief marketing officer, "Hungerithm hit the exact digital sweet spot we were going for. [It] managed to create a real-life connection to the product that captured everyone's attention and imagination."

Sources: Emily Abrams, "7 Surprising Facts Every Snickers Lover Should Know," *Swirled*, February 14, 2018, https://swirled.com/snickers-facts/; Erik Oster, "Clemenger BBDO Melbourne Programs 'Hungerithm' for Snickers," *Adweek*, May 26, 2016, www.adweek.com/agencyspy/clemenger-bbdo-melbourne-programs-hungerithm-for-snickers/110055; T. L. Stanley, "How Snickers Used Social Media Outrage to Fuel the Year's Most Innovative Media Plan," *Adweek*, September 17, 2017, p. 14; Karlene Lukovitz, "Snickers Brings 'Hungerithm' to the U.S.," *Mediapost*, November 27, 2017, www.mediapost.com/publications/article/310600/snickers-brings-hungerithm-to-the-us.html; and www.mediacom.com/en/work/hungerithm, accessed September 2018.

Using social media might involve something as simple as a contest or promotion to garner Facebook Likes, tweets, Instagram "regrams," or YouTube postings. But more often these days, brands create large-scale, carefully integrated social media programs. For example, energy drink maker Red Bull uses a broad mix of social media to connect and inspire its enthusiastic fan base. It now has more than 50 million followers on Facebook, 2 million on Twitter, and 8 million on Instagram. Red Bull's high-energy social media pages hardly mention the company's products at all. Instead, they promote Red Bull's pedal-to-the-metal lifestyle and provide a place where fans can connect with the brand and each other to share their common interests in extreme sports, music, and entertainment. More than just an energy drink maker, "Red Bull is now a top brand for sporting activities and action shots," says an analyst, "and users follow them on social for their adrenaline-filled feed."[33]

Mobile Marketing

Mobile marketing is perhaps the fastest-growing digital marketing platform. Smartphones are ever present, always on, finely targeted, and highly personal. This makes them ideal for engaging customers anytime, anywhere as they move through the buying process. For example, Starbucks customers can use their mobile devices for everything from finding the nearest Starbucks and learning about new products to placing and paying for orders, perhaps through the coffee merchant's artificial intelligence-powered, voice-activated My Starbucks Barista virtual assistant.

Four out of five smartphone users use their phones to shop—browsing product information through apps or the mobile web, making price comparisons, reading online product reviews, and making purchases from home, from work, or even in stores. Almost 35 percent of all online purchases are now made from mobile devices. As a result, to reach mobile shoppers, mobile advertising is surging and now accounts for 75 percent of all digital ad spending.[34]

Marketers use mobile channels to stimulate immediate buying, make shopping easier, enrich the brand experience, reach on-the-go consumers, or all of these. >> For example, Taco Bell uses mobile advertising to reach consumers at what it calls mobile "moments that matter."[35]

> As part of its ongoing push to promote Taco Bell's breakfast in 2016, the chain used carefully targeted mobile advertising to reach consumers just as they were starting their day. It targeted mobile ads based on specific behaviors such as which apps consumers use first in the morning, their favorite news apps, or what time of day they've looked at a breakfast recipe. "We're weaving into morning behaviors," said an executive of the agency who led media buying for the campaign. Taco Bell has also targeted mobile ads geographically using navigation and traffic apps such as Google's Waze to zero in on specific customer locations, even providing step-by-step directions to nearby stores. In these ways, Taco Bell has been able to customize mobile ads according to each customer's actions, experiences, and environment. In marketing Taco Bell's breakfasts, said the agency director, mobile lets Taco Bell be "present on experiences that consumers turn to when they first open their eyes in the morning."

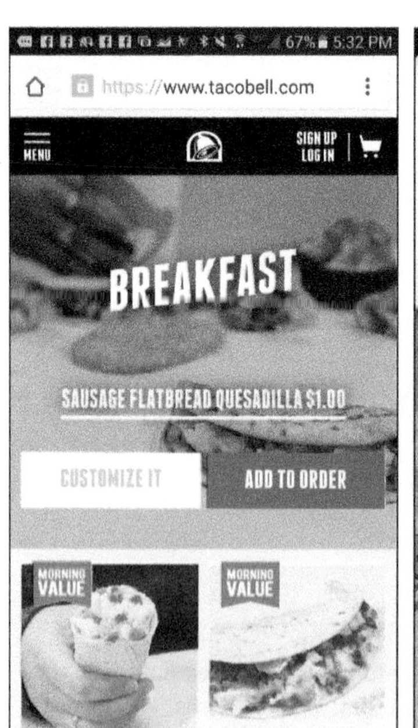

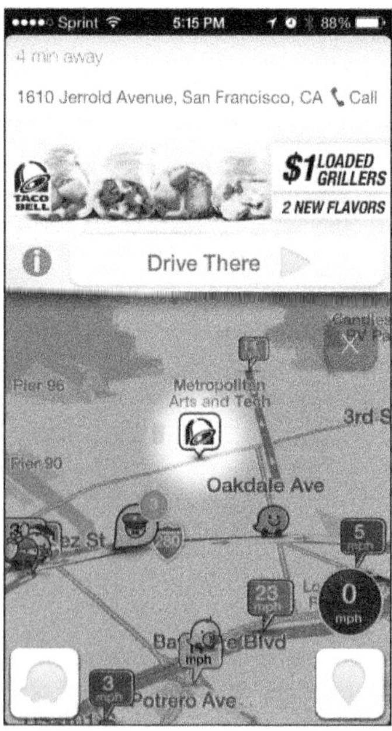

>> Mobile marketing: Carefully-targeted mobile advertising lets Taco Bell reach breakfast customers at "moments that matter."

Taco Bell Corp. and Google

Although online, social media, and mobile marketing offer huge potential, most marketers are still learning how to use them effectively. The key is to blend the new digital approaches with traditional marketing to create a smoothly integrated marketing strategy and mix. We will examine digital, mobile, and social media marketing throughout the text—they touch almost every area of marketing strategy and tactics. Then, after we've covered the marketing basics, we'll look more deeply into digital and direct marketing in Chapter 14.

Big Data and Artificial Intelligence (AI)

With the explosion in digital technologies, marketers can now amass mountains of data. They are tapping information sources ranging from customer transactions to real-time data flowing from website and social media monitoring, connected Internet of Things (IoT) devices, and many others. Brands can use such *big data* to gain deep customer insights, personalize marketing offers, and improve customer engagements and service.

To make sense of all this big data and use it to benefit their brands and customers, marketers are turning to ever-more-advanced marketing analytics. For example, *artificial intelligence (AI)* has burst onto the marketing scene. AI involves machines that think and learn in a way that looks and feels human but with a lot more analytical capacity. Marketers can use AI to analyze data at lightning speed and apply the insights to engage customers in real time and help them through the buying process.

AI-empowered applications include everything from customer-service chat bots and virtual assistants like Amazon Echo's Alexa or Apple's Siri to IBM's almost-human AI supercomputer Watson. For example, one medicine maker recently used Watson to shape personalized mobile ads to individual allergy medication customers based on real-time weather data and pollen counts in their areas. We will discuss the fascinating developments in big data and artificial intelligence more deeply in Chapter 4.

The Growth of Not-for-Profit Marketing

In recent years, marketing has also become a major part of the strategies of many not-for-profit organizations, such as colleges, hospitals, museums, zoos, symphony orchestras, foundations, and even churches. The nation's not-for-profits face stiff competition for support and membership. Sound marketing can help them attract membership, funds, and support.

>> For example, not-for-profit St. Jude Children's Research Hospital has a special mission: "Finding cures. Saving children." It directly serves some 7,500 patients each year plus countless thousands more through its affiliations and clinical trials in places across the country and around the world. Families never receive a bill from St. Jude, for treatment, travel, housing, or food. To accomplish this mission, St. Jude raises the funds for its $2 million-plus daily operating budget through powerhouse marketing.[36] Fundraising efforts include everything from public service announcements, celebrity endorsements, corporate partnerships, and an extensive online presence to events such as Trike-a-thons, Math-a-thons, an Up 'Til Dawn student challenge, and the St. Jude Dream Home Giveaway. St. Jude works with more than 70 corporate partners such as Target, Domino's, Williams-Sonoma, Regal Cinemas, and Expedia that participate in its annual Thanks and Giving campaign, which asks consumers to "give thanks

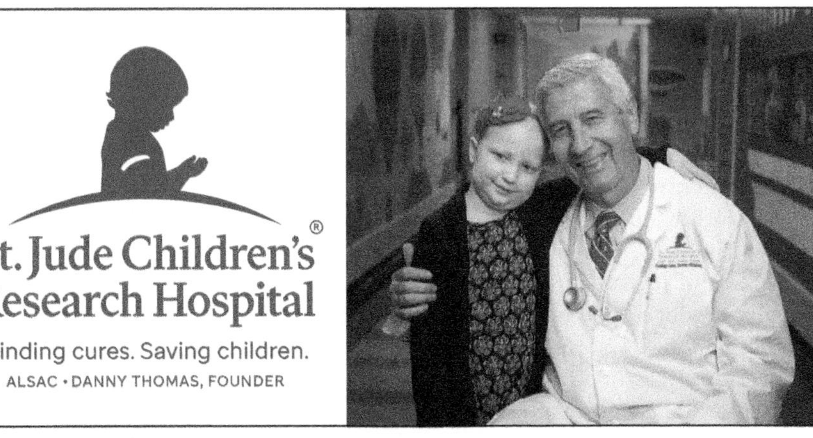

>> Not-for-profit marketing: St. Jude Children's Research Hospital aggressively markets its powerful mission: "Finding cures. Saving children."

Used with permission of ALSAC | St. Jude. St. Jude Children's Research Hospital® and Finding Cures. Saving Children® are registered trademarks of American Lebanese Syrian Associated Charities, Inc. (ALSAC).

for the healthy kids in your life, and give to those who are not." The result is a pervasive brand that brings in more than $1.3 billion each year from private donors—ranging from preschoolers and professionals to eighth-graders and 80-year-olds.

Another example is the World Wildlife Fund (WWF), a global not-for-profit conservation organization whose mission is to conserve nature and protect the world's wildlife. WWF uses sophisticated marketing to raise the considerable resources it needs to accomplish its sweeping mission. Just one example is the WWF's recent cost-efficient but effective #LastSelfie Snapchat campaign:

> The idea behind the WWF #Last Selfie campaign is that the world's endangered wildlife species are disappearing from the earth as quickly as a Snapchat snap. To make the point, WWF sent nine-second snaps of endangered animals to WWF followers worldwide with the message "Don't let this be my #LastSelfie," urging recipients to take a screenshot. Within only eight hours, the campaign generated 5,000 tweets viewed on 6 million timelines. Within only a week, there were 40,000 tweets reaching 120 million users. In all, the #LastSelfie campaign reached more than half of all Twitter users. It also helped WWF to meet its monthly donation target in just three days and led to a record number of animal adoptions through WWF's website. More broadly, thanks to such marketing efforts and despite its limited marketing budget, WWF raised nearly $290 million in funds last year, more than a third of it from individual donors.

Government agencies have also shown an increased interest in marketing. For example, the U.S. military has a marketing plan to attract recruits to its different services, and various government agencies are now designing social marketing campaigns to encourage energy conservation and concern for the environment or discourage smoking, illegal drug use, and obesity. Even the once-stodgy U.S. Postal Service has developed innovative marketing to sell commemorative stamps, promote its Priority Mail services, and lift its image as a contemporary and competitive organization. In all, the U.S. government is the nation's 40th largest advertiser.[37]

Rapid Globalization

As they are redefining their customer relationships, marketers are also taking a fresh look at the ways in which they relate with the broader world around them. Today, almost every company, large or small, is touched in some way by global competition. A neighborhood florist buys its flowers from Mexican nurseries, and a large U.S. electronics manufacturer competes in its home markets with giant Korean rivals. A fledgling internet retailer finds itself receiving orders from all over the world at the same time that an American consumer goods producer introduces new products into emerging markets abroad.

American firms have been challenged at home by the skillful marketing of European and Asian multinationals. Companies such as Toyota, Nestlé, and Samsung have often outperformed their U.S. competitors in American markets. Similarly, U.S. companies in a wide range of industries have developed truly global operations, making and selling their products worldwide. Quintessentially American McDonald's now serves 69 million customers daily in more than 36,000 local restaurants in more than 100 countries worldwide—75 percent of its corporate revenues come from outside the United States. Similarly, Nike markets in 190 countries, with non-U.S. sales accounting for 53 percent of its worldwide sales.[38] Today, companies are not just selling more of their locally produced goods in international markets; they are also sourcing more supplies and components abroad and developing new products for specific markets around the world.

Thus, managers in countries around the world are increasingly taking a global, not just local, view of the company's industry, competitors, and opportunities. They are asking: What is global marketing? How does it differ from domestic marketing? How do global competitors and forces affect our business? To what extent should we "go global"? We will discuss the global marketplace in more detail in Chapter 15.

Sustainable Marketing—The Call for More Environmental and Social Responsibility

Marketers are reexamining their relationships with social values and responsibilities and with the very earth that sustains us. As the worldwide consumerism and environmentalism movements mature, today's marketers are being called on to develop sustainable marketing practices. Corporate ethics and social responsibility have become hot topics for almost every business. And few companies can ignore the renewed and very demanding environmental movement. Every company action can affect customer relationships. Today's customers expect companies to deliver value in a socially and environmentally responsible way.

The social responsibility and environmental movements will place even stricter demands on companies in the future. Some companies resist these movements, budging only when forced by legislation or organized consumer outcries. Forward-looking companies, however, readily accept their responsibilities to the world around them. They view sustainable marketing as an opportunity to do well by doing good. They seek ways to profit by serving immediate needs and the best long-run interests of their customers and communities.

Some companies, such as Patagonia, Timberland, Ben & Jerry's, Warby Parker, and others, practice caring capitalism, setting themselves apart by being civic minded and responsible. They build social and environmental responsibility into their company value and mission statements. >> For example, Warby Parker—the highly successful online marketer of low-priced prescription glasses—sells "eyewear with a purpose":[39]

>> Sustainable marketing: Warby Parker sells eyewear with a purpose. "Companies can do good in the world while still being profitable," says the company's co-founder.

Warby Parker

> Warby Parker was founded with a lofty objective: "to offer designer eyewear at a revolutionary price while leading the way for socially conscious businesses." For starters, by cutting out distributors, designing its own glasses in-house, and engaging customers directly online, the company sells high-quality eyewear at very low prices. Buying glasses from Warby Parker "should leave you happy and good-looking, with money in your pocket."
>
> But beyond bringing value to its customers, Warby Parker has a broader social mission. It notes that nearly one billion people worldwide who need glasses lack access to them. To help fix that problem, Warby Parker's Buy a Pair, Give a Pair program promises that for every pair of glasses it sells, another pair will be distributed to someone in need. So far, more than 3 million pairs of glasses have been distributed through the program. "We believe that everyone has the right to see," says the company. Beyond being socially admirable, Warby Parker's Buy a Pair, Give a Pair program also makes good economic sense, for both the company and its customers. After only eight years, the company has grown to more than $250 million in annual sales and a company valuation of $1.75 billion. "Companies can do good in the world while still being profitable," says Warby Parker co-founder Neil Blumenthal. "Good eyewear, good outcome."

Sustainable marketing presents both opportunities and challenges for marketers. We will revisit the topic of sustainable marketing in greater detail in Chapter 16.

So, What Is Marketing? Pulling It All Together

Author Comment
Remember Figure 1.1 outlining the marketing process? Now, based on everything we've discussed in this chapter, we'll expand that figure to provide a road map for learning marketing throughout the remainder of the text.

At the start of this chapter, Figure 1.1 presented a simple model of the marketing process. Now that we've discussed all the steps in the process, >> **Figure 1.6** presents an expanded model that will help you pull it all together. What is marketing? Simply put, marketing is the process of engaging customers and building profitable customer relationships by creating value for customers and capturing value in return.

The first four steps of the marketing process focus on creating value for customers. The company first gains a full understanding of the marketplace by researching customer needs and managing marketing information. It then designs a customer-driven marketing

Figure 1.6 An Expanded Model of the Marketing Process

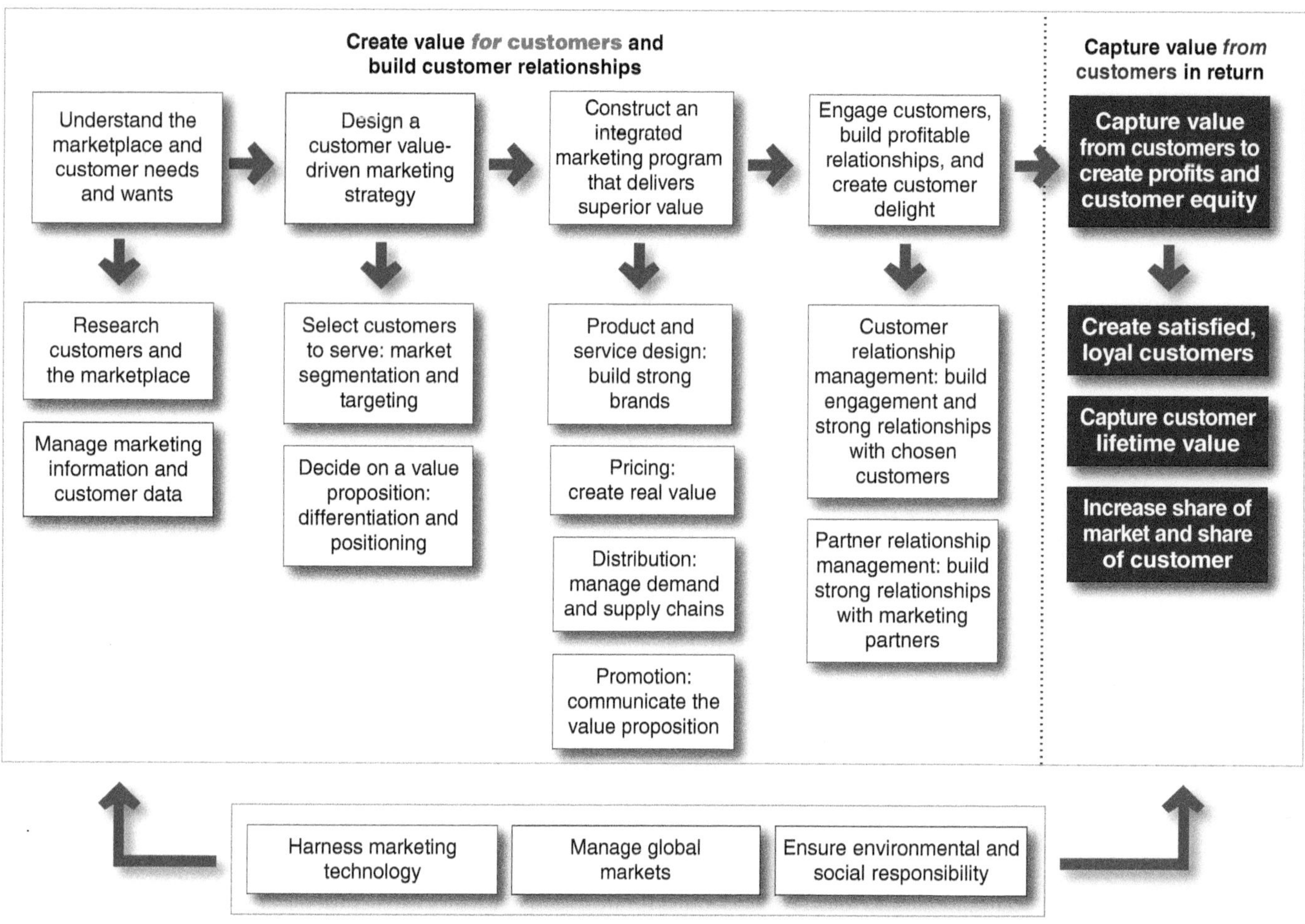
Create value for customers and build customer relationships
Capture value from customers in return
Understand the marketplace and customer needs and wants
Design a customer value-driven marketing strategy
Construct an integrated marketing program that delivers superior value
Engage customers, build profitable relationships, and create customer delight
Capture value from customers to create profits and customer equity
Research customers and the marketplace
Manage marketing information and customer data
Select customers to serve: market segmentation and targeting
Decide on a value proposition: differentiation and positioning
Product and service design: build strong brands
Pricing: create real value
Distribution: manage demand and supply chains
Promotion: communicate the value proposition
Customer relationship management: build engagement and strong relationships with chosen customers
Partner relationship management: build strong relationships with marketing partners
Create satisfied, loyal customers
Capture customer lifetime value
Increase share of market and share of customer
Harness marketing technology
Manage global markets
Ensure environmental and social responsibility

This expanded version of Figure 1.1 at the beginning of the chapter provides a good road map for the rest of the text. The underlying concept of the entire text is that marketing creates value for customers in order to capture value from customers in return.

strategy based on the answers to two simple questions. The first question is "What consumers will we serve?" (market segmentation and targeting). Good marketing companies know that they cannot serve all customers in every way. Instead, they need to focus their resources on the customers they can serve best and most profitably. The second marketing strategy question is "How can we best serve targeted customers?" (differentiation and positioning). Here, the marketer outlines a value proposition that spells out what values the company will deliver to win target customers.

With its marketing strategy chosen, the company now constructs an integrated marketing program—consisting of a blend of the four marketing mix elements, the four Ps—that transforms the marketing strategy into real value for customers. The company develops product offers and creates strong brand identities for them. It prices these offers to create real customer value and distributes the offers to make them available to target consumers. Finally, the company designs promotion programs that engage target customers, communicate the value proposition, and persuade customers to act on the market offering.

Perhaps the most important step in the marketing process involves building value-laden, profitable relationships with target customers. Throughout the process, marketers practice customer relationship management to create customer satisfaction and delight. They engage customers in the process of creating brand conversations, experiences, and community. In creating customer value and relationships, however, the company cannot go it alone. It must work closely with marketing partners both inside the company and throughout its marketing system. Thus, beyond practicing good customer relationship management and customer-engagement marketing, firms must also practice good partner relationship management.

The first four steps in the marketing process create value for customers. In the final step, the company reaps the rewards of its strong customer relationships by capturing value from customers. Delivering superior customer value creates highly satisfied customers who will buy more, buy again, and advocate for the brand. This helps the company capture customer lifetime value and greater share of customer. The result is increased long-term customer equity for the firm.

Finally, in the face of today's changing marketing landscape, companies must consider three additional factors. In building customer and partner relationships, they must harness marketing technologies in the new digital age, take advantage of global opportunities, and ensure that they act sustainably in an environmentally and socially responsible way.

Figure 1.6 provides a good road map to future chapters of this text. Chapters 1 and 2 introduce the marketing process, with a focus on building customer relationships and capturing value from customers. Chapters 3 through 5 address the first step of the marketing process—understanding the marketing environment, managing marketing information, and understanding consumer and business buyer behavior. In Chapter 6, we look more deeply into the two major marketing strategy decisions: selecting which customers to serve (segmentation and targeting) and determining a value proposition (differentiation and positioning). Chapters 7 through 14 discuss the marketing mix variables one by one. The final two chapters examine special marketing considerations: global marketing and sustainable marketing.

Developing Skills for Your Career

Marketing is an exciting, fast-changing discipline that offers a wide range of rewarding careers. See Appendix 4, Careers in Marketing, to see if one of these careers is right for you. But even if you're not planning a career in marketing or business, the lessons you learn in this course will help you in whatever career to choose and in your life more generally. You will acquire and apply many of the skills that employers have identified as critical to success in the workplace, which will contribute to your employability.

In studying this text, you'll sharpen your *critical-thinking* and *problem-solving* skills as you learn about and assess marketing strategies and issues. You'll expand your persuasive *communication* skills as you study and report on how marketers create advertising, digital, social media, and other promotional campaigns that engage consumers and create brand relationships. You'll see how *technology and marketing analytics* are dramatically reshaping the marketing world and even apply some of these technologies in completing your own analyses of marketing problems. You'll learn the importance of *collaboration and teamwork* as you see how marketers work closely with others on their marketing teams and with managers in other company areas to develop overall organizational strategies and tactics. And you'll learn more about *business ethics and social responsibility*, from sections in the very first chapter through the final chapter on sustainable marketing.

During the course, your professors will help you to improve your critical thinking, analytical, communication, presentation, and teamwork skills through meaningful assignments, perhaps from the end-of-chapter exercises, cases, or appendixes in this text. Finally, beyond business applications, you'll see that marketing applies to your life more generally. For the rest of your life, you will be marketing yourself to others. In fact, a favorite tactic of some employers during job interviewers is to give you this challenge: "Pretend you are a product and market yourself to me." After taking this course and studying this text, you should have ready answers.

REVIEWING AND EXTENDING THE CONCEPTS

CHAPTER REVIEW AND KEY TERMS

Objectives Review

Today's successful companies—whether large or small, for-profit or not-for-profit, domestic or global—share a strong customer focus and a heavy commitment to marketing. The goal of marketing is to engage customers and manage profitable customer relationships.

OBJECTIVE 1-1 Define marketing and outline the steps in the marketing process. (pp 4–6)

Marketing is the process by which companies engage customers, build strong customer relationships, and create customer value in order to capture value from customers in return. The marketing process involves five steps. The first four steps create value for customers. First, marketers need to understand the marketplace and customer needs and wants. Next, marketers design a customer value-driven marketing strategy with the goal of getting, engaging, and growing target customers. In the third step, marketers construct a marketing program that actually delivers superior value. All of these steps form the basis for the fourth step: engaging customers, building profitable customer relationships, and creating customer delight. In the final step, the company reaps the rewards of strong customer relationships by capturing value from customers.

OBJECTIVE 1-2 Explain the importance of understanding the marketplace and customers and identify the five core marketplace concepts. (pp 6–10)

Outstanding marketing companies go to great lengths to learn about and understand their customers' needs, wants, and demands. This understanding helps them to design want satisfying market offerings and build value-laden customer relationships by which they can capture customer lifetime value and greater share of customer. The result is increased long-term customer equity for the firm. The core marketplace concepts are needs, wants, and demands; market offerings (products, services, and experiences); value and satisfaction; exchange and relationships; and markets. Companies address needs, wants, and demands by putting forth a value proposition, a set of benefits that they promise to consumers to satisfy their needs. The value proposition is fulfilled through a market offering, which delivers customer value and satisfaction, resulting in long-term exchange relationships with customers.

OBJECTIVE 1-3 Identify the key elements of a customer value-driven marketing strategy and discuss the marketing management orientations that guide marketing strategy. (pp 10–14)

To design a winning marketing strategy, the company must first decide whom it will serve. It does this by dividing the market into segments of customers (market segmentation) and selecting which segments it will cultivate (target marketing). Next, the company must decide how it will serve targeted customers (how it will differentiate and position itself in the marketplace).

Marketing management can adopt one of five competing market orientations. The production concept holds that management's task is to improve production efficiency and bring down prices. The product concept holds that consumers favor products that offer the most in quality, performance, and innovative features; thus, little promotional effort is required. The selling concept holds that consumers will not buy enough of an organization's products unless it undertakes a large-scale selling and promotion effort. The marketing concept holds that achieving organizational goals depends on determining the needs and wants of target markets and delivering the desired satisfactions more effectively and efficiently than competitors do. The societal marketing concept holds that generating customer satisfaction and long-run societal well-being through sustainable marketing strategies is key to both achieving the company's goals and fulfilling its responsibilities.

OBJECTIVE 1-4 Discuss customer relationship management and identify strategies for creating value for customers and capturing value from customers in return. (pp 15–23)

Broadly defined, customer relationship management is the process of engaging customers and building and maintaining profitable customer relationships by delivering superior customer value and satisfaction. Customer-engagement marketing aims to make a brand a meaningful part of consumers' conversations and lives through direct and continuous customer involvement in shaping brand conversations, experiences, and community. The aim of customer relationship management and customer engagement is to produce high customer equity, the total combined customer lifetime values of all the company's customers. The key to building lasting relationships is the creation of superior customer value and satisfaction. In return for creating value for targeted customers, the company captures value from customers in the form of profits and customer equity.

OBJECTIVE 1-5 Describe the major trends and forces that are changing the marketing landscape in this age of relationships. (pp 23–31)

Dramatic changes are occurring in the marketing arena. The digital age has created exciting new ways to learn about, engage, and relate to individual customers. As a result, advances in digital, social, and mobile media have taken the marketing world by storm. Online, mobile, and social media marketing offer exciting new opportunities to target customers more selectively and engage them more deeply. And today's big data and improved marketing analytics, such as artificial intelligence, are enhancing how marketers learn about and interact with customers. The key is to blend the new digital technologies and approaches with traditional marketing to create a smoothly integrated marketing strategy and mix.

In recent years, marketing has become a major part of the strategies for many not-for-profit organizations, such as colleges, hospitals, museums, zoos, symphony orchestras, foundations, and even churches. Also, in an increasingly smaller world, many marketers are now connected globally with their customers, marketing partners, and competitors. Finally, today's marketers are also reexamining their sustainability responsibilities. Marketers are being called on to take greater responsibility for the social and environmental impacts of their actions.

Pulling it all together, as discussed throughout the chapter, the major new developments in marketing can be summed up in a single concept: engaging customers and creating and capturing customer value. Today, marketers of all kinds are taking advantage of new opportunities for building value-laden relationships with their customers, their marketing partners, and the world around them.

Key Terms

Objective 1-1
Marketing (p 5)

Objective 1-2
Needs (p 6)
Wants (p 6)
Demands (p 6)
Market offerings (p 7)
Marketing myopia (p 7)
Exchange (p 9)
Market (p 9)

Objective 1-3
Marketing management (p 10)
Production concept (p 11)
Product concept (p 12)
Selling concept (p 12)
Marketing concept (p 12)
Societal marketing concept (p 13)

Objective 1-4
Customer relationship management (p 15)
Customer-perceived value (p 15)
Customer satisfaction (p 16)
Customer-engagement marketing (p 17)
Consumer-generated marketing (p 19)
Partner relationship management (p 20)
Customer lifetime value (p 20)
Share of customer (p 21)
Customer equity (p 21)

Objective 1-5
Digital and social media marketing (p 24)

DISCUSSION AND CRITICAL THINKING

Discussion Questions

1-1. How does the marketing process create value for customers and the company? (AACSB: Written and Oral Communication; Reflective Thinking)

1-2. What is a market offering? Give a recent example of a market offering that has satisfied your need or want. (AACSB: Written and Oral Communication; Reflective Thinking)

1-3. Define marketing management, and explain how marketing managers design winning marketing strategies. (AACSB: Written and Oral Communication; Reflective Thinking)

1-4. Discuss the concept of customer satisfaction. How do customer relationship management and customer-perceived value impact customer satisfaction? (AACSB: Written and Oral Communication; Reflective Thinking)

1-5. What are the outcomes of creating superior customer value? Why should companies pay attention to these outcomes? (AACSB: Written and Oral Communication; Reflective Thinking)

1-6. Explain the growing importance of digital and social media marketing. (AACSB: Written and Oral Communication; Reflective Thinking)

Critical Thinking Exercises

1-7. In small groups, using the five core customer and marketplace concepts, discuss how the following companies address the first step in the marketing process: (a) Uber, (b) Dunkin', (c) Dannon, and (d) McDonald's. (AACSB: Written and Oral Communication; Information Technology; Reflective Thinking)

1-8. Examine how your college or university creates value for the customers it serves. How does your institution differentiate and position itself? Outline its integrated marketing program from your own perspective. Is it successful? Why or why not? (AACSB: Written and Oral Communication; Analytical Thinking)

1-9. Visit http://tide.com/en-us. Scroll to the bottom of the page, and notice how Tide is currently connecting with customers on social media platforms including Facebook, Twitter, Pinterest, and YouTube. Click on one or more of the platforms to view ways in which Tide is building and maintaining customer linkages while illustrating value and providing information about the brand. Evaluate Tide's effectiveness in creating customer engagement. (AACSB: Written and Oral Communication, Information Technology, Reflective Thinking)

MINICASES AND APPLICATIONS

Online, Mobile, and Social Media Marketing The ALS Ice Bucket Challenge

In the summer of 2014, people with connections to ALS (Lou Gehrig's disease) raised awareness of the condition by urging people to post videos of themselves dumping buckets of ice water over their heads and to challenge others to do the same. The efforts raised millions of dollars in online donations to the ALS Association for enhanced research and patient services. This real-time marketing campaign generated 17 million videos uploaded to social media platforms from 159 countries. Celebrities posting videos available on YouTube included Will Smith, Bill Gates, Oprah Winfrey, and Mark Zuckerberg. The Ice Bucket Challenge generated 70 billion video views and raised $220 million. The best part? Zero dollars were spent to promote the Ice Bucket Challenge, yet 440 million people saw it. The ALS Association has now expanded the wildly successful challenge into several opportunities to support the fight against ALS. For more information, visit http://alsa.org/fight-als/teamchallengeals and alsa.org/fight-als/challenge.

1-10. Real-time marketing lets marketers digitally link brands to important moments in customers' lives. Explain how real-time marketing was used in the Ice Bucket Challenge. Why was this campaign successful? (AACSB: Written and Oral Communication; Reflective Thinking)

1-11. Create a real-time marketing campaign for a product or service of your choice to create customer engagement using online, mobile, and social media. How would you measure the success of your campaign? (AACSB: Written and Oral Communication; Reflective Thinking)

Marketing Ethics Is Big Brother Watching?

Retailers commonly track their customer's shopping patterns and target them with special offers. For example, CVS has an Extracare card that, when swiped at checkout, applies discounts to purchases and provides rebates called Extra Bucks to be used as cash on future purchases. Behind the scenes, CVS is gathering data on customers' purchases and using aggregated data to target individuals with special offers. Customers who haven't recently shopped may receive a discount in the mail or an online offer to incentivize them to return. Frequent shoppers can scan their Extracare cards to get discounts and offers in the store.

1-12. Is it right for marketers to track consumer purchases? Should consumers be concerned with what information is being used? (AACSB: Written and Oral Communication; Ethical Understanding and Reasoning; Reflective Thinking)

1-13. Discuss other examples of marketers using data collection to sell products. Is this ethical? (AACSB: Written and Oral Communication; Ethical Understanding and Reasoning)

Marketing by the Numbers Gillette Trying to Shave Off Competition

Gillette, Procter & Gamble's powerhouse razor brand, is experiencing challenges from consumer trends and upstart digital competitors. Gillette and close competitor Schick have focused on product innovation and higher prices. Indeed, their cartridges first contained two blades, then three, and now five. Razors now have swiveling balls that let the blades pivot, some used to vibrate, and Gillette recently applied for a patent for a razor that heats up. And with each addition, prices have increased accordingly. Even though Gillette produces excellent products that garnered $1.5 billion in sales last year, it faces threats posed by the continuing consumer trend of "beardedness," such as the "scruff" or "stubble" look that's not likely to go away soon. Online upstarts like Dollar Shave Club, Harry's, and 800Razor.com are also eating away at Gillette's sales. And when Gillette's patent expired on its Mach3 razor, rival Schick came out with a less expensive compatible refill blade cartridge. Although Gillette still captures more than 50 percent market share in the men's grooming market, its market share has dropped from 70 percent in 2010. To help win back share, Gillette launched its own Gillette Shave Club in 2016. But the brand's most significant change was to focus less on product innovation and implement an average 12 percent across-the-board price cut.

1-14. Assuming a contribution margin of 60 percent, what sales would be necessary to break even (that is, maintain the current total contribution) on the 12 percent across-the-board price reduction? Refer to Financial Analysis of Marketing Tactics: Price Decrease in Appendix 3: Marketing by the Numbers to learn how to perform this analysis. (AACSB: Written and Oral Communication; Analytical Thinking)

1-15. What absolute increase and percentage increase in sales does this represent? (AACSB: Written and Oral Communication; Analytical Thinking)

Company Cases 1 Chick-fil-A/4 Qualtrics/11 Bass Pro Shops

See Appendix 1 for cases appropriate for this chapter.

Case 1, Chick-fil-A: Getting Better before Getting Bigger. Chick-fil-A has quietly become the largest chicken chain by holding tenaciously to the philosophy that the most sustainable way to do business is to provide the best possible customer experience.

Case 4, Qualtrics: Managing the Complete Customer Experience. Qualtrics pioneered the online survey. Now, it employs online surveys toward managing customer experience.

Case 11, Bass Pro Shops: Creating Nature's Theme Park for People Who Hate to Shop. Bass Pro Shops became the largest sporting goods retailer by providing the broadest assortment of products and enticing customers with engaging experiences.

Video Case Eskimo Joe's

To view this video case and its accompanying questions, please visit MyLab Marketing.

Since 1975, Eskimo Joe's has been a popular watering hole in Stillwater, Oklahoma. Through word of mouth and a popular logo spread via T-shirts, it rapidly became a favorite place to grab a beer for students at Oklahoma State. But what started as a basic beer joint has grown into something much more. When the drinking age changed from 18 to 21 in the 1980s, Eskimo Joe's had to decide how it would move forward. That challenge helped the company to recognize that its product is much more than just a cold mug of beer. Instead, people flocked to Eskimo Joe's for the fun atmosphere and customer-friendly service. This realization led to an expansion into different businesses that have now spread the Eskimo Joe's logo all over the planet.

Writing Assignments

1-16. Compare and contrast needs, wants, and demands. Which one(s) can marketers influence? (AACSB: Communication; Reflective Thinking)

1-17. Is it fair to single out specific products for restrictions such as when New York City proposed size cap on soft drinks? Discuss this argument from all sides of this issue: government, soft drink marketers, and consumers. (AACSB: Written and Oral Communication; Reflective Thinking)

2 Company and Marketing Strategy

Partnering to Build Customer Engagement, Value, and Relationships

Objectives Outline

- OBJECTIVE 2-1 **Explain company-wide strategic planning and its four steps.** See: Company-Wide Strategic Planning: Defining Marketing's Role (pp 38–40)
- OBJECTIVE 2-2 **Discuss how to design business portfolios and develop growth strategies.** See: Designing the Business Portfolio (pp 40–46)
- OBJECTIVE 2-3 **Explain marketing's role in strategic planning and how marketing works with its partners to create and deliver customer value.** See Planning Marketing: Partnering to Build Customer Relationships (pp 46–48)
- OBJECTIVE 2-4 **Describe the elements of a customer value-driven marketing strategy and mix and the forces that influence them.** See: Marketing Strategy and the Marketing Mix (pp 48–54)
- OBJECTIVE 2-5 **List the marketing management functions, including the elements of a marketing plan, and discuss the importance of measuring and managing marketing return on investment.** See: Managing the Marketing Effort and Marketing Return on Investment (pp 54–59)

Previewing the Concepts

In the first chapter, we explored the marketing process by which companies create value for customers to capture value from them in return. In this chapter, we dig deeper into steps two and three of that process: designing customer value-driven marketing strategies and constructing marketing programs. First, we look at the organization's overall strategic planning, which guides marketing strategy and planning. Next, we discuss how, guided by the strategic plan, marketers partner closely with others inside and outside the firm to engage customers and create value for them. We then examine marketing strategy and planning—how marketers choose target markets, position their market offerings, develop a marketing mix, and manage their marketing programs. Finally, we look at the important step of measuring and managing marketing return on investment (marketing ROI).

First, let's look at Starbucks, a good company and a good marketing strategy story. Starbucks met with enormous early success by focusing not just on coffee but on the coffee-drinking experience. The company has since taken a bumpy ride from boom to bust and back to boom again. Along the way, it learned that good marketing strategy means more than just growth, sales, and profits. It means skillfully engaging customers and creating value for them. At its core, Starbucks doesn't sell just coffee, it sells "The Starbucks Experience."

First Stop

Starbucks's Marketing Strategy: Delivering "The Starbucks Experience"

More than 30 years ago, Howard Schultz transformed the coffee industry by bringing a European-style coffeehouse to America. He believed that people needed to slow down—to "smell the coffee" and to enjoy life a little more. The result was Starbucks, founded with a whole new strategy for engaging customers and creating customer value.

Starbucks didn't sell just coffee, it sold "The Starbucks Experience"—"an uplifting experience that enriches people's lives one moment, one human being, one extraordinary cup of coffee at a time." Starbucks gave customers what it calls a "third place"—a place away from home and away from work. At Starbucks, the smells, the sound of beans grinding, and watching baristas blend and brew the brand's specialty coffees all became as much or more a part of the customer experience as the coffee itself.

» More than just coffee, Starbucks sells "The Starbucks Experience," one that "enriches people's lives one moment, one human being, one extraordinary cup of coffee at a time."

Andrew Aitchison/Alamy Stock Photo

Over the next two decades, customers flocked to Starbucks cafés. By 2007, some 15,000 Starbucks stores dotted the nation and globe, and the company's sales and profits rose like steam off a mug of hot java. However, Starbucks's enormous success drew a host of competitors. It seemed that every rival—from independent coffeehouses to fast-food restaurants—was peddling its own brand of premium coffee.

To maintain its phenomenal growth in the increasingly overcaffeinated marketplace, Starbucks brewed up an ambitious growth strategy. It opened new stores at a breakneck pace, seemingly everywhere. For example, one three-block stretch in Chicago contained six of the trendy coffee bars. In New York City, there were two Starbucks in one Macy's store. In fact, cramming so many stores so close together caused one satirical publication to run this headline: "A New Starbucks Opens in the Restroom of Existing Starbucks." The company also blanketed the country with Starbucks kiosks and coffee stands in everything from Target stores and supermarkets to hotel lobbies, and service businesses from airlines to car dealerships proclaimed, "We proudly serve Starbucks coffee."

The more Starbucks grew, however, the more it drifted away from the core mission and values that had made it so successful. The company's almost obsessive focus on growth for growth's sake began to take a toll on the prized Starbucks Experience. Far from its roots as a warm and intimate coffeehouse, Starbucks began to evolve into more of a caffeine filling station. More and more, the premium brand found itself competing with the likes of—gasp!—McDonald's for many of the same customers.

Founder Howard Schultz, who had stepped down as CEO in 2000, expressed concern. In a 2007 memo to Starbucks management, Schultz lamented that the company's push for growth had "led to the watering down of the Starbucks Experience" and that Starbucks was "losing its soul." Schultz was right that something was wrong. By early 2008, when Schultz reassumed his role as Starbucks president and CEO, the company found itself in hot water. For the first time ever, the average number of transactions per U.S. store fell off, and same-store sales growth slowed. Within just the previous two years, Starbucks's stock had tumbled nearly 80 percent. According to one analyst, "The financial vultures circled. Obituaries were drafted."

Instead of presiding over the brand's demise, however, Schultz reacted quickly to restore its luster. He cooled the pace of Starbucks's growth, closed underperforming locations, and replaced most of the company's top executives. Most important, Schultz laid plans to reestablish the brand's core mission and values and to refocus the company on giving customers the authentic Starbucks Experience. "As we grew rapidly and had phenomenal success," Shultz announced, "we started to lose sight of our focus on the customer and our commitment to continually and creatively enhance the Starbucks Experience." Starbucks needed to shift its focus back to customers—to "reignite the emotional attachment with customers."

Starbucks has become America's—the world's—largest coffeehouse by skillfully engaging customers and delivering superior customer value. At its core, Starbucks doesn't sell just coffee. It sells "The Starbucks Experience."

To emphasize the point, at a cost of $30 million, Schultz transported 10,000 Starbucks store managers to New Orleans for a morale-building reorientation. A short time later, Starbucks dramatically closed all of its U.S. locations for three hours to conduct nationwide employee training on the basics of producing satisfying customer experiences.

Those early actions began a process of continual renewal by which Starbucks has reignited the Starbucks customer experience through new products, innovative store formats, and new platforms for engaging customers. Beyond improvements in its signature coffee products, Starbucks has developed new products that take the Starbucks Experience into new areas. For example, a few years ago, Starbucks successfully launched Via, an instant coffee that's as good at home as fresh-brewed is in stores. Since then, Starbucks has developed or acquired various brands that it sells throughout the Starbucks chain including Fizzio (freshly carbonated and handcrafted sodas), Teavana (bottled craft iced teas), and Evolution Fresh (cold-pressed fruit and vegetable juices). To round out the Starbucks experience, the chain has also broadened its premium food options. It now offers everything from hot breakfast entrees to sandwiches and paninis, protein boxes and bowls, and yogurts and fruits. Starbucks expects to double its food business in the next three years.

The company is also rolling out new store formats, such as the high-end Starbucks Reserve Roasteries—part café, part shrine, and part working roaster. Schultz, now chairman emeritus of Starbucks, describes these interactive stores as "Niketown meets Apple meets Starbucks"—think of it as the Starbucks Experience on steroids. These flagship stores are rolling out slowly and only in the world's most cosmopolitan cities, including Shanghai, Milan, New York, Tokyo, and Chicago. In other areas, Starbucks is also creating more than 30 Starbucks Reserve Bars—smaller-scale, more intimate roasteries described as "perfect places to pick up Starbucks Reserve whole bean coffee, enjoy a handcrafted Starbucks Reserve beverage, and chat with a barista about all things coffee."

Beyond employee training, new products, and innovative store formats, Starbucks has been a leader in building customer engagement and brand community through digital and mobile platforms. Its highly successful Starbucks Rewards loyalty program boasts 15 million members. With the Starbucks mobile app, members can order ahead, pay, earn rewards, and learn about new products and special offers. The app now accounts for 20 percent of all in-store transactions. Starbucks thinks of its mobile app as "a direct, real-time, personalized, two-way digital relationship with its customers."

Today, a rejuvenated Starbucks is once again fully engaged with customers and delivering the one-of-a-kind Starbucks Experience. And once again, sales and profits are really perking. Every week, 238,000 Starbucks employees serve more than 75 million customers face-to-face in more than 27,000 stores in 75 countries. Over the past five years, Starbucks's annual revenues have grown by double digits, and profits are at an all-time high.

The moral of the Starbucks story: Good marketing strategy means keeping your eye squarely on delivering customer value. The objective isn't just growth or sales or profits; it's engaging customers in a meaningful way and creating value for them. If a company takes care of customer engagement and value, good performance will result. "It's not just about ringing a register and performing a task," says Schultz. "It's also about creating an emotional, enduring relationship and connection with our . . . customers. At our core, we celebrate the interaction between us and our customers through the coffee experience. Life happens over coffee."[1]

Author Comment
Company-wide strategic planning guides marketing strategy and planning. Like marketing strategy, the company's broader strategy must also be customer focused.

Company-Wide Strategic Planning: Defining Marketing's Role

OBJECTIVE 2-1 Explain company-wide strategic planning and its four steps.

Strategic planning
The process of developing and maintaining a strategic fit between the organization's goals and capabilities and its changing marketing opportunities.

Each company must find the game plan for long-run survival and growth that makes the most sense given its specific situation, opportunities, objectives, and resources. This is the focus of **strategic planning**—the process of developing and maintaining a strategic fit between the organization's goals and capabilities and its changing marketing opportunities.

Strategic planning sets the stage for the rest of planning in the firm. Companies usually prepare annual plans, long-range plans, and strategic plans. The annual and long-range plans deal with the company's current businesses and how to keep them going. In contrast, the strategic plan involves adapting the firm to take advantage of opportunities in its constantly changing environment.

At the corporate level, the company starts the strategic planning process by defining its overall purpose and mission (see >> **Figure 2.1**). This mission is then turned into detailed supporting objectives that guide the entire company. Next, headquarters decides what portfolio of businesses and products is best for the company and how much support to give each one. In turn, each business and product develops detailed marketing and other departmental plans that support the company-wide plan.

Like the marketing strategy, the broader company strategy must be customer focused.

Corporate level

Defining the company mission → Setting company objectives and goals → Designing the business portfolio → Planning marketing and other functional strategies

>> Figure 2.1 Steps in Strategic Planning

Thus, marketing planning occurs at the business-unit, product, and market levels. It supports company strategic planning with more detailed plans for specific marketing opportunities.

Defining a Market-Oriented Mission

An organization exists to accomplish something, and this purpose should be clearly stated. Forging a sound mission begins with the following questions: What *is* our business? Who is the customer? What do consumers value? What *should* our business be? These simple-sounding questions are among the most difficult the company will ever have to answer. Successful companies continuously raise these questions and answer them carefully and completely.

Many organizations develop formal mission statements that answer these questions. A **mission statement** is a statement of the organization's purpose—what it wants to accomplish in the larger environment. A clear mission statement acts as an "invisible hand" that guides people in the organization.

Mission statement
A statement of the organization's purpose—what it wants to accomplish in the larger environment.

Some companies define their missions myopically in product or technology terms ("We make and sell furniture" or "We are a chemical-processing firm"). But mission statements should be *market oriented* and defined in terms of satisfying basic customer needs. Products and technologies eventually become outdated, but basic market needs may last forever. For example, social scrapbooking site Pinterest doesn't define itself as just an online place to post pictures. Its mission is to give people a social media platform for collecting, organizing, and sharing things they love. And Microsoft's mission isn't to create the world's best software, technologies, and devices. It's to empower people across the world to achieve more. >> **Table 2.1** provides several examples of product-oriented versus market-oriented business definitions.[2]

Mission statements should be meaningful and specific yet motivating. Too often, mission statements are written for public relations purposes and lack specific, workable guidelines. Instead, they should emphasize the company's strengths and tell forcefully how it intends to win in the marketplace.

Finally, as we discovered in the chapter-opening Starbucks story, a company's mission should not be stated as making more sales or profits; profits are only a reward for creating

Table 2.1 Product- versus Market-Oriented Business Definitions

Company	Product-Oriented Definition	Market-Oriented Definition
Starbucks	We sell coffee and snacks.	We sell "The Starbucks Experience," one that enriches people's lives one moment, one human being, one extraordinary cup of coffee at a time.
Panera	We sell fast-casual food in our restaurants.	We give customers "Food as it should be": food that tastes good; food that feels good; food that does good things for them and the world around them.
Instagram	We are a social networking app for posting photos and videos.	We help people capture and share the world's moments.
Home Depot	We sell tools and home repair and improvement items.	We empower consumers to achieve the homes of their dreams.
NPR	We are a public radio network.	We create a more informed public—one challenged and invigorated by a deeper understanding and appreciation of events, ideas, and cultures.
Sephora	We are a beauty products retailer.	We sell lifestyle and self-expression by helping customers to unlock their beauty potential.
Ritz-Carlton Hotels & Resorts	We rent rooms.	We create "The Ritz-Carlton experience"—a memorable stay that far exceeds guests' already-high expectations.
Walmart	We run discount stores.	We deliver low prices every day and give ordinary folks the chance to buy the same things as rich people. "Save Money. Live Better."

value for customers. Instead, the mission should focus on customers and the customer experience the firm seeks to create. For example, Ritz-Carlton Hotels & Resorts doesn't see itself as just renting out rooms. It's on a mission to create "The Ritz-Carlton Experience," one that "enlivens the senses, instills well-being, and fulfills even the unexpressed wishes and needs of our guests." Ritz-Carlton follows up this mission with specific steps of service by which every employee can help to turn the mission into reality.[3] Similarly, Airbnb doesn't just help people find places to rent. It lets them "Belong Anywhere"—be insiders when they travel and immerse themselves in local cultures and experiences (see Marketing at Work 2.1).

Setting Company Objectives and Goals

The company needs to turn its broad mission into detailed supporting objectives for each level of management. Each manager should have objectives and be responsible for reaching them. For example, most Americans know CVS as a chain of retail pharmacies selling prescription and over-the-counter medicines, personal care products, and a host of convenience and other items. But CVS Health has a much broader mission. >> It views itself as a "pharmacy innovation company," one that is "helping people on their path to better health." The company's motto: "Health is everything."[4]

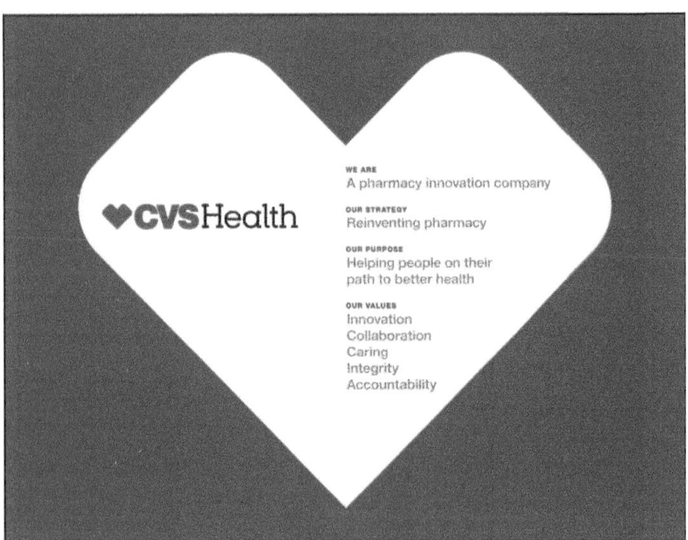

>> CVS Health's overall mission is to be a "pharmacy innovation company," one that is "helping people on their way to better health." Its marketing strategies and programs must support this mission.

CVS Caremark Corporation

CVS Health's broad mission leads to a hierarchy of objectives, including business objectives and marketing objectives. CVS Health's overall business objective is to increase access, lower costs, and improve the quality of care. It does this through the products it sells at its retail pharmacies and by taking a more active role in overall health-care management through research, consumer outreach and education, and support of health-related programs and organizations.

However, such activities are expensive and must be funded through improved profits, so improving profits becomes another major objective for CVS Health. Profits can be improved by increasing sales or by reducing costs. Sales can be increased by improving customer engagement and raising the company's share of the health-care market. These goals then become the company's current marketing objectives.

Marketing strategies and programs must be developed to support these marketing objectives. To increase customer engagement, sales, and market share, CVS Health has reshaped and broadened its lines of products and services. For example, it recently stopped selling tobacco products, items not compatible with its "better health" mission. And it has placed CVS MinuteClinic locations in more than 1,100 of its 9,600 stores, providing walk-in medical care for more than 34 million patient visits since 2000. CVS Health has also broadened its range of customer contact activities to include tailored advising to customers managing chronic and specialty health conditions.

These are CVS Health's broad marketing strategies. Each marketing strategy must then be defined in greater detail. For example, the company's rapidly expanding MinuteClinic services will require more advertising and promotional efforts, and such efforts will need to be spelled out carefully. In this way, CVS Health's broad mission is translated into a set of specific short-term objectives and marketing plans.

Designing the Business Portfolio

OBJECTIVE 2-2 Discuss how to design business portfolios and develop growth strategies.

Business portfolio
The collection of businesses and products that make up the company.

Guided by the company's mission statement and objectives, management now must plan its business portfolio—the collection of businesses and products that make up the company. The best **business portfolio** is the one that best fits the company's strengths and weaknesses to opportunities in the environment.

MARKETING AT WORK 2.1

Airbnb's Mission: Belong Anywhere—Don't Stay There. Live There.

Airbnb has revolutionized the hospitality industry. In little over 10 years, the tech startup that popularized staying at the homes of strangers has built a global network of 4.5 million listings and 300 million guests in 191 countries. That's stunning, especially when compared to the size of the world's largest hotel chain—90-year-old Marriott International—with its 1.2 million rooms across 6,500 properties in 122 countries. Airbnb has become so pervasive that many customers use the brand as a verb—as in "Let's go to Chicago for the weekend. We'll Airbnb a place downtown!"

It all started when Airbnb founders Brian Chesky and Joe Gebbia decided to make some extra income to help pay the rent on their modest San Francisco loft apartment by renting out three air mattresses on the apartment's floor at $40 a night each (hence the "air" in Airbnb). Chesky and Gebbia quickly realized that people who booked their air mattresses got a lot more than just a cheap place to stay. They got an authentic "live-like-the-locals" experience. The idea blossomed into Airbnb, an online lodgings marketplace that matches people who need a place to stay with property owners who have room to spare.

The basic Airbnb model is conceptually simple. It starts with *hosts*—Airbnb's official term for property owners with space to rent—who register and are vetted for legitimacy. Listings can include anything from a couch, single room, suite of rooms, or apartment to moored yachts, entire houses, or even a castle. Some hosts even rent space in their yards for guests to pitch a tent. Each location is as unique as its owner.

For *guests*, using Airbnb is like buying or booking almost anything else online. Registered users search by city, room type, price range, amenities, host language, and other options. Most listings provide photos and details that give potential guests a good idea of what their stay will be like. Guests can contact potential hosts with questions before booking. Bookings are made through Airbnb, so money changes hands only through a secure interface. When guests arrive at the property, the host either greets them or arranges for entry.

At first, Airbnb attracted mostly venturesome travelers looking for cheap and cool places to stay. Other potential customers shied away, unwilling to accept the risk or discomfort of staying with strangers. But the concept caught on and Airbnb grew rapidly. More than the cookie-cutter rooms and impersonal travel experiences offered by conventional hotels, people warmed to Airbnb's authenticity and the unique experiences that Airbnb lodgings offered.

That realization marked a major turning point for Airbnb and its founders. Chesky and Gebbia came to realize that Airbnb provided much more than just spaces to rent. They began a search for the brand's soul, asking difficult but important questions: "We asked ourselves, 'What is our mission? What is the big idea that truly defines Airbnb?'" says Chesky.

To find answers, the Airbnb team interviewed hundreds of guests and hosts around the world. Time and again, they heard

» Belong Anywhere: Airbnb's mission is to help create a world where you can belong anywhere, and where people can live a place instead of just travelling to it. The brand's bélo logo is "the universal symbol of belonging."

M4OS Photos/Alamy Stock Photo

guests say that the last thing they wanted was to be tourists. Instead, Airbnb customers wanted to be insiders; to engage with people and immerse themselves in local cultures. According to the company, 86 percent of users picked Airbnb because they wanted to live more like a local. They wanted to *belong*.

So in 2014, Airbnb launched a new company mission: To help create a world where you can belong anywhere, and where people can live a place instead of just travelling to it. The new mission inspired a new brand tagline—"Belong Anywhere"—and a new brand symbol, the bélo. Carefully conceived to contain the "A" in Airbnb, a heart, and a location pin, Airbnb casts the bélo as "the universal symbol of belonging."

Airbnb's "Belong Anywhere" mission is more than just a plaque on the wall at corporate headquarters or an inspirational statement on the About page of its website. Instead, the mission drives everything the company does, from its travel offerings to its marketing campaigns. Airbnb sees itself not just as a rooms provider but as a curator of unique and authentic "belonging" experiences.

The essence of the Airbnb experience is rooted in the company's hosts, which Airbnb sees as its first-line customers. The company has nurtured a huge global community of lodging providers who are true believers in the Airbnb vision. Airbnb encourages hosts to follow certain guidelines. However, although the guidelines may suggest certain services to guests, such as airport pickup or walking tours, Airbnb gives hosts complete autonomy to shape unique guest experiences. The overriding rule: create belonging.

Shortly after launching the new mission, Chesky addressed a crowd of hosts in Paris at Airbnb's annual host event, called the Airbnb Open. He gave this advice: "What's special in your world isn't just the home you have. It's your whole life." As part of his presentation, Chesky shared pictures relating the experiences of his own parents in Paris as they attended that year's Airbnb Open. On the first day, they did the usual touristy stuff, hosted by typical tourist guides. "Every year, 30 million people go to Paris," noted Chesky. "They look at everything and they see nothing." Chesky then showed images from his parents' second day in Paris—guided by some of Airbnb's top hosts—where they experienced the city from the perspective of locals. They had coffee at an authentic sidewalk café, took a walk in a garden, and drank and danced at a cozy Parisian nightclub. "Maybe we should not *travel to* Paris," suggested Chesky. "Maybe what we should do is *live in* Paris."

Airbnb is quick to point out that "belonging" doesn't have to be about having tea and cookies with a host. Many hosts don't live in the lodgings they share, and many guests don't actually want to meet the host. More broadly, belonging means hanging out in someone else's space and having a local experience "hosted" by that person, even if the host is not present. It means venturing into local spots guests might not otherwise see and doing things they might not otherwise do. Airbnb sees the optimal "belonging" experience as a transformational journey.

To broaden its offerings under the new mission, Airbnb introduced Experiences, a platform that lets customers book not just lodging but also one- or two-day excursions with locals, ranging from hiking with wolves in a nature conservatory to singing in a Harlem gospel choir to making a from-scratch pasta meal with two chefs in Florence. "These aren't tours," says Chesky, "You immerse yourself, you join the local communities."

Airbnb has also launched an expanded array of lodging experiences. Airbnb Plus offers a selection of high-quality, well-equipped homes with hosts known for great reviews and attention to detail. And for really discerning customers, Airbnb Beyond offers premium luxury in extravagant homes with high-end options, such as booking a butler or personal chef.

Airbnb's mission and positioning are embodied by the company's "Don't go there. Live there!" ad campaign. Different ads feature people experiencing an artist loft in Tokyo, a quiet Los Angeles retreat, or a cozy Paris apartment. But the ads suggest that guests are getting much more than just a place to stay. The first ad opens with people doing ho-hum standard tours of Paris landmarks like the Eiffel Tower and the Arc de Triomphe, admonishing, "Don't go to Paris. Don't tour Paris, and please don't do Paris." Instead, as it cuts to warm scenes of people letting loose and hanging out like locals, the ad urges "*Live* in Paris. Even if it's just for a day." For Airbnb, that's mission accomplished. With Airbnb, you "Belong Anywhere."

Sources: Leigh Gallagher, "How Airbnb Found a Mission and a Brand," *Fortune*, January 1, 2017, pp. 56–62; Leigh Gallagher, "Here's How 'Experiences' Are Doing So Far," *Fortune*, October 23, 2017, http://fortune.com/2017/10/23/airbnb-ceo-experiences-new-york/; Katie Richards, "Put Away the Selfie Stick and Live Like a Local, Urges Airbnb's New Campaign," *Adweek*, April 19, 2016, www.adweek.com/brand-marketing/put-away-selfie-stick-and-live-local-urges-airbnbs-new-campaign-170920/; Ruth Reader, "On Its 10th Birthday, Airbnb Just Launched High-End Options to Lure Discerning Travelers," *Fast Company*, February 22, 2018, www.fastcompany.com/40534726/on-its-10th-birthday-airbnb-just-launched-high-end-options-to-lure-discerning-travelers; Max Chafkin, "Airbnb Opens Up the World?" *Fast Company*, February 2016, pp. 76-95; and additional information from www.airbnb.com and https://blog.atairbnb.com/belong-anywhere/, accessed September 2018.

Most large companies have complex portfolios of businesses and brands. » For example, you probably know Mars Inc. as the world's number one candy maker. The giant $35 billion company makes some of the world's best-loved confectionary brands, including M&M's, Snickers, Mars, Twix, Skittles, Starburst, Altoids, and Wrigley and Orbit gums. It also owns the Uncle Ben's rice brand.

» Complex business portfolios: You probably know Mars Inc. as the world's number one candy maker. But did you know that it's also a world-leading pet nutrition and health-care company?

Randy Duchaine/Alamy Stock Photo

But did you know that Mars is also a world-leading pet nutrition and health-care company? Its leading pet food brands include Iams, Royal Canin, Eukanuba, Whiskas, and Pedigree—the world's number one dog food brand. It also owns several pet hospital, doggie daycare, and veterinary services companies, including Banfield, Blue Pearl, and VCA pet hospitals. Mars even has growing businesses in canine DNA testing and GPS pet tracking and monitoring. In all, Mars sells more pet care products and services than candy. Strategic and marketing planning for such a complex business portfolio can be a daunting but critical task. Through skillful portfolio management, however, Mars profitably manages its broad portfolio under its founding mission of "doing business for the betterment of all" and five guiding principles: "quality, responsibility, mutuality, efficiency, and freedom."[5]

Business portfolio planning involves two steps. First, the company must analyze its *current* business portfolio and determine which businesses should receive more, less, or no investment. Second, it must shape the *future* portfolio by developing strategies for growth and downsizing.

Analyzing the Current Business Portfolio

Portfolio analysis
The process by which management evaluates the products and businesses that make up the company.

The major activity in strategic planning is business **portfolio analysis**, whereby management evaluates the products and businesses that make up the company. The company will want to put strong resources into its more profitable businesses and phase down or drop its weaker ones.

Management's first step is to identify the key businesses that make up the company, called *strategic business units* (SBUs). An SBU can be a company division, a product line within a division, or sometimes a single product or brand. The company next assesses the attractiveness of its various SBUs and decides how much support each deserves. When designing a business portfolio, it's a good idea to add and support products and businesses that fit closely with the firm's core philosophy and competencies.

The purpose of strategic planning is to find ways in which the company can best use its strengths to take advantage of attractive opportunities in the environment. For this reason, most standard portfolio analysis methods evaluate SBUs on two important dimensions: the attractiveness of the SBU's market or industry and the strength of the SBU's position in that market or industry. The best-known portfolio-planning method was developed by the Boston Consulting Group, a leading management consulting firm.[6]

The Boston Consulting Group Approach

Growth-share matrix
A portfolio-planning method that evaluates a company's SBUs in terms of market growth rate and relative market share.

Using the now-classic Boston Consulting Group (BCG) approach, a company classifies all its SBUs according to the **growth-share matrix**, as shown in >> **Figure 2.2**. On the vertical axis, *market growth rate* provides a measure of market attractiveness. On the horizontal axis, *relative market share* serves as a measure of company strength in the market. The growth-share matrix defines four types of SBUs:

1. ***Stars.*** Stars are high-growth, high-share businesses or products. They often need heavy investments to finance their rapid growth. Eventually their growth will slow down, and they will turn into cash cows.
2. ***Cash cows.*** Cash cows are low-growth, high-share businesses or products. These established and successful SBUs need less investment to hold their market share. Thus, they produce a lot of the cash that the company uses to pay its bills and support other SBUs that need investment.

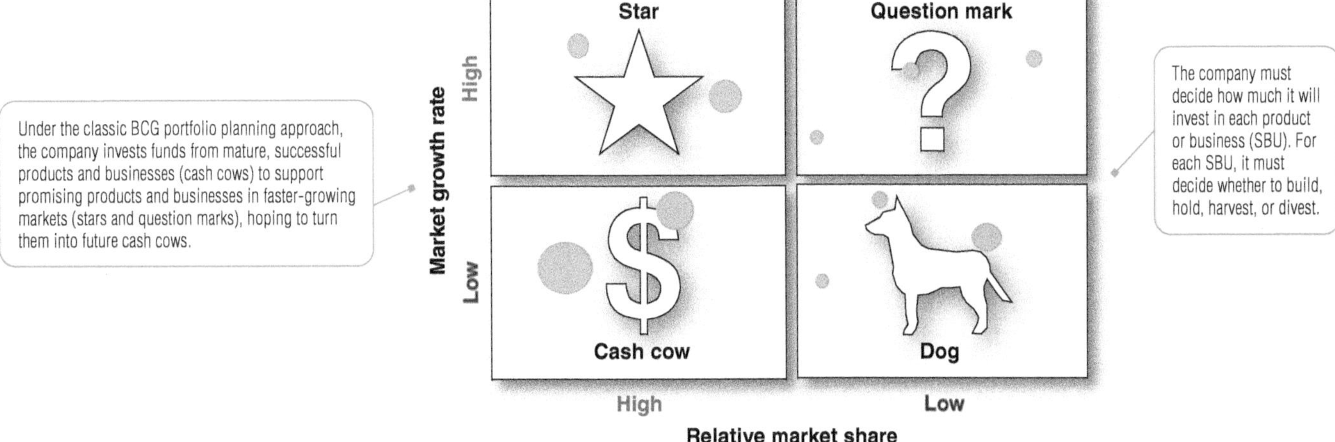
Under the classic BCG portfolio planning approach, the company invests funds from mature, successful products and businesses (cash cows) to support promising products and businesses in faster-growing markets (stars and question marks), hoping to turn them into future cash cows.
Market growth rate
High
Low
Star
Question mark
Cash cow
Dog
High
Low
Relative market share
The company must decide how much it will invest in each product or business (SBU). For each SBU, it must decide whether to build, hold, harvest, or divest.

>> **Figure 2.2 The BCG Growth-Share Matrix**

3. ***Question marks.*** Question marks are low-share business units in high-growth markets. They require a lot of cash to hold their share, let alone increase it. Management has to think hard about which question marks it should try to build into stars and which should be phased out.
4. ***Dogs.*** Dogs are low-growth, low-share businesses and products. They may generate enough cash to maintain themselves but do not promise to be large sources of cash.

The 10 circles in the growth-share matrix represent the company's 10 current SBUs. The company has two stars, two cash cows, three question marks, and three dogs. The area of each circle is proportional to the SBU's dollar sales. This company is in fair shape, although not in good shape. It wants to invest in the more promising question marks to make them stars and maintain the stars so that they will become cash cows as their markets mature. Fortunately, it has two good-sized cash cows. Income from these cash cows will help finance the company's question marks, stars, and dogs. The company should take some decisive action concerning its dogs and its question marks.

Once it has classified its SBUs, the company must determine what role each will play in the future. It can pursue one of four strategies for each SBU. It can invest more in the business unit to *build* its share. Or it can invest just enough to *hold* the SBU's share at the current level. It can *harvest* the SBU, milking its short-term cash flow regardless of the long-term effect. Finally, it can *divest* the SBU by selling it or phasing it out and using the resources elsewhere.

As time passes, SBUs change their positions in the growth-share matrix. Many SBUs start out as question marks and move into the star category if they succeed. They later become cash cows as market growth falls and then finally die off or turn into dogs toward the end of the life cycle. The company needs to add new products and units continuously so that some of them will become stars and, eventually, cash cows that will help finance other SBUs.

Problems with Matrix Approaches

The BCG and other formal methods revolutionized strategic planning. However, such centralized approaches have limitations: They can be difficult, time consuming, and costly to implement. Management may find it difficult to define SBUs and measure market share and growth. In addition, these approaches focus on classifying current businesses but provide little advice for future planning.

Because of such problems, many companies have dropped formal matrix methods in favor of more customized approaches that better suit their specific situations. Moreover, unlike former strategic planning efforts that rested mostly in the hands of senior managers at company headquarters, today's strategic planning has been decentralized. Increasingly, companies are placing responsibility for strategic planning in the hands of cross-functional teams of divisional managers who are close to their markets. In this digital age, such managers have rich and current data at their fingertips and can adapt their plans quickly to meet changing conditions and events in their markets.

Portfolio planning can be challenging. >> For example, consider GE, the giant $124 billion industrial conglomerate operating with a broad portfolio of products in dozens of consumer and business markets:[7]

>> **Business portfolio management: Managing GE's vast and complex portfolio of businesses and its mission to become The Digital Industrial Company will require plenty of skill and lots of GE's famed "Imagination at work."**

Cum Okolo/Alamy Stock Photo

> When most consumers see the familiar GE logo, they think of home appliances and lighting products. But in recent years, GE has dramatically shifted its vast and complex portfolio away from consumer products and financial services toward the goal of becoming "The Digital Industrial Company," one that's more focused on a mission to "invent the next digital industrial era, to build, move, power, and cure the world." A broad array of GE units—such as GE Transportation, GE Power, GE Renewable Energy, GE Aviation, GE Healthcare, and others—offer products

and services ranging from jet engines, diesel-electric locomotives, wind turbines, and offshore drilling solutions to aerospace systems and medical imaging equipment. GE Capital offers a breadth of financial products and services.

Currently, less than 2 percent of GE's annual revenues come from consumer products. The company is in the midst of selling off its huge GE Capital financial services arm, and it recently sold its entire GE Appliances division to Haier. Such portfolio decisions have huge implications for the company's future. For example, prior to the sale of its appliances unit, GE's appliance and lighting businesses alone generated $8.8 billion in annual revenues, more than the total revenues of companies such as JetBlue, Campbell's Soup, Harley-Davidson, or Hershey. Managing GE's broad and complex portfolio will take plenty of management skill and—as GE's long-running corporate slogan suggests—lots of "Imagination at work." In fact, GE has struggle mightily recently to find the right mix of businesses. "We need to continue to move with purpose to reshape GE."

Developing Strategies for Growth and Downsizing

Beyond evaluating current businesses, designing the business portfolio involves finding businesses and products the company should consider in the future. Companies need growth if they are to compete more effectively, satisfy their stakeholders, and attract top talent. At the same time, a firm must be careful not to make growth itself an objective. The company's objective must be to manage "profitable growth."

Marketing has the main responsibility for achieving profitable growth for the company. Marketing needs to identify, evaluate, and select market opportunities and lay down strategies for capturing them. One useful device for identifying growth opportunities is the **product/market expansion grid**, shown in >> **Figure 2.3**.[8] We apply it here to Starbucks.

Product/market expansion grid
A portfolio-planning tool for identifying company growth opportunities through market penetration, market development, product development, or diversification.

As noted in our chapter-opening story, in only three decades, Starbucks has grown at an astounding pace from a small Seattle coffee shop to an over $22 billion powerhouse with more than 27,000 retail stores in more than 75 countries. Growth is the engine that keeps Starbucks perking. To maintain its incredible growth in an increasingly overcaffeinated marketplace, Starbucks must brew up an ambitious, multipronged growth strategy.[9]

Market penetration
Company growth by increasing sales of current products to current market segments without changing the product.

First, Starbucks' management might consider whether the company can achieve deeper **market penetration**—making more sales to current customers without changing its original products. It might add new stores in current market areas to make it easier for customers to visit. In fact, Starbucks opened more than 800 new U.S. stores last year. Starbucks can add new features to its mobile app to enhance customer engagement and loyalty. For example, the recently added My Starbucks Barista feature lets customers order via voice commands or messaging to an artificial intelligence-powered virtual barista. And improvements in Starbucks's advertising, prices, service, store design, or menu selection might encourage customers to stop by more often, stay longer, or buy more during each visit. Thanks to an ever-expanding food menu, sales of breakfast items alone have doubled in the past four years, and food sales currently account for 20 percent of Starbucks' total revenue.

Market development
Company growth by identifying and developing new market segments for current company products.

Second, Starbucks might consider possibilities for **market development**—identifying and developing new markets for its current products. For instance, managers could review new demographic markets. Perhaps new groups—such as seniors—could be encouraged to visit Starbucks shops for the first time or to buy more from them. Managers could also

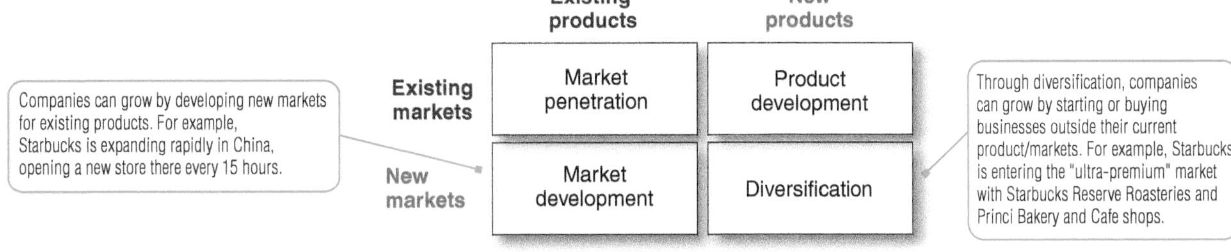

Existing products
New products
Existing markets
New markets
Market penetration
Product development
Market development
Diversification
Companies can grow by developing new markets for existing products. For example, Starbucks is expanding rapidly in China, opening a new store there every 15 hours.
Through diversification, companies can grow by starting or buying businesses outside their current product/markets. For example, Starbucks is entering the "ultra-premium" market with Starbucks Reserve Roasteries and Princi Bakery and Cafe shops.

>> **Figure 2.3 The Product/Market Expansion Grid**

» Strategies for growth: To maintain its incredible growth, Starbucks has brewed up an ambitious, multipronged growth strategy including swift expansion in non-U.S. markets like China.

Jens Kalaene/picture-alliance/dpa/AP Images

review new geographic markets. Starbucks is now expanding swiftly in non-U.S. markets, especially Asia. » For example, the number of Starbucks stores in China has grown from 800 to 3,200 in the past five years, with an average of one new store opening every 15 hours. Starbucks plans to open more than 5,000 stores in China by 2021.

Third, Starbucks could consider **product development** offering modified or new products to current markets. For example, to capture a piece of the fast-growing single-serve beverage market, Starbucks developed Via instant coffee, and it sells its coffees and Tazo teas in K-Cup packs that fit Keurig at-home brewers. And Starbucks continues to expand it lines of ready-to-drink beverages sold in grocery stores, such as Starbucks Doubleshot, Iced Expresso Classics, and Starbucks Refreshers caffeinated pick-me-up drinks.

Finally, Starbucks might consider **diversification**—starting up or buying businesses beyond its current products and markets. For example, the company recently created the ultra-premium Starbucks Reserve brand, with Starbucks Reserve Roasteries and Starbucks Reserve Bars featuring high-end immersive experiences. And within its Starbucks Reserve locations, the company is opening Princi Bakery and Café shops, offering artisan Italian food—from fresh-baked bread and pastries to flakey cornetti to focaccia sandwiches—based on the recipes of famed Italian baker Rocco Princi. Starbucks is also experimenting with stand-alone boutique Princi bakery stores, taking the company beyond coffee and snack shops. Such diversification into premium food and beverage fits well with the brand's "Starbuck Experience" positioning.

Product development
Company growth by offering modified or new products to current market segments.

Diversification
Company growth through starting up or acquiring businesses outside the company's current products and markets.

Companies must develop not only strategies for growing their business portfolios but also strategies for *downsizing* them. There are many reasons that a firm might want to abandon products or markets. A firm may have grown too fast or entered areas where it lacks experience. The market environment might change, making some products or markets less profitable. For example, in difficult economic times, many firms prune out weaker, less-profitable products and markets to focus their more limited resources on the strongest ones. Finally, some products or business units simply age and die.

When a firm finds brands or businesses that are unprofitable or that no longer fit its overall strategy, it must carefully prune, harvest, or divest them. For example, in past years, P&G has sold off dozens of major brands—from Crisco, Folgers, Jif, and Pringles to Duracell batteries, Right Guard deodorant, Aleve pain reliever, CoverGirl and Max Factor cosmetics, Wella and Clairol hair care products, and its Iams and other pet food brands—allowing the company to focus on household care and beauty and grooming products. And in recent years, GM has pruned several underperforming brands from its portfolio, including Oldsmobile, Pontiac, Saturn, Hummer, and Saab. Weak businesses usually require a disproportionate amount of management attention. Managers should focus on promising growth opportunities, not fritter away energy trying to salvage fading ones.

Author Comment
Marketing can't go it alone in creating customer value. Under the company-wide strategic plan, marketing must work closely with other departments to form an effective internal company value chain and with other companies in the marketing system to create an external value delivery network that jointly serves customers.

Planning Marketing: Partnering to Build Customer Relationships

OBJECTIVE 2-3 Explain marketing's role in strategic planning and how marketing works with its partners to create and deliver customer value.

The company's strategic plan establishes what kinds of businesses the company will operate and its objectives for each. Then, within each business unit, more detailed planning takes place. The major functional departments in each unit—marketing, finance, accounting, purchasing, operations, information systems, human resources, and others—must work together to accomplish strategic objectives.

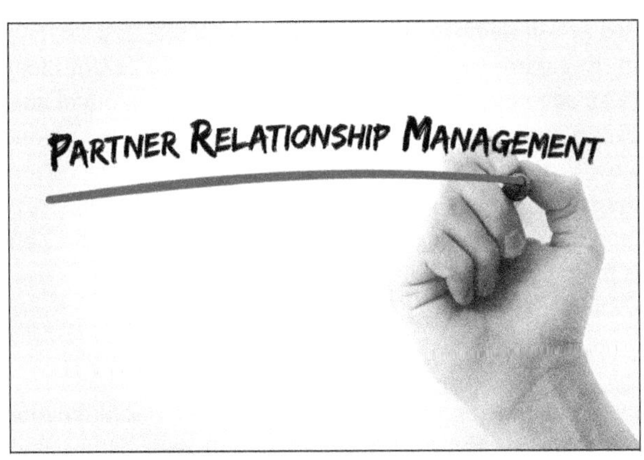

>> Partner relationship management: Marketers must work closely with others inside and outside the company to jointly carry out customer value-creating activities.

dizain/Shutterstock

Marketing plays a key role in the company's strategic planning in several ways. First, marketing provides a guiding *philosophy*—the marketing concept—that suggests the company strategy should revolve around creating customer value and building profitable relationships with important consumer groups. Second, marketing provides *inputs* to strategic planners by helping to identify attractive market opportunities and assessing the firm's potential to take advantage of them. Finally, within individual business units, marketing designs *strategies* for reaching the unit's objectives. Once the unit's objectives are set, marketing's task is to help carry them out profitably.

Customer engagement and value are the key ingredients in the marketer's formula for success. However, as noted in Chapter 1, although marketing plays a leading role, it cannot act alone. It can be only a partner in attracting, engaging, and growing customers. >> In addition to *customer relationship management*, marketers must also practice *partner relationship management*. They must work closely with partners in other company departments to form an effective internal *value chain* that serves customers. Moreover, they must partner effectively with other companies in the marketing system to form a competitively superior external *value delivery network*. We now take a closer look at the concepts of a company value chain and a value delivery network.

Partnering with Other Company Departments

Value chain
The series of internal departments that carry out value-creating activities to design, produce, market, deliver, and support a firm's products.

Each company department can be thought of as a link in the company's internal **value chain**.[10] That is, each department carries out value-creating activities to design, produce, market, deliver, and support the firm's products. The firm's success depends not only on how well each department performs its work but also on how well the various departments coordinate their activities.

For example, True Value Hardware's goal is to create customer value and satisfaction by providing shoppers with the hardware and home improvement products they need at affordable prices along with top-notch customer service. Marketers at the retail-owned cooperative play an important role. They learn what customers need and help the 3,500 independent True Value retailers stock their store shelves with the desired products at competitive prices. They prepare advertising and merchandising programs and assist shoppers with customer service. Through these and other activities, True Value marketers help deliver value to customers.

However, True Value's marketers, both at the home office and in stores, need help from the company's other functions. True Value's ability to help you "Start Right. Start Here." depends on purchasing's skill in developing the needed suppliers and buying from them at low cost. True Value's information technology people must provide fast and accurate information about which products are selling in each store. And its operations people must provide effective, low-cost merchandise handling and delivery.

A company's value chain is only as strong as its weakest link. Success depends on how well each group performs its work of adding customer value and on how the company coordinates the activities of various functions. True Value's marketing campaign—"Behind Every Project Is a True Value"—recognizes the importance of having everyone in the organization—from in-store managers and employees to home-office operations managers and marketing research analysts—understand the needs and aspirations of the chain's do-it-yourself customers and help them handle home improvement projects.

Ideally, then, a company's different functions should work in harmony to produce value for consumers. But, in practice, interdepartmental relations are full of conflicts and misunderstandings. The marketing department takes the consumer's point of view. But when marketing tries to improve customer satisfaction, it can cause other departments to do a poorer job *in their terms*. Marketing department actions can increase purchasing costs, disrupt production schedules, increase inventories, and create budget headaches. Thus, other departments may resist the marketing department's efforts.

Yet marketers must find ways to get all departments to "think consumer" and develop a smoothly functioning value chain. Engaging customers today requires a whole-company commitment. Thus, whether you're an accountant, an operations manager, a financial analyst, an IT specialist, or a human resources manager, you need to understand marketing and your role in creating customer value. "From finance to customer service to manufacturing, every employee should see how their role plays a part in the customer experience," says one marketer. "Customer experience doesn't depend solely on the...marketing team, but [marketing] sets the tone and leads the way for all other departments."[11]

Partnering with Others in the Marketing System

In its quest to engage customers and create customer value, the firm needs to look beyond its own internal value chain and into the value chains of its suppliers, its distributors, and, ultimately, its customers. Consider fast-food chain Subway. People do not eat at Subway only because they love the chain's sandwiches. Consumers flock to the Subway *system*. Throughout the nation, Subway's finely tuned value delivery system consistently delivers fresh, fast, and tasty made-to-order sandwiches at affordable prices. Subway is effective only to the extent that it successfully partners with its franchisees, suppliers, and others to jointly carry out its "Make It What You Want" positioning promise.

More companies today are partnering with other members of the supply chain—suppliers, distributors, and, ultimately, customers—to improve the performance of the customer **value delivery network**. Competition no longer takes place only between individual competitors. Rather, it takes place between the entire value delivery network created by these competitors. Thus, Ford's performance against Toyota depends on the quality of Ford's overall value delivery network versus Toyota's. Even if Ford makes the best cars, it might lose in the marketplace if Toyota's dealer network provides a more customer-satisfying sales and service experience.

Value delivery network
A network composed of the company, suppliers, distributors, and, ultimately, customers who partner with each other to improve the performance of the entire system in delivering customer value.

LINKING THE CONCEPTS

Pause here for a moment to apply what you've read in the first part of this chapter.

- Why are we talking about company-wide strategic planning in a marketing text? What *does* strategic planning have to do with marketing?
- What are Starbucks's strategy and mission? What role does marketing play in helping Starbucks to accomplish its strategy and mission?
- What roles do other Starbucks departments play and how can the company's marketers partner with these departments to maximize overall engagement and customer value? What roles do Starbucks's suppliers play?

Author Comment
Now that we've set the context in terms of company-wide strategy, it's time to discuss customer value-driven marketing strategies and programs.

Marketing Strategy and the Marketing Mix

OBJECTIVE 2-4 **Describe the elements of a customer value-driven marketing strategy and mix and the forces that influence them.**

The strategic plan defines the company's overall mission and objectives. Marketing's role is shown in >> **Figure 2.4**, which summarizes the major activities involved in managing a customer-driven marketing strategy and the marketing mix.

Consumers are at the center. The goal is to create value for customers and build profitable customer relationships. Next comes **marketing strategy**—the marketing logic by which the company hopes to create this customer value and achieve these profitable relationships. The company decides which customers it will serve (segmentation and targeting) and how (differentiation and positioning). It identifies the total market and then divides it into smaller segments, selects the most promising segments, and focuses on serving and satisfying the customers in these segments.

Marketing strategy
The marketing logic by which the company hopes to create customer value and achieve profitable customer relationships.

Figure 2.4 Managing Marketing Strategies and the Marketing Mix

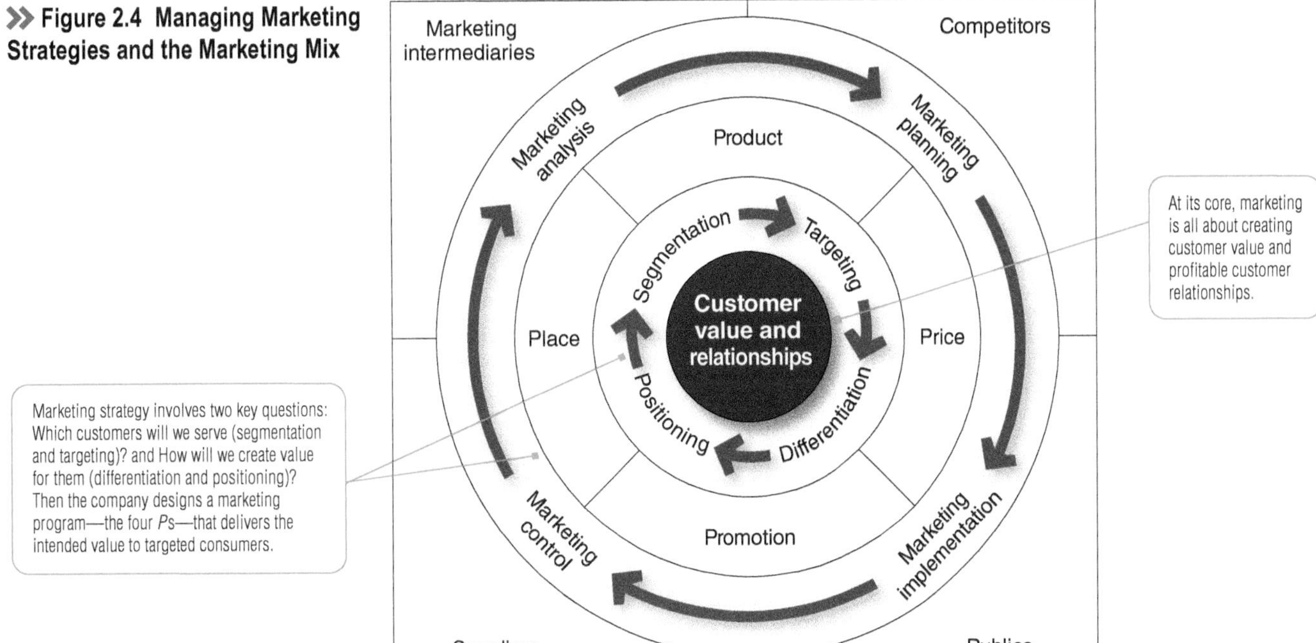
Marketing intermediaries
Competitors
Suppliers
Publics
Marketing analysis
Marketing planning
Marketing implementation
Marketing control
Product
Price
Place
Promotion
Segmentation
Targeting
Differentiation
Positioning
Customer value and relationships
At its core, marketing is all about creating customer value and profitable customer relationships.
Marketing strategy involves two key questions: Which customers will we serve (segmentation and targeting)? and How will we create value for them (differentiation and positioning)? Then the company designs a marketing program—the four *Ps*—that delivers the intended value to targeted consumers.

Guided by marketing strategy, the company designs an integrated *marketing mix* made up of factors under its control—product, price, place, and promotion (the four Ps). To find the best marketing strategy and mix, the company engages in marketing analysis, planning, implementation, and control. Through these activities, the company watches and adapts to the actors and forces in the marketing environment. We will now look briefly at each activity. In later chapters, we will discuss each one in more depth.

Customer Value-Driven Marketing Strategy

To succeed in today's competitive marketplace, companies must be customer centered. They must win customers from competitors and then engage and grow them by delivering greater value. But before it can satisfy customers, a company must first understand customer needs and wants. Thus, sound marketing requires careful customer analysis.

Companies know that they cannot profitably serve all consumers in a given market—at least not all consumers in the same way. There are too many different kinds of consumers with too many different kinds of needs. Most companies are in a position to serve some segments better than others. Thus, each company must divide up the total market, choose the best segments, and design strategies for profitably serving chosen segments. This process involves *market segmentation, market targeting, differentiation*, and *positioning*.

Market Segmentation

The market consists of many types of consumers, products, and needs. The marketer must determine which segments offer the best opportunities. Consumers can be grouped and served in various ways based on geographic, demographic, psychographic, and behavioral factors. The process of dividing a market into distinct groups of buyers who have different needs, characteristics, or behaviors and who might require separate marketing strategies or mixes is called **market segmentation**.

Market segmentation
Dividing a market into distinct groups of buyers who have different needs, characteristics, or behaviors and who might require separate marketing strategies or mixes.

Every market has segments, but not all ways of segmenting a market are equally useful. For example, Tylenol would gain little by distinguishing between low-income and high-income pain-relief users if both respond the same way to marketing efforts. A **market segment** consists of consumers who respond in a similar way to a given set of marketing efforts. In the car market, for example, consumers who want the biggest, most comfortable car regardless of price make up one market segment. Consumers who care

Market segment
A group of consumers who respond in a similar way to a given set of marketing efforts.

mainly about price and operating economy make up another segment. It would be difficult to make one car model that was the first choice of consumers in both segments. Companies are wise to focus their efforts on meeting the distinct needs of individual market segments.

Market Targeting

Market targeting
Evaluating each market segment's attractiveness and selecting one or more segments to serve.

After a company has defined its market segments, it can enter one or many of these segments. **Market targeting** involves evaluating each market segment's attractiveness and selecting one or more segments to enter. A company should target segments in which it can profitably generate the greatest customer value and sustain it over time.

A company with limited resources might decide to serve only one or a few special segments or market niches. Such nichers specialize in serving customer segments that major competitors overlook or ignore. For example, McLaren sold only 3,340 of its very-high-performance cars last year but at very high prices—such as its 570S model at $188,000 or a made-to-order FI model starting at an eye-popping $837,000. Most nichers aren't quite so exotic. Profitable low-cost airline Allegiant Air avoids direct competition with larger major airline rivals by targeting smaller, neglected markets and new fliers. Nicher Allegiant "goes where they ain't."

Alternatively, a large company (for example, car companies such as Honda and Ford) might decide to offer a complete range of products to serve all market segments. Or a company might choose to serve several related segments—perhaps those with different kinds of customers but with the same basic wants. Gap Inc., for example, targets different age, income, and lifestyle clothing and accessory segments with six different store and online brands: Gap, Banana Republic, Old Navy, Athleta, and INTERMIX. The Gap store brand breaks its segment down into even smaller niches, including Gap, GapKids, babyGap, GapMaternity, and GapBody.[12]

Most companies enter a new market by serving a single segment; if this proves successful, they add more segments. For example, Southwest Airlines entered the crowded airline market almost 50 years ago as an upstart, no-frills commuter airline serving selected second-tier airports in Texas and other Southwestern states. Based on its early success in niche markets, Southwest has grown to become the nation's second-largest airline, serving 100 major destinations in the United States and 10 additional countries. The successful $21 billion airline has pulled in 45 straight years of profits.[13] More recently, Tesla broke into an auto industry dominated by well-established, deep-pocketed competitors by first concentrating on a narrow, high-tech market niche and then expanded to more-mass-market models (see Marketing at Work 2.2).

Market Differentiation and Positioning

Positioning
Arranging for a product to occupy a clear, distinctive, and desirable place relative to competing products in the minds of target consumers.

After a company has decided which market segments to enter, it must determine how to differentiate its market offering for each targeted segment and what positions it wants to occupy in those segments. **Positioning** is arranging for a product to occupy a clear, distinctive, and desirable place relative to competing products in the minds of target consumers. Marketers plan positions that distinguish their products from competing brands and give them the greatest advantage in their target markets.

For example, Panera gives you "Food as it should be"; at Wendy's, "Quality Is Our Recipe." Netflix invites you to "See what's next"; Hulu says "Come TV with us"; and with HBO Go, "It's HBO. Anywhere." Car sharing service Lyft positions itself as "your friend with a car"; >> Uber is "Everyone's private driver." And BMW promises "Sheer driving pleasure"; Subaru is "Confidence in motion."

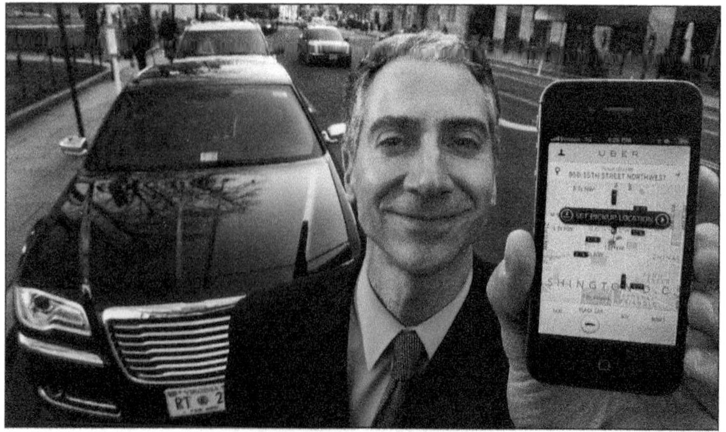

>> Positioning: Car sharing service Uber positions itself as "Everyone's private driver." This simple statement provides the backbone for its marketing strategy.
PAUL J. RICHARDS/AFP/Getty Images

Such deceptively simple statements form the backbone of a product's marketing strategy. For example, the "confidence" in Subaru's "Confidence in Motion" positioning reflects the brand's long-standing commitment to

MARKETING AT WORK 2.2

Tesla: On a Fast Track from Upstart Nicher to Mass-Market Brand

Breaking into the modern auto industry is an almost impossible task. The industry is characterized by well-entrenched and deep-pocketed competitors, extremely high startup costs, and stifling regulations. Some companies have tried—remember DeLorean in the early 1980s? That one failed after producing only 9,000 units. And even mighty GM failed after only 10 years with Saturn, launched as "A new kind of car. A new kind of car company."

Then along comes Tesla, another startup with lofty ambitions. But rather than tackling the likes of Toyota, Ford, Honda, and GM head-on, Tesla began by sneaking in the back door. While the auto industry majors were still peddling mostly traditional internal combustion vehicles, Tesla began by focusing on a narrow sliver of the market—high-performance all-electric vehicles (EVs) targeted toward a small segment of affluent, technology-obsessed buyers. Founded by tech entrepreneur and businessman Elon Musk, Tesla Motors introduced its first vehicle—the Roadster—in 2008. A two-seat, convertible sports car, the Roadster shocked the auto world. At the time, the major auto companies were already dabbling in all-electric vehicles. But most EVs were little more than glorified golf carts that appealed mostly to environmentally conscious buyers. They were underpowered, slow to recharge, and limited in operating range.

>> Upstart Tesla entered the competitive auto industry by first concentrating on a narrow, all-electric vehicle sliver of the market. It now offers an expanded lineup of EV models.

Joby Sessions/T3 Magazine/Getty Images (car); imageBROKER/Alamy Stock Photo (logo)

By contrast, the Tesla Roadster was a real sports car. It featured chassis components licensed from Lotus. It had a powerful all-electric drivetrain and became the first production EV to employ lithium ion battery cells. With a range of more than 200 miles, it could fully recharge in just four hours with a home-installed quick charger. And more than just eye candy, the Roadster went from 0 to 60 miles per hour in less than four seconds, faster than all but the fastest production supercars. Despite a base price of $109,000 and long waits while Roadsters dribbled of the assembly line, the rich and famous snatched them up. Tesla sold 2,450 Roadsters in 30 countries before phasing out the model in 2012.

From the start, Tesla planned to broaden its EV niche. Based on the early success of the Roadster, in 2012 Tesla launched the Model S, a luxury four-door sedan that could park respectably next to a BMW 7-series or a Mercedes S-class. At a starting price of about $70,000, the Model S boasted a range of 335 miles. And with new supercharging technologies, it could recharge 180 miles of range in as little as 15 minutes.

Although range and recharging were still perceived as disadvantages versus conventional internal combustion vehicles, the sleek Model S offered a dazzling array of pluses for its targeted segment of adventuresome, tech-forward luxury buyers. On the practical side, Model S owners chuckled as they showed surprised friends the car's "frunk," Tesla's name for the extra storage area under the front hood where you'd expect the engine to be. The Model S also offered a rear-facing third row of kid-friendly seats, making it the only four-door sedan that could seat seven passengers.

But it was the Model S's extreme performance and alluring technology that really set it apart. First, the Model S is super-fast. Placed in "Ludicrous Mode," the car rockets from 0 to 60 in only 2.275 seconds, faster than a Lamborghini, Ferrari, or any other exotic sports car save the Porsche 918 Spyder. Second, the Model S is super high-tech. For example, it comes with a range of self-driving capabilities, including features such as self-parking, smart cruise control, and even taking the wheel for short periods of time. Tesla claims that all its vehicles come with the hardware needed to be fully self-driving and will automatically self-upgrade as software and regulations allow. Moreover, owners have an almost personal relationship with their Teslas. They communicate intimately with their cars through an app that lets them track and manage every nuance of the car's settings and performance.

To expand its EV niche even further, Tesla added the Model X, a midsized, luxury crossover SUV boasting innovative features similar to those of the Model S. Both Tesla models have done well. Tesla sales have grown steadily with combined sales of more than 300,000 units so far. That makes Tesla the world's top seller of all-electric vehicles. Still, it's a drop in the bucket compared with the numbers churned out by the world's major automakers. Tesla has its sights on even bigger things.

Not content to be a high-end nicher, Tesla next plunged headlong into creating a mass market EV line. In 2015 it announced plans to develop the Model 3, a compact sports sedan about the same size as the Audi A4 and the BMW 3 Series. Although less luxurious than other Tesla models, the Model 3 promised "everything—range, affordability, and performance" at a base price of only $35,000.

Public reaction was swift. By the time the Model 3 previewed at the 2016 Paris Auto Show, anticipation had reached a fever pitch. Within one week, Tesla had taken 325,000 preorders, each with a refundable deposit of $1,000, representing $14 billion in future sales and providing $325 million in much-needed capital for development and production. Tesla announced that it would begin delivering the first Model 3s in late 2017 and that it would quickly ramp up production to as many as 10,000 vehicles per week. The still-upstart brand also announced a jaw-dropping goal of 500,000 total EVs for 2018.

By the time it delivered the first Model 3 in July 2017, Tesla had more than 450,000 orders in hand. The innovative car had no front grill (no engine to be cooled, so no grill needed) and a dashboard devoid of any gauges or displays other than a single, centrally mounted 15-inch LED screen (the car is designed eventually to be fully self-driving). Initial customers and auto journalists raved about every aspect of the car—from its advanced technology and driving experience to its high-quality fit and finish. Said one *Road & Track* journalist: "It's one thing to discover driving joy in a sports car that was painstakingly engineered to tickle the pleasure neurons of autocrossers and track rats. Finding that in a family sedan—a car aimed at entry-luxury four-door buyers—is an unexpected delight." The Model 3 has even been compared to the Ford Model T for its significance and potential impact on human transportation.

The biggest problem with the Model 3: Tesla can't make them fast enough. Major factory setbacks have kept production far below planned numbers, leaving preorders unfilled and the company far short of its 500,000-vehicle goal. And Tesla faces a potentially busy and bumpy roadway ahead as the established automakers meet the Tesla challenge by pouring resources into developing their own EVs. For example, Volkswagen—the world's largest automaker with its VW, Audi, Bentley, Porsche, and Lamborghini brands—by itself plans to launch 50 EV models and achieve annual EV sales of three million units by 2025.

However, despite potential bumps in the road, Tesla continues its journey from upstart nicher to full mass-market brand. It is further diversifying its vehicle portfolio with self-driving EV semi-trucks and a new Roadster slated for 2020—one that promises to shatter more records for speed, acceleration, range, and coolness. And although the future remains uncertain, Tesla has already gone further, faster than any other vehicle startup in history. Tesla is to cars what Apple has long been to consumer electronics, with the same kind of innovative leadership and cult brand following. Despite the potholes, Tesla's current and wannabe customers remain unwavering in their enthusiasm for the brand.

Sources: Bob Sorokanich, "Can Tesla's Most Affordable Model Kick-Start the Electric Car Revolution?" *Road & Track*, January 12, 2018; John Rosevear, "Volkswagen's Electric-Car Program Is about to Blow Right Past Tesla," *Forbes*, March 14, 2018, www.fool.com/investing/2018/03/17/volkswagens-electric-car-program-is-about-to-blow.aspx; Jeff Dyer and Hal Gregersen, "Tesla's Innovations Are Transforming the Industry," *Forbes*, August 24, 2016, www.forbes.com/sites/innovatorsdna/2016/08/24/teslas-innovations-are-transforming-the-auto-industry/#3d71735219f7; J. Jennings Moss, "Musk: Tesla Model 3 Production 'Incredibly Difficult and Painful,'" *Silicon Valley Business Journal*, April 11, 2018, www.bizjournals.com/sanjose/news/2018/04/11/musk-telsa-model-3-production-elon-musk-tsla.html; and other information from www.tesla.com, accessed September 2018.

building trust through safety, reliability, and durability—to both the enjoyment and peace of mind of owning a Subaru. The brand's long-running "Love" campaign promotes to a safe, loving lifestyle: "Love. It's what makes a Subaru a Subaru," says the company. The "in motion" aligns with Subaru's targeting of Millennials and their on-the-go, ever-changing lifestyles.[14]

In positioning its brand, a company first identifies possible customer value differences that provide competitive advantages on which to build the position. A company can offer greater customer value by either charging lower prices than competitors or offering more benefits to justify higher prices. But if the company *promises* greater value, it must then *deliver* that greater value. Thus, effective positioning begins with **differentiation**—actually *differentiating* the company's market offering to create superior customer value. Once the company has chosen a desired position, it must take strong steps to deliver and communicate that position to target consumers. The company's entire marketing program should support the chosen positioning strategy.

Differentiation
Actually differentiating the market offering to create superior customer value.

Developing an Integrated Marketing Mix

After determining its overall marketing strategy, the company is ready to begin planning the details of the **marketing mix**, one of the major concepts in modern marketing. The marketing mix is the set of tactical marketing tools that the firm blends to produce the response it wants in the target market. The marketing mix consists of everything the firm

Marketing mix
The set of tactical marketing tools—product, price, place, and promotion—that the firm blends to produce the response it wants in the target market.

can do to engage consumers and deliver customer value. The many possibilities can be collected into four groups of variables—the four Ps. >> **Figure 2.5** shows the marketing tools under each P.

- *Product* means the goods-and-services combination the company offers to the target market. Thus, a Ford Escape consists of nuts and bolts, spark plugs, pistons, headlights, and thousands of other parts. Ford offers several Escape models and dozens of optional features. The car comes fully serviced and with a comprehensive warranty that is as much a part of the product as the tailpipe.
- *Price* is the amount of money customers must pay to obtain the product. For example, Ford calculates suggested retail prices that its dealers might charge for each Escape. But Ford dealers rarely charge the full sticker price. Instead, they negotiate the price with each customer, offering discounts, trade-in allowances, and credit terms. These actions adjust prices for the current competitive and economic situations and bring them into line with the buyer's perception of the car's value.
- *Place* includes company activities that make the product available to target consumers. Ford partners with a large body of independently owned dealerships that sell the company's many different models. Ford selects its dealers carefully and strongly supports them. The dealers keep an inventory of Ford automobiles, demonstrate them to potential buyers, negotiate prices, close sales, and service the cars after the sale.
- *Promotion* refers to activities that communicate the merits of the product and persuade target customers to buy it. Ford spent nearly $2.4 billion last year on U.S. advertising to tell consumers about the company and its many products.[15] Dealership salespeople assist potential buyers and persuade them that Ford is the best car for them. Ford and its dealers offer special promotions—sales, cash rebates, and low financing rates—as added purchase incentives. And Ford's Facebook, Twitter, YouTube, Instagram, and other social media platforms engage consumers with the brand and with other brand fans.

An effective marketing program blends the marketing mix elements into an integrated marketing program designed to achieve the company's marketing objectives by engaging consumers and delivering value to them. The marketing mix constitutes the company's tactical tool kit for establishing strong positioning in target markets.

>> **Figure 2.5 The Four Ps of the Marketing Mix**

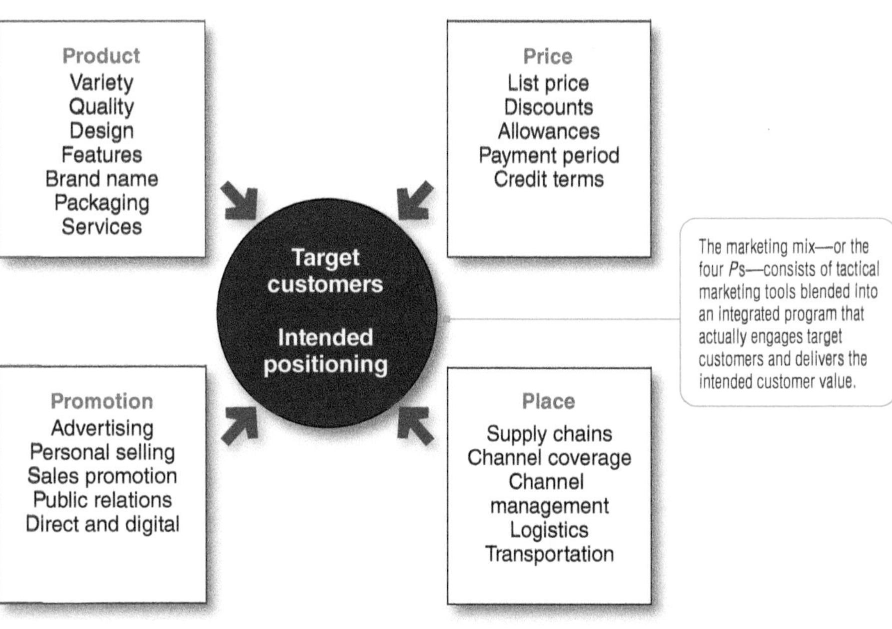

Some critics think that the four Ps may omit or underemphasize certain important activities. For example, they ask, "Where are services? Just because they don't start with a *P* doesn't justify omitting them." The answer is that services, such as banking, airline, and retailing services, are products too. We might call them *service products*. "Where is packaging?" the critics might ask. Marketers would answer that they include packaging as one of many product decisions. All said, as Figure 2.5 suggests, many marketing activities that might appear to be left out of the marketing mix are included under one of the four Ps. The issue is not whether there should be four, six, or ten Ps so much as what framework is most helpful in designing integrated marketing programs.

There is another concern, however, that is valid. It holds that the four Ps concept takes the seller's view of the market, not the buyer's view. From the buyer's viewpoint, in this age of customer value and relationships, the four Ps might be better described as the four As:[16]

Four Ps	Four As
Product	Acceptability
Price	Affordability
Place	Accessibility
Promotion	Awareness

Under this more customer-centered framework, *acceptability* is the extent to which the product exceeds customer expectations; *affordability* the extent to which customers are willing and able to pay the product's price; *accessibility* the extent to which customers can readily acquire the product; and *awareness* the extent to which customers are informed about the product's features, persuaded to try it, and reminded to repurchase. The four As relate closely to the traditional four Ps. Product design influences acceptability, price affects affordability, place affects accessibility, and promotion influences awareness. Marketers would do well to think through the four As first and then build the four Ps on that platform.

Author Comment
So far we've focused on the marketing in marketing management. Now, let's turn to the management.

Managing the Marketing Effort and Marketing Return on Investment

OBJECTIVE 2-5 List the marketing management functions, including the elements of a marketing plan, and discuss the importance of measuring and managing marketing return on investment.

Managing the Marketing Effort

In addition to being good at the *marketing* in marketing management, companies also need to pay attention to the *management*. Managing the marketing process requires the five marketing management functions shown in >> **Figure 2.6**—*analysis, planning, implementation, organization, and control*. The company first develops company-wide strategic plans and then translates them into marketing and other plans for each division, product, and brand. Through implementation and organization, the company turns the plans into actions. Control consists of measuring and evaluating the results of marketing activities and taking corrective action where needed. Finally, marketing analysis provides the information and evaluations needed for all the other marketing activities.

Marketing Analysis

SWOT analysis
An overall evaluation of the company's strengths (S), weaknesses (W), opportunities (O), and threats (T).

Managing the marketing function begins with a complete analysis of the company's situation. The marketer should conduct a **SWOT analysis** (pronounced "swat analysis"), by which it evaluates the company's overall strengths (S), weaknesses (W), opportunities (O), and threats (T) (see >> **Figure 2.7**). Strengths include internal capabilities, resources, and positive situational factors that may help the company serve its customers and achieve its objectives. Weaknesses include internal limitations and negative situational factors that may interfere with the company's performance. Opportunities are favorable factors or

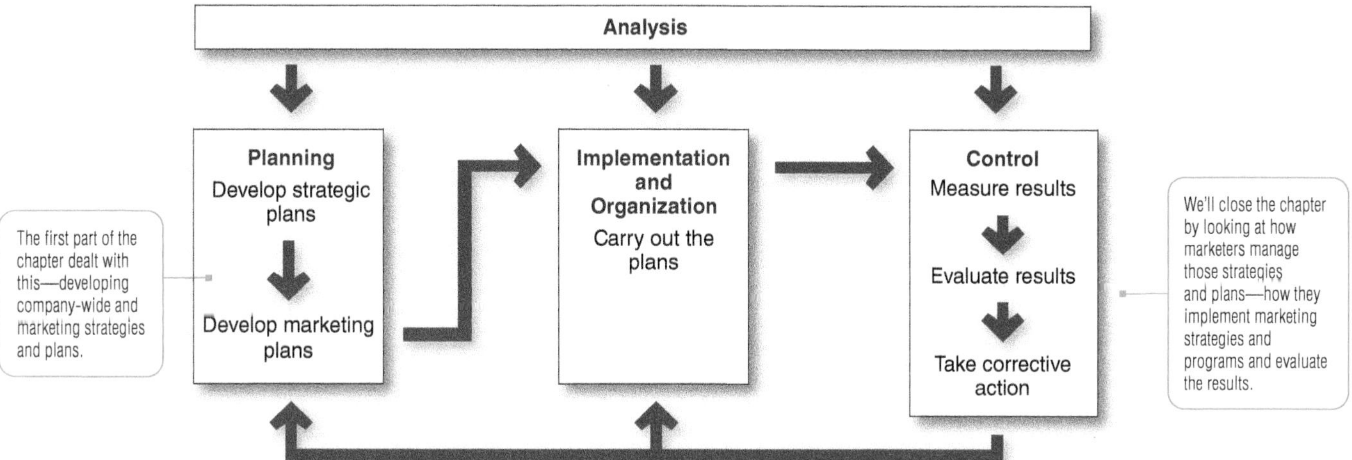

>> **Figure 2.6 Managing Marketing: Analysis, Planning, Implementation, and Control**

trends in the external environment that the company may be able to exploit to its advantage. And threats are unfavorable external factors or trends that may present challenges to performance.

The company should analyze its markets and marketing environment to find attractive opportunities and identify threats. It should analyze company strengths and weaknesses as well as current and possible marketing actions to determine which opportunities it can best pursue. The goal is to match the company's strengths to attractive opportunities in the environment while simultaneously eliminating or overcoming the weaknesses and minimizing the threats. Marketing analysis provides inputs to each of the other marketing management functions. We discuss marketing analysis more fully in Chapter 3.

Marketing Planning

Through strategic planning, the company decides what it wants to do with each business unit. Marketing planning involves choosing marketing strategies that will help the company attain its overall strategic objectives. A detailed marketing plan is needed for each business, product, or brand. What does a marketing plan look like? Our discussion focuses on product or brand marketing plans.

>> **Table 2.2** outlines the major sections of a typical product or brand marketing plan. (See Appendix 2 for a sample marketing plan.) The plan begins with an executive summary that quickly reviews major assessments, goals, and recommendations. The main section of the plan presents a detailed SWOT analysis of the current marketing situation as well as potential threats and opportunities. The plan next states major objectives for the brand and outlines the specifics of a marketing strategy for achieving them.

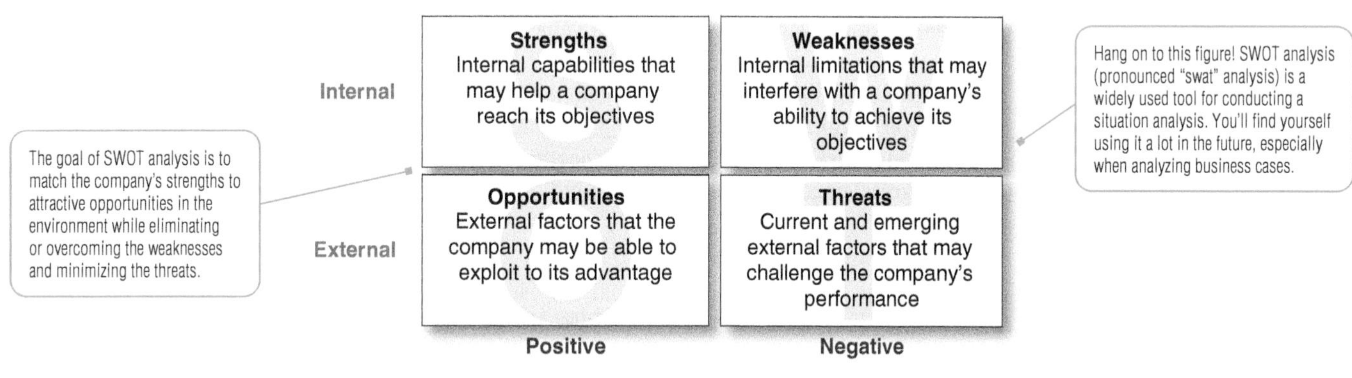

>> **Figure 2.7 SWOT Analysis: Strengths (S), Weaknesses (W), Opportunities (O), and Threats (T)**

Table 2.2 Contents of a Marketing Plan

Section	Purpose
Executive summary	Presents a brief summary of the main goals and recommendations of the plan for management review, helping top management find the plan's major points quickly.
Current marketing situation	Describes the target market and the company's position in it, including information about the market, product performance, competition, and distribution. This section includes the following: • A *market description* that defines the market and major segments and then reviews customer needs and factors in the marketing environment that may affect customer purchasing. • A *product review* that shows sales, prices, and gross margins of the major products in the product line. • A review of *competition* that identifies major competitors and assesses their market positions and strategies for product quality, pricing, distribution, and promotion. • A review of *distribution* that evaluates recent sales trends and other developments in major distribution channels.
Threats and opportunities analysis	Assesses major threats and opportunities that the product might face, helping management to anticipate important positive or negative developments that might have an impact on the firm and its strategies.
Objectives and issues	States the marketing objectives that the company would like to attain during the plan's term and discusses key issues that will affect their attainment.
Marketing strategy	Outlines the broad marketing logic by which the business unit hopes to engage customers, create customer value, and build customer relationships, plus the specifics of target markets, positioning, and marketing expenditure levels. How will the company create value for customers in order to capture value from customers in return? This section also outlines specific strategies for each marketing mix element and explains how each responds to the threats, opportunities, and critical issues spelled out earlier in the plan.
Action programs	Spells out how marketing strategies will be turned into specific action programs that answer the following questions: *What* will be done? *When* will it be done? *Who* will do it? *How* much will it cost?
Budgets	Details a supporting marketing budget that is essentially a projected profit-and-loss statement. It shows expected revenues and expected costs of production, distribution, and marketing. The difference is the projected profit. The budget becomes the basis for materials buying, production scheduling, personnel planning, and marketing operations.
Controls	Outlines the controls that will be used to monitor progress, allow management to review implementation results, and spot products that are not meeting their goals. It includes measures of return on marketing investment.

A *marketing strategy* consists of specific strategies for target markets, positioning, the marketing mix, and marketing expenditure levels. It outlines how the company intends to engage target customers and create value in order to capture value in return. In this section, the planner explains how each strategy responds to the threats, opportunities, and critical issues spelled out earlier in the plan. Additional sections of the marketing plan lay out an *action program* for implementing the marketing strategy along with the details of a supporting *marketing budget*. The last section outlines the *controls* that will be used to monitor progress, measure return on marketing investment, and take corrective action.

Marketing Implementation

Planning good strategies is only a start toward successful marketing. A brilliant marketing strategy counts for little if the company fails to implement it properly. **Marketing implementation** is the process that turns marketing *plans* into marketing *actions* to accomplish strategic marketing objectives. Whereas marketing planning addresses the *what* and *why* of marketing activities, implementation addresses the *who, where, when*, and *how*.

Marketing implementation
Turning marketing strategies and plans into marketing actions to accomplish strategic marketing objectives.

Many managers think that "doing things right" (implementation) is as important as, or even more important than, "doing the right things" (strategy). The fact is that both are critical to success, and companies can gain competitive advantages through effective implementation. One firm can have essentially the same strategy as another yet win in the marketplace through faster or better execution. Still, implementation is difficult—it is often easier to think up good marketing strategies than it is to carry them out.

In an increasingly connected world, people at all levels of the marketing system must work together to implement marketing strategies and plans. At John Deere, for example, marketing implementation for the company's residential, commercial, agricultural, and industrial equipment requires day-to-day decisions and actions by thousands of people both inside and outside the organization. Marketing managers make decisions about target segments, branding, product development, pricing, promotion, and distribution. They talk with engineering about product design, with manufacturing about production and inventory levels, and with finance about funding and cash flows. They also connect with outside people, such as advertising agencies to plan ad campaigns and the news media to obtain publicity support. The sales force urges and supports independent John Deere dealers and large retailers like Lowe's in their efforts to convince residential, agricultural, and industrial customers that "Nothing Runs Like a Deere."

Marketing Department Organization

The company must design a marketing organization that can carry out marketing strategies and plans. If the company is very small, one person might do all the research, selling, advertising, customer service, and other marketing work. As the company expands, however, a marketing department emerges to plan and carry out marketing activities. In large companies, this department contains many specialists—product and market managers, sales managers and salespeople, market researchers, and advertising and social media experts, among others.

To head up such large marketing organizations, many companies have now created a *chief marketing officer* (or CMO) position. This person heads up the company's entire marketing operation and represents marketing on the company's top management team. The CMO position puts marketing on equal footing with other "C-level" executives, such as the chief operating officer (COO) and the chief financial officer (CFO). As a member of top management, the CMO's role is to champion the customer's cause. To that end, many companies call their top marketer the "Chief Customer Experience Officer" or the "Chief Customer Value Officer." "Today's customer experiences must align with business strategy—and the CMO is the best candidate to drive these programs across the company," says one marketing analyst. "Instead of [just] creating big-picture marketing campaigns, CMOs are now responsible for the entire customer experience."[17]

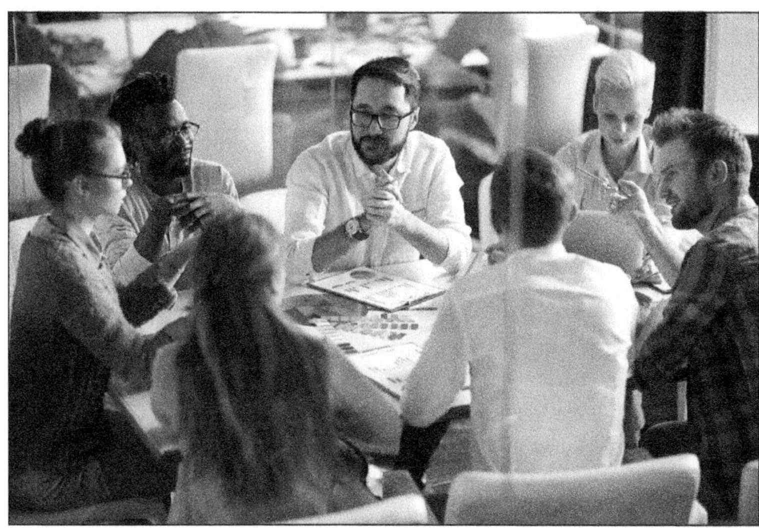

>> Marketers must continually plan their analysis, implementation, and control activities.

Dmitriy Shironosov/123 RF

Modern marketing departments can be arranged in several ways. The most common form of marketing organization is the *functional organization*, under which different marketing activities are headed by a functional specialist—a sales manager, an advertising manager, a marketing research manager, a customer service manager, or a new product manager. A company that sells across the country or internationally often uses a *geographic organization*, assigning sales and marketing people to specific countries, regions, and districts. Companies with many very different products or brands often create a *product management organization*. For companies that sell one product line to many different types of markets and customers who have different needs and preferences, a *market* or *customer management organization* might be best. Large companies that produce many different products flowing into many different geographic and customer markets usually employ some *combination* of the functional, geographic, product, and market organization forms.

Marketing organization has become an increasingly important issue in recent years. More and more, companies are shifting their brand management focus toward *customer management*—moving away from managing only product or brand profitability and toward managing customer profitability and customer equity. They think of themselves not as managing portfolios of brands but as managing portfolios of customers. And rather than managing the fortunes of a brand, they see themselves as managing customer–brand engagement, experiences, and relationships.

Marketing Control

Marketing control
Measuring and evaluating the results of marketing strategies and plans and taking corrective action to ensure that the objectives are achieved.

Because many surprises occur during the implementation of marketing strategies and plans, marketers must practice constant **marketing control**—evaluating results and taking corrective action to ensure that the objectives are attained. Marketing control involves four steps. Management first sets specific marketing goals. It then measures its performance in the marketplace and evaluates the causes of any differences between expected and actual performance. Finally, management takes corrective action to close the gaps between goals and performance. This may require changing the action programs or even changing the goals.

Operating control involves checking ongoing performance against the annual plan and taking corrective action when necessary. Its purpose is to ensure that the company achieves the sales, profits, and other goals set out in its annual plan. It also involves determining the profitability of different products, territories, markets, and channels. *Strategic control* involves looking at whether the company's basic strategies are well matched to its opportunities. Marketing strategies and programs can quickly become outdated, and each company should periodically reassess its overall approach to the marketplace.

Author Comment
Measuring marketing return on investment has become a major emphasis. But it can be difficult. For example, a Super Bowl ad reaches more than 100 million consumers but may cost more than $4 million for 30 seconds of airtime. How do you measure the return on such an investment in terms of sales, profits, and building customer engagement and relationships?

Measuring and Managing Marketing Return on Investment

Marketing managers must ensure that their marketing dollars are being well spent. In the past, many marketers spent freely on big, expensive marketing programs and flashy advertising campaigns, often without thinking carefully about the financial returns on their spending. Their goal was often a general one—to "build brands and consumer preference." They believed that marketing produces intangible creative outcomes, which do not lend themselves readily to measures of productivity or return.

However, those free-spending days have been replaced by a new era of marketing measurement and accountability. More than ever, today's marketers are being held accountable for linking their strategies and tactics to measurable marketing performance outcomes. One important marketing performance measure is **marketing return on investment** (or **marketing ROI**). *Marketing ROI* is the net return from a marketing investment divided by the costs of the marketing investment. It measures the profits generated by investments in marketing activities.

Marketing return on investment (marketing ROI)
The net return from a marketing investment divided by the costs of the marketing investment.

Marketing ROI can be difficult to measure. In measuring financial ROI, both the *R* and the *I* are uniformly measured in dollars. For example, when buying a piece of equipment, the productivity gains resulting from the purchase are fairly straightforward. As of yet, however, there is no consistent definition of marketing ROI. For instance, returns such as engagement, advertising, and brand-building impact aren't easily put into dollar returns.

A company can assess marketing ROI in terms of standard marketing performance measures, such as brand awareness, sales, or market share. Many companies are assembling such measures into *marketing dashboards*—meaningful sets of marketing performance measures in a single display used to monitor strategic marketing performance. Just as automobile dashboards present drivers with details on how their cars are performing, the marketing dashboard gives marketers the detailed measures they need to assess and adjust their marketing strategies. For example, VF Corporation uses a marketing dashboard to track the performance of its more than 30 lifestyle apparel brands—including Wrangler, Lee, The North Face, Vans, Nautica, 7 For All Mankind, Timberland, and others. VF's marketing dashboard tracks brand equity and trends, share of voice, market share, online sentiment, and marketing ROI in key markets worldwide, not only for VF brands but also for competing brands.[18]

Increasingly, however, beyond standard performance measures, marketers are using customer-centered measures of marketing impact, such as customer acquisition, customer engagement, customer experience, customer retention, customer lifetime value, and customer equity. These measures capture not only current marketing performance but also future performance resulting from stronger customer relationships. >> **Figure 2.8** views marketing expenditures as investments that produce returns in the form of more profitable customer relationships.[19] Marketing investments result in improved customer value, engagement, and satisfaction, which in turn increase customer attraction and retention. This increases individual customer lifetime values and the firm's overall customer equity. Increased customer equity, in relation to the cost of the marketing investments, determines return on marketing investment.

As one chief marketing officer says, "You have to be able to move on to those deeper engagement metrics, which show that for the money that I'm spending, here are the various programs that are working in terms of driving engagement with customers and ultimately driving purchase behavior and revenue."[20]

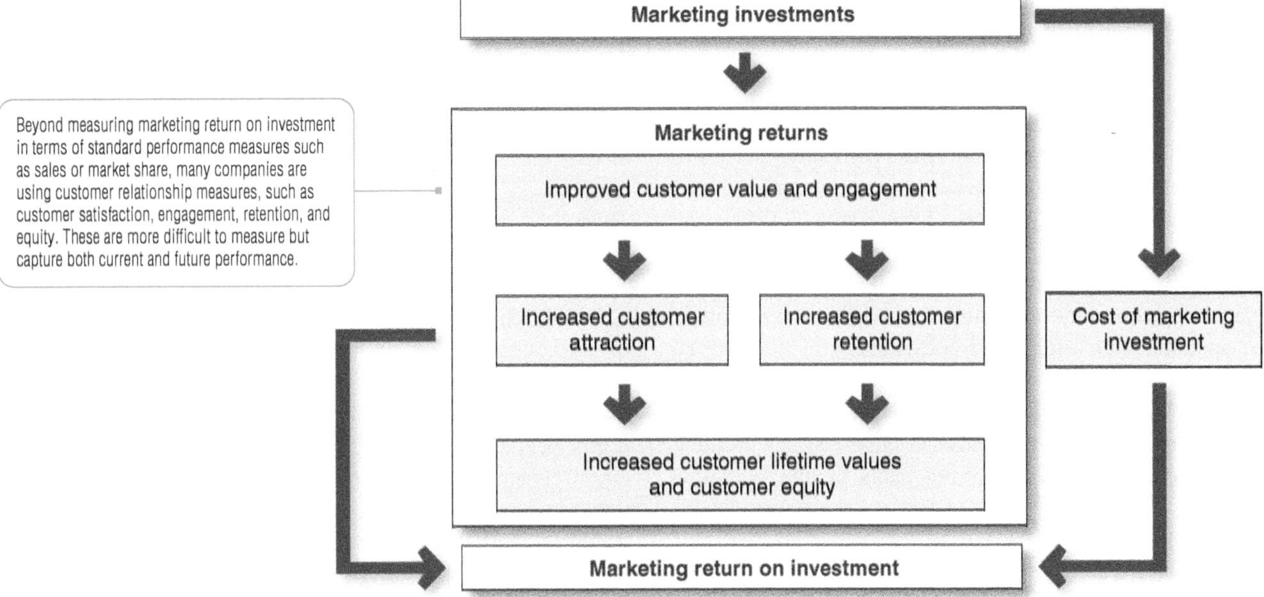

>> **Figure 2.8 Marketing Return on Investment**

Source: Adapted from Roland T. Rust, Katherine N. Lemon, and Valerie A. Zeithaml, "Return on Marketing: Using Consumer Equity to Focus Marketing Strategy," *Journal of Marketing*, January 2004, p. 112. Used with permission.

REVIEWING AND EXTENDING THE CONCEPTS

CHAPTER REVIEW AND KEY TERMS

Objectives Review

In Chapter 1, we defined marketing and outlined the steps in the marketing process. In this chapter, we examined company-wide strategic planning and marketing's role in the organization. Then we looked more deeply into marketing strategy and the marketing mix and reviewed the major marketing management functions. So you've now had a pretty good overview of the fundamentals of modern marketing.

OBJECTIVE 2-1 Explain company-wide strategic planning and its four steps. (pp 38–40)

Strategic planning sets the stage for the rest of the company's planning. Marketing contributes to strategic planning, and the overall plan defines marketing's role in the company.

Strategic planning involves developing a strategy for long-run survival and growth. It consists of four steps: (1) defining the company's mission, (2) setting objectives and goals, (3) designing a business portfolio, and (4) developing functional plans. The company's mission should be market oriented, realistic, specific, motivating, and consistent with the market environment. The mission is then transformed into detailed supporting goals and objectives, which in turn guide decisions about the business portfolio. Then each business and product unit must develop detailed marketing plans in line with the company-wide plan.

OBJECTIVE 2-2 Discuss how to design business portfolios and develop growth strategies. (pp 40–46)

Guided by the company's mission statement and objectives, management plans its business portfolio, or the collection of businesses and products that make up the company. The firm wants to produce a business portfolio that best fits its strengths and weaknesses to opportunities in the environment. To do this, it must analyze and adjust its current business portfolio and develop growth and downsizing strategies for adjusting the future portfolio. The company might use a formal portfolio-planning method. But many companies are now designing more-customized portfolio-planning approaches that better suit their unique situations.

OBJECTIVE 2-3 Explain marketing's role in strategic planning and how marketing works with its partners to create and deliver customer value. (pp 46–48)

Under the strategic plan, the major functional departments—marketing, finance, accounting, purchasing, operations, information systems, human resources, and others—must work together to accomplish strategic objectives. Marketing plays a key role in the company's strategic planning by providing a marketing concept philosophy and inputs regarding attractive market opportunities. Within individual business units, marketing designs strategies for reaching the unit's objectives and helps to carry them out profitably.

Marketers alone cannot produce superior value for customers. Marketers must practice partner relationship management, working closely with partners in other departments to form an effective *value chain* that serves the customer. And they must also partner effectively with other companies in the marketing system to form a competitively superior value delivery network.

OBJECTIVE 2-4 Describe the elements of a customer value–driven marketing strategy and mix and the forces that influence them. (pp 48–54)

Customer engagement, value, and relationships are at the center of marketing strategy and programs. Through market segmentation, targeting, differentiation, and positioning, the company divides the total market into smaller segments, selects segments it can best serve, and decides how it wants to bring value to target consumers in the selected segments. It then designs an integrated marketing mix to produce the response it wants in the target market. The marketing mix consists of product, price, place, and promotion decisions (the four Ps).

OBJECTIVE 2-5 List the marketing management functions, including the elements of a marketing plan, and discuss the importance of measuring and managing marketing return on investment. (pp 54–59)

To find the best strategy and mix and to put them into action, the company engages in marketing analysis, planning, implementation, and control. The main components of a marketing plan are the executive summary, the current marketing situation, threats and opportunities, objectives and issues, marketing strategies, action programs, budgets, and controls. Planning good strategies is often easier than carrying them out. To be successful, companies must also be effective at implementation—turning marketing strategies into marketing actions.

Marketing departments can be organized in one way or a combination of ways: functional marketing organization, geographic organization, product management organization, or market management organization. In this age of customer relationships, more and more companies are now changing their organizational focus from product or territory management to customer relationship management. Marketing organizations carry out marketing control, both operating control and strategic control.

More than ever, marketing accountability is the top marketing concern. Marketing managers must ensure that their marketing dollars are being well spent. In a tighter economy, today's marketers face growing pressures to show that they are adding value in line with their costs. In response, marketers are developing better measures of marketing return on investment. Increasingly, they are using customer-centered measures of marketing impact as a key input into their strategic decision making.

Key Terms

Objective 2-1
Strategic planning (p 38)
Mission statement (p 39)

Objective 2-2
Business portfolio (p 40)
Portfolio analysis (p 43)
Growth-share matrix (p 43)
Product/market expansion grid (p 45)
Market penetration (p 45)
Market development (p 45)
Product development (p 46)
Diversification (p 46)

Objective 2-3
Value chain (p 47)
Value delivery network (p 48)

Objective 2-4
Marketing strategy (p 48)
Market segmentation (p 49)
Market segment (p 49)
Market targeting (p 50)
Positioning (p 50)
Differentiation (p 52)
Marketing mix (p 52)

Objective 2-5
SWOT analysis (p 54)
Marketing implementation (p 56)
Marketing control (p 58)
Marketing return on investment (marketing ROI) (p 58)

DISCUSSION AND CRITICAL THINKING

Discussion Questions

2-1. Discuss the role marketing plays in the company-wide strategic planning process. (AACSB: Written and Oral Communications)

2-2. How does a firm evaluate and analyze its business portfolio? (AACSB: Written and Oral Communications; Reflective Thinking)

2-3. Describe the differences between a value chain and a value delivery network. (AACSB: Written and Oral Communication, Reflective Thinking)

2-4. Why do companies use market segmentation, market targeting, differentiation, and positioning in implementing an effective marketing strategy? (AACSB: Written and Oral Communication)

2-5. What is an integrated marketing mix, and why is it important for a firm's marketing strategy? (AACSB: Written and Oral Communication; Reflective Thinking)

2-6. Describe the five marketing management functions. How are they related to one another? (AACSB: Written and Oral Communication)

Critical Thinking Exercises

2-7. Go to www.kellogs.com, and examine the brands offered by Kellogg's. Using the BCG growth-share matrix, classify 10 brands as stars, question marks, cash cows, or dogs. Find at least one product you believe fits into each of the four quadrants. Support your position. (AACSB: Written and Oral Communication; Reflective Thinking)

2-8. Examine Starbucks, and determine how its marketers have positioned the company relative to the competition. How has Starbucks used differentiation to create customer value? (AACSB: Written and Oral Communication)

2-9. Locate the mission statements for the following organizations: (a) USAA, (b) United Airlines, (c) South Carolina State University (SC State), and (d) IKEA. Evaluate each statement using the criteria for creating a sound mission statement. What could be done to improve each organization's mission statement? (AACSB: Written and Oral Communication; Reflective Thinking)

MINICASES AND APPLICATIONS

Online, Mobile, and Social Media Marketing Diff Eyewear

Diff Eyewear is a successful business built around a socially conscious mission. The company makes and sells stylish eyewear with comparable quality but a significantly lower price than luxury eyewear brands. The best part of Diff is its "buy one, get one free" charitable mission. For every pair of Diff sunglasses purchased, the company donates a pair of reading glasses to someone in need. Diff has provided more than 180,000 pairs of reading glasses to underserved communities throughout Africa. Additionally, through its Sabo Project "Pouch Program," Diff provides fair wages to artisans in Uganda who make protective eyewear carrying cases. It invests the proceeds of that program in a local school and provides health and literacy workshops for community members. Diff promotes its products and mission via a range of social media platforms, primarily Instagram, Facebook, Snapchat, Pinterest, Twitter, and YouTube. It also enlists celebrities such as Demi Lovato and Jessie James Decker. Visit www.diffeyewear.com for more information.

2-10. Research Diff Eyewear to learn more about its products and to review its mission statement. What recommendations would you make to Diff regarding the visibility of its mission statement on various social media outlets? Explain. (AACSB: Written and Oral Communication; Reflective Thinking)

2-11. Create a new social media campaign for Diff that highlights its socially conscious mission. (AACSB: Written and Oral Communication; Reflective Thinking)

Marketing Ethics Creating Value or Distracting Consumers?

In early 2014, Chipotle Mexican Grill announced that it would stop using genetically modified ingredients (GMOs) in its restaurants. Many observers applauded this move. However, critics of the fast-food chain cited a lack of evidence to support its anti-GMO stance. They suspected that Chipotle's anti-GMO claim was simply a ploy to distract consumers from a larger issue: the company's risky sanitation practices. Chipotle's anti-GMO policies may have won the burrito chain some health-conscious customers, but at the same time customers were becoming sick after eating at some Chipotle locations, calling into question the firm's food handling and safety practices.

Steve Ells, founder and co-CEO of Chipotle, said the GMO decision was "another step toward the visions we have of changing the way people think about and eat fast food. Just because food is served fast doesn't mean it has to be made with cheap raw ingredients, highly processed with preservatives and fillers and stabilizers and artificial colors and flavors." However, ridding Chipotle's supply chain of genetically altered components proved difficult. The chain discovered GMOs in basic ingredients such as baking powder, cornstarch, canola and soy oils, cornmeal, and sugar. And many non-GMO ingredients were in short supply. For example, at one point, Chipotle found that it could not supply all its locations with enough non-GMO pork to make carnitas. Given the supply chain challenges, Chipotle decided to use non-GMO products in its food preparation but to continue to serve some soft drinks with sweeteners derived from genetically engineered corn.

2-12. Has Chipotle's focus on eliminating GMOs created value for its customers? Defend this market strategy. (AACSB: Written and Oral Communication; Ethical Understanding and Reasoning)

2-13. From an ethics standpoint, discuss Chipotle's focus on sourcing non-GMO food products rather than attention to food safety. The company's oversights in food safety resulted in numerous customers becoming ill (E. coli, norovirus, and salmonella). Discuss the challenges Chipotle still faces in overcoming the negative image that resulted. (AACSB: Written and Oral Communication; Reflective Thinking; Ethical Understanding and Reasoning)

Marketing by the Numbers Facebook versus Google

Facebook and Google are both giants in the tech industry. However, if you just compare sales, you would think that Google is a far better marketer than Facebook, considering Google's sales last year were almost triple Facebook's sales. Comparing net profits, Facebook bests Google by a slim margin. Sales and profits provide information to compare the profitability of companies, but between these numbers is information regarding the efficiency of marketing efforts in creating those sales and profits. Appendix 3: Marketing by the Numbers, Marketing Performance Measures, discusses other marketing profitability measures beyond the return on marketing investment (marketing ROI) measure described in this chapter. Review the appendix to answer the questions using the following information from the two companies' incomes statements (all numbers are in thousands):

	Facebook	Google
Sales	$40,653,000	$110,855,000
Gross Profit	$35,199,000	$65,272,000
Marketing Expenses	$5,431,501	$16,875,750
Net Income (Profit)	$15,920,000	$12,662,000

2-14. Calculate profit margin, net marketing contribution, marketing return on sales (or marketing ROS), and marketing return on investment (or marketing ROI) for each company. Which company is performing better? (AACSB: Written and Oral Communication; Information Technology; Analytical Thinking)

2-15. Go to Yahoo! Finance (http://finance.yahoo.com/), and find the income statements for two other competing companies. Perform the same analyses for these companies that you performed for the previous question. Which company is doing better overall and with respect to marketing? For marketing expenses, use 75 percent of the company's reported "Selling General and Administrative" expenses, as not all of the expenses in that category are marketing expenses. (AACSB: Written and Oral Communication; Analytical Thinking; Reflective Thinking)

Video Case Konica Minolta

To view this video case and its accompanying questions, please visit MyLab Marketing.

Konica Minolta has been in business since 1873. For decades, it was a successful photo company selling cameras, equipment, and supplies primarily to final consumers. But dramatic changes in the marketing environment forced the company to reevaluate its marketing strategy and ultimately to abandon what had been its primary industry.

Today, Konica Minolta has a successful business-to-business strategy centered on office equipment and print products for commercial printers. The company has also developed a health-care and medical group, an optics group, and a division that produces components for mobile phones and televisions. With the advent and growth of social media, Konica Minolta's marketing strategy continues to evolve.

Company Cases 2 Facebook/8 Bose/13 Procter & Gamble

See Appendix 1 for cases appropriate for this chapter.

Case 2, Facebook: Making the World More Open and Connected. Facebook has amassed more than two billion active monthly users by focusing on its mission—"to give people the power to share and make the world more open and connected."

Case 8, Bose: Better Products by Focusing on the Product. Bose has been successful for more than 50 years by focusing on a strategy of creating superior products.

Case 13, Procter & Gamble: Selling Through Customer Business Development. Using a sales strategy it calls Customer Business Development, P&G succeeds by ensuring that its retail customers succeed.

Writing Assignments

2-16. Explain the roles of market segmentation, market targeting, differentiation, and positioning in implementing an effective marketing strategy. (AACSB: Communication)

2-17. Marketers are increasingly held accountable for demonstrating marketing success.Research the various marketing metrics, in addition to those described in the chapter and Appendix 3, used by marketers to measure marketing performance. Write a brief report of your findings. (AACSB: Written and Oral Communication; Reflective Thinking)

3 Analyzing the Marketing Environment

Objectives Outline

OBJECTIVE 3-1 **Describe the environmental forces that affect the company's ability to serve its customers.** See: The Microenvironment and Macroenvironment (pp 66–70)

OBJECTIVE 3-2 **Explain how changes in the demographic and economic environments affect marketing decisions.** See: The Demographic and Economic Environments (pp 70–78)

OBJECTIVE 3-3 **Identify the major trends in the firm's natural and technological environments.** See: The Natural and Technological Environments (pp 79–83)

OBJECTIVE 3-4 **Explain the key changes in the political and cultural environments.** See: The Political–Social and Cultural Environments (pp 83–89)

OBJECTIVE 3-5 **Discuss how companies can react to the marketing environment.** See: Responding to the Marketing Environment (pp 89–92)

Previewing the Concepts

So far, you've learned about the basic concepts of marketing and the steps in the marketing process for engaging and building profitable relationships with targeted consumers. Next, we'll begin digging deeper into the first step of the marketing process—understanding the marketplace and customer needs and wants. In this chapter, you'll see that marketing operates in a complex and changing environment. Other actors in this environment—suppliers, intermediaries, customers, competitors, publics, and others—may work with or against the company. Major environmental forces—demographic, economic, natural, technological, political, and cultural—shape marketing opportunities, pose threats, and affect the company's ability to engage customers and build customer relationships. To develop effective marketing strategies, a company must first understand the environment in which marketing operates.

To start, let's look at Microsoft, the technology giant that dominated the computer software world throughout the 1990s and much of the 2000s. Its Windows and Office products have long been must-haves in the PC market. But with the decline in stand-alone personal computers and the surge in digitally connected devices—everything from smartphones and tablets to internet-connected TVs—mighty Microsoft found itself struggling to find its place in a fast-changing environment. However, the tech giant has now reinvented itself as a relevant brand that consumers can't live without in the post-PC era.

First Stop

Microsoft: Adapting to the Fast-Changing Marketing Environment

Twenty years ago, talking high-tech meant talking about the almighty personal computer. Intel provided the PC microprocessors while manufacturers such as Dell and HP built and marketed the machines. But it was Microsoft that really ruled the PC industry—it made the operating systems that kept most PCs humming. As the dominant software developer, Microsoft put its Windows operating system and Office productivity suite on almost every computer sold.

The huge success of Windows drove Microsoft's revenues, profits, and stock price to dizzying heights. By the start of the 2000s, Microsoft's was the most valuable company in corporate history. In those heady days, no company was more relevant than Microsoft. And from a competitive standpoint, no company was more powerful.

But times change. Moving through the first decade of the new millennium, PC sales growth flattened as the world fell in love with a rush of alluring new digital devices and technologies. The computing industry shifted rapidly from stationary stand-alones like the PC to connected mobile devices that linked users to an ever-on, ever-changing world of information, entertainment, and socialization options. But unlike PCs, those mobile devices didn't need Microsoft Windows.

In the new digitally connected world, Microsoft found itself lagging more-glamorous competitors such as Google, Apple, Samsung, and even Amazon and Facebook, which provided a complete slate of things digital—not just the software but also the smart devices, connecting technologies, and even digital destinations. Although still financially strong and still the world's dominant PC software maker, Microsoft lost some of its luster. In turn, the company's growth stalled and profits languished at early-2000s levels for a dozen years or more. Microsoft needed to change with the times—and fast.

So Microsoft began a sweeping transformation to align itself better with the new digital world order. More than just a PC software developer, Microsoft set out to become a full-line digital competitor. In tune with the times, the company pursued a new "mobile first, cloud first" strategy. It developed a mobile version of its Windows operating system—the longtime company cash cow. And it created Office 365—a cloud-based subscription version of its market-dominating suite of productivity apps.

At the same time, Microsoft unleashed a flurry of new, improved, or acquired digital products and services. These included an upgraded version of Skype, a OneDrive cloud storage solution, and even an innovative new digital hardware line—Microsoft Surface tablets and Microsoft Surface Book laptops—that it hoped would lead the way to even more innovative Windows devices. Microsoft also dabbled seriously with mobile phones, first buying then selling phone maker Nokia and then rumored to be soon introducing its own Windows-based Surface phone. Microsoft hoped that the Surface line, along with its Xbox console, would give it better access to three important digital screens beyond the PC—tablets, TVs, and phones.

But even with these new initiatives, Microsoft found itself still chasing rather than leading the pack of new digital competitors. The Microsoft Windows operating system still dominates the declining PC market, but its mobile versions capture only a sliver of the mobile operating system market dominated by Apple iOS and Google Android. Although its Surface tablets and laptops have done well, they still lag far behind those of Apple and Samsung. And Microsoft has yet to introduce a successful Surface phone.

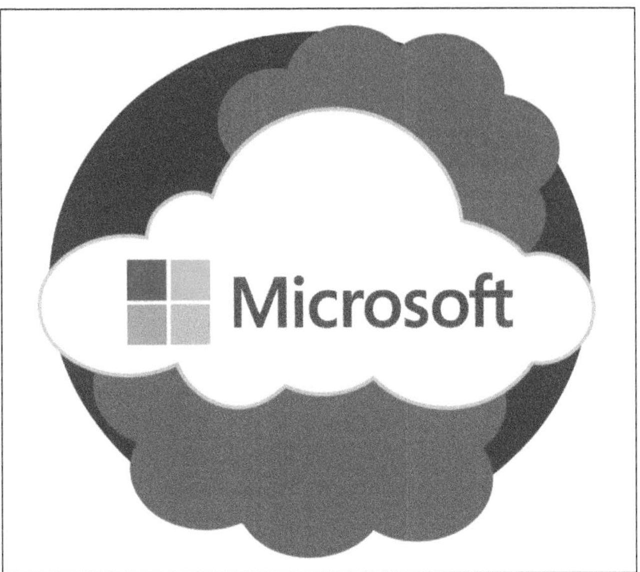

» In the fast-changing digital marketing environment, Microsoft has transformed itself into a brand that consumers can't live without in the post-PC world.

imageBROKER/Alamy Stock Photo

Thus, to continue its massive makeover, Microsoft has made yet another significant shift. It started with a new mission. Microsoft's early mission was to "put a computer on every desk in every home." Not until 2013 did that change to a grander but still-product-centered mission: "to create a family of devices and services for individuals and businesses that empower people around the globe at home, at work, and on the go." Then in 2015, Microsoft announced a simpler mission: "to empower every person and every organization on the planet to achieve more."

Microsoft has undergone a dramatic transformation to better align itself with the new digital world in the post-PC era. More than just making the software that makes PCs run, Microsoft now wants to empower every person and every organization on the planet to achieve more, regardless of what device or operating system they use.

The new mission focuses not on devices and services but on outcomes. Rather than chasing competitors in mobile devices and operating systems, Microsoft now intends to lead them in productivity tools. And instead of clinging to Windows as the linchpin in its future, Microsoft is taking its productivity apps and services headlong into the cloud. The old Microsoft didn't care what apps you ran as long as you ran them on Windows. In a dramatic shift, the new Microsoft doesn't care what operating system you run as long as you're using Microsoft apps and services.

At the center of Microsoft's cloud offerings is good old Microsoft Office, with its Word, Excel, PowerPoint, and other productivity apps. Although competitors Google and Apple have word processing, spreadsheet, and presentation apps, Office is still far and away the gold standard for getting things done, whether for large corporations, small businesses, students, or home users. In the old days, Office came bundled with Windows. But the plan now is to make Office accessible to anyone and everyone. Office 365 subscription services can be accessed from the cloud and run on any device or operating system—iOS, Android, or Windows.

Accessibility is only the start. Microsoft's goal is to make Office 365 the center for a whole new family of cloud-based online services that work seamlessly together. To that end, in addition to mobile versions of Word, Excel, and PowerPoint, Microsoft has been adding an ever-expanding set of mobile productivity apps to the Office 365 portfolio, such as Outlook Mobile (email) and To-Do (task management). Moreover, the cloud-based Office 365 increases the likelihood that subscribers will sign up for other Microsoft services, such as Skype, OneDrive cloud services, or Power BI data analytics and insights tools.

Another key part of Microsoft's new direction is artificial intelligence (AI)—the latest battleground for digital giants Amazon, Google, Samsung, and IBM. For example, Microsoft's Windows 10 AI voice assistant—Cortana, already installed on hundreds of millions of Windows devices worldwide—is currently no match for Amazon's Alexa, Apple's Siri, or Google's "OK, Google." However, Microsoft recently partnered with Amazon to let their formerly competing voice assistants work with and through each other. The partnership gives Amazon Echo users access to Microsoft's productivity apps. In turn, it gives Cortana users access to Alexa's smart home capabilities, such as streaming music and controlling smart home devices.

So this is not your grandfather's Microsoft. With its sweeping transformation well under way, Microsoft now seems to be making the right moves to stay ahead of the times. As a result, sales and profit growth have rebounded. Although the Windows operating system remains a key component of Microsoft's current success, the company's future now lies in the cloud. And with nearly $19 billion in commercial cloud revenues last year, more than 20 percent of its total revenues, Microsoft is now winning the cloud wars, ahead of Amazon, IBM, and a host of others.

Still, continued success will depend on Microsoft's ability to effectively adapt to—or even lead—the lightning-quick changes occurring in the marketing environment. "The opportunity ahead for Microsoft is vast," says Microsoft's CEO, "but to seize it, we must focus clearly, move faster, and continue to transform."[1]

Marketing environment
The actors and forces outside marketing that affect marketing management's ability to build and maintain successful relationships with target customers.

A company's **marketing environment** consists of the actors and forces outside marketing that affect marketing management's ability to build and maintain successful relationships with target customers. Like Microsoft, companies must constantly watch and adapt to the changing environment—or, in many cases, lead those changes.

More than any other group in the company, marketers must be environmental trend trackers and opportunity seekers. Although every manager in an organization should watch the outside environment, marketers have two special aptitudes. They have disciplined methods—marketing research, marketing intelligence, and marketing analytics—for collecting information and developing insights about the marketing environment. They also spend more time in customer and competitor environments. By carefully studying the environment, marketers can adapt their strategies to meet new marketplace challenges and opportunities.

Author Comment
The microenvironment includes all the actors close to the company that affect, positively or negatively, its ability to engage with and create value for customers.

The Microenvironment and Macroenvironment

OBJECTIVE 3-1 Describe the environmental forces that affect the company's ability to serve its customers.

The marketing environment consists of a *microenvironment* and a *macroenvironment*. The **microenvironment** consists of the actors close to the company that affect its ability to engage and serve its customers—the company, suppliers, marketing intermediaries, customer markets, competitors, and publics. The **macroenvironment** consists of the larger societal forces that affect the microenvironment—demographic, economic, natural, technological, political, and cultural forces. We look first at the company's microenvironment.

Microenvironment
The actors close to the company that affect its ability to serve its customers—the company, suppliers, marketing intermediaries, customer markets, competitors, and publics.

Macroenvironment
The larger societal forces that affect the microenvironment—demographic, economic, natural, technological, political, and cultural forces.

The Microenvironment

Marketing management's job is to build relationships with customers by creating customer value and satisfaction. However, marketing managers cannot do this alone. >> **Figure 3.1** shows the major actors in the marketer's microenvironment. Marketing success requires building relationships with other company departments, suppliers, marketing intermediaries, competitors, various publics, and customers, which combine to make up the company's value delivery network.

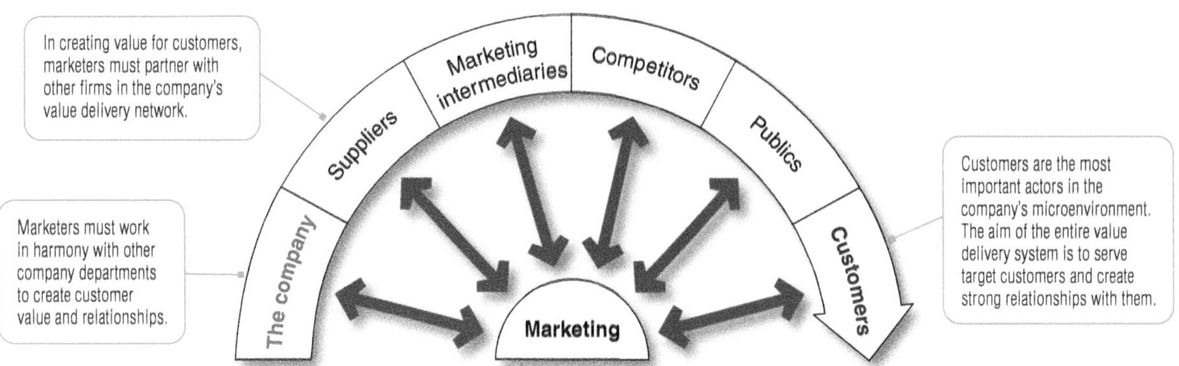
In creating value for customers, marketers must partner with other firms in the company's value delivery network.
Marketers must work in harmony with other company departments to create customer value and relationships.
The company
Suppliers
Marketing intermediaries
Competitors
Publics
Customers
Marketing
Customers are the most important actors in the company's microenvironment. The aim of the entire value delivery system is to serve target customers and create strong relationships with them.

>> Figure 3.1 Actors in the Microenvironment

The Company

In designing marketing plans, marketing management takes other company groups into account—groups such as top management, finance, research and development (R&D), purchasing, operations, human resources, and accounting. All of these interrelated groups form the internal environment. Top management sets the company's mission, objectives, broad strategies, and policies. Marketing managers make decisions within these broader strategies and plans. Then, as we discussed in Chapter 2, marketing managers must work closely with other company departments. With marketing taking the lead, all departments—from manufacturing and finance to legal and human resources—share the responsibility for understanding customer needs and creating customer value.

Suppliers

Suppliers form an important link in the company's overall customer value delivery network. They provide the resources needed by the company to produce its goods and services. Supplier problems can seriously affect marketing. Marketing managers must watch supply availability and costs. Supply shortages or delays, natural disasters, and other events can cost sales in the short run and damage customer satisfaction in the long run. Rising supply costs may force price increases that can harm the company's sales volume.

Most marketers today treat their suppliers as partners in creating and delivering customer value. >> For example, home furnishings retailer IKEA knows the importance of building close relationships with its extensive network of suppliers:[2]

IKEA

>> Suppliers: Giant furniture retailer IKEA doesn't just buy from its suppliers. It involves them deeply in the process of delivering trendy but simple and affordable home furnishings to create a better everyday life for its customers.

IKEA, the world's largest furniture retailer, is the quintessential global cult brand. Last year, the Scandinavian retailer attracted more than 936 million visits to its 403 huge stores in 49 world markets plus an additional 2.3 *billion* website visits, generating more than $47 billion in sales. And IKEA is growing at a healthy clip—sales have climbed 24 percent in only the past three years. But the biggest obstacle to growth isn't opening new stores and attracting customers. Rather, it's finding enough of the right kinds of *suppliers* to help design and produce the billions of dollars of goods that those customers will carry out of its stores. IKEA currently relies on about 1,000 suppliers in 51 countries to stock its shelves. At its current rate of growth, that number might have to double over the next decade.

IKEA's mission is to create a better everyday life for customers by offering trendy but simple and practical home furnishings at prices so low that as many people as possible can afford them. But before it can sell the billions of dollars' worth of products its customers covet, IKEA must first develop a robust and reliable network of supplier–partners who can help it design and make all those products. IKEA does more than just buy from suppliers. The design process for a new IKEA product can take up to three years. IKEA's designers start with a basic customer value proposition and then work closely with key suppliers throughout the process to bring that proposition to life—refining the design, improving function, and reducing costs. "What makes the IKEA design process unique is that our suppliers play a very important role," says the company. It's a mutually beneficial partnership from start to finish, what IKEA refers to as "growing together as partners with passion for [creating] a better life at home. We strive to be the good link between suppliers and customers."

Marketing Intermediaries

Marketing intermediaries
Firms that help the company to promote, sell, and distribute its goods to final buyers.

Marketing intermediaries help the company promote, sell, and distribute its products to final buyers. They include resellers, physical distribution firms, marketing services agencies, and financial intermediaries. *Resellers* are distribution channel firms that help the company find customers or make sales to them. These include wholesalers and retailers that buy and resell merchandise. *Physical distribution firms* help the company stock and move goods from their points of origin to their destinations. *Marketing services agencies* are the marketing research firms, advertising agencies, media firms, and marketing consulting firms that help the company target and promote its products to the right markets. *Financial intermediaries* include banks, credit companies, insurance companies, and other businesses that help finance transactions or insure against the risks associated with the buying and selling of goods.

Like suppliers, marketing intermediaries form an important component of the company's overall value delivery network. Thus, today's marketers recognize the importance of working with their intermediaries as partners rather than simply as channels through which they sell their products. >> For example, when Coca-Cola signs on as the exclusive beverage provider for a fast-food chain, such as McDonald's, Wendy's, or Subway, it provides much more than just soft drinks. It also pledges powerful marketing support:[3]

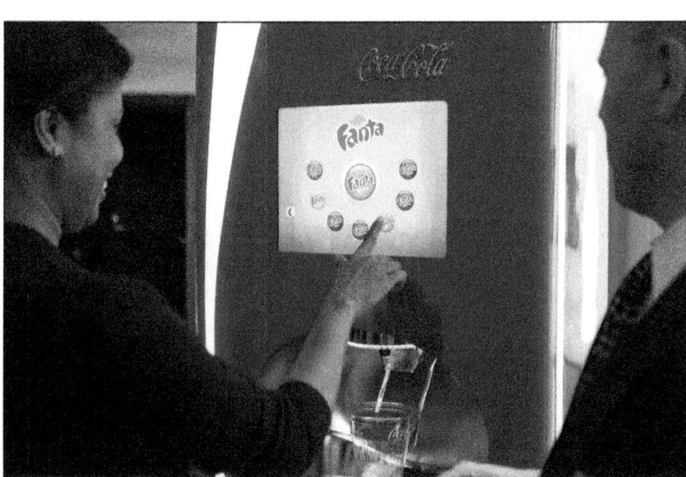

>> Partnering with intermediaries: Coca-Cola provides its retail partners with much more than just soft drinks. It also pledges powerful marketing support.

Andrew Harrer/Bloomberg/Getty Images

> Coca-Cola assigns cross-functional teams dedicated to understanding the finer points of each retail partner's business. It conducts a staggering amount of research on beverage consumers and shares these insights with its partners. It analyzes the demographics of U.S. zip code areas and helps partners determine which Coke brands are preferred in their areas. Coca-Cola has even studied the design of drive-through menu boards to better understand which layouts, fonts, letter sizes, colors, and visuals induce consumers to order more food and drink. Based on such insights, the Coca-Cola food service solutions group develops marketing programs and merchandising tools that help its retail partners improve their beverage sales and profits. Its website, www.CokeSolutions.com, provides retailers with a wealth of information, business solutions, merchandising tips, advice on digital and social media marketing, and techniques on how to go green. Such intense partnering has made Coca-Cola a runaway leader in the U.S. fountain-soft-drink market.

Competitors

The marketing concept states that, to be successful, a company must provide greater customer value and satisfaction than its competitors do. Thus, marketers must do more than simply adapt to the needs of target consumers. They also must gain strategic advantage by positioning their offerings strongly against competitors' offerings in the minds of consumers.

No single competitive marketing strategy is best for all companies. Each firm should consider its own size and industry position compared with those of its competitors. Large firms with dominant positions in an industry can use certain strategies that smaller firms cannot afford. But being large is not enough. There are winning strategies for large firms, but there are also losing ones. And small firms can develop strategies that give them better rates of return than large firms enjoy.

Publics

Public
Any group that has an actual or potential interest in or impact on an organization's ability to achieve its objectives.

The company's marketing environment also includes various publics. A **public** is any group that has an actual or potential interest in or impact on an organization's ability to achieve its objectives. We can identify seven types of publics:

- ***Financial publics.*** This group influences the company's ability to obtain funds. Banks, investment analysts, and stockholders are the major financial publics.
- ***Media publics.*** This group carries news, features, editorial opinions, and other content. It includes television stations, newspapers, magazines, and blogs and other social media.
- ***Government publics.*** Management must take government developments into account. Marketers must often consult the company's lawyers on issues of product safety, truth in advertising, and other matters.
- ***Citizen-action publics.*** A company's marketing decisions may be questioned by consumer organizations, environmental groups, minority groups, and others. Its public relations department can help it stay in touch with consumer and citizen groups.
- ***Internal publics.*** This group includes workers, managers, volunteers, and the board of directors. Large companies use newsletters and other means to inform and motivate their internal publics. When employees feel good about the companies they work for, this positive attitude spills over to the external publics.
- ***General public.*** A company needs to be concerned about the general public's attitude toward its products and activities. The public's image of the company affects its buying behavior.
- ***Local publics.*** This group includes local community residents and organizations. Large companies usually work to become responsible members of the local communities in which they operate.

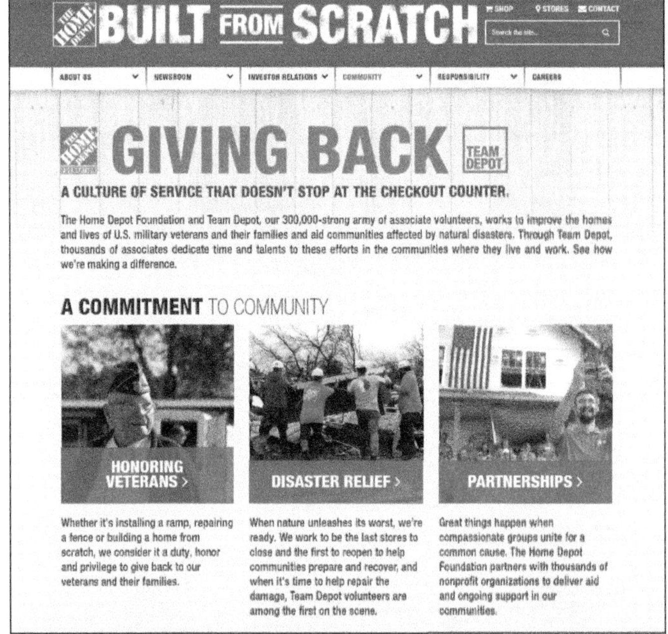

>> Publics: The Home Depot Foundation gives back to local communities through support for local nonprofits, grants, and countless Team Depot volunteer hours. Its mission is simple: improve the homes and lives of people.

A company can prepare marketing plans and programs for major publics as well as for customer markets. >> For example, home-improvement retailer The Home Depot gives back to its local publics through its charitable giving arm, The Home Depot Foundation:[4]

> The Home Depot Foundation has a simple mission: improve the homes and lives of people. Through its support for local nonprofits, grants, and countless employee volunteer hours, in addition to natural disaster relief, the foundation focuses on repairing and refurbishing homes and facilities for military veterans who face growing financial and physical hardships as they return to civilian life. The goal is "to ensure every veteran has a safe place to call home." To that end, the foundation provides Veteran Housing Grants to nonprofits that help develop and repair housing for veterans. And through Team Depot—the company's employee-led volunteer program—dedicated Home Depot employees volunteer their time in local communities to create a meaningful impact on veterans' lives. Since 2011, The Home Depot Foundation has improved more than 37,000 veteran homes and facilities.

Customers

Customers are the most important actors in the company's microenvironment. The aim of the entire value delivery network is to engage target customers and create strong relationships with them. The company might target any or all of five types of customer markets. *Consumer markets* consist of individuals and households that buy goods and services for personal consumption. *Business markets* buy goods and services for further processing or use in their production processes, whereas *reseller markets* buy goods and services to resell at a profit. *Government markets* consist of government agencies that buy goods and services to produce public services or transfer the goods and services to others who need them. Finally, *international markets* consist of these buyers in other countries, including consumers, producers, resellers, and governments. Each market type has special characteristics that call for careful study by the seller.

Author Comment
The macroenvironment consists of broader forces that affect the actors in the microenvironment.

The Macroenvironment

The company and all the other actors operate in a larger macroenvironment of forces that shape opportunities and pose threats to the company. >> **Figure 3.2** shows the six major forces in the company's macroenvironment. Even the most dominant companies can be vulnerable to the often turbulent and changing forces in the marketing environment. Some of these forces are unforeseeable and uncontrollable. Others can be predicted and handled through skillful management. Companies that understand and adapt well to their environments can thrive. Those that don't can face difficult times. One-time dominant market leaders such as Xerox, Sears, Sony, and Kodak have learned this lesson the hard way. In the remaining sections of this chapter, we examine these forces and show how they affect marketing plans.

Author Comment
Changes in demographics mean changes in markets, so they are very important to marketers. We first look at the biggest demographic trend—the changing age structure of the population.

The Demographic and Economic Environments

OBJECTIVE 3-2 Explain how changes in the demographic and economic environments affect marketing decisions.

The Demographic Environment

Demography
The study of human populations in terms of size, density, location, age, gender, race, occupation, and other statistics.

Demography is the study of human populations in terms of size, density, location, age, gender, race, occupation, and other statistics. The demographic environment is of major interest to marketers because it involves people, and people make up markets. The world population is growing at an explosive rate. It now exceeds 7.4 billion people and is expected to grow to more than 8.6 billion by the year 2030.[5] The world's large and highly diverse population poses both opportunities and challenges.

Changes in the world demographic environment have major implications for business. Thus, marketers keep a close eye on demographic trends and developments in their markets. They analyze changing age and family structures, geographic population shifts, educational characteristics, and population diversity. Here, we discuss the most important demographic trends in the United States.

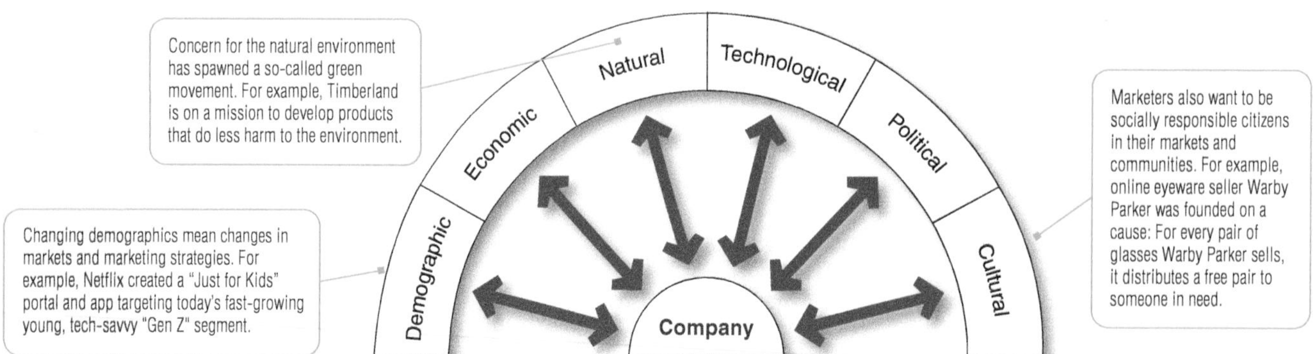

>> **Figure 3.2 Major Forces in the Company's Macroenvironment**

The Changing Age Structure of the Population

The U.S. population currently stands at more than 327 million and may reach almost 360 million by 2030.[6] The single most important demographic trend in the United States is the changing age structure of the population. Primarily because of falling birthrates and longer life expectancies, the U.S. population is rapidly getting older. In 1970, the median age was 28; by 2016, it was 38.[7] This aging of the population will have a significant impact on markets and those who service them.

The U.S. population contains several generational groups. Here, we discuss the four largest groups—the baby boomers, Generation X, the millennials, and Generation Z—and their impact on today's marketing strategies.

Baby boomers
The 74 million people born during the years following World War II and lasting until 1964.

The Baby Boomers. There are currently 74 million U.S. **baby boomers**, people born during the post–World War II baby boom from 1946 to 1964. Over the years, the baby boomers have been one of the most powerful forces shaping the marketing environment. The youngest boomers are now in their 50s; the oldest are in their early 70s and well into retirement.

The baby boomers are the wealthiest generation in U.S. history. Today's baby boomers account for about 22 percent of the U.S. population but control 42 percent of the spending power.[8] The boomers constitute a lucrative market for financial services, new housing and home remodeling, new cars, travel and entertainment, eating out, health and fitness products, and just about everything else.

It's fashionable for some marketers these days to look past the boomers, instead targeting the highly coveted millennial generation. Some may stereotype the older boomers as stuck in the past, out of touch, and not interested in new products. However, it would be a mistake to think of older boomers as phasing out or slowing down. Rather than viewing themselves that way, many of today's boomers see themselves as entering new life phases.

More active boomers have no intention of abandoning their youthful lifestyles as they age. For example, adults over 50 now account for 80 percent of luxury travel spending in America. Contrary to the popular belief that they are staid in their ways, one recent survey found that 82 percent of boomers are open to new brands. Anything but tech-phobic, boomers are also digitally active and increasingly social media savvy. Some 70 percent of baby boomers now use mobile internet. And they are the fastest-growing shopper demographic online, outspending younger generations two to one.[9]

Thus, although boomers may buy lots of products that help them deal with issues of aging—from vitamins to blood pressure monitors to Good Grips kitchen tools—they tend to appreciate marketers who appeal to their youthful thinking rather than their advancing age. For example, after its research showed that older consumers were "perplexed, annoyed, and amused" by how little brands seemed to understand them, insurance company Sun Life ran a "Welcome to life over 50" campaign challenging the stereotypes. In one ad, a distinguished older gentleman exits a boring cruise via a zip line into a cocktail bar, while a sunbathing beauty turns heads before removing her floppy hat to reveal that she is a "woman of 62."[10]

Similarly, Walgreens recently launched a campaign called "Carpe Med Diem," telling older boomers how to "seize the day" to get more out of life and their Medicare Part D prescription coverage at Walgreens, not just with savings on prescriptions but also with products that make them look and feel good.[11] One "Carpe Med Diem" ad features an active and stylish boomer-age woman with purple highlights in her hair and the headline "Who says blonds have more fun." In another ad, two boomer women pick up their prescriptions at Walgreens but also load up on sunscreen before heading out to a nude beach, where they drop their clothes and enjoy some fun in the sun. "Walgreen's has you covered," says the ad. "Who says that being on Medicare has to stop you from being edgy?"

Generation X
The 55 million people born between 1965 and 1980 in the "birth dearth" following the baby boom.

Generation X. The baby boom was followed by a "birth dearth," creating another generation of 55 million people born between 1965 and 1980.[12] Author Douglas Coupland calls them **Generation X** because they lie in the shadow of the boomers.

Considerably smaller than the boomer generation that precedes them and the millennials who follow, the Generation Xers are a sometimes-overlooked "in-between" consumer group. Although they seek success, they are less materialistic than the other groups; they prize experience, not acquisition. For many of the Gen Xers who are parents and homeowners, family comes first—both children and their aging parents—and career second.

From a marketing standpoint, the Gen Xers are a more skeptical bunch. They are sensible shoppers who research products heavily before they consider a purchase, prefer quality to quantity, and tend to be less receptive to overt marketing pitches. But once they find a brand, they tend to be more loyal than other generational groups. They are more receptive to irreverent ad pitches that make fun of convention and tradition. Many Gen Xers grew up before the internet and adapted to digital technology during young adulthood. Most are now fully connected and embrace the benefits of new technology.

The Gen Xers, now in their 40s and early 50s, have grown up and are taking over. They have increasingly displaced the lifestyles, culture, and values of the baby boomers. They are firmly into their careers, and many are proud homeowners with growing families. They are the most educated generation to date, and they possess hefty annual purchasing power. Although Gen Xers make up less than a quarter of all U.S. adults, they pull in 29 percent of the nation's total income.[13]

>> Targeting Gen Xers: Lowe's markets heavily to Gen X homeowners with ideas and advice on home-improvement projects and problems, urging them to "Never Stop Improving."

Bryan Bedder/Stringer/Getty Images

With so much potential, many brands and organizations focus on Gen Xers as a prime target segment. For example, a full 82 percent of Gen Xers own their own homes, making them an important segment for home-and-hearth marketers. >> Home-improvement retailer Lowe's markets heavily to Gen X homeowners, urging them to "Never Stop Improving." Through ads, online videos, and a substantial social media presence, Lowe's provides ideas and advice on a wide range of indoor and outdoor home-improvement projects and problems, providing solutions that make life simpler for busy Gen X homeowners and their families. Its myLowe's app is like a 24/7 home-improvement concierge that lets customers build room-by-room profiles of their homes, archive their Lowe's purchases, build product lists with photos, receive reminders for things like changing furnace filters, and even consult with store employees online as they plan out home-improvement projects.[14]

Millennials (or Generation Y)
The 75 million children of the baby boomers born between 1981 and 1997.

Millennials. Both the baby boomers and Gen Xers will one day be passing the reins to the **millennials** (also called **Generation Y** or the echo boomers). Born between 1981 and 1997, these children of the baby boomers number 75 million or more, dwarfing the Gen Xers and now larger than the baby boomer segment. The 20- to 30-something millennials, by their sheer numbers, wield substantial buying power and make up a huge and attractive market, both now and in the future.

One thing that all millennials have in common is their comfort with digital technology. They don't just embrace technology; it's a way of life. The millennials were the first generation to grow up in a world filled with computers, mobile phones, satellite TV, iPods and iPads, and online social media. As a result, they engage with brands in an entirely new way, such as with mobile or social media. In one recent survey of millennials, when asked where they do most of their shopping, 75 percent said online mobile or online laptop. Ninety-two percent preferred to do their banking over a web or mobile device.[15]

More than sales pitches from marketers, millennials seek authenticity, value, and opportunities to shape their own brand experiences and share them with others. Compared with other generational groups, they tend to be frugal, practical, connected, mobile, and impatient. "The millennials are open to connecting with brands, drawn to bite-size content (paid or not), and intrigued by new information, product-wise," notes one analyst. "However, the main [caution] is that it all needs to get done in an [efficient], digestible, and fluid manner."[16]

Many brands are now fielding specific products and marketing campaigns aimed at millennial needs and lifestyles. For example, many financial services firms are shedding their once-stodgy images to make their brands more appealing to mobile-first millennial consumers. >> Consider Fifth Third Bank:[17]

>> **Targeting millennials: Fifth Third Bank's "No Waiting" campaign engages impatient, social-media-savvy millennials with anything-but-stodgy videos demonstrating how its mobile app takes the wait out of banking.**

M4OS Photos/Alamy Stock Photo

> Fifth Third Bank knows that waiting is hard for time-crunched millennials. So it launched a new campaign called "No Waiting" that showed how its mobile app takes the wait out of banking. The campaign targeted younger consumers who are increasingly put off by the traditional banking world. The "No Waiting" campaign included TV spots but also a full slate of digital video and social media content, even a novel mobile game, aimed at engaging impatient, social-media-savvy millennials. The anything-but-stodgy digital videos provided humorous side-by-side comparisons showing that a check could be deposited using the Fifth Third Bank app faster than a hamster could eat five cheese balls or faster than an accordion player could play "Mary Had a Little Lamb." The campaign also featured an animated mobile game, "TXTvsTXT," that tested a user's texting speed. Something you wouldn't expect from a bank, the mobile game offered a quirky way for text-savvy millennials to test their finger-clicking skills, challenge friends on Facebook, and earn badges ranging from "molasses hands" to "turbo twiddler." Millennials "want it fast, whether in a text conversation or checking your balance on the Fifth Third Bank mobile app," said Fifth Third's chief marketer. "Our mobile banking takes the wait out of banking and we believe [this campaign told] that story in a fun engaging way."

Generation Z
People born between 1997 and 2016 who make up the kids, tweens, and teens markets.

Generation Z. Hard on the heels of the millennials is **Generation Z**, young people born between 1997 and 2016. The approximately 80 million Gen Zers make up the important kids, tweens, and teens markets. They spend an estimated $43 billion to $143 billion annually of their own money and influence up to $333 billion of family spending.[18] These young consumers also represent tomorrow's markets—they are now forming brand relationships that will affect their buying well into the future.

Even more than the millennials, the defining characteristic of Gen Zers is their utter fluency and comfort with digital technologies. Generation Z takes Wi-Fi, smartphones, tablets, internet-connected game consoles, and digital and social media for granted—they've always had them—making this group highly mobile, connected, and social. "If they're awake, they're online," quips one analyst. They have "digital in their DNA," says another.[19]

Gen Zers blend the online and offline worlds seamlessly as they socialize and shop. According to recent studies, despite their youth, more than half of all Generation Z tweens and teens do product research before buying a product or having their parents buy it for them. Some 39 percent of Gen Zer girls find shopping inspiration from social media, 35 percent read newsletters from brands, and 33 percent don't mind when brands work with influencers they like. Of Gen Zers who shop online, more than half *prefer* shopping online in categories ranging from electronics, books, music, sports equipment, and beauty products to clothes, shoes, and fashion accessories.[20]

Companies in almost all industries market products and services aimed at Generation Z. However, marketing to Gen Zers and their parents presents special challenges. Traditional media are still important to this group. But marketers know they must meet Gen Zers where they hang out and shop. Increasingly, that's in the online and mobile worlds. Although the under-13 set remains barred from social media such as Periscope, Snapchat, and Instagram, at least officially, social media plays a crucial marketing role for older Gen Zers. Today's youth are notoriously fickle and hard to pin down. The key is to engage these young consumers and let them help to define their brand experiences. For example, to engage young consumers more deeply, The North Face even invited them to help design its outdoor apparel and gear:[21]

> The North Face Youth Design Team held focus groups at summer camps with tweens 9- to 12-year-olds and their parents to get their input on the brand's outdoor clothing for kids. "We

find that these kids are just beginning to have their own personal style and are also beginning to influence their parents in their purchases," said a North Face marketer. To engage kids even further, The North Face launched a design contest in which it invited young would-be artists ages 6 to 12 to submit new apparel and gear designs that represent what the brand's "Never Stop Exploring" mantra meant to them. The winners saw their artwork featured in the brand's youth collection. "Kids are our main source of inspiration," said a Youth Design Team marketer. "It's important that we make things that are 'fun,' and how fun would it be to have kids help design our product?" Such engagement efforts have helped to make The North Face one of today's hottest brands among teens and tweens.

An important Generation Z marketing concern involves children's privacy and their vulnerability to marketing pitches. Companies marketing to this group must do so responsibly or risk the wrath of parents and public policy makers.

Generational Marketing. Do brands need to create separate products and marketing programs for each generation? Some experts warn that marketers need to be careful about turning off one generation each time they craft a product or message that appeals effectively to another. Others caution that each generation spans decades of time and many socioeconomic levels. For example, Generation Z spans kids through tweens and teens to early 20s, each group with its own beliefs and behaviors.

Thus, marketers need to form more precise age-specific segments within each group. More important, defining people by their birth date may be less effective than segmenting them by lifestyle, life stage, or the common values they seek in the products they buy. We will discuss many other ways to segment markets in Chapters 5 and 6.

The Changing American Family

The traditional household consists of a husband, wife, and children (and sometimes grandparents). Yet the historic American ideal of the two-child, two-car suburban family has lately been losing some of its luster.

In the United States, fewer than half of today's households contain married couples, down from 76 percent in 1940. Married couples with children under 18 represent only 20 percent of the nation's 125.8 million households. Married couples without children represent 30 percent, and single parents are another 9 percent. A full 35 percent are nonfamily households—singles living alone or unrelated adults of one or both sexes living together.[22]

More people are divorcing or separating, choosing not to marry, marrying later, remarrying, or marrying without intending to have children. Currently, 17 percent of all new marriages are interracial or interethnic, and 17 percent of married, same-sex couple households are raising children.[23] » The changing composition of today's modern American families is increasingly reflected in popular movies and television shows, such as *Modern Family* and Amazon's *Transparent*. Marketers must consider the special needs of nontraditional households because they are now growing more rapidly than traditional households. Each group has distinctive needs and buying habits.

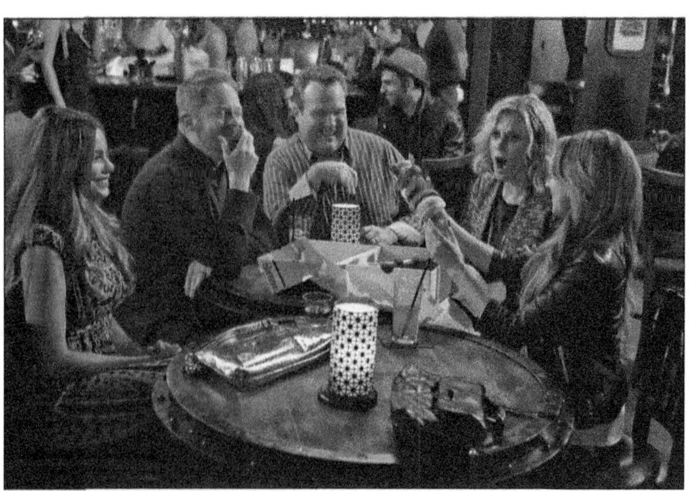

» The American family: The changing composition of American families is increasingly reflected in popular movies and television shows, such as *Modern Family*, the award-winning TV sitcom about an extended nontraditional family.

Mitch Haddad/Getty Images

The number of working women has also increased greatly, growing from 38 percent of the U.S. workforce in 1970 to 47 percent of the workforce today. American women now make up 42 percent of primary family breadwinners in households with children under 18. Among households made up of married couples with children, 60 percent are dual-income households; only the husband works in 27 percent. Meanwhile, more men also stay home with their children and manage the household while their wives go to work.[24]

Companies are now adapting their marketing to reflect the changing dynamics of American families. For example, whereas fathers were once ignored or portrayed as dolts in family-oriented ads, today's advertisers are showing more caring and capable dads. For example, nobody puts much thought into a commodity like toilet paper, but Georgia-Pacific created emotional involvement for its Angel Soft brand and its "Be soft. Be strong." positioning with a heart-warming commercial featuring a single father raising a daughter, from infant to young adulthood. The ad shows the sensitive and caring dad alone helping his daughter though the full range of childhood and teenage hurdles, closing with this advice: "When you're raising a child, be soft. When you're doing it alone, be strong. Life takes softness and strength." Another ad in the series showed a caring dad advising and consoling his teenage son after the break-up of his first true love.[25]

Other ads reflect the evolving diversity in modern American households. For example, Campbell Soup's recent "Your Father" commercial—part of the brand's "Made for Real. Real Life" campaign—featured a real-life same-sex couple feeding their son Campbell's Star Wars soup as they mimicked Darth Vader's famous Star Wars line "I am your father." The commercial, like others in the campaign, aligned the brand with the company's purpose: "Real food that matters for real life moments." Similarly, General Mills ran a series of commercials for Cheerios featuring an interracial couple and their daughter portraying typical young family scenarios—from the daughter pouring Cheerios on her sleeping dad's chest after learning that Cheerios are good for your heart to her negotiating for a new puppy after learning that she is going to have a baby brother. Said a General Mills marketer, "At Cheerios, we know there are many kinds of families and we celebrate them all."[26]

Geographic Shifts in Population

Americans are a mobile people, with about 11 percent of all U.S. residents moving each year. Over the past few decades, the U.S. population has shifted from the Snowbelt states to the Sunbelt states. The West and South have grown, whereas the Midwest and Northeast states have lost population.[27] Such population shifts interest marketers because people in different regions buy differently.

Also, for more than a century, Americans have been moving from rural to metropolitan areas. In the 1950s, they made a massive exit from the cities to the suburbs. Today, the migration to the suburbs continues. And more and more Americans are moving to "micropolitan areas," small cities located beyond congested metropolitan areas, such as Minot, North Dakota; Boone, North Carolina; Traverse City, Michigan; and Concord, New Hampshire. These smaller micros offer many of the advantages of metro areas—jobs, restaurants, diversions, community organizations—but without the population crush, traffic jams, high crime rates, and high property taxes often associated with heavily urbanized areas.[28]

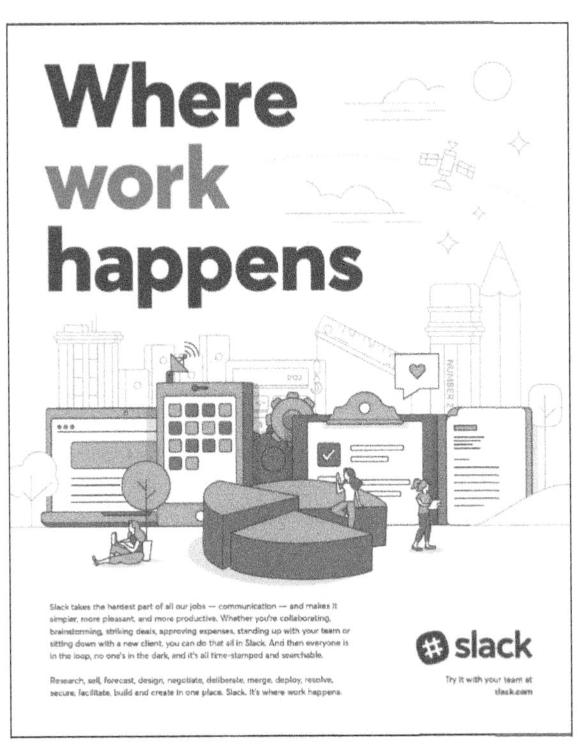

>> Working remotely: Apps like Slack let people work remotely and collaborate anywhere and everywhere through the internet and mobile devices.

Slack Technologies, Inc.

The shift in where people live has also caused a shift in where they work. For example, the migration to micropolitan and suburban areas has resulted in a rapid increase in the number of people who "telecommute"—working remotely at home or in a remote office with the help of PCs, tablets, smartphones, and broadband internet access. One recent study found that 43 percent of employed Americans spend at least some time working remotely.[29]

Many marketers are actively courting the lucrative telecommuting market. For example, online applications such as Citrix's GoToMeeting and Cisco's WebEx help people who telecommute or work remotely connect. And companies ranging from Salesforce.com to Google, IBM, and Slack offer cloud computing applications that let people collaborate from anywhere and everywhere through the internet and mobile devices. >> For example, Slack has been described as "a messaging app on steroids." It provides a shared digital workspace that connects people across remote offices and remote teams through real-time individual and group messaging, chat rooms, file sharing, video calls, and integrations with other cloud-based apps and services. Slack (an acronym for Searchable Log of All Conversations and Knowledge) is "where work happens, for millions of people around the world, every day."[30]

Additionally, for telecommuters who can't work fully at home, companies such as ShareDesk, DaVinci, and Regus rent out fully equipped shared office space. For a daily, monthly, or yearly fee, telecommuters who work away from a main office can rent shared space that includes the same amenities of a regular office, from networked computers, printers, and copiers to conference rooms and lounge spaces.

A Better-Educated, More White-Collar, More Professional Population

The U.S. population is becoming better educated. For example, in 2015, 90 percent of the U.S. population over age 25 had completed high school and 34 percent had a bachelor's degree or better, compared with 66 percent and 16 percent, respectively, in 1980.[31] The workforce also is becoming more white-collar. Job growth is now strongest for professional workers and weakest for manufacturing workers. Between 2014 and 2024, of 30 occupations projected to have the fastest employment growth, most require some type of postsecondary education.[32] The rising number of educated professionals affects not just what people buy but also how they buy.

Increasing Diversity

Countries vary in their ethnic and racial makeup. The United States has often been called a melting pot, where diverse groups from many nations and cultures have melted into a single, more homogenous whole. Instead, the United States seems to have become more of a "salad bowl" in which various groups have mixed together but have maintained their diversity by retaining and valuing important ethnic and cultural differences.

Marketers now face increasingly diverse markets, both at home and abroad, as their operations become more international in scope. The U.S. population is about 61 percent non-Hispanic white, with Hispanics at almost 18 percent, African Americans at over 13 percent, and Asian Americans at about 6 percent, with the remaining groups being Native Hawaiian, Pacific Islander, American Indian, Eskimo, or Aleut. The nation's ethnic populations are expected to explode in coming decades. By 2060, Hispanics will be about 28 percent of the population, African Americans will be about 14 percent, and Asian Americans will increase to 9 percent.[33]

Most large companies, from P&G, Walmart, and McDonald's to Toyota and Marriott, now target specially designed products, ads, and promotions to one or all of these diverse groups. For example, consider Marriott:[34]

> As part of its #LoveTravels campaign, Marriott launched a social media effort targeted specifically at Hispanic consumers. In a YouTube video series, Hispanic stars shared inspiring stories about their pride of heritage and related what travel means to them. In addition to YouTube videos, Marriott rolled out web and mobile ads on Pandora, Facebook, Twitter, and Instagram, hoping to inspire genuine and real conversations regarding culture and travel in the Hispanic community.
>
> More broadly, the long-running, award-winning Marriott #Love Travels campaign features inclusive efforts targeting a wide range of diverse groups, ranging from Hispanics, whites, blacks, and Asians to same-sex couples with kids and the transgender community. The #LoveTravels website links visitors to more than a dozen inspiring video portraits of diverse Americans and their love of travel. "Marriott welcomes all," say the website. "Love is a universal language understood by all, and when it travels, it has the power to bridge cultures and inspire discovery around the world—connecting people, place, and purpose."

Diversity goes beyond ethnic heritage. For example, many major companies explicitly target gay and lesbian consumers. According to one estimate, the 7 percent of U.S. adults who identify themselves as lesbian, gay, bisexual, or transgender (LGBT) have buying power of nearly $1 trillion.[35] As a result of TV shows such as *Modern Family, Transparent,* and *Gotham*; movies like *Brokeback Mountain* and *Carol*; and openly gay celebrities and public figures such as Neil Patrick Harris, Ellen DeGeneres, David Sedaris, and Apple CEO Tim Cook, the LGBT community has increasingly emerged in the public eye.

Brands in a wide range of industries are now targeting the LGBT community with gay-specific ads and marketing efforts. For example, Macy's and Best Buy run regular ads for their wedding registries featuring same-sex couples. Starbucks recently ran a holiday ad showing a same-sex couple leaning in for a kiss while holding a Starbucks cup together. Frito-Lay launched a limited-edition Doritos Rainbows, multicolored chips demonstrating the brand's "expression of inclusion and support for individuality." And Wells Fargo became one of the first banks to feature an LGBT couple in a national TV ad campaign. The heartwarming commercial, featuring a lesbian couple adopting a deaf child, is part of a nine-commercial series that also spotlights other diverse customer groups. Says a Wells Fargo representative, "We ... embrace diversity in every aspect, internally and externally. This [campaign] is a very important and natural progression of [that value] in how we serve our customers."[36]

Another attractive diversity segment is individuals with disabilities. One in five U.S. adults has a disability, representing a market of anywhere from $200 to $550 billion in annual spending power. Most individuals with disabilities are active consumers. For example, one study found that the segment spends $17.3 billion on 73 million business or leisure trips every year.[37] How are companies trying to reach consumers with disabilities? Many marketers now recognize that the worlds of people with disabilities and those without disabilities are one in the same. Marketers such as McDonald's, Verizon Wireless, Nike, Samsung, Nordstrom, Toyota, and Apple have featured people with disabilities in their mainstream marketing.

For instance, a recent Apple iPad Air commercial features real-life travel writer Chérie King traveling the world with her iPad Air in hand, helping her along as she travels through diverse global settings. She communicates back home, posts photos, writes articles, and lets her iPad translate what she wants to say to shopkeepers and others who don't speak English. Only at the very end of the commercial is her disability revealed—she is deaf.[38]

» As another example, Toyota's "Start Your Impossible" campaign, which ran during the most recent Olympic and Paralympic Winter Games, included ads highlighting inspirational real-life stories of athletes who overcame mobility challenges. One ad—titled "Good Odds"—featured Canadian Para alpine skier Lauren Woolstencroft, born missing her left arm below the elbow as well as both legs below the knees, overcoming tremendous odds to become a legendary Paralympic gold medalist. "Toyota believes that mobility goes beyond cars," says the company. "It is about enabling everyone the freedom of movement."[39]

As the population in the United States grows more diverse, successful marketers will continue to diversify their marketing programs to take advantage of opportunities in fast-growing segments.

» Targeting consumers with disabilities: Toyota's "Start Your Impossible" campaign included ads highlighting inspirational real-life stories of athletes who overcame mobility challenges, such Paralympic gold medalist alpine skier Lauren Woolstencroft.

Donald Miralle/Getty Images (photo); Editorial/Alamy Stock Photo (logo)

LINKING THE CONCEPTS

Stop here and think about how deeply these demographic factors impact all of us and, as a result, marketing strategies.

- Apply these demographic developments to your own life. Discuss some specific examples of how changing demographic factors affect you and your buying behavior.
- Identify a specific company that has done a good job of reacting to the shifting demographic environment—generational segments (baby boomers, Gen Xers, millennials, or Gen Zers), the changing American family, and increased diversity. Compare this company to one that's done a poor job.

Author Comment
The economic environment can offer both opportunities and threats. For example, in the post–Great Recession era of more sensible consumer spending, "value" has become the marketing watchword.

The Economic Environment

Economic environment
Economic factors that affect consumer purchasing power and spending patterns.

Markets require buying power as well as people. The **economic environment** consists of economic factors that affect consumer purchasing power and spending patterns. Economic factors can have a dramatic effect on consumer spending and buying behavior. For example, the Great Recession of 2008 to 2009 and its aftermath hit American consumers hard. After two decades of overspending, new economic realities forced consumers to bring their consumption back in line with their incomes and rethink their buying priorities.

In today's post-recession era, consumer spending is again on the rise. However, even as the economy has strengthened, rather than reverting to their old free-spending ways, Americans are retaining an enthusiasm for frugality. Each generational group faces financial challenges. For example, many boomers are watching their retirement accounts; many Gen Xers are facing the financial responsibilities of raising families, sending kids to college, and supporting aging parents; and many millennials are saddled with the expenses of paying back student loans and buying new homes.

As a result, consumers have now adopted a back-to-basics sensibility in their lifestyles and spending patterns that will likely persist for years to come. The new, more frugal spending values don't mean that people have resigned themselves to lives of deprivation. As the economy has improved, consumers are again indulging in luxuries and bigger-ticket purchases, just more sensibly. They are looking for greater value in the things they do buy. In turn, companies in all industries—from discounters such as Target to luxury brands such as Lexus and Tiffany—are focusing on value for the money, practicality, and durability in their product offerings and marketing pitches.

>> Economic environment: Consumers adopted a new back-to-basics sensibility in their lifestyles and spending patterns. To serve the tastes of these more financially frugal buyers, companies like Target are emphasizing the "pay less" side of their value propositions.

Justin Sullivan/Getty Images

>> For example, for years discount retailer Target focused increasingly on the "Expect More" side of its "Expect More. Pay Less." value proposition. Its carefully cultivated "upscale-discounter" image successfully differentiated it from Walmart's more hard-nosed "lowest-price" position. But when the economy soured and as buyers increasingly shifted toward low-priced and convenient online retailers such as Amazon, many consumers worried that Target's trendier assortments and hip marketing also meant higher prices. So Target has shifted its balance more toward the "Pay Less" half of the slogan, making certain that its prices are in line with Walmart's and that customers know it. Although still chic and trendy, Target's marketing now emphasizes practical price and savings appeals. Offering "more for your money" holds a prominent place in the Target mission. "We think a lot about your budget and how to give you the best value every time you shop with us," says the company.[40]

In adjusting to the economy, companies may be tempted to cut their marketing budgets and slash prices to coax customers into opening their wallets. However, although cutting costs and offering selected discounts can be important marketing tactics, smart marketers understand that making cuts in the wrong places can damage long-term brand images and customer relationships. The challenge is to balance the brand's value proposition with the current times while also enhancing its long-term equity. Thus, rather than slashing prices in uncertain economic times, many marketers hold the line on prices and instead explain why their brands are worth it.

Marketers should pay attention changes in major economic variables that have a large impact on the marketplace, such as income, cost of living, and savings and borrowing patterns. Companies watch and predict these variables using economic forecasting. Businesses do not have to be wiped out by an economic downturn or caught short in a boom. With adequate warning, they can take advantage of changes in the economic environment.

Author Comment
Today's enlightened companies are developing environmentally sustainable strategies in an effort to create a world economy that the planet can support indefinitely.

The Natural and Technological Environments

OBJECTIVE 3-3 Identify the major trends in the firm's natural and technological environments.

The Natural Environment

Natural environment
The physical environment and the natural resources that are needed as inputs by marketers or that are affected by marketing activities.

The **natural environment** involves the physical environment and the natural resources that are needed as inputs by marketers or that are affected by marketing activities. At the most basic level, unexpected happenings in the physical environment—anything from weather to natural disasters—can affect companies and their marketing strategies. For example, during a recent cold winter—in which the term *polar vortex* gusted into the American vocabulary—sales suffered across a wide range of businesses, from florists and auto dealers to restaurants, airlines, and tourist destinations. In contrast, the severe weather boosted demand for products such as salt, snowblowers, winter clothing, and auto repair centers.

Although companies can't prevent such natural occurrences, they should prepare for dealing with them. For example, shipping companies such as FedEx and UPS maintain corps of meteorologists on their staffs to anticipate weather conditions that might inhibit on-time deliveries around the world. "Someone awaiting a package in Bangkok doesn't care if it snowed in Louisville, Kentucky," says a UPS meteorologist. "They want their stuff."[41]

At a broader level, environmental sustainability concerns have grown steadily over the past several decades. In many cities around the world, air and water pollution have reached dangerous levels. World concern continues to mount about the possibilities of global warming, and many environmentalists fear that we soon will be buried in our own trash.

Marketers should be aware of several trends in the natural environment. The first involves growing *shortages of raw materials*. Air and water may seem to be infinite resources, but some groups see long-run dangers. Air pollution chokes many of the world's large cities, and water shortages are already a big problem in some parts of the United States and the world. By 2030, more than one in three people in the world will not have enough water to drink.[42] Renewable resources, such as forests and food, also have to be used wisely. Nonrenewable resources, such as oil, coal, and various minerals, pose a serious problem. Firms making products that require these scarce resources face large cost increases even if the materials remain available.

A second environmental trend is *increased pollution*. Industry will almost always damage the quality of the natural environment. Consider the disposal of chemical and nuclear wastes; the dangerous mercury levels in the ocean; the quantity of chemical pollutants in the soil and food supply; and the littering of the environment with nonbiodegradable bottles, plastics, and other packaging materials.

A third trend is *increased government intervention* in natural resource management. The governments of different countries vary in their concern and efforts to promote a clean environment. Some, such as the German government, vigorously pursue environmental quality. Others, especially many poorer nations, do little about pollution, largely because they lack the needed funds or political will.

In the United States, the Environmental Protection Agency (EPA) was created in 1970 to create and enforce pollution standards and conduct pollution research. In the future, companies doing business in the United States can expect continued strong controls from government and pressure groups. Instead of opposing regulation, many marketers are now helping to develop solutions to the materials and energy problems facing the world.

Environmental sustainability
Developing strategies and practices that create a world economy that the planet can support indefinitely.

Concern for the natural environment has spawned an **environmental sustainability** movement. Today, enlightened companies go beyond what government regulations dictate. They are developing strategies and practices that create a world economy that the planet can support indefinitely. Environmental sustainability means meeting present needs without compromising the ability of future generations to meet their needs.

Many companies are responding to consumer demands with more environmentally responsible products. Others are developing recyclable or biodegradable packaging, recycled materials and components, better pollution controls, and more energy-efficient operations. Consider

>> The natural environment: Walmart has emerged in recent years as the world's super "eco-nanny" through its own sustainability practices and its impact on the actions of its huge network of suppliers.

grzegorz knec/Alamy Stock Photo (logo); beboy/Shutterstock (illustration)

Walmart, for example. >> Through its own environmental sustainability actions and its impact on the actions of suppliers, Walmart has emerged in recent years as the world's super "eco-nanny":[43]

> When it comes to sustainability, perhaps no company in the world is doing more good these days than Walmart. That's right—big, bad Walmart. The giant retailer is now one of the world's biggest crusaders for the cause of saving the world for future generations. For starters, Walmart is rolling out new high-efficiency stores, each one saving more energy than the last. These stores use wind turbines to generate energy, high-output linear fluorescent lighting to reduce what energy stores do use, and native landscaping to cut down on watering and fertilizer. Store heating systems burn recovered cooking oil from the deli fryers and motor oil from the Tire and Lube Express centers. All organic waste, including produce, meats, and paper, is hauled off to a company that turns it into mulch for the garden. Walmart is committed to eventually using 100 percent renewable energy in all of its stores and distribution centers (it's currently at 26 percent) and sending zero waste to landfills (currently down to just 19 percent).
>
> Walmart not only is greening up its own operations but also has laid down the eco-law to its vast network of suppliers to get them to do the same, asking them to examine the carbon life cycles of their products and rethink how they source, manufacture, package, and transport these goods. It has developed the Walmart Sustainability Index program, which helps suppliers understand, monitor, and enhance the sustainability of their products and the supply chain. As a result, Walmart suppliers have cut energy, water, materials, toxic ingredients, and other inputs while creating less waste and fewer emissions—for themselves as well as for Walmart stores and consumers. With its immense buying power, Walmart can humble even the mightiest supplier. When imposing its environmental demands on suppliers, Walmart has even more clout than government regulators. Whereas the EPA can only level nominal fines, Walmart can threaten a substantial chunk of a supplier's business.

Companies are learning that what's good for customer well-being and the planet can also be good business. For example, Walmart's eco-charge is about more than just doing the right thing. It also makes good business sense. More efficient operations and less wasteful products are not only good for the environment but also save Walmart money. "From a brass tack standpoint," says Walmart's Director of Sustainability, "the efficiency gains that you get through programs like energy efficiency and operating a smarter, better system, result in some real financial savings." Lower costs, in turn, let Walmart do more of what it has always done best—save customers money.

Many companies today are looking to do more than just good deeds. More and more, companies are making environmental sustainability a part of their core missions. For example, outdoor apparel and equipment maker Patagonia donates 1 percent of its revenue annually to environmental causes and adheres fiercely to a "Five Rs" mantra: "reduce, repair, reuse, recycle, and reimagine." But more than just implementing sustainability practices, Patagonia wants to "reimagine a world where we take only what nature can replace." It recently took sustainability to a whole new level when it told its customers, "Don't buy our products" (see Marketing at Work 3.1).

Author Comment
Technological advances are perhaps the most dramatic forces affecting today's marketing strategies. Just think about the tremendous impact on marketing of digital technologies—which have exploded in recent years. You'll see examples of the fast-growing world of online, mobile, and social media marketing throughout every chapter, and we'll discuss them in detail in Chapter 14.

The Technological Environment

The **technological environment** is perhaps the most dramatic force now shaping our world. Technology has released such wonders as antibiotics, air travel, the internet, smartphones, artificial intelligence, and driverless cars. It also has released such horrors as nuclear missiles and assault rifles. Our attitude toward technology depends on whether we are more impressed with its wonders or its blunders.

Technological environment
Forces that create new technologies, creating new product and market opportunities.

Digital technologies and the dawn of the Internet of Things (IoT) have created a brave new world of marketing. The seemingly unending barrage of digital advances is affecting every aspect of how consumers learn about, shop for, buy, and experience brands. In turn,

MARKETING AT WORK 3.1

Patagonia's "Conscious Consumption"—Telling Consumers to Buy Less

Patagonia—the high-end outdoor clothing and gear company—was founded on a mission of using business to help save the planet. More than 40 years ago, mountain-climber entrepreneur Yvon Chouinard started the company with this enduring mission: "Build the best product, cause no unnecessary harm, use business to inspire and implement solutions to the environmental crisis." Now, Chouinard and Patagonia are taking that mission to new extremes. They're actually telling consumers "don't buy our products."

It started several years ago with a full-page *New York Times* ad on Black Friday, the day after Thanksgiving and busiest shopping day of the year, showing Patagonia's best-selling R2 jacket and pronouncing "Don't Buy This Jacket." Patagonia backed the ad with messaging in its retail stores and at its website and social media pages. To top things off, Patagonia customers received a follow-up email prior to Cyber Monday—the season's major online shopping day—reasserting the brand's buy less message. Here's part of what it said:

> Because Patagonia wants to be in business for a good long time—and leave a world inhabitable for our kids—we want to do the opposite of every other business today. We ask you to buy less and to reflect before you spend a dime on this jacket or anything else.
>
> The environmental cost of everything we make is astonishing. Consider the R2 Jacket shown, one of our best sellers. To make it required 135 liters of water, enough to meet the daily needs (three glasses a day) of 45 people. Its journey from its origin as 60% recycled polyester to our Reno warehouse generated nearly 20 pounds of carbon dioxide, 24 times the weight of the finished product. This jacket left behind, on its way to Reno, two-thirds its weight in waste. And this is a 60% recycled polyester jacket, knit and sewn to a high standard. But, as is true of all the things we can make and you can buy, this jacket comes with an environmental cost higher than its price.
>
> There is much to be done and plenty for us all to do. Don't buy what you don't need. Think twice before you buy anything. [Work with us] to reimagine a world where we take only what nature can replace.

>> **Environmental sustainability: A for-profit firm telling its customers to buy *less* sounds crazy. But it's right on target with Patagonia's reason for being. The company wants to "reimagine a world where we take only what nature can replace."**

A for-profit firm telling its customers to buy *less*? It sounds crazy. But that message is right on target with Patagonia's reason for being. Founder Chouinard contends that capitalism is on an unsustainable path. Today's companies and customers are wasting the world's resources by making and buying low-quality goods that they buy mindlessly and throw away too quickly. Instead, Chouinard and his company are calling for *conscious consumption,* asking customers to think before they buy and to stop consuming for consumption's sake.

Coming from Patagonia, a company that spends almost nothing on traditional advertising, the paradoxical "Don't Buy This Jacket" ad had tremendous impact. The internet was soon ablaze with comments from online journalists, bloggers, and customers regarding the meaning and motivation behind Patagonia's message. Analysts speculated about whether the ad would help or harm sales—whether it would engage customers and build loyalty or be perceived as little more than a cheap marketing gimmick.

But to Patagonia, far from a marketing gimmick, the campaign expressed the brand's deeply held philosophy of sustainability. The purpose was to increase awareness of and participation in the Patagonia Common Threads Initiative, which urges customers to take a pledge to work together with the company to consume more responsibly. Common Threads rests on five Rs of joint action toward sustainability:

> *Reduce*: **WE** make useful gear that lasts a long time. **YOU** don't buy what you don't need.
>
> *Repair*: **WE** help you repair your Patagonia gear. **YOU** pledge to fix what's broken.

Reuse: **WE** help find a home for Patagonia gear you no longer need. **YOU** sell or pass it on.

Recycle: **WE** take back your Patagonia gear that is worn out. **YOU** pledge to keep your stuff out of the landfill and incinerator.

Reimagine: **TOGETHER** we reimagine a world where we take only what nature can replace.

So Patagonia's conscious consumption solution seems pretty simple. Making, buying, repairing, and reusing higher-quality goods results in less consumption, which in turn uses fewer resources and lowers costs for everyone. Patagonia has always been committed to the idea of quality as a cure for overconsumption. It makes durable products with timeless designs, products that customers can keep and use for a long time. Then, through programs like its Worn Wear Initiative, Patagonia uses social media to let customers share stories about their long-lasting gear and to inspire people to keep their clothing in circulation for as long as possible. In Patagonia's words:

> At the end of the day, we can tinker with our supply chain, improve sourcing, use all-recycled fabrics, and give away millions of dollars to environmental organizations until the cows come in, but nothing is more important and impactful than keeping our clothing in use for as long as possible.

So on that Black Friday weekend, while other companies were inundating customers with promotions that encouraged them to "buy, buy, buy," Patagonia stood on its founding principles. It said, "Hey, look: Only purchase what you need," explains Rob BonDurant, vice president of marketing and communications at Patagonia. "The message, 'Don't buy this jacket,' is obviously super counterintuitive to what a for-profit company would say, especially on a day like Black Friday, but honestly [it] is what we really were after, [communicating] this idea of evolving capitalism and conscious consumption that we wanted to effect."

Not just any company can pull off something like this—such a message can only work if it is real. Patagonia didn't just suddenly stick an ad in the *New York Times* on Black Friday. It had been sending—and living—this message for decades. Can other companies follow Patagonia's lead? "If it is [just] a marketing campaign, no," says BonDurant. "If it is a way they live their lives and do their business, absolutely. You can't just apply it to your messaging or to a particular window of time. It has to be done 24 hours a day, 365 days a year."

Pushing conscious consumption doesn't mean that Patagonia wants customers to stop buying its products. To the contrary, like other for-profit brands, Patagonia really does care about doing well on Black Friday and the rest of the holiday season. As a company that sells products mostly for cold-weather activities, Patagonia reaps a whopping 40 percent of its revenues during the final two months of the year. But to Patagonia, business is about more than making money. And according to BonDurant, the "Don't Buy This Jacket" campaign has more than paid for itself with the interest and involvement it created for the Common Threads Initiative. As an added bonus, however, the campaign also boosted sales. During the first year of the campaign, Patagonia's sales surged by almost a third.

"It is not enough just to make good products anymore," says BonDurant. "There also has to be a message that people can buy into, that people feel they are a part of, that they can be solutions-based. That is what [Patagonia's "buy only what you need"] communication efforts are really all about." But what's good for customers and the planet is also good for Patagonia. Says founder Chouinard, "I know it sounds crazy, but every time I have made a decision that is best for the planet, I have made money. Our customers know that—and they want to be part of that environmental commitment."

Sources: Based on information from Danielle Sacks, "Any Fight Worth Fighting—That's the Attitude We Take," *Fast Company,* February 2015, pp. 34–36; Ryan Bradley, "The Tao Rose," *Fortune,* September 15, 2015, pp. 155–160; Katherine Ling, "Walking the Talk," *Marketing News,* March 15, 2012, p. 24, https://issuu.com/hennessydesigngroup/docs/marketingnews; Kyle Stock, "Patagonia's 'Buy Less' Plea Spurs More Buying," *Bloomberg Businessweek,* August 28, 2013, www.businessweek.com/printer/articles/147326-patagonias-buy-less-plea-spurs-more-buying; "How a Clothing Company's Anti-Consumerist Message Boosted Business," *PBS,* August 20, 2015, www.pbs.org/newshour/bb/clothing-companys-anti-consumerist-message-boosted-business/; Marisa Meltzer, "Patagonia and The North Face: Saving the World—One Puffer Jacket at a Time," March 17, 2017, https://www.theguardian.com/business/2017/mar/07/the-north-face-patagonia-saving-world-one-puffer-jacket-at-a-time; Jeff Beer, "Patagonia Is Launching a New Digital Platform for Environmental Activism," *Fast Company,* February 6, 2018, https://www.fastcompany.com/40527501/patagonia-is-launching-a-new-digital-platform-for-environmental-activism and www.patagonia.com/us/common-threads?src=112811_mt1; and http://wornwear.patagonia.com/and www.patagonia.com/us/environmentalism, accessed September 2018.

the digital age gives marketers exciting opportunities for understanding consumers, creating new products, and engaging customers in more direct and meaningful ways. Two decades ago, even wide-eyed futurists would have had difficulty envisioning today's digital world:

> Digital has become an inseparable part of everything we do as consumers. You see it in the products we buy—from wearable technology like Fitbits and Apple watches; to connected IoT smart home devices such as Nest monitors, Sonos wireless speakers, and Google smart home gadgets; to digital-centric cars like the Tesla that can even self-drive for short periods. You see it in the ways we buy—from the massive shift from in-store to web and mobile shopping, to our reliance on apps and chatbots, to the way we relish brand experiences enhanced by augmented reality and other digital wizardry. It's evident in the ways we engage with brands, through digital brand communities, web and mobile apps, and our constant companions, the social media. Need more shopping information or assistance? Just ask Amazon's Alexa or Apple's Siri, or even let them do the buying for you. Today, our consumer lives—our lives in general—are inexorably linked to all things digital. It has become a part of us, almost like in a Dan Brown novel in which

a futurist predicts that humans will eventually evolve into beings that are half human and half artificial intelligence–fueled machines. Fiction? Far-fetched? Who knows.

Disney takes full advantage of digital technology in creating magical customer experiences at its Walt Disney World Resort. Five years ago, it introduced My Disney Experience, a web and mobile app that helps guests plan their trips and then manage their visits in real time while at the resort. >> At the heart of the experience is an RFID-embedded wristband called the "MagicBand":[44]

>> Marketing technology: Disney takes full advantage of digital technology in creating magical customer experiences at its Walt Disney World Resort.

Bob Croslin

Wearing a MagicBand at the Walt Disney World Resort opens up a whole new level of Disney's famed magic. After registering for cloud-based MyMagic+ services, with the flick of your wrist you can enter a park or attraction, buy dinner or souvenirs, skip lines at certain attractions, or even unlock your hotel room. But Disney has only begun to tap the MagicBand's potential for personalizing guest experiences. Future applications could be truly magical. Imagine, for example, the wonder of a child who receives a warm hug from Mickey Mouse or a bow from Prince Charming, who then greets the child by name and wishes her a happy birthday. Imagine animatronics that interact with nearby guests based on personal information supplied in advance. You get separated from family or friends? No problem. A quick scan of your MagicBand at a nearby directory could pinpoint the locations of your entire party. Linked to your Disney phone app, the MagicBand could trigger in-depth information about park features, ride wait times, FastPass check-in alerts, and your reservations schedule. Of course, the MagicBand also offers Disney a potential mother lode of digital data on guest activities and movements in minute detail, helping to improve guest logistics, services, and sales. If all this seems too Big Brother-ish, there will be privacy options—for example, letting parents opt out of things like characters knowing children's names. In all, such digital technologies promise to enrich the Disney experience for both guests and the company.

The technological environment changes rapidly, creating new markets and opportunities. However, every new technology replaces an older technology. Transistors hurt the vacuum-tube industry, digital photography hurt the film business, and digital downloads and streaming are hurting the DVD and book businesses. When old industries fight or ignore new technologies, their businesses decline. Marketers should watch the technological environment closely. Companies that do not keep up will soon find their products outdated. If that happens, they will miss new product and market opportunities.

As products and technologies become more complex, the public needs to know that these items are safe. Thus, government agencies investigate and ban potentially unsafe products. In the United States, the Food and Drug Administration (FDA) has created complex regulations for testing new drugs. The Consumer Product Safety Commission (CPSC) establishes safety standards for consumer products and penalizes companies that fail to meet them. Such regulations have resulted in much higher research costs and longer times between new product ideas and their introduction. Marketers should be aware of these regulations when applying new technologies and developing new products.

Author Comment
Even the strongest free-market advocates agree that the system works best with at least some regulation. But beyond regulation, most companies want to be socially responsible. We'll dig deeper into marketing and social responsibility in Chapter 20.

The Political–Social and Cultural Environments

OBJECTIVE 3-4 **Explain the key changes in the political and cultural environments.**

The Political and Social Environment

Marketing decisions are strongly affected by developments in the political environment. The **political environment** consists of laws, government agencies, and pressure groups that influence or limit various organizations and individuals in a given society.

Political environment
Laws, government agencies, and pressure groups that influence and limit various organizations and individuals in a given society.

Legislation Regulating Business

Even the strongest advocates of free-market economies agree that the system works best with at least some regulation. Well-conceived regulation can encourage competition and ensure fair markets for goods and services. Thus, governments develop *public policy* to guide commerce—sets of laws and regulations that limit business for the good of society as a whole. Almost every marketing activity is subject to a wide range of laws and regulations.

Legislation affecting business around the world has increased steadily over the years. The United States and many other countries have many laws covering issues such as competition, fair-trade practices, environmental protection, product safety, truth in advertising, consumer privacy, packaging and labeling, pricing, and other important areas (see **>> Table 3.1**).

Understanding the public policy implications of a particular marketing activity is not a simple matter. In the United States, there are many laws created at the national, state, and local levels, and these regulations often overlap. For example, aspirin products sold in Dallas are governed by both federal labeling laws and Texas state advertising laws. Moreover, regulations are constantly changing; what was allowed last year may now be prohibited, and what was prohibited may now be allowed. Marketers must work hard to keep up with changes in regulations and their interpretations.

Business legislation has been enacted for a number of reasons. The first is to *protect companies* from each other. Although business executives may praise competition, they sometimes try to neutralize it when it threatens them. Therefore, laws are passed to define and prevent unfair competition. In the United States, such laws are enforced by the Federal Trade Commission (FTC) and the Antitrust Division of the Attorney General's office.

The second purpose of government regulation is to *protect consumers* from unfair business practices. Some firms, if left alone, would make shoddy products, invade consumer privacy, mislead consumers in their advertising, and deceive consumers through their packaging and pricing. Rules defining and regulating unfair business practices are enforced by various agencies.

The third purpose of government regulation is to *protect the interests of society* against unrestrained business behavior. Profitable business activity does not always create a better quality of life. Regulation arises to ensure that firms take responsibility for the social costs of their production or products.

International marketers will encounter dozens, or even hundreds, of agencies set up to enforce trade policies and regulations. In the United States, Congress has established federal regulatory agencies, such as the FTC, the FDA, the Federal Communications Commission, the Federal Energy Regulatory Commission, the Federal Aviation Administration, the Consumer Product Safety Commission, the Environmental Protection Agency, and hundreds of others. Because such government agencies have some discretion in enforcing the laws, they can have a major impact on a company's marketing performance.

New laws and their enforcement will continue to increase. Business executives must watch these developments when planning their products and marketing programs. Marketers need to know about the major laws protecting competition, consumers, and society. They need to understand these laws at the local, state, national, and international levels.

Increased Emphasis on Ethics and Socially Responsible Actions

Written regulations cannot possibly cover all potential marketing abuses, and existing laws are often difficult to enforce. However, beyond written laws and regulations, business is also governed by social codes and rules of professional ethics.

Socially Responsible Behavior. Enlightened companies encourage their managers to look beyond what the regulatory system allows and simply "do the right thing." These socially responsible firms actively seek out ways to protect the long-run interests of their consumers and the environment.

Almost every aspect of marketing involves ethics and social responsibility issues. Unfortunately, because these issues usually involve conflicting interests, well-meaning people can honestly disagree about the right course of action in a given situation. Thus, many industrial and professional trade associations have suggested codes of ethics. And more companies are now developing policies, guidelines, and other responses to complex social responsibility issues.

Table 3.1 Major U.S. Legislation Affecting Marketing

Legislation	Purpose
Sherman Antitrust Act (1890)	Prohibits monopolies and activities (price-fixing, predatory pricing) that restrain trade or competition in interstate commerce.
Federal Food and Drug Act (1906)	Created the Food and Drug Administration (FDA). It forbids the manufacture or sale of adulterated or fraudulently labeled foods and drugs.
Clayton Act (1914)	Supplements the Sherman Act by prohibiting certain types of price discrimination, exclusive dealing, and tying clauses (which require a dealer to take additional products in a seller's line).
Federal Trade Commission Act (1914)	Established the Federal Trade Commission (FTC), which monitors and remedies unfair trade methods.
Robinson-Patman Act (1936)	Amends the Clayton Act to define price discrimination as unlawful. Empowers the FTC to establish limits on quantity discounts, forbid some brokerage allowances, and prohibit promotional allowances except when made available on proportionately equal terms.
Wheeler-Lea Act (1938)	Makes deceptive, misleading, and unfair practices illegal regardless of injury to competition. Places advertising of food and drugs under FTC jurisdiction.
Lanham Trademark Act (1946)	Protects and regulates distinctive brand names and trademarks.
National Traffic and Safety Act (1958)	Provides for the creation of compulsory safety standards for automobiles and tires.
Fair Packaging and Labeling Act (1966)	Provides for the regulation of the packaging and labeling of consumer goods. Requires that manufacturers state what the package contains, who made it, and how much it contains.
Child Protection Act (1966)	Bans the sale of hazardous toys and articles. Sets standards for child-resistant packaging.
Federal Cigarette Labeling and Advertising Act (1967)	Requires that cigarette packages contain the following statement: "Warning: The Surgeon General Has Determined That Cigarette Smoking Is Dangerous to Your Health."
National Environmental Policy Act (1969)	Establishes a national policy on the environment. The 1970 Reorganization Plan established the Environmental Protection Agency (EPA).
Consumer Product Safety Act (1972)	Establishes the Consumer Product Safety Commission (CPSC) and authorizes it to set safety standards for consumer products as well as exact penalties for failing to uphold those standards.
Magnuson-Moss Warranty Act (1975)	Authorizes the FTC to determine rules and regulations for consumer warranties and provides consumer access to redress, such as the class action suit.
Children's Television Act (1990)	Limits the number of commercials aired during children's programs.
Nutrition Labeling and Education Act (1990)	Requires that food product labels provide detailed nutritional information.
Telephone Consumer Protection Act (1991)	Establishes procedures to avoid unwanted telephone solicitations. Limits marketers' use of automatic telephone dialing systems and artificial or prerecorded voices.
Americans with Disabilities Act (1991)	Makes discrimination against people with disabilities illegal in public accommodations, transportation, and telecommunications.
Children's Online Privacy Protection Act (2000)	Prohibits websites or online services operators from collecting personal information from children without obtaining consent from a parent and allowing parents to review information collected from their children.
Do-Not-Call Implementation Act (2003)	Authorizes the FTC to collect fees from sellers and telemarketers for the implementation and enforcement of a national Do-Not-Call Registry.
CAN-SPAM Act (2003)	Regulates the distribution and content of unsolicited commercial email.
Financial Reform Law (2010)	Created the Bureau of Consumer Financial Protection, which writes and enforces rules for the marketing of financial products to consumers. It is also responsible for enforcement of the Truth-in-Lending Act, the Home Mortgage Disclosure Act, and other laws designed to protect consumers.

The boom in online, mobile, and social media marketing has created a new set of social and ethical issues. Critics worry most about online privacy issues. There has been an explosion in the amount of personal digital data available. Users themselves supply some of it. They voluntarily place highly private information on social media sites, such as Facebook or LinkedIn, or on genealogy sites that are easily searched by anyone with a computer or a smartphone.

However, much of the information is systematically developed by businesses seeking to learn more about their customers, often without consumers realizing that they are under the microscope. Legitimate businesses track consumers' online browsing and buying behavior and collect, analyze, and share digital data from every move consumers make at their online sites. Critics worry that these companies may now know *too* much and might use digital data to take unfair advantage of consumers.

Although most companies fully disclose their internet privacy policies and most try to use data to benefit their customers, abuses do occur. In recent years, consumer data breaches of major companies such as Facebook, Yahoo!, credit agency Equifax, Target, Uber, Sony, and many others have threatened the privacy of hundreds of millions or even billions of individuals.[45] As a result, companies are tightening their data security and public policy makers are acting to protect consumer privacy. In Chapters 4 and 16, we discuss these and other societal marketing issues in greater depth.

Cause-Related Marketing. To exercise their social responsibility and build more positive images, many companies are now linking themselves to worthwhile causes. These days, every product seems to be tied to some cause. For example, AT&T joined forces with competitors Verizon, Sprint, and T-Mobile to spearhead the "It Can Wait" campaign, which addresses the texting-while-driving epidemic by urging people of all ages to take the pledge to never text and drive. State Farm reinforces its "Good Neighbor" positioning with a "Neighborhood of Good" program that encourages policyholders to volunteer at charitable organizations in their communities. Lacoste partnered with the International Union for Conservation of Nature to offer limited-edition polo shirts on which it replaced its iconic crocodile logo with depictions of 10 threatened animal species; the proceeds supported the organization's animal protection efforts. And Whirlpool's Care Counts program places washing machines and dryers in schools so that at-risk kids can have clean clothes, increasing both their confidence and their attendance. The program boosted the attendance of 90 percent of participating children.[46]

>> Cause-related marketing: Ben & Jerry's three-part "linked prosperity" mission drives it to make fantastic ice cream (product mission), manage the company for sustainable financial growth (economic mission), and use the company "in innovative ways to make the world a better place" (social mission). Both Ben & Jerry's and its products are "Made of Something Better."

Clark Brennan/Alamy Stock Photo

Some companies are founded on cause-related missions. Under the concept of "values-led business" or "caring capitalism," their mission is to use business to make the world a better place. >> For example, Ben & Jerry's, a division of Unilever, has long prided itself on being a "values-led business," one that creates "linked prosperity" for everyone connected to the brand—from suppliers to employees to customers and communities:[47]

> Under its three-part mission, Ben & Jerry's wants to make fantastic ice cream (product mission), manage the company for sustainable financial growth (economic mission), and use the company "in innovative ways to make the world a better place" (social mission). Ben & Jerry's backs its mission with actions. For example, the company is committed to using wholesome, natural, non-GMO, fair-trade-certified ingredients and buys from local farms. It employs business practices "that respect the earth and the environment," investing in wind energy, solar usage, travel offsets, and carbon neutrality. Its Caring Dairy program helps farmers develop more sustainable practices on the farm ("Caring Dairy means happy cows, happy farmers, and a happy planet"). The Ben & Jerry's Foundation awards nearly $2 million annually in grassroots grants to community service organizations and projects in communities across the nation. Ben & Jerry's also operates 14 PartnerShops, scoop shops that are independently owned and operated by community-based not-for-profit organizations. The company waives standard franchise fees for these shops.

Cause-related marketing has become a primary form of corporate giving. It lets companies "do well by doing good" by linking purchases of the company's products or services with benefiting worthwhile causes or charitable organizations. Beyond being socially admirable, cause-related marketing can make good economic sense for the company. For example, despite its values-led mission, or more probably because of it, Ben & Jerry's is the nation's second-largest ice cream brand behind only Breyers, with close to half a billion dollars in annual sales. And in addition to boosting school attendance, Whirlpool's Care Counts program also boosted the company's image, earning 350 million media impressions, more than 12 million video views across Facebook and YouTube, and a significant lift in purchase intent for the brand.[48]

Cause-related marketing has also stirred some controversy. Critics worry that cause-related marketing is more a strategy for selling than a strategy for giving—that "cause-related" marketing is really "cause-exploitative" marketing. Thus, companies using cause-related marketing might find themselves walking a fine line between an improved image and perceptions of exploitation or inauthenticity. However, if handled well, cause-related marketing can greatly benefit both the company and the cause. The company gains an effective marketing tool while building a more positive public image. The charitable organization or cause gains greater visibility and important new sources of funding and support. Spending on cause-related marketing in the United States skyrocketed from only $120 million in 1990 to more than $2 billion in 2018.[49]

Author Comment

Cultural factors strongly affect how people think and how they consume, so marketers are keenly interested in the cultural environment.

The Cultural Environment

The **cultural environment** consists of institutions and other forces that affect a society's basic values, perceptions, preferences, and behaviors. People grow up in a particular society that shapes their basic beliefs and values. They absorb a worldview that defines their relationships with others. The following cultural characteristics can affect marketing decision making.

Cultural environment
Institutions and other forces that affect society's basic values, perceptions, preferences, and behaviors.

The Persistence of Cultural Values

People in a given society hold many beliefs and values. Their core beliefs and values have a high degree of persistence. For example, most Americans believe in individual freedom, hard work, getting married, and achievement and success. These beliefs shape more specific attitudes and behaviors found in everyday life. *Core* beliefs and values are passed on from parents to children and are reinforced by schools, businesses, religious institutions, and government.

Secondary beliefs and values are more open to change. Believing in marriage is a core belief; believing that people should get married early in life is a secondary belief. Marketers have some chance of changing secondary values but little chance of changing core values. For example, family-planning marketers could argue more effectively that people should get married later than not get married at all.

Shifts in Secondary Cultural Values

Although core values are fairly persistent, cultural swings do take place. Consider the impact of popular music groups, movie personalities, and other celebrities on young people's hairstyle and clothing norms. Marketers want to predict cultural shifts to spot new opportunities or threats. The major cultural values of a society are expressed in people's views of themselves and others as well as in their views of organizations, society, nature, and the universe.

People's Views of Themselves. People vary in their emphasis on serving themselves versus serving others. Some people seek personal pleasure, wanting fun, change, and escape. Others seek self-realization through religion, recreation, or the avid pursuit of careers or other life goals. Some people see themselves as sharers and joiners; others see themselves as individualists. People use products, brands, and services as a means of self-expression, and they buy products and services that match their views of themselves.

Marketers can position their brands to appeal to specific self-view segments. For example, consider Sperry, maker of storied Sperry Top-Sider boat shoes:[50]

> Sperry first introduced its iconic Top-Sider shoes in 1935 as the perfect non-slip boat shoe for rough seas and slippery decks. That nautical legacy remains an important part of Sperry's positioning. The brand's recent "Odysseys Await" marketing campaign confirms that the sure-footed shoes are built for adventurous soles who can't stay put. The campaign targets "intrepid consumers"—active millennials who view themselves as adventurous, authentic, bold, and creative. "There's a certain section of millennials that really look at life as an opportunity," says a Sperry marketer. They "want to have meaningful experiences and align with brands that provide opportunities for such." The "Odysseys Await" campaign reconnects the brand with the sea, featuring intrepid consumers having nautical adventures, jumping off boats, sailing, and diving off cliffs. Headlines such as "The best stories are written with your feet," "Keep your laces tight and your plans loose," "Try living for a living," and "If Earth has an edge, find it" suggest that Sperry Top-Siders are more than just shoes. They are the embodiment of customers' self-views and lifestyles.

People's Views of Others. People's attitudes toward and interactions with others shift over time. In recent years, some analysts have voiced concerns that the digital age would result in diminished human interaction, as people buried themselves in social media pages or emailed and texted rather than interacting personally. Instead, today's digital technologies seem to be allowing allow people to connect more than ever. Basically, the more people meet, network, text, and socialize online, the more likely they are to eventually meet up with friends and followers in the real world.

However, these days, even when people are together, they are often "alone together." » Groups of people may sit or walk in their own little bubbles, intensely connected to tiny screens and keyboards. One expert describes the latest communication skill as "maintaining eye contact with someone while you text someone else; it's hard but it can be done," she says. "Technology-enabled, we are able to be with one another, and also 'elsewhere,' connected to wherever we want to be."[51] Thus, whether the new technology-driven communication is a blessing or a curse is a matter of much debate.

» People's views of others: These days, even when people are together, they are often "alone together."

Dmitriy Shironosov/123RF

This new way of interacting strongly affects how companies market their brands and communicate with customers. Consumers increasingly tap digitally into networks of friends and online brand communities to learn about and buy products and to shape and share brand experiences. As a result, it is important for brands to participate in these networks too.

People's Views of Organizations. People vary in their attitudes toward corporations, government agencies, trade unions, universities, and other organizations. By and large, people are willing to work for major organizations and expect them, in turn, to carry out society's work.

The past two decades have seen a sharp decrease in confidence in and loyalty toward America's business and political organizations and institutions. In the workplace, there has been an overall decline in organizational loyalty. Waves of company downsizings bred cynicism and distrust. In just the past decade, major corporate scandals, consumer data breaches, stories of Wall Street bankers' greed and incompetence, and other unsettling activities have resulted in a further loss of confidence in big business. Many people today see work not as a source of satisfaction but as a required chore to earn money to enjoy their nonwork hours. This trend suggests that organizations need to find new ways to win consumer and employee confidence.

People's Views of Society. People vary in their attitudes toward their society—patriots defend it, reformers want to change it, and malcontents want to leave it. People's orientation to their society influences their consumption patterns and attitudes toward the marketplace.

American patriotism has been increasing gradually for the past two decades. One annual consumer survey shows that some brands are highly associated with patriotism, such as Jeep, Levi Strauss, Disney, Coca-Cola, and Ford. Marketers respond with renewed "Made in America" pitches and ads with patriotic themes. For example, Coca-Cola launched a limited-edition red, white, and blue flag can surrounding the July 4 holiday with the patriotic song lyric "I'm proud to be an American" on the label. Companies ranging from The Home Depot and Buffalo Wild Wings to *National Geographic* ran Veteran's Day ads and promotions honoring American veterans. And Jeep's patriotic "Portraits" ad in a recent Super Bowl—which featured famous and ordinary faces of Americans who've driven Jeeps through 75 years of wars, peace, boom times, and bust—resonated strongly with Americans. "We don't make Jeep," concludes the ad, "you do."[52]

Although most such marketing efforts are tasteful and well received, waving the red, white, and blue can sometimes prove tricky. Flag-waving promotions can be viewed as corny or as token attempts to cash in on the nation's emotions.

>> **Riding the natural and organic foods trend, Annie's is out to create a happier and healthier world with nourishing products that are "forever kind to the planet." It puts its "rabbit seal of approval" on every product and promises that its products are "Made with Goodness!"**

Sheila Fitzgerald/Shutterstock

People's Views of Nature. People vary in their attitudes toward the natural world—some feel ruled by it, others feel in harmony with it, and still others seek to master it. A long-term trend has been people's growing mastery over nature through technology and the belief that nature is bountiful. More recently, however, people have recognized that nature is finite and fragile; it can be destroyed or spoiled by human activities.

This renewed love of things natural has created a sizable market of consumers who seek out everything from natural, organic, and nutritional products to fuel-efficient cars and alternative medicines. For example, the U.S. organic/natural food market now generates $47 billion in annual retail sales and will grow by an estimated 14 percent per year through 2021.[53] >> Annie's Homegrown, a General Mills company, caters to this market with sustainable, all-natural food products—from mac and cheese to pizzas, pastas, snacks, soups, cereals, yogurt, and salad dressings—made and sold in a sustainable way:[54]

> Annie's is out to create a happier and healthier world with nourishing foods and responsible conduct that is "forever kind to the planet." Annie's products are made from simple, natural ingredients grown by its farm partners. The products contain "no artificial anything," says the company. "If it's not real, it's not Annie's." The company works closely with its food-supply-system partners to jointly raise the bar for sustainability and organics. Annie's also makes sustainable practices a top priority with its packaging—more than 90 percent of Annie's packaging by weight is recyclable. Finally, Annie's gives back to the community through programs such as sustainable agriculture scholarships, school garden programs, and support for like-minded organizations dedicated to making the planet a better place to live and eat. Annie's puts its "rabbit seal of approval" on every product and promises "organic for everybunny." Creating good food for humans has also been good for Annie's; the brand's sales have nearly doubled to almost one-half billion dollars in just the past four years.

People's Views of the Universe. Finally, people vary in their beliefs about the origins of the universe and their place in it. Although most Americans practice religion, religious conviction and practice have been dropping off gradually through the years. According to a recent study, almost one in four (24 percent) Americans now say they are not affiliated with any particular faith, up from about 16 percent just one decade earlier. Among Americans under age 30, more than one-third say they are not currently affiliated with any particular religion.[55]

However, the fact that people are dropping out of organized religion doesn't mean that they are abandoning their faith. Some futurists have noted a renewed interest in spirituality, perhaps as a part of a broader search for a new inner purpose. People have been moving away from materialism and dog-eat-dog ambition to seek more permanent values—family, community, earth, faith—and a more certain grasp of right and wrong. Rather than calling it "religion," they call it "spirituality." One recent survey found that whereas Americans have become less religious in recent years, the share of people who feel a deep sense of "spiritual peace and well-being" as well as a deep sense of "wonder about the universe" has risen.[56] This changing spiritualism affects consumers in everything from the television shows they watch and the books they read to the products and services they buy.

Responding to the Marketing Environment

Author Comment
Rather than simply watching and reacting to the marketing environment, companies should take proactive steps.

OBJECTIVE 3-5 Discuss how companies can react to the marketing environment.

Someone once observed, "There are three kinds of companies: those who make things happen, those who watch things happen, and those who wonder what's happened." Many companies view the marketing environment as an uncontrollable element to which they must react and adapt. They passively accept the marketing environment and do not try to change it. They analyze environmental forces and design strategies that will help the company avoid the threats and take advantage of the opportunities the environment provides.

Other companies take a *proactive* stance toward the marketing environment. Rather than assuming that strategic options are bounded by the current environment, these firms develop strategies to change the environment. Companies and their products often create and shape new industries and their structures, products such as Ford's Model T car, Apple's iPod and iPhone, Google's search engine, and Amazon's online marketplace.

Even more, rather than simply watching and reacting to environmental events, proactive firms take aggressive actions to affect the publics and forces in their marketing environment. Such companies hire lobbyists to influence legislation affecting their industries and stage media events to gain favorable press coverage. They take to the social media and run blogs to shape public opinion. They press lawsuits and file complaints with regulators to keep competitors in line, and they form contractual agreements to better control their distribution channels.

By taking action, companies can often overcome seemingly uncontrollable environmental events. For example, whereas some companies try to hush up negative talk about their products, others proactively counter false information. Newell Rubbermaid's Crock-Pot slow cooker brand did this when an episode of a hit TV show wrongly portrayed the product as a potential home fire hazard:[57]

> It happened in a recent episode of NBC's hit show *This Is Us*. The show's beloved patriarch died when the family's Pittsburgh home burned down in a fire caused by a faulty slow cooker much like your grandmother's 1970s' Crock-Pot. The incident went viral, creating a crisis for the Crock-Pot brand. Thousands of viewers took to Twitter to express both their grief and their intentions to toss out their Crock-Pots. As one fan tweeted: "Gee thanks #thisisus for ruining #CROCKPOT cooking. Now every time I use mine I'll be sad AND afraid."
>
> Rather than sitting back, Crock-Pot reacted quickly with both humor and facts. It created its first-ever Twitter account—CrockPotCares—and posted a humorous "spoiler alert" to Facebook and other social media channels, complete with broken heart emojis and a Pittsburgh Steeler–branded Crock-Pot. "America's favorite dad and husband deserved a better exit and Crock-Pot shares in your devastation," read the message. "Don't further add to this tragedy by throwing your Crock-Pot Slow Cooker away ... (grandma won't be too happy)." In the week that followed, Crock-Pot continued listening and responding online, expressing concern but with a bit of levity (#CrockPotIsInnocent). The brand also followed up with the facts. Media releases and social media posts noted, "For nearly 50 years, with over 100 million Crock-Pots sold, we have never received any consumer complaints similar to the fictional event portrayed in last night's episode." Thanks to its rapid "We miss him, too. But here are the facts" response, the Crock-Pot brand escaped with little or no long-term damage.

Marketing management cannot always control environmental forces. In many cases, it must settle for simply watching and reacting to the environment. For example, a company would have little success trying to influence geographic population shifts, the economic environment, or major cultural values. But whenever possible, smart marketing managers take a *proactive* rather than *reactive* approach to the marketing environment (see Marketing at Work 3.2).

MARKETING AT WORK 3.2

In the Social Media Age: When the Dialogue Gets Nasty

Marketers have hailed the internet and social media as the great new way to engage customers and nurture customer relationships. In turn, today's more-empowered consumers use the digital media to share their brand experiences with companies and with each other. All of this back and forth helps both the company and its customers. But sometimes, the dialogue can get nasty. Consider the following examples:

- KFC has one of its worse weeks in history. It runs out of chicken. The blunder forces the company to close most of its 900 restaurants in England. Customers are not happy, igniting a social media firestorm. News crews interview angry customers, post the clips online, and then sit back and watch them go viral. In one, a woman rants that she was forced to eat at Burger King! In another, a young girl points to the closed KFC behind her and says, "Look at them. They're just chillin'. They're happy. Sorry, but I'm mad at them."

- Whole Foods Market is no stranger to folks taking online aim at its expensive gourmet products. But one experiment in the produce section causes quite a viral stir. Responding to high demand for convenience, the grocery chain puts single pre-peeled oranges in individual plastic containers at the eye-popping price of $5.99 a pound. But a single tweet puts the company on notice. Seeing a picture of the enshrined citrus at online image sharing community Imgur, customer Nathalie Gordon reposts the photo on Twitter with the quote "If only nature would find a way to cover these oranges so we didn't need to waste so much plastic on them." The hashtag #OrangeGate quickly takes flight, populated with negative Whole Foods Market potshots and memes.
- The airline industry thrives by overbooking flights. But one overbooked flight turns into a nightmare for United Airlines. With the boarding process complete, every seat is occupied by ticketed passengers. But United wants four seats for employees needing to make a connection to service another flight. After United's pleas for volunteers to give up their seats fail, the flight crew informs four passengers that they must vacate the plane. One man, a 67-year-old physician who claims he has to get home to work the next morning, refuses. The crew calls in the airport police, who forcibly remove the man, injuring him in the process, and drag him kicking and screaming from the plane. Within hours, video clips posted by troubled fellow passengers go viral, creating a well-earned image nightmare for United.

Extreme events? Not anymore. The internet and social media have turned the traditional power relationship between businesses and consumers upside down. In the good old days, disgruntled consumers could do little more than bellow at a company service rep or shout out their complaints from a street corner. Now, armed with only a smartphone or tablet, they can take it public, airing their gripes to millions on social media sites, blogs, or even hate sites devoted exclusively to their least favorite corporations. "A consumer's megaphone is now [sometimes] more powerful than a brand's," says one ad agency executive. "Individuals can bring a huge company to its knees ... simply by sharing their experiences and opinions on Facebook, Instagram, Twitter, Yelp, or other social forums."

Some online attacks air legitimate complaints that should be addressed. Others, however, are little more than anonymous, vindictive slurs that unfairly ransack brands and corporate reputations. Some of the attacks are only a passing nuisance; others can draw serious attention and create real headaches.

How should companies react to online attacks? The real quandary for targeted companies is figuring out how far they can go to protect their images without fueling the already-raging fire. One point on which all experts seem to agree: Don't try to retaliate in kind. "It's rarely a good idea to lob bombs at the fire starters," says one analyst. "Preemption, engagement, and diplomacy are saner tools." Such criticisms are often based on real consumer concerns and unresolved anger. Hence, the best strategy might be to proactively monitor and respond sincerely to the concerns they express.

For example, after its initial attempts to cool down angry British KFC customers with lighthearted Twitter posts only made them madder, KFC got serious and joined customers by talking a surprising shot at itself. It took out a full-page ad featuring an empty KFC bucket on which the letters in its brand were scrambled to form "FCK." The ad followed with a humble and sincere apology: "We're sorry. A chicken restaurant without chicken. It's not ideal. A huge apology to our customers....Thank you for bearing with us." Although the ad might have been highly controversial in many countries, it was a perfect match for the British sense of humor. The artful response drew high praise in the social media, and when KFC restaurants reopened within the following week, they were once again serving chicken to throngs of cheerful customers.

Similarly, Whole Foods responded to #OrangeGate within hours with a response to the customer's viral tweet. "Definitely our mistake. These have been pulled. We hear you, and we will leave them in their natural packaging: the peel." The next day, Whole Foods even posted a humorous self-critical meme of its own. Over an image of four oranges in glass jars, the caption read, "IS THIS MORE A PEELING?" Whole Foods's prompt response derailed the negative #OrangeGate momentum and earned the company praise.

United Airlines's response to viral outrage over its forcible removal of a passenger was neither artful nor well-received. United's CEO fueled additional viral fury by taking 24 hours to

>> Today's empowered consumers: Whole Foods Market's decision to put single pre-peeled oranges in individual plastic containers caused a viral storm of #OrangeGate tweets. However, the retailer averted the potential PR disaster by responding within hours with its own humorous, self-critical social media posts admitting its mistake.

Nathalie Gordon

issue a half-hearted apology only for "having to re-accommodate passengers," a response considered by both consumers and experts as "cold," "callous," and "a painfully-bad, jargony response." To make matters worse, the CEO circulated an internal memo to employees in which he referred to the removed passenger as "disruptive" and "belligerent." Within 48 hours, United's social sentiment had dropped 160 percent and its stock price had plummeted.

Many companies have now created teams of specialists who monitor online conversations and engage unhappy consumers. For example, Southwest Airlines has a state-of-the art social media listening center, staffed by 40 customer service experts who listen and respond 24/7 to customers online. They track Twitter comments, monitor Facebook groups, interact with bloggers, and check the company's presence on sites such as YouTube, Instagram, Flickr, and LinkedIn. So if someone posts an online comment, the company can respond promptly in a personal way.

Not long ago, Southwest's team helped avert what could have been a PR catastrophe when an engine exploded on a New York-to-Dallas flight, sending shrapnel through a window and leading to the airline's first-ever passenger fatality. Renowned for its emergency response strategy, only minutes after the incident, even as videos, images, and tweets of the incident were being posted by passengers on the flight, the Southwest listening center staff reacted. They crafted sincere, heartfelt responses and channeled the social media posts to people in various departments to assist in the response effort. The posting passengers were soon praising the company. "Southwest is a great company and they took really good care of us," said a firefighter who was onboard the flight. "There's no question in my mind as to who I'll be flying with again."

Thus, by monitoring and proactively responding to seemingly uncontrollable events in the environment, companies can prevent the negatives from spiraling out of control or even turn them into positives.

Sources: David Kerley, "Behind the Scenes with Southwest Airlines' Social Media 'Listening Center,'" *ABC News*, November 21, 2017, http://abcnews.go.com/US/scenes-southwest-airlines-social-media-listening-center/story?id=51297908; Conor Shine, "Southwest's Heavy Heart: How The LUV Airline Is Responding to the Worst Accident in Its History," *Dallas News*, April 22, 2018, www.dallasnews.com/business/southwest-airlines/2018/04/22/southwests-heavy-heart-luv-airline-responded-worst-accident-history; Sherry Smith, "United Airlines and the 'Re-Accommodation' Debacle," *Clarity*, November 30, 2017, http://clarity.pr/best-worst-2017s-pr-disasters-2-united-airlines-re-accomodation-debacle/; Alanna Petroff, "United Airlines Shows How to Make a PR Crisis a Total Disaster," *CNN Money*, April 11, 2017, http://money.cnn.com/2017/04/11/news/united-passenger-pr-disaster/index.html; Jennifer Earl, "Whole Foods Responds to $6 Pre-Peeled Orange Twitterstorm," *CBS News*, March 8, 2016, www.cbsnews.com/news/whole-foods-responds-to-6-pre-peeled-orange-twitterstorm/; Chris Matyszczyk, "Many KFCs Are Still Closed Because They Have No Chicken," *Inc.*, February 18, 2018, www.inc.com/chris-matyszczyk/kfc-is-still-short-of-chicken-one-customer-just-let-colonel-know-how-big-of-a-mistake-hes-made.html; Robbie Abed, "KFC Just Handled a Public Relations Crisis Perfectly with a Single Picture," *Inc.*, February 23, 2018, www.inc.com/robbie-abed/kfc-just-handled-a-public-relations-crisis-perfectly-with-a-single-picture.html.

REVIEWING AND EXTENDING THE CONCEPTS

CHAPTER REVIEW AND KEY TERMS

Objectives Review

In this and the next two chapters, you'll examine the environments of marketing and how companies analyze these environments to better understand the marketplace and consumers. Companies must constantly watch and manage the *marketing environment* to seek opportunities and ward off threats. The marketing environment consists of all the actors and forces influencing the company's ability to transact business effectively with its target market.

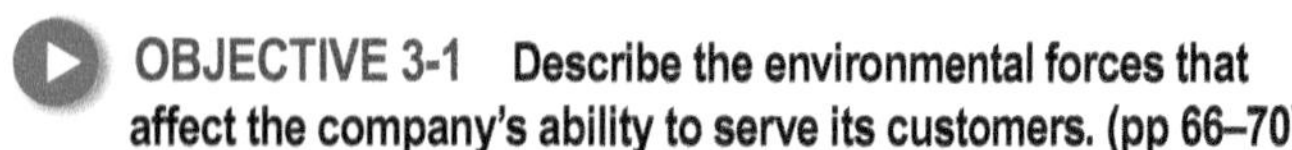

OBJECTIVE 3-1 Describe the environmental forces that affect the company's ability to serve its customers. (pp 66–70)

The company's *microenvironment* consists of actors close to the company that combine to form its value delivery network or that affect its ability to serve customers. It includes the company's *internal environment*—its several departments and management levels—as it influences marketing decision making. *Marketing channel firms*—suppliers, marketing intermediaries, physical distribution firms, marketing services agencies, and financial intermediaries—cooperate to create customer value. *Competitors* vie with the company in an effort to serve customers better. Various *publics* have an actual or potential interest in or impact on the company's ability to meet its objectives. Finally, five types of customer *markets* exist: consumer, business, reseller, government, and international markets.

The *macroenvironment* consists of larger societal forces that affect the entire microenvironment. The six forces making up the company's macroenvironment are demographic, economic, natural, technological, political/social, and cultural forces. These forces shape opportunities and pose threats to the company.

 **OBJECTIVE 3-2 Explain how changes in the demographic and economic environments affect marketing decisions. (pp 70–78)**

Demography is the study of the characteristics of human populations. Today's *demographic environment* shows a changing age structure, shifting family profiles, geographic population shifts, a better-educated and more white-collar population, and increasing diversity. The *economic environment* consists of factors that affect buying power and patterns. The economic environment is characterized by more frugal consumers who are seeking greater value—the right combination of good quality and service at a fair price. In turn, many companies—from discounters such as Target to luxury brands such as Lexus—are focusing on value for the money, practicality, and durability in their product offerings and marketing pitches.

 **OBJECTIVE 3-3 Identify the major trends in the firm's natural and technological environments. (pp 79–83)**

The *natural environment* shows three major trends: shortages of certain raw materials, higher pollution levels, and more government intervention in natural resource management. Environmental concerns create marketing opportunities for alert companies. The *technological environment* creates both opportunities and challenges. The barrage of digital advances is affecting every aspect of how consumers learn about, shop for, buy, and experience brands. In turn, the digital age gives marketers exciting opportunities for understanding consumers, creating new products, and engaging customers in more direct and meaningful ways. Companies that fail to keep up with technological change will miss out on new product and marketing opportunities.

OBJECTIVE 3-4 Explain the key changes in the political and cultural environments. (pp 83–89)

The *political environment* consists of laws, agencies, and groups that influence or limit marketing actions. The political environment has undergone changes that affect marketing worldwide: increasing legislation regulating business, strong government agency enforcement, and greater emphasis on ethics and socially responsible actions. The *cultural environment* consists of institutions and forces that affect a society's values, perceptions, preferences, and behaviors. The environment shows trends toward new technology-enabled communication, a lessening trust of institutions, increasing patriotism, greater appreciation for nature, a changing spiritualism, and the search for more meaningful and enduring values.

OBJECTIVE 3-5 Discuss how companies can react to the marketing environment. (pp 89–92)

Companies can passively accept the marketing environment as an uncontrollable element to which they must adapt, avoiding threats and taking advantage of opportunities as they arise. Or they can take a *proactive* stance, working to change the environment rather than simply reacting to it. Whenever possible, companies should try to be proactive rather than reactive.

Key Terms

Objective 3-1
Marketing environment (p 66)
Microenvironment (p 66)
Macroenvironment (p 66)
Marketing intermediaries (p 68)
Public (p 69)

Objective 3-2
Demography (p 70)
Baby boomers (p 71)
Generation X (p 71)
Millennials (Generation Y) (p 72)
Generation Z (p 73)
Economic environment (p 78)

Objective 3-3
Natural environment (p 79)
Environmental sustainability (p 79)
Technological environment (p 80)

Objective 3-4
Political environment (p 83)
Cultural environment (p 87)

DISCUSSION AND CRITICAL THINKING

Discussion Questions

3-1. Define *marketing environment,* and discuss the two parts that make up a company's marketing environment. (AACSB: Written and Oral Communication)

3-2. What are marketing intermediaries, and are they important for marketers? (AACSB: Written and Oral Communication; Reflective Thinking)

3-3. Discuss the impact of the changing age structure of the population on consumer spending and buying behavior. Why is this trend important to marketers? (AACSB: Written and Oral Communication; Reflective Thinking)

3-4. Describe the challenges marketers face with changing economic conditions. What factors should marketers consider in offer value to today's customers? (AACSB: Written and Oral Communication)

3-5. Discuss the natural environment and the three trends that will impact future marketing plans. (AACSB: Written and Oral Communication)

3-6. Why should marketers pay close attention to the cultural environment? (AACSB: Written and Oral Communication)

Critical Thinking Exercises

3-7. Many companies today are looking to do more than just good deeds. More and more, companies are making environmental sustainability a part of their core missions. Research companies that make environmental sustainability part of their values. Write a report to present your findings. (AACSB: Written and Oral Communication; Reflective Thinking)

3-8. Form a small group, and discuss cultural trends in the United States. Research one of them in depth, and create a presentation on the trend's impact on marketing. (AACSB: Written and Oral Communication; Reflective Thinking)

3-9. Technological advances are perhaps the most dramatic forces affecting today's marketing strategies. Imagine you are in the marketing department of a major brand familiar to you. How might new technologies affect the development of a marketing campaign for this brand targeting baby boomers? A campaign targeting Generation Z? (AACSB: Written and Oral Communication; Information Technology)

MINICASES AND APPLICATIONS

Online, Mobile, and Social Media Marketing #MeToo

Recent times have seen the rise of the #MeToo movement, focused on creating awareness and change relating to sexual harassment, assault, and violence in the workplace. At first, the movement centered on female Hollywood celebrities, such as Rose McGowan and Alyssa Milano, who alleged misconduct by producer Harvey Weinstein. However, once the silence was broken in Hollywood, many women around the world began using the #MeToo hashtag on Twitter and Facebook, pointing to their own experiences with workplace harassment or misconduct.

The #MeToo movement emboldened many women to step forward and speak out about toxic workplace environments and company cultures in high-profile companies. As a result, many companies are reacting or taking proactive steps in response to the #MeToo movement. For example, after allegations surfaced regarding a toxic "bro culture" at ride-sharing service Uber, founder Travis Kalanick stepped down as CEO, and the company fired many top-level executives. Newly hired CEO Dara Khosrowshahi took to LinkedIn to post Uber's new cultural norms.

3-10. Many businesses have now crafted responses to the #MeToo movement. Discuss what online or social media platforms they are using. Are they communicating the message clearly and effectively? (AACSB: Written and Oral Communication; Information Technology; Reflective Thinking)

3-11. Is the #MeToo movement a marketing issue? How are customers likely to react to allegations of workplace harassment? How should companies deal with the issue, whether reactively or proactively? (AACSB: Written and Oral Communication; Reflective Thinking)

Marketing Ethics How Young Is Too Young?

Walmart rolled out a cosmetics line aimed at girls as young as 9 years old. According to the *Wall Street Journal,* Walmart introduced this line—called geoGirl—to meet the demands of "tween" girls. The geoGirl line was developed free of chemicals (phthalates and parabens), synthetic colors, and fragrances, allowing marketers to promote the "environmentally friendly" product offering to parents. Capitalizing on this demand trend, Target launched the Hello Kitty line. Tween boys are not to be left out; Axe markets a line of chocolate-scented body spray, and Old Spice developed Swagger body wash. Recently, focus has been placed on girls' self-images as they near the teen years. Some child development experts say that makeup for young girls places too much emphasis on appearance, while others say a little lipstick shouldn't cause much concern.

3-12. Is it an appropriate business strategy to use a popular movement such as environmentalism to market an unrelated product? (AACSB: Written and Oral Communication; Ethical Understanding and Reasoning)

3-13. Apart from the question of placing undue emphasis on a child's appearance, what factors should marketers consider in developing a campaigns for these types of products? (AACSB: Ethical Understanding and Reasoning)

Marketing by the Numbers An Aging America

As marketers focus on millennials embarking on major first-time consumption decisions related to careers, homes, and families, another generation should not be forgotten: the aging baby boomers. The U.S. 65-and-older population will increase to almost 100 million people by 2060. One reason for this trend is the sheer size of the cohort to begin with—76 million people born between 1946 and 1964. Another major factor is that Americans are living longer. In 1950, the average life span was 68 years, but it is now 78.7 years. And the life-span gap between men and women is decreasing because of reduced smoking rates among men. In addition to longer life spans, families are spreading out—as children embark on careers and start their own families they are no longer staying close to their hometowns. These factors contribute to a greater need for caregiver support for the elderly. There is already a proliferation of services such as Visiting Angels and A Place for Mom. The number of boomers needing nursing home care could increase 75 percent by 2030, and the number of people with Alzheimer's disease could triple by 2050. The chart below shows the population estimates for the 65-and-over population for 2011 and 2016, the latest years for which data are available:

	2011	2016
Both sexes	41,364,093	49,244,195
Males	17,932,803	21,792,826
Females	23,431,290	27,451,369

3-14. Calculate the percentage change in the 65-and-over population between 2011 and 2016 for both sexes, males, and females. (AACSB: Analytical Thinking)

3-15. How many more females than males aged 65 and over were there in 2011 and 2016? What percentage of the population did females make up in each year? Draw some conclusions regarding this data. (AACSB: Written and Oral Communication; Analytical Thinking)

Video Case Burger King

To view this video case and its accompanying questions, please visit MyLab Marketing.

In the fast-food burgers business, french fries are perhaps more important than the burgers themselves. System-wide, Burger King sells 56 million orders of french fries every month—one order of fries for every two customers. But nothing is exempt from the impact of marketing environment forces. As health trends drove some companies to cut back on fatty foods, Burger King saw its french fry sales dip.

So Burger King decided to let people have their fries and eat them, too. To bring health-conscious customers back to the counter, Burger King introduced Satisfries—french fries with 30 percent less fat and 20 percent fewer calories than its regular fries. In a product category that has seen little if any innovation, Satisfries could be a big game changer. Still, reduced fat and calories may not be enough to make a difference to health-food lovers. And at 30 to 40 cents more per item, Satisfries may end up as little more than a fry fiasco.

Company Cases 3 Fitbit/7 MINI/14 OfferUp

See Appendix 1 for cases appropriate for this chapter.

Case 3, Fitbit: Riding the Fitness Wave to Glory. How did Fitbit create the fast-growing category of wearable tech? By coming up with the right product at the right time.

Case 7, MINI: Focus on the Essential—Maximize the Experience. BMW has a hit on its hands with MINI, achieving success by remaining true to the original brand while simultaneously keeping up with a changing marketing environment.

Case 14, OfferUp: A Mobile Solution for the Mobile Era. By focusing on the local second-hand marketplace with a modern approach, OfferUp now poses a real threat to the aging Craigslist platform.

Writing Assignments

3-16. What is environmental sustainability and why has it grown in importance for marketers? (AACSB: Communication)

3-17. Discuss a recent change in the technological environment that impacts marketing. How has it affected buyer behavior and how has it changed marketing? (AACSB: Written and Oral Communication; Reflective Thinking)

Managing Marketing Information

to Gain Customer Insights

Objectives Outline

- OBJECTIVE 4-1 **Explain the importance of information in gaining insights about the marketplace and customers.** See: Marketing Information and Customer Insights (pp 98–100)
- OBJECTIVE 4-2 **Define the marketing information system and discuss its parts.** See: Assessing Information Needs and Developing Data (pp 100–103)
- OBJECTIVE 4-3 **Outline the role of marketing research and the steps in the marketing research process.** See: Marketing Research (pp 103–117)
- OBJECTIVE 4-4 **Explain how companies analyze and use marketing information.** See: Analyzing and Using Marketing Information (pp 117–122)
- OBJECTIVE 4-5 **Discuss the special issues some marketing researchers face, including public policy and ethics issues.** See: Other Marketing Information Considerations (pp 122–126)

Previewing the Concepts

In this chapter, we continue our exploration of how marketers gain insights into consumers and the marketplace. We look at how companies develop and manage information about important marketplace elements: customers, competitors, products, and marketing programs. To succeed in today's marketplace, companies must know how to turn mountains of marketing information from a slew of new sources into fresh customer insights that will help them engage customers and deliver greater value to them. As you'll see as the chapter unfolds, the marketing information and research industry is undergoing a major transformation. Traditional marketing research is giving way to an onslaught of new digital, online, mobile, and analytical technologies that enhance the marketer's ability to gather, analyze, communicate, and gain insights from data about consumers and markets.

Let's start with a story about marketing research and customer insights in action. Procter & Gamble has long been considered the world's premier consumer packaged goods company. P&G's success over the decades has resulted from creating and marketing transformational brands that meet consumer needs and wants. But to meet consumer needs and wants, P&G must first discover and deeply understand them. And that understanding comes from thorough marketing research.

First Stop

Marketing Research at P&G: Creating Irresistibly Superior Experiences

P&G makes and markets an impressive list of food, beauty, and household products, including such familiar megabrands as Tide, Gillette, Bounty, Pampers, Always, Febreze, Charmin, Crest, Pantene, Vicks, and Old Spice. In all, P&G markets 65 top-selling consumer brands serving nearly 5 billion consumers in 180 countries, bringing in $65 billion in annual revenues. P&G's brand portfolio includes 23 billion-dollar-plus brands. Year in and year out, P&G is also the world's leading advertiser.

P&G's goal is to create innovative brands that give consumers an "irresistibly superior experience." In these fast-changing times, however, to create such irresistibly superior experiences, P&G must first create a steady flow of deep, fresh insights into consumers' constantly changing needs and behaviors and into just what it is that will make the company's brands irresistibly superior.

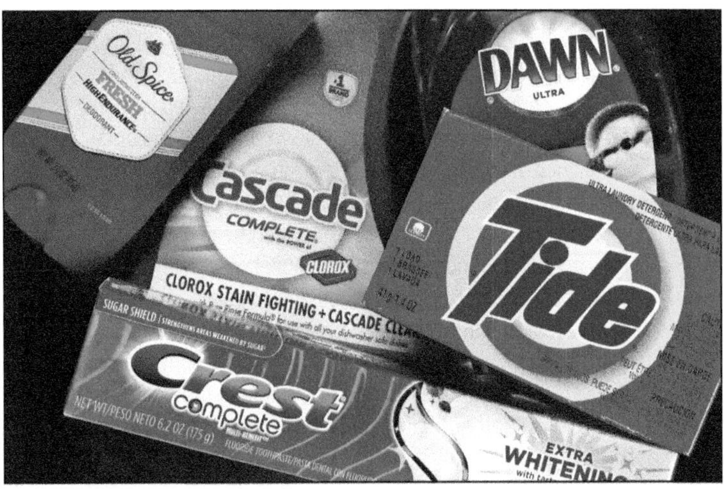

» To gain deep consumer insights, P&G employs a wide range of marketing research approaches—from traditional large-scale surveys and small-scale focus groups to real-time social media listening, mobile surveys, and big data analytics.

Charles Krupa/AP Images

How does P&G gain these insights? Through marketing research—*lots* of marketing research. Each year, the company invests some $350 million on marketing research, conducting more than 15,000 research studies and interacting with more than 5 million consumers, amassing mountains of information and insights into what its consumers need and how they think, act, and buy. P&G employs a wide range of research approaches, ranging from traditional large-scale consumer surveys, small-scale focus groups, and in-store studies to online panels, real-time social media listening, mobile surveys, and big data analytics.

Over the years, P&G's marketing research has resulted in an impressive stream of innovative new-product and marketing successes. Consider P&G's Febreze odor remover. Febreze was developed as an "odor neutralizer," a groundbreaking innovation in a category filled with "odor masking" air fresheners. But after only a few years, Febreze's sales were tanking. To find out why, P&G conducted in-home usage tests in which small teams of P&G researchers observed and interviewed Febreze users and nonusers. The teams came up with a key consumer insight: Most Febreze purchasers weren't using the product to eliminate specific odors—say, in those smelly old sneakers or a pet bed. Instead, they were using it after normal cleaning—for example, spraying a carpet after vacuuming a room—as a further confirmation of cleanliness.

Based on that insight, P&G reworked the product and its positioning. It added mild but refreshing scents to reinforce Febreze's odor neutralizing qualities. Currently positioned as "Odors out. Freshness in. Go ahead, breathe happy," Febreze now comes in a variety of scents including fresh-cut pine, bamboo ("a hint of misty bamboo") and Big Sur ("so your home smells like it's perched on the limb of a sandalwood tree"). P&G then launched an award-winning "Breathe Happy" repositioning campaign that dramatically demonstrated Febreze's ability to "clean away odors." Febreze grew quickly to become one of P&G's billion-dollar brands.

P&G long ago mastered the art and science of consumer immersion research—called "Living It"—in which small teams of P&G staffers live, work, and shop with consumers to gain deep insights into what they think, feel, need, and do. For example, some years ago, P&G used immersion research to find out why Ariel Ultra, the super-concentrated version of its non-U.S. flagship detergent brand, wasn't selling well in Mexico. Ariel Ultra, which delivered more cleaning power at half the quantity per load, was targeted toward middle-class Mexican households, a value-oriented segment that had little room to store bulky detergent containers. However, after only a few months of disappointing sales, P&G temporarily pulled Ariel Ultra from store shelves while it reconsidered its strategy.

Traditional surveys and focus groups provided some of the answers. First, Mexican consumers simply didn't believe that smaller amounts of concentrated Ariel Ultra could provide the same cleaning power. Second, for Mexican women, suds are a sign that the detergent was doing its job, but Ariel Ultra didn't suds up. "We should have understood. We didn't, so we failed," says a P&G manager. "We had to get out of our offices and become immersed in the real world and daily routines of consumers."

> **P&G uses innovative marketing research—lots and lots of it—to dig out deep and fresh consumer insights and then uses the insights to create transformational brands and marketing that deliver irresistibly superior experiences for consumers.**

So P&G's researchers dug deeper with "Living It" studies. The research teams learned that laundry is the most important household task for Mexican homemakers, who want to ensure that their clothing lasts and presents their family well outside the home. The researchers also noted that 90 percent of Mexican women use fabric softener, a product that P&G managers had assumed was little used. Finally, they saw that millions of rural Mexican homes had no running water or had it for only a few hours a day. Women either washed clothing by hand or with semi-automatic machines that required changing water manually, employing two rinse cycles after washing and two more after softening.

Armed with these deeper insights, P&G reformulated Ariel Ultra to require less rinsing and less water. It also introduced Downey Single Rinse. The combination reduced the previous six-step laundry process to three steps—wash, add softener, and then rinse once. P&G then launched a promotional campaign that emphasized how P&G laundry products could save women time, effort, and water. The relaunched brand dramatically increased P&G's share of the laundry market in low- and middle-income Mexican households.

Beyond traditional research approaches, P&G has also perfected today's digital research platforms, from online panels, web tracking, and mobile surveys to big data collection and analytics. Some of this research consists of digital adaptations of traditional methods. For example, when P&G learned that it was losing Pampers customers to competing brands when they switched to bigger sizes, it developed a mobile app that tracked participating customers' use of the brand through everyday diaries. The mobile app data showed that the next-size-up brand switching had nothing to do with perceived diaper performance. Instead, because the bigger size Pampers were shaped so differently, parents perceived potential fit problems. Parents also had a tough time in stores figuring out which size of Pampers was next. These research insights led to simple solutions—minor diaper design changes for better perceived fit and packaging modifications to more quickly and clearly communicate needed sizing information. The modifications lead to reductions in brand switching and increases in Pampers market share.

P&G researchers have also mastered today's "big data." For example, the company reaps massive amounts of data from its thousands of consumer-facing websites around the world, which it combs constantly for customer insights. And P&G closely monitors the online, mobile, and social media environments to research and respond in real time to what consumers are doing, thinking, and talking about. For example, when Tide was doused on the NASCAR Daytona 500 track to clean up fuel spilled after a wreck, allowing the race to continue, Tide researchers picked up the flood of social media response and quickly aired ads capitalizing on the event.

P&G uses sophisticated analytics to dig out actionable consumer insights from its big data. It then delivers the insights into the hands of P&G marketers via "decision cockpits," interfaces on their computers that let them drill down into important information. P&G has also set up more than 50 "Business Spheres" worldwide, high-tech digital centers where managers can immerse themselves in real-time information viewed on large displays. Such real-time research analytics help P&G marketers make faster and better decisions in their quick-changing environments.

So how does P&G go about creating those irresistibly superior experiences? By gaining deep and fresh insights into what consumers need and want. And how does P&G gain those consumer insights? Through marketing research—*lots* and *lots* of marketing research.[1]

As the P&G story highlights, good products and marketing programs begin with good customer information and insights. Companies also need an abundance of information on competitors, resellers, and other actors and marketplace forces. But more than just gathering information, marketers must *use* the information to gain powerful *customer and market insights*.

Author Comment
Marketing information by itself has little value. The value is in the *customer insights* gained from the information and how marketers use these insights to make better decisions.

Marketing Information and Customer Insights

OBJECTIVE 4-1 Explain the importance of information in gaining insights about the marketplace and customers.

To create value for customers and build meaningful relationships with them, marketers must first gain fresh, deep insights into what customers need and want. Such customer insights come from good marketing information. Companies use these customer insights to develop a competitive advantage.

Although customer and market insights are important for building customer value and engagement, these insights can be very difficult to obtain. Customer needs and buying motives are often anything but obvious—consumers themselves usually can't tell you exactly what they need and why they buy. To gain good customer insights, marketers must effectively manage marketing information from a wide range of sources.

Marketing Information and Today's "Big Data"

With the recent explosion of information technologies, companies can now generate and find marketing information in great quantities. The marketing world is filled to the brim with information from innumerable sources—not just data collected from the company's marketing research and internal customer transaction data but real-time data flowing in from social media monitoring, connected devices, and other digital sources.

Consumers themselves are now generating tons of marketing information. Through their smartphones, PCs, and tablets—via online browsing and blogging, apps and social media interactions, texting and video, and geolocation data—consumers now volunteer a tidal wave of bottom-up information to companies and to each other.

Big data
The huge and complex data sets generated by today's sophisticated information generation, collection, storage, and analysis technologies.

Far from lacking information, most marketing managers are overloaded with data and often overwhelmed by it. This problem is summed up in the concept of **big data**. The term *big data* refers to the huge and complex data sets generated by today's sophisticated information generation, collection, storage, and analysis technologies. Every day, the people and systems of the world generate nearly 2.3 trillion gigabytes of data. That's enough data to fill 5.68 trillion good old CD-ROMs, a stack tall enough to go to the moon and back nine times. Roughly 90 percent of the data in the world today has been created in only the past two years.[2]

Big data presents marketers with both big opportunities and big challenges. Companies that effectively tap this glut of data can gain rich, timely customer insights. However, accessing and sifting through so much data is a daunting task. For example, when a large consumer brand such as Coca-Cola or Apple monitors online discussions about its brand in tweets, blogs, social media posts, and other sources, it might take in a stunning 6 million public conversations a day, more than 2 billion a year. That's far more information than any manager can digest.

Thus, marketers don't need *more* information; they need *better* information. And they need to make better *use* of the information they already have. "When it rains, you can't just drink the water. It must be collected, purified, bottled, and delivered for consumption," observes a data expert. "Big data works the same way. It's a raw resource that is a few important steps away from being useful."[3]

Managing Marketing Information

Customer insights
Fresh marketing information-based understandings of customers and the marketplace that become the basis for creating customer value, engagement, and relationships.

The real value of marketing information lies in how it is used—in the **customer insights** that it provides. Based on such thinking, companies ranging from PepsiCo, Starbucks, and McDonald's to Google and GEICO have restructured their marketing information and research functions. They have created *customer insights teams*, whose job it is to develop actionable insights from marketing information and work strategically with marketing decision makers to apply those insights. >> Consider PepsiCo:[4]

Years ago, PepsiCo's various marketing research departments were mainly data providers. But not anymore. Today they are integrated "customer insights teams" charged with delivering insights at the center of the brand, the business, and consumers. The teams gather insights from a rich and constantly evolving variety of sources—ranging from grocery store cash registers, focus groups and surveys, and subconscious measures to mingling with and observing customers in person and monitoring their digital and social media behaviors. The teams continually evaluate new methods for uncovering consumer truths that might predict market behavior. Then the insights teams use the data and observations, tempered by intuitive judgment, to form actionable consumer insights with real business implications. Finally, they share these insights with brand teams from Pepsi, Mountain Dew, Aquafina, and other PepsiCo brands to help them make better decisions.

Beyond just transmitting data and findings through traditional fact-based presentations, reports, and spreadsheets, the Consumer Insights teams share their insights in more engaging, accessible, and digestible ways. For example, the PepsiCo North America Beverages (NAB) Consumer Insights team has even developed a consumer insights app that disseminates custom-designed data and content to marketing and brand decision makers. More than just collecting and distributing data, the PepsiCo consumer insights teams are strategic marketing partners. "We drive decisions that ultimately lead to sustainable growth," says a senior PepsiCo consumer strategy and insights executive. "And everything we do impacts the bottom line."

>> Consumer insights: PepsiCo's "consumer insights teams" wring actionable insights out of the glut of marketing data. They have even developed a consumer insights app to share custom-designed content with brand decision makers.

Vasiliy Baziuk/AP Images

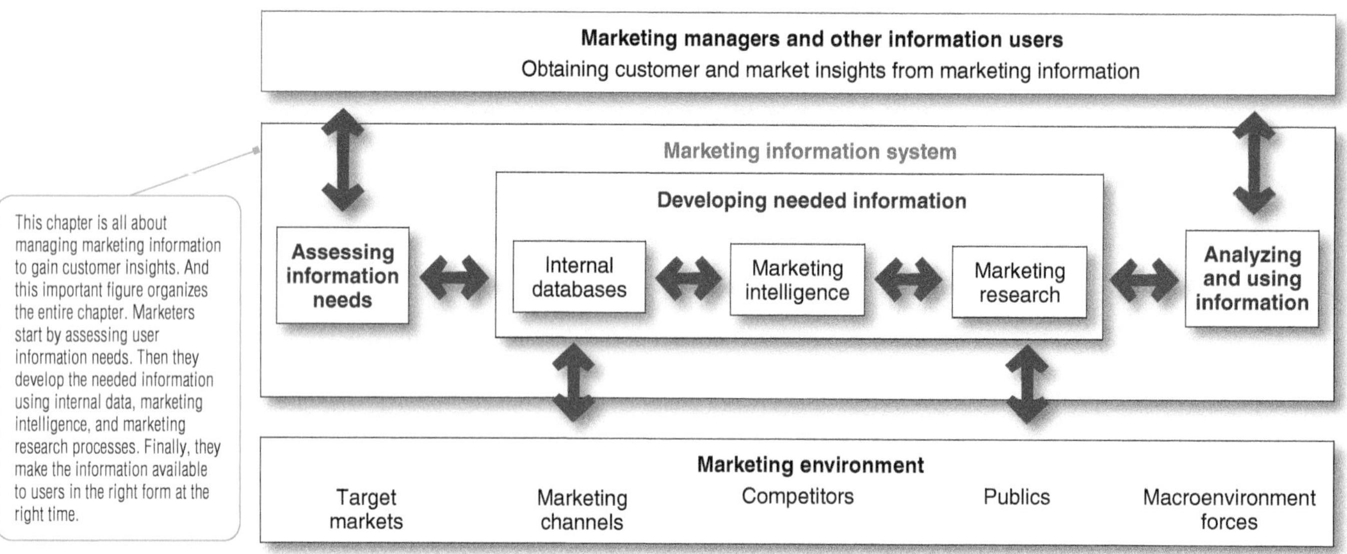
Marketing managers and other information users
Obtaining customer and market insights from marketing information
Marketing information system
Developing needed information
Assessing information needs
Internal databases
Marketing intelligence
Marketing research
Analyzing and using information
Marketing environment
Target markets
Marketing channels
Competitors
Publics
Macroenvironment forces
This chapter is all about managing marketing information to gain customer insights. And this important figure organizes the entire chapter. Marketers start by assessing user information needs. Then they develop the needed information using internal data, marketing intelligence, and marketing research processes. Finally, they make the information available to users in the right form at the right time.

Figure 4.1 The Marketing Information System

Marketing information system (MIS) People and procedures dedicated to assessing information needs, developing the needed information, and helping decision makers to use the information to generate and validate actionable customer and market insights.

Thus, companies must design effective marketing information systems that give managers the right information, in the right form, at the right time and help them to use this information to create customer value, engagement, and stronger customer relationships. A **marketing information system (MIS)** consists of people and procedures dedicated to assessing information needs, developing the needed information, and helping decision makers use the information to generate and validate actionable customer and market insights.

Figure 4.1 shows that the MIS begins and ends with information users—marketing managers, internal and external partners, and others who need marketing information and insights. First, it interacts with these information users to assess information needs. Next, it interacts with the marketing environment to develop needed information through internal company databases, marketing intelligence activities, and marketing research. Finally, the MIS helps users to analyze and use the information to develop customer insights, make marketing decisions, and manage customer engagement and relationships.

Author Comment
The marketing information system begins and ends with users—assessing their information needs and then delivering information and insights that meet those needs.

Assessing Information Needs and Developing Data

OBJECTIVE 4-2 Define the marketing information system and discuss its parts.

Assessing Marketing Information Needs

The marketing information system primarily serves the company's marketing and other managers. However, it may also provide information to external partners, such as suppliers, resellers, or marketing services agencies. For example, Walmart's Retail Link system gives key suppliers access to information on everything from customers' buying patterns and store inventory levels to how many items they've sold in which stores in the past 24 hours.[5]

A good marketing information system balances the information users would like to have against what they really need and what is feasible to offer. Some managers will ask for whatever information they can get without thinking carefully about what they really need. And in this age of big data, some managers will want to collect and store vast amounts of digital data simply because technology lets them. But too much information can be as harmful as too little. In contrast, other managers may omit things they ought to know, or they may not know to ask for some types of information they should have. The MIS must monitor the marketing environment to provide decision makers with information and insights they should have to make key marketing decisions.

Finally, the costs of obtaining, analyzing, storing, and delivering information can mount quickly. The company must decide whether the value of insights gained from additional information is worth the costs of providing it, and both value and cost are often hard to assess.

Author Comment
The problem isn't *finding* information; in this "big data" age, the world is bursting with information from a glut of sources. The real challenge is to find the *right* information—from inside and outside sources—and turn it into customer insights.

Developing Marketing Information

Marketers can obtain the needed information from *internal data, marketing intelligence,* and *marketing research.*

Internal Data

Internal databases
Collections of consumer and market information obtained from data sources within the company network.

Many companies build extensive **internal databases**, collections of consumer and market information obtained from data sources within the company's network. Information in an internal database can come from many sources. The marketing department furnishes information on customer characteristics, in-store and online sales transactions, and web and social media site visits. The customer service department keeps records of customer satisfaction or service problems. The accounting department provides detailed records of sales, costs, and cash flows. Operations reports on production, shipments, and inventories. The sales force reports on reseller reactions and competitor activities, and marketing channel partners provide data on sales transactions. Harnessing such information can provide powerful customer insights and competitive advantage.

For example, insurance and financial services provider USAA uses its internal database to create incredibly loyal customers:[6]

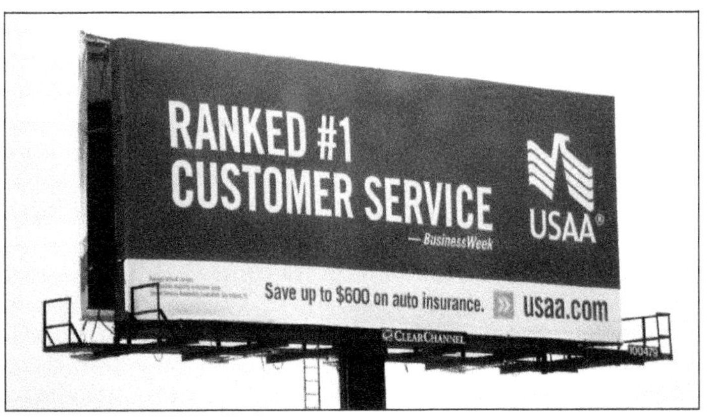

>> Internal data: Financial services provider USAA uses its extensive database to tailor its services to the specific needs of individual customers, creating incredible loyalty.
Courtney Young

>> USAA provides financial services to U.S. military personnel and their families, largely through direct marketing via the phone, the internet, and mobile channels. It maintains a huge customer database built from customer purchasing histories and information collected directly through customer surveys, transaction data, and browsing behavior at its web and social media sites. USAA uses the database to tailor direct marketing offers to the needs of individual customers. For example, for customers looking toward retirement, it sends information on estate planning. If the family has college-age children, USAA sends those children information on how to manage their credit cards.

One delighted reporter, a USAA customer, recounts how USAA even helped him teach his 16-year-old daughter to drive. Just before her birthday, but before she received her driver's license, USAA sent a "package of materials, backed by research, to help me teach my daughter how to drive, help her practice, and help us find ways to agree on what constitutes safe driving later on, when she gets her license." Through such skillful use of its database, USAA serves each customer uniquely, resulting in legendary levels of customer satisfaction and loyalty. More important, the $27 billion company retains 98 percent of its customers.

Internal databases usually can be accessed more quickly and cheaply than other information sources, but they also present some problems. Because internal information is often collected for other purposes, it may be incomplete or in the wrong form for making marketing decisions. Data also age quickly; keeping the database current requires a major effort. Finally, managing and mining the mountains of information that a large company produces require highly sophisticated equipment and techniques.

Competitive Marketing Intelligence

Competitive marketing intelligence
The systematic monitoring, collection, and analysis of publicly available information about consumers, competitors, and developments in the marketing environment.

Competitive marketing intelligence is the systematic monitoring, collection, and analysis of publicly available information about consumers, competitors, and developments in the marketplace. The goal of competitive marketing intelligence is to improve strategic decision making by understanding the consumer environment, assessing and tracking competitors' actions, and providing early warnings of opportunities and threats.

Marketing intelligence techniques range from observing consumers firsthand to quizzing the company's own employees, benchmarking competitors' products, online research, and real-time monitoring of social and mobile media.

Good marketing intelligence can help marketers gain insights into how consumers talk about and engage with their brands. Many companies send out teams of trained observers to mix and mingle personally with customers as they use and talk about the company's products. Other companies have set up state-of-the-art social media command centers that routinely monitor real-time brand-related online consumer and marketplace social and mobile media activity. Such centers can scour the digital environment, analyze brand-related conversations in real time to gain marketing insights, and respond quickly and appropriately.

>> For example, Mastercard's digital intelligence command center—called the Conversation Suite—monitors, analyzes, and responds in real time to millions of online conversations around the world:[7]

>> **Competitive marketing intelligence: Mastercard's digital intelligence command center—called the Conversation Suite—monitors, analyzes, and responds in real time to millions of brand-related conversations across 56 markets and 27 languages around the world.**

Mastercard

The Conversation Suite monitors online brand-related conversations across 56 markets and 27 languages. It tracks social networks, blogs, online and mobile video, and traditional media—any and every digital place that might contain relevant content or commentary on Mastercard. At Mastercard's Purchase, New York, headquarters, Conversation Suite staff huddle with managers from various Mastercard departments and business units in front of a giant 40-foot LED screen that displays summaries of ongoing global brand conversations, refreshed every four minutes. A rotating group of marketing and customer service people spends two or three hours a day in the command center. "It's a real-time focus group," says a Mastercard marketing executive. "We track all mentions of Mastercard and any of our products, plus the competition."

Mastercard uses what it sees, hears, and learns in the Conversation Suite to improve its products and marketing, track brand performance, and spark meaningful customer conversations and engagement. Mastercard even trains "social ambassadors," who can join online conversations and engage customers and brand influencers directly. "Today, almost everything we do [across the company] is rooted in insights we're gathering from the Conversation Suite," says another manager. "[It's] transforming the way we do business."

Companies also need to actively monitor competitors' activities. They can monitor competitors' web and social media sites. For example, Amazon's Competitive Intelligence arm routinely purchases merchandise from competing sites to analyze and compare their assortment, speed, and service quality. Companies can use the internet to search specific competitor names, events, or trends and see what turns up. And tracking consumer conversations about competing brands is often as revealing as tracking conversations about the company's own brands.

Firms use competitive marketing intelligence to gain early insights into competitor moves and strategies and to prepare quick responses. For example, Samsung routinely monitors real-time social media activity surrounding the introductions of Apple's latest iPhones, iPads, and other devices to quickly shape marketing responses for its own Galaxy S smartphones and tablets. At the same time that Apple CEO Tim Cook is onstage unveiling the latest much-anticipated new models, Samsung marketing strategists are huddled around screens in a war room hundreds of miles away watching the introductions unfold. They carefully monitor not only each new device feature as it is presented but also the gush of online consumer commentary flooding blogs and social media channels. Even as the real-time consumer and competitive data surge in, the Samsung team is posting responses. Within only a few days, just as Apple's new models are hitting store shelves, Samsung is already airing TV, print, and social media responses that rechannel the excitement toward its own Galaxy line.[8]

Much competitor intelligence can be collected from people inside the company—executives, engineers and scientists, purchasing agents, and the sales force. The company can also obtain important intelligence information from suppliers, resellers, and key customers. Intelligence seekers can also pour through any of thousands of online databases. Some are free. For example, the U.S. Securities and Exchange Commission's database provides a huge stockpile of financial information on public competitors, and the U.S. Patent Office and Trademark database reveals patents that competitors have filed. For a fee, companies can also subscribe to any of the more than 3,000 online databases and information search services, such as D&B Hoover's, LexisNexis, and Dun & Bradstreet. Today's marketers have an almost overwhelming amount of competitor information only a few keystrokes away.

The intelligence and monitoring game goes both ways. Facing determined competitive marketing intelligence efforts by competitors, most companies take steps to protect their own information. Companies should try conducting marketing intelligence investigations of themselves, looking for potentially damaging information leaks. They should start by "vacuuming up" everything they can find in the public record, including job postings, court records, company advertisements and blogs, web pages, press releases, online business reports, social media site postings by customers and employees, and other information available to inquisitive competitors.

The growing use of marketing intelligence also raises ethical issues. Some intelligence-gathering techniques may involve questionable ethics. Clearly, companies should take advantage of publicly available information. However, they should not stoop to snoop. With all the legitimate intelligence sources now available, a company does not need to break the law or accepted codes of ethics to get good intelligence.

Author Comment
Whereas marketing intelligence involves actively scanning the general marketing environment, marketing research involves more focused studies to gain customer insights related to specific marketing decisions.

Marketing Research

OBJECTIVE 4-3 Outline the role of marketing research and the steps in the marketing research process.

In addition to marketing intelligence information about general consumer, competitor, and marketplace happenings, marketers often need formal studies that provide customer and market insights for specific marketing situations and decisions. For example, Starbucks wants to know how customers would react to a new breakfast menu item. Google wants to know how online and mobile searchers will react to a proposed redesign of its site. Or Samsung wants to know how many and what kinds of people will buy its next-generation, ultrathin televisions. In such situations, managers will need marketing research.

Marketing research
The systematic design, collection, analysis, and reporting of data relevant to a specific marketing situation facing an organization.

Marketing research is the systematic design, collection, analysis, and reporting of data relevant to a specific marketing situation facing an organization. Companies use marketing research in a wide variety of situations. For example, marketing research gives marketers insights into customer motivations, purchase behavior, and satisfaction. It can help them to assess market potential and market share or measure the effectiveness of pricing, product, distribution, and promotion activities.

Some large companies have their own research departments that work with marketing managers on marketing research projects. In addition, these companies—like their smaller counterparts—frequently hire outside research specialists to consult with management on specific marketing problems and to conduct marketing research studies. Sometimes firms simply purchase data collected by outside firms to aid in their decision making.

Traditional Marketing Research in Transition

In recent years, as a host of new digital data-gathering technologies have burst onto the scene, traditional marketing research has undergone a major transformation. Traditional mainstays such as research surveys and focus groups, although still prevalent and powerful, are now giving way to newer, more agile, more immediate, and less costly digital data

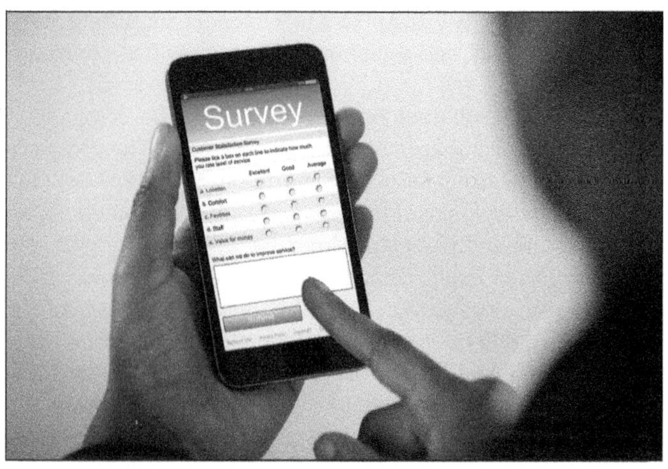

>> Marketing research in transition: Traditional mainstays such as research surveys, although still prevalent and powerful, are now giving way to newer, more agile, more immediate, and less costly digital data gathering methods.

Andriy Popov/123RF

gathering methods. These new approaches—ranging from real-time social media, website, and online feedback monitoring to mobile device tracking—pose a threat to traditional marketing >> research. "The market research industry, as we have known it for decades, is disappearing," proclaims one industry observer. "It is being absorbed into a rapidly transforming collection of market intelligence subdisciplines."[9]

Today's fast and agile decision making often calls for fast and agile marketing information and research—call it *just-in-time research*. In such situations, speed often matters more than research rigor and precision. "If marketing managers can, at the tap of a button, see the views, clicks, likes, and shares of a new ad campaign, as well as listen to the roar—or silence, depending upon its success—of social media comments; then why would they be willing to wait four weeks for a [market research study's] bar chart to tell them that their spontaneous awareness has gone up?" asks an analyst. "Traditional research is in danger of being not only slower but also less insightful than other sources of information."[10] Marketing researchers must adjust to the new pace of information.

Although its role is changing, however, traditional marketing research is still widely used and very important. For many marketing decisions, information quality and rigor are more important than speed, convenience, and lower cost. The traditional research approaches, although often more time-consuming and expensive, can allow for deeper, more focused probing, especially into the whys and wherefores of consumer attitudes and behavior.

Thus, along with the threats, the rise of new digital research platforms also presents the marketing research industry with tremendous opportunities. When combined, the traditional and new digital approaches can greatly enhance the marketer's ability to gather, analyze, communicate, and gain insights from data about consumers and markets.

The key for marketers is to blend the traditional and new approaches into a unified marketing information system that yields agile but deep and complete marketing information and insights. New digital approaches can provide immediate and affordable access to real-time data on the wants, whens, wheres, and hows of consumer buying activities and responses. That frees traditional marketing research approaches to dig more deeply and rigorously into the whys. "In spite of all the benefits digital approaches can deliver," says an analyst, they "should be viewed not solely as a substitute for existing methods but as a new approach that can complement and enhance what has come before."[11]

The marketing research process has four steps (see >> **Figure 4.2**): defining the problem and research objectives, developing the research plan, implementing the research plan, and interpreting and reporting the findings.

Defining the Problem and Research Objectives

Marketing managers and researchers must work together closely to define the problem and agree on research objectives. The manager best understands the decisions for which information is needed, whereas the researcher best understands marketing research and how to obtain the information. Defining the problem and research objectives is often the hardest step in the research process. The manager may know that something is wrong without knowing the specific causes.

This first step is probably the most difficult but also the most important one. It guides the entire research process. It's frustrating and costly to reach the end of an expensive research project only to learn that you've addressed the wrong problem!

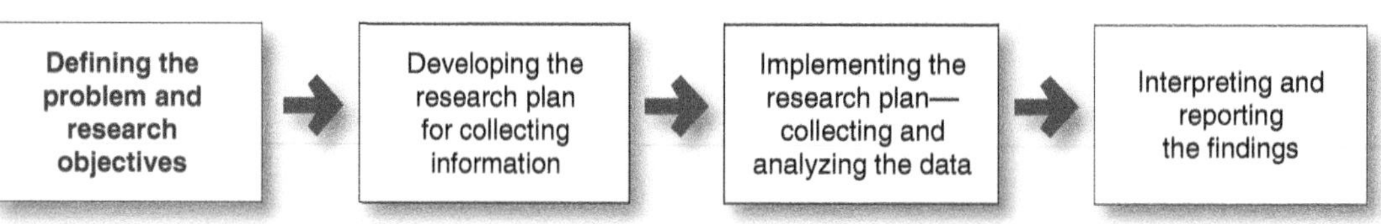

>> Figure 4.2 The Marketing Research Process

After the problem has been defined carefully, the manager and the researcher must set the research objectives. A marketing research project might have one of three types of objectives. The objective of **exploratory research** is to gather preliminary information that will help define the problem and suggest hypotheses. The objective of **descriptive research** is to describe things, such as the market potential for a product or the demographics and attitudes of consumers who buy the product. The objective of **causal research** is to test hypotheses about cause-and-effect relationships. For example, would a 10 percent decrease in tuition at a private college result in an enrollment increase sufficient to offset the reduced tuition? Managers often start with exploratory research and later follow with descriptive or causal research.

Exploratory research
Marketing research to gather preliminary information that will help define problems and suggest hypotheses.

Descriptive research
Marketing research to better describe marketing problems, situations, or markets, such as the market potential for a product or the demographics and attitudes of consumers.

Causal research
Marketing research to test hypotheses about cause-and-effect relationships.

The statement of the problem and research objectives guides the entire research process. The manager and the researcher should put the statement in writing to be certain that they agree on the purpose and expected results of the research.

Developing the Research Plan

Once researchers have defined the research problem and objectives, they must determine the exact information needed, develop a plan for gathering it efficiently, and present the plan to management. The research plan outlines sources of existing data and spells out the specific research approaches, contact methods, sampling plans, and instruments that researchers will use to gather new data.

Research objectives must be translated into specific information needs. >> For example, suppose that Chick-fil-A wants to know how consumers would react to the addition of vegan "chicken" tenders to its menu. According to a recent report, more than 6 percent of Americans now identify themselves as vegan, up from only 1 percent three years ago. Yet vegan offerings at fast-food chains are usually limited to sides, such as fries or salads with no cheese.[12] Adding vegan meals could help attract new sales and allow Chick-fil-A to become a market leader for vegan offerings. The proposed research might call for the following specific information:

- The demographic, economic, and lifestyle characteristics of current Chick-fil-A customers: Do current customers have family members who don't eat meat? Or would Chick-fil-A need to target a new segment of consumers?
- The characteristics and usage patterns of the broader population of fast-food and fast-casual diners: What do they need and expect from such restaurants? Where, when, and how do they use them, and what existing quality, price, and service levels do they value? The new Chick-fil-A offering would require strong, relevant, and distinctive positioning in the crowded fast-food market.
- Impact on the Chick-fil-A customer experience: Would vegan "chicken" offerings be consistent in quality with its famous chicken sandwich?
- Chick-fil-A employee reactions to vegan "chicken": Would restaurant employees buy into such a nontraditional product? Would they be able to prepare and present it properly?
- Forecasts of vegan "chicken" sales and profits: Would vegan "chicken" create enough new sales to make it a lasting and profitable menu item?

>> A decision by Chick-fil-A to add vegan "chicken" would call for marketing research that provides lots of specific information.
Allen Creative/Steve Allen/Alamy Stock Photo

Chick-fil-A's marketers would need these and many other types of information to decide whether to introduce vegan "chicken" tenders and, if so, the best way to do it.

The research plan should be presented in a *written proposal*. A written proposal is especially important when the research project is large and complex or when an outside firm carries it out. The proposal should cover the management problems addressed, the research objectives, the information to be obtained, and how the results will help management's decision making. The proposal also should include estimated research costs.

To meet the manager's information needs, the research plan can call for gathering secondary data, primary data, or both. **Secondary data** consist of information that already exists somewhere, having been collected for another purpose. **Primary data** consist of information collected for the specific purpose at hand.

Secondary data
Information that already exists somewhere, having been collected for another purpose.

Primary data
Information collected for the specific purpose at hand.

Gathering Secondary Data

Researchers usually start by gathering secondary data. The company's internal database provides a good starting point. However, the company can also tap into a wide assortment of external information sources.

Companies can buy secondary data from outside suppliers. For example, Nielsen sells shopper insight data from a consumer panel of more than 250,000 households in 25 countries worldwide, with measures of trial and repeat purchasing, brand loyalty, and buyer demographics. Experian Simmons carries out a full spectrum of consumer studies that provide a comprehensive view of the American consumer. The U.S. MONITOR service by Kantar Futures sells information on important social and lifestyle trends. Kantar's Cultural Streetscapers can give marketers "an on-the-ground view of anything that's shaping the marketplace of tomorrow (and today): from broad societal shifts to breakthrough trends and unique consumer segments." These and other firms supply high-quality data to suit a wide variety of marketing information needs.[13]

Using *commercial online databases*, marketing researchers can conduct their own searches of secondary data sources. General database services such as ProQuest and LexisNexis put an incredible wealth of information at the fingertips of marketing decision makers. Beyond commercial services offering information for a fee, almost every industry association, government agency, business publication, and news medium offers free information to those tenacious enough to find their websites or apps.

Internet search engines can also be a big help in locating relevant secondary information sources. However, they can also be very frustrating and inefficient. For example, a Chick-fil-A marketer Googling "fast-food vegan chicken" would come up with more than 42 million hits. Still, well-structured, well-designed online searches can be a good starting point to any marketing research project.

Secondary data can usually be obtained more quickly and at a lower cost than primary data. Also, secondary sources can sometimes provide data an individual company cannot collect on its own—information that either is not directly available or would be too expensive to collect. For example, it would be too expensive for a consumer products brand such as Coca-Cola or Tide to conduct a continuing retail store audit to find out about the market shares, prices, and displays of its own and competitors' brands. But those marketers can buy store sales and audit data from IRI, which provides data from more than 100,000 retail stores in markets around the nation.[14]

Secondary data can also present problems. Researchers can rarely obtain all the data they need from secondary sources. For example, Chick-fil-A will not find existing information regarding consumer reactions about vegan chicken tenders in the fast-food setting. Even when data can be found, the information might not be very usable. The researcher must evaluate secondary information carefully to make certain it is *relevant* (fits the research project's needs), *accurate* (reliably collected and reported), *current* (up-to-date enough for current decisions), and *impartial* (objectively collected and reported).

Primary Data Collection

Secondary data provide a good starting point for research and often help to define research problems and objectives. In most cases, however, the company must also collect primary data. >> **Table 4.1** shows that designing a plan for primary data collection calls for decisions on *research approaches*, *contact methods*, the *sampling plan*, and *research instruments*.

Table 4.1 Planning Primary Data Collection

Research Approaches	Contact Methods	Sampling Plan	Research Instruments
Observation	Mail	Sampling unit	Questionnaire
Survey	Telephone	Sample size	Mechanical instruments
Experiment	Personal	Sampling procedure	
	Online		

Research Approaches

Research approaches for gathering primary data include observation, surveys, and experiments. We discuss each one in turn.

Observational research
Gathering primary data by observing relevant people, actions, and situations.

Observational Research. **Observational research** involves gathering primary data by observing relevant people, actions, and situations. For example, food retailer Trader Joe's might evaluate possible new store locations by checking traffic patterns, neighborhood conditions, and the locations of competing Whole Foods, Fresh Market, and other retail chains.

Researchers often observe consumer behavior to glean customer insights they can't obtain by simply asking customers questions. For instance, many new menu items at pizza giant Domino's come from its stores, where franchisees observe special requests from customers and fiddle accordingly to adapt existing offerings. >> The new menu ideas then come to corporate test kitchens, where they are tested using the company's 12 "sensory booths." Each booth is outfitted with a slot for sliding pizza slices to subjects and devices for getting feedback about product appearance, taste, and preferences. Beyond testing new products, Domino's also uses the observation booths to test improvements in existing products and reactions to ingredients from new suppliers.[15]

Ethnographic research
A form of observational research that involves sending trained observers to watch and interact with consumers in their "natural environments."

Marketers not only observe what consumers do but also observe what consumers are saying. As discussed earlier, marketers now routinely listen in on consumer conversations on social media, blogs, and websites. Observing such naturally occurring feedback can provide inputs that simply can't be gained through more structured and formal research approaches.

A wide range of companies also use **ethnographic research**. Ethnographic research involves sending observers to watch and interact with consumers in their "natural environments." The observers might be trained anthropologists and psychologists or company researchers and managers. Consider Intuit, maker of Turbo Tax and QuickBooks financial software:[16]

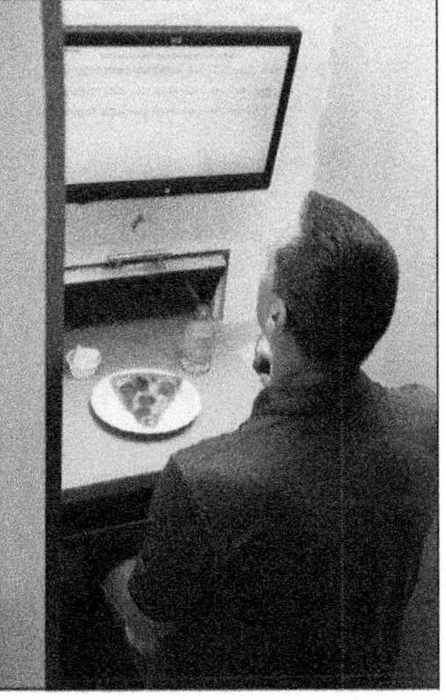

>> **Observational research: Domino's observes special customer requests in its stores and turns them into potential new menu items, which are then tested in the company's test kitchens using "sensory observation booths."**

Domino's Pizza, Inc.

> Most companies want to get close to their customers, but Intuit caries it to extremes. Under the company's "follow-me-home" program, small, well-trained teams of employees visit customers' homes and offices to watch customers experience the company's products in real life—everything from removing the shrink-wrap to applying the software. The

teams don't interview the customers; they simply observe. After each visit, the teams debrief immediately "so you get a complete picture faster," says Intuit CEO Brand Smith. Intuit conducts some 10,000 hours of follow-me-home visits a year; Smith himself devotes 60 to 100 hours a year to such visits. "The underlying reality is that you can't [always] believe what customers tell you," notes one observer. "Customer behavior is the truth." CEO Smith agrees: "What you get from a follow-me-home you can't get from a data stream. You've gotta look somebody in the eye and feel the emotion."

Similarly, global branding firm Landor launched Landor Families, an ongoing ethnographic study that has followed 11 French families intensely for the past seven years. Landor researchers visit the families twice a year in their homes, diving deeply into both their refrigerators and their food shopping behaviors and opinions. The researchers also shop with the families at their local supermarkets and look over their shoulders while they shop online. The families furnish monthly online reports detailing their shopping behaviors and opinions. The Landor Families study provides rich behavioral insights for Landor clients such as Danone, Kraft Foods, and P&G. Today's big data analytics can provide important insights into the whats, whens, and wheres of consumer buying. The Landor Families program is designed to explore the whys. According to Landor, "There is no better way to understand people than to observe them in real life."[17]

Observational and ethnographic research often yields the kinds of details that just don't emerge from traditional research questionnaires or focus groups. Whereas traditional quantitative research approaches seek to test known hypotheses and obtain answers to well-defined product or strategy questions, observational research can generate fresh customer and market insights that people are unwilling or unable to provide. It provides a window into customers' unconscious actions and unexpressed needs and feelings.

However, some things simply cannot be observed, such as attitudes, motives, or private behavior. Long-term or infrequent behavior is also difficult to observe. Finally, observations can be very difficult to interpret. Because of these limitations, researchers often use observation along with other data collection methods.

Survey research
Gathering primary data by asking people questions about their knowledge, attitudes, preferences, and buying behavior.

Survey Research. Long the backbone traditional marketing research, **survey research** is the most widely used method for primary data collection. Survey research is best suited for gathering descriptive information. A company that wants to know about people's knowledge, attitudes, preferences, or buying behavior can often find out by asking them directly.

The major advantage of survey research is its flexibility; it can be used to obtain many kinds of information in many different situations. Surveys addressing almost any marketing question or decision can be conducted by phone or mail, online, or in person.

However, survey research also presents some problems. Sometimes people are unable to answer survey questions because they cannot remember or have never thought about what they do and why they do it. People may be unwilling to respond to unknown interviewers or about things they consider private. Respondents may answer survey questions even when they do not know the answer just to appear smarter or more informed. Or they may try to help the interviewer by giving pleasing answers. Finally, busy people may not take the time, or they might resent the intrusion into their privacy.

Experimental research
Gathering primary data by selecting matched groups of subjects, giving them different treatments, controlling related factors, and checking for differences in group responses.

Experimental Research. Whereas observation is best suited for exploratory research and surveys for descriptive research, **experimental research** is best suited for gathering causal information. Experiments involve selecting matched groups of subjects, giving them different treatments, controlling unrelated factors, and checking for differences in group responses. Thus, experimental research tries to explain cause-and-effect relationships.

For example, before adding a new sandwich to its menu, McDonald's might use experiments to test the effects on sales of two different prices it might charge. It could introduce the new sandwich at one price in one city and at another price in another city. If the cities are similar and if all other marketing efforts for the sandwich are the same, then differences in sales in the two cities could be related to the price charged.

>> Experimental research: Online experiments can be simple and inexpensive. For example, an online "A/B test" for Microsoft's Bing search engine formatting yielded performance-enhancing results in only hours.

One photo/Shutterstock

Online controlled experiments can be simple and inexpensive to run with immediate and revealing results. >> For example, to test a possible change in the way its Bing search engine displays ad headlines, Microsoft conducted an online "A/B test" or "split-run test" in which one group of users saw the old headline format (version A) while another group saw the new format (version B). Within only hours, the new headline variation was producing an astonishing 12 percent ad revenue increase without harming the user experience. Needless to say, Microsoft adopted the new format. Today, Microsoft and other digital companies such as Amazon, Google, and Facebook each conduct thousands of controlled experiments involving millions of users annually.[18]

Contact Methods

Information can be collected by mail, by telephone, by personal interview, or online. Each contact method has its own particular strengths and weaknesses.

Mail, Telephone, and Personal Interviewing. *Mail questionnaires* can be used to collect large amounts of information at a low cost per respondent. Respondents may give more honest answers on a mail questionnaire than to an unknown interviewer in person or over the phone. Also, no interviewer is involved to bias respondents' answers. However, mail questionnaires are not very flexible; all respondents answer the same questions in a fixed order. And mail surveys usually take longer to complete and response rates are often low. As a result, more and more marketers are now shifting to faster, more flexible, and lower-cost email, online, and mobile phone surveys.

Telephone interviewing can be used by gather information quickly, and it provides greater flexibility than mail questionnaires. Interviewers can explain difficult questions and, depending on the answers they receive, skip some questions or probe on others. Response rates tend to be higher than with mail questionnaires, and interviewers can ask to speak to respondents with the desired characteristics or even by name.

However, with telephone interviewing, the cost per respondent is higher than with mail, online, or mobile questionnaires. Also, people may not want to discuss personal questions with an interviewer. The method introduces interviewer bias—the way interviewers talk, how they ask questions, and other differences that may affect respondents' answers. Finally, in this age of do-not-call lists, promotion-harassed consumers, caller ID, and mobile phones, potential survey respondents are increasingly not answering or hanging up on telephone interviewers rather than talking with them. As a result, although telephone interviewing remains a valuable marketing research methodology, its use has declined in recent years.[19]

Personal interviewing takes two forms: individual interviewing and group interviewing. *Individual interviewing* involves talking with people in their homes or offices, on the street, or in shopping malls. Such interviewing is flexible. Trained interviewers can guide interviews, explain difficult questions, and explore issues as the situation requires. They can show subjects actual products, packages, advertisements, or videos and observe reactions and behavior. However, individual personal interviews may cost three to four times as much as telephone interviews.

Focus Group Interviewing. *Group interviewing* consists of inviting small groups of people to meet with a trained moderator to talk about a product, service, or organization. Participants normally are paid a small sum for attending. A moderator encourages free and easy discussion, hoping that group interactions will bring out deeper feelings and thoughts. At the same time, the moderator "focuses" the discussion—hence the name **focus group interviewing**.

Focus group interviewing
Personal interviewing that involves inviting small groups of people to gather for a few hours with a trained interviewer to talk about a product, service, or organization. The interviewer "focuses" the group discussion on important issues.

In traditional focus groups, researchers and marketers watch the focus group discussions from behind a one-way mirror and video-record sessions for later study. Through videoconferencing and internet technology, marketers in far-off locations can look in and listen, even participate, as a focus group progresses.

Focus group interviewing remains one of the major qualitative marketing research tools for gaining fresh insights into consumer thoughts and feelings. In focus group settings, researchers not only hear consumer ideas and opinions, they also can observe facial expressions, body movements, group interplay, and conversational flows. However, focus group studies present some challenges. They usually employ small samples to keep time and costs down, and it may be hard to generalize from the results. Moreover, consumers in focus groups are not always open and honest about their real feelings, behaviors, and intentions in front of other people.

To overcome these problems, many researchers are tinkering with the focus group design. Some companies are changing the environments in which they conduct focus groups to help consumers relax and elicit more authentic responses. For example, Lexus hosts "An Evening with Lexus" dinners in customers' homes with groups of luxury car buyers to learn up close and personal why they did or did not buy a Lexus. Other companies use *immersion groups*—small groups of consumers who interact directly and informally with product designers without a focus group moderator present.

>> Research and innovation consultancy The Mom Complex uses such immersion groups to help brand marketers from companies such as Unilever, Johnson & Johnson, Kimberly-Clark, Kellogg, Playskool, and Walmart understand and connect with their "mom customers":[20]

> According to The Mom Complex, America's 80 million moms control 85 percent of the nation's $2.4 trillion in household purchases, yet three out of four moms say marketers have no idea what it's like to be a mother. To change that, The Mom Complex arranges "Mom Immersion Sessions," in which brand marketers interact directly with groups of mothers, who receive $100 in compensation for a two-hour session. Rather than the usual focus group practice of putting the marketers behind a one-way mirror to observe groups of moms discussing their brands, the participants and marketers sit in the same room. Guided by a discussion facilitator, the moms begin by educating the marketers about the realities of motherhood—"the raw, real ugly truth about being a mom." Then the moms and marketers work together to address specific brand issues—whether it's new product ideas, current product problems, or positioning and communications strategy. The goal is to "turn the challenges of motherhood into growth opportunities for brands."

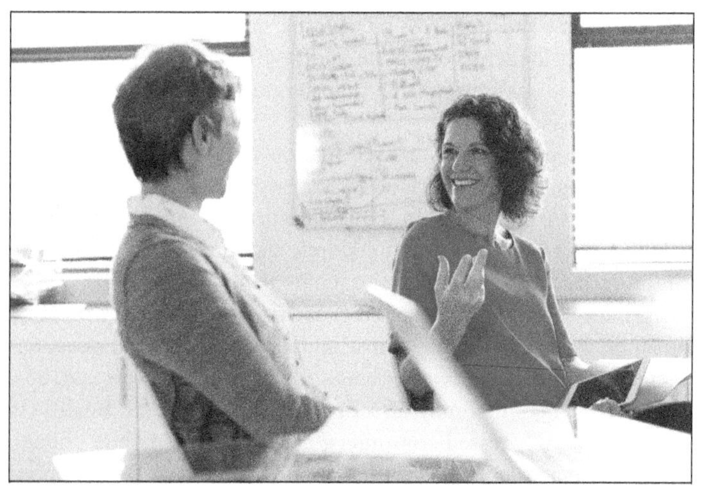

>> New focus group designs: The Mom Complex uses "Mom Immersion Sessions" to help brand marketers understand and connect directly with their "mom customers" on important brand issues.

caia image/Alamy Stock Photo

Individual and focus group interviews can add a personal touch as opposed to more numbers-oriented, big data–driven research. They can provide rich insights into the motivations and feelings behind the numbers and analytics. Things really come to life when you hear people say them. For that reason, focus groups are still the most widely used qualitative research tool.

Online marketing research
Collecting primary data through internet and mobile surveys, online focus groups, consumer tracking, experiments, and online panels and brand communities.

Online Marketing Research. The internet has had a dramatic impact on how marketing research is conducted. Increasingly, researchers are collecting primary data through **online marketing research**: internet and mobile surveys, online focus groups, consumer tracking, experiments, and online panels and brand communities.

Online research can take many forms. A company can use the internet or mobile technology as a survey medium: It can include a questionnaire on its web or social media sites or use email or mobile devices to invite people to answer questions. It can create online panels that provide regular feedback or conduct live discussions or online focus groups. Researchers can also conduct online experiments. They can experiment with different prices, headlines, or product features on different web or mobile sites or at different times to learn the relative effectiveness of their offers. They can set up virtual shopping environments and use them to test new products and marketing programs. Or a company can learn about the behavior of online customers by following their click streams as they visit the online site and move to other sites.

The internet is especially well suited to *quantitative* research—for example, conducting marketing surveys and collecting data. Almost 90 percent of all Americans now use the internet, making it a fertile channel for reaching a broad cross-section of consumers.[21] As response rates for traditional survey approaches decline and costs increase, the internet is quickly replacing mail and the telephone as the dominant data collection methodology.

Internet-based survey research offers many advantages over traditional phone, mail, and personal interviewing approaches. The most obvious advantages are speed and low costs. By going online, researchers can quickly and easily distribute surveys to thousands of respondents simultaneously via email or by posting them on selected online, social media, and mobile sites. Responses can be almost instantaneous, and because respondents themselves enter the information, researchers can tabulate, review, and share research data as the information arrives.

Online research also usually costs much less than research conducted through mail, phone, or personal interviews. Using the internet eliminates most of the postage, phone, interviewer, and data-handling costs associated with the other approaches. Moreover, sample size and location have little impact on costs. Once the questionnaire is set up, there's little difference in cost between 10 respondents and 10,000 respondents on the internet or between local or globally distant respondents.

Its low cost puts online research well within the reach of almost any business, large or small. In fact, with the internet, what was once the domain of research experts is now available to almost any would-be researcher. >> Even smaller, less sophisticated researchers can use online survey services such as Google Surveys (www.google.com/analytics/surveys), Snap Surveys (www.snapsurveys.com), and SurveyMonkey (www.surveymonkey.com) to create, publish, and distribute their own custom online or mobile surveys in minutes.

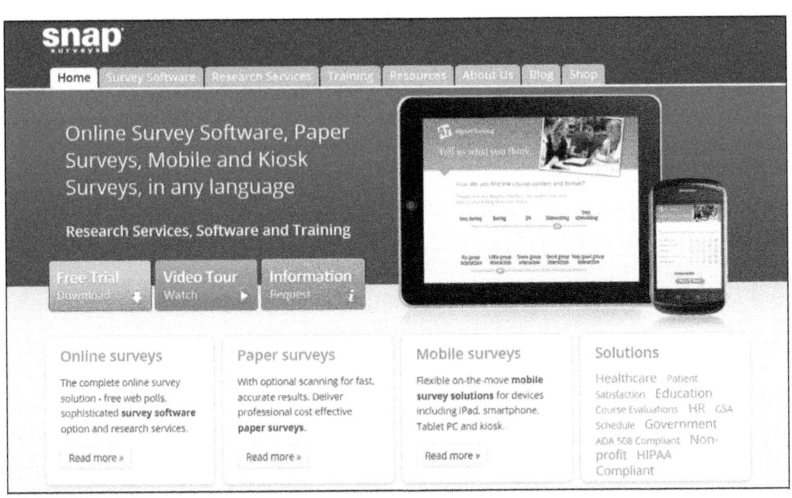

>> **Online research: Thanks to survey services such as Snap Surveys, almost any business, large or small, can create, publish, and distribute its own custom online or mobile surveys in minutes.**

Reproduced with permission from Snap Surveys. www.snapsurveys.com

Internet-based surveys also tend to be more interactive and engaging, easier to complete, and less intrusive than traditional phone or mail surveys. As a result, they usually garner higher response rates. The internet is an excellent medium for reaching the hard-to-reach consumer—for example, the often-elusive teen, single, affluent, and well-educated audiences. It's also good for reaching people who lead busy lives, from working mothers to on-the-go executives. Such people are well represented online, and they can respond in their own space and at their own convenience.

Just as marketing researchers have rushed to use the internet for quantitative surveys and data collection, they are now also adopting *qualitative* internet-based research approaches, such as online focus groups, blogs, and social networks. The internet can provide a fast, low-cost way to gain qualitative customer insights.

Online focus groups
Gathering a small group of people online with a trained moderator to chat about a product, service, or organization and gain qualitative insights about consumer attitudes and behavior.

A primary qualitative internet-based research approach is **online focus groups**. >> For example, online research firm FocusVision offers its InterVu service, which lets companies connect with customers through interactive video and online focus groups. Groups can include participants at remote locations, anywhere in the world, at any time. InterVu participants can log on to focus sessions from their homes or offices and see, hear, and react to each other in real-time, face-to-face discussions. Researchers can capture thoughts and emotions through verbal and nonverbal responses, zeroing in on facial expressions and body language.[22] Such focus groups can be conducted in any language and viewed with simultaneous translation. They work well for bringing together people from different parts of the country or world at low cost. Researchers can view the sessions in real time from just about anywhere, eliminating travel, lodging, and facility costs. Finally, although online focus groups require some advance scheduling, results are almost immediate.

Although growing rapidly, both quantitative and qualitative internet-based research have some drawbacks. One major problem is controlling who's in the online sample. Without seeing respondents, it's difficult to know who they really are. To overcome such sample and context problems, many online research firms use opt-in communities and respondent panels.

» Online focus groups: FocusVision's InterVu service lets focus group participants at remote locations see, hear, and react to each other in real-time, face-to-face discussions.

Image provided courtesy of FocusVision, the leading research technology software provider for simple to sophisticated qualitative and quantitative projects.

Alternatively, many companies have now developed their own "insight communities" from which they obtain customer feedback and insights. For example, ESPN has a long-standing digital insights community called FANography:[23]

> ESPN FANography consists of 12,000 dedicated ESPN fans who provide ongoing feedback across a wide range of topics—everything from marketing and advertising campaigns to program content. For example, when ESPN wanted to understand if fans were still enjoying NBA Christmas Day promotions, which featured Santa Claus at NBA press conferences, reactions from FANography members showed that the promos were well liked—in fact, fans clamored for more. In another case, ESPN wanted to know whether inconsistencies in NFL player jersey colors depicted in *Monday Night Football* promotions confused viewers. So it invited FANography members to participate in a rapid-fire response test to identify team jersey color associations. Based on feedback from the insight community, ESPN reworked future promotions.
>
> ESPN works to make FANography members feel like real insiders. It sends them custom-designed quarterly FANewsletters showing how others in the community responded to questions and how their feedback is being used. ESPN also hosts a private Facebook group for FANography members, with round-the-clock sports conversations and sneak peeks into breaking company news. "Our insight community provides quick yet deep customer insight to numerous ESPN divisions," says a brand marketing executive.

Online Behavioral and Social Tracking and Targeting. Thus, the internet has become an important tool for conducting research and developing customer insights. But today's marketing researchers are going even further—well beyond online surveys, focus groups, and online communities. Increasingly, they are listening to and watching consumers by actively mining the rich veins of unsolicited, unstructured, "bottom-up" customer information already coursing around the internet. Whereas traditional marketing research provides more logical consumer responses to structured and intrusive research questions, online listening provides the passion and spontaneity of unsolicited, real-time consumer opinions.

Tracking consumers online might be as simple as scanning customer reviews and comments on the company's brand site or on shopping sites such as Amazon.com or BestBuy.com. Or it might mean using sophisticated online-analysis tools to deeply analyze the mountains of consumer brand-related comments and messages found in blogs or on social media sites.

Listening to and engaging customers online can provide valuable insights into what consumers are saying or feeling about a brand. It can also provide opportunities for building positive brand experiences and relationships. Many companies now excel at listening online and responding quickly and appropriately. As noted previously, more and more companies are setting up social media command centers with which they scour the digital environment and analyze brand-related comments and conversations to gain marketing insights.

Information about what consumers do while trolling the vast digital expanse—what searches they make, the online and mobile sites they visit, how they shop, and what they buy—is pure gold to marketers. And today's marketers are busy mining that gold. Then, in a practice called **behavioral targeting**, marketers use the online data to target ads and offers to specific consumers. Even further, they use *social targeting,* mining individual online social networking activity for the purpose of target ads and marketing efforts.

Behavioral targeting
Using online consumer tracking data and analytics to target advertisements and marketing offers to specific consumers.

Online listening, behavioral targeting, and social targeting can help marketers to harness the massive amounts of consumer information swirling around the internet. However, as marketers get more adept at trolling social media, shopping sites, and other internet and mobile domains, many critics worry about consumer privacy. At what point does sophisticated online research cross the line into consumer stalking? Although behavioral and social targeting can benefit consumers with more relevant ads and products, if overdone and done badly, it can also strike customers as more than just a little creepy (see Marketing at Work 4.1).

MARKETING AT WORK 4.1

Behavioral and Social Targeting: Sophisticated Marketing or Just a Little Creepy?

Thanks to the burgeoning world of web browsing, social media, mobile apps, online shopping, and other internet activities, marketers now have real-time access to a flood of online consumer information. It's all there for the digging—what sites consumers visit, what searches they make, what apps they use, how they shop, what they buy, with whom they interact—digitally revealed as they navigate the internet.

Marketers routinely employ sophisticated big data tools to analyze the churning mass of online and mobile data in precise detail, using the resulting insights to target and personalize marketing ads and offers. On today's internet, everyone knows who you are. By combining online and offline data, marketers know your age, your gender, where you live, that you love dogs, what you bought recently at Amazon.com, and that you spent one hour and 21 minutes last Sunday morning browsing college basketball news and scores at ESPN.com.

Marketers use all that data to deliver ads and offers aimed squarely at individual consumers, wherever they travel on the internet, or even in stores. It's called *behavioral targeting*—tracking consumers' online behavior and using it to target ads and offers to them. So, for example, if you do a Google search for a Samsung TV you're thinking about buying, you'll probably see an ad for that very type of TV on your next visit to Facebook or your favorite buying site. Or as you're shopping in one section of your local Walgreen's, you might receive a real-time notification on your phone of a deal in another section of the store.

All this is amazing enough, but web analytics and targeting take online eavesdropping even further—from *behavioral* targeting to *social* targeting. Whereas behavioral targeting tracks consumer movements across online sites, social targeting also mines individual online social media connections and conversations. Research shows that consumers shop a lot like their friends and are five times more likely to respond to ads from brands friends use. Social targeting links customer data to social interaction data from social networking sites.

So, instead of just having a Zappos.com ad for running shoes pop up because you've recently searched for running shoes (behavioral targeting), an ad for a specific pair of running shoes pops up because a friend that you're connected to via Instagram or Twitter just bought those shoes from Zappos.com last week (social targeting).

Social targeting can even capture the dynamics of real-time conversations. For example, beyond just targeting 24- to 26-year-old males who are both sports fans and car enthusiasts, Chevrolet made its ad message even more relevant by targeting those consumers while they are talking about football on a mobile Twitter app during the Super Bowl. When they checked the

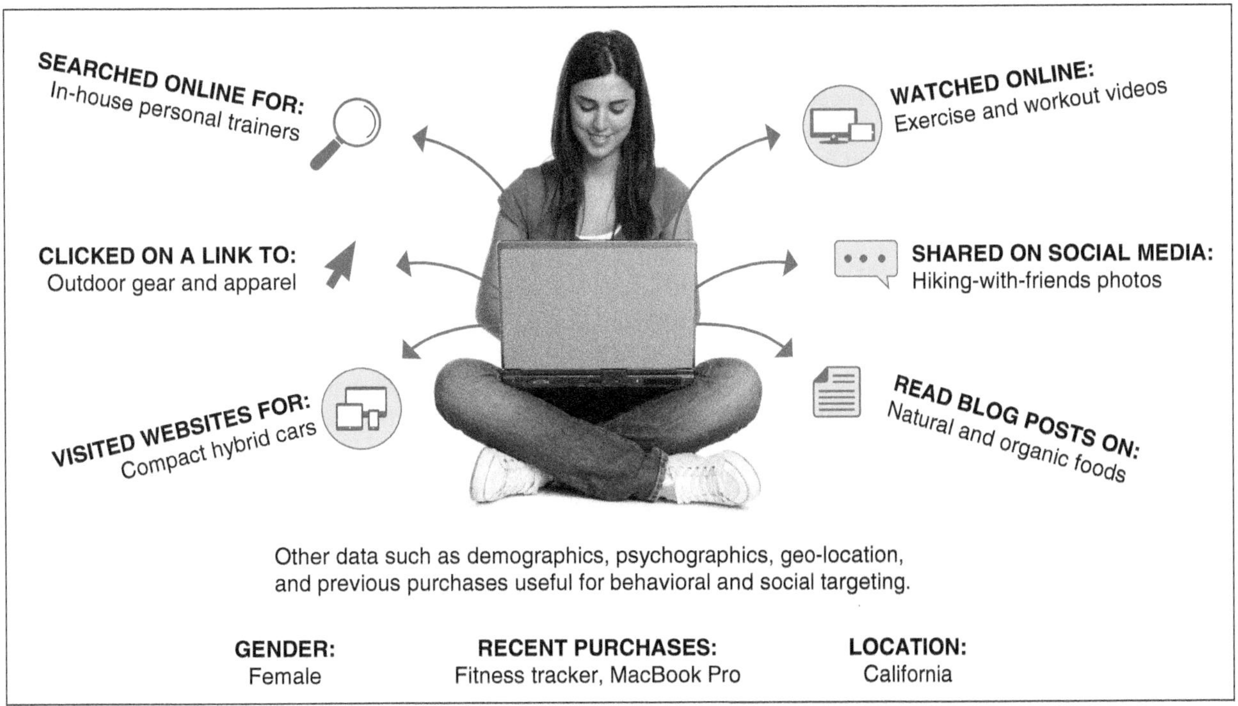

>> On today's internet, with today's advanced analytics, everyone knows who you are. Marketers use such insights to personalize online shopping experiences. But is it sophisticated marketing or "just a little creepy"?

Rido/Shutterstock

app, targeted consumers saw an ad that prompted them to check out Chevy's Super Bowl video on YouTube.

Behavioral and social targeting require sophisticated analytics, so many marketers enlist the services of specialized ad networks with exotic names like Taboola, PulsePoint, and Adknowledge. These digital advertising networks obtain user browsing data by partnering with hundreds or even thousands of websites. The partners supply gobs of data on user browsing histories, web and mobile site usage, electronic shopping cart contents, and other details of what users do, where, and when.

The ad networks then apply high-powered big data analytics to identify consumers with similar interests, needs, behavior, and internet habits. This lets them merge audience data from one group of sites with ad placements on another. Armed with that information, the networks then work with advertisers to purchase ads that target the right customers. So if you're browsing lawn and garden sites, don't be surprised to see ads for Scotts lawn products the next time you visit Weather.com. Or if you seek car-buying advice at sites such as Edmunds.com or nadaguides.com, you might well see ads for the cars you researched the next time you visit Google News to catch up on what's happening around the nation and world.

The major social media have also gotten into behavioral targeting in a big way. Facebook, Google, Instagram, Twitter, Snapchat, and other social media dig deeply into user data to help their advertisers target more sharply. For example, some 2 billion people use Facebook every month. However, based on sophisticated analytics, Facebook offers powerful audience selection tools that help its advertisers target the right customer groups or even individuals on Facebook.

Advertisers can target Facebook users based on demographics (age, gender, education, relationship status, or even job titles), location (where they live, or maybe within a radius around a store), interests (say, hobbies or favorite entertainment), or behaviors (what they buy, device usage, or other activities). Or Facebook can help advertisers create "custom audiences" by finding and reaching existing customers and contacts who also use Facebook. Advertisers can even build what Facebook calls "lookalike audiences," people on Facebook whose behaviors mirror those of their target customers. Thanks to such sophisticated targeting capabilities, Facebook now captures more that 20 percent of all online advertising dollars, second only to Google's more than 40 percent.

Online analytics. Behavioral targeting. Social targeting. All of these are great for marketers as they work to mine customer insights from the massive amounts of consumer information swirling around the internet. The biggest question? You've probably already guessed it. As marketers get more adept at trolling web and mobile sites, social media, and other digital domains, what happens to consumer privacy? Yup, that's the downside. At what point does sophisticated online research cross the line into unwelcome invasions of privacy?

Proponents claim that behavioral and social targeting benefit more than abuse consumers by feeding back ads and products that are more relevant to their interests. But to many consumers and public advocates, following consumers online and stalking them with ads feels more than just a little creepy. "Marketers must find a sweet spot between personalization and surveillance," says one analyst. "Customers can be creeped out when brands cross the thin line between knowing them like a friend and knowing them like a stalker."

Despite such concerns, behavior and social targeting continue to grow and to get smarter. And, with appropriate safeguards, they promise benefits for both companies and customers. Marketers who can plumb the depths of customer data and respond in meaningful, valuable ways without crossing the line will thrive. But it can be a delicate balance. As Snapchat's Privacy Center states, "We want you to feel understood. We want to understand what's relevant to you and your life, and we want to show you things that you'll care about. At the same time, we don't want to serve ads that are so custom-tailored that they feel invasive or uncomfortable."

Sources: See Hal Conick, "Where Does Convenience Turn Creepy?" *Marketing News,* April/May 2017, p. 10; Lara O'Reilly, "Snapchat Is About to Introduce Something Advertisers Have Been Wanting for Ages: Behavioral Targeting," *Business Insider,* August 26, 2016, www.businessinsider.com/snapchat-to-launch-behavioral-targeting-for-advertisers-2016-8; "Google and Facebook Tighten Their Grip on US Digital Ad Market," *eMarketer,* September 21, 2017, www.emarketer.com/Article/Google-Facebook-Tighten-Grip-on-US-Digital-Ad-Market/1016494; and "Choose Your Audience," www.facebook.com/business/products/ads/ad-targeting, accessed September 2018.

Regulators and others are stepping in. The Federal Trade Commission (FTC) has recommended the creation of a "Do Not Track" system (the online equivalent to the "Do Not Call" registry), which would let people opt out of having their actions monitored online. However, progress has been mixed and slow. Meanwhile, many major internet browsers and social media have heeded the concerns and added extended privacy features to their services.[24]

Sampling Plan

Sample
A segment of the population selected for marketing research to represent the population as a whole.

Marketing researchers usually draw conclusions about large groups of consumers by studying a small sample of the total consumer population. A **sample** is a segment of the population selected for marketing research to represent the population as a whole. Ideally, the sample should be representative so that the researcher can make accurate estimates of the thoughts and behaviors of the larger population.

Designing the sample requires three decisions. First, *who* is to be studied (what *sampling unit*)? The answer to this question is not always obvious. For example, to learn about the decision-making process for a family automobile purchase, should the subject be the husband, the wife, other family members, dealership salespeople, or all of these? Second, *how many* people should be included (what *sample size*)? Large samples give more

Table 4.2 Types of Samples

Probability Sample	
Simple random sample	Every member of the population has a known and equal chance of selection.
Stratified random sample	The population is divided into mutually exclusive groups (such as age groups), and random samples are drawn from each group.
Cluster (area) sample	The population is divided into mutually exclusive groups (such as blocks), and the researcher draws a sample of the groups to interview.
Nonprobability Sample	
Convenience sample	The researcher selects the easiest population members from which to obtain information.
Judgment sample	The researcher uses his or her judgment to select population members who are good prospects for accurate information.
Quota sample	The researcher finds and interviews a prescribed number of people in each of several categories.

reliable results than small samples. However, larger samples usually cost more, and it is not necessary to sample the entire target market or even a large portion to get reliable results.

Finally, *how* should the people in the sample be *chosen* (what *sampling procedure*)? >> **Table 4.2** describes different kinds of samples. Using *probability samples*, each population member has a known chance of being included in the sample, and researchers can calculate confidence limits for sampling error. But when probability sampling costs too much or takes too much time, marketing researchers often take *nonprobability samples* even though their sampling error cannot be measured. These varied ways of drawing samples have different costs and time limitations as well as different accuracy and statistical properties. Which method is best depends on the needs of the research project.

Research Instruments

In collecting primary data, marketing researchers have a choice of two main research instruments: *questionnaires* and *mechanical devices.*

Questionnaires. The questionnaire is by far the most common instrument, whether administered in person, by phone, by email, or online. Questionnaires are very flexible—there are many ways to ask questions. Closed-ended questions include all the possible answers, and subjects make choices among them. Examples include multiple-choice questions and scale questions. Open-ended questions allow respondents to answer in their own words. In a survey of airline users, Southwest Airlines might simply ask, "What is your opinion of Southwest Airlines?" Or it might ask people to complete a sentence: "When I choose an airline, the most important consideration is . . . " These and other kinds of open-ended questions often reveal more than closed-ended questions because they do not limit respondents' answers.

Open-ended questions are especially useful in exploratory research, when the researcher is trying to find out *what* people think but is not measuring *how many* people think in a certain way. Closed-ended questions, on the other hand, provide answers that are easier to interpret and tabulate.

Researchers should also use care in the *wording* and *ordering* of questions. They should use simple, direct, and unbiased wording. Questions should be arranged in a logical order. The first question should create interest if possible, and difficult or personal questions should be asked last so that respondents do not become defensive.

Mechanical Instruments. Although questionnaires are the most common research instrument, researchers also use mechanical instruments to monitor consumer behavior. For example, Nielsen Media Research attaches people meters to television sets in selected homes to record who watches which programs. Retailers use checkout scanners to record shoppers' purchases. Other marketers use mobile phone GPS technologies to track consumer movements in and near their stores.

Today's big data, Internet of Things (IoT) world has produced a flood of information from internet-connected devices. There are now more than 50 billion IoT-connected devices worldwide, not counting computers and phone.[25] They include everything from smart TVs and smart home devices to digital cameras, in-car navigation systems, and even robotic vacuum cleaners. Internet-connected devices offer huge potential for gathering data on consumer movements, actions, and activities.

Still other researchers apply *neuromarketing*, using EEG and MRI technologies to track brain electrical activity to learn how consumers feel and respond. Neuromarketing measures, often combined with *biometric* measures (such as heart rates, respiration rates, sweat levels, and facial and eye movements), can provide companies with insights into what turns consumers on and off regarding their brands and marketing. For example, research firm Nielsen and the Ad Council used neuromarketing to improve the effectiveness of an ad for the Shelter Pet Project, a public service campaign focused on increasing adoption rates for pets in shelters:[26]

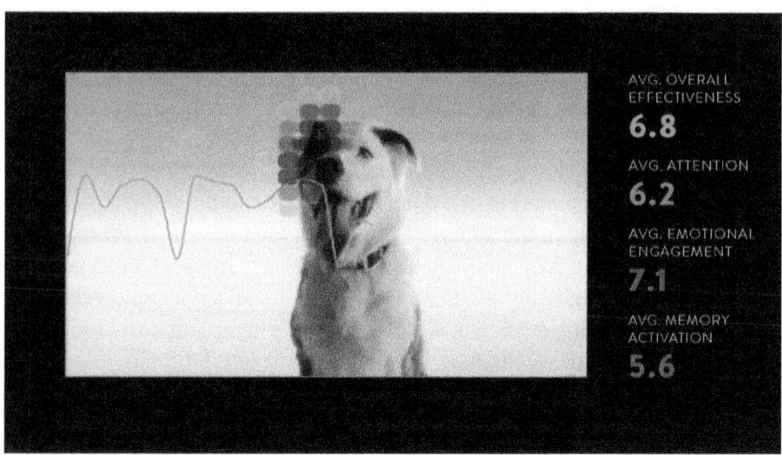

>> Neuromarketing helped improve the effectiveness of ads for the Shelter Pet Project, increasing viewer attention, emotional engagement, and memory recall and more than doubling traffic to the organization's website.

>> Using neuroscience methods, Nielsen charted how people's brains responded to an existing Shelter Pet Project public service ad and the ad's canine star, Jules the dog. Researchers used a combination of EEG and eye-tracking measurements to determine the second-by-second, scene-by-scene impact of the ad on viewer attention, emotional engagement, and memory activation. They discovered that viewer attention and emotional engagement jumped when Jules was on the screen. They also learned that the end of the ad caused confusion, with Jules, the logo, and the website URL all competing for viewer attention. The creative team re-edited the ad, increasing Jules's on-screen moments and sharpening the ad's ending and call to action. A second round of neuroscience tests showed that the recrafted ad held viewers' attention better, kept them more consistently engaged, and improved ad recall. As a result, in the first three months after the launch of the refreshed ad, traffic to the Shelter Pet Project website more than doubled, a change that may have real life-or-death implications for shelter pets.

Although neuromarketing techniques can measure consumer involvement and emotional responses second by second, such brain responses can be difficult to interpret. Thus, neuromarketing is usually used in combination with other research approaches to gain a more complete picture of what goes on inside consumers' heads.

Implementing the Research Plan

The researcher next puts the marketing research plan into action. This involves collecting, processing, and analyzing the information. Data collection can be carried out by the company's marketing research staff or outside firms. Researchers should watch closely to make sure that the plan is implemented correctly. They must guard against problems with data collection techniques and technologies, data quality, and timeliness.

Researchers must also process and analyze the collected data to isolate important information and insights. They need to check data for accuracy and completeness and code them for analysis. The researchers then tabulate the results and compute statistical measures.

Interpreting and Reporting the Findings

The market researcher must now interpret the findings, draw conclusions, and report them to management. The researcher should not try to overwhelm managers with numbers and fancy statistical techniques. Rather, the researcher should present important findings and insights that are useful in the major decisions faced by management.

However, interpretation should not be left only to researchers. Although they are often experts in research design and statistics, the marketing manager knows more about the problem and the decisions that must be made. The best research means little if the manager blindly accepts faulty interpretations from the researcher. Similarly, managers may be biased. They might tend to accept research results that show what they expected and reject those that they did not expect or hope for. In many cases, findings can be interpreted in different ways, and discussions between researchers and managers will help point to the best interpretations. Thus, managers and researchers must work together closely when interpreting research results, and both must share responsibility for the research process and resulting decisions.

LINKING THE CONCEPTS

Whew! We've covered a lot of territory. Hold up a minute, take a breather, and see if you can apply the marketing research process you've just studied.

- What specific kinds of research can Chick-fil-A marketing managers use to learn more about its customers' preferences and buying behaviors? Sketch out a brief research plan for assessing potential reactions to potential new menu items.
- Could you use the marketing research process to analyze your career opportunities and job possibilities? (Think of yourself as a "product" and employers as potential "customers.") If so, what would your research plan look like?

Author Comment

We've talked generally about managing customer relationships throughout the book. But here, *customer relationship management* (CRM) has a much narrower data-management meaning. It refers to capturing and using customer data from all sources to manage customer interactions, engage customers, and build customer relationships.

Analyzing and Using Marketing Information

OBJECTIVE 4-4 **Explain how companies analyze and use marketing information.**

Information gathered from internal databases, competitive marketing intelligence, and marketing research usually requires additional analysis. Managers may need help applying the information to gain customer and market insights that will improve their marketing decisions. This help may include advanced analytics to learn more about the relationships within sets of data. Information analysis might also involve the application of analytical models that will help marketers make better decisions.

Once the information has been processed and analyzed, it must be made available to the right decision makers at the right time. In the following sections, we look deeper into analyzing and using marketing information.

Customer Relationship Management (CRM)

The question of how best to analyze and use individual customer data presents special problems. In the current *big data* era, most companies are awash in information about their customers and the marketplace. Still, smart companies capture information at every possible customer *touch point*. These touch points include customer purchases, sales force contacts, service and support calls, web and social media site visits, satisfaction surveys, credit and payment interactions, market research studies—every contact between a customer and a company.

Unfortunately, this information is usually scattered widely across the organization or buried deep in separate company databases. To overcome such problems, many companies are now turning to **customer relationship management (CRM)** to manage detailed information about individual customers and carefully manage customer touch points to maximize customer loyalty.

Customer relationship management (CRM)
Managing detailed information about individual customers and carefully managing customer touch points to maximize customer loyalty.

CRM consists of sophisticated software and analysis tools from companies such as Salesforce.com, Oracle, Microsoft, and SAS that integrate customer and marketplace information from all sources, analyze it, and apply the results to build stronger customer relationships. CRM integrates everything that a company's sales, service, and marketing teams know about individual customers, providing a 360-degree view of the customer relationship. For example, MetLife employs a CRM system that it calls "The MetLife Wall":[27]

One of the biggest customer service challenges for MetLife's sales and service reps used to be quickly finding and getting to customer information—different records, transactions, and interactions stored in dozens of different company data locations and formats. The MetLife Wall solves that problem. The Wall uses a Facebook-like interface to serve up a consolidated view of each MetLife customer's service experience. The innovative CRM system draws customer data from 70 different MetLife systems containing 45 million customer agreements and 140 million transactions. It puts all of a given customer's information and related links into a single record on a single screen, updated in near real time. Now, thanks to The MetLife Wall—with only a single click instead of the 40 clicks it used to take—sales and service reps can see a complete view of a given customer's various policies, transactions, and claims filed and paid along with a history of all the interactions the customer has had with MetLife across the company's many touch points, all on a simple timeline. The Wall has given a big boost to MetLife's customer service and cross-selling efforts. According to a MetLife marketing executive, it's also had "a huge impact on customer satisfaction."

By using CRM to understand customers better, companies can provide higher levels of customer service and develop deeper customer relationships. They can use CRM to pinpoint high-value customers, target them more effectively, cross-sell the company's products, and create offers tailored to specific customer requirements.

Big Data, Marketing Analytics, and Artificial Intelligence

As noted at the start of the chapter, today's big data can yield big results. But simply collecting and storing huge amounts of data has little value. Marketers must sift through the mountains of data to mine the gems—the bits that yield customer insights. As one marketing executive puts it, "It's actually [about getting] *big insights* from big data. It's throwing away 99.999 percent of that data to find things that are actionable." Says another data expert, "*right* data trumps *big* data."[28] That's the job of *marketing analytics*.

Marketing analytics
The analysis tools, technologies, and processes by which marketers dig out meaningful patterns in big data to gain customer insights and gauge marketing performance.

Marketing analytics consists of the analysis tools, technologies, and processes by which marketers dig out meaningful patterns in big data to gain customer insights and gauge marketing performance. Marketers apply marketing analytics to the large and complex sets of data they collect from web, mobile, and social media tracking; customer transactions and engagements; and other big data sources. >> For example, Netflix uses sophisticated big data analytics to gain consumer insights, which it then uses to give customers exactly what they want:[29]

Netflix streams more movie and program content by far than any other video service. Worldwide, Netflix's 110 million paid subscribers watch some 250 million hours of movies, TV programs, and original Netflix content a day. But while avid Netflixers are busy watching Netflix videos, Netflix is also busy watching *them*—watching them very, very closely. Every day, Netflix tracks and parses member data on tens of millions of searches, ratings, and "plays." The company's bulging database contains every viewing detail for each individual subscriber—real-time data on what shows they watch, at what times, on what devices, at what locations, even when they hit the pause, rewind, or fast-forward buttons during programs. Netflix also employs experts to classify each video on hundreds of characteristics, such as talent, action, tone, genre, color, volume, scenery, and many, many others. Netflix supplements this already-massive database with consumer information purchased from Nielsen, Facebook, Twitter, and other sources.

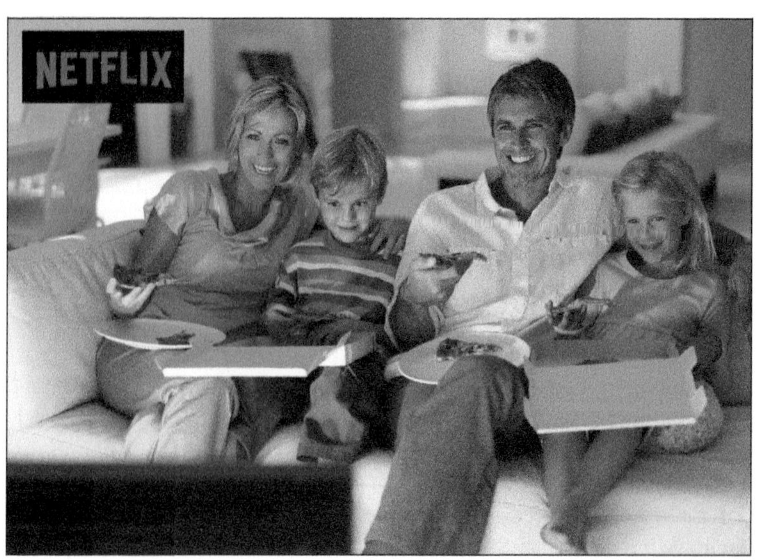

>> Netflix, big data, and CRM: While members are busy watching Netflix videos, Netflix is busy watching them—watching them very, very closely. Then it uses the big data insights to give customers exactly what they want.
Chris Ryan/OJO Images Ltd/Alamy Stock Photo (photo); dennizn/Shutterstock (logo)

Using this rich base of big data, Netflix builds detailed individual subscriber profiles and then uses these profiles to tailor each customer's viewing experience and make personalized recommendations. As one analyst puts it, "No more 'there's nothing on TV tonight' or 'I don't know which show to watch.' Instead, you get a personal feed, with suggestions based on what you watched before." According to Netflix, there are 110 million different versions of Netflix, one for each individual subscriber worldwide. Netflix also uses the data to assess what additional content it should obtain or produce itself. "We always use our in-depth knowledge about what our members love to watch to decide what's available on Netflix," says a Netflix marketer. "If you keep watching, we'll keep adding more of what you love."

Artificial intelligence (AI)
Technology by which machines think and learn in a way that looks and feels human but with a lot more analytical capacity.

Such analytics employ **artificial intelligence (AI)**, technology by which machines think and learn in a way that looks and feels human but with a lot more analytical capacity. Artificial intelligence has taken the marketing—and about everything else in the world—by storm. Marketers are now using AI for everything from big data analytics to engaging customers to crafting personalized advertising and selling efforts. Although still in its infancy, AI offers vast potential for marketing. As Google's CEO suggests, AI "is more profound than fire or electricity." That's saying a great deal (see Marketing at Work 4.2).[30]

The benefits of customer relationship management, big data analytics, and artificial intelligence don't come without costs or risks. The most common mistake is to view CRM, marketing analytics, and AI as technology processes only. Managers get buried in the big data details and miss the big picture. Or they can let machines make decisions rather than putting on their own thinking caps.[31] Yet technology alone cannot build profitable customer relationships. Companies can't improve customer relationships by simply installing some new software. Instead, marketers should start with the fundamentals of managing customer relationships and *then* employ high-tech data and analytics solutions. They should focus first on the R—it's the *relationship* that CRM is all about.

Distributing and Using Marketing Information

Marketing information has no value until it is used to make better marketing decisions. Thus, the marketing information system must make information readily available to managers and others who need it, when they need it. In some cases, this means providing managers with regular performance reports, intelligence updates, and reports on the results of research studies.

But marketing managers may also need access to nonroutine information for special situations and on-the-spot decisions. For example, a sales manager having trouble with a large customer may want a summary of the account's sales and profitability over the past year. Or a brand manager may want to get a sense of the amount of the social media buzz surrounding the recent launch of a new product. These days, therefore, information distribution involves making information available in a timely, user-friendly way.

Many firms use company *intranet* and internal CRM systems to facilitate this process. These systems provide ready access to research and intelligence information, customer transaction and experience information, shared reports and documents, and more. For example, the CRM system at phone and online gift retailer 1-800-Flowers.com gives customer-facing employees real-time access to customer information. When a repeat customer calls, the system immediately pulls up data on previous transactions and other contacts, helping reps make the customer's experience easier and more relevant. For instance, if a customer usually buys tulips for his wife, the rep can talk about the best tulip selections and related gifts. Such connections result in greater customer satisfaction and loyalty and greater sales for the company. "We can do it in real time," says a 1-800-Flowers.com executive, "and it enhances the customer experience."[32]

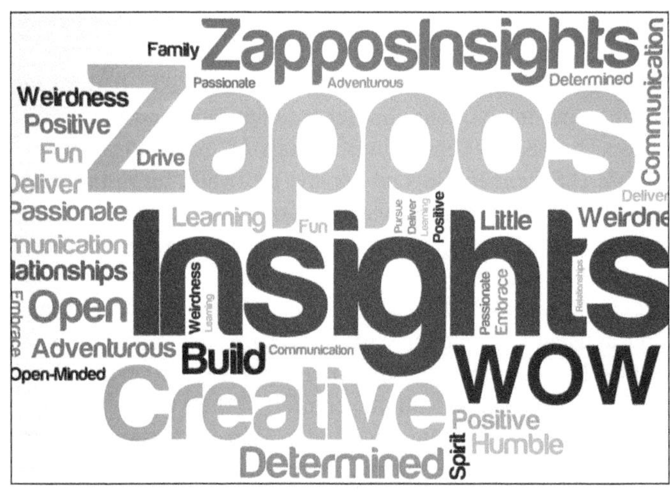

» Extranets: Zappos shares marketing information and insights with suppliers through its ZUUL extranet. It considers suppliers to be "part of the Zappos family."

Zappos

In addition, companies are increasingly allowing key customers and value-network members to access account, product, and other data on demand through *extranets*. Suppliers, customers, resellers, and select other network members may access a company's extranet to update their accounts, arrange purchases, and check orders against inventories to improve customer service.

» For example, online shoes and accessories retailer Zappos considers suppliers to be "part of the Zappos family" and a key component in its quest to deliver "WOW" through

MARKETING AT WORK 4.2

Artificial Intelligence in Marketing: "A Bigger Deal Than Fire or Electricity"

It's early morning, you're headed out to start your day, and you feel the urge for that first jolt of caffeine. As you get in your car, you tap the Starbucks app on your phone and ask for "the usual." Your Starbucks virtual barista replies in her familiar, cheerful voice: "One tall caramel latte!" She then politely suggests a breakfast snack—a Vermont maple nut muffin—not your usual, but it sure sounds good. You agree. "Thanks! Your order will be ready for pickup in five to seven minutes minutes at University and 28th," she confirms. "Would you like to pay for that with your credit card on file?" You step inside the store, bypass the long lines, and grab your order—no fuss, no muss. Welcome to the world of artificial intelligence (AI).

This is just one example of how AI has exploded onto the marketing scene. Starbucks has long been into cutting-edge technology—a full 25 percent of its transactions are already placed through its smartphone apps. But My Starbucks Barista is more than just an ordering app. It uses artificial intelligence to create personalized customer experiences and manage real-time customer interactions, based on everything from customers' past transactions and preferences to demographics, store trends and inventories, and local traffic and weather conditions.

» Artificial intelligence: The My Starbucks Barista uses artificial intelligence to create personalized customer experiences and manage real-time customer interactions, based on everything from customers' past transactions and preferences to local traffic and weather conditions.

Elias Stein Illustration

Artificial intelligence is sweeping the world. It involves machines that think and learn in a way that looks and feels human but with a lot more analytical capacity. The engine behind the AI's explosive growth is big data. Raw data is flowing in from everywhere: customer transaction and interaction data, web and social media data, news and environmental data, and data from more than 50 billion connected devices—everything from consumer wearables and GPS technology to household thermostats, washing machines, and cars. Companies need to make sense of all that data for their brands and consumers.

The human mind simply can't grapple with today's glut of big data. But machines can. However, more than just collecting and tabulating mountains of data, AI analyzes it at lightning speed to gain deep insights and apply them to accomplish designated tasks. AI learns as it goes along—the more data it ingests, the smarter and more accurate it gets. "AI is the planet we're headed to," says one AI expert. "Machine learning is the rocket that's going to get us there. And big data is the fuel."

Marketers use AI to assess, address, service, and sell to customers. In turn, AI can help customers manage their lives and their buying. It might be requesting a ride from Lyft via chat (Facebook Messenger or Slack) or voice (Amazon Echo's Alexa virtual assistant). Lyft's chatbot lets you know the current location of your driver along with a picture of the license plate and car model. Or it might be IBM's Watson supercomputer combing through vast amounts of data to unearth customer and market insights that help marketers sharpen their targeting, personalize customer engagements, design new products, and even craft better ads in real time.

Today's machines are smart and eerily human. IBM's Watson "is loquacious; it can tell jokes, answer questions, and write songs," notes one observer. "Google's AI can now read lips better than a professional and can master video games within hours. MIT's AI can predict action on video two seconds before it begins. Tesla's AI powers [its] innovative self-driving car."

Companies like Amazon have mastered AI, harnessing insights and interactions that let it understand and serve customers. Amazon's Echo brings Alexa's AI magic to nearly 50 million U.S. homes. Beyond serving as a valet for duties such as adjusting household appliances, controlling music, keeping shopping lists, sending text messages, and answering questions on about any subject, Echo and other similar AI devices, such as Google Home, have become voice-activated personal shopping assistants. Companies ranging from P&G and Clorox to 1-800-Flowers are hard at work perfecting ways to tap into Echo users who voice-shop from the comfort of their own kitchens.

At Amazon's shopping and video sites, AI powers recommendations that help consumers decide what to buy and what to watch. "Increasingly, Amazon will be selling you things you didn't even know you needed because it has learned what you like and are most inclined to buy," says an analyst. Amazon is so good at this that it's even considering what it calls "predictive delivery," sending consumers stuff they haven't even ordered yet. If customers don't want it, they would just keep it for free. Although such deliveries may still be a while off, Amazon uses such AI predictions to keep the right stock in warehouses or even on trucks to support its ever-more-popular one-day or even one-hour delivery promise.

Hosts of retailers are employing AI to improve how they service and sell to their customers. For example, in select California stores, home improvement retailer Lowe's is rolling out LoweBots—five-foot something, fully mobile, AI-powered robots that roam stores helping customers. The LoweBots detect customers who might need assistance and engage them through voice and touchscreens. The AI robots tap store and external data to answers customer questions, offer solutions, lead customers to merchandise in the store (or order online merchandise that's not in stock). They even offer text and video tutorials. Meanwhile, the LoweBots keep tabs on store-level data and analyze customer shopping patterns. They're "learning things that we never knew before," says a Lowe's Innovation Labs manager, like "what is happening at 3 o'clock on a Tuesday" in any given store.

AI does more than just serve customers. It also helps marketing managers shape marketing strategies and tactics. For example, IBM has formed a new division called Watson Advertising, built around its AI supercomputer Watson, which first gained public recognition when it bested human contestants and won $1 million on *Jeopardy*. Watson can ingest hundreds of millions of pages of data each second. IBM is now turning Watson's talents toward marketing. For example, factoring in emotion, tone, language, sentiment, purchase history, and social media interactions, Watson "can generate a psycholinguistic profile of an individual in literally milliseconds," explains an IBM executive.

Using such analytics, Watson can give marketers precise, real-time views of customers and put the insights it learns into action, using its AI powers for everything from data analysis and media planning to audience targeting and actual content creation. According to one account:

> As part of a Toyota campaign, for example, Watson became a copywriter, crafting messaging for the carmaker's Mirai model based on [big data analysis of] tech and science fans' interests. Earlier this year, it transformed into a doctor, promoting Theraflu while answering questions about various flu symptoms. For Campbell's, Watson put on its chef's hat, personalizing recipes within display ads using data about consumers' locations and what ingredients they had on hand. For a major partnership with H&R Block, Watson turned into a tax expert, deploying an AI smart assistant to help clients find tax deductions.

IBM recently bought The Weather Company, which produces forecasts for 2.2 billion locations every 15 minutes, letting Watson munch on troves of data to gauge how weather affects consumers' moods, health, and buying. It recently used a combination of this weather data, consumer Google searches, and pollen counts to advise a medicine maker on which media to use in various markets and when.

Despite all these remarkable applications, AI is still in its early stages. "We're still in the dawn of AI adoption," says a technology expert. "It's a new frontier and one that will redefine the relationship between consumers and brands." As an industry, AI will skyrocket from current annual revenues of $650 million to nearly $40 billion by 2025. And that doesn't include the trillions of dollars' worth of retail sales that AI will facilitate. "AI is going to be like electricity or the internet," says the Lowe's technology manager. "It becomes so interwoven ... it takes all of this other stuff that we've been doing for so long and it makes it better than the sum of its parts." Google's CEO puts it more simply: "It's more profound than fire or electricity."

Sources: "Google CEO: AI Is a Bigger Deal than Fire or Electricity," *Fast Company*, January 19, 2018, www.fastcompany.com/40519204/google-sundar-pichai-ai-is-a-bigger-deal-than-fire-or-electricity; Hal Conick, "The Past, Present, and Future of AI in Marketing," *Marketing News*, December 29, 2016, pp. 27–35; Erik Wander, "Welcome to the Machine," *Adweek*, December 4, 2017, p. 16; Marty Swant, "As IBM Ramps Up Its AI-Powered Advertising, Can Watson Crack the Code of Digital Marketing," *Adweek*, September 25, 2017, pp. 19–23; Lauren Johnson, "5 Bleeding-Edge Brands That Are Infusing Retail with Artificial Intelligence," *Adweek*, January 2, 2017, www.adweek.com/digital/5-bleeding-edge-brands-are-infusing-retail-artificial-intelligence-175312/; and Lauren Hirsch and Michelle Castillo, "Amazon Has Big Plans for Alexa Ads in 2018," *CNBC*, January 2, 2018, www.cnbc.com/2018/01/02/amazon-alexa-is-opening-up-to-more-sponsored-product-ads.html.

great customer service. So it treats suppliers as valued partners, including sharing information with them. Through its ZUUL extranet (Zappos Unified User Login), thousands of suppliers are given full access to brand-related Zappos's inventory levels, sales figures, and even profitability. Suppliers can also use ZUUL to interact with the Zappos creative team and to enter suggested orders for Zappos buyers to approve.[33]

Thanks to modern technology, today's marketing managers can gain direct access to a company's information system at any time and from virtually anywhere. They can tap into the system from a home office, customer location, airport, or the local Starbucks—anyplace they can connect on a laptop, tablet, or smartphone. Such systems allow managers to get the information they need directly and quickly and tailor it to their own needs.

LINKING THE CONCEPTS

Let's stop here, think back, and be certain that you've got the "big picture" concerning marketing information systems.

- What's the overall goal of a marketing information system? How are the individual components linked and what does each contribute? Take another look at Figure 4.1—It provides a good organizing framework for the entire chapter.
- Apply the MIS framework to Converse (a Nike company). How might Converse go about assessing marketing managers' information needs, developing the needed information, and helping managers to analyze and use the information to gain actionable customer and market insights?

Author Comment
We finish this chapter by examining three special marketing information topics.

Other Marketing Information Considerations

OBJECTIVE 4-5 **Discuss the special issues some marketing researchers face, including public policy and ethics issues.**

This section discusses marketing information in two special contexts: marketing research in small businesses and nonprofit organizations and international marketing research. Then we look at public policy and ethics issues in marketing research.

Marketing Research in Small Businesses and Nonprofit Organizations

Just like larger firms, small businesses and not-for-profit organizations need market information and the customer insights that it can provide. However, large-scale research studies are beyond the budgets of most small organizations. Still, many of the marketing research techniques discussed in this chapter can be used by smaller organizations in a less formal manner and at little or no expense.

Small businesses can obtain much useful market and customer insight without spending a lot of money. >> Consider GoldieBlox:[34]

> As an engineering student at Stanford, Debbie Sterling was bothered by how few women were entering the engineering profession. So she founded GoldieBlox, a media and toy company that makes and sells interactive books, apps, videos, and construction toys designed to encourage girls to love science, technology, engineering, and math (STEM). GoldieBlox's mission is to "disrupt the pink aisle and inspire future generations of female engineers."
>
> But before starting the company, in line with her sparse self-funded budget, Sterling began with informal, affordable marketing research. She spent a year digging into published research on how girls learn best. She studied the toy industry and talked with neuroscientists and preschool teachers. She observed children at play and haunted the "pink aisles" of toy stores looking for inspiration and ideas. Through her research, Sterling discovered several truths about how girls play and what they prefer in their toys. Her findings served as a basis for GoldieBlox's founding concepts, product designs, and marketing. Sterling's basic research paid off. To date, GoldieBlox has had more than 1 million app downloads and sold more than 1 million narrative-driven construction toys across more than 6,000 major retail outlets worldwide.

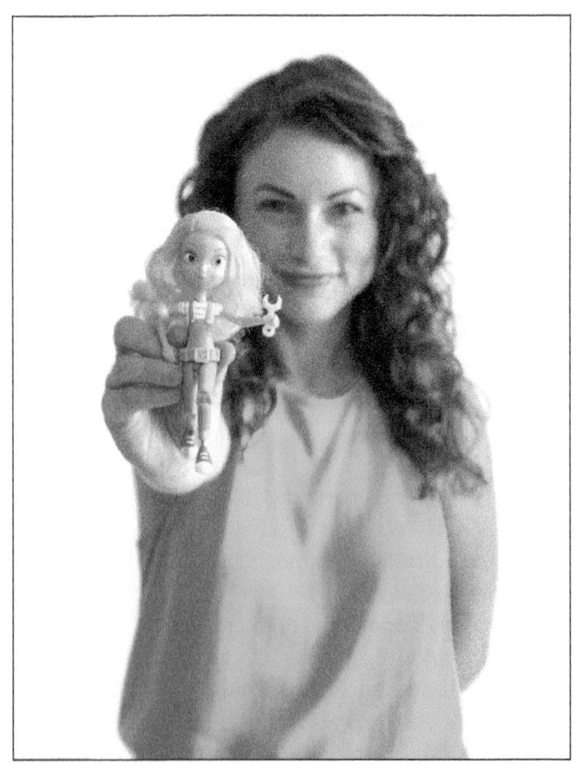

>> **Before starting GoldieBlox, in line with her sparse self-funded budget, founder and CEO Debbie Sterling began with informal, affordable marketing research.**
GoldieBlox, Inc.

Thus, small businesses and not-for-profit organizations can obtain good marketing insights through observation, secondary data searches, or informal surveys using small convenience samples. Also, many associations, local media, and government agencies provide special help to small organizations. For example, the U.S. Small Business Administration offers dozens of free publications and a website (www.sba.gov) that give advice on topics ranging from starting, financing, and expanding a small business to ordering business cards. Other excellent research resources for small businesses include the U.S. Census Bureau (www.census.gov) and the Bureau of Economic Analysis (www.bea.gov).

Finally, small businesses can collect a considerable amount of information at very little cost online. They can check out online product and service review sites, use internet search engines to research specific companies and issues, and scour competitor and customer web, mobile, and social media sites.

In summary, secondary data collection, observation, surveys, and experiments can all be used effectively by small organizations with small budgets. However, although these informal research methods are less complex and less costly, they still must be conducted with care. Managers must think carefully about the objectives of the research, formulate questions in advance, recognize the biases introduced by smaller samples and less skilled researchers, and conduct the research systematically.[35]

International Marketing Research

International researchers follow the same steps as domestic researchers, from defining the research problem and developing a research plan to interpreting and reporting the results. However, these researchers often face more and different problems. Whereas domestic researchers deal with fairly homogeneous markets within a single country, international researchers deal with diverse markets in many different countries. These markets often vary greatly in their levels of economic development, cultures and customs, and buying patterns.

In many foreign markets, the international researcher may have a tough time finding good secondary data. Whereas U.S. marketing researchers can obtain reliable secondary data from dozens of domestic research services, many countries have almost no research services at all. Some of the largest international research services operate in many countries. >> For example, the Nielsen Company (the world's largest marketing research company) has offices in more than 100 countries, from Schaumburg, Illinois, to Hong Kong to Nicosia, Cyprus.[36] However, most research firms operate in only a relative handful of countries. Thus, even when secondary information is available, it usually must be obtained from many varied sources on a country-by-country basis, making the information difficult to combine or compare.

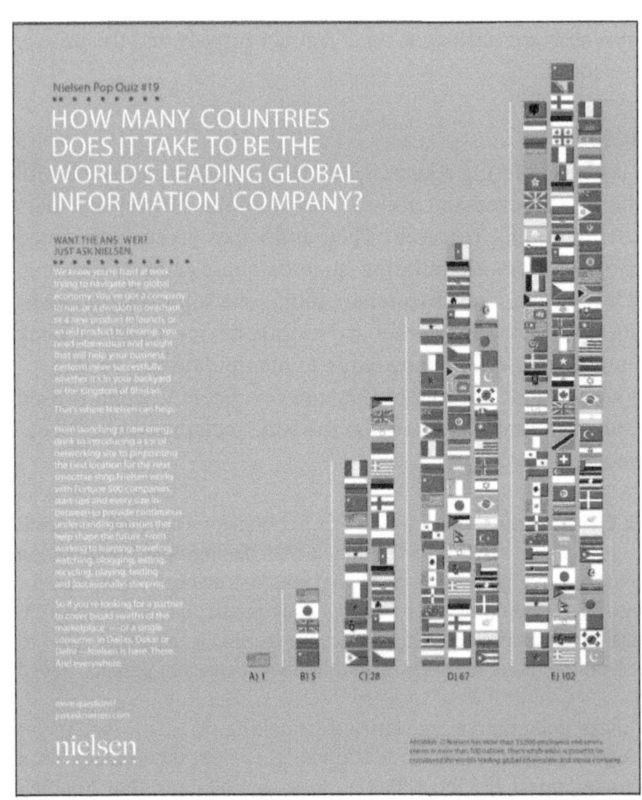

>> Some of the largest research services firms have large international organizations. Nielsen has offices in more than 100 countries.

Because of the scarcity of good secondary data, international researchers often must collect their own primary data. However, obtaining primary data may be no easy task. For example, it can be difficult simply to develop good samples. U.S. researchers can use current telephone directories, email lists, census tract data, and any of several sources of socioeconomic data to construct samples. However, such information is largely lacking in many countries.

Once the sample is drawn, the U.S. researcher usually can reach most respondents easily via any of multiple platforms—by phone, by mail, in person, or through online, social, or mobile media. However, reaching respondents by mail or phone is often not so easy in other parts of the world. As a result, digital surveys have now become the major means for conducting international research. However, the adoption of digital technologies varies greatly worldwide. For example, much digital research in the United States is designed to run on desktops or laptops. However, most consumers in emerging markets, such as India or Africa, leapfrogged those technologies and are accessing the internet for the first time largely from mobile devices. Survey research in such markets must be designed specifically for mobile, with all its inherent limitations.[37]

Cultural differences from country to country cause additional problems for international researchers. Language is the most obvious obstacle. For example, questionnaires must be prepared in one language and then translated into the languages of each country researched. Responses then must be translated back into the original language for analysis and interpretation. This adds to research costs and increases the risks of error. Even within a given country, language can be a problem. For example, in India, English is the language of business, but consumers may use any of 14 "first languages," with many additional dialects.

Translating a questionnaire from one language to another is anything but easy. Many idioms, phrases, and statements mean different things in different cultures. For example, a Danish executive noted, "Check this out by having a different translator put back into English what you've translated from English. You'll get the shock of your life. I remember [an example in which] 'out of sight, out of mind' had become 'invisible things are insane.'"[38]

Consumers in different countries also vary in their attitudes toward marketing research. People in one country may be very willing to respond; in other countries, nonresponse can be a major problem. Customs in some countries may prohibit people from talking with strangers. In certain cultures, research questions often are considered too personal. For example, in many Muslim countries, mixed-gender focus groups are taboo, as is videotaping female-only focus groups. In some countries, even when respondents are *willing* to respond, they may not be *able* to because of high functional illiteracy rates.

Despite these problems, as global marketing grows, global companies have little choice but to conduct these types of international marketing research. Although the costs and problems associated with international research may be high, the costs of not doing it—in terms of missed opportunities and mistakes—might be even higher. Once recognized, many of the problems associated with international marketing research can be overcome or avoided.[39]

Public Policy and Ethics in Marketing Research

Most marketing research benefits both the sponsoring company and its consumers. Through marketing research, companies gain insights into consumers' needs, resulting in more satisfying products and services and stronger customer relationships. However, the misuse of marketing research can also harm or annoy consumers. Two major public policy and ethics issues in marketing research are intrusions on consumer privacy and the misuse of research findings.

Intrusions on Consumer Privacy

Many consumers feel positive about marketing research and believe that it serves a useful purpose. Some actually enjoy being surveyed and giving their opinions. However, others strongly resent or even mistrust marketing research. They don't like being interrupted by researchers. They worry that marketers are building huge databases full of personal information about customers. Or they fear that researchers might use sophisticated techniques to probe our deepest feelings, track our internet and mobile device usage, or peek over our shoulders as we shop and then use this knowledge to manipulate our buying.

For example, Target made some of its customers very uneasy recently when it used their buying histories to figure out that they had a baby on the way, including eerily accurate estimates of child gender and due date:[40]

> Target gives every customer a Guest ID number, tied to his or her name, credit card, or email address. It then tracks the customer's purchases in detail, along with demographic information from other sources. By studying the buying histories of women who'd previously signed up for its baby registries, Target found that it could develop a "pregnancy prediction" score for each customer based on her purchasing patterns across 25 product categories. It used this score to start sending personalized books of coupons for baby-related items to expectant parents, keyed to their pregnancy stages.
>
> The strategy seemed to make good marketing sense—by hooking parents-to-be, Target could turn them into loyal buyers as their families developed. However, the strategy hit a snag when an angry man showed up at his local Target store, complaining that his high school–aged daughter was receiving Target coupons for cribs, strollers, and maternity clothes. "Are you trying to encourage her to get pregnant?" he demanded. The Target store manager apologized. But when he called to apologize again a few days later, he learned

>> **Consumer privacy: Target made some customers uneasy when it used their buying histories to figure out things about them that even their family and friends didn't know. The chain's bull's-eye logo may now "send a shiver . . . down the closely-watched spines of some Target shoppers."**

MiraMira/Mira/Alamy Stock Photo

that Target's marketers had, in fact, known about the young woman's pregnancy before her father did. It turns out that many other customers were creeped out that Target knew about their pregnancies before they'd told even family and close friends. And they wondered what else Target might be tracking and profiling. >> As one reporter concluded: "The store's bull's-eye logo may now send a shiver...down the closely-watched spines of some [Target shoppers]."

When mining customer information, marketers must be careful not to cross over the privacy line. But there are no easy answers when it comes to marketing research and privacy. For example, is it a good or bad thing that some retailers use mannequins with cameras hidden in one eye to record customer demographics and shopping behavior in order to serve them better? Should we applaud or resent companies that monitor consumer posts on Facebook, Twitter, Instagram, YouTube, or other social media in an effort to be more responsive? Should we worry when marketers track consumers' mobile phone usage to issue location-based information, ads, and offers? Consider this example:[41]

> SAP's Consumer Insight 365 service helps mobile service providers to "extract data about subscribers [and their] mobile-centric lifestyles." It ingests as many as 300 mobile web surfing, text messaging, phone call, and other mobile events per day for each of 20 to 25 million mobile subscribers across multiple carriers. The data tell marketers in detail where customers are coming from and where they go. According to one analyst, by combining the mobile data with other information, the service can tell businesses "whether shoppers are checking out competitor prices on their phones or just emailing friends. It can tell them the age ranges and genders of people who visited a store location between 10 a.m. and noon, and link location and demographic data with shoppers' web browsing histories. Retailers might use the information to arrange store displays to appeal to certain customer segments at different times of the day, or to help determine where to open new locations." Although such information can help marketers target customers with more useful offers, it might be "a little too close for comfort" from a consumer privacy viewpoint.

Increasing consumer privacy concerns have become a major problem for the marketing research industry. Companies face the challenge of unearthing valuable but potentially sensitive consumer data while also maintaining consumer trust. At the same time, consumers wrestle with the trade-offs between personalization and privacy. They want to receive relevant, personalized offers that meet their needs, but they worry or resent that companies may track them too closely. The key question: When does a company cross the line in gathering and using customer data?

Failure to address privacy issues could result in angry, less cooperative consumers and increased government intervention. As a result, the marketing research industry is considering several options for responding to intrusion and privacy issues. One example is the Marketing Research Association's "Your Opinion Counts" and "Respondent Bill of Rights" initiatives to educate consumers about the benefits of marketing research and distinguish it from telephone selling and database building.[42]

Most major companies—including Facebook, Apple, Microsoft, IBM, American Express, and even the U.S. government—have now appointed a chief privacy officer (CPO), whose job is to safeguard the privacy of customers. In the end, however, if researchers provide value in exchange for information, customers will gladly provide it. For example, Amazon's customers don't mind if the firm builds a database of previous purchases as a way to provide future product recommendations. This saves time and provides value. The best approach is for researchers to ask only for the information they need, use it responsibly to provide customer value, and avoid sharing information without the customer's permission.

Misuse of Research Findings

Research studies can be powerful persuasion tools; companies often use study results as claims in their advertising and promotion. Today, however, many research studies appear to be little more than vehicles for pitching the sponsor's products. In fact, in some cases, research surveys appear to have been designed just to produce the intended effect. For example, a Black Flag survey once asked: "A roach disk...poisons a roach slowly. The dying roach returns to the nest and after it dies is eaten by other roaches. In turn these roaches become poisoned and die. How effective do you think this type of product would be in killing roaches?" Not surprisingly, 79 percent said effective.

Few advertisers openly rig their research designs or blatantly misrepresent the findings—most abuses tend to be more subtle "stretches." Or disputes arise over the validity, interpretation, and use of research findings. Almost any research results can be variously interpreted depending on the researchers' bias and viewpoints.

Recognizing that marketing research can be abused, several associations—including the American Marketing Association, the Marketing Research Association, and the Council of American Survey Research Organizations (CASRO)—have developed codes of research ethics and standards of conduct. For example, the CASRO Code of Standards and Ethics for Survey Research outlines researcher responsibilities to respondents, including confidentiality, privacy, and avoidance of harassment. It also outlines major responsibilities in reporting results to clients and the public.[43]

In the end, however, unethical or inappropriate actions cannot simply be regulated away. Each company must accept responsibility for policing the conduct and reporting of its own marketing research to protect consumers' best interests as well as its own.

REVIEWING AND EXTENDING THE CONCEPTS

CHAPTER REVIEW AND KEY TERMS

Objectives Review

To create value for customers and build meaningful relationships with them, marketers must first gain fresh, deep insights into what customers need and want. Such insights come from good marketing information. Because of the recent explosion of "big data" and digital technologies, companies can now obtain great quantities of information, often even too much. Consumers themselves are now generating a tidal wave of bottom-up information through their smartphones, PCs, and tablets via online browsing, apps and social media interactions, texting and video, and geolocation data. The challenge is to transform today's vast volume of consumer information into actionable customer and market insights.

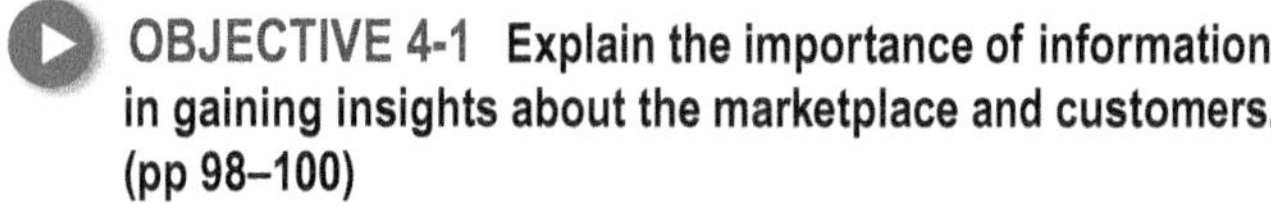

OBJECTIVE 4-1 Explain the importance of information in gaining insights about the marketplace and customers. (pp 98–100)

The marketing process starts with a complete understanding of the marketplace and consumer needs and wants. Thus, the company needs to turn sound consumer information into meaningful *customer insights* by which it can produce superior value for its customers. The company also requires information on competitors, resellers, and other actors and forces in the marketplace. Increasingly, marketers are viewing information not only as an input for making better decisions but also as an important strategic asset and marketing tool.

OBJECTIVE 4-2 Define the marketing information system and discuss its parts. (pp 100–103)

The *marketing information system (MIS)* consists of people and procedures for assessing information needs, developing the needed information, and helping decision makers use the information to generate and validate actionable customer and market insights. A well-designed information system begins and ends with users.

The MIS first *assesses information needs.* The MIS primarily serves the company's marketing and other managers, but it may also provide information to external partners. Then the MIS *develops information* from internal databases, marketing intelligence activities, and marketing research. *Internal databases* provide information on the company's own operations and departments. Such data can be obtained quickly and cheaply but often need to be adapted for marketing decisions. *Marketing intelligence* activities supply everyday information about developments in the external marketing environment, including listening and responding to the vast and complex digital environment. *Market research* consists of collecting information relevant to a specific marketing problem faced by the company. Last, the marketing information system helps users analyze and use the information to develop customer insights, make marketing decisions, and manage customer relationships.

OBJECTIVE 4-3 Outline the role of marketing research and the steps in the marketing research process. (pp 103–117)

In recent years, as a host of new digital data gathering technologies have burst onto the scene, traditional marketing research has undergone a major transformation. Traditional mainstays such as research surveys and focus groups, although still prevalent and powerful approaches, are now giving way to newer, more agile, more immediate, and less costly digital data gathering methods. Although its role is changing, however, traditional marketing research is still widely used and important.

The first step in the marketing research process involves *defining the problem and setting the research objectives*, which may be exploratory, descriptive, or causal research. The second step consists of *developing a research plan* for collecting data from primary and secondary sources. The third step calls for *implementing the marketing research plan* by gathering, processing, and analyzing the information. The fourth step consists of *interpreting and reporting the findings.* Additional information analysis helps marketing managers apply the information and provides them with sophisticated statistical procedures and models from which to develop more rigorous findings.

Both *internal* and *external* secondary data sources often provide information more quickly and at a lower cost than primary data sources, and they can sometimes yield information that a company cannot collect by itself. However, needed information might not exist in secondary sources. Researchers must also evaluate secondary information to ensure that it is *relevant, accurate, current*, and *impartial.*

Primary research must also be evaluated for these features. Each primary data collection method—*observational, survey*, and *experimental*—has its own advantages and disadvantages. Similarly, each of the various research contact methods—mail, telephone, personal interview, and online—has its own advantages and drawbacks.

OBJECTIVE 4-4 Explain how companies analyze and use marketing information. (pp 117–122)

Information gathered in internal databases and through marketing intelligence and marketing research usually requires more analysis. To analyze individual customer data, many companies have now acquired or developed special software and analysis techniques—called *customer relationship management (CRM)*—that integrate, analyze, and apply the mountains of individual customer data to gain a 360-degree view of customers and build stronger the customer relationships. They apply *marketing analytics* to dig out meaningful patterns in big data and gain customer insights and gauge marketing performance.

Marketing information has no value until it is used to make better marketing decisions. Thus, the MIS must make the information available to managers and others who make marketing decisions or deal with customers. In some cases, this means providing regular reports and updates; in other cases, it means making nonroutine information available for special situations and on-the-spot decisions. Many firms use company intranets and extranets to facilitate this process. Thanks to modern technology, today's marketing managers can gain direct access to marketing information at any time and from virtually any location.

OBJECTIVE 4-5 Discuss the special issues some marketing researchers face, including public policy and ethics issues. (pp 122–126)

Some marketers face special marketing research situations, such as those conducting research in small business, not-for-profit, or international situations. Marketing research can be conducted effectively by small businesses and nonprofit organizations with limited budgets. International marketing researchers follow the same steps as domestic researchers but often face more and different problems. All organizations need to act responsibly concerning major public policy and ethical issues surrounding marketing research, including issues of intrusions on consumer privacy and misuse of research findings.

Key Terms

Objective 4-1
Big data (p 99)
Customer insights (p 99)
Marketing information system (MIS) (p 100)

Objective 4-2
Internal databases (p 101)
Competitive marketing intelligence (p 101)

Objective 4-3
Marketing research (p 103)
Exploratory research (p 105)
Descriptive research (p 105)
Causal research (p 105)
Secondary data (p 106)
Primary data (p 106)
Observational research (p 107)
Ethnographic research (p 107)
Survey research (p 108)
Experimental research (p 108)
Focus group interviewing (p 109)
Online marketing research (p 110)
Online focus groups (p 111)
Behavioral targeting (p 112)
Sample (p 114)

Objective 4-4
Customer relationship management (CRM) (p 117)
Marketing analytics (p 118)
Artificial intelligence (AI) (p 119)

DISCUSSION AND CRITICAL THINKING

Discussion Questions

4-1. Why is it important for companies to understand and use customer insights in managing marketing information? (AACSB: Written and Oral Communication; Reflective Thinking)

4-2. Explain how marketing intelligence differs from marketing research. Which is more valuable to a company? Why? (AACSB: Written and Oral Communication; Reflective Thinking)

4-3. Marketers make heavy use of both primary and secondary data. What is primary data? What is secondary data? What are possible benefits or drawbacks of using each of these data types? (AACSB: Written and Oral Communication, Reflective Thinking)

4-4. Discuss the advantages of conducting online marketing research. (AACSB: Written and Oral Communication)

4-5. What is customer relationship management (CRM), and how is it related to big data, marketing analytics, and artificial intelligence? Provide an example of a company using artificial intelligence. (AACSB: Written and Oral Communication, Reflective Thinking)

Critical Thinking Exercises

4-6. Imagine you own a pet grooming business. You want to use market research to identify how you can grow your business, but you are on a limited budget. Review the marketing research techniques outlined in the chapter to determine which ones can be used for your small business. What information will you need, and how will you obtain it? (AACSB: Written and Oral Communication; Reflective Thinking)

4-7. Suppose you are conducting market research for your favorite soda brand. Sales have been lagging for two quarters, and you are determined to find out why. You decide to host an in-person focus group to gain customer insights into your brand's current product offerings. You also want to obtain feedback on a new product that your brand plans to launch in the next six months. Determine the makeup of your focus group. Who should be invited to the focus group and why? What types of information would you want to obtain? Identify possible questions to present to the focus group. (AACSB: Written and Oral Communication; Reflective Thinking)

4-8. Market research is critical for companies that want to grow their markets. Companies can hire outside market research firms or create their own internal market research positions or teams. There are many career opportunities in this field. Go to Indeed.com or another nationwide or worldwide job site. Determine what jobs are available in the market research industry. Create a table comparing jobs, areas/regions, and salaries. Include a job description and title for at least three different jobs. Compare average salaries in small, medium-sized, and large cities. (AACSB: Written and Oral Communication; Information Technology; Reflective Thinking)

MINICASES AND APPLICATIONS

Online, Mobile, and Social Media Marketing The Trail You Leave Behind

Marketers want to collect as much valuable data as possible regarding customer Likes, preferences, and trends. Web activity and social media platforms such as Twitter, Facebook, Instagram, and various blog sites are gold mines for marketers. All these access points create information that can be aggregated and used to a company's competitive advantage, allowing firms to stay in tune with what is currently trending in the marketplace. Businesses can also use these access points to track competitor activity, which can then be used in competitive marketing intelligence.

4-9. Marketers are always looking for digital footprints—traceable sources of online activities. Have you thought about what data you leave behind online for marketers to collect? Visit www.internetsociety.org/your-digital-footprint-matters, and review the various resources available. Select one of the tutorials, and present what you learned from the video. (AACSB: Written and Oral Communication; Information Technology; Reflective Thinking)

4-10. After reviewing the tutorials at www.internetsociety.org/your-digital-footprint-matters, do you plan to alter your online habits? Are you concerned about your digital footprint and the data trail you leave behind, and do you plan to actively manage them? Why or why not? (AACSB: Written and Oral Communication; Information Technology; Reflective Thinking)

Marketing Ethics Facebook's Cambridge Analytica Data Scandal

In early 2018, Facebook faced a firestorm of criticism when it was learned that a political data firm hired by Donald Trump's election campaign—Cambridge Analytica—had gained access to private data on as many as 87 million Facebook users. The Facebook profiles contained information on user identities, friend networks, Likes, and other data that could be used to target American voters and influence their behavior. The data breach raised important questions about how the social media giant protects the huge amounts of user information it amasses and employs for its own market targeting activities. Facebook founder and CEO Mark Zuckerberg admitted that Facebook had made a "huge mistake" in not adequately protecting user data from exploitation. Said Zuckerberg, "The reality of a lot of this is, when you're building something like Facebook that is unprecedented in the world, there are going to be things that you mess up" (see http://fortune.com/2018/04/04/facebook-mark-zuckerberg-data-cambridge-analytica/)

4-11. Is it wrong for Facebook and other companies to use customer profile information to market products and services? Does it help customers or harm them? Explain your thinking. Discuss other examples of companies targeting consumers by using consumer data collected online. (AACSB: Written and Oral Communication; Ethical Understanding and Reasoning)

4-12. In today's digital environment, what steps should Facebook take to update its data usage practices to better protect users? What types of protections do you value most as a consumer? (AACSB: Written and Oral Communication; Ethical Understanding and Reasoning)

Marketing by the Numbers The Value of Information

Conducting research is costly, and the costs must be weighed against the value of the information gathered. Consider a company faced with a competitor's price reduction. Should the company also reduce price in order to keep market share or should the company maintain its current price? The company has conducted preliminary research showing the financial outcomes of each decision under two competitor responses: the competition maintains its price or the competition lowers its price further. The company is not very confident that the competitor cannot lower its price even further and assigns that outcome a probability (p) of 0.6, which means the other outcome that the competitor would maintain its price would have a 40 percent chance of occurring $1 - p = 0.4$. These outcomes are shown in the table below:

	Competitive Response	
Company Action	**Reduce Price Further** $p = 0.6$	**Maintain Price** $1 - p = 0.4$
Reduce Price	$150,000	$180,000
Maintain Price	$100,000	$200,000

For example, if the company reduces its price and the competitor reduces its price again, the company would realize $150,000, and so on. From this information, the expected monetary value (EMV) of each company action (reduce price or maintain price) can be determined using the following equation:

$$EMV = (p)(\text{financial outcome}_p) + (1 - p)(\text{financial outcome}_{(1-p)})$$

The company would select the action expected to deliver the greatest EMV. More information might be desirable, but is it worth the cost of acquiring it? One way to assess the value of additional information is to calculate the expected value of perfect information (EMV_{PI}) using the following equation:

$$EMV_{PI} = EMV_{certainty} - EMV_{best\ alternative}$$

where

$$EMV_{certainty} = (p)(\text{highest financial outcome}_p) + (1 - p)(\text{highest financial outcome}_{(1-p)})$$

If the value of perfect information is more than the cost of conducting the research, then the research should be undertaken (that is, $EMV_{PI} >$ cost of research). However, if the value of the additional information is less than the cost of obtaining more information, the research should not be conducted.

4-13. Calculate the expected monetary value (EMV) of both company actions. Which action should the company take? (AACSB: Written and Oral Communication; Analytical Thinking)

4-14. What is the expected value of perfect information (EMV_{PI})? Management suggests conducting more research costing $5,000. Should the research be conducted? (AACSB: Written and Oral Communication; Analytical Thinking)

Video Case Nielsen

To view this video case and its accompanying questions, please visit MyLab Marketing.

Most people know Nielsen as the TV ratings company. In reality, however, Nielsen is a multiplatform market research company that has constantly been evolving since 1923. Its goal is to measure and track a wide range of consumer activity in order to establish a 360-degree view of individuals and market segments. To accomplish this, Nielsen has to follow consumers wherever they may be—watching TV, online, in their homes, or in stores.

How does Nielsen track all this activity? The veteran research firm has established effective methods of recording consumer activity, from retail scanner data to household panels to monitoring social networks. As data are captured, they are transferred to a Nielsen data warehouse, where they are matched to the right individual and added to the terabytes of information Nielsen already possesses. Through data sorting and analytics, Nielsen cuts through billions of daily transactions to deliver clear consumer insights to clients.

Company Cases 4 Qualtrics/7 MINI/12 LinkedIn

See Appendix 1 for cases appropriate for this chapter.

Case 4, Qualtrics: Managing the Complete Customer Experience. Qualtrics pioneered the online survey. Now, it employs online surveys toward managing customer experience.

Case 7, MINI: Focus on the Essential—Maximize the Experience. BMW has a hit on its hands with MINI, achieving success by remaining true to the original brand while responding to current consumer needs.

Case 12, LinkedIn: Crushing the White-Collar Stereotype with IMC. With its first mass-media IMC campaign, LinkedIn is out to change widely held perceptions that its services are white collar only.

Writing Assignments

4-15. What is neuromarketing and how is it useful in marketing research? Why is this research approach usually combined with other approaches? (AACSB: Communication)

4-16. Describe an example in which marketing research could cause harm to participants. Many companies have a review process similar to that required for following the government's "Common Rule." Write a brief report explaining this rule and how you would apply it to your example. (AACSB: Written and Oral Communication; Reflective Thinking)

5 Understanding Consumer and Business Buyer Behavior

Objectives Outline

- OBJECTIVE 5-1 **Understand the consumer market and the major factors that influence consumer buyer behavior.** See: Consumer Markets and Consumer Buyer Behavior (pp 134–148)
- OBJECTIVE 5-2 **Identify and discuss the stages in the buyer decision process.** See: The Buyer Decision Process (pp 148–151)
- OBJECTIVE 5-3 **Describe the adoption and diffusion process for new products.** See: The Buyer Decision Process for New Products (pp 151–153)
- OBJECTIVE 5-4 **Define the business market and identify the major factors that influence business buyer behavior.** See: Business Markets and Business Buyer Behavior (pp 153–159)
- OBJECTIVE 5-5 **List and define the steps in the business buying decision process.** See: The Business Buyer Decision Process (pp 159–161)
- OBJECTIVE 5-6 **Discuss how online, mobile, and social media have changed business-to-business marketing.** See: Engaging Business Buyers with Digital and Social Marketing (pp 161–165)

Previewing the Concepts

You've studied how marketers obtain, analyze, and use information to develop customer insights and assess marketing programs. In this chapter, we take a closer look at the most important element of the marketplace—customers. The aim of marketing is to engage customers and affect how they think and act. To affect the *whats, whens*, and *hows* of buyer behavior, marketers must first understand the *whys*. We first look at *final consumer* buying influences and processes and then at the buyer behavior of *business customers*. You'll see that understanding buyer behavior is an essential but very difficult task.

To get a better sense of the importance of understanding consumer behavior, we begin with Shinola, the Detroit-based premium goods maker. Shinola's name and its Detroit roots seem incongruous with the premium-priced luxury goods it makes and sells. But dig deeper and you find that everything about Shinola binds together strongly under a carefully crafted, all-American brand image that aligns well with the deeply held emotions and motivations that underlie its customers' buying behavior.

First Stop

Shinola: Nobody's Confusing Sh*t with Shinola Anymore

Not long ago, a comedy sketch on Jimmy Kimmel Live featured a mock TV game show that presented each of two contestants with a pair of luxury products and asked, "Which of these products is sh*t, and which is Shinola?" It wasn't much of a challenge. One product in each pair really did look like it was made from poop, whereas the other items were genuine products from the hot new American luxury brand, Shinola. The contestants ended up taking home "all this beautiful sh*t from Shinola." The idea for the gag came from the very company that was the butt of the joke, Detroit-based luxury goods maker Shinola.

Shinola opened for business less than a decade ago with a line of premium watches priced between $550 and $850. Its unlikely name derives from the old Shinola shoe polish brand that became a household word following a widely circulated story during World War II that a soldier had polished his commander's boots with poop because "he doesn't know sh*t from Shinola."

The strong emotions, values, and motivations that underlie the buying behavior of Shinola customers are captured in the brand's recent "Let's Roll Up Our Sleeves" advertising campaign.

Andrew Harrer/Bloomberg via Getty Images

The original Shinola company closed its doors in 1960, but the founders of the current company purchased the rights to the unique Shinola name, replete with its mildly crude but colorful associations. In another seemingly surprising move, Shinola chose to headquarter itself in Detroit, the once-iconic symbol of gritty American manufacturing and ingenuity that had since fallen into bankruptcy and desperately hard times. Together with the company logo, every Shinola product bears the simple phrase "Built in Detroit."

Since its founding, Shinola has expanded rapidly into other product categories including high-end bicycles, apparel, leather accessories, and audio equipment. Its sales are booming, up from $20 million in 2013 to $125 million last year. You'll find Shinola's products in nearly 1,000 stores worldwide, including high-end department stores such as Nordstrom, Neiman Marcus, Saks Fifth Avenue, and Bloomingdale's. The company has opened 27 stores of its own and faces exploding online demand for its products. And, it seems, Shinola is just getting started.

Such success might seem surprising. At first blush, Shinola's name and its Detroit roots seem incongruous with the premium-priced luxury goods it makes and sells. But dig deeper and you find that everything about Shinola binds together strongly under a carefully crafted, all-American brand image. In an age of products "made in China," Shinola is on a mission to revive old-time American values.

Why the Shinola name and why the Detroit location? "We're starting with the reinvigoration of a storied American brand, and a storied American city," says the company. Shinola "is a brand committed to turning out high-quality products in America with. . . American suppliers and American labor," says one analyst. "To drive home that commitment, the company selected Detroit—the buckle of the American rust belt—as its base." By linking the brand with Detroit's legacy of hardworking people, resilience, and craftsmanship, Shinola is selling more than watches and bicycles—it's selling a made-in-America comeback story.

The roots of American ingenuity and manufacturing are evident in every facet of Shinola's products and branding, from its Wright Brothers Limited Edition Runwell bike ($2,950) to its Bluetooth player with Gramophone speaker ($400 with a waiting list of buyers) to its limited-edition Great American Series Mohammad Ali watch, a tribute to the six principles that shaped the life of the famed fighter: conviction, respect, dedication, confidence, giving, and spirituality. Despite their premium prices, Shinola's new and limited-edition products often sell out.

Shinola products are at once both classic and modern, with clean, functional, and authentically American designs, craftsmanship, and quality. Backed by a lifetime guarantee, they are meant to be handed down from generation to generation rather than to end up in a landfill after a few years of use. Many owners think of their Shinola products as works of art worthy of display.

> **Shinola is selling much more than just watches or bikes or leather accessories. It's selling gritty Detroit, authentically American values, emotions, and a roll-up-our-sleeves lifestyle, things that lie at the heart consumers' feelings and behavior toward the brand.**

More than just its products, Shinola's manufacturing and supplier operations also support its authentically American image. In another throwback to a bygone era, Shinola is committed to its employees. It prides itself on creating American jobs. Shinola began operations with about 100 local manufacturing employees and brought in the world's best Swiss watchmakers to train them how to build watches the old-fashioned way—by hand.

Shinola pays its people above-market wages and provides amazing benefits. All its 600 employees spend time in the company's retail stores to gain a clear understanding of what motivates the customers for whom they are making products. Shinola has a promote-from-within policy. Today, many of Shinola's operations managers are people who started with the company as security guards, janitors, and delivery people. "We build our goods to last," says Shinola, "but of all the things we make, American jobs might just be the thing we're most proud of."

As the company has expanded into other lines, it has remained committed to working with mostly U.S.-based suppliers. Leather goods come from the Horween tannery in Chicago, bike frames and forks are hand-built by Wisconsin-based Waterford, and parts for turntables are sourced from New Jersey's VPI Industries. We are "creating a community that will thrive through excellence of craft and pride of work," says the company, "where we will reclaim the making of things that are made well and define American luxury through American quality."

Consistent with the vibe of its products, Shinola's retail stores are the ultimate embodiment of its brand image. Store interiors have an industrial feel—weathered brick, varnished wood, glass, stainless steel, and exposed iron trusswork. Visitors are encouraged to look, touch, listen, and drool. But more than just place to buy stuff, the stores are warm and inviting activity centers, with permanent coffee bars and period events like whisky tastings or barbershops, where customers are encouraged to hang out.

The strong emotions and motivations that underlie the buying behavior of Shinola customers are perhaps best captured in the brand's recent "Let's Roll Up Our Sleeves" advertising campaign. The campaign "delivers an inspiring rallying cry to. . . come together and work hard for the greater good," says an advertising analyst. It "upholds the values of labor, sweat, and dedication with impassioned lines including 'Working together. The job big enough for all of us'; 'Plant it, grow it, build it, weld it'; and 'Whatever color your collar might be.'" Many ads in the campaign show only the words themselves in black and white, without glossy product shots or other embellishments. Other ads feature people who have given back to their communities through their own hard work.

Thus, Shinola is selling much more than just watches or bikes or leather accessories. It's selling gritty Detroit, authentically American values, emotions, and a roll-up-our-sleeves lifestyle, things that lie at the heart of consumers' feelings and behavior toward the brand. "There's really nothing else like Shinola," says one marketing professor. "It's a brilliant thing they did, this association with Detroit, a very authentic look, and this authentic story." Shinola's marketing director agrees. "Consumers want something real, something authentic. You want to feel proud about something. We have good timing, a good product, and a good story." In short, nobody's confusing sh*t with Shinola anymore.[1]

The Shinola example shows that factors at many levels affect consumer buying behavior. Buying behavior is never simple, yet understanding it is an essential task of marketing management. First we explore the dynamics of the consumer market and the consumer buyer behavior. We then examine business markets and the business buyer process.

Author Comment
In some ways, consumer and business markets are similar in their buyer behavior. But in many other ways, they differ a lot. We start by digging into consumer buyer behavior. Later in the chapter, we'll tackle business buyer behavior

Consumer Markets and Consumer Buyer Behavior

OBJECTIVE 5-1 Understand the consumer market and the major factors that influence consumer buyer behavior.

Consumer buyer behavior
The buying behavior of final consumers—individuals and households that buy goods and services for personal consumption.

Consumer market
All the individuals and households that buy or acquire goods and services for personal consumption.

Consumer buyer behavior refers to the buying behavior of final consumers—individuals and households that buy goods and services for personal consumption. All of these final consumers combine to make up the **consumer market**. The American consumer market consists of more than 327 million people who consume more than $12 trillion worth of goods and services each year, making it one of the most attractive consumer markets in the world.[2]

Consumers around the world vary tremendously in age, income, education level, and tastes. They also buy an incredible variety of goods and services. How these diverse consumers relate with each other and with other elements of the world around them affects their choices among various products, services, and companies. Here we examine the fascinating array of factors that affect consumer behavior.

Model of Consumer Behavior

Author Comment
Despite the simple-looking model in Figure 5.1, understanding the whys of buying behavior is very difficult. Says one expert, "The mind is a whirling, swirling, jumbled mass of neurons bouncing around...."

Consumers make many buying decisions every day, and the buying decision is the focal point of the marketer's effort. Most large companies research consumer buying decisions in great detail to answer questions about what consumers buy, where they buy, how and how much they buy, when they buy, and why they buy. Marketers can study actual consumer purchases to find out what they buy, where, and how much. But learning about the

>> Figure 5.1 The Model of Buyer Behavior

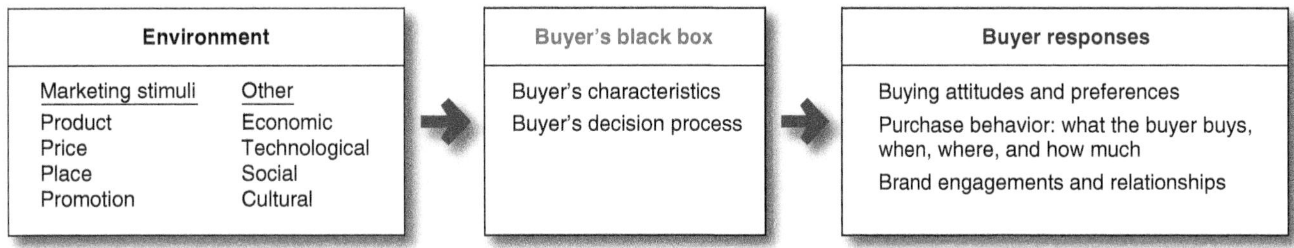

We can measure the whats, wheres, and whens of consumer buying behavior. But it's very diffcult to "see" inside the consumer's head and figure out the whys of buying behavior (that's why it's called the black box). Marketers spend a lot of energy and dollars trying to figure out what makes customers tick.

whys behind consumer buying behavior is not so easy—the answers are often locked deep within the consumer's mind. Often, consumers themselves don't know exactly what influences their purchases.

The central question for marketers is this: How do consumers respond to various marketing efforts the company might use? The starting point is the stimulus-response model of buyer behavior shown in **>> Figure 5.1**. This figure shows that marketing and other stimuli enter the consumer's "black box" and produce certain responses.

Marketers want to understand how the stimuli are changed into responses inside the consumer's black box, which has two parts. First, the buyer's characteristics influence how he or she perceives and reacts to the stimuli. These characteristics include a variety of cultural, social, personal, and psychological factors. Second, the buyer's decision process itself affects his or her behavior. This decision process—from need recognition, information search, and alternative evaluation to the purchase decision and postpurchase behavior—begins long before the actual purchase decision and continues long after. We look first at buyer characteristics as they affect buyer behavior and then discuss the buyer decision process.

Author Comment
Many levels of factors affect our buying behavior—from broad cultural and social influences to motivations, beliefs, and attitudes lying deep within us.

Characteristics Affecting Consumer Behavior

Consumer purchases are influenced strongly by cultural, social, personal, and psychological characteristics, as shown in **>> Figure 5.2**. For the most part, marketers cannot control such factors, but they must take them into account.

Cultural Factors

Cultural factors exert a broad and deep influence on consumer behavior. Marketers need to understand the role played by the buyer's *culture, subculture*, and *social class*.

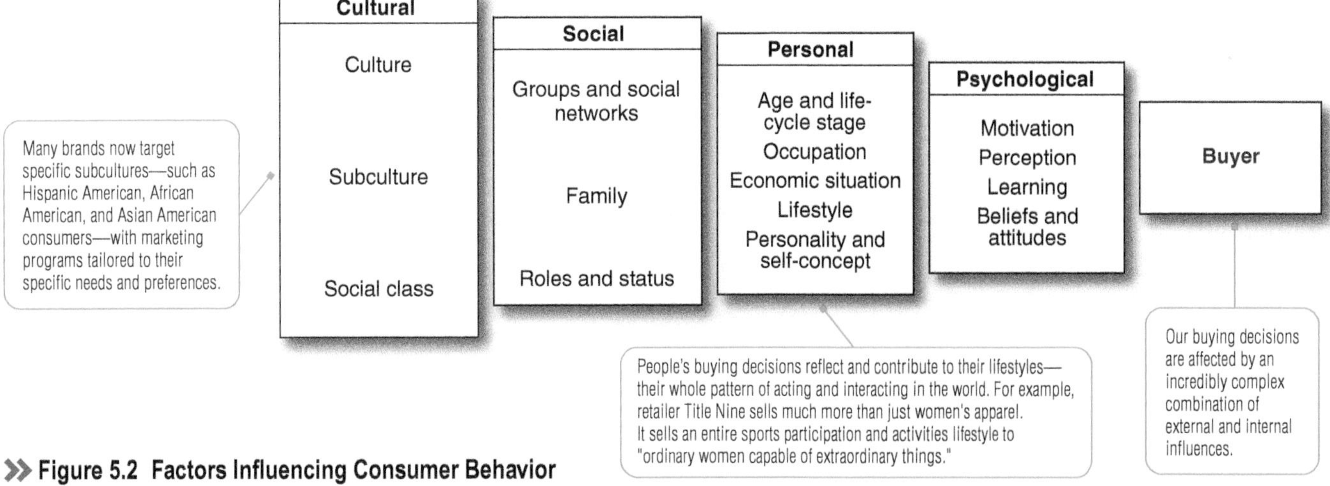

>> Figure 5.2 Factors Influencing Consumer Behavior

Culture
The set of basic values, perceptions, wants, and behaviors learned by a member of society from family and other important institutions.

Culture. **Culture** is the most basic cause of a person's wants and behavior. Human behavior is largely learned. Growing up in a society, a child learns basic values, perceptions, wants, and behaviors from his or her family and other important institutions. A child in the United States normally is exposed to the following values: achievement and success, freedom, individualism, hard work, activity and involvement, efficiency and practicality, material comfort, youthfulness, and fitness and health. Every group or society has a culture, and cultural influences on buying behavior may vary greatly from both county to county and country to country.

Marketers are always trying to spot *cultural shifts* to discover new products that might be wanted. For example, the cultural shift toward greater concern about health and fitness has created a huge industry for health-and-fitness services, exercise equipment and clothing, organic foods, and a variety of diets.

Subculture
A group of people with shared value systems based on common life experiences and situations.

Subculture. Each culture contains smaller **subcultures**, or groups of people with shared value systems based on common life experiences and situations. Subcultures include nationalities, religions, racial groups, and geographic regions. Many subcultures make up important market segments, and marketers often design products and marketing programs tailored to their needs. Examples of three such important subculture groups are Hispanic American, African American, and Asian American consumers.

Hispanics represent a large, fast-growing market. The nation's more than 59 million Hispanic consumers have total annual buying power of $1.7 trillion. The U.S. Hispanic population will surge in coming decades, growing to represent nearly 29 percent of the total U.S. population by 2060. Hispanics are a youthful segment, with a median age of just 29 years old.[3] Within the Hispanic market, there exist many distinct subsegments based on nationality, age, income, and other factors. A company's product or message may be more relevant to one nationality over another, such as Mexicans, Costa Ricans, Argentineans, or Cubans.

Although Hispanic consumers share many characteristics and behaviors with the mainstream buying public, there are also distinct differences. They tend to be deeply family oriented and make shopping a family affair—children have a big say in what brands they buy. And befitting their youthfulness, Hispanics are more active on mobile and social networks than other segments, making digital media ideal for reaching this segment.

Companies ranging from P&G, McDonald's, AT&T, Walmart, and State Farm to Google, Amazon, and L'Oréal have developed special targeting efforts for this fast-growing consumer segment. For example, working with its longtime Hispanic advertising agency Conill, Toyota has developed numerous Hispanic marketing campaigns that have helped make it the favorite automobile brand among Hispanic buyers. Consider its award-winning "Más Que un Auto" campaign:[4]

To celebrate its 10th year as America's most-loved auto brand among Hispanics, Toyota ran a Hispanic campaign themed "Más Que un Auto" (translation: "More Than a Car"). The campaign appealed to Hispanics' special love for their cars and their penchant for giving everything and anything a superpersonal nickname, including their cars. >> The campaign offered Hispanic customers free nameplates featuring their unique car names, made with the same typeface and materials as the official Toyota nameplates. Now, along with the Toyota and model names, they could adorn their cars with personalized, official-looking brand badges of their own—whether Pepe, El Niño, Trueno ("Thunder"), Monster, or just plain Oliver, Ellie, or Rolly the Corolla.

>> Targeting Hispanic consumers: Toyota's award-winning "Más Que un Auto" campaign created a strong emotional connection between Hispanics and their Toyotas with free, official-looking, personalized nameplates for their much-loved cars—here, Pepe.

Toyota Motor Sales, U.S.A. Inc.

The award-winning "Más Que un Auto" campaign created a strong emotional connection between Hispanics and their Toyotas. Since the start of the campaign, customers have ordered more than 150,000 customer nameplates, far exceeding the goal of 25,000. Brand fans by the thousands posted pictures and shared their car love stories on campaign sites and other social media. Toyota is now shaping new phases of the "Más Que un Auto" campaign, such as turning some of the fan car stories into ads or asking customers to imagine what a commercial featuring their beloved ride might look like and then picking the best idea to produce for a real broadcast ad.

The U.S. *African American* population is growing in affluence and sophistication. The nation's nearly 47 million black consumers wield $1.5 trillion in annual buying power. Blacks are strongly motivated by quality and selection. Brands are important. African American consumers are heavy users of digital and social media, providing access through a rich variety of marketing channels.[5]

Many companies develop special products, appeals, and marketing programs for African American consumers—from carmakers like Ford, Toyota, and Hyundai to consumer products companies like P&G to even not-for-profits and government agencies such as the U.S. Forest Service. >> For example, the U.S. Forest Service and the Ad Council joined forces to create the "Discover the Forest" public service campaign to raise awareness among urban families of the benefits for children of getting outside and enjoying nature. A recent round of the campaign specifically targeted African American families:[6]

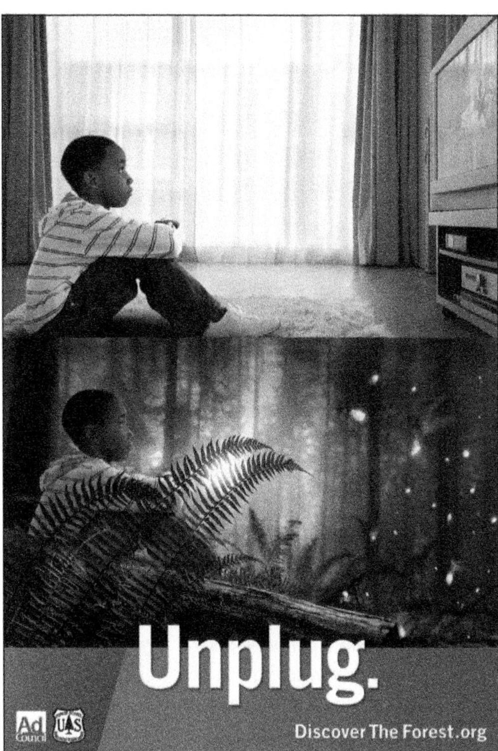

>> Targeting African American consumers: The U.S. Forest Service and the Ad Council joined forces to create the "Discover the Forest" public service campaign to raise awareness among African American families of the benefits for children of getting outside and enjoying nature.

The Forest Service, an agency of the U.S. Department of Agriculture, and the Ad Council

> More than 245 million Americans live within 100 miles of a national forest or grassland. However, research shows that only 37 percent of African American children ages 6 to 12 participate frequently in outdoor activities, compared with 67 percent of the broader U.S. population in that age group. To help close that gap, the U.S. Forest Service and the Ad Council created a series of "Discover the Forest" public service messages. With headlines such as "Unplug," "Where Curiosity Blooms," and "Connected," ads targeting African American families promote the health and well-being benefits of connecting with the great outdoors. The recent "Connected" campaign features a clever play on familiar social media terms such as "streaming," "connected," "tweet," and others to highlight the natural adventures awaiting families who disconnect from technology for a while.

Asian Americans are the most affluent U.S. demographic segment. A relatively well-educated segment, they now number more than 20 million, with annual buying power of $1 trillion. Asian Americans are the nation's fastest-growing subsegment. And like the other subsegments, they are a diverse group. Chinese Americans constitute the largest group, followed by Filipinos, Asian Indians, Vietnamese, Korean Americans, and Japanese Americans. Yet, unlike Hispanics who all speak various dialects of Spanish, Asians speak many different languages. For example, ads for the 2010 U.S. Census ran in languages ranging from Japanese, Cantonese, Khmer, Korean, and Vietnamese to Thai, Cambodian, Hmong, Hinglish, and Taglish.[7]

As a group, Asian American consumers shop frequently and are the most brand conscious of all the ethnic groups. They can be fiercely brand loyal, especially to brands that work to build relationships with them. As a result, many firms now target the Asian American market. For example, many retailers, especially luxury retailers such as Bloomingdale's, now feature themed events and promotions during the Chinese New Year, a spending season equivalent to the Christmas holidays for Chinese American consumers. They hire Mandarin-speaking staff, offer Chinese-themed fashions and other merchandise, and feature Asian cultural presentations. Bloomingdale's has even introduced seasonal, limited edition pop-up shops in many stores around the country:[8]

> Richly designed in red, gold, and black motifs, Chinese colors of good fortune, the Bloomingdale's pop-up boutiques feature high-end Chinese-themed fashions and other merchandise created especially for the Chinese New Year celebration. Some locations sponsor entertainment such as lion dancers, Chinese tarot card readings, calligraphy, lantern making, tea tastings, and free Zodiac nail art. Shoppers in some stores are invited to select Chinese red envelopes with prizes such as gift cards in denominations of $8, $88, or $888 (eight is a lucky number in Chinese culture). In addition to the pop-up boutiques, Bloomingdale's celebrates the days and weeks leading up to the Chinese New Year with Chinese-language ads and promotions in carefully targeted traditional and online media. The retailer also has 175 Chinese-speaking associates across the country. "Chinese customers, including both tourists as well as Chinese Americans, are an important part of the overall Bloomingdale's business," says the retailer's CEO.

Total market strategy
Integrating ethnic themes and cross-cultural perspectives within a brand's mainstream marketing, appealing to consumer similarities across subcultural segments rather than differences.

Total Marketing Strategy. Beyond targeting segments such as Hispanics, African Americans, and Asian Americans with specially tailored efforts, many marketers now embrace a **total market strategy**—the practice of integrating ethnic themes and cross-cultural perspectives within their mainstream marketing. An example is general-market commercials for brands such as Cheerios and IKEA that feature interracial and blended families and couples. A total market approach appeals to consumer similarities across subcultural segments rather than differences.[9]

Toyota uses a total market strategy that includes both ads targeting specific subcultural segments and cross-cultural ads aimed at the general market:[10]

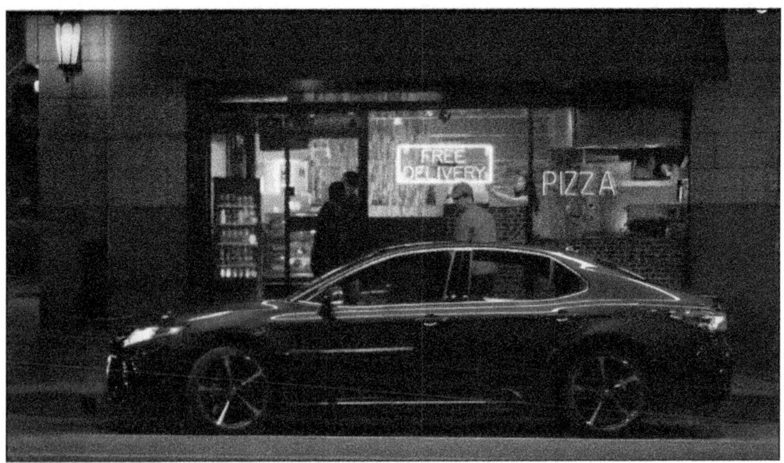

>> **Total marketing strategy: Toyota's recent Camry "Sensations" campaign includes both ads targeting specific subcultural segments and cross-cultural ads aimed at the general market. Here the "Strut" commercial targets African Americans with "cool slice of style" appeals.**

Toyota Motor Sales, U.S.A., Inc.

A portion of the recent Toyota Camry "Sensations" marketing campaign features ads targeting Hispanic, African American, and Asian American subsegments, prepared by specialized, ethnic-focused ad agencies. For example, a commercial titled "Captivating" captures the bond between a Chinese American father and daughter as they share the thrilling technology features of their new Camry, emphasizing the importance of family and technology to Asian American consumers. Another ad titled "Rebellious"—aired in both English and Spanish—shows a young Hispanic man in a red Camry hesitating before declining a call on his phone from his mother. It's an edgy move based on Hispanic generational insights. >> Still another ad, "Strut," features an African American man transforming a routine run to pick up pizza into "a cool slice of style." "We found that with African-Americans style really comes to the forefront in how we look at cars," says an executive at the agency that created the ad.

At the same time, the "Sensations" campaign also features overarching mainstream ads prepared by Toyota's general-market ad agency. These ads appeal to what Toyota's national manager of brand, multicultural, and crossline marketing strategy calls "the total transcultural market." They employ a diverse mix of actors and environments under a single, overall theme that focuses on shared, cross-cultural consumer values rather than cultural differences.

So, Toyota appears to cover all its bases under a comprehensive total marketing strategy. In the mainstream ads, "people like to see people of all ethnicities in what they're seeing because that's the life they're living in most of the U.S. today," says a Toyota brand executive. At the same time, in the ethnic-focused ads, "if a person of any group is looking for communication that is like them, that looks like them specifically, the good news is because of the breadth of something like a Camry campaign, they can find it."

Social class
Relatively permanent and ordered divisions in a society whose members share similar values, interests, and behaviors.

Social Class. Almost every society has some form of social class structure. **Social classes** are society's relatively permanent and ordered divisions whose members share similar values, interests, and behaviors. Social scientists have identified seven American social classes: upper-upper class, lower-upper class, upper-middle class, middle class, working class, upper-lower class, and lower-lower class.

Social class is not determined by a single factor, such as income, but is measured as a combination of occupation, income, education, wealth, and other variables. In some social systems, members of different classes are reared for certain roles and cannot change their social positions. In the United States, however, the lines between social classes are not fixed and rigid; people can move to a higher social class or drop into a lower one.

Marketers are interested in social class because people within a given social class tend to exhibit similar buying behavior. Social classes show distinct product and brand preferences in areas such as clothing, home furnishings, travel and leisure activity, financial services, and automobiles.

Reference group
A group that serves as direct or indirect point of comparison or reference in forming a person's attitudes or behavior.

Opinion leader
A person within a reference group who, because of special skills, knowledge, personality, or other characteristics, exerts social influence on others.

Word-of-mouth influence
The impact of the personal words and recommendations of trusted friends, family, associates, and other consumers on buying behavior.

Influencer marketing
Enlisting established influencers or creating new influencers to spread the word about a company's brands.

Online social networks
Online social communities—blogs, online social media, brand communities, and other online forums—where people socialize or exchange information and opinions.

Social Factors

A consumer's behavior also is influenced by social factors, such as the consumer's *groups and social networks*, *family*, and *social roles and status*.

Groups and Social Networks. Many groups influence a person's behavior. Groups that have a direct influence and to which a person belongs are called *membership groups*. In contrast, **reference groups** serve as direct (face-to-face interactions) or indirect points of comparison or reference in forming a person's attitudes or behavior. People often are influenced by reference groups to which they do not belong. For example, an *aspirational group* is one to which the individual wishes to belong, as when a young basketball player hopes to someday emulate basketball star LeBron James and play in the NBA.

Marketers try to identify the reference groups of their target markets. Reference groups expose a person to new behaviors and lifestyles, influence the person's attitudes and self-concept, and create pressures to conform that may affect the person's product and brand choices. The importance of group influence varies across products and brands. It tends to be strongest when the product is visible to others whom the buyer respects.

Marketers of brands subjected to strong group influence must figure out how to reach **opinion leaders**—people within a reference group who, because of special skills, knowledge, personality, or other characteristics, exert social influence on others. Marketers try to identify opinion leaders for their brands and direct marketing efforts toward them.

Word-of-mouth influence can have a powerful impact on consumer buying behavior. The personal words and recommendations of trusted friends, family, associates, and other consumers tend to be more credible than those coming from commercial sources, such as advertisements or salespeople. Most word-of-mouth influence happens naturally: Consumers start chatting about a brand they use or feel strongly about one way or the other. Often, however, rather than leaving it to chance, marketers can help to create positive conversations about their brands.

Influencer marketing involves enlisting established influencers or creating new influencers to spread the word about a company's brands. » For example, giant cosmetics maker CoverGirl has built its "I Am What I Make Up" ad campaign around a new, diverse team of well-known "badass" brand influencers—barrier-breaking women who bring the brand slogan to life. The influencer team includes, among others, Katy Perry; Issa Rae, star of the HBO series *Insecure*; Food Network host Ayesha Curry; fitness guru Massy Arias; 69-year-old model Maye Musk; and professional motorcycle racer Shelina Moreda. In the campaign, the influential CoverGirl ambassadors explain in their own words, in a personal and authentic way, what "I Am What I Make Up" means to them.[11]

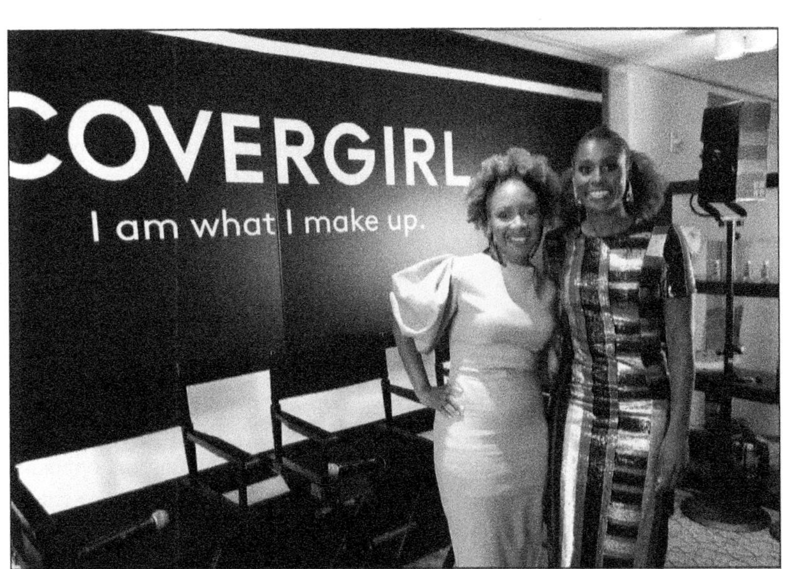

» Influencer marketing: CoverGirl's "I Am What I Make Up" campaign uses a diverse team of influential brand ambassadors who explain authentically in their own words what the slogan means to them.

Craig Barritt/Getty Images

Other marketers are shaping influence by tapping into the **online social networks**, online communities where people socialize or exchange information and opinions. Social networking communities range from blogs (Mashable, Engadget, Gizmodo) and message boards (Craigslist) to social media sites (Facebook, Twitter, YouTube, Instagram, Snapchat, LinkedIn) and even communal shopping sites (Amazon.com and Etsy). Marketers are working to harness the power of these social networks and other "word-of-web" influence opportunities to promote their products and build closer customer relationships. They hope to use digital, mobile, and social media to become an interactive part of consumers' conversations and lives.

Many influencer marketing campaigns involve building relationships with the army of self-made influencers already plying the internet, from social media personalities to independent bloggers. The key is to find online influencers who have strong networks of relevant followers, a credible voice, and a good fit with the brand. For example, Target's children's apparel line Art Class, designed by kids for kids, leaned heavily on popular young online influencers for design inspiration and marketing. Teen social media stars such as 15-year-old Loren Gray (6.5 million Instagram followers), 16-year-old Nia Sioux (4.5 million Instagram followers), and Jacob Martin (309,000 Instagram followers) shared stories with their online their audiences about the joys of working with Target to create unique, personal Art Class designs. Their posts drew hundreds of thousands of likes and a slew of comments such as this one: "I swear I'm going to persuade my mom to buy it."[12]

Similarly, you'll no doubt cross paths with the likes of climbers and skiers blogging for Patagonia, bikers blogging for Harley-Davidson, and foodies blogging for Whole Foods Market or Trader Joe's. And companies such as P&G, McDonald's, Walmart, and Disney work closely with influential "mom bloggers" or "social media moms," turning them into brand advocates (see Marketing at Work 5.1).

We will dig deeper into online and social media as marketing tools in Chapter 14. However, although much current influencer marketing discussion focuses on digital, mobile, and social media, most brand conversations still take place the old-fashioned way—face-to-face. So effective word-of-mouth marketing programs usually begin with generating person-to-person brand conversations and integrating both offline and online social influence strategies. The goal is to get customers involved with brands, turn them into brand advocates, and help them share their brand passions and experiences with others in both their real and digital worlds.

Family. Family members can strongly influence buyer behavior. The family is the most important membership reference group and consumer buying organization in society. It has been researched extensively. Marketers are interested in the roles and influence of the husband, wife, and children on the purchase of different products and services.

Husband–wife involvement varies widely by product category and by stage in the buying process. Buying roles change with evolving consumer lifestyles. For example, in the United States, the wife traditionally has been considered the main purchasing agent for the family in the areas of food, household products, and clothing. But with 71 percent of all mothers now working outside the home and the willingness of husbands to do more of the family's purchasing, all this has changed in recent years. Recent surveys show that 41 percent of men are now the primary grocery shoppers in their households, 39 percent handle most of their household's laundry, and about one-quarter say they are responsible for all of their household's cooking. At the same time, today women outspend men three to two on new technology purchases and influence more than 80 percent of all new car purchases.[13]

Such shifting roles signal a new marketing reality. Marketers in industries that have traditionally sold their products to only women or only men—from groceries and personal care products to cars and consumer electronics—are now carefully targeting the opposite sex. For example, a recent General Mills "How to Dad" campaign for Cheerios presents a dad as a multitasking superhero around the house, a departure from the bumbling dad stereotypes often shown in food ads. This dad does all the right things, including feeding his children healthy Cheerios breakfasts. Similarly, a 90-second ad for Barbie, shown during an NFL playoff game, shows heartwarming scenes of dads and daughters playing together with Barbies. The ad concludes, "Time spent in her imaginary world is an investment in her real world."[14]

Children may also have a strong influence on family buying decisions. The nation's kids and tweens influence up to 80 percent of all household purchases, to the tune of

MARKETING AT WORK 5.1

Tapping Social Media Moms as Brand Ambassadors

America's moms constitute a huge market. Women account for 85 percent of all consumer purchases, and the nation's 85 million moms account $2.4 trillion worth of annual consumer spending. Moms are also heavy social media sharers and shoppers. They are 20 percent more likely than the general population to use social media, and 44 percent of moms have made a purchase on their smartphones within the past week.

Moreover, many moms rely heavily on social media to share experiences with other moms, including brand and buying experiences. For example, there are as many as 14.2 million U.S. mothers who blog, and some 4.4 million mom bloggers influence a million or more followers. Go-to social media platforms for mom bloggers include Instagram ("Instamoms"), Facebook, and Twitter, but Pinterest and YouTube are also popular. Such mom influencers are important. Some 55 percent of moms on social media regularly base their buying decisions on personal stories, recommendations, and product reviews that they find in blogs and other social media.

Given these pretty amazing figures, it's not surprising that many marketers now harness the power of mom-to-mom influence by creating or tapping into networks of influential social media moms and turning them into brand ambassadors. Here are just three examples: McDonald's, Walmart, and Disney.

McDonald's Mom Bloggers. McDonald's systematically reaches out to key "mom bloggers," those who influence the nation's homemakers, who in turn influence their families' eating-out choices. For example, McDonald's recently hosted 15 influential mom bloggers on an all-expenses-paid tour of its Chicago-area headquarters. The bloggers toured the facilities (including the test kitchens), met McDonald's USA president, and had their pictures taken with Ronald at a nearby Ronald McDonald House.

McDonald's knows that these mom bloggers have loyal followings and talk a lot about McDonald's in their blogs. So it's turning the bloggers into believers by giving them a behind-the-scenes view. McDonald's doesn't try to tell the bloggers what to say in their social media posts about the visit. It simply asks them to write one honest recap of their trip. However, the resulting posts (each acknowledging the blogger's connection with McDonald's) were mostly very positive. Thanks to this and other such efforts, mom bloggers around the country are now more informed about and connected with McDonald's. "I know they have smoothies and they have yogurt and they have other things that my kids would want," says one prominent blogger. "I really couldn't tell you what Burger King's doing right now," she adds. "I have no idea."

Walmart Moms. Nine years ago, Walmart enlisted a group of 11 influential mom bloggers—originally called the ElevenMoms but quickly growing in number to 22—to "represent the voice of all moms." Later called simply the "Walmart Moms," these influential social media moms provided input to Walmart on behalf of all moms and in turn represented Walmart to their large social media followings.

Described by Walmart as "moms like you," the Walmart Moms represented a cross-section of American moms in terms of geography, ethnicity, and age. "Walmart Moms are pretty much like most moms out there," said Walmart. They "know what it's like to balance family, work, errands, searching for missing softball mitts, and everything else in between. And [they're] always looking for ways to save money and live better."

The Walmart Moms became important and influential Walmart brand ambassadors. Through surveys, focus groups, and in-store events, the mom bloggers and their readers provided Walmart and its suppliers with key customer insights regarding its stores and products. Going the other way, the Walmart Moms created relevant stories, pictures, and videos—everything from money-saving tips to product reviews to craft suggestions and recipes—shared on social media and through links on Walmart's online and social media sites.

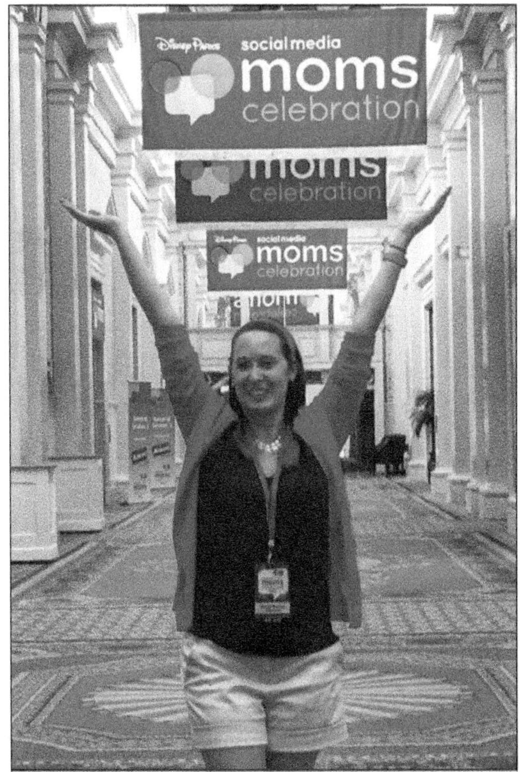

>> Harnessing the power of mom-to-mom influence: Each year, Disney invites 175 to 200 moms and their families to its Disney Social Media Moms Celebration in Florida, an affair that's a mix of public relations event, educational conference, and family vacation with plenty of Disney magic for these important mom influencers.

Mindy Marzec

Walmart Moms received product samples and compensation. Their posts often referred to products sold by Walmart and included links to the products on Walmart sites. But both Walmart and the Walmart Moms knew that their strength depended on their authenticity and in the trust they built with their followers. So with Walmart's urging and full support, the moms posted whatever they pleased and shared their sincere opinions. "Walmart does not require anything of us but to be ourselves and remain authentic to our own voice," said one mom blogger. Without that, what the Walmart Moms posted would be viewed as little more than paid promotions.

After eight years, Walmart bid farewell to its official ElevenMoms program. However, based on the valuable lessons learned, Walmart actively engages much broader base of mom-to-mom social media influencers.

Disney Social Media Moms. The Walt Disney Company has long recognized the power of moms in social media and the importance moms play in planning family vacations. Seven years ago, the company assembled a group called Disney Social Media Moms, roughly 1,300 carefully selected mom bloggers (and some dads), travel bloggers, and active Disney-focused social media posters.

Disney looks for influential moms who fit the brand's family-friendly focus, use social media heavily, and are active in their communities offline as well as online. One example is Rachel Pitzel, a mother of two and former CEO of Club Momme, a social and educational group that sponsors events for moms, expectant parents, and families and maintains an active blog. Another is Wendy Wright, a homeschooling mother of two and a prolific blogger. Wendy describes herself as a "Disney nut" (she named her cats Mickey and Minnie), and she fills her blog with advice for planning Disney park visits, tips for holding Disney-themed parties, and reviews of Disney movies.

Disney Social Media Moms aren't paid; they participate because of their passion and enthusiasm for all things Disney. However, they do receive special educational attention from Disney, inside information, and occasional perks. For example, every year, Disney invites 175 to 200 of the moms and their families for a deeply discounted, four-day trip to attend its annual Disney Social Media Moms Celebration in Florida. The celebration is a mix of public relations event, educational conference, and family vacation with plenty of Disney magic for these important mom influencers.

The Disney Social Media Moms are under no obligation to post anything about Disney, and the company doesn't tell them what to say when they do post. However, the most recent celebration generated 28,500 tweets, 4,900 Instagram photos, and 88 blog posts full of ride reviews, videos of families meeting Disney characters, and a host of overwhelmingly positive comments. "For a big chunk of our guests, it's the moms who are making [travel] decisions," says a top Disney executive. The Disney Social Media Moms effort costs the company very little but effectively harnesses the power of mom-to-mom influence to help sprinkle Disney's magical pixie dust on an important group of buyers.

Sources: Holly Pavlika, "Millennial Moms Are Asked 9.6 Times a Month for Recommendations," *MediaPost*, November 10, 2017, www.mediapost.com/publications/article/310052/millennial-moms-are-asked-96-times-a-month-for-re.html; Neil Patel, "9 Things We Can Learn from the Mom Blog Industry," *Forbes*, November 3, 2016, www.forbes.com/sites/neilpatel/2016/11/03/9-things-we-can-learn-from-the-mom-blog-industry/#1ac630062181; Keith O'Brien, "How McDonald's Came Back Bigger Than Ever," *New York Times*, May 6, 2012, p. MM44; "How Walmart Made 11 Moms Become Its Brand Ambassadors," October 14, 2015, http://crezeo.com/how-11-moms-became-walmart-brand-ambassadors/; Lisa Richwine, "Disney's Powerful Marketing Force: Social Media Moms," *Reuters*, June 15, 2015, www.reuters.com/article/us-disney-moms-insight-idUSKBN0OV0DX20150615; John Andrews, "Influencer Marketing 2018: The Rise of the Personal Influencer," *Good Audience*, December 31, 2017, https://blog.goodaudience.com/influencer-marketing-2018-the-rise-of-the-personal-influencer-81f0c514eec3; and "Social Media Moms," https://twitter.com/disneymoms?lang=en, accessed September 2018.

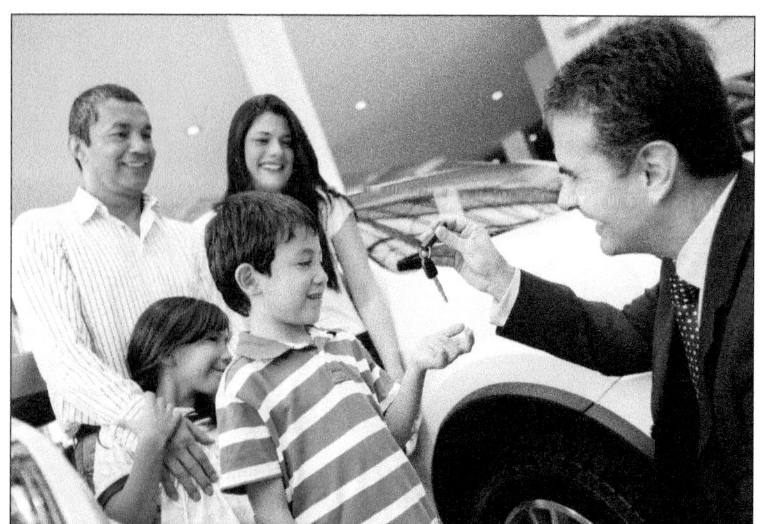

>> Family buying influences: Children may weigh in heavily on family purchases for everything from restaurants and vacation destinations to mobile devices and even car purchases.

Andres Rodriguez/123RF

$1.2 trillion of spending annually. >> In one recent survey, parents with teens reported that their children weigh in heavily on everything from where they eat out (95 percent) and take vacations (82 percent) to what mobile devices they use (63 percent) and cars they buy (45 percent).[15]

Marketers across a wide range of industries recognize such family influences in their marketing programs. For example, one ad for Honda's Odyssey minivan, titled "Keep the Peace," touts innovative features that satisfy the entire family. "When kids are happy, parents are happy, so the goal of this new campaign is to communicate that the all-new Honda Odyssey has the connectivity, functionality, flexibility, and fun-to-drive handling to keep everyone in the family happy," says a Honda marketer.[16]

Roles and Status. A person belongs to many groups—family, clubs, organizations, online communities. The person's position in each group can be defined in terms of both role and status. A role consists of the activities people are expected to perform according to the people around them. Each role carries a status reflecting the general esteem given to it by society.

People usually choose products appropriate to their roles and status. Consider the various roles a working mother plays. In her company, she may play the role of a brand manager; in her family, she plays the role of wife and mother; at her favorite sporting events, she plays the role of avid fan. As a brand manager, she will buy the kind of clothing that reflects her role and status in her company. At the game, she may wear clothing supporting her favorite team.

Personal Factors

A buyer's decisions also are influenced by personal characteristics such as the buyer's *occupation, age and stage, economic situation, lifestyle*, and *personality and self-concept.*

Occupation. A person's occupation affects the goods and services bought. Blue-collar workers tend to buy more rugged work clothes, whereas executives buy more business suits. Marketers try to identify the occupational groups that have an above-average interest in their products and services. A company can even specialize in making products needed by a given occupational group. For example, Red Kap makes rugged, durable work clothes and uniform apparel for the automotive and construction industries. Since 1923, the brand has lived up to its "Done Right" slogan—it makes "Workwear. Built Better." It tells customers, "You didn't get where you are today by taking the easy way out. . . .You know great work starts with a little sweat, determination, and pride. That's what sets us apart. That's what makes our workwear tougher, smarter, better." Red Kap currently outfits "16 million Americans who apply their hands and hearts to all kinds of jobs."[17]

Age and Life Stage. People change the goods and services they buy over their lifetimes. Tastes in food, clothes, furniture, and recreation are often age related. Buying is also shaped by the stage of the family life cycle—the stages through which families might pass as they mature over time. Life-stage changes usually result from demographics and life-changing events—marriage, having children, purchasing a home, divorce, children going to college, changes in personal income, moving out of the house, and retirement. Marketers often define their target markets in terms of life-cycle stage and develop appropriate products and marketing plans for each stage.

One of the leading life-stage segmentation systems is the Nielsen PRIZM Lifestage Groups system. PRIZM classifies every American household into one of 66 distinct life-stage segments, which are organized into 11 major life-stage groups based on affluence, age, and family characteristics. The classifications consider a host of demographic factors such as age, education, income, occupation, family composition, ethnicity, and housing; and behavioral and lifestyle factors such as purchases, free-time activities, and media preferences.

The major PRIZM Lifestage groups carry names such as "Striving Singles," "Midlife Success," "Young Achievers," "Sustaining Families," "Affluent Empty Nests," and "Conservative Classics," which in turn contain subgroups such as "Bright Lights, Li'l City," "Kids & Cul-de-Sacs," "Gray Power," and "Big City Blues." The "Young Achievers" group consists of hip, single 20-somethings who rent apartments in or close to metropolitan neighborhoods. Their incomes range from working class to well-to-do, but the entire group tends to be politically liberal, listen to alternative music, and enjoy lively nightlife.[18]

Life-stage segmentation provides a powerful marketing tool for marketers in all industries to better find, understand, and engage consumers. Armed with data about the makeup of consumer life stages, marketers can create targeted, actionable, personalized campaigns based on how people consume and interact with brands and the world around them.

Economic Situation. A person's economic situation will affect his or her store and product choices. Marketers watch trends in spending, personal income, savings, and interest rates. In today's value-conscious times, most companies have taken steps to create more customer value by redesigning, repositioning, and repricing their products and services. For example, in recent years, upscale discounter Target has put more emphasis on the "Pay Less" side of its "Expect More. Pay Less." positioning promise. And soon after Amazon purchased Whole Foods, the online giant took a knife to the upscale grocery chain's high prices. To help blunt the chain's "Whole Foods. Whole Paycheck." image, Amazon quickly slashed Whole Foods prices as much as 40 percent in key categories.[19]

Lifestyle
A person's pattern of living as expressed in his or her activities, interests, and opinions.

Lifestyle. People coming from the same subculture, social class, and occupation may have quite different lifestyles. **Lifestyle** is a person's pattern of living as expressed in his or her psychographics. It involves measuring consumers' major AIO dimensions—*activities* (work, hobbies, shopping, sports, social events), *interests* (food, fashion, family, recreation), and *opinions* (about themselves, social issues, business, products). Lifestyle captures something more than the person's social class or personality. It profiles a person's whole pattern of acting and interacting in the world.

When used carefully, the lifestyle concept can help marketers understand changing consumer values and how they affect buyer behavior. Consumers don't just buy products; they buy the values and lifestyles those products represent. >> For example, Title Nine markets much more than just women's apparel:

> Named after the federal act that helped end gender discrimination in high school and collegiate sports, Title Nine markets "adventure-ready athletic and sportswear" that fits a sports participation and activities lifestyle. "We are evangelical about women's participation in sports and fitness," says T9. Title Nine fills its web and social media sites, catalogs, and blog with images of strong, confident, and active women running on trails wearing reflective gear, snowshoeing with their dogs, stand-up paddle boarding in tropical lagoons, and running errands in ski resort towns wearing more casual, playful clothing. Title Nine's models are all real people, and T9 highlights their lifestyles and stories through an active social media presence plus local activities sponsored by its retail shops. "They are ordinary women capable of extraordinary things," says the company. "And, like many of you, they somehow manage to weave sports and fitness into their hectic lives." That's the T9 lifestyle.

>> Lifestyles: Title Nine markets much more than just women's apparel. It sells the T9 sports participation and activities lifestyle of "ordinary women capable of extraordinary things."
Photograph by Virginia Nowell

Marketers look for lifestyle segments with needs that can be served through special products or marketing approaches. Such segments might be defined by anything from family characteristics or outdoor interests to the foods people eat.

Personality
The unique psychological characteristics that distinguish a person or group.

Personality and Self-Concept. Each person's distinct personality influences his or her buying behavior. **Personality** refers to the unique psychological characteristics that distinguish a person or group. Personality is usually described in terms of traits such as self-confidence, dominance, sociability, autonomy, defensiveness, adaptability, and aggressiveness. Personality can be useful in analyzing consumer behavior for certain product or brand choices.

The idea is that brands also have personalities, and consumers are likely to choose brands with personalities that match their own. A *brand personality* is the specific mix of human traits that may be attributed to a particular brand. One researcher identified five brand personality traits: *sincerity* (down-to-earth, honest, wholesome, and cheerful), *excitement* (daring, spirited, imaginative, and up-to-date), *competence* (reliable, intelligent, and successful), *sophistication* (glamorous, upper class, charming), and *ruggedness* (outdoorsy and tough). "Your personality determines what you consume, what TV shows you watch, what products you buy, and [most] other decisions you make," says one consumer behavior expert.[20]

Most well-known brands are strongly associated with a particular trait: the Ford F150 with "ruggedness," Apple with "excitement," the *Washington Post* with "competence," Method with "sincerity," and Gucci with "class and sophistication." Many brands build their positioning and brand stories around such traits. For example, as we learned in the chapter-opening story, fast-growing lifestyle brand Shinola has crafted an "authentic, Detroit" persona that has made it one of America's hottest brands.

Many marketers use a concept related to personality—a person's *self-concept* (also called *self-image*). The idea is that people's possessions contribute to and reflect their identities—that

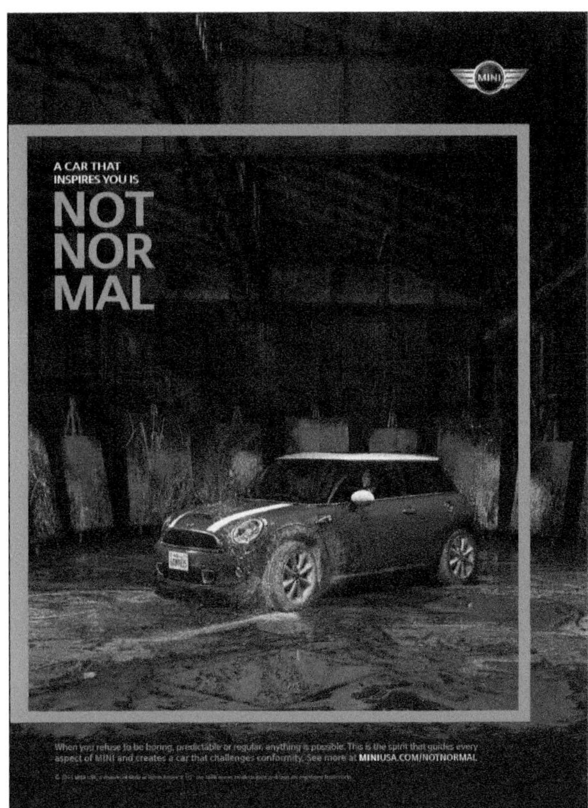

>> **Brand personality: MINI markets to personality segments of people who are "adventurous, individualistic, open-minded, creative, tech-savvy, and young at heart"—anything but "normal"—just like the car.**

Used with permission of MINI Division of BMW of North America, LLC

is, "we are what we consume." Thus, to understand consumer behavior, marketers must first understand the relationship between consumer self-concept and possessions.

Hence, brands will attract people who are high on the same personality traits. >> For example, the MINI automobile has an instantly recognizable personality as a clever and sassy but powerful little car. MINI owners—who sometimes call themselves "MINIacs"—have a strong and emotional connection with their cars. More than targeting specific demographic segments, MINI appeals to personality segments—to people who are "adventurous, individualistic, open-minded, creative, tech-savvy, and young at heart," just like the car.[21]

Psychological Factors

A person's buying choices are further influenced by four major psychological factors: *motivation, perception, learning*, and *beliefs and attitudes*.

Motivation. A person has many needs at any given time. Some are biological, arising from states of tension such as hunger, thirst, or discomfort. Others are psychological, arising from the need for recognition, esteem, or belonging. A need becomes a motive when it is aroused to a sufficient level of intensity. A **motive** (or **drive**) is a need that is sufficiently pressing to direct the person to seek satisfaction. Psychologists have developed theories of human motivation. Two of the most popular—the theories of Sigmund Freud and Abraham Maslow—carry quite different meanings for consumer analysis and marketing.

Sigmund Freud assumed that people are largely unconscious about the real psychological forces shaping their behavior. His theory suggests that a person's buying decisions are affected by subconscious motives that even the buyer may not fully understand. Thus, an aging baby boomer who buys a sporty BMW convertible might explain that he simply likes the feel of the wind in his thinning hair. At a deeper level, he may be trying to impress others with his success. At a still deeper level, he may be buying the car to feel young and independent again.

Motive (drive)
A need that is sufficiently pressing to direct the person to seek satisfaction of the need.

Consumers often don't know or can't describe why they act as they do. Thus, many companies employ teams of psychologists, anthropologists, and other social scientists to carry out *motivation research* that probes the subconscious motivations underlying consumers' emotions and behaviors toward brands. One ad agency routinely conducts one-on-one, therapy-like interviews to delve the inner workings of consumers. Another company asks consumers to describe their favorite brands as animals or cars (say, a Mercedes versus a Chevy) to assess the prestige associated with various brands. Still others rely on hypnosis, dream therapy, or soft lights and mood music to plumb the murky depths of consumer psyches.

Such projective techniques might seem pretty goofy, and some marketers dismiss such motivation research as mumbo jumbo. But many marketers use such touchy-feely approaches, now sometimes called *interpretive consumer research*, to dig deeper into consumer psyches and develop better marketing strategies.

Abraham Maslow sought to explain why people are driven by particular needs at particular times. Why does one person spend a lot of time and energy on personal safety and another on gaining the esteem of others? Maslow's answer is that human needs are arranged in a hierarchy, as shown in >> **Figure 5.3**, from the most pressing at the bottom to the least pressing at the top.[22] They include *physiological* needs, *safety* needs, *social* needs, *esteem* needs, and *self-actualization* needs.

A person tries to satisfy the most important need first. When that need is satisfied, it will stop being a motivator, and the person will then try to satisfy the next most important need. For example, starving people (physiological need) will not take an interest in the latest happenings in the art world (self-actualization needs) nor in how they are seen or esteemed by others (social or esteem needs) nor even in whether they are breathing clean

Figure 5.3 Maslow's Hierarchy of Needs

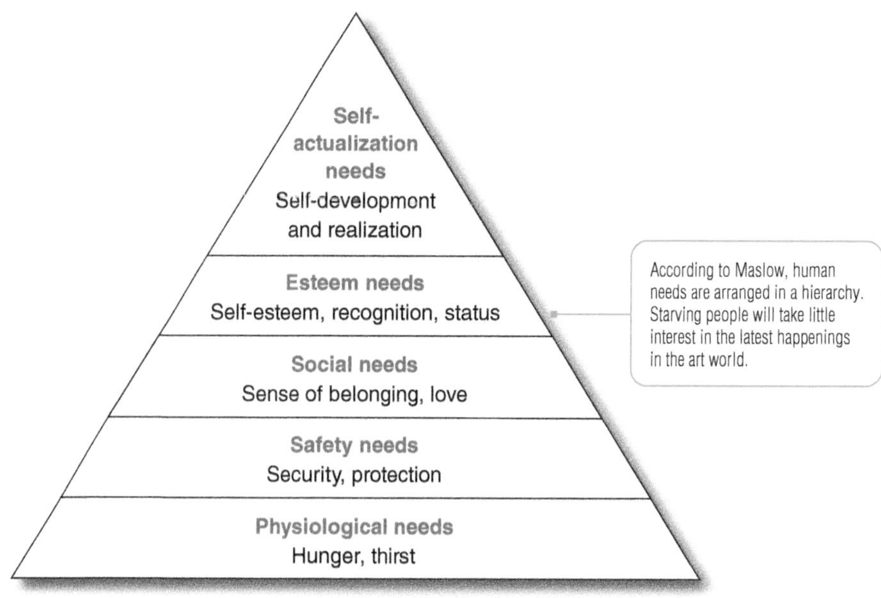

air (safety needs). But as each important need is satisfied, the next most important need will come into play.

Perception. A motivated person is ready to act. How the person acts is influenced by his or her own perception of the situation. All of us learn by the flow of information through our five senses: sight, hearing, smell, touch, and taste. However, each of us receives, organizes, and interprets this sensory information in an individual way. **Perception** is the process by which people select, organize, and interpret information to form a meaningful picture of the world.

Perception
The process by which people select, organize, and interpret information to form a meaningful picture of the world.

People can form different perceptions of the same stimulus because of three perceptual processes: selective attention, selective distortion, and selective retention. People are exposed to a huge number of stimuli every day. For example, individuals are exposed to an estimated 3,000 to 10,000 ad messages daily—from TV and magazine ads to billboards to social media ads and smartphones posts.[23] People can't possibly pay attention to all the competing stimuli surrounding them. *Selective attention*—the tendency for people to screen out most of the information to which they are exposed—means that marketers must work especially hard to attract the consumer's attention.

Even noticed stimuli do not always come across in the intended way. Each person fits incoming information into an existing mindset. *Selective distortion* describes the tendency of people to interpret information in a way that supports what they already believe. People also will forget much of what they learn. They tend to retain information that supports their attitudes and beliefs. *Selective retention* means that consumers are likely to remember good points made about a brand they favor and forget good points made about competing brands. Because of selective attention, distortion, and retention, marketers must work hard just to get their messages through.

Interestingly, although most marketers worry about whether their offers will be perceived at all, some consumers worry that they will be affected by marketing messages without even knowing it—through *subliminal advertising*. More than 50 years ago, a researcher announced that he had flashed the phrases "Eat popcorn" and "Drink Coca-Cola" on a screen in a New Jersey movie theater every five seconds for 1/300th of a second. He reported that although viewers did not consciously recognize these messages, they absorbed them subconsciously and bought 58 percent more popcorn and 18 percent more Coke. Suddenly advertisers and consumer-protection groups became intensely interested in subliminal perception. Although the researcher later admitted to making up the data, the

>> This classic ad from the American Association of Advertising Agencies pokes fun at subliminal advertising. "So-called 'subliminal advertising' simply doesn't exist," says the ad. "Overactive imaginations, however, most certainly do."
American Association of Advertising Agencies

issue has not died. Some consumers still fear that they are being manipulated by subliminal messages.

Numerous studies by psychologists and consumer researchers have found little or no link between subliminal messages and consumer behavior. Recent brain-wave studies have found that in certain circumstances, our brains may register subliminal messages. However, it appears that subliminal advertising simply doesn't have the power attributed to it by its critics.[24] Moreover, mainstream marketers simply don't insert such messages into their advertising content. >> One classic ad from the American Association of Advertising Agencies pokes fun at subliminal advertising. "So-called 'subliminal advertising' simply doesn't exist," says the ad. "Overactive imaginations, however, most certainly do."

Learning. When people act, they learn. **Learning** describes changes in an individual's behavior arising from experience. Learning theorists say that most human behavior is learned. Learning occurs through the interplay of drives, stimuli, cues, responses, and reinforcement.

A *drive* is a strong internal stimulus that calls for action. A drive becomes a motive when it is directed toward a particular *stimulus object*. For example, a person's drive for self-actualization might motivate him or her to look into buying a camera. The consumer's response to the idea of buying a camera is conditioned by the surrounding cues. *Cues* are minor stimuli that determine when, where, and how the person responds. The camera buyer might spot several camera brands in a shop window, hear of a special sale price, see buyer reviews on Amazon.com, or discuss cameras with a friend. These are all cues that might influence a consumer's *response* to his or her interest in buying the product.

Suppose the consumer buys a Nikon camera. If the experience is rewarding, the consumer will probably use the camera more and more, and his or her response will be *reinforced*. Then the next time he or she shops for a camera, or for binoculars or some similar product, the probability is greater that he or she will buy a Nikon product. The practical significance of learning theory for marketers is that they can build up demand for a product by associating it with strong drives, using motivating cues, and providing positive reinforcement.

Learning
Changes in an individual's behavior arising from experience.

Belief
A descriptive thought that a person holds about something.

Attitude
A person's consistently favorable or unfavorable evaluations, feelings, and tendencies toward an object or idea.

Beliefs and Attitudes. Through doing and learning, people acquire beliefs and attitudes. These, in turn, influence their buying behavior. A **belief** is a descriptive thought that a person holds about something. Beliefs may be based on real knowledge, opinion, or faith and may or may not carry an emotional charge. Marketers are interested in the beliefs that people formulate about specific products and services because these beliefs make up product and brand images that affect buying behavior. If some of the beliefs are wrong and prevent purchase, the marketer will want to launch a campaign to correct them.

People have attitudes regarding religion, politics, clothes, music, food, and almost everything else. **Attitude** describes a person's relatively consistent evaluations, feelings, and tendencies toward an object or idea. Attitudes put people into a frame of mind of liking or disliking things, of moving toward or away from them. Our camera buyer may hold attitudes such as "Buy the best," "The Japanese make the best camera products in the world," and "Creativity and self-expression are among the most important things in life." If so, the Nikon camera would fit well into the consumer's existing attitudes.

Attitudes are difficult to change. A person's attitudes fit into a pattern; changing one attitude may require difficult adjustments in many others. Thus, a company should usually try to fit its products into existing attitude patterns rather than attempt to change attitudes. Of course, there are exceptions. Repositioning or extending a brand calls for changing attitudes. So does introducing an innovative new brand that counters conventional thinking.

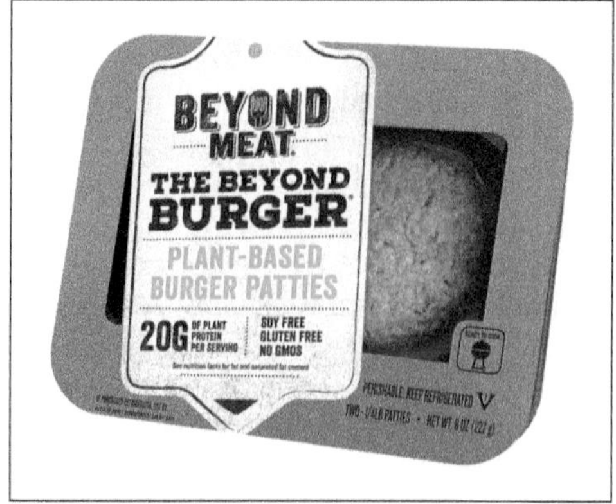

» Changing consumer attitudes and beliefs can be difficult. But Beyond Meat is off to a good start with its plant-based meat products. The Beyond Burger "cooks like a beef patty. It sizzles, it oozes. And sizzle, we know, is what sells."

Beyond Meat

» For example, consider Beyond Meat, a startup company that is trying to disrupt the huge meat industry by creating healthier, eco-friendlier, plant-based alternatives to beef and chicken:[25]

> Beyond Meat claims that it has invented a vegetarian burger—The Beyond Burger—that tastes like beef. To most skeptical Americans, however, at least at first, the idea seems too good to be true. Beyond Meat has a worthy mission. It seeks "a better way to feed the planet" by replacing animal protein with plant protein. With its plant-based "meat," which doesn't rely on livestock that requires more land, water, and other resources, Beyond Meat is "dedicated to improving human health, positively impacting climate change, conserving natural resources, and respecting animal welfare."
>
> That all sounds great on a broad, societal level. However, changing firmly ingrained individual consumer attitudes toward meat will present real challenges. Americans love their meat—they are among the highest per capita meat eaters in the world. But if the taste is right, products such as The Beyond Burger offer huge market potential. And Beyond Meat is off to a good start. After only one year, the meatless meat was available in more than 5,000 grocery stores—including Whole Foods and Safeway—as well as restaurants such as BurgerFi's and TGI Friday. And for many consumers, the product's taste is a real attitude changer. "If the idea of building a juicy, tasty, 'I-can't-believe-it's a' veggie burger in a lab sounds totally sci-fi, then the future is here," says one food critic. Says another, "It 'cooks' like a beef patty. It sizzles, it oozes. And sizzle, we know, is what sells."

We can now appreciate the many forces acting on consumer behavior. The consumer's choice results from the complex interplay of cultural, social, personal, and psychological factors.

Author Comment
The actual purchase decision is part of a much larger buying process—from recognizing a need through postpurchase behavior. Marketers want to be involved throughout the entire buyer decision process.

The Buyer Decision Process

OBJECTIVE 5-2 Identify and discuss the stages in the buyer decision process.

Now that we have looked at the influences that affect buyers, we are ready to look at how consumers make buying decisions. » **Figure 5.4** shows that the buyer decision process consists of five stages: *need recognition, information search, evaluation of alternatives*, the *purchase decision*, and *postpurchase behavior*. Clearly, the buying process starts long before the actual purchase and continues long after. Marketers need to focus on the entire buying process rather than on the purchase decision only.

Figure 5.4 suggests that consumers pass through all five stages with every purchase in a considered way. But buyers may pass quickly or slowly through the buying decision process. And in more routine purchases, consumers often skip or reverse some of the stages. Much depends on the nature of the buyer, the product, and the buying situation. A person buying a regular brand of toothpaste would recognize the need and go right to the purchase decision, skipping information search and evaluation. However, we use the model in Figure 5.4 because it shows all the considerations that arise when a consumer faces a new and complex purchase situation.

Need Recognition

The buying process starts with need recognition—the buyer recognizes a problem or need. The need can be triggered by *internal stimuli* when one of the person's normal needs—for example, hunger or thirst—rises to a level high enough to become a drive. A need can also be triggered by *external stimuli*. For example, an advertisement or a chat with a friend might get you thinking about buying a new car. At this stage, the marketer should research consumers to find out what kinds of needs or problems arise, what brought them about, and how they led the consumer to this particular product.

The buying process starts long before the actual purchase and continues long after. In fact, it might result in a decision not to buy. Therefore, marketers must focus on the entire buying process, not just the purchase decision.

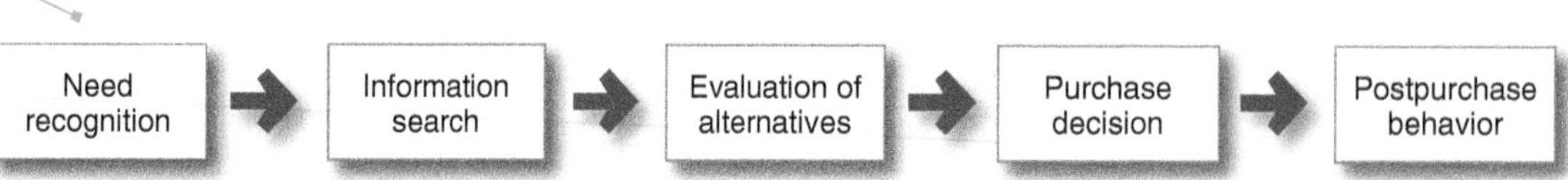

» Figure 5.4 Buyer Decision Process

Information Search

An interested consumer may or may not search for more information. If the consumer's drive is strong and a satisfying product is near at hand, he or she is likely to buy it then. If not, the consumer may store the need in memory or undertake an information search related to the need. For example, once you've decided you need a new car, at the least, you will probably pay more attention to car ads, cars owned by friends, and car conversations. Or you may actively search online, talk with friends, and gather information in other ways.

Consumers can obtain information from any of several sources. These include *personal sources* (family, friends, neighbors, acquaintances), *commercial sources* (advertising, salespeople, dealer and manufacturer web and mobile sites, packaging, displays), *public sources* (mass media, consumer rating organizations, social media, online searches and peer reviews), and *experiential sources* (examining and using the product). The relative influence of these information sources varies with the product and the buyer.

Traditionally, consumers have received the most information about a product from commercial sources—those controlled by the marketer. The most effective sources, however, tend to be personal. Commercial sources normally *inform* the buyer, but personal sources *legitimize* or *evaluate* products for the buyer. Few advertising campaigns can be as effective as a next-door neighbor leaning over the fence and raving about a wonderful experience with a product you are considering.

Increasingly, that "neighbor's fence" is a digital one. Today, consumers share product opinions, images, and experiences freely across social media. And buyers can find an abundance of user-generated reviews alongside the products they are considering at sites ranging from Amazon.com or BestBuy.com to Yelp, TripAdvisor, and Epicurious. >> For example, Yelp's goal is "to connect people with great local businesses" by maintaining a huge, searchable collection of candid reviews from people who've used those businesses. Over the past decade, Yelpers have written more than 163 million reviews of local restaurants, service business, arts and entertainment activities, and other service in cities across the nation. The site receives some 175 million unique visitors per month seeking reviews and ratings.[26] Although individual user reviews at Yelp and other sites vary widely in quality, an entire body of reviews often provides a reliable product assessment—straight from the fingertips of people like you who've actually purchased and experienced the product. "Reviews for anything you could need," says Yelp. "We know just the place."

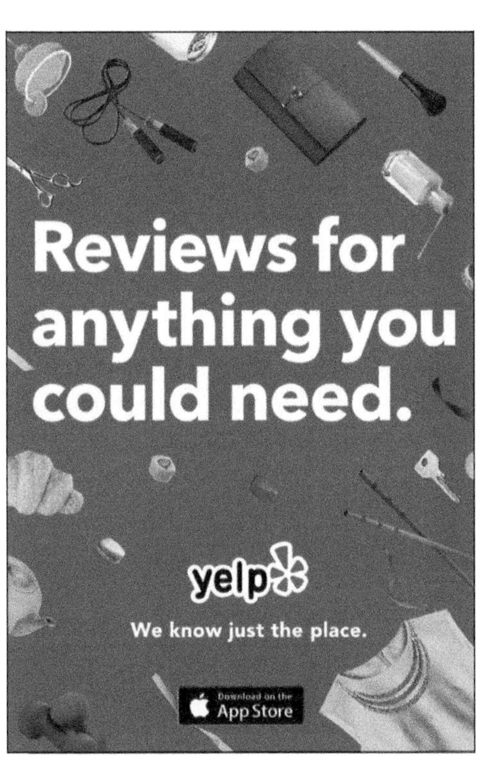

>> Information sources: Yelp's goal is "to connect people with great local businesses" by maintaining a huge, searchable collection of candid reviews from people who've used those businesses. "Reviews for anything you could need," says Yelp. "We know just the place."

Yelp, Inc.

As more information is obtained, the consumer's awareness and knowledge of the available brands and features increase. In your car information search, you may learn about several brands that are available. The information might also help you to drop certain brands from consideration. A company must design its marketing mix to make prospects aware of and knowledgeable about its brand. It should carefully identify consumers' sources of information and the importance of each source.

Evaluation of Alternatives

We have seen how consumers use information to arrive at a set of final brand choices. Next, marketers need to know about alternative evaluation, that is, how consumers process information to choose among alternative brands. Unfortunately, consumers do not use a simple and single evaluation process in all buying situations. Instead, several evaluation processes are at work.

How consumers go about evaluating purchase alternatives depends on the individual consumer and the specific buying situation. In some cases, consumers use careful calculations and logical thinking. At other times, the same consumers do little or no evaluating. Instead, they buy on impulse and rely on intuition. Sometimes consumers make buying decisions on their own; sometimes they turn to friends, online reviews, or salespeople for buying advice.

Suppose you've narrowed your car choices to three brands. And suppose that you are primarily interested in four attributes—price, style, operating economy, and performance. By this time, you've probably formed beliefs about how each brand rates on each attribute. Clearly, if one car rated best on all the attributes, the marketer could predict that you would choose it. However, the brands will no doubt vary in appeal. You might base your buying decision mostly on one attribute, and your choice would be easy to predict. If you wanted style above everything else, you would buy the car that you think has the most style. But most buyers consider several attributes, each with different importance. By knowing the importance that you assigned to each attribute, the marketer could predict and affect your car choice more reliably.

Marketers should study buyers to find out how they evaluate brand alternatives. If marketers know what evaluative processes go on, they can take steps to influence the buyer's decision.

Purchase Decision

In the evaluation stage, the consumer ranks brands and forms purchase intentions. Generally, the consumer's purchase decision will be to buy the most preferred brand, but two factors can come between the purchase *intention* and the purchase *decision*. The first factor is the *attitudes of others*. If someone important to you thinks that you should buy the lowest-priced car, then the chances of you buying a more expensive car are reduced.

The second factor is *unexpected situational factors*. The consumer may form a purchase intention based on factors such as expected income, expected price, and expected product benefits. However, unexpected events may change the purchase intention. For example, the economy might take a turn for the worse, a close competitor might drop its price, or a friend might report being disappointed in your preferred car. Thus, preferences and even purchase intentions do not always result in an actual purchase choice.

Postpurchase Behavior

Cognitive dissonance
Buyer discomfort caused by postpurchase conflict.

The marketer's job does not end when the product is bought. After purchasing the product, the consumer will either be satisfied or dissatisfied and will engage in postpurchase behavior of interest to the marketer. What determines whether the buyer is satisfied or dissatisfied with a purchase? The answer lies in the relationship between the *consumer's expectations* and the product's *perceived performance*. If the product falls short of expectations, the consumer is disappointed; if it meets expectations, the consumer is satisfied; if it exceeds expectations, the consumer is delighted. The larger the negative gap between expectations and performance, the greater the consumer's dissatisfaction. This suggests that sellers should promise only what their brands can deliver so that buyers are satisfied.

>> Postpurchase cognitive dissonance: Postpurchase customer satisfaction is a key to building profitable customer relationships. Most marketers go beyond merely meeting the customer expectations—they aim to delight customers.

Dusit/Shutterstock

Almost all major purchases, however, result in **cognitive dissonance**, or discomfort caused by postpurchase conflict. After the purchase, consumers are satisfied with the benefits of the chosen brand and are glad to avoid the drawbacks of the brands not bought. However, every purchase involves compromise. So consumers feel uneasy about acquiring the drawbacks of the chosen brand and about losing the benefits of the brands not purchased. Thus, consumers feel at least some postpurchase dissonance for every purchase.

Why is it so important to satisfy the customer? Customer satisfaction is a key to building profitable relationships with consumers—to keeping and growing consumers and reaping their customer lifetime value. Satisfied customers buy a product again, talk favorably to others about the product, pay less attention to competing brands and advertising, and buy other products from the company. >> Many marketers go beyond merely *meeting* the expectations of customers—they aim to *delight* customers.

A dissatisfied consumer responds differently. Bad word of mouth often travels farther and faster than good word of mouth. It can quickly damage consumer attitudes about a company and its products. But companies cannot simply wait for dissatisfied customers to volunteer their complaints. Most unhappy customers never tell the company about their problems. Therefore, a company should measure customer satisfaction regularly. It should set up systems that *encourage* customers to complain. In this way, the company can learn how well it is doing and how it can improve.

By studying the overall buyer decision process, marketers may be able to find ways to help consumers move through it. For example, if consumers are not buying a new product because they do not perceive a need for it, marketing might launch advertising messages that trigger the need and show how the product solves customers' problems. If customers know about the product but are not buying because they hold unfavorable attitudes toward it, marketers must find ways to change either the product or consumer perceptions.

Author Comment
Here we look at some special considerations in new product buying decisions.

The Buyer Decision Process for New Products

OBJECTIVE 5-3 Describe the adoption and diffusion process for new products.

We now look at how buyers approach the purchase of new products. A **new product** is a good, service, or idea that is perceived by some potential customers as new. It may have been around for a while, but our interest is in how consumers learn about products for the first time and make decisions on whether to adopt them. We define the **adoption process** as the mental process through which an individual passes from first learning about an innovation to final adoption. *Adoption* is the decision by an individual to become a regular user of the product.[27]

New product
A good, service, or idea that is perceived by some potential customers as new.

Adoption process
The mental process through which an individual passes from first hearing about an innovation to final adoption.

Stages in the Adoption Process

Consumers go through five stages in the process of adopting a new product:

Awareness. The consumer becomes aware of the new product but lacks information about it.

Interest. The consumer seeks information about the new product.

Evaluation. The consumer considers whether trying the new product makes sense.

Trial. The consumer tries the new product on a small scale to improve his or her estimate of its value.

Adoption. The consumer decides to make full and regular use of the new product.

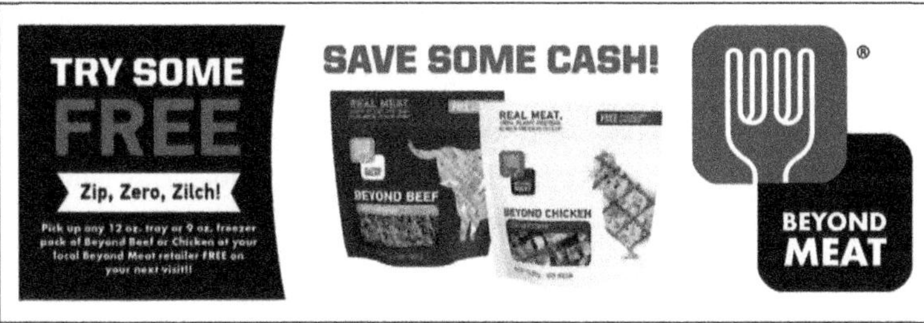

>> The adoption process: To help get tentative consumers over the buying decision hump, Beyond Meat invited consumers to "try some free—zip, zero, zilch" at their local grocery store.
Beyond Meat

This model suggests that marketers should think about how to help consumers move through these stages. For example, if a company finds that many consumers are considering its products but are still tentative about buying one, it might offer sales prices or special promotions that help get consumers over the decision hump. >> For instance, when Beyond Meat first entered the supermarket aisles, the company offered "Try Some Free" coupons for free packages of its Beyond Beef and Beyond Chicken products at local supermarkets. The promotion helped get interested consumers to take the next step and try the product.

Individual Differences in Innovativeness

People differ greatly in their readiness to try new products. In each product area, there are "consumption pioneers" and early adopters. Other individuals adopt new products much later. People can be classified into the adopter categories shown in >> **Figure 5.5.**[28] As shown by the curve, after a slow start, an increasing number of people adopt the new product. As successive groups of consumers adopt the innovation, it eventually reaches its cumulative saturation level. Innovators are defined as the first 2.5 percent of buyers to

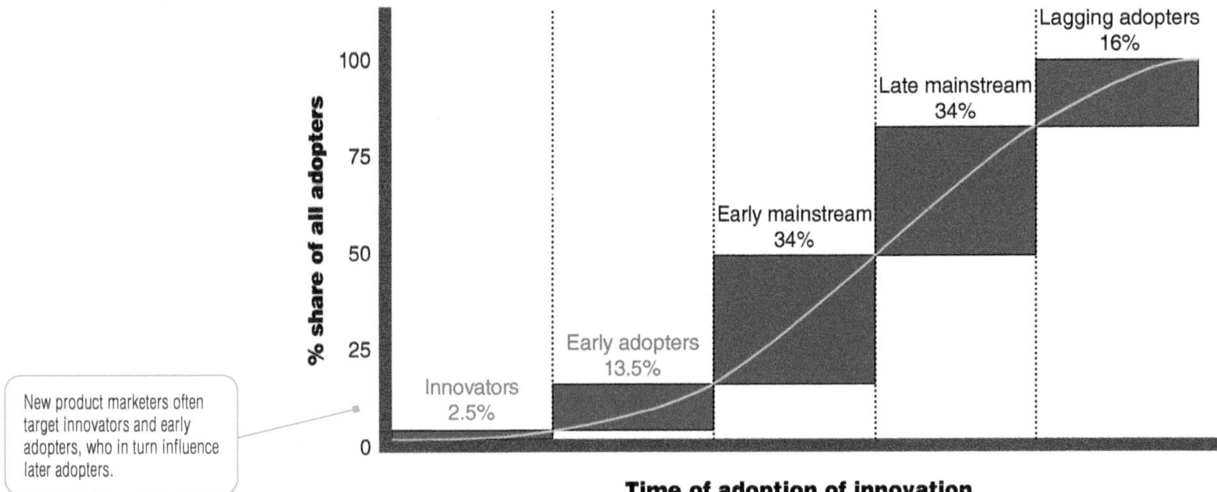

Figure 5.5 Adopter Categories Based on Relative Time of Adoption of Innovations

adopt a new idea (those beyond two standard deviations from mean adoption time); the early adopters are the next 13.5 percent (between one and two standard deviations); and then come early mainstream, late mainstream, and lagging adopters.

The five adopter groups have differing values. *Innovators* are venturesome—they try new ideas at some risk. *Early adopters* are guided by respect—they are opinion leaders in their communities and adopt new ideas early but carefully. *Early mainstream* adopters are deliberate—although they rarely are leaders, they adopt new ideas before the average person. *Late mainstream* adopters are skeptical—they adopt an innovation only after a majority of people have tried it. Finally, *lagging adopters* are tradition bound—they are suspicious of changes and adopt the innovation only when it has become something of a tradition itself.

This adopter classification suggests that an innovating firm should research the characteristics of innovators and early adopters in their product categories and direct initial marketing efforts toward them.

Influence of Product Characteristics on Rate of Adoption

The characteristics of the new product affect its rate of adoption. Some products catch on almost overnight. For example, Apple's iPod, iPhone, and iPad flew off retailers' shelves at an astounding rate from the day they were first introduced. Others take a longer time to gain acceptance. For example, all-electric cars were first introduced in the United States in 2010, led by models such as the Nissan Leaf and the Tesla Model S. However, although sales have picked up lately, electric vehicles still account for far less than 1 percent of total U.S. automobile sales. It will likely be years or even decades before they replace gasoline-powered cars.[29]

Five characteristics are especially important in influencing an innovation's rate of adoption. For example, consider the characteristics of all-electric vehicles in relation to their rate of adoption:

Relative advantage. The degree to which the innovation appears superior to existing products. All-electric cars require no gas and use clean, less costly energy. This will accelerate their rate of adoption. However, they have limited driving range before recharging and cost more initially, which will slow the adoption rate.

Compatibility. The degree to which the innovation fits the values and experiences of potential consumers. Electric cars are driven the same way as gas-powered cars. However, they are not compatible with the nation's current refueling network. Plug-in electric charging stations are few and far between. Increased adoption will depend on the development of a national network of recharging stations, which may take considerable time.

Complexity. The degree to which the innovation is difficult to understand or use. Electric cars are not different or complex to drive, which will help to speed up adoption.

However, the "conceptual complexity" of the new technologies and concerns about how well they will likely work slow down the adoption rate.

Divisibility. The degree to which the innovation may be tried on a limited basis. Consumers can test-drive electric cars, a positive for the adoption rate. However, current high prices to own and fully experience these new technologies will likely slow adoption.

Communicability. The degree to which the results of using the innovation can be observed or described to others. To the extent that electric cars lend themselves to demonstration and description, their use will spread faster among consumers.

Other characteristics influence the rate of adoption, such as initial and ongoing costs, risk and uncertainty, and social approval. The new product marketer must research all these factors when developing the new product and its marketing program.

LINKING THE CONCEPTS

Here's a good place to pause and apply the concepts you've examined in the first part of this chapter.

- Think about a specific major purchase you've made recently. What buying process did you follow? What major factors influenced your decision?
- Pick a company or brand that we've discussed in a previous chapter—Amazon, Nike, Microsoft, Starbucks, Netflix, Apple, P&G, or another. How does the company you chose use its understanding of customers and their buying behavior to build better customer relationships?
- Think about companies such as Intel or GE, which sell their products to other businesses rather than directly to final consumers. How would Intel's and GE's marketing to business customers differ from Apple's marketing to final consumers? The second part of the chapter deals with this issue.

Author Comment
Business markets operate "behind the scenes" to most consumers. Most of the things you buy involve many sets of business purchases before you ever see them.

Business Markets and Business Buyer Behavior

OBJECTIVE 5-4 Define the business market and identify the major factors that influence business buyer behavior.

In one way or another, most large companies sell to other organizations. Companies such as IBM, Boeing, DuPont, Caterpillar, GE, and countless other firms sell *most* of their products to other businesses. Even large consumer products companies, which make products used by final consumers, must first sell their products to other businesses. For example, General Mills makes many familiar consumer brands—Big G cereals (Cheerios, Wheaties, Trix, Chex, Total, Fiber One), baking products (Pillsbury, Betty Crocker, Bisquick, Gold Medal flour), snacks (Nature Valley, Bugles, Chex Mix), Yoplait yogurt, Häagen-Dazs ice cream, and many others. But to sell these products to consumers, General Mills must first sell them to its wholesaler and retailer customers, who in turn serve the consumer market.

Business buyer behavior
The buying behavior of organizations that buy goods and services for use in the production of other products and services that are sold, rented, or supplied to others.

Business buying process
The decision process by which business buyers determine which products and services their organizations need to purchase and then find, evaluate, and choose among alternative suppliers and brands.

Business buyer behavior refers to the buying behavior of organizations that buy goods and services for use in the production of other products and services that are sold, rented, or supplied to others. It also includes the behavior of retailing and wholesaling firms that acquire goods to resell or rent to others at a profit. In the **business buying process**, business buyers determine which products and services their organizations need to purchase and then find, evaluate, and choose among alternative suppliers and brands. *Business-to-business (B-to-B) marketers* must do their best to understand business markets and business buyer behavior. Then, like businesses that sell to final buyers, they must engage business customers and build profitable relationships with them by creating superior customer value.

Business Markets

The business market is *huge*. In fact, business markets involve far more dollars and items than do consumer markets. For example, think about the large number of business transactions involved in the production and sale of a single set of Goodyear tires. Various suppliers sell Goodyear the rubber, steel, equipment, and other goods that it needs to produce tires. Goodyear then sells the finished tires to retailers, which in turn sell them to consumers. Thus, many sets of *business* purchases were made for only one set of *consumer* purchases. In addition, Goodyear sells tires as original equipment to manufacturers that install them on new vehicles and as replacement tires to companies that maintain their own fleets of company cars, trucks, or other vehicles.

In some ways, business markets are similar to consumer markets. Both involve people who assume buying roles and make purchase decisions to satisfy needs. However, business markets differ in many ways from consumer markets. The main differences are in *market structure and demand*, the *nature of the buying unit*, and the *types of decisions and the decision process* involved.

Market Structure and Demand

The business marketer normally deals with *far fewer but far larger buyers* than the consumer marketer does. Even in large business markets, a few buyers often account for most of the purchasing. For example, when Goodyear sells replacement tires to final consumers, its potential market includes millions of car owners around the world. But its fate in business markets depends on getting orders from only a handful of large automakers.

Further, many business markets have *inelastic and more fluctuating demand*. The total demand for many business products is not much affected by price changes, especially in the short run. A drop in the price of leather will not cause shoe manufacturers to buy much more leather unless it results in lower shoe prices that, in turn, increase consumer demand for shoes. And the demand for many business goods and services tends to change more—and more quickly—than does the demand for consumer goods and services. A small percentage increase in consumer demand can cause large increases in business demand.

Derived demand
Business demand that ultimately comes from (derives from) the demand for consumer goods.

Finally, business demand is **derived demand**—it ultimately derives from the demand for consumer goods. >> For example, demand for Gore-Tex fabrics derives from consumer purchases of outdoor apparel brands made from Gore-Tex. If consumer demand for these products increases, so does the demand for the Gore-Tex fabrics they contain. So to boost demand for Gore-Tex, Gore advertises to final consumers to educate them on the benefits of Gore-Tex fabrics in the brands they buy. It also directly markets brands containing Gore-Tex—from Rukka, Marmot, The North Face, Burton and L.L. Bean to Adidas, Under Armour, and New Balance—on its own website (www.gore-tex.com). As a result, consumers around the world have learned to look for the familiar Gore-Tex brand label, and both Gore and its partner brands win.[30]

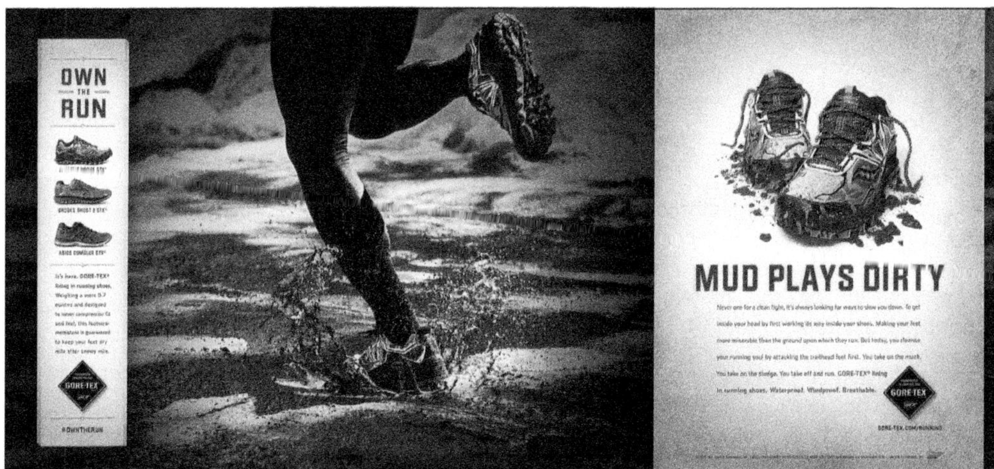

>> Derived demand: To increase demand for Gore-Tex fabrics, Gore markets directly buyers of the outdoor and athletic apparel brands made using its products and technologies. Both Gore and its partner brands win. For example, "This ad encourages runners to 'take on the muck, . . .take on the sludge, . . .take off and run,' thanks to Gore-Tex technology in their running shoes."

Courtesy: Gore-Tex, Shine United, Eric Cook (art director), James Breen (copywriter), John Krull (creative director), Michael Kriefski (executive creative director), Mike Tittle (photographer), and Scott Lanza (photographer).

Nature of the Buying Unit

Compared with consumer purchases, a business purchase usually involves *more decision participants* and a *more professional purchasing effort*. Often, business buying is done by trained purchasing agents who spend their working lives learning how to buy better. The more complex the purchase, the more likely it is that several people will participate in the decision-making process. Buying committees composed of technical experts and top management are common in the buying of major goods. Beyond this, B-to-B marketers now face a new breed of higher-level, better-trained supply managers. Therefore, companies must have well-trained marketers and salespeople to deal with these well-trained buyers.

Types of Decisions and the Decision Process

Business buyers usually face *more complex* buying decisions than do consumer buyers. Business purchases often involve large sums of money, complex technical and economic considerations, and interactions among people at many levels of the buyer's organization. The business buying process also tends to be *longer* and *more formalized*. Large business purchases usually call for detailed product specifications, written purchase orders, careful supplier searches, and formal approval.

Finally, in the business buying process, the buyer and seller are often much *more dependent* on each other. B-to-B marketers may roll up their sleeves and work closely with customers during all stages of the buying process—from helping customers define problems to finding solutions to supporting after-sale operation. In the short run, sales go to suppliers who meet buyers' immediate product and service needs. In the long run, however, business-to-business marketers keep customers by meeting current needs *and* by partnering with them to help solve their problems. >> For example, consider agricultural and food giant Cargill's Cocoa & Chocolate division:[31]

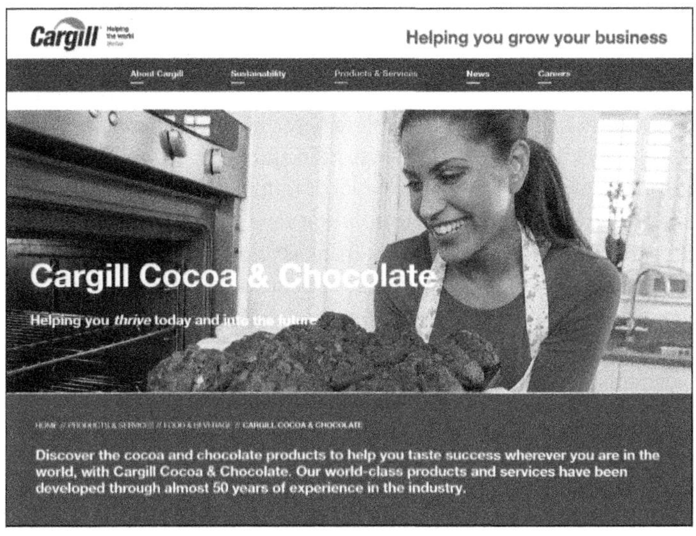

>> The business buyer decision process: Cargill's Cocoa & Chocolate division does more than sell its products to manufacturers. It partners closely with customers to help them use its products to serve their own customers better and more profitably.

Cargill

Cargill's Cocoa & Chocolate division sells cocoa and chocolate products to business customers around the world, including giants such as Mars and Mondelēz. But its success lies in doing much more than just selling its products *to* such major customers. Instead, Cargill partners closely them, applying its deep chocolate expertise and broad food knowledge to help customers *use* its products to serve their own customers better and more profitably. For example, Cargill's researchers keep customers up-to-date on the latest global consumer food trends. Its research and development teams give customers personalized product development support. And its technical services specialists provide help in resolving customer ingredient and applications challenges. "Whether you need laboratory or pilot work on finished products or help with production start-up, sustainability solutions, price services, or raw material price movement" says the company, "Cargill's applications experts can assist you—from developing new end-product recipes, achieving better pricing for your products, or getting to market more quickly." Thus, more than just selling cocoa and chocolate, Cargill sells customer success in using those products. Its goal is to "[apply] our deep chocolate expertise and broad food knowledge. . . to provide you with more opportunities to grow your business across a wide range of cocoa and chocolate products and applications. . . helping you *thrive*, today and into the future."

As in Cargill's case, in recent years, relationships between most customers and suppliers have been changing from downright adversarial to close and chummy. In fact, many customer companies are now practicing **supplier development**, systematically developing networks of supplier-partners to ensure a dependable supply of the products and materials that they use in making their own products or reselling to others. For example, Walmart doesn't have a "Purchasing Department"; it has a "Supplier Development Department." The giant retailer knows that it can't just rely on spot suppliers who might be available when needed. Instead, Walmart manages a huge network of supplier-partners that help provide the hundreds of billions of dollars of goods that it sells to its customers each year.

Supplier development
Systematic development of networks of supplier-partners to ensure an appropriate and dependable supply of products and materials for use in making products or reselling them to others.

Author Comment
Business buying decisions can range from routine to incredibly complex, involving only a few or very many decision makers and buying influences.

Business Buyer Behavior

At the most basic level, marketers want to know how business buyers will respond to various marketing stimuli. >> **Figure 5.6** shows a model of business buyer behavior. In this model, marketing and other stimuli affect the buying organization and produce certain buyer responses. To design good marketing strategies, marketers must understand what happens within the organization to turn stimuli into purchase responses.

Within the organization, buying activity consists of two major parts: the *buying center,* composed of all the people involved in the buying decision; and the *buying decision process.* The model shows that the buying center and the buying decision process are influenced by internal organizational, interpersonal, and individual factors as well as external environmental factors.

The model in Figure 5.6 suggests four questions about business buyer behavior: What buying decisions do business buyers make? Who participates in the business buying process? What are the major influences on buyers? How do business buyers make their buying decisions?

Major Types of Buying Situations

Straight rebuy
A business buying situation in which the buyer routinely reorders something without modifications.

Modified rebuy
A business buying situation in which the buyer wants to modify product specifications, prices, terms, or suppliers.

New task
A business buying situation in which the buyer purchases a product or service for the first time.

Systems selling (or solutions selling)
Buying a packaged solution to a problem from a single seller, thus avoiding all the separate decisions involved in a complex buying situation.

There are three major types of buying situations.[32] In a **straight rebuy**, the buyer reorders something without any modifications. It is usually handled on a routine basis by the purchasing department. To keep the business, "in" suppliers try to maintain customer engagement and product and service quality. "Out" suppliers try to find new ways to add value or exploit dissatisfaction so that the buyer will consider them.

In a **modified rebuy**, the buyer wants to modify product specifications, prices, terms, or suppliers. The "in" suppliers may become nervous and feel pressured to put their best foot forward to protect an account. "Out" suppliers may see the modified rebuy situation as an opportunity to make a better offer and gain new business.

A company buying a product or service for the first time faces a **new task** situation. In such cases, the greater the cost or risk, the larger the number of decision participants and the greater the company's efforts to collect information. The new task situation is the marketer's greatest opportunity and challenge. The marketer not only tries to reach as many key buying influences as possible but also provides help and information. The buyer makes the fewest decisions in the straight rebuy and the most in the new task decision.

Many business buyers prefer to buy a complete solution to a problem from a single seller rather than buying separate products and services from several suppliers and putting them together. The sale often goes to the firm that engages business customers deeply and provides the most complete *system* for meeting a customer's needs and solving its problems. Such **systems selling** (or **solutions selling**) is often a key business marketing strategy for winning and holding accounts. Consider IBM and its customer Six Flags Entertainment Corporation:[33]

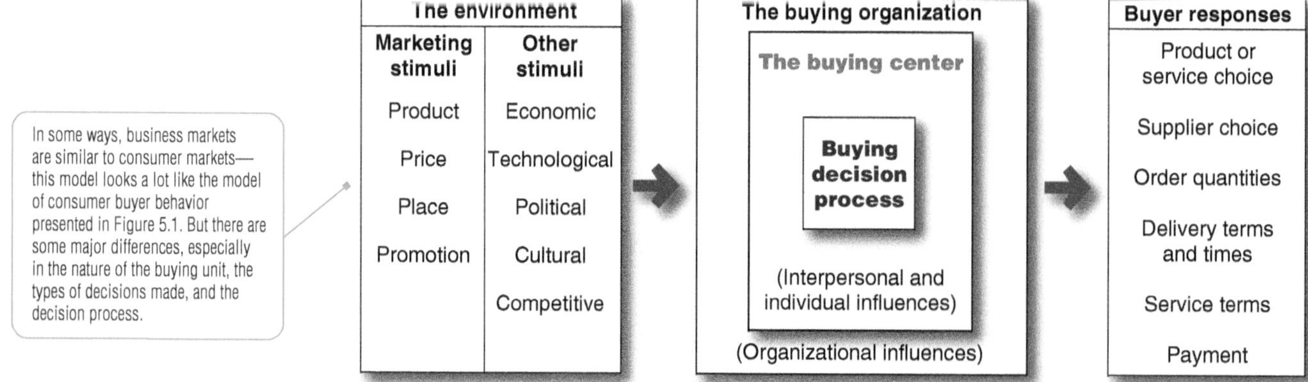

>> **Figure 5.6 A Model of Business Buyer Behavior**

>> **Solutions selling: Delivering a fun and safe experience for Six Flags guests requires careful and effective management of thousands of park assets across its 19 regional theme parks. IBM works hand in hand with Six Flags to provide not just software but a complete solution.**

Matthew Imaging/WireImage/Getty Images

Six Flags operates 19 regional theme parks across North America featuring exciting rides and water attractions, world-class roller coasters, and special shows and concerts. >> To deliver a fun and safe experience for guests, Six Flags must carefully and effectively manage thousands of park assets—from rides and equipment to buildings and other facilities. Six Flags needed a tool for managing all those assets efficiently and effectively across its far-flung collection of parks. So it turned to IBM, which has software—called Maximo Asset Management software—that handles that very problem well.

But IBM didn't just hand the software over to Six Flags with best wishes for happy implementation. Instead, IBM's Maximo Professional Services group combined the software with an entire set of services designed to get and keep the software up and running. IBM worked hand in hand with Six Flags to customize the application and strategically implement and run it across Six Flags's far-flung facilities, along with on-site immersion training and planning workshops. Thus, IBM isn't just selling the software; it's selling a complete solution to Six Flags's complex asset management problem.

Participants in the Business Buying Process

Buying center
All the individuals and units that play a role in the purchase decision-making process.

Who does the buying of the trillions of dollars' worth of goods and services needed by business organizations? The decision-making unit of a buying organization is called its **buying center**. It consists of all the individuals and units that play a role in the business purchase decision-making process. This group includes the actual users of the product or service, those who make the buying decision, those who influence the buying decision, those who do the actual buying, and those who control buying information.

The buying center is not a fixed and formally identified unit within the buying organization. It is a set of buying roles assumed by different people for different purchases. Within the organization, the size and makeup of the buying center will vary for different products and for different buying situations. For some routine purchases, one person—say, a purchasing agent—may assume all the buying center roles and serve as the only person involved in the buying decision. For more complex purchases in large companies, the buying center may include 20, 30, or even more people from different levels and departments in the organization.

The buying center concept presents a major marketing challenge. The business marketer must learn who participates in the decision, each participant's relative influence, and what evaluation criteria each decision participant uses. This can be difficult.

The buying center usually includes some obvious participants who are involved formally in the buying decision. For example, the decision to buy a corporate jet will probably involve the company's CEO, the chief pilot, a purchasing agent, some legal staff, a member of top management, and others formally charged with the buying decision. It may also involve less obvious, informal participants, some of whom may actually make or strongly affect the buying decision. Sometimes, even the people in the buying center are not aware of all the buying participants. For example, the decision about which corporate jet to buy may actually be made by a corporate board member who has an interest in flying and who knows a lot about airplanes. This board member may work behind the scenes to sway the decision. Many business buying decisions result from the complex interactions of ever-changing buying center participants.

Major Influences on Business Buyers

Business buyers are subject to many influences when they make their buying decisions. Some marketers assume that the major influences are economic. They think buyers will favor the supplier who offers the lowest price or the best product or the most service. They

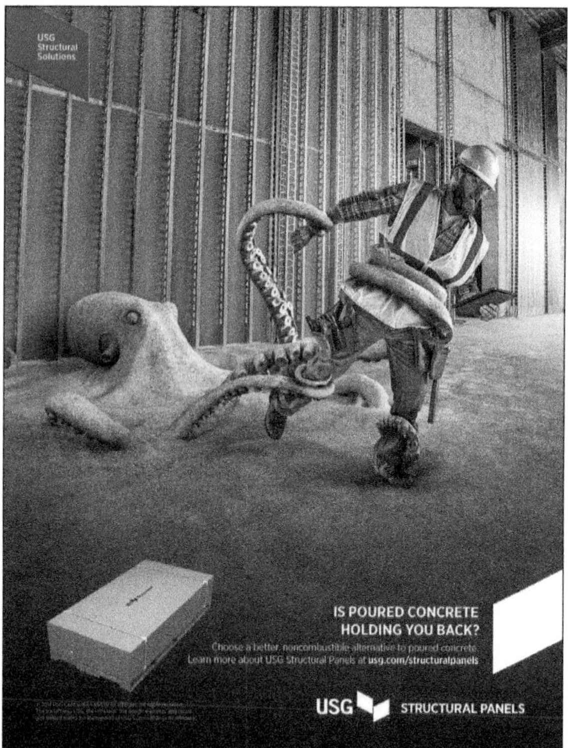

>> Ads like this one for USG concrete structural panels suggest that emotions play a role even in heavily performance-based business-to-business decision making.
USG

concentrate on offering strong economic benefits to buyers. Such economic factors are very important to most buyers, especially in a tough economy. However, business buyers actually respond to both economic and personal factors. Far from being cold, calculating, and impersonal, business buyers are human and social as well. They react to both reason and emotion.

Today, most B-to-B marketers recognize that emotion plays an important role in business buying decisions. Consider this example:[34]

>> USG Corporation is a leading manufacturer of building materials for the construction and remodeling industries. Given its construction contractor, architect, and builder audience, you might expect USG's B-to-B ads to focus heavily on detailing performance features and benefits, such as strength, impact resistance, ease of installation, and costs. USG does promote these benefits. However, the imagery in its B-to-B ads packs a decided emotional wallop. For example, overall sales and marketing for USG's concrete structural panels stresses durability, light weight, and ease of installation versus traditional poured concrete, which is comparatively heavy, slow, and expensive. But rather than state these benefits directly, a USG ad for its structural panels features a dramatic image of a structural engineer caught hand and foot in the grasp of the tentacles of a concrete octopus emerging from a poured concrete floor. The ad asks, "Is poured concrete holding you back?" and then refers customers to USG's website for detailed performance features and comparisons. This and other USG ad recognize that emotions can play a role even in heavily performance-based decisions.

>> **Figure 5.7** lists various groups of influences on business buyers—environmental, organizational, interpersonal, and individual. Business buyers are heavily influenced by factors in the current and expected *economic environment*, such as the level of primary demand, the economic outlook, and the cost of money. Another environmental factor is the *supply* of key materials. Business buyers also are affected by *technological, political,* and *competitive* developments in the environment. Finally, *culture and customs* can strongly influence business buyer reactions to the marketer's behavior and strategies, especially in the international marketing environment. The business buyer must watch these factors, determine how they will affect the buyer, and try to turn these challenges into opportunities.

Organizational factors are also important. Each buying organization has its own objectives, strategies, structure, systems, and procedures, and the business marketer must understand these factors well. Questions such as these arise: How many people are involved in the buying decision? Who are they? What are their evaluative criteria? What are the company's policies and limits on its buyers?

The buying center usually includes many participants who influence each other, so *interpersonal factors* also influence the business buying process. However, it is often difficult to assess such interpersonal factors and group dynamics. Buying center participants do not wear tags that label them as "key decision maker" or "not influential."

Like consumer buying decisions in Figure 5.2, business buying decisions are affected by an incredibly complex combination of environmental, interpersonal, and individual influences, but with an extra layer of organizational factors thrown into the mix.

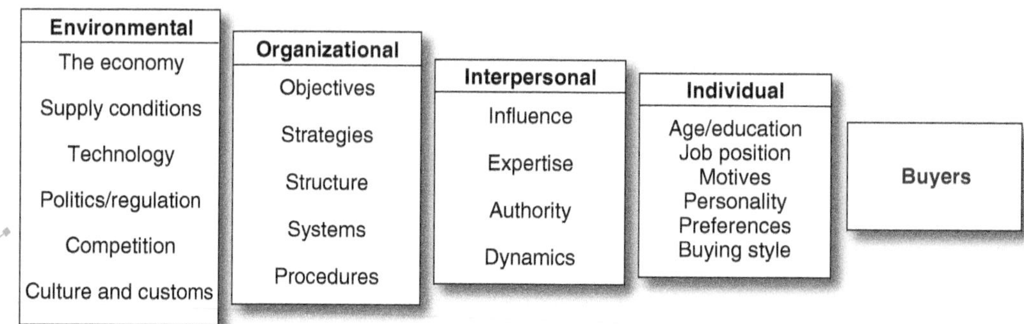

>> Figure 5.7 Major Influences on Business Buyer Behavior

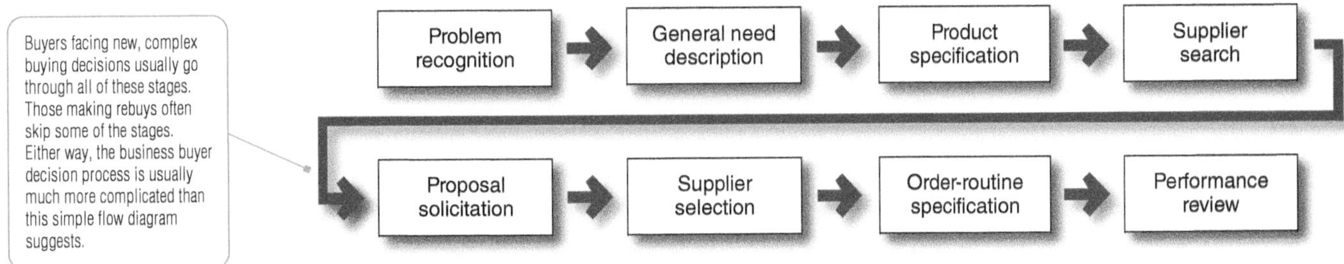

>> Figure 5.8 Stages of the Business Buyer Decision Process

Nor do buying center participants with the highest rank always have the most influence. Participants may influence the buying decision because they control rewards and punishments, are well liked, have special expertise, or have a special relationship with other important participants. Interpersonal factors are often very subtle. Whenever possible, business marketers must try to understand these factors and design strategies that take them into account.

Each participant in the business buying decision process brings in personal motives, perceptions, and preferences. These *individual factors* are affected by personal characteristics such as age, income, education, professional identification, personality, and attitudes toward risk. Also, buyers have different buying styles. Some may be technical types who make in-depth analyses of competitive proposals before choosing a supplier. Other buyers may be intuitive negotiators who are adept at pitting the sellers against one another for the best deal.

The Business Buyer Decision Process

OBJECTIVE 5-5 List and define the steps in the business buying decision process.

>> Figure 5.8 lists the eight stages of the business buyer decision process.[35] Buyers who face a new task buying situation usually go through all stages of the buying process. Buyers making modified or straight rebuys, in contrast, may skip some of the stages. We will examine these steps for the typical new task buying situation.

Problem Recognition

The buying process begins when someone in the company recognizes a problem or need that can be met by acquiring a specific product or service. Problem recognition can result from internal or external stimuli. Internally, the company may decide to launch a new product that requires new production equipment and materials. Or a machine may break down and need new parts. Perhaps a purchasing manager is unhappy with a current supplier's product quality, service, or prices. Externally, the buyer may get some new ideas at a trade show, see an ad or website, or receive a call from a salesperson who offers a better product or a lower price.

In fact, business marketers often alert customers to potential problems and then show how their products and services provide solutions. **>>** For example, consulting firm Accenture's award-winning "High Performance. Delivered." B-to-B ads do this. One Accenture ad points to the urgent need for a business to get up to speed with digital technology. "Accenture Digital can help you attract more customers." the ad states, showing moths drawn to a brightly lit smartphone screen. Accenture's solution: "Our industry expertise, coupled with our integrated capabilities across interactive, analytics, and mobility, can help you take advantage of the opportunity to

>> Problem recognition: This Accenture ad alerts customers to the problem of getting up to speed with digital technology and then suggests a solution. It promises "High Performance. Delivered."

Accenture

innovate and compete." Other ads in the series tell success stories of how Accenture has helped client companies recognize and solve a variety of other problems.[36]

General Need Description

Having recognized a need, the buyer next prepares a general need description that describes the characteristics and quantity of the needed item. For standard items, this process presents few problems. For complex items, however, the buyer may need to work with others—-engineers, users, consultants—to define the item. The team may want to rank the importance of reliability, durability, price, and other attributes desired in the item. In this phase, the alert business marketer can help the buyers define their needs and provide information about the value of different product characteristics.

Product Specification

The buying organization next develops the item's technical product specifications, often with the help of a value analysis engineering team. *Product value analysis* is an approach to cost reduction in which components are studied carefully to determine if they can be redesigned, standardized, or made by less costly methods of production. The team decides on the best product characteristics and specifies them accordingly. Sellers, too, can use value analysis as a tool to help secure a new account. By showing buyers a better way to make an object, outside sellers can turn straight rebuy situations into new task situations that give them a chance to obtain new business.

Supplier Search

The buyer now conducts a supplier search to find the best vendors. The buyer can compile a small list of qualified suppliers by reviewing trade directories, doing online searches, or phoning other companies for recommendations. Today, more and more companies are turning to the internet to find suppliers. For marketers, this has leveled the playing field—the internet gives smaller suppliers many of the same advantages as larger competitors. The newer the buying task and the more complex and costly the item, the greater the amount of time the buyer will spend searching for suppliers. The supplier's task is to get listed in major directories and build a good reputation in the marketplace. Salespeople should watch for companies in the process of searching for suppliers and make certain that their firm is considered.

Proposal Solicitation

In the proposal solicitation stage of the business buying process, the buyer invites qualified suppliers to submit proposals. In response, some suppliers will refer the buyer to their website or promotional materials or send a salesperson to call on the prospect. However, when the item is complex or expensive, the buyer will usually require a detailed written proposal or formal presentation from each potential supplier.

Business marketers must be skilled in researching, writing, and presenting proposals in response to buyer proposal solicitations. Proposals should be marketing documents, not just technical documents. Presentations should inspire confidence and should make the marketer's company stand out from the competition.

Supplier Selection

The members of the buying center now review the proposals and select a supplier or suppliers. During supplier selection, the buying center often will draw up a list of the desired supplier attributes and their relative importance. Such attributes include product and service quality, reputation, on-time delivery, ethical corporate behavior, honest communication, and competitive prices. The members of the buying center will rate suppliers against these attributes and identify the best suppliers.

Buyers may attempt to negotiate with preferred suppliers for better prices and terms before making the final selections. In the end, they may select a single supplier or a few suppliers. Many buyers prefer multiple sources of supplies to avoid being totally dependent on one supplier and to allow comparisons of prices and performance of several suppliers over time. Today's supplier development managers want to develop a full network of supplier-partners that can help the company bring more value to its customers.

Order-Routine Specification

The buyer now prepares an order routine specification. It includes the final order with the chosen supplier or suppliers and lists items such as technical specifications, quantity needed, expected delivery time, return policies, and warranties. In the case of maintenance, repair, and operating items, buyers may use blanket contracts rather than periodic purchase orders. A blanket contract creates a long-term relationship in which the supplier promises to resupply the buyer as needed at agreed prices for a set time period.

Many large buyers now practice *vendor-managed inventory*, in which they turn over ordering and inventory responsibilities to their suppliers. Under such systems, buyers share sales and inventory information directly with key suppliers. The suppliers then monitor inventories and replenish stock automatically as needed. For example, most major suppliers to large retailers such as Walmart, Target, Home Depot, and Lowe's assume vendor-managed inventory responsibilities.

Performance Review

In this stage, the buyer reviews supplier performance. The buyer may contact users and ask them to rate their satisfaction. The performance review may lead the buyer to continue, modify, or drop the arrangement. The seller's job is to monitor the same factors used by the buyer to make sure that the seller is giving the expected satisfaction.

In all, the eight-stage buying-process model shown in Figure 5.8 provides a simple view of the business buying as it might occur in a new task buying situation. However, the actual process is usually much more complex. In the modified rebuy or straight rebuy situation, some of these stages would be compressed or bypassed. Each organization buys in its own way, and each buying situation has unique requirements.

Different buying center participants may be involved at various stages of the process. Although certain buying-process steps usually do occur, buyers do not always follow them in the same order, and they may add other steps. Often, buyers will repeat certain stages of the process. Finally, a customer relationship might involve many different types of purchases ongoing at a given time, all in different stages of the buying process. The seller must manage the total *customer relationship*, not just individual purchases.

Author Comment
As in consumer marketing, in recent years, digital technologies and online, mobile, and social media marketing have exploded onto the B-to-B marketing scene.

Engaging Business Buyers with Digital and Social Marketing

OBJECTIVE 5-6 Discuss how online, mobile, and social media have changed business-to-business marketing.

As in every other area of marketing, the explosion of information technologies and online, mobile, and social media has changed the face of the B-to-B buying and marketing process. In the following sections, we discuss two important technology advancements: *e-procurement and online purchasing* and *B-to-B digital and social media marketing.*

E-procurement and Online Purchasing

E-procurement
Purchasing through electronic connections between buyers and sellers—usually online.

Advances in information technology have dramatically affected the face of the B-to-B buying process. » Online purchasing, often called **e-procurement**, has grown rapidly in recent years. Virtually unknown two decades ago, online purchasing is standard procedure for most companies today. In turn, business marketers can connect with

Online procurement is standard procedure for most companies today, letting business marketers connect with customers online to sell products and services, provide customer support services, and maintain ongoing customer relationships.

icetray/123RF

customers online to share marketing information, sell products and services, provide customer support services, and maintain ongoing customer relationships.

Companies can do e-procurement in any of several ways. They can conduct *reverse auctions*, in which they put their purchasing requests online and invite suppliers to bid for the business. Or they can engage in online *trading exchanges*, through which companies work collectively to facilitate the trading process. Companies also can conduct e-procurement by setting up their own *company buying sites*. For example, GE operates a company trading site on which it posts its buying needs and invites bids, negotiates terms, and places orders. Or companies can create *extranet links* with key suppliers. For instance, they can create direct procurement accounts with suppliers such as Dell or Staples through which company buyers can purchase equipment, materials, and supplies directly. Staples operates a business-to-business procurement division called Staples Business Advantage, which serves the office supplies and services buying needs of businesses of any size, from 10 employees to the *Fortune* 1000.

Business-to-business e-procurement yields many benefits. First, it shaves transaction costs and results in more efficient purchasing for both buyers and suppliers. E-procurement reduces the time between order and delivery. And an online-powered purchasing program eliminates the paperwork associated with traditional requisition and ordering procedures and helps an organization keep better track of all purchases. Finally, beyond the cost and time savings, e-procurement frees purchasing people from a lot of drudgery and paperwork. Instead, they can focus on more-strategic issues, such as finding better supply sources and working with suppliers to reduce costs and develop new products.

The rapidly expanding use of e-procurement, however, also presents some problems. For example, although the internet makes it possible for suppliers and customers to share business data and even collaborate on product design, it can also erode decades-old customer–supplier relationships. Many buyers now use the power of the internet to pit suppliers against one another and search out better deals, products, and turnaround times on a purchase-by-purchase basis.

Business-to-Business Digital and Social Media Marketing

In response to business customers' rapid shift toward online buying, today's B-to-B marketers are now using a wide range of digital and social media marketing approaches—from websites, blogs, mobile apps, e-newsletters, and proprietary online networks to mainstream social media such as Facebook, LinkedIn, YouTube, Google+, and Twitter—to engage business customers and manage customer relationships anywhere, anytime.

B-to-B digital and social media marketing isn't just growing, it's exploding. Digital and social media marketing have rapidly become the new space for engaging business customers. Consider Maersk Line, the world's leading container shipping and transport company, serving business customers through 374 offices in 160 countries:[37]

> You might not expect much by way of new-age marketing from an old-line container shipping company, but think again. Maersk Line is one of the most forward-looking and accomplished B-to-B digital and social media marketers in any industry. Maersk Line has sailed full steam ahead into the social media waters with eight global accounts on primary social media networks including Facebook, LinkedIn, Twitter, and YouTube. Maersk Line has more than 1.1 million Facebook followers with an average engagement of 7 percent per post, making Facebook a platform for engaging a broad audience of customers and other stakeholders interested in the brand. On Instagram, the company shares customer and employee images and stories to help visualize the brand. On YouTube it posts informational and educational videos detailing Maersk Line's activities, services, and people. Maersk Line's Twitter feed presents the latest news and events, creating conversation and buzz with and among its more than 133,000 Twitter followers. The company's LinkedIn account, with more than 147,500 followers, lets Maersk Line engage customers, opinion leaders, and industry influencers,

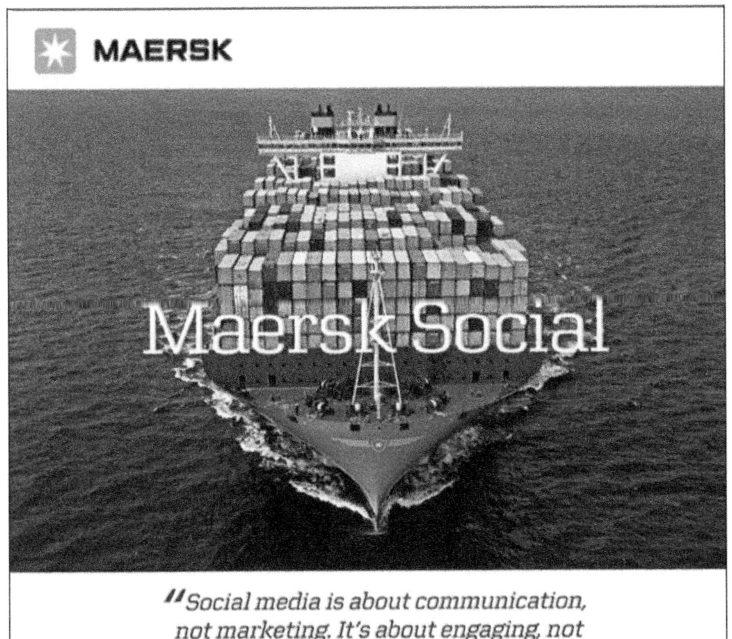

MAERSK
Maersk Social
"Social media is about communication, not marketing. It's about engaging, not pushing. And social media is definitely not just about the media side.

>> **Container shipping giant Maersk Line engages business customers through a boatload of digital and social media. "The goal is to get closer to our customers."**

A.P. Møller-Mærsk A/S

who share information and discuss industry challenges and opportunities with shipping and logistics experts. Why all this social media? "The goal is to use social media to get closer to our customers," says Maersk Line.

Compared with traditional media and sales approaches, digital and social media can create greater customer engagement and interaction. B-to-B marketers know that they aren't really targeting *businesses*, they are targeting *individuals* in those businesses who affect buying decisions. And today's business buyers are always connected via their digital devices—whether it's computers, tablets, or smartphones.

Digital and social media play an important role in engaging these always-connected business buyers in a way that personal selling alone cannot. Instead of the old model of sales reps calling on business customers at work or maybe meeting up with them at trade shows, the new digital approaches facilitate anytime, anywhere connections between a wide range of people in the selling and customer organizations. It gives both sellers and buyers more control of and access to important information. B-to-B marketing has always been social network marketing, but today's digital environment offers an exciting array of new networking tools and applications.

Some B-to-B companies mistakenly assume that today's digital and social media are useful primarily to consumer products and services companies. But no matter what the industry, digital platforms can be powerful tools for engaging customers and other important publics. For example, industrial powerhouse GE uses a wide array of digital and social media, not just to engage and support its business customers directly but also to tell the compelling GE brand story more broadly and to keep the company relevant, contemporary, and accessible (see Marketing at Work 5.2).

MARKETING AT WORK 5.2

GE: A Model for B-to-B Digital and Social Media Marketing

Few brands are more familiar than GE. For more than 130 years, we've packed our homes with GE products—from good ol' GE light bulbs to refrigerators, ranges, clothes washers and dryers, microwave ovens, and hundreds of other products bearing the familiar GE script logo. But here's a fact that might startle you. In recent years, the company has sold off almost all its consumer product businesses. Less than a meager 2 percent of GE's $120 billion in annual sales now come from consumer products.

Almost all of GE's sales come from industrial products and services across a wide range of energy, transportation, and health-care industries. Far beyond light bulbs, GE sells everything from jet aircraft engines, giant wind turbines, and diesel locomotives to water processing systems and high-tech medical imaging equipment. GE bills itself as "The Digital Industrial Company," one that's on a mission to "invent the next industrial era, to build, move, power, and cure the world."

Jet engines? Diesel locomotives? Power turbines? Yawn. To many people, "industrial" translates to "dull." It's hardy the fodder for stimulating digital and social media content. But GE doesn't see it that way. GE has a brand story to tell—a story of big, bad machines and innovative technologies that are changing the world and how we live in it. And it sees digital as an ideal platform for sharing that story. As a result, GE has become a model for B-to-B use of digital and social media.

At a core level, GE covers the digital basics well through a wide variety of platforms that inform and engage business customers directly, connect them with GE salespeople, and promote customer purchasing and relationships. For example, GE's various divisions—from GE Aviation to GE Healthcare and GE Energy—offer dozens of industry-specific websites, containing thousands of individual site areas and tens of thousands of pages that provide B-to-B customers with

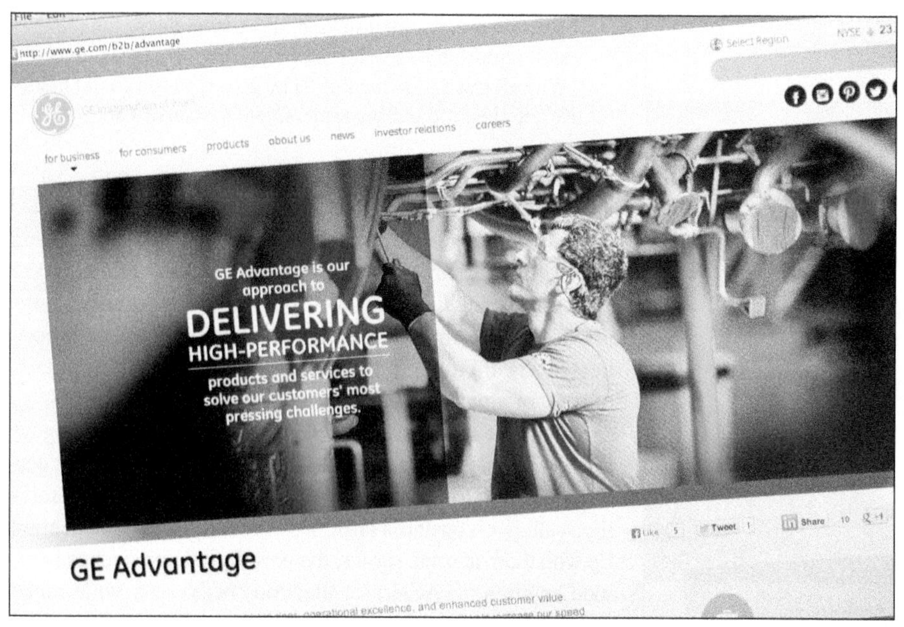

>> Through its inspired use of digital and social media, industrial powerhouse GE engages customers and keeps the GE brand relevant, contemporary, and accessible to important publics in today's digital industrial era.

GE

purchasing solutions, product overviews, detailed technical information, online videos and webinars, live chats, and real-time customer support.

GE also helps its sales force engage business customers more deeply through a comprehensive presence in major social media such as Facebook, Twitter, LinkedIn, Google+, Salesforce.com, and even Instagram and Pinterest. At its core, GE believes that business is social.

But GE's most inspired use of digital and social media goes well beyond the basics of engaging and supporting customers directly. GE also uses digital platforms to reach out to other important publics. "The more people know GE, the more they like GE," says the company's director of global media. "So our [digital] content strategy is about uncovering and telling great stories about innovation, technology, big data, developing healthcare, and so on." The goal is to make the GE brand relevant, contemporary, and accessible, a task ideally suited to digital and social media. "No one remembers product specs and features," says GE's CMO. But "compelling stories bring a brand to life—they make us relevant, poignant, vibrant, droll, and hopefully memorable."

To that end, over the past several years, GE has unleashed a remarkable array of digital content that connects the brand with consumers and positions the 130-year-old company as a youthful, contemporary technology leader in the new digital industrial era. For example, one of GE's first and most successful social media campaigns was #sixsecondscience, a program launched on Twitter's now-defunct Vine asking people to share their favorite science experiments in video clips of six seconds or less. The campaign drew in 400 videos in a week, including demonstrations of everything from how to make a volcano using a pile of sand, vinegar, and baking soda to a homemade Tesla coil in action. The Vine campaign, which now resides on Tumblr, won awards and accolades. More important, it got people to spend time with the GE brand.

You'll find GE actively engaged on all the major social media. For example, GE's Instagram, Snapchat, Facebook, Pinterest, YouTube, and other social media sites introduce tech enthusiasts to the raw beauty of the company's innovative industrial products and technologies. As an example, when GE recently rigged an active Nicaraguan volcano with sensors that provide real-time data about atmospheric pressure, gravity, and gaseous activity for an early warning detection system that would help predict when the volcano will erupt, it used social media to capture the process. It cataloged the journey to the center of the volcano on Snapchat and then turned it into a video series on Instagram, all while conducting live Q&A sessions on Facebook.

According to the CMO, GE's social media efforts show "the majesty and scale of our big machines. It's GE at our badass best." In fact, the very first board at the GE Pinterest site is "Badass Machines." Others include "From the Factory Floor," "Minds and Machines," and "Brilliant Machines."

GE also publishes an innovative daily online B-to-B blog, called GE Reports, which features science fiction-like stories on topics such as moon power, digital pathology, and 3D printing done by hand. The blog includes original content from various GE sources, including GE Garages—an initiative designed to reinvigorate innovation and manufacturing by providing a collaborative space where technologists, entrepreneurs, and everyday Americans can engage in hands-on experiences with 3D printers, computer-controlled milling machines, laser cutters, and injection molders. As with GE's other digital content, GE Reports offers easily digestible material that gets people excited about the future of technology and science while positioning GE as a company that is leading them into that future.

GE has also mastered the art of digital video content. An example is the company's award-winning "Childlike Imagination" campaign, a series of magical video ads that show the scope of GE's product lines through the eyes of an amazed young girl whose mom works at GE. "My mom? She makes underwater fans that are powered by the moon," declares the girl. "My mom makes airplane engines that can talk." Although these videos can be shown as ads on traditional TV, they drive substantial online traffic through GE's social media channels.

Thus, in its digital efforts, GE acts less like an advertiser and more like a brand content publisher—creating, curating, and shaping brand content and conversations in real time. "We don't sit around saying 'how are we going to be cool today?', because if you work here you think the stuff we do is pretty damn cool," jokes GE's CMO. "We think about who shares our passion and our interest in science, technology, and engineering and we go after that." Through diverse social media platforms, she says, "we try to find ways to bring it to life, to tell that story in fresh, unexpected, human, and relatable ways that don't diminish the fact that we're working on things like bringing electricity to a billion people around the world."

In all, few companies do digital and social media better than GE. "When it comes to innovative social media campaigns," says one analyst, GE is "often light-years ahead of most marketers," regardless of industry.

Sources: Charlotte Rogers, "GE's CMO on Redefining Marketing at the 'Pretty Damn Cool' Brand," *Marketing Week,* January 11, 2017, www.marketingweek.com/2017/01/11/general-electric-cmo-redefining-marketing/; Katie Richards, "GE's Chief Marketing Officer on Storytelling in the New Digital Industrial Era," *Adweek,* October 12, 2015, pp. 11–12; Bill Sobel, "GE's Linda Boff: Content Created to Help Is What Sells," *CMSWire,* September 24, 2015, www.cmswire.com/cms/customer-experience/ges-linda-boff-content-created-to-help-is-what-sells-027470.php; Robert Elder, "General Electric's Social Media Strategy Erupts," *Business Insider,* August 5, 2016, www.businessinsider.com/general-electrics-social-media-strategy-erupts-2016-8; Emily Copp, "Learn About GE's Winning Social Media Strategy—Direct from the CMO," *Hootsuite,* June 1, 2017, https://blog.hootsuite.com/hootcast-ge-linda-boff/; and www.youtube.com/watch?v=Co0qkWRqTdM, www.gereports.com, www.pinterest.com/generalelectric/, www.ge.com, and www.ge.com/investor-relations, accessed September 2018.

REVIEWING AND EXTENDING THE CONCEPTS

CHAPTER REVIEW AND KEY TERMS

Objectives Review

This chapter is the last of three chapters that address understanding the marketplace and consumers. Here, we've looked closely at *consumer* and *business buyer behavior.* The American consumer market consists of more than 327 million people who consume more than $12 trillion worth of goods and services each year, making it one of the most attractive consumer markets in the world. The business market involves even more dollars and items than the consumer market. Understanding buyer behavior is one of the biggest challenges marketers face.

OBJECTIVE 5-1 Understand the consumer market and the major factors that influence consumer buyer behavior. (pp 134–148)

The *consumer market* consists of all the individuals and households that buy or acquire goods and services for personal consumption. A simple model of consumer behavior suggests that marketing stimuli and other major forces enter the consumer's "black box." This black box has two parts: buyer characteristics and the buyer's decision process. Once in the black box, the inputs result in buyer responses, such as buying attitudes and preferences and purchase behavior.

Consumer buyer behavior is influenced by four key sets of buyer characteristics: cultural, social, personal, and psychological. Understanding these factors can help marketers to identify interested buyers and to shape products and appeals to serve consumer needs better. *Culture* is the most basic determinant of a person's wants and behavior. People in different cultural, subcultural, and social class groups have different product and brand preferences. *Social factors*—such as small group, social network, and family influences—strongly affect product and brand choices, as do *personal characteristics,* such as age, life stage, occupation, economic circumstances, lifestyle, and personality. Finally, consumer buying behavior is influenced by four major sets of *psychological factors*—motivation, perception, learning, and beliefs and attitudes. Each of these factors provides a different perspective for understanding the workings of the buyer's black box.

OBJECTIVE 5-2 Identify and discuss the stages in the buyer decision process. (pp 148–151)

When making a purchase, the buyer goes through a decision process consisting of need recognition, information search, evaluation of alternatives, purchase decision, and postpurchase behavior. During *need recognition,* the consumer recognizes a problem or need that could be satisfied by a product or service. Once the need is recognized, the consumer moves into the *information search* stage. With information in hand, the consumer proceeds to *alternative evaluation* and assesses brands in the choice set. From there, the consumer makes a *purchase decision* and actually buys the product. In the final stage of the buyer decision process, *postpurchase behavior,* the consumer takes action based on satisfaction or dissatisfaction. The marketer's job is to understand the buyer's behavior at each stage and the influences that are operating.

 **OBJECTIVE 5-3 Describe the adoption and diffusion process for new products. (pp 151–153)**

The product *adoption process* is made up of five stages: awareness, interest, evaluation, trial, and adoption. New product marketers must think about how to help consumers move through these stages. Regarding the *diffusion process* for new products, consumers respond at different rates, depending on consumer and product characteristics. Consumers may be innovators, early adopters, early mainstream, late mainstream, or lagging adopters. Each group may require different marketing approaches. Marketers often try to bring their new products to the attention of potential early adopters, especially those who are opinion leaders.

 **OBJECTIVE 5-4 Define the business market and identify the major factors that influence business buyer behavior. (pp 153–159)**

The *business market* is composed of all organizations that buy goods and services for use in the production of other products and services or for the purpose of reselling or renting them to others at a profit. As compared to consumer markets, business markets usually have fewer, larger buyers who are more geographically concentrated. Business demand is derived demand, and the business buying decision usually involves more, and more professional, buyers.

Business buyers make decisions that vary with the three types of *buying situations:* straight rebuys, modified rebuys, and new tasks. The decision-making unit of a buying organization—the *buying center*—can consist of many different people playing many different roles. The business marketer needs to know the following: Who are the major buying center participants? In what decisions do they exercise influence and to what degree? What evaluation criteria does each decision participant use? The business marketer also needs to understand the major environmental, organizational, interpersonal, and individual influences on the buying process.

 **OBJECTIVE 5-5 List and define the steps in the business buyer decision process. (pp 159–161)**

The *business buyer decision process* itself can be quite involved, with eight basic stages: problem recognition, general need description, product specification, supplier search, proposal solicitation, supplier selection, order-routine specification, and performance review. Buyers who face a new task buying situation usually go through all stages of the buying process. Buyers making modified or straight rebuys may skip some of the stages. Companies must manage the overall customer relationship, which often includes many different buying decisions in various stages of the buying decision process.

 **OBJECTIVE 5-6 Discuss how online, mobile, and social media have changed business-to-business marketing. (pp 161–165)**

Recent advances in information and digital technology have given birth to "e-procurement," by which business buyers are purchasing all kinds of products and services online. Business marketers are increasingly connecting with customers online and through digital, mobile, and social media to engage customers, share marketing information, sell products and services, provide customer support services, and maintain ongoing customer relationships. Instead of the old model of sales reps calling on business customers at work or maybe meeting up with them at trade shows, the new digital approaches facilitate anytime, anywhere connections between a wide range of people in the selling and customer organizations.

Key Terms

Objective 5-1
Consumer buyer behavior (p 134)
Consumer market (p 134)
Culture (p 136)
Subculture (p 136)
Total market strategy (p 138)
Social class (p 138)
Reference group (p 139)
Opinion leader (p 139)
Word-of-mouth influence (p 139)
Influencer marketing (p 139)
Online social networks (p 139)
Lifestyle (p 144)
Personality (p 144)
Motive (drive) (p 145)
Perception (p 146)
Learning (p 147)
Belief (p 147)
Attitude (p 147)

Objective 5-2
Cognitive dissonance (p 150)

Objective 5-3
New product (p 151)
Adoption process (p 151)

Objective 5-4
Business buyer behavior (p 153)
Business buying process (p 153)
Derived demand (p 154)
Supplier development (p 155)
Straight rebuy (p 156)
Modified rebuy (p 156)
New task (p 156)
Systems selling (solutions selling) (p 156)
Buying center (p 157)

Objective 5-6
E-procurement (p 161)

DISCUSSION AND CRITICAL THINKING

Discussion Questions

5-1. Discuss the characteristics affecting consumer behavior that marketers must be aware of in evaluating consumers' purchase decisions. (AACSB: Written and Oral Communication; Reflective Thinking)

5-2. What is a *total market strategy*, and why do marketers use this approach? Provide a recent example of a product or service that uses the total market strategy approach, and discuss the components that make it effective or ineffective. (AACSB: Written and Oral Communication; Diverse and Multicultural Work Environments; Reflective Thinking)

5-3. What four psychological factors influence a customer's purchase behavior? Name and explain each of the four factors. (AACSB: Written and Oral Communication; Diverse and Multicultural Work Environments; Reflective Thinking)

5-4. What are the stages in the adoption process? Describe how a student goes through the adoption process when choosing a college or university? (AACSB: Written and Oral Communication; Reflective Thinking)

5-5. Briefly discuss a business buyer's straight rebuy and modified rebuy strategies. What are the similarities and differences? When might it be beneficial to use one approach over the other? (AACSB: Written and Oral Communication; Reflective Thinking)

5-6. Describe the tools B-to-B marketers use to engage customers. What are the challenges with B-to-B social media marketing? (AACSB: Written and Oral Communication; Reflective Thinking)

Critical Thinking Exercises

5-7. Identify a new product that you have recently adopted into your daily lifestyle. Discuss each step of the consumer buyer decision process as it relates to the purchase decision with your adopted new product. Then review the stages in the adoption process. When purchasing your new product, did you follow the decision process stages outlined in the chapter? Why or why not? (AACSB: Written and Oral Communication; Reflective Thinking)

5-8. The characteristics of a new product affect its rate of adoption. Identify the five characteristics that influence the rate of adoption, and describe how each factor will influence the rate of adoption of the Apple Watch. (AACSB: Written and Oral Communication; Reflective Thinking)

5-9. Business buying can be a very involved process. Many companies employ procurement or purchasing experts dedicated to managing the firm's buying process. Visit www.glassdoor.com/Salaries and www.indeed.com/salary to conduct a search of the salary ranges for "procurement specialists," "procurement manager," or similar positions in purchasing. Present your findings. Can e-procurement help to streamline the buying process? Might it eventually replace employees in these careers? Discuss whether it is possible for all buying functions to be performed through e-procurement. (AACSB: Written and Oral Communication; Reflective Thinking; Information Technology)

MINICASES AND APPLICATIONS

Online, Mobile, and Social Media Marketing E-procurement and Mobile Procurement

Gone are the days of tedious, paper-laden, labor-intensive B-to-B procurement duties. E-procurement is changing the way buyers and sellers do business, specifically via mobile procurement that offers cloud-based platforms that reduce the search, order, and approval cycle. Most large companies have adopted some form of e-procurement. A recent study found that almost 70 percent of companies utilize some form of e-procurement, mobile procurement, or supply chain management applications. A leading industry platform, Coupa, provides a suite of cloud-based applications for finance, including accounts payable, sourcing, procurement, and expense management that allows customers full functionality from their mobile devices. Employees now enjoy the flexibility and time savings of viewing, approving, or denying requisitions, purchase orders, and invoices. One of Coupa's large retail clients claimed a reduction from 10 days to only 5 hours in its requisition-approval-process cycle by implementing Coupa's mobile procurement platform. Talk about savings! Visit www.coupa.com/software/procurement/to learn more about how this company is revolutionizing the e-procurement and mobile procurement environments.

5-10. Discuss the advantages of e-procurement to both buyers and sellers. What are the disadvantages? (AACSB: Written and Oral Communication; Reflective Thinking)

5-11. Research mobile procurement, and discuss the roles in the buying center that are impacted most by this technology. (AACSB: Written and Oral Communication; Reflective Thinking)

Marketing Ethics Ultimate Water

Water is water, right? Not so! Beverly Hills 90H20 claims to be designed "by a world-class team of experts, including a water sommelier." The winner of the World's Best Water Award, this water is sourced in the California mountains. At $72 for a case of 24 bottles, this is not your everyday drinking water. The 7.5 alkalinity "silky" water is loaded with minerals and electrolytes. It is available in fine restaurants, gourmet markets, and luxury hotels but sold only in California. Beverly Hills 90H20 isn't the only luxury water, and it's actually somewhat of a bargain. Fillico Beverly Hills (from Japan) costs $100 per bottle. That's without the gold or silver crown cap—double the price if you want that. Acqua di Cristallo Tributo a Modigliani gold-bottled water tops them all at $60,000 per bottle!

5-12. What buying factors most likely have the biggest influence on consumers who purchase luxury bottle water? (AACSB: Written and Oral Communication; Reflective Thinking)

5-13. Discuss the ethical issues surrounding the bottled water industry. (AACSB: Written and Oral Communication; Ethical Understanding and Reasoning)

Marketing by the Numbers Evaluating Alternatives

One way consumers can evaluate alternatives is to identify important attributes and assess how alternative choices perform on those attributes. Consider a consumer deciding among various fitness centers. Each attribute considered, such as price, class offerings, and so on, is given a score to reflect its level of importance to that consumer. In this example, the consumer gives each attribute a score of 1 to 10 to reflect how important that attribute is to him. Then the consumer evaluates each alternative on each attribute (that is, his belief about how an alternative performs on each attribute). For example, in the table below, location (with an importance score of 9) is the most important attribute for this consumer. This consumer believes that Peak Fitness performs best on this attribute because it is closest to his home, rating it 8 (higher ratings indicate better perceived performance), but he also believes this alternative to be the most expensive (belief rating of 3). He believes Revolution Fitness offers the best price, but it is located relatively far away. Class offerings are the least important attribute for this consumer.

A score can be calculated for each alternative by multiplying the importance rating for each attribute by the alternative's perceived rating on that attribute. These scores are then summed to determine the score for that brand. For example, $\text{Score}_{\text{Revolution}} = (5 \times 10) + (9 \times 5) + (6 \times 5) + (2 \times 6) = 50 + 45 + 30 + 12 = 137$. This consumer will calculate the scores for each brand in a similar way and select the brand with the highest score.

5-14. Calculate the scores for 24/7 Fitness and Peak Fitness. Which fitness center would this consumer likely choose? (AACSB: Written and Oral Communication; Analytical Thinking)

5-15. Which brand is this consumer least likely to select? Discuss two ways the marketer of this alternative can enhance consumer likelihood of joining its fitness club. (AACSB: Written and Oral Communication; Reflective Thinking; Analytic Thinking)

		Alternatives Considered		
Attributes Considered	**Importance of Each Attribute**	**Revolution Fitness Beliefs**	**24/7 Fitness Beliefs**	**Peak Fitness Beliefs**
Price	5	10	7	3
Location	9	5	6	8
Hours of operation	6	5	10	4
Class offerings	2	6	3	8

Video Case IMG Worldwide

To view this video case and its accompanying questions, please visit MyLab Marketing.

IMG Worldwide is the world's largest sports entertainment media company. In years past, IMG was all about professional golf and tennis marketing. But today, IMG handles sales and marketing activities for 70 to 80 colleges, making college sports marketing the company's highest-growth business. In short, IMG handles anything and everything that touches the college sports consum or short of actually playing games on the court or field.

Although you might think that all college sports fans are created equal, IMG finds that nothing could be further from the truth. How different fans consume sports and sports-related activities is affected by geographical, generational, and institutional factors. IMG focuses on comprehensively understanding the process that consumers go through to view or attend a sporting event. It then connects with consumers at each and every stage.

Company Cases 5 Spanx/1 Chick-fil-A/11 Bass Pro Shops

See Appendix 1 for cases appropriate for this chapter.

Case 5, Spanx: Changing the Way an Industry Thinks about Underwear. In order to revolutionize the world of women's undergarments, Spanx first had to change the way women think about shapewear.

Case 1, Chick-fil-A: Getting Better before Getting Bigger. Chick-fil-A has quietly become the largest chicken chain by knowing who its customers are and by understanding what drives them.

Case 11, Bass Pro Shops: Creating Nature's Theme Park for People Who Hate to Shop. Bass Pro Shops became the largest sporting goods retailer by making shopping enticing to everyone, even people who hate to shop.

Writing Assignments

5-16. Discuss how lifestyle influences consumers' buying behavior and how marketers measure lifestyle. (AACSB: Communication; Reflective Thinking)

5-17. Describe the characteristics of a new product that affect its rate of adoption. Which characteristics will affect how quickly the new digital and social media services described above will be accepted by consumers in the United States? (AACSB: Written and Oral Communication; Reflective Thinking)

Customer Value-Driven Marketing Strategy

Creating Value for Target Customers

Objectives Outline

OBJECTIVE 6-1 **Define the major steps in designing a customer value-driven marketing strategy: market segmentation, targeting, differentiation, and positioning.** See: Marketing Strategy (pp 172–173)

OBJECTIVE 6-2 **List and discuss the major bases for segmenting consumer and business markets.** See: Market Segmentation (pp 173–182)

OBJECTIVE 6-3 **Explain how companies identify attractive market segments and choose a market-targeting strategy.** See: Market Targeting (pp 182–189)

OBJECTIVE 6-4 **Discuss how companies differentiate and position their products for maximum competitive advantage.** See: Differentiation and Positioning (pp 189–197)

Previewing the Concepts

So far, you've learned what marketing is and about the importance of understanding consumers and the marketplace. We now delve deeper into marketing strategy and tactics. This chapter looks further into key customer value-driven marketing strategy decisions—dividing markets into meaningful customer groups (*segmentation*), choosing which customer groups to serve (*targeting*), creating market offerings that best serve targeted customers (*differentiation*), and positioning the offerings in the minds of consumers (*positioning*). The chapters that follow explore the tactical marketing tools—the four Ps—by which marketers bring these strategies to life.

To open our discussion of segmentation, targeting, differentiation, and positioning, let's look at Dunkin', which has expanded rapidly in recent years into a national powerhouse, on par with Starbucks. But Dunkin' is no Starbucks. In fact, it doesn't want to be. It targets a very different kind of customer with a very different value proposition. Grab yourself a cup of coffee and read on.

First Stop

Dunkin': Targeting the Average Joe

Some years back, Dunkin' paid dozens of faithful customers in cities around the country $100 a week to buy coffee at Starbucks instead. At the same time, the coffee chain paid Starbucks customers to make the opposite switch. When it later debriefed the two groups, Dunkin' says it found them so polarized that company researchers dubbed them "tribes," each of which loathed the very things that made the other tribe loyal to their coffee shop. Dunkin' fans viewed Starbucks as pretentious and trendy, whereas Starbucks loyalists saw Dunkin' as plain and unoriginal. "I don't get it," one Dunkin' regular told researchers after visiting Starbucks. "If I want to sit on a couch, I stay at home."

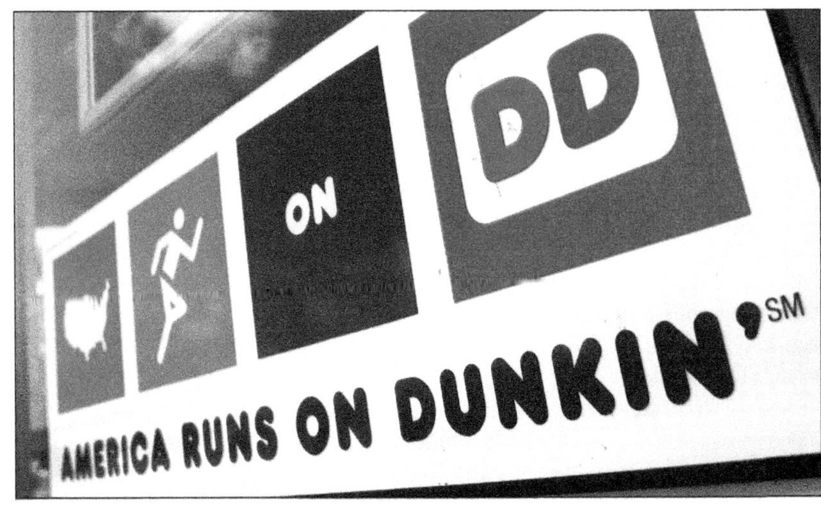

» Dunkin' targets everyday Joes who just don't get what Starbucks is all about. Its targeting and positioning are pretty well summed up in its long-running ad slogan "America Runs on Dunkin'."

Tim Boyle/Getty Images

Dunkin' has rapidly expanded into a national coffee powerhouse, on par with Starbucks, the nation's largest coffee chain. But the research confirmed a simple fact: Dunkin' is *not* Starbucks. In fact, it doesn't want to be. To prosper, Dunkin' must have its own clear vision of just which customers it wants to serve and how. Dunkin' and Starbucks target very different customers who want very different things from their favorite coffee shops. Starbucks is strongly positioned as a sort of highbrow "third place"—outside the home and office—featuring couches, eclectic music, and art-splashed walls. Dunkin' has a decidedly more low-brow, "everyman" kind of appeal.

The Dunkin' research showed that its brand fans were largely bewildered and turned off by the atmosphere at Starbucks. They groused that crowds of laptop users made it difficult to find a seat. They didn't like Starbucks's "tall," "grande," and "venti" lingo for small, medium, and large coffees. And they couldn't understand why anyone would pay so much for a cup of coffee. "It was almost as though they were a group of Martians talking about a group of Earthlings," says an executive from Dunkin's advertising agency. The Starbucks customers that Dunkin' paid to switch were equally uneasy in Dunkin' shops. "The Starbucks people couldn't bear that they weren't special anymore," says the ad executive.

Such opposing opinions aren't surprising, given the differences in the two stores' customers. Dunkin's customers include more middle-income blue- and white-collar workers across all age, race, and income demographics. By contrast, Starbucks targets a higher-income, more professional group. But Dunkin' researchers concluded that it was more the ideal, rather than income, that set the two tribes apart: Dunkin's tribe members want to be part of a crowd, whereas members of the Starbucks tribe want to stand out as individuals. "You could open a Dunkin' Donuts right next to Starbucks and get two completely different types of consumers," says one retailing expert.

Dunkin' built its positioning on serving simple fare at reasonable prices to working-class customers. It gained a reputation as a morning pit stop where everyday folks could get their daily donut and caffeine fix. But to broaden its appeal and fuel expansion, the chain began been moving upscale a bit. It spiffed up its stores and added new menu items, such as lattes, smoothies, peach and caramel flavor coffee shots, and non-breakfast items like a steak wrap and chicken bacon afternoon sandwich. Dunkin' also made dozens of store and atmosphere redesign changes, big and small, ranging from adding free Wi-Fi, digital menu boards, and more electrical outlets for laptops and smartphones to playing relaxing background music. And it let Dunkin' franchisees redecorate their stores in any of four Starbucks-esque color schemes, including "Dark Roast," "Cappuccino Blend," and "Jazz Brew."

As it inched upscale, however, Dunkin' tried not to alienate its traditional customer base. There were no couches in the remodeled stores. Dunkin' even renamed a new hot sandwich a "stuffed melt" after customers complained that calling it a "panini" was too fancy; it then dropped it altogether when faithful customers thought it was too messy. "We're walking [a fine] line," said the chain's vice president of consumer insights at the time. "The thing about the Dunkin' tribe is, they see through the hype."

Dunkin' targets the "Dunkin' tribe"—not the Starbucks coffee snob but the average Joe. Fast-growing Dunkin' isn't like competitor Starbucks; it doesn't want to be.

Over the past several years, both Dunkin' and Starbucks have grown rapidly, each targeting its own tribe of customers and riding the wave of America's growing thirst for coffee. Although still smaller than Starbucks—which captures a 40 percent U.S. market share versus Dunkin's roughly 22 percent share—Dunkin' is currently the nation's fastest-growing snack and coffee chain. It hopes that continued repositioning and upgrades will help keep that momentum going. Signaling its shifting positioning, Dunkin' recently announced that it would drop the Donuts from its former Dunkin' Donuts name. "Just call us Dunkin'," says the chain. Dunkin' plans eventually to double its number of stores from the current about 9,000 locations to 18,000 (compared with Starbucks's 14,000 U.S. outlets).

However, in pursuing growth, Dunkin' must stay true to the needs and preferences of the Dunkin' tribe. Dunkin' is "not going after the Starbucks coffee snob," says one analyst, it's "going after the average Joe." In fact, after recent surveys showed that Dunkin customers thought that its menu and operations were getting too complicated, and maybe a little too pretentious, the company announced a new wave of menu and location redesign decisions. The aim is to take the brand back to the basics, giving core customers what they want without many frills.

Dunkin' now says simply that it wants to be an "on-the-go, beverage-led brand and a coffee leader." It's streamlining its menu—phasing out items such as smoothies, flavored coffee shots, bagel and flatbread options, and a wide array of baked goods and afternoon sandwiches. Dunkin' is even simplifying its bloated donut selection, from about 30 varieties to the 18 "core donuts" that its best customers like best. The refined positioning emphasizes beverages (an expanded coffee selection), speed and convenience (adding drive-throughs, Grab & Go sections, and on-the-go ordering through its mobile app), and value ("half the price" of more upscale chains).

Dunkin's targeting and positioning are pretty well summed up in its long-running ad slogan "America Runs on Dunkin'." The brand remains committed to keep America running with its great coffee, donuts and other edibles, simple but friendly environment, and solid value. According to Dunkin's chief marketer, Dunkin' remains a place where, "everyday folks who keep America running keep themselves running every day."

So far, so good. For the past 11 years, Dunkin' has topped the coffee category in a leading customer loyalty and engagement survey, ahead of number two Starbucks. According to the survey, Dunkin' has been the top brand for consistently meeting or exceeding customer expectations with respect to taste, quality, and customer service. Nothing too fancy—just meeting the everyday needs of the Dunkin' tribe.[1]

Companies today recognize that they cannot appeal to all buyers in the marketplace—or at least not to all buyers in the same way. Buyers are too numerous, widely scattered, and varied in their needs and buying practices. Moreover, companies themselves vary widely in their abilities to serve different market segments. Instead, like Dunkin', companies must identify the parts of the market they can serve best and most profitably. They must design customer-driven marketing strategies that build the right relationships with the right customers. Thus, most companies have moved away from mass marketing and toward *target marketing:* identifying market segments, selecting one or more of them, and developing products and marketing programs tailored to each.

Marketing Strategy

OBJECTIVE 6-1 Define the major steps in designing a customer value-driven marketing strategy: market segmentation, targeting, differentiation, and positioning.

Market segmentation
Dividing a market into distinct groups of buyers who have different needs, characteristics, or behaviors and who might require separate marketing strategies or mixes.

» **Figure 6.1** shows the four major steps in designing a customer value-driven marketing strategy. In the first two steps, the company selects the customers that it will serve. **Market segmentation** involves dividing a market into distinct groups of buyers who have different needs, characteristics, or behaviors and who might require separate marketing strategies or mixes. The company identifies different ways to segment the market and develops profiles

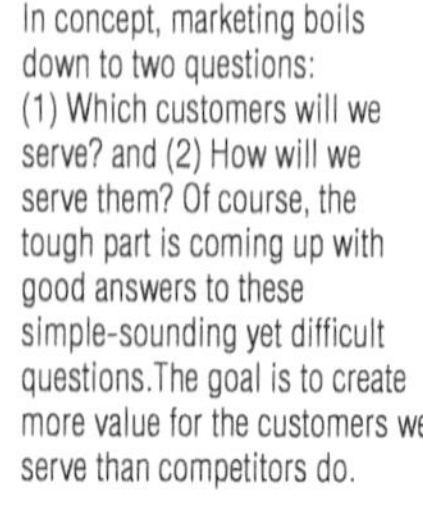

In concept, marketing boils down to two questions:
(1) Which customers will we serve? and (2) How will we serve them? Of course, the tough part is coming up with good answers to these simple-sounding yet difficult questions. The goal is to create more value for the customers we serve than competitors do.

» **Figure 6.1 Designing a Customer-Driven Marketing Strategy**

Market targeting (targeting)
Evaluating each market segment's attractiveness and selecting one or more segments to serve.

Differentiation
Actually differentiating the market offering to create superior customer value.

Positioning
Arranging for a market offering to occupy a clear, distinctive, and desirable place relative to competing products in the minds of target consumers.

of the resulting market segments. **Market targeting (or targeting)** consists of evaluating each market segment's attractiveness and selecting one or more market segments to enter.

In the final two steps, the company decides on a value proposition—how it will create value for target customers. **Differentiation** involves actually differentiating the firm's market offering to create superior customer value. **Positioning** consists of arranging for a market offering to occupy a clear, distinctive, and desirable place relative to competing products in the minds of target consumers. We discuss each of these steps in turn.

Author Comment
Market segmentation addresses the first simple-sounding marketing question: What customers will we serve?

Market Segmentation

OBJECTIVE 6-2 List and discuss the major bases for segmenting consumer and business markets.

Buyers in any market differ in their wants, resources, locations, buying attitudes, and buying practices. Through market segmentation, companies divide large, diverse markets into smaller segments that can be reached more efficiently and effectively with products and services that match their unique needs. In this section, we discuss four important segmentation topics: segmenting consumer markets, segmenting business markets, segmenting international markets, and the requirements for effective segmentation.

Segmenting Consumer Markets

There is no single way to segment a market. A marketer has to try different segmentation variables, alone and in combination, to find the best way to view market structure. » **Table 6.1** outlines variables that might be used in segmenting consumer markets. Here we look at the major *geographic, demographic, psychographic*, and *behavioral* variables.

Geographic Segmentation

Geographic segmentation
Dividing a market into different geographical units, such as nations, states, regions, counties, cities, or even neighborhoods.

Geographic segmentation calls for dividing the market into different geographical units, such as nations, regions, states, counties, cities, or even neighborhoods. A company may decide to operate in one or a few geographical areas or operate in all areas but pay attention to geographical differences in needs and wants. Moreover, many companies today are localizing their products, services, advertising, promotion, and sales efforts to fit the needs of individual regions, cities, and other localities.

For example, many large retailers—from Target and Walmart to Kohl's and Staples—are now opening smaller-format stores designed to fit the needs of smaller markets or densely packed urban neighborhoods in larger cities not suited to their typical large suburban superstores. For example, Target is opening more than 100 small-format stores over the next three years in college towns and crowded urban areas. The stores are about one-fifth the size of a regular Target. These smaller stores carry a limited assortment of products carefully tailored toward local patrons to create personalized shopper experiences. For example, its campus stores are designed to fit the on-the-go,

Table 6.1 Major Segmentation Variables for Consumer Markets

Segmentation Variable	Examples
Geographic	Nations, regions, states, counties, cities, neighborhoods, population density (urban, suburban, rural), climate
Demographic	Age, life-cycle stage, gender, income, occupation, education, religion, ethnicity, generation
Psychographic	Lifestyle, personality
Behavioral	Occasions, benefits, user status, usage rate, loyalty status

budget-conscious lifestyles of college students. Each small-format store analyzes its customers' characteristics, purchases, and feedback to shape assortments. A Target campus store at Florida State would be very different from one near the Northwestern University campus. Target's Chicago Belmont store features Chicago Cubs gear and gay pride banners in the front window to match fit its location near Wrigley Field and a local gay community.[2]

>> Hyperlocal social marketing: Dunkin' drinkers in local communities can use the brand's Waze app to navigate to the nearest store, order ahead, and have their order waiting when they arrive.

The surge in digital and mobile technology has caused a corresponding surge in *hyperlocal social marketing*—location-based targeting to consumers in local communities or neighborhoods using digital and social media. >> For example, to get coffee and promotions to customers faster, Dunkin' has partnered with traffic and navigation app Waze. No matter where they are, Dunkin' drinkers can open the Waze app, locate the nearest Dunkin' (map included), order ahead using the app, and have their order waiting when they arrive.

Alternatively, many of the major social media, such as Facebook and Instagram, let advertisers select audiences by geographic location. Companies can sign up with Google Maps to show their locations and ads in response to "near me" or "nearby" Google searches. For instance, a search of "auto repairs near me" brings up several ads for anything from your local Sears service center to local auto repair shops. If you search "hotels in Poughkeepsie, NY," the search results are topped by ads for Expedia.com, Booking.com. Tripadvisor.com, and KAYAK.com, followed by several specific hotel listings with site links and a map showing each location. Such hyperlocal targeting lets advertisers refine tailor their marketing content to local consumer locations and search intent.

Demographic Segmentation

Demographic segmentation
Dividing the market into segments based on variables such as age, life-cycle stage, gender, income, occupation, education, religion, ethnicity, and generation.

Demographic segmentation divides the market into segments based on variables such as age, life-cycle stage, gender, income, occupation, education, religion, ethnicity, and generation. Demographic factors are the most popular bases for segmenting customer groups. One reason is that consumer needs, wants, and usage rates often vary closely with demographic variables. Another is that demographic variables are easier to measure than most other types of variables. Even when marketers first define segments using other bases, such as benefits sought or behavior, they must know a segment's demographic characteristics to assess the size of the target market and reach it efficiently.

Age and life-cycle segmentation
Dividing a market into different age and life-cycle groups.

Age and Life-Cycle Stage. Consumer needs and wants change with age. Some companies use **age and life-cycle segmentation**, offering different products or using different marketing approaches for different age and life-cycle groups. For example, P&G's Crest White Brilliance toothpaste targets seniors and older adults—it helps "seniors turn their tooth stains into a brighter, whiter smile." By contrast, Crest Pro Health Jr. toothpaste targets young children by featuring packages adorned with *Frozen* and *Star Wars* characters and offering a Magic Timer App "to help even the most reluctant child to brush longer."[3]

Marketers must be careful to guard against stereotypes when using age and life-cycle segmentation. For example, although some 80-year-olds fit the stereotypes of doddering shut-ins with fixed incomes, others ski and play tennis. Similarly, whereas some 40-year-old couples are sending their children off to college, others are just beginning new families. Thus, age is often a poor predictor of a person's life cycle, health, work or family status, needs, and buying power.

Gender segmentation
Dividing a market into different segments based on gender.

Gender. **Gender segmentation** has long been used in marketing clothing, cosmetics, toiletries, toys, and magazines. For example, P&G was among the first to use gender segmentation with Secret, a deodorant brand specially formulated for a woman's chemistry, packaged and advertised to reinforce the female image.

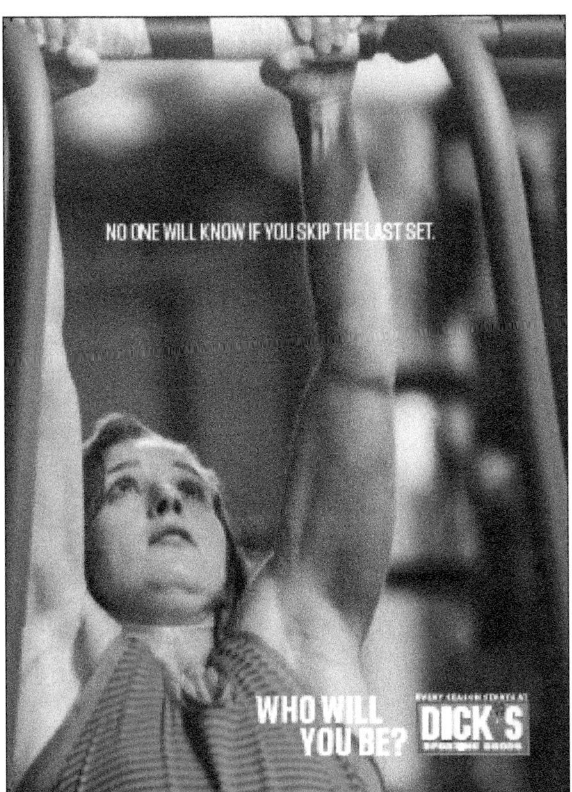

>> **Gender segmentation: In line with the "athleisure" trend that has more women wearing workout gear as everyday fashion, Dick's Sporting Goods recently launched its first-ever ads aimed directly at fitness-minded women.**
DICK'S Sporting Goods

More recently, the men's personal care industry has exploded, and many cosmetics brands that previously catered mostly to women—from L'Oréal, Nivea, and Sephora to Unilever's Dove brand—now successfully market men's lines. For example, Dove's Men+Care believes that "Care makes a stronger man." The brand provides a full line of body washes, body bars, deodorants, face care, and hair care.[4]

Going in the other direction, brands that have traditionally targeted men are now targeting women. For example, in line with the "athleisure" trend in which more women are wearing workout gear as everyday fashion, sports apparel makers and retailers—from Nike and Under Armour to Dick's Sporting Goods—are boosting their marketing efforts aimed at women buyers. Women now make up half of all sporting good shoppers.

>> Dick's Sporting Goods recently launched its first-ever ads aimed directly at fitness-minded women, as part of its broader "Who Will You Be?" campaign. The ads feature women who must juggle their busy lives to meet their fitness goals. The first ad in the series showed one mom jogging rather than driving to pick up her sons at school. Another mom jogs on a treadmill while listening to her baby monitor. "Who will you be?" asks the ad. "Every run. Every workout. Every day. Every choice. Every season begins with Dick's Sporting Goods." Dick's wants women buyers to know that "we understand the choices that they have to make every single day... to fit in fitness," says the retailer's chief marketer.[5]

Income segmentation
Dividing a market into different income segments.

Income. The marketers of products and services such as automobiles, clothing, cosmetics, financial services, and travel have long used **income segmentation**. Many companies target affluent consumers with luxury goods and convenience services. For example, credit card companies target affluent customers with premium cards that offer luxury and more perks but at hefty annual fees. For example, the American Express Platinum card costs members $550 per year. It comes with perks such as special airport lounge access, airline fee credits, Uber credits, elite status at hotel and car rental chains, and extra bonus airline travel points. But for the really well heeled, American Express offer the Centurion Black Card, perhaps the world's most exclusive credit card. The Amex Centurion Black Card targets high-net-worth individuals who earn at least $1 million annually and charge at least $100,000 to $450,000 a year. Application is by invitation only, and cardholders pay an initiation fee of $7,500 plus a $2,500 annually. Black Card members receive exclusive experiences—many kept secret—not available to Platinum Card holders. For example, it includes the Centurion Concierge, a kind of personal assistant who tends to every need, such as priority seating in hot restaurants, first-dibs on show tickets, and research for that exotic vacation. And, of course, the Amex Black Card comes with status and bragging rights that you just can't get with other cards.[6]

Not all companies that use income segmentation target the affluent. For example, many retailers—such as the Dollar General, Family Dollar, and Dollar Tree store chains—successfully target low- and middle-income groups. The core market for such stores is represented by families with incomes under $30,000. When Family Dollar real estate experts scout locations for new stores, they look for lower-middle-class neighborhoods where people wear less-expensive shoes and drive old cars that drip a lot of oil. With their low-income strategies, dollar stores are now the fastest-growing retailers in the nation.

Psychographic Segmentation

Psychographic segmentation
Dividing a market into different segments based on lifestyle or personality characteristics.

Psychographic segmentation divides buyers into different segments based on lifestyle or personality characteristics. People in the same demographic group can have very different psychographic characteristics.

In Chapter 5, we discussed how the products people buy reflect their *lifestyles*. As a result, marketers often segment their markets by consumer lifestyles and base their marketing strategies on lifestyle appeals. For example, retailer Anthropologie, with its whimsical,

"French flea market" store atmosphere, sells a Bohemian-chic lifestyle to which its young women customers aspire. And Athleta sells an urban-active lifestyle to women with its yoga, running, and other athletic clothing along with urban-causal, post-workout apparel.

Fast-casual restaurant Panera caters to a lifestyle segment of people who want more than just good-tasting food—they want food that's good for them, too. To better meet the needs of this healthy-living lifestyle segment, Panera recently announced that it would soon banish more than 150 artificial preservatives, sweeteners, colors, and flavors from its food. It then launched a marketing campaign tagged "Food as it should be," showing happy customers eating better at Panera. >> "100% of our food is 100% clean," says one ad. According to Panera, food should do more than just fill your stomach. "Food should taste good. It should feel good. It should do good things for you and the world around you. That's food as it should be." If that kind of thinking fits your lifestyle, suggests Panera's head of marketing, "then yeah, come on in... that's why we're here."[7]

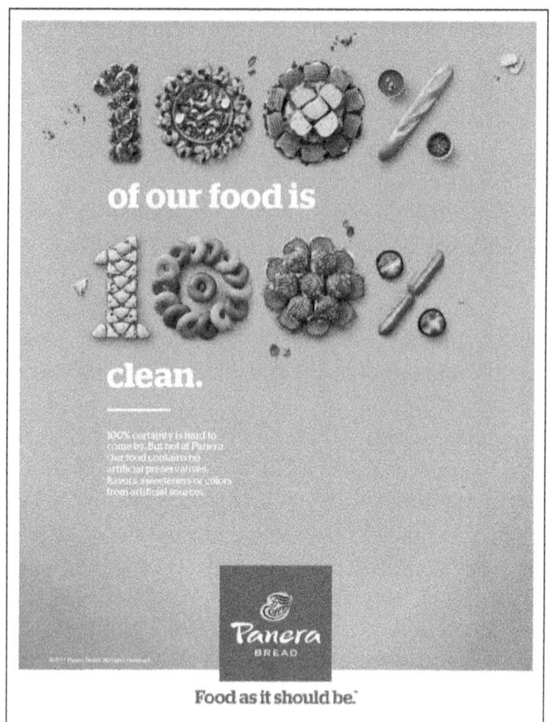

>> **Lifestyle segmentation: Panera caters to a healthy-eating lifestyle segment of people who want more than just good-tasting food—they want food that's good for them, too.**

Panera LLC

Marketers also use *personality* variables to segment markets. For example, Loews, a luxury-boutique hotel chain that offers high-level personal service, targets "personas" segments, such as "weekend explorer couples," "confident business travelers," "serious planners," "luxury jet-setters," "vacationing families" and "Loews loyalists." The chain creates personalized offers, messages, and media plans for each segment, keyed to stages of planning and staying at a Loews hotel—what Loews calls a "SmartJourney." For example, communications aimed at luxury jetsetters might start with an email offering opportunities to enhance their experiences with special room upgrades. Next come Loews app notifications offering additional pre-stay options, such as reservations for fine dining. Once on site, the travelers in this persona group receive high-touch, personal attention tailored to their preferences, say, app notifications of a special "chef's tasting" or spa treatments. In the year following the start of the SmartJourney approach, Lowes customer email engagement rates improved 40 percent and rebookings were up 20 percent.[8]

Behavioral Segmentation

Behavioral segmentation
Dividing a market into segments based on consumer knowledge, attitudes, uses of a product, or responses to a product.

Behavioral segmentation divides buyers into segments based on their knowledge, attitudes, uses, or responses to a product. Many marketers believe that behavior variables are the best starting point for building market segments.

Occasion segmentation
Dividing the market into segments according to occasions when buyers get the idea to buy, actually make their purchase, or use the purchased item.

Occasions. Buyers can be grouped according to occasions when they get the idea to buy, actually make their purchases, or use the purchased items. **Occasion segmentation** can help firms build up product usage. Campbell's advertises its soups more heavily in the cold winter months. And for more than a dozen years, Starbucks has welcomed the autumn season with its pumpkin spice latte (PSL). Sold only in the fall, PSLs pull in $80 million in revenues for Starbucks each year.[9]

Still other companies try to boost consumption by promoting usage during nontraditional occasions. For example, most consumers drink orange juice in the morning, but orange growers have promoted drinking orange juice as a cool, healthful refresher at other times of the day. Similarly, whereas consumers tend to drink soft drinks later in the day, Mountain Dew introduced Mtn Dew A.M. (a mixture of Mountain Dew and orange juice) to increase morning consumption. And Taco Bell attempts to build morning business by promoting Mtn Dew A.M. (available only at Taco Bell) along with the chain's A.M. Crunchwrap and other breakfast items as a great way to start the day.

Benefit segmentation
Dividing the market into segments according to the different benefits that consumers seek from the product.

Benefits Sought. A powerful form of segmentation is grouping buyers according to the different *benefits* that they seek from a product. **Benefit segmentation** requires finding the major benefits people look for in a product class, the kinds of people who look for each benefit, and the major brands that deliver each benefit.

For example, people who buy wearable health and activity trackers are looking for a variety of benefits, everything from counting steps taken and calories burned to heart rate monitoring and high-performance workout tracking and reporting. To meet these varying benefit preferences, Fitbit makes health and fitness tracking devices aimed at buyers in three major benefit segments: Everyday Fitness, Active Fitness, and Performance Fitness:[10]

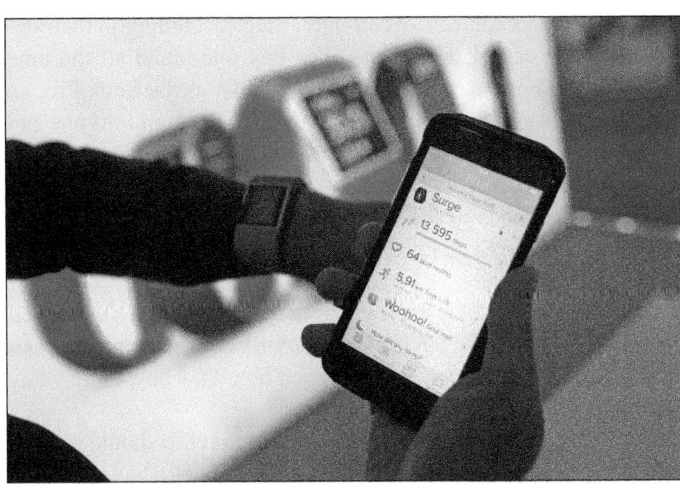

>> Benefit segmentation: Within Fitbit's family of health and fitness tracking products and apps, no matter what bundle of benefits one seeks, "There's a Fitbit for Everyone."

Chris Ratcliffe/Bloomberg via Getty Images

> Everyday Fitness buyers want only very basic fitness tracking. So Fitbit's simplest device, the Fitbit Zip, offers these consumers "Get fit. Have fun with Zip." It tracks steps taken, distance traveled, calories consumed, and active minutes. At the other extreme, for the Performance Fitness segment, the high-tech Fitbit Ionic watch is "the watch designed for your life." It offers more advanced features such as GPS tracking, heart rate monitoring, all-day activity tracking, automatic workout tracking and recording, sleep monitoring, digital pay, text notification, music control, personal guidance and insights, and wireless synching to Fitbit's smartphone and computer apps. >> In all, within Fitbit's family of fitness products and apps, no matter what bundle of benefits one seeks, there's a Fitbit product for everyone.

User Status. Markets can be segmented into nonusers, ex-users, potential users, first-time users, and regular users of a product. Marketers want to reinforce and retain regular users, attract targeted nonusers, and reinvigorate relationships with ex-users. Included in the potential users group are consumers facing life-stage changes—such as new parents and newlyweds—who can be turned into heavy users. For example, to get new parents off to the right start, P&G makes certain that its Pampers Swaddlers are the diaper most U.S. hospitals provide for newborns and then promotes them as "the #1 choice of hospitals."[11]

Usage Rate. Markets can also be segmented into light, medium, and heavy product users. Heavy users are often a small percentage of the market but account for a high percentage of total consumption. >> For instance, fast-growing Southeastern fast-food chain Bojangles' Famous Chicken 'n Biscuits targets everything it does toward the tastes and tendencies of its core of regulars.[12]

> The company calls them Bo Fanatics or Bo'lievers, people who crave lots and lots of Bojangles' signature fried chicken, made-from-scratch biscuits, and "Legendary Sweet Tea." North Carolinian Brandon Sanders, a 36-year-old basketball trainer, is a typical Bo'liever. Brandon has eaten in more than 100 of Bojangles' 715 stores. "He picks up on the subtle differences between locations like a fried chicken sommelier," notes a reporter. Brandon's Bojangles' obsession began with childhood family meals. His father's side of the family eats regular Bojangles' takeout; his mother's side ate often in the restaurant. So Brandon got Bojangles' on both sides. As an adult, he's cut back—he's now down to only two or three Bo visits per week. He could eat at KFC or some other fried chicken place, but "they don't have the soul for it." The brand has even created Bomojis, including one featuring a Bo'liever kneeling and holding a Bo Box of chicken toward the heavens as thanks to the gods. For hungry Bo'lievers, the company's long-time brand slogan says it all. No matter where or when; rain or shine; morning, noon, or night; "It's Bo Time!"

>> Targeting heavy users: Fast-growing Southeastern fast-food chain Bojangles' Famous Chicken 'n Biscuits targets everything it does toward the tastes and tendencies of hungry regulars.

Luke Sharrett/Bloomberg via Getty Images

Loyalty Status. A market can also be segmented by consumer loyalty. Consumers can be loyal to brands (Tide), stores

(Target), and companies (Apple). Buyers can be divided into groups according to their degree of loyalty. Some consumers are completely loyal—they buy one brand all the time and can't wait to tell others about it. For example, whether they own a MacBook Pro, an iPhone, or an iPad, Apple devotees are granitelike in their devotion to the brand. At one end are the quietly satisfied Apple users, folks who own one or several Apple devices and use them for browsing, texting, email, and social networking. At the other extreme, however, are the Apple zealots—the so-called MacHeads or Macolytes—who can't wait to tell anyone within earshot of their latest Apple gadget. Such loyal Apple devotees are at the forefront of Apple's huge iPhone, iPad, and iTunes empire.

Other consumers are somewhat loyal—they are loyal to two or three brands of a given product or favor one brand while sometimes buying others. Still other buyers show no loyalty to any brand—they either want something different each time they buy, or they buy whatever's on sale.

A company can learn a lot by analyzing loyalty patterns in its market. It should start by studying its own loyal customers. Highly loyal customers can be a real asset. They often promote the brand through personal word of mouth and social media. Instead of just marketing to loyal customers, companies should engage them fully and make them partners in building the brand and telling the brand story. For example, Mountain Dew has turned its loyal customers into a "Dew Nation" of passionate superfans who have made it the nation's number three soft drink brands behind only Coca-Cola and Pepsi (see Marketing at Work 6.1).

Some companies actually put loyalists to work for the brand. For example, Patagonia relies on its most tried-and-true customers—what it calls Patagonia ambassadors—to field-test products in harsh environments, provide input for "ambassador-driven" lines of apparel and gear, and share their product experiences with others.[13] In contrast, by studying its less-loyal buyers, a company can detect which brands are most competitive with its own. By looking at customers who are shifting away from its brand, the company can learn about its marketing weaknesses and take actions to correct them.

>> Using Acxiom's Personicx segmentation system, marketers can paint a surprisingly precise picture of who you are and what you buy. Personicx clusters carry such colorful names as "Skyboxes and Suburbans," "Shooting Stars," "Hard Chargers," "Soccer and SUVs," "Raisin' Grandkids," "Truckin' and Stylin'," "Pennywise Mortgagees," and "Cartoons and Carpools."

Acxiom Corporation

Using Multiple Segmentation Bases

Marketers rarely limit their segmentation analysis to only one or a few variables. Rather, they often use multiple segmentation bases in an effort to identify smaller, better-defined target groups. Several business information services—such as Nielsen, Acxiom, Esri, and Experian—provide multivariable segmentation systems that merge geographic, demographic, lifestyle, and behavioral data to help companies segment their markets down to zip codes, neighborhoods, and even households.

>> For example, Acxiom's Personicx Lifestage system classifies U.S. households into one of 70 distinct clusters within 21 life stage groups.[14] Personicx segments carry colorful descriptive names such as "Summit Estates," "Skyboxes and Suburbans," "Hard Chargers," "Toys and Tots," "Country Single," "Raisin' Grandkids," "Truckin' and Stylin'," "Farmland Families," "Downtown Dwellers," "Pennywise Mortgagees," and "Cartoons and Carpools."

Each segment has its own pattern of demographics, lifestyles, likes and dislikes, and purchase behaviors. Using the Personicx system, marketers can paint a surprisingly precise picture of who consumers are and what they might buy. For instance, the Personicx "Cartoons and Carpools" cluster consists of solidly middle-income, married, mid-30s couples with children of all ages. They lay dead center in terms of income,

MARKETING AT WORK 6.1

Mountain Dew: "Doin' the Dew" with Brand Superfans

Perhaps no brand has built a more passionately loyal and engaged following than PepsiCo's high-flying Mountain Dew. For example, take Jason Hemperly, the shy high school kid who had his grandmother make him a tuxedo for his prom out of flattened Mountain Dew cans. And Chester Atkins and his wife Amy who sport matching Mountain Dew tattoos and who toasted their marriage proposal with champagne flutes filled with the citrusy green drink. Then there's Chris Whitley from Jackson, Mississippi, who drinks some 40 cans of Mountain Dew a week, keeps a copious collection of Mountain Dew T-shirts and hats, and absolutely worships recently retired NASCAR driver and Mountain Dew spokesman Dale Earnhardt Jr. "It's pretty much a religious obsession for me, I guess," says Whitley about Mountain Dew. "I just don't drink anything else."

Such fiercely loyal customers—who collectively make up the "Dew Nation"—have made Mountain Dew one of PepsiCo's best-selling brands. Mountain Dew's avid superfans make up only 20 percent of its customers but consume a mind-boggling 70 percent of the brand's total volume. Thanks to such fans, even as overall soft drink sales have lost their fizz during the past decade, Mountain Dew's sales are holding steady. The hugely popular $9 billion brand is now the nation's number-three soft drink, behind only behemoths Coca-Cola and Pepsi.

Such loyalty and sales don't just flow automatically out of bottles and pop-top cans. Mountain Dew markets heavily to its superfans. The brand's long-running "Do the Dew" slogan—what Mountain Dew calls its "iconic rallying cry and brand credo"—headlines the extreme moments and excitement behind the brand's positioning. Mountain Dew spends an estimated more than $80 million per year on "Do the Dew" advertising and other brand content, 45 percent of it in digital media.

But marketing to the Dew Nation explains only one part of Mountain Dew's success. The real story revolves around the brand's skill in fueling customer loyalty by actively engaging brand superfans and creating close brand community. Mountain Dew doesn't just market *to* loyal customers; it makes them partners in building the brand and being part of the brand story.

For example, over the years, through several "DEWmocracy" campaigns, the company has involved Mountain Dew lovers in shaping the brand at all levels. Under DEWmocracy, the Dew Nation has participated via online and social media in everything from choosing and naming new flavors and designing the cans to submitting and selecting TV commercials and even picking an ad agency and media. DEWmocracy has produced hit flavors such as Voltage and White Out. More important, DEWmocracy has been a perfect forum for getting youthful, digitally-savvy Dew drinkers engaged with each other and the company, making the brand their own.

In creating engagement and community among loyal brand fans, Mountain Dew views itself as the ultimate lifestyle brand. Offline, for more than a decade, Mountain Dew has teamed with NBC Sports to sponsor the Dew Tour, a slate of summer and winter action sports events in major cities across the country. At a Dew Tour, superfans can experience the adrenaline-packed Mountain Dew lifestyle firsthand and share their experiences with others in the Dew Nation.

According to Mountain Dew's chief marketer, the "Do the Dew" slogan is "about enjoying the moment you're in," something highly relevant to the brand's young, largely millennial-male target market. "Besides their love of Mountain Dew, what truly unites [the Dew Nation] is the idea of chasing a feeling. A feeling you only get from doing something exhilarating," he says. "Whether it's the thrill you get when you land a kickflip or the rush from completing a set on stage, this campaign is a celebration of the feeling of doing."

Online, Mountain Dew's dozens of web, mobile, and social media sites provide more by way of entertainment and community building than product information. For example, the main "Do the Dew" website serves as a lifestyle hub where super-passionate fans can check out the latest #dothedew programs, ads, and videos; hang out in the gaming section; and follow the adventures of Mountain Dew's action sports athletes in skateboarding (Nick Tucker, Sean Malto, and Theotis Beasley),

>> Mountain Dew has turned its loyal customers into a "Dew Nation" of passionate superfans who avidly adhere to the brand's iconic "Do the Dew" rallying cry.

PepsiCo

snowboarding (Danny Davis and Julia Marino), basketball (Russell Westbrook), and even fishing (Gerald Swindle).

But the ultimate digital hangout for Mountain Dew superfans is a place called Green Label, a web and social media community created by Mountain Dew as a hub for youth culture, covering Dew-related content on sports, music, art, and style. Green Label "welcomes all kinds: derelict skaters, music nerds, and art doodlers, and focuses on the genetically modified cross-pollination that occurs at the intersection of skate, music, and art."

Green Label produces a constant flow of engaging content that gets superfans interacting with the brand. Green Label has also spawned ambitious projects such *Mountain Dew's Green Label Experience*—a cable TV series showcasing action sports from the Dew Tour—and *We Are Blood*—a feature-length film that follows amateur and pro skaters around the world, "celebrating the unconditional bond created by the simple act of skateboarding." The main GreenLabel.com site now draws five times more traffic than MountainDew.com.

In all, few brands can match Mountain Dew when it comes to engaging loyal customers and involving them with the brand. In turn, the cult-like loyalty of the Dew Nation has kept Mountain Dew flowing even as competitors face declines. "The thing that really makes it different from a lot of other drinks, certainly from a lot of other carbonated soft drinks, is its incredibly loyal and passionate consumer base," says Mountain Dew's top marketer. To such loyal fans, Mountain Dew is more than just a something you drink. In the words of PepsiCo's CEO, to Dew fans, Mountain Dew is "an attitude. It's a fantastic attitude."

Just ask a superfan like 20-year-old Steven Kearney, who's been drinking Mountain Dew every day since eighth grade. Kearney has a collection of 80 vintage cans and bottles—he collects a new can as a memento every time a new flavor is released. He always starts the show he hosts on his college radio station by popping open a can of Mountain Dew, and he hangs out with a group of friends he calls "The Mountain Dew buddies." Will he ever outgrow his yen to "Do the Dew"? "I feel like it will definitely be something I'm going to drink for the rest of my life," he says.

Sources: Peter Hartlaub, "Sweet! America's Top 10 Brands of Soda," *NBC News*, www.nbcnews.com/id/42255151/ns/business-us_business/t/sweet-americas-top-brands-soda/#.Wm-X76inGw4, accessed March 2018; Joshua Hughes, "Mountain Dew Launches New 'Do the Dew' Campaign," *World Branding Forum*, January 10, 2017, https://brandingforum.org/advertising/mountain-dew-launches-new-dew-campaign/; Jillian Berman, "Here's Why Mountain Dew Will Survive the Death of Soda," *Huffington Post*, January 25, 2015, www.huffingtonpost.com/2015/01/26/mountain-dew-regions_n_6524382.html; Venessa Wong, "Nobody Knows What Mountain Dew Is, and That's the Key to Its Success," *Buzzfeed*, November 1, 2015, www.buzzfeed.com/venessawong/what-is-mountain-dew#.ikdN7aw8X; "Advertising Spending on Selected Beverage Brands in the United States," *Statista*, www.statista.com/statistics/264985/ad-spend-of-selected-beverage-brands-in-the-us/, accessed September 2018; and www.mountaindew.com and www.greenlabel.com, accessed September 2018.

education, and home values and provide comfortably for their families. The cluster has a high concentration of Hispanics and blue-collar occupations. "Cartoons and Carpools" consumers drive minivans and pickups, buy lots of clothes and shoes for their kids, and enjoy family activities such as visiting zoos, going to theme parks, and camping.[15]

Personicx and other such systems can help marketers to segment people and locations into marketable groups of like-minded consumers. Such rich segmentation provides a powerful tool for marketers of all kinds. It can help companies identify and better understand key customer segments, reach them more efficiently, and tailor market offerings and messages to their specific needs.

Segmenting Business Markets

Consumer and business marketers use many of the same variables to segment their markets. Business buyers can be segmented geographically, demographically (industry, company size), or by benefits sought, user status, usage rate, and loyalty status. Yet business marketers also use some additional variables, such as customer *operating characteristics*, *purchasing approaches*, *situational factors*, and *personal characteristics*.

Almost every company serves at least some business markets. For example, Starbucks has developed distinct marketing programs for various commercial segments, such as colleges and universities, government and military, and office coffee. In the office coffee segment, Starbucks Branded Solutions markets a variety of workplace coffee services to businesses of any size, helping them to make Starbucks coffee and related products available to their employees in their workplaces. Starbucks helps these business customers design the best office solutions involving its coffees (the Starbucks, Seattle's Best, and Torrefazione Italia brands), syrups, and branded paper products and methods of serving them—brewed, premium self-service, or ready to drink. The college and university segment offers various platforms of providing Starbucks products, such as premium-self-service, ready to drink, and licensed stores.

Starbucks provides not only the coffee, tea, and paper products to its business customers but also equipment, training, and marketing and merchandising support.[16]

Many companies establish separate systems for dealing with larger or multiple-location customers. For example, Steelcase, a major producer of office furniture systems, first divides customers into several segments: health-care, education, hospitality, legal, U.S. and Canadian governments, and state and local governments. Next, company salespeople work with independent Steelcase dealers to handle smaller, local, or regional Steelcase customers in each segment. But many national, multiple-location customers, such as ExxonMobil or IBM, have special needs that may reach beyond the scope of individual dealers. Therefore, Steelcase uses national account managers to help its dealer networks handle national accounts and global account managers who deal with accounts that operate across both national and international regions.[17]

Segmenting International Markets

Few companies have either the resources or the will to operate in all, or even most, of the countries that dot the globe. Although some large companies, such as Coca-Cola or Unilever, sell products in more than 200 countries, most international firms focus on a smaller set. Different countries, even those that are close together, can vary greatly in their economic, cultural, and political makeup. Thus, just as they do within their domestic markets, international firms need to group their world markets into segments with distinct buying needs and behaviors.

Companies can segment international markets using one or a combination of several variables. They can segment by *geographic location*, grouping countries by regions such as Western Europe, the Pacific Rim, South Asia, or Africa. Geographic segmentation assumes that nations close to one another will have many common traits and behaviors. Although this is sometimes the case, there are many exceptions. For example, some U.S. marketers lump all Central and South American countries together. However, the Dominican Republic is no more like Brazil than Italy is like Sweden. Many Central and South Americans don't even speak Spanish, including more than 200 million Portuguese-speaking Brazilians and the millions in other countries who speak a variety of indigenous languages.

Intermarket (cross-market) segmentation
Forming segments of consumers who have similar needs and buying behaviors even though they are located in different countries.

World markets can also be segmented based on *economic factors*. Countries might be grouped by population income levels or by their overall level of economic development. A country's economic structure shapes its population's product and service needs and therefore the marketing opportunities it offers. For example, many companies are now targeting the BRICS countries—Brazil, Russia, India, China, and South Africa—which are fast-growing developing economies with rapidly increasing buying power.

Countries can also be segmented by *political and legal factors* such as the type and stability of government, receptivity to foreign firms, monetary regulations, and amount of bureaucracy. *Cultural factors* can also be used, grouping markets according to common languages, religions, values and attitudes, customs, and behavioral patterns.

>> Intermarket segmentation: Coca-Cola targets teens the world over through universal teen themes, such as music and fun.
Godong/UIG via Getty Images

Segmenting international markets based on geographic, economic, political, cultural, and other factors presumes that segments should consist of clusters of countries. However, today's marketers can define and reach segments of like-minded consumers no matter where in the world they are thanks to technologies such as social media, mobile phones, and satellite TV. Using **intermarket segmentation** (also called **cross-market segmentation**), marketers form segments of consumers who have similar needs and buying behaviors even though they are located in different countries. For example, retailer H&M targets fashion-conscious but frugal shoppers in 43 countries with its low-priced, trendy apparel and accessories. And Coca-Cola creates special programs to target teens, core consumers of its soft drinks the world over. By 2020, one-third of the world's population—some 2.5 billion people—will be under 18 years of age. >> Coca-Cola reaches this important market through the universal teen themes, such as music and fun. For example, during the 2016 Olympics Games, Coca-Cola launched the #ThatsGold social media campaign, which engaged 13- to 20-year-olds with a steady stream of content filled with influencers, musicians, and Olympic athletes. The campaign created millions of views, impressions, comments, and shares.[18]

Requirements for Effective Segmentation

Clearly, there are many ways to segment a market, but not all segmentations are effective. For example, buyers of table salt could be divided into blonde and brunette customers. But hair color obviously does not affect the purchase of salt. Furthermore, if all salt buyers bought the same amount of salt each month, believed that all salt is the same, and wanted to pay the same price, the company would not benefit from segmenting this market.

To be useful, market segments must be

- ***Measurable.*** The size, purchasing power, and profiles of the segments can be measured.
- ***Accessible.*** The market segments can be effectively reached and served.
- ***Substantial.*** The market segments are large or profitable enough to serve. A segment should be the largest possible homogeneous group worth pursuing with a tailored marketing program. It would not pay, for example, for an automobile manufacturer to develop cars especially for people whose height is greater than seven feet.
- ***Differentiable.*** The segments are conceptually distinguishable and respond differently to different marketing mix elements and programs. If men and women respond similarly to marketing efforts for soft drinks, they do not constitute separate segments.
- ***Actionable.*** Effective programs can be designed for attracting and serving the segments. For example, although one small airline identified seven market segments, its staff was too small to develop separate marketing programs for each segment.

LINKING THE CONCEPTS

Pause for a bit and think about segmentation. How do the companies you do business with employ the segmentation concepts you're reading about here?

- Can you identify specific companies, other than the examples already mentioned, that practice the different types of segmentation just discussed?
- Using the segmentation bases you've just read about, segment the U.S. footwear market. Describe each of the major segments and subsegments. Keep these segments in mind as you read the next section on market targeting.

Author Comment
After dividing the market into segments, it's time to answer that first seemingly simple marketing strategy question we raised in Figure 6.1: Which customers will the company serve?

Market Targeting

OBJECTIVE 6-3 Explain how companies identify attractive market segments and choose a market-targeting strategy.

Market segmentation reveals the firm's market segment opportunities. The firm then has to evaluate the various segments and decide how many and which segments it can serve best. We now look at how companies evaluate and select target segments.

Evaluating Market Segments

In evaluating different market segments, a firm must look at three factors: segment size and growth, segment structural attractiveness, and company objectives and resources. First, a company wants to select segments that have the right size and growth characteristics. But "right size and growth" is a relative matter. The largest, fastest-growing segments are not always the most attractive ones for every company. Smaller companies may lack the skills and resources needed to serve larger segments. Or they may find these segments too competitive. Such companies may target segments that are smaller and less attractive, in an absolute sense, but that are potentially more profitable for them.

The company also needs to examine major structural factors that affect long-run segment attractiveness.[19] For example, a segment is less attractive if it already contains many strong and aggressive *competitors* or if it is easy for *new entrants* to come into the segment. The existence of many actual or potential *substitute products* may limit prices and the profits that can be earned in a segment. The relative *power of buyers* also affects segment attractiveness. Buyers with strong bargaining power relative to sellers will try to force prices down, demand more services, and set competitors against one another—all at the expense of seller profitability. Finally, a segment may be less attractive if it contains *powerful suppliers* that can control prices or reduce the quality or quantity of ordered goods and services.

Even if a segment has the right size and growth and is structurally attractive, the company must consider its own objectives and resources. Some attractive segments can be dismissed quickly because they do not mesh with the company's long-run objectives. Or the company may lack the skills and resources needed to succeed in an attractive segment. For example, the economy segment of the automobile market is large and growing. But given its objectives and resources, it would make little sense for luxury-performance carmaker Mercedes-Benz to enter this segment. A company should only enter segments in which it can create superior customer value and gain advantages over its competitors.

Selecting Target Market Segments

Target market
A set of buyers who share common needs or characteristics that a company decides to serve.

After evaluating different segments, the company must decide which and how many segments it will target. A **target market** consists of a set of buyers who share common needs or characteristics that a company decides to serve. Market targeting can be carried out at several different levels. >> **Figure 6.2** shows that companies can target very broadly (*undifferentiated marketing*), very narrowly (*micromarketing*), or somewhere in between (*differentiated or concentrated marketing*).

Undifferentiated Marketing

Undifferentiated (mass) marketing
A market-coverage strategy in which a firm decides to ignore market segment differences and go after the whole market with one offer.

Using an **undifferentiated marketing** (or **mass marketing**) strategy, a firm might decide to ignore market segment differences and target the whole market with one offer. Such a strategy focuses on what is *common* in the needs of consumers rather than on what is *different*. The company designs a product and a marketing program that will appeal to the largest number of buyers.

This figure covers a broad range of targeting strategies, from mass marketing (virtually no targeting) to individual marketing (customizing products and programs to individual customers). An example of individual marketing: At mymms.com you can order a batch of M&M's with your face and personal message printed on each little candy.

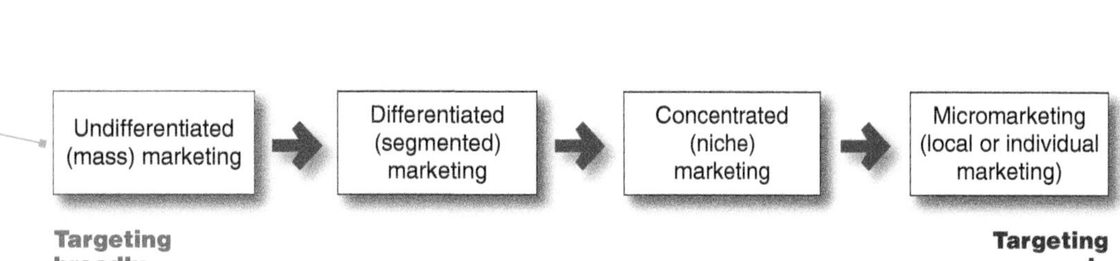

>> **Figure 6.2 Market-Targeting Strategies**

As noted earlier in the chapter, most modern marketers have strong doubts about this strategy. Difficulties arise in developing a product or brand that will satisfy all consumers. Moreover, mass marketers often have trouble competing with more-focused firms that do a better job of satisfying the needs of specific segments and niches.

Differentiated Marketing

Differentiated (segmented) marketing A market-coverage strategy in which a firm targets several market segments and designs separate offers for each.

Using a **differentiated marketing** (or **segmented marketing**) strategy, a firm decides to target several market segments and designs separate offers for each. For example, P&G markets at least six different laundry detergent brands in the United States (Tide, Gain, Cheer, Era, Dreft, and Bold), which compete with each other on supermarket shelves. Then P&G further segments each detergent brand to serve even narrower niches. For example, you can buy any of dozens of versions of Tide—from Tide Original, Tide Plus Coldwater Clean, or Tide Pods to Tide Free & Gentle, Tide Simply Clean, or Tide Plus a Touch of Downy.

>> Differentiated marketing: P&G markets multiple laundry detergent brands and then further segments each brand to service even narrower niches. As a result, it's really cleaning up in the U.S. laundry detergent market, with an almost 60 percent market share.

© Torontonian/Alamy Stock Photo

By offering product and marketing variations to segments, companies hope for higher sales and a stronger position within each market segment. Developing a stronger position within several segments creates more total sales than undifferentiated marketing across all segments. >> Thanks to its differentiated approach, P&G is really cleaning up in the $15 billion U.S. laundry detergent market, capturing a 61 percent market share. Incredibly, by itself, the Tide family of brands captures about 40 percent of all North American detergent sales.[20]

But differentiated marketing also increases the costs of doing business. A firm usually finds it more expensive to develop and produce, say, 10 units of 10 different products than 100 units of a single product. Developing separate marketing plans for separate segments requires extra marketing research, forecasting, sales analysis, promotion planning, and channel management. And trying to reach different market segments with different advertising campaigns increases promotion costs. Thus, the company must weigh increased sales against increased costs when deciding on a differentiated marketing strategy.

Concentrated Marketing

Concentrated (niche) marketing A market-coverage strategy in which a firm goes after a large share of one or a few segments or niches.

When using a **concentrated marketing** (or **niche marketing**) strategy, instead of going after a small share of a large market, a firm goes after a large share of one or a few smaller segments or niches. >> For example, consider nicher Stance:[21]

> "Rihanna designs them, Jay Z sings about them, and the rest of the world can't seem to get enough of Stance socks," says one observer. They've even become the official on-court sock of the NBA and a favorite of many professional players on game day. Nicher Stance sells socks, and mostly just socks. Yet it's thriving in the shadows of much larger competitors who sell socks only as a sideline. Seven years ago, Stance's founders discovered socks as a large but largely overlooked and undervalued market. While walking through the sock section a local Target store, says Stance's CEO and cofounder, Jeff Kearl, "It was like, black, white, brown, and gray—with some argyle—in plastic bags. I thought, we could totally [reinvent] socks, because everyone was ignoring them."
>
> So Stance set out to breathe new life into the sock category by creating technically superior socks that also offered fun, style, and status. Mission accomplished. You'll now find colorful displays of Stance's comfortable but quirky socks in stores in more than 40 countries, from the local surf shop to Foot Locker to Nordstrom, Bloomingdale's, and Macy's. Selling at prices ranging from $10 to $40 a pair, in its first four years Stance has now sold more than 36 million pairs of socks. That's small potatoes for giant competitors such as Hanes or Nike, but it's nicely profitable for nicher Stance. Next up? Another often overlooked niche—Stance men's underwear.

>> **Concentrated marketing: Innovative nicher Stance Socks thrives in the shadows of larger competitors.**

Stance, Inc.

Through concentrated marketing, the firm achieves a strong market position because of its greater knowledge of consumer needs in the niches it serves and the special reputation it acquires. It can market more *effectively* by fine-tuning its products, prices, and programs to the needs of carefully defined segments. It can also market more *efficiently*, targeting its products or services, channels, and communications programs toward only consumers that it can serve best and most profitably.

Niching lets smaller companies focus their limited resources on serving niches that may be unimportant to or overlooked by larger competitors. Many companies start as nichers to get a foothold against larger, more resourceful competitors and then grow into broader competitors. For example, Southwest Airlines began by serving intrastate, no-frills commuters in Texas but is now one of the nation's largest airlines. Enterprise Rent-A-Car began by building a network of neighborhood offices rather than competing with Hertz and Avis in airport locations but is now the nation's largest car rental company. And Amazon began by selling books online but now sells anything and everything as the nation's largest online emporium.

Concentrated marketing can be highly profitable. At the same time, it involves higher-than-normal risks. Companies that rely on one or a few segments for all of their business will suffer greatly if the segment turns sour. Or larger competitors may decide to enter the same segment with greater resources. In fact, many large companies develop or acquire niche brands of their own. For example, Coca-Cola's Venturing & Emerging Brands unit markets a cooler full of niche beverages. Its brands include Honest Tea (the nation's number one organic bottled tea brand), NOS (an energy drink popular among auto enthusiasts), FUZE (a fusion of tea, fruit, and other flavors), Topo-Chico (premium sparkling mineral water), Zico (pure premium coconut water), Odwalla (natural beverages and bars that "bring goodness to your life"), Fairlife (ultra-filtered milk), and many others. Such brands let Coca-Cola compete effectively in smaller, specialized markets, and some will grow into future powerhouse brands. In fact, the Coca-Cola Venturing & Emerging Brands unit's mission is "to identify and nurture brands with billion-dollar potential."[22]

Micromarketing

Micromarketing
Tailoring products and marketing programs to the needs and wants of specific individuals and local customer segments; it includes local marketing and individual marketing.

Differentiated and concentrated marketers tailor their offers and marketing programs to meet the needs of various market segments and niches. At the same time, however, they do not customize their offers to each individual customer. **Micromarketing** is the practice of tailoring products and marketing programs to suit the tastes of specific individuals and local customer segments. Rather than seeing a customer in every individual, micromarketers see the individual in every customer. Micromarketing includes *local marketing* and *individual marketing*.

Local marketing
Tailoring brands and marketing to the needs and wants of local customer segments—cities, neighborhoods, and even specific stores.

Local Marketing. **Local marketing** involves tailoring brands and promotions to the needs and wants of local customers. For example, Marriott's Renaissance Hotels has a Navigator program, which hyper-localizes guest experiences at each of its more than 160 lifestyle hotels around the world:[23]

> Renaissance Hotels' Navigator program puts a personal and local face on each location by "micro-localizing" recommendations for guests' food, shopping, entertainment, and cultural experiences at each destination. The program is anchored by on-site Renaissance Hotels "Navigators" at each location. >> It might be Jennifer Portuhondo, a restaurant-loving Manhattanite at the Renaissance New York Times Square Hotel who "lives and breathes New York." Navigators are

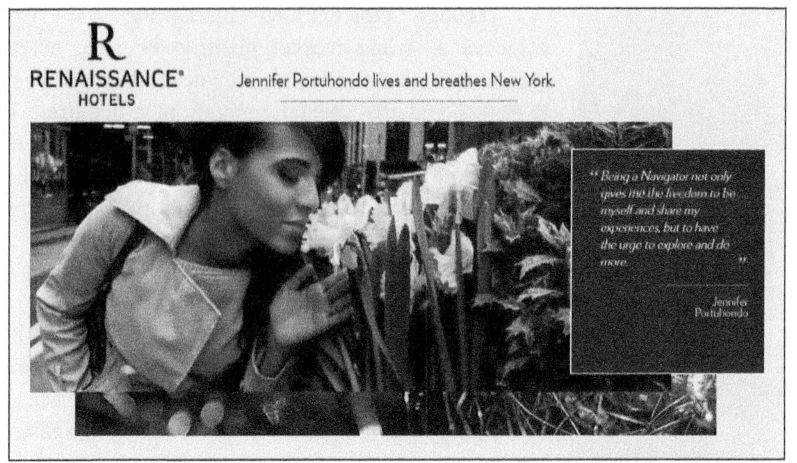

R
RENAISSANCE®
HOTELS
Jennifer Portuhondo lives and breathes New York.
"Being a Navigator not only gives me the freedom to be myself and share my experiences, but to have the urge to explore and do more."
Jennifer Portuhondo

Geographic segmentation: Marriott's Renaissance Hotels' Navigator program helps guests experience "the hidden gems throughout the neighborhood of each hotel through the eyes of those who know it best." Navigator Jennifer Portuhondo at the Renaissance New York Times Square Hotel "lives and breathes New York."

Renaissance Hotels, Marriott International, Marriott Rewards. Renaissance is a registered trademark of Marriott International, Inc.

extensively trained locals who are deeply passionate about the destination and often have a personal connection to the locale. Based on hours of intense training plus their own personal experiences and ongoing research, they work with guests personally to help them experience the hidden gems in the neighborhood of each hotel through their own experienced eyes.

In addition, Renaissance Hotels engages locals in each city to participate by inviting them to follow their local Navigator via social media as well as adding their own favorites to the system, creating each hotel's own version of Yelp. Navigators then cull through submitted tips and feature the best recommendations alongside their own for sharing on its web, mobile, and social media channels or in the hotel lobby on a tablet or in a printed Local Navigator Guide. The hotels also offer an R Navigator phone app that lets guests "uncover the most authentic hidden gems the city you're visiting has to offer. Eat, drink, shop and more—at locations handpicked and continually updated by our local Navigators themselves."

Advances in communications technology have given rise to new high-tech versions of location-based marketing. Thanks to the explosion in smartphones and tablets that integrate geolocation technology, companies can now track consumers' whereabouts closely and engage them on the go with localized deals and information fast, wherever they may be. Retailers ranging from REI and Starbucks to Walgreens and Macy's have jumped onto the hyperlocal bandwagon. For example, Walgreens uses its mobile app to beam in-store notifications and personalized offers to shoppers as they navigate the store's aisles, based on shopper demographics and previous buying patterns.

Local marketing has some drawbacks, however. It can drive up manufacturing and marketing costs by reducing the economies of scale. It can also create logistics problems as companies try to meet the varied requirements of different local markets. Still, as companies face increasingly fragmented markets and as new supporting digital technologies develop, the advantages of local marketing often outweigh the drawbacks.

Individual marketing
Tailoring products and marketing programs to the needs and preferences of individual customers.

Individual Marketing. In the extreme, micromarketing becomes **individual marketing**—tailoring products and marketing programs to the needs and preferences of individual customers. Individual marketing has also been labeled one-to-one marketing, mass customization, and markets-of-one marketing.

The widespread use of mass marketing has obscured the fact that for centuries consumers were served as individuals: The tailor custom-made a suit, the cobbler designed shoes for an individual, and the cabinetmaker made furniture to order. Today, new technologies are permitting many companies to return to customized marketing. Detailed databases, robotic production and flexible manufacturing, and interactive technologies such as smartphones and online and social media have combined to foster mass customization. *Mass customization* is the process by which firms interact one to one with masses of customers to design products, services, and marketing programs tailor-made to individual needs.

Companies these days are hyper-customizing everything from food, artwork, earphones, and sneakers to high-end luxury products. At one end of the spectrum, candy lovers can go to mymms.com and buy M&Ms with personalized messages or pictures embossed on each little candy. Visit Nike ID or Puma Factory online to design and order your very own personalized sneakers. JH Audio in Orlando makes customized earphones based on molds of customers' ears to provide optimized fit and better and safer sound. The company even laser-prints designs on the tiny ear buds—some people request a kid for each ear; others prefer a dog.

At the other extreme are "bespoke" luxury goods (a fancy word for "custom-made" or "made to order"). For the right price, well-heeled customers can buy custom-designed goods ranging from bespoke fashions and accessories by Hermès and Gucci to bespoke cars from Aston Martin or Rolls-Royce.[24]

>> Individual marketing: The Rolls-Royce Bespoke design team works closely with individual customers to help them create their own unique Rolls-Royces. "Outside of compromising the safety of the car—or disfiguring the Spirit of Ecstasy—we won't say no."
WENN Ltd/Alamy Stock Photo

>> Ninety-five percent of Rolls-Royce buyers customize their cars in some way. Customers can sit down with a Rolls-Royce Bespoke design team—color experts, leather-smiths, master woodworkers—in a lounge filled with images, materials, and other inspirational elements to design their own unique Rolls-Royces. Want to match the exterior paint and interior leather to your favorite pale pink leather gloves? No problem. Want to customize your door handles, have your initials and a meaningful logo stitched into the headrests, or install mother-of-pearl inlays, crocodile skin seating, rabbit-pelt linings, or mahogany trim? Easily done. One customer even wanted his car's interior trim to be made from a favorite tree that had recently fallen on his estate. After analyzing a sample, a Rolls-Royce craftsman deemed the wood acceptable and the customer's tree will now live forever in the dash and door panels of his custom Rolls-Royce. "Outside of compromising the safety of the car—or disfiguring the Spirit of Ecstasy—we won't say no," says a Rolls-Royce executive.

Beyond customizing products, marketers also personalize advertising messages, marketing offers, and service encounters on a one-to-one basis. Given today's data and analytics technologies, almost any customer engagement can be fine-tuned to individual customer characteristics, preferences, and behaviors.

Choosing a Targeting Strategy

Companies need to consider many factors when choosing a market-targeting strategy. Which strategy is best depends on the company's resources. When the firm's resources are limited, concentrated marketing makes the most sense. The best strategy also depends on the degree of product variability. Undifferentiated marketing is more suited for uniform products, such as grapefruit or steel. Products that can vary in design, such as cameras and cars, are more suited to differentiation or concentration. The product's life-cycle stage also must be considered. When a firm introduces a new product, it may be practical to launch one version only, and undifferentiated marketing or concentrated marketing may make the most sense. In the mature stage of the product life cycle, however, differentiated marketing often makes more sense.

Another factor is *market variability*. If most buyers have the same tastes, buy the same amounts, and react the same way to marketing efforts, undifferentiated marketing is appropriate. Finally, *competitors' marketing strategies* should be considered. When competitors use differentiated or concentrated marketing, undifferentiated marketing can be suicidal. Conversely, when competitors use undifferentiated marketing, a firm can gain an advantage by using differentiated or concentrated marketing, focusing on the needs of buyers in specific segments.

Socially Responsible Target Marketing

Smart targeting helps companies become more efficient and effective by focusing on the segments that they can satisfy best and most profitably. Targeting also benefits consumers—companies serve specific groups of consumers with offers carefully tailored to their needs. However, target marketing sometimes generates controversy and concern.

The biggest issues usually involve the targeting of vulnerable or disadvantaged consumers with controversial or potentially harmful products.

For example, fast-food chains have generated controversy over the years by their attempts to target inner-city minority consumers. They've been accused of pitching their high-fat, salt-laden fare to low-income, urban residents who are much more likely than suburbanites to be heavy consumers. Similarly, big banks and mortgage lenders have been criticized for targeting consumers in poor urban areas with attractive adjustable-rate home mortgages that they can't really afford.

Children are seen as an especially vulnerable audience. Marketers in a wide range of industries—from cereal, soft drinks, and fast food to toys and fashion—have been criticized for their marketing efforts directed toward children. Critics worry that enticing premium offers and high-powered advertising appeals will overwhelm children's defenses. In recent years, for instance, McDonald's has been criticized by some health advocates and parent groups concerned that its popular Happy Meals offers—featuring items tied in with popular children's movies and TV shows—create a too-powerful connection between children and less-healthy eating. McDonald's has responded by putting the Happy Meal on a diet, cutting the overall calorie count by 20 percent, adding fruit to every meal, and promoting Happy Meals only with milk, water, and juice. It has also cut down on sugar, offering organic apple juice that is only 8 grams of sugar versus the previous 19.[25]

Digital technologies may make children even more vulnerable to targeted marketing messages. Traditional child-directed TV and print ads usually contain fairly obvious pitches that are easily detected and controlled by parents. » However, marketing in digital media may be subtly embedded within the content and viewed by children on personal, small-screen devices that are beyond even the most watchful parent's eye. In digital platforms, the lines between educational, entertainment, and commercial content are often blurred. Thus, as children consume increasing amounts of online and digital content, experts advise close parental supervision of children using digital devices.

More broadly, the growth of the internet, smartphones, and other carefully targeted direct media has raised fresh concerns about potential targeting abuses. The internet and mobile marketing allow more precise targeting, letting the makers of questionable products or deceptive advertisers zero in on the most vulnerable audiences. Unscrupulous marketers can now send tailor-made, deceptive messages by email directly to millions of unsuspecting consumers. For example, the Federal Bureau of Investigation's Internet Crime Complaint Center website alone received almost 300,000 complaints last year.[26]

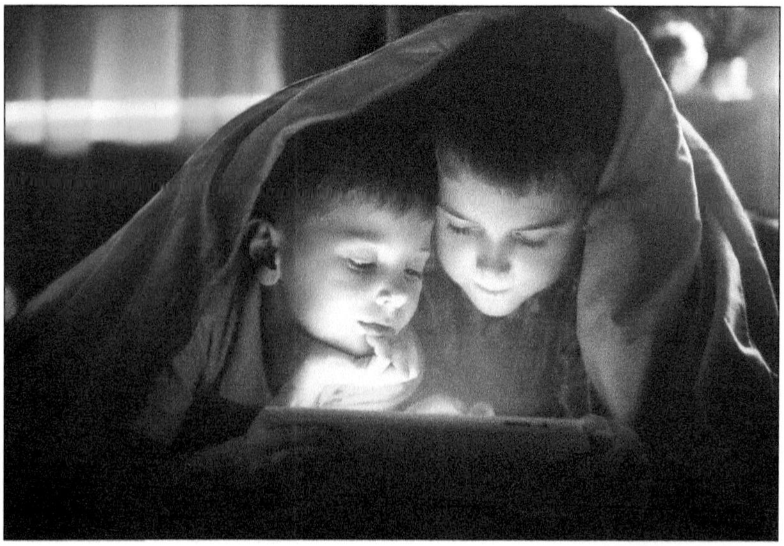

» **Socially responsible targeting: Digital technologies may make children even more vulnerable to targeted marketing messages.**

subbotina/123RF

Today's marketers are also using sophisticated analytical techniques to track consumers' digital movements and to build amazingly detailed customer profiles containing highly personal information. Such profiles can then be used to hypertarget individual consumers with personalized brand messages and offers. However, with such targeting, marketers often walk a fine line between serving customers better and stalking them:

> How well does your smartphone know you? What stories could your laptop tell? In truth, your digital devices probably know more about you than you know about yourself. Smartphones and other digital equipment have become fundamental extensions of our lives. Whatever you do—at work, at play, socializing, shopping—your phone, tablet, laptop, or desktop is almost always a part of the action. These

devices go where you go, entertain you, connect you with friends, take you browsing and shopping, feed you news and information, and listen in on even your most intimate voice, text, and email conversations. And more and more, these devices are sharing all that personal information with marketers. Companies have now developed sophisticated new ways that border on wizardry to extract intimate insights about consumers. For brands and marketers, such information is pure gold.

Marketers argue that using all of this up-close-and-personal information better serves both customers and a company. Customers receive tailored, relevant information and offers from brands that really understand and interest them. However, many consumers and privacy advocates are concerned that such intimate information in the hands of unscrupulous marketers could result in more harm than benefit to consumers. They often view big data and hypertargeting less as "getting to know consumers better to serve them better" and more as "stalking" consumers and "profiling" them. Although most consumers are willing to share some personal information if it means getting better service or deals, many consumers worry that marketers might go too far.

Thus, in target marketing, the issue is not really *who* is targeted but rather *how* and for *what*. Controversies arise when marketers attempt to profit at the expense of targeted segments—when they unfairly target vulnerable segments or target them with questionable products or tactics. Socially responsible marketing calls for segmentation and targeting that serve not just the interests of the company but also the interests of those targeted.

LINKING THE CONCEPTS

It's time to pause and take stock.

- At the last Linking the Concepts, you segmented the U.S. footwear market. Refer to Figure 6.2 and select two companies that serve the footwear market. Describe their segmentation and targeting strategies. Can you come up with a company that targets many different segments versus another that focuses on only one or a few segments?
- How does each company you chose differentiate its market offering and image? Has each done a good job of establishing this differentiation in the minds of targeted consumers? The final section in this chapter deals with such positioning issues.

Author Comment
At the same time that a company is answering the first simple-sounding question (Which customers will we serve?), it must also be asking the second question (How will we serve them?).

Differentiation and Positioning

OBJECTIVE 6-4 Discuss how companies differentiate and position their products for maximum competitive advantage.

Beyond deciding which segments of the market it will target, the company must decide on a *value proposition*—how it will create differentiated value for targeted segments and what positions it wants to occupy in those segments. A **product position** is the way a product is *defined by consumers* on important attributes—the place the product occupies in consumers' minds relative to competing products. Products are made in factories, but brands happen in the minds of consumers.

Product position
The way a product is defined by consumers on important attributes—the place it occupies in consumers' minds relative to competing products.

In the automobile market, the Honda Fit and Nissan Versa are positioned on economy, Mercedes and Cadillac on luxury, and Porsche and BMW on performance. Your Visa card is "Everywhere you want to be"; with American Express, "The Journey Never Stops." Gillette is "The best a man can get," but with Dollar Shave Club you "Shave time. Shave money." >> And whereas Bose gives you "Better sound through research," Sonos unleashes "All the music on earth, in every room of your house, wirelessly." Such simple sounding statements form the backbone of a brand's value proposition.

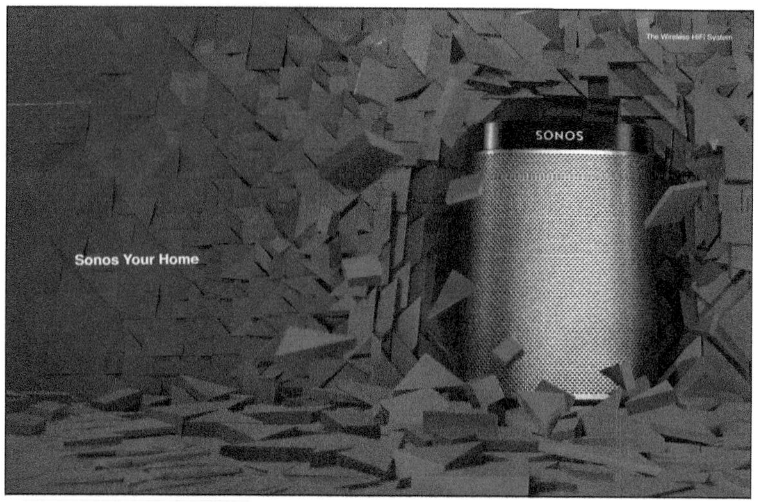

>> Positioning: Sonos does more than just sell speakers; it unleashes "All the music on earth, in every room of your house, wirelessly."

The Advertising Archives/Alamy Stock Photo

Consumers are overloaded with information about products and services. They cannot reevaluate products every time they make a buying decision. To simplify the buying process, consumers organize products, brands, and companies into categories and "position" them in their minds. A product's position is the complex set of perceptions, impressions, and feelings that consumers have for the product compared with competing products.

Consumers position products with or without the help of marketers. But marketers do not want to leave their products' positions to chance. They must *plan* positions that will give their products the greatest advantage in selected target markets, and they must design marketing mixes to create these planned positions.

Positioning Maps

In planning their differentiation and positioning strategies, marketers often prepare *perceptual positioning maps* that show consumer perceptions of their brands versus those of competing products on important buying dimensions. **>> Figure 6.3** shows a positioning map for the U.S. large luxury SUV market.[27] The position of each circle on the map indicates the brand's perceived positioning on two dimensions: price and orientation (luxury versus performance). The size of each circle indicates the brand's relative market share.

Thus, customers view the market-leading Cadillac Escalade as a moderately priced, large, luxury SUV with a balance of luxury and performance. The Escalade is positioned on urban luxury, and in its case, "performance" probably means power and safety performance. You'll find no mention of off-road adventuring in an Escalade ad.

Choosing a Differentiation and Positioning Strategy

Some firms find it easy to choose a differentiation and positioning strategy. For example, a firm well known for quality in certain segments will go after this position in a new segment if there are enough buyers seeking quality. But in many cases, two or more firms will go after the same position. Then each will have to find other ways to set itself apart. Each firm

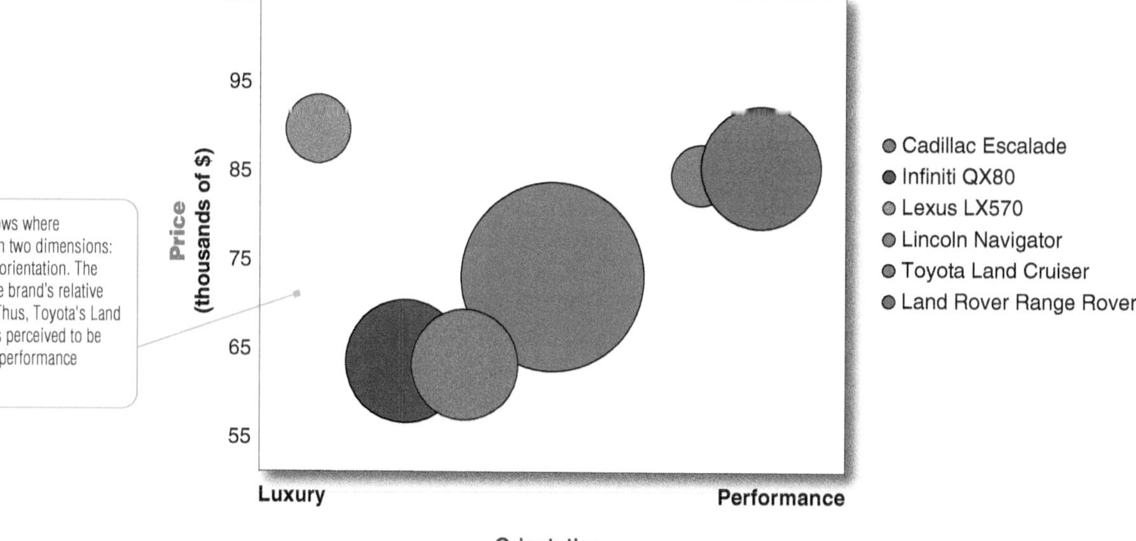

The location of each circle shows where consumers position a brand on two dimensions: price and luxury-performance orientation. The size of each circle indicates the brand's relative market share in the segment. Thus, Toyota's Land Cruiser is a niche brand that is perceived to be relatively expensive and more performance oriented.

>> Figure 6.3 Positioning Map: Large Luxury SUVs

must differentiate its offer by building a unique bundle of benefits that appeal to a substantial group within the segment.

Above all else, a brand's positioning must serve the needs and preferences of well-defined target markets. For example, as discussed in the chapter-opening story, although both Dunkin' and Starbucks are coffee and snack shops, they target very different customers who want very different things from their favorite coffee seller. Starbucks targets more upscale professionals with more high-brow positioning. In contrast, Dunkin' targets the "average Joe" with a decidedly more low-brow, "everyman" kind of positioning. Yet each brand succeeds because it creates just the right value proposition for its unique mix of customers.

The differentiation and positioning task consists of three steps: identifying a set of differentiating competitive advantages on which to build a position, choosing the right competitive advantages, and selecting an overall positioning strategy. The company must then effectively communicate and deliver the chosen position to the market.

Identifying Possible Value Differences and Competitive Advantages

To build profitable relationships with target customers, marketers must understand customer needs and deliver more customer value better than competitors do. To the extent that a company can differentiate and position itself as providing superior customer value, it gains **competitive advantage**.

Competitive advantage
An advantage over competitors gained by offering greater customer value either by having lower prices or providing more benefits that justify higher prices.

But solid positions cannot be built on empty promises. If a company positions its product as *offering* the best quality and service, it must actually differentiate the product so that it *delivers* the promised quality and service. Companies must do much more than simply shout out their positions with slogans and taglines. They must first *live* the slogan. For example, online shoes and accessories seller Zappos's "powered by service" positioning would ring hollow if not backed by truly outstanding customer care. Zappos aligns its entire organization and all of its people around providing the best possible customer service. The online seller's number one core value: "Deliver WOW through service."[28]

To find points of differentiation, marketers must think through the customer's entire experience with the company's product or service. An alert company can find ways to differentiate itself at every customer contact point. In what specific ways can a company differentiate itself or its market offer? It can differentiate along the lines of *product, services, channels, people*, or *image*.

Through *product differentiation*, brands can be differentiated on features, performance, or style and design. Thus, premium audio brand Bose positions its audio products on the innovative, high-quality listening experiences it gives users. Bose promises "better sound through research." And BMW positions itself as "The Ultimate Driving Machine" that's "designed for driving pleasure."

Beyond differentiating its physical product, a firm can also differentiate the services that accompany the product. Some companies gain *services differentiation* through speedy, convenient service. >> QuickenLoans' Rocket Mortgage unit doesn't just offer mortgage loans; its online-only website or mobile app interface lets users easily upload financial details and get a loan decision in only minutes. Other firms promise high-quality customer service. For example, in an age where customer satisfaction with airline service is in constant decline, Singapore Airlines sets itself apart through extraordinary customer care and the grace of its flight attendants.

Firms that practice *channel differentiation* gain competitive advantage through the way they design their channel's coverage, expertise, and performance. Amazon and GEICO, for example, set

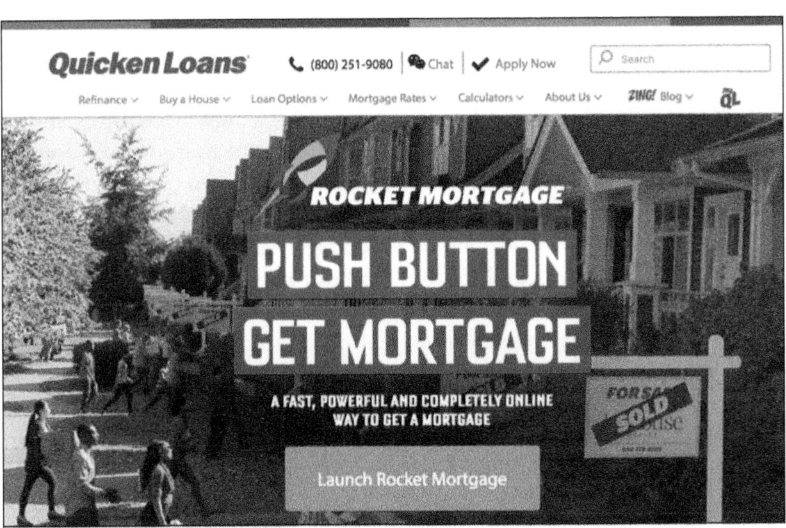

>> Services differentiation: QuickenLoans' Rocket Mortgage doesn't just offer mortgage loans; its online-only interface lets users get a loan decision in only minutes.
Quicken Loans

themselves apart with their smooth-functioning direct channels. Companies can also gain a strong competitive advantage through *people differentiation*—hiring and training better people than their competitors do. People differentiation requires that a company select its customer-contact people carefully and train them well. For example, East Coast supermarket chain Wegmans has long been recognized as a customer service champ with a cult-like loyalty among its shoppers. The secret to its extraordinary customer service lies in its carefully selected, superbly trained, happy employees, who personify Wegmans's commitment to customers: "Everyday You Get Our Best." For example, the chain's cashiers aren't allowed to interact with customers until they've had at least 40 hours of training. "Our employees are our number one asset," says the chain's vice president for human resources.[29]

Even when competing offers look the same, buyers may perceive a difference based on company or brand *image differentiation*. A company or brand image should convey a product's distinctive benefits and positioning. Developing a strong and distinctive image calls for creativity and hard work. A company cannot develop an image in the public's mind overnight by using only a few ads. If Ritz-Carlton means quality, this image must be supported by everything the company is, says, and does.

Symbols, such as the McDonald's golden arches, the colorful Google logo, the Twitter bird, the Nike swoosh, or Apple's "bite mark" logo, can provide strong company or brand recognition and image differentiation. The company might build a brand around a famous person, as Nike did with its Michael Jordan, Kobe Bryant, and LeBron James basketball shoe and apparel collections. Some companies even become associated with colors, such as Coca-Cola (red), IBM (blue), or UPS (brown). The chosen symbols, characters, and other image elements must be communicated through advertising that conveys the company's or brand's personality.

Choosing the Right Competitive Advantages

Suppose a company is fortunate enough to discover several potential differentiations that provide competitive advantages. It now must choose the ones on which it will build its positioning strategy. It must decide how many differences to promote and which ones.

How Many Differences to Promote. Many marketers think that companies should aggressively promote only one benefit to the target market. Former advertising executive Rosser Reeves, for example, said a company should develop a *unique selling proposition (USP)* for each brand and stick to it. Each brand should pick an attribute and tout itself as "number one" on that attribute. Buyers tend to remember number one better, especially in this overcommunicated society. Thus, Walmart promotes its unbeatable low prices and Burger King promotes personal choice—"have it your way."

Other marketers think that companies should position themselves on more than one differentiator. This may be necessary if two or more firms are claiming to be best on the same attribute. >> For example, as noted previously, Toyota positions its Land Cruiser on both luxury and off-road performance. The Land Cruiser began in 1951 as a four-wheel-drive, jeep-like vehicle designed to conquer the world's most grueling terrains and climates. In recent years, the vehicle has retained this adventure and performance positioning but with luxury added. Its website brags of a "timeless icon," with "a sophisticated blend of off-road prowess, on-road comfort, and unparalleled refinement."[30] Toyota's challenge is to convince buyers that one brand can provide both luxury and off-road performance.

>> Positioning on multiple competitive advantages: Toyota positions its Land Cruiser as "a sophisticated blend of off-road prowess, on-road comfort, and unparalleled refinement."

Toyota Motor Sales, U.S.A., Inc.

Today, in a time when the mass market is fragmenting into many small segments, companies and brands are trying to broaden their positioning strategies to appeal to more segments.

Which Differences to Promote. Not all brand differences are meaningful or worthwhile, and each difference has the potential to create company costs as well as customer benefits. A difference is worth establishing to the extent that it satisfies the following criteria:

- ***Important.*** The difference delivers a highly valued benefit to target buyers.
- ***Distinctive.*** Competitors do not offer the difference, or the company can offer it in a more distinctive way.
- ***Superior.*** The difference is superior to other ways that customers might obtain the same benefit.
- ***Communicable.*** The difference is communicable and visible to buyers.
- ***Preemptive.*** Competitors cannot easily copy the difference.
- ***Affordable.*** Buyers can afford to pay for the difference.
- ***Profitable.*** The company can introduce the difference profitably.

Many companies have introduced differentiations that failed one or more of these tests. When the Westin Stamford Hotel in Singapore once advertised itself as the world's tallest hotel, it was a distinction that was not important to most tourists; in fact, it turned many off. Similarly, Coca-Cola's classic product failure—New Coke—failed the superiority and importance tests among core Coca-Cola drinkers:

> Extensive blind taste tests showed that 60 percent of all soft drink consumers chose a new, sweeter Coca-Cola formulation over the original Coke, and 52 percent chose it over Pepsi. So the brand dropped its original-formula Coke and, with much fanfare, replaced it with New Coke, a sweeter, smoother version. However, in its research, Coca-Cola overlooked the many intangibles that have made Coca-Cola so popular for 130 years. To loyal Coke drinkers, the original beverage stands alongside baseball, apple pie, and the Statue of Liberty as an American institution. As it turns out, Coca-Cola differentiates its brand not just by taste but by tradition. By dropping the original formula, Coca-Cola trampled on the sensitivities of the huge core of loyal Coke drinkers who loved Coke just the way it was. After only three months, the company brought the classic Coke back.

Thus, choosing competitive advantages on which to position a product or service can be difficult, yet such choices are crucial to success. Choosing the right differentiators can help a brand stand out from the pack of competitors.

Selecting an Overall Positioning Strategy

Value proposition
The full positioning of a brand—the full mix of benefits on which it is positioned.

The full positioning of a brand is called the brand's **value proposition**—the full mix of benefits on which a brand is differentiated and positioned. It is the answer to the customer's question "Why should I buy your brand?" BMW's "ultimate driving machine/designed for driving pleasure" value proposition hinges on performance but also includes luxury and styling, all for a price that is higher than average but seems fair for this mix of benefits.

>> **Figure 6.4** shows possible value propositions on which a company might position its products. In the figure, the five green cells on the top and right represent winning value propositions—differentiation and positioning that give the company a competitive advantage. The red cells at the lower left, however, represent losing value propositions. The center cell represents at best a marginal proposition. In the following sections, we discuss the five winning value propositions: more for more, more for the same, the same for less, less for much less, and more for less.

More for More. *More-for-more* positioning involves providing the most upscale product or service and charging a higher price to cover the higher costs. A more-for-more market offering not only offers higher quality, it also gives prestige to the buyer. It symbolizes status and a loftier lifestyle. Four Seasons hotels, Patek Philippe watches, Starbucks coffee,

>> Figure 6.4 Possible Value Propositions

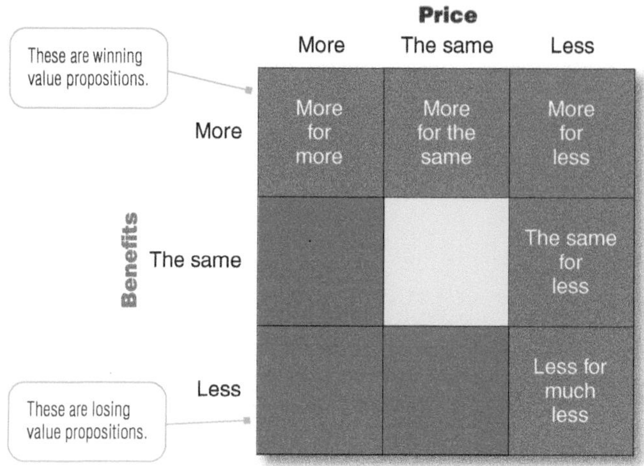

Louis Vuitton handbags, Mercedes automobiles, SubZero appliances—each claims superior quality, craftsmanship, durability, performance, or style and therefore charges a higher price.

Similarly, the marketers of Hearts On Fire diamonds have created a more-for-more niche as "The World's Most Perfectly Cut Diamond." >> Hearts On Fire diamonds have a unique "hearts and arrow" design. When viewed under magnification from the bottom, a perfect ring of eight hearts appears; from the top comes a perfectly formed Fireburst of light. Hearts On Fire diamonds aren't for everyone, says the company. "Hearts On Fire is for those who expect more and give more in return." The brand commands a 15 to 20 percent price premium over comparable competing diamonds.[31]

Although more-for-more can be profitable, this strategy can also be vulnerable. It often invites imitators who claim the same quality but at a lower price. For example, more-for-more brand Starbucks now faces "gourmet" coffee competitors ranging from McDonald's to the local corner coffee roaster. Also, luxury goods that sell well during good times may be at risk during economic downturns when buyers become more cautious in their spending.

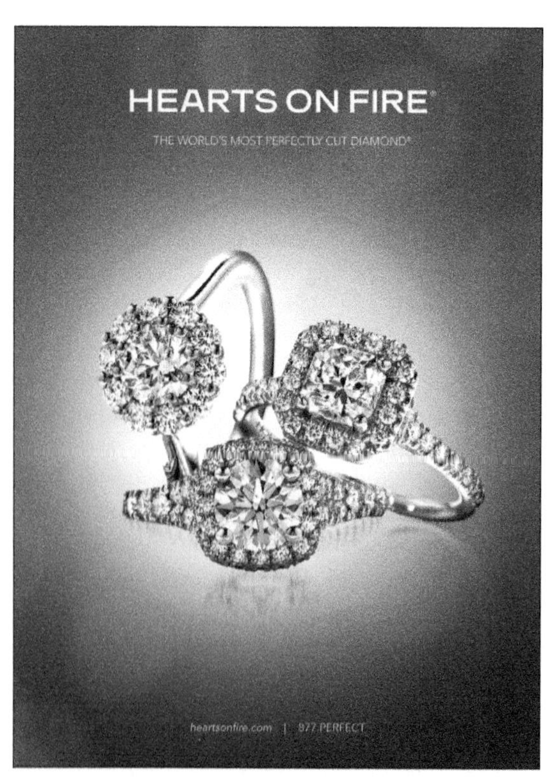

>> More-for-more positioning: Hearts On Fire diamonds have created a more-for-more niche as "The World's Most Perfectly Cut Diamond—for those who expect more and give more in return."

More for the Same. A company can attack a competitor's value proposition by positioning its brand as offering more for the same price. For example, Target positions itself as the "upscale discounter." It claims to offer more in terms of store atmosphere, service, stylish merchandise, and classy brand image but at prices comparable to those of Walmart, Kohl's, and other discounters.

The Same for Less. Offering *the same for less* can be a powerful value proposition—everyone likes a good deal. Discount stores such as Walmart and "category killers" such as Costco, PetSmart, and DSW Shoes use this positioning. They don't claim to offer different or better products. Instead, they offer many of the same brands as department stores and specialty stores but at deep discounts based on superior purchasing power and lower-cost operations. Other companies develop imitative but lower-priced brands in an effort to lure customers away from the market leader. For example, Amazon's Kindle Fire tablets sell for less than 40 percent of the price of the Apple iPad or Samsung Galaxy tablet. Amazon claims that it offers "Premium products at non-premium prices."

Less for Much Less. A market almost always exists for products that offer less and therefore cost less. Few people need, want, or can afford "the very best" in everything they buy. In many cases, consumers will gladly settle for less-than-optimal performance or give up some of the bells and whistles in exchange for a lower price. For example, many travelers seeking lodgings prefer not to pay for what they consider unnecessary extras, such as a pool, an attached restaurant, or mints on the pillow. Hotel chains such as Ramada Limited, Holiday Inn Express, and Motel 6 suspend some of these amenities and charge less accordingly.

Less-for-much-less positioning involves meeting consumers' lower performance or quality requirements at a much lower price. For example, Costco warehouse stores offer less merchandise selection and consistency and much lower levels of service; as a result, they charge rock-bottom prices. Similarly, at ALDI grocery stores, customers pay super-low prices but must settle for less in terms of the service extras. "You can't eat frills," says ALDI, "so why pay for them?" (See Marketing at Work 6.2.)

More for Less. Of course, the winning value proposition would be to offer *more for less*. Many companies claim to do this. And, in the short run, some companies can actually achieve such lofty positions. For example, when it first opened for business, Home Depot had arguably the best product selection, the best service, *and* the lowest prices compared with local hardware stores and other home-improvement chains.

Yet in the long run, companies will no doubt find it very difficult to sustain such best-of-both positioning. Offering more usually costs more, making it difficult to deliver on the "for-less" promise. Companies that try to deliver both may lose out to more focused competitors. For example, facing determined competition from Lowe's stores, Home Depot must now decide whether it wants to compete primarily on superior service or on lower prices.

All said, each brand must adopt a positioning strategy designed to serve the needs and wants of its target markets. *More for more* will draw one target market, *less for much less* will draw another, and so on. In any market, there is usually room for many different companies, each successfully occupying different positions. The important thing is that each company must develop its own winning positioning strategy, one that makes the company special to its target consumers.

Positioning statement
A statement that summarizes company or brand positioning using this form: To (target segment and need) our (brand) is (concept) that (point of difference).

Developing a Positioning Statement

Company and brand positioning should be summed up in a **positioning statement**. The statement should follow the form: To (target segment and need) our (brand) is (concept) that (point of difference).[32] >> Here is an example using the popular digital information management application Evernote: "To busy multitaskers who need help remembering things, Evernote is a digital content management application that makes it easy to capture, organize, and share moments and ideas from your everyday or business life using your computer, phone, tablet, and the web."

Note that the positioning statement first states the product's membership in a category (digital content management application) and then shows its point of difference from other members of the category (easily capture and organize moments and ideas to remember and share later). Evernote is "your second brain" lets you create notes, capture photos, create to-do lists, and record voice reminders and then makes them easy to find, access, and share using just about any device, anywhere—at home, at work, or on the go.

Placing a brand in a specific category suggests similarities that it might share with other products in the category. But the case for the brand's

>> **Positioning statement: Evernote is positioned as a digital content management application that helps busy people to capture and remember moments and ideas and find them fast later.**

Evernote Corporation

MARKETING AT WORK 6.2

ALDI's Less-for-Much-Less Value Proposition: You Can't Eat Frills, So Why Pay for Them?

When asked to name the world's largest grocery chains, you'd probably come up with Walmart, the world's largest retailer, and maybe Kroger, the largest U.S. grocery-only merchant. One name that probably wouldn't come to mind is Germany-based discount grocer ALDI. Yet, surprisingly, with more than $84 billion in global sales, ALDI is the world's eighth-largest retailer overall and the second-largest grocery-only retailer behind Kroger. What's more, ALDI is taking the United States and other country markets by storm, growing faster than any of its larger rivals.

How does ALDI do it? With a simple less-for-much-less value proposition. At ALDI you get less, but you pay much less for it. The chain gives customers a basic assortment of good-quality everyday items with no-frills service at everyday extra-low prices. These days, many grocers brag about low prices. But at ALDI, they are an absolute fact. The rapidly expanding chain promises customers "Simply Smarter Shopping." ALDI has redesigned the food shopping experience to reduce costs and give customers prices that it claims are up to 50 percent lower than those of rival supermarkets.

>> Good-value pricing: ALDI keeps costs low so that it can offer customers "impressively high quality at impossibly low prices" every day.
AKP Photos/Alamy Stock Photo

To get those super-low prices, however, ALDI customers must settle for less in terms of many of the extras they've come to expect from competitors. For example, they get a smaller selection. To keep costs and prices down, ALDI operates smaller, energy-saving stores (about one-third the size of traditional supermarkets), and each store carries only about 1,800 of the fastest-moving grocery items (the typical supermarket carries about 40,000 items). ALDI also carries fewer national brands; some 90 percent of its items are ALDI store brands. (ALDI claims customers are paying for the product itself, not national brand advertising and marketing.) ALDI does no promotional pricing or price matching—it just sticks with its efficient everyday very low prices. "We don't match other stores' prices because that would mean raising ours," say ALDI.

In trimming costs and passing savings along to customers, ALDI leaves no stone unturned. Even customers themselves help to keep costs low: They bring their own bags (or purchase them from ALDI for a small charge), bag their own groceries (ALDI provides no baggers), and return shopping carts on their own (to get back a 25-cent deposit). But to ALDI fans, even though they get less in terms of selection and services, the savings make it all worthwhile. ALDI tells customers "You can't eat frills, so why pay for them?"

Whereas ALDI cuts operating costs to the bone, it doesn't scrimp on quality. With its preponderance of store brands, ALDI exercises complete control over the quality of the products on its shelves, and the chain promises that everything it sells is certifiably fresh and tasty. ALDI backs this promise with a Double Guarantee on all items: "If for any reason you are not 100-percent satisfied with any product, we will gladly replace the product *and* refund your money."

To improve the quality of its assortment, ALDI has progressively added items that aren't usually associated with "discounted" groceries. Beyond the typical canned, boxed, and frozen food basics, ALDI carries fresh meat, baked goods, and fresh produce. It also carries an assortment of regular and periodic specialty goods, such as Mama Cozzi's Pizza Kitchen Meat Trio Focaccia, Appetitos Spinach Artichoke Dip, and All Natural Mango Salsa. ALDI even offers a selection of gluten-free and organic foods. With such items and with its clean, bright stores, ALDI targets not just low-income customers but frugal middle-class and upper-middle-class customers as well.

None of this is news to German shoppers, who have loved ALDI for decades. In Germany, the chain operates more than 4,200 stores and is the country's discount grocery leader. That might explain why Walmart gave up in Germany just nine years after entering the market. Against competitors like ALDI, Walmart's normally low prices were just too expensive for frugal German consumers.

ALDI's no-frills, less-for-much-less approach isn't for everyone. Whereas some shoppers love the low prices, basic assortments, and simple store atmosphere, others can't imagine life without at least some of the luxuries and amenities offered by rivals. But most people who shop at ALDI quickly become true believers. Testimonials from converts litter the internet. "I just recently switched to ALDI from a 'premium' grocery store...and the savings blow me away!" proclaims one customer. Another fervent fan, a mother shopping on a tight budget for her family, used to scour the papers for coupons and shop at two or three different stores on a typical grocery trip. Now, she gets everything on her list in a single stop at ALDI, with money left over for extra items not on the list. "I cannot believe how much I saved!" she says. "ALDI is now my immediate go-to grocery store! I'm totally team ALDI."

With tradition behind it and its can't-lose value proposition, ALDI is expanding rapidly in the United States. The chain currently operates 1,750 U.S. stores in 35 states and plans to increase that number to 2,500 stores by 2022. During that time, it's estimated U.S. sales will grow from as much as $27 billion to as much as $40 billion. That's a huge accomplishment in the saturated U.S. grocery industry where most supermarket chains are stagnating or declining. Even star performer Kroger's impressive 13-year streak of same-store sales increases came to an end last year. "We're growing at a time when other retailers are struggling," says ALDI's chief executive.

That's good news for ALDI but also for customers. When ALDI comes to your neighborhood, says the less-for-much-less grocer, "Your wallet and taste buds are in for a treat."

Sources: "Global Powers of Retailing 2018," Deloitte, www2.deloitte.com/content/dam/Deloitte/uk/Documents/consumer-business/deloitte-uk-global-powers-of-retailing-2018.pdf; Haley Peterson, "The Retail Apocalypse Is Heading Straight for Kroger, Whole Foods, and Aldi," *Business Insider,* August 5, 2017, www.businessinsider.com/retail-apocalypse-coming-for-grocery-stores-2017-8; Craig Rosenblum, "Aldi's Jason Hart: Relentless Focus on Cutting Costs," *Supermarket News,* December 16, 2015, http://supermarketnews.com/limited-assortment/aldis-jason-hart-relentless-focus-cutting-costs#ixzz3wb9dWnMj; Jeff Daniels, "US Grocery Battle Heats Up with German Retailer Seen as 'Disruptive' Force," *CNBC,* June 14, 2017, www.cnbc.com/2017/06/14/us-grocery-battle-heats-up-with-german-players.html; "German Grocery Chain Aldi to Invest $34 Billion to Expand U.S. Stores," *Fortune,* June 12, 2017, http://fortune.com/2017/06/12/german-grocery-chain-aldi-expand-stores/; Barbara Thau, "What Aldi, BJ's, and Ethan Allen Aim to Do in 2018," *Forbes,* January 26, 2018, www.forbes.com/sites/barbarathau/2018/01/26/aldi-bjs-ethan-allen-ceos-outline-top-2018-goals-what-you-didnt-hear-at-the-big-retail-show/#124e9e8f1349; and www.aldi.us, accessed September 2018.

superiority is made on its points of difference. For example, the U.S. Postal Service ships packages just like UPS and FedEx, but it differentiates its Priority Mail from competitors with convenient, low-price, flat-rate shipping boxes and envelopes. "If it fits, it ships," promises USPS.

Communicating and Delivering the Chosen Position

Once it has chosen a position, the company must take strong steps to deliver and communicate the desired position to its target consumers. All the company's marketing mix efforts must support the positioning strategy.

Positioning the company calls for concrete action, not just talk. If the company decides to build a position on better quality and service, it must first *deliver* that position. Designing the marketing mix—product, price, place, and promotion—involves working out the tactical details of the positioning strategy. Thus, a firm that seizes on a more-for-more position knows that it must produce high-quality products, charge a high price, distribute through high-quality dealers, and advertise in high-quality media. It must hire and train more service people, find retailers that have a good reputation for service, and develop sales and advertising content that supports its superior offer. This is the only way to build a consistent and believable more-for-more position.

Companies often find it easier to come up with a good positioning strategy than to implement it. Establishing a position or changing one usually takes a long time. In contrast, positions that have taken years to build can quickly be lost. Once a company has built the desired position, it must take care to maintain the position through consistent performance and communication. It must closely monitor and adapt the position over time to match changes in consumer needs and competitors' strategies. However, the company should avoid abrupt changes that might confuse consumers. Instead, a product's position should evolve gradually as it adapts to the ever-changing marketing environment.

REVIEWING AND EXTENDING THE CONCEPTS

CHAPTER REVIEW AND KEY TERMS

Objectives Review

In this chapter, you learned about the major elements of a customer value-driven marketing strategy: segmentation, targeting, differentiation, and positioning. Marketers know that they cannot appeal to all buyers in their markets—or at least not to all buyers in the same way. Therefore, most companies today practice *target marketing*—identifying market segments, selecting one or more of them, and developing products and marketing mixes tailored to each.

OBJECTIVE 6-1 Define the major steps in designing a customer value-driven marketing strategy: market segmentation, targeting, differentiation, and positioning. (pp 172–173)

A customer value-driven marketing strategy begins with selecting which customers to serve and determining a value proposition that best serves the targeted customers. It consists of four steps. *Market segmentation* is the act of dividing a market into distinct groups of buyers who have different needs, characteristics, or behaviors and who might require separate marketing strategies or mixes. Once the groups have been identified, *market targeting* evaluates each market segment's attractiveness and selects one or more segments to serve. *Differentiation* involves actually differentiating the market offering to create superior customer value. *Positioning* consists of positioning the market offering in the minds of target customers. A customer value-driven marketing strategy seeks to build the *right relationships* with the *right customers*.

OBJECTIVE 6-2 List and discuss the major bases for segmenting consumer and business markets. (pp 173–182)

There is no single way to segment a market. Therefore, the marketer tries different variables to see which give the best segmentation opportunities. For consumer marketing, the major segmentation variables are geographic, demographic, psychographic, and behavioral. In *geographic segmentation*, the market is divided into different geographical units, such as nations, regions, states, counties, cities, or even neighborhoods. In *demographic segmentation*, the market is divided into groups based on demographic variables, including age, life-cycle stage, gender, income, occupation, education, religion, ethnicity, and generation. In *psychographic segmentation*, the market is divided into different groups based on social class, lifestyle, or personality characteristics. In *behavioral segmentation*, the market is divided into groups based on consumers' knowledge, attitudes, uses, or responses concerning a product.

Business marketers use many of the same variables to segment their markets. But business markets also can be segmented by business *demographics* (industry, company size), *operating characteristics, purchasing approaches, situational factors*, and *personal characteristics*. The effectiveness of the segmentation analysis depends on finding segments that are *measurable, accessible, substantial, differentiable*, and *actionable*.

OBJECTIVE 6-3 Explain how companies identify attractive market segments and choose a market-targeting strategy. (pp 182–189)

To target the best market segments, the company first evaluates each segment's size and growth characteristics, structural attractiveness, and compatibility with company objectives and resources. It then chooses one of four market-targeting strategies—ranging from very broad to very narrow targeting. The seller can ignore segment differences and target broadly using *undifferentiated* (or *mass*) *marketing*. This involves mass producing, mass distributing, and mass promoting the same product in about the same way to all consumers. Or the seller can adopt *differentiated marketing*—developing different market offers for several segments. *Concentrated marketing* (or *niche marketing*) involves focusing on one or a few market segments only. Finally, *micromarketing* is the practice of tailoring products and marketing programs to suit the tastes of specific individuals and locations. Micromarketing includes *local marketing* and *individual marketing*. Which targeting strategy is best depends on company resources, product variability, product life-cycle stage, market variability, and competitive marketing strategies.

OBJECTIVE 6-4 Discuss how companies differentiate and position their products for maximum competitive advantage. (pp 189–197)

Once a company has decided which segments to enter, it must decide on its *differentiation and positioning strategy*. The differentiation and positioning task consists of three steps: identifying a set of possible differentiations that create competitive advantage, choosing advantages on which to build a position, and selecting an overall positioning strategy.

The brand's full positioning is called its *value proposition*—the full mix of benefits on which the brand is positioned. In general, companies can choose from one of five winning value propositions on which to position their products: more for more, more for the same, the same for less, less for much less, or more for less. Company and brand positioning are summarized in positioning statements that state the target segment and need, the positioning concept, and specific points of difference. The company must then effectively communicate and deliver the chosen position to the market.

Key Terms

Objective 6-1
Market segmentation (p 172)
Market targeting (targeting) (p 173)
Differentiation (p 173)
Positioning (p 173)

Objective 6-2
Geographic segmentation (p 173)
Demographic segmentation (p 174)
Age and life-cycle segmentation (p 174)
Gender segmentation (p 174)
Income segmentation (p 175)
Psychographic segmentation (p 175)
Behavioral segmentation (p 176)
Occasion segmentation (p 176)
Benefit segmentation (p 176)
Intermarket (cross-market) segmentation (p 181)

Objective 6-3
Target market (p 183)
Undifferentiated (mass) marketing (p 183)
Differentiated (segmented) marketing (p 184)
Concentrated (niche) marketing (p 184)
Micromarketing (p 185)
Local marketing (p 185)
Individual marketing (p 186)

Objective 6-4
Product position (p 189)
Competitive advantage (p 191)
Value proposition (p 193)
Positioning statement (p 195)

DISCUSSION AND CRITICAL THINKING

Discussion Questions

6-1. Name and briefly describe the four major steps in designing a customer value-driven marketing strategy. (AACSB: Written and Oral Communication)

6-2. How is demographic segmentation used in consumer markets? Provide an example where marketers have used demographic segmentation. (AACSB: Written and Oral Communication; Reflective Thinking)

6-3. Describe how marketers segment business markets. How do business segmentation strategies differ from consumer segmentation strategies? (AACSB: Written and Oral Communication)

6-4. Compare the three levels of market targeting that companies can use in choosing how many segments to target. Provide an example for each of the three targeting options. (AACSB: Written and Oral Communication; Reflective Thinking)

6-5. How can a company gain competitive advantage through differentiation? Describe an example of a company that illustrates each type of differentiation discussed in the chapter. (AACSB: Written and Oral Communication)

6-6. What is a value proposition? Discuss the five winning value propositions on which a company might position its products, and give an example of each. (AACSB: Written and Oral Communication)

Critical Thinking Exercises

6-7. Identify a product you use every day. Assume you are the marketer of the product and want to convey the ways your product differs from competing products in the marketplace. Create a differentiation strategy to promote your product and create a competitive advantage. (AACSB: Written and Oral Communication; Reflective Thinking)

6-8. The breakfast cereal market is highly competitive, and marketers for the many varieties of cereal attempt to differentiate their brands to appeal to specific segments. Choose five different breakfast cereal brands, and match them with the segmentation variables that marketers might be using to target a specific market. Explain why you matched each cereal with the specific segmentation variables. (AACSB: Written and Oral Communication; Reflective Thinking)

6-9. In a small group, identify a new business that has emerged in your community or online in the past few years. Using the steps described in the chapter, describe the company's customer value-driven marketing strategy. Write as a positioning statement for this business. (AACSB: Written and Oral Communication; Reflective Thinking)

MINICASES AND APPLICATIONS

Online, Mobile, and Social Media Marketing Get Your Groupon

Local marketing is an effective tool used by marketers to reach intended market segments. Groupon has capitalized on this concept by tailoring brands and marketing to the needs and wants of local customer segments—cities, neighborhoods, and even specific stores. According to its website, Groupon "offers a vast mobile and online marketplace where people discover and save on amazing things to do, see, eat, and buy. By enabling real-time commerce across local businesses, travel destinations, consumer products, and live events, shoppers can find the best a city has to offer. Groupon is redefining how small businesses attract and retain customers by providing them with customizable and scalable marketing tools and services to profitably grow their businesses." This concept lies at the heart of Groupon's mission: "to connect local commerce, increasing consumer buying power while driving more business to local merchants through price and discovery." To help consumers make those connections, Groupon offers a mobile app, online marketplace, and social media touch points where customers can readily access information on its daily deals.

6-10. Discuss the ways in which small businesses utilize local marketing in your community. (AACSB: Written and Oral Communication; Information Technology; Reflective Thinking)

6-11. Do you use Groupon? Is it effective in helping local businesses to meet the challenges of local marketing? Why or why not? (AACSB: Written and Oral Communication; Reflective Thinking)

Marketing Ethics Allegiant Airlines: Value Creation or Flying Public at Risk?

With millions of American passengers selecting air travel to reach their intended destination, Allegiant Airlines has cornered the market by providing exceptionally low fares, consistent customer service, and excellent returns for investors. While Allegiant is known for its bargain fares, it is also now known for its in-flight breakdowns and mechanical failures. According to a *60 Minutes* investigation in 2018, Allegiant Airlines, which has the oldest fleet of airplanes in the industry, experienced more than 100 serious mechanical incidents between January 2016 and October 2017, ranging from engine failures and fires, aborted takeoffs, and smoke and fumes in the passenger cabin to rapid descents and flight control malfunctions. Experts believe that Allegiant's problems stem from its aggressive cost-reduction business practices, which have produced 60 consecutive quarters of profitability, with profit margins near 30 percent. To achieve these results, Allegiant has maintained or decreased costs as much as possible and kept its fleet flying as often as possible. To view the full video and clips, visit www.cbsnews.com/news/allegiant-air-the-budget-airline-flying-under-the-radar/.

6-12. Companies have long struggled to balance the need for profit with consumer value. How has Allegiant differentiated and positioned itself in the airline industry? How has this differentiation and positioning strategy impacted its corporate decision making? (AACSB: Written and Oral Communication; Ethical Understanding and Reasoning)

6-13. Give an example of another airline that positions itself in a way that differentiates it from Allegiant. Which airline would you rather fly? (AACSB: Written and Oral Communication; Reflective Thinking)

Marketing by the Numbers See the Clot, Bust the Clot, Save a Life

Stroke is the fifth-leading cause of death among Americans, claiming more than 130,000 lives each year. Almost 800,000 people suffer a stroke each year in the United States, one every 40 seconds. These grim statistics are actually not as grim as they used to be. New technologies and treatments are increasing the survival rate among sufferers of the most common type of stroke caused by a clot blocking a blood vessel supplying blood to the brain. A procedure known as thrombectomy busts or removes clots and increases survival rates if patients are treated within six to 24 hours of symptom presentation. However, fewer than 5 percent of patients present symptoms within this short time window. Neural Analytics, Inc. has a solution—its Lucid Robotic System. The system is a combination of two products: transcranial ultrasound and a robotic system. The ultrasound, taken from a natural "window into the brain" near a patient's ear, lets medical professionals see if a clot is blocking blood flow. The robotic system, using artificial intelligence (AI), then compares the image to thousands of stored images of severe strokes to identify candidates for the life-saving thrombectomy procedure. This device will help hospital emergency departments to better identify the 10 to 15 percent of stroke patients who qualify for a thrombectomy and send them to one of the country's 100 certified stroke centers. Neural Analytics plans to market its Lucid Robotic System to hospitals first, with the ultimate goal of getting a lower-priced portable system into every emergency response vehicle in the United States.

6-14. There are 5,534 certified hospitals in the United States, and 95 percent have emergency departments. Assuming the price of the Lucid Robotic System is $50,000 and that hospitals with emergency departments purchase one system, use the chain ratio method described in Market Potential and Sales Estimates in Appendix 3: Marketing by the Numbers to calculate the market potential for this product. (AACSB: Analytical Thinking)

6-15. There are approximately 50,000 emergency response vehicles operated by private ambulance companies, municipal fire departments, and hospitals. Assuming the price of the portable Lucid Robotic System is $5,000 and that each emergency response vehicle would be equipped with one system, calculate the market potential of this target market. (AACSB: Analytical Thinking)

Video Case Sprout

To view this video case and its accompanying questions, please visit MyLab Marketing.

In the world of children's television programming, Sprout is a relative newcomer. Owned by NBCUniversal, Sprout airs PBS Kids programming as well as additional acquired material. A true multi-platform network, Sprout can be accessed as regular cable programming, as on-demand programming through Comcast, and online through Sproutonline.com.

Sprout does not target only kids, however. It targets preschool families—households that have one or more preschool-age children. Parents need to be involved with their children's viewing of interactive content, multiple access points, and 24-hour programming. For this reason, Sprout's promotional efforts are geared toward parents as well as children.

Company Cases 6 5-Hour Energy/7 MINI/15 L'Oréal

See Appendix 1 for cases appropriate for this chapter.

Case 6, 5-Hour Energy: Hours of Energy without the Beverage. To break into the crowded world of caffeinated beverages, 5-Hour Energy focused first on targeting the right customer with unmet needs.

Case 7, MINI: Focus on the Essential—Maximize the Experience. BMW has a hit on its hands with MINI, achieving success by remaining true to the original brand while positioning the brand for today's customer.

Case 15, L'Oréal: The United Nations of Beauty. L'Oréal has become the world's largest cosmetics company by achieving the best balance between standardizing its brands for global impact and adapting them to meet local needs and desires.

Writing Assignments

6-16. Describe how marketers segment international markets. What is intermarket segmentation? (AACSB: Communication)

6-17. Discuss ideas for applications of the Google Glass device among the business and institutional markets. How can these applications be incorporated into online, mobile, and social media marketing? (AACSB: Written and Oral Communication; Information Technology; Reflective Thinking)

PART 1: DEFINING MARKETING AND THE MARKETING PROCESS (CHAPTERS 1–2)
PART 2: UNDERSTANDING THE MARKETPLACE AND CONSUMER VALUE (CHAPTERS 3–5)
PART 3: DESIGNING A CUSTOMER VALUE-DRIVEN STRATEGY AND MIX (CHAPTERS 6–14)
PART 4: EXTENDING MARKETING (CHAPTERS 15–16)

Products, Services, and Brands

Building Customer Value

Objectives Outline

OBJECTIVE 7-1 **Define product and describe the major classifications of products and services.** See: What Is a Product? (pp 204–209)

OBJECTIVE 7-2 **Describe the decisions companies make regarding their individual products and services, product lines, and product mixes.** See: Product and Service Decisions (pp 209–218)

OBJECTIVE 7-3 **Identify the four characteristics that affect the marketing of services and the additional marketing considerations that services require.** See: Services Marketing (pp 219–224)

OBJECTIVE 7-4 **Discuss branding strategy—the decisions companies make in building and managing their brands.** See: Branding Strategy: Building Strong Brands (pp 224–233)

Previewing the Concepts

After examining customer value-driven marketing strategy, we now take a deeper look at the marketing mix: the tactical tools that marketers use to implement their strategies, engage customers, and deliver superior customer value. In this and the next chapter, we study how companies develop and manage products, services, and brands. Then, in the chapters that follow, we look at pricing, distribution, and marketing communication tools. The product and brand are usually the first and most basic marketing consideration. We start with a seemingly simple question: What *is* a product? As it turns out, the answer is not so simple.

To dig a little deeper into the question of "What is a product?", we begin by looking at Nike. Nike is the world's leading sports apparel company and one of the best-known brands on the planet. Nike makes good products. But to its customers, the Nike "product" is much, much more than just innovative running shoes and sports apparel. Deep down, Nike is sports inspiration, a just-do-it attitude, and the total brand experience. The brand's outstanding success results from deep brand–customer engagement and close brand community with and among customers.

First Stop

Nike: More Than Just Innovative Sports Gear—a Total Brand Experience

The Nike "swoosh"—it's everywhere! Just for fun, try counting the swooshes whenever you pick up the sports pages or watch a basketball game or tune into a televised soccer match. Over the past 50 years, through innovative marketing, Nike has built the ever-present swoosh into one of the world's best-known brand symbols.

Product innovation has always been a cornerstone of Nike's success. Nike makes outstanding shoes, clothing, and gear, whether for basketball, football, and baseball or golf, skateboarding, bicycling, and hiking. But from the start, Nike revolutionized sports marketing. To build image and market share, the brand lavishly outspent competitors on big-name endorsements, splashy promotional events, and big-budget, in-your-face "Just Do It" ads. Whereas competitors stressed technical performance, Nike built customer engagement and relationships.

Beyond shoes, Nike markets a way of life, a genuine passion for sports, a "just-do-it" attitude. Customers don't just wear their Nikes, they *experience* them. As the company once stated, "Nike has always known the truth—it's not so much the shoes but where they take you." Nike's mission isn't to "make better products," it's to "bring inspiration and innovation to every athlete in the world." Few brands have become more ever-present and valued than Nike in their customers' lives and conversations.

Whether customers connect with Nike through big media ads, in-person events at Niketown stores, a local Nike running club, Nike+ mobile apps, or one of the company's profusion of community web and social media sites, more and more people are bonding closely with the Nike brand. Connecting with customers once required simply outspending competitors on big media ads and celebrity endorsers that talk *at* them. But in these digital times, Nike is forging a new kind of brand–customer connection—a deeper, more personal, more engaging one. While the company still invests heavily in traditional advertising, Nike now spends the lion's share of its marketing budget on cutting-edge digital and social media marketing that interacts *with* customers to build brand engagement, experiences, and community.

Nike's innovative use of digital marketing recently earned the brand the title of "top genius" in "digital IQ" among 70 activewear companies in one digital consultancy's rankings. Another firm ranked Nike the number one apparel brand in social media. It's little wonder. Nike maintains a massive presence on social media platforms such as Instagram, Facebook, Twitter, and YouTube. For example, the main Nike Facebook page has more than 29 million Likes. The Nike Football (soccer) page adds another 45 million, the Nike Basketball page 8.5 million more, and the Nike+ Run Club another 17 million. Nike has more than 79 million Instagram followers, second only to National Geographic.

More than just numbers, Nike's social media presence engages customers deeply, gets them talking with each other about the brand, and weaves the brand into their daily lives. More than just selling shoes, Nike uses emotion-filled stories and other content to "define moments" that capture people who are achieving more by believing in more. An example is the image of double-amputee Blake Leeper stretching on a track with his prosthetic running blades next to him and the caption "Anyone can find excuses to stop. Find a reason to keep going." Or the shot of the U.S. women's soccer team, arm in arm, after winning the last FIFA World Cup, captioned "It takes more than one star to bring home your third." Such defining moments routinely earn Nike more than 500,000 Likes apiece. Such marketing content never mentions the Nike "product" as such—it's all about being part of something bigger.

» The Nike swoosh—it's everywhere. Nike's outstanding success results from creating deep brand–customer engagement, valued brand experiences, and close brand community with and among customers.

Eric D ricochet69/Alamy Stock Photo

To customers, the Nike brand means much more than just innovative running shoes and apparel. Deep down, Nike means sports inspiration, a just-do-it attitude, and a total brand experience.

Nike draws on a wide range of experiences to connect with consumers. For example, it scored a coup by luring rapper Kendrick Lamar away from Reebok and into its fold of celebrity endorsers. To engage Lamar's massive social media following, Nike created a special version of its original Cortez running shoe, dubbed the Cortez Kenny. Teaser posts for the new shoe grabbed millions of views leading up to the sneaker's introduction on the eve of the 2018 Grammy Awards, in which Lamar took home the award for the best rap album of the year.

Last year, Nike blanketed the social media with one of its most ambitious content creation efforts yet. It produced "Breaking2," a moonshot attempt to achieve what most running experts consider impossible—breaking the two-hour marathon barrier. Nike spent years planning every detail of Breaking2. It recruited three of the world's fastest runners, including Kenya's Eliud Kipchoge. It paid them to skip other marathons to focus on the record-breaking attempt. It equipped the runners with specially designed versions of lightweight Nike Zoom Vaporfly Elite shoes. It chose the location—Monza Italy's Formula 1 Grand Prix course—for optimal temperature, wind, and elevation conditions, along with its flat oval shape and gradual turns. Nike also assembled a team of 30 world-class runners to serve as "pacers" and "drafters." The teams even ran wind tunnel experiments to set the best drafting formation. When the Breaking2 race was over, Kipchoge had logged a time of 2:00:25—25 seconds short of the two-hour goal but a whopping 2 minutes and 32 seconds faster than the previous world record.

Breaking2 created a surge in Nike brand engagement with the world's running community. Exclusive live broadcasts and posts on Facebook, Instagram, Twitter, and YouTube chalked up nearly 6 million views. In the weeks and months that followed, the #breaking2 hashtag sparked substantial online chatter, especially as inspiration for morning runs. And a Breaking2 documentary drew another more than 1.7 million views. "We're already discussing other moonshots, perhaps related to female athletes," says the VP of the Nike Sport Research Lab.

Nike has also created customer brand community through groundbreaking mobile apps. For example, its Nike+ and Nike+ Run Club apps have helped Nike become a part of the daily fitness routines of millions of customers around the world. Whether your activity is running, jumping, baseball, skating, dancing, stacking sports cups, or chasing chickens, you can use the Nike+ family of apps to "unlock your potential." Nike+ apps let everyday athletes design their workouts, access training tools, track personal progress, get extra inspiration on the go, and share and compare experiences with friends and others in the Nike community. Nike+ has created a huge global brand community, with tens of millions of registered users worldwide.

Thus, the Nike "product" is much more than just sports shoes and apparel. To customers, Nike represents an attitude, a sports passion, and a deep kinship and sense of community surrounding the brand. More than just something to wear, Nike has become a valued part of customers' lives and times. As a result, Nike remains the world's largest sports apparel company, more than 40 percent larger than rival adidas. Even more impressive, despite mounting competitive pressures, Nike captures 46.5 percent of the U.S. sports footwear market versus number two adidas at 11.3 percent. During the past decade, even as an often-shaky retail market has left many sports apparel rivals gasping for breath, Nike's global sales and income have nearly doubled.[1]

As the Nike story shows, in their quest to create customer relationships, marketers must build and manage products and brands that connect with customers. This chapter begins with a deceptively simple question: *What is a product?* After addressing this question, we look at ways to classify products in consumer and business markets. Then we discuss the important decisions that marketers make regarding individual products, product lines, and product mixes. Next, we examine the characteristics and marketing requirements of a special form of product—services. Finally, we look into the critically important issue of how marketers build and manage product and service brands.

What Is a Product?

Author Comment
As you'll see, this deceptively simple question has a very complex answer. For example, think back to the opening Nike story. What is the Nike "product"?

OBJECTIVE 7-1 Define product and describe the major classifications of products and services.

We define a **product** as anything that can be offered to a market for attention, acquisition, use, or consumption that might satisfy a want or need. Products include more than just tangible objects, such as cars, clothing, or mobile phones. Broadly defined, products also include services, events, persons, places, organizations, and ideas or a mixture of these. Throughout this text, we use the term *product* broadly to include any or all these entities. Thus, an Apple iPhone, a Toyota Camry, and a Caffé Mocha at Starbucks are products. But so are a trip to Las Vegas, Schwab online investment services, your Instagram account, and advice from your family doctor.

Product
Anything that can be offered to a market for attention, acquisition, use, or consumption that might satisfy a want or need.

Because of their importance in the world economy, we give special attention to services. **Services** are a form of product that consists of activities, benefits, or satisfactions offered for sale that are essentially intangible and do not result in the ownership of anything. Examples include banking, hotel, airline travel, retail, wireless communication, and home-repair services. We will look at services more closely later in this chapter.

Service
An activity, benefit, or satisfaction offered for sale that is essentially intangible and does not result in the ownership of anything.

Products, Services, and Experiences

Products are a key element in the overall *market offering*. Marketing mix planning begins with building an offering that brings value to target customers. This offering becomes the basis on which the company builds profitable customer relationships.

>> Creating customer experiences: More than just selling products, Apple's highly successful retail stores create engaging life-feels-good brand experiences.

Area 52 Advertising Inc/Getty Images

A company's market offering often includes both tangible goods and services. At one extreme, the market offer may consist of a *pure tangible good*, such as soap, toothpaste, or salt; no services accompany the product. At the other extreme are *pure services*, for which the market offer consists primarily of a service. Examples include a doctor's exam and financial services. Between these two extremes, however, many goods-and-services combinations are possible.

Today, as products and services become more commoditized, many companies are moving to a new level in creating value for their customers. To differentiate their offers, beyond simply making products and delivering services, they are creating and managing customer *experiences* with their brands or companies.

Experiences have always been an important part of marketing for some companies. Disney has long manufactured dreams and memories through its movies and theme parks—it wants theme park cast members to deliver a thousand "small wows" to every customer. And Nike has long declared, "It's not so much the shoes but where they take you." Today, however, all kinds of firms are recasting their traditional goods and services to create experiences. >> For example, Apple's highly successful retail stores don't just sell the company's products. They create an engaging Apple brand experience:[2]

Apple's retail stores are very seductive places, where "life-feels-good" experiences abound. The store design is clean, simple, and just oozing with style—much like an Apple iPad or a featherweight MacBook Air. The bustling stores feel more like community centers than retail outlets, with crowds of customers sampling the goods and buzzing excitedly about all things Apple. The stores encourage a lot of purchasing, to be sure. But they also encourage lingering, with tables full of fully functioning Macs, iPads, and iPhones sitting out for visitors to try and dozens of laid-back Apple employees close at hand to answer questions and cater to every whim. The stores offer expert technical assistance at the Genius Bar and a full schedule of workshops where customers at all experience levels can learn about their Apple devices and explore their creative sides. You don't just visit an Apple store—you experience it in a way that no other consumer electronics company can match. As one Apple retail executive explains, "I don't want to be sold to when I walk into a store. Don't sell! No! Because that's a turn-off. Build an amazing brand experience, and then [sales] will just naturally happen."

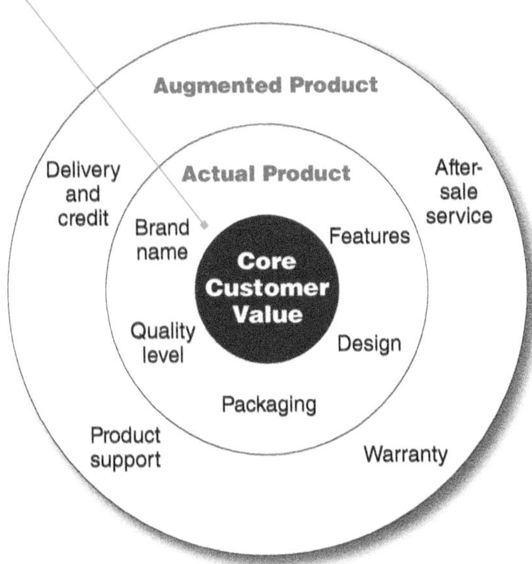
At the most basic level, the company asks, "What is the customer really buying?" For example, people who buy an Apple iPad are buying more than just a tablet computer. They are buying entertainment, self-expression, productivity, and connectivity—a mobile and personal window to the world.
Augmented Product
Actual Product
Delivery and credit
After-sale service
Brand name
Features
Core Customer Value
Quality level
Design
Packaging
Product support
Warranty

>> Figure 7.1 Three Levels of Product

Levels of Product and Services

Product planners need to think about products and services on three levels (see >> **Figure 7.1**). Each level adds more customer value. The most basic level is the *core customer value*, which addresses the question: *What is the buyer really buying?* When designing products, marketers must first define the core, problem-solving benefits, services, or experiences that consumers seek. A woman buying lipstick buys more than lip color. Charles Revson of Revlon saw this early: "In the factory, we make cosmetics; in the store, we sell hope." And people who buy a Harley-Davidson motorcycle are buying much more than a machine that gets them from point A to point B:[3]

>> Core product: People who buy a Harley-Davidson are buying more than just a motorcycle. They are buying self-expression, lifestyles, aspirations, and dreams.
Scott Olson/Getty Images NEWS/Getty Images

Remove the helmets and the leathers of a hardcore Harley enthusiast, and there's no telling whom you'll find. It might be a guy with tattoos and unruly hair, but it's just as likely to be a CEO, investment banker, or gourmet chef. The average Harley customer is a 50-something male with a median household income of $87,000. More than 12 percent of Harley purchasers today are women. "Harley brings together all walks of life," says Harley's chief marketing officer. "You'll find a neurosurgeon talking and riding with a janitor. It's a family."

But no matter who they are, Harley-Davidson disciples share a common, deeply held attraction to the brand. >> The core Harley appeals are these: freedom, independence, power, and authenticity. Harley-Davidson doesn't just sell motorcycles. It sells self-expression, lifestyles, aspirations, and dreams. A Harley renews your spirits and announces your freedom and independence. "It's all about the *experience*," says an analyst, "one forged in heavy metal thunder, living free, and peeling wheel down Route 66. It's an experience that allows middle-aged accountants to don black, studded leather and forget about debits and credits for a little while."

At the second level, product planners must turn the core benefit into an *actual product*. They need to develop product and service features, a design, a quality level, a brand name, and packaging. For example, a Harley-Davidson motorcycle is an actual product. Its name, styling, features, sounds, parts, and other attributes have all been carefully combined to deliver the core customer values of freedom and independence.

Finally, product planners must build an *augmented product* around the core benefit and actual product by offering additional consumer services and benefits. Thus, when consumers buy a Harley, Harley-Davidson and its dealers also give buyers a warranty on parts and workmanship, quick repair services when needed, a showroom full of accessories, and web and mobile sites to use if they have problems or questions. The Harley Owners Group (H.O.G.) provides additional benefits such as roadside assistance, H.O.G. rallies and other events, and regular issues of HOG Magazine, packed with H.O.G. news, product information, riding stories, and more.

Consumers see products as complex bundles of benefits that satisfy their needs. When developing products, marketers first must identify the *core customer value* that consumers seek from the product. They must then design the *actual* product and find ways to *augment* it to create customer value and a full and satisfying brand experience.

Product and Service Classifications

Products and services fall into two broad classes based on the types of consumers who use them: *consumer products* and *industrial products*. Broadly defined, products also include other marketable entities such as experiences, organizations, persons, places, and ideas.

Consumer Products

Consumer product
A product bought by final consumers for personal consumption.

Consumer products are products and services bought by final consumers for personal consumption. Marketers usually classify these products and services further based on how consumers go about buying them. Consumer products include *convenience products, shopping products, specialty products*, and *unsought products*. These products differ in the ways consumers buy them and, therefore, in how they are marketed (see >> **Table 7.1**).

Table 7.1 Marketing Considerations for Consumer Products

Marketing Considerations	Type of Consumer Product: Convenience	Shopping	Specialty	Unsought
Customer buying behavior	Frequent purchase; little planning, little comparison or shopping effort; low customer involvement	Less frequent purchase; much planning and shopping effort; comparison of brands on price, quality, and style	Strong brand preference and loyalty; special purchase effort; little comparison of brands; low price sensitivity	Little product awareness or knowledge (or, if aware, little or even negative interest)
Price	Low price	Higher price	Highest price	Varies
Distribution	Widespread distribution; convenient locations	Selective distribution in fewer outlets	Exclusive distribution in only one or a few outlets per market area	Varies
Promotion	Mass promotion by the producer	Advertising and personal selling by both the producer and resellers	More carefully targeted promotion by both the producer and resellers	Aggressive advertising and personal selling by the producer and resellers
Examples	Toothpaste, magazines, and laundry detergent	Major appliances, televisions, furniture, and clothing	Luxury goods, such as Rolex watches or fine crystal	Life insurance and Red Cross blood donations

Convenience product
A consumer product that customers usually buy frequently, immediately, and with minimal comparison and buying effort.

Shopping product
A consumer product that the customer, in the process of selecting and purchasing, usually compares on such attributes as suitability, quality, price, and style.

Specialty product
A consumer product with unique characteristics or brand identification for which a significant group of buyers is willing to make a special purchase effort.

Unsought product
A consumer product that the consumer either does not know about or knows about but does not normally consider buying.

Convenience products are consumer products and services that customers usually buy frequently, immediately, and with minimal comparison and buying effort. Examples include laundry detergent, candy, magazines, and fast food. Convenience products are usually low priced, and marketers place them in many locations to make them readily available when customers need or want them.

Shopping products are less frequently purchased consumer products and services that customers compare carefully on suitability, quality, price, and style. When buying shopping products and services, consumers spend much time and effort in gathering information and making comparisons. Examples include furniture, clothing, major appliances, and hotel services. Shopping product marketers usually distribute their products through fewer outlets but provide deeper sales support to help customers in their comparison efforts.

Specialty products are consumer products and services with unique characteristics or brand identifications for which a significant group of buyers is willing to make a special purchase effort. Examples include specific brands of cars, high-priced photography equipment, designer clothes, gourmet foods, and the services of medical or legal specialists. A Lamborghini automobile, for example, is a specialty product because buyers are usually willing to travel great distances to buy one. Buyers normally do not compare specialty products. They invest only the time needed to reach dealers carrying the wanted brands.

Unsought products are consumer products that a consumer either does not know about or knows about but does not normally consider buying. Most major new innovations are unsought until consumers become aware of them through marketing. Classic examples of known but unsought products and services are life insurance, preplanned funeral services, and blood donations to the Red Cross. By their very nature, unsought products require a lot of promoting, personal selling, and other marketing efforts.

Industrial Products

Industrial product
A product bought by individuals and organizations for further processing or for use in conducting a business.

Industrial products are those products purchased for further processing or for use in conducting a business. Thus, the distinction between a consumer product and an industrial product is based on the *purpose* for which the product is purchased. If a consumer buys a lawn mower for use around home, the lawn mower is a consumer product. If the same consumer buys the same lawn mower for use in a landscaping business, the lawn mower is an industrial product.

The three groups of industrial products and services are materials and parts, capital items, and supplies and services. *Materials and parts* include raw materials as well as manufactured materials and parts. Raw materials consist of farm products (wheat, cotton, livestock, fruits, vegetables) and natural products (fish, lumber, crude petroleum, iron ore). Manufactured materials and parts consist of component materials (iron, yarn, cement, wires) and component parts (small motors, tires, castings). Most manufactured materials and parts are sold directly to industrial users. Price and service are the major marketing factors; branding and advertising tend to be less important.

Capital items are industrial products that aid in the buyer's production or operations, including installations and accessory equipment. Installations consist of major purchases such as buildings (factories, offices) and fixed equipment (generators, drill presses, large computer systems, elevators). Accessory equipment includes portable factory equipment and tools (hand tools, lift trucks) and office equipment (computers, fax machines, desks). These types of equipment have shorter lives than do installations and simply aid in the production process.

The final group of industrial products is *supplies and services*. Supplies include operating supplies (lubricants, coal, paper, pencils) and repair and maintenance items (paint, nails, brooms). Supplies are the convenience products of the industrial field because they are usually purchased with a minimum of effort or comparison. Business services include maintenance and repair services (window cleaning, computer repair) and business advisory services (legal, management consulting, advertising). Such services are usually supplied under contract.

Organizations, Persons, Places, and Ideas

In addition to tangible products and services, marketers have broadened the concept of a product to include other market offerings: organizations, persons, places, and ideas.

Organizations often carry out activities to "sell" the organization itself. *Organization marketing* consists of activities undertaken to create, maintain, or change the attitudes and behavior of target consumers toward an organization. Both profit and not-for-profit organizations practice organization marketing.

Business firms sponsor public relations or corporate image marketing campaigns to market themselves, their images, and their ideals. For example, GE's long-running "Imagination at Work" campaign markets the industrial giant as a company whose imaginative industrial products and technologies are making a difference in the world. Consider one award-winning TV spot, called "Childlike Imagination." The whimsical ad brings GE's products—from jet engines and diesel locomotives to giant wind turbines and hospital diagnostics machines—to life through the eyes of a wide-eyed young girl whose mom works at GE. GE is "Building, powering, moving, and curing the world," says the company. "Not just imagining. Doing. GE works."[4]

People can also be thought of as products. *Person marketing* consists of activities undertaken to create, maintain, or change attitudes or behavior toward particular people. People ranging from presidents, entertainers, and sports figures to professionals such as doctors, lawyers, and architects use person marketing to build their reputations. And businesses, charities, and other organizations use well-known personalities to help sell their products or causes. For example, Nike spends almost $10 billion annually on endorsement deals with a stable of stars spanning almost every conceivable sport worldwide, including headliners such as tennis greats Maria Sharapova and Rodger Federer, world soccer superstars Cristiano Ronaldo and Neymar, and current and former NBA all-stars Michael Jordan, LeBron James, and Kevin Durant.[5]

Place marketing involves activities undertaken to create, maintain, or change attitudes or behavior toward particular places. Cities, states, regions, and even entire nations compete to attract tourists, new residents, conventions, and company offices and factories. For example, Detroit's city website celebrates Detroit as "American's Great Comeback City" and promotes the best places to eat, things to do, and events to attend. Tourism Australia advertises that "There's Nothing Like Australia" and provides a website and smartphone app complete with videos, holiday ideas, destination information, and about anything else travelers might need to plan an Australian vacation.[6]

Social marketing
The use of traditional business marketing concepts and tools to encourage behaviors that will create individual and societal well-being.

Ideas can also be marketed. In one sense, all marketing is the marketing of an idea, whether it is the general idea of brushing your teeth or the specific idea that Crest toothpastes "improve the health of your smile." Here, however, we narrow our focus to the marketing of *social ideas*. This area has been called **social marketing** and consists of using traditional business marketing concepts and tools to encourage behaviors that will create individual and societal well-being.

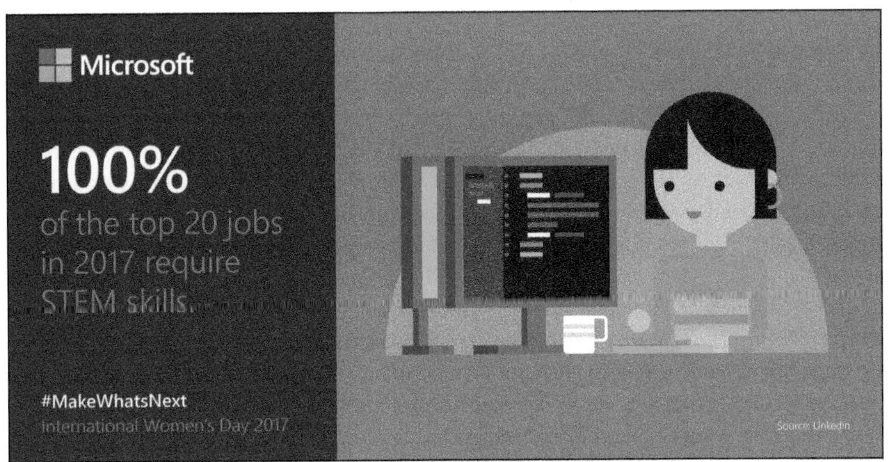

>> Marketing ideas: Microsoft's "Make What's Next campaign" markets the company's support for the idea of encouraging girls to enter tech and science fields.

Microsoft

Many companies engage in social marketing to support ideas they believe in. >> Microsoft's "Make What's Next" campaign encourages girls to enter tech and science fields. The company promotes the program with inspirational ads, social media videos and events, and a dedicated website. The website also offers an experiential tool called Career Explorer, powered by professional networking site LinkedIn, that shows girls how to pursue their passions and skills in specific areas. "When we encourage girls to pursue science, technology, engineering, and math (STEM)," says Microsoft, "we double the potential to solve problems. If she stays in STEM, she could be the one to change the world."[7]

Social marketing programs cover a wide range of issues. The Ad Council of America (www.adcouncil.org), for example, has developed dozens of social advertising campaigns involving issues ranging from health care, education, and environmental sustainability to preventing teen bullying and confronting sexual harassment. But social marketing involves much more than just advertising. It involves a broad range of marketing strategies and marketing mix tools designed to bring about beneficial social change.[8]

Author Comment
Now that we've answered the "What is a product?" question, we dig into the specific decisions that companies must make when designing and marketing products and services.

Product and Service Decisions

OBJECTIVE 7-2 Describe the decisions companies make regarding their individual products and services, product lines, and product mixes.

Marketers make product and service decisions at three levels: individual product decisions, product line decisions, and product mix decisions. We discuss each in turn.

Individual Product and Service Decisions

>> **Figure 7.2** shows the important decisions in the development and marketing of individual products and services. We will focus on decisions about *product attributes, branding, packaging, labeling and logos*, and *product support services*.

Product and Service Attributes

Developing a product or service involves defining the benefits that it will offer. These benefits are communicated and delivered by product attributes such as *quality, features*, and *style and design*.

Product quality
The characteristics of a product or service that bear on its ability to satisfy stated or implied customer needs.

Product Quality. **Product quality** is one of the marketer's major positioning tools. Quality affects product or service performance; thus, it is closely linked to customer value and satisfaction. In the narrowest sense, quality can be defined as "no defects." But most marketers go beyond this narrow definition. Instead, they define quality in terms of creating customer value and satisfaction. The American Society for Quality defines quality as the characteristics of a product or service that bear on its ability to satisfy stated or implied customer

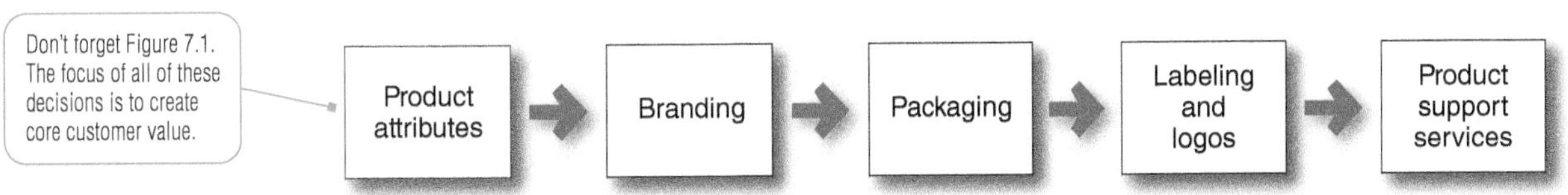

>> **Figure 7.2 Individual Product Decisions**

needs. Similarly, Siemens defines quality this way: "Quality is when our customers come back and our products don't."[9]

Total quality management (TQM) is an approach in which all the company's people are involved in constantly improving the quality of products, services, and business processes. For most top companies, customer-driven quality has become a way of doing business. Today, companies are taking a *return-on-quality* approach, viewing quality as an investment and holding quality efforts accountable for bottom-line results.

Product quality has two dimensions: level and consistency. In developing a product, the marketer must first choose a *quality level* that will support the product's positioning. Here, product quality means *performance quality*—the product's ability to perform its functions. For example, a Rolls-Royce provides higher performance quality than a Chevrolet: It has a smoother ride, lasts longer, and provides more handcraftsmanship, custom design, luxury, and "creature comforts." Companies rarely try to offer the highest possible performance quality level; few customers want or can afford the high levels of quality offered in products such as a Rolls-Royce automobile, a Viking range, or a Rolex watch. Instead, companies choose a quality level that matches target market needs and the quality levels of competing products.

Beyond quality level, high quality also can mean high levels of quality consistency. Here, product quality means *conformance quality*—freedom from defects and consistency in delivering a targeted level of performance. All companies should strive for high levels of conformance quality. In this sense, a Chevrolet can have just as much quality as a Rolls-Royce. Although a Chevy doesn't perform at the same level as a Rolls-Royce, it can just as consistently deliver the quality that customers pay for and expect.

Similarly, Americas Best Value Inn—the fast-growing economy hotel chain—doesn't aspire to provide a luxury Ritz-Carlton experience. However, it consistently delivers on its promise to gives customers "The Best Bang for Your Buck." Its locally owned and operated hotels consistently "provide an honest stay and reliable service." As one satisfied guest confirms: "Awesome for the price! We stayed for 5 nights with our two doggies. Got a great rate on a no-frills but clean and comfortable room. The front desk managers are super friendly and very down to earth. Couldn't ask for any better service!" By consistently meeting and exceeding customer quality expectations, Americas Best Value Inn recently earned the J.D. Power Award for highest customer satisfaction among the nation's economy hotels. "A good stay doesn't require any complicated formula," says the hotel. "We focus on a comfortable bed to sleep in, complimentary breakfast each morning, and the promise of a great day ahead. It is that simple."[10]

Product Features. A product can be offered with varying features. A stripped-down model, one without any extras, is the starting point. The company can then create higher-level models by adding more features. Features are a competitive tool for differentiating the company's product from competitors' products. Being the first producer to introduce a valued new feature is one of the most effective ways to compete.

How can a company identify new features and decide which ones to add? It should periodically survey buyers who have used the product and ask these questions: How do you like the product? Which specific features of the product do you like most? Which features could we add to improve the product? The answers to these questions provide the company with a rich list of feature ideas. The company can then assess each feature's *value* to customers versus its *cost* to the company. Features that customers value highly in relation to costs should be added.

Product Style and Design. Another way to add customer value is through distinctive *product style and design*. Design is a larger concept than style. *Style* simply describes the appearance of a product. Styles can be eye catching or yawn producing. A sensational style may grab attention and produce pleasing aesthetics, but it does not necessarily make the product *perform* better. Unlike style, *design* is more than skin deep—it goes to the very heart of a product. Good design contributes to a product's usefulness as well as to its looks.

Good design doesn't start with brainstorming new ideas and making prototypes. Design begins with observing customers, understanding their needs, and shaping their product-use experience. Product designers should think less about technical product specifications and more about how customers will use and benefit from the product. For example, using smart design based on consumer needs, Sonos created a wireless, internet-enabled speaker system that's easy to use and fills a whole house with great sound.[11]

> In the past, setting up a whole-house entertainment or sound system required routing wires through walls, floors, and ceilings, creating a big mess and lots of expense. And if you moved, you couldn't take it with you. Enter Sonos, which took home-audio and theater systems to a new level worthy of the digital age. The innovative company created a wireless speaker system that's not just stylish but also easy to set up, easy to use, and easy to move to meet changing needs. With Sonos, you can stream high-quality sound through a variety of stylish speakers anywhere in your home with just an app and a tap on your smartphone. Smart design has paid off handsomely for Sonos. Founded in 2002, the company's sales have grown to an estimated $1 billion a year.

Branding

Brand
A name, term, sign, symbol, or design, or a combination of these, that identifies the products or services of one seller or group of sellers and differentiates them from those of competitors.

Perhaps the most distinctive skill of professional marketers is their ability to build and manage brands. A **brand** is a name, term, sign, symbol, or design or a combination of these that identifies the maker or seller of a product or service. Consumers view a brand as an important part of a product, and branding can add value to a consumer's purchase. Customers attach meanings to brands and develop brand relationships. As a result, brands have meaning well beyond a product's physical attributes. Consider this story:[12]

> One Tuesday evening in January, Joshua Bell, one of the world's finest violinists, played at Boston's stately Symphony Hall before a packed audience who'd paid an average of $100 a seat. Based on the well-earned strength of the "Joshua Bell brand," the talented musician routinely drew standing-room-only audiences at all of his performances around the world. Three days later, however, as part of a *Washington Post* social experiment, Bell found himself standing in a Washington, DC, metro station, dressed in jeans, a T-shirt, and a Washington Nationals baseball cap. As morning commuters streamed by, Bell pulled out his $4 million Stradivarius violin, set the open case at his feet, and began playing the same revered classics he'd played in Boston. During the next 45 minutes, some 1,100 people passed by but few stopped to listen. Bell earned a total of $32. No one recognized the "unbranded" Bell, so few appreciated his artistry. What does that tell you about the meaning of a strong brand?

Branding has become so strong that today hardly anything goes unbranded. Salt is packaged in branded containers, common nuts and bolts are packaged with a distributor's label, and automobile parts—spark plugs, tires, filters—bear brand names that differ from those of the automakers. Even fruits, vegetables, dairy products, and poultry are branded—Cuties mandarin oranges, Dole Classic salads, Wonderful Pistachios, Perdue chickens, Eggland's Best eggs, and Avocados From Mexico.

Branding helps buyers in many ways. Brand names help consumers identify products that might benefit them. Brands also say something about product quality and consistency—buyers who always buy the same brand know that they will get the same features, benefits, and quality each time they buy. Branding also gives the seller several advantages. The seller's brand name and trademark provide legal protection for unique product features that otherwise might be copied by competitors. Branding helps the seller to segment markets. For example, rather than offering just one general product to all consumers, Toyota can offer the different Lexus, Toyota, and Scion brands, each with numerous subbrands—such as Avalon, Camry, Corolla, Prius, Yaris, Tundra, and Land Cruiser.

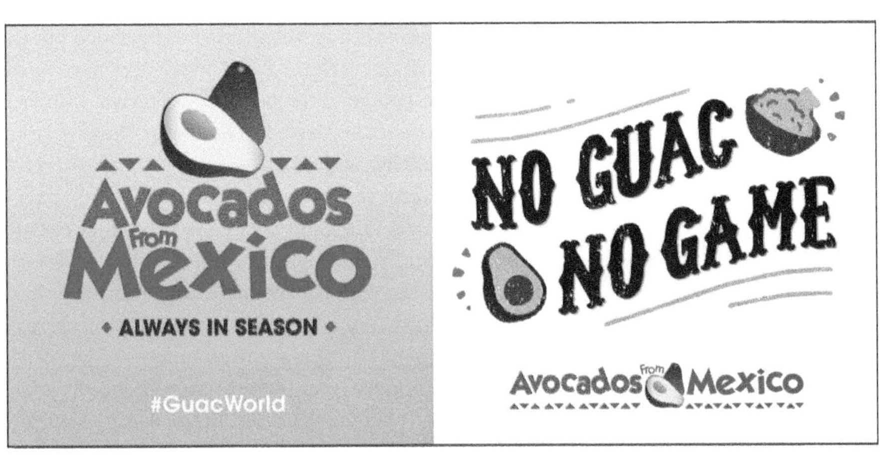

>> **Branding has become so strong that today hardly anything goes unbranded. The Avocados From Mexico brand now accounts for 80 percent of all U.S. avocado sales.**

Avocados From Mexico

Finally, a brand name becomes the basis on which a whole story can be built about a product's special qualities. >> For example, the goal of Avocados From Mexico—a not-for-profit organization that represents both Mexican avocado growers and packers and U.S. importers and packers—is to convince U.S. consumers that avocados are a must-have snack ("No Guac. No Game!"). What's more, it wants consumers to know that the Avocados From Mexico brand stands for great avocados that make for good times, good food, and good health. To promote the brand, the organization spends $20 million a year on advertising, including big-budget ads in four consecutive Super Bowls. During last year's Super Bowl, Avocados From Mexico was the most mentioned advertiser across Instagram and Twitter and #Guacworld was the most used hashtag. As a result of such brand building, U.S. avocado sales have seen double-digit growth during the past few years, and the Avocados From Mexico brand now accounts for nearly 80 percent of all U.S. avocado sales.[13] We will discuss branding strategy in more detail later in the chapter.

Packaging

Packaging
The activities of designing and producing the container or wrapper for a product.

Packaging involves designing and producing the container or wrapper for a product. Traditionally, the primary function of the package was to hold and protect the product. In recent times, however, packaging has become an important marketing tool as well. Increased competition and clutter on retail store shelves means that packages must now perform many sales tasks—from attracting buyers to communicating brand positioning to closing the sale. Not every customer will see a brand's advertising, social media pages, or other marketing content. However, all consumers who buy and use a product will interact regularly with its packaging. Thus, the humble package represents prime marketing space.

Companies realize the power of good packaging to create immediate consumer recognition of a brand. For example, an average supermarket stocks about 38,000 items; the average Walmart supercenter carries 142,000 items. And according to a recent study, 55 percent of shoppers decide what brand to buy while shopping. In this highly competitive environment, the package may be the seller's best and last chance to influence buyers. So the package itself becomes an important promotional medium.[14]

Innovative packaging can give a company an advantage over competitors and boost sales. Distinctive packaging may even become an important part of a brand's identity. For example, an otherwise plain brown carton imprinted with the familiar curved arrow from the Amazon.com logo—variously interpreted as "a to z" or even a smiley face—leaves no doubt as to who shipped the package sitting at your doorstep. And Tiffany's distinctive blue boxes have come to embody the exclusive jewelry retailer's premium legacy and positioning. As the company puts it, "Glimpsed on a busy street or resting in the palm of a hand, Tiffany Blue Boxes make hearts beat faster and epitomize Tiffany's great heritage of elegance, exclusivity, and flawless craftsmanship."[15]

» Innovative Child Guard safety packaging likely saved P&G's fast-growing Tide PODS and other unit-dose laundry detergent brands.
Gary Armstrong

Poorly designed packages can cause headaches for consumers and lost sales for the company. Think about all those hard-to-open packages, such as packaging with finger-splitting wire twist-ties or sealed plastic clamshell containers that cause "wrap rage" and send thousands of people to the hospital each year with lacerations and puncture wounds. Another packaging issue is overpackaging—as when a tiny USB flash drive in an oversized cardboard and plastic display package is delivered in a giant corrugated shipping carton. Overpackaging creates an incredible amount of waste, frustrating those who care about the environment.

In making packaging decisions, the company also must heed growing environmental concerns. Fortunately, many companies have gone "green" by reducing their packaging and using environmentally responsible packaging materials. Product safety has also become a major packaging concern in recent years. » For example, consider P&G's Tide

PODS unit-dose laundry detergent packets. To prevent children from accidentally eating the colorful, candy-looking but toxic packets, P&G spent three years perfecting a Child-Guard Pack, a flexible pouch with a child-resistant zipper, and Child-Guard Tub, featuring a child-resistant squeeze-and-twist lid. These packaging innovations likely saved P&G's Tide PODS and other unit-dose brands. Unit-dose products have accounted for 90 percent of recent laundry detergent category growth and about 15 percent of total category sales. P&G's Tide PODS and Gain Flings! hold nearly 80 percent of those unit-dose sales.[16]

Labeling and Logos

Labels and logos range from simple tags attached to products to complex graphics that are part of the packaging. They perform several functions. At the very least, the label *identifies* the product or brand, such as the name Sunkist stamped on oranges. The label might also *describe* several things about the product—who made it, where it was made, when it was made, its contents, how it is to be used, and how to use it safely. Finally, the label might help to *promote* the brand and engage customers. For many companies, labels have become an important element in broader marketing campaigns.

Labels and brand logos can support the brand's positioning and add personality to the brand. In fact, they can become a crucial element in the brand–customer connection. Customers often become strongly attached to logos as symbols of the brands they represent. Consider the feelings evoked by the logos of companies such as Google, Coca-Cola, Twitter, Apple, and Nike. Logos must be redesigned from time to time. For example, brands ranging from Yahoo!, eBay, and Southwest Airlines to Wendy's, Pizza Hut, Black+Decker, and Hershey have successfully adapted their logos to keep them contemporary and to meet the needs of new digital devices and interactive platforms such as the mobile apps and social media (see Marketing at Work 7.1).

However, companies must take care when changing such important brand symbols. Customers often form strong connections to the visual representations of their brands and may react strongly to changes. » For example, a few years ago when Gap introduced a more contemporary redesign of its familiar old logo—the well-known white text on a blue square—customers went ballistic and imposed intense online pressure. Gap reinstated the old logo after only one week.

Along with the positives, there has been a long history of legal concerns about labels and packaging. The Federal Trade Commission Act of 1914 held that false, misleading, or deceptive labels or packages constitute unfair competition. Labels can mislead customers, fail to describe important ingredients, or fail to include needed safety warnings. As a result, several federal and state laws regulate labeling. The most prominent is the Fair Packaging and Labeling Act of 1966, which set mandatory labeling requirements, encouraged voluntary industry packaging standards, and allowed federal agencies to set packaging regulations in specific industries. The Nutritional Labeling and Educational Act of 1990 requires sellers to provide detailed nutritional information on food products, and recent sweeping actions by the Food and Drug Administration (FDA) regulate the use of health-related terms such as *low fat, light, high fiber,* and *organic*. Sellers must ensure that their labels contain all the required information.

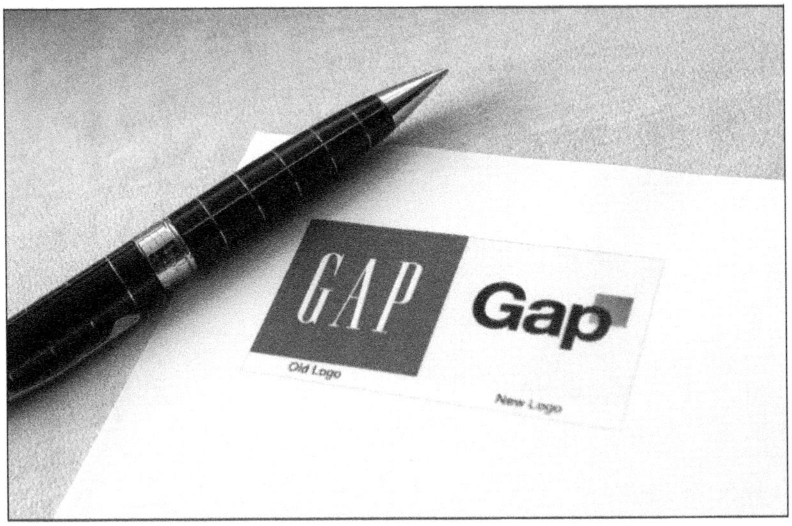

» Brand labels and logos: When Gap tried to modernize its familiar old logo, customers went ballistic, highlighting the powerful connection people have to the visual representations of their beloved brands.

Jean Francois FREY/PHOTOPQR/L'ALSACE/Newscom

Product Support Services

Customer service is another element of product strategy. A company's offer usually includes some support services, which can be a minor part or a major part of the total offering. Later in this chapter, we will discuss services as products in themselves. Here, we discuss services that augment actual products.

MARKETING AT WORK 7.1

Brand Logo Makeovers for the Digital Age

It seems like everyone is doing it these days—giving their logos major makeovers. From Google, Hershey, Audi, Pizza Hut, and American Airlines to Southwest and IHOP, it's out with the old and in with the new. Such logo redesigns can be risky. Brand logos can be like a pair of old shoes—familiar and comforting—and customers often don't take kindly to changes. Given the risks, why are so many companies reworking their logos?

Companies have always taken great care to craft simple, easily recognized logos that quickly identify their brands and trigger positive consumer associations. However, in today's digital world, brand logos are being asked to do much more. A logo is no longer just a static symbol placed on a printed page, package, TV ad, billboard, or store display. Instead, todays logos must also meet the demands of an ever-more-diverse set of digital devices and media. A brand logo that looks great and communicates well on a package or in a magazine ad might fail miserably in a social media setting on a smartphone screen.

Today's logos must stand out visually on screens of all sizes, from big-screen TVs to tablets, mobile phones, and even smartwatches. Often, they must also function as interactive icons or animated activity indicators on website, mobile, and social media pages. As a result, companies are adapting their logos to keep them in sync with the rapidly evolving digital times.

Most logo modifications focus on creating simpler, brighter, more modern designs that present better on digital screens and platforms. For example, Hershey flipped its colors from light letters on a dark field to dark letters on a white field, while also replacing its long-standing image of a Hershey's Kiss wrapped in silver foil with a more contemporary silhouette version. Pizza Hut's new logo consists of a simple pizza-shaped medallion with the brand name and familiar roof symbol reversed out in white. And Southwest went from black all-capital letters beneath a jumbo jet image to bright blue letters in title format accompanied by its signature heart icon in rainbow colors.

Such redesigns have multiple aims, but the primary objective is to make the logos more digital device-friendly. For example, the old IHOP logo had white letters placed on a blue field with a downward-curving red banner containing the word "restaurant." Now, IHOP's letters are blue on a white field, a design that stands out better against the white backgrounds on most web, mobile, and social media sites. The new logo also replaces the old frown-like "restaurant" banner with an upward curving red line under the "o" and the "p," creating a smiley face that adds a burst of happiness to the brand.

Many logos today are wordless, using only a brand symbol with no mention of the brand name at all. Think Apple, Twitter, Nike, and Airbnb. Carmaker Audi recently redesigned its logo, dropping the red Audi wordmark altogether. It turned its signature four 3D interlocking chrome rings to flat black and let the rings themselves become the logo. The new logo seems plainer but is also less restrictive and more interactive across today's digital formats, from screens inside the car to Audi's website, mobile apps, and even wearables. No longer tied to the Audi wordmark, the flat black logo can be used with any number of positioning phrases and interactive features. "The overall design ... is bold, minimal, confident, and luxurious in a way that matches Audi's cars," says one analyst. "It's a living interface that interacts with human beings," says Audi.

Some logo redesigns go much, much deeper. For example, consider recent changes to Google's familiar blue, red, green, and yellow logo. At first glance, the changes seem minor—you might not even have noticed them. The letter colors remain largely the same, as does the childlike quality that we've come to associate with the Google brand. The biggest difference is

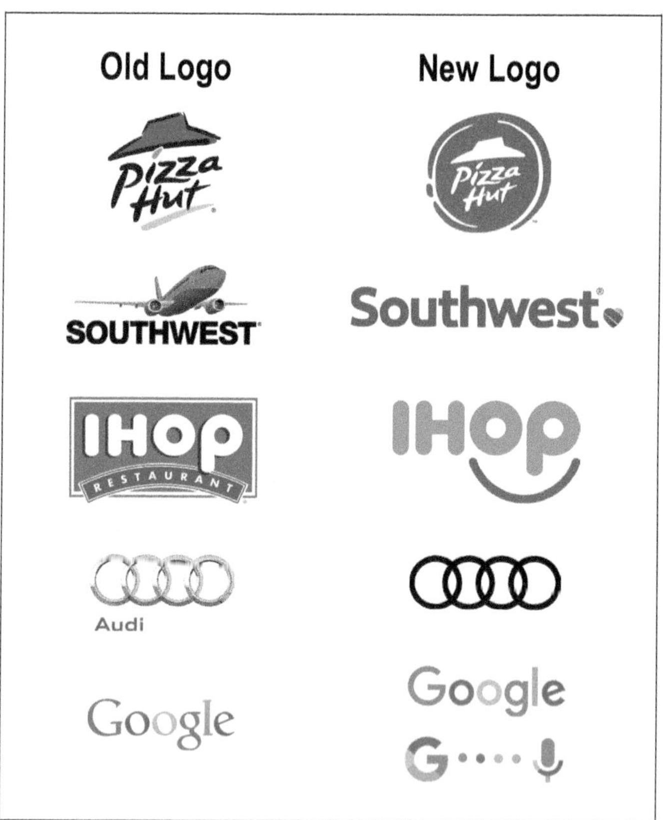

» Brand logo makeovers: Many companies are redesigning their logos to keep them in sync with the rapidly evolving digital times.

Pizza Hut, Inc.; Southwest Airlines; International House of Pancakes, LLC; Audi of America; Google and the Google logo are registered trademarks of Google Inc., used with permission.

the new typeface—Google changed its old serif typeface (with little lines and squiggles at the ends of letters) to a sans serif typeface (without the lines and squiggles). The result is a simpler, cleaner, more readable logo. The streamlined font shrinks down more legibly than fancier fonts, so it transfers more readily across all kinds of screens. Google claims that its new logo can be read just as well on a 2.5-inch Android Wear watch as it can on a 50-inch TV screen.

But Google didn't just change the logo typeface. It created a full kit of new brand logo tools befitting the digital age. For example, recognizing that six letters are just too many for some uses, Google also revised its "favicon" (short for "favorite icon" but also known as a website icon, tab icon, or URL icon), a "G" in the new sans typeface, partitioned into the four familiar Google colors. It also fashioned a contemporary four-color microphone icon that users can tap to access voice recognition on an Android device. It crafted a set of four animated dots (one in each color) for use during interactive and transitional moments to indicate activities such as waiting, thinking, speaking, and replying.

All the Google logo elements now work seamlessly together. So, for example, when you pick up your phone and activate the Google microphone icon, "the Google logo will morph from 'Google' into the dots, which undulate like water in anticipation of your query," notes one reporter. "As you talk, the dots will become an equalizer, reacting to the sound of your vocalizations. Then when you're done talking, the waveform becomes dots again, which spin as Google looks up your results. Then once the results are presented, the dots return to good old 'Google' again." Thus, the Google logo is no longer just a static emblem that sits atop an online search bar. It's a full set of dynamic symbols that bring the brand and its many functions to life across today's digital screens and platforms.

Companies need to tread carefully when making changes to their brand logos. Such changes often require a huge investment. For example, Southwest's seemingly simple logo redesign requires sweeping changes that touch almost every aspect of the company's operations. Just think of all the places you see Southwest's logo—from its advertising, web, and social media activities to the graphics on its airplanes and the design of its airport gates to its corporate letterhead. Everything must be redone to reflect the new logo look, a process that requires resources and must be carried out with strategic precision.

Perhaps more important, the old logos closely link brands to the hearts and minds of consumers. Studies show that the stronger their attachments to a brand, the more resistant consumers are to logo changes. For example, although most experts would agree that the new Hershey logo is a vast improvement, some consumers balked, suggesting that the silhouette Kiss resembles a lump of poop. "All I can see is the emoji poo," says one perplexed observer. "With apologies to Hershey: Your new logo kinda stinks." And when American Airlines replaced its familiar 45-year-old "AA eagle" logo with a more modern version, the new logo became a flashpoint for both brand fans and detractors. Although the redesign was probably overdue, fans lamented the loss of the classic design, whereas detractors claimed that the millions spent on repainting all of American's planes should have been invested in improving the airline's customer service.

Such examples highlight the powerful connections people have to the visual representations of their brands. When logo changes are required—as they most certainly will be at some point—the best course is to alert customers to the upcoming changes and to explain why they are needed. Google did that in a widely distributed video showing the evolution of its logo and the reasons behind the most recent redesign. That's one reason that its massive logo makeover went so smoothly. As the video explains, "We think we've taken the best of Google (simple, uncluttered, colorful, friendly), and recast it not just for the Google of today, but for the Google of tomorrow."

Sources: Miriam Harris, "The Biggest Logo Redesigns of 2017/2018," *Digital Arts*, January 12, 2018, www.digitalartsonline.co.uk/news/graphic-design/biggest-logo-redesigns-of-2017-18/#7; Mark Wilson, "Google's New Logo Is Its Biggest Update in 16 Years," *Fast Company*, September 1, 2015, www.fastcodesign.com/3050613/googles-new-logo-is-its-biggest-update-in-16-years; "Four Rings to Rule Them All," *Brand New*, April 27, 2017, www.underconsideration.com/brandnew/archives/new_global_identity_for_audi_by_strichpunkt_and_kms_team.php; Richard Feloni, "Did You Notice That These 20 Companies Changed Their Logos This Year?" *Business Insider*, October 27, 2015, www.businessinsider.com/corporate-logo-changes-2015-10; Lauren Entis, "Why We Hate Logo Redesigns," *Entrepreneur*, September 11, 2015, www.entrepreneur.com/article/250559; "You Like Your Logo, but Does Joe Consumer," *Advertising Age*, October 30, 2017, pp. 14–15; "Google, Evolved," www.youtube.com/watch?v=olFEpeMwgHk, accessed September 2018; and www.youtube.com/watch?v=0PU7KX3i2pM and www.usatoday.com/videos/tech/2015/09/01/71532636/, accessed September 2018.

Support services are an important part of the customer's overall brand experience. Lexus knows that good marketing doesn't end with making a sale. Keeping customers happy *after* the sale is the key to building lasting relationships. Lexus believes that if you delight the customer, and continue to delight the customer, you will have a customer for life. So Lexus dealers across the country will go to almost any lengths to take care of customers and keep them coming back:[17]

> The typical Lexus dealership is, well, anything but typical. For example, in addition to its Starbucks coffee shop, one Florida Lexus dealership features four massage chairs, two putting greens, two customer lounges, and a library. But at Lexus, customer service goes much deeper than just dealership amenities. From the very start, Lexus set out to revolutionize the auto ownership experience.

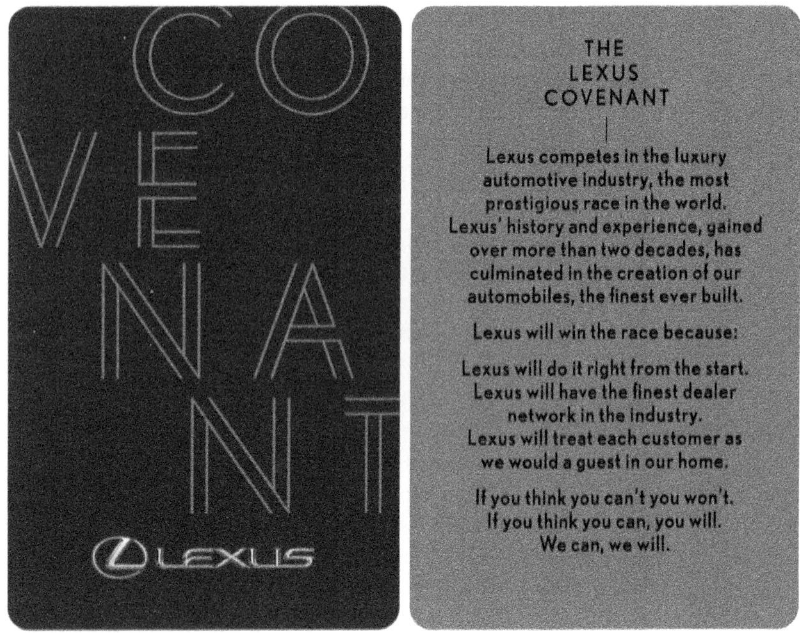

COVENANT
LEXUS
THE LEXUS COVENANT
Lexus competes in the luxury automotive industry, the most prestigious race in the world.
Lexus' history and experience, gained over more than two decades, has culminated in the creation of our automobiles, the finest ever built.
Lexus will win the race because:
Lexus will do it right from the start.
Lexus will have the finest dealer network in the industry.
Lexus will treat each customer as we would a guest in our home.
If you think you can't you won't.
If you think you can, you will.
We can, we will.

>> Customer service: From the start, under the Lexus Covenant, Lexus's high-quality support services create an unmatched car ownership experience and some of the world's most satisfied car owners.

Toyota Motor Sales, USA, Inc.

Of course, Lexus knows that the best dealership visit is the one you never have to make. So it builds customer-pleasing cars to start with. >> In its "Lexus Covenant," the company vows that it will make "the finest cars ever built"—high-quality cars that need little servicing. However, the covenant also vows to value customers as important individuals and "treat each customer as we would a guest in our own home." So, when a car does need servicing, Lexus goes out of its way to make it easy and painless. Many dealers will even pick up a car and then return it when the maintenance is finished. And the car comes back spotless, thanks to a complimentary cleaning. You might even be surprised to find that they've touched up a door ding to help restore the car to its fresh-from-the-factory luster.

By all accounts, Lexus has lived up to its ambitious customer-satisfaction promise. It has created what appear to be the world's most satisfied car owners. Lexus regularly tops not just the industry quality ratings but also customer-satisfaction ratings in both the United States and globally. "My wife will never buy another car except a Lexus," says one satisfied Lexus owner. "They come to our house, pick up the car, do an oil change, spiff it up, and bring it back. She's sold for life."

The first step in designing support services is to survey customers periodically to assess the value of current services and obtain ideas for new ones. Once the company has assessed the quality of various support services to customers, it can take steps to fix problems and add new services that will both delight customers and yield profits to the company.

Many companies now use a sophisticated mix of phone, email, online, social media, mobile, and interactive voice and data technologies to provide support services that were not possible before. For example, home-improvement store Lowe's offers a vigorous dose of customer service at both its store and online locations that makes shopping easier, answers customer questions, and handles problems. Customers can access Lowe's extensive support by phone, email (CareTW@lowes.com), website, mobile app, and Twitter via @LowesCares. The Lowe's website and mobile app link to a buying guide and how-to library. In its stores, Lowe's has equipped employees with iPhones filled with custom apps and add-on hardware, letting them perform service tasks such as checking inventory at nearby stores, looking up specific customer purchase histories, sharing how-to videos, and checking competitor prices—all without leaving the customer's side. In some of its California stores, Lowe's is even experimenting with putting interactive, talking, moving AI robots (called LoweBots) in stores that can greet customers as they enter, answer even their most vexing questions, and guide them to whatever merchandise they are seeking.[18]

Product Line Decisions

Product line
A group of products that are closely related because they function in a similar manner, are sold to the same customer groups, are marketed through the same types of outlets, or fall within given price ranges.

Beyond decisions about individual products and services, product strategy also calls for building a product line. A **product line** is a group of products that are closely related because they function in a similar manner, are sold to the same customer groups, are marketed through the same types of outlets, or fall within given price ranges. For example, Nike produces several lines of athletic shoes and apparel, and Marriott offers several lines of hotels.

The major product line decision involves *product line length*—the number of items in the product line. The line is too short if the manager can increase profits by adding items; the line is too long if the manager can increase profits by dropping items. Managers need to analyze their product lines periodically to assess each item's sales and profits and understand how each item contributes to the line's overall performance.

A company can expand its product line in two ways: by *line filling* or *line stretching*. *Product line filling* involves adding more items within the present range of the line. There are several reasons for product line filling: reaching for extra profits, satisfying dealers, using excess capacity, being the leading full-line company, and plugging holes to keep out competitors. However, line filling is overdone if it results in cannibalization (eating up sales of the company's own existing products) and customer confusion. The company should ensure that new items are noticeably different from existing ones.

Product line stretching occurs when a company lengthens its product line beyond its current range. The company can stretch its line downward, upward, or both ways. Companies located at the upper end of the market can stretch their lines *downward*. For example, Mercedes has stretched downward with the CLA line to draw in younger, first-time buyers. A company may stretch downward to plug a market hole that otherwise would attract a new competitor or to respond to a competitor's attack on the upper end. Or it may add low-end products because it finds faster growth taking place in the low-end segments. Companies can also stretch their product lines *upward*. Sometimes, companies stretch upward to add prestige to their current products or to reap higher margins. P&G did that with brands such as Cascade dishwashing detergent and Dawn dish soap by adding "Platinum" versions at a higher price points.

As they grow and expand, many companies both stretch and fill their product lines. Consider BMW:[19]

> Over the years, BMW Group has transformed itself from a single-brand, five-model automaker into a powerhouse with three brands, 14 "Series," and dozens of distinct models. The company has expanded downward with its MINI Cooper line and upward with Rolls-Royce. Its BMW line brims with models from the low end to the high end to everything in between. The brand's seven "Series" lines range from the entry-level 1-Series subcompact to the luxury-compact 3-Series to the midsize 5-Series sedan to the luxurious full-size 7-Series. In between, BMW has filled the gaps with X1, X3, X4, X5, and X6 SUVs; M-Series performance models; and the i3 and i8 hybrids. >> Thus, through skillful line stretching and filling, while staying within its premium positioning, BMW now has brands and lines that successfully appeal to the rich, the super-rich, and the hope-to-be-rich.

>> Product line stretching and filling: Through skillful line stretching and filling, BMW now has brands and lines that successfully appeal to the rich, the super-rich, and the hope-to-be-rich.

dpa picture alliance archive/Alamy Stock Photo

Product Mix Decisions

Product mix (or product portfolio)
The set of all product lines and items that a particular seller offers for sale.

An organization with several product lines has a product mix. A **product mix** (or **product portfolio**) consists of all the product lines and items that a particular seller offers for sale. For example, Colgate-Palmolive is perhaps best known for its toothpaste and other oral care products. But, in fact, Colgate is a $15.2 billion consumer products company that makes and markets a full product mix consisting of dozens of familiar lines and brands. Colgate divides its overall product mix into four major lines: oral care, personal care, home care, and pet nutrition. Each product line consists of many brands and items.[20]

A company's product mix has four important dimensions: width, length, depth, and consistency. Product mix *width* refers to the number of different product lines the company carries. >> For example, Colgate markets a fairly wide product mix, consisting of

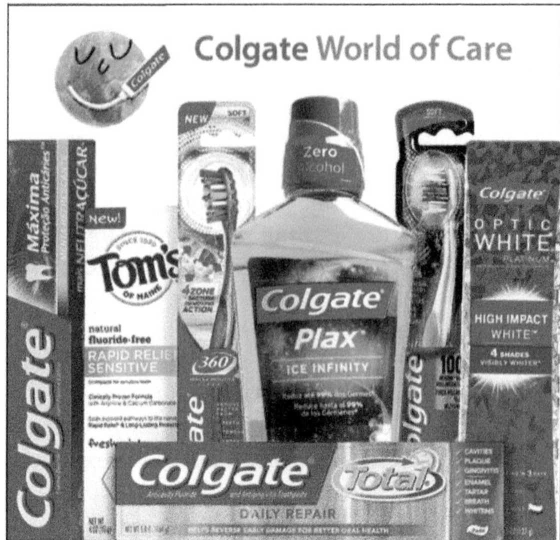

>> The product mix: Colgate-Palmolive's nicely consistent product mix contains dozens of brands that constitute the "Colgate World of Care"—products that "every day, people like you trust to care for themselves and the ones they love."

Colgate-Palmolive Company

dozens of brands that constitute the "Colgate World of Care"—products that "every day, people like you trust to care for themselves and the ones they love."

Product mix *length* refers to the total number of items a company carries within its product lines. Colgate carries several brands within each line. For example, its personal care line includes Softsoap liquid soaps and body washes, Tom's of Maine, Irish Spring bar soaps, Speed Stick deodorants, Afta, and Colgate toiletries and shaving products, among others. The Colgate home care line includes Palmolive and AJAX dishwashing products, Suavitel fabric conditioners, and Murphy Oil Soap cleaners. The pet nutrition line houses the Hill's Science Diet pet food brand.

Product line *depth* refers to the number of versions offered of each product in the line. Colgate toothpastes come in numerous varieties, ranging from Colgate Total, Colgate Optic White, and Colgate Tartar Protection to Colgate Sensitive, Colgate Enamel Health, Colgate PreviDent, and Colgate Kids. Then each variety comes in its own special forms and formulations. For example, you can buy Colgate Total in regular, clean mint, advanced whitening, deep clean, total daily repair, 2in1 liquid gel, or any of several other versions.

Finally, the *consistency* of the product mix refers to how closely related the various product lines are in end use, production requirements, distribution channels, or some other way. Colgate's product lines are consistent insofar as they are consumer products that go through the same distribution channels. The lines are less consistent insofar as they perform different functions for buyers.

These product mix dimensions provide the handles for defining the company's product strategy. A company can increase its business in four ways. It can add new product lines, widening its product mix. In this way, its new lines build on the company's reputation in its other lines. A company can lengthen its existing product lines to become a more full-line company. It can add more versions of each product and thus deepen its product mix. Finally, a company can pursue more product line consistency—or less—depending on whether it wants to have a strong reputation in a single field or in several fields.

From time to time, a company may also have to streamline its product mix to pare out marginally performing lines and to regain its focus. For example, P&G pursues a megabrand strategy built around 23 billion-dollar-plus brands in the food, household care, beauty, and grooming categories. During the past decade, the consumer products giant has sold off dozens of major brands that no longer fit either its evolving focus or the billion-dollar threshold, ranging from Jif peanut butter, Crisco shortening, Folgers coffee, Pringles snack chips, and Sunny Delight drinks to Noxzema skin care products, Right Guard deodorant, Aleve pain reliever, Duracell batteries, CoverGirl and Max Factor cosmetics, Wella and Clairol hair care products, and Iams and other pet food brands. These divestments allow P&G to focus investment and energy on the 65 core brands that yield most of its sales and profits. "Less [can] be much more," says P&G's CEO.[21]

LINKING THE CONCEPTS

Slow down for a minute. To get a better sense of how large and complex a company's product offering can become, investigate Procter & Gamble's product mix.

- Using P&G's website (www.pg.com), its annual report, or other sources, develop a list of all the company's product lines and individual products. What surprises you about this list of products?
- Is P&G's product mix consistent? What products has P&G dropped or sold recently? What overall strategy or logic appears to have guided the shaping of this product mix?

Author Comment
As noted at the start of this chapter, services are "products," too—intangible ones. So all the product topics we've discussed so far apply to services as well as to physical products. However, in this section, we focus on the special characteristics and marketing needs that set services apart.

Services Marketing

OBJECTIVE 7-3 Identify the four characteristics that affect the marketing of services and the additional marketing considerations that services require.

Services have grown dramatically in recent years. Services now account for more than 80 percent of the U.S. gross domestic product (GDP). Services are growing even faster in the world economy, making up almost 63 percent of the gross world product.[22]

Service industries vary greatly. *Governments* offer services through courts, employment services, hospitals, military services, police and fire departments, the postal service, and schools. *Private not-for-profit organizations* offer services through museums, charities, churches, colleges, foundations, and hospitals. In addition, a large number of *business organizations* offer services—airlines, banks, hotels, insurance companies, consulting firms, medical and legal practices, entertainment and telecommunications companies, real estate firms, retailers, and others.

The Nature and Characteristics of a Service

A company must consider four special service characteristics when designing marketing programs: intangibility, inseparability, variability, and perishability (see **>> Figure 7.3**).

Service intangibility
Services cannot be seen, tasted, felt, heard, or smelled before they are bought.

Service intangibility means that services cannot be seen, tasted, felt, heard, or smelled before they are bought. For example, people undergoing cosmetic surgery cannot see the result before the purchase. Airline passengers have nothing but a ticket and a promise that they and their luggage will arrive safely at the intended destination, hopefully at the same time. To reduce uncertainty, buyers look for *signals* of service quality. They draw conclusions about quality from the place, people, price, equipment, and communications that they can see. Therefore, the service provider's task is to make the service tangible in one or more ways and send the right signals about quality. Oscar Health does this well:[23]

> To most people, traditional health insurance companies are little more than faceless corporate entities. And for individuals who don't get their health insurance through an employer, buying insurance in the open marketplace can be a complex and uncertain process. >> Fast-growing startup Oscar Insurance Corporation is changing all that. "Insurance is confusing. Oscar makes it simple," says the company. Oscar gives you "health insurance that won't make your head explode, … and if it does, you're covered."
>
> Predominantly web-based Oscar targets young, digitally savvy consumers with simple, affordable health insurance plans. It offers a slew of high-tech features that make the user experience more personal and tangible. For example, every member is assigned a dedicated Oscar concierge team: "You talk to the same people each time, so you get personalized help when you need it." Oscar's innovative web and mobile apps make it easier for members to manage their health care. They can use the aps for everything from accessing their health histories and account information to finding a doctor, having a free virtual visit, and getting prescriptions.

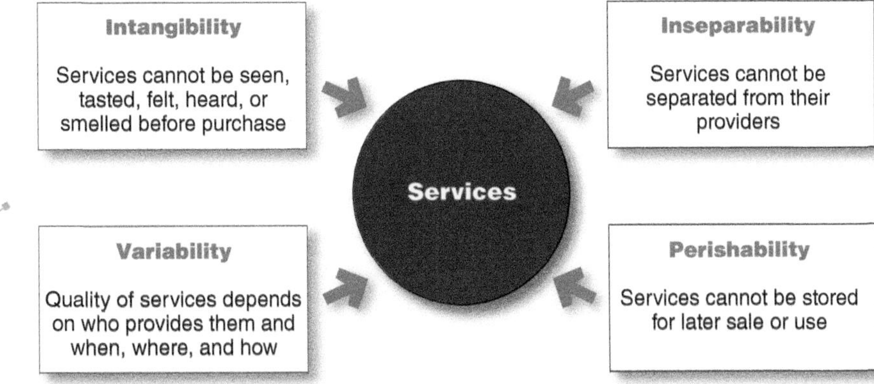

Intangibility
Services cannot be seen, tasted, felt, heard, or smelled before purchase
Inseparability
Services cannot be separated from their providers
Services
Variability
Quality of services depends on who provides them and when, where, and how
Perishability
Services cannot be stored for later sale or use

Although services are "products" in a general sense, they have special characteristics and marketing needs. The biggest differences come from the fact that services are essentially intangible and that they are created through direct interactions with customers. Think about your experiences with an airline or Google versus Nike or Apple.

>> Figure 7.3 Four Service Characteristics

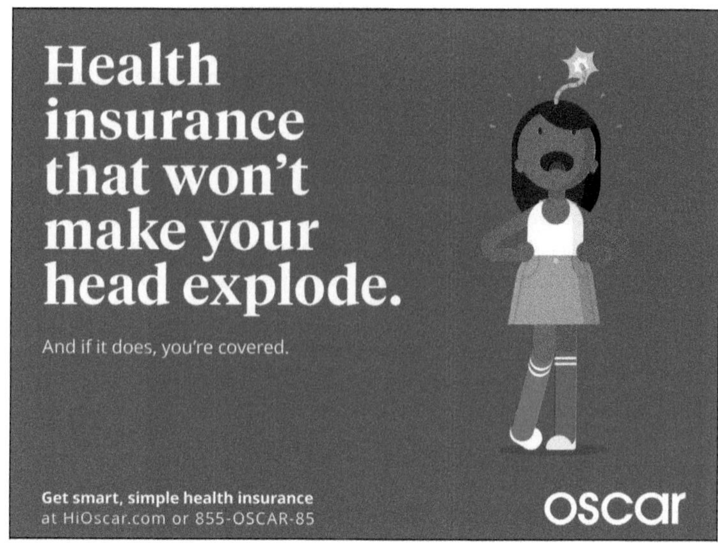

Health insurance that won't make your head explode.
And if it does, you're covered.
Get smart, simple health insurance
at HiOscar.com or 855-OSCAR-85
oscar

>> **Oscar Insurance Corporation personalizes and tangibilizes heath care in an industry that is notoriously complex and difficult to navigate. The young company's business is booming.**

Oscar

Oscar also offers free 24/7 doctor consultation and telemedicine services. It's "stupidly easy," says the company. Just open the Oscar app, request a call from a doctor, and get a call back in about 10 minutes. You can even attach a picture of your symptoms.

Personalizing and tangibilizing the user experience has paid off for Oscar. At a time when larger health insurance companies are scaling back on individual healthcare, Oscar is surging. During the past three years, its business has soared from 40,000 members and $200 million in yearly revenues to an estimated 250,000 members and $1 billion in revenues.

Physical goods are produced, then stored, then later sold, and then still later consumed. In contrast, services are first sold and then produced and consumed at the same time. **Service inseparability** means that services cannot be separated from their providers, whether the providers are people or machines. If a service employee provides the service, then the employee becomes a part of the service. And customers don't just buy and use a service; they play an active role in its delivery. Customer coproduction makes *provider–customer interaction* a special feature of services marketing. Both the provider and the customer affect the service outcome.

Service inseparability
Services are produced and consumed at the same time and cannot be separated from their providers.

Service variability
The quality of services may vary greatly depending on who provides them and when, where, and how they are provided.

Service perishability
Services cannot be stored for later sale or use.

Service variability means that the quality of services depends on who provides them as well as when, where, and how they are provided. For example, some hotels—say, Marriott—have reputations for providing better service than others. Still, within a given Marriott hotel, one registration-counter employee may be cheerful and efficient, whereas another standing just a few feet away may be grumpy and slow. Even the quality of a single Marriott employee's service varies according to his or her energy and frame of mind at the time of each customer encounter.

Service perishability means that services cannot be stored for later sale or use. Some doctors charge patients for missed appointments because the service value existed only at that point and disappeared when the patient did not show up. The perishability of services is not a problem when demand is steady. However, when demand fluctuates, service firms often have difficult problems. For example, because of rush-hour demand, public transportation companies must own much more equipment than they would if demand were even throughout the day. Thus, service firms often design strategies for producing a better match between demand and supply. Hotels and resorts charge lower prices in the off-season to attract more guests. And restaurants hire part-time employees to serve during peak periods.

Marketing Strategies for Service Firms

Just like manufacturing businesses, good service firms use marketing to position themselves strongly in chosen target markets. Enterprise Rent-A-Car says, "You drive. We'll take care of the rest"; Zipcar offers "Wheels when you want them." At CVS Pharmacy, "Health is everything"; Walgreens meets you "at the corner of happy & healthy." And St. Jude Children's Hospital is "Finding cures. Saving children." These and other service firms establish their positions through traditional marketing mix activities. However, because services differ from tangible products, they often require additional marketing approaches.

The Service Profit Chain

In a service business, the customer and the front-line service employee *interact* to co-create the service. Effective interaction, in turn, depends on the skills of front-line service employees and on the support processes backing these employees. Thus, successful

Service profit chain
The chain that links service firm profits with employee and customer satisfaction.

service companies focus their attention on both their customers and their employees. They understand the **service profit chain**, which links service firm profits with employee and customer satisfaction. This chain consists of five links:[24]

- *Internal service quality.* Superior employee selection and training, a quality work environment, and strong support for those dealing with customers, which results in ...
- *Satisfied and productive service employees.* More satisfied, loyal, and hardworking employees, which results in ...
- *Greater service value.* More effective and efficient customer value creation, engagement, and service delivery, which results in ...
- *Satisfied and loyal customers.* Satisfied customers who remain loyal, make repeat purchases, and refer other customers, which results in ...
- *Healthy service profits and growth.* Superior service firm performance.

>> For example, at Four Seasons Hotels and Resorts, creating delighted customers involves much more than just crafting a lofty customer-focused marketing strategy and handing it down from the top. At Four Seasons, satisfying customers is everybody's business. And it all starts with satisfied employees:[25]

Four Seasons has perfected the art of high-touch, carefully crafted service. Whether it's at the tropical island paradise at the Four Seasons Resort Mauritius or the luxurious sub-Saharan "camp" at the Four Seasons Safari Lodge Serengeti, guests paying $1,000 or more a night expect to have their minds read. For these guests, Four Seasons doesn't disappoint. As one Four Seasons Maui guest once told a manager, "If there's a heaven, I hope it's run by Four Seasons." What makes Four Seasons so special? It's really no secret. It's the quality of the Four Seasons staff. Four Seasons knows that happy, satisfied employees make for happy, satisfied customers. So just as it does for customers, Four Seasons respects and pampers its employees.

Four Seasons hires the best people, pays them well, orients them carefully, instills in them a sense of pride, and rewards them for outstanding service deeds. It treats employees as it would its most important guests. For example, all employees—from the maids who make up the rooms to the general manager—dine together (free of charge) in the hotel cafeteria. Perhaps best of all, every employee receives free stays at other Four Seasons resorts, six free nights per year after one year with the company. The room stays make employees feel as important and pampered as the guests they serve and motivate employees to achieve even higher levels of service in their own jobs. Says one Four Seasons staffer, "You come back from those trips on fire. You want to do so much for the guests." As a result of such actions, the annual turnover for full-time employees at Four Seasons is only 18 percent, half the industry average. Four Seasons has been included for 20 straight years on *Fortune* magazine's list of 100 Best Companies to Work For. That's the biggest secret to Four Seasons' success.

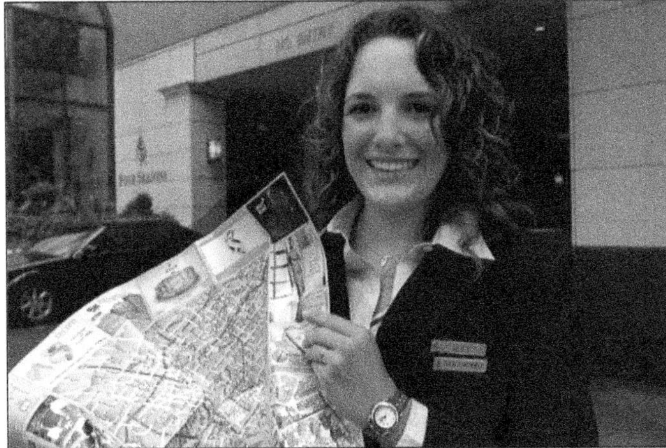

>> The service-profit chain: Four Seasons' excels at delighting customers, and it all starts with satisfied employees—from the pool manager to the concierge. "If there's a heaven," says one customer, "I hope it's run by Four Seasons."

Dick Loek/Toronto Star/Getty Images

Internal marketing
Orienting and motivating customer-contact employees and supporting service employees to work as a team to provide customer satisfaction.

Interactive marketing
Training service employees in the fine art of interacting with customers to satisfy their needs.

Services marketing requires more than just traditional external marketing using the four Ps. >> **Figure 7.4** shows that services marketing also requires *internal marketing* and *interactive marketing*. **Internal marketing** means that the service firm must orient and motivate its customer-contact employees and supporting service people to work as a team to provide customer satisfaction. Marketers must get everyone in the organization to be customer centered. In fact, internal marketing must *precede* external marketing. For example, Four Seasons starts by hiring the right people and carefully orienting and inspiring them to give unparalleled customer service. The idea is to make certain that employees themselves believe in the brand so that they can authentically deliver the brand's promise to customers.

Interactive marketing means that service quality depends heavily on the quality of the buyer–seller interaction during the service encounter. In product marketing, product quality often depends little on how the product is obtained. But in services marketing, service quality

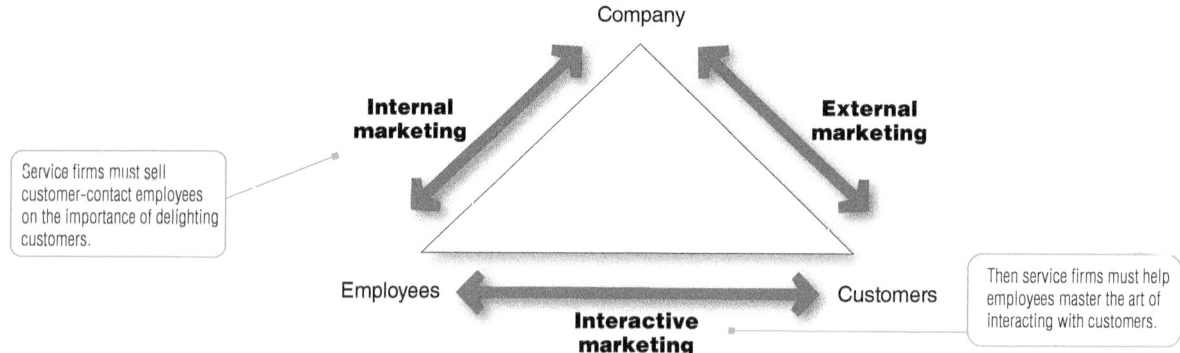
Company
Internal marketing
External marketing
Service firms must sell customer-contact employees on the importance of delighting customers.
Employees
Customers
Interactive marketing
Then service firms must help employees master the art of interacting with customers.

>> Figure 7.4 Three Types of Services Marketing

depends on both the service deliverer and the quality of delivery. Service marketers, therefore, have to master interactive marketing skills. Thus, Four Seasons hires only the people who fit the company's culture and instructs them carefully in the fine art of interacting with customers to satisfy their every need. All new hires—at all levels of the company—complete three months of training on how to interact with customers and meet their needs.

Today, as competition and costs increase and as productivity and quality decrease, more services marketing sophistication is needed. Service companies face three major marketing tasks: They want to increase their *service differentiation, service quality*, and *service productivity*.

Managing Service Differentiation

In these days of intense price competition, service marketers often complain about the difficulty of differentiating their services from those of competitors. To the extent that customers view the services of different providers as similar, they care less about the provider than the price. The solution to price competition is to develop a differentiated offer, delivery, and image.

The *offer* can include innovative features that set one company's offer apart from competitors' offers. >> For example, Emirates recently added first-class suites to its Boeing 777 airplanes featuring door-to-ceiling sliding doors, closets for hanging clothes, wireless tablets with 2,500 channels, 32-inch TV screens, personal minibars, and "inspiration kits" containing moisturizing pajamas and skincare kits. Some retailers differentiate themselves with offerings that take you well beyond the products they stock. At any of several large REI stores, consumers can get hands-on experience with merchandise before buying it via the store's mountain bike test trail, gear-testing stations, a huge rock climbing wall, or an in-store simulated rain shower.

SUITE 2A

>> Service differentiation: Emirates offers first-class suites in its Boeing 777 airplanes featuring door-to-ceiling sliding doors, closets for hanging clothes, wireless tablets with 2,500 channels, 32-inch TV screens, personal minibars, and "inspiration kits" containing moisturizing pajamas and skincare kits.

Christian Charisius/picture-alliance/dpa/AP Images

Service companies can differentiate their service *delivery* by having more able and reliable customer-contact people, developing a superior physical environment in which the service product is delivered, or designing a superior delivery process. For example, many grocery chains now offer online ordering with curbside pick-up or home delivery as a better way to shop than having to drive, park, wait in line, and tote groceries home. CVS Health offers fast and convenient walk-in medical services through Minute Clinics in its own and Target stores, saving you a trip and long wait at the doctor's office for immunizations, treatment of minor illnesses, and other health-care needs. Minute Clinic gives you "The care you need on your schedule."

Finally, service companies also can work on differentiating their *images* through symbols and branding. Well-known service characters and symbols include the GEICO gecko, Progressive Insurance's Flo, McDonald's golden arches, Allstate's "good hands," the Twitter bird, and the freckled, red-haired, pig-tailed Wendy's girl. The KFC Colonel has become a popular pop culture figure, portrayed in a series of delightfully awful ads over the past few years by a dozen or more celebrities, from Rob Lowe, George Hamilton, and Norm McDonald to country singer Reba McEntire.

Managing Service Quality

A service firm can differentiate itself by delivering consistently higher quality than its competitors provide. Like manufacturers before them, most service industries have now joined the customer-driven quality movement. And like product marketers, service providers need to identify what target customers expect in regard to service quality.

Unfortunately, service quality is harder to define and judge than product quality. For instance, it is harder to agree on the quality of a haircut than on the quality of a hair dryer. Customer retention is perhaps the best measure of quality; a service firm's ability to hang onto its customers depends on how consistently it delivers value to them.

Top service companies set high service-quality standards. They watch service performance closely, both their own and that of competitors. They do not settle for merely good service—they strive for 100 percent defect-free service. A 98 percent performance standard may sound good, but using this standard, the U.S. Postal Service would lose or misdirect 353,000 pieces of mail each hour, and U.S. pharmacies would misfill more than 1.5 million prescriptions each week.[26]

Unlike product manufacturers who can adjust their machinery and inputs until everything is perfect, service quality will always vary, depending on the interactions between employees and customers. As hard as they may try, even the best companies will have an occasional late delivery, burned steak, or grumpy employee. However, good *service recovery* can turn angry customers into loyal ones. In fact, good recovery can win more customer purchasing and loyalty than if things had gone well in the first place.

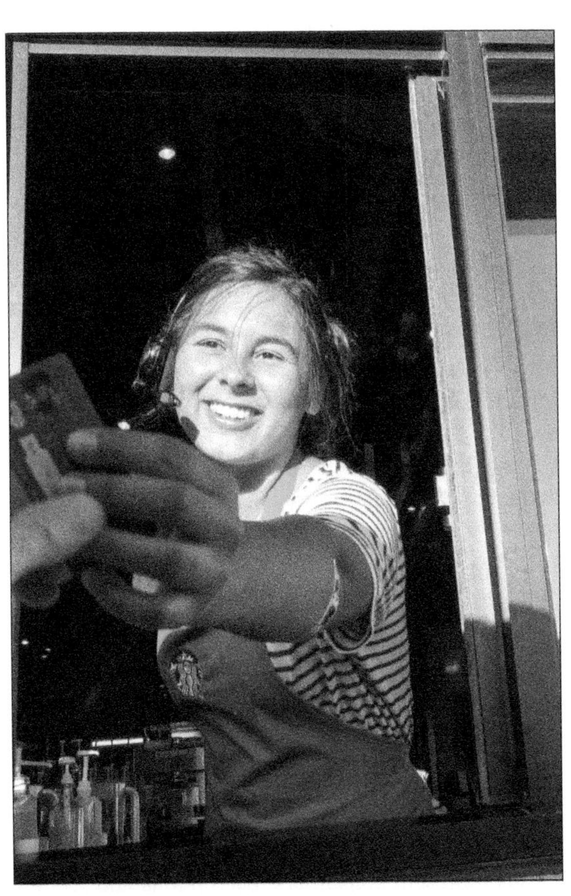

>> Service quality: Good service recovery can turn angry customer into loyal ones. Starbucks trains its employees to "LATTE" upset customers: Listen, Acknowledge, Take action, Thank them, and Explain what happened.

B.O'Kane/Alamy Stock Photo

Many companies train their frontline employees in the art of service recovery. >> For example, Starbucks Baristas learn the LATTE method for recognizing disgruntled customers and addressing their concerns in positive ways. LATTE stands for *Listen* to the customer, *Acknowledge* their complaint, *Take action* by solving the problem, *Thank* them, and then *Explain* why the problem occurred. By listening and taking positive action, Starbucks employees can often turn upset customers into delighted ones.[27]

These days, social media such as Facebook, Instagram, and Twitter can help companies root out and remedy customer dissatisfaction with service. As discussed in Chapter 4, companies now monitor the digital space to spot customer issues quickly and respond in real time. For example, Southwest Airlines has a dedicated team of 29 people who respond to roughly 80,000 Facebook and Twitter posts monthly. Southwest and other airlines have become adept at responding quickly to social media inquiries and comments. A recent study shows that Southwest's response time to customers on Twitter averages just 6 minutes and 36 seconds. A quick and thoughtful response can turn a dissatisfied customer into a brand advocate.[28]

Managing Service Productivity

With their costs rising rapidly, service firms are under great pressure to increase service productivity. They can do so in several ways. They can train current employees better or hire new ones who will work harder or more skillfully. Or they can increase the quantity of their service by giving up some quality. Finally, a service provider can harness the power of technology. Although we often think of technology's power to save time and costs in manufacturing companies, it also has great—and often untapped—potential to make service workers more productive.

However, companies must avoid pushing productivity so hard that doing so reduces quality. Attempts to streamline a service or cut costs can make a service company more efficient in the short run. But that can also reduce its longer-run ability to innovate, maintain service quality, or respond to consumer needs and desires. For example, some airlines have learned this lesson the hard way as they attempt to economize in the face of rising costs. Passengers on most airlines now encounter "time-saving" check-in kiosks rather than personal counter service. And most airlines have stopped offering even the little things for free—such as in-flight snacks—and now charge extra for everything from checked luggage to aisle seats. The result is a plane full of disgruntled customers. In their attempts to improve productivity, many airlines have mangled customer service.

Thus, in attempting to improve service productivity, companies must be mindful of how they create and deliver customer value. They should be careful not to take *service* out of the service. In fact, a company may purposely lower service productivity to improve service quality, in turn allowing it to maintain higher prices and profit margins.

LINKING THE CONCEPTS

Let's pause here for a moment. We've said that although services are "products" in a general sense, they have special characteristics and marketing needs. To get a better grasp of this concept, select a traditional product brand, such as Nike or Honda. Next, select a service brand, such as JetBlue Airlines or McDonald's. Then compare the two.

- How are the characteristics and marketing needs of the product and service brands you selected similar?
- How do the characteristics and marketing needs of the two brands differ? How are these differences reflected in each brand's marketing strategy? Keep these differences in mind as we move into the final section of the chapter.

Author Comment
A brand represents everything that a product or service means to consumers. As such, brands are valuable assets to a company. For example, when you hear someone say "Coca-Cola," what do you think, feel, or remember? What about "Target"? Or "Google"?

Branding Strategy: Building Strong Brands

OBJECTIVE 7-4 Discuss branding strategy—the decisions companies make in building and managing their brands.

Some analysts see brands as *the* major enduring asset of a company, outlasting the company's specific products and facilities. John Stewart, former CEO of Quaker Oats, once said, "If this business were split up, I would give you the land and bricks and mortar, and I would keep the brands and trademarks, and I would fare better than you." A former CEO of McDonald's declared, "If every asset we own, every building, and every piece of equipment were destroyed in a terrible natural disaster, we would be able to borrow all the money to replace it very quickly because of the value of our brand.... The brand is more valuable than the totality of all these assets."[29]

Thus, brands are powerful assets that must be carefully developed and managed. In this section, we examine the key strategies for building and managing product and service brands.

Brand Equity and Brand Value

Brands are more than just names and symbols. They are a key element in the company's relationships with consumers. Brands represent consumers' perceptions and feelings about a product and its performance—everything that the product or the service *means* to consumers. In the final analysis, brands exist in the heads of consumers. As one well-respected marketer once said, "Products are created in the factory, but brands are created in the mind."[30]

Brand equity
The differential effect that knowing the brand name has on customer response to the product or its marketing.

A powerful brand has high *brand equity*. **Brand equity** is the differential effect that knowing the brand name has on customer response to the product and its marketing. It's a measure of the brand's ability to capture consumer preference and loyalty. A brand has positive brand equity when consumers react more favorably to it than to a generic or unbranded version of the same product. It has negative brand equity if consumers react less favorably than to an unbranded version.

Brands vary in the amount of power and value they hold in the marketplace. Some brands—such as Coca-Cola, Nike, Disney, Apple, McDonald's, Harley-Davidson, and others—become larger-than-life icons that maintain their power in the market for years, even generations. Other brands—such as Amazon, Google, Instagram, Airbnb, Uber, and Waze—create fresh consumer excitement and loyalty. These brands win in the marketplace not simply because they deliver unique benefits or reliable service. Rather, they succeed because they forge deep connections with customers.

People really do have relationships with brands. >> For example, to the world's more than 800 million Instagram users, the Instagram brand stands for something much more than just a photo and video sharing service. Instagram stands for sharing important moments with friends through pictures as they happen. It means growing closer to friends and family through shared experiences in the moment, whether it's a new puppy, someone getting married, your kid's first steps, or seeing a beautiful double rainbow in Hawaii.[31]

>> **Consumers' relationships with brands: To devoted Instagram users, the brand stands for much more than just a photo sharing service. It means growing closer to friends and family through shared experiences in the moment.**

Alex Segre/Alamy Stock Photo

Ad agency Young & Rubicam's BrandAsset Valuator measures brand strength along four consumer perception dimensions: *differentiation* (what makes the brand stand out), *relevance* (how consumers feel it meets their needs), *knowledge* (how much consumers know about the brand), and *esteem* (how highly consumers regard and respect the brand). Brands with strong brand equity rate high on all four dimensions. The brand must be distinct, or consumers will have no reason to choose it over other brands. However, the fact that a brand is highly differentiated doesn't necessarily mean that consumers will buy it. The brand must stand out in ways that are relevant to consumers' needs. Even a differentiated, relevant brand is far from a shoo-in. Before consumers will respond to the brand, they must first know about and understand it. And that familiarity must lead to a strong, positive consumer-brand connection.[32]

Thus, positive brand equity derives from consumer feelings about and connections with a brand. A brand with high brand equity is a very valuable asset. **Brand value** is the total financial value of a brand. Measuring such value is difficult. However, according to one estimate, the brand value of Google is a whopping $246 billion, with Apple at $235 billion, Microsoft at $143 billion, Amazon at $140 billion, Facebook at $130 billion, and AT&T at $115 billion. Other brands rating among the world's most valuable include Visa, Tencent, IBM, McDonald's, and Verizon.[33]

Brand value
The total financial value of a brand.

High brand equity provides a company with many competitive advantages. A powerful brand enjoys a high level of consumer brand awareness and loyalty. Because consumers expect stores to carry the particular brand, the company has more leverage in bargaining with resellers. Because a brand name carries high credibility, the company can more easily launch line and brand extensions. A powerful brand also offers the company some defense against fierce price competition and other competitor marketing actions.

Above all, however, a powerful brand forms the basis for building strong and profitable customer engagement and relationships. The fundamental asset underlying brand equity is *customer equity*—the value of customer relationships that the brand creates. A powerful brand is important, but what it really represents is a profitable set of loyal customers. The proper focus of marketing is building customer equity, with brand management serving as a major marketing tool. Companies need to think of themselves not as portfolios of brands but as portfolios of customers.

Figure 7.5 Major Brand Strategy Decisions

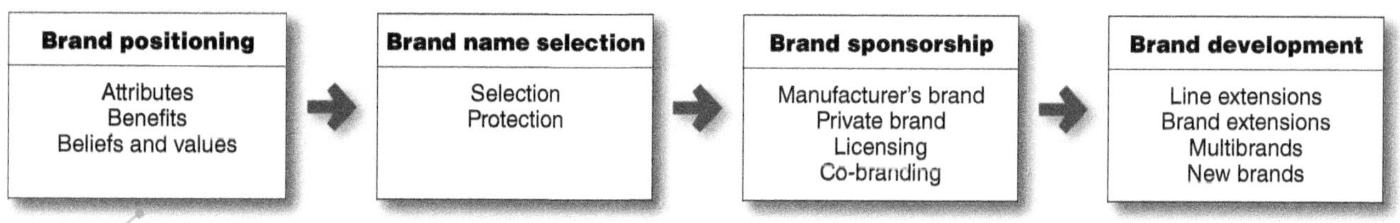

Brands are powerful assets that must be carefully developed and managed. As this figure suggests, building strong brands involves many challenging decisions.

Building Strong Brands

Branding poses challenging decisions to the marketer. **Figure 7.5** shows that the major brand strategy decisions involve *brand positioning, brand name selection, brand sponsorship*, and *brand development.*

Brand Positioning

Marketers need to position their brands clearly in target customers' minds. They can position brands at any of three levels.[34] At the lowest level, they can position the brand on *product attributes*. For example, Whirlpool can position its major home appliance products on attributes such as quality, selection, style, and innovative features. In general, however, attributes are the least desirable level for brand positioning. Competitors can easily copy attributes. More important, customers are not interested in attributes as such—they are interested in what the attributes will do for them.

A brand can be better positioned by associating its name with a desirable *benefit*. Thus, Whirlpool can go beyond technical product attributes and talk about benefits such as taking the hassle out of cooking and cleaning, better energy savings, or more stylish kitchens. For example, for years, Whirlpool positioned its washing machines as having "the power to get more done." Some successful brands positioned on benefits are FedEx (guaranteed on-time delivery), Walmart (save money), and Instagram (capturing and sharing moments).

The strongest brands go beyond attribute or benefit positioning. They are positioned on strong *beliefs and values,* engaging customers on a deep, emotional level. For example, Whirlpool's research showed that home appliances are more than just "cold metal" to customers. They have a deeper meaning connected with the value that they play in customers' lives and relationships. So Whirlpool launched a major positioning campaign—called "Every Day, Care"—based on the warm emotions of taking care of the people you love with Whirlpool appliances. One ad shows a father leaving a note in his son's lunch, accompanied by Johnny Cash singing "You Are My Sunshine" in the background. Another ad centers on a mom's interactions with her daughter around their Whirlpool washer-dryer, and still another shows a couple cooking dinner together with the wish "May your 'tatoes be fluffy and white." Warming up cold metal worked wonders for Whirlpool. Within just six months, the brand's sales rose 6.6 percent, market share increase 10 percent, and positive social media sentiment surged sixfold.[35]

Brand positioning: Some brands—such as Disney—have become lovemarks, products or services that pack an emotional wallop and "inspire loyalty beyond reason."

Art of Drawing/Alamy Stock Photo

Advertising agency Saatchi & Saatchi suggests that brands should strive to become *lovemarks*, products or services that "inspire loyalty beyond reason." Brands ranging from Disney, Apple, Nike, and Coca-Cola to Trader Joe's, Google, and Pinterest have achieved this status with many of their customers. Lovemark brands pack an emotional wallop. Customers don't just like these brands; they have strong emotional connections with them and love them unconditionally.[36] For example, Disney is a classic lovemark brand. As one Walt Disney World Resort regular affirms: "I have a deep love and bond to all things Disney. Walking down Main Street and seeing Cinderella's castle for the first time always makes my heart jump. It's a moment I can guarantee and rely on. A constant in my life. No matter what I'm going through... suddenly the world is filled with magic and wonder and possibilities all over again and I feel a wave of happiness flow over me and a smile creep back onto my face easily, not forced or painted on. A real, true smile."[37]

When positioning a brand, the marketer should establish a mission for the brand and a vision of what the brand must be and do. A brand is the company's promise to deliver a specific set of features, benefits, services, and experiences consistently to buyers. The brand promise must be clear, simple, and honest. Motel 6, for example, offers clean rooms, low prices, and good service but does not promise expensive furnishings or large bathrooms. In contrast, the Ritz-Carlton offers luxurious rooms and a truly memorable experience but does not promise low prices.

Brand Name Selection

A good name can add greatly to a product's success. However, finding the best brand name is a difficult task. It begins with a careful review of the product and its benefits, the target market, and proposed marketing strategies. After that, naming a brand becomes part science, part art, and a measure of instinct.

Desirable qualities for a brand name include the following: (1) It should suggest something about the product's benefits and qualities: Beautyrest, Slimfast, Facebook, Airbnb. (2) It should be easy to pronounce, recognize, and remember: iPad, Tide, Jelly Belly, Twitter, JetBlue. (3) The brand name should be distinctive: Panera, Swiffer, Zappos, Nest. (4) It should be extendable—Amazon.com began as an online bookseller but chose a name that would allow expansion into other categories. (5) The name should translate easily into foreign languages: Coca-Cola translates in Chinese to "Ke Kou Ke Le," which means "tasty fun." (6) It should be capable of registration and legal protection. A brand name cannot be registered if it infringes on existing brand names.

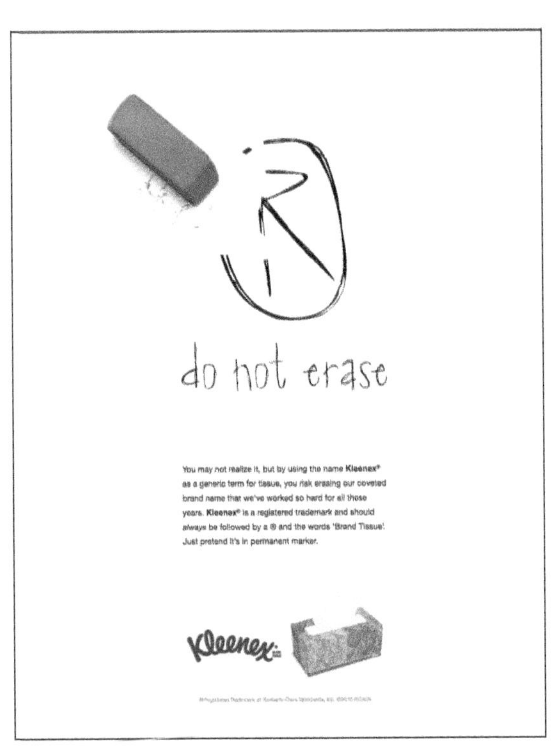
do not erase
You may not realize it, but by using the name Kleenex® as a generic term for tissue, you risk erasing our coveted brand name that we've worked so hard for all these years. Kleenex® is a registered trademark and should always be followed by a ® and the words 'Brand Tissue'. Just pretend it's in permanent marker.
Kleenex

>> Protecting the brand name: This ad asks advertisers and others to always add the registered trademark symbol and the words "Brand Tissue" to the Kleenex name, helping to keep from "erasing our coveted brand name that we've worked so hard for all these years."

Choosing a new brand name is hard work. After a decade of choosing quirky names (Yahoo!, Google) or trademark-proof made-up names (Novartis, Aventis, Accenture), today's style is to build brands around names that have real meaning. For example, names like Silk (soy milk), Method (home products), Smartwater (beverages), and Snapchat (photo messaging app) are simple and make intuitive sense. But with trademark applications soaring, *available* new names can be hard to find. Try it yourself. Pick a product and see if you can come up with a better name for it. How about Moonshot? Tickle? Purple? Treehugger? Avocado? Simplicity? Mindbender? Google them and you'll find that they are already taken.

Once chosen, the brand name must be protected. Many firms try to build a brand name that will eventually become identified with the product category. Brand names such as Kleenex, JELL-O, BAND-AID, Scotch Tape, Velcro, Formica, Magic Marker, Post-it Notes, and Ziploc have succeeded in this way. However, their very success may threaten the company's rights to the name. Many originally protected brand names—such as cellophane, aspirin, nylon, kerosene, linoleum, yo-yo, trampoline, escalator, thermos, and shredded wheat—are now generic names that any seller can use.

To protect their brands, marketers present them carefully using the word *brand* and the registered trademark symbol, as in "BAND-AID® Brand Adhesive Bandages." Even the long-standing "I am stuck on BAND-AID 'cause BAND-AID's stuck on me" jingle has now become "I am stuck on BAND-AID brand 'cause BAND-AID's stuck on me." >> Similarly, a recent Kleenex ad advises advertisers and others that the name Kleenex should always be followed by the registered trademark symbol and the words "Brand Tissue." "You may not realize it, but by using the name Kleenex® as a generic term for tissue," says the ad, "you risk erasing our coveted brand name that we've worked so hard for all these years."

Companies often go to great lengths to protect their names and brand symbols. For example, insurance company Travelers zealously pursues companies that infringe in even the slightest way on its familiar trademarked red umbrella symbol. It recently threatened a tiny consulting firm in Anchorage, Alaska—Human Resource Umbrella—with legal action for hanging an umbrella above the two *l*'s in its name. Such actions might seem unneeded, but they are serious business to Travelers. "Mary Poppins might want to consider lawyering up," quips one industry lawyer.[38]

Brand Sponsorship

A manufacturer has four sponsorship options. The product may be launched as a *national brand* (or *manufacturer's brand*), as when Samsung and Kellogg sell their output under their own brand names (the Samsung Galaxy tablet or Kellogg's Frosted Flakes). Or the manufacturer may sell to resellers who give the product a *private brand* (also called a *store brand*). Although most manufacturers create their own brand names, others market licensed brands. Finally, two companies can join forces and *co-brand* a product. We discuss each of these options in turn.

Store brand (or private brand)
A brand created and owned by a reseller of a product or service.

National Brands versus Store Brands. National brands (or manufacturers' brands) have long dominated the retail scene. In recent times, however, increasing numbers of retailers and wholesalers have created their own **store brands** (or **private brands**). Store brands have been gaining strength for decades, but recent years have seen a store-brand boom.

Many large retailers skillfully market a deep assortment of store-brand merchandise. For example, Kroger's private brands—the Kroger house brand, Private Selection, Heritage Farm, Simple Truth (natural and organic), Psst, Check This Out (savings), and others—add up to a whopping 25 percent of the giant grocery retailer's sales, nearly $23 billion worth annually. At thrifty grocery chain ALDI, more than 90 percent of sales come from private brands such as Baker's Choice, Friendly Farms, Simply Nature, and Mama Cozzi's Pizza Kitchen. Even online retailer Amazon has developed a stable of private brands, including AmazonBasics (mostly electronics), Amazon Elements (nutritional supplements), Strathwood (outdoor furniture), GoodThreads (menswear), and Denali (tools).[39]

Once known as "generic" or "no-name" brands, today's store brands have shed their image as cheap knockoffs of national brands. Store brands now offer much greater selection, and they are rapidly achieving name-brand quality. In fact, retailers such as Target and Trader Joe's are out-innovating many of their national-brand competitors. >> Kroger even offers a Kroger brand guarantee—"Try it, like it, or get the national brand free." As a result, consumers are becoming loyal to store brands for reasons besides price. In some cases, consumers are even willing to pay more for store brands that have been positioned as gourmet or premium items. Beyond just price and value, the customer experience has become an important motive behind store brand success (see Marketing at Work 7.2).

>> Store brands: Kroger's store brands—from Private Selection to Simple Truth—account for 25 percent of the grocery retailer's sales. Kroger even offers a "Try it, like it, or get the national brand for free" guarantee.
Al Behrman/AP Images

In the so-called *battle of the brands* between national and private brands, retailers have many advantages. They control what products they stock, where they go on the shelf, what prices they charge, and which ones they will feature in local promotions. Retailers often price their store brands lower than comparable national brands and feature the price differences in side-by-side comparisons on store shelves. Although store brands can be hard to establish and costly to stock and promote, they also yield higher profit margins for the reseller. And they give resellers exclusive products that cannot be bought from competitors, resulting in greater store traffic and loyalty. Retailer Trader Joe's, which carries approximately 90 percent store brands, largely controls its own brand destiny rather than relying on producers to make and manage the brands it needs to serve its customers best.

MARKETING AT WORK 7.2

Store Brands: Price Is Important, but It's More about the Customer Experience

Store brands are surging, grabbing market share from national brands in categories ranging from groceries and apparel to household goods, consumer electronics, and tools. Saving money is part of the reason. But gone are the days when store brands were little more than cheap, no-name knockoffs. Today's store brands often equal national brands in quality, and they are backed by retailers with reputations that match or exceed those of national brand manufacturers. For example, who do you have a closer relationship with, Kraft or Trader Joe's? Wrangler or Target?

Beyond offering good value, large retailers offer something else that brand-name manufacturers can't—shopping convenience and selection across a wide range of products. Store brands help take the work out of buying. Today's shoppers are often overwhelmed with options. Store brands can reduce the time and mental effort needed to make brand choices. For example, Costco affixes its highly successful Kirkland Signature brand to products in a dozen or more categories, from food and clothing to health and beauty items, household and cleaning goods, and even pet supplies. So whether you're buying laundry detergent, baby wipes, or sockeye salmon, brand choice at Costco is easier.

Similarly, a single trip to Target brings customers face-to-face with a broad selection of store brands that includes Archer Farms and Market Pantry (food and grocery), Wondershop (holiday snacks), Simply Balanced (organic and healthy foods), Threshold (premium home goods), Room Essentials (budget-friendly home goods), Goodfellow & Co, (menswear), JoyLab (women's fashion performance), Cat & Jack (children's apparel), and Up & Up (low-priced essentials in various categories). If you like Target, chances are good that you will like its store brands too. Whereas Target has struggled in recent years in the murky retail market, its store brands have been a beacon. Target now boasts more than 20 store brands, 10 of them billion-dollar-a-year brands. Launched only a few years ago, for example, its Cat & Jack children's apparel line now leads the industry with more than $2 billion in revenues.

Unlike the early days, consumers have learned to trust major store brands, just as they trust the stores that sell them. For example, customers flock to Trader Joe's *because* of its store brands, which are about all that the trendy retailer sells. Trader Joe's sells novel brands that you just can't get anywhere else, at great value for the price and backed by a no-questions-asked refund policy.

Are Trader Joe's brands really as good as private brands? In many cases, they are produced by the same manufacturers. Trader Joe's makes very few if any of the products it sells. Instead, it partners with third-party producers, many of them national brand manufacturers who agree to sell some of their products under Trader Joe's labels. Although the retailer is notoriously tight-lipped about the identity of its suppliers, analysts have sleuthed out likely makers of many Trader Joe's products. These include Wonderful Pistachios, Naked Juice, Tate's Bake Shop, Tribe Mediterranean Foods, Snack Factory, Stauffer's, and big conglomerates like ConAgra (maker of Hunt's brand foods). But Trader Joe's fans don't think of the retailer's wares as "generics" sourced elsewhere. "[They think] 'it's Trader Joe's—that's the brand,'" says an analyst, "and it's a special brand you can only get here."

When it comes to marketing their brands, retailers have another big advantage over brand-name marketers—direct customer access and control over the customer experience. Perhaps no retailer knows this better than Amazon. Amazon got into store brands just over a decade ago when it introduced its Kindle e-reader. Since then, Amazon has launched a blitz of private brands in almost every imaginable category. That makes good sense. Once on Amazon.com, customers have access to a broad selection of Amazon store brands that reduce buying uncertainty and make filling their shopping carts a lot easier. Why spend time evaluating a long list of brands when you can just buy an AmazonBasics cable or batteries and trust that you'll be getting good quality and value (confirmed by customer reviews)?

Amazon's bread-and-butter store brand is AmazonBasics, which accounts for 85 percent of the company's total private label revenues. It covers a wide range of everyday electronics and household items, from electronics accessories and batteries to bed sheets, bath towels, knife sets, and yoga mats. The Amazon Essentials brand covers basic clothing items, and Amazon Elements includes vitamins, supplements, and other health and exercise-related items.

But Amazon is now moving rapidly beyond basics, essentials, and elements toward store brands with more fashion and flair. Its more-recently launched store brands include the likes of Lark & Ro (sleek women's wear), Mae (intimate apparel), Franklin Tailored (men's dress wear), Buttoned Down (men's dress shirts), Goodthreads (men's casual wear), Scout + Ro (children's clothing), Pinzon (décor-related linens and bath accessories), Presto! (bio-based household cleaners), Mama Bear (baby products), and Wickedly Prime and Happy Belly (gourmet snack foods).

Despite their newness, Amazon's store brands are soaring. Last year alone, sales of Amazon-owned brands grew by an average of 90 percent. For example, sales of AmazonBasics batteries grew 93 percent last year and now account for 94 percent of all batteries sold on Amazon. Amazon Elements Baby Wipes grew 266 percent and are poised to outsell Pampers and Huggies soon. Lark & Ro sales also doubled last year.

Its store brands are helping Amazon to dominate retail sales in some unexpected categories. For example, including sales of its own and national brands, Amazon now captures a surprising 40 percent share of all U.S. apparel and footwear sales. Experts predict that Amazon will soon pass Walmart as the nation's largest clothing retailer, with apparel sales reaching $85 billion by 2020. And an increasing share of those sales will come from Amazon's store brands.

It's easy to understand the dramatic growth of store brands that have Amazon in the name—AmazonBasics, Amazon Essentials, and Amazon Elements. When shoppers see the trusted Amazon name on an everyday product, they believe that they'll get good quality at a fair price. Amazon Prime will deliver it to their doorsteps within a few hours or a few days, and if they have issues with the product, Amazon will fix things without question.

But for store brands that don't include its name, Amazon must build customer trust, satisfaction, and advocacy. In its usual fashion, with its store brands, Amazon is putting the customer experience before short-term profits. As just one example, Amazon representatives recently met with fashion designer Jackie Wilson to discuss making a women's knit top that would be sold under an Amazon private label. Wilson later reported that Amazon's quality specifications are on par with those of name-brand apparel sellers. "They are not concerned at all about how many units they sell, and they're not focused on margins," says Wilson, whose company makes clothing for Kohl's, American Eagle Outfitters, and J.C. Penney. "They're concerned about customer satisfaction. They want five-star reviews."

Sources: Daphne Howland, "AmazonBasics Is Crushing Other Private Brands," *Retail Dive*, September 29, 2017, www.retaildive.com/news/amazonbasics-is-crushing-other-private-brands/506116/; Tony Garcia, "Amazon's Apparel Business Could Grow to as Much as $85 Billion in Sales by 2020," *Market Watch*, December 10, 2017, www.marketwatch.com/story/amazons-apparel-business-could-to-grow-to-as-much-as-85-billion-in-sales-by-2020-2017-12-05; Matthew Boyle, "How Private Labels Caught the Public Eye," *Bloomberg BusinessWeek*, December 18, 2017, pp. 13–14; Tara Johnson, "The Complete List of Amazon's Private Label Brands," *CPC Strategy*, July 5, 2017, www.cpcstrategy.com/blog/2017/07/amazons-private-label-brands/; Vince Dixon, "What Brands Are Actually behind Trader Joe's Snacks," *Eater*, August 9, 2017, www.eater.com/2017/8/9/16099028/trader-joes-products; and www.amazon.com/amazonbasics, https://www.amazon.com/Amazon-Elements-Premium-products-Transparent-origins-Exclusive-to-Prime/b?ie=UTF8&node=10166275011, and www.amazon.com/stores/page/F8FB6F3C-F896-455C-BC52-7879F4CEF0CF, accessed September 2018.

>> Store brands: Amazon has launched a blitz of private brands in almost every imaginable category. Why spend time evaluating a long list of brands when you can just buy an AmazonBasics product and trust that you'll be getting good quality and value (confirmed by customer reviews)?

Gary Armstrong

To compete with store brands, national brands must sharpen their value propositions, especially when appealing to today's more frugal consumers. Many national brands are fighting back by rolling out more discounts and coupons to defend their market share. In the long run, however, leading brand marketers must compete by investing in new brands, new features, and quality improvements that set them apart. They must design strong advertising programs to maintain high awareness and preference. And they must find ways to partner with major distributors to find distribution economies and improve joint performance.

Licensing. Most manufacturers take years and spend millions to create their own brand names. However, some companies license names or symbols previously created by other manufacturers, names of well-known celebrities, or characters from popular movies and books. For a fee, any of these can provide an instant and proven brand name.

Apparel and accessories sellers pay large royalties to adorn their products—from blouses to ties and linens to luggage—with the names or initials of well-known fashion innovators such as Calvin Klein, Tommy Hilfiger, Gucci, or Armani. Sellers of children's products attach an almost endless list of character names to clothing, toys, school supplies, linens, dolls, lunch boxes, cereals, and other items. Licensed character names range from classics such as Sesame Street, Disney, Star Wars, Scooby Doo, Hello Kitty, SpongeBob SquarePants, and Dr. Seuss characters to the more recent Doc McStuffins, Monster High, Frozen, and Minions. And currently, numerous top-selling retail toys are products based on television shows and movies.

>> Licensing can be a highly profitable business for companies: Nickelodeon's hugely popular SpongeBob SquarePants character by itself has generated billions of dollars of retail sales over the years.

Gary Armstrong

Name and character licensing has grown rapidly in recent years. Annual retail sales of licensed products worldwide have grown from only $4 billion in 1977 to $55 billion in 1987 and more than $272 billion today. >> Licensing can be a highly profitable business for many companies. For example, Nickelodeon's hugely popular SpongeBob SquarePants character by itself has generated some $12 billion worth of endorsement deals over the past 15 years. Disney is the world's biggest licensor with a studio full of popular characters, from the Disney Princesses and Disney Fairies to heroes from *Toy Story* and *Star Wars* and classic characters such as Mickey and Minnie Mouse. Disney characters reaped a reported $56.6 billion in worldwide merchandise sales last year.[40]

Co-branding
The practice of using the established brand names of two different companies on the same product.

Co-branding. **Co-branding** occurs when two established brand names of different companies are used on the same product. Co-branding offers many advantages. Because each brand operates in a different category, the combined brands create broader consumer appeal and greater brand equity. For example, Google partnered with Oreo to name a latest version of its Android operating system Android Oreo, creating a fun association with great buzz value for both brands. Sherwin-Williams and Pottery Barn joined forces to create a special collection of Sherwin-Williams paint colors designed to perfectly coordinate with Pottery Barn's furnishings and accents. And Taco Bell and Doritos teamed up to create the Doritos Locos Taco. Taco Bell sold more than 100 million of the tacos in just the first 10 weeks. It quickly added Cool Ranch and Fiery versions and has since sold more than a billion. More than just co-branding, these companies are "co-making" these products.

Co-branding can take advantage of the complementary strengths of two brands. It also allows a company to expand its existing brand into a category it might otherwise have difficulty entering alone. For example, Nike and Apple co-branded the Nike+iPod Sport Kit, which lets runners link their Nike shoes with their iPods to track and enhance running performance in real time. The Nike+iPod arrangement gave Apple a presence in the sports and fitness market. At the same time, it helps Nike bring new value to its customers.

Line extension
Extending an existing brand name to new forms, colors, sizes, ingredients, or flavors of an existing product category.

Co-branding can also have limitations. Such relationships usually involve complex legal contracts and licenses. Co-branding partners must carefully coordinate their advertising, sales promotion, and other marketing efforts. Finally, when co-branding, each partner must trust that the other will take good care of its brand. If something damages the reputation of one brand, it can tarnish the co-brand as well.

Brand Development

A company has four choices when it comes to developing brands (see >> **Figure 7.6**). It can introduce *line extensions, brand extensions, multibrands*, or *new brands*.

This is a very handy framework for analyzing brand development opportunities. For example, what strategy did Toyota use when it introduced the Toyota Camry Hybrid? When it introduced the Toyota Prius? The Lexus?

Brand name \ Product category	Existing	New
Existing	Line extension	Brand extension
New	Multibrands	New brands

>> **Figure 7.6 Brand Development Strategies**

Line Extensions. **Line extensions** occur when a company extends existing brand names to new forms, colors, sizes, ingredients, or flavors of an existing product category. For example, over the years, KFC has extended its "finger lickin' good" chicken lineup well beyond original recipe, bone-in Kentucky fried chicken. It now offers grilled chicken, boneless fried chicken, chicken tenders, hot wings, chicken bites, chicken popcorn nuggets, chicken sandwiches, and KFC Go Cups—chicken and potato wedges in a handy car-cup holder that lets customers snack on the go.

A company might introduce line extensions as a low-cost, low-risk way to introduce new products. Or it might want to meet consumer desires for variety, use excess capacity, or simply command more shelf space from resellers. However, line extensions involve some risks. An overextended brand name might cause consumer confusion or lose some of its specific meaning.

At some point, additional extensions might add little value to a line. For instance, the original Doritos Tortilla Chips have morphed into a U.S. roster of more than 20 different types of chips and flavors, plus dozens more in foreign markets. Flavors include everything from Nacho Cheese and Taco flavor to Tapatio, Chile Limon, and Salsa Verde. Or how about spicy chicken flavored Late Night or garlic shrimp favored Royal (Japan)? Although the line is doing great—Doritos is the number two chip brand in the United States (Lay's is number one)—the original Doritos chips now seem like just another flavor.[41] And how much would adding yet another flavor steal from Doritos' own sales versus those of competitors? A line extension works best when it takes sales away from competing brands, not when it "cannibalizes" the company's other items.

Brand extension
Extending an existing brand name to new product categories.

Brand Extensions. A **brand extension** extends a current brand name to new or modified products in a new category. For example, Google-owned Nest—which began as a maker of stylish, connected, learning thermostats that can be controlled remotely by phone—has extended its line with a host of smart and stylish smart-home products, including a smoke and carbon monoxide alarm, home monitoring cameras, a home security alarm system, and a video doorbell that lets you know who's calling. >> And it's extending the Nest line to include "Works with Nest," applications developed with a variety of partners that let its smart devices interact with and control everything from keyless door locks and home lighting to home appliances and fitness tracking bands. All of the extensions fit together under Nest's smart homes mission.[42]

>> **Brand extensions: Nest has extended its line to include a host of its own smart-home products, along with "Works with Nest" applications developed with a variety of partners.**
Nest Labs

These days, a large majority of new products are extensions of already-successful brands. Compared with building new brands, extensions can create immediate new-product familiarity and acceptance at lower development costs. For example, it's not just any new wireless charging mat for your mobile devices, it's a Duracell Powermat. And it's not just a new, no-name over-the-counter sleep aid, it's Vicks ZzzQuil. Extensions such as the Duracell Powermat and Vicks ZzzQuil make good sense—they connect well with the core brand's values and build on its strengths.

At the same time, a brand extension strategy involves some risk. The extension may confuse the image of the main brand—for example, how about Zippo perfume or Fruit of the Loom laundry detergent? Brand extensions such as Cheetos lip balm, Heinz pet food, Colgate ready meals, and Life Savers gum met early deaths.[43] Furthermore, a brand name may not be appropriate to a particular new product, even if it is well made and satisfying—would you consider flying on Hooters Air or wearing an Evian water-filled padded bra (both failed)? And if a brand extension fails, it may harm consumer attitudes toward other products carrying the same brand name. Thus, a company can't just take a familiar brand name and slap it on a product in another category. Instead, a good brand extension should fit the parent brand, and the parent brand should give the extension competitive advantage in its new category.

Multibrands. Companies often market many different brands in a given product category. For example, in the United States, PepsiCo markets at least eight brands of carbonated soft drinks (Pepsi, Sierra Mist, Mountain Dew, Manzanita Sol, Mirinda, IZZE, Tropicana Twister, and Mug root beer), three brands of sports and energy drinks (Gatorade, AMP Energy, Starbucks Refreshers), five brands of bottled teas and coffees (Brisk, Pure Leaf, SoBe, Starbucks, Tazo), five brands of bottled waters (Aquafina, H2OH!, Ocean Spray PACt, Propel, SoBe), and nine brands of fruit drinks (Brisk, Dole, IZZE, Looza, Ocean Spray, Tropicana, and others). Each brand includes a long list of sub-brands. For instance, Aquafina includes regular Aquafina, Aquafina Flavorsplash, and Aquafina Sparkling.

Multibranding offers a way to establish different features that appeal to different customer segments, lock up more reseller shelf space, and capture a larger market share. For example, although PepsiCo's many brands of beverages compete with one another on supermarket shelves, the combined brands reap a much greater overall market share than any single brand ever could. Similarly, by positioning multiple brands in multiple segments, Pepsi's eight soft drink brands combine to capture much more market share than any single brand could capture by itself.

A major drawback of multibranding is that each brand might obtain only a small market share, and none may be very profitable. The company may end up spreading its resources over many brands instead of building a few brands to a highly profitable level. These companies should reduce the number of brands they sell in a given category and set up tighter screening procedures for new brands. This happened to GM, which in recent years has cut numerous brands from its portfolio, including Saturn, Oldsmobile, Pontiac, Hummer, and Saab.

New Brands. A company might believe that the power of its existing brand name is waning so a new brand name is needed. Or it may create a new brand name when it enters a new product category for which none of its current brand names is appropriate. For example, Toyota created the separate Lexus brand aimed at luxury car consumers.

As with multibranding, offering too many new brands can result in a company spreading its resources too thin. And in some industries, such as consumer packaged goods, consumers and retailers have become concerned that there are already too many brands with too few differences between them. Thus, P&G, PepsiCo, Kraft, GA, and other large marketers of consumer products are now pursuing megabrand strategies—weeding out weaker or slower-growing brands and focusing their marketing dollars on brands that can achieve the number one or number two market share positions with good growth prospects in their categories.

Managing Brands

Companies must manage their brands carefully. First, the brand's positioning must be continuously communicated to consumers. Major brand marketers often spend huge amounts on advertising to create brand awareness and build preference and loyalty. For example, worldwide, Coca-Cola spends $4 billion annually to advertise its many brands, GM spends nearly $5.3 billion, Unilever spends $8.6 billion, and P&G spends an astounding $10.5 billion.[44]

Such advertising campaigns can help create name recognition, brand knowledge, and perhaps even some brand preference. However, the fact is that brands are not maintained by advertising but by customers' *engagement* with brands and customers' *brand experiences*. Today, customers come to know a brand through a wide range of contacts and touch points. These include advertising but also personal experience with the brand, word of mouth and social media, company websites and mobile apps, and many others. The company must put as much care into managing these touch points as it does into producing its ads. As one former Disney top executive put it: "A brand is a living entity, and it is enriched or undermined cumulatively over time, the product of a thousand small gestures."[45]

The brand's positioning will not take hold fully unless everyone in the company lives the brand. Therefore, the company needs to train its people to be customer centered. Even better, the company should carry on internal brand building to help employees understand and be enthusiastic about the brand promise. Many companies go even further by training and encouraging their distributors and dealers to serve their customers well.

Finally, companies need to periodically audit their brands' strengths and weaknesses. They should ask: Does our brand excel at delivering benefits that consumers truly value? Is the brand properly positioned? Do all our consumer touch points support the brand's positioning? Do the brand's managers understand what the brand means to consumers? Does the brand receive proper, sustained support? The brand audit may turn up brands that need more support, brands that need to be dropped, or brands that must be rebranded or repositioned because of changing customer preferences or new competitors.

REVIEWING AND EXTENDING THE CONCEPTS

CHAPTER REVIEW AND KEY TERMS

Objectives Review

A product is more than a simple set of tangible features. Each product or service offered to customers can be viewed on three levels. The *core customer value* consists of the core problem-solving benefits that consumers seek when they buy a product. The *actual product* exists around the core and includes the quality level, features, design, brand name, and packaging. The *augmented product* is the actual product plus the various services and benefits offered with it, such as a warranty, free delivery, installation, and maintenance.

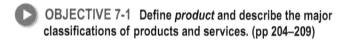

OBJECTIVE 7-1 Define *product* and describe the major classifications of products and services. (pp 204–209)

Broadly defined, a *product* is anything that can be offered to a market for attention, acquisition, use, or consumption that might satisfy a want or need. Products include physical objects but also services, events, persons, places, organizations, ideas, or mixtures of these entities. *Services* are products that consist of activities, benefits, or satisfactions offered for sale that are essentially intangible, such as banking, hotel, tax preparation, and home-repair services.

Products and services fall into two broad classes based on the types of consumers who use them. *Consumer products*—those bought by final consumers—are usually classified according to consumer shopping habits (convenience products, shopping products, specialty products, and unsought products). *Industrial products*—those purchased for further processing or for use in conducting a business—include materials and parts, capital items, and supplies and services. Other marketable entities—such as organizations, persons, places, and ideas—can also be thought of as products.

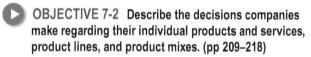

OBJECTIVE 7-2 Describe the decisions companies make regarding their individual products and services, product lines, and product mixes. (pp 209–218)

Individual product decisions involve product attributes, branding, packaging, labeling, and product support services. *Product attribute* decisions involve product quality, features, and style and design. *Branding* decisions include selecting a brand name and developing a brand strategy. *Packaging* provides many key benefits, such as protection, economy, convenience, and promotion. Package decisions often include designing *labels and logos*, which identify, describe, and possibly promote the product. Companies also develop *product support services* that enhance customer service and satisfaction and safeguard against competitors.

Most companies produce a product line rather than a single product. A *product line* is a group of products that are related in function, customer-purchase needs, or distribution channels. All product lines and items offered to customers by a particular seller make up the *product mix*. The mix can be described by four dimensions: width, length, depth, and consistency. These dimensions are the tools for developing the company's product strategy.

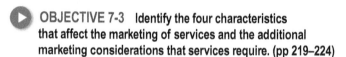

OBJECTIVE 7-3 Identify the four characteristics that affect the marketing of services and the additional marketing considerations that services require. (pp 219–224)

Services are characterized by four key aspects: they are *intangible, inseparable, variable*, and *perishable*. Each characteristic poses problems and marketing requirements. Marketers work to find ways to make the service more tangible, increase the productivity of providers who are inseparable from their products, standardize quality in the face of variability, and improve demand movements and supply capacities in the face of service perishability.

Good service companies focus attention on *both* customers and employees. They understand the *service profit chain*, which links service firm profits with employee and customer satisfaction. Services marketing strategy calls not only for external marketing but also for *internal marketing* to motivate employees and *interactive marketing* to create service delivery skills among service providers. To succeed, service marketers must create *competitive differentiation*, offer high *service quality*, and find ways to increase *service productivity*.

OBJECTIVE 7-4 Discuss branding strategy—the decisions companies make in building and managing their brands. (pp 224–233)

Some analysts see brands as *the* major enduring asset of a company. Brands are more than just names and symbols; they embody everything that the product or the service *means* to consumers. *Brand equity* is the positive differential effect that knowing the brand name has on customer response to the product or the service. A brand with strong brand equity is a very valuable asset.

In building brands, companies need to make decisions about brand positioning, brand name selection, brand sponsorship, and brand development. The most powerful *brand positioning* builds around strong consumer beliefs and values. *Brand name selection* involves finding the best brand name based on a careful review of product benefits, the target market, and proposed marketing strategies. A manufacturer has four *brand sponsorship* options: It can launch a *national brand* (or manufacturer's brand), sell to resellers that use a *private brand*, market *licensed brands*, or join forces with another company to *co-brand* a product. A company also has four choices when it comes to developing brands. It can introduce *line extensions, brand extensions, multibrands*, or *new brands*.

Companies must build and manage their brands carefully. The brand's positioning must be continuously communicated to consumers. Advertising can help. However, brands are not maintained by advertising but by customers' *brand experiences*. Customers come to know a brand through a wide range of contacts and interactions. The company must put as much care into managing these touch points as it does into producing its ads. Companies must periodically audit their brands' strengths and weaknesses.

Key Terms

Objective 7-1
Product (p 204)
Service (p 204)
Consumer product (p 206)
Convenience product (p 207)
Shopping product (p 207)
Specialty product (p 207)
Unsought product (p 207)
Industrial product (p 207)
Social marketing (p 208)

Objective 7-2
Product quality (p 209)
Brand (p 211)
Packaging (p 212)
Product line (p 216)
Product mix (or product portfolio) (p 217)

Objective 7-3
Service intangibility (p 219)
Service inseparability (p 220)
Service variability (p 220)
Service perishability (p 220)
Service profit chain (p 221)
Internal marketing (p 221)
Interactive marketing (p 221)

Objective 7-4
Brand equity (p 225)
Brand value (p 225)
Store brand (or private brand) (p 228)
Co-branding (p 231)
Line extension (p 231)
Brand extension (p 232)

DISCUSSION AND CRITICAL THINKING

Discussion Questions

7-1. Define *consumer products*. Describe the characteristics of each type of consumer product, and give examples of each. (AACSB: Written and oral communication; Reflective thinking)

7-2. Name and explain the five important decisions that marketers must make in developing and marketing individual products and services. (AACSB: Written and oral communication)

7-3. Explain the difference between a *product line* and a *product mix*, and provide examples to illustrate each one. (AACSB: Written and oral communication)

7-4. Describe the service profit chain. Provide an example. (AACSB: Written and oral communication, Reflective thinking)

7-5. Discuss brand equity and brand value. How do marketers use these to build powerful brands? (AACSB: Written and oral communication, Reflective thinking)

7-6. Explain the four choices a company has when developing brands, and illustrate each with an example. (AACSB: Written and oral communication, Reflective thinking)

Critical Thinking Exercises

7-7. Walt Disney created the Disney brand from humble beginnings based on his love of drawing and animation. The Walt Disney Company has since expanded successfully into a global entertainment and media brand. Using the internet, research the brands that make up the Walt Disney Company, and discuss how Disney has expanded its product mix. (AACSB: Written and oral communication; Information technology; Reflective thinking)

7-8. Companies must consider four special service characteristics when designing service marketing programs. Discuss a recent service experience using the four characteristics. Compare your service experience with that of a classmate. How do they differ? (AACSB: Written and oral communication, Reflective thinking)

7-9. There are four types of consumer products—products and services bought by final consumers for personal consumption. Identify a product or service in each consumer product category that you or someone you know has purchased. What did you purchase, and where did you purchase it? Explain the purchase decision using the consumer product characteristics outlined in the Table 7.1, Marketing Considerations for Consumer Products. (AACSB: Written and oral communication; Reflective thinking)

MINICASES AND APPLICATIONS

Online, Mobile, and Social Media Marketing Feeding Buddy from Your Smartphone

People lead busy lives, sometimes taking time away from their pets. Petnet has developed the Smartfeeder, allowing pet owners to schedule feeding times, monitor food intake, and personalize pet nutrition information. The Smartfeeder measures out the appropriate amount of food for a pet based on age, activity, and weight. Additional features include the ability to conveniently store five to seven pounds of pet food in the attached hopper. Petnet has also seamlessly integrated its products with a smartphone app. Pet owners can now control feeding times, portion sizes, and food supply and even order pet food to be delivered directly to their homes, all from a mobile device.

7-10. What type of product is Petnet's Smartfeeder? How should this type of product be marketed? (AACSB: Written and oral communication; Reflective thinking)

7-11. What are customers really buying when they purchase a Petnet Smartfeeder? Identify the core, actual, and augmented product levels for this product. (AACSB: Written and oral communication; Reflective thinking)

Marketing Ethics Permission to Unlock? Amazon In-Home/In-Car Delivery Service

With online shopping growing rapidly, delivering packages securely to their final destinations and reducing parcel theft are growing concerns. Amazon has recognized these needs and is bridging the gap for its 85 million Prime members. Rather than delivering a parcel to your front doorstep, the online retail giant now offers secure in-home and in-car delivery services. It recently launched Amazon Key, which uses a smart lock and cloud-based security cameras to allow Amazon delivery staff to drop off packages inside customers' homes when they aren't there. The setup kit for Amazon Key costs $250. Amazon is also testing a free in-car package delivery service that works with cars equipped with GM's On-Star or Volvo's On-Call technology. To make in-car deliveries, Amazon employees must have access to a car's GPS location and license plate number.

Such Amazon services seem to offer many benefits. However, some consumers will decline this service. They will worry that Amazon's cloud-based camera for in-home deliveries might be hacked and that no such video monitoring is available for in-car deliveries. Amazon insists that customers remain in control at all times, with multiple notifications and the option to block access at any time.

7-12. Would you use the Amazon Key services? Why or why not? When would you be most likely to use this service? (AACSB: Written and oral communication; Reflective thinking)

7-13. What ethical issues must Amazon address before consumers will consider adopting this service? (AACSB: Written and oral communication; Reflective thinking; Ethical understanding and reasoning)

Marketing by the Numbers Diet Coke with Fiber

Coca-Cola launched Coca-Cola Plus in a limited market in Japan last year and now plans to launch it nationwide in that country. Coca-Cola Plus is a zero-calorie soda (essentially Diet Coke) with five grams of an indigestible dietary fiber called dextrin. Although some might just call it Diet Coke with a laxative, Coca-Cola Plus is touted in Japan as a health food that suppresses the absorption of fat and keeps blood triglycerides at moderate levels. In fact, the product has earned the Japanese government's "gold label," designating it as a government-approved Food of Specific Health Use (FOSHU). Although the new Coca-Cola Plus reaps a higher wholesale price for the company ($1.20 per 470-milliliter bottle versus $1.15 per bottle for the original Diet Coke), it also comes with higher variable costs ($0.65 per bottle versus $0.55 per bottle for the original product). Although some Diet Coke drinkers will switch to Coca-Cola Plus, the company believes the new product will attract new customers because of its health benefits. Coca-Cola is no stranger to introducing new products in Japan. The company released Coca-Cola Coffee Plus last year and recently introduced its first alcoholic beverage called Lemon Do.

7-14. What brand development strategy is Coca-Cola undertaking? (AACSB: Written and oral communication; Reflective thinking)

7-15. Assume the company expects to sell 5 million bottles of Coca-Cola Plus in the first year after introduction but that 60 percent of those sales will come from buyers who would normally purchase Diet Coke (that is, cannibalized sales). Assuming the sales of Diet Coke are normally 300 million bottles per year and that the company will incur an increase in fixed costs of $500,000 during the first year to launch Coca-Cola Plus, will the new product be profitable for the company? Refer to the Financial Analysis of Marketing Tactics: Extend the Product Line section in Appendix 3: Marketing by the Numbers for an explanation regarding how to conduct this analysis. (AACSB: Written and oral communication; Analytical thinking)

Video Case Plymouth Rock Assurance

To view this video case and its accompanying questions, please visit MyLab Marketing.

Plymouth Rock Assurance is an insurance company with a branding tale to tell. What started as a single Massachusetts-based auto insurance company in the early 1980s quickly grew into a group of separate companies that write and manage property and casualty insurance in various states. To streamline operations, cut costs, and better serve customers, the company undertook a rebranding process to combine three distinct auto insurance brands—Plymouth Rock, High Point, and Palisades—into one.

Rather than remaking the brand overnight, the company carried out a gradual transformation that retained existing brand equity and put customers' minds at ease. With Plymouth Rock as the parent brand and High Point and Palisades as sub-brands, the company transitioned the three into a single brand in incremental steps.

Company Cases 7 MINI/5 Spanx/12 LinkedIn

See Appendix 1 for cases appropriate for this chapter.

Case 7, MINI: Focus on the Essential—Maximize the Experience. BMW has a hit on its hands with MINI, achieving success by remaining true to the original brand while simultaneously keeping up with changing customer dynamics.

Case 5, Spanx: Changing the Way an Industry Thinks about Underwear. Spanx revolutionized the world of women's undergarments with a spicy new brand built around a superior product.

Case 12, LinkedIn: Crushing the White-Collar Stereotype with IMC. With its first mass-media IMC campaign, LinkedIn is out to change widely held perceptions that its services are white collar only.

Writing Assignments

7-16. Describe how marketers manage service differentiation, other than through pricing, and describe an example of a service provider that has successfully differentiated its offering from competitors. (AACSB: Communication, Reflective Thinking)

7-17. A product's package must satisfy many criteria, such as sustainability, convenience, safety, efficiency, functionality, and marketing. Research "packaging awards" and develop a presentation analyzing an award-winning product packaging effort. Describe the organization hosting the award competition, the criteria for selecting winners, and one of the award-winning packages. (AACSB: Written and Oral Communication; Information Technology)

Developing New Products

and Managing the Product Life Cycle

Objectives Outline

OBJECTIVE 8-1 **Explain how companies find and develop new product ideas.** See: New Product Development Strategy (pp 240–241)

OBJECTIVE 8-2 **List and define the steps in the new product development process and the major considerations in managing this process.** See: The New Product Development Process (pp 241–251)

OBJECTIVE 8-3 **Describe the stages of the product life cycle and how marketing strategies change during a product's life cycle.** See: Product Life-Cycle Strategies (pp 251–258)

OBJECTIVE 8-4 **Discuss two additional product issues: socially responsible product decisions and international product and services marketing.** See: Additional Product and Service Considerations (pp 258–260)

Previewing the Concepts

In the previous chapter, you learned how marketers manage and develop products and brands. In this chapter, we examine two additional product topics: developing new products and managing products through their life cycles. New products are the lifeblood of an organization. However, new product development is risky, and many new products fail. So, the first part of this chapter lays out a process for finding and growing successful new products. Once introduced, marketers then want their products to enjoy long and happy lives. In the second part of the chapter, you'll see that every product passes through several life-cycle stages, and each stage poses new challenges requiring different marketing strategies and tactics. Finally, we wrap up our product discussion by looking at two additional considerations: social responsibility in product decisions and international product and services marketing.

For openers, consider Samsung, a world-leading consumer electronics maker and one of the world's most innovative companies. Over the past two decades, Samsung has transformed itself by creating a culture of customer-focused innovation and a seemingly endless flow of inspired new products that feature stunning design, innovative technology, life-enriching features, and a big dose of "Wow!"

First Stop

Samsung: Enriching Customers' Lives through New-Product Innovation

You're probably familiar with the Samsung brand. Maybe you own one of Samsung's hot new Galaxy smartphones, or maybe you've seen one of its dazzling new QLED Smart TVs that can produce more than a billion colors. Samsung produces "gotta have" electronics in just about every category, from TVs and flat-screen monitors, tablets and mobile phones, and wearable technology to smart-home devices and even a full range of home appliances.

But 25 years ago, Samsung was barely known, and it was anything but cutting-edge. Back then, Samsung was a Korean copycat brand that you bought off a shipping pallet at Costco if you couldn't afford a Sony, then the world's most coveted consumer electronics brand. However, in 1993 Samsung made an inspired decision. It turned its back on cheap knockoffs and set out to overtake rival Sony. To dethrone the consumer electronics giant, however, Samsung first had to change its entire culture, from copycat to leading-edge. To out*sell* Sony, Samsung decided, it first had to out-*innovate* Sony.

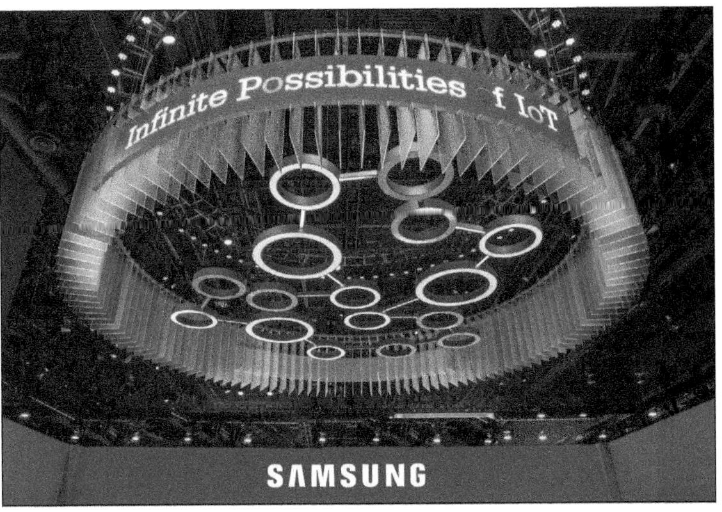

» Beyond cutting-edge technology and stylish design, Samsung puts the customer at the core of its innovation movement. Its new products "bring genuine change to people's lives."

Kobby Dagan/Shutterstock

So Samsung set out to become a premier brand and a trailblazing product leader. It hired a crop of fresh, young designers and managers, who unleashed a torrent of new products—not humdrum, me-too products but sleek, bold, and beautiful products targeted to high-end users. Samsung called them "lifestyle works of art." Every new product had to pass the "Wow!" test: If it didn't get a "Wow!" reaction during market testing, it went straight back to the design studio. Beyond cutting-edge technology and stylish designs, Samsung put the customer at the core of its innovation movement. Its primary innovation goal was to improve the customer experience and bring genuine change to people's lives in everything it did.

With its fresh customer-centered new-product focus, Samsung overtook Sony in less than 10 years. Today, Samsung's annual revenues of $174 billion are two and a half times Sony's revenues. But more than just being bigger, Samsung has also achieved the new-product Wow! factor it sought. For example, Samsung has been dominant in recent years at the International Design Excellence Awards (IDEA) presentations—the Academy Awards of the design world—which judges new products based on appearance, functionality, and inspirational thinking.

In this digital, connected, and mobile era, Samsung now competes less with the Sonys of the world and more with innovation pacesetters like Apple. And against Apple, Samsung is more than holding its own. In mobile devices, for example, Samsung has surged to the top of the market. Just a few years ago, Samsung's goal was to double its market share of smartphones from 5 percent to 10 percent. But the success of its Galaxy line catapulted Samsung's global share to 26 percent, ahead of Apple's 17 percent worldwide. What's more, Samsung earned billions of dollars last year from the success of Apple's newest iPhone—it supplies the OLED displays, NAND flash, and DRAM chips for Apple's smartphones.

Samsung holds another piece of the technology puzzle that Apple doesn't—big screens. In fact, Samsung has been the global leader in television sales for 11 straight years. Its smart TVs not only offer gesture control, voice control, and face recognition but also provide seamless connectivity that has TV users Facebooking, Skyping, streaming online content, controlling their appliances, and using their favorite apps. Control of so many kinds of screens gives Samsung a leg up against more-focused competitors in this connected age. This year, Samsung will update all its TVs with Bixby, Samsung's Alexa-challenging digital voice assistant.

But Samsung also realizes that today's "gotta have it" products can be tomorrow's has-beens. Future growth will come not just from bigger TVs and better smartphones. Rather, the electronics powerhouse is constantly on the prowl for the next "big thing," regardless of the product category. To that end, Samsung's market intelligence and product innovation teams around the globe continually research product usage, purchase behavior, and lifestyle trends, looking for consumer insights and innovative new ways to meet consumer needs.

Samsung has become one of the world's leading consumer electronics companies through customer-focused innovation and new products that enrich customers' lives. At Samsung, every new product has to pass the consumer "Wow!" test.

For instance, Samsung is investing heavily in the "Internet of Things" (IoT), or, as Samsung likes to call it, the "Intelligence of Things," a global environment where everything—from home electronics and appliances to automobiles, buildings, and even clothing—is digitally connected to everything else. "We believe IoT should be as easy as flipping a switch," says a Samsung executive. Samsung wants to "help consumers realize the benefits of a seamless and simple connected life."

Given that Samsung already makes products in almost every electronics category, IoT provides fertile territory for future innovation and growth. Samsung is developing a "web of connectivity" that links its products to the rest of the world. The goal is to develop Samsung IoT products and technologies that are "In Sync with Life." The company has already introduced numerous "smart" products—including its entire Smart TV lineup, dozens of household appliances, smart hubs and sensors, and mobile apps—that connect devices to each other and to those who use them. The company will soon launch its own SmartThings Cloud—a single ecosystem for all its IoT products and services.

Samsung's current IoT lineup is just the tip of the iceberg. According to one estimate, the number of networked devices has surged from about a billion just a few years ago to more than 20 billion today. All indications are that the number of IoT devices will swell to more than 30 billion by 2020, representing an almost $9 trillion market. By that time, Samsung claims that 100 percent of its products will be internet-connected.

Such innovation provides Samsung with much more than just new products to sell. Samsung used to be a "break and fix" brand, one that customers came to only when their products needed to be fixed or replaced. But with its growing IoT presence, Samsung now focuses on building meaningful customer relationships in every part of customers' lives every day. "The idea is that as customers become more connected with their devices, they can also become more connected to the brand," says an analyst. "More devices means there is more chance to build loyal Samsung customers for life."

Twenty-five years ago, few people would have predicted that Samsung would transform itself so completely from a low-cost copycat manufacturer into a world-leading innovator of stylish, high-performing, and industry-leading products. But through a dedication to customer-focused new-product innovation, that's exactly what Samsung has done. Even recently, few would have predicted that Samsung would be a driving force behind creating an interconnected world. Yet Samsung seems well on its way to accomplishing that as well.

"We have to show consumers what's in it for them and what the Internet of Things can achieve," says Samsung's CEO, "to transform our economy, society, and how we live our lives." Adds another Samsung executive: "We will focus on creating amazing experiences, [on doing] what is right by customers." In short, whatever gets that "Wow!"[1]

As the Samsung story suggests, companies that excel at developing and managing new products reap big rewards. Every product seems to have a life cycle: It is born, goes through several phases, and eventually dies as newer products come along that create new or greater value for customers.

This product life cycle presents two major challenges: First, because all products eventually decline, a firm must be good at developing new products to replace aging ones (the challenge of *new product development*). Second, a firm must be good at adapting its marketing strategies in the face of changing tastes, technologies, and competition as products pass through stages (the challenge of *product life-cycle strategies*). We first look at the problem of finding and developing new products and then at the problem of managing them successfully over their life cycles.

Author Comment
New products are the lifeblood of a company. As old products mature and fade away, companies must develop new ones to take their place. For example, the iPhone and iPad have been around for little over a decade but are now Apple's two top-selling products.

New Product Development Strategy

OBJECTIVE 8-1 Explain how companies find and develop new product ideas.

A firm can obtain new products in two ways. One is through *acquisition*—by buying a whole company, a patent, or a license to produce someone else's product. The other is through the firm's own **new product development** efforts. By *new products* we mean original products, product improvements, product modifications, and new brands that the firm develops through its own product development. In this chapter, we concentrate on new product development.

New product development
The development of original products, product improvements, product modifications, and new brands through the firm's own product development efforts.

New products are important to both customers and the marketers who serve them: They bring new solutions and variety to customers' lives, and they are a key source of growth for companies. In today's fast-changing environment, many companies rely on new products for the majority of their growth. For example, 3M's CEO estimates that 40 percent of the company's revenues last year came from products that did not exist five years ago. And new products have almost completely transformed Apple in recent years. The iPhone and iPad—introduced little more than a decade ago—are now the company's two biggest-selling products, with the iPhone alone bringing in more than 70 percent of Apple's total global revenues and 93 percent of device unit sales.[2]

Yet innovation can be very expensive and very risky. New products face tough odds. For example, by one estimate, 60 percent of all new consumer packaged products introduced by established companies fail; two-thirds of new product concepts are never even launched.[3] Why do so many new products fail? There are several reasons. Although an idea may be good, the company may overestimate market size. The actual product may be poorly designed. Or it might be incorrectly positioned, launched at the wrong time, priced too high, or poorly advertised. A high-level executive might push a favorite idea despite poor marketing research findings. Sometimes the costs of product development are higher than expected, and sometimes competitors fight back harder than expected.

So, companies face a problem: They must develop new products, but the odds weigh heavily against success. To create successful new products, a company must understand its consumers, markets, and competitors and develop products that deliver superior value to customers.

Author Comment
Companies can't just hope that they'll stumble across good new products. Instead, they must develop a systematic new product development process.

The New Product Development Process

OBJECTIVE 8-2 List and define the steps in the new product development process and the major considerations in managing this process.

Rather than leaving new products to chance, a company must carry out strong new product planning and set up a systematic, customer-driven *new product development process* for finding and growing new products. >> **Figure 8.1** shows the eight major steps in this process.

Idea Generation

Idea generation
The systematic search for new product ideas.

New product development starts with **idea generation**—the systematic search for new product ideas. A company typically generates hundreds—even thousands—of ideas to find a few good ones. Major sources of new product ideas include internal sources and external sources such as customers, competitors, distributors and suppliers, and others.

Internal Idea Sources

Using *internal sources*, the company can find new ideas through formal R&D. For example, Ford operates an innovation and mobility center in Silicon Valley staffed by engineers, app developers, and scientists working on everything from driverless cars to Works with Nest apps that let consumers control home heating, lighting, and appliances from their vehicles. Chick-fil-A has set up three large innovation centers. The first, called Hatch, is an idea hatchery where Chick-fil-A staff and partners explore new ideas in food, design, and service. It's a place to "ideate, explore, and imagine the future," to hatch new food and restaurant ideas and bring them to life.[4]

Beyond its internal R&D process, a company can pick the brains of its own people—from executives to salespeople to scientists, engineers, and manufacturing staff. Many companies have developed successful internal social networks and *intrapreneurial* programs that encourage employees to develop new product ideas. For example, AT&T has set up an internal online innovation community called The Innovation Pipeline (TIP), through which AT&T employees from all areas and levels of the company submit, discuss, and vote on new product and service ideas. Each quarter, the "founders" of top vote-getting ideas pitch them to AT&T senior executives, who select the best three for further funding and

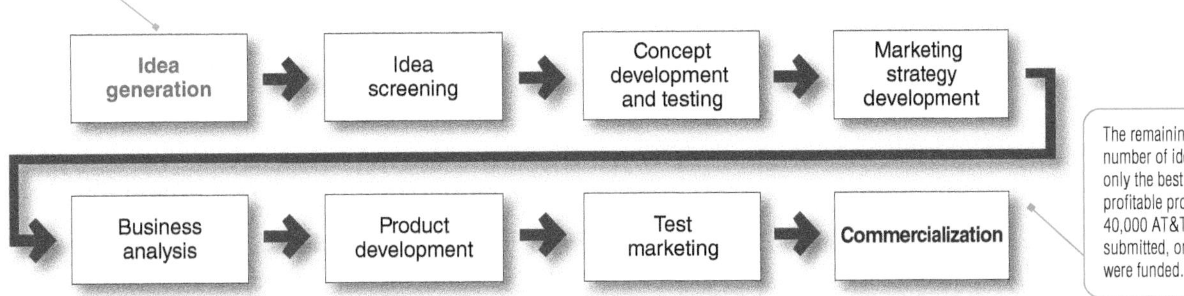
New product development starts with good new product ideas—lots ofthem. For example, during the past decade, AT&T's The Innovation Pipeline (TIP) employee crowdsourcing program has attracted more than 40,000 innovation ideas from members in all 50 states and 54 countries.
Idea generation
Idea screening
Concept development and testing
Marketing strategy development
Business analysis
Product development
Test marketing
Commercialization
The remaining steps reduce the number of ideas and develop only the best ones into profitable products. Of the 40,000 AT&T TIP ideas submitted, only 80 TIP projects were funded.

>> **Figure 8.1 Major Stages in New Product Development**

>> Internal new product ideas: Many companies—such as Facebook—use hackathons to pick the brains of their own employees for innovative ideas.

Hero Images Inc./Alamy Stock Photo

development. Since its inception in 2009, AT&T employees have submitted more than 40,000 ideas to the TIP community, and the company has funded more than 80 TIP projects ranging from customer service enhancements to new product offerings.[5]

Many companies sponsor periodic internal "hackathons," in which employees take a day or a week away from their day-to-day work to develop new ideas. >> Such hackathons are legendary at Facebook. During a Facebook hackathon, "a few hundred of our engineers unleash their talents in epic, all-night coding sessions and often end up with products that hit the internal and external versions of the site within weeks," says one Facebook employee. The social media giant's hackathons have produced major innovations such as the "Like" button or friend tagging. Such events not only produce fresh new ideas, they can also boost employee morale and engagement. As the employee explains, "the camaraderie, productivity, and occasional insanity of hackathons have helped make Facebook what it is."[6]

External Idea Sources

Companies can also obtain good new product ideas from any of a number of external sources. For example, *distributors and suppliers* can contribute ideas. Distributors are close to the market and can pass along information about consumer problems and new product possibilities. Suppliers can tell the company about new concepts, techniques, and materials that can be used to develop new products.

Competitors are another important source. Companies watch competitors' ads to get clues about their new products. They buy competing new products, take them apart to see how they work, analyze their sales, and decide whether they should bring out a new product of their own. Other idea sources include trade magazines, shows, websites, and seminars; government agencies; advertising agencies; marketing research firms; university and commercial laboratories; and inventors.

Crowdsourcing
Inviting broad communities of people—customers, employees, independent scientists and researchers, and even the public at large—into the new product innovation process.

Perhaps the most important sources of new product ideas are *customers* themselves. The company can analyze customer questions and complaints to find new products that better solve consumer problems. Or it can invite customers to share suggestions and ideas. >> For example, Salesforce—the leading customer relationship management solutions company—hosts an online IdeaExchange, where it invites customers to suggest, discuss, and vote on new software features and product enhancements. Over the past 10 years, customers have submitted more than 60,000 ideas and cast millions of votes. Often, the best results come more from the ensuing collaboration and brainstorming than from the initial idea. A Salesforce executive estimates that one-third of a product management team's thinking is influenced by IdeaExchange. The system also greatly improves the customer experience. It builds two-way relationships where customers feel listened to and valued.[7]

>> New product ideas from customers: Salesforce's IdeaExchange invites customers to suggest, discuss, and vote on new software features and product enhancements. Over the past 10 years, customers have submitted more than 60,000 ideas and cast millions of votes.

salesforce.com inc

Crowdsourcing

More broadly, many companies are now developing crowdsourcing or open-innovation new product idea programs. Through **crowdsourcing**, a company invites broad communities of people—customers, employees, independent scientists and researchers, and even the public at large—into the innovation process. Tapping into a breadth of sources—both inside and outside the company—can produce unexpected and powerful new ideas.

Companies large and small, across all industries, are crowdsourcing product innovation ideas rather than relying only on their own R&D labs. >> For example, sports apparel maker Under Armour knows that no matter how many top-notch developers it has inside, sometimes the only way to produce good outside-the-box ideas is by going outside the company. So in its quest to find the Next Big Thing, Under Armour sponsors an annual crowdsourcing competition called the Future Show Innovation Challenge:[8]

> The Future Show challenge invites entrepreneurs and inventors from around the nation to submit new product ideas. Then, from thousands of entries, an Under Armour team culls 12 finalists who go before a panel of seven judges to pitch their products in a splashy, *Shark Tank*–like reality TV setting. The winner earns $50,000 and a contract to work with Under Armour to help develop the winning product. The goal of the Future Show Challenge is to "cajole top innovators to come to Under Armour first with gee-whizzers," says CEO Kevin Plank. The first winner, and Plank's favorite so far, is a made-for-athletes zipper—the UA MagZip—that can be zipped easily with only one hand. Under Armour's internal R&D team had been trying to develop a better zipper for two years, but "we couldn't get it to work," says the company's vice president of innovation. That simple zipper is just one of dozens of creative new product ideas from the Future Show. But by itself, it makes the entire crowdsourcing effort worthwhile. "We need to be humble enough to know that the next great thing might come from some kid playing college football who happens to have a better idea," says the Under Armour innovation chief.

>> Crowdsourcing: Under Armour sponsors an annual crowdsourcing competition called the Future Show Innovation Challenge, in which it invites outside innovators to pitch new product ideas in a splashy, *Shark Tank*–like reality TV setting.
ZUMA Press, Inc./Alamy Stock Photo

Thus, truly innovative companies don't rely only on one source or another for new product ideas. Instead, they develop extensive innovation networks that capture ideas and inspiration from every possible source, from employees and customers to outside innovators and multiple points beyond.

Idea Screening

Idea screening
Screening new product ideas to spot good ones and drop poor ones as soon as possible.

The purpose of idea generation is to create a large number of ideas. The purpose of the succeeding stages is to *reduce* that number. The first idea-reducing stage is **idea screening**, which helps spot good ideas and drop poor ones as soon as possible. Product development costs rise greatly in later stages, so the company wants to go ahead only with those product ideas that will turn into profitable products.

Many companies require their executives to write up new product ideas in a standard format that can be reviewed by a new product committee. The write-up describes the product or the service, the proposed customer value proposition, the target market, and the competition. It makes some rough estimates of market size, product price, development time and costs, manufacturing costs, and rate of return. The committee then evaluates the idea against a set of general criteria.

One marketing expert describes an R-W-W ("real, win, worth doing") new product screening framework that asks three questions.[9] First, *Is it real?* Is there a real need and desire for the product, and will customers buy it? Is there a clear product concept, and will such a product satisfy the market? Second, *Can we win?* Does the product offer a sustainable competitive advantage? Does the company have the resources to make such a product a success? Finally, *Is it worth doing?* Does the product fit the company's overall growth strategy? Does it offer sufficient profit potential? The company should be able to answer yes to all three R-W-W questions before developing the new product idea further.

Concept Development and Testing

Product concept
A detailed version of the new product idea stated in meaningful consumer terms.

An attractive idea must then be developed into a **product concept**. It is important to distinguish between a product idea, a product concept, and a product image. A *product idea* is an idea for a possible product that the company can see itself offering to the market. A *product concept* is a detailed version of the idea stated in meaningful consumer terms. A *product image* is the way consumers perceive an actual or potential product.

Concept Development

Suppose a car manufacturer has developed a practical battery-powered, all-electric car. Its initial models were a sleek, sporty roadster convertible selling for more than $100,000, followed by a full-size sports sedan priced at $71,000.[10] >> However, it now plans to introduce a more-affordable, mass-market compact version that will compete with recently introduced hybrid-electric or all-electric cars such as the Nissan Leaf, Chevy Volt, KIA Soul EV, and Chevy Bolt EV. This 100 percent plug-in electric car will accelerate from 0 to 60 miles per hour in five seconds, travel up to 310 miles on a single charge, recharge in two hours from a normal 120-volt electrical outlet, and cost about one penny per mile to power.

>> All-electric cars: This is Tesla's initial all-electric full-sized sedan. Its more recent Model 3 compact will travel up to 310 miles on a single charge and costs pennies per mile to operate.

Photo by Salwan Georges/The Washington Post via Getty Images

Looking ahead, the marketer's task is to develop this new product into alternative product concepts, find out how attractive each concept is to customers, and choose the best one. It might create the following product concepts for this all-electric car:

- *Concept 1.* An affordably priced compact car designed as a second family car to be used around town for running errands and visiting friends.
- *Concept 2.* A mid-priced sporty compact appealing to young singles and couples.
- *Concept 3.* A "green" everyday car appealing to environmentally conscious people who want practical, no-polluting transportation.
- *Concept 4.* A compact crossover SUV appealing to those who love the space SUVs provide but lament the poor gas mileage.

Concept Testing

Concept testing
Testing new product concepts with a group of target consumers to find out if the concepts have strong consumer appeal.

Concept testing calls for testing new product concepts with groups of target consumers. The concepts may be presented to consumers symbolically or physically. Here, in more detail, is concept 3:

> An efficient, fun-to-drive, battery-powered compact car that seats five. This 100 percent electric wonder provides practical and reliable transportation with no pollution. It goes 310 miles on a single charge and costs pennies per mile to operate. It's a sensible, responsible alternative to today's pollution-producing gas-guzzlers. Its fully equipped base price is $35,000.

Many firms routinely test new product concepts with consumers before attempting to turn them into actual new products. For some concept tests, a word or picture description might be sufficient. However, a more concrete and physical presentation of the concept will increase the reliability of the concept test. After being exposed to the concept, consumers then may be asked to react to it by answering questions similar to those in >> **Table 8.1**.

The answers to such questions will help the company decide which concept has the strongest appeal. For example, the last question asks about the consumer's intention to buy. Suppose 2 percent of consumers say they "definitely" would buy and another 5 percent say "probably." The company could project these figures to the full population in this target group to estimate sales volume. Even then, however, the estimate is uncertain because people do not always carry out their stated intentions.

Marketing Strategy Development

Marketing strategy development
Designing an initial marketing strategy for a new product based on the product concept.

Suppose the carmaker finds that concept 3 for the new electric car model tests best. The next step is **marketing strategy development**, designing an initial marketing strategy for introducing this car to the market.

Table 8.1 Questions for the All-Electric Car Concept Test

1. Do you understand the concept of a battery-powered electric car?
2. Do you believe the claims about the car's performance?
3. What are the major benefits of an all-electric car compared with a conventional car?
4. What are its advantages compared with a hybrid gas-electric car?
5. What improvements in the car's features would you suggest?
6. For what uses would you prefer an all-electric car to a conventional car?
7. What would be a reasonable price to charge for the car?
8. Who would be involved in your decision to buy such a car? Who would drive it?
9. Would you buy such a car (definitely, probably, probably not, definitely not)?

The *marketing strategy statement* consists of three parts. The first part describes the target market; the planned value proposition; and the sales, market-share, and profit goals for the first few years. Thus:

> The target market is younger, well-educated, moderate- to high-income individuals, couples, or small families seeking stylish but practical and environmentally responsible transportation. The car will be positioned as more fun to drive and less polluting than today's internal combustion engine or hybrid cars. The company will aim to sell 50,000 cars in the first year, at a loss of not more than $15 million. In the second year, the company will aim for sales of 90,000 cars and a profit of $25 million.

The second part of the marketing strategy statement outlines the product's planned price, distribution, and marketing budget for the first year:

> The battery-powered all-electric car will be offered in three colors—red, white, and blue—and will have a full set of accessories as standard features. It will sell at a base retail price of $35,000, with 15 percent off the list price to dealers. Dealers who sell more than 10 cars per month will get an additional discount of 5 percent on each car sold that month. A marketing budget of $50 million will be split 30-40-30 among a national media campaign, online and social media marketing, and local event marketing. Advertising, the web and mobile sites, and various social media content will emphasize the car's fun spirit, high status, and low emissions. During the first year, $200,000 will be spent on marketing research to find out who is buying the car and what their satisfaction levels are.

The third part of the marketing strategy statement describes the planned long-run sales, profit goals, and marketing mix strategy:

> We intend to capture a 3 percent long-run share of the total auto market and realize an after-tax return on investment of 15 percent. To achieve this, product quality will start high and be improved over time. Price will be raised in the second and third years if competition and the economy permit. The total marketing budget will be raised each year by about 10 percent. Marketing research will be reduced to $60,000 per year after the first year.

Business Analysis

Business analysis
A review of the sales, costs, and profit projections for a new product to find out whether these factors satisfy the company's objectives.

Once management has decided on its product concept and marketing strategy, it can evaluate the business attractiveness of the proposal. **Business analysis** involves a review of the sales, costs, and profit projections for a new product to find out whether they satisfy the company's objectives. If they do, the product can move to the product development stage.

To estimate sales, the company might look at the sales history of similar products and conduct market surveys. It can then estimate minimum and maximum sales to assess the range of risk. After preparing the sales forecast, management can estimate the expected costs and profits for the product, including marketing, R&D, operations, accounting, and finance costs. The company then uses the sales and cost figures to analyze the new product's financial attractiveness.

Product Development

Product development
Developing the product concept into a physical product to ensure that the product idea can be turned into a workable market offering.

For many new product concepts, a product may exist only as a word description, a drawing, or perhaps a crude mock-up. If the product concept passes the business test, it moves into **product development**. Here, R&D or engineering develops the product concept into a physical product. The product development step, however, now calls for a huge jump in investment. It will show whether the product idea can be turned into a workable product.

The R&D department will develop and test one or more physical versions of the product concept. R&D hopes to design a prototype that will satisfy and excite consumers and that can be produced quickly and at budgeted costs. Developing a successful prototype can take days, weeks, months, or even years depending on the product and prototype methods.

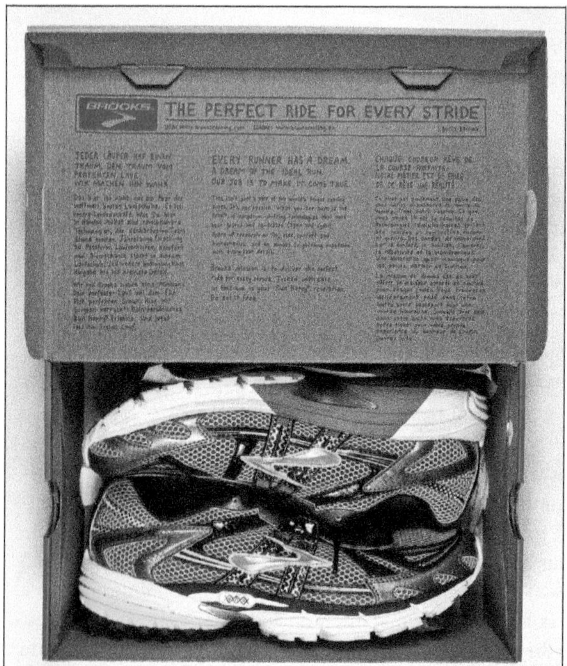

>> Product testing: Brooks has enlisted an army of users it calls Lab Rats and Wear Testers to test its products. "Your feedback is what helps determine fit, function, and design of all our future products."

Paul Vidler/Alamy Stock Photo

Often, products undergo rigorous tests to make sure that they perform safely and effectively or that consumers will find value in them. Companies can do their own product testing or outsource testing to other firms that specialize in testing.

Marketers often involve actual customers in product development and testing. >> For example, Brooks, maker of high-performance running gear and apparel, has enlisted an army of users it calls Lab Rats and Wear Testers to test its products. It studies the Lab Rats in its Biomechanics Lab at headquarters, where it places them on treadmills wearing Brooks gear and watches how they run, making sure that Brooks products enhance rather than impede performance. The Wear Testers use Brooks running shoes and gear in the field and report back regarding fit, design, style, and function. "It's pretty simple," says Brooks. "We send you gear, you use it. You use it on morning jogs, on race days, in the sun and in the snow. Any time and any place you run and then let us know how it worked (or didn't work) for you. Your feedback is what helps determine fit, function, and design of all our future products."[11]

A new product must have the required functional features and also convey the intended psychological characteristics. The all-electric car, for example, should strike consumers as being well built, comfortable, and safe. Management must learn what makes consumers decide that a car is well built. To some consumers, this means that the car has "solid-sounding" doors. To others, it means that the car can withstand a heavy impact in crash tests. Consumer tests are conducted in which consumers test-drive the car and rate its attributes.

Test Marketing

Test marketing
The stage of new product development in which the product and its proposed marketing program are tested in realistic market settings.

If the product passes both the concept test and the product test, the next step is **test marketing**, the stage at which the product and its proposed marketing program are tested in realistic market settings. Test marketing gives the marketer experience with marketing a product before going to the great expense of full introduction. It lets the company test the product and its entire marketing program—targeting and positioning strategy, advertising, distribution, pricing, branding and packaging, and budget levels.

The amount of test marketing needed varies with each new product. When introducing a new product requires a big investment, when the risks are high, or when management is not sure of the product or its marketing program, a company may do a lot of test marketing. For instance, Taco Bell took three years and 45 prototypes before introducing Doritos

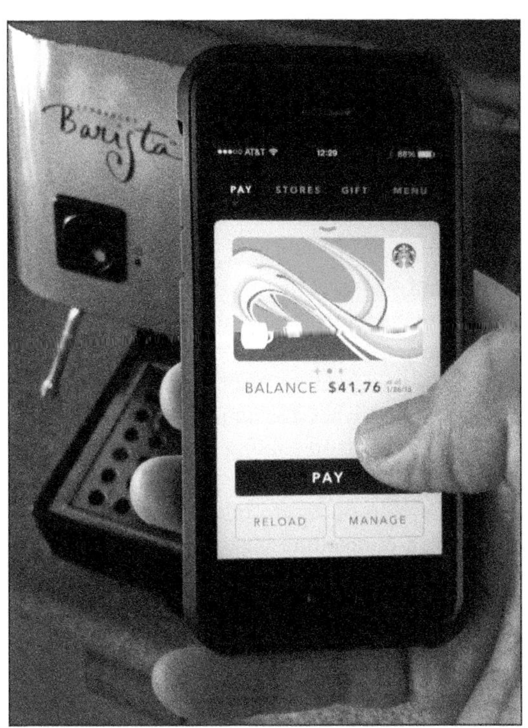

>> **Companies sometimes shorten or skip test marketing to take advantage of fast-changing market developments, as Starbucks did with its hugely successful mobile payments app.**

Kevin Schafer/Getty Images

Locos Tacos, now the most successful product launch in the company's history. And Starbucks spent 20 years developing Starbucks VIA instant coffee—one of its most risky product rollouts ever—and several months testing the product in Starbucks shops in Chicago and Seattle before releasing it nationally. Starbucks VIA is now a best-selling coffee brand.[12]

However, test marketing costs can be high, and testing takes time that may allow market opportunities to slip by or competitors to gain advantages. A company may do little or no test marketing when the costs of developing and introducing a new product are low or when management is already confident about the new product. For example, companies often do not test-market simple line extensions or copies of competitors' successful products.

Companies may also shorten or skip testing in the face of fast-changing market developments. >> For example, to take advantage of digital and mobile trends, Starbucks quickly introduced a less-than-perfect mobile payments app and then worked out the flaws during the six months after launch. Mobile payments through the Starbucks app now account for more than 30 percent of all Starbucks U.S. transactions. "We don't think it is okay if things aren't perfect," says Starbucks' chief digital officer, "but we're willing to innovate and have speed to market trump a 100 percent guarantee that it'll be perfect."[13]

As an alternative to extensive and costly standard test markets, companies can use controlled test markets or simulated test markets. In *controlled test markets*, new products and tactics are tested among controlled panels of shoppers and stores. By combining information on each test consumer's purchases with consumer demographic and media viewing information, the company can assess the impact of in-store and in-home marketing efforts. Using *simulated test markets*, researchers measure consumer responses to new products and marketing tactics in laboratory stores or simulated online shopping environments. Both controlled test markets and simulated test markets reduce the costs of test marketing and speed up the process.

Commercialization

Commercialization
Introducing a new product into the market.

Test marketing gives management the information needed to make a final decision about whether to launch the new product. If the company goes ahead with **commercialization**—introducing the new product into the market—it will face high costs. For example, the company may need to build or rent a manufacturing facility. And, in the case of a major new consumer product, it may spend hundreds of millions of dollars for advertising, sales promotion, and other marketing efforts in the first year. For instance, Nintendo spent an estimated $18 million in a single month on TV advertising to introduce its Nintendo Switch console/hand-held hybrid game system. Tide spent $150 million on a campaign to launch Tide Pods in the highly competitive U.S. laundry detergent market. And to introduce the original Surface tablet, Microsoft spent close to $400 million on an advertising blitz that spanned TV, print, radio, outdoor, the internet, events, public relations, and sampling.[14]

A company launching a new product must first decide on introduction *timing*. If the new product will eat into the sales of other company products, the introduction may be delayed. If the product can be improved further or if the economy is down, the company may wait until the following year to launch it. However, if competitors are ready to introduce their own competing products, the company may push to introduce its new product sooner.

Next, the company must decide *where* to launch the new product—in a single location, a region, the national market, or the international market. Some companies may quickly introduce new models into the full national market. Companies with international distribution systems may introduce new products through swift global rollouts. For example, in its fastest-ever global rollout, Apple launched the iPhone X in 55 countries on the same day.[15]

Author Comment
Above all else, new product development must focus on creating customer value. Says a senior Samsung executive, "We get our ideas from the market. The market is the driver."

Managing New Product Development

The new product development process shown in Figure 8.1 highlights the important activities needed to find, develop, and introduce new products. However, new product development involves more than just going through a set of steps. Companies must take a holistic approach to managing this process. Successful new product development requires a customer-centered, team-based, and systematic effort.

Customer-Centered New Product Development

Above all else, new product development must be customer centered. When looking for and developing new products, companies often rely too heavily on technical research in their R&D laboratories. But like everything else in marketing, successful new product development begins with a thorough understanding of what consumers need and value. **Customer-centered new product development** focuses on finding new ways to solve customer problems and create more customer-satisfying experiences.

Customer-centered new product development
New product development that focuses on finding new ways to solve customer problems and create more customer-satisfying experiences.

One study found that the most successful new products are ones that are differentiated, solve major customer problems, and offer a compelling customer value proposition. Another study showed that companies that directly engage their customers in the new product innovation process had twice the return on assets and triple the growth in operating income of firms that did not. Thus, customer involvement has a positive effect on the new product development process and product success.

>> Leading toymaker The LEGO Group is a strong proponent of customer-centered new product development:[16]

>> Customer-centered new product development: Toymaker LEGO listens to its customers and actively taps its user community for new product ideas, making it what one observer calls "the Apple of Toys."

Photo by S. Clyde/U.S. Department of Transportation, Federal Highway Administration

Fifteen years ago, The LEGO Group (TLG) was near bankruptcy, spiraling downward and losing money. In the age of the internet, video games, mobile devices, and high-tech playthings, traditional toys such as LEGO bricks had been pushed to the back of the closet. So TLG set out to rebuild its aging product lines, brick by brick. The LEGO makeover, however, didn't start with engineers working in design labs. It started with listening to and engaging customers.

For example, TLG embedded researchers with families, observed children at play, interviewed parents, and shopped with customers. The research produced a lot of "Aha! Moments." For example, TLG had long offered only basic, unstructured building sets that it thought would foster creativity. But in today's tech-rich world, children get bored easily and welcome more-structured play experiences. So TLG now offers a seemingly endless selection of themed, specialized kits with detailed instructions by which kids can construct anything from fire trucks and helicopters to crave-worthy ninja castles. Research also showed that, for children today, the digital and physical worlds blend as one. This insight led to TLG's "One Reality" products, which combine digital and real-world play experiences that involve building with LEGO bricks alongside software running on a phone or tablet app.

TLG also actively taps its avid user community for new customer insights and ideas. For example, the LEGO Ideas website, a kind of branded version of Kickstarter, invites customers to submit ideas and to evaluate and vote on the ideas of others. On average, four new customer-inspired products come out of LEGO Ideas each year. Such customer co-creation resulted in TLG's most popular product ever, LEGO MINDSTORMS, a series of building sets complete with hardware and software for making customizable robots that are programmable from a smartphone app. Thanks to customer-centered new product development, LEGO now runs neck-and-neck with Mattel as the world's largest toymaker. As one analyst concludes, "LEGO has grown into nothing less than the Apple of Toys."

Thus, today's innovative companies get out of the research lab and connect with customers in search of fresh ways to meet customer needs. Customer-centered new product development begins and ends with understanding customers and involving them in the process.

Team-Based New Product Development

Good new product development also requires a total-company, cross-functional effort. Some companies organize their new product development process into the orderly sequence of steps shown in Figure 8.1, starting with idea generation and ending with commercialization. Under this *sequential product development* approach, one company department works individually to complete its stage of the process before passing the new product along to the next department and stage. This orderly, step-by-step process can help bring control to complex and risky projects. But it can also be dangerously slow. In fast-changing, highly competitive markets, such slow-but-sure product development can result in product failures, lost sales and profits, and crumbling market positions.

Team-based new product development New product development in which various company departments work closely together, overlapping the steps in the product development process to save time and increase effectiveness.

To get their new products to market more quickly, many companies use a **team-based new product development** approach. Under this approach, company departments work closely together in cross-functional teams, overlapping the steps in the product development process to save time and increase effectiveness. Instead of passing the new product from department to department, the company assembles a team of people from various departments that stays with the new product from start to finish. Such teams usually include people from the marketing, finance, design, manufacturing, and legal departments and even supplier and customer companies. In the sequential process, a bottleneck at one phase can seriously slow an entire project. In the team-based approach, however, if one area hits snags, it works to resolve them while the team moves on.

The team-based approach does have some limitations, however. For example, it sometimes creates more organizational tension and confusion than the more orderly sequential approach. However, in rapidly changing industries facing increasingly shorter product life cycles, the rewards of fast and flexible product development far exceed the risks. Companies that combine a customer-centered approach with team-based new product development gain a big competitive edge by getting the right new products to market faster.

Systematic New Product Development

Finally, the new product development process should be holistic and systematic rather than compartmentalized and haphazard. Otherwise, few new ideas will surface, and many good ideas will sputter and die. To avoid these problems, a company can install an *innovation management system* to collect, review, evaluate, and manage new product ideas.

The company can appoint a respected senior person to be its innovation manager. It can set up web-based idea management software and encourage all company stakeholders—employees, suppliers, distributors, dealers—to become involved in finding and developing new products. It can assign a cross-functional innovation management committee to evaluate proposed new product ideas and help bring good ideas to market. It can also create recognition programs to reward those who contribute the best ideas.

The innovation management system approach yields two favorable outcomes. First, it helps create an innovation-oriented company culture. It shows that top management supports, encourages, and rewards innovation. Second, it will yield a larger number of new product ideas, among which will be found some especially good ones. The good new ideas will be more systematically developed, producing more new product successes. No longer will good ideas wither for the lack of a sounding board or a senior product advocate.

Thus, new product success requires more than simply thinking up a few good ideas, turning them into products, and finding customers for them. It requires a holistic approach for finding new ways to create valued customer experiences, from generating and screening new product ideas to creating and rolling out want-satisfying products to customers.

More than this, successful new product development requires a whole-company commitment. At companies known for their new product prowess, such as Samsung, Google, Apple, 3M, P&G, and GE, the entire culture encourages, supports, and rewards innovation. For example, at Google and its parent company Alphabet, innovation is more just than a process—it's part of the company's DNA (see Marketing at Work 8.1).

MARKETING AT WORK 8.1

Google (. . .er, Alphabet): The New Product Moonshot Factory

Google is wildly innovative. Over the past decade and a half, it has become a top-five fixture in every list of most-innovative companies. Google simply refuses to get comfortable with the way things are. Instead, it innovates constantly, plunging into new markets and taking on new competitors.

Google began as an online search company with a mission "to organize the world's information and make it universally accessible and useful." In accomplishing that mission, Google has been spectacularly successful. Despite formidable competition from giants such as Microsoft and Yahoo!, Google's U.S. share of online search stands at a decisive 63 percent. It grabs a breathtaking 94 percent share of mobile search. Google also dominates in paid online and mobile search-related advertising revenue, which accounted for 86 percent of its $110.9 billion in revenues last year. And Google is growing at a blistering rate—its revenues have more than doubled in just the past four years.

But Google has rapidly become much more than just an online search and advertising company. In Google's view, information is a kind of natural resource—one to be mined, refined, and universally distributed. That broad mission gives Google's engineers and developers a blank canvas, a broad brush, and plenty of incentive to innovate. At many companies, new product development is a cautious, step-by-step affair that might take years to unfold. In contrast, Google's freewheeling new product development process moves at the speed of light. The nimble innovator implements major new products and services in less time than it takes most competitors to refine and approve an initial idea. Google would rather see projects fail quickly than see a carefully planned, drawn-out project fail. When Google developers face two paths and aren't sure which one to take, they invariably take the quickest one.

Google's famously chaotic innovation process has unleashed a seemingly unending flurry of diverse products, many of which are market leaders in their categories. Although diverse, many of these innovations are tied in one way or another to Google's Internet-related information mission. Google's mega-hits include an email service (Gmail), projects for mapping and exploring the world (Google Maps and Google Earth), a digital media store (Google Play), an online payment service (Google Wallet), a photo sharing service (Google Photos), a mobile operating system (Google Android), a suite of cloud computing services (Google Cloud), an online social network (Google+), and a cloud-friendly Internet browser (Chrome).

Although Google has traditionally focused on software-based innovations, it has recently moved into hardware with Pixel phones, tablets, and laptops; an AI virtual assistant (Google Home and Google Assistant); connected smart-home devices (Nest), a state-of-the-art virtual reality headset (Daydream VR); and a small, wireless smart camera (Google Clips). Google seamlessly connects its hardware with its vast information world by infusing otherwise ordinary hardware with sophisticated algorithms and artificial intelligence. For example, its Pixel 2 phone can turn standard snapshots into beautiful portraits even though it has only one camera. The Pixel Buds are more than just wireless headphones—they interface with Google Assistant and put Google Translate front and center, letting people to talk to others in multiple languages. And Google Clips uses AI to automatically recognize great expressions, lighting, and framing to capture spontaneous images.

Google acquired Nest Labs as its entry into the Internet of Things (IoT). The subsequent development of Google Home and Google Assistant has added voice control and AI technology to Nest's fast-growing smart-home presence. Nest now includes its own expanding portfolio of smart and stylish home control and monitoring devices, along with "Works with Nest" smart products from other companies, from LED light bulbs, electrical switches, and sprinkler systems to a host of kitchen and household appliances. Backed by Google's huge innovation prowess, Nest will soon be helping consumers run their entire homes, an enormous potential market.

Google's wild-eyed innovation process has also taken the company down paths that are far afield from its main information mission—everything from self-driving cars to Earth-imaging satellites and even a crusade to increase human lifespan. In fact, Google has innovated into so many diverse new ventures that it created a broader organization—a parent holding company called Alphabet—to contain them all.

Google is the largest Alphabet company—it continues to house information and Internet-related software and hardware products. But along with Google, Alphabet provides an independent home for the company's more far-reaching collection

>> Google and parent company Alphabet are wildly innovative. The company's innovation machine is renowned for producing new product "moonshots," futuristic long shots that, if successful, will profoundly change how people live.

of projects and businesses. These include what Alphabet calls "moonshots"—futuristic, breathtakingly idealistic longshots that, if successful, will profoundly change how people live. To foster moonshots, the company created X—a secretive innovation lab and kind of nerd heaven charged with developing things that seem audacious, even for Alphabet.

The X innovation lab is Alphabet's incubator for earth-shaking projects that may or may not pay for themselves in the long run. To get the green light at X, a project must address a huge problem that affects millions or even billions of people, propose a radical solution to that problem, and require a breakthrough technology to bring about that solutions. Those stringent requirements "cause us to throw out more than 99 percent of our ideas," says X's director, whose official title is Captain of Moonshots. Secreted behind X's curtain are numerous exotic projects, such as Project Loon (a Wi-Fi-distributing high-altitude balloons network), Project Malta (salt-based thermal storage system), Project Wing (a drone product delivery system), and Project Makani (kite-like wind-energy production).

In addition to X, Alphabet includes Fiber, the ultrafast fiber-optic internet service that is rolling out across the country; and Waymo, the self-driving car project that's on a mission to make it safe and easy to for people and things to move around. Lesser-known Alphabet companies include investment arms GV (funding for bold new startups) and CapitalG (funding for long-term tech projects); Verily (health-care projects, such as glucose-monitoring contact lenses); and Calico (research into fighting age-related disease and increasing life span). According to Google co-founder Larry Page, Alphabet's goal is "to keep tremendous focus on the extraordinary opportunities" that exist and will exist within Google and the other companies.

In the end, at Google (and at parent company Alphabet), innovation is more than a process—it's part of the company's DNA. "Where does innovation happen at Google? It happens everywhere," says a Google research scientist.

> Talk to Googlers at various levels and departments, one powerful theme emerges: These people feel that their work can change the world. The marvel of Google is its ability to continue to instill a sense of creative fearlessness and ambition in its employees. Prospective hires are often asked, "If you could change the world using Google's resources, what would you build?" But here, this isn't a goofy or even theoretical question: Google wants to know because thinking—and building—on that scale is what Google does. When it comes to innovation, Google is different. But the difference isn't tangible. It's in the air—in the spirit of the place.

Sources: David Pierce, "One Man's Quest to Make Google's Gadgets Great," *Wired*, February 8, 2018, www.wired.com/story/one-mans-quest-to-make-googles-gadgets-great/; Rob Price and Mike Nudelman, "Google's Parent Company, Alphabet, Explained in One Chart," *Business Insider*, January 12, 2016, www.businessinsider.com/chart-of-alphabet-google-parent-company-infographic-x-gv-2016-1?r=UK&IR=T; Chuck Salter, "Google: The Faces and Voices of the World's Most Innovative Company," *Fast Company*, March 2008, pp. 74–88; Alan Boyle, "Inside the X 'Moonshot Factory': Here's Where Google's Ideas Take Flight (or Fizzle)," *Geek Wire*, November 26, 2017, www.geekwire.com/2017/inside-x-moonshot-factory-heres-googles-ideas-take-flight-flop/; Nick Statt, "Nest Is Rejoining Google to Better Compete with Amazon and Apple," *The Verge*, February 9, 2018, www.theverge.com/2018/2/7/16987002/nest-google-alphabet-smart-home-competition-amazon-alexa-apple; and https://abc.xyz/and http://investor.google.com, accessed September 2018.

LINKING THE CONCEPTS

Take a break. Think about new products and how companies find and develop them.

- Suppose that you're on a panel to nominate the "best new products of the year." What products would you nominate and why? See what you can learn about the new product development process for one of these products.
- Applying the new product development process you've just studied, develop an idea for an innovative new snack-food product and sketch out a brief plan for bringing it to market. Loosen up and have some fun with this.

Author Comment
A company's products are born, grow, mature, and then decline, just as living things do. To remain vital, the firm must continually develop new products and manage them effectively throughout their life cycles.

Product Life-Cycle Strategies

OBJECTIVE 8-3 Describe the stages of the product life cycle and how marketing strategies change during a product's life cycle.

After launching the new product, management wants that product to enjoy a long and happy life. Although it does not expect the product to sell forever, the company wants to earn a decent profit to cover all the effort and risk that went into launching it. Management is aware that each product will have a life cycle, although its exact shape and length are not known in advance.

Product life cycle (PLC)
The course of a product's sales and profits over its lifetime.

>> **Figure 8.2** shows a typical **product life cycle (PLC)**, the course that a product's sales and profits take over its lifetime. The PLC has five distinct stages:

1. Product development begins when the company finds and develops a new product idea. During product development, sales are zero, and the company's investment costs mount.

>> Figure 8.2 Sales and Profits over the Product's Life from Inception to Decline

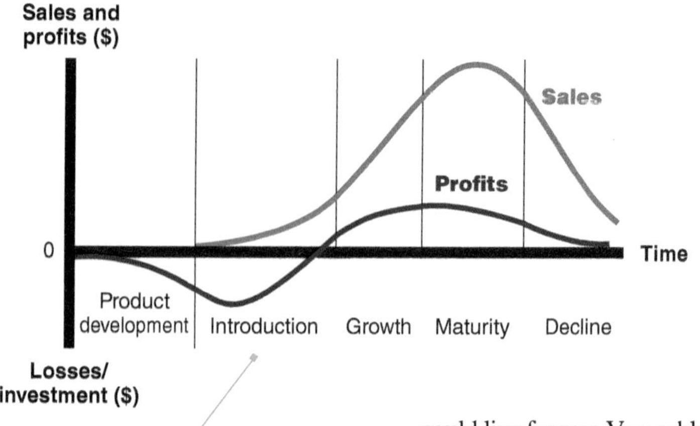

Some products die quickly; others stay in the mature stage for a long, long time. For example, Crayola Crayons have been around for more than 115 years. However, to keep the brand young, the company has added a continuous stream of contemporary new products, such as Color Alive, which lets kids color cartoons, scan them, and then watch as an app animates them.

2. Introduction is a period of slow sales growth as the product is introduced in the market. Profits are nonexistent in this stage because of the heavy expenses of product introduction.
3. Growth is a period of rapid market acceptance and increasing profits.
4. Maturity is a period of slowdown in sales growth because the product has achieved acceptance by most potential buyers. Profits level off or decline because of increased marketing outlays to defend the product against competition.
5. Decline is the period when sales fall off and profits drop.

Not all products follow all five stages of the PLC. Some products are introduced and die quickly; others stay in the mature stage for a long, long time. Some enter the decline stage and are then cycled back into the growth stage through strong promotion or repositioning. It seems that a well-managed brand could live forever. Venerable brands like Coca-Cola, Gillette, IBM, American Express, Wells Fargo, Heinz, and Quaker, for instance, are still going strong after more than 100 years. Guinness beer has been around for more than 250 years, and 149-year-old TABASCO sauce brags that it's "over 140 years old and still able to totally whup your butt!"

The PLC concept can describe a *product class* (gasoline-powered automobiles), a *product form* (SUVs), or a *brand* (the Ford Escape). The PLC concept applies differently in each case. Product classes have the longest life cycles; the sales of many product classes stay in the mature stage for a long time. Product forms, in contrast, tend to have the standard PLC shape. Product forms such as dial telephones, VHS tapes, and film cameras passed through a regular history of introduction, rapid growth, maturity, and decline.

A specific brand's life cycle can change quickly because of changing competitive attacks and responses. For example, although laundry soaps (product class) have enjoyed a long life cycle, the life cycles of laundry product forms and specific brands have tended to be shorter. Powdered detergents (product form) have increasingly given way to liquids and pods. And today's leading U.S. brands of laundry detergent are Tide and Gain; the leading brands 100 years ago were Fels-Naptha and Octagon.

Style
A basic and distinctive mode of expression.

Fashion
A currently accepted or popular style in a given field.

Fad
A temporary period of unusually high sales driven by consumer enthusiasm and immediate product or brand popularity.

The PLC concept also can be applied to what are known as styles, fashions, and fads. Their special life cycles are shown in **>> Figure 8.3**. A **style** is a basic and distinctive mode of expression. For example, styles appear in homes (colonial, ranch, transitional), clothing (formal, casual), and art (realist, surrealist, abstract). Once a style is invented, it may last for generations, passing in and out of vogue. A style has a cycle showing several periods of renewed interest.

A **fashion** is a currently accepted or popular style in a given field. For example, the more formal "business attire" look of corporate dress of the 1980s and 1990s gave way to the "business casual" look of the 2000s and 2010s. Fashions tend to grow slowly, remain popular for a while, and then decline slowly.

Fads are temporary periods of unusually high sales driven by consumer enthusiasm and immediate product or brand popularity.[17] A fad may be part of an otherwise normal life cycle, as in the case of recent surges in the sales of poker chips and accessories. Or the fad may comprise a brand's or product's entire life cycle.

>> Figure 8.3 Styles, Fashions, and Fads

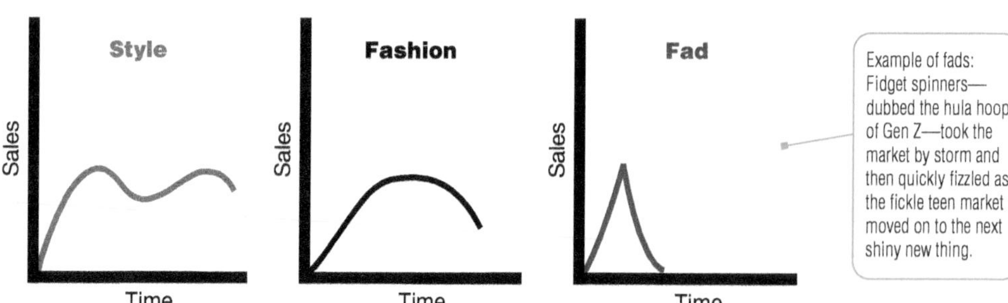

Example of fads: Fidget spinners—dubbed the hula hoop of Gen Z—took the market by storm and then quickly fizzled as the fickle teen market moved on to the next shiny new thing.

» **Fads: Dubbed the "hula hoop of Gen Z," fidget spinners took the preteen and teen market by storm. However, like most fads, sales quickly fizzled as fickle teens moved on to the next shiny new thing.**

3Baboons/Shutterstock

» An example is the fidget spinner—the small, three-pronged ball-bearing device that you flick and spin to relieve stress or just because it's fun to do. Dubbed the "hula hoop of Gen Z," the spinners took the preteen and teen market by storm in early 2017. By early May of that year, the gizmos accounted for an amazing 17 percent of daily online toy sales. However, like most fads, sales quickly started to fizzle. By June, then widely sold by mass merchants like Toys "R" Us and Walmart, the gadgets were becoming too common to be cool. It didn't help that schools began banning the toys as distractions. Notoriously fickle teens lost interest and moved on to the next shiny new thing. Other examples of fads include selfie sticks, Silly Bandz, and Pokemon Go.[18]

Marketers can apply the product life-cycle concept as a useful framework for describing how products and markets work. And when used carefully, the PLC concept can help in developing good marketing strategies for the different life-cycle stages. However, using the PLC concept for forecasting product performance or developing marketing strategies presents some practical problems. For example, in practice, it is difficult to forecast the sales level at each PLC stage, the length of each stage, and the shape of the PLC curve. Using the PLC concept to develop marketing strategy also can be difficult because strategy is both a cause and a result of the PLC. The product's current PLC position suggests the best marketing strategies, and the resulting marketing strategies affect product performance in later stages.

Moreover, marketers should not blindly push products through the traditional product life-cycle stages. Instead, marketers often defy the "rules" of the life cycle and position or reposition their products in unexpected ways. By doing this, they can rescue mature or declining products and return them to the growth phase of the life cycle. Or they can leapfrog obstacles that slow consumer acceptance and propel new products forward into the growth phase.

The moral of the product life cycle is that companies must continually innovate; otherwise, they risk extinction. To grow, the company must develop a steady stream of new products that bring new value to customers. And no matter how successful its current product lineup, a company must skillfully manage the life cycles of existing products for future success. Financial-software maker Intuit does this well. Rather than sitting on its successful products, it systematically reinvents them before competitors can. So Intuit's products stay in a perpetual PLC growth stage and never reach maturity or go into decline (see Marketing at Work 8.2).

We looked at the product development stage of the PLC in the first part of this chapter. We now look at strategies for each of the other life-cycle stages.

Introduction Stage

Introduction stage
The PLC stage in which a new product is first distributed and made available for purchase.

The **introduction stage** starts when a new product is first launched. Introduction takes time, and sales growth is apt to be slow. Well-known products such as frozen foods, HDTVs, and all-electric cars lingered for many years before they entered a stage of more rapid growth.

In this stage, as compared to other stages, profits are negative or low because of the low sales and high distribution and promotion expenses. Much money is needed to attract distributors and build their inventories. Promotion spending is relatively high to inform consumers of the new product and get them to try it. Because the market is not generally ready for product refinements at this stage, the company and its few competitors produce basic versions of the product. These firms focus their selling on those buyers who are the most ready to buy.

A company, especially the *market pioneer*, must choose a launch strategy that is consistent with the intended product positioning. It should realize that the initial strategy is just the first step in a grander marketing plan for the product's entire life cycle. If the pioneer chooses its launch strategy to make a "killing," it may be sacrificing long-run revenue for the sake of short-run gain. The pioneer has the best chance of building and retaining market leadership if it plays its cards correctly from the start.

MARKETING AT WORK 8.2

Intuit: Reinvention and the Product Life Cycle

When Intuit first set up shop in 1983 with its Quicken personal-finance software, it jumped into a fiercely competitive market fueled by the surging growth of personal computers. Of its original financial-software competitors, only Intuit still survives. And more than just surviving, Intuit now dominates. Last year, it sold more than $5 billion worth of software. Its revenues have been growing at double-digit rates, and profits are at an all-time high. Intuit's QuickBooks now captures an 80 percent market share in small-business accounting software. And last year, customers used Intuit's TurboTax to prepare some 35 million U.S. individual income tax returns, almost twice the 19 million prepared by H&R Block's software and services.

What's behind Intuit's long-running success? Intuit thrives on a product life-cycle strategy of "creative destruction." Rather than protecting and nurturing its successful products, Intuit systematically reinvents them before competitors can. So Intuit's products stay in a perpetual PLC growth stage and never reach maturity or go into decline.

To fuel its creative-destruction machine, Intuit proactively and obsessively studies its customers and the marketplace. It looks for unanticipated or unexplained findings—what it calls "savoring the surprise"—and turns them into opportunities. For example, early surveys of users of Quicken personal-finance software yielded a surprising result. When asked whether they used Quicken at home or at the office, half reported using it at the office. Researchers might have assumed this meant that Quicken users were taking time at work to balance their checkbooks and pay their bills. But digging deeper, Intuit learned that Quicken users weren't doing their personal finances at work; they were using Quicken to run their small-business finances. Scared off by business accounting software that employed big-company accounting methods, small business owners were using the less sophisticated but also less complex Quicken software in their businesses.

So, although Quicken was still selling very well to this segment, Intuit created QuickBooks, user-friendly small-business finance software. QuickBooks had fewer than half the features of the market-leading business accounting software and sold at $99, twice the price. But it hit the market sweet spot, overtaking the market leader in only two months. Today, with its 80 percent market share, QuickBooks accounts for half of Intuit's revenues.

More recently, Intuit researchers noticed that some users of the company's Mint online money management system were behaving differently from the other young professionals that Mint targets. These customers were using Mint to manage self-employment income and spending. Many were "gig" workers—such as Uber or Lyft drivers, Airbnb hosts, or the like—independent contractors or freelancers hired by companies for short-term gigs or engagements. So Intuit created a version of QuickBooks for independent contractors, now the company's fastest-growing product in the exploding "gig economy."

Whereas many companies wait for a crisis or competitive disruption before messing with a successful product, Intuit wants to be the cause of its own disruption. Over the years, the company has routinely reinvented its products to meet market changes that drove competitors into decline. For example, when Microsoft introduced Windows in the late 1980s, Intuit quickly added compatible versions of Quicken and QuickBooks, even though most of the market was still using the old MS-DOS operating system. A few years, later during the earliest days of the World Wide Web, Intuit smoothly took its products online. And as the mobile age dawned, Intuit reconceived its products yet again, perfecting mobile applications long before smartphones and tablets had saturated the market. "It all seems obvious in retrospect," says an analyst, "but each transformation was a mind bender at the time—[I mean,] doing taxes on a phone?—which Intuit achieved."

Intuit is now undertaking one of the most far-reaching reinventions in its history. Rather than simply selling software products and services, Intuit is becoming an open platform. The transformation began five years ago with a seemingly simple insight: "The average small business uses 16 to 20 apps, and we make three," recalls Intuit's CEO. "We had to open up our platform and trust that this would make our customers more loyal to us and also would give us insights into problems we could go solve."

As a result, Intuit created an online platform where outside developers could contribute apps designed to work with Intuit products. For example, American Express now offers a free app that automatically transfers AmEx card transactions to a user's

>> **Skillful PLC management: Rather than sitting on successful products, Intuit reinvents them before competitors can, keeping them out of maturity and decline.**

Michael Nagle/Bloomberg via Getty Images

QuickBooks Online account. Something Intuit could never have developed on its own, the Amex app benefits both companies by making things easier for their shared customers.

The open platform poses risks—it relinquishes control to outside forces, some of which are potential competitors. Yet it's working well. In only five years, the number of apps that work with Intuit products shot up from 3 to 1,400. The open collaboration has transformed Intuit into an ecosystem—a brand community where customers, accountants, app developers, and Intuit can interact to the benefit of all.

For example, Intuit learned that small businesses that work with accountants enjoy better success. And Intuit already has relationships with some 600,000 accountants who use its tax software. Recognizing this opportunity, Intuit created a matchmaking feature to connect QuickBooks Online users with the accountants. Last year alone, the feature helped 600,000 small businesses obtain professional accountant services. "That's a huge win-win for both of them," says the Intuit CEO. It's also a huge win for Intuit. The accountant matchmaking feature has helped increase the QuickBooks Online customer renewal rate from 75 percent to a whopping 91 percent.

Competitors cannot easily duplicate Intuit's creative destruction process—reinvention is deeply ingrained in Intuit's culture and operations. To support innovation, Intuit spends 19.3 percent of its revenue on R&D, compared with 15.5 percent spent by Google/Alphabet and 14.5 percent by Microsoft. To nurture a climate of innovation and reinvention, Intuit urges employees at all levels—including top management—to admit and learn from mistakes and failures. Intuit has also assembled an internal community of "Innovation Catalysts," employees trained to coach, mentor, and inspire other employees to innovate. And it encourages people across the company to spend 10 percent of their time on unstructured projects in search of innovative new ideas.

Intuit's reinvention process, culture, and success have earned it the number eight spot on *Fortune* magazine's most recent Future 50 list of companies best prepared to thrive and grow their revenue rapidly in coming years. As a *Fortune* writer concludes, "No company tries harder to find the next big disruption before it finds them. Intuit understands that in the digital world there are no final victories but plenty of final defeats, and success is always tenuous. That's how a tech oldster lands on the Future 50." Under its creative destruction and reinvention mantras, Intuit welcomes each new challenge. Says the CEO, "It's another opportunity to change before it's needed."

Sources: Geoff Colvin, "How Intuit Reinvents Itself," *Fortune*, October 20, 2017, http://fortune.com/2017/10/20/how-intuit-reinvents-itself/; Rich Karlgaard, "How 34-Year-Old Intuit Became Tech's Resilient Force," *Forbes*, April 25, 2017, www.forbes.com/sites/richkarlgaard/2017/04/25/how-34-year-old-intuit-became-techs-resilient-force/#22a67a4864b2; Thomas Lockwood and Edgar Papke, "How Intuit Used Design Thinking to Boost Sales by $10 Million in a Year," *Forbes*, October 31, 2017, www.fastcodesign.com/90147434/how-intuit-used-design-thinking-to-boost-sales-by-10m-in-a-year; "Innovation Catalysts," www.intuitlabs.com/innovationcatalysts/, accessed September 2018; and information from www.intuit.com, accessed September 2018.

Growth Stage

Growth stage
The PLC stage in which a product's sales start climbing quickly.

If the new product satisfies the market, it will enter a **growth stage** in which sales will start climbing quickly. The early adopters will continue to buy, and later buyers will start following their lead, especially if they hear favorable word of mouth. Attracted by the opportunities for profit, new competitors will enter the market. They will introduce new product features and the market will expand. The increase in competitors leads to an increase in the number of distribution outlets, and sales jump just to build reseller inventories. Prices remain where they are or decrease only slightly. Companies keep their promotion spending at the same or a slightly higher level. Educating the market remains a goal, but now the company must also meet the competition.

Profits increase during the growth stage as promotion costs are spread over a large volume and as unit manufacturing costs decrease. The firm uses several strategies to sustain rapid market growth for as long as possible. It improves product quality and adds new product features and models. It enters new market segments and new distribution channels. It shifts some advertising from building product awareness to building product conviction and purchase, and it lowers prices at the right time to attract more buyers.

In the growth stage, the firm faces a trade-off between high market share and high current profit. By spending a lot of money on product improvement, promotion, and distribution, the company can capture a dominant position. In doing so, however, it gives up maximum current profit, which it hopes to make up in the next stage.

Maturity Stage

Maturity stage
The PLC stage in which a product's sales growth slows or levels off.

At some point, a product's sales growth will slow down, and it will enter the **maturity stage**. This maturity stage normally lasts longer than the previous stages, and it poses strong challenges to marketing management. Most products are in the maturity stage of the life cycle, and therefore most of marketing management deals with the mature product.

The slowdown in sales growth results in many producers with many products to sell. In turn, this overcapacity leads to greater competition. Competitors begin marking down prices, increasing their advertising and sales promotions, and upping their product development budgets to find better versions of the product. These steps lead to a drop in profit. Some of the weaker competitors start dropping out, and the industry eventually contains only well-established competitors.

Although many products in the mature stage appear to remain unchanged for long periods, most successful ones are actually evolving to meet changing consumer needs. Product managers should do more than simply ride along with or defend their mature products—a good offense is the best defense. They should consider modifying the market, product offering, and marketing mix.

In *modifying the market*, the company tries to increase consumption by finding new users and new market segments for its brands. For example, brands such as Harley-Davidson and Axe fragrances, which have typically targeted male buyers, have created products and marketing programs aimed at women. Conversely, Weight Watchers and Bath & Body Works, which have typically targeted women, have created products and programs aimed at men.

The company may also look for ways to increase usage among present customers. For example, Campbell encourages people to use more of its soups and other product by offering meal ideas and recipes. Using the Campbell's Kitchen website or phone app (www.campbells.com/kitchen/), meal planners can search for or exchange recipes, create their own personal recipe box, learn ways to eat healthier, calculate meal costs, and sign up for a daily or weekly Meal Mail program. At the Campbell's Facebook, Pinterest, and Twitter sites, consumers can join in and share on Campbell's Kitchen Community conversations.

The company might also try *modifying the product*—changing characteristics such as quality, features, style, packaging, or technology platforms to retain current users or attract new ones. Thus, to freshen up their products for today's technology-obsessed children, many classic toy and game makers are creating new digital versions or add-ons for old favorites. For example, the venerable, 115-year-old Crayola brand has modernized its product line to meet the technology tastes of the new generation. And with the Crayola My Virtual Fashion Show drawing kit and app, children first design fashions using the provided color pencils and sketchpad. They then take photos of the designs with their smartphones or tablets and watch their original creations magically come to life inside the app on 3D models who walk virtual runways in Milan, New York, and Paris.[19]

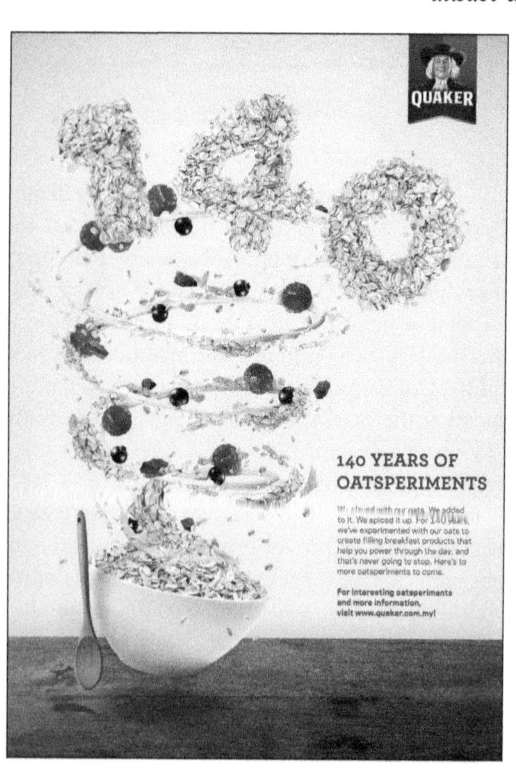

>> Managing the product life cycle: The 140-year-old Quaker brand is acting anything but its age. Through what it calls "oatsperiments," the brand has added a kitchen cabinet full of contemporary new products and a full slate of modern marketing approaches.

Provided courtesy of The Quaker Oat Company.

Finally, the company can try *modifying the marketing mix*—improving sales by changing one or more marketing mix elements. The company can offer new or improved services to buyers. It can cut prices to attract new users and competitors' customers. It can launch a better advertising campaign or use aggressive sales promotions—trade deals, cents-off, premiums, and contests. In addition to pricing and promotion, the company can also move into new marketing channels to help serve new users.

PepsiCo has use all these market, product, and marketing mix modification approaches to continually reinvigorate its venerable Quaker Oats brand:[20]

>> The 140-year-old Quaker brand is acting anything but its age. In recent years, far beyond its legacy oatmeal products, Quaker has added a kitchen cabinet full of contemporary new products and a full slate of modern marketing approaches. According to a recent Malaysian ad, "We played with our oats. We spiced it up. For 140 years, we've experimented with our oats to create filling breakfast products that help you power through the day, and that's never going to stop." To that end, Quaker offers a full and ever-evolving line of energy-packed hot and cold cereals, snack bars, cookies, and other products that give contemporary families healthy lifestyle choices.

More than just new product additions, Quaker modernizes every other element of the brand to keep it fresh. Befitting the more mobile and connected lifestyles of the young families it targets, Quaker's marketing campaigns incorporate healthy doses of digital media, including mobile ads, extensive social media content, and an information-packed www.quaker.com.my community website.

Decline Stage

The sales of most product forms and brands eventually dip. The decline may be slow, as in the cases of postage stamps and mainframe computers, or rapid, as in the case of VHS tapes. Sales may plunge to zero, or they may drop to a low level where they continue for many years. This is the **decline stage**.

Decline stage
The PLC stage in which a product's sales fade away.

Sales decline for many reasons, including technological advances, shifts in consumer tastes, and increased competition. As sales and profits decline, some firms withdraw from the market. Those remaining may prune their product offerings. In addition, they may drop smaller market segments and marginal trade channels, or they may cut the promotion budget and reduce their prices further.

Carrying a weak product can be very costly to a firm, and not just in profit terms. There are many hidden costs. A weak product may take up too much of management's time. It often requires frequent price and inventory adjustments. It requires advertising and sales-force attention that might be better used to make "healthy" products more profitable. A product's failing reputation can cause customer concerns about the company and its other products. The biggest cost may well lie in the future. Keeping weak products delays the search for replacements, creates a lopsided product mix, hurts current profits, and weakens the company's foothold on the future.

For these reasons, companies must identify products in the decline stage and decide whether to maintain, harvest, or drop them. Management may decide to *maintain* its brand, repositioning or reinvigorating it in hopes of moving it back into the growth stage of the product life cycle. >> Radio Flyer—the 100-year-old iconic red wagon maker—did this:[21]

> Less than 20 years ago, Radio Flyer was declining and unprofitable. But rather giving in to the product life cycle, the brand engineered a turnaround. It sent designers out to visit homes, playgrounds, and side-street sidewalks around the country to watch firsthand how today's kids were using wagons, tricycles, and other items that Radio Flyer makes. At headquarters, it built a Play Lab with a test-track sidewalk, where it videotaped how kids ride. It also studied parents. "We'll say to Mom, 'OK, take this wagon and put it into your trunk,' and then we watch: Is it clumsy? Is it awkward?" says Radio Flyer's CEO.
>
> Such customer-focused new product development paid off. For example, after watching small children ride the toys, the Radio Flyer team came up with a scooter that had a wider deck, two front wheels, and a less-wobbly ride. "We went from not having a product in this category to becoming the number one brand...in scooters for little kids," says the CEO. Thanks to this and other products successes, Radio Flyer is now once again rolling and profitable, recently earning it a spot on the *Forbes* list of America's Best Small Companies.

>> Reinvigorating an iconic brand: Thanks to customer-centered new product development, the 100-year-old Radio Flyer is once again growing and profitable.

Courtesy of Radio Flyer, Inc.

Management may decide to *harvest* the product, which means reducing various costs (plant and equipment, maintenance, R&D, advertising, sales force), hoping that sales hold up. If successful, harvesting will increase the company's profits in the short run. Finally, management may decide to *drop* the product from its line. The company can sell the product to another firm or simply liquidate it at salvage value. In recent years, P&G has sold off several declining brands and brands that no longer fit strategically, such as Folgers coffee, Crisco oil, Comet cleanser, Sure deodorant, Noxzema, Duncan Hines cake mixes, CoverGirl and Max Factor cosmetics, Duracell batteries, Iams pet foods, and others.

>> **Table 8.2** summarizes the key characteristics of each stage of the PLC. The table also lists the marketing objectives and strategies for each stage.[22]

Table 8.2 Summary of Product Life-Cycle Characteristics, Objectives, and Strategies

	Introduction	Growth	Maturity	Decline
Characteristics				
Sales	Low sales	Rapidly rising sales	Peak sales	Declining sales
Costs	High cost per customer	Average cost per customer	Low cost per customer	Low cost per customer
Profits	Negative	Rising profits	High profits	Declining profits
Customers	Innovators	Early adopters	Mainstream adopters	Lagging adopters
Competitors	Few	Growing number	Stable number beginning to decline	Declining number
Marketing objectives				
	Create product engagement and trial	Maximize market share	Maximize profit while defending market share	Reduce expenditure and milk the brand
Strategies				
Product	Offer a basic product	Offer product extensions, service, and warranty	Diversify brand and models	Phase out weak items
Price	Use cost-plus	Price to penetrate market	Price to match or beat competitors	Cut price
Distribution	Build selective distribution	Build intensive distribution	Build more intensive distribution	Go selective: phase out unprofitable outlets
Advertising	Build product awareness among early adopters and dealers	Build engagement and interest in the mass market	Stress brand differences and benefits	Reduce to level needed to retain hard-core loyals
Sales promotion	Use heavy sales promotion to entice trial	Reduce to take advantage of heavy consumer demand	Increase to encourage brand switching	Reduce to minimal level

Source: Based on Philip Kotler and Kevin Lane Keller, *Marketing Management*, 15th ed. (Hoboken, NJ: Pearson Education, 2016), p. 358. © 2016. Printed and electronically reproduced by permission of Pearson Education, Inc., Hoboken, New Jersey.

Author Comment
Let's look at just a few more product topics, including regulatory and social responsibility issues and the special challenges of marketing products internationally.

Additional Product and Service Considerations

OBJECTIVE 8-4 Discuss two additional product issues: socially responsible product decisions and international product and services marketing.

We wrap up our discussion of products and services with two additional considerations: social responsibility in product decisions and issues of international product and services marketing.

Product Decisions and Social Responsibility

Marketers should carefully consider public policy issues and regulations regarding acquiring or dropping products, patent protection, product quality and safety, and product warranties.

Regarding new products, the government may prevent companies from adding products through acquisitions if the effect threatens to lessen competition. Companies dropping products must be aware that they have legal obligations, written or implied, to their suppliers, dealers, and customers who have a stake in the dropped product. Companies must also obey U.S. patent laws when developing new products. A company cannot make its product illegally similar to another company's established product.

Manufacturers must comply with specific laws regarding product quality and safety. The Federal Food, Drug, and Cosmetic Act protects consumers from unsafe and adulterated food, drugs, and cosmetics. Various acts provide for the inspection of sanitary conditions in the meat- and poultry-processing industries. Safety legislation has been passed to regulate fabrics, chemical substances, automobiles, toys, and drugs and poisons. The Consumer Product Safety

Act of 1972 established the Consumer Product Safety Commission, which has the authority to ban or seize potentially harmful products and set severe penalties for violation of the law.

If consumers have been injured by a product with a defective design, they can sue manufacturers or dealers. A recent survey of manufacturing companies found that product liability was the second-largest litigation concern, behind only labor and employment matters. Tens of thousands of product liability suits are now tried in U.S. district courts each year. Although manufacturers are found to be at fault in only a small percentage of all product liability cases, when they are found guilty, awards can run into the tens or even hundreds of millions of dollars. Class-action suits can run into the billions. For example, after admitting that it had rigged its diesel engine cars to cheat on emissions test, it revealed it fudged the results of the emissions tests on its 2.0 liter diesel engines, Volkswagen faced a class action lawsuit involving 475,000 owners and lessees and an estimated settlement of $15 billion.[23]

This litigation phenomenon has resulted in huge increases in product liability insurance premiums, causing big problems in some industries. Some companies pass these higher rates along to consumers by raising prices. Others are forced to discontinue high-risk product lines. Some companies are now appointing *product stewards*, whose job is to protect consumers from harm and the company from liability by proactively ferreting out potential product problems.

International Product and Services Marketing

International product and services marketers face special challenges. First, they must figure out what products and services to introduce and in which countries. Then they must decide how much to standardize or adapt their products and services for world markets.

On the one hand, companies would like to standardize their offerings. Standardization helps a company develop a consistent worldwide image. It also lowers the product design, manufacturing, and marketing costs of offering a large variety of products. On the other hand, markets and consumers around the world differ widely. Companies must usually respond to these differences by adapting their product offerings.

For example, McDonald's operates in more than 100 countries, with sometimes widely varying local food preferences. So although you'll find its signature burgers and fries in most locations around the world, the chain has added menu items that meet the unique taste buds of customers in local markets. McDonald's serves salmon burgers in Norway, mashed-potato burgers in China, shrimp burgers in Japan, a Samurai Pork Burger in Thailand, chicken porridge in Malaysia, and Spam and eggs in Hawaii. In a German McDonald's, you'll find the Nürnburger (three large bratwurst on a soft roll with lots of mustard, of course); in Israel, there's the McFalafel (chickpea fritters, tomatoes, cucumber, and cheese topped with tahini and wrapped in lafa). And menus in Turkey feature a chocolate orange fried pie (Brazil adds banana, Egypt taro, and Hawaii pineapple).

In many major global markets, McDonald's adapts more than just its menu. It also adjusts its restaurant design and operations. >> For example, McDonald's France has redefined itself as a French company that adapts to the needs and preferences of French consumers:[24]

>> Global product adaption: By adapting its menu and operations to the needs and preferences of French consumers and ther culture, McDonald's has turned France into its second-most-profitable world market.

PRM/SIPA/Newscom

> "France—the land of haute cuisine, fine wine, and cheese—would be the last place you would expect to find a thriving [McDonald's]," opines one observer. Yet the fast-food giant has turned France into its second-most profitable world market. Although a McDonald's in Paris might at first seem a lot like one in Chicago, McDonald's has carefully adapted its French operations to the preferences of local customers. At the most basic level, although a majority of revenues still come from burgers and fries, McDonald's France has changed its menu to please the French palate. For instance, it offers up burgers with French cheeses such as chevre, cantel, and bleu, topped off with whole-grain French mustard sauce. And French consumers love baguettes, so McDonald's bakes them fresh in its restaurants and sells them in oh-so-French McBaguette sandwiches.
>
> But perhaps the biggest difference isn't in the food but in the design of the restaurants themselves, which have been adapted to suit

French lifestyles. For example, French meal times tend to be longer, with more food consumed per sitting. So McDonald's has refined its restaurant interiors to create a comfortable, welcoming environment where customers want to linger and perhaps order an additional coffee or dessert. McDonald's even provides tableside service. As a result, the average French McDonald's customer spends about four times what an American customer spends per visit.

Service marketers also face special challenges when going global. Some service industries have a long history of international operations. For example, the commercial banking industry was one of the first to grow internationally. Banks had to provide global services to meet the foreign exchange and credit needs of their home-country clients who wanted to sell overseas. In recent years, many banks have become truly global. Germany's Deutsche Bank, for example, serves more than 28 million customers through 2,400 branches in more than 70 countries. For its clients around the world who wish to grow globally, Deutsche Bank can raise money not only in Frankfurt but also in Zurich, London, Paris, Tokyo, and Moscow.[25]

Retailers are among the latest service businesses to go global. As their home markets become saturated, American retailers such as Walmart, Office Depot, and Saks Fifth Avenue are expanding into faster-growing markets abroad. For example, Walmart now has more than 11,700 stores in 28 countries; its international division's sales account for 24 percent of total sales. Foreign retailers are making similar moves. Asian shoppers can now buy American products in French-owned Carrefour stores. Carrefour—the world's seventh-largest retailer behind the likes of Walmart, Costco, Kroger, Germany's Schwarz, Walgreens, and The Home Depot—now operates more than 12,000 stores in more than 30 countries. It is the leading retailer in Europe, Brazil, and Argentina and the largest foreign retailer in China.[26]

The trend toward growth of global service companies will continue, especially in banking, airlines, telecommunications, and professional services. Today, service firms are no longer simply following their manufacturing customers. Instead, they are taking the lead in international expansion.

REVIEWING AND EXTENDING THE CONCEPTS

CHAPTER REVIEW AND KEY TERMS

Objectives Review

A company's current products face limited life spans and must be replaced by newer products. But new products can fail—the risks of innovation are as great as the rewards. The key to successful innovation lies in a customer-focused, holistic, total-company effort; strong planning; and a systematic new product development process.

OBJECTIVE 8-1 Explain how companies find and develop new product ideas. (pp 240–241)

Companies find and develop new product ideas from a variety of sources. Many new product ideas stem from *internal sources*. Companies conduct formal R&D, or they pick the brains of their employees, urging them to think up and develop new product ideas. Other ideas come from *external sources*. Companies track *competitors'* offerings and obtain ideas from *distributors and suppliers* who are close to the market and can pass along information about consumer problems and new product possibilities.

Perhaps the most important sources of new product ideas are *customers* themselves. Companies observe customers, invite them to submit their ideas and suggestions, or even involve customers in the new product development process. Many companies are now developing *crowdsourcing* or *open-innovation* new product idea programs, which invite broad communities of people—customers, employees, independent scientists and researchers, and even the general public—into the new product innovation process. Truly innovative companies do not rely only on one source for new product ideas.

OBJECTIVE 8-2 List and define the steps in the new product development process and the major considerations in managing this process. (pp 241–251)

The new product development process consists of eight sequential stages. The process starts with *idea generation*. Next comes *idea screening*, which reduces the number of ideas based on the company's own criteria. Ideas that pass the screening stage continue through *product concept development,* in which a detailed version of the new product idea is stated in meaningful consumer terms. This stage includes *concept testing,* in which new product concepts are tested with a group of target consumers to determine whether the concepts have strong consumer appeal. Strong concepts proceed to *marketing strategy development,* in which an initial marketing strategy for the new product is developed from the product concept. In the *business-analysis* stage, a review of the sales, costs, and profit projections for a new product is conducted to determine whether the new product is likely to satisfy the company's objectives. With positive results here, the ideas become more concrete through *product development* and *test marketing* and finally are launched during *commercialization.*

New product development involves more than just going through a set of steps. Companies must take a systematic, holistic approach to managing this process. Successful new product development requires a customer-centered, team-based, systematic effort.

OBJECTIVE 8-3 Describe the stages of the product life cycle and how marketing strategies change during a product's life cycle. (pp 251–258)

Each product has a *life cycle* marked by a changing set of problems and opportunities. The sales of the typical product follow an S-shaped curve made up of five stages. The cycle begins with the *product development* stage in which the company finds and develops a new product idea. *The introduction stage* is marked by slow growth and low profits as the product is distributed to the market. If successful, the product enters a *growth stage,* which offers rapid sales growth and increasing profits. Next comes a *maturity stage* in which the product's sales growth slows down and profits stabilize. Finally, the product enters a *decline stage* in which sales and profits dwindle. The company's task during this stage is to recognize the decline and decide whether it should maintain, harvest, or drop the product. The different stages of the PLC require different marketing strategies and tactics.

OBJECTIVE 8-4 Discuss two additional product issues: socially responsible product decisions and international product and services marketing. (pp 258–260)

Marketers must consider two additional product issues. The first is *social responsibility.* This includes public policy issues and regulations involving acquiring or dropping products, patent protection, product quality and safety, and product warranties. The second involves the special challenges facing international product and services marketers. International marketers must decide how much to standardize or adapt their offerings for world markets.

Key Terms

Objective 8-1
New product development (p 240)

Objective 8-2
Idea generation (p 241)
Crowdsourcing (p 242)
Idea screening (p 243)
Product concept (p 243)
Concept testing (p 244)
Marketing strategy development (p 244)
Business analysis (p 245)
Product development (p 246)
Test marketing (p 246)
Commercialization (p 247)
Customer-centered new product development (p 248)
Team-based new product development (p 249)

Objective 8-3
Product life cycle (PLC) (p 251)
Style (p 252)
Fashion (p 252)
Fad (p 252)
Introduction stage (p 253)
Growth stage (p 255)
Maturity stage (p 255)
Decline stage (p 257)

DISCUSSION AND CRITICAL THINKING

Discussion Questions

8-1. Explain how firms obtain new products and why it is an important process for companies and customers. (AACSB: Written and Oral Communication; Reflective Thinking)

8-2. Why do so many new products fail? (AACSB: Written and Oral Communication)

8-3. What is idea generation? List and explain the sources of new product ideas. (AACSB: Written and Oral Communication; Reflective Thinking)

8-4. How does a *product idea* differ from a *product concept* and a *product image*? Where do these concepts fit in the new product development process? (AACSB: Written and Oral Communication)

8-5. Name and explain the five stages in the product life cycle (PLC). What message does the product life cycle hold for marketers? (AACSB: Written and Oral Communication)

8-6. Discuss the special challenges faced by companies when marketing products internationally. (AACSB: Written and Oral Communication)

Critical Thinking Exercises

8-7. Companies large and small, across all industries, are crowdsourcing product innovation ideas. Research three crowdsourcing campaigns that companies have used within the past two years. Were they successful? Explain. (AACSB: Written and Oral Communication; Information Technology; Reflective Thinking)

8-8. In small groups, research the Owlet Smart Sock. Where is it in the new product life cycle? After examining the company website, assess what the company does well. What challenges will it face? (AACSB: Written and Oral Communication; Information Technology; Reflective Thinking)

8-9. Review the five stages in the product life cycle (PLC). Select products that fit into each of the introduction, growth, maturity, and decline stages, and support your reasoning using the summary of key characteristics in Table 8.2. What objectives and strategies should the company use as next steps for each product? Support your opinion. (AACSB: Written and Oral Communication; Reflective Thinking)

MINICASES AND APPLICATIONS

Online, Mobile, and Social Media Marketing No Excuses. Work Out in Your Home

About 24 million people in the United States did yoga at least once in 2013, and participation has been increasing by 6.5 percent annually, according to the Sports and Fitness Industry Association. A survey commissioned by Yoga Journal revealed that more than 44 percent of people who don't practice yoga are interested in trying it.

Enter Adriene Mishler, an actress, yoga teacher, and entrepreneur from Austin, Texas. Adriene co-founded Find What Feels Good (www.yogawithadriene.vhx.tv/members-only), a video subscription website that provides creative yoga and yoga lifestyle content to some 2 million subscribers. In addition, Adriene also produces and hosts Yoga With Adriene (YWA), a successful online community that provides high quality yoga instruction at no cost to inspire people of all shapes and sizes across the globe. The development of free yoga videos came from Mishler's mission to get the tools of yoga into schools and homes (www.yogawithadriene.com). YWA has been recognized by Google as the most searched workout, has been recognized by the *Wall Street Journal*, and was awarded a Streamy in Health and Wellness.

8-10. Research the exploding online fitness and health industry, and describe two companies offering fitness or wellness services. Discuss the pros and cons of offering fitness services this way online. (AACSB: Written and Oral Communication; Reflective Thinking)

8-11. In what stage of the product life cycle is online fitness? What role has mobile technology played in evolution of this industry? Explain. (AACSB: Written and Oral Communication; Reflective Thinking)

Marketing Ethics Autonomous Autos

The road to autonomous cars could be right around the corner, but automakers will likely face twists and turns getting there as these vehicles make their way to the marketplace. Companies like Waymo, General Motors, Tesla, and even Uber and Lyft are piloting various autonomous vehicle technologies that will likely be seen on streets within the next three years. In one futuristic forecast, Goldman Sachs predicts that "robo-taxis will help the ride-hailing and ride-sharing business grow from $5 billion in revenue today to $285 billion by 2030...Without drivers, operating margins could be in the 20 percent range, more than twice what carmakers generate right now. If that kind of growth and profit come to pass—very big ifs—it would be almost three times what GM makes in a year." As this potentially lucrative technology looms on the horizon, consumers and industry groups, such as the Insurance Institute for Highway Safety, are concerned about safety measures and developing realistic consumer expectations. Test programs of self-driving vehicles on public roads have produced some high-profile accidents, some resulting in fatalities.

8-12. Discuss the ethical issues surrounding the testing and introduction of self-driving vehicles. Is there sufficient research to support the claims and safety of these new products? (AACSB: Written and Oral Communication; Ethical Understanding and Reasoning)

8-13. Would you use such a product? Why or why not? Support your answer. (AACSB: Written and Oral Communication; Reflective Thinking)

Marketing by the Numbers Dental House Calls

With the population aging and patients who dread sitting in a sterile dental office, dentists are finding an opportunity in dental house calls. The Blende Dental Group has taken its services on the road in San Francisco and New York City, performing everything from routine exams and cleanings to root canals. Some patients are wealthy and prefer the personal service, whereas others are disabled or elderly homebounds who cannot get to the dentist's office. Recreating a dental office in a home requires additional equipment, such as a portable X-ray machine that looks like a ray gun, sterile water tanks, a dental drill, lights, and a laptop in addition to a vehicle. A portable X-ray machine alone costs $8,000. Refer to Increase Distribution Coverage in Appendix 3: Marketing by the Numbers to answer the following questions.

8-14. What types of fixed costs are associated with this service? Assuming fixed costs of adding this mobile service will increase by $36,000 and a desired contribution margin of 60 percent, determine the amount of sales necessary to break even on this increase in fixed costs to offer this additional service. (AACSB: Written and Oral Communication; Analytical Thinking)

8-15. What other factors must a dentist consider before offering this service in addition to his or her in-office service? (AACSB: Written and Oral Communication; Reflective Thinking)

Video Case Day2Night Convertible Heels

To view this video case and its accompanying questions, please visit MyLab Marketing.

Many women love the fashionable looks and heightening effects of high-heeled shoes. But every woman knows the problems associated with wearing them. For example, they are very uncomfortable for anything more than light walking for short distances. For other activities, you'd better be packing a second pair of shoes.

That's where Day2Night Convertible Heels comes in. Created by a woman who had an epiphany after a hard night of dancing, Day2Night's shoes instantly convert to any one of four heel sizes, from low-heeled pumps to spiked-heeled stilettos. An interchangeable heel makes these high heels a high-tech proposition. Beyond launching a line of shoes, Day2Night is looking to license the technology to other shoe manufacturers.

Company Cases 8 Bose/3 Fitbit/6 5-Hour Energy

See Appendix 1 for cases appropriate for this chapter.

Case 8, Bose: Better Products by Focusing on the Product. Bose became the most trusted consumer electronics brand by focusing on creating superior products over maximizing profits.

Case 3, Fitbit: Riding the Fitness Wave to Glory. How did Fitbit create the fast-growing category of wearable tech? By coming up with the right product at the right time.

Case 6, 5-Hour Energy: Hours of Energy without the Beverage. To break into the crowded world of caffeinated beverages, 5-Hour Energy created an entirely new kind of product.

Writing Assignments

8-16. Discuss how a company can maintain success for products in the mature stage of the product life cycle and give examples not already described in the chapter. (AACSB: Communication)

8-17. What decisions must be made once a company decides to go ahead with commercialization for a new product? (AACSB: Written and Oral Communication)

Pricing

Understanding and Capturing Customer Value

Objectives Outline

- OBJECTIVE 9-1 **Define price, identify the three major pricing strategies, and discuss the importance of understanding customer-value perceptions, company costs, and competitor strategies when setting prices.** See: Major Pricing Strategies (pp 267–274)
- OBJECTIVE 9-2 **Identify and define the other important external and internal factors affecting a firm's pricing decisions.** See: Other Internal and External Considerations Affecting Price Decisions (pp 274–278)
- OBJECTIVE 9-3 **Describe the major strategies for pricing new products.** See: New Product Pricing Strategies (p 279)
- OBJECTIVE 9-4 **Explain how companies find a set of prices that maximizes the profits from the total product mix.** See: Product Mix Pricing Strategies (pp 280–281)
- OBJECTIVE 9-5 **Discuss how companies adjust and change their prices to take into account different types of customers and situations.** See: Price Adjustment Strategies and Price Changes (pp 282–292)
- OBJECTIVE 9-6 **Discuss the major public policy concerns and key pieces of legislation that affect pricing decisions.** See: Public Policy and Pricing (pp 292–295)

Previewing the Concepts

In this chapter, we look at the second major marketing mix tool—pricing. If effective product development, promotion, and distribution sow the seeds of business success, effective pricing is the harvest. Firms successful at creating customer value with the other marketing mix activities must still capture some of this value in the prices they earn. In this chapter, we discuss the importance of pricing, dig into three major pricing strategies, and look at internal and external considerations that affect pricing decisions. Finally, we examine some additional pricing considerations and approaches.

For openers, let's examine Apple's premium pricing strategy. Apple sets its prices substantially above those of even its highest-priced competitors. But Apple's appeal to customers has never been about prices. Instead, Apple's vision has always been to provide innovative designs and superior user experiences that make its prices secondary in the minds of customers who covet Apple products.

First Stop

Apple: Premium Priced and Worth It

» **Apple earns the premium prices it charges. Avid Apple fans have long anointed the brand as the keeper of all things cool.**

Thomas Kurmeier/Getting Images

Apple is the prototypical premium pricer. Whether it's an iPhone, iPad, Mac laptop, or Apple Watch, customers pay more for an Apple than for competing devices—a lot more. For example, the Apple iPhone's average selling price last year approached $800, almost three times higher than the overall industry average. Similarly, a standard MacBook Pro costs $300 more than a comparable Dell or HP computer.

Yet despite such sky-high prices, Apple's products continue to fly off shelves, as eager customers get in line to snap up the latest models. That leaves Apple in an envious position: It charges the highest prices and still captures market-leading revenue shares in most of its product categories. How does Apple pull that off?

For Apple, success has never been about prices. Instead, it's been about the Apple user experience. Many tech companies make products that just occupy space and complete the tasks at hand. By contrast, Apple creates "life-feels-good" experiences. Ask Apple users and they'll tell you that their Apple devices simply work better and are easier to use. And they love Apple's clean, simple designs that ooze style.

Apple's obsession with deepening the user experience shows up in everything the company does. From the beginning, Apple was an innovative leader, churning out one cutting-edge product after another. Making products customers want—usually before consumers themselves even know what they want—has resulted in one Apple-led revolution after another. Apple has always had a genius for wrapping technology beautifully around human needs in a way that puts its customers at the front of the crowd.

In turn, Apple has built a huge corps of avid Apple enthusiasts. For more than four decades, its customers have anointed Apple as the undisputed keeper of all things cool. When you buy an Apple product, you join a whole community of fervent fellow believers. Say the word *Apple* in front of hard-core fans, and they'll go into raptures about the superiority of the brand. Such enthusiasm and support create demand for Apple products beyond the limits of price. Not only are Apple fans willing to pay more, they believe deep down that the value they receive is well worth the higher price.

One of the best illustrations of Apple's premium pricing power is the Apple Watch. Apple was hardly a pioneer in introducing a smartwatch. Dozens of companies were already selling wearables across a broad range of price points. In the year prior to the launch of the Apple Watch, competitors sold 6.8 million smartwatches at an average price of $189. Apple unveiled its own smartwatch in three versions. The least expensive version, the basic Apple Watch Sport, sold for $349, nearly twice the average industry price. At the other extreme was the ultra-premium Apple Watch Edition, made of solid 18-karat gold with sapphire crystal glass. Fully loaded, it sold for as much as $17,000. Such high prices have done anything but scare away buyers. Apple now sells some 13 million Apple Watches a year and holds an almost 50 percent share of the greatly expanded smartwatch market.

More broadly, Apple's ability to command higher prices has produced stunning revenue and profit results. In smartphones, for example, Apple captures a 15.2 percent global unit market share, second to Samsung's 21.9 percent unit share. However, thanks to its much higher prices and margins, in the fourth quarter of last year, Apple grabbed an impressive 51 percent share of global smartphone revenues, compared to Samsung's 15.7 percent. And it reaped a stunning 72 percent of global smartphone profits, three times Samsung's 24 percent. Similarly, Apple captures only 7 percent of the personal computer market but a commanding 60 percent of profits.

Under its premium pricing strategy, Apple sets its prices above those of even its highest-priced competitors. Yet Apple's sales remain hot and its profits even hotter.

Overall, in just the past four years, Apple's sales have risen 34 percent to $229 billion, placing the company at number three on the list of *Fortune* 500 companies, ahead of traditional industrial giants such as GM and GE. Brand tracker Interbrand recently rated Apple as the world's most valuable brand. And the company's soaring stock prices have made Apple the world's most valuable company, edging out Google parent Alphabet.

Even with all this success, however, Apple's premium pricing strategy does present some risks. For example, in some markets—especially the world's rapidly growing emerging markets—Apple's high prices make it vulnerable to low-price competitors. Consider China, an incredibly competitive smartphone market that accounts for a full one-third of all device sales worldwide. In China, Apple now places fifth in market share behind fast-growing, low-priced local competitors such as Huawei and Xiaomi.

Chinese market leader Huawei has grown quickly in recent years to become the world's third-largest smartphone producer behind Apple and Samsung. Huawei offers a wide range of phones with the same or similar features as Apple but at much lower prices. Similarly, Xiaomi has come from nowhere in just the past five years by producing low-cost smartphones, laptops, and other devices that are modeled closely after Apple devices. Xiaomi packs potent technology and stunning design into dirt-cheap phones that sell at a fraction of Apple's prices. For instance, an entry-level iPhone sells in China for $833—that's more than a month's wages for the average Chinese buyer. By contrast, the average Xiaomi smartphone goes for only $149.

With its smart designs and lower prices, Xiaomi is targeting the "technically inclined, geeky, typically younger sort of customer who can't afford a top-of-the-line Apple or Samsung phone," says one tech blogger. Such consumers make up the fastest-rising tech segment not just in China but also in other emerging markets such as India and Brazil. And so far, Apple neither has nor intends to have an affordable answer for that type of consumer. Low-end products simply don't fit Apple's operating style or premium positioning.

However, Apple is still thriving in China and other emerging economies by catering to the also-burgeoning numbers of more-affluent consumers in those markets who want and can afford the luxury and status associated with Apple. Just like anywhere else, if you can afford it, an Apple device is well worth the premium price. In China, according to one analyst, "It's a price people have been willing to pay, specifically because it is expensive." For instance, remember that exorbitantly priced Apple Watch Edition? It sold out in China in less than an hour.

Thus, whether here or abroad, Apple's premium pricing strategy will likely remain a winner. "The dominance of Apple is something that is very hard to overcome," says an industry executive. "Apple has to stumble somehow or another, and I don't think that's going to happen." The lesson is simple: Truly premium products earn premium prices.[1]

>> Pricing: No matter what the state of the economy, companies should sell value, not price.

magicoven/Shutterstock.com

Price
The amount of money charged for a product or service, or the sum of the values that customers exchange for the benefits of having or using the product or service.

Companies today face a fierce and fast-changing pricing environment. Value-seeking customers have put increased pricing pressure on many companies. Thanks to tight economic times in recent years, the pricing power of the internet, and value-driven retailers such as Walmart and Amazon, today's consumers are pursuing more frugal spending strategies. In response, it seems that almost every company has been looking for ways to cut prices.

>> Yet cutting prices is often not the best answer. Reducing prices unnecessarily can lead to lost profits and damaging price wars. It can cheapen a brand by signaling to customers that price is more important than the customer value a brand delivers. Instead, in both good economic times and bad, companies should sell value, not price. In some cases, that means selling lesser products at rock-bottom prices. But in most cases, it means persuading customers that paying a higher price for the company's brand is justified by the greater value they gain.

In the narrowest sense, **price** is the amount of money charged for a product or a service. More broadly, price is the sum of all the values that customers give up to gain the benefits of having or using a product or service. Historically, price has been the major factor affecting buyer choice. In recent decades, however, nonprice factors have gained increasing importance. Even so, price remains one of the most important elements that determine a firm's market share and profitability.

Price is the only element in the marketing mix that produces revenue; all other elements represent costs. Price is also one of the most flexible marketing mix elements. Unlike product features and channel commitments, prices can be changed quickly. At the same time, pricing is the number one problem facing many marketing executives, and many companies do not handle pricing well. Some managers view pricing as a big headache, preferring instead to focus on other marketing mix elements.

However, smart managers treat pricing as a key strategic tool for creating and capturing customer value. Prices have a direct impact on a firm's bottom line. A small percentage improvement in price can generate a large percentage increase in profitability. More important, as part of a company's overall value proposition, price plays a key role in creating customer value and building customer relationships. So, instead of shying away from pricing, smart marketers are embracing it as an important competitive asset.[2]

Author Comment
Setting the right price is one of the marketer's most difficult tasks. A host of factors come into play. But as the opening story about Apple illustrates, finding and implementing the right pricing strategy is critical to success.

Major Pricing Strategies

OBJECTIVE 9-1 Define price, identify the three major pricing strategies, and discuss the importance of understanding customer-value perceptions, company costs, and competitor strategies when setting prices.

The price the company charges will fall somewhere between one that is too low to produce a profit and one that is too high to produce any demand. >> **Figure 9.1** summarizes the major considerations in setting prices. Customer perceptions of the product's value set the ceiling for its price. If customers perceive that the product's price is greater than its value, they will not buy the product. Likewise, product costs set the floor for a product's price. If the company prices the product below its costs, the company's profits will suffer. In setting its price between these two extremes, the company must consider several external and internal factors, including competitors' strategies and prices, the overall marketing strategy and mix, and the nature of the market and demand.

Figure 9.1 suggests three major pricing strategies: customer value-based pricing, cost-based pricing, and competition-based pricing.

Author Comment
Like everything else in marketing, good pricing starts with customers and their perceptions of value.

Customer Value–Based Pricing

In the end, the customer will decide whether a product's price is right. Pricing decisions, like other marketing mix decisions, must start with customer value. When customers buy a product, they exchange something of value (the price) to get something of value (the benefits of having or using the product). Effective customer-oriented pricing involves understanding how much value consumers place on the benefits they receive from the product and setting a price that captures that value.

Customer value-based pricing
Setting price based on buyers' perceptions of value rather than on the seller's cost.

Customer value–based pricing uses buyers' perceptions of value as the key to pricing. Value-based pricing means that the marketer cannot design a product and marketing program and then set the price. Price is considered along with all other marketing mix variables *before* the marketing program is set.

>> **Figure 9.2** compares value-based pricing with cost-based pricing. Although costs are an important consideration in setting prices, cost-based pricing is often product driven. The company designs what it considers to be a good product, adds up the costs of making the product, and sets a price that covers costs plus a target profit. Marketing must then convince buyers that the product's value at that price justifies its purchase. If the price turns out to be too high, the company must settle for lower markups or lower sales, both resulting in disappointing profits.

Value-based pricing reverses this process. The company first assesses customer needs and value perceptions. It then sets its target price based on customer perceptions of value. The targeted value and price drive decisions about what costs can be incurred and the resulting product design. As a result, pricing begins with analyzing consumer needs and value perceptions, and the price is set to match perceived value.

If customers perceive that a product's price is greater than its value, they won't buy it. If the company prices the product below its costs, profits will suffer. Between the two extremes, the "right" pricing strategy is one that delivers both value to the customer and profits to the company.

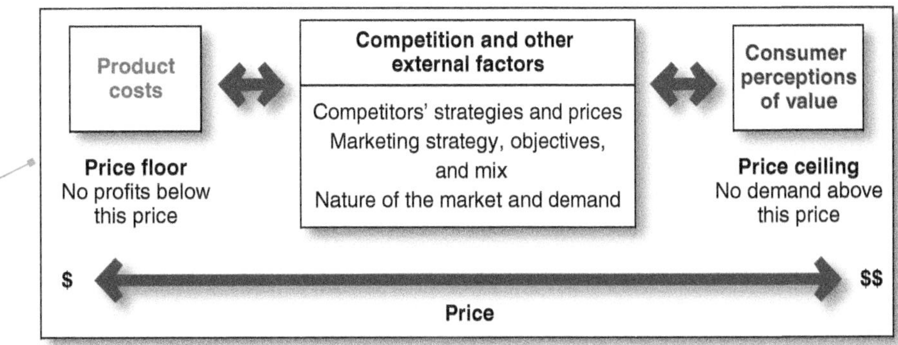

>> **Figure 9.1 Considerations in Setting Price**

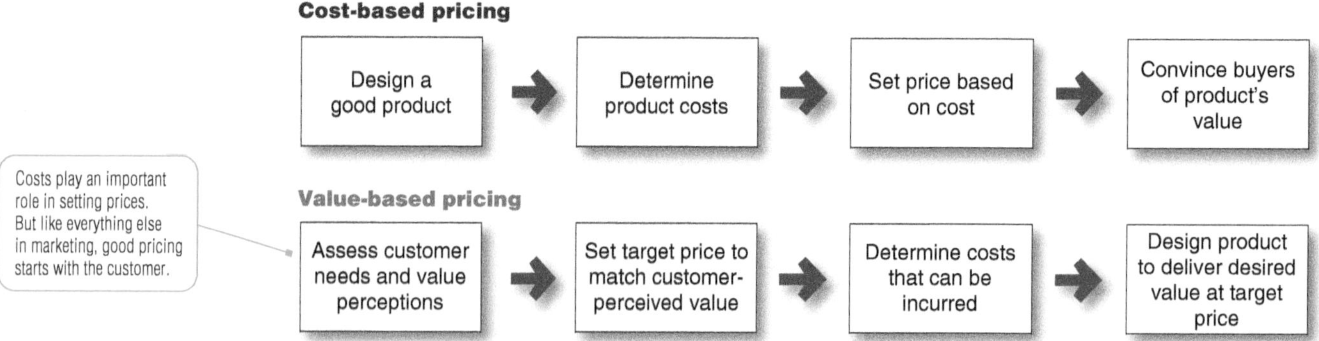

Costs play an important role in setting prices. But like everything else in marketing, good pricing starts with the customer.

>> Figure 9.2 Value-Based Pricing versus Cost-Based Pricing

It's important to remember that "good value" is not the same as "low price." >> For example, some owners consider a luxurious Patek Philippe watch a real bargain, even at eye-popping prices ranging from $20,000 to $500,000:[3]

> Listen up here because I'm about to tell you why a certain watch costing $20,000, or even $500,000, isn't actually expensive but is in fact a tremendous value. Every Patek Philippe watch is handmade by Swiss watchmakers from the finest materials and can take more than a year to make. Still not convinced? Beyond keeping precise time, Patek Philippe watches are also good investments. They carry high prices but retain or even increase their value over time. Many models achieve a kind of cult status that makes them the most coveted timepieces on the planet. But more important than just a means of telling time or a good investment is the sentimental and emotional value of possessing a Patek Philippe. Says the company's president: "This is about passion. I mean—it really is a dream. Nobody needs a Patek." These watches are unique possessions steeped in precious memories, making them treasured family assets. According to the company, "The purchase of a Patek Philippe is often related to a personal event—a professional success, a marriage, or the birth of a child—and offering it as a gift is the most eloquent expression of love or affection." A Patek Philippe watch is made not to last just one lifetime but many. Says one ad: "You never actually own a Patek Philippe, you merely look after it for the next generation." That makes it a real bargain, even at twice the price.

>> Perceived value: Some owners consider a luxurious Patek Philippe watch a real bargain, even at eye-popping prices ranging from $20,000 to $500,000.
FABRICE COFFRINI/AFP/Getty Images

A company will often find it hard to measure the value customers attach to its product. For example, calculating the cost of ingredients in a meal at a fancy restaurant is relatively easy. But assigning value to other measures of satisfaction such as taste, environment, relaxation, conversation, and status is very hard. Such value is subjective; it varies both for different consumers and different situations.

Still, consumers will use these perceived values to evaluate a product's price, so the company must work to measure them. Sometimes, companies ask consumers how much they would pay for a basic product and for each benefit added to the offer. Or a company might conduct experiments to test the perceived value of different product offers. According to an old Russian proverb, there are two fools in every market—one who asks too much and one who asks too little. If the seller charges more than the buyers' perceived value, the company's sales will suffer. If the seller charges less, its products will sell very well, but they will produce less revenue than they would if they were priced at the level of perceived value.

We now examine two types of value-based pricing: *good-value pricing* and *value-added pricing*.

Good-Value Pricing

Recent years have seen a shift in consumer attitudes toward price and quality. Increasingly, consumers want to know that they are getting good value for their money. In response,

Mercedes-Benz
Vehicles
Shopping Tools
AMG
CLA-Class Coupes
Inspiring design. Inviting price.
Starting at $31,500* MSRP
The art of seduction. At a price reduction.
The Concept Style Coupe set the auto show circuit abuzz with its dramatic design and athletic presence. Showgoers had only one request: Build it. The CLA brings an international sensation to life with nothing lost in translation, from its diamond-block grille to its frameless door glass to its sweeping taillamps, all at a down-to-earth price.

>> Good-value pricing: Even premium brands can launch good-value versions. The Mercedes CLA Class gives customers "The Art of Seduction. At a price reduction."

many companies have changed their pricing approaches to bring them in line with changing price and value perceptions. More and more, marketers have adopted the strategy of **good-value pricing**—offering the right combination of quality and good service at a fair price.

Good-value pricing
Offering just the right combination of quality and good service at a fair price.

In many cases, this has involved introducing less-expensive versions of established brand name products or new lower-price lines. For example, Kroger carries three low-priced product lines—Heritage Farm, Check This Out, and Psst, which offers thrift-conscious customers rock-bottom prices on grocery staples such as chicken, toilet paper, and sugar. Good-value prices are a relative thing—even premium brands can launch value versions. >> Mercedes-Benz released its CLA Class, entry-level models starting at $31,500. From its wing-like dash and diamond-block grille to its 208-hp turbo inline-4 engine, the CLA Class gives customers "The Art of Seduction. At a price reduction."[4]

In other cases, good-value pricing involves redesigning existing brands to offer more quality for a given price or the same quality for less. Some companies even succeed by offering less value but at very low prices. For example, Spirit Airlines gives customers "Bare Fare" pricing, by which they get less but don't pay for what they don't get (see Marketing at Work 9.1).

An important type of good-value pricing at the retail level is called *everyday low pricing (EDLP)*. EDLP involves charging a constant, everyday low price with few or no temporary price discounts. The Lidl supermarket chain practices EDLP, value proposition that promises "Big on quality, Lidl on pricing." Perhaps the king of EDLP is Walmart, which practically defined the concept. Except for a few sale items every month, Walmart promises everyday low prices on everything it sells. In contrast, *high-low pricing* involves charging higher prices on an everyday basis but running frequent promotions to lower prices temporarily on selected items. Department stores such as Kohl's and JCPenney practice high-low pricing by having frequent sale days, early-bird savings, and bonus earnings for store credit-card holders.

Value-added pricing
Attaching value-added features and services to differentiate a company's offers and charging higher prices.

Value-Added Pricing

Value-based pricing doesn't mean simply charging what customers want to pay or setting low prices to meet competition. Instead, many companies adopt **value-added pricing** strategies. Rather than cutting prices to match competitors, they add quality, services, and value-added features to differentiate their offers and thus support their higher prices.

>> For example, premium audio brand Bose doesn't try to beat out its competition by offering discounts or by selling lower-end, more affordable versions of its speakers, headphones, and home theater system products. Instead, for more than 50 years, Bose has poured resources into research and innovation to create high-quality products that merit the premium prices it charges. Bose's goal is to create "better sound through research—an innovative, high-quality listening experience," says the company. "We're passionate engineers, developers, researchers, retailers, marketers ... and dreamers. One goal unites us—to create products and experiences our customers simply can't get anywhere else." As a result, Bose has hatched a long list of groundbreaking innovations and high-quality products that bring added value to its customers. Despite its premium prices, or perhaps because of them, Bose remains a consistent leader in the markets it serves.[5]

>> Value-added pricing: Premium audio brand Bose creates "better sound through research—an innovative, high-quality listening experience," adding value that merits its premium prices.

MARKETING AT WORK 9.1

Good Value at Spirit Airlines: Getting Less but Paying Much Less for It

"@SpiritAirlines worst, most devious, nickel-and-diming I've ever experienced. I will NEVER fly with you again. #lessonlearned."

This tweet, and a flood of similar social media comments posted regularly by dissatisfied Spirit Airlines customers, isn't the kind of feedback most companies want to hear. What's more, adding to such negative social media testimonials, Spirit Airlines has earned the dubious distinction of being the lowest-rated airline on the American Consumer Satisfaction Index for three years in a row.

So Spirit Airlines must be headed down the path to bankruptcy and ruin, right? To the contrary, Spirit is one of the nation's fastest-growing carriers—last year it grew its revenue passenger miles at twice the rate of its major competitors. It fills almost every available seat on every flight. And it turns a healthy profit every quarter—a difficult feat in the up-and-down airline industry. How does Spirit Airlines do it? By mastering the art and science of extreme good-value pricing. Spirit's value proposition: "Less money. More go."

Spirit Airlines is an unrivaled "ultra low-cost carrier," resulting in prices much lower than those of competitors—up to 90 percent lower in some cases. But to cash in on such rock-bottom fares, customers must accept less in return. Buying a ticket on a Spirit flight gets you one thing and one thing only—a seat on a plane to your destination. If you want more, you pay for it. Under what it calls "Bare Fare" pricing, Spirit charges extra for everything. *Everything.* You get only what you pay for—and not one peanut more.

For example, whereas most airlines provide free beverages, Spirit charges $3 for a bottle of water or can of soda. Want a pillow or a blanket? Glad to oblige—that'll be $7, please. Getting a seat assignment costs $15, and it will cost you $10 extra to have a check-in agent print out your boarding pass. A full-size carry-on bag runs another $55. Adding insult to injury, seats on Spirit flights are crammed much closer together (what Spirit calls "a little cozier seating"), and the seats don't recline. If you do want a little more breathing room—you guessed it—for a fee you can get an exit row or first-class-sized front-row seat.

Spirit refers to its pricing practices as "Frill Control," claiming that it gives customers more control over what they pay for and what they don't. It points out that the so-called free sodas and extra legroom on other airlines aren't really free. Customers are forced to pay for them in the all-inclusive ticket price whether they want them or not. On Spirit, passengers have the option. Although this approach sounds refreshing, some customers view it as cheap nickel-and-diming or, worse, as unfair and deceitful. The social media are filled with tales of unwary customers who say they ended up paying more for extras than they saved on the initial ticket.

Spirit Airlines takes a hardline approach in responding to customer complaints. When customers request pricing exceptions, Spirit agents stand their ground. The extra charges are optional, not mandatory, the airline explains. The base ticket price includes everything passengers need to get to their destinations. "We've rejected, for example, charging for bathrooms," says Spirit's CEO. "We're never going to do that. That's not an optional thing."

Rather than hiding from its poor customer service record, Spirit Airlines seems almost to wear it as a badge of honor. When one recent study showed that Spirit ranked dead last in complaints made to the U.S. Department of Transportation, Spirit turned it into bragging rights. Over the five years of the study, the airline averaged only eight complaints per 100,000 customers. Spirit celebrated by offering $24 discounts. "That's right, over 99.99 percent of our customers did not file a complaint with the Department of Transportation," Spirit declared in a press release. "To the 0.01 percent—that's OK, we know we aren't the airline for everyone (though we'd love for you to save by flying with us again!)."

The company further defends its pricing by noting that, for customers who take the time to look, it provides plenty of up-front information about what its fares cover. In fact, Spirit's online site offers "Spirit 101: Your Simple Guide to the Way We Fly," a detailed guide on what you get for what you pay and how to make the Spirit Bare Fare system work to your advantage. Despite the angst of the vocal few who think they are being fleeced, most Spirit customers seem to know exactly what they are getting and are happy with that. When asked if she resented paying $3 for water on a Spirit flight, one passenger replied, "Not at all. They're trying to cover their costs." That attitude is

>> **Good-value pricing: Fast-growing Spirit Airlines thrives on giving customers less but charging them less for it. Under its "Bare Fare" pricing, you don't pay for what you don't get.**

Larry MacDougal via AP

shared by most Spirit customers, who seem more than happy to give up the extras to get the super-cheap fares.

To see what all the fuss was about, one airline analyst put Spirit Airlines to the test, eyes wide open. After paying only $63 for a one-way flight from Detroit to LaGuardia—roughly $300 less than the same fare offered by Delta, American, or United—he reported on his experience. "After we landed I turned to my friend and said, 'I don't get it—what ... are people complaining about?'" He concluded that most dissatisfaction stems from misconceptions—that if people are aware of Spirit's policies ahead of time, they can avoid unpleasant surprises and add-ons they don't want. If you want entertainment, he suggests, bring along your own on a mobile device. Plan ahead and buy snacks and beverages before boarding. Think ahead and add in the fees for carry-ons or checked bags to calculate the true fare. Or pack light and jam everything into a small carry-on bag or backpack you can take on for free. And prepare yourself mentally that you might "be able to determine the shampoo used by the person in the row ahead of you." For flights no longer than three hours, being a little squished isn't all that bad.

For those customers who complain that the extras add up to more than the savings, official numbers suggest otherwise. Spirit's total flight price (all fees included) is still the lowest in the industry—an average of 40 percent below competitors' prices. Even at those super-low prices, thanks to its industry-lowest cost per seat-mile, Spirit Airlines still reaps industry-leading profit margins. For example, Spirit's total revenue per passenger is less than half of what United Airlines needs per passenger just to break even. Over the past four years, despite renewed challenges from its large competitors, Spirit's annual revenues shot up 60 percent to more than $2.6 billion; net income soared almost 237 percent. Tellingly, more than half its revenues come from non-ticket sales.

Thus, Spirit Airlines is thriving with its ultra-low-cost approach. True, you don't get much when you fly Spirit. Then again, you don't pay for what you don't get. And you end up with more money in your pocket to spend at your destination. If paying for the extras bothers you, don't buy them. Or just fly another airline and pay the full up-front fare. But Spirit won't be giving away those extras for free anytime soon. "[We won't] add costs for things that most customers don't value as much as our low fares just to reduce the complaints of a few customers," says the CEO. "Doing that would raise prices for everyone, compromising our commitment to what our customers have continuously told us they truly value—the lowest possible price."

Sources: Based on information from Adam Levine, "Could Rising Fuel Prices Lift Spirit Airlines in 2018?" *The Motley Fool*, January 2, 2018, www.fool.com/investing/2018/01/02/could-rising-fuel-prices-lift-spirit-airlines-2018.aspx; "Company Case Spirit Airlines: The Lowest Possible Price—At All Costs," accessed at www.chegg.com/homework-help/questions-and-answers/company-case-spirit-airlines-lowest-possible-price-costs-note-planet-earth----never-fly-sp-q16992319, July 2018; "If Spirit Airlines Is So Unpopular, Why Are Its Flights So Full?" *CBS News*, March 23, 2014, www.cbsnews.com/news/if-spirit-airlines-is-so-unpopular-why-are-its-flights-so-full/; Jared Blank, "3 Myths about Spirit Airlines," *Online Travel Review*, September 10, 2012, www.onlinetravelreview.com/2012/09/10/3-myths-about-spirit-airlines-or-my-flight-on-spirit-was-perfectly-fine-really/; Justin Bachman, "Spirit Airlines Sees All Those Passenger Complaints as Mere Misunderstandings," *Bloomberg Businessweek*, April 18, 2014, www.businessweek.com/articles/2014-04-18/spirit-airlines-passenger-complaints-part-of-its-business-model; Kathryn Vasel, "America's Least Favorite Airline (Hint: It's Not United)," *CNN*, April 25, 2017, http://money.cnn.com/2017/04/25/pf/best-worst-airline-customer-satisfaction/index.html; and http://marketing.spirit.com/how-to-fly-spirit-airlines/en/, http://ir.spirit.com/financials.cfm, and www.spirit.com, accessed October 2018.

Cost-Based Pricing

> Author Comment
> Costs set the floor for price, but the goal isn't always to minimize costs. In fact, many firms invest in higher costs so that they can claim higher prices and margins (think back about Patek Philippe watches or Bose audio products). The key is to manage the spread between costs and prices—how much the company makes for the customer value it delivers.

Whereas customer value perceptions set the price ceiling, costs set the floor for the price that the company can charge. **Cost-based pricing** involves setting prices based on the costs of producing, distributing, and selling the product plus a fair rate of return for the company's effort and risk. A company's costs may be an important element in its pricing strategy.

Cost-based pricing
Setting prices based on the costs of producing, distributing, and selling the product plus a fair rate of return for effort and risk.

Some companies, such as Walmart or Spirit Airlines, work to become the *low-cost producers* in their industries. Companies with lower costs can set lower prices that result in smaller margins but greater sales and profits. However, other companies—such as Apple, BMW, and Steinway—intentionally pay higher costs so that they can add value and claim higher prices and margins. For example, it costs more to make a "handcrafted" Steinway piano than a Yamaha production model. But the higher costs result in higher quality, justifying an average $87,000 price. To those who buy a Steinway, price is nothing; the Steinway experience is everything. The key is to manage the spread between costs and prices—how much the company makes for the customer value it delivers.

Types of Costs

Fixed costs (overhead)
Costs that do not vary with production or sales level.

Variable costs
Costs that vary directly with the level of production.

A company's costs take two forms: fixed and variable. **Fixed costs** (also known as **overhead**) are costs that do not vary with production or sales level. For example, a company must pay each month's bills for rent, heat, interest, and executive salaries regardless of the company's level of output. **Variable costs** vary directly with the level of production. Each smartphone or tablet produced by Samsung involves a cost of computer chips, wires, plastic, packaging, and other inputs. Although these costs tend to be the same for each unit produced, they are called variable costs because the total varies with the number of units produced. **Total costs** are the sum of the fixed and variable costs for any given level of production. Management wants to charge a price that will at least cover the total production costs at a given level of production.

Total costs
The sum of the fixed and variable costs for any given level of production.

The company must watch its costs carefully. If it costs the company more than its competitors to produce and sell a similar product, the company will need to charge a higher price or make less profit, putting it at a competitive disadvantage.

Cost-Plus Pricing

Cost-plus pricing (markup pricing)
Adding a standard markup to the cost of the product.

The simplest pricing method is **cost-plus pricing (or markup pricing)**—adding a standard markup to the cost of the product. For example, an electronics retailer might pay a manufacturer $20 for a gaming controller and mark it up to sell at $30, a 50 percent markup on cost. The retailer's gross margin is $10. If the store's operating costs amount to $8 per controller sold, the retailer's profit margin will be $2. The manufacturer that made the controller probably used cost-plus pricing, too. If the manufacturer's standard cost of producing the gaming controller was $16, it might have added a 25 percent markup, setting the price to the retailers at $20.

Does using standard markups to set prices make sense? Generally, no. Any pricing method that ignores consumer demand and competitor prices is not likely to lead to the best price. Still, markup pricing remains popular for many reasons. First, sellers are more certain about costs than about demand. By tying the price to cost, sellers simplify pricing. Second, when all firms in the industry use this pricing method, prices tend to be similar and price competition is minimized.

Break-even pricing (target return pricing)
Setting price to break even on the costs of making and marketing a product or setting price to make a target return.

Another cost-oriented pricing approach is **break-even pricing**, or a variation called **target return pricing**. The firm tries to determine the price at which it will break even or make the target return it is seeking. Target return pricing uses the concept of a *break-even chart*, which shows the total cost and total revenue expected at different sales volume levels. >> **Figure 9.3** shows a break-even chart for the gaming controller manufacturer discussed previously. Fixed costs are $6 million regardless of sales volume, and variable costs are $5 per unit. Variable costs are added to fixed costs to form total costs, which rise with volume. The slope of the total revenue curve reflects the price. Here, the price is $15 (for example, the company's revenue is $12 million on 800,000 units, or $15 per unit).

At the $15 price, the manufacturer must sell at least 600,000 units to *break even* (break-even volume = fixed costs ÷ (price − variable costs) = $6,000,000 ÷ ($15 − $5) = 600,000). That is, at this level, total revenues will equal total costs of $9 million, producing no profit. If the controller manufacturer wants a target return of $2 million, it must sell at least 800,000 units to obtain the $12 million of total revenue needed to cover the costs of $10 million plus the $2 million of target profits. In contrast, if the company charges a higher price, say $20, it will not need to sell as many units to break even or to achieve its target profit. In fact, the higher the price, the lower the manufacturer's break-even point will be.

>> **Figure 9.3 Break-Even Chart for Determining Target Return Price and Break-Even Volume**

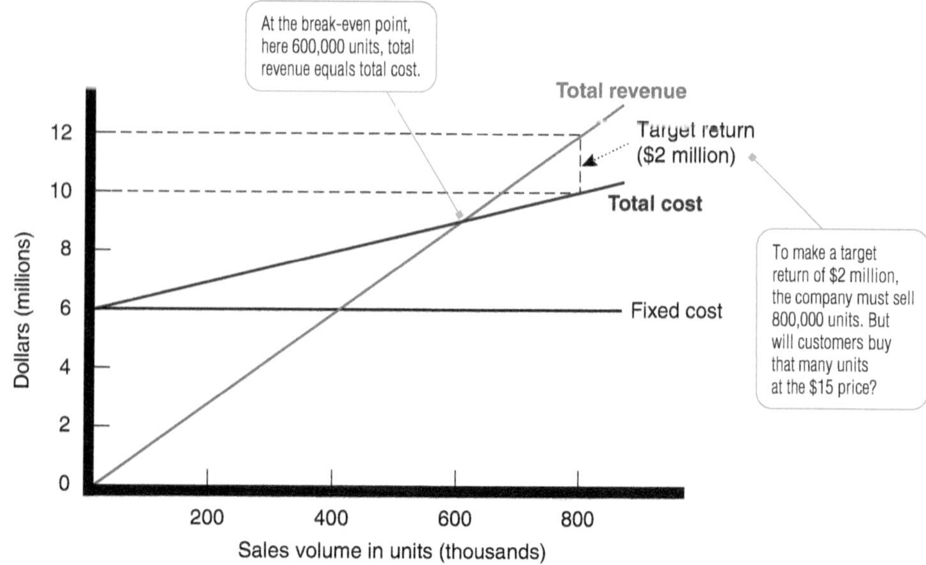
At the break-even point, here 600,000 units, total revenue equals total cost.
Total revenue
Target return ($2 million)
Total cost
Fixed cost
To make a target return of $2 million, the company must sell 800,000 units. But will customers buy that many units at the $15 price?
Dollars (millions)
0
2
4
6
8
10
12
200
400
600
800
Sales volume in units (thousands)

The major problem with this analysis, however, is that it fails to consider customer value and the relationship between price and demand. As the *price* increases, *demand* decreases, and the market may not buy even the lower volume needed to break even at the higher price. For example, suppose the gaming controller manufacturer calculates that, given its current fixed and variable costs, it must charge a price of $30 for the product in order to earn its desired target profit. But marketing research shows that few consumers will pay more than $25. In this case, the company must trim its costs to lower the break-even point so that it can charge the lower price consumers expect.

Thus, although break-even analysis and target return pricing can help the company to determine the minimum prices needed to cover expected costs and profits, they do not take the price–demand relationship into account. When using this method, the company must also consider the impact of price on the sales volume needed to realize target profits and the likelihood that the needed volume will be achieved at each possible price.

Author Comment
In setting prices, the company must also consider competitors' prices. No matter what price it charges—high, low, or in between—the company must be certain to give customers superior value for that price.

Competition-Based Pricing

Competition-based pricing involves setting prices based on competitors' strategies, costs, prices, and market offerings. Consumers will base their judgments of a product's value on the prices that competitors charge for similar products.

Competition-based pricing
Setting prices based on competitors' strategies, prices, costs, and market offerings.

In assessing competitors' pricing strategies, a company should ask several questions. First, how does the company's market offering compare with competitors' offerings in terms of customer value? If consumers perceive that the company's product or service provides greater value, the company can charge a higher price. If consumers perceive less value relative to competing products, the company must either charge a lower price or change customer perceptions to justify a higher price.

Next, how strong are current competitors, and what are their current pricing strategies? If the company faces a host of smaller competitors charging high prices relative to the value they deliver, it might charge lower prices to drive weaker competitors from the market. If the market is dominated by larger, lower-price competitors, a company may decide to target unserved market niches by offering value-added products and services at higher prices.

Importantly, the goal is not to match or beat competitors' prices. Rather, the goal is to set prices according to the relative value. If a company creates greater value for customers, higher prices are justified. >> For example, Caterpillar makes high-quality, heavy-duty construction and mining equipment. It dominates its industry despite charging higher prices than competitors such as Komatsu. When a commercial customer once asked a Caterpillar dealer why it should pay $500,000 for a big Caterpillar bulldozer when it could get an "equivalent" Komatsu dozer for $420,000, the Caterpillar dealer famously provided an analysis like the following:

$420,000	the Caterpillar's price if equivalent to the competitor's bulldozer
$50,000	the value added by Caterpillar's superior reliability and durability
$40,000	the value added by Caterpillar's lower lifetime operating costs
$40,000	the value added by Caterpillar's superior service
$20,000	the value added by Caterpillar's longer parts warranty
$570,000	the value-added price for Caterpillar's bulldozer
–$70,000	discount
$500,000	final price

>> **Pricing versus competitors: Caterpillar dominates the heavy equipment industry despite charging premium prices. Customers believe that Caterpillar gives them a lot more value for the price over the lifetime of its machines.**
Kristoffer Tripplaar/Alamy Stock Photo

Thus, although the customer pays an $80,000 price premium for the Caterpillar bulldozer, it's actually getting $150,000 in added value over the product's lifetime. The customer chose the Caterpillar bulldozer.

What principle should guide decisions about prices to charge relative to those of competitors? The answer is simple in concept but often difficult in practice: No matter what price you charge—high, low, or in between—be certain to give customers superior value for that price.

Author Comment
Now that we've looked at the three general pricing strategies—value-, cost-, and competitor-based pricing—let's dig into some of the many other factors that affect pricing decisions.

Other Internal and External Considerations Affecting Price Decisions

OBJECTIVE 9-2 Identify and define the other important external and internal factors affecting a firm's pricing decisions.

Beyond customer value perceptions, costs, and competitor strategies, the company must consider several additional internal and external factors. Internal factors affecting pricing include the company's overall marketing strategy, objectives, and marketing mix as well as other organizational considerations. External factors include the nature of the market and demand and other environmental factors.

Overall Marketing Strategy, Objectives, and Mix

Price is only one element of the company's broader marketing strategy. So, before setting price, the company must decide on its overall marketing strategy for the product or service. If a company has selected its target market and positioning carefully, then its marketing mix strategy, including price, will be fairly straightforward. For example, Tesla targets high-end, technology-driven buyers with sophisticated all-electric cars that "accelerate the advent of sustainable transportation." Such elevated targeting and positioning dictate charging premium prices.

By contrast, sometimes a company's builds its strategy around its price and value story. >> For example, grocery retailer Trader Joe's unique price-value positioning has earned it an almost cult-like following of devoted customers who love what they get for the prices they pay:[6]

> Trader Joe's has put its own special twist on the food price-value equation—call it "cheap gourmet." It offers gourmet-caliber, one-of-a-kind products at bargain prices, all served up in a festive, vacation-like atmosphere that makes shopping fun. Trader Joe's is a gourmet foodie's delight, featuring everything from kettle corn cookies, organic strawberry lemonade, creamy Valencia peanut butter, and fair-trade coffees to kimchi fried rice and triple-ginger ginger snaps. The assortment is uniquely Trader Joe's—90 percent of the store's brands are private labels. The prices aren't all that low in absolute terms, but they're a real bargain compared with what you'd pay for the same quality and coolness elsewhere. "It's not complicated," says Trader Joe's. "We just focus on what matters—great food + great prices = value. So you can afford to be adventurous without breaking the bank."

>> Trader Joe's unique price-value strategy has earned it an almost cult-like following of devoted customers who love what they get for the prices they pay.

© Lannis Waters/The Palm Beach Post/ZUMAPRESS.com/Alamy Live News

Pricing may play an important role in helping to accomplish company objectives at many levels. A firm can set prices to attract new customers or profitably retain existing ones. It can set prices low to prevent competition from entering the market or set prices at competitors' levels to stabilize the market. It can price to keep the loyalty and support of resellers or avoid government intervention. Prices can be reduced temporarily to create excitement for a brand. Or one product may be priced to help the sales of other products in the company's line.

Price decisions must be coordinated with product design, distribution, and promotion decisions to form a consistent and effective integrated marketing mix program. Decisions made for other marketing mix variables may affect pricing decisions. For example, a decision to position the product on high-performance quality will mean that the seller must charge a higher price to cover higher costs. And producers whose resellers are expected to support and promote their products may have to build larger reseller margins into their prices.

Target costing
Pricing that starts with an ideal selling price, then targets costs that will ensure that the price is met.

Companies often position their products on price and then tailor other marketing mix decisions to the prices they want to charge. Here, price is a crucial product-positioning factor that defines the product's market, competition, and design. Many firms support such price-positioning strategies with a technique called **target costing**. Target costing reverses the usual process of first designing a new product, determining its cost, and then asking, "Can we sell it for that?" Instead, it starts with an ideal selling price based on customer value considerations and then targets costs that will ensure that the price is met. For example, when Honda initially designed the Honda Fit, it began with a $13,950 starting price point and highway mileage of 33 miles per gallon firmly in mind. It then designed a stylish, peppy little car with costs that allowed it to give target customers those values.

Other companies deemphasize price and use other marketing mix tools to create *nonprice* positions. Often, the best strategy is not to charge the lowest price but rather to differentiate the marketing offer to make it worth a higher price. >> For example, Sleep Number puts high value into its mattresses and charges a higher price to match that value.

> At the most basic level, a Sleep Number mattress lets you adjust each side to your ideal level of firmness and support. Add SleepIQ technology and you can track and optimize for the best possible night's sleep. Sleep Number lets you "Know. Adjust. Sleep." SleepIQ technology inside the bed monitors restful sleep time, heart rate, breathing rate, movements, and other factors. Then the SleepIQ app reports on your night's SleepIQ score and how you slept. The app even recommends adjustments that will change your sleep for the better. The Sleep Number children's mattress line helps parents track how their kids sleep. It even lets parents know when their kids get out of bed at night and includes a head tilt for stuffy heads, star-based rewards for sleep habits, and a clever "monster detector." Sleep Number beds cost more than a traditional mattresses—models run from $900 to more than $7,000 compared with good-quality traditional mattresses at $1,000 or less. But Sleep Number's satisfied customers are willing to pay more to get more. After all, it's hard to put a price on a good night's sleep.[7]

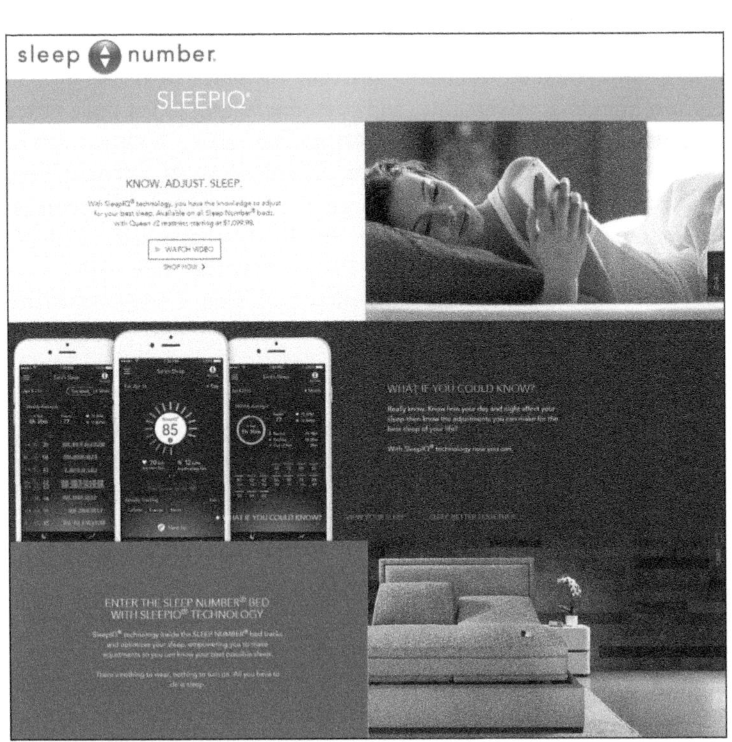

>> **Nonprice positioning: Sleep Number beds cost more than traditional mattresses, but the brand's highly satisfied customers are willing to pay more to get more. After all, it's hard to put a price on a good night's sleep.**
Select Comfort Corporation

Thus, marketers must consider the total marketing strategy and mix when setting prices. But again, even when featuring price, marketers need to remember that customers rarely buy on price alone. Instead, they seek products that give them the best value in terms of benefits received for the prices paid.

Organizational Considerations

Management must decide who within the organization should set prices. Companies handle pricing in a variety of ways. In small companies, prices are often set by top management rather than by the marketing or sales departments. In large companies, pricing is typically handled by divisional or product managers. In industrial markets, salespeople may be allowed to negotiate with customers within certain price ranges. Even so, top management sets the pricing objectives and policies, and it often approves the prices proposed by lower-level management or salespeople.

In industries in which pricing is a key factor (airline, aerospace, steel, railroads, and oil companies), companies often have pricing departments to set the best prices or help others set them. These departments report to the marketing department or top management. Others who have an influence on pricing include sales managers, production managers, finance managers, and accountants.

The Market and Demand

As noted earlier, good pricing starts with understanding how customers' perceptions of value affect the prices they are willing to pay. Both consumer and industrial buyers balance the price of a product or service against the benefits of owning it. Thus, before setting prices, the marketer must understand the relationship between price and demand for the company's product. In this section, we take a deeper look at the price–demand relationship and how it varies for different types of markets. We then discuss methods for analyzing the price–demand relationship.

Pricing in Different Types of Markets

The seller's pricing freedom varies with different types of markets. Economists recognize four types of markets, each presenting a different pricing challenge.

Under *pure competition*, the market consists of many buyers and sellers trading in a uniform commodity, such as wheat, copper, or financial securities. No single buyer or seller has much effect on the going market price. In a purely competitive market, marketing research, product development, pricing, advertising, and sales promotion play little or no role. Thus, sellers in these markets do not spend much time on marketing strategy.

Under *monopolistic competition*, the market consists of many buyers and sellers trading over a range of prices rather than a single market price. A range of prices occurs because sellers can differentiate their offers to buyers. Because there are many competitors, each firm is less affected by competitors' pricing strategies than in oligopolistic markets. Sellers try to develop differentiated offers for different customer segments and, in addition to price, freely use branding, advertising, and personal selling to set their offers apart. >> Thus, Google attempts to set its Pixel smartphones apart from the profusion of other phones not by price but by the power of its brand and the host of differentiating features. Pixel ads tell consumers to "Ask more of your phone." Its Pixel phones promise a more ultra-vivid display, more beautiful portraits, the best smartphone camera, faster battery charging, water resistance, free cloud storage, Google Lens, more help from Google Assistant, more fun, more memories, and more, more, more, more ... Google spent close to $40 million in one month on TV advertising alone to introduce the Pixel 2 and drive home these differentiating features.[8]

>> Pricing in monopolistic competition markets: Google attempts to set its Pixel smartphones apart not by price but by the power of its brand and the host of differentiating features. Pixel ads tell consumers to "Ask more of your phone."

Under *oligopolistic competition*, the market consists of only a few large sellers. For example, only a handful of providers—Comcast, Spectrum, AT&T, and Dish Network—control a lion's share of the cable/satellite television market. Because there are few sellers, each seller is alert and responsive to competitors' pricing strategies and marketing moves. In the battle for subscribers, price becomes a major competitive tool. For example, to woo customers away from competitors, they offers special discounts, free equipment upgrades, and lock-in prices.

In a *pure monopoly*, the market is dominated by one seller. The seller may be a government monopoly (the U.S. Postal Service), a private regulated monopoly (a power company), or a private unregulated monopoly (De Beers and diamonds). Pricing is handled differently in each case.

Analyzing the Price–Demand Relationship

Demand curve
A curve that shows the number of units the market will buy in a given time period, at different prices that might be charged.

Each price the company might charge will lead to a different level of demand. The relationship between the price charged and the resulting demand level is shown in the **demand curve** in **>> Figure 9.4**. The demand curve shows the number of units the market will buy in a given time period at different prices that might be charged. In the normal case, demand and price are inversely related—that is, the higher the price, the lower the demand. Thus, the company would sell less if it raised its price from P_1 to P_2. In short, consumers with limited budgets probably will buy less of something if its price is too high.

Understanding a brand's price-demand curve is crucial to good pricing decisions. ConAgra Foods has learned this lesson when pricing its Banquet frozen dinners:[9]

> Banquet has charged about $1 per dinner since its start way back in 1953. And that's what customers still expect. The $1 price is a key component in the brands appeal. Six years ago, when ConAgra tried to cover higher commodity costs by raising the list price of Banquet dinners from $1 to $1.25, consumers turned up their noses to the higher price. Sales dropped sharply, forcing ConAgra to sell off excess dinners at discount prices and drop its prices back to a buck a dinner. To make money at that price, ConAgra tried to do a better job of managing costs by shrinking portions and substituting less expensive ingredients for costlier ones. But as commodity prices continue to rise, Banquet just can't make a decent dinner for a dollar anymore. So it's cautiously raising prices again. Some smaller meals are still priced at $1. For example, the chicken finger meal still comes with macaroni and cheese but no longer includes a brownie. But classic meals such as Salisbury steak are now back up to $1.25, and ConAgra has introduced Banquet Select Recipes meals at a startling $1.50. The brand has seen some initial sales declines since the price increase but not as severe as feared. Banquet is an entry-point brand, notes ConAgra's CEO, but "that doesn't mean it's married to a dollar. It [just] needs to be the best value for our core customer."

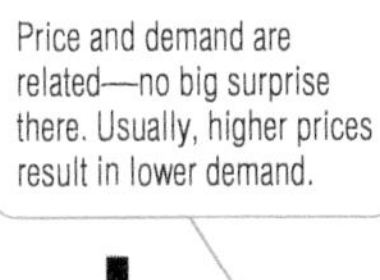

Price and demand are related—no big surprise there. Usually, higher prices result in lower demand.

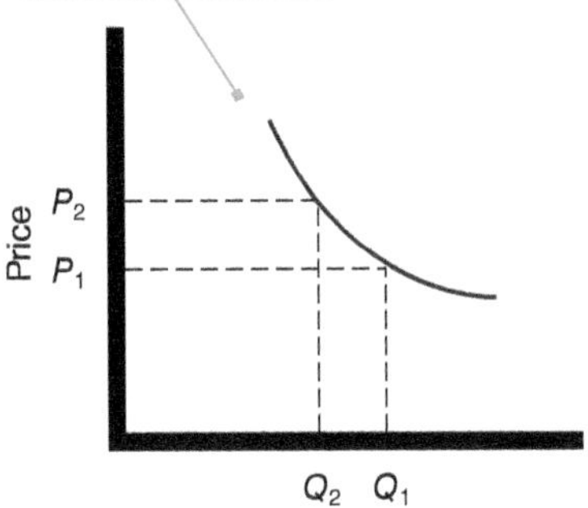

>> Figure 9.4 Demand Curve

Most companies try to measure their demand curves by estimating demand at different prices. The type of market makes a difference. In a monopoly, the demand curve shows the total market demand resulting from different prices. If the company faces competition, its demand at different prices will depend on whether competitors' prices stay constant or change with the company's own prices.

Price Elasticity of Demand

Price elasticity
A measure of the sensitivity of demand to changes in price.

Marketers also need to know **price elasticity**—how responsive demand will be to a change in price. If demand hardly changes with a small change in price, we say demand is *inelastic*. If demand changes greatly, we say the demand is *elastic*.

If demand is elastic rather than inelastic, sellers will consider lowering their prices. A lower price will produce more total revenue. This practice makes sense as long as the extra costs of producing and selling more do not exceed the extra revenue. At the same time, most firms want to avoid pricing that turns their products into commodities. In recent years, forces such as deregulation and the instant price comparisons afforded by the internet and mobile and other technologies have increased consumer price sensitivity, turning products ranging from phones and computers to new automobiles into commodities in some consumers' eyes.

The Economy

Economic conditions can have a strong impact on the firm's pricing strategies. Economic factors such as a boom or recession, inflation, and interest rates affect pricing decisions because they affect consumer spending, consumer perceptions of the product's price and value, and the company's costs of producing and selling a product.

In the aftermath of the Great Recession of 2008–2009, many consumers rethought the price-value equation. They tightened their belts and become more value conscious. Consumers have continued their thriftier ways well beyond the economic recovery. As a result, many marketers have increased their emphasis on value-for-the-money pricing strategies.

The most obvious response to the new economic realities is to cut prices and offer discounts. Thousands of companies have done just that. Lower prices make products more affordable and help spur short-term sales. However, such price cuts can have undesirable long-term consequences. Lower prices mean lower margins. Deep discounts may cheapen a brand in consumers' eyes. And once a company cuts prices, it's difficult to raise them again when the economy recovers.

Rather than cutting prices on their main-market brands, many companies are holding their price positions but redefining the "value" in their value propositions. Other companies have developed "price tiers," adding both more affordable lines and premium lines that span the varied means and preferences of different customer segments. >> For example, for cost-conscious customers with tighter budgets, P&G has added lower-price versions of its brands, such as "Basic" versions of Bounty and Charmin and a lower-priced version of Tide called Tide Simply Clean and Fresh. At the same time, at the higher end, P&G has launched upscale versions of some of its brands, such as Bounty DuraTowel and Cascade Platinum dishwasher detergent, which offer superior performance at up to twice the price of the middle-market versions.

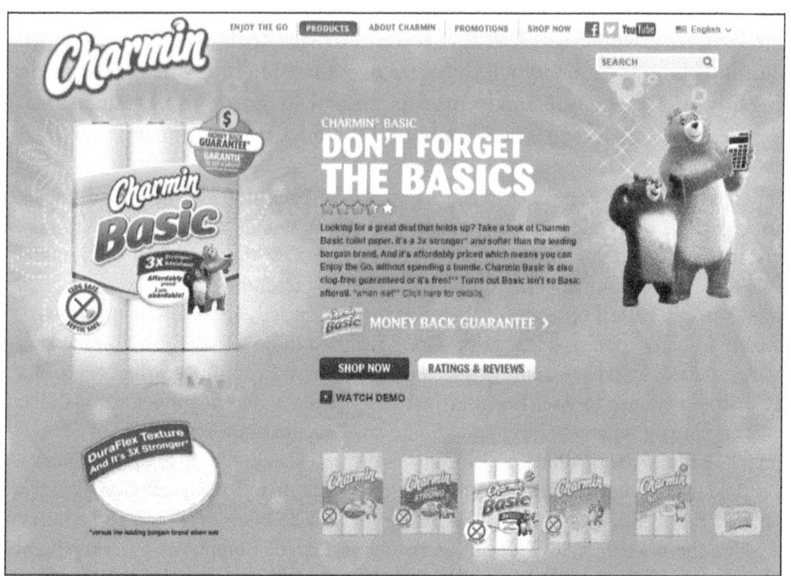

>> Pricing and the economy: Many companies have developed "price tiers." For example, P&G offers economically priced versions of many brands—such as Charmin Basic above—but also premium versions that offer superior performance and higher prices.

The Procter & Gamble Company

Remember, even in tough economic times, consumers do not buy based on prices alone. They balance the price they pay against the value they receive. For example, despite selling its shoes for as much as $200 a pair, Nike commands the highest consumer loyalty of any brand in the footwear segment. Customers perceive the value of Nike's products and the Nike ownership experience to be well worth the price. Thus, no matter what price they charge—low or high—companies need to offer great *value for the money*.

Other External Factors

Beyond the market and the economy, the company must consider several other factors in its external environment when setting prices. It must know what impact its prices will have on other parties in its environment. How will *resellers* react to various prices? The company should set prices that give resellers a fair profit, encourage their support, and help them to sell the product effectively. The *government* is another important external influence on pricing decisions. Finally, *social concerns* may need to be taken into account. In setting prices, a company's short-term sales, market share, and profit goals may need to be tempered by broader societal considerations. We will examine public policy issues later in this chapter.

LINKING THE CONCEPTS

The concept of customer value is critical to good pricing and to successful marketing in general. Pause for a minute and be certain that you appreciate what value really means.

- An earlier example states that although the average Steinway piano costs $87,000, to those who own one, a Steinway is a great value. Does this fit your idea of value?
- Pick two competing brands from a familiar product category (watches, perfume, consumer electronics, restaurants)—one low priced and the other high priced. Which, if either, offers the greatest value?
- Does "value" mean the same thing as "low price"? How do these concepts differ?

Author Comment
Pricing new products can be especially challenging. Just think about all the things you'd need to consider in pricing a new smartphone, say, the first Apple iPhone. Even more, you need to start thinking about the price—along with many other marketing considerations—at the very beginning of the design process.

New Product Pricing Strategies

OBJECTIVE 9-3 Describe the major strategies for pricing new products.

Pricing strategies usually change as the product passes through its life cycle. The introductory stage is especially challenging. Companies bringing out a new product face the challenge of setting prices for the first time. They can choose between two broad strategies: *market-skimming pricing* and *market-penetration pricing*.

Market-Skimming Pricing

Market-skimming pricing (price skimming)
Setting a high price for a new product to skim maximum revenues layer by layer from the segments willing to pay the high price; the company makes fewer but more profitable sales.

Many companies that invent new products set high initial prices to *skim* revenues layer by layer from the market. Apple frequently uses this strategy, called **market-skimming pricing** (or **price skimming**). With each new generation of Apple iPhone, iPad, or Mac computer, new models start at a high price then work their way down as newer models are introduced. In this way, Apple skims the maximum amount of revenue and margins from the various segments of the market. For example, as noted in the chapter-opening story, through smart premium pricing, Apple vacuums up as much as 72 percent of all global smartphone profits.

Market skimming makes sense only under certain conditions. First, the product's quality and image must support its higher price, and enough buyers must want the product at that price. Second, the costs of producing a smaller volume cannot be so high that they cancel the advantage of charging more. Finally, competitors should not be able to enter the market easily and undercut the high price.

Market-penetration pricing
Setting a low price for a new product in order to attract a large number of buyers and a large market share.

Market-Penetration Pricing

Rather than setting a high initial price to skim off small but profitable market segments, some companies use **market-penetration pricing**. Companies set a low initial price to *penetrate* the market quickly and deeply—to attract a large number of buyers quickly and win a large market share. The high sales volume results in falling costs, allowing companies to cut their prices even further. For example, AGIT Global used penetration pricing to quickly build demand for its Wavestorm surfboards:[10]

>> **Penetration pricing: An entry-level, 8-foot, blue-and-white Wavestorm surfboard at Costco sells for only $99.99.**
AGIT Global North America

> Before Wavestorm, surfers and would-be surfers typically bought custom-made or high-end surfboards at local surf shops, where entry-level boards typically run $800 to $1,000. AGIT Global had a different idea. With a mission to make surfing more accessible for both adults and children, it began 10 years ago mass-producing good-quality soft-foam surfboards and selling them through big-box stores at penetration prices. >> For example, it initially sold an entry-level, eight-foot, blue-and-white Wavestorm board at Costco for only $99.99. Ten years later, the boards still sell at Costco for only $149.99. Thanks to penetration pricing, Wavestorm is now the market leader, selling an estimated five times more boards than the other largest surfboard brands.The inexpensive boards have even become favorites of advanced surfers, who buy them for their friends or children. "Margins are slim at Costco," says AGIT's vice president of sales. "But we pump out volume and get paid on time."

Several conditions must be met for this low-price strategy to work. First, the market must be highly price sensitive so that a low price produces more market growth. Second, production and distribution costs must decrease as sales volume increases. Finally, the low price must help keep out the competition, and the penetration pricer must maintain its low-price position. Otherwise, the price advantage may be only temporary.

Author Comment
Most individual products are part of a broader product mix and must be priced accordingly. For example, Gillette prices its Fusion razors low. But once you buy the razor, you're a captive customer for its higher-margin replacement cartridges.

Product Mix Pricing Strategies

OBJECTIVE 9-4 Explain how companies find a set of prices that maximizes the profits from the total product mix.

The strategy for setting a product's price often has to be changed when the product is part of a product mix. In this case, the firm looks for a set of prices that maximizes its profits on the total product mix. Pricing is difficult because the various products have related demand and costs and face different degrees of competition. We now take a closer look at the five product mix pricing situations summarized in >> **Table 9.1**: *product line pricing, optional-product pricing, captive-product pricing, by-product pricing*, and *product bundle pricing*.

Product Line Pricing

Product line pricing
Setting the price steps between various products in a product line based on cost differences between the products, customer evaluations of different features, and competitors' prices.

Companies usually develop product lines rather than single products. In **product line pricing**, management must determine the price steps to set between the various products in a line. The price steps should take into account cost differences between products in the line. More important, they should account for differences in customer perceptions of the value of different features.

For example, Intuit offers an entire line of Quicken financial management software versions, including Starter, Deluxe, Premier, and Home and Business versions priced at \$59.99, \$89.99, \$129.99, \$159.99, respectively. Although it costs Quicken no more to produce the Premier version than the Starter version, many buyers happily pay more to obtain additional Premier features, such as financial-planning, retirement, and investment-monitoring tools. Quicken's task is to establish perceived value differences that support the price differences.

Optional-Product Pricing

Optional-product pricing
The pricing of optional or accessory products along with a main product.

Many companies use **optional-product pricing**—pricing optional or accessory products along with the main product. For example, a car buyer may choose to order a navigation system and premium entertainment system. Refrigerators come with optional ice makers. And when you order a new laptop, you can select from a bewildering array of processors, hard drives, docking systems, software options, and service plans. Pricing these options is a sticky problem. Companies must decide which items to include in the base price and which to offer as options.

Captive-Product Pricing

Captive-product pricing
Setting a price for products that must be used along with a main product, such as blades for a razor and games for a video-game console.

Companies that make products that must be used along with a main product are using **captive-product pricing**. Examples of captive products are razor blade cartridges, video games, printer cartridges, single-serve coffee pods, and e-books. Producers of the main

Table 9.1 Product Mix Pricing

Pricing Situation	Description
Product line pricing	Setting prices across an entire product line
Optional-product pricing	Pricing optional or accessory products sold with the main product
Captive-product pricing	Pricing products that must be used with the main product
By-product pricing	Pricing low-value by-products to get rid of or make money on them
Product bundle pricing	Pricing bundles of products sold together

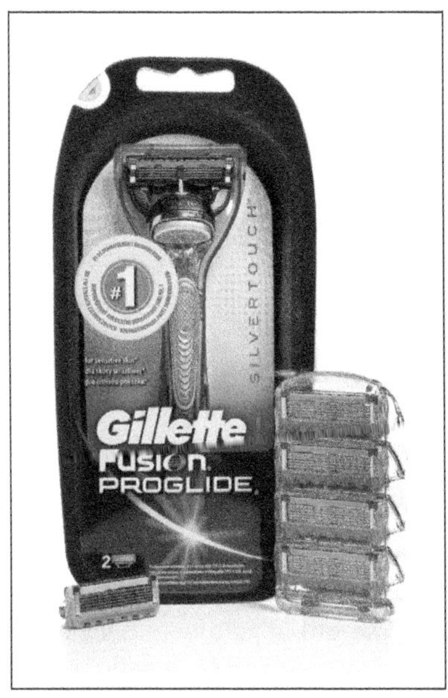

>> **Captive-product pricing: Gillette has long sold razor handles at low prices and made its money on higher-price, higher-margin replacement blade cartridges.**

Melica/Shutterstock

products (razors, video-game consoles, printers, single-cup coffee brewing systems, and tablet computers) often price them low and set high markups on the supplies. For example, Amazon makes little or no profit on its Kindle readers and tablets. It's eight-inch Fire tablet is priced at less than $80 versus an eight-inch iPad tablet at more than $300. However, Amazon hopes to more than make up for thin margins through sales of more Amazon Prime memberships, digital books, music, movies, subscription services, and other content for the devices. "We want to make money when people use our devices, not when they buy our devices," declares Amazon CEO Jeff Bezos.[11]

Captive products can account for a substantial portion of a brand's sales and profits. >> For example, Gillette has long sold razor handles at low prices and made its money on higher-price, higher-margin replacement blade cartridges. "The razor business is all about the blades," says an analyst. "Get consumers hooked on your razor, and they buy the highly profitable refill blades forever." Last year, Gillette sold well over half a billion dollars' worth of refill blades at prices ranging up to a hefty $5 per cartridge.

However, companies that use captive-product pricing must be careful. Finding the right balance between the main-product and captive-product prices can be tricky. Even more, consumers trapped into buying expensive captive products may come to resent the brand that ensnared them. For example, Gillette has lost market share in recent years as price-fatigued customers have shifted to lower-priced private-label upstarts such as Dollar Shave Club and Harry's. To compete, it was recently forced to slash cartridge prices across the board by 15 to 20 percent.[12]

In the case of services, captive-product pricing is called *two-part pricing*. The price of the service is broken into a *fixed fee* plus a *variable usage rate*. Thus, at Six Flags and other amusement parks, you pay a daily ticket or season pass charge plus additional fees for food and other in-park features.

By-Product Pricing

By-product pricing
Setting a price for by-products to help offset the costs of disposing of them and help make the main product's price more competitive.

Producing products and services often generates by-products. If the by-products have no value and if getting rid of them is costly, this will affect the pricing of the main product. Using **by-product pricing**, the company seeks a market for these by-products to help offset the costs of disposing of them and help make the price of the main product more competitive.

The by-products themselves can even turn out to be profitable—turning trash into cash. For example, cheese makers in Wisconsin have discovered a use for their leftover brine, a salt solution used in the cheese-making process. Instead of paying to have it disposed of, they now sell it to local city and county highway departments, which use it in conjunction with salt to melt icy roads. It doesn't stop there. In New Jersey, pickle makers sell their leftover brine for similar uses. In Tennessee, distilleries sell off potato juice, a by-product of vodka distillation. And on many highways across the nation, highway crews use a product called Beet Heet, which is made from—you guessed it—beet juice brine by-products. The only side effect of these brine solutions is a slight odor. Says one highway department official about cheese brine, "If you were behind a snow plow, you'd immediately smell it."[13]

Product Bundle Pricing

Product bundle pricing
Combining several products and offering the bundle at a reduced price.

Using **product bundle pricing**, sellers often combine several products and offer the bundle at a reduced price. For example, fast-food restaurants bundle a burger, fries, and a soft drink at a "combo" price. Microsoft Office is sold as a bundle of computer software, including Word, Excel, PowerPoint, and Outlook. And Comcast, AT&T, Spectrum, Verizon, and other telecommunications companies bundle TV, phone, and high-speed internet services at a low combined price. Price bundling can promote the sales of products consumers might not otherwise buy, but the combined price must be low enough to get them to buy the bundle.

Author Comment

Setting the base price for a product is only the start. The company must then adjust the price to account for customer and situational differences. When was the last time you paid the full suggested retail price for something?

Price Adjustment Strategies and Price Changes

OBJECTIVE 9-5 Discuss how companies adjust and change their prices to take into account different types of customers and situations.

Companies usually adjust their basic prices to account for various customer differences and changing situations. Here we examine the seven price adjustment strategies summarized in >> **Table 9.2**: *discount and allowance pricing, segmented pricing, psychological pricing, promotional pricing, geographical pricing, dynamic pricing*, and *international pricing*.

Discount and Allowance Pricing

Most companies adjust their basic price to reward customers for certain responses, such as paying bills early, volume purchases, and off-season buying. These price adjustments—called *discounts* and *allowances*—can take many forms.

Discount
A straight reduction in price on purchases during a stated period of time or of larger quantities.

One form of **discount** is a *cash discount*, a price reduction to buyers who pay their bills promptly. A typical example is "2/10, net 30," which means that although payment is due within 30 days, the buyer can deduct 2 percent if the bill is paid within 10 days. A *quantity discount* is a price reduction to buyers who buy large volumes. A seller offers a *functional discount* (also called a *trade discount*) to trade-channel members who perform certain functions, such as selling, storing, and record keeping. A *seasonal discount* is a price reduction to buyers who buy merchandise or services out of season.

Allowance
Promotional money paid by manufacturers to retailers in return for an agreement to feature the manufacturer's products in some way.

Allowances are another type of reduction from the list price. For example, *trade-in allowances* are price reductions given for turning in an old item when buying a new one. Trade-in allowances are most common in the automobile industry, but they are also given for other durable goods. *Promotional allowances* are payments or price reductions that reward dealers for participating in advertising and sales-support programs.

Segmented Pricing

Segmented pricing
Selling a product or service at two or more prices, where the difference in prices is not based on differences in costs.

Companies will often adjust their basic prices to allow for differences in customers, products, and locations. In **segmented pricing**, the company sells a product or service at two or more prices, even though the difference in prices is not based on differences in costs.

Segmented pricing takes several forms. Under *customer-segment pricing*, different customers pay different prices for the same product or service. For example, museums, movie theaters, and retail stores may charge lower prices for students, people in the military, and senior citizens. Lowe's offers a 10 percent military discount to active service personnel and veterans. And Walgreens holds periodic Senior Discount Day events, offering

Table 9.2 Price Adjustments

Strategy	Description
Discount and allowance pricing	Reducing prices to reward customer responses such as volume purchases, paying early, or promoting the product
Segmented pricing	Adjusting prices to allow for differences in customers, products, or locations
Psychological pricing	Adjusting prices for psychological effect
Promotional pricing	Temporarily reducing prices to spur short-run sales
Geographical pricing	Adjusting prices to account for the geographic location of customers
Dynamic pricing	Adjusting prices continually to meet the characteristics and needs of individual customers and situations
International pricing	Adjusting prices for international markets

20 percent price reductions to AARP members and to its Balance Rewards members age 55 and over. "Grab Granny and go shopping!" advises one Walgreens ad.

Under *product form pricing*, different versions of the product are priced differently but not according to differences in their costs. For instance, a round-trip economy seat on a flight from New York to London might cost $1,100, whereas a business-class seat on the same flight might cost $6,500 or more. Although business-class customers receive roomier, more comfortable seats and higher-quality food and service, the differences in costs to the airlines are much less than the additional prices to passengers. However, to passengers who can afford it, the additional comfort and services are worth the extra charge.

Using *location-based pricing*, a company charges different prices for different locations, even though the cost of offering each location is the same. For instance, state universities charge higher tuition for out-of-state students, and theaters vary their seat prices because of audience preferences for certain locations. Finally, using *time-based pricing*, a firm varies its price by the season, the month, the day, and even the hour. For example, movie theaters charge matinee pricing during the daytime, and resorts give weekend and seasonal discounts.

For segmented pricing to be an effective strategy, certain conditions must exist. The market must be segmentable, and segments must show different degrees of demand. The costs of segmenting and reaching the market cannot exceed the extra revenue obtained from the price difference. Of course, the segmented pricing must also be legal.

Most important, segmented prices should reflect real differences in customers' perceived value. Consumers in higher price tiers must feel that they're getting their extra money's worth for the higher prices paid. Otherwise, segmented pricing practices can cause consumer resentment. For example, buyers reacted negatively when a New York City Department of Consumer Affairs (DCA) investigation found that women consumers often pay a "pink tax," paying more for female versions of products that are virtually identical to male versions except for gender-specific packaging:[14]

> The DCA compared the prices of male and female versions for nearly 800 products—including children's toys and clothing, adult apparel, personal care products, and home goods. It found that items marketed to girls and women cost an average of 7 percent more than similar items aimed at boys and men. In the hair care category, women paid 48 percent more for products such shampoo, conditioner, and gel; razor cartridges cost women 11 percent more. For example, a major drug store chain sold a blue box of Schick Hydro 5 razor cartridges for $14.99; virtually identical cartridges for the Schick Hydro "Silk," a purple-boxed sister brand, sold for $18.49. In another case, Target sold red Radio Flyer scooters for boys at $24.99; the same scooter in pink for girls was priced at $49.99. Target lowered its price for the pink scooter after the DCA report was released, calling the price mismatch a "system error." Although no laws prohibit gender-based pricing differences, such glaring disparities can damage a brand's credibility and reputation.

Companies must also be careful not to treat customers in lower price tiers as second-class citizens. Otherwise, in the long run, the practice will lead to customer resentment and ill will. For example, in recent years, the airlines have incurred the wrath of frustrated customers at both ends of the airplane. Passengers paying full fare for business- or first-class seats often feel that they are being gouged. At the same time, passengers in lower-priced coach seats feel that they're being ignored or treated poorly.

Psychological Pricing

Price says something about the product. For example, many consumers use price to judge quality. A $100 bottle of perfume may contain only $3 worth of scent, but some people are willing to pay the $100 because this price indicates something special.

Psychological pricing
Pricing that considers the psychology of prices and not simply the economics; the price is used to say something about the product.

In using **psychological pricing**, sellers consider the psychology of prices, not simply the economics. For example, consumers usually perceive higher-priced products as having higher quality. When they can judge the quality of a product by examining it or by calling on past experience with it, they use price less to judge quality. But when they cannot judge quality because they lack the information or skill, price becomes an important quality signal. For instance, who's the better lawyer, one who charges $50 per hour or one who charges $500 per hour? You'd have to do a lot of digging into the respective lawyers' credentials to answer this question objectively; even then, you might not be able to judge accurately. Most of us would simply assume that the higher-priced lawyer is better.

Reference prices
Prices that buyers carry in their minds and refer to when they look at a given product.

Another aspect of psychological pricing is **reference prices**—prices that buyers carry in their minds and refer to when looking at a given product. The reference price might be formed by noting current prices, remembering past prices, or assessing the buying situation. Sellers can influence or use these consumers' reference prices when setting price. For example, a grocery retailer might place its store brand of bran flakes and raisins cereal priced at $2.49 next to Kellogg's Raisin Bran priced at $3.79. Or a company might offer more expensive models that don't sell very well to make its less expensive but still-high-priced models look more affordable by comparison. For example, Williams-Sonoma once offered a fancy bread maker at the steep price of $279. However, it then added a $429 model. The expensive model flopped, but sales of the cheaper model doubled.[15]

For most purchases, consumers don't have all the skill or information they need to figure out whether they are paying a good price. They don't have the time, ability, or inclination to research different brands or stores, compare prices, and get the best deals on every item they buy. Instead, they may rely on certain cues that signal whether a price is high or low. Interestingly, such pricing cues are often provided by sellers, in the form of sales signs, price-matching guarantees, loss-leader pricing, and other helpful hints.

Even small differences in price can signal product differences. A 9 or 0.99 at the end of a price often signals a bargain. You see such prices everywhere. For example, browse the online sites of top discounters such as Target, Best Buy, or Overstock.com, where almost every price ends in 9. In contrast, high-end retailers might favor prices ending in a whole number (for example, $6, $25, or $200). Others use 00-cent endings on regularly priced items and 99-cent endings on discount merchandise.

>> Premium phone maker Apple uses 9-endings to take a little of the psychological sting out of its highest-in-market phone prices. For instance, when it introduced the iPhone X, it assigned a starting price of $999, keeping it just under the then-key market threshold of $1,000. The $1 difference is surprisingly bigger in psychological terms. Interestingly, Apple set the initial starting price of the iPhone X at £999 in the United Kingdom (almost $1,400).[16]

>> Psychological pricing: Apple uses 9-ending prices to take a little of the psychological sting out of its highest-market prices. There is a surprising psychological difference between $999 and $1,000.

Photo by Qi Heng/VCG via Getty Images

Although actual price differences might be small, the impact of such psychological tactics can be big. For example, in one study, people were asked how likely they were to choose among LASIK eye surgery providers based only on the prices they charged: $299 or $300. The actual price difference was only $1, but the study found that the psychological difference was much greater. Preference ratings for the providers charging $300 were much higher. Subjects perceived the $299 price as significantly less, but the lower price also raised stronger concerns about quality and risk. Some psychologists even argue that each digit has symbolic and visual qualities that should be considered in pricing. Thus, eight (8) is round and even and creates a soothing effect, whereas seven (7) is angular and creates a jarring effect.[17]

Promotional Pricing

Promotional pricing
Temporarily pricing products below the list price, and sometimes even below cost, to increase short-run sales.

With **promotional pricing**, companies will temporarily price their products below list price—and sometimes even below cost—to create buying excitement and urgency. Promotional pricing takes several forms. A seller may simply offer *discounts* from normal prices to increase sales and reduce inventories. Sellers also use *special-event pricing* in certain seasons to draw more customers. Thus, TVs and other consumer electronics are promotionally priced in November and December to attract holiday shoppers into the stores. *Limited-time offers*, such as online *flash sales*, can create buying urgency and make buyers feel lucky to have gotten in on the deal.

Manufacturers sometimes offer *cash rebates* to consumers who buy the product from dealers within a specified time; the manufacturer sends the rebate directly to the customer. Rebates have been popular with automakers and producers of mobile phones and small appliances, but they are also used with consumer packaged goods. Some manufacturers offer *low-interest financing, longer warranties*, or *free maintenance* to reduce the consumer's "price." This practice has become another favorite of the auto industry.

» **Promotional pricing: Some marketers bombard consumers with endless price promotions, eroding the brand's value. "Shopping with a coupon at Bed Bath & Beyond has begun to feel like a given instead of like a special treat."**

Keri Miksza

Promotional pricing can help move customers over humps in the buying decision process. For example, to encourage consumers to convert to its Windows 10 operating system, Microsoft ran an Easy Trade-Up promotion offering buyers $200 trade-ins on their old devices when purchasing new Windows 10 PCs costing $599 or more at the Microsoft Store. It sweetened the deal to $300 for trade-ins of Apple MacBooks or iMacs. In the past, Microsoft has offered customers up to $650 toward the purchase of a Surface Pro when they trade in a MacBook Air. Such aggressive price promotions can provide powerful buying and switching incentives.

Promotional pricing, however, can have adverse effects. During most holiday seasons, for example, it's an all-out bargain war. Marketers bombard consumers with deals, causing buyer wear-out and pricing confusion. Constantly reduced prices can erode a brand's value in the eyes of customers. And used too frequently, price promotions can create "deal-prone" customers who wait until brands go on sale before buying them. » For example, ask most regular shoppers at home goods retailer Bed Bath & Beyond, and they'll likely tell you that they never shop there without a stack of 20-percent-off or 5-dollar-off coupons in hand. As one reporter put it: "Shopping with a coupon at Bed Bath & Beyond has begun to feel like a given instead of like a special treat, and that's bad news for the chain's bottom line." In fact, greater recent coupon redemption rates have increasingly eaten into the retailer's profit margins.[18]

Geographical Pricing

Geographical pricing
Setting prices for customers located in different parts of the country or world.

A company also must decide how to price its products for customers located in different parts of the United States or the world. Should the company risk losing the business of more-distant customers by charging them higher prices to cover the higher shipping costs? Or should the company charge all customers the same prices regardless of location? We will look at five **geographical pricing** strategies for the following hypothetical situation:

> The Peerless Paper Company is located in Atlanta, Georgia, and sells paper products to customers all over the United States. The cost of freight is high and affects the companies from which customers buy their paper. Peerless wants to establish a geographical pricing policy. It is trying to determine how to price a $10,000 order to three specific customers: Customer A (Atlanta), Customer B (Bloomington, Indiana), and Customer C (Compton, California).

One option is for Peerless to ask each customer to pay the shipping cost from the Atlanta factory to the customer's location. All three customers would pay the same factory price of $10,000, with Customer A paying, say, $100 for shipping; Customer B, $150; and Customer C, $250. Called *FOB-origin pricing*, this practice means that the goods are placed *free on board* (hence, *FOB*) a carrier. At that point, the title and responsibility pass to the customer, who pays the freight from the factory to the destination. Because each customer picks up its own cost, supporters of FOB pricing feel that this is the fairest way to assess freight charges. The disadvantage, however, is that Peerless will be a high-cost firm to distant customers.

Uniform-delivered pricing is the opposite of FOB pricing. Here, the company charges the same price plus freight to all customers, regardless of their location. The freight charge is set at the average freight cost. Suppose this is $150. Uniform-delivered pricing therefore results in a higher charge to the Atlanta customer (who pays $150 freight instead of $100) and a lower charge to the Compton customer (who pays $150 instead of $250). Although the Atlanta customer would prefer to buy paper from another local paper company that uses FOB-origin pricing, Peerless has a better chance of capturing the California customer.

Zone pricing falls between FOB-origin pricing and uniform-delivered pricing. The company sets up two or more zones. All customers within a given zone pay a single total price; the more distant the zone, the higher the price. For example, Peerless might set up an East Zone and charge $100 freight to all customers in this zone, a Midwest Zone in which it charges $150, and a West Zone in which it charges $250. In this way, the customers within a given price zone receive no price advantage from the company. For example, customers in Atlanta and Boston pay the same total price to Peerless. The complaint, however, is that the Atlanta customer is paying part of the Boston customer's freight cost.

Using *basing-point pricing*, the seller selects a given city as a "basing point" and charges all customers the freight cost from that city to the customer location, regardless of the city from which the goods are actually shipped. For example, Peerless might set Chicago as the basing point and charge all customers $10,000 plus the freight from Chicago to their locations. This means that an Atlanta customer pays the freight cost from Chicago to Atlanta, even though the goods may be shipped from Atlanta. If all sellers used the same basing-point city, delivered prices would be the same for all customers, and price competition would be eliminated.

Finally, the seller who is anxious to do business with a certain customer or geographical area might use *freight-absorption pricing*. Using this strategy, the seller absorbs all or part of the actual freight charges to get the desired business. The seller might reason that if it can get more business, its average costs will decrease and more than compensate for its extra freight cost. Freight-absorption pricing is used for market penetration and to hold on to increasingly competitive markets.

Dynamic and Personalized Pricing

Throughout most of history, prices were set by negotiation between buyers and sellers. A *fixed-price* policy—setting one price for all buyers—is a relatively modern idea that arose with the development of large-scale retailing at the end of the nineteenth century. Today, most prices are set this way. However, many companies are now reversing the fixed-pricing trend. They are using **dynamic pricing**—adjusting prices continually to meet the characteristics and needs of individual customers and situations.

Dynamic pricing
Adjusting prices continually to meet the characteristics and needs of individual customers and situations.

Dynamic pricing offers many advantages for marketers. Services ranging from retailers, airlines, and hotels to sports teams change prices on the fly to optimize sales according to changes in demand, costs, or competitor pricing, adjusting what they charge for specific items on a daily, hourly, or even continuous basis.

Marketers also use dynamic pricing to adjust their prices and personalize offers to customers. These days, it seems every seller knows what prices competitors are charging—for anything and everything it sells, minute by minute, and down to the penny. For example, in this age of big data, online sellers such as Amazon, L.L.Bean, or Apple can mine their databases to gauge a specific shopper's desires, measure his or her means, check out competitors' prices, and instantaneously personalize offers to fit that shopper's situation and behavior, pricing products accordingly.

These days, online offers and prices might well be based on what specific customers search for and buy, how much they pay for other purchases, and whether they might be willing and able to spend more. For example, a consumer who recently went online to purchase a first-class ticket to Paris or customize a new Mercedes coupe might later get a higher quote on a new Bose Wave Radio. By comparison, a friend with a more modest online search and purchase history might receive an offer of 5 percent off and free shipping on the same radio.

Dynamic pricing doesn't happen only online. For example, many store retailers and other organizations now adjust prices by the day, hour, or even minute. For example, Kohl's uses electronic price tags in its stores to adjust prices instantly based on supply, demand, and store traffic factors. It can now stage sales that last only hours instead of days, much as its online competitors do.

Ride-sharing services such as Uber and Lyft adjust their fares dynamically during slow or peak times, a practice called "surge pricing." Similarly, supply and demand dictates minute-to-minute price adjustments these days for everything from theater tickets to parking spots and golf course greens fees. Tollways in Texas even shift toll prices every five minutes depending on traffic—the fare for one 11-mile stretch, for example, ranges between 94 cents and $8.38 depending on the speed of the traffic.[19]

Dynamic pricing makes sense in many contexts—it adjusts prices according to market forces and consumer preferences. However, done poorly, it can trigger margin-eroding price wars and damage customer relationships and trust. Companies must be careful not to cross the fine line between smart dynamic pricing strategies and damaging ones. Customers may resent what they see as unfair pricing practices or price gouging. For example, consumers reacted badly to reports that Coca-Cola was proposing smart vending machines that would adjust prices depending on outside temperatures. Poorly executed dynamic pricing can also cause shopper confusion or disgruntlement. >> For example, according to one source, Amazon's automated dynamic pricing system changes the price on as many as 80 million items on its site throughout a given day, based on a host of marketplace factors. Consider this Amazon shopper's experience:[20]

>> Dynamic pricing: Amazon's automated dynamic pricing system reportedly changes the price on as many as 80 million items on its site in a given day based on a host of marketplace factors.

© webpics/Alamy

> Nancy Plumlee had just taken up mahjong, a Chinese game of tiles similar to rummy. She browsed Amazon.com and, after sifting through several pages of options, settled on a set for $54.99. She placed it in her [shopping cart] and continued shopping for some scorecards and game accessories. A few minutes later, she scanned the cart and noticed the $54.99 had jumped to $70.99. Plumlee thought she was going crazy. She checked her computer's viewing history and, indeed, the game's original price was listed at $54.99. Determined, she cleared out the cart and tried again. [This time,] the game's price jumped from $54.99 to $59.99. "That just doesn't feel like straight-up business honesty. Shame on Amazon," said Plumlee, who called [Amazon] and persuaded the online retailer to refund her $5.

Just as dynamic and personalized pricing can benefit sellers, however, consumers can use it to their own benefit. Thanks to the internet, consumers with smartphones can now routinely compare prices online while at home, in stores, or anywhere in between. They can get instant product and price comparisons from mobile apps such as ShopSavvy, Amazon's Price Check, or Price.com. In fact, retailers are finding that ready online access to comparison prices is giving consumers *too* much of an edge. Such information lets alert shoppers take advantage of the constant price skirmishes among sellers, snap up good deals, leverage retailer price-matching policies, or simply buy items online at lower prices.

Store retailers are now implementing strategies to combat such cross-channel price comparisons and shopping or, better, to turn it into an advantage. For example, Best Buy now has a "Price Match Guarantee" where it will match the prices of major online merchants or store competitors. Once it has neutralized price as a buying factor, Best Buy reasons, it can convert shoppers into in-store buyers with its nonprice advantages, such as immediacy, convenient locations, personal assistance by well-trained associates, and the ability to order goods online and pick up or return them in the store. Best Buy has also sharpened its own online and mobile marketing.

International Pricing

Companies that market their products internationally must decide what prices to charge in different countries. In some cases, a company can set a uniform worldwide price. For example, Boeing sells its jetliners at about the same price everywhere, whether the buyer is in the United States, Europe, or a third-world country. However, most companies adjust their prices to reflect local market conditions and cost considerations.

The price that a company should charge in a specific country depends on many factors, including economic conditions, competitive situations, laws and regulations, and the nature of the wholesaling and retailing system. Consumer perceptions and preferences also may vary from country to country, calling for different prices. Or the company may have different marketing objectives in various world markets, which require changes in pricing strategy.

For example, Apple uses a premium pricing strategy to introduce sophisticated, feature-rich, premium smartphones in carefully segmented mature markets in developed countries and to affluent consumers in emerging markets. By contrast, it's now under pressure to discount older models and develop cheaper, more basic phone models for sizable but less affluent markets in developing countries, where even discounted older Apple phones sell at prices three to five times those of those of competing low-price models. >> For example, Apple's latest premium phones sell well and profitably in China to affluent consumers. However, says one analyst, "If Apple wants to grow iPhone volume higher in China in the future, it will have to push down, not up, the pricing curve, to target more mid-range consumers who can no longer afford a full-featured iPhone."[21]

>> International prices: Companies often must change their pricing strategies from country to country. For example, Apple sells its latest phones at premium prices to affluent Chinese customers but is under pressure to target China's mid-range customers with lower priced phones.

FRED DUFOUR/AFP/Getty Images

Costs play an important role in setting international prices. Travelers abroad are often surprised to find that goods that are relatively inexpensive at home may carry outrageously higher price tags in other countries. A pair of Levi's 501 selling for $54 in Los Angeles might go for $118 in Paris. A McDonald's Big Mac selling for $5.04 in the United States might cost $7.85 in Norway or $5.65 in Brazil, and an Oral-B toothbrush selling for $2.49 at home may cost $10 in China. Conversely, a Gucci handbag going for only $140 in Milan, Italy, might fetch $240 in the United States.

In some cases, such *price escalation* may result from differences in selling strategies or market conditions. In most instances, however, it is simply a result of the higher costs of selling in another country—the additional costs of operations, product modifications, shipping and insurance, exchange-rate fluctuations, and physical distribution. Import tariffs and taxes can also add to costs. For example, China imposes duties as high as 25 percent on imported Western luxury products such as watches, designer dresses, shoes, and leather handbags. It also levies consumption taxes of 30 percent for cosmetics and 20 percent on high-end watches. As a result, Western luxury goods bought in mainland China carry prices as much as 50 percent higher than in Europe.[22]

Price has become a key element in the international marketing strategies of companies attempting to enter less affluent emerging markets. Typically, entering such markets has meant targeting the exploding middle classes in developing countries such as China, India, Russia, and Brazil, whose economies have been growing rapidly. More recently, however, as the weakened global economy has slowed growth in both domestic and emerging markets, many companies are shifting their sights to include a new target—the so-called "bottom of the pyramid," the vast untapped market consisting of the world's poorest consumers.

Not long ago, the preferred way for many brands to market their products in developing markets—whether consumer products or cars, computers, and smartphones—was to paste new labels on existing models and sell them at higher prices to the privileged few who could afford them. However, such a pricing approach put many products out of the reach of the tens of millions of poor consumers in emerging markets. As a result, many companies developed smaller, more basic and affordable product versions for these markets. For example, Unilever—the maker of such brands as Dove, Sunsilk, Lipton, and Vaseline—shrunk its packaging and set low prices that even the world's poorest consumers could afford. It developed single-use packages of its shampoo, laundry detergent, face cream, and other products that it could sell profitably for just pennies a pack. As a result, today, 57 percent of Unilever's revenues come from emerging economies.[23]

Although this strategy has been successful for Unilever, most companies are learning that selling profitably to the bottom of the pyramid requires more than just repackaging or stripping down existing products and selling them at low prices. Just like more well-to-do consumers, low-income buyers want products that are both functional *and* aspirational. Thus, companies today are innovating to create products that not only sell at very low prices but also give bottom-of-the-pyramid consumers more for their money, not less.

International pricing presents many special problems and complexities. We discuss international pricing issues in more detail in Chapter 15.

Price Changes

Author Comment
When and how should a company change its price? What if costs rise, putting the squeeze on profits? What if the economy sags and customers become more price sensitive? Or what if a major competitor raises or drops its prices? As Figure 9.5 suggests, companies face many price-changing options.

After developing their pricing structures and strategies, companies often face situations in which they must initiate price changes or respond to price changes by competitors.

Initiating Price Changes

In some cases, the company may find it desirable to initiate either a price cut or a price increase. In both cases, it must anticipate possible buyer and competitor reactions.

Initiating Price Cuts. Several situations may lead a firm to consider cutting its price. One such circumstance is excess capacity. Another is falling demand in the face of strong price competition or a weakened economy. In such cases, the firm may aggressively cut prices to boost sales and market share. But as the airline, fast-food, automobile, retailing, and other industries have learned in recent years, cutting prices in an industry loaded with excess capacity may lead to price wars as competitors try to hold on to market share.

A company may also cut prices in a drive to dominate the market through lower costs. Either the company starts with lower costs than its competitors, or it cuts prices in the hope of gaining market share that will further cut costs through larger volume. For example, computer and electronics maker Lenovo uses an aggressive low-cost, low-price strategy to increase its share of the PC market in developing countries. Similarly, Chinese low-price phone maker Huawei has now become China's smartphone market leader, and the low-cost producer is making rapid inroads into India and other emerging markets, as well as in the United States.[24]

Initiating Price Increases. A successful price increase can greatly improve profits. For example, if the company's profit margin is 3 percent of sales, a 1 percent price increase will boost profits by 33 percent if sales volume is unaffected. A major factor in price increases is cost inflation. Rising costs squeeze profit margins and lead companies to pass cost increases along to customers. Another factor leading to price increases is over-demand: When a company cannot supply all that its customers need, it may raise its prices, ration products to customers, or both.

When raising prices, the company must avoid being perceived as a *price gouger*. For example, when gasoline prices rise rapidly, angry customers often accuse the major oil companies of enriching themselves at the expense of consumers. Customers have long memories, and they will eventually turn away from companies or even whole industries that they perceive as charging excessive prices. In the extreme, claims of price gouging may even bring about increased government regulation.

There are some techniques for avoiding these problems. One is to maintain a sense of fairness surrounding any price increase. Price increases should be supported by company communications telling customers why prices are being raised.

Wherever possible, the company should consider ways to meet higher costs or demand without raising prices. For example, it might consider more cost-effective ways to produce or distribute its products. It can "unbundle" its market offering, removing features, packaging, or services and separately pricing elements that were formerly part of the offer. Or it can shrink the product or substitute less-expensive ingredients instead of raising the price, a process sometimes called "shrinkflation." Kimberly-Clark raised Kleenex prices by "desheeting"—reducing the number of sheets of toilet paper or facial tissues in each same-priced package. >> And Mondelez recently cut the size of its popular Toblerone chocolate bar by about 12 percent in the UK, not by shortening the bar but by increasing the spacing between its signature triangles. "Shrinkflation is actually quite a successful tactic because a lot of shoppers are more sensitive to a price change than to a weight change," says a pricing expert. However, British consumers found the too-obvious change to Toblerone's iconic shape hard to stomach, sparking online outrage.[25]

>> Brands must be careful when raising prices. When Mondelez reduced the amount of chocolate in its Toblerone bar (effectively raising the price), British consumers found the change in Toblerone's iconic shape hard to stomach, sparking online outrage.

DARREN STAPLES/REUTERS

Buyer Reactions to Price Changes. Customers do not always interpret price changes in a straightforward way. A price *increase*, which would normally lower sales, may have some positive meanings for buyers. For example, what would you think if Rolex *raised* the price of its latest watch model? On the one hand, you might think that the watch is even more exclusive or better made. On the other hand, you might think that Rolex is simply being greedy by charging what the traffic will bear.

Similarly, consumers may view a price *cut* in several ways. For example, what would you think if Rolex were to suddenly cut its prices? You might think that you are getting a better deal on an exclusive product. More likely, however, you'd think that quality had been reduced, and the brand's luxury image might be tarnished. A brand's price and image are often closely linked. A price change, especially a drop in price, can adversely affect how consumers view the brand.

Competitor Reactions to Price Changes. A firm considering a price change must worry about the reactions of its competitors as well as those of its customers. Competitors are most likely to react when the number of firms involved is small, when the product is uniform, and when the buyers are well informed about products and prices.

How can the firm anticipate the likely reactions of its competitors? The problem is complex because, like the customer, the competitor can interpret a company price cut in many ways. It might think the company is trying to grab a larger market share or that it's doing poorly and trying to boost its sales. Or it might think that the company wants the whole industry to cut prices to increase total demand.

The company must assess each competitor's likely reaction. If all competitors behave alike, this amounts to analyzing only a typical competitor. In contrast, if the competitors do not behave alike—perhaps because of differences in size, market shares, or policies—then separate analyses are necessary. However, if some competitors will match the price change, there is good reason to expect that the rest will also match it.

Responding to Price Changes

Here we reverse the question and ask how a firm should respond to a price change by a competitor. The firm needs to consider several issues: Why did the competitor change the price? Is the price change temporary or permanent? What will happen to the company's market share and profits if it does not respond? Are other competitors going to respond? Besides these issues, the company must also consider its own situation and strategy and possible customer reactions to price changes.

>> **Figure 9.5** shows the ways a company might assess and respond to a competitor's price cut. Suppose a company learns that a competitor has cut its price and decides that this price cut is likely to harm its sales and profits. It might simply decide to hold its current price and profit margin. The company might believe that it will not lose too much market share or that it would lose too much profit if it reduced its own price. Or it might decide that it should wait and respond when it has more information on the effects of the competitor's price change. However, waiting too long to act might let the competitor get stronger and more confident as its sales increase.

If the company decides that effective action can and should be taken, it might make any of four responses. First, it could *reduce its price* to match the competitor's price. It may decide that the market is price sensitive and that it would lose too much market share to the lower-priced competitor. However, cutting the price will reduce the company's profits in the short run. Some companies might also reduce their product quality, services, and marketing communications to retain profit margins, but this will ultimately hurt long-run market share. The company should try to maintain its quality as it cuts prices.

Alternatively, the company might maintain its price but *raise the perceived value* of its offer. It could improve its communications, stressing the relative value of its product over that of the lower-price competitor. The firm may find it cheaper to maintain price and spend money to improve its perceived value than to cut price and operate at a lower margin. Or the company might *improve quality* and *increase price*, moving its brand into a higher price–value position. The higher quality creates greater customer value, which justifies the higher price. In turn, the higher price preserves the company's higher margins.

Finally, the company might launch a *low-price "fighter brand"*—adding a lower-price item to the line or creating a separate lower-price brand. This is necessary if the particular market segment being lost is price sensitive and will not respond to arguments of higher quality.

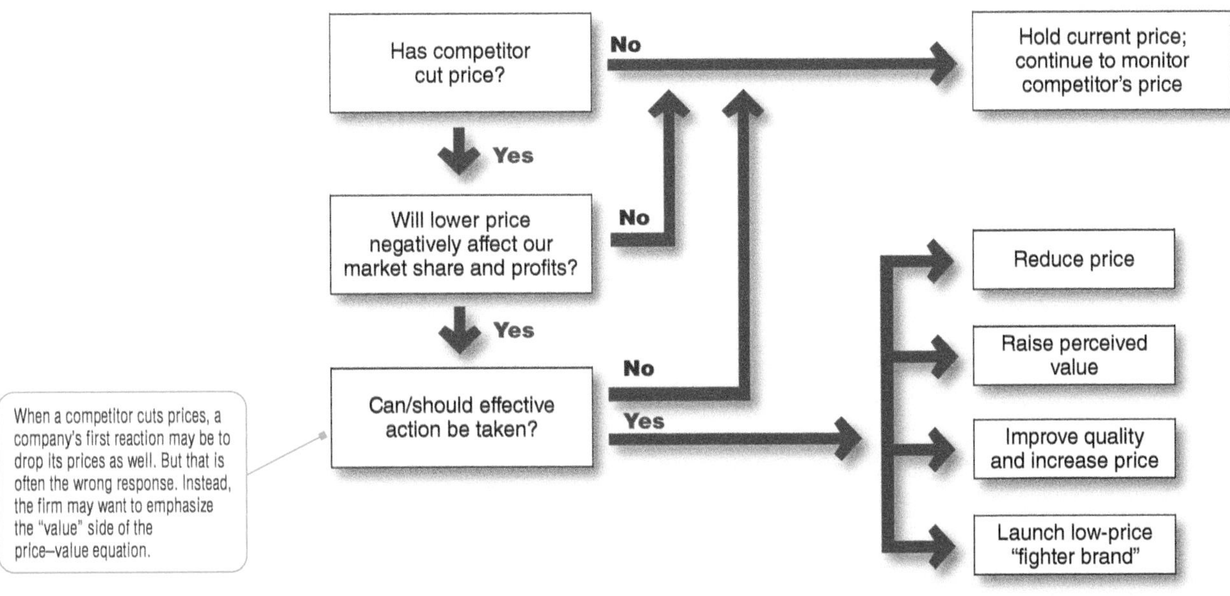

>> **Figure 9.5 Responding to Competitor Price Changes**

>> Fighter brands: Whole Foods Market created its offshoot 365 by Whole Foods Market chain of smaller, value-driven stores as an answer to Trader Joe's and lower-price challengers such as Lidl and Aldi.

Patrick T. Fallon/Bloomberg via Getty Images

>> Whole Foods did this when it began experimenting with its offshoot 365 chain of smaller, value-driven stores named after the chain's 365 Everyday Value brand. 365 is Whole Foods' answer to Trader Joe's and lower-price challengers such as Lidl and Aldi. It targets smart, tech-oriented, but frugal young shoppers who think of Whole Foods as an unnecessary extravagance. 365 promises a grocery shopping experience that's "good for your body, your budget, your lifestyle, and the planet."[26]

To counter store brands and other low-price entrants in a tighter economy, P&G turned a number of its brands into fighter brands. Luvs disposable diapers give parents "premium leakage protection for less than pricier brands." And P&G offers popular budget-priced basic versions of several of its major brands. For example, Charmin Basic "holds up at a great everyday price," and Puffs Basic gives you "Everyday softness. Everyday value." Tide Simply Clean & Fresh is about 35 percent cheaper than regular Tide detergent—it's "tough on odors and easy on your wallet." However, companies must use caution when introducing fighter brands, as such brands can tarnish the image of the main brand. In addition, although they may attract budget buyers away from lower-priced rivals, they can also take business away from the firm's higher-margin brands.

Author Comment
Pricing decisions are often constrained by social and legal issues. For example, think about the pharmaceuticals industry. Are rapidly rising prescription drug prices justified? Or are the drug companies unfairly lining their pockets by gouging consumers who have few alternatives? Should the government step in?

Public Policy and Pricing

OBJECTIVE 9-6 Discuss the major public policy concerns and key pieces of legislation that affect pricing decisions.

Price competition is a core element of our free-market economy. In setting prices, companies usually are not free to charge whatever prices they wish. Many federal, state, and even local laws govern the rules of fair play in pricing. In addition, companies must consider broader societal pricing concerns. In setting their prices, for example, pharmaceutical firms must balance their development costs and profit objectives against the sometimes life-and-death needs of prescription drug consumers (see Marketing at Work 9.2).

The most important pieces of legislation affecting pricing are the Sherman Act, the Clayton Act, and the Robinson-Patman Act, initially adopted to curb the formation of monopolies and regulate business practices that might unfairly restrain trade. Because these federal statutes can be applied only to interstate commerce, some states have adopted similar provisions for companies that operate locally.

>> **Figure 9.6** shows the major public policy issues in pricing. These include potentially damaging pricing practices within a given level of the channel (price-fixing and predatory pricing) and across levels of the channel (retail price maintenance, discriminatory pricing, and deceptive pricing).[27]

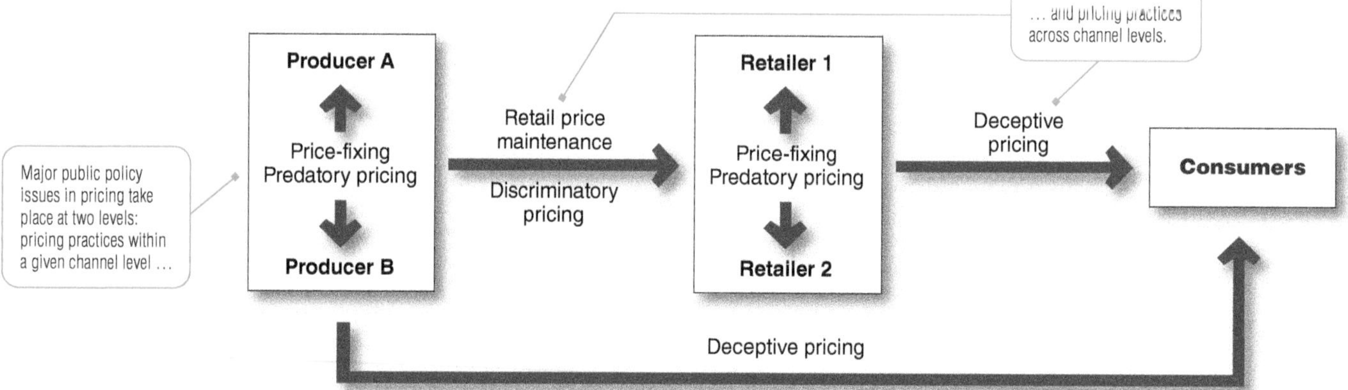

>> Figure 9.6 Public Policy Issues in Pricing

Source: Adapted from Dhruv Grewal and Larry D. Compeau, "Pricing and Public Policy: A Research Agenda and Overview of the Special Issue," *Journal of Public Policy and Marketing*, Spring 1999, pp. 3–10.

MARKETING AT WORK 9.2

Pharmaceutical Pricing: No Easy Answers

The U.S. pharmaceutical industry has historically been one of the nation's most profitable industries. Over the past five years, returns for the S&P Pharmaceuticals Select Industry Index have doubled those of the broader S&P 500. In most situations, we'd applaud such high-performing companies and industries. However, when it comes to pharmaceutical firms, critics claim, healthy sales and profits may not be so healthy for consumers.

Somehow, learning that major pharmaceutical companies such as Johnson & Johnson, Roche, Pfizer, Novartis, Merck, and GlaxoSmithKline are reaping big profits leaves a bad taste in the mouths of many consumers. It's like learning that the oil companies are profiting when gas prices rocket upward. Although most consumers appreciate the steady stream of beneficial drugs produced by pharmaceutical companies, they worry that the industry's huge success may be coming at their own expense—literally.

Americans spent about $457 billion last year on prescription medications, up 5.8 percent from the prior year. Prescription prices have risen rapidly over the years, and health-care costs continue to jump. For example, the price of popular brand name drugs jumped 208 percent between 2008 and 2016.

The critics claim that competitive forces don't operate well in the pharmaceuticals market, allowing the pharmaceutical companies to charge excessive prices. Unlike purchases of other consumer products, drug purchases cannot be postponed. And consumers don't usually shop for the best deals on medicines—they simply take what the doctor orders. Because physicians who write the prescriptions don't pay for the medicines they recommend, they have little incentive to be price conscious. Moreover, third-party payers—insurance companies, health plans, and government programs—often pay all or part of the bill. Finally, because of patent protection and the huge investment and time needed to develop and test new drugs, there are fewer competing brands to force lower prices.

The critics claim that these market factors leave pharmaceutical companies free to practice monopoly pricing, sometimes resulting in unfair practices or even seemingly outlandish cases of price gouging. One classic case made headlines when entrepreneur Martin Shkreli and his company Turing Pharmaceuticals acquired Daraprim, a 62-year-old, lifesaving medication used by AIDS patients. Turing immediately jacked up the price of Daraprim from $13.50 per pill to an astounding $750 per pill, a more than 5,000 percent increase. The pill itself costs only about a dollar to produce.

Major drug companies would never commit such atrocities. "He is not us," said Merck's CEO of Turing's Shkreli. Nevertheless, mainstream pharmaceutical makers routinely boost the prices of their cancer, diabetes, MS, and cholesterol-reducing drugs by 10 percent or more per year, much faster than inflation. As just one example, take Gleevec, a drug sold by Novartis to treat blood-based cancer. Gleevec seemed pretty expensive when it first came to market in 2001 at about $30,000 for a year's supply. Yet, for reasons unknown, Novartis has since more than tripled Gleevec's price, leading one industry economist to remark that she could find no economic theory to explain how pharmaceutical companies set or raise their drug prices.

The prices of some new lifesaving drugs seem more than exorbitant. For example, Bavencio, a recently approved new cancer drug, costs patients about $156,000 a year. And a new muscular dystrophy drug recently debuted at an eye-popping $300,000 annually. But even older drugs that have been on the market for a long time have seen major price increases. For example, despite no changes, insulin tripled in price between 2002 and 2013. And the price of 40-year-old EpiPen, a lifesaving allergy medication, increase 500 percent over the past decade, sparking public outrage.

To add insult to injury, the critics say, drug companies pour more than $6.4 billion a year into direct-to-consumer advertising and spend another $24 billion on marketing to doctors. These marketing efforts dictate higher prices at the same time that they build demand for more expensive remedies. Thus, the severest critics say, the big drug companies may be profiting unfairly—or even at the expense of human life—by promoting and pricing products beyond the reach of many people who need them.

But there's another side to the drug-pricing issue. Industry proponents point out that, over the years, the drug companies have developed a steady stream of medicines that transform people's lives. Developing such new drugs is risky and expensive, involving legions of scientists, expensive technology, and years of effort with no certainty of success. The top 10 pharmaceutical companies combined last year to spend more than

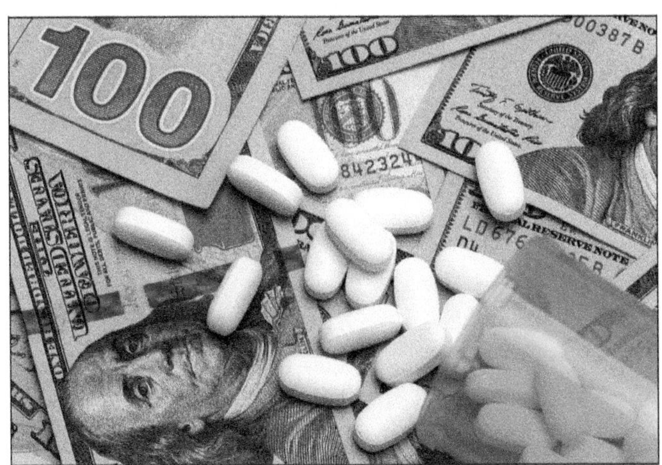

>> Responsible pharmaceutical pricing: Most consumers understand that they'll have to pay the price for beneficial drugs. They just want to be treated fairly in the process.

pixelrobot/123RF

$76 billion on R&D, more than 65 percent of sales. On average, it takes 12 to 15 years and costs between $660 million and $2.7 billion to bring a new drug to market. Thus, the proponents say, although the prices of new prescription drugs seem high, they're needed to fund the development of important future drugs. As one recent Pfizer ad states: "It takes an average of 1,600 scientists 12 years to bring one Pfizer medicine to life. That's a lot of collective brain power dedicated to finding medicines that improve lives." GlaxoSmithKline (GSK) says it this way: "Inventing new medicines isn't easy, but it's worth it.... Today's medicines finance tomorrow's miracles."

And so the controversy continues. As drug prices climb, the pharmaceutical companies face pressures from the federal government, insurance companies, managed-care providers, and consumer advocacy groups to exercise restraint in setting prices. However, rather than waiting for tougher legislation on prices—or simply because it's the right thing to do—many of the drug companies are taking action on their own. For example, some companies have committed to keeping their average price hikes at or below inflation. Others employ tiered pricing—selling their medicines in different countries at varying prices based on ability to pay in each country. Most pharmaceutical companies now sponsor patient assistance programs that provide prescription medicines free or at low cost to people who cannot afford them, and they regularly donate free medicines in response to disaster relief efforts around the globe.

In all, pharmaceutical pricing is no easy issue. For the pharmaceutical companies, it's more than a matter of sales and profits. In setting prices, short-term financial goals must be tempered by broader societal considerations. For example, GSK's heartfelt mission is "to help people do more, feel better, live longer." Accomplishing this mission won't come cheap. Most consumers understand that. One way or another, they know, they'll have to pay the price. All they really ask is that they be treated fairly in the process.

Sources: "Why Our Drugs Cost So Much," *AARP Bulletin,* May 2017, www.aarp.org/health/drugs-supplements/info-2017/rx-prescription-drug-pricing.html; "U.S. Oncologists Decry High Cost of Cancer Drugs," *Health Day,* July 23, 2015, http://consumer.healthday.com/cancer-information-5/mis-cancer-news-102/u-s-oncologists-speak-out-on-high-cost-of-cancer-drugs-701616.html; Rafi Mohammed, "It's Time to Rein In Exorbitant Pharmaceutical Prices," *Harvard Business Review,* September 22, 2015, https://hbr.org/2015/09/its-time-to-rein-in-exorbitant-pharmaceutical-prices; Benjamin Siegel and Mary Bruce, "Former Pharma Big Martin Shkreli Boasted '$1 Bn Here We Come,' Documents Say," February 2, 2016, http://abcnews.go.com/Politics/pharma-big-martin-shkreli-boasted-bn-documents/story?id=36671216; Nancy Yu, Zachary Helms, and Peter Bach, "R&D Costs for Pharmaceutical Companies Do Not Explain Elevated US Drug Prices," *Health Affairs,* March 7, 2017, www.healthaffairs.org/do/10.1377/hblog20170307.059036/full/; Richard Harris, "R&D Costs for Cancer Drugs Are Likely Much Less Than Industry Claims, Study Finds," *NPR,* September 11, 2017, www.npr.org/sections/health-shots/2017/09/11/550135932/r-d-costs-for-cancer-drugs-are-likely-much-less-than-industry-claims-study-finds; and "Our Mission and Strategy," http://us.gsk.com/en-us/about-us/our-mission-and-strategy/, accessed October 2018. For more on the biopharmaceutical industry viewpoint, see www.goboldly.com, accessed October 2018.

Pricing within Channel Levels

Federal legislation on *price-fixing* states that sellers must set prices without talking to competitors. Otherwise, price collusion is suspected. Price-fixing is illegal per se—that is, the government does not accept any excuses for price-fixing. Recently, governments at the state and national levels have been aggressively enforcing price-fixing regulations in industries ranging from gasoline, insurance, and concrete to credit cards, computer chips, and e-books. Companies found guilty of price-fixing practices can pay heavy penalties. For example, Apple paid $450 million in fines for conspiring with publishers to fix prices on e-books. And four major U.S. airlines—United, Delta, Southwest, and American—now face a potentially costly class action suit and U.S. Department of Justice investigation for conspiring to artificially inflate air fares to "reap huge profits."[28]

Sellers are also prohibited from using *predatory pricing*—selling below cost with the intention of punishing a competitor or gaining higher long-run profits by putting competitors out of business. This protects small sellers from larger ones that might sell items below cost temporarily or in a specific locale to drive them out of business. The biggest problem is determining just what constitutes predatory pricing behavior. Selling below cost to unload excess inventory is not considered predatory; selling below cost to drive out competitors is. Thus, a given action may or may not be predatory depending on intent, and intent can be very difficult to determine or prove.

>> Predatory pricing: Some industry critics have accused Amazon.com of pricing books at fire-sale prices that harm competing booksellers. But is it predatory pricing or just plain good competitive marketing?
imageBROKER/Alamy Stock Photo

In recent years, several large and powerful companies have been accused of predatory pricing. However, turning an accusation into a lawsuit can be difficult. >> For example, many publishers and booksellers have expressed concerns about Amazon.com's predatory practices, especially its book pricing:[29]

> Many booksellers and publishers complain that Amazon's book pricing policies are destroying their industry. Amazon routinely sells best-selling hardback books as loss leaders at cut-rate prices. And it peddles e-books at fire-sale prices in order to win customers for its Kindle e-reader and tablets. Such very low book prices have caused considerable damage to competing booksellers, many of whom view Amazon's pricing actions as predatory. According to some industry groups, such practices "harm the interests of America's readers, impoverish the book industry as a whole, and impede the free flow of ideas in our society." Still, no predatory pricing charges have ever been filed against Amazon. It would be extremely difficult to prove that such loss-leader pricing is purposefully predatory as opposed to just plain good competitive marketing. "But wait a minute," states one analyst. "Isn't that what business is supposed to do—compete to lower prices?"

Pricing across Channel Levels

The Robinson-Patman Act seeks to prevent unfair *price discrimination* by ensuring that sellers offer the same price terms to customers at a given level of trade. For example, every retailer is entitled to the same price terms from a given manufacturer, whether the retailer is REI or a local bicycle shop. However, price discrimination is allowed if the seller can prove that its costs are different when selling to different retailers—for example, that it costs less per unit to sell a large volume of bicycles to REI than to sell a few bicycles to the local dealer.

The seller can also discriminate in its pricing if the seller manufactures different qualities of the same product for different retailers. The seller has to prove that these differences are proportional. Price differentials may also be used to "match competition" in "good faith," provided the price discrimination is temporary, localized, and defensive rather than offensive.

Laws also prohibit *retail (or resale) price maintenance*—a manufacturer cannot require dealers to charge a specified retail price for its product. Although the seller can propose a manufacturer's *suggested* retail price to dealers, it cannot refuse to sell to a dealer that takes independent pricing action, nor can it punish the dealer by shipping late or denying advertising allowances. For example, the Florida attorney general's office investigated Nike for allegedly fixing the retail price of its shoes and clothing. It was concerned that Nike might be withholding items from retailers who were not selling its most expensive shoes at prices the company considered suitable.

Deceptive pricing occurs when a seller states prices or price savings that mislead consumers or are not actually available to consumers. This might involve bogus reference or comparison prices, as when a retailer sets artificially high "regular" prices and then announces "sale" prices close to its previous everyday prices. For example, luxury apparel and accessories retailer Michael Kors recently settled a class action lawsuit alleging that it used deceptive pricing at its outlet stores. The retailer was charged with tagging products with false "manufacturer's suggested retail prices" to make its supposed discounted prices more appealing when, in fact, the products were sold only in the outlet stores. Such artificial comparison pricing is widespread in retailing.[30]

Although comparison pricing claims are legal if they are truthful, the Federal Trade Commission's "Guides against Deceptive Pricing" warn sellers not to advertise (1) a price reduction unless it is a savings from the usual retail price, (2) "factory" or "wholesale" prices unless such prices are what they are claimed to be, and (3) comparable value prices on imperfect goods.[31]

Other deceptive pricing issues include *scanner fraud* and price confusion. The widespread use of scanner-based computer checkouts has led to increasing complaints of retailers overcharging their customers. Most of these overcharges result from poor management, such as a failure to enter current or sale prices into the system. Other cases, however, involve intentional overcharges.

Many federal and state statutes regulate against deceptive pricing practices. For example, the Automobile Information Disclosure Act requires automakers to attach a statement on new vehicle windows stating the manufacturer's suggested retail price, the prices of optional equipment, and the dealer's transportation charges. However, reputable sellers go beyond what is required by law. Treating customers fairly and making certain that they fully understand prices and pricing terms are an important part of building strong and lasting customer relationships.

REVIEWING AND EXTENDING THE CONCEPTS

CHAPTER REVIEW AND KEY TERMS

Objectives Review

Pricing decisions are subject to an incredibly complex array of company, environmental, and competitive forces.

OBJECTIVE 9-1 Define price, identify the three major pricing strategies, and discuss the importance of understanding customer-value perceptions, company costs, and competitor strategies when setting prices. (pp 267–274)

Price can be defined as the sum of all the values that customers give up in order to gain the benefits of having or using a product or service. The three major pricing strategies include customer value-based pricing, cost-based pricing, and competition-based pricing. Good pricing begins with a complete understanding of the value that a product or service creates for customers and setting a price that captures that value.

Customer perceptions of the product's value set the ceiling for prices. If customers perceive that the price is greater than the product's value, they will not buy the product. At the other extreme, company and product costs set the floor for prices. If the company prices the product below its costs, its profits will suffer. Between these two extremes, consumers will base their judgments of a product's value on the prices that competitors charge for similar products. Thus, in setting prices, companies need to consider all three factors, customer perceived value, costs, and competitors pricing strategies.

Costs are an important consideration in setting prices. However, cost-based pricing is often product driven. The company designs what it considers to be a good product and sets a price that covers costs plus a target profit. If the price turns out to be too high, the company must settle for lower markups or lower sales, both resulting in disappointing profits. Value-based pricing reverses this process. The company assesses customer needs and value perceptions and then sets a target prices to match targeted value. The targeted value and price then drive decisions about product design and what costs can be incurred. As a result, price is set to match customers' perceived value.

OBJECTIVE 9-2 Identify and define the other important external and internal factors affecting a firm's pricing decisions. (pp 274–278)

Other *internal* factors that influence pricing decisions include the company's overall marketing strategy, objectives, and marketing mix, as well as organizational considerations. Price is only one element of the company's broader marketing strategy. If the company has selected its target market and positioning carefully, then its marketing mix strategy, including price, will be fairly straightforward. Common pricing objectives might include customer retention and building profitable customer relationships, preventing competition, supporting resellers and gaining their support, or avoiding government intervention. Price decisions must be coordinated with product design, distribution, and promotion decisions to form a consistent and effective marketing program. Finally, in order to coordinate pricing goals and decisions, management must decide who within the organization is responsible for setting price.

Other *external* pricing considerations include the nature of the market and demand and environmental factors such as the economy, reseller needs, and government actions. Ultimately, the customer decides whether the company has set the right price. The customer weighs the price against the perceived values of using the product—if the price exceeds the sum of the values, consumers will not buy. So the company must understand concepts like demand curves (the price-demand relationship) and price elasticity (consumer sensitivity to prices).

Economic conditions can have a major impact on pricing decisions. The Great Recession caused consumers to rethink the price-value equation. Marketers have responded by increasing their emphasis on value-for-the-money pricing strategies. Even in tight economic times, however, consumers do not buy based on prices alone. Thus, no matter what price they charge—low or high—companies need to offer superior value for the money.

OBJECTIVE 9-3 Describe the major strategies for pricing new products. (p 279)

Pricing is a dynamic process. Companies design a *pricing structure* that covers all their products. They change this structure over time and adjust it to account for different customers and situations. Pricing strategies usually change as a product passes through its life cycle. In pricing innovative new products, a company can use *market-skimming pricing* by initially setting high prices to "skim" the maximum amount of revenue from various segments of the market. Or it can use *market-penetrating pricing* by setting a low initial price to penetrate the market deeply and win a large market share.

OBJECTIVE 9-4 Explain how companies find a set of prices that maximizes the profits from the total product mix. (pp 280–281)

When the product is part of a product mix, the firm searches for a set of prices that will maximize the profits from the total mix. In *product line pricing*, the company decides on price steps for the entire set of products it offers. In addition, the company must set prices for *optional products* (optional or accessory products included with the main product), *captive products* (products that are required for use of the main product), *by-products* (waste or residual products produced when making the main product), and *product bundles* (combinations of products at a reduced price).

 **OBJECTIVE 9-5 Discuss how companies adjust and change their prices to take into account different types of customers and situations. (pp 282–292)**

Companies apply a variety of *price adjustment strategies* to account for differences in consumer segments and situations. One is *discount and allowance pricing*, whereby the company establishes cash, quantity, functional, or seasonal discounts, or varying types of allowances. A second strategy is *segmented pricing*, where the company sells a product at two or more prices to accommodate different customers, product forms, locations, or times. Sometimes companies consider more than economics in their pricing decisions, using *psychological pricing* to better communicate a product's intended position. In *promotional pricing*, a company offers discounts or temporarily sells a product below list price as a special event, sometimes even selling below cost as a loss leader. Another approach is *geographical pricing*, whereby the company decides how to price to near or distant customers. In *dynamic pricing*, companies adjust prices continually to meet the characteristics and needs of individual customers and situations. Finally, *international pricing* means that the company adjusts its price to meet different conditions and expectations in different world markets.

When a firm considers initiating a *price change*, it must consider customers' and competitors' reactions. There are different implications to *initiating price cuts* and *initiating price increases*. Buyer reactions to price changes are influenced by the meaning customers see in the price change. Competitors' reactions flow from a set reaction policy or a fresh analysis of each situation.

There are also many factors to consider in responding to a competitor's price changes. The company that faces a price change initiated by a competitor must try to understand the competitor's intent as well as the likely duration and impact of the change. If a swift reaction is desirable, the firm should preplan its reactions to different possible price actions by competitors. When facing a competitor's price change, the company might sit tight, reduce its own price, raise perceived quality, improve quality and raise price, or launch a fighting brand.

 **OBJECTIVE 9-6 Discuss the major public policy concerns and key pieces of legislation that affect pricing decisions. (pp 292–295)**

Price competition is a core element of our free-market economy. In setting prices, companies usually are not free to charge whatever prices they wish. Marketers must heed federal, state, and local laws govern pricing. In addition, companies must consider broader societal pricing concerns. The major public policy issues in pricing include potentially damaging pricing practices within a given level of the channel (price-fixing and predatory pricing) and across levels of the channel (retail price maintenance, discriminatory pricing, and deceptive pricing). Reputable marketers go beyond what is required by law. Treating customers fairly and making certain that they fully understand prices and pricing terms are an important part of building strong and lasting customer relationships.

Key Terms

Objective 9-1
Price (p 266)
Customer value-based pricing (p 267)
Good-value pricing (p 269)
Value-added pricing (p 269)
Cost-based pricing (p 271)
Fixed costs (overhead) (p 271)
Variable costs (p 271)
Total costs (p 272)
Cost-plus pricing (markup pricing) (p 272)
Break-even pricing (target return pricing) (p 272)
Competition-based pricing (p 273)

Objective 9-2
Target costing (p 275)
Demand curve (p 277)
Price elasticity (p 277)

Objective 9-3
Market-skimming pricing (price skimming) (p 279)
Market-penetration pricing (p 279)

Objective 9-4
Product line pricing (p 280)
Optional-product pricing (p 280)
Captive-product pricing (p 280)
By-product pricing (p 281)
Product bundle pricing (p 281)

Objective 9-5
Discount (p 282)
Allowance (p 282)
Segmented pricing (p 282)
Psychological pricing (p 283)
Reference prices (p 284)
Promotional pricing (p 284)
Geographical pricing (p 285)
Dynamic pricing (p 286)

DISCUSSION AND CRITICAL THINKING

Discussion Questions

9-1. Why is finding and implementing the right pricing strategy critical to a company's success? (AACSB: Written and Oral Communication)

9-2. What is cost-based pricing? How do companies use fixed and variable costs in cost-based pricing models? (AACSB: Written and Oral Communication)

9-3. Explain the price–demand relationship. What factors must sellers consider when setting prices in different types of markets? (AACSB: Written and Oral Communication)

9-4. Discuss the two new product pricing strategies, and provide an example to illustrate each. Discuss the challenges faced by companies launching new products under each of these strategies. (AACSB: Written and Oral Communication)

9-5. Why might the strategy for setting a product's price need to be changed when a product is part of a product mix? What are the five product mix pricing strategies? Provide an example for each. (AACSB: Written and Oral Communication; Reflective Thinking)

9-6. Compare fixed pricing with dynamic pricing. Illustrate how and when each of these strategies is used. (AACSB: Written and Oral Communication)

Critical Thinking Exercises

9-7. Congratulations! You just won your state lottery and will be receiving a check for $1 million. You have always wanted to own your own business and have noticed the increase in the number of food trucks in your local area. A new food truck with a kitchen and related equipment costs about $100,000. Other fixed costs include salaries, gas for the truck, and license fees and are estimated to be about $50,000 per year. You decide to offer traditional Mediterranean cuisine. Variable costs include food and beverages estimated at $6 per platter (meat, rice, vegetable, and pita bread). Meals will be priced at $10. Calculate the break-even for your food truck business. After reviewing your break-even, what changes would you consider? Is this how you want to spend your lottery winnings? (AACSB: Written and Oral Communication; Reflective Thinking)

9-8. Alicia is a self-employed hair stylist who owns her own salon. She has asked you to consult with her on how to generate more revenue. Using the price adjustment strategies discussed in the chapter, advise Alicia on her options to increase overall sales. (AACSB: Written and Oral Communication; Reflective Thinking)

9-9. Your company has developed a new weight-loss breakfast shake that has proven to be successful in the test market phase. Users have experienced an average weight loss of two pounds per week. You hold a patent on the product. The cost to produce the shake is relatively low, with a total manufacturing costs running about $0.05 per ounce. Each shake is eight ounces. What pricing strategy do you recommend for this product? (AACSB: Written and Oral Communication; Information Technology; Reflective Thinking)

MINICASES AND APPLICATIONS

Online, Mobile, and Social Media Marketing Krazy Coupon Lady

Price-conscious consumers are all about finding the best deal. Some even make a sport out of it! Krazy couponers Heather and Joanie have been showcased on many national television shows and in web and print articles. The two friends run a highly successful company that works tirelessly to uncover the best deals, enabling families to save money. Posted on their website, www.krazycouponlady.com, is the company mantra "You'd be krazy not to be one of us!" The website features promotions and alerts to special pricing on products as well as coupons and discounts to help consumers stretch their dollars. Also featured are retailers with sale-priced merchandise, coupons, and promotions. Community members post their best deals in the brag section.

9-10. Visit www.krazycouponlady.com, and browse a deal you would consider purchasing. After identifying the deal, conduct an online price comparison at various retailers to determine the range of prices you would typically pay for the product. Present your conclusions. (AACSB: Written and Oral Communication; Information Technology; Reflective Thinking)

9-11. Using www.krazycouponlady.com, click on Stores, Coupons, and Deals on the navigation bar, and make a list of the featured products. Identify the pricing strategy used by the retailer. (AACSB: Written and Oral Communication; Information Technology; Reflective Thinking)

Marketing Ethics Less Bang for Your Buck

Over the past several years, careful shoppers may be spending about the same amount of money at the grocery store but leaving the store with a lighter load in their grocery bags. Food prices on many items have increased, and food manufacturers are facing the same challenges as consumers. With increases in raw materials and transportation, making a profit requires a very sharp pencil. According to Phil Lempert, editor of SupermarketGuru.com, "The reality is, if you look at USDA projections, food is going to get more expensive. And as a result, food companies are going to do one of two or three things: Raise prices and keep packages the same, or reduce the quantity in the package. Or do a little of both."

9-12. Week after week, consumers shop for many of the same groceries. At some point, the product may be priced the same and look the same as before but with less in the package. If consumers are not made aware of the change, is this deception? Is this different from deceptive pricing? Explain. (AACSB: Written and Oral Communication; Ethical Understanding and Reasoning; Reflective Thinking)

9-13. Develop a list of the products you buy from a grocery store, dollar store, or convenience store where one of two things has occurred: the price has increased or the quantity in the package has decreased. Were you aware of the change? Explain. (AACSB: Written and Oral Communication; Reflective Thinking)

Marketing by the Numbers Rock Bottom Promotional Pricing

Rock Bottom Golf is an online golf equipment retailer that sells clubs, shoes, balls, and all the other gadgets golfers could ever need. Rock Bottom's prices are lower than those of most brick-and-mortar golf and sporting goods retailers, but they often go even lower with limited-time promotional pricing, especially around major holidays. For example, the Father's Day promotion offers $50 off Rock Bottom's already low price on select clubs and range finders that normally cost hundreds of dollars. One current offer is $50 off the Tour Edge EX10 Driver that Rock Bottom normally sells for $249.99. To get the word out about the offer, Rock Bottom spent $10,000 on banner ads on golf-related websites like www.golfchannel.com and www.pga.com. Rock Bottom understands that promotional pricing cuts into its profits for each sale but also knows that such pricing generates excitement and a sense of urgency among buyers because of the limited time the promotional price is available. In fact, Rock Bottom's research of past Father's Day promotions shows that it's mostly men buying the clubs and gadgets for themselves!

9-14. Assuming Rock Bottom's cost of goods sold (COGS) is 60 percent, calculate Rock Bottom's margin per driver before the $50 off promotional price and after the promotional price. What effect does the promotional pricing have on the margin Rock Bottom earns for every driver sold? Refer to Break-Even and Margin Analysis in Appendix 3: Marketing by the Numbers to learn how to perform this analysis. (AACSB: Written and Oral Communication; Analytical Thinking; Reflective Thinking)

9-15. How many additional drivers must Rock Bottom sell to break even on this promotion? Assume the $10,000 spent on banner ads is the only fixed cost associated with this promotion. (AACSB: Analytical Thinking)

Video Case Fast-Food Discount Wars

To view this video case and its accompanying questions, please visit MyLab Marketing.

Fast-food chains are locked in a fierce battle that has them practically giving food away. McDonald's, Wendy's, Burger King, and others are constantly trying to lure customers at the low end of the price spectrum with tempting menu options that can serve as a snack or a meal. Although this technique is nothing new, it's more popular today than ever. The tactic has even found its way into full-service restaurant chains such as Olive Garden.

But are bargain-basement options a sustainable path for restaurant chains? This video takes a look at the various ways discount menus are executed. It also considers the reasons for using discount menu tactics as well as the possible negative outcomes.

Company Cases 9 Trader Joe's/5 Spanx/10 Target

See Appendix 1 for cases appropriate for this chapter.

Case 9, Trader Joe's: Cheap Gourmet—Putting a Special Twist on the Price-Value Equation. Trader Joe's provides superior customer value by providing the perfect ratio of benefits to prices.

Case 5, Spanx: Changing the Way an Industry Thinks about Underwear. Spanx revolutionized the world of women's undergarments with a premium product at a premium price.

Case 10, Target: A Serious Contender in the Same-Day Delivery Business. Struggling to maintain growth in the world of discount retailing, Target recently scored a coup by acquiring same-day delivery startup Shipt.

Writing Assignments

9-16. Describe the cost-plus pricing method and discuss why marketers use it even if it is not the best method for setting prices. (AACSB: Communication)

9-17. Compare and contrast fixed costs and variable costs and discuss their importance in setting prices. (AACSB: Written and Oral Communication; Reflective Thinking)

10 Marketing Channels

Delivering Customer Value

Objectives Outline

OBJECTIVE 10-1 **Explain why companies use marketing channels and discuss the functions these channels perform.** See: Supply Chains and the Value Delivery Network (pp 302–306)

OBJECTIVE 10-2 **Discuss how channel members interact and how they organize to perform the work of the channel.** See: Channel Behavior and Organization (pp 306–313)

OBJECTIVE 10-3 **Identify the major channel alternatives open to a company.** See: Channel Design Decisions (pp 314–317)

OBJECTIVE 10-4 **Explain how companies select, motivate, and evaluate channel members.** See: Channel Management Decisions (pp 317–321)

OBJECTIVE 10-5 **Discuss the nature and importance of marketing logistics and integrated supply chain management.** See: Marketing Logistics and Supply Chain Management (pp 321–328)

Previewing the Concepts

We now look at the third marketing mix tool—distribution. Companies rarely work alone in engaging customers, creating customer value, and building profitable customer relationships. Instead, most are only a single link in a larger supply chain and marketing channel. As such, a firm's success depends not only on how well *it* performs but also on how well its *entire marketing channel* competes with competitors' channels. The first part of this chapter explores the nature of marketing channels and the marketer's channel design and management decisions. We then examine physical distribution—or logistics—an area that has grown dramatically in importance and sophistication. In the next chapter, we'll look more closely at two major channel intermediaries: retailers and wholesalers.

We start by looking at Netflix. Through innovative distribution, Netflix has become the world's largest video subscription service. But as baseball great Yogi Berra, known more for his mangled phrasing than for his baseball prowess, once said, "The future ain't what it used to be." To stay atop the churning video distribution industry, Netflix must continue to innovate at a break-neck pace or risk being pushed aside.

First Stop

Netflix's Channel Innovation: Finding the Future by Abandoning the Past

» **Netflix's innovative distribution strategy: From DVDs by mail to Watch Instantly to streaming on almost any device and creating original content, Netflix has lead the howling pack by doing what it does best—revolutionize distribution. What's next?**

sitthiphong/Shutterstock

Time and again, Netflix has innovated its way to the top in video entertainment distribution. In the early 2000s, Netflix's revolutionary DVD-by-mail service put all but the most powerful movie-rental stores out of business. In 2007, Netflix's then-groundbreaking move into digital streaming once again revolutionized how people accessed movies and other video content. Since then, Netflix has continued to break new ground by making its services available through any and all digital and mobile devices and by creating its own original content. With Netflix leading the pack, video distribution has now become a roiling pot of emerging technologies and high-tech competitors, one that offers both mind-bending opportunities and stomach-churning risks.

Just ask Blockbuster, the former brick-and-mortar movie-rental chain that once flat-out owned the industry. Then along came Netflix, the fledgling DVD-by-mail service. First thousands, then millions, of subscribers were drawn to Netflix's innovative distribution model, catching market-leading Blockbuster off guard and eventually pulling the rug out from under it. In 2010, as Netflix surged, once-mighty Blockbuster fell into bankruptcy.

The Blockbuster riches-to-rags story underscores the turmoil that typifies the video distribution business today. In only the past few years, a glut of video access options has materialized. At the same time that Netflix ascended and Blockbuster plunged, Coinstar's Redbox came out of nowhere to build a novel national network of $1-a-day DVD-rental kiosks. Then high-tech venues such as Hulu and Crackle began pushing on-demand digital streaming through a model of ad-supported free viewing.

All along the way, Netflix has acted boldly to stay ahead of the competition. For example, by 2007, Netflix had mailed out its one-billionth DVD. But rather than rest on success, Netflix and its CEO, Reed Hastings, set their sights on a then-revolutionary new video distribution model: Deliver Netflix to any and every Internet-connected screen—from laptops to Internet-ready TVs to smartphones and other Wi-Fi-enabled devices. Netflix launched its Watch Instantly service, which let members stream movies to their internet-connected devices as part of their monthly fee, even if it came at the expense of the company's still-hot DVD-by-mail business.

Although Netflix didn't pioneer digital streaming, it poured resources into improving the technology and building the largest streaming content library. It built a huge subscriber base, and sales and profits soared. With its massive physical DVD library and a streaming library of more than 20,000 high-definition movies accessible via 200 different devices, it seemed that nothing could stop Netflix.

But Netflix's stunning success drew a slew of resourceful competitors. Video giants such as Google's YouTube and Apple's iTunes began renting movie downloads, and Hulu and Amazon expanded their libraries and added subscription-based streaming services with Hulu Plus and Amazon Prime Video. To stay ahead, even to survive, Netflix needed to keep the innovation pedal to the metal. So in the summer of 2011, in an ambitious but risky move, CEO Hastings made an all-in bet on digital streaming. He split off Netflix's still-thriving DVD-by-mail service into a separate business with a separate subscription fee.

Time and again, Netflix has innovated its way to the top in the distribution of video entertainment. But to stay atop its boiling, roiling industry, Netflix must keep the distribution innovation pedal to the metal.

Although subscribership dipped temporarily as some customers jumped ship, Hastings had made a visionary move. Now more than ever, Netflix's heavy focus is on streaming video. Some 96.5 percent of the company's current 118 million paid subscribers are now streaming-only customers. Netflix subscribers stream an astounding 4.2 billion hours of movies and TV programs every month. On an average weeknight, Netflix commands one-third of all internet traffic in North American homes. And the company has expanded globally into more than 190 countries. Streaming now accounts for nearly all of Netflix's fast-growing revenues.

Despite its sustained success, Netflix knows that it can't rest its distribution innovation machine. Competition continues to move at a blurring rate. For example, Amazon's Prime Instant Video offers streaming access to its ever-expanding library of movies and TV shows to Prime members at no extra cost. YouTube's Red subscription service, backed by parent Google's deep pockets, offers ad-free access to videos and to members-only original shows and movies from top YouTubers. And even as Netflix has been the prime force behind the cord-cutting trend—in which consumers abandon traditional cable or satellite TV services in favor of over-the-top video streaming—the traditional networks and services are fighting back with their own subscription streaming options, such as Comcast's Xfinity Streampix, HBO Now, CBS All Access, and DirectTV Now, to name only a few. Some services even provide streaming access to live TV.

For years, as the industry has settled into streaming as the main delivery model, Netflix has known that content—not just delivery—is key to staying ahead in video distribution. Given its head start, Netflix remains ahead in the content race. But with more competitors working feverishly to sign contracts with big movie and television content providers, content-licensing deals are harder and more expensive to get and keep.

So, in yet another innovative twist, to decrease its reliance on content from outside sources, Netflix has been producing and distributing its own original content at a torrid pace. Seven years ago, it shocked the industry when it paid $100 million to out-bid HBO and AMC for exclusive rights to air the first two seasons of *House of Cards*. The show was a huge success, and Netflix moved rapidly to develop other original series, including *Master of None, Unbreakable Kimmy Schmidt, Daredevil,* and *Orange Is the New Black*.

Although Netflix's streaming competitors have once again followed the leader by creating their own original content, Netflix still has the upper hand. Last year it released an estimated 126 original series or films, more than any single network or cable channel. Netflix puts out a mountain of content monthly, and its library bulges with an exploding array of original series, movies, documentaries, comedy specials, and even a talk show series with retired late-night legend David Letterman.

Such efforts have left the rest of the industry scrambling to keep up. And Netflix is just getting started. In the coming year, Netflix will spend an astounding $8 billion on original content. It plans to release a staggering 80 original motion pictures, more than the output of all the major Hollywood studios combined. The intent is clear: in a more tumultuous video environment, Netflix intends to control its own destiny by locking down ownership of its content. According to Netflix executives, within a year, half of the company's vast video library will be its own original content.

Thus, from DVDs by mail, to Watch Instantly, to video streaming on almost any device, to dominating with original content, Netflix has stayed ahead of the howling pack by doing what it does best—innovate and revolutionize distribution. In *Fast Company*'s most recent list of the 50 most innovative companies, Netflix is number two, trailing only Apple. Its revenues and streaming subscribership have doubled in just the past three years, and its stock price has surged 1,000 percent in the past five years.

What's next? No one really knows. But one thing seems certain: Whatever's coming, if Netflix doesn't lead the change, it risks being left behind—and quickly. In this fast-changing business, new tricks grow old in a hurry. To stay ahead, as one headline suggests, Netflix must "find its future by abandoning its past."[1]

As the Netflix story shows, good distribution strategies can contribute strongly to customer value and create competitive advantage for a firm. But firms cannot bring value to customers by themselves. Instead, they must work closely with other firms in a larger value delivery network.

Author Comment
These are pretty hefty terms for a really simple concept: A company can't go it alone in creating customer value. It must work within a broader network of partners to accomplish this task. Individual companies and brands don't compete; their entire value delivery networks do.

Supply Chains and the Value Delivery Network

OBJECTIVE 10-1 Explain why companies use marketing channels and discuss the functions these channels perform.

Producing a product or service and making it available to buyers requires building relationships not only with customers but also with key suppliers and resellers in the company's *supply chain*. This supply chain consists of upstream and downstream partners. Upstream from the company is the set of firms that supply the raw materials, components, parts, information, finances, and expertise needed to create a product or service. Marketers, however, have traditionally focused on the downstream side of the supply chain—the *marketing channels* (or *distribution channels*) that look toward the customer. Downstream marketing channel partners, such as wholesalers and retailers, form a vital link between the firm and its customers.

The term *supply chain* may be too limited, as it takes a *make-and-sell* view of the business. It suggests that raw materials, productive inputs, and factory capacity

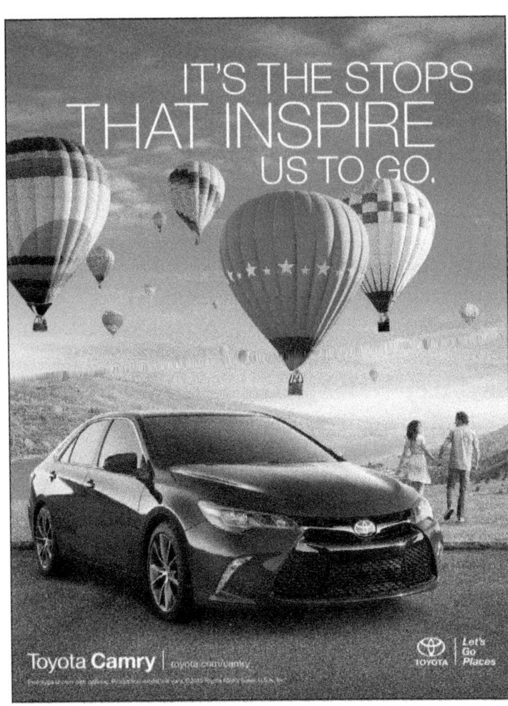
IT'S THE STOPS
THAT INSPIRE
US TO GO.
Toyota Camry
TOYOTA
Let's
Go
Places

>> Value delivery network: In making and marketing its lines of cars, Toyota manages a huge network of people within the company plus thousands of outside suppliers, dealers, and marketing service firms that work together to deliver the brand's "Let's Go Places" promise.

Toyota Motor Sales

should serve as the starting point for market planning. A better term would be *demand chain* because it suggests a *sense-and-respond* view of the market. Under this view, planning starts by identifying the needs of target customers, to which the company responds by organizing a chain of resources and activities with the goal of creating customer value.

Yet even a demand chain view of a business may be too limited because it takes a step-by-step, linear view of purchase-production-consumption activities. Instead, most large companies today are engaged in building and managing a complex, continuously evolving value delivery network. As defined in Chapter 2, a **value delivery network** is made up of the company, suppliers, distributors, and, ultimately, customers who "partner" with each other to improve the performance of the entire system. >> For example, Toyota makes great cars. But to make and market just one of its many lines—say, its best-selling Camry model—Toyota manages a huge network of people within the company, from marketing and sales people to folks in finance and operations. It also coordinates the efforts of thousands of suppliers, dealers, and advertising agencies and other marketing service firms. The entire network must function together to create customer value and establish the brand's "Let's Go Places" positioning.

This chapter focuses on marketing channels—on the downstream side of the value delivery network. We examine four major questions concerning marketing channels: What is the nature of marketing channels, and why are they important? How do channel firms interact and organize to do the work of the channel? What problems do companies face in designing and managing their channels? What role do physical distribution and supply chain management play in attracting and satisfying customers? In the next chapter, we will look at marketing channel issues from the viewpoints of retailers and wholesalers.

Author Comment

In this section, we look at the downstream side of the value delivery network—the marketing channel organizations that connect the company and its customers. To understand their value, imagine life without retailers—say, without grocery stores or department stores.

The Nature and Importance of Marketing Channels

Few producers sell their goods directly to final users. Instead, most use intermediaries to bring their products to market. They try to forge a **marketing channel** (or **distribution channel**)—a set of interdependent organizations that help make a product or service available for use or consumption by the consumer or business user.

A company's channel decisions directly affect every other marketing decision. Pricing depends on whether the company works with national discount chains, uses high-quality specialty stores, or sells directly to consumers online. The firm's sales force and communications decisions depend on how much persuasion, training, motivation, and support its channel partners need. Whether a company develops or acquires certain new products may depend on how well those products fit the capabilities of its channel members.

Companies often pay too little attention to their distribution channels—sometimes with damaging results. In contrast, many companies have used imaginative distribution systems to gain a competitive advantage. Enterprise Rent-A-Car revolutionized the car-rental business by setting up off-airport rental offices. Apple turned the retail music business on its head by selling music for the iPod via the internet on iTunes. FedEx's creative and imposing distribution system made it a leader in express package delivery. Uber and Airbnb, with the sharing models, have disrupted the taxi and hospitality businesses. And Amazon.com forever changed the face of retailing and became the Walmart of the internet by selling anything and everything without using physical stores.

Distribution channel decisions often involve long-term commitments to other firms. For example, companies such as Ford, McDonald's, or Nike can easily change their

Value delivery network
A network composed of the company, suppliers, distributors, and, ultimately, customers who partner with each other to improve the performance of the entire system in delivering customer value.

Marketing channel (distribution channel)
A set of interdependent organizations that help make a product or service available for use or consumption by the consumer or business user.

advertising, pricing, or promotion programs. They can scrap old products and introduce new ones as market tastes demand. But when they set up distribution channels through contracts with franchisees, independent dealers, or large retailers, they cannot readily replace these channels with company-owned stores or internet sites if the conditions change. Therefore, management must design its channels carefully, with an eye on both today's likely selling environment and tomorrow's as well.

How Channel Members Add Value

Why do producers give some of the selling job to channel partners? After all, doing so means giving up some control over how and to whom they sell their products. Producers use intermediaries because they create greater efficiency in making goods available to target markets. Through their contacts, experience, specialization, and scale of operation, intermediaries usually offer the firm more than it can achieve on its own.

>> **Figure 10.1** shows how using intermediaries can provide economies. Figure 10.1A shows three manufacturers, each using direct marketing to reach three customers. This system requires nine different contacts. Figure 10.1B shows the three manufacturers working through one distributor, which contacts the three customers. This system requires only six contacts. In this way, intermediaries reduce the amount of work that must be done by both producers and consumers.

From the economic system's point of view, the role of marketing intermediaries is to transform the assortments of products made by producers into the assortments wanted by consumers. Producers make narrow assortments of products in large quantities, but consumers want broad assortments of products in small quantities. Marketing channel members buy large quantities from many producers and break them down into the smaller quantities and broader assortments desired by consumers.

For example, Unilever makes millions of bars of Dove Beauty Bar soap each week. However, you most likely want to buy only a few bars at a time. Therefore, big food, drug, and discount retailers, such as Safeway, Walgreens, and Target, buy Dove by the truckload and stock it on their stores' shelves. In turn, you can buy a single bar of Dove along with a shopping cart full of small quantities of toothpaste, shampoo, and other related products as you need them. Thus, intermediaries play an important role in matching supply and demand.

Marketing channel intermediaries make buying a lot easier for consumers. Again, think about life without grocery retailers. How would you go about buying that 12-pack of Coke or any of the hundreds of other items that you now routinely drop into your shopping cart?

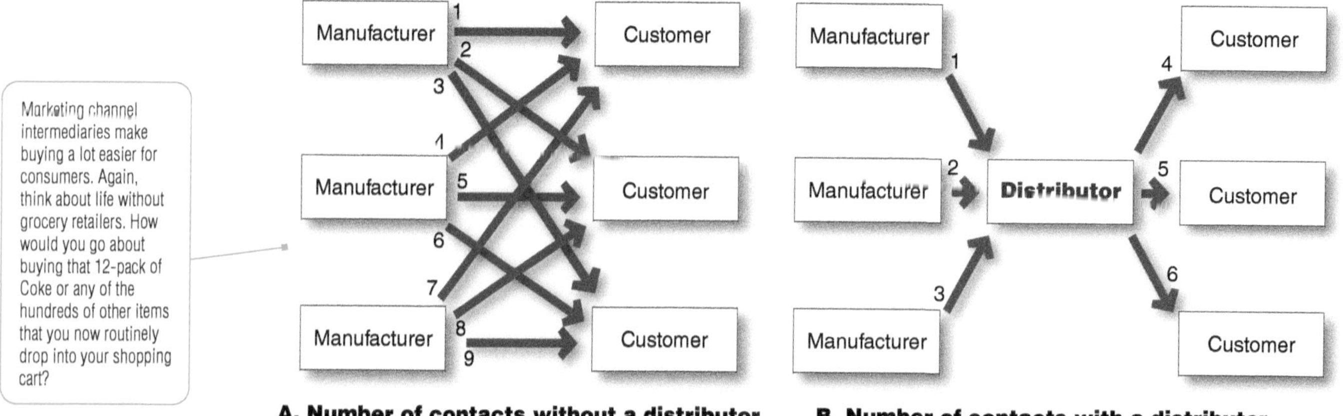

>> **Figure 10.1 How a Distributor Reduces the Number of Channel Transactions**

In making products and services available to consumers, channel members add value by bridging the major time, place, and possession gaps that separate goods and services from those who use them. Members of the marketing channel perform many key functions. Some help to complete transactions:

- ***Information.*** Gathering and distributing information about consumers, producers, and other actors and forces in the marketing environment needed for planning and aiding exchange.
- ***Promotion.*** Developing and spreading persuasive communications about an offer.
- ***Contact.*** Finding and engaging customers and prospective buyers.
- ***Matching.*** Shaping offers to meet the buyer's needs, including activities such as manufacturing, grading, assembling, and packaging.
- ***Negotiation.*** Reaching an agreement on price and other terms so that ownership or possession can be transferred.

Others help to fulfill the completed transactions:

- ***Physical distribution.*** Transporting and storing goods.
- ***Financing.*** Acquiring and using funds to cover the costs of the channel work.
- ***Risk taking.*** Assuming the risks of carrying out the channel work.

The question is not *whether* these functions need to be performed—they must be—but rather *who* will perform them. To the extent that the manufacturer performs these functions, its costs go up; therefore, its prices must be higher. When some of these functions are shifted to intermediaries, the producer's costs and prices may be lower, but the intermediaries must charge more to cover the costs of their work. In dividing the work of the channel, the various functions should be assigned to the channel members that can add the most value for the cost.

Number of Channel Levels

Channel level
A layer of intermediaries that performs some work in bringing the product and its ownership closer to the final buyer.

Companies can design their distribution channels to make products and services available to customers in different ways. Each layer of marketing intermediaries that performs some work in bringing the product and its ownership closer to the final buyer is a **channel level**. Because both the producer and the final consumer perform some work, they are part of every channel.

Direct marketing channel
A marketing channel that has no intermediary levels.

Indirect marketing channel
A marketing channel containing one or more intermediary levels.

The *number of intermediary levels* indicates the *length* of a channel. **>> Figure 10.2** shows both consumer and business channels of different lengths. Figure 10.2A shows several common consumer distribution channels. Channel 1, a **direct marketing channel**, has no intermediary levels—the company sells directly to consumers. For example, Pampered Chef, Mary Kay Cosmetics, and Amway sell their products through home and office sales parties and online websites and social media; companies ranging from GEICO insurance to Quicken Loans to Omaha Steaks sell directly to customers via internet, mobile, and telephone channels. The remaining channels in Figure 10.2A are **indirect marketing channels**, containing one or more intermediaries.

Figure 10.2B shows some common business distribution channels. The business marketer can use its own sales force to sell directly to business customers. Or it can sell to various types of intermediaries, which in turn sell to these customers. Although consumer and business marketing channels with even more levels can sometimes be found, these are less common. From the producer's point of view, a greater number of levels means less control and greater channel complexity. Moreover, all the institutions in the channel are connected by several types of *flows*. These include the *physical flow* of products, the *flow of ownership*, the *payment flow*, the *information flow*, and the *promotion flow*. These flows can make even channels with only one or a few levels very complex.

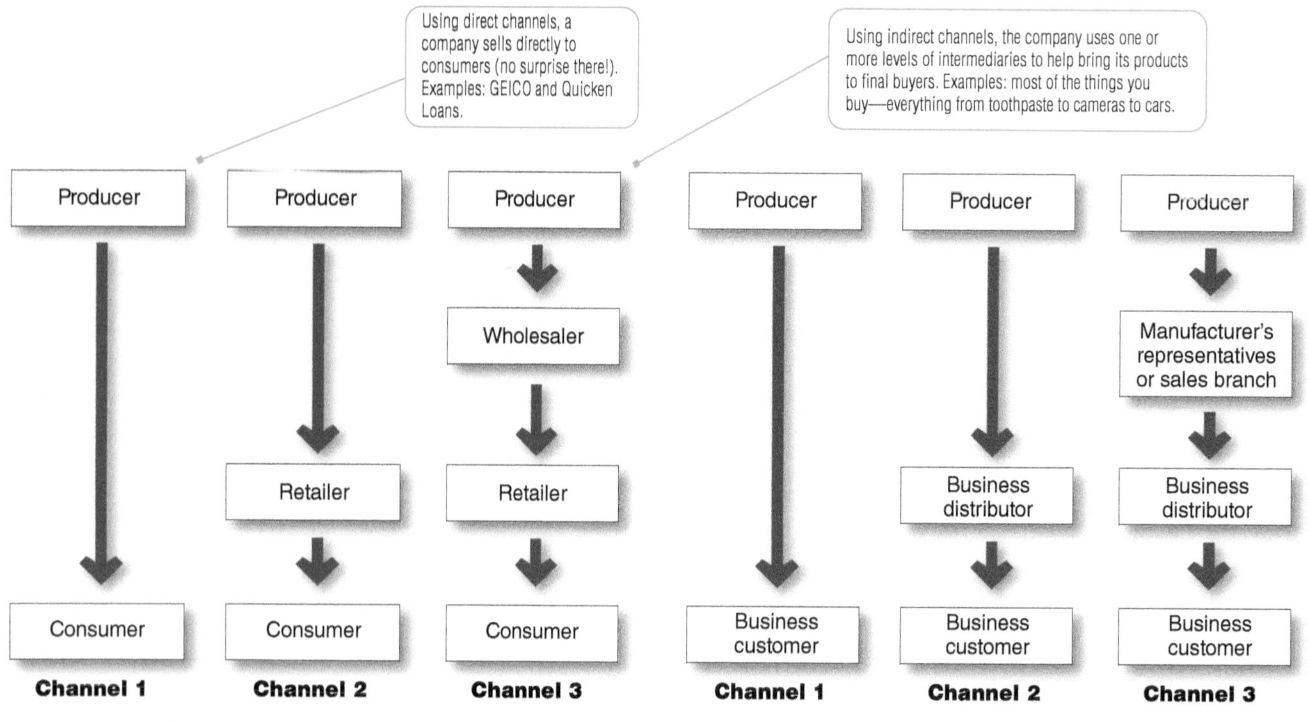

Figure 10.2 Consumer and Business Marketing Channels

Author Comment
Channels are made up of more than just boxes and arrows on paper. They are behavioral systems consisting of real companies and people who interact to accomplish their individual and collective goals. Like groups of people, sometimes they work well together and sometimes they don't.

Channel Behavior and Organization

OBJECTIVE 10-2 Discuss how channel members interact and how they organize to perform the work of the channel.

Distribution channels are more than simple collections of firms tied together by various flows. They are complex behavioral systems in which people and companies interact to accomplish individual, company, and channel goals. Some channel systems consist of only informal interactions among loosely organized firms. Others consist of formal interactions guided by strong organizational structures. Moreover, channel systems do not stand still—new types of intermediaries emerge and whole new channel systems evolve. Here we look at channel behavior and how members organize to do the work of the channel.

Channel Behavior

A marketing channel consists of firms that have partnered for their common good. Each channel member depends on the others. For example, a Ford dealer depends on Ford to design cars that meet customer needs. In turn, Ford depends on the dealer to engage customers, persuade them to buy Ford cars, and service the cars after the sale. Each Ford dealer also depends on other dealers to provide good sales and service that will uphold the brand's reputation. In fact, the success of individual Ford dealers depends on how well the entire Ford marketing channel competes with the channels of Toyota, GM, Honda, and other auto manufacturers.

Each channel member plays a specialized role in the channel. For example, Samsung's role is to produce electronics products that consumers will covet and create demand through national advertising. Best Buy's role is to display these Samsung products in convenient locations, answer buyers' questions, and complete sales. The channel will be most effective when each member assumes the tasks it can do best.

Ideally, because the success of individual channel members depends on the overall channel's success, all channel firms should work together smoothly. They should understand and accept their roles, coordinate their activities, and cooperate to attain overall channel goals.

Channel conflict
Disagreements among marketing channel members on goals, roles, and rewards—who should do what and for what rewards.

However, individual channel members rarely take such a broad view. Cooperating to achieve overall channel goals sometimes means giving up individual company goals. Although channel members depend on one another, they often act alone in their own short-run best interests. They often disagree on who should do what and for what rewards. Such disagreements over goals, roles, and rewards generate **channel conflict**.

Horizontal conflict occurs among firms at the same level of the channel. For instance, some Ford dealers in Chicago might complain that other dealers in the city steal sales from them by pricing too low or advertising outside their assigned territories. Or Holiday Inn franchisees might complain about other Holiday Inn operators overcharging guests or giving poor service, hurting the overall Holiday Inn image.

Vertical conflict, conflict between different levels of the same channel, is even more common. >> For example, McDonald's has recently faced growing conflict with its corps of 3,100 independent franchisees:[2]

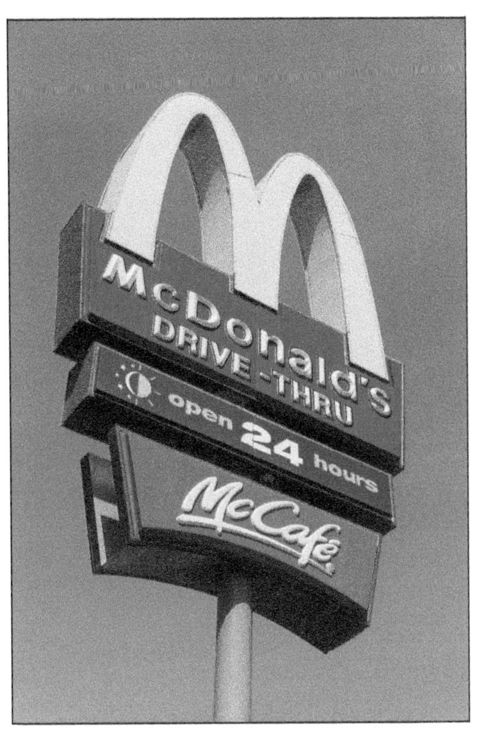

>> **Channel conflict: A high level of franchisee discontent is worrisome to McDonald's. Franchisees operate more than 80 percent of the chain's restaurants, and there's a huge connection between franchisee satisfaction and customer service.**

© Greg Balfour Evans/Alamy

> Recent surveys of McDonald's franchise owners have reflected substantial franchisee discontent with the corporation. Some of the conflict has stemmed from a slowdown in system-wide sales in recent years that put both sides on edge. The most basic conflicts are financial. McDonald's makes its money from franchisee royalties based on total system sales. In contrast, franchisees make money on margins—what's left over after their costs. To reverse slumping sales, McDonald's increased its emphasis on aggressive discounting—in the form of value menus—a strategy that increases corporate sales but squeezes franchisee profits. Franchisees also grumble about adding popular but more complex menu items—such as customizable burgers, fresh beef, McCafé beverages, and all-day breakfasts—that increase the top-line growth for McDonald's but add preparation, equipment, and staffing costs for franchisees while slowing down service. McDonald's has also asked franchisees to make costly restaurant upgrades and overhauls, such as order kiosks. In all, despite recently rebounding sales, franchisees remain disgruntled. The most recent survey rates McDonald's current franchisee relations at an all-time low 1.81 out of a possible 5, in the "fair" to "poor" range. That's worrisome for McDonald's, whose franchise owners operate more that 80 percent of its locations. Studies show that there's a huge connection between franchisee satisfaction and customer service.

Some conflict in the channel takes the form of healthy competition. Such competition can be good for the channel; without it, the channel could become passive and noninnovative. For example, the McDonald's conflict with its franchisees might represent normal give-and-take over the respective rights of the channel partners. However, severe or prolonged conflict can disrupt channel effectiveness and cause lasting harm to channel relationships. McDonald's should manage the channel conflict carefully to keep it from getting out of hand.

Vertical Marketing Systems

For the channel as a whole to perform well, each channel member's role must be specified, and channel conflict must be managed. The channel will perform better if it includes a firm, agency, or mechanism that provides leadership and has the power to assign roles and manage conflict.

Conventional distribution channel
A channel consisting of one or more independent producers, wholesalers, and retailers, each a separate business seeking to maximize its own profits, perhaps even at the expense of profits for the system as a whole.

Historically, *conventional distribution channels* have lacked such leadership and power, often resulting in damaging conflict and poor performance. One of the biggest channel developments over the years has been the emergence of *vertical marketing systems* that provide channel leadership. >> **Figure 10.3** contrasts the two types of channel arrangements.

A **conventional distribution channel** consists of one or more independent producers, wholesalers, and retailers. Each is a separate business seeking to maximize its own profits, perhaps even at the expense of the system as a whole. No channel member has much control over the other members, and no formal means exists for assigning roles and resolving channel conflict.

Vertical marketing system (VMS)
A channel structure in which producers, wholesalers, and retailers act as a unified system. One channel member owns the others, has contracts with them, or has so much power that they all cooperate.

In contrast, a **vertical marketing system (VMS)** consists of producers, wholesalers, and retailers acting as a unified system. One channel member owns the others, has

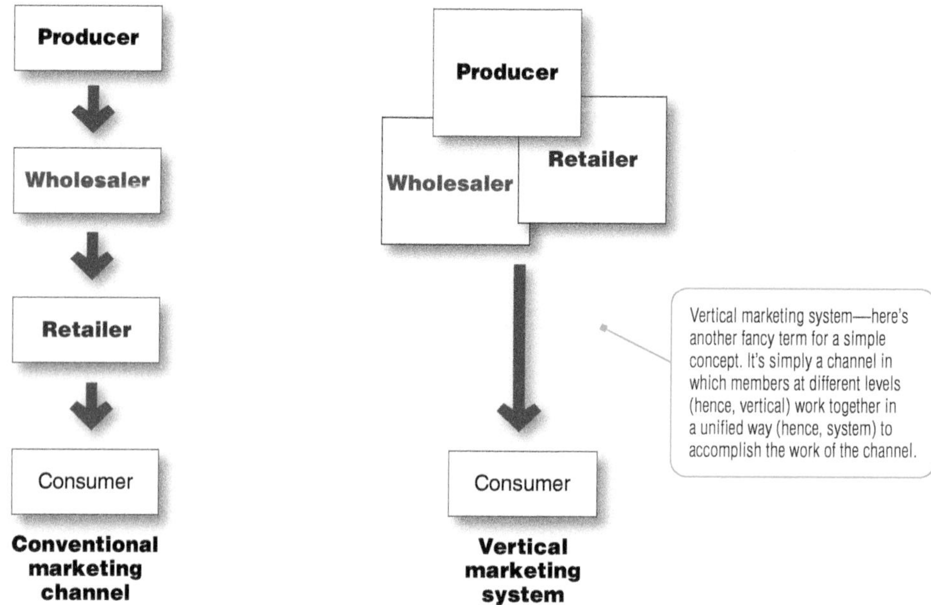

>> Figure 10.3 Comparison of Conventional Distribution Channel with Vertical Marketing System

contracts with them, or wields so much power that they must all cooperate. The VMS can be dominated by the producer, the wholesaler, or the retailer.

We look now at three major types of VMSs: *corporate, contractual*, and *administered*. Each uses a different means for setting up leadership and power in the channel.

Corporate VMS

Corporate VMS
A vertical marketing system that combines successive stages of production and distribution under single ownership—channel leadership is established through common ownership.

A **corporate VMS** integrates successive stages of production and distribution under single ownership. Coordination and conflict management are attained through regular organizational channels. For example, grocery giant Kroger owns and operates 38 food product plants—17 dairies, seven bakery plants, five grocery plants, one deli plant, two frozen dough plants, two beverage plants, two cheese plants, and two meat plants. That gives it factory-to-store channel control more than 40 percent of the 13,000 private-label items found on its shelves.[3]

Similarly, little-known Italian eyewear maker Luxottica produces many famous eyewear brands—including its own Ray-Ban, Oakley, Persol, and Vogue Eyewear brands and licensed brands such as Burberry, Chanel, Polo Ralph Lauren, Dolce & Gabbana, DKNY, Prada, Versace, and Michael Kors. Luxottica then controls the distribution of these brands through some of the world's largest optical chains—LensCrafters, Pearle Vision, Sunglass Hut, Target Optical, Sears Optical—which it also owns. In all, through vertical integration, Luxottica controls an estimated 60 to 80 percent of the U.S. eyewear market. And Luxottica recently merged with Essilor, the world's biggest manufacturer of lenses, giving it even more vertical control over its supply chain.[4]

Contractual VMS

Contractual VMS
A vertical marketing system in which independent firms at different levels of production and distribution join together through contracts.

A **contractual VMS** consists of independent firms at different levels of production and distribution that join together through contracts to obtain more economies or sales impact than each could achieve alone. Channel members coordinate their activities and manage conflict through contractual agreements.

Franchise organization
A contractual vertical marketing system in which a channel member, called a franchisor, links several stages in the production-distribution process.

The **franchise organization** is the most common type of contractual relationship. In this system, a channel member called a *franchisor* links several stages in the production-distribution process. In the United States alone, almost 746,000 franchise outlets account for $425 billion of economic output.[5] Almost every kind of business has been franchised—from motels and fast-food restaurants to dental centers and dating services, from wedding consultants and handyman services to funeral homes, fitness centers, moving services, and hair salons. Franchising allows entrepreneurs with good business concepts

GET IN LINE, ONLINE.
SPORTCLIPS.COM/
CHECKIN

GUY-SMART STYLISTS. SPORTS ON TV. NO APPOINTMENTS.

>> Franchising systems: Through franchising, Sports Clips—where you can "Get your hair in the game"—has grown rapidly to more than 1,700 locations.

Sports Clips, Inc.

to grow their businesses quickly and profitably. **>>** For example, consider Sports Clips Haircuts, the sports-themed hair salon that caters to men and boys, a place where you can "Get your hair in the game." Through franchising, since the mid-1990s, Sports Clips has grown rapidly and now has more than 1,700 locations across the United States and Canada pulling in more than $600 million in annual systemwide sales. Last year, Sports Clips ranked number 10 on the *Entrepreneur* Franchise 500 list of top franchise opportunities, just below franchising heavyweights such as McDonald's, 7-Eleven, Dunkin', and Taco Bell.[6]

There are three types of franchises. The first type is the *manufacturer-sponsored retailer franchise system*—for example, Ford and its network of independent franchised dealers. The second type is the *manufacturer-sponsored wholesaler franchise system*—Coca-Cola licenses bottlers (wholesalers) in various world markets that buy Coca-Cola syrup concentrate and then bottle and sell the finished product to retailers locally. The third type is the *service-firm-sponsored retailer franchise system*—for example, Jimmy Johns and its more than 2,600 franchisee-operated restaurants in the United States. Other examples can be found in everything from auto rentals (Hertz, Avis), apparel retailers (The Athlete's Foot, Plato's Closet), and motels (Holiday Inn, Hampton Inn) to supplemental education (Huntington Learning Center, Kumon Math & Reading Centers) and personal services (Two Men and a Truck, Mr. Handyman, Anytime Fitness).

The fact that most consumers cannot tell the difference between contractual and corporate VMSs shows how successfully the contractual organizations compete with corporate chains. The next chapter on retailing presents a fuller discussion of the various contractual VMSs.

Administered VMS

Administered VMS
A vertical marketing system that coordinates successive stages of production and distribution through the size and power of one of the parties.

In an **administered VMS**, leadership is assumed not through common ownership or contractual ties but through the size and power of one or a few dominant channel members. Manufacturers of a top brand can obtain strong trade cooperation and support from resellers. For example, P&G and Apple can command unusual cooperation from many resellers regarding displays, shelf space, promotions, and price policies. In turn, large retailers such as Walmart, Home Depot, Kroger, and Walgreens can exert strong influence on the many manufacturers that supply the products they sell.

For example, in the normal push and pull between Walmart and its consumer goods suppliers, giant Walmart—the biggest grocer in the United States with a more than 21 percent share of all U.S. grocery sales—usually gets its way. Take supplier Clorox, for instance. Although The Clorox Company's strong consumer brand preference gives it significant negotiating power, Walmart simply holds more cards. Sales to Walmart make up 27 percent of Clorox's sales, whereas Clorox products account for only one-third of 1 percent of Walmart's purchases, making Walmart by far the dominant partner. And it's not just Clorox. Cal-Maine Foods and its Eggland's Best brand relies on Walmart for almost 30 percent of its sales yet tallies only about one-tenth of 1 percent of Walmart's volume. For such brands, maintaining a strong relationship with the giant retailer is crucial.[7]

Horizontal Marketing Systems

Horizontal marketing system
A channel arrangement in which two or more companies at one level join together to follow a new marketing opportunity.

Another channel development is the **horizontal marketing system**, in which two or more companies at one level join together to follow a new marketing opportunity. By working together, companies can combine their financial, production, or marketing resources to accomplish more than any one company could alone.

CVS pharmacy
TARGET

>> **Horizontal marketing systems: Target partners with CVS Health, which operates store-within-store pharmacies to the benefit of all—Target, the partners, and their mutual customers.**

Veronica Wong/Alamy Stock Photo

Companies might join forces with competitors or noncompetitors. They might work with each other on a temporary or permanent basis, or they may create a separate company. >> For example, Target partners with noncompetitor Starbucks to place coffee stands in its stores. Starbucks benefits from Target's heavy store traffic, and Target keeps its shoppers caffeinated and ready to shop. Target also partners with CVS Health, which operates CVS pharmacies and Minute Clinics in Target stores through a store-within-a-store format. The partnership gives CVS Health more than 1,700 pharmacies and 80 clinics at prime locations inside Target stores. At the same time, it frees up Target focus on its core product design, merchandising, and marketing strengths while still offering customers the expert pharmacy and healthcare services they want.[8]

Horizontal channel arrangements also work well globally. For example, most of the world's major airlines have joined to together in one of three major global alliances: Star Alliance, Skyteam, or Oneworld. Star Alliance consists of 28 airlines "working in harmony," including United, Air Canada, Lufthansa, Air China, Turkish Airlines, and almost two dozen others. It offers more than 18,500 combined daily departures to more than 1,300 airports around the world. Such alliances tie the individual carriers into massive worldwide air travel networks with joint branding and marketing, co-locations at airports, interline scheduling and smoother global flight connections, and shared rewards and membership privileges.[9]

Multichannel Distribution Systems

Multichannel distribution system
A distribution system in which a single firm sets up two or more marketing channels to reach one or more customer segments.

In the past, many companies used a single channel to sell to a single market or market segment. Today, with the proliferation of customer segments and channel possibilities, more and more companies have adopted **multichannel distribution systems**. Such multichannel marketing occurs when a single firm sets up two or more marketing channels to reach one or more customer segments.

>> Figure 10.4 shows a multichannel marketing system. In the figure, the producer sells directly to consumer segment 1 using catalogs and online and mobile channels and reaches consumer segment 2 through retailers. It sells indirectly to business segment 1 through distributors and dealers and to business segment 2 through its own sales force.

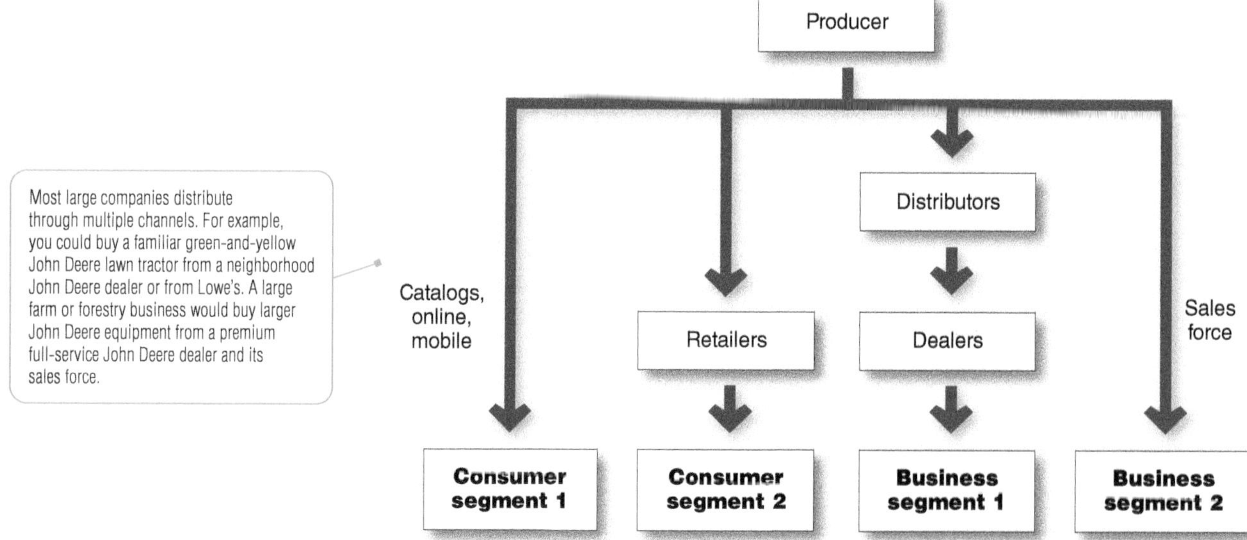
Most large companies distribute through multiple channels. For example, you could buy a familiar green-and-yellow John Deere lawn tractor from a neighborhood John Deere dealer or from Lowe's. A large farm or forestry business would buy larger John Deere equipment from a premium full-service John Deere dealer and its sales force.
Producer
Catalogs, online, mobile
Retailers
Distributors
Dealers
Sales force
Consumer segment 1
Consumer segment 2
Business segment 1
Business segment 2

>> **Figure 10.4 Multichannel Distribution System**

These days, almost every large company and many small ones distribute through multiple channels. For example, John Deere sells its familiar green-and-yellow lawn and garden tractors, mowers, and outdoor power products to consumers and commercial users through several channels, including John Deere retailers, Lowe's home improvement stores, and online. It sells and services its tractors, combines, planters, and other agricultural equipment through its premium John Deere dealer network. And it sells large construction and forestry equipment through selected large, full-service John Deere dealers and their sales forces.

Multichannel distribution systems offer many advantages to companies facing large and complex markets. With each new channel, the company expands its sales and market coverage and gains opportunities to tailor its products and services to the specific needs of diverse customer segments. But such multichannel systems are harder to control, and they can generate conflict as more channels compete for customers and sales. For example, when John Deere first began selling selected consumer products through Lowe's home improvement stores, many of its independent dealers complained loudly. To avoid such conflicts in its online marketing channels, the company routes all of its online sales to John Deere dealers.

Changing Channel Organization

Disintermediation
The cutting out of marketing channel intermediaries by product or service producers or the displacement of traditional resellers by radical new types of intermediaries.

Changes in technology and the explosive growth of direct and online marketing are having a profound impact on the nature and design of marketing channels. One major trend is toward **disintermediation**—a big term with a clear message and important consequences. Disintermediation occurs when product or service producers cut out intermediaries and go directly to final buyers or when radically new types of channel intermediaries displace traditional ones.

Thus, in many industries, traditional intermediaries are dropping by the wayside, as is the case with online marketers taking business from traditional brick-and-mortar retailers. For example, online music download services such as iTunes and Amazon pretty much put traditional music-store retailers out of business, with physical music sales now capturing less than 22 percent of music market revenues. In turn, however, streaming music services such as Spotify, Amazon Prime Music, and Apple Music are now disintermediating digital download services. Music downloads now account for an ever-shrinking 24 percent of music industry revenues compared with streaming's 51 percent.[10]

Disintermediation presents both opportunities and problems for producers and resellers. Channel innovators who find new ways to add value in the channel can displace traditional resellers and reap the rewards. For example, app-based ride-hailing services Lyft and Uber have recently stormed onto the scene, rapidly disintermediating traditional taxi and car-for-hire services by offering better customer experiences at lower fares (see Marketing at Work 10.1).

In turn, traditional intermediaries must continue to innovate to avoid being swept aside. >> For example, Toys "R" Us pioneered the superstore format that once made it the go-to place for buying toys and baby products, driving most small independent toy stores out of business. But in recent years, Toys "R" Us has failed to adapt to major shifts in toy market sales, first toward big discounters such as Walmart and Target and then toward online merchants like Amazon. By 2021, an estimated 28 percent of toy and baby product purchases will be made online, where Toys "R" Us lags badly. Amazon now captures three times the online toys sales of Toys "R" Us, with Walmart hot on Amazon's digital heels. As a result, Toy "R" Us recently closed down operations and shuttered its stores.[11]

>> Disintermediation: Toys "R" Us pioneered the superstore format that once made it the go-to place for buying toys. But after falling victim to shifts in toy market sales to big discounters like Walmart and online merchants like Amazon, the retail giant was forced to close down operations and shutter its stores.
Sundry Photography/Shutterstock

Like resellers, to remain competitive, product and service producers must develop new channel opportunities, such as the internet, mobile, and other direct channels. However, developing these new channels often brings them into direct competition with their established channels, resulting in conflict. To ease this problem, companies often look for ways to make going direct a plus for the entire channel. For example, to avoid conflicts in its online and mobile channels, motorcycle maker Harley-Davidson routes all its online sales through its independent dealers:[12]

MARKETING AT WORK 10.1

Lyft: Disrupting and Disintermediating Urban Transportation Channels

It's rare. But every now and then a company comes along that completely disrupts the traditional ways of distributing a product or service. FedEx revolutionized small package delivery channels, Amazon radically transformed retailing, and Apple's iTunes and iPod turned music distribution on its ear. Now, here come Lyft and Uber, app-based ride services that are revolutionizing urban transportation. These fast-growing startups are rapidly disintermediating conventional taxicab and car-for-hire services.

When it comes to app-based urban ride-hailing, you probably think first of market leader Uber. But it was number two Lyft that pioneered the ridesharing concept. Before Uber's tires ever hit the road, Lyft began as Zimride, a carpool app aimed at college students looking for rides home for weekends and holidays. However, by the time Zimride morphed into Lyft, Uber was already well financed and strongly established. Although Lyft is now growing much faster than Uber, it still plays tortoise to Uber's hare, capturing about a third of the U.S. ridesharing market versus Uber's two-thirds.

Why are so many customers now bypassing good old taxicabs in favor of newcomers like Lyft and Uber? It's all about convenience and peace of mind. Lyft's smartphone app lets passengers hail the nearest car from any location and then track it on a map as it approaches. The Lyft app gives riders an accurate estimate of the fare in advance (usually much less than that charged by a regular cab), eliminating guesswork and uncertainty. After the ride, passengers simply exit and walk away. Lyft automatically charges the passenger's credit card, eliminating the often-awkward moment of payment. And it's the same process anywhere in the country, from New York to San Francisco to Ashville, North Carolina, or Athens, Georgia.

From the get-go, Lyft has been all about the customer experience. Conventional urban transportation channels have long been ruled by cartel-like relationships between cab companies and local governments, characterized by high fares for poor service. By contrast, under its founding mission of "reconnecting people and communities," Lyft hit the streets with ordinary cars driven by ordinary people giving friendly service at reasonable fares. It encouraged riders to sit up front and exchange conversation and fist bumps with its drivers. Lyft brags of "Happy drivers. Happy riders."

Compare the Lyft experience to the often-unsettling experience of using a standard taxicab. One business reporter describes waiting in line at a taxi stand while a driver tried to convince another would-be passenger—a total stranger—to share the cab, thereby increasing his fare. The cab itself was ancient and filthy, with ripped and worn seats. During the entire ride, the cabbie carried on a phone conversation via his headset, causing safety concerns while distractedly navigating busy city streets. The driver spoke only poor, hard-to-understand English. "That turned out to be a good thing," says the reporter, "because I couldn't understand what he was trying to say when he insulted me for not tipping him enough."

Thus, Lyft's disruptive innovation brought a breath of fresh air to an industry begging for change. As one economics professor points out, the taxicab industry "was ripe for entry [by startups] because everybody hates it." And although competition between Lyft and Uber has intensified, each company benefits from the other's success. The more consumers accept the ride-hailing model, the more the new channel will grow and thrive versus traditional channels, creating opportunities for both companies. The biggest threat is to traditional taxicab and car-for-hire companies, who are now losing both customers and drivers to Lyft and Uber.

Lyft won't likely catch Uber any time soon. With its first-mover advantage and deep-pocket investor financing, Uber grew quickly to capture a 90 percent share of the U.S. ride-hailing market. Uber has also expanded rapidly worldwide—it now serves more than 60 countries and 400 cities globally. Lyft is just beginning to go global. But in 2017, Uber was rocked by a series of scandals—from public misdeeds by its co-founder and then-CEO Travis Kalanick to charges of unfair treatment of Uber drivers, stolen technologies, and sexual harassment within a toxic corporate culture. Uber customers responded with the social media–driven #deleteUber campaign, costing Uber customers and market share.

Uber's misfortunes left Lyft looking like what one reporter called "the more moral choice among ride-hailing companies." As Uber's market share fell, Lyft's surged. Although Uber's sales recovered and grew modestly during the year, Lyft emerged from Uber's shadow, doubling its number of drivers and passengers.

>> Lyft and other innovative app-based ride services are rapidly disintermediating conventional taxicab and urban transportation systems.

Josh Edelson/AP Images for Lyft

"It felt like the year in which the public really got to know us for our mission and our values," says Lyft's VP of Operations.

The future is bright for Lyft. Its market continues to grow as consumers shift not only from taxis to the new ride-hailing services but also from public transportation. Some people are even ditching their cars and using car-hailing apps like Lyft and Uber as their sole means of car transportation. Nearly a quarter of U.S. adults sold or traded in a car during the past year. Almost 10 percent of that group didn't replace their old car with a new one, opting instead to depend on Lyft or Uber to get them around. And beyond just delivering people to their destinations, Lyft and Uber are moving toward using their driver networks to deliver about anything else—from takeout food to retail packages. As one executive puts it, "Once you're delivering cars in five minutes, there are a lot of other things you can deliver in five minutes."

But looking ahead, Lyft knows that disintermediation is a two-edged sword. The ride-hailing companies that are now wreaking havoc on conventional urban transportation services are themselves vulnerable to disruption by the next big thing. In this case, that next big this is self-driving cars. Once a distant fantasy, widespread use of driverless cars is now a foregone conclusion—it's just a matter of when. And what better way to move people around than with a fleet of self-driving cars? So both Lyft and Uber are investing heavily in driverless vehicle technology, hoping to disrupt their own innovative ride-hailing channel before new-wave competitors can.

The driverless car industry is in a huge state of flux. Giants ranging from GM and Ford to Google and Amazon are developing their own driverless fleets and have even investigated setting up their own ride-hailing and delivery services. For example, GM's Cruise Automation division has already experimented with a ride-hailing app to let San Francisco employees access its driverless vehicles. Partnerships with Lyft or Uber, which already have established ride-hailing customer bases, might help these companies get up and running faster.

Recognizing that it lacks the resources to go it alone, Lyft is seeking collaboration. It has launched partnerships with several driverless technology developers, including GM's Cruise, Ford, and Google's Waymo self-driving car project. In its biggest move yet, Lyft is creating its own self-driving technology development program that will develop an open self-driving platform that carmakers could plug into any car, turning it into a driverless Lyft provider.

Thus, even as Lyft's innovative ride-hailing model is disrupting and replacing conventional competitors, the young company itself faces disruption from even newer technologies. To thrive, or even survive, Lyft must continue to innovate, disintermediating its own distribution model before competitors can.

Sources: Brett Williams, "Americans Have Started to Ditch Their Cars for Uber and Lyft," *Mashable*, May 26, 2017, https://mashable.com/2017/05/25/cars-replaced-by-ride-hailing-poll/#Z0bZc.OFoOqY; Michal Lev-Ram, "Scandals and Missteps at Uber Have Given Lyft a Chance to Catch Up in the Ride-Sharing Race," *Fortune*, July 19, 2017, http://fortune.com/2017/07/19/uber-vs-lyft-race/; Jim Edwards, "Uber Has Changed My Life and as God Is My Witness I Will Never Take a Taxi Again" *Business Insider*, January 22, 2014, www.businessinsider.com/uber-has-changed-my-life-and-as-god-is-my-witness-i-will-never-take-a-taxi-again-where-available-2014-1#ixzz3TYF7ZY29; David Z. Morris, "Lyft Could Have One-Third of the U.S. Rideshare Market by Christmas," *Fortune*, November 12, 2017, http://fortune.com/2017/11/12/lyft-us-rideshare-market-report/; Biz Carson, "Lyft Doubled Rides in 2017 as Its Rival Uber Stumbled," *Forbes*, January 16, 2018, www.forbes.com/sites/bizcarson/2018/01/16/lyft-doubled-rides-in-2017/#5afda477d6be; Olivia Solon, "Is Lyft Really the 'Woke' Alternative to Uber?", *The Guardian*, March 29, 2017, www.theguardian.com/technology/2017/mar/29/is-lyft-really-the-woke-alternative-to-uber; Arian Marshall, "The Ride-Hailing Business Is Now Way Bigger Than Uber and Lyft," *Wired*, February 28, 2018, www.wired.com/category/transportation/; and www.lyft.com, accessed October 2018.

Harley-Davidson sells more than $1.1 billion worth of parts, accessories, branded apparel, and other general merchandise each year to devoted Harley fans, accounting for more than 20 percent of its total annual revenue. So it makes sense to sell such products online to reach even more customers. However, by selling online, Harley-Davidson risks alienating its more than 700 independent U.S. dealers, who count on the sales of such high-margin items in their stores. To avoid dealer conflict, the company sells products online but only "on behalf of and as agent for participating dealerships." When Harley-Davidson takes online orders, it asks customers to select a Harley dealer from which to make the purchase, keeping the dealer at the center of the customer experience. Then, whether the items are shipped by Harley, shipped by the store, or picked up at the store by the customer, the dealer receives credit for the sale. Thus, Harley's direct and mobile marketing benefits both the company and its channel partners.

LINKING THE CONCEPTS

Stop here for a moment and apply the distribution channel concepts we've discussed so far.

- Compare the GEICO and Ford channels. Draw a diagram that shows the types of intermediaries in each channel. What kind of channel system does each company use?
- What are the roles and responsibilities of the members in each channel? How well do these channel members work together toward overall channel success?

Author Comment
Like everything else in marketing, good channel design begins with analyzing customer needs. Remember, marketing channels are really customer value delivery networks.

Channel Design Decisions

OBJECTIVE 10-3 Identify the major channel alternatives open to a company.

We now look at several channel design decisions manufacturers face. In designing marketing channels, manufacturers struggle between what is ideal and what is practical. A new firm with limited capital usually starts by selling in a limited market area. In this case, deciding on the best channels might not be a problem: The problem might simply be how to convince one or a few good intermediaries to handle the line.

If successful, the new firm can branch out to new markets through existing intermediaries. In smaller markets, the firm might sell directly to retailers; in larger markets, it might sell through distributors. In one part of the country, it might grant exclusive franchises; in another, it might sell through all available outlets. Then it might add an online store that sells directly to hard-to-reach customers. In this way, channel systems often evolve to meet market opportunities and conditions.

Marketing channel design
Designing effective marketing channels by analyzing customer needs, setting channel objectives, identifying major channel alternatives, and evaluating those alternatives.

For maximum effectiveness, however, channel analysis and decision making should be more purposeful. **Marketing channel design** calls for analyzing consumer needs, setting channel objectives, identifying major channel alternatives, and evaluating the alternatives.

Analyzing Consumer Needs

As noted previously, marketing channels are part of the overall *customer value delivery network*. Each channel member and level adds value for the customer. Thus, designing the marketing channel starts with finding out what target consumers want from the channel. Do consumers want to buy nearby, or are they willing to travel to more centralized locations? Would customers rather buy in person, by phone, or online? Do they value breadth of assortment, or do they prefer specialization? Do consumers want many add-on services (delivery, installation, repairs), or will they obtain these services elsewhere? The faster the delivery, the greater the assortment provided, and the more add-on services supplied, the greater the channel's service level.

Providing the fastest delivery, the greatest assortment, and the most services, however, may not be possible, practical, or desired. The company and its channel members may not have the resources or skills needed to provide all the desired services. Also, higher levels of service result in higher costs for the channel and higher prices for consumers. The success of modern discount retailing shows that consumers often accept lower service levels in exchange for lower prices. For example, Walmart typically rates near the bottom in rankings of grocery retailers on customer shopping experience and satisfaction compared to the likes of Wegmans, Publix, Kroger, Trader Joe's, Whole Foods, or about any other grocery retailer. Yet it captures a 21.5 percent share of the U.S. grocery market.[13]

Many companies, however, position themselves on higher service levels, and customers willingly pay the higher prices. >> For example, whereas Walmart typically rates near the bottom in rankings of grocery retailer customer satisfaction, East Coast supermarket chain Wegmans consistently ranks at the top:[14]

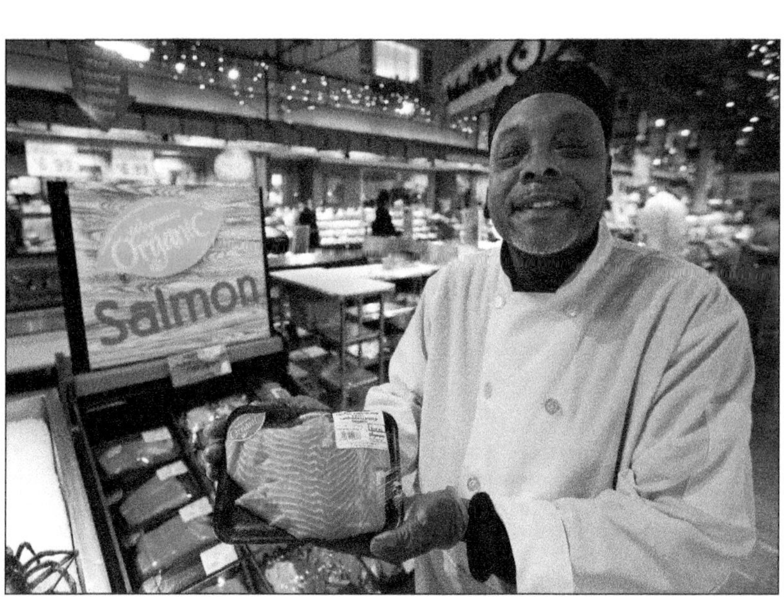

>> Meeting customers' channel service needs: Wegmans is the "best supermarket around, hands down." To devoted Wegmans shoppers, the retailer's extraordinary people and service are well worth its somewhat higher prices.
Alex Brandon/AP Images

> Wegmans prides itself on its broad and deep selection, clean stores, very high service levels, and well-trained and friendly employees. "Best supermarket around, hands down," says one customer in a Yelp review. "The knowledge and helpfulness of the workers is beyond amazing." Says another, "Aside from the overwhelming options of everything on the planet to choose from, it's an amazing place. I walk around thinking... OK, I'm impressed!" The result is avidly

loyal customers. Actor Alec Baldwin's mother reportedly refused to move from New York to Los Angeles because she didn't want to abandon her favorite Wegmans store. So even though they could probably save money by shopping at Walmart, to devoted Wegmans shoppers, the higher quality and extraordinary service are well worth the somewhat-higher prices.

Thus, companies must balance consumer needs not only against the feasibility and costs of meeting these needs but also against customer price preferences.

Setting Channel Objectives

Companies should state their marketing channel objectives in terms of targeted levels of customer service. Usually, a company can identify several segments wanting different levels of service. The company should decide which segments to serve and the best channels to use in each case. In each segment, the company wants to minimize the total channel cost of meeting customer service requirements.

The company's channel objectives are also influenced by the nature of the company, its products, its marketing intermediaries, its competitors, and the environment. For example, the company's size and financial situation determine which marketing functions it can handle itself and which it must give to intermediaries. Companies selling perishable products, for example, may require more direct marketing to avoid delays and too much handling.

In some cases, a company may want to compete in or near the same outlets that carry competitors' products. For example, Maytag and other appliance makers want their products displayed alongside competing brands to facilitate comparison shopping. In other cases, companies may avoid the channels used by competitors. The Pampered Chef, for instance, sells high-quality kitchen tools directly to consumers through its corps of more than 60,000 consultants worldwide rather than going head-to-head with other kitchen tool makers for scarce positions in retail stores. And Stella & Dot sells quality jewelry through more than 50,000 independent reps—called stylists—who hold Tupperware-like in-home "trunk shows."[15] GEICO and USAA primarily market insurance and banking products to consumers via phone and internet channels rather than through agents.

Finally, environmental factors such as economic conditions and legal constraints may affect channel objectives and design. For example, in a depressed economy, producers will want to distribute their goods in the most economical way, using shorter channels and dropping unneeded services that add to the final price of the goods.

Identifying Major Alternatives

When the company has defined its channel objectives, it should next identify its major channel alternatives in terms of the *types* of intermediaries, the *number* of intermediaries, and the *responsibilities* of each channel member.

Types of Intermediaries

A firm should identify the types of channel members available to carry out its channel work. Most companies face many channel member choices. For example, Dell initially sold directly to final consumers and business buyers only through its sophisticated phone and online marketing channel. It also sold directly to large corporate, institutional, and government buyers using its direct sales force. However, to reach more consumers and match competitors such as Samsung and Apple, Dell now sells indirectly through retailers such as Best Buy, Staples, and Walmart. It also sells indirectly through *value-added resellers*, independent distributors and dealers that develop computer systems and applications tailored to the special needs of small and medium-sized business customers.

Using many types of resellers in a channel provides both benefits and drawbacks. For example, by selling through retailers and value-added resellers in addition to its own direct channels, Dell can reach more and different kinds of buyers. However, these are more difficult to manage and control. In addition, the direct and indirect channels compete with each other for many of the same customers, causing potential conflict. In fact, Dell often finds itself "stuck in the middle," with its direct sales reps complaining about competition from retail stores, whereas its value-added resellers complain that the direct sales reps are undercutting their business.

Intensive distribution
Stocking the product in as many outlets as possible.

Exclusive distribution
Giving a limited number of dealers the exclusive right to distribute the company's products in their territories.

Number of Marketing Intermediaries

Companies must also determine the number of channel members to use at each level. Three strategies are available: intensive distribution, exclusive distribution, and selective distribution. Producers of convenience products and common raw materials typically seek **intensive distribution**—a strategy in which they stock their products in as many outlets as possible. These products must be available where and when consumers want them. For example, toothpaste, candy, and other similar items are sold in millions of outlets to provide maximum brand exposure and consumer convenience. P&G, Coca-Cola, Kimberly-Clark, and other consumer goods companies distribute their products in this way.

By contrast, some producers purposely limit the number of intermediaries handling their products. The extreme form of this practice is **exclusive distribution**, in which the producer gives only a limited number of dealers the exclusive right to distribute its products in their territories. Exclusive distribution is often found in the distribution of luxury brands. Breitling watches—positioned as "Instruments for Professionals" and selling at prices from $5,000 to more than $100,000—are sold by only a few authorized dealers in any given market area. For example, the brand sells through only one jeweler in Chicago and only six jewelers in the entire state of Illinois. Exclusive distribution enhances Breitling's distinctive positioning and earns greater dealer support and customer service.

Between intensive and exclusive distribution lies **selective distribution**—the use of more than one but fewer than all of the intermediaries who are willing to carry a company's products. Most consumer electronics, furniture, and home appliance brands are distributed in this manner. >> For example, outdoor power equipment maker STIHL doesn't sell its chain saws, blowers, hedge trimmers, and other products through mass merchandisers such as Lowe's, Home Depot, or Sears. Instead, it sells through a select corps of independent hardware and lawn and garden dealers. By using selective distribution, STIHL can develop good working relationships with dealers and expect a better-than-average selling effort. Selective distribution also enhances the STIHL brand's image and allows for higher markups resulting from greater value-added dealer service. "We count on our select dealers every day and so can you," says one STIHL ad.

Why is the world's number one selling brand of chain saw not sold at Lowe's or The Home Depot?

STIHL

>> Selective distribution: STIHL sells its products through a select corps of independent retailers. "We count on them every day and so can you."
STIHL Incorporated

Selective distribution
The use of more than one but fewer than all of the intermediaries that are willing to carry the company's products.

Responsibilities of Channel Members

The producer and intermediaries need to agree on the terms and responsibilities of each channel member. They should agree on price policies, conditions of sale, territory rights, and the specific services to be performed by each party. The producer should establish a list price and a fair set of discounts for the intermediaries. It must define each channel member's territory, and it should be careful about where it places new resellers.

Mutual services and duties need to be spelled out carefully, especially in franchise and exclusive distribution channels. For example, Subway provides franchisees with access to proprietary formulas and operational systems, promotional and advertising support, intensive training, site selection assistance, and general management guidance. In turn, franchisees must meet company standards for physical facilities and food quality, provide requested information, buy specified food products, cooperate with new promotion programs and pay and advertising fund fee, and pay an 8 percent royalty to Subway.[16]

Evaluating the Major Alternatives

Suppose a company has identified several channel alternatives and wants to select the one that will best satisfy its long-run objectives. Each alternative should be evaluated against economic, control, and adaptability criteria.

Using *economic criteria*, a company compares the likely sales, costs, and profitability of different channel alternatives. What will be the investment required by each channel alternative, and what returns will result? The company must also consider *control issues*.

Using intermediaries usually means giving them some control over the marketing of the product, and some intermediaries take more control than others. Other things being equal, the company prefers to keep as much control as possible. Finally, the company must apply *adaptability criteria*. Channels often involve long-term commitments, yet the company wants to keep the channel flexible so that it can adapt to environmental changes. Thus, to be considered, a channel involving long-term commitments should be greatly superior on economic and control grounds.

Designing International Distribution Channels

International marketers face many additional complexities in designing their channels. Each country has its own unique distribution system that has evolved over time and changes very slowly. These channel systems can vary widely from country to country. Thus, global marketers must usually adapt their channel strategies to the existing structures within each country.

There are large differences in the numbers and types of intermediaries serving each country market and in the transportation infrastructure serving these intermediaries. For example, whereas large-scale retail chains dominate the U.S. scene, most of the retailing in other countries is done by small, independent retailers. In India or Indonesia, millions of retailers operate tiny shops or sell in open markets.

Even in world markets containing similar types of sellers, retailing practices can vary widely. For example, you'll find plenty of Walmarts, Carrefours, Tescos, and other retail superstores in major Chinese cities. But whereas consumer brands sold in such stores in Western markets rely largely on self-service, brands in China hire armies of uniformed in-store promoters—called "promoter girls" or "push girls"—to dispense samples and pitch their products person to person. In a Beijing Walmart, on any given weekend, you might find 100 or more such promoters acquainting customers with products from Kraft, Unilever, P&G, Johnson & Johnson, and a slew of local competitors. "Chinese consumers know the brand name through media," says the director of a Chinese retail marketing service, "but they want to feel the product and get a detailed understanding before they make a purchase."[17]

>> International distribution: To overcome distribution infrastructure problems in Brazil's Amazon River basin, Nestlé even launched a floating supermarket to take goods directly to customers.

Marcia Zoet/Bloomberg/Getty Images

When selling in emerging markets, companies must often overcome distribution infrastructure and supply challenges. For example, in Nigeria, Domino's Pizza has had to dig wells and install water-treatment plants behind many of its restaurants to obtain clean water. Similarly, after having difficulty sourcing quality beef in South Africa, rather than buying scarce beef from scrawny cattle raised by local herdsmen, Burger King finally invested $5 million in its own local cattle ranch.[18] >> And to serve northeast Brazil's Amazon River basin, which lacks a solid network of good roads, Nestlé has even launched a floating supermarket to take goods directly to customers. The boat served 800,000 consumers in 18 riverside towns with 300 different Nestlé products, spending one day at each stop.[19]

Author Comment
Now it's time to implement the chosen channel design and work with selected channel members to manage and motivate them.

Channel Management Decisions

OBJECTIVE 10-4 Explain how companies select, motivate, and evaluate channel members.

Once the company has reviewed its channel alternatives and determined the best channel design, it must implement and manage the chosen channel. **Marketing channel management** calls for selecting, managing, and motivating individual channel members and evaluating their performance over time.

Marketing channel management
Selecting, managing, and motivating individual channel members and evaluating their performance over time.

Selecting Channel Members

Producers vary in their ability to attract qualified marketing intermediaries. Some producers have no trouble signing up channel members. For example, when Toyota first introduced its Lexus line in the United States, it had no trouble attracting new dealers. In fact, it had to turn down many would-be resellers.

At the other extreme are producers that have to work hard to line up enough qualified intermediaries. For example, when Timex first tried to sell its inexpensive watches through regular jewelry stores, most jewelry stores refused to carry them. The company then managed to get its watches into mass-merchandise outlets. This turned out to be a wise decision because of the rapid growth of mass merchandising.

>> Selecting channels: Even established brands may have difficulty getting desired channels. For example, Amazon refuses to sell many Google-branded products.
BigTunaOnline/Shutterstock

Even established brands may have difficulty gaining and keeping their desired distribution, especially when dealing with powerful resellers. >> For example, Amazon.com refuses to sell Google's line of Nest smart home products, its Google Home voice assistant speakers, or its Pixel smartphone, saying that they compete with its own Amazon Echo and other products. In turn, Google has removed its YouTube from Amazon's FireTV and Echo show/Spot streaming products. The feud between the two digital giants deprives both companies of significant distribution opportunities while also inconveniencing their mutual customers.[20]

When selecting intermediaries, the company should determine what characteristics distinguish the better ones. It will want to evaluate each channel member's years in business, other lines carried, location, growth and profit record, cooperativeness, and reputation.

Managing and Motivating Channel Members

Once selected, channel members must be continuously managed and motivated to do their best. The company must sell not only *through* the intermediaries but also *to* and *with* them. Most companies see their intermediaries as first-line customers and partners. They practice strong *partner relationship management* to forge long-term partnerships with channel members. This creates a value delivery system that meets the needs of both the company *and* its marketing partners.

In managing its channels, a company must convince suppliers and distributors that they can succeed better by working together as a part of a cohesive value delivery system. Companies must work in close harmony with others in the channel to find better ways to bring value to customers. Thus, Amazon and P&G work closely to accomplish their joint goal of selling consumer package goods profitably online. And companies ranging from automaker Toyota to cosmetics maker L'Oréal forge beneficial relationships with their large networks of suppliers to gain mutual competitive advantage (see Marketing at Work 10.2).

For example, heavy-equipment manufacturer Caterpillar works hand in hand with its superb dealer network—together they dominate the world's construction, mining, and logging equipment business:

> Heavy-equipment manufacturer Caterpillar produces innovative, high-quality industrial equipment products. But ask anyone at Caterpillar, and they'll tell you that the most important reason for Caterpillar's dominance is its outstanding distribution network of 172 independent dealers around the world. Dealers are the ones on the front line. Once the product leaves the factory, the dealers take over. They're the ones that customers see. So rather than selling to or through its dealers, Caterpillar treats dealers as inside partners. When a big piece of Caterpillar equipment breaks down, customers know that they can count on both Caterpillar and its dealer network for support. A strong dealer network makes for a strong Caterpillar, and the other way around. On a deeper level, dealers play a vital role in almost every aspect of Caterpillar's operations,

MARKETING AT WORK 10.2

Working with Channel Partners to Create Value for Customers

Today's successful companies know that they can't go it alone in creating value for customers. Instead they must create effective value delivery systems, consisting of suppliers, producers, and distributors who work together to get the job done. Partnering with suppliers and distributors can yield big competitive advantages. Consider these examples.

Toyota

Achieving satisfying supplier relationships has been a cornerstone of Toyota's stunning success. Historically, Toyota's U.S. competitors often alienated their suppliers through self-serving, heavy-handed dealings. "The [U. S. automakers] set annual cost-reduction targets [for the parts they buy]," said one supplier. "To realize those targets, they'll do anything. [They've unleashed] a reign of terror, and it gets worse every year." Says another, "[One automaker] seems to send its people to 'hate school' so that they learn how to hate suppliers."

By contrast, Toyota has long known the importance of building close relationships with suppliers. Rather than bullying them, Toyota partners with suppliers and helps them to meet its very high expectations. It learns about their businesses, conducts joint improvement activities, helps train supplier employees, gives daily performance feedback, and actively seeks out supplier concerns. It even recognizes top suppliers with annual performance awards.

As a result, for 15 of the past 17 years, Toyota has received the top supplier relations score in the respected North American Automotive Supplier Working Relations Index Study. The study rates companies on financial dealings with suppliers, valuing suppliers and treating them fairly, open and honest communication, and providing opportunities to make profits. The study suggests that Toyota suppliers consider themselves true partners with the automotive giant.

Such high supplier satisfaction means that Toyota can rely on suppliers to help it improve its own quality, reduce costs, and develop new products quickly. For example, when Toyota once launched a program to reduce prices by 30 percent on 170 parts that it would buy for its next generation of cars, suppliers didn't complain. Instead, they pitched in, trusting that Toyota will help them achieve the targeted reductions, in turn making them more competitive and profitable in the future. In all, creating satisfied suppliers helps Toyota produce lower-cost, higher-quality cars, which in turn results in more satisfied customers. As Toyota puts it on their supplier website, "not everything our diverse suppliers do is easily seen... but everything they do shows in every Toyota."

L'Oréal

L'Oréal is the world's largest cosmetics maker, with 35 global brands ranging from Maybelline and Kiehl's to Lancôme and Redken. Like Toyota, L'Oréal's extensive supplier network—which supplies everything from polymers and fats to spray cans and packaging to production equipment and office supplies—is crucial to its success.

As a result, L'Oréal treats suppliers as respected partners. On the one hand, it expects a lot from suppliers in terms of design innovation, quality, and socially responsible actions. The company carefully screens new suppliers and regularly assesses the performance of current suppliers. On the other hand, L'Oréal works closely with suppliers to help them meet its exacting standards. Whereas some companies make unreasonable demands of their suppliers and "squeeze" them for short-term gains, L'Oréal builds long-term supplier relationships based on mutual benefit and growth.

According to the company's extensive supplier website, "L'Oréal does not simply buy products and services from its suppliers. The group has a deep respect for suppliers, their corporate culture, their growth, and their employees." L'Oréal seeks to create "solid and sustainable" supplier relationships, "based on trust, mutual interest, and high standards." The goal is to "invent together the beauty of tomorrow." As a result, more than 75 percent of L'Oréal's supplier partners have been working with the company for 10 years or more and the majority of them for several decades. Says the company's head of purchasing, "The CEO wants to make L'Oréal a top performer and one of the world's most respected companies. Being respected also means being respected by our suppliers."

Amazon–P&G

Until recently, if you ordered Bounty paper towels, Pampers diapers, Charmin toilet paper, or any of the dozens of other P&G consumer products from Amazon.com, they probably came to your doorstep by a circuitous distribution route. The paper

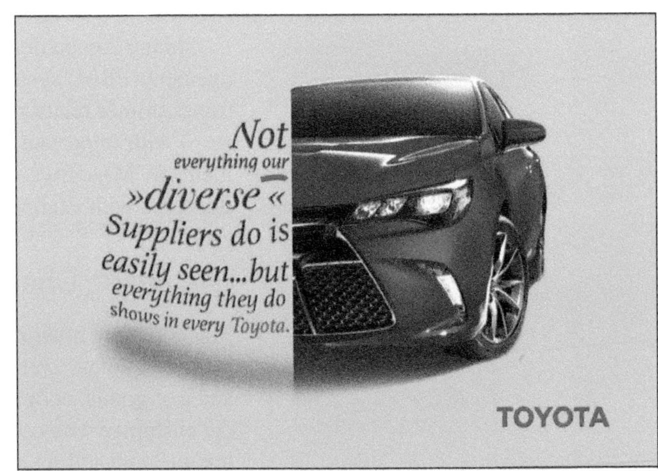

» **Partnering in the distribution channel: Toyota works closely with and values its suppliers. "Not everything our diverse suppliers do is easily seen... but everything they do shows in every Toyota."**
Toyota Motor Sales

towels, for example, might well have been produced in P&G's large northeastern Pennsylvania factory and shipped by the trailer-truck load to its nearby Tunkhannock warehouse, where they were unloaded and repacked with other P&G goods and shipped to Amazon's Dinwiddie, Virginia, fulfillment center. At the fulfillment center, they were unloaded and shelved and then finally picked and packed by Amazon employees for shipment to you via UPS, FedEx, or the USPS.

But these days, Amazon and P&G have partnered to blaze a new, simpler, lower-cost distribution trail for such goods. Now, for example, at the Pennsylvania warehouse, rather than reloading truckloads of P&G products and shipping them to Amazon fulfillment centers, P&G employees simply cart the goods to a fenced-off area inside their own warehouse. The fenced-in area is run by Amazon. From there, Amazon employees pack, label, and ship items directly to customers who've ordered them online. Amazon calls this venture Vendor Flex—and it's revolutionizing how people buy low-priced, low-margin everyday household products.

Amazon's Vendor Flex program takes channel partnering to an entirely new level. Co-locating "in the same tent" creates advantages for both partners. For Amazon, Vendor Flex reduces the costs of storing bulky items in its own distribution centers, and it frees up space for more higher-margin goods. The sharing arrangement lets Amazon extend its consumer package goods selection without building more distribution center space. For example, the P&G warehouse also stocks other popular P&G household brands, from Gillette razors to Pantene shampoo to Tide laundry detergent. Finally, locating at the source guarantees Amazon immediate availability and facilitates quick delivery of P&G products to customers.

P&G also benefits from the Vendor Flex partnership. It saves money by cutting out the costs of transporting goods to Amazon's fulfillment centers, which in turn lets it charge more competitive prices to the e-commerce giant. And although P&G is a superb in-store brand marketer, it is still a relative newcomer to online selling, one of the company's top priorities. Through Vendor Flex, P&G gets Amazon's expert help in moving its brands online.

So the Amazon–P&G partnership looks like an ideal match for both companies. If P&G wants to do better at selling its brands online, what better partner than Amazon, the undisputed master of online retailing? If Amazon wants to do better at selling household staples, what better partner than P&G, the acknowledged master of consumer package goods marketing? Together, under Amazon's Vendor Flex, these respective industry leaders can flex their distribution muscles to their own benefit and to the benefit of the consumers they jointly serve.

Sources: George Anderson, *"Why Amazon Is Trying to Convince CPG Giants to Go Direct-to-Consumers," Forbes, April 7, 2017, www.forbes.com/sites/retailwire/2017/04/07/why-amazon-is-trying-to-convince-cpg-giants-to-go-consumer-direct/#789427a94607;* Jeffery K. Liker and Thomas Y. Choi, "Building Deep Supplier Relationships," *Harvard Business Review,* 2004, pp.104–113; Alex Short, "Amazon and P&G Blow Business Collaboration Wide Open!" *Vizibl,* July 21, 2015, http://blog.vizibl.co/amazon-pg-blow-business-collaboration-wide-open/; Serena Ng, "Soap Opera: Amazon Moves In with P&G," *Wall Street Journal,* October 15, 2013, p. A1; "GM Jumps to Third Place, Nissan Falls to Last, in Annual Study of Automakers' Relations with Suppliers," May 15, 2017, www.ppi1.com/wp-content/uploads/2017/11/2017-wri-press-release-05-15-17-final.pdf; and www.toyotasupplier.com, https://toyotasupplierdiversity.com/, and www.loreal.com/_en/_ww/html/suppliers/, accessed October 2018.

from product design and delivery to service and support. As a result of its close partnership with dealers, Caterpillar dominates the world's markets for heavy construction, mining, and logging equipment. Its familiar yellow tractors, crawlers, loaders, bulldozers, and trucks capture a commanding share of the worldwide heavy-equipment business, nearly twice that of number two Komatsu.

Many companies are now installing integrated high-tech partnership relationship management (PRM) systems to coordinate their whole-channel marketing efforts. Just as they use customer relationship management (CRM) software systems to help manage relationships with important customers, companies can now use PRM and supply chain management (SCM) software to help recruit, train, organize, manage, motivate, and evaluate relationships with channel partners.

Evaluating Channel Members

The company must regularly check channel member performance against standards such as sales quotas, average inventory levels, customer delivery time, treatment of damaged and lost goods, cooperation in company promotion and training programs, and services to the customer. The company should recognize and reward intermediaries that are performing well and adding good value for consumers. Those that are performing poorly should be assisted or, as a last resort, replaced. Finally, companies need to be sensitive to the needs of their channel partners. Those that treat their partners poorly risk not only losing their support but also causing some legal problems. The next section describes various rights and duties pertaining to companies and other channel members.

Public Policy and Distribution Decisions

For the most part, companies are legally free to develop whatever channel arrangements suit them. In fact, the laws affecting channels seek to prevent the exclusionary tactics of some companies that might keep another company from using a desired channel. Most channel law deals with the mutual rights and duties of channel members once they have formed a relationship.

Many producers and wholesalers like to develop exclusive channels for their products. When the seller allows only certain outlets to carry its products, this strategy is called *exclusive distribution*. When the seller requires that these dealers not handle competitors' products, its strategy is called *exclusive dealing*. Both parties can benefit from exclusive arrangements: The seller obtains more loyal and dependable outlets, and the dealers obtain a steady source of supply and stronger seller support. But exclusive arrangements also exclude other producers from selling to these dealers. This situation brings exclusive dealing contracts under the scope of the Clayton Act of 1914. They are legal as long as they do not substantially lessen competition or tend to create a monopoly and as long as both parties enter into the agreement voluntarily.

Exclusive dealing often includes *exclusive territorial agreements*. The producer may agree not to sell to other dealers in a given area, or the buyer may agree to sell only in its own territory. The first practice is normal under franchise systems as a way to increase dealer enthusiasm and commitment. It is also perfectly legal—a seller has no legal obligation to sell through more outlets than it wishes. The second practice, whereby the producer tries to keep a dealer from selling outside its territory, has become a major legal issue.

Producers of a strong brand sometimes sell it to dealers only if the dealers will take some or all of the rest of its line. This is called *full-line forcing*. Such *tying agreements* are not necessarily illegal, but they violate the Clayton Act if they tend to lessen competition substantially. The practice may prevent consumers from freely choosing among competing suppliers of these other brands.

Finally, producers are free to select their dealers, but their right to terminate dealers is somewhat restricted. In general, sellers can drop dealers "for cause." However, they cannot drop dealers if, for example, the dealers refuse to cooperate in a doubtful legal arrangement, such as exclusive dealing or tying agreements.

LINKING THE CONCEPTS

Time for another pause. This time, compare the Caterpillar and McDonald's channel systems.

- Diagram the Caterpillar and McDonald's channel systems. How do they compare in terms of channel levels, types of intermediaries, channel member roles and responsibilities, and other characteristics? How well is each system designed?
- Assess how well Caterpillar and McDonald's have managed and supported their channels. With what results?

Author Comment
Marketers used to call this plain-old "physical distribution." But as these titles suggest, the topic has grown in importance, complexity, and sophistication.

Marketing Logistics and Supply Chain Management

OBJECTIVE 10-5 Discuss the nature and importance of marketing logistics and integrated supply chain management.

In today's global marketplace, selling a product is sometimes easier than getting it to customers. Companies must decide on the best way to store, handle, and move their products and services so that they are available to customers in the right assortments, at the right time, and in the right place. Logistics effectiveness has a major impact on both customer satisfaction and company costs. Here we consider the nature and importance of logistics management in the supply chain, the goals of the logistics system, major logistics functions, and the need for integrated supply chain management.

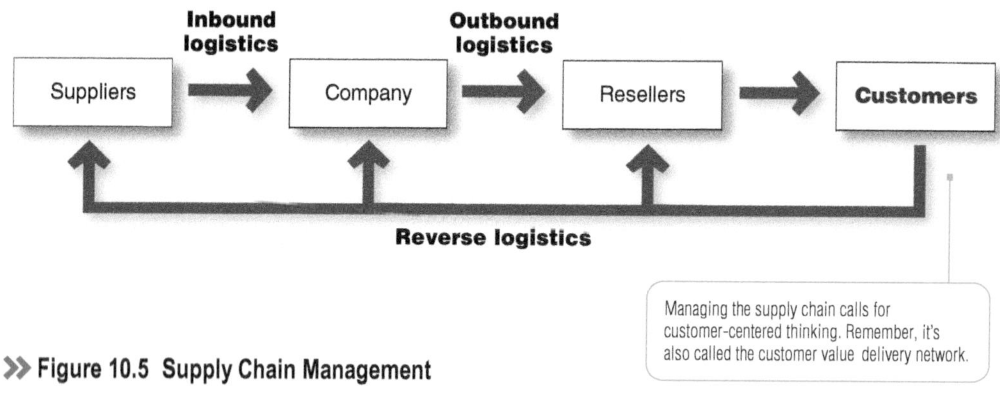

Managing the supply chain calls for customer-centered thinking. Remember, it's also called the customer value delivery network.

Figure 10.5 Supply Chain Management

Nature and Importance of Marketing Logistics

Marketing logistics (physical distribution)
Planning, implementing, and controlling the physical flow of materials, final goods, and related information from points of origin to points of consumption to meet customer requirements at a profit.

Supply chain management
Managing upstream and downstream value-added flows of materials, final goods, and related information among suppliers, the company, resellers, and final consumers.

To some managers, marketing logistics means only trucks and warehouses. But modern logistics is much more than this. **Marketing logistics**—also called **physical distribution**—involves planning, implementing, and controlling the physical flow of goods, services, and related information from points of origin to points of consumption to meet customer requirements at a profit. In short, it involves getting the right product to the right customer in the right place at the right time profitably.

In the past, physical distribution planners typically started with products at the plant and then tried to find low-cost solutions to get them to customers. However, today's *customer-centered* logistics starts with the marketplace and works backward to the factory or even to sources of supply. Marketing logistics involves not only *outbound logistics* (moving products from the factory to resellers and ultimately to customers) but also *inbound logistics* (moving products and materials from suppliers to the factory) and *reverse logistics* (reusing, recycling, refurbishing, or disposing of broken, unwanted, or excess products returned by consumers or resellers). That is, it involves the entirety of **supply chain management**—managing upstream and downstream value-added flows of materials, final goods, and related information among suppliers, the company, resellers, and final consumers, as shown in **Figure 10.5**.

The logistics manager's task is to coordinate the activities of suppliers, purchasing agents, marketers, channel members, and customers. These activities include forecasting, information systems, purchasing, production planning, order processing, inventory, warehousing, and transportation planning.

Companies today are placing greater emphasis on logistics for several reasons. First, companies can gain a powerful competitive advantage by using improved logistics to give customers better service or lower prices. Second, improved logistics can yield tremendous cost savings to both a company and its customers. As much as 20 percent of an average product's price is accounted for by shipping and transport alone.

American companies spend $1.39 trillion each year—about 7.5 percent of GDP—to wrap, bundle, load, unload, sort, reload, and transport goods. That's more than the total national GDPs of all but 19 countries worldwide. By itself, General Motors has hundreds of millions of tons of finished vehicles, production parts, and aftermarket parts in transit at any given time, running up an annual logistics bill of about $8 billion. Shaving off even a small fraction of logistics costs can mean substantial savings. For example,

The importance of logistics: At any given time, GM has hundreds of millions of tons of finished vehicles and parts in transit, running up an annual logistics bill of about $8 billion. Even small savings can be substantial.

SeongJoon Cho/Bloomberg via Getty Images

GM recently announced a logistical overhaul that would save nearly $2 billion over two years in North America alone.[21]

Third, the explosion in product variety has created a need for improved logistics management. For example, in 1916 the typical Piggly Wiggly grocery store carried only 605 items. Today, a Piggly Wiggly carries a bewildering stock of between 20,000 and 35,000 items, depending on store size. A Walmart Supercenter store carries 142,000 products, 30,000 of which are grocery products.[22] Ordering, shipping, stocking, and controlling such a variety of products presents a sizable logistics challenge.

Improvements in information technology have also created opportunities for major gains in distribution efficiency. Today's companies are using sophisticated supply chain management software, internet-based logistics systems, point-of-sale scanners, RFID tags, satellite tracking, and electronic transfer of order and payment data. Such technology lets them quickly and efficiently manage the flow of goods, information, and finances through the supply chain.

Finally, more than almost any other marketing function, logistics affects the environment and a firm's environmental sustainability efforts. Transportation, warehousing, packaging, and other logistics functions are typically the biggest supply chain contributors to the company's environmental footprint. Therefore, many companies are now developing *green supply chains*.

Sustainable Supply Chains

Companies have many reasons for reducing the environmental impact of their supply chains. For one thing, if they don't green up voluntarily, a host of sustainability regulations enacted around the world will soon require them to. For another, many large customers—from Walmart and Nike to the federal government—are demanding it. Even consumers are demanding it: According to one survey, 73 percent of millennials are willing to pay more for sustainable products.[23] Thus, environmental sustainability has become an important factor in supplier selection and performance evaluation. But perhaps even more important than *having* to do it, designing sustainable supply chains is simply the *right* thing to do. It's one more way that companies can contribute to saving our world for future generations.

But that's all pretty heady stuff. As it turns out, companies have a more immediate and practical reason for turning their supply chains green. >> Not only are sustainable channels good for the world, they're also good for a company's bottom line. The very logistics activities that create the biggest environmental footprint—such as transportation, warehousing, and packaging—also account for a lion's share of logistics costs. Companies green up their supply chains through greater efficiency, and greater efficiency means lower costs and higher profits. In other words, developing a sustainable supply chain is not only environmentally responsible, it can also be profitable. Consider Levi Strauss & Co.:[24]

>> Green supply chains: Developing a sustainable supply chain is not only environmentally responsible, it can also be profitable.

christianchan/123RF

Water is essential to every step in Levi Strauss's jeans-making process. Making just one pair of Levi's 501's jeans consumes 3,781 liters of water—about three days' worth of water for one U.S. household. To conserve water, Levi's launched a series of innovative techniques called Water<Less, which saves up to 96 percent of the water in the denim finishing process alone. So far, Water<Less innovations have save more than 2 billion liters of water. But more than being good for the planet, Water<Less has also been good for Levi Strauss's bottom line, saving the company more than $1.6 million. Says Levi's vice president of Sustainability, "Sustainability should actually cost less, because, by definition, if you're more sustainable, you're consuming fewer resources, which means you have fewer input costs."

Beyond manufacturing, however, the greatest environmental impact from a pair of jeans occurs in after-purchase care. So to save even more water, Levi Strauss launched a Water<Less line of jeans made specifically to require no machine washing. The company tells consumers that washing their jeans less, washing them in cold water, and line drying them can reduce the full life-cycle climate change impact of a pair of jeans by as much as 50 percent. Once again, what's good for consumers is also good for Levi Strauss. "Being known as a progressive brand also has helped carry Levi's through difficult business times," says the executive. "After all, consumers love a sustainable company."

Goals of the Logistics System

Some companies state their logistics objective as providing maximum customer service at the least cost. Unfortunately, as nice as this sounds, no logistics system can *both* maximize customer service *and* minimize distribution costs. Maximum customer service implies rapid delivery, large inventories, flexible assortments, liberal returns policies, and other services—all of which raise distribution costs. In contrast, minimum distribution costs imply slower delivery, smaller inventories, and larger shipping lots—which represent a lower level of overall customer service.

The goal of marketing logistics should be to provide a *targeted* level of customer service at the least cost. A company must first research the importance of various distribution services to customers and then set desired service levels for each segment. The objective is to maximize *profits*, not sales. Therefore, the company must weigh the benefits of providing higher levels of service against the costs. Some companies offer less service than their competitors and charge a lower price. Other companies offer more service and charge higher prices to cover higher costs.

Major Logistics Functions

Given a set of logistics objectives, the company designs a logistics system that will minimize the cost of attaining these objectives. The major logistics functions are *warehousing, inventory management, transportation*, and *logistics information management*.

Warehousing

Production and consumption cycles rarely match, so most companies must store their goods while they wait to be sold. For example, Snapper, Toro, and other lawn mower manufacturers run their factories all year long and store up products for the heavy spring and summer buying seasons. The storage function overcomes differences in needed quantities and timing, ensuring that products are available when customers are ready to buy them.

A company must decide on *how many* and *what types* of warehouses it needs and *where* they will be located. The company might use either *storage warehouses* or *distribution centers*. Storage warehouses store goods for moderate to long periods. In contrast, **distribution centers** are designed to move goods rather than just store them. They are large and highly automated warehouses designed to receive goods from various plants and suppliers, take orders, fill them efficiently, and deliver goods to customers as quickly as possible.

Distribution center
A large, highly automated warehouse designed to receive goods from various plants and suppliers, take orders, fill them efficiently, and deliver goods to customers as quickly as possible.

For example, Amazon operates more than 70 giant distribution centers in the United States, called fulfillment centers, which fill online orders and handle returns. These centers are huge and highly automated. For example, the Amazon fulfillment center in Tracy, California, covers 1.2 million square feet (equivalent to 27 football fields). At the center, 4,000 employees control an inventory of 21 million items and ship out up to 700,000 packages a day to Amazon customers in Northern California and parts of the Pacific Northwest. During last year's Cyber Monday, Amazon's fulfillment center network filled customer orders at a rate of more than 740 items per second globally.[25]

Like almost everything else these days, warehousing has seen dramatic changes in technology in recent years. Outdated materials-handling methods are steadily being replaced

» **High-tech distribution centers: Amazon employs teams of super-retrievers—Day-Glo-orange Kiva robots—to keep its fulfillment centers humming.**

Bloomberg via Getty Images

by newer, automated systems requiring fewer employees. Computers and scanners read orders and direct lift trucks, electric hoists, or robots to gather goods, move them to loading docks, and issue invoices. » For example, Amazon uses an army of robots to make its fulfillment centers more efficient:[26]

> When you buy from Amazon, the chances are good that your order will still be plucked and packed by human hands. However, the humans in Amazon's fulfillment centers are now assisted by an army of more than 100,000 squat, ottoman-size, Day-Glo-orange robots, developed by the digital giant's own Amazon Robotics division. The robots bring racks of merchandise to workers, who in turn fill boxes with orders. The robots make warehouse work less tedious and physically taxing for employees while also creating efficiencies let that a customer order something as small as dental floss and receive it within two days. Dubbed the "magic shelf," racks of items simply materialize in front of workers, with red lasers pointing to items to be picked. The robots then drive off and new shelves appear. The super-efficient robots work tirelessly 16 hours a day, seven days a week. They never complain about the workload or ask for pay raises, and they are pretty much maintenance free. "The robot will work the same all day long," says an Amazon warehouse supervisor. And "their stomachs don't grumble."

Inventory Management

Inventory management also affects customer satisfaction. Here, managers must maintain the delicate balance between carrying too little inventory and carrying too much. With too little stock, the firm risks not having products when customers want to buy. To remedy this, the firm may need costly emergency shipments or production. Carrying too much inventory results in higher-than-necessary inventory-carrying costs and stock obsolescence. Thus, in managing inventory, firms must balance the costs of carrying larger inventories against resulting sales and profits.

Many companies have greatly reduced their inventories and related costs through *just-in-time* logistics systems. With such systems, producers and retailers carry only small inventories of parts or merchandise, often enough for only a few days of operations. New stock arrives exactly when needed rather than being stored in inventory until being used. Just-in-time systems require accurate forecasting along with fast, frequent, and flexible delivery so that new supplies will be available when needed. However, these systems result in substantial savings in inventory-carrying and inventory-handling costs.

When it comes to managing inventories, Walmart doesn't mess around with its suppliers. With the goal of having just enough but not too much inventory on its shelves, Walmart demands "On-Time, In-Full" deliveries to its stores. Suppliers who miss the designated delivery window pay the price. "Two days late? That'll earn you a fine," says an analyst. "One day early? That's a fine, too. Right on time but good aren't packed properly? You guessed it—fine." While this delivery policy seems severe, Walmart pays a huge price for having too little inventory (lost sales) or too much (inventory carrying costs). Inventory "variability is the No. 1 killer in the supply chain," says a Walmart operations manager.[27]

Marketers are always looking for new ways to make inventory management more efficient. For example, many companies now use some form of RFID or "smart tag" technology, by which small transmitter chips are embedded in or placed on products, packaging, and shipping pallets for everything from flowers, fashions, and razors to tires. Such smart tags can make the entire supply chain—which accounts for up to 75 percent of a product's cost—intelligent and automated. Many large and resourceful marketing companies, such as Walmart, Macy's, P&G, and IBM, are investing heavily to make the full use of RFID technology a reality.

Transportation

The choice of transportation carriers affects the pricing of products, delivery performance, and the condition of goods when they arrive—all of which will affect customer satisfaction. » In shipping goods to its warehouses, dealers, and customers, the company can choose among five main transportation modes: truck, rail, water, pipeline, and air along with an alternative mode for digital products—the internet.

Trucks have increased their share of transportation steadily and now account for 64 percent of total tons transported in the United States. Trucks are highly flexible in their routing and time schedules, and they can usually offer faster service than railroads. They are efficient for short hauls of high-value merchandise. Trucking firms have evolved in recent years to become full-service providers of global transportation services. For example, large trucking firms now offer everything from satellite tracking, internet-based shipment management, and logistics planning software to cross-border shipping operations.[28]

» **Transportation: In shipping goods to their warehouses, dealers, and customers, companies can choose among many transportation modes, including truck, rail, water, pipeline, and air. Much of today's shipping requires multiple modes.**

Thanapun/Shutterstock

Railroads account for 10 percent of the total tons shipped. They are one of the most cost-effective modes for shipping large amounts of bulk products—coal, sand, minerals, and farm and forest products—over long distances. In recent years, railroads have increased their customer services by designing new equipment to handle special categories of goods, providing flatcars for carrying truck trailers by rail (piggyback), and providing in-transit services such as the diversion of shipped goods to other destinations en route and the processing of goods en route.

Water carriers, which account for 4 percent of goods transported, transport large amounts of goods by ships and barges on U.S. coastal and inland waterways. Although the cost of water transportation is very low for shipping bulky, low-value, nonperishable products such as sand, coal, grain, oil, and metallic ores, water transportation is the slowest mode and may be affected by the weather. *Pipelines*, which account for 18 percent of the tonnage transported, are a specialized means of shipping petroleum, natural gas, and chemicals from sources to markets. Most pipelines are used by their owners to ship their own products.

Although *air* carriers transport less than 1 percent of the of the nation's goods, they are an important transportation mode. Airfreight rates are much higher than rail or truck rates, but airfreight is ideal when speed is needed or distant markets have to be reached. Among the most frequently airfreighted products are perishables (such as fresh fish, cut flowers) and high-value, low-bulk items (technical instruments, jewelry). Companies find that airfreight also reduces inventory levels, packaging costs, and the number of warehouses needed.

The *internet* carries digital products from producer to customer via satellite, cable, phone wire, or wireless signal. Software firms, the media, music and video companies, and education all make use of the internet to deliver digital content. The internet holds the potential for lower product distribution costs. Whereas planes, trucks, and trains move freight and packages, digital technology moves information bits.

Multimodal transportation
Combining two or more modes of transportation.

Shippers also use **multimodal transportation**—combining two or more modes of transportation. *Piggyback* describes the use of rail and trucks; *fishyback*, water and trucks; *trainship*, water and rail; and *airtruck*, air and trucks. Combining modes provides advantages that no single mode can deliver. Each combination offers advantages to the shipper. For example, not only is piggyback cheaper than trucking alone, but it also provides flexibility and convenience. Numerous logistics companies provide single-source multimodal transportation solutions.

Logistics Information Management

Companies manage their supply chains through information. Channel partners often link up to share information and make better joint logistics decisions. From a logistics perspective, flows of information, such as customer transactions, billing, shipment and inventory levels, and even customer data, are closely linked to channel performance. Companies need simple, accessible, fast, and accurate processes for capturing, processing, and sharing channel information.

Information can be shared and managed in many ways, but most sharing takes place through *electronic data interchange* (*EDI*), the digital exchange of data between organizations, which primarily is transmitted via the internet. Walmart, for example, requires EDI links with its more than 100,000 suppliers through its Retail Link sales data system. If new suppliers don't have the required EDI capability, Walmart will work with them to find and implement the needed tools.[29]

In some cases, suppliers might actually be asked to generate orders and arrange deliveries for their customers. Many large retailers—such as Walmart and Home Depot—work closely with major suppliers such as P&G or Moen to set up *vendor-managed inventory (VMI)* systems or *continuous inventory replenishment* systems. Using VMI, the customer shares real-time data on sales and current inventory levels with the supplier. The supplier then takes full responsibility for managing inventories and deliveries. Some retailers even go so far as to shift inventory and delivery costs to the supplier. Such systems require close cooperation between the buyer and seller.

Integrated Logistics Management

Integrated logistics management
The logistics concept that emphasizes teamwork—both inside the company and among all the marketing channel organizations—to maximize the performance of the entire distribution system.

Today, more and more companies are adopting the concept of **integrated logistics management**. This concept recognizes that providing better customer service and trimming distribution costs require *teamwork*, both inside the company and among all the marketing channel organizations. Inside, the company's various departments must work closely together to maximize its own logistics performance. Outside, the company must integrate its logistics system with those of its suppliers and customers to maximize the performance of the entire distribution network.

Cross-Functional Teamwork Inside the Company

Most companies assign responsibility for various logistics activities to many different departments—marketing, sales, finance, operations, and purchasing. Too often, each function tries to optimize its own logistics performance without regard for the activities of the other functions. However, transportation, inventory, warehousing, and information management activities interact, often in an inverse way. Lower inventory levels reduce inventory-carrying costs. But they may also reduce customer service and increase costs from stockouts, backorders, special production runs, and costly fast-freight shipments. Because distribution activities involve strong trade-offs, decisions by various functions must be coordinated to achieve better overall logistics performance.

The goal of integrated supply chain management is to harmonize all of the company's logistics decisions. Close working relationships among departments can be achieved in several ways. Some companies have created permanent logistics committees composed of managers responsible for different physical distribution activities. Companies can also create supply chain manager positions that link the logistics activities of functional areas. For example, P&G has created product supply managers who manage all the supply chain activities for each product category. Many companies have a vice president of logistics or a supply chain VP with cross-functional authority.

Finally, companies can employ sophisticated, system-wide supply chain management software, now available from a wide range of software enterprises large and small, from Oracle and SAP to Logility. >> For example, Oracle's supply chain management software solutions help companies to "gain sustainable advantage and drive innovation by transforming their traditional supply chains into integrated value chains."[30] It coordinates every aspect of the supply chain, from value chain collaboration to inventory optimization to transportation and logistics management. The important thing is that the company must coordinate its logistics, inventory investments, demand forecasting, and marketing activities to create high market satisfaction at a reasonable cost.

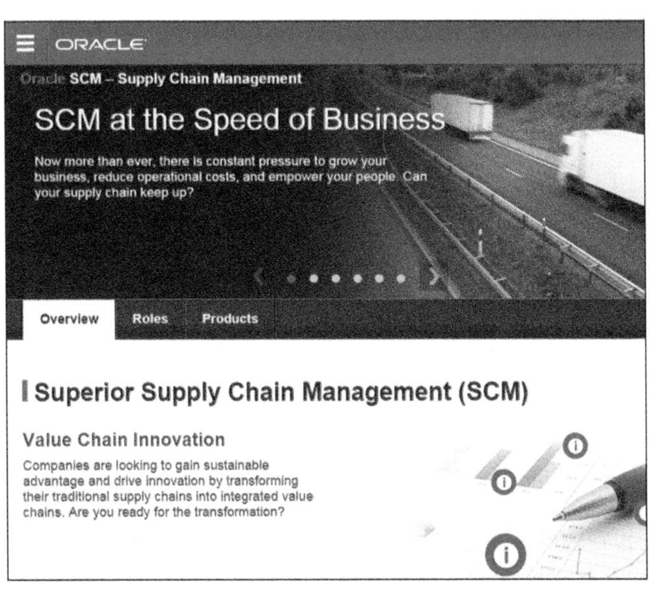

>> Integrated logistics management: Oracle's supply chain management software solutions help companies to "gain sustainable advantage and drive innovation by transforming their traditional supply chains into integrated value chains."
Oracle Corporation

Building Logistics Partnerships

Companies must do more than improve their own logistics. They must also work with other channel partners to improve whole-channel distribution. The members of a marketing channel are linked closely in creating customer value and building customer relationships. One company's distribution system is another company's supply system. The success of each channel member depends on the performance of the entire supply chain. For example, furniture retailer IKEA can create its stylish but affordable furniture and deliver the "IKEA lifestyle" only if its entire supply chain—consisting of thousands of merchandise designers and suppliers, transport companies, warehouses, and service providers—operates at maximum efficiency and with customer-focused effectiveness.

Smart companies coordinate their logistics strategies and forge strong partnerships with suppliers and customers to improve customer service and reduce channel costs. Many companies have created *cross-functional, cross-company teams*. For example, Nestlé's Purina pet food unit has a team of dozens of people working in Bentonville, Arkansas, the home base of Walmart. The Purina Walmart team members work jointly with their counterparts at Walmart to find ways to squeeze costs out of their distribution system. Working together benefits not only Purina and Walmart but also their shared, final consumers.

Other companies partner through *shared projects*. For example, many large retailers conduct joint in-store programs with suppliers. Home Depot allows key suppliers to use its stores as a testing ground for new merchandising programs. The suppliers spend time at Home Depot stores watching how their product sells and how customers relate to it. They then create programs specially tailored to Home Depot and its customers. Clearly, both the supplier and the customer benefit from such partnerships. The point is that all supply chain members must work together in the cause of bringing value to final consumers.

Third-Party Logistics

Although most big companies love to make and sell their products, many loathe the associated logistics "grunt work." They detest the bundling, loading, unloading, sorting, storing, reloading, transporting, customs clearing, and tracking required to supply their factories and get products to their customers. They hate it so much that many firms outsource some or all of their logistics to **third-party logistics (3PL) providers** such as Ryder, Penske Logistics, BAX Global, DHL Logistics, FedEx Logistics, and UPS Business Solutions.

Third-party logistics (3PL) provider
An independent logistics provider that performs any or all of the functions required to get a client's product to market.

For example, UPS knows that, for many companies, logistics can be a real nightmare. But logistics is exactly what UPS does best. To UPS, logistics is today's most powerful force for creating competitive advantage. To its supply chain customers, UPS stands for "United Problem Solvers." At one level, UPS can simply handle a company's package shipments. But on a deeper level, UPS can help businesses sharpen their own logistics systems to cut costs and serve customers better. At a still deeper level, companies can let UPS take over and manage part or all of their logistics operations.

For example, UPS not only delivers packages for online retailer Overstock.com, it also manages Overstock's complex order returns process in an efficient, customer-pleasing way. Consumer electronics maker Toshiba lets UPS handle its entire laptop PC repair process—lock, stock, and barrel. Individuals simply drop their computers off at a nearby UPS store, which forwards them to a special UPS facility next to its Worldport central hub for repair. The UPS–Toshiba computer repair process is so efficient that laptops brought in one day can often be sent back to the owner the next day. "Customers are expecting the world from you," says UPS. "We can help you deliver."[31]

3PL providers like UPS can help clients tighten up sluggish, overstuffed supply chains; slash inventories; and get products to customers more quickly and reliably. According to one report, 90 percent of *Fortune* 500 companies now use 3PL (also called *outsourced logistics* or *contract logistics*) services, compared to only 46 percent in 2001. General Motors, P&G, and Walmart each use 50 or more 3PLs.[32]

Companies use third-party logistics providers for several reasons. First, because getting the product to market is their main focus these providers can often do it more efficiently and at lower cost. Second, outsourcing logistics frees a company to focus more intensely on its core business. Finally, integrated logistics companies understand increasingly complex logistics environments.

REVIEWING AND EXTENDING THE CONCEPTS

CHAPTER REVIEW AND KEY TERMS

Objectives Review

Some companies pay too little attention to their distribution channels; others, however, have used imaginative distribution systems to gain a competitive advantage. A company's channel decisions directly affect every other marketing decision. Management must make channel decisions carefully, incorporating today's needs with tomorrow's likely selling environment.

OBJECTIVE 10-1 Explain why companies use marketing channels and discuss the functions these channels perform. (pp 302–306)

In creating customer engagement and value, a company can't go it alone. It must work within an entire network of partners—a value delivery network—to accomplish this task. Individual companies and brands don't compete; their entire value delivery networks do.

Most producers use intermediaries to bring their products to market. They forge a *marketing channel* (or *distribution channel*)—a set of interdependent organizations involved in the process of making a product or service available for use or consumption by the consumer or business user. Through their contacts, experience, specialization, and scale of operation, intermediaries usually offer the firm more than it can achieve on its own.

Marketing channels perform many key functions. Some help *complete transactions* by gathering and distributing *information* needed for planning and aiding exchange, developing and spreading persuasive *communications* about an offer, performing *contact* work (finding and communicating with prospective buyers), *matching* (shaping and fitting the offer to the buyer's needs), and entering into *negotiation* to reach an agreement on price and other terms of the offer so that ownership can be transferred. Other functions help to *fulfill* the completed transactions by offering *physical distribution* (transporting and storing goods), *financing* (acquiring and using funds to cover the costs of the channel work), and *risk taking* (assuming the risks of carrying out the channel work.

OBJECTIVE 10-2 Discuss how channel members interact and how they organize to perform the work of the channel. (pp 306–313)

The channel will be most effective when each member assumes the tasks it can do best. Ideally, because the success of individual channel members depends on overall channel success, all channel firms should work together smoothly. They should understand and accept their roles, coordinate their goals and activities, and cooperate to attain overall channel goals. By cooperating, they can more effectively sense, serve, and satisfy the target market.

In a large company, the formal organization structure assigns roles and provides needed leadership. But in a distribution channel composed of independent firms, leadership and power are not formally set. Traditionally, distribution channels have lacked the leadership needed to assign roles and manage conflict. In recent years, however, new types of channel organizations have appeared that provide stronger leadership and improved performance.

OBJECTIVE 10-3 Identify the major channel alternatives open to a company. (pp 314–317)

Channel alternatives vary from direct selling to using one, two, three, or more intermediary *channel levels*. Marketing channels face continuous and sometimes dramatic change. Three of the most important trends are the growth of *vertical, horizontal*, and *multichannel marketing systems*. These trends affect channel cooperation, conflict, and competition.

Channel design begins with assessing customer channel service needs and company channel objectives and constraints. The company then identifies the major channel alternatives in terms of the *types* of intermediaries, the *number* of intermediaries, and the *channel responsibilities* of each. Each channel alternative must be evaluated according to economic, control, and adaptive criteria. *Channel management* calls for selecting qualified intermediaries and motivating them. Individual channel members must be evaluated regularly.

OBJECTIVE 10-4 Explain how companies select, motivate, and evaluate channel members. (pp 317–321)

Producers vary in their ability to attract qualified marketing intermediaries. Some producers have no trouble signing up channel members, whereas others have to work hard to line up enough qualified intermediaries. When selecting intermediaries, the company should evaluate each channel member's qualifications and select those that best fit its channel objectives.

Once selected, channel members must be continuously motivated to do their best. The company must sell not only *through* the intermediaries but also *with* them. It should forge strong partnerships with channel members to create a marketing system that meets the needs of both the manufacturer *and* the partners.

OBJECTIVE 10-5 Discuss the nature and importance of marketing logistics and integrated supply chain management. (pp 321–328)

Marketing logistics (or *physical distribution*) is an area of potentially high cost savings and improved customer satisfaction. Marketing logistics addresses not only *outbound logistics* but also *inbound logistics* and *reverse logistics*. That is, it involves the entire *supply chain management*—managing value-added flows between suppliers, the company, resellers, and final users. No logistics system can both maximize customer service and minimize distribution costs. Instead, the goal of logistics management is to provide a *targeted* level of service at the least cost. The major logistics functions are *warehousing, inventory management, transportation*, and *logistics information management*.

The *integrated supply chain management concept* recognizes that improved logistics requires teamwork in the form of close working relationships across functional areas inside the company and across various organizations in the supply chain. Companies can achieve logistics harmony among functions by creating cross-functional logistics teams, integrative supply manager positions, and senior-level logistics executive positions with cross-functional authority. Channel partnerships can take the form of cross-company teams, shared projects, and information-sharing systems. Today, some companies are outsourcing their logistics functions to third-party logistics (3PL) providers to save costs, increase efficiency, and gain faster and more effective access to global markets.

Key Terms

Objective 10-1
Value delivery network (p 303)
Marketing channel (distribution channel) (p 303)
Channel level (p 305)
Direct marketing channel (p 305)
Indirect marketing channel (p 305)

Objective 10-2
Channel conflict (p 307)
Conventional distribution channel (p 307)
Vertical marketing system (VMS) (p 307)
Corporate VMS (p 308)
Contractual VMS (p 308)
Franchise organization (p 308)
Administered VMS (p 309)
Horizontal marketing system (p 309)
Multichannel distribution system (p 310)
Disintermediation (p 311)

Objective 10-3
Marketing channel design (p 314)
Intensive distribution (p 316)
Exclusive distribution (p 316)
Selective distribution (p 316)

Objective 10-4
Marketing channel management (p 317)

Objective 10-5
Marketing logistics (physical distribution) (p 322)
Supply chain management (p 322)
Distribution center (p 324)
Multimodal transportation (p 326)
Integrated logistics management (p 327)
Third-party logistics (3PL) provider (p 328)

DISCUSSION AND CRITICAL THINKING

Discussion Questions

10-1. Describe a value delivery network. How does it differ from a supply chain? Explain. (AACSB: Written and Oral Communication; Reflective Thinking)

10-2. Discuss direct marketing channels and indirect marketing channels. Provide examples of each type of marketing channel. (AACSB: Written and Oral Communication)

10-3. Explain the difference between a conventional distribution channel, a vertical marketing system, and a horizontal marketing system. (AACSB: Written and Oral Communication)

10-4. What channel design decisions do manufacturers face for maximum effectiveness? (AACSB: Written and Oral Communication; Reflective Thinking)

10-5. How do logistics managers effectively manage the supply chain? Why do companies need to pay close attention to managing logistics? (AACSB: Written and Oral Communication; Reflective Thinking)

10-6. Define *integrated logistics management*, and discuss its importance in a firm achieving its corporate goals. (AACSB: Written and Oral Communication; Reflective Thinking)

Critical Thinking Exercises

10-7. The franchise organization is the most common type of contractual vertical marketing system. Vertical conflict, conflict between different levels of the same channel, is common in this channel. Research the possible causes of conflict in the franchisee–franchisor relationship and the best strategies for resolving that conflict. Report on your findings. (AACSB: Written and Oral Communication; Information Technology; Reflective Thinking)

10-8. Review the strategies available to companies when determining how to best distribute their products: intensive, exclusive, and selective distribution. Select five products (in more than one category) that you or someone you know has recently purchased. Describe the product, the manufacturer, where you purchased it, and which distribution strategy was used. (AACSB: Written and Oral Communication; Reflective Thinking)

10-9. Multimodal transportation is a crucial component of the logistics industry. Search the internet to find the largest multimodal facilities in the United States. Review the key features offered at these terminals, and report your findings on their similarities and differences. (AACSB: Written and Oral Communication; Information Technology; Reflective Thinking)

MINICASES AND APPLICATIONS

Online, Mobile, and Social Media Marketing Fabletics Changing Channels

According to the Fabletics company website, www.fabletics.com, JustFab Inc. co-CEOs Don Ressler and Adam Goldenberg launched Fabletics with Kate Hudson after they saw a gap in the activewear marketplace. There were plenty of luxury brands, but none that offered stylish and high-quality gear at an accessible price point. These three unstoppable innovators joined forces to create the Fabletics brand in 2013. Fabletics, a division of Just-Fab, offers affordable, high-quality, and stylish workout clothes including yoga pants, leggings, joggers, tops, tees, and more for women and men at every fitness level. After being in business just a few short years, the company ranked number 98 in the Internet Retailer 2015 Top 500 Guide with revenues of $150 million. Although initially internet-based, Fabletics moved into brick-and-mortar retailing in 2015. It plans to open 75 to 100 stores by 2020.

10-10. Conduct research to learn more about Fabletics. Discuss how Fabletics is meeting customer needs through its value delivery network. What controversy surrounds the company? (AACSB: Written and Oral Communication; Reflective Thinking; Information Technology)

10-11. What type of marketing channel is Fabletics using? What is its distribution strategy? Did opening brick-and-mortar stores make sense for Fabletics? Explain. (AACSB: Written and Oral Communication; Reflective Thinking; Information Technology)

Marketing Ethics Single-Pilot Cargo Planes?

A possible shift is in the works in the aviation industry. The Federal Aviation Administration and members of the U.S. Congress are investigating legislation to allow cargo pilots to operate single-pilot flights. Research is being conducted into what technologies would be necessary to enable single-pilot planes. Airline pilots are pushing back. The International Brotherhood of Teamsters Airline Division says that single-pilot flights would be unsafe and would put valuable freight assets and the public at risk. Also, they would affect staffing levels at major logistics carriers, such as UPS and FedEx. If this idea takes off and is embraced by lawmakers and the public, the practice could make its way to passenger airlines as well. Even autonomous planes could be a possibility. However, industry safety groups say that members of the public are watching what happens with autonomous vehicles to determine whether such technology is practicable.

10-12. Discuss the pros and cons of single-pilot cargo planes. Explain your answer. (AACSB: Written and Oral Communication; Reflective Thinking)

10-13. What ethical conflicts could airline pilots face if the industry moves to single-pilot flights? (AACSB: Written and Oral Communication; Reflective Thinking)

Marketing by the Numbers Drinking from the Source

The post-Prohibition "three-tier system" requires the separation of the production, distribution, and retailing of alcohol in most states. That wasn't much of an issue for craft brewers during the explosive growth years between 2011 and 2015 when craft beers doubled their percentage of the beer market and could hardly keep up with demand. However, craft beer volume through the three-tier system grew by just 1.6 percent last year, causing craft brewers to turn to direct distribution for growth. Adding direct distribution, mainly through operating taprooms and brewpubs, resulted in 24 percent volume growth. Taprooms are located in working breweries where consumers can buy beer, and brewpubs are restaurants with a brewery. Now, such establishments account for almost 10 percent of all U.S. bar traffic and for as much as 35 percent of traffic in Denver and San Diego. Some craft beer bar chains are closing locations in states like Texas because of lost sales following a 2013 law that relaxed the three-tier system and allowed breweries to sell 5,000 barrels a year for on-site consumption. Small craft brewers are excited about this trend—they make higher margins selling direct compared to using an indirect channel of distributors and bars. A brewer's average cost per keg of craft beer is $60, and a keg sells to distributors for $90. The distributor then resells the keg to a bar for $120. Each keg contains more than 100 14.5-ounce glasses, the amount typically poured into a 16-ounce glass at a bar to accommodate a foam head. A bar's cost per glass of craft beer poured is $0.88 per glass. The standard in the bar industry is to have 20 percent liquor cost, meaning 20 percent of the price to consumers represents the bar's cost of goods sold, leaving 80 percent for the bar's margin.

10-14. Calculate the price at which a bar will sell one 14.5-ounce glass of craft beer if the desired 80 percent margin is based on selling price. What is the bar's dollar markup on a glass of craft beer? Refer to Setting Price Based on External Factors in Appendix 3: Marketing by the Numbers to learn how to do this analysis. (AACSB: Analytical Thinking)

10-15. Determine the brewer's cost per 14.5-ounce serving (one glass). What price would a brewer sell that glass of beer for to achieve an 80 percent margin based on its selling price at its own taproom or brewpub? What dollar and percentage margin would a brewer realize if the glass of beer was sold for the same price as it is sold in bars? Is the brewer better off using the direct channel compared to the "three-tiered system" indirect channel? (AACSB: Written and Oral Communication; Analytical Thinking; Reflective Thinking)

Video Case Progressive

To view this video case and its accompanying questions, please visit MyLab Marketing.

Progressive has attained top-tier status in the insurance industry by focusing on innovation. Progressive was the first company to offer drive-in claims service, installment payment of premiums, and 24/7 customer service. But perhaps Progressive's most innovative moves involve its channels of distribution. Whereas most insurance companies distribute via intermediary agents or direct-to-consumer methods, Progressive was one of the first to see value in doing both. In the late 1980s, it augmented its agency distribution with a direct 800-number channel.

Two decades ago, Progressive moved into the digital future by becoming the first major insurer to launch a website. Soon after, it allowed customers to buy auto insurance policies online in real time. Today, customers can use Progressive's website to do everything from managing their own account information to reporting claims directly. Progressive even offers one-stop concierge claim service.

Company Cases 10 Target/3 Fitbit/14 OfferUp

See Appendix 1 for cases appropriate for this chapter.

Case 10, Target: A Serious Contender in the Same-Day Delivery Business. Struggling to maintain growth in the world of discount retail, Target recently scored a coup by acquiring same-day delivery startup Shipt.

Case 3, Fitbit: Riding the Fitness Wave to Glory. How did Fitbit create the fast-growing category of wearable tech? By coming up with the right product at the right time.

Case 14, OfferUp: A Mobile Solution for the Mobile Era. By focusing on the local secondhand marketplace with a purely mobile approach that overcomes the shortcomings of Craigslist, OfferUp now poses a real threat to the classified ads leader.

Writing Assignments

10-16. Why does channel conflict occur? Name and describe the various types of channel conflict. (AACSB: Communication)

10-17. Should retailers be responsible for safety conditions in garment supplier factories in other countries? Discuss. (AACSB: Written and Oral Communication; Reflective Thinking; Ethical Understanding and Reasoning)

11 Retailing and Wholesaling

Objectives Outline

OBJECTIVE 11-1 **Explain the role of retailers in the distribution channel and describe the major types of retailers.** See: Retailing (pp 336–344)

OBJECTIVE 11-2 **Discuss how retailers are using omni-channel retailing to meet the cross-channel shopping behavior of today's digitally connected consumers.** See: Omni-Channel Retailing: Blending In-Store, Online, Mobile, and Social Media Channels (pp 345–346)

OBJECTIVE 11-3 **Describe the major retailer marketing decisions.** See: Retailer Marketing Decisions (pp 346–351)

OBJECTIVE 11-4 **Discuss the major trends and developments in retailing.** See: Retailing Trends and Developments (pp 351–357)

OBJECTIVE 11-5 **Explain the major types of wholesalers and their marketing decisions.** See: Wholesaling (pp 357–362)

Previewing the Concepts

We now look more deeply into the two major intermediary marketing channel functions: retailing and wholesaling. You already know something about retailing—retailers of all shapes and sizes serve you every day, both in stores and online. However, you probably know much less about the hoard of wholesalers working behind the scenes. In this chapter, we examine the characteristics of different kinds of retailers and wholesalers, the marketing decisions they make, and trends for the future.

When it comes to retailers, you have to start with Walmart. This megaretailer's phenomenal success has resulted from an unrelenting focus on bringing value to its customers. Day in and day out, Walmart lives up to its promise: "Save money. Live better." But with recent massive shifts toward digital and mobile buying, the giant store retailer now finds itself locked in the fight of its life with another, more recent retail titan—Amazon.

First Stop

Walmart: A Battle between Titans in the New World of Retail

Walmart is almost unimaginably big. It's the world's largest retailer—the world's largest *company*. It rang up an incredible $485 billion in sales last year—more than triple the sales of competitors Target, Macy's, Sears, JCPenney, and Kohl's combined. If Walmart were a country, its sales would rank it 24th in the world in GDP, just behind Sweden and ahead of Poland.

Walmart is the number-one seller in numerous consumer product categories, including groceries, apparel, toys, and pet care products. On average, Walmart serves more than 260 million customers per week through more than 11,600 stores in 28 countries. It's also hard to fathom Walmart's impact on the U.S. economy. It's the nation's largest employer—one out of every 219 working-age people in the United States is a Walmart associate.

Walmart is passionately dedicated to its long-time, low-price value proposition and what those low prices mean to customers: "Save money. Live better." The iconic retailer grew rapidly by offering a broad selection of goods at "unbeatable low prices," day in and day out. No other retailer has come nearly so close to mastering everyday low prices and one-stop shopping. Underlying those low prices, Walmart is a lean, mean distribution machine—it has the lowest cost structure in the industry. Walmart's low costs result from efficient distribution, sophisticated information technology, and good-old "tough buying" from suppliers.

For the past several decades, Walmart has dominated retailing. Yet, despite its incredible success, in recent years mighty Walmart has faced challenges. Having grown so big, the maturing giant has had difficulty maintaining the rapid growth rates of its youth. Its same-store sales growth has stagnated over the past few years. Think about this: To grow just 6 percent next year, Walmart will have to add more than $29 billion in new sales. That's a sales *increase* greater than the *total* sales of all but the top 100 or so companies on the *Fortune* 500, including companies such as McDonald's, Goodyear, Macy's, Facebook, or about two General Mills.

But more than just its size, Walmart's recent malaise is the result of a massive shift in how consumers buy. Although Walmart still dominates *store* retailing and outperforms most of its store-based rivals, consumers are increasingly shifting toward digital and mobile buying. Thus, Walmart is now locked in the fight of its life with another retail titan—online seller Amazon.

Whereas overall U.S. retail sales are inching up only a few percent per year, online sales are surging at 15 percent per year. And Amazon captures an amazing 44 percent of all U.S. online sales. Whereas Walmart's revenues are growing by only a percent or two a year, Amazon's sales have more than double to $177 billion in just the past three years. Unthinkable as it might have seemed only a few years ago, by some estimates, Amazon could overtake Walmart in total revenues in less than 10 years.

Walmart's recent twists and turns—and the colossal battle raging between giants Walmart and Amazon—provide a vivid example of what's happening in today's retailing world—or even in today's broader world. Digital and online technologies have reshaped the

>> Walmart has invested heavily to build its omni-channel capabilities to better serve today's mobile-first, omni-channel consumers.

Eyal Dayan - Photography

very foundations of how the world works. Walmart is now feverishly at work reinventing its strategies to meet the needs of today's mobile-first, omni-channel consumers—buyers who shop readily across digital platforms from home, from work, in stores, or anywhere in between.

In the battle of the titans, each has advantages. No company does store retailing better than Walmart. In turn, no company does online retailing better than Amazon. Now, however, each is invading the other's domain, hoping to give customers the seamless blend of the in-store and digital options they seek. In short, Walmart wants to become Amazon before Amazon can become Walmart.

Walmart has long dominated retailing. It's the world's largest retailer—the world's largest company. But with recent massive shifts toward digital and mobile buying, Walmart is now redefining how it delivers on its "Save money. Live better." promise.

For its part, Amazon is adding bricks and mortar to its powerful online empire. For example, it acquired upscale grocery chain Whole Foods Market, which will not only accelerate its push into grocery retailing but will also provide a physical store platform for selling and delivering other kinds of goods. Amazon is also opening tech-forward physical bookstores and experimenting with futuristic Amazon Go grocery stores, which use cameras and sensors to detect what customers take from shelves and let customers "just walk out," automatically charging purchases to their accounts. Amazon has formed a partnership with Kohl's, by which Kohl's processes Amazon returns at many of its stores. And it's testing Amazon store-within-a-store concepts at some Kohl's and other locations. All these brick-and-mortar moves employ large doses of digital, online, and mobile technology that help Amazon connect the digital and physical worlds.

Walmart still has a huge physical store advantage. And it continues to bolster that advantage by spiffing up its stores and expanding its private label lines of goods you simply can't buy at Amazon.com. But during the past few years, Walmart has also invested heavily to build its omni-channel capabilities. It wants to better serve today's "busy families"—busy, money-challenged households with two working parents who are tethered to their phones at home and at work and are looking for even more convenience and savings.

First, Walmart has expanded its online and mobile options. It has upgraded its websites and mobile apps to improve the online shopping experience. In just one year, it tripled the number of items it offers online from 20 million to 70 million. Walmart has even aligned with Google for voice shopping via Google Home (take that, Alexa!) and is a featured retailer on Google's Google Express shopping site. Further, to bolster its online presence and learn more about doing things digital, Walmart has been on an acquisitions spree. It began by paying $3.3 billion for innovative online discount retailer Jet.com and then scooped up a slew of trendy niche sites: men's apparel retailer Bonobos, women's vintage-style fashions retailer ModCloth, footwear seller ShoeBuy, outdoor gear site Moosejaw, and home furnishings merchant Hayneedle.

Second, to make buying online from Walmart easier and to leverage its store locations, the company is linking online and mobile services to its massive network of stores. It now offers free two-day shipping without an Amazon Prime–like membership fee and is exploring new options for same-day delivery. Walmart has added drive-through or curbside pickup of online grocery orders at one-quarter of its U.S. stores, and many stores now feature "Pickup Towers" inside stores where customers can grab online-ordered items by simply scanning their order numbers. Walmart has also reinvented its returns process with Mobile Express Returns, by which customers can initiate returns on the Walmart app and then fast-track through a mobile express lane at the store.

More and more, everything Walmart does is becoming part of a unified online-offline, omni-channel proposition. The new Walmart is summed up in its recent "More Ways to Walmart" marketing campaign, with ads showing busy families ordering everyday items with ease on their mobile apps and then picking up goods curbside or having them delivered to their doorsteps in bright blue Walmart boxes.

Walmart's omni-channel efforts are paying off. Its online sales are growing at mid-double-digit rates, putting it well ahead of its major discount and department store rivals. Although Walmart still lags far behind Amazon online, Amazon can't come close to matching Walmart's mammoth network of stores. In the long run, however, it won't matter much who has more stores or more online. The future of retailing belongs to the merchant that best merges the digital and physical worlds into a seamless omni-channel experience that fits the ways that today's consumers shop.

In redefining how it delivers on its long-standing "Save money. Live better." promise, Walmart is acting more like a startup than an aging giant. "We are building a business," says Walmart's CEO. "We are learning something new."[1]

The Walmart story sets the stage for examining the fast-changing world of today's resellers. This chapter looks at *retailing* and *wholesaling*. In the first section, we look at the nature and importance of retailing, the major types of retailers, the decisions retailers make, and the future of retailing. In the second section, we discuss these same topics as they apply to wholesalers.

Author Comment
You already know a lot about retailers. You deal with them every day—store retailers, service retailers, online and mobile retailers, and others.

Retailing

OBJECTIVE 11-1 Explain the role of retailers in the distribution channel and describe the major types of retailers.

What is retailing? We all know that Costco, Home Depot, Macy's, and Trader Joe's are retailers, but so are Amazon.com, the local Hampton Inn, and a doctor seeing patients. **Retailing** includes all the activities involved in selling products or services directly to final consumers for their personal, nonbusiness use. Many institutions—manufacturers, wholesalers, and retailers—do retailing. But most retailing is done by **retailers**, businesses whose sales come *primarily* from retailing. Retailing plays a very important role in most marketing channels. Last year, retailers accounted for more than $5 trillion of sales to final consumers.[2]

Retailing
All the activities involved in selling goods or services directly to final consumers for their personal, nonbusiness use.

Retailer
A business whose sales come *primarily* from retailing.

Retailing: Connecting Brands with Consumers

Retailers connect brands with consumers throughout the buying process and at the point of purchase. In fact, many marketers are now embracing the concept of **shopper marketing**, focusing the entire marketing process—from product and brand development to logistics, promotion, and merchandising—toward turning shoppers into buyers as they move along toward the point of sale. Of course, every well-designed marketing effort focuses

Shopper marketing
Focusing the entire marketing process on turning shoppers into buyers as they move along toward the point of sale, whether during in-store, online, or mobile shopping.

on customer buying behavior. What differentiates the concept of shopper marketing is the suggestion that these efforts should be coordinated around the consumer's buying journey itself.

Shopper marketing builds around what P&G has long called the "First Moment of Truth"—the critical three to seven seconds that a shopper considers a product on a store shelf. However, with the dramatic growth of online and mobile shopping, the retailing "moment of truth" no longer takes place only in stores. Instead, Google defines a "zero moment of truth" and "micro-moments," brief seconds of decision making when consumers turn to their online or mobile devices to search for, learn about, or buy something. According to Google, consumers have no brand in mind during 90 percent of their micro-moments. And 73 percent of consumers make a purchase decision based which brand is most useful during micro-moments of retail research.[3] Thus, these days, shopper marketing and the "point of purchase" go well beyond in-store buying.

The Shifting Retailing Model

Online and mobile technologies have caused a massive shift in how and where people buy. Today's consumers are increasingly *omni-channel buyers,* who make little distinction between in-store and online shopping, and for whom the path to a retail purchase runs across multiple channels.

Consumers are increasingly "mobile-first" shoppers who begin—and sometimes end—their buying processes on mobile devices. Purchases often consist of researching a product online and buying it from an online retailer without ever setting foot in a retail store. Or they might involve using a smartphone to research a purchase on the fly or while in retail store aisles. Although 90 percent of all purchases are still made in stores, one recent study found that mobile devices drive more than half of all retail sales. By 2021, smartphone retail sales will represent 24 percent of online sales. "The retail customer journey is now almost unrecognizable from just a few years ago," says a retail analyst.[4]

Such dramatic shifts in buying have caused a massive upheaval in the retailing industry. Increased online buying means less need for physical stores and shopping malls. As Amazon and other online merchants have boomed, traditional store retailers have struggled. Amazon has grown by three Sears in just the past six years. In what some analysts have called a "retail apocalypse," retail bankruptcies and store closings have soared to record levels recent years. Even as overall retail spending grows, retail icons ranging from Sears, JC Penney, and Macy's to Kohl's and The Limited have shuttered stores as their sales have stagnated and profits have shrunk. Even retail stars like Walmart, Target, and Best Buy are scrambling to adapt to the new retailing challenges posed by today's connected customers.[5]

Omni-channel retailing
Creating a seamless cross-channel buying experience that integrates in-store, online, and mobile shopping.

Given these incredible shifts in consumer buying, some experts are predicting an end to retailing as we know it today and perhaps even the eventual death of physical stores altogether. That's not likely. The Amazons of the world aren't likely to swallow up the brick-and-mortar retailing world. But it's no longer a matter of online sellers *versus* brick-and-mortar stores. >> Instead, successful retailers of the future must adopt **omni-channel retailing**, creating a seamless cross-channel buying experience that integrates in-store, online, and mobile shopping. Thus, to meet the needs of customers who work across multiple channels as they shop, traditional store retailers are rapidly integrating digital, online, and mobile shopping into their operations. And many once-online-only retailers—such as Amazon, Warby Parker, and Blue Nile—are setting up physical stores.

We discuss online and omni-channel retailing in detail later in this chapter and in Chapter 14. But first, because a large majority of retailing still happens in stores, we examine the various types of store retailers.

>> The new retailing model: Digital technologies have caused a massive shift in how and where people buy. Today's retailers must adopt omni-channel retailing that integrates in-store, online, and mobile shopping.

Stanisic Vladimir/123RF

Types of Store Retailers

Retailer stores come in all shapes and sizes—from your local hairstyling salon or family-owned restaurant to national specialty chain retailers such as REI or Williams-Sonoma to megadiscounters such as Costco or Walmart. The most important types of retail stores are described in Table 13.1 and discussed in the following sections. They can be classified in terms of several characteristics, including the *amount of service* they offer, the breadth and depth of their *product lines*, the *relative prices* they charge, and how they are *organized*.

Amount of Service

Different types of customers and products require different amounts of service. To meet these varying service needs, retailers may offer one of three service levels: self-service, limited service, and full service.

Self-service retailers serve customers who are willing to perform their own *locate-compare-select* process to save time or money. Self-service is the basis of all discount operations and is typically used by retailers selling convenience goods (such as supermarkets) and nationally branded, fast-moving shopping goods (such as Target or Kohl's). *Limited-service retailers*, such as Sears or JCPenney, provide more sales assistance because they carry more shopping goods about which customers need information. Their increased operating costs result in higher prices.

Full-service retailers, such as high-end specialty stores (for example, Tiffany or Williams-Sonoma) and first-class department stores (such as Nordstrom or Neiman Marcus), assist customers in every phase of the shopping process. Full-service stores usually carry more specialty goods for which customers need or want assistance or advice. They provide more services, which results in much higher operating costs. These higher costs are passed along to customers as higher prices.

Product Line

Specialty store
A retail store that carries a narrow product line with a deep assortment within that line.

Department store
A retail store that carries a wide variety of product lines, each operated as a separate department managed by specialist buyers or merchandisers.

Supermarket
A large, low-cost, low-margin, high-volume, self-service store that carries a wide variety of grocery and household products.

Retailers can also be classified by the length and breadth of their product assortments. Some retailers, such as **specialty stores**, carry narrow product lines with deep assortments within those lines. Today, specialty stores are flourishing. The increasing use of market segmentation, market targeting, and product specialization has resulted in a greater need for stores that focus on specific products and segments.

By contrast, **department stores** carry a wide variety of product lines. In recent years, mainstream department stores have been squeezed between more focused and flexible specialty stores on the one hand and more efficient, lower-priced discounters on the other. In response, many have added promotional pricing to meet the discount threat. Others have stepped up the use of store brands and single-brand *shop-in-shop* concepts to compete with specialty stores. High-end department stores such as Nordstrom, Saks, and Neiman Marcus are emphasizing exclusive merchandise and high-quality service.

The shift toward online and mobile buying has also hit department stores hard, causing many major chains—from Sears and JC Penney to Macy's and Dillard's—to close stores and adapt their strategies. Most major chains have added direct and online selling but still have a long way to go to catch up with the Amazons of the retailing world. "The world is moving faster than department stores are adapting," says a store retailing executive.[6]

Supermarkets are the most frequently visited type of retail store. Today, however, they are facing slow sales growth because of slower population growth and an increase in competition from discounters (Walmart, Costco, and Dollar General) on the one hand and specialty food stores (Whole Foods Market, Trader Joe's, ALDI, Sprouts, Lidl) on the other. Like department stores, supermarkets are also facing challenges from Amazon and other online shopping options, such as food and recipe delivery services like Blue Apron and HelloFresh. Online grocery shopping will capture an estimated 20 percent of total grocery retail sales by 2025. And more than half of all grocery purchases are now impacted by what consumers have seen or researched online.[7]

In the battle for "share of stomach," some supermarkets are competing head-on with large discounters such as Costco and Walmart by cutting costs, establishing more-efficient

>> In the battle for "share of stomach," regional discount-grocery chain WinCo is rapidly becoming "Walmart's worst nightmare."

Francis Joseph Dean/Deanpictures/Newscom (top); ZUMA Press, Inc./Alamy Stock Photo (bottom)

operations, and lowering prices. >> An example is WinCo, the fast-growing regional discount-grocery chain in the western United States that positions itself directly against mighty Walmart as "The Supermarket Low Price Leader." WinCo's large, efficient, no-frills stores carry a limited assortment of basic fast-moving merchandise, and customers help to keep costs down by bagging their own groceries and paying cash (no credit cards accepted). As a result, WinCo doesn't just match Walmart's prices; it often undercuts them.

Other supermarkets have moved upscale, providing improved store environments and higher-quality food offerings, such as from-scratch bakeries, gourmet deli counters, natural and organic foods, and fresh seafood departments. Still others are adding online buying options, such as online ordering for home delivery, in-store pickup, or curbside pickup. They are beefing up their websites and mobile apps shopping list creators, recipes and meal ideas, and other features.

Convenience store
A small store, located near a residential area, that is open long hours seven days a week and carries a limited line of high-turnover convenience goods.

Convenience stores are small stores that carry a limited line of high-turnover convenience goods. After several years of stagnant sales due to fewer cigarette sales and rising gas prices, these stores are now experiencing growth. Many convenience store chains have expanded beyond their primary market of young, blue-collar men by redesigning their stores to attract female shoppers. They are shedding the image of a "truck stop" where men go to buy gas, beer, cigarettes, or shriveled hot dogs on a roller grill and are instead offering freshly prepared foods and cleaner, safer, more-upscale environments.

Many convenience stores are expanding their offerings to attract "fill-in" shoppers—people looking to pick up a few items between major grocery store trips. For example, Midwestern convenience chain Kwik Trip has expanded its offerings to become the one quick stop customers need to help get dinner on the table when they're rushing home from work:[8]

> Walk into a Kwik Trip and you can buy everything from buns, bread, and milk to fresh produce, salads, and fresh meat. Yes, fresh meat like ground beef, brats, chicken, and steaks—whatever's in demand. It's not always easy to persuade customers to buy fresh groceries in stores better known for selling cigarettes, beer, and lottery tickets. Kwik Trip strategically places a cold case of meat, fresh vegetables, and fruits near the front of its stores to help convince shoppers that a Kwik Trip is their "neighborhood market"—a valid place to stop and buy what they need for dinner. It offers the basics in fresh groceries but also seasonal produce such as fresh cherries, preaches, and strawberries, "just to keep it interesting for our guests," says one of Kwik Trips registered dieticians. The "fill-in" approach has been successful for Kwik Trip, especially in rural areas where the chain helps fill the gap left by the decline of rural grocery stores.

Superstore
A store much larger than a regular supermarket that offers a large assortment of routinely purchased food products, nonfood items, and services.

Category killer
A giant specialty store that carries a very deep assortment of a particular line.

Service retailer
A retailer whose product line is actually a service; examples include hotels, airlines, banks, colleges, and many others.

Superstores are much larger than regular supermarkets and offer a large assortment of routinely purchased food products, nonfood items, and services. Walmart, Target, Meijer, and other discount retailers offer *supercenters*, very large combination food and discount stores. Whereas a traditional grocery store brings in about $397,500 a week in sales, a Walmart supercenter brings in about $1.25 million a week.[9]

Recent years have also seen the rapid growth of superstores that are actually giant specialty stores, the so-called **category killers** (for example, Best Buy, Home Depot, Petco, and Bed Bath & Beyond). They feature stores the size of airplane hangars that carry a very deep assortment of a particular line. Category killers are found in a wide range of categories, including electronics, home-improvement products, books, baby gear, toys, home goods, party goods, sporting goods, and even pet supplies.

Finally, for many retailers, the product line is actually a service. **Service retailers** include hotels and motels, banks, airlines, restaurants, colleges, hospitals, movie theaters, tennis clubs, bowling alleys, repair services, hair salons, and dry cleaners. Service retailers in the United States are growing faster than product retailers.

Relative Prices

Retailers can also be classified according to the prices they charge (see » **Table 11.1**). Most retailers charge regular prices and offer normal-quality goods and customer service. Others offer higher-quality goods and service at higher prices. Retailers that feature low prices are discount stores and "off-price" retailers.

Discount store
A retail operation that sells standard merchandise at lower prices by accepting lower margins and selling at higher volume.

Discount Stores. A **discount store** (for example, Target, Kohl's, or Walmart) sells standard merchandise at lower prices by accepting lower margins and selling higher volume. The early discount stores cut expenses by offering few services and operating in warehouse-like facilities in low-rent, heavily traveled districts. Today's discounters have improved their store environments and increased their services while at the same time keeping prices low through lean, efficient operations.

Leading "big-box" discounters, such as Walmart and Target, now dominate the retail scene. However, even "small-box" discounters are thriving in the current economic environment. For example, dollar stores are now today's fastest-growing retail format. Back in the day, dollar stores sold mostly odd-lot assortments of novelties, factory overruns, closeouts, and outdated merchandise—most priced at $1. Not anymore. » Dollar General, the nation's largest small-box discount retailer, makes a powerful value promise for the times: "Save time. Save money. Every day":[10]

> Dollar General's slogan isn't just for show. It's a careful statement of the store's value promise. The retailer's goal is to keep shopping simple by offering only a selected assortment of popular brands at everyday low prices in small and convenient locations. Dollar General's slimmed-down product line and smaller stores (you could fit more than 25 Dollar General stores inside the average Walmart supercenter) add up to a quick trip—the average customer is in and out of the store in

Table 11.1 Major Store Retailer Types

Type	Description	Examples
Specialty store	A store that carries a narrow product line with a deep assortment, such as apparel stores, sporting-goods stores, furniture stores, florists, and bookstores.	REI, Sunglass Hut, Sephora, Williams-Sonoma
Department store	A store that carries several product lines—typically clothing, home furnishings, and household goods—with each line operated as a separate department managed by specialist buyers or merchandisers.	Macy's, Sears, Neiman Marcus
Supermarket	A relatively large, low-cost, low-margin, high-volume, self-service operation designed to serve the consumer's total needs for grocery and household products.	Kroger, Publix, Safeway, SuperValu
Convenience store	A relatively small store located near residential areas, open 24/7, and carrying a limited line of high-turnover convenience products at slightly higher prices.	7-Eleven, Circle K, Speedway, Sheetz
Superstore	A very large store that meets consumers' total needs for routinely purchased food and nonfood items. This includes *supercenters*, combined supermarket and discount stores, and *category killers*, which carry a deep assortment in a particular category.	Walmart Supercenter, SuperTarget, Meijer (discount stores); Best Buy, Petco, Staples, Bed Bath & Beyond (category killers)
Discount store	A store that carries standard merchandise sold at lower prices with lower margins and higher volumes.	Walmart, Target, Kohl's
Off-price retailer	A store that sells merchandise bought at less-than-regular wholesale prices and sold at less than retail. These include *factory outlets* owned and operated by manufacturers; *independent off-price retailers* owned and run by entrepreneurs or by divisions of larger retail corporations; and *warehouse (or wholesale) clubs* selling a limited selection of goods at deep discounts to consumers who pay membership fees.	Mikasa (factory outlet); TJ Maxx (independent off-price retailer); Costco, Sam's Club, BJ's (warehouse clubs)

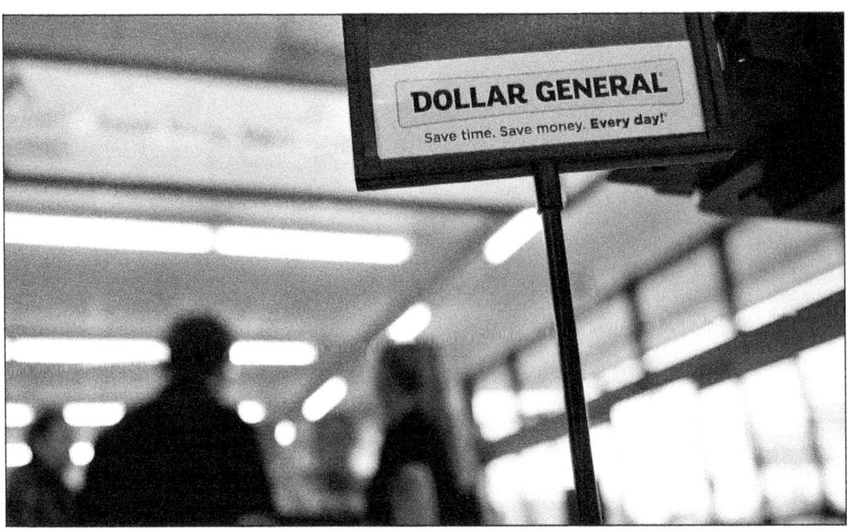

>> **Discounter Dollar General, the nation's largest small-box discount retailer, makes a powerful value promise for the times: "Save time. Save money. Every day!"**

Daniel Acker/Bloomberg/Getty Images

less than 10 minutes. And its prices on the popular brand-name products it carries are an estimated 20 to 40 percent lower than grocery store prices and on par with Walmart. Put it all together, and performance is strong at Dollar General. Whereas other retailers are closing stores at record rates and getting crushed by Amazon and Walmart, Dollar General is opening new stores at a rate of more than 900 a year and its revenues are growing at double-digit rates. Convenience and low prices, it seems, never go out of style.

Off-Price Retailers. As the major discount stores traded up, a new wave of **off-price retailers** moved in to fill the ultralow-price, high-volume gap. Ordinary discounters buy at regular wholesale prices and accept lower margins to keep prices down. By contrast, off-price retailers buy at less-than-regular wholesale prices and charge consumers less than retail. Off-price retailers can be found in all areas, from food, clothing, and electronics to no-frills banking and discount brokerages.

Off-price retailer
A retailer that buys at less-than-regular wholesale prices and sells at less than retail.

Independent off-price retailer
An off-price retailer that is independently owned and operated or a division of a larger retail corporation.

Factory outlet
An off-price retailing operation that is owned and operated by a manufacturer and normally carries the manufacturer's surplus, discontinued, or irregular goods.

The three main types of off-price retailers are *independents, factory outlets*, and *warehouse clubs*. **Independent off-price retailers** either are independently owned and run or are divisions of larger retail corporations. Although many off-price operations are run by smaller independents, most large off-price retailer operations are owned by bigger retail chains. Examples include store retailers such as TJ Maxx, Marshalls, and HomeGoods, all owned by TJX Companies, and online sellers such as Overstock.com. TJ Maxx promises brand-name and designer fashions for 20 to 60 percent off department store prices. How does it fulfill this promise? Its buyers are constantly on the lookout for deals. "So when a designer overproduces and department stores overbuy," says the company, "we swoop in, negotiate the lowest possible price, and pass the savings on."[11]

Factory outlets—manufacturer-owned and operated stores by firms such as J.Crew, Gap, Levi Strauss, and others—sometimes group together in *factory outlet malls* and *value-retail centers*. At these centers, dozens of outlet stores offer prices as much as 50 percent below retail on a wide range of mostly surplus, discounted, or irregular goods. Whereas outlet malls consist primarily of manufacturers' outlets, value-retail centers combine manufacturers' outlets with off-price retail stores and department store clearance outlets.

These malls in general are now moving upscale—and even dropping *factory* from their descriptions. A growing number of outlet malls now feature luxury brands such as Coach, Polo Ralph Lauren, Dolce & Gabbana, Giorgio Armani, Burberry, and Versace. As consumers become more value-minded, even upper-end retailers are accelerating their factory outlet strategies, placing more emphasis on outlets such as Nordstrom Rack, Neiman Marcus Last Call, Bloomingdale's Outlets, and Saks Off 5th. Many companies now regard outlets not simply as a way of disposing of problem merchandise but as an additional way of gaining business for fresh merchandise. The combination of highbrow brands and lowbrow prices found at outlets provides powerful shopper appeal, especially in thriftier times.

Warehouse club
An off-price retailer that sells a limited selection of brand name grocery items, appliances, clothing, and other goods at deep discounts to members who pay annual membership fees.

Warehouse clubs (also known as *wholesale clubs* or *membership warehouses*), such as Costco, Sam's Club, and BJ's, operate in huge, warehouse-like facilities and offer few frills. In exchange for the bare-bones environment, they offer ultralow prices and surprise deals on selected branded merchandise. Warehouse clubs have grown rapidly in recent years. These retailers appeal not only to low-income consumers seeking bargains on bare-bones products but also to all kinds of customers shopping for a wide range of goods, from necessities to extravagances.

Consider Costco, now the world's second-largest retailer behind only Walmart. Low price is an important part of Costco's equation, but what really sets Costco apart is the products it carries and the sense of urgency that it builds into the Costco shopper's store experience (see Marketing at Work 11.1).

MARKETING AT WORK 11.1

Costco: Merchandising Magic that Competitors Can't Match

Giant Walmart is used to beating up on competitors. It gives Best Buy migraines in consumer electronics, sells more dog food than PetSmart or Petco, and dresses more people than Gap, American Eagle Outfitters, and Abercrombie & Fitch combined. With more than 14 percent of the U.S. grocery market, it sells twice the groceries of leading grocery-only retailer Kroger. Almost every retailer, no matter what the category, has its hands full devising strategies by which it can compete with Walmart and survive.

But this isn't a story about Walmart. It's about Costco, the red-hot warehouse retailer that competes head-on with Walmart's Sam's Club—and wins. Sam's Club is huge. With 600-plus stores and $57 billion in revenues, if Sam's Club were a separate company, it would be the eighth-largest U.S. retailer. But when it comes to warehouse retailing, it's Costco that's the bully, not the other way around.

With only about 20 percent more locations than Sam's Club, Costco has more than twice the revenues, and the revenue gap grows bigger every year. Costco's $129 billion in sales makes it the world's second-largest retailer, behind only Walmart. This year Costco moved up to number 16 among *Fortune* 500 companies. And unlike Sam's Club, whose revenues are flat or falling, Costco's sales are growing rapidly. In just the past four years, Costco's revenues have climbed 23 percent; profits are up 35 percent. How is Costco beating Sam's Club at its own low-price game? The two retailers are very similar in many ways. But inside the store, Costco adds a certain merchandising magic that Sam's Club just can't match.

Let's start with the similarities. Both Costco and Sam's Club are warehouse retailers. They offer a limited selection of nationally branded and private-label products in a wide range of categories at very low prices to shoppers who pay an annual membership fee. Both retailers stock about 4,000 items, often only jumbo sizes (a typical supermarket stocks 40,000 items; a Walmart supercenter about 150,000). And to keep costs and prices low, both operate out of big, drafty, bare bones stores and use their substantial buying power to wring low prices from suppliers.

Price is an important part of the equation, and both Costco and Sam's Club seem addicted to selling every item at the lowest possible price. But more than just focusing on low discount prices, Costco focuses on high value through low mark-ups, regardless of the ultimate price. From the beginning, *discount* has been a bad word at Costco—it denotes "cheap." Instead, Costco's strategy is to give customers the best value through low margins, whether it's on a pantry staple or a high-priced wine. Costco's operating profit margins average a razor-thin 3.2 percent. Then again, Sam's Club's margins are only 3.5 percent.

Thus, both Costco and Sam's Club excel at low-cost operations and low prices. What is it, then, that really sets Costco apart? It has to do with Costco's differentiated value proposition—with the products it carries and sense of urgency that it builds into the shopping experience. Whereas Sam's Club and other wholesale retailers stand for low prices, Costco is a retail treasure hunt where both low-end and high-end products meet deep-discount prices. Alongside the gallon jars of peanut butter, four packs of toothpaste, and 2,250-count packs of Q-Tips that make other warehouse clubs popular, Costco offers an ever-changing assortment of high-quality products—even luxuries—all at tantalizingly low margins.

Last year, Costco sold more than 110 million hot dog–soda combos (still only $1.50, as they have been for more than three decades). At the same time, it sold more than 100,000 carats of diamonds at up to $100,000 per item. Costco is the nation's biggest baster of poultry (nearly 70,000 rotisserie chickens a day at $4.99 and a million whole turkeys during a holiday season), but it's also the country's biggest seller of fine wines (including the likes of a Chateau Cheval Blanc Premier Grand Cru Classe at $1,750 a bottle). Just for the fun of it, a Costco in Arizona once sold an extremely limited-edition bottle of Macallan Lalique single-malt scotch for $17,000 (actually a $6,000 discount). And Costco.com once offered a Pablo Picasso drawing at only $129,999.99!

Costco brings flair to an otherwise-dreary setting. Mixed in with its regular stock of staples, Costco features a glittering, constantly shifting array of one-time specials on brands such as Andrew Marc, Calvin Klein, Chanel, Prada, and Breitling—deals you just won't get anywhere else. It finds the best deals on premium electronics and appliances, then sells them at rock-bottom prices. In fact, 25 percent of the items that Costco

» **Warehouse clubs: Costco is a retail treasure hunt, where both low-end and high-end products meet deep-discount prices.**

Oleksiy Maksymenko Photography/Alamy Stock Photo

carries are designated as "treasure items" (Costco's words). The deals come and go quickly, and the changing assortment and great prices keep people coming back, wallets in hand.

Once inside, many customers fall prey to "the Costco effect"—spending more than they'd planned to. "When people say, 'I hate you guys, I came in to buy four things and I spent $400,' that's what we like," says Costco's CEO. Some customers even become "Costcoholics," as one reporter's story illustrates:

> A good friend of mine was raving about Costco recently, going on about how she couldn't resist shopping there at least two to three times a week. She said sometimes she doesn't even plan on buying anything. She just loves wandering around in the enormous, double-football-field-sized warehouse, hunting for what's new. She is also obsessed by what the big luxury "surprise" of the week might be—stuff like Waterford Crystal, Coach handbags, or Omega watches, to name a few, all selling out quickly at shock-and-awe low prices. And even though she may have shopped with no intention of purchasing, she says she always finds something that seduces her to buy.

There was a time when only the great unwashed masses shopped at off-price retailers. But Costco has changed all that. Even people who don't have to pinch pennies shop there. Not by accident, Costco's stores tend to be located in more affluent locations than Sam's Clubs. The average Costco member has a household income of nearly $100,000.

Costco's flair even extends to its store brand—Kirkland Signature. Whereas the Sam's Club Member's Mark store brand covers a limited assortment of generic-priced food, household, and apparel lines, Costco puts the Kirkland Signature brand on a much wider range of goods. Customers seek out Kirkland Signature products not just for price but also for quality. Costco customers can buy anything from a $19 bottle of Kirkland Signature Series Mendoza Malbec red wine to a $2,299 Kirkland Signature Braeburn five-piece woven fire pit patio set to a $3,799-per-person, seven-day Kirkland Signature river cruise package in France.

So, in its own warehouse club retailing backyard, it's Costco, not Walmart, that's beating up on competitors. In fact, mighty but frustrated Walmart has spent years trying to make Sam's Club more Costco-like. Costco is much more than a big-box store that "stacks 'em high and sells 'em cheap"—more than just a place to load up on large sizes of consumer staples. Each Costco store is a theater of retail that creates buying urgency and excitement for customers.

Sources: Benjamin Romano, "Booming Costco Courts Millennials with Online and Delivery, but Stores Still Rule," *Seattle Times,* February 1, 2018, www.seattletimes.com/business/retail/booming-costco-courts-millennials-with-online-and-delivery-but-stores-still-rule/; Robin Lewis, "'Costoholics': Costco's $113.7 Billion Addicts," *Forbes,* February 16, 2016, www.forbes.com/sites/robinlewis/2016/02/16/costcoholics-costcos-113-7-billion-addicts/#179cdc9b5f73; "Global Powers of Retailing 2018," Deloitte, www2.deloitte.com/global/en/pages/consumer-business/articles/global-powers-of-retailing.html, accessed May 2018; Stan Laegreid, "The Choreography of Design, Treasure Hunts, and Hot Dogs that Have Made Costco So Successful," *Fast Company,* January 24, 2014, www.fastcompany.com/3025312; "There Is Something Off with Costco," *Seeking Alpha,* December 9, 2017, https://seekingalpha.com/article/4130830-something-costco; and information from www.corporate.walmart.com, www.costco.com, and http://phx.corporate-ir.net/phoenix.zhtml?c=83830&p=irol-newsArticle&ID=2305024, accessed October 2018.

Organizational Approach

Although many retail stores are independently owned, others band together under some form of corporate or contractual organization. >> **Table 11.2** describes four major types of retail organizations—*corporate chains, voluntary chains, retailer cooperatives,* and *franchise organizations.*

Table 11.2 Major Types of Retail Organizations

Type	Description	Examples
Corporate chain	Two or more outlets that are commonly owned and controlled. Corporate chains appear in all types of retailing but they are strongest in department stores, discount stores, food stores, drugstores, and restaurants.	Macy's (department stores), Target (discount stores), Kroger (grocery stores), CVS (drugstores)
Voluntary chain	Wholesaler-sponsored group of independent retailers engaged in group buying and merchandising.	Independent Grocers Alliance (IGA), Western Auto (auto supply), True Value (hardware)
Retailer cooperative	Group of independent retailers who jointly establish a central buying organization and conduct joint promotion efforts.	Associated Grocers (groceries), Ace Hardware (hardware)
Franchise organization	Contractual association between a franchisor (a manufacturer, wholesaler, or service organization) and franchisees (independent businesspeople who buy the right to own and operate one or more units in the franchise system).	McDonald's, Subway, Pizza Hut, Jiffy Lube, Meineke Mufflers, 7-Eleven

Corporate chains
Two or more outlets that are commonly owned and controlled.

Corporate chains are two or more outlets that are commonly owned and controlled. They have many advantages over independents. Their size allows them to buy in large quantities at lower prices and gain promotional economies. They can hire specialists to deal with areas such as pricing, promotion, merchandising, inventory control, and sales forecasting.

The great success of corporate chains caused many independents to band together in one of two forms of contractual associations. One is the *voluntary chain*—a wholesaler-sponsored group of independent retailers that engages in group buying and common merchandising. Examples include the Independent Grocers Alliance (IGA), Western Auto, and True Value hardware stores. The other type of contractual association is the *retailer cooperative*—a group of independent retailers that bands together to set up a jointly owned, central wholesale operation and conduct joint merchandising and promotion efforts. Examples are Associated Grocers and Ace Hardware. These organizations give independents the buying and promotion economies they need to meet the prices of corporate chains.

Franchise
A contractual association between a manufacturer, wholesaler, or service organization (a franchisor) and independent businesspeople (franchisees) who buy the right to own and operate one or more units in the franchise system.

Another form of contractual retail organization is a **franchise**. The main difference between franchise organizations and other contractual systems (voluntary chains and retail cooperatives) is that franchise systems are normally based on some unique product or service; a method of doing business; or the trade name, goodwill, or patent that the franchisor has developed. Franchising has been prominent in fast-food restaurants, motels, health and fitness centers, auto sales and service dealerships, and real estate agencies.

However, franchising covers a lot more than just burger joints and fitness centers. Franchises have sprung up to meet just about any need. For example, Mad Science Group franchisees put on science programs for schools, scout troops, and birthday parties. Soccer Shots offers programs that give kids ages two to eight an introduction to basic soccer skills at daycare centers, schools, and parks. Mr. Handyman provides repair services for homeowners, while Merry Maids tidies up their houses and Mosquito Joe rids their yards of mosquitos. >> H&R Block franchises provide tax-preparation services. Over one-third of H&R Block's more than10,000 retail offices are owned and operated by franchisees.[12]

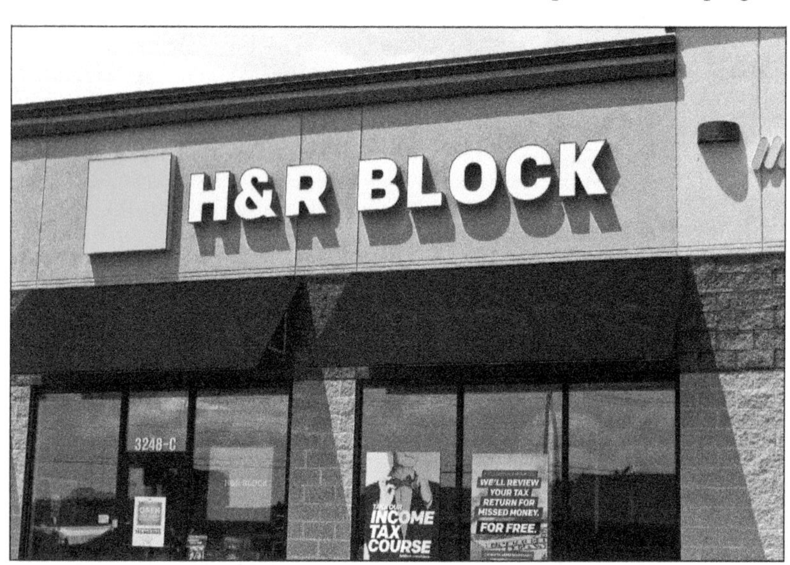

>> Franchising covers a lot more than just burger joints and fitness centers. More than one-third of H&R Block's 12,000 retail offices are owned and operated by franchisees.

Jonathan Weiss/Shutterstock

Franchises now command about 45 percent of all retail sales in the United States. These days, it's nearly impossible to stroll down a city block or drive on a city street without seeing a McDonald's, Subway, Jiffy Lube, or Hampton Inn. One of the best-known and most successful franchisers, McDonald's, now has more than 36,000 stores in more than 100 countries, including more than 14,000 in the United States. It serves 69 million customers a day and racks up more than $94 billion in annual system-wide sales. More than 80 percent of McDonald's restaurants worldwide are owned and operated by franchisees.[13]

LINKING THE CONCEPTS

Pause here to think about all the different kinds of retailers you deal with regularly, many of which overlap in the products they carry.

- Pick a familiar product: a camera, microwave oven, lawn tool, or something else. Shop for this product at two very different store types—say, a discount store or category killer on the one hand and a department store or smaller specialty store on the other. Then shop for it online. Compare the three shopping outlets on product assortment, services, and prices. If you were going to buy the product, where would you buy it and why?
- What does your shopping trip suggest about the futures of the competing store formats that you sampled?

Author Comment
To succeed in this age of retail upheaval, traditional retailers must adapt to the ways that today's digitally connected customers shop, providing seamless, cross-channel buying experiences.

Omni-Channel Retailing: Blending In-Store, Online, Mobile, and Social Media Channels

OBJECTIVE 11-2 Discuss how retailers are using omni-channel retailing to meet the cross-channel shopping behavior of today's digitally connected consumers.

As discussed earlier in the chapter, the retail shopping process has changed radically in recent years. Not all that long ago, shopping consisted mostly of going store to store—or perhaps flipping through catalogs—to gather product information, make price comparisons, and purchase goods. That was then. Now—in this age of websites, smartphones, mobile apps, social media, and other things digital—shopping typically involves a dazzling array of channels and platforms.

Online retailing is thriving. Although it currently accounts for only about 9 percent of total U.S. retail sales, online buying is growing at a much brisker pace than retail buying as a whole. Last year's U.S. online retail sales grew 16 percent over the previous year versus a 4.4 percent increase in overall retail sales. Beyond direct online sales, retailer online sites, mobile apps, and social media also influence a large amount of in-store buying. It's estimated that more than half of total U.S. retail sales are either transacted directly or influenced by online research.[14]

Today's omni-channel consumers readily research products and prices online, shopping digitally from home, from work, in stores, or anywhere in between. They scour retailer websites and social media for buying ideas, inspiration, and advice. They might see products in stores and order them online, see products online then buy them in stores, or buy goods online for in-store pickup or home delivery. According to a recent study, nearly 60 percent of shoppers research product information on their smartphone while shopping and 54 percent compare prices while shopping.[15]

This massive shift in how people shop calls for massive changes in how store retailers operate. Omni-channel *buying* calls for omni-channel *retailing*, integrating all available shopping channels and devices into a seamless customer shopping experience. The boundaries between in-store and online retailing are rapidly blurring. For most customers, it's no longer a matter of deciding whether to shop in a store *or* to shop online. Today's omni-channel buyers shift seamlessly across online and in-store channels throughout the buying process. They've gotten used to researching and buying anywhere, anytime—whether it's in the store, online, on the go, or even online while in the store.

An increasing share of the growth in online sales is being captured by omni-channel retailers who successfully merge the virtual and physical worlds. Physical store operators are expanding to the digital world via websites, mobiles apps, and the social media. Meanwhile, many online merchants—including Amazon—are moving into the physical world with showrooms, pop-up shops, their own stores, and other ways of meeting shoppers face-to-face.

Retailers have learned that shoppers with smartphones are doing far more than just checking online prices. More often, they are filling in the information gap. "The consumer has never been more informed, and that information comes from their phone," says a senior marketer at outdoor-gear retailer REI. "We love when someone enters the store holding their phone saying, 'I want this tent. I want this bike. Help me find this.'" This type of activity shows how digital and store retailing can come together to make a sale.

But omni-channel retailing goes way beyond just helping in-store customers as they cross-shop on mobile devices. It requires carefully integrating the entire range of available shopping channels, both in-store and out, from discovery to purchase in the buying process. To that end, most large retailers are now boosting their own online and digital selling options and linking them with stores.

For example, Walmart has upped its emphasis on in-store pickups and free two-day delivery. It tells customers that they can order from its Walmart.com site, pick up items on the same day, avoid shipping fees, and easily return items to the store if not satisfied. Customers now pick up half of all Walmart.com purchases in stores, often buying additional merchandise during the visit. Similarly, Target recently acquired same-day delivery service Shipt. As with Amazon's Prime, Target customers in major urban areas can pay an annual membership to have same-day delivery of online orders.

In addition to websites, omni-channel retailers are integrating other digital shopping channels. Walmart, Target, Macy's, and other major retailers offer handy mobile apps that pull customers to both their websites and stores, let them prepare shopping lists, help them locate merchandise inside stores, and send daily alerts and exclusive discounts to their phones. A recent study showed that 44 percent of shoppers regularly or occasionally purchase on their phones from within a retail store from that store's website. Ten percent of Walmart purchases via mobile devices are made from inside a Walmart store.[16]

Social media also play an important part in omni-channel retailing. Thirty percent of shoppers made purchases via social media last year, 44 percent discovered new products via social networks, and 49 percent made purchases based on referrals from social media. In turn, most large store retailers now use social media extensively to engage customers, build community, and link buyers to their websites and stores.[17]

But simply creating a digital-friendly store, high-powered website, and extensive social media presence doesn't constitute good omni-channel retailing. The key is to integrate these elements to create that critical seamless, anywhere, anytime, omni-channel shopping experience that today's customers seek. >> Consider athletic footwear and apparel giant Foot Locker, which operates several chains, including Foot Locker and Champs Sports:[18]

Foot Locker has mastered omni-channel retailing. Its online and mobile efforts link seamlessly with store operations, offering options such as "buy online, ship from store" and "buy online, reserve in store" for pickup. And you'll find Foot Locker everywhere in social media, with more than 150 million total followers across Instagram, Facebook, Snapchat, Twitter, YouTube, and Pinterest, where it builds customer community and pulls customers to its online and store locations.

Foot Locker's omni-channel prowess comes to life inside its Foot Locker, Champs Sports, and other stores. The chain gives sales associates the same mobile research capabilities that customers have. Tablets in hand, using online information about products and competitor offers, associates work with and educate customers. Foot Locker trains store employees to go beyond prices and engage customers in ways that add value through personal touches. With 3,300 stores and Foot Locker's own substantial online presence, the store retailer can help customers to shape almost any kind of shopping experience, including a broad choice of service, payment, and delivery options not available from online-only retailers. Thanks to its omni-channel mastery, whereas other shoe and apparel retailers have had trouble fending off web-only sellers like online star Zappos, Foot Locker's online sales have been a bright spot. It now gets 12 percent of its sales online, half of that from mobile buying, and its online sales are growing at a steady 20 percent annually.

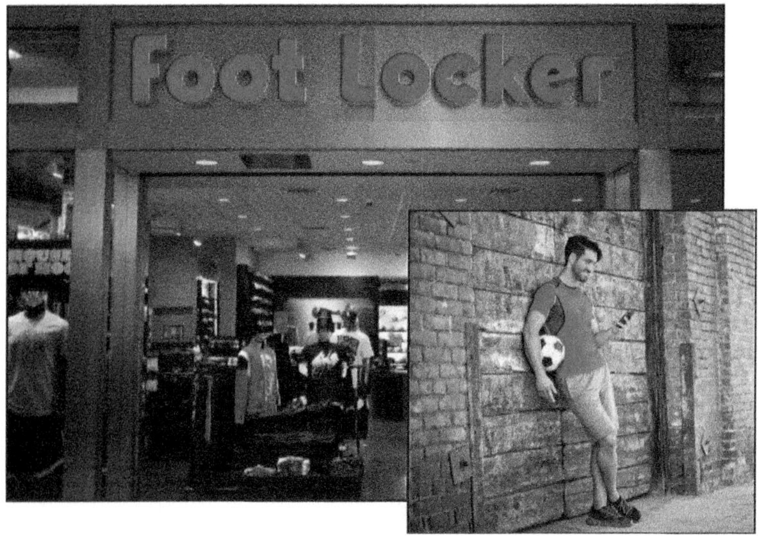

>> Athletic footwear and apparel giant Foot Locker has mastered omni-channel retailing. It skillfully integrates its in-store environment, high-powered websites, and extensive social media presence to create the seamless, anytime, anywhere, omni-channel shopping experience that today's customers seek.

Luke Sharrett/Bloomberg/Getty Images; Tony Garcia/Image Source/Getty Images

Author Comment
Not surprisingly, retailers must make the same types of segmentation, positioning, and marketing mix of decisions as any other marketer.

Retailer Marketing Decisions

OBJECTIVE 11-3 Describe the major retailer marketing decisions.

Retailers are always searching for new marketing strategies to attract and hold customers. In the past, retailers attracted customers with unique product assortments and more or better services. Today, the assortments and services of various retailers are looking more and more alike. You can find most consumer brands not only in department stores but also in mass-merchandise discount stores, in off-price discount stores, and all over the internet. Thus, it's now more difficult for any one retailer to offer exclusive merchandise.

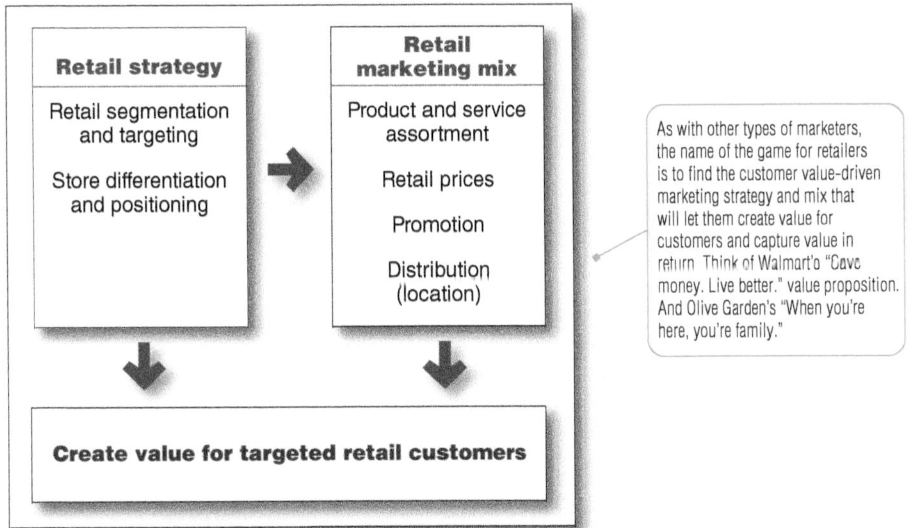

>> **Figure 11.1 Retailer Marketing Strategies**

Service differentiation among retailers has also eroded. Many department stores have trimmed their services, whereas discounters have increased theirs. In addition, customers have become smarter and more price sensitive. They see no reason to pay more for identical brands, especially when service differences are shrinking. For all these reasons, many retailers today are rethinking their marketing strategies.

As shown in >> **Figure 11.1**, retailers face major marketing decisions about *segmentation and targeting, store differentiation and positioning*, and the *retail marketing mix*.

Segmentation, Targeting, Differentiation, and Positioning Decisions

Retailers must first segment and define their target markets and then decide how they will differentiate and position themselves in these markets. Should they focus on upscale, midscale, or downscale shoppers? Do target shoppers want variety, depth of assortment, convenience, or low prices? Until they define and profile their markets, retailers cannot make consistent decisions about product assortment, services, pricing, advertising, store décor, online and mobile site design, or any of the other decisions that must support their positions.

Successful retailers define their target markets well and position themselves strongly. For example, Trader Joe's has established its "cheap gourmet" value proposition. Walmart is powerfully positioned on low prices and what those always-low prices mean to its customers. And highly successful outdoor products retailer Bass Pro Shops positions itself strongly as being "as close to the Great Outdoors as you can get indoors!"

With solid targeting and positioning, a retailer can compete effectively against even the largest and strongest competitors. >> For example, compare small In-N-Out Burger to giant McDonald's. In-N-Out now has under 400 stores in a handful of states, with estimated sales of about $600 million. McDonald's has 36,000 stores in more than 100 countries, racking up more than $94 *billion* of annual system-wide sales. How does In-N-Out compete with the world's largest fast-food chain? It doesn't—at least not directly. In-N-Out succeeds by carefully positioning itself *away* from McDonald's:[19]

> In-N-Out has never wanted to be like McDonald's, growing rapidly and expanding both its menu and locations. Instead, In-N-Out thrives by doing the unthinkable: growing slowly and not changing. From the start, In-N-Out's slogan has been, "Quality you can taste." Burgers are made from 100 percent pure beef—no additives, fillers, or preservatives—and they're always fresh, not frozen. Fries are made from whole potatoes, and, yes, milkshakes are made from real ice cream. You won't find a freezer, heating lamp, or microwave oven in an In-N-Out restaurant. And unlike McDonald's unending stream of new menu items, In-N-Out

>> **Retail targeting and positioning: In-N-Out Burger thrives by positioning itself *away* from McDonald's. The chain stays with what it does best: making really good hamburgers, really good fries, and really good shakes—that's it.**

© E. J. Baumeister Jr./Alamy

stays with what the chain has always done well: making really good hamburgers, really good fries, and really good shakes—that's it.

Moreover, far from standardized fare, In-N-Out gladly customizes any menu item. Menu modifications have become so common at In-N-Out that a "secret" ordering code has emerged that isn't posted on menu boards. Customers in the know can order their burgers "animal style" (pickles, extra spread, grilled onions, and a mustard-fried patty). And whereas the "Double-Double" (double meat, double cheese) is on the menu, burgers can also be ordered 3x3 or 4x4. Fries can also be ordered animal style (two slices of cheese, grilled onions, and spread), well done, or light. This secret menu makes customers feel special. Another thing that makes them feel special is In-N-Out's outgoing, enthusiastic, and capable employees, who deliver unexpectedly friendly service. You won't find that at McDonald's. Finally, in contrast to McDonald's obsession to grow, grow, grow, In-N-Out's slow-and-steady growth means that you won't find one on every corner. The scarcity of In-N-Out stores only adds to its allure. Customers regularly go out of their way and drive long distances to get their In-N-Out fix.

So, In-N-Out can't match McDonald's massive economies of scale, incredible volume purchasing power, ultra-efficient logistics, and low prices. Then again, it doesn't even try. By positioning itself away from McDonald's and other large competitors, In-N-Out has developed a cult-like following. When it comes to customer satisfaction, In-N-Out regularly posts the highest customer satisfaction scores of any fast-food restaurant in its markets. Long lines snake out the door of any location at lunchtime, and In-N-Out's average per-store sales are double the industry average.

Product Assortment and Services Decision

Retailers must decide on three major product variables: product assortment, services mix, and store atmosphere. These decisions, more than any other, can help store retailers differentiate themselves from online sellers. Of course, store retailers must add effective online elements to their marketing mixes. But they must also leverage assets that the Amazons of retailing can't match, such as their own private brands, personal service, and store experiences.

"When Amazon zigs, retailers must zag," says a retailing expert. "The...bigger Amazon gets, the more opportunity it creates for fresh, local alternatives. The more Amazon pushes robot-powered efficiency, the more space there is for warm and individualized service. The more that people interact with Amazon through its AI-based assistant Alexa, the more they will crave the insight and personal connection of fellow humans."[20]

The retailer's *product assortment* should differentiate it while matching target shoppers' expectations. One strategy is to offer a highly targeted product assortment: Lane Bryant carries plus-size clothing; Five Below offers "hot stuff. cool prices."—all priced at $1 to $5; and Battery Depot offers about every imaginable kind of replacement battery. Alternatively, a retailer can differentiate itself by offering merchandise that no other competitor carries, such as store brands or national brands on which it holds exclusive rights. For example, Kohl's gets exclusive rights to carry well-known labels such as Simply Vera by Vera Wang and a Food Network–branded line of kitchen tools, utensils, and appliances. Kohl's also offers its own private-label lines, such as Sonoma, Croft & Barrow, Candies, and Apt. 9.

The *services mix* can also help set one retailer apart from another. For example, some retailers invite customers to ask questions or consult service representatives in person or via phone or tablet. Home Depot offers a diverse mix of services to do-it-yourselfers, from "how-to" classes and "do-it-herself" and kid workshops to a proprietary credit card. Nordstrom delivers top-notch service and promises to "take care of the customer, no matter what it takes."

>> **Experiential retailing: Furnishings retailer Restoration Hardware has unleashed a new generation of furniture galleries that are part store, part interior design studio, and part restaurant. In these new stores, you don't just see the furnishings, you *experience* them.**

Mike Dupre/Stringer/Getty Images

The *store's atmosphere* is another important element in the reseller's product arsenal. Retailers want to create a unique store experience, one that suits the target market and moves customers to buy. Many retailers practice *experiential retailing*. >> For example, up-scale home furnishings retailer Restoration Hardware has unleashed a new generation of furniture galleries in Chicago, Atlanta, Denver, Tampa, and Hollywood that are part store, part interior design studio, part restaurant, and part home:[21]

> Picture this: You're sipping a glass of good wine, surrounded by plush furnishings and crystal chandeliers with soothing music playing in the background. You're not sure whether to order another glass of wine, a light lunch, or both. Instead, you decide to buy the furniture upon which you are sitting. You're not in a fancy restaurant; you're in RH Chicago, a new retail concept by Restoration Hardware. Most retail furniture stores do little more than display their wares in functional fashion. Not so at RH galleries. "We wanted to blur the lines between residential and retail, and to create a sense of place that is more home than store," says Restoration Hardware's CEO. The RH Atlanta gallery is a massive 70,000-square-foot, six-story estate on two acres, complete with a 40-foot-tall entry rotunda flanked by a double staircase, gardens, terraces, a 50-foot-long reflecting pool, and a rooftop park. Its rooms and outdoor places serve as showrooms for the goods that Restoration Hardware sells, from glasses to furniture to rugs to items for the garden. But it feels more like a grand home. You don't just see the furnishings, you *experience* them. "We created spaces where guests who visit our new homes are saying 'I want to live here,'" says the CEO. "I've been in retail almost 40 years and I've never heard anyone say they wanted to live in a retail store, until now."

Successful retailers carefully orchestrate virtually every aspect of the consumer store experience. The next time you step into a retail store—whether it sells consumer electronics, hardware, food, or high fashion—stop and carefully consider your surroundings. Think about the store's layout and displays. Listen to the background music. Check out the colors. Smell the smells. Chances are good that everything in the store, from the layout and lighting to the music and even the colors and smells, has been carefully orchestrated to help shape the customers' shopping experiences—and open their wallets.

For example, many large retailers have developed signature scents that you smell only in their stores.[22] Anytime Fitness pipes in "Inspire," a eucalyptus-mint fragrance to create a uniform scent from store to store and mask that "gym" smell. Bloomingdale's uses different essences in different departments: the soft scent of baby powder in the baby store, coconut in the swimsuit area, lilacs in intimate apparel, and sugar cookies and evergreen scent during the holiday season. Scents can subtly reinforce a brand's imagery and positioning. For example, the Hard Rock Café Hotel in Orlando added a scent of the ocean in its lobby to help guests imagine checking into a seaside resort (even though the hotel is located an hour from the coast). To draw customers into the hotel's often-overlooked downstairs ice cream shop, the hotel put a sugar cookie aroma at the top of the stairs and a whiff of waffle cone at the bottom. Ice cream sales jumped 45 percent in the following six months.

Such experiential retailing confirms that retail stores are much more than simply assortments of goods. They are environments to be experienced by the people who shop in them.

Price Decision

A retailer's price policy must fit its target market and positioning, product and service assortment, the competition, and economic factors. All retailers would like to charge high markups and achieve high volume, but the two seldom go together. Most retailers seek *either* high markups on lower volume (most specialty stores) *or* low markups on higher volume (mass merchandisers and discount stores).

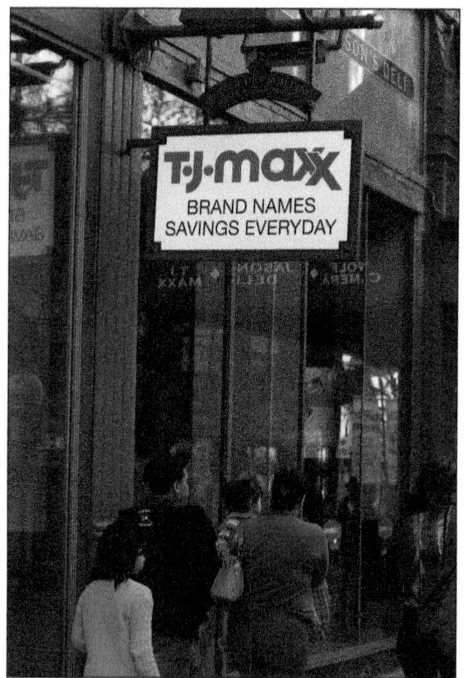

>> Retail price positioning: TJ Maxx sells brand-name clothing at everyday discount prices aimed at middle Americans.

Matthew Staver/Bloomberg/Getty Images

Thus, 120-year-old Bergdorf Goodman caters to the upper crust by selling apparel, shoes, and jewelry created by designers such as Chanel, Prada, Hermès, and Jimmy Choo. The upmarket retailer pampers its customers with services such as a personal shopper and in-store showings of the upcoming season's trends with cocktails and hors d'oeuvres. >> By contrast, TJ Maxx sells brand-name clothing at everyday discount prices aimed at middle-class Americans. As it stocks new products each week, the discounter provides a treasure hunt for bargain shoppers. "No sales. No gimmicks." says the retailer. "Just brand name and designer fashions for you...for up to 60 percent off department store prices."

Retailers must also decide on the extent to which they will use sales and other price promotions. Some retailers use no price promotions at all, competing instead on product and service quality rather than on price. For example, it's difficult to imagine Bergdorf Goodman holding a two-for-the-price-of-one sale on Chanel handbags, even in a tight economy. Other retailers—such as Walmart, Costco, ALDI, and Family Dollar—practice *everyday low pricing (EDLP)*, charging constant, everyday low prices with few sales or discounts.

Still other retailers practice *high-low pricing*—charging higher prices on an everyday basis coupled with frequent sales and other price promotions to increase store traffic, create a low-price image, or attract customers who will buy other goods at full prices (Macy's, Kohl's, JCPenney, for example). Recent fierce retail competition, both online and offline, has caused a rash of high-low pricing, as retailers have poured on price cuts and promotions to coax bargain-hunting customers into their stores. Which pricing strategy is best depends on the retailer's overall marketing strategy, the pricing approaches of its competitors, and the economic environment.

Promotion Decision

Retailers use various combinations of the five promotion tools—advertising, personal selling, sales promotion, public relations, and direct and social media marketing—to reach consumers. They advertise in newspapers and magazines and on radio and television. Advertising may be supported by newspaper inserts and catalogs. Store salespeople greet customers, meet their needs, and build relationships. Sales promotions may include in-store demonstrations, displays, sales, and loyalty programs. PR activities, such as new-store openings, special events, newsletters and blogs, store magazines, and public service activities, are also available to retailers. Most retailers also interact digitally with customers using websites and digital catalogs, online ads and video, social media, mobile ads and apps, blogs, and email. Almost every retailer, large or small, maintains a full social media presence.

Digital promotions let retailers personalize offers to individual customers with carefully targeted messages. >> For example, CVS/pharmacy distributes personalized versions of its weekly circulars to the chain's 80 million ExtraCare loyalty program members. Called myWeekly Ad, customers can view their circulars by logging into their personal accounts on CVS.com or through the CVS app on their phones. Based on ExtraCare members' characteristics and previous purchases, the personalized promotions highlight sales items and special offers of special interest to each specific customer. For example, if a customer buys a certain shampoo, CVS will highlight that shampoo when it's on sale in the myWeekly Ad. Or customers with allergies might receive special ads and promotions on their apps when the pollen count is high in their areas. CVS ExtraCare members who access their personal digital promotions tend to save three times more than customers who don't.[23]

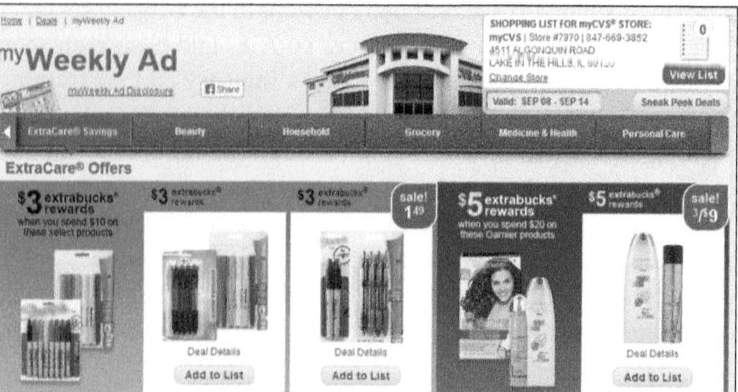

>> Retailer promotion: Most retailers interact digitally with customers using websites and digital catalogs, mobile and social media, and other digital platforms. CVS's myWeekly Ad program distributes personalized versions of its weekly circulars to the chain's ExtraCare loyalty program members.

CVS Health

Place Decision

Store retailers often point to three critical factors in retailing success: location, location, and location! It's very important that retailers select locations that are accessible to the target market in areas that are consistent with the retailer's positioning. For example, Apple locates its stores in high-end malls and trendy shopping districts—such as the Magnificent Mile on Chicago's Michigan Avenue or Fifth Avenue in Manhattan—not low-rent strip malls on the edge of town. By contrast, to keep costs down and support its "cheap gourmet" positioning, Trader Joe's places its stores in lower-rent, out-of-the-way locations. Small retailers may have to settle for whatever locations they can find or afford. Large retailers, however, usually employ specialists who use advanced methods to select store locations.

Most stores today cluster together to increase their customer pulling power and give consumers the convenience of one-stop shopping. Central business districts were the main form of retail cluster until the 1950s. Every large city and town had a central business district with department stores, specialty stores, banks, and movie theaters. When people began moving to the suburbs, however, many of these central business districts, with their traffic, parking, and crime problems, began to lose business. In recent years, many cities have joined with merchants to revive downtown shopping areas, generally with only mixed success.

Shopping center
A group of retail businesses built on a site that is planned, developed, owned, and managed as a unit.

A **shopping center** is a group of retail businesses built on a site that is planned, developed, owned, and managed as a unit. A *regional shopping center*, or *regional shopping mall*, the largest and most dramatic shopping center, has from 50 to more than 100 stores, including two or more full-line department stores. It is like a covered mini-downtown and attracts customers from a wide area. A *community shopping center* contains between 15 and 50 retail stores. It normally contains a branch of a department store or variety store, a supermarket, specialty stores, professional offices, and sometimes a bank. Most shopping centers are *neighborhood shopping centers* or *strip malls* that generally contain between 5 and 15 stores. These centers, which are close and convenient for consumers, usually contain a supermarket, perhaps a discount store, and several service stores—dry cleaner, drugstore, hardware store, local restaurant, or other stores.[24]

Power centers are huge unenclosed shopping centers consisting of a long strip of retail stores, including large, freestanding anchors such as Walmart, Home Depot, Costco, Best Buy, Michaels, PetSmart, and Office Depot. Each store has its own entrance with parking directly in front for shoppers who wish to visit only one store. By contrast, *lifestyle centers* are smaller, open-air malls with upscale stores, convenient locations, and nonretail activities, such as a playground, skating rink, hotel, dining establishments, and a movie theater complex.

The past few years have brought hard times for many shopping centers. The country has long been "overmalled"—between 1970 and 2015, U.S. malls grew at twice the rate of the population. More recently, online shopping has siphoned off shoppers and reduced the need for mall-going. And as embattled department store and specialty chains have announced record store closings, vacancy rates at the nation's enclosed malls have soared.

Although the largest and best regional malls are still prospering, many weaker and smaller regional malls are suffering. Power centers have also been hard hit hard as their big-box retailer tenants such as Kmart, Circuit City, Borders, Mervyns, and Linens N Things have gone out of business and others such as Best Buy, Barnes & Noble, and Office Depot have reduced the number or size of their stores. In all, according to one prediction, one out of every four U.S. malls could be out of business by 2022.[25]

Despite these grim predictions, the future for the stronger malls is bright. Traditional malls are reinventing themselves to meet the changing needs of shoppers. They are adding lifestyle elements—such as fitness centers, restaurants, children's play areas, common areas, and multiplex theaters—to make themselves more social and welcoming. In all, today's centers are more like places to hang out rather than just places to shop.

Author Comment
Retailers must constantly adapt their marketing strategies and mixes to today's challenging, fast-changing retail environment.

Retailing Trends and Developments

OBJECTIVE 11-4 Discuss the major trends and developments in retailing.

Retailers operate in a harsh and fast-changing environment, which offers threats as well as opportunities. Consumer demographics, lifestyles, and spending patterns are changing rapidly, as are retailing technologies. To be successful, retailers need to choose target segments carefully and position themselves strongly. They need to take the following retailing developments into account as they plan and execute their competitive strategies.

Tighter Consumer Spending

Following many years of good economic times, the Great Recession of 2008–2009 turned many relatively free-spending consumers into value-seeking ones. Even as the economy has recovered, retailers will feel the effects of changed consumer spending patterns well into the future.

Some retailers actually benefit from more frugal consumer spending. For example, as consumers cut back and looked for ways to spend less on what they bought, big discounters such as Costco scooped up new business from bargain-hungry shoppers. And price-oriented and off-price retailers such as ALDI, Dollar General, and TJ Maxx have attracted greater shares of more frugal buyers.

For other retailers, however, tighter consumer spending has required marketing strategy and tactics adjustments. As the economy has improved and as consumers have retained their thriftier ways, many retailers have added new value pitches to their positioning. For example, Home Depot replaced its older "You can do it. We can help." theme with a thriftier one: "More saving. More doing." Retailers ranging from Walmart to Macy's to Kroger and Whole Foods Market have boosted their emphasis on more economical private-label brands. And to compete with the boom in fast-casual restaurants such as Panera Bread and Chipotle, traditional sit-down restaurants have added value offerings of their own. For example, Applebee's has a 2 for $20 menu—two meals and one appetizer, all for just $20. >> TGI Fridays offers Fridays 5, "a selection of delicious drinks and appetizers, all for $5 each, . . . all the options you could want, whenever you want, even late night."

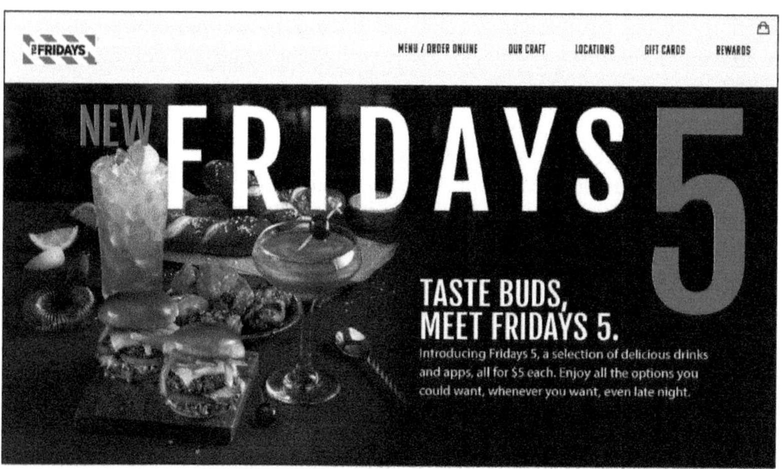

>> Value positioning: To attract today's more value-oriented consumers, TGI Fridays offers Fridays 5, "a selection of delicious drinks and appetizers, all for $5 each . . . whenever you want."

When reacting to economic shifts, retailers must be careful that their short-run actions don't damage their long-run images and positions. For example, cost-cutting and drastic price discounting can increase immediate sales but damage brand loyalty. One analyst calls this "death by discount" and suggests that "virtually every retailer—at both the high and the low end—has fallen so deeply into the trap that discounting has become an expectation of customers rather than a bonus."[26] A stroll through your local shopping mall confirms this assessment.

Iconic retailer Macy's has fallen into this trap. To prop up sales, it offers a never-ending stream of deep discounts, damaging its profit margins. To prop up its profits, it has centralized its merchandising and reduced its sales staff, resulting in less customer service. "Macy's has worked very hard to kill their points of difference—sales help," laments one consultant. "The sales professionals who knew their customers got trashed in the name of efficiency." Because of such actions, Macy's sales and profits have declined steadily over the past several years.[27] Instead of relying on cost-cutting and price reductions, Macy's and other retailers should focus on building greater customer value within their long-term store positioning strategies.

New Retail Forms, Shortening Retail Life Cycles, and Retail Convergence

New retail forms continue to emerge to meet new situations and consumer needs, but the life cycle of new retail forms is getting shorter. Department stores took about 100 years to reach the mature stage of the life cycle; more recent forms, such as warehouse stores, reached maturity in about 10 years. In such an environment, seemingly solid retail positions can crumble quickly. Of the top 10 discount retailers in 1962 (the year that the first Walmart, Kmart, Target, and Kohl's stores opened), not one still exists today. Even the most successful retailers can't sit back with a winning formula. To remain successful, they must keep adapting.

>> New retail forms: Roosevelt Field mall in Long Island, New York, has set up a permanent section for pop-up stores, primarily for online retailers that want to experiment with reaching consumers who may hesitate to buy online without seeing and touching the goods.

Simon Property Group, Inc.

New retail forms are always emerging. As discussed, one of the most recent blockbuster retailing trends is the advent of online retailing, by both online-only and store retailers, via websites, mobile apps, and social media. But other innovations occur regularly. For example, many retailers now use limited-time *pop-up stores* that let them promote their brands to seasonal shoppers and create buzz in busy, high-rent areas. Shopping malls are also jumping in with pop-up options to freshen their store mixes. >> Large mall operator Simon has set up a permanent section for pop-ups—called "The Edit @ Roosevelt Fields"—in one of its New York area malls. Offering short-term leases (versus standard five- to ten-year leases), The Edit @ Roosevelt Fields hosts numerous pop-ups, primarily online-only retailers that want to experiment with retail to reach consumers who may hesitate to buy online without seeing and touching the goods. The mix of retailers at The Edit @ Roosevelt Fields is rotated periodically. Recent pop-ups at The Edit @ Roosevelt Fields include Lively (bras), Beltology (belts), Raden (luggage), JARS (desserts), and Winky Lux (cosmetics).[28]

The online and mobile equivalent of pop-ups is online *flash sales*. Originally found on flash sale-only sites, such as Gilt and Zulily, flash sales can help move inventory or create buzz and excitement. For example, Target has one-day only flash sales on specific product lines, such as Halloween costumes on a day in October. And Amazon runs flash sales—called Lightning Deals—throughout the year and especially during the holiday season. The Lightning Deals are offered in limited quantities for a short period of time, one per customer, until available inventory runs out.[29]

Today's retail forms appear to be converging. Increasingly, different types of retailers now sell the same products at the same prices to the same consumers thanks in part to the price transparency the internet provides. For example, you can buy brand-name home appliances at department stores, discount stores, home-improvement stores, off-price retailers, electronics superstores, and a slew of online sites that all compete for the same customers. If you can't find the microwave oven you want at Home Depot or Lowe's, you can step across the street and find one for a better price at Target or Best Buy—or just order one online from Amazon.com or Build.com. This merging of consumers, products, prices, and retailers is called *retail convergence*. Such convergence means greater competition for retailers and greater difficulty in differentiating the product assortments of various types of retailers.

The Rise of Megaretailers

The rise of huge mass merchandisers and specialty superstores, the formation of vertical marketing systems, the rapid growth of online retailers like Amazon, and a rash of retail mergers and acquisitions have created a core of superpower megaretailers. With their size and buying power, these giant retailers can offer better merchandise selections, good service, and strong price savings to consumers. As a result, they grow even larger by squeezing out their smaller, weaker competitors.

The megaretailers have shifted the balance of power between retailers and producers. A small handful of retailers now controls access to enormous numbers of consumers, giving them the upper hand in their dealings with manufacturers. For example, you may never have heard of specialty coatings and sealants manufacturer RPM International, but you've probably used one or more of its many familiar do-it-yourself brands—such as Rust-Oleum paints, Plastic Wood and Dap fillers, Mohawk and Watco finishes, and Testors hobby cements and paints—all of which you can buy at your local Home Depot store. Home Depot is a very important customer to RPM, accounting for a significant share of its consumer sales. However, Home Depot's sales of $94.6 billion are almost 20 times RPM's sales of $4.8 billion. As a result, the giant retailer can, and often does, use this power to wring concessions from RPM and thousands of other smaller suppliers.[30]

Growing Importance of Retail Technology

As digital and omni-channel shopping become the norm, retail technologies have become critically important as competitive tools. Progressive retailers are using advanced information technology and software systems to produce better forecasts, control inventory costs, interact digitally with suppliers, send information between stores, and even sell to customers within stores. They have adopted sophisticated systems for checkout scanning, RFID inventory tracking, merchandise handling, information sharing, and customer interactions.

Perhaps the most startling advances in retail technology concern the ways in which retailers are assessing and connecting with consumers. In this age of big data, retailers large and small can apply advanced analytics to mountains of in-store and online data to gain insights into customer needs and behaviors. Using artificial intelligence, they can tailor merchandise, promotions, recommendations, and service to individual customer profiles.

As the surge in online and mobile shopping has changed retail customer shopping behavior and expectations, a wide range of store retailers are merging the physical and digital worlds to create new-age experiential retailing environments. For example, at AT&T's new flagship store in Chicago, customers can sit at any of dozens of stations, sampling the latest phone apps and electronic gadgetry. Enthusiastic, iPad-wielding associates mingle with customers, talking tech and dispensing hands-on help and advice. With 130 digital screens and an 18-foot video wall, every aspect of the open space is designed to engage customers about future wireless technologies and services and let them experience the impact of AT&T's devices and services on their lives. It's "like walking into a website," says AT&T's president of retail.[31]

Many other advanced technologies are finding their way into retail showrooms. One is beacon technology, Bluetooth connections that greet and engage customers via their smartphones as they shop around in stores. For example, when opted-in customers enter a Target store, a beacon signal wakes up the Target app on their smartphones. The app then shows shoppers' locations on a map as they move through the store. It also shows the locations of items on their shopping lists and identifies nearby Cartwheel deals. The beacon-based Target technology may one day soon also offer a scan-and-go feature that simply tracks what items customers select and automatically charges them to a credit card without going through checkout. "I want our digital experiences to be every bit as delightful as shopping in one of our stores," says Target's chief information and digital officer.[32]

Other retailers are experimenting with *augmented (AR)* and *virtual reality (VR)* to enhance the shopping experience. » For example, customers at North Face's Manhattan store can don virtual-reality headsets that transport them to remote hiking, climbing, or even base-jumping locations where they can experience gutsy jumps off a 420-foot cliff, all while using North Face gear. Marriott guests can put on virtual-reality goggles for up-close tours of destinations such as Hawaii or London. Intel has developed a "smart" dressing room, dubbed the MemoryMirror, in which shoppers, using augmented reality, can change outfits and colors with a wave of the hand. Although augmented and virtual reality technologies are difficult and expensive to implement now, they hold exciting promise for the future (see Marketing at Work 11.2).[33]

» Retail technology: Retailers are experimenting with virtual reality to enhance the in-store shopping experience. At North Face's Manhattan store, customers can don virtual-reality headsets that transport them to remote outdoor experiences, such as a gutsy jump off a 420-foot cliff.

The Washington Post/Contributor

Green Retailing

Today's retailers are increasingly adopting environmentally sustainable practices. They are greening up their stores and operations, promoting more environmentally responsible products, launching programs to help customers be more responsible, and working with channel partners to reduce their environmental impact.

MARKETING AT WORK 11.2

AR and VR in Retailing: Extending and Enhancing the Shopping Experience

Remodeling a dated kitchen or bathroom can be a Herculean task, and many customers simply throw up their hands and say, "Forget it!" To help solve this customer dilemma, home improvement retailer Lowe's created a virtual reality program called Holoroom, which lets customers in some stores redo rooms and see how they look without ever knocking down a wall.

Dubbed "Minecraft for Moms," Holoroom lets customers use an in-store tablet app to design their dream room, selecting cabinets, countertops, faucets, appliances, tile, and paint colors in endless configurations (all with Lowe's products, of course). Customers then don an Oculus Rift headset and find themselves standing in the middle of the redesigned space in 3D virtual reality. Based on what they see, they can fine-tune the design until it looks just right. Then they can export it to YouTube 360 for sharing and viewing at home with Google Cardboard.

Welcome to the fast-growing world of augmented and virtual reality in retailing. Retailers are increasingly using sophisticated digital technologies to extend and enhance the customer shopping experience, bring the outside world into their stores, and bring their stores to the outside world. They are using augmented reality (AR) and virtual reality (VR), fueled by artificial intelligence (AI), to create enhanced, personalized, and highly engaging retail experiences that transcend real world limits.

Augmented reality merges digitally augmented objects with real world images. AR can help consumers design, try out, and visualize products before buying them. For example, Sephora's Virtual Artist makeup app scans a customer's face and lets her experiment with different combinations of eye, lip, and cheek makeup until she finds one she likes. It also offers "virtual tutorials" that show customers how to apply makeup and digitally overlays the results on their faces. Similarly, Sherwin-Williams Color Visualizer app lets you "Color It Before You Paint It!" by uploading actual room images and painting them virtually. And at its Nike By You Studio in New York City, Nike is experimenting with technology that lets invited customers design their own one-of-a-kind Nikes and walk out the door with them in less than 90 minutes. Customers first put on a blank version of Nike Presto X shoes. Then as they select custom options—colors, text, and patterns—the designs are instantly brought to life right on their feet using projection and object tracking technologies. Such AR applications can greatly enrich and personalize customer shopping experiences.

Whereas AR augments customers' existing environments, virtual reality immerses them in whole new virtual environments. For example, automaker Audi has installed VR in many dealer showrooms. Customers use tablets to select any Audi model and customize each element. They then put on a headset and earphones to experience the sights and sounds of their customized car in virtual reality. They can move around the outside of the car, open the trunk and doors, check under the hood, and even sit in the driver's seat. Future versions may even add the cool feel of the leather upholstery and the rich new car smells.

Retailers can use virtual reality to help customers experience products in simulated real-world environments. For example, Walmart is experimenting with VR applications that enhance "the contextual shopping experience." The retail giant's innovation arm—called Store No. 8 (named after an early Walmart store remembered by founder Sam Walton as an "experiment")—recently demonstrated a VR app that allows shoppers try out camping gear in a virtual Yosemite National Park. "You can see the tent in the environment in which you'll use it," says the head of Store No. 8. "You can unzip the opening, get inside, lay on the ground and say, 'You know what? this is too tight,' then swipe your hand to try another tent." While Walmart doesn't have room to set up even one or two tents in its physical stores, with virtual reality, it can let customers experience its entire inventory. "The ability to have a real-life experience, to see how the tent's fabric is woven and what type of zipper it's using, has the potential to be the next generation of merchandising," adds the Walmart developer.

Beyond using VR to draw shoppers into stores or to give them out-of-store experiences, retailers can use it to bring their stores to shoppers, wherever they might be. For example, you won't likely find a Nike store in a small town. But Nike could

» AR and VR in retailing: Car maker Audi has installed virtual reality in many of its showrooms, letting customers put on a headset and earphones to experience the sights and sounds of their customized car in realistic virtual environments.

Audi of America

create a virtual Nike store and put it anywhere. Using artificial intelligence, such virtual stores could provide interactive experiences personalized to each shopper's demographics, preferences, purchase histories, and actions while navigating the store. Steph Curry fans might see store shelves full of Warriors merchandise; Patriots fans could gorge on Tom Brady goods. Because some VR gear can track exactly what a user is viewing, virtual store apps could use AI to adapt an individual shopper's experience based on what he or she is most interested in. "Right now stores have zero customization, so they're trying to appeal to everyone," says the analyst. "VR solves that."

Wild-eyed VR futurists envision virtual stores—or even real stores—populated by AI-driven salespeople synched to individual shopper characteristics and preferences. Customers in some stores or situations might prefer assistance from a man, others from a woman. Some might need salespeople with a specific look or knowledge set. A physical store can only hire so many salespeople. With virtual reality, stores can create whatever the customer wants. "Imagine walking into a real Tesla showroom and being approached by a holographic [Tesla founder and CEO] Elon Musk," says the head of a startup firm that creates photo-realistic human holograms used inside VR environments. "You could ask virtual Elon [anything and] it would understand what you're saying and respond as the real Elon might."

AR and VR are still in their infancy. The hardware remains expensive and awkward, and the impact of virtual apps on shoppers is still untested and uncertain. Thus, retailers are still only experimenting with these potentially powerful technologies for attracting and engaging customers. But most retailers view AR and VR, fueled by AI, as the wave of the future. Says a VR consultant, "When you take a three-dimensional world like VR or AR and combine that with a smart [AI] system that can replicate a human, suddenly the experience is leaps and bounds ahead of where we've been."

Sources: Based on information from Dan Tynan, "Find Your Virtual Intelligence," *Adweek,* December 4, 2017, pp. 18–19; Tim Nudd, "Future of Retail? Nike's Cool New Toy Lets You Design and Print Customer Sneakers in an Hour," *Adweek,* September 6, 2017, www.adweek.com/creativity/future-of-retail-nikes-cool-new-toy-lets-you-design-and-print-custom-sneakers-in-an-hour/; "Real-Time Retail," *Adweek,* June 20, 2016, pp. 23–25; Ashley Carman, "Sephora's Latest App Update Let's You Try Virtual Makeup on at Home with AR," *The Verge,* March 16, 2017, www.theverge.com/2017/3/16/14946086/sephora-virtual-assistant-ios-app-update-ar-makeup; "Audi Launches Virtual Reality Technology in Dealerships," October 30, 2017, www.audi-mediacenter.com/en/press-releases/audi-launches-virtual-reality-technology-in-dealerships-9270; Carolanne Mangies, "Is Marketing Ready for VR/AR in 2018?," *Smart Insights,* January 11, 2018, www.smartinsights.com/digital-marketing-platforms/video-marketing/is-marketing-ready-for-vr-ar-in-2018/; and "Lowe's Holoroom, Virtual Reality for Retail—3D Furniture Cloud VR Showroom," www.marxentlabs.com/ar-videos/lowes-holoroom-retail/, accessed October 2018.

At the most basic level, most large retailers are making their stores more environmentally friendly through sustainable building design, construction, and operations. >> For example, under its "People & Planet Positive" sustainability strategy, home furnishings retailer IKEA's long-term goal is to become 100 percent sustainable:[34]

>> Green retailing: Under its "People & Planet Positive" sustainability strategy, home furnishings retailer IKEA's long-term goal is to become 100% sustainable, both in its operations and in the products it sells.

Used with the permission of Inter IKEA Systems B.V.

> The "People & Planet Positive" strategy begins with making IKEA's 355 giant stores in 29 countries more energy independent and efficient. To power its stores, IKEA has committed to owning and operating 416 wind turbines and has installed 750,000 solar panels—90 percent of its U.S. stores have solar panels. By 2020, IKEA will generate as much energy as it uses from renewable sources. Inside its stores, IKEA uses only energy-efficient LED lighting. Most stores also sort food waste from in-store customer restaurants for composting or send it to treatment centers where it is turned into animal feed or biogas to fuel cars and buses. Some IKEAs offer customer recycling centers for products such as plastic, paper, CFL light bulbs, batteries, and even end-of-life appliances.

Retailers are also greening up their product assortments. For example, IKEA now sells only LED lighting products in its stores, and a growing proportion of the home furnishing products it sells are made from sustainable and renewable cotton, wood, and other resources. IKEA suppliers must adhere to the retailer's IWAY supplier code of conduct sustainability standards. IKEA's goal is have all of its home furnishings made from renewable, recyclable, or recycled materials. "At IKEA, sustainability is central to our business," says the company, "to ensure that we have a positive impact on people and the planet."

Many retailers have also launched programs that help consumers make more environmentally responsible decisions. Staples's Easy Sustainability Program helps customers to identify green products sold in its stores and to recycle printer cartridges, mobile phones, computers, and other office technology products. Staples recycles some 30 million printer cartridges and 10 million pounds of old technology each year.[35]

Finally, many large retailers are joining forces with suppliers and distributors to create more sustainable products, packaging, and distribution systems. For example, Amazon.com works closely with the producers of many of the products it sells to reduce and simplify their packaging. And beyond its own substantial sustainability initiatives, Walmart wields its huge buying power to urge its army of suppliers to improve their environmental impact and practices. The retailer has even developed a worldwide Sustainable Product Index by which it rates suppliers. It plans to translate the index into a simple rating for consumers to help them make more sustainable buying choices.

Green retailing yields both top- and bottom-line benefits. Sustainable practices lift a retailer's top line by attracting consumers looking to support environmentally friendly sellers and products. They also help the bottom line by reducing costs. For example, Amazon.com's reduced-packaging efforts increase customer convenience and eliminate "wrap rage" while at the same time saving packaging costs. And IKEA's more energy-efficient buildings not only appeal to customers and help save the planet but also cost less to operate.

Global Expansion of Major Retailers

Retailers with unique formats and strong brand positions are increasingly moving into other countries. Many are expanding internationally to escape saturated home markets. Over the years, some giant U.S. retailers, such as McDonald's and Walmart, have become globally prominent because of their marketing prowess.

However, some U.S. retailers are still significantly behind Europe and Asia when it comes to global expansion. Although 10 of the world's top 20 retailers are U.S. companies, only five of these retailers have set up operations outside North America (Walmart, Home Depot, Walgreens, Amazon, and Costco). Of the 10 non-U.S. retailers in the world's top 20, eight have stores in at least 10 countries. Foreign retailers that have gone global include France's Carrefour, Groupe Casino, and Groupe Auchan; Germany's Metro, Lidl, and ALDI chains; Britain's Tesco; and Japan's Seven & I.[36]

International retailing presents challenges as well as opportunities. Retailers can face dramatically different retail environments when crossing countries, continents, and cultures. Simply adapting the operations that work well in the home country is usually not enough to create success abroad. Instead, when going global, retailers must understand and meet the needs of local markets.

LINKING THE CONCEPTS

Time out! So-called experts have long predicted that online retailing eventually will replace store retailing as our primary way to shop. What do you think?

- Shop for a good book at the Barnes & Noble website (www.bn.com), taking time to browse the site and see what it has to offer. Next, shop at a nearby Barnes & Noble or other bookstore. Compare the two shopping experiences. Where would you rather shop? On what occasions? Why?
- A Barnes & Noble store creates a "community" where people can "hang out." How does its website compare on this dimension?
- Do Barnes & Noble's various social media efforts create community for the retailer and its customers? For example, see www.facebook.com/barnesandnoble, www.instagram.com/barnesandnoble/, and www.pinterest.com/barnesandnoble.

Author Comment
Whereas retailers primarily sell goods and services directly to final consumers for personal use, wholesalers sell primarily to those buying for resale or business use. Because wholesalers operate behind the scenes, they are largely unknown to final consumers. But they are very important to their business customers.

Wholesaling

OBJECTIVE 11-5 Explain the major types of wholesalers and their marketing decisions.

Wholesaling
All the activities involved in selling goods and services to those buying for resale or business use.

Wholesaler
A firm engaged *primarily* in wholesaling activities.

Wholesaling includes all the activities involved in selling goods and services to those buying them for resale or business use. Firms engaged *primarily* in wholesaling activities are called **wholesalers**.

Wholesalers buy mostly from producers and sell mostly to retailers, industrial consumers, and other wholesalers. As a result, many of the nation's largest and most important wholesalers are largely unknown to final consumers. For example, how much do you know about McKesson, the huge $191 billion diversified health-care-services provider and the nation's leading wholesaler of pharmaceutical, health and beauty care, home health-care, and medical supply and equipment products? Or how about wholesaler Arrow Electronics, which supplies $24 billion worth of computer chips, capacitors, and other electronics and computer components annually to more than 125,000 original equipment manufacturers and commercial customers through a global network of more than 465 locations serving over 90 countries? >> And you may never have heard of a company called Grainger, even though it is very well known and much valued by its more than 3.2 million business and institutional customers in more than 150 countries:[37]

>> **Wholesaling: Many of the nation's largest and most important wholesalers—like Grainger—are largely unknown to final consumers. But they are very well known and much valued by the business customers they serve.**

Kristoffer Tripplaar/Alamy Stock Photo

Grainger may be the biggest market leader you've never heard of. It's a $10 billion business that offers more than 1.6 million maintenance, repair, and operating (MRO) products from 5,000 manufacturers to more than 3.2 million active customers. Through its branch network, service centers, sales reps, catalog, and online and social media sites, Grainger links customers with the supplies they need to keep their facilities running smoothly—everything from light bulbs, cleaners, and display cases to nuts and bolts, motors, valves, power tools, test equipment, and safety supplies. Grainger's nearly 600 branches, 33 strategically located distribution centers, more than 25,000 employees, and innovative web and mobile sites handle more than 100,000 transactions a day. Grainger's customers include organizations ranging from factories, garages, and grocers to schools and military bases.

Grainger operates on a simple value proposition: to make it easier and less costly for customers to find and buy MRO supplies. It starts by acting as a one-stop shop for products needed to maintain facilities. On a broader level, it builds lasting relationships with customers by helping them find *solutions* to their overall MRO problems. Acting as consultants, Grainger sales reps help buyers with everything from improving their supply chain management to reducing inventories and streamlining warehousing operations.

So, how come you've never heard of Grainger? Perhaps it's because the company operates in the not-so-glamorous world of MRO supplies, which are important to businesses but not so important to consumers. More likely, it's because Grainger is a wholesaler. And like most wholesalers, it operates behind the scenes, selling mostly to other businesses.

Why are wholesalers important to sellers? For example, why would a producer use wholesalers rather than selling directly to retailers or consumers? Simply put, wholesalers add value by performing one or more of the following channel functions:

- ***Selling and promoting.*** Wholesalers' sales forces help manufacturers reach many small customers at a low cost. The wholesaler has more contacts and is often more trusted by the buyer than the distant manufacturer.
- ***Buying and assortment building.*** Wholesalers can select items and build assortments needed by their customers, thereby saving much work.
- ***Bulk breaking.*** Wholesalers save their customers money by buying in carload lots and breaking bulk (breaking large lots into small quantities).
- ***Warehousing.*** Wholesalers hold inventories, thereby reducing the inventory costs and risks of suppliers and customers.
- ***Transportation.*** Wholesalers can provide quicker delivery to buyers because they are closer to buyers than are producers.
- ***Financing.*** Wholesalers finance their customers by giving credit, and they finance their suppliers by ordering early and paying bills on time.
- ***Risk bearing.*** Wholesalers absorb risk by taking title and bearing the cost of theft, damage, spoilage, and obsolescence.
- ***Market information.*** Wholesalers give information to suppliers and customers about competitors, new products, and price developments.

- ***Management services and advice.*** Wholesalers often help retailers train their salesclerks, improve store layouts and displays, and set up accounting and inventory control systems.

Merchant wholesaler
An independently owned wholesale business that takes title to the merchandise it handles.

Types of Wholesalers

Wholesalers fall into three major groups (see >> **Table 11.3**): *merchant wholesalers, brokers and agents*, and *manufacturers' and retailers' branches and offices*. **Merchant wholesalers**

Table 11.3 Major Types of Wholesalers

Type	Description
Merchant wholesalers	Independently owned businesses that take title to all merchandise handled. There are full-service wholesalers and limited-service wholesalers.
Full-service wholesalers	Provide a full line of services: carrying stock, maintaining a sales force, offering credit, making deliveries, and providing management assistance. Full-service wholesalers include wholesale merchants and industrial distributors.
Wholesale merchants	Sell primarily to retailers and provide a full range of services. General merchandise wholesalers carry several merchandise lines, whereas general line wholesalers carry one or two lines in great depth. Specialty wholesalers specialize in carrying only part of a line.
Industrial distributors	Sell to manufacturers rather than to retailers. Provide several services, such as carrying stock, offering credit, and providing delivery. May carry a broad range of merchandise, a general line, or a specialty line.
Limited-service wholesalers	Offer fewer services than full-service wholesalers. Limited-service wholesalers are of several types:
Cash-and-carry wholesalers	Carry a limited line of fast-moving goods and sell to small retailers for cash. Normally do not deliver.
Truck wholesalers (or truck jobbers)	Perform primarily a selling and delivery function. Carry a limited line of semiperishable merchandise (such as milk, bread, snack foods), which is sold for cash as deliveries are made to supermarkets, small groceries, hospitals, restaurants, factory cafeterias, and hotels.
Drop shippers	Do not carry inventory or handle the product. On receiving an order, drop shippers select a manufacturer, who then ships the merchandise directly to the customer. Drop shippers operate in bulk industries, such as coal, lumber, and heavy equipment.
Rack jobbers	Serve grocery and drug retailers, mostly in nonfood items. Rack jobbers send delivery trucks to stores, where the delivery people set up toys, paperbacks, hardware items, health and beauty aids, or other items. Rack jobbers price the goods, keep them fresh, set up point-of-purchase displays, and keep inventory records.
Producers' cooperatives	Farmer-owned members that assemble farm produce for sale in local markets. Producers' cooperatives often attempt to improve product quality and promote a co-op brand name, such as Sun-Maid raisins, Sunkist oranges, or Diamond nuts.
Mail-order or web wholesalers	Send catalogs to or maintain websites for retail, industrial, and institutional customers featuring jewelry, cosmetics, specialty foods, and other small items. Its primary customers are businesses in small outlying areas.
Brokers and agents	Do not take title to goods. The main function is to facilitate buying and selling, for which they earn a commission on the selling price. Generally specialize by product line or customer type.
Brokers	Bring buyers and sellers together and assist in negotiation. Brokers are paid by the party who hired the broker and do not carry inventory, get involved in financing, or assume risk. Examples include food brokers, real estate brokers, insurance brokers, and security brokers.
Agents	Represent either buyers or sellers on a more permanent basis than brokers do. There are four types:
Manufacturers' agents	Represent two or more manufacturers of complementary lines. Often used in such lines as apparel, furniture, and electrical goods. A manufacturer's agent is hired by small manufacturers who cannot afford their own field sales forces and by large manufacturers who use agents to open new territories or cover territories that cannot support full-time salespeople.
Selling agents	Have contractual authority to sell a manufacturer's entire output. The selling agent serves as a sales department and has significant influence over prices, terms, and conditions of sale. Found in product areas such as textiles, industrial machinery and equipment, coal and coke, chemicals, and metals.

(Continued)

Type	Description
Purchasing agents	Generally have a long-term relationship with buyers and make purchases for them, often receiving, inspecting, warehousing, and shipping the merchandise to buyers. Purchasing agents help clients obtain the best goods and prices available.
Commission merchants	Take physical possession of products and negotiate sales. Used most often in agricultural marketing by farmers who do not want to sell their own output. Take a truckload of commodities to a central market, sell it for the best price, deduct a commission and expenses, and remit the balance to the producers.
Manufacturers' and retailers' branches and offices	Wholesaling operations conducted by sellers or buyers themselves rather than operating through independent wholesalers. Separate branches and offices can be dedicated to either sales or purchasing.
Sales branches and offices	Set up by manufacturers to improve inventory control, selling, and promotion. Sales branches carry inventory and are found in industries such as lumber and automotive equipment and parts. Sales offices do not carry inventory and are most prominent in the dry goods and notions industries.
Purchasing offices	Perform a role similar to that of brokers or agents but are part of the buyer's organization. Many retailers set up purchasing offices in major market centers, such as New York and Chicago.

are the largest single group of wholesalers, accounting for roughly 50 percent of all wholesaling. Merchant wholesalers include two broad types: full-service wholesalers and limited-service wholesalers. *Full-service wholesalers* provide a full set of services, whereas the various *limited-service wholesalers* offer fewer services to their suppliers and customers. The different types of limited-service wholesalers perform varied specialized functions in the distribution channel.

Broker
A wholesaler who does not take title to goods and whose function is to bring buyers and sellers together and assist in negotiation.

Agent
A wholesaler who represents buyers or sellers on a relatively permanent basis, performs only a few functions, and does not take title to goods.

Manufacturers' and retailers' branches and offices
Wholesaling by sellers or buyers themselves rather than through independent wholesalers.

Brokers and *agents* differ from merchant wholesalers in two ways: They do not take title to goods, and they perform only a few functions. Like merchant wholesalers, they generally specialize by product line or customer type. A **broker** brings buyers and sellers together and assists in negotiation. **Agents** represent buyers or sellers on a more permanent basis. *Manufacturers' agents* (also called *manufacturers' representatives*) are the most common type of agent wholesaler. The third major type of wholesaling is that done in **manufacturers' and retailers' branches and offices** by sellers or buyers themselves rather than through independent wholesalers.

Wholesaler Marketing Decisions

Wholesalers now face growing competitive pressures, more-demanding customers, new technologies, and more direct-buying programs on the part of large industrial, institutional, and retail buyers. As a result, they have taken a fresh look at their marketing strategies. As with retailers, their marketing decisions include choices of segmentation and targeting, differentiation and positioning, and the marketing mix—product and service assortments, price, promotion, and distribution (see >> **Figure 11.2**).

>> **Figure 11.2 Wholesaler Marketing Strategies**

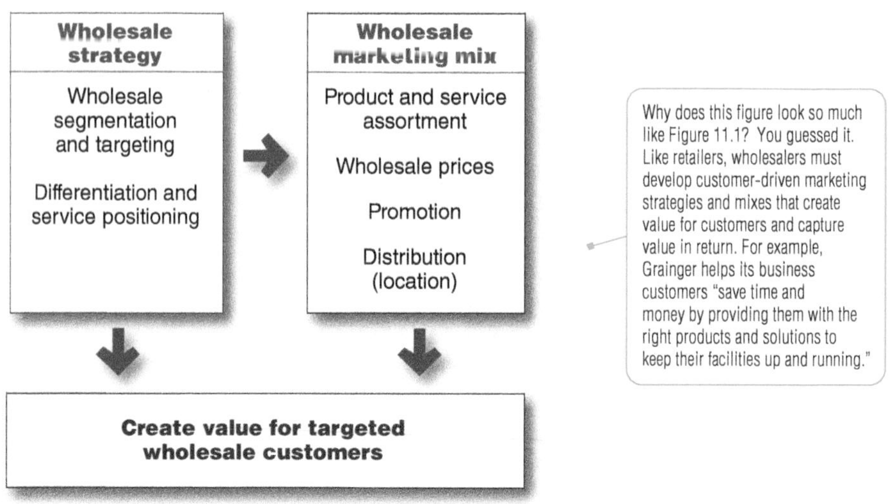
Wholesale strategy
Wholesale segmentation and targeting
Differentiation and service positioning
Wholesale marketing mix
Product and service assortment
Wholesale prices
Promotion
Distribution (location)
Create value for targeted wholesale customers
Why does this figure look so much like Figure 11.1? You guessed it. Like retailers, wholesalers must develop customer-driven marketing strategies and mixes that create value for customers and capture value in return. For example, Grainger helps its business customers "save time and money by providing them with the right products and solutions to keep their facilities up and running."

Segmentation, Targeting, Differentiation, and Positioning Decisions

Like retailers, wholesalers must segment and define their target markets and differentiate and position themselves effectively—they cannot serve everyone. They can choose a target group by size of customer (for example, large retailers only), type of customer (convenience stores only), the need for service (customers who need credit), or other factors. Within the target group, they can identify the more profitable customers, design stronger offers, and build better relationships with them. They can propose automatic reordering systems, establish management-training and advisory systems, or even sponsor a voluntary chain. They can discourage less-profitable customers by requiring larger orders or adding service charges to smaller ones.

Marketing Mix Decisions

Like retailers, wholesalers must decide on product and service assortments, prices, promotion, and place. Wholesalers add customer value though the *products and services* they offer. They are often under great pressure to carry a full line and stock enough for immediate delivery. But this practice can damage profits. Wholesalers today are cutting down on the number of lines they carry, choosing to carry only the more profitable ones. They are also rethinking which services count most in building strong customer relationships and which should be dropped or paid for by the customer. The key for companies is to find the mix of services most valued by their target customers.

Price is also an important wholesaler decision. Wholesalers usually mark up the cost of goods by a standard percentage and operate on small margins. As retail and industrial customers face increasing costs and margins pressures, they turn to wholesalers, looking for lower prices. Wholesalers may, in turn, cut their margins on some lines to keep important customers. They may also ask suppliers for special price breaks in cases when they can turn them into an increase in the supplier's sales.

Although *promotion* can be critical to wholesaler success, most wholesalers are not promotion minded. They have historically used largely scattered and unplanned trade advertising, sales promotion, personal selling, and public relations. Like other business-to-business marketers, wholesalers need to make a team effort to sell, build, and service major accounts. Wholesalers also need to adopt some of the nonpersonal promotion techniques used by retailers. They need to develop an overall promotion strategy and make greater use of supplier promotion materials and programs.

Digital and social media are playing an increasingly important role in wholesaler promotion. For example, Grainger maintains an active presence on Facebook, YouTube, Twitter, LinkedIn, and Instagram. It also provides a feature-rich mobile app. On its YouTube channel, Grainger lists more than 700 videos on topics ranging from the company and its products and services to keeping down inventory costs.

Finally, *distribution* (location) is important. Wholesalers must choose their locations, facilities, and other locations carefully. There was a time when wholesalers could locate in low-rent, low-tax areas and invest little money in their buildings, equipment, and systems. Today, however, as technology zooms forward, such behavior results in outdated systems for material handling, order processing, and delivery.

Instead, today's large and progressive wholesalers have reacted to rising costs by investing in automated warehouses and IT systems. Orders are fed from the retailer's information system directly into the wholesaler's, and the items are picked up by mechanical devices and automatically taken to a shipping platform where they are assembled. Most large wholesalers use technology to carry out accounting, billing, inventory control, and forecasting. Modern wholesalers are adapting their services to the needs of target customers and finding cost-reducing methods of doing business. They are also transacting more business online. For example, e-commerce is Grainger's fastest-growing sales channel. Online and mobile purchasing now account for almost half of the wholesaler's total sales.[38]

Trends in Wholesaling

Today's wholesalers face considerable challenges. The industry remains vulnerable to one of its most enduring trends—the need for ever-greater efficiency. Tight economic conditions and retailer woes have led to demands for even lower prices and the winnowing out of suppliers who are not adding value based on cost and quality. Progressive wholesalers constantly watch for better ways to meet the changing needs of their suppliers and target customers. They recognize that their only reason for existence comes from adding value, which occurs by increasing the efficiency and effectiveness of the entire marketing channel.

As with other types of marketers, the goal is to build value-adding customer relationships. >> For example, consider Sysco, the $55 billion wholesale food distribution company that operates behind the scenes to supply more than 425,000 restaurants, schools, hospitals, colleges, and other commercial customers that prepare meals away from home.[39]

>> **Giant food distribution wholesaler Sysco lives up to its "Good things come from Sysco" motto by procuring and delivering food and food service supplies more dependably, efficiently, and cheaply than customers could ever hope to do on their own.**
Sysco Corporation

Whether it's a hot dog from Reliant Stadium in Houston, the original Italian sub from Jersey Mike's, crab cakes from a Hilton Hotel, or a ham and cheese sandwich at the local hospital cafeteria, the chances are good that the ingredients were supplied by Sysco, the nation's top food supplier. Sysco supplies anything and everything needed to run an eating establishment, from boxes of seafood, chicken, and beef to 25-pound bags of rice or pasta to gallon jars of ketchup or salsa to boxes of plastic gloves and jugs of dishwashing detergent. What makes Sysco so valuable to its customers is that it procures and delivers these supplies more dependably, efficiently, and cheaply than customers could ever hope to do on their own.

For example, Lowell's, the iconic restaurant in Seattle's Pike Place Market, procures almost all of its products conveniently through the Sysco Market online ordering system. Its orders are processed quickly and accurately at Sysco's automated distribution center. Then Lowell's—by itself or with the help of Sysco sales associates and dispatchers—can track the location of individual deliveries via the My Sysco Truck program. Sysco constantly seeks new ways to add more value and build trust, from product traceability for safety to sourcing products from local, small- to mid-sized farms, ranches, and processors to serve the needs of customers whose businesses are positioned on sustainability and community. In short, Sysco more than lives up to its motto: "Good things come from Sysco."

The distinction between large retailers and large wholesalers continues to blur. Many retailers now operate formats such as wholesale clubs and supercenters that perform many wholesale functions. In return, some large wholesalers are setting up their own retailing operations. For example, SuperValu is one of the nation's largest food wholesalers, and it's also one of the country's largest food retailers. About one-third of the company's sales come from its Cub Foods, Farm Fresh, Hornbacher's, Shop 'n Save, and Shoppers stores.[40]

Wholesalers will continue to increase the services they provide to retailers—retail pricing, cooperative advertising, marketing and management information services, accounting services, online transactions, and others. However, both the more value-focused environment and the demand for increased services have put the squeeze on wholesaler profits. Wholesalers that do not find efficient ways to deliver value to their customers will soon drop by the wayside. Fortunately, the increased use of computerized, automated, and internet-based systems will help wholesalers contain the costs of ordering, shipping, and inventory holding, thus boosting their productivity.

REVIEWING AND EXTENDING THE CONCEPTS

CHAPTER REVIEW AND KEY TERMS

Objectives Review

Retailing and wholesaling consist of many organizations bringing goods and services from the point of production to the point of use. In this chapter, we examined the nature and importance of retailing, the major types of retailers, the decisions retailers make, and the future of retailing. We then examined these same topics for wholesalers.

OBJECTIVE 11-1 Explain the role of retailers in the distribution channel and describe the major types of retailers. (pp 336–344)

Retailing includes all the activities involved in selling goods or services directly to final consumers for their personal, nonbusiness use. Retailers play an important role in connecting brands to consumers in the final phases of the buying process. *Shopper marketing* involves focusing the entire marketing process on turning shoppers into buyers as they move along toward the point of sale, whether during in-store, online, or mobile shopping.

Recent dramatic shifts in how today's connected consumers shop and buy have caused a massive upheaval in the retailing industry. Today's buyers are omni-channel consumers who work across multiple channels as they shop, changing the role of retail stores in the buying process. As Amazon and other online merchants have boomed, traditional store retailers have struggled. Successful retailers of the future must adopt *omni-channel retailing*, creating a seamless cross-channel buying experience that integrates in-store, online, and mobile shopping.

Retail stores come in all shapes and sizes, and new retail types keep emerging. Store retailers can be classified by the *amount of service* they provide (self-service, limited service, or full service), *product line sold* (specialty stores, department stores, supermarkets, convenience stores, superstores, and service businesses), and *relative prices* (discount stores and off-price retailers). Today, many retailers are banding together in corporate and contractual *retail organizations* (corporate chains, voluntary chains, retailer cooperatives, and franchise organizations).

OBJECTIVE 11-2 Discuss how retailers are using omni-channel retailing to meet the cross-channel shopping behavior of today's digitally connected consumers. (pp 345–346)

The retail shopping process has changed radically in this age of websites, smartphones, mobile apps, social media, and other things digital. Today's omni-channel buyers shift easily across online and in-store channels throughout the buying process. They readily research products and prices online, shopping digitally from home, from work, in stores, or anywhere in between. This massive shift in how people shop calls for massive changes in how store retailers operate. Omni-channel *buying* calls for omni-channel *retailing*, integrating all available shopping channels and devices into a seamless customer shopping experience.

Omni-channel retailing goes beyond just helping in-store customers as they cross-shop on mobile devices. It requires carefully integrating the entire range of available shopping channels, both in-store and out, from discovery to purchase in the buying process. To that end, most large retailers are now boosting their online and digital selling options and linking them with stores. The key is to integrate these elements to create the critical seamless, anywhere, anytime, omni-channel shopping experience that today's customers seek.

OBJECTIVE 11-3 Describe the major retailer marketing decisions. (pp 346–351)

Retailers are always searching for new marketing strategies to attract and hold customers. They face major marketing decisions about segmentation and targeting, store differentiation and positioning, and the retail marketing mix.

Retailers must first segment and define their target markets and then decide how they will differentiate and position themselves in these markets. Those that try to offer "something for everyone" end up satisfying no market well. By contrast, successful retailers define their target markets well and position themselves strongly.

Guided by strong targeting and positioning, retailers must decide on a retail marketing mix—product and services assortment, price, promotion, and place. Retail stores are much more than simply an assortment of goods. Beyond the products and services they offer, today's successful retailers carefully orchestrate virtually every aspect of the consumer store experience. A retailer's price policy must fit its target market and positioning, products and services assortment, and competition. Retailers use various combinations of the five promotion tools—advertising, personal selling, sales promotion, PR, and direct and digital marketing—to reach consumers. Online, mobile, and social media tools are playing an ever-increasing role in helping retailers to engage customers. Finally, it's very important that retailers select locations that are accessible to the target market in areas that are consistent with the retailer's positioning.

 **OBJECTIVE 11-4 Discuss the major trends and developments in retailing. (pp 351–357)**

Retailers operate in a harsh and fast-changing environment, which offers threats as well as opportunities. Following years of good economic times, retailers have now adjusted to the new economic realities and more thrift-minded consumers. New retail forms continue to emerge. At the same time, however, different types of retailers are increasingly serving similar customers with the same products and prices (retail convergence), making differentiation more difficult. Other trends in retailing include the rise of megaretailers, the growing importance of retail technology, a surge in green retailing, and the global expansion of major retailers.

 **OBJECTIVE 11-5 Explain the major types of wholesalers and their marketing decisions. (pp 357–362)**

Wholesaling includes all the activities involved in selling goods or services to those who are buying for resale or business use. Wholesalers fall into three groups. First, *merchant wholesalers* take possession of the goods. They include *full-service wholesalers* and *limited-service wholesalers.* Second, *brokers* and *agents* do not take possession of the goods but are paid a commission for aiding companies in buying and selling. Finally, *manufacturers' and retailers' branches and offices* are wholesaling operations conducted by non-wholesalers to bypass the wholesalers.

Like retailers, wholesalers must target carefully and position themselves strongly. And, like retailers, wholesalers must decide on product and service assortments, prices, promotion, and place. Progressive wholesalers constantly watch for better ways to meet the changing needs of their suppliers and target customers. They recognize that, in the long run, their only reason for existence comes from adding value, which occurs by increasing the efficiency and effectiveness of the entire marketing channel. As with other types of marketers, the goal is to build value-adding customer relationships.

Key Terms

Objective 11-1
Retailing (p 336)
Retailer (p 336)
Shopper marketing (p 336)
Omni-channel retailing (p 337)
Specialty store (p 338)
Department store (p 338)
Supermarket (p 338)
Convenience store (p 339)
Superstore (p 339)
Category killer (p 339)
Service retailer (p 339)
Discount store (p 340)
Off-price retailer (p 341)
Independent off-price retailer (p 341)
Factory outlet (p 341)
Warehouse club (p 341)
Corporate chains (p 344)
Franchise (p 344)

Objective 11-3
Shopping center (p 351)

Objective 11-5
Wholesaling (p 357)
Wholesaler (p 357)
Merchant wholesaler (p 359)
Broker (p 360)
Agent (p 360)
Manufacturers' and retailers' branches and offices (p 360)

DISCUSSION AND CRITICAL THINKING

Discussion Questions

11-1. Define *omni-channel retailing,* and explain its connection to *shopper marketing.* (AACSB: Written and Oral Communication)

11-2. Discuss the four characteristics by which retail stores are classified. (AACSB: Written and Oral Communication)

11-3. Explain the various marketing decisions retailers must consider in designing strategies to attract and hold customers. (AACSB: Written and Oral Communication)

11-4. What major trends and developments are retailers facing? How do these developments impact their competitive strategies? (AACSB: Written and Oral Communication; Reflective Thinking)

11-5. List and describe the functions wholesalers perform that add value to both retailers and consumers. (AACSB: Written and Oral Communication)

11-6. Discuss the marketing mix decisions faced by wholesalers. What current challenges do wholesalers face? (AACSB: Written and Oral Communication)

Critical Thinking Exercises

11-7. You need a new pair of jeans, and you have many retail options. Using the information in your text, choose three different major store retailer types, and select a specific store for each type chosen. Visit each store (in person or online), and describe each store's segmentation and positioning strategy and retail marketing mix—product, price, place, and promotion. How do the product assortments differ? What is each store's pricing approach? What promotional tools are used? Discuss store locations. (AACSB: Written and Oral Communication; Reflective Thinking; Information Technology)

11-8. In a small group, present a plan for a new retail store. Who is the store's target market? Describe the merchandise, atmospherics, price points, services provided, location, and how you would promote your retail store. Describe how you will differentiate your store from competitors. (AACSB: Written and Oral Communication; Reflective Thinking)

11-9. Identify a retailer that is successfully using an omni-channel strategy. What is this retailer doing that sets it apart from the competition? (AACSB: Written and Oral Communication; Reflective Thinking)

MINICASES AND APPLICATIONS

Online, Mobile, and Social Media Marketing Skipping the Checkout Line

The convenience of running to the store for a few grocery items can be hampered by long checkout lines. The creative geniuses at Selfycart solved this issue by developing an app that allows shoppers to browse, scan, and pay for products in participating stores using their mobile devices without waiting in line. Selfycart's technology continues to change, including a virtual shopping cart, shopping lists, historical purchase information, list sharing, and a coupon portal that virtually clips coupons. Selfycart also developed a daily deal section that offers discounts and special offers specific to each store. Selfycart will eventually introduce online ordering, so consumers can add products to a virtual shopping cart, pay, and arrange store pickup at a specified time. Selfycart continues to discover new ways to create value for its users. Suddenly, skipping the line is an extremely appealing prospect!

11-10. Investigate the Selfycart app. What benefits and challenges will stores face in introducing Selfycart or any other mobile checkout app? (AACSB: Written and Oral Communication; Information Technology; Reflective Thinking)

11-11. If Selfycart or a similar mobile checkout app were available at your grocery store, would you use it? What benefits would you gain by using this new technology? Discuss the challenges you would face. (AACSB: Written and Oral Communication; Reflective Thinking)

Marketing Ethics Embracing What's Good at Costco

As a *Fortune* 500 company, warehouse retailing giant Costco has successfully positioned itself as a progressive retailer that serves its membership base with quality products and services at low prices. Costco also has built a reputation for attracting, taking care of, and retaining its employees. With operations in eight countries and more than 225,000 employees globally, Costco has taken cutting-edge employer actions such as extending health-care coverage to part-time workers and raising its average pay rate. The national average hourly pay rate for retail workers is $11.39. Costco's starting hourly pay is $11.50, but the average hourly pay for most of its employees is around $21.00. More than 85 percent of Costco employees have company-offered health-care coverage. Costco CEO Craig Jelinek believes that if employees have good health care and make a living wage, more money is pumped into local economies. It is also interesting to note that more than 70 percent of Costco's employees are promoted to higher positions with the company via Costco's promote-from-within policy. Additionally, Costco seeks to hire veterans and diverse team members that represent the communities where stores are located. Beyond its positive workplace culture, Costco has implemented broad sustainability practices aimed at minimizing environmental impact, including waste management, food donations, using sustainable fisheries, protecting animals, and building LEED-certified warehouses. All of these factors contributed to landing Costco at number 5 on the *Forbes* list of "America's Best Employers" and 86 on its list of "World's Most Valuable Brands."

11-12. What can other companies learn from Costco's socially responsible and ethical business practices? (AACSB: Written and Oral Communication; Ethical Understanding and Reasoning)

11-13. Discuss the benefits and limitations warehouse clubs face when offering a limited selection of products? (AACSB: Written and Oral Communication; Reflective Thinking)

Marketing by the Numbers Grocery Stores Offering Meal Kits

Half of Americans' food dollars are spent eating out, and many meals eaten at home are not actually cooked there, trends that are eating into grocery store sales. More recently, firms such as Blue Apron, Plated, Hello Fresh, and others have begun delivering meal kits that include premeasured ingredients to be cooked at home, further eroding grocery store sales. Although the meal kit industry has exploded to $2 billion in annual sales, it has had problems achieving scale and profitability. To combat this, Hello Fresh and Blue Apron are distributing meals kits through supermarkets and wholesale clubs. Others meal kit firms are being acquired by grocery chains. For example, Kroger, the largest U.S. supermarket chain, just announced its purchase of Home Chef, the largest privately owned meal kit company. In addition to increasing its online delivery, Kroger also intends to sell meal kits in its stores. However, the meal kit business could be difficult for Kroger. Online subscription meal kit operators have found that it's not good to offer too many recipe options. But how many different recipes are optimal? Kroger thinks that its no-subscription requirement and price ($14 to $18 for a two-person meal kit compared to $50 or more for regular home-delivery meal kits) will attract more sales. But finding the right balance of kit offerings and stocking levels is challenging. Not stocking enough merchandise—in this case varied meal kits—results in lost sales. But carrying too much inventory increases costs and lowers margins, especially because of perishability. Both conditions reduce profits. One measure of a reseller's inventory management effectiveness is its *stockturn rate* (also called *inventory turnover rate* for manufacturers). Retailers want to realize a large volume of sales on as little inventory as possible while maintaining enough stock to meet customer demand. To determine this, Kroger plans to run short-term market tests in selected stores to determine the optimum inventory levels.

11-14. Using the data, determine Kroger's weekly stockturn rate for meal kits during one of the market tests. Refer to Analytic Ratios in Appendix 3: Marketing by the Numbers to learn how to calculate stockturn rate. (AACSB: Analytical Thinking)

11-15. Interpret your answers in question 11-14. Is Kroger's weekly stockturn rate good or bad? What factors should be considered to determine this? (AACSB: Written and Oral Communication; Reflective Thinking)

Video Case Kmart

To view this video case and its accompanying questions, please visit MyLab Marketing.

Once the leader in discount retailing, Kmart long ago took a back seat to Walmart, Target, and others discount chains. But recent efforts to provide value to customers through innovation show that the veteran retailer may still have its edge. To gain a competitive one-up, Kmart started a unique program that combined the benefits of online and brick-and-mortar shopping. When an item that customers wanted to purchase was not in stock at one of its stores, Kmart would ship the item to the customer's home for free.

To launch this program, Kmart unveiled an ad campaign that illustrated an uncharacteristic relevance to younger, tech-savvy customers. With the slight-of-mouth message that customers could "ship their pants" (or any of the other 65 million items in Kmart's inventory) for free, the ad went viral. As a result, Kmart got its message out in spades, entertaining many while offending a few along the way.

Company Cases 11 Bass Pro Shops/9 Trader Joe's/10 Target

See Appendix 1 for cases appropriate for this chapter.

Case 11, Bass Pro Shops: Creating Nature's Theme Park for People Who Hate to Shop. Bass Pro Shops became the largest sporting goods retailer by providing the broadest assortment of products and enticing customers with engaging experiences.

Case 9, Trader Joe's: Cheap Gourmet—Putting a Special Twist on the Price-Value Equation. Trader Joe's provides superior customer value by providing the perfect ratio of benefits to prices.

Case 10, Target: A Serious Contender in the Same-Day Delivery Business. Struggling to maintain growth in the world of discount retailing, Target recently scored a coup by acquiring same-day delivery startup Shipt.

Writing Assignments

11-16. Describe the types of shopping centers and identify specific examples in your community or a nearby city. (AACSB: Communication; Reflective Thinking)

11-17. The atmosphere in a retail store is carefully crafted to influence shoppers. Select a retailer that has both a physical store and an online store. Describe the elements of the physical store's atmosphere, such as the colors, lighting, music, scents, and décor. What image is the store's atmosphere projecting? Is that image appropriate given the merchandise assortment and target market of the store? Which elements of the physical store's atmosphere are part of its online store atmosphere? Does the retailer integrate the physical store's atmosphere with its online presence? Explain. (AACSB: Written and Oral Communication; Information Technology; Reflective Thinking)

12 Engaging Consumers and Communicating Customer Value

Advertising and Public Relations

Objectives Outline

- OBJECTIVE 12-1 **Define the five promotion mix tools for communicating customer value.** See: The Promotion Mix (pp 370–371)
- OBJECTIVE 12-2 **Discuss the changing communications landscape and the need for integrated marketing communications.** See: Integrated Marketing Communications (pp 371–378)
- OBJECTIVE 12-3 **Describe and discuss the major decisions involved in developing an advertising program.** See: Advertising and Major Advertising Decisions (pp 379–396)
- OBJECTIVE 12-4 **Explain how companies use public relations to communicate with their publics.** See: Public Relations (pp 396–398)

Previewing the Concepts

In this and the next two chapters, we'll examine the last of the marketing mix tools—promotion. Companies must do more than just create customer value. They must also clearly and persuasively communicate that value. Promotion is not a single tool but rather a mix of several tools. Ideally, under the concept of *integrated marketing communications,* a company will carefully coordinate these promotion elements to engage customers and build a clear, consistent, and compelling message about an organization and its products.

We'll begin by introducing the various promotion mix tools. Next, we'll examine the rapidly changing communications environment—especially the addition of digital, mobile, and social media—and the need for integrated marketing communications. Finally, we'll look more closely at two of the promotion tools—advertising and public relations. In the next chapter, we'll visit two other promotion mix tools—sales promotion and personal selling. Then, in Chapter 14, we'll explore direct, online, mobile, and social media marketing.

Let's start by looking at a good integrated marketing communications campaign. In the fiercely competitive snack and candy industry, where well-established brands are fighting for survival, the inspired-yet-durable Snickers "You're not you when you're hungry" campaign has given the iconic brand new life. No matter where you see the message—on TV, on a mobile screen, in a friend's post, or even on a Snickers candy bar wrapper—the imaginative campaign clearly and consistently drives home the brand's "Snickers satisfies" and "You're not you when you're hungry" positioning in an engaging and memorable way. It has also made Snickers the world's leading sweet snack.

First Stop

Snickers: "You're Not You When You're Hungry"

It all started with a now-classic Snickers ad in the 2010 Super Bowl. In the ad, during a neighborhood pickup football game, then-octogenarian Golden Girl Betty White appeared as a football player who was "playing like Betty White"—that is, very poorly. But after biting into a Snickers bar, she morphed back into a young, athletic footballer who played more like his usual self. The ad ended with the now-familiar slogan "You're not you when you're hungry" followed by the tagline "Snickers satisfies."

The Betty White ad generated tremendous buzz, reinvigorating the then-stagnant Snickers candy bar brand. According to Nielsen, it was the "best-liked spot" of that year's Super Bowl, and it achieved the highest score on the *USA Today* Ad Meter rankings. The ad went viral, racking up tens of millions of views online and earning seemingly endless media attention. The "You're not you when you're hungry" slogan went on to become the cornerstone of a long-running, highly successful integrated marketing communications campaign that has propelled Snickers to the top of the global confectionary market.

» The Snickers "You're not you when you're hungry" mantra taps into a powerful and universal emotional appeal—hunger. Everyone can relate to how being hungry changes who you are.

Judy Unger/Alamy Stock Photo

Every great marketing communications campaign starts with a unique brand message, something that sets the brand apart. For decades, Mars has positioned Snickers on one overriding brand attribute: Snickers is satisfying. Heartier than most candy bars, Snickers combines ingredients like chocolate, nougat, and caramel with the protein power of peanuts. The "Snickers satisfies" tagline emphasizes the bar's stomach-filling properties. Before the current campaign, Snickers pitched the bar to young athletic males as a meal alternative. One classic print ad, for example, showed an approving mother sending her son off to football practice with a Snickers bar.

But by the early 2000s, Snickers was in a rut. Its positioning had grown stale; its sales and market share had flattened. The brand needed a new creative concept—-something that would rejuvenate Snickers and broaden its market appeal. Rather than abandoning its established positioning, however, Mars extended it with the fresh new "You're not you when you're hungry" theme. So while "Snickers satisfies" remains the brand's baseline positioning, "You're not you" is the creative "big idea" that now brings the positioning to life in a clever and engaging way.

"You're not you when you're hungry" taps into a powerful and universal emotional appeal—hunger. It reaches a broad market. Almost everyone can relate to how being hungry changes who you are. The positioning is as powerful for women as for men; for older generations as for younger ones; for office workers, factory workers, or students. It works across global cultural lines. Finally, the "You're not you" theme lends itself to no end of imaginative and entertaining ads and executions across varied media platforms.

From that first Betty White Super Bowl ad, the "You're not you" campaign has spawned a host of creative ads in more than 80 countries. One memorable TV ad featured the late Robin Williams as a football coach instructing his team to "kill them—with kindness" by making balloon animals and tea cosies. Then there was the Snickers *Brady Bunch* ad for Super Bowl XLIX in which roughneck Danny Trejo portrayed a snarling Marcia and quirky Steve Buscemi played a disgruntled Jan. That ad ranked third-highest among that year's Super Bowl ads in terms of earned impressions and went on to win a first-ever Super Clio (the Academy Awards of advertising). During Super Bowl 50, another Snickers ad mimicked the iconic photo shoot featuring Marilyn Monroe in a white dress standing over a breezy subway grate—only this time, the updraft revealed grumpy-faced Willem Dafoe's bony legs and tighty-whiteys. That ad pulled in more than 11 million views on the Snickers YouTube channel alone.

The "You're not you" campaign also works well in print. One print ad shows three sprinters in start position on a track, one of them facing the wrong direction. Another shows four soccer players in position to block a free kick, all with their cupped hands protecting important body parts save one who is unguarded, hands above his head with his jersey pulled over his face. Still another ad gets the point across without using humans at all. In a reversal of roles, it shows a zebra in hot pursuit of a lion. Each simple visual is accompanied by a cross-section of a Snickers bar and the phrase "You're not you when you're hungry. Snickers satisfies."

The enduring Snickers "You're not you when you're hungry" integrated marketing communications campaign clearly and consistently drives the brand's "Snickers satisfies" positioning in an engaging and memorable way, helping to make Snickers the world's leading sweet snack.

Beyond TV and print ads, the "You're not you" campaign is fully integrated across a range of digital, mobile, positional, and other media, even packaging. Snickers's "Hunger Bar" candy wrappers directly reinforce the campaign message, with labels containing mood descriptors such as Cranky, Loopy, Spacey, Whiny, Snippy, Curmudgeon, Goofball, and Drama Mama. Snickers urges customers to call out contrarian-acting friends with an appropriately labeled Snickers bar. Mars even created a clever two-minute mini-reality-show video highlighting a Snickers hotline operator who dispatches bike messengers to deliver the wrappers to deserving candidates.

The Snickers "You're not you when you're hungry" campaign's numerous digital elements are designed to engage customers and trigger consumer-generated content. For example, a "Snap a Selfie with your Snickers Bar" contest invited the brand's more than 11 million Facebook followers to share photos of "who R U when U R hungry"—the winner received $100,000 and his own personalized Snickers bars. A Snickers "You're Not YouTube" campaign signed up 13 influential YouTubers, with a combined following of 7 million subscribers, to illustrate their own "You're not you" moments. And a global Twitter campaign asking users what happens #WhenYouAreHungry drew nearly 5 million tweets in only one week.

In yet another digital campaign, this one in the United Kingdom, British celebrities posted four "out-of-character" tweets—such as professional soccer player Rio Ferdinand tweeting "Really getting into knitting!!!" or glamor model Katie Price tweeting "Large scale quantitative easing could distort liquidity of government bond market"—followed by a fifth tweet promoting Snickers bars and quoting the campaign slogan #yourenotyouwhenyourehungry. Such digital efforts effectively engage and entertain the brand's digitally savvy fans while reinforcing the Snickers mantra.

Despite its diversity, no matter what the platform—whether print or packaging or TV, laptop, and mobile screens or something else—the Snickers campaign is much more than just a scattered collection of clever content. What makes the campaign so powerful is that all its pieces are carefully integrated under the brand's "Snickers satisfies" and "You're not you when you're hungry" positioning. The message strikes a core human emotion—that you're likely to get a little out of sorts when you haven't eaten for a while—in an engaging and memorable way. No matter where you are in the world or how you receive the message, the campaign delivers a clear and consistent brand message.

Thus, after more than eight years, the popular Snickers "You're not you" campaign is still packing energy. Prior to the campaign, Snickers was losing market share. However, not long after Betty White made her Super Bowl debut, Snickers surpassed Mars's own M&Ms to become the planet's best-selling candy, a position it still holds today. With an expanded lineup that now includes Snickers Almond, Snickers Peanut Butter Squared, Snickers Bites, and Snickers Ice Cream bars, the $3.5 billion Snickers brand now contributes more than 10 percent of giant Mars, Inc.'s total annual revenues. Thanks in large part to the innovative "You're not you when you're hungry" integrated marketing communications campaign, the brand's long-standing claim holds truer than ever, for both the company and its customers: "Snickers satisfies."[1]

Author Comment
The promotion mix is the marketer's bag of tools for engaging and communicating with customers and other stakeholders. To deliver a clear and compelling message, each tool must be carefully coordinated under the concept of integrated marketing communications (IMC).

Building good customer relationships calls for more than just developing a good product, pricing it attractively, and making it available to target customers. Companies must also engage consumers and communicate their value propositions to customers, and what they communicate should not be left to chance. All communications must be planned and blended into carefully integrated programs. Just as good communication is important in building and maintaining any other kind of relationship, it is a crucial element in a company's efforts to engage customers and build profitable customer relationships.

The Promotion Mix

OBJECTIVE 12-1 Define the five promotion mix tools for communicating customer value.

Promotion mix (marketing communications mix)
The specific blend of promotion tools that the company uses to persuasively communicate customer value and build customer relationships.

Advertising
Any paid form of nonpersonal presentation and promotion of ideas, goods, or services by an identified sponsor.

Sales promotion
Short-term incentives to encourage the purchase or sale of a product or a service.

A company's total **promotion mix**—also called its **marketing communications mix**—consists of the specific blend of advertising, public relations, personal selling, sales promotion, and direct and digital marketing tools that the company uses to engage consumers, persuasively communicate customer value, and build customer relationships. The five major promotion tools are defined as follows:[2]

- **Advertising**. Any paid form of nonpersonal presentation and promotion of ideas, goods, or services by an identified sponsor.
- **Sales promotion**. Short-term incentives to encourage the purchase or sale of a product or service.
- **Personal selling**. Personal customer interactions by the firm's sales force to engage customers, make sales, and build customer relationships.
- **Public relations (PR)**. Building good relations with the company's various publics by obtaining favorable publicity, building up a good corporate image, and handling or heading off unfavorable rumors, stories, and events.
- **Direct and digital marketing**. Engaging directly with carefully targeted individual consumers and customer communities to both obtain an immediate response and build lasting customer relationships.

Personal selling
Personal presentation by the firm's sales force for the purpose of engaging customers, making sales, and building customer relationships.

Public relations (PR)
Building good relations with the company's various publics by obtaining favorable publicity, building up a good corporate image, and handling or heading off unfavorable rumors, stories, and events.

Direct and digital marketing
Engaging directly with carefully targeted individual consumers and customer communities to both obtain an immediate response and build lasting customer relationships.

Each category involves specific promotional tools that are used to communicate with customers. For example, *advertising* includes broadcast, print, online, mobile, outdoor, and other forms. *Sales promotion* includes discounts, coupons, displays, demonstrations, and events. *Personal selling* includes sales presentations, trade shows, and incentive programs. *Public relations* includes press releases, sponsorships, events, and webpages. And *direct and digital marketing* includes direct mail, email, catalogs, online and social media, mobile marketing, and more.

At the same time, marketing communication goes beyond these specific promotion tools. The product's design, its price, the shape and color of its package, and the stores that sell it—*all* communicate something to buyers. Thus, although the promotion mix is the company's primary engagement and communications activity, the entire marketing mix—promotion *and* product, price, and place—must be coordinated for greatest impact.

Author Comment
Integrated marketing communications—IMC—is a really hot topic these days. No other area of marketing is changing so quickly and profoundly. A big part of the reason is the huge surge in customer engagement through digital media—online, mobile, and social media marketing.

Integrated Marketing Communications

OBJECTIVE 12-2 Discuss the changing communications landscape and the need for integrated marketing communications.

In past decades, marketers perfected the art of mass marketing: selling highly standardized products to masses of customers. In the process, they developed effective mass-media communication techniques to support these strategies. Large companies now routinely invest millions or even billions of dollars in television, magazine, or other mass-media advertising, reaching tens of millions of customers with a single ad. Today, however, marketing managers face some new marketing communications realities. Perhaps no other area of marketing is changing so profoundly as marketing communications, creating both exciting and challenging times for marketing communicators.

The New Marketing Communications Model

Several major factors are changing the face of today's marketing communications. First, *consumers* are changing. In this digitally connected, mobile age, consumers are better informed and more communications empowered. Rather than relying on marketer-supplied information, they can use the internet, social media, and other technologies to find information on their own. They can connect easily with other consumers to exchange brand-related information or even create their own brand messages and experiences.

Second, *marketing strategies* are changing. As mass markets have fragmented, marketers are shifting away from mass marketing. More and more, they are developing focused marketing programs designed to engage customers and build customer relationships in more narrowly defined micromarkets.

Finally, sweeping advances in *digital technology* are causing remarkable changes in the ways companies and customers communicate with each other. The digital age has spawned a host of new information and communication tools—from to smartphones and tablets to the many faces of the internet (brand websites, email, blogs, streamed content, social media and online communities, the mobile web, and so much more). Just as mass marketing once gave rise to a new generation of mass-media communications, the new digital and social media have given birth to a more targeted, social, and engaging marketing communications model.

Although network television, magazines, newspapers, and other traditional mass media remain very important, their dominance is declining. In their place, advertisers are now adding a broad selection of more-specialized and highly targeted media to engage smaller customer communities with more personalized, interactive content. The new media range from specialty cable television channels and made-for-the-web videos to online ads, email and texting, blogs, mobile catalogs and coupons, and a burgeoning list of social media. Such new media have taken marketing by storm.

Some advertising industry experts even predict that the old mass-media communications model will eventually become obsolete. Mass-media costs are rising, audiences are shrinking, ad clutter is increasing, and viewers are gaining control of message exposure through technologies such as video streaming or DVRs that let them skip disruptive television commercials. As a result, the skeptics suggest, marketers are shifting ever-larger portions of their marketing budgets away from old-media mainstays and to online, social, and mobile media.

In recent years, although TV remains a potent advertising medium, TV ad spending growth has flattened or declined. Ad spending in magazines, newspapers, and radio has also lost ground. Meanwhile, spending in digital media has surged. Growing at a rate of more than 18 percent annually, total digital ad spending surpassed TV spending worldwide in 2017. By 2020, digital media will capture an estimated 50 percent of all ad spending. By far the fastest-growing digital category is mobile, which grew 39 percent last year now accounts for 75 percent of all digital ad spending.[3]

More and more, large advertisers—from Nike and P&G to Unilever—are moving toward a "digital-first" approach to building their brands. For example, Unilever, one of the world's largest advertisers, now spends as much as 30 percent of its more than $9 billion global marketing budget on digital media. In countries such as the United States and China, digital media account for closer to 50 percent of its marketing budget.[4] Some marketers now rely almost entirely on digital and social media. » For example, adidas has now abandoned TV altogether and uses only digital channels to reach younger consumers. "It's clear that the younger consumer engages with us predominantly over the mobile device," says adidas's CEO.[5]

» The new marketing communications model: Marketers are shifting ever-larger portions of their marketing budgets away from old-media mainstays to online, social, and mobile media. Adidas now uses only digital channels to engage its younger consumers.

Dan Freebairn

In the new marketing communications world, rather than using old approaches that interrupt customers and force-feed them mass messages, new media formats let marketers reach smaller communities of consumers in more engaging ways. For example, think about television viewing these days. Consumers can now watch their favorite programs on just about anything with a screen—on televisions but also tablets, smartphones, or laptops. And they can choose to watch programs whenever and wherever they wish, often without commercials. Increasingly, programs, ads, and videos are being produced only for online viewing.

Despite the shift toward digital media, however, traditional mass media still capture a sizable share of the promotion budgets of most major marketing firms, a fact that probably won't change quickly. Thus, rather than the old-media model collapsing completely, most marketers foresee a shifting mix of both traditional mass media and online, mobile, and social media that engage more-targeted consumer communities in a more personalized way. In the end, regardless of the communications channel, the key is to integrate all of these media in a way that best engages customers, communicates the brand message, and enhances the customer's brand experiences.

Content marketing
Creating, inspiring, and sharing brand messages and conversations with and among consumers across a fluid mix of paid, owned, earned, and shared channels.

As the marketing communications environment shifts, so will the role of marketing communicators. Rather than just creating and placing "TV ads" or "print ads" or "Snapchat brand stories," many marketers now view themselves more broadly as **content marketing** managers. As such, they create, inspire, and share brand messages and conversations with and among customers across a fluid mix of *paid, owned, earned,* and *shared* communication channels. These channels include media that are both traditional and new as well as controlled and not controlled. It's not just advertising anymore, notes one ad agency executive. "It's about [communications] context and channels now, rather than just the message itself. It's about mapping the customer journey to start a conversation with consumers, one that leads to engagement, purchase, loyalty, and advocacy at different touchpoints against this integrated journey" (see Marketing at Work 12.1).[6]

MARKETING AT WORK 12.1

Just Don't Call It Advertising: It's Content Marketing

In the good old days, life seemed so simple for advertisers. When a brand needed an advertising campaign, everybody knew what that meant. The brand team and ad agency came up with a creative strategy, developed a media plan, produced and placed a set of TV commercials and magazine or newspaper ads, and maybe issued a press release to stir up some news. But in these digital times, the old practice of placing "advertisements" in well-defined "media" within the tidy framework of a carefully managed "advertising campaign" just doesn't work anymore.

Instead, the lines are rapidly blurring between traditional advertising and new digital content. To be relevant, today's brand messages must be social, mobile, interactively engaging, and multi-platformed. Says one industry insider: "Today's media landscape keeps getting more diverse—it's broadcast, cable, and streaming; it's online, tablet, and smartphone; it's video, rich media, social media, branded content, banners, apps, in-app advertising, and interactive technology products."

The new digital landscape has called into question the very definition of advertising. "What Is Advertising Anyway?" asks one provocative headline. Call it whatever you want, admonishes another, but "Just *Don't* Call It Advertising." Instead, according to many marketers these days, it's "content marketing," creating and distributing a broad mix of compelling content that engages customers, builds relationships with and among them, and moves them to act and advocate the brand to others. To feed today's digital and social media machinery and to sustain "always-on" consumer conversations, brands need a constant supply of fresh content across a breadth of traditional and digital platforms.

Many advertisers and marketers now view themselves more broadly as *content marketing managers* who create, inspire, share, and curate marketing content—both their own content and that created by consumers and others. Rather than using traditional media breakdowns, they subscribe to a new framework that builds on how and by whom marketing content is created, controlled, and distributed. The new classification identifies four major types of media: paid, owned, earned, and shared (POES):

Paid media—promotional channels paid for by the marketer, including traditional media (such as TV, radio, print, or outdoor) and online and digital media (paid search ads, web and social media display ads, mobile ads, or email marketing).

Owned media—promotional channels owned and controlled by the company, including company websites, corporate blogs, owned social media pages, proprietary brand communities, sales forces, and events.

Earned media—PR media channels, such as television, newspapers, blogs, online video sites, and other media not directly paid for or controlled by the marketer but that include the content because of viewer, reader, or user interest.

Shared media—media shared by consumers with other consumers, such as social media, blogs, mobile media, and viral channels as well as traditional word-of-mouth.

In the past, advertisers have focused on traditional paid (broadcast, print) or earned (public relations) media. Now, however, content marketers have rapidly added the new digital generation of owned (websites, blogs, brand communities) and shared (online social, mobile, email) media. Whereas a successful paid ad used to be an end in itself, marketers are now developing integrated marketing content that leverages the combined power of all the POES channels. Thus, many TV ads often aren't just TV ads any more. They're "video content" you might see anywhere—on a TV screen but also on a tablet or phone. Other video content looks a lot like TV advertising but was never intended for TV, such as made-for-online videos posted

>> Content marketing: Tecate's content-rich, skillfully integrated "Soccer Gentleman" campaign produced striking results across POES media by helping men to balance the two true loves of their lives: women and World Cup soccer.

Cervecería Cuauhtémoc Moctezuma, SA de CV

on websites or social media. Similarly, printed brand messages and pictures no longer appear only in carefully crafted magazine ads or catalogs. Instead, such content, created by a variety of sources, pops up in anything from formal ads and online brand pages to mobile and social media and independent blogs.

The new "content marketing" campaigns look a lot different from the old "advertising" campaigns. For example, consider Tecate—Heineken-Mexico's leading beer brand. In Mexico, Tecate stands for all things male, including soccer, Mexico's favorite sport. But Tecate faced a tough creative challenge during a recent soccer World Cup. It wanted to tap into the fan fever surrounding the tournament but couldn't directly mention either the World Cup or the Mexican national team, both sponsored by competitor Corona. So instead of just running big-budget TV ads filled with the usual clichés, Tecate launched a novel, content-rich "Soccer Gentleman" campaign that went well beyond traditional media:

> Tecate's "Soccer Gentleman" campaign recognized that during the World Cup a real Tecate man must balance the two true loves of his life: women and soccer. So the campaign set out to help men successfully juggle their love lives and watching soccer nonstop by being "perfect gentlemen." The campaign was built around a beautifully penned, 185-page love letter that took 90 minutes to read (which just happens to be the length of a soccer match).
>
> In an opening TV spot aired a minute before a big match, a man touchingly presents the lengthy letter to his beloved and implores her to read it right away. Enchanted by his romantic gesture, she settles in to read his heartfelt words, so enrapt that she fails to notice as he races off to watch the World Cup match with his friends without interruption. During the match, five more TV spots, a campaign website, and 47 Facebook posts follow the reading of the letter in real time, with updates such as "She is now halfway through your 90-minute letter." A final post-game ad shows the man racing home just in time to greet his love as she emerges from her rapture and falls into his arms. Men could then download the entire letter for the next match and customize it by changing the woman's name; 16,000 people did so and lived the experience of reading the actual letter.
>
> In another part of the campaign, a Tecate man refuses his new girlfriend's invitation to come inside after a first date, proclaiming his deep affection for her and his honorable intentions to be a perfect gentleman by defying the "macho culture" and the temptations of a one-night stand. As she swoons, he races off to catch the next game. "Watching World Cup soccer and being loved for it?" concludes Tecate. "Life doesn't get much better than that."

Skillfully integrated across POES channels, the "Soccer Gentleman" content campaign produced striking results. Tecate sales increased 11 percent during the World Cup period. During the four-month campaign, the brand saw a 228 percent increase in YouTube followers, added 1.2 million Facebook fans, and generated a flurry of media coverage and social media buzz. The campaign's ads and videos garnered 17 million YouTube views and accounted for two of YouTube's 10 most-watched ads during the World Cup. "Soccer Gentleman" was named by ad industry publication *Advertising Age* as the year's best integrated marketing communications campaign. "Soccer Gentleman" has "become a cultural phenomenon in Mexico," says a Tecate marketer. "The phrase is part of the popular culture; with memes, videos, and T-shirts. You hear it in restaurants and taxis. During the World Cup, without being able to say anything, we took everything!"

So, we can't just call it "advertising" anymore. Today's shifting and sometimes chaotic marketing communications environment calls for more than just creating and placing ads in well-defined and controlled media spaces. Rather, today's marketing communicators must be marketing content strategists, creators, connectors, and catalysts who manage brand conversations with and among customers and help those conversations catch fire across a fluid mix of channels. That's a tall order, but with today's new thinking, anything is POES-ible!

Sources: See Evelyn Timson, "Understanding Paid, Owned, Earned and Shared Media," Business West, February 7, 2018, www.businesswest.co.uk/blog/understanding-paid-owned-earned-and-shared-media; "How PESO Makes Sense in Influencer Marketing," *PR Week*, June 8, 2015, www.prweek.com/article/1350303/peso-makes-sense-influencer-marketing; Randall Rothenberg, "What Is Advertising Anyway?" *Adweek*, September 16, 2013, p. 15; Laurel Wentz, "Integrated Campaign of the Year: 'Soccer Gentleman' for Tecate," *Advertising Age*, August 3, 2015, http://adage.com/article/print/299755; Gini Dietrich, "Why and How PR Pros Should Adopt the PESO Model," *PR Daily*, January 23, 2018, https://www.prdaily.com/mediarelations/Articles/Why_and_how_PR_pros_should_adopt_the_PESO_model_23870.aspx; and "Soccer Gentlemen," *Facebook Studio*, www.facebook-studio.com/gallery/submission/soccer-gentlemen-4, accessed October 2018.

The Need for *Integrated* Marketing Communications

The shift toward a richer mix of media and content approaches poses a problem for marketers. Consumers today are bombarded by brand messages from a broad range of sources. But all too often, companies fail to integrate their various communication channels. Mass-media ads say one thing, whereas company's website, social media pages and posts, videos, or emails say something altogether different.

One problem is that marketing content often comes from different parts of the company. Advertising messages are prepared by the advertising department or an ad agency. Other company departments or agencies prepare public relations messages, sales promotion events, and web, mobile, or social media content. However, consumers don't distinguish between content sources the way marketers do. In the consumer's mind, brand-related content from different sources—whether it's a Super Bowl ad, in-store display, mobile app, or friend's social media post—all merge into a single message about the brand or company.

Conflicting content from these different sources can result in confused company images, brand positions, and customer relationships.

Thus, the explosion of online, mobile, and social media marketing presents tremendous opportunities but also big challenges. It gives marketers rich new tools for understanding and engaging customers. At the same time, it complicates and fragments overall marketing communications. The challenge is to bring it all together in an organized way. To that end, most companies practice the concept of **integrated marketing communications (IMC)**. Under this concept, as illustrated in >> **Figure 12.1**, the company carefully integrates its many communication channels to deliver a clear, consistent, and compelling message about the organization and its brands.

Integrated marketing communications (IMC)
Carefully integrating and coordinating the company's many communications channels to deliver a clear, consistent, and compelling message about the organization and its products.

Often, different media play unique roles in engaging, informing, and persuading consumers. For example, a recent study showed that more than two-thirds of advertisers and their agencies are planning video ad campaigns that stretch across multiple viewing platforms, such as traditional TV and digital, mobile, and social media. Such *cross-platform* campaigns combine TV's core strength—vast reach—with digital's better targeting, interaction, and engagement. These varied media and roles must be carefully coordinated under the overall integrated marketing communications plan.

One good example of a well-integrated marketing communications effort is automaker Land Rover's "Above and Beyond" marketing campaign, which integrates the clout and reach of traditional media with the power of digital media to create deep customer engagement:[7]

> The 70-year-old Range Rover brand uses plenty of good old traditional media. It runs big-budget television ads—including Super Bowl spots—that drive home its luxury performance and outdoor adventure positioning. It supports those mass-market ads with more targeted broadcast ads on AMC, ESPN, Food Network, and NFL Network and print ads in *Architectural Digest, GQ, Wired, Vogue*, and *The Wall Street Journal.*
>
> But the Range Rover campaign also includes a carefully integrated flow of web and social media content that enriches the customer experience in ways that traditional media can't. For example, the Land Rover Stories section of the brand's website features travelogues in which adventure photographers relate their personal experiences riding Land Rovers through rugged and picturesque landscapes, each story illustrated with stunning visuals. But that's just a start. The brand recently produced a video series capturing the adventures of a couple and their young child during a trip across Europe in a Land Rover Discovery, and it created a 360-degree video by which viewers could sail with the Land Rover team in Bermuda ahead of the 35th America's Cup.
>
> Land Rover shares such video stories and other carefully crafted content with brand fans via social media. The brand boasts 15.9 million Facebook followers, 195,000 YouTube subscribers, 680,000 Twitter followers, and 3.5 million Instagram faithful who engage by the

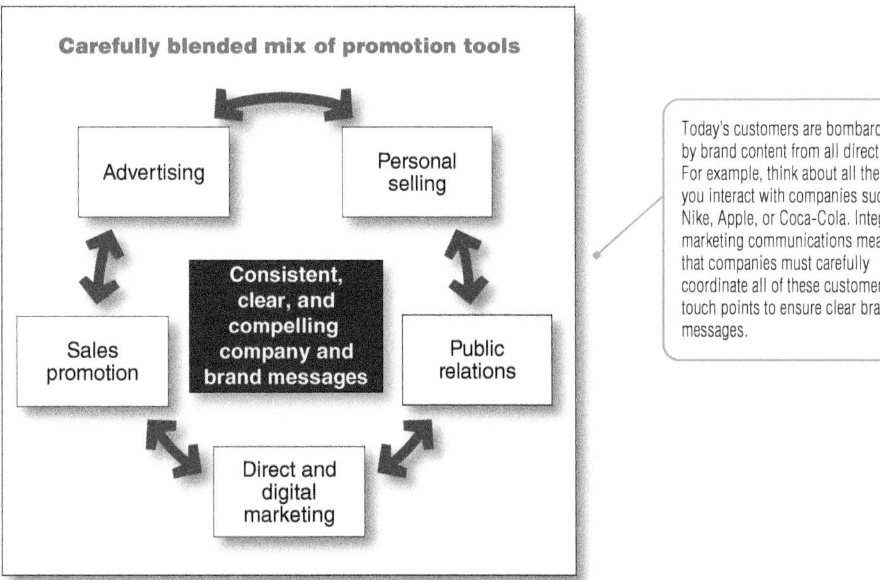

>> **Figure 12.1 Integrated Marketing Communications**

thousands with every post. The social media followings of competitors pale by comparison (for example, competitor Toyota Landcruiser has only 310,000 Facebook followers and 32,000 Instagram fans). No matter what the platform, all content—from television spots to web videos to Instagram posts—is carefully coordinated under Range Rover's "Above and Beyond" luxury adventure mantra. The integrated marketing campaign seems less about selling vehicles and more about reinforcing the Range Rover experience and keeping customers deeply engaged.

In the past, no one person or department was responsible for thinking through the communication roles of the various promotion tools and coordinating the promotion mix. To help implement integrated marketing communications, many companies now appoint a marketing communications director who has overall responsibility for the company's communications efforts. This helps to produce better communications consistency and greater sales impact. It places the responsibility in someone's hands to unify the company's image as it is shaped across ever-expanding cross-platform communications activities.

Author Comment
In this section, we'll look at how marketers blend the various marketing communication tools into a smooth-functioning, integrated, and engaging promotion mix.

Shaping the Overall Promotion Mix

The concept of integrated marketing communications suggests that the company must blend the promotion tools carefully into a coordinated *promotion mix*. But how does it determine what mix of promotion tools to use? Companies within the same industry differ greatly in the design of their promotion mixes. For example, cosmetics maker Mary Kay spends most of its promotion funds on personal selling and direct marketing, whereas competitor CoverGirl spends heavily on consumer advertising. We now look at factors that influence the marketer's choice of promotion tools.

The Nature of Each Promotion Tool

Each promotion tool has unique characteristics and costs. Marketers must understand these characteristics in shaping the promotion mix.

Advertising. Advertising can reach masses of geographically dispersed buyers at a low cost per exposure, and it enables the seller to repeat a message many times. Television advertising can reach huge audiences. For example, more than 103 million Americans watched the most recent Super Bowl, and as many as 26 million avid fans tuned in each week for the latest season of *This Is Us*. What's more, a popular TV ad's reach can be extended through online and social media. >> For example, consider the Super Bowl XLIX commercial for Supercell's popular mobile game "Clash of Clans: Revenge" starring Liam Neeson. In addition to the more than 100-plus million TV viewers during the big game, the ad became the most-viewed Super Bowl commercial on YouTube for the year, capturing a stunning 82 million YouTube views by year's end. Thus, for companies that want to reach a mass audience, TV is the place to be.[8]

>> TV has vast reach: Supercell's "Clash of Clans: Revenge" ad during Super Bowl XLIX drew 100-plus million TV viewers and triggered tens of millions of online views and shares.
IanDagnall Computing/Alamy Stock Photo

Beyond its reach, large-scale advertising says something positive about the seller's size, popularity, and success. Because of advertising's public nature, consumers tend to view advertised products as more legitimate. Advertising is also very expressive; it allows the company to dramatize its products through the artful use of visuals, print, sound, and color. On the one hand, advertising can be used to build up a long-term image for a product (such as Coca-Cola ads). On the other hand, advertising can trigger quick sales (as when Kohl's advertises weekend specials).

Advertising also has some drawbacks. Although it reaches many people quickly, mass-media advertising is impersonal and lacks the direct persuasiveness of company salespeople. For the most part, advertising can carry on only a one-way communication with an audience, and the audience does not feel that it has to pay attention or respond. In addition, advertising can be very costly. Although some advertising forms—such as newspaper, radio, or online advertising—can be done on smaller budgets, other forms, such as network TV advertising, require very large budgets. For example, the 90-second Amazon Echo "Alexa Loses Her Voice" Super Bowl ad cost $14.9 million for media time alone—more than $165,000 per tick of the clock—not counting the costs of producing the ad.

Personal Selling. Personal selling is the most effective tool at certain stages of the buying process, particularly in building up buyers' preferences, convictions, and actions. It involves personal interaction between two or more people, so each person can observe the other's needs and characteristics and make quick adjustments. Personal selling also allows all kinds of customer relationships to spring up, ranging from matter-of-fact selling relationships to personal friendships. An effective salesperson keeps the customer's interests at heart to build a long-term relationship by solving a customer's problems. Finally, with personal selling, the buyer usually feels a greater need to listen and respond, even if the response is a polite "No, thank you."

These unique qualities come at a cost, however. A sales force requires a longer-term commitment than does advertising—advertising can be turned up or down, but the size of a sales force is harder to change. Personal selling is also the company's most expensive promotion tool, costing companies on average $600 or more per sales call, depending on the industry.[9] U.S. firms spend up to three times as much on personal selling as they do on advertising.

Sales Promotion. Sales promotion includes a wide assortment of tools—coupons, contests, discounts, premiums, and others—all of which have many unique qualities. They attract consumer attention, engage consumers, offer strong incentives to purchase, and can be used to dramatize product offers and boost sagging sales. Sales promotions invite and reward quick response. Whereas advertising says, "Buy our product," sales promotion says, "Buy it now." Sales promotion effects can be short lived, however, and often are not as effective as advertising or personal selling in building long-run brand preference and customer relationships.

Public Relations. Public relations is very believable—news stories, features, sponsorships, and events seem more real and believable to readers than ads do. PR can also reach many prospects who avoid salespeople and advertisements—the message gets to buyers as "news and events" rather than as a sales-directed communication. And, as with advertising, public relations can dramatize a company or product. Marketers tend to underuse public relations or use it as an afterthought. Yet a well-thought-out public relations campaign used with other promotion mix elements can be very effective and economical.

Direct and Digital Marketing. The many forms of direct and digital marketing—from traditional direct mail, catalogs, and telephone marketing to newer online, mobile, and social media—all share some distinctive characteristics. Direct marketing is more targeted: It's usually directed to a specific customer or customer community. Direct marketing is immediate and personalized: Messages can be prepared quickly—even in real time—and tailored to appeal to individual consumers or brand groups. Finally, direct marketing is interactive: It allows a dialogue between the marketing team and the consumer, and messages can be altered depending on the consumer's response. Thus, direct and digital marketing are well suited to highly targeted marketing efforts, creating customer engagement, and building one-to-one customer relationships.

Promotion Mix Strategies

Push strategy
A promotion strategy that calls for using the sales force and trade promotion to push the product through channels. The producer promotes the product to channel members who in turn promote it to final consumers.

Marketers can choose from two basic promotion mix strategies: *push* promotion or *pull* promotion. >> **Figure 12.2** contrasts the two strategies. The relative emphasis given to the specific promotion tools differs for push and pull strategies. A **push strategy** involves "pushing" the product through marketing channels to final consumers. The producer directs its marketing activities (primarily personal selling and trade promotion) toward channel members to induce them to carry the product and promote it to final consumers.

Figure 12.2 Push versus Pull Promotion Strategy

For example, John Deere does very little promoting of its lawn mowers, garden tractors, and other residential consumer products to final consumers. Instead, John Deere's sales force works with Lowe's, Home Depot, independent dealers, and other channel members, who in turn push John Deere products to final consumers.

Pull strategy
A promotion strategy that calls for spending a lot on consumer advertising and promotion to induce final consumers to buy the product, creating a demand vacuum that "pulls" the product through the channel.

Using a **pull strategy**, the producer directs its marketing activities (primarily advertising, consumer promotion, and direct and digital media) toward final consumers to induce them to buy the product. For example, P&G promotes its Tide laundry products directly to consumers using TV and print ads, web and social media brand sites, and other channels. If the pull strategy is effective, consumers will then demand the brand from retailers such as Walmart, Target, Kroger, Walgreens, or Amazon, which will in turn demand it from P&G. Thus, under a pull strategy, consumer demand "pulls" the product through the channels.

Some industrial-goods companies use only push strategies; likewise, some direct marketing companies use only pull strategies. However, most large companies use some combination of both. For example, P&G spends more than $4.3 billion each year on U.S. consumer advertising to create brand preference and pull customers into stores that carry its products.[10] At the same time, it uses its sales force and trade promotions to push its brands through the channels so that they will be available on store shelves when consumers come calling.

Companies consider many factors when designing their promotion mix strategies, including the type of product and market. For example, the importance of different promotion tools varies between consumer and business markets. Business-to-consumer companies usually pull more, putting more of their funds into advertising, followed by sales promotion, personal selling, and then public relations. In contrast, business-to-business marketers tend to push more, putting more of their funds into personal selling, followed by sales promotion, advertising, and public relations.

LINKING THE CONCEPTS

Pause here for a few minutes. Flip back through and link the parts of the chapter you've read so far.

- How does the *integrated marketing communications (IMC)* concept relate to the *promotion mix* concept?
- How has the changing communications environment affected the ways companies communicate with you about their products and services? If you were in the market for a new car, where might you hear about various available models? Where would you *search* for information?

Author Comment
You already know a lot about advertising—you are exposed to it every day. But here we'll look behind the scenes at how companies make advertising decisions.

Advertising and Major Advertising Decisions

OBJECTIVE 12-3 Describe and discuss the major decisions involved in developing an advertising program.

Advertising can be traced back to the very beginnings of recorded history. Archaeologists working in countries around the Mediterranean Sea have dug up signs announcing various events and offers. The Romans painted walls to announce gladiator fights, and the Phoenicians painted pictures on large rocks to promote their wares along parade routes. During the golden age in Greece, town criers announced the sale of cattle, crafted items, and even cosmetics. An early "singing commercial" went as follows: "For eyes that are shining, for cheeks like the dawn/For beauty that lasts after girlhood is gone/For prices in reason, the woman who knows/Will buy her cosmetics from Aesclyptos."

Modern advertising, however, is a far cry from these early efforts. U.S. advertisers now run up an estimated annual bill of more than $200 billion on measured advertising media; worldwide ad spending is an estimated $558 billion. P&G, the world's largest advertiser, spent more than $4.3 billion on U.S. advertising and $10.5 billion worldwide.[11]

Although advertising is used mostly by business firms, a wide range of not-for-profit organizations, professionals, and social agencies also use advertising to promote their causes to various target publics. In fact, the 46th-largest U.S. advertising spender is a not-for-profit organization—the U.S. government, which advertises in many ways. For example, the U.S. Army alone spends some $400 million a year to attract new recruits.[12] Advertising is a good way to engage, inform, and persuade, whether the purpose is to sell Coca-Cola worldwide, help smokers kick the habit, or educate people in developing nations on how to lead healthier lives.

Marketing management must make four important decisions when developing an advertising program (see >> **Figure 12.3**): *setting advertising objectives, setting the advertising budget, developing advertising strategy (message decisions and media decisions),* and *evaluating advertising effectiveness.*

Setting Advertising Objectives

Advertising objective
A specific communication task to be accomplished with a specific target audience during a specific period of time.

The first step is to set *advertising objectives*. These objectives should be based on past decisions about the target market, positioning, and the marketing mix, which define the job that advertising must do in the total marketing program. The overall advertising objective is to help engage customers and build customer relationships by communicating customer value. Here, we discuss specific advertising objectives.

An **advertising objective** is a specific communication *task* to be accomplished with a specific *target* audience during a specific period of *time*. Advertising objectives can be classified by their primary purpose—to *inform, persuade*, or *remind*. >> **Table 12.1** lists examples of each of these specific objectives.

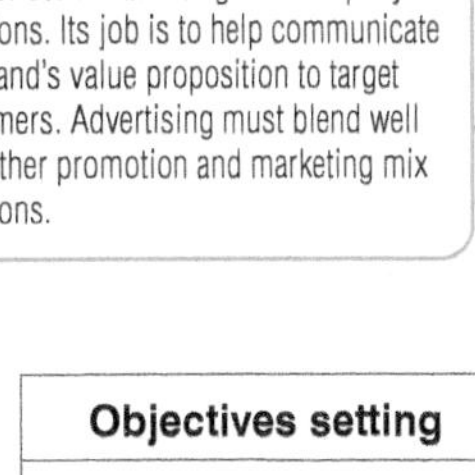

Don't forget—advertising is only part of a broader set of marketing and company decisions. Its job is to help communicate the brand's value proposition to target customers. Advertising must blend well with other promotion and marketing mix decisions.

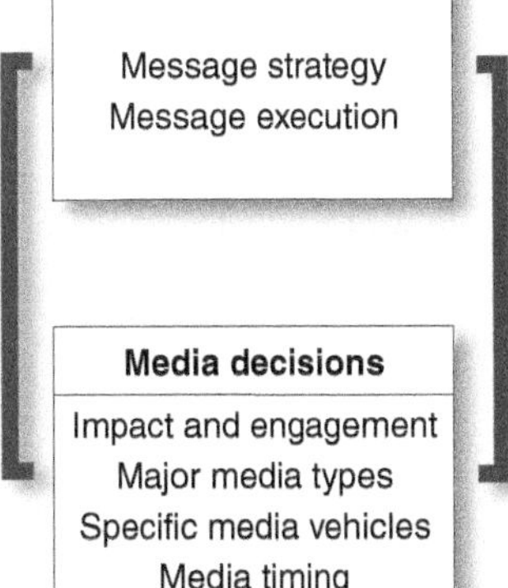

>> **Figure 12.3 Major Advertising Decisions**

Table 12.1 Possible Advertising Objectives

Informative Advertising	
Communicating customer value	Suggesting new uses for a product
Building a brand and company image	Informing the market of a price change
Telling the market about a new product	Describing available services and support
Explaining how a product works	Correcting false impressions
Persuasive Advertising	
Building brand preference	Persuading customers to purchase now
Encouraging switching to a brand	Creating customer engagement
Changing customer perceptions of product value	Building brand community
Reminder Advertising	
Maintaining customer relationships	Reminding consumers where to buy the product
Reminding consumers that the product may be needed in the near future	Keeping the brand in a customer's mind during off-seasons

Informative advertising is used heavily when introducing a new product category. In this case, the objective is to build primary demand. Thus, early producers of all-electric vehicles (EVs) have first had to inform consumers of the economic and performance benefits of the new class of products. *Persuasive advertising* becomes more important as competition increases. Here, the company's objective is to build selective demand. For example, as EVs catch on, GM is now trying to persuade consumers that its Chevy Bolt offers more value for the price than the Tesla Model 3, Toyota Prius Prime, or Nissan Leaf. Such advertising wants to engage customers and create brand preference.

Some persuasive advertising has become *comparative advertising* (or *attack advertising*), in which a company directly or indirectly compares its brand with one or more other brands. You see examples of comparative advertising in almost every product category, ranging from soft drinks and fast food to car rentals, credit cards, and wireless phone services. For example, Pepsi has long fielded comparative ads that take direct aim at rival Coca-Cola:[13]

> It began years ago with the long-running "Pepsi Challenge" campaign, where Pepsi ads showed blind taste tests in shopping malls and other public places in which consumers invariably preferred the taste of Pepsi to that of Coca-Cola. Since then, Pepsi has run regular comparative ads tweaking its larger competitor, ranging from an ad showing Santa Claus (long associated with Coca-Cola advertising) choosing a Pepsi over a Coke to one in which a Pepsi delivery driver snaps a candid photo of a Coke driver covertly draining a cold can of Pepsi. In another ad, a happy Pepsi drinker mocks a Coke buyer by telling him, "You've still got the polar bear" (another Coca-Cola ad symbol). A scraggly polar bear then sadly pets the Coke drinker. Such comparison ads have been popular with Pepsi fans. "There are few things that grab our fans' attention as much as seeing our beloved blue and that red next to each other," says Pepsi's brand marketing and digital director. "It's done well for us in the past, and it's just something that we know works and that they love to see."

Comparative advertising campaigns often create controversy. Many times, that's the point of using them. Whereas established market leaders want to exclude other brands from the consumer's choice set, challengers want to shake things up, inject their brands into the consumer conversation, and put themselves on equal footing with the leader. For example, Microsoft has a long history of successful comparative advertising, both in initiating challenges against market-leading rivals and fending off attacks by challengers (see Marketing at Work 12.2).

Still, advertisers should use comparative advertising with caution. All too often, such ads invite competitor responses, resulting in an advertising war that neither competitor can win. Upset competitors might also take more drastic action, such as filing complaints

MARKETING AT WORK 12.2

Microsoft's Comparative Advertising: "I Couldn't Do That on My Mac"

For as long as there's been advertising, challenger brands have squared off against market leaders with comparative ads. There was Avis versus Hertz ("We're #2 so we try harder"), Pepsi versus Coke (The Pepsi Challenge), Dunkin' versus Starbucks ("Friends don't let friends drink Starbucks"), and countless more. But few companies have made more or better use of challenge campaigns than Microsoft, which has gone toe to toe time and again over the past decade with worthy rivals such as Apple and Google.

It all started well over a decade ago when Apple set out to loosen Microsoft's iron grip on the personal computer market. Microsoft-powered PCs had long dominated the market, with Apple's Macs competing for niche segments. So Apple fired the first direct salvo at Microsoft by launching the now-classic "Get a Mac" comparative campaign.

"Get a Mac" ads featured two characters—"Mac" and "PC"—sparring over the relative advantages of the Apple Mac versus Microsoft Windows-based PCs. The ads portrayed Mac as a young, hip, laid-back guy in a hoodie, whereas PC was a stodgy, befuddled, error-prone, middle-aged nerd in baggie khakis, a brown sport coat, and unfashionable glasses. Not surprisingly, Mac always got the best of outdated and inflexible PC. Over the next few years, Apple unleashed a nonstop barrage of Mac versus PC ads that bashed Windows-based machines—and their owners—as outmoded and dysfunctional.

The smug "Get a Mac" ads hit their mark. Within two years, the Mac's share of the U.S. personal computer market had doubled, and consumer value perceptions of Apple computers had skyrocketed. Even though its computers were viewed as more expensive, at one point Apple scored a whopping 70 on the BrandIndex (which tracks consumer perceptions of brand value on a scale of −100 to 100). Microsoft, meanwhile, floundered below zero.

Microsoft needed to do something dramatic. So two years after the Apple "Get a Mac" onslaught began, Microsoft counterpunched with its own cheeky "I'm a PC" campaign, featuring a dead-on look-alike of Apple's PC character. In the first ad, dressed in PC's dorky outfit, Microsoft's character opened with "I'm a PC. And I've been made into a stereotype." He was followed by a parade of everyday PC users—from environmentalists, political bloggers, mixed martial arts fighters, and mash-up DJs to budget-conscious laptop shoppers and remarkably tech-savvy preschoolers—each proclaiming, "I'm a PC."

The Microsoft "I'm a PC" campaign struck a chord with Windows users, who no longer had to sit back and take Apple's jibes. Microsoft quickly extended the "I'm a PC" campaign with a new pitch, one more in tune with the then-troubled economy. Part advertising and part reality TV, the new comparative campaign—called "Laptop Hunters"—tagged along with real consumers as they shopped for computers. The task? Find a laptop with everything a person could want for under $1,000. Shopper after shopper visited PC and Apple retailers, only to find that getting a decent Mac for that price was impossible, whereas fully loaded Windows-driven laptops came in well under the mark.

If previous "I'm a PC" ads started a shift in perceptions, the "Laptop Hunters" series really moved the needle. The ads spoke volumes in a difficult economy, portraying Apple as too expensive, "too cool," and out of touch with mainstream consumers. The provocative ads bumped Microsoft's BrandIndex score from less than zero to 46, while Apple's score dropped from its previous high of 70 to only 12. Apple struck back with one of its most negative comparative Mac versus PC ads yet. Called "Broken Promises," it featured a skeptical Mac attacking PC about whether the newest Windows version would eliminate problems associated with previous Window's versions. Many analysts thought that the biting tone of the ad suggested that Apple was feeling the heat and getting defensive. Uncharacteristically, Mac seemed to be losing his cool.

The Microsoft–Apple ad skirmish continued for another two years, with neither combatant gaining much new headway. In fact, the constant bickering seemed to wear thin with consumers of both brands. So both companies eventually turned down the comparative advertising heat, instead fielding ads that focused on their own positives rather than the rival's negatives.

A few years later, however, when it introduced its Bing search engine, Microsoft once again turned to comparative advertising, this time as the attacker rather than the attacked. To get Bing—a distant also-ran to search leader Google—into consumers' choice sets, Microsoft launched an aggressive campaign called "Bing It On." The campaign challenged users to make direct side-by-side comparisons of Bing search results to Google search results without knowing which results were from which search engine. According to Microsoft, to the surprise of many people, those making the comparison chose Bing over Google by a two-to-one margin.

Microsoft pressed on against Google with an even more aggressive "Scroogled" campaign, which attacked Google's search engine for "Scroogling" users by exploiting their personal data with everything from invasive ads in Gmail to sharing data with app developers to maximize advertising profits. "For an honest search engine," said the Scroogled ads, "try Bing." Although controversial, the Scroogled campaign got many consumers to look at Bing and other Microsoft products in a new light versus Google. Research showed that following a visit to Scroogled.com, Google's favorability gap over Bing faded from 45 points to just 5. And after watching a Scroogled ad, the chance of a viewer recommending Bing to a friend rose 7 percent.

In a more recent comparative campaign, this one for Microsoft's Surface tablet, Microsoft once again turned its sights on Apple, which dominates the high-end tablet market. But rather than going after Apple's wildly successful iPad, the

Surface campaign directly challenged Apple's MacBook Air laptop, positioning the Surface Pro as a laptop alternative rather than an iPad killer. For example, one online video ad made a direct and convincing side-by-side comparison of the Microsoft Surface Pro with the Apple MacBook Air, concluding that the Surface is "the tablet that can replace your laptop." A Surface Pro print ad proclaimed, "Powerful as a laptop, lighter than Air." And in a Surface Pro TV ad, reminiscent of the original Mac versus PC ads, a MacBook Air owner at first gloats over his Apple. But after watching one after another Surface Pro user, the dejected MacBook owner confesses, "I like your Surface Pro. No, seriously, where can I get one?"

Although the Bing It On, Scroogled, and Surface Pro comparative campaigns have now faded into history, each accomplished its purpose—to bring a new Microsoft product, whether Bing or the Surface Pro or something else, into the competitive set against established rivals. The comparative campaigns have created controversy along with heated debate about the relative merits of, say, Bing versus Google or the Surface Pro versus the MacBook Air. But that's the point. Whereas established market leaders want to maintain the status quo and monopolize the conversation, market challengers want to shake things up and put their products on equal footing with the leader. That's what a good comparative advertising campaign does.

Comparative advertising must be working for Microsoft. New ads and videos for its Microsoft Surface Pro 4 and kick-off content for its new Microsoft Surface Book hybrid laptop/tablet—which features "the power of touch"—took up where previous comparative campaigns left off. They took direct aim at competing Apple models, positioning the Surface line as equipment that "does more. Just like you." One online video showed a happy user working magic on her Microsoft Surface Pro touchscreen, concluding, "I couldn't do that on my Mac."

Sources: Mitchel Broussard, "Microsoft's Surface Book Ads Borrow Music from Apple to Focus on Things a Mac 'Just Can't Do,'" *MacRumors,* March 9, 2016, www.macrumors.com/2016/03/09/microsoft-surface-book-ads/; Alex Wilhelm, "Microsoft's Scroogled Ad Campaign Appears to Be Working," *TechCrunch,* October 15, 2013, http://techcrunch.com/2013/10/15/microsofts-scroogled-ad-campaign-appears-to-be-working/; Tom Spring, "Microsoft Amps Up Apple Attack with Switch to Surface Campaign," *CRN,* December 20, 2014, www.crn.com/news/mobility/300075218/microsoft-amps-up-apple-attack-with-switch-to-surface-campaign.htm; Brian Fagioli, "Microsoft Acting Like Donald Trump by Attacking Apple MacBook in New Surface Book Videos," *betanews,* March 3, 2016, http://betanews.com/2016/03/07/microsoft-donald-trump-attack-apple-macbook-pro-surface-videos/; and https://mspoweruser.com/check-out-the-new-video-ads-for-surface-book-2-and-surface-pro/, accessed October 2018.

>> Microsoft has a long history of successful comparative advertising. Says the happy user in this video ad for the Microsoft Surface Pro, "I couldn't do that on my Mac." The Surface Pro 4 does more.

Microsoft and Melissa Arnot

with the self-regulatory National Advertising Division of the Council of Better Business Bureaus or even filing false-advertising lawsuits. Consider the reactions of competitors to recent comparative ads by Chobani:[14]

> One Chobani Simply 100 yogurt ad shows a woman scrutinizing the label on a container of Yoplait Greek 100 yogurt and promptly discarding it as the ad voiceover says, "Potassium sorbate? Really? That stuff is used to kill bugs." The ad concludes by noting that Chobani Simply 100 Greek yogurt contains zero preservatives. Another ad portrays a woman sitting poolside tossing a container of Dannon Light and Fit into the trash as a voiceover declares, "Sucralose, why? That stuff has chlorine added to it. Chobani Simply 100 is the only 100-calorie yogurt sweetened naturally." Competitors didn't take kindly to the jabs. Yoplait maker General Mills filed a lawsuit against Chobani for misleading advertising. And Dannon's lawyers sent Chobani a cease-and-desist letter asking it to discontinue the campaign. In turn, Chobani sued Dannon asking the courts to confirm that Chobani's advertising is not misleading. In both lawsuits, the courts that the information about competitors was misleading and rule that Chobani could not run the ads.

Reminder advertising is important for mature products; it helps to maintain customer relationships and keep consumers thinking about the product. For example, a recent ad campaign for Silk soymilk tells consumers to "Fall back in love with Soymilk," reminding them of the many reasons that "Silk helps you bloom." And expensive Coca-Cola television ads primarily build and maintain the Coca-Cola brand relationship rather than inform consumers or persuade them to buy it in the short run.

Advertising's goal is to help move consumers through the buying process. Some advertising is designed to move people to immediate action. For example, a direct-response television ad by Weight Watchers urges consumers to go online and sign up right away, and a Walgreens mobile ad with promoting weekend specials encourages immediate store visits. However, many ads focus on building or strengthening long-term customer relationships. For example, a Nike television ad in which well-known athletes work through extreme challenges in their Nike gear never directly asks for a sale. Instead, the goal is to engage customers and somehow change the way they think or feel about the brand.

Setting the Advertising Budget

Advertising budget
The dollars and other resources allocated to a product or a company advertising program.

After determining its advertising objectives, the company next sets its **advertising budget** for each product. Here, we look at four common methods used to set the total budget for advertising: the *affordable method*, the *percentage-of-sales method*, the *competitive-parity method*, and the *objective-and-task method*.

Affordable Method

Affordable method
Setting the promotion budget at the level management thinks the company can afford.

Some companies use the **affordable method**: They set the promotion budget at the level they think the company can afford. Small businesses often use this method, reasoning that the company cannot spend more on advertising than it has. They start with total revenues, deduct operating expenses and capital outlays, and then devote some portion of the remaining funds to advertising.

Unfortunately, this method of setting budgets completely ignores the effects of promotion on sales. It tends to place promotion last among spending priorities, even in situations in which advertising is critical to the firm's success. It leads to an uncertain annual promotion budget, which makes long-range market planning difficult. Although the affordable method can result in overspending on advertising, it more often results in underspending.

Percentage-of-Sales Method

Percentage-of-sales method
Setting the promotion budget at a certain percentage of current or forecasted sales or as a percentage of the unit sales price.

Other companies use the **percentage-of-sales method**, setting their promotion budget at a certain percentage of current or forecasted sales. Or they budget a percentage of the unit sales price. The percentage-of-sales method is simple to use and helps management think about the relationships between promotion spending, selling price, and profit per unit.

Despite these claimed advantages, however, the percentage-of-sales method has little to justify it. It wrongly views sales as the *cause* of promotion rather than as the *result*. Although studies have found a positive correlation between promotional spending and brand strength, this relationship often turns out to be effect and cause, not cause and effect. Stronger brands with higher sales can afford the biggest ad budgets.

Thus, the percentage-of-sales budget is based on the availability of funds rather than on opportunities. It may prevent the increased spending sometimes needed to turn around falling sales. Because the budget varies with year-to-year sales, long-range planning is difficult. Finally, the method does not provide any basis for choosing a *specific* percentage, except what has been done in the past or what competitors are doing.

Competitive-Parity Method

Competitive-parity method
Setting the promotion budget to match competitors' outlays.

Still other companies use the **competitive-parity method**, setting their promotion budgets to match competitors' outlays. They monitor competitors' advertising or get industry promotion spending estimates from publications or trade associations and then set their budgets based on the industry average.

Two arguments support this method. First, competitors' budgets represent the collective wisdom of the industry. Second, spending what competitors spend helps prevent promotion wars. Unfortunately, neither argument is valid. There are no grounds for believing that the competition has a better idea of what a company should be spending on promotion than does the company itself. Companies differ greatly, and each has its own special promotion needs. Finally, there is no evidence that budgets based on competitive parity prevent promotion wars.

Objective-and-Task Method

Objective-and-task method
Developing the promotion budget by (1) defining specific promotion objectives, (2) determining the tasks needed to achieve these objectives, and (3) estimating the costs of performing these tasks. The sum of these costs is the proposed promotion budget.

The most logical budget-setting method is the **objective-and-task method**, whereby the company sets its promotion budget based on what it wants to accomplish with promotion. This budgeting method entails (1) defining specific promotion objectives, (2) determining the tasks needed to achieve these objectives, and (3) estimating the costs of performing these tasks. The sum of these costs is the proposed promotion budget.

The advantage of the objective-and-task method is that it forces management to spell out its assumptions about the relationship between dollars spent and promotion results. But it is also the most difficult method to use. Often, it is hard to figure out which specific tasks will achieve the stated objectives. For example, suppose Samsung wants a 95-percent-awareness level for its latest smartphone model during the six-month introductory period. What specific advertising messages, marketing content, and media schedules should Samsung use to attain this objective? How much would this content and media cost? Samsung management must consider such questions, even though they are hard to answer.

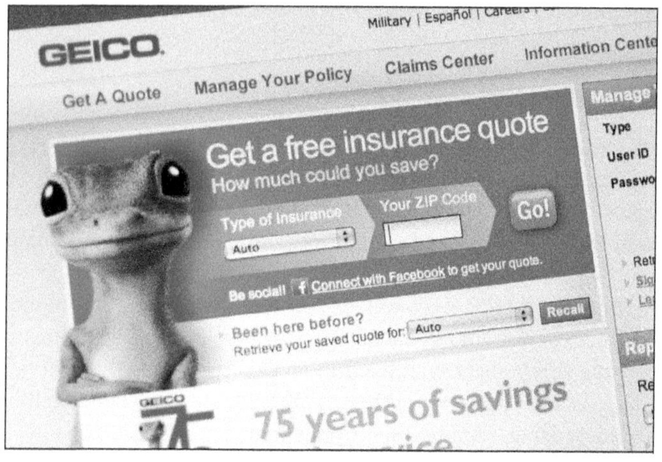

>> **Setting the advertising budget is one of the hardest decisions facing a company. For example, GEICO spends more than $1 billion a year on its award-winning ad campaigns, but is that too little, just right, or too much?**

NetPhotos/Alamy Stock Photo

No matter what method is used, setting the advertising budget is no easy task. How does a company know if it is spending the right amount? Because so many factors affect advertising effectiveness, some controllable and others not, measuring the results of advertising spending remains an inexact science. >> For example, GEICO spends more than $1 billion a year on its award-winning advertising campaigns, but is that too little, just right, or too much? In most cases, marketers must rely on large doses of judgment along with more quantitative analysis when setting advertising budgets.

As a result, advertising is one of the easiest budget items to cut when economic times get tough. Cuts in brand-building advertising appear to do little short-term harm to sales. In the long run, however, slashing ad spending may cause long-term damage to a brand's image and market share. In fact, companies that can maintain or even increase their advertising spending while competitors are decreasing theirs can gain competitive advantage.

Developing Advertising Strategy

Advertising strategy
The strategy by which the company accomplishes its advertising objectives. It consists of two major elements: creating advertising messages and selecting advertising media.

Advertising strategy consists of two major elements: creating advertising *messages* and selecting advertising *media*. In the past, companies often viewed media planning as secondary to the message-creation process. After the creative department created good advertisements, the media department then selected and purchased the best media for carrying those advertisements to the desired target audiences. This often caused friction between creatives and media planners.

Today, however, soaring media costs, more-focused target marketing strategies, and the blizzard of new online, mobile, and social media have promoted the importance of the media-planning function. The decision about which media to use for an ad campaign—television, newspapers, magazines, video, a website, social media, mobile devices, or email—is now sometimes more critical than the creative elements of the campaign. Also, brand content is now often co-created through interactions with and among consumers. As a result, most advertisers orchestrate a close harmony between their messages and the media that deliver them. As discussed earlier in the chapter, the goal is to create and manage brand content across a full range of media, whether they are paid, owned, earned, or shared.

Creating the Advertising Message and Brand Content

No matter how big the budget, advertising can succeed only if it engages consumers and communicates well. Good advertising messages and content are especially important in today's costly and cluttered advertising environment.

Today, the average U.S. household receives more than 200 TV channels and consumers have more than 7,200 magazines from which to choose.[15] Add in the countless radio stations and a continuous barrage of catalogs, direct mail, out-of-home media, email, and online, mobile, and social media exposures, and consumers are being bombarded with ads and brand content at home, work, and all points in between. For example, Americans are exposed to an estimated 5.3 trillion online ad impressions each year and a daily diet of 500 million tweets, 576,000 hours of YouTube videos, 95 million photos shared on Instagram, 5 million article pins on Pinterest, and 4.75 billion pieces of shared content on Facebook.[16]

Breaking Through the Clutter. If all this clutter bothers some consumers, it also causes huge headaches for marketers. Take the situation facing network television advertisers. They pay an average of $350,000 to produce a single 30-second commercial. Then each time they show it, they pay an average of $123,000 for 30 seconds of advertising time during a popular primetime program. They pay even more if it's an especially popular program, such as *Sunday Night Football* ($700,000), *This Is Us* ($394,000), *Empire* ($437,000), or a mega-event such as the Super Bowl (averaging $5 million per 30 seconds!). Then their ads are sandwiched in with a clutter of other commercials, network promotions, and other nonprogram material totaling as much as 20 minutes per primetime hour, with long commercial breaks coming every six minutes on average. Such clutter in television and other ad media has created an increasingly hostile advertising environment.[17]

>> **Advertising clutter: Today's consumers can easily skip, mute, or block TV and digital content they don't want to watch. And, increasingly, they are choosing not to watch ads.**

cgstock/Shutterstock

It used to be that television viewers were pretty much a captive audience for advertisers. But today's viewers have a rich new set of information and entertainment options—the internet, video streaming, social and mobile media, tablets and smartphones, and others. More and more consumers are becoming "cord cutters"—dropping their cable and satellite subscriptions in favor of often ad-free internet-based or wireless streaming. >> Today's consumers can easily skip, mute, or block TV and digital content they don't want to watch. And, increasingly, they are choosing not to watch ads.

Thus, advertisers can no longer force-feed the same old cookie-cutter messages and content to captive consumers through traditional media. Simply interrupting or disrupting consumers no longer works. Unless ads provide content that is engaging, useful, or entertaining, many consumers will simply ignore or skip them.

Madison & Vine
A term that has come to represent the merging of advertising and entertainment in an effort to break through the clutter and create new avenues for reaching customers with more engaging messages.

Merging Advertising and Entertainment. To break through the clutter, many marketers are now a merging of advertising and entertainment, a practice dubbed "**Madison & Vine.**" You've probably heard of Madison Avenue, the New York City street that houses the headquarters of many of the nation's largest advertising agencies. You may also have heard of Hollywood & Vine, the intersection of Hollywood Avenue and Vine Street in Hollywood, California, long the symbolic heart of the U.S. entertainment industry. Now, Madison Avenue and Hollywood & Vine have come together to form a new intersection—-Madison & Vine—that represents the merging of advertising and entertainment to create new avenues for reaching consumers with more engaging messages.

This merging of advertising and entertainment takes one of two forms: advertainment or brand integrations. The aim of *advertainment* is to make ads and brand content themselves so entertaining or so useful that people *want* to watch them. There's no chance that you'd watch ads on purpose, you say? Think again. For example, the Super Bowl has become an annual advertainment showcase. Tens of millions of people tune in to the Super Bowl each year, as much to watch the entertaining ads as to see the game. And ads and related content posted online before and after the big game draw tens of millions of views. These days, it's common to see an entertaining ad on YouTube long before you see it on TV.

Advertisers are also creating content forms that look less like ads and more like short films or shows. A range of brand messaging platforms—from webisodes and blogs to long-form online videos and social media posts—now blur the line between ads and other consumer content. For example, consider Marriott's highly successful "Two Bellmen" video series:[18]

> Marriott's long-form "Two Bellmen" videos follow the action-packed adventures of two Marriott bellmen as they foil the evil plots of "bio bots," robots who represent the dehumanization of personalized service. Shot on location in Marriott cities such as Los Angeles, Dubai, and Seoul, South Korea, the "Two Bellmen" episodes are more entertainment than advertising. However, Marriott is featured prominently throughout, communicating the spirit of the brand rather than traditional, product-focused advertising. Produced by the chain's own Marriott Content Studios, the award-winning videos have captured both critical acclaim and consumer engagement: The videos typically claim 5 to 8 million views on YouTube within a few months of their release. The most recent video drove an impressive 247 million PR impressions, worth some $34 million in advertising value. "Marketing as interruption is over," says Marriott's VP of Creative and Content Marketing. "Our short films are creating raving brand fans and driving commerce for our hotels .... In a world filled with so many screens and marketing messages, [we are] on a mission to stop interrupting consumers and instead use storytelling to reach them where they are already."

Marketers have tested all kinds of novel ways to break through today's clutter and engage consumers. For example, P&G's recent Super Bowl "It's a Tide Ad" ads featured *Stranger Things* actor David Harbour asking viewers to question every ad they saw during the game. If they were seeing clean clothes, it was a Tide ad. A 45-second ad run in the first quarter of the game set things up. It featured various teaser scenarios of car, beer, shaving, and other ads before revealing, "No, it's a Tide ad." How do you know? "Look at those clean clothes." Ads in each subsequent quarter began like typical ads for other products before revealing, "It's a Tide ad." Throughout the game, the clever takeover campaign had many viewers asking during the opening seconds whether other commercials were actual ads or just another Tide ad.[19]

Other brands have also used unexpected twists to earn engagement. For example, JCPenney once posted incoherent tweets, grabbing widespread attention and leading to speculation that the retailer's social media person was either drunk or had been hacked. Instead, says JCPenney, the person was tweeting with mittens on to promote its winter merchandise. P&G's Charmin brand's #tweetfromtheseat Twitter campaign used irreverent humor to create engagement and drive buzz, with questions such as "Charmin asks: What are your thoughts on streaming while streaming?" and "There's no toilet paper left on the roll, do you yell for help, wiggle and air dry, text someone for help?"[20]

Brand integrations (or *branded entertainment*) involve making the brand an inseparable part of some other form of entertainment or content. The most common form of brand integration is product placements—embedding brands as props within other programming. It might be characters drinking from Starbucks cups in episodes of *Will & Grace*, Jimmy Dean sausage in a scene on *Young Sheldon,* or characters in *The Big Bang Theory* working at the Cheesecake Factory. It could be scenes from the latest *Avengers* movie in which Black Widow rides a Harley-Davidson Livewire.

Or the product placement might be scripted into a movie or episodes of TV shows. For example, a storyline in one episode of *Black-ish* was built around a Buick Encore, which characters Dre and Bow purchased for their daughter, Zoey. Another episode was scripted around a super-competitive game of Hasbro's Monopoly, which brings out the worst competitive instincts of each family member. In yet another show, Dre's ad agency discusses an ad campaign for P&G. Then there's the one in which Dre learns to deal with his newly discovered type 2 diabetes—ads between segments feature Tresiba Long-Lasting Insulin and diabetes management drug Victoza, both developed and marketed by pharmaceutical giant Novo Nordisk. Other *Black-ish* episodes feature storylines built around brands ranging State Farm Insurance to Disney.

>> **Branded entertainment: The highly acclaimed *The LEGO Movie* was pretty much a 100-minute product placement for iconic LEGO construction bricks, what one writer calls "product-placement perfection."**

Pictorial Press Ltd/Alamy

Originally created with TV in mind, brand integration spread quickly into other sectors of the entertainment industry. If you look carefully, you'll see product placements in movies, video games, comic books, Broadway musicals, and even pop music. >> For example, the highly acclaimed film *The LEGO Movie* was pretty much a 100-minute product placement for iconic LEGO construction bricks. According to one writer, "The audience happily sits through a cinematic sales pitch...that shows off the immense versatility of the product while placing it in a deeply personal context. The majority of the film is a breathtaking display of what LEGO bricks are capable of as creative tools, but the personal element is what really elevates this film to product-placement perfection." *The LEGO Movie* boosted The LEGO Group's sales by 13 percent the year after it opened.[21]

Native advertising
Advertising or other brand-produced online content that looks in form and function like the other natural content surrounding it on a web or social media platform.

A related form of brand integration is so-called **native advertising** (also called *sponsored content*), advertising or other brand-produced online content that appears to be "native to" the web or social media site in which it is placed. The brand content looks in form and function like the other natural content surrounding it. It might be an article on a website such as *The Huffington Post, BuzzFeed, Mashable,* or even *The New York Times* or *The Wall Street Journal* that is paid for, written by, and placed by an advertiser but uses the same format as articles written by the editorial staff. Or it might be brand-prepared videos, pictures, posts, or pages integrated into social media such as Facebook, YouTube, Instagram, Pinterest, or Twitter that match the form and feel of native content on those media. Examples include Twitter's promoted tweets, Facebook's promoted stories, *BuzzFeed*'s sponsored posts, or Snapchat's "brand story" ads, branded posts that appear in the app's "Stories" feed.

Native advertising is an increasingly popular form of brand content. It lets advertisers create relevant associations between brand and consumer content. It bypasses ad-blockers but seems less intrusive than pop-up ads or banners. One recent study found that viewers pay 53 percent more attention to native advertising that to banner ads. As a result, one optimistic forecast estimates that advertisers over the next four years will be moving 25 percent of their marketing budgets from traditional advertising to native and content marketing.[22]

Thus, Madison & Vine is now the meeting place for advertising, brand content, and entertainment. The goal is to make brand messages a part of the broader flow of consumer content and conversation rather than an intrusion or interruption of it. As advertising agency JWT puts it, "We believe advertising needs to stop *interrupting* what people are interested in and *be* what people are interested in." However, advertisers must be careful that the new intersection itself doesn't become too congested. With all the new brand content formats and integration, Madison & Vine threatens to create even more of the very clutter that it was designed to break through. At that point, consumers might decide to take yet a different route.

Message and Content Strategy. The first step in creating effective advertising content is to plan a message strategy—the general message that will be communicated to consumers. The purpose of advertising and other content is to get consumers to engage with or react to the product or company in a certain way. People will engage and react only if they believe they will benefit from doing so. Thus, developing an effective message strategy begins with identifying customer *benefits* that can be used as content appeals. Ideally, the message strategy will follow directly from the company's broader positioning and customer value-creation strategies.

Creative concept
The compelling "big idea" that will bring an advertising message strategy to life in a distinctive and memorable way.

Message strategy statements tend to be plain, straightforward outlines of benefits and positioning points that the advertiser wants to stress. The advertiser must next develop a compelling **creative concept**—or *big idea*—that will bring the message strategy to life in a distinctive and memorable way. At this stage, simple message ideas become great ad

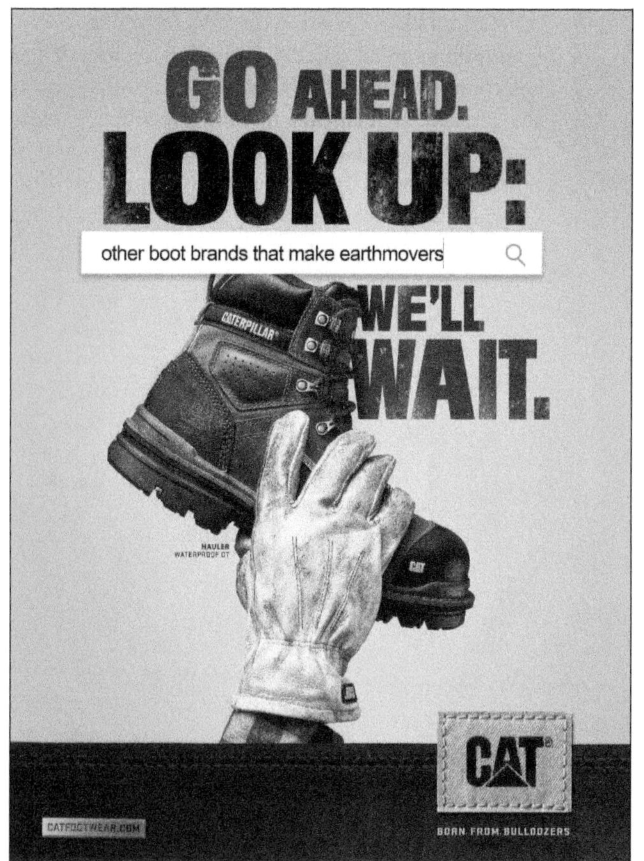
GO AHEAD.
LOOK UP:
other boot brands that make earthmovers
WE'LL
WAIT.
CAT
CATFOOTWEAR.COM
BORN FROM BULLDOZERS

» Distinctive advertising appeals: Wolverine sets its Cat Earthmovers footwear apart through its association with the well-respected Caterpillar brand. Cat Earthmovers boots are "born from bulldozers."

Courtesy Young & Laramore and Cat Footwear

campaigns. Usually, a copywriter and an art director will team up to generate many creative concepts, hoping that one of these concepts will turn out to be the big idea. The creative concept may emerge as a visualization, a phrase, or a combination of the two.

The creative concept will guide the choice of specific appeals to be used in an advertising campaign. *Advertising appeals* should have three characteristics. First, they should be *meaningful*, pointing out benefits that make the product more desirable or interesting to consumers. Second, appeals must be *believable*. Consumers must believe that the product or service will deliver the promised benefits.

However, the most meaningful and believable benefits may not be the best ones to feature. Appeals should also be *distinctive*. They should tell how the product is better than competing brands. For example, the most meaningful benefit of owning a wristwatch is that it keeps accurate time, yet few watch ads feature this benefit. For years, Timex has been the affordable watch that "takes a licking and keeps on ticking." In contrast, Rolex ads talk about the brand's "obsession with perfection" and the fact that "Rolex has been the preeminent symbol of performance and prestige for more than a century."

Similarly, the most meaningful benefits of work boots are ruggedness and durability. » But Wolverine sets its Cat Earthmovers footwear apart through its association with the well-respected Caterpillar construction equipment brand. Cat Earthmovers boots are "born from bulldozers."[23] "Cat Footwear comes from a world of industry and action," says the brand. "A world where you can build anything. Where effort is everything. Where hard work pays off. Where others see obstacles, we see opportunity. We are Earthmovers."

Message Execution. The advertiser now must turn the big idea into an actual ad execution that will capture the target market's attention and interest. The creative team must find the best approach, style, tone, words, and format for executing the message. The message can be presented in various **execution styles**, such as the following:

Execution style
The approach, style, tone, words, and format used for executing an advertising message.

- *Slice of life.* This style shows one or more "typical" people using the product in a normal setting. For example, IKEA content—from microsites and Instagram posts to print ads and television commercials—features people living in rooms furnished with IKEA furniture and household goods.
- *Lifestyle.* This style shows how a product fits in with a particular lifestyle. For example, an ad for Athleta activewear shows a woman in a complex yoga pose and states: "If your body is your temple, build it one piece at a time."
- *Fantasy.* This style creates a fantasy around the product or its use. For example, an ad for Nestle Pure Life water shows a young girl diving into a water-filled fantasy land where children blow bubbles high on a gondola lift and paddle a boat through the clouds, suggesting "a future full of possibilities starts by drinking pure bottled water now."
- *Mood or image.* This style builds a mood or image around the product or service, such as beauty, love, intrigue, serenity, or pride. Few claims are made about the product or service except through suggestion. For example, a warm, soul-stirring three-minute "Little Moments" ad for HP's phone-sized Sprocket printer captures through printed images the evolving relationship between a father and his moody 12-year-old daughter as she starts sixth grade. "Hold onto the ones you love," the ad urges. "Reinvent memories."
- *Musical.* This style shows characters singing about the product. For example, as part of its "Insure Carefully, Dream Fearlessly" campaign, American Family Insurance sends Grammy Award winner Jennifer Hudson to the streets of Atlanta

to help make a dream come true by singing a surprise duet with an aspiring street performer. "With the right support, any dream is possible," the ad concludes. In another musical ad, Hudson surprises the Morehouse College Glee Club.

- *Personality symbol.* This style creates a character that represents the product. The character might be animated (Mr. Clean, the GEICO Gecko, or the Travelocity Gnome) or real (perky Progressive Insurance spokeswoman Flo, KFC's Colonel Sanders, or Ronald McDonald).
- *Technical expertise.* This style shows the company's expertise in making the product. Thus, Jim Koch of the Boston Beer Company tells about his many years of experience in brewing Samuel Adams beer.
- *Scientific evidence.* This style presents survey or scientific evidence that the brand is better or better liked than one or more other brands. For years, Crest toothpaste has used scientific evidence to convince buyers that Crest is better than other brands at fighting cavities.
- *Testimonial evidence or endorsement.* This style features a highly believable or likable source endorsing the product. It could be ordinary people saying how much they like a given product. For example, Whole Foods features a variety of real customers in its Values Matter marketing campaign. Or it might be a celebrity presenting the product, such as Taylor Swift for Diet Coke or NBA star Stephen Curry for Under Armour.

The advertiser also must choose a *tone* for the ad. For example, P&G always uses a positive tone: Its ads say something very positive about its products. Other advertisers now use edgy humor to break through the commercial clutter. Doritos and Burger King commercials are famous for this.

The advertiser must use memorable and attention-getting *words* in the ad. For example, rather than just saying that its prescription sunglass lenses protect your eyes and look good at the same time, a LensCrafters ad announces, "Sunblock Never Looked So Good." Rather than claiming that "a BMW is a well-engineered automobile," BMW uses more creative and higher-impact phrasing: "The ultimate driving machine." And instead of stating plainly that Hanes socks last longer than less expensive ones, Hanes suggests, "Buy cheap socks and you'll pay through the toes."

>> Novel formats can make an advertisement stand out. This Rocket Mortgage by Quicken Loans ad compels readers to flip the ad, where they get the brand's "Go Waitless" message.

Quicken Loans

Finally, *format* elements make a difference in an ad's impact as well as in its cost. A small change in an ad's design can make a big difference in its effect. In a print or display ad, the *illustration* is the first thing the reader notices—it must be strong enough to draw attention. Next, the *headline* must effectively entice the right people to read the copy. Finally, the *copy*—the main block of text in the ad—must be simple but strong and convincing. Moreover, these three elements must effectively work *together* to engage customers and persuasively present customer value. However, novel formats can help an ad stand out from the clutter. >> For example, in an ad for Rocket Mortgage by Quicken Loans, the headline and subhead are upside down, suggesting that the person in the ad is floating weightlessly above the ground. Curious readers are compelled to flip the ad and the headline becomes clear: "Go Waitless—Don't get held down by an outdated mortgage process. Go completely online for a fast, convenient approval."

Consumer-Generated Content. Taking advantage of today's digital and social media technologies, many companies are now tapping consumers for marketing content, message ideas, or even actual ads and videos. Sometimes the results are outstanding; sometimes they are forgettable. If done well, however, user-generated content can incorporate the voice of the customer into brand messages and generate greater customer engagement.

Perhaps the best-known consumer-generated content effort is the former "Crash the Super Bowl Challenge" held annually by

PepsiCo's Doritos brand. For more than a decade, Doritos invited consumers to create their own 30-second video ads, with winners receiving cash awards and having their ads run during the Super Bowl. Based on the success of the "Crash the Super Bowl" contest, Doritos now runs new campaigns that create fun fan-made ads and other content throughout the year.[24]

Consumer-generated content can make customers an everyday part of the brand. For example, trendy home furnishings maker West Elm runs a campaign called #MyWestElm. The campaign collects user-generated photos of West Elm products shared online and uses them in promotional posts on its web, Facebook, Instagram, and Pinterest sites along with links to similar products on the company's online store. It even includes user-generated photos on its product pages to show buyers how fellow customers use the products in the real world. The click-through rate for these user-generated photos is 2.6 times higher than for traditional, professionally produced photos.[25]

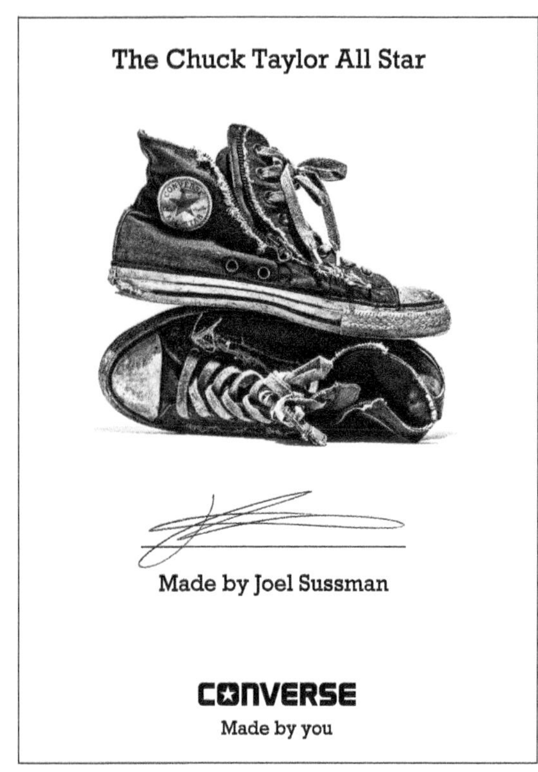

The Chuck Taylor All Star
Made by Joel Sussman
CONVERSE
Made by you

>> Today's Converse brand is built less on big-budget marketing campaigns and more on consumer-generated content by which customers express themselves and share their brand experiences. The Converse brand is "Made By You."

Courtesy of Converse Inc., Anomaly, and Joel Sussman

>> As another example, rather than relying on high-powered advertising, shoe brand Converse steps aside and lets customers themselves co-create the brand and co-author the brand story:[26]

> Converse recognizes that today's young consumers don't want a brand that's neatly defined and handed to them; they want to experience a brand, help shape it, and share it with other like-minded people. That was the idea behind its 2015 "Made By You" campaign, which celebrated individuality and self-expression by inviting people to share photos of their uniquely customized Converse All Stars along with stories of their Converse experiences.
>
> "Made By You" was inspired by the reality that consumers by the thousands were already sharing pictures, videos, and other content of themselves in their Chucks via social media. The campaign simply helped inspire and organize the consumer-generated content process. It assembled photos of customized Converse sneakers submitted by fans from around the world and made them available in a curated online collection. The collection included photos from notable celebrities such as Patti Smith and Andy Warhol. But the bulk of the creative images come from ordinary but impassioned Converse consumers. Converse sums up "Made By You" this way: We make them, but "as soon as you put them on and start doing your thing, their true life begins. You define them. You determine their journey. They become a one-of-a-kind celebration of your individuality and self-expression. They become a part of you. They're Made by you."

Not all consumer-generated content efforts, however, are successful. As many big companies have learned, ads and other content made by amateurs can be... well, pretty amateurish. If done well, however, consumer-generated content efforts can produce new creative ideas and fresh perspectives on the brand from consumers who actually experience it. Such campaigns can boost consumer engagement and get customers talking about a brand and its value to them.

Selecting Advertising Media

Advertising media
The vehicles through which advertising messages are delivered to their intended audiences.

The major steps in **advertising media** selection are (1) determining *reach, frequency, impact,* and *engagement*; (2) choosing among major *media types*; (3) selecting specific *media vehicles*; and (4) choosing *media timing*.

Determining Reach, Frequency, Impact, and Engagement. To select media, the advertiser must determine the reach and frequency needed to achieve the advertising objectives. *Reach* is a measure of the *percentage* of people in the target market who are exposed to an ad campaign during a given period of time. For example, the advertiser might try to reach 70 percent of the target market during the first three months of a campaign. *Frequency* is a measure of how many *times* the average person in the target market is exposed to a message. For example, the advertiser might want an average exposure frequency of three.

But advertisers want to do more than just reach a given number of consumers a specific number of times. The advertiser also must determine the desired *media impact*—the *qualitative value* of message exposure through a given medium. For example, the same message in one magazine (say, *Leisure+Travel*) may be more believable than in another

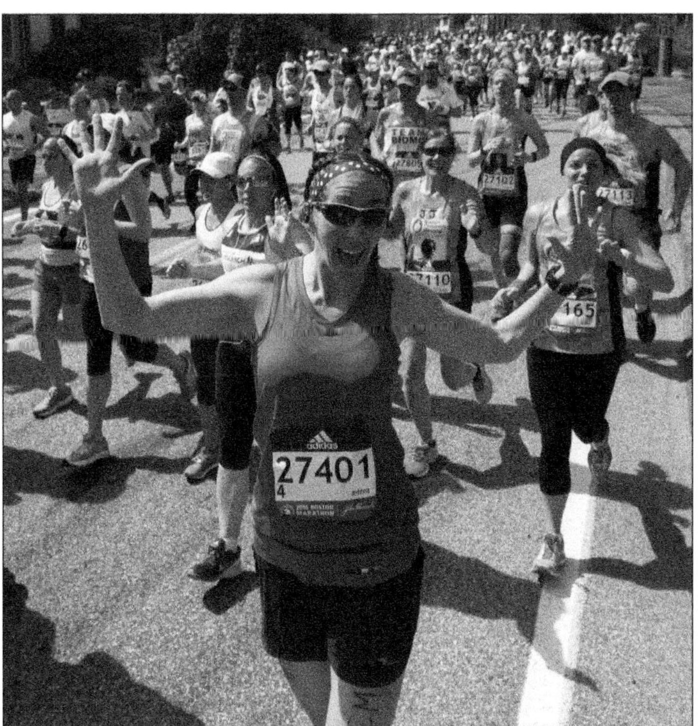

>> **Engaging the right consumers with the right media: The "Here to Create Legend" Boston Marathon campaign created ultrapersonalized highlight videos for each of 30,000 marathon participants, identified by RFID chips on their adidas bibs, and made available online within hours.**

Marcio Jose Bastos Silva/Shutterstock

(say, the *National Enquirer*). For products that need to be demonstrated, television ads or online videos may have more impact than radio messages because they use sight, motion, *and* sound. Products for which consumers provide input on design or brand experiences might be better promoted at a website or social media page than in a direct mailing.

More generally, an advertiser wants to choose media that will *engage* consumers rather than simply reach them. Using any medium, the relevance of ad content for its audience is often much more important than how many people it reaches. >> For example, when adidas wanted to connect personally with avid runners and influencers, it launched a "Here to Create Legend" Boston Marathon campaign that created personalized highlight videos for each of 30,000 marathon participants. Using data generated by RFID chips on bibs worn by runners and video footage captured by seven cameras along the 26.2-mile course, adidas blended personal highlights with general race day scenes and inspriational music, creating 30,000 unique videos for 30,000 runners. Participants could retrieve their videos at an adidas "Here to Create Legend" website within hours of the race and share them via Facebook, Twitter, Instagram, and other social media. Although the campaign didn't deliver the big audience numbers of a TV ad campaign, such ultrapersonalization and engagement could be achieved only with digital media.[27]

Although Nielsen is beginning to measure *media engagement* levels for some television, radio, and social media, such measures are still hard to find in most cases. Current media measures are things such as ratings, readership, listenership, and click-through rates. However, engagement happens inside the head of the consumer. It's hard enough to measure how many people are exposed to a given television ad, video, or social media post, let alone measure the depth of engagement with that content. Still, marketers need to know how customers connect with an ad and brand idea as a part of the broader brand relationship.

Engaged consumers are more likely to act upon brand messages and even share them with others. Thus, rather than simply tracking consumer impressions for a media placement—how many people see, hear, or read an ad—Coca-Cola now also tracks the consumer expressions that result, such as a comment, a "Like," uploading a photo or video, or sharing brand content on social networks. Today's empowered consumers often generate more messages about a brand than a company can.

Choosing among Major Media Types. As summarized in >> **Table 12.2**, the major media types are television; digital, mobile, and social media; newspapers; direct mail; magazines; radio; and outdoor. Each medium has its advantages and its limitations. Media planners want to choose a mix of media that will effectively and efficiently present the advertising message to target customers. Thus, they must consider each medium's impact, message effectiveness, and cost.

As discussed earlier in the chapter, traditional mass media still make up a majority of today's media mixes. However, as mass-media costs rise and audiences shrink, companies have now added digital, mobile, and social media that cost less, target more effectively, and engage consumers more fully. Today's marketers are assembling a full mix of *paid, owned, earned, and shared media* that create and deliver engaging brand content to target consumers.

In addition to the explosion of online, mobile, and social media, cable and satellite television systems are thriving. Such systems allow narrow programming formats, such as all sports, all news, nutrition, arts, home improvement and gardening, cooking, travel, history, finance, and others that target select groups. Comcast and other cable operators are even testing systems that will let them target specific types of ads to TVs in specific neighborhoods or individually to specific types of customers. For example, ads for a

Table 12.2 Profiles of Major Media Types

Medium	Advantages	Limitations
Television	Good mass-marketing coverage; low cost per exposure; combines sight, sound, and motion; appealing to the senses	High absolute costs; high clutter; fleeting exposure; less audience selectivity
Digital, mobile, and social media	High selectivity; low cost; immediacy; engagement capabilities	Potentially low impact; high audience control of content and exposure
Newspapers	Flexibility; timeliness; good local market coverage; broad acceptability; high believability	Short life; poor reproduction quality; small pass-along audience
Direct mail	High audience selectivity; flexibility; no ad competition within the same medium; allows personalization	Relatively high cost per exposure; "junk mail" image
Magazines	High geographic and demographic selectivity; credibility and prestige; high-quality reproduction; long life and good pass-along readership	Long ad purchase lead time; high cost; no guarantee of position
Radio	Good local acceptance; high geographic and demographic selectivity; low cost	Audio only; fleeting exposure; low attention ("the half-heard" medium); fragmented audiences
Outdoor	Flexibility; high repeat exposure; low cost; good positional selectivity	Little audience selectivity; creative limitations

Spanish-language channel would run in only Hispanic neighborhoods, or only pet owners would see ads from pet food companies.

Finally, in their efforts to find less costly and more highly targeted ways to reach consumers, advertisers have discovered a dazzling collection of *alternative media*. These days, no matter where you go or what you do, you will probably run into some new form of advertising:

> Tiny billboards attached to shopping carts urge you to buy Pampers, while ads roll by on the store's checkout conveyor touting your local Chevy dealer. Step outside, and there goes a city trash truck sporting an ad for Glad trash bags or a school bus displaying a Little Caesar's pizza ad. A nearby fire hydrant is emblazoned with advertising for KFC's "fiery" chicken wings. You escape to the ballpark, only to find billboard-size video screens running Budweiser ads while a blimp with an electronic message board circles lazily overhead. >> On a rainy day, as thunder booms and the rain begins, groundskeepers cover the infield with a colorful Skittles-branded "Taste the Rainbow" tarp.
>
> These days, you're likely to find ads—well—anywhere. Taxicabs sport electronic messaging signs tied to GPS location sensors that can pitch local stores and restaurants wherever they roam. Ad space is being sold on parking-lot tickets, airline boarding passes, subway turnstiles, highway toll booth gates, ATMs, municipal garbage cans, and even police cars, doctors' examining tables, and church bulletins. One company even sells space on toilet paper furnished free to restaurants, stadiums, and malls—the paper carries advertiser logos, coupons, and codes you can scan with your smartphone to download digital coupons or link to advertisers' social media pages. Now that's a captive audience.

>> Marketers have discovered as dazzling array of alternative media, like this colorful Skittles-branded "Taste the Rainbow" infield groundcover tarp.

AP Photo/Carolyn Kaster

Such alternative media seem a bit far-fetched, and they sometimes irritate consumers who resent it all as "ad nauseam." But for many marketers, these media can save money and provide a way to hit selected consumers where they live, shop, work, and play.

Another important trend affecting media selection is the rapid growth in the number of *media multitaskers*, people who absorb more than one medium at a time. For example, it's not uncommon to find someone watching TV with a smartphone in hand, tweeting, Snapchatting with friends, and chasing down product information on Google. One recent survey found that 70 percent of consumers regularly use another digital device while watching TV. Another study found that millennials and Gen X consumers engage in an average of three additional media activities while watching television, including online browsing, text messaging, and reading email. Although some of this multitasking is related to TV viewing—such as looking up related product and program information—most multitasking involves tasks unrelated to the shows or ads being watched. Marketers need to take such media interactions into account when selecting the types of media they will use.[28]

Selecting Specific Media Vehicles. Media planners must also choose the best media vehicles—specific media within each general media type. For example, television vehicles include *Modern Family* and *ABC World News Tonight.* Magazine vehicles include *People, Better Homes and Gardens*, and *ESPN The Magazine.* Online and mobile vehicles include Twitter, Facebook, Instagram, and YouTube.

Media planners must compute the cost per 1,000 persons reached by a vehicle. For example, if a full-page, four-color advertisement in the U.S. national edition of *Forbes* costs $163,413 and *Forbes*'s readership is 900,000 people, the cost of reaching each group of 1,000 persons is about $181. The same advertisement in *Bloomberg Businessweek*'s global edition may cost only $114,640 but reach only 600,000 people—at a cost per 1,000 of about $191.[29] The media planner ranks each magazine by cost per 1,000 and often favors those magazines with the lower cost per 1,000 for reaching target consumers. In the previous case, if a marketer is targeting global business managers, *Bloomberg Businessweek* might be the more cost-effective buy, even at a higher cost per thousand.

Media planners must also consider the costs of producing ads for different media. Whereas newspaper ads may cost very little to produce, flashy television ads can be very costly. Many online and social media ads cost little to produce, but costs can climb when producing made-for-the-web video and ad series.

In selecting specific media vehicles, media planners must balance media costs against several media effectiveness factors. First, the planner should evaluate the media vehicle's audience quality. For a Huggies disposable diapers ad, for example, *Parents* magazine would have a high exposure value; men's lifestyle magazine *Maxim* would have a low exposure value. Second, the media planner should consider audience engagement. Readers of *Vogue*, for example, typically pay more attention to ads than do *People* readers. Third, the planner should assess the vehicle's editorial quality. *People* and *The Wall Street Journal* are more believable and prestigious than *Star* or the *National Enquirer*.

Deciding on Media Timing. An advertiser must also decide how to schedule the advertising over time. Suppose sales of a product peak in December and drop in March (for winter outdoor gear, for instance). The firm can vary its advertising to follow the seasonal pattern, oppose the seasonal pattern, or be the same all year. Most firms do some seasonal advertising. For example, weight-loss product and service marketers tend to heavy up after the first of the year, targeting consumers who let their appetites get the better of them over the holiday season. Weight Watchers, for instance, spends more than a quarter of its annual advertising budget in January. >> By contrast, Peeps, the perennial Easter favorite marshmallow chicks and bunnies candies, launched an "Every Day Is a Holiday" campaign to broaden demand beyond Easter, which accounts for an estimated 70 percent of the brand's business. The campaign now promotes new versions of Peeps at Valentine's Day, Halloween, Thanksgiving, Christmas, and other holiday seasons. Some marketers do *only* seasonal advertising: For instance, P&G advertises its Vicks NyQuil only during the cold and flu season.[30]

>> Peeps "Every Day Is a Holiday" campaign promotes new versions of the favorite marshmallow candies all year, not just at Easter. Shown here are gingerbread men for the winter holiday season.
Keith Homan/Alamy Stock Photo

Today's online and social media let advertisers create ads that respond to events in real time. In a classic example, Oreos reacted in a timely way to a power outage during Super Bowl XLVII with an outage-related "Power out? No problem. You can still dunk in the dark" tweet ad. The fast-reaction ad was re-tweeted and shared tens of thousands of times in only 15 minutes, attracting more attention for Oreo than the brand's extravagant first-quarter advertisement. On a more local scale, Red Roof Inn regularly links airline flight data from flight tracking service FlightAware with Google's online search ads to beam real-time ads to stranded travelers facing flight cancellations. For example, when Chicago's O'Hare Airport recently experienced a major bout of flight cancellations, Red Roof managed to secure the top ad spot in three-quarters of the Google search results for "hotels near O'Hare," resulting in a 60 percent jump in bookings from those searches.[31]

Evaluating Advertising Effectiveness and the Return on Advertising Investment

Return on advertising investment
The net return on advertising investment divided by the costs of the advertising investment.

Measuring advertising effectiveness and the **return on advertising investment** has become a hot issue for most companies. Top management at many companies is asking marketing managers, "How do we know that we're spending the right amount on advertising?" and "What return are we getting on our advertising investment?"

Advertisers should regularly evaluate two types of advertising results: the communication effects and the sales and profit effects. Measuring the *communication effects* of an ad or ad campaign tells whether the ads and media are communicating the ad message well. Individual ads can be tested before or after they are run. Before an ad is placed, the advertiser can show it to consumers, ask how they like it, and measure message recall or attitude changes resulting from it. After an ad is run, the advertiser can measure how the ad affected consumer recall or product awareness, engagement, knowledge, and preference. Pre- and post-evaluations of communication effects can be made for entire advertising campaigns as well.

Advertisers have gotten pretty good at measuring the communication effects of their ads and ad campaigns. However, *sales and profit* effects of advertising and other content are often much harder to measure. For example, what sales and profits are produced by an ad campaign that increases brand awareness by 20 percent and brand preference by 10 percent? Sales and profits are affected by many factors other than advertising—such as product features, price, and availability.

One way to measure the sales and profit effects of advertising is to compare past sales and profits with past advertising expenditures. Another way is through experiments. For example, to test the effects of different advertising spending levels, Coca-Cola could vary the amount it spends on advertising in different market areas and measure the differences in the resulting sales and profit levels. More complex experiments could be designed to include other variables, such as differences in the ads or media used.

However, because so many factors affect advertising effectiveness, some controllable and others not, pretesting ads and measuring the results of advertising spending remains an inexact science. Managers often must rely on large doses of judgment along with quantitative analysis when assessing content and advertising performance. That's especially true in this content-hungry digital age, where large quantities of ads and other content are produced and run on a virtual real-time basis. Thus, whereas companies tend to carefully pretest traditional big-budget media ads before running them, digital marketing content often goes untested.

Other Advertising Considerations

In developing advertising strategies and programs, the company must address two additional questions. First, how will the company organize its advertising and content function—who will perform which advertising tasks? Second, how will the company adapt its advertising strategies and programs to the complexities of international markets?

Organizing for Advertising

Different companies organize in different ways to handle advertising. In small companies, advertising might be handled by someone in the sales department. Large companies have advertising departments whose job it is to set the advertising budget, work with ad agencies, and handle other advertising not done by an agency. However, most large companies use outside advertising agencies because they offer several advantages.

Advertising agency
A marketing services firm that assists companies in planning, preparing, implementing, and evaluating all or portions of their advertising programs.

How does an **advertising agency** work? Advertising agencies originated in the mid- to late 1800s from salespeople and brokers who worked for the media and received a commission for selling advertising space to companies. As time passed, the salespeople began to help customers prepare their ads. Eventually, they formed agencies and grew closer to the advertisers than to the media.

Today's agencies employ specialists who can often perform advertising and brand content tasks better than the company's own staff can. Agencies also bring an outside point of view to solving the company's problems along with lots of experience from working with different clients and situations. So, today, even companies with strong advertising departments of their own use advertising agencies.

Some ad agencies are huge; the largest U.S. agency group, Y&R, has annual gross U.S. revenues of $3.6 billion. In recent years, many agencies have grown by gobbling up other agencies, thus creating huge agency holding companies. The largest of these megagroups, WPP, includes several large advertising, PR, digital, and promotion agencies with combined worldwide revenues of more than $19 billion.[32]

Most large advertising agencies have the staff and resources to handle all phases of an advertising campaign for their clients, from creating a marketing plan to developing ad and content campaigns and preparing, placing, and evaluating ads and content. Large brands commonly employ several agencies that handle everything from mass-media advertising campaigns to shopper marketing to social media content.

International Advertising Decisions

International advertisers face many complexities not encountered by domestic advertisers. The most basic issue concerns the degree to which global advertising should be adapted to the unique characteristics of various country markets.

Some advertisers have attempted to support their global brands with highly standardized worldwide advertising, with campaigns that work as well in Bangkok as they do in Baltimore. For example, Coca-Cola follows a "one brand" strategy under which it unifies its creative elements and brand presentation under a global "Taste the Feeling" theme. Oreo's latest "Open Up with Oreo" runs in 50 global markets with a simple universal message—"Open your heart to people who are different and you will discover similarities." >> And five years ago, Chevrolet swapped out its previous, American-focused "Chevy Runs Deep" positioning and advertising theme with a more global "Find New Roads" theme. The new theme "works in all markets," says a GM marketing executive. "The theme has meaning in mature markets like the U.S. as well as emerging markets like Russia and India, where the potential for continued growth is the greatest." The time was right for a more globally consistent Chevy brand message. Chevrolet sells cars in more than 140 countries, and nearly two-thirds of its sales are now outside the United States, compared with only about one-third a decade ago.[33]

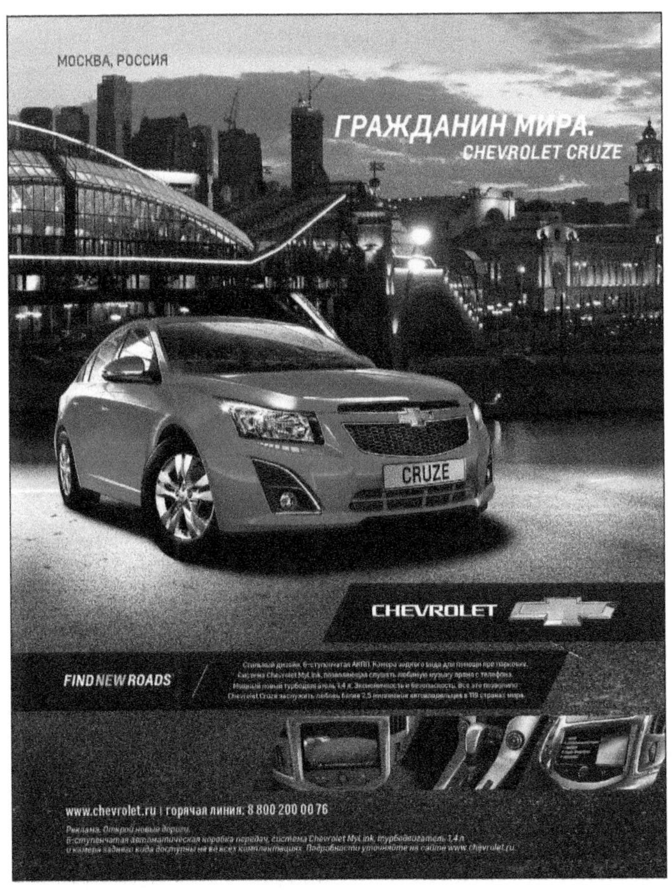

>> International advertising: Chevrolet unifies its global advertising under a "Find New Roads" theme that has meaning in all markets, here Russia.
General Motors

In recent years, the increased popularity of online marketing and social media sharing has boosted the need for advertising standardization for global brands. Connected consumers can now zip easily across borders via the internet and social media, making it difficult for advertisers to roll out adapted campaigns in a controlled, orderly fashion. As a result, at the very least, most global consumer brands coordinate their digital sites internationally. For example, Coca-Cola web and social media sites around the world, from Australia and Argentina to France, Romania, and Russia, are surprisingly uniform. All feature splashes of familiar Coke red, iconic Coke bottle shapes, and Coca-Cola's music and "Taste the Feeling" themes.

Standardization produces many benefits—lower advertising costs, greater global advertising coordination, and a more consistent worldwide image. But it also has drawbacks. Most important, it ignores the fact that country markets differ greatly in their cultures, demographics, and economic conditions. Thus, most international advertisers "think globally but act locally." They develop global advertising *strategies* that make their worldwide efforts more efficient and consistent. Then they adapt their advertising *programs* to make them more responsive to consumer needs and expectations within local markets. For example, although Visa employs its "Everywhere you want to be" theme globally, ads in specific locales employ local language and inspiring local imagery that make the theme relevant to the local markets in which they appear.

Global advertisers face several special problems. For instance, advertising media costs and availability differ vastly from country to country. Countries also differ in the extent to which they regulate advertising practices. Many countries have extensive systems of laws restricting how much a company can spend on advertising, the media used, the nature of advertising claims, and other aspects of the advertising program. Such restrictions often require advertisers to adapt their campaigns from country to country.

Thus, although advertisers may develop global strategies to guide their overall advertising efforts, specific advertising programs must usually be adapted to meet local cultures and customs, media characteristics, and regulations.

Author Comment
Not long ago, public relations was considered a marketing stepchild because of its limited marketing use. That situation is changing fast, however, as more marketers recognize PR's brand building, customer engagement, and social power.

Public Relations

OBJECTIVE 12-4 Explain How Companies Use Public Relations to Communicate With Their Publics.

Another major promotion tool, public relations, consists of activities designed to engage and build good relations with the company's various publics. PR may include any or all of the following functions:[34]

- Press relations or press agency. Creating and placing newsworthy information in the news media to attract attention to a person, product, or service.
- Product and brand publicity. Publicizing specific products and brands.
- Public affairs. Building and maintaining national or local community relationships.
- Lobbying. Building and maintaining relationships with legislators and government officials to influence legislation and regulation.
- Investor relations. Maintaining relationships with shareholders and others in the financial community.
- Development. Working with donors or members of nonprofit organizations to gain financial or volunteer support.

Public relations is used to promote products, people, places, ideas, activities, organizations, and even nations. Companies use PR to build good relations with consumers, investors, the media, and their communities. PR is often used to build support for newsworthy company events and actions. For example, a few years ago when CVS Health announced its bold decision to stop selling cigarettes and tobacco products in its stores, even though it meant sacrificing $2 billion in tobacco-related revenues, it knew that the decision would make headlines. But it left little to chance about how the full story would be told. Instead, CVS crafted a comprehensive "CVS Quits for Good" public relations campaign to tell consumers, Wall Street, and the health-care community that the decision would benefit both customers and the company:[35]

> The "CVS Quits" PR campaign kicked off with full-page ads in *The New York Times, The Wall Street Journal*, the *Boston Globe*, and other major newspapers along with multimedia news releases featuring video announcements from CVS's president and other company leaders. The ads and releases explained that dropping tobacco products "is simply the right thing to do for the good of our customers and our company," consistent "with our purpose—helping people on their path to better health." CVS also created an information-packed cvsquits.com microsite along with a #cvsquits hashtag and banners announcing the decision on the company's many

web and social media sites. The "CVS Quits" story was snapped up by major print and broadcast media, creating some 2,557 broadcast mentions and more than 218 million total media impressions. The news also went viral online, becoming a top trending topic on both Facebook and Twitter and generating 200,000 social media mentions and 152,000 shares.

On the day the decision was activated, CVS's CEO rang the New York Stock Exchange bell, and CVS Health executives snuffed out a 50-foot-high cigarette at an event in New York City's Bryant Park. Both events received substantial media coverage. Finally, at the same time that it nixed tobacco products, CVS launched a nationwide campaign to help smokers kick the habit, cementing the company's message of "helping people on their path to better health" and generating even more positive news.

The "CVS Quits" PR campaign achieved impressive results. On Capitol Hill, eight U.S. senators, 12 House members, and other influential leaders released statements urging other retailers to follow in CVS's footsteps. CVS's stock price jumped 9.2 percent in the three weeks following the announcement. And a survey showed that one in four consumers not currently shopping at CVS pharmacies said they would switch their prescriptions there after it quit tobacco. "CVS Quits" was named *PR Week*'s campaign of the year. "This is a new standard in PR," said one judge. "Great business decision that led to amazing PR results [that had] a real business impact on stock value, consumer behavior, and brand reputation."

The Role and Impact of PR

Like other promotional forms, public relations has the power to engage consumers and make a brand part of their lives and conversations. However, public relations can have a strong impact at a much lower cost than advertising can. Interesting brand stories, events, videos, or other content can be picked up by different media or shared virally by consumers, giving it the same or even greater impact than advertising that would cost millions of dollars. Consider recent PR moves by Burger King:[36]

The Floyd Mayweather–Manny Pacquiao fight in Las Vegas was a commercial-free pay-per-view event. So when "The King"—Burger King's quirky, ceramic-headed robed mascot—appeared as part of Mayweather's entourage during the walkout prior the "Fight of the Century," it caused quite a stir. Beyond the 4.4 million viewers who watched the fight live worldwide, The King's appearance was all over Facebook and Twitter, generating big-time buzz for the burger chain. Burger King paid Mayweather an estimated $1 million, but that was a small fraction of the $5 million companies spend for a single 30-second Super Bowl ad. » A month later, the bearded mascot popped up at the Belmont Stakes in an owner's box behind trainer Bob Baffert, whose horse American Pharoah ran for the coveted Triple Crown that day. As TV cameras panned Baffert before the race, The King stole the show, once again sparking a social media frenzy. The Belmont appearance reportedly cost Burger King only a $200,000 donation to a racing-related charity.

In yet another clever PR move, Burger King issued an invitation to rival McDonald's to call a cease-fire on Peace Day. In a full slate of online content, as well as full-page ads in *The New York Times* and the *Chicago Tribune,* Burger King publicly proposed that the chains jointly develop and sell a McWhopper, containing "all the tastiest bits of your Big Mac and our Whopper, united in one delicious, peace-loving burger," with all the proceeds benefiting the Peace One Day organization. McDonald's refused, but the gesture generated hugely positive PR for Burger King. Through these and other PR moves, Burger King has found a way to inject itself into daily social media conversations. "Burger King has really found a way to get attention by doing the unexpected and somewhat irreverent," says one expert. "They're generating an enormous amount of publicity at a very modest cost." Says another expert, "If you have the right spark, it will generate more buzz than paid media."

» Public relations moves: Burger King's quirky, ceramic-headed "The King" mascot pops up in unexpected places—here in American Pharoah's owner's box at the Belmont Stakes—sparking media attention and big-time social media buzz.

Gary Gershoff/Stringer/Getty Images

Despite its potential strengths, public relations is occasionally described as a marketing stepchild because of its sometimes limited and scattered use. The PR department is often located at corporate headquarters or handled by a third-party agency. Its staff is so busy dealing with various publics—stockholders, employees, legislators, and the press—that PR programs to support product marketing objectives may be ignored. Moreover, marketing managers and PR practitioners do not always speak the same language. Whereas many PR practitioners see their jobs as simply communicating, marketing managers tend to be much more interested in how advertising and PR affect brand building, sales and profits, and customer engagement and relationships.

This situation is changing, however. Although public relations still captures only a modest portion of the overall marketing budgets of many firms, PR can be a powerful brand-building tool. Especially in this digital age, the lines between advertising, PR, and other content are becoming more and more blurred. For example, are brand websites, blogs, video content, and social media activities advertising, PR, or something else? All are marketing content. And as the use of earned and shared digital content grows rapidly, PR is playing a bigger role in marketing content management.

More than any other department, PR has always been responsible for creating relevant marketing content that draws consumers to a brand rather than pushing messages out. "PR pros are an organization's master storytellers. In a word, they *do* content," says one expert. "The rise of social media [is] moving public relations professionals from the backroom, crafting press releases and organizing events, to the forefront of brand development and customer engagement," says another. PR professionals "have an edge because they have always had to earn attention, while [ad people] have bought attention."[37] The point is that PR should work hand in hand with advertising within an integrated marketing communications program to help build customer engagement and relationships.

Major Public Relations Tools

Public relations uses several tools. One of the major tools is *news*. PR professionals find or create favorable news about the company and its products or people. Sometimes news stories occur naturally; sometimes the PR person can suggest events or activities that would create news. Another common PR tool is *special events*, ranging from news conferences and speeches, brand tours, and sponsorships to multimedia presentations or educational programs designed to reach and interest target publics.

Public relations people also prepare *written materials* to reach and influence their target markets. These materials include annual reports, brochures, articles, and company newsletters and magazines. *Audiovisual materials*, such as videos, are being used increasingly as communication tools. *Corporate identity materials* can also help create a corporate identity that the public immediately recognizes. Logos, stationery, brochures, signs, business forms, business cards, buildings, uniforms, and company cars and trucks all become marketing tools when they are attractive, distinctive, and memorable. Finally, companies can improve public goodwill by contributing money and time to *public service activities*.

As previously discussed, the web and social media are also important PR channels. Websites, blogs, and social media such as YouTube, Facebook, Instagram, Snapchat, Pinterest, and Twitter provide ways to reach and engage people. As noted, storytelling and engagement are core PR strengths, and that plays well into the use of online, mobile, and social media.

As with the other promotion tools, in considering when and how to use product public relations, management should set PR objectives, choose the PR messages and vehicles, implement the PR plan, and evaluate the results. The firm's PR should be blended smoothly with other promotion activities within the company's overall integrated marketing communications effort.

REVIEWING AND EXTENDING THE CONCEPTS

CHAPTER REVIEW AND KEY TERMS

Objectives Review

In this chapter, you've learned how companies use integrated marketing communications (IMC) to engage customers and communicate customer value. You've also explored two of the major marketing communications mix elements—advertising and public relations. Modern marketing calls for more than just creating customer value by developing a good product, pricing it attractively, and making it available to target customers. Companies also must clearly and persuasively *communicate* that value to current and prospective customers. To do this, they must blend five communication mix tools, guided by a well-designed and implemented integrated marketing communications strategy.

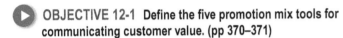

OBJECTIVE 12-1 Define the five promotion mix tools for communicating customer value. (pp 370–371)

A company's total *promotion mix*—also called its *marketing communications mix*—consists of the specific blend of *advertising, personal selling, sales promotion, public relations,* and *direct and digital marketing* tools that the company uses to engage customer, persuasively communicate customer value, and build customer relationships. Advertising includes any paid form of nonpersonal presentation and promotion of ideas, goods, or services by an identified sponsor. In contrast, public relations focuses on building good relations with the company's various publics. Personal selling is personal presentation by the firm's sales force for the purpose of making sales and building customer relationships. Firms use sales promotion to provide short-term incentives to encourage the purchase or sale of a product or service. Finally, firms seeking immediate response from targeted individual consumers and consumer communities use direct and digital marketing tools to engage consumers and cultivate relationships with them.

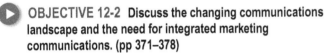

OBJECTIVE 12-2 Discuss the changing communications landscape and the need for integrated marketing communications. (pp 371–378)

Explosive developments in communications technology and changes in marketer and customer communication strategies have had a dramatic impact on marketing communications. Digital and social media have given birth to a more targeted, social, and engaging marketing communications model. Along with traditional media, advertisers now use a broad selection of more-specialized and highly targeted media to engage smaller customer segments with more-personalized, interactive content. As they adopt richer but more fragmented media and promotion mixes to reach their diverse markets, however, they risk creating a communications hodgepodge for consumers. To prevent this, companies must adopt the concept of *integrated marketing communications (IMC)*. Guided by an overall IMC strategy, the company works out the roles that the various promotional tools will play and the extent to which each will be used. It carefully coordinates the promotional activities and the timing of when major campaigns take place.

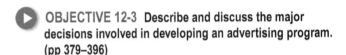

OBJECTIVE 12-3 Describe and discuss the major decisions involved in developing an advertising program. (pp 379–396)

Advertising—the use of paid, owned, earned, and shared media by a seller to inform, persuade, and remind about its products or organization—is a strong promotion tool that takes many forms and has many uses. *Advertising decision making* involves decisions about the objectives, the budget, the message, the media, and, finally, the evaluation of results. Advertisers should set clear *objectives* as to whether the advertising is supposed to inform, persuade, or remind buyers. The advertising *budget* can be based on what is affordable, on sales, on competitors' spending, or on advertising objectives and tasks. The *message decision* calls for planning a creative concept (or "big idea") and message strategy and executing it effectively. The *media decision* involves defining reach, frequency, impact, and engagement goals; choosing major media types; selecting media vehicles; and deciding on media timing. Message and media decisions must be closely coordinated for maximum campaign effectiveness. Finally, *evaluation* calls for evaluating the communication and sales effects of advertising and other brand content before, during, and after it is placed and measuring advertising return on investment.

OBJECTIVE 12-4 Explain how companies use public relations to communicate with their publics. (pp 396–398)

Public relations involves building good relations with the company's various publics. Its functions include *press agentry, product publicity, public affairs, lobbying, investor relations,* and *development*. Public relations can have a strong impact on public awareness at a much lower cost than advertising can. In this digital age, the lines between advertising, PR, and other content are becoming more and more blurred. And as the use of earned and shared digital content grows rapidly, PR is playing a bigger role in marketing content management. Public relations tools include *news, special events, written materials, audiovisual materials, corporate identity materials,* and *public service activities*. In considering when and how to use product PR, management should set PR objectives, choose the PR messages and vehicles, implement the PR plan, and evaluate the results. Public relations should be blended smoothly with other promotion activities within the company's overall integrated marketing communications effort.

Key Terms

Objective 12-1
Promotion mix (marketing communications mix) (p 370)
Advertising (p 370)
Sales promotion (p 370)
Personal selling (p 371)
Public relations (PR) (p 371)
Direct and digital marketing (p 371)
Content marketing (p 372)

Objective 12-2
Integrated marketing communications (IMC) (p 375)
Push strategy (p 377)
Pull strategy (p 378)

Objective 12-3
Advertising objective (p 379)
Advertising budget (p 383)
Affordable method (p 383)
Percentage-of-sales method (p 383)
Competitive-parity method (p 383)
Objective-and-task method (p 384)
Advertising strategy (p 384)
Madison & Vine (p 385)
Native advertising (p 387)
Creative concept (p 387)
Execution style (p 388)
Advertising media (p 390)
Return on advertising investment (p 394)
Advertising agency (p 395)

DISCUSSION AND CRITICAL THINKING

Discussion Questions

12-1. How do marketers use the five promotional tools to deliver a clear and consistent message to consumers? (AACSB: Written and Oral Communication)

12-2. Define *content marketing* and *integrated marketing communications* (IMC). How do marketers blend these concepts to reach customers? (AACSB: Written and Oral Communication)

12-3. What major decisions should a marketing manager consider when developing an advertising program? (AACSB: Written and Oral Communication)

12-4. Name and explain the two major elements in developing advertising strategy. (AACSB: Written and Oral Communication)

12-5. Define *public relations,* and explain the many public relations functions. (AACSB: Written and Oral Communication)

12-6. Discuss the major tools used by the public relations team to communicate relevant marketing content. (AACSB: Written and Oral Communication)

Critical Thinking Exercises

12-7. Identify a new consumer food or beverage product. Using the major promotion tools, design a promotion campaign for the product. Identify how you are using both push and pull strategies. (AACSB: Written and Oral Communication; Information Technology; Reflective Thinking)

12-8. Search YouTube for three of your favorite television commercials, each using a different execution style. For each ad, identify the execution style used and the audience targeted. Is it a good ad? Be prepared to present the commercials and support your conclusions. (AACSB: Written and Oral Communication; Information Technology; Reflective Thinking)

12-9. In early 2016, the Wounded Warrior Project suffered a major blow to its fundraising when reports surfaced suggesting that the nonprofit organization spent too much of its money on travel, conferences, and high-end events rather than direct assistance to wounded veterans. Research this case. Was the Wounded Warrior Project's public relations response to the alleged misspending accusations effective in reaching out to its donors and other audiences? Why or why not? How is social media changing the public relations process? (AACSB: Written and Oral Communication; Information Technology; Reflective Thinking)

MINICASES AND APPLICATIONS

Online, Mobile, and Social Media Marketing Facebook Audience Network

Facebook has more than 2 billion monthly active users. What started as an online social network allowing people to connect with each other has transformed into a behemoth media mogul and a real game-changer in mobile advertising. Facebook's mobile ad platform—called Audience Network—delivers targeted mobile ads for advertisers. While there are other mobile ad platforms (Google is the dominant player), Facebook has a treasure trove of data that is useful for advertisers. Google is strong in search data, but Facebook is part of our lives. Facebook has been placing ads on its site for advertisers but now pushes those ads to third-party apps. This is a win-win-win situation for advertisers, app developers, and Facebook because advertisers get their mobile ads to people based on very personal information, app developers get ad revenue, and Facebook gets a cut of the ad revenue for placing the ad. And it's no small cut—in just the last quarter of 2015, Facebook earned $8 billion in mobile ad revenue. That's 87 percent of Facebook's overall ad revenue.

12-10. Compare Facebook's, Google's, and Twitter's ad networks. Which is most effective for advertisers? (AACSB: Written and Oral Communication; Reflective Thinking)

12-11. Mobile advertising is one of the fastest-growing sectors of digital advertising, but how is mobile advertising effectiveness measured? Research this issue, and create a report of your findings. (AACSB: Written and Oral Communication; Reflective Thinking)

Marketing Ethics An Ethical Promotion?

A Unilever brand in Thailand ran into some problems with one of its promotion campaigns, the "Citra 3D Brightening Girls Search." Citra Pearly White UV Body Lotion is marketed as a skin-whitening product. Skin whitening is popular in many Asian countries because lighter skin color is associated with higher economic status. However, this belief is not created by marketers. Anthropologists point out that Asian cultures, and Thailand in particular, have long histories of associating darker skin tones with outdoor peasants and field workers and lighter skin tones with higher socioeconomic status. Citra's advertising was criticized because it showed two female students—one lighter-skinned than the other—and asked them what would make them "outstanding in uniform." The darker girl seemed confused and didn't answer, while the lighter girl answered with Citra's product slogan. After considerable social media outcry, Citra pulled the ad, but it did not stop a related scholarship competition. The competition offered a 100,000 baht ($3,200) prize for the college student best demonstrating "product efficacy"—that is, the whitest skin. The company claims its products help people feel good about themselves and enhance their self-esteem.

12-12. Since lighter skin and skin whitening are popular in Thailand, is it wrong for marketers to offer and promote products that encourage this belief and behavior? Explain why or why not. (AACSB: Written and Oral Communication; Reflective Thinking; Ethical Understanding and Reasoning)

12-13. Find other examples of marketers creating controversy by promoting culture-based products that could be viewed as inappropriate by others outside that culture. (AACSB: Written and Oral Communication; Reflective Thinking)

Marketing by the Numbers Never-Ending Cola War

Although consumption of carbonated beverages has been decreasing, it is still an $81 billion industry in North America, which far exceeds alternatives such as water ($23 billion) and sports drinks ($9.4 billion). That's why Coca-Cola and Pepsi still battle it out. Coca-Cola's market share increased from 17.3 percent to 17.8 percent during the past decade. That might not seem like much, but one share point equals 1 percent of market sales, so a half a share point represents $405 million. Pepsi's market share decreased from 10.3 percent to 8.4 percent during the same period—a loss of 1.9 share points or $1.5 billion. The war is not yet over, though. PepsiCo announced that it would increase its advertising budget for 2018. Many marketers budget an upcoming year's advertising expenditures using a percentage-of-sales method based on past or projected sales. The industry average advertising-to-sales ratio for beverages is 4.1 percent of sales. Below are the worldwide advertising expenditures and sales revenues for the two combatants (all numbers are in billions of dollars):

	PepsiCo		Coca-Cola	
Year	Advertising	Sales	Advertising	Sales
2013	$2.4	$66.42	$3.27	$46.85
2014	$2.3	$66.68	$3.50	$46.00
2015	$2.4	$63.06	$3.98	$44.29
2016	$2.5	$62.80	$4.00	$41.86
2017	$2.4	$63.53	$3.96	$35.41

12-14. Calculate both companies' advertising-to-sales ratios for each year. What is each company's average ratio over the five-year period? Refer to the percentage-of-sales method in the chapter to learn about this method. (AACSB: Analytical Thinking)

12-15. PepsiCo decided to base its 2018 advertising budget on the industry average advertising-to-sales ratio for beverages, which is 4.1 percent. How much would PepsiCo have budgeted for advertising if the company based expenditures on last year's sales? How much of an increase is that? (AACSB: Analytical Thinking)

Video Case Kmart

To view this video case and its accompanying questions, please visit MyLab Marketing.

On the heels of its wildly popular "Ship My Pants" ads, Kmart struck again with an ad that was considered hilarious by some, offensive by others, and a stroke of genius by advertising critics. Its latest ad, "Big Gas Savings," was launched on YouTube prior to airing on television. And like its "Ship My Pants" predecessor, the ad also went viral.

In addition to relying on potty humor to pull its sales out of the toilet, Kmart struck a very timely note in the tune of customer value—saving money on gasoline. Customers could save 30 cents a gallon on gas by spending $50 or more in its stores. Millions of customers took advantage of the offer, driving traffic into Kmart stores.

Company Cases 12 LinkedIn/2 Facebook/14 OfferUp

See Appendix 1 for cases appropriate for this chapter.

Case 12, LinkedIn: Crushing the White-Collar Stereotype with IMC. With its first mass-media IMC campaign, LinkedIn is out to change the widely held perception that its services are white collar only.

Case 2, Facebook: Making the World More Open and Connected. Facebook has amassed more than 2 billion active monthly users by focusing on its mission: "to give people the power to share and make the world more open and connected."

Case 14, OfferUp: A Mobile Solution for the Mobile Era. By focusing on the local secondhand marketplace with a purely mobile approach that overcomes the shortcomings of Craigslist, OfferUp now poses a real threat to the classified ads leader.

Writing Assignments

12-16. Name and describe the various execution styles for presenting messages and provide an example of each style different from the ones in the chapter. (AACSB: Communication)

12-17. Discuss the major advertising objectives and describe an advertisement that is attempting to achieve each objective. (AACSB: Written and Oral Communication; Reflective Thinking)

13 Personal Selling and Sales Promotion

Objectives Outline

OBJECTIVE 13-1 **Discuss the role of a company's salespeople in engaging customers, creating customer value, and building customer relationships.** See: Personal Selling (pp 406–408)

OBJECTIVE 13-2 **Identify and explain the six major sales force management steps.** See: Managing the Sales Force (pp 408–419)

OBJECTIVE 13-3 **Discuss the personal selling process, distinguishing between transaction-oriented marketing and relationship marketing.** See: The Personal Selling Process (pp 419–423)

OBJECTIVE 13-4 **Explain how sales promotion campaigns are developed and implemented.** See: Sales Promotion (pp 423–429)

Previewing the Concepts

In the previous chapter, you learned about engaging customers and communicating customer value through integrated marketing communications (IMC) and two elements of the promotion mix: advertising and public relations. In this chapter, we examine two more IMC elements: personal selling and sales promotion. Personal selling is the interpersonal arm of marketing communications, in which the sales force engages customers and prospects to build relationships and make sales. Sales promotion consists of short-term incentives to encourage the purchase or sale of a product or service. Although this chapter presents personal selling and sales promotion as separate tools, they must be carefully integrated with the other elements of the promotion mix.

First, let's look at a real-life sales force. When you think of salespeople, perhaps you think of pushy retail sales clerks, "yell and sell" TV pitchmen, or the stereotypical glad-handing "used-car salesman." But such stereotypes don't fit the reality of most of today's salespeople—sales professionals who succeed not by taking advantage of customers but by listening to their needs and helping to forge solutions. Consider Salesforce—the industry leader in customer relationship management solutions. Salesforce not only produces market-leading sales management software services, it also excels at practicing what it preaches—effective personal selling.

First Stop

Salesforce: You Need a Great Sales Force to Sell Salesforce

Salesforce is way out front in the $25 billion market for customer relationship management (CRM) solutions. The Salesforce logo, set inside the image of a puffy cloud, underscores Salesforce's highly successful cloud-based computing model (no software to install or own). Cloud-based systems are common today, but they were state-of-the art when Salesforce pioneered the concept nearly 20 years ago. Since then, the company has established itself as a leading innovator, constantly finding new ways to help client companies connect with customers and achieve greater sales force effectiveness using the latest online, mobile, social, artificial intelligence (AI), and cloud technologies.

>> Salesforce's cloud-based "Customer Success Platform" provides a wide array of customer relationship management tools that help its customers "supercharge their sales."

Bloomberg/Getty Images

Salesforce helps businesses to "supercharge their sales." It supplies what it calls a "Customer Success Platform," a wide array of cloud-based sales management software tools that gather, organize, analyze, and disseminate in-depth data about a company's customers, sales, and individual sales rep and overall sales force performance. Salesforce's Einstein artificial intelligence system even lets clients predict customer outcomes based on sales data without their own data science teams. From its home in the cloud, Salesforce makes all these data and analyses readily available anytime, from anywhere, on any device with online access—desktops, laptops, tablets, or smartphones. Salesforce also integrates with major social media, providing tools for social media monitoring and real-time customer engagement and collaboration on its Salesforce Chatter platform, a kind of Facebook for enterprises.

Salesforce's innovative products have made it the world's number one and fastest-growing CRM platform, ahead of blue-chip competitors such as Microsoft, Oracle, SAP, and IBM. The company's revenues hit $10.4 billion last year, up an impressive 25 percent over the previous year and more than three times what they were just five years ago. Salesforce has placed first or second on the *Forbes* World's Most Innovative Company list for seven straight years. With the ongoing digital transformation causing a surge in the CRM market, Salesforce has set a bold target of $20 billion in annual revenue by 2022.

Innovative products and platforms have played a major role in Salesforce's stunning success. But even the best products don't sell themselves. You need a great sales force to sell Salesforce, and the company excels at practicing what it preaches—effective personal selling. Like the companies that buy its services, Salesforce has its own army of experienced, well-trained, highly motivated sales reps who take the company's products to customers. In many respects, Salesforce's own sales force serves as a model for the products and services it sells—not just for using the Salesforce cloud but more generally for achieving the "supercharged" sales force results that the company promises its clients.

At Salesforce, developing an outstanding sale force starts with recruiting and hiring top-notch salespeople. Salesforce's aggressive but highly selective recruiting program skims the cream off the top of the global sales rep candidate pool. Each year on average, Salesforce hires only 4.5 percent of the more than 100,000 candidates who apply. Experience counts. Salesforce expects a minimum of two years of prior sales experience for small-business sales reps and up to two decades of experience for sales execs assigned to major accounts. To find such experienced candidates, Salesforce freely raids rival companies for new hires, counting on its high-energy culture and strong compensation packages to lure successful salespeople into the Salesforce fold.

Salesforce leads the market in sales force automation and customer relationship management solutions. But even Salesforce's innovative products won't sell themselves. The company knows that it needs a great sales force to sell Salesforce.

Once hired, as you might expect, Salesforce salespeople have access to all the latest high-tech selling tools. In fact, the first major assignment of new hires is to study 20 hours of at-home video that teaches them the ins and outs of the Salesforce technologies that they won't be just selling but also using. But Salesforce would be the first to tell you that, although its cloud wizardry can help to optimize customer contact and the selling process, it doesn't take the place of good personal selling skills. So in training and fine-tuning its own sales force, the company starts by preaching tried-and-true selling fundamentals, tempered by its own modern twists.

The first fundamental of good selling at Salesforce is to listen and learn. As new recruits go through Salesforce's weeklong selling boot camp, taught at the company's Salesforce U, they learn that they should begin building customer relationships by asking probing questions and getting customers to talk, seeking to understand everything they can about a customer's situation and needs. "Eighty-five percent of salespeople don't slow down enough to really understand their customer's business," says a senior Salesforce sales executive.

Understanding the customer leads to a second selling fundamental: empathize—let customers know that you understand their issues and feel their pain. Empathy builds rapport and trust, an important step toward closing sales and building long-term customer relationships. Listening, learning, and empathizing are important first steps, but more is needed. "If all you are is responsive and helpful, then all you are is an administrative assistant," says the Salesforce sales executive.

So the next important step is to offer solutions—to show how Salesforce's cloud-based solutions will help clients make their sales forces more effective and productive in connecting with and selling to customers. Salesforce believes that the best way to offer solutions is by telling good stories that highlight other customers' successes with its products. "Storytelling is very, very important," says Salesforce's sales productivity manager. "It can be the foundation of things like the corporate pitch and your interactions with your customers and prospects." When it comes to handling objections—such as "I don't trust putting our data in the cloud," "My current system is working fine," or "It costs too much"—Salesforce tells its salespeople that stories can be the most powerful tools they have. "When faced with objections, we always relate it back to a customer story," says a Salesforce marketing manager. "We're not the hero in our customer's stories," says another manager. "It's how the customer succeeded, not how we saved them."

When it comes to competitors, Salesforce's salespeople are ferocious. But Salesforce reps are trained to take the high road—to sell Salesforce's strengths, not competitors' weaknesses. "Internally, we have these posters: Crush Microsoft and Obliterate Oracle," says the Salesforce marketing manager. But, he adds, "when you go out to your customers, you have to be careful that you're guiding them and not just stepping on Microsoft. Even though we all want to."

Thus, effective professional selling is about much more than glad-handing and back-slapping on the one hand or plying high-tech CRM tools and data analytics on the other. Even though Salesforce boasts the best sales and customer connection tools in the business, backed by big data and combined with AI and plenty of other new-school techniques, its sales reps stay focused on old-school selling principles. At Salesforce—or anywhere else—good selling starts with the fundamentals of engaging and listening to customers, understanding and empathizing with their problems, and building relationships by offering meaningful solutions for mutual gain. That's how you build an incredibly successful sales force and Salesforce.[1]

In this chapter, we examine two more promotion mix tools: *personal selling* and *sales promotion*. Personal selling consists of interpersonal interactions with customers and prospects to make sales and maintain customer relationships. Sales promotion involves using short-term incentives to encourage customer purchasing, reseller support, and sales force efforts.

Author Comment
Personal selling is the interpersonal arm of the promotion mix. A company's sales force creates and communicates customer value by personally engaging customers and building customer relationships.

Personal Selling

OBJECTIVE 13-1 Discuss the role of a company's salespeople in engaging customers, creating customer value, and building customer relationships.

Robert Louis Stevenson once noted, "Everyone lives by selling something." Companies around the world use sales forces to sell products and services to business customers and final consumers. But sales forces are also found in many other kinds of organizations. For example, colleges use recruiters to attract new students. Museums and fine arts organizations use fundraisers to contact donors and raise money. Even governments use sales forces. The U.S. Postal Service, for instance, uses a sales force to sell Express Mail and other shipping and mailing solutions to corporate customers. In the first part of this chapter, we examine personal selling's role in the organization, sales force management decisions, and the personal selling process.

The Nature of Personal Selling

Personal selling
Personal presentations by the firm's sales force for the purpose of engaging customers, making sales, and building customer relationships.

Personal selling is one of the oldest professions in the world. The people who do the selling go by many names, including salespeople, sales representatives, agents, district managers, account executives, sales consultants, and sales engineers.

People hold many stereotypes of salespeople—including some unfavorable ones. *Salesman* may bring to mind the image of Dwight Schrute, the opinionated Dunder Mifflin paper salesman from the old TV show *The Office*, who lacks both common sense and social skills. Or you may think of the real-life "yell and sell" TV pitchmen, who hawk everything from the Flex Seal to the INSANITY Workout and the Power Air Fryer in infomercials. However, the majority of salespeople are a far cry from these unfortunate stereotypes.

As the opening Salesforce story shows, most salespeople are well-educated and well-trained professionals who add value for customers and maintain long-term customer relationships. They listen to their customers, assess customer needs, and organize the company's efforts to solve customer problems. The best salespeople are the ones who work closely with customers for mutual gain. >> Consider GE's diesel locomotive business:

>> Professional selling: It takes more than fast talk and a warm smile to sell expensive GE locomotives. GE's real challenge is to win and keep business by building day-in, day-out, year-in, year-out partnerships with customers.
GE

> It takes more than fast talk and a warm smile to sell a batch of $2 million high-tech locomotives. A single big sale can easily run into the hundreds of millions of dollars. GE salespeople head up an extensive team of company specialists, all dedicated to finding ways to satisfy the needs of large customers. The selling process can be nerve-rackingly slow, involving dozens or even hundreds of decision makers from all levels of the buying organization and layer upon layer of subtle and not-so-subtle buying influences. A major sale can take years from the first sales presentation to the day the sale is announced. After getting the order, salespeople then must stay in almost constant touch to keep track of the account's equipment needs and to make certain the customer stays satisfied. The real challenge is to win and keep buyers' business by building day-in, day-out, year-in, year-out partnerships with them based on superior products and close collaboration.

Salesperson
An individual who represents a company to customers by performing one or more of the following activities: prospecting, communicating, selling, servicing, information gathering, and relationship building.

The term **salesperson** covers a wide range of positions. At one extreme, a salesperson might be largely an *order taker*, such as the department store salesperson standing behind the counter. At the other extreme are *order getters*, whose positions demand *creative selling, social selling,* and *relationship building* for products and services ranging from appliances, industrial equipment, and airplanes to insurance and IT services. In this chapter, we focus on the more creative types of selling and the process of building and managing an effective sales force.

The Role of the Sales Force

Personal selling is the interpersonal arm of the promotion mix. It involves interpersonal interactions and engagement between salespeople and individual customers—whether face-to-face, by phone, via email or social media, through video or online conferences, or by other means. Personal selling can be very effective in complex selling situations. Salespeople can probe customers to learn more about their problems and then adjust the marketing offer and presentation to fit each customer's special needs.

The role of personal selling varies from company to company. Some firms have no salespeople at all—for example, companies that sell only online or companies that sell through manufacturers' reps, sales agents, or brokers. In most firms, however, the sales force plays a major role. In companies that sell business products and services, such as IBM, DuPont, or GE, salespeople work directly with customers. In consumer product companies such as P&G or Nike, the sales force plays an important behind-the-scenes role. It works with wholesalers and retailers to gain their support and help them be more effective in selling the company's products to final buyers.

Linking the Company with Its Customers

The sales force serves as a critical link between a company and its customers. In many cases, salespeople serve two masters—the seller and the buyer. First, they *represent the*

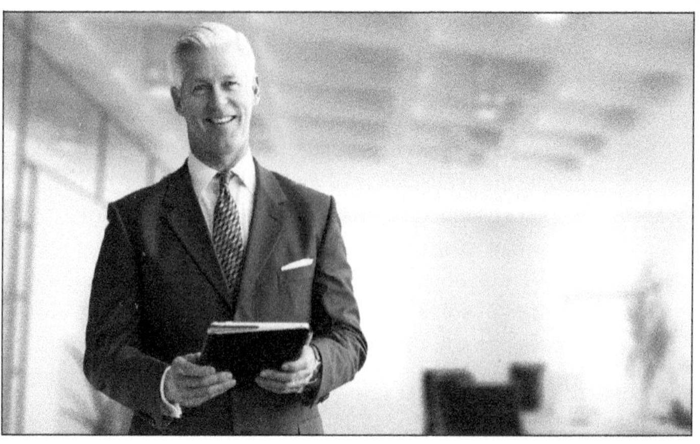

>> **Salespeople link the company with its customers. To many customers, the salesperson is the company.**

dotshock/Shutterstock

company to customers. They find and develop new customers and communicate information about the company's products and services. They sell products by engaging customers and learning about their needs, presenting solutions, answering objections, negotiating prices and terms, closing sales, servicing accounts, and maintaining account relationships.

At the same time, salespeople *represent customers to the company*, acting inside the firm as "champions" of customers' interests and managing the buyer–seller relationship. Salespeople relay customer concerns about company products and actions back inside to those who can handle them. They learn about customer needs and work with other marketing and nonmarketing people in the company to develop greater customer value.

>> In fact, to many customers, the salesperson *is* the company—the only tangible manifestation of the company that they see. Hence, customers may become loyal to salespeople as well as to the companies and products they represent. This concept of *salesperson-owned loyalty* lends even more importance to the salesperson's customer-relationship-building abilities. Strong relationships with the salesperson will result in strong relationships with the company and its products. Conversely, poor salesperson relationships will probably result in poor company and product relationships.

Coordinating Marketing and Sales

Ideally, the sales force and other marketing functions (marketing planners, brand managers, marketing content managers, and researchers) should work together closely to jointly create value for customers. Unfortunately, however, some companies still treat sales and marketing as separate functions. When this happens, the separate sales and marketing groups may not get along well. When things go wrong, marketers blame the sales force for its poor execution of what they see as an otherwise splendid strategy. In turn, the sales team blames the marketers for being out of touch with what's really going on with customers. Neither group fully values the other's contributions. However, if not repaired, such disconnects between marketing and sales can damage customer relationships and company performance.

A company can take several actions to help bring its marketing and sales functions closer together. At the most basic level, it can increase communications between the two groups by arranging joint meetings and spelling out communication channels. It can create opportunities for salespeople and marketers to work together. Brand managers and researchers can tag along on sales calls or sit in on sales planning sessions. In turn, salespeople can sit in on marketing planning sessions and share their firsthand customer knowledge.

A company can also create joint objectives and reward systems for sales and marketing teams or appoint marketing-sales liaisons—people from marketing who "live with the sales force" and help coordinate marketing and sales force programs and efforts. Finally, it can appoint a high-level marketing executive to oversee both marketing and sales. Such a person can help infuse marketing and sales with the common goal of creating value for customers to capture value in return.[2]

Author Comment

Here's another definition of sales force management: "planning, organizing, leading, and controlling personal contact programs designed to achieve profitable customer relationships." Once again, the goal of every marketing activity is to create customer value, engage customers, and build profitable customer relationships.

Managing the Sales Force

OBJECTIVE 13-2 Identify and explain the six major sales force management steps.

We define **sales force management** as analyzing, planning, implementing, and controlling sales force activities. It includes designing sales force strategy and structure as well as recruiting, selecting, training, compensating, supervising, and evaluating the firm's salespeople. These major sales force management decisions are shown in >> **Figure 13.1** and discussed in the following sections.

Sales force management
Analyzing, planning, implementing, and controlling sales force activities.

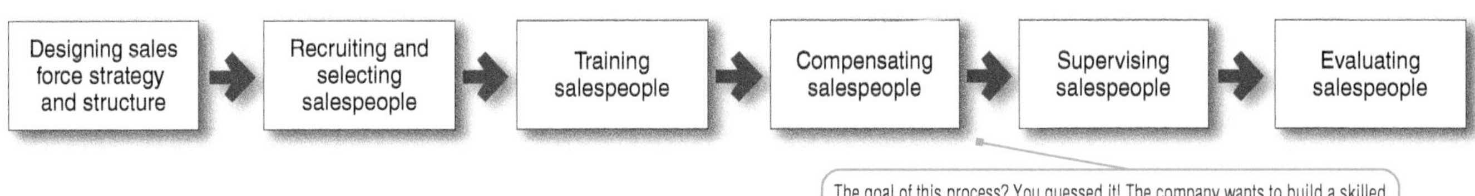
Designing sales force strategy and structure
Recruiting and selecting salespeople
Training salespeople
Compensating salespeople
Supervising salespeople
Evaluating salespeople
The goal of this process? You guessed it! The company wants to build a skilled and motivated sales team that will help to create customer value, engage customers, and build strong customer relationships.

Figure 13.1 Major Steps in Sales Force Management

Designing the Sales Force Strategy and Structure

Marketing managers face several sales force strategy and design questions. How should salespeople and their tasks be structured? How big should the sales force be? Should salespeople sell alone or work in teams with other people in the company? Should they sell in the field, by phone, or using online and social media? We address these issues next.

The Sales Force Structure

A company can divide sales responsibilities along any of several lines. The structure decision is simple if the company sells only one product line to one industry with customers in many locations. In that case the company would use a *territorial sales force structure*. However, if the company sells many products to many types of customers, it might need a *product sales force structure*, a *customer sales force structure*, or a combination of the two.

Territorial sales force structure
A sales force organization that assigns each salesperson to an exclusive geographic territory in which that salesperson sells the company's full line.

Product sales force structure
A sales force organization in which salespeople specialize in selling only a portion of the company's products or lines.

Customer (or market) sales force structure
A sales force organization in which salespeople specialize in selling only to certain customers or industries.

In the **territorial sales force structure**, each salesperson is assigned to an exclusive geographic area and sells the company's full line of products or services to all customers in that territory. This organization clearly defines each salesperson's job and fixes accountability. It also increases the salesperson's desire to build local customer relationships that, in turn, improve selling effectiveness. Finally, because each salesperson travels within a limited geographic area, travel expenses are relatively small. A territorial sales organization is often supported by many levels of sales management positions. For example, individual territory sales reps may report to area managers, who in turn report to regional managers, who report to a director of sales.

If a company has numerous and complex products, it can adopt a **product sales force structure**, in which the sales force specializes along product lines. For example, GE employs different sales forces for and within different product and service divisions of its major businesses. For instance, the company has separate sales forces for aviation, energy, transportation, and healthcare products and technologies. Within GE Healthcare, the company employs different sales forces for diagnostic imaging, life sciences, and integrated IT products and services. No single salesperson can become expert in all of these product categories, so product specialization is required. In all, a company as large and complex as GE might have dozens of separate sales forces serving its diverse product and service portfolio.

Using a **customer (or market) sales force structure**, a company organizes its sales force along customer or industry lines. Separate sales forces may be set up for different industries, serving current customers versus finding new ones, and serving major accounts versus regular accounts. Organizing the sales force around customers can help a company build closer relationships with important customers. Many companies even have special sales forces to handle the needs of individual large customers. For example, P&G sales reps are integrated into Customer Business Development (CBD) teams. Each CBD team is assigned to a major P&G customer, such as Walmart, Safeway, or CVS Health. >> P&G's Walmart CBD team consists of more than 200 P&Gers who partner with Walmart

P&G
Walmart

>> **Customer sales force structure: P&G's Walmart Customer Business Development sales team consists of hundreds of P&Gers who work closely with Walmart buyers in Walmart's hometown of Bentonville, Arkansas.**

grzegorz knec/Alamy

buyers in Walmart's hometown of Bentonville, Arkansas. The CBD organization places the focus on serving the complete needs of each major customer. It lets P&G "grow business by working as a 'strategic partner' with our accounts," not just as a supplier.[3]

When a company sells a wide variety of products to many types of customers over a broad geographic area, it often employs a *complex sales force structure,* which combines several types of organization. Salespeople can be specialized by customer and territory; product and territory; product and customer; or territory, product, and customer. For example, P&G specializes its sales force by customer (with different sales teams for Walmart, Safeway, CVS Health, or other large customers) *and* by territory for each key customer group (territory CBD representatives, territory managers, regional managers, and so on). No single structure is best for all companies and situations. Each company should select a sales force structure that best serves the needs of its customers and fits its overall marketing strategy.

Sales Force Size

Once the company has set its structure, it is ready to consider *sales force size.* Sales forces may range in size from only a few salespeople to tens of thousands. Some sales forces are huge—for example, IBM's employs almost 40,000 salespeople around the world; Microsoft, 18,300; Pfizer, 13,500; and Samsung Electronics, 10,200.[4] Salespeople constitute one of the company's most productive—and most expensive—assets. Therefore, increasing their numbers will increase both sales and costs.

A company might use some form of *workload approach* to set sales force size. Using this approach, a company first groups accounts into different classes according to size, account status, or other factors related to the amount of effort required to maintain the account. It then determines the number of salespeople needed to call on each class of accounts the desired number of times.

The company might think as follows: Suppose we have 1,000 A-level accounts and 2,000 B-level accounts. A-level accounts require 36 calls per year, and B-level accounts require 12 calls per year. In this case, the sales force's *workload*—the number of calls it must make per year—is 60,000 calls [(1,000 × 36) + (2,000 × 12) = 36,000 + 24,000 = 60,000]. Suppose our average salesperson can make 1,000 calls a year. Thus, we need 60 salespeople (60,000 ÷ 1,000).

Other Sales Force Strategy and Structure Issues

Sales management must also determine who will be involved in the selling effort and how various sales and sales-support people will work together.

Outside sales force (or field sales force)
Salespeople who travel to call on customers in the field.

Inside sales force
Salespeople who conduct business from their offices via telephone, online and social media interactions, or visits from prospective buyers.

Outside and Inside Sales Forces. A company may have an **outside sales force (or field sales force)**, an **inside sales force**, or both. Outside salespeople travel to call on customers in the field. In contrast, inside salespeople conduct business from their offices via phone, online and social media interactions, or visits from buyers. The use of inside sales has grown in recent years as a result of increased outside selling costs and the surge in online, mobile, and social media technologies.

Some inside salespeople provide support for the outside sales force, freeing them to spend more time selling to major accounts and finding new prospects. For example, *technical sales-support people* provide technical information and answers to customers' questions. Sales assistants provide research and administrative backup for outside salespeople. They track down sales leads, call ahead and confirm appointments, follow up on deliveries, and answer customers' questions when outside salespeople cannot be reached. Using such combinations of inside and outside salespeople can help serve important customers better. The inside rep provides daily access and support, whereas the outside rep provides face-to-face collaboration and relationship building.

Other inside salespeople do more than just provide support. Telemarketers and online sellers use the phone, internet, and social media to find new leads, learn about customers and their business, or sell and service accounts directly. Telemarketing and online selling can be very effective, less costly ways to sell to smaller, harder-to-reach customers. Depending on the complexity of the product and customer, for example, a telemarketer can make from 20 to 33 decision-maker contacts a day compared with the average of four that an outside salesperson can make. In addition, whereas the cost of a business-to-business (B-to-B) field sales call can average close to $600, a routine industrial telemarketing or online contact might average only $25 to $75.[5]

Although the federal government's Do Not Call Registry put a dent in telephone sales to consumers, telemarketing remains a vital tool for most B-to-B marketers. For some smaller companies, telephone and online selling may be the primary sales approaches. However, most of the larger companies also use these tactics extensively, either to sell directly to small and midsize customers or to assist their sales forces in selling to larger ones.

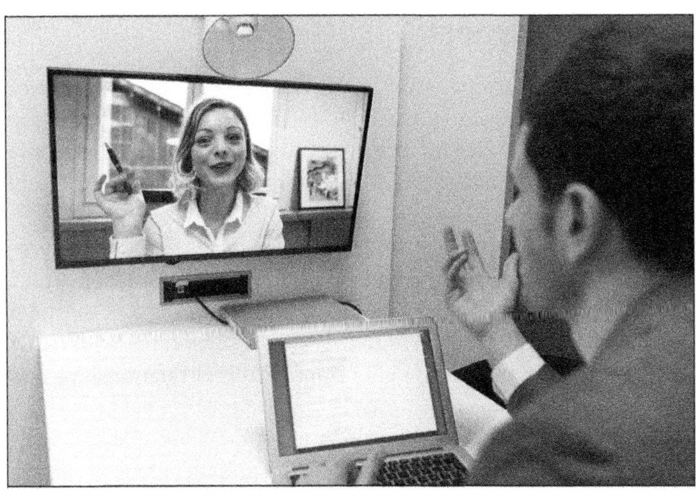

>> Outside and inside sales: In today's digital, mobile, and social media environment, inside selling is growing much faster than in-person selling. And a growing proportion of outside selling is now done over a phone or mobile device.

LDProd/Shutterstock

>> In addition to costs savings, in today's digital, mobile, and social media environments, many buyers are more receptive to—or even prefer—phone and online contact versus the high level of face-to-face contact once required. Today's customers are more inclined to gather their own information online—one study showed that a typical buyer reports contacting a sales rep only after independently completing about 60 percent of the buying process. Then buyers routinely use the phone, online meetings, and social media interactions to engage sellers and close deals.

As a result of these trends, telephone and online selling are growing much faster than in-person selling. One recent study found that inside sales positions are growing 300 times faster than outside sales positions. More than 28 percent of sales professionals in large companies are now inside reps; in small companies, a full 47 percent are inside. Moreover, the lines are blurring between outside and inside selling, creating a new breed of "hybrid sales reps"—a modern cross between a field sales rep and an inside rep—who often work from remote locations. Today's outside sales reps spend nearly half their time selling remotely rather than in face-to-face meetings, an 80 percent increase in just the past four years.[6]

Team selling
Using teams of people from sales, marketing, engineering, finance, technical support, and even upper management to service large, complex accounts.

Team Selling. As products become more complex and as customers grow larger and more demanding, a single salesperson simply can't handle all of a large customer's needs. Instead, most companies now use **team selling** to service large, complex accounts. Sales teams can unearth problems, solutions, and sales opportunities that no individual salesperson could. Such teams might include experts from any area or level of the selling firm—sales, marketing, technical and support services, research and development, engineering, operations, finance, and others.

In many cases, the move to team selling mirrors similar changes in customers' buying organizations. Many large customer companies have implemented team-based purchasing, requiring marketers to employ equivalent team-based selling. When dealing with large, complex accounts, one salesperson can't be an expert in everything the customer needs. Instead, selling is done by strategic account teams, quarterbacked by senior account managers or customer business managers.

For example, the 200-person P&G Walmart Customer Business Development team is a complete, multifunctional customer service unit. The team includes a CBD manager and several CBD account executives (each responsible for a specific P&G product category), supported by specialists in marketing strategy, product development, operations, information systems, logistics, finance, and human resources.

Team selling does have some pitfalls, however. For example, salespeople are by nature competitive and have often been trained and rewarded for outstanding individual performance. Salespeople who are used to having customers all to themselves may have trouble learning to work with and trust others on a team. In addition, selling teams can confuse or overwhelm customers who are used to working with only one salesperson. Finally, difficulties in evaluating individual contributions to the team-selling effort can create some sticky compensation issues.

Recruiting and Selecting Salespeople

At the heart of any successful sales force operation is the recruitment and selection of good salespeople. The performance difference between an average salesperson and a top salesperson can be substantial. In a typical sales force, the top 30 percent of the salespeople might bring in 60 percent of the sales. Thus, careful salesperson selection can greatly increase overall sales force performance.

Beyond the differences in sales performance, poor selection results in costly turnover. When a salesperson quits, the costs of finding and training a new salesperson—plus the costs of lost sales—can be very high. One sales consulting firm calculates the total 12-month cost of a bad sales hire at a whopping $475,000.[7] Also, a sales force with many new people is less productive, and turnover disrupts important customer relationships and sales team morale.

What sets great salespeople apart from all the rest? In an effort to profile top sales performers, Gallup Consulting, a division of the well-known Gallup polling organization, has interviewed hundreds of thousands of salespeople. Its research suggests that the best salespeople possess four key talents: intrinsic motivation, a disciplined work style, the ability to close a sale, and, perhaps most important, the ability to build relationships with customers.[8]

Super salespeople are motivated from within—they have an unrelenting drive to excel. Some salespeople are driven by money, a desire for recognition, or the satisfaction of competing and winning. Others are driven by the desire to provide service and build relationships. The best salespeople possess some of each of these motivations. However, another analysis found that the best salespeople are driven by a strong sense of purpose: "The salespeople who sold with noble purpose, who truly want to make a difference to customers, consistently outsold the salespeople focused on sales goals and money." Selling with such a sense of customer-related purpose is not only more successful, it's also more profitable and more satisfying to salespeople.[9]

>> Great salespeople: The best salespeople possess intrinsic motivation, a disciplined work style, the ability to close a sale, and, perhaps most important, the ability to build relationships with customers.

nd3000/Shutterstock

Super salespeople also have a disciplined work style. They lay out detailed, organized plans and then follow through in a timely way. But motivation and discipline mean little unless they result in closing more sales and building better customer relationships. Super salespeople build the skills and knowledge they need to get the job done. >> Perhaps most important, top salespeople are excellent customer problem solvers and relationship builders. They understand their customers' needs. Talk to sales executives and they'll describe top performers in these terms: good listeners, empathetic, patient, caring, and responsive. Top performers can put themselves on the buyer's side of the desk and see the world through their customers' eyes. They don't want just to be liked; they want to add value for their customers.

That said, there is no one right way to sell. Each successful salesperson uses a different approach, one that best applies his or her unique strengths and talents. For example, some salespeople enjoy the thrill of a harder sell in confronting challenges and winning people over. Others might apply "softer" talents to reach the same goal. "The truth is, no two great sales reps are alike," says one sales consultant. "You might thrive on fierce competition, while a colleague wins by being a super-analytical problem solver. Or maybe you have a tremendous talent for building relationships, while your fellow top performer is a brilliant strategist. What's most important is that you win business your way."[10]

When recruiting, a company should analyze the sales job itself and the characteristics of its most successful salespeople to identify the traits needed by a successful salesperson in its industry. Then it must recruit the right salespeople. The human resources department looks for applicants by getting names from current salespeople, using employment agencies, searching the internet and online social media, posting ads and notices on its website and industry media, and working through college placement services. Another source is to attract top salespeople from other companies. Proven salespeople need less training and can be productive immediately.

Recruiting will attract many applicants from which the company must select the best. The selection procedure can vary from a single informal interview to lengthy testing and interviewing. Many companies give formal tests to sales applicants. Tests typically measure sales aptitude, analytical and organizational skills, personality traits, and other characteristics. But test scores provide only one piece of information in a set that includes personal characteristics, references, past employment history, and interviewer reactions.

Training Salespeople

New salespeople may spend anywhere from a few weeks or months to a year or more in training. After the initial training ends, most companies provide continuing sales training via seminars, sales meetings, and online learning throughout the salesperson's career. According to one source, U.S. firms spend approximately $70 billion on sales training each year. Although training can be expensive, it can also yield important returns.[11]

Training programs have several goals. First, salespeople need to know about customers and how to build relationships with them. Therefore, the training program must teach them about different types of customers and their needs, buying motives, and buying habits. It must also teach them how to sell effectively and train them in the basics of the selling process. Salespeople also need to know and identify with the company, its products, and its competitors. Therefore, an effective training program teaches them about the company's objectives, organization, products, and the strategies of major competitors.

Today, many companies are adding digital components to their sales training programs. Online training may range from simple self-paced text- and video-based product training and internet-based sales exercises that build sales skills to sophisticated simulations that recreate the dynamics of real-life sales calls. Training online instead of on-site can cut travel and other training costs, and it takes up less of a salesperson's selling time. It also makes on-demand training available to salespeople, letting them train as little or as much as needed, whenever and wherever needed. Although most online training is web-based, companies now offer on-demand training from anywhere via almost any mobile device.

Many companies are now using imaginative new digital techniques to make sales training more efficient and effective—and sometimes even more fun. For example, learning solutions company Bottom-Line Performance has developed a digital game-based sales-training tool called Knowledge Guru, which helps salespeople learn and remember key product, company, and customer facts as well as selling skills and processes.[12]

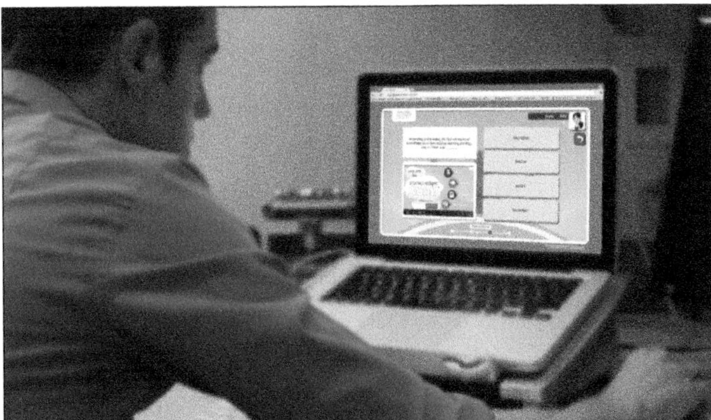

>> E-training can make sales training more effective—and more engaging. BLP's game-based sales-training tool—called Knowledge Guru—helps sales people learn key product, company, and customer facts as well as selling skills and processes.

Bottom-Line Performance

Using Knowledge Guru, companies can create single-pass games that teach foundational knowledge to new salespeople or for new products or extended-play games with performance challenges for teaching new selling skills. >> Salespeople can play the learning games alone or in competition with others, offline or online on a smartphone, tablet, or desktop. All the while, sales trainers can track individual salesperson learning performance. Several *Fortune* 500 companies use Knowledge Guru to add fun and engagement to training tasks that can sometimes be dull or intimidating. For example, IT networking company Cisco Systems uses Knowledge Guru as part of each module within its certified sales associate program. According to a Cisco program manager who helped introduce Knowledge Guru into the program, "Before they can work with customers, new [sales] associates must obtain a deep knowledge of our architectures and technologies. Knowledge Guru is essential to reinforcing this technical knowledge, and participants have rated Knowledge Guru highly as a learning tool." Most important, the game really works, helping salespeople achieve an average retention rate of 87 percent against training objectives across all Cisco users.

Compensating Salespeople

To attract good salespeople, a company must have an appealing compensation plan. Compensation consists of four elements: a fixed amount, a variable amount, expenses, and fringe benefits. The fixed amount, usually a salary, gives the salesperson some stable income. The variable amount, which might be commissions or bonuses based on sales performance, rewards the salesperson for greater effort and success.

>> A sales force compensation plan can both motivate salespeople and direct their activities. Compensation should direct salespeople toward activities that are consistent with the overall sales force and marketing objectives. For example, if the strategy is to acquire new business, grow rapidly, and gain market share, the compensation plan might include a larger commission component, coupled with a new account bonus to encourage high sales performance and new account development. In contrast, if the goal is to maximize current account profitability, the compensation plan might contain a larger base-salary component with additional incentives for current account sales or customer satisfaction.

>> Sales force compensation: A good compensation plan both motivates salespeople and directs their activities.

Luca Bertolli/123RF

In fact, more and more companies are moving away from high-commission plans that may drive salespeople to make short-term grabs for business. They worry that a salesperson who is pushing too hard to close a deal may ruin the customer relationship. Instead, companies are designing compensation plans that reward salespeople for building customer relationships and growing the long-run value of each customer.

When times get tough economically, some companies are tempted to cut costs by reducing sales compensation. However, although some cost-cutting measures make sense when business is sluggish, cutting sales force compensation across the board is usually an action of last resort. Top salespeople are always in demand, and paying them less might mean losing them at a time when they are needed most. Thus, short-changing key salespeople can result in short-changing important customer relationships. If the company must reduce its compensation expenses, rather than making across-the-board cuts, companies should continue to pay top performers well while turning loose low performers.

Supervising and Motivating Salespeople

New salespeople need more than a territory, compensation, and training—they need supervision and motivation. The goal of *supervision* is to help salespeople "work smart" by doing the right things in the right ways. The goal of *motivation* is to encourage salespeople to "work hard" and energetically toward sales force goals. If salespeople work smart and work hard, they will realize their full potential—to their own and the company's benefit.

Supervising Salespeople

Companies vary in how closely they supervise their salespeople. Many help salespeople identify target customers and set call objectives. Some may also specify how much time the sales force should spend prospecting for new accounts and set other time management priorities. One tool is the weekly, monthly, or annual *call plan* that shows which customers and prospects to call on and which activities to carry out. Another tool is *time-and-duty analysis*.

In addition to time spent selling, the salesperson spends time planning, traveling, in meetings, processing orders, and doing administrative chores. Surprisingly, studies show that, on average, salespeople spend only 37 percent of their time on active selling.[13] Companies are always looking for ways to save time—simplifying administrative duties, developing better sales-call and routing plans, supplying more and better customer information, and using phone, email, online, or mobile conferencing instead of traveling.

>> **Sales force automation: To help salespeople work more efficiently and effectively anytime, anywhere, companies routinely equip their salespeople with laptops or tablets, smartphones, wireless connections, videoconferencing technologies, and customer relationship management software.**
kantver/123RF

Many firms have adopted *sales force automation systems*: computerized, digitized sales force operations that let salespeople work more effectively anytime, anywhere. >> Companies now routinely equip their salespeople with laptops or tablets, smartphones, wireless connections, videoconferencing technologies, and customer-contact and relationship management software. Armed with these technologies, salespeople can more effectively and efficiently profile customers and prospects, analyze and forecast sales, engage customers, make presentations, prepare sales and expense reports, and manage account relationships. The result is better time management, improved customer service, lower sales costs, and higher sales performance. In all, technology has reshaped the ways in which salespeople carry out their duties and engage customers.

Motivating Salespeople

Beyond directing salespeople, sales managers must also motivate them. Some salespeople will do their best without any special urging from management. To them, selling may be the most fascinating job in the world. But selling can also be frustrating. Salespeople often work alone, and they must sometimes travel away from home. They may also face aggressive competing salespeople and difficult customers. Therefore, salespeople often need special encouragement to do their best.

Management can boost sales force morale and performance through its organizational climate, sales quotas, and positive incentives. *Organizational climate* describes the feeling that salespeople have about their opportunities, value, and rewards for a good performance. Some companies treat salespeople as if they are not very important, so performance suffers accordingly. Other companies treat their salespeople as valued contributors and allow virtually unlimited opportunity for income and promotion. Not surprisingly, these companies enjoy higher sales force performance and less turnover.

Sales quota
A standard that states the amount a salesperson should sell and how sales should be divided among the company's products.

Many companies motivate their salespeople by setting **sales quotas**—standards stating the amount they should sell and how sales should be divided among the company's products. Compensation is often related to how well salespeople meet their quotas. Companies also use various *positive incentives* to increase the sales force effort. *Sales meetings* provide social occasions, breaks from the routine, chances to meet and talk with "company brass," and opportunities to air feelings and identify with a larger group. Companies also sponsor *sales contests* to spur the sales force to make a selling effort above and beyond what is normally expected. Other incentives include honors, merchandise and cash awards, trips, and profit-sharing plans.

Evaluating Salespeople and Sales Force Performance

We have thus far described how management communicates what salespeople should be doing and how it motivates them to do it. This process requires good feedback, which means getting regular information about salespeople to evaluate their performance.

Management gets information about its salespeople in several ways. The most important source is *sales reports*, including weekly or monthly work plans and longer-term territory marketing plans. Salespeople also write up their completed activities on *call reports* and turn in *expense reports* for which they are partly or wholly reimbursed. The company can also monitor the sales and profit performance data in the salesperson's territory. Additional information comes from personal observation, customer surveys, and talks with other salespeople.

Using various sales force reports and other information, sales management evaluates the members of the sales force. It evaluates salespeople on their ability to "plan their work and work their plan." Formal evaluation forces management to develop and communicate clear standards for judging performance. It also provides salespeople with constructive feedback and motivates them to perform well.

On a broader level, management should evaluate the performance of the sales force as a whole. Is the sales force accomplishing its customer relationship, sales, and profit objectives? Is it working well with other areas of the marketing and company organization? Are sales force costs in line with outcomes? As with other marketing activities, the company wants to measure its *return on sales investment.*

Author Comment
Like just about everything else these days, selling has been affected in a big way by digital technologies. Today's sales forces are mastering the use of online, mobile, and social media tools to engage business customers, build relationships, and make sales.

Social Selling: Online, Mobile, and Social Media Tools

Social selling
Using online, mobile, and social media to engage customers, build stronger customer relationships, and augment sales performance.

The fastest-growing sales trend is the explosion in **social selling**—the use of online, mobile, and social media to engage customers, build stronger customer relationships, and augment sales performance. Digital sales force technologies are creating exciting avenues for connecting with and engaging customers. Some analysts even predict that the internet will mean the death of person-to-person selling, as salespeople are ultimately replaced by websites, online social media, mobile apps, video and conferencing technologies, AI-driven sales assistants, and other tools that allow direct customer contact. Such predictions are much overstated. Online and social media technologies won't likely make salespeople obsolete (see Marketing at Work 13.1). However, digital technologies are rapidly changing the role of face-to-face selling.

When used properly, digital technologies can make salespeople more productive and effective. They provide powerful tools for identifying and learning about prospects, engaging customers, creating customer value, closing sales, and nurturing customer relationships. Social selling technologies can produce big organizational benefits for sales forces. They help conserve salespeople's valuable time, save travel dollars, and give salespeople new vehicles for selling and servicing accounts.

Social selling hasn't really changed the fundamentals of selling. Sales forces have always taken the primary responsibility for reaching out to and engaging customers and managing customer relationships. Now, more of that is being done digitally. However, because online and social media are dramatically changing the customer buying process, they are also changing the selling process. In today's digital world, many customers no longer rely as much as they once did on information and assistance provided by salespeople. Instead, they carry out more of the buying process on their own—especially the early stages. Increasingly, they use online and social media resources to analyze their own problems, research solutions, get advice from colleagues, and rank buying options before ever speaking to a salesperson. One study of business buyers found that 94 percent of buyers start their searches online and that, on average, buyers completed nearly 60 percent of the buying process before contacting a supplier.[14]

Thus, today's customers have much more control over the sales process than they had in the days when brochures, pricing, and product advice were available only from sales reps. Customers can now browse corporate websites and social media sites to identify and qualify sellers. They can hobnob with other buyers on social media such as LinkedIn, Twitter, or Facebook to share experiences, identify solutions, and evaluate products they are considering.

As a result, if and when salespeople do enter the buying process, customers often know almost as much about a company's products as the salespeople do. And when customers do call in salespeople, they are more often doing it digitally, with the expectation of real-time engagement. These days, they want more than product and pricing information from salespeople—they want problem solving and solutions. "Today, 68 percent of B2B buyers prefer doing business online versus with a salesperson," says one sales consultant, "and when they engage with sales, they want that experience to be in a more problem-solving, consultative manner."[15]

In response to this new digital buying environment, sellers are reorienting their selling processes around the new customer buying process. They are "going where customers are"—social media, web forums, online communities, blogs—in order to engage customers earlier. They are engaging customers not just where and when they are buying but also where and when they are learning about and evaluating what they will buy.

Salespeople now routinely use digital tools that monitor customer social media exchanges to spot trends, identify prospects, and learn what customers would like to

MARKETING AT WORK 13.1

B-to-B Salespeople: In This Digital and Social Media Age, Who Needs Them Anymore?

It's hard to imagine a world without salespeople. But according to some analysts, there will be a lot fewer of them a decade from now. With the explosion of the internet, mobile devices, social media, and other technologies that link customers directly with companies, they reason, who needs face-to-face selling anymore? According to the doubters, salespeople are rapidly being replaced by websites, email, mobile apps, blogs, video sharing, virtual trade shows, social media, AI agents, and a host of other digital-age interaction tools.

Research firm Forrester recently predicted a 22 percent decline in the number of B-to-B sales reps in the United States within five years—that's one in five sales reps out of a job. "The world no longer needs salespeople," one doomsayer boldly proclaimed. "Sales is a dying profession and soon will be as outmoded as oil lamps and the rotary phone."

So, is business-to-business selling really dying? Will the internet, mobile technologies, social media, and AI reps replace the age-old art of selling face-to-face? To most sales analysts, the answer is a resounding "no." "A lot of people who are experts in sales... would predict the fall of the sales rep," says one sales expert. "I hear people say that and I think, 'no way.'"

Most experts do agree on one thing: Technology is radically transforming the selling profession. Today's revolutionary changes in how people communicate are affecting every aspect of business, and selling is no exception. But digital technologies won't soon replace person-to-person buying and selling. Technology can greatly enhance the selling process but it can't replace many of the functions that salespeople perform. "The internet can take orders and disseminate content, but what it can't do is discover customer needs," says another sales expert. "It can't build relationships, and it can't prospect on its own." Adds another, "Someone must define the company's value proposition and unique message and communicate it to the market, and that person is the sales rep."

What is dying, however, is the account-maintenance role—the order taker who stops by the customer's office on Friday and says, "Hey, got anything for me?" Likewise, there's not much of a future for explainers, reps who simply convey product and service information that can be obtained more quickly and easily online. Such salespeople are not creating value and can easily be replaced by automation. However, salespeople who excel at new customer acquisition, relationship management, problem solving, and account growth with existing customers will always be in high demand. And digital technologies will only make those salespeople better.

There's no doubt about it—technology is transforming the selling profession. Instead of relying on salespeople for basic information and education, customers can now do much of their own prepurchase research via websites, online searches, phone apps, social media contacts, and other venues. Many customers now start the sales process online and do their homework about problems, competing products, and suppliers before the first sales meeting ever takes place.

According to one survey, business buyers are at least 60 percent of the way through the buying process by the time they reach out to a vendor. They don't need basic information or product education; they need solutions and new insights. So today's salespeople need to excel at solving customer problems and building relationships. In fact, even as lower-order sales jobs disappear in coming years, jobs for such consultant-type sales reps are expected to grow at a healthy clip.

Beyond the mechanics of the selling process, buying and selling involve emotional exchanges as well as transactional

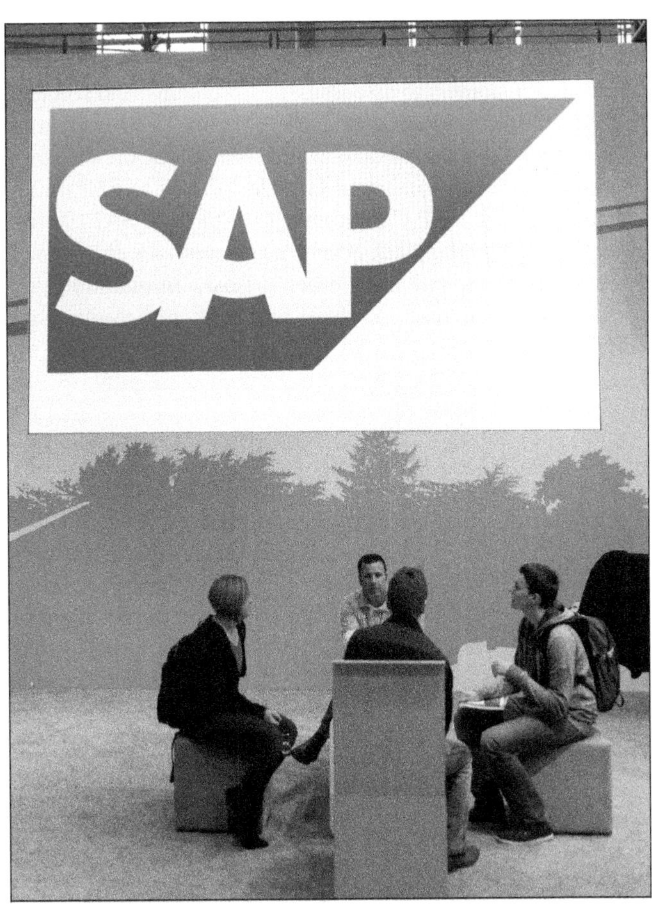

>> B-to-B online selling: SAP's online, community-powered social media and mobile marketplace—called SAP Community—can help to build customer engagement and generate buying interest and sales. But rather than replacing salespeople, such efforts extend their reach and effectiveness.

FocusEurope/Alamy Stock Photo

ones. Even with new artificial intelligence applications that put an almost-human face on sales force automation, digital technologies still can't replace the human touch—the empathy, instinct, and understanding that's essential to good selling. Rather than replacing salespeople, technology is augmenting them. Today's top salespeople aren't really doing anything fundamentally new. They've always done customer research, problem solving, social networking, and relationship building. Today, however, they are doing it on steroids, using a new kit of high-tech digital tools and applications.

For example, many companies have moved rapidly into online-community-based selling. Case in point: Enterprise-software company SAP has created its own online, community-powered social media and mobile marketplace called SAP Community. It consists of customers, SAP software experts, partners, and almost anyone else who wants to join. Established less than a decade ago, SAP Community grew quickly, today consisting of millions of users in more than 200 countries, extending across a broad online spectrum—a dedicated website, mobile apps, Twitter channels, LinkedIn groups, Facebook and Google+ pages, YouTube channels, and more. SAP Community has grown into hundreds of "solution storefronts," where visitors can "discover, evaluate, and buy" software solutions and services from SAP and its partners. SAP Community also lets users rate and share the solutions and advice they get from other community members.

As SAP Community has grown, what was originally seen as a place for customers to discuss issues, problems, and solutions has turned into a significant point of sale. The information, give-and-take discussions, and conversations at the site draw in customers, even for big-ticket sales of $20 to $30 million or more. In fact, SAP Community gave birth to SAP Store, a gigantic SAP marketplace where customers can engage with SAP, its partners, and each other to share information, post comments and reviews, discover problems, and evaluate and buy SAP solutions.

However, although the SAP Store draws in new potential customers and takes them through many of the initial stages of product discovery and evaluation, it doesn't replace SAP's or its partners' salespeople. Instead, it extends their reach and effectiveness. Its real value is the flood of sales leads it creates for the SAP and partner sales forces. Once prospective customers have discovered, discussed, and evaluated SAP solutions online, SAP invites them to initiate contact, request a proposal, or start the negotiation process. That's where the person-to-person selling begins.

All this suggests that B-to-B selling isn't dying, it's just changing. Now more than ever, salespeople must blend more traditional approaches with new digital experiences. The tools and techniques may be different as sales forces leverage and adapt to selling in the digital and social media age. But B-to-B marketers still need strong sales teams comprised of salespeople who can engage customers, discover customer needs, solve customer problems, and build relationships. Especially for those big-ticket B-to-B sales, "all the new technology may make it easier to sell by building strong ties to customers even before the first sit-down, but when the signature hits the dotted line, there will be a sales rep there."

Sources: Tim Colter, "What the Future Science of B2B Sales Growth Looks Like," McKinsey, January 2018, accessed at www.mckinsey.com/business-functions/marketing-and-sales/our-insights/what-the-future-science-of-b2b-sales-growth-looks-like; Ian Altman, "Are Salespeople Becoming Obsolete," *Forbes*, May 16, 2017, www.forbes.com/sites/ianaltman/2017/05/16/are-sales-people-becoming-obsolete/#198567e03e93; Lain Chroust Ehmann, "Sales Up!," *SellingPower*, January/February 2011, p. 40; Robert McGarvey, "Sales Up!" *SellingPower*, March 7, 2011, p. 48; John Ellett, "SAP's Success Formula for B2B Social Selling," *Forbes*, April 1, 2016, www.forbes.com/sites/johnellett/2016/04/01/saps-success-formula-for-btob-social-selling/#1ecd7ec213cb; Kurt Shaver, "How SAP Is Winning with Social Selling," *Vengreso*, November 10, 2017, https://vengreso.com/blog/how-sap-is-winning-social-selling; Andy Hoar, "The Death of a (B2B) Salesman," Forrester, May 11, 2017, https://go.forrester.com/what-it-means/ep12-death-b2b-salesman/; and www.sapstore.com/and www.sap.com/community.html, accessed October 2018.

---

buy, how they feel about a vendor, and what it would take to make a sale. They generate lists of prospective customers from online databases and social networking sites, such as InsideView, Hoovers, and LinkedIn. They create dialogues when prospective customers visit their web and social media sites through live chats with the sales team. They use internet conferencing tools such as WebEx, Zoom, GoToMeeting, or TelePresence to talk live with customers about products and services. They provide videos and other information on their YouTube channels and Facebook pages.

Today's sales forces have also ramped up their own use of digital content and social media to engage customers throughout the buying process. A recent survey of business-to-business marketers found that, although they have recently cut back on traditional media and event spending, they are investing more in social media, ranging from proprietary online customer communities to webinars and social media and mobile applications. Consider Makino, a leading manufacturer of metal cutting and machining technology:[16]

>> There's a hot new video on YouTube these days, featured at the Makino Machine Tools YouTube channel. It shows a Makino five-axis vertical machining center in action, with metal chips flying as the machinery mills a new industrial part. Sound exciting? Probably not to you. But to the right industrial customer, the video is downright spellbinding. YouTube is just one of a wide variety of

>> Social selling: Machine tool manufacturer Makino engages customers through extensive digital content and social media, which complement sales force efforts to engage customers and build product–customer relationships.

Courtesy of Makino

social media initiatives that Makino uses to complement its salespeople in their efforts to engage and inform customers and enhance customer relationships. For example, Makino hosts an ongoing series of industry-specific webinars that position the company as an industry thought leader. Makino produced and archived hundreds webinars on topics ranging from how to get the most out of your machine tools to how metal-cutting processes are done. Webinar content is tailored to specific industries, such as aerospace or medical, and is promoted through carefully targeted online ads and email invitations. The webinars help to build Makino's customer database, generate sales leads, build customer relationships, and prepare the way for salespeople by serving up relevant information and educating customers online. Makino also uses Facebook, YouTube, and Twitter to inform customers and prospects about the latest Makino innovations and events and to demonstrate the company's machines in action. Such digital content and social media don't replace salespeople. Instead, they help salespeople build even more fruitful customer relationships. When it comes to B-to-B selling these days, Makino has learned, social marketing is *the* space to be.

Ultimately, social selling technologies are helping to make sales forces more efficient, cost-effective, and productive. The technologies help salespeople do what good salespeople have always done—build customer relationships by solving customer problems—but do it better, faster, and cheaper.

However, social selling also has some drawbacks. For starters, it's not cheap. But even more, there are some things you just can't present or teach via the internet—things that require personal engagement, insight, and interaction. For these reasons, some technology experts recommend that sales executives use online and social media technologies to spot prospects and opportunities, provide information, maintain customer contact, and make preliminary client sales presentations but resort to old-fashioned, face-to-face meetings when the time draws near to close a big deal.

LINKING THE CONCEPTS

Take a break to reexamine your thoughts about salespeople and sales management.

- Again, when someone says "salesperson," what image comes to mind? Have your perceptions of salespeople changed after what you've read in the chapter so far? If so, how? Be specific.
- Find and talk with someone employed in professional sales. Ask about and report on how this salesperson's company designs its sales force and recruits, selects, trains, compensates, supervises, and evaluates its salespeople. Would you like to work as a salesperson for this company?

Author Comment
So far, we've examined how sales management develops and implements overall sales force strategies and programs. In this section, we'll look at how individual salespeople and sales teams sell to customers and build relationships with them.

The Personal Selling Process

OBJECTIVE 13-3 Discuss the personal selling process, distinguishing between transaction-oriented marketing and relationship marketing.

Selling process
The steps that salespeople follow when selling, which include prospecting and qualifying, preapproach, approach, presentation and demonstration, handling objections, closing, and follow-up.

We now turn from designing and managing a sales force to the personal selling process. The **selling process** consists of several steps that salespeople must master. These steps focus on the goal of getting new customers and obtaining orders from them. However, most salespeople spend much of their time maintaining existing accounts and building long-term customer relationships. We will discuss the relationship aspect of the personal selling process in a later section.

Steps in the Selling Process

As shown in >> **Figure 13.2**, the selling process consists of seven steps: prospecting and qualifying, preapproach, approach, presentation and demonstration, handling objections, closing, and follow-up.

Prospecting and Qualifying

Prospecting
The sales step in which a salesperson or company identifies qualified potential customers.

The first step in the selling process is **prospecting**—identifying qualified potential customers. Approaching the right customers is crucial to selling success. Salespeople don't want to call on just any potential customers. They want to call on those who are most likely to appreciate and respond to the company's value proposition—those the company can serve well and profitably.

A salesperson must often approach many prospects to get only a few sales. Although the company supplies some leads, salespeople need skill in finding their own. The best source is referrals. Salespeople can ask current customers for referrals and cultivate other referral sources, such as suppliers, dealers, noncompeting salespeople, and online or social media contacts. They can also search for prospects in directories or on the internet and track down leads using the phone, email, and social media. Or, as a last resort, they can drop in unannounced on various offices (a practice known as *cold calling*).

Salespeople also need to know how to *qualify* leads—that is, how to identify the good ones and screen out the poor ones. Prospects can be qualified by looking at their financial ability, volume of business, special needs, location, and possibilities for growth.

Preapproach

Preapproach
The sales step in which a salesperson learns as much as possible about a prospective customer before making a sales call.

Before calling on a prospect, the salesperson should learn as much as possible about the organization (what it needs, who is involved in the buying) and its buyers (their characteristics and buying styles). This step is known as **preapproach**. A successful sale begins long before the salesperson makes initial contact with a prospect. Preapproach begins with good research and preparation. The salesperson can consult standard industry and online sources, acquaintances, and others to learn about the company. He or she can scour the prospect's web and social media sites for information about its products, buyers, and buying processes. Then the salesperson must apply the research gathered to develop a customer strategy.

The salesperson should set *call objectives*, which may be to qualify the prospect, gather information, or make an immediate sale. Another task is to determine the best approach, which might be a personal visit, a phone call, an email, or a text or tweet. The ideal timing should be considered carefully because many prospects are busiest at certain times of the day or week. Finally, the salesperson should give thought to an overall sales strategy for the account.

Approach

Approach
The sales step in which a salesperson meets the customer for the first time.

During the **approach** step, the salesperson should know how to meet and greet the buyer and get the relationship off to a good start. The approach might take place offline or online,

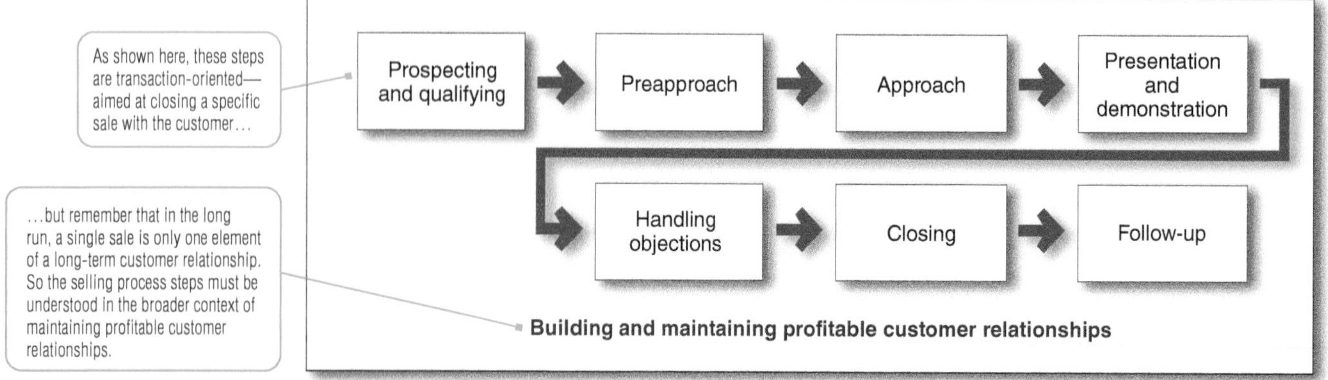

>> **Figure 13.2 Steps in the Selling Process**

in-person or via digital conferencing or social media. This step involves the salesperson's appearance, opening lines, and follow-up remarks. The opening lines should be positive to build goodwill from the outset. This opening might be followed by some key questions to learn more about the customer's needs or by showing a display or sample to attract the buyer's attention and curiosity. As in all stages of the selling process, listening to the customer is crucial.

Presentation and Demonstration

Presentation
The sales step in which a salesperson tells the "value story" to the buyer, showing how the company's offer solves the customer's problems.

During the **presentation** step of the selling process, the salesperson tells the "value story" to the buyer, showing how the company's offer solves the customer's problems. The *customer-solution approach* fits better with today's relationship marketing focus than does a hard sell or glad-handing approach.

The goal should be to show how the company's products and services fit the customer's needs. Buyers today want insights and solutions, not smiles; results, not razzle-dazzle. Moreover, buyers don't want just products; they want to know how those products will add value to their businesses. They want salespeople who listen to their concerns, understand their needs, and respond with the right products and services.

But before salespeople can *present* customer solutions, they must *develop* solutions to present. The solutions approach calls for good listening and problem-solving skills. The qualities that buyers *dislike most* in salespeople include being pushy, late, deceitful, unprepared, disorganized, or overly talkative. The qualities they *value most* include good listening, empathy, honesty, dependability, thoroughness, and follow-through. >> Great salespeople know how to sell, but more important, they know how to listen and build strong customer relationships. According to an old sales adage, "You have two ears and one mouth. Use them proportionally." A classic ad from office products maker Boise Cascade makes the listening point. It shows a Boise salesperson with huge ears drawn on. "With Boise, you'll notice a difference right away, especially with our sales force," says the ad. "At Boise ... our account representatives have the unique ability to listen to your needs."

>> **Great salespeople know how to sell, but more important, they know how to listen and build strong customer relationships.**

Tony Garcia/Getty Images

Finally, salespeople must also plan their presentation methods. Good interpersonal communication skills count when it comes to engaging customers and making effective sales presentations. However, the current media-rich and cluttered communications environment presents many new challenges for sales presenters. Today's information-overloaded customers demand richer presentation experiences. For their part, presenters now face multiple distractions during presentations from mobile phones, text messages, and other digital competition. As a result, salespeople must deliver their messages in more engaging and compelling ways.

Thus, today's salespeople are employing advanced presentation technologies that allow for full multimedia presentations to only one or a few people. The venerable old sales presentation flip chart has been replaced with tablets, sophisticated presentation software, online presentation technologies, interactive whiteboards, and digital projectors.

Handling Objections

Handling objections
The sales step in which a salesperson seeks out, clarifies, and overcomes any customer objections to buying.

Customers almost always have objections during the presentation or when asked to place an order. The objections can be either logical or psychological, and they are often unspoken. In **handling objections**, the salesperson should use a positive approach, seek out hidden objections, ask the buyer to clarify any objections, take objections as opportunities to provide more information, and turn the objections into reasons for buying. Every salesperson needs training in the skills of handling objections.

Closing

Closing
The sales step in which a salesperson asks the customer for an order.

After handling the prospect's objections, the salesperson next tries to close the sale. However, some salespeople do not get around to **closing** or don't handle it well. They may lack confidence, feel guilty about asking for the order, or fail to recognize the right moment to close the sale. Salespeople should know how to recognize closing signals from the buyer, including physical actions, comments, and questions. For example, the customer might sit forward and nod approvingly or ask about prices and credit terms.

Salespeople can use any of several closing techniques. They can ask for the order, review points of agreement, offer to help write up the order, ask whether the buyer wants this model or that one, or note that the buyer will lose out if the order is not placed now. The salesperson may offer the buyer special reasons to close, such as a lower price, an extra quantity at no charge, or additional services.

Follow-Up

Follow-up
The sales step in which a salesperson follows up after the sale to ensure customer satisfaction and repeat business.

The last step in the selling process—**follow-up**—is necessary if the salesperson wants to ensure customer satisfaction and repeat business. Right after closing, the salesperson should complete any details on delivery time, purchase terms, and other matters. The salesperson then should schedule a follow-up call after the buyer receives the initial order to make sure proper installation, instruction, and servicing occur. This visit would reveal any problems, assure the buyer of the salesperson's interest, and reduce any buyer concerns that might have arisen since the sale.

Personal Selling and Managing Customer Relationships

The steps in the just-described selling process are *transaction oriented*—their aim is to help salespeople close a specific sale with a customer. But in most cases, the company is not simply seeking a sale. Rather, it wants to engage the customer over the long haul in a mutually profitable *relationship*. The sales force usually plays an important role in customer relationship building. Thus, as shown in Figure 13.2, the selling process must be understood in the context of building and maintaining profitable customer relationships. Moreover, as discussed in a previous section, today's buyers are increasingly moving through the early stages of the buying process themselves, before ever engaging sellers. Salespeople must adapt their selling process to match the new buying process. That means discovering and engaging customers on a relationship basis rather than a transaction basis.

Successful sales organizations recognize that winning and keeping accounts requires more than making good products and directing the sales force to close lots of sales. If the company wishes only to close sales and capture short-term business, it can do this by simply slashing its prices to meet or beat those of competitors. Instead, most companies want their salespeople to practice *value selling*—demonstrating and delivering superior customer value and capturing a return on that value that is fair for both the customer and the company.

Unfortunately, in the heat of closing sales, salespeople too often take the easy way out by cutting prices rather than selling value. >> Sales management's challenge is to transform salespeople from customer advocates for price cuts into company advocates for value. Here's how Rockwell Automation sells value and relationships rather than price:[17]

>> Value selling: Sales management's challenge is to transform salespeople from customer advocates for price cuts into company advocates for value.
almagami/123RF

> Under pressure from Walmart to lower its prices, a condiment producer asked several competing supplier representatives—including Rockwell Automation sales rep Jeff Policicchio—to help it find ways to reduce its operating costs. After spending a day in the customer's plant, Policicchio quickly put his finger on the major problem: Production was suffering because of downtime due to poorly performing pumps on the customer's 32 large

condiment tanks. Quickly gathering cost and usage data, Policicchio used his Rockwell Automation laptop value-assessment tool to develop an effective solution for the customer's pump problem.

The next day, as he and competing reps presented their cost-reduction proposals to plant management, Policicchio offered the following value proposition: "With this Rockwell Automation pump solution, through less downtime, reduced administrative costs in procurement, and lower spending on repair parts, your company will save at least $16,268 per pump—on up to 32 pumps—relative to our best competitor's solution." Compared with competitors' proposals, Policicchio's solution carried a higher initial price. However, no competing rep offered more than fuzzy promises about possible cost savings. Most simply lowered their prices.

Impressed by Policicchio's value proposition—despite its higher initial price—the plant managers opted to buy and try one Rockwell Automation pump. When the pump performed even better than predicted, the customer ordered all of the remaining pumps. By demonstrating tangible value rather than simply selling on price, Policicchio not only landed the initial sale but also earned a loyal future customer.

Thus, value selling requires listening to customers, understanding their needs, and carefully coordinating the whole company's efforts to create lasting relationships based on customer value.

Author Comment
Sales promotion is the most short-term of the promotion mix tools. Whereas advertising or personal selling says "buy," sales promotions say "buy now."

Sales Promotion

OBJECTIVE 13-4 Explain how sales promotion campaigns are developed and implemented.

Personal selling and advertising often work closely with another promotion tool: sales promotion. **Sales promotion** consists of short-term incentives to encourage the purchase or sales of a product or service. Whereas advertising offers reasons to buy a product or service, sales promotion offers reasons to buy *now*.

Sales promotion
Short-term incentives to encourage the purchase or sale of a product or a service.

Examples of sales promotions are found everywhere. A freestanding insert in the Sunday newspaper contains a coupon offering $2 off Seventh Generation laundry detergent. >> A Sunday newspaper ad from your local Orange Leaf frozen yogurt store offers "Buy 1 Get 1 Free" and "20% off your next purchase." The end-of-the-aisle display in the local supermarket tempts impulse buyers with a wall of Coca-Cola cases—four 12-packs for $12. Buy a new Samsung tablet and get a free memory upgrade. A hardware store chain receives a 10 percent discount on selected Stihl power lawn and garden tools if it agrees to advertise them in local newspapers. Sales promotion includes a wide variety of promotion tools designed to stimulate earlier or stronger market response.

>> Sales promotions are found everywhere. For example, your Sunday newspaper or favorite magazine is loaded with offers like this one that promote a strong and immediate response.

Orange Leaf Holdings, LLC

The Rapid Growth of Sales Promotion

Sales promotion tools are used by most organizations, including manufacturers, distributors, retailers, and not-for-profit institutions. They are targeted toward final buyers (*consumer promotions*), retailers and wholesalers (*trade promotions*), business customers (*business promotions*), and members of the sales force (*sales force promotions*). In all, by one estimate, sales promotion spending by consumer packaged-goods companies accounts for about 54 percent of all marketing spending.[18]

Several factors have contributed to these high sales promotion levels, particularly in consumer markets. First, inside the company, product managers face great pressures to increase current sales, and they view promotion as an effective short-run sales tool. Second, externally, the company faces stiff competition, and competing brands are increasingly less differentiated. Sales promotion can help to differentiate their offers.

Third, advertising efficiency has declined because of rising costs, media clutter, and legal restraints. Finally, consumers have become very deal oriented. Consumers are demanding lower prices and better deals. Sales promotions can help attract today's more value-oriented consumers.

The heavy use of sales promotion has resulted in *promotion clutter*, which is similar to advertising clutter. With so many products being sold on deal these days, a given promotion runs the risk of being lost in a sea of other promotions, weakening its ability to trigger an immediate purchase. Manufacturers are now searching for ways to rise above the clutter, such as offering larger coupon values, creating more dramatic point-of-purchase displays, or delivering promotions through digital, mobile, and social media. Digital promotions can help drive both in-store and online sales.

In developing a sales promotion program, a company must first set sales promotion objectives and then select the best tools for accomplishing these objectives.

Sales Promotion Objectives

Sales promotion objectives vary widely. Sellers may use *consumer promotions* to urge short-term customer buying or boost customer-brand engagement. Objectives for *trade promotions* include getting retailers to carry new items and more inventory, buy ahead, or promote the company's products and give them more shelf space. *Business promotions* are used to generate business leads, stimulate purchases, reward customers, and motivate salespeople. For the sales force, objectives include getting more sales force support for current or new products and getting salespeople to sign up new accounts.

Sales promotions are usually used together with advertising, personal selling, direct and digital marketing, or other promotion mix tools. Consumer promotions must usually be advertised and can add excitement and pulling power to ads and other marketing content. Trade and business sales promotions support the firm's personal selling process.

When the economy tightens and sales lag, it's tempting to offer deep promotional discounts to spur consumer spending. In general, however, rather than creating only short-term sales or temporary brand switching, sales promotions should help to reinforce the product's position and build long-term customer relationships. If properly designed, every sales promotion tool has the potential to build both short-term excitement and long-term consumer engagement and relationships. Marketers should avoid "quick fix," price-only promotions in favor of promotions that are designed to build brand equity. Examples include the various *frequency marketing programs* and loyalty cards. Most hotels, supermarkets, and airlines offer frequent-guest/buyer/flier programs that give rewards to regular customers to keep them coming back. Such promotional programs can build loyalty through added value rather than discounted prices.

» Customer loyalty programs: An REI membership gives customers exclusive access to deals and limited-edition products and events. More important, it makes them feel like a genuine part of the REI outdoor adventure community.

Keri Miksza

For example, at outdoor outfitter REI, customers can pay a $20 one-time fee to become a lifetime member. » Once members, they receive members-only coupons and deals, access to exclusive limited-edition products and events, and special pricing on certain REI-sponsored travel, services, and classes. Another membership perk is the REI Dividend—an annual year-end 10 percent back on all their eligible purchases. Beyond the perks, the success of REI's membership program lies in its ability to make members feel like a genuine part of the REI outdoor adventure community.

Major Sales Promotion Tools

Many tools can be used to accomplish sales promotion objectives. Descriptions of the main consumer, trade, and business promotion tools follow.

Consumer Promotions

Consumer promotions
Sales promotion tools used to boost short-term customer buying and engagement or enhance long-term customer relationships.

Consumer promotions include a wide range of tools—from samples, coupons, refunds, premiums, and point-of-purchase displays to contests, sweepstakes, and event sponsorships.

Samples are offers of a trial amount of a product. Sampling is the most effective—but most expensive—way to introduce a new product or create new excitement for an existing one. Some samples are free; for others, the company charges a small amount to offset its cost. The sample might be sent by mail, handed out in a store or at a kiosk, attached to another product, or featured in an ad, email, or mobile offer. Samples are sometimes combined into sample packs, which can then be used to promote other products and services. Sampling can be a powerful promotional tool. >> For example, for the past 37 years, Ben & Jerry's has set aside one day each year as Free Cone Day, on which it invites customers to stop by its scoop shops to sample any of a variety of the brand's classic ice cream flavors for free. Around the country, the unique sampling promotion is a huge success, with lines stretching out the doors and around the block at most shops. Officially, Ben & Jerry's uses Free Cone Day to thank its customers for being "so uniquely awesome." But the sampling program also generates tons of buzz and draws new customers into its shops, something that Ben & Jerry's hopes will turn into a habit.

>> **Consumer samples can be a powerful promotion tool. Ben & Jerry's annual Free Cone Day thanks customers for being "so uniquely awesome" and also generates tons of buzz and draws new customer into its scoop shops.**

Helen H. Richardson/Denver Post/Getty Images

Coupons are certificates that save buyers money when they purchase specified products. Most consumers love coupons. U.S. consumer packaged-goods companies distributed 302 billion coupons last year. Consumers redeemed more than 2.1 billion of them for a total savings of more than $3.1 billion.[19] Coupons can promote early trial of a new brand or stimulate sales of a mature brand. However, to combat the increase in coupon clutter, most major consumer goods companies are issuing fewer coupons and targeting them more carefully.

Marketers are also cultivating new outlets for distributing coupons, such as supermarket shelf dispensers, electronic point-of-sale coupon printers, and online and mobile coupon programs. Digital coupons represent today's fastest-growing coupon segment. Digital coupons can be individually targeted and personalized in ways that print coupons can't. Whether printed at home, loaded to a loyalty card, or redeemed via smartphone or other mobile device, digital coupon redemptions are growing much more rapidly the traditional coupon redemptions.[20]

Rebates (or *cash refunds*) are like coupons except that the price reduction occurs after the purchase rather than at the retail outlet. The customer sends proof of purchase to the manufacturer, which then refunds part of the purchase price by mail. For example, Toro ran a clever preseason promotion on some of its snowblower models, offering a rebate if the snowfall in the buyer's market area turned out to be below average. Competitors were not able to match this offer on such short notice, and the promotion was very successful.

Price packs (also called *cents-off deals*) offer consumers savings off the regular price of a product. The producer marks the reduced prices directly on the label or package. Price packs can be single packages sold at a reduced price (such as two for the price of one) or two related products banded together (such as a toothbrush and toothpaste). Price packs are very effective—even more so than coupons—in stimulating short-term sales.

Premiums are goods offered either free or at low cost as an incentive to buy a product, ranging from toys included with kids' products to phone cards and DVDs. A premium may come inside the package (in-pack), outside the package (on-pack), or through the mail. For example, over the years, McDonald's has offered a variety of premiums in its Happy Meals—from Shopkins to Pokemon characters. Customers can visit www.happymeal.com to play games, read e-books, and watch commercials associated with the current Happy Meal sponsor.[21]

Advertising specialties, also called *promotional products*, are useful articles imprinted with an advertiser's name, logo, or message that are given as gifts to consumers. Typical items include T-shirts and other apparel, pens, coffee mugs, calendars, key rings, tote bags, coolers, golf balls, and caps. U.S. marketers spent more than $21 billion on advertising specialties last year. Such items can be very effective. The "best of them stick around for months, subtly burning a brand name into a user's brain," notes a promotional products expert.[22]

Point-of-purchase (POP) promotions include displays and demonstrations that take place at the point of sale. Think of your last visit to the local Costco, Walmart, or Bed Bath & Beyond. Chances are good that you were tripping over aisle displays, promotional signs, "shelf talkers," or demonstrators offering free tastes of featured food products. Unfortunately, many retailers do not like to handle the hundreds of displays, signs, and posters they receive from manufacturers each year. Manufacturers have therefore responded by offering better POP materials, offering to set them up, and tying them in with television, print, or online messages.

Contests, sweepstakes, and *games* give consumers the chance to win something, such as cash, trips, or goods, by luck or through extra effort. A *contest* calls for consumers to submit an entry—a jingle, guess, suggestion—to be judged by a panel that will select the best entries. A *sweepstakes* calls for consumers to submit their names for a drawing. A *game* presents consumers with something—bingo numbers, missing letters—every time they buy, which may or may not help them win a prize.

All kinds of companies use sweepstakes and contests to create brand attention and boost consumer involvement. For example, furniture retailer West Elm ran a "$5,000 Room Redo Contest" inviting entrants to send short videos showcasing themselves and their spaces with a changed to win a complete one-room makeover valued up to $5,000. And for the past several years, Google's "Doodle 4 Google" contest has invited kids to design a Google logo based on themes such as "If I could invent one thing to make the world a better place" or "What inspires me," with prizes ranging from T-shirts and tablets to a $30,000 college scholarship or $50,000 for the technology program at the winner's school or organization.[23]

Event marketing (or event sponsorships)
Creating a brand-marketing event or serving as a sole or participating sponsor of events created by others.

Finally, marketers can promote their brands through **event marketing (or event sponsorships)**. They can create their own brand-marketing events or serve as sole or participating sponsors of events created by others. The events might include anything from mobile brand tours to festivals, reunions, marathons, concerts, or other sponsored gatherings. Event marketing is huge, and it may be the fastest-growing area of promotion. Effective event marketing links events and sponsorships to a brand's value proposition. And with the social sharing power of today's digital media, even local events can have far-reaching impact. For example, Delta Faucet used an imaginative event to promote its H2Okinetic low-flow showerheads—which use 40 percent less water but work just as well as competing higher-flow models—to its fitness and family-oriented target audience.[24]

> Delta's #HappiMess promotion campaign is based on the insight that some of its customers' happiest moments came from making and overcoming big messes. To show target consumers firsthand how well its low-flow showerheads work under really tough conditions, Delta partnered with Warrior Dash, which sponsored several 5K mud run races around the country over the summer. >> At each event, Delta built a huge custom shower station, complete with 184 Delta showerheads, where mud-soaked competitors could meet and wash off after the race. "Warrior Dash is a great example of a place where people are having fun getting messy," says a senior Delta Faucet senior brand manager. "We want people to celebrate those fun moments having confidence that we have products that will help transform them back to clean." At one event in Indiana, 331 people gathered to shower, setting a Guinness World Record for most people showering simultaneously. After experiencing the showerheads, 75 percent of runners surveyed said they'd consider buying one. The shower stations also included a selfie station. As a result, the event boosted social media activity around Delta's #HappiMess campaign by 85 percent and gave the brand a 50 percent sales lift.

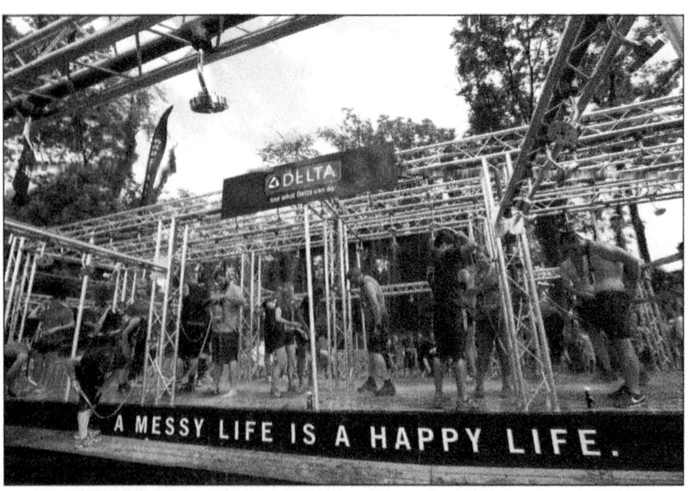

>> Event marketing: As part of its #HappiMess campaign, Delta Faucet used an imaginative event to show target consumers firsthand how well its low-flow showerheads worked under really tough conditions—following a 5K mud run race.

AP Images for Delta Faucet Company

All kinds of brands now hold events. But one-time events are rarely as effective as well-planned event campaigns that tie into a brand's broader promotions and positioning. Consider energy drink maker Red Bull. Called by one business reporter the "mother of all event marketers," Red Bull holds hundreds of events around the globe each year designed to bring the high-octane world of Red Bull to its community of enthusiasts (see Marketing at Work 13.2).

MARKETING AT WORK 13.2

Red Bull: The Mother of All Event Marketers

There's no question: Coca-Cola and PepsiCo dominate the global beverage industry. Each boasts leading brands in almost every category, from carbonated soft drinks to enhanced juice drinks to bottled waters. Last year, Coca-Cola sold more than $35 billion worth of beverages worldwide; PepsiCo was a solid runner-up at nearly $30 billion. Both companies spend hundreds of millions of dollars annually on sophisticated marketing and advertising programs. So how does a smaller company compete effectively with such global powerhouses? The best answer: It doesn't—at least not directly. Instead, it uses a unique marketing approach and runs where the big dogs don't.

That's what Red Bull does. When Red Bull first introduced its energy drink more than 30 years ago, few imagined that it would become the $6.5 billion-a-year success that it is today. Red Bull has succeeded by avoiding head-to-head promotional battles with giants like Coca-Cola and Pepsi. Instead, it has energized brand fans with a unique product, brand personality, and event-marketing approach.

Back in 1987, energy drinks simply didn't exist. If you wanted a quick pick-me-up, about the only options were caffeinated soft drinks or a good old cup of coffee. But Red Bull formulated a new beverage containing a hefty dose of caffeine along with little-known ingredients such as taurine and glucuronolactone. It tasted terrible. But it packed the right punch, producing unique physical-energy and mental-clarity benefits. To make the new beverage even more distinctive, the founders gave it a unique name (Red Bull) and packaged it in a slim 8.3-ounce blue-and-silver can with a distinct red-and-yellow logo. Thus was born a whole new beverage category—energy drinks—with Red Bull as its only player.

The unique Red Bull product demanded equally unique brand positioning and personality, a declaration that this was no ordinary beverage. Red Bull's marketing didn't disappoint. The brand's first and still-only slogan—"Red Bull Gives You Wings"—communicated the product's energy-inducing benefits. More important, it tapped into the forces that moved the brand's narrow target segment—customers seeking to live life in the adrenaline-stoked fast lane.

To reinforce the "Gives You Wings" brand promise and in line with the new brand's meager early finances, Red Bull shunned the big-budget, mass-media advertising common in the beverage industry at the time. Instead, it relied on grassroots, high-octane sports and event marketing. It sponsored extreme sports events and athletes who were overlooked by big beverage competitors but were spiking in popularity with Red Bull's target customers, events such as snowboarding and freestyle motocross and athletes like Shaun White and Travis Pastrana.

In the years since, Red Bull has turned event marketing into a science. Today, the brand holds hundreds of events each year in dozens of sports around the world. Each event features off-the-grid experiences designed to bring the high-octane world of Red Bull to its impassioned community of enthusiasts. Red Bull owns Formula 1 car racing teams and soccer clubs. Its name is plastered all over events such as the Red Bull Crashed Ice World Championship and the annual Red Bull Rampage freeride mountain bike competition. Beyond sports, the company also sponsors lifestyle events in music, dance, fashion, and art.

Red Bull is perhaps best known by some for its massive, highly promoted events intended to reach as many viewers as possible. A classic example was the Red Bull Stratos project, in which extreme skydiver Felix Baumgartner jumped from a helium balloon 128,000 feet (more than 24 miles) above the earth, breaking the sound barrier and numerous other records in the process. The jump also set records for consumer brand engagement. Baumgartner diving into space fit perfectly with Red Bull's "Gives You Wings" brand message. And both Baumgartner's capsule and his space-age jumpsuit were emblazoned with the Red Bull name and logo. More than 8 million people watched the event live on 40 TV stations and 130 digital channels. For months before and after the event, you couldn't see or hear anything about Baumgartner without thinking about Red Bull. And by one estimate, 90 million people worldwide followed the campaign on social media, creating 60 million trusted brand impressions. You just can't buy that kind of consumer engagement in traditional media.

Although Red Bull is known for such massive viral hits, the real bread and butter comes from its constant menu of smaller events. And the bigger purpose of behind Red Bull's non-stop

>> **Event marketing: Red Bull has turned event marketing into a science. It hosts hundreds of events each year designed to bring the high-octane world of Red Bull to its community of enthusiasts.**

Mi Pan/Shutterstock

event machine is to create action-filled fodder for its massive video library. Visitors to the brand's www.redbull.com website won't find so much as a single picture of a Red Bull beverage. Instead, they'll find a cleanly designed, carefully curated video showcase, with a seemingly unending selection of video clips organized by events, athletes, moods, and seasons. With a little browsing, they can view videos of everything from 27-meter ocean cliff dives at its Red Bull's Cliff Diving Series event in Grimstad, Norway, to daredevil freeskiing feats at its Red Bull Cold Rush event in the Colorado mountain peaks, to video documentaries on their extreme sports heroes, to absolutely breathtaking wing suit flights at Red Bull events staged in exotic locations from Monterrey, Mexico, to Hunan Province, China.

Individually, the smaller events and videos don't pack the wallop of the Red Bull Stratos project. The average Red Bull video gets a modest 500,000 views in its first 30 days. But the torrent of events adds up to massive impact. During a recent one-year period, Red Bull uploaded 4,331 videos to 23 channels. Combined, these videos generated more than 2.5 billion views and over 50 million engagements. That's equivalent to more than 60 space jumps every year. That made Red Bull the nation's most-viewed brand for nine of the year's 12 months.

More than just a beverage company, Red Bull today has become a close-knit brand community. Red Bull's event marketing has produced a steady stream of absorbing brand content that engages and entertains brand fans in relevant ways. During the past few years, Red Bull's Media House unit has filmed movies, signed a deal with NBC for a show called *Red Bull Signature Series*, developed reality-TV ideas with big-name producers, become one of the biggest producers of original content on YouTube and Facebook, and loaded its own web and mobile sites with unique content features. "Whenever we [have done] any event, or signed an athlete or executed a project, everything has been put on film or photographed. Stories have been told," says the head of the Red Bull Media House unit. "It's part of the DNA of the brand."

Thus, Red Bull can't compete directly across the board with big-budget brands like Coca-Cola and PepsiCo—it doesn't even try. Then again, given the depth of consumer engagement and loyalty that Red Bull engenders in its own corner of the beverage world, Coke and Pepsi have found it even more difficult to compete with Red Bull in the energy drink segment. Red Bull still owns around 40 percent of the global energy drink category it created, with Coke and Pepsi also-rans.

In the end, although Red Bull events draw large crowds and plenty of media coverage, it's about more than just the events—it's about customer engagement. Event marketing is about creating tactile engagements where people can feel, touch, taste, and experience the brand face-to-face rather than simply reading about or watching it. Red Bull doesn't just sponsor an event—it *is* the event. The brand experience is often as much of the story as the event itself. Through smart event marketing, Red Bull has given its customers—and itself—new wings and a big shot of energy. As one observer puts it, Red Bull is the "mother of all event marketers."

Sources: Mack Collier, "The Power of Being Second: How Red Bull Is Winning the (Content) Marketing Wars," *MackCollier.com*, February 1, 2018, http://tubularinsights.com/red-bull-video-marketing-strategy/; Greg Jarboe, "How Red Bull Quietly Changed Its Video Marketing Strategy," *Tubular Insights*, January 13, 2017, http://tubularinsights.com/red-bull-video-marketing-strategy/; Bruce Weinstein, "Do Not Dump: Make Your Marketing Strategy Story-Based, Not Fact-Based," *Forbes*, April 4, 2018, www.forbes.com/sites/bruceweinstein/2018/04/04/do-not-dump-make-your-marketing-strategy-story-based-not-fact-based/#2bef49bd5427; and www.coca-colacompany.com/investors, www.pepsico.com/investors, and www.redbull.com, accessed October 2018.

Trade Promotions

Trade promotions
Sales promotion tools used to persuade resellers to carry a brand, give it shelf space, and promote it in advertising.

Consumer package goods manufacturers spend nearly four times as much on trade sales promotion as on consumer sales promotion.[25] **Trade promotions** can persuade resellers to carry a brand, give it shelf space, promote it in advertising, and push it to consumers. Shelf space is so scarce these days that manufacturers often have to offer price-offs, allowances, buy back guarantees, or free goods to retailers and wholesalers to get products on the shelf and, once there, to keep them on it.

Manufacturers use several trade promotion tools. Many of the tools used for consumer promotions—contests, premiums, displays—can also be used as trade promotions. Or the manufacturer may offer a straight *discount* off the list price on each case purchased during a stated period of time (also called a *price-off, off-invoice*, or *off-list*). Manufacturers also may offer an *allowance* (usually so much off per case) in return for the retailer's agreement to feature the manufacturer's products in some way. For example, an advertising allowance compensates retailers for advertising the product, whereas a display allowance compensates them for using special displays.

Manufacturers may offer *free goods*, which are extra cases of merchandise, to resellers who buy a certain quantity or who feature a certain flavor or size. They may also offer *push money*—cash or gifts to dealers or their sales forces to "push" the manufacturer's goods. Manufacturers may give retailers free *specialty advertising items* that carry the company's name, such as pens, calendars, memo pads, flashlights, and tote bags.

Business Promotions

Business promotions
Sales promotion tools used to generate business leads, stimulate purchases, reward customers, and motivate salespeople.

Companies spend billions of dollars each year on promotion geared toward industrial customers. **Business promotions** are used to generate business leads, stimulate purchases, reward customers, and motivate salespeople. Business promotions include many of the same tools used for consumer or trade promotions. Here, we focus on two additional major business promotion tools: conventions and trade shows and sales contests.

Many companies and trade associations organize *conventions and trade shows* to promote their products. Firms selling to the industry show their products at the trade show. Vendors at these shows receive many benefits, such as opportunities to find new sales leads, contact customers, introduce new products, meet new customers, sell more to present customers, and educate customers with publications and audiovisual materials. Trade shows also help companies reach many prospects that are not reached through their sales forces.

>> Some trade shows are huge. At this year's Bauma mining and construction equipment trade show, more than 3,400 exhibitors from 58 countries presented their latest product innovations to more than 583,000 attendees from more than 210 countries.

dpa picture alliance/Alamy Stock Photo

Some trade shows are huge. For example, at this year's International Consumer Electronics Show, more than 4,000 exhibitors attracted some 180,000 professional visitors. >> Even more impressive, at the Bauma mining and construction equipment trade show in Munich, Germany, more than 3,400 exhibitors from 58 countries presented their latest product innovations to over 583,000 attendees from more than 210 countries. Total exhibition space equaled about 6.5 million square feet (more than 112 football fields).[26]

A *sales contest* is a contest for salespeople or dealers to motivate them to increase their sales performance over a given period. Sales contests motivate and recognize good company performers, who may receive trips, cash prizes, or other gifts. Some companies award points for performance, which the receiver can turn in for any of a variety of prizes. Sales contests work best when they are tied to measurable and achievable sales objectives (such as finding new accounts, reviving old accounts, or increasing account profitability).

Developing the Sales Promotion Program

Beyond selecting the types of promotions to use, marketers must make several other decisions in designing the full sales promotion program. First, they must determine the *size of the incentive*. A certain minimum incentive is necessary if the promotion is to succeed; a larger incentive will produce more sales response. The marketer also must set *conditions for participation*. Incentives might be offered to everyone or only to select groups.

Marketers must determine how to promote and distribute the promotion program itself. For example, a $2-off coupon could be given out in a package, in an advertisement, at the store, via a website or social media, or in a mobile download. Each distribution method involves a different level of reach and cost. Increasingly, marketers are blending several media into a total campaign concept. The length of the promotion is also important. If the sales promotion period is too short, many prospects (who may not be buying during that time) will miss it. If the promotion runs too long, the deal will lose some of its "act now" force.

Evaluation is also very important. Marketers should work to measure the returns on their sales promotion investments, just as they should seek to assess the returns on other marketing activities. The most common evaluation method is to compare sales before, during, and after a promotion. Marketers should ask: Did the promotion attract new customers or more purchasing from current customers? Can we hold onto these new customers and purchases? Will the long-run customer relationship and sales gains from the promotion justify its costs?

Clearly, sales promotion plays an important role in the total promotion mix. To use it well, the marketer must define the sales promotion objectives, select the best tools, design the sales promotion program, implement the program, and evaluate the results. Moreover, sales promotion must be coordinated carefully with other promotion mix elements within the overall IMC program.

REVIEWING AND EXTENDING THE CONCEPTS

CHAPTER REVIEW AND KEY TERMS

Objectives Review

This chapter is the second of three chapters covering the final marketing mix element—promotion. The previous chapter dealt with overall integrated marketing communications and with advertising and public relations. This chapter investigated personal selling and sales promotion. Personal selling is the interpersonal arm of the communications mix. Sales promotion consists of short-term incentives to encourage the purchase or sale of a product or service.

OBJECTIVE 13-1 Discuss the role of a company's salespeople in engaging customers, creating customer value, and building customer relationships. (pp 406–408)

Most companies use salespeople, and many companies assign them an important role in the marketing mix. For companies selling business products, the firm's sales force works directly with customers. Often, the sales force is the customer's only direct contact with the company and therefore may be viewed by customers as representing the company itself. In contrast, for consumer product companies that sell through intermediaries, consumers usually do not meet salespeople or even know about them. The sales force works behind the scenes, dealing with wholesalers and retailers to obtain their support and helping them become more effective in selling the firm's products.

As an element of the promotion mix, the sales force is very effective in achieving certain marketing objectives and carrying out such activities as prospecting, communicating, selling and servicing, and information gathering. But with companies becoming more market oriented, a customer-focused sales force also works to produce both customer satisfaction and company profit. The sales force plays a key role in engaging customers and developing and managing profitable customer relationships.

OBJECTIVE 13-2 Identify and explain the six major sales force management steps. (pp 408–419)

High sales force costs necessitate an effective sales management process consisting of six steps: designing sales force strategy and structure, recruiting and selecting, training, compensating, supervising, and evaluating salespeople and sales force performance.

In designing a sales force, sales management must address various issues, including what type of sales force structure will work best (territorial, product, customer, or complex structure), sales force size, who will be involved in selling, and how various salespeople and sales-support people will work together (inside or outside sales forces and team selling).

Salespeople must be recruited and selected carefully. In recruiting salespeople, a company may look to the job duties and the characteristics of its most successful salespeople to suggest the traits it wants in new salespeople. It must then look for applicants through recommendations of current salespeople, ads, and the internet and social media as well as college recruitment/placement centers. After the selection process is complete, training programs familiarize new salespeople not only with the art of selling but also with the company's history, its products and policies, and the characteristics of its customers and competitors.

The sales force compensation system helps to reward, motivate, and direct salespeople. In addition to compensation, all salespeople need supervision, and many need continuous encouragement because they must make many decisions and face many frustrations. Periodically, the company must evaluate their performance to help them do a better job. In evaluating salespeople, the company relies on information gathered from sales reports, personal observations, customer surveys, and conversations with other salespeople.

The fastest-growing sales trend is the explosion in social selling—using online, mobile, and social media in selling. Digital technologies are providing salespeople with powerful tools for identifying and learning about prospects, engaging customers, creating customer value, closing sales, and nurturing customer relationships. Many of today's customers no longer rely as much on assistance provided by salespeople. Instead, increasingly, they use online and social media resources to analyze their own problems, research solutions, get advice from colleagues, and rank buying options before ever speaking to a salesperson. In response, sellers are reorienting their selling processes around the new customer buying process. They are using social media, mobile devices, web forums, online communities, blogs, and other digital tools to engage customers earlier and more fully. Ultimately, online, mobile, and social media technologies are helping to make sales forces more efficient, cost-effective, and productive.

OBJECTIVE 13-3 Discuss the personal selling process, distinguishing between transaction-oriented marketing and relationship marketing. (pp 419–423)

Selling involves a seven-step process: prospecting and qualifying, preapproach, approach, presentation and demonstration, handling objections, closing, and follow-up. These steps help marketers close a specific sale and, as such, are transaction oriented. However, a seller's dealings with customers should be guided by the larger concept of relationship marketing. The company's sales force should help to orchestrate a whole-company effort to develop profitable long-term relationships with key customers based on superior customer value and satisfaction.

 **OBJECTIVE 13-4 Explain how sales promotion campaigns are developed and implemented. (pp 423–429)**

Sales promotion campaigns call for setting sales promotion objectives (in general, sales promotions should be *consumer relationship building*); selecting tools; and developing and implementing the sales promotion program by using *consumer promotion tools* (from coupons, refunds, premiums, and point-of-purchase promotions to contests, sweepstakes, and events), *trade promotion tools* (from discounts and allowances to free goods and push money), and *business promotion tools* (conventions, trade shows, and sales contests) as well as determining such things as the size of the incentive, the conditions for participation, how to promote and distribute the promotion package, and the length of the promotion. After this process is completed, the company must evaluate its sales promotion results.

Key Terms

Objective 13-1
Personal selling (p 406)
Salesperson (p 407)

Objective 13-2
Sales force management (p 408)
Territorial sales force structure (p 409)
Product sales force structure (p 409)
Customer (or market) sales force structure (p 409)
Outside sales force (or field sales force) (p 410)
Inside sales force (p 410)
Team selling (p 411)
Sales quota (p 415)
Social selling (p 416)

Objective 13-3
Selling process (p 419)
Prospecting (p 420)
Preapproach (p 420)
Approach (p 420)
Presentation (p 421)
Handling objections (p 421)
Closing (p 422)
Follow-up (p 422)

Objective 13-4
Sales promotion (p 423)
Consumer promotions (p 425)
Event marketing (or event sponsorships) (p 426)
Trade promotions (p 428)
Business promotions (p 429)

DISCUSSION AND CRITICAL THINKING

Discussion Questions

13-1. Define *personal selling,* and discuss its role in a company's promotion mix. (AACSB: Written and Oral Communication; Reflective Thinking)

13-2. Name and explain the major steps in sales force management. (AACSB: Written and Oral Communication)

13-3. What is *social selling*? How are salespeople using digital technologies to benefit their companies? (AACSB: Written and Oral Communication; Reflective Thinking)

13-4. Describe the steps in the personal selling process. How does this process work with engaging customers and building relationships? (AACSB: Written and Oral Communication; Reflective Thinking)

13-5. What is *sales promotion*? Discuss its growth as a short-term consumer promotion tool. (AACSB: Written and Oral Communication)

13-6. Discuss the differences among consumer promotions, trade promotions, and business promotions. Provide examples of the different sales promotion tools that could be used in each promotion campaign. (AACSB: Written and Oral Communication)

Critical Thinking Exercises

13-7. Using the internet, research the characteristics of a successful salesperson. Then think about a recent interaction with a salesperson where you purchased a product. Using the steps in the selling process, outline how the salesperson followed (or did not follow) each of the steps. Did your salesperson have the characteristics of a successful salesperson? (AACSB: Written and Oral Communication; Information Technology; Reflective Thinking)

13-8. You are the district manager for Pureation Beverage Group, a beer and wine distributor. The company has experienced rapid growth and needs to add additional salespeople to its team. Using the sales force management steps in your text, discuss what needs to be done to effectively manage your sales force. Support your position. (AACSB: Written and Oral Communication; Reflective Thinking)

13-9. Evaluate the sales promotion activities of a grocery store in your area. What consumer sales promotions is it using? Is it successful at reaching its target market with effective promotions? (AACSB: Written and Oral Communication; Reflective Thinking)

MINICASES AND APPLICATIONS

Online, Mobile, and Social Media Marketing Kohl's App and Wallet

As consumers increasingly use social media and mobile apps to save money, companies must "go where the consumers are" and offer digital coupons and other sales promotions in those locations. Digital coupons are today's fastest-growing coupon segment. They can be individually targeted and personalized in ways that print coupons can't. Whether printed at home, loaded to a store loyalty card, or redeemed in the store via smartphone app, digital coupon redemptions are growing much more rapidly than traditional coupon redemptions. Retailer Kohl's is cashing in on the trend and sweetening consumer deals by offering digital coupons, Kohl's Cash, and other special online and mobile offers. For example, Kohl's might offer a promotion for $20 off a purchase of $100 or more via an online coupon code to be scanned from a mobile device. Other promotions let shoppers earn Kohl's Cash based on a previous purchase that can be applied to a future purchase. Kohl's Cash can be stacked with other sales in-store and online discounts, giving consumers even deeper discounts on everything from home goods to shoes and apparel for the family. In giving consumers access to so many special savings opportunities, organization and access are key. The Kohl's app houses all coupons, gift cards, special offers, and Kohl's Cash and lets consumers keep all savings options together in one location, making it as easy as possible for shoppers to spend their hard earned money.

13-10. Visit www.kohls.com or download the Kohl's app and choose a product you want to purchase. What coupon codes, deals, or promotions are available? How is the sales promotion program structured? Is this an effective tactic to target consumers? (AACSB: Written and Oral Communication, Information Technology, Reflective Thinking)

13-11. Research other types of apps that rely on smartphones to redeem a sales promotion offer. Explain how they work. (AACSB: Written and Oral Communication; Information Technology; Reflective Thinking)

Marketing Ethics Walking the Customer

In years past, employees at Staples have faced a challenging work environment. According to *The New York Times*, Staples maintained an internal reporting system nicknamed "Market Basket" that carefully tracked all equipment and protection plan add-ons that each sales staff member sold. Staples expected that each salesperson would upsell each transaction by $200 with additional merchandise and warranty contracts. Staples salespeople were trained to push until they got at least three objections. This was a classic hard-sell technique. Sales staff who did not meet their goals were coached. If that didn't work, the underperforming employees faced disciplinary action that could lead to more night and weekend shifts, reduced work hours, or even termination.

Store managers also faced intense scrutiny. They received a clear message that to avoid bringing down a store's Market Basket averages, salespeople should "walk the customer" if they could not be successfully upsold. The customer was informed that the merchandise was not in stock and then would leave the store empty-handed. Salespeople had another option: They could escort customers to an in-store kiosk to place an online order. Online orders were not subject to Staples's key performance indicators (KPI) and were not reported to a store's Market Basket. (For more reading, see David Haggler, "Selling It with Extras, or Not at All," www.nytimes.com/2012/09/09/your-money/sales-incentives-at-staples-draw-complaints-the-haggler.html.)

13-12. A company's sales force creates and communicates customer value by personally engaging customers and building customer relationships. With its Market Basket approach, was Staples focusing on building customer value and relationships? Explain. (AACSB: Written and Oral Communication, Ethical Understanding and Reasoning)

13-13. Find and read Staples's code of ethics online. Is the sales policy outlined above consistent with Staples's ethics policies? Is "walking the customer" a violation of the ethics code? Provide specific examples. (AACSB: Written and Oral Communication, Ethical Understanding and Reasoning)

Marketing by the Numbers Buy One, Get Something Free!

Mountain Goat Cyclery is an independent bicycle retailer in Colorado specializing in mountain bikes. It offers a full line of mountain bikes for men, women, and children as well as accessories and bike repair services. Like many local retailers, it advertises in local media such as newspapers, radio, magazines, and the local news. The owner is considering spending $500 to advertise a summer sales promotion premium offer. For every Diamondback Lux bicycle purchased, the retailer is offering a free Fox Flux mountain bike helmet. It sells the bike for $500, and the retail value of the helmet is $100.

13-14. If Mountain Goat's markup percentage on selling prices is 35 percent, what margin will the retailer realize for each bike purchased during the premium offer? How many additional bikes would Mountain Goat need to sell to break even on this premium offer? Refer to Break-Even and Margin Analysis in Appendix 3: Marketing by the Numbers to learn how to perform this analysis. (AACSB: Communication; Analytic Reasoning; Reflective Thinking)

13-15. Mountain Goat ran the promotion and sold 15 bikes during the promotional period. Assuming the $500 spent on advertising is the only marketing cost associated with this promotion, calculate the net marketing contribution of the promotion. Was the promotion successful? Refer to Net Marketing Contribution in Appendix 3: Marketing by the Numbers to learn how to do this analysis. (AACSB: Analytic Reasoning)

Video Case First Flavor

To view this video case and its accompanying questions, please visit MyLab Marketing.

First Flavor is a start-up company with a unique product. It manufactures great-tasting edible film that can replicate the flavor of just about anything, from an eight-topping pizza to an alcoholic beverage. If you're wondering why a company would make such a product, think of the endless possibilities it allows for consumers to sample the taste of a food or beverage before purchasing it.

Although First Flavor first replicated flavors on thin film in order to market the product as a new method for product sampling, the company is now evaluating many other applications of the technology. This video demonstrates how one product can be marketed in multiple ways.

Company Cases 13 Procter & Gamble/11 Bass Pro Shops

See Appendix 1 for cases appropriate for this chapter.

Case 13, Procter & Gamble: Selling Through Customer Business Development. Using a sales strategy it calls Customer Business Development, P&G succeeds by ensuring that its retail customers succeed.

Case 11, Bass Pro Shops: Creating Nature's Theme Park for People Who Hate to Shop. Bass Pro Shops drives traffic to its super stores by enticing customers with engaging experiences, including special events.

Writing Assignments

13-16. What is social selling, and how is it affecting the sales function in organizations? (AACSB: Communication; Reflective Thinking)

13-17. What is team selling, and why has it become more important? Are there any pitfalls to this approach? (AACSB: Communication; Reflective Thinking)

14 Direct, Online, Social Media, and Mobile Marketing

Objectives Outline

- OBJECTIVE 14-1 **Define *direct and digital marketing* and discuss their rapid growth and benefits to customers and companies.** See: Direct and Digital Marketing (pp 436–438)
- OBJECTIVE 14-2 **Identify and discuss the major forms of direct and digital marketing.** See: Forms of Direct and Digital Marketing (pp 438–439)
- OBJECTIVE 14-3 **Explain how companies have responded to the internet and the digital age with various online marketing strategies.** See: Marketing, the Internet, and the Digital Age (pp 439–445)
- OBJECTIVE 14-4 **Discuss how companies use social media and mobile marketing to engage consumers and create brand community.** See: Social Media and Mobile Marketing (pp 445–453)
- OBJECTIVE 14-5 **Identify and discuss the traditional direct marketing forms and overview public policy and ethical issues presented by direct marketing.** See: Traditional Direct Marketing Forms (pp 453–460)

Previewing the Concepts

In the previous two chapters, you learned about engaging consumers and communicating customer value through integrated marketing communication and about four elements of the marketing communications mix: advertising, publicity, personal selling, and sales promotion. In this chapter, we examine direct marketing and its fastest-growing form: digital marketing (online, social media, and mobile marketing). Today, spurred by the surge in internet usage and buying as well as rapid advances in digital technologies—from smartphones, tablets, and other digital devices to the spate of online mobile and social media—direct marketing has undergone a dramatic transformation. As you read this chapter, remember that although direct and digital marketing are presented as separate tools, they must be carefully integrated with each other and with other elements of the promotion and marketing mixes.

Let's start by looking at Coca-Cola, a company famous for its advertising. Its classic mass-media advertising campaigns have informed and entertained generations of consumers over many decades. But as the times have changed in this digital age, so has the way Coca-Cola communicates with and engages consumers. Although it still relies heavily on massive advertising campaigns to position the brand and tell the brand story, Coca-Cola has also mastered digital, social, and mobile media to engage consumers directly, spark brand conversations, and make the brand a part of consumers' lives.

First Stop

Coca-Cola's Digital Marketing: Making the Brand a Part of the Customer's Story

Down through the decades, Coca-Cola has been an undisputed master of mass-media advertising and marketing. The company has produced an impressive string of big-budget campaigns built around classic slogans such as "The Pause that Refreshes," "Things Go Better with Coke," "I'd Like to Teach the World to Sing," "Have a Coke and a Smile," and the current "Taste the Feeling." The campaigns have featured memorable characters ranging from Michael Jordan to Santa Claus and the iconic Coca-Cola Polar Bears. Coca-Cola now spends an eye-popping $4 billion a year on advertising worldwide—10 percent of its revenues.

Its huge advertising presence has made Coca-Cola one of the world's best-known brands—according to one source, the word *Coca-Cola* is the second most recognized word in the world, after *okay*. But you know all that. What you might not have realized is that, as the world has shifted massively toward digital, so has Coca-Cola. Although the brand is still the king of mass-media marketing, Coca-Cola has shifted with the times to become a leading-edge digital, social media, and mobile marketer as well.

In the old days, Coca-Cola's advertising objective was to build the brand's image and positioning through mass-media impressions. Brand messages flowed from the company to consumers. A single Super Bowl ad could create hundreds of millions of consumer impressions worldwide. That's still important. But today's digital media let the brand take consumer engagement a big step farther. In addition to creating *impressions*, Coca-Cola now seeks to create consumer "*expressions*," brand-related exchanges and responses such as comments, retweets, photo uploads, advocating the brand, and sharing brand content on social media.

Coca-Cola has learned that today's empowered consumers often generate more content about a brand than a company can. For example, Coca-Cola estimates that of the hundreds of millions of views of Coca-Cola-related content on YouTube each year, only about 18 percent are from content created by Coca-Cola. The other 82 percent are from content created by engaged consumers. So, many Coca-Cola marketing campaigns are aimed at sparking brand-related consumer expressions rather than just impressions.

For instance, the brand's "Share a Coke" campaign—in which it swaps out the company's iconic logo on 20-ounce Coke bottles for one of more than 1,000 of the nation's most popular names—encourages Coca-Cola fans to share the bottles with friends and family. Consumers can also go online and order multi-packs with custom labels or create virtual custom Coke bottles they can save, post, or share. They can also share their Coca-Cola photos, stories, and experiences online using the hashtag #ShareaCoke, with selected posts featured on the brand's websites and across company billboards.

"Share a Coke" has become one of Coca-Cola's most successful campaigns ever. After only one year, it resulted in more than 500,000 photos and 6 million virtual Coke bottles shared online, along with a boost of nearly 25 million Coca-Cola Facebook followers. Now in its fifth year, the campaign has a new twist. The "Share a Coke" name labels on bottles are now stickers that customers can be peel off and stick to clothes, backpacks, phones, cars, or anywhere else, providing even more opportunities to share brand conversations and photos in social media.

Coca-Cola digital, mobile, and social media campaigns spark brand conversations, build brand community, and make the brand a part of consumers' lives.

Barry Tuck/Stockimo/Alamy Stock Photo

In its efforts to create a "connected Coke" and spur consumer co-creation and sharing of brand content, Coca-Cola maintains a massive digital footprint. In addition to hundreds of websites around the world, the brand hosts 70 Facebook pages, 35 Twitter handles, 21 Instagram accounts, and 10 YouTube channels. Its home Facebook page has 107 million fans. It draws 3.5 million Twitter followers, 2.5 million Instagram followers, and 2.3 million YouTube subscribers. Coca-Cola fills its always-on, endlessly connected websites and social media pages with interactive content designed to connect consumers with the brand and get them to share their brand experiences.

Long known for its classic mass-media advertising campaigns, Coca-Cola has shifted its communications to fit the digital times. It has now also mastered digital, social media, and mobile content that engages consumers directly and interactively.

For example, a few years ago, Coca-Cola transformed its corporate website into a dynamic digital magazine, called Coca-Cola Journey. The highly journalistic site contains magazine-style feature stories, brought to life with compelling photography, video and audio formats, and eye-catching graphics that are "Refreshing the world, one story at a time." On any given day, you'll find real-time stories about company happenings, new products, and the company's views on key current issues. But you'll also find features written by staff, employees, and customers on topics ranging from the history of Coca-Cola advertising slogans and how to order a Coke bottle with your name on it to what it's like to work at Coca-Cola and even how to bake a Coca-Cola cake (complete with a video).

The site also invites visitors to "join the journey," to "share you're your Coke moments" and "spread happiness" by uploading photos or videos. "Puppy dog eyes ... a walk in the woods ... sharing ice cream and laughs with a friend—those are a few of our Journey staffers' favorite things," says the site. "So we'd like to know what makes you happy!" Selected fan submissions are featured on Coca-Cola Journey. Thus, anything but a typically staid and stale corporate website, Coca-Cola Journey brims with engaging and sharable brand content.

Coca-Cola also makes extensive use of mobile marketing. For example, it offers more than a dozen mobile apps of its own, from its mainstay Coca-Cola app to Coke Studio (streaming music), Coca-Cola Happy Shopmate (finding and redeeming exciting local Coke deals, perks, and freebies on mobile), Simply Tasty (providing everyday recipes and "food adventures"), and even Coca-Cola Freestyle (a mixology app that lets customers blend and save their own favorite Coke concoctions and then order them digitally at a local Coke Freestyle vending machine).

Coca-Cola also produces a steady stream of mobile campaigns, designed to deliver "snackable, portable content" for today's time-pressed, highly mobile consumers. An example is Coca-Cola's "The Ahh Effect" campaign, launched a few years ago as one of the brand's first digital-led efforts. Optimized for mobile, "The Ahh Effect" campaign provided easily digestible, mobile-friendly bits of content designed to engage the world's teens, an audience known for its short attention span. "Think amusing videos and GIFs that teens [could] choose to spend only a few seconds viewing to get the message and simple games that they [could] play for two or three minutes," says a digital marketing analyst. "They [could] dip in, dip out, and move on," says a senior Coca-Cola marketing executive, "and if you look at the way teens consume tweets and posts and texts, that's pretty much their behavior." The "Ahh Effect" content came not only from Coca-Cola but also from teens themselves. And it was updated regularly, "continuously tapping into a teen's desire for discovery, constant stimulation, and novelty," says the marketer.

Thus, Coca-Cola is still a prolific traditional mass-media advertiser; its massive advertising campaigns position the brand and tell the brand story. But Coca-Cola is also a leader in creating digital, social media, and mobile content. Digital content doesn't just *tell* the brand story, it makes the brand part of the *consumer's* story. It engages consumers directly and personally, fuels brand conversations, and makes the brand a part of consumers' lives.[1]

Many of the marketing and promotion tools that we've examined in previous chapters were developed in the context of *mass marketing*: targeting broad markets with standardized messages and offers distributed through intermediaries. Today, however, with the trend toward narrower targeting and the surge in digital and social media technologies, many companies are shifting toward *direct marketing*, either as a primary marketing approach or as a supplement to other approaches. In this section, we explore the exploding world of direct marketing and its fastest-growing form—digital marketing using online, social media, and mobile marketing channels.

> Author Comment
> For most companies, direct and digital marketing are supplemental channels or media. But for many other companies today—such as Amazon, GEICO, or Travelocity—direct marketing is a complete way of doing business.

Direct and Digital Marketing

OBJECTIVE 14-1 Define *direct and digital marketing* and discuss their rapid growth and benefits to customers and companies.

Direct and digital marketing
Engaging directly with carefully targeted individual consumers and customer communities to both obtain an immediate response and build lasting customer relationships.

Direct and digital marketing involve engaging directly with carefully targeted individual consumers and customer communities to both obtain an immediate response and build lasting customer relationships. Companies use direct marketing to tailor their offers and content to the needs and interests of narrowly defined segments or individual buyers. In this way, they build customer engagement, brand community, and sales.

For example, Amazon.com interacts directly with customers via its website or mobile app to help them discover and buy almost anything and everything online. Similarly, GEICO interacts directly with customers—by phone, through its website or smartphone app, or on its Facebook, Twitter, and YouTube pages—to build individual brand relationships, give insurance quotes, sell policies, or service customer accounts.

The New Direct Marketing Model

Early direct marketers—catalog companies, direct mailers, and telemarketers—gathered customer names and sold goods mainly by mail and telephone. Today, however, spurred by the surge in internet usage and buying and by rapid advances in digital technologies—from smartphones, tablets, and other digital devices to the spate of online social and mobile media—direct marketing has undergone a dramatic transformation.

In previous chapters, we discussed direct marketing as direct distribution—as marketing channels that contain no intermediaries. We also included direct and digital marketing elements of the promotion mix—as an approach for engaging consumers directly and creating brand community. In actuality, direct marketing is both of these things and much more.

Most companies still use direct marketing as a supplementary channel or medium. Thus, most department stores, such as Macy's or Kohl's, sell the majority of their merchandise off their store shelves, but they also sell through websites and online catalogs, direct mail, and social media pages. Pepsi's Mountain Dew brand markets heavily through mass-media advertising and its retail partners' channels. However, it also supplements these channels with a heavy dose of direct marketing. For example, the brand aired blockbuster television ads during the most recent Super Bowl. But it also spent heavily on digital media to engage its passionately loyal fan base in the weeks leading up to and following the big game. "Close to 40 percent of our investment [was] on digital because that's where consumers are having conversations," says Pepsi's chief marketer. We spent "big dollars on the Super Bowl game day. But that itself is not enough to have a two-way conversation with a consumer."[2] Mountain Dew also engages fans digitally though a heavy website and social media presence.

However, for many companies today, direct and digital marketing are more than just supplementary channels or advertising media—they constitute a complete model for doing business. Firms employing this direct model use it as the only approach. Online giants such as Amazon, Netflix, GEICO, and Expedia have successfully built their entire approaches to the marketplace around direct and digital marketing.

>> For example, Expedia Group is a huge collection of online-only travel businesses, including such familiar brands as Expedia, Travelocity, Hotels.com, Hotwire, trivago, Orbitz, and HomeAway. With combined revenues of $10.1 billion in 2017, the company does business through more than 200 travel booking sites and over 150 mobile websites. Its Travelocity unit was one of the first online travel companies that let customers find and book travel arrangements without the help of travel agents or brokers. Now itself one of the world's largest travel brands, Travelocity and its famous Roaming Gnome help customers to "Wander Wisely," making their travel experiences both simple and memorable.[3]

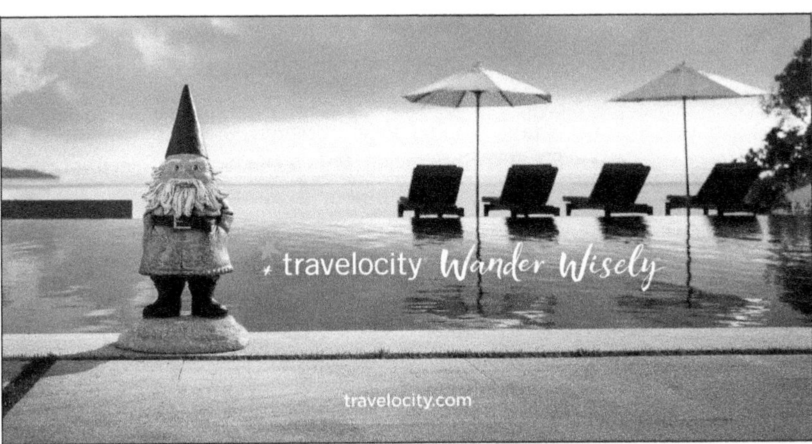

>> The new direct marketing model: Online travel company Expedia Group has successfully built its entire approach to the marketplace around direct and digital marketing. Its Travelocity.com unit and the famous Roaming Gnome make it easy for customer to "Wander Wisely."

Rapid Growth of Direct and Digital Marketing

Direct and digital marketing have become the fastest-growing form of marketing. And as direct marketing continues to shift online, digital direct marketing is claiming a surging share of marketing spending and sales. Total digital advertising spending—including online display and search advertising, social media, mobile, video, email, and other—now accounts for the largest share of media spending, with digital media expenditures running 20 percent ahead of spending on runner-up television. And as consumers spend more and more time on their tablets and smartphones, ad spending on mobile media is exploding. Mobile ad spending now accounts for 70 percent of all digital ad spending.[4]

Benefits of Direct and Digital Marketing to Buyers and Sellers

For buyers, direct and digital marketing are convenient, easy, and private. They give buyers anywhere, anytime access to an almost unlimited assortment of goods and a wealth of product and buying information. For example, on its website and mobile app, Amazon.

com offers more information than most consumers can digest, ranging from top 10 product lists, extensive product descriptions, and expert and user product reviews to recommendations based on customers' previous searches and purchases.

Through direct marketing, buyers can interact with sellers by phone or on the seller's website or mobile app to create exactly the configuration of information, products, or services they want and then order them on the spot. Finally, for consumers who want it, digital marketing through online, mobile, and social media provides a sense of brand engagement and community—a place to share brand information and experiences with other brand fans.

For sellers, direct marketing often provides a low-cost, efficient, speedy alternative for reaching their markets. Today's direct marketers can target small groups or individual customers. Because of the one-to-one nature of direct marketing, companies can interact with customers by phone or online, learn more about their needs, and personalize products and services to specific customer tastes. In turn, customers can ask questions and volunteer feedback.

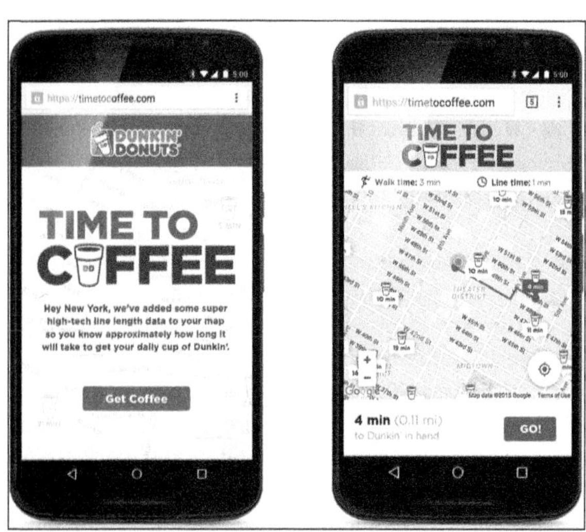

>> Direct and digital marketing let brands create immediate and timely customer engagement, as when Dunkin' beams maps and wait times for nearby locations to people who search "coffee near me" on their phones.

Courtesy of Dunkin' Brands

Direct and digital marketing also offer sellers greater flexibility. They let marketers make ongoing adjustments to prices and programs or to create immediate, timely, and personal engagement and offers. For example, home improvement retailer Lowe's online "How-Tos Library" links consumers to hundreds of in-depth how-to videos, project planning guides, cost calculators, and other helpful information on almost any project, from building a backyard patio or installing in a lawn sprinkler system to hanging drywall or even getting rid of mice. The guides are available whenever projects pop up and, of course, provide detailed lists of supplies available at a nearby Lowe's store.[5]

Especially in today's digital environment, direct marketing provides opportunities for *real-time marketing* that links brands to important moments and trending events in customers' lives. It is a powerful tool for moving customers through the buying process and for building customer engagement, community, and personalized relationships. For example, in some locations, Dunkin' engages people who search "coffee near me" on their phones using Google Search or Google Maps with mobile ads that say, "Find the fastest coffee." >> Clicking on the ad brings up a map and wait times at nearby Dunkin' locations. On a broader level, brands ranging from Ben & Jerry's or Starbucks to the Red Cross use Twitter or Instagram to communicate with consumers in real time about important events, promotions, announcements, and even trending news.

Author Comment
Direct marketing is rich in tools, from traditional favorites such as direct mail and catalogs to newer digital tools such as online, mobile, and social media.

Forms of Direct and Digital Marketing

OBJECTIVE 14-2 Identify and discuss the major forms of direct and digital marketing.

The major forms of direct and digital marketing are shown in **>> Figure 14.1**. Traditional direct marketing tools include face-to-face selling, direct-mail marketing, catalog marketing, telemarketing, direct-response television marketing, and kiosk marketing. In recent

We'll begin with the exciting new digital forms of direct marketing. But remember that the traditional forms are still heavily used and that the new and old must be integrated for maximum impact.

>> Figure 14.1 Forms of Direct and Digital Marketing

years, however, newer digital direct marketing tools have burst onto the marketing scene, including online marketing (websites, online ads and promotions, email, online videos, and blogs), social media marketing, and mobile marketing.

We'll begin by examining direct digital and social media marketing tools that now receive so much attention. Then we'll look at the still heavily used and very important traditional direct marketing tools. As always, however, it's important to remember that all of these tools—both the new digital and the more traditional forms—must be blended into a fully integrated marketing communications program.

Digital and social media marketing Using digital marketing tools such as websites, social media, mobile apps and ads, online video, email, and blogs that engage consumers anywhere, anytime via their digital devices.

As noted earlier, **digital and social media marketing** is the fastest-growing form of direct marketing. It uses digital marketing tools such as websites, online video, email, blogs, social media, mobile ads and apps, and other digital platforms to directly engage consumers anywhere, anytime via their computers, smartphones, tablets, internet-ready TVs, and other digital devices. The widespread use of the internet and digital technologies has had a dramatic impact on both buyers and the marketers who serve them.

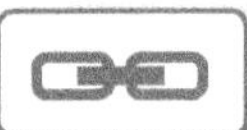

LINKING THE CONCEPTS

Hold up a moment and think about the impact of direct and digital marketing on your life.

- Think back about a major purchase that you made recently via direct or digital marketing. What did you buy, and why did you buy it direct? Think about a recent major purchase you made in a store rather than direct. Why did you not by direct? Based on these experiences, what advice would you give to direct marketers?
- For the next week, keep track of all the direct and digital marketing offers that come your way via direct mail and catalogs, email and mobile ads, online and social media marketing offers, and others. Then analyze the offers by type, source, and what you liked or disliked about each offer and the way it was delivered. Which offer best hit its target (you)? Which missed by the widest margin?

Marketing in the Digital Age

Author Comment
Direct digital and social media marketing is surging and grabbing all the headlines these days, so we'll start with it. But the traditional direct marketing tools are still heavily used. We'll dig into them later in the chapter.

OBJECTIVE 14-3 Explain how companies have responded to the internet and the digital age with various online marketing strategies.

These days, people connect digitally with information, brands, and each other at almost any time and from almost anywhere. In the age of the "Internet of Things" (IoT), it seems that everything and everyone will soon be connected digitally to everything and everyone else. The digital age has fundamentally changed customers' notions of convenience, speed, price, product information, service, and brand interactions. As a result, it has given marketers a whole new way to create customer value, engage customers, and build customer relationships.

Digital usage and impact continues to grow steadily. More than 88 percent of all U.S. adults use the internet, and the average U.S. internet user spends almost six hours a day consuming digital media, primarily via mobile devices. Worldwide, more than 54 percent of the population has internet access. And 32 percent has access to the mobile internet.[6]

As a result, more than half of all U.S. households now regularly shop online, and digital buying continues to grow at a healthy double-digit rate. U.S. online retail sales were an estimated $454 billion last year, a 16.6 percent one-year increase and 13 percent of total retail sales. By 2027, as consumers continue to shift their spending from physical to digital stores, online sales are expected to grow to more than $1 trillion. Perhaps even more important, an estimated more than one-half of all U.S. retail sales were either transacted directly online or influenced by internet research.[7] As today's omni-channel consumers become more and more adept at blending online, mobile, and in-store shopping, digital channels will come into play for an ever-larger proportion of their purchases.

To reach this burgeoning market, most companies now market online. Some companies operate *only* online. They include a wide array of firms, from *e-tailers* such as Amazon,

Quicken Loans, and Expedia.com that sell products and services directly to final buyers via the internet to *search engines and portals* (such as Google, Bing, and Yahoo!), *transaction sites* (eBay, Craigslist), *content sites* (the *New York Times*, ESPN.com, and Wikipedia), and *online social media* (Facebook, Twitter, Instragram, YouTube, and Snapchat).

Today, however, it's hard to find a company that doesn't have a substantial online presence. Even companies that have traditionally operated offline have now created their own online sales, marketing, and brand community channels. Traditional store retailers are reaping increasingly larger proportions of their sales online. For example, Macy's is now the world's 10th-largest e-tailer, with nearly 18 percent of its revenues online. Target captures about 23 percent of its sales online; at Nordstrom, it's 22 percent.[8]

Omni-channel retailing
Creating a seamless cross-channel buying experience that integrates in-store, online, and mobile shopping.

In fact, **omni-channel retailing** companies are having as much online success as their online-only competitors. For example, home-improvement retailer Home Depot has nearly 2,000 U.S. stores. But its hottest growth area in recent years has been online sales, which grew almost 22 percent last year:[9]

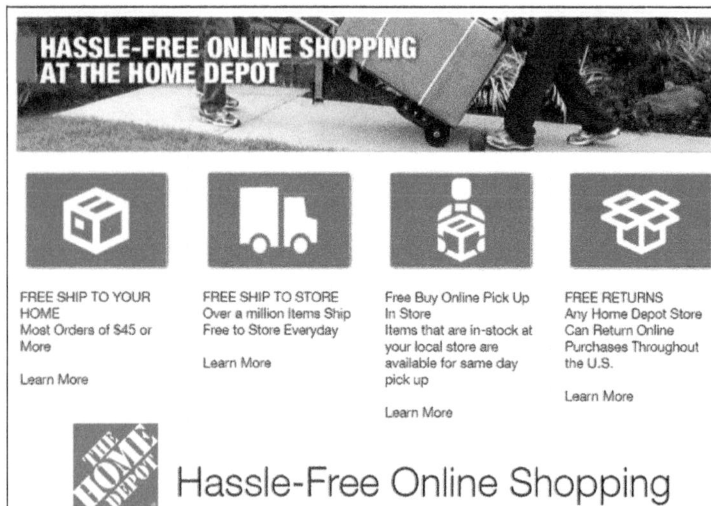

>> Omni-channel retailing: Home Depot's goal is to provide "a seamless and frictionless experience no matter where our customers shop, be it in the digital world, our brick and mortar stores, at home, or on the job site. Anywhere the customer is, we need to be there."

Although it might be hard to imagine selling sheets of plywood, pre-hung doors, dishwashers, or vinyl siding online, Home Depot does that and much more these days. Last year, Home Depot sold almost $6.8 billion worth of goods online, an amount equal to the total retail revenues of retailers such as Staples, Barnes & Noble, Tiffany, or Williams-Sonoma. Home Depot is now one of the nation's top 10 online merchants. Its online inventory exceeds 1 million products, compared with only about 35,000 in a typical Home Depot store.

Home Depot now offers its customers multiple contact points and delivery modes. Of course, customers can buy products off the shelf in Home Depot stores. >> But they can also order online from home, a job site, or anywhere in between on their computers, tablets, or smartphones and then have goods shipped or pick them up at a store. More than 46 percent of online orders are now picked up inside a Home Depot store. Finally, in the store, associates armed with tablets can help customers order out-of-stock items for later pickup or delivery. In all, Home Depot uses online as a sales channel to drive both online and in-store sales and to improve the customer experience by providing product, project, and other information. "Our customers are changing the way they shop and how they engage with us," says Home Depot. The goal is to provide "a seamless and frictionless experience no matter where our customers shop, be it in the digital world, our brick-and-mortar stores, at home, or on the job site. Anywhere the customer is, we need to be there."

Direct digital and social media marketing takes any of the several forms shown in Figure 14.1. These forms include online marketing, social media marketing, and mobile marketing. We discuss each in turn, starting with online marketing.

Online Marketing

Online marketing
Marketing via the internet using company websites, online ads and promotions, email, online video, and blogs.

Online marketing refers to marketing via the internet using company websites, online advertising and promotions, email marketing, online video, and blogs. Social media and mobile marketing also take place online and must be closely coordinated with other forms of digital marketing. However, because of their special characteristics, we discuss the fast-growing social media and mobile marketing approaches in separate sections.

Websites and Branded Web Communities

Marketing website
A website that engages consumers to move them closer to a direct purchase or other marketing outcome.

For most companies, the first step in conducting online marketing is to create a website. Websites vary greatly in purpose and content. Some websites are primarily **marketing websites**, designed to engage customers and move them closer to a direct purchase or other marketing outcome.

For example, car companies like Hyundai operate marketing websites. Once a potential customer clicks in to Hyundai's site, the carmaker wastes no time trying to turn the inquiry into a sale and then into a long-term relationship. The site opens with a promotional message and then offers a garage full of useful information and interactive selling features, including detailed descriptions of current Hyundai models, tools for designing your own Hyundai, an area to calculate the trade-in value of your current car, information on dealer locations and services, and even a place to request a quote online. Inventory search and schedule a test drive features encourage customers to take the plunge and visit a Hyundai dealership.

Brand community website
A website that presents brand content that engages consumers and creates customer community around a brand.

In contrast, **brand community websites** do much more than just sell products. Instead, their primary purpose is to present brand content that engages consumers and creates customer-brand community. Such sites typically offer a rich variety of brand information, videos, blogs, activities, and other features that build closer customer relationships and generate engagement with and between the brand and its customers. >> For example, you can't buy anything at ESPN.com. Instead, the site creates a vast branded sports community:[10]

>> **Brand community websites: You can't buy anything at ESPN.com. Instead, the site creates a vast branded sports community.**

NetPhotos/Alamy

At ESPN.com, sports fans can access an almost overwhelming repository of sports information, statistics, and game updates. They can customize site content by sport, team, players, and authors to match their own special sports interests and team preferences. The site engages fans in contests and fantasy games (everything from fantasy football, baseball, basketball, and hockey to poker). Sports fans from around the world can participate in discussions with other fans and celebrities before, during, and after sporting events. They can friend and message other users and post comments on message boards and blogs. By downloading various apps, fans can customize their ESPN experience and carry it with them wherever they go. In all, ESPN's website creates a virtual brand community without walls, a must-have experience that keeps fans coming back again and again. Last March, more than 73 million fans spent a total of 5.9 billion minutes at ESPN digital sites.

Creating a website is one thing; getting people to *visit* the site is another. To attract visitors, companies aggressively promote their websites in offline print and broadcast advertising and through ads and links on other sites. But today's web users are quick to abandon any website that doesn't measure up. The key is to create enough engaging and valued content to get consumers to come to the site, stick around, and come back again.

At the very least, a website should be easy to use and visually appealing. Ultimately, however, websites must also be *useful*. When it comes to online browsing and shopping, most people prefer substance over style and function over flash. For example, ESPN's site isn't all that flashy, and it's pretty heavily packed and congested. But it connects customers quickly and effectively to all the sports information and involvement they are seeking. Thus, effective websites contain deep and useful information, interactive tools that help find and evaluate content of interest, links to other related sites, changing promotional offers, and entertaining features that lend relevant excitement.

Online Advertising

Online advertising
Advertising that appears while consumers are browsing online, including display ads and search-related ads.

As consumers spend more and more time online, companies are shifting more of their marketing dollars to **online advertising** to build brand sales or attract visitors to their internet, mobile, and social media sites. Online advertising has become a major promotional medium. The main forms of online advertising are display ads and search-related ads. Together, display and search-related ads account for the largest portion of firms' digital marketing budgets.

Online display ads might appear anywhere on an internet user's screen and are often related to the information being viewed. For example, while browsing espn.com on a warm summer day, users might see the web content wrapped at the top and both sides by a large banner ad for RTIC Coolers, touting the product's durability and ice-keeping prowess. Clicking on the banner or on an inset display ad nearby takes them to brand's website.

>> Online display advertising: To create anticipation for a summer promotion, Sonic paired a real-time countdown clock with an interactive quiz that "made it easy to say 'yes!' to half-price summer treats from Sonic."

Courtesy SONIC Drive-In

Display ads have come a long way in recent years in terms of engaging consumers and moving them along the path to purchase. Today's rich media ads incorporate animation, video, sound, and interactivity. For example, Boeing recently ran a display ad featuring a breathtaking, rotating 3D view of the International Space Station. >> At the other extreme, when Sonic restaurants wanted to create awareness and anticipation for a summer promotion making its shakes and ice cream slushes half price after 8 p.m., it created an online display ad featuring a real-time daily countdown clock. The ad paired the clock with an interactive quiz to help customers decide in advance their perfect flavor, and a store locator helped them find the nearest Sonic restaurant. "In other words," says a Sonic marketer, "we made it easy to say 'yes!' to half-price summer treats from Sonic."[11]

Using *search-related ads* (or *contextual advertising*), text- and image-based ads and links appear atop or alongside search engine results on sites such as Google, Yahoo!, and Bing. For example, search Google for "LED TVs." At the top and side of the resulting search list, you'll see inconspicuous ads for 10 or more advertisers, ranging from Samsung and Panasonic to Best Buy, Amazon.com, Walmart.com, Crutchfield, and CDW. Eighty-six percent of Google's $110.9 billion in revenues last year came from ad sales. Search is an always-on kind of medium, and the results are easily measured.[12]

A search advertiser buys search terms or keywords from the search site and pays only if consumers click through to its site. The average cost per click-through for Google Search Network keywords is about $2.70. The most expensive and competitive keywords can cost $50 or more per click. Search advertising is a large component in the digital advertising mix of most brands. Large retailers might easily spend $50 million or more per year on paid search advertising. In all, search advertising accounts for 42 percent of all digital advertising spending.[13]

Email Marketing

Email marketing
Sending highly targeted, highly personalized, relationship-building marketing messages via email.

Email marketing remains an important and growing digital marketing tool. Around the world, people send out more than 186 million emails every minute of every day. According to one survey, 77 percent of consumers prefer getting permission-based marketing messages via email versus direct mail, text, or social media. And 76 percent of consumers agree that retail brands send relevant emails that accurately reflect their shopping preferences, locations, or purchase histories. Email is an important business-to-business tool—86 percent of business professionals prefer to use email when communicating for business purposes, and email rates as the third most influential source of information for B-to-B audiences. What's more, email is now an on-the-go medium—55 percent of all emails are now opened on mobile devices. Not surprisingly, given its low costs and targetability, email can yield a very high return on investment.[14]

When used properly, email can be the ultimate direct marketing medium. Today's emails are anything but the staid, text-only messages of the past. Instead, they are colorful, inviting, and interactive. Email lets marketers send highly targeted, tightly personalized, relationship-building messages. For example, toymaker Fisher-Price uses email to send timely check-ins, updates, and birthday wishes to subscribers. A mother might receive a colorful, personalized "happy birthday to your baby" email on her child's first birthday that contains links to age-related playtime ideas, parenting tips, and product information.[15]

Similarly, eyewear brand Warby Parker sends a sequence of nine informational and promotional emails to home try-on customers. Each is personally addressed and keyed to steps in the trial process, from initial registration and order confirmation to offers of selection assistance and instructions for returning frames. "The magical part was feeling like Warby Parker was right there with me throughout the process," says one customer. Warby Parker also sends cheerful after-purchase follow-up and announcement emails.

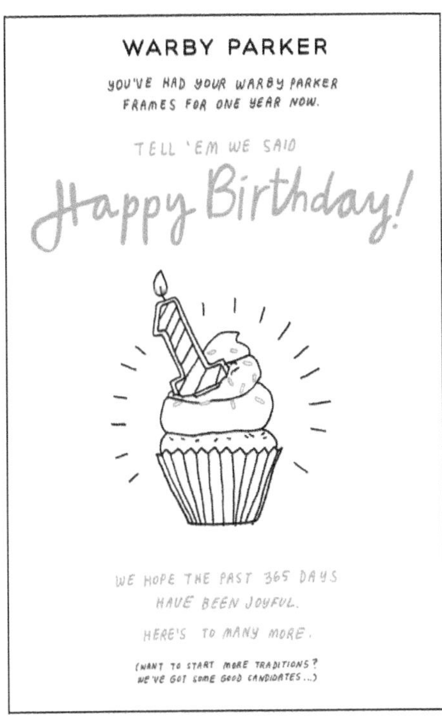
WARBY PARKER
YOU'VE HAD YOUR WARBY PARKER FRAMES FOR ONE YEAR NOW.
TELL 'EM WE SAID
Happy Birthday!
WE HOPE THE PAST 365 DAYS HAVE BEEN JOYFUL.
HERE'S TO MANY MORE.

>> **Email marketing: Eyewear brand Warby Parker sends personalized emails to home try-on customers throughout the purchase and after-purchase process. "You've had your Warby Parker frames for one year now. Tell 'em we said Happy Birthday!"**

Courtesy of Warby Parker

>> For example, it sends personalized emails to customers on the first anniversary of their purchase, with the message "You've had your Warby Parker frames for one year now. Tell 'em we said Happy Birthday! We hope the first 365 days have been joyful." And just in case the customer wants "to start more traditions," the email also includes a link to Warby Parker's website.[16]

But there's a dark side to the use of email marketing. The explosion of **spam**—unsolicited, unwanted commercial email messages that clog up our email boxes—has produced consumer irritation and frustration. According to one source, spam now accounts for about 55 percent of the billions of emails sent worldwide each day. American office workers receive an average of 200 emails per day and spend nearly two and a half hours reading and replying to them.[17] Email marketers walk a fine line between adding value for consumers and being intrusive and annoying.

Spam
Unsolicited, unwanted commercial email messages.

To address these concerns, most legitimate marketers now practice *permission-based email marketing*, sending email pitches only to customers who "opt in." Many companies use configurable email systems that let customers choose what they want to get. For example, Amazon targets opt-in customers with a limited number of helpful "we thought you'd like to know" messages based on their expressed preferences and previous purchases. Few customers object, and many actually welcome such promotional messages. Amazon benefits through higher return rates and by avoiding alienating customers with emails they don't want.

Online Videos

Another form of online marketing is posting digital video content on brand websites or on social media sites such as YouTube, Facebook, Instagram, Twitter, and others. Some videos are made specifically for the web and social media. Such videos range from "how-to" instructional videos and public relations pieces to brand promotions and brand-related entertainment. Other videos are ads that a company makes primarily for TV or other media but posts online before or after an advertising campaign to extend their reach and impact.

Good online videos can engage consumers by the tens of millions. The online video audience is soaring. Almost 85 percent of the U.S. population has viewed online videos. YouTube users now upload more than 300 hours of video every minute. Facebook alone generates more than 30 billion video views per day worldwide; Snapchat adds another 10 billion views. By one estimate, video accounted for 69 percent of all internet traffic last year. "Over the past few years," notes one analyst, "the internet has evolved from a text-based medium to the new TV."[18]

Many brands produce multiplatform video campaigns that bridge traditional TV, online, and mobile media. For example, video versions of and promotions for most Super Bowl ads attract huge audiences before and after the big game airs. Consider Amazon's humorous "Alexa loses her voice" ad shown during Super Bowl LII. In the ad, a host of big-name celebrities fill in when the tech-giant's AI assistant loses her voice and can't fulfill requests. The 90-second ad ranked number one in the *USA Today* ad meter ratings, making more than 81 million TV ad impressions and earning more than 8 million online views on game day. But short-form teaser videos and prerelease versions of the ad grabbed more than 20 million online views in the days leading up to the game and tens of millions more views in the days following. By one account, the Amazon ad and related videos ranked number four in online "digital buzz" prior to the game.[19]

Viral marketing
The digital version of word-of-mouth marketing: videos, ads, and other marketing content that is so infectious that customers will seek it out or pass it along to friends.

Marketers hope that some of their videos will go viral. **Viral marketing**, the digital version of word-of-mouth marketing, involves creating videos, ads, and other marketing content that are so infectious that customers will seek them out or pass them along to their friends. Because customers find and pass along the content, viral marketing can be very inexpensive. And when content comes from a friend, the recipient is much more likely to view or read it.

All kinds of videos can go viral, producing engagement and positive exposure for a brand. >> For example, Google Android launched a compellingly sharable video called "Friends Furever," which featured unlikely pairings of animals—an orangutan and a dog, a bear and a tiger, a cat and a duckling—being pals and enjoying life together. The video was the latest installment in Android's "Be together. Not the same." marketing campaign. The campaign highlights how people can be different and still be stronger together, in line with Android's core competency of running on diverse devices, each with its own design and features. The heartwarming "Friends Furever" video went viral in a big way. It captured more than 24 million YouTube views and was shared more than 6.4 million times across Facebook, Twitter, and the blogosphere in its first nine months, making it one of the most-shared videos of all time.[20]

Despite these viral successes, it's important to note that marketers usually have little control over where their viral messages end up. They can seed content online, but that does little good unless the message itself strikes a chord with consumers. Says one creative director, "You hope that the creative is at a high enough mark where the seeds grow into mighty oaks. If they don't like it, it ain't gonna move. If they like it, it'll move a little bit; and if they love it, it's gonna move like a fast-burning fire through the Hollywood hills."[21]

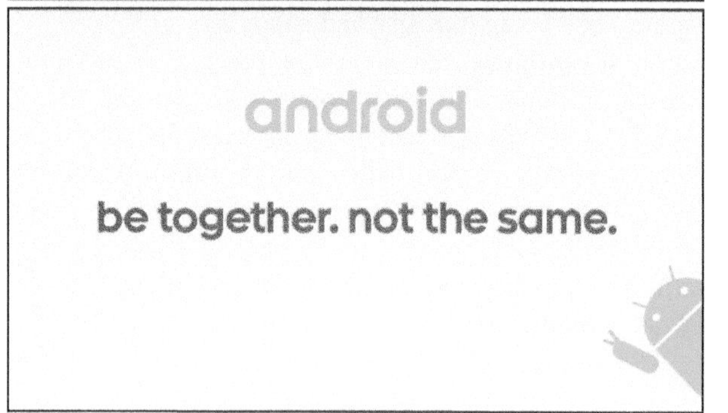

>> Viral marketing: Google Android's "Friends Furever" video went viral in a big way. It was shared more than 6.4 million times across Facebook, Twitter, and the blogosphere in its first nine months, making it the most-shared video of all time.

Blogs and Other Online Forums

Brands also conduct online marketing through various digital forums that appeal to specific special-interest groups and brand communities. **Blogs** (or web logs) are online forums where people and companies post their thoughts and other content, usually related to narrowly defined topics. Blogs can be about anything, from politics or baseball to haiku, car repair, brands, or the latest television series. Many bloggers use social networks such as Twitter, Facebook, Tumblr, and Instagram to promote their blogs, giving them huge reach. Such reach can give blogs—especially those with large and devoted followings—substantial influence.

Blogs
Online forums where people and companies post their thoughts and other content, usually related to narrowly defined topics.

Most marketers are now tapping into the blogosphere with their own brand-related blogs that reach customer communities. For example, on the Netflix Blog, members of the Netflix team (themselves rabid movie fans) tell about the latest Netflix features, share tricks for getting the most out of the Netflix experience, and collect feedback from subscribers. The creative Nuts About Southwest blog, written by Southwest Airline employees, fosters a two-way dialogue that gives customers a look inside the company's culture and operations. At the same time, it lets Southwest engage customers directly and get feedback from them. >> And Patagonia's blog, The Cleanest Line, shares stories about the environment, tells where the company stands on key issues, and spreads the brand's "Build the best product, cause no unnecessary harm" message rather than promoting sales. Patagonia uses its popular social media sites, especially Instagram (with more than 3.4 million followers), to steer fans to the blog's longer-form stories and videos.

>> Company blogs: Patagonia's blog, The Cleanest Line, shares stories about the environment and spreads the brand's "Build the best product, cause no unnecessary harm" message rather than promoting sales.

Beyond their own brand blogs, many marketers use third-party blogs to help get their messages out. For example, some fashion bloggers have amassed millions of followers, with fan bases larger even than the blogs and social media accounts of major fashion magazines. For example, 26-year-old Danielle Bernstein started the We Wore What fashion blog as an undergraduate at the Fashion Institute of Technology in New York City. The blog and Instagram account are now a source of daily outfit inspiration to a fan base of more than 1.7 million. Because of such large followings, brands flock to Bernstein and other fashion blog influencers such as BryanBoy, The Blonde Salad, Song of Style, and Gal Meets Glam, paying them $15,000 or more to post and tag product images in their blog, Facebook, and

Instagram sites. Bernstein posts images that contain sponsored products from small brands such as Schultz Shoes and Revolve Clothing to large brands such as Nike, Lancôme, and Nordstrom.[22]

As a marketing tool, blogs offer some advantages. They can offer a fresh, original, personal, and cheap way to enter into consumer online and social media conversations. However, the blogosphere is cluttered and difficult to control. And although companies can sometimes leverage blogs to engage customers in meaningful relationships, blogs remain largely a consumer-controlled medium. Whether or not they actively participate in the blogs, companies should monitor and listen to them. Marketers can use insights from consumer online conversations to improve their marketing programs.

Author Comment
As in about every other area of our lives, digital media and mobile technologies have taken the marketing world by storm. They offer some amazing marketing possibilities. But truth be told, many marketers are still sweating over how to use them most effectively.

Social Media and Mobile Marketing

OBJECTIVE 14-4 Discuss how companies use social media and mobile marketing to engage consumers and create brand community.

Social Media Marketing

Social media
Independent and commercial online social networks where people congregate to socialize and share messages, opinions, pictures, videos, and other content.

As we've discussed throughout the text, the surge in internet usage and digital technologies and devices has spawned a dazzling array of online **social media** and other digital communities. Countless independent and commercial social networks have arisen where people congregate to socialize and share messages, opinions, pictures, videos, and other content. These days, it seems, almost everyone is buddying up on Facebook, checking in with Twitter, tuning into the day's hottest videos at YouTube, pinning images on social scrapbooking site Pinterest, or sharing photos with Instagram and Snapchat. And, of course, wherever consumers congregate, marketers will surely follow.

Most marketers are now riding the huge social media wave. Almost all businesses large and small use at least one social media channel. Large brands usually have a huge social media presence. For example, according to one source, Nike maintains at least 108 Facebook pages, 104 Twitter handles, 16 Instagram accounts, and 41 YouTube channels.[23]

Interestingly, just as marketers are mastering the use of social media to engage customers, the social media themselves are learning how to make their communities a suitable platform for marketing content, in a way that benefits both social media users and brands. Most social media, even the most successful ones, still face a monetization issue: how they can profitably tap the marketing potential of their massive communities to make money without driving off loyal users. Exceptions are Facebook and massively successful Facebook-owned Instagram (see Marketing at Work 14.1).

Using Social Media

Marketers can engage in social media in two ways: They can use existing social media or they can set up their own. Using existing social media seems the easiest. Thus, most brands—large and small—have set up shop on a host of social media sites. Check the websites of brands ranging from Coca-Cola, Nike, and Victoria's Secret to the Chicago Bulls or even the U.S. Forest Service, and you'll find links to each brand's Facebook, Twitter, Instagram, YouTube, Spotify, or other social media pages. Such social media can create substantial brand communities. For example, the Chicago Bulls have more the 18 million Facebook fans; Coca-Cola has an eye-popping 107 million Facebook fans.

Some of the major social networks are huge. Nearly 2.2 billion people access Facebook every month, almost five times the population of the United States. Twitter has more than 330 million active monthly users. And YouTube's more than 1 billion users upload 300 hours of video every minute of every day. The list goes on: Instagram has 800 million active users, LinkedIn 500 million, SnapChat 187 million, and Pinterest 175 million.[24]

MARKETING AT WORK 14.1

Instagram: A Win-Win-Win for the Company, Advertisers, and Instagrammers

Social media giant Facebook acquired a young startup called Instagram six years ago for the then-mind-blowing sum of $1 billion—a record price paid for any app and far more than Facebook had ever spent on an acquisition. Experts were shocked, and some critics mocked Facebook's sanity. At the time, Instagram had zero revenue, only 30 million users, and no idea how it would make money. But Facebook saw potential in the fledgling Instagram that others overlooked.

As the world has rapidly gone social and mobile, social networks have played a huge role. Whether it's on massive platforms such as Facebook, Twitter, and YouTube or lesser-known niche sites, it's common to see people everywhere these days, heads down with devices in hand, connecting, posting, messaging, and sharing. On Facebook alone, every day, 1.57 billion of the network's 2.2 billion active users worldwide watch 8 billion videos, generate 4.5 billion Likes, and share 4.75 billion pieces of content.

However, even as social media networks have achieved incredible success in terms of numbers of users and sheer content volume, a nagging problem still plagues them. It's called *monetization*. How can social media profitably tap the marketing potential of their massive communities to make money without driving off their legions of loyal users? Most social media still struggle to make a profit. Last year, Twitter lost $108 million; Snapchat lost $720 million. Although each generates revenue, neither has ever made a profit.

Facebook was the first social medium to solve the profitability issue, and it's the only one yet to do that on a large scale. Last year, Facebook netted $16 billion in profits on revenues of just over $40 billion—an amazing 39 percent margin. And although Facebook began making money only six years ago, its revenues have grown by an average more than 50 percent annually, and profits have grown by 89 percent a year. How does Facebook succeed where so many other social media still wrestle with the issue of monetization? It's all about advertising. Facebook rakes in money by providing effective ways for companies to target and engage its gigantic user community with relevant ads and other brand content.

Perhaps nowhere is this monetization success more apparent than at massively successful Instagram. Launched as a private startup in 2010, Instagram differentiated itself from other apps in two ways: It was mobile-only, and it was designed with a single simple function in mind—sharing photos. Instagram's simplicity and the wide appeal of communicating through images made it an instant hit. Within only two months, the photo-sharing app had amassed its first million users; in less than a year it had 10 million users. Instagram quickly became the preferred social network for then-young millennials to communicate with their friends, out of the sight of their parents' watchful eyes.

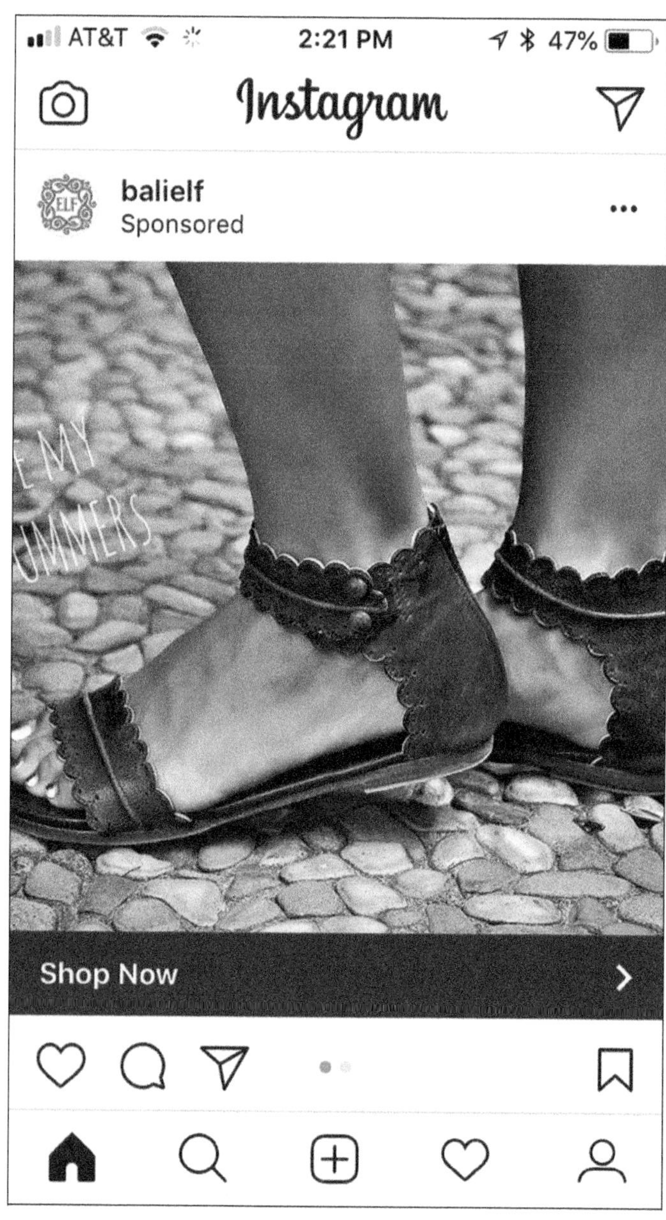

>> Hugely successful Instagram has figured out how to integrate advertising with consumer content in a way that satisfies users, advertisers, and its own bottom line, here bohemian chic, handmade clothing and accessory brand Elf.

ELF

The Facebook acquisition came less than two years after Instagram's launch. Although small at the time, Instagram's youthful audience complemented Facebook's aging one. A year later, Instagram introduced paid advertising. The decision was controversial. Like most social media users, Instagrammers cherished the free (and commercial-free) sharing culture of their digital community. If not well conceived, commercial content would be an unwelcome intrusion that could alienate users and drive them away. The challenge for Instagram, as for all social media, was to inject brand content alongside user content without upsetting the community dynamic.

But even as more and more advertisers have jumped aboard Instagram—first hundreds, then thousands, then millions—Instagram's user base has continued to explode. In fact, although still much smaller, Instagram's growth rates rival those of parent Facebook. Every day, 800 million Instagrammers now share more than 100 million photos and videos and hit the Like button more than 4.2 billion times. And Instagram's advertiser base has grown in harmony with its user base. Instagram is one of the world's premier digital, social media, and mobile advertising channels, now attracting 2 million monthly advertisers, ranging from marketing heavyweights like Nike, Disney, and P&G to your local restaurant or fitness center.

Instagram's unique user base makes it an ideal fit for the content strategies of many brands. The Instagram community is big and youngish—59 percent of Instagram users are 18- to 29-year-olds—but spans a wide demographic range that allows for precision targeting. Instagram's audience is also brand loyal, with 80 percent of users following one or more brands on the app and 60 percent saying they discover new products there. What's more, some 75 percent of Instagram users take action after looking at an advertising post, such as visiting a website or checking out an offer.

Instagram's design makes it easy for advertisers to blend their brand content naturally with the flow of user content. As a result, rather than disrupting the Instagrammer experience, brand content often enhances it. Beyond their own Instagram feeds, advertisers can choose from several content formats. Using photo ads—Instagram's first and most basic ad format—advertisers can post high-impact images on the app's "clean, simple, and beautiful creative canvas." Video ads inject the power of sound and motion in brand videos up to 60 seconds long. Carousel ads bring more depth, letting users swipe to view additional photos or videos in a single ad. Finally, with Stories ads, advertisers can present brand content in the same way that Instagrammers use the Stories feature—weaving photos and videos together, enhancing them with text and doodles, and presenting them in full-screen slideshows that stay around for 24 hours.

Designed for sharing photos and videos, Instagram's presentation formats let users process the visual content quickly and efficiently, with more emotional impact, befitting today's in-the-moment mobile generation. Instagram ad content creates high levels of consumer engagement compared with other social media. For example, whereas as closest competitor Snapchat's disappearing content makes brand-consumer connections fleeting, Instagram's format lets consumers scroll through, linger over, and share content on their own time terms. Beyond Snapchat comparisons, one recent study revealed that brands get as much as 30 times more engagement on Instagram than on Twitter and three times more engagement than on Facebook. In one example, Mercedes recently posted social media teasers for the world premiere of its new A-Class hatchback. On Facebook, the post racked up a respectable 10,000 Likes. By comparison, however, the very same image on Instagram generated 150,000 Likes. Thus, Instagram reaps levels of engagement that older, more text-based social media often can't match.

Beyond its ability to engage consumers with impactful brand content, Instagram is now setting its sights on the next step of the customer journey—purchase. Brands can now create storefronts on Instagram, where users can click through to a company's web or mobile site to place orders. Instagram is even working on ways to accept payments and place orders without having to leave the network.

Thus, it didn't take long for Facebook to turn Instagram into a moneymaker. Although Facebook doesn't report Instagram financial information separately, by one estimate, Instagram will generate about $7 billion in advertising revenue this year. Another analysis values Instagram at more than $100 billion as a standalone company—100 times what Facebook paid for it just six years ago. In short, no one is mocking Facebook's Instagram purchase anymore.

Instagram is soaring because it has figured out how to integrate advertising with consumer content in a way that satisfies everyone. Far from resenting brand content as intrusive, many Instagrammers appear to welcome it, making social media advertising a win-win-win for Instagram, its advertisers, and its user community.

Sources: Ryan Holmes, "As Facebook Shifts, Instagram Emerges as a New Home for Brands," *Forbes*, February 1, 2018, www.forbes.com/sites/ryanholmes/2018/02/01/as-facebook-shifts-instagram-emerges-as-a-new-home-for-brands/#567780a37834; Yoni Heisler, "Once Mocked, Facebook's $1 Billion Acquisition of Instagram Was a Stroke of Genius," *BGR*, December 29, 2016, http://bgr.com/2016/12/29/facebook-instagram-acquisition-1-billion-genius/; David Meyer, "Instagram Is Starting to Take Payments—but Not for Products Just Yet," *Fortune*, May 4, 2018, http://fortune.com/2018/05/04/instagram-app-payments-e-commerce/; Jessica Wade, "20 Instagram Statistics Every Marketer Should Know About for 2018," *Smart Insights*, February 2, 2018, www.smartinsights.com/social-media-marketing/instagram-marketing/instagram-statistics/; Mary Lister, "Instagram Is Worth Over $100 Billion," *Mediakix*, http://mediakix.com/2017/12/how-much-is-instagram-worth-market-cap/#gs.unG4ykE; and www.statista.com/statistics/271633/annual-revenue-of-instagram/, https://business.instagram.com/blog/welcoming-two-million-advertisers, and https://business.instagram.com/advertising/, accessed October 2018.

Although these large, general-interest social media networks grab most of the headlines, countless niche and interest-based social media have also emerged. These online social networks cater to the needs of smaller communities of like-minded people, making them ideal vehicles for marketers who want to target special-interest groups. There's at least one social media network for just about every interest, hobby, or group. Goodreads is a social network where 65 million avid readers can "Meet your next favorite book" and discuss it with friends, whereas moms share advice and commiseration at CafeMom.com. FarmersOnly.com provides online dating for down-to-earth "country folks" who enjoy "blue skies, living free and at peace in wide open spaces, raising animals, and appreciating nature"—"because city folks just don't get it." At Birdpost.com, avid bird watchers can keep an online list of birds they've seen and share bird sightings with other members using modern satellite maps.[25]

Social Media Marketing Advantages and Challenges

Using social media presents both advantages and challenges. On the plus side, social media are *targeted* and *personal*—they allow marketers to create and share tailored brand content with individual consumers and customer communities. Social media are *interactive*, making them ideal for starting and participating in customer conversations and listening to customer feedback. Social media are also *immediate* and *timely*. They can be used to reach customers anytime, anywhere with timely and relevant marketing content regarding brand happenings and activities. As discussed earlier in the chapter, the rapid growth in social media usage has caused a surge in *real-time marketing*, allowing marketers to create and join consumer conversations around situations and events as they occur. Consider JetBlue:[26]

> A man once tweeted JetBlue while waiting at the airport to ask why he was charged $50 for taking an earlier flight. JetBlue responded to his Tweet within several minutes, and the customer seemed satisfied. But the JetBlue social media crew didn't stop there. Instead, it forwarded the exchange to the JetBlue staff at the airport. The airport staff studied the man's Twitter profile picture and then walked around the terminal until they found him so they could follow up in person. In another case, one JetBlue customer jokingly tweeted that she expected a "welcome parade" at the gate when she arrived in Boston. Much to the delighted customer's surprise, when she arrived at her destination, the JetBlue airport staff welcomed her with fanfare, including marching band music and handmade signs.
>
> Of course, JetBlue can't surprise every customer in this way. >> However, the airline is legendary for the speed and quality of its social media interactions. It receives 2,500 to 2,600 Twitter mentions every day, and the JetBlue social media team reads and responds to every single one, with an impressive average response time of 10 minutes. Beyond engaging customers and keeping them happy, such social media interactions provide valuable customer feedback. "We're all about people," says JetBlue's Manager of Customer Commitment, "and being on social media is just a natural extension of that."

>> JetBlue is legendary for the speed and quality of its social media responses. For example, the JetBlue social media team responds to every single Twitter mention it receives, with an impressive average response time of 10 minutes.

JetBlue

Social media can be very *cost-effective*. Although creating and administering social media content can be costly, many social media are free or inexpensive to use. Thus, returns on social media investments are often high compared with those of expensive traditional media such as television or print. The low cost of social media puts them within easy reach of even small businesses and brands that can't afford the high costs of big-budget marketing campaigns.

Perhaps the biggest advantage of social media is their *engagement and social sharing capabilities*. Social media are especially well suited to creating customer engagement and community—for getting customers involved with the brand and with each other. More than any other channels, social media can involve customers in shaping and sharing brand content, experiences, information, and ideas.

For example, consider Etsy—the online craft marketplace that's "Your place to buy and sell all things handmade." Etsy uses its web and mobile sites and a host of social media to create an Etsy lifestyle community, where buyers congregate to learn about, explore, exchange, and share ideas about handmade and vintage products and related topics. In addition to its active Facebook, Twitter, and YouTube pages, Etsy engages 1.7 million brand followers on photo-sharing site Instagram, where the Etsy community shares photos of creative ideas and projects. It also engages over a million followers on social scrapbooking site Pinterest, with boards on topics ranging from "DIY Projects," "Entertaining," and "Stuff We Love" to "Etsy Weddings" and even "Yum! Recipes to Share," where the community posts favorite recipes. Etsy sells few of the ingredients that go into the recipes, but it's all part of the Etsy lifestyle. Through its extensive online and social media presence, Etsy has created an active and engaged worldwide community of 33.4 million shoppers and 1.9 million sellers worldwide in what it calls "The marketplace we make together."[27]

Social media marketing also presents challenges. First, many companies are still experimenting with how to use them effectively and results are hard to measure. Second, such social networks are largely user controlled. The company's goal in using social media is to make the brand a part of consumers' conversations and their lives. However, marketers can't simply muscle their way into consumers' digital interactions—they need to earn the right to be there. Rather than intruding, marketers must become a valued part of the online experience by developing a steady flow of engaging content.

Also, because consumers have so much control over social media content, even a seemingly harmless social media campaign can backfire. The social media highway is littered with well-intentioned campaigns that were hijacked by consumers who turned #hashtags into #bashtags. There's a clear message. With social media, "you're going into the consumer's backyard. This is their place," warns one social marketer. "Social media is a pressure cooker," says another. "The hundreds of thousands, or millions, of people out there are going to take your idea, and they're going to try to shred it or tear it apart and find what's weak or stupid in it."[28]

Integrated Social Media Marketing

Using social media might be as simple as posting some messages and promotions on a brand's Facebook or Twitter pages or creating brand buzz with videos or images on YouTube, Instagram, or Pinterest. However, most large companies are now designing full-scale social media efforts that blend with and support other elements of a brand's marketing content strategy and tactics. More than making scattered efforts and chasing Likes and retweets, companies that use social media successfully are integrating a broad range of diverse media to create brand-related social sharing, engagement, and customer community.

Managing a brand's social media efforts can be a major undertaking. For example, Starbucks is one of the world's most successful social media marketers. Its core social media team connects with its fans through 30 accounts on five different social platforms. Frappuccino drinks alone have more than 14 million followers on Facebook, Twitter, and Instagram. Managing and integrating all that social media content is challenging, but the results are worth the investment. Customers can and do engage with Starbucks by the tens of millions digitally, without ever setting foot in a store. One recent study found that Starbucks tallied 17 times the Facebook and Instagram engagement of nearest competitor Dunkin'.[29]

But more than just creating online engagement and community, Starbucks' social media presence also drives customers into its stores. For example, in its first big social media promotion several years ago, Starbucks offered a free pastry with a morning drink purchase. A million people showed up. A more recent "Tweet-a-Coffee" promotion, which let customers give a $5 gift card to a friend by putting both #tweetacoffee and the friend's handle in a tweet, resulted in $180,000 in purchases within little more than one month. And when Starbucks introduced the Unicorn Frappuccino last spring—a limited-time drink that changed colors when swirled—it was perfectly crafted to catch the attention of Instagrammers, who posted some 180,000 Instagram photos of the drink in only a week. Although offered for one week, many Starbucks locations ran out of supplies sooner. Social media "are not just about engaging and telling a story and connecting," says Starbucks's head of global digital marketing. "They can have a material impact on the business."[30]

Mobile Marketing

Mobile marketing
Marketing messages, promotions, and other content delivered to on-the-go consumers through their mobile devices.

Mobile marketing features marketing messages, promotions, and other marketing content delivered to on-the-go consumers through their mobile devices. Marketers use mobile marketing to engage customers anywhere, anytime during the buying and relationship-building processes. The widespread adoption of mobile devices and the surge in mobile web traffic have made mobile marketing a must for most brands.

With the recent proliferation of mobile phones, smartphones, and tablets, mobile device penetration is now greater than 100 percent in the United States (many people possess more than one mobile device). More than 75 percent of people in the United States own a smartphone, and more than half of all U.S. households are currently mobile-only households with no landline phone. The mobile apps market, little more than a decade old, has exploded globally: There are millions of apps available, and the average smartphone owner uses nine apps a day.[31]

Most people love their phones and rely heavily on them. According to one study, nearly 90 percent of consumers who own smartphones, tablets, computers, and TVs would give up all of those other screens before giving up their phones. On average, Americans check their smartphones 80 times a day and spend five hours a day on their mobile devices using apps, talking, texting, and browsing the web. Thus, although TV is still a big part of people's lives, mobile is rapidly becoming their "first screen." Away from home, it's their only screen.[32]

>> For consumers, a smartphone or tablet can be a handy shopping companion. It can provide on-the-go product information, price comparisons, advice and reviews from other consumers, access to instant deals, and fast and convenient avenues to purchase. One recent study found that more than 90 percent of smartphone-toting shoppers have used their phone while shopping and 62 percent of shoppers have made a purchase using a mobile device. Mobile buying now accounts for nearly 40 percent of all e-commerce sales.[33] Mobile provides a rich platform for engaging consumers more deeply as they move through the buying process with tools ranging from mobile ads, coupons, and texts to apps and mobile websites.

>> For consumers, a smartphone or tablet can be a handy shopping companion. As a result, mobile advertising spending is surging.
George Rudy/Shutterstock

As a result, mobile advertising spending in the United States is surging. It is projected to grown 20 percent this year and will account for more than 75 percent of all digital advertising spending.[34] Mobile ad spending by itself is expected to overtake TV ad spending by next year. Almost every major marketer—from Nike, P&G, and Macy's to your local supermarket to nonprofits such as the Red Cross—is now integrating mobile marketing into its direct marketing programs.

Companies use mobile marketing to stimulate immediate buying, make shopping easier, enrich the brand experience, or all of these. It lets marketers provide consumers with information, incentives, and choices at the moment they are expressing an interest or when they are most likely to make a buying choice (see Marketing at Work 14.2). Today's rich-media mobile ads can create substantial engagement and impact. For example, Gatorade put mobile marketing's timely engagement potential to good use during a recent Super Bowl:[35]

MARKETING AT WORK 14.2

Mobile Marketing: Engaging Consumers in Moments That Matter

It seems like whatever you want to do these days, "there's an app for that." The mobile app market has exploded in recent years. Apple's App Store now boasts 2.2 million apps; the Google Play Store leads with more than 2.8 million apps. Mobile has become today's brave new marketing frontier, especially for brands courting younger consumers. Mobile devices are very personal, ever-present, and always on. That makes them an ideal medium for obtaining quick responses to individualized, time-sensitive offers. Mobile marketing lets brands engaged consumers in moments that matter.

Some mobile apps are brand-specific—they help consumers navigate the brand's products, services, special offers, and community. For example, the Sephora app "Makes Beauty Mobile," providing "instant, on-the-go access to daily inspiration, exclusive offers, and more." The Chick-fil-A One app gives customers "Endless Awesome"—it makes ordering easier, lets them bypass lines and scan to pay, and gives them some surprising treats. Is that Redbox kiosk too slow? Download the Redbox app—it lets you find and reserve a DVD using your mobile device and have it waiting for you at the kiosk.

Other apps help consumers navigate the marketplace and access other companies' offers. The Angie's List app provides on-the-go access to lists, ratings, and reviews of best local services providers, from roofers, plumbers, and mechanics to doctors and dentists. The coupon organizing Flipp app delivers weekly store flyer deals to consumers' phones even as they shop; the AwardWallet app helps users track and manage points and awards from all their rewards accounts in one place.

In today's cluttered mobile environment, successful mobile marketing goes well beyond just texting out a coupon or a link to buy. Instead, it engages customers in the moment with relevant features and offers that enhance brand relationships and buying experiences. Google's Waze app does more than just help users navigate from point A to point B and find local stops along way. It also pinpoints traffic jams, accidents, speed traps, and fuel prices in real time, faithfully updated by Waze's 100 million active users. REI's Powder Project app gives users "backcountry, sidecountry, and secret stashes" ski slope information for locations throughout the United States and Canada. Beyond just the basics like snow conditions, number of open lifts, and trail maps, the app offers webcam views, GPS routing, elevation profiles, forums, and a host of interactive features plus links to REI for times when you decide you can't live without a new set of K2 skis or a two-man Hubba Hubba tent.

Consumers have come to expect frictionless mobile buying experiences from marketing giants like Amazon. But with recent rapid advances in mobile capabilities, more and more companies are becoming the Amazons of their industries. Consider travel company TripAdvisor. What started mostly as a hotel and restaurant review website has now become "your ultimate travel companion." TripAdvisor's mobile apps give users anytime, anywhere, as-they-travel access to comprehensive crowd-sourced reviews, photos and videos, maps, and descriptive information about hotels, restaurants, air travel options, places to go, and things to see worldwide. The easy-to-use apps include lots of useful features, such as smartphone lock screen notifications that call out nearby points of interest as you travel. And booking options for hotels, restaurants, and flights are always just a tap away.

One user likens the TripAdvisor app to a best friend who's an endlessly knowledgeable travel expert and helps you make all your vacation travel arrangements. And then she goes along with you on your vacation as your own personal travel guide, sharing just the right information about local points of interest, finding and reviewing good places to eat, and providing digital maps to help you get where you're going. In turn, TripAdvisor is a great place for travel- and hospitality-related brands to link up with 375 million engaged and connected travelers a month who are actively traveling or planning trips. TripAdvisor took in $1.5 billion in revenues from mobile advertising and bookings last year.

Mobile marketing lets brands personalize promotions and weave them into relevant everyday customer experiences. For example, Kiip (pronounced "keep") is a mobile rewards network that specializes in helping brands provide

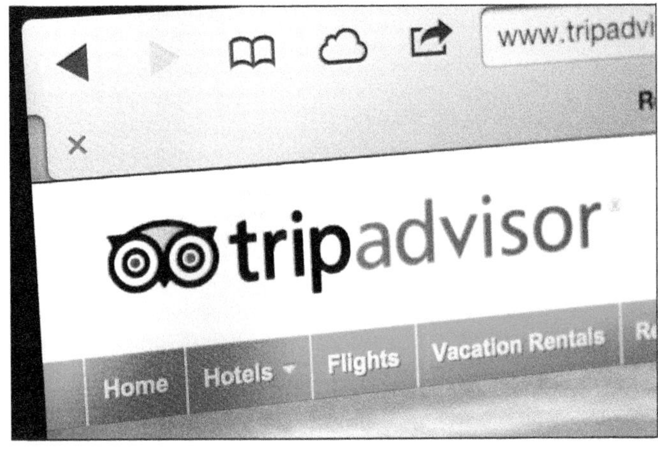

>> Mobile marketing: TripAdvisor's mobile app—"your ultimate travel companion"—gives users as-they-travel access to crowd-sourced information about hotels, restaurants, places to go, and things to see worldwide. And booking options are always just a tap away.

Ian Dagnall/Alamy Stock Photo

customers with just the right rewards at just the right times based on their everyday activities. Kiip started by embedding its technology into video game apps, rewarding gamers who reached new game levels or met other goals with coupons for one of their favorite brands, such as Coca-Cola. It now helps brands across a range of categories to use mobile rewards to engage customers at key brand-related moments. Kiip has worked with 500 brands—including Coca-Cola, Kellogg's, Johnson & Johnson, McDonald's, Taco Bell, and MasterCard—and is now embedded in more than 6,000 mobile apps.

Kiip works with brands to help them map out "demand moments"—times when consumers might be most receptive to brand engagement and messages. It then uses the here-and-now power of mobile to let brands be right there when the behavior is occurring. For fitness apps like MapMyRun and productivity apps like Any.do, Kiip ties rewards to real-life achievements. When users cross things off their to-do lists or achieve a running goal, they get a reward from a relevant brand. For example, P&G's Secret deodorant rewarded female MapMyRun users with free song downloads for their workout playlists. And snack giant Mondelez rewarded Any.do users with free packs of Trident when they set new personal records.

Kiip helped spirits company Campari America with a corporate responsibility campaign designed to connect consumers with the brand while promoting responsible drinking. Kiip identified probable drinking occasions—as when customers were doing mobile searches for happy hours, consulting cocktail recipes, or checking game scores while at sports bars during the wee hours. Campari then offered users coupons for discounted or even free rides from ride-hailing service Lyft to help them return home safely.

Unlike typical banner ads, pop-ups, or emails, Kiip's offers enhance a user's regular activities rather than interrupting them. According to Kiip's founder and CEO, Kiip "is less about real-time marketing and more about real-time-needs addressing." In fact, he asserts, Kiip isn't really in the mobile ad business at all—it's in the happiness business. "We want to capitalize on happiness," he says. "Everything's better when you're happy." Mobile timeliness, relevance, and happiness pay off in terms of consumer response. Across its entire network, Kiip's average engagement rate—people claiming a reward, clicking on it, or watching a video related to it—is 10 percent but can reach as high as 50 percent. That's impressive given that engagement rates for typical app ads run below one percent.

Many consumers are still initially skeptical about mobile marketing. But they often change their minds if mobile offers deliver useful, in-the-moment brand and shopping information, entertaining content, or timely coupons and discounted prices. Most mobile efforts target only consumers who voluntarily opt in or download apps. But in the increasingly cluttered mobile marketing space, customers just won't do that unless they see real value in it. The challenge for marketers: develop valued mobile offers, ads, and apps that make customers want to come calling.

Sources: See Henry Burrell, "The Best Travel Apps for Android & iOS," *Tech Advisor*, April 26, 2018, www.techadvisor.co.uk/feature/software/best-travel-apps-3676191/; "Kiip CEO: Engage Consumers in the Moments that Matter," *Wall Street Journal*, January 9, 2018, http://deloitte.wsj.com/cmo/2018/01/09/kiip-ceo-engage-consumers-in-the-moments-that-matter/; John Corpuz, "25 Essential Travel Apps," *Toms Guide*, December 13, 2017, www.tomsguide.com/us/pictures-story/491-best-travel-apps.html#s16; Felicia Tanasoiu, "Mobile App Success Story: How TripAdvisor Did It," *Appsamurai*, September 25, 2017, https://appsamurai.com/mobile-app-success-story-how-tripadvisor-did-it/; and information from www.powderproject.com/, www.kiip.me/brands/, www.sephora.com/mobile, and www.tripadvisor.com/MediaKit, accessed October 2018.

Gatorade wanted to recreate the iconic Gatorade dunk moment—the tradition of dousing a sports coach with a cooler of ice cold Gatorade after a big win—but make it a personal moment, one that individual fans could enjoy and share during and after the game. So it worked with Snapchat to create a Snapchat filter that made it look like a cooler of the sports drink was spilling over users' heads while fans cheered in the background. The result? Fans created more than 8.2 million videos of themselves getting virtually dunked with more than 165 million views in 48 hours. Although it never appeared on TV, it was the most viewed and interacted-with ad of the Super Bowl. "We've always been a little hesitant to activate against the dunk because it's such a natural moment that happens in the game," says a Gatorade marketer. But "this ended up feeling like the right opportunity because it's not about what happens on the field—it's about the fans being able to participate."

Most marketers have created their own mobile online sites. Others have created useful or entertaining mobile apps to engage customers with their brands and help them shop. For example, the Benjamin Moore Color Capture app lets customers take photos of colorful objects and then match them to any of 3,500 Benjamin Moore paint colors. Starbucks's mobile app lets customers use their phones as a Starbucks card to make fast and easy purchases. And Charles Schwab's mobile apps let customers get up-to-the-minute investment news, monitor their accounts, and make trades at any time from any location—it helps you "stay connected with your money."

As with other forms of direct marketing, however, companies must use mobile marketing responsibly or risk angering already ad-weary consumers. Most people don't want to be interrupted regularly by advertising, so marketers must be smart about how they engage people on mobile devices. The key is to provide genuinely useful information and offers that will make consumers want to engage. And many marketers target mobile ads on an opt-in-only basis.

In all, digital direct marketing—online, social media, and mobile marketing—offers both great promise and many challenges for the future. Its most ardent apostles still envision a time when the internet and digital marketing will replace magazines, newspapers, and even stores as sources for information, engagement, and buying. Most marketers, however, hold a more realistic view. For most companies, digital, mobile, and social media marketing will remain important approaches to the marketplace that work alongside other approaches in a fully integrated marketing mix.

LINKING THE CONCEPTS

Stop now and think about how online, social media, and mobile marketing affect your brand buying behavior and preferences.

- How much of your product research, shopping, and actual buying take place online? How much of that is conducted on a mobile device? How and how much do your digital and in-store buying activities interact?
- How much and what kinds of online, social media, and mobile marketing do you encounter? Do you benefit from such marketing or is it more of an unwelcome intrusion? In what ways?
- Do you engage directly with any brands or brand communities through online sites, social media, or phone apps? Do your online, social media, or mobile interactions influence your brand preferences and buying? Discuss.

Author Comment
Although online, social media, and mobile direct marketing seem to be getting much of the attention these days, traditional direct media still carry a lot of the direct marketing freight. Just think about your often-overstuffed mailbox.

Traditional Direct Marketing Forms

OBJECTIVE 14-5 Identify and discuss the traditional direct marketing forms and overview public policy and ethical issues presented by direct marketing.

Although the fast-growing digital, social, and mobile marketing tools have grabbed most of the headlines lately, traditional direct marketing tools are very much alive and still heavily used. We now examine the traditional approaches shown on the right side of Figure 14.1.

The major traditional forms of direct marketing are face-to-face or personal selling, direct-mail marketing, catalog marketing, telemarketing, direct-response television (DRTV) marketing, and kiosk marketing. We examined personal selling in depth in Chapter 13. Here, we look into the other forms of traditional direct marketing.

Direct-Mail Marketing

Direct-mail marketing
Marketing that occurs by sending an offer, announcement, reminder, or other item directly to a person at a particular address.

Direct-mail marketing involves sending an offer, announcement, reminder, or other item to a person at a particular address. Using highly selective mailing lists, direct marketers send out millions of mail pieces each year—letters, catalogs, ads, brochures, samples, videos, and other "salespeople with wings." U.S. marketers spend an estimated $42 billion annually on direct mail (including both catalog and noncatalog mail), which accounts for 26 percent of all direct marketing spending.[36]

Direct mail is well suited to direct, one-to-one communication. It permits high target market selectivity, can be personalized, is flexible, and allows the easy measurement of results. Although direct mail costs more per thousand people reached than mass media such as television or magazines, the people it reaches are much better prospects. Direct mail has proved successful in promoting all kinds of products, from books, insurance, travel, gift items, gourmet foods, clothing, and other consumer goods to industrial products of all kinds. Charities also use direct mail heavily to raise billions of dollars each year.

Some analysts have predicted the eventual demise of traditional forms of direct mail in the coming years as marketers switch to newer digital forms, such as email and online, social media, and mobile marketing. The newer digital direct marketing approaches deliver messages at incredible speeds and lower costs compared to the U.S. Post Office's "snail mail" pace.

However, although the volume of traditional direct mail has decreased during the past decade, it is still heavily used by most marketers. Mail marketing offers some distinct advantages over digital forms. It provides something tangible for people to hold and keep, and it can be used to send samples. "Mail makes it real," says one analyst. It "creates an emotional connection with customers that digital cannot. They hold it, view it, and engage with it in a manner entirely different from their [digital] experiences." In contrast, email and other digital forms are easily ignored, filtered, or trashed. With spam filters and ad blockers filtering out email and mobile ads these days, says a direct marketer, "sometimes you have to lick a few stamps."[37]

Traditional direct mail can be an effective component of a broader integrated marketing campaign. For example, GEICO relies heavily on TV advertising to establish broad customer awareness and positioning. However, it also uses lots of good old direct mail to break through the glut of insurance advertising clutter on TV. GEICO uses direct mail offers that invite carefully targeted customers act immediately to save money on their auto insurance by visiting geico.com, calling 1-800-947-AUTO, or contacting a local GEICO agent. GEICO makes its direct mailers as unskippable as its TV and digital ads. >> For example, potential customers might receive a personally addressed mail piece with a "save money" message and scannable code on the front of the envelope, inviting them to look inside or simply scan the code with their smartphone. Scanning the code takes them directly to GEICO's mobile site where they received additional information and calls to action.

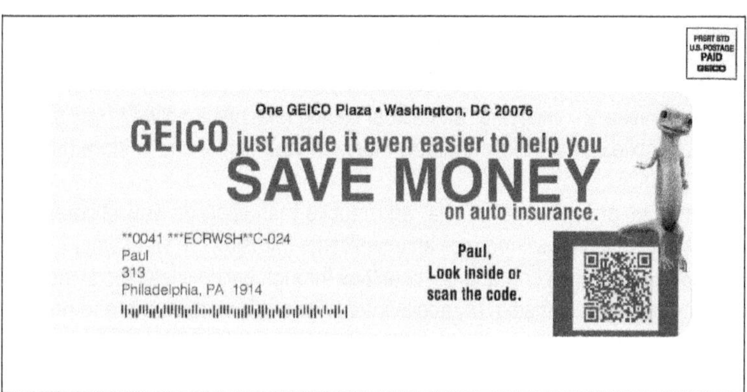

>> Direct-mail marketing: GEICO uses lots of good old direct mail to break through the glut of insurance advertising clutter.

Direct mail may be resented as *junk mail* if sent to people who have no interest in it. For this reason, smart marketers are targeting their direct mail carefully so as not to waste their money and recipients' time. They are designing permission-based programs that send direct mail only to those who want to receive it.

Catalog Marketing

Catalog marketing
Direct marketing through print, video, or digital catalogs that are mailed to select customers, made available in stores, or presented online.

Advances in technology, along with the move toward personalized, one-to-one marketing, have resulted in exciting changes in **catalog marketing**. *Catalog Age* magazine used to define a *catalog* as "a printed, bound piece of at least eight pages, selling multiple products, and offering a direct ordering mechanism." That definition must now be revamped to meet changing times.

With the stampede to the internet and digital marketing, more and more catalogs are going digital. A variety of online-only catalogers have emerged and most print catalogers have added web-based catalogs and mobile catalog apps to their marketing mixes. For example, catalogs from retailers such as Macy's, Anthropologie, L.L. Bean, Williams-Sonoma, Restoration Hardware, J. Crew, Bonobos, or West Elm are only a finger swipe away on a mobile device.

Digital catalogs eliminate printing and mailing costs. They also allow real-time merchandising. Whereas printed catalogs are frozen in time, digital catalogs let sellers add or remove products and features as needed and adjust prices instantly to match demand. And whereas space is limited in a print catalog, online catalogs can offer an almost unlimited amount of merchandise. Customers can carry digital catalogs anywhere they go, even when shopping in stores. Digital catalogs can be interactive, and they can offer a broader assortment of presentation formats, including search, video, and augmented reality (AR). For example, IKEA's catalog app contains 3D and AR features that let customers experiment with room designs and colors schemes and even virtually place furniture and other IKEA products in their homes to see how they might look or to share them with others via social media.

Despite the advantages of digital catalogs, however, as your overstuffed mailbox may suggest, printed catalogs are still thriving. U.S. direct marketers mailed out almost 10 billion catalogs last year.[38] Although that's less than half the number mailed out a decade ago, it's still a lot of catalogs.

Beyond their ability to drive immediate sales, paper catalogs create emotional connections with customers. >> Somehow, turning actual catalog pages engages consumers in a way that digital images simply can't. And most of today's catalogs are much more than just big books full of product pictures and prices. For example, Anthropologie calls its catalogs "journals" and fills them with lifestyle images. Although the retailer has been expanding its digital marketing, it realizes that "there is something special about holding a beautiful book of imagery in your hands," says an Anthropologie marketer. "Years ago, [a catalog] was a selling tool, and now it's become an inspirational source," says another direct marketer. "We know our customers love a tactile experience."[39]

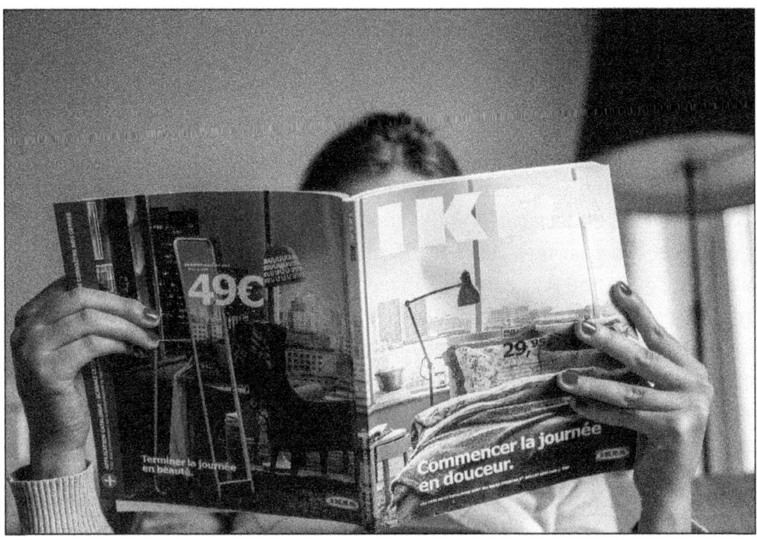

>> Despite the rapid growth of digital catalogs, printed catalogs are still thriving. Somehow, turning actual catalog pages engages consumers in a way that digital images simply can't.

Hadrian/Shutterstock

Importantly, printed catalogs are one of the best ways to drive in-store, online, and mobile sales. For example, one survey found that 75 percent of Lands' End shoppers say they look at a catalog before heading to the retailer's online or mobile site to buy. And menswear company Bonobos discovered that 30 percent of its first-time online customers are inspired to shop there after receiving a catalog, and those buyers spend 50 percent more than catalog-free Bonobos shoppers. Furniture retailer Restoration Hardware says that its catalogs, which it calls "source books," are "a key driver of sales through both our websites and retail stores." "I think their catalog is a work of art," says a retail consultant. "It's very, very high end. People end up wanting to see the products [in stores] because of how beautiful they look on the page." Catalogs and online sales together make up 45 percent of Restoration Hardware's revenues.[40] Thus, the key to catalog marketing today is to carefully integrate catalogs with online and store marketing efforts.

Telemarketing

Telemarketing
Using the telephone to sell directly to customers.

Telemarketing involves using the telephone to sell directly to consumers and business customers. We're all familiar with telephone marketing directed toward consumers, but business-to-business marketers also use telemarketing extensively. Marketers use *outbound* telephone marketing to sell directly to consumers and businesses. They also use *inbound* toll-free numbers to receive orders referred from television and print ads, direct mail, catalogs, websites, and phone apps.

Properly designed and targeted telemarketing provides many benefits, including purchasing convenience and increased product and service information. However, the explosion in unsolicited outbound telephone marketing over the years annoyed many consumers, who objected to the almost daily "junk phone calls." In 2003, U.S. lawmakers responded with the National Do Not Call Registry, which is managed by the Federal Trade Commission (FTC). The legislation bans most telemarketing calls to registered phone numbers (although people can still receive calls from nonprofit groups, politicians, and companies with which they have recently done business). Consumers responded enthusiastically. To date, more than 229 million home and mobile phone numbers have been registered at www.donotcall.gov or by calling 888-382-1222.[41] Businesses that break do-not-call laws can be fined more than $40,000 per violation. As a result, the program has been very successful.

Do-not-call legislation has hurt parts of the consumer telemarketing industry. Outgoing consumer telemarketing has dropped off substantially in recent years. However, two major forms of telemarketing—inbound consumer telemarketing and outbound B-to-B telemarketing—remain strong and growing. Telemarketing also remains a major fundraising tool for nonprofit and political groups. Interestingly, do-not-call regulations appear to be helping some direct marketers more than hurting them. Rather than making unwanted calls, many of these marketers are developing "opt-in" calling systems, in which they provide useful information and offers to customers who have invited the company to contact them by phone or email. The opt-in model provides better returns for marketers than the formerly invasive one.

Direct-Response Television Marketing

Direct-response television (DRTV) marketing
Direct marketing via television that persuasively describes a product and give customers a toll-free number or an online site for ordering.

Using **direct-response television (DRTV) marketing**, direct marketers air television spots, often 60 or 120 seconds in length, which persuasively describe a product and give customers a toll-free number or an online site for ordering. It also includes full 30-minute or longer advertising programs, called *infomercials*, for a single product.

Successful direct-response television advertising campaigns can ring up big sales. For example, little-known infomercial maker Guthy-Renker has helped propel Proactiv acne treatment, Crepe Erase, Meaningful Beauty, and other "transformational" beauty products into multimillion-dollar power brands. Guthy-Renker combines DRTV with social media campaigns using Facebook, Pinterest, Twitter, and YouTube to create a powerful integrated direct marketing channel that builds consumer involvement and buying.[42]

DRTV ads are often associated with somewhat loud or questionable pitches for cleaners, stain removers, kitchen gadgets, and nifty ways to stay in shape without working very hard at it. For example, over the past few years "yell and-sell" TV pitchmen like Anthony Sullivan (Swivel Sweeper, Awesome Auger) and Vince Offer (ShamWow, SlapChop) have racked up billions of dollars in sales of "As Seen on TV" products. Brands like OxiClean, ShamWow, and the Snuggie (a blanket with sleeves) have become DRTV cult classics. And direct marketer Beachbody brings in more than $1.3 billion annually via an army of workout videos—from P90X and T-25 to Insanity and Hip Hop Abs—that it advertises on TV using before-and-after stories, clips of the workout, and words of encouragement from the creators.[43]

In recent years, however, a number of large companies—from P&G, Disney, Revlon, and Apple to Toyota, Coca-Cola, Sears, Home Depot, *The Economist*, and even the U.S. Navy—have begun using infomercials to sell their wares, refer customers to retailers, recruit members, or attract buyers to their online, mobile, and social media sites.

Increasingly, as the lines continue to blur between TV and other screens, direct response ads and infomercials are appearing not just on TV, but also on mobile, online, and social media platforms, adding even more TV-like interactive direct marketing venues. Also, most TV ads these days routinely feature web, mobile, and social media links that let multiscreen consumers connect in real time to obtain and share more information about advertised brands.

Kiosk Marketing

As consumers become more and more comfortable with digital and touchscreen technologies, many companies are placing information and ordering machines—called *kiosks* (good old-fashioned vending machines but so much more)—in stores, airports, hotels, college campuses, and other locations. Kiosks are everywhere these days, from self-service hotel and airline check-in devices, to unmanned product and information kiosks in malls, to in-store ordering devices that let you order merchandise not carried in the store. Many modern "smart kiosks" are now wireless-enabled. And some machines can even use facial recognition software that lets them guess gender and age and make product recommendations based on those data.

In-store Kodak, Fuji, and HP kiosks let customers transfer pictures from memory cards, mobile phones, and other digital storage devices; edit them; and make high-quality color prints. Coinstar kiosks in grocery, drug, and mass merchandise stores convert your mountains of coins into paper cash, gift certificates for retailers such as Amazon and Home Depot, or donations to your favorite charity. Redbox operates more than 40,000 movie and video game rental kiosks in McDonald's, Walmart, Walgreens, CVS, Family Dollar, and other retail outlets. Customers make their selections on a touchscreen and then swipe a credit or debit card to rent DVDs and games for less than $3 a day.

ZoomSystems creates small, freestanding kiosks called ZoomShops for retailers ranging from Proactiv, Uniqlo, and Nespresso to Macy's and Best Buy. For example, 100 Best Buy Express ZoomShop kiosks across the country—conveniently located in airports, busy malls, military bases, retail stores, and resorts—automatically dispense an assortment of

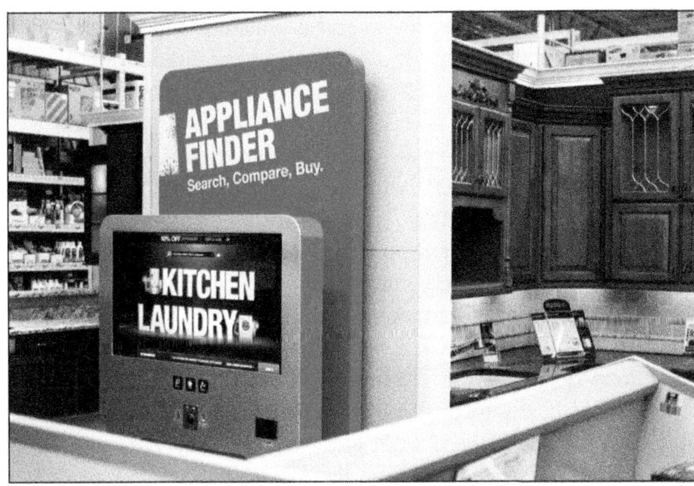

>> **Kiosk marketing: The in-store Home Depot Appliance Finder kiosk helps customers find and buy the products they want on the spot. Sales associates can also use the kiosk as a sales tool.**

Image Manufacturing Group

portable media players, digital cameras, gaming consoles, headphones, phone chargers, travel gadgets, and other popular products. According to ZoomSystems, today's automated retailing "offers [consumers] the convenience of online shopping with the immediate gratification of traditional retail."[44]

Retailers can also use kiosks inside their store to improve the customer shopping experience or assist their salespeople. >> An example is Home Depot's in-store Appliance Finder virtual inventory kiosk. Because appliances are a big purchase, customers often do online research to determine their brand and feature preferences but then come to Home Depot to make the purchase. However, the Home Depot stores can stock only about 5 percent of the appliances available for sale, so customers may browse the store and not find what they want. The Home Depot Appliance Finder kiosk helps such customers find and buy the products they want on the spot. On their own, customers can digitally navigate Home Depot's entire catalog, view informative content including photos and videos, narrow in a product that's right for them, and then pay for and set up delivery of their selection. Sales associates can also use the kiosk as a sales tool. The Home Depot stores featuring the Appliance Finder have seen a 10 to 12 percent increase in appliance sales.[45]

Author Comment

Although we mostly benefit from direct and digital marketing, like most other things in life, they have a dark side as well. Marketers and customers alike must guard against irritating or harmful direct and digital marketing practices.

Public Policy Issues in Direct and Digital Marketing

Direct marketers and their customers usually enjoy mutually rewarding relationships. Occasionally, however, a darker side emerges. The aggressive and sometimes shady tactics of a few direct marketers can bother or harm consumers, giving the entire industry a black eye. Abuses range from simple excesses that irritate consumers to instances of unfair practices or even outright deception and fraud. The direct marketing industry has also faced growing privacy concerns, and online marketers must deal with internet and mobile security issues.

Irritation, Unfairness, Deception, and Fraud

Direct marketing excesses sometimes annoy or offend consumers. For example, most of us dislike direct-response TV commercials that are too loud, long, and insistent. Our mailboxes fill up with unwanted junk mail, our email inboxes bulge with unwanted spam, and our computer, phone, and tablet screens flash with unwanted online or mobile display ads, pop-ups, or pop-unders.

Beyond irritating consumers, some direct marketers have been accused of taking unfair advantage of impulsive or less-sophisticated buyers. Television shopping channels, enticing websites, and program-long infomercials targeting television-addicted shoppers seem to be the worst culprits. They feature smooth-talking hosts, elaborately staged demonstrations, claims of drastic price reductions, flash sales, "while they last" time limitations, and unequaled ease of purchase to inflame buyers who have low sales resistance.

Fraudulent schemes, such as investment scams or phony collections for charity, have also multiplied in recent years. *Internet fraud*, including identity theft and financial scams, has become a serious problem. >> According to the Internet Crime Complaint Center, since 2005, internet scam complaints have more than tripled to almost 280,000 per year. Last year, the monetary loss of scam complaints exceeded $1.3 billion.[46]

One common form of internet fraud is *phishing*, a type of identity theft that uses deceptive emails and fraudulent web and online mobile sites to fool users into divulging their personal data. For example, consumers may receive an email, supposedly from their bank or credit card company, saying that their account's security has been compromised. The sender asks them to log on to a provided web address and confirm their account number, password, and perhaps even their Social Security number. By following the instructions, users are actually turning this sensitive information over to scam artists. Although most

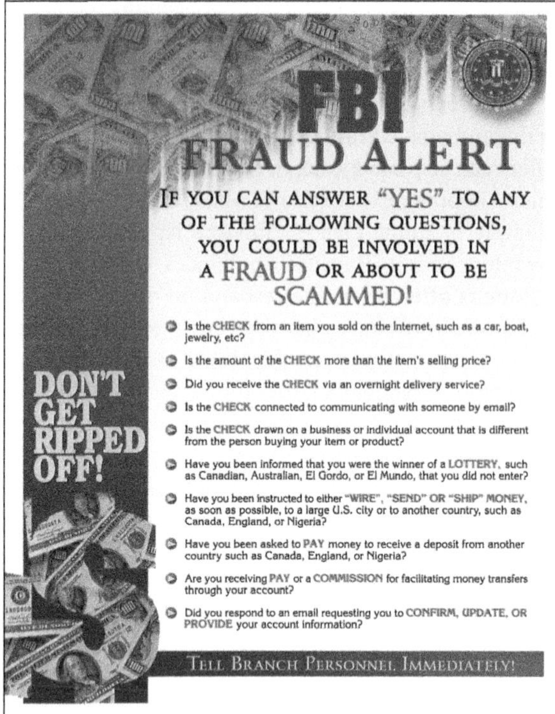

>> Internet fraud has multiplied in recent years. The FBI's Internet Crime Complaint Center provides consumers with a convenient way to alert authorities to suspected violations.

FBI

consumers are now aware of such schemes, phishing can be extremely costly to those caught in the net. It also damages the brand identities of legitimate online marketers who have worked to build user confidence in digital interactions.

Many consumers also worry about *online and digital security*. They fear that unscrupulous snoopers will eavesdrop on their online transactions and social media postings, picking up personal information or intercepting credit and debit card numbers. Although online and mobile shopping are now commonplace, one recent study indicated that 75 percent of participants were still concerned about identity theft. Such concerns are often justified in this age of massive consumer data breaches by organizations ranging from retailers, social media, telecommunications services, and banks to health-care providers and the government. According to one source, there were almost 1,600 major data security breaches in the United States last year alone, a 45 percent increase over the year prior.[47]

Another internet marketing concern is that of *access by vulnerable or unauthorized groups*. For example, marketers of adult-oriented materials and sites have found it difficult to restrict access by minors. Although Facebook, Snapchat, Twitter, Instagram, and other social networks allow no children under age 13 to have profiles, all have significant numbers of underage users. Young social media users can be especially vulnerable to identity theft schemes, revealing personal information, negative experiences, and other online dangers. Concerned state and national lawmakers are currently debating bills that would help better protect children online. Unfortunately, this requires the development of technology solutions, and as Facebook puts it, "That's not so easy."[48]

Consumer Privacy

Invasion of privacy is perhaps the toughest public policy issue now confronting the direct marketing industry. Consumers often benefit from database marketing; they receive more offers that are closely matched to their interests. However, many critics worry that marketers know *too* much about consumers' lives and that they may use this knowledge to take unfair advantage of consumers. At some point, they claim, the extensive use of databases intrudes on consumer privacy. Consumers, too, worry about their privacy. Although they are now much more willing to share personal information and preferences with marketers via digital and social media, they are still nervous about it. One recent survey found that 78 percent of U.S. internet users worry about their privacy online. Another found that 70 percent of Americans feel they have lost control over the collection and use by companies of their personal data and information.[49]

In these days of "big data," it seems that almost every time consumers post something on social media or send a tweet, visit a website, enter a sweepstakes, apply for a credit card, or order products by phone or online, their names, profiles, and behaviors are entered into some company's already bulging database. Using sophisticated big data analytics, direct marketers can mine these databases to "microtarget" their selling efforts. For example, using mobile phone usage data supplied by mobile operators, SAP's Consumer Insight 365 unit gleans and sells customer insights from up to 300 mobile call, web surfing, and text messaging events per day for each of 20 million to 25 million mobile subscribers.[50]

Most marketers have become highly skilled at collecting and analyzing detailed consumer information both online and offline. Even the experts are sometimes surprised by how much marketers can learn. For example, got a Google account? Consider what Google alone likely knows about you:[51]

> Google knows everything you've ever searched, across all your devices. It knows where you've been—it stores your location every time you turn on your phone. It knows what apps you use, when, and how often. And it stores your YouTube history, from which it can likely glean your

family status, religion, favorite sports, political leanings, and the fact, say, that you recently sought instructions on fixing your dishwasher. Google creates an advertising profile of you based on things like your location, age, gender, interests, career, income, and a host of other variables. Google lets you download all the data it stores about you at google.com/takeout; one reporter was stunned to learn that his download file was 5.5GB big (roughly 3 million Word documents). "This link includes your bookmarks, emails, contacts, your Google Drive files, your YouTube videos, the photos you've taken on your phone, the businesses you've bought from, [and] the products you've bought through Google," says the reporter. Google also has "data from your calendar, your Google hangout sessions, your location history, the music you listen to, the Google books you've purchased, the Google groups you're in, the websites you've created, the phones you've owned, the pages you've shared, how many steps you walk in a day . . ." He concludes, "Manage to gain access to someone's Google account? Perfect, you have a diary of everything that person has done."

Facebook and many other social media can construct similar profiles. And then there's Amazon and most other sellers who track details of consumer online browsing and purchase transactions. Add the data held by credit reporting agencies such as Equifax, which was recently breeched, and the potential for consumer abuse can be frightening.

A Need for Action

To curb direct marketing excesses, various government agencies are investigating not only do-not-call lists but also do-not-mail lists, do-not-track-online lists, and Can Spam legislation. In response to online privacy and security concerns, the federal government has considered numerous legislative actions to regulate how online, social media, and mobile operators obtain and use consumer information. For example, Congress is drafting legislation that would give consumers more control over how online information is used. In addition, the FTC is taking a more active role in policing online privacy.

All of these concerns call for strong actions by marketers to monitor and prevent privacy abuses before legislators step in to do it for them. For example, to head off increased government regulation, six advertiser groups—the American Association of Advertising Agencies, the American Advertising Federation, the Association of National Advertisers, the Data & Marketing Association, the Interactive Advertising Bureau, and the Network Advertising Initiative—issued a set of online advertising principles through the Digital Advertising Alliance. Among other measures, the self-regulatory principles call for online and mobile marketers to provide transparency and choice to consumers if online data are collected or used for targeting interest-based advertising. >> The ad industry uses an *advertising option icon*—a little "i" inside a triangle—that it adds to behaviorally targeted online ads to tell consumers why they are seeing a particular ad and allowing them to opt out.

>> Consumer privacy: The ad industry has agreed on an *advertising option icon* that will tell consumers why they are seeing a particular ad and allow them to opt out.

Digital Advertising Alliance

Of special concern are the privacy rights of children. In 1998, Congress passed the Children's Online Privacy Protection Act (COPPA), which requires online operators targeting children to post privacy policies on their sites. They must also notify parents about any information they're gathering and obtain parental consent before collecting personal information from children under age 13. With the subsequent advent of online social media, mobile phones, and other digital technologies, Congress in 2013 extended COPPA to include "identifiers such as cookies that track a child's activity online, as well as geolocation information, photos, videos, and audio recordings." The main concern is the amount of data mined by third parties from social media as well as social media's own hazy privacy policies.[52]

Many companies have responded to consumer privacy and security concerns with actions of their own. Still others are taking an industry-wide approach. For example, TRUSTe, a nonprofit self-regulatory organization, works with many large corporate sponsors, including Microsoft, Yahoo!, AT&T, Facebook, Disney, and Apple, to audit privacy and security measures and help consumers navigate the internet safely. According to the company's website, "TRUSTe believes that an environment of mutual trust and openness will help make and keep the internet a free, comfortable, and richly diverse community for everyone." To reassure consumers, the company lends its TRUSTe privacy seal to websites, mobile apps, email marketing, and other online and social media channels that meet its privacy and security standards.[53]

The direct marketing industry as a whole is also addressing public policy issues. For example, in an effort to build consumer confidence in shopping direct, the Data & Marketing Association—the largest association for businesses practicing direct, database, and interactive marketing, including nearly half of the *Fortune* 100 companies—launched a "Privacy Promise to American Consumers." The Privacy Promise requires that all DMA members adhere to a carefully developed set of consumer privacy rules. Members must agree to notify customers when any personal information is rented, sold, or exchanged with others. They must also honor consumer requests to opt out of receiving further solicitations or having their contact information transferred to other marketers. Finally, they must abide by the DMA's Preference Service by removing the names of consumers who do not wish to receive mail, phone, or email offers.[54]

Direct marketers know that, if left untended, such direct marketing abuses will lead to increasingly negative consumer attitudes, lower response and engagement rates, and calls for more restrictive state and federal legislation. Most direct marketers want the same things that consumers want: honest and well-designed marketing offers targeted only toward consumers who will appreciate and respond to them. Direct marketing is just too expensive to waste on consumers who don't want it.

REVIEWING AND EXTENDING THE CONCEPTS

CHAPTER REVIEW AND KEY TERMS

Objectives Review

This chapter is the last of three chapters covering the final marketing mix element—promotion. The previous chapters dealt with advertising, public relations, personal selling, and sales promotion. This one investigates the burgeoning field of direct and digital marketing, including online, social media, and mobile marketing.

OBJECTIVE 14-1 Define *direct and digital marketing* and discuss their rapid growth and benefits to customers and companies. (pp 436–438)

Direct and digital marketing involve engaging directly with carefully targeted individual consumers and customer communities to both obtain an immediate response and build lasting customer relationships. Companies use direct marketing to tailor their offers and content to the needs and interests of narrowly defined segments or individual buyers to build direct customer engagement, brand community, and sales. Today, spurred by the surge in internet usage and buying and by rapid advances in digital technologies—from smartphones, tablets, and other digital devices to the spate of online social and mobile media—direct marketing has undergone a dramatic transformation.

For buyers, direct and digital marketing are convenient, easy to use, and private. They give buyers anywhere, anytime access to an almost unlimited assortment of products and buying information. Direct marketing is also immediate and interactive, allowing buyers to create exactly the configuration of information, products, or services they desire and then order them on the spot. Finally, for consumers who want it, digital marketing through online, mobile, and social media provides a sense of brand engagement and community—a place to share brand information and experiences with other brand fans. For sellers, direct and digital marketing are powerful tools for building customer engagement and close, personalized, interactive customer relationships. They also offer greater flexibility, letting marketers make ongoing adjustments to prices and programs or make immediate, timely, and personal announcements and offers.

OBJECTIVE 14-2 Identify and discuss the major forms of direct and digital marketing. (pp 438–439)

The main forms of direct and digital marketing include traditional direct marketing tools and the new digital marketing tools. Traditional direct approaches are face-to-face personal selling, direct-mail marketing, catalog marketing, telemarketing, direct response TV marketing, and kiosk marketing. These traditional tools are still heavily used and very important in most firms' direct marketing efforts. In recent years, however, a new set of direct digital marketing tools has burst onto the marketing scene, including online marketing (websites, online ads and promotions, email, online videos, and blogs), social media marketing, and mobile marketing. The chapter first discusses the fast-growing new digital direct marketing tools and then examines the traditional tools.

OBJECTIVE 14-3 Explain how companies have responded to the internet and the digital age with various online marketing strategies. (pp 439–445)

The internet and digital age have fundamentally changed customers' notions of convenience, speed, price, product information, service, and brand interactions. As a result, they have given marketers a whole new way to create customer value, engage customers, and build customer relationships. The internet now influences a large proportion of total sales—including sales transacted online plus those made in stores but encouraged by online research. To reach this burgeoning market, most companies now market online.

Online marketing takes several forms, including company websites, online advertising and promotions, email marketing, online video, and blogs. Social media and mobile marketing also take place online. But because of their special characteristics, we discuss these fast-growing digital marketing approaches in separate sections. For most companies, the first step in conducting online marketing is to create a website. The key to a successful website is to create enough value and engagement to get consumers to come to the site, stick around, and come back again.

Online advertising has become a major promotional medium. The main forms of online advertising are display ads and search-related ads. Email marketing is also an important form of digital marketing. Used properly, email lets marketers send highly targeted, tightly personalized, relationship-building messages. Another important form of online marketing is posting digital video content on brand websites or social media. Marketers hope that some of their videos will go viral, engaging consumers by the tens of millions. Finally, companies can use blogs as effective means of reaching customer communities. They can create their own blogs and advertise on existing blogs or influence content there.

OBJECTIVE 14-4 Discuss how companies use social media and mobile marketing to engage consumers and create brand community. (pp 445–453)

In the digital age, countless independent and commercial social media have arisen that give consumers online places to congregate, socialize, and exchange views and information. Most marketers are now riding this huge social media wave. Brands can use existing social media or they can set up their own. Using existing social media seems the easiest. Thus, most brands—large and small—have set up shop on a host of social media sites. Some of the major social networks are huge; other niche social media cater to the needs of smaller communities of like-minded people. Beyond these independent social media, many companies have created their own online brand communities. More than making just scattered efforts and chasing Likes and tweets, most companies are integrating a broad range of diverse media to create brand-related social sharing, engagement, and customer community.

Using social media presents both advantages and challenges. On the plus side, social media are targeted and personal, interactive, immediate and timely, and cost-effective. Perhaps the biggest advantage is their engagement and social sharing capabilities, making them ideal for creating customer community. On the down side, consumers' control over social media content makes social media difficult to control.

Mobile marketing features marketing messages, promotions, and other content delivered to on-the-go consumers through their mobile devices. Marketers use mobile marketing to engage customers anywhere, anytime during the buying and relationship-building processes. The widespread adoption of mobile devices and the surge in mobile web traffic have made mobile marketing a must for most brands, and almost every major marketer is now integrating mobile marketing into its direct marketing programs. Many marketers have created their own mobile online sites. Others have created useful or entertaining mobile apps to engage customers with their brands and help them shop.

OBJECTIVE 14-5 Identify and discuss the traditional direct marketing forms and overview the public policy and ethical issues presented by direct marketing. (pp 453–460)

Although the fast-growing digital marketing tools have grabbed most of the headlines lately, traditional direct marketing tools are very much alive and still heavily used. The major forms are face-to-face or personal selling, direct-mail marketing, catalog marketing, telemarketing, direct-response television (DRTV) marketing, and kiosk marketing.

Direct-mail marketing consists of the company sending an offer, announcement, reminder, or other item to a person at a specific address. Some marketers rely on catalog marketing—selling through catalogs mailed to a select list of customers, made available in stores, or accessed online. Telemarketing consists of using the telephone to sell directly to consumers. DRTV marketing involves television advertising that persuasively describes a product and gives customers a toll-free number or an online site for ordering. Kiosks are information and ordering machines that direct marketers place in stores, airports, hotels, and other locations.

Direct marketers and their customers usually enjoy mutually rewarding relationships. Sometimes, however, direct marketing presents a darker side. The aggressive and sometimes shady tactics of a few direct marketers can bother or harm consumers, giving the entire industry a black eye. Abuses range from simple excesses that irritate consumers to instances of unfair practices or even outright deception and fraud. The direct marketing industry has also faced growing concerns about invasion-of-privacy and internet security issues. Such concerns call for strong action by marketers and public policy makers to curb direct marketing abuses. In the end, most direct marketers want the same things that consumers want: honest and well-designed marketing offers targeted only toward consumers who will appreciate and respond to them.

Key Terms

Objective 14-1
Direct and digital marketing (p 436)

Objective 14-2
Digital and social media marketing (p 439)

Objective 14-3
Omni-channel retailing (p 440)
Online marketing (p 440)
Marketing website (p 440)
Branded community website (p 441)
Online advertising (p 441)
Email marketing (p 442)
Spam (p 443)
Viral marketing (p 443)
Blogs (p 444)

Objective 14-4
Social media (p 445)
Mobile marketing (p 450)

Objective 14-5
Direct-mail marketing (p 453)
Catalog marketing (p 454)
Telemarketing (p 455)
Direct-response television (DRTV) marketing (p 456)

DISCUSSION AND CRITICAL THINKING

Discussion Questions

14-1. Compare and contrast the new direct marketing model with the traditional direct marketing model. (AACSB: Written and Oral Communication)

14-2. List the major forms of direct and digital marketing. Has there been a shift in how marketers use direct marketing? (AACSB: Written and Oral Communication)

14-3. Describe the two types of company websites. What challenges do marketers face when using websites to market their products and services? (AACSB: Written and Oral Communication)

14-4. How can marketers use social media and mobile marketing to engage customers? What challenges do marketers face? (AASCB: Written and Oral Communication)

14-5. Discuss how the traditional forms of direct marketing continue to be important promotion tools. (AACSB: Written and Oral Communication)

14-6. What are marketers doing to address consumer privacy in their company's direct marketing campaigns? (AACSB: Written and Oral Communication)

Critical Thinking Exercises

14-7. In a small group, search the internet to locate a controversial or failed social media campaign. Present an analysis of the failed campaign. Make a recommendation on how to address the controversy. (AACSB: Information Technology; Written and Oral Communication; Reflective Thinking)

14-8. Real-time marketing is being used by marketers to connect with consumers. Search the web for real-time marketing examples, and describe three. Why were they successful? (AACSB: Written and Oral Communication; Information Technology; Reflective Thinking)

14-9. Traditional direct marketing is still used by marketers to reach targeted consumers. Using the major forms of traditional direct marketing, select three forms, and prepare a presentation using examples of how companies connected with you, their customer. What was your response? (AACSB: Written and Oral Communication; Information Technology; Reflective Thinking)

MINICASES AND APPLICATIONS

Online, Mobile, and Social Media Marketing Positioning QVC to Compete

With many online retailers having to look giants Amazon and Walmart directly in the eye, QVC is rethinking how it can compete and stay relevant in a tight retail marketplace. The infamous home shopping network that began in 1986 has grown to an $8.8 billion-plus global shopping organization. One aspect QVC is focusing on is its social media interaction with consumers and the social experience of shopping—a shell that Amazon has not been able to crack.

Many Americans have "cut the cord" due to the high costs of cable television subscriptions, which has negatively impacted QVC's access to television audiences over time. However, the organization has overcome this obstacle by livestreaming its shopping content on its own website and also on other platforms like Roku, AppleTV, and Facebook Live. The company boasts more than 100 hours per week in simulcast video. QVC hosts even have their own Facebook Fan pages that shoppers can follow.

QVC reaps strong advantages from this strategy. Because QVC is a historically known entity, consumers' trust levels are high, consumer engagement is high, and the company can track what's working—or not—on its marketing dashboard. QVC has found that it is able to convert consumers from product awareness to actual purchase very quickly with 93 percent of sales coming from repeat customers.

14-10. Discuss the shift in strategy QVC has made. What competitive advantages can now be achieved? (AACSB: Written and Oral Communication; Reflective Thinking)

14-11. Visit www.qvc.com, and connect to one or more of their social media links. What about their social media presence engages you the most as a potential customer? (AACSB Written and Oral Communication; Reflective Thinking; Information Technology)

Marketing Ethics #Fail

According to one survey, 92 percent of U.S. companies now claim that social media marketing is important for their businesses. Fashion designer Kenneth Cole took advantage of the trend in 2011 by posting the following tweet: "Millions are in uproar in #Cairo. Rumor is they heard our new spring collection is now available online at http://bit.ly/KCairo -KC." Kenneth Cole was criticized on social media for capitalizing on the strife of the Egyptian revolution to promote his website. The offensive tweet was deleted, and Cole apologized by tweeting: "Re Egypt tweet: we weren't intending to make light of a serious situation. We understand the sensitivity of this historic moment -KC."

Most marketers would not make the same mistake twice. However, in September 2013, as the United States deliberated military action in Syria, Cole tweeted the following: "'Boots on the ground' or not, let's not forget about sandals, pumps and loafers. #Footwear." To justify this action, Cole told *Details* magazine, "Billions of people read my inappropriate, self-promoting tweet. I got a lot of harsh responses, and we hired a crisis management firm. If you look at lists of the biggest Twitter gaffes ever, we're always one through five. But our stock went up that day, our e-commerce business was better, the business at every one of our stores improved, and I picked up 3,000 new followers on Twitter. So on what criteria is this a gaffe? Within hours, I tweeted an explanation, which had to be vetted by lawyers. I'm not even sure I used the words I'm sorry—because I wasn't sorry."

14-12. Kenneth Cole believes that his controversial tweets improve business and provoke conversation and awareness. Is this an effective use of social media to engage customers with the brand? Why or why not? (AACSB: Written and Oral Communication; Reflective Thinking)

14-13. Many marketers are still learning how to use social media platforms effectively to engage customers in meaningful relationships. Locate three social media platforms used by the Kenneth Cole brand to engage customers. Is the brand's marketing message consistent across all platforms? Explain. (AACSB: Written and Oral Communication; Information Technology; Reflective Thinking)

Marketing by the Numbers Uniqlo's Digital Marketing Campaigns

Uniqlo is a Japanese retail brand that has grown into a global brand in 15 countries thanks to digital marketing campaigns. Founder Tadashi Yamai inherited a chain of men's tailoring retail stores, so he was no stranger to fashion retailing. But he wanted to bring affordable, fashionable, casual clothing to all people, so he created Uniqlo in 1984 to offer casual clothing for all. The philosophy of the brand is "UNIQLO clothes are MADE FOR ALL." The company focuses on its signature innovative clothing lines that have names like HeatTech, UV Cut, LifeWear, and AIRism. In 2007, its pioneering "Uniqlock" viral marketing campaign won dozens of advertising awards, including the coveted Grand Prix award at Cannes. The company continues to run digital marketing campaigns, and while awards are nice, results are better. Marketers measure all sorts of metrics related to digital campaigns, from impressions and click-throughs to purchases. Consider one of its most recent digital campaigns running in the United States to increase brand awareness and sales of its LifeWear line of clothing:

Measures	Value
Impressions	4,000,000
Click-through to site	150,000
Cost of campaign	$45,000
Number of orders	10,250
Revenue generated	$750,000
Abandoned shopping cart	650
Average cost of goods sold (%)	45%
Shipping and handling costs (per order)	$8.50

Performance Metric	Equation
Click-through rate (CTR)	(Click-throughs ÷ Impressions) × 100
Cost per click (CPC)	Cost of campaign ÷ Click-throughs
Conversion ratio	(Number of orders ÷ Click throughs) × 100
Cost per conversion	Cost of campaign ÷ Number of orders
Average order value (AOV)	Revenue generated ÷ Number of orders
Shopping cart abandonment rate	(Abandoned shopping cart ÷ Click-throughs) × 100

14-14. Calculate the performance metrics listed in the table above. Based on these metrics, evaluate the campaign. (AACSB: Oral and Written Communication; Analytic Reasoning; Reflective Thinking)

14-15. Calculate the net marketing contribution (NMC), marketing return on sales (marketing ROS), and marketing return on investment (marketing ROI). Was the campaign successful? Refer to Marketing Profitability Metrics in Appendix 3: Marketing by the Numbers to learn how to do this analysis. (AACSB: Oral and Written Communication; Reflective Thinking; Analytic Reasoning)

Video Case Nutrisystem

To view this video case and its accompanying questions, please visit MyLab Marketing.

You've probably heard of Nutrisystem, a company that produced $800 million in revenues last year by selling weight-loss products. What started as a small effort based on an e-commerce marketing plan has evolved into a multipronged marketing campaign that not only has expanded the business but also provides substantial return-on-investment potential.

The key to Nutrisystem's efforts is its direct-to-consumer platform. Using various advertising outlets, from magazines to television, Nutrisystem's promotions all have one thing in common—they let customers make direct contact with the company. Inserting a unique URL or 800 number in every ad also lets Nutrisystem track the success of each and every effort.

Company Cases 14 OfferUp/2 Facebook/4 Qualtrics

See Appendix 1 for cases appropriate for this chapter.

Case 14, OfferUp: A Mobile Solution for the Mobile Era. By focusing on the local secondhand marketplace with a purely mobile approach that overcomes the shortcomings of Craigslist, OfferUp now poses a real threat to the classified ads leader.

Case 2, Facebook: Making the World More Open and Connected. Facebook has amassed more than 2 billion active monthly users by focusing on its mission: "to give people the power to share and make the world more open and connected."

Case 4, Qualtrics: Managing the Complete Customer Experience. Qualtrics pioneered the online survey. Now, it employs online surveys toward managing customer experience.

Writing Assignments

14-16. Compare and contrast a marketing website and a branded community website. (AACSB: Communication)

14-17. Review the FTC's guidelines on disclosure in online, social media, and mobile advertisements at www.ftc.gov/os/2013/03/130312dotcomdisclosures.pdf. Will the FTC's requirements regarding ads and endorsements make Twitter less effective as an advertising medium?

15 The Global Marketplace

Objectives Outline

OBJECTIVE 15-1 **Discuss how the international trade system and the economic, political-legal, and cultural environments affect a company's international marketing decisions.** See: Global Marketing Today (pp 468–480)

OBJECTIVE 15-2 **Describe three key approaches to entering international markets.** See: Deciding How to Enter the Market (pp 480–483)

OBJECTIVE 15-3 **Explain how companies adapt their marketing strategies and mixes for international markets.** See: Deciding on the Global Marketing Program (pp 483–490)

OBJECTIVE 15-4 **Identify the three major forms of international marketing organization.** See: Deciding on the Global Marketing Organization (pp 490–491)

Previewing the Concepts

You've now learned the fundamentals of how companies develop competitive marketing strategies to engage customers, create customer value, and build lasting customer relationships. In this chapter, we extend these fundamentals to global marketing. Although we've discussed global topics in each previous chapter—it's difficult to find an area of marketing that doesn't contain at least some international elements—here we'll focus on special considerations that companies face when they market their brands globally. Advances in communication, transportation, and digital technologies have made the world a much smaller place. Today, almost every firm, large or small, faces international marketing issues. In this chapter, we will examine six major decisions marketers make in going global.

To start our exploration of global marketing, let's look at Scandinavian furniture and housewares retailer IKEA. IKEA operates successfully in more than 50 countries, engaging consumers across vastly different means, languages, and cultures. IKEA follows a highly standardized international operating model designed to create good-quality, functional furniture at low prices that everyday people can afford. However, IKEA has learned that, when it comes to global markets, one size rarely fits all.

First Stop

IKEA: Just the Right Balance between Global Standardization and Local Adaptation

IKEA, the world's largest furniture retailer, is the quintessential global cult brand. Last year, shoppers made more than 936 million visits to the Scandinavian retailer's 400-plus locations in over 50 countries, generating revenues of more than $47 billion. That's an average of more than $100 million per store annually, more than double Walmart's average per-store sales. IKEA is big and getting bigger—its revenues have doubled during the past decade.

IKEA offers a classic model for how to do business in a global environment. Far more than just a big furniture merchant, IKEA has achieved global success by engaging consumers of all nationalities and cultures. From Beijing to Moscow to Middletown, Ohio, customers are drawn to the IKEA lifestyle, one built around trendy but simple and practical furniture at affordable prices. IKEA's mission worldwide is to "create a better everyday life for the many people... by offering a wide range of well-designed, functional home furnishing products at prices so low that as many people as possible will be able to afford them."

IKEA succeeds globally by striking just the right balance between global standardization and local market adaptation. No matter where in the world you shop at IKEA, you'll find huge stores, the familiar blue-and-yellow brand logo and signage, large selections of contemporary Scandinavian-design furnishings, and affordable prices. At the same time, IKEA carefully adapts its merchandise assortments, store operations, and marketing to cater to the unique needs of customers in different global markets characterized by vastly different means, languages, and cultures.

Many aspects of IKEA's strategy are standard worldwide. For starters, all of its products are rooted in Swedish, contemporary design. Its classic, simple designs have a timeless, near-universal appeal. Low prices are another constant in IKEA's global formula. As a benchmark, every IKEA product is designed to sell for half the price of similar competing products. IKEA keeps its prices low through a relentless focus on cost cutting. Selling largely standardized products worldwide helps keep costs down. So does IKEA's space-saving "flat-pack" approach—selling furniture in pieces to be assembled by customers at home.

IKEA's stores around the world share a standardized design. All are gigantic. At an average size of 300,000 square feet, the average IKEA store is 50 percent larger than an average Walmart Supercenter. To offset such massive size, IKEA stores everywhere are divided into three main sections: *Showrooms* display furnishings in real-room settings, the *marketplace* houses small items, and the *warehouse* makes it easy for customers to pull their own furniture items in flat-pack boxes and cart them to checkout. At any IKEA in the world, parents can drop off their children in the IKEA Småland play area and feed the entire family in the snack bar or the three-meal-a-day restaurant, making it easy to hang around and shop for hours.

Although IKEA tries to standardize its operations as much as possible, it has learned that, in global marketing, one size rarely fits all. IKEA found this out the hard way in the early 1980s when it opened its first U.S. store in Philadelphia and stocked it by importing the same goods it sold in Europe. Americans weren't much impressed. For example, IKEA's beds were too small and too firm for American tastes. Sales suffered, and IKEA considered pulling out of the U.S. market altogether.

No matter where in the world you shop at IKEA, you'll find the huge and familiar blue-and-yellow stores and large selections of Scandinavian-design furnishings at affordable prices. At the same time, IKEA carefully adapts its merchandise and marketing to the unique needs of customers in specific global markets.

LIU JIN/Stringer/Getty Images

Instead, the company made a decision that would become the cornerstone for its expansions into all new international markets—study the market intensely and adapt accordingly. "The more far away we go from our culture, the more we need to understand, learn, and adapt," says IKEA's head of research. Fueled by a better understanding of U.S. consumers, IKEA changed the composition of its mattresses and added king-size beds. After similar changes storewide, sales took off. The United States is now IKEA's second-largest market behind only Germany.

IKEA, the world's largest furniture retailer, is the quintessential global brand. Operating in more countries than Walmart, IKEA is a model for global standardization versus local adaptation in international markets.

IKEA now routinely adjusts its product designs and assortments worldwide to meet the distinct needs and tastes of local consumers. For example, although IKEA stores in China carry many of the same items found in other parts of the world, they also heavy up on rice cookers and chopsticks. The Chinese love a good, hard mattress, so IKEA sells mostly firmer ones there. And because the average living space in China's crowded cities is much smaller than in Europe and the United States, Chinese IKEAs stock smaller appliances and products geared toward saving space and organizing a household.

But there are limits to how much IKEA can adapt product designs and assortments without increasing costs. Says one analyst, "The IKEA model, remember, is volume, volume, volume: It needs vast economies of scale to keep costs low, and that means creating one-size-fits-all solutions as often as possible." So instead of making wholesale product changes around the globe, IKEA often simply adapts its marketing and merchandising to show locals how IKEA's standard products fit with their lives and cultures. "IKEA has gotten awfully good at showing how the same product can mesh with different regional habitats," says the analyst.

For example, showrooms in Japan and the Netherlands may feature the same beds and cabinets, but the Japanese display might show tatami mats while the Dutch room incorporates slanted ceilings. In the United States, those same beds will be covered with decorative pillows. Similarly, the heavily circulated IKEA catalog (more than 203 million printed each year) is customized to show standard IKEA products in localized settings. IKEA publishes 67 versions of the catalog in 32 languages, each one carefully prepared to reflect local tastes and preferences.

Beyond adapting designs, assortments, and merchandising, IKEA often adjusts its basic store operations to turn local cultural nuances into competitive advantages. For example, IKEA's Chinese stores are a big draw for up-and-coming Chinese consumers. But IKEA customers in China want a lot more from its stores then just affordable Scandinavian-designed furniture.

In Chinese, IKEA is known as Yi Jia. Translated, it means "comfortable home," a concept taken literally by the millions of consumers who visit one of IKEA's 20 huge Chinese stores each year. "Customers come on family outings, hop into display beds and nap, pose for snapshots with the décor, and hang out for hours to enjoy the air conditioning and free soda refills," notes one observer. On a typical Saturday afternoon, for example, display beds and other furniture in a huge Chinese IKEA store are occupied, with customers of all ages lounging or even fast asleep. One Chinese IKEA has even hosted several weddings.

Whereas this might be considered as unwanted loitering in the United States or other Western markets, IKEA managers in China encourage such behavior, figuring that familiarity with the store will result in later purchasing when shoppers' incomes eventually rise to match their aspirations. "Maybe if you've been visiting IKEA, eating meatballs, hot dogs, or ice cream for 10 years, then maybe you will consider IKEA when you get yourself a sofa," says the company's Asia-Pacific president. In fact, that seems to be the case. Thanks to such cultural understandings coupled with competitively low prices, China is now IKEA's fastest-growing market. Eight of the world's 10 biggest IKEA stores are in China. What do Chinese consumers think of Swedish meatballs? "They love them," says IKEA China's marketing director.[1]

In the past, U.S. companies paid little attention to international trade. If they could pick up some extra sales via exports, that was fine. But the big market was at home, and it teemed with opportunities. The home market was also much safer. Managers did not need to learn other languages, deal with strange and changing currencies, face political and legal uncertainties, or adapt their products to different customer needs and expectations. Today, however, the situation is much different. Organizations of all kinds, from Coca-Cola, Apple, and Nike to Google, Airbnb, and even the NBA, have gone global.

Author Comment
The rapidly changing global environment provides both opportunities and threats. It's difficult to find a marketer today that isn't affected in some way by global developments.

Global Marketing Today

OBJECTIVE 15-1 Discuss how the international trade system and the economic, political-legal, and cultural environments affect a company's international marketing decisions.

The world is shrinking rapidly with the advent of faster digital communication, transportation, and financial flows. Products developed in one country—McDonald's hamburgers, Netflix video service, Samsung electronics, Zara fashions, Caterpillar construction equipment, German BMWs, Facebook social networking—have found enthusiastic acceptance in other countries. It would not be surprising to hear about a German businessman wearing an Italian suit meeting an English friend at a Japanese restaurant who later returns home to drink Russian vodka while watching *The Big Bang Theory* on TV and checking Facebook posts from friends around the world.

International trade has boomed over the past three decades. Since 1990, the number of multinational corporations in the world has more than tripled to over 100,000. Some of these multinationals are true giants. In fact, of the largest 150 economies in the world, only about half are countries. The rest are multinational corporations. Walmart, the world's largest company (based on a weighted average of sales, profits, assets, and market value), has annual revenues greater than the gross domestic product (GDP) of all but the world's 25 largest countries.[2] The global trade of products and services last year was valued at more than $20 trillion, about 25 percent of GDP worldwide.[3]

>> Many American companies have now made the world their market. KFC's Colonel Sanders is almost as familiar in Shanghai, China (above), or Tokyo, Japan, as he is in Boise, Idaho.

Gary Armstrong

>> Many U.S. companies have long been successful at international marketing: Coca-Cola, McDonald's, Starbucks, KFC, Nike, GE, Google, Caterpillar, Boeing, and dozens of other American firms have made the world their market. In the United States, non-American brands such as Toyota, Samsung, Nestlé, IKEA, Canon, and adidas have become household words. Other products and services that appear to be American are, in fact, produced or owned by foreign companies, such as Ben & Jerry's ice cream, Budweiser beer, Purina pet foods, 7-Eleven, Universal Studios, and Motel 6. Michelin, the oh-so-French tire manufacturer, now does 36 percent of its business in North America; J&J, the maker of quintessentially all-American products such as BAND-AIDs and Johnson's Baby Shampoo, does almost half of its business abroad. America's own Caterpillar belongs more to the wider world, with 53.5 percent of its sales coming from outside North America. Once all-American McDonald's captures nearly two-thirds of its revenues in foreign markets. KFC's Colonel Sanders is almost as familiar in Shanghai, China, or Tokyo, Japan, as he is in Boise, Idaho. And with more than 4,100 products worldwide, American favorite Coca-Cola now lets consumers "taste the feeling" more than 1.9 billion times a day in over 200 countries.[4]

But as global trade grows, global competition is also intensifying. Foreign firms are expanding aggressively into new international markets, and home markets are no longer as rich in opportunity. Few industries are currently safe from foreign competition. If companies delay taking steps toward internationalizing, they risk being shut out of growing markets in Western and Eastern Europe, China and Southeast Asia, Russia, India, Brazil, and elsewhere. Firms that stay at home to play it safe might not only lose their chances to enter other markets but also risk losing their home markets. Domestic companies that never thought about foreign competitors suddenly find these competitors in their own backyards.

Ironically, although the need for companies to go abroad is greater today than in the past, so are the risks. Companies that go global may face highly unstable governments and currencies, restrictive government policies and regulations, and high trade barriers. The recently dampened global economic environment has also created big global challenges. In addition, corruption is an increasing problem; officials in several countries often award business not to the best bidder but to the highest briber.

Global firm
A firm that, by operating in more than one country, gains R&D, production, marketing, and financial advantages in its costs and reputation that are not available to purely domestic competitors.

A **global firm** is one that, by operating in more than one country, gains marketing, production, research and development (R&D), and financial advantages that are not available to purely domestic competitors. Because the global company sees the world as one market, it minimizes the importance of national boundaries and develops global brands. The global company raises capital, obtains materials and components, and manufactures and markets its goods wherever it can do the best job.

For example, U.S.-based Otis Elevator, the world's largest elevator maker, is headquartered in Farmington, Connecticut. However, it sells and maintains elevators and escalators in more than 200 countries and achieves more than 80 percent of its sales from outside the United States. It gets elevator door systems from France, small-geared parts from Spain, electronics from Germany, and special motor drives from Japan. It operates manufacturing facilities in the Americas, Europe, and Asia and engineering and test centers in the United States, Austria, Brazil, China, Czech Republic, France, Germany, India, Italy, Japan, Korea, and Spain. In turn, Otis Elevator is a wholly owned subsidiary of global commercial and aerospace giant United Technologies Corporation.[5] Many of today's global corporations—both large and small—have become truly borderless.

This does not mean, however, that every firm must operate in dozens of countries to succeed. Smaller firms can practice global niching. But the world is becoming smaller, and every company operating in a global industry—whether large or small—must assess and establish its place in world markets.

Figure 15.1 Major International Marketing Decisions

It's a big and beautiful but threatening world out there for marketers! Most large American firms have made the world their market. For example, once all-American McDonald's now captures two-thirds of its sales from outside the United States.

The rapid move toward globalization means that all companies will have to answer some basic questions: What market position should we try to establish in our country, in our economic region, and globally? Who will our global competitors be and what are their strategies and resources? Where should we produce or source our products? What strategic alliances should we form with other firms around the world?

As shown in **Figure 15.1**, a company faces six major decisions in international marketing. We discuss each decision in detail in this chapter.

Author Comment
As if operating within a company's own borders wasn't difficult enough, going global adds many layers of complexities. For example, Coca-Cola markets its products in hundreds of countries around the globe. It must understand the varying trade, economic, cultural, and political environments in each market.

Elements of the Global Marketing Environment

Before deciding whether to operate internationally, a company must understand the international marketing environment. That environment has changed a great deal in recent decades, creating both new opportunities and new problems.

The International Trade System

U.S. companies looking abroad must start by understanding the international *trade system.* When selling to another country, a firm may face restrictions on trade between nations. Governments may charge *tariffs* or *duties*, taxes on certain imported products designed to raise revenue or protect domestic firms. Tariffs and duties are often used to force favorable trade behaviors from other nations.

For example, to rein in its large and growing $375 billion annual trade deficit with China, the United States recently began charging 30 percent tariffs on imported solar panels and residential washing machines, most of which come from China. It also placed import duties on steel and aluminum from China and selected other countries. In response, China increased tariffs by up to 28 percent on 128 U.S. products ranging from pork and soybeans to wine, airplanes, and automobiles. In turn, the United States retaliated with new tariffs on 1,300 Chinese industrial, technology, transport, and medical products. Such trade spats between nations are part of wider international dynamics. However, they can cause major difficulties for companies trying to market their goods across international borders.[6]

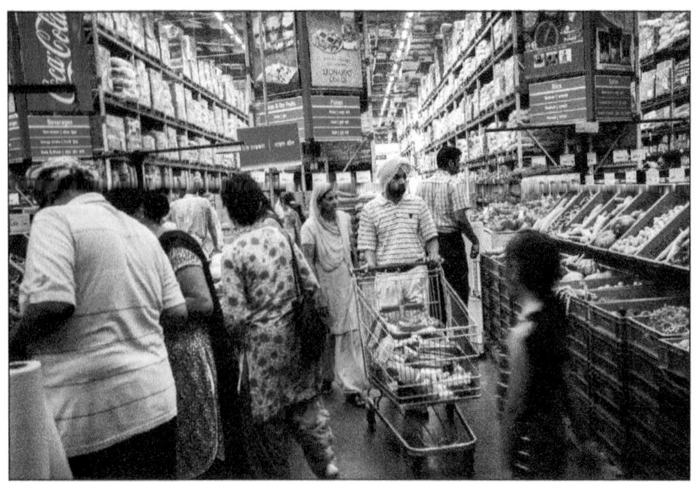

Nontariff trade barriers: Because of nontariff obstacles, Walmart recently scaled down its once-ambitious plans to expand in India's huge but fragmented retail market.

Bloomberg via Getty Images

Countries may set quotas, limits on the amount of imports that they will accept in certain product categories. The purpose of a quota is to conserve on foreign exchange and protect local industry and employment. Firms may also encounter exchange controls, which limit the amount of foreign exchange and the exchange rate against other currencies.

A company also may face nontariff trade barriers, such as biases against its bids, restrictive product standards, or excessive host-country regulations or enforcement. For example, Walmart recently scaled back its once-ambitious plans to expand into India's huge but fragmented retail market by opening hundreds of Walmart superstores there. Beyond difficult market conditions, such as spotty electricity and poor roads, India is notorious for throwing up nontariff obstacles to protect the nation's own predominately mom-and-pop retailers, which control 91 percent of India's $670 billion in retail sales.[7] One such obstacle is a government regulation requiring foreign retailers in India to buy 30 percent of the merchandise they sell from local small businesses. Such a requirement is nearly impossible for Walmart because small suppliers can't produce the quantities of goods needed by the giant retailer. Further, India's few large domestic retailers are not bound by the same rule, making it difficult for Walmart to compete profitably. Walmart recently purchased Flipkart, India's biggest ecommerce company, as a way to supplement slow store growth and help it crack the mammoth Indian market.[8]

At the same time, certain other forces can *help* trade between nations. Examples include the World Trade Organization (WTO) and various regional free trade agreements.

The World Trade Organization. The General Agreement on Tariffs and Trade (GATT), established in 1947 and modified in 1994, was designed to promote world trade by reducing tariffs and other international trade barriers. It established the World Trade Organization (WTO), which replaced GATT in 1995 and now oversees the original GATT provisions. WTO and GATT member nations (currently numbering 164) have met in eight rounds of negotiations to reassess trade barriers and establish new rules for international trade. The WTO also imposes international trade sanctions and mediates global trade disputes. Its actions have been productive. The first seven rounds of negotiations reduced the average worldwide tariffs on manufactured goods from 45 percent to just 5 percent. And the WTO's trade dispute mechanism has been used extensively. Over the past two decades, members have filed more than 500 disputes, most of which were settled within the WTO framework.[9]

Economic community
A group of nations organized to work toward common goals in the regulation of international trade.

Regional Free Trade Zones. Certain countries have formed *free trade zones* or **economic communities**. These are groups of nations organized to work toward common goals in the regulation of international trade. One such community is the *European Union (EU)*. Formed in 1957, the EU set out to create a single European market by reducing barriers to the free flow of products, services, finances, and labor among member countries and developing policies on trade with nonmember nations. Today, the EU represents one of the world's largest single markets. >> Currently, it has 28 member countries containing 516 million consumers and accounting for almost 20 percent of the world's imports and exports.[10] The EU offers tremendous trade opportunities for U.S. and other non-European firms.

For almost 20 years, 19 EU member nations have adopted the euro as a common currency. Widespread adoption of the euro decreased much of the currency risk associated with doing business in Europe, making member countries with previously weak currencies more attractive markets. However, the adoption of a common currency has also caused problems, as European economic powers such as Germany and France have had to step in recently to prop up weaker economies such as those of Greece, Portugal, and Cyprus. This ongoing "euro crisis" has led some analysts to predict the possible breakup of the euro zone as it is now set up.[11]

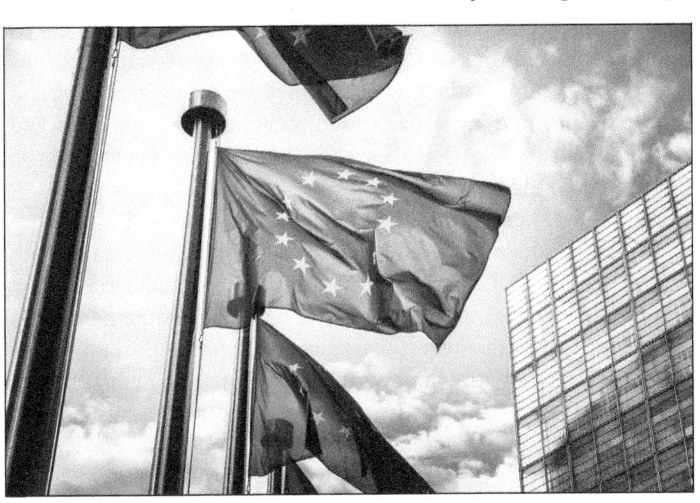

>> Economic communities: The European Union represents one of the world's largest single markets. It contains more than half a billion consumers and accounts for almost 20 percent of the world's imports and exports.
Paul Grecaud/123RF

It is unlikely that the EU will ever go against 2,000 years of tradition and become the "United States of Europe." A community with more than two dozen different languages and cultures and a history of sometimes strained relationships will always have difficulty coming together and acting as a single entity. For example, in a 2016 national referendum, the people of the United Kingdom voted to exit the European Union. The UK is set to depart the EU in early 2019 with a 21-month "transition period" to smooth the way to post-Brexit relations with the remaining EU countries. The so-called "Brexit" has sent aftershocks across Europe and the world, raising concerns about the future of European economic and political unity. Still, with a post-Brexit combined annual GDP of more than $15 trillion, the EU remains a potent economic force.[12]

In 1994, the North American Free Trade Agreement (NAFTA) established a free trade zone among the United States, Mexico, and Canada. The agreement created a single market of 487 million people who produce and consume $23.5 trillion worth of goods and services annually. Over the past 25 years, NAFTA has eliminated trade barriers and investment restrictions among the three countries. Total trade among the NAFTA countries nearly tripled from $288 billion in 1993 to more than $1.2 trillion a year.[13]

Following the apparent success of NAFTA, in 2005 the Central American Free Trade Agreement (CAFTA-DR) established a free trade zone between the United States and Costa Rica, the Dominican Republic, El Salvador, Guatemala, Honduras, and Nicaragua. Other free trade areas have formed in Latin America and South America. For example, the Union of South American Nations (UNASUR), modeled after the EU, was formed in 2004 and formalized by a constitutional treaty in 2008. Consisting of 12 countries, UNASUR makes up the largest trading bloc after NAFTA and the EU, with a population of more than 420 million and a combined economy of more than $6.5 trillion. Similar to NAFTA and the EU, UNASUR aims to eliminate all tariffs between nations.[14]

Two other major world trade agreements are the Comprehensive and Progressive Agreement for Trans-Pacific Partnership (CPTPP) and the Transatlantic Trade and Investment Partnership (T-TIP). The recently signed CPTPP promises to lower trade barrier and increase economic cooperation among 11 Pacific Rim countries: Australia, Brunei, Canada, Chile, Japan, Malaysia, Mexico, New Zealand, Peru, Singapore, and Vietnam. The T-TIP agreement between the United States and the European Union is still under negotiation. These major trade agreements will have a significant and sometimes controversial economic and political impact. For example, the 11 CPTPP countries have a collective population of 500 million people, more than NAFTA, and account for 13 percent of all world trade.[15]

Each nation has unique features that must be understood. A nation's readiness for different products and services and its attractiveness as a market to foreign firms depend on its economic, political-legal, and cultural environments.

Economic Environment

The international marketer must study each country's economy. Two economic factors reflect the country's attractiveness as a market: its industrial structure and its income distribution.

The country's industrial structure shapes its product and service needs, income levels, and employment levels. For example, in subsistence economies, most people engage in simple agriculture, consume most of their output, and barter the rest for simple goods and services. These economies offer few market opportunities. Many African countries fall into this category. At the other extreme, industrial economies are major importers and exporters of manufactured goods and services. Their varied manufacturing activities and large middle classes make them rich markets for all sorts of goods. The United States, Japan, and the Western European countries are examples.

Emerging economies are those experiencing rapid economic growth and industrialization. Examples include the BRICS countries—Brazil, Russia, India, China, and South Africa—and MENA countries (the Middle East and North Africa region). Industrialization typically creates a new rich class and a growing middle class, both demanding new types of goods and services. As more-developed markets stagnate and become increasingly competitive, many marketers are now targeting growth opportunities in emerging markets.

The second economic factor is the country's income distribution. Industrialized nations may have low-, medium-, and high-income households. In contrast, countries with subsistence economies consist mostly of households with very low family incomes. Still other countries may have households with either very low or very high incomes. Even poor or emerging economies may be attractive markets for all kinds of goods. In recent years, as growth has slowed in both domestic and emerging markets, many companies have shifted their sights to the so-called "bottom of the economic pyramid," the vast untapped market consisting of the world's poorest consumers (see Marketing at Work 15.1).

MARKETING AT WORK 15.1

International Marketing: Targeting the Bottom of the Economic Pyramid

Many companies have now awakened to a shocking statistic. Of the more than 7 billion people on this planet, more than 3 billion live on less than $2.50 a day. Known as the "bottom of the pyramid," the world's poor might not seem like a promising market. However, despite their paltry incomes, as a group, these consumers represent an eye-popping $5 trillion in annual purchasing power. Moreover, this vast segment is largely untapped. The world's poor often have little or no access to even the most basic products and services taken for granted by more affluent consumers. Companies are increasingly looking to the bottom of the pyramid for fresh growth opportunities.

But how can a company sell profitably to consumers with incomes below the poverty level? For starters, the *price* has got to be right. And in this case, says one analyst, "right" means "lower than you can imagine." With this in mind, many companies have made their products more affordable simply by offering smaller package sizes or lower-tech versions of current products. For example, in Nigeria, P&G sells a Gillette razor for 23 cents, a 1-ounce package of Ariel detergent for about 10 cents, and a 10-count pack of one-diaper-a-night Pampers for $2.30. Although there isn't much margin on products selling for pennies apiece, P&G is succeeding through massive volume.

Consider Pampers: Nigeria alone produces some 6 million newborns each year, almost 50 percent more than the United States, a country with twice the population. Nigeria's astounding birthrate created a huge, untapped market for Pampers diapers, P&G's top-selling brand. However, the typical Nigerian mother spends only about 5,000 naira a month, about $30, on all household purchases. P&G's task was to make Pampers affordable to this mother and to convince her that Pampers were worth some of her scarce spending. To keep costs and prices low in markets like Nigeria, P&G invented an absorbent diaper with fewer features. Although much less expensive, the diaper still functioned at a high level. When creating such affordable new products, says an R&D manager at P&G, "Delight, don't dilute." That is, the diaper needed to be priced low, but it also had to do what other cheap diapers didn't—keep a baby comfortable and dry for 12 hours.

Even with the right diaper at the right price, selling Pampers in Nigeria presented a challenge. In the West, babies typically go through numerous disposable diapers a day. In Nigeria, however, most babies were in cloth diapers. To make Pampers more acceptable and even more affordable for Nigerians, P&G marketed the diapers as a one-a-day item. According to company ads, "One Pampers equals one dry night." The campaign told mothers that keeping babies dry at night helped them to get a good night's sleep, which in turn helped them to grow and achieve. The message tapped into a deep sentiment among Nigerians, unearthed by P&G researchers, that their children would have a better life than they do. Thus, thanks to affordable pricing, a product that met customers' needs, and relevant positioning, Pampers sales boomed. In Nigeria, the name Pampers became synonymous with diapers. And despite the recent emergence of numerous competing products, P&G's Pampers remains a dominant brand there.

As P&G has learned, in most cases, selling profitably to the bottom of the pyramid takes much more than just developing single-use packets and pennies-apiece pricing. It requires broad-based innovation that produces not just lower prices but also new products that give people in poverty more for their money, not less. As another example, consider how Indian appliance company Godrej & Boyce used customer-driven innovation to successfully tap the market for low-priced refrigerators in India:

> Because of their high cost to both buy and operate, traditional compressor-driven refrigerators had penetrated only 18 percent of the Indian market. But rather than just produce a cheaper, stripped-down version of its higher-end refrigerators, Godrej assigned a team to study the needs of Indian consumers with poor or no refrigeration. The semi-urban and rural people that the team observed typically earned 5,000 to 8,000 rupees (about $125 to $200) a month, lived in single-room dwellings with four or five family members, and changed residences frequently. Unable to afford conventional refrigerators, these consumers were making do with communal, usually secondhand ones. But even the shared fridges usually contained only a few items. Their users tended to shop daily and buy only small quantities of vegetables and milk. Moreover, electricity was unreliable, putting even the little food they wanted to keep cool at risk.
>
> Godrej concluded that the low-end segment had little need for a conventional high-end refrigerator; it needed a fundamentally new product. So Godrej invented the ChotuKool ("little cool"), a

>> Selling to the world's poor: At only $88, Godrej's ChotuKool ("little cool") does a better job of meeting the needs of low-end Indian consumers at half the price of even the most basic conventional refrigerator.

Courtesy Godrej & Boyce Mfg. Co. Ltd.

candy red, top-opening, highly portable, dorm-size unit that has room for the few items users want to keep fresh for a day or two. Rather than a compressor and refrigerant, the miserly little unit uses a chip that cools when current is applied, and its top-opening design keeps cold air inside when the lid is opened. In all, the ChotuKool uses less than half the energy of a conventional refrigerator and can run on a battery during the power outages common in rural villages. The best part: At only $88, "little cool" does a better job of meeting the needs of low-end consumers at half the price of even the most basic traditional refrigerator. Godrej sold 100,000 ChotuKools in its second full year on the market.

Thus, the bottom of the pyramid offers large untapped opportunities to companies that can develop the right products at the right prices. And companies such as P&G are moving aggressively to capture these opportunities. P&G has set lofty goals for acquiring new customers in the developing economies of Asia and Africa. But successfully tapping these new developing markets will require more than just shipping out cheaper versions of existing products. "Our innovation strategy is not just diluting the top-tier product for the lower-end consumer," says P&G's CEO. "You have to discretely innovate for every one of those consumers on that economic curve, and if you don't do that, you'll fail."

Sources: See "Co-Creating with Rural Consumers Helps Achieve Inclusive Growth," *Innosight,* www.innosight.com/client_impact_story/godrej/, accessed July 2018; Purvita Chatterjee, "Godrej Appliances to Go Rural to Get Growth Back Post-Demonetization," *Hindu Business Line,* February 22, 2017, www.thehindubusinessline.com/companies/godrej-appliances-to-go-rural-to-get-growth-back-postdemonetisation/article9555646.ece; Erik Simanis and Duncan Duke, "Profits at the Bottom of the Pyramid," *Harvard Business Review,* October 2014, pp. 87–93; Matthew J. Eyring, Mark W. Johnson, and Hari Nair, "New Business Models in Emerging Markets," *Harvard Business Review,* January–February 2011, pp. 89–95; Mya Frazier, "How P&G Brought the Diaper Revolution to China," *CBS News,* January 7, 2010, www.cbsnews.com/8301-505125_162-51379838/; David Holthaus, "Health Talk First, Then a Sales Pitch," April 17, 2011, *Cincinnati.com,* http://news.cincinnati.com/article/20110417/BIZ01/104170344/; Danielle le Clus-Rossouw, "Baby Diapers in Nigeria," *Nonwovens Industry,* January 5, 2018, www.nonwovens-industry.com/issues/2018-01/view_features/baby-diapers-in-nigeria; and "The State of Consumption Today," *Worldwatch Institute,* www.worldwatch.org/node/810, accessed October 2018.

These days, companies in a wide range of industries—from cars to computers to soft drinks—are increasingly targeting middle-income or low-income consumers in subsistence and emerging economies. For example, as soft drink sales growth has lost its fizz in North America and Europe, Coca-Cola has had to look elsewhere to meet its ambitious growth goals. So the company has set its sights on Africa, with its promising though challenging long-term growth opportunities. Many Western companies view Africa as an untamed final frontier, plagued by poverty, political instability, unreliable transportation, and shortages of fresh water and other essential resources. But Coca-Cola sees plenty of opportunity to justify the risks. The African continent has a growing population of more than 1.3 billion people, a just-emerging middle class, and $3.3 trillion of GDP and spending power. Five of the world's 10 fastest-growing markets are in Africa:[16]

Coca-Cola has operated in Africa since 1929 and holds a dominant 29 percent market share in Africa and the Middle East, compared with Pepsi's 15 percent share. However, there's still plenty of room for Coca-Cola to grow there. For example, annual per capita consumption of Coke and other soft drinks is about 13 times less in Africa than in North America. Still, marketing in Africa is very different from marketing in more developed regions. Beyond just marketing through traditional channels in larger African cities, Coca-Cola is now invading smaller communities with more grassroots tactics.

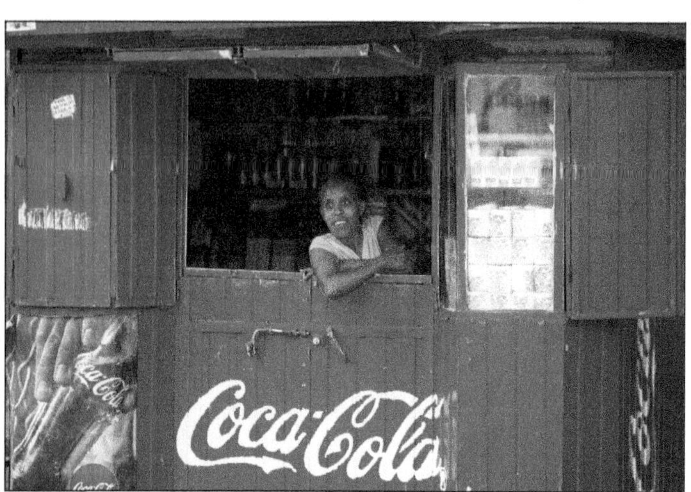

» With sales stagnating in its mature markets, Coca-Cola is looking to emerging markets—such as Africa—to meet its ambitious growth goals. Its African distribution network is rudimentary but effective.

John Wollwerth/Shutterstock

» Small stores play a big role in helping Coca-Cola to grow in Africa. In countless poor neighborhoods across the continent, crowded streets are lined with shops painted Coke red, selling low-priced Coca-Cola products by the bottle out of Coke-provided, refrigerated coolers. Such shops are supplied by a rudimentary but effective network of Coca-Cola distributors, whose crews often deliver crates of Coke products by hand-pulled trolleys or even a crate at a time carried on their heads. Because of the poor roads crowded with traffic, moving drinks by hand is often the best method. The company's first rule is to get its products "cold and close." "If they don't have roads to move products long distances on trucks, we will use boats, canoes, or trolleys," says the president of Coca-Cola South Africa. For example, in Nigeria's Makako district—a maze of stilt houses on the Lagos lagoon—women crisscross the waterways in canoes selling Coca-Cola directly to residents.

Political-Legal Environment

Nations differ greatly in their political-legal environments. In considering whether to do business in a given country, a company should consider factors such as the country's attitudes toward international buying, government bureaucracy, political stability, and monetary regulations.

Some nations are very receptive to foreign firms; others are less accommodating. For example, India has tended to bother foreign businesses with import quotas, currency restrictions, foreign investment limits, and other limitations that make operating there a challenge. In contrast, neighboring Asian countries such as Singapore, Vietnam, and Thailand court foreign investors and shower them with incentives and favorable operating conditions. Political and regulatory stability is another issue. For example, Russia is consumed by corruption and governmental red tape, which the government finds difficult to control. The country's recent geopolitical conflicts with Europe, the United States, and other countries have made doing business in Russia difficult and risky.[17]

Companies must also consider a country's monetary regulations. Sellers want to take their profits in a currency of value to them. Ideally, the buyer can pay in the seller's currency or in other world currencies. Short of this, sellers might accept a blocked currency—one whose removal from the country is restricted by the buyer's government—if they can buy other goods in that country that they need or can sell elsewhere for a needed currency. In addition to currency limits, a changing exchange rate also creates high risks for the seller.

Most international trade involves cash transactions. Yet many nations have too little hard currency to pay for their purchases from other countries. They may want to pay with other items instead of cash. *Barter* involves the direct exchange of goods or services. For example, Indonesia recently bartered coffee, tea, rubber, and palm oil for military aircraft from Russia. And South Korea bartered apples for coffee from Vietnam to help balance an apple surplus against a burgeoning coffee demand.[18]

Cultural Environment

Each country has its own folkways, norms, and taboos. When designing global marketing strategies, companies must understand how culture affects consumer reactions in each of its world markets. In turn, they must also understand how their strategies affect local cultures.

The Impact of Culture on Marketing Strategy. Sellers must understand the ways that consumers in different countries think about and use certain products before planning a marketing program. There are often surprises. For example, the average French man uses almost twice as many cosmetics and grooming aids as his wife. The Germans and the French eat more packaged, branded spaghetti than Italians do. A clock makes a nice gift in Western countries but is inappropriate in China, where such a gift is associated with death and funerals. Most American women let down their hair and take off makeup at bedtime, whereas some Chinese women style their hair at bedtime and even put *on* makeup.[19]

Companies that violate cultural norms and differences can make some very expensive and embarrassing mistakes. Here are just two examples:[20]

> Nike inadvertently offended Chinese officials when it ran an ad featuring LeBron James crushing a number of culturally revered Chinese figures in a kung fu–themed television ad. The Chinese government found that the ad violated regulations to uphold national dignity and respect the "motherland's culture" and yanked the multimillion-dollar campaign. With egg on its face, Nike released a formal apology.
>
> >> Marriott International recently stumbled in China when its website listed Tibet, Hong Kong, Macau, and Taiwan as "countries." Officially, the first three locations are "autonomous regions" of China; Hong Kong and Macau are "special administrative regions." And China considers Taiwan to be a "breakaway province" controlled by an illegitimate government. What seemed like an innocent mistake led to harsh penalties in China, where Marriott operates 124 large properties. Although Marriott apologized and corrected the error, the Chinese government shut down Marriott's Chinese website and app for more than a week, preventing online sales and bookings in China.

>> **Culture and marketing strategy: Marriott International recently stumbled in China when its website listed Tibet, Hong Kong, Macau, and Taiwan as "countries." The Chinese government shut down Marriott's Chinese website and app for more than a week.**

Imagine China/Newscom

Business norms and behaviors also vary from country to country. For example, American executives like to get right down to business and engage in fast and tough face-to-face bargaining. However, Japanese and other Asian businesspeople often find this behavior offensive. They prefer to start with polite conversation, and they rarely say no in face-to-face conversations.

As another example, firm handshakes are a common and expected greeting in most Western countries; in some Middle Eastern countries, however, handshakes might be refused if offered. Microsoft founder Bill Gates once set off a flurry of international controversy when he shook the hand of South Korea's president with his right hand while keeping his left hand in his pocket, something that Koreans consider highly disrespectful. In some countries, when being entertained at a meal, not finishing all the food implies that it was somehow substandard. In other countries, in contrast, wolfing down every last bite might be taken as a mild insult, suggesting that the host didn't supply enough quantity.[21] American business executives need to understand these kinds of cultural nuances before conducting business in another country.

By the same token, companies that understand cultural nuances can use them to their advantage in global markets. For example, when British clothing retailer Marks & Spencer decided to open its first standalone lingerie and beauty store, to the surprise of many it bypassed Paris, London, and New York and instead chose Saudi Arabia. Operating in Saudi Arabia requires some significant but worthwhile cultural adjustments:[22]

> The Saudi retail market is booming, and the country has a fast-growing and affluent consumer class. However, the conservative Islamic kingdom has no end of restrictive cultural and religious rules, especially when it involves retailing to women. In Saudi Arabia, women cover themselves in full-length black cloaks—called *abaya*—when they go out in public and must have a male chaperone, usually a relative. However, because they typically wear Western clothes at home or when traveling abroad, Western-style fashion stores are still very popular.
>
> When selling to Saudi women, Marks & Spencer must adhere to rigorously enforced religious and cultural strictures. For example, by government decree, its lingerie stores must employ an exclusively female sales staff. Because women's faces can't be shown and certain public dress is prohibited, Marks & Spencer uses tamer in-store marketing photos and video displays requiring separate photo shoots. Music is forbidden in Saudi malls and stores, so Marks & Spencer has eliminated the usual background compositions. Thanks to these and many other cultural adaptations, Saudi Arabia has become one of Marks & Spencer's highest-grossing emerging markets, well worth the additional costs of operating there. Marks & Spencer now has six lingerie and beauty stores in Saudi Arabia along with 16 full department stores. It has even gone so far as to use headless or faceless female mannequins to display its lingerie. "Unfortunately," says one Marks & Spencer marketer, "even the mannequins are not allowed to show faces."

Thus, understanding cultural traditions, preferences, and behaviors can help companies not only avoid embarrassing mistakes but also take advantage of cross-cultural opportunities.

The Impact of Marketing Strategy on Cultures. Whereas marketers worry about the impact of global cultures on their marketing strategies, others may worry about the impact of marketing strategies on global cultures. For example, social critics contend that large American multinationals, such as McDonald's, Coca-Cola, Starbucks, Nike, Google, Disney, and Facebook, aren't just globalizing their brands; they are Americanizing the world's cultures. Other elements of American culture have become pervasive worldwide. For instance, more people now study English in China than speak it in the United States. If you assemble businesspeople from Brazil, Germany, and China, they'll likely transact in English. And the thing that binds the world's teens together in a kind of global community, notes one observer, "is American culture—the music, the Hollywood fare, the electronic games, Google, Facebook, American consumer brands. The . . . rest of the world is becoming [evermore] like us—in ways good and bad."[23]

Critics worry that, under such "McDomination," countries around the globe are losing their individual cultural identities. Teens in Turkey watch MTV, connect with others globally through Facebook and Twitter, and ask their parents for more Westernized clothes and other symbols of American pop culture and values. Grandmothers in small European villas no longer spend each morning visiting local meat, bread, and produce markets to gather the ingredients for dinner. Instead, they now shop at Walmart. Women in Saudi Arabia see American films, question their societal roles, and shop at any of the country's growing number of Victoria's Secret boutiques. In China, most people never drank coffee before Starbucks entered the market. Now Chinese consumers rush to Starbucks stores because it symbolizes a new kind of lifestyle. Similarly, in China, where McDonald's plans to expand from 2,500 to 4,500 locations within five years, nearly half of all children identify the chain as a domestic brand.[24]

Such concerns have sometimes led to a backlash against American globalization. Well-known U.S. brands have become the targets of boycotts and protests in some international markets. As symbols of American capitalism, companies such as Coca-Cola, McDonald's, Nike, and KFC have been singled out by protestors and governments in hot spots around the world, especially when anti-American sentiment peaks. For example, following Russia's annexation of Crimea and the resulting sanctions by the West, Russian authorities initiated a crackdown on McDonald's franchises (even though most were Russian-owned), forcing some to close for uncertain reasons. McDonald's flagship store in Moscow was shut down for several weeks by the Russian Food Safety Authority. And the three McDonald's in Crimea were permanently shuttered, with at least one becoming a nationalist chain outlet called Rusburger, serving "Czar Cheeseburgers" where Quarter Pounders once flowed.[25]

Despite such problems, defenders of globalization argue that concerns of Americanization and the potential damage to American brands are overblown. U.S. brands are doing very well internationally. In the most recent Millward Brown BrandZ brand value survey of global consumer brands, 21 of the top 25 global brands were American owned, including megabrands such as Google, Apple, IBM, Microsoft, McDonald's, Coca-Cola, GE, Amazon.com, and Walmart.[26]

Many iconic American brands are soaring globally. For example, most international markets covet American fast food. Consider KFC in Japan. On the day that KFC introduced its outrageous Double Down sandwich—bacon, melted cheese, and a "secret sauce" between two deep-fried chicken patties—in one of its restaurants in Japan, fans formed long lines and slept on the sidewalks outside to get a taste. "It was like the iPhone," says the CMO of KFC International, "people [were] crazy." The U.S. limited-time item has since become a runaway success worldwide, from Canada to Australia, the Philippines, and Malaysia. >> More broadly, KFC has become its own cultural institution in Japan. For instance, the brand has long been one of Japan's leading Christmas dining traditions, with the iconic Colonel Sanders standing in as a kind of Japanese Father Christmas:[27]

> Japan's KFC Christmas tradition began more than 40 years ago when the company unleashed a "Kentucky for Christmas" advertising campaign in Japan to help the brand get off the ground. Now, eating Kentucky Fried Chicken has become one of the country's most popular holiday traditions. Each KFC store displays a life-size Colonel Sanders statue, adorned in a traditional fur-trimmed red suit and Santa hat. A month in advance, Japanese customers order their special Christmas meal—a special bucket of fried chicken with wine and cake for about $40. Some 3.6 million Japanese households have a KFC Christmas feast each year. Those who don't preorder risk standing in lines that snake around the block or having to go without KFC's coveted blend of 11 herbs and spices altogether. Christmas Eve is KFC's most successful sales day of the year in Japan, and December monthly sales run as much as 10 times greater than sales in other months.

>> American brands in other cultures: KFC has become one of Japan's leading Christmas dining traditions, with the iconic Colonel Sanders standing in as a kind of Japanese Father Christmas.

Anthea Freshwater

More fundamentally, the cultural exchange goes both ways: America gets as well as gives cultural influence. True, Hollywood dominates the global movie market, but British TV originated the programming that was Americanized into such hits as *American Idol, Dancing with the Stars,* and *Hell's Kitchen.* Although Chinese and Russian youth are donning NBA superstar jerseys, the increasing popularity of soccer in America has deep international roots.

Even American childhood has been increasingly influenced by European and Asian cultural imports. Most kids know all about imports such as Hello Kitty, Pokemon, or any of a host of Nintendo or Sega game characters. And J. K. Rowling's so-very-British Harry Potter books shaped the thinking of a generation of American youngsters, not to mention the millions of American oldsters who fell under their spell as well. For the moment, English remains the dominant language of the internet, and having web and mobile access often means that third-world youth have greater exposure to American popular culture. Yet these same technologies let Eastern European students studying in the United States hear webcast news and music from Poland, Romania, or Belarus.

Thus, globalization is a two-way street. If the world is eating Big Macs and drinking Coca-Cola, it is also talking on a Samsung smartphone, buying furniture at IKEA, driving a Toyota Camry, and watching a British-inspired show on an LG OLED television.

Deciding Whether to Go Global

Not all companies need to venture into international markets to survive. For example, most local businesses need to market well only in their local marketplaces. Operating domestically is easier and safer. Managers don't need to learn another country's language and laws. They don't have to deal with unstable currencies, face political and legal uncertainties, or redesign their products to suit different customer expectations. However, companies that operate in global industries, where their strategic positions in specific markets are affected strongly by their overall global positions, must compete on a regional or worldwide basis to succeed.

Any of several factors might draw a company into the international arena. For example, global competitors might attack the company's home market by offering better products or lower prices. The company might want to counterattack these competitors in their home markets to tie up their resources. The company's customers might be expanding abroad and require international servicing. Or, most likely, international markets might simply provide better opportunities for growth. For example, as noted previously, Coca-Cola has emphasized international growth in recent years to offset stagnant or declining U.S. soft drink sales. Today, non-North America markets account for 80 percent of Coca-Cola's unit case volume, and the company is making major pushes into 90 emerging markets, such as China, India, and the entire African continent.[28]

Before going abroad, the company must weigh several risks and answer many questions about its ability to operate globally. Can the company learn to understand the preferences and buyer behavior of consumers in other countries? Can it offer competitively attractive products? Will it be able to adapt to other countries' business cultures and deal effectively with foreign nationals? Do the company's managers have the necessary international experience? Has management considered the impact of regulations and the political environments of other countries?

Deciding Which Markets to Enter

Before going abroad, a company should try to define its international *marketing objectives and policies*. It should decide what *volume* of foreign sales it wants. Most companies start small when they go abroad. Some plan to stay small, seeing international sales as a small part of their business. Other companies have bigger plans, however, seeing international business as equal to—or even more important than—their domestic business.

The company also needs to choose in *how many* countries it wants to market. Companies must be careful not to spread themselves too thin or expand beyond their

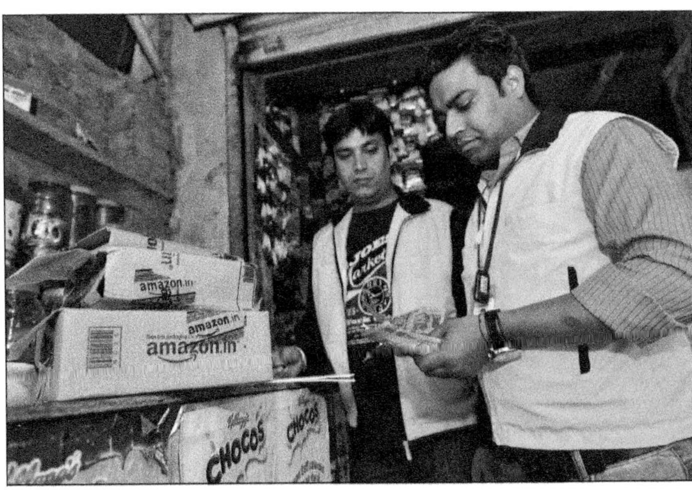

>> **Entering new global markets: Amazon's entry into India seems like a no-brainer. But it's also a very large and complex undertaking. The challenge is summed up by this slogan: "Transforming the way India sells, transforming the way India buys."**

Pradeep Gaur/Mint/Hindustan Times/Getty Images

capabilities by operating in too many countries too soon. Next, the company needs to decide on the *types* of countries to enter. A country's attractiveness depends on the product, geographical factors, income and population, political climate, and other considerations. In recent years, many major new markets have emerged, offering both substantial opportunities and daunting challenges.

After listing possible international markets, the company must carefully evaluate each one. It must consider many factors. >> For example, Amazon's decision to expand into India seems like a no-brainer. The online merchant is already doing well in such global markets as Germany, Japan, and the United Kingdom. International sales account for nearly a third of Amazon's total revenues and are growing by about 25 percent per year. India is now the world's fastest-growing economy, with a population of 1.35 billion people, four times the U.S. population and 2.5 times Europe's. What's more, only one-quarter of India's population now has access to the internet and only a small proportion of Indians have ever shopped online, leaving explosive room for growth in online shopping.[29]

However, as Amazon considers expanding into new markets such as India, it must ask some important questions. Can it compete effectively with local competitors? Can it master the varied cultural and buying differences of Indian consumers? Will it be able to meet environmental and regulatory hurdles in each country? Can it overcome some daunting infrastructure problems?

In entering India, Amazon is facing many challenges. For example, it confronts two established local competitors there—Flipkart (now owned by Walmart) and Snapdeal—plus a slew of smaller Indian start-ups. Flipkart currently leads India's e-commerce with Amazon playing catch-up. Amazon also faces a tangle of Indian regulations, including a law that forbids foreign companies from selling directly to Indians. Thus, rather than buying goods and reselling them as it does in the United States, Amazon in India will be only a platform for vendors, similar to its "fulfillment by Amazon" operations in the West.

Package delivery is another major obstacle. India is characterized by muddy, potholed rural roads or congested city streets with arcane address systems, and there are no reliable delivery services such FedEx, UPS, or the postal service. To make speedy deliveries, Amazon has had to set up its own motorcycle delivery service, consisting of thousands of motorbike riders with large black backpacks who race around the country delivering packages. Still another concern is payment. Twenty percent of Indians have no bank accounts, and only a small fraction on Indians have credit cards. Most customers pay cash for home-delivered purchases or when they collect their packages from local shops across the country that serve as pickup and payment points. The small local shops also serve as online ordering spots for the majority of Indian consumers who have no internet connections. Store owners guide customers through Amazon's site, write down their orders, and collect the cash when orders are picked up from the shop.

Thus, Amazon's decision to enter India is, in fact, a no-brainer. "The size of the opportunity is so large it will be measured in trillions, not billions—trillions of dollars, that is, not rupees," says Amazon's senior vice president for international retail. But it's also a very large and complex undertaking. A slogan posted on the wall in Amazon's Hyderabad warehouse sums up the challenge: "Transforming the way India sells, transforming the way India buys."[30]

Possible global markets should be ranked on several factors, including market size, market growth, the cost of doing business, competitive advantage, and risk level. The goal is to determine the potential of each market, using indicators such as those shown in >> **Table 15.1**. Then the marketer must decide which markets offer the greatest long-run return on investment.

Table 15.1 Indicators of Market Potential

Demographic Characteristics	Sociocultural Factors
Education Population size and growth Population age composition	Consumer lifestyles, beliefs, and values Business norms and approaches Cultural and social norms Languages
Geographic Characteristics	**Political and Legal Factors**
Climate Country size Population density—urban, rural Transportation structure and market accessibility	National priorities Political stability and compatibility Government attitudes toward global trade Government bureaucracy Monetary and trade regulations
Economic Factors	
GDP size and growth Income distribution Industrial infrastructure Natural resources Financial and human resources	

Author Comment
A company has many options for entering an international market, from simply exporting its products to working jointly with foreign companies to setting up its own foreign-based operations.

Deciding How to Enter the Market

OBJECTIVE 15-2 Describe three key approaches to entering international markets.

Once a company has decided to sell in a foreign country, it must determine the best mode of entry. Its choices are *exporting, joint venturing*, and *direct investment*. **Figure 15.2** shows the three market entry strategies along with the options each one offers. As the figure shows, each succeeding strategy involves more commitment and risk but also more control and potential profits.

Exporting

Exporting
Entering foreign markets by selling goods produced in the company's home country, often with little modification.

The simplest way to enter a foreign market is through **exporting**. The company may passively export its surpluses from time to time, or it may make an active commitment to expand exports to a particular market. In either case, the company produces all its goods in its home country. It may or may not modify them for the export market. Exporting involves the least change in the company's product lines, organization, investments, or mission.

Companies typically start with *indirect exporting*, working through independent international marketing intermediaries. Indirect exporting involves less investment because the firm does not require an overseas marketing organization or network. It also involves less

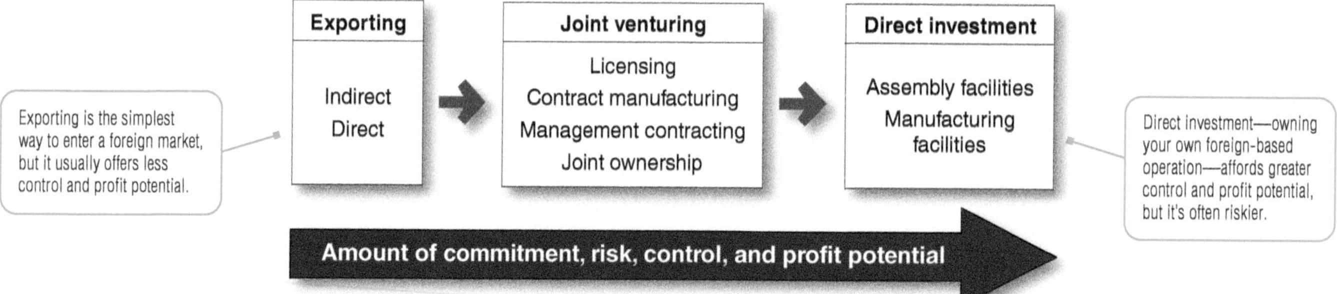

Figure 15.2 Market Entry Strategies

Joint venturing
Entering foreign markets by joining with foreign companies to produce or market a product or service.

risk. International marketing intermediaries bring know-how and services to the relationship, so the seller normally makes fewer mistakes. Sellers may eventually move into *direct exporting*, whereby they handle their own exports. The investment and risk are somewhat greater in this strategy, but so is the potential return.

Joint Venturing

A second method of entering a foreign market is by **joint venturing**—joining with foreign companies to produce or market products or services. Joint venturing differs from exporting in that the company joins with a host country partner to sell or market abroad. It differs from direct investment in that an association is formed with someone in the foreign country. There are four types of joint ventures: *licensing, contract manufacturing, management contracting*, and *joint ownership*.

Licensing
Entering foreign markets through developing an agreement with a licensee in the foreign market.

Licensing

Licensing is a simple way for a manufacturer to enter international marketing. The company enters into an agreement with a licensee in the foreign market. For a fee or royalty payments, the licensee buys the right to use the company's manufacturing process, trademark, patent, trade secret, or other item of value. The company thus gains entry into a foreign market at little risk; at the same time, the licensee gains production expertise or a well-known product or name without having to start from scratch.

In Japan, Budweiser beer flows from Kirin breweries, and Mizkan produces Sunkist lemon juice, drinks, and dessert items. >> Tokyo Disney Resort is owned and operated by Oriental Land Company under license from The Walt Disney Company. The 45-year license gives Disney licensing fees plus a percentage of admissions and food and merchandise sales. And Coca-Cola markets internationally by licensing bottlers around the world and supplying them with the syrup needed to produce the product. Its global bottling partners range from the Coca-Cola Bottling Company of Saudi Arabia to beer maker SABMiller in Africa to Europe-based Coca-Cola Hellenic, which bottles and markets 136 Coca-Cola brands to 600 million people in 28 countries, from Italy and Greece to Nigeria and Russia.[31]

>> International licensing: The Tokyo Disney Resort is owned and operated by Oriental Land Company (a Japanese development company) under license from The Walt Disney Company.
David Harding/Alamy Stock Photo

Licensing has potential disadvantages, however. The firm has less control over the licensee than it would over its own operations. Furthermore, if the licensee is very successful, the firm has given up these profits, and if and when the contract ends, it may find it has created a competitor.

Contract Manufacturing

Contract manufacturing
A joint venture in which a company contracts with manufacturers in a foreign market to produce its product or provide its service.

Another option is **contract manufacturing**, in which the company makes agreements with manufacturers in the foreign market to produce its product or provide its service. For example, P&G serves 650 million consumers across India with the help of nine contract manufacturing sites there. And Volkswagen contracts with Russia's largest auto manufacturer, GAZ Group, to make Volkswagen Jettas for the Russian market as well as its Škoda (VW's Czech Republic subsidiary) Octavia and Yeti models sold there.[32] The drawbacks of contract manufacturing are decreased control over the manufacturing process and loss of potential profits on manufacturing. The benefits are the chance to start faster with less risk and the later opportunity either to form a partnership with or buy out the local manufacturer. Contract manufacturing can also reduce plant investment, transportation, and tariff costs while at the same time helping to meet the host country's local manufacturing requirements.

Management Contracting

Management contracting
A joint venture in which the domestic firm supplies the management know-how to a foreign company that supplies the capital; the domestic firm exports management services rather than products.

Under **management contracting**, the domestic firm provides the management know-how to a foreign company that supplies the capital. In other words, the domestic firm exports management services rather than products. Hilton uses this arrangement in managing hotels around the world. For example, the hotel chain operates DoubleTree by Hilton hotels in countries ranging from the UK and Italy to Peru and Costa Rica to China, Russia, and Tanzania. The properties are locally owned, but Hilton manages the hotels with its world-renowned hospitality expertise.[33]

Management contracting is a low-risk method of getting into a foreign market, and it yields income from the beginning. The arrangement is even more attractive if the contracting firm has an option to buy some share in the managed company later on. The arrangement is not sensible, however, if the company can put its scarce management talent to better uses or if it can make greater profits by undertaking the whole venture. Management contracting also prevents the company from setting up its own operations for a period of time.

Joint Ownership

Joint ownership
A cooperative venture in which a company creates a local business with investors in a foreign market who share ownership and control.

Joint ownership ventures consist of one company joining forces with foreign investors to create a local business in which they share possession and control. A company may buy an interest in a local firm, or the two parties may form a new business venture. Joint ownership may be needed for economic or political reasons. For example, the firm may lack the financial, physical, or managerial resources to undertake the venture alone. Alternatively, a foreign government may require joint ownership as a condition for entry. Disney's Hong Kong Disneyland and Shanghai Disneyland are both joint ownership ventures with the Chinese government-owned Shanghai Shendi Group. Disney owns 43 percent of the Shanghai resort; the Shanghai Shendi Group owns 57 percent.[34]

Often, companies form joint ownership ventures to merge their complementary strengths in developing a global marketing opportunity. >> For example, Walmart's purchase of a 77 percent stake in Flipkart, India's leading online marketplace, helped the U.S.-based retailer navigate India's strict foreign investment restrictions. The arrangement also gave Walmart a big head start over Amazon in market share and online retailing expertise in India. In turn, Flipkart benefits from Walmart's deep pockets and distribution experience. Similarly, joint ownership ventures have helped Kellogg move quickly and strongly into emerging markets in West Africa. For instance, Kellogg purchased 50-percent stakes in Tolaram Africa Foods, a leading manufacturer of packaged foods in Nigeria and Ghana, and Multipro, the largest foods distributor in those countries. The joint ownership investments will help Kellogg to better understand West African consumers and to master the region's complex distribution environment.[35]

>> Joint ownership: Walmart's joint ownership stake in Flipkart, India's leading online marketplace, helps the retailer to navigate India's strict foreign investment restrictions.
grzegorz knec/Alamy Stock Photo (Walmart); Farbentek/123RF (Flipkart).

Joint ownership has certain drawbacks, however. The partners may disagree over investment, marketing, or other policies. Whereas many U.S. firms like to reinvest earnings for growth, local firms often prefer to take out these earnings; whereas U.S. firms emphasize the role of marketing, local investors may rely on selling.

Direct Investment

Direct investment
Entering a foreign market by developing foreign-based assembly or manufacturing facilities.

The biggest involvement in a foreign market comes through **direct investment**—the development of foreign-based assembly or manufacturing facilities. For example, in addition to joint ownership ventures in China, Intel has also made substantial investments in its own manufacturing and research facilities there. It recently spent \$1.6 billion upgrading its decade-old chip factory in the central Chinese city of Chengdu and another \$2.5 billion to build a shiny new fabrication plant in Dalian, a port city in China's northeast. "China is our fastest-growing major market," says Intel's CEO, "and we believe it's critical that we invest in markets that will provide for future growth to better serve our customers."[36]

If a company has gained experience in exporting and if the foreign market is large enough, foreign production facilities offer many advantages. The firm may have lower costs in the form of cheaper labor or raw materials, foreign government investment incentives, and freight savings. The firm may also improve its image in the host country because it creates jobs. Generally, a firm develops a deeper relationship with the government, customers, local suppliers, and distributors, allowing it to adapt its products to the local market better. Finally, the firm keeps full control over the investment and therefore can develop manufacturing and marketing policies that serve its long-term international objectives.

The main disadvantage of direct investment is that the firm faces many risks, such as restricted or devalued currencies, falling markets, or government changes. In some cases, a firm has no choice but to accept these risks if it wants to operate in the host country.

LINKING THE CONCEPTS

Slow down here and think about McDonald's global marketing issues.

- To what extent can McDonald's standardize for the Chinese market? What marketing strategy and program elements can be similar to those used in the United States and other parts of the Western world? Which ones must be adapted? Be specific.
- To what extent can McDonald's standardize its strategy, products, and programs for the Canadian market? What elements can be standardized and which must be adapted?
- To what extent are McDonald's "globalization" efforts contributing to "Americanization" of countries and cultures around the world? What are the positives and negatives of such cultural developments?

Author Comment
The major global marketing decision usually boils down to this: How much, if at all, should a company adapt its marketing strategy and programs to local markets? How might the answer differ for Boeing versus McDonald's?

Deciding on the Global Marketing Program

OBJECTIVE 15-3 Explain how companies adapt their marketing strategies and mixes for international markets.

Standardized global marketing
A global marketing strategy that basically uses the same marketing strategy and mix in all of the company's international markets.

Adapted global marketing
A global marketing approach that adjusts the marketing strategy and mix elements to each international target market, which creates more costs but hopefully produces a larger market share and return.

Companies that operate in one or more foreign markets must decide how much, if at all, to adapt their marketing strategies and programs to local conditions. At one extreme are global companies that use **standardized global marketing**, essentially using the same marketing strategy approaches and marketing mix worldwide. At the other extreme is **adapted global marketing**. In this case, the producer adjusts the marketing strategy and mix elements to each target market, resulting in more costs but hopefully producing a larger market share and return.

The question of whether to adapt or standardize the marketing strategy and program has been much debated over the years. On the one hand, some global marketers believe that technology is making the world a smaller place, and consumer needs around the world are becoming more similar. This paves the way for global brands and standardized global marketing. Global branding and standardization, in turn, result in greater brand power and reduced costs from economies of scale.

On the other hand, the marketing concept holds that marketing programs will be more engaging if tailored to the unique needs of each targeted customer group. If this concept applies within a country, it should apply even more across international markets. Despite global convergence, consumers in different countries still have widely varied cultural backgrounds. They still differ significantly in their needs and wants, spending power, product preferences, and shopping patterns. Because these differences are hard to change, most marketers today adapt their products, prices, channels, and promotions to fit consumer desires in each country.

However, global standardization is not an all-or-nothing proposition. It's a matter of degree. Most international marketers suggest that companies should "think globally but act locally." They should seek a balance between standardization and adaptation, leveraging global brand recognition but adapting their marketing, products, and operations to specific markets.

Consider L'Oréal, the world's biggest cosmetics maker. L'Oréal and its brands are truly global in scope and appeal. The company's well-known brands originated in a half dozen or more different cultures, including French (L'Oréal Paris, Garnier, Lancôme), American (Maybelline, Kiehl's, SoftSheen-Carson, Ralph Lauren, Urban Decay, Clarisonic, Redken), British (The Body Shop), Italian (Giorgio Armani), and Japanese (Shu Uemura). But the company's outstanding international success comes from achieving a global-local balance, one that adapts and differentiates L'Oréal's well-known brands to meet local needs while also integrating them across world markets to optimize their global impact:[37]

> L'Oréal digs deep to understand what beauty means to consumers in different parts of the world, with research insights gained through everything from in-home visits to observations made in "bathroom laboratories" equipped with high-tech gadgetry. How many minutes does a Chinese woman devote to her morning beauty routine? How do people wash their hair in Bangkok? How many brush strokes does a Japanese woman or a French woman use to apply mascara? L'Oréal then uses such detailed insights to create products and positioning for brands in local markets. For example, more than 260 scientists work in L'Oréal's Shanghai research center, tailoring products ranging from lipstick to herbal cleaners to cucumber toners for Chinese tastes.
>
> L'Oréal also adapts brand positioning and marketing to international needs and expectations. For example, more than 20 years ago, the company bought stodgy American makeup producer Maybelline. To reinvigorate and globalize the brand, it moved the unit's headquarters from Tennessee to New York City and added "New York" to the label. The resulting urban, street-smart, Big Apple image played well with the midprice positioning of the workaday makeup brand globally. The makeover soon earned Maybelline a 20 percent market share in its category in Western Europe. The young urban positioning also hit the mark in Asia, where few women realized that the trendy "New York" Maybelline brand belonged to a French cosmetics giant. >> L'Oréal's CEO sums up the company's global approach this way: "We have global brands, but we need to adapt them to local needs." When a former CEO once addressed a UNESCO conference, nobody batted an eyelid when he described L'Oréal as "The United Nations of Beauty."

>> Global–local balance: Cosmetics and beauty care giant L'Oréal balances local brand responsiveness and global brand impact, making it "The United Nations of Beauty."

Marc Piasecki/Stringer/Getty Images

Collectively, local brands still account for the overwhelming majority of consumer purchases. Most consumers, wherever they live, lead very local lives. So a global brand must engage consumers at a local level, respecting the culture and becoming a part of it. For example, 7-Eleven has become the world's largest convenience store chain by skillfully adapting its operations in each global market to match widely differing local definitions of just what "convenience" means (see Marketing at Work 15.2).

Product

Five strategies are used for adapting product and marketing communication strategies to a global market (see **>> Figure 15.3**).[38] We first discuss the three product strategies and then turn to the two communication strategies.

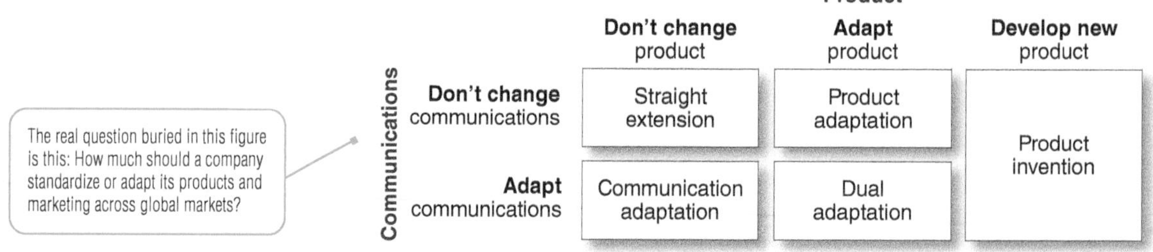

>> Figure 15.3 Five Global Product and Communications Strategies

MARKETING AT WORK 15.2

7-Eleven: Making Life a Little Easier for People around the Globe

Americans love convenience stores. There's one just around the corner, and they're open long hours, seven days a week. Whether it's big chains like 7-Eleven and Circle K or more-local favorites like Illinois based Moto-Mart, Nebraska's Bucky's, or Minnesota's own Pump 'N Munch, convenience stores have become an American mainstay for buying snacks, gas, or a few fill-in items between major grocery store trips. It's hard to imagine a convenience store being anything else.

But as it turns out, the convenience store concept doesn't translate in a standard way across international borders. Just ask 7-Eleven, a chain that's sweeping the planet. 7-Eleven is America's largest convenience store chain, with more than 9,000 U.S. stores in 34 states. But it's also the *world's* biggest convenience chain, with more than 66,000 stores in 17 countries generating nearly $96 billion in annual worldwide sales. 7-Eleven's global success results from carefully adapting its overall convenience format to unique market-by-market needs.

7-Eleven began in 1927 when "Uncle Johnny" Jefferson Green started selling milk, bread, and eggs from the dock of the Southland Ice Company where he worked, often on Sundays and evenings when regular grocery stores were closed. Within 10 years, Southland Ice Company had opened 60 such outlets selling basic staples—everything from canned goods to cold watermelon. As the chain grew, the convenience store concept took root—small stores in convenient locations, a limited line of high-demand products, speedy transactions, and friendly service.

In 1946, the fast-growing chain boldly established longer store hours—you guessed it, 7 a.m. to 11 p.m.—a practice unheard of at the time. And to cement its convenience positioning, it changed its name to 7-Eleven. To support its breakneck expansion, 7-Eleven also adopted a franchise model by which franchisees shared some of the financial and operational burdens of growth. In return, 7-Eleven granted franchisees lots of flexibility in catering to local tastes in their stores. The company calls this "retailer initiative" and considers it a key competitive advantage. Catering to local tastes would later become the cornerstone of 7-Eleven's international expansion.

In 1969, 7-Eleven became the first convenience chain to go global, first in Canada, then in Mexico, and soon in Japan and other Asian markets. In each global market, the chain has retained its key strategy elements—the small-store format, convenience positioning, and global brand identity—you'll see the familiar 7-Eleven logo and orange, red, white, and green stripes on every 7-Eleven store anywhere in the world. At first glance, a 7-Eleven in Tokyo looks pretty much like one in Teaneck, New Jersey. But true to its "retailer initiative" philosophy, 7-Eleven skillfully adapts its operations in each global market to match widely differing local definitions of just what "convenience" means.

Consider Japan, one of 7-Eleven's first international ventures. 7-Elevens are everywhere in Japan, more the 20,000 of them—2,300 in Tokyo alone. Japan is now by far the company's largest market. Once you get past the familiar signage on the outside of a Japanese 7-Eleven, you'll find some pretty stark contrasts on the inside. More than just a place to grab a loaf of bread or a Slurpee, Big Gulp, or Big Bite, 7-Eleven in Japan has become the country's most popular eatery.

Around mealtime, the aisles at every Japanese 7-Eleven are packed with long lines of patrons who are treated to some of the finest prepared foods in the world. Typical offerings include salmon on rice with butter and soy sauce, hashed beef doria in a red wine demi-glace, and ground chicken with ginger and a side of spinach coleslaw. Fresh sushi abounds, and the ongiri (rice balls with seaweed) is wrapped in a way that keeps the seaweed crispy and the rice moist. 7-Eleven in Japan also offers a wide selection of beverages, including soft drinks, beer, sake, Champagne, single-malt scotch, wine, and more than 20 varieties of iced coffee.

This is not your typical American 7-Eleven. Stores receive several food deliveries each day, keeping shelves well stocked with fresh goods and ensuring that everything is locally made. Food is served in open display cases in a manner that's more Trader Joe's than convenience store. Japanese customers can even order food and groceries online and have them delivered at work or home. The chain also meets other customer service needs. At 7-Eleven, customers can pay their phone or utility

» Global–local balance: At first glance, a 7-Eleven in Tokyo looks pretty much like one in Teaneck, New Jersey. However, 7-Eleven skillfully adapts its operations in each global market to match widely differing local definitions of just what "convenience" means.

Rodrigo Reyes Marin/AFLO/Alamy Live News

bills, pick up their mail and parcel deliveries, and even buy baseball tickets from the copy machine.

For 7-Eleven, Japan now represents far more than just a booming international market. Since the early 1990s, Japan has become 7-Eleven's home market. When Dallas-based 7-Eleven encountered financial difficulties in 1991, its own highly successful Japanese subsidiary bailed it out, buying a majority stake. In 2005, 7-Eleven Japan created Tokyo-based Seven & I Holdings, which acquired the remaining shares of 7-Eleven. Then, in a case of the student becoming the teacher, the new parent corporation applied its well-honed "retailer initiative" skills to strengthen the U.S. division.

Wherever it operates, 7-Eleven seeks to become a part of the local culture. For example, in tech-crazed Taiwan, 7-Elevens are stocked full of purchasable electronics like iPads. They serve as a place to pay everything from credit card and utility bills to traffic tickets and property taxes. Some will even do your dry cleaning. Conversely, on weekends in Hong Kong, you'll find people hanging around and drinking at the local "Club 7"—yes, we're talking about the 7-Eleven. "Young locals and 'gweilo' (foreigners) swarm these places, drinks in hand, making the convenience store look like an open-aired bar," notes an observer. In Hawaii, where people are obsessed with Spam canned cooked meat, 7-Elevens serve up a positively sinful dish called Spam musubi, a slice of fried Spam on top of a bed of rice and wrapped in nori dried seaweed.

In stark contrast, in Denmark, the chain's health-conscious customers are more inclined toward crunchy granola and paleo salads. Whereas American customers enjoy neon-color Slurpees, calorie-rich Big Gulps, and roller dogs, 7-Elevens in Denmark offer freshly prepared sandwiches on artisan-style bread and fresh-cooked kebabs. Snacks include protein-packed muesli bars, hummus, a variety of healthy salads, and lots of other fast, healthy options. "Denmark is ranked as the happiest country in the world," says an analyst. "7-Eleven, of all places, is aiming to make it the healthiest, too."

Thus, 7-Eleven's fine-tuned global marketing strategy has made it the world's largest convenience store chain. Wherever 7-Eleven operates, its overall brand identity and convenience positioning remain constant: "At 7-Eleven, our purpose and mission is to make life a little easier for our guests," says the company, by "giving customers what they want, when and where they want it." But 7-Eleven knows that those whats, whens, and wheres can shift dramatically from market to market. The real secret is to weave the global 7-Eleven strategy into the fabric of each local culture.

Sources: See "Reitan Servicehandel (7-Eleven HQ)," www.facebook.com/pages/Reitan-Servicehandel-7-Eleven-HQ/304390909574505, accessed July 2018; "Seven & I: The World's Best Convenience Stores Are in Denmark," *Seeking Alpha,* April 7, 2016, https://seekingalpha.com/article/3963695-seven-worlds-best-convenience-stores-denmark?page=2; Taryn Stenvei, "What 7-Elevens in Tokyo Taught Me about Japan," *AWOL,* September 11, 2014, http://awol.com.au/what-7-elevens-in-tokyo-taught-me-about-japan/98; Justin Moyer, "In Honor of 7/11: How Japan Slurped Up 7-Eleven," *Washington Post,* July 11, 2014, www.washingtonpost.com/news/morning-mix/wp/2014/07/11/in-honor-of-711-how-japan-slurped-up-7-eleven/; Margot Huber, "Hangout Haven," *Business Today,* May 26, 2013, http://businesstoday.intoday.in/story/london-business-school-case-study-on-7-eleven/1/194769.html; Kelsey Richardson, "Around the World in Seven 7-Elevens," *Klook,* September 1, 2015, www.klook.com/blog/around-the-world-in-seven-7-elevens/; and http://corp.7-eleven.com/corp/7-eleven-profile, www.sej.co.jp/company/en/g_stores.html. and http://franchise.7-eleven.com/franchise/our-iconic-brand, accessed October 2018.

Straight product extension
Marketing a product in a foreign market without making any changes to the product.

Straight product extension means marketing a product in a foreign market without making significant changes to the product. Top management tells its marketing people, "Take the product as is and find customers for it." The first step, however, should be to find out whether foreign consumers use that product and what form they prefer.

Straight extension has been successful in some cases and disastrous in others. Apple iPads, Gillette razors, and Black & Decker tools are all sold successfully in about the same form around the world. But when General Foods introduced its standard powdered JELL-O in the British market, it discovered that British consumers prefer a solid wafer or cake form. Likewise, Philips began to make a profit in Japan only after it reduced the size of its coffeemakers to fit into smaller Japanese kitchens and its shavers to fit smaller Japanese hands. And Panasonic's refrigerator sales in China surged tenfold in a single year after it shaved the width of its appliances by 15 percent to fit smaller Chinese kitchens.[39] Straight extension is tempting because it involves no additional product development costs, manufacturing changes, or new promotion. But it can be costly in the long run if products fail to satisfy consumers in specific global markets.

Product adaptation
Adapting a product to meet local conditions or wants in foreign markets.

Product adaptation involves changing the product to meet local requirements, conditions, or wants. >> For example, In the United States, Amazon's Echo-based virtual voice assistant Alexa speaks a soft but precise version of American English. Alexa knows that Independence Day falls on July 4 and that Americans love turkey with all the fixings at Thanksgiving. But what happens when Alexa goes global? Amazon's Echo speakers and Alexa must be carefully adapted to the particulars of each new global culture. Consider Echo in India:[40]

>> **Product adaptation: Amazon carefully adapts its Echo-based virtual voice assistant Alexa to each new global culture. In India, Alexa speaks Hinglish—a blend of Hindi and English—with an unmistakable Indian accent.**

Zapp2Photo/Shutterstock

Before introducing Alexa in India, teams of linguists, speech scientists, and developers gave her a decidedly local makeover. In India, Alexa speaks Hinglish—a blend of Hindi and English—with an unmistakable Indian accent. "She knows Independence Day is August 15, not July 4, and wishes listeners "Happy Diwali and a prosperous New Year!" says one business reporter. "She also refers to the living room as 'drawing room' and can add jeera (cumin), haldi (turmeric) and atta (flour) to your shopping list." Alexa's many "skills" cover a wide range of Indian interests, notes another reporter—"chants for cricket enthusiasts, recitations of the Gayatri Mantra,... daily horoscopes, Bollywood quizzes, Indian flute music, and even cooking instructions based on late celebrity chef Tarla Dalal's recipes."

Mastering Hinglish is critical. Although many Indians understand both English and Hindi, they feel more comfortable with an Alexa who sounds like them. Having Alexa understand the nuances of Hinglish and local subcultures is especially important as Amazon expands beyond India's big cities. A greater proportion of rural Indians speaks only Hindi or another local language, and lower literacy rates mean more people prefer voice controls to typing. "Alexa is not going to be a visiting American who is going to come to India for a few days and go back," says Amazon's country manager, Alexa Skills, India. "She is as Indian as it gets."

Product invention
Creating new products or services for foreign markets.

Product invention consists of creating something new to meet the needs of consumers in a given country. As markets have gone global, companies ranging from appliance manufacturers and carmakers to candy and soft drink producers have developed products that meet the special purchasing needs of low-income consumers in developing economies.

For example, Chinese appliance producer Haier developed sturdier washing machines for rural users Africa, India, and other emerging markets, where it found that lighter-duty machines often became clogged with mud when farmers used them to clean vegetables as well as clothes. And solar lighting manufacturer d.light Solar has developed affordable solar-powered home lighting systems for the hundreds of millions of people in the developing world who don't have access to reliable power. d.light's hanging lamps and portable lanterns require no energy source other than the sun and can last up to 15 hours on one charge. The company has already sold close to 20 million solar light and power products in 62 countries, reaching 82 million users.[41]

Promotion

Companies can either adopt the same communication strategy they use in the home market or change it for each local market. Consider advertising messages. Some global companies use a standardized advertising theme around the world. For example, Coca-Cola unifies its global advertising around a "Taste the Feeling" theme. Of course, even in highly standardized communications campaigns, some adjustments might be required for language and cultural differences. Ads for Coca-Cola's "Taste the Feeling" campaign have a similar look worldwide but are adapted in different global markets to feature local consumers, languages, celebrities, and events.

Global companies often have difficulty crossing the language barrier, with results ranging from mild embarrassment to outright failure. Seemingly innocuous brand names and advertising phrases can take on unintended or hidden meanings when translated into other languages. For example, Interbrand of London, the firm that created household names such as Prozac and Acura, recently developed a brand name "hall of shame" list, which contained these and other foreign brand names you're never likely to see inside the local Kroger supermarket: Krapp toilet paper (Denmark), Plopp chocolate (Scandinavia), Crapsy Fruit cereal (France), Poo curry powder (Argentina), and Pschitt lemonade (France). Similarly, advertising themes often lose—or gain—something in the translation. In Chinese, the KFC slogan "finger-lickin' good" came out as "eat your fingers off." And Motorola's Hellomoto ringtone sounds like "Hello, Fatty" in India.

Marketers must be watchful to avoid such mistakes, taking great care when localizing their brand names and messages to specific global markets. In important but culturally different markets such as China, finding just the right name can make or break a brand:

> After a long day's work, an average upscale Beijinger can't wait to dash home, lace on a comfortable pair of Enduring and Persevering, pop the top on a refreshing can of Tasty Fun, and then hop into his Dashing Speed and head to the local tavern for a frosty glass of Happiness Power with friends. Translation? In China, those are the brand name meanings for Nike, Coca-Cola, Mercedes, and Heineken, respectively. To Westerners, such names sound pretty silly, but to brands doing business in China, they are no laughing matter. Perhaps more than anywhere else in the world, brand names in China take on deep significance.
>
> Ideally, to maintain global consistency, the Chinese name should sound similar to the original while at the same time conveying the brand's benefits in meaningful symbolic terms. Nike's Chinese brand name, Nai ke, does this well. Not only does it sound the same when pronounced in Chinese, its "enduring and persevering" meaning powerfully encapsulates the "Just Do It" essence of the Nike brand the world over. Similarly, P&G's Tide is Taizi in China, which translates to "gets out the dirt," a perfect moniker for a tough-acting detergent. Other names that wear well on Chinese ears while also conveying a brand's essence include Lay's snack foods—Le shi ("happy things"); Reebok—Rui bu ("quick steps"); and Colgate—Gau lu jie ("revealing superior cleanliness").[42]

Communication adaptation
A global communication strategy of fully adapting advertising messages to local markets.

Rather than standardizing their advertising globally, other companies follow a strategy of **communication adaptation**, adapting their advertising messages to local markets. For example, in the United States and most Western countries, parents view play as beneficial to child development and creativity. However, Chinese parents tend view play negatively, as a distraction from schoolwork that doesn't contribute to learning and development. As a result, although China has almost five times the population of the United States, Chinese parents spend less than half of what U.S. parents spend on toys.

To meet this challenge, U.S. toymakers adapt their Chinese communications campaigns to emphasize how play helps children to succeed in life by boosting their knowledge, skills, and creativity. For example, LEGO shared a WeChat post showing a father who is a Silicon Valley engineer using LEGO bricks to teach his son math skills. A Crayola campaign featured a virtual children's art gallery showing how children will grow up "creating not just art, but also ideas, products, and scientific progress." A Mattel campaign reframed the value of play by, for example, showing how Hot Wheels can teach children about physics. >> And an Asia video for Mattel's Barbie, based on the brand's "You can be anything" theme, countered Chinese stereotypes about play being a waste of time by showing how playing with Barbie made girls more self-confident, creative, and emotionally intelligent. The video drew 7.5 million views.[43]

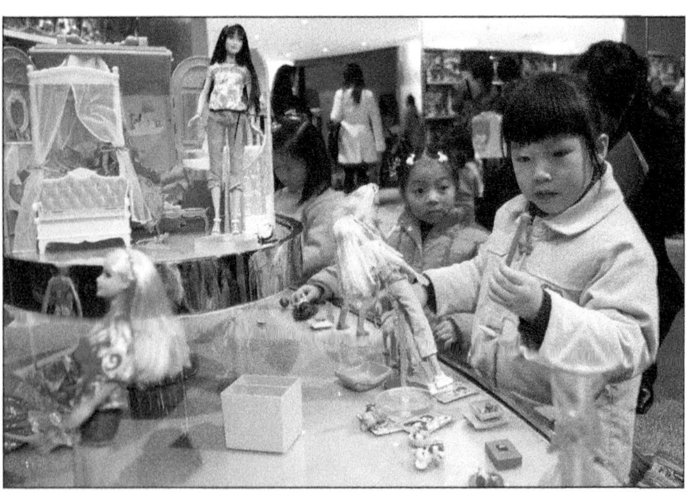

>> **Communication adaptation: To counter negative Chinese stereotypes about play, Mattel created a campaign showing how playing with Barbie made girls more self-confident, creative, and emotionally intelligent.**
AP Photo/Eugene Hoshiko

Media also need to be adapted internationally because media availability and regulations vary from country to country. While TV advertising has few regulations in the United States, TV advertising time is very limited in Europe. For instance, France has banned retailers from advertising on TV and Sweden forbids TV advertising to children. However, mobile phone ads are much more widely accepted in Europe and Asia than in the United States. Newspapers are national in the United Kingdom, only local in Spain, and the leading advertising medium in Germany. India has nearly 300 newspapers, but because of paper shortages, ads must be booked up to six months in advance.[44]

Price

Companies also face many considerations in setting their international prices. For example, how might Makita price its power tools globally? It could set a uniform price globally, but this amount would be too high of a price in poor countries and not high enough in rich ones. It could charge what consumers in each country would bear, but this strategy ignores differences in the actual costs from country to country. Finally, the company could use a standard markup of its costs everywhere, but this approach might price Makita out of the market in some countries where costs are high.

Regardless of how companies go about pricing their products, their foreign prices probably will be higher than their domestic prices for comparable products. An Apple 10.5" iPad Pro that sells for $649 in the United States goes for $888 in the United Kingdom. Why? Apple faces a *price escalation* problem. It must add the cost of transportation, tariffs, importer margin, wholesaler margin, and retailer margin to its factory price. Depending on these added costs, a product may have to sell for two to five times as much in another country to make the same profit.

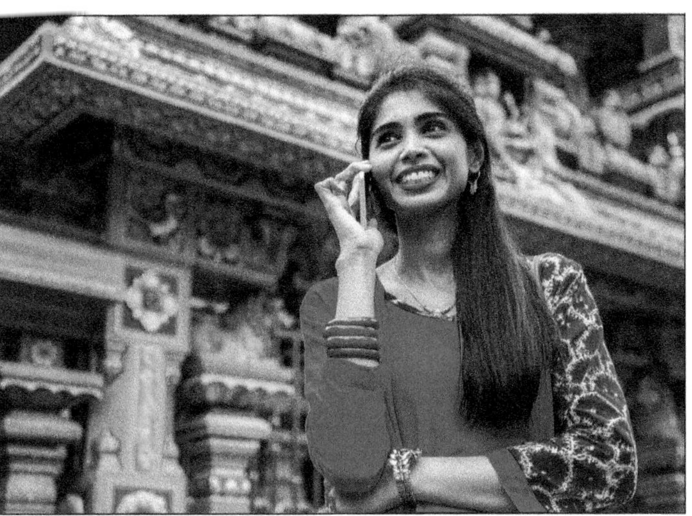

>> **International pricing: To compete with low-end competitors in emerging economies, Samsung developed its low-priced Galaxy J line, which carries the Galaxy name and style but with few high-end features.**
rawpixel/123RF

To overcome this problem when selling to less-affluent consumers in emerging markets, many companies make simpler or smaller versions of their products available that can be sold at lower prices. For example, Apple still sells its older 5S model online in India for less than $250 to compete with other low-price competitors such as Motorola, Xiaomi, Lenovo, and Samsung. And a subscription to Apple Music service in India is priced at only $2 per month versus $10 in the United States. >> Similarly, to compete with low-end competitors in Indonesia, India, Pakistan, and other emerging economies, Samsung developed its low-priced Galaxy J line. The J models, priced under $150, carry the Galaxy name and style but with few high-end features.[45]

Recent economic and technological forces have had an impact on global pricing. For example, the internet is making global price differences more obvious. When firms sell their wares over the internet, customers can see how much products sell for in different countries. They can even order a given product directly from the company location or dealer offering the lowest price. This is forcing companies toward more standardized international pricing.

Distribution Channels

Whole-channel view
Designing international channels that take into account the entire global supply chain and marketing channel, forging an effective global value delivery network.

An international company must take a **whole-channel view** of the problem of distributing products to final consumers. >> **Figure 15.4** shows the two major links between the seller and the final buyer. The first link, *channels between nations*, moves company products from points of production to the borders of countries within which they are sold. The second link, *channels within nations*, moves products from their market entry points to the final consumers. The whole-channel view takes into account the entire global supply chain and marketing channel. It recognizes that to compete well internationally, the company must effectively design and manage an entire *global value delivery network.*

In some markets, the distribution system is complex, competitive, and hard to penetrate. For example, many Western companies find India's distribution system difficult to navigate. Large discount, department store, and supermarket retailers still account for only a small portion of the huge Indian market. Instead, most shopping is done in small neighborhood

Distribution channels can vary dramatically around the world. For example, in the U.S., Coca-Cola distributes products through sophisticated retail channels. In less-developed countries, it delivers Coca-Cola products using everything from push carts to delivery donkeys.

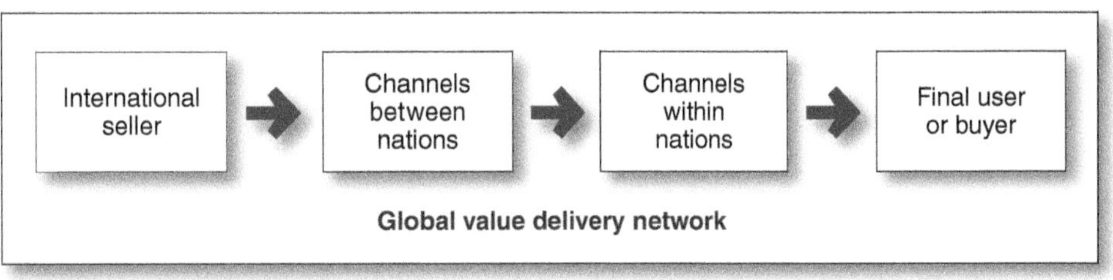

>> **Figure 15.4 Whole-Channel Concept for International Marketing**

>> McDelivery: In big cities in Asia and Africa, where crowded streets and high real estate costs make drive-thrus impractical, legions of McDonald's motorbike delivery drivers dispense Big Macs and fries to customers who call in.

Sorbis/Shutterstock

stores called *kirana* shops, run by their owners and popular because they offer personal service and credit. In addition, large Western retailers have difficulty dealing with India's complex government regulations and poor infrastructure.

Distribution systems in developing countries may be scattered, inefficient, or altogether lacking. For example, China's rural markets are highly decentralized, made of many distinct submarkets, each with its own subculture. And, because of inadequate distribution systems, most companies can profitably access only a small portion of China's massive population located in affluent cities. China's distribution system is so fragmented that logistics costs to wrap, bundle, load, unload, sort, reload, and transport goods amount nearly 15 percent of the nation's GDP, far higher than in most other countries. (In comparison, U.S. logistics costs account for about 7.5 percent of the nation's GDP.)[46]

Sometimes local conditions can greatly influence how a company distributes products in global markets. For example, in low-income neighborhoods in Brazil where consumers have limited access to supermarkets, Nestlé supplements its distribution an army of self-employed salespeople who sell Nestlé products from refrigerated carts door to door. >> And in big cities in Asia and Africa, where crowded streets and high real estate costs make drive-throughs impractical, fast-food restaurants such as McDonald's and KFC offer delivery. Legions of motorbike delivery drivers in colorful uniforms dispense Big Macs and buckets of chicken to customers who call in. McDonald's reaped more than $1 billion in delivery sales worldwide for last year.[47]

Thus, international marketers face a wide range of channel alternatives. Designing efficient and effective channel systems between and within various country markets poses a difficult challenge.

Deciding on the Global Marketing Organization

Author Comment

Many large companies, regardless of their "home country," now think of themselves as truly global organizations. They view the entire world as a single borderless market. For example, although headquartered in Chicago, Boeing is as comfortable selling planes to Lufthansa or Air China as to American Airlines.

OBJECTIVE 15-4 Identify the three major forms of international marketing organization.

Companies manage their international marketing activities in at least three different ways: Most companies first organize an export department, then create an international division, and finally become a global organization.

A firm normally gets into international marketing by simply shipping out its goods. If its international sales expand, the company will establish an *export department* with a sales manager and a few assistants. As sales increase, the export department can expand to include various marketing services so that it can actively go after business. If the firm moves into joint ventures or direct investment, the export department will no longer be adequate.

Many companies get involved in several international markets and ventures. A company may export to one country, license to another, have a joint ownership venture in a third, and own a subsidiary in a fourth. Sooner or later it will create *international divisions* or subsidiaries to handle all its international activity.

International divisions are organized in a variety of ways. An international division's corporate staff consists of marketing, manufacturing, research, finance, planning, and personnel specialists. It plans for and provides services to various operating units, which can be organized in one of three ways. They can be *geographical organizations*, with country managers who are responsible for salespeople, sales branches, distributors, and licensees in their respective countries. Or the operating units can be *world product groups*, each responsible for worldwide sales of different product groups. Finally, operating units can be *international subsidiaries*, each responsible for their own sales and profits.

Many firms have passed beyond the international division stage and are truly global organizations. For example, as discussed previously, despite its French origins, L'Oréal no longer has a clearly defined home market. Nor does it have a home-office staff. Instead, the company is famous for building global brand teams around managers who have deep backgrounds in several cultures. L'Oréal managers around the world bring diverse cultural perspectives to their brands as if they were, say, German or American or Chinese—or all three at once. As explained by one Indian-American-French manager of a team that launched a men's skin care line in Southeast Asia: "I cannot think about things one way. I have a stock of references in different languages: English, Hindi, and French. I read books in three different languages, meet people from different countries, eat food from different [cultures], and so on."[48]

Global organizations don't think of themselves as national marketers that sell abroad but as global marketers. The top corporate management and staff plan worldwide manufacturing facilities, marketing policies, financial flows, and logistical systems. The global operating units report directly to the chief executive or the executive committee of the organization, not to the head of an international division. Executives are trained in worldwide operations, not just domestic *or* international operations. Global companies recruit management from many countries, buy components and supplies where they cost the least, and invest where the expected returns are greatest.

Today, major companies must become more global if they hope to compete. As foreign companies successfully invade their domestic markets, companies must move more aggressively into foreign markets. They will have to change from companies that treat their international operations as secondary to companies that view the entire world as a single borderless market.

REVIEWING AND EXTENDING THE CONCEPTS

CHAPTER REVIEW AND KEY TERMS

Objectives Review

Companies today can no longer afford to pay attention only to their domestic market, regardless of its size. Many industries are global industries, and firms that operate globally achieve lower costs and higher brand awareness. At the same time, global marketing is risky because of variable exchange rates, unstable governments, tariffs and trade barriers, and several other factors. Given the potential gains and risks of international marketing, companies need a systematic way to make their global marketing decisions.

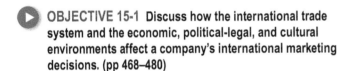

OBJECTIVE 15-1 Discuss how the international trade system and the economic, political-legal, and cultural environments affect a company's international marketing decisions. (pp 468–480)

A company must understand the *global marketing environment*, especially the international trade system. It should assess each foreign market's *economic, political-legal*, and *cultural characteristics*. The company can then decide whether it wants to go abroad and consider the potential risks and benefits. It must decide on the volume of international sales it wants, how many countries it wants to market in, and which specific markets it wants to enter. These decisions call for weighing the probable returns against the level of risk.

OBJECTIVE 15-2 Describe three key approaches to entering international markets. (pp 480–483)

The company must decide how to enter each chosen market—whether through *exporting, joint venturing*, or *direct investment*. Many companies start as exporters, move to joint ventures, and finally make a direct investment in foreign markets. In *exporting*, the company enters a foreign market by sending and selling products through international marketing intermediaries (indirect exporting) or the company's own department, branch, or sales representatives or agents (direct exporting). When establishing a *joint venture*, a company enters foreign markets by joining with foreign companies to produce or market a product or service. In *licensing*, the company enters a foreign market by contracting with a licensee in the foreign market and offering the right to use a manufacturing process, trademark, patent, trade secret, or other item of value for a fee or royalty.

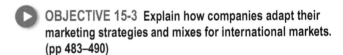

OBJECTIVE 15-3 Explain how companies adapt their marketing strategies and mixes for international markets. (pp 483–490)

Companies must also decide how much their marketing strategies and their products, promotion, price, and channels should be adapted for each foreign market. At one extreme, global companies use *standardized global marketing* worldwide. Others use *adapted global marketing*, in which they adjust the marketing strategy and mix to each target market, bearing more costs but hoping for a larger market share and return. However, global standardization is not an all-or-nothing proposition. It's a matter of degree. Most international marketers suggest that companies should "think globally but act locally"—that they should seek a balance between globally standardized strategies and locally adapted marketing mix tactics.

OBJECTIVE 15-4 Identify the three major forms of international marketing organization. (p 490–491)

The company must develop an effective organization for international marketing. Most firms start with an *export department* and graduate to an *international division*. Large companies eventually become *global organizations*, with worldwide marketing planned and managed by the top officers of the company. Global organizations view the entire world as a single, borderless market.

Key Terms

Objective 15-1
Global firm (p 469)
Economic community (p 471)

Objective 15-2
Exporting (p 480)
Joint venturing (p 481)
Licensing (p 481)
Contract manufacturing (p 481)
Management contracting (p 482)
Joint ownership (p 482)
Direct investment (p 482)

Objective 15-3
Standardized global marketing (p 483)
Adapted global marketing (p 483)
Straight product extension (p 486)
Product adaptation (p 486)
Product invention (p 487)
Communication adaptation (p 488)
Whole-channel view (p 489)

DISCUSSION AND CRITICAL THINKING

Discussion Questions

15-1. Discuss the benefits and challenges companies face as they navigate the rapidly changing global environment. (AACSB: Written and Oral Communication)

15-2. What environmental factors must international marketers consider when entering foreign markets? (AACSB: Written and Oral Communication)

15-3. Name and explain a company's market entry options for international markets. (AACSB: Written and Oral Communication)

15-4. Name and discuss the two marketing strategies global companies can use to adapt to foreign markets. What are the benefits of each strategy? (AACSB: Written and Oral Communication; Reflective Thinking)

15-5. Briefly outline the strategies used for adapting products to a global market. Provide an example for each strategy. (AACSB: Written and Oral Communication)

15-6. Explain the two major links between the seller and the final buyer in the global value delivery network. Why is a whole-channel view important for a firm's distribution choices? (AACSB: Written and Oral Communication; Reflective Thinking)

Critical Thinking Exercises

15-7. The chapter describes the global marketing presence of McDonald's, IKEA, and Amazon. Select two additional global companies, and identify their market entry strategies. Support your position. (AACSB: Written and Oral Communication; Information Technology; Reflective Thinking)

15-8. For the past several years, Procter & Gamble has seen significant growth from emerging markets. Visit the P&G website at www.pg.com. Pick three global brands. Using Figure 15.3, identify which of the five global product and communications strategies the company has use with each brand. Support your conclusions. (AACSB: Written and Oral Communication; Reflective Thinking)

15-9. You have been asked to consult with a small business owner who wants to expand her company overseas. She has asked you to develop a global marketing strategy. You are not certain if the owner thoroughly understands the international expansion process and the challenges involved. Prior to meeting with the owner next week, create a presentation listing the factors she will need to consider prior to her company going global. (AACSB: Written and Oral Communication; Information Technology; Reflective Thinking)

MINICASES AND APPLICATIONS

Online, Mobile, and Social Media Marketing China's Great Firewall

China has emerged as an enormous social media market. With more than 1.35 billion people and 635 million internet users, internet usage in China is growing explosively at about 30 percent annually. That makes it an extremely attractive market for Western social media companies such as Facebook, Google, Twitter, and YouTube. However, under what has come to be called the "Great Firewall of China"—an extensive level of control and censorship of websites and internet activities by the Chinese government—many Western social media and other online marketers have been largely blocked from operating in China. According to *The Diplomat*, eight of the top 25 most-visited global sites are now blocked in China. However, even with constant government monitoring of internet activities, China has become one of the world's most active social media environments. Chinese consumers can connect though carefully controlled local social networking platforms such as Renren (everyone's website), Baidu (Google-like search engine), Youku (China's answer to YouTube), Weixin (instant messaging), Jiepang (similar to Foursquare), microblogging sites such as Sina Weibo (like Twitter), and Dianping (similar to Yelp).

As more marketers enter the social media landscape in China, strategies to reach consumers must be carefully shaped to the country's culture, consumers, content, platforms, and regulations. Online marketers must understand Chinese culture, translations, and etiquette to help craft better messages and marketing content that will resonate with Chinese consumers. At the same time, they must navigate under the watchful eye of the Chinese government.

15-10. Research the Great Firewall of China. How will such government control impact social media marketing in China? Report on a Western online company now operating in China. How is it able to work within and around Chinese regulations? (AACSB: Written and Oral Communication; Reflective Thinking)

15-11. Suppose that your company is preparing to enter the Chinese market with a product line that you believe will have great success. What is the best mode of entry for your company? Review the economic and political climates. Is the timing right for entering China? (AACSB: Written and Oral Communication; Information Technology; Reflective Thinking)

Marketing Ethics Unlicensed and Counterfeit Products

Fake products make up 5 to 7 percent of world trade and include everything from counterfeit electronics, medications, pirated DVDs, and computer software to toys, cosmetics, and household products. Counterfeit name-brand apparel and sportswear, shoes, and accessories are exceptionally common. According to the *Global Brand Counterfeiting Report, 2018*, the total amount of global counterfeiting has reached $1.2 trillion annually. Luxury brands such as Louis Vuitton, Chanel, Manolo Blahnik, and Christian Louboutin have seen an upsurge in trademark violations and fraudulent products hitting the market.

Counterfeit products are big business globally. So big, in fact, that Chinese industry regulators are hesitant to shut the practice down; the counterfeit goods market comprises millions of desperately needed jobs within China's economy. But companies lose an estimated $20 billion in revenue annually because of fake goods. Moreover, many worldwide consumers are not getting what they pay for—consumers may get the brand name or label they want but an inferior product.

15-12. Discuss worldwide organizations that assist companies in developing and abiding by global standards for marketing, consumer protection, and regulatory compliance. (AACSB: Written and Oral Communication; Reflective Thinking)

15-13. Is there any justification for companies to profit by creating counterfeit products that create local jobs and provide consumers with access to products they typically would not be able to buy? Support your answer. (AACSB: Written and Oral Communication; Ethical Understanding and Reasoning)

Marketing by the Numbers Peloton Pedals to the UK

The word *peloton* means "the main group of cyclists in a race." But Peloton means something different to the million or so fanatics in the United States who've shelled out $1,995 for an internet-connected indoor exercise bike and who pay $39 a month to stream live and on-demand classes from Peloton's New York City studio to the tablet connected to the bike. Peloton streams 12 hours of live content every day and offers more than 8,000 on-demand cycling classes and other "Beyond the Ride" classes such as yoga, arms, legs, and core strengthening. Riders can select their favorite instructor, class length, class type, and even music genre, and they can follow and compete with others. Peloton's success comes from being more than an exercise bike, studio, or cycling class—it's an experience that has created a cult-like following among its subscribers. Peloton's closed Facebook group boasts more than 90,000 members. More than 3,000 of those members descended on New York City during Peloton's Home Rider Invasion weekend where they eagerly paid $50 to attend a cocktail party and two studio classes with Peloton's celebrity-like instructors. Now Peloton wants to expand globally, beginning with the United Kingdom, the world's second-largest fitness market. With today's technologies, Peloton could distribute the service to consumers worldwide from its New York studio. But instead, the company intends to recreate the entire experience in the United Kingdom, with a studio in London, British instructors, and retail showrooms just like in the United States. Bikes will be priced at £1,995 and class subscriptions will run £39.50 per month. Peloton sells the bikes at cost because it knows that the real money comes from selling the associated services.

15-14. How many bikes must Peloton sell to break even on this international expansion if total fixed costs are £30 million per year, variable costs are £1,995 per bike (Peloton sells them at cost), and monthly service variable costs are £5? Assume that a consumer purchasing a bike at the price of £1,995 will also subscribe for 12 months of the streaming service at £39.50 per month. Refer to Break-Even and Margin Analysis in Appendix 3: Marketing by the Numbers to learn how to perform this analysis. (AACSB: Analytical Thinking)

15-15. What U.S. dollar sales does your answer in question 15-14 represent? Use a currency exchange calculator, such as the one at www.xe.com/currencyconverter/, to convert from British pounds to U.S. dollars. (AACSB: Analytical Thinking; Information Technology)

Video Case Monster Worldwide

To view this video case and its accompanying questions, please visit MyLab Marketing.

Monster.com is one of the most visited employment sites in the United States and one of the largest in the world. Now a part of parent company Monster Worldwide, Monster.com pioneered job recruiting on the Internet. Today, it is the only online recruitment provider that can service job seekers and job posters on a truly global basis. With a presence in 50 countries around the world, Monster has unparalleled international reach. Even through tough economic times, Monster continued to invest heavily in order to maintain and expand its global presence.

Monster's international expansion included the purchase of ChinaHR.com, giving it a strong presence in the world's largest country. Monster already gets about 45 percent of its annual revenue of $1.3 billion from outside the United States. But it expects to become even more global in the coming years. To back that geographic expansion, Monster is also investing heavily in search technologies and Web design in order to appeal to clients everywhere.

Company Cases 15 L'Oréal/7 MINI

See Appendix 1 for cases appropriate for this chapter.

Case 15, L'Oréal: The United Nations of Beauty. L'Oréal has become the world's largest cosmetics company by achieving the best balance between standardizing its brands for global impact and adapting them to meet local needs and desires.

Case 7, MINI: Focus on the Essential—Maximize the Experience. MINI is one of the most iconic automotive brands in the world, thriving for more than 50 years through six owners.

Writing Assignments

15-16. What is the World Trade Organization? What is its purpose, and what has it accomplished? (AACSB: Communication)

15-17. Visit www.ikea.com and compare a catalog from one country to that of another. Note the prices of some of the products. Convert some of the foreign prices to U.S. dollars and compare them to the prices in the U.S. catalog. Are the prices equivalent? Are they consistently higher or lower? (AACSB: Written and Oral Communication; Reflective Thinking)

16 Sustainable Marketing

Social Responsibility and Ethics

Objectives Outline

OBJECTIVE 16-1 Define sustainable marketing and discuss its importance. See: Sustainable Marketing (pp 498–500)

OBJECTIVE 16-2 Identify the major social criticisms of marketing. See: Social Criticisms of Marketing (pp 500–509)

OBJECTIVE 16-3 Define *consumerism* and *environmentalism* and explain how they affect marketing strategies. See: Consumer Actions to Promote Sustainable Marketing (pp 509–513)

OBJECTIVE 16-4 Describe the principles of sustainable marketing. See: Business Actions toward Sustainable Marketing (pp 513–517)

OBJECTIVE 16-5 Explain the role of ethics in marketing. See: Marketing Ethics and the Sustainable Company (pp 518–520)

Previewing the Concepts

In this final chapter, we'll examine the concept of sustainable marketing, meeting the needs of consumers, businesses, and society—now and in the future—through socially and environmentally responsible marketing actions. We'll start by defining sustainable marketing and then look at some common criticisms of marketing as it affects individual consumers as well as public actions that promote sustainable marketing. Finally, we'll see how companies themselves can benefit from proactively pursuing sustainable marketing practices that bring value to not only individual customers but also society as a whole. Sustainable marketing actions are more than just the right thing to do; they're also good for business.

First, let's look at an example of sustainable marketing in action at Unilever, the world's third-largest consumer products company. For 19 years running, Unilever has been named a sustainability leader in the food and beverage industry by the Dow Jones Sustainability Indexes. Nearly a decade ago, the company launched its 10-year Sustainable Living Plan, by which it intended to double its size while at the same time reducing its impact on the planet and increasing the social benefits arising from its activities. That's an ambitious goal.

First Stop

Sustainability at Unilever: Creating a Better Future Every Day

When Paul Polman took over as CEO of Unilever nearly a decade ago, the foods, home, and personal care products company was a slumbering giant. Despite its stable of star-studded brands—including the likes of Dove, Axe, Noxzema, Sunsilk, OMO, Hellmann's, Knorr, Lipton, and Ben & Jerry's—Unilever had experienced a decade of stagnant sales and profits. The company needed renewed energy and purpose. "To drag the world back to sanity, we need to know why we are here," said Polman.

To answer the "why are we here" question and find a more energizing mission, Polman looked beyond the usual corporate goals of growing sales, profits, and shareholder value. Instead, he asserted, growth results from accomplishing a broader social and environmental mission. Unilever exists "for consumers, not shareholders," he said. "If we are in sync with consumer needs and the environment in which we operate, and take responsibility for our [societal impact], then the shareholder will also be rewarded."

Evaluating and working on sustainability impact is nothing new at Unilever. Prior to Polman taking the reins, the company already had multiple programs in place to manage the impact of its products and operations. But the existing programs and results—while good—simply didn't go far enough for Polman. So in late 2010 Unilever launched its Sustainable Living Plan—an aggressive long-term plan that takes capitalism to the next level. Under the plan, the company set out to "create a better future every day for people around the world: the people who work for us, those we do business with, the billions of people who use our products, and future generations whose quality of life depends on the way we protect the environment today." According to Polman, Unilever's long-run commercial success depends on how well it manages the social and environmental impact of its actions.

The Sustainable Living Plan set out three major social and environmental objectives to be accomplished by 2020: "(1) To help more than one billion people take action to improve their health and well-being; (2) to halve the environmental footprint of the making and use of our products; and (3) to enhance the livelihoods of millions of people as we grow our business." The Sustainable Living Plan pulled together all of the work Unilever had already been doing and set ambitious new sustainability goals. These goals span the entire value chain, from how the company sources raw materials to how consumers use and dispose of its products. "Our aim is to make our activities more sustainable and also encourage our customers, suppliers, and others to do the same," says the company.

On the "upstream supply side," more than half of Unilever's raw materials come from agriculture, so the company is helping suppliers develop sustainable farming practices that meet its own high expectations for environmental and social impact. Unilever assesses suppliers against two sets of standards. The first is the Unilever Supplier Code, which calls for socially responsible actions regarding human rights, labor practices, product safety, and care for the environment. Second, specifically for agricultural suppliers, the Unilever Sustainable Agriculture Code details Unilever's expectations for sustainable agriculture practices so that it and its suppliers "can commit to the sustainability journey together."

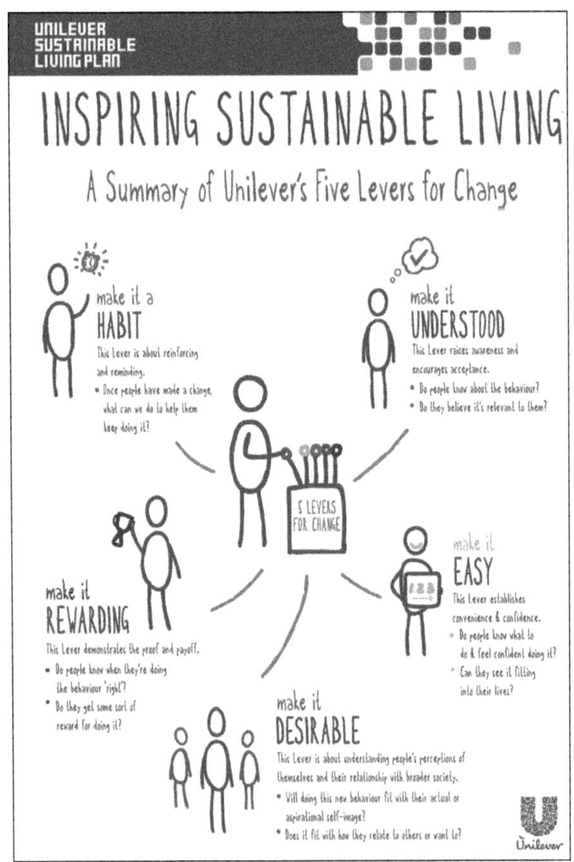

» Under its Sustainable Living Plan, Unilever is working with billions of customers worldwide to improve the social and environmental impact of its products. "Small actions. Big difference."

But Unilever's Sustainable Living Plan goes far beyond simply creating more responsible supply and distribution chains. Approximately 68 percent of the total greenhouse gas footprint of Unilever's products and 50 percent of the water footprint occur during post-purchase consumer use. So Unilever is also working with its customers to improve the environmental impact of its products in use. On any given day, about 2.5 billion people in 190 global markets use a product from one of Unilever's more than 400 brands. Therefore, small everyday consumer actions can add up to a big difference. Unilever sums it up with this equation: "Unilever brands × small everyday actions × billions of consumers = big difference."

Under Unilever's Sustainable Living Plan, the consumer goods giant has set out to "create a better future every day for people around the world." Unilever's long-run commercial success depends on how well it manages the social and environmental impact of its actions.

For example, almost one-third of households worldwide use Unilever laundry products to do their washing—approximately 125 billion washes every year. Therefore, under its Sustainable Living Plan, Unilever is both creating more eco-friendly laundry products and motivating consumers to improve their laundry habits.

Around the world, for instance, Unilever is encouraging consumers to wash clothes at lower temperatures and use the correct dosage of detergent. Unilever products such as OMO and Persil Small & Mighty concentrated laundry detergents use less packaging, making them cheaper and less polluting to transport. More important, they've been reformulated to wash efficiently at lower temperatures, using less energy and water. Unilever estimates that these changes have achieved a 15 percent reduction in greenhouse gas emissions. Another Unilever product, Comfort One Rinse fabric conditioner, was created for handwashing clothes in developing and emerging markets where water is often in short supply. The innovative product requires only one bucket of water for rinsing rather than three, saving consumers time, effort, and 30 liters of water per wash.

Such energy and water savings don't show up on Unilever's income statement, but they are extremely important to the people and the planet. "Ultimately," says the company, "we will only succeed if we inspire people around the world to take small, everyday actions that can add up to a big difference for the world." To meet this objective, Unilever has identified "Five Levers for Change"—things that its marketers can do to inspire people to adopt specific sustainable behaviors. The model helps marketers identify the barriers and triggers for change. The levers for change are: make it understood, make it easy, make it desirable, make it rewarding, and make it a habit.

Will Unilever's Sustainable Living Plan produce results for the company? So far, so good. Unilever is making excellent progress on its overall mission of "making sustainable living commonplace" and on its 79 aggressive Sustainable Living Plan goals. The company has already achieved 16 specific targets, is right on pace with 56 more, and is making good progress on the other seven. And despite volatility in its global markets, Unilever's profits continue to grow. In the past two years alone, Unilever's revenues have increased 22 percent while profits have shot up a whopping 48 percent. Even more telling, Unilever's 26 Sustainable Living Brands grew 46 percent faster than the rest of its business, and 22 are among the company's top 40 brands.

Thus, claims Polman, the sustainability plan is not just the right thing to do for people and the environment, it's also right for Unilever. The quest for sustainability saves money by reducing energy use and minimizing waste. It fuels innovation, resulting in new products and new consumer benefits. And it creates new market opportunities: More than half of Unilever's sales are from developing countries, the very places that face the greatest sustainability challenges.

In all, Polman predicts, the sustainability plan is helping Unilever double in size while also creating a better future for billions of people without increasing the environmental footprint. "We do not believe there is a conflict between sustainability and profitable growth," he concludes. "The daily act of making and selling consumer goods drives economic and social progress. There are billions of people around the world who deserve the better quality of life that everyday products like soap, shampoo, and tea can provide. Sustainable living is not a pipedream. It can be done, and there is very little downside."[1]

Responsible marketers discover what consumers want and respond with market offerings that create value for buyers and capture value in return. The *marketing concept* is a philosophy of customer value and mutual gain. Its practice leads the economy by an invisible hand to satisfy the many and changing needs of consumers.

Not all marketers follow the marketing concept, however. In fact, some companies use questionable marketing practices that serve their own rather than consumers' interests. Moreover, even well-intentioned marketing actions that meet the current needs of some consumers may cause immediate or future harm to other consumers or the larger society. Responsible marketers must consider whether their actions are sustainable in the longer run.

This chapter examines sustainable marketing and the social and environmental effects of private marketing practices. First, we address the question: What is sustainable marketing, and why is it important?

Author Comment
Marketers must think beyond immediate customer satisfaction and business performance toward sustainable strategies that preserve the world for future generations.

Sustainable Marketing

OBJECTIVE 16-1 **Define sustainable marketing and discuss its importance.**

Sustainable marketing
Socially and environmentally responsible marketing that meets the present needs of consumers and businesses while also preserving or enhancing the ability of future generations to meet their needs.

Sustainable marketing calls for socially and environmentally responsible actions that meet the present needs of consumers and businesses while also preserving or enhancing the ability of future generations to meet their needs. >> **Figure 16.1** compares the sustainable marketing concept with marketing concepts we studied in earlier chapters.

The *marketing concept* recognizes that organizations thrive by determining the current needs and wants of target customers and fulfilling them more effectively and efficiently than competitors do. It focuses on meeting the company's short-term sales, growth, and

>> **Figure 16.1 Sustainable Marketing**

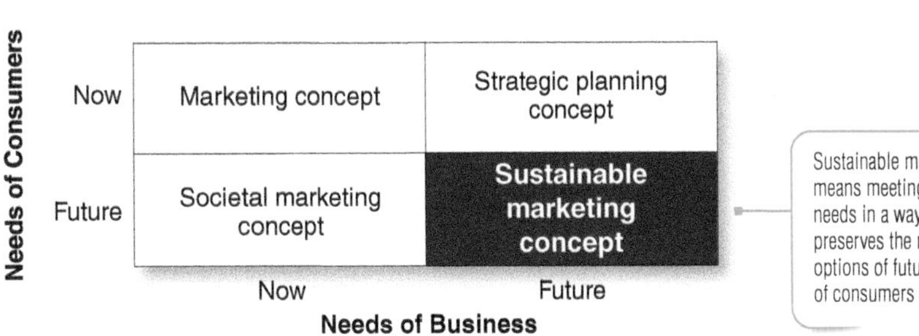

The marketing concept means meeting the current needs of both customers and the company. But that can sometimes mean compromising the future of both.
Needs of Consumers
Now
Future
Marketing concept
Strategic planning concept
Societal marketing concept
Sustainable marketing concept
Now
Future
Needs of Business
Sustainable marketing means meeting current needs in a way that preserves the rights and options of future generations of consumers and businesses.

profit needs by engaging customers and giving them what they want now. However, satisfying consumers' immediate needs and desires doesn't always serve the future best interests of either customers or the business.

For example, McDonald's early decisions to market tasty but fat- and salt-laden fast foods created immediate satisfaction for customers as well as sales and profits for the company. However, critics assert that McDonald's and other fast-food chains contributed to a longer-term national obesity epidemic, damaging consumer health and burdening the national health system. They worried that McDonald's Happy Meals created poor eating habits in children that carried forward into their later years. In turn, many consumers began looking for healthier eating options, causing a slump in the sales and profits of the fast-food industry.

Beyond issues of ethical behavior and social welfare, McDonald's was also criticized for the sizable environmental footprint of its vast global operations, everything from wasteful packaging and solid waste creation to inefficient energy use in its stores. Thus, McDonald's strategy was not sustainable in the long run in terms of either consumer or company benefit.

Whereas the *societal marketing concept* identified in Figure 16.1 considers the future welfare of consumers and the *strategic planning concept* considers future company needs, the *sustainable marketing concept* considers both. Sustainable marketing calls for socially and environmentally responsible actions that meet both the immediate and future needs of customers and the company.

For example, for more than a decade, McDonald's has responded to these challenges with a more sustainable strategy of diversifying into salads, fruits, grilled chicken, low-fat milk, and other healthy fare. The company has also sponsored major education campaigns to help consumers better understand the keys to living balanced, active lifestyles. >> It announced a list of "Commitments to Offer Improved Nutrition Choices" and has been working with the Alliance for a Healthier Generation to make improvements to the Happy Meal, offering more balanced meals and simpler ingredients. McDonald's points out that 80 percent of the items on its national menu fall into its "favorites under 400 calories" category—from a basic cheeseburger to products such as Fruit & Maple Oatmeal and the Egg White Delight McMuffin, made with eight grams of whole grain, 100 percent egg whites, and extra-lean Canadian bacon.[2]

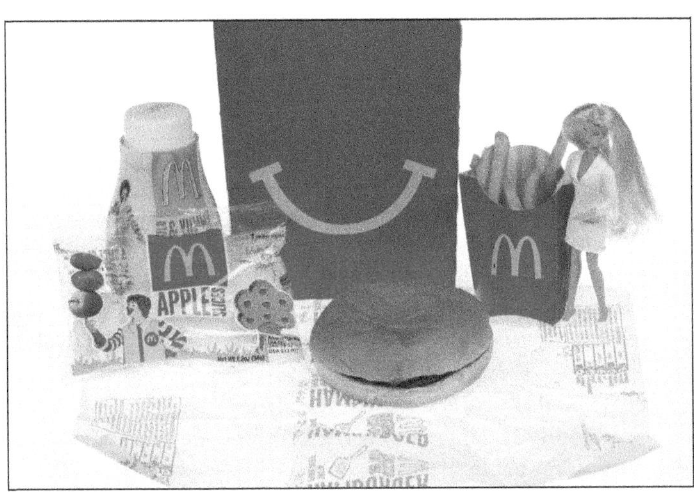

APPLE

>> **Sustainability: McDonald's has responded to sustainability challenges with a more sustainable strategy of diversifying into salads, fruits, grilled chicken, low-fat milk, and other healthy fare, including Happy Meals offering more balanced meals with simpler ingredients.**

Michael Neelon(misc)/Alamy Stock Photo

McDonald's sustainability initiatives also address environmental issues. It calls for food-supply sustainability, reduced and environmentally sustainable packaging, reuse and recycling, and more responsible store designs. For example, McDonald's has made the commitment to source all packaging from renewable or certified resources and make recycling an option at all locations by 2025.[3] Thus, McDonald's is now well positioned for a sustainably profitable future.

Truly sustainable marketing requires a smooth-functioning marketing system in which consumers, companies, public policy makers, and others work together to ensure socially and environmentally responsible marketing actions. Unfortunately, however, the marketing system doesn't always work smoothly. The following sections examine several sustainability questions: What are the most frequent social criticisms of marketing? What steps have private citizens taken to curb marketing ills? What steps have legislators and government agencies taken to promote sustainable marketing? What steps have enlightened companies taken to carry out socially responsible and ethical marketing that creates sustainable value for both individual customers and society as a whole?

Author Comment

In most ways, we all benefit greatly from marketing activities. However, like most other human endeavors, marketing has its flaws. Here we present both sides of some of the most common criticisms of marketing.

Social Criticisms of Marketing

OBJECTIVE 16-2 Identify the major social criticisms of marketing.

Marketing receives much criticism. Some of this criticism is justified; much is not. Social critics claim that certain marketing practices hurt individual consumers, society as a whole, and other business firms.

Marketing's Impact on Individual Consumers

Consumers have many concerns about how well the American marketing system serves their interests. Surveys usually show that consumers hold mixed or even slightly unfavorable attitudes toward marketing practices. Consumer advocates, government agencies, and other critics have accused marketing of harming consumers through high prices, deceptive practices, high-pressure selling, shoddy or unsafe products, planned obsolescence, and poor service to disadvantaged consumers. Such questionable marketing practices are not sustainable in terms of long-term consumer or business welfare.

High Prices

Many critics charge that the American marketing system causes prices to be higher than they would be under more "sensible" systems. Such high prices are hard to swallow, especially when the economy gets tight. Critics point to three factors—high costs of distribution, high advertising and promotion costs, and excessive markups.

A long-standing charge is that greedy marketing channel members mark up prices beyond the value of their services. As a result, distribution costs too much and consumers pay for these excessive costs in the form of higher prices. Resellers respond that intermediaries do work that would otherwise have to be done by manufacturers or consumers. Their prices reflect services that consumers want—more convenience, larger stores and assortments, more service, longer store hours, return privileges, and others. In fact, they argue, retail competition is so intense that margins are actually quite low. And discounters such as Walmart, Costco, and others pressure their competitors to operate efficiently and keep their prices down.

Modern marketing is also accused of pushing up prices to finance unneeded advertising, sales promotion, and packaging. >> For example, a heavily promoted national brand sells for much more than a virtually identical store-branded product. Critics charge that much of this promotion and packaging adds only psychological, not functional, value. Marketers respond that although advertising adds to product costs, it also adds value by informing potential buyers of the availability and merits of a brand. Brand name products may cost more, but branding assures buyers of consistent quality. Moreover, although consumers can usually buy functional versions of products at lower prices, they *want* and are willing to pay more for products that also provide psychological benefits—that make them feel wealthy, attractive, or special.

Critics also charge that some companies mark up goods excessively. They point to the drug industry, where a pill

>> A heavily promoted national brand sells for much more than a virtually identical non-branded or store-branded product. Critics charge that promotion adds only psychological value to the product rather than functional value.

Keri Miksza

costing five cents to make may cost the consumer $2 to buy, and to the high charges for auto repairs and other services. Marketers respond that most businesses try to price fairly to consumers because they want to build customer relationships and repeat business. Also, they assert, consumers often don't understand the reasons for high markups. For example, pharmaceutical markups help cover the costs of making and distributing existing medicines plus the high costs of developing and testing new medicines. As pharmaceuticals company GlaxoSmithKline has stated in its ads, "Today's medicines finance tomorrow's miracles."

Deceptive Practices

Marketers are sometimes accused of deceptive practices that lead consumers to believe they will get more value than they actually do. Deceptive practices fall into three groups: promotion, packaging, and pricing. *Deceptive promotion* includes practices such as misrepresenting the product's features or performance or luring customers to the store for a bargain that is out of stock. *Deceptive packaging* includes exaggerating package contents through subtle design, using misleading labeling, or describing size in misleading terms.

Deceptive pricing includes practices such as falsely advertising "factory" or "wholesale" prices or a large price reduction from a phony high retail "list price." For example, retailers from JCPenney and Kohl's to Neiman Marcus and Nordstrom were hit with lawsuits alleging that they used inflated original prices. A class action suit against Macy's accused the retailer of duping customers with a "phantom markdown scheme" and of "purporting to offer steep discounts off of fabricated, arbitrary, and false former or purported original, regular or 'compare at' prices."[4] And Overstock.com was recently fined $6.8 million by a California court as a result of a fraudulent pricing lawsuit filed by the attorneys general of eight California counties. The suit charged that the online giant routinely advertised its prices as lower than fabricated "list prices." It recites one example in which Overstock sold a patio set for $449 while claiming that the list price was $999. When the item was delivered, the customer found that it had a Walmart sticker stating a price of $247.[5]

Deceptive practices have led to legislation and other consumer protection actions. For example, in 1938 Congress enacted the Wheeler-Lea Act, which gave the Federal Trade Commission (FTC) power to regulate "unfair or deceptive acts or practices." The FTC has since published several guidelines listing deceptive practices.

Despite regulations, however, some critics argue that deceptive claims are still common, even for well-known brands. >> For example, identity theft protection company LifeLock recently paid a record $100 million relating to FTC charges of deceptive advertising. The FTC accused LifeLock—which claims that it is "relentlessly protecting your identity"—of falsely advertising that it protected consumers' sensitive data with the same high-level safeguards as financial institutions and that it falsely claimed it protected consumers' identity around the clock by providing alerts "as soon as" it received any indication there was a problem. Said one reporter, "It's bad enough that people have to worry about their personal data getting stolen. Now they have to worry about the companies responsible for protecting their data not doing their job."[6]

>> **Deceptive advertising: The FTC accused LifeLock—which claims that it is "relentlessly protecting your identity"—of making false advertising claims.**

FOOTAGE VECTOR PHOTO/Shutterstock

The toughest problem often is defining what is "deceptive." For instance, an advertiser's claim that its chewing gum will "rock your world" isn't intended to be taken literally. Instead, the advertiser might claim, it is "puffery"—innocent exaggeration for effect. However, others claim that puffery and alluring imagery can harm consumers in subtle ways. Think about the popular and long-running MasterCard "Priceless" commercials that once painted pictures of consumers fulfilling their priceless dreams despite the costs. The ads suggested that your credit card could make it happen. But critics charge that such imagery by credit card companies encourages a spend-now-pay-later attitude that causes many consumers to *over*use their cards.

Marketers argue that most companies avoid deceptive practices. Because such practices harm a company's business in the long run, they simply aren't sustainable. Profitable customer relationships are built on a foundation of value and trust. If consumers do not get what they expect, they will switch to more reliable products. In addition, consumers usually protect themselves from deception. Most consumers recognize a marketer's selling intent and are careful when they buy, sometimes even to the point of not believing completely true product claims.

High-Pressure Selling

Salespeople are sometimes accused of high-pressure selling that persuades people to buy goods they had no thought of buying. It is often said that insurance, real estate, and used cars are *sold*, not *bought*. Salespeople are trained to deliver smooth, canned talks to entice purchases. They sell hard because sales contests promise big prizes to those who sell the most. Similarly, TV infomercial pitchmen use "yell and sell" presentations that create a sense of consumer urgency that only those with strong willpower can resist.

But in most cases, marketers have little to gain from high-pressure selling. Although such tactics may work in one-time selling situations for short-term gain, most selling involves building long-term relationships with valued customers. High-pressure or deceptive selling can seriously damage such relationships. For example, imagine a P&G account manager trying to pressure a Walmart buyer or an IBM salesperson trying to browbeat an information technology manager at GE. It simply wouldn't work.

Shoddy, Harmful, or Unsafe Products

Another criticism concerns poor product quality or function. One complaint is that, too often, products and services are not made well or do not perform well. A second complaint concerns product safety. Product safety has been a problem for several reasons, including company indifference, increased product complexity, and poor quality control. A third complaint is that many products deliver little benefit or may even be harmful.

For example, think about the soft drink industry. For years, industry critics have blamed the plentiful supply of sugar-laden, high-calorie soft drinks for the obesity epidemic and other health issues in the United States. They are quick to fault what they see as greedy beverage marketers for cashing in on vulnerable consumers, turning us into a nation of Big Gulpers. Although U.S. consumption of soft drinks has dropped in recent years, beverage companies are now looking to emerging markets for growth. >> According to a report by the Center for Science in the Public Interest (CSPI) titled "Carbonating the World," in 2008 emerging markets such as China, India, and Mexico accounted for just over half of global soft drink consumption. Now, however, nearly 70 percent of soft drinks are sold in such markets. The CPSI accuses beverage companies of behaving much like the tobacco industry, marketing their harmful products to countries already struggling to provide health care to their citizens.[7]

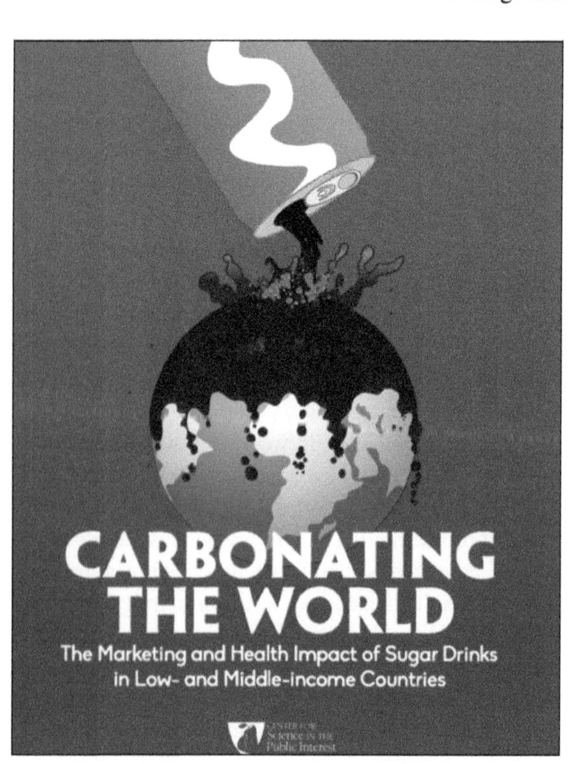

>> Harmful products: Is the soft drink industry being irresponsible by promoting harmful products in emerging markets, or is it simply serving the wants of consumers while letting them make their own consumption choices?

Center for Science in the Public Interest

Is the soft drink industry being socially irresponsible by aggressively promoting overindulgence to ill-informed or unwary consumers in emerging markets? Or is it simply serving the wants of customers by offering products that ping consumer taste buds while letting consumers make their own consumption choices? Is it the industry's job to police public tastes? As in many matters of social responsibility, what's right and wrong may be a matter of opinion. Whereas some analysts criticize the industry, others suggest that responsibility lies with consumers. Maybe companies shouldn't sell Big Gulps. Then again, nobody is forced to buy and drink one.

Most manufacturers *want* to produce quality goods. After all, the way a company deals with product quality and safety problems can harm or help its reputation. Companies selling poor-quality or unsafe products risk damaging conflicts with consumer groups and regulators. Unsafe products can result in product liability suits and large awards for damages. More fundamentally, consumers who are unhappy with a firm's products may avoid future purchases and talk other consumers into doing the same. In today's social media and online review environment, word of poor quality can spread like wildfire. Thus, quality missteps are not consistent with sustainable marketing. Today's marketers know that good quality results in customer value and satisfaction, which in turn create sustainable customer relationships.

Planned Obsolescence

Critics also have charged that some companies practice *planned obsolescence*, causing their products to become obsolete before they actually should need replacement. They accuse some producers of using materials and components that will break, wear, rust, or rot sooner than they should. And if the products themselves don't wear out fast enough, other companies are charged with *perceived obsolescence*—continually changing consumer concepts of acceptable styles to encourage more and earlier buying. An obvious example is the fast-fashion industry with its constantly changing clothing fashions, which some critics claim creates a wasteful disposable clothing culture. "Too many garments end up in landfill sites," bemoans one designer. "They are deemed aesthetically redundant and get discarded at the end of the season when there are often years of wear left."[8]

Still others are accused of introducing planned streams of new products that make older models obsolete, turning consumers into "serial replacers." Critics claim that this occurs in the consumer electronics industries. If you're like most people, you probably have a drawer full of yesterday's hottest technological gadgets—from mobile phones and cameras to iPods and flash drives—now reduced to the status of fossils. It seems that anything more than a year or two old is hopelessly out of date. >> Apple was even accused recently of deliberately slowing down older iPhones through software updates to encourage customers to upgrade to newer models. Apple admitted slowing some phones but said it was doing so to "prolong the life" of the devices with ageing batteries.[9]

>> Planned obsolescence: Apple was accused recently of deliberately slowing down older iPhones through software updates to encourage customers to upgrade to newer models.

Halfpoint/Shutterstock

Marketers respond that consumers *like* style changes; they get tired of the old goods and want a new look in fashion. Or they *want* the latest high-tech innovations, even if older models still work. No one has to buy a new product, and if too few people like it, it will simply fail. Finally, most companies do not design their products to break down earlier because they do not want to lose customers to other brands. Instead, they seek constant improvement to ensure that products will consistently meet or exceed customer expectations.

Much of the so-called planned obsolescence is the working of the competitive and technological forces in a free society—forces that lead to ever-improving goods and services. For example, if Samsung produced a new Galaxy phone or tablet that would last 10 years, few consumers would want it. Instead, buyers want the latest technological innovations. "Obsolescence isn't something companies are forcing on us," confirms one analyst. "It's progress, and it's something we pretty much demand. As usual, the market gives us exactly what we want."[10]

Poor Service to Disadvantaged Consumers

Finally, the American marketing system has been accused of poorly serving disadvantaged consumers. For example, critics claim that the urban poor often have to shop in smaller stores that carry inferior goods and charge higher prices. The presence of large national chain stores in low-income neighborhoods would help to keep prices down. However, the critics accuse major chain retailers of *redlining*, drawing a red line around disadvantaged neighborhoods and avoiding placing stores there.

For example, the nation's poor areas have 30 percent fewer supermarkets than affluent areas do. As a result, many low-income consumers find themselves in "food deserts," which are awash with small markets offering frozen pizzas, Cheetos, Moon Pies, and Cokes but where fruits and vegetables or fresh fish and chicken are out of reach. The U.S. Department of Agriculture has identified more than 6,500 food deserts in rural and urban areas of the United States. Currently, more than 17 million Americans—5.6 percent of the population—live in low-income areas where a supermarket is over a mile away in an urban area and 20 miles away in a rural area. In turn, the lack of access to healthy, affordable fresh foods has a negative impact on the health of underserved consumers in these areas.[11]

Many national chains, such as Walmart, Walgreens, SuperValu, and even Whole Foods Market have recently agreed to open or expand more stores that bring nutritious and fresh foods to underserved communities. Other retailers have found that they can act responsibly and even operate profitably by focusing on low-income areas ignored by other companies. For example, Starbucks is now opening stores in low-income urban areas (see Marketing at Work 16.1). And consider Brown's Super Stores, Inc. in Philadelphia:[12]

MARKETING AT WORK 16.1

Starbucks: Serving the Underserved—Doing Good *and* Doing Well

Starbucks has long been famous for its pricey premium coffee and upscale "Starbucks Experience," targeted largely toward well-off professionals. Some 83 percent of Starbucks's U.S. stores are located in predominately white middle-class or higher-than-middle-class communities. There's been a distinct underrepresentation of Starbucks stores in the nation's lowest income areas populated by minorities. In recent years, however, Starbucks has been experimenting with stores in such underserved communities. In part, this initiative stems from Starbucks's long-held social responsibility mission. But beyond doing good, Starbucks believes that such stores also provide good opportunities for growth and profits.

Starbucks's move into underserved communities began in the mid-1990s when the company hooked up with retired Los Angeles Lakers basketball superstar Earvin "Magic" Johnson. Johnson was on a mission to take big business into depressed urban areas. More than just a philanthropic attempt to "give back," Johnson saw genuine marketing opportunities in inner-city "commerce deserts" largely ignored by big brands. He started with a few Pepsi bottling plants and then expanded into shopping centers and movie theater complexes.

Johnson soon found a kindred spirit in Starbucks founder and executive chairman Howard Schultz. "I said, 'Look Howard, Latinos and black folks. We like coffee too,'" Johnson later revealed. After seeing the success of Johnson's urban theaters, Schultz agreed that putting Starbucks in underserved low-income communities made good business sense. The two struck a deal for a 50-50 Starbucks–Johnson venture to build Starbucks shops in urban neighborhoods.

Targeting urban consumers required adapting the Starbucks model, everything from the menu to the music. "I had to take the scones out of my Starbucks and put in things like sweet potato pie and sock-it-to-me cake," Johnson said. Over the next 12 years, Starbucks built 105 Magic Johnson Enterprises stores. The stores were an unqualified success. When Johnson liquidated his business holdings a few years ago, Starbucks paid handsomely for full ownership of all 105 stores.

The Starbucks–Johnson stores were no big stretch for Starbucks. From its earliest days, the chain maintained a strong corporate culture of social responsibility. Schultz saw "doing good" as an essential prerequisite to "doing well." There is a great need "to achieve the fragile balance between profit, social impact, and a moral obligation," said Schultz. Companies must "enhance the lives of our employees and the communities we serve." And the best way to have strong social impact is to achieve strong financial performance.

To further serve the underserved, Starbucks recently committed to opening 15 "community stores" in low-income urban areas such as East Baltimore; the Jamaica neighborhood of Queens, New York; and Englewood on Chicago's Southside. The Starbucks Community Store initiative began after the 2014 riots in Ferguson, Missouri, part of greater metropolitan St. Louis. Schultz led a team of Starbucks executives on a tour of Ferguson, an urban community with a population that is 70 percent African-American, where 22 percent of residents live below the poverty line and unemployment among young black males nears 50 percent. Schultz told the executives, "We're absent from this community… but we have a responsibility and an opportunity to be here."

Opening a store in Ferguson made sense from a social responsibility perspective. But from a business point of view, most analysts were skeptical. They viewed Ferguson as an urban economic dead zone. The riots had only made things worse, leaving behind 37 damaged businesses, 17 of which were completely destroyed. Increasing the risk, Starbucks met with substantial resistance locally. "Many people told us, 'You do not have a role here,'" says Starbucks's global responsibility chief. As it turned out, the Ferguson store was among the top performers of the hundreds of new stores opened by Starbucks that year, and it had 15 percent sales growth in the second year. Today, Starbucks considers the Ferguson store "a blueprint for the future" of its community stores.

How has a store that most businesses would never have opened been successful? A visit to the store tells the story. On the wall hangs a framed photo of a yard sign that reads, "WE LOVE ALL OF FERGUSON." A homeless woman who routinely parks her shopping cart outside sleeps at a table. Diedric Cook—a 21-year-old barista who was living out of his car before being hired a year ago—places a cup of tea on her table for when she wakes up. Around lunchtime, a dozen men and women gather in the shop's designated community room for a free job-skills training class led by members of the Urban League. The

» Serving the underserved: Starbucks is opening new stores in low-income urban areas often overlooked by other big companies. "There's a bigger purpose here than just coffee."

Photo by Jahi Chikwendiu/The Washington Post via Getty Image room serves as a community center, hosting job fairs, school board meetings, and poetry readings. Young, green apron–clad employees combine bright and hopeful personalities with hard knowledge of life on the street, creating an environment where they interact naturally among themselves and with customers.

Although employees in the Ferguson store appear carefree, a deeper look reveals how they struggle to keep things together. Cordell Lewis—the tattooed, mohawk-shorn manager who was recruited from the video game store across the street—will tell you that Cook isn't the only employee who's lived out of his car. Lewis himself had done that as a child. Referring to another young employee who had slept in her car in a Walmart parking lot the night before, Lewis says, "How am I ever going to get on that person and say, 'You're late, you're not in dress code'?" He continues, "If [such employees] were in a bad spot I would take care of it. Starbucks would take care of it."

Ironically, the situations that render these employees "unemployable" to most other companies are key ingredients in the mix that makes inner-city Starbucks locations work. "Seeing your manager care about you that much makes it where you like coming to work," Cook points out. "He's like a dad around here," says another employee of Lewis. "This is our home away from home." That kind of employee commitment creates a place where local customers also feel at home.

By being one of the first to set up shop in underserved communities, Starbucks has inspired other businesses to follow suit. Since it opened the Ferguson store, 41 other new businesses have opened there, creating a vibrant economic center. "When one person steps out from the crowd, others will follow," says a local city council member. "Starbucks said, 'We are going to Ferguson. We are going to help this community recover.' Once Starbucks stepped out of the crowd, everybody began to follow."

Fifteen Starbucks community stores hardly make a dent in the massive network of Starbucks locations in well-heeled communities around the world. Nor do 105 former Magic Johnson shops. But it's a start. And Starbucks's rapid expansion has led to saturation in many markets. If the company wants to continue growing, it must find new pockets of opportunity. As it ponders where to place the 10,000 new stores it plans to open in the next five years, Starbucks's community store successes suggest that it can both do good *and* do well by serving underserved communities. Says the manager of the new community store in the Bedford–Stuyvesant area of Brooklyn, New York, "There's a bigger purpose here than just coffee."

Sources: Tanya Mohn, "Howard Schultz, Starbucks, and a History of Corporate Responsibility," *New York Times*, November 15, 2015, www.nytimes.com/2017/11/15/business/dealbook/howard-schultz-starbucks-corporate-responsibility.html; Biz Carson, "The Vital Lesson Magic Johnson Taught Starbucks CEO Howard Schultz," *Business Insider*, February 9, 2016, www.businessinsider.com/magic-johnson-nba-star-to-businessman-2016-2; Vince Dixon, "What Do Starbucks Locations Really Say about Income and Diversity in America?" *Eater*, November 20, 2015, www.eater.com/a/starbucks-income-map; Kate Taylor, "As the American Middle Class Shrinks, Starbucks Sees Ferguson Store as a Blueprint for the Future," *Business Insider*, April 27, 2017, www.businessinsider.com/starbucks-in-ferguson-is-a-blueprint-for-the-future-2017-4; Chris Isidore, "Starbucks Says Ferguson Store Is One of Its Top New Locations," *Money*, September 7, 2016, http://money.cnn.com/2016/09/07/news/companies/ferguson-starbucks-schultz/index.html; Karen Valby, "Starbucks Is Bringing Hope—and Profit—to the Communities America's Forgotten," *Fast Company*, July 31, 2017, www.fastcompany.com/40438365/starbucks-is-bringing-hope-and-profit-to-the-communities-americas-forgotten; Jennifer Warnick, "A Dream Grows in Brooklyn: Starbucks Opens Tenth Community Store in Bed-Stuy," March 8, 2018, https://news.starbucks.com/news/starbucks-opens-tenth-community-store-in-bed-stuy; and www.starbucks.com/about-us/company-information/starbucks-company-timeline, www.starbucks.com/responsibility, and www.starbucks.com/about-us/company-information, accessed October 2018.

>> When Jeff Brown opened his first grocery store in a low-income Southwest Philly neighborhood, most people thought he was crazy. How could he make money in a food desert? But Brown now operates seven profitable ShopRite stores in low-income areas in and around Philadelphia. Brown knows that serving consumers in low-income areas takes more than just opening a store and stocking it with healthy foods. Prices have to be low. At the same time, food quality and service have to be good. So Brown takes cues from high-end grocers by doing things like hand-stacking fresh fruits and produce to avoid bruising and make it more eye-catching. His ShopRite stores also hire skilled butchers, fishmongers, and in-store chefs to entice shoppers to choose healthier options, such as "fire-grilled chicken," cooked right in the store.

>> Serving underserved consumers: Jeff Brown's seven ShopRite stores operate profitably in low-income Philadelphia neighborhoods by becoming a part of the communities they serve.

Steven M. Falk/Philadelphia Inquirer

Perhaps most important, Brown's ShopRite stores have become parts of the communities in which they operate. Brown and his associates work with local leaders even before a store opens to learn exactly what they seek in a neighborhood grocery store. They research neighborhood demographics and tailor offerings to community preferences. Brown's ShopRite stores are also community gathering places, providing community center space in stores for local meetings and events. The company even works with local nonprofits to provide free services such as credit unions, social workers, and health clinics. Such services help the community but also help Brown's ShopRites by building a more frequent and loyal customer base. "In the end, it's really about putting the supermarket at the center of the community," concludes one food retailing expert.

Clearly, better marketing systems must be built to service disadvantaged consumers. In fact, like Brown's, marketers in many industries profitably target such consumers with legitimate goods and services that create real value. In cases where marketers do not step in to fill the void, the government likely will. For example, the FTC has taken action against sellers that advertise false values, wrongfully deny services, or charge disadvantaged customers too much.

LINKING THE CONCEPTS

Hold up for a moment. Few marketers want to abuse or anger consumers—it's simply not good business. Still, some marketing abuses do occur.

- Think back over the past three months or so and list any instances in which you've suffered a marketing abuse such as those just discussed. Analyze your list: What kinds of companies were involved? Were the abuses intentional? What did the situations have in common?
- Pick one of the instances you listed and describe it in detail. How might you go about righting this wrong? Write out an action plan and then do something to remedy the abuse. If we all took such actions when wronged, there would be far fewer wrongs to right!

Marketing's Impact on Society as a Whole

The American marketing system has been accused of adding to several "evils" in American society at large, such as creating too much materialism, too few social goods, and a glut of cultural pollution.

False Wants and Too Much Materialism

Critics have charged that the marketing system urges too much interest in material possessions, and that America's love affair with worldly possessions is not sustainable. Too often, people are judged by what they *own* rather than by who they *are*. The critics do not view this interest in material things as a natural state of mind but rather as a matter of false wants created by marketing. Marketers, they claim, stimulate people's desires for goods and create materialistic models of the good life. Thus, marketers have created an endless cycle of mass consumption based on a distorted interpretation of the "American dream."

In this view, marketing's purpose is to promote consumption, and the inevitable outcome of successful marketing is unsustainable *over*consumption. According to the critics, more is not always better. Some groups have taken their concerns straight to the public. For example, New Dream is a nonprofit organization founded on a mission to empower "individuals, communities, and organizations to transform the ways they consume to improve well-being for people and the planet." Through educational videos, services, and marketing campaigns such as "More fun! Less stuff!" the organization works to counter the commercialization of culture and promote positive changes in the way goods are produced and consumed.[13]

Marketers respond that such criticisms overstate the power of business to create needs. They claim people have strong defenses against advertising and other marketing tools. Marketers are most effective when they appeal to existing wants rather than when they attempt to create new ones. Furthermore, people seek information when making important purchases and often do not rely on single sources. Even minor purchases that may be affected by advertising messages lead to repeat purchases only if the product delivers the promised customer value. Finally, the high failure rate of new products shows that companies are not able to control demand.

On a deeper level, our wants and values are influenced not only by marketers but also by family, peer groups, religion, cultural background, and education. If Americans are highly materialistic, these values arose out of basic socialization processes that go much deeper than business and marketing could produce alone. Consumption patterns and attitudes are also subject to larger forces, such as the economy.

These days consumers are also more supportive of environmental and social sustainability efforts by companies. As a result, instead of encouraging today's more sensible and conscientious consumers to overspend or spend wastefully, many marketers are working to help them

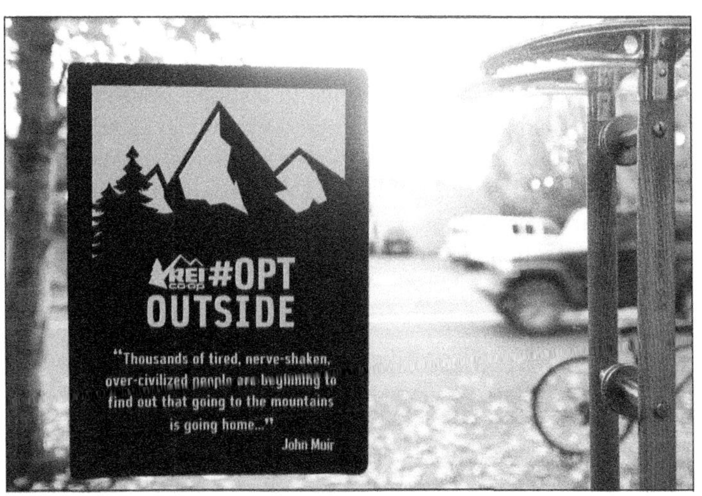

>> **Materialism: Some marketers are urging "conscious consumption." REI closes its stores on Black Friday and encourages customers to #OptOutside.**

Alex Milan Tracy/Sipa USA/Newscom

find greater value with less. For example, Patagonia's "conscious consumption" campaigns actually urge its customers to buy less, telling them, "Don't buy what you don't need." and "Think twice before you buy anything." >> Similarly, for several years REI has closed its stores on Black Friday while its #OptOutside campaign urges customers to enjoy the outdoors instead of shopping. And L.L.Bean's "When" campaign encourages customers to buy and hang onto products that last rather than always buying new ones. It asks, "When did disposable become our default?" The answer: "At L.L.Bean, it never did. When you buy something from us, we want you to like it for a long time #lasting."[14]

Too Few Social Goods

Business has been accused of overselling private goods at the expense of public goods. As private goods increase, they require more public services that are usually not forthcoming. For example, private automobile ownership (private good) requires highways, traffic control, parking spaces, and police services (public goods). The overselling of private goods results in social costs. For cars, some of the social costs include traffic congestion, gasoline shortages, and air pollution. For example, American travelers lose, on average, 42 hours a year in traffic jams, costing the United States more than $160 billion a year—$960 per commuter. In the process, they waste 3.1 billion gallons of fuel (enough to fill the New Orleans Superdome more than four times).[15]

A way must be found to restore a balance between private and public goods. One option is to make producers bear the full social costs of their operations. For example, the government is requiring automobile manufacturers to build cars with more efficient engines and better pollution-control systems. Automakers will then raise their prices to cover the extra costs. If buyers find the price of some car models too high, these models will disappear. Demand will then move to those producers that can support the sum of the private and social costs.

A second option is to make consumers pay the social costs. For example, many cities around the world are now levying congestion tolls and other charges in an effort to reduce traffic congestion. The island nation of Singapore—about the size of three and a half Washington, DCs—has taken such measures to extremes:[16]

> To control traffic congestion and pollution, Singapore's government makes car ownership very expensive. New car purchases are taxed at 100 percent or more of their market value, and buyers must purchase a "certificate of entitlement," which costs tens of thousands of dollars. As a result, a Toyota Corolla purchased in Singapore runs close to $96,000; a Toyota Prius goes for about $154,000. That plus the high cost of gas and "Electronic Road Pricing" tolls collected automatically as cars are driven around the country makes car ownership prohibitively expensive for most Singaporeans. Only about 15 percent of the population owns a car, keeping congestion, pollution, and other auto evils to a minimum and making Singapore one of the greenest urban areas in Asia.

Cultural Pollution

Critics charge the marketing system with creating *cultural pollution*. They feel our senses are being constantly assaulted by marketing and advertising. Commercials interrupt serious programs; pages of ads obscure magazines; billboards mar beautiful scenery; spam fills our email inboxes; flashing display ads intrude on our online and mobile screens. What's more, the critics claim, these interruptions continually pollute people's minds with messages of materialism, sex, power, or status. Some critics call for sweeping changes.

Marketers answer the charges of commercial noise with these arguments: First, they hope that their ads primarily reach the target audience. But because of mass-communication channels, some ads are bound to reach people who have no interest in the product and are therefore bored or annoyed. People who buy magazines they like or who opt in to email, social media, or mobile marketing programs rarely complain about the ads because they involve products and services of interest.

Second, because of ads, many television, online, and social media sites are free to users. Ads also help keep down the costs of magazines and newspapers. Many people think viewing ads is a small price to pay for these benefits. In addition, consumers find many television commercials entertaining and seek them out; for example, ad viewership during the Super Bowl usually equals or exceeds game viewership. Finally, today's consumers have alternatives. For example, they can zip or zap TV commercials on recorded programs or avoid them altogether on many paid cable, satellite, and online streaming channels. Thus, to hold consumer attention, advertisers are making their ads more entertaining and informative.

Marketing's Impact on Other Businesses

Critics also charge that a company's marketing practices can harm other companies and reduce competition. They identify three problems: acquisitions of competitors, marketing practices that create barriers to entry, and unfair competitive marketing practices.

Critics claim that firms are harmed and competition is reduced when companies expand by acquiring competitors rather than by developing their own new products. The large number of acquisitions and the rapid pace of industry consolidation over the past several decades have caused concern that vigorous young competitors will be absorbed, thereby reducing competition. In virtually every major industry—store and online retailing, entertainment, financial services, utilities, transportation, automobiles, telecommunications, health care—the number of major competitors is shrinking.

Acquisition is a complex subject. In some cases, acquisitions can be good for society. The acquiring company may gain economies of scale that lead to lower costs and lower prices. In addition, a well-managed company may take over a poorly managed company and improve its efficiency. An industry that was not very competitive might become more competitive after the acquisition. But acquisitions can also be harmful and therefore are closely regulated by the government.

Critics have also charged that marketing practices bar new companies from entering an industry. Large marketing companies can use patents and heavy promotion spending or tie up suppliers or dealers to keep out or drive out competitors. Those concerned with antitrust regulation recognize that some barriers are the natural result of the economic advantages of doing business on a large scale. Existing and new laws can challenge other barriers. For example, some critics have proposed a progressive tax on advertising spending to reduce the role of selling costs as a major barrier to entry.

Finally, some firms have, in fact, used unfair competitive marketing practices with the intention of hurting or destroying other firms. They may set their prices below costs, threaten to cut off business with suppliers, discourage the buying of a competitor's products, or use their size and market dominance to unfairly damage rivals. Although various laws work to prevent such predatory competition, it is often difficult to prove that the intent or action was really predatory. It's often difficult to differentiate predatory practices from effective competitive strategy and tactics.

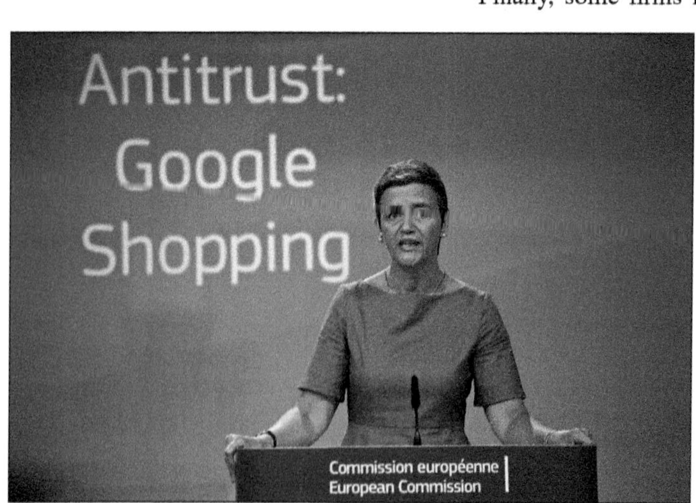

» **Competitive marketing practices: The European Commission recently fined Google heavily for illegally using its search dominance to manipulate the results of its Google Shopping search comparison services to favor its own shopping services at the expense of rivals.**

Alexandros Michailidis/Shutterstock

In recent years, search giant Google has been accused of using predatory practices at the expense of smaller competitors. » For example, the European Commission found Google of guilty of using its search dominance to manipulate the results of its Google Shopping search comparison services to favor its own shopping services at the expense of rivals. The Commission fined Google a record-breaking $2.7 billion for the violations. "Google has come up with many innovative products and services that have made a difference to our lives. That's a good thing," said the EU's competition commissioner. "But Google's strategy for its comparison shopping service wasn't just about attracting customers by making its product better than those of its rivals. Instead,

Google abused its market dominance as a search engine by promoting its own comparison shopping service in its search results and demoting those of competitors. . . . That's illegal under EU antitrust rules." Google has appealed the decision.[17]

Author Comment
Sustainable marketing isn't something that only businesses and governments do. Through consumerism and environmentalism, consumers themselves can play an important role.

Consumer Actions to Promote Sustainable Marketing

OBJECTIVE 16-3 Define *consumerism* and *environmentalism* and explain how they affect marketing strategies.

Sustainable marketing calls for more responsible actions by both businesses and consumers. Because some people view businesses as the cause of many economic and social ills, grassroots movements have arisen from time to time to keep businesses in line. Two major movements have been *consumerism* and *environmentalism*.

Consumerism

Consumerism
An organized movement of citizens and government agencies designed to improve the rights and power of buyers in relation to sellers.

Consumerism is an organized movement of citizens and government agencies to improve the rights and power of buyers in relation to sellers. Traditional *sellers' rights* include the following:

- The right to introduce any product in any size and style, provided it is not hazardous to personal health or safety, or, if it is, to include proper warnings and controls
- The right to charge any price for the product, provided no discrimination exists among similar kinds of buyers
- The right to spend any amount to promote the product, provided it is not defined as unfair competition
- The right to use any product message, provided it is not misleading or dishonest in content or execution
- The right to use buying incentive programs, provided they are not unfair or misleading

Traditional buyers' rights include the following:

- The right not to buy a product that is offered for sale
- The right to expect the product to be safe
- The right to expect the product to perform as claimed

In comparing these rights, many believe that the balance of power lies on the seller's side. True, the buyer can refuse to buy. But critics feel that the buyer has too little information, education, and protection to make wise decisions when facing sophisticated sellers. Consumer advocates call for the following additional consumer rights:

- The right to be well informed about important aspects of the product
- The right to be protected against questionable products and marketing practices
- The right to influence products and marketing practices in ways that will improve "quality of life"
- The right to consume now in a way that will preserve the world for future generations of consumers

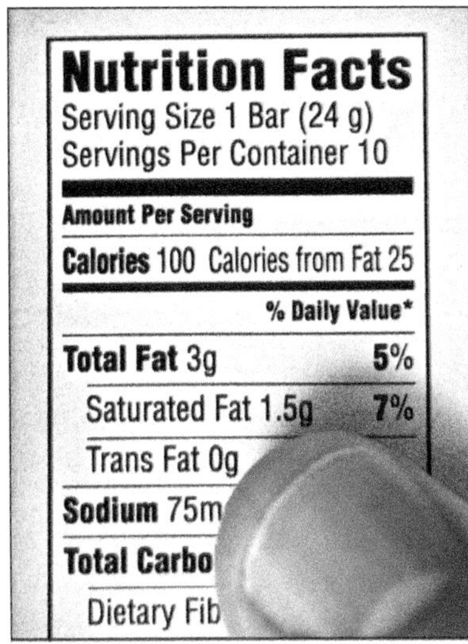

>> Consumer desire for more information led to package labels with loads of useful facts.
Jon Schulte/Shutterstock

Each proposed right has led to more specific proposals by consumerists and consumer protection actions by the government. >> The right to be informed includes the right to know the true interest on a loan (truth in lending), the true cost per unit of a brand (unit pricing), the ingredients in a product (ingredient labeling), the nutritional value of foods (nutritional labeling), product freshness (open dating), and the true benefits of a product (truth in advertising).

Proposals related to consumer protection include strengthening consumer rights in cases of business fraud and financial protection, requiring greater product safety, ensuring information privacy, and giving more power to government agencies. Proposals relating to quality of life include controlling the ingredients that go into certain products and packaging and reducing the level of advertising "noise." Proposals for preserving the world for future consumption include promoting the use of sustainable ingredients, recycling and reducing solid wastes, and managing energy consumption.

Sustainable marketing applies not only to businesses and governments but also to consumers. Consumers have not only the right but also the responsibility to protect themselves instead of leaving this function to the government or someone else. Consumers who believe they got a bad deal have several remedies available, including contacting the company; making their case through the media or social media; contacting federal, state, or local agencies; and going to small-claims courts. Consumers should also make good consumption choices, rewarding companies that act responsibly while punishing those that don't. Ultimately, the move from irresponsible consumption to sustainable consumption is in the hands of consumers.

Environmentalism

Environmentalism
An organized movement of concerned citizens, businesses, and government agencies designed to protect and improve people's current and future living environment.

Whereas consumerists consider whether the marketing system is efficiently serving consumer wants, environmentalists are concerned with marketing's effects on the environment and the environmental costs of serving consumer needs and wants. **Environmentalism** is an organized movement of concerned citizens, businesses, and government agencies designed to protect and improve people's current and future living environment.

Environmentalists are not against marketing and consumption; they simply want people and organizations to operate with more care for the environment. They call for doing away with what sustainability advocate and Unilever CEO Paul Polman calls "mindless consumption." According to Polman, "The road to well-being doesn't go via reduced consumption. It has to be done via more responsible consumption."[18] The marketing system's goal, environmentalists assert, should not be to maximize consumption, consumer choice, or consumer satisfaction but rather to maximize life quality. Life quality means not only the quantity and quality of consumer goods and services but also the quality of the environment, now and for future generations.

Environmentalism is concerned with damage to the ecosystem caused by global warming, resource depletion, toxic and solid wastes, the availability of fresh water, and other problems. Other issues include the loss of recreational areas and the increase in health problems caused by bad air, polluted water, and chemically treated food.

Over the past several decades, such concerns have resulted in federal and state laws and regulations governing industrial commercial practices affecting the environment. Some companies have strongly resented and resisted such environmental regulations, claiming that they are too costly and have made their industries less competitive. These companies responded to consumer environmental concerns by doing only what was required to avert new regulations or keep environmentalists quiet.

Environmental sustainability
A management approach that involves developing strategies that both sustain the environment and produce profits for the company.

In recent years, however, most companies have accepted responsibility for doing no harm to the environment. They have shifted from protest to prevention and from regulation to responsibility. More and more companies are now adopting policies of environmental sustainability. Simply put, **environmental sustainability** is about generating profits while helping to save the planet. Today's enlightened companies are taking action not because someone is forcing them to or to reap short-run profits but because it's the right thing to do—because it's for their customers' well-being, the company's well-being, and the planet's environmental future.

>> **Figure 16.2** shows a grid that companies can use to gauge their progress toward environmental sustainability. It includes both internal and external *greening* activities that will pay off for the firm and environment in the short run and *beyond greening* activities that will pay off in the longer term.

At the most basic level, a company can practice *pollution prevention*. This involves more than pollution control—cleaning up waste after it has been created. Pollution prevention means eliminating or minimizing waste *before* it is created. Companies emphasizing prevention have responded with internal green marketing programs—designing and

>> Figure 16.2 Environmental Sustainability and Sustainable Value

Source: Based on Stuart L. Hart, "Sustainable Value," www.stuartlhart.com/sustainablevalue.html, October 2016.

	Today: Greening	Tomorrow: Beyond Greening
Internal	**Pollution prevention** Eliminating or reducing waste before it is created	**New clean technology** Developing new sets of environmental skills and capabilities
External	**Product stewardship** Minimizing environmental impact throughout the entire product life cycle	**Sustainability vision** Developing a strategy framework for creating sustainable value

This framework addresses more than just natural environmental challenges. It also points to opportunities for creating sustainable value for markets and the firm through environmentally sustainable strategies and practices.

developing ecologically safer products, recyclable and biodegradable packaging, better pollution controls, and more energy-efficient operations.

>> For example, in creating new products, athletic shoe and apparel maker adidas considers their environmental impact before ever producing them. This results in low-waste footwear and apparel, such as Duramo shoes, which yield both performance and sustainability benefits. With their simplified design—the upper is only made of four pieces—the lightweight shoes give athletes a more natural run while at the same time cutting down on materials, waste, and energy use in production. On a broader scale, adidas has developed a restricted substances list for product design and manufacturing: no PVCs, no materials from endangered or threatened species, and fewer materials from non-sustainable sources. adidas has also set ambitious internal goals for reducing greenhouse emissions and energy, water, and paper consumption in its operations. And it has set up Green Teams at locations around the world whose members promote adidas's environmental programs internally and urge their colleagues to "think green," such as reducing office waste going to landfills.[19]

>> Environmental sustainability: adidas sets ambitious goals for sustainable products and operations. In creating new products, such as the Duramo, the company considers their environmental impact before ever producing them.

Michael Dechev/Shutterstock

At the next level, companies can practice *product stewardship*—minimizing not only pollution from production and product design but also all environmental impacts throughout the full product life cycle while at the same time reducing costs. Many companies have adopted *design for environment (DFE)* and *cradle-to-cradle* practices. This involves thinking ahead to design products that are easier to recover, reuse, recycle, or safely return to nature after usage, thus becoming part of the ecological cycle. DFE and cradle-to-cradle practices not only help to sustain the environment, but they can also be highly profitable for the company.

For example, IBM started a business—IBM Global Asset Recovery Services—designed to reuse and recycle parts from returned mainframe computers and other equipment. Last year, IBM processed more than 1.33 million end-of-life IT products worldwide, stripping down old equipment to recover chips and valuable metals. Since 1999 it has processed more than 17.5 million units. IBM Global Asset Recovery Services finds uses for more than 99 percent of what it takes in, sending less than 1 percent to landfills and incineration facilities. What started out as an environmental effort has now grown into a multibillion-dollar IBM business that profitably recycles electronic equipment at 22 sites worldwide.[20]

Today's *greening* activities focus on improving what companies already do to protect the environment. The *beyond greening* activities identified in Figure 16.2 look to the future. First, internally, companies can plan for *new clean technology*. Many organizations that have made good sustainability headway are still limited by existing technologies. To create fully sustainable strategies, they will need to develop and employ innovative new technologies. For example, energy technology giant Siemens has committed to becoming fully carbon neutral by 2030. Making that happen requires lots of innovation:[21]

> With more than 340,000 employees in 200 countries, 150-year-old Siemens is reducing its carbon footprint by transferring from "combustification" to "electrification." As just one example, it's 50-year-old production facility in Kalawa, India, now uses 6,000 solar panels to supply 25 percent of its electricity use—the equivalent of 62,000 newly planted trees. To cut

employee bottled water consumption, the plant installed a high-tech water-treatment facility that further cleans city water to make it drinkable and dispenses it to employees at 50 locations around the plant, saving more than 2 million single-use plastic water bottles per year. The water facility also treats all industrial water used at the plant and recycles it for everything from cleaning streets and flushing toilets to watering green areas. Finally, the plant's state-of-the-art waste segregation depot separates waste into 45 categories and readies it to be processed by recyclers. Siemens's carbon neutrality innovations will not only help save the environment, they will also save the company money. The technology project will pay for itself in just five years and will generate $20 million in annual savings thereafter.

Finally, companies can develop a *sustainability vision*, which serves as a guide to the future. It shows how the company's products and services, processes, and policies must evolve and what new technologies must be developed to get there. This vision of sustainability provides a framework for pollution control, product stewardship, and new environmental technology for the company and others to follow. It addresses not just challenges in the natural environment but also strategic opportunities for using environmental strategies to create sustainable value for the firm and its markets.

Most companies today focus on the upper-left quadrant of the grid in Figure 16.2, investing most heavily in pollution prevention. Some forward-looking companies practice product stewardship and are developing new environmental technologies. However, emphasizing only one or two quadrants in the environmental sustainability grid can be shortsighted. Investing only in the left half of the grid puts a company in a good position today but leaves it vulnerable in the future. In contrast, a heavy emphasis on the right half suggests that a company has good environmental vision but lacks the skills needed to implement it. Thus, companies should work at developing all four dimensions of environmental sustainability.

The North Face, for example, is doing just that through its own environmental sustainability actions and its impact on the actions of suppliers and consumers:[22]

The North Face's headquarters building in Alameda, California, comes complete with solar panels and wind turbines that generate more electricity than the building uses. The building employs an evaporating cooling system that eliminates the need for emissions-heavy coolants. The company's other regional headquarters and distribution centers also incorporate solar or water-saving features. In manufacturing, The North Face works closely with suppliers to achieve its goal to use polyester—which makes up 80 percent of its clothing lines—from 100 percent recycled content. The North Face also partners with suppliers to reduce waste and chemical, water, and energy usage in their mills. Since 2010, The North Face's suppliers have removed more than 100 tanker trucks of chemicals and more than 230 Olympic swimming pools of water from their manufacturing processes.

In addition, The North Face has dedicated itself to inspiring customers to reduce the waste generated by today's fast-fashion era. The company's lifetime apparel and gear warranty results in the return and repair of more than 80,000 products annually. >> The North Face also runs a program called "Clothes the Loop," by which it collects worn-out or unwanted used clothing of any brand from customers for recycling or renewal. Items dropped in its collection bins are sent to a recycling center where they are carefully sorted, then repurposed for reuse to extend their life or recycled into raw materials for use in making other products. Proceeds from the program benefit the Conservation Alliance, which funds community-based campaigns to protect shared wilderness and recreation areas.

>> Sustainability vision: At The North Face, sustainability is about more than just doing the right thing—it also makes good business sense. Sustainability efforts such as its "Clothes the Loop" program are good for the company, its customers, *and* the planet.

VF Corporation

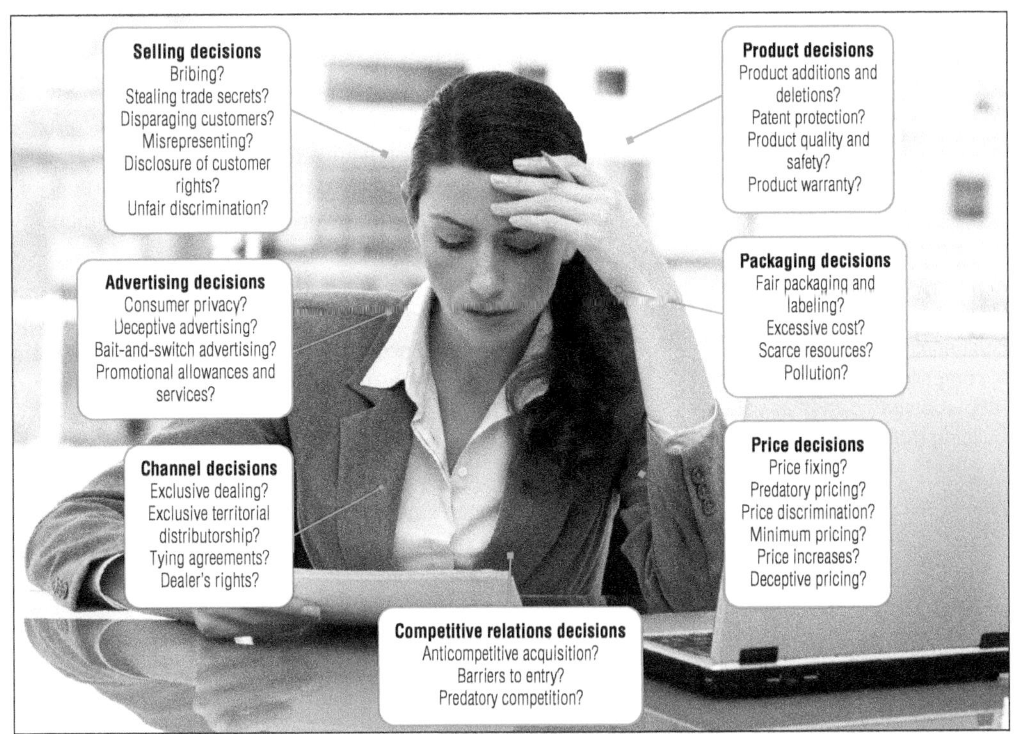

>> Figure 16.3 Major Marketing Decision Areas That May Be Called into Question under the Law

Wavebreakmedia/Shutterstock (photo)

For The North Face, being environmentally sustainable is about more than just doing the right thing. It also makes good business sense. More efficient operations and less wasteful products not only are good for the environment but also save The North Face money, helping it to deliver more value to customers. It's a winning combination. "At the heart of The North Face is a mission to inspire a global movement of outdoor exploration and conservation," says the brand. "We believe the success of our business is fundamentally linked to having a healthy planet."[23]

Public Actions to Regulate Marketing

Citizen concerns about marketing practices will usually lead to public attention and legislative proposals. Many of the laws that affect marketing were identified in Chapter 3. The task is to translate these laws into a language that marketing executives understand as they make decisions about competitive relations, products, price, promotion, and distribution channels. **>> Figure 16.3** illustrates the major legal issues facing marketing management.

Author Comment
In the end, marketers themselves must take responsibility for sustainable marketing. That means operating in a responsible and ethical way to bring both immediate and future value to customers.

Business Actions toward Sustainable Marketing

OBJECTIVE 16-4 Describe the principles of sustainable marketing.

At first, many companies opposed consumerism, environmentalism, and other elements of sustainable marketing. They thought the criticisms were either unfair or unimportant. But by now, most companies have grown to embrace sustainability principles as a way to create both immediate and future customer value and strengthen customer relationships.

Sustainable Marketing Principles

Under the sustainable marketing concept, a company's marketing should support the best long-run performance of the marketing system. It should be guided by five sustainable marketing principles: *consumer-oriented marketing, customer value marketing, innovative marketing, sense-of-mission marketing*, and *societal marketing*.

Consumer-Oriented Marketing

Consumer-oriented marketing
A company should view and organize its marketing activities from the consumer's point of view.

Consumer-oriented marketing means that the company should view and organize its marketing activities from the consumer's point of view. It should work hard to sense, serve, and satisfy the needs of a defined group of customers—both now and in the future. The good marketing companies that we've discussed throughout this text have had this in common: an all-consuming passion for delivering superior value to carefully chosen customers. Only by seeing the world through its customers' eyes can the company build sustainable and profitable customer relationships.

Customer Value Marketing

Customer value marketing
A company should put most of its resources into customer value–building marketing investments.

According to the principle of **customer value marketing**, the company should put most of its resources into customer value-building marketing investments. Many things marketers do—one-shot sales promotions, cosmetic product changes, direct-response advertising—may raise sales in the short run but add less *value* than would actual improvements in the product's quality, features, or convenience. Enlightened marketing calls for building long-run consumer engagement, loyalty, and relationships by continually improving the value consumers receive from the firm's market offering. By creating value *for* consumers, the company can capture value *from* consumers in return.

Innovative Marketing

Innovative marketing
A company should seek real product and marketing improvements.

The principle of **innovative marketing** requires that the company continuously seek real product and marketing improvements. The company that overlooks new and better ways to do things will eventually lose customers to another company that has found a better way.

Innovative marketers never stop looking for new and better ways to create customer value. For example, fast and dependable delivery is highly important to online shoppers. So Amazon delighted customers by being the first to innovate with free shipping on orders over $50. But Amazon didn't stop there. It next introduced Amazon Prime, by which customers could receive their packages within only two days for no extra charge or in one day for a small additional fee. >> Still not satisfied, Amazon innovated with Amazon Prime Now, which offers super-fast same-day delivery—or even one-hour delivery—on tens of thousands of items in major metropolitan areas. In its never-ending quest to shorten delivery times, Amazon has even invested heavily in research on drones, driverless vehicles, and robots. This and a seemingly endless list of other innovations over the years—from Recommendations for You, Customer Reviews, and 1-Click Ordering features to the Amazon Marketplace, Kindle e-readers, and Amazon Cloud services—have helped Amazon to enhance the shopping customer experience and dominate online retailing.

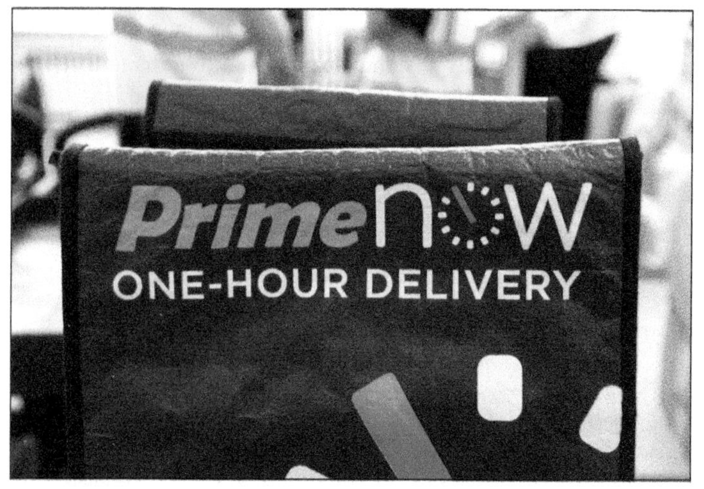

>> Innovative marketing: Amazon never stops looking for new ways to create customer value, such as Amazon Prime Now, which gives same-day—or even one-hour—delivery of customer orders.

creativep/Alamy Stock Photo

Sense-of-Mission Marketing

Sense-of-mission marketing
A company should define its mission in broad social terms rather than narrow product terms.

Sense-of-mission marketing means that the company should define its mission in broad *social* terms rather than narrow *product* terms. When a company defines a social mission, employees feel better about their work and have a clearer sense of direction. Brands linked with broader missions can serve the best long-run interests of both the brand and consumers.

For example, Pedigree makes good dog food but that's not what the brand is really all about. Instead, at its core, the brand is about loving and caring for dogs. "Dogs bring out the good in us. Pedigree brings out the good in them. Feed the good," says Pedigree. "The lovable innocence found in every dog helps us reconnect with our true selves and teaches us valuable life lessons. Simply put, dogs make us better people. And that has a profound impact on the world in which we live." In line with this sweeping brand philosophy, beyond making nutritious dog food, Pedigree backs a substantial effort to support dogs in need. Through its "You buy. We give." program, for every customer purchase, the brand donates healthy meals to shelter dogs. And to further fulfill its brand promise, the company created the Pedigree Foundation, which has raised millions of dollars for helping "shelter dogs" find homes. Sense-of-mission marketing has made Pedigree the world's number one dog food brand.[24]

Some companies define their overall corporate missions in broad societal terms. For example, under its buy-one-give-one model, shoemaker TOMS seeks both profits and to make the world a better place. Thus, at TOMS, "doing good" and "doing well" go hand in hand. To achieve its social change mission, TOMS has to make money. At the same time, the brand's social mission gives customers a powerful reason to buy.

However, having a *double bottom line* of values and profits isn't easy. Over the years, brands such as Ben & Jerry's, Timberland, The Body Shop, and Burt's Bees—all known and respected for putting "principles before profits"—have at times struggled with less-than-stellar financial returns. In recent years, however, a new generation of social entrepreneurs has emerged, well-trained business managers who know that to *do good*, they must first *do well* in terms of profitable business operations.

Moreover, today, socially responsible business is no longer the sole province of small, socially conscious entrepreneurs. Many large, established companies and brands—from Walmart and Nike to Starbucks, Coca-Cola, and CVS Health—have adopted substantial social and environmental responsibility missions. Rather than being at odds with revenues and profits, purpose-driven missions can drive them. For example, sense-of-mission marketing and doing what's right for customers has helped transform CVS into the nation's largest health-care company (see Marketing at Work 16.2).

Societal marketing
A company should make marketing decisions by considering consumers' wants, the company's requirements, consumers' long-run interests, and society's long-run interests.

Deficient products
Products that have neither immediate appeal nor long-run benefits.

Pleasing products
Products that give high immediate satisfaction but may hurt consumers in the long run.

Salutary products
Products that have low immediate appeal but may benefit consumers in the long run.

Desirable products
Products that give both high immediate satisfaction and high long-run benefits.

Societal Marketing

Following the principle of **societal marketing**, a company makes marketing decisions by considering consumers' wants, the company's requirements, consumers' long-run interests, and society's long-run interests. Companies should be aware that neglecting consumer and societal long-run interests is a disservice to consumers and society. Alert companies view societal problems as opportunities.

Sustainable marketing calls for products that are not only pleasing but also beneficial. The difference is shown in >> **Figure 16.4**. Products can be classified according to their degree of immediate consumer satisfaction and long-run consumer benefit.

Deficient products, such as bad-tasting and ineffective medicine, have neither immediate appeal nor long-run benefits. **Pleasing products** give high immediate satisfaction but may hurt consumers in the long run. Examples include cigarettes and junk food. **Salutary products** have low immediate appeal but may benefit consumers in the long run, for instance, bicycle helmets or some insurance products. **Desirable products** give both high immediate satisfaction and high long-run benefits, such as a tasty *and* nutritious breakfast food.

Companies should try to turn all of their products into desirable products. The challenge posed by pleasing products is that they sell very well but may end up hurting the

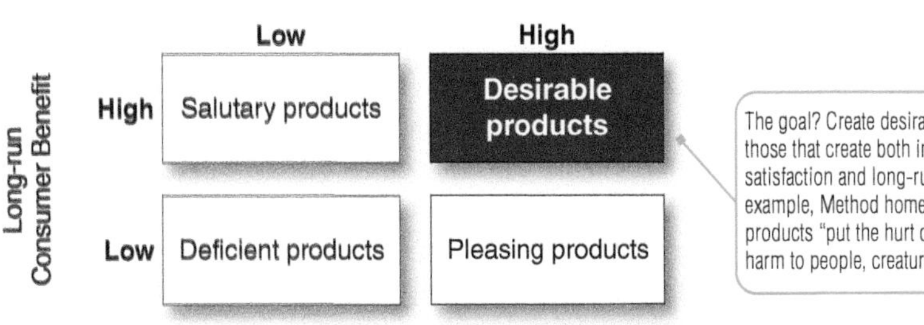
Immediate Satisfaction
Low
High
Long-run Consumer Benefit
High
Low
Salutary products
Desirable products
Deficient products
Pleasing products
The goal? Create desirable products—those that create both immediate customer satisfaction and long-run benefit. For example, Method home and personal cleaning products "put the hurt on dirt without doing harm to people, creatures, or the planet."

>> **Figure 16.4 Societal Classification of Products**

MARKETING AT WORK 16.2

CVS Health: Balancing Purpose with Profit

In 2014, CVS made the bold decision to stop selling cigarettes and other tobacco products. It was a risky decision. Although it won high praise from health advocates and public officials, stubbing out cigarettes resulted in the immediate loss of $2 billion in annual tobacco sales, and it risked driving a significant portion of CVS's smoking customers to competitors such as Walgreens, Walmart, or Kroger, all of which continued to sell cigarettes.

But to CVS, dropping tobacco was pretty much a no-brainer. CVS is on an important mission: "Millions of times a day, close to home and across the country, we're helping people on their path to better health," says CVS. Selling cigarettes *and* helping people on their path to better health? The two simply didn't jibe with one another. So CVS pulled tobacco products from its shelves. "CVS quits for good," the company announced. "This is the right thing to do."

Stopping tobacco sales was a landmark moment for CVS. And it was the event that received most of the headlines. However, the ban on tobacco was only one step in a more sweeping purpose-driven transformation. Consistent with its broader mission, CVS has been on a decade-long shift from being the traditional "drug store on the corner" to becoming a "multi-spectrum health care company." In fact, CVS no longer considers itself just a retail pharmacy. Rather, it sees itself as a pharmacy innovation company. "We're reinventing pharmacy to have a more active, supportive role in each person's unique health experience and in the greater health care environment," says the company.

Underscoring this commitment, at the same time that CVS suspended tobacco sales, it changed its name from CVS Caremark to CVS Health. And true to its mission and new name, CVS Health now offers a full range of products and services that help people on their path to better health. It all starts, of course, with CVS Health's network of 9,800 retail pharmacies, which sell an extensive assortment of prescription and nonprescription pharmaceuticals, personal care products, health and beauty aids, and general merchandise. CVS/pharmacy dispenses more prescriptions than any other drugstore chain, and prescriptions account for 71 percent of the chain's retail sales. More than 1,100 CVS locations also house a CVS MinuteClinic, where medical professionals treat minor health conditions and provide other walk-in care.

CVS Health's pursuit of its "path to better health" mission extends well beyond retail pharmacies. For example, the company's CVS Caremark division provides Pharmacy Benefits Management (PBM) services that help big companies and insurers manage their prescription-drug programs. CVS Caremark helps clients to manage costs while improving health outcomes for 94 million Caremark members. CVS Health recently acquired Coram, which provides home infusion services to homebound patients, and Omnicare, a distributor of prescription drugs to nursing home and assisted-living facilities. The company has also broadened its range of customer contact activities to include tailored in-store and phone advising to customers managing chronic and specialty health conditions. In all, these days, CVS likes to think of itself as a kind of one-stop shop for health care. In fact, retail sales now account for only 43 percent of the company's annual revenue.

Beyond these products and services, CVS Health also takes an active role in health-care management through research, consumer outreach and education, and support of health-related programs and organizations. For example, it has joined forces with a variety of organizations in efforts to curb tobacco use in the United States. It has partnered with the American Cancer Society and the National Urban League to lobby for anti-tobacco legislation and with the American Academy of Pediatrics, the Campaign for Tobacco-Free Kids, and Scholastic, Inc. on tobacco-related education.

CVS recently launched a five-year, $50 million "Be the First" campaign by which it will work with national health organizations and youth groups to combat smoking through education, advocacy, tobacco control, and healthy behavior programming.

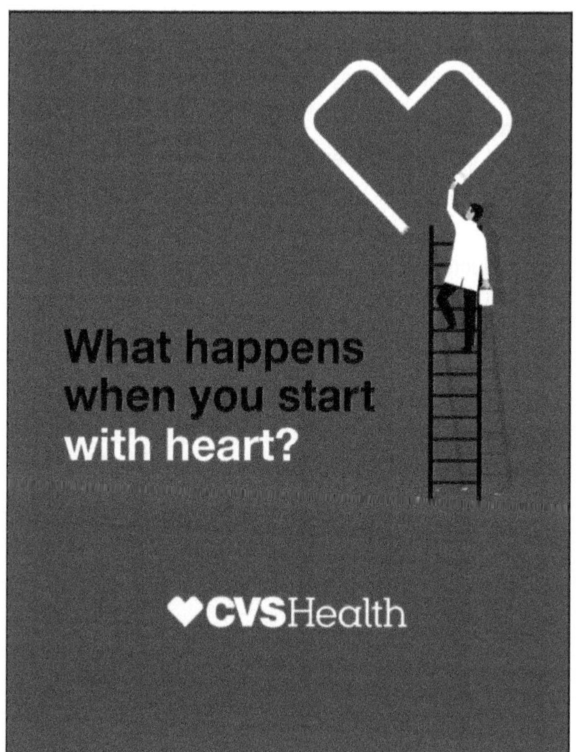

What happens
when you start
with heart?
CVSHealth

>> **Sense-of-mission marketing: CVS Health is on a mission of helping people on their path to better health. It succeeds by "delivering what's right for people every day in a way that creates economic value for the business."**

CVS Health

"We are at a critical moment in our nation's efforts to end the epidemic of tobacco use that ... threatens the health and well-being of our next generation," says CVS Health's chief medical officer. "We're partnering with experts across the public health community ... to move us one step closer to delivering the first tobacco-free generation."

So how is sense-of-mission marketing working for CVS Health? An interesting thing happened after the company stopped selling tobacco products. Although front-of-store sales dropped that year, overall CVS revenues increased by nearly 10 percent. And in the following year, revenues jumped another 10 percent. It appears that the loss of revenues from tobacco products has been more than offset by revenues from new sources, including those resulting from the decision to quit selling cigarettes.

Strange as it sounds, one source of new sales is smokers themselves. In turns out that 70 percent of smokers want to quit. At the same time that CVS Health pulled cigarettes off its shelves, it launched a "Let's Quit Together" assistance program to help smokers kick the habit, complete with an information-packed website offering tips, testimonials, and other resources. By the end of the first year, CVS prescriptions for smoking cessation products grew by 63 percent and CVS Smoking Cessation Hubs received nearly one million visits. CVS is now becoming the retailer of choice for those seeking smoking cessation products and services. Its MinuteClinic "Start to Stop" program provides in-store personal counseling with a nurse practitioner and other services to help smokers quit.

Probably more significant, however, CVS's decision to purge tobacco products gave its reputation a boost, earning new business from nonsmoking consumers on the one hand and PBM partners and clients on the other. Although it's difficult to track benefits from such sources, in the months following the elimination of tobacco from its shelves, revenues from CVS's pharmacy benefits services rose by 12 percent and the company lined up $11 billion worth of new contracts for its PBM business.

The decision to quit tobacco may have led to another important opportunity for CVS. About a year later, when Target went looking for a partner to buy and operate the pharmacies in 1,700 of its stores, CVS was a natural choice. Target had stopped selling cigarettes and tobacco products almost a decade earlier. CVS's new image and sense-of-mission strategy fit perfectly with the like-minded "no tobacco" mentality of Target and its customers.

Thus, CVS Health is on a mission. Its genuine concern for "helping people on their path to better health" reaches far beyond just revenues and profits. But as it turns out, doing good and doing well are not at odds. To the contrary, rather than stunting sales, CVS's lofty mission is driving new growth and profits. No longer just the "drugstore on the corner," CVS Health is now a $185 billion health-care giant, number seven among the *Fortune* 500 and the nation's largest health care–related company. And the CVS Health transformation is still a work in progress. Its recent $69 billion purchase of managed-health-care company Aetna, its biggest step yet in fulfilling its broadened mission, makes CVS Health the *world's* largest health-care company.

As for that decision to quit tobacco? "I cannot think of another example in corporate America where a company sacrificed $2 billion of revenue for what they felt was the right thing to do," says CVS's chief marketer. "It's a stunning thing, [and] it proved out for us in [so may] ways." For CVS Health, he says, success means "delivering what's right for people every day in a way that creates economic value for the business."

Sources: Bruce Japsen, "CVS Kicks In Another $50 Million for Anti-Tobacco Push," *Forbes*, March 10, 2016, www.forbes.com/sites/brucejapsen/2016/03/10/cvs-kicks-in-another-50m-to-anti-tobacco-push/#41c6eb5f11f3; Phil Wahba, "She Thanks You for Not Smoking," *Fortune*, September 11, 2015, http://fortune.com/2015/09/11/cvs-health-helena-foulkes/; Kristina Monllos, "CVS Health's Marketing Chief on Turning the Pharmacy Brand into a Healthcare Player," *Adweek*, March 28, 2016, www.adweek.com/print/170437; Emma Court, "CVS-Aetna Merger Is Not about the Minute Clinic," Market Watch, May 22, 2018, www.marketwatch.com/story/cvs-aetna-merger-is-not-about-the-minute-clinic-aetna-ceo-says-2018-05-22; and information from www.cvs.com/shop/health-medicine/stop-smoking, www.cvs.com/minuteclinic/resources/smoking-cessation, cvshealth.com/about/facts-and-company-information, http://investors.cvshealth.com, and https://cvshealth.com/about/purpose-statement, accessed October 2018.

consumer. The product opportunity, therefore, is to add long-run benefits without reducing the product's pleasing qualities. The challenge posed by salutary products is to add some pleasing qualities so that they will become more desirable in consumers' minds.

Consider Method, the "people against dirty" brand of household and personal cleaning products. Many effective household cleaning products contain chemicals or even toxic ingredients that can be harmful to people and the environment. But Method products are formulated with naturally derived, biodegradable, nontoxic ingredients. "We prefer ingredients that come from plants, not chemical plants," says the brand. Method also uses recycled and recyclable packaging, and it works with suppliers to reduce the carbon intensity of producing its products. Method uses renewable energy sources such as wind turbines and solar trees to help power its Chicago manufacturing facility. In all, "Method cleaners put the hurt on dirt without doing harm to people, creatures, or the planet," says the company. As Method's cofounder and "chief greenskeeper" puts it: "Beautiful design and environmental responsibility are equally important when creating a product and we shouldn't have to trade functionality for sustainability."[25]

Marketing Ethics and the Sustainable Company

OBJECTIVE 16-5 Explain the role of ethics in marketing.

Marketing Ethics

Good ethics are a cornerstone of sustainable marketing. In the long run, unethical marketing harms customers and society as a whole. Further, it eventually damages a company's reputation and effectiveness, jeopardizing its very survival. Thus, the sustainable marketing goals of long-term consumer and business welfare can be achieved only through ethical marketing conduct.

Conscientious marketers face many moral dilemmas. The best thing to do is often unclear. Because not all managers have fine moral sensitivity, companies need to develop *corporate marketing ethics policies*—broad guidelines that everyone in the organization must follow. These policies should cover distributor relations, advertising standards, customer service, pricing, product development, and general ethical standards.

The finest guidelines cannot resolve all the difficult ethical situations the marketer faces. **>> Table 16.1** lists some difficult ethical issues marketers could face during their careers. If marketers choose immediate-sales-producing actions in all of these cases, their marketing behavior might well be described as immoral or even amoral. If they refuse to go along with *any* of the actions, they might be ineffective as marketing managers and unhappy because of the constant moral tension. Managers need a set of principles that will help them figure out the moral importance of each situation and decide how far they can go in good conscience.

But *what* principle should guide companies and marketing managers on issues of ethics and social responsibility? One philosophy is that the free market and the legal system should decide such issues. Under this principle, companies and their managers are not responsible for making moral judgments. Companies can in good conscience do whatever the market and legal systems allow. However, history provides a long list of examples of company actions that were legal but highly irresponsible.

A second philosophy puts responsibility not on the system but in the hands of individual companies and managers. This more enlightened philosophy suggests that a company should have a social conscience. Companies and managers should apply high standards of ethics and morality when making corporate decisions, regardless of "what the system allows."

Each company and marketing manager must work out a philosophy of socially responsible and ethical behavior. Under the societal marketing concept, each manager must look beyond what is legal and allowed and develop standards based on personal integrity, corporate conscience, and long-run consumer welfare.

Dealing with issues of ethics and social responsibility in a proactive, open, and forthright way helps to build and maintain strong customer relationships based on honesty and trust. For example, think about SC Johnson, maker of familiar home-products brands such as Pledge, Shout, Windex, Ziploc, and Saran Wrap. SC Johnson believes deeply that "Integrity is part of our DNA. It's been our family way since 1886." Based on that belief, the company has a long tradition of doing what's right, even at the expense of sales. Just one example involves Saran Wrap, a longtime market leader and one of SC Johnson's best-known and biggest brands:[26]

> For more than 50 years, Saran Wrap was made with polyvinylidene chloride (PVDC), an ingredient responsible for the product's two major differentiating features: impenetrable odor barrier qualities and superior microwavability. Without PVDC, Saran Wrap would have been no better than competing wraps by Glad and Reynolds, which did not contain PVDC. In the early 2000s, however, regulators, environmentalists, and consumers began to voice concerns about materials containing chlorine, specifically polyvinyl chloride (PVC). In fact, SC Johnson's own Greenlist analysis—by which it rates product ingredients based on their impact on environmental and human health—confirmed the hazards of PVCs, and the company quickly pledged to eliminate them from its products and packaging.

Table 16.1 Some Morally Difficult Situations in Marketing

1. Your R&D department has changed one of your company's products slightly. It is not really "new and improved," but you know that putting this statement on the package and in advertising will increase sales. What would you do?
2. You have been asked to add a stripped-down model to your line that could be advertised to pull customers into the store. The product won't be very good but salespeople will be able to switch buyers who come into the store up to higher-priced units. You are asked to give the green light for the stripped-down version. What would you do?
3. You are thinking of hiring a product manager who has just left a competitor's company. She would be more than happy to tell you all the competitor's plans for the coming year. What would you do?
4. One of your top dealers in an important territory recently has had family troubles and his sales have slipped. It looks like it will take him a while to straighten out his family problems. Meanwhile, you are losing many sales. Legally, on performance grounds, you can terminate the dealer's franchise and replace him. What would you do?
5. You have a chance to win a big account in another country that will mean a lot to you and your company. The purchasing agent hints that a "gift" would influence the decision. Such gifts are common in that country and some of your competitors will probably make one. What would you do?
6. You have heard that a competitor has a new product feature that will make a big difference in sales. The competitor will demonstrate the feature in a private dealer meeting at the annual trade show. You can easily send a snooper to this meeting to learn about the new feature. What would you do?
7. You have to choose between three advertising and social media campaigns outlined by your agency. The first (a) is a soft-sell, honest, straight-information campaign. The second (b) uses emotion-loaded appeals then exaggerate the product's benefits. The third (c) involves a noisy, somewhat irritating commercial and pop-ups that are sure to gain audience attention. Pretests show that the campaigns are effective in the following order: c, b, and a. What would you do?
8. You are interviewing a capable female applicant for a job as salesperson. She is better qualified than the men who have been interviewed. Nevertheless, you know that in your industry some important customers prefer dealing with men and you will lose some sales if you hire her. What would you do?

But SC Johnson took things a step further. In 2004, it also eliminated PVDCs, even though that important ingredient had not yet come under scrutiny. The company developed a PVDC-free polyethylene version of Saran Wrap, an admittedly less effective product. Sure enough, Saran Wrap's market share dropped from 18 percent in 2004 to only 11 percent today. Over the years, however, even though such decisions have sometimes hurt sales, they have helped SC Johnson to earn and keep the trust of customers. "I don't regret the decision," says SC Johnson's CEO. "Despite the cost, it was the right thing to do, and . . . I sleep better at night because of it. We gained a surer sense of who we are as a company and what we want SC Johnson to represent."

As with environmentalism, the issue of ethics presents special challenges for international marketers. Business standards and practices vary a great deal from one country to the next. For example, bribes and kickbacks are illegal for U.S. firms, and various treaties against bribery and corruption have been signed and ratified by more than 60 countries. Yet these are still standard business practices in many countries. The International Monetary Fund estimates that bribes totaling more than $2 trillion per year are paid out worldwide.[27] The question arises as to whether a company must lower its ethical standards to compete effectively in countries with lower standards. The answer is no. Companies should make a commitment to a common set of shared standards worldwide.

Many industrial and professional associations have suggested codes of ethics, and many companies are now adopting their own codes. For example, the American Marketing Association, an international association of marketing managers and scholars, developed a code of ethics that calls on marketers to adopt the following ethical norms:[28]

- ***Do no harm.*** This means consciously avoiding harmful actions or omissions by embodying high ethical standards and adhering to all applicable laws and regulations in the choices we make.

- ***Foster trust in the marketing system.*** This means striving for good faith and fair dealing so as to contribute toward the efficacy of the exchange process as well as avoiding deception in product design, pricing, communication, and delivery or distribution.
- ***Embrace ethical values.*** This means building relationships and enhancing consumer confidence in the integrity of marketing by affirming these core values: honesty, responsibility, fairness, respect, transparency, and citizenship.

Companies are also developing programs to teach managers about important ethical issues and help them find the proper responses. They hold ethics workshops and seminars and create ethics committees. Furthermore, most major U.S. companies have appointed high-level ethics officers to champion ethical issues and help resolve ethics problems and concerns facing employees. And most companies have established their own codes of ethical conduct.

For example, Under Armour's Code of Conduct urges all employees ("teammates") to "Protect this house—Make the right call." regarding issues of ethics and social responsibility. All Under Armour teammates make decisions daily that can affect the brand's well-being. The detailed code's core message: "It's as simple as it sounds," states the code. "Whenever you're faced with a decision—big or small—always do what you know is ethically right, and, of course, always follow the law."

The Under Armour Code of Conduct covers in detail a wide range of topics, from gifts and bribery to honest and fair dealing. But it stresses that it can't cover *every* issue, so teammates "should be sensitive to situations and activities and know that if something looks wrong and feels wrong, it's probably wrong." If employees see or hear about any situation that might violate the ethics code, are urged to report it to their management, senior leaders in the Human Resources organization, or directly anyone to on Under Armour's Global Ethics & Compliance team. Or they call report issue on Under Armour's phone hotline or hotline website, both monitored 24 hours a day, seven days a week, with an option to report anonymously. "We're an aggressive brand, and we're going to stay that way," concludes Under Armour CEO and founder Kevin Plank in the code's introduction. "We all want to win—it's why we're here. [But] we're committed to winning the right way. Period."[29]

Still, written codes and ethics programs do not ensure ethical behavior. Ethics and social responsibility require a total corporate commitment. They must be a component of the overall corporate culture.

The Sustainable Company

At the foundation of marketing is the belief that companies that fulfill the needs and wants of customers will thrive. Companies that fail to meet customer needs or that intentionally or unintentionally harm customers, others in society, or future generations will decline.

Says one observer, "Sustainability is an emerging business megatrend, like electrification and mass production, that will profoundly affect companies' competitiveness and even their survival." Says another, "increasingly, companies and leaders will be assessed not only on immediate results but also on ... the ultimate effects their actions have on societal well-being. This trend has been coming in small ways for years but now is surging. So pick up your recycled cup of fair-trade coffee, and get ready."[30]

Sustainable companies are those that create value for customers through socially, environmentally, and ethically responsible actions. Sustainable marketing goes beyond caring for the needs and wants of today's customers. It means having concern for tomorrow's customers in ensuring the survival and success of the business, shareholders, employees, and the broader world in which they all live. It means pursuing the mission of shared value and a triple bottom line: people, planet, profits. Sustainable marketing provides the context in which companies can engage customers and build profitable relationships with them by creating value *for* customers in order to capture value *from* customers in return—now and in the future.

REVIEWING AND EXTENDING THE CONCEPTS

CHAPTER REVIEW AND KEY TERMS

Objectives Review

In this chapter, we addressed many of the important *sustainable marketing* concepts related to marketing's sweeping impact on individual consumers, other businesses, and society as a whole. Sustainable marketing requires socially, environmentally, and ethically responsible actions that bring value to not only present-day consumers and businesses but also future generations and society as a whole. Sustainable companies are those that act responsibly to create value for customers in order to capture value from customers in return—now and in the future.

OBJECTIVE 16-1 Define *sustainable marketing* and discuss its importance. (pp 498–500)

Sustainable marketing calls for meeting the present needs of consumers and businesses while preserving or enhancing the ability of future generations to meet their needs. Whereas the marketing concept recognizes that companies thrive by fulfilling the day-to-day needs of customers, sustainable marketing calls for socially and environmentally responsible actions that meet both the immediate and future needs of customers and the company. Truly sustainable marketing requires a smooth-functioning marketing system in which consumers, companies, public policy makers, and others work together to ensure responsible marketing actions.

OBJECTIVE 16-2 Identify the major social criticisms of marketing. (pp 500–509)

Marketing's *impact on individual consumer welfare* has been criticized for its high prices, deceptive practices, high-pressure selling, shoddy or unsafe products, planned obsolescence, and poor service to disadvantaged consumers. Marketing's *impact on society* has been criticized for creating false wants and too much materialism, too few social goods, and cultural pollution. Critics have also denounced marketing's *impact on other businesses* for harming competitors and reducing competition through acquisitions, practices that create barriers to entry, and unfair competitive marketing practices. Some of these concerns are justified; some are not.

OBJECTIVE 16-3 Define *consumerism* and *environmentalism* and explain how they affect marketing strategies. (pp 509–513)

Concerns about the marketing system have led to citizen action movements. *Consumerism* is an organized social movement intended to strengthen the rights and power of consumers relative to sellers. Alert marketers view it as an opportunity to serve consumers better by providing more consumer information, education, and protection. *Environmentalism* is an organized social movement seeking to minimize the harm done to the environment and quality of life by marketing practices. Most companies are now accepting responsibility for doing no environmental harm. They are adopting policies of *environmental sustainability*—developing strategies that both sustain the environment and produce profits for the company. Both consumerism and environmentalism are important components of sustainable marketing.

OBJECTIVE 16-4 Describe the principles of sustainable marketing. (pp 513–517)

Many companies originally resisted these social movements and laws, but most now recognize a need for positive consumer information, education, and protection. Under the sustainable marketing concept, a company's marketing should support the best long-run performance of the marketing system. It should be guided by five sustainable marketing principles: *consumer-oriented marketing, customer value marketing, innovative marketing, sense-of-mission marketing*, and *societal marketing*.

OBJECTIVE 16-5 Explain the role of ethics in marketing. (pp 518–520)

Increasingly, companies are responding to the need to provide company policies and guidelines to help their managers deal with questions of *marketing ethics*. Of course, even the best guidelines cannot resolve all the difficult ethical decisions that individuals and firms must make. But there are some principles from which marketers can choose. One principle states that the free market and the legal system should decide such issues. A second and more enlightened principle puts responsibility not on the system but in the hands of individual companies and managers. Each firm and marketing manager must work out a philosophy of socially responsible and ethical behavior. Under the sustainable marketing concept, managers must look beyond what is legal and allowable and develop standards based on personal integrity, corporate conscience, and long-term consumer welfare.

Key Terms

Objective 16-1
Sustainable marketing (p 498)

Objective 16-3
Consumerism (p 509)
Environmentalism (p 510)
Environmental sustainability (p 510)

Objective 16-4
Consumer-oriented marketing (p 514)
Customer value marketing (p 514)
Innovative marketing (p 514)
Sense-of-mission marketing (p 514)
Societal marketing (p 515)
Deficient products (p 515)
Pleasing products (p 515)
Salutary products (p 515)
Desirable products (p 515)

DISCUSSION AND CRITICAL THINKING

Discussion Questions

16-1. Explain how sustainable marketing meets consumers' needs. (AACSB: Written and Oral Communication)

16-2. What are the major social criticisms of marketing? How do marketers respond to these criticisms? (AACSB: Written and Oral Communication; Reflective Thinking)

16-3. How do marketing efforts impact society? Discuss both sides of this issue. (AACSB: Written and Oral Communication; Reflective Thinking)

16-4. Discuss the two major grassroots movements that work to keep companies' sustainability efforts in line. (AACSB: Written and Oral Communication)

16-5. Describe the sustainability principles marketers can use to operate in a responsible and ethical manner. (AACSB: Written and Oral Communication)

16-6. What guidelines should firms follow when developing corporate marketing ethics policies? (AACSB: Written and Oral Communication)

Critical Thinking Exercises

16-7. Figure 16.4 outlines a societal classification of products. Identify two products for each of the four categories, and explain why they are deficient, pleasing, salutary, or desirable products. (AACSB: Written and Oral Communication; Reflective Thinking)

16-8. Suppose that you are leading PepsiCo's environmental sustainability efforts. How would you gauge the effectiveness of these programs? How would you communicate your efforts to loyal consumers of your brand? (AACSB: Written and Oral Communication; Information Technology; Reflective Thinking)

16-9. Using the internet, research current practices on employee use of social media at work. Write an ethics policy to govern social media use by employees. (AACSB: Written and Oral Communication; Information Technology; Ethical Reasoning)

MINICASES AND APPLICATIONS

Online, Mobile, and Social Media Marketing Greenwashing: Embellishment or Eco-Friendly?

Greenwashing is the practice of promoting a product by misleading consumers about its environmentally beneficial aspects. Products might be labeled as "natural," "green," "environmentally friendly," or "biodegradable" but have little or no environmental benefits. Many companies are doing their best to communicate their sustainable and environmentally friendly business practices to consumers. The Greenwashing Index (www.greenwashingindex.com) provides a website location where consumers can review sustainability claims that companies are touting to determine if what they say is true or bogus.

16-10. Visit www.greenwashingindex.com/ads, and select an ad for a company of your choice. View the ad. In your opinion, is the company's product or business practice sustainable, or is this ad an example of greenwashing? Explain your answer. (AACSB: Written and Oral Communication; Information Technology; Ethical Reasoning)

16-11. Choose a product you are familiar with, and trace its entire life cycle. Where does the product originate? What resources go into manufacturing and production? How it is transported and sold? Analyze the economic, environmental, and ethical costs and benefits associated with the product. (AACSB: Written and Oral Communication; Ethical Reasoning; Information Technology)

Marketing Ethics Milking the International Market

Since the 1970s, Nestlé and other companies have faced criticism about their marketing of infant formula to families in developing countries. Their marketing has positioned formula as superior to breast milk and as a more modern way to feed babies despite emerging research findings that breast milk usually led to healthier outcomes for babies. Third-world women grew dependent on infant formula but began watering it down to make it last longer and save money, often with contaminated water. This too often resulted in child malnourishment and other serious health problems and even death in some cases.

Nestlé has been accused by some child watchdog groups of using overly aggressive marketing tactics to sell its infant formula products. Nestlé targeted many new mothers with tactics such as providing samples, promoting products directly in hospitals and communities, and giving gifts to health-care workers and new moms. Other infant formula companies even hired saleswomen in nurses' uniforms to drop by homes unannounced and sell potential customers on using baby formula rather than breastfeeding.

In April 2012, Nestlé acquired Pfizer's infant nutrition unit, making it the biggest player in the infant formula market. According to *The Guardian*, this business unit generates approximately 85 percent of its revenues from emerging markets, demonstrating that Nestlé and other infant formula companies are still capitalizing on consumers in emerging economies. An International Nestlé Boycott Committee began in 1984 to address this global issue and is still active today.

16-12. In a small group, conduct research on this topic and formulate a sustainable, responsible marketing plan for marketing infant formula across the globe. Present your plan. (AACSB: Written and Oral Communication; Information Technology; Ethical Reasoning)

16-13. Is it wrong for marketers to create wants where none exist in the marketplace in order to make profits? Support your answer. (AACSB: Written and Oral Communication; Ethical Reasoning)

Marketing by the Numbers Gouging Their Eyes Out

MyEye 2.0 is a thumb drive–sized device that weighs less than an ounce and attaches magnetically to the stem of almost any pair of glasses. It helps people with impaired vision to "see." It recognizes paper money dominations, faces based on stored images, surroundings, and almost anything else to which the user points a finger. MyEye 2.0 can read a menu or package label and softly tell the wearer what's for dinner via a small speaker near the user's ear. For almost 8 million visually impaired Americans and 253 million visually impaired people worldwide, this could be a game-changer. However, for many, the $4,500 price tag is a game-stopper. Many smartphones equipped with AI technology have apps that can do many of the same things as MyEye 2.0, although they are not wearable. Some believe this wearability does not add enough value to justify MyEye 2.0's outrageous price, especially considering that some 58 percent of U.S. adults with significant vision impairment are unemployed and that percentage is likely higher worldwide. Apple's iPhone X—with Face ID, Siri, and its other AI sensors, camera, speaker, and app capabilities—can do many of the things the MyEye 2.0 can do. It carries a price tag of $999 with the estimated cost of goods sold (COGS) of $360. In contrast, MyEye 2.0's COGS is estimated at $200 per device.

16-14. Calculate the gross margin dollars and percentage for the MyEye 2.0 and the iPhone X. Refer to The Profit-and-Loss Statement and Marketing Budget in Appendix 3: Marketing by the Numbers to learn how to calculate gross margins. (AACSB: Analytical thinking)

16-15. Discuss the pros and cons of the company's decision to price the MyEye 2.0 so high. Is the company following the principle of societal marketing? Should it? (AACSB: Written and Oral Communication; Reflective thinking)

Video Case Honest Tea

To view this video case and its accompanying questions, please visit MyLab Marketing.

Honest Tea, the Coca-Cola brand that produced $130 million in global revenues last year, got its start because cofounder Seth Goldman didn't like the options in the beverage coolers at convenience stores. So with the help of a former professor, he launched Honest Tea—the nation's first fully organic bottled tea.

But the company's drive for success was not based not as much on profits as on a desire to change the world. With social responsibility steeped deep into its business model, Honest Tea set out to help develop the economic structure of impoverished nations. Honest Tea purchased raw ingredients from Native American and South African farmers and invested in its supplier-farmers to help them become self-reliant. Although Honest Tea has been a wholly owned subsidiary of the Coca-Cola Company since 2011, it continues to operate on the principles of social responsibility established by its founders.

Company Cases 16 LEGO/12 LinkedIn

See Appendix 1 for cases appropriate for this chapter.

Case 16, LEGO: Making the World a Better Place—One Brick at a Time. The LEGO Group has become the biggest toy company in the world while also becoming one of the most socially responsible.

Case 12, LinkedIn: Crushing the White Collar Stereotype with IMC. With its first mass-media IMC campaign, LinkedIn is out to forge an image of diversity and inclusiveness.

Writing Assignments

16-16. What is consumerism? What rights do consumers have, and why do some critics feel buyers need more protection? (AACSB: Communication)

16-17. Discuss the philosophies that might guide marketers facing ethical issues. (AACSB: Written and Oral Communication)

Appendix 1 Company Cases

Company Case 1

Chick-fil-A: Getting Better before Getting Bigger

Chick-fil-A is dominating the U.S. fast-food market. Whereas McDonald's, Subway, Burger King, and Taco Bell trudge along at the top of the heap, Chick-fil-A has quietly grown from a Southeast regional favorite into the largest chicken chain and the eighth-largest quick-service food purveyor in the country. The chain sells significantly more food per restaurant than any of its competitors—three times that of Taco Bell or Wendy's and more than four times what the KFC Colonel fries up. And it does this without even opening its doors on Sundays. With annual revenues of $8 billion and annual average growth of 16 percent, the chicken champ from Atlanta shows no signs of slowing down.

How does Chick-fil-A do it? By focusing on customers. Since the first Chick-fil-A restaurant opened for business in the late 1960s, the chain's founders have held tenaciously to the philosophy that the most sustainable way to do business is to provide the best possible customer experience.

Applying Some Pressure

Chick-fil-A founder S. Truett Cathy was no stranger to the restaurant business. Owning and operating restaurants in Georgia in the 1940s, '50s, and '60s, he was led by his experience to investigate a better (and faster) way to cook chicken. He discovered a pressure fryer that could cook a chicken breast in the same amount of time it took to cook a fast-food burger. Developing the chicken sandwich as a burger alternative, he registered the name "Chick-fil-A, Inc." and opened the first Chick-fil-A restaurant in 1967.

The company began expanding immediately, although at a much slower pace than the market leaders. Even today, Chick-fil-A adds only about 100 new stores each year. Although it now has more than 2,200 stores throughout the United States, that number is relatively small compared to KFC's 4,100, McDonald's 14,000, and Subway's 27,000. Chick-fil-A's controlled growth ties directly to its "customer first" mantra. As a family-owned operation, the company has never deviated from its core value to "focus on getting better before getting bigger." The slow-growth strategy has enabled that ability to "get better."

As another way to perfect its business, the company has also stuck to a limited menu. The original breaded chicken sandwich remains at the core of Chick-fil-A's menu today—"a boneless breast of chicken seasoned to perfection, hand-breaded, pressure cooked in 100% refined peanut oil and served on a toasted, buttered bun with dill pickle chips." In fact, the company's trademarked slogan—"We didn't invent the chicken, just the chicken sandwich"—has kept the company on track for decades. Although it has carefully and strategically added other items to the menu, it's the iconic chicken sandwich in all its varieties that primarily drives the brand's image and the company's revenues. This focus has helped the company give customers what they want year after year without being tempted to develop a new flavor of the month.

Getting It Right

Also central to Chick-fil-A's mission is to "have a positive influence on all who come in contact with Chick-fil-A." Although seemingly a tall order to fill, this sentiment permeates every aspect of its business. Not long ago, current Chick-fil-A CEO Dan Cathy was deeply affected by a note that his wife taped to their refrigerator. In a recent visit to a local Chick-fil-A store, she had not only received the wrong order, she had been overcharged. She circled the amount on her receipt, wrote "I'll be back when you get it right" next to it, and posted it on the fridge for her husband to see.

That note prompted Dan Cathy to double down on customer service. He initiated a program by which all Chick-fil-A employees were retrained to go the "second mile" in providing service to everyone. That "second mile" meant not only meeting basic standards of cleanliness and politeness but going above and beyond by delivering each order to the customer's table with unexpected touches such as a fresh-cut flower or ground pepper for salads.

The experience of a recent patron illustrates the level of service Chick-fil-A's customers have come to expect as well as the innovative spirit that makes such service possible:

> My daughter and I stopped at Chick-fil-A on our way home. The parking lot was full, the drive-thru was packed... but the love we have for the chicken sandwiches and waffle potato fries! So we decided it was worth the wait. As we walked up the sidewalk, there were two staff members greeting every car in the drive-thru and taking orders on little tablets. A manager was making his rounds around the building outside smiling and waving at cars as they were leaving.
>
> When we came inside, the place was packed! We were greeted immediately by the cashiers. Seth happened to take our order. He had a big smile, wonderful manners, spoke clearly and had great energy as a teenager! He gave us a number and said he'd be right out with our drinks. We were able to sit at a table as the other guests were leaving and before we could even get settled our drinks were on the table! While Seth started to walk away, our food was delivered by another very friendly person. Both myself and my 15-year-old daughter commented on how fast it all happened. We were so shocked that we started commenting on the large groups arriving behind us, and began watching in amazement, not only inside but outside!

> Everyone behind the counter worked together, used manners, and smiled. The teamwork was amazing! Then Ron, a gray headed friendly man, made his way from table to table, checking on guests, giving drink refills, and trading coloring books for small ice cream cones with sprinkles for little kids. He checked on us twice and filled our drinks once.

Recently, the company instituted the "parent's valet service," inviting parents juggling small children to go through the drive-through, place their order, park, and make their way inside the store. By the time the family gets inside, its meal is waiting on placemats at a table with high chairs in place. But beyond the tactics that are taught as a matter of standard policy, Chick-fil-A also trains employees to look for special ways to serve—such as retrieving dental appliances from dumpsters or delivering smartphones and wallets that customers have left behind.

Give Them Something to Do

Beyond high levels of in-store service, Chick-fil-A has focused on other brand-building elements that enhance the customer experience. The brand got a big boost when the Chick-fil-A cows made their promotional debut as three-dimensional characters on billboards with the now famous slogan "EAT MORE CHIKIN." The beloved bovines and their self-preservation message have been a constant across Chick-fil-A promotional materials for more than 23 years. They've also been the lynchpin for another Chick-fil-A customer experience enhancing strategy—engage customers by giving them something to do.

When it comes to giving customers "something to do," Chick-fil-A doesn't fool around. For starters, there's "Cow Appreciation Day"—a day set aside every July when customers who go to any Chick-fil-A store dressed as a cow get a free entree. Last year, the 12th anniversary of this annual event, about 1.8 million cow-clad customers cashed in on the offer.

Another tradition for brand loyalists is to camp out prior to the opening of a new restaurant. Chick-fil-A encourages this ardent activity with its "First 100" promotion—an officially sanctioned event in which the company presents vouchers for a full year's worth of Chick-fil-A meals to the first 100 people in line for each new restaurant opening. Dan Cathy himself has been known to camp out with customers, signing T-shirts, posing for pictures, and personally handing coupons to the winners. And whereas some customer-centric giveaways are regular events, others pop up randomly. Take the most recent "family challenge," which awards free ice cream cones to any dine-in customers who relinquish their smartphones to a "cell phone coop" for the duration of their meals.

To keep customers engaged when they aren't in the stores, Chick-fil-A has become an expert in social and digital media. It's app, Chick-fil-A One, jumped to the number one spot on iTunes only hours after being announced. Nine days later, more than a million customers had downloaded the app, giving them the ability to place and customize their orders, pay in advance, and skip the lines at the register. And in a recent survey by social media tracker Engagement Labs, Chick-fil-A was ranked number one and crowned the favorite American brand on all major social media platforms, including Facebook, Twitter, and Instagram.

Every year, as the accolades roll in, it is apparent that Chick-fil-A's customer-centric culture is more than just talk. Among the many competitors, Chick-fil-A was ranked number one in customer service in the most recent American Customer Service Satisfaction Index (ACSI) for fast-food chains. Chick-fil-A took the same top spot in surveys by the Temkin Group and Consumer Reports. The most cited reason for these achievements was employees described as having a "pleasant demeanor," making eye contact, and saying "please" and "thank you."

After decades of phenomenal growth and success, Chick-fil-A is giving the cows a break. "The cows are an integral part of the brand. They're our mascot, if you will," says Jon Bridges, chief marketing officer for Chick-fil-A. "But they aren't the brand. The brand is bigger than that." The cows haven't disappeared, they've just changed pastures as the brand's promotional messages have shifted to tell engaging stories about the food, people, and service that make the brand so special. It's a risky move. With Chick-fil-A growing faster than any other major fast-food chain, it begs the question as to whether such a drastic change in the brand's symbolism will sustain its current growth for years to come or send customers out cow tipping.

Prior to this recent announcement, one estimate has Chick-fil-A on track to leapfrog Dunkin', Taco Bell, Burger King, Wendy's, and Subway to become the third-largest fast-food chain in the United States. by 2020. At that point, Chick-fil-A will trail only Starbucks and McDonald's. Clearly, all this growth is no accident. As one food industry analyst states, "It's about trying to maintain high levels of service, high quality, not deviating dramatically, and giving customers an idea of what to expect." As long as Chick-fil-A continues to make customers the number one priority, we can expect to find more and more access to those scrumptious chicken sandwiches.

Questions for Discussion

1. Give examples of needs, wants, and demands of Chick-fil-A customers, differentiating these three concepts.
2. Describe Chick-fil-A in terms of the value it provides customers. How does Chick-fil-A engage customers?
3. Evaluate Chick-fil-A's performance relative to customer expectations.
4. Which of the five marketing management orientations best applies to Chick-fil-A?
5. Will Chick-fil-A's change in promotional strategy affect its level of growth and success?

Sources: Cheyenne Buckingham, "Fast Food Chains with the Best (and Worst) Service," *24/7 Wall St.*, July 26, 2018, https://247wallst.com/special-report/2017/07/26/fast-food-chains-with-the-best-and-worst-service/2/; "The QSR 50," www.qsrmagazine.com/content/qsr50-2017-top-50-chart, accessed June 2018; Jessica Wohl, "Chick-fil-A Drops the Richards Group after 22 Years," *Advertising Age*, July 21, 2016, http://adage.com/article/cmo-strategy/chick-fil-a-drops-richards-group-after-22-years/305057/; Michael Bartiromo, "Chick-fil-A to Become Nation's Third-Largest Fast Food Restaurant by 2020, Analysts Say," *Fox News*, April 3, 2018, www.foxnews.com/food-drink/2018/04/03/chick-fil-to-become-nations-third-largest-fast-food-restaurant-by-2020-analysts-say.html;

"Consumer Conversations about Chick-fil-A, Wendy's and In-N-Out Heat Up," *Engagement Labs*, November 16, 2017, www.engagementlabs.com/press/consumer-conversations-chick-fil-wendys-n-heat-coffee-chains-starbucks-dunkin-donuts-freeze/; Cameron Sperance, "'Everybody Wants Chick-fil-A': Why the Chicken Chain Is Dominating Fast Food," *Bisnow*, June 7, 2018, www.bisnow.com/national/news/retail/how-2020-will-be-the-year-of-the-chick-fil-a-89287; Alicia Kelso, "Chick-fil-A's Growth Trajectory Fueled by Demand for Simplicity," *Forbes*, April 3, 2018, www.forbes.com/sites/aliciakelso/2018/04/03/chick-fil-as-growth-trajectory-fueled-by-demand-for-simplicity/#4a963905612b; and www.chick-fil-a.com/About/Who-We-Are, accessed October 2018.

Company Case 2

Facebook: Making the World More Open and Connected

The world has rapidly gone online, social, and mobile. And no company is more online, social, and mobile than Facebook. Despite the growing number of social media options, Facebook continues to dominate. In little more than a decade, it has accumulated 2.2 billion active monthly users—approximately 30 percent of the world's total population—and some 1.7 billion people now access the network on a mobile device. More than 1.5 billion Facebook members already log on daily, and eight new Facebook profiles are created every second. In the United States, more collective time is spent on Facebook than on any other website. Together, the Facebook community uploads 350 million photos, "Likes" 5.8 billion items, and shares 4.75 billion pieces of content daily.

Having achieved such phenomenal impact in such a short period of time, Facebook can attribute its success to a tenacious focus on its mission—"to give people the power to share and make the world more open and connected." It's a place where friends and family meet, share their stories, display their photos, pass along information, and chronicle their lives. Hordes of people have made Facebook their digital home 24/7.

From Simple Things

Initially, carrying out this mission was relatively simple. When CEO Mark Zuckerberg and friends launched "thefacebook.com" in 2004, it was for Harvard students only. Still, with its clean design ("No Disneyland, no 'Live nude girls.'"), the fledgling site attracted a lot of attention when it racked up more than 1,200 registered users by the end of the first day. Within the first month, more than half of Harvard's undergraduate student body had joined. The massive response demonstrated tremendous untapped demand. At first, the social network grew one university campus at a time. But it wasn't long before Facebook was open to the public and people everywhere were registering by the millions.

As it grew, Facebook's interface was a work in progress. Features were added and modified to appeal to everyone. The network's growth and development also gave it the ability to target specific kinds of content to well-defined user segments. However, Facebook's "all things to all people" approach left many users, especially younger ones, visiting Facebook less and shifting time to more specialized competing social networks. To meet that growing threat, Facebook shifted gears from a "one site for all" approach to a multi-app strategy of providing "something for any and every individual." According to Zuckerberg, "Our vision for Facebook is to create a set of products that help you share any kind of content you want with any audience you want."

As the first move under its multi-app strategy, Facebook paid a then-stunning $1 billion to acquire Instagram, the surging photo-sharing app. Although Facebook already had its own photo-sharing features, the Instagram acquisition brought a younger, 27-million-strong user base into the Facebook fold. And rather than incorporating Instagram as just another Facebook feature, Facebook maintained Instagram as an independent brand with its own personality and user base. Instagram and Facebook customers can choose their desired level of integration, including Instagram membership without a Facebook account. "The fact that Instagram is connected to other services beyond Facebook is an important part of the experience," says Zuckerberg. The strategy has worked. Instagram's userbase has exploded to more than 800 million in just six years.

On the heels of the Instagram acquisition came another stunning Facebook mega-acquisition. Dwarfing its Instagram deal, Facebook paid a shocking $19 billion for standalone messaging app WhatsApp. Facebook's own Messenger had already grown quickly to 200 million users. But similar to Instagram, WhatsApp immediately gave Facebook something it could not easily build on its own—an independent brand with more than 450 million registered international users, many of whom were not on Facebook. Now, four years after the acquisition, 1.5 billion worldwide WhatsApp users send 60 billion messages every day.

By developing and acquiring such new products and apps, Facebook is doing what it does best—growing its membership and giving its diverse users more ways and reasons to connect and engage. Facebook's fuller portfolio lets users meet their individual needs within the broadening Facebook family.

To the Stratosphere

As Facebook develops more reasons for more users to connect and engage, it also pursues technologies that might leave some observers scratching their heads. For example, a few years ago, the social media giant paid $2 billion to acquire Oculus VR, the virtual reality startup. In the past year, Facebook has also developed its own 360-degree stereoscopic 3D video camera with 17 lenses—a device it calls Facebook Surround360. Why these acquisitions and developments? According to Zuckerberg, it has to do with "first steps."

When Zuckerberg took his first steps, his parents noted the event in his baby book. When one of his cousins first walked some time later, Mom and Dad captured the moment with a photo. When his niece learned to walk, the video camera was rolling. But for his own daughter, Zuckerberg wanted to take it to the next level. "When Max takes her first step, we'll be able to capture the whole scene, not just write down the date or take a photo or take a little 2D video," Zuckerberg says. "The people we want to share this with... can go there. They can experience *that moment*."

Zuckerberg's wanting to broadcast his daughter's first steps as though others were there is just one more example of how Facebook constantly focuses on its central mission—to connect the world. "Over time, people get richer and richer tools to communicate and express what they care about," says Zuckerberg. Facebook anticipates that this kind of video could lead to an entirely new mode of communication, one that could extend to Facebook's own Oculus virtual reality headset.

As much as 3D virtual reality video sounds like a long shot, it's easy pickings compared to Facebook's biggest current initiative. Zuckerberg has been spanning the globe, addressing everyone from global leaders to fellow entrepreneurs and making a case for what he sees as the most critical social endeavor or our time—making the internet a basic human right, like health care or clean water. As he tells it, lack of free and open access to information is the greatest barrier to prosperity for the world's impoverished. But three and a half billion people are not yet connected to the internet. Zuckerberg and the Facebook team aim to eliminate that barrier by making the internet accessible to all.

To this end, Facebook has created its own innovation think tank called the Connectivity Lab. This group is working on putting satellites into orbit as a means of providing broadband internet service to remote regions of the world. But satellites are expensive, so the group is working on other options as well. The most promising option is known internally as Aquila—a sleek, boomerang-shaped drone that has a wingspan wider than a Boeing 737, flies at altitudes up to 90,000 feet in a 31-mile radius, and can to stay aloft for three months at a time. Aquila receives radio signals from a ground station, relays those signals via lasers to transponders on the ground, and converts the signals to Wi-Fi or 4G networks. Aquila has already completed multiple test flights successfully, and Facebook's vision is to eventually have thousands of the drone wings flying the friendly skies around planet Earth.

Giving It All Away

Although Facebook spent more than five years building its user base and paying almost no attention to generating income, it is now making up for lost time. In the past five years, Facebook's annual revenues have gone viral—from $7.87 billion to $40.65 billion, a fivefold increase to its top line. With a profit margin of nearly 40 percent, its bottom line isn't doing too badly either. And although Facebook has experimented with various ways to generate income, the vast majority of its income comes via tried-and-true online advertising.

With all the development of fancy technologies such as drones, lasers, virtual reality, and 3D video, you might think that Facebook intends to diversify into new businesses that could generate cash and profits. But nothing could be further from the truth. In fact, as Facebook launches these and other technologies, it is giving away the designs for free. Years ago when Facebook built its own servers and data centers, it promptly open-sourced the designs and let the world have them for nothing. It did the same with big data analytics tools such as Cassandra and Hadoop. Although that might seem like throwing away money, it's right in line with Facebook's mission. Whereas most companies define themselves by a craft, such as making the best consumer electronic gadgets or solving companies' efficiency problems, Facebook has been built around a single-minded goal of connecting everyone in the world and giving them the tools they need "to share anything and everything in a natural way."

For that reason, Facebook focuses on what it does best—being the best social network. Rather than becoming distracted by developing multiple business units and trying to make money through diversified means, it remains focused on building its user base and treating its core social media products as works in process. To those who view the projects coming out of the Connectivity Lab as unrelated, Zuckerberg points out, "They're actually incredibly focused in terms of the mission. The real goal is to build the community. A lot of times, the best way to advance the technology is to work on it as a community."

With many companies already working on the very technologies that Facebook is trying to advance, it might seem that Facebook isn't adding much. But Zuckerberg is impatient, and he feels that the tech world is providing too little, too late. For example, Facebook's laser drones will be able to shower entire rural areas, villages, and cities with extremely high bandwidth at higher speeds with more economical costs than the systems currently being employed and developed by telecom companies. "We need certain technologies to exist in the world, so we will build those," says Zuckerberg. "We're not selling [servers] or cameras or connectivity services. But if no one else is building them, we're going to."

Whatever its future, Facebook seems to have barely scratched the surface when it comes to fulfilling its mission. Its new multi-app, multi-segment strategy, combined with its massive, closely knit social structure, gives Facebook staggering potential. And moving the world toward internet access for all will help make Facebook's portfolio of apps and products available to everyone. For years, a popular saying around Facebook has been "We are one percent done with our mission." These days, those who manage Facebook might concede that they've made progress—say, to maybe two percent. For skeptics, consider how Facebook got started:

> It was a few nights after [Zuckerberg] launched the website. He and his computer science buddy were getting pizza and talking. Zuckerberg told his friend that someone was going to build a social network, because it was too important not to exist. But he didn't guess, back then, that he'd be the guy to do it. There were older people and bigger companies. So why, then, was Zuckerberg the one to build Facebook? "I think it's because we cared. A lot of times, caring about something and believing in it trumps," he says. "I couldn't connect the dots going forward on Facebook from the beginning. To me, that's a lot of the story of [Facebook's future] too."

Questions for Discussion

1. Is Facebook's mission statement market oriented? Explain.
2. How is Facebook's strategy driven by its mission?
3. Is it wise for Facebook to give away it technologies for free? Why or why not?
4. As it moves forward in fulfilling its mission, what challenges does Facebook face in the future?

Sources: Based on information from Eric Mack, "Is Facebook Secretly Building an Internet Satellite?" *CNET*, May 3, 2018, www.cnet.com/news/is-facebook-secretly-building-an-internet-satellite-athena/; Luke Stangel, "Facebook Wants to Test Experimental Internet Drones in New Mexico," *Silicon Valley Business Journal*, April 23, 2018, www.bizjournals.com/sanjose/news/2018/04/23/facebook-internet-drones-aquila-project-new-mexico.html; Cade Metz, "How Will Zuckerberg Rule the World? By Giving Facebook's Tech Away," *Wired*, April 12, 2016, www.wired.com/2016/04/mark-zuckerberg-giving-away-facebooks-tech-free/; Josh Constine, "WhatsApp Hits 1.5 Billion Monthly Users. $19 B? Not So Bad," *Techcrunch*, January 31, 2018, https://techcrunch.com/2018/01/31/whatsapp-hits-1-5-billion-monthly-users-19b-not-so-bad/; and information from https://zephoria.com/top-15-valuable-facebook-statistics/, accessed October 2018.

Company Case 3

Fitbit: Riding the Fitness Wave to Glory

It was 2009. James Park and Eric Friedman were at a breaking point. They'd been flitting around Asia for months, setting up the supply chain for their company's first product, the Fitbit Tracker. Having raised capital to launch the product with nothing more than a circuit board in a balsa wood box, they were now on the verge of pushing the button to start the assembly line. But with thousands of orders to fill, they discovered that the device's antenna wasn't working properly. They stuck a piece of foam on the circuit board and called it "good enough." Five thousand customers received shiny new Fitbit Trackers just in time for the holidays.

Getting a startup company off the ground is challenging. Getting a hardware startup to succeed is near impossible, especially when you're the pioneer. But with so many changes in the marketing environment, Park and Friedman knew they had something special. Pedometers had been selling for years, following personal fitness and wellness trends. But those devices were low-tech and limited in the information they provided consumers. And with the seemingly endless demand for high-tech gadgetry, Park and Friedman saw big potential for using sensors in small, wearable devices.

The two entrepreneurs were correct. Fitbit has now marketed more than a dozen different products and sold millions of units. Six years after launching its first device, the company shipped 21 million devices and rang up $1.86 billion in annual revenues and $116 million in profits. Fitbit created a fast-growing segment—wearable tech. In 2015, Fitbit went public with an initial public offering of $4.1 billion. How did the company go from a balsa wood box to sitting atop an exploding industry? To hear Park tell it, "It was the right product at the right time at the right price point."

A Magical Device

Although Park's response may seem simplistic, it's right on. Coming up with a product that delivers the right benefits to consumers at precisely the time they need them is the key to any new product launch. In Fitbit's case, consumers were hungry for this small device that could not only track steps taken but calculate distance walked, calories burned, floors climbed, and activity duration and intensity, all from an unobtrusive spot—clipped on a pants pocket. What's more, the Fitbit Tracker could track sleep quality based on periods of restlessness, the amount of time before falling asleep, and the amount of time actually sleeping.

Even more enticing to consumers, the device could upload data to a computer and make it available on the Fitbit website. At the site, users could overview their physical activity, set and track goals, and keep logs of food eaten and additional activities not tracked by the device. To top things off, the explosion of social media and sharing personal information went hand in hand with what users were uploading. By design, Park and Friedman put more into Fitbit's software than its own hardware, recognizing that other hardware device companies like Garmin had shortchanged the software aspect.

But Fitbit's success can also be attributed to new models. Recognizing that gadgets have a limited life span and that competition would attempt to improve on its offerings, Fitbit has made development a constant process. From the original Tracker to its current Blaze smart watch with GPS, heart-rate monitor, and the ability to display smartphone notifications for calls, texts, and calendar alerts, Fitbit has stayed ahead in giving consumers what they want.

An Unexpected Opportunity

Still, Fitbit's path to success has been challenging. One big challenge the company has faced from the start is customer retention. Like many diets and pieces of exercise equipment, users are drawn to the "wow" factor of something that can improve their health and wellness but then quickly fizzle out. And if users stop using a device, they are far less likely to purchase the "new-and-improved" version, much less recommend it to anyone else. But an interesting thing happened as Fitbit got things rolling. The company received a flood of calls and messages from corporate human resource departments. Perplexed as to why businesses would want to buy Fitbit devices in bulk, the company assigned a point person to find out.

It turned out that corporate America was going through a push to enroll employees in wellness programs. The reasons for this push extended far beyond concerns about employee health and well-being. Healthy employees provide major benefits for a company. They call in sick less often and are generally more productive. They also cost less in terms of health-care benefits. And although diet and exercise can't erase every poor health condition, they can have a big effect on health factors such as blood pressure, cholesterol levels, and blood sugar levels—conditions related to common diseases such as heart disease, stroke, and diabetes. So it's no wonder that companies have an incentive to do whatever they can to motivate employees to take better care of themselves.

As Fitbit talked to companies, it discovered that most were struggling to enroll even a small proportion of employees in their workforce wellness programs—many had less than 20 percent compliance. One problem was that—even as the latest fitness wearables from Fitbit and its competitors were showing up around offices everywhere—participation in corporate wellness programs often required the use of a bulky corporate-issued tracker, better known as an analog pedometer. "Can you imagine asking engineers to wear a janky old pedometer and write down their steps?" mused Amy McDonough, Fitbit's corporate point person. Fitbit, of course, offered a much more high-tech option, letting individuals easily track more complex data and letting HR departments easily compile and analyze the data as well. Fitbit's bulk sales to corporations started rolling in.

Much to Fitbit's pleasant surprise, Fitbit products sold through corporations versus those sold to individuals had noticeably higher retention rates. Fitness trackers in corporate wellness programs were often used in wellness challenges—maintain a minimum of 10,000 steps a day and get free vacation days or a discount on health insurance premiums. It might seem logical that people would stop using their devices once a challenge ended. But when IBM gave out 40,000 Fitbits to employees over a two-year period, it found not only that 96 percent of employees routinely logged their health data and eating habits but that 63 percent of employees continued to wear their Fitbits months after the challenge concluded.

Other companies noted even greater tangible benefits. Cloud-services startup Appirio bought Fitbit devices for 400 employees. Armed with data from the wearables, Appirio was able to convince its health insurance provider, Anthem, that the increased health benefits were translating into lower health-care costs. This gave Appirio the leverage to negotiate lower premiums, shaving $280,000 off its annual bill.

Today, Fitbit's wellness division offers tools specifically designed for employers, such as dashboards, dedicated service support, and webinars. Corporate clients include BP America, Kimberly-Clark, Time Warner, and Barclays. Target offered Fitbit Zip trackers to 335,000 of its employees. Corporate sales currently account for 10 percent of Fitbit revenues. But the corporate share of the sales will increase, as adoption in that sector is growing faster than in consumer markets. Founder Park claims that the use of Fitbits in employee wellness programs is having an impact not only on health and well-being but on job safety as well. Companies have also experienced improvements in office cultures as a result of the unified effort among coworkers to achieve fitness goals together, a factor that is also likely boosting retention numbers in the corporate setting.

Encountering Hurdles

With Fitbit's high growth rates and plenty of market potential, it would seem that the sky is the limit for Fitbit. But Fitbit still faces numerous obstacles. For starters, privacy issues have increased as technology creates new ways to gather and share information. In Fitbit's early days, information logged by users was public by default. That meant that as users integrated their information into social networks, their fitness, eating, sleeping, and in some cases sexual activities were being posted for all to see. That was easily remedied by making "private" the default setting. But general concerns about what happens with uploaded personal data remain, even amid assurances from Fitbit that it does not analyze individual data and or sell or share consumer data.

But other privacy matters haven't been so easily managed. Fitness trackers and the data they generate are not regulated. That means that any organization bound by compliance with the U.S. Health Insurance Portability and Accountability Act (HIPAA) have had to tread lightly when adopting a digital tracking device. Fitbit has always been proactive on privacy and information security issues, leading the industry by working with congress on legislation in this area. Fitbit recently achieved HIPAA compliance, which goes a long way toward putting employers' fears about privacy and security to rest.

But other concerns remain on the part of both employers and employees. Even as Fitbit and its corporate customers do all they can to allay privacy concerns, many employees have expressed concerns that companies will misuse the data. Uncertainty about what data is being collected and how it is being used has led some employees to wonder whether their Fitbits could be telling employers if they are recovering from a wild night of partying, are calling in sick when they really aren't, are feeling nervous in a meeting, or even become pregnant.

Although the overall benefits of integrating a Fitbit device into wellness programs and the associated challenges seem clear, there are negative outcomes as well. Health experts point to the potential for a cultural divide between the "dos" and the "do nots." Employees with disabilities, chronic ailments, or even unhealthy habits may opt out of such programs. Particularly in programs that use leaderboards and group incentives, the result can be to celebrate the fit but demoralize those who are not. And rewards given to those who participate as well as those who succeed are viewed as penalties for those who opt out.

Cheaters are also a concern. Yes, some participants in wellness programs have found ways to fool their Fitbits. For example, a dog can trigger 13,000 to 30,000 steps per day with a Fitbit attached to its collar, easily exceeding the standard 10,000-step goal. Social media sites have erupted with shared practices. "Want to cheat your Fitbit? Try a puppy or a power drill," suggests one Tweet with a link to instructions. Other methods for logging steps include putting it in the dryer, shaking the fist, attaching it to small children, playing the piano, leading music, and whisking a bowl of chocolate-chip cookie batter. Even the vibrations from riding a Harley or a lawnmower can do the trick.

Beyond these concerns that stand in the way of more widespread acceptance and use, perhaps Fitbit's greatest challenge is competition. With a dominant market share in the rapidly growing product category that it created, Fitbit seems to have it made. However, as digital technologies advance on all fronts, fitness trackers have been a hot target. Only a few short years after Fitbit's cutting-edge launch, companies like Xiaomi and Garmin commoditized the market with cheaper devices. And when Apple and Samsung launched pricey smartwatches with built-in fitness tracking capabilities, it became painfully apparent that "fitness tracking" could be minimized as a feature of more complex devices. And on the software and analytics side, Apple Health and Google Fit emerged with compatibility across mobile platforms.

Last year, Fitbit watched as its revenues plummeted by 25 percent to $1.6 billion and fell into a dead heat with Xiaomi for the position of market leader. But Fitbit is hard at work differentiating its wares and positioning itself as more than just a maker of fitness trackers. With the recent launch of Ionic, its first full-featured smartwatch, Fitbit is taking on Apple with a product that touts a lower price and longer battery life. And its "next big leap" is to move beyond fitness tracking into medical diagnosis. By partnering with organizations that can link Fitbit's products with more detailed clinical research, Fitbit devices could soon replace blood glucose meters and even alert users to dangerous health conditions and disease. If Fitbit can successfully position itself on strengths that competitors have a hard time replicating, the sky may still be the limit.

Questions for Discussion

1. What microenvironmental factors have affected Fitbit since it opened for business?
2. What macroenvironmental factors have affected Fitbit?
3. How should Fitbit overcome the threats and obstacles it faces?
4. What factors in the marketing environment not mentioned in this case could affect Fitbit?

Sources: Based on information from Matthew Lynley, "Fitbit Posted a Weaker-Than-Expected First Quarter and Its Shares Are Crashing," *Techcrunch*, February 26, 2018, https://techcrunch.com/2018/02/26/fitbit-posted-a-weaker-than-expected-quarter-and-its-shares-are-crashing/; "Fitbit Gains from Partnerships, Market Share Loss a Concern," *Nasdaq*, January 2, 2018, www.nasdaq.com/article/fitbit-gains-from-partnerships-market-share-loss-a-concern-cm899734; Leo Sun, "Why 2017 Was a Year to Forget for Fitbit," *The Motley Fool*, www.fool.com/investing/2017/11/03/why-2017-was-a-year-to-forget-for-fitbit-inc.aspx; Christina Farr, "Fitbit at Work," *Fast Company*, May 2016, pp. 27–30; Robert Hof, "How Fitbit Survived as a Hardware Startup," *Forbes*, February 4, 2014, forbes.com/sites/roberthof/2014/02/04/how-fitbit-survived-as-a-hardware-startup/#5e2a544e4f42; and Jen Wieczner, "Fitbit Users Are Finding Creative Ways to Cheat," *Fortune*, June 10, 2016, http://fortune.com/2016/06/10/fitbit-hack-cheat/.

Company Case 4

Qualtrics: Managing the Complete Customer Experience

Over the past few decades, the practice of gathering customer feedback data has been changing as new technologies have let marketers dig deeper. For example, take customer satisfaction surveys. A common scenario involves retail cashiers promoting online surveys to customers by pointing out links on receipts, often accompanied by enticing incentives such as gift certificates.

In fact, everywhere customers turn, retailers and brands are emailing, texting, and handing out links to online surveys in hopes that customers will provide them with valuable feedback. But what most customers don't know is that few if any of those companies are managing their own surveys. Instead, many marketers turn to a handful of experts to handle all aspects of online surveys and how such surveys fit into the bigger picture of their customer intelligence programs.

For companies like Lowe's, Ford, Verizon, 3M, and Disney, the expert they turn to is Qualtrics—the leader of the fast-growing online survey industry. In fact, more than 8,500 of the world's leading brands trust Qualtrics to power customer data collection, including 80 of the *Fortune* 100 and 99 of the top 100 business schools. But to characterize Qualtrics's services as "online surveys" is an oversimplification. Ask anyone at Qualtrics what business they're in and they'll say it's all about "experience management."

Pioneering the Online Survey

Today, gathering survey data online seems like no-brainer. But to fully understand what Qualtrics is and does for its clients, you have to go back more than 20 years when online surveys didn't exist. The company's beginnings are a classic example of a tech startup at the turn of the millennium. But instead of a garage in Silicon Valley, Qualtrics started in the basement of a house on a cul-de-sac in Provo, Utah.

The house belonged to BYU marketing professor, Scott Smith. In 1997 he came up with the idea to develop a digital survey engine that would facilitate his own research. Back then, the standard process for collecting survey data was distributing a paper-and-pencil questionnaire in person or through the mail. As such, it was a costly process in terms of both time and money to create a survey, collect responses from respondents, code data, and enter data into a computer. "The first survey that we collected online—within 48 hours, our data was in the computer," says Smith, noting that the process would normally have taken months using traditional methods. "All of a sudden, the light clicks on and you're like, this is something wonderful. It's quick, it's easy, it's more accurate."

Smith enlisted his sons, Ryan and Jared, to help develop and launch one of the first online survey services. What started as SurveyPro became Qualtrics in 2002. Initially targeting the academic community, the team soon recognized its software's potential as a marketing research tool. Honing the software over several years, Qualtrics expanded its client base in 2008 to include organizations of all kinds—business and academic, for-profit and not-for-profit. But before long, the majority of Qualtrics's business was coming from corporations.

From the start, Qualtrics differentiated its offering by making it user-friendly. The goal was to help anyone with a non-tech background quickly and easily create and manage an online survey. With Qualtrics, clients could use simple question-generating tools to draw from various types of questions, including sliding scales with endpoints such as "happy" and "sad" or grades from "A" to "F." An early Qualtrics innovation was heat maps that let respondents click on a particular location in a retail facility, indicating preferences for certain types of product or service experiences, such as the preferred seating in a theater. Users could also choose from numerous types of graphs to summarize results.

Qualtrics was one of the first to use an online-only model, eliminating the need to install software on individual computers. Once registered, customers can develop, tweak, and adapt their own custom surveys without asking Qualtrics to do it for them. Along the way, Qualtrics has added features that not only increase the flexibility of survey creation but make it easier to aggregate and analyze collected data. The online do-it-yourself Qualtrics approach not only saves users a great deal of time compared with more traditional methods, it's also considerably cheaper.

Experience Management—the Pioneering Continues

Today, the original basic Qualtrics survey engine has evolved into what the company dubs the Experience Management (XM) Platform—a suite of products that lets clients use a single interface to manage the four core business experiences—customer experience, brand experience, product experience, and employee experience. According to Mike Maughan, head of global insights at Qualtrics, the four core experiences used to be managed separately by corporations, if at all. But the Qualtrics XM platform integrates them and manages them simultaneously, helping companies gain a holistic view of customers and develop accurate customer profiles.

"In every instance, the focus is on breaking down data silos to make sure organizations are able to provide the best experience possible," Maughan says. "For example, we all know that how employees act directly impacts the experience customers have. A common saying is that disengaged employees are firing your customers."

The single, integrated Qualtrics data analysis platform allows organizations to "bridge the experience gap." To illustrate, consider a 2005 Bain and Company study that revealed that 80 percent of CEOs believed their company was delivering a superior customer experience. However, notes Maughan, "when their customers were asked if they felt they were receiving a superior customer experience, only eight percent agreed." Qualtrics XM narrows this experience gap by measuring stakeholder experiences to establish a baseline, predicting and prioritizing stakeholder needs, initiating a plan of action, and tracking progress in narrowing the gap between the baseline and the need. If used correctly, the XM platform drives continuous experience improvement.

AI Comes to Experience Management

A few years ago, the company introduced Qualtrics iQ as part of the XM platform. This innovative new product uses artificial intelligence (AI) to automatically identify trends, statistically validate key consumer drivers, and identify the appropriate statistical tests that should be used to deliver results. "Qualtrics iQ hunts down experience gaps automatically, predicting what customers want and helping organizations find and address issues before they negatively impact the business," says Webb Stevens, head of product at Qualtrics. "Machine learning helps automate tasks that were previously time consuming or impossible to scale, like analyzing open text feedback or finding key drivers buried in your data."

With XM and innovations such as Qualtrics iQ, Qualtrics clients are seeing real results and strong return on marketing investment. JetBlue choose Qualtrics because it offered total control over all phases of customer experience management. By combining relational data (brand purchase drivers) with transactional data (experience and satisfaction) into a centralized hub, JetBlue was able to easily identify the biggest customer impact areas and immediately execute changes that made a difference.

For example, JetBlue found that the vast majority of passengers didn't care about free bags, instead preferring cheaper ticket prices. Based on the data, JetBlue increased revenue by rolling out different rate structures and pricing options. In Philadelphia, JetBlue was able to trace dissatisfaction to the lack of airport shops and amenities open in the early morning hours. The fix was simple—pass out water, juice, and coffee at the gate. And in another airport, negative customer comments and lower-than-normal satisfaction scores at a particular gate were traced to a defective terminal speaker, making it impossible for waiting passengers to hear gate agent announcements. JetBlue immediately sent an automated alert to the airport maintenance crew. The problem was fixed the same day, and survey responses returned to normal.

Cases of client success using Qualtrics's XM platform are abundant. This year, Morgan Stanley bestowed its prestigious CTO Innovation award on Qualtrics. "We're putting clients first in everything we do, and Qualtrics has become an integral partner in our journey," said Chris Kovel, managing director at the global financial services firm. "Starting out as a satisfaction scoring tool for our institutional clients, we are now leveraging their insights to gauge the perceptions of our external and internal clients across the business, which will ultimately shape and improve our overall performance as a firm."

Today, many companies are competing for a slice of the growing experience management industry. Not the least of these is IBM, which applies its Watson artificial and predictive intelligence capabilities to experience analysis. But Qualtrics argues that IBM's technology is too complex, insisting that its XM software provides predictive intelligence that is more easily consumed by the customer experience masses.

Clients seem to agree. By making market research more comprehensive as well as more accessible, the company has turned a profit and doubled its revenue each year since it made its online survey software available to the public. The company has resisted selling out to another company multiple times, refusing offers as high as $500 million. That decision proved farsighted—Qualtrics was recently valued at $2.8 billion. As long as Qualtrics continues to innovate its experience management products in meaningful ways, it will continue to be the one that other companies follow.

Questions for Discussion

1. How does Qualtrics fit in with the big data trend?
2. Discuss how Qualtrics's services facilitate the discovery of customer insights.
3. Which components of the marketing information system do Qualtrics's tools facilitate?
4. Discuss Qualtrics's tools in the context of research approaches.
5. What challenges does Qualtrics face in the future?

Sources: "Qualtrics Selected for Prestigious Innovation Award by Morgan Stanley," *PR Newswire*, June 07, 2018, www.prnewswire.com/news-releases/qualtrics-selected-for-prestigious-innovation-award-by-morgan-stanley-300661768.html; Ee Chien Chua, "Professors Find Success," *Daily Universe*, March 12, 2013, universe.byu.edu/2013/03/12/nutty-wealthy-professors/; Alex Konrad, "Qualtrics Inches Closer to IPO by Acquiring the Startup Behind Ratings for Postmates and Uber," *Forbes*, April 12, 2018, www.forbes.com/sites/alexkonrad/2018/04/12/qualtrics-acquires-delighted/#4cff93eb27a2; Jennifer Post, "Experience Management Software: What Small Businesses Need to Know," *Business News Daily*, May 18, 2018, www.businessnewsdaily.com/10791-experience-management-software-small-business.html; and information from www.qualtrics.com/customers/jetblue/ and www.qualtrics.com/about/, accessed October 2018.

Company Case 5

Spanx: Changing the Way an Industry Thinks about Underwear

As Sara Blakely got ready to go out for a night on the town, she stood looking into her closet, trying to decide what to wear. There were her favorite dress pants—an elegant pair of unlined cream-colored Arden B. designer slacks. She loved them enough that she'd paid full price for them—$98—a real stretch given the modest income she earned selling fax machines to businesses. But there they hung, almost never worn. And on that evening, they would remain in her closet.

Why would Sara rarely wear her favorite article of clothing? "Every time I would go to wear them, you could see the undergarment," Blakely reveals. "Regular underwear left a panty line. The thong wasn't a great solution—it also left marks that you could see. And then, the shapewear—the girdles were so thick and overdone!" Thick waistbands caused ripples, and ungainly leg bands left rumples.

There had to be something that could smooth Blakely's shape to the point where she would feel comfortable wearing the pants she loved so much. This line of thinking led her to invent Spanx—shapewear that revolutionized women's undergarments and other apparel.

Blakely was not alone in experiencing the dilemma of garment–body compatibility. Women of all shapes and sizes often felt the same way. And this dilemma was nothing new. For centuries, women have wrestled with how to get their bodies to fit into fashionable clothing. From the 16th century through the 19th century, women commonly used corsets made of cloth and reinforced with wood, whale bone, or even steel. Such undergarments cinched women's waists so tightly they impaired the ability to breath properly and could even cause a broken rib or two. By the 1900s, girdles gave women some relief and became a standard undergarment. But they were still thick, uncomfortable, and inconvenient and didn't conform to changing fashions of the latter 20th century.

As a working professional, Blakely wore pantyhose every day on the job. But when it came to stepping out on her own time, like most women, she detested them. Although hosiery had been standard attire for women from the 1920s through the 1960s, it began to diminish in popularity as the feminist movement gave women the power to take control of their attire. Too hot, inconvenient, prone to runs, and generally considered unattractive by modern standards (especially with open-toed shoes), hosiery began a long and slow decline during the late 1900s.

That's when Blakely had her epiphany. Control-top pantyhose provided a valuable benefit. Although not perfect, they smoothed out her midsection to the point that her favorite cream-colored pants looked good on her. But what to do about the ugly foot seams and reinforcements that showed through her open-toed shoes? Sara simply cut out the feet. That wouldn't work for skirts, but for pants, no one would be the wiser. So why couldn't someone design an undergarment that would take the "control top" concept to a higher level, perfecting the midsection and eliminating the feet and lower legs?

A Focus Group of One

With no good options, many women often chose not to wear or even buy certain articles of clothing. So Blakely got to work on her miracle garment. She performed exhaustive patent research to ensure that no one else had the rights to the type of garment she had in mind. Satisfied that the path was clear, she tested the potential market. She went into the women's department at a local Neiman Marcus and asked a saleswoman if she thought there was a need for the type of shapewear she envisioned. The woman's face lit up as she told Blakely that many of her customers already created their own homemade versions of such an undergarment by cutting the feet out of control top panty hose.

That was all the data Blakely needed to design a prototype. With the prototype created and no money to produce the garment in any quantity, she set out find a manufacturer that would take a chance for a small piece of the action. One after another, doors slammed in her face. "The manufacturing plants didn't get it at all," Blakely recalls. "I found it interesting that all I was meeting with were men, and then it kind of became clear to me why [women] had been so uncomfortable for so long—the people that were making [undergarments] weren't spending all day in them!" Blakely also faced the challenge that her idea threatened to upend an entire industry that had been looking at a product in one way, even as sales for the product continued to decline year after year.

But after asking each of his three adult daughters what they thought of Blakely's prototype, Sam Kaplan, co-owner of hosiery manufacturer Highland Mills, called Blakely back. Although Kaplan still could not entirely wrap his head around the idea, Blakely's conviction and his daughters' reactions were enough for him to take a gamble. Blakely decided to call her creation "Spanx"—kind of funny, kind of naughty, all about the rear end. And having heard somewhere that incorrect spellings for products do better than real words, she thought Spanx seemed like the perfect brand name.

Blakely's next hurdle was finding retail outlets. Her first stop was the corporate headquarters for Neiman Marcus. But during the initial sales meeting, Blakely could tell that she wasn't getting through to the woman in charge of purchasing hosiery for the premium retailer. So Blakely took a big chance. She invited the buyer to go with her to the restroom. The woman was taken aback, but Blakely clarified, "I want to show you my own product before and after." Once in the restroom, Blakely modeled the very cream-colored pants that started the whole project, first without Spanx and then with them. The Neiman Marcus buyer placed an order on the spot for Spanx to be sold on a trial basis in seven of the chain's stores.

It's All about Context

With a quality product, a catchy brand name, and a premium retailer all lined up, one might think that consumer would be a given. After all, women everywhere were begging for such a product. But Blakely found that changing the mind-set of customers was just as challenging as getting through to manufacturers and retailers. Sara shipped Spanx to Neiman Marcus in packaging designed by a friend—bright red with stylish illustrations and the motto "Don't worry, we've got your butt covered." Neiman placed Spanx in the hosiery department, allotting a single slot near the bottom of one rack. Combined with a price tag that was many times higher than even the most expensive pantyhose, Spanx sat on the rack just as Blakely's cream-colored pants had stayed in her closet.

If Spanx was going to change how women perceived undergarments and their clothing, Blakely would have to take matters into her own hands. Without asking permission, Blakely went into each of the seven Neiman Marcus stores that carried Spanx and moved them from the hosiery department to the ready-to-wear department. After all, hosiery was designed for how it looked on women's legs. Spanx was designed for what it did to women's abdomens. Blakely created small displays from racks she had purchased, complete with "before/after" pictures, locating her product next to cash registers. Spanx started to sell.

Blakely realized that to change their perceptions, women not only had to see what Spanx could do, they had to consider it in the right context. With no money to advertise, Blakely went about promoting her product any way she could. She sent samples to every celebrity on the planet in hopes one or more would start wearing Spanx and get the word out. She sent multiple gift baskets to Oprah Winfrey, and one day Oprah's hairdresser finally draped a pair of Spanx over the chair in Oprah's dressing room. Oprah not only wore the product and sang its praises on her internationally distributed show, she also selected Spanx as her favorite product of the year. Having battled with weight gain and loss for years, Oprah felt comfortable and confident in Spanx. "Oprah made it okay to talk about whether your bra fits, and that shapewear is the fastest 10-minute fix you'll ever find," said one online retailing executive.

With Oprah's endorsement, Spanx took off. Other A-list celebrities such as Kate Winslet, Brooke Shields, and Julia Roberts started strutting their Spanx-clad bodies across the media, singing the shapewear's praises for slimming panty lines under unforgiving couture gowns. In one red-carpet interview, Gwyneth Paltrow even claimed that Spanx helped her post-baby body look better.

Neiman Marcus put Spanx in all their stores, followed by Saks Fifth Avenue and other retailers. But Blakely knew Spanx needed to reach more audiences. So Blakely took Spanx to QVC, ignoring the advice of many that doing so would kill the premium image of the Spanx brand that had developed while the product sold only in high-end department stores. But Blakely disagreed, going on the home shopping outlet herself to ensure that she could control the message. On its first appearance, Spanx sold 8,000 units in five minutes.

Now, after only 20 years, Sara Blakely maintains 100 percent ownership of the company she started. Today, Spanx makes all kinds of shapewear including bodysuits, camis, slips, hosiery, and leggings. With expansion into bras, panties, shorts, and jeans—not to mention sub-brands such as Bra-llelujah! and Slim Cognito—Spanx is now a full-line brand of women's apparel. The company has even started making shapewear for men. Although revenue numbers are closely held, Blakely's personal net worth is an indication of the company's success. In 2012, only 14 years after Spanx first went on sale, *Forbes* named her the youngest self-made female billionaire.

More important, Spanx has given new life to an industry once in decline—experts predict that by 2022, the global shapewear market will be worth $5.5 billion a year. With every apparel company from traditional undergarment brands to Nike and Under Armour now making shapewear, Spanx has changed the way companies view and women shop for clothing. "Shapewear is the canvas and the clothes are the art," Blakely declares. "I know things are right on me by the way I feel." Spanx and shapewear in general have now given new life to ill-fitting clothing that have sat dormant in the back of women's closets.

Questions for Discussion

1. Of the factors that influence consumer behavior, which category or categories (cultural, social, personal, or psychological) best explain the success of Spanx? Why?
2. Choose the specific consumer behavior factor (for example, culture, family, occupation, attitudes) that most accounts for Spanx acceptance by the market.
3. Based on the principles of consumer behavior, explain the challenges faced by Spanx in its early years.
4. Discuss the buyer decision process as it relates to women and shopping for clothing. How did Spanx change the way women go through the steps of the buyer decision process?
5. Has Spanx changed the world? Explain.

Sources: Danielle Wiener-Bronne, "She Was Too Short to Play Goofy. Then She Invented Spanx. Now She's a Billionaire," *CNN Money*, April 2, 2018, http://money.cnn.com/2018/04/02/news/companies/sara-blakely-rebound/index.html; Ali Montag, "How an Embarrassing Moment Led to Spanx Billionaire Sara Blakely's Huge Success," *CNBC*, August 15, 2017, www.cnbc.com/2017/08/15/billionaire-sarah-blakelys-embarrassing-moment-led-to-spanx-success.html; Lynn Yaeger, "The Bottom Line: A Profile on Spanx Founder Sara Blakely," *Vogue*, March 19, 2012, www.vogue.com/article/the-bottom-line-spanx-founder-sara-blakely; Guy Raz, "Spanx: Sara Blakely," *How I Built This*, September 11, 2016, https://one.npr.org/?sharedMediaId=493169696:493311384; "Compression Wear and Shapewear Market to Reach $5,576 Million, Globally, by 2022," *Allied Market Research*, www.alliedmarketresearch.com/press-release/compression-wear-shapewear-market.html, accessed October 2018.

Company Case 6

5-Hour Energy: Hours of Energy without the Beverage

You've no doubt heard of 5-Hour Energy—the small red bottles filled with an energy-infused elixir, located alongside the candy and gum near the checkout at most grocery and convenience stores. Chances are good that you've tried one. You may even be among the more than 4 million people in the United States who have collectively consumed 9 million bottles of 5-Hour Energy in just the past seven days. This upstart brand has had a huge impact on the beverage industry. How did 5-Hour Energy become so big so fast? By targeting the right kinds of customers with a product that gives them exactly what they want at precisely the right moment.

Discovering an Unmet Need

It all started in the early 2000s. India-born Manoj Bhargava had sold his company—an outdoor furniture components maker—and retired to Michigan with his wife and son. But after only a couple of months, he grew tired of doing nothing and began looking for a product he could license and turn into the "next big thing." With that in mind, he attended a natural products trade show in Anaheim, California.

Amid meetings with numerous companies, he happened upon the booth for an energy drink developed by a group of PhDs. The 16-ounce concoction claimed to boost energy for hours. Knowing he faced meetings until 10 p.m. that evening, Bhargava was concerned that he not would be able to stay awake, let alone pay attention. So, he tried a can of the energy drink. The results were almost instantaneous. "For the next six or seven hours, I was in great shape," Bhargava recalls. Not only was he wide awake, but his levels of focus and awareness were enhanced. "I thought, 'Wow, this is amazing. I can sell this.'"

But when he talked with the drink's owners to discuss potential partnerships, Bhargava learned that they were not interested in selling or even licensing the rights for the product. He looked over the label and made a mental note of its ingredients and thought, "How hard can it be?" Whereas most people with no science or nutrition background would never dream of trying to come up with their own recipe for a product intended for human consumption, Bhargava was not deterred. He got to work setting up his own lab and forming a company he called Living Essentials.

Bhargava quickly realized that a 16-ounce beverage would not succeed in a market saturated with long-standing brands peddled by deep-pocketed companies. As an energy-giving beverage, the new product would have to compete for refrigerator and shelf space with an ever-increasing batch of brands led by Red Bull. It would also face off against some of the most established brands in the world put out by the likes of the Coca-Cola and PepsiCo.

But Bhargava's new concoction didn't have to be a 16-ounce beverage or, for that matter, a beverage at all. "If I'm tired, am I also thirsty? Is that like having a headache and a stomachache," mused Bhargava. After all, Tylenol didn't sell a 16-ounce single serving version of its pain-killing product. As he developed the formula through trial and error—he always tried the experimental versions out on himself—he contemplated the customer he was trying to reach and how the product could be positioned to appeal to them.

Profile of an Unfulfilled Customer

In defining that customer, he thought about himself at the trade show. He needed energy to stay awake. But he also needed to be able to pay attention—to focus on what was happening as he met with various people from various companies. He needed energy and focus quickly, preferably in a form that wouldn't weigh him down or produce unwanted side effects. Once he thought in those terms, he considered other types of people who also need those benefits—people working two jobs to make ends meet, truck drivers who spend hours at a time behind the wheel, the Wall Street trader grinding out 16-hour days, or the person who works on a Hollywood movie set. All those people have two things in common—they work long hours, and they need to be able to focus on their work.

From his own experience and observation, Bhargava knew that energy drinks, caffeinated soft drinks, and even coffee all focused on providing energy and the ability to stay awake. But consuming enough of any of those beverages to get the right amount of energy put a lot of liquid in people's bellies, tending to weigh them down and make them feel sluggish. Additionally, product's containing sugar might produce an initial jolt of energy, but that spike is short-lived, followed by a carbohydrate-induced crash into grogginess.

With the target customer in mind, Bhargava set the form—a sugar-free two-ounce shot that contained enough caffeine—200 milligrams by some estimates—to produce a substantial boost in energy along with a blend of vitamins and amino acids known to increase the human brain's ability to focus. The small dose of liquid wasn't so much a beverage as it was a delivery system.

Positioning through the Marketing Mix

With the product's form established, Bhargava created the name: 5-Hour Energy—simple and functional, communicating the product benefit exactly. The product's form was important for ease of consumption and for differentiating it from the beverage options. But it was necessary for another key component of Bhargava's marketing mix strategy—to get the product into stores in its own spot, away from the refrigerated beverages and right next to the cash registers.

The first retail chain that 5-Hour Energy's marketing team targeted for distribution was GNC—the largest chain of vitamin and nutrition stores in the country. 5-Hour Energy was a perfect fit for GNC's customers—fitness- and health-oriented people who spent hours working out each day on top of their jobs and other life pursuits. GNC's buyers agreed, placing 5-Hour Energy in a small display next to the cash register.

After the first week, however, 5-Hour Energy sold only 200 bottles across GNC's 1,200 stores. The premium price of more than $3 for the little shot was a hurdle. But Bhargava wasn't worried. He knew that the product was sound, the location was perfect, and the price was right to establish an image as a quality product. His hunches were right. After six months, 5-Hour Energy was selling 10,000 bottles a week.

That success gained 5-Hour Energy entry into Walgreen's, CVS, and various convenience store chains throughout the country. With increased distribution, the company ran ads on TV and the internet. The ads were simple—even low budget—in appearance. But the message was right on. "You know what 2:30 in the afternoon feels like, right? Sleepy? Groggy? Dying for a nap?" said a young, hip, white-collar worker, navigating his way around a typical corporate office. "What do you do? Run for the coffee? Grab a soda? But how long does that last, before you're back for more?" After detailing the benefits provided by 5-Hour Energy, the ad ended with the tagline "Hours of energy now, no 2:30 feeling later."

Adding multiple flavors in regular, extra strength, and even decaf forms, 5-Hour Energy rose to new heights with distribution in Walmart and every other major U.S. grocery chain. By that time, many of other companies were taking notice of the upstart brand and opportunities in the new energy shot category. If 5-Hour Energy had been created by a guy with no background in the business, they could do it better.

Soon, Coca-Cola, Pepsi, Red Bull, Monster, and host of other established beverage makers to begin distributing their own versions of the two-ounce shot, pressing for their share of limited counter space next to cash registers. And they weren't the only new entrants. At one point, there were literally hundreds of brands of two-ounce shots on the market, most from small, opportunistic companies looking to score a quick buck. Almost all came in at cheaper price points than 5-Hour Energy. And the deep-pocketed veteran brands threw their muscle into distribution channels and promoting their newest offerings.

Initially, the new competition made a dent in 5-Hour Energy's fortunes. Within months, the brand's market share dropped from 93 percent to 67 percent. "Everybody tried their products," reports Bhargava. "However, the one thing they all forgot was, you have to have a great product." Bhargava remains a big believer in product quality. "It's not the little bottle. It's not the placement. It's the product. You can con people one time, but nobody pays $3 twice."

As the energy shot market has evolved, Bhargava has been proven right. Even as the market has continued to grow in overall volume, competitors have dropped be the wayside. With little repeat purchase and not enough incentive to stay in the game, even the big brands have decided the battle isn't worth it.

Today, 5-Hour Energy again commands more than 90 percent of the category it created. The number two brand? NVE Pharmaceutical's "Stacker," at just over 3 percent of the market. When asked what other brand 5-Hour Energy most resembles, Bhargava replies, "WD-40." He considers the two brands to be similar in that they are both brands without categories. "Usually, to be a category, there have to be at least two major players. This shot area... it's really not so much a category as a brand."

As a private company, Living Essentials doesn't disclose its performance. But analysis of scanner data puts 5-Hour Energy's annual retail sales at more than $1.2 billion—a number that has gone up every year since the brand's inception. About 25 percent of that retail figure filters down to Living Essential's net profit. That's enough for Bhargava to have amassed a net worth that analysts put somewhere between $1.5 billion and $4 billion. And yet, with its rapid growth and market domination, Bhargava sees much more potential before the market becomes saturated. "If we sold 5-Hour Energy to everyone who needs it, we'd be selling twenty times more."

Questions for Discussion

1. Consider the variables commonly used to segment markets. Which of these best represents how the makers of 5-Hour Energy segmented the market?
2. Which market targeting strategy is 5-Hour Energy following? Justify your answer.
3. Write a positioning statement for 5-Hour Energy.
4. What are the potential challenges 5-Hour Energy faces in the future?

Sources: "Do 5-Hour Energy Shots Actually Work?," *Stack*, June 29, 2018, www.stack.com/a/do-5-hour-energy-shots-actually-work; Clare O'Connor, "The Mystery Monk Makes Billions with 5-Hour Energy,"

Forbes, February 8, 2012, www.forbes.com/sites/clareoconnor/2012/02/08/manoj-bhargava-the-mystery-monk-making-billions-with-5-hour-energy/#30b89c0927ae; Robert Klara, "How This Tiny, Caffeine-Packed Bottle Became the Boost of Choice for 7 Million Americans," *Adweek*, October 3, 2016, pp. 35–36; and information from https://5hourenergy.com/facts/, www.statista.com/statistics/477374/5-hour-energy-consumption-usa/, and https://one.npr.org/?sharedMediaId=519514841:519712175, accessed July 2018.

Company Case 7

MINI: Focus on the Essential—Maximize the Experience

Long-term brands face a balancing act. On the one hand, they must remain true to the characteristics that endear them to their throngs of loyal customers. On the other hand, the longer a brand remains, the more it must develop new attributes that appeal to new generations of customers. Maintaining this balance between consistency and relevancy is difficult. Brands that can do this for decades are truly special. Take BMW's MINI—the modern representation of the iconic British people's car. MINIs continue to roll off the assembly line after almost 60 years. Not only has MINI remained true to the original brand while keeping up with changing customer dynamics, it has done so despite having been owned by six different companies.

A Classic Is Born

In 1956, the Suez Crisis brought on a major worldwide fuel shortage. As a result, the demand for small, fuel-efficient vehicles spiked. The British Motor Corporation (BMC) gave Sir Alec Issigonis the job of designing a vehicle with a unique challenge—minimize dimensions and amenities while maximizing efficiency and utility. That challenge became the heart and soul of the MINI brand.

Measuring only 10 feet long, four and a half feet wide, and four and a half feet high, the original MINI rode on tiny 10-inch wheels. But with its wheels pushed out to the extreme corners and its 40-horsepower engine mounted sideways, the tiny car could seat four people comfortably with room in the back for cargo. It was fuel efficient and boasted a sturdy frame and suspension. The innovative design of the original MINI gave it nimble reflexes and go kart–like handing. Available in a variety of basic colors, the car offered optional niceties such as adjustable seats, opening rear side windows, rubber mats, and a heater.

Customers were thrilled with the MINI and its small-on-size-big-on-function design. Those initial characteristics of the brand were soon enhanced even further through a partnership between BMC and John Cooper, the legendary Formula One driver and race car designer. Recognizing the MINI's potential as a race car based on its small size, low weight, and stiff chassis, Cooper designed performance modifications for the drivetrain, suspension, and brakes. Cooper's hunches were right. MINI won the Monte Carlo Rally three times between 1958 and 1962 against veteran racing brands such as Ferrari, Maserati, and Lotus. With Cooper performance modifications added to the options list, the MINI was poised to deliver more value than ever.

Based on its design and options, key characteristics of the brand began to emerge. Round headlights and a "smiley face" bumper contributed to a friendly and fun brand personality. As the options offered by BMC and by aftermarket companies evolved, MINI soon became one of the most customizable car brands, giving it a strong appeal to those who wanted a car that would express their individuality.

MINI fast became a favorite of the young and the young at heart—the perfect blend of practical and cool that was irresistible to everyone, regardless of class and culture. MINI's popularity really took off as iconic celebrities became fans. Model Twiggy and actor Steve McQueen were photographed driving MINIs. The car played a central role in the 1969 Michael Caine film *The Italian Job*. And all four Beatles were counted among the growing body of MINI owners.

Under BMC during its first decade, the MINI was sold in coupe, wagon, and van versions as a sub-brand of various marks (Morris MINI-Minor and the Austin Seven MINI, among others). In 1969, MINI became a standalone brand. But as BMC experienced financial difficulties in the late 1960s, MINI bounced from one company to another for the better part of 25 years—first to British Motor Holdings, then British Leyland, followed by the Rover Group. The Rover Group was acquired by British Aerospace before finding its final resting place with BMW in 1994.

Although the MINI's pedigree is confusing, the car changed very little, staying true to the original design. But after 41 years, safety and emissions regulations as well as changing consumer needs brought MINI production to a halt. In October 2000, MINI number 5,387,862—a red Cooper Sport—was driven off the line and immediately parked in the Heritage Motor Centre in Gaydon, England, right alongside the first MINI ever made—a tribute to the most popular British car of all time. Just one year before, a jury of 126 automotive experts from 32 countries had voted the MINI the runner-up as they selected Ford's Model T as the Car of the Century.

Redesigning an Iconic Brand

Although the writing was on the wall signaling the end of the original MINI design, BMW was hard at work designing its replacement. The brand had far too much equity and heritage to let it die. However, BMW faced a challenge in recreating one of the most iconic automobiles ever made. Modern customers called for more—more power, larger size, safer design, and more features and options. But the heritage of the brand demanded an automobile for the new millennium that was unmistakably a MINI.

In 2001, the first of the new two-door MINI hatchbacks rolled off the assembly line in England and hit showroom floors. Although the length and width of the new MINI were substantially greater than the original (22 inches longer and 11 inches wider), the new MINI was very small relative to average vehicles of the time. Various engine options delivered between 75 and 245 horsepower. BMWs recreation delivered on fuel efficiency, practicality, and driving performance. With nimble reflexes and rally-car handling, it was easy to drive and park. Yet taller-than-average occupants found plenty of headroom and legroom, not to mention superb visibility in any direction. Round headlights and a happy-face grill gave the new design a look that was unmistakably MINI.

Sticking with the original MINI's appeal to individuality, BMW provided a lengthy list of options with various wheel packages, paint schemes, and latex appliques that could be fitted to give the roof, mirrors, hood, and hatch seemingly endless appearance options. Within a few years, the two-door hatch spawned convertible and wagon variants.

The goal of the new MINI's branding was to sell "lifestyles defined by freedom, good cheer, and camaraderie." To that end, MINI unleashed the "Let's Motor" campaign, employing a rich mix of unconventional media, carefully integrated to create personality for the car and excited buzz among consumers. The company put MINIs in all kinds of imaginative places. It mounted them atop Ford SUVs and drove them around 22 major cities, highlighting the car's sensible size. It set up "MINI Ride" displays outside department stores, featuring an actual MINI that looked like a children's ride. Displays in airport terminals featured oversize newspaper vending machines showing the undersized MINI and proclaiming, "Makes everything else seem too big."

The car was also promoted on the internet, in ads painted on city buildings, and on baseball card–like handouts at auto shows. In addition, BMW created MINI games, MINI booklets, and MINI suitcases. It worked closely with selected magazines to create memorable print ads—like the cardboard foldout of a MINI in *Wired* magazine that suggested readers assemble it and drive it around their desks making "putt-putt" noises.

The "Let's Motor" campaign not only won awards, it was a smashing success in achieving BMW's goals. Together with company-sponsored owner events, MINI developed a cult-like following of devoted owners. Although the new MINI didn't please all purists, many were impressed. Like the original, the new MINI drew drivers of all demographics despite the fact that BMW targeted drivers between the ages of 20 and 30 who enjoyed the pleasure of driving. Sales were initially strong and steadily increased to more than 300,000 units sold in 2012—a figure that rivaled the best sales years ever of the classic MINI.

The Soul of the Brand Lives On

With the MINI's popularity stronger than ever, in the summer of 2015 BMW announced that it would again reinvent the brand, complete with new designs, a new logo, and a new positioning for its cars. "Things are going extremely well for MINI, so why is it reinventing itself now?" asked BMW board director Peter Schwarzenbauer, addressing the question on everyone's minds. "To explain this, we have to look at a comparison between 2001 and 2015." BMW had discovered that its target customer—affluent urban dwellers in their 20s and 30s who enjoy fun, freedom, and individuality—had changed considerably. From a time when consumers were brimming with confidence from a booming world economy, "Rapid technological change, geo-political uncertainty, and the financial crash of 2008 have combined to fundamentally alter consumer behaviors," Schwarzenbauer explained. "People are more focused on 'the essential' and I believe that no other car brand is better positioned than MINI to meet this new focus on things that count."

The new MINI logo was toned down from the 3D version to a more simple 2D black and white rendition. MINI's approach to advertising was also simplified. Gone were the tongue-in-cheek creatives that broke with convention. Instead, new MINI ads were simpler, focusing on the features and functions of the cars. The MINI website was also updated with videos and visuals that helped customers better understand the benefits of the car. These branding changes were designed to communicate that MINI was authentic, practical, and ready to play a bigger role in society.

As part of the new branding philosophy, BMW planned to roll out complete revisions of each of its five models—now referring to them as the "Five Superheroes"—the Hardtop 2 Door, the Hardtop 4 Door, the Convertible, the wagon-esque Clubman, and the all-wheel drive Countryman crossover. All models would receive substantial technological updates. In a departure from the past, branding efforts for each new model would emphasize a unique identity, including color schemes and aesthetics tailored to each car. The purpose of this approach was to create a MINI brand with five product lines that appealed to a broader range of customers. For example, the Clubman was aimed at attracting more families to the brand. Advertising focused on the car's functionality and elegant design. And at over 14 feet in length and six feet in width, it was MINI's largest and roomiest car ever.

Did this brand redesign signal the abandonment of the MINI brand original values? Not according to Marc Lengning, head of brand management at MINI. "With our five 'superheroes' we want to make it very clear that each of those cars has its own character," Lengning explains. "The Clubman is the most extreme example in terms of moving in a direction away from the past, but you should still expect a lot of fun from the different models as each character emerges." Those at the company emphasize that MINI's brand values are still in line with the minimizing, practical instincts of Issigonis on the one hand contrasted with the maximizing, performance-driven approach of Cooper on the other.

"MINI has always been about new ideas, inspiration, and a lot of passion, and these things are not going to change," says Schwarzenbauer. This year, MINI has added customer MINI Connected Concierge services, wireless smartphone charging, and other options like anti-dazzle adaptive headlights with a matrix high beam—a rarity on small city cars. And in an even bolder move, buyers of new MINIs can custom design interior appointments like dashboard inserts, side scuttles, and door sills that are produced on 3D printers and installed in the car before the buyer takes ownership.

Based on MINI's recent sales numbers, it seems that the new direction is right on the money. For each of the past three years, MINI has set a worldwide record, moving more than 370,000 vehicles into garages around the world last year. As MINI moves boldly into the future with efforts to stay relevant in a changing world, it must also cling to the qualities that have made it iconic for so long. The folks at MINI seem to get that. "Mini crosses cultures, class, gender, and age," says MINI's head of design, Anders Warming. "Anyone who buys a MINI feels immediately younger while driving it. It just puts a smile on your face."

Questions for Discussion

1. Discuss how MINI has endured for 60 years as a brand despite being owned by various companies.
2. Does MINI have high brand equity? Explain.
3. Over the years, has MINI been positioned based on attributes, benefits, or values? Explain.
4. Do you think BMW is taking MINI in the right direction with its current branding strategy? Why or why not?

Sources: Jonathan Bacon, "Mini: Reinventing a Brand Icon," *Marketing Week*, July 8, 2015, www.marketingweek.com/2015/07/08/how-mini-is-reinventing-itself-to-remain-iconic/; Nargess Banks, "New MINI as Personal Gadget: Tech Advanced with Novel 3D Print Service," *Forbes*, January 10, 2018, www.forbes.com/sites/nargessbanks/2018/01/10/new-mini/#7b93db3177d8; Hannah Elliott, "Fifty Years of Mini Love," *Forbes*, July 29, 2009, www.forbes.com/2009/07/29/bmw-mini-cooper-lifestyle-vehicles-mini-car-50.html#2a21eb2ccb74; Gabriel Bridger, "2017 MINI Sales Had a Record Year," *Motoring File*, January 12, 2018, www.motoringfile.com/2018/01/12/2017-mini-sales-hit-record-worldwide/.

Company Case 8

Bose: Better Products by Focusing on the Product

In a survey by brand strategy firm Lippincott, the most trusted brand in consumer electronics was not Apple. Nor was it Samsung, Sony, or Microsoft. It was Bose, the still relatively small, privately held corporation that has been making innovative audio devices for more than 50 years. In consumer electronics, Bose's $4 billion worth of annual headphone, speaker, and other product sales is "relatively small"—think Apple, which rang up $228 billion worth of techno gadgets and goodies. But when it comes to the passion customers feel for their brands, the Massachusetts-based technology company outshines even Apple. Bose forges that deep consumer connection based on the brand's design simplicity and brilliant functionality.

Bose adheres religiously to a set of values that have guided the company since its origins. Most companies today focus heavily on building revenues, profits, and stock prices. They try to outdo competitors by differentiating product lines with features and attributes that other companies don't have. Although Bose doesn't ignore such factors, its competitive advantage is rooted in its unique corporate philosophy—the product comes first. "We are not in it strictly to make money," says a Bose spokesperson. "The business is almost a secondary consideration." From its earliest days, the strategy at Bose has been to make the most innovative products by focusing on research and design.

The Bose Philosophy

To understand Bose the company, you must first look at Bose the man. In the 1950s, founder Amar Bose was working on his third degree at the Massachusetts Institute of Technology. He had a keen interest in research and studied various areas of electrical engineering. He also had a strong interest in music. When he purchased his first hi-fi system—a model that he believed had the best specifications—he was disappointed in the system's ability to reproduce realistic sound. It was then that Bose began heavily researching the problem to find his own solution. Thus began a stream of research that would ultimately lead to the founding of the Bose Corporation in 1964. It also led to the development of the long-standing Bose slogan, "Better Sound Through Research."

From those early days, Amar Bose worked around certain core principles that have guided the philosophy of the company. In conducting his first research on speakers and sound, he did something that has since been repeated time and time again at Bose. He ignored existing technologies and started entirely from scratch, something not common in product development strategies.

In another departure from typical corporate strategies, Amar Bose put all of the privately held company's profits back into research and development, a practice that reflected his avid love of research and his drive to produce the highest-quality products. In doing so, he also bypassed the process of figuring out what customers wanted. Instead, Bose kept research confined to the laboratory and centered on the technical specifications of creating a superior product.

Today, this approach is considered heresy in the innovation world. Amar pursued this approach because he could. He often pointed out that publicly held companies have long lists of constraints that don't apply to privately held companies, noting that "if I worked for another company, I would have been fired a long time ago." For this reason, Bose always vowed that he would never take the company public. "Going public for me would have been the equivalent of losing the company. My real interest is research—that's the excitement—and I wouldn't have been able to do long-term projects with Wall Street breathing down my neck."

Innovating the Bose Way

The company that started so humbly now has a breadth of product lines beyond its core home audio line. Additional lines target a variety of applications that captured Amar Bose's creative attention over the years, including military, automotive, homebuilding/remodeling, aviation, and professional and commercial sound systems. It even has a division that markets testing equipment to research institutions, universities, medical device companies, and engineering companies worldwide. The following are just a few of the products that illustrate the innovative breakthroughs produced by the company.

Speakers

Bose's first product was a speaker introduced in 1965. Expecting to sell $1 million worth of speakers that first year, Bose made 60 but sold only 40. The original Bose speaker evolved into the 901 Direct/Reflecting speaker system launched in 1968. That speaker system was designed around the concept that live sound reaches the human ear via direct as well as reflected channels (off walls, ceilings, and other objects). The speakers featured a completely unorthodox configuration. Shaped like one-eighth of a sphere and mounted facing into a room's corner, the audio waves reflected off the walls and filled the room with sounds that seem to be everywhere but come from nowhere in particular. The speakers had no woofers or tweeters, composed instead of eight four-and-a-half-inch midrange drivers. The speakers were also very small compared to the high-end speakers of the day. The design came much closer to the essence and emotional impact of live music than anything else on the market and won immediate industry acclaim. The reflective approach, although groundbreaking at the time, is commonly found in home theater systems throughout the industry today.

Back then, however, Bose had a hard time convincing customers of the merits of these innovative speakers. At a time when size meant everything, the 901 series initially flopped. In 1968, a retail salesperson explained to Amar Bose why the speakers weren't selling:

> Look, I love your speaker but I cannot sell it because it makes me lose all my credibility as a salesman. I can't explain to anyone why the 901 doesn't have any woofers or tweeters. A man came in and saw the small size, and he started looking in the drawers for the speaker cabinets. I walked over to him, and he said, "Where are you hiding the woofer?" I said to him, "There is no woofer." So he said, "You're a liar," and he walked out.

To resolve this credibility problem, Bose developed another core competency—identifying and targeting the right customer with the products it was confident were superior to even the best offerings. For Bose, this generally meant targeting higher-income customers who aren't audio buffs but want a good product and are willing to pay a premium price for it. For the 901, this included using innovative display and demonstration tactics. Throughout its history, this approach has served Bose well. Although hardcore audiophiles scoff at Bose products as little more than smoke and mirrors, customers whose expectations haven't been shaped by preconceived specifications perceive Bose products to be exceptional. So far as the 901 is concerned, the product became so successful that Amar Bose credited the speaker series with building the company.

The list of major speaker innovations at Bose is a long one. In the 1970s, the company introduced concert-like sound in the bookshelf-size 301 Direct/Reflecting speaker system. Fourteen years of research lead to the development of acoustic waveguide speaker technology, a technology today found in the award-winning Wave music systems.

In the 1980s, the company again changed conventional thinking about the relationship between speaker size and sound. The Acoustimass system employed a remote subwoofer, enabling palm-size speakers to produce audio quality equivalent to that of much larger high-end systems. This concept is just another example of how Bose influenced the industry as the subwoofer/satellite speaker configuration became the standard for home theater systems.

Recently, Bose again introduced the state-of-the-art with the Computer MusicMonitor, a pair of compact computer speakers that rival the sound of three-piece subwoofer systems. And Bose has led the way in developing wireless speaker systems—a move quickly followed by all competitors. Not only was each of these speaker systems ground-breaking when introduced, each was so technologically advanced that Bose still sells it today—even the original 901 series. And with cutting-edge products in the categories of smart speakers, wearable speakers, portable speakers, multi-room speakers, and home theater, Bose continues to set the standard.

Headphones

Over a period of nearly two decades, Bose invested tens of million of dollars developing headset technology before ever selling a single pair. Now, headsets are one of the company's core products. Initially, Bose focused on noise reduction technologies to make headphones for pilots that would block out the high levels of noise interference generated by aircraft. Bose headphones didn't just muffle noise, they electronically canceled ambient noise so that pilots wearing them heard nothing but the intended sound coming through the phones. Bose quickly discovered that airline passengers could benefit as much as pilots from its headphone technology. Today, the Bose QuietComfort series, used in a variety of consumer applications, sets the benchmark in noise-canceling headphones. One journalist considers this product to be so significant that it made his list of "101 gadgets that changed the world"—right up there with aspirin, paper, and the light bulb.

Automotive Suspensions

Since 1980, the inquisitively innovative culture at Bose has even led the company down the path of developing automotive suspensions. Amar Bose's interest in suspensions dates back to the 1950s when he bought both a Citroen and a Pontiac, each riding on unconventional air suspension systems. Thereafter, he was obsessed with the engineering challenge of achieving good cornering capabilities without sacrificing a smooth ride.

The system Bose developed was based on electromagnetic motors installed at each wheel. Based on inputs from road sensing monitors, the motor could retract and extend almost instantaneously. For a bump in the road, the suspension reacted by "jumping" over it. For a pothole, the suspension allowed the wheel to extend downward, retracting it quickly enough that the pothole wouldn't be felt by passengers. In addition to these comfort-producing capabilities, the wheel motors were designed to keep a car completely level during an aggressive maneuver such as cornering or stopping. The system achieved Amar Bose's vision to provide better handling than any sports car while simultaneously giving vehicle occupants the most comfortable ride imaginable.

Bose invested more than $100 million over 30 years in the groundbreaking suspension. In the end, the system was simply too heavy and too expensive for use in passenger cars. Rather than shelf the product, however, Bose did what it has often done. It found a market where the technology could be used to provide genuine customer value. The company now markets a smaller, lighter version of the Bose suspension as the Bose Ride seat system for heavy-duty trucks. Surpassing current air ride and other conventional technologies in performance, its $6,000 price tag also exceeded the going price of a truck seat by five to ten times. Although most companies and drivers were skeptical at first, drivers reported that using Bose Ride was a transformational experience—like floating down the highway, detached from the truck, regardless of the road surface quality.

Bose's commitment to research and development has produced state-of-the-art products that have contributed to the trust that Bose customers have in the company. Customers know that the company cares more about their interests—about making the best products—than about maximizing profits. But for a company not driven by the bottom line, Bose does just fine in that department as well. In the personal headphone market, five companies control two-thirds of the global market. Bose is second only to Beats and is the only company besides the market leader with a double-digit share.

Amar Bose passed away a few years ago at the age of 83. With the passion of a genuine scientist, he worked every day well into his 80s. "He's got more energy than an 18-year-old," one of Bose' colleagues once revealed. "Every one of the naysayers only strengthens his resolve." This work ethic illustrates the passion of the man who shaped one of today's most innovative and most trusted companies. His philosophies have produced Bose's long list of groundbreaking innovations. Even today, the company continues to achieve success by following another one of Amar Bose's basic philosophies: "The potential size of the market? We really have no idea. We just know that we have a technology that's so different and so much better that many people will want it."

Questions for Discussion

1. Based on concepts discussed in this chapter, describe the factors that have contributed to Bose's new product success.
2. Is Bose's product development process customer centered? Explain.
3. How is Bose unique with respect to product life cycle management?
4. With respect to the product life cycle, what challenges does Bose face in managing its product portfolio?
5. Can Bose continue to maintain its innovative culture without Amar Bose?

Sources: "Apple's Next Big Thing Could Be High-End Headphones to Rival Beats and Bose," *Time*, March 5, 2018, http://time.com/5185613/apple-headphones-beats-bose/; "The Global Earphones and Headphones Market," *PRNewswire*, January 22, 2018, www.prnewswire.com/news-releases/the-global-earphones-and-headphones-market-is-expected-to-grow-at-a-cagr-of-731-during-20172023-300585974.html; DavidCarnoy, "Bose's New Beat," *CNET*, February 3, 2016, www.cnet.com/news/bose-new-beat-ceo-maresca-profile/; Brian Dumaine, "Amar Bose," *Fortune Small Business*, September 1, 2004, http://money.cnn.com/magazines/fsb/fsb_archive/2004/09/01/8184686/; Olga Kharif, "Selling Sound: Bose Knows," *Bloomberg*, May 14, 2006, www.bloomberg.com/news/articles/2006-05-14/selling-sound-bose-knows; and http://bose.com/en_us/about_bose.html, accessed October 2018.

Company Case 9

Trader Joe's: Cheap Gourmet—Putting a Special Twist on the Price-Value Equation

Apple Store openings aren't the only place where long lines form these days. Early on a summer morning, there's a crowd gathered, eagerly awaiting the opening of a Trader Joe's outpost. The waiting shoppers discuss all things Trader Joe's, including their favorite items. One customer suggests the chain will be good for the neighborhood even though there are already plenty of grocery stores around, including various upscale food boutiques.

This is a scene that plays out every time Southern California–based Trader Joe's opens a new store—something that only happens a handful of times each year. Within moments of a new opening, a deluge of customers makes it almost impossible to navigate the aisles. They line up 10 deep at checkouts with carts full of Trader Joe's exclusive $2.99 Charles Shaw wine—aka "Two-Buck Chuck"—and an assortment of other exclusive gourmet products at impossibly low prices. Amid hanging plastic lobsters and hand-painted signs, a Hawaiian shirt–clad manager (the "captain") and employees (the "crew") explain to first timers that the prices are not grand-opening specials. They are everyday prices.

What is it about Trader Joe's that has consumers everywhere waiting with such anxious anticipation? Trader Joe's seems to have cracked the customer value code by providing the perfect blend of benefits to prices.

High on Benefits

Trader Joe's isn't really a gourmet food store. Then again, it's not a discount food store either. It's actually a bit of both. One of America's hottest retailers, Trader Joe's has put its own special twist on the food price-value equation—call it "cheap gourmet." It offers gourmet-caliber, one-of-a-kind products at bargain prices, all served up in a festive, vacation-like atmosphere that makes shopping fun. Trader Joe's isn't low end, it isn't high end, and it certainly isn't mainstream. "Their mission is to be a nationwide chain of neighborhood specialty grocery stores," said one business professor who does research on the company. However you define it, Trader Joe's inventive price-value positioning has earned it an almost cult-like following of devoted customers who love what they get from Trader Joe's for the prices they pay.

Trader Joe's describes itself as an "island paradise" where "value, adventure, and tasty treasures are discovered, every day." Shoppers bustle and buzz amid cedar plank–lined walls and fake palm trees as a ship's bell rings out occasionally at checkout, alerting them to special announcements. Unfailingly helpful and cheery associates in aloha shirts chat with customers about everything from the weather to menu suggestions for dinner parties. Customers don't just shop at Trader Joe's; they experience it.

Shelves bristle with an eclectic assortment of gourmet-quality grocery items. Trader Joe's stocks only a limited assortment of about 4,000 products (compared with the 45,000 items found in an average supermarket). However, the assortment is uniquely Trader Joe's, including special concoctions of gourmet packaged foods and sauces, ready-to-eat soups, fresh and frozen entrees, snacks, and desserts—all free of artificial colors, flavors, and preservatives.

Trader Joe's is a gourmet foodie's delight, featuring everything from organic broccoli slaw, organic strawberry lemonade, creamy Valencia peanut butter, and fair-trade coffees to corn-and-chile tomato-less salsa and triple-ginger ginger snaps. Trader Joe's sells various items that are comparable to other stores, like organic vanilla yogurt, almond milk, extra-pulp orange juice, smoked gouda cheese, and roasted garlic hummus. But the quirky retailer also maintains pricing power by selling things that are uniquely Trader Joe's. Try finding Ginger Cats cookies, quinoa and black bean tortilla chips, or mango coconut popcorn at any other store.

More than 80 percent of the store's brands are private label goods, sold exclusively by Trader Joe's. If asked, almost any customer can tick off a ready list of Trader Joe's favorites that they just can't live without—a list that quickly grows. People go into the store intending to buy a few favorites and quickly fill a cart. "I think consumers look at it and think, 'I can go and get things that I can't get elsewhere,'" says one food industry analyst. "They just seem to turn their customers on."

Low on Prices

A special store atmosphere, exclusive gourmet products, helpful and attentive associates—this all sounds like a recipe for high prices. Not so at Trader Joe's. Whereas upscale competitors such as Whole Foods Market charge upscale prices to match their wares ("Whole Foods, Whole Paycheck"), Trader Joe's amazes customers with its relatively frugal prices. The prices aren't all that low in absolute terms, but they're a real bargain compared with what you'd pay for the same quality and coolness elsewhere. "At Trader Joe's, we're as much about value as we are about great food," says the company. "So you can afford to be adventurous without breaking the bank."

All that low-price talk along with consumers' perceptions is valid. A recent report from Deutsche Bank compared prices at Trader Joe's with those at Whole Foods for a basket of 77 products—a mix of perishable items, private-label products, and non-food items. Trader Joe's was 21 percent cheaper than Whole Foods and had the lowest price on 78 percent of the items. Even when comparing private-label brands, Trader Joe's was 15 percent cheaper. What's more, Trader Joe's price advantage has been increasing, a point that is particularly telling given that Whole Foods, now an Amazon company, has focused strategically on lowering its prices over the past few years.

How does Trader Joe's keep its gourmet prices so low? By maintaining a sound strategy based on price and adjusting the nonprice elements of the marketing mix accordingly. For starters, Trader Joe's has lean operations and a near-fanatical focus on saving money. To keep costs down, Trader Joe's typically locates its stores in low-rent, out-of-the-way locations, such as suburban strip malls. Notorious for small parking lots that are always packed, Trader Joe's points out that spacious parking lots require more real estate and that costs money. Its small stores with small back rooms and limited product assortment result in reduced facilities and inventory costs. Trader Joe's saves money by eliminating large produce sections and expensive on-site bakery, butcher, deli, and seafood shops. And for its private label brands, Trader Joe's buys directly from suppliers and negotiates hard on price.

Finally, the frugal retailer saves money by spending almost nothing on advertising. Also, it offers no coupons, discount cards, or special promotions of any kind. Trader Joe's unique combination of quirky products and low prices produces so much word-of-mouth promotion that the company doesn't really need to advertise. The closest thing to an official promotion is the company's *The Fearless Flyer* website page and a newsletter mailed out monthly to people who opt in.

In the absence of traditional advertising, Trader Joe's most potent promotional weapon is its army of faithful followers. If you doubt the importance and impact of fanatical Trader Joe's fans, just check out the numerous fan sites (such as traderjoesfan.com, whatsgoodattraderjoes.com, clubtraderjoes.com, livingtraderjoes.com, and cooktj.com) where the faithful unite to discuss new products and stores, trade recipes, and swap their favorite Trader Joe's stories.

Something Extra

Although the simple calculation of benefits to prices equates to strong value, there's something bigger that plays in Trader Joe's favor. Beyond all the wonderful and unique products, friendly staff, quirky store design, the combination of all these things produces synergy. It adds up to an atmosphere and kind of trust that eludes most companies. One industry observer who is not a fan of grocery shopping sums it up this way:

> Walking into a Trader Joe's, my demeanor is noticeably different than when I'm shopping anywhere else. Somehow I don't mind going there. At times—and it's still hard for me to believe I'd say this about shopping—I actually look forward to it. Trader Joe's does something pleasant for my brain, as it does for millions of others. There's more transparency in my dealings with TJ's than most other places. Authenticity is something you can feel—it's crucial to the

buzz. Trader Joe's proves that even when you get the other elements of the experience right, people still matter most.

Finding the right price-value formula has made Trader Joe's one of the nation's fastest-growing and most popular food stores. Its 504 stores in 48 states (plus the District of Columbia) now reap annual sales of at least $13 billion by one analyst's estimate (the private company is tight-lipped about its financial results), an amount that has quadrupled in the past decade. Trader Joe's stores pull in an amazing $1,750 per square foot, more than twice the supermarket industry average. In *Consumer Reports*'s "Best Supermarket Chain" review, Trader Joe's has occupied one of the top three spots every year for the past five years.

It's all about value and price—what you get for what you pay. Just ask Trader Joe's regular Chrissi Wright, found early one morning browsing her local Trader Joe's in Bend, Oregon.

> Chrissi expects she'll leave Trader Joe's with eight bottles of the popular Charles Shaw wine priced at $2.99 each tucked under her arms. "I love Trader Joe's because they let me eat like a yuppie without taking all my money," says Wright. "Their products are gourmet, often environmentally conscientious and beautiful... and, of course, there's Two-Buck Chuck—possibly the greatest innovation of our time."

Questions for Discussion

1. Under the concept of customer value-based pricing, explain Trader Joe's success.
2. Does Trader Joe's employ good-value pricing or value-added pricing? Explain.
3. Does Trader Joe's pricing strategy truly differentiate it from the competition?
4. Is Trader Joe's pricing strategy sustainable? Explain.
5. What changes—if any—would you recommend that Trader Joe's make?

Sources: Megan McArdle, "What's Not to Love about Trader Joe's," *Washington Post*, March 30, 2018, www.washingtonpost.com/blogs/post-partisan/wp/2018/03/30/whats-not-to-love-about-trader-joes/?noredirect=on&utm_term=.cd7f8ae8939d; Tom Foster, "Whole Foods' Latest Gamble? Go After Trader Joe's an a Big Way," *Inc.*, April 28, 2017, www.inc.com/tom-foster/inside-whole-foods-big-bet-to-turn-around-slowing-sales.html; Kathryn Vasel, "Price Wars: Trader Joe's Is Beating Whole Foods," *CNNMoney*, March 31, 2016, http://money.cnn.com/2016/03/31/pf/trader-joes-whole-foods-prices/; David DiSalvo, "What Trader Joe's Knows about Making Your Brain Happy," *Forbes*, February 19, 2015, http://forbes.com/sites/daviddisalvo/2015/02/19/what-trader-joes-knows-about-making-your-brain-happy/#27f0f6f41539; Sarah Berger, "The Surprising Story Behind Trader Joe's 19 Cent Bananas," *CNBC*, May 3, 2018, www.cnbc.com/2018/05/03/why-trader-joes-sells-cheap-bananas.html; Alan Liddle, "Meet the 2018 Top 75," *Supermarket News*, February 27, 2018, http://supermarketnews.com/rankings-research/top-75-retailers-wholesalers; and www.traderjoes.com, accessed October 2018.

Company Case 10

Target: A Serious Contender in the Same-Day Delivery Business

Once upon a time, there were two major forces dominating the discount retail market: Walmart and Target. The two retailers offered very similar merchandise assortments, and their stores were close to one another—often facing off from opposite sides of major boulevards. The two were constantly compared—the press rarely covered one without mentioning the other.

Walmart was far and away the market leader. But although Target was a distant runner-up, its stylish "cheap chic" positioning and "Expect More. Pay Less." mantra made it a formidable challenger to Walmart's always-lowest-price positioning. In fact, Target grew at a faster rate than Walmart for years, nibbling away at the giant's market share and posing a genuine threat.

But what a difference a decade makes. Since the Great Recession of 2008, Walmart's annual revenues have increased by more than $120 billion while Target's have barely moved. In fact, Target's $72 billion in total sales last year was lower than six years before. Not only has Walmart improved its game, but increased competition from Amazon, Costco, Kohl's, and dollar stores have flattened Target's growth. Still, Target hasn't given up. It has doubled down on improving its customer experience while at the same time cutting corporate costs. So far, however, its efforts haven't seemed to make much difference.

All that may soon change. Today, Target is making a major investment that it hopes will help it regain its edge in the retail world and restore its growth. For a cool $550 million in cash, Target recently acquired Shipt, the exploding four-year-old startup with a thriving same-day delivery network across 80 U.S. markets. The future of retail favors companies that can deliver goods fast and cheap, and Target is serious about establishing a competitive advantage in delivery. With the Shipt acquisition, Target plans not only to increase sales of its current inventory but also to become a major player in an area of retail where it has languished—groceries.

A New Way to Deliver Groceries

Founded in 2014 by a 32-year-old high school dropout, Shipt quickly established itself as a force in the home delivery business. After a few failed models, Shipt focused on groceries. Members get unlimited same-day grocery delivery on orders of $35 or more for just $99 a year—a fee now reduced to $49 for the first year. The Shipt app and website offer users a seamless experience for ordering and receiving groceries and general merchandise.

But Shipt is not a grocer. It's a home delivery service. Rather than invest in its own inventory, Shipt has partnered with grocery chains such as Kroger, Publix, and, of course, Target. When a customer places an order, employees at partner stores don't have to do anything. Instead, one of Shipt's personal shoppers—a veritable army that now exceeds 40,000—goes to the store, plucks the products from shelves, and delivers them to the customer's home. Shipt shoppers wear green T-shirts with the company logo. But similar to Uber and Lyft, they are independent contractors. They drive their own vehicles and work when they want to. A Shipt personal shopper makes $22 an hour on average. By the end of this year, Shipt projects that its army of shoppers will exceed 100,000 and its total revenue will eclipse $1 billion.

Experts have predicted a reliable model for home grocery delivery to the masses for the past 20 years. Until now, however, efforts have moved slowly, leaving behind many casualties. Today, same-day grocery delivery is a rapidly growing sector with many large retail competitors entering the fray. Fueled by the explosion in mobile devices and consumer expectations for instant everything, same-day grocery delivery is more in demand than ever. "One-stop shopping was convenient in the 1990s," says one retail analyst. "But for today's families you have to be able to do instant food delivery as well." According to a recent report, online grocery shopping could expand fivefold during the next 10 years. That means U.S. consumers will be spending well over $100 billion on grocery items by then.

Why Partner When You Can Buy?

Although the acquisition of Shipt may seem sudden for Target, it was actually a long time coming. Target has always striven to stand out from the rest of the discount retail world by offering a more high-end customer experience. With Amazon and Walmart fast establishing their same-day grocery delivery capabilities, Target knew it had to make a move or risk falling further behind. But why buy Shipt instead of simply partnering with it? For starters, the acquisition sends a strong signal to competitors and customers that Target is serious about the grocery business and about delivering its goods better and faster than larger competitors.

Purchasing rather than partnering with Shipt also gives Target more control. The acquisition lets the company take full advantage of the Shipt technology platform across its entire network of stores, letting it to provide faster and more convenient same-day delivery on a wide variety of goods. Now, just six months after the acquisition, Target customers can take delivery via Shipt of groceries, home goods, and electronics, among other things. "By the end of 2019, we'll offer same-day delivery on all major product categories at Target," claims John Mulligan, Target's chief operating officer.

Prior to the acquisition, Target was already partnering with Shipt rival Instacart. But the strong compatibility between Target and Shipt was apparent to both companies. "What sets us apart, and really one of the big reasons we were drawn to Target, is the value we place on delivering quality, personalized experiences to our customers," notes Shipt's founder. "Our localized network of... shoppers goes above and beyond to make sure our customers are well served."

In the Race or Out in Front?

The Shipt purchase was primarily prompted by developments at Target's main competitors. Walmart now offers same-day grocery delivery in only six U.S. markets. But it recently announced that by the end of this year, it will expand service to 800 of its stores in 100 markets reaching 40 percent of U.S. households. For same-day delivery, Walmart customers pay a flat fee of $9.95 on minimum orders of $30. Similar to Shipt, Walmart also uses personal shoppers to assemble orders from shelves. But these shoppers are actual Walmart employees who also pick orders for its curbside pickup. All orders are taken to a designated holding area at the front of the store. But while Shipt uses the same delivery mechanism systemwide, Walmart's store-to-household delivery is still fragmented. It is using a mix of methods to fuel the rapid growth of its delivery service, including Uber, Postmates, and even its own subsidiary Jet.com.

Amazon is also establishing itself as a leader in same-day grocery delivery. As the owner of Whole Foods Market, the dominant ecommerce retailer now has a bigger stake in the grocery business. And with its Amazon Fresh service, Prime members who pay an additional $14.99 per month can get same-day grocery delivery on minimum orders of $50. Customers can even have orders auto-delivered every two weeks. Available in numerous markets throughout the United States, Amazon Fresh warehouses groceries in its own facilities. In some markets, delivery is carried out by Amazon drivers and a fleet of big green Amazon Fresh box trucks. In other markets, Amazon Fresh is delivered by the U.S. Postal Service.

So far, the quality of Amazon Fresh delivery has been spotty, prompting complaints by loyal Amazon customers about late orders, missed orders, and missing items. "I feel like Amazon now has two very distinct divisions," said one Los Angeles customer. "While I love Amazon Prime and even Prime Now, I don't know what's going on with Amazon Fresh. It really leaves a bad taste in my mouth, because there are other companies that do grocery so much better." The disruptions have led Amazon to pull back temporarily, halting Amazon Fresh service in nine states where it relied on the USPS. But Amazon assures the public that it is regrouping, promising more cooperation over time between Whole Foods, Amazon Fresh, and Prime Now.

Although Target now owns Shipt, its business as usual at the Birmingham-based startup. Target is allowing Shipt to continue to operate independently, and Shipt will continue to service its other clients and Target competitors. For now, that's just fine by Target. It gains an immediate strength in the same-day delivery business through one of the strongest players in the market. For Shipt, the acquisition provides a big boost to its already growing network.

So how does Target stack up against its larger competitors? Target may now be in the best position of all grocers to establish reliable nationwide same-day delivery. According to one Moody's analyst, "The fact that Target will have this service in place during 2018 will significantly improve its online competitive position." Based on calculations for the average home, Shipt's service is the cheapest compared to Walmart and Amazon. As of now, Shipt also delivers to more markets. And most important, the consistency and reliability of the Shipt delivery system gives Target the highest quality customer experience.

With the capability to extend its services in a more modern and flexible way, Target is making one thing clear—it won't simply fade away. It will continue to do whatever it takes to serve its customer base. The competition in the same-day grocery sector gives even more options to shoppers looking for time savings and convenience. For customers, that's good news. For the retailers, only time will tell.

Questions for Discussion

1. As completely as possible, diagram the value delivery network for Target's grocery business, from raw materials to finished consumer goods.
2. Is Target a producer, a consumer, or an intermediary? How about Shipt? Explain.
3. Discuss Target's channel management procedures.
4. Regarding the same-day delivery venture, why are Target's partnerships important?
5. Will Target's acquisition of Shipt result in growing revenues in the coming years? Explain.

Sources: Anne D'Innocenzio, "Walmart Prepares to Roll Out Online Same-Day Grocery Delivery to 100 Cities," *Chicago Tribune*, March 14, 2018, www.chicagotribune.com/business/ct-walmart-online-same-day-grocery-delivery-20180314-story.html; Sarah Berger, "How This 32-Year-Old High School Dropout Built a Business that Sold to Target for $550," *CNBC*, March 29, 2018, www.cnbc.com/2018/03/29/how-bill-smith-founded-shipt-and-sold-it-to-target.html; Dennis Green, "Amazon's Struggles with Its Fresh Grocery Service Show a Huge Liability for Prime," *Business Insider*, July 1, 2018, www.businessinsider.com/amazon-fresh-struggles-show-a-huge-liability-in-prime-2018-7; Matthew Boyle "Target to Buy Shipt for $550 Million in Challenge to Amazon," *Bloomberg*, December 13, 2017, www.bloomberg.com/news/articles/2017-12-13/target-to-buy-shipt-for-550-million-in-bet-on-same-day-delivery; Yoni Blumberg "Amazon, Walmart and Target Are Competing to Deliver Your Groceries—Here's How Their Offers Stack Up" *CNBC*, March 19, 2018, www.cnbc.com/2018/03/19/how-amazon-Walmart-and-target-compare-on-grocery-delivery-services.html; "Here's How Acquiring Shipt Will Bring Same-Day Delivery to About Half of Target Stores in Early 2018," December 13, 2017, https://corporate.target.com/article/2017/12/target-acquires-shipt.

Company Case 11

Bass Pro Shops: Creating Nature's Theme Park for People Who Hate to Shop

Outdoor-products megaretailer Bass Pro Shops has seemingly been breaking the rules of retailing for nearly 50 years and basking in the spoils as a result. With more than 95 retail stores throughout the United States and Canada, the privately held Springfield, Missouri–based company reeled in $4.6 billion in revenues during the most recent year—nearly $50 million per store—making it the number one outdoor retailer. Going against common retail wisdom, Bass Pro Shops stores are enormous and packed to the gills with overhead. Even more daring, the chain has achieved retail success by targeting customers who hate to shop! The typical Bass Pro Shops customer is a reclusive male outdoorsman who yearns for the great outdoors but detests jostling crowds and shopping.

Over the past few decades, Bass Pro Shops has evolved from a popular mail-order catalog business into one of the nation's hottest store retailers. Despite Bass Pro Shops often-remote locations, customers flock to its superstores to buy hunting, fishing, and outdoor gear. More than 120 million people visit a Bass Pro Shops store every year—almost double the number that attended a game put on by the NFL, NBA, and MLB combined. In a true display of "destination retail," customers drive an average of more than 50 miles to get to a Bass Pro Shops store (some drive hundreds of miles) and stay an average of two hours. Schools, churches, and senior centers even send in people by the busload.

Filling a Gap in the Market

So how do you explain Bass Pro Shops's climb to the top? Bass Pro Shops's ability to attract these hordes of otherwise reluctant shoppers to its stores is part of a double-hook strategy that dates back to the company's beginning. First, each store guarantees a product assortment that is as wide as the Mississippi River and as deep as the Mariana Trench. In 1971, Johnny Morris—a tournament fisherman and avid outdoorsman—was frustrated by the lack of decent fishing tackle in sporting goods stores. With the ink on his college diploma barely dry, he rented a U-Haul trailer and headed out on a cross-country road trip, filling the trailer with latest and greatest in premium fishing tackle. Returning to Springfield, he set up shop in his father's liquor store near Table Rock Lake. With that, Bass Pro Shops was born.

That first Bass Pro Shops store quickly outgrew the liquor store. And within a few years, Morris's vision of what he wanted Bass Pro Shops to become began to take shape. At the time, the sporting goods retail sector was fragmented with lots of independent retail shops catering to different outdoor activities. To meet the needs of customers across the country, Bass Pro Shops printed its first catalog in 1974. The company's catalog business has been a mainstay ever since.

But the company simultaneously moved to fill a gap in brick-and-mortar retail. With no national chain that could serve the outdoor masses, Bass Pro Shops quickly moved beyond fishing, adding hunting, camping, outdoor cooking gear, outdoor footwear and apparel, and nature-themed gifts. During this expansion, Bass Pro Shops not only carried the leading national brands, it also developed a portfolio of store brands, including its first brand, Bass Tracker—the first dedicated bass boat and still the market leader. By manufacturing and selling direct, Bass Pro Shops could not only pass on huge savings to customers, it could compete on price with just about any company.

Growing rapidly throughout the 1970s, the second hook of Bass Pro Shops's strategy solidified with the opening of the first Outdoor World showroom adjacent to its headquarters. From that day on, it was clear that Bass Pro Shops was to be much more than a chain of stores that sells lots of cool stuff—it was to be a place that provided engaging customer *experiences* for all who would visit. To that end, Bass Pro Shops has created what amounts to a natural history theme park for outdoor enthusiasts—the "Disney World" of sporting goods.

Nature's Theme Park

Take the store in Memphis, Tennessee, for example—Bass Pro Shops at the Pyramid. Former home of the Memphis Grizzlies, the 535,000-square-foot, 32-story glass-and-steel Pyramid now houses the largest Bass Pro Shops store. The store is dominated by various representations of wildlife, from the deer, duck, turkey, bear, bobcat, and wolf tracks imprinted in the concrete floors to the hand-painted murals from renowned artists depicting nature scenes reflecting the local geography.

But the Pyramid also brings wildlife to life in three dimensions. Each store features lifelike, museum-quality taxidermy animals in action poses—everything from prairie dogs, deer, elk, and caribou to brown bears, polar bears, musk oxen, and mountain goats—set in natural dioramas that make customers feel like they're on location in some of the most striking outdoor landscapes. And while these animals are stuffed, the Pyramid store boasts 600,000 gallons of water features, stocked with live fish and other wildlife. Consider the cypress swamp with an 84,000-gallon alligator habitat (live feedings every Saturday) surrounded by 100-foot-tall trees, various aquariums, and the Live Duck Aviary—a four-pond multi-habitat home to five species of ducks.

The carefully planned and orchestrated wildlife displays set the structure for the rest of what amounts to one of the most dynamic and captivating retail adventures in the world. Visitors can ride the nation's tallest freestanding glass elevator to the Lookout—a breathtaking glass-floored cantilevering observation deck at the top of the Pyramid. From there, visitors can survey the view outside the store as well as the one inside. And there is plenty to see inside, including the arcade shooting gallery, archery and pistol ranges, fudge shop, Beretta Fine Gun Center, interactive Ducks Unlimited Waterfowling Heritage Center, and the 103-room Big Cypress Lodge.

Because visitors to the Pyramid store often make a day of it, there are two full-service restaurants on site, including Uncle Buck's Fishbowl & Grill. One of six company-owned restaurant chains, Uncle Buck's is a nautical-themed dining experience with a saltwater aquarium that weaves in and around the restaurant, offering diners full view of exotic and tropical fish. And before or after the meal, diners can work up an appetite or work off calories in the Fishbowl's 13-lane ocean-themed bowling alley where the balls are returned right through a shark's gaping jaws.

Half the Size with All the Fun

While Bass Pro Shops at the Pyramid is larger and more fantastic than any of the chain's other stores, each Outdoor World store is designed to shower its guests with the same captivating experience. Most stores have but one restaurant and no hotel and are just under 200,000 square feet—about the size of the average Walmart supercenter. But the rest of the formula plays out in magnificent splendor across the many Bass Pro Shops outlets in North America. One mother sums up the Bass Pro Shops experience:

> We recently had a visiting family group that included two 5-year-olds. They thoroughly enjoyed our trip to Bass Pro Shop! It's half retail store and half wildlife museum. There was plenty to see for any outdoor sports enthusiast. The kids loved seeing real fish and ducks, as well as plenty of inanimate displays. There were boats they could sit on and "trees" they could hide in. The store includes a restaurant. They offer plenty of merchandise for every budget, but you don't really have to spend money to enjoy the visit. Highly recommended!

With its retail design that builds theater and entertainment into every store, Bass Pro Shops is not only a haven for the reluctant male outdoorsman, it's enjoyable for everyone. "First off, I am not an outdoor person so Bass Pro isn't a shop for me," says a recent store visitor. "That being said, I loved this store. I felt like I was in a museum and aquarium."

Bass Pro Shops provides even more reasons to visit with various special events such as Family Summer Camp, Professional Bull Riders Event, Fall Hunting Classic, and Halloween Bass Pro Style. Each event is filled with demonstrations and activities, including seminars for fishing and hunting featuring national and local experts. But no other Bass Pro Shops event compares to Santa's Wonderland, a six-week extravaganza that transforms each Bass Pro Shops outlet into a veritable Christmas village featuring rustic cabins, moving model trains, animated Christmas characters, interactive talking caribou, and live elves set among snow-covered hills and illuminated Christmas trees. Kids are free to hang out in the play zone and get their hands on old-time model trains, RC trucks, slot cars, and both laser and foam-dart guns. Families can spend time at various activity tables and make decorations and crafts to take home. They can also enjoy one of various seasonal goodies. And, of course, Santa's Wonderland wouldn't be complete without a visit from the big guy himself, the event's main feature that includes a free studio-quality photo.

As amazing as Bass Pro Shops's retail design is, the chain is not alone in its approach to marketing the great outdoors. Nebraska-based Cabela's got its start just before Bass Pro Shops, has almost as many stores, and pulls in nearly as much in revenues. Beyond the similarities on paper, the Cabela's retail experience is nearly identical to that of Bass Pro Shops, right down to the aquariums, animal-filled dioramas, and shooting galleries. In fact, the two chains have so much in common that Bass Pro Shops bought Cabela's two years ago. That's right. The number one outdoor retailer acquired number two. As much as Bass Pro Shops had been thriving financially, Cabela's had suffered declining sales and losses. With few markets playing host to both chains, the promise of economy-of-scale advantages, and the elimination of its largest competitor, Bass Pro Shops made the acquisition with confidence that it could turn the Cabela's chain around.

How is the marriage going? So far, so good. While Bass Pro has certainly taken advantage of the combined company to merge certain aspects of its operations, it has continued to operate

Cabela's stores as a separate chain. The merger gives Bass Pro a combined total of 177 stores, $10 billion in annual revenue, and one of the fastest-growing online businesses in retail. Regardless of the brand on the sign out front, the company does business the same way it has for decades—by wowing customers with the unsurpassed retail experience of its nature's theme parks. "People spend time there when they go," said Morris of Bass Pro Shops stores. "They can't wait to see what's around the next aisle. It's an experience. It's about creating memories. It's about being with friends and family. It's about having fun."

Questions for Discussion

1. Define Bass Pro Shops's targeting strategy. Does it provide a truly differentiated experience?
2. Describe how Bass Pro Shops became the nation's leading outdoor retailer based on the retail marketing mix.
3. Based on the major types of retailers, how would you classify Bass Pro Shops?
4. How is it possible that Bass Pro Shops was succeeding while Cabela's was floundering?
5. Was it a good idea for Bass Pro Shops to acquire Cabela's? Explain.

Sources: Taylor Stanton, "Bass Pro Shop's $5 Billion Acquisition Nets Fastest-Growing Online Outfitter," *Slice Intelligence*, April 25, 2018, http://intelligence.slice.com/blog/2016/bass-pro-shops-5-billion-aquisition-nets-fastest-growing-online-outfitter; Matt Olberding, "Bass Pro Give Details on Buyouts, Cabela's Future in Sidney," *Lincoln Journal Star*, March 8, 2018, https://journalstar.com/business/local/bass-pro-gives-details-on-buyouts-cabela-s-future-in/article_dbd7e03f-74f9-58f3-8b31-209f13185017.html; Lee Tolliver, "Money Hasn't Change Humble Bass Pro Founder," *The Virginian-Pilot*, January 16, 2011, http://pilotonline.com/sports/outdoors/money-hasn-t-changed-humble-bass-pro-founder/article_939a1378-026d-517b-9875-dd01ddc69b8e.html; and http://tripadvisor.com, www.cabelas.com/, and http://basspro.com, accessed October 2018.

Company Case 12

LinkedIn: Crushing the White-Collar Stereotype with IMC

Social media networks seem numberless these days, but only an elite few that started in the early days of the World Wide Web still survive. One of those is LinkedIn, a social media site that debuted in 2002. Today, more than just surviving, LinkedIn is thriving. The professional networking social media platform provides a venue for companies and individuals to interact in a business context. It has grown year after year, amassing more than 560 million members in more than 200 countries. Today, only a handful of social networks are larger. And of the major social media platforms active today, none have been around as long as LinkedIn.

But a few years ago, LinkedIn's marketers recognized that their popular professional networking platform had a problem. It had developed an constraining image best described as "the place where white collars meet." Even more limiting, "white collar" tended to be defined as "Caucasian," "male," and "old." What's more, success in this group was defined as "moving up the corporate ladder." In other words, LinkedIn was perceived by the masses as stiff and stoic. This image prevailed despite the fact that LinkedIn's membership spanned a diverse range of people and businesses. As the realization of public perception settled in, many at LinkedIn felt that the company had strayed from its true nature and mission.

To correct this stereotype, LinkedIn did something it had never before done. Although it had traditionally done very little advertising, the company launched its first-ever major–media integrated marketing campaign. The aim of LinkedIn's "In It Together" campaign was to recast the professional social network's brand image by sending a message of diversity across TV, outdoor, radio, online video, digital display, podcast, search engine, and other media channels.

Developing the Message

As LinkedIn marketers began developing the brand repositioning campaign, they first asked themselves what work meant to them and how important work is. The company also engaged researchers to ask LinkedIn members the same questions. What they discovered astounded them. There were nearly as many unique answers as there were respondents. As researchers combed through the data, certain themes began to emerge. For some, work symbolizes a sense of purpose. For others, it means a deep passion. Some members defined work as a way to give back. Others viewed work more pragmatically, as a means of providing.

Regardless of people's motivations or reasons for working, one overriding theme emerged. "No one wants to go it alone," says Melissa Selcher, LinkedIn's vice president of brand marketing and corporate communications. "Whatever you're in it for, you want to know there is a community of people to help, support, inspire, and push you." As the data revealed more and more people with nontraditional backgrounds, another theme also became clear. People hold different beliefs about what it means to succeed. However, regardless of how each person defines success, the importance of succeeding seems universal.

From these insights, LinkedIn's marketers developed a central campaign message. In short, LinkedIn boiled down a large and complex concept to a simple theme: Success is as diverse as the people trying to achieve it. With that, the campaign needed to communicate the professional network's key positioning point—that LinkedIn provides a community where people meet, understand, and support each other. And beyond just being a detached corporation that offers a professional meeting place, LinkedIn partners with organizational and individual members to help them succeed. To establish the "partner" image, the campaign needed to show that LinkedIn doesn't want to mold people into something they aren't but rather provides the tools needed for members to forge their own individual paths. In all, LinkedIn and its entire community are "In It Together" to create member success.

Executing the Theme

To bring this "In It Together" positioning to life, LinkedIn's marketers decided to showcase actual members. Stacy Peralta, director for the campaign's video content, explains:

> I knew from the first reading of the boards that this was one of those rare opportunities. They asked us to tell real stories about real people; they wanted it shot in black and white; and they wanted energy, enthusiasm, and candor from the people involved. We found and documented many of the unique people who use the platform. We found avant-garde musicians, MMA fighters, physics teachers, animators, chefs, and real-life cowboys, all of whom not only use LinkedIn but rave about its effect on their careers.

In developing the "In It Together" campaign, LinkedIn invited its 11,000 employees to visit a microsite to share why they are "in it." They also asked employees to nominate LinkedIn members to be subjects for the campaign's content.

Of the LinkedIn members chosen for the campaign—all of whom volunteered to participate without compensation—one thought he was just the recipient of a mass email when he received the invitation. "I'm not the typical financial advisor," said Eszylfie Taylor, founder and president of Taylor Insurance and Financial Services. "I'm still young. I'm African-American. And my story is not one that's told commonly." As someone who perceived himself as atypical, Taylor was excited to "share the reasons behind what I do and the role I play in people's lives on a grand scale."

To monitor the campaign's effectiveness, LinkedIn rolled out the "In It Together" campaign sequentially, with the initial 12-week effort targeted at four core markets—Atlanta, Philadelphia, Los Angeles, and San Francisco. It compared outcomes in these markets against performance in control markets not exposed to the campaign. It next launched a TV spot during the Golden Globes award show—an uncharacteristic media channel and vehicle but one LinkedIn thought perfect for making clear its intentions to shatter current perceptions of its brand image.

That first ad, along with other video content, incorporated raw, black-and-white video and stills in a documentary style. The ads featured a variety of real LinkedIn members telling their success stories in their own unique environments. Moreover, LinkedIn created different versions of the ad so that each market saw an ad featuring people from that market. The simple ad-production approach allowed the powerful message to shine.

The "In It Together" message unfolded in bits and pieces across the montage of individuals. "Mixed martial arts is literally the hardest thing I have ever done in my life," said member Colleen Schneider, to images of her working out and sparring. "It brings me a lot of pride knowing that I can help expand human knowledge," said physics researcher and lecturer Lamar Glover against a backdrop of formulas on a blackboard. "Being a rancher's not what I do, it's who I am," commented Mike Williams on a cold morning as he herded cattle. "It's pretty simple really." Other quotes included, "I'm living my life, doing what I love for a living," "Nobody in my family tried to take that leap of faith—so I decided to do it," and "My definition of success is changing lives for the better."

The ad continued with responses to a question posed by Ms. Schneider. "What am I in it for?" The answers from various members came quickly—"'Cause I believe in science," "because it's in my blood," "to crush it," "to inspire," "because I love fixing problems," "to create magic," "to be a pioneer," and "to do what I love." As the ad came to an end, a voice narrated the conclusive tagline "Whatever you're in it for, we're in it together."

The campaign received a considerable amount of attention from the marketing press. Four months into 2018, the Digital Marketing Institute dubbed it one of the top three most creative marketing campaigns of the year. Part of the campaign's impact can be attributed to perfect timing. Shortly before the launch of LinkedIn's message of partnership and trust, the global press reported widely on cases of sexual harassment that evolved into the "#MeToo" movement. Shortly after the campaign's launch, the world learned of the data breaches involving Facebook and Cambridge Analytica.

Although the campaign is still young and LinkedIn has remained tight-lipped about measured outcomes, the workplace social network has now moved past the opening 12-week phase, increasing the campaign's scope across North America, Europe, and India. And even though the campaign has gone global, it remains local by showcasing people and stories from each region. For those unfamiliar with LinkedIn, the campaign introduces the network with the desired image of diversity and partnership. For those already familiar with the brand, the campaign erases undesirable perceptions. Either way, it is likely that LinkedIn will expand its membership across ethnicities and career types in the near future.

Questions for Discussion

1. Analyze the "In It Together" ads based on the process of creating an advertising message as outlined in the text (see www.youtube.com/user/LinkedIn/playlists).
2. Discuss issues of selecting advertising media for the "In It Together" campaign. How might this process differ from that of campaigns for other companies?
3. Based on the information in this case, how might LinkedIn measure the effectiveness of the "In It Together" campaign?
4. Will the "In It Together" campaign be effective? Support your answer.

Sources: "Three of the Most Creative Marketing Campaigns of 2018 (So Far)," *Digital Marketing Institute*, May 2, 2018, http://digitalmarketinginstitute.com/en-us/blog/05-02-18-3-of-the-most-creative-marketing-campaigns-of-2018; David Cohen, 'LinkedIn's New Integrated Marketing Campaign Seeks to Smash Its 'White Collar' Stereotype," *Adweek*, January 8, 2018, www.adweek.com/digital/linkedins-new-integrated-marketing-campaign-seeks-to-smash-its-white-collar-stereotype/; Emily Tan, "LinkedIn Readies Consumer Ads Featuring Real Members," *Campaign*, June 15, 2018,www.campaignlive.com/article/linkedin-readies-consumer-ads-featuring-real-members/1485051; and www.ourstory.linkedin.com/, accessed October 2018.

Company Case 13

Procter & Gamble: Selling through Customer Business Development

When it comes to personal selling, the term *win-win* gets thrown around so much that it has become a cliché. But at Procter & Gamble, the selling concept that the company benefits only if the customer benefits has long been a way of life. Since William Procter and James Gamble formed a family-operated soap and candle company in 1837, P&G has understood that if the customer doesn't do well, neither will the company.

So although P&G boasts a massive sales force of more than 5,000 employees in the United States alone, P&Gers rarely utter the term *sales*. Instead, at P&G, they call it *customer business development*, or *CBD*. The title pretty much says it all. Rather than just selling detergent or toothpaste, P&G's philosophy is to grow its own business by growing the business of its customers, the thousands of retailers and wholesalers that distribute P&G's brands throughout the world. To these customers, P&G isn't just a supplier. It's a strategic business partner. "We depend on them as much as they depend on us," says Jeff Weedman, a CBD manager.

The Core Competency of Customer Business Development

As today's big retailers get bigger and bigger, they also grow more complex. Take companies such as Walmart, Kroger, or Amazon. How can a vendor like P&G ever fully understand such giant customers? These complex organizations have so many arms and legs that it becomes nearly impossible to get a full and firm grasp on their operations and needs.

To deal with such customer complexities, P&G organizes its sales representatives into customer business development teams. Rather than assigning reps to specific geographic regions or products, it assigns each CBD team to a P&G customer. For the company's biggest customer, Walmart (which accounts for 16 percent of all P&G sales) the CBD team consists of more than 300 employees. For a customer such as Family Dollar, the nation's second-largest dollar store chain, the CBD team has a comparatively few 30 employees.

Regardless of the team's size, the strength of the CBD concept derives from the fact that each team, in and of itself, is a complete customer-service unit, containing at least one support specialist for every important business function. In addition to an overall CBD manager and several sales account executives (each responsible for a specific category of P&G products), each CBD team includes specialists in marketing strategy, operations, information systems, logistics, finance, and human resources. This "multi-functional" structure enables each team to meet the multiple and vast needs of its customer, whether the needs revolve around those of a chief finance officer or an entire IT department.

A real strength of the CBD teams is that team members function as a collaborative whole rather than as individuals performing their own tasks in isolation. Team members share information, organizational capabilities, and technologies. "I have all the resources I need right here," says Amy Fuschino, a HealthCare and Cosmetics account executive. "If I need to, I can go right down the hall and talk with someone in marketing about doing some kind of promotional deal. It's that simple."

But the multi-functional nature of the CBD team also means that collaboration extends far beyond internal interactions. Each time a CBD team member contacts the customer, he or she represents the entire team. For example, if during a customer call a CBD account executive receives a question about a promotional, logistical, or financial matter, the account executive acts as the liaison with the appropriate CBD specialist. So, although not each CBD member has specialized knowledge in every area, the CBD team as a unit does.

Competitors have attempted to implement some aspects of P&G's multi-functional approach. However, P&G pioneered the CBD structure. And it has built in some unique characteristics that have allowed it to leverage more power from its team structure than its rivals can.

The True Advantage

For starters, P&G's CBD structure is broader and more comprehensive, making it more multi-functional than similar team structures employed by other companies. But perhaps more important, P&G's structure is designed to accomplish four key objectives. So important are these objectives that they are referred to internally as the "core work" of CBD. These four objectives are:

- ***Align strategy:*** Create opportunities for both P&G and the customer to benefit by collaborating in strategy development.
- ***Create demand:*** To build profitable sales volume for P&G and the customer through consumer value and shopper satisfaction.
- ***Optimize supply:*** To maximize the efficiency of the supply chain from P&G to the point of purchase to optimize cost and responsiveness.
- ***Enable the organization***: To develop capabilities to maximize business results by creating the capacity for frequent breakthrough.

More than just corporate catchphrases jotted down in an employee handbook, these are words to live by for CBD employees. P&G trains sales employees in methods of achieving each objective and evaluates their effectiveness in meeting the objectives. In fact, the CBD concept came about through the recognition that, in order to develop true win-win relationships with each customer, P&G would need to accomplish the first objective. According to Bill Warren, a CBD senior account executive, "The true competitive advantage is achieved by taking a multi-functional approach from basic selling to strategic customer collaboration!"

Strategic collaboration starts with annual joint business planning. Both the P&G team and the customer come to the table focused on the most important thing: how can each best provide value for the final consumer? The team and customer give much attention during this planning phase to how products can best be presented and placed in the retail setting. This is because P&G and its customers know that the end consumer assesses value within the first three to seven seconds of seeing that product on the shelf. At P&G, this is known as "winning the first moment of truth." If customers quickly perceive that a product will meet their needs, they will likely purchase it.

CBD team members are very good at demonstrating to the retailer that the best way to win the first moment of truth is most often with a P&G product. But P&G is so committed to developing the *customer's* business as a means of developing its own that it is open to the possibility that the best way to serve the customer may be through a competitor's product. The CBD team's primary goal is to help the customer win in each product category. Sometimes, analysis shows that the best solution for the customer is "the other guy's product." For P&G, that's OK. P&G knows that creating the best situation for the retailer ultimately brings in more customer traffic, which in turn will likely result in increased sales for other P&G products in the same category. Because most of P&G's brands are market leaders, P&G stands to benefit more from the increased traffic than competitors. Again, it's a win-win situation. This type of honesty also helps to build trust and strengthen the company/customer relationships.

The collaborative efforts between P&G and each of its customers often involve more than joint planning and the sharing of information. They may also involve cooperative efforts to share the costs of different activities. "We'll help customers run these commercials or do those merchandising events, but there has to be a return-on-investment," explains Amy Fuschino. "Maybe its helping us with a new distribution or increasing space for fabric care. We're very willing if the effort creates value for us in addition to creating value for the customer and the consumer."

If the CBD team can effectively accomplish the first objective of aligning strategy and collaborating on strategic development, accomplishing the other three objectives will follow more easily. For example, if strategic planning leads to winning the first moment of truth, not only does the consumer benefit, but both the retailer and P&G achieve higher revenues and profits as well. Through proper strategic planning, it is also more likely that both P&G and the customer will create greater efficiencies in the supply chain.

It's Better to Give... *Then* to Receive

By collaborating with customers, P&G receives as much or more than it gives. Among other things, P&G receives information that helps in achieving the fourth CBD objective, enabling the organization to achieve innovation. Where the research and development process is concerned, this means creating better products. This is one reason why, at the 2017 Product of the Year awards held in New York City, P&G cleaned up, winning five of the 13 categories in which it competes.

In recent years, the consumer products industry has been hit hard by tough economic times and a rise in popularity of store brands. But P&G has weathered the storm. Over the past few years, P&G has divested most many low-performing brands in order to strengthen its best brands. P&G remains the world's largest consumer products firm with $65 billion in revenues and a whopping 23 brands that *each* bring in over $1 billion every year. Last year, Pampers sales alone exceeded $8.5 billion, a figure that by itself would have placed the leading diaper brand as number 344 on *Fortune*'s prestigious 500 list.

Many factors have contributed to P&G's growth and success. But the role that CBD plays can't be overestimated. And as P&G moves forward, Mr. Weedman's words that "We depend on them as much as they depend on us" ring ever truer. As P&G's mega-customers grow in size and power, developing P&G's business means first developing its customers' businesses. And the CBD sales organization lies at the heart of that effort.

Questions for Discussion

1. Which of the sales force structures discussed in the text best describes P&G's CBD structure?
2. From the perspective of team selling, discuss the positive as well as possible negative aspects to the customer business development sales organization.
3. Discuss ways that the CBD structure may be more effective than a single sales rep for each step in the personal selling process.
4. It seems that P&G has the most effective sales force structure of any company in its industry. Why have competitors not been able to match it?

Sources: Based on information from numerous P&G managers; Jen Birkhofer, "These Are the 2018 Product of the Year Award Winners," *Today*, February 21, 2018, www.today.com/home/these-are-2018-product-year-award-winners-t122831; with additional information from "Selling Power 500 Largest Sales Forces (2017)," *Selling Power*, www.sellingpower.com/resources/2017/selling-power-500, www.pginvestor.com/CustomPage/Index?keyGenPage=1073748359, and www.pg.com/vn/careers/our_functions/customer_business_development.shtml, accessed October 2018.

Company Case 14

OfferUp: A Mobile Solution for the Mobile Era

When people think of buying and selling things online locally, most think automatically of Craigslist, the classified ad marketplace that has dominated that business for the past two decades. But as the rest of the world has gone mobile, Craigslist has not. In fact, the familiar but cluttered collection of blue hyperlinks has changed very little over the years. Some critics suggest that Craigslist has taken its monopoly for granted. One industry observer refers to Craigslist as "the cockroach of the internet age—an ugly but effective e-commerce platform that... emerged unscathed from technology shifts that crippled mightier contemporaries like Netscape and Yahoo."

In the new landscape of digital disruption, one thing seems certain: What dominates today could be under threat tomorrow.

That tomorrow may already be here for Craigslist as numerous, more user-friendly competitors have emerged to challenge the classified ad champ. Enter OfferUp—a relatively new mobile app for buying and selling items that is taking the digital marketplace by storm. OfferUp is not only challenging Craigslist as the go-to platform by which individuals and businesses sell goods and services in local markets, it's also starting to challenge the likes of eBay and even Amazon by flexing its muscles beyond local market boundaries. Unexpectedly, OfferUp now rivals the most popular social media apps in terms of time spent by users.

About a decade ago, as the mobile device revolution began to explode, Seattle resident Nick Huzar was frustrated as he tried to unload unwanted household items in preparation for his soon-to-be-born daughter's nursery. He didn't have time to post all these items on Craigslist, which required multiple steps that pretty much required a desktop or laptop to complete. Instead, he went to Goodwill, where he always found a line to drop donations. With a smartphone in his hand, he recognized the potential for an online marketplace that made posting, monitoring, and browsing items for sale in a local market as simple as social media interactions. That led to a partnership with friend Arean van Veelen and the ultimate launch of OfferUp in 2011.

A Different Kind of Marketplace

The main thing that differentiates OfferUp from Craigslist and other traditional online marketplace platforms is that it's designed exclusively for mobile channels. For sellers, that means that posting an item is as simple as posting a photo to Facebook—point, shoot, add a description, and click. Each local ad defaults to a 30-mile radius, and standard ads are free. OfferUp's goal is to have the process take no more than 30 seconds. For sellers, it's painless with little risk.

For shoppers, the interface is also very appealing, with a Pinterest-like vibe that is primarily visual. The bottomless scroll entices users, luring them in to a virtual treasure hunt. People typically access the OfferUp app looking for one thing but discover a trove of unexpected goodies. This element of surprise has users spending an average of 25 minutes a day on OfferUp, the same as Snapchat and Instagram. "It's not like Amazon where it's very intent-based—where you know what you want," says Huzar. "OfferUp is more discovery-based. You go in there and you kind of look around and you find that thing you didn't think you wanted that you end up buying."

Beyond the Pinterest-like feel, OfferUp also boasts the strong sense of community that is normally reserved for dedicated social media sites. The foundation of this community is trust and reputation. Take the user profile and rating system for example. Users are not random, anonymous users but *community* members. A user can create a profile and upload a photo. What's more, users can take it a step further and apply for TruYou verification, submitting a mobile phone number, a picture, and a state-issued ID. Once verified, a Trubadge is displayed as part of the user's profile.

Beyond TruYou, a user's status can be enhanced through various achievements—positive reviews, average response time, and trusted connections, to name a few. Users can also personalize their background images and profile descriptions, just as they can on social media sites. And when it comes to communicating, OfferUp includes a chat-like message function that lets users communicate with each other without revealing personal contact information. If that isn't enough, OfferUp facilitates Community MeetUp Spots for users to make their exchanges. Partnering with local businesses and police forces, Community MeetUp Spots provide well-lit, video-monitored places that are safe for buyers and sellers to make exchanges—a stark contrast to Craigslist's traditional and laissez-faire approach.

All this does more than just help people feel connected or even develop social networks within OfferUp. It eliminates some of Craiglist's biggest security issues. For starters, because phone numbers and email addresses are typically shared on Craigslist, users are commonly targeted by scam artists. What's more, meeting someone in person for a transaction has led to robberies, assaults, and even murders. That's right. Dozens of people have suffered death at the hands of the person they were meeting to conduct a Craigslist transaction.

During its first five years, OfferUp focused on building its user base while putting little effort into generating revenue, the typical strategy for online marketplaces. In fact, with 18 million downloads and fifth-year transactions totaling more than $14 billion, OfferUp hadn't made a dime for itself. With very marketing expense and a growth rate that exceeded Craigslist and eBay in their early years, OfferUp was able to raise money through investors—first in the tens and then in the hundreds of millions of dollars.

From Mobile App to Mobile Marketer

But OfferUp eventually began addressing the issue of how to make money off all those users and transactions. Like Craigslist, OfferUp developed naturally as a platform for consumer-to-consumer transactions as well as business-to-consumer and even business-to-business transactions. Although there were various options for starting a revenue stream, OfferUp first focused on businesses. For starters, it designed two optional premium features to facilitate targeting customers—Bump and Feature. With Bump, a seller can put an item at the top of browsing and search results for new items. Feature, on the other hand, allows sellers to promote items and makes them appear in special promotional spots within the top 50 search, browse, and category results. Both of these features can be purchased for runs of three, seven, or 14 days. While these features appeal primarily to business sellers, they can be selected by anyone.

Recently, OfferUp made two big moves to increase its value to national brands and to increase the company's income base. First, it introduced paid advertising. Marketers can now target specific users based on their network, browsing, and posting activities. So when a user searches for a home theater system among the local offerings by individuals and businesses, for example, that shopper will likely see ads for relevant offerings by online retailers such as eBay, Amazon, and Walmart as well as by marketers such as Sony or Samsung that sell their products directly.

In its biggest move yet, OfferUp has expanded its marketplace beyond local boundaries by adding a shipping option. When an item is sold through this new nationwide shipping feature, the seller is charged a 7.9 percent fee—lower than eBay or Amazon. The buyer pays between $5 and $20 for shipping, depending on the size of the product. This new transaction fee offers far more value to companies and brands of all sizes and locations while also increasing the utility of the platform for shoppers. For OfferUp, advertising and transaction fees represent substantial new revenue streams over the paid tools for promoting items for sale.

OfferUp's strategies appear to be working. Craigslist reported 55 million unique visitors for the most recent month, a huge audience but one that was down 10 percent from the year before. That decline wasn't all due to OfferUp. Rival LetGo offers a similar mobile marketplace and is doing just about as much business as OfferUp in the United States. And while OfferUp plans to eventually take its app international, LetGo is already doing business in multiple countries. LetGo has also raised nearly double the amount of venture capital as OfferUp and is spending aggressively on advertising, whereas OfferUp has relied more on word of mouth. In addition to LetGo, other new marketplace apps are also vying for a piece of the online local marketplace pie. Even Facebook is getting into the game. With its rapidly growing Marketplace as an avenue for local buying and selling, it need only engage a fraction of its user base to make a large dent in the market.

While Huzar recognizes the competition posed by LetGo, Facebook, Craigslist, and others, he has a different perspective than most. He believes that the business of online marketplaces—whether local, national, or global—is not a zero-sum game. In his view, OfferUp doesn't need to steal business from Craigslist in order to thrive. Instead, along with LetGo and other entrants, OfferUp needs to attract a new generation of mobile device users that never even considered Craigslist as a shopping or selling platform. Huzar may be right. Although it's nearly impossible to calculate the sales volume that flows through Craigslist (the company leaves all money-changing to the buyers and sellers), OfferUp and LetGo will combine for an estimated total of more than $40 billion worth of goods and services sold in the United States this year. Compare that to eBay's total global volume of $61 billion last year or even Amazon's North American sales of just over $100 billion. The new entrants are having a substantial impact.

Ultimately, although OfferUp faces some stiff challenges ahead, its future looks bright. With its focus on an easy-to-use interface made for today's mobile users as well as a growing and safe community, OfferUp will continue disrupt the world of digital marketplaces. Huzar takes the challenges seriously but tries not to let it bother him too much. "I don't lose much sleep at night over it," referring to the competition. Indeed, Huzar is counting on OfferUp being around in a decade when it's time to buy his daughter her first car.

Questions for Discussion

1. As a mobile marketplace, how does OfferUp provide value to shoppers? Sellers?
2. Analyze OfferUp's business model relative to the different forms of digital and online marketing covered in this chapter.
3. Describe the value of OfferUp to national brands and retailers as a channel for mobile marketing. Does OfferUp also pose a threat these companies?
4. Compare the competitive relationship between OfferUp and LetGo to that of Uber and Lyft. Based on this comparison, what does the future hold for OfferUp?
5. Do you agree with Nick Huzar that OfferUp can succeed without taking business away from Craigslist? Explain.

Sources: Sarah Perez. "Local Marketplace OfferUp Takes on EBay with Launch of Nationwide Shipping," *TechCrunch*, May 1, 2018, http://techcrunch.com/2018/05/01/local-marketplace-offerup-takes-on-ebay-with-launch-of-nationwide-shipping/; Jason Del Rey, "OfferUp Went Head to Head with Craigslist to Build a Following. Now It's Going after Ebay to Build a Business," *Recode*, May 1, 2018, www.recode.net/2018/5/1/17305648/offerup-shipping-feature-ebay-letgo-facebook-marketplace; and Ryan Mac, "Can Craigslist Be Killed? These Startups Are Taking Aim," *Forbes*, May 2, 2017, www.forbes.com/sites/ryanmac/2017/05/02/offerup-letgo-killing-craigslist/#5ed619256ff7.

Company Case 15

L'Oréal: The United Nations of Beauty

How does a French company successfully market an American version of a Korean skin beautifier under a French brand name in Australia? Ask L'Oréal, which sells more than $30 billion worth of cosmetics, hair care products, skin care concoctions, and fragrances each year in 150 countries, making it the world's biggest cosmetics marketer. L'Oréal's success is based on a concept it calls "universalization." It sells its brands globally by understanding how they appeal to varied cultural nuances of beauty in specific local markets. Then it finds the best balance between standardizing its brands for global impact and adapting them to meet local needs and desires.

L'Oréal is as global as a company gets. With offices spread throughout the world and more than half of its sales coming from markets outside Europe and North America, the company no longer has a clearly defined home market. L'Oréal's 34 brands originated in a half dozen or more different cultures, including French (L'Oréal Paris, Garnier,

Lancôme), American (Maybelline, Kiehl's, SoftSheen-Carson, Ralph Lauren, Urban Decay, Clarisonic, Redken), British (The Body Shop), Italian (Giorgio Armani), and Japanese (Shu Uemura). With these and many other well-known brands, the master global marketer is the uncontested world leader in makeup, skin care, and hair coloring and second only to P&G in hair care.

Because I'm Worth It

L'Oréal's strategy of universalization is tied to its mission—"beauty for all." If there is one thing that L'Oréal has discovered about women worldwide, it is that they want to feel good about themselves. And how they feel is inherently connected to how they care for themselves and their appearance. This universal characteristic holds true regardless of ethnicity, culture, age, or socioeconomic status. For this reason, "beauty for all" has L'Oréal focused on providing the ultimate in luxury beauty for the masses.

While the Paris-based giant has been peddling cosmetics for more than a century, the relevance of its mission became more apparent than ever in the 1970s. The company launched Superior Preference hair color with an advertisement that presented a woman's point of view and ended with four words—"Because I'm Worth It." From the moment the ad hit, those words struck a chord with women. Here was a brand with a message about what a woman thought—about her self-confidence, her decisions, her style.

Originally just a tagline, those four words have transcended their intended purpose and have even become part of the social fabric. They have been written into global language, used by women for any situation where she wants to stand up for herself and proclaim her self-worth. Today, 80 percent of women worldwide recognize and respond to this phrase in a positive and powerful way. And today, "Because I'm Worth It" is translated into action every day by L'Oréal.

Beauty from Multiple Perspectives

To achieve "beauty for all" globally, L'Oréal's starts with a corps of highly multicultural managers. The company is famous for building global brand teams around managers who have deep backgrounds in several cultures. Unlike many global corporations that set up an international structure composed of autonomous subsidiaries, divisions, and management teams in different parts of the world, L'Oréal knew that such a structure would not provide the balance between standardization and adaptation that is critical in today's cosmetics industry. Instead, the company built global teams around individual managers with deep backgrounds in multiple cultures, allowing them to switch easily among them.

Able to see things from multiple perspectives, a truly multicultural manager can think at any moment as if he or she were German, American, or Chinese—or all three at once. The Indian-American-French manager of a team that launched a men's skin care line in Southeast Asia explains. "I have a stock of references in different languages: English, Hindi, and French. I read books in three different languages, meet people from different countries, eat food from different [cultures], and so on. I cannot think about things one way."

For example, a French-Irish-Cambodian manager working on skin care noticed that, in Europe, face creams tended to be either "tinted" (and considered as makeup) or "lifting" (and considered as skin care). But in Asia, many face creams combined the two traits. Recognizing the growing popularity of Asian beauty trends in Europe, this manager guided his team in developing a tinted cream with lifting effects for the French market, a product that proved to be highly successful. As the global environment has created a greater need for this type of knowledge integration across cultures, L'Oréal's strategic use of multicultural managers provides built-in shortcuts. This management structure has given L'Oréal a critical competitive advantage in new-product development.

Diving Deep for Beauty

L'Oréal digs deep to understand what beauty means to consumers in different parts of the world. It outspends all major competitors on R&D, painstakingly researching beauty and personal care behaviors unique to specific locales. One of the goals of its global R&D efforts is to gain an in-depth understanding of the behaviors of women and men around the world with respect to beautifying and taking care of themselves. L'Oréal explains the need for this worldwide approach to beauty rituals:

> How many minutes does a Chinese woman devote to her morning beauty routine? How do people wash their hair in Bangkok? How many brush strokes does a Japanese woman or a French woman use to apply mascara? These beauty rituals, repeated thousands of times, are inherently cultural. Passed on by tradition, influenced by climate and by local living conditions, they strive to achieve an ideal of perfection that is different from one country and from one continent to the next. They provide an incredibly rich source of information for L'Oréal Research. Behind these rituals, there are physiological realities: fine, straight and short eyelashes cannot be made up the same way as thick, curled, and long lashes.

To facilitate this major R&D effort, L'Oréal has set up centers all over the world, developing a science of local observation it calls "geocosmetics." This science is fueled with insight gained through in-home visits as well as observations made in "bathroom laboratories." Equipped with high-tech gadgetry, these labs enable teams to study consumer behavior around the world.

L'Oréal's R&D program produces very precise information about regional rituals of hygiene and beauty as well as local conditions and constraints that affect the use of products, such as humidity and temperature. These insights feed R&D teams in the process of creating products for local markets. Combined with insights from global locations, such products can be adapted for multiple markets.

For example, consider Elséve Total Reparação, a hair care line initially developed at L'Oréal's labs in Rio de Janeiro to address specific hair problems described by Brazilian women.

In Brazil, more than half of all women have long, dry, dull, and very curly hair, resulting from the humid Brazilian climate, exposure to the sun, frequent washing, and smoothing and straightening treatments. Elséve Total Reparação was an immediate hit in Brazil, and L'Oréal quickly rolled it out to other South American and Latin American markets. The company then tracked down other global locales with climate characteristics and hair care rituals similar to those faced by Brazilian women. Subsequently, L'Oréal launched the brand as Elséve Total Repair in numerous European, Indian, and other South East Asian markets, where consumers greeted it with similar enthusiasm.

Such adaptation often plays out across multiple L'Oréal brands—which takes us back to that Korean skin beautifier sold under a French brand in Australia mentioned in the opening paragraph. Blemish balm cream (BB cream) was originally created by dermatologists in Korea to soothe skin and hide minor blemishes. It quickly became a high-flying Korean brand. However, applying their deep knowledge of skin colors, treatments, and makeup worldwide, L'Oréal researchers developed a successful new-generation BB cream adapted to conditions and skin colors in U.S. markets (where BB stands for "beauty balm") and launched it under the Maybelline New York brand. Still not finished, L'Oréal created yet another local version for Europe under the Garnier brand, which it also introduced in other world markets, including Australia.

L'Oréal's global R&D efforts have produced a "geography of skin colors"—a proprietary mapping of the world that makes it possible to adapt cosmetic products to the needs of women around the world. In a similar manner, the company has expanded the traditional classification of three hair types (African, Asian, and European) to eight different categories, based on a scientific measurement of curl characteristics that include the diameter of the curvature, the curl index, the number of waves, and tendrils.

L'Oréal doesn't just adapt its product formulations globally. It also adapts brand positioning and marketing to international needs and expectations. For example, more than 20 years ago, the company bought stodgy American makeup producer Maybelline. To reinvigorate and globalize the brand, it moved the unit's headquarters from Tennessee to New York City and added "New York" to the label. The resulting urban, street-smart, Big Apple image played well globally with the mid-price positioning of the workaday makeup brand. The makeover soon earned Maybelline a 20 percent market share in its category in Western Europe. The young urban positioning also hit the mark in Asia, where few women realized that the trendy "New York" Maybelline brand belonged to French cosmetics giant L'Oréal.

By acquiring brands such as Maybelline, L'Oréal also gains brands that have immediate recognition and products already made for a given market. This gives the company an immediate point-of-entry to a market at a cost that is lower than building a brand from scratch. Such is the case with Yue-Sai Cosmetics, a Chinese company that uses herbs in its creams. L'Oréal bought it a decade ago. Sales of Yue-Sai have been on the rise ever since.

L'Oréal and its brands are truly global and will become even more so when it launches an augmented reality digital beauty assistant later this year. The new service will allow women all over the world to livestream a consultation session designed to mimic those offered at L'Oreal makeup counters. This continued effort to provide luxury beauty for the masses is working. Even as the Western European market growth has slowed and Brazil is in a slump, L'Oréal's revenues have increased every year over the past seven years for a total increase of 30 percent.

L'Oréal's huge international success comes from achieving a global–local balance that adapts and differentiates brands in local markets while optimizing their impact across global markets. L'Oréal is one of few companies that has achieved both local brand responsiveness and global brand integration. "We respect the differences among our consumers around the world," says L'Oréal's CEO. "We have global brands, but we need to adapt them to local needs." When a former CEO once addressed a UNESCO conference, nobody batted an eyelid when he described L'Oréal as "The United Nations of Beauty."

Questions for Discussion

1. Of the five global product and communications strategies, which best describes L'Oréal's approach?
2. On a scale of one to five, to what degree does L'Oréal adapt its offering in each global market? Support your answer.
3. What are the disadvantages to L'Oréal's global approach?
4. Which strategy does L'Oréal employ for entering a new market? How does the company benefit from this approach?
5. Will L'Oréal continue to succeed at such a high level? Why or why not?

Sources: Based on information from Kristina Monllos, "L'Oreal Is Bringing the Makeup Counter Experience into Your Home with AR and Livestreaming," *Adweek*, June 18, 2018, www.adweek.com/brand-marketing/loreal-is-bringing-the-makeup-counter-experience-into-your-home-with-ar-and-livestreaming/; "Our Mission Is 'Beauty for All,' Says L'Oréal Global CEO Jean-Paul," *The Economic Times*, January 30, 2015, https://economictimes.indiatimes.com/magazines/corporate-dossier/our-mission-is-beauty-for-all-says-loreal-global-ceo-jean-paul/articleshow/46053691.cms; Hae-Jung Hong and Yves Doz, "L'Oréal Masters Multiculturalism," *Harvard Business Review*, June, 2013, pp. 114–119; Liza Lin, "L'Oréal Puts on a Happy Face in China," *Bloomberg Businessweek*, April 1–7, 2013, pp. 25–26; "A Worldwide Approach to Beauty Rituals," www.loreal.com/research-innovation/when-the-diversity-of-types-of-beauty-inspires-science/a-world-wide-approach-to-beauty-rituals.aspx, accessed June 2018; and additional information and quotes from www.lorealparisusa.com/en/about-loreal-paris/overview.aspx and www.loreal-finance.com/eng/annual-report, accessed October 2018.

Company Case 16

LEGO: Making the World a Better Place—One Brick at a Time

Classic LEGO plastic bricks have been fixtures in homes around the world for more than 70 years. Just 15 years ago, The LEGO Group (TLG) was near bankruptcy, spiraling downward and losing money at a rate of $1 million a day. But after a massive restructuring and implementation of a new strategic plan, TLG has been on the rise ever since. In fact, TLG is now the world's largest toy company, besting powerhouses Mattel and Hasbro. Last year, The LEGO Group (TLG) produced 3,700 different types of LEGO bricks and a record 75 *billion* total bricks, enough to construct a continuous line stretching around the world more than 27 times. All those bricks went into more than 100 million LEGO sets that found their way into the eager hands of customers in 140 countries, putting over $5.6 billion into TLG's coffers.

Perhaps more notable than becoming the global toy market leader is the fact that TLG has achieved this feat while also establishing an unsurpassed commitment to social responsibility. In fact, in an annual study published by *Forbes*, based on ratings of social responsibility from consumers in 15 countries, LEGO came out on top last year, moving up from its fifth-place showing the year before. In the study conducted by the Reputation Institute, LEGO topped all other companies in perceptions that it behaves ethically, operates transparently, conducts business fairly, protects the environment, and supports worthy causes. These consumer perceptions reflect TLG's actions. According to Stephen Hahn-Griffiths, Chief Research Officer for the Reputation Institute, TLG "has embraced corporate social responsibility from top to bottom."

When TLG developed its plan to bounce back from the brink of bankruptcy, it also took the opportunity to reevaluate its company values. As a result, a social responsibility strategy became a key component of TLC's turnaround plan, driven by a desire to have a more positive impact on the world. To demonstrate its commitment, TLG became the first toy company to join the United Nations Global Compact—the world's largest social responsibility initiative—and committed to support the 17 United Nations Sustainable Development Goals.

It's for the Children

TLG's social responsibility goals are organized into three key areas—children, people, and the environment. According to Thomas Kirk Kristiansen, great-grandson of company TLG founder Ole Kirk Kristiansen, "Children are our role models." TLG has always sought to inspire children through the power of play by facilitating a child's natural approach to learning. The idea is to enable children to build valuable life skills while having fun. This supports TLG's vision—"to inspire and develop the builders of tomorrow." In addition, one of the driving pillars of TLG's responsibility strategy is "leaving the best possible world for children to inherit."

TLG's very ownership structure demonstrates its commitment to children. The LEGO Foundation owns 25 percent of the company. Dedicated to carrying out TLG's vision, the LEGO Foundation acts as an internal watchdog, ensuring that the profits from every LEGO product sold help bring learning through play to children. To this end, the LEGO Foundation conducts research and carries out Local Community Engagement activities all over the world. Such activities include working with partners to execute early childhood programs, launch Play Labs, and establish early childhood centers.

Recognizing "play" as a child's right, TLG worked with the LEGO Foundation and partner UNICEF to give children a voice during World Children's Day, bringing kids in to take over key roles at TLG. Additionally, TLG motivated employees to volunteer to work with children around the world in a program to engage them in environmental and social issues as well as help them build ideas to make the world a better place. Through these and other activities, the LEGO Foundation engaged 1.3 million children last year.

Caring for People: A Company Value

The initiatives mentioned above aren't only about children—they focus on TLG's responsibility toward people as well. For such initiatives, TLG engages employees as well as local community members to take part. For example, TLG encourages employees to become "Play Agents," training and educating them to understand the role and significance of play and providing them with the tools needed to inspire children through Local Community Engagement activities. Last year, the LEGO Foundation trained almost 1,200 Play Agents, bringing the total to 3,000. TLG believes that engaging employees in the company mission and vision is an important part of creating "the best place to work."

But when it comes to caring for people, TLG goes much deeper than mixing work and play. TLG has high standards for treating employees with respect, paying fair wages, maintaining a safe work environment, and ensuring reasonable working hours. These standards do not stop at the walls of the company's own facilities. Under the LEGO Code of Conduct, all suppliers must comply with strict guidelines for child labor, forced labor, discrimination, wages and benefits, health and safety, and other aspects of ethical treatment of employees. During the past year, TLG audited 100 percent of suppliers with respect to the LEGO Code of Conduct, including suppliers in high-risk countries. What's more, TLG requires that each supplier provide written assurance that their own suppliers comply with the same standards.

Leaving the Planet Better for Tomorrow's Children

The final component of TLG's social responsibility strategy is caring for the environment. Although setting goals to reduce a company's environmental footprint is pretty much mandatory these days, TLG sees it as an extension of its mission. That is, TLG's work to inspire children and help them achieve their full potential through play applies to the children of tomorrow as much as to the children of today. And TLG recognizes that for children of future generations to enjoy the fruits of its mission, they must inherit a planet with a healthy environment. As with the other components of its social responsibility code, TLG has high standards for both itself and its suppliers when it comes to minimizing CO_2 emissions, waste, and pollution. It has also established goals for developing renewable energy and sustainable materials.

Recently, TLG achieved a major environmental milestone when it announced that the first LEGO pieces made from sustainable plant-based plastic will go on sale this year. Specifically, polyethylene—a soft, durable, and flexible plastic made with ethanol extracted from sugar cane material—will be the sole plastic used to make botanical elements such as leaves, bushes, and trees included in LEGO building sets. As a bioplastic, these pieces will also be recyclable and biodegradable.

Until now, LEGO elements have always been made entirely from petroleum-based plastic. The first bioplastic LEGO pieces to hit the shelves will comprise only about two percent of all LEGO elements produced. However, according to Tim Brooks, vice president of environmental responsibility at TLG, "This is a great first step in our ambitious commitment of making all LEGO bricks using sustainable materials." To move toward this goal, TLG has joined forces with the World Wide Fund for Nature and the Bioplastic Feedstock Alliance to support and build demand for sustainably sourced plastic and ensure fully sustainable sourcing of raw materials for the bioplastics industry.

Just a few years ago, TLG set a goal to achieve 100 percent sustainable materials in its bricks and packaging by 2030. However, it recently moved its deadline for its goal for packaging materials forward to 2025. Already, 75 percent of the cardboard used in its packaging comes from recycled material. Additionally, the company is focused on other environmental benefits that can be achieved through innovations in packaging. For example, reducing the average size of a LEGO box by 14 percent over the past four years saved 7,000 tons of cardboard, in turn eliminating the need for 3,000 truckloads.

When a major global corporation makes even a small social or environmental improvement, the scale of the company magnifies the impact. But TLG is not satisfied to achieve big impacts through small improvements. Can you imagine the impact of 700 million LEGO tires being made from bioplastic instead of oil-based plastic? TLG can. And TLG expects that the impact of such actions will not only result in direct benefits, they will be felt throughout the toy industry and beyond.

Questions for Discussion

1. Give as many examples as you can for how TLG defies the common social criticisms of marketing.
2. Of the five sustainable marketing principles discussed in the text, which one best describes TLG's approach?
3. Analyze TLG's business using the Societal Classification of Products (Figure 16.4).
4. Would TLG be more financially successful if it were not so focused on social responsibility? Explain.

Sources: "First Sustainable LEGO Pieces to Go on Sale," *The Guardian*, March 2, 2018, www.theguardian.com/lifeandstyle/2018/mar/02/first-sustainable-lego-pieces-to-go-on-sale; Karsten Strauss, "The Companies with the Best CSR Reputations in 2017," *Forbes*, February 8, 2018, www.forbes.com/sites/karstenstrauss/2018/02/08/the-companies-with-the-best-csr-reputations-in-2017/#788c20333873; Simon Mainwaring, "How LEGO Rebuilt Itself as a Purposeful and Sustainable Brand," *Forbes*, August 11, 2016, www.forbes.com/sites/simonmainwaring/2016/08/11/how-lego-rebuilt-itself-as-a-purposeful-and-sustainable-brand/#2bbd44e46f3c; and additional information from www.lego.com/en-us/aboutus/news-room, www.lego.com/en-us/aboutus/lego-group/code-of-conduct, and www.lego.com/en-us/aboutus/responsibility/story/report, accessed October 2018.

Appendix 2 Marketing Plan

The Marketing Plan: An Introduction

As a marketer, you will need a good marketing plan to provide direction and focus for your brand, product, or company. With a detailed plan, any business will be better prepared to launch a new product or build sales for existing products. Nonprofit organizations also use marketing plans to guide their fund-raising and outreach efforts. Even government agencies put together marketing plans for initiatives such as building public awareness of proper nutrition and stimulating area tourism.

The Purpose and Content of a Marketing Plan

Unlike a business plan, which offers a broad overview of the entire organization's mission, objectives, strategy, and resource allocation, a marketing plan has a more limited scope. It serves to document how the organization's strategic objectives will be achieved through specific marketing strategies and tactics, with the customer as the starting point. It is also linked to the plans of other departments within the organization. Suppose, for example, a marketing plan calls for selling 200,000 units annually. The production department must gear up to make that many units, the finance department must arrange funding to cover the expenses, the human resources department must be ready to hire and train staff, and so on. Without the appropriate level of organizational support and resources, no marketing plan can succeed.

Although the exact length and layout will vary from company to company, a marketing plan usually contains the sections described in Chapter 2. Smaller businesses may create shorter or less formal marketing plans whereas corporations frequently require highly structured marketing plans. To guide implementation effectively, every part of the plan must be described in considerable detail. Sometimes a company will post its marketing plans on an intranet site, which allows managers and employees in different locations to consult specific sections and collaborate on additions or changes.

The Role of Research

Marketing plans are not created in a vacuum. To develop successful strategies and action programs, marketers need up-to-date information about the environment, the competition, and the market segments to be served. Often, analysis of internal data is the starting point for assessing the current marketing situation, supplemented by marketing intelligence and research investigating the overall market, the competition, key issues, and threats and opportunities. As the plan is put into effect, marketers use a variety of research techniques to measure progress toward objectives and identify areas for improvement if results fall short of projections.

Finally, marketing research helps marketers learn more about their customers' requirements, expectations, perceptions, and satisfaction levels. This deeper understanding provides a foundation for building competitive advantage through well-informed segmenting, targeting, differentiating, and positioning decisions. Thus, the marketing plan should outline what marketing research will be conducted and how the findings will be applied.

The Role of Customer Involvement and Relationships

The marketing plan shows how the company will establish and maintain profitable customer engagement and relationships. In the process, however, it also shapes a number of internal and external relationships. First, it affects how marketing personnel work with each other and with other departments to deliver value and satisfy customers. Second, it affects how the company works with suppliers, distributors, and strategic alliance partners to achieve the objectives listed in the plan. Third, it influences the company's dealings with other stakeholders, including government regulators, the media, and the community at large. All of these relationships are important to the organization's success, so they should be considered when a marketing plan is being developed.

From Marketing Plan to Marketing Action

Companies generally create yearly marketing plans, although some plans cover a longer period. Marketers start planning well in advance of the implementation date to allow time for marketing research, thorough analysis, management review, and coordination between departments. Then, after each action program begins, marketers monitor ongoing results, compare them with projections, analyze any differences, and take corrective steps as needed. Some marketers also prepare contingency plans for implementation if certain conditions emerge. Because of inevitable and sometimes unpredictable environmental changes, marketers must be ready to update and adapt marketing plans at any time.

For effective implementation and control, the marketing plan should define how progress toward objectives will be measured. Managers typically use budgets, schedules, and performance standards for monitoring and evaluating results. With budgets, they can compare planned expenditures with actual expenditures for a given week, month, or other period. Schedules allow management to see when tasks were supposed to be completed—and when they were actually completed. Performance standards track the outcomes of marketing programs to see whether the company is moving toward its objectives. Some examples of performance standards are market share, sales volume, product profitability, and customer satisfaction.

Sample Marketing Plan: Chill Beverage Company

Executive Summary

The Chill Beverage Company is preparing to launch a new line of vitamin-enhanced water called NutriWater. Although the bottled water market is maturing, the functional water category—and more specifically the vitamin-enhanced water category—is still growing. NutriWater will be positioned by the slogan "Expect more"—indicating that the brand offers more in the way of desirable product features and benefits at a competitive price. Chill Beverage is taking advantage of its existing experience and brand equity among its loyal current customer base of millennials who consume its Chill Soda soft drink. NutriWater will target similar millennials who are maturing and looking for an alternative to soft drinks and high-calorie sugared beverages.

The primary marketing objective is to achieve first-year U.S. sales of $50 million, roughly 2 percent of the functional water market. Based on this market share goal, the company expects to sell more than 26 million units the first year and break even in the final quarter of the year.

Current Marketing Situation

The Chill Beverage Company—founded in 2010—markets niche and emerging products in the beverage industry. Rather than directly challenging established beverage giants like the Coca-Cola Company and PepsiCo, the Chill Beverage Company has focused on the fringes of the industry. Its Chill Soda soft drink brand hit the market with six unique flavors in glass bottles. The company now markets dozens of Chill Soda flavors, many unique to the brand. Over the past few years, Chill has successfully introduced new lines including natural juice drinks and iced teas. Chill Beverage has grown its business every year since it was founded. In the most recent year, it achieved $230 million in revenue and net profits of $18.6 million. As part of its future growth strategy, Chill Beverage plans to introduce new lines of beverages to continue to take advantage of emerging trends in the industry. Currently, it is preparing to launch a line of vitamin-enhanced waters.

For years, U.S. consumers have imbibed more carbonated soft drinks than any other bottled beverage. But concerns over health and obesity have taken the fizz out of the soda market—sales have declined for the past 13 years in a row. Meanwhile, bottled water consumption is on a growth trajectory that shows no sign of slowing down. In fact, bottled water passed carbonated soft drinks as the number one beverage by volume two years ago. People in the United States now consumer more bottled water than any other beverage, including carbonated soft drinks, coffee, beer, and milk.

Currently, the average person in the United States consumes more than 42 gallons of bottled water every year and experts expect that volume to rise to 50 gallons by 2020. In contrast, per capita consumption of carbonated soft drinks is down to 37.5 gallons and will continue to decline. Supporting bottled water's new position as the market leader, a recent study found that among U.S. consumers, bottled water is their most preferred beverage. An $18.5 billion market, bottled water revenues in the United States are expected to increase by more than 40 percent during the next four years.

Competition is more intense now than ever as the industry consolidates and new types of bottled water emerge. The U.S. market is dominated by three global corporations. With a global portfolio of more than 50 brands (including Poland Spring, Nestlé Pure Life, Arrowhead, Deer Park, and Ice Mountain), Nestlé leads the market for with a 28 share of all water sales (sparkling, functional water, flavored water, and so on). Coca-Cola is number two with more than 24 percent and PepsiCo follows at a distant third with approximately 13 percent. Private labels account for 22 percent of the market.

While bottled water as a whole is strong, the market for the sub-category of functional waters is even stronger, growing by 11 percent for the most recent year. In the current market environment, functional waters have thrived based on the promise of incremental benefits for health-conscious consumers based on the infusion of ingredients such as vitamins, minerals (including electrolytes), herbs, and other additives. Functional waters, therefore, carry the standard benefits of taste and convenience with an increased appeal to lifestyle and wellbeing. Most functional waters are sweetened and flavored and are distinguished from sports drinks that have the primary purpose of maximizing hydration by replenishing electrolytes.

To break into this market dominated by huge global corporations and littered with dozens of other small players, Chill Beverage must carefully target specific segments with features and benefits valued by those segments.

Market Description

The bottled water market consists of many different types of water. Varieties of plain water include spring, purified, mineral, and distilled. Although these different types of water are sold as consumer products, they also serve as the core ingredient for the various types of functional waters. The flexibility of bottled water as a category seems to be endless.

Although some consumers may not perceive much of a difference between brands, others are drawn to specific product features and benefits provided by different brands. For example, some consumers may perceive spring water as healthier than other types of water. Some may look for water that is optimized for hydration. Others seek additional nutritional benefits claimed by bottlers that enhance their brands with vitamins, minerals, herbs, and other additives. Still other consumers make selections based on flavor. A recent study revealed that the most important attribute driving the choice of bottled water is *all natural ingredients* (57 percent) followed by *vitamin-enhanced* (33 percent), *antioxidants* (31 percent), and *flavors* (31 percent).

The industry as a whole has positioned bottled water of all kinds as a low-calorie, healthy alternative to soft drinks, sports drinks, energy drinks, and other types of beverages. This positioning is working—94 percent of Americans believe bottled water is healthier than soda. Bottled water brands also distinguish themselves by size and type of container, multipacks, and refrigeration at point-of-sale.

Chill Beverage's market for NutriWater consists of consumers of single-serving-sized bottled beverages who are looking for a healthy yet flavorful alternative. *Healthy* in this

Table A2.1 Segment Needs and Corresponding Features/Benefits of NutriWater

Targeted Segment	Customer Need	Corresponding Features/Benefits
Athletes	• Hydration and replenishment of essential minerals • Energy to maximize performance	• Electrolytes and carbohydrates • B vitamins, carbohydrates
Health conscious	• Maintain optimum weight • Optimize nutrition levels • Avoid harmful chemicals and additives • Desire to consume a tastier beverage than water	• Half the calories of fully sugared beverages • Higher levels of vitamins A, B, C, E, zinc, chromium, and folic acid than other products; vitamins unavailable in other products • All natural ingredients • Six new-age flavors
Socially conscious	• Support causes that help solve world's social problems	• 25-cent donation from each purchase to Vitamin Angels
Millennials	• Aversion to mass-media advertising/technologically savvy • Counter-culture attitude • Diet enhancement due to fast-paced lifestyle	• Less-invasive online and social networking promotional tactics • Small, privately held company • Full RDA levels of essential vitamins and minerals

context means natural ingredients, enhanced nutritional content, and low calories. This market includes traditional soft drink consumers who want to improve their health as well as non–soft drink consumers who want an option other than plain bottled water. Specific segments that Chill Beverage will target during the first year include athletes, the health conscious, the socially responsible, and millennials who favor independent corporations. The Chill Soda brand has established a strong base of loyal customers, primarily among millennials. This generational segment is becoming a prime target as it matures and seeks alternatives to full-calorie soft drinks. >> **Table A2.1** shows how NutriWater addresses the needs of targeted consumer segments.

Product Review

Chill Beverage's new line of NutriWater vitamin-enhanced water offers the following features:

- Six new-age flavors including Peach Mango, Berry Pomegranate, Kiwi Dragonfruit, Mandarin Orange, Blueberry Grape, and Key Lime.
- Single-serving size, 20-ounce, PET recyclable bottles.
- Formulated for wellness, replenishment, and optimum energy.
- Full recommended daily allowance (RDA) of essential vitamins and minerals (including electrolytes).
- Higher vitamin concentration—vitamin levels are two to ten times higher than-market-leading products, with more vitamins and minerals than any other brand.
- Additional vitamins—vitamins include A, E, and B2 as well as folic acid—none of which are contained in the market-leading products.
- All natural—no artificial flavors, colors, or preservatives.
- Sweetened with pure cane sugar and Stevia, a natural zero-calorie sweetener.
- Twenty-five cents from each purchase will be donated to Vitamin Angels, a nonprofit organization with a mission to prevent vitamin deficiency in at-risk children.

Competitive Review

More than a decade before Chill launched its first product, bottled water entered a strong growth phase. New types of plain water emerged, followed by new subcategories. These included flavored waters—such as Aquafina's Flavorsplash—as well as functional waters. Functional waters emerged to bridge the gap between soft drinks and waters, appealing to people who knew they should drink more water and less soft drinks but still wanted flavor. Initially, development of brands for this product variation occurred in startup and boutique beverage companies such as SoBe and Glacéau, creator of Vitaminwater. In the 2000s, major beverage corporations acquired the most successful smaller brands, providing the bigger firms with a solid market position in this category and diversification in bottled waters in general. Backed by the marketing expertise and budgets of the leading beverage companies, functional water grew at a rate exceeding that of plain water.

At one point, Coca-Cola's Vitaminwater was the fourth-largest bottled water brand, behind Nestlé Pure Life, Coca-Cola's Dasani, and Pepsi's Aquafina. After taking a hit in the press for the low amount of vitamins and high amount of sugar contained in most brands of vitamin-enhanced waters, sales for Vitaminwater temporarily slipped. But Coca-Cola lost no ground as sales for Smartwater—Vitaminwater's non-flavored sibling—filled the void, rising to the fourth largest brand. Industry insiders expect growth of functional waters to outpace non-functional waters in the coming years.

The fragmentation of this category, combined with domination by the market leaders, has created a severely competitive environment. Although there is indirect competition posed by all types of bottled waters and even other types of beverages (soft drinks, energy drinks, juices, teas, and flavor drops), this competitive analysis focuses on direct competition from leading functional water brands. Functional water brands are either sweetened and flavored, just flavored, or neither sweetened nor flavored. Sweetened varieties use blend traditional sugars with zero-calorie sweeteners. The types of sweeteners used create a point of differentiation. The result is a range of sugar content, carbohydrates, and calories as high as half that of regular soft drinks and other sweetened beverages and as low as zero.

Pricing for this product is consistent across brands and varies by type of retail outlet, with convenience stores typically charging more than grocery stores. The price for a 20-ounce bottle ranges from $1.00 to $1.99, with some niche brands costing slightly more. Smartwater—a plain still water enhanced with electrolytes—is the leading functional water brand. Chill Beverage's NutriWater will focus on competition posed by flavored and enhanced water brands, include the following:

- ***Vitaminwater:*** Created in 2000 as a new product for Energy Brands' Glacéau, which was also the developer of Smartwater (distilled water with electrolytes). Coca-Cola purchased Energy Brands for $4.1 billion in 2007. Vitaminwater is sold in regular, zero-calorie, and *active* varieties. With 22 bottled varieties—10 regular, 9 zero-calorie, and 3 active—as well as availability in fountain form, Vitaminwater offers more options than any brand on the market. Whereas Vitaminwater varieties are distinguished by flavor, they are named to invoke perceptions of benefits such as Refresh, Power-C, Focus, and Revive. The brand's current slogan is "Drink Outside the Lines." Vitaminwater is vapor distilled, de-ionized, and/or filtered and is sweetened with crystalline fructose (corn syrup) and cane sugar or erythritol and stevia. Vitaminwater exceeds $700 million in annual sales and commands approximately one-third of the functional water market.
- ***Propel:*** Gatorade created Propel in 2000, just one year prior to PepsiCo's purchase of this leading sports drink marketer. It marketed Propel as "Hydration for Your Workout," PepsiCo recently tied its fitness water brand to its market-leading sports drink brand with the tagline, "How Gatorade Does Water." Propel was originally available in regular and zero-calorie varieties. However, it is now available only as a zero-calorie beverage. Propel comes in nine flavored varieties as well as in unflavored form. Each variety of Propel contains the same blend of B vitamins, vitamin C, vitamin E, antioxidants, and electrolytes. Flavored versions are sweetened with sucralose. Propel is available in a wide variety of sizes, with 16.9 and 24-ounce PET bottles and multipacks. Propel is also marketed in powder form to be added to bottled water. With more than $200 million in revenues and double-digit growth during the past three years, Propel is the number three functional water brand behind Smartwater and Vitaminwater.

Table A2.2 Sample of Competitive Products

Competitor	Brand	Features
Coca-Cola	Vitaminwater	Regular and zero-calorie versions; 22 varieties; each flavor provides a different function based on blend of vitamins and minerals; vapor distilled, de-ionized, and/or filtered; sweetened with crystalline fructose and cane sugar; 20-ounce single-serve or multi-pack, fountain, and drops.
PepsiCo	Propel	Zero-calorie only; ten flavors; fitness positioning based on "Hydration for Your Workout"; B vitamins, vitamin C, vitamin E, antioxidants, and electrolytes; sweetened with sucralose; 16.9-ounce and 24-ounce PET bottles and multipacks; powdered packets; liquid enhancer.
PepsiCo	SoBewater	Zero calories, vitamins, minerals, and herbs; Pure—mildly flavored, sweetened with Stevia; 20-ounce single-serve and multi-packs.

- ***SoBewater:*** PepsiCo bought SoBe in 2000 and introduced Lifewater in 2008 as an answer to Coca-Cola's Vitaminwater. Now rebranded as SoBewater, the brand includes multiple zero-calorie varieties. Each variety is infused with a formulation of vitamins, minerals, and herbs designed to provide a claimed benefit. Sweetened with Stevia-based PureVia, SoBewater contains no artificial flavors or colors. SoBewater is sold in 20-ounce PET bottles and multipacks. With more than $150 million in annual revenues, SoBewater is the fourth-largest functional water brand with a 7 percent share.
- ***Niche brands:*** The market for functional waters includes companies that market their wares on a small scale through independent retailers: Assure, Zico, Ayala Herbal Water, and Skinny Water. Some brands feature exotic additives and/or artistic glass bottles.

Despite the strong competition, NutriWater believes it can create a relevant brand image and gain recognition among the targeted segments. The brand offers strong points of differentiation with higher and unique vitamin content, all-natural ingredients, and support for a relevant social cause. With other strategic assets, Chill Beverage is confident that it can establish a competitive advantage that will allow NutriWater to grow in the market. >> **Table A2.2** shows a sample of competing products.

Channels and Logistics Review

With the three main brands now owned by Coca-Cola and PepsiCo, there is a huge hole in the independent distributor system. NutriWater will be distributed through an independent distributor to a network of retailers in the United States. This strategy will avoid some of the head-on competition for shelf space with the Coca-Cola and PepsiCo brands and will also directly target likely NutriWater customers. As with the rollout of the core Chill Soda brand, this strategy will focus on placing coolers in retail locations that will exclusively hold NutriWater. These retailers include:

- ***Grocery chains:*** Regional grocery chains such as HyVee in the Midwest, Wegman's in the east, and WinCo in the west.
- ***Health and natural food stores:*** Chains such as Whole Foods as well as local health food co-ops.
- ***Fitness centers:*** National fitness center chains such as 24-Hour Fitness, Gold's Gym, and other regional chains.

As the brand gains acceptance, channels will expand into larger grocery chains, convenience stores, and unique locations relevant to the target customer segment.

Strengths, Weaknesses, Opportunities, and Threats Analysis

NutriWater has several powerful strengths on which to build, but its major weakness is lack of brand awareness and image. Major opportunities include a growing market and consumer trends targeted by NutriWater's product traits. Threats include barriers to entry posed

Table A2.3 NutriWater's Strengths, Weaknesses, Opportunities, and Threats

Strengths	Weaknesses
• Superior quality • Expertise in alternative beverage marketing • Social responsibility • Anti-establishment image	• Lack of brand awareness • Limited budget
Opportunities	**Threats**
• Market growth • Gap in the distribution network • Health trends • Anti-establishment image	• Limited shelf space • Image of enhanced waters • Environmental issues

by limited retail space as well as image issues for the bottled water industry. >> **Table A2.3** summarizes NutriWater's main strengths, weaknesses, opportunities, and threats.

Strengths

NutriWater can rely on the following important strengths:

1. ***Superior quality:*** NutriWater boasts the highest levels of added vitamins of any enhanced water, including full RDA levels of many vitamins. It is all natural with no artificial flavors, colors, or preservatives. It is sweetened with both pure cane sugar and the natural zero-calorie sweetener Stevia.
2. ***Expertise in alternative beverage marketing:*** The Chill Soda brand went from nothing to a successful and rapidly growing soft drink brand with fiercely loyal customers in a matter of only one decade. This success was achieved by starting small and focusing on gaps in the marketplace.
3. ***Social responsibility:*** Every customer will have the added benefit of helping malnourished children throughout the world. Although the price of NutriWater is in line with other competitors, low promotional costs allow for the substantial charitable donation of 25 cents per bottle while maintaining profitability.
4. ***Anti-establishment image:*** The big brands have decent products and strong distribution relationships. But they also carry the image of the large, corporate establishments. Chill Beverage has achieved success with an underdog image while remaining privately held. Vitaminwater, Propel, and SoBe were built on this same image but are now owned by major multinational corporations.

Weaknesses

1. ***Lack of brand awareness:*** As an entirely new brand, NutriWater will enter the market with limited or no brand awareness. The affiliation with Chill Soda will be kept at a minimum in order to prevent associations between NutriWater and soft drinks. This issue will be addressed through promotion and distribution strategies.
2. ***Limited budget:*** As a smaller company, Chill Beverage has much smaller funds available for promotional and research activities.

Opportunities

1. ***Market growth:*** Functional water as a category is growing at a rate of about 12 percent annually. Of the top six beverage categories, soft drinks, beer, milk, and fruit drinks experienced declines. The growth for coffee was less than 1 percent.
2. ***Gap in the distribution network:*** The market leaders distribute directly to retailers. This gives them an advantage in large national chains. However, no major enhanced water brands are currently being sold through independent distributors.

3. ***Health trends:*** Weight and nutrition continue to be issues for consumers in the United States. The country has the highest obesity rate for developed countries at 34 percent, with well over 60 percent of the population officially "overweight." Those numbers continue to rise. Additionally, Americans get 21 percent of their daily calories from beverages, a number that has tripled in the last three decades. Consumers still desire flavored beverages but look for lower calorie alternatives.
4. ***Anti-establishment image:*** Millennials (born between 1981 and 1997) maintain a higher aversion to mass marketing messages and global corporations than do Gen Xers and baby boomers.

Threats

1. ***Limited shelf space:*** Whereas competition is generally a threat for any type of product, competition in retail beverages is particularly high because of limited retail space. Carrying a new beverage product requires retailers to reduce shelf or cooler space already occupied by other brands.
2. ***Image of enhanced waters:*** The image of enhanced waters took a hit as Coca-Cola recently fought a class-action lawsuit accusing it of violating FDA regulations by promoting the health benefits of Vitaminwater. The lawsuit exposed the number one functional water brand as basically sugar water with minimal nutritional value. Each of the major brands is strengthening its zero-calorie lines. They no longer promote health benefits on the labels. Although this is potentially a threat, it is also an opportunity for Chill to exploit.
3. ***Environmental issues:*** Environmental groups continue to educate the public on the environmental costs of bottled water, including landfill waste, carbon emissions from production and transportation, and harmful effects of chemicals in plastics.

Objectives and Issues

Chill Beverage has set aggressive but achievable objectives for NutriWater for the first and second years of market entry.

First-year Objectives

During the first year on the market, Chill Beverage aims for NutriWater to achieve a 2 percent share of the functional water market, or approximately $50 million in sales, with break-even achieved in the final quarter of the year. With an average retail price of $1.89, that equates with a sales goal of 26,455,026 bottles.

Second-year Objectives

During the second year, Chill Beverage will unveil additional NutriWater flavors, including zero-calorie varieties. The second-year objective is to double sales from the first year, to $100 million.

Issues

In launching this new brand, the main issue is the ability to establish brand awareness and a meaningful brand image based on positioning that is relevant to target customer segments. Chill Beverage will invest in nontraditional means of promotion to accomplish these goals and to spark word-of-mouth. Establishing distributor and retailer relationships will also be critical in order to make the product available and provide point-of-purchase communications. Brand awareness and knowledge will be measured in order to adjust marketing efforts as necessary.

Marketing Strategy

NutriWater's marketing strategy will involve developing a "more for the same" positioning based on extra benefits for the price. The brand will also establish channel differentiation, as it will be available in locations where major competing brands are not. The primary target segments are millennials—born between 1981 and 1997. NutriWater will focus specifically on the young adult market. Subsets of this generational segment include athletes, the health conscious, and the socially responsible.

Positioning

NutriWater will be positioned on an "Expect more" value proposition. This will allow for differentiating the brand based on product features (expect more vitamin content and all-natural ingredients), desirable benefits (expect greater nutritional benefits), and values (do more for a social cause). Marketing will focus on conveying that NutriWater is more than just a beverage: It gives customers much more for their money in a variety of ways.

Product Strategy

NutriWater will be sold with all the features described in the Product Review section. As awareness takes hold and retail availability increases, more varieties will be made available. A zero-calorie version will be added to the product line, providing a solid fit with the health benefits sought by consumers. Chill Beverage's considerable experience in brand-building will be applied as an integral part of the product strategy for NutriWater. All aspects of the marketing mix will be consistent with the brand.

Pricing

There is little price variation in the enhanced waters category, particularly among leading brands. For this reason, NutriWater will follow a competition-based pricing strategy. Given that NutriWater claims superior quality, it must be careful not to position itself as a lower-cost alternative. Manufacturers do not quote list prices on this type of beverage, and prices vary considerably based on type of retail outlet and whether or not the product is refrigerated. Regular prices for single 20-ounce bottles of competing products are as low as $1.00 in discount-retailer stores and as high as $1.99 in convenience stores. Because NutriWater will not be targeting discount retailers and convenience stores initially, this will allow Chill Beverage to set prices at the average to higher end of the range for similar products in the same outlets. For grocery chains, this should be approximately $1.69 per bottle, with that price rising to $1.99 at health food stores and fitness centers, where prices tend to be higher.

Distribution Strategy

NutriWater will employ a selective distribution strategy with well-known regional grocers, health and natural food stores, and fitness centers. This distribution strategy will be executed through a network of independent beverage distributors, as there are no other major brands of enhanced water following this strategy. Chill Beverage gained success for its core Chill Soda soft drink line using this method. It also placed coolers with the brand logo in truly unique venues such as skate, surf, and snowboarding shops; tattoo and piercing parlors; fashion stores; and music stores—places that would expose the brand to target customers. Then, the soft drink brand expanded by getting contracts with retailers such as Panera, Barnes & Noble, Target, and Starbucks. This same approach will be taken with NutriWater by starting small, then expanding into larger chains. NutriWater will not target all the same stores used originally by Chill Soda, as many of those outlets were unique to the positioning and target customer for the Chill Soda soft drink brand.

Marketing Communication Strategy

As with the core Chill Soda brand, the marketing communication strategy for NutriWater will not follow a strategy based on traditional mass-communication advertising. Initially, there will be no broadcast or print advertising. Promotional resources for NutriWater will focus on three areas:

- ***Online and mobile marketing:*** The typical target customer for NutriWater spends more time online than with traditional media channels. A core component for this strategy will be building web and mobile brand sites and driving traffic to those sites by creating a presence on social networks, including Facebook, Twitter, Instagram, and Snapchat. The NutriWater brand will also incorporate location-based services by Foursquare and Facebook to help drive traffic to retail locations. A mobile phone ad campaign will provide additional support to the online efforts.

- ***Trade promotions:*** Like the core Chill Soda brand, NutriWater's success will rely on relationships with retailers to create product availability. Primary incentives to retailers will include point-of-purchase displays, branded coolers, and volume incentives and contests. This push marketing strategy will combine with the other pull strategies.
- ***Event marketing:*** NutriWater will deploy teams in brand-labeled RVs to distribute product samples at events such as skiing and snowboarding competitions, golf tournaments, and concerts.

Marketing Research

To remain consistent with the online promotional approach as well as using research methods that will effectively reach target customers, Chill Beverage will monitor online discussions. In this manner, the company will gauge customer perceptions of the brand, the products, and general satisfaction. For future development of the product and new distribution outlets, crowdsourcing methods will be utilized.

Action Programs

NutriWater will be introduced in February. The following are summaries of action programs that will be used during the first six months of the year to achieve the stated objectives.

January: Chill Beverage representatives will work with both independent distributors and retailers to educate them on the trade promotional campaign, incentives, and advantages for selling NutriWater. Representatives will also ensure that distributors and retailers are educated on product features and benefits as well as instructions for displaying point-of-purchase materials and coolers. The brand website and other sites such as Facebook will present teaser information about the product as well as availability dates and locations. Buzz will be enhanced by providing product samples to selected product reviewers, opinion leaders, influential bloggers, and celebrities.

February: On the date of availability, product coolers and point-of-purchase displays will be placed in retail locations. The full brand website and social network campaign will launch with full efforts on Facebook, Twitter, Instagram, and Snapchat. This campaign will drive the "Expect more" slogan as well as illustrate the ways that NutriWater delivers more than expected on product features, desirable benefits, and values by donating to Vitamin Angels and the social cause of battling vitamin deficiency in children.

March: To enhance the online and social marketing campaign, location-based services Foursquare and Facebook Location Services will be employed to drive traffic to retailers. Point-of-purchase displays and signage will be updated to support these efforts and to continue supporting retailers. The message of this campaign will focus on all aspects of "Expect more."

April: A mobile ad campaign will provide additional support, driving traffic to the brand website and social network sites as well as driving traffic to retailers.

May: A trade sales contest will offer additional incentives and prizes to the distributors and retailers that sell the most NutriWater during a four-week period.

June: An event marketing campaign will mobilize a team of NutriWater representatives in NutriWater RVs to concerts and sports events. This will provide additional visibility for the brand as well as giving customers and potential customers the opportunity to sample products.

Budgets

Chill Beverage has set a first-year retail sales goal of $50 million with a projected average retail price of $1.89 per unit for a total of 26,455,026 units sold. With an average wholesale price of 95 cents per unit, this provides revenues of $25.1 million. Chill Beverage expects to break even during the final quarter of the first year. A break-even analysis assumes per-unit wholesale revenue of 95 cents per unit, a variable cost per unit of 22 cents, and estimated first-year fixed costs of $12,500,000. Based on these assumptions, the break-even calculation is:

$$\frac{\$12{,}500{,}000}{\$0.95/\text{unit} - \$0.22/\text{unit}} = 17{,}123{,}287$$

Controls

Chill Beverage is planning tight control measures to closely monitor product quality, brand awareness, brand image, and customer satisfaction. This will enable the company to react quickly in correcting any problems that may occur. Other early warning signals that will be monitored for signs of deviation from the plan include monthly sales (by segment and channel) and monthly expenses. Given the market's volatility, contingency plans are also in place to address fast-moving environmental changes such as shifting consumer preferences, new products, and new competition.

Sources: "Bottled Water Holds Steady at No. 1," *Beverage Industry*, July 2018, p. SOI 15; "Global Flavored and Functional Water Market: Growing Incidence of Obesity to Stimulate Growth," *Transparency Market Research*, June 2017, www.transparencymarketresearch.com/pressrelease/flavored-functional-water.htm; Jeff Beer, "Propel Water's New Brand Strategy Is Hyping Its Gatorade Roots," *Fast Company*, March 29, 2018, www.fastcompany.com/40551566/propel-waters-new-brand-strategy-is-hyping-its-gatorade-roots; and product and market information obtained from http://vitaminwater.com, http://propelwater.com, and http://nestle-watersna.com, July 2018.

Appendix 3 Marketing by the Numbers

Marketing managers are facing increased accountability for the financial implications of their actions. This appendix provides a basic introduction to measuring marketing financial performance. Such financial analysis guides marketers in making sound marketing decisions and in assessing the outcomes of those decisions.

The appendix is built around a hypothetical manufacturer of home automation products—Wise Domotics ("domotics" refers to information technology in the home). The company is introducing a device that allows users to control all internet-connected smart devices in their homes. Users will be able to control lighting, temperature, multimedia, security systems, appliances, windows and doors, phones, and any other smart devices in their homes that are connected to the internet. In this appendix, we will analyze the various decisions Wise Domotics's marketing managers must make before and after the new product launch.

The appendix is organized into *three sections*. The *first section* introduces pricing, break-even, and margin analysis assessments that will guide the introduction of Wise Domotics's new product. The *second section* discusses demand estimates, the marketing budget, and marketing performance measures. It begins with a discussion of estimating market potential and company sales. It then introduces the marketing budget, as illustrated through a *pro forma* profit-and-loss statement followed by the actual profit-and-loss statement. Next, we discuss marketing performance measures, with a focus on helping marketing managers to better defend their decisions from a financial perspective. In the *third section,* we analyze the financial implications of various marketing tactics.

Each of the three sections ends with a set of quantitative exercises that provide you with an opportunity to apply the concepts you learned to situations beyond Wise Domotics.

Pricing, Break-Even, and Margin Analysis

Pricing Considerations

Determining price is one of the most important marketing mix decisions. The limiting factors are demand and costs. Demand factors, such as buyer-perceived value, set the price ceiling. The company's costs set the price floor. In between these two factors, marketers must consider competitors' prices and other factors such as reseller requirements, government regulations, and company objectives.

Most current competing home automation products sell at retail prices between $100 and $500. We first consider Wise Domotics's pricing decision from a cost perspective. Then we consider consumer value, the competitive environment, and reseller requirements.

Determining Costs

Fixed costs
Costs that do not vary with production or sales level.

Variable costs
Costs that vary directly with the level of production.

Total costs
The sum of the fixed and variable costs for any given level of production.

Recall from Chapter 9 that there are different types of costs. **Fixed costs** do not vary with production or sales levels and include costs such as rent, interest, depreciation, and clerical and management salaries. Regardless of the level of output, the company must pay these costs. Whereas total fixed costs remain constant as output increases, the fixed cost per unit (or average fixed cost) will decrease as output increases because the total fixed costs are spread across more units of output. **Variable costs** vary directly with the level of production and include costs related to the direct production of the product (such as costs of goods sold—COGS) and many of the marketing costs associated with selling it. Although these costs tend to be uniform for each unit produced, they are called variable because their total varies with the number of units produced. **Total costs** are the sum of the fixed and variable costs for any given level of production.

Wise Domotics has invested $10 million in refurbishing an existing facility to manufacture the new home automation product. Once production begins, the company estimates that it will incur fixed costs of $20 million per year. The variable cost to produce each device is estimated to be $125 and is expected to remain at that level for the output capacity of the facility.

Setting Price Based on Costs

Cost-plus pricing (or markup pricing)
A standard markup to the cost of the product.

Wise Domotics starts with the cost-based approach to pricing discussed in Chapter 9. Recall that the simplest method, **cost-plus pricing (or markup pricing)**, simply adds a standard markup to the cost of the product. To use this method, however, Wise Domotics must specify expected unit sales so that total unit costs can be determined. Unit variable costs will remain constant regardless of the output, but *average unit fixed costs* will decrease as output increases.

To illustrate this method, suppose Wise Domotics has fixed costs of $20 million, variable costs of $125 per unit, and expected unit sales of 1 million devices. Thus, the cost per unit is given by:

$$\text{Unit cost} = \text{variable cost} + \frac{\text{fixed costs}}{\text{unit sales}} = \$125 + \frac{\$20{,}000{,}000}{1{,}000{,}000} = \$145$$

Relevant costs
Costs that will occur in the future and that will vary across the alternatives being considered.

Note that we do *not* include the initial investment of $10 million in the total fixed cost figure. It is not considered a fixed cost because it is not a *relevant* cost. **Relevant costs** are those that will occur in the future and that will vary across the alternatives being considered. Wise Domotics's investment to refurbish the manufacturing facility was a one-time cost that will not reoccur in the future. Such past costs are *sunk costs* and should not be considered in future analyses.

Break-even price
The price at which total revenue equals total cost and profit is zero.

Also notice that if Wise Domotics sells its product for $145, the price is equal to the total cost per unit. This is the **break-even price**—the price at which total revenue equals total cost and profit is zero.

Suppose Wise Domotics does not want to merely break even but rather wants to earn a 25% markup on sales. Wise Domotics's markup price is:[i]

$$\text{Markup price} = \frac{\text{unit cost}}{(1 - \text{desired return on sales})} = \frac{\$145}{1 - 0.25} = \$193.33$$

This is the price at which Wise Domotics would sell the product to resellers such as wholesalers or retailers to earn a 25% profit on sales.

Return on investment (ROI) pricing (or target-return pricing)
A cost-based pricing method that determines price based on a specified rate of return on investment.

Another approach Wise Domotics could use is called **return on investment (ROI) pricing (or target-return pricing)**. In this case, the company *would* consider the initial $10 million investment, but only to determine the dollar profit goal. Suppose the company wants a 30% return on its investment. The price necessary to satisfy this requirement can be determined by:

$$\text{ROI price} = \text{unit cost} + \frac{\text{ROI} \times \text{investment}}{\text{unit sales}} = \$145 + \frac{0.3 \times \$10{,}000{,}000}{1{,}000{,}000} = \$148$$

That is, if Wise Domotics sells its product for $148, it will realize a 30% return on its initial investment of $10 million.

In these pricing calculations, unit cost is a function of the expected sales, which were estimated to be 1 million units. But what if actual sales were lower? Then the unit cost would be higher because the fixed costs would be spread over fewer units, and the realized percentage markup on sales or ROI would be lower. Alternatively, if sales are higher than the estimated 1 million units, unit cost would be lower than $145, so a lower price would produce the desired markup on sales or ROI. It's important to note that these cost-based pricing methods are *internally* focused and do not consider demand, competitors' prices, or reseller requirements. Because Wise Domotics will be selling this product to consumers through wholesalers and retailers offering competing brands, the company must consider markup pricing from this perspective.

Setting Price Based on External Factors

Whereas costs determine the price floor, Wise Domotics also must consider external factors when setting price. Wise Domotics does not have the final say concerning the final price of its product to consumers—retailers do. So it must start with its suggested retail price and work back. In doing so, Wise Domotics must consider the markups required by resellers that sell the product to consumers.

Markup
The difference between a company's selling price for a product and its cost to manufacture or purchase it.

In general, a dollar **markup** is the difference between a company's selling price for a product and its cost to manufacture or purchase it. For a retailer, then, the markup is the difference between the price it charges consumers and the cost the retailer must pay for the product. Thus, for any level of reseller:

$$\text{Dollar markup} = \text{selling price} - \text{cost}$$

Markups are usually expressed as a percentage, and there are two different ways to compute markups—on *cost* or on *selling price*:

$$\text{Markup percentage on cost} = \frac{\text{dollar markup}}{\text{cost}}$$

$$\text{Markup percentage on selling price} = \frac{\text{dollar markup}}{\text{selling price}}$$

To apply reseller margin analysis, Wise Domotics must first set the suggested retail price and then work back to the price at which it must sell the product to a wholesaler. Suppose retailers expect a 30% margin and wholesalers want a 20% margin based on their respective selling prices. And suppose that Wise Domotics sets a manufacturer's suggested retail price (MSRP) of $299.99 for its product.

Wise Domotics selected the $299.99 MSRP because it is lower than most competitors' prices but is not so low that consumers might perceive it to be of poor quality. And the company's research shows that it is below the threshold at which more consumers are willing to purchase the product. By using buyers' perceptions of value and not the seller's cost to determine the MSRP, Wise Domotics is using **value-based pricing**. For simplicity, we will use an MSRP of $300 in further analyses.

Value-based pricing
Offering just the right combination of quality and good service at a fair price.

To determine the price Wise Domotics will charge wholesalers, we must first subtract the retailer's margin from the retail price to determine the retailer's cost ($300 − ($300 × 0.30) = $210). The retailer's cost is the wholesaler's price, so Wise Domotics next subtracts the wholesaler's margin ($210 − ($210 × 0.20) = $168). Thus, the **markup chain** representing the sequence of markups used by firms at each level in a channel for Wise Domotics's new product is:

Markup chain
The sequence of markups used by firms at each level in a channel.

Suggested retail price:	$300
minus retail margin (30%):	−$ 90
Retailer's cost/wholesaler's price:	$210
minus wholesaler's margin (20%):	−$ 42
Wholesaler's cost/Wise Domotics's price:	$168

By deducting the markups for each level in the markup chain, Wise Domotics arrives at a price for the product to wholesalers of $168.

Break-Even and Margin Analysis

The previous analyses derived a value-based price of $168 for Wise Domotics's product. Although this price is higher than the break-even price of $145 and covers costs, that price assumed a demand of 1 million units. But how many units and what level of dollar sales must Wise Domotics achieve to break even at the $168 price? And what level of sales must be achieved to realize various profit goals? These questions can be answered through break-even and margin analysis.

Determining Break-Even Unit Volume and Dollar Sales

Break-even analysis
Analysis to determine the unit volume and dollar sales needed to be profitable given a particular price and cost structure.

Unit contribution
The amount that each unit contributes to covering fixed costs—the difference between price and variable costs.

Contribution margin
The unit contribution divided by the selling price.

Based on an understanding of costs, consumer value, the competitive environment, and reseller requirements, Wise Domotics has decided to set its price to wholesalers at $168. At that price, what sales level will be needed for Wise Domotics to break even or make a profit on its product? **Break-even analysis** determines the unit volume and dollar sales needed to be profitable given a particular price and cost structure. At the break-even point, total revenue equals total costs and profit is zero. Above this point, the company will make a profit; below it, the company will lose money. Wise Domotics can calculate break-even volume using the following formula:

$$\text{Break-even volume} = \frac{\text{fixed costs}}{\text{price} - \text{unit variable cost}}$$

The denominator (price – unit variable cost) is called **unit contribution** (sometimes called contribution margin). It represents the amount that each unit contributes to covering fixed costs. Break-even volume represents the level of output at which all (variable and fixed) costs are covered. In Wise Domotics's case, break-even unit volume is:

$$\text{Break-even volume} = \frac{\text{fixed cost}}{\text{price} - \text{variable cost}} = \frac{\$20{,}000{,}000}{\$168 - \$125} = 465{,}116.2 \text{ units}$$

Thus, at the given cost and pricing structure, Wise Domotics will break even at 465,117 units.

To determine the break-even dollar sales, simply multiply unit break-even volume by the selling price:

$$\text{BE sales} = \text{BE}_{\text{vol}} \times \text{price} = 465{,}117 \times \$168 = \$78{,}139{,}656$$

Another way to calculate dollar break-even sales is to use the percentage contribution margin (hereafter referred to as **contribution margin**), which is the unit contribution divided by the selling price:

$$\text{Contribution margin} = \frac{\text{price} - \text{variable cost}}{\text{price}} = \frac{\$168 - \$125}{\$168} = 0.256 \text{ or } 25.6\%$$

Then,

$$\text{Break-even sales} = \frac{\text{fixed costs}}{\text{contribution margin}} = \frac{\$20{,}000{,}000}{0.256} = \$78{,}125{,}000$$

Note that the difference between the two break-even sales calculations is due to rounding.

Such break-even analysis helps Wise Domotics by showing the unit volume needed to cover costs. If production capacity cannot attain this level of output, then the company should not launch this product. However, the unit break-even volume is well within Wise Domotics's capacity. Of course, the bigger question concerns whether Wise Domotics can sell this volume at the $168 price. We'll address that issue a little later.

Understanding contribution margin is useful in other types of analyses as well, particularly if unit prices and unit variable costs are unknown or if a company (say, a retailer) sells many products at different prices and knows the percentage of total sales variable costs represent. Whereas unit contribution is the difference between unit price and unit variable costs, total contribution is the difference between total sales and total variable costs. The overall contribution margin can be calculated by:

$$\text{Contribution margin} = \frac{\text{total sales} - \text{total variable costs}}{\text{total sales}}$$

Regardless of the actual level of sales, if the company knows what percentage of sales is represented by variable costs, it can calculate contribution margin. For example, Wise Domotics's unit variable cost is $125, or 74% of the selling price ($125 ÷ $168 = 0.74). That means for every $1 of sales revenue for Wise Domotics, $0.74 represents variable costs, and the difference ($0.26) represents contribution to fixed costs. But even if the company doesn't know its unit price and unit variable cost, it can calculate the contribution margin from total sales and total variable costs or from knowledge of the total cost structure. It can set total sales equal to 100% regardless of the actual absolute amount and determine the contribution margin:

$$\text{Contribution margin} = \frac{100\% - 74\%}{100\%} = \frac{1 - 0.74}{1} = 1 - 0.74 = 0.26 \text{ or } 26\%$$

Note that this matches the percentage calculated from the unit price and unit variable cost information. This alternative calculation will be very useful later when analyzing various marketing decisions.

Determining "Break-Even" for Profit Goals

Although it is useful to know the break-even point, most companies are more interested in making a profit. Assume Wise Domotics would like to realize a \$5 million profit in the first year. How many units must it sell at the \$168 price to cover fixed costs and produce this profit? To determine this, Wise Domotics can simply add the profit figure to fixed costs and again divide by the unit contribution to determine unit sales:

$$\text{Unit volume} = \frac{\text{fixed cost} + \text{profit goal}}{\text{price} - \text{variable cost}} = \frac{\$20{,}000{,}000 + \$5{,}000{,}000}{\$168 - \$125} = 581{,}395.3 \text{ units}$$

Thus, to earn a \$5 million profit, Wise Domotics must sell 581,396 units. Multiply by price to determine dollar sales needed to achieve a \$5 million profit:

$$\text{Dollar sales} = 581{,}396 \text{ units} \times \$168 = \$97{,}674{,}528$$

Or use the contribution margin:

$$\text{Sales} = \frac{\text{fixed cost} + \text{profit goal}}{\text{contribution margin}} = \frac{\$20{,}000{,}000 + \$5{,}000{,}000}{0.256} = \$97{,}656{,}250$$

Again, note that the difference between the two break-even sales calculations is due to rounding.

As we saw previously, a profit goal can also be stated as a return on investment goal. For example, recall that Wise Domotics wants a 30% return on its \$10 million investment. Thus, its absolute profit goal is \$3 million (\$10,000,000 × 0.30). This profit goal is treated the same way as in the previous example:[ii]

$$\text{Unit volume} = \frac{\text{fixed cost} + \text{profit goal}}{\text{price} - \text{variable cost}} = \frac{\$20{,}000{,}000 + \$3{,}000{,}000}{\$168 - \$125} = 534{,}884 \text{ units}$$

$$\text{Dollar sales} = 534{,}884 \text{ units} \times \$168 = \$89{,}860{,}512$$

Or

$$\text{Dollar sales} = \frac{\text{fixed cost} + \text{profit goal}}{\text{contribution margin}} = \frac{\$20{,}000{,}000 + \$3{,}000{,}000}{0.256} = \$89{,}843{,}750$$

Finally, Wise Domotics can express its profit goal as a percentage of sales, which we also saw in previous pricing analyses. Assume Wise Domotics desires a 25% return on sales. To determine the unit and sales volume necessary to achieve this goal, the calculation is a little different from the previous two examples. In this case, we incorporate the profit goal into the unit contribution as an additional variable cost. Look at it this way: If 25% of each sale must go toward profits, that leaves only 75% of the selling price to cover fixed costs. Thus, the equation becomes:

$$\text{Unit volume} = \frac{\text{fixed cost}}{\text{price} - \text{variable cost} - (0.25 \times \text{price})} \text{ or } \frac{\text{fixed cost}}{(0.75 \times \text{price}) - \text{variable cost}}$$

So,

$$\text{Unit volume} = \frac{\$20{,}000{,}000}{(0.75 \times \$168) - \$125} = 20{,}000{,}000 \text{ units}$$

$$\text{Dollar sales necessary} = 20{,}000{,}000 \text{ units} \times \$168 = \$3{,}360{,}000{,}000$$

Thus, Wise Domotics would need more than $3 billion in sales to realize a 25% return on sales given its current price and cost structure! Could it possibly achieve this level of sales? The major point is this: Although break-even analysis can be useful in determining the level of sales needed to cover costs or to achieve a stated profit goal, it does not tell the company whether it is *possible* to achieve that level of sales at the specified price. To address this issue, Wise Domotics needs to estimate demand for this product.

Before moving on, however, let's stop here and practice applying the concepts covered so far. Now that you have seen pricing and break-even concepts in action as they relate to Wise Domotics's new product, here are several exercises for you to apply what you have learned in other contexts.

Marketing by the Numbers Exercise Set One

Now that you've studied pricing, break-even, and margin analysis as they relate to Wise Domotics's new product launch, use the following exercises to apply these concepts in other contexts.

1.1 Lawn King, a manufacturer of riding lawn mowers, realizes a cost of $450 for every unit it produces. Its total fixed costs equal $6 million. If the company manufactures 1 million units, compute the following:
   a. unit cost
   b. markup price if the company desires a 30% return on sales
   c. ROI price if the company desires a 60% return on an investment of $2 million

1.2 A sporting goods retailer purchases items to sell in his store. He purchases a kayak for $250 and sells it for $625. Determine the following:
   a. dollar markup
   b. markup percentage on cost
   c. markup percentage on selling price

1.3 A consumer purchases a bicycle from a retailer for $150. The retailer's markup is 40%, and the wholesaler's markup is 15%, both based on selling price. For what price does the manufacturer sell the product to the wholesaler?

1.4 A furniture manufacturer has a unit cost of $100 on an end table and wishes to achieve a margin of 60% based on selling price. If the manufacturer sells directly to a retailer who then adds a set margin of 50% based on selling price, determine the retail price charged to consumers.

1.5 Home Solutions manufactures internet-connected doorbells and sells them to intermediaries in the channel of distribution for $55. Each doorbell costs Home Solutions $15 to manufacture in addition to $550,000 in fixed costs. Calculate the following:
   a. contribution per unit and contribution margin percentage
   b. break-even volume in units and dollars
   c. unit volume and dollar sales necessary if Home Solution's profit goal is $3 million
   d. unit volume and dollar sales necessary if Home Solution's profit goal is 10% profit on sales

Demand Estimates, the Marketing Budget, and Marketing Performance Measures

Market Potential and Sales Estimates

Wise Domotics has now calculated the sales needed to break even and to attain various profit goals on its new product. However, the company needs more information regarding demand in order to assess the feasibility of attaining the needed sales levels. This information is also needed for production and other decisions. For example, production schedules need to be developed and marketing tactics need to be planned.

Total market demand
The total volume that would be bought by a defined consumer group in a defined geographic area in a defined time period in a defined marketing environment under a defined level and mix of industry marketing effort.

Market potential
The upper limit of market demand.

The **total market demand** for a product or service is the total volume that would be bought by a defined consumer group in a defined geographic area in a defined time period in a defined marketing environment under a defined level and mix of industry marketing effort. Total market demand is not a fixed number but a function of the stated conditions. For example, next year's total market demand for this type of product will depend on how much other producers spend on marketing their brands. It also depends on many environmental factors, such as government regulations, economic conditions, and the level of consumer confidence in a given market. The upper limit of market demand is called **market potential**.

One general but practical method that Wise Domotics might use for estimating total market demand uses three variables: (1) the number of prospective buyers, (2) the quantity purchased by an average buyer per year, and (3) the price of an average unit. Using these numbers, Wise Domotics can estimate total market demand as follows:

$$Q = n \times q \times p$$

where

Q = total market demand
n = number of buyers in the market
q = quantity purchased by an average buyer per year
p = price of an average unit

Chain ratio method
Estimating market demand by multiplying a base number by a chain of adjusting percentages.

A variation of this approach is the **chain ratio method**. This method involves multiplying a base number by a chain of adjusting percentages. For example, Wise Domotics's product is designed to automate operation of multiple internet-connected smart devices in a home. Thus, only consumers who have broadband internet access and Wi-Fi in their homes will be able to use the product. Finally, not all Wi-Fi internet households will be willing and able to purchase this product. Wise Domotics can estimate U.S. demand using a chain of calculations like the following:

Total number of U.S. households
× The percentage of U.S. households with broadband internet
× The percentage of internet households with Wi-Fi
× The percentage of these households willing and able to buy this device

The U.S. Census Bureau estimates that there are approximately 120 million households in the United States, and other research indicates that 70 percent of U.S. households have broadband internet and 71 percent of those have Wi-Fi in their homes.[iii] Finally, the company's research also reveals that 35 percent of households possess the discretionary income needed and are willing to buy a product such as this. Then the total number of households willing and able to purchase this product is:

120 million households × 0.70 × 0.71 × 0.35 = 20.9 million households

Households need to purchase only one device to control all other smart devices throughout the household. Assuming the average retail price across all brands is $350 for this type of product, the estimate of total market demand is as follows:

20.9 million households × 1 device per household × $350 = $7,315,000,000

This simple chain of calculations gives Wise Domotics only a rough estimate of potential demand. However, more detailed chains involving additional segments and other qualifying factors would yield more accurate and refined estimates. Still, these are only *estimates* of market potential. They rely heavily on assumptions regarding adjusting percentages, average quantity, and average price. Thus, Wise Domotics must make certain that its assumptions are reasonable and defendable. As can be seen, the overall market potential in dollar sales can vary widely given the average price used. For this reason, Wise Domotics will use unit sales potential to determine its sales estimate for next year. Market potential in terms of units is 20.9 million (20.9 million households × 1 device per household).

Assuming that Wise Domotics forecasts it will have a 3.56% market share in the first year after launching this product, then it can forecast unit sales at 20.9 million units × 0.0356 = 744,040 units. At a selling price of $168 per unit, this translates into sales of $124,998,720 (744,040 units × $168 per unit). For simplicity, further analyses will use forecasted sales of $125 million.

This unit volume estimate is well within Wise Domotics's production capacity and exceeds not only the break-even estimate (465,117 units) calculated earlier but also the volume necessary to realize a $5 million profit (581,396 units) or a 30% return on investment (534,884 units). However, this forecast falls well short of the volume necessary to realize a 25% return on sales (20 million units!) and may require that Wise Domotics revise expectations.

To assess expected profits, we must now look at the budgeted expenses for launching this product. To do this, we will construct a pro forma profit-and-loss statement.

The Profit-and-Loss Statement and Marketing Budget

Pro forma (or projected) profit-and-loss statement (or income statement or operating statement)
A statement that shows projected revenues less budgeted expenses and estimates the projected net profit for an organization, product, or brand during a specific planning period, typically a year.

All marketing managers must account for the profit impact of their marketing strategies. A major tool for projecting such profit impact is a **pro forma** (or projected) **profit-and-loss statement** (also called an **income statement** or **operating statement**). A pro forma statement shows projected revenues less budgeted expenses and estimates the projected net profit for an organization, product, or brand during a specific planning period, typically a year. It includes direct product production costs, marketing expenses budgeted to attain a given sales forecast, and overhead expenses assigned to the organization or product. A profit-and-loss statement typically consists of several major components (see >> **Table A3.1**):

- ***Net sales***—gross sales revenue minus returns and allowances (for example, trade, cash, quantity, and promotion allowances). Wise Domotics's net sales for 2019 are estimated to be $125 million, as determined in the previous analysis.
- ***Cost of goods sold***—(sometimes called *cost of sales*)—the actual cost of the merchandise sold by a manufacturer or reseller. It includes the cost of inventory, purchases, and other costs associated with making the goods. Wise Domotics's cost of goods sold is estimated to be 50% of net sales, or $62.5 million.

Table A3.1 Pro Forma Profit-and-Loss Statement for the 12-Month Period Ended December 31, 2019

			Percent of Sales
Net Sales		$125,000,000	100%
Cost of Goods Sold		62,500,000	50%
Gross Margin		$ 62,500,000	50%
Marketing Expenses			
Sales expenses	$17,500,000		
Promotion expenses	15,000,000		
Freight	12,500,000	45,000,000	36%
General and Administrative Expenses			
Managerial salaries and expenses	$ 2,000,000		
Indirect overhead	3,000,000	5,000,000	4%
Net Profit before Income Tax		$ 12,500,000	10%

- ***Gross margin (or gross profit)***—the difference between net sales and cost of goods sold. Wise Domotics's gross margin is estimated to be $62.5 million.
- ***Operating expenses***—the expenses incurred while doing business. These include all other expenses beyond the cost of goods sold that are necessary to conduct business. Operating expenses can be presented in total or broken down in detail. Here, Wise Domotics's estimated operating expenses include *marketing expenses* and *general and administrative expenses.*

Marketing expenses include sales expenses, promotion expenses, and distribution expenses. The new product will be sold through Wise Domotics's sales force, so the company budgets $5 million for sales salaries. However, because sales representatives earn a 10% commission on sales, Wise Domotics must also add a variable component to sales expenses of $12.5 million (10% of $125 million net sales), for a total budgeted sales expense of $17.5 million. Wise Domotics sets its advertising and promotion to launch this product at $10 million. However, the company also budgets 4% of sales, or $5 million, for cooperative advertising allowances to retailers who promote Wise Domotics's new product in their advertising. Thus, the total budgeted advertising and promotion expenses are $15 million ($10 million for advertising plus $5 million in co-op allowances). Finally, Wise Domotics budgets 10% of net sales, or $12.5 million, for freight and delivery charges. In all, total marketing expenses are estimated to be $17.5 million + $15 million + $12.5 million = $45 million.

General and administrative expenses are estimated at $5 million, broken down into $2 million for managerial salaries and expenses for the marketing function and $3 million of indirect overhead allocated to this product by the corporate accountants (such as depreciation, interest, maintenance, and insurance). Total expenses for the year, then, are estimated to be $50 million ($45 million marketing expenses + $5 million in general and administrative expenses).

- ***Net profit before taxes***—profit earned after all costs are deducted. Wise Domotics's estimated net profit before taxes is $12.5 million.

In all, as Table A3.1 shows, Wise Domotics expects to earn a profit on its new product of $12.5 million in 2016. Also note that the percentage of sales that each component of the profit-and-loss statement represents is given in the right-hand column. These percentages are determined by dividing the cost figure by net sales (that is, marketing expenses represent 36% of net sales determined by $45 million ÷ $125 million). As can be seen, Wise Domotics projects a net profit return on sales of 10% in the first year after launching this product.

Marketing Performance Measures

Profit-and-loss statement (or income statement or operating statement)
A statement that shows actual revenues less expenses and net profit for an organization, product, or brand during a specific planning period, typically a year.

Now let's fast-forward a year. Wise Domotics's product has been on the market for one year, and management wants to assess its sales and profit performance. One way to assess this performance is to compute performance ratios derived from Wise Domotics's **profit-and-loss statement** (or **income statement** or **operating statement**).

Whereas the pro forma profit-and-loss statement shows *projected* financial performance, the statement given in **» Table A3.2**) shows Wise Domotics's *actual* financial performance based on actual sales, cost of goods sold, and expenses during the past year. By comparing the profit-and-loss statement from one period to the next, Wise Domotics can gauge performance against goals, spot favorable or unfavorable trends, and take appropriate corrective action.

The profit-and-loss statement shows that Wise Domotics lost $1 million rather than making the $12.5 million profit projected in the pro forma statement. Why? One obvious reason is that net sales fell $25 million short of estimated sales. Lower sales translated into lower variable costs associated with marketing the product. However, both fixed costs and the cost of goods sold as a percentage of sales exceeded expectations. Hence, the product's contribution margin was 21% rather than the estimated 26%. That is, variable costs represented 79% of sales (55% for cost of goods sold, 10% for sales commissions, 10% for freight, and 4% for co-op allowances). Recall that contribution margin can be

Table A3.2 Profit-and-Loss Statement for the 12-Month Period Ended December 31, 2019

			Percent of Sales
Net Sales		$100,000,000	100%
Cost of Goods Sold		55,000,000	55%
Gross Margin		$ 45,000,000	45%
Marketing Expenses			
Sales expenses	$15,000,000		
Promotion expenses	14,000,000		
Freight	10,000,000	39,000,000	39%
General and Administrative Expenses			
Managerial salaries and expenses	$ 2,000,000		
Indirect overhead	5,000,000	7,000,000	7%
Net Profit before Income Tax		–$ 1,000,000	–1%

calculated by subtracting that fraction from one ($1 - 0.79 = 0.21$). Total fixed costs were $22 million, $2 million more than estimated. Thus, the sales that Wise Domotics needed to break even given this cost structure can be calculated as:

$$\text{Break-even sales} = \frac{\text{fixed costs}}{\text{contribution margin}} = \frac{\$22{,}000{,}000}{0.21} = \$104{,}761{,}905$$

If Wise Domotics had achieved another $5 million in sales, it would have earned a profit.

Although Wise Domotics's sales fell short of the forecasted sales, so did overall industry sales for this product. Overall industry sales were only $2.5 billion. That means that Wise Domotics's **market share** was 4% ($\$100 \text{ million} \div \$2.5 \text{ billion} = 0.04 = 4\%$), which was higher than forecasted. Thus, Wise Domotics attained a higher-than-expected market share, but the overall market sales were not as high as estimated.

Market share
Company sales divided by market sales.

Analytic Ratios

The profit-and-loss statement provides the figures needed to compute some crucial **operating ratios**—the ratios of selected operating statement items to net sales. These ratios let marketers compare the firm's performance in one year to that in previous years (or with industry standards and competitors' performance in that year). The most commonly used operating ratios are the gross margin percentage, the net profit percentage, and the operating expense percentage. The inventory turnover rate and return on investment (ROI) are often used to measure managerial effectiveness and efficiency.

Operating ratios
The ratios of selected operating statement items to net sales.

The **gross margin percentage** indicates the percentage of net sales remaining after cost of goods sold that can contribute to operating expenses and net profit before taxes. The higher this ratio, the more a firm has left to cover expenses and generate profit. Wise Domotics's gross margin ratio was 45%:

Gross margin percentage
The percentage of net sales remaining after cost of goods sold—calculated by dividing gross margin by net sales.

$$\text{Gross margin percentage} = \frac{\text{gross margin}}{\text{net sales}} = \frac{\$45{,}000{,}000}{\$100{,}000{,}000} = 0.45 = 45\%$$

Note that this percentage is lower than estimated, and this ratio is seen easily in the percentage of sales column in Table A3.2. Stating items in the profit-and-loss statement as a percent of sales allows managers to quickly spot abnormal changes in costs over time. If there was previous history for this product and this ratio was declining, management should examine it more closely to determine why it has decreased (that is, because of a decrease in sales volume or price, an increase in costs, or a combination of these). In Wise Domotics's case, net sales were $25 million lower than estimated, and cost of goods sold was higher than estimated (55% rather than the estimated 50%).

Net profit percentage
The percentage of each sales dollar going to profit—calculated by dividing net profits by net sales.

The **net profit percentage** shows the percentage of each sales dollar going to profit. It is calculated by dividing net profits by net sales:

$$\text{Net profit percentage} = \frac{\text{net profit}}{\text{net sales}} = \frac{-\$1{,}000{,}000}{\$100{,}000{,}000} = -0.01 = -1.0\%$$

This ratio is easily seen in the percent of sales column. Wise Domotics's new product generated negative profits in the first year, not a good situation given that before the product launch net profits before taxes were estimated at more than $12 million. Later in this appendix, we will discuss further analyses the marketing manager should conduct to defend the product.

Operating expense percentage
The portion of net sales going to operating expenses—calculated by dividing total expenses by net sales.

The **operating expense percentage** indicates the portion of net sales going to operating expenses. Operating expenses include marketing and other expenses not directly related to marketing the product, such as indirect overhead assigned to this product. It is calculated by:

$$\text{Operating expense percentage} = \frac{\text{total expenses}}{\text{net sales}} = \frac{\$46{,}000{,}000}{\$100{,}000{,}000} = 0.46 = 46\%$$

This ratio can also be quickly determined from the percent of sales column in the profit-and-loss statement by adding the percentages for marketing expenses and general and administrative expenses (39% + 7%). Thus, 46 cents of every sales dollar went for operations. Although Wise Domotics wants this ratio to be as low as possible, and 46% is not an alarming amount, it is of concern if it is increasing over time or if a loss is realized.

Inventory turnover rate (or stockturn rate)
The number of times an inventory turns over or is sold during a specified time period (often one year)—calculated based on costs, selling price, or units.

Another useful ratio is the **inventory turnover rate** (also called **stockturn rate** for resellers). The inventory turnover rate is the number of times an inventory turns over or is sold during a specified time period (often one year). This rate tells how quickly a business is moving inventory through the organization. Higher rates indicate that lower investments in inventory are made, thus freeing up funds for other investments. It may be computed on a cost, selling price, or unit basis. The formula based on cost is:

$$\text{Inventory turnover rate} = \frac{\text{cost of goods sold}}{\text{average inventory at cost}}$$

Assuming Wise Domotics's beginning and ending inventories were $30 million and $20 million, respectively, the inventory turnover rate is:

$$\text{Inventory turnover rate} = \frac{\$55{,}000{,}000}{(\$30{,}000{,}000 + \$20{,}000{,}000)/2} = \frac{\$55{,}000{,}000}{\$25{,}000{,}000} = 2.2$$

That is, Wise Domotics's inventory turned over 2.2 times in 2019. Normally, the higher the turnover rate, the higher the management efficiency and company profitability. However, this rate should be compared with industry averages, competitors' rates, and past performance to determine if Wise Domotics is doing well. A competitor with similar sales but a higher inventory turnover rate will have fewer resources tied up in inventory, allowing it to invest in other areas of the business.

Return on investment (ROI)
A measure of managerial effectiveness and efficiency—net profit before taxes divided by total investment.

Companies frequently use **return on investment (ROI)** to measure managerial effectiveness and efficiency. For Wise Demotics, ROI is the ratio of net profits to total investment required to manufacture the new product. This investment includes capital investments in land, buildings, and equipment (here, the initial $10 million to refurbish the manufacturing facility) plus inventory costs (Wise Domotics's average inventory totaled $25 million), for a total of $35 million. Thus, Wise Domotics's ROI for this product is:

$$\text{Return on investment} = \frac{\text{net profit before taxes}}{\text{investment}} = \frac{-\$1{,}000{,}000}{\$35{,}000{,}000} = -.0286 = -2.86\%$$

ROI is often used to compare alternatives, and a positive ROI is desired. The alternative with the highest ROI is preferred to other alternatives. Wise Domotics needs to be concerned with the ROI realized. One obvious way Wise Domotics can increase ROI is to increase net profit by reducing expenses. Another way is to reduce its investment, perhaps by investing less in inventory and turning it over more frequently.

Marketing Profitability Metrics

Given the above financial results, you may be thinking that Wise Domotics should drop this new product. But what arguments can marketers make for keeping or dropping this product? The obvious arguments for dropping the product are that first-year sales were well below expected levels and the product lost money, resulting in a negative return on investment.

So what would happen if Wise Domotics did drop this product? Surprisingly, if the company drops the product, the profits for the total organization will decrease by \$4 million! How can that be? Marketing managers need to look closely at the numbers in the profit-and-loss statement to determine the *net marketing contribution* for this product. In Wise Domotics's case, the net marketing contribution for the product is \$4 million, and if the company drops this product, that contribution will disappear as well. Let's look more closely at this concept to illustrate how marketing managers can better assess and defend their marketing strategies and programs.

Net Marketing Contribution

Net marketing contribution (NMC) A measure of marketing profitability that includes only components of profitability controlled by marketing.

Net marketing contribution (NMC), along with other marketing metrics derived from it, measures *marketing* profitability. It includes only components of profitability that are controlled by marketing. Whereas the previous calculation of net profit before taxes from the profit-and-loss statement includes operating expenses not under marketing's control, NMC does not. Referring back to Wise Domotics's profit-and-loss statement given in Table A3.2, we can calculate net marketing contribution for the product as:

$$\begin{aligned} \text{NMC} &= \text{net sales} - \text{cost of goods sold} - \text{marketing expenses} \\ &= \$100\text{ million} - \$55\text{ million} - \$41\text{ million} = \$4\text{ million} \end{aligned}$$

The marketing expenses include sales expenses (\$15 million), promotion expenses (\$14 million), freight expenses (\$10 million), and the managerial salaries and expenses of the marketing function (\$2 million), which total \$41 million.

Thus, the product actually contributed \$4 million to Wise Domotics's profits. It was the \$5 million of indirect overhead allocated to this product that caused the negative profit. Further, the amount allocated was \$2 million more than estimated in the pro forma profit-and-loss statement. Indeed, if only the estimated amount had been allocated, the product would have earned a *profit* of \$1 million rather than losing \$1 million. If Wise Domotics drops the product, the \$5 million in fixed overhead expense will not disappear—it will simply have to be allocated elsewhere. However, the \$4 million in net marketing contribution *will* disappear.

Marketing Return on Sales and Investment

To get an even deeper understanding of the profit impact of marketing strategy, we'll now examine two measures of marketing efficiency—*marketing return on sales* (marketing ROS) and *marketing return on investment* (marketing ROI).[iv]

Marketing return on sales (or marketing ROS) The percent of net sales attributable to the net marketing contribution—calculated by dividing net marketing contribution by net sales.

Marketing return on sales (or **marketing ROS**) shows the percent of net sales attributable to the net marketing contribution. For our product, ROS is:

$$\text{Marketing ROS} = \frac{\text{net marketing contribution}}{\text{net sales}} = \frac{\$4{,}000{,}000}{\$100{,}000{,}000} = 0.04 = 4\%$$

Thus, out of every \$100 of sales, the product returns \$4 to Wise Domotics's bottom line. A high marketing ROS is desirable. But to assess whether this is a good level of performance, Wise Domotics must compare this figure to previous marketing ROS levels for the product, the ROSs of other products in the company's portfolio, and the ROSs of competing products.

Marketing return on investment (or marketing ROI)
A measure of the marketing productivity of a marketing investment—calculated by dividing net marketing contribution by marketing expenses.

Marketing return on investment (or **marketing ROI**) measures the marketing productivity of a marketing investment. In Wise Domotics's case, the marketing investment is represented by $41 million of the total expenses. Thus, marketing ROI is:

$$\text{Marketing ROI} = \frac{\text{net marketing contribution}}{\text{marketing expenses}} = \frac{\$4{,}000{,}000}{\$41{,}000{,}000} = 0.0976 = 9.76\%$$

As with marketing ROS, a high value is desirable, but this figure should be compared with previous levels for the given product and with the marketing ROIs of competitors' products. Note from this equation that marketing ROI could be greater than 100%. This can be achieved by attaining a higher net marketing contribution and/or a lower total marketing expense.

In this section, we estimated market potential and sales, developed profit-and-loss statements, and examined financial measures of performance. In the next section, we discuss methods for analyzing the impact of various marketing tactics. However, before moving on to those analyses, here's another set of quantitative exercises to help you apply what you've learned to other situations.

Marketing by the Numbers Exercise Set Two

2.1 Determine the market potential for a product that has 10 million prospective buyers who purchase an average of five per year and price averages $5.

2.2 Develop a profit-and-loss statement for a company that had $50 million in net sales last year. Cost of goods sold represents 45% of net sales. Marketing expenses include selling expenses, promotion expenses, and freight. Selling expenses include sales salaries totaling $2 million per year and sales commissions (10% of sales). The company spent $2 million on advertising last year, and freight costs were 5% of sales. Other costs include $500,000 for managerial salaries and expenses for the marketing function and another $2 million for indirect overhead allocated to the division.

2.3 Using the profit-and-loss statement you developed in question 2.2 and assuming that the company's beginning inventory was $15 million, ending inventory was $6 million, and total investment was $30 million including inventory, determine the following:

a. gross margin percentage
b. net profit percentage
c. operating expense percentage
d. inventory turnover rate
e. return on investment (ROI)
f. net marketing contribution
g. marketing return on sales (marketing ROS)
h. marketing return on investment (marketing ROI)
i. Is the company doing well? Explain your answer.

Financial Analysis of Marketing Tactics

Although the first-year profit performance for Wise Domotics's new product was less than desired, management feels that this attractive market has excellent growth opportunities. Although the sales of Wise Domotics's product were lower than initially projected, they were not unreasonable given the size of the current market. Thus, Wise Domotics wants to explore new marketing tactics to help grow the market for this product and increase sales for the company.

For example, the company could increase advertising to promote more awareness of the new product and its category. It could add salespeople to secure greater product distribution. Wise Domotics could decrease prices so that more consumers could afford its product. Finally, to expand the market, Wise Domotics could introduce a lower-priced model in addition to the higher-priced original offering. Before pursuing any of these tactics, Wise Domotics must analyze the financial implications of each.

Increase Advertising Expenditures

Wise Domotics is considering boosting its advertising to make more people aware of the benefits of this device in general and of its own brand in particular. What if Wise Domotics's marketers recommend increasing national advertising by 50% to $15 million (assume no change in the variable cooperative component of promotional expenditures)? This represents an increase in fixed costs of $5 million. What increase in sales will be needed to break even on this $5 million increase in fixed costs?

A quick way to answer this question is to divide the increase in fixed cost by the contribution margin, which we found in a previous analysis to be 21%:

$$\text{Increase in sales} = \frac{\text{increase in fixed cost}}{\text{contribution margin}} = \frac{\$5{,}000{,}000}{0.21} = \$23{,}809{,}524$$

Thus, a 50% increase in advertising expenditures must produce a sales increase of almost $24 million to just break even. That $24 million sales increase translates into an almost 1 percentage point increase in market share (1% of the $2.5 billion overall market equals $25 million). That is, to break even on the increased advertising expenditure, Wise Domotics would have to increase its market share from 4% to 4.95% ($123,809,524 ÷ $2.5 billion = 0.0495, or 4.95% market share). All of this assumes that the total market will not grow, which might or might not be a reasonable assumption.

Increase Distribution Coverage

Wise Domotics also wants to consider hiring more salespeople in order to call on new retailer accounts and increase distribution through more outlets. Even though Wise Domotics sells directly to wholesalers, its sales representatives call on retail accounts to perform other functions in addition to selling, such as training retail salespeople. Currently, Wise Domotics employs 70 sales reps who earn an average of $60,000 in salary plus 10% commission on sales. The product is currently sold to consumers through 1,875 retail outlets. Suppose Wise Domotics wants to increase that number of outlets to 2,500, an increase of 625 retail outlets. How many additional salespeople will Wise Domotics need, and what sales will be necessary to break even on the increased cost?

Workload method
An approach to determining sales force size based on the workload required and the time available for selling.

One method for determining what size sales force Wise Domotics will need is the **workload method**. The workload method uses the following formula to determine the salesforce size:

$$NS = \frac{NC \times FC \times LC}{TA}$$

where

NS = number of salespeople
NC = number of customers
FC = average frequency of customer calls per customer
LC = average length of customer call
TA = time an average salesperson has available for selling per year

Wise Domotics's sales reps typically call on accounts an average of 20 times per year for about two hours per call. Although sales reps work 2,000 hours per year (50 weeks per year × 40 hours per week), they spent about 15 hours per week on nonselling activities such as administrative duties and travel. Thus, the average annual available selling time per sales rep per year is 1,250 hours (50 weeks × 25 hours per week). We can now calculate how many sales reps Wise Domotics will need to cover the anticipated 2,500 retail outlets:

$$NS = \frac{2{,}500 \times 20 \times 2}{1{,}250} = 80 \text{ salespeople}$$

Therefore, Wise Domotics will need to hire 10 more salespeople. The cost to hire these reps will be $600,000 (10 salespeople × $60,000 salary per salesperson).

What increase in sales will be required to break even on this increase in fixed costs? The 10% commission is already accounted for in the contribution margin, so the contribution margin remains unchanged at 21%. Thus, the increase in sales needed to cover this increase in fixed costs can be calculated by:

$$\text{Increase in sales} = \frac{\text{increase in fixed cost}}{\text{contribution margin}} = \frac{\$600{,}000}{0.21} = \$2{,}857{,}142$$

That is, Wise Domotics's sales must increase by almost $3 million to break even on this tactic. So, how many new retail outlets will the company need to secure to achieve this sales increase? The average revenue generated per current outlet is $53,333 ($100 million in sales divided by 1,875 outlets). Wise Domotics would need about 54 new outlets to break even on this tactic ($2,857,142 ÷ $53,333 = 53.6 outlets), or about 5-6 outlets per new rep. Given that current reps cover about 27 outlets apiece (1,875 outlets ÷ 70 reps), it seems very reasonable that Wise Domotics can break even on this tactic.

Decrease Price

Wise Domotics is also considering lowering its price to increase sales revenue through increased volume. The company's research has shown that demand for most types of consumer electronics products is elastic—that is, the percentage increase in the quantity demanded is greater than the percentage decrease in price.

What increase in sales would be necessary to break even on a 10% decrease in price? That is, what increase in sales will be needed to maintain the total contribution that Wise Domotics realized at the higher price? The current total contribution can be determined by multiplying the contribution margin by total sales:[v]

$$\text{Current total contribution} = \text{contribution margin} \times \text{sales} = 0.21 \times \$100 \text{ million} = \$21 \text{ million}$$

Price changes result in changes in unit contribution and contribution margin. Recall that the contribution margin of 21% was based on variable costs representing 79% of sales. Therefore, unit variable costs can be determined by multiplying the original price by this percentage: $168 × 0.79 = $132.72 per unit. If price is decreased by 10%, the new price is $151.20. However, variable costs do not change just because price decreased, so the contribution and contribution margin decrease as follows:

	Old	**New (Reduced 10%)**
Price	$168	$151.20
− Unit variable cost	$132.72	$132.72
= Unit contribution	$35.28	$18.48
Contribution margin	$35.28/$168 = 0.21 or 21%	$18.48/$151.20 = 0.12 or 12%

So a 10% reduction in price results in a decrease in the contribution margin from 21% to 12%.[vi] To determine the sales level needed to break even on this price reduction, we calculate the level of sales that must be attained at the new contribution margin to achieve the original total contribution of $21 million:

$$\text{New contribution margin} \times \text{new sales level} = \text{original total contribution}$$

So,

$$\text{New sales level} = \frac{\text{original contribution}}{\text{new contribution margin}} = \frac{\$21{,}000{,}000}{0.12} = \$175{,}000{,}000$$

Thus, sales must increase by $75 million ($175 million − $100 million) just to break even on a 10% price reduction. This means that Wise Domotics must increase market share to 7% ($175 million ÷ $2.5 billion) to achieve the current level of profits (assuming no increase in the total market sales). The marketing manager must assess whether or not this is a reasonable goal.

Extend the Product Line

Cannibalization
The situation in which one product sold by a company takes a portion of its sales from other company products.

As a final option, Wise Domotics is considering extending its product line by offering a lower-priced model. Of course, the new, lower-priced product would steal some sales from the higher-priced model. This is called **cannibalization**—the situation in which one product sold by a company takes a portion of its sales from other company products. If the new product has a lower contribution than the original product, the company's total contribution will decrease on the cannibalized sales. However, if the new product can generate enough new volume, it is worth considering.

To assess cannibalization, Wise Domotics must look at the incremental contribution gained by having both products available. Recall that in the previous analysis we determined that unit variable costs were $132.72 and unit contribution was just over $35. Assuming costs remain the same next year, Wise Domotics can expect to realize a contribution per unit of approximately $35 for every unit of the original product sold.

Assume that the first model offered by Wise Domotics is called Wise Domotics1 and the new, lower-priced model is called Wise Domotics2. Wise Domotics2 will retail for $250, and resellers will take the same markup percentages on price as they do with the higher-priced model. Therefore, Wise Domotics2's price to wholesalers will be $140 as follows:

Retail price:	$250
minus retail margin (30%):	–$ 75
Retailer's cost/wholesaler's price:	$175
minus wholesaler's margin (20%):	–$ 35
Wholesaler's cost/Wise Domotics's price	$140

If Wise Domotics2's variable costs are estimated to be $120, then its contribution per unit will equal $20 ($140 − $120 = $20). That means for every unit that Wise Domotics2 cannibalizes from Wise Domotics1, Wise Domotics will *lose* $15 in contribution toward fixed costs and profit (that is, $\text{contribution}_{\text{Wise Domotics2}} - \text{contribution}_{\text{Wise Domotics1}} = \$20 - \$35 = -\$15$). You might conclude that Wise Domotics should not pursue this tactic because it appears as though the company will be worse off if it introduces the lower-priced model. However, if Wise Domotics2 captures enough *additional* sales, Wise Domotics will be better off even though some Wise Domotics1 sales are cannibalized. The company must examine what will happen to *total* contribution, which requires estimates of unit volume for both products.

Originally, Wise Domotics estimated that next year's sales of Wise Domotics1 would be 600,000 units. However, with the introduction of Wise Domotics2, it now estimates that 200,000 of those sales will be cannibalized by the new model. If Wise Domotics sells only 200,000 units of the new Wise Domotics2 model (all cannibalized from Wise Domotics1), the company would lose $3 million in total contribution (200,000 units × −$15 per cannibalized unit = −$3 million)—not a good outcome. However, Wise Domotics estimates that Wise Domotics2 will generate the 200,000 of cannibalized sales plus an *additional* 500,000 unit sales. Thus, the contribution on these additional Wise Domotics2 units will be $10 million (i.e., 500,000 units × $20 per unit = $10 million). The net effect is that Wise Domotics will gain $7 million in total contribution by introducing Wise Domotics2.

The following table compares Wise Demotics' total contribution with and without the introduction of Wise Domotics2:

	Wise Domotics1 only	Wise Domotics1 and Wise Domotics2
Wise Domotics1 contribution	600,000 units × $35 = $ 21,000,000	400,000 units × $35 = $14,000,000
Wise Domotics2 contribution	0	700,000 units × $20 = $14,000,000
Total contribution	$21,000,000	$28,000,000

The difference in the total contribution is a net gain of $7 million ($28 million − $21 million). Based on this analysis, Wise Domotics should introduce the Wise Domotics2 model because it results in a positive incremental contribution. However, if fixed costs will increase by more than $7 million as a result of adding this model, then the net effect will be negative and Wise Domotics should not pursue this tactic.

Now that you have seen these marketing tactic analysis concepts in action as they relate to Wise Domotics's new product, here are several exercises for you to apply what you have learned in this section in other contexts.

Marketing by the Numbers Exercise Set Three

3.1 Synegys, Inc. manufactures accent lighting that is sold to consumers through retail outlets in the southern United States. The company's sales are $1 million and contribution margin is 30%. The company is considering options to increase sales.

a. The marketing manager has suggested increasing consumer advertising by $50,000. By how much would dollar sales need to increase to break even on this expenditure? What percentage increase in sales does this represent?

b. Another suggestion is to make a 5% across-the-board price reduction. By how much would dollar sales need to increase to maintain Synegys's current contribution? (See endnote 6 to calculate the new contribution margin percentage.) What percentage increase in sales does this represent?

3.2 A company currently has 2,000 industrial customer accounts and wants to expand to another geographic market to acquire 3,000 more. It currently has ten sales representatives who earn $60,000 per year and 5% commission on sales. Each customer account is visited six times per year and sales reps spend an hour and a half on each call (that is, 1.5 hours). An average salesperson works 2,000 hours per year (50 weeks per years × 50 hours per week), but each will spend 10 hours a week on nonselling activities, such as administrative tasks and travel. The company's contribution margin is 40% and each customer generates an average $50,000 in sales for the company.

a. How many salespeople will the company need to hire?

b. What increase in sales is needed to cover the increased cost of an additional sales representative? How much must sales increase to break even on the number of sales representatives the company needs to hire?

c. How many customers must the company acquire to break even on this tactic?

3.3 BriteSmile brand of teeth whitening products is considering adding a modified version of the product—a gel product in addition to its regular paste product. Variable costs and prices to wholesalers are:

	Current paste product	New gel product
Unit selling price	$4.00	$4.50
Unit variable costs	$1.70	$2.50

BriteSmile expects to sell 1 million units of the new gel product in the first year after introduction, but it estimates that only 45% of those sales will come from buyers who do not already purchase the company's paste product (that is, new customers). BriteSmile estimates that it would sell 1.5 million units of the current paste product if it did not introduce the gel. If the fixed costs of launching the new gel product will be $250,000 during the first year, should BriteSmile add the new gel product to its line? Why or why not?

Appendix 4 Careers in Marketing

You may have decided you want to pursue a marketing career because it offers constant challenge, stimulating problems, the opportunity to work with people, and excellent advancement opportunities. But you still may not know which part of marketing best suits you—marketing is a very broad field offering a wide variety of career options.

This appendix helps you discover what types of marketing jobs best match your special skills and interests, shows you how to conduct the kind of job search that will get you the position you want, describes marketing career paths open to you, and suggests other information resources.

Marketing Careers Today

The marketing field is booming, with nearly a third of all working Americans now employed in marketing-related positions. Marketing salaries may vary by company, position, and region, and salary figures change constantly. In general, entry-level marketing salaries usually are only slightly below those for engineering and chemistry, but equal or exceed starting salaries in economics, finance, accounting, general business, and the liberal arts. Moreover, if you succeed in an entry-level marketing position, it's likely that you will be promoted quickly to higher levels of responsibility and salary. In addition, because of the consumer and product knowledge you will gain in these jobs, marketing positions provide excellent training for the highest levels in an organization.

Overall Marketing Facts and Trends

In conducting your job search, consider the following facts and trends that are changing the world of marketing:

Focus on customers. More and more, companies are realizing that they win in the marketplace only engaging customers and creating superior value for them. To capture value from customers, they must first find new and better ways to engage customers, solve customer problems, and improve customer brand experiences. This increasing focus on the customer puts marketers at the forefront in many of today's companies. As the primary customer-facing function, marketing's mission is to get all company departments to "think customer."

Technology. Technology is changing the way marketers work. For example, internet, social media, mobile, and other digital technologies are rapidly changing the ways marketers interact with and service customers. They are also changing everything from the ways marketers create new products and advertise them to how marketers access information and recruit personnel. Whereas advertising firms have traditionally recruited "generalists" in account management, *generalist* has now taken on a whole new meaning—advertising account executives must now have both broad and specialized knowledge.

Diversity. The number of women and minorities in marketing continues to grow, and women and minorities also are advancing rapidly into marketing management. For example, women now outnumber men as advertising account executives. As marketing becomes more global, the need for diversity in marketing positions will continue to increase, opening new opportunities.

Global. Companies such as Coca-Cola, McDonald's, Google, Walmart, IBM, Facebook, and Procter & Gamble have become multinational, with manufacturing and marketing operations in hundreds of countries. Indeed, such companies often make more profit from sales outside the United States than from within. And it's not just the big companies that are involved in international marketing. Organizations of all sizes have moved into the global arena. Many new marketing opportunities and careers will be directly linked to the expanding global marketplace. The globalization of business also means that you will need more cultural, language, and people skills in the marketing world of the twenty-first century.

Not-for-profit organizations. Increasingly, colleges, arts organizations, libraries, hospitals, and other not-for-profit organizations are recognizing the need for effectively marketing their "products" and services to various publics. This awareness has led to new marketing positions—with these organizations hiring their own marketing directors and marketing vice presidents or using outside marketing specialists.

Looking for a Job in Today's Marketing World

To choose and find the right job, you will need to apply the marketing skills you've learned in this course, especially marketing analysis and planning. Follow these eight steps for marketing yourself: (1) Conduct a self-assessment and seek career counseling; (2) examine job descriptions; (3) explore the job market, follow up, and assess opportunities; (4) develop search strategies; (5) prepare résumés; (6) write a cover letter and assemble supporting documents; (7) interview for jobs; and (8) take a follow-up interview.

Conduct a Self-Assessment and Seek Career Counseling

If you're having difficulty deciding what kind of marketing position is the best fit for you, start out by doing some self-testing or seeking career counseling. Self-assessments require that you honestly and thoroughly evaluate your interests, strengths, and weaknesses. What do you do well (your best and favorite skills) and not so well? What are your favorite interests? What are your career goals? What makes you stand out from other job seekers?

The answers to such questions may suggest which marketing careers you should seek or avoid. For help in completing an effective self-assessment, look for the following books in your local bookstore or online: Nicholas Lore, *The Pathfinder: How to Choose or Change Your Career for a Lifetime of Satisfaction and Success* (Touchstone, 2012) and Richard Bolles, *What Color Is Your Parachute? 2018* (Ten Speed Press, 2017; also see www.eparachute.com). Many online sites also offer self-assessment tools, such as the Keirsey Temperament Theory and the Temperament Sorter, a free but broad assessment available at Keirsey.com. For a more specific evaluation, CareerLeader.com offers a complete online business career self-assessment program designed by the Directors of MBA Career Development at Harvard Business School. You can use this for a fee.

For help in finding a career counselor to guide you in making a career assessment, Richard Bolles's *What Color Is Your Parachute? 2018* contains a useful state-by-state sampling. CareerLeader.com also offers personal career counseling. (Some counselors can help you in your actual job search, too.) You can also consult the career counseling, testing, and placement services at your college or university.

Examine Job Descriptions

After you have identified your skills, interests, and desires, you need to see which marketing positions are the best match for them. Two U.S. Labor Department publications available in your local library or online—the *Occupation Outlook Handbook* (www.bls.gov/ooh) and the *Dictionary of Occupational Titles* (www.occupationalinfo.org)—describe the duties involved in various occupations, the specific training and education needed, the availability of jobs in each field, possibilities for advancement, and probable earnings.

Your initial career shopping list should be broad and flexible. Look for different ways to achieve your objectives. For example, if you want a career in marketing management, consider the public as well as the private sector and local and regional as well as national and international firms. Be open initially to exploring many options, and then focus on specific industries and jobs, listing your basic goals as a way to guide your choices. Your list might include "a job in a startup company, near a big city on the West Coast, doing new product planning with a computer software firm."

Explore the Job Market and Assess Opportunities

At this stage, you need to look at the market and see what positions are actually available. You do not have to do this alone. Any of the following may assist you.

Career Development Centers

Your college's career development center and its website are excellent places to start. For example, the websites of the undergraduate career services center provide lists of career links that can help to focus your job search. Most schools also provide career coaches and career education courses. Also check the National Association of Colleges and Employers website (www.naceweb.org). It publishes a national forecast of hiring intentions of employers as they relate to new college graduates (search: "Job Outlook").

In addition, find out everything you can about the companies that interest you by consulting company websites, business magazine articles and online sites, annual reports, business reference books, faculty, career counselors, and others. Try to analyze the industry's and the company's future growth and profit potential, advancement opportunities, salary levels, entry positions, travel time, and other factors of significance to you.

Job Fairs

Career development centers often work with corporate recruiters to organize on-campus job fairs. You might also use the internet to check on upcoming career fairs in your region. For example, visit National Career Fairs at www.nationalcareerfairs.com or Choice Career Fairs listings at https://choicecareerfairs.com.

Networking

Networking—asking for job leads from friends, family, people in your community, and career centers—is one of the best ways to find a marketing job. Studies estimate that 60 to 90 percent of jobs are found through networking. The idea is to spread your net wide, contacting anybody and everybody.

Internships

An internship is filled with many benefits, such as gaining experience in a specific field of interest and building up a network of contacts. The biggest benefit: the potential of being offered a job shortly before or soon after graduation. According to a recent survey by the National Association of Colleges and Employers, employers converted more than 51 percent of last year's interns into full-time hires. In addition, 62 percent of the seniors who had paid internship experience and applied for a job received at least one job offer. Conversely, only 43 percent of seniors without internship experience who applied for a job received an offer. In addition, survey results show that the median accepted salary offer for seniors with a paid internship was 27 percent higher than the median accepted salary offered to non-intern seniors.

Many company internet sites have separate internship areas. For example, check out Internships.com, InternshipPrograms.com, MonsterCollege (college.monster.com/education), CampusCareerCenter.com, InternJobs.com, and GoAbroad.com (www.goabroad.com/intern-abroad). If you know of a company for which you wish to work, go to that company's corporate website, enter the human resources area, and check for internships. If none are listed, try emailing the human resources department, asking if internships are offered.

Job Hunting on the Internet

A constantly increasing number of sites on the internet deal with job hunting. You can also use the internet to make contacts with people who can help you gain information on and research companies that interest you. CareerBuilder, Indeed, Monster, and ZipRecruiter are good general sites for seeking job listings. Other helpful sites are Disability.gov and Diversity.com, which contain information on opportunities for individuals with disabilities and minorities, respectively.

Most companies have their own online sites on which they post job listings. This may be helpful if you have a specific and fairly limited number of companies that you are keeping your eye on for job opportunities. But if this is not the case, remember that to find out what interesting marketing jobs the companies themselves are posting, you may have to visit hundreds of corporate sites.

Professional Networking Sites

Many companies have now begun to take advantage of social networking sites to find talented applicants. From LinkedIn to Facebook to Google+, social networking has become professional networking. For example, companies ranging from P&G to BASF have jobs pages on LinkedIn (www.linkedin.com/company/procter-and-gamble/jobs/and www.linkedin.com/company/basf/jobs/) to find potential candidates for entry-level positions. And professional organizations, such as the Public Relations Society of America and the American Advertising Federation, have job listings on their websites. For job seekers, online professional networking offers more efficient job targeting and reduces associated costs as compared with traditional interaction methods such as traveling to job fairs and interviews, printing résumés, and other expenses.

However, although the internet offers a wealth of resources for searching for the perfect job, be aware that it's a two-way street. Just as job seekers can search the internet to find job opportunities, employers can search for information on job candidates. Jobs searches can sometimes be derailed by information mined by potential employers from online social networking sites that reveals unintended or embarrassing anecdotes and photos. Internet searches can sometimes also reveal inconsistencies and résumé inflation. A recent study found that more than half of recruiters surveyed have reconsidered a candidate based on their social profile.

Develop Search Strategies

Once you've decided which companies you are interested in, you need to contact them. One of the best ways is through on-campus interviews. However, not every company you are interested in will visit your school. In such instances, you can write, email, or phone the company directly or ask marketing professors or school alumni for contacts.

Prepare Résumés

A résumé is a concise yet comprehensive written summary of your qualifications, including your academic, personal, and professional achievements, that showcases why you are the best candidate for the job. Because an employer will spend on average only 15 to 20 seconds reviewing your résumé, you want to be sure that you prepare a good one.

In preparing your résumé, remember that all information on it must be accurate and complete. Résumés typically begin with the applicant's full name, telephone number, and mail and email addresses. A simple and direct statement of career objectives generally appears next, followed by work history and academic data (including awards and internships) and then by personal activities and experiences applicable to the job sought.

The résumé sometimes ends with a list of references the employer may contact (at other times, references may be listed separately). If your work or internship experience is limited, nonexistent, or irrelevant, then it is a good idea to emphasize your academic and nonacademic achievements, showing skills related to those required for excellent job performance.

There are three main types of résumés. Reverse *chronological* résumés, which emphasize career growth, are organized in reverse chronological order, starting with your most recent job. They focus on job titles within organizations, describing the responsibilities and accomplishments for each job. *Functional* résumés focus less on job titles and work history and more on assets and achievements. This format works best if your job history is scanty or discontinuous. *Mixed,* or *combination,* résumés take from each of the other two formats. First, the skills used for a specific job are listed, and then the job title is stated. This format works best for applicants whose past jobs are in other fields or seemingly unrelated to the position. For further explanation and examples of these types of résumés, see the Résumé Resource format page (www.resume-resource.com/format.html).

Many books can assist you in developing your résumé. A popular guide is Molly Mapes, *Cracking the Code: A Practical Guide to Getting You Hired* (Difference Press, 2016). Websites such as MyPerfectResume (www.myperfectresume.com) provide sample résumés and ready-to-use phrases while guiding you through the résumé preparation process. CareerOneStop (www.careeronestop.org/resumeguide/introduction.aspx) offers a step-by-step résumé tutorial, and Monster (http://career-advice.monster.com) offers résumé advice and writing services. Finally, you can even create your own personalized online résumé at sites such as optimalresume.com.

Online Résumés

The internet is now a widely used job-search environment, so it's a good idea to have your résumé ready for the online environment. You can forward it to networking contacts or recruiting professionals through email. You can also post it in online databases with the hope that employers and recruiters will find it.

Successful internet-ready résumés require a different strategy than that for paper résumés. For instance, when companies search résumé banks, they search key words and industry buzz words that describe a skill or the core work required for each job, so nouns are much more important than verbs. Two good resources for preparing internet-ready résumés are GCF (www.gcflearnfree.org/resumewriting/9/print) and LiveCareer (www.livecareer.com/career/advice/resume/e-resumes).

After you have written your internet-ready résumé, you need to post it. Indeed and LinkedIn are good locations to star. However, use caution when posting your résumé on various sites. In this era of identity theft, you need to select sites with care so as to protect your privacy. Limit access to your personal contact information, and don't use sites that offer to "blast" your résumé into cyberspace.

Résumé Tips

- Communicate your worth to potential employers in a concrete manner, citing examples whenever possible.
- Be concise and direct.
- Use active verbs to show you are a doer.
- Do not skimp on quality or use gimmicks. Spare no expense in presenting a professional résumé.
- Have someone critique your work. A single typo can eliminate you from being considered.
- Customize your résumé for specific employers. Emphasize your strengths as they pertain to your targeted job.
- Keep your résumé compact, usually one page.
- Format the text to be attractive, professional, and readable. Times New Roman is often the font of choice. Avoid too much "design" or gimmicky flourishes.

Write Cover Letter, Follow Up, and Assemble Supporting Documents

Cover Letter

You should include a cover letter informing the employer that a résumé is enclosed. But a cover letter does more than this. It also serves to summarize in one or two paragraphs the contents of the résumé and explains why you think you are the right person for the position.

The goal is to persuade the employer to look at the more detailed résumé. A typical cover letter is organized as follows: (1) the name and position of the person you are contacting; (2) a statement identifying the position you are applying for, how you heard of the vacancy, and the reasons for your interest; (3) a summary of your qualifications for the job; (4) a description of what follow ups you intend to make, such as phoning in two weeks to see if the résumé has been received; and (5) an expression of gratitude for the opportunity of being a candidate for the job.

CareerOneStop (www.careeronestop.org/ResumeGuide/Writeeffectivecoverletters.aspx) offers a step-by-step tutorial on how to create a cover letter, and Susan Ireland's website contains more than 50 cover letter samples (susanireland.com/letter/cover-letter-examples). Another popular site, Resume Genius, can build a cover letter for you (https://resumegenius.com/cover-letter-builder). A popular guide to check out is Jeremy Schifeling, *Get It Done: Write a Cover Letter* (Adams Media, 2016).

Follow Up

Once you send your cover letter and résumé to prospective employers via the method they prefer—email, their website, or regular mail—it's often a good idea to follow up. In today's market, job seekers can't afford to wait for interviews to find them. A quality résumé and an attractive cover letter are crucial, but a proper follow-up may be the key to landing an interview. However, before you engage your potential employer, be sure to research the company. Knowing about the company and understanding its place in the industry will help you shine. When you place a call, send an email, or mail a letter to a company contact, be sure to restate your interest in the position, check on the status of your résumé, and ask employers about any questions they may have.

Letters of Recommendation

Letters of recommendation are written references by professors, former and current employers, and others that testify to your character, skills, and abilities. Some companies may request letters of recommendation, to be submitted either with the résumé or at the interview. Even if letters of recommendation aren't requested, it's a good idea to bring them with you to the interview. A good reference letter tells why you would be an excellent candidate for the position. In choosing someone to write a letter of recommendation, be confident that the person will give you a good reference. In addition, do not assume the person knows everything about you or the position you are seeking. Rather, provide the person with your résumé and other relevant data. As a courtesy, allow the reference writer at least a month to complete the letter and enclose a stamped, addressed envelope with your materials.

In the packet containing your résumé, cover letter, and letters of recommendation, you may also want to attach other relevant documents that support your candidacy, such as academic transcripts, graphics, portfolios, and samples of writing.

Interview for Jobs

As the old saying goes, "The résumé gets you the interview; the interview gets you the job." The job interview offers you an opportunity to gather more information about the organization, while at the same time allowing the organization to gather more information about you. You'll want to present your best self. The interview process consists of three parts: before the interview, the interview itself, and after the interview. If you pass through these stages successfully, you will be called back for the follow-up interview.

Before the Interview

In preparing for your interview, do the following:

1. Understand that interviewers have diverse styles, including the "chitchat," let's-get-to-know-each-other style; the interrogation style of question after question; and the tough-probing "why, why, why" style, among others. So be ready for anything.

2. With a friend, practice being interviewed and then ask for a critique. Or video yourself in a practice interview so that you can critique your own performance. Your college placement service may also offer "mock" interviews to help you.
3. Prepare at least five good questions whose answers are not easily found in the company literature, such as "What is the future direction of the firm?" "How does the firm differentiate itself from competitors?" or "Do you have a new-media division?"
4. Anticipate possible interview questions, such as "Why do you want to work for this company?" or "Why should we hire you?" Prepare solid answers before the interview. Have a clear idea of why you are interested in joining the company and the industry to which it belongs.
5. Avoid back-to-back interviews—they can be exhausting, and it is unpredictable how long each will last.
6. Prepare relevant documents that support your candidacy, such as academic transcripts, letters of recommendation, graphics, portfolios, and samples of writing. Bring multiple copies to the interview.
7. Dress conservatively and professionally. Be neat and clean.
8. Arrive 10 minutes early to collect your thoughts and review the major points you intend to cover. Check your name on the interview schedule, noting the name of the interviewer and the room number. Be courteous and polite to office staff.
9. Approach the interview enthusiastically. Let your personality shine through.

During the Interview

During the interview, do the following:

1. Shake hands firmly in greeting the interviewer. Introduce yourself, using the same form of address that the interviewer uses. Focus on creating a good initial impression.
2. Keep your poise. Relax, smile when appropriate, and be upbeat throughout.
3. Maintain eye contact and good posture and speak distinctly. Don't clasp your hands or fiddle with jewelry, hair, or clothing. Sit comfortably in your chair.
4. Along with the copies of relevant documents that support your candidacy, carry extra copies of your résumé with you.
5. Have your story down pat. Present your selling points. Answer questions directly. Avoid either one-word or too-wordy answers.
6. Let the interviewer take the initiative but don't be passive. Find an opportunity to direct the conversation to things about yourself that you want the interviewer to hear.
7. To end on a high note, make your most important point or ask your most pertinent question during the last part of the interview.
8. Don't hesitate to "close." You might say, "I'm very interested in the position and I have enjoyed this interview."
9. Obtain the interviewer's business card or address, email address, and phone number so that you can follow up later.

A tip for acing the interview: Before you open your mouth, find out *what it's like* to be a brand manager, sales representative, market researcher, advertising account executive, social media analyst, or other position for which you're interviewing. See if you can find a "mentor"—someone in a position similar to the one you're seeking, perhaps with another company. Talk with this mentor about the ins and outs of the job and industry.

After the Interview

After the interview, do the following:

1. Record the key points that arose. Be sure to note who is to follow up and when a decision can be expected.
2. Analyze the interview objectively, including the questions asked, the answers to them, your overall interview presentation, and the interviewer's responses to specific points.

3. Immediately send a thank-you letter or email, mentioning any additional items and your willingness to supply further information.
4. If you do not hear from the employer within the specified time, call, email, or write the interviewer to determine your status.

Follow-Up Interview

If your first interview takes place off-site, such as at your college or at a job fair, and if you are successful with that initial interview, you will be invited to visit the organization. The in-company interview will probably run from several hours to an entire day. The organization will examine your interest, maturity, enthusiasm, assertiveness, logic, and company and functional knowledge. You should ask questions about issues of importance to you. Find out about the working environment, job role, responsibilities, opportunities for advancement, current industrial issues, and the company's personality. The company wants to discover if you are the right person for the job, whereas you want to find out if it is the right job for you. The key is to determine if the right *fit* exists between you and the company.

Marketing Jobs

This section describes some of the key marketing positions.

Advertising

Advertising is one of the most exciting fields in marketing, offering a wide range of career opportunities.

Job Descriptions

Key advertising positions include copywriter, art director, production manager, account executive, account planner, digital and social media content managers, and media planner/buyer.

- *Copywriters* write advertising copy and help find the concepts behind the written words and visual images of advertisements.
- *Art directors,* the other part of the creative team, help translate the copywriters' ideas into dramatic visuals called "layouts." Agency artists develop print layouts, package designs, television and video layouts (called "storyboards"), corporate logotypes, trademarks, and symbols.
- *Production managers* are responsible for physically creating ads, either in-house or by contracting through outside production houses.
- *Account development executives* research and understand clients' markets and customers and help develop marketing and advertising strategies to impact them.
- *Account executives* serve as liaisons between clients and agencies. They coordinate the planning, creation, production, and implementation of an advertising campaign for the account.
- *Account planners* serve as the voice of the consumer in the agency. They research consumers to understand their needs and motivations as a basis for developing effective ad campaigns.
- *Digital and social media content managers* plan and place digital and social media marketing and advertising content and coordinate it with traditional media content.
- *Media planners (or buyers)* determine the best mix of television, radio, newspaper, magazine, digital, and other media for the advertising campaign.

Skills Needed, Career Paths, and Typical Salaries

Work in advertising requires strong people skills in order to interact closely with an often-difficult and demanding client base. In addition, advertising attracts people with strong skills in planning, problem solving, creativity, communication, initiative, leadership, and presentation. Advertising involves working under high levels of stress and pressure created by unrelenting deadlines. Advertisers frequently have to work long hours to meet deadlines for a presentation. But work achievements are very apparent, with the results of creative strategies observed by thousands or even millions of people.

Positions in advertising sometimes require an MBA. But most jobs only require a business, graphic arts, or liberal arts degree. Advertising positions often serve as gateways to higher-level management. Moreover, with large advertising agencies opening offices all over the world, there is the possibility of eventually working on global campaigns.

Starting advertising salaries are relatively low compared to those of some other marketing jobs because of strong competition for entry-level advertising jobs. Compensation will increase quickly as you move into account executive or other management positions. For more facts and figures, see the online pages of *Advertising Age,* a key ad industry publication (www.adage.com, click on the Jobs link) and the American Association of Advertising Agencies (www.aaaa.org).

Brand and Product Management

Brand and product managers plan, direct, and control business and marketing efforts for their products. They are involved with research and development, packaging, manufacturing, sales and distribution, advertising, promotion, market research, digital marketing, and business analysis and forecasting.

Job Descriptions

A company's brand management team consists of people in several positions:

- *Brand managers* guide the development of marketing strategies for a specific brand.
- *Assistant brand managers* are responsible for certain strategic components of the brand.
- *Product managers* oversee several brands within a product line or product group.
- *Product category managers* direct multiple product lines in the product category.
- *Market analysts* research the market and provide important strategic information to the project managers.
- *Project directors* are responsible for collecting market information on a marketing or product project.
- *Research directors* oversee the planning, gathering, and analyzing of all organizational research.

Skills Needed, Career Paths, and Typical Salaries

Brand and product management requires high problem-solving, analytical, presentation, communication, and leadership skills as well as the ability to work well in a team. Product management requires long hours and involves the high pressure of running large projects. In consumer goods companies, the newcomer—who usually needs an MBA—joins a brand team as an assistant and learns the ropes by doing numerical analyses and assisting senior brand people. This person eventually heads the team and later moves on to manage a larger brand, then several brands.

Many industrial goods companies also have product managers. Product management is one of the best training grounds for future corporate officers. Product management also offers good opportunities to move into international marketing. Product managers command relatively high salaries. Because this job category encourages or requires a master's degree, starting pay tends to be higher than in other marketing categories such as advertising or retailing.

Sales and Sales Management

Sales and sales management opportunities exist in a wide range of profit and not-for-profit organizations and in product and service organizations, including financial, insurance, consulting, and government organizations.

Job Descriptions

Key jobs include consumer sales, industrial sales, national account managers, service support, sales trainers, and sales management

- *Consumer sales* involves selling consumer products and services through retailers.
- *Industrial sales* involves selling products and services to other businesses.
- *National account managers (NAMs)* oversee a few very large accounts.
- *Service support* personnel support salespeople during and after the sale of a product.
- *Sales trainers* train new hires and provide refresher training for all sales personnel.
- *Sales management* includes a sequence of positions ranging from district manager to vice president of sales.

Salespeople enjoy active professional lives, working outside the office and interacting with others. They manage their own time and activities. And successful salespeople can be very well paid. Competition for top jobs can be intense. Every sales job is different, but some positions involve extensive travel, long workdays, and working under pressure. You can also expect to be transferred more than once between company headquarters and regional offices. However, most companies are now working to bring good work–life balance to their salespeople and sales managers.

Skills Needed, Career Paths, and Typical Salaries

Selling is a people profession in which you will work with people every day, all day long. In addition to people skills, sales professionals need sales and communication skills. Most sales positions also require strong problem-solving, analytical, presentation, and leadership abilities as well as creativity and initiative. Teamwork skills are increasingly important.

Career paths lead from salesperson to district, regional, and higher levels of sales management and, in many cases, to the top management of the firm. Today, most entry-level sales management positions require a college degree. Increasingly, people seeking selling jobs are acquiring sales experience in an internship capacity or from a part-time job before graduating. Sales positions are great springboards to leadership positions, with more CEOs starting in sales than in any other entry-level position. This might explain why competition for top sales jobs is intense.

Starting base salaries in sales may be moderate but compensation is often supplemented by significant commission, bonus, or other incentive plans. In addition, many sales jobs include a company car or car allowance. Successful salespeople are among most companies' highest paid employees.

Other Marketing Jobs

Marketing Research

Marketing researchers interact with managers to define problems and identify the information needed to resolve them. They design research projects, prepare questionnaires and samples, analyze data, prepare reports, and present their findings and recommendations to management. They must understand statistics, data analytics tools, consumer behavior, psychology, and sociology. As more and more marketing research goes digital, they must also understand the ins and outs of obtaining and managing online information. A master's degree helps. Career opportunities exist with manufacturers, retailers, some wholesalers, trade and industry associations, marketing research firms, advertising agencies, and governmental and private nonprofit agencies.

Marketing Data Science

A marketing data scientist's job is to analyze marketing data to gain actionable customer insights. Data scientists collect big data sets and apply marketing analytics to discover actionable insights and marketing solutions. They share these insights and solutions with marketing managers to help them make better marketing decisions. Being a marketing data scientist often requires math, statistics, analytical, and computer science skills, along with an understanding of marketing strategy. Most data scientists have at least a master's degree.

Digital and Social Media Management

The exploding use of digital and social media has created a wide range of marketing positions and careers, from digital and social media strategists and managers to social media planners, digital content producers, data scientists and big data analysts, and online community managers. These positions involve varying degrees of helping to develop digital and social media campaigns, developing and managing digital content across social media platforms, managing online brand communities, mining customer insights from social media data, and engaging and interacting with customers via websites, mobile, and social media. Such positions require a knowledge of digital technologies and social media platforms such as Twitter, Facebook, Instagram, YouTube, LinkedIn, Pinterest, and Snapchat.

Retailing

Retailing provides an early opportunity to assume marketing responsibilities. Key jobs include store manager, regional manager, buyer, department manager, and salesperson. *Store managers* direct the management and operation of an individual store. *Regional managers* manage groups of stores across several states and report performance to headquarters. *Buyers* select and buy the merchandise that the store carries. The *department manager* acts as store manager of a department, such as clothing, but on the department level. The *salesperson* sells merchandise to retail customers. Retailing can involve relocation, but generally there is little travel, unless you are a buyer. Retailing requires high people and sales skills because retailers are constantly in contact with customers. Enthusiasm, willingness, and communication skills are very helpful for retailers, too.

Retailers work long hours, but their daily activities are often more structured than in some types of marketing positions. Starting salaries in retailing tend to be low but pay increases as you move into management or a retailing specialty job.

New Product Planning

People interested in new product planning can find opportunities in many types of organizations. They usually need a good background in marketing, marketing research, and sales forecasting; they need organizational skills to motivate and coordinate others; and they may need a technical background. Usually, these people work first in other marketing positions before joining the new product department.

Marketing Logistics (Physical Distribution)

Marketing logistics, or physical distribution, is a large and dynamic field, with many career opportunities. Major transportation carriers, manufacturers, wholesalers, and retailers all employ logistics specialists. Increasingly, marketing teams include logistics specialists, and marketing managers' career paths include marketing logistics assignments. Coursework in quantitative methods, finance, accounting, and marketing will provide you with the necessary skills for entering the field.

Public Relations

Most organizations have a public relations staff to anticipate problems with various publics, handle complaints, deal with media, and build the corporate image. People interested in public relations should be able to speak and write clearly and persuasively, and they should have a background in journalism, communications, or the liberal arts. The challenges in this job are highly varied and very people-oriented.

Not-for-Profit Services

The key jobs in not-for-profits include marketing director, director of development, event coordinator, publication specialist, and intern/volunteer. The *marketing director* is in charge of all marketing activities for the organization. The *director of development* organizes, manages, and directs the fundraising campaigns that keep a not-for-profit in existence. An *event coordinator* directs all aspects of fundraising events, from initial planning through implementation. The *publication specialist* oversees publications designed to promote awareness of the organization. Although typically an unpaid position, the *intern/volunteer* performs various marketing functions, and this work can be an important step to gaining a full-time position.

The not-for-profit sector is typically not for someone who is money-driven. Rather, most not-for-profits look for people with a strong sense of community spirit and the desire to help others. Therefore, starting pay is usually lower than in other marketing fields. However, the bigger the not-for-profit, the better your chance of rapidly increasing your income when moving into upper management.

Other Resources

Professional marketing associations and organizations are another source of information about careers. Marketers belong to many such societies. You may want to contact some of the following in your job search:

American Advertising Federation, 1101 Vermont Avenue NW, 5th Floor, Washington, DC 20005. (202) 898-0089 (www.aaf.org)

American Marketing Association, 130 E Randolph Street, 22nd Floor, Chicago, IL 60601. (800) AMA-1150 (www.marketingpower.com)

The Association of Women in Communications, 1717 E Republic Road, Suite A, Springfield, MO 65804. (417) 886-8606 (www.womcom.org)

The Insights Association, 1156 15th Street NW, Suite 302, Washington, DC 20005. (202) 800-2545 (www.insightsassociation.org/)

National Association of Sales Professionals, 555 Friendly Street, Bloomfield Hills, MI 48341. (866) 365-1520 (www.nasp.com)

National Management Association, 2210 Arbor Boulevard, Dayton, OH 45439. (937) 294-0421 (www.nma1.org)

National Retail Federation, 1101 New York Avenue NW, Washington, DC 20005. (800) 673-4692 (www.nrf.com)

Product Development and Management Association, 1000 Westgate Drive, Suite 252, St. Paul, MN 55114. (651) 290-6280 (www.pdma.org)

Public Relations Society of America, 120 Wall St, 21st Floor, New York, NY 10005. (212) 460-1400 (www.prsa.org)

Sales and Marketing Executives International, PO Box 1390, Sumas, WA, 98295. (312) 893-0751 (www.smei.org)

She Runs It, 28 West 44th Street, Suite 912, New York, NY 10036. (212) 221-7969 (https://sherunsit.org)

Glossary

Adapted global marketing A global marketing approach that adjusts the marketing strategy and mix elements to each international target market, which creates more costs but hopefully produces a larger market share and return.

Adoption process The mental process through which an individual passes from first hearing about an innovation to final adoption.

Advertising Any paid form of nonpersonal presentation and promotion of ideas, goods, or services by an identified sponsor.

Advertising agency A marketing services firm that assists companies in planning, preparing, implementing, and evaluating all or portions of their advertising programs.

Advertising budget The dollars and other resources allocated to a product or a company advertising program.

Advertising media The vehicles through which advertising messages are delivered to their intended audiences.

Advertising objective A specific communication *task* to be accomplished with a specific *target* audience during a specific period of *time*.

Advertising strategy The strategy by which the company accomplishes its advertising objectives. It consists of two major elements: creating advertising messages and selecting advertising media.

Affordable method Setting the promotion budget at the level management thinks the company can afford.

Age and life-cycle segmentation Dividing a market into different age and life-cycle groups.

Agent A wholesaler who represents buyers or sellers on a relatively permanent basis, performs only a few functions, and does not take title to goods.

Allowance Promotional money paid by manufacturers to retailers in return for an agreement to feature the manufacturer's products in some way.

Approach The sales step in which a salesperson meets the customer for the first time.

Artificial intelligence (AI) Technology by which machines think and learn in a way that looks and feels human but with a lot more analytical capacity.

Attitude A person's consistently favorable or unfavorable evaluations, feelings, and tendencies toward an object or idea.

Baby boomers The 74 million people born during the years following World War II and lasting until 1964.

Behavioral segmentation Dividing a market into segments based on consumer knowledge, attitudes, uses of a product, or responses to a product.

Behavioral targeting Using online consumer tracking data and analytics to target advertisements and marketing offers to specific consumers.

Belief A descriptive thought that a person holds about something.

Benefit segmentation Dividing the market into segments according to the different benefits that consumers seek from the product.

Big data The huge and complex data sets generated by today's sophisticated information generation, collection, storage, and analysis technologies.

Blogs Online forums where people and companies post their thoughts and other content, usually related to narrowly defined topics.

Brand A name, term, sign, symbol, or design, or a combination of these, that identifies the products or services of one seller or group of sellers and differentiates them from those of competitors.

Brand community website A website that presents brand content that engages consumers and creates customer community around a brand.

Brand equity The differential effect that knowing the brand name has on customer response to the product or its marketing.

Brand extension Extending an existing brand name to new product categories.

Brand value The total financial value of a brand.

Break-even analysis Analysis to determine the unit volume and dollar sales needed to be profitable given a particular price and cost structure.

Break-even price The price at which total revenue equals total cost and profit is zero.

Break-even pricing (target return pricing) Setting price to break even on the costs of making and marketing a product or setting price to make a target return.

Broker A wholesaler who does not take title to goods and whose function is to bring buyers and sellers together and assist in negotiation.

Business analysis A review of the sales, costs, and profit projections for a new product to find out whether these factors satisfy the company's objectives.

Business buyer behavior The buying behavior of organizations that buy goods and services for use in the production of other products and services that are sold, rented, or supplied to others.

Business buying process The decision process by which business buyers determine which products and services their organizations need to purchase and then find, evaluate, and choose among alternative suppliers and brands.

Business portfolio The collection of businesses and products that make up the company.

Business promotions Sales promotion tools used to generate business leads, stimulate purchases, reward customers, and motivate salespeople.

Buying center All the individuals and units that play a role in the purchase decision-making process.

By-product pricing Setting a price for by-products to help offset the costs of disposing of them and help make the main product's price more competitive.

Cannibalization The situation in which one product sold by a company takes a portion of its sales from other company products.

Captive-product pricing Setting a price for products that must be used along with a main product, such as blades for a razor and games for a video-game console.

Catalog marketing Direct marketing through print, video, or digital catalogs that are mailed to select customers, made available in stores, or presented online.

Category killer A giant specialty store that carries a very deep assortment of a particular line.

Causal research Marketing research to test hypotheses about cause-and-effect relationships.

Chain ratio method Estimating market demand by multiplying a base number by a chain of adjusting percentages.

Closing The sales step in which a salesperson asks the customer for an order.

Co-branding The practice of using the established brand names of two different companies on the same product.

Cognitive dissonance Buyer discomfort caused by postpurchase conflict.

Commercialization Introducing a new product into the market.

Communication adaptation A global communication strategy of fully adapting advertising messages to local markets.

Competition-based pricing Setting prices based on competitors' strategies, prices, costs, and market offerings.

Competitive advantage An advantage over competitors gained by offering greater customer value either by having lower prices or providing more benefits that justify higher prices.

Competitive marketing intelligence The systematic monitoring, collection, and analysis of publicly available information about consumers, competitors, and developments in the marketing environment.

Competitive-parity method Setting the promotion budget to match competitors' outlays.

Concentrated (niche) marketing A market-coverage strategy in which a firm goes after a large share of one or a few segments or niches.

Concept testing Testing new product concepts with a group of target consumers to find out if the concepts have strong consumer appeal.

Consumer buyer behavior The buying behavior of final consumers—individuals and households that buy goods and services for personal consumption.

Consumer market All the individuals and households that buy or acquire goods and services for personal consumption.

Consumer product A product bought by final consumers for personal consumption.

Consumer promotions Sales promotion tools used to boost short-term customer buying and engagement or enhance long-term customer relationships.

Consumer-generated marketing Brand exchanges created by consumers themselves—both invited and uninvited—by which consumers are playing an increasing role in shaping their own brand experiences and those of other consumers.

Consumer-oriented marketing A company should view and organize its marketing activities from the consumer's point of view.

Consumerism An organized movement of citizens and government agencies designed to improve the rights and power of buyers in relation to sellers.

Content marketing Creating, inspiring, and sharing brand messages and conversations with and among consumers across a fluid mix of paid, owned, earned, and shared channels.

Contract manufacturing A joint venture in which a company contracts with manufacturers in a foreign market to produce its product or provide its service.

Contribution margin The unit contribution divided by the selling price.

Convenience product A consumer product that customers usually buy frequently, immediately, and with minimal comparison and buying effort.

Convenience store A small store, located near a residential area, that is open long hours seven days a week and carries a limited line of high-turnover convenience goods.

Corporate chains Two or more outlets that are commonly owned and controlled.

Cost-based pricing Setting prices based on the costs of producing, distributing, and selling the product plus a fair rate of return for effort and risk.

Cost-plus pricing (markup pricing) Adding a standard markup to the cost of the product.

Creative concept The compelling "big idea" that will bring an advertising message strategy to life in a distinctive and memorable way.

Crowdsourcing Inviting broad communities of people—customers, employees, independent scientists and researchers, and even the public at large—into the new product innovation process.

Cultural environment Institutions and other forces that affect society's basic values, perceptions, preferences, and behaviors.

Culture The set of basic values, perceptions, wants, and behaviors learned by a member of society from family and other important institutions.

Customer-centered new product development New product development that focuses on finding new ways to solve customer problems and create more customer-satisfying experiences.

Customer-engagement marketing Making the brand a meaningful part of consumers' conversations and lives by fostering direct and continuous customer involvement in shaping brand conversations, experiences, and community.

Customer-perceived value The customer's evaluation of the difference between all the benefits and all the costs of a marketing offer relative to those of competing offers.

Customer (or market) sales force structure A sales force organization in which salespeople specialize in selling only to certain customers or industries.

Customer equity The total combined customer lifetime values of all of the company's customers.

Customer insights Fresh marketing information-based understandings of customers and the marketplace that become the basis for creating customer value, engagement, and relationships.

Customer lifetime value The value of the entire stream of purchases a customer makes over a lifetime of patronage.

Customer relationship management (CRM) Managing detailed information about individual customers and carefully managing customer touch points to maximize customer loyalty.

Customer relationship management The overall process of building and maintaining profitable customer relationships by delivering superior customer value and satisfaction.

Customer satisfaction The extent to which a product's perceived performance matches a buyer's expectations.

Customer value marketing A company should put most of its resources into customer value–building marketing investments.

Customer value–based pricing Setting price based on buyers' perceptions of value rather than on the seller's cost.

Decline stage The PLC stage in which a product's sales fade away.

Deficient products Products that have neither immediate appeal nor long-run benefits.

Demand curve A curve that shows the number of units the market will buy in a given time period, at different prices that might be charged.

Demands Human wants that are backed by buying power.

Demographic segmentation Dividing the market into segments based on variables such as age, life-cycle stage, gender, income, occupation, education, religion, ethnicity, and generation.

Demography The study of human populations in terms of size, density, location, age, gender, race, occupation, and other statistics.

Department store A retail store that carries a wide variety of product lines, each operated as a separate department managed by specialist buyers or merchandisers.

Derived demand Business demand that ultimately comes from (derives from) the demand for consumer goods.

Descriptive research Marketing research to better describe marketing problems, situations, or markets, such as the market potential for a product or the demographics and attitudes of consumers.

Desirable products Products that give both high immediate satisfaction and high long-run benefits.

Differentiated (segmented) marketing A market-coverage strategy in which a firm targets several market segments and designs separate offers for each.

Differentiation Actually differentiating the market offering to create superior customer value.

Digital and social media marketing Using digital marketing tools such as websites, social media, mobile apps and ads, online video, email, and blogs to engage consumers anywhere, at any time, via their digital devices.

Direct and digital marketing Engaging directly with carefully targeted individual consumers and customer communities to both obtain an immediate response and build lasting customer relationships.

Direct investment Entering a foreign market by developing foreign-based assembly or manufacturing facilities.

Direct-mail marketing Marketing that occurs by sending an offer, announcement, reminder, or other item directly to a person at a particular address.

Direct-response television (DRTV) marketing Direct marketing via television that persuasively describes a product and give customers a toll-free number or an online site for ordering.

Discount A straight reduction in price on purchases during a stated period of time or of larger quantities.

Discount store A retail operation that sells standard merchandise at lower prices by accepting lower margins and selling at higher volume.

Diversification Company growth through starting up or acquiring businesses outside the company's current products and markets.

Dynamic pricing Adjusting prices continually to meet the characteristics and needs of individual customers and situations.

E-procurement Purchasing through electronic connections between buyers and sellers—usually online.

Economic community A group of nations organized to work toward common goals in the regulation of international trade.

Economic environment Economic factors that affect consumer purchasing power and spending patterns.

Email marketing Sending highly targeted, highly personalized, relationship-building marketing messages via email.

Environmental sustainability A management approach that involves developing strategies that both sustain the environment and produce profits for the company.

Environmental sustainability Developing strategies and practices that create a world economy that the planet can support indefinitely.

Environmentalism An organized movement of concerned citizens, businesses, and government agencies designed to protect and improve people's current and future living environment.

Ethnographic research A form of observational research that involves sending trained observers to watch and interact with consumers in their "natural environments."

Event marketing (or event sponsorships) Creating a brand-marketing event or serving as a sole or participating sponsor of events created by others.

Exchange The act of obtaining a desired object from someone by offering something in return.

Execution style The approach, style, tone, words, and format used for executing an advertising message.

Experimental research Gathering primary data by selecting matched groups of subjects, giving them different treatments, controlling related factors, and checking for differences in group responses.

Exploratory research Marketing research to gather preliminary information that will help define problems and suggest hypotheses.

Exporting Entering foreign markets by selling goods produced in the company's home country, often with little modification.

Factory outlet An off-price retailing operation that is owned and operated by a manufacturer and normally carries the manufacturer's surplus, discontinued, or irregular goods.

Fad A temporary period of unusually high sales driven by consumer enthusiasm and immediate product or brand popularity.

Fashion A currently accepted or popular style in a given field.

Fixed costs (overhead) Costs that do not vary with production or sales level.

Focus group interviewing Personal interviewing that involves inviting small groups of people to gather for a few hours with a trained interviewer to talk about a product, service, or organization. The interviewer "focuses" the group discussion on important issues.

Follow-up The sales step in which a salesperson follows up after the sale to ensure customer satisfaction and repeat business.

Franchise A contractual association between a manufacturer, wholesaler, or service organization (a franchisor) and independent businesspeople (franchisees) who buy the right to own and operate one or more units in the franchise system.

Gender segmentation Dividing a market into different segments based on gender.

Generation X The 55 million people born between 1965 and 1980 in the "birth dearth" following the baby boom.

Generation Z People born between 1997 and 2016 who make up the kids, tweens, and teens markets.

Geographic segmentation Dividing a market into different geographical units, such as nations, states, regions, counties, cities, or even neighborhoods.

Geographical pricing Setting prices for customers located in different parts of the country or world.

Global firm A firm that, by operating in more than one country, gains R&D, production, marketing, and financial advantages in its costs and reputation that are not available to purely domestic competitors.

Good-value pricing Offering just the right combination of quality and good service at a fair price.

Gross margin percentage The percentage of net sales remaining after cost of goods sold—calculated by dividing gross margin by net sales.

Growth stage The PLC stage in which a product's sales start climbing quickly.

Growth-share matrix A portfolio-planning method that evaluates a company's SBUs in terms of market growth rate and relative market share.

Handling objections The sales step in which a salesperson seeks out, clarifies, and overcomes any customer objections to buying.

Idea generation The systematic search for new product ideas.

Idea screening Screening new product ideas to spot good ones and drop poor ones as soon as possible.

Income segmentation Dividing a market into different income segments.

Independent off-price retailer An off-price retailer that is independently owned and operated or a division of a larger retail corporation.

Individual marketing Tailoring products and marketing programs to the needs and preferences of individual customers.

Industrial product A product bought by individuals and organizations for further processing or for use in conducting a business.

Influencer marketing Enlisting established influencers or creating new influencers to spread the word about a company's brands.

Innovative marketing A company should seek real product and marketing improvements.

Inside sales force Salespeople who conduct business from their offices via telephone, online and social media interactions, or visits from prospective buyers.

Integrated marketing communications (IMC) Carefully integrating and coordinating the company's many communications channels to deliver a clear, consistent, and compelling message about the organization and its products.

Interactive marketing Training service employees in the fine art of interacting with customers to satisfy their needs.

Intermarket (cross-market) segmentation Forming segments of consumers who have similar needs and buying behaviors even though they are located in different countries.

Internal databases Collections of consumer and market information obtained from data sources within the company network.

Internal marketing Orienting and motivating customer-contact employees and supporting service employees to work as a team to provide customer satisfaction.

Introduction stage The PLC stage in which a new product is first distributed and made available for purchase.

Inventory turnover rate (or stockturn rate) The number of times an inventory turns over or is sold during a specified time period (often one year)—calculated based on costs, selling price, or units.

Joint ownership A cooperative venture in which a company creates a local business with investors in a foreign market who share ownership and control.

Joint venturing Entering foreign markets by joining with foreign companies to produce or market a product or service.

Learning Changes in an individual's behavior arising from experience.

Licensing Entering foreign markets through developing an agreement with a licensee in the foreign market.

Lifestyle A person's pattern of living as expressed in his or her activities, interests, and opinions.

Line extension Extending an existing brand name to new forms, colors, sizes, ingredients, or flavors of an existing product category.

Local marketing Tailoring brands and marketing to the needs and wants of local customer segments—cities, neighborhoods, and even specific stores.

Macroenvironment The larger societal forces that affect the microenvironment—demographic, economic, natural, technological, political, and cultural forces.

Madison & Vine A term that has come to represent the merging of advertising and entertainment in an effort to break through the clutter and create new avenues for reaching customers with more engaging messages.

Management contracting A joint venture in which the domestic firm supplies the management know-how to a foreign company that supplies the capital; the domestic firm exports management services rather than products.

Manufacturers' and retailers' branches and offices Wholesaling by sellers or buyers themselves rather than through independent wholesalers.

Market The set of all actual and potential buyers of a product or service.

Market development Company growth by identifying and developing new market segments for current company products.

Market offerings Some combination of products, services, information, or experiences offered to a market to satisfy a need or want.

Market penetration Company growth by increasing sales of current products to current market segments without changing the product.

Market potential The upper limit of market demand.

Market segment A group of consumers who respond in a similar way to a given set of marketing efforts.

Market segmentation Dividing a market into distinct groups of buyers who have different needs, characteristics, or behaviors and who might require separate marketing strategies or mixes.

Market share Company sales divided by market sales.

Market targeting (targeting) Evaluating each market segment's attractiveness and selecting one or more segments to serve.

Market-penetration pricing Setting a low price for a new product in order to attract a large number of buyers and a large market share.

Market-skimming pricing (price skimming) Setting a high price for a new product to skim maximum revenues layer by layer from the segments willing to pay the high price; the company makes fewer but more profitable sales.

Marketing The process by which companies engage customers, build strong customer relationships, and create customer value in order to capture value from customers in return.

Marketing analytics The analysis tools, technologies, and processes by which marketers dig out meaningful patterns in big data to gain customer insights and gauge marketing performance.

Marketing concept A philosophy in which achieving organizational goals depends on knowing the needs and wants of target markets and delivering the desired satisfactions better than competitors do.

Marketing control Measuring and evaluating the results of marketing strategies and plans and taking corrective action to ensure that the objectives are achieved.

Marketing environment The actors and forces outside marketing that affect marketing management's ability to build and maintain successful relationships with target customers.

Marketing implementation Turning marketing strategies and plans into marketing actions to accomplish strategic marketing objectives.

Marketing information system (MIS) People and procedures dedicated to assessing information needs, developing the needed information, and helping decision makers to use the information to generate and validate actionable customer and market insights.

Marketing intermediaries Firms that help the company to promote, sell, and distribute its goods to final buyers.

Marketing management The art and science of choosing target markets and building profitable relationships with them.

Marketing mix The set of tactical marketing tools—product, price, place, and promotion—that the firm blends to produce the response it wants in the target market.

Marketing myopia The mistake of paying more attention to the specific products a company offers than to the benefits and experiences produced by these products.

Marketing research The systematic design, collection, analysis, and reporting of data relevant to a specific marketing situation facing an organization.

Marketing return on investment (marketing ROI) The net return from a marketing investment divided by the costs of the marketing investment.

Marketing return on sales (or marketing ROS) The percent of net sales attributable to the net marketing contribution—calculated by dividing net marketing contribution by net sales.

Marketing strategy The marketing logic by which the company hopes to create customer value and achieve profitable customer relationships.

Marketing strategy development Designing an initial marketing strategy for a new product based on the product concept.

Marketing website A website that engages consumers to move them closer to a direct purchase or other marketing outcome.

Markup The difference between a company's selling price for a product and its cost to manufacture or purchase it.

Markup chain The sequence of markups used by firms at each level in a channel.

Maturity stage The PLC stage in which a product's sales growth slows or levels off.

Merchant wholesaler An independently owned wholesale business that takes title to the merchandise it handles.

Microenvironment The actors close to the company that affect its ability to serve its customers—the company, suppliers, marketing intermediaries, customer markets, competitors, and publics.

Micromarketing Tailoring products and marketing programs to the needs and wants of specific individuals and local customer segments; it includes *local marketing* and *individual marketing*.

Millennials (or Generation Y) The 75 million children of the baby boomers born between 1981 and 1997.

Mission statement A statement of the organization's purpose—what it wants to accomplish in the larger environment.

Mobile marketing Marketing messages, promotions, and other content delivered to on-the-go consumers through their mobile devices.

Modified rebuy A business buying situation in which the buyer wants to modify product specifications, prices, terms, or suppliers.

Motive (drive) A need that is sufficiently pressing to direct the person to seek satisfaction of the need.

Native advertising Advertising or other brand-produced online content that looks in form and function like the other natural content surrounding it on a web or social media platform.

Natural environment The physical environment and the natural resources that are needed as inputs by marketers or that are affected by marketing activities.

Needs States of felt deprivation.

Net marketing contribution (NMC) A measure of marketing profitability that includes only components of profitability controlled by marketing.

Net profit percentage The percentage of each sales dollar going to profit—calculated by dividing net profits by net sales.

New product A good, service, or idea that is perceived by some potential customers as new.

New product development The development of original products, product improvements, product modifications, and new brands through the firm's own product development efforts.

New task A business buying situation in which the buyer purchases a product or service for the first time.

Objective-and-task method Developing the promotion budget by (1) defining specific promotion objectives, (2) determining the tasks needed to achieve these objectives, and (3) estimating the costs of performing these tasks. The sum of these costs is the proposed promotion budget.

Observational research Gathering primary data by observing relevant people, actions, and situations.

Occasion segmentation Dividing the market into segments according to occasions when buyers get the idea to buy, actually make their purchase, or use the purchased item.

Off-price retailer A retailer that buys at less-than-regular wholesale prices and sells at less than retail.

Omni-channel retailing Creating a seamless cross-channel buying experience that integrates in-store, online, and mobile shopping.

Online advertising Advertising that appears while consumers are browsing online, including display ads and search-related ads.

Online focus groups Gathering a small group of people online with a trained moderator to chat about a product, service, or organization and gain qualitative insights about consumer attitudes and behavior.

Online marketing Marketing via the internet using company websites, online ads and promotions, email, online video, and blogs.

Online marketing research Collecting primary data through internet and mobile surveys, online focus groups, consumer tracking, experiments, and online panels and brand communities.

Online social networks Online social communities—blogs, online social media, brand communities, and other online forums—where people socialize or exchange information and opinions.

Operating expense percentage The portion of net sales going to operating expenses—calculated by dividing total expenses by net sales.

Operating ratios The ratios of selected operating statement items to net sales.

Opinion leader A person within a reference group who, because of special skills, knowledge, personality, or other characteristics, exerts social influence on others.

Optional-product pricing The pricing of optional or accessory products along with a main product.

Outside sales force (or field sales force) Salespeople who travel to call on customers in the field.

Packaging The activities of designing and producing the container or wrapper for a product.

Partner relationship management Working closely with partners in other company departments and outside the company to jointly bring greater value to customers.

Percentage-of-sales method Setting the promotion budget at a certain percentage of current or forecasted sales or as a percentage of the unit sales price.

Perception The process by which people select, organize, and interpret information to form a meaningful picture of the world.

Personal selling Personal presentation by the firm's sales force for the purpose of engaging customers, making sales, and building customer relationships.

Personality The unique psychological characteristics that distinguish a person or group.

Pleasing products Products that give high immediate satisfaction but may hurt consumers in the long run.

Political environment Laws, government agencies, and pressure groups that influence and limit various organizations and individuals in a given society.

Portfolio analysis The process by which management evaluates the products and businesses that make up the company.

Positioning Arranging for a market offering to occupy a clear, distinctive, and desirable place relative to competing products in the minds of target consumers.

Positioning statement A statement that summarizes company or brand positioning using this form: To (target segment and need) our (brand) is (concept) that (point of difference).

Preapproach The sales step in which a salesperson learns as much as possible about a prospective customer before making a sales call.

Presentation The sales step in which a salesperson tells the "value story" to the buyer, showing how the company's offer solves the customer's problems.

Price The amount of money charged for a product or service, or the sum of the values that customers exchange for the benefits of having or using the product or service.

Price elasticity A measure of the sensitivity of demand to changes in price.

Primary data Information collected for the specific purpose at hand.

Product Anything that can be offered to a market for attention, acquisition, use, or consumption that might satisfy a want or need.

Product adaptation Adapting a product to meet local conditions or wants in foreign markets.

Product bundle pricing Combining several products and offering the bundle at a reduced price.

Product concept A detailed version of the new product idea stated in meaningful consumer terms.

Product concept The idea that consumers will favor products that offer the most quality, performance, and features; therefore, the organization should devote its energy to making continuous product improvements.

Product development Company growth by offering modified or new products to current market segments.

Product development Developing the product concept into a physical product to ensure that the product idea can be turned into a workable market offering.

Product invention Creating new products or services for foreign markets.

Product life cycle (PLC) The course of a product's sales and profits over its lifetime.

Product line A group of products that are closely related because they function in a similar manner, are sold to the same customer groups, are marketed through the same types of outlets, or fall within given price ranges.

Product line pricing Setting the price steps between various products in a product line based on cost differences between the products, customer evaluations of different features, and competitors' prices.

Product/market expansion grid A portfolio-planning tool for identifying company growth opportunities through market penetration, market development, product development, or diversification.

Product mix (or product portfolio) The set of all product lines and items that a particular seller offers for sale.

Product position The way a product is defined by consumers on important attributes—the place it occupies in consumers' minds relative to competing products.

Product quality The characteristics of a product or service that bear on its ability to satisfy stated or implied customer needs.

Product sales force structure A sales force organization in which salespeople specialize in selling only a portion of the company's products or lines.

Production concept The idea that consumers will favor products that are available and highly affordable; therefore, the organization should focus on improving production and distribution efficiency.

Pro forma (or projected) profit-and-loss statement (or income statement or operating statement) A statement that shows projected revenues less budgeted expenses and estimates the projected net profit for an organization, product, or brand during a specific planning period, typically a year.

Profit-and-loss statement (or income statement or operating statement) A statement that shows actual revenues less expenses and net profit for an organization, product, or brand during a specific planning period, typically a year.

Promotion mix (marketing communications mix) The specific blend of promotion tools that the company uses to persuasively communicate customer value and build customer relationships.

Promotional pricing Temporarily pricing products below the list price, and sometimes even below cost, to increase short-run sales.

Prospecting The sales step in which a salesperson or company identifies qualified potential customers.

Psychographic segmentation Dividing a market into different segments based on lifestyle or personality characteristics.

Psychological pricing Pricing that considers the psychology of prices and not simply the economics; the price is used to say something about the product.

Public Any group that has an actual or potential interest in or impact on an organization's ability to achieve its objectives.

Public relations (PR) Building good relations with the company's various publics by obtaining favorable publicity, building up a good corporate image, and handling or heading off unfavorable rumors, stories, and events.

Pull strategy A promotion strategy that calls for spending a lot on consumer advertising and promotion to induce final consumers to buy the product, creating a demand vacuum that "pulls" the product through the channel.

Push strategy A promotion strategy that calls for using the sales force and trade promotion to push the product through channels. The producer promotes the product to channel members who in turn promote it to final consumers.

Reference group A group that serves as direct or indirect point of comparison or reference in forming a person's attitudes or behavior.

Reference prices Prices that buyers carry in their minds and refer to when they look at a given product.

Relevant costs Costs that will occur in the future and that will vary across the alternatives being considered.

Retailer A business whose sales come *primarily* from retailing.

Retailing All the activities involved in selling goods or services directly to final consumers for their personal, nonbusiness use.

Return on advertising investment The net return on advertising investment divided by the costs of the advertising investment.

Return on investment (ROI) A measure of managerial effectiveness and efficiency—net profit before taxes divided by total investment.

Return on investment (ROI) pricing (or target-return pricing) A cost-based pricing method that determines price based on a specified rate of return on investment.

Sales force management Analyzing, planning, implementing, and controlling sales force activities.

Sales promotion Short-term incentives to encourage the purchase or sale of a product or a service.

Sales quota A standard that states the amount a salesperson should sell and how sales should be divided among the company's products.

Salesperson An individual who represents a company to customers by performing one or more of the following activities: prospecting, communicating, selling, servicing, information gathering, and relationship building.

Salutary products Products that have low immediate appeal but may benefit consumers in the long run.

Sample A segment of the population selected for marketing research to represent the population as a whole.

Secondary data Information that already exists somewhere, having been collected for another purpose.

Segmented pricing Selling a product or service at two or more prices, where the difference in prices is not based on differences in costs.

Selling concept The idea that consumers will not buy enough of the firm's products unless the firm undertakes a large-scale selling and promotion effort.

Selling process The steps that salespeople follow when selling, which include prospecting and qualifying, preapproach, approach, presentation and demonstration, handling objections, closing, and follow-up.

Sense-of-mission marketing A company should define its mission in broad social terms rather than narrow product terms.

Service An activity, benefit, or satisfaction offered for sale that is essentially intangible and does not result in the ownership of anything.

Service inseparability Services are produced and consumed at the same time and cannot be separated from their providers.

Service intangibility Services cannot be seen, tasted, felt, heard, or smelled before they are bought.

Service perishability Services cannot be stored for later sale or use.

Service profit chain The chain that links service firm profits with employee and customer satisfaction.

Service retailer A retailer whose product line is actually a service; examples include hotels, airlines, banks, colleges, and many others.

Service variability The quality of services may vary greatly depending on who provides them and when, where, and how they are provided.

Share of customer The portion of the customer's purchasing that a company gets in its product categories.

Shopper marketing Focusing the entire marketing process on turning shoppers into buyers as they move along toward the point of sale, whether during in-store, online, or mobile shopping.

Shopping center A group of retail businesses built on a site that is planned, developed, owned, and managed as a unit.

Shopping product A consumer product that the customer, in the process of selecting and purchasing, usually compares on such attributes as suitability, quality, price, and style.

Social class Relatively permanent and ordered divisions in a society whose members share similar values, interests, and behaviors.

Social marketing The use of traditional business marketing concepts and tools to encourage behaviors that will create individual and societal well-being.

Social media Independent and commercial online social networks where people congregate to socialize and share messages, opinions, pictures, videos, and other content.

Social selling Using online, mobile, and social media to engage customers, build stronger customer relationships, and augment sales performance.

Societal marketing A company should make marketing decisions by considering consumers' wants, the company's requirements, consumers' long-run interests, and society's long-run interests.

Societal marketing concept The idea that a company's marketing decisions should consider consumers' wants, the company's requirements, consumers' long-run interests, and society's long-run interests.

Spam Unsolicited, unwanted commercial email messages.

Specialty product A consumer product with unique characteristics or brand identification for which a significant group of buyers is willing to make a special purchase effort.

Specialty store A retail store that carries a narrow product line with a deep assortment within that line.

Standardized global marketing A global marketing strategy that basically uses the same marketing strategy and mix in all of the company's international markets.

Store brand (or private brand) A brand created and owned by a reseller of a product or service.

Straight product extension Marketing a product in a foreign market without making any changes to the product.

Straight rebuy A business buying situation in which the buyer routinely reorders something without modifications.

Strategic planning The process of developing and maintaining a strategic fit between the organization's goals and capabilities and its changing marketing opportunities.

Style A basic and distinctive mode of expression.

Subculture A group of people with shared value systems based on common life experiences and situations.

Supermarket A large, low-cost, low-margin, high-volume, self-service store that carries a wide variety of grocery and household products.

Superstore A store much larger than a regular supermarket that offers a large assortment of routinely purchased food products, non-food items, and services.

Supplier development Systematic development of networks of supplier-partners to ensure an appropriate and dependable supply of products and materials for use in making products or reselling them to others.

Survey research Gathering primary data by asking people questions about their knowledge, attitudes, preferences, and buying behavior.

Sustainable marketing Socially and environmentally responsible marketing that meets the present needs of consumers and businesses while also preserving or enhancing the ability of future generations to meet their needs.

SWOT analysis An overall evaluation of the company's strengths (S), weaknesses (W), opportunities (O), and threats (T).

Systems selling (or solutions selling) Buying a packaged solution to a problem from a single seller, thus avoiding all the separate decisions involved in a complex buying situation.

Target costing Pricing that starts with an ideal selling price, then targets costs that will ensure that the price is met.

Target market A set of buyers who share common needs or characteristics that a company decides to serve.

Team selling Using teams of people from sales, marketing, engineering, finance, technical support, and even upper management to service large, complex accounts.

Team-based new product development New product development in which various company departments work closely together, overlapping the steps in the product development process to save time and increase effectiveness.

Technological environment Forces that create new technologies, creating new product and market opportunities.

Telemarketing Using the telephone to sell directly to customers.

Territorial sales force structure A sales force organization that assigns each salesperson to an exclusive geographic territory in which that salesperson sells the company's full line.

Test marketing The stage of new product development in which the product and its proposed marketing program are tested in realistic market settings.

Total costs The sum of the fixed and variable costs for any given level of production.

Total market demand The total volume that would be bought by a defined consumer group in a defined geographic area in a defined time period in a defined marketing environment under a defined level and mix of industry marketing effort.

Total market strategy Integrating ethnic themes and cross-cultural perspectives within a brand's mainstream marketing, appealing to consumer similarities across subcultural segments rather than differences.

Trade promotions Sales promotion tools used to persuade resellers to carry a brand, give it shelf space, and promote it in advertising.

Undifferentiated (mass) marketing A market-coverage strategy in which a firm decides to ignore market segment differences and go after the whole market with one offer.

Unit contribution The amount that each unit contributes to covering fixed costs—the difference between price and variable costs.

Unsought product A consumer product that the consumer either does not know about or knows about but does not normally consider buying.

Value-added pricing Attaching value-added features and services to differentiate a company's offers and charging higher prices.

Value-based pricing Offering just the right combination of quality and good service at a fair price.

Value chain The series of internal departments that carry out value-creating activities to design, produce, market, deliver, and support a firm's products.

Value delivery network A network composed of the company, suppliers, distributors, and, ultimately, customers who partner with each other to improve the performance of the entire system in delivering customer value.

Value proposition The full positioning of a brand—the full mix of benefits on which it is positioned.

Variable costs Costs that vary directly with the level of production.

Viral marketing The digital version of word-of-mouth marketing: videos, ads, and other marketing content that is so infectious that customers will seek it out or pass it along to friends.

Wants The form human needs take as they are shaped by culture and individual personality.

Warehouse club An off-price retailer that sells a limited selection of brand name grocery items, appliances, clothing, and other goods at deep discounts to members who pay annual membership fees.

Whole-channel view Designing international channels that take into account the entire global supply chain and marketing channel, forging an effective global value delivery network.

Wholesaler A firm engaged *primarily* in wholesaling activities.

Wholesaling All the activities involved in selling goods and services to those buying for resale or business use.

Word-of-mouth influence The impact of the personal words and recommendations of trusted friends, family, associates, and other consumers on buying behavior.

Workload method An approach to determining sales force size based on the workload required and the time available for selling.

References

Chapter 1

1. Jeff Haden, "20 Years Ago, Jeff Bezos Said This One Thing Separates People Who Achieve Lasting Success from Those Who Don't," *Inc.*, November 6, 2017, www.inc.com/jeff-haden/20-years-ago-jeff-bezos-said-this-1-thing-separates-people-who-achieve-lasting-success-from-those-who-dont.html; Craig Smith, "130 Amazing Amazon Statistics and Facts," *DMR*, January 3, 2018, https://expandedramblings.com/index.php/amazon-statistics/; Morten T. Hansen, Herminia Ibarra, and Urs Peyer, "The Best-Performing CEOs in the World," *Harvard Business Review*, January–February 2013, pp. 81–86; Noah Robischon, "Why Amazon Is the World's Most Innovative Company of 2017," *Fast Company*, March 2017, www.fastcompany.com/3067455/why-amazon-is-the-worlds-most-innovative-company-of-2017; "Benchmarks by Company: Amazon," ACSI, www.theacsi.org/index.php?option=com_content&view=article&id=149&catid=&Itemid=214&c=Amazon&i=Internet+Retail, accessed September 2018; and annual reports and other information found at www.amazon.com, accessed September 2018.
2. See http://newsroom.fb.com/company-info/; www.facebook.com/pg/Amazon/about/; and www.starbucks.com/about-us/company-information/mission-statement, accessed September 2018.
3. See Philip Kotler and Kevin Lane Keller, *Marketing Management*, 15th ed. (Hoboken, NJ: Pearson Education, 2016), p. 5.
4. The American Marketing Association offers the following definition: "Marketing is the activity, set of institutions, and processes for creating, communicating, delivering, and exchanging offerings that have value for customers, clients, partners, and society at large." See www.marketingpower.com/_layouts/Dictionary.aspx?dLetter=M, accessed September 2018.
5. See Phil Wahba, "Back on Target," *Fortune*, March 1, 2015, p. 86–94; Jackie Crosby, "Target CEO Brian Cornell Visiting Homes of Customers," *Star Tribune*, January 20, 2016, www.startribune.com/target-to- add-1-000-technology-jobs-in-year-ahead/365965181/; and Leah Fessler, "Airbnb Is Defined by Its CEO's Obsessive Perfection," *Quartz*, February 21, 2018, https://work.qz.com/1214411/airbnb-ceo-brian-chesky-wants-to-do-home-visits-to-check-your-wifi/.
6. See and Tim Nudd, "The 10 Best Ads of 2017," *Adweek*, December 10, 2017, www.adweek.com/creativity/the-10-best-ads-of-2017.
7. See Theodore Levitt's classic article, "Marketing Myopia," *Harvard Business Review*, July–August 1960, pp. 45–56. For more recent discussions, see Roberto Friedmann, "What Business Are You In?" *Marketing Management*, Summer 2011, pp. 18–23; Al Ries, "'Marketing Myopia' Revisited: Perhaps a Narrow Vision Is Better Business," *Advertising Age*, December 4, 2013, http://adage.com/print/245511; and Amy Gallo, "A Refresher on Marketing Myopia," *Harvard Business Review*, August 22, 2016, https://hbr.org/2016/08/a-refresher-on-marketing-myopia.
8. See "130 Amazing Walt Disney World Facts and Statistics (February 2018), *Disney News*, February 6, 2018, https://disneynews.us/walt-disney-world-statistics-fun-facts/; and https://disneyworld.disney.go.com/, accessed September 2018.
9. Dan Caplinger, "Henry Ford's 10 Best Quotes," *Motley Fool*, October 16, 2016, www.fool.com/investing/2016/10/16/henry-fords-10-best-quotes.aspx; and "Steve Jobs: Quotable Quotes," *Goodreads*, www.goodreads.com/quotes/988332-some-people-say-give-the-customers-what-they-want-but, accessed September 2018.
10. "Steve Jobs: Quotable Quotes," *Goodreads*, www.goodreads.com/quotes/988332-some-people-say-give-the-customers-what-they-want-but, accessed September 2018.
11. See Michael E. Porter and Mark R. Kramer, "Creating Shared Value," *Harvard Business Review*, January–February 2011, pp. 63–77; Marc Pfitzer, Valerie Bockstette, and Mike Stamp, "Innovating for Shared Value," *Harvard Business Review*, September 2013, pp. 100–107; "About Shared Value," Shared Value Initiative, http://sharedvalue.org/about-shared-value, accessed September 2018; and "Shared Value," www.fsg.org, accessed September 2018.
12. Kara Stiles, "How Jeni's Splendid Ice Creams Flavor-Finessed Its Way to the Top," *Forbes*, December 15, 2017, www.forbes.com/sites/karastiles/2017/12/15/how-jenis-splendid-ice-creams-flavor-finessed-its-way-to-the-top/#1c6472694807; Hanna Snyder, "Community, Quality and Creativity: Jeni's Splendid Ice Cream Founder Shares the Scoop on Her B-Corp Business," *Yellow/Co.*, December, 29, 2017, https://yellowco.co/blog/2017/12/29/jenis-ice-cream-b-corp-business/; and https://jenis.com/about/, accessed September 2018.
13. See "Steinway & Sons," www.pianobuyer.com/Resources/Piano-Brands-Profiles/Detail/ArticleId/109/Brand/STEINWAY-SONS, accessed September 2018; "Steinway Composes Global Campaign to Reach Cultured Achievers," *Luxury Daily*, April 13, 2016, www.luxurydaily.com/steinway-composes-global-campaign-to-reach-cultured-achievers/; and www.steinway.com/about and www.steinwaypianos.com/kb/artists, accessed September 2018.
14. Based on information from www.llbean.com/llb/shop/516917?lndrNbr=516884&nav=leftnav-cust and other pages at www.llbean.com, accessed September 2018. Also see "L.L. Bean Beats Amazon.com, Once Again, for Best Customer Service," *Forbes*, August 3, 2017, www.forbes.com/sites/forbesinsights/2017/08/03/l-l-bean-beats-amazon-com-once-again-for-best-customer-service/#7923b45050f6; and Shep Hyken, "L.L. Bean Discontinues Lifetime Guarantee," *Forbes*, February 18, 2018, www.forbes.com/sites/shephyken/2018/02/18/l-l-bean-discontinues-lifetime-guarantee/#5a149cd3714d.
15. "Delighting the Customer Doesn't Pay," *Sales & Marketing Management*, November 11, 2013, http://salesandmarketing.com/content/delighting-customers-doesnt-pay; Patrick Spenner, "Why Simple Brands Are Profitable Brands," *Forbes*, February 20, 2014, www.forbes.com/sites/patrickspenner/2014/02/20/why-simple-brands-are-profitable-brands-2/#2b28be11b097; and Amy Sandys, "Why Brands Should Embrace Simplicity," *Transform*, November 21, 2017, www.transformmagazine.net/articles/2017/why-brands-should-embrace-simplicity/.
16. See "JetBlue TrueBlue: The Ultimate Guide," *LoungeBuddy*, www.loungebuddy.com/blog/jetblue-trueblue-ultimate-guide/, accessed September 2018; and www.jetblue.trueblue.com, accessed September 2018.
17. See Sami Main, "Why BarkBox Uses Comedians Instead of Marketers to Create Engaging Content," *Adweek*, December 4, 2017, www.adweek.com/tv-video/why-barkbox-uses-comedians-instead-of-marketers-to-create-engaging-content; Sami Main, "The 22 Most Engaging Pieces of Brand Content on Social Media in 2017," *Adweek*, December 27, 2017, www.adweek.com/creativity/the-22-most-engaging-pieces-of-brand-content-on-social-media-in-2017; and www.bark.co, accessed September 2018.
18. See https://mondelez.promo.eprize.com/myoreocreation/ and https://ideas.starbucks.com/, accessed September 2018.
19. See Tim Nudd, "Tesla Crowned This Commercial as the Winner of Its Fan-Made Ad Contest," *Adweek*, July 31, 2017, www.adweek.com/brand-marketing/tesla-crowned-this-commercial-as-the-winner-of-its-fan-made-ad-contest/; Darrell Etherington, "Tesla's Top 10 Project Loveday Videos Reveal Truly Dedicated Fans," *Tech Crunch*, July 26, 2017, https://techcrunch.com/2017/07/26/teslas-top-10-project-loveday-videos-reveal-truly-dedicated-fans/; and www.youtube.com/watch?v=oSnoYEzZnUg and www.tesla.com/project-loveday, accessed September 2018.
20. Lauren Johnson, "Mountain Dew Turns Tweets into Online Ads with the Return of Baja Blast," *Adweek*, April 9, 2015, www.adweek.com/print/163979.
21. See "#Bashtag: Avoiding User Outcry in Social Media," *WordStream*, March 8, 2013, www.wordstream.com/blog/ws/2013/03/07/bashtag-avoiding-social-media-backlash; "What Is Hashtag Hijacking?" *Small Business Trends*, August 18, 2013, http://smallbiztrends.com/2013/08/what-is-hashtag-hijacking-2.html; and "HBD #Hashtag! What Brands Can Learn from a Decade of Hashtagging," *Social Media Week*, August 23, 2017, https://socialmediaweek.org/blog/2017/08/hashtag-ten-years-old/.
22. See www.stewleonards.com/how-it-all-began/, accessed September 2018.
23. See Mai Erne, "Calculating Customer Lifetime Value," HaraPartners, www.harapartners.com/blog/calculating-lifetime-value/, accessed September 2018. For more on calculating customer value, see V. Kumar, "A Theory of Customer Valuation: Concepts, Metrics, Strategy, and Implementation," *Journal of Marketing*, January 2018, pp. 1–19.
24. See Eugene Kim, "Amazon Just Shared New Numbers That Give a Clue about How Many Prime Members It Has," *Business Insider*,

February 13, 2017, www.businessinsider.com/amazon-gives-clue-number-of-prime-users-2017-2?utm_source=feedly&utm_medium=referral; Carl Richards, "4 Steps to Manage Your Desire for Instant Gratification," *The Motley Fool,* April 24, 2013, www.fool.com/investing/general/2013/04/24/4-steps-to-manage-your-desire-for-instant-gratific.aspx; and Caroline Cakebread, "With 90 Million Subscribers, Amazon Prime May Be One of Jeff Bezos Best Ideas Yet," *Business Insider,* October 19, 2017, www.businessinsider.in/With-90-million-subscribers-Amazon-Prime-might-be-one-of-Jeff-Bezos-best-ideas-yet/articleshow/61147211.cms; and www.amazon.com/prime, accessed September 2018.

25. For more discussions on customer equity, see Roland T. Rust, Valerie A. Zeithaml, and Katherine N. Lemon, *Driving Customer Equity* (New York: Free Press, 2000); Roland T. Rust, Katherine N. Lemon, and Valerie A. Zeithaml, "Return on Marketing: Using Customer Equity to Focus Marketing Strategy," *Journal of Marketing,* January 2004, pp. 109–127; Christian Gronroos and Pekka Helle, "Return on Relationships: Conceptual Understanding and Measurement of Mutual Gains from Relational Business Engagements," *Journal of Business & Industrial Marketing,* Vol. 27, No. 5, 2012, pp. 344–359; and V. Kumar, "A Theory of Customer Valuation: Concepts, Metrics, Strategy, and Implementation," *Journal of Marketing,* January 2018, pp. 1–19.
26. This example is based on one found in Rust, Lemon, and Zeithaml, "Where Should the Next Marketing Dollar Go?" *Marketing Management,* September–October 2001, pp. 24–28; with information from Grant McCracken, "Provocative Cadillac, Rescuing the Brand from Bland," *Harvard Business Review,* March 4, 2014, http://blogs.hbr.org/2014/03/provocative-cadillac-rescuing-the-brand-from-bland/; "Cadillac Is Reinventing Its Entire Lineup after Years of Losing US Market Share," *CNBC,* March 23, 2018, www.cnbc.com/2018/03/23/cadillac-is-reinventing-its-lineup-after-years-of-lost-us-market-share.html; and www.dare-greatly.com, accessed September 2018.
27. Based on Werner Reinartz and V. Kumar, "The Mismanagement of Customer Loyalty," *Harvard Business Review,* July 2002, pp. 86–94. Also see Chris Lema, "Not All Customers Are Equal—Butterflies & Barnacles," April 18, 2013, http://chrislema.com/not-all-customers-are-equal-butterflies-barnacles/; Jill Avery, Susan Fournier, and John Wittenbraker, "Unlock the Mysteries of Your Customer Relationships," *Harvard Business Review,* July–August 2014, pp. 72–81, "Telling Customers 'You're Fired,'" Sales and Marketing.com, September/October 2014, p. 8; and Michele McGovern, "6 Rules for Firing a Customer," *Customer Insight Experience,* January 6, 2016, www.customerexperienceinsight.com/6-rules-for-firing-a-customer/.
28. Khadeeja Sadar, "How Your Returns Are Used against You at Best Buy, Other Retailers," *Wall Street Journal,* March 13, 2018, www.wsj.com/articles/how-your-returns-are-used-against-you-at-best-buy-other-retailers-1520933400.
29. Adam Lella, "U.S. Smartphone Penetration Surpassed 80 Percent in 2016," *comScore,* February 3, 2017, www.comscore.com/Insights/Blog/US-Smartphone-Penetration-Surpassed-80-Percent-in-2016; and "Internet Usage Statistics," *Internet World Stats,* www.internetworldstats.com/stats.htm; accessed September 2018.
30. Amanda Kooser, "Sleep with Your Smartphone in Hand? You're Not Alone," *CNET,* June 30, 2015, www.cnet.com/news/americans-like-to-snooze-with-their-smartphones-says-survey/; Lee Raine, "About 6 in 10 Young Adults in U.S. Primarily Use Online Streaming to Watch TV," *Pew Research,* September 13, 2017, www.pewresearch.org/fact-tank/2017/09/13/about-6-in-10-young-adults-in-u-s-primarily-use-online-streaming-to-watch-tv/; and "Quarterly Retail E-Commerce Sales 4th Quarter 2017," U.S. Census Bureau, February 16, 2018, www.census.gov/retail/mrts/www/data/pdf/ec_current.pdf.
31. See http://community.us.playstation.com/, https://ideas.lego.com, and www.sephora.com/about-beauty-insider, accessed September 2018.
32. Darrell Etherington, "Instagram Now Has 800 Million Monthly and 500 Million Daily Active Users," *TechCrunch,* September 25, 2017, https://techcrunch.com/2017/09/25/instagram-now-has-800-million-monthly-and-500-million-daily-active-users/; Matthew Lynley, "Pinterest Crosses 200 Million Monthly Active Users," *TechCrunch,* September 14, 2017, https://techcrunch.com/2017/09/14/pinterest-crosses-200-million-monthly-active-users/; and https://newsroom.fb.com/company-info/, www.cafemom.com, and ravelry.com, accessed September 2018.
33. See Alexandra Zamfir, "5 Brands that Built Authentic Social Media Communities," *Falcon,* January 18, 2016, www.falcon.io/insights-hub/topics/customer-engagement/5-brands-who-built-authentic-social-media-communities/#CS; and www.redbull.com, https://twitter.com/redbull, and www.facebook.com/redbull, accessed September 2018.
34. John Koetsier, "Mobile Advertising Will Drive 75% of All Digital Ad Spend in 2018: Here's What's Changing," *Forbes,* February 23, 2018, www.forbes.com/sites/johnkoetsier/2018/02/23/mobile-advertising-will-drive-75-of-all-digital-ad-spend-in-2018-heres-whats-changing/#b7eece4758be; and "U.S. Mobile Retail Commerce Sales as a Percentage of Retail E-commerce Sales from 2017 to 2021," *Statista,* www.statista.com/statistics/249863/us-mobile-retail-commerce-sales-as-percentage-of-e-commerce-sales/, accessed September 2018.
35. Lauren Johnson, "Taco Bell's Mobile Ads Are Highly Targeted to Make Users Crave Its Breakfast Menu," *Adweek,* March 14, 2016, www.adweek.com/print/170155; And Johnson, "Taco Bell Beefs Up Mobile Advertising Play to Drive In-Store Foot Traffic," *Mobile Marketer,* www.mobilemarketer.com/ex/mobilemarketer/cms/news/advertising/13229.html, accessed September 2018.
36. Information from "The 100 Largest U.S. Charities: St. Jude Children's Research Hospital," *Forbes,* www.forbes.com/companies/st-jude-childrens-research-hospital/, accessed September 2018; and various pages at www.stjude.org, accessed September 2018. Finding Cures. Saving Children®, Up 'Til Dawn®, St. Jude Dream Home® Giveaway, and St. Jude Thanks and Giving® are registered trademarks of American Lebanese Syrian Associated Charities, Inc. (ALSAC).
37. See "United States Advertisers/Agencies," *Ad Brands,* www.adbrands.net/us/top-us-advertisers.htm, accessed September 2018.
38. See www.aboutmcdonalds.com/mcd and www.nikeinc.com, accessed September 2018.
39. See Jason Del Rey, "Warby Parker Is Valued at $1,75 Billion after a Pre-IPO Investment of $75 Million," *Recode,* March 14, 2018, www.recode.net/2018/3/14/17115230/warby-parker-75-million-funding-t-rowe-price-ipo; Tom Foster, "Warby Parker Grew to $250 Million in Sales through Disciplined Growth. Now It's Time to Get Aggressive," *Inc.,* June 2017, www.inc.com/magazine/201706/tom-foster/warby-parker-eyewear.html; and www.warbyparker.com, www.warbyparker.com/history, and www.warbyparker.com/buy-a-pair-give-a-pair, accessed September 2018.

Chapter 2

1. Alicia Kelso, "Starbucks' Plans to Double Food Offerings Could Further Disrupt Traditional QSRs," *Forbes,* March 27, 2018, www.forbes.com/sites/aliciakelso/2018/03/27/starbucks-plans-to-double-food-offerings-could-further-disrupt-traditional-qsrs/#45c2e66a4f0f; Julie Jargon, "New Starbucks CEO Sees Growth in Suburbs, Midwest and Lunch," *Wall Street Journal,* April 3, 2017, www.wsj.com/articles/new-ceo-on-where-starbucks-sees-growth-suburbs-midwest-lunch-1491192060; Laura Lorenzetti, "Fortune's World's Most Admired Companies: Starbucks, Where Innovation Is Always Brewing," *Fortune,* October 30, 2014, http://fortune.com/2014/10/30/starbucks-innovation-cafe-to-classroom/; David Kaplan, "Starbucks: The Art of Endless Transformation," *Inc.,* June, 2014, pp. 82–86+; Kate Taylor, "Starbucks Just Quietly Made a Change That Reveals the Future of the Company," *Business Insider,* March 27, 2018, www.businessinsider.com/starbucks-mobile-order-and-pay-for-all-customers-2018-3; and Starbucks annual reports and other information accessed at www.starbucks.com, September 2018.
2. The NASA mission statement is from www.nasa.gov/about/whats_next.html, accessed September 2018.
3. See www.ritzcarlton.com/en/about/gold-standards, accessed September 2018. For more mission statement examples, see www.missionstatements.com/fortune_500_mission_statements.html, accessed September 2018.
4. Information about CVS Health and its mission and activities from www.cvshealth.com/about, www.cvshealth.com/about/our-story, www.cvs.com/minuteclinic/visit/about-us/history, and www.cvshealth.com/about/our-offerings, accessed September 2018.
5. See www.mars.com/global and www.mars.com/global/about-us, accessed September 2018.
6. The following discussion is based in part on information found at www.bcg.com/documents/file13904.pdf, accessed September 2018.
7. See Matt Egan, "GE Could Break Itself Apart as Cash Crisis Deepens," *CNN Money,* January 16, 2018, http://money.cnn.com/2018/01/16/investing/ge-breakup-stock/index.html; and Kevin McCoy, "GE Weighs a Breakup of Iconic U.S. Conglomerate amid Insurance Problem," *USA Today,* January 16, 2018, www.usatoday.com/story/money/2018/01/16/ge-weighs-breakup-iconic-us-conglomerate-amid-insurance-problem/1036258001/; and www.ge.com, accessed September 2018.
8. H. Igor Ansoff, "Strategies for Diversification," *Harvard Business Review,* September–October 1957, pp. 113–124.
9. Information about Starbucks in this section is from "Starbucks CEP Kevin Johnson Unveils Innovative Growth Strategy at 2018 Annual Meeting," March 21, 2018, https://news.starbucks.com/press-releases/starbucks-unveils-innovative-growth-strategy-at-2018-annual-meeting; Sarah Whitten, "Starbucks Opens First Princi Location, Teases More to Come in 2018," *CNBC,* November 7, 2017, www.cnbc.com/2017/11/07/starbucks-opens-first-princi-location-teases-more-to-come-in-2018.html; and various pages at www.starbucks.com, accessed September 2018.

10. See Michael E. Porter, *Competitive Advantage: Creating and Sustaining Superior Performance* (New York: Free Press, 1985); and Michael E. Porter, "What Is Strategy?" *Harvard Business Review*, November–December 1996, pp. 61–78. Also see "The Value Chain," www.quickmba.com/strategy/value-chain, accessed September 2018; and Philip Kotler and Kevin Lane Keller, *Marketing Management*, 15th ed. (Hoboken, NJ: Prentice Hall, 2016), Chapter 2.
11. Blake Morgan, "When the CMO Owns the Customer Experience: 10 Top CMOs Share Their POV," *Forbes,* August 29, 2017, www.forbes.com/sites/blakemorgan/2017/08/29/when-the-cmo-owns-customer-experience-10-top-cmos-share-their-pov/#65afabf469d2.
12. See www.gapinc.com/content/gapinc/html/aboutus/ourbrands/gap.html, accessed September 2018.
13. See www.swamedia.com/pages/corporate-fact-sheet, accessed September 2018.
14. See Elizabeth Petra, "Love. It's What Makes a Subaru a Subaru," *Huffington Post,* May 31, 2017, www.huffingtonpost.com/entry/love-its-what-makes-a-subaru-a-subaru_us_592ee9abe4b0d80e3a8a3241; and www.subaru.co.jp/en/csr/about.html and www.subaru.ie/subaru-life/confidence-in-motion/, accessed September 2018.
15. "Leading National Advertisers Fact Pack," *Advertising Age*, June 26, 2017, http://adage.com/d/resources/system/files/resource/LNA%20Fact%20Pack%202017-online.pdf.
16. The four Ps classification was first suggested by E. Jerome McCarthy, *Basic Marketing: A Managerial Approach* (Homewood, IL: Irwin, 1960). The four As are discussed in Jagdish Sheth and Rajendra Sisodia, *The 4 A's of Marketing: Creating Value for Customer, Company and Society* (New York: Routledge, 2012); and Philip Kotler and Kevin Lane Keller, *Marketing Management,* 15th ed. (Hoboken, NJ: Pearson Education, 2016), p. 26.
17. Blake Morgan, "When the CMO Owns the Customer Experience: 10 Top CMOs Share Their POV," *Forbes,* August 29, 2017, www.forbes.com/sites/blakemorgan/2017/08/29/when-the-cmo-owns-customer-experience-10-top-cmos-share-their-pov/#65afabf469d2.
18. For more on marketing dashboards and financial measures of marketing performance, see Ofer Mintz and Imran S. Currim, "What Drives Managerial Use of Marketing Financial Metrics and Does Metric Use Affect Performance of Marketing-Mix Activities?" *Journal of Marketing,* March 2013, pp. 17–40; and "Marketing Dashboard Examples," *Klipfolio,* www.klipfolio.com/resources/dashboard-examples, accessed September 2018.
19. For a full discussion of this model and details on customer–centered measures of marketing return on investment, see Roland T. Rust, Katherine N. Lemon, and Valerie A. Zeithaml, "Return on Marketing: Using Customer Equity to Focus Marketing Strategy," *Journal of Marketing*, January 2004, pp. 109–127; Roland T. Rust, Katherine N. Lemon, and Das Narayandas, *Customer Equity Management* (Upper Saddle River, NJ: Prentice Hall, 2005); Roland T. Rust, "Seeking Higher ROI? Base Strategy on Customer Equity," *Advertising Age,* September 10, 2007, pp. 26–27; Andreas Persson and Lynette Ryals, "Customer Assets and Customer Equity: Management and Measurement Issues," *Marketing Theory*, December 2010, pp. 417–436; and Kirsten Korosec, "'Tomato, Tomäto'? Not Exactly," *Marketing News*, January 13, 2012, p. 8.
20. Molly Soat, "More Companies Require Revenue-Focused Marketing ROI Measures, Study Finds," *Marketing News Weekly,* www.ama.org/publications/eNewsletters/Marketing-News-Weekly/Pages/more-companies-require-revenue-focused-marketing-roi-measures.aspx, accessed September 2018.

Chapter 3

1. See Bob Evans, "Microsoft, Amazon, and IBM: Which Cloud Powerhouse Will Top Q1 Revenue Charts?," *Forbes,* April 9, 2018, www.forbes.com/sites/bobevans1/2018/04/09/microsoft-amazon-and-ibm-which-cloud-powerhouse-will-top-q1-revenue-charts/#47d6f73b14dc; Aaron Tilley, "The Microsoft-Amazon Alliance in Voice Assistants Puts Pressure on Google," *Forbes,* August 30, 2017, www.forbes.com/sites/aarontilley/2017/08/30/microsoft-cortana-amazon-alexa-alliance/#1247b17022bf; Matt Weinberger, "Microsoft CEO Satya Nadella's Genius Plan: To Swap One Monopoly for Another," *Business Insider,* August 29, 2015; www.businessinsider.com/microsoft-ceo-satya-nadella-focus-on-office-2015-8; Tom Vander Ark, "Hit Refresh: How a Growth Mindset Culture Tripled Microsoft's Value," *Forbes,* April 18, 2018, www.forbes.com/sites/tomvanderark/2018/04/18/hit-refresh-how-a-growth-mindset-culture-tripled-microsofts-value/#4904470652ad; and www.microsoft.com and www.microsoft.com/en-us/investor/, accessed July 2018.
2. See https://preview.thenewsmarket.com/Previews/IKEA/DocumentAssets/493700.pdf, www.ikea.cn/ms/en_CN/about_ikea/the_ikea_way/our_business_idea/a_better_everyday_life.html, www.ikea.com/gb/en/this-is-ikea/people-planet/people-communities/suppliers/, and https://preview.thenewsmarket.com/Previews/IKEA/DocumentAssets/493700.pdf, accessed September 2018.
3. Information from Robert J. Benes, Abbie Jarman, and Ashley Williams, "2007 NRA Sets Records," www.chefmagazine.com, accessed September 2007; "Thought Leadership Begins with Experience," *fishbowl,* February 20, 2015, www.fishbowl.com/coca-cola-offers-restaurant-customers-new-digital-marketing-solutions-powered-by-fishbowl/; and www.cokesolutions.com, accessed September 2018.
4. See https://corporate.homedepot.com/community, accessed September 2018.
5. U.S. and World POP Clock, U.S. Census Bureau, www.census.gov/popclock/, accessed September 2018. This website provides continuously updated projections of the U.S. and world populations.
6. See "Population Projections for the United States from 20-15 to 2060," *Statista,* www.statista.com/statistics/183481/united-states-population-projection/, accessed September 2018.
7. "U.S. Population," *Worldometers,* www.worldometers.info/world-population/us-population/, accessed September 2018.
8. Population numbers in this section are based on Richard Fry, "Millennials Overtake Baby Boomers as America's Largest Generation," *Pew Research,* April 25, 2016, www.pewresearch.org/fact-tank/2016/04/25/millennials-overtake-baby-boomers/. Also see "Baby Boomers Slip to 74.1 Million in U.S.," *Cleveland.com,* April 24, 2017, www.cleveland.com/datacentral/index.ssf/2017/04/baby_boomers_slip_to_741_milli.html; Paul Davidson, "The Economy Is Still About—Who Else?—Boomers," *USA Today,* July 17, 2017, www.usatoday.com/story/money/2017/07/17/economy-still-all-who-else-boomers/476908001.
9. "Generational Marketing: Tips for Reaching Baby Boomers," July 16, 2015, www.mayecreate.com/2015/07/generational-marketing-tips-for-reaching-baby-boomers/; Janet Morrissey, "Baby Boomers to Advertisers: Don't Forget about Us," *New York Times,* October 15, 2017, www.nytimes.com/2017/10/15/business/media/baby-boomers-marketing.html?mtrref=undefined; Chloe Aiello, "Tech Companies Will Increasingly Look to Aging Baby Boomers for Growth, Says Evercore Analyst," *CNBC,* January 26, 2018, www.cnbc.com/2018/01/26/tech-companies-will-increasingly-look-to-aging-baby-boomers-for-growth.html.
10. See Alexandra Jardine, "After the Rise of 'Femvertising,' Is 'Oldvertising' the Next Big Thing?" *Advertising Age,* April 5, 2017, http://adage.com/article/creativity/fem-vertising-vertising/308527/.
11. "Last Night's Ads: Walgreens Reassures Baby Boomers They Can Still Be Cool," *Advertising Age,* January 4, 2016, http://adage.com/print/301976/; "Walgreens TV Commercial, 'Carpe Med Diem,'" www.ispot.tv/ad/A7LR/walgreens-carpe-med-diem, accessed September 2018; and www.walgreens.com/topic/pharmacy/medicarepartd-info.jsp, accessed September 2018.
12. The specific date ranges for the generations varies by source. The ones used here are from the Pew Research Center. See www.pewresearch.org/fact-tank/2018/03/01/millennials-overtake-baby-boomers/.
13. Robert Klara, "5 Reasons Marketers Have Largely Overlooked Generation X," *Adweek,* April 4, 2016, www.adweek.com/brand-marketing/5-reasons-marketers-have-largely-overlooked-generation-x-170539/; Richard Fry, "Millennials Projected to Overtake Baby Boomers as America's Largest Generation," Pew Research, March 1, 2018, www.pewresearch.org/fact-tank/2018/03/01/millennials-overtake-baby-boomers/.
14. See Michelle Markelz, "Why You Should Be Marketing to Gen X," American Marketing Association, www.ama.org/publications/eNewsletters/Marketing-News-Weekly/Pages/why-you-should-be-marketing-to-gen-x.aspx, accessed September 2018; www.lowes.com/mobile, www.lowes.com, www.youtube.com/watch?v=zbFX7p6ZGTk, and www.pinterest.com/lowes/, accessed September 2018.
15. Carrie Cummings, "Blue Ribbon Millennials," *Adweek,* April 11, 2018, p. 13.
16. See Emma Brazilian, "Millennial Movers," *Adweek,* February 27, 2017, p. 9. Also see "Millennials," Pew Research Center, www.pewresearch.org/topics/millennials/, accessed September 2018.
17. "Fifth Third Bank Invites You to 'Lose the Wait,'" Leo Burnett, February 12, 2016, http://leoburnett.us/chicago/article/fifth-third-bank-invites-you-to-lose-the-wait-/; and Adrianne Pasqarelli, "Another Bank Chases Millennials with Digital Games, Ads," *Advertising Age*, January 21, 2016, http://adage.com/print/302263/. Also see https://financialinsights.53.com/financial-planning-millennials/ and www.youtube.com/watch?v=jaKosB4F1OU, accessed September 2018.
18. See Josh Perlstein, "Engaging Generation Z: Marketing to a New Brand of Consumer," *Adweek*, November 27, 2017, www.adweek.com/digital/josh-perlstein-response-media-guest-post-generation-z/; Libby Kane, "Meet Generation Z, the 'Millennials on Steroids' Who Could Lead the Change in the US," *Business Insider*, December 4, 2017, www.businessinsider.com/generation-z-profile-2017-9; and "The Power of Gen Z

Influence," Barkley Report, January 2018, www.millennialmarketing.com/wp-content/uploads/2018/01/Barkley_WP_GenZMarketSpend_Final.pdf.

19. See "GenZ: Digital in Their DNA"; Shannon Bryant, "'Generation Z' Children More Tech-Savvy; Prefer Gadgets, Not Toys," *Marketing Forecast,* April 3, 2013, www.ad-ology.com/tag/tech-savvy-children/#.U5d9avldV8E; Brett Relander, "How to Market to Gen Z," *Entrepreneur,* November 4, 2014, www.entrepreneur.com/article/238998; Josh Perlstein, "Engaging Generation Z: Marketing to a New Brand of Consumer," *Adweek,* November 27, 2017, www.adweek.com/digital/josh-perlstein-response-media-guest-post-generation-z/; and "Redesigning Retail for the Next Generation," Accenture, www.accenture.com/us-en/insight-redesigning-retail-next-generation, accessed September 2018.
20. Carrie Cummings, "Infographic: Here's How Gen Z Girls Prefer to Shop and Socialize Online," *Adweek,* May 8, 2016, www.adweek.com/brand-marketing/infographic-heres-how-gen-z-girls-prefer-shop-and-socialize-online-171328/; and "13 Strategies for Marketing to Generation Z," *Forbes,* February 22, 2018, www.forbes.com/sites/forbesbusinessdevelopmentcouncil/2018/02/22/13-strategies-for-marketing-to-generation-z/#2f6cf90731c3.
21. See http://neverstopexploring.com/2016/02/18/12068/ and http://neverstopexploring.com/2015/08/25/the-north-face-youth-design-team-seeks-inspiration-from-kids/, accessed September 2016.
22. For statistics on family composition, see U.S. Census Bureau, "Family Households," Table F1, and "Households by Type, Age of Members, Region of Residence, and Age of Householder: 2016," Table H2, www.census.gov/data/tables/2016/demo/families/cps-2016.html, accessed September 2018.
23. "Interracial Marriage across the U.S. by Metro Area," *Pew Research,* May 18, 2017, www.pewsocialtrends.org/interactives/intermarriage-across-the-u-s-by-metro-area/; "The Changing American Family," *CBS News,* May 11, 2014, www.cbsnews.com/videos/the-changing-american-family/; and U.S. Census Bureau, "Table 1. Household Characteristics of Opposite-Sex and Same-Sex Couple Households," www.census.gov/data/tables/time-series/demo/same-sex-couples/ssc-house-characteristics.html, accessed September 2018.
24. See Department of Labor, "Facts Over Time: Women in the Labor Force," www.dol.gov/wb/stats/facts_over_time.htm; Pew Research Center, "Breadwinner Moms," May 29, 2013, www.pewsocialtrends.org/2013/05/29/breadwinner-moms/; U.S. Census Bureau, "America's Families and Living Arrangements: 2016," Table FG1, www.census.gov/hhes/families/data/cps2015FG.html, accessed September 2018; and U.S. Census Bureau, "Parents and Children in Stay at Home Parent Family Groups: 1994 to Present," Table SHP-1, www.census.gov/hhes/families/data/families.html, accessed September 2018.
25. See T.L. Stanley, "Angel Soft Continues to Build Ads around Quiet, Relatable Moments in People's Lives," *Adweek,* January 11, 2017, www.adweek.com/creativity/angel-soft-continues-build-ads-around-quiet-relatable-moments-peoples-lives-175479/; "Best of Dad Ads," *Ad Forum,* www.adforum.com/creative-work/best-of/13299/best-of-dad-ads/play#34540302, accessed September 2018; and www.youtube.com/watch?v=r7tRf0dtK7E, accessed September 2018.
26. See Cord Jefferson, "Cheerios Ad Starring Interracial Family Predictably Summons Bigot Wave," *Gawker,* May 30, 2013, http://gawker.com/cheerios-ad-starring-interracial-family-predictably-sum-510591871; Jessica Wohl, "Campbell Soup Shows 'Real, Real Life' in New Brand Campaign," *Advertising Age,* October 5, 2016, http://adage.com/print/300750; and www.youtube.com/watch?v=Z01qH-jqGBY and www.youtube.com/watch?v=7rZOMY2sOnE, accessed September 2018.
27. Tim Henderson, "Americans Are Moving South, West Again," Pew Charitable Trusts, January 8, 2016, www.pewtrusts.org/en/research-and-analysis/blogs/stateline/2016/01/08/americans-are-moving-south-west-again; U.S. Census Bureau, "Declining Mover Rate Drive by Renters, Census Bureau Reports," November 15, 2017, www.census.gov/newsroom/press-releases/2017/mover-rates.html; and U.S. Census Bureau, "Migration/Geographical Mobility," www.census.gov/population/www/socdemo/migrate.html, accessed September 2018.
28. See U.S. Census Bureau, "Metropolitan and Micropolitan Statistical Areas," www.census.gov/population/metro/data/index.html/, accessed September 2018; Mike Maciag, "Population Growth Shifts to Suburban America," *Governing,* June 2017, www.governing.com/topics/urban/gov-suburban-population-growth.html; and "List of Micropolitan Statistical Areas," *Wikipedia,* http://en.wikipedia.org/wiki/List_of_Micropolitan_Statistical_Areas, accessed September 2018.
29. Niraj Chokshi, "Out of the Office: More People Are Working Remotely, Survey Finds." *New York Times,* February 15, 2017, www.nytimes.com/2017/02/15/us/remote-workers-work-from-home.html.
30. See www.slack.com, accessed September 2018.
31. U.S. Census Bureau, "Educational Attainment," www.census.gov/data/tables/2017/demo/education-attainment/cps-detailed-tables.html, accessed June 2018.
32. See U.S. Department of Labor, "Employment Projections: 2014–2024 Summary," www.bls.gov/emp/ep_table_103.htm, accessed September 2018.
33. See U.S. Census Bureau, "Projections of the Size and Composition of the U.S. Population: 2014 to 2060," March 2015, www.census.gov/content/dam/Census/library/publications/2015/demo/p25-1143.pdf; "Multicultural Consumers by the Numbers," *Advertising Age,* April 6, 2015, p. 20; U.S. Census Bureau, "The Nation's Older Population Is Still Growing, Census Bureau Reports," June 22, 2017, www.census.gov/newsroom/press-releases/2017/cb17-100.html; and Census Quick Facts, www.census.gov/quickfacts/fact/table/US/PST045217, accessed September 2018.
34. See Brielle Jaekel, "Marriott Celebrates Latino Love of Travel in Social Media Campaign," *Mobile Marketer,* www.mobilemarketer.com/ex/mobilemarketer/cms/news/advertising/21118.html, accessed September 2018; Parker Morse, "3 Hispanic Marketing Campaigns That Are Awesome," *Media Post,"* December 6, 2017, https://www.mediapost.com/publications/article/311189/3-hispanic-marketing-campaigns-that-are-awesome.html; and http://lovetravelswithme.com/, accessed September 2018.
35. Jeff Green, "LGBT Purchasing Power Near $1 Trillion Rivals other Minorities," *Bloomberg,* July 20, 2016, www.bloomberg.com/news/articles/2016-07-20/lgbt-purchasing-power-near-1-trillion-rivals-other-minorities; and "The LGBT Economy Is America's Future," *Advocate,* January 2, 2018, www.advocate.com/commentary/2018/1/02/lgbt-economy-americas-future.
36. For more discussion, see Jacob Passy, "Wells Fargo: Ad with Gay Couple Reflects 'Demographic Reality,'" *American Banker,* June 23, 2015, www.americanbanker.com/news/consumer-finance/wells-fargo-ad-with-gay-couple-reflects-demographic-reality-1075043-1.html; and https://www.youtube.com/watch?v=DxDsx8HfXEk, accessed September 2018.
37. "Institute on Disability, "2016 Disability Statistics Annual Report," https://disabilitycompendium.org/sites/default/files/user-uploads/2016_AnnualReport.pdf; "What Is the Disability Market," http://returnondisability.com/disability-market/, accessed September 2018; and "Disability Travel Generates $17.3 Billion in Annual Spending," *PR Newswire,* July 31, 2015, www.prnewswire.com/news-releases/disability-travel-generates-173-billion-in-annual-spending-300121930.html; and Michael Kimmelman, "How Design for One Turns into Design for All," *New York Times,* January 24, 2018, www.nytimes.com/2018/01/24/arts/design/cooper-hewitt-access-ability.html.
38. "We Can Change Attitudes with Disability in Advertising," *Advertising and Disability,* February 18, 2016, http://-advertisinganddisability.com/2016/02/18/we-can-change-attitudes-with-disability-in-advertising/.
39. Katie Richards, "Toyota Is Betting on the Olympics with 7 New Pieces of Creative for Its First Global Campaign," *Adweek,* February 9, 2018, www.adweek.com/brand-marketing/toyota-is-betting-big-on-the-olympics-with-7-new-pieces-of-creative-for-its-first-global-campaign/; "Toyota Rolls Out 'Start Your Impossible' Global Campaign That Reflects the Olympic and Paralympic Spirit of Encouragement, Challenge and Progress," Toyota Newsroom, February 9, 2018, https://newsroom.toyota.co.jp/en/corporate/21064838.html; and www.youtube.com/watch?v=38PMmAbR_e4, accessed September 2018.
40. See "Purpose & Beliefs," https://corporate.target.com/about/purpose-beliefs, accessed September 2018.
41. Drew Harwell, "Meet the Secret Army of Meteorologists Who Keep Your Holiday Deliveries on Time," *The Washington Post,"* December 8, 2014, www.washingtonpost.com/business/economy/meet-the-secret-army-of-meteorologists-who-keep-your-holiday-deliveries-on-time/2014/12/08/2d9d3c82-759d-11e4-9d9b-86d397daad27_story.html; and Steve Banker, "Using Weather Data to Improve Supply Chain Resiliency," *Forbes,* June 29, 2016, www.forbes.com/sites/stevebanker/2016/06/29/using-weather-to-improve-supply-chain-resiliency/#5da581be23f2.
42. Sarah Begley, "UN Report Warns of Serious Water Shortages within 15 Years," *Time,* March 20, 2015, http://time.com/3752643/un-water-shortage-2030/; Tim Smedley, "Is the World Running Out of Fresh Water," *BBC,* April 12, 2017, www.bbc.com/future/story/20170412-is-the-world-running-out-of-fresh-water; and "The World's Water," *Pacific Institute,* www.worldwater.org/data.html, accessed September 2018.
43. See Joel Makower, "Walmart Sustainability at 10: The Birth of a Notion," *GreenBiz,* November 16, 2016, www.greenbiz.com/article/walmart-sustainability-10-birth-notion; Joel Makower, "Walmart Sustainability at 10: An Assessment," *GreenBiz,* November 17, 2016, www.greenbiz.com/article/walmart-sustainability-10-assessment; Luna Atamian, "Why Is Walmart a Sustainability Leader?" *Huffington Post,* December 14, 2017, www.huffingtonpost.com/entry/why-is-walmart-a-sustainability-leader_us

_5a329da5e4b00caf3d59eae8; and http://corporate.walmart.com/global-responsibility/sustainability/ and www.walmartsustainabilityhub.com/, accessed September 2018.

44. See "A $1 Billion Project to Remake the Disney World Experience, Using RFID," http://www.fastcodesign.com/1671616/a-1-billion-project-to-remake-the-disney-world-experience-using-rfid#1; and Arthur Levine, "Disney Park Upgrades Make Visiting More Convenient," *USA Today*, February 27, 2018, www.usatoday.com/story/travel/experience/america/theme-parks/2018/02/27/disney-parks-magicbands-fastpasses-app/374588002/.
45. See, for example, Taylor Armerding, "The 17 Biggest Data Breaches of the 21st Century," *CSO*, January 26, 2018, www.csoonline.com/article/2130877/data-breach/the-biggest-data-breaches-of-the-21st-century.html; and Sarah Frier, "Facebook Just Doubled the Number of People Exposed in Data Breach," *Time*, April 4, 2018, http://time.com/money/5228277/facebook-cambridge-analytica-data-breach-numbers/.
46. See Angela Natividid, "Lacoste's Iconic Crocodile Makes Room for 10 Endangered Species on Brand's Polo Shirts," *Adweek*, February 28, 2018, www.adweek.com/brand-marketing/lacostes-iconic-crocodile-makes-room-for-10-endangered-species-on-brands-polo-shirts/; and https://carecounts.whirlpool.com/ and www.itcanwait.com, accessed September 2018.
47. See www.benjerry.com/values, www.benandjerrysfoundation.org and www.unilever.com/brands-in-action/detail/ben-and-jerrys/291995, accessed July 2018.
48. See David Gianatasio, "A New Cycle," *Adweek*, September 11, 2017, p. 13; and "Top Ice Cream Brands of the United States," *Statista*, www.statista.com/statistics/190426/top-ice-cream-brands-in-the-united-states/, accessed July 2018.
49. See "Social Impact Statistics You Should Know," http://engageforgood.com/guides/statistics-every-cause-marketer-should-know/, accessed July 2018.
50. Kristina Monllos, "Sperry Goes Back to Basics with a Campaign for Adventurous Millennials," *Adweek*, February 19, 2015, www.adweek.com/print/162983; Erik Oster, "mono Rebrands Sperry with 'Odysseys Await,'" *Adweek*, February 19, 2015, www.adweek.copm/print/81123; and www.sperry.com/en/our-story/ and https://mono-1.com/work/sperry-odysseys-await, accessed July 2018.
51. Sherry Turkle, "The Flight from Conversation," *New York Times*, April 22, 2012, p. SR1; and Turkle, "Stop Googling. Let's Talk," *New York Times*, September 27, 2015, p. SR1.
52. See Tim Nudd, "What the Famous Faces from Jeep's Super Bowl Ad Really Had to Do with the Vehicle," *Advertising Age*, February 7, 2016, www.adage.com/print/169489; "Apple Kicks Off 'Made in USA' Marketing Push with High-End Mac Pro," *Advertising Age*, December 19, 2013, http://adage.com/print/245765/; E. J. Schultz, "Coke Joins Patriotic Branding Boom with Flag Can," *Advertising Age*, May 26, 2016, www.adage.com/print/304186; "5 Veteran's Day Campaigns to Honor Those Who Served," *Campaign Live*, November 10, 2017, www.campaignlive.co.uk/article/5-veterans-day-campaigns-honor-served/1449776; and www.youtube.com/watch?v=wKn5K5V7tRo, accessed September 2018.
53. See Emily Monaco, "Organic Food and Beverage Market Growth Projected at 14 Percent Before 2021," *Organic Authority*, January 3, 2018, www.organicauthority.com/organic-food-and-beverage-market-growth-projected-at-14-percent-before-2021/; and Frank Giles, "Future Looks Bright for Organic Produce Growth," *Growing Produce*, February 15, 2018, www.growingproduce.com/fruits/future-looks-bright-organic-produce-growth/.
54. See Elaine Watson, "Annie's President: 'Over the Last Two Years We've Added Four Million New Households Each Year,'" *Food Navigator*, March 21, 2017, www.foodnavigator-usa.com/Article/2017/03/21/Annie-s-sales-set-to-reach-400m-in-fiscal-2017; and various pages at www.annies.com, accessed July 2018.
55. The Pew Forum on Religion & Public Life, "Nones on the Rise," www.pewforum.org/Unaffiliated/nones-on-the-rise.aspx, accessed October 9, 2012; "America's Changing Religious Landscape," May 12, 2015, www.pewforum.org/2015/05/12/americas-changing-religious-landscape/; Daniel Cox and Robert P. Jones, "America's Changing Religious Identity," PRRI, September 6, 2017, www.prri.org/research/american-religious-landscape-christian-religiously-unaffiliated/; and www.pewforum.org/religious-landscape-study/, accessed July 2018.
56. For more discussion, see David Masci and Michael Lipka, "Americans May Be Getting Less Religious, but Feelings of Spirituality Are on the Rise," Pew Research Center, January 21, 2016, www.pewresearch.org/fact-tank/2016/01/21/americans-spirituality/.
57. See Gini Dietrich, "5 Crisis Lessons from Crock-Pot and 'This Is Us,'" *PR Daily*, February 19, 2017, www.prdaily.com/mediarelations/Articles/5_crisis_lessons_from_CrockPot_and_This_Is_Us_23990.aspx; and Amy George, "Crock-Pot's Response to Its Tragic Role in 'This Is Us' Is a Lesson in Smart PR," *Inc.*, January 29, 2018, www.inc.com/amy-george/crock-pots-response-to-angry-this-is-us-fans-shows-why-every-company-needs-a-pr-crisis-plan.html.

Chapter 4

1. See Jack Neff, "Do You Find P&G Irresistible?" *Advertising Age*, May 1, 2017, p. 6; George Kuhn, "How Market Research Saved Febreze: A Case Study," *Drive Research*, November 2, 2016, www.driveresearch.com/single-post/2016/11/03/How-Market-Research-Saved-Febreze-Consumer-Behavior-Case-Study; www.febreze.com/en-us, accessed September 2018; A.G. Lafley and Ram Charan, "The Consumer Is Boss," *Fortune*, March 10, 2008, http://archive.fortune.com/2008/03/07/news/companies/lafley_charan.fortune/index.htm?postversion=2008031012; Michael Barnett, "Data Analysis: Hidden Treasure," *Marketing Week*, November 13, 2013, www.marketingweek.com/2013/11/13/data-analysis-hidden-treasure/; and www.pginvestor.com/Cache/1001226104.PDF?O=PDF&T=&Y=&D=&FID=1001226104&iid=4004124, http://news.pg.com/about/core_strengths, www.pg.com/en_PH/company/core_strengths.shtml, and www.pgscience.com/home/the_innovation_process/consumer_research.html, accessed September 2018.
2. See Tom Hale, "How Much Data Does the World Generate Every Minute?" *IFLSCIENCE*, July 2017, www.iflscience.com/technology/how-much-data-does-the-world-generate-every-minute/; Bernard Marr, "9 Technology Mega Trends That Will Change the World in 2018," *Forbes*, December 4, 2017, www.forbes.com/sites/bernardmarr/2017/12/04/9-technology-mega-trends-that-will-change-the-world-in-2018/#43d299b75eed; and "Big Data," *Wikipedia*, http://en.wikipedia.org/wiki/Big_data, accessed June 2018.
3. See Jordan Bitterman, "Let's Clear Up the Data Forecast," *Adweek*, December 12, 2016, p. W1.
4. Based on information from Shareen Pathak, "How PepiCo Sweetens Up Consumer Insights," *Digiday*, June 8, 2015, http://digiday.com/brands/pepsico-sweetens-consumer-insights/.
5. See https://corporate.walmart.com/suppliers, accessed September 2018; and "What Is Retail Link For?" 8th & Walton, https://blog.8thandwalton.com/2015/08/what-is-retail-link-for//.
6. See Micah Solomon, "Crushing It via Customer-Centricity: How USAA Insurance Succeeds without Geckos and Flying Pigs," *Forbes*, August 13, 2015, www.forbes.com/sites/-micahsolomon/2015/08/13/-crushing-it-via-customer-centricity-not-geckos-and-flying-pigs-the-usaa-model/; Scott Horstein, "Use Care with That Database," *Sales & Marketing Management*, May 2006, p. 22; Jeff Ross, "Top 7 Best Auto Insurance Companies of 2018," *Goof Financial Cents*, January 5, 2018, www.goodfinancialcents.com/best-auto-insurance-companies/#usaa; and www.usaa.com and www.usaa.com/inet/pages/reporttomembers_financialhighlights_landing, accessed September 2018.
7. See, "Mastercard Conversation Suite Video," http://newsroom.mastercard.com/videos/mastercard-conversation-suite-video/, accessed September 2018; Sheila Shayon, "Mastercard Harnesses the Power of Social with Innovative Conversation Suite," *brandchannel*, May 7, 2013, www.brandchannel.com/home/post/2013/05/07/Mastercard-Conversation-Suite-050713.aspx; and "Mastercard's, Conversation Suite: Bringing Insights and Analytics to Social," http://shortyawards.com/7th/mastercards-conversation-suite-bringing-insights-and-analytics-to-social, accessed September 2018.
8. See Tom Warren, "Samsung Returns to Mock iPhone X Buyers in Latest Commercial," *The Verge*, November 6, 2017, www.theverge.com/2017/11/6/16611758/samsung-mocks-iphone-x-commercial; and "Samsung: Growing Up," www.theverge.com/2017/11/6/16611758/samsung-mocks-iphone-x-commercial, accessed September 2018.
9. Michael Brereton and Diane Bowers, "The 2017 AMA Gold Global Top 25 Market Research Firms," *Marketing News*, October 1, 2017, www.ama.org/publications/MarketingNews/Pages/2017-ama-gold-global-report.aspx.
10. Patrick Young, "Embracing an Era of Just-in-Time Research," *Marketing*, October 19, 2017, www.marketing-interactive.com/embracing-an-era-of-just-in-time-research/.
11. Amanda Lacey, "The New Age of Market Research Is Here," *CMO Magazine*, May 4, 2016, www.theceomagazine.com/business/the-new-age-of-market-research-is-here/.
12. Global Data, "Top Trends in Prepared Foods 2017: Exploring Trends in Meat, Fish, Seafood; Pasta, Noodle and Rice; Prepared Meals; Savory Deli Food; Soup; and Meat Substitutes," June 2017, www.reportbuyer.com/product/4959853/top-trends-inprepared-foods-2017-exploring-

trends-in-meat-fish-and-seafood-pasta-noodles-and-rice-prepared-meals-savory-deli-food-soup-and-meat-substitutes.html.

13. For more on research firms that supply marketing information, see Michael Brereton and Diane Bowers, "The 2017 AMA Gold Global Top 25 Market Research Companies," *Marketing News*, October 1, 2017, www.ama.org/publications/MarketingNews/Pages/2017-ama-gold-global-report.aspx. Other information from www.nielsen.com/us/en/solutions/measurement/retail-measurement.html and www.kantarfutures.com/products/subscriptions/, accessed September 2018.
14. See www.iriworldwide.com, accessed September 2018.
15. Kai Ryssdal and Tommy Andres, "Domino's CEO Patrick Doyle: Tech with a Side of Pizza," *Marketplace*, September 24, 2015, www.marketplace.org/2015/09/24/business/corner-office/dominos-ceo-patrick-doyle-tech-side-pizza.
16. See Geoff Colvin, "How Intuit Reinvents Itself," *Fortune*, November 12, 2017, pp. 76–82.
17. See Birkner, "C'est La Vie"; and "Landor Families," http://landor.com/#!/talk/articles-publications/articles/landor-families/, accessed September 2018.
18. Ron Kohavi and Stefan Thomke, "The Surprising Power of Experiments," *Harvard Business Review*, September-October 2017, pp. 74–82.
19. See Scott Keeter and others, "What Low Response Rates Mean for Telephone Surveys," Pew Research Center, May 15, 2017, www.pewresearch.org/2017/05/15/what-low-response-rates-mean-for-telephone-surveys/; and Jackie Lorch, "There Is Plenty of Life Left in Telephone Research Methodology," *Research Now*, September 24, 2017, www.surveysampling.com/blog/plenty-life-left-telephone-research-methodology/.
20. See Rebecca Greenfield, "How the Deepest, Darkest Secrets of Moms Shape the Products in Aisle 6," *Fast Company*, December 19, 2014, www.fastcompany.com/3039798/most-creative-people/how-the-deepest-darkest-secrets-of-moms-shape-the-products-in-aisle-6?utm_source; Chrisine Michel Carter, "Meet the Company Decoding How to Market to Millennial Moms," Forbes, May 1, 2017, www.forbes.com/sites/christinecarter/2017/05/01/marketing-to-millennial-moms-where-there-is-pain-there-is-profit/#2fc67df35201; and www.momcomplex.com, accessed September 2018.
21. See "Internet World Stats," www.internetworldstats.com/stats14.htm#north, accessed September 2018.
22. For more information, see www.focusvision.com/products/intervu/, accessed September 2018.
23. See Giselle Tsirulnik, "ESPN Is Mobile Publisher of the Year," *Mobile Marketing*, www.mobilemarketer.com/ex/mobilemarketer/cms/news/media/7846.html, accessed September 2018; and Vision Critical, "ESPN: How the Sports Media Company Delivers What Fans Want—and Saves Resources," www.visioncritical.com/customer-stories/espn/, accessed September 2017.
24. For more discussion, see "S.2404 (114th): Do Not Track Online Act of 2015," January 17, 2018, www.govtrack.us/congress/bills/114/s2404; and "Do Not Track Legislation," http://en.wikipedia.org/wiki/Do_Not_Track_legislation, accessed September 2018.
25. "Internet of Things (IoT) Connected Devices Base Worldwide from 2015 to 2025 (in Billions)," *Statista*, www.statista.com/statistics/471264/iot-number-of-connected-devices-worldwide/, accessed September 2018.
26. Michael E. Smith, "The Brains behind Better Ads: Optimizing the Cute and Cuddly," June 18, 2014, www.nielsen.com/us/en/insights/news/2014/the-brains-behind-better-ads-optimizing-the-cute-and-cuddly.html; "The Shelter Pet Project," 2015 ARF Awards, www.youtube.com/watch?v=PtRxJsGWMFo; and www.theshelterpetproject.org, accessed September 2018.
27. See Jennifer Alsever, "Technology Is the Best Policy," *Fortune*, November 18, 2013; "MetLife Wall—Customer Focus by Leveraging Big Data," KPMG, www.the-digital-insurer.com/dia/metlife-wall-customer-focus-by-leveraging-big-data/, accessed September 2018; and "Rethinking the Customer Experience at MetLife," MongoDB, www.mongodb.com/customers/metlife, accessed September 2018.
28. Andrew Nusca, "Despite High Tech, the Future of Marketing Is Exactly the Same: Focus on Customers," *Fortune*, July 15, 2014, http://fortune.com/2014/07/15/big-data-future-marketing-customer-focus.
29. See Kate Jones, "What Can Associations Learn from Netflix about Member Analytics?" *Informz*, November 9, 2016, www.informz.com/blog/associations/associations-learn-member-analytics/; "How Netflix Uses Bid Data to Keep You Entertained," *Cumul.io*, May 12, 2017, https://blog.cumul.io/2017/12/05/how-netflix-uses-big-data/; Dana Feldman, "Netflix Is on Track to Exceed $11B in Revenue This Year," *Forbes*, October 16, 2017, www.forbes.com/sites/danafeldman/2017/10/16/netflix-is-on-track-to-exceed-11b-in-revenue-this-year/#6f4fd5c865dd; and www.netflix.com, accessed September 2018.
30. "Google CEO: AI Is a Bigger Deal Than Fire or Electricity," *Fast Company*, January 19, 2018, www.fastcompany.com/40519204/google-sundar-pichai-ai-is-a-bigger-deal-than-fire-or-electricity.
31. For examples, Peter Horst and Robert Duboff, "Don't Let Big Data Bury Your Brand," *Harvard Business Review*, November 2015, pp. 79–86; and Roger L. Martin and Tony Golsby-Smith, "Management Is Much More Than a Science," *Harvard Business Review*, September–October, 2017, pp. 129–135.
32. "Customer Loyalty Blossoms with Analytics," www.sas.com/en_us/customers/1-800-flowers.html, accessed September 2018.
33. See Daryl Travis, "The Best Omni-Channel Brands Look More Like a Cause Than a Business," *The Hub*, August 2014, www.hubmagazine.com/the-hub-magazine/zappos-omnivalues-082014/; and https://zuul.zappos.com/zuul, accessed September 2018.
34. See Elana Lyn Gross, "How the Founder of GoldieBlox Is Creating the Next Generation of Women in STEM," *Forbes*, October 11, 2017, www.forbes.com/sites/elanagross/2017/10/11/how-the-founder-of-goldieblox-is-creating-the-next-generation-of-women-in-stem/#3a9851e4e132; Mara Leighton, "This Toy Company for Girls Is Out to Disrupt the 'Pink Aisle' and Create More Female Engineers," *Insider*, June 13, 2017, www.thisisinsider.com/goldieblox-stem-toys-for-girls-disrupt-pink-aisle-2017-6; Gigi DeVault, "Young Women Entrepreneurs Conduct Market Research," *The Balance*, October 14, 2017, www.thebalance.com/young-women-entrepreneurs-conduct-market-research-2296719; and www.goldieblox.com, accessed September 2018.
35. For some good advice on conducting market research in a small business, search "conducting market research" at www.sba.gov or see "Researching Your Market," *Entrepreneur*, www.entrepreneur.com/article/43024-1, accessed September 2018.
36. See "The 2017 AMA Gold Global Top 25 Report," *Marketing News*, October 2017, pp. 36+; and www.nielsen.com/us/en/about-us.html and www.nielsen.com/us/en/about-us.html, accessed September 2018.
37. See Zach Brooke, "When Surveys Get Lost in Translation," *Marketing News*, October 2017, pp. 12–13.
38. Subhash C. Jain, *International Marketing Management*, 3rd ed. (Boston: PWS-Kent, 1990), p. 338. For more discussion on international marketing research issues and solutions, see Warren J. Keegan and Mark C. Green, *Global Marketing*, 8th ed. (Upper Saddle River, NJ: Pearson, 2015), pp. 170–201.
39. For more on problems and solutions in international marketing research, see Caitlin Sanford, "Tips for Market Research in Emerging Markets," *Medium*, August 1, 2017, https://medium.com/facebook-research/tips-for-market-research-in-emerging-markets-695bed660517.
40. See Charles Duhigg, "Psst, You in Aisle 5," *New York Times*, February 19, 2012, p. MM30; Kashmir Hill, "How Target Figured Out a Teen Girl Was Pregnant before Her Father Did," *Forbes*, February 16, 2012, www.forbes.com/sites/-kashmirhill/2012/02/16/-how-target-figured-out-a-teen-girl-was-pregnant-before-her-father-did/; "7 Big Data Blunders You're Thankful Your Company Didn't Make," Umbel, October 22, 2014, www.umbel.com/blog/big-data/7-big-data-blunders/?utm_content=buffer6a719&utm_medium=social&utm_source=twitter.com&utm_campaign=buffer; and Leslie K. John, Tami Kim, and Kate Barasz, "Ads That Don't Overstep," *Harvard Business Review*, January–February 2018, pp. 62–69.
41. See Kate Kaye, "The $24 Billion Data Business That Telcos Don't Want to Talk About," *Advertising Age*, October 26, 2015, pp. 12–14; and "Mobile Data Analysis with SAP Consumer Insight 365," https://experience.sap.com/designservices/work/mobile-data-analysis-with-sap-consumer-insight-365, accessed September 2018.
42. See "Respondent Bill of Rights," www.marketingresearch.org/issues-policies/best-practice/respondent-bill-rights, accessed September 2018.
43. See www.insightsassociation.org/issues-policies/casro-code-standards-and-ethics, accessed September 2018.

Chapter 5

1. See Frank Witsil, "Shinola Touts 'Roll Up Our Sleeves' Ad Campaign," *Detroit Free Press*, March 21, 2017, www.freep.com/story/money/business/michigan/2017/03/21/shinola-advertising-roll-up-sleeves/99447088/; Dennis Green, "The Real Story Behind the Watch Obama Just Gave to David Cameron," *Business Insider*, May 17, 2016, www.businessinsider.com/the-real-story-behind-shinola-detroit-2016-5; Robert Klara, "How Shinola

Went from Shoe Polish to the Coolest Brand in America," *Adweek*, June 22, 2015, pp. 23–25; Helen Heller, "The Luxury-Goods Company Shinola Is Capitalizing on Detroit," *Washington Post,* November 17, 2014, www.washingtonpost.com/lifestyle/style/the-luxury-goods-company-shinola-is-capitalizing-on-detroit/2014/11/17/638f88a4-6a8f-11e4-b053-65cea7903f2e_story.html; Ann-Christine Diaz, "Shinola Puts a Lot of 'Work' into Its New Campaign," *Advertising Age,* March 20, 2017, http://creativity-online.com/work/shinola-roll-up-our-sleeves/51303; and www.shinola.com/our-story and www.shinola.com/about-shinola, accessed September 2018.

2. Consumer expenditure figures from "United States Consumer Spending Forecast," *Trading Economics,* https://tradingeconomics.com/united-states/consumer-spending/forecast, accessed September 2018. Population figures from the World POPClock, U.S. Census Bureau, www.census.gov/popclock, accessed September 2018. This website provides continuously updated projections of U.S. and world populations.
3. "Advertising Age Hispanic Fact Pack," August 21, 2017, pp. 6, 22; Antonio Flores, "How the U.S. Hispanic Population Is Changing," Pew Research, September 18, 2017, www.pewresearch.org/fact-tank/2017/09/18/how-the-u-s-hispanic-population-is-changing/; and "Buying Power of Hispanic Consumers in the United States," *Statista,* www.statista.com/statistics/251438/hispanics-buying-power-in-the-us/, accessed September 2018
4. Ann-Christine Diaz, "Toyota's 'Mas Que un Auto' Is More Than Your Average Campaign," *Advertising Age*, April 7, 2015, http://adage.com/print/297904/; Laurel Wentz, "U.S. Hispanic Awards Honor Toyota, Volvo, California Milk," *Advertising Age*, April 29, 2015, http://adage.com/print/298296/; "Toyota Unveils the Book of Names in Honor of 'Mas Que Un Auto' Loyalty Campaign," February 3, 2017, www.hispanicprblog.com/toyota-unveils-the-book-of-names-in-honor-of-mas-que-un-auto-loyalty-campaign/; and www.masqueunauto.com, accessed September 2018.
5. See Ellen McGirt, "A New Report Shows Black Women's Influence at Work and on the Web," *Fortune,* http://fortune.com/2017/09/21/consumer-spending-black-women-nielsen/; Bill Chappell, "Census Finds a More Diverse America, as Whites Lag Growth," *NPR,* June 22, 2017, www.npr.org/sections/thetwo-way/2017/06/22/533926978/census-finds-a-more-diverse-america-as-whites-lag-growth; and U.S. Census Bureau, "U.S. Population Projections," www.census.gov/topics/population.html/, accessed September 2018.
6. "Discovering Nature (African-American Market)," www.adcouncil.org/Our-Campaigns/Family-Community/Discovering-Nature-African-American-Market, accessed September 2018; "Discover the Forest: Connected," www.multivu.com/players/English/8171051-new-ad-council-u-s-forest-services-discover-the-forest-psa/, accessed September 2018; and www.discovertheforest.org, accessed September 2018.
7. See "Nielsen: Asian-American Buying Power Increased by More than $50 Billion in One Year—Expected to Hit $1 Trillion by 2018," Nielsen, June 11, 2015; and Gustavo Lopez, Neil G. Ruiz, and Eileen Patten, "Key Facts About Asian Americans, a Diverse and Growing Population," Pew Research, September 8, 2017, www.pewresearch.org/fact-tank/2017/09/08/key-facts-about-asian-americans/.
8. See Hannah Madans, "Retailers Step Up Luxury Goods during Lunar New Year as Asians Celebrate a Season of Shopping," *McClatchy-Tribune Business News*, February 24, 2015; Mitch Moxley, "Global Luxury Retailers Gear Up for Chinese New Year Shoppers," *Jing Daily,* January 29, 2014, https://-jingdaily.com/global-luxury-retailers-gear-up-for-chinese-new-year-shoppers/#.Vmc1bnarRhF; and Tori Telfer, "Bloomingdale's Will Celebrate the Chinese New Year Again This Year," *Chicago Magazine,* www.chicagomag.com/style-shopping/January2015/Bloomingdales-Will-Celebrate-Chinese-New-Years-Again-This-Year/.
9. See Yuriy Boykiv, "What Leaders Need to Know About the 'Total Market' Approach to Diverse Audiences," *Inc.,* November 10, 2014, www.inc.com/yuriy-boykiv/what-leaders-need-to-know-about-the-total-market-approach-to-diverse-audiences.html; Laurel Wentz, "Welcome to the Multicultural Mainstream," *Advertising Age,* April 6, 2015, pp. 18+.
10. See ANA, "Totally Sold on Total Marketing?" 2017 ANA Multicultural Thought Leadership Supplement, www.portada-online.com/wp-content/uploads/2017/guides/2017-ANA-MULTICULTURAL/docs/17-POR-003_Issue_FINAL_singles.pdf; Sapna Maheshwari, "Different Ads, Different Ethnicities, Same Car," *New York Times,* October 12, 2017, www.nytimes.com/interactive/2017/10/12/business/media/toyota-camry-ads-different-ethnicities.html; and "All-New Toyota Camry Ignites the Senses," September 1, 2017, http://toyotanews.pressroom.toyota.com/releases/all+new+toyota+camry+ignites+senses.htm.
11. Nicole Laporte, "How CoverGirl Built an Ad Campaign Around Multicultural Badassness," *Fast Company,* October 30, 2017, www.fastcompany.com/40485716/how-covergirl-built-an-ad-campaign-around-multicultural-badassness; Kelsey Castanon, "CoverGirl Is Getting a Makeover—& These Women Are Leading the Charge," *Refinery29,* October 10, 2017, www.refinery29.com/2017/10/175599/covergirl-new-slogan-no-easy-breezy-beautiful; and Elana Gross, "CoverGirl Just Dropped Its 'Easy, Breezy, Beautiful, CoverGirl' Slogan," *Allure,* October 10, 2017, www.allure.com/story/covergirl-drops-easy-breezy-beautiful-covergirl-slogan.
12. Kristina Monllos, "Going All-In on Influencers," *Adweek,* September 18, 2017, p. 8.
13. Chris Slocumb, "Women Outspend Men 3 to 2 on Technology Purchases," *ClarityQuest*, January 3, 2013, www.clarityqst.com/women-outspend-men-3-to-2-on-technology-purchases/; "More Men Are Grocery Shopping, but They Do So Grudgingly, Reports NPD," November 12, 2014, www.npd.com/wps/portal/npd/us/news/press-releases/more-men-are-grocery-shopping-but-they-do-so-grudgingly/; Sarwant Singh, "Women in Cars: Overtaking Men on the Fast Lane," *Forbes,* May 23, 2014, www.forbes.com/sites/sarwantsingh/2014/05/23/women-in-cars-overtaking-men-on-the-fast-lane/; and "Women Make Up 85% of All Consumer Purchases," *BloombergBusiness,* June 22, 2015, www.bloomberg.com/news/videos/b/9e28517f-8de1-4e59-bcda-ce536aa50bd6.
14. See "Cheerios Leverages the Power of 'Dadvertising," *Marketing News,* February 2015, pp. 4–5; and Mary Bowerman, "Dad Plays with Barbie in Sweet Commercial Aired During the Playoffs," *USA Today,* January 23, 2017, www.usatoday.com/story/money/nation-now/2017/01/23/dads-play-barbie-sweet-commercial-aired-during-nfl-playoffs/96948886/.
15. See "Kids Spending and Influencing Power: $1.2 Trillion Says Leading Ad Firm," Center for Digital Democracy, November 1, 2012, www.democraticmedia.org/kids-spending-and-influencing-power-12-trillion-says-leading-ad-firm; and "How Much Influence Do Teens Wield over Their Parents' Purchase Decisions?" *Marketing Charts,* June 23, 2015, www.marketingcharts.com/traditional/-how-much-influence-do-teens-wield-over-their-parents-purchase-decisions-56068/.
16. Tanyua Gazdik, "Honda Odyssey Helps 'Keep the Peace,'" *Marketing Daily,* June 13, 2017, www.mediapost.com/publications/article/302750/honda-odyssey-helps-keep-the-peace.html.
17. See www.redcap.com and www.redkapautomotive.com/Home/Our-Story, accessed September 2018.
18. For more on the Nielsen PRIZM, visit https://segmentationsolutions.nielsen.com/mybestsegments/Default.jsp?ID=0&menuOption=home&pageName=Home, accessed September 2018.
19. Jennifer Kaplan and Matthew Boyle, "Amazon Cuts Whole Foods Prices as Much as 43% on First Day, *Bloomberg Businessweek,* August 28, 2017, www.bloomberg.com/news/articles/2017-08-28/amazon-cuts-prices-at-whole-foods-as-much-as-50-on-first-day; and Jordan Valinsky, *CNN Money,* "Amazon Is Cutting Prices at Whole Foods Again," November 15, 2017, http://money.cnn.com/2017/11/15/news/companies/amazon-whole-foods-price-cuts/index.html.
20. See Jennifer Aaker, "Dimensions of Measuring Brand Personality," *Journal of Marketing Research*, August 1997, pp. 347–356; and Philip Kotler and Kevin Lane Keller, *Marketing Management*, 15th ed. (Upper Saddle River, New Jersey: Pearson Publishing, 2016), p. 163.
21. Deborah Malone, *The Reinvention of Marketing* (New York: The Internationalist Press, 2014), Kindle location 142; and "Which Mini Cooper Persona Are You?" June 9, 2016, www.schompmini.com/mini-cooper-persona/.
22. See Abraham H. Maslow, "A Theory of Human Motivation," *Psychological Review, 50* (1943), pp. 370–396. Also see Maslow, *Motivation and Personality*, 3rd ed. (New York: HarperCollins Publishers, 1987); Michael R. Solomon, *Consumer Behavior,* 12th ed. (Hoboken, NJ: Pearson Publishing, 2017), pp. 156–157.
23. See "The Myth of 5,000 Ads," http://cbi.hhcc.com/writing/the-myth-of-5000-ads/, accessed September 2016; and Joshua Saxon, "Why Your Customers' Attention Is the Scarcest Resource in 2017," www.ama.org/partners/content/Pages/why-customers-attention-scarcest-resources-2017.aspx, accessed November 2017.
24. See Ian Zimmerman, "Subliminal Ads, Unconscious Influence, and Consumption," *Psychology Today,* June 2014, www.psychologytoday.com/blog/sold/201406/subliminal-ads-unconscious-influence-and-consumption and "Does Subliminal Advertising Actually Work?" *BBC,* January 20, 2015, www.bbc.com/news/magazine-30878843.
25. See Ronald Holden, "Where's Da Beef? Safeway to Add Meatless 'Beyond Meat' Burger," *Forbes,* May 30, 2017, www.forbes.com/sites/ronaldholden/2017/05/30/wheres-da-beef-safeway-to-add-meatless-beyond-meat-burger/#3dea30d8746e; Larissa Zimmeroff, "Fabulous

Fakes," *Rachael Ray Every Day*, June 2017, http://beyondmeat.com/media/pdfs/Every_Day_with_Rachael_Ray_June%202017.pdf; Leanna Garfield, "Leonardo DiCaprio Just Invested in the Bill Gates-Backed Veggie Burger That 'Bleeds' Like Beef—Here's How It Tastes," *Business Insider*, October 17, 2017, www.businessinsider.com/review-leonardo-dicaprio-beyond-meat-veggie-plant-burger-2017-10.

26. See www.yelp.com and www.yelp.com/about, accessed September 2018.
27. The following discussion draws from the work of Everett M. Rogers. See his *Diffusion of Innovations*, 5th ed. (New York: Free Press, 2003).
28. Based on Rogers, *Diffusion of Innovation*, p. 281. For more discussion, see http://en.wikipedia.org/wiki/Everett_Rogers, accessed September 2018.
29. See Jess Shankleman, "Electric Car Sales Are Surging, IEA Reports," *Bloomberg Businessweek*, June 7, 2017, www.bloomberg.com/news/articles/2017-06-07/electric-car-market-goes-zero-to-2-million-in-five-years; "Electric Car Use by Country," *Wikipedia*, http://en.wikipedia.org/wiki/Electric_car_use_by_country, accessed September 2018; and "Plug-In Vehicle Tracker: What's Coming, When," www.pluginamerica.org/vehicles, accessed September 2018.
30. See Scott Lanza, "Shine United, Gore-Tex ads," January 24, 2017, www.scottlanza.com/posts/shine-united-gore-tex-ads/; and www.gore-tex.com, accessed September 2018.
31. Based on information from www.cargill.com, www.cargill.com/food-beverage/cocoa-and-chocolate, and www.cargillcocoachocolate.com/innovation/product-development-support/index.htm, accessed September 2018.
32. This classic categorization was first introduced in Patrick J. Robinson, Charles W. Faris, and Yoram Wind, *Industrial Buying Behavior and Creative Marketing* (Boston: Allyn & Bacon, 1967). Also see Philip Kotler and Kevin Lane Keller, *Marketing Management* (Hoboken, NJ: Pearson Publishing, 2016), pp. 192–193.
33. Based on information from "Six Flags Entertainment Corporation: Improving Business Efficiency with Enterprise Asset Management," July 12, 2012, www-01.ibm.com/software/success/cssdb.nsf/CS/LWIS-8W5Q84?OpenDocument&Site=default&cty=en_us; www-01.ibm.com/software/tivoli/products/maximo-asset-mgmt/, accessed September 2016; and "Maximize Your Investment in IBM Maximo," www.ibm.com/internet-of-things/business-solutions/asset-management/maximo-case-studies, accessed September 2018.
34. See "USG Corporation: Structural Panels—Octopus," *Ads of the World*, Juley 18, 2017, www.adsoftheworld.om/media/print/usg_corporation_structural_panels_octopus; and USG Structural Solutions, "A New Level of Performance," http://info.usg.com/structuralpanels.html, accessed September 2018.
35. Robinson, Faris, and Wind, *Industrial Buying Behavior*, p. 14. Also see Kotler and Keller, *Marketing Management*, pp. 198–204.
36. For more ads in this series, see www.accenture.com/id-en/advertising-index, accessed September 2018.
37. See David Moth, "Q&A: How Maersk Line Created a Brilliant B2B Social Media Strategy," September 9, 2015, https://econsultancy.com/blog/66901-q-a-how-maersk-line-created-a-brilliant-b2b-social-media-strategy; Laurence Hebberd, "How Maersk Line Uses Social Media," October 19, 2015, http://linkhumans.com/case-study/maersk-line; and www.maerskline.com/ar-sa/social/our-social-media, accessed September 2018.

Chapter 6

1. Quotes and other information from Danielle Wiener-Bronner, "Dunkin' Donuts Wants to Double the Number of Stores," *CNN Money*, January 8, 2018, http://money.cnn.com/2018/01/09/news/companies/dunkin-brands-double-us-stores/index.html; Nik DeCosta-Klipa, "Everything You Need to Know about the Changes Happening at Dunkin' Donuts," *The Boston Globe*, November 16, 2017, www.boston.com/news/restaurants/2017/11/16/everything-you-need-to-know-about-the-changes-happening-at-dunkin-donuts; Janet Adamy, "Battle Brewing: Dunkin' Donuts Tries to Go Upscale, but Not Too Far," *Wall Street Journal*, April 8, 2006, p. A1; Christine Champagne and Teressa Iezzi, "Dunkin' Donuts and Starbucks: A Tale of Two Coffee Marketing Giants," *Fast Company*, August 21, 2014, www.fastcocreate.com/3034572; "Brand Keys Names Dunkin' Donuts #1 in Coffee Customer Loyalty for 11th Consecutive Year," Dunkin' Donuts Newsroom, January 26, 2017, https://news.dunkindonuts.com/news/brand-keys-names-dunkin-donuts; "Dunkin' Drops the Donuts as It Tests New Store Brand," *CBS News*, January 15, 2018, www.cbsnews.com/news/dunkin-drops-the-donuts-as-it-tests-new-store-brand/; Brett Molina, "Dunkin' Officially Drops Donuts from its Name," *USA Today*, September 25, 2018, www.usatoday.com/story/money/nation-now/2018/09/25/dunkin-donuts-drops-donuts-brand-name/1422584002/; and www.dunkindonuts.com and www.dunkinbrands.com, accessed September 2018.
2. Corinne Ruff, "How Target Is Using Small-Format Stores to Score with Younger Shoppers," *Retail Dive*, August 24, 2017, www.retaildive.com/news/how-target-is-using-small-format-stores-to-score-with-younger-shoppers/503362/; and Tonya Garcia, "Target's Small-Format Stores Are Turning into a Big Winner for the Retailer," August 19, 2017, www.marketwatch.com/story/targets-small-format-stores-are-turning-into-a-big-win-for-the-retailer-2017-08-16.
3. Seed https://crest.com/en-us/products/kids and https://crest.com/en-us/products/crest-3d-white-brilliance-toothpaste, accessed September 2018.
4. See www.dove.com/us/en/men-care.html, accessed September 2018.
5. Michael McCarthy, "Ad of the Day: Dick's Sporting Goods Goes the Extra Mile in Its First Campaign for Women," April 30, 2015, www.adweek.com/print/164418; Alana Vagianos, "'Who Will You Be?' Campaign Celebrates the Raw Strength of Women's Bodies," *Huffington Post*, May 8, 2015, www.huffingtonpost.com/2015/05/08/who-will-you-be-campaign-dicks-sporting-goods_n_7242320.html; and www.youtube.com/watch?v=Mf0_G1FS0l4, accessed September 2018.
6. See Johnny Jet, "American Express Centurion Black Card Review," *Forbes*, July 28, 2017, www.forbes.com/sites/johnnyjet/2017/07/28/american-express-centurion-black-card-review/#2a3e997d7055; "What Super Rich People Do to Show Their Status in Style?" *LinkedIn*, November 4, 2017, www.linkedin.com/pulse/what-super-rich-people-do-show-status-style-property-find; and Bryan Kelly, "Travel Secrets of the World's Most Exclusive Travel Card," *Travel+Leisure*, www.travelandleisure.com/travel-tips/points-miles/american-express-black-card, accessed September 2018.
7. Jessica Wohl, "Panera Bread Cleans Up Its Act," *Advertising Age*, January 6, 2017, http://adage.com/article/307387/; Andrew McMains, "Ad of the Day: Panera Gets into Lifestyle Branding with Manifesto about Healthy Living," *Adweek*, June 15, 2015, and www.panerabread.com/en-us/our-beliefs/food-as-it-should-be-nopt.html, accessed September 2018.
8. "Loews, Elicit, Spotify Win People-Based Marketing Awards," *Media Daily News*, September 25, 2017, www.mediapost.com/publications/article/307818/loews-elicit-spotify-win-people-based-marketing.html.
9. "Will the Fall Season Add (Pumpkin) Spice to Starbucks' Earnings" *Seeking Alpha*, September 14, 2017, https://seekingalpha.com/article/4106931-will-fall-season-add-pumpkin-spice-starbucks-earnings?page=2.
10. Based on information from www.fitbit.com, accessed September 2018.
11. See wwww.pampers.com/Diapers/Swaddlers, accessed September 2018.
12. See Jeremy Markovich, "The Bo-lievers," *Our State*, April 2017, pp. 114–122; and www.annualreports.com/Company/bojangles-inc and www.bojangles.com, accessed September 2018.
13. See www.patagonia.com/us/ambassadors, accessed September 2018.
14. See https://isapps.acxiom.com/personicx/personicx.aspx and www.acxiom.com/what-we-do/consumer-segmentation-personicx/, accessed September 2018.
15. See http://c.ymcdn.com/sites/dema.site-ym.com/resource/resmgr/Member_Resources/Lifestage_Clustering.pdf and https://isapps.acxiom.com/personicx/personicx.aspx, accessed September 2018.
16. See www.starbucks.com/business and https://solutions.starbucks.com, accessed September 2018.
17. See www.wayup.com/i-j-Steelcase-168484129000263/, accessed September 2018.
18. Ilyse Liffreing, "How Coca-Cola Targeted Teens during the 2016 Olympic Games," *Campaign*, August 19, 2016, www.campaignlive.com/article/coca-cola-targeted-teens-during-2016-olympic-games/1406187.
19. See Michael Porter, *Competitive Advantage* (New York: Free Press, 1985), pp. 4–8, 234–236. For a more recent discussion, see Philip Kotler and Kevin Lane Keller, *Marketing Management*, 15th ed. (Hoboken, NJ: Pearson, 2016), pp. 263–264.
20. Michael McCoy, "P&G and Henkel Go Head to Head in the Laundry Aisle," *Chemical and Engineering News*, January 23, 2017, https://cen.acs.org/articles/95/i4/PG-Henkel-head-head-laundry.html?h=1384844903; and A.G. Lafley and Roger L. Martin, "Customer Loyalty Is Overrated," *Harvard Business Review*, January-February 2017, https://hbr.org/2017/01/customer-loyalty-is-overrated.
21. See "Socks FW18/19," *Broad Sport Source*, http://www.boardsportsource.com/trend-report/socks-fw18-19/, accessed September 2018; Evie Nagy, "Putting Its Best Foot Forward," *Fast Company*, October 2015, pp. 46–48; Adam Tschorn, "How Stance Socks Got to Be on Rihanna's and NBA Players Feet," *Los Angeles Times*, October 19, 2015, www.latimes.com/fashion/la-ig-stance-20151018-story.html; and www.stance.com and www.stance.com/about/, accessed September 2018.
22. See Journey Staff, "10 Years Strong. Coca-Cola's Venturing & Emerging Brands Takes on New Territory," February 23, 2017, www.coca-colacompany.com/stories/10-years-strong-coca-colas-venturing-emerging-

brands-takes-on-new-territory; and www.vebatcoke.com/, accessed September 2018.

23. See https://renaissance-hotels.marriott.com/, http://renaissance-hotels.marriott.com/navigators, and http://www.marriott.com/renaissance-hotels/mobile-apps.mi, accessed September 2018.
24. Alanis King, "This Oddball Rolls-Royce Could Be the Most Expensive Ever," *Jalopnik*, May 27, 2017, https://jalopnik.com/this-oddball-rolls-royce-could-be-the-new-most-expensive-1795605881, Hannah Elliot, "With Bespoke Details, You Can Make Your Aston Martin or Rolls-Royce as Ugly as You Want," *Bloomberg Business*, February 18, 2015, www.bloomberg.com/news/articles/2015-02-18/with-bespoke-details-you-can-make-your-aston-martin-or-rolls-royce-as-ugly-as-you-want; Harvey Briggs, "For Rolls-Royce the Future Is Bespoke," *Purist*, http://pursuitist.com/for-rolls-royce-the-future-is-bespoke/, accessed September 2018; and www.rolls-roycemotorcars.com/en-US/bespoke.html, accessed September 2018.
25. See Zlati Meyer, "How McDonald's Happy Meals Are Changing," *USA Today*, September 18, 2017, www.usatoday.com/story/money/2017/09/17/mcdonalds-switch-organic-less-sugary-apple-juice-happy-meals/675181001/.
26. See "2016 Internet Crime Report," May 2017, https://pdf.ic3.gov/2016_IC3Report.pdf.
27. SUV sales data furnished by www.WardsAuto.com, accessed September 2018. Price data from www.edmunds.com, accessed September 2018.
28. See "Zappos Family Core Values," http://about.zappos.com/our-unique-culture/zappos-core-values; and http://about.zappos.com/, accessed September 2018.
29. David Rohde, "The Anti-Walmart: The Secret Sauce of Wegans Is People," *The Atlantic*, March 23, 2012, www.theatlantic.com/business/archive/2012/03/the-anti-walmart-the-secret-sauce-of-wegmans-is-people/254994/; and www.wegmans.com and https://jobs.wegmans.com/diversity, accessed September 2018.
30. See www.toyota.com/landcruiser/, accessed September 2018.
31. See www.heartsonfire.com/Learn-About-Our-Diamonds.aspx, accessed September 2018.
32. See Bobby J. Calder and Steven J. Reagan, "Brand Design," in Dawn Iacobucci, ed., *Kellogg on Marketing* (New York: John Wiley & Sons, 2001), p. 61. For more discussion, see Philip Kotler and Kevin Lane Keller, *Marketing Management*, 15th ed. (Hoboken, NJ: Pearson, 2016), Chapter 10.

Chapter 7

1. See Tobias Matthews, "How Nike Uses Instagram and Is Winning," *Fourthsource*, January 13, 2018, www.fourthsource.com/instagram/nike-uses-instagram-marketing-20141; "L2 Digital IQ Index," March 3, 2017, www.l2inc.com/research/activewear-2017#brands; Tracey Greenstein, "Study: Nike Ranked Number One in Social Media Traffic," *WWD*, September 1, 2017, http://wwd.com/business-news/retail/nike-ranked-number-one-in-social-media-traffic-10969406/; L. Roberts, "Adidas Has Nearly Doubled Its Sneaker Market Share—at Nike's Expense," *Yahoo! Finance*, June 23, 2017, https://finance.yahoo.com/news/adidas-nearly-doubled-us-sneaker-market-share-nikes-expense-153106743.html; Angela Natividad, "The Story Behind Nike's Ambitious Effort to Run a Marathon in Less Than 2 Hours," *Adweek*, May 8, 2017, www.adweek.com/brand-marketing/the-story-behind-nikes-ambitious-effort-to-run-a-marathon-in-less-than-2-hours/; Nikki Ogunnaike, "Kendrick Lamar's Nike Cortez Sneaker Is How We're All Feeling," *Elle*, January 9, 2018, www.elle.com/fashion/a14913133/kendrick-lamars-nike-cortez-sneaker-is-how-were-all-feeling/; and information from www.adidas.com and www.nike.com, accessed September 2018.
2. See "'Today at Apple' Bringing New Experiences to Every Apple Store," Apple press release, April 25, 2017, www.apple.com/newsroom/2017/04/today-at-apple-bringing-new-experiences-to-every-apple-store/; "How Online Retailers Are Creating Immersive Brand Experiences in the Real World," *Advertising Age*, March 25, 2015, www.adage.com/print/297750; and www.apple.com/retail/ and www.apple.com/retail/learn/, accessed September 2018.
3. See Rich Duprey, "12 Motorcycle Statistics that Will Floor You," *The Motley Fool*," March 5, 2017, Susanna Hamner, "Harley, You're Not Getting Any Younger," *New York Times*, March 22, 2009, p. BU1; www.fool.com/investing/2017/03/05/7-motorcycle-statistics-thatll-floor-you.aspx; Tim Clark, "Harley-Davidson Goes Whole Hog with Customer Insight," *Forbes*, www.forbes.com/sites/sap/2011/06/29/harley-davidson-goes-whole-hog-with-customer-insight/#3803c03250eb; and various pages at www.harley-davidson.com, accessed September 2018.
4. See www.ge.com and www.ge.com/news/advertising, accessed June 2018.
5. Darren Griffin, "Nike Spent Almost $10 Billion on Endorsements in 2016," *NiceKicks.com*, October 13, 2016, www.nicekicks.com/nike-spent-almost-10-billion-endorsements-2016/.
6. See https://visitdetroit.com and www.tourism.australia.com/en/about/our-campaigns/theres-nothing-like-australia/campaign-assets/print-ads.html, accessed September 2018.
7. See Lindsey Stein, "Microsoft's New 'Makes What's Next' Ad Shows Girls How to Pursue STEM Careers," *Advertising Age*, March 7, 2017, http://adage.com/article/cmo-strategy/microsoft-s-make-ad-shows-pursue-stem/308189/; and www.microsoft.com/en-us/philanthropies/make-whats-next, accessed September 2018.
8. For more on social marketing, see Nancy Lee and Philip Kotler, *Social Marketing: Changing Behaviors for Good*, 5th ed. (Thousand Oaks, CA: SAGE Publications, 2015); and www.adcouncil.org and www.i-socialmarketing.org, accessed September 2018.
9. Quotes and definitions from Philip Kotler, *Marketing Insights from A to Z* (Hoboken, NJ: Wiley, 2003), p. 148; and www.asq.org/glossary/q.html, accessed September 2018.
10. See "Award Recipient: Americas Best Value Inn," J.D. Power, www.jdpower.com/ratings/study/North-America-Hotel-Guest-Satisfaction-Study/2572ENG/Economy/2672, accessed September 2018; and www.americasbestvalueinn.com, accessed September 2018.
11. See Nathaniel Wice, "Sonos: The Best Wireless Speakers," *Barrons*, January 3, 2015, http://online.barrons.com/articles/sonos-the-best-wireless-speakers-1420260626; Aaron Tilley, "Connected Speaker Market Heats Up with Super High-End Devialet Phantom," *Forbes*, June 8, 2015, www.forbes.com/sites/aarontilley/2015/06/18/super-high-end-speaker-devialet-phantom-looks-to/; and www.sonos.com, accessed September 2018.
12. See Gene Weingarten, "Pearls before Breakfast," *Washington Post*, April 8, 2007, www.washingtonpost.com/wp-dyn/content/-article/2007/04/04/AR2007040401721.html; Jessica Contrera, "Joshua Bell's Metro Encore Draws a Crowd," *Washington Post*, September 30, 2014, www.washingtonpost.com/lifestyle/style/joshua-bells-metro-encore-draws-a-crowd/2014/09/30/c28b6c50-48d5-11e4-a046-120a8a855cca_story.html; and "Stop and Hear the Music," www.youtube.com/watch?v=hnOPu0_YWhw, accessed September 2018.
13. See Michael Castillo. "The Most Talked About Super Bowl Advertiser Online Was Avocados From Mexico," *CNBC*, February 5, 2018, www.cnbc.com/2018/02/05/the-most-talked-about-super-bowl-ad-online-was-about-avocados-.html; Patrick Coffee, "Avocados From Mexico Puts Its Account in Review Ahead of 4th Straight Super Bowl Campaign," *Adweek*, February 1, 2018, www.adweek.com/agencyspy/avocados-from-mexico-goes-into-review-ahead-of-4th-straight-super-bowl-campaign/142907; and https://avocadosfrommexico.com/, accessed September 2018.
14. See "FMI—Supermarket Facts," www.fmi.org/our-research/supermarket-facts, accessed September 2018; Christina Ng, "The Drivers behind Shoppers' Purchasing Decisions," *Project Nosh*, April 30, 2015, www.projectnosh.com/news/2015/the-drivers-behind-shoppers-purchasing-decisions; and "Our Retail Divisions," http://news.walmart.com/news-archive/2005/01/07/our-retail-divisions, accessed September 2018.
15. See www.tiffany.com/WorldOfTiffany/TiffanyStory/Legacy/BlueBox.aspx, accessed September 2018.
16. See "Procter & Gamble (PG) Q3 2017 Results," *MSN*, April 4, 2017, www.msn.com/en-us/money/news/procter-and-gamble-pg-q3-2017-results-earnings-call-transcript/ar-BBAp8wZ; "Keep Your Home and Loved Ones Safe," P&G, https://tide.com/en-us/safety, accessed September 2018.
17. "Lexus Places First in the 2017 J.D. Power Customer Service Index," *Lexus Enthusiast*, March 17, 2017, https://lexusenthusiast.com/2017/03/17/lexus-places-first-in-2017-j-d-power-customer-service-index-study/; Bill Taylor, "More Lessons from Lexus—Why It Pays to Do the Right Thing," *Harvard Business Review*, December 12, 2007, https://hbr.org/2007/12/more-lessons-from-lexuswhy-it; Bennett Bennett, "Lexus Gets Conceptual, Create Perceptual Origami Art to Celebrate Customer Service," *The Drum*, March 8, 2018, www.thedrum.com/news/2018/03/08/lexus-gets-conceptual-creates-perceptual-origami-art-celebrate-customer-service; and www.lexuslearn.com/covenant accessed September 2018.
18. See "Lowe's Is Augmenting Retail Reality with VR & Robot Assistants," *Future Stores*, https://futurestoreseast.wbresearch.com/lowes-vr-robot-creates-future-retail-experience-ty-u, accessed September 2018; Anna Rose Welch, "Lowe's Leverages Mobile Initiatives to Improve Customer Experience," *Integrated Solutions for Retailers*, November 21, 2013, www.retailsolutionsonline.com/doc/lowe-s-leverages-mobile-initiatives-to-improve-customer-experience-0001; Greg Petro, "Lowe's: The Home Improvement Retailer of the Future," *Forbes*, April 1, 2015, www.forbes.com/sites/-gregpetro/2015/04/01/lowes-the-home-improvement-retailer-of-

the-future/; and www.lowes.com/webapp/wcs/stores/servlet/ContactUsLandingPageView, www.lowes.com/how-to-library, and https://twitter.com/LowesCares, accessed September 2018.

19. See www.bmwgroup.com/com/en/brands/bmw.html and www.bmw.com/en, accessed September 2018.
20. Information on the Colgate-Palmolive product mix is from www.colgatepalmolive.com/en-us/brands, accessed September 2018.
21. Devika Krishna Kumar, "P&G to Sell Up to 100 Brands to Revive Sales, Cut Costs," *Reuters,* August 1, 2014, www.reuters.com/article/2014/08/01/procter-gamble-results-idUSL4N0Q745T20140801; and https://us.pg.com/our-brands, accessed September 2018.
22. See CIA World Fact Book, www.cia.gov/library/publications/the-world-factbook, accessed September 2018; and "List of Countries by GDP Sector Composition," https://en.wikipedia.org/wiki/List_of_countries_by_GDP_sector_composition, accessed September 2018.
23. See Bruce Japson, "Oscar Health's Obamacare Enrollment Surges Past 250K," *Forbes,* December 21, 2017, www.forbes.com/sites/brucejapsen/2017/12/21/oscar-healths-2018-obamacare-enrollment-surges-past-250k/#5ef8520b2fff; "10 Things to Know about Oscar Health Insurance: Will It Be the Uber of Health Plans," *Becker's Healthcare Review,* August 4, 2015, www.beckershospitalreview.com/payer-issues/10-things-to-know-about-oscar-health-insurance-will-it-be-the-uber-of-health-plans.html; Sarah Buhr, "Oscar Health Expects to Generate $1 Billion in Revenue and Sign Up 250,000 Members in 2018," *Tech Crunch,* December 21, 2017, https://techcrunch.com/2017/12/21/oscar-health-expects-to-generate-1-billion-in-revenue-and-sign-up-250000-members-in-2018/; and www.hioscar.com/about, accessed September 2018.
24. See James L. Heskett, W. Earl Sasser Jr., and Leonard A. Schlesinger, *The Service Profit Chain: How Leading Companies Link Profit and Growth to Loyalty, Satisfaction, and Value* (New York: Free Press, 1997); and Heskett, Sasser, and Schlesinger, *The Value Profit Chain: Treat Employees Like Customers and Customers Like Employees* (New York: Free Press, 2003). Also see Jay Doerksen, "How Employee Satisfaction Drives the Service-Profit Chain and Improves the Customer Experience," *Vision Critical,* May 11, 2017, www.visioncritical.com/employee-satisfaction-service-profit-chain/; and The Service-Profit Chain Institute, http://serviceprofitchain.com/, accessed September 2018.
25. "Four Seasons Hotels and Resorts Named 'Great Place to Work Legend' Honouring 20 Consecutive Years in Fortune's '100 Best Places to Work For' List,'" March 9, 2017, https://press.fourseasons.com/news-releases/2017/fortune-100-best-companies-to-work-for/; Jeffrey O'Brien, "A Perfect Season," *Fortune,* February 1, 2008, http://archive.fortune.com/2008/01/18/news/companies/fourseasons.fortune/index.htm; and http://jobs.fourseasons.com and www.fourseasons.com/about_us/, accessed September 2018.
26. See "United States: Prescription Drugs," www.kff.org/state-category/health-costs-budgets/, accessed September 2018; and "Postal Facts," http://about.usps.com/who-we-are/postal-facts/welcome.htm, accessed September 2018.
27. Micah Solomon, "Thanks a Latte: How to Fix a Customer Service Failure, per Starbucks, Marriott, and Me," *Forbes,* November 29, 2017, www.forbes.com/sites/micahsolomon/2017/11/19/thanks-a-latte-how-to-fix-a-customer-service-failure-per-starbucks-marriott-and-me/#4a1a1873462a.
28. See Martha White, "Lost Bags, at 140 Characters, and Airlines Respond," *New York Times,* October 20, 2015, p. B6; and Leslie Josephs, "Between Five Minutes and Five Hours: How Long Airlines Take to Respond to Your Complaint on Twitter," *CNBC,* January 9, 2018, https://www.cnbc.com/2018/01/09/how-long-airlines-take-to-respond-to-your-complaints-on-twitter.html.
29. See "McAtlas Shrugged," *Foreign Policy*, May–June 2001, pp. 26–37; and Philip Kotler and Kevin Lane Keller, *Marketing Management*, 15th ed. (Upper Saddle River, NJ: Pearson Publishing, 2016), p. 316.
30. See "For Sale: Hessian, A Brand without a Product," *Fast Company,* February 12, 2013, www.fastcodesign.com/1671819/for-sale-hessian-a-brand-without-a-product.
31. See Kevin Systrom, "On Instagram's Big Moves," *Fast Company,* March 3, 2018, www.fastcompany.com/3069066/kevin-systrom-on-instagrams-big-moves-its-almost-riskier-not-to-disrupt-yo; and www.instagram.com/about/us/, accessed September 2018.
32. For more on BrandAsset Valuator, see Kotler and Keller, *Marketing Management,* Chapter 11; and "BrandAsset Valuator," www.yr.com/BAV, accessed September 2018.
33. See Kantar Millward Brown, "BrandZ Top 100 Most Valuable Global Brands," www.millwardbrown.com/brandz/top-global-brands/2017, accessed September 2018.
34. See Scott Davis, *Brand Asset Management*, 2nd ed. (San Francisco: Jossey-Bass, 2002). For more on brand positioning, see Kotler and Keller, *Marketing Management*, Chapter 10.
35. See Jack Neff, "How Whirlpool Heated Up Sales by Warming Up 'Cold Metal,'" *Advertising Age,* June 15, 2015, p. 38; "Every Day Care," www.multivu.com/players/English/7318751-whirlpool-announced-launch-of-every-day-take-the-chore-out-of-household-responsibilities/, accessed September 2016; and www.whirlpool.com/everydaycare/, accessed September 2018.
36. See Doug Grisaffe, "Feeling the Brand Love," *Marketing News,* February 2014, pp. 26–27; Simon Goodley, "Marketing Is Dead, Says Saatchi & Saatchi Boss—Long Live Lovemarks," *The Guardian,* March 3, 2015, www.theguardian.com/media/2015/mar/03/advertising-is-dead-says-saatchi-saatchi-boss-long-live-lovemarks; and www.saatchi.com/the_lovemarks_company and www.lovemarks.com, accessed September 2018.
37. "Why I Love Walt Disney World," https://ithoughtyouweresshorter.wordpress.com/2012/11/15/why-i-love-walt-disney-world/, accessed September 2016.
38. Leslie Scism, "Travelers Doesn't Want to Share Its Umbrella Logo," *Wall Street Journal,* May 25, 2015, www.wsj.com/articles/travelers-doesnt-want-to-share-its-umbrella-logo-1432598794.
39. See Alexander Coolidge, "The Simple Truth: Private Selection, and Other Kroger Brands Drive Sales," *Cincinnati Enquirer,* July 26, 2017, www.cincinnati.com/story/money/2017/07/27/kroger-gins-up-own-goods-win-thrifty-consumers/472740001/; Nandita Bose, "Exclusive Aldi Raises Stakes in U.S. Price War with Walmart," *Reuters,* May 11, 2017, www.reuters.com/article/us-aldi-walmart-pricing-exclusive/exclusive-aldi-raises-stakes-in-u-s-price-war-with-wal-mart-idUSKBN1870EN.
40. "Top 150 Global Licensors," *Global License*, April 1, 2017, www.licensemag.com/license-global/top-150-global-licensors-3.
41. See Gill Hyslop, "Top 10 US Salty Snack Brands in 2017 So Far: Sales Soar for Frito-Lay's Ruffles Brand," *Bakery and Snacks,* July 14, 2017, www.bakeryandsnacks.com/Article/2017/07/13/Top-10-US-snack-brands-Sales-soar-for-Frito-Lay-s-Ruffles-brand; and www.fritolay.com/our-snacks/doritos.html, accessed September 2018.
42. See www.nest.com and https://nest.com/works-with-nest/, accessed September 2018.
43. For interesting lists of good and bad brand extension candidates, see Christina Austin, "See the 10 Worst Brand Extensions Currently on the Market," *Business Insider,* February 9, 2013, www.businessinsider.com/the-10-worst-brand-extensions-2013-2?op=1; Brad Tuttle, "Why Some Brand Extensions Are Brilliant and Others Are Just Awkward," *Time,* February 7, 2013, http://business.time.com/2013/02/07/-why-some-brand-extensions-are-brilliant-and-others-are-just-awkward/; and "12 Brand Extensions the World Would Like to See," *Attest,* November 13, 2017, http://insights.askattest.com/12-brand-extensions-consumers-would-love-to-see.
44. "World's 25 Biggest Advertisers," *AdAge Marketing Fact Pack 2018,* December 18, 2017, p. 9.
45. Stephen Cole, "Value of the Brand," *CA Magazine*, May 2005, pp. 39–40. Also see "The Power of Customer Service," *Fortune,* December 3, 2012, www.timeincnewsgroupcustompub.com/-sections/121203_Disney.pdf; and "Customer Engagement," http://thewaltdisneycompany.com/citizenship/community/consumer-engagement, accessed September 2018.

Chapter 8

1. Shara Tibken, "Samsung's Next Big Thing Isn't Something You Can Buy," *CNET*, January 8, 2018, www.cnet.com/news/the-next-big-thing-from-samsung-at-ces-isnt-actually-a-thing/; Blake Morgan, "The Connected Customer with Samsung," *Forbes*, January 29, 2018, www.forbes.com/sites/blakemorgan/2018/01/29/the-connected-customer-with-samsung/#6a9b9c4c38e4; Louis Columbus, "2017 Roundup of Internet of Things Forecasts," *Forbes,* December 10, 2017, www.forbes.com/sites/louiscolumbus/2017/12/10/2017-roundup-of-internet-of-things-forecasts/#5e238f261480; Corinne Reichert, "Samsung Smart TVs Will All Be IoT Compatible from 2016," *ZDNet,* December 29, 2015, www.zdnet.com/article/samsung-smart-tvs-will-all-be-iot-compatible-from-2016/; Jared Newman, "Samsung's $100 Million Internet of Things Bet Is Even Crazier than You Think," *Fast Company,* January 28, 2015, www.fastcompany.com/3041104/app-economy/samsungs-100-million-internet-of-things-bet-is-even-crazier-than-you-think; Don Reisinger, "Samsung Is Back Atop the Smartphone Market," *Fortune,* April 11, 2017, http://fortune.com/2017/04/11/samsung-apple-market-share/; Rae Johnston, "Samsung Is Connecting All of Your Appliances in a Big Appliance Orgy," *Gizmodo,* January 11, 2018, www.gizmodo.com.au/2018/01/bixby-in-your-vase-in-your-fridge-in-your-car-samsungs-vision-of-the-future-is-becoming-a-reality; and www.samsung.com, accessed September 2018.
2. Kurt Schroeder, "Why So Many New Products Fail (and It's Not the Product)," *The Business Journals,* March 14, 2017, https://

www.bizjournals.com/bizjournals/how-to/marketing/2017/03/why-so-many-new-products-fail-and-it-s-not-the.html; and "Apple 2017 10-K Filing," November 3, 2017, http://investor.apple.com/sec.cfm?DocType=Annual.

3. David Meer, Edward C. Landry, and Samrat Sharma, "Creating What Consumers Want," *Forbes*, January 26, 2015, www.forbes.com/sites/strategyand/2015/01/26/creating-what-consumers-want/.
4. See Michael Martinez, "Ford Opens Silicon Valley Innovation Center," *The Detroit News*, January 22, 2015, www.detroitnews.com/story/business/autos/ford/2015/01/22/ford-silicon-valley/22165837/; "Chick-fil-A Goes High Tech at Tech Square," March 8, 2017, https://thechickenwire.chick-fil-a.com/News/Chick-fil-A-Goes-High-Tech-at-Tech-Square; and http://corporate.ford.com/innovation/research-and-innovation-center.html, accessed September 2018.
5. http://about.att.com/innovation/tlp, accessed September 2018.
6. See "Dominic Powell, "Want to Run Your First Hackathon? Here Are Some Tips from KPMG," *Smart Company*, August 15, 2017, www.smartcompany.com.au/startupsmart/advice/want-run-first-internal-hackathon-tips-kpmg/; Matt Weinberger, "'There Are Only Two Rules'—Facebook Explains How 'Hackathons,' One of Its Oldest Traditions, Is Also One of Its Most Important," *Business Insider*, January 11, 2017, www.businessinsider.com/facebook-hackathons-2017-6; and www.facebook.com/hackathon/, accessed September 2018.
7. Blake Morgan, "Customer Collaboration with Salesforce's Mike Rosenbaum," *Forbes*, January 3, 2017, www.forbes.com/sites/blakemorgan/2017/01/03/customer-collaboration-with-salesforces-mike-rosenbaum/#464b47ce7403; Erica Kuhl, "4 Tips to Turn Customer Feedback into Action," *Salesforce Blog*, December 15, 2016, www.salesforce.com/blog/2016/12/4-tips-to-turn-customer-feedback-into-action.html; and Salesforce IdeaExchange, https://success.salesforce.com/ideaSearch, accessed September 2018.
8. See Jeff Beer, "Why Under Armour's Future Show Is Key to Its Brand Innovation Strategy," *Fast Company*, October 14, 2015, www.fastcocreate.com/3052298/why-under-armours-future-show-is-key-to-its-brand-innovation-strategy#13; Bruce Horovitz, "Under Armour Seeks Ideas for Its Next Big Thing," *USA Today*, October 20, 2013; and http://ideahouse.ua.com/shows#future-show, September 2018.
9. See George S. Day, "Is It Real? Can We Win? Is It Worth Doing?" *Harvard Business Review*, December 2007, pp. 110–120.
10. This example is based on Tesla Motors and information obtained from www.teslamotors.com and www.tesla.com/model3, accessed September 2018; and "Electric Car," *Wikipedia*, http://en.wikipedia.org/wiki/Electric_car, accessed September 2018.
11. See www.brooksrunning.com/en_us/programs/beta-runners, accessed September 2018.
12. See Maureen Morrison, "Marketer of the Year: Taco Bell," *Advertising Age*, September 2, 2013, pp. 15–16; Susan Berfield, "Baristas, Patrons Steaming over Starbucks VIA," *Bloomberg BusinessWeek*, November 13, 2009; and Tamara Walsh, "Starbucks Makes a Big Bet on New Product Mix in 2014," *The Motley Fool*, January 8, 2014, www.fool.com/investing/general/2014/01/08/starbucks-makes-a-big-bet-on-new-product-mix-in-20.aspx.
13. Austin Carr, "Starbucks Leap of Faith," *Fast Company*, June 2013, pp. 46–48; Taylor Soper, "Starbucks Misses Revenue Expectations as Mobile Order-Ahead Accounts for 10% of U.S. Transactions," *GeekWire*, November 2, 2017, www.geekwire.com/2017/starbucks-misses-revenue-expectations-mobile-order-ahead-accounts-10-u-s-transactions; and www.starbucks.com/coffeehouse/mobile-apps, accessed September 2018.
14. See Jack Neff, "P&G Reinvents Laundry with $150 Million Tide Pods Launch," *Advertising Age*, April 26, 2011, www.adage.com/print/227208/; Sheila Shayon, "Microsoft Unleashes Global Marketing Blitz for Windows 8, New Devices," *BrandChannel*, October 25, 2012, www.brandchannel.com/home/post/2012/10/25/Microsoft-Global-Windows-8-Launch-102512.aspx; and Thomas Whitehead, "Nintendo of America Spent Big on Switch Advertising in March," *Nintendo Life*, May 2, 2017, www.nintendolife.com/news/2017/05/nintendo_of_america_spent_big_on_switch_tv_advertising_in_march.
15. "iPhone X Available for Pre-Order on Friday, October 27," October 24, 2017, www.apple.com/newsroom/2017/10/iphone-x-available-for-pre-order-on-friday-october-27/.
16. Jonathon Ringen, "When It Clicks, It Clicks," *Fast Company*, February 2015, pp. 72–78+; Andrew Jack, "How LEGO Took to Anthropology," *Financial Times*, February 26, 2014, www.ft.com/cms/s/0/b071990c-9d4c-11e3-a599-00144feab7de.html#axzz3N8u6XIPH; Christian Madsbjerg and Mikkel B. Rasmussen, "An Anthropologist Walks into a Bar...," *Harvard Business Review*, March, 2014, pp. 80–88; Jeff Beer, "The Secret of Lego's Social Media Success Is in the Creative Power of Crowds," *Fast Company*, June 20, 2017, www.fastcompany.com/40432685/the-secret-to-legos-social-media-success-is-in-the-creative-power-of-crowds; and https://ideas.lego.com/dashboard and www.lego.com/en-us, accessed September 2018.
17. This definition is based on one found in Bryan Lilly and Tammy R. Nelson, "Fads: Segmenting the Fad-Buyer Market," *Journal of Consumer Marketing*, Vol. 20, No. 3, 2003, pp. 252–265.
18. See Lisa Fu, "The Fidget Spinner Trend Is Ending and You Missed It," *Fortune*, June 13, 2017, http://fortune.com/2017/06/13/the-fidget-spinner-trend-is-ending-and-you-missed-it/; and www.crazyfads.com, accessed September 2018.
19. See Robert Klara, "Perspective: Crayola Crayons," *Adweek*, September 4, 2017, pp. 46–47; and www.crayola.com/splash/products/ColorAlive and www.crayola.com/fashionshow/, accessed September 2016.
20. See www.quakeroats.com and www.quaker.com.my, accessed September 2018.
21. Sheila Marikar, "How One Iconic American Brand Got Back on a Roll," *Inc.*, March 2016, p. 32; and Robert Klara, "How an Immigrant Cabinetmaker Accidentally Invented the Toy that Defined America," *Adweek*, March 21, 2017, www.adweek.com/brand-marketing/how-an-immigrant-cabinetmaker-accidentally-invented-the-toy-that-defined-american-childhood/; and www.radioflyer.com/content/about-us/, accessed September 2018.
22. For more discussion of marketing strategies over the course of the PLC, see Philip Kotler and Kevin Lane Keller, *Marketing Management*, 15th ed. (Hoboken, NJ: Pearson Education, 2016), pp. 358.
23. Chris Isadore and David Goldman, "Volkswagen Agrees to Record $14.7 Billion over Emissions Cheating," *CNN*, June 28, 2016, http://money.cnn.com/2016/06/28/news/companies/volkswagen-fine/index.html; and Alison Frankel, "VW Class Counsel: Nationwide Deal Won't Be Undone by 9th Circuit's Hyundai Ruling," *Reuters*, January 25, 2018, www.reuters.com/article/legal-us-otc-volkswagen/vw-class-counsel-nationwide-deal-wont-be-undone-by-9th-circuits-hyundai-ruling-idUSKBN1FE2WI.
24. Information on McDonald's menus and operations found in Lucy Fancourt, Bredesen Lewis, and Nicholas Majka, "Born in the USA, Made in France: How McDonald's Succeeds in the Land of Michelin Stars," Knowledge @Wharton, January 3, 2012, http://knowledge.wharton.upenn.edu/article.cfm?articleid=2906; Richard Vines and Caroline Connan, "McDonald's Wins Over French Chef with McBaguette Sandwich," *Bloomberg*, January 15, 2013, www.bloomberg.com/news/2013-01-15/mcdonald-s-wins-over-french-chef-with-mcbaguette-sandwich.html; Rob Wile, "The True Story of How McDonald's Conquered France," *Business Insider*, August 22, 2014, www.businessinsider.com/how-mcdonalds-conquered-france-2014-8; and "McDonald's Food You Can't Get Here," *Chicago Tribune*, www.chicagotribune.com/business/ct-biz-mcdonalds-food-around-the-world,0,5168632.photogallery, accessed September 2018.
25. Information from www.db.com, accessed September 2018.
26. See "Global Powers of Retailing 2017," www.deloitte.com/content/dam/Deloitte/global/Documents/consumer-industrial-products/gx-cip-2017-global-powers-of-retailing.pdf; "Walmart Corporate International," http://corporate.walmart.com/our-story/locations, accessed September 2018; and information from www.walmart.com and www.carrefour.com, accessed September 2018.

Chapter 9

1. Donna Fuscaldo, "Apple's World Smartphone Market Share Above 50%," *Investopedia*, February 16, 2018, www.investopedia.com/news/apple-global-smartphone-market-share-more-50-first-time/; Chuck Jones, "No Surprise that Apple's iPhone Dominates Smartphone Profits," *Forbes*, November 20, 2017, www.forbes.com/sites/chuckjones/2017/11/20/no-surprise-that-apples-iphone-dominates-smartphone-profits/#5c9bd1ecbf8c; Kristijan Lucic, "Price Gap between Apple & Samsung Smartphones Reach $465," *Android Headlines*, May 5, 2017, www.androidheadlines.com/2017/05/price-gap-apple-samsung-smartphones-reaches-465.html; "With 7% of Market, the Mac Captures 60% of Profit," *Ped30*, November 3, 2016, www.ped30.com/2016/11/03/apple-dediu-macbook-pro/; "Apple Trails Samsung in Smartphone Market—and Won't Catch Up in 2018," *Fortune*, February 13, 2018, http://fortune.com/2018/02/13/apple-iphone-samsung-market-share/; Arjun Kharpal, "Apple's iPhone 7 Plus Was the Second-Best Selling Phone in China Last Year," *CNBC*, January 15, 2018, www.cnbc.com/2018/01/15/apple-iphone-7-plus-second-best-selling-phone-in-china-in-2017.html; and information from www.apple.com and http://investor.apple.com/financials.cfm, accessed October 2018.
2. For more on the importance of sound pricing strategy, see Thomas T. Nagle and Georg Muller, *The Strategy and Tactics of Pricing: A Guide to Growing More Profitably*, 6th ed. (New York: Routledge, 2018), Chapter 1.

3. See Megan Willett, "How Swiss Watchmaker Patek Philippe Handcrafts Its Famous $500,000 Watches," *Business Insider,* July 12, 2013, www.businessinsider.com/how-a-patek-philippe-watch-is-made-2013-7; Stacy Perman, "Patek Philippe Crafts Its Future," *Fortune,* June 16, 2014, pp. 37–44; and www.patek.com/contents/default/en/values.html, accessed October 2018.
4. See www.mbusa.com/mercedes/vehicles/class/class-CLA/bodystyle-CPE, accessed October 2018.
5. See www.bose.com, accessed October 2018.
6. See Vince Dixon, "What Brands Are Actually Behind Trader Joe's Snacks," *Eater,* August 9, 2017, www.eater.com/2017/8/9/16099028/trader-joes-products; and www.traderjoes.com/our-story and www.traderjoes.com, accessed October 2018.
7. See www.sleepnumber.com, accessed October 2018.
8. "Watch the Newest Ads on TV from Amazon, Honda, Google, and More," *Advertising Age,* December 12, 2017, http://adage.com/article/media/watchnewest-tv-ads-amazon-honda-google/311610/; and https://store.google.com/us/product/pixel_2?hl=en-US, accessed October 2018.
9. See Joseph Weber, "Over a Buck for Dinner? Outrageous," *BusinessWeek,* March 9, 2009, p. 57; Tom Mulier and Matthew Boyle, "Dollar Dinners from ConAgra's Threatened by Costs," *Bloomberg Businessweek,* August 19, 2010, www.businessweek.com; and Jessica Wohl, "ConAgra's Banquet Raises Prices, Brings Back Commercials," *Advertising Age,* December 9, 2015, www.adage.com/print/301684.
10. See David Sax, "Hang $99.99," *Bloomberg Businessweek,* November 2–8, 2015, pp. 43–44; Chris Ahrens, "The Advantage of a Custom Board," *San Diego Reader,* January 2, 2018, www.sandiegoreader.com/news/2018/jan/02/waterfront-advantage-custom-board/#; "The 7 Best Beginner Surfboards Reviewed & Rated [2018]," *Outside Pursuits,* accessed October 2018; and www.wavestormboards.com/about-us/, accessed October 2018.
11. Nick Wingfield, "Amazon Has a Potent Weapon in the Tablet Wars: Low Prices," *New York Times,* September 8, 2016, www.nytimes.com/2016/09/09/technology/amazon-has-a-potent-weapon-in-the-tablet-wars-low-prices.html.
12. Thomas Heath, "How Hipster Brands Have the King of Razors on the Run," *Washington Post,* April 5, 2017, www.washingtonpost.com/business/capitalbusiness/how-hipster-brands-have-the-king-of-razors-on-the-run/2017/04/05/edca3af6-1a27-11e7-9887-1a5314b56a08_story.html?utm_term=.4736a3a073d0; and "Sales of the Leading Cartridge Razor Blade Brands in the United States," *Statista,* www.statista.com/statistics/276535/leading-men-s-cartridge-razor-blade-brands-sales/, accessed October 2018.
13. See Bill Campbell, "Cheese to the Rescue: Surprising Spray Melts Road Ice," *NPR,* January 21, 2014, www.npr.org/blogs/thetwo-way/2014/01/21/264562529/cheese-to-the-rescue-surprising-spray-melts-road-ice; "Four Foods That Help Prevent Slippery Roads," *AccuWeather.com,* January 22, 2015, www.accuweather.com/en/weather-news/beet-cheese-and-potatoes-roads/22447484; and Nicholas Johansen, "Beet Juice Battles Road Ice," *Castanet.net,* November 22, 2017, www.castanet.net/news/BC/212141/Beet-juice-battles-road-ice.
14. See Danielle Paquette, "Why You Should Always Buy the Men's Version of Almost Anything," *Washington Post,* December 22, 2015, www.washingtonpost.com/news/wonk/wp/2015/12/22/women-really-do-pay-more-for-razors-and-almost-everything-else/; Rafi Mohammed, "You Can Charge Women More, but Should You?" *Harvard Business Review,* January 29, 2016, https://hbr.org/2016/01/you-can-charge-women-more-but-should-you?cm_sp=Article-_-Links-_-Comment; and Anne-Marcelle Ngabirano, "'Pink Tax' Forces Women to Pay More Than Men," *USA Today,* March 27, 2017, www.usatoday.com/story/money/business/2017/03/27/pink-tax-forces-women-pay-more-than-men/99462846/.
15. For this and other examples and explanations, see Peter Coy, "Why the Price Is Rarely Right," *Bloomberg Businessweek,* February 1 & 8, 2010, pp. 77–78; and Utpal Dholakia, "What Shoppers Should Know about Reference Prices," *Psychology Today,* September 8, 2015, www.psychologytoday.com/blog/the-science-behind-behavior/201509/what-shoppers-should-know-about-reference-prices.
16. See Emmie Martin, "There's a Sneaky Reason Why the New iPhone X Costs $999 Instead of $1,000," *CNBC,* September 13, 2017, www.cnbc.com/2017/09/13/why-iphone-x-costs-999-instead-of-1000.html; and "Subdued Sales May Force Apple to Call Time on the iPhone X," *The Times,* January 24, 2018, www.thetimes.co.uk/article/subdued-sales-may-force-apple-to-call-time-on-the-iphone-x-3wzbtxd2d.
17. See Anthony Allred, E. K. Valentin, and Goutam Chakraborty, "Pricing Risky Services: Preference and Quality Considerations," *Journal of Product and Brand Management,* Vol. 19, No. 1, 2010, p. 54; Kenneth C. Manning and David E. Sprott, "Price Endings, Left-Digit Effects, and Choice," *Journal of Consumer Research,* August 2009, pp. 328–336; Bouree Lam, "The Psychological Difference between $12.00 and $11.67," *The Atlantic,* January 30, 2015, www.theatlantic.com/business/archive/2015/01/the-psychological-difference-between-1200-and-1167/384993/; and Darian Kovacs, "4 Psychological Techniques That Can Improve Your Product Pricing," *Entrepreneur,* November 15, 2017, www.entrepreneur.com/article/304687.
18. Sarah Halzack, "The Trouble with Those 20 Percent Off Coupons from Bed Bath & Beyond," *Washington Post,* September 30, 2015, www.washingtonpost.com/news/business/wp/2015/09/30/the-trouble-with-those-20-percent-off-coupons-from-bed-bath-beyond/; and Wayne Duggan, "Bed Bath & Beyond Struggles to Adapt," *US News,* December 21, 2017, https://money.usnews.com/investing/stock-market-news/articles/2017-12-21/bed-bath-beyond-inc-bbby.
19. Alex Samuels, "Texans Drive Mad as Tolls Burn Holes in Their Wallets," *Texas Tribune,* November, 17, 2017, www.texastribune.org/2017/11/17/texans-driven-mad-tolls-burn-holes-their-wallets/.
20. See Laura Gunderson, "Amazon's 'Dynamic' Prices Get Some Static," *The Oregonian,* May 5, 2012, http://blog.oregonlive.com/complaintdesk/2012/05/amazons_dynamic_prices_get_som.html; and Kathy Kristof, "How Amazon Uses Surge Pricing Just Like Uber," *CBS News,* July 24, 2017, www.cbsnews.com/news/amazon-surge-pricing-are-you-getting-ripped-off-small-business/.
21. Ralph Jennings, "Why Apple Will Lose China Marketing Share in 2008, despite the Success of the iPhone X," *Forbes,* February 25, 2018, www.forbes.com/sites/ralphjennings/2018/02/25/why-apple-despite-the-iphone-x-will-lose-china-market-share-in-2018/#7a927675462e.
22. Liza Lin, "Shhh...Luxury Goods Are Discounted in China," *Bloomberg Businessweek,* August 21, 2014, pp. 28–29; and "China's Grey Market Threatened by New Tax Regime," *Reuters,* April 5, 2016, http://fortune.com/2016/04/03/chinas-grey-luxury-market-taxes/.
23. Scheherazade Daneshkhu, "Unilever Boosted by Higher Prices in Emerging Markets," *FT.com,* July 20, 2017, www.ft.com/content/573f2b26-6d21-11e7-bfeb-33fe0c5b7eaa.
24. "Huawei to Launch First AI Enabled Phone in India," *Hindu Business Line,* December 8, 2017, www.thehindubusinessline.com/info-tech/huawei-to-launch-first-artificial-intelligence-phone-in-india/article9986902.ece; and "Huawei to Enter the US Market with Mate 10 Pro on AT&T, Negotiating with Verizon as Well," *Phones Arena,* December 12, 2017, www.phonearena.com/news/Huawei-to-enter-the-US-market-with-Mate-10-Pro-on-AT-T-negotiating-with-Verizon-as-well_id100667.
25. See Katy Allen, "Shrinking Sweets? 'You're Not Imagining It,' ONS Tells Shopper," *The Guardian,"* July 24, 2017, www.theguardian.com/business/2017/jul/24/sweets-are-shrinking-youre-not-imagining-it-ons-tells-shoppers.
26. See "Here's Where (and Why) Whole Foods Is Opening 365 Stores," http://media.thinknum.com/articles/heres-where-whole-foods-is-opening-365-locations/, accessed February 2018; and Craig Giammona, "Whole Foods' 365 Offshoot Moving Ahead under Amazon," *Bloomberg,* February 1, 2018, https://www.bloomberg.com/news/articles/2018-02-01/whole-foods-365-offshoot-moving-ahead-under-amazon-ownership.
27. For discussions of these issues, see Dhruv Grewal and Larry D. Compeau, "Pricing and Public Policy: A Research Agenda and Overview of the Special Issue," *Journal of Public Policy and Marketing,* Spring 1999, pp. 3–10; Walter L. Baker, Michael V. Marn, and Craig C. Zawada, *The Price Advantage* (Hoboken, NJ: John Wiley & Sons, 2010), Appendix 2; and Thomas T. Nagle, John Hogan, and Joseph Zale, *The Strategy and Tactics of Pricing: A Guide to Growing More Profitably,* 5th ed. (Upper Saddle River, NJ: Prentice Hall, 2011).
28. See Joe Rossignol, "Apple Loses Appeal in E-books Price Fixing Lawsuit, Ordered to Pay $450 Million Fine," *MacRumors,* June 30, 2015, www.macrumors.com/2015/06/30/apple-ebooks-appeal-rejected-450m-fine; "Airlines Accused of Price-Fixing Conspiracy in Dallas Class-Action Lawsuit," *PRNewswire,* July 8, 2015, www.prnewswire.com/news-releases/airlines-accused-of-price-fixing-conspiracy-in-dallas-class-action-lawsuit-300110405.html; "U.S. Airlines Lose Bid to Dismiss Price-Fixing Lawsuit," *Fortune,* October 30, 2016, http://fortune.com/2016/10/30/airlines-price-fixing-lawsuit/.
29. Roger Lowenstein, "Why Amazon Monopoly Accusations Deserve a Closer Look," *Fortune,* July 23, 2015, http://fortune.com/2015/07/23/why-amazon-monopoly-accusations-deserve-a-closer-look/.
30. Jonathan Stempel, "Michael Kors Settles U.S. Lawsuit Alleging Deceptive Price Tags," *Reuters,* June 12, 2015, www.reuters.com/article/us-michaelkors-settlement-idUSKBN0OS2AU20150612.
31. "FTC Guides against Deceptive Pricing," www.ecfr.gov/cgi-bin/text-idx?c=ecfr&sid=dfafb89837c306cf5b010b5bde15f041&rgn=div5&view=text&node=16:1.0.1.2.16&idno=16, accessed October 2018.

Chapter 10

1. Rani Molla, "Netflix Now Has Nearly 118 Million Streaming Subscribers Globally," *Recode,* January 22, 2018, www.recode.net/2018/1/22/16920150/netflix-q4-2017-earnings-subscribers; Nick Statt, "Netflix Plans to Spend $8 Billion to Make Its Library 50 Percent Original by 2018," *The Verge,* October 16, 2017, www.theverge.com/2017/10/16/16486436/netflix-original-content-8-billion-dollars-anime-films; Rian Barrett, "Netflix Is Turning 20—but Its Birthday Doesn't Matter," *Wired,* August 29, 2017, www.wired.com/story/netflix-20th-anniversary/; "The World's Most Innovative Companies—2018," *Fast Company,* February 21, 2018, www.fastcompany.com/most-innovative-companies/2018; and www.netflix.com, accessed October 2018.
2. See Bryan Gruley and Leslie Patton, "McRevolt: The Frustrating Life of the McDonald's Franchisee: Not Lovin' It," *Bloomberg Business,* September 16, 2015, www.bloomberg.com/features/2015-mcdonalds-franchises/; "Is McDonald's Broken? Franchisees Are Furious," *Yahoo! Finance,* April 15, 2015, http://finance.yahoo.com/news/mcdonalds-broken-franchisees-furious-133644537.html; Paul R. La Monica, "McDonald's: A Great American McComeback?" *CNN Money,* January 22, 2016, http://money.cnn.com/2016/01/22/investing/mcdonalds-earnings-comeback/; Sarah Whitten, "Owners of McDonalds Aren't Happy with Headquarters as Promotions Pick Up and Remodeling Costs Rise," *CNBC,* January 23, 2018, www.cnbc.com/2018/01/23/owners-of-mcdonalds-arent-happy-with-headquarters.html.
3. See "The Kroger Co. Fact Book," http://ir.kroger.com/CorporateProfile.aspx?iid=4004136, accessed October 2018.
4. See "Is Competition in the Eyewear Segment Preying over Luxottica's Bottom Line?" GuruFocus, February 24, 2015, www.gurufocus.com/news/318329; "EU Unconditionally Approves Luxottica-Essilor Merger," *Financial Times,* March 1, 2018, www.ft.com/content/319367b8-1d46-11e8-956a-43db76e69936; and www.luxottica.com/en/company/quick_view, October 2018.
5. "Franchise Business Economic Outlook for 2017," August 2017, https://franchiseeconomy.com/files/Franchise_Business_Outlook_Aug_2017.pdf.
6. See Entrepreneur Franchised 500 2018, *Entrepreneur,* www.entrepreneur.com/franchise500/2018, accessed October 2018; and www.sportclipsfranchise.com/facts-stats/no1-haircare-franchise/ and https://sportclips.com/about-us/our-story, accessed October 2018.
7. See Eric Platt, "22 Companies That Are Addicted to Walmart," June 13, 2012, *Business Insider,* www.businessinsider.com/22-companies-who-are-completely-addicted-to-walmart-2012-6#; Ben Levisohn, "Colgate, Clorox & Procter: The Uninvestable," *Barron's,* April 19, 2017, www.barrons.com/articles/colgate-clorox-procter-the-uninvestable-1492615711; Jeff Daniels, "Walmart Regaining Grocery Share from Competitors at 'Accelerating Rate,'" *CNBC,* May 24, 2017, www.cnbc.com/2017/05/24/wal-mart-regaining-grocery-share-from-competitors-at-accelerating-rate.html; Cal-Maine Foods Annual Reports, http://calmainefoods.com/investors/financial-reports/, accessed October 2018.
8. Daphne Howland, "Why Target Sold Out to CVS," *Retail Dive,* February 11, 2016, www.retaildive.com/news/why-target-sold-out-to-cvs/413432/; and www.cvs.com/target-pharmacy, accessed October 2018.
9. See www.staralliance.com, www.oneworld.com, and www.skyteam.com, accessed October 2018.
10. Scott Wilson, "Streaming Overtakes Downloads and Physical Sales for the First Time Ever in Bumper Year for Music Industry," *FACT,* March 31, 2017, www.factmag.com/2017/03/31/streaming-overtakes-downloads-physical-sales-2016/.
11. See Dennis Green and Mike Nudelman, "Why Amazon Is Still Such a Threat to Toys R Us, in One Chart," *Business Insider,* September 20, 2017, www.businessinsider.com/amazon-beat-toys-r-us-online-sales-2017-9; and Joan Verdon, "Toys R Us Said to Be Preparing for Liquidation," March 9, 2018, www.usatoday.com/story/money/business/2018/03/08/toys-r-us-preparing-liquidation-sources-say/408975002/.
12. See www.harley-davidson.com/shop/check-store-availability?storeId=10152&catalogId=10051&langId=-1, www.harley-davidson.com/store/CustomerCareContentDisplayView?catalogId=10051&langId=-1&storeId=10152&emsName=ES_CS_StoreFAQs&linkName=ourSite§ionName=storeFAQ§ion=Store%20FAQs, and http://investor.harley-davidson.com/static-files/df9257e2-6c11-4c14-8c00-4468aa1b5d1c, accessed October 2018.
13. "Better, Faster, Cheaper: The Grocery Shopping Revolution," *Consumer Reports,* May 23, 2017, www.consumerreports.org/grocery-stores-supermarkets/faster-fresher-cheaper-grocery-shopping-revolution/; Jeff Daniels, "Walmart Regaining Grocery Share from Competitors at an Accelerating Rate," *CNBC,* May 24, 2017, www.cnbc.com/2017/05/24/wal-mart-regaining-grocery-share-from-competitors-at-accelerating-rate.html; and "Benchmarks by Industry: Supermarkets," *ACSI,* www.theacsi.org/index.php?option=com_content&view=article&id=147&catid=&Itemid=212&i=Supermarkets, accessed October 2018.
14. See "Faster, Fresher, Cheaper: The Grocery Shopping Revolution," *Consumer Reports,* May 23, 2017, www.consumerreports.org/grocery-stores-supermarkets/faster-fresher-cheaper-grocery-shopping-revolution/; Ashley Lutz, "17 Reasons Why Wegmans Is America's Best Grocery Store," *Business Insider,* April 2, 2014, www.businessinsider.com/wegmans-grocery-is-americas-best-2014-4; "The 100 Best Companies to Work For," *Fortune,* March 2017, http://fortune.com/best-companies/; and "Wegmans," *Yelp,* www.yelp.com/biz/wegmans-fairfax, accessed October 2018.
15. See Alexis Sobel Fitts, "Inside the Startup Luring Thousands of Women into the Gig Economy," *Wired,* www.wired.com/2017/03/inside-the-startup-luring-thousands-of-women-into-the-gig-economy/; http://new.pamperedchef.com/company-facts and www.stelladot.com/trunkshow, accessed October 2018.
16. See "Subway: Be Part of a Winning Team with the #1 Franchise," www.franchisesolutions.com/franchise/subway, accessed October 2018.
17. Anita Chang Beattie, "Catching the Eye of a Chinese Shopper," *Advertising Age,* December 10, 2012, pp. 20–21.
18. Drew Hinshaw, "Burgers Face a Tough Slog in Africa," *Wall Street Journal,* December 10, 2013, www.wsj.com/articles/SB10001424052702304607104579214133498585594.
19. See Leanna Garfield, "Nestle Sponsored a River Barge to Create a 'Floating Supermarket' the Sold Candy and Chocolate Pudding to the Backwoods of Brazil," *Business Insider,* September 17, 2017, www.businessinsider.com/nestle-expands-brazil-river-barge-2017-9.
20. Chris Welch, "Amazon Will Soon Stop Selling All Nest Products," *The Verge,* March 3, 2018, www.theverge.com/2018/3/3/17074844/amazon-stopping-nest-sales.
21. See Marcus Williams, "Cutting Logistics Costs Key to GM Profit Targets," *Automotive Logistics,* October 2014, http://automotivelogistics.media/news/cutting-logistics-costs-key-to-gm-profit-targets; and "28th Annual State of Logistics Report: Accelerating into Uncertainty," June 20, 2017, https://cscmp.org/CSCMP/Products/State_of_Logistics_Report/28th_Annual_State_of_Logistics_Report.aspx?WebsiteKey=0b3f453d-bd90-4121-83cf-172a90b226a9.
22. Andy Brack, "Piggly Wiggly Center Offers Info-Packed Field Trip," *Charleston Currents,* January 4, 2010, www.charlestoncurrents.com/issue/10_issues/10.0104.htm; and information from http://en.wikipedia.org/wiki/Piggly_wiggly and http://corporate.walmart.com/_news_/news-archive/2005/01/07/our-retail-divisions, accessed October 2018.
23. Sarah Landrum, "Millennials Driving Brands to Practice Socially Responsible Marketing," *Forbes,* March 17, 2017, www.forbes.com/sites/sarahlandrum/2017/03/17/millennials-driving-brands-to-practice-socially-responsible-marketing/#2c2d4dc94990.
24. "Levi's How Can 'Clean' Begin with 'Design?'" IPE, August 16, 2017, http://wwwen.ipe.org.cn/GreenSupplyChain/BrandStoryDetail.aspx?id=20; Gaylen Davenport, "Levi's Water Conservation Efforts Actually Save the Company Money," *Worldwide Energy,* February 24, 2015, www.worldwideenergy.com/levis-water-conservation-efforts-actually-save-company-money/; Anna Sanina, "Levi's Asks People Not to Wash Their Jeans," *Popsop,* March 22, 2012, http://popsop.com/2012/03/levis-asks-people-not-to-wash-their-jeans/; and www.levistrauss.com/sustainability/products/waterless/ and www.levi.com/US/en_US/features/sustainability#process, accessed October 2018.
25. "SoCal Amazon Warehouse Fulfilling Millions of Cyber Monday Orders," *ABC* 7, November 27, 2017, http://abc7.com/business/socal-amazon-warehouse-fulfilling-millions-of-cyber-monday-orders/2703057; and "Tour an Amazon Fulfillment Center," http://amazonfctours.com/, accessed October 2018.
26. See Nick Wingfield, "As Amazon Pushes Forward with Robots, Workers Find New Roles," September 10, 2017, www.nytimes.com/2017/09/10/technology/amazon-robots-workers.html; and www.amazonrobotics.com, accessed October 2018.
27. Matthew Boyle, "Walmart Cracks the Whip on Suppliers," *Bloomberg Businessweek,* July 24, 2017, pp. 14-15.
28. Bureau of Transportation Statistics, "Pocket Guide to Transportation 2017," January 2017, www.rita.dot.gov/bts/sites/rita.dot.gov.bts/files/publications/pocket_guide_to_transportation/2017/3_Moving_Goods/table3_1.
29. See Walmart's supplier requirements at http://corporate.walmart.com/suppliers, accessed October 2018.
30. www.oracle.com/webfolder/assets/infographics/value-chain/index.html, accessed October 2018.
31. For this and other UPS examples and information, see "Moving Returns Forward with Overstock.com," www.ups-scs.com/solutions/case_studies/cs_

Overstock.pdf, accessed October 2018; Daniel Goure, "United Parcel Service Is on the Forefront of the Revolution in Healthcare," Lexington Institute, September 14, 2017, www.lexingtoninstitute.org/united-parcel-service-forefront-revolution-healthcare/; and www.ups-scs.com/solutions/ and https://solvers.ups.com/ accessed October 2018.

32. Jennifer McKevitt, "Fortune 500 Companies Are Using 3PLs More, Study Finds," *Supply Chain Dive*, May 30, 2017, www.supplychaindive.com/news/third-party-logistics-3pl-increase-large-companies-2017/443710/.

Chapter 11

1. Anne D'Innocenzio and Michelle Chapman, "Walmart Sees the Future and It Is Digital," *Chicago Tribune*, October 10, 2017, www.chicagotribune.com/business/ct-biz-walmart-shareholders-digital-future-20171010-story.html; Jack Neff, "How Walmart Found Its Footing in the Amazon Era," *Advertising Age*, September 27, 2017, http://adage.com/article/cmo-strategy/walmart-found-footing-amazon-era/310599/; "44% of U.S. E-Commerce Sales in 2017 Went to Amazon," *Motley Fool*, January 8, 2018, www.fool.com/investing/2018/01/08/44-of-us-e-commerce-sales-in-2017-went-to-amazon.aspx; Michael Corkery, "Walmart's Online Sales Growth Lags as It Confronts Challenges," *New York Times*, February 20, 2018, www.nytimes.com/2018/02/20/business/walmart-fourth-quarter-results.html; and information from https://corporate.walmart.com/, accessed October 2018.
2. See "Monthly and Annual Retail Trade," U.S. Census Bureau, www.census.gov/retail/, accessed October 2018.
3. See "Just Released: P&G 2014 Annual Report," P&G Corporate Newsroom, August 20, 2014, http://news.pg.com/blog/company-strategy/just-released-pg-2014-annual-report; "Procter & Gamble," *Growth Champions*, March 2016, http://growthchampions.org/growth-champions/procter-gamble/; and "Zero Moment of Truth (ZMOT)," *Think with Google*, www.thinkwithgoogle.com/marketing-resources/micro-moments/zero-moment-truth/ and www.thinkwithgoogle.com/marketing-resources/micro-moments/, accessed October 2018.
4. Hal Conick, "The End of Retail (as We Knew It)," *Marketing News*, September 27, 2017, pp. 38–47.
5. For more on the current struggles of traditional retailers, see "Derek Thompson, "What in the World Is Causing the Retail Meltdown," *The Atlantic*, April 10, 2017, www.theatlantic.com/business/archive/2017/04/retail-meltdown-of-2017/522384/; Phil Wahba, "The Death of Retail Is Greatly Exaggerated," *Fortune*, June 25, 2017, pp. 33–34; and Steve Dennis, "Retail 2018: Now Comes the Real Reckoning," *Forbes*, January 12, 2018, www.forbes.com/sites/stevendennis/2018/01/12/retail-2018-now-comes-the-real-reckoning/#46bed5a55f54.
6. Phil Wahba, "Everything Must Go," *Fortune*, March 1, 2017, pp. 95–100.
7. Daniel B. Kline, "Grocery Stores Are Facing a New Challenge and It's Not Just Amazon," *Business Insider*, September 14, 2017, www.businessinsider.com/grocery-stores-are-facing-a-new-challenge-and-its-not-just-amazon-2017-9; Pamela Danziger, "Online Grocery Sale to Reach $100 Billion in 2025; Amazon Is Current and Future Leader," *Forbes*, January 18, 2018, www.forbes.com/sites/pamdanziger/2018/01/18/online-grocery-sales-to-reach-100-billion-in-2025-amazon-set-to-be-market-share-leader/#683ed44462f3.
8. Mike Tighe, "Kwik Trip Aims to Fill Grills with Fresh Meat Offerings," *LaCrosse Tribune*, May 16, 2014, http://lacrossetribune.com/news/local/kwik-trip-aims-to-fill-grills-with-fresh-meat-offerings/article_0d23f455-1c56-5b94-884f-013d22b78fa9.html; Amanda Baltazar, "C-Stores Challenge Perceptions about Grocery," *CSP Magazine*, October 2017, www.cspdailynews.com/print/csp-magazine/article/c-stores-challenge-consumer-perceptions-about-grocery; and www.kwiktrip.com, accessed September 2018.
9. "Store Productivity—Walmart US," *eMarketer*, https://retail-index.emarketer.com/company/data/5374f24d4d4afd2bb4446614/5374f3094d4afd2bb444a93c/lfy/false/wal-mart-stores-inc-walmart-us, accessed October 2018; and "Supermarket Facts," www.fmi.org/research-resources/supermarket-facts, accessed October 2018.
10. See Hayley Peterson, "Dollar General Is Defying the Retail Apocalypse and Opening 900 Stores," *Business Insider*, February 24, 2018, www.businessinsider.com/dollar-general-opening-stores-photos-details-2018-2; and http://investor.shareholder.com/dollar/financials.cfm, accessed October 2018.
11. "How We Do It," http://tjmaxx.tjx.com/store/jump/topic/how-we-do-it/2400087, accessed May 2018.
12. See "H&R Block," *Entrepreneur*, www.entrepreneur.com/franchises/hrblock/330827, accessed October 2018; and www.hrblock.com/corporate/our-company, accessed October 2018.
13. Company and franchising information from "Top 200 Franchise Systems," *Franchise Times*, October 2017, www.franchisetimes.com/Top-200/; www.score.org/resources/should-i-buy-franchise; and www.aboutmcdonalds.com/mcd/our_company.html, accessed October 2018.
14. "Quarterly Retail E-Commerce Sales 4th Quarter 2017," U.S. Census Bureau, February 16, 2018, www.census.gov/retail/mrts/www/data/pdf/ec_current.pdf.
15. Sandy Skrovan, "How Shoppers Use Their Smartphones in Stores," *Retail Dive*, June 7, 2017, https://www.retaildive.com/news/how-shoppers-use-their-smartphones-in-stores/444147.
16. Erik Wander, "Meet the Omnishopper," *Adweek*, September 12, 2017, p. 10.
17. "Online or In-Store? How about a Little of Both?" *Washington Post*, November 28, 2014, p. A01; and "Social Media 2018: It's Influence in the Path to Purchase," *eMarketer*, December 18, 2017, www.emarketer.com/Report/Social-Commerce-2018-Its-Influence-Path-Purchase/2002175.
18. See www.footlocker-inc.com/investors.cfm?page=annual-reports and www.footlocker-inc.com, accessed October 2018.
19. Dina Berrta, "The Power List: Lynsi Snyder—Growing the Cult Chain Slow and Steady," *Nation's Restaurant News*, January 19, 2016, http://nrn.com/power-list-2016-Lynsi-Snyder; Robert Klara, "How In-N-Out Became the Small Burger Chain with the Massive Following," *Adweek*, November 17, 2015, www.adweek.com/print/168120; Daniel P. Smith, "The Secret to In-N-Out's Cult Following," *QSR*, August 2017, www.qsrmagazine.com/competition/secret-n-out-s-cult-following; and www.in-n-out.com, accessed October 2018.
20. Austin Carr, "The Future of Retailing in the Age of Amazon," *Fast Company*, December 2017–January 2018, pp. 84–101.
21. See Betsy Riley, "A Sneak Peek at Buckhead's New Restoration Hardware Gallery," *Atlanta Magazine*, November 20, 2014, www.atlantamagazine.com/decorating/a-sneak-peek-at-buckheads-new-restoration-hardware-gallery/; Richard Mullins, "Restoration Hardware Building Meg-Mansion 'Gallery' in Tampa," *Tampa Tribune*, January 4, 2015, www.tbo.com/news/business/restoration-hardware-building-mega-mansion-gallery-in-tampa-20150104/; and Bridget Brennan, "Would You Like Champagne with That Sofa? Restoration Hardware Bets Big on Experiential Retail," *Forbes*, November 13, 2015, www.forbes.com/sites/bridgetbrennan/2015/11/13/would-you-like-champagne-with-that-sofa-restoration-hardware-bets-big-on-experiential-retail/#7b46683e579e67def966579e; Hadley Keller, "RH Expands New Gallery Retail Strategy with West Palm Store," *Architectural Digest*, December 4, 2017, www.architecturaldigest.com/story/rh-expands-new-gallery-retail-strategy-west-palm-beach; and www.restorationhardware.com/content/promo.jsp?id=557012, accessed October 2018.
22. See Alexandra Sifferlin, "My Nose Made Me Buy It," *Time*, December 16, 2013, http://healthland.time.com/2013/12/16/my-nose-made-me-buy-it-how-retailers-use-smell-and-other-tricks-to-get-you-to-spend-spend-spend/; Cassandra Girard, "Meet the Scent Marketing Firm Winning the Battle for Your Nose," *NBC News*, July 24, 2017, www.nbcnews.com/business/your-business/meet-scent-marketing-firm-winning-battle-your-nose-n783761; and www.scentair.com, accessed October 2018.
23. Elyse Dupre, "Personalization at the Heart of CVS's ExtraCare Loyalty Program," *DMN*, May 9, 2017, www.dmnews.com/multichannel-marketing/personalization-is-at-the-heart-of-cvss-extracare-loyalty-program/article/656057/and www.cvs.com, accessed October 2018.
24. For definitions of these and other types of shopping centers, see "Dictionary," *American Marketing Association*, www.marketingpower.com/_layouts/Dictionary.aspx, accessed October 2018.
25. Josh Sanburn, "Why the Death of Malls Is about More Than Shopping," *Time*, July 10, 2017, http://time.com/4865957/death-and-life-shopping-mall/; Laura Sanicola, "America's Malls Are Rotting Away," *CNN Money*, December 12, 2017, www.bloomberg.com/news/articles/2018-01-08/why-some-shopping-malls-may-be-in-deeper-trouble-than-you-think; and Sarah Mulholland, "Why Some Shopping Malls May Be in Deeper Trouble Than You Think," *Bloomberg*, January 8, 2018, www.bloomberg.com/news/articles/2018-01-08/why-some-shopping-malls-may-be-in-deeper-trouble-than-you-think.
26. Jennifer Reingold and Phil Wahba, "Where Have All the Shopper Gone?" *Fortune*, September 3, 2014, http://fortune.com/2014/09/03/where-have-all-the-shoppers-gone/.
27. See Susan Berfield, "Shop Today," *Bloomberg Businessweek*, November 27, 2017, pp. 46–51, Phil Wahba, "Macy's Make-or-Break Christmas," *Fortune*, December 1, 2017, pp. 79–84; and http://investors.macysinc.com/phoenix.zhtml?c=84477&p=irol-reportsannual, accessed October 2018.
28. See Laia Garcia, "The Edit at Roosevelt Field Mall Brings Your URL Favs IRL," *Refinery*, November 30, 2017, www.refinery29.com/the-edit-store-experience-roosevelt-field-mall; Daniel Keyes, "Malls Look to Pop-Up

Shops to Boost Their Appeal," *Business Insider*, December 1, 2017, www.businessinsider.com/malls-look-to-pop-up-shops-to-boost-their-appeal-2017-12; and www.simon.com/the-edit, accessed October 2018.

29. See www.gilt.com, www.zulily.com, www.target.com, and www.amazon.com/gp/help/customer/display.html?nodeId=201134080, accessed October 2018.
30. See www.rpminc.com/leading-brands/consumer-brands, accessed October 2018.
31. See Jacqueline Renfrow, "AT&T Turns Michigan Avenue Flagship into a Museum," *Fierce Retail,* March 11, 2015, www.fierceretail.com/story/att-turns-michigan-avenue-flagship-museum/2015-03-11; Christopher Heine, "The Store of the Future Has Arrived," *Adweek*, June 3, 2013, www.adweek.com/print/149900; and www.callison.com/projects/att-%E2%80%93-michigan-avenue, accessed October 2016.
32. Sarah Perez, "Target Rolls Out Bluetooth Beacon Technology in Stores to Power New Indoor Maps in Its App," *Tech Crunch,* September 20, 2017, https://techcrunch.com/2017/09/20/target-rolls-out-bluetooth-beacon-technology-in-stores-to-power-new-indoor-maps-in-its-app/; "There's More in Store with the Target App," *A Bullseye View,* September 20, 2017, https://corporate.target.com/article/2017/09/target-app-mike-mcnamara; and Keith Wright, "Say Hello to Our Little Friends: How New Beacons May Save Old Retail," *Marketing Insider,* January 3, 2018, www.mediapost.com/publications/article/312422/say-hello-to-our-little-friends-how-new-beacons-m.html.
33. See Nikki Baird, "In Retail, AR Is for Shoppers and VR Is for Business," *Forbes*, April 26, 2017, www.forbes.com/sites/nikkibaird/2017/04/26/in-retail-ar-is-for-shoppers-and-vr-is-for-business/#2197c621618f; and Carolanne Mangies, "Is Marketing Ready for VR/AR in 2018?" Smart Insights, January 11, 2018, www.smartinsights.com/digital-marketing-platforms/video-marketing/is-marketing-ready-for-vr-ar-in-2018/.
34. "Green MashUP: 7 Trends Transforming Retail Sustain ability," *The Fifth Estate,* February 17, 2015, www.thefifthestate.com.au/business/trends/green-mashup-7-trends-transforming-retail-sustain-ability/71455; "The IKEA Group Yearly Summary FY2017 Report," www.ikea.com/ms/en_US/pdf/yearly_summary/IKEA_Group_Yearly_Summary_2017.pdf, accessed October 2018; and "The IKEA Group Approach to Sustainability," www.ikea.com/ms/en_US/pdf/sustainability_report/group_approach_sustainability_fy11.pdf, accessed October 2018.
35. See www.staples.com/sbd/cre/marketing/sustainability-center/?icid=SustainabilityCenter:topnav:1:home:20170901, accessed October 2018.
36. See "Global Powers of Retailing 2018," *Deloitte*, January 2018, accessed at www2.deloitte.com/content/dam/Deloitte/at/Documents/about-deloitte/global-powers-of-retailing-2018.pdf.
37. Grainger facts and other information are from the http://pressroom.grainger.com/phoenix.zhtml?c=194987&p=irol-mediakit and www.grainger.com, accessed October 2018.
38. Paul Demery, "Grainger's E-Commerce Sales Are Even Higher Than Reported," *Digital Commerce 360*, March 1, 2017, www.digitalcommerce360.com/2017/03/01/graingers-e-commerce-sales-are-even-higher-reported/; and www.grainger.com, accessed October 2018.
39. See http://investors.sysco.com/~/media/Files/S/Sysco-IR/documents/quarterly-results/1q18-factsheet.pdf and www.sysco.com/, accessed October 2018.
40. See www.supervalu.com, accessed October 2018.

Chapter 12

1. Jeff Haden, "A Marketing Expert Names the Top 5 Super Bowl Commercials of All Time," *Inc.,* February 21, 2018, www.inc.com/jeff-haden/an-expert-marketer-picks-top-5-super-bowl-commercials-of-all-time-and-dissects-why-they-were-so-effective.html; E. J. Schultz, "Behind the Snickers Campaign That Launched a Global Comeback," *Advertising Age,* October 4, 2013, www.adage.com/print/244593; Robert Klara, "How Snickers Fired a Quarterback, Hired a Zebra, and Tweaked One of Advertising's Most Famous Tag Lines," *Adweek,* February 27, 2014, www.adweek.com/print/155873; Ria Sharma, "Snickers Returns with a Brilliant Ad Campaign!" Einfach Digital, December 18. 2017, http://einfachdigital.com/snickers-returns-brilliant-ad-campaign/; and www.mars.com, www.youtube.com/snickers, www.facebook.com/snickers, http://snickers.tumblr.com/, and https://twitter.com/snickers/status/875116720356298752?lang=en, accessed October 2018.
2. For other definitions, see www.ama.org/resources/Pages/Dictionary.aspx, accessed October 2016.
3. See Dana Feldman, "U.S. TV Ad Spend Drops as Digital Ad Spend Climbs to $107B in 2018," *Forbes,* March 28, 2018, www.forbes.com/sites/danafeldman/2018/03/28/u-s-tv-ad-spend-drops-as-digital-ad-spend-climbs-to-107b-in-2018/#18c5ddb87aa6; and John Koetsier, "Mobile Advertising Will Drive 75% of All Digital Ad Spend in 2018: Here's What's Changing," *Forbes,* February 23, 2018, www.forbes.com/sites/johnkoetsier/2018/02/23/mobile-advertising-will-drive-75-of-all-digital-ad-spend-in-2018-heres-whats-changing/#b7eece4758be.
4. Julia Kollewe, "Marmite Maker Unilever Threatens to Pull Ads from Facebook and Google," *The Guardian,* February 12, 2018, www.theguardian.com/media/2018/feb/12/marmite-unilever-ads-facebook-google.
5. Karen Gilchrist, "Adidas Steps Away from TV Advertising as It Targets $4 Billion Growth," *CNBC,* March 15, 2017, www.cnbc.com/2017/03/15/adidas-steps-away-from-tv-advertising-as-it-targets-4-billion-growth.html; and Daphne Howland, "Adidas Ditching TV Ads to Reach Generation Z on Mobile," *Marketing Dive,* March 16, 2017, www.marketingdive.com/news/adidas-ditching-tv-ads-to-reach-generation-z-on-mobile/438291/.
6. See Lesley Bielby, "The 'A' Word—Does Advertising Still Exist?" *Advertising Age,* April 22, 2016, www.adage.com/print/303678 and Michael Strober, "We Interrupt This Interruption for an Important Message," *Advertising Age,* September 25, 2018, pp. 62–63.
7. See "The NewsCred Top 50 Awards," *NewsCred,* https://insights.newscred.com/best-content-marketing-brands/#about, accessed October 2018; and www.landroverusa.com/experiences/stories/index.html, www.instagram.com/landrover/, www.youtube.com/user/landrover, www.facebook.com/landrover/, and https://twitter.com/LandRover?ref_src=twsrc%5Egoogle%7Ctwcamp%5Eserp%7Ctwgr%5Eauthor, accessed October 2018.
8. See "Nielsen's Top Programs for Jan. 29–Feb.4," *Associated Press,* February 6, 2018, www.washingtonpost.com/entertainment/tv/nielsens-top-programs-for-jan-29-feb-4/2018/02/06/c770f692-0b80-11e8-998c-96deb18cca19_story.html?utm_term=.04b3ea218423; Todd Spangler, "Super Bowl Ads: YouTube Reveals Most Viewed Spots," *Variety,* February 5, 2018; and www.youtube.com/watch?v=J6-8DQALGt4, accessed February 9, 2018.
9. See discussions at Mike Ishmael, "The Cost of a Sales Call," October 22, 2012, http://4dsales.com/the-cost-of-a-sales-call/; Jeff Green, "The New Willy Loman Survives by Staying Home," *Bloomberg Businessweek,* January 14–20, 2013, pp. 16–17; Scott Tousley, "107 Mind-Blowing Sales Statistics That Will Help You Sell Smarter," *HubSpot,* September 14, 2015, http://blog.hubspot.com/sales/sales-statistics; and "What Is the Real Cost of a B2B Sales Call?" www.marketing-playbook.com/sales-marketing-strategy/what-is-the-real-cost-of-a-b2b-sales-call, accessed October 2018.
10. "Marketing Fact Pack 2018," *Advertising Age,* December 18, 2017, p. 8.
11. For these and other advertising spending facts, see "Marketing Fact Pack 2018," *Advertising Age,* December 18, 2017, pp. 4–8.
12. See Patrick Coffee, "U.S. Army Audit Claims 'Ineffective Marketing Programs' Have Wasted Millions in Taxpayer Dollars Each Year," *Adweek,* January 3, 2018, www.adweek.com/agencies/u-s-army-audit-claims-ineffective-marketing-programs-have-wasted-millions-in-taxpayer-dollars-each-year/.
13. See E. J. Schultz, "Pepsi Ads Take Shot at Share-A-Coke, Polar Bears," *Advertising Age,* June 15, 2015, www.adage.com/print/298985; and Brian Steinberg, "Coke, Pepsi Go to Super Bowl Battle Armed with Similar Pitches," *Variety,* February 1, 2018, http://variety.com/2018/tv/news/super-bowl-commercials-coca-cola-pepsi-advertising-1202684017/.
14. See Michael Addady, "General Mills Sues Chobani for Advertising That Yoplait Contains 'Bug Spray,'" *Fortune,* January 12, 2016, http://fortune.com/2016/01/12/general-mills-sues-chobani/; Christine Birkner, "'Scare Tactics' Used in Its Ads: Spots Imply Yoplait and Dannon Contain Pesticides, Chlorine," *Advertising Age,* January 20, 2016, www.adweek.com/print/169107; "United States Courts Opinions: United States District Court Eastern District of New York: Chobani, LLC, Plaintiff, v The Dannon Company, Inc., Defendant," April 25, 2016; and Graig Giammona, "Why Big Brands Couldn't Stop Chobani from Winning the Yogurt War," *Bloomberg,* March 9, 2017, www.bloomberg.com/news/articles/2017-03-09/yogurt-war-exposes-big-food-s-flaws-as-chobani-overtakes-yoplait.
15. "Who's Watching How Many TV Channels?," *Marketing Charts,* October 3, 2018, www.marketingcharts.com/television-71258; and "Number of Magazines in the United States from 2002 to 2016," *Statista,* www.statista.com/statistics/238589/number-of-magazines-in-the-united-states/, accessed October 2018.
16. Kelsey Libert and Kristen Tynski, "Research: The Emotions That Make Marketing Campaigns Go Viral," *HBR Blog Network,* October 24, 2013,

http://blogs.hbr.org/2013/10/research-the-emotions-that-make-marketing-campaigns-go-viral/; and data from YouTube, Facebook, Instagram, and Twitter, accessed October 2018.

17. "Figuring Out a Production Budget These Days Is Complicated," *Advertising Age,* May 1, 2015, http://adage.com/lookbook/article/production-companies/figuring-a-production-budget-days-complicated/298390/; Maggie Aland, "TV Advertising Costs and How to Advertise on a Budget," *FitSmallBusiness.com,* November 28, 2017, https://fitsmallbusiness.com/tv-advertising/; and "Cost for a 30-Second Commercial," Marketing Fact Pack 2018, *Advertising Age,* December 18, 2017, p. 18.
18. See Bree Brouwer, "Marriott Starts Production on 'Two Bellmen Two' Starring Freida Pinto," *Tubefilter,* November 10, 2015, www.tubefilter.com/2015/11/10/marriott-content-studio-two-bellmen-two-frieda-pinto/; Sarah Parker, "Marriott's Video Marketing Stays Strong with Two Bellmen Three," *Union Metrics,* January 21, 2017, https://unionmetrics.com/blog/2017/01/marriotts-video-marketing-stays-strong-two-bellmen-three/# "Two Bellmen: Winner in Hospitality," Shorty Awards, http://shortyawards.com/8th/two-bellmen, accessed October 2018; and www.youtube.com/watch?v=ZOgteFrOKt8 and www.youtube.com/channel/UCNs4ZSULeve-iGEFthwAfAQ, accessed October 2018.
19. Marty Swant, "Every Ad Is a Tide Ad: Inside Saatchi and P&G's Clever Super Bowl Takeover Starring David Harbour," *Advertising Age,* February 4, 2018, www.adweek.com/brand-marketing/every-ad-is-a-tide-ad-inside-saatchi-and-pgs-clever-super-bowl-takeover-starring-david-harbour/; and Lauren Johnson, "5 Takeaways from Tide's Full-Blown Super Bowl Blitz," *Adweek,* February 5, 2018, www.adweek.com/digital/5-takeaways-from-tides-full-blown-super-bowl-blitz/.
20. See Lindsay Kolowich, "Funny Tweets and Social Media Examples from 17 Real Brands," Hubspot, February 4, 2016, http://blog.hubspot.com/blog/tabid/6307/bid/33488/14-Funny-Brands-You-Can-t-Help-But-Follow-in-Social-Media.aspx.
21. "Why *The Lego Movie* Is the Perfect Piece of Product Placement," A.V. Club, February 11, 2014, www.avclub.com/article/why-the lego-movie-is-the-perfect-piece-of-product-201102; and Katarina Gustafsson, "LEGO Movie Helps Full-Year Revenue Growth Beat Rivals," *Bloomberg Business,* February 25, 2015, www.bloomberg.com/news/articles/2015-02-25/lego-movie-helps-toymaker-s-full-year-sales-growth-beat-rivals.
22. See Timothy Nichols, "How to Get the Best Visibility with Native Ads," *Forbes,* February 8, 2018, www.forbes.com/sites/forbesagencycouncil/2018/02/08/how-to-get-the-best-visibility-with-native-ads/#1db31d54766f; and Adam Abelin, "5 Global Native Advertising Trends 2018," Native Advertising Institute, https://nativeadvertisinginstitute.com/blog/5-global-native-advertising-trends-2018/, accessed October 2018.
23. See www.adsoftheworld.com/media/print/cat_footwear_go_ahead_look_up and www.wolverineworldwide.com/our-brands/cat/, accessed October 2018.
24. Benjamin Snyder, "Here's Why Doritos Is Ending Its 'Crash the Super Bowl' Contest," Fortune, January 29, 2016, http://fortune.com/2016/01/29/doritos-crash-the-super-bowl-contest/.
25. Christopher Heine, "West Elm Is Lifting Sales by Using Customer's Instagram Photos in Facebook Carousel Ads," *Adweek,* June 17, 2016, www.adweek.com/digital/west-elm-lifting-sales-using-customers-instagram-photos-facebook-carousel-ads-172076/; and Daniela Forte, "West Elm's Pinterest Style Finder Lets Customers Aid in Design," *Multichannel Merchant,* August 25, 2017, http://multichannelmerchant.com/marketing/west-elms-pinterest-style-finder-lets-customers-aid-design/.
26. See www.converse.com and https://help-en-us.nike.com/app/answer/article/converse-story/a_id/64073/country/us, accessed October 2018.
27. "Adidas Introduces 'Here to Create Legend' 2018 Boston Marathon Campaign Featuring Personal Highlight Videos Delivered to 30K Runners within Hours," *Adidas News Stream,* April 5, 2018, https://news.adidas.com/US/Latest-News/adidas-introduces-here-to-create-legend-2018-boston-marathon-campaign-featuring-30k-personal-hig/s/118fc950-53c9-406c-98ff-34881adb6f0f; and Laura McQuarrie, *Trend Hunter,* April 20, 2018, www.trendhunter.com/trends/running-videos.
28. See "Multitasking Is Changing Media Consumption Habits," Screen Media Daily, April 8, 2016, http://screenmediadaily.com/multitasking-is-changing-media-consumption-habits; and "Few Viewers Are Giving the TV Set Their Undivided Attention," eMarketer, November 7, 2017, www.emarketer.com/Article/Few-Viewers-Giving-TV-Set-Their-Undivided-Attention/1016717?ecid=NL1001.
29. *Forbes* and *Bloomberg Businessweek* cost and circulation data found online at www.bloombergmedia.com/specs/ and www.forbes.com/forbes-media/advertising/, accessed October 2018.
30. Natalie Tadena, "With the New Year Approaching, Weight Loss Ad Barrage Has Commenced," *Wall Street Journal,* December 30, 2014, http://blogs.wsj.com/cmo/2014/12/30/with-the-new-year-approaching-weight-loss-ad-barrage-has-commenced/; and T. L. Stanley, "Popular at Easter, Peeps Candy Extends to the Quirky Holidays," *New York Times,* June 18, 2014, www.nytimes.com/2014/06/19/business/media/popular-at-easter-peeps-candy-extends-to-the-quirky-holidays.html.
31. For these and other examples, see "Marketing in the Moments, to Reach Customers Online," *New York Times,* January 18, 2016, p. B5; and Tanya Dua, "You Can Still Dunk in the Dark, but You Don't Need a War Room," *Digiday,* February 4, 2016, http://digiday.com/agencies/super-bowl-war-room-rip/.
32. Information on advertising agency revenues from "Agency Report," *Advertising Age,* May 1, 2017, pp. 22–23.
33. Jeffrey N. Ross, "Chevrolet Will 'Find New Roads' as Brand Grows Globally: Aligns around the World behind Singular Vision," January 8, 2013, http://media.gm.com/media/us/en/gm/news.detail.html/content/Pages/news/us/en/2013/Jan/0107-find-new-roads.html; and Dale Buss, "Chevy Wins at Sochi by Giving Dimension to 'Find New Roads,'" *Forbes,* February 24, 2014, www.forbes.com/sites/dalebuss/2014/02/24/chevrolet-wins-at-sochi-as-find-new-roads-theme-gets-traction/.
34. Based on Glen Broom and Bey-Ling Sha, *Cutlip & Center's Effective Public Relations,* 11th ed. (Upper Saddle River, NJ: Prentice Hall, 2013), Chapter 1.
35. See "Healthcare Campaign of the Year 2015," *PR Week,* March 20, 2015, www.prweek.com/article/1337832; "CVS Health: CVS Quits for Good Campaign," *(add)ventures,* www.addventures.com/cvs-quits-good-campaign, accessed October 2018; and www.cvs.com/quit-smoking/, accessed October 2018.
36. See Craig Giammona, "Long Live the King," Bloomberg Businessweek, October 5–11, 2015, pp. 23–24; Krushbu Shah, "Burger King Mascot Steals Show at Belmont Stakes," Eater, June 8, 2015, www.eater.com/2015/6/8/8746047/burger-king-mascot-steals-show-at-belmont-stakes; and http://mcwhopper.com/, accessed October 2016.
37. Quotes from Sarah Skerik, "An Emerging PR Trend: Content PR Strategy and Tactics," January 15, 2013, http://blog.prnewswire.com/2013/01/15/an-emerging-pr-trend-content-pr-strategy-tactics/; Mary Teresa Bitti, "The New Mad Men: How Publics Relations Firms Have Emerged from the Shadows," *Financial Post,* December 28, 2014, http://business.financialpost.com/entrepreneur/the-changing-role-of-public-relations-firms; and Nelson Granados, "How Public Relations Agencies Are Becoming Top Creators of Digital Video Content," *Forbes,* January 9, 2018, www.forbes.com/sites/nelsongranados/2018/01/09/how-public-relations-agencies-are-becoming-top-creators-of-digital-video-content/#540e1b986626.

Chapter 13

1. Based on information from Bob Evans, "Why Salesforce Is Soaring in the Cloud," *Forbes,* March 5, 2018, www.forbes.com/sites/bobevans1/2018/03/05/20-eye-popping-stats-from-salesforce-com-as-it-soars-on-digital-transformation-boom/; David Whitford, "Salesforce.com: The Software and the Story," *Inc.*, September 2014, pp. 113–117; Whitford, "Selling, the Story: Four Strategies Salesforce.com Uses to Stay on Top," *Inc.,* September 2014, p. 116; Dan Gallagher, "Salesforce Won't Let Age Slow It Down," *Wall Street Journal,* November 9, 2017, www.wsj.com/articles/salesforce-wont-let-age-slow-it-down-1510240677; "The World's Most Innovative Companies," *Forbes,* www.forbes.com/innovative-companies/list/, accessed October 2018; and information from www.statista.com and www.salesforce.com, accessed October 2018.
2. See Jack Neff, "Why the Wall Is Crumbling between Sales, Marketing," *Advertising Age,* April 4, 2016, pp. 30–31; Jonathan Gray, "Why You Can't Afford to Keep Sales and Marketing in Silos," *Sales & Marketing Management,* July 18, 2016, https://salesandmarketing.com/node/6661; and Philip Kotler and Kevin Lane Keller, *Marketing Management,* 15th ed. (Hoboken, NJ: Pearson Education, 2016), p. 644.
3. See "Walmart and Amazon Rachet Up Pressure on Suppliers," *Seeking Alpha,* March 31, 2017, https://seekingalpha.com/article/4059526-wal-mart-amazon-ratchet-pressure-suppliers; and "Customer Business Development," www.pg.com/vn/careers/our_functions/customer_business_development.shtml, accessed October 2018.
4. "The World's Largest Sales Forces," *Sales Benchmark Index,* Spring 2016, pp. 34–35, https://salesbenchmarkindex.com/wp-content/uploads/2016/07/201602-SBIMag_e2e_Online_LR.pdf.
5. See Gabe Larsen, "Inside vs. Outside Sales: How to Structure a Sales Team for Success," *HubSpot,* March 21, 2018, https://blog.hubspot.com/sales/inside-vs-outside-sales; and "What Is the Real Cost of a B2B Sales Call?" www.marketing-playbook.com/sales-marketing-strategy/what-is-the-real-cost-of-a-b2b-sales-call, accessed October 2018.

6. See "The State of Sales," InsideSales.com Labs, 2017, www.insidesales.com/wp-content/uploads/2017/09/State-of-Sales-9_15_17-Exec-Summary.pdf?27a428&27a428.
7. Chris Young, "Hiring Costs Are Just the Tip of the Iceberg," *Rainmaker Group Sales Wolf Blog,* January 19, 2016, www.therainmakergroupinc.com/human-capital-strategy-blog/the-ugly-truth-the-real-costs-of-a-bad-sales-hire.
8. For this and more information and discussion, see www.gallupaustralia.com.au/consulting/118729/sales-force-effectiveness.aspx, accessed October 2012; Brittney Helmrich, "8 Important Traits of Successful Salespeople," *Business News Daily,* January 25, 2016, www.businessnewsdaily.com/4173-personality-traits-successful-sales-people.html; and Heather R. Morgan, "The Most Successful Salespeople All Have This One Thing in Common," *Forbes,* January 26, 2018. www.forbes.com/sites/heathermorgan/2018/01/16/the-most-successful-salespeople-all-have-this-one-thing-in-common/#bb4b8256d221.
9. See Steve Denning, "The One Thing the Greatest Salespeople All Have," *Forbes,* November 29, 2012, www.forbes.com/sites/stevedenning/2012/11/29/the-one-thing-the-greatest-salespeople-all-have/.
10. "Strengths Based Selling," www.gallup.com/press/176651/strengths-based-selling.aspx, accessed October 2018.
11. Frank V. Cespedes and Yuchun Lee, "Your Sales Training Is Probably Lackluster. Here's How to Fix It," *Harvard Business Review,* June 12, 2017, https://hbr.org/2017/06/your-sales-training-is-probably-lackluster-heres-how-to-fix-it.
12. See www.theknowledgeguru.com, www.theknowledgeguru.com/testimonials/case-studies/, and www.theknowledgeguru.com/solution/, accessed October 2018.
13. See "Sales Reps Spend Only 37% of Time Selling According to Research from InsideSales.com," *Business Wire,* November 190, 2017, www.businesswire.com/news/home/20171110005551/en/Sales-Reps-Spend-37-Time-Selling-Research.
14. See Shelly Cernel, "Selling to the Modern B2B Buyer," *Salesforce.com Blog*, June 16, 2016, www.salesforce.com/blog/2016/06/selling-to-the-modern-b2b-buyer.html; Brian Signorelli, "How Google Killed 1 Million Sales Jobs—and How to Keep Yours," *HubSpot*, May 2, 2017, https://blog.hubspot.com/sales/how-google-killed-1-million-sales-jobs; and Tim Colter, "What the Future Science of B2B Sales Growth Looks Like," McKinsey, January 2018, accessed at www.mckinsey.com/business-functions/marketing-and-sales/our-insights/what-the-future-science-of-b2b-sales-growth-looks-like.
15. Andy Hoar, "The Death of a (B2B) Salesman," Forrester, May 11, 2017, https://go.forrester.com/what-it-means/ep12-death-b2b-salesman/.
16. Neil Davey, "Using Social Media Marketing in B2B Markets," *SmartInsights,* February 16, 2015, www.smartinsights.com/b2b-digital-marketing/b2b-social-media-marketing/b2bsocialmediamarketing/. For more on Makino's social networking efforts, see www.facebook.com/Makino Machine, www.youtube.com/user/Makino MachineTools, and http://twitter.com/#!/makinomachine, accessed October 2018.
17. Example based on information from James C. Anderson, Nirmalya Kumar, and James A. Narus, "Become a Value Merchant," *Sales & Marketing Management*, May 6, 2008, pp. 20–23; and "Business Market Value Merchants," *Marketing Management*, March/April 2008, pp. 31+. For more discussion and examples, Larry Myler, "B2B Sales Insights for Commoditized Markets," *Forbes,* November 7, 2017, www.forbes.com/sites/larrymyler/2017/11/07/b2b-sales-insights-for-commoditized-markets/#7d74b1d8b63d; and Eric Almquist, Jamie Cleghorn, and Lori Sherer, "The B@B Elements of Value," *Harvard Business Review,* April 2018, https://hbr.org/2018/03/the-b2b-elements-of-value.
18. Jack Neff, "Study: CPG Now Spends More on Digital Than Traditional Ads, but Shoppers Doubt They Work," *Advertising Age*, February 23, 2017, http://adage.com/article/cmo-strategy/study-cpg-spends-digital-traditional-advertising-combined/308077/
19. "2017 Marks the Demise of Print-at-Home Coupons as Digital Redemption Climbs 67%," Inmar Press Release, February 6, 2018, https://globenewswire.com/news-release/2018/02/06/1333761/0/en/2017-Marks-the-Demise-of-Print-at-Home-Coupons-as-Digital-Redemption-Climbs-67.html.
20. See "2017 Marks the Demise of Print-at-Home Coupons as Digital Redemption Climbs 67%," Inmar Press Release, February 6, 2018, https://globenewswire.com/news-release/2018/02/06/1333761/0/en/2017-Marks-the-Demise-of-Print-at-Home-Coupons-as-Digital-Redemption-Climbs-67.html.
21. See www.happymeal.com, accessed October 2018.
22. See "The 2016 Estimate of Promotional Products Distributor Sales," *PPAI,* www.ppai.org/media/2534/ppai2016salesvolumestudysummary.pdf.
23. See www.infinitesweeps.com/sweepstake/155913-West-Elm-The-5000-Room.html and https://doodles.google.com/d4g/rules.html, accessed October 2018.
24. Rachael Kirkpatrick, "Delta Sets Record with Mass Shower at Warrior Dash," *Event Marketer,* July 10, 2015, www.eventmarketer.com/-article/delta-sets-new-world-record-331-person-shower-warrior-dash/; "Mud Shower Station," *Adweek,* September 7, 2015, p. 38; and "Delta Faucet Embraces Muddy Mess Makers, Celebrates Shower Singers," *PR Newswire,* August 2, 2017, www.prnewswire.com/news-releases/delta-faucet-embraces-muddy-mess-makers-celebrates-shower-singers-300303609.html.
25. Cadent Consulting Group, "2017 Marketing Spending Industry Study," http://cadentcg.com/wp-content/uploads/2017-Marketing-Spending-Study.pdf, accessed October 2018.
26. See "CES Attendee Audit Summary Results," www.ces.tech/About-CES/CES-by-the-Numbers.aspx, accessed October 2018; "The Greatest and Most Fascinating Show on Earth," www.bauma.de/trade-fair/information/about-bauma/index.html, accessed October 2018.

Chapter 14

1. See E. J. Schultz, "Why Coke Is Adding Last Names to 'Share a Coke,'" *Advertising Age,* April 18, 2017, http://adage.com/article/cmo-strategy/coke-adding-names-share-a-coke/308678/; Alex Samuely, "Coca-Cola Uses Snackable Mobile Content for Refreshing Marketing Approach," *Mobile Marketer,* www.mobilemarketer.com/ex/mobilemarketer/cms/news/content/22824.html, accessed October 2018; Christine Champagne, "Coca-Cola Goes Full Digital in Multisite Campaign to Reach Teens," *Fast Company,* April 23, 2013, www.fastcompany.com/1682843/coca-cola-goes-full-digital-in-multi-site-campaign-to-reach-teens; Joe Tripodi, "Coca-Cola Marketing Shifts from Impressions to Expressions," *Harvard Business Review,* April 27, 2011, https://hbr.org/2011/04/coca-colas-marketing-shift-fro; "A Deep Dive into the Social Media Habits and Performance of Coca-Cola," *Unmetric,* https://unmetric.com/brands/coca-cola, accessed October 2018; Larissa Faw, "Coca-Cola Adds New Features to 'Share a Coke' Campaign," *MediaPost,* May 10, 2018, www.mediapost.com/publications/article/319083/coca-cola-adds-new-features-to-share-a-coke-camp.html?edition=108997; and www.coca-colacompany.com, http://uploader.coca-colacompany.com/jump-in-ugc-image-uploader, www.coca-colacompany.com/our-company/about-coca-cola-journey, and www.coca-colacompany.com/tags/share-a-coke, https://buy.shareacoke.com/, accessed October 2018.
2. Lauren Johnson, "Q&A: PepsiCo's CMOs on Why 40% of Its Super Bowl Budget Is Going to Digital," *Adweek,* January 28, 2018, www.adweek.com/digital/qa-pepsicos-cmos-why-40-its-super-bowl-budget-going-digital-169270/.
3. See www.expediagroup.com, www.expediagroup.com/about, www.expediagroup.com/brands/travelocity/, and www.travelocity.com/inspire/, accessed October 2018.
4. See Greg Sterling, "Digital Advertising Pulling Away from TV on Global Basis," *Marketing Land,* March 26, 2018, https://marketingland.com/forecast-digital-advertising-pulling-away-from-tv-on-global-basis-236977; and Bruce Biegel, "Outlook for Data-Drive Marketing—First Look for 2018," Winterberry Group, January 10, 2018, www.winterberrygroup.com/our-insights/outlook-data-driven-marketing-2018.
5. See www.lowes.com/how-to-library, accessed October 2018.
6. See "US Adults Now Spend 12 Hours 7 Minutes a Day Consuming Media," *eMarketer,* May 1, 2017, www.emarketer.com/Article/US-Adults-Now-Spend-12-Hours-7-Minutes-Day-Consuming-Media/1015775; "Internet Usage Statistics," *Internet World Stats,* www.internetworldstats.com/stats.htm; accessed October 2018; "Mobile Phone Users Worldwide," *Statista,* www.statista.com/statistics/330695/number-of-smartphone-users-worldwide/, accessed October 2018.
7. See Greg Sterling, "Reports: Digital, Especially Mobile, Driving Trillions in Offline Retail Spending," *Marketing Land*, February 17, 2017, https://marketingland.com/reports-digital-especially-mobile-driving-trillions-offline-retail-spending-207037; "U.S. Online Retail Sales Likely to Surpass $1 Trillion by 2027," *Reuters,* October 17, 2017, www.reuters.com/article/us-usa-retail-internet/u-s-online-retail-sales-likely-to-surpass-1-trillion-by-2027-fti-idUSKBN1CM1LW; and Stefany Zarboan, "U.S. E-commerce Sales Grow 16.0% in 2017," *Internet Retailer,* February 16, 2018, www.digitalcommerce360.com/article/us-ecommerce-sales/.
8. See Arthur Zaczkiewcz, "Amazon, Wal-Mart an Apple Top List of Biggest E-commerce Retailers," *WWD,* April 7, 2017, http://wwd.com/business-news/business-features/amazon-wal-mart-apple-biggest-e-commerce-retailers-10862796/; and "2017 Top 50-E-retailers Chart," *NRF,* January 16, 2017, https://nrf.com/blog/2017-top-250-global-powers-of-retailing.

9. Bill Briggs, "Home Depot's Online Sales Grow 21.5% in Fiscal 2017," *Digital Commerce 360,* February 21, 2018, www.digitalcommerce360.com/2018/02/21/home-depots-online-sales-grow-21-5-fiscal-2017/; Mark Brohan, "Home Depot Hammers Away at Online Growth," *Digital Commerce 360,* January 20, 2016, www.digitalcommerce360.com/2016/01/20/home-depot-hammers-away-online-growth/; Matthew Cochrane, "3 Big Takeaways from Home Depot's Fourth Quarter," *Motley Fool,* March 2, 2018, www.fool.com/investing/2018/03/02/3-big-takeaways-from-home-depots-fourth-quarter.aspx; and Home Depot annual reports and other information found at http://ir.homedepot.com/financial-reports/annual-reports/recent, accessed October 2018.
10. See Kevin Ota, "ESPN Digital: No. 1 in March across All Key Metrics" ESPN press release, April 17, 2018, https://espnmediazone.com/us/press-releases/2018/04/espn-digital-no-1-in-march-across-all-key-metrics/; and www.espn.com, accessed October 2018.
11. See "IAC Internet Advertising Competition," www.iacaward.org/iac/winner/17152/21st-century-fox-truex-sonic-wins-2018-iac-award-for-sonic-.html, accessed October 2018.
12. Alphabet annual reports, https://abc.xyz/investor/, accessed October 2018.
13. Rani Molla, "Advertisers Will Spend $40 Billion more on IOnternet Ads Than on TV Ads This Year," *Recode,* March 26, 2018, www.recode.net/2018/3/26/17163852/online-internet-advertisers-outspend-tv-ads-advertisers-social-video-mobile-40-billion-2018; Dan Shewan, "How Much Does Google AdWords Cost?" *WordStream,* December 11, 2017, www.wordstream.com/blog/ws/2015/05/21/how-much-does-adwords-cost; Allen Finn, "35 Marketing Statistics That Should Change Your Strategy in 2018," *Word Stream,* March 22, 2018, www.wordstream.com/blog/ws/2018/02/05/marketing-statistics.
14. See Allen Finn, "35 Face-Melting Email Marketing Stats for 2018," *WordStream,* March 22, 2018, www.wordstream.com/blog/ws/2017/06/29/email-marketing-statistics; Jess Nelson, "Majority of Emails Read on Mobile Devices," *MediaPost,* July 21, 2017, www.mediapost.com/publications/article/304735/majority-of-emails-read-on-mobile-devices.html; "2017 Consumer Email Habits Report: What Do Your Customers Really Want?" *Campaign Monitor,* www.campaignmonitor.com/resources/guides/insights-research-report/, accessed October 2018; and The Radicati Group, "Email Statistics Report 2017–2021," www.radicati.com/wp/wp-content/uploads/2017/01/Email-Statistics-Report-2017-2021-Executive-Summary.pdf, accessed October 2018.
15. See "The Top 100 Email Marketing Campaigns," www.campaignmonitor.com/best-email-marketing-campaigns/, accessed October 2018.
16. See Lindsey Kolowich, "12 of the Best Email Marketing Examples You've Ever Seen (and Why They're Great)," *Hubspot,* March 5, 2015, http://blog.hubspot.com/marketing/email-marketing-examples-list; and "The Top 100 Email Marketing Campaigns," www.campaignmonitor.com/best-email-marketing-campaigns/, accessed October 2018.
17. Anabel Acton, "How to Stop Wasting 2.5 Hours on Email Every Day," *Forbes,* July 13, 2017, www.forbes.com/sites/annabelacton/2017/07/13/innovators-challenge-how-to-stop-wasting-time-on-emails/#7ca30e049788; and Symantec Security Response Publications, www.symantec.com/security_response/publications/monthlythreatreport.jsp, accessed October 2018.
18. James G. Brooks, "Here's How Social Video Will Evolve in 2018," *Venture Beat,* November 19, 2017, https://mashable.com/2017/12/05/how-facebook-watch-will-overtake-youtube-as-biggest-video-platform/#CkdhCWfv35qG; Brendan Gahan, "Facebook Watch Will Overtake YouTube as the Biggest Video Platform." *Mashable,* December 5, 2017, https://mashable.com/2017/12/05/how-facebook-watch-will-overtake-youtube-as-biggest-video-platform/#CkdhCWfv35qG; Salman Aslam, "Snapchat by the Numbers," Omnicore Agency, February 13, 2018, www.omnicoreagency.com/snapchat-statistics/; Aaron Smith and Monica Anderson, "Social Media Use in 2018," Pew Research, March 1, 2018, www.pewinternet.org/2018/03/01/social-media-use-in-2018/; and "Statistics and Facts about Online Video Usage," *Statista,* www.statista.com/topics/1137/online-video/, accessed October 2018.
19. "Being Heard: The Top 10 Super Bowl Ads by Digital Share of Voice," *Advertising Age,* Fbruary 5, 2018, http://adage.com/article/special-report-super-bowl/top-10-super-bowl-ads-digital-share-voice/312257/; "Amazon Rolls Out Celebs for 90-Seconde Alexa Super Bowl Commercial," *Seattle Times,* February 2, 2018, www.seattletimes.com/business/amazon/amazon-rolls-out-celebs-for-90-second-alexa-super-bowl-commercial/; and "2018 Ad Meter Results," http://admeter.usatoday.com/results/2018.
20. See Tim Nudd, "The 20 Most Viral Ads of 2015," *Adweek,* November 19, 2015, www.adweek.com/news-gallery/advertising-branding/20-most-viral-ads-2015-168213; Abner Li, "Latest 'Be together. Not the same.' Android Ad Has a Strong and Charming Message," *9TO5 Google,* February 29, 2016, http://9to5google.com/2016/02/29/latest-be-together-not-the-same-ad/; and www.youtube.com/watch?v=q-NKpDTwMms, accessed October 2018.
21. Troy Dreier, "The Force Was Strong with This One," *Streaming Media Magazine,* April/May 2011, pp. 66–68. Also see "Why Certain Things Go Viral," *HBR Video,* January 2016, https://hbr.org/video/4698519638001/why-certain-things-go-viral; and Christine DesMarais, "Want Your Video to Go Viral? The Rules Have A ll Changed," *Inc,* February 5, 2018, www.inc.com/christina-desmarais/5-steps-to-a-viral-video-according-to-a-guy-behind-youtubes-number-one-ad-of-decade.html.
22. Kayleen Schafer, "How Bloggers Make Money on Instagram," *Harpers Bazaar,* May 20, 2015; Caitlin Keating, "The Fashion Blogger behind We Wore What," *New York Times,* January 20, 2016, www.nytimes.com/2016/01/21/fashion/weworewhat-danielle-bernstein.html; Laureen Indvik, "The 20 Most Influential Personal Style Bloggers: 2016 Edition," *Fashionista,* March 14, 2016; Claire Coghlan, "How 'We Wore What' Blogger Danielle Bernstein Went from Sophomore to 6 Figures in Under 6 Years," *Forbes,* August 23, 2017, www.forbes.com/sites/clairecoghlan/2017/08/23/how-we-wore-what-blogger-danielle-bernstein-went-from-sophomore-to-seven-figures-in-under-6-years/#415d42275843; and http://weworewhat.com/, accessed October 2018.
23. "A Deep Dive into the Social Media Habits and Performance of Nike," *Unmetric,* https://unmetric.com/brands/nike, accessed October 2018.
24. See http://newsroom.fb.com/company-info, www.youtube.com/yt/press/statistics.html, and www.statista.com/statistics/282087/number-of-monthly-active-twitter-users/, accessed October 2018.
25. For these and other examples, see www.goodreads.com, www.farmersonly.com, www.birdpost.com, and www.cafemom.com, accessed October 2018.
26. See Mary Blacklston, "Why JetBlue Is the Best Example of Customer Service," *Success Agency Growth HQ Blog,* October 18, 2017, www.successagency.com/growth/2017/10/18/jetblue-best-customer-service/; and Lindsay Kolowich, "Delighting People in 140 Characters: An Inside Look at JetBlue's Customer Service Success," *Hubspot,* https://blog.hubspot.com/marketing/jetblue-customer-service-twitter, accessed October 2018.
27. See www.instagram.com/etsy/, www.pinterest.com/etsy/, and www.etsy.com/about, accessed October 2018.
28. Michael Bourne, "Sailing of 14 Social Cs," *Mullen Advertising,* February 13, 2012.
29. David Cohen, "What Dunkin' Donuts Can Learn from Starbucks' Social Strategy," *Adweek,* April 3, 2018, www.adweek.com/digital/what-dunkin-donuts-can-learn-from-starbucks-social-strategy/.
30. Kate Taylor, "The Unicorn Frappuccino Completely Revolutionized How Starbucks Invents New Drinks," *Business Insider,* July 2, 2017, www.businessinsider.com/starbucks-new-unicorn-frappuccino-inspired-era-2017-6; Todd Wassermann, "Starbucks 'Tweet-a-Coffee' Campaign Prompted $180,000 in Purchases," *Mashable,* December 13, 2013, http://mashable.com/2013/12/05/starbuckss-tweet-a-coffee-180000/; and www.facebook.com/Starbucks and https://twitter.com/Starbucks, accessed October 2018.
31. Facts in this paragraph are from "Why Nearly 46 Percent of Households Still Have Landlines," *Associated Press,* May 4, 2017, https://nypost.com/2017/05/04/why-nearly-46-percent-of-household-still-have-landlines/; Sara Perez, "Report: Smartphone Owners Are Using 9 Apps per Day, 30 per Month," *Tech Crunch,* May 4, 2017, https://techcrunch.com/2017/05/04/report-smartphone-owners-are-using-9-apps-per-day-30-per-month/; and "Mobile Fact Sheet," *Pew Research Center,* February 5, 2018, www.pewinternet.org/fact-sheet/mobile/.
32. Sarah Perez, "U.S. Consumers Now Spend More Time in Apps Than Watching TV," *Tech Crunch,* September 10, 2015, http://techcrunch.com/2015/09/10/u-s-consumers-now-spend-more-time-in-apps-than-watching-tv/; "Americans Check Their Phones 80 Times a Day," *New York Post,* November 8, 2017, https://nypost.com/2017/11/08/americans-check-their-phones-80-times-a-day-study/; and Chris Klotzbach and Lali Kesiraju, "Flurry State of Mobile 2017: With Captive Mobile Audiences, New App Growth Stagnates," *Flurry Blog,* January 10, 2018, http://flurrymobile.tumblr.com/post/169545749110/state-of-mobile-2017-mobile-stagnates.
33. "U.S. Mobile Retail Commerce Sales as Percentage of Retail E-Commerce from 2017 to 20121," *Statista,* www.statista.com/statistics/249863/us-mobile-retail-commerce-sales-as-percentage-of-e-commerce-sales/, accessed October 2018; "Deloitte: 93 Percent of Consumers Use Their Phone while Shopping," *Apparel,* December 13, 2016, https://apparelmag.com/deloitte-93-percent-consumers-use-their-phone-while-shopping; and Justin Smith, "Mobile eCommerce Stats in 2018 and the Future Trends of

mCommerce," *OuterBox Blog,* January 11, 2018, www.outerboxdesign.com/web-design-articles/mobile-ecommerce-statistics.

34. See John Koetsier, "Mobile Advertising Will Drive 75% of All Digital Ad Spend in 2018," *Forbes,* February 23, 2018, www.forbes.com/sites/johnkoetsier/2018/02/23/mobile-advertising-will-drive-75-of-all-digital-ad-spend-in-2018-heres-whats-changing/2/#705b42e01b43.
35. See "Check Out the 26 Boldly Inventive Campaigns That Won This Year's Project Isaac Awards," *Adweek,* August 21, 2016, www.adweek.com/brand-marketing/check-out-26-boldly-inventive-campaigns-won-years-project-isaac-awards-173060/; Lauren Johnson, "How Brands Are Using Instagram and Snapchat for Their Super Bowl Campaigns," *Adweek,* February 5, 2017, www.adweek.com/digital/how-brands-are-using-instagram-and-snapchat-for-their-super-bowl-campaigns/; and "Gatorade Super Bowl Dunk," www.jeffschroer.com/filter/Cannes/Gatorade Super-Bowl Dunk, accessed October 2018.
36. See Ginger Conlon, "Will Digital Media Spend Surpass Offline Spend in 2018?," *MKTG Insight*, www.mktginsight.com/winterberry-outlook-2018-data, accessed October 2018; Bruce Biegel, "Outlook for Data-Driven Marketing–First Look for 2018," Winterberry Group, January 10, 2018, www.winterberrygroup.com/our-insights/outlook-data-driven-marketing-2018.
37. "Direct Mail Statistics," Data & Marketing Association, https://thedma.org/marketing-insights/marketing-statistics/direct-mail-statistics/, accessed October 2018; Julie Liesse, "When Times Are Hard, Mail Works," *Advertising Age*, March 30, 2009, p. 14; Lois Geller, "If Direct Mail Is Dying, It's Sure Taking Its Time about It," *Forbes,* December 4, 2013, www.forbes.com/sites/loisgeller/2013/12/04/if-direct-mail-is-dying-its-sure-taking-its-time-about-it/; Craig Simpson, "4 Reasons to Use Direct Mail Marketing Instead of Email," *Entrepreneur,* February 17, 2015, www.entrepreneur.com/article/242731; and Allen Abbott, "It's 2017 and Direct Mail Still Exists," *Navistone Blog*, February 1, 2017, www.navistone.com/blog/its-2017-and-direct-mail-marketing-still-isnt-dead.
38. "Data & Marketing Association Direct Mail Statistics," Data & Marketing Association, https://thedma.org/marketing-insights/marketing-statistics/direct-mail-statistics/, accessed October 2018; and Ben Unglesbee, "Why Paper Catalogs Still Matter," *Retail Dive,* Oct. 6, 2017, www.retaildive.com/news/why-paper-catalogs-still-matter/506298/.
39. Molly Soat, "In the Mood to Peruse," *Marketing News,* July 2015, pp. 41–49; and Ronald D. White, "The Old-Fashioned Mail-Order Catalog Is Making a Comeback," *Los Angeles Times,* November 23, 2017, www.latimes.com/business/la-fi-catalogs-return-20171123-story.html.
40. Mike Ryan, "Print Is Dead? J.C. Penney Catalog Crunches the Data, Returns to Print," *Businesss2Community*, July 30, 2015, www.business2community.com/consumer-marketing/print-is-dead-j-c-penney-catalog-crunches-the-data-returns-to-print-01289952#kDooq0brVHlyjgym.97; Ronald White, "The Old-Fashioned Mail-Order Catalog Is Making a Comeback," *Los Angeles Times,* November 23, 2017, www.latimes.com/business/la-fi-catalogs-return-20171123-story.html; and "Data & Marketing Association Direct Mail Statistics," https://thedma.org/marketing-insights/marketing-statistics/direct-mail-statistics/, accessed September 2018.
41. See Federal Trade Commission, "FTC Issues FY 2017 National Do Not Call Registry Data," December 18, 2017, www.ftc.gov/news-events/press-releases/2017/12/ftc-releases-fy-2017-national-do-not-call-registry-data-book-dnc; and www.donotcall.gov, accessed October 2018.
42. See "This Skin Care Company Grew Sales by Almost 400% Last Quarter," *Yahoo! Finance*, January 26, 2017; and www.guthy-renker.com/ and www.proactiv.com, accessed October 2018.
43. Michael Hickins, "Beachbody Expanding while Its Customers' Waistlines Shrink," *Forbes,* January 23, 2017, www.forbes.com/sites/oracle/2017/01/23/beachbody-expanding-while-its-customers-waistlines-shrink/#18a559724628.
44. "Best Buy: Consumer Electronics Retailing on the Go," www.zoomsystems.com/our-partners/partner-portfolio/; and www.zoomsystems.com/about-us, accessed October 2018.
45. See "The Home Depot Appliance Finder," Image Manufacturng Group, http://imgarchitectural.com/case-studies/2014/3/26/the-home-depot-appliance-finder; and "Customer Experience Is the New Marketing," August 21, 2017, Momentum Worldwide, www.momentumww.com/news/2017/8/16/customer-experience-is-the-new-marketing.
46. See Internet Crime Complaint Center, www.ic3.gov, accessed October 2018.
47. See Generali Global Assistance, "Three-Quarters of Americans Concerned about Identity Theft during Holiday Shopping Season," November 2, 2017, www.prnewswire.com/news-releases/three-quarters-of-americans-concerned-about-identity-theft-during-holiday-shopping-season-300547979.html; and "The IRTC 2017 Annual Report," *Identity Theft Resource Center*, www.idtheftcenter.org/About-ITRC/itrc-corporate-overview.html, accessed October 2018.
48. See Jenny Anderson, "When Will Social Media Companies Get Seriosus about Their Effect on Young Kids," *Quartz,* January 15, 2018, https://qz.com/1179894/when-will-social-media-companies-like-facebook-and-snapchat-get-serious-about-their-effect-on-young-kids/; and "21 Completely Insane Social Media Statistics," *Content Factory,* www.contentfac.com/more-people-own-cell-phone-than-toothbrush-10-crazy-social-media-statistics/, accessed October 2018.
49. See Bree Fowler, "Americans Want More Say in the Privacy of Personal Data," *Consumer Reports,* May 18, 2017, www.consumerreports.org/privacy/americans-want-more-say-in-privacy-of-personal-data/; and William E Gibson, "Online Privacy a Major Concern, AARP Survey Shows," *AARP,* May 17, 2017, www.aarp.org/home-family/personal-technology/info-2017/survey-shows-online-privacy-concerns-fd.html.
50. "Unleash Mobile Data Analytics on Carrier Networks," http://go.sap.com/product/crm/mobile-data-analytics.html#item_0, accessed October 2018.
51. Dylan Currin, "Are You Ready? Here Is All the Data Facebook and Google Have on You," *The Guardian,* March 28, 2018, www.theguardian.com/commentisfree/2018/mar/28/all-the-data-facebook-google-has-on-you-privacy; and Ben Popken, "Google Sells the Future, Powered byYour Personal Data," *NBC News,* May 10, 2018, www.nbcnews.com/tech/tech-news/google-sells-future-powered-your-personal-data-n870501.
52. See Richard Byrne Reilly, "Feds to Mobile Marketers: Stop Targeting Kids, or Else," *Venture Beat,* March 27, 2014, http://venturebeat.com/2014/03/27/feds-to-mobile-marketers-stop-targeting-kids-or-else-exclusive/; and www.business.ftc.gov/privacy-and-security/childrens-privacy, accessed October 2018.
53. Information on TRUSTe at www.truste.com, accessed October 2018.
54. Information on the DMA Privacy Promise at https://thedma.org/resources/consumer-resources/ and https://thedma.org/privacy-policy/, accessed October 2018.

Chapter 15

1. See Tim Nudd, "11 Ikea Ads That Show What a Brilliant Year the Brand Had Creatively," *Adweek,* December 8, 2017, www.adweek.com/creativity/11-ikea-ads-that-show-what-a-brilliant-year-the-brand-had-creatively/; Beth Kowitt, "It's IKEA's World," *Fortune,* March 15, 2015, pp. 166–175; Richard Milne in Leiden, "IKEA Thinks Outside the Big Box," *Financial Times,* December 4, 2015, www.ft.com/cms/s/2/44a495f6-9a68-11e5-bdda-9f13f99fa654.html#axzz47Ft78U7Q; Michael Wei, "In IKEA's China Stores, Loitering Is Encouraged," *Bloomberg Businessweek,* November 1, 2010, pp. 22–23; Emily Raulhala, "No, IKEA Hasn't Banned Customers from Sleeping in Its Chinese Stores," *Time*, April 10, 2015, http://time.com/3814935/ikea-china-customers-sleeping/; Anne Quinto, "How the IKEA Catalogue Cracked What 'Domestic Bliss' Means in Different Cultures," *Quartzy,* July 25, 2017, https://quartzy.qz.com/1036380/ikea-catalogue-2017-defining-domestic-bliss-in-different-cultures; and https://highlights.ikea.com/2017/facts-and-figures, accessed October 2018.
2. Data from "*Fortune* 500," *Fortune*, June 2017, http://fortune.com/fortune500/; United Nations Conference on Trade and Development, "World Investment Report 2017: Key Messages and Overview," http://unctad.org/en/Pages/DIAE/World%20Investment%20Report/World_Investment_Report.aspx, accessed April 2018; and "List of Countries by GDP: List by the CIA World Factbook," *Wikipedia,* http://en.wikipedia.org/wiki/List_of_countries_by_GDP_(nominal), accessed October 2018.
3. See "World Trade Statistical Review 2017," *WTO,* www.wto.org/english/res_e/statis_e/wts2017_e/wts2017_e.pdf; and "Gross Domestic Product (GDP) at Current Prices from 2012 to 2022," *Statista,* www.statista.com/statistics/268750/global-gross-domestic-product-gdp/, accessed October 2018.
4. Information from www.michelin.com/eng/finance/financial-results/2017-annual-results, www.jnj.com, www.caterpillar.com, http://corporate.mcdonalds.com/, www.coca-colacompany.com/contact-us/faqs, and www.coca-colacompany.com/our-company/infographic-coca-cola-at-a-glance, accessed October 2018.
5. See www.otisworldwide.com/d1-about.html and UTC Annual Report, www.utc.com/Investors/Pages/Annual-Reports-and-Proxy-Statements.aspx, accessed October 2018.
6. Max Bouchet and Joseph Parilla, "How Trump's Steel and Aluminium Tariffs Could Affect State Economies," *Brookings,* March 6, 2018, www.brookings.edu/blog/the-avenue/2018/03/06/how-trumps-steel-and-aluminum-tariffs-could-affect-state-economies/; and Rishi Iyengar, "US-China Trade Battle: How We Got Here," *CNN,* April 4, 2018, http://money.cnn.com/2018/04/04/news/economy/trump-china-us-tariffs-trade-timeline/index.html.

7. "Retail Industry in India," India Brand Equity Foundation, www.ibef.org/industry/retail-india.aspx, accessed October 2018.
8. Suneera Tandon, "Why Walmart Isn't Getting to Play India's $670 Billion Retail Game," *Quartz India,* January 16, 2018, https://qz.com/1177373/why-walmart-isnt-getting-to-play-indias-670-billion-retail-game/; Paul Ausick, "Walmart Still Struggles in India," *247wallst,* April 8, 2014, http://247wallst.com/retail/2014/04/08/walmart-still-struggles-in-india/; Adi Narayan and Harichandan Arakali, "Walmart's Flipkart Buy Rekindles Hopes for Relaxation of India's FDA Rules," *Forbes,* May 10, 2018, www.forbesindia.com/article/special/walmarts-flipkart-buy-rekindles-hopes-for-relaxation-of-indias-fdi-rules/50149/1.
9. See James McBride, "What's Next for the WTO?" Council on Foreign Relations, March 23, 2018, www.cfr.org/backgrounder/whats-next-wto; and "What Is the WTO?" www.wto.org/english/thewto_e/whatis_e/whatis_e.htm, accessed October 2018.
10. "The EU at a Glance," http://europa.eu/about-eu/index_en.htm; "EU Statistics and Opinion Polls," http://europa.eu/documentation/statistics-polls/index_en.htm; and "EU Position in World Trade," http://ec.europa.eu/trade/policy/eu-position-in-world-trade/, all accessed October 2018.
11. Chris Giles, "Former BoE Chief King Predicts Collapse of Eurozone," *Financial Times,* February 19, 2016, www.ft.com/intl/cms/s/0/5726e610-dec0-11e5-b7fd-0dfe89910bd6.html#axzz4720ff4j3; Luis Marti, "Eurozone: The Shocks from the Eternal Return to the Proposal of Euro Exit," *Corner,* April 9, 2018; http://thecorner.eu/news-europe/eurozone-the-shocks-from-the-eternal-return-to-the-proposal-of-euro-exit/72207/; and "European Union: The Euro," http://europa.eu/about-eu/basic-information/money/euro/, accessed October 2018.
12. Alex Hunt and Brian Wheeler, "All You Need to Know about the UK Leaving the EU," *BBC,* May 10, 2018, www.bbc.com/news/uk-politics-32810887; CIA, *The World Factbook,* https://www.cia.gov/library/publications/resources/the-world-factbook/index.html, and "The Economy," https://europa.eu/european-union/about-eu/figures/economy_en, accessed October 2018.
13. Statistics and other information from "How NAFTA Changed U.S. Trade with Canada and Mexico," *New York Times,* August 15, 2017, www.nytimes.com/interactive/2017/business/nafta-canada-mexico.html; and CIA, *The World Factbook;* and North America Free Trade Agreement, accessed October 2018.
14. See "Explainer: What Is UNASUR?" www.as-coa.org/articles/explainer-what-unasur; and http://en.wikipedia.org/wiki/Union_of_South_American_Nations, accessed October 2018.
15. "Eleven Asia-Pacific Countries Signed a Trans-Pacific Partnership in Chile," *Merco Press,* March 9, 2018, http://en.mercopress.com/2018/03/09/eleven-asia-pacific-countries-signed-a-trans-pacific-partnership-in-chile; and "Transatlantic Trade and Investment Partnership," Office of the United States Trade Representative, https://ustr.gov/ttip, accessed October 2018..
16. See Zeenat Moorad, "The Coca-Cola Company: Tapping Africa's Fizz," *Financial Mail,* May 4, 2015, www.financialmail.co.za/coverstory/2015/04/30/the-coca-cola-company-tapping-africas-fizz; Annaleigh Vallie, "Coke Turns 125 and Has Much Life Ahead," *Business Day,* May 16, 2011, www.bdlive.co.za/articles/2011/05/16/coke-turns-125-and-has-much-more-life-ahead; Kate Taylor, "Coca-Cola Has Discovered an Untapped Market to Save the Soda Business," *Business Insider,* February 7, 2016, www.businessinsider.com/africa-is-the-future-of-coca-cola-2016-2;Prableen Bajpal, "5 Fastest Growing Economies in the World," *Nasdaq,* April 13, 2017, www.nasdaq.com/article/5-fastest-growing-economies-in-the-world-cm773771; and Coca-Cola annual reports and other information from www.thecoca-colacompany.com, accessed October 2018.
17. See "2017 Investment Climate Statement—Russia," U.S. Bureau of Economic and Business Affairs, May 2017, www.state.gov/e/eb/rls/othr/ics/investmentclimatestatements/index.htm?year=2017&dlid=269946; and "Russia County Commercial Guide," www.export.gov/article?series=a0pt0000000PAulAAG&type=Country_Commercial__kav, accessed October 2018.
18. "Indonesia Barters Coffee and Palm Oil for Russian Fighter Jets," *Bloomberg,* August 7, 2017, www.bloomberg.com/news/articles/2017-08-07/indonesia-barters-coffee-palm-oil-for-russian-fighter-jets; and "South Korean Organisation Proposes Coffee-Barter Trade with Vietnam," *International Comunicaffe,*March14,2018,www.comunicaffe.com/south-korean-organisation-proposes-coffee-barter-trade-with-vietnam/.
19. For these and other examples, see Emma Hall, "Do You Know Your Rites? BBDO Does," *Advertising Age,* May 21, 2007, p. 22; Michael R. Czinkota and Ilkka A. Ronkainen, *International Marketing* (Cincinnati, OH: South-Western College Publishing, 2013), Chapter 3; and "13 Unusual International Customs You Never Knew Existed," *Reader's Digest,* www.readersdigest.ca/travel/travel-tips/13-unusual-international-customs-you-never-knew-existed/, accessed October 2018.
20. Mason Hinsdale, "International Brands," *Jing Daily,* January 13, 2018, https://jingdaily.com/marriotts-blunder-a-warning-in-dealing-with-beijings-understanding-of-history/; Sui-Lee Wee, "Marriott to China: We Do Not Support Separatists," *New York Times,* January 11, 2018, www.nytimes.com/2018/01/11/business/china-marriott-tibet-taiwan.html. JamieBryan, "The Mintz Dynasty," *Fast Company,* April 2006, pp. 56–61.
21. For these and other examples, see Bill Chappell, "Bill Gates' Handshake with South Korea's Park Sparks Debate," *NPR,* April 23, 2013, www.npr.org/blogs/thetwo-way/2013/04/23/178650537/bill-gates-handshake-with-south-koreas-park-sparks-debate; "Managing Quality across the (Global) Organization, Its Stakeholders, Suppliers, and Customers," Chartered Quality Institute, www.thecqi.org/Knowledge-Hub/Knowledge-portal/Corporate-strategy/Managing-quality-globally, accessed October 2018.
22. See Rory Jones, "Foreign Retailers Bend to Conform to Saudi Religious Rules," *Wall Street Journal,* June 16, 2015, www.wsj.com/articles/foreign-retailers-bend-to-conform-to-saudi-religious-rules-1434421369; and www.marksandspencer.com, accessed October 2018.
23. Andres Martinez, "The Next American Century," *Time,* March 22, 2010, p. 1.
24. Emily Feng, "McDonald's to Double Number of China Restaurants," *Financial Times,* August 8, 2017, www.ft.com/content/ae5b2e96-7c1c-11e7-9108-edda0bcbc928; and Clarissa Wei, "Why China Loves American Chain Restaurants So Much," *Eater,* March 20, 2018, www.eater.com/2018/3/20/16973532/mcdonalds-starbucks-kfc-china-pizza-hut-growth-sales.
25. Adam Chandler, "How McDonald's Became a Target for Protest," *The Atlantic,* April 16, 2015, www.theatlantic.com/business/archive/2015/04/setting-the-symbolic-golden-arches-aflame/390708/; and "McDonald's Set for Russia Expansion," *New Europe Investor,* August 26, 2015, www.neweuropeinvestor.com/news/mcdonalds-set-for-russia-expansion10522/. Also see "Russia Could Ban US Imports," *Reuters,* April 4, 2018, www.newshub.co.nz/home/world/2018/04/russia-could-ban-us-imports.html.
26. "2017 BrandZ Top 100 Global Brands," Millward Brown, http://brandz.com/charting/51.
27. See Rachael Tepper, "Yum! Brands' International Product Strategy: How the Double Down Went Global," *Huffington Post,* March 11, 2013, www.huffingtonpost.com/2013/03/11/yum-brands-international-product-strategy_n_2814360.html; Molly Osberg, "How Colonel Sanders Became Father Christmas in Japan," *TPM,* December 23, 2014, http://talkingpointsmemo.com/theslice/kfc-christmas-in-japan-colonel-sanders-history-12-23-2014; and Kate Taylor, "How KFC Made Christmas All about Fried Chicken—in Japan," *Business Insider,* December 25, 2017, www.businessinsider.com/how-kfc-became-a-christmas-tradition-in-japan-2016-12?r=UK&IR=T.
28. See annual reports and other financial and review data from www.coca-colacompany.com/our-company/ and www.coca-colacompany.com/our-company/infographic-coca-cola-at-a-glance/, accessed October 2018.
29. See Amazon's 2017 annual report, http://phx.corporate-ir.net/phoenix.zhtml?c=97664&p=irol-reportsannual; and "Population of the World," www.livepopulation.com/country/india.html, accessed October 2018.
30. For this and other information in this section on Amazon in India, see Vivienne Walt, "Amazon Invades India," *Fortune,* January 1, 2016, pp. 63–72; Jan Dawson, "Amazon's International Growth Challenge," *Re/Code,* May 11, 2015, http://recode.net/2015/05/11/amazons-international-growth-challenge/; Wang Qionghui, "In Tough China Market, Amazon Sells the World," *Caixin Online,* November 2, 2015, http://english.caixin.com/2015-11-02/100869131.html; Leena Rao, "Amazon May Face Regulatory Hurdles in India," *Fortune,* April 8, 2016, http://fortune.com/2016/04/08/amazon-regulatory-hurdles-india/; and Shareen Sharma, "19% of Indian Population Remains Unbanked,"*Businessworld,* July 24, 2017, http://businessworld.in/article/19-Of-Indian-Population-Remains-Unbanked/24-07-2017-122715/, and Rishi Iyengar, "Amazon vs. Walmart: The Fight for India Is Just Beginning," *CNN Money,* May 11, 2018, http://money.cnn.com/2018/05/11/investing/amazon-walmart-flipkart-india-what-next/index.html.
31. See Kate Taylor, "Coca-Cola Has Discovered an Untapped Market to Save the Soda Business," *Business Insider,* February 7, 2016, www.businessinsider.com/africa-is-the-future-of-coca-cola-2016-2; and https://coca-colahellenic.com/en/about-us/coca-cola-hbc-at-a-glance/, accessed October 2018.
32. See "Volkswagen Group Rus and GAZ Group Extend Their Cooperation in Russia," June 15, 2017, www.volkswagen-media-services.com/en/detailpage/-/detail/Volkswagen-Group-Rus-and-GAZ-Group-extend-their-cooperation-in-Russia/view/5145928/7a5bbec13158edd433c6630f

5ac445da?p_p_auth=kiEFZdL3; and www.pg.com/en_IN/company/pg-india.shtml, accessed October 2018.

33. See "HP Hotels Picks Up Management of DoubleTree in Tulsa, Okla," January 10, 2018, www.hotelmanagement.net/operate/hp-hotels-picks-up-management-doubletree-downtown-tulsa-okla; and http://en.wikipedia.org/wiki/Doubletree, accessed October 2018.
34. Rick Munarriz, "Shanghai Disney Hits a Few Hiccups," *The Motley Fool,* March 28, 2016, www.fool.com/investing/general/2016/03/28/shanghai-disney-hits-a-few-hiccups.aspx; and Seth Kubersky, "Who Owns the Disney Parks around the World," *Attractions Magazine*, February 12, 2017, http://attractionsmagazine.com/owns-disney-parks-around-world/.
35. See Adam Levy, "3 Reasons Walmart's Flipkart Acquisition Is Its Most Important Yet," *The Motley Fool,* May 15, 2018, www.fool.com/investing/2018/05/15/3-reasons-walmarts-flipkart-acquisition-is-its-mos.aspx; and "Kellogg Tops Profit Estimates, Makes West Africa Investment," *Reuters,* May 3, 2018, www.reuters.com/article/us-kellogg-results/kellogg-tops-profit-estimates-makes-west-africa-investment-idUSKBN1I41E9.
36. "Intel in China," *iLook China,* May 28, 2010, http://ilookchina.net/2010/05/page/2/;Christina Larson, "Intel Buys Its Way Deeper into China," *Bloomberg Businessweek,* March 8, 2015, pp. 33–34; and Stacey Higginbotham, "Qualcomm Forms Joint Venture in China to Take on Intel," *Fortune,* January 17, 2016, http://fortune.com/2016/01/17/qualcomm-server-china/; and Jeffrey Burt, "Chip Makers and the China Challenge," *Next Platform,* February 2, 2017, www.nextplatform.com/2017/02/02/chip-makers-china-challenge/.
37. Based on information from "Our Mission Is 'Beauty for All,' Says L'Oréal Global CEO Jean-Paul," *The Economic Times,"* January 30, 2015, http://articles.economictimes.indiatimes.com/2015-01-30/news/58625572_1_l-oreal-loreal-jean-paul-agon; Hae-Jung Hong and Yves Doz, "L'Oréal Masters Multiculturalism," *Harvard Business Review*, June, 2013, pp. 114–119; Liza Lin, "L'Oréal Puts on a Happy Face in China," *Bloomberg Businessweek*, April 1–7, 2013, pp. 25–26; and www.lorealusa.com/Article.aspx?topcode=CorpTopic_RI_CustomerInnovation, www.lorealusa.com/research-innovation/when-the-diversity-of-types-of-beauty-inspires-science/stories-of-multicultural-innovations.aspx, and www.loreal-finance.com/eng/-annual-report, accessed October 2018.
38. See Warren J. Keegan and Mark C. Green, *Global Marketing*, 9th ed. (Hoboken, NJ: Pearson, 2017), pp. 322–329.
39. Toshiro Wakayama, Junjiro Shintaku, and Tomofumi Amano, "What Panasonic Learned in China," *Harvard Business Review,* December 2012, pp. 109–113.
40. See Saritha Rai, "Amazon Teaches Alexa to Speak Hinglish. Apple's Siri Is Next," *Bloomberg Businessweek,* October 30, 2017, www.bloomberg.com/news/articles/2017-10-30/amazon-teaches-alexa-to-speak-hinglish-apple-s-siri-is-next; and J. Vignesh, "Amazon Intent on Making Alexa 'As Indian as It Gets,'" *Economic Times,* March 29, 2018, https://economictimes.indiatimes.com/small-biz/startups/newsbuzz/for-amazon-alexa-shines-new-light-on-india/articleshow/63525866.cms.
41. See www.dlight.com/ and www.dlight.com/about-us/, accessed October 2018.
42. See Sophia Yan, "What's in a Brand Name? In China, Everything," *CNN Money,* September 7, 2015, http://money.cnn.com/2015/09/07/news/foreign-firms-china-branding/; Michael Wines, "Picking Brand Names in China Is a Business Itself," *New York Times,* November 12, 2011, p. A4; Carly Chalmers, "12 Amazing Translations of Chinese Brand Names," *todaytranslations,* August 27, 2013, www.todaytranslations.com/blog/12-amazing-translations-of-chinese-brand-names/; and Alfred Maskeroni, "Can You Identify All These Famous Logos Redesigned by an Artist into Chinese?" *Adweek,* February 10, 2015, www.adweek.com/print/162867.
43. For these and other examples, see "How Crayola Used WeChat and Alibaba to Grow Sales in China," *Advertising Age,* May 30, 2016, p. 27; and Angela Doland, "How to Sell Toys in a Culture Where Play Is Viewed Negatively," *Advertising Age,* March 20, 2017, http://adage.com/article/cmo-strategy/sell-toys-a-culture-parents-playtime/308340/.
44. See Warren J. Keegan and Mark C. Green, *Global Marketing*, 9th ed. (Hoboken, NJ: Pearson Publishing, 2017), pp. 423–424.
45. Rob Wile, "This Country Is Getting Discounts on iPhones that America Will Never See," *Time*, June 12, 2017, http://time.com/money/4814424/iPhone-discount-deals-apple-india-smartphones/; Gordon Gottsegen, "Samsung Makes the Cheap Galaxy J5 and J7 Official," *CNET*, June 6, 2017, www.cnet.com/news/samsung-unveils-galaxy-j5-j7-2017/; and Shannon Liao, "Apple May Start Making iPhone 6S in India to Slash Its Prices," *The Verge*, April 13, 2018, www.theverge.com/circuit-breaker/2018/4/13/17234466/apple-iPhone-6s-plus-india-tariffs.
46. See "China's Logistics Sector Continues to Grow in 2016," *Xinhuanet.com*, March 9, 2017, http://news.xinhuanet.com/english/2017-03/09/c_136115835.htm; and "Total US Logistics Spend Dipped in 2016, Says CSCMP," *Transport Topics,* June 20, 2017, http://www.ttnews.com/articles/total-us-logistics-spend-dipped-2016-says-cscmp.
47. See http://corporate.mcdonalds.com/mcd/investors/financial-information/annual-report.html, accessed October 2018.
48. Hae-Jung Hong and Yves Doz, "L'Oréal Masters Multiculturalism," *Harvard Business Review,* June, 2013, pp. 114–119; and "L'Oréal around the World," www.loreal.com/group/our-activities/l%E2%80%99or%C3%A9al-around-the-world, accessed October 2018.

Chapter 16

1. See "Unilever Tops High-Profile Sustainability Ranking," July 9, 2017, www.unilever.com/news/news-and-features/Feature-article/2017/unilever-tops-high-profile-sustainability-ranking.html; Andrew Saunders, "Paul Polman of Unilever," *Management Today,* March 2011, pp. 42–47; Adi Ignatius, "Captain Planet," *Harvard Business Review,* June 2012, pp. 2–8; Dale Buss, "Unilever's Sustainable Living Brands," *Brand Channel,* May 10, 2018, www.brandchannel.com/2018/05/10/unilever_sustainable_living_brands_good_business/; Alyssa Danigelis, "Unilever's Sustainable Living Brands Pay Off with Big Growth," *Environmental Leader,* May 14, 2018, www.environmentalleader.com/2018/05/unilever-sustainable-living-brands/; and www.unilever.com/sustainable-living/ and www.unilever.com/about/who-we-are/about-Unilever/, accessed October 2018.
2. See "McDonald's Announces Global Commitment to Support Families with Increased Focus on Happy Meals," February 18, 2018, http://news.mcdonalds.com/news-releases/news-release-details/mcdonalds-announces-global-commitment-support-families-0; www.mcdonalds.com/us/en-us/about-our-food/quality-food.html; http://corporate.mcdonalds.com/corpmcd/scale-for-good/using-our-scale-for-good.html; and www.mcdonalds.com/us/en-us/about-our-food/nutrition-calculator.html, accessed October 2018.
3. Melissa Locker, "If McDonald's Keeps Its Promise, Your Happy Meal Could Be Green within Seven Years," *Fast Company*, January 16, 2017, www.fastcompany.com/40517145/mcdonalds-promises-to-start-recycling-its-packaging-by-2025.
4. Brad Tuttle, "More Retailers Accused of Misleading Customers with Fake Price Schemes," *Money,* January 7, 2016, http://time.com/money/4171081/macys-jc-penney-lawsuit-original-prices/; and Hannah Taylor, "Proposed Settlement of Neiman Marcus 'Compare To' Deceptive Pricing Class Actions," *Mondaq,* April 30, 2018, www.mondaq.com/unitedstates/x/696826/advertising+marketing+branding/Proposed+Settlement+Of+Neiman+Marcus+Compare+To+Deceptive+Pricing+Class+Action.
5. Tony T Liu, "Overstock.com Receives $6.8 Million Fine for False Advertising," *Orange Country Business Attorney Blog,* February 11, 2014, www.orangecountybusinessattorneyblog.com/2014/02/11/overstock-com-receives-6-8-million-fine-false-advertising/; David Streitfeld, "It's Discounted, but Is It a Deal? How List Prices Lost Their Meaning," *New York Times,* March 6, 2016, p. A1; and Paul Tassin, "Overstock Must Pay $6.8 Million Penalty in 'Compare At' Pricing Lawsuit," *Top Class Actions,* June 7, 2017, https://topclassactions.com/lawsuit-settlements/lawsuit-news/722412-overstock-must-pay-6-8m-penalty-compare-pricing-lawsuit/.
6. Jonathan Vanian, "LifeLock Pays Big to Settle FTC Suit over Weak Data Security," *Fortune,* December 17, 2015; and "LifeLock to Pay $100 Million in FTC Settlement," *Practical Law*, January 21, 2016, https://content.next.westlaw.com/Document/I02f47330a46e11e598dc8b09b4f043e0/View/FullText.html?originationContext=document&transitionType=DocumentItem&contextData=(sc.Default).
7. Dan Mitchell, "Americans Don't Buy Enough Soda—Here's the New Targets," *Fortune,* February 19, 2016, http://fortune.com/2016/02/19/soda-emerging-nations-sales/; Trefis Team, "How Coca-Cola Plans to Make India Its Third Largest Market," *Forbes*, September 7, 2017, https://www.forbes.com/sites/greatspeculations/2017/09/07/how-coca-cola-plans-to-make-india-its-third-largest-market/#5114de2e848b; and Center for Science in the Public Interest, "Carbonating the World," www.cspinet.org/carbonating/, accessed October 2018.
8. Brian Clark Howard, "Planned Obsolescence: 8 Products Designed to Fail," *Popular Mechanics,* www.popularmechanics.com/-technology/planned-obsolescence-460210#slide-5, accessed September 2015. Also see Linda Simpson, "Is There a Cure for Society's Affluenza?" *Huffington Post,* January 10, 2018, www.huffingtonpost.ca/linda-simpson/is-there-a-cure-for-our-societys-affluenza_a_23329763/.
9. "Apple Apologizes for Slowing Older iPhones Dawn," *Reuters,* December 29, 2018, www.bbc.com/news/technology-42508300; and "Apple Inves-

tigated by France for 'Planned Obsolescence,'" *BBC,* January 8, 2018, www.bbc.com/news/world-europe-42615378.

10. Rob Walker, "Replacement Therapy," *Atlantic Monthly,* September 2011, p. 38. For other interesting discussions, see Homa Khaleeli, "End of the Line for Stuff That's Built to Die?" *The Guardian,* March 3, 2015, www.theguardian.com/technology/shortcuts/2015/mar/03/has-planned-obsolesence-had-its-day-design.
11. See U.S. Department of Agriculture, "Food Access Research Atlas: Documentation," www.ers.usda.gov/data-products/food-access-research-atlas/documentation/, accessed October 2018.
12. See Maanvi Singh, "Why a Philadelphia Grocery Chain Is Thriving in Food Deserts," *NPR,* May 14, 2015, www.npr.org/sections/thesalt/2015/05/14/406476968/why-one-grocery-chain-is-thriving-in-philadelphias-food-deserts; and "Brown's Super Stores," https://vimeo.com/216220650, accessed October 2018.
13. See www.newdream.org/ and www.newdream.org/about/mission, accessed October 2018.
14. See Erik Oster, "Erwin Penland, L.L. Bean Take on Disposable Fashion with 'When,'" *Adweek,* April 21, 2016, www.adweek.com/print/107497; Rose Marcario, "The End of Consumerism," *LinkedIn,* November 24, 2017, www.linkedin.com/pulse/end-consumerism-rose-marcario/; and Kevin Moss, "Don't Read This Article: How Ads Against Consumerism Help Sustainability," *World Resources Institute,* February 5, 2018, www.wri.org/blog/2018/02/dont-read-article-how-ads-against-consumerism-help-sustainability.
15. See Texas Transportation Institute, "Urban Mobility Scorecard," https://mobility.tamu.edu/ums/, accessed October 2018.
16. Mimi Kirk, "A Prius Costs $154,000 in Singapore and People Are Still Buying Them," *Quartz,* June 18, 2013, http://qz.com/95429/a-prius-costs-154000-in-singapore-and-people-are-still-buying-them/; and Jeff Cuellar, "What Is the True Cost of Owning a Car in Singapore? You Don't Want to Know," MoneySmart.sg, August 21, 2014, http://blog.moneysmart.sg/car-ownership/the-true-cost-of-owning-a-car-in-singapore/; and Julian Wong, "How Much It Really Costs to Own a Car in Singapore," *Channel NewsAsia,* November 24, 2017, www.channelnewsasia.com/news/brandstudio/how-much-it-really-costs-to-own-a-car-in-singapore-9346730.
17. See Natasha Lomas, "Google Fined $2.7BN for EU Antitrust Violations over Shopping Searches," *Tech Crunch,* June 27, 2017, https://techcrunch.com/2017/06/27/google-fined-e2-42bn-for-eu-antitrust-violations-over-shopping-searches/; and Terry Collins, "Google Appeals Record $2.7 Billion EU Antitrust Fine," *CNET,* September 11, 2017, https://www.cnet.com/news/google-is-appealing-record-2-7-billion-eu-antitrust-fine/.
18. See Philip Kotler, "Reinventing Marketing to Manage the Environmental Imperative," *Journal of Marketing,* July 2011, pp. 132–135; and Kai Ryssdal, "Unilever CEO: For Sustainable Business, Go against 'Mindless Consumption,'" *Marketplace,* June 11, 2013, www.marketplace.org/topics/sustainability/consumed/unilever-ceo-paul-polman-sustainble-business.
19. Andrew Lord, "Adidas Created a Shoe That Is Literally Made Out of Trash," *Huffington Post,* June 30, 2016, www.huffingtonpost.com/2015/06/30/adidas-shoe-made-of-ocean-trash_n_7699632.html; "Adidas Group Sustainable Materials," www.adidas-group.com/en/sustainability/products/materials/#/recyceltes-polystyrol/sustainable-better-cotton/pvc-and-phthalates/, accessed October 2018; and www.adidas-group.com/en/sustainability/managing-sustainability/general-approach/ and www.adidas-group.com/en/sustainability/products/sustainability-innovation/, accessed October 2018.
20. See Alan S. Brown, "The Many Shades of Green," *Mechanical Engineering,* January 2009, http://memagazine.asme.org/Articles/2009/January/Many_Shades_Green.cfm; Linda Demmler, "It's Earth Day. Why Care?," www.ibm.com/blogs/ibm-global-financing/2018/04/its-earth-day-why-care/, April 18, 2018; and www.ibm.com/financing/asset-buyback/global-asset-recovery-services, accessed October 2018.
21. See "Decarbonization," www.siemens.com/global/en/home/company/sustainability/decarbonization.html, and "Green, Greener Kalwa," www.siemens.com/global/en/home/company/about/businesses/real-estate/green-greener-kalwa.html, accessed October 2018.
22. Information from Leon Kaye, "The North Face Sustainability Report," Triple Pundit, July 29, 2014, www.triplepundit.com/2014/07/the-north-face-sustainability/; and www.thenorthface.com/about-us/responsibility.html, accessed October 2018.
23. See www.thenorthface.com/about-us/responsibility.html, accessed October 2018.
24. See "Market Share of Leading Brands of Dry Dog Food in the United States in 2017," Statista, www.statista.com/statistics/188670/top-dry-dog-food-brands-in-the-united-states/, accessed October 2018; and www.pedigree.com/why-pedigree/about-us and www.pedigreefoundation.org/about-us-2/, accessed October 2018.
25. See "Leading Cleaning Products Company Method Commits Majority of its Product Lineup to Cradle to Cradle Product Certification," April 9, 2014, www.c2ccertified.org/news/article/leading_cleaning_products_company_method_commits_majority_of_its_product_li; and https://methodhome.com/, https://methodhome.com/about-us/our-story/, and https://methodhome.com/blog/category/people-against-dirty/, accessed October 2018.
26. "SC Johnson's CEO on Doing the Right Thing, Even When It Hurts Business," *Harvard Business Review,* April 2015, pp. 33–36; and "We Commit to What Matters Most," http://scjohnson.com/en/commitment/overview.aspx, accessed October 2018.
27. See International Monetary Fund Staff Team from the Fiscal Affairs Department the Legal Department, "Corruption: Costs and Mitigating Strategies," May 2016, www.imf.org/external/pubs/ft/sdn/2016/sdn1605.pdf. Also see Michael Montgomery, "The Cost of Corruption," *American RadioWorks,* http://americanradioworks.publicradio.org/features/corruption/, accessed October 2018.
28. See www.marketingpower.com/AboutAMA/Pages/Statement%20of%20Ethics.aspx, accessed October 2018.
29. See "Protect This House: The Under Armour Code of Conduct. Make the Right Call," http://files.shareholder.com/downloads/UARM/6278599929x0x873823/38F030C7-5348-4CC6-B8CD-81D68B2F496C/Code_of_Conduct_2016.pdf, accessed October 2018.
30. David A. Lubin and Daniel C. Esty, "The Sustainability Imperative," *Harvard Business Review,* May 2010, pp. 41–50; and Roasbeth Moss Kanter, "It's Time to Take Full Responsibility," *Harvard Business Review,* October 2010, p. 42.

Appendix 3

i. This is derived by rearranging the following equation and solving for price: Percentage markup = (price – cost) ÷ price.

ii. Using the basic profit equation, we set profit equal to ROI × I: ROI × I = (P × Q) – TFC – (Q × UVC). Solving for Q gives Q = (TFC + (ROI × I)) ÷ (P – UVC).

iii. YCharts (2018), "US Households," available at ycharts.com/indicators/us_households; Pew Research Center (2018), "US Households," available at www.pewinternet.org/fact-sheet/internet-broadband/; and Parks Associates (2017), "Internet/Broadband Fact Sheet," available at www.parksassociates.com/blog/article/pr-01102017).

iv. See Roger J. Best, *Market-Based Management,* 6th ed. (Upper Saddle River, NJ: Prentice Hall, 2013).

v. Total contribution can also be determined from the unit contribution and unit volume: Total contribution = unit contribution unit sales. Total units sold in 2019 were 595,238 units, which can be determined by dividing total sales by price per unit ($100 million ÷ $168). Total contribution = $35.28 contribution per unit × 595,238 units = $20,999,996.64 (difference due to rounding).

vi. Recall that the contribution margin of 21% was based on variable costs representing 79% of sales. Therefore, if we do not know price, we can set it equal to $1.00. If price equals $1.00, 79 cents represents variable costs and 21 cents represents unit contribution. If price is decreased by 10%, the new price is 90 cents. However, variable costs do not change just because price decreased, so the unit contribution and contribution margin decrease as follows:

	Old	New (Reduced 10%)
Price	$1.00	$0.90
– Unit variable cost	$0.79	$0.79
= Unit contribution	$0.21	$0.11
Contribution margin	$0.21/$1.00 = 0.21 or 21%	$0.11/$0.90 = 0.12 or 12%

Indexes

Brand, Name, and Organization Index

In this index, *f* refers to figures, *p* refers to pictures, and *t* refers to tables.

A

AARP, 283
ABC World News Tonight television show, 393
Abercrombie & Fitch, 342
Accenture, 159, 159*p*
Ace Hardware, 344
Acqua di Cristallo Tributo a Modigliani, 168
Acxiom Personicx segmentation system, 178, 178*p*, 180
Ad Council of America, 116, 137*p*, 209
adidas, Inc., 14, 154, 204, 372, 372*p*, 391, 391*p*, 511, 511*p*
Adknowledge ad networks, 114
Advertising Age, 374
Afta (Colgate-Palmolive), 218
AGIT Global, 279, 279*p*
Airbnb, 6, 40–42, 41*p*, 214, 225, 227, 254, 303, 468
Air Canada, 310
Air China, 310
AJAX dishwashing products (Colgate-Palmolive), 218
ALDI grocery stores, 16, 195–197, 196*p*, 228, 292, 338, 350, 352, 357
Aleve pain reliever, 46, 218
Allegiant Airlines, 50, 200
All Natural salsa, 196
Allstate insurance, 222
Alphabet (Google parent co.), 249–251, 250*p*, 255, 265
ALS (Lou Gehrig's disease), 34
Altoids (Mars, Inc.), 42
Always feminine hygiene products (P&G), 97
AmazonBasics brand (Amazon), 228–230, 230*p*
Amazon.com, 3–4, 3*p*, 11, 16, 21, 23, 65–66, 74, 78, 82, 90, 102, 109, 113, 125, 136, 139, 143, 149, 185, 191–192, 194, 212, 225, 227, 229–230, 266, 281, 286–287, 287*p*, 295, 301–303, 311, 312, 313, 318–320, 318*p*, 324–325, 325*p*, 335–338, 345, 348, 353, 357, 377, 378, 437–438, 439, 442, 443, 451, 456, 463, 477, 479, 479*p*, 482, 486–487, 487*p*, 492, 514, 514*p*
Amazon Echo, 27, 120–121
Amazon Elements brand, 228–230
Amazon Essentials, 229–230
Amazon Key, 236
Amazon Prime, 230, 236
AMC, 302, 375
American Academy of Pediatrics, 516
American Advertising Federation, 459
American Airlines, 214–215, 271, 294
American Association of Advertising Agencies, 147, 147*p*, 459
American Best Value Inn, 210
American Cancer Society, 516
American Consumer Satisfaction Index, 270
American Eagle Outfitters, 230, 342
American Express, 125, 175, 189, 252, 254–255
American Family Insurance, 388
American Idol television show, 478
American Marketing Association, 126, 519–520
American Society for Quality, 209
America's Cup, 375
Amex Centurion Black Card (American Express), 175
Amway, 304
Android Oreo operating systems, 231
Android Wear watch, 215
Angel Soft (Georgia-Pacific), 75
Angie's List, 451
Annie Homegrown, 89, 89*p*
Anthropologie, 175–176, 454–455
Antitrust Division, of Attorney General's office, 84
Any.do app, 452
Anytime Fitness, 349
A Place for Mom, 95
Appetitos Dips, 196
Apple, Inc., 13, 38, 52, 65–66, 76–77, 82, 90, 99, 102–103, 125, 144, 152, 167, 178, 192, 194, 204–205, 205*p*, 213–214, 225–226, 227, 231, 239, 247, 249, 265–266, 265*p*, 271, 279, 284, 284*p*, 286, 288, 288*p*, 294, 301–302, 309, 311–312, 315, 351, 381–382, 456, 459, 468, 477, 486, 489, 489*p*, 503, 503*p*, 523
Applebee's, 352
Apple iPad Air, 77
Apple Siri, 27
AppleTV, 463
Apple Watch, 265–266
Appliance Finder kiosk (Home-Depot), 457, 457*p*
Apt. 9 brand (Kohl's), 348
Aquafina (PepsiCo), 232
Archer Farms (Target Stores, Inc.), 229
Architectural Digest, 375
Arias, Massy, 139
Ariel detergent (P&G), 473
Ariel Ultra (P&G), 97–98
Armani, 230
Arrow Electronics, 358
Art Class brand (Target Stores, Inc.), 140
Asics, Inc, 14
Associated Grocers, 344
Association of National Advertisers, 459
Aston Martin, 187
Athleta activewear, 50, 176, 388
Atkins, Amy, 179
Atkins, Chester, 179
AT&T, Inc., 86, 136, 225, 241–242, 281, 354, 459
Attorney General's office, Antitrust Division, 84
Audience Network (Facebook.com), 401
Audi Motor Co., 52, 214, 214*p*, 355, 355*p*
Avengers (film), 386
Avis car rentals, 185, 381
Avocados from Mexico, 211–212, 211*p*
Axe fragrances, 256

B

babyGap (Gap), 50
Baffert, Bill, 397
Baidu (Chinese search engine), 493
Baja Blast (Mountain Dew), 19
Baker's Choice brand (ALDI), 228
Baldwin, Alec, 315
Banana Republic, 50
BAND-AID, 227
Banfield veterinary services (Mars, Inc.), 42
Banquet frozen dinners (ConAgra), 277
Barkbox subscriptions, 18, 18*p*
Barnes & Noble, 351, 440
Bass Pro Shops, 35, 169, 347, 367, 433
Bath & Body Works, 256
Battery Depot, 348
Bauma mining and construction equipment trade show, 429, 429*p*
Baumgartner, Felix, 427
BAX Global, 328
Beachbody, 456
Bean, Leon Leonwood, 16
Beasley, Theotis, 179
Beautyrest mattresses, 227
Bed Bath & Beyond, 285, 285*p*, 339, 426
Beet Heet, 281
Bell, Joshua, 211
Belmont Stakes, 397*p*
Beltology at Roosevelt Field mall (NY), 353
Benjamin Moore Color Capture app, 450
Ben & Jerry's, 29, 86–87, 86*p*, 425, 425*p*, 438, 515
Bentley Motors, 52
Bergdorf Goodman, 350
Bernstein, Danielle, 444
Berra, Yogi, 23
Best Buy, 23, 76–77, 149, 284, 287, 306, 315, 337, 339, 342, 351, 353, 442, 456
Better Business Bureau, 382
Better Homes and Gardens magazine, 393
Beverly Hills 90H20, 168
Beyond Meat, 148, 148*p*, 151, 151*p*
Bezos, Jeff, 3–4, 281
Big Bang Theory television show, 386, 468
Bing search engine (Microsoft Corp.), 109, 109*p*, 381–382, 440, 442
Birdpost.com, 24, 448
BJ's warehouse club, 341
Black & Decker tools, 213, 486
Black Flag, 126
Black-ish television show, 386
Blende Dental Group, 263
Blockbuster rental chain, 301
Blonde Salad blog, 444
Bloomberg Businessweek, 393
Bloomingdale's, 133, 137, 184
Bloomingdale's Outlets, 341
Blue Apron meal kits, 338, 366
Blue Nile, 337
Blue Pearl veterinary services (Mars, Inc.), 42
Blumenthal, Neil, 29
BMW, 22, 50–52, 95, 131, 145, 189, 191, 193, 201, 217, 217*p*, 237, 271, 389, 468
Body Shop, The, 515
Boeing, Inc., 153, 222, 288, 442, 469
Boise Cascade, 421
Bojangles fast food, 177, 177*p*
Bold detergent (P&G), 184
BonDurant, Rob, 82
Bonobos, 336, 454–455
Booking.com, 174
Borders Books, 351
Bose audio, 63, 189, 191, 263, 269, 269*p*, 287
Boston Beer Company, 389
Boston Consulting Group, 43–44
Boston Globe, 396

Boston Marathon, 391, 391*p*
Bottom Line Performance learning solutions, 413, 413*p*
Bounty paper towels (P&G), 97, 278, 319
Brady, Tom, 356
Brady Bunch television show, 369
BrandAsset Valuator (Young & Rubicam), 225
BrandIndex, 381
Breitling watches, 316
Breyers, 87
Brokeback Mountain (film), 76
Brooks running gear, 246, 246*p*
Brown, Don, 82
Brown, Jeff, 505, 505*p*
Brown's Super Stores, Inc., 503
BryanBoy blog, 444
Bryant, Kobe, 192
Bucky's convenience stores, 485
Budweiser beer, 392, 469, 481
Buffalo Wild Wings, 7–9, 8*p*, 89
Buick Motor Co., 386, 386*p*
Build.com, 353
Burberry, 308, 341
Bureau of Economic Analysis, 123
BurgerFi's, 148
Burger King, 90–91, 95, 141, 192, 299, 317, 389, 397, 397*p*
Burton brand, 154
Burt's Bees, 515
Buscemi, Steve, 369
Buy a Pair, Give a Pair program (Warby Parker), 29
BuzzFeed, 387

C

Cadillac Motor Co., 21–22, 22*p*, 189–190
CafeMom.com, 24, 448
Cal-Maine Foods, 309
Calvin Klein apparel, 230
Cambridge Analytica, 129
Campaign for Tobacco-Free Kids, 516
Campari America, 452
Campbell's Soup, 45, 75, 121, 176, 256
Camry (Toyota Motor Co.), 303, 303*p*
Candies brand (Kohl's), 348
Canon, 469
Caremark (CVS Health), 516
Cargill's Cocoa & Chocolate division, 155, 155*p*
Caring Dairy program (Ben & Jerry's), 86
Carol (film), 76
Carrefour stores (France), 260, 316, 357
Cascade dishwashing detergent (P&G), 217, 278
Cash, Johnny, 226
Catalog Age magazine, 454
CAT Earthmovers footwear (Wolverine), 388, 388*p*
Caterpillar equipment, 153, 273–274, 273*p*, 318, 320, 388, 468–469
Cat & Jack (Target Stores, Inc.), 229
CBS All Access, 302
CDW, 442
Center for Science in the Public Interest (CSPI), 502, 502*p*
Champs Sports (Foot Locker), 346
Chanel, 308, 350, 493
Charles Schwab investments, 452
Charmin bath tissue (P&G), 97, 278, 278*p*, 292, 319, 386
Check This Out brand (Kroger), 228, 269
Cheer detergent (P&G), 184
Cheerios (General Mills), 75, 138, 140
Cheesecake Factory, 386
Chesky, Brian, 6, 41–42
Chevrolet Motor Co., 145, 210, 244, 392, 395, 395*p*
Chevy Bolt (GM), 380
Chicago Bulls, 445
Chicago Cubs, 174
Chicago Tribune, 397
Chick-fil-A, 16, 35, 105–106, 105*p*, 169, 241, 451
Child Guard safety packaging (P&G), 212–213, 212*p*
ChinaHR.com (Monster.com), 494
Chipolte Mexican Grill, 62, 352
Chobani yogurt, 382
Chouinard, Yvon, 81–82
Christian Louboutin, 493
Circle K convenience stores, 485
Circuit City, 351
Cisco's WebEx, 75
Cisco Systems, 413
Citra Pearly White UV Lotion (Unilever), 401
Citrix's GoToMeeting, 75
CLA Class (Mercedes Benz), 269, 269*p*
Clairol hair care, 46, 218
Cleanest Line blog (Patagonia), 444, 444*p*
Clorox Company, 120, 309
Club Momme, 142
Coach leather goods, 341
Coca-Cola Co., 4, 68, 68*p*, 88–89, 99, 100, 178, 179, 181–182, 181*p*, 185, 192–193, 213, 225–226, 227, 233, 236–237, 252, 287, 309, 316, 376, 379–381, 383, 389, 391, 394–395, 401, 423, 427–428, 435–437, 435*p*, 445, 452, 456, 468–469, 474, 474*p*, 476–478, 481, 487–488, 515, 524
Coca-Cola Hellenic, 481
Coca-Cola Plus, 236
Coinstar, 456
Coinstar's Redbox, 301
Colgate-Palmolive, 217–218, 218*p*, 488
Comcast cable, 201, 276, 281, 302, 391
Comet cleanser, 257
ConAgra Foods, 229, 277
Conill advertising agency, 136
Conservation Alliance, 512
Consumer Product Safety Commission (CPSC), 83, 84, 259
Conversation Suite, at MasterCard, 102, 102*p*
Converse shoes, 14, 390, 390*p*
Cook, Diedric, 503
Cook, Tim, 76, 102
Cornell, Brian, 6, 6*p*
Corona beer, 374
Cortez Kenny running shoes (Nike), 203
Costco, 194–195, 229, 239, 260, 279, 336, 338, 341–343, 342*p*, 350–352, 357, 365–366, 426, 500
Council of American Survey Research Organizations (CASRO), 126
Council of Better Business Bureaus, 382
Coupa cloud applications, 167–168
Coupland, Douglas, 71
CoverGirl cosmetics, 46, 139, 218, 257, 376
Crackle streaming service, 301
Craigslist.com, 95, 139, 332, 402, 440
Crayola Crayons, 252, 256, 488
Crepe Erase, 456
Crest toothpaste (P&G), 97, 97*p*, 174, 208, 389
Crisco shortening, 46, 218, 257
Crock-Pot slow cooker (Newell Rubbermaid), 90
Croft & Barrow (Kohl's), 348
Crutchfield, 442
Cub Foods, 362
Cultural Streetscapers (Kantar Futures), 106
Curry, Ayesha, 139
Curry, Steph, 356
Curry, Steve, 389
Customer Success Platform (Salesforce.com), 405, 405*p*
Cuties mandarin oranges, 211
CVS Extracare card, 34
CVS Health, 40, 40*p*, 222, 310, 310*p*, 396–397, 409, 456, 515–517, 516*p*
CVS MinuteClinics, 40
CVS/pharmacy, 220, 350, 350*p*
Cyber Monday, 324

D

Dafoe, Willem, 369
Dancing with the Stars television show, 478
Dannon brand, 34
Danone, 108
Dap fillers (RPM International), 353
Data & Marketing Association, 459–460
DaVinci, 76
Davis, Danny, 180
Dawn dish soap (P&G), 217
Day2Night Convertible Heels, 263
Daydream VR (Google), 250
D&B Hoover's, 103
De Beers, 277
Decker, Jesse James, 62
DeGeneres, Ellen, 76
Dell Computer, 65, 162, 315
Delta Airlines, 271, 294
Delta Faucet, 426, 426*p*
Denali brand (Amazon), 228
Details magazine, 463
Detroit, marketing of, 208
Deutsche Bank, 260
DHL Logistics, 328
Dianping (Chinese microblogging site), 493
Dick's Sporting Goods, 175, 175*p*
Diet Coke (Coca-Cola Co.), 236–237
Diff Eyewear, 62
Digital Advertising Alliance, 459
Dillard's department stores, 338
Diplomat, The, 493
DirectTV, 302
Dish Network, 276
Disney. *See* Walt Disney Company
"Disneyland of Dairy Stores" (Stew Leonard's), 21
Disney Social Media Moms Celebration, 141–142, 141*p*
DKNY, 308
d.light Solar, 487
Doc McStuffins branded merchandise, 230
Dolce & Gabbana, 308, 341
Dole Classic salads, 211
Dollar General, 11, 175, 338, 340–341, 341*p*, 352
Dollar Shave Club, 35, 189, 281
Dollar Tree, 175
Domino's Pizza, 27, 107, 107*p*, 317
Doritos Locos Tacos (Taco Bell), 246–247
Doritos snacks (PepsiCo), 231–232, 389–390
Dove personal care products (Unilever), 175, 304
Dow Jones Sustainability Indexes, 496
Downey Single Rinse (P&G), 98
Dreft detergent (P&G), 184
Dr. Seuss branded merchandise, 230
Drucker, Peter, 5
DSW Shoes, 194
Dun & Bradstreet, 103
Duncan Hines cake mixes, 257
Dunkin', 34, 171–172, 171*p*, 174, 174*p*, 191, 309, 381, 438, 438*p*, 449
DuPont Co., Inc., 153, 407
Duracell batteries, 46, 218, 232, 257
Durant, Kevin, 208

E

Earnhardt, Dale, Jr., 179
Easy Sustainability Program (Staples), 356
eBay.com, 213, 440
EcoHub (SAP), 417
Economist, The, 456
Edgadget, 139
The Edit at Roosevelt Field mall (NY), 353, 353*p*
Edmunds.com, 114
Eggland's Best (Cal-Maine Foods), 211, 309
800Razor, 35
Einstein artificial intelligence system (Salesforce.com), 405
Elf clothing, 446*p*
Ells, Steve, 62
Emirates Airlines, 222, 222*p*
Empire television show, 385
Enterprise Rent-A-Car, 185, 303
Entrepreneur Franchise 500, 309
Epicurious.com, 149
Equifax, 86
Era detergent (P&G), 184
Eskimo Joe's, 35
ESPN, 112–113, 375
ESPN.com, 440, 441, 441*p*
ESPN The Magazine, 393
Esri, 178
Essilorl, 308
Etsy marketplace, 139, 448
Eukanuba (Mars, Inc.), 42
European Union (EU), 508, 508*p*
Evernote application, 195, 195*p*
Evolution Fresh juice (Starbucks), 38
Expedia Group, 27, 174, 437, 437*p*, 440
Experian credit rating service, 178
Experian Simmons, 106
Experiences platform (Airbnb), 42
ExtraCare loyalty program (CVS/pharmacy), 350, 350*p*
ExxonMobil, 181

F

Fabletics, 331
Facebook.com, 4, 18, 24, 25–26, 53, 62–63, 65, 73, 76, 86, 87, 90–92, 109, 114, 118, 125, 129, 139, 141, 162, 164, 174, 203, 223, 225, 227, 239, 242, 242*p*, 256, 335, 346, 370, 375–376, 387, 390–391, 393, 397, 401–402, 405, 416, 418–419, 428, 435, 440, 443–447, 449, 456, 458, 459, 465, 468, 476–477, 493, 494
Facebook Live, 463
Facebook Messenger, 120
Fairlife (Coca-Cola Co.), 185
Family Dollar, 175, 350, 456
FANography (ESPN), 112
FarmersOnly.com, 448
Farm Fresh stores, 362
Fashion Institute of Technology, 444
Fast Company, 302
Febreze products (P&G), 97
Federal Aviation Administration (FAA), 84, 331
Federal Bureau of Investigation (FBI), 457, 457*p*
Federal Bureau of Investigation's Internet Crime Complaint Center, 188
Federal Communications Commission (FCC), 84
Federal Energy Regulatory Commission, 84
Federal Trade Commission (FTC), 84, 114, 295, 455, 459, 501
Federer, Rodger, 208
FedEx, Inc., 4, 79, 197, 226, 303, 312, 320, 331, 479
FedEx Logistics, 328
Fels-Naptha detergent, 252
Ferdinand, Rio, 370
Ferrari Motor Co., 51
Fiber Internet service (Alphabet), 251
Fidgit spinners, 253, 253*p*
FIFA World Cup soccer, 203
Fifth Third Bank, 73, 73*f*
Fillico Beverly Hills, 168
Find What Feels Good yoga, 262
Fisher-Price, 442
Fitbit, 82, 95, 177, 177*p*, 263, 332
5-Hour Energy drink, 201, 263
Five Below, 348
Fizzio soda (Starbucks), 38
Flex Seal, 407
Flickr.com, 92
FlightAware, 394
Flipkart e-commerce co. (Walmart Stores, Inc.), 471, 479, 482, 482*p*
Flipp app, 451
Florida State University, 174
Focus Vision research, 111, 112*p*
Folgers coffee, 46, 218, 257
Food and Drug Administration (FDA), 83–84
Food Network, 139, 348, 375
Foot Locker, 184, 346, 346*p*
Forbes magazine, 257, 365, 393, 405
Ford, Henry, 13
Ford Motor Co., 10, 48, 51–52, 53, 88, 90, 137, 144, 252, 303, 306–307, 309, 313
Formica, 227
Formula 1 Grand Priz course, Monza, Italy, 204
Forrester Research, 417
Fortune 100, 460
Fortune 500, 265, 328, 335, 342, 365, 413, 517
Fortune 1000, 162
Fortune magazine, 221
Fortune magazine Future 50, 255
Four Seasons Hotels and Resorts, 193, 221–222, 221*f*
Fresh Market, 107
Freud, Sigmund, 145
Friendly Farms brand (ALDI), 228
Frito-Lay, 77
Frozen branded merchandise, 230
Fuji photography, 456
Future Show Innovation Challenge (Under Armour), 243, 243*p*
FUZE (Coca-Cola Co.), 185

G

Gain detergent (P&G), 184, 232
Gain Flings! (unit-dose laundry detergent packets, P&G), 213
Galaxy smartphones (Samsung), 239
Gallup Consulting, 412
Gal Meets Glam blog, 444
Gap, Inc., 50, 213, 213*p*, 341, 342
GapBody, 50
GapKids, 50
GapMaternity, 50
Gates, Bill, 34, 476
Gatorade, 450, 452
GAZ Group (Russia), 481
GE Appliances, 45
GE Aviation, 44
Gebbia, Joe, 6, 41
GEICO insurance, 191–192, 222, 304, 315, 384, 384*p*, 437, 454, 454*p*
General Electric (GE), 13, 44–45, 44*p*, 153, 163–165, 164*p*, 208, 249, 265, 407, 407*p*, 409, 469, 477, 502
GE Capital, 45
GE Healthcare, 44
GE Power, 44
GE Renewable Energy, 44
GE Reports, 164
GE Transportation, 44
General Foods, 486
General Mills, 75, 89, 140, 153, 335
General Motors (GM), 46, 51, 233, 236, 262, 265, 313, 322–323, 322*p*, 328, 380, 395
Georgia-Pacific, 74–75
Gillette razors (P&G), 35, 97, 189, 252, 281*p*, 320, 473, 486
Gilt.com flash sale site, 353
Giorgio Armani, 341
Gizmodo, 139
Glad trash bags, 392
glassdoor.com, 167
GlaxoSmithKline Pharmaceuticals, 293–294, 501
Gleevec (Novartis), 293
Godrej & Boyce, 473–474, 473*p*
Goldenberg, Adam, 331
GoldieBlox, 122, 122*p*
Goldman, Seth, 524
Goldman Sachs, 262
Goodfellow & Co. (Target Stores, Inc.), 229
Good Grips kitchen tools, 71
Goodreads, 448
GoodThreads brand (Amazon), 228
Goodyear, Inc., 153–154, 335
Google+, 24, 162, 164, 418
Google Android, 443–444, 444*p*
Google Cardboard, 355
Google.com, 4, 13, 25, 26, 62–63, 65–66, 75, 82, 90, 99, 103, 106, 109, 113–114, 119, 120–121, 136, 192, 213–215, 214*p*, 225–226, 231–232, 249–251, 250*p*, 255, 262, 276, 301–302, 313, 318, 336, 337, 381–382, 393, 394, 401, 426, 440, 442, 458–459, 468–469, 476, 477, 493, 508–509, 508*p*
Google Maps, 174
Google News, 114
Google Play Store, 451
Google Surveys, 111
Google+YouTube.com, 18
Gordon, Nathalie, 91
Gore-Tex fabrics, 154, 154*p*
Gorman, Leon, 16
Gotham television show, 76
GoToMeeting conferencing tools, 418
GQ magazine, 375
Grainger MRO products, 358, 358*p*, 361
Grammy Awards, 203, 388
Gray, Lauren, 140
Green, Jefferson "Uncle Johnny," 485
Green Label (Mountain Dew), 180
Greenwashing Index, 522
Groupe Auchan (France), 357
Groupe Casino (France), 357
Groupon, 200
Guardian, The, 523
Gucci, 144, 187, 230, 288
Guinness beer, 252
Guinness World Record, 426
Guthy-Renker, 456

H

Haier appliances, 11, 45, 487
Hamilton, George, 223
Hampton Inn, 336, 344
Hanes, 184, 389
Happy Meal (McDonald's), 19
Harbour, David, 386
Hard Rock Café Hotel (Orlando), 349
Harley-Davidson, 45, 140, 205–206, 206*p*, 225, 256, 311, 313, 386
Harley Owners Group (H.O.G.), 206
Harris, Neil Patrick, 76
Harry's, 35, 281
Hasbro toy co.., 387
Hastings, Reed, 301
Hayneedle, 336
HBO, 139
HBO Go, 50
HBO Now, 302
Hearts On Fire diamonds, 194, 194*p*

Heineken beer, 488
Heineken-Mexico beer, 374
Heinz, 252
HelloFresh meal kits, 338, 366
Hello Kitty branded merchandise, 230
Hell's Kitchen television show, 478
Hemperly, Jason, 179
Heritage Farm brand (Kroger), 228, 269
Hermès, 187, 350
Hershey Foods, 45, 213–215
Hertz car rentals, 185, 381
High Point insurance, 237
Hill's Science Diet pet food (Colgate-Palmolive), 218
Hilton Hotels, 11, 362, 482
H&M retail, 181–182
Holiday Inn, 307
Holiday Inn Express, 195
Holoroom (Lowe's Home Improvement Stores), 355
HomeAway (Expedia Group), 437
Home Chef meal kits, 366
Home Depot, 39*t*, 69, 89, 195, 260, 309, 316, 327, 328, 336, 339, 348, 351–353, 357, 440, 440*p*, 456–457, 457*p*
Home Depot Foundation, 69, 69*p*
HomeGoods, 341
Homewood Suites by Hilton, 11
Honda Fit, 275
Honda Motor Co., 51, 142, 189
Honest Tea (Coca-Cola Co.), 185, 524
Hong Kong Disneyland, 482
Hoovers.com, 418
Hornbacher's stores, 362
Horween tannery, 134
Hotels.com (Expedia Group), 437
Hotwire.com (Expedia Group), 437
HP, Inc., 65, 456
HP Sprocke printer, 388
H&R Block, 121, 254, 344, 344*p*
Huawei (China), 266, 289
Hudson, Jennifer, 388–389
Hudson, Kate, 331
Huffington Post, 387
Huggies diapers, 393
Hulu streaming service, 50, 301
Human Resources Umbrella, 228
Hummer Motors, 46
Hunt's brand foods, 229
Hyatt Regency Hilton Hotels, 11
Hyundai Motor Co., 137, 441

I

Iams pet food (Mars, Inc.), 42, 218
IBM, Inc., 13, 66, 75, 125, 153, 156–157, 157*p*, 181, 192, 252, 325, 405, 407, 410, 477, 502
IBM Global Asset Recovery Services, 511
IBM Watson supercomputer, 27, 120–121
Ice Bucket Challenge for ALS (Lou Gehrig's disease), 34
Iced Expresso Classics (Starbucks), 46
Idea Exchange (Salesforce.com), 242, 242*p*
IHOP, 214, 214*p*
IKEA, 61, 67–68, 67*p*, 138, 328, 356–357, 356*p*, 388, 454–455, 455*p*, 467–469, 467*p*, 478, 492
IMG sports entertainment, 169
Imgur, 91
Indeed.com, 129
Independent Grocers Alliance (IGA), 344
In-N-Out Burger, 347–348, 348*p*
INSANITY Workout, 407
Insecure television show, 139
InsideView.com, 418
Instagram.com, 18, 24, 26, 39*t*, 53, 62, 73, 76, 91, 92, 113–114, 125, 129, 139–141, 164, 174, 203–204, 212, 223, 225–226, 225*p*, 346, 375, 387, 390, 391, 393, 435, 440, 443, 445–447, 446*p*, 449, 458
Insurance Institute for Highway Safety, 262
Intel, Inc., 354, 482
Interactive Advertising Bureau, 459
Interbrand of London, 487
INTERMIX, 50
International Brotherhood of Teamsters Airline Division, 331
International Consumer Electronics trade show, 429
International Design Excellence Awards (IDEA), 239
International Monetary Fund (IMF), 519
International Nestlé Boycott Committee, 523
International Space Station, 442
International Union for Conservation of Nature, 86
Internet Crime Complaint Center (FBI), 457, 458*p*
Internet Retailer 2015 Top 500 Guide, 331
InterVu service (Focus Vision research), 111, 112*p*
Intuit, Inc., 107–108, 254–255, 254*p*, 280
IRI, 106
Irish Spring soap (Colgate-Palmolive), 218

J

James, LeBron, 139, 192, 208, 475
JARS at Roosevelt Field mall (NY), 353
Jasansky, Sonja, 19, 19*p*
Jay Z, 184
JCPenney, Inc., 230, 269, 335, 337–338, 350, 386, 501
J.Crew, 341, 454
J.D. Power Award, 210
Jeep (GM), 88–89
Jelinek, Craig, 365
JELL-O (General Foods), 227, 486
Jelly Belly, 227
Jeni's Splendid Ice Creams, 13–14, 14*p*
Jersey Mike's, 362
JetBlue Airways, 11, 16–17, 45, 227, 448, 448*p*
Jet.com, 336
JH Audio, 186
Jiepang (Chinese Foursquare site), 493
Jiffy Lube, 344
Jif peanut butter, 46, 218
Jimmy Choo shoes, 350
Jimmy Dean sausage, 386
Jimmy Johns restaurants, 309
Jimmy Kimmel Live television show, 133
Jobs, Steve, 13
John Deere, Inc., 57, 311
Johnson, Earvin "Magic," 503–504
Johnson & Johnson, 13, 110, 293, 317, 452, 469
Jordan, Michael, 192, 208, 435
JoyLab (Target Stores, Inc.), 229
JustFab, Inc., 331
JWT advertising agency, 387

K

Kalanick, Travis, 95, 312
Kantar Futures, 106
KAYAK.com, 174
Kearl, Jeff, 184
Kearney, Steven, 180
Kelleher, Herb, 12
Kellogg's, 61, 110, 228, 284, 452, 482
Kenneth Cole, Inc., 463
Keurig brewers, 46
KFC International, 90–91, 177, 223, 231, 392, 469*p*, 477, 477*p*, 487, 490
Khosrowshahi, Dara, 95
KIA Motors, 244
Kiehl's (L'Oréal), 319
Kiip app, 451–452
Kimberly-Clark, 110, 290, 316
Kindle Fire tablet (Amazon), 194
Kindle readers (Amazon), 281
King, Chérie, 77
Kipchoge, Eliud, 204
Kirin brewers, 481
Kirkland Signature brand (Costco), 229, 343
Kiva robots, 325, 325*p*
Kleenex (Kimberly-Clark), 227, 227p, 290
Kmart Stores, Inc., 351, 366, 402
Knowledge Guru (Bottom Line Performance learning solutions), 413, 413*p*
Koch, Jim, 389
Kodak, 70, 456
Kohl's Stores, Inc., 173, 194, 230, 269, 287, 335, 337–338, 340, 348, 350, 432, 437, 501
Komatsu equipment, 273
Konica Minolta, 63
Kraft Foods, 108, 229, 233, 316
KrazyCouponLady.com, 298
Kroger Co., Inc., 17, 196–197, 228, 228*p*, 260, 269, 308, 309, 314, 342, 352, 366, 378, 487, 500*p*, 516
Kwik Trip convenience stores, 339

L

Lab Rats, to test Brooks running gear, 246, 246*p*
Lacoste, 86
Lamar, Kendrick, 203
Lamborghini, 51–52, 207
Lancôme (L'Oréal), 319, 445
Land Cruiser (Toyota Motor Co.), 192, 192*p*
Landor global branding, 108
Land Rover, 375
Lands' End, 455
Lane Bryant, 348
Last Selfie Snapchat campaign, World Wildlife Fund (WWF), 28
Lay's snacks, 488
Lee (VF Corporation), 58
LEGO Group, 248, 248*p*, 488, 524
LEGO Movie, 387, 387*p*
Lempert, Phil, 298
Lenovo electronics, 11, 289, 489
LensCrafters, 308, 389
Leonard, Stew, 20–21, 20*p*
"Let's Quit Together" assistance program (CVS Health), 517
Levi Strauss & Co., 88, 288, 323–324, 341
Lewis, Cordell, 503
LexisNexis, 103, 106
Lexus (Toyota Motor Co.), 78, 110, 211, 215–216, 216*p*, 318
LG OLED television, 478
Lidl grocery stores (Germany), 269, 292, 338, 357
LifeLock, 501, 501*p*
Lightning Deals (Amazon), 353
The Limited stores, 337
Linens N' Things, 351
LinkedIn.com, 86, 92, 94, 131, 139, 162, 164, 237, 402, 416, 418, 445, 524
Little Caesar's pizza, 392
Lively at Roosevelt Field mall (NY), 353
L.L. Bean, 16, 16*p*, 154, 286, 454, 507
Loews hotels, 176
Logic, 7
L'Oréal, 136, 175, 201, 318–319, 484, 484*p*, 490–491, 495
Lotus, 51
Louis Vuitton, 194, 493
Lovato, Demi, 62
Lowe, Rob, 223
Lowell's restaurant (Seattle), 362
Lowe's Home Improvement Stores, 57, 71, 71*p*, 121, 195, 216, 282, 311, 316, 355, 438

Lucid Robotic System (Neural Analytics, Inc.), 200–201
Lufthansa Airlines, 310
Luvs diapers (P&G), 292
Luxottica eyewear, 308
Lyft ride sharing, 50, 120, 254, 262, 287, 312–313, 312*p*, 452

M

Macy's, 37, 76–77, 184, 186, 325, 335–338, 346, 350, 352, 437, 440, 450, 454, 456, 501
Mad Science Group franchise, 344
Maersk Line container shipping, 162–163, 163*p*
Magic Band, at Walt Disney World Resort, 83, 83*p*
Magic Markers, 227
Makino machine tools, 418–419, 419*p*
Makita power tools, 488–489
Malto, Sean, 179
Mama Cozzi's Pizza Kitchen (ALDI), 196, 228
Manolo Blahnik footwear, 493
MapMyRun app, 452
Marino, Julia, 180
Marketing Research Association, 125–126
Market Pantry (Target Stores, Inc.), 229
Marks & Spencer, 476
Marmot brand, 154
Marriott Content Studios, 386
Marriott Hotels, 76, 185–186, 186*p*, 216, 220, 354, 386
Marriott International, 475, 476*p*
Mars, Inc., 24–26, 42, 42*p*, 155, 369–370
Marshalls, Inc., 341
Martin, Jacob, 140
Mary Kay Cosmetics, 304, 376
Mashable, 139, 387
Maslow, Abraham, 145, 145
MasterCard, 102, 102*p*, 452, 501
Mattel toys, 488, 488*p*
Max Factor cosmetics, 46, 218, 257
Maxim magazine, 393
Maximo Asset Management software (IBM), 157
Maybelline Cosmetics (L'Oréal), 319, 484
Maytag appliance, 315
Mayweather, Floyd, 397
McDonald, Norm, 223
McDonald's, Inc., 19, 28, 34, 76, 77, 136, 141, 188, 192, 194, 222, 224–225, 259–260, 259*p*, 288, 299, 303, 307, 307*p*, 309, 335, 344, 347, 357, 397, 425, 452, 456, 468–469, 476–478, 490, 490*p*, 492, 499, 499*p*
McEntire, Reba, 223
McGowan, Rose, 94
McKesson health care services, 357–358
McLaren cars, 50
Meaningful Beauty, 456
Medicare, 71
Meijer, Inc., 339
Member's Mark brand (Sam's Club), 343
MemoryMirror (Intel), 354
Mercedes Benz, 51, 145, 183, 189, 194, 217, 268, 269, 269*p*, 287, 447, 488
Merck Pharmaceuticals, 293
Merry Maids franchise, 344
Mervyns stores, Inc., 351
Method household cleaning products, 517
MetLife insurance, 117–118
#MeToo movement, 94
Metro (Germany), 357
Michael Kors, Inc., 295, 308
Michaels Crafts, 351
Michelin tires, 469
Mickey Mouse merchandise (Walt Disney Company), 231
Microsoft Corp., 4, 39, 39*t*, 65–66, 65*p*, 109, 109*p*, 117, 125, 209, 209*p*, 225, 247, 250, 254–255, 281, 285, 380–382, 405–406, 410, 459, 477
Milano, Alyssa, 94
Millward Brown BrandZ survey, 477
MINDSTORMS sets (LEGO Group), 248
MINI Cooper (BMW), 145, 145*p*, 201, 217, 237, 495
Minions branded merchandise, 230
Minnie Mouse merchandise (Walt Disney Company), 231
Mint money management system (Intuit, Inc.), 254
Minute Clinics (CVS Health), 222, 516–517
Mishler, Adriene, 262
MIT (Massachusetts Institute of Technology), 25
Mizkan, 481
M&Ms candy (Mars, Inc.), 42, 186, 370
ModCloth, 336
Modern Family television show, 74, 76, 76*p*, 393
Moen, 327
Mohawk finishes (RPM International), 353
Mom Complex consultancy, 110, 110*p*
Mondelez snacks, 155, 290, 452
Monopoly (Hasbro), 386
Monroe, Marilyn, 369
Monster.com employment site, 494
Monster High branded merchandise, 230
Moosejaw, 336
Moreda, Shelina, 139
Morehouse College, 389
Mosquito Joe franchise, 344
Motel 6, 195, 227, 469
Moto-Mart convenience stores, 485
Motorola, 487, 489
Mountain Dew (PepsiCo), 19, 176, 178–180, 179*p*, 437
Mr. Handyman franchise, 344
MTV, 477
Multipro food distribution, 482
Murphy Oil Soap cleaners (Colgate-Palmolive), 218
Musk, Elon, 51, 356
Musk, Maye, 139
MyEye 2.0, 523
MyStarbucks Barista, 26, 45, 120, 120*p*

N

Naked Juice (Trader Joe's), 229
NASCAR, 98, 179
National Advertising Division of the Council of Better Business Bureaus, 382
National Enquirer, 391, 393
National Geographic, 89
National Suicide Prevent Lifeline (NSPL), 7
National Urban League, 516
Nautica (VF Corporation), 58
NBA (National Basketball Association), 139, 468, 478
NBC Sports, 179
NBC-TV, 90
NBCUniversal, 201
Neeson, Liam, 376
Neiman Marcus, 133, 338, 501
Neiman Marcus Last Call, 341
Nespresso, 456
Nest (Amazon), 82, 227, 232, 232*p*
Nestlé, 28, 317, 317*p*, 328, 469, 490, 523
Nestlé Pure Life water, 388
Netflix, 50, 118–119, 118*p*, 301–302, 301*p*, 437, 444, 468
Network Advertising Initiative, 459
Neural Analytics, Inc., 200–201
New Balance, Inc., 14, 154
New Dream, 506
Newell Rubbermaid, 90
New York City Department of Consumer Affairs (DCA), 283
New York Stock Exchange, 397
New York Times, 81–82, 387, 396–397, 432, 440
New York Yankees, 23
Next Labs (Google), 250, 318
Neymar, 208
NFL (National Football League), 140
NFL Network, 375
Nickelodeon, 231
Nielsen Media Research, 106, 115–116, 116*p*, 118, 123, 123*p*, 130, 178, 391
Nielsen PRIZM Lifestage Groups system, 143
Nike, Inc., 14, 28, 38, 77, 175, 184, 186, 192, 202–205, 203*p*, 208, 213, 214, 216, 225–226, 231, 278, 295, 303, 323, 355–356, 372, 383, 407, 445, 447, 450, 468–469, 475, 476–477, 488, 515
Nike Zoom Vaporfly Elite shoes, 204
Nikon cameras, 147
Nintendo game systems, 247
Nissan Motor Co., 152, 189, 244, 380
Nivea personal care products, 175
Nordstrom department stores, 11, 16, 77, 133, 184, 338, 348, 440, 445, 501
Nordstrom Rack, 341
North American Automotive Supplier Working Relations Index Study, 319
North Face (VF Corporation), 58, 73–74, 154, 354, 354*p*, 512–513, 512*p*
Northwestern University, 174
NOS (Coca-Cola Co.), 185
Novartis Pharmaceuticals, 293
Novo Nordisk, 386
Noxema skin care products, 218, 257
NPR (National Public Radio), 39*t*
NSPL (National Suicide Prevention Lifeline), 7
Nutrisystem, 464
Nuts About Southwest blog (Southwest Airlines), 444

O

Oakley (Luxottica), 308
Octagon detergent, 252
Oculus Rift headset, 355
Odwalla (Coca-Cola Co.), 185
Offer, Vince, 456
OfferUp.com, 95, 332, 402, 465
Office Depot, 260, 351
The Office television show, 406
Office 365 (Microsoft Corp.), 65–66
O'Hare Airport (Chicago), 394
Oklahoma State University, 35
Old Navy stores (Gap), 50
Oldsmobile (GM), 46
Old Spice products (P&G), 97, 97*p*
Olive Garden restaurants, 299
Olympic Games, 182
Omaha Steaks, 304
OneDrive cloud storage (Microsoft Corp.), 65–66
1-800-Flowers, 120
"One Reality" products (LEGO Group), 248
Oneworld (airline alliance), 310
Oracle Corp., 117, 327, 327*p*, 405–406
Oral-B dental products, 288
Orange Leaf yogurt, 423, 423*p*
Orbit gum (Mars, Inc.), 42
Orbitz.com (Expedia Group), 437
Oreo cookies, 19, 231, 393–394
Oriental Land Company, 481, 481*p*
Oscar Health, 219–220, 220*p*
Otis Elevator, 469
Overstock.com, 284, 328, 341, 501
OxiClean, 456

P

Pacquiao, Manny, 397
Page, Larry, 251
Palisades insurance, 237
Palmolive dishwashing products (Colgate-Palmolive), 218
Pampered Chef, 304, 315
Pampers diapers (P&G), 97–98, 392, 473
Pampers Swaddlers (P&G), 177
Panasonic, 442, 486
Pandora.com, 76
Panera Bread, 39*t*, 50, 176, 176*p*, 227, 352
Pantene hair care products (P&G), 97, 320
Paraolympic Winter Games, 77, 77*p*
Parents magazine, 393
Paris Auto Show, 52
PartnerShops (Ben & Jerry's), 86–87
Patagonia, Inc., 29, 80–82, 81*p*, 140, 178, 444, 444*p*, 507
Patagonia Common Threads Initiative, 81
Patek Philippe watches, 193, 268, 268*p*
PBS Kids, 201
Peace Day organization, 397
Pearle Vision, 308
Pedigree dog food (Mars, Inc.), 42, 514–515
Pedigree Foundation, 515
Peeps candy, 393, 393*p*
Peloton exercise bikes, 494
Penske Logistics, 328
People magazine, 393
People & Planet Positive sustainability strategy (IKEA), 356
PepsiCo, Inc., 99, 99*p*, 178–179, 232–233, 256, 380–381, 389–390, 401, 427–428, 437, 503
Perdue chicken, 211
Periscope.com, 73
Perry, Katy, 139
Persol (Luxottica), 308
PetCo pet stores, 339, 342
Petnet, 236
PetSmart, 194, 342, 351
Pfizer infant nutrition unit, 523
Pfizer Pharmaceuticals, 293–294, 410
Pharmacy Benefits Management (PBM) services (CVS Health), 516–517
Philips appliances, 486
Piggly-Wiggly grocery stores, 323
Pinterest.com, 24, 34, 39, 39t, 62, 141, 164, 226, 256, 346, 387, 390, 445, 456
Pitzel, Rachel, 142
Pixel electronics (Google), 250, 276, 276*p*, 318
Pizza Hut, 213–214, 214*p*
Plank, Kevin, 243, 520
Plastic Wood fillers (RPM International), 353
Plated meal kits, 366
Platinum Card (American Express), 175
Playskool, 110
PlayStation Community (Sony), 24, 24*p*
Plumlee, Nancy, 287
Plymouth Rock Assurance, 237
Pohlman, Paul, 497–498, 510
Policicchio, Jeff, 422–423
Polo Ralph Lauren, 308, 341
Pontiac Motors (GM), 46
Porsche Motor Co., 51–52, 189
Portuhondo, Jennifer, 185–186, 186*p*
Post-It Notes (3M), 227
Pottery Barn, 231
Powder Project app (REI), 451
Power Air Fryer, 407
Power BI data analytics (Microsoft Corp.), 66
Powermat (Duracell), 232
Prada, 308, 350
Preference Service (Data & Marketing Association), 460
Price, Katie, 370
Price Check (Amazon), 287
Price.com, 287
Pringles snacks, 46, 218
Private Selection brand (Kroger), 228
Proactiv acne treatment, 456
Procter & Gamble (P&G), 4, 17, 35, 46, 63, 76, 96–98, 97*p*, 108, 120, 136–137, 140, 174, 177, 184, 184*p*, 212–213, 212*p*, 217–218, 233, 249, 257, 278, 292, 309, 316–320, 325, 327–328, 337, 378, 386, 389, 393, 407, 409–411, 409*p*, 433, 447, 450, 452, 456, 473–474, 481, 488, 492, 502
Progressive insurance, 222, 332
ProQuest, 106
PR Week, 397
Psst brand (Kroger), 228, 269
Publix Stores, Inc., 314
Puffs facial tissue (P&G), 292
PulsePoint ad networks, 114
Puma, Inc., 14, 186
Pump 'N Munch convenience stores, 485
Purina pet food (Nestlé), 328, 469

Q

QLED Smart TV (Samsung), 239
Quaker Oats, 224, 252, 256, 256*p*
Qualtrics surveys, 35, 131, 465
QuickBooks (Intuit, Inc.), 107
Quicken financial software (Intuit, Inc.), 254–255, 280
Quicken Loans, 304, 389, 389*p*, 439, 440
QuickenLoans' Rocket Mortgage, 191, 191*p*
QVC, 463

R

Raden at Roosevelt Field mall (NY), 353
Radio Flyer wagons, 257, 257*p*, 283
Rae, Issa, 139
Ramada Limited, 195
Ravelry.com, 24
Ray-Ban (Luxottica), 308
Redbox, 451, 456
Red Bull, 26, 426–428, 427*p*
Cliff Diving Series event, 428
Cold Rush event, 428
Crashed Ice World Championship, 427
Rampage freeride mountain bike competition, 427
Signature Series reality TV, 428
Stratos project, 427–428
Red Cross, 207, 438, 450
Reddit.com, 24
Red Kap, 143
Redken (L'Oréal), 319
Red Roof Inn, 394
Reebok, Inc., 14, 203, 488
Reeves, Rosser, 192
Regal Cinemas, 27
Regus, 76
REI, Inc., 186, 295, 338, 345, 423, 423*p*, 507, 507*p*
Reliant Stadium (Houston), 362
Renren (Chinese social networking platform), 493
REO stores, 222
Ressler, Don, 331
Restoration Hardware, 349, 349*p*, 454–455
Retail Equation, 23
Retail Link data system (Walmart Stores, Inc.), 327
Revlon Cosmetics, 205, 456
Revolve Clothing, 445
Revson, Charles, 205
Right Guard deodorant, 46, 218
Rihanna, 184
Ritz-Carlton Hotels & Resorts, 39*t*, 40, 192, 210, 227
Road & Track, 52
Roche Pharmaceuticals, 293
Rock Bottom Golf, 299
Rockwell Automation, 422–423
Roku platform, 463
Rolex watches, 210, 290, 388
Rolls-Royce (BMW), 187, 187*p*, 210, 217
Ronald McDonald House, 141
Ronaldo, Cristiano, 208
Room Essentials (Target Stores, Inc.), 229
Roosevelt Field mall (NY), 353, 353*p*
Rowling, J. K., 478
Royal Canin (Mars, Inc.), 42
RPM International, 353
RTIC Coolers, 441
Rukka brand, 154
Russian Food Safety Authority, 477
Rust-Oleum paints (RPM International), 353
Ryder truck rental, 328

S

Saab Motors, 46
Saatchi & Saatchi advertising, 226
SABMiller beer, 481
Sabo Project (Diff Eyewear), 62
Safeway Stores, Inc., 148, 304, 409
Saks Fifth Avenue, 133, 260, 338
Saks Off 5th, 341
Salesforce Chatter platform (Salesforce.com), 405
Salesforce.com, 75, 117, 164, 242, 242*p*, 405–406, 405*p*
Sam Adams beer (Boston Beer Company), 389
Sam's Club (Walmart), 341–342
Samsung Electronics, 28, 65, 77, 102–103, 113, 194, 228, 239–240, 249, 265–266, 271, 306, 315, 384, 410, 423, 442, 468–469, 478, 489, 503
Sanders, Brandon, 177
SAP Community, 417–418
SAP Consumer Insight 365 service, 125, 458
SAP software, 327, 405, 417–418, 417*p*
SAP Store online marketplace, 417–418
SAS software, 117
Saturn Motors, 46, 51
Schick Hydro 5 razor, 283
Schick razors, 35
Scholastic, Inc., 516
Schrute, Dwight, 406
Schultz, Howard, 37–38, 503
Schultz Shoes, 445
Schwab online investment services, 204
Schwarz stores, 260
Scion (Toyota), 211
SC Johnson Co., 518–519
Scooby Doo branded merchandise, 230
Scotch Tape, 227
Scotts lawn products, 114
Sears, Inc., 70, 174, 316, 335, 337, 338, 456
Sears Optical, 308
Seattle's Best (Starbucks), 180
Secret deodorant (P&G), 174
Sedaris, David, 76
Selfycart app, 365
Sephora Beauty Insider Community, 24
Sephora Cosmetics, 39*t*, 175, 355, 451
Sesame Street, 230
7-Eleven convenience stores, 25, 309, 469, 484–486, 485*p*
7 For All Mankind (VF Corporation), 58

Seven & I Holdings (Japan), 357, 486
Seventh Generation detergent, 423
ShamWow, 456
Shanghai Disneyland, 482
Shanghai Shendi Group, 482
Sharapova, Maria, 208
ShareDesk, 76
Shelter Pet Project, 116, 116*p*
Sherwin-Williams, 231, 355
Shinola, 133–134, 133*p*, 144
Shipt delivery service (Target Stores, Inc.), 299, 343, 367
Shkreli, Martin, 293
ShoeBuy, 336
Shop 'n Save stores, 362
Shoppers stores, 362
ShopRite Stores, 505, 505*p*
ShopSavvy app, 287
Siemens, 511–512
Silk soymilk, 383
Simple Truth brand (Kroger), 228
Simply Balanced (Target Stores, Inc.), 229
Simply Nature brand (ALDI), 228
Simply Vera by Vera Wang, 348
Sina Weibo (Chinese microblogging site), 493
Singapore Airlines, 191
Sioux, Nia, 140
Six Flags Entertainment Corp., 156–157, 157*p*, 281
60 *Minutes* television news program, 200
Skittles candy, 391, 392, 392*p*
Škoda auto manufacturing (Czech Republic), 481
Skype (Microsoft Corp.), 65–66, 239
Skyteam (airline alliance), 310
Slack, 75, 75*p*, 120
Sleep Number beds, 275, 275*p*
Slimfast diet, 227
SmartJourney (Loews), 176
SmartThings Cloud (Samsung), 240
Smith, Brad, 108
Smith, Patti, 390
Smith, Will, 34
Smoking Cessation Hubs (CVS Health), 517
Snack Factory (Trader Joe's), 229
Snapchat.com, 18, 24, 62, 73, 139, 164, 346, 372, 387, 393, 440, 443, 445–447, 458
Snapchat Privacy Center, 114
Snapdeal, 479
Snap Surveys, 111, 111*p*
Snickers candy (Mars, Inc.), 24–26, 25*p*, 42, 369–370, 369*p*
Snuggie, 456
Soccer Shots franchise, 344
Softsoap (Colgate-Palmolive), 218
Song of Style blog, 444
Sonic restaurants, 442, 442*p*
Sonoma brand (Kohl's), 348
Sonos sound systems, 11, 11*p*, 82, 189, 190*p*, 211
Sony, Inc., 24, 24*p*, 70, 86, 239
South Carolina State University, 61
Southland Ice Company, 485
Southwest Airlines, 12, 50, 92, 115, 185, 213–215, 214*p*, 223, 294, 444
Spanx underwear, 169, 237, 299
Spectrum cable, 276, 281
Speed Stick (Colgate-Palmolive), 218
Sperry, Inc., 88
S&P 500, 293
S&P Pharmaceuticals Select Industry Index, 293
Spirit Airlines, 11, 269–271, 270*p*
SpongeBob SquarePants branded merchandise, 230–231, 231*p*
Sport Clips Haircuts, 309, 309*p*
Sports and Fitness Industry Association, 262
Spotify.com, 311, 445
Sprint, Inc., 86
Sprouts grocery, 338
Sprout television programming (NBCUniversal), 201
Stance socks, 184, 185*p*
Stanford University, 122
Staples Business Advantage, 162
Staples Office Stores, 173, 315, 356, 432, 440
Star, 393
Star Alliance (airline alliance), 310
Starbucks, 19, 21, 26, 37–39, 37*p*, 39*t*, 45–46, 46*p*, 61, 77, 103, 120, 120*p*, 171, 176, 180–181, 186, 191, 193–194, 204, 223, 223*p*, 310, 310*p*, 381, 386, 438, 449–450, 452, 469, 476–477, 503–505, 504*p*, 515
  Community Store initiative, 503
  Doubleshot, 46
  mobile payments app, 247, 247*p*
  Refreshers, 46
  Reserve Bars, 38, 46
  Reserve Roasteries, 38, 46
  VIA instant coffee, 247
Starburst (Mars, Inc.), 42
Star Wars branded merchandise (Walt Disney Company), 230–231
State Farm Insurance, 86, 136, 386
Stauffer's (Trader Joe's), 229
Steelcase office furniture, 181
Steinway pianos, 15, 15*p*, 271
Stella & Dots jewelry, 315
Sterling, Debbie, 122, 122*p*
Stewart, John, 224
STIHL equipment, 316, 316*p*, 423
St. Jude's Children's Research Hospital, 27, 27*p*, 220
Stranger Things television show, 386
Strathwood brand (Amazon), 228
Suavital fabric conditioners (Colgate-Palmolive), 218
Subaru Motors, 50, 52
Subway, Inc., 48, 316, 344
SubZero appliances, 194
Sullivan, Anthony, 456
Sunday Night Football, 385
Sunglass Hut, 308
Sunkist juice, 481
Sun Life, 71
Sunny Delight drinks, 218
Super Bowl, 58, 89, 113–114, 212, 369–370, 374, 376–377, 385, 390, 393, 397, 435, 437, 443, 450, 452, 508
Supercell games, 376
Super Clo awards for advertising, 369
SupermarketGuru.com, 298
SuperValu food wholesalers, 362, 503
Sure deodorant, 257
Surface Pro (Microsoft Corp.), 381–382, 382*p*
Surface tablet (Microsoft Corp.), 65, 247, 285
Survey Monkey, 111
Sustainable Living Plan (Unilever), 497–498, 497*p*
Swiffer, 227
Swift, Taylor, 389
Swindle, Gerald, 180
Sysco food distribution, 362, 362*p*

T

TABASCO, 252
Taboola ad networks, 114
Taco Bell, 26, 26*p*, 176, 231, 246–247, 309, 452
Target Optical, 308
Target Stores, Inc., 4, 6*p*, 27, 78, 78*p*, 86, 94, 124, 140, 143, 173–174, 178, 184, 194, 222, 228, 229, 283–284, 299, 304, 310, 310*p*, 311, 332, 335, 337–340, 345–346, 353, 354, 366–367, 378, 440
Tate's Bake Shop (Trader Joe's), 229
Teavana tea (Starbucks), 38
Tecate beer, 373*p*, 374
TelePresence conferencing tools, 418
Tencent, Inc., 225
Tesco (UK), 316, 357
Tesla Motor Co., 19, 19*p*, 50–52, 51*p*, 82, 152, 164, 244*p*, 262, 274, 356, 380
Testors cement and paints (RPM International), 353
TGI Friday's, 148, 352, 352*p*
Thanks and Giving campaign, St. Jude's Children's Research Hospital, 27–28
This Is Us television show, 90, 376, 385
3M, Inc., 240
Threshold (Target Stores, Inc.), 229
Tide detergent (P&G), 17, 34, 97–98, 97*p*, 106, 177, 184, 184*p*, 227, 247, 252, 278, 292, 320, 378, 386, 488
Tide Pods unit-dose laundry detergent packets (P&G), 212–213, 212*p*
Tiffany's, 78, 212, 338, 440
Timberland (VF Corporation), 29, 58, 515
Timex watches, 318, 388
Title Nine stores, 144, 144*p*
TJ Maxx, 341, 350, 350*p*, 352
TJX Companies, 341
T-Mobile, Inc., 86
Toblerone chocolates (Mondelez), 290
Tokyo Disney Resorts (Oriental Land Company), 481, 481*p*
Tolaram Africa Foods, 482
Tommy Hilfiger, 230
Tom's of Maine (Colgate-Palmolive), 218
TOMS shoes, 515
Topo-Chico (Coca-Cola Co.), 185
Top-Siders (Sperry), 88
Toro equipment, 425
Torrefazione Italia (Starbucks), 180
Toshiba electronics, 328
Tourism Australia, 208
Toyota Motor Co., 28, 48, 51, 76, 77, 77*p*, 121, 136–138, 136*p*, 192, 192*p*, 204, 303, 303*p*, 318–319, 319*p*, 376, 380, 456, 469, 478, 507
Toys "R" Us, 253, 311, 311*p*
Toy Story merchandise (Walt Disney Company), 231
Trader Joe's, 107, 140, 226, 228–229, 274, 274*p*, 292, 299, 314, 336, 338, 347, 351, 367, 485
Transparent television show, 74, 76
Travelers insurance, 228
Travelocity.com (Expedia Group), 437, 437*p*
Trejo, Danny, 369
Tresiba (Novo Nordisk), 386
Tribe Mediterranean Foods (Trader Joe's), 229
TripAdvisor.com, 149, 174, 451, 451*p*
Triple Crown stakes, 397
trivago.com (Expedia Group), 437
TrueBlue loyalty program (JetBlue Airways), 17, 17*p*
True Value Hardware stores, 47, 344
Trump, Donald, 129
TRUSTe, 459
Tucker, Nick, 179
Tumblr.com, 164, 444
Tupperware, 315
TurboTax software (Intuit, Inc.), 107, 254
Turing Pharmaceuticals, 293
Turkish Airlines, 310

Twitter.com, 18, 19, 24, 25–26, 28, 34, 53, 62, 76, 90–92, 94, 113–114, 118, 125, 129, 139, 141, 162, 164, 192, 203, 212–214, 216, 222–223, 227, 256, 346, 370, 375, 386, 387, 391, 393, 397, 401, 416, 418–419, 435, 438, 440, 443–448, 456, 458, 463, 477, 493
Twix (Mars, Inc.), 42
Tylenol, 49

U
UA MagZip (Under Armour), 243
Uber ride sharing, 34, 50, 50*p*, 86, 94, 225, 254, 262, 287, 303, 312
Uncle Ben's rice (Mars, Inc.), 42
Under Armour, 154, 175, 243, 243*p*, 389, 520
Unilever, 13, 86, 110, 175, 181, 233, 289, 304, 316, 372, 401, 497–498, 497*p*, 510
Uniqlo retail, 456, 464
United Airlines, 61, 91–92, 271, 294, 310
United Technologies Corporation, 469
Universal Studios, 469
UPS, Inc., 4, 79, 192, 197, 320, 331, 479
UPS Business Solutions, 328
Up & Up (Target Stores, Inc.), 229
Urban League, 503
USAA insurance, 101, 101*p*, 315
U.S. Army, 379
USA Today, 443
USA Today Ad Meter, 369
U.S. Census Bureau, 123
U.S. Congress, 331
U.S. Department of Agriculture, 298, 503
U.S. Department of Justice, 294
U.S. Department of Transportation, 270
U.S. Food and Drug Administration, 213
U.S. Forest Service, 137, 137*p*, 445
USG Corporation, 158, 158*p*
U.S. military services, 28
U.S. MONITOR, 106
U.S. Navy, 456
U.S. Patent Office, 103
U.S. Postal Service, 4, 28, 197, 223, 277, 320, 406, 453
U.S. Securities and Exchange Commission (SEC), 103
U.S. Small Business Administration, 122–123

V
Vans (VF Corporation), 58
VCA veterinary services (Mars, Inc.), 42
Velcro fasteners, 227
Vendor Flex program (Amazon), 320
Verizon, Inc., 86, 225, 281
Verizon Wireless, 77
Versace, 308, 341
VF Corporation, 58
Via instant coffee (Starbucks), 37, 46
Vicks Nyquil (P&G), 393
Vicks products (P&G), 97
Vicks ZzzQuil (P&G), 232
Victoria's Secret, 445, 477
Victoza (Novo Nordisk), 386
Viking range, 210
Visa credit services, 189, 225, 396
Visiting Angels, 95
Vogue Eyewear (Luxottica), 308
Vogue magazine, 375, 393
Volkswagen Motor Co., 52, 259
Volvo Motors, 236
VPI Industries, 134

W
Walgreens Stores, Inc., 71, 113, 186, 220, 260, 282, 304, 309, 357, 378, 456, 503, 516
Wall Street Journal, 94, 262, 375, 387, 396
Walmart Stores, Inc., 3–4, 10, 13, 17, 39*t*, 76, 78, 80, 80*p*, 94, 110, 136, 140, 141–142, 155, 173, 192, 194, 196, 226, 229, 253, 260, 266, 269, 271, 303, 309, 311, 314–316, 323, 325, 327–328, 335–343, 335*p*, 345–347, 350–352, 355, 357, 366, 378, 409–411, 409*p*, 422–423, 426, 442, 456, 463, 467–468, 470–471, 470*p*, 477, 479, 482, 482*p*, 500–503, 515–516
Walt Disney Company, 88, 140–142, 205, 225–227, 226*p*, 230–231, 233, 235, 386, 447, 456, 459, 476, 481–482, 481*p*
Walt Disney World, 7, 7*p*, 83, 83*p*
Walton, Sam, 355
Warby Parker, 29, 29*p*, 337, 442–443, 443*p*
Warhol, Andy, 390
Washington Nationals baseball team, 211
Washington Post, 144, 211
Watco finishes (RPM International), 353
Waterford, 134
Watson Advertising (IBM), 121
Wavestorm surfboards (AGIT Global), 279, 279*p*
Waymo, 262
Waze app (Google), 451
Waze navigation app, 26, 174, 174*p*, 225
Wear Testers, to test Brooks running gear, 246
Weather.com, 114
Weather Company, The, 121
WebEx conferencing tools, 418
Wegmans Stores, Inc., 314–315, 314*p*
Wegmans supermarkets, 192
Weight Watchers, 256, 383, 393
Weinstein, Harvey, 94
Weixin (Chinese instant messaging site), 493
Wella hair care, 46, 218
Wells Fargo, 77, 252
Wendy's, 50, 213, 223, 299
Westbrook, Russell, 180
West Elm, 390, 426, 454
Western Auto, 344
Westin Stamford Hotel, 193
What We Wore fashion blog (Bernstein), 444
Whirlpool appliances, 226
Whirlpool's Care Counts program, 86–87
Whiskas (Mars, Inc.), 42
White, Betty, 369–370
Whitley, Chris, 179
Whole Foods Market, 4, 91, 91*p*, 107, 140, 143–144, 148, 292, 292*p*, 314, 335, 338, 352, 389, 503
Wikipedia.com, 440
Will & Grace television show, 386
Williams, Robin, 369
Williams-Sonoma, 27, 284, 338, 440, 454
Wilson, Jackie, 230
WinCo discount grocery, 339, 339*p*
Windows Operating System (Microsoft Corp.), 65
Winfrey, Oprah, 34
Winky Lux at Roosevelt Field mall (NY), 353
Wired magazine, 375
Wolverine footwear, 388, 388*p*
Wonderful Pistachios (Trader Joe's), 211, 229
Wondershop (Target Stores, Inc.), 229
Woolstencroft, Lauren, 77, 77*p*
World Cup soccer, 374
World's Most Innovative Company list (*Forbes* magazine), 405
World Trade Organization (WTO), 471
World Wildlife Fund (WWF), 28
Wounded Warrior Project, 400
WPP advertising agency, 395
Wrangler (VF Corporation), 58, 229
Wright, Wendy, 142
Wrigley Field, 174
Wrigley gum (Mars, Inc.), 42

X
Xerox Corp., 70
Xfinity Streampix (Comcast), 302
Xiaomi electronics (China), 266, 489
X innovation lab (Alphabet), 251

Y
Yahoo!.com, 86, 213, 250, 440, 442, 459
Yahoo! Finance, 63
Yamaha pianos, 271
Yelp.com, 91, 149, 149*p*, 186, 314
Yoga With Adriene, 262
Yoplait yogurt, 382
Yosemite National Park, 355
Youku (Chinese social networking site), 493
Young & Rubicam, 225
Young Sheldon television show, 386
YouTube.com, 18, 19, 24, 25–26, 34, 53, 62, 76, 87, 92, 114, 125, 139, 141, 162, 164, 203, 301–302, 318, 346, 355, 369, 375, 376, 385–387, 393, 400, 418–419, 428, 435, 440, 443, 445–446, 449, 456, 458, 493
Y&R advertising agency, 395

Z
Zappos.com, 16, 113, 119, 119*p*, 121, 191, 227, 346
Zara fashions, 468
Zico (Coca-Cola Co.), 185
Zipcar car sharing, 220
Ziploc storage bags, 227
Zoom conferencing tools, 418
ZoomSystems, 456–457
Zuckerberg, Mark, 34, 129
Zulily.com flash sale site, 353
ZUUL extranet (Zappos.com), 119*p*, 121

Subject Index

In this index, *f* refers to figures, *p* refers to pictures, and *t* refers to tables.

A
Acceptability, 54
Accessibility
  in four As of marketing, 54
  Office 365 (Microsoft Corp.) for, 66
Acquisition of competitors, 508
Actual product, in product levels, 206
Adaptation of products for international markets, 467–468, 483–486, 485*p*
Administered vertical marketing systems (VMS), 309
Adoption of new products, 151–153, 151*p*, 152*f*
Advertainment (merging entertainment and advertising), 385–386
Advertising agencies, 395
Advertising and public relations, 368–403
  budget for, 383–384
  in commercialization of products, 247
  corporate spending on, 233
  cross-cultural, 138, 138*p*
  deceptive, 501, 501*p*
  digital advertising networks, 113–114
  example of, 369–370

Ford Motor Co. spending on, 53
functions of PR, 370–371, 396–397
Google profiles of consumers for, 459
Instagram introduction of paid, 447
in integrated marketing communications, 371–378
international, 395–396, 488
in mature stage of product life cycle, 256
media strategy for, 390–394
message and brand content strategy for, 385–390
objectives for, 379–383, 379*f*, 380*t*
online, 441–442, 442*p*
organizing for, 394–395
in promotion mix, 370–371
proposed progressive tax on, 508
return on advertising investment, 394
role and impact of PR, 397–398
search-related ads, 442
subliminal, 146–147
tools for PR, 398
underuse of PR, 377
Advertising option icon, 459, 459*p*
Advertising specialties, 425, 428
Affluent consumers, 175
Affordability, 54
Affordable method, of advertising budgeting, 383
African American subculture, 76, 137–138, 137*p*
Agents and brokers, 359*t*–360*t*, 360
Age structure of population
changes in, 71–74
life stage, buying behavior and, 143
market segmentation by, 174
AI (artificial intelligence). *See* Artificial intelligence (AI)
Airtruck multimodal transportation, 326
All-electric vehicles (EVs), 51
Allowances and discounts
consumer expectations of, 352
in pricing, 282, 307
in trade promotions, 428
Alternative media, 392, 392*p*
American family, changes in, 74–75
"Americanization" of world cultures, 476
Antitrust regulations, 508, 508*p*
AR (augmented reality), 354–356, 355*p*, 454–455
Artificial intelligence (AI)
customer relationship management solutions with, 405
in marketing analytics, 119–121, 120*p*
as new direction for "digital giants," 66
overview, 27
for tailoring offers to customers, 354–356, 355*p*
in wearable devices, 523
Asian American subculture, 76, 137–138
Attack advertising, 380
Attention, selective, 146
Attitudes, in buying behavior, 147–148, 150
Attributes of products, 209–211
Augmented product, in product levels, 206
Augmented reality (AR), 354–356, 355*p*, 454–455
Automated warehousing, 361
Automobile Information Disclosure Act, 295
Awareness, in four As of marketing, 54

B

Baby boomers, 71, 145
Back-to-basics economics sensibility, 78
Barnacles, as customer classification, 22–23, 22*f*
Barter, in international trade, 475
Basing-point pricing, 286
Beacon technology for apps, 354
Behavioral segmentation of markets, 176–178
Behavioral targeting of consumers online, 112–114, 113*p*
Beliefs, buying behavior affected by, 147–148
Benefits sought, segmentation of markets by, 176–177, 177*p*
Beyond greening activities, 511
"Big box" discount stores, 340
Big data
artificial intelligence and, 120
dynamic pricing based on, 286
marketing analytics and, 118–119
in marketing information, 97*p*, 98–99
overview, 27
as "stalking" customers, 189
Biometric measures in marketing, 116
Blogs and forums, 444–445, 444*p*
Bluetooth technology, 354
"Bottom of the pyramid" markets, 288–289, 473–474
Brand advocacy, 18, 140–142
Brand content, in advertising, 385–390
Branded web communities, 440–441, 441*p*
Branding strategy
brand-building advertising, 384
"break and fix," 240
customer engagement in, 203
development, 231–233
equity and value, 224–225, 225*p*
managing, 233
name selection, 227–228
positioning, 226–227
product, 211–212, 211*p*
sponsorship, 228, 230–231
store brands, 229–230
See also Products; Services
Brand integrations (branded entertainment), 386–387
Brand personality, 144
"Break and fix" brands, 240
Break-even pricing, 272–273, 272*f*
Brexit (UK exiting European Union), 471–472
Bribes and kickbacks, 519
BRICS countries (Brazil, Russia, India, China, and South Africa), 181, 472
Brokers and agents, as wholesalers, 359*t*–360*t*, 360
B-to-B marketing. *See* Business-to-business companies; Buyers, behavior of
Budget for advertising and public relations, 383–384
Business analysis, in product development, 241*f*, 245–246
Business distribution channels, 305, 306*f*. *See also* Channels
Business markets, 70. *See also* Business-to-business companies; Buyers, behavior of; Marketing strategies, customer value-driven
Business portfolio
analyzing current, 43
Boston Consulting Group approach, 43–45
example of, 41–42
growth and downsizing strategies, 45–46
Business promotions, 424, 429, 429*p*
Business-to-business companies
email marketing to, 442
online purchasing by, 416–417
push strategies used by, 378
See also Personal selling
Business-to-consumer companies, 378. *See also* Personal selling
Butterflies, as customer classification, 22, 22*f*
Buyer behavior, 132–169
business market, 153–159, 156*f*
decision process, 159–161, 159*f*
digital and social marketing, 161–165
consumer market
cultural factors in, 135–138, 135*f*
model of, 134–135, 135*f*
personal factors in, 135*f*, 143–144
psychological factors in, 135*f*, 145–148
social factors in, 135*f*, 139–142
consumer decision process, 148–151
example of, 133–134
new product decision process, 151–153
By-product pricing, 281

C

CAFTA-DR (Central American Free Trade Agreement), 472
Call plan, for sales, 414
Cannibalization, 217
Capital items, 208
Captive product pricing, 280–281, 280*t*, 281*p*
Carbonating the World (Center for Science in the Public Interest), 502, 502*p*
Carbon footprint reduction, 511–512
Careers in marketing, 31
Caring capitalism, 29, 86
Cash cows, in growth-share matrix, 43–44
Cash discounts, 282
Catalog marketing, 454–455, 454*p*
Category killers, 194, 339
Causal research, 105
Cause-related marketing, 86–87, 86*p*
CBD (Customer Business Development) teams, 409–411
Celebrity endorsements, 203, 208
Censorship, 493
Central American Free Trade Agreement (CAFTA-DR), 472
Central business districts, 351
Changing prices, 289–292, 290*p*, 291*f*, 292*p*
Channel differentiation, 191–192
Channel levels, pricing in, 294–295
Channels, 300–333
design decisions in, 314–317
horizontal marketing systems, 309–310
innovation in, 301–302
for international markets, 489–490, 489*f*
management decisions about, 317–321
marketing logistics
functions of, 324–327, 325*p*, 326*p*
importance of, 321–323, 322*f*, 322*p*
integrated management of, 327–328, 327*p*
member roles in, 306–307
multichannel distribution systems, 310–311
omni-channel retailing, 345–346, 346*p*
organization of, 311–313
pricing in levels of, 294–295
supply chain management, 323–324, 323*p*
supply chains and value delivery network, 302–306
vertical marketing systems, 307–309
in wholesaling, 361
Chat bots, for customer service, 27
Checkout scanning technology, 354

Chief financial officer (CFO), 57
Chief marketing officer (CMO), 57, 59
Chief operating officer (COO), 57
Chief privacy officer (CPO), 125
Children
  in international markets, 488, 488*p*
  target marketing to, 188, 188*p*
  vulnerability on social media of, 458
Children's Online Privacy Protection Act (COPPA), 459
Citizen-action publics, 69
Class-action lawsuits, 259
Classifying customers, 22, 22*f*
Clayton Act of 1914, 292, 321
Clean technology, 511–512, 511*f*
Closed-ended questions, 115
Cloud-based computing services
  Amazon.com, 3
  collaboration with, 75
  Salesforce.com, 405–406
Cluster sample, 115*t*
Clutter, promotion, 424
Co-branding, 231
Co-creation of products, with customers, 248, 248*p*
Cognitive dissonance, in buying decision, 150–151, 150*p*
Collaboration, cloud computing for, 75
Commercialization of products, 241*f*, 247
Commercial online databases, 106
Commercial sources of information, 149
Commission-based compensation, for sales, 414
Communicability of new products, 153
Communication adaptations, for international markets, 488, 488*p*
Communications. *See* Advertising and public relations
Company buying sites, for e-procurement, 162
Company profits, consumer wants, society needs and, 13, 13*f*
Comparative advertising, 380–382, 382*p*
Compatibility of new products, 152
Compensation
  sales force, 409*f*, 414, 414*p*
  sales quotas and, 415
  team selling situations, 412
Competition
  business buying and, 158
  in content licensing, 302
  distribution decisions limiting, 321
  dynamic pricing based on, 286
  freight-absorption pricing and, 286
  high-low pricing in response to, 350
  in international markets, 469
  marketing-caused reductions of, 508
  in mature stage of product life cycle, 256
  in microenvironment, 68–69
  price change impacts on, 290–291, 291*f*
  product development ideas from, 242
  pure, monopolistic, and oligopolistic, 276, 276*p*
  retail convergence and more, 353
  See also Advertising and public relations
Competition-based pricing, 273–274, 273*p*
Competitive advantage, 191–193, 318
Competitive marketing intelligence, 101–103
Competitive-parity method, of advertising budgeting, 383–384
Complexity of new products, 152–153
Complex sales force structure, 410
Comprehensive and Progressive Agreement for Trans-Pacific Partnership (CPTPP), 472
Concentrated target marketing, 184–185, 185*p*
Concept development and testing, 243–244, 245*t*
Conformance quality, 210
Consumer-generated marketing, 19, 19*p*
Consumer immersion research, 97
Consumer insights. *See* Marketing information
Consumerism, 509–510, 509*p*
Consumer-oriented marketing, 514
Consumer Product Safety Act of 1972, 258–259
Consumer promotions
  advertising specialties, 425
  contests, sweepstakes, and games, 426
  coupons, 425
  event marketing, 426–428
  point-of-purchase (POP) promotions, 426
  premiums, 425
  price packs, 425
  rebates, 425
  samples, 425, 425*p*
Consumers
  advertising content generated by, 389–390
  affluent, 175
  at bottom of economic pyramid, 473–474
  brand strength perceptions of, 225
  government agencies for protecting, 84
  markets for, 70
  omni-channel, 439
  post-recession spending behavior, 352, 352*p*
  privacy of, 124–125, 458–459
  products for, 206–207
  retailing and, 336–337, 352
  social costs paid by, 507
  tracking and targeting of, 112–114, 124–125
  See also Advertising and public relations; Buyers, behavior of; Customers
Contact methods, in marketing research, 109–114
Content
  advertising as marketing, 372–374, 373*p*
  brand, 385–390
  consumer-generated, 389–390
  licensing of, 302
  public relations generation of, 398
  streaming, 239
Contests, sweepstakes, and games, 426
Contextual advertising, 442
Continuous inventory replenishment systems, 327
Contract logistics, 328
Contract manufacturing, 481
Contractual vertical marketing systems (VMS), 308–309
Control, marketing, 58
Controlled test marketing, 247
Convenience products, 207, 207*t*
Convenience sample, 115*t*
Convenience stores, 339, 340*t*
Conventional distribution channels, 307, 308*f*
Convergence of markets, 353, 485–486
"Cord cutters" (dropping cable and satellite subscriptions), 385, 385*p*
Core cultural values, 87
Core customer value, 205–206
Corporate chain retail organization, 343*t*, 344
Corporate identity materials, 398
Corporate vertical marketing systems (VMS), 308
Corporation scandals, 88
Cost-based pricing, 268*f*, 271–273, 272*f*
Cost-plus pricing, 272–274, 272*f*
Counterfeit products, 493
Coupons, as consumer promotions, 425
Cradle-to-cradle practices, 511
Creative concept, in advertising, 387–388, 388*p*
"Creative destruction" strategy, 254–255
Critical thinking skills, 31
CRM (customer relationship management). *See* Customer relationship management (CRM)
Cross-functional, cross-company teams, 328
Crowdsourcing, 242–243, 243*p*
Culture
  business buying and, 158, 158*f*
  consumer buying and, 135–138
  international marketing and, 475–478, 480*t*
  marketing-caused pollution of, 507–508
  marketing research and, 124
  market segmentation by, 181
  overview, 87–89
Customer Business Development (CBD) teams, 409–411
Customer-centered logistics, 322
Customer-centered new product development, 248, 248*p*, 257, 257*p*
Customer-driven marketing, 13
Customer-engagement marketing, 17–18
Customer management organization of marketing departments, 57–58
Customer-perceived value, 15
Customer relationship management (CRM)
  building blocks for, 15–16
  consumer-generated marketing, 19
  in digital, mobile, and social media, 17–18
  levels and tools for, 17
  overview, 117–119
  partner relationship management and, 20
  in personal selling, 422–423
  Salesforce.com for, 405–406
Customers
  Amazon's attention to, 3
  artificial intelligence for tailoring offers to, 354–356
  brand engagement and experiences of, 233
  classifying, 22, 22*f*
  creating value for, 30
  disadvantaged, poor service received by, 503–506
  engagement in brands, 203
  interaction with providers, in services, 220
  lovemark brands and, 226–227
  marketing channels to meet needs of, 314–315, 314*p*
  marketing strategy driven by, 49–52
  in microenvironment, 69–70
  mobile marketing and, 345
  needs of, 6–10, 6*f*, 6*p*
  partner relationship management for, 46–48
  Patagonia Common Threads Initiative and, 81–82
  personal retail promotion for, 350, 350*p*
  product development ideas from, 242, 242*p*
  retention of, 223
  sales force as link from company to, 407–408, 408*p*
  sales force structured by, 411

store brands and, 229–230
value delivery network for, 47–48
value-driven marketing strategy for, 10–14
value from, 20–23
See also Advertising and public relations; Buyers, behavior of; Customer relationship management (CRM); Marketing information; Marketing strategies, customer value-driven
Customer-segment pricing, 282
Customer service, chat bots for, 27
Customer value-based pricing, 267–271, 268*f*, 268*p*, 269*p*, 270*p*
Customer-value marketing, 514

D

Dashboards, marketing, 58
"Death by discount" trap, 352
Deceptive advertising, 501
Deceptive prices, 295, 501–502
Deceptive promotion, 501
Decision process
for business buyers, 155, 155*p*, 159–161
for consumers, 148–151
for individual products, 209–216, 209*f*, 211*p*, 212*p*, 213*p*, 214*p*, 216*p*
for new products, 151–153
for product lines, 216–217, 217*p*
for product mix, 217–218, 218*p*
Deficient products, 515
"Delivering the Starbucks experience" example of strategic planning, 37–38
Delivery services, 479
Demand
in business markets, 154
channel intermediaries match supply to, 304
elasticity of, 277
forecasting, 327
in pricing decision, 276–277, 276*p*, 277*f*
wants and needs *versus*, 6
Demand curve, pricing and, 277, 277*f*
Demographic environment
changing age structure, 71–74, 95
changing American family, 74–75
diversity, 76–77
education and, 76
geographic shifts, 75–76
international marketing and, 480*t*
in market development, 45–46
overview, 70
for segmentation of markets, 174–175
Department stores, 338, 340*t*
Derived demand, 154, 154*p*
Descriptive research, 105
Design for environment (DFE) practices, 511
Design of marketing channels, 314–317, 314*p*, 316*p*, 317*p*
Desirable products, 515–516
Differentiated target marketing, 184
Differentiation and positioning
brand strength measured by, 225
communicating and delivering, 197
competitive advantages, 191–193
definition of, 173
overview, 50–52
positioning maps in, 190
retail convergence and, 353
in retailing, 347–348
of services, 191, 191*p*, 222–223, 222*p*
statement of, 195–197
strategy for, 193–195
in value proposition, 342
in wholesaling, 361
Digital catalogs, 454–455
Digital coupons, 425, 432
Digital data gathering methods, 103–104, 104*p*, 123
Digital footprints, 129
Digital marketing, 434–455
big data and artificial intelligence for, 27
blogs and forums, 444–445, 444*p*
business buyers in, 161–165, 163*p*, 164*p*
buyer and seller benefits from, 437–438, 438*p*
description of, 23–24
direct marketing model in, 436–437
email marketing, 442–443, 442*p*
example of, 435–436
forms of, 438–439, 438*f*
growth of direct marketing and, 437
logo adaptation for, 213–215
on mobile devices, 26–27, 450–453
online advertising, 441–442, 442*p*
online videos, 443–444
in promotion mix, 370–371, 372*p*
public policy issues in, 457–460
skipped, muted, or blocked, 385*p*
on social media, 24–26, 445–450
strategies for, 439–440, 440*p*
for targeted marketing, 377
"top genius" award, 203
websites and branded web communities, 440–441, 441*p*
See also Direct marketing; Technology
Digital "neighbor's fence," 149
Digital security, 458
Direct exporting, 481
Direct investment as entry to international markets, 480*f*, 482–483
Direct marketing
catalog marketing, 454–455, 454*p*
channels for, 305, 306*f*
digital marketing model of, 436–437
direct-mail marketing, 453–454, 453*p*
direct-response television marketing (DRTV), 456
growth of, 437
kiosk marketing, 456–457, 457*p*
in promotion mix, 370–371, 377
public policy issues in, 457–460
pull strategies used by, 378
telemarketing, 455
See also Digital marketing; Technology
Disabilities, marketing to individuals with, 77, 77*p*
Disadvantaged customers, service for, 503–506
Discounts and allowances
consumer expectations of, 352
in pricing, 282, 307
in trade promotions, 428
Discount stores, 340, 340*t*, 341*p*
Discrimination, price, 295
Disintermediation (cutting out channel intermediaries), 311–313, 311*p*
Disrupting channels, 312–313
Distortion, selective, 146
Distribution
distribution centers, 324–325, 325*p*
multichannel systems for, 310–311, 310*f*
in product development, 242, 245
in wholesaling, 361
See also Channels
Diversification, 46
Diversity, in demographic environment, 76–77
Divisibility of new products, 153
Dogs, in growth-share matrix, 43–44
Do Not Call Registry, 411, 455
Do Not Track system, 114
Double bottom line of values and profits, 515
Downsizing strategies, 45–46, 88
Driverless vehicles, 4, 313
Drones, delivery by, 4
Dropping products, in life cycle, 257
DRTV (direct-response television marketing), 456
Duties, on international trade, 470
Dynamic pricing, 286–287, 287*p*

E

Earned media, 373–374, 391
E-commerce, in wholesaling, 361. *See also* Digital marketing
Economics
bottom of economic pyramid, countries in, 473–474
business buying affected by, 158, 158*f*
buying behavior affected by, 143–144
channel design affected by, 315
discount store growth and, 340
of distribution channel alternatives, 316–317
in emerging markets, 289, 317, 472
"gig economy," 254
intermediary use for, 304, 304*f*
in international markets, 469, 472–474, 480*t*
marketing affected by, 78
market segmentation by, 181
pricing and, 277–278, 278*p*
EDLP (everyday low pricing), 269, 350
Educational increases, in demographic environment, 76
Elasticity of demand, 277
Electronic data interchange (EDI), 327
Electronic order and payments transfer, 323
Email marketing, 442–443, 442*p*
Emergency response, corporate, 92
Emerging economies, 289, 317, 472
Empowerment of consumers, 18
EMV (expected monetary value), 130
Endorsement advertising messages, 389
Energy drinks, as product category, 427
Energy efficiency, 79–80
Engagement
in advertising media strategy, 391, 391*p*
customer-engagement marketing, 17–18
of customers in brand experiences, 233
of customers in branding strategy, 203
Instagram strength in, 449
in social media, 53
Entertainment, advertising merged with, 385–386
Environmental influences on business buying, 158, 158*f*
Environmental responsibility, 28
Environmental sustainability movement, 79–82, 81*p*, 510–513, 511*f*, 511*p*
E-procurement, 161–162, 162*p*
Equity, brand, 224–225
Equity, customer, 21–22
Esteem, brand strength measured by, 225
E-tailers, 439–440
Ethics
autonomous autos, issues of, 262
codes of, 84, 86, 126
in marketing, 29, 34
in marketing intelligence, 103
in marketing research, 124–126
for sustainability, 365–366, 518–520, 519*t*
Ethnographic research, 107–108, 107*p*
European Union (EU), 471, 471*p*
Evaluating salespeople, 415–416

Evaluation of alternatives, 149–150
Event marketing, 426–428
Everyday low pricing (EDLP), 269, 350
Exchange, relationships and, 9
Exchange controls, as obstacles to trade, 470
Exclusive dealing, 321
Exclusive distribution, 316, 321
Exclusive territorial agreements, 321
Execution of advertising messages, 388–389
Expected monetary value (EMV), 130
Experiences, for customers, 205
Experiential retailing, 349, 349*p*, 354
Experiential sources of information, 149
Experimental research, 108–109, 109*p*
Exploratory research, 105
Exporting, 480–481, 480*f*
Extensions of brands, 231*f*, 232, 232*p*
External idea sources, 242, 242*p*
External marketing, in services firms, 221, 222*f*
Extranet links, for e-procurement, 162

F

Factory outlets, 341
Fads, product life cycle and, 252–253, 252*f*, 253*p*
Fair Packaging and Labeling Act of 1966, 213
Family, as buying influence, 140, 142, 142*p*
Family structure, changes in, 74–75
Fantasy advertising messages, 388
Fashion, product life cycle and, 252, 252*f*
Features, of products, 210
Federal Food, Drug, and Cosmetic Act, 258
Federal Trade Commission Act of 1914, 213
"Fighter brand," 291–292, 292*p*
"Fill-in" approach, at convenience stores, 339
Filling product lines, 217, 217*p*
Financial intermediaries, as marketing intermediaries, 68
Financial publics, 69
Fishyback multimodal transportation, 326
Five Rs of joint action toward sustainability (Patagonia), 81–82
Fixed costs, 271
Flash sales, 285, 353
Flows, in business distribution channels, 305
Fluctuating demand, in business markets, 154
FOB (free on board)-origin pricing, 285–286
Focus group interviewing, 109–111, 124
Food deserts, 503
Forums and blogs, 444–445, 444*p*
Four As of marketing, 54
Four Ps of marketing, 14, 53–54, 53*f*. *See also* Pricing; Retailing
Franchise organizations
  as contractual VMS, 308–309, 309*p*
  mutual services and duties of, 316
  overview, 343*t*, 344, 344*p*
  relations with, 307, 307*p*
Fraud, 457–458, 457*p*, 493
Free goods, as trade promotions, 428
Freight-absorption pricing, 286
Frequency, in advertising media strategy, 390
Frequency marketing programs, 17, 424
Full-line forcing, 321
Full-service retailers, 338
Full-service wholesalers, 359–360, 359*t*
Functional discounts, 282
Functional organization of marketing departments, 57

G

GDP (gross domestic product). *See* Gross domestic product (GDP)
Gender, market segmentation by, 174–175, 175*p*
General Agreement on Tariffs and Trade (GATT), 471
General public, 69
Generational marketing, 74
Generation X
  demographics of, 71–72, 72*p*, 78
  as media multitaskers, 393
Generation Z, demographics of, 73–74, 74*p*
Geographical characteristics, 480*t*
Geographical pricing, 285–286
Geographic organization
  for international marketing, 490
  of marketing departments, 57
Geographic segmentation of markets, 173–174, 181
Geographic shifts, in demographic environment, 75–76
"Gig economy," 254
Global Brand Counterfeiting Report, 2018, 493
Globalization, 28
Global marketplace. *See* International markets
Good-value pricing, 268–269, 269*p*
Gouging prices, 289
Government intervention
  in advertising claims, 396
  censorship as, 493
  in consumer tracking and targeting, 114
  corporate lobbyists to influence, 90
  marketing-related legislation as, 85*t*
  in natural resources management, 79
  in pricing, 278
  in product safety, 83
  for sustainable marketing, 513, 513*f*
Government markets, 70
Government publics, 69
Great Firewall of China, 493
Great Recession of 2008–2009, 78, 277, 352
Greening activities, 511
Green retailing, 354, 356–357, 356*p*
Green supply chains, 323–324, 323*p*
Greenwashing (deceptive promotion), 522
Gross domestic product (GDP)
  of European Union, 472
  logistics costs proportion in Chinese, 490
  multinational corporations and, 468
  services as proportion of, 219
Groups, as social networks, 139, 142–143
Growth-share matrix (Boston Consulting Group), 43–44, 43*f*
Growth strategies, 45–46

H

"Hackathons," 242, 242*p*
Hard-sell techniques, 432
Harvesting products, in life cycle, 257
High-low pricing, 269, 350
High-pressure selling, 502
Hispanic subculture, 76, 136–138, 136*p*
Horizontal conflict in marketing channel, 307
Horizontal marketing systems, 309–310, 310*p*
Hungerithm algorithm (Mars, Inc.), 24
Hyperlocal social marketing, 174, 186

I

Idea generation, 241–243, 241*f*
Ideas as products, 208–209
Idea screening, 243
Image advertising messages, 388
Image differentiation, 192
IMC (integrated marketing communications). *See* Integrated marketing communications (IMC)
Immersion groups, in marketing research, 110
Impact, in advertising media strategy, 390–391
Implementation, marketing, 56–57
Incentives, sales, 415, 429
Income, market segmentation by, 175
Independent off-price retailers, 341
Indirect marketing, 305, 306*f*, 480–481
Individual influences on business buying, 158*f*, 159
Individual interviewing, 109
Individual marketing, 186–187, 187*p*
Industrialization of emerging economies, 472
Industrial products, 207–208
Inelastic demand, in business markets, 154
Influencer marketing, 139–140, 139*p*
Infomercials, 407, 456
Information search, 148*f*, 149, 149*p*
Informative advertising, 380
Innovation. *See* Product development
Innovative marketing principle, 514
Innovativeness, 151–152
Inseparability of services, 219*f*, 220
Inside and outside sales force, 410–411, 411*p*. *See also* Personal selling
Instruments to collect marketing research data, 115–116
Intangibility of services, 219, 219*f*
Integrated marketing communications (IMC)
  content marketing in, 372–374, 373*p*
  model of, 371–372
  need for, 374–376, 375*f*
  in promotion mix, 376–378
Integrated marketing mix, 52–54
Integrated marketing plan, 14
Integrated shopping channels, 345
Integrated social media marketing, 449–450
Intensive distribution, 316
Interactive marketing, 221–222, 222*f*
Intermarket segmentation, 181–182, 181*p*
Intermediaries. *See* Channels
Internal data for marketing, 101
Internal idea sources, 241–242
Internal marketing, 221, 222*f*
Internal publics, 69
International markets, 466–495
  advertising and public relations in, 395–396, 395*p*
  in commercialization of products, 247
  cultural environment of, 475–478
  decision to go global, 478
  decision which markets to enter, 478–480, 480*t*
  direct investment as market entry, 480*f*, 482–483
  distribution channels for, 317, 317*p*, 489–490

economic environment and, 472–474
exporting as market entry to, 480–481, 480*f*
government agencies enforcing trade regulations in, 84
joint venturing as market entry to, 480*f*, 481–482, 481*p*, 482*p*
for major retailers, 357
marketing decisions for, 468–470, 470*f*
marketing organization for, 490–491
marketing program for, 483–484
marketing research in, 123–124
overview, 70
political-legal environment and, 475
pricing for, 288–289, 288*p*, 488–489
product development and, 259–260, 259*p*
products for, 484–487
promotion for, 487–488
segmentation of, 181–182
standardization *versus* local adaptation to, 467–468
trade system for, 470–472
International subsidiaries, 490
Internet
censorship of, 493
customer-engagement marketing and, 18
fraud from digital and direct marketing on, 457–458, 457*p*
international marketing and, 479
job recruiting on, 494
logistics systems based on, 323
marketing to vulnerable audiences via, 188–189
online marketing research, 110–112, 112*p*
online purchasing, 161–162
online social networks, 139–140
Peloton exercise classes streamed on, 494
search engines on, 106
Snickers Hungerithm social media campaign, 24–25
See also Digital marketing; online activities listed separately; Technology
Internet of Things (IoT)
Amazon involvement in, 3
as big data source, 27
"brave new world" of marketing, 80
consumer data gathered from, 115–116
corporate investment in, 239–240
digital connections in, 23
marketing and, 439
Next Labs and, 250
Interpersonal influences on business buying, 158, 158*f*
Interpretive consumer research, 145
Intranets, 119
Intrapreneurial programs, 241
Invention of products for international markets, 487
Inventory management, 325, 327
Inventory tracking, 354
Inventory turnover rate, 366

J

Joint in-store programs, 328
Joint ownership, 482
Joint venturing, in international markets, 480*f*, 481–482, 481*p*, 482*p*
Judgment sample, in marketing research, 115*t*
Junk mail, 454
Just-in-time logistics systems, 325
Just-in-time research, 104

K

Key performance indicators (KPIs), 432
Kickbacks and bribes, 519
Kiosk marketing, 456–457, 457*p*
Knowledge, brand strength measured by, 225

L

Labeling and logos on products, 213–215, 213*p*, 214*p*
Language barriers, in marketing research, 123–124
Launch strategy for new products, 253
Learning, buying behavior affected by, 147
LEED certification, 365
Legal factors, market segmentation by, 181
Legislation affecting marketing, 85*t*
LGBT (lesbian, gay, bisexual, and transgender) population, 76–77
Liability, product, 259
Licensing, 230–231, 231*p*, 481, 481*p*
Life-cycle product strategies
decline stage, 257–258
growth stage, 255
introduction stage, 253–255
maturity stage, 255–256
overview, 251–253, 258*f*
shortened retail, 352–353
Life-cycle stages, 143, 174
Lifestyle advertising messages, 388
Lifestyle shopping centers, 351
Lifestyles of consumers, 144, 144*p*, 175–176, 176*p*
Lifetime value of customers, 20–21
Limited-service retailers, 338
Limited-service wholesalers, 359*t*, 360
Limited-time offers, 285
Line extensions, 231–232, 231*f*
Line filling or stretching, 217, 217*p*
Lobbyists, 90
Local adaptation for international markets, 467–468, 483–486, 485*p*
Local marketing, 185–186, 186*p*
Local publics, 69
Location-based pricing, 283
Logistics. *See* Marketing logistics
Logistics information management, 326–327
Logos, 192, 213–215, 213*p*, 214*p*
Lovemarks, brands as, 226, 226*p*
Loyalty
in positioning, 352
retention of customers based on, 20–21
rewards programs for, 17, 424, 424*p*
salesperson-owned, 408, 408*p*
segmentation of markets by status of, 177–178

M

Machine learning, 120
Macroenvironment, 70, 70*f*
"Madison & Vine" (merging entertainment and advertising), 385–387
Mail questionnaires, 109
Management contracting, 482
Managing
branding strategy, 233
brands, 233
channels, 317–321
inventory, 325
marketing effort, 54–58
marketing information, 99–100
marketing strategies, 49, 49*f*
product development, 248–251
product quality, 210
service differentiation, 222–223, 222*p*
service quality, 223
Manufactured materials, as industrial products, 208
Manufacturers' and retailers' branches and offices, 360, 360*t*
Manufacturer-sponsored retailer franchise system, 309
Manufacturer-sponsored wholesaler franchise system, 309
Market(s)
development of, 45–46
as exchanges, 9
international, decision to enter, 478–480
pricing affected by, 276–277, 276*p*, 277*f*
sales force structured by, 409
See also International markets
Marketing
careers in, 31
company cases, 35
customer needs and marketplace, 6–10
customer relationship management, 15–20
customer value-driven marketing strategy, 10–14
decisions for international markets, 468–470
description of, 4–6
ethics in, 34
event, 427–428
globalization and, 28
integrated marketing plan, 14
market share numbers in, 35
not-for-profit, 27–28
online, mobile, social, and social media, 34
overview of, 29–31
sales coordinated with, 408
sustainable, 29
test, 241*f*, 246–247
value from customers, 20–23
See also Channels
Marketing, social criticisms of
competition reduced by, 508
cultural pollution, 507–508
deceptive prices resulting from, 501–502
few social goods, 507
high-pressure selling from, 502
high prices resulting from, 500–501
materialism growth from, 506–507
planned obsolescence from, 503
poor service to disadvantaged customers, 503–506
shoddy, harmful, or unsafe products from, 502
Marketing analytics, 118–119, 118*p*
Marketing concept, 12, 13*f*
Marketing environment, 64–96
cultural environment, 87–89
demographic environment, 70–77
economic environment, 78
fast-changing, 65–66
macroenvironment, 70
microenvironment, 66–70
natural environment, 79–80
political and social environment, 83–87
responding to, 89–92
technological environment, 80–83
Marketing information, 96–131
analyzing and using, 117–122
assessing needs for, 100–101
big data in, 98–99
developing, 101–103
managing, 99–100
marketing research
example of, 97–98
findings from, 116–117
implementation of, 116
international, 123–124
objectives of, 104–105
plan development for, 105–106
primary data collection, 107–116. *See also* Marketing research, primary data
public policy and ethics in, 124–126
secondary data collection for, 106
in small business and non-profits, 122–123
in transition, 103–104

Marketing information system (MIS), 100, 100*f*
Marketing intermediaries, 68
Marketing logistics
  functions of, 324–327, 325*p*, 326*p*
  importance of, 321–323, 322*f*, 322*p*
  integrated management of, 327–328, 327*p*
Marketing management, 10–14
Marketing mix
  customers in center of, 48–49, 49*f*
  differentiation and positioning of market, 50–52
  four Ps, 53–54, 53*f*
  integrated, 52–54
  modifying to extend product life cycle, 256
  overview, 14
  in pricing, 274–275, 274*p*, 275*p*
  in product development, 245
  segmentation of market, 49–50
  targeting of market, 50
  in wholesaling, 361
Marketing research
  example of, 97–98
  implementation plans for, 116
  international, 123–124
  interpreting findings of, 116–117, 126
  interpretive consumer, 145
  objectives of, 104–105
  plan development, 105–106
  primary data
    approaches to, 107–109
    contact methods in, 109–114
    overview, 106–107, 107*f*
    research instruments, 115–116
    sampling plan, 114–115
  process of, 104*f*
  public policy and ethics in, 124–126
  secondary data collection, 106
  in small business and non-profits, 122–123
  in transition, 103–104
Marketing services agencies, 68
Marketing strategies
  marketing mix and, 48–54
  in marketing plan, 56
  post-Great Recession of 2008–2009, 352
  pricing, 274–275, 274*p*, 275*p*
  retailer, 347–351, 347*f*, 348*p*, 349*p*, 350*p*
  services, 220
  sustainability and, 354, 356–357, 356*p*
  total, 138, 138*p*
  wholesaling, 360–361, 360*f*
Marketing strategies, customer value-driven, 170–201
  differentiation and positioning
    communicating and delivering, 197
    competitive advantages, identifying, 191–193
    positioning maps in, 190
    statement of, 195–197
    strategy for, 193–195
    effective segmentation in, 182
  example of, 171–172
  overview, 172–173, 172*f*
  segmentation
    of business markets, 180–181
    of consumers, 173–180
    evaluation of, 183
    of international markets, 181–182
  selecting target market segments, 183–189
Marketing systems
  elements of, 10, 10*f*
  horizontal, 309–310
  in marketing process, 30–31, 30*f*
  vertical, 307–309
Market management organization of marketing departments, 57
Market offering, products in, 204–205
Market penetration, 45, 286
Market-penetration pricing, 279, 279*p*
Market pioneers, 253
Market-skimming pricing, 279
Markup, in retail pricing decision, 349–350
Markup pricing, 272–273, 272*f*, 350*p*
Maslow's hierarchy of needs, 146*f*
Mass customization, in marketing, 186–187
Mass media communications model, 371–372
Mass-media marketing, 435
Mass merchandising, as channel, 318
Materialism growth from marketing, 506–507
Materials and parts, as industrial products, 207–208
Mechanical instruments, in marketing research, 115–116
Media
  advertising strategy for, 390–394, 392*t*
  in international markets, 488
  paid, owned, earned, and shared (POES), 373–374, 391
  publics of, 69
Media multitaskers, 393
Megabrand strategies, 233
Megaretailers, 353
Merchandise handling technology, 354
Merchant wholesalers, 359–360, 359*t*
Mergers and acquisitions, 353
Message strategy for advertising, 385–390
Microenvironment, 66–70
  actors in, 67*f*
  company in, 67
  competitors in, 68–69
  customers in, 69–70
  marketing intermediaries in, 68
  publics in, 69
  suppliers in, 67
Micromarketing, 186–187
"Micro-moments," in buying decision, 337
"Micropolitan areas," 75
Millennials (Generation Y), 72–73, 73*p*, 393
Mining customer information, 125
Mission statement, market-oriented, 39–40, 39*t*
Mobile marketing
  consumers tracked for, 125
  digital marketing by, 450–453, 451*p*
  example of, 34
  Instagram focus on, 446–447
  in integrated marketing communications, 372, 372*p*
  in international markets, 123, 488
  logo adaptation for, 213–215
  mobile payments app, 247, 247*p*
  overview, 26–27
  for research while shopping, 345
  retail model shifts from, 337
  retail store apps for, 346
  selling on, 416–419
  by smartphone apps, 5*p*
  to vulnerable audiences, 188–189
Modified rebuy, in business buying, 156
Modifying the market, in product life cycle, 256
Modifying the marketing mix, 256
Modifying the product, in product life cycle, 256
"Mom bloggers," 140–142
Monetization of social media, 445–447
Monopolies, 276–277, 292
Monopolistic competition, 276
Mood advertising messages, 388
More-for-more positioning, 193–194
Motivating sales force, 409*f*, 415
Motivation, buying behavior affected by, 145
Multibrands, 231*f*, 232–233
Multichannel distribution systems, 310–311, 310*f*
Multimodal transportation, 326, 326*p*
Musical advertising messages, 388–389
Music streaming, 3

N

NAFTA (North American Free Trade Agreement), 472
Name selection, in branding, 227–228
National brands, 228
National Do Not Call Registry, 411, 455
Native advertising, 387
Natural environment, 79–80, 89
Needs
  in business buying, 160
  Maslow's hierarchy of, 145, 146*f*
  recognition of, 148, 148*f*
  wants and demands *versus*, 6
Neuromarketing, 116, 116*p*
New brands, 231*f*, 233
New task, in business buying, 156
Niche marketing, 184–185, 185*p*
Nonprice positioning, 275
Nonprobability sample, in marketing research, 115*t*
Non-profit organizations, marketing research in, 122–123
Nonrenewable resources, 79
Nontariff obstacles to trade, 470–471, 470*p*
North American Free Trade Agreement (NAFTA), 472
Not-for-profit marketing, 27–28
Nutritional Labeling and Educational Act of 1990, 213

O

Objective-and-task method, advertising budgeting, 384, 384*p*
Observational research, 107–108
Occasions, segmentation of markets by, 176
Occupation, buying behavior affected by, 143
Off-price retailers, 341, 341*t*
Oligopolistic competition, 276
Omni-channel consumers, 439
Omni-channel retailing, 336–337, 337*p*, 345–346, 346*p*, 440
"One brand" strategy, for international advertising, 395
Online grocery shopping, 338
Online marketing
  advertising, 441–442, 442*p*
  blogs and forums, 444–445, 444*p*
  email marketing, 442–443, 442*p*
  overview, 24, 24*p*, 34
  in retail, 353
  videos, 443–444, 443*p*
  websites and branded communities, 440–441, 441*p*
Online marketing research, 110–112, 111*p*
Online purchasing, wholesale, 361
Online retailing, 161–162, 345, 351
Online security, 458
Online selling, 410, 416–419
Online social networks, 139–140
Open-ended questions, in marketing research, 115
Opinion leaders, 139
Optional product pricing, 280, 280*t*
Order-routine specification, in business buying, 161
Organization, as product, 208–209
Organizational climate, for sales, 415
Organizational considerations in pricing, 275–276
Organizational influences on business buying, 158, 158*f*
Organization of marketing departments, 57–58, 57*p*

Outside and inside sales force, 410–411, 411*p*. *See also* Personal selling
Outsourcing logistics, 328
Overhead costs, 271
"Overmalled" shopping center situation, 351
Owned media, 373–374, 391

P

Packaging
product, 212–213, 212*p*
promotion campaign message on, 369
sustainable marketing movement against, 499, 501
Paid, owned, earned, and shared media (POES), 373–374, 391
Partner relationship management, 20, 46–48, 47*p*, 318–320
Patronage discounts, 17
People, as products, 208–209
People differentiation, 192
Percentage-of-sales method, of advertising budgeting, 383
Perceptions, buying behavior affected by, 146
Performance quality, 210
Performance review, in business buying, 161
Perishability of services, 219*f*, 220
Permission-based email marketing, 443
Personal factors in consumer buyer behavior, 143–144
Personal interviewing, 109
Personality, in marketing, 144, 176
Personality symbol advertising messages, 389
Personalized pricing, 286–287, 287*p*
Personal selling, 404–423
approach in, 420–421, 420*f*
closing in, 420*f*, 422
customer relationship management in, 422–423
follow-up in, 420*f*, 422
high-pressure, 502
nature of, 406–407
objection handling in, 420*f*, 421
outside and inside sales force, 410–411
preapproach in, 420, 420*f*
presentation and demonstration in, 420*f*, 421, 421*p*
in promotion mix, 370–371, 377
prospecting and qualifying in, 420, 420*f*
social selling, 416–419
team selling, 411
technology for, 405–406
See also Sales promotion
Personal selling, sales force and
compensation, 414
motivation, 415
performance, 415–416
recruiting, 412–413
role of sales force, 407–408
size, 410
structure, 409–410
supervision, 414–415
training, 413
Personal sources of information, 149
Persuasive advertising, 380
"Phantom markdown schemes," 501
Pharmaceutical industry, pricing in, 293–294, 293*p*
Phishing fraud, 457–458
Physical distribution firms, 68
Piggyback multimodal transportation, 326
Place
in four Ps of marketing, 14, 53
as product, 208–209
retail decisions on, 350–351
Planned obsolescence, 503
Planning, marketing, 55–56, 55*f*, 56*t*
Pleasing products, 515
POES (paid, owned, earned, and shared media), 373–374, 391
Point-of-purchase (POP) promotions, 426
Point-of-sale scanners, 323
Pokemon Go, 253
Political environment, 83–84
Political-legal environment
business buying affected by, 158, 158*f*
in international markets, 475, 480*t*
market segmentation by, 181
Pollution, increases in, 79
POP (point-of-purchase) promotions, 426
Pop-up stores, 353, 353*p*
Portfolio
analysis of, 43–45
product, 217–218, 218*p*
Positioning
in branding strategy, 226–227, 226*f*, 233
communicating and delivering, 197
competitive advantages, identifying, 191–193
definition of, 173
loyalty and value building, 352
nonprice, 275
overview, 50–52
positioning maps in, 190, 190*f*, 190*p*
price-value, 274
quality level for, 210
in retailing, 347–348, 348*p*
statement of, 195–197, 195*p*
strategy for, 193–195
in wholesaling, 361
Postpurchase behavior, 150–151, 150*p*
Power shopping centers, in suburbs, 351
Predatory pricing, 294–295, 294*p*
"Pregnancy prediction" by Target Stores, Inc., 124–125
Premium pricing, 265–266, 265*p*
Premiums, as consumer promotions, 425
Price confusion, 295
Price-demand relationship, 277
Price escalation, 288
Price fixing, 294
Price packs, as consumer promotions, 425
Pricing, 264–299
by-product, 280*t*, 281
captive product, 280–281, 280*t*, 281*p*
changes in, 289–292, 290*p*, 291*f*, 292*p*
competition-based, 222, 225, 273–274, 273*p*
for consumers below poverty level, 473
cost-based, 268*f*, 271–273, 272*f*
customer value-based, 267–271, 268*f*, 268*p*, 269*p*, 270*p*
deceptive, 501–502
discounts and allowances in, 25, 282
dynamic and personalized, 286–287, 287*p*
economic factors and, 277–278, 278*p*
in four Ps of marketing, 14, 53
geographical, 285–286
international, 288–289, 288*p*, 488–489
market and demand considerations in, 276–277, 276*p*, 277*f*
marketing channel impact on, 303
marketing resulting in high, 500–501
marketing strategy, objectives, and mix in, 274–275, 274*p*, 275*p*
market-penetration, 279, 279*p*
market-skimming, 279
optional product, 280, 280*t*
organizational considerations in, 275–276
overview, 266
premium, 265–266, 265*p*
product bundle, 280*t*, 281
in product development, 245
product line, 280, 280*t*
promotional, 284–285, 285*p*
psychological, 283–284, 284*p*
public policy and, 292–295, 292*f*
retail, 340–343, 349–350, 350*p*
segmented, 282–283
warehouse store, 341–342
wholesaling decision about, 361
Primary data, in marketing research
approaches to, 107–109
contact methods in, 109–114
overview, 106–107
research instruments, 115–116
sampling plan, 114–115
Privacy
digital advertising networks *versus*, 114
invasion of, 458–459
marketing research as intrusion on, 124–125
of vulnerable audiences, 189
Private brands, 228–230
Proactive approach to environmental changes, 89–90
Probability sample, in marketing research, 115*t*
Problem recognition, in business buying, 159–160, 159*p*
Problem solving skills, for marketing careers, 31
Product(s)
attributes of, 209–211
branding of, 211–212
consumer, 206–207
counterfeit, 493
deficient, 515
desirable, 515–516
example of, 202–204
in four Ps of marketing, 14, 53
industrial, 207–208
for international markets, 484–487, 484*f*
labeling and logos on, 213–215
in market offering, 204–205
market-oriented business definitions *versus*, 39*t*
Product(s) (*Continued*)
organizations, persons, places, and ideas as, 208–209
packaging of, 212–213
pleasing, 515
product line decisions, 216–217, 217*p*
product mix decisions, 217–218, 218*p*
retail assortment of, 348–349
retail decisions about, 338–339
sales force structured by, 409
salutary, 515
shoddy, harmful, or unsafe, 502
support services for, 213, 215–216
three levels of, 205–206
wholesaling decision about, 361
See also Branding strategy; Services
Product bundle pricing, 281
Product concept, in marketing management, 12
Product development, 238–263
business analysis for, 245–246
commercialization of, 247
example of, 239–240
international marketing of services and, 259–260
life-cycle strategies for
decline stage, 257–258
growth stage, 255
introduction stage, 253–255
maturity stage, 255–256
overview, 251–253, 252*f*
managing, 248–251
marketing channel impact on, 303
marketing strategy in, 244–245
overview, 46

Product development (*continued*)
  process of, 241–244, 246
  social responsibility decisions, 258–259
  strategy for, 240–241
  test marketing in, 246–247
Product differentiation, 191
Product form pricing, 283
Production concept, in marketing management, 10–11
Productivity, 66, 223–224
Product line pricing, 280, 280*t*
Product management organization of marketing departments, 57
Product/market expansion grid, 45, 45*f*
Product placement, 387
Product specification, in business buying, 160
Product stewardship, 259, 511–512, 511*f*
Professional population, in demographic environment, 76
Profits, in product development, 245
Promotion
  advertising and public relations in, 370–371
  deceptive, 501, 523
  flag-waving, 89
  in four Ps of marketing, 14, 53
  higher prices based on, 500
  integrated marketing communications for, 376–378
  for international markets, 487–488
  retail decisions on, 350, 350*p*
  wholesaling less oriented to, 361
Promotional allowances, 282
Promotional pricing, 284–285, 285*p*
Proposals, in business buying, 160
Psychographic segmentation of markets, 175–176
Psychological factors in consumer buyer behavior, 145–148
Psychological pricing, 283–284, 284*p*
Public policy
  in digital and direct marketing, 457–460
  distribution decisions and, 321
  marketing research and, 124–126
  pricing and, 292–295, 292*f*
Public relations. *See* Advertising and public relations
Public service activities, 398
Publics in microenvironment, 69
Public sources of information, 149
Pull strategy, 377–378, 378*f*
Purchase decision, 150
Purchasing online, 161–162
Pure competition, 276
Pure monopoly, 276–277
Pure services, 205
Push strategy, 377–378, 378*f*

Q

Quality, 209–210, 223, 223*p*
Quantitative research, 110
Quantity discounts, 282
Question marks, in growth-share matrix, 43–44
Questionnaires, marketing research, 115, 123–124
Quotas
  in marketing research, 115*t*
  as obstacles to trade, 470
  for sales, 415

R

Radio-frequency identification (RFID) technology, 83, 83*p*, 323, 325, 354, 391
Raw materials, 79, 207–208
Reach, in advertising media strategy, 390
Real-time marketing, 438
Real-time research analytics, 98–99
Rebates, as consumer promotions, 425
Recovery, service, 223
Recruiting sales force, 405, 409*f*, 412–413, 412*p*
Redlining, 503
Reference groups, 139
Reference prices, 284
Regional free trade zones, 471
Registered trademarks and brandnames, 227, 227*p*
Regulations affecting marketing, 85*t*
Relative advantage of new products, 152
Relevance, brand strength measured by, 225
Religion, 89
Reminder advertising, 383
Remotely, working, 75
Renewable resources, 79
Research. *See* Marketing research
Resellers
  as marketing intermediaries, 68, 315–316
  markets for, 70
  pricing and, 278
  See also Channels
"Respondent Bill of Rights" initiatives, 125
Retailer cooperative retail organization, 343*t*, 344
Retailing
  consumers connected to brands in, 336–337
  consumer spending decreases and, 352
  convergence in, 352–353
  global expansion of, 357
  green, 354, 356–357
  international operations in, 260
  marketing decisions in, 346–351, 347*f*
  megaretailers, 353
  model of, 337
  new world of, 335–336
  omni-channel, 345–346
  organizational approach, 343–344
  price maintenance in, 295
  pricing, 340–343
  product line, 338–339
  service level, 338
  technology in, 354–356
  See also Wholesaling
Retention, selective, 146
Retention of customers, 223
Return behavior, of customers, 23
Return on advertising investment, 394
Return on investment (ROI), from marketing, 58–59, 59*f*
Return-on-quality approach, 210
Return on sales investment, 416
Return on social media investment, 448–449
Reverse auctions, 162
RFID inventory tracking, 354
RFID tags, 323, 325
RFID (radio-frequency identification) technology, 83, 83*p*, 391
Robinson-Patman Act, 292, 295
Roles, buying behavior affected by, 142–143
R-W-W (real, win, worth doing) framework for Idea screening, 243

S

Sales
  channel partners handling, 304
  contests to increase, 429
  in marketing management, 12, 13*f*
  in product development, 245
Sales force automation systems, 415, 415*p*
Sales force management. *See* Personal selling
Sales promotion
  growth of, 423–424
  objectives of, 424
  program development, 429
  in promotion mix, 370–371, 377
  tools of, 424–429
  See also Personal selling
Salutary products, 515
Samples, as consumer promotions, 425
Sampling plan, in marketing research, 114–115, 115*t*
Satellite tracking, 323
Satisfaction, customer, 7–9, 15–16, 150–151
SBUs (strategic business units), 43
Scan-and-go technology, 354
Scanner fraud, 295
Scents, for retail store ambiance, 349
Science, technology, engineering, and math (STEM), 122, 209, 209*p*
Scientific evidence advertising messages, 389
Search-related ads, 442
Seasonal discounts, 282
Secondary cultural values, 87–89
Secondary data collection, in marketing research, 106, 123
Segmentation
  of business markets, 180–181
  of consumer markets, 173–180, 173*t*
  effective, 182
  of international markets, 181–182
  by life stage, 143
  overview, 49–50
  in pricing, 282–283
  in retailing, 347–348
  selecting target markets from, 183–189
  in wholesaling, 361
Selective attention, distortion, and retention, 146
Selective distribution, 316, 316*p*
Self-concept, buying behavior and, 144
Selfie sticks, 253
Self-service retailers, 338
Selling. *See* Personal selling; Sales
Sense-of-mission marketing principle, 514–515
Service(s)
  characteristics of, 219–220
  differentiating, 191, 191*p*, 222–223, 222*p*
  as industrial products, 208
  international operations of, 260
  marketing mix for, 54
  marketing strategies for, 220
  in market offering, 204–205
  as retail differentiation, 348–349
  retail level of, 338
  service profit chain, 220–224, 221*p*
  See also Branding strategy; Products
Service-firm-sponsored retailer franchise system, 309
Service retailers, 339
Shared media, 373–374, 391
Shared projects, cross company, 328
Shared value concept, 13
Share of customer, 21
Share of market, 35
Sharing models, as marketing channel, 303
Sherman Anti-Trust Act, 292
Shopper marketing, 336
Shopping centers, in suburbs, 351
Shopping products, 207, 207*t*
"Shrinkflation," 290
Silly Bandz, 253
Simple random sample, 115*t*
Simulated test marketing, 247
Situational factors, in buying decision, 150
Slice of life advertising messages, 388
Small business, marketing research in, 122–123
Small-format stores, 173–174
"Smart" dressing rooms, 354
Social classes, 138
Social criticisms of marketing. *See* Marketing, social criticisms of
Social environment, 84–87

Social factors, in consumer buyer behavior, 139–142
Social goods, 507
Social media
  brands and, 233
  for customer engagement, 53, 203
  Generation Z orientation toward, 73
  Millennial orientation toward, 72
  in omni-channel retailing, 346
  retail promotion on, 350
  for selling, 419*p*
  selling on, 416–419
  sharing capabilities of, 449
  trolling by marketers, 112
  in wholesaling, 361
  See also Digital marketing
Social media listening, 90, 92, 97*p*
Social media marketing
  business-to-business, 161–165, 163*p*, 164*p*
  customer-engagement marketing and, 18
  digital marketing in, 439, 445–450
  example of, 34
  hyperlocal, 174, 186
  overview, 24–26, 208–209, 209*p*
  targeted, 448, 448*p*
"Social media moms," 140–142, 141*p*
Social networks, 139–140
Social responsibility
  overview, 28
  in product development, 258–259
  for sustainability, 365–366
  in target marketing, 187–189, 188*p*
  See also Sustainable marketing
Social targeting, 113–114
Societal marketing, 13, 13*f*, 515–516, 515*f*
Solutions selling, in business buying, 156, 157*p*
Spam, negative response to, 443
Special event pricing, 284–285
Specialty products, 207, 207*t*
Specialty stores, 338, 340*t*
Spending patterns, back-to-basics, 78
Split-run test, as experimental research, 109
Sponsored content, in advertising, 387
Sponsorship, in branding, 228, 230–231
Standardization, 396, 467–468, 483–486
Stars, in growth-share matrix, 43–44
Status, buying behavior affected by, 142–143
STEM (science, technology, engineering, and math), 122, 209, 209*p*
Stimulus object, 147
Stockturn rate, 366
Store brands, 228–230, 500, 500*p*
Straight product extensions, 486
Straight rebuy, in business buying, 156
Strangers, as customer classification, 22, 22*f*
Strategic business units (SBUs), 43
Strategic planning, 36–63
  business portfolio in, 40–46
  "delivering the Starbucks experience" example, 37–38
  marketing effort, managing, 54–58
  marketing mix in, 48–54
  marketing return on investment, 58–59
  marketing role in, 38–40, 38*f*
  partnering for customer relationships in, 46–48
Strategies. *See* Branding strategy; Life-cycle product strategies; Marketing strategies; Strategic planning
Stratified random sample, in marketing research, 115*t*
Streaming content, 239, 301, 385
Strengths, weaknesses, opportunities, and threats (SWOT) analysis, 54–55, 55*f*
Stretching product lines, 217, 217*p*
Style, product life cycle and, 252, 252*f*
Style and design, of products, 210–211
Subculture, buyer behavior and, 136–137, 136*p*
Subliminal advertising, 146–147
"Superfans" of certain brands, 179
Supermarkets, 338, 340*t*
Superstores, 339, 340*t*
Supervising sales force, 409*f*, 414–415
Suppliers
  business buying decision and, 160–161
  development of, 155
  marketing information provided to, 119–121, 119*p*
  in microenvironment, 67
  product development ideas from, 242
  sustainable marketing and, 497
  See also Channels
Supplies and services, as industrial products, 208
Supply chain
  in channels, 302–306
  management of, 20, 322*f*, 323–324, 323*p*
  software solutions for, 327, 327*p*
Support services for products, 213, 215–216, 216*p*
Survey research, 108, 123, 126
Sustainable marketing, 496–524
  business actions to promote, 513–517
  companies thriving with, 520
  consumerism to promote, 509–510
  description of, 498–500, 499*f*, 499*p*
  environmentalism to promote, 510–513
  environmental issues in, 79–82, 80*p*, 81*p*
  example of, 497–498
  marketing ethics for, 518–520
  overview, 29
  regulations and, 513
  in retailing, 354, 356–357, 356*p*, 365
  social criticisms of marketing
    competition reduced by, 508
    cultural pollution, 507–508
    deceptive prices resulting from, 501–502
    few social goods, 507
    high-pressure selling from, 502
    high prices resulting from, 500–501
    materialism growth from, 506–507
    planned obsolescence from, 503
    poor service to disadvantaged customers, 503–506
    shoddy, harmful, or unsafe products from, 502
  supply chains and, 323–324, 323*p*
  See also Social responsibility
SWOT (strengths, weaknesses, opportunities, and threats) analysis, 54–55, 55*f*
Symbols, for image differentiation, 192
Systematic new product development, 249
Systems selling, in business buying, 156

T

Tangible goods, 205, 205*p*
Target costing, 275
Target marketing
  bottom of economic pyramid, 473–474
  concentrated, 184–185
  differentiated, 184
  digital marketing suited for, 377
  evaluating segmentation, 183
  micromarketing, 186–187
  online, 112–114
  overview, 50, 173
  precision, 447
  in product development, 245
  in retailing, 347–348, 348*p*
  socially responsible, 187–189, 188*p*
  strategies for, 183*f*, 187
  undifferentiated, 183–184
  in wholesaling, 361
Target return pricing, 272–273, 272*f*
Tariffs, on international trade, 470
Team-based new product development, 249
Team selling, 411. *See also* Personal selling
Technical expertise advertising messages, 389
Technical sales-support people, 410
Technology
  business buying affected by, 158, 158*f*
  clean, 511–512, 511*f*
  for delivery services, 236
  for distribution centers, 324–325, 325*p*
  individual marketing made possible by, 186–187
  interacting in, 88, 88*p*
  marketing communications model affected by, 371–372, 372*p*
  marketing in, 80–83
  marketing to vulnerable audiences and, 188–189
  perceived obsolescence *versus*, 503
  for personal selling, 405–406
  in retailing, 335, 337, 354–356
  RFID, 83, 323, 325, 354, 391
  sales force automation systems, 415
  for service productivity, 223–224
  social selling, 416–419
  wholesaling use of, 361
  See also Digital marketing; Internet
Telecommuters, 75–76
Telemarketing, 410–411, 411*p*, 455
Telephone interviewing, 109
Territorial sales force structure, 409–410
Testimonial evidence advertising messages, 389
Test marketing of products, 241*f*, 246–247, 246*p*
Texting-while-driving epidemic, 86
The Innovation Pipeline (TIP), at AT&T, 241–242
Third-party logistics (3PL), 328
360-degree view of customer relationships, 117–118
Three levels of products, 205–206
Three-tier system for beverage alcohol, 332
Tiered pricing, 294
Time-and-duty analysis, for sales, 414
Time-based pricing, 283
Tobacco products, CVS refusal to sell, 516
Total costs, 272
Total marketing strategy, 138, 138*p*
Total quality management (TQM), 210
Touch points for customers and brands, 233
Tracking consumers, 112–114, 124–125
Trade discounts, 282
Trademarks, violations of, 493
Trade promotions, 424, 428
Trade shows, 429, 429*p*
Trade system for international markets, 470–472
Trading exchanges, 162
Training sales force, 405, 409*f*, 413

Trainship multimodal transportation, 326
Transatlantic Trade and Investment Partnership (T-TIP), 472
Transportation, 326, 326*p*
True friends, as customer classification, 22, 22*f*
Tying agreements, 321

U

Unauthorized access to data, 458
Undifferentiated target marketing, 183–184
Uniform-delivered pricing, 286
Union of South American Nations (UNASUR), 472
Unique selling proposition (USP), 192
Unsought goods, selling concept used with, 12
Unsought products, 207, 207*t*
Usage rate, segmentation of markets by, 177, 177*p*
U.S. Environmental Protection Agency (EPA), 79, 84
User status, market segmentation by, 177

V

Value
- brand, 224–225
- channel member additions t, 304, 304*f*
- core customer, 205–206
- cultural, 87–89
- customer-perceived, 15
- for customers, 30
- from customers, 20–23
- customer-value marketing, 514
- as driver in marketing strategy, 10–14
- global value delivery network, 489
- of information, 130
- lifetime value of customers, 20–21
- selling, 266–271, 266*p*, 268*f*, 268*p*, 269*p*, 270*p*
- shared value concept, 13
- *See also* Advertising and public relations; Marketing strategies, customer value-driven

Value-added pricing, 269, 269*p*, 271
Value chain, 47
Value delivery network, 47–48, 302–306, 303*p*
Value propositions
- differentiated, 342
- Great Recession of 2008–2009 impact on, 78, 277–278, 278*p*
- less for much less, 194–195, 194*f*
- more for less, 194*f*, 195
- more for more, 193–194, 194*f*, 194*p*
- more for the same, 194, 194*f*
- overview, 11
- same for less, 194, 194*f*
- *See also* Differentiation and positioning

Value selling, 422–423, 422*p*
Values-led business, 86
Variability of services, 219*f*, 220
Variable costs, 271–272
Vendor-managed inventory (VMI) systems, 327
Vertical conflict in marketing channel, 307, 307*p*
Vertical marketing systems (VMS), 307–309, 308*f*
Videos, online, 443–444, 443*p*
Video streaming, 3
Viral marketing, 443–444
Virtual reality (VR), 354–356, 354*p*, 355*p*
Virtual stores, 356
Voice shopping, 336
Voluntary chain retail organization, 343*t*, 344

W

Walmart Sustainability Index program, 80, 80*p*
Wants, demands and needs *versus*, 6
Warehouse clubs, as off-price retailers, 341–343, 342*p*
Warehousing, 324–325, 325*p*, 361
Wearable electronics, 265
Weather, markets affected by, 79
Websites and branded web communities, 440–441, 441*p*, 493
Wheeler-Lea Act of 1938, 501
White-collar professions, in demographic environment, 76
Whole channel view of international distribution, 489
Wholesaling
- overview, 357–359, 358*p*
- trends in, 361–362
- types of, 359–361
- voluntary chain of independent retailers based on, 342
- *See also* Retailing

Women
- market segmentation and, 174–175, 175*p*
- proportion working outside the home, 74
- purchasing influence of, 140–142

Word-of-mouth influence, 139
"Word-of-web" influence, 139–140
Working, telecommuting and, 75–76, 76*p*
World product groups, for international marketing, 490
"Wrap rage," 357

Y

"Yell and sell" TV pitchmen, 404, 406

Z

Zone pricing, 286

Continuous Distrib

Beta

$0 < \alpha$

$0 < \beta$

$$f(x) = \frac{\Gamma(\alpha + \beta)}{\Gamma(\alpha)\Gamma(\beta)} x^{\alpha-1}(\ldots$$

$$\mu = \frac{\alpha}{\alpha + \beta}, \qquad \sigma^2 = \frac{\alpha\beta}{(\alpha + \beta + 1)(\alpha + \beta)^2}$$

Chi-square

$\chi^2(r)$

$r = 1, 2, \ldots$

$$f(x) = \frac{1}{\Gamma(r/2)2^{r/2}} x^{r/2-1} e^{-x/2}, \qquad 0 \le x < \infty$$

$$M(t) = \frac{1}{(1 - 2t)^{r/2}}, \qquad t < \frac{1}{2}$$

$$\mu = r, \qquad \sigma^2 = 2r$$

Exponential

$0 < \theta$

$$f(x) = \frac{1}{\theta} e^{-x/\theta}, \qquad 0 \le x < \infty$$

$$M(t) = \frac{1}{1 - \theta t}, \qquad t < \frac{1}{\theta}$$

$$\mu = \theta, \qquad \sigma^2 = \theta^2$$

Gamma

$0 < \alpha$

$0 < \theta$

$$f(x) = \frac{1}{\Gamma(\alpha)\theta^\alpha} x^{\alpha-1} e^{-x/\theta}, \qquad 0 \le x < \infty$$

$$M(t) = \frac{1}{(1 - \theta t)^\alpha}, \qquad t < \frac{1}{\theta}$$

$$\mu = \alpha\theta, \qquad \sigma^2 = \alpha\theta^2$$

Normal

$N(\mu, \sigma^2)$

$-\infty < \mu < \infty$

$0 < \sigma$

$$f(x) = \frac{1}{\sigma\sqrt{2\pi}} e^{-(x-\mu)^2/2\sigma^2}, \qquad -\infty < x < \infty$$

$$M(t) = e^{\mu t + \sigma^2 t^2/2}$$

$$E(X) = \mu, \qquad \mathrm{Var}(X) = \sigma^2$$

Uniform

$U(a, b)$

$-\infty < a < b < \infty$

$$f(x) = \frac{1}{b - a}, \qquad a \le x \le b$$

$$M(t) = \frac{e^{tb} - e^{ta}}{t(b - a)}, \qquad t \ne 0; \qquad M(0) = 1$$

$$\mu = \frac{a + b}{2}, \qquad \sigma^2 = \frac{(b - a)^2}{12}$$

Probability
and
Statistical Inference

PROBABILITY AND STATISTICAL INFERENCE

EIGHTH EDITION

Robert V. Hogg
University of Iowa

Elliot A. Tanis
Hope College

Prentice Hall
is an imprint of

Upper Saddle River, NJ 07458

Library of Congress Cataloging-in-Publication Data

Hogg, Robert V.
Probability and statistical inference/Robert V. Hogg, Elliot A. Tanis.–8th ed.
p. cm.
Includes bibliographical references and index.
ISBN 0-321-58475-9 (978-0-321-58475-5)
1. Probabilities. 2. Mathematical statistics. I. Tanis, Elliot A. II. Title.
QA273.H694 2010
519.2–dc22

2008043025

Editor-in-Chief: *Deirdre Lynch*
Acquisitions Editor: *Christopher Cummings*
Assistant Editor: *Christina Lepre*
Project Manager: *Raegan Keida Heerema*
Associate Managing Editor: *Bayani Mendoza deLeon*
Senior Managing Edior: *Linda Mihatov Behrens*
Senior Operations Supervisor: *Diane Peirano*
Editorial Assistant: *Dana Jones*
Marketing Manager: *Alex Gay*
Marketing Assistant: *Kathleen DeChavez*
Art Director: *Jayne Conte*
Cover Designer: *Bruce Kenselaar*
Art Studio/Formatter: *Laserwords*
Cover Image: *The image on the cover shows the joint p.d.f. of the sum of two U-shaped random variables (see Figure 5.6-4 on page 261) and a single U-shaped random variable*

Prentice Hall
is an imprint of

Pearson Prentice Hall
Pearson Education, Inc.
Upper Saddle River, New Jersey 07458

Printed in the United States of America

10 9 8 7 6 5 4 3 2 1

ISBN-10: 0-321-58475-9
ISBN-13: 978-0-321-58475-5

Pearson Education Ltd., *London*
Pearson Education Singapore, Pte. Ltd.
Pearson Education Canada, Inc.
Pearson Education—Japan
Pearson Education Australia Pty. Limited, *Sydney*
Pearson Education North Asia Ltd., *Hong Kong*
Pearson Educación de Mexico, S.A. de C.V.
Pearson Education Malaysia, Pte. Ltd.
Pearson Education, Inc., Upper Saddle River, New Jersey

Contents

Preface ix

Prologue xiii

1 Probability 1

1.1 Basic Concepts 1
1.2 Properties of Probability 11
1.3 Methods of Enumeration 20
1.4 Conditional Probability 29
1.5 Independent Events 38
1.6 Bayes's Theorem 45

2 Discrete Distributions 51

2.1 Random Variables of the Discrete Type 51
2.2 Mathematical Expectation 61
2.3 The Mean, Variance, and Standard Deviation 67
2.4 Bernoulli Trials and the Binomial Distribution 78
2.5 The Moment-Generating Function 89
2.6 The Poisson Distribution 99

3 Continuous Distributions 111

3.1 Continuous-Type Data 111
3.2 Exploratory Data Analysis 121
3.3 Random Variables of the Continuous Type 131
3.4 The Uniform and Exponential Distributions 141
3.5 The Gamma and Chi-Square Distributions 149
3.6 The Normal Distribution 157
3.7 Additional Models 168

4 Bivariate Distributions . . . 179

4.1 Distributions of Two Random Variables . . . 179
4.2 The Correlation Coefficient . . . 190
4.3 Conditional Distributions . . . 197
4.4 The Bivariate Normal Distribution . . . 207

5 Distributions of Functions of Random Variables . . . 215

5.1 Functions of One Random Variable . . . 215
5.2 Transformations of Two Random Variables . . . 224
5.3 Several Independent Random Variables . . . 234
5.4 The Moment-Generating Function Technique . . . 242
5.5 Random Functions Associated with Normal Distributions . . . 246
5.6 The Central Limit Theorem . . . 255
5.7 Approximations for Discrete Distributions . . . 263

6 Estimation . . . 273

6.1 Point Estimation . . . 273
6.2 Confidence Intervals for Means . . . 283
6.3 Confidence Intervals for the Difference of Two Means . . . 291
6.4 Confidence Intervals for Variances . . . 302
6.5 Confidence Intervals for Proportions . . . 307
6.6 Sample Size . . . 314
6.7 A Simple Regression Problem . . . 321
6.8 More Regression . . . 333

7 Tests of Statistical Hypotheses . . . 343

7.1 Tests about Proportions . . . 343
7.2 Tests about One Mean . . . 353
7.3 Tests of the Equality of Two Means . . . 363
7.4 Tests for Variances . . . 373
7.5 One-Factor Analysis of Variance . . . 379
7.6 Two-Factor Analysis of Variance . . . 389
7.7 Tests Concerning Regression and Correlation . . . 399

8 Nonparametric Methods . . . 407

8.1 Chi-Square Goodness-of-Fit Tests . . . 407
8.2 Contingency Tables . . . 417
8.3 Order Statistics . . . 428
8.4 Distribution-Free Confidence Intervals for Percentiles . . . 436
8.5 The Wilcoxon Tests . . . 443
8.6 Run Test and Test for Randomness . . . 455

8.7 Kolmogorov–Smirnov Goodness-of-Fit Test 461
8.8 Resampling Methods 467

9 Bayesian Methods 477

9.1 Subjective Probability 477
9.2 Bayesian Estimation 483
9.3 More Bayesian Concepts 490

10 Some Theory 497

10.1 Sufficient Statistics 497
10.2 Power of a Statistical Test 505
10.3 Best Critical Regions 512
10.4 Likelihood Ratio Tests 519
10.5 Chebyshev's Inequality and Convergence in Probability 525
10.6 Limiting Moment-Generating Functions 529
10.7 Asymptotic Distributions of Maximum Likelihood Estimators . . . 535

11 Quality Improvement through Statistical Methods 541

11.1 Time Sequences 541
11.2 Statistical Quality Control 547
11.3 General Factorial and 2^k Factorial Designs 558
11.4 Understanding Variation 564

APPENDICES

A References 571

B Tables 573

C Answers to Selected Odd-Numbered Exercises 601

D Review of Selected Mathematical Techniques . . . . CD-ROM

Index 615

Preface

We are pleased with the reception that was given to the first seven editions of *Probability and Statistical Inference*. We believe, after seven trys, that this is our best edition for students at the junior level who have taken a good standard course in calculus. While the text is designed for a two-semester course, we've provided suggestions on how it can be adapted for a one-semester course around four semester hours. Of course, no previous study of probability or statistics is needed. The material in this text is taught by many departments of mathematics or statistics and is actually required of many students who want to major in one of those departments.

One of the authors has been associated with the excellent program in actuarial science at the University of Iowa for a long time and no doubt has been influenced by the needs of actuarial students. However, we certainly have not designed the text for their needs only, but have written it to reflect what we believe is the best course for all students taking probability and mathematical statistics at this level. We must note, however, that actuarial students who truly understand the first five chapters, including the sections on Bayes's theorem and additional models, and who can work the exercises should be able to pass the first actuarial examination. This exam is now called Exam P by the Society of Actuaries and Exam 1 by the Casualty Actuarial Society. The first four chapters of the book contain material that most statisticians believe provides an excellent course in probability and in probability distributions of the discrete and continuous types, both of one and two random variables. In Chapter 5, these concepts are extended to many random variables, particularly those which are independent. This important chapter includes transformations of random variables and the moment-generating function technique, which leads to the central limit theorem, although its proof is given in Chapter 10, which is titled "Some Theory."

For a two-semester course, we assume that the instructor will cover most, if not all, of the sections included in the first seven chapters. Chapter 6 is a fine one on estimation, both point and interval, with a clear explanation concerning the sample size required to achieve a certain accuracy. Chapter 7 is about the other aspect of statistical inference, namely, tests of statistical hypotheses, and goes through elementary analysis of variance and simple linear regression. The connection between tests of statistical hypotheses and confidence intervals is clearly explained, including that between one-sided tests and confidence intervals.

Then, to complete the course, the instructor can select topics of his or her interests from the chapters titled "Nonparametric Methods," "Bayesian Methods," "Some

Theory," and "Quality Improvement Through Statistical Methods." We believe that we have included those additional topics which will appeal to most instructors' interests.

Chapter 8 on nonparametric methods include the topic of order statistics, leading to distribution-free confidence intervals for percentiles, resampling methods, and many standard methods in this area. Bayesian methods are in the substantial, but brief Chapter 9, which includes an interesting discussion of subjective probability. We decided to collect much of the theory given in a mathematical statistics course in Chapter 10. This includes consideration of sufficient statistics, the power of statistical tests, best critical regions, likelihood ratio tests, and many limiting ideas, including a proof of the central limit theorem. Many instructors might want to include these theoretical concepts in their course. Finally, Chapter 11 gives some basic ideas about quality improvement in the workplace via statistical methods, with a short description of the Six Sigma program.

For the one-semester course, we believe that instructors can select sections from the first seven chapters.

We have tried to make the eighth edition more "user-friendly;" yet we do want to reinforce certain basic concepts of mathematics, particularly calculus. To help the student with methods used in the algebra of sets and in calculus, we include Appendix D, a "Review of Selected Mathematical Techniques," on the companion CD-ROM bound into the back of this book. This review includes a method that makes integration by parts easier. Also, we derive the important "Rule of 72," which provides an approximation to the number of years necessary for money to double.

Some Special Features

- There is a better and more logical flow in this edition, and that is one of the reasons we believe it to be our best. For example, the normal distribution has been moved to the end of Chapter 3. Now all of the usual one-variable distributions which are used by statisticians are in Chapters 2 and 3.
- In the first five chapters, we have included several "real" probability examples and exercises that will appeal to students of actuarial science, finance, economics, and so on. We are less dependent upon problems involving coins, cards, and dice, although we find that students are interested in some of the latter problems.
- Chapter 6 on estimation and Chapter 7 on tests of hypotheses are now back-to-back. Furthermore, confidence intervals and tests of hypotheses are tied together.
- There is a short, but excellent, Bayesian chapter, including real examples and an indication of how Bayesians prove theorems by establishing "Dutch books." The technique was pointed out to us by George Woodworth.
- There is a very good coverage of conditional distributions, correlation, and distributions that are mixtures of the discrete and continuous cases.
- At the end of each chapter, we have added interesting historical comments, such as one that explains how the normal distribution was discovered.
- In the section on bootstrapping, there is an explanation of the origin of this word.
- Examples are given of Simpson's paradox.
- An explanation of the Six Sigma program is given in Chapter 11.
- The figures include the use of color.

- The companion CD-ROM includes not only all of the data sets in several formats—ASCII files, Minitab worksheets, as text files, and a format used by *Maple*—but also many more applications of Minitab and *Maple*, as well as Appendix D, a Review of Selected Mathematical Techniques of the book.
- Illustrations of *Maple* as a computer algebra system are given in the text and on the CD-ROM.

Important Points in This Edition

We recognize the importance of technology in modern statistics by including supplements that actively engage students in using the computer. Some of these supplements illustrate the use of Minitab for calculating probabilities, analyzing data, and applying statistical inference in the form of tests of hypotheses and confidence intervals. The power of a computer algebra system (CAS) for theoretical computations is illustrated with *Maple*. The importance of simulation is also demonstrated. Some of the illustrations are printed in the text. There are also new illustrations on the CD-ROM and you are encouraged to check these out.

There are many exercises in the text illustrating the mathematics of probability and statistics but a great number are concerned with applications. We've included applications in the areas of biology, education, economics, engineering, environmental studies, exercise science, health science, manufacturing, opinion polls, psychology, sociology, and sports.

Throughout the book, figures and real applications will help the student understand probability and statistics and what they can accomplish. For some exercises, it is assumed that calculators or computers are available; thus, the solutions will not always involve "nice" numbers. Data sets for all of the exercises are available on the companion CD-ROM. The data are provided in different formats so that they should be accessible to most computer programs. Finally, in the first part of the book, concerning probability, supplementary comments are inserted about statistics and computation.

Ancillaries

An **Instructor's Solutions Manual** containing worked-out solutions to the even-numbered exercises in the text is available for download from Pearson Education's online catalog. Many of the numerical exercises were solved with *Maple*. For additional exercises that involve simulations, a separate manual, *Probability & Statistics: Explorations with MAPLE*, second edition, by Zaven Karian and Elliot Tanis, is available for download from Pearson Education's online catalog. Several exercises in that manual also make use of the power of *Maple* as a computer algebra system.

The **CD-ROM** contains all of the data sets in various formats. There are also applications of Minitab for drawing figures, calculating probabilities, calculating characteristics of a sample, and statistical inference. One folder contains some supplementary *Maple* programs that are useful in probability and statistics. These programs were used to construct the figures in this text and for other applications. *Maple* was also used to animate some of the figures in the text. All you need is a browser. Simply load in the directory and you can pull up these animations. Appendix D, a "Review of Selected Mathematical Techniques," is also available on the CD-ROM.

If you find any errors in this text, please send them to tanis@hope.edu so that they can be corrected in a future printing. These **errata** will also be posted on http://www.math.hope.edu/tanis/.

Acknowledgments

We wish to thank our colleagues, students, and friends for many suggestions and for their generosity in supplying data for exercises and examples. In particular we would like to acknowledge the excellent suggestions from our copy editor, Brian Baker, and the fine work of our accuracy checkers, Tom Wegleitner and Roxane Barrows. We also thank the University of Iowa and Hope College for providing office space and encouragement. Finally, our families, through eight editions, have been most understanding during the preparation of all of this material. We would especially like to thank our wives, Ann and Elaine. We truly appreciate their patience and needed their love.

Robert V. Hogg
Elliot A. Tanis
tanis@hope.edu

Prologue

The discipline of statistics deals with the collection and analysis of data. Advances in computing technology, particularly in relation to changes in science and business, have increased the need for more statistical scientists to examine the huge amount of data being collected. We know that data are not equivalent to information. Once data (hopefully of high quality) are collected, there is a strong need for statisticians to make sense of them. That is, data must be analyzed, in order to provide information upon which decisions can be made. In light of this great demand, opportunities for the discipline of statistics have never been greater, and there is a special need for more bright young persons to go into statistical science.

If we think of fields in which data play a major part, the list is almost endless: accounting, actuarial science, atmospheric science, biological science, economics, educational measurement, environmental science, epidemiology, finance, genetics, manufacturing, marketing, medicine, pharmaceutical industries, psychology, sociology, sports, and on and on. Because statistics is useful in all of these areas, it really should be taught as an applied science. Nevertheless, to go very far in such an applied science, it is necessary to understand the importance of creating models for each situation under study. Now, no model is ever exactly right, but some are extremely useful as an approximation to the real situation. Most appropriate models in statistics require a certain mathematical background in probability. Accordingly, while alluding to applications in the examples and the exercises, this textbook is really about the mathematics needed for the appreciation of probabilistic models necessary for statistical inferences.

In a sense, statistical techniques are really the heart of the scientific method. Observations are made that suggest conjectures. These conjectures are tested, and data are collected and analyzed, providing information about the truth of the conjectures. Sometimes the conjectures are supported by the data, but often the conjectures need to be modified and more data must be collected to test the modifications, and so on. Clearly, in this iterative process, statistics plays a major role with its emphasis on proper design and analysis of experiments and the resulting inferences upon which decisions can be made. Through statistics, information is provided that is relevant to taking certain actions, including improving manufactured products, providing better services, marketing new products or services, forecasting energy needs, classifying diseases better, and so on.

Statisticians recognize that there are often small errors in their inferences, and they attempt to make the probabilities of those mistakes as small as possible. That these uncertainties even exist is due to the fact that there is variation in the data. Even though experiments are repeated under seemingly the same conditions, the results vary from trial to trial. We try to improve the quality of the data by making them as reliable as possible, but the data simply do not fall on given patterns. In light of this uncertainty, the statistician tries to determine the pattern in the best possible way, always explaining the error structures of the statistical estimates.

This is an important lesson to be learned: Variation is almost everywhere. It is the statistician's job to understand variation. Often, as in manufacturing, the desire is to reduce variation because the products will be more consistent. In other words, car doors will fit better in the manufacturing of automobiles if the variation is decreased by making each door closer to its target values.

Many statisticians in industry have stressed the need for "statistical thinking" in everyday operations. This need is based upon three points (two of which have been mentioned in the preceding paragraph): (1) Variation exists in all processes, (2) understanding and reducing undesirable variation is a key to success, and (3) all work occurs in a system of interconnected processes. W. Edwards Deming, an esteemed statistician and quality improvement "guru," stressed these three points, particularly the third one. He would carefully note that you could not maximize the total operation by maximizing the individual components unless they are independent of each other. However, in most instances, they are highly dependent, and persons in different departments must work together in creating the best products and services. If not, what one unit does to better itself could very well hurt others. He often cited an orchestra as an illustration of the need for the members to work together to create an outcome that is consistent and desirable.

Any student of statistics should understand the nature of variability and the necessity for creating probabilistic models of that variability. We cannot avoid making inferences and decisions in the face of this uncertainty; however, these inferences and decisions are greatly influenced by the probabilistic models selected. Some persons are better model builders than others and accordingly will make better inferences and decisions. The assumptions needed for each statistical model are carefully examined; it is hoped that thereby the reader will become a better model builder.

Finally, we must mention how modern statistical analyses have become dependent upon the computer. Statisticians and computer scientists really should work together in areas of exploratory data analysis and "data mining." Statistical software development is critical today, for the best of it is needed in complicated data analyses. In light of this growing relationship between these two fields, it is good advice for bright students to take substantial offerings in statistics and in computer science.

Students majoring in statistics, computer science, or a joint program are in great demand in the workplace and in graduate programs. Clearly, they can earn advanced degrees in statistics or computer science or both. But, more importantly, they are highly desirable candidates for graduate work in other areas: actuarial science, industrial engineering, finance, marketing, accounting, management science, psychology, economics, law, sociology, medicine, health sciences, etc. So many fields have been "mathematized" that their programs are begging for majors in statistics or computer science. Often, such students become "stars" in these other areas. We truly hope that we can interest students enough that they want to study more statistics. If they do, they will find that the opportunities for very successful careers are numerous.

Probability and Statistical Inference

Probability

CHAPTER 1

1.1 BASIC CONCEPTS
1.2 PROPERTIES OF PROBABILITY
1.3 METHODS OF ENUMERATION
1.4 CONDITIONAL PROBABILITY
1.5 INDEPENDENT EVENTS
1.6 BAYES'S THEOREM

1.1 BASIC CONCEPTS

It is usually difficult to explain to the general public what statisticians do. Many think of us as "math nerds" who seem to enjoy dealing with numbers. And there is some truth to that concept. But if we consider the bigger picture, many recognize that statisticians can be extremely helpful in many investigations.

Consider the following:

1. There is some problem or situation that needs to be considered; so statisticians are often asked to work with investigators or research scientists.
2. Suppose that some measure (or measures) are needed to help us understand the situation better. The measurement problem is often extremely difficult, and creating good measures is a valuable skill. As an illustration, in higher education, how do we measure good teaching? This is a question to which we have not found a satisfactory answer, although several measures, such as student evaluations, have been used in the past.
3. After the measuring instrument has been developed, we must collect data through observation, possibly the results of a survey or an experiment.
4. Using these data, statisticians summarize the results, often with descriptive statistics and graphical methods.
5. These summaries are then used to analyze the situation. Here it is possible that statisticians make what are called statistical inferences.
6. Finally a report is presented, along with some recommendations that are based upon the data and the analysis of them. Frequently such a recommendation might be to perform the survey or experiment again, possibly changing some of

the questions or factors involved. This is how statistics is used in what is referred to as the scientific method, because often the analysis of the data suggests other experiments. Accordingly, the scientist must consider different possibilities in his or her search for an answer and thus performs similar experiments over and over again.

The discipline of statistics deals with the *collection* and *analysis of data*. When measurements are taken, even seemingly under the same conditions, the results usually vary. Despite this variability, a statistician tries to find a pattern; yet due to the "noise," not all of the data fit into the pattern. In the face of the variability, the statistician must still determine the best way to describe the pattern. Accordingly, statisticians know that mistakes will be made in data analysis, and they try to minimize those errors as much as possible and then give bounds on the possible errors. By considering these bounds, decision makers can decide how much confidence they want to place in the data and in their analysis of them. If the bounds are wide, perhaps more data should be collected. If, however, the bounds are narrow, the person involved in the study might want to make a decision and proceed accordingly.

Variability is a fact of life, and proper statistical methods can help us understand data collected under inherent variability. Because of this variability, many decisions have to be made that involve uncertainties. In medical research, interest may center on the effectiveness of a new vaccine for mumps; an agronomist must decide whether an increase in yield can be attributed to a new strain of wheat; a meteorologist is interested in predicting the probability of rain; the state legislature must decide whether decreasing speed limits will result in fewer accidents; the admissions officer of a college must predict the college performance of an incoming freshman; a biologist is interested in estimating the clutch size for a particular type of bird; an economist desires to estimate the unemployment rate; an environmentalist tests whether new controls have resulted in a reduction in pollution.

In reviewing the preceding (relatively short) list of possible areas of applications of statistics, the reader should recognize that good statistics is closely associated with careful thinking in many investigations. As an illustration, students should appreciate how statistics is used in the endless cycle of the scientific method. We observe nature and ask questions, we run experiments and collect data that shed light on these questions, we analyze the data and compare the results of the analysis with what we previously thought, we raise new questions, and on and on. Or if you like, statistics is clearly part of the important "plan–do–study–act" cycle: Questions are raised and investigations planned and carried out. The resulting data are studied and analyzed and then acted upon, often raising new questions.

There are many aspects of statistics. Some people get interested in the subject by collecting data and trying to make sense out of their observations. In some cases the answers are obvious and little training in statistical methods is necessary. But if a person goes very far in many investigations, he or she soon realizes that there is a need for some theory to help describe the error structure associated with the various estimates of the patterns. That is, at some point, appropriate probability and mathematical models are required to make sense out of complicated data sets. Statistics and the probabilistic foundation on which statistical methods are based can provide the models to help people do this. So in this book, we are more concerned with the mathematical, rather than the applied, aspects of statistics. Still, we give enough real examples so that the reader can get a good sense of a number of important applications of statistical methods.

In the study of statistics, we consider experiments for which the outcome cannot be predicted with certainty. Such experiments are called **random experiments**. Each experiment ends in an outcome that cannot be determined with certainty before the experiment is performed. However, the experiment is such that the collection of every possible outcome can be described and perhaps listed. This collection of all outcomes is called the **outcome space**, the **sample space**, or, more simply, the **space** S. The following examples will help illustrate what we mean by random experiments, outcomes, and their associated spaces.

EXAMPLE 1.1-1 Two dice are cast, and the total number of spots on the sides that are "up" are counted. The outcome space is $S = \{2, 3, 4, 5, 6, 7, 8, 9, 10, 11, 12\}$. ■

EXAMPLE 1.1-2 Each of six students has a standard deck of playing cards, and each student selects one card randomly from his or her deck. We are interested in whether at least two of these six cards match (M) or whether all are different (D). Thus, $S = \{M, D\}$. ■

EXAMPLE 1.1-3 A fair coin is flipped successively at random until the first head is observed. If we let x denote the number of flips of the coin that are required, then $S = \{x : x = 1, 2, 3, 4, \ldots\}$, which consists of an infinite, but countable, number of outcomes. ■

EXAMPLE 1.1-4 A box of breakfast cereal contains one of four different prizes. The purchase of one box of cereal yields one of the prizes as the outcome, and the sample space is the set of four different prizes. ■

EXAMPLE 1.1-5 In Example 1.1-4, assume that the prizes are put into the boxes randomly. A family continues to buy this cereal until it obtains a complete set of the four different prizes. The number of boxes of cereal that must be purchased is one of the outcomes in $S = \{b : b = 4, 5, 6, \ldots\}$. ■

EXAMPLE 1.1-6 A fair coin is flipped successively at random until heads is observed on two successive flips. If we let y denote the number of flips of the coin that are required, then $S = \{y : y = 2, 3, 4, \ldots\}$. ■

EXAMPLE 1.1-7 To determine the percentage of body fat on a person, one measurement that is made is a person's weight under water. If w denotes this weight in kilograms, then the sample space could be $S = \{w : 0 < w < 7\}$, as we know from past experience that this weight does not exceed 7 kilograms. ■

EXAMPLE 1.1-8 An ornithologist is interested in the clutch size (number of eggs in a nest) for gallinules, a species of bird that lives in a marsh. If we let c equal the clutch size, then a possible sample space would be $S = \{c : c = 0, 1, 2, \ldots, 15\}$, as 15 is the largest known clutch size. ■

Note that the outcomes of a random experiment can be numerical, as in Examples 1.1-3, 1.1-6, 1.1-7, and 1.1-8, but they do not have to be, as shown by Examples 1.1-2 and 1.1-4. Often we "mathematize" those latter outcomes by assigning numbers to them. For instance, in Example 1.1-2, we could denote the outcome

$\{D\}$ by the number zero and the outcome $\{M\}$ by the number one. In general, measurements on outcomes associated with random experiments are called **random variables**, and these are usually denoted by some capital letter toward the end of the alphabet, such as X, Y, or Z.

Note the numbers of outcomes in the sample spaces in these examples. In Examples 1.1-1, 1.1-4, and 1.1-8, the number of outcomes is finite. In Examples 1.1-3 and 1.1-6, the number of possible outcomes is infinite but countable. That is, there are as many outcomes as there are counting numbers (positive integers). The space for Example 1.1-7 is different from that of the other examples in that the set of possible outcomes is an interval of numbers. Theoretically the weight could be any one of an infinite number of possible weights; here the number of possible outcomes is not countable. However, from a practical point of view, reported weights are selected from a finite number of possibilities because we can read and record the answer only to an accuracy determined by our scale. Many times, however, it is better to conceptualize the space as an interval of outcomes, and Example 1.1-7 is an example of a space of the continuous type.

If we consider a random experiment and its space, we note that under repeated performances of the experiment, some outcomes occur more frequently than others. For instance, in Example 1.1-3, if this coin-flipping experiment is repeated over and over, the first head is observed on the first flip more often than on the second flip. If we can somehow, by theory or observations, determine the fractions of times a random experiment ends in the respective outcomes, we have described a **distribution of the random variable** (sometimes called a **population**). Often we cannot determine this distribution through theoretical reasoning, but must actually perform the random experiment a number of times to obtain guesses or **estimates** of these fractions. The collection of the observations that are obtained from such repeated trials is often called a **sample**. The making of a conjecture about the distribution of a random variable based on the sample is called a **statistical inference**. That is, in statistics, we try to infer from the sample to the population. To understand the background behind statistical inferences that are made from the sample, we need a knowledge of some probability, basic distributions, and sampling distribution theory; these topics are considered in the early part of this book.

Given a sample or set of measurements, we would like to determine methods for describing the data. Suppose that we have some **counting** or **discrete data**. For example, you record the number of children in the families of each of your classmates. Or perhaps your state, on a regular basis, selects 5 integers out of the first 37 positive integers for the state lottery; you could count the number of odd integers among the 5 that were chosen.

In general, suppose we repeat a random experiment a number of times—say, n. If a certain outcome—say, A—has occurred $f = \mathcal{N}(A)$ times in these n trials, then the number $f = \mathcal{N}(A)$ is called the **frequency** of the outcome A. The ratio $f/n = \mathcal{N}(A)/n$ is called the **relative frequency** of the outcome. A relative frequency is usually very unstable for small values of n, but it tends to stabilize about some number—say, p—as n increases. The number p is called the **probability** of the outcome.

To develop an understanding of a particular set of discrete data, we can summarize the data in a frequency table and then construct a histogram of the data. A **frequency table** provides the number of occurrences of each possible outcome. A **histogram** presents the tallied data graphically, as illustrated in the next example.

EXAMPLE 1.1-9 In Table 1.1-1, the number of children in each family of 100 students in two statistics classes is recorded.

TABLE 1.1-1: Number of Children per Family

2	2	5	3	4	4	3	3	6	4	3	4	4	4	4	2	5	9	2	3
1	3	5	2	4	4	4	3	3	2	2	4	2	2	6	6	1	3	3	3
3	2	3	4	7	3	3	3	2	2	2	2	3	2	3	2	3	2	5	2
3	2	2	2	4	3	3	2	3	2	4	3	3	3	4	2	4	1	2	2
2	4	3	3	3	5	2	3	3	2	2	3	3	4	2	2	2	7	2	3

We shall construct a frequency table in which we tally the number of times that each outcome was observed. We also add a column that gives the relative frequency of each outcome.

TABLE 1.1-2: Frequency Table of Number of Children per Family

Number of Children	Tabulation	Frequency	Relative Frequency
1	|||	3	0.03
2	𝍸 𝍸 𝍸 𝍸 𝍸 𝍸 ||||	34	0.34
3	𝍸 𝍸 𝍸 𝍸 𝍸 𝍸 ||||	34	0.34
4	𝍸 𝍸 𝍸 |||	18	0.18
5	𝍸	5	0.05
6	|||	3	0.03
7	||	2	0.02
8		0	0.00
9	|	1	0.01
Totals		100	1.00

In a table of numbers like Table 1.1-1, it is often difficult to detect features of the measurements, such as the minimum, the maximum, or the measurement that occurs most often (known as the typical value). Often this typical value is called the **mode**. The frequency table, Table 1.1-2, helps to point out these features. A more visual way to present such data is with a **histogram**. To construct a **frequency histogram**, center a rectangle with a base of length 1 at each observed integer value and make the height equal to the frequency of this integer. To construct a **relative frequency histogram** or a **density histogram**—say, $h(x)$—make the height of each rectangle equal to the relative frequency of the outcome. Note that since each base equals 1, the area of each rectangle is the respective relative frequency of the midpoint of the base and the total area of a relative frequency histogram is equal to 1. This relationship is illustrated in Figure 1.1-1 on next the page. ■

One reason for constructing histograms is to picture the data more easily. Also, a histogram helps us to use the observed data to say something about the source of the data or the population from which the data were selected, provided that the data were selected randomly. For example, these 100 observations of number of children could perhaps help us say something about the number of children in families having

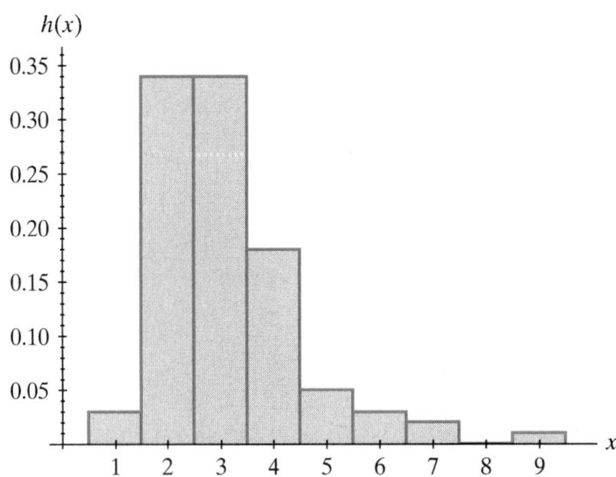

FIGURE 1.1-1: Relative frequency histogram of number of children per family

a student at Hope College. If we would like to say something about the number of children in families in the United States, we should select a representative sample of many families and look at the number of children in those families. Note that 0 is a possible outcome for this latter experiment, while that is not true of families sending at least one of their children to Hope College.

We have noted that the relative frequency of x—say, $f/n = \mathcal{N}(x)/n$—is very unstable for small n but tends to stabilize around some probability p as n increases. Since the relative frequency histogram $h(x)$ represents the relative frequencies of various values of x, we would believe that as n increases, $h(x)$ approaches some ideal function $f(x)$ that represents the probabilities of the respective values of x. That is, if x_0 is one of the possible x values with frequency $f_0 = \mathcal{N}(x_0)$, then, as n increases,

$$h(x_0) = \frac{f_0}{n} = \frac{\mathcal{N}(x_0)}{n} \rightarrow p_0 = f(x_0),$$

where p_0 is that probability about which $f_0/n = \mathcal{N}(x_0)/n$ stabilizes. Suppose that we have a certain function $f(x)$ that serves as a model for the probabilities of the outcomes of a random experiment. If we repeat that random experiment a large number of times and construct the corresponding relative frequency histogram $h(x)$, we would anticipate that $h(x)$ would be approximately equal to $f(x)$. We call this function, $f(x)$, the **probability mass function** and abbreviate it **p.m.f.** In order to graphically compare $h(x)$ and $f(x)$, we construct a **probability histogram** of $f(x)$. This is a graphical representation that has a rectangle of height $f(x)$ and a base of length 1, centered at each $x \in S$, where $x \in S$ means "x belongs to the space S." Since each base is equal to 1, the area of each rectangle is equal to the probability $f(x)$.

Let us consider a simple example in which we can intuitively assign a reasonable probability model to the outcomes of a given random experiment.

EXAMPLE 1.1-10 Place 10 chips of the same size in a bowl. The number 1 is placed on one of the chips, the number 2 on two of the chips, the number 3 on three of the chips, and finally the number 4 on four of the chips. The experiment is to select one chip at random and read the number x on the chip. Here $S = \{1, 2, 3, 4\}$. If this experiment is performed in a "fair" manner, most of us would intuitively assign the probabilities 1/10, 2/10,

3/10, and 4/10 to the respective x values $x = 1$, $x = 2$, $x = 3$, $x = 4$. That is, our model is given by the p.m.f.

$$f(1) = \frac{1}{10}, \qquad f(2) = \frac{2}{10}, \qquad f(3) = \frac{3}{10}, \qquad f(4) = \frac{4}{10}$$

or, equivalently, by

$$f(x) = \frac{x}{10}, \qquad x = 1, 2, 3, 4.$$

In Figure 1.1-2, we plot the probability histogram associated with the p.m.f. $f(x)$ on the left. To simulate this experiment, we used the random numbers in Table IX in the appendix. There are 1260 digits in this table. We assigned the digit $\{0\}$ to $x = 1$, the digits $\{1,2\}$ to $x = 2$, the digits $\{3,4,5\}$ to $x = 3$, and the digits $\{6,7,8,9\}$ to $x = 4$. The respective frequencies of $x = 1, 2, 3$, and 4 are 119, 254, 376, and 511. The respective relative frequencies are

$$h(1) = \frac{119}{1260}, \quad h(2) = \frac{254}{1260}, \quad h(3) = \frac{376}{1260}, \quad h(4) = \frac{511}{1260}.$$

In Figure 1.1-2 on the right, we plot the relative frequency histogram $h(x)$ with the p.m.f. superimposed. The top of $f(x)$ is dashed. Note that $h(x)$ approximates $f(x)$ very well—almost too well. ■

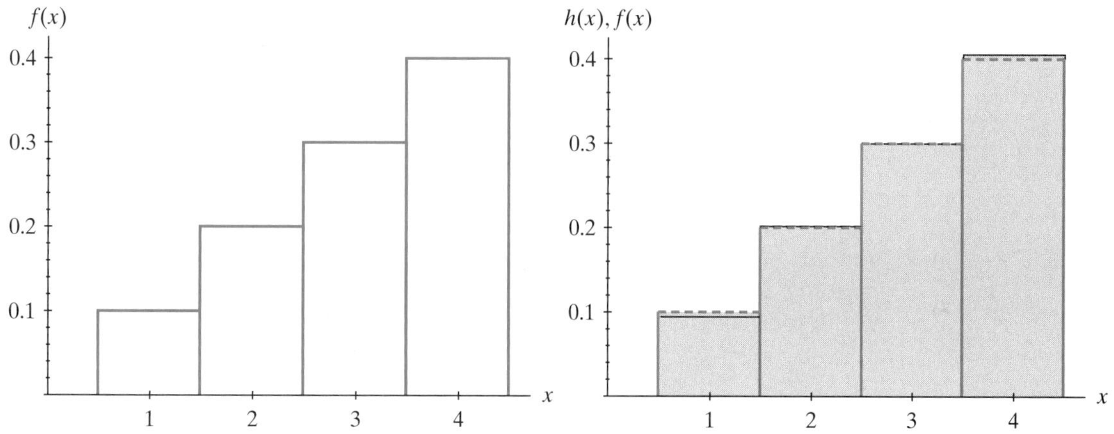

FIGURE 1.1-2: Probability histogram alone and with relative frequency histogram

The value of x that has a greatest probability (or highest relative frequency) is called the **mode** of the distribution (or of the histogram determined by the data). So in the last example, $x = 4$ is the mode.

EXAMPLE 1.1-11 A student in a statistics class was asked to write down a string of one-digit numbers $(0, 1, 2, \ldots, 9)$ that seemed to her to be random. She recorded the following 40 numbers in this order:

8, 2, 6, 0, 3, 9, 1, 6, 5, 8, 7, 4, 9, 5, 0, 5, 2, 7, 5, 2
4, 8, 1, 3, 6, 5, 2, 8, 4, 1, 0, 8, 1, 2, 7, 6, 1, 9, 4, 0

Let us count the number of times she recorded the same number next to itself (like 5, 5), the number of times adjacent numbers were next to each other (like 7, 6 and, say, 9, 0 are next to each other) and the number of times neither of these occurred. If the 40 numbers were truly selected at random, consecutive numbers would be the same about 10% of the time, consecutive numbers would differ by one about 20% of the time (recall that 9 and 0 differ by one in this example), and consecutive numbers would differ by more than one 70% of the time. The student's results were as follows:

	Frequency	Relative Frequency
Same	0	0/39 = 0.00
Differ by one	6	6/39 = 0.15
Differ by more than one	33	33/39 = 0.85
Totals	39	39/39 = 1.00

It seems as if 0.00 differs too much from 0.10, 0.15 is fairly close to 0.20, and 0.85 is somewhat higher than the expected 0.70. Intuitively, her sequence does not seem to be a very good approximation to a sequence of random digits. Later in the text, you will study a statistical method to test for the difference. ■

In many applied problems, not just those associated with probability, we want to find a model that describes the reality of the situation as well as possible. In truth, no model is exactly right, but often models are close enough to being correct that they are extremely useful in practice. However, before they can be used, models must be tested with data collected from the real situation. In this text, we are interested in constructing probability models for different random experiments. In the next few chapters, we study enough probability that allows us to assign certain reasonable probability models to important cases. Often we do not know everything about these models; that is, they frequently have unknown parameters. Thus, we must observe the results of several trials of the experiment to make further inferences about the models; in particular, we must estimate the unknown parameter(s). This process of refining a model by using the data is referred to as making a **statistical inference** and is the focus of the latter part of the text.

STATISTICAL COMMENTS (**Simpson's Paradox**) While most of the first five chapters are about probability and probability distributions, from time to time we will mention certain statistical concepts. As an illustration, the relative frequency, f/n, is called a **statistic** and is used to **estimate** a probability p, which is usually unknown. For example, if a major league batter gets $f = 152$ hits in $n = 500$ official at bats during the season, then the relative frequency $f/n = 0.304$ is an estimate of his probability of getting a hit and is called his batting average for that season.

Once while speaking to a group of coaches, one of us (Hogg) made the comment that it would be possible for batter A to have a higher average than batter B for each season during their careers and yet B could have a better overall average at the end of their careers. While no coach spoke up, you could tell that they were thinking, "And that guy is supposed to know something about math."

Of course, the following simple example convinced them that the statement was true: Suppose A and B played only two seasons, with these results:

Season	Player A			Player B		
	AB	Hits	Average	AB	Hits	Average
1	500	126	0.252	300	75	0.250
2	300	90	0.300	500	145	0.290
Totals	800	216	0.270	800	220	0.275

Clearly, A beats B in the two individual seasons, but B has a better overall average. Note that during their better season (the second) B had more at bats than did A. This kind of result is often called **Simpson's paradox** and it can happen in real life. (See Exercises 1.1-11, 1.1-12, and 1.1-13.)

EXERCISES

1.1-1. Describe the outcome space for each of the following experiments:

(a) A student is selected at random from a statistics class, and the student's ACT score in mathematics is determined. HINT: ACT test scores in mathematics are integers between 1 and 36, inclusive.

(b) A candy bar with a 20.4-gram label weight is selected at random from a production line and is weighed.

(c) A coin is tossed three times, and the sequence of heads and tails is observed.

1.1-2. Describe the outcome space for each of the following experiments:

(a) Consider families that have three children each, and select one such family at random. Describe the sample space S in terms of their children as 3-tuples, agreeing, for example, that "gbb" would indicate that the youngest is a girl and the two oldest are boys.

(b) A rat is selected at random from a cage, and its sex is determined.

(c) A state selects a three-digit integer at random for one of its lottery games.

1.1-3. The State of Arizona generates a three-digit number at random six days a week for its daily lottery. The numbers are generated one digit at a time. Consider the following set of 50 three-digit numbers as 150 one-digit integers that were generated at random from May 1, 2000 to July 3, 2000:

```
951  728  818  922  850  835  003  406  203  603
011  217  803  776  397  019  785  185  632  245
945  929  508  849  516  729  306  305  278  100
089  860  918  124  675  220  728  751  786  609
076  320  732  911  913  556  367  897  540  979
```

Let X denote the outcome when a single digit is generated.

(a) With true random digits, what probability would you assign to each digit? That is, what is the p.m.f. of X?

(b) For the 150 observations, determine the relative frequencies of 0, 1, 2, 3, 4, 5, 6, 7, 8, and 9, respectively.

(c) Construct a probability histogram and a relative frequency histogram like those in Figure 1.1-2.

(d) A set of 32 three-digit numbers was generated from May 4, 1998 to June 9, 1998. Answer (b) and (c) for these data. What is true about the fit of the probability model to the data? (For a more complete discussion of these numbers, see "The Case of the Missing Lottery Number," by W. D. Kaigh, in *The College Mathematics Journal*, January, 2001, pages 15–19.) The numbers are as follows:

```
287  215  846  873  485  812  432  415  348  383
334  075  655  871  824  704  533  014  822  477
880  316  012  010  557  881  222  256  282  704
111  124
```

1.1-4. Some ornithologists were interested in the clutch size of the common gallinule. They observed the number of eggs in each of 117 nests, yielding the following data:

7	5	13	7	7	8	9	9	9	8	8	9	9	7	7
5	9	7	7	4	9	8	8	10	9	7	8	8	8	7
9	7	7	10	8	7	9	7	10	8	9	7	11	10	9
9	4	8	6	8	9	9	9	8	8	5	8	8	9	9
14	10	8	9	9	9	8	7	9	7	9	10	10	7	6
11	7	7	6	9	7	7	6	8	9	4	6	9	8	9
7	9	9	9	9	8	8	8	9	9	9	8	10	9	9
8	5	7	8	7	6	7	7	7	6	5	9			

(a) Construct a frequency table for these data.
(b) Draw a histogram.
(c) What is the mode (the typical clutch size)?

1.1-5. Noticing that some of the gallinules in the last exercise had a second brood during the summer, the ornithologists became interested in comparing the clutch sizes for the second brood with those for the first brood. They were able to collect the following clutch sizes for the second brood:

4	4	6	5	5	9	6	5	6	9	7	9	4	8	6	5	9
8	8	7	6	8	8	9	10	9	9	7	4	6	8	7	5	

(a) Construct a frequency table for these data.
(b) Draw a histogram.
(c) Is there a typical clutch size for second broods?

1.1-6. Before buying enough cereal to obtain a set of four prizes (Example 1.1-4), a family decided to use simulation to estimate the number of boxes it would have to buy. Each member of the family rolled a four-sided die until he or she observed each face at least once. The family members repeated this exercise 100 times and recorded the numbers of rolls needed as follows:

8	6	6	4	13	11	19	13	4	15	8	13	5	8	9
16	9	5	12	6	4	8	6	6	6	11	6	5	10	5
6	5	8	4	5	14	5	7	5	7	5	8	4	9	8
9	13	8	14	5	24	4	5	6	7	5	4	8	7	6
11	4	5	6	5	10	10	4	5	14	10	15	6	9	8
7	10	14	10	8	8	10	7	9	10	8	10	9	7	5
12	7	16	6	5	11	4	11	5	5					

(a) Construct a frequency table for these data.
(b) Draw a histogram.

1.1-7. For a Texas lottery game, Cash Five, 5 integers are selected randomly out of the first 37 positive integers. The following table lists the numbers of odd integers out of each set of five integers selected in 100 consecutive drawings in 2007:

3	2	2	2	2	3	3	2	4	2	4	2	2	3	2	3	1	3	2	3
4	3	3	4	5	3	2	1	2	0	2	2	2	3	1	2	1	3	3	1
2	5	4	0	3	3	0	1	3	3	3	5	2	2	3	1	4	4	3	3
4	3	3	1	2	3	1	3	2	3	3	2	2	3	3	4	3	2	1	5
3	0	1	2	2	4	3	3	3	1	2	4	4	1	1	4	4	1	1	3

(a) Construct a frequency table for these data.
(b) Draw a histogram.

1.1-8. Consider a bowl containing 10 chips of the same size such that 2 are marked "one," 3 are marked "two," 3 are marked "three," and 2 are marked "four." Select a chip at random and read the number. Here $S = \{1, 2, 3, 4\}$.

(a) Assign a reasonable p.m.f. $f(x)$ to the outcome space.
(b) Simulate this experiment at least $n = 100$ times and find the relative frequency histogram $h(x)$. HINT: Here you can use a com-

puter to perform the simulation; or simply use the table of random numbers (Table IX in the appendix), start at a random spot, and let an integer in the set $\{0,1\} = 1$, in $\{2,3,4\} = 2$, in $\{5,6,7\} = 3$, in $\{8,9\} = 4$.

(c) Plot $f(x)$ and $h(x)$ on the same graph.

1.1-9. Toss two coins at random and count the number of heads that appear "up." Here $S = \{0,1,2\}$. In Chapter 2, we discover that a reasonable probability model is given by the p.m.f. $f(0) = 1/4$, $f(1) = 1/2$, $f(2) = 1/4$. Repeat this experiment at least $n = 100$ times, and plot the resulting relative frequency histogram $h(x)$ on the same graph with $f(x)$.

1.1-10. Let the random variable X be the number of tosses of a coin needed to obtain the first head. Here $S = \{1,2,3,4,\ldots\}$. In Chapter 2, we find that a reasonable probability model is given by the p.m.f. $f(x) = (1/2)^x$, $x \in S$. Do this experiment a large number of times, and compare the resulting relative frequency histogram $h(x)$ with $f(x)$.

1.1-11. In 1985, Al Bumbry of the Baltimore Orioles and Darrell Brown of the Minnesota Twins had the following numbers of hits (H) and official at bats (AB) on grass and artificial turf:

Playing Surface	Bumbry			Brown		
	AB	H	BA	AB	H	BA
Grass	295	77		92	18	
Artificial Turf	49	16		168	53	
Total	344	93		260	71	

(a) Find the batting averages BA (namely, H/AB) of each player on grass.
(b) Find the BA of each player on artificial turf.
(c) Find the season batting averages for the two players.
(d) Interpret your results.

1.1-12. In 1985, Kent Hrbek of the Minnesota Twins and Dion James of the Milwaukee Brewers had the following numbers of hits (H) and official at bats (AB) on grass and artificial turf:

Playing Surface	Hrbek			James		
	AB	H	BA	AB	H	BA
Grass	204	50		329	93	
Artificial Turf	355	124		58	21	
Total	559	174		387	114	

(a) Find the batting averages BA (namely, H/AB) of each player on grass.
(b) Find the BA of each player on artificial turf.
(c) Find the season batting averages for the two players.
(d) Interpret your results.

1.1-13. If we had a choice of two airlines, we would possibly choose the airline with the better "on-time performance." So consider Alaska Airlines and America West, using data reported by Arnold Barnett (see references):

Airline	Alaska Airlines	America West
Destination	Relative Frequency on Time	Relative Frequency on Time
Los Angeles	$\frac{497}{559}$	$\frac{694}{811}$
Phoenix	$\frac{221}{233}$	$\frac{4840}{5255}$
San Diego	$\frac{212}{232}$	$\frac{383}{448}$
San Francisco	$\frac{503}{605}$	$\frac{320}{449}$
Seattle	$\frac{1841}{2146}$	$\frac{201}{262}$
Five-City Total	$\frac{3274}{3775}$	$\frac{6438}{7225}$

(a) For each of the five cities listed, which airline has the better on-time performance?
(b) Combining the results, which airline has the better on-time performance?
(c) Interpret your results.

1.2 PROPERTIES OF PROBABILITY

In Section 1.1, the collection of all possible outcomes (the **universal set**) of a random experiment is denoted by S and is called the **outcome space**. Given an outcome space S, let A be a part of the collection of outcomes in S; that is, $A \subset S$. Then A is called an **event**. When the random experiment is performed and the outcome of the experiment is in A, we say that **event A has occurred**.

Since, in studying probability, the words *set* and *event* are interchangeable, the reader might want to review **algebra of sets**, found in Appendix D on the CD-ROM. For convenience, however, here we remind the reader of some terminology:

- $\emptyset$ denotes the **null** or **empty** set;
- $A \subset B$ means A is a **subset** of B;
- $A \cup B$ is the **union** of A and B;
- $A \cap B$ is the **intersection** of A and B;
- A' is the **complement** of A (i.e., all elements in S that are not in A).

Some of these sets are depicted by the shaded region in Figure 1.2-1, in which S is the interior of the rectangles. Such figures are called **Venn diagrams**.

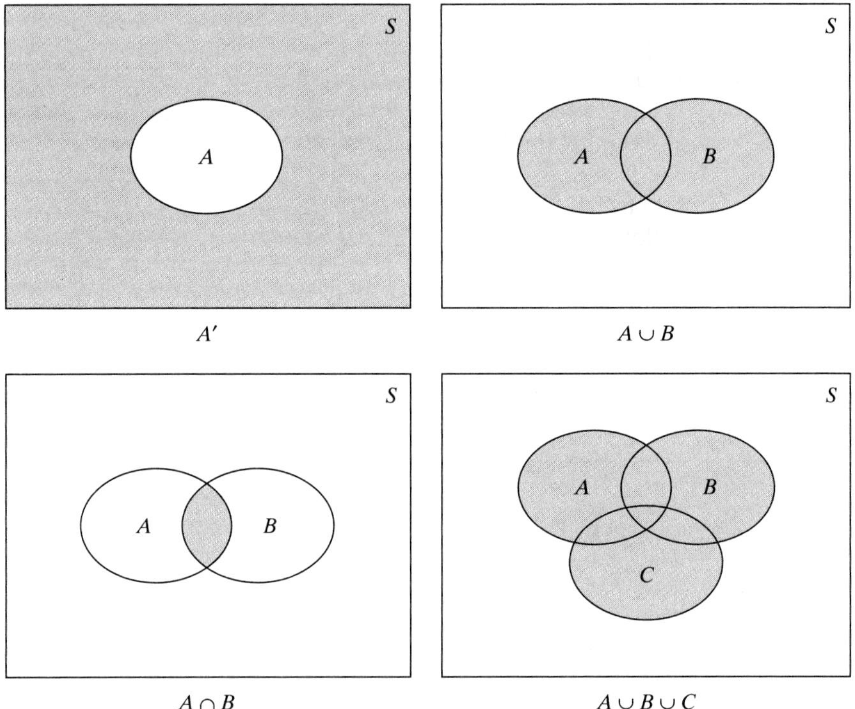

FIGURE 1.2-1: Algebra of sets

Special terminology associated with events that is often used by statisticians includes the following:

1. $A_1, A_2, \ldots, A_k$ are **mutually exclusive events** means that $A_i \cap A_j = \emptyset, i \neq j$, that is, $A_1, A_2, \ldots, A_k$ are disjoint sets;
2. $A_1, A_2, \ldots, A_k$ are **exhaustive events** means that $A_1 \cup A_2 \cup \cdots \cup A_k = S$.

So if $A_1, A_2, \ldots, A_k$ are **mutually exclusive and exhaustive** events, we know that $A_i \cap A_j = \emptyset, i \neq j$, and $A_1 \cup A_2 \cup \cdots \cup A_k = S$.

We are interested in defining what is meant by the probability of event A, denoted by $P(A)$ and often called the chance of A occurring. To help us understand what is meant by the probability of A, consider repeating the experiment a number of times—say, n times. Count the number of times that event A actually occurred throughout these n performances; this number is called the frequency of event A and is denoted by $\mathcal{N}(A)$. The ratio $\mathcal{N}(A)/n$ is called the **relative frequency** of event A

in these n repetitions of the experiment. A relative frequency is usually very unstable for small values of n, but it tends to stabilize as n increases. This suggests that we associate with event A a number—say, p—that is equal to or approximately equal to the number about which the relative frequency tends to stabilize. This number p can then be taken as the number that the relative frequency of event A will be near in future performances of the experiment. Thus, although we cannot predict the outcome of a random experiment with certainty, we can, for a large value of n, predict fairly accurately the relative frequency associated with event A. The number p assigned to event A is called the **probability** of event A and is denoted by $P(A)$. That is, $P(A)$ represents the proportion of outcomes of a random experiment that terminate in the event A as the number of trials of that experiment increases without bound.

The next example will help to illustrate some of the ideas just presented.

EXAMPLE 1.2-1 A fair six-sided die is rolled six times. If the face numbered k is the outcome on roll k for $k = 1, 2, \ldots, 6$, we say that a match has occurred. The experiment is called a success if at least one match occurs during the six trials. Otherwise, the experiment is called a failure. The sample space is $S = \{\text{success, failure}\}$. Let $A = \{\text{success}\}$. We would like to assign a value to $P(A)$. Accordingly, this experiment was simulated 500 times on a computer. Figure 1.2-2 depicts the results of this simulation, and the following table summarizes a few of the results:

n	$\mathcal{N}(A)$	$\mathcal{N}(A)/n$
50	37	0.740
100	69	0.690
250	172	0.688
500	330	0.660

The probability of event A is not intuitively obvious, but it will be shown in Example 1.5-6 that $P(A) = 1 - (1 - 1/6)^6 = 0.665$. This assignment is certainly supported by the simulation (although not proved by it). ■

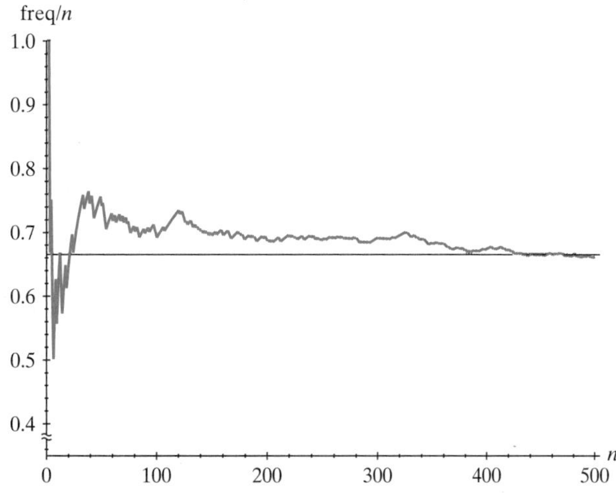

FIGURE 1.2-2: Fraction of experiments having at least one match

Example 1.2-1 shows that at times intuition cannot be used to assign probabilities, although simulation can perhaps help to assign a probability empirically. The next example illustrates where intuition can help in assigning a probability to an event.

EXAMPLE 1.2-2 A disk 2 inches in diameter is thrown at random on a tiled floor, where each tile is a square with sides 4 inches in length. Let C be the event that the disk will land entirely on one tile. In order to assign a value to $P(C)$, consider the center of the disk. In what region must the center lie to ensure that the disk lies entirely on one tile? If you draw a picture, it should be clear that the center must lie within a square having sides of length 2 and with its center coincident with the center of a tile. Since the area of this square is 4 and the area of a tile is 16, it makes sense to let $P(C) = 4/16$. ■

Sometimes the nature of an experiment is such that the probability of A can be assigned easily. For example, when a state lottery randomly selects a three-digit integer, we would expect each of the 1000 possible three-digit numbers to have the same chance of being selected, namely, 1/1000. If we let $A = \{233, 323, 332\}$, then it makes sense to let $P(A) = 3/1000$. Or if we let $B = \{234, 243, 324, 342, 423, 432\}$, then we would let $P(B) = 6/1000$, the probability of the event B. Probabilities of events associated with many random experiments are perhaps not quite as obvious and straightforward as was seen in Example 1.2-1.

So we wish to associate with A a number $P(A)$ about which the relative frequency $\mathcal{N}(A)/n$ of the event A tends to stabilize with large n. A function such as $P(A)$ that is evaluated for a set A is called a **set function**. In this section, we consider the probability set function $P(A)$ and discuss some of its properties. In succeeding sections, we shall describe how the probability set function is defined for particular experiments.

To help decide what properties the probability set function should satisfy, consider properties possessed by the relative frequency $\mathcal{N}(A)/n$. For example, $\mathcal{N}(A)/n$ is always nonnegative. If $A = S$, the sample space, then the outcome of the experiment will always belong to S, and thus $\mathcal{N}(S)/n = 1$. Also, if A and B are two mutually exclusive events, then $\mathcal{N}(A \cup B)/n = \mathcal{N}(A)/n + \mathcal{N}(B)/n$. Hopefully, these remarks will help to motivate the following definition.

DEFINITION 1.2-1 **Probability** is a real-valued set function P that assigns, to each event A in the sample space S, a number $P(A)$, called the probability of the event A, such that the following properties are satisfied:

(a) $P(A) \geq 0$,

(b) $P(S) = 1$,

(c) If $A_1, A_2, A_3, \ldots$ are events and $A_i \cap A_j = \emptyset, i \neq j$, then

$$P(A_1 \cup A_2 \cup \cdots \cup A_k) = P(A_1) + P(A_2) + \cdots + P(A_k)$$

for each positive integer k, and

$$P(A_1 \cup A_2 \cup A_3 \cup \cdots) = P(A_1) + P(A_2) + P(A_3) + \cdots$$

for an infinite, but countable, number of events.

The theorems that follow give some other important properties of the probability set function. When one considers these theorems, it is important to understand the theoretical concepts and proofs. However, if the reader keeps the relative frequency concept in mind, the theorems should also have some intuitive appeal.

THEOREM 1.2-1

For each event A,

$$P(A) = 1 - P(A').$$

Proof. We have

$$S = A \cup A' \qquad \text{and} \qquad A \cap A' = \emptyset.$$

Thus, from properties (b) and (c), it follows that

$$1 = P(A) + P(A').$$

Hence,

$$P(A) = 1 - P(A'). \qquad \square$$

EXAMPLE 1.2-3

A fair coin is flipped successively until the same face is observed on successive flips. Let $A = \{x : x = 3, 4, 5, \ldots\}$; that is, A is the event that it will take three or more flips of the coin to observe the same face on two consecutive flips. To find $P(A)$, we first find the probability of $A' = \{x : x = 2\}$, the complement of A. In two flips of a coin, the possible outcomes are $\{HH, HT, TH, TT\}$, and we assume that each of these four points has the same chance of being observed. Thus,

$$P(A') = P(\{HH, TT\}) = \frac{2}{4}.$$

It follows from Theorem 1.2-1 that

$$P(A) = 1 - P(A') = 1 - \frac{2}{4} = \frac{2}{4}. \qquad \blacksquare$$

THEOREM 1.2-2

$P(\emptyset) = 0.$

Proof. In Theorem 1.2-1, take $A = \emptyset$ so that $A' = S$. Then

$$P(\emptyset) = 1 - P(S) = 1 - 1 = 0. \qquad \square$$

THEOREM 1.2-3

If events A and B are such that $A \subset B$, then $P(A) \le P(B)$.

Proof. We have

$$B = A \cup (B \cap A') \qquad \text{and} \qquad A \cap (B \cap A') = \emptyset.$$

Hence, from property (c),

$$P(B) = P(A) + P(B \cap A') \ge P(A)$$

because, from property (a),

$$P(B \cap A') \geq 0. \qquad \square$$

THEOREM 1.2-4 For each event A, $P(A) \leq 1$.

Proof. Since $A \subset S$, we have, by Theorem 1.2-3 and property (b),

$$P(A) \leq P(S) = 1,$$

which gives the desired result. $\square$

Property (a), along with Theorem 1.2-4, shows that, for each event A,

$$0 \leq P(A) \leq 1.$$

THEOREM 1.2-5 If A and B are any two events, then

$$P(A \cup B) = P(A) + P(B) - P(A \cap B).$$

Proof. The event $A \cup B$ can be represented as a union of mutually exclusive events, namely,

$$A \cup B = A \cup (A' \cap B).$$

Hence, by property (c),

$$P(A \cup B) = P(A) + P(A' \cap B). \qquad (1.2\text{-}1)$$

However,

$$B = (A \cap B) \cup (A' \cap B),$$

which is a union of mutually exclusive events. Thus,

$$P(B) = P(A \cap B) + P(A' \cap B)$$

and

$$P(A' \cap B) = P(B) - P(A \cap B).$$

If the right-hand side of this equation is substituted into Equation 1.2-1, we obtain

$$P(A \cup B) = P(A) + P(B) - P(A \cap B),$$

which is the desired result. $\square$

EXAMPLE 1.2-4 A faculty leader was meeting two students in Paris, one arriving by train from Amsterdam and the other arriving by train from Brussels at approximately the same time. Let A and B be the events that the respective trains are on time. Suppose we know from past experience that $P(A) = 0.93$, $P(B) = 0.89$, and $P(A \cap B) = 0.87$. Then

$$\begin{aligned} P(A \cup B) &= P(A) + P(B) - P(A \cap B) \\ &= 0.93 + 0.89 - 0.87 = 0.95 \end{aligned}$$

is the probability that at least one train is on time. ■

THEOREM 1.2-6 If A, B, and C are any three events, then

$$\begin{aligned} P(A \cup B \cup C) = P(A) + P(B) + P(C) - P(A \cap B) \\ - P(A \cap C) - P(B \cap C) + P(A \cap B \cap C). \end{aligned}$$

Proof. Write

$$A \cup B \cup C = A \cup (B \cup C)$$

and apply Theorem 1.2-5. The details are left as an exercise. □

EXAMPLE 1.2-5 A survey was taken of a group's viewing habits of sporting events on TV during the last year. Let $A = \{\text{watched football}\}$, $B = \{\text{watched basketball}\}$, $C = \{\text{watched baseball}\}$. The results indicate that if a person is selected from the group surveyed, then $P(A) = 0.43$, $P(B) = 0.40$, $P(C) = 0.32$, $P(A \cap B) = 0.29$, $P(A \cap C) = 0.22$, $P(B \cap C) = 0.20$, and $P(A \cap B \cap C) = 0.15$. It then follows that

$$\begin{aligned} P(A \cup B \cup C) &= P(A) + P(B) + P(C) - P(A \cap B) - P(A \cap C) \\ &\quad - P(B \cap C) + P(A \cap B \cap C) \\ &= 0.43 + 0.40 + 0.32 - 0.29 - 0.22 - 0.20 + 0.15 \\ &= 0.59 \end{aligned}$$

is the probability that this person watched at least one of these sports. ■

Let a probability set function be defined on a sample space S. Let $S = \{e_1, e_2, \ldots, e_m\}$, where each e_i is a possible outcome of the experiment. The integer m is called the total number of ways in which the random experiment can terminate. If each of these outcomes has the same probability of occurring, we say that the m outcomes are **equally likely**. That is,

$$P(\{e_i\}) = \frac{1}{m}, \qquad i = 1, 2, \ldots, m.$$

If the number of outcomes in an event A is h, then the integer h is called the number of ways that are favorable to the event A. In this case, $P(A)$ is equal to the number of ways favorable to the event A divided by the total number of ways in which the experiment can terminate. That is, under this assumption of equally likely outcomes, we have

$$P(A) = \frac{h}{m} = \frac{N(A)}{N(S)},$$

where $h = N(A)$ is the number of ways A can occur and $m = N(S)$ is the number of ways S can occur. Exercise 1.2-19 considers this assignment of probability in a more theoretical manner.

It should be emphasized that in order to assign the probability h/m to the event A, we must assume that each of the outcomes $e_1, e_2, \ldots, e_m$ has the same probability $1/m$. This assumption is then an important part of our probability model; if it is not realistic in an application, then the probability of the event A cannot be computed in this way. Actually, we have used this result in the simple case given in Example 1.2-3 because it seemed realistic to assume that each of the possible outcomes in $S = \{HH, HT, TH, TT\}$ had the same chance of being observed.

EXAMPLE 1.2-6 Let a card be drawn at random from an ordinary deck of 52 playing cards. Then the sample space S is the set of $m = 52$ different cards, and it is reasonable to assume that each of these cards has the same probability of selection, 1/52. Accordingly, if A is the set of outcomes that are kings, then $P(A) = 4/52 = 1/13$ because there are $h = 4$ kings in the deck. That is, 1/13 is the probability of drawing a card that is a king, provided that each of the 52 cards has the same probability of being drawn. ■

In Example 1.2-6, the computations are very easy because there is no difficulty in the determination of the appropriate values of h and m. However, instead of drawing only one card, suppose that 13 are taken at random and without replacement. Then we can think of each possible 13-card hand as being an outcome in a sample space, and it is reasonable to assume that each of these outcomes has the same probability. For example, to use the preceding method to assign the probability of a hand consisting of seven spades and six hearts, we must be able to count the number h of all such hands, as well as the number m of possible 13-card hands. In these more complicated situations, we need better methods of determining h and m. We discuss some of these counting techniques in Section 1.3.

EXERCISES

1.2-1. Of a group of patients having injuries, 28% visit both a physical therapist and a chiropractor and 8% visit neither. Say that the probability of visiting a physical therapist exceeds the probability of visiting a chiropractor by 16%. What is the probability of a randomly selected person from this group visiting a physical therapist?

1.2-2. An insurance company looks at its auto insurance customers and finds that (a) all insure at least one car, (b) 85% insure more than one car, (c) 23% insure a sports car, and (d) 17% insure more than one car, including a sports car. Find the probability that a customer selected at random insures exactly one car and it is not a sports car.

1.2-3. Draw one card at random from a standard deck of cards. The sample space S is the collection of the 52 cards. Assume that the probability set function assigns 1/52 to each of the 52 outcomes. Let

$$A = \{x : x \text{ is a jack, queen, or king}\},$$
$$B = \{x : x \text{ is a 9, 10, or jack and } x \text{ is red}\},$$
$$C = \{x : x \text{ is a club}\},$$
$$D = \{x : x \text{ is a diamond, a heart, or a spade}\}.$$

Find (a) $P(A)$, (b) $P(A \cap B)$, (c) $P(A \cup B)$, (d) $P(C \cup D)$, and (e) $P(C \cap D)$.

1.2-4. A coin is tossed four times, and the sequence of heads and tails is observed.

(a) List each of the 16 sequences in the sample space S.

(b) Let events A, B, C, and D be given by $A = \{\text{at least 3 heads}\}$, $B = \{\text{at most 2 heads}\}$, $C = \{\text{heads on the third toss}\}$, and $D = \{\text{1 head and 3 tails}\}$. If the probability set function assigns 1/16 to each outcome in the sample space, find (i) $P(A)$, (ii) $P(A \cap B)$, (iii) $P(B)$,

(iv) $P(A \cap C)$, (v) $P(D)$, (vi) $P(A \cup C)$, and (vii) $P(B \cap D)$.

1.2-5. A field of beans is planted with three seeds per hill. For each hill of beans, let A_i be the event that i seeds germinate, $i = 0, 1, 2, 3$. Suppose that $P(A_0) = 1/64$, $P(A_1) = 9/64$, and $P(A_2) = 27/64$. Give the value of $P(A_3)$.

1.2-6. Consider the trial on which a 3 is first observed in successive rolls of a six-sided die. Let A be the event that 3 is observed on the first trial. Let B be the event that at least two trials are required to observe a 3. Assuming that each side has probability 1/6, find (a) $P(A)$, (b) $P(B)$, and (c) $P(A \cup B)$.

1.2-7. A fair eight-sided die is rolled once. Let $A = \{2, 4, 6, 8\}$, $B = \{3, 6\}$, $C = \{2, 5, 7\}$, and $D = \{1, 3, 5, 7\}$. Assume that each face has the same probability.

(a) Give the values of (i) $P(A)$, (ii) $P(B)$, (iii) $P(C)$, and (iv) $P(D)$.
(b) Give the values of (i) $P(A \cap B)$, (ii) $P(B \cap C)$, and (iii) $P(C \cap D)$.
(c) Give the values of (i) $P(A \cup B)$, (ii) $P(B \cup C)$, and (iii) $P(C \cup D)$, using Theorem 1.2-5.

1.2-8. If $P(A) = 0.4$, $P(B) = 0.5$, and $P(A \cap B) = 0.3$, find (a) $P(A \cup B)$, (b) $P(A \cap B')$, and (c) $P(A' \cup B')$.

1.2-9. Given that $P(A \cup B) = 0.76$ and $P(A \cup B') = 0.87$, find $P(A)$.

1.2-10. During a visit to a primary care physician's office, the probability of having neither lab work nor referral to a specialist is 0.21. Of those coming to that office, the probability of having lab work is 0.41 and the probability of having a referral is 0.53. What is the probability of having both lab work and a referral?

1.2-11. Roll a fair six-sided die three times. Let $A_1 = \{1 \text{ or } 2 \text{ on the first roll}\}$, $A_2 = \{3 \text{ or } 4 \text{ on the second roll}\}$, and $A_3 = \{5 \text{ or } 6 \text{ on the third roll}\}$. It is given that $P(A_i) = 1/3$, $i = 1, 2, 3$; $P(A_i \cap A_j) = (1/3)^2, i \neq j$; and $P(A_1 \cap A_2 \cap A_3) = (1/3)^3$.

(a) Use Theorem 1.2-6 to find $P(A_1 \cup A_2 \cup A_3)$.
(b) Show that $P(A_1 \cup A_2 \cup A_3) = 1 - (1 - 1/3)^3$.

1.2-12. Prove Theorem 1.2-6.

1.2-13. For each positive integer n, let $P(\{n\}) = (1/2)^n$. Consider the events $A = \{n : 1 \leq n \leq 10\}$, $B = \{n : 1 \leq n \leq 20\}$, and $C = \{n : 11 \leq n \leq 20\}$. Find (a) $P(A)$, (b) $P(B)$, (c) $P(A \cup B)$, (d) $P(A \cap B)$, (e) $P(C)$, and (f) $P(B')$.

1.2-14. Let x equal a number that is selected randomly from the closed interval from zero to one, $[0, 1]$. Use your intuition to assign values to

(a) $P(\{x : 0 \leq x \leq 1/3\})$.
(b) $P(\{x : 1/3 \leq x \leq 1\})$.
(c) $P(\{x : x = 1/3\})$.
(d) $P(\{x : 1/2 < x < 5\})$.

1.2-15. A typical roulette wheel used in a casino has 38 slots that are numbered $1, 2, 3, \ldots, 36, 0, 00$, respectively. The 0 and 00 slots are colored green. Half of the remaining slots are red and half are black. Also, half of the integers between 1 and 36 inclusive are odd, half are even, and 0 and 00 are defined to be neither odd nor even. A ball is rolled around the wheel and ends up in one of the slots; we assume that each slot has equal probability of 1/38, and we are interested in the number of the slot into which the ball falls.

(a) Define the sample space S.
(b) Let $A = \{0, 00\}$. Give the value of $P(A)$.
(c) Let $B = \{14, 15, 17, 18\}$. Give the value of $P(B)$.
(d) Let $D = \{x : x \text{ is odd}\}$. Give the value of $P(D)$.

1.2-16. The five numbers 1, 2, 3, 4, and 5 are written respectively on five disks of the same size and placed in a hat. Two disks are drawn without replacement from the hat, and the numbers written on them are observed.

(a) List the 10 possible outcomes of this experiment as unordered pairs of numbers.
(b) If each of the 10 outcomes has probability 1/10, assign a value to the probability that the sum of the two numbers drawn is (i) 3; (ii) between 6 and 8 inclusive.

1.2-17. Divide a line segment into two parts by selecting a point at random. Use your intuition to assign a probability to the event that the longer segment is at least two times longer than the shorter segment.

1.2-18. Let the interval $[-r, r]$ be the base of a semicircle. If a point is selected at random from this interval, assign a probability to the event that the length of the perpendicular segment from the point to the semicircle is less than $r/2$.

1.2-19. Let $S = A_1 \cup A_2 \cup \cdots \cup A_m$, where events $A_1, A_2, \ldots, A_m$ are mutually exclusive and exhaustive.

(a) If $P(A_1) = P(A_2) = \cdots = P(A_m)$, show that $P(A_i) = 1/m$, $i = 1, 2, \ldots, m$.

(b) If $A = A_1 \cup A_2 \cup \cdots \cup A_h$, where $h < m$, and (a) holds, prove that $P(A) = h/m$.

1.2-20. Let p_n, $n = 0, 1, 2, \ldots$, be the probability that an automobile policyholder will file for n claims in a five-year period. The actuary involved makes the assumption that $p_{n+1} = (1/4)p_n$. What is the probability that the holder will file two or more claims during this period?

1.3 METHODS OF ENUMERATION

In this section, we develop counting techniques that are useful in determining the number of outcomes associated with the events of certain random experiments. We begin with a consideration of the multiplication principle.

Multiplication Principle: Suppose that an experiment (or procedure) E_1 has n_1 outcomes and, for each of these possible outcomes, an experiment (procedure) E_2 has n_2 possible outcomes. Then the composite experiment (procedure) E_1E_2 that consists of performing first E_1 and then E_2 has n_1n_2 possible outcomes.

EXAMPLE 1.3-1 Let E_1 denote the selection of a rat from a cage containing one female (F) rat and one male (M) rat. Let E_2 denote the administering of either drug A (A), drug B (B), or a placebo (P) to the selected rat. Then the outcome for the composite experiment can be denoted by an ordered pair, such as (F, P). In fact, the set of all possible outcomes, namely, $(2)(3) = 6$ of them, can be denoted by the following rectangular array:

(F, A) (F, B) (F, P)
(M, A) (M, B) (M, P) ■

Another way of illustrating the multiplication principle is with a tree diagram like that in Figure 1.3-1. The diagram shows that there are $n_1 = 2$ possibilities (branches) for the sex of the rat and that, for each of these outcomes, there are $n_2 = 3$ possibilities (branches) for the drug.

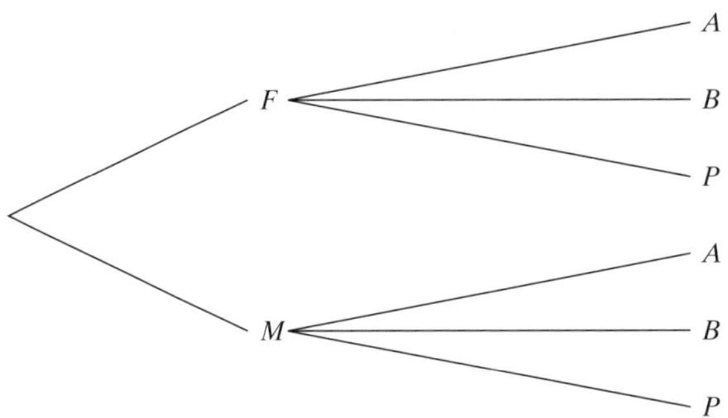

FIGURE 1.3-1: Tree diagram

Clearly, the multiplication principle can be extended to a sequence of more than two experiments or procedures. Suppose that the experiment E_i has n_i ($i = 1, 2, \ldots, m$) possible outcomes after previous experiments have been performed. Then the composite experiment $E_1E_2 \cdots E_m$ that consists of performing E_1, then $E_2, \ldots,$ and finally E_m has $n_1n_2 \cdots n_m$ possible outcomes.

EXAMPLE 1.3-2 A certain food service gives the following choices for dinner: E_1, soup or tomato juice; E_2, steak or shrimp; E_3, French fried potatoes, mashed potatoes, or a baked potato; E_4, corn or peas; E_5, jello, tossed salad, cottage cheese, or coleslaw; E_6, cake, cookies, pudding, brownie, vanilla ice cream, chocolate ice cream, or orange sherbet; E_7, coffee, tea, milk, or punch. How many different dinner selections are possible if one of the listed choices is made for each of $E_1, E_2, \ldots,$ and E_7? By the multiplication principle, there are

$$(2)(2)(3)(2)(4)(7)(4) = 2688$$

different combinations. ■

Although the multiplication principle is fairly simple and easy to understand, it will be extremely useful as we now develop various counting techniques.

Suppose that n positions are to be filled with n different objects. There are n choices for filling the first position, $n - 1$ for the second, ..., and 1 choice for the last position. So, by the multiplication principle, there are

$$n(n - 1)\cdots(2)(1) = n!$$

possible arrangements. The symbol $n!$ is read "n factorial." We define $0! = 1$; that is, we say that zero positions can be filled with zero objects in one way.

DEFINITION 1.3-1 Each of the $n!$ arrangements (in a row) of n different objects is called a **permutation** of the n objects.

EXAMPLE 1.3-3 The number of permutations of the four letters a, b, c, and d is clearly $4! = 24$. However, the number of possible four-letter code words using the four letters a, b, c, and d if letters may be repeated is $4^4 = 256$, because in this case each selection can be performed in four ways. ■

If only r positions are to be filled with objects selected from n different objects, $r \le n$, then the number of possible ordered arrangements is

$${}_nP_r = n(n - 1)(n - 2)\cdots(n - r + 1).$$

That is, there are n ways to fill the first position, $(n - 1)$ ways to fill the second, and so on, until there are $[n - (r - 1)] = (n - r + 1)$ ways to fill the rth position.

In terms of factorials, we have

$${}_nP_r = \frac{n(n - 1)\cdots(n - r + 1)(n - r)\cdots(3)(2)(1)}{(n - r)\cdots(3)(2)(1)} = \frac{n!}{(n - r)!}.$$

DEFINITION 1.3-2 Each of the ${}_nP_r$ arrangements is called a **permutation of n objects taken r at a time.**

EXAMPLE 1.3-4 The number of possible four-letter code words, selecting from the 26 letters in the alphabet, in which all four letters are different is

$${}_{26}P_4 = (26)(25)(24)(23) = \frac{26!}{22!} = 358{,}800.$$ ■

EXAMPLE 1.3-5 The number of ways of selecting a president, a vice president, a secretary, and a treasurer in a club consisting of 10 persons is

$$_{10}P_4 = 10 \cdot 9 \cdot 8 \cdot 7 = \frac{10!}{6!} = 5040. \qquad \blacksquare$$

Suppose that a set contains n objects. Consider the problem of drawing r objects from this set. The order in which the objects are drawn may or may not be important. In addition, it is possible that a drawn object is replaced before the next object is drawn. Accordingly, we give some definitions and show how the multiplication principle can be used to count the number of possibilities.

DEFINITION 1.3-3 If r objects are selected from a set of n objects, and if the order of selection is noted, then the selected set of r objects is called an **ordered sample of size r**.

DEFINITION 1.3-4 **Sampling with replacement** occurs when an object is selected and then replaced before the next object is selected.

By the multiplication principle, the number of possible ordered samples of size r taken from a set of n objects is n^r when sampling with replacement.

EXAMPLE 1.3-6 A die is rolled five times. The number of possible ordered samples is $6^5 = 7776$. Note that rolling a die is equivalent to sampling with replacement. ■

EXAMPLE 1.3-7 An urn contains 10 balls numbered $0, 1, 2, \ldots, 9$. If 4 balls are selected one at a time and with replacement, then the number of possible ordered samples is $10^4 = 10{,}000$. Note that this is the number of four-digit integers between 0000 and 9999, inclusive. ■

DEFINITION 1.3-5 **Sampling without replacement** occurs when an object is not replaced after it has been selected.

By the multiplication principle, the number of possible ordered samples of size r taken from a set of n objects without replacement is

$$n(n-1)\cdots(n-r+1) = \frac{n!}{(n-r)!},$$

which is equivalent to $_nP_r$, the number of permutations of n objects taken r at a time.

EXAMPLE 1.3-8 The number of ordered samples of 5 cards that can be drawn without replacement from a standard deck of 52 playing cards is

$$(52)(51)(50)(49)(48) = \frac{52!}{47!} = 311{,}875{,}200. \qquad \blacksquare$$

Often the order of selection is not important, and interest centers only on the selected set of r objects. That is, we are interested in the number of subsets of size r that can be selected from a set of n different objects. In order to find the number of (unordered) subsets of size r, we count, in two different ways, the number of ordered subsets of size r that can be taken from the n distinguishable objects. Then, by equating the two answers, we are able to count the number of (unordered) subsets of size r.

Let C denote the number of (unordered) subsets of size r that can be selected from n different objects. We can obtain each of the ${}_nP_r$ ordered subsets by first selecting one of the C unordered subsets of r objects and then ordering these r objects. Since the latter ordering can be carried out in $r!$ ways, the multiplication principle yields $(C)(r!)$ ordered subsets; so $(C)(r!)$ must equal ${}_nP_r$. Thus, we have

$$(C)(r!) = \frac{n!}{(n-r)!},$$

or

$$C = \frac{n!}{r!\,(n-r)!}.$$

We denote this answer by either ${}_nC_r$ or $\binom{n}{r}$; that is,

$${}_nC_r = \binom{n}{r} = \frac{n!}{r!\,(n-r)!}.$$

Accordingly, a set of n different objects possesses

$$\binom{n}{r} = \frac{n!}{r!\,(n-r)!}$$

unordered subsets of size $r \le n$.

We could also say that the number of ways in which r objects can be selected without replacement from n objects when the order of selection is disregarded is $\binom{n}{r} = {}_nC_r$, and the latter expression can be read as "n choose r." This result motivates the next definition.

DEFINITION 1.3-6

Each of the ${}_nC_r$ unordered subsets is called a **combination of n objects taken r at a time**, where

$${}_nC_r = \binom{n}{r} = \frac{n!}{r!\,(n-r)!}.$$

EXAMPLE 1.3-9

The number of possible 5-card hands (in 5-card poker) drawn from a deck of 52 playing cards is

$${}_{52}C_5 = \binom{52}{5} = \frac{52!}{5!\,47!} = 2{,}598{,}960.$$

■

EXAMPLE 1.3-10 The number of possible 13-card hands (in bridge) that can be selected from a deck of 52 playing cards is

$$_{52}C_{13} = \binom{52}{13} = \frac{52!}{13!\,39!} = 635{,}013{,}559{,}600. \quad \blacksquare$$

The numbers $\binom{n}{r}$ are frequently called **binomial coefficients**, since they arise in the expansion of a binomial. We illustrate this property by giving a justification of the binomial expansion

$$(a + b)^n = \sum_{r=0}^{n} \binom{n}{r} b^r a^{n-r}. \tag{1.3-1}$$

In the expansion of

$$(a + b)^n = (a + b)(a + b)\cdots(a + b),$$

either an a or a b is selected from each of the n factors. One possible product is then $b^r a^{n-r}$; this occurs when b is selected from each of r factors and a from each of the remaining $n - r$ factors. But the latter operation can be completed in $\binom{n}{r}$ ways, which then must be the coefficient of $b^r a^{n-r}$, as shown in Equation 1.3-1.

The binomial coefficients are given in Table I in the appendix for selected values of n and r. Note that for some combinations of n and r, the table uses the fact that

$$\binom{n}{r} = \frac{n!}{r!\,(n - r)!} = \frac{n!}{(n - r)!\,r!} = \binom{n}{n - r}.$$

That is, the number of ways in which r objects can be selected out of n objects is equal to the number of ways in which $n - r$ objects can be selected out of n objects.

EXAMPLE 1.3-11 Assume that each of the $\binom{52}{5} = 2{,}598{,}960$ five-card hands drawn from a deck of 52 playing cards has the same probability of being selected. Then the number of possible 5-card hands that are all spades (event A) is

$$N(A) = \binom{13}{5}\binom{39}{0},$$

because the 5 spades can be selected from the 13 spades in $\binom{13}{5}$ ways, after which zero nonspades can be selected in $\binom{39}{0} = 1$ way. We have

$$\binom{13}{5} = \frac{13!}{5!8!} = 1287$$

from Table I in the appendix. Thus, the probability of an all-spade 5-card hand is

$$P(A) = \frac{N(A)}{N(S)} = \frac{1287}{2{,}598{,}960} = 0.000495.$$

Suppose now that the event B is the set of outcomes in which exactly 3 cards are kings and exactly 2 cards are queens. We can select the three kings in any one of $\binom{4}{3}$ ways and the two queens in any one of $\binom{4}{2}$ ways. By the multiplication principle, the number of outcomes in B is

$$N(B) = \binom{4}{3}\binom{4}{2}\binom{44}{0},$$

where $\binom{44}{0}$ gives the number of ways in which 0 cards are selected out of the nonkings and nonqueens and of course is equal to 1. Thus,

$$P(B) = \frac{N(B)}{N(S)} = \frac{\binom{4}{3}\binom{4}{2}\binom{44}{0}}{\binom{52}{5}} = \frac{24}{2{,}598{,}960} = 0.0000092.$$

Finally, let C be the set of outcomes in which there are exactly two kings, two queens, and one jack. Then

$$P(C) = \frac{N(C)}{N(S)} = \frac{\binom{4}{2}\binom{4}{2}\binom{4}{1}\binom{40}{0}}{\binom{52}{5}} = \frac{144}{2{,}598{,}960} = 0.000055$$

because the numerator of this fraction is the number of outcomes in C. ■

Now suppose that a set contains n objects of two types: r of one type and $n - r$ of the other type. The number of permutations of n different objects is $n!$. However, in this case, the objects are not all distinguishable. To count the number of distinguishable arrangements, first select r out of the n positions for the objects of the first type. This can be done in $\binom{n}{r}$ ways. Then fill in the remaining positions with the objects of the second type. Thus, the number of distinguishable arrangements is

$${}_nC_r = \binom{n}{r} = \frac{n!}{r!\,(n-r)!}.$$

DEFINITION 1.3-7 Each of the ${}_nC_r$ permutations of n objects, r of one type and $n - r$ of another type, is called a **distinguishable permutation**.

EXAMPLE 1.3-12 A coin is flipped 10 times and the sequence of heads and tails is observed. The number of possible 10-tuplets that result in four heads and six tails is

$$\binom{10}{4} = \frac{10!}{4!\,6!} = \frac{10!}{6!\,4!} = \binom{10}{6} = 210.$$

■

EXAMPLE 1.3-13 In an orchid show, seven orchids are to be placed along one side of the greenhouse. There are four lavender orchids and three white orchids. Considering only the color of the orchids, we see that the number of lineups of the orchids is

$$\binom{7}{4} = \frac{7!}{4!\,3!} = 35.$$

If the colors of the seven orchids are white, lavender, yellow, mauve, crimson, orange, and pink, the number of different displays is $7! = 5040$. ■

The foregoing results can be extended. Suppose that in a set of n objects, n_1 are similar, n_2 are similar, ..., n_s are similar, where $n_1 + n_2 + \cdots + n_s = n$. Then the number of distinguishable permutations of the n objects is (see Exercise 1.3-18)

$$\binom{n}{n_1, n_2, \ldots, n_s} = \frac{n!}{n_1!\,n_2!\,\cdots\,n_s!}. \tag{1.3-2}$$

EXAMPLE 1.3-14 Among nine orchids for a line of orchids along one wall, three are white, four lavender, and two yellow. The number of different color displays is then

$$\binom{9}{3, 4, 2} = \frac{9!}{3!\,4!\,2!} = 1260.$$ ■

The argument used in determining the binomial coefficients in the expansion of $(a + b)^n$ can be extended to find the expansion of $(a_1 + a_2 + \cdots + a_s)^n$. The coefficient of ${a_1}^{n_1}{a_2}^{n_2}\cdots{a_s}^{n_s}$ is

$$\binom{n}{n_1, n_2, \ldots, n_s} = \frac{n!}{n_1!\,n_2!\,\cdots\,n_s!}.$$

This is sometimes called a **multinomial coefficient**.

When r objects are selected out of n objects, we are often interested in the number of possible outcomes. We have seen that for ordered samples, there are n^r possible outcomes when sampling with replacement and ${}_nP_r$ outcomes when sampling without replacement. For unordered samples, there are ${}_nC_r$ outcomes when sampling without replacement. Each of the preceding outcomes is equally likely, provided that the experiment is performed in a fair manner.

REMARK Although not needed in the study of probability, it is interesting to count the number of possible samples of size r that can be selected out of n objects when the order is irrelevant and when sampling with replacement. For example, if a six-sided die is rolled 10 times (or 10 six-sided dice are rolled once), how many possible unordered outcomes are there? To count the number of possible outcomes, think of listing r 0's for the r objects that are to be selected. Then insert $(n - 1)$ |'s to partition the r objects into n sets, the first set giving objects of the first kind, and so on. So if $n = 6$ and $r = 10$ in the die illustration, a possible outcome is

$$0\,0\,|\,|\,0\,0\,0\,|\,0\,|\,0\,0\,0\,|\,0,$$

which says there are two 1's, zero 2's, three 3's, one 4, three 5's, and one 6. In general, each outcome is a permutation of r 0's and $(n - 1)$ |'s. Each distinguishable permutation is equivalent to an unordered sample. The number of distinguishable permutations, and hence the number of unordered samples of size r that can be selected out of n objects when sampling with replacement, is

$$_{n-1+r}C_r = \frac{(n - 1 + r)!}{r!\,(n - 1)!}.$$

■

EXERCISES

1.3-1. A boy found a bicycle lock for which the combination was unknown. The correct combination is a four-digit number, $d_1d_2d_3d_4$, where d_i, $i = 1, 2, 3, 4$, is selected from 1, 2, 3, 4, 5, 6, 7, and 8. How many different lock combinations are possible with such a lock?

1.3-2. How many different orchid displays in a line are possible using four orchids of different colors if exactly three orchids are used?

1.3-3. How many different license plates are possible if a state uses

(a) Two letters followed by a four-digit integer (leading zeros are permissible and the letters and digits can be repeated)?
(b) Three letters followed by a three-digit integer? (In practice, it is possible that certain "spellings" are ruled out.)

1.3-4. In designing an experiment, the researcher can often choose many different levels of the various factors in order to try to find the best combination at which to operate. As an illustration, suppose the researcher is studying a certain chemical reaction and can choose four levels of temperature, five different pressures, and two different catalysts.

(a) To consider all possible combinations, how many experiments would need to be conducted?
(b) Often in preliminary experimentation, each factor is restricted to two levels. With the three factors noted, how many experiments would need to be run to cover all possible combinations with each of the three factors at two levels? (NOTE: This is often called a 2^3 design.)

1.3-5. How many four-letter code words are possible using the letters in HOPE if

(a) The letters may not be repeated?
(b) The letters may be repeated?

1.3-6. The "eating club" is hosting a make-your-own sundae at which the following are provided:

Ice Cream Flavors	Toppings
Chocolate	Caramel
Cookies-n-cream	Hot fudge
Strawberry	Marshmallow
Vanilla	M&M's
	Nuts
	Strawberries

(a) How many sundaes are possible using one flavor of ice cream and three different toppings?
(b) How many sundaes are possible using one flavor of ice cream and from zero to six toppings?
(c) How many different combinations of flavors of three scoops of ice cream are possible if it is permissible to make all three scoops the same flavor?

1.3-7. In a state lottery, four digits are drawn at random one at a time with replacement from 0 to 9. Suppose that you win if any permutation of your selected integers is drawn. Give the probability of winning if you select

(a) 6, 7, 8, 9.
(b) 6, 7, 8, 8.
(c) 7, 7, 8, 8.
(d) 7, 8, 8, 8.

1.3-8. From a collection of nine paintings, four are to be selected to hang side by side on a gallery wall in positions 1, 2, 3, and 4. In how many ways can this be done?

1.3-9. Some albatrosses return to the world's only mainland colony of royal albatrosses, on Otago Peninsula near Dunedin, New Zealand, every two years to nest and raise their young. In order to learn more about the albatross, colored plastic bands are placed on their legs so that they can be identified from a distance. Suppose that three bands are placed on one leg, with the color of the band selected from the colors red, yellow, green, white, and blue. Find the number of different color codes that are possible for banding an albatross if

(a) The three bands are of different colors.
(b) Repeated colors are permissible.

1.3-10. Hope and Calvin play volleyball until one team wins three games. Using **H** for a Hope victory and **C** for a Calvin victory, and considering the possible orderings for the winning team, in how many ways could the volleyball match end?

1.3-11. The World Series in baseball continues until either the American League team or the National League team wins four games. How many different orders are possible (e.g., *ANNAAA* means the American League team wins in six games) if the series goes

(a) Four games?
(b) Five games?
(c) Six games?
(d) Seven games?

1.3-12. How many different varieties of pizza can be made if you have the following choices: small, medium, or large size; thin 'n crispy, hand-tossed, or pan crust; and 12 toppings (cheese is automatic), from which you may select from 0 to 12?

1.3-13. A cafe lets you order a deli sandwich your way. There are six choices for bread, four choices for meat, four choices for cheese, and 12 different garnishes (condiments). How many different sandwich possibilities are there if you choose

(a) One bread, one meat, and one cheese?
(b) One bread, one meat, one cheese, and from 0 to 12 garnishes?
(c) One bread; 0, 1, or 2 meats; 0, 1, or 2 cheeses; and from 0 to 12 garnishes?

1.3-14. Pascal's triangle gives a method for calculating the binomial coefficients; it begins as follows:

```
              1
           1     1
        1     2     1
     1     3     3     1
  1     4     6     4     1
1    5    10    10     5    1
.    .     .     .     .    .
.    .     .     .     .    .
.    .     .     .     .    .
```

The nth row of this triangle gives the coefficients for $(a + b)^{n-1}$. To find an entry in the table other than a 1 on the boundary, add the two nearest numbers in the row directly above. The equation

$$\binom{n}{r} = \binom{n-1}{r} + \binom{n-1}{r-1},$$

called **Pascal's equation**, explains why Pascal's triangle works. Prove that this equation is correct.

1.3-15. Three students (S) and six faculty members (F) are on a panel discussing a new college policy.

(a) In how many different ways can the nine participants be lined up at a table in the front of the auditorium?
(b) How many lineups are possible, considering only the labels S and F?
(c) For each of the nine participants, you are to decide whether the participant did a good job or a poor job stating his or her opinion of the new policy; that is, give each of the nine participants a grade of G or P. How many different "scorecards" are possible?

1.3-16. Prove:

$$\sum_{r=0}^{n}(-1)^r\binom{n}{r} = 0 \qquad \text{and} \qquad \sum_{r=0}^{n}\binom{n}{r} = 2^n.$$

HINT: Consider $(1 - 1)^n$ and $(1 + 1)^n$, or use Pascal's equation and proof by induction.

1.3-17. A poker hand is defined as drawing 5 cards at random without replacement from a deck of 52 playing cards. Find the probability of each of the following poker hands:

(a) Four of a kind (4 cards of equal face value and 1 card of a different value).
(b) Full house (one pair and one triple of cards with equal face value).
(c) Three of a kind (three equal face values plus 2 cards of different values).
(d) Two pairs (two pairs of equal face value plus 1 card of a different value).
(e) One pair (one pair of equal face value plus 3 cards of different values).

1.3-18. Prove Equation 1.3-2. HINT: First select n_1 positions in $\binom{n}{n_1}$ ways. Then select n_2 from the remaining $n - n_1$ positions in $\binom{n-n_1}{n_2}$ ways, and so on. Finally, use the multiplication rule.

1.3-19. There are three teams in a cross-country race. Team A has five runners, team B has six runners, and team C has seven runners. In how many ways can the runners cross the finish line if we are interested only in the team for which they run? That is, what is the number of distinguishable permutations of five A's, six B's, and seven C's? (Note that, for scoring purposes, only the scores of the first five runners for each team count.)

1.3-20. A box of candy hearts contains 52 hearts, of which 19 are white, 10 are tan, 7 are pink, 3 are purple, 5 are yellow, 2 are orange, and 6 are green. If you select 9 pieces of candy randomly from the box, without replacement, give the probability that

(a) Three of the hearts are white.

(b) Three are white, 2 are tan, 1 is pink, 1 is yellow, and 2 are green.

1.3-21. An office furniture manufacturer that makes modular storage files offers its customers two choices for the base and four choices for the top, and the modular storage files come in five different heights. The customer may choose any combination of the five different-sized modules so that the finished file has a base, a top, and one, two, three, four, five, or six storage modules.

(a) How many choices does the customer have if the completed file has four storage modules, a top, and a base? The order in which the four modules are stacked is irrelevant.

(b) In its advertising, the manufacturer would like to use the number of different files that are possible—selecting one of the two bases, one of the four tops, and then either one, two, three, four, five, or six storage modules. The manufacturer may select any combination of the five different sizes, with the order of stacking irrelevant. What is the number of possibilities?

1.3-22. A bag of 36 dum-dum pops (suckers) contains up to 10 flavors. That is, there are from 0 to 36 suckers of each of 10 flavors in the bag. How many different flavor combinations are possible?

1.4 CONDITIONAL PROBABILITY

We introduce the idea of conditional probability by means of an example.

EXAMPLE 1.4-1 Suppose that we are given 20 tulip bulbs that are similar in appearance and told that 8 will bloom early, 12 will bloom late, 13 will be red, and 7 will be yellow, in accordance with the various combinations listed in Table 1.4-1. If one bulb is selected at random, the probability that it will produce a red tulip (R) is given by $P(R) = 13/20$, under the assumption that each bulb is "equally likely." Suppose, however, that close examination of the bulb will reveal whether it will bloom early (E) or late (L). If we consider an outcome only if it results in a tulip bulb that will bloom early, only eight outcomes in the sample space are now of interest. Thus, under this limitation, it is natural to assign the probability 5/8 to R; that is, $P(R \mid E) = 5/8$, where $P(R \mid E)$ is read as the probability of R given that E has occurred. Note that

$$P(R \mid E) = \frac{5}{8} = \frac{N(R \cap E)}{N(E)} = \frac{N(R \cap E)/20}{N(E)/20} = \frac{P(R \cap E)}{P(E)},$$

where $N(R \cap E)$ and $N(E)$ are the numbers of outcomes in events $R \cap E$ and E, respectively. ■

TABLE 1.4-1: Tulip Combinations

	Early (E)	Late (L)	Totals
Red (R)	5	8	13
Yellow(Y)	3	4	7
Totals	8	12	20

This example illustrates a number of common situations. That is, in some random experiments, we are interested only in those outcomes which are elements of a subset B of the sample space S. This means, for our purposes, that the sample space is effectively the subset B. We are now confronted with the problem of defining a probability set function with B as the "new" sample space. That is, for a given event A, we want to define $P(A \mid B)$, the probability of A, considering only those outcomes of the random experiment that are elements of B. The previous example gives us the clue to that definition. That is, for experiments in which each outcome is equally likely, it makes sense to define $P(A \mid B)$ by

$$P(A \mid B) = \frac{N(A \cap B)}{N(B)},$$

where $N(A \cap B)$ and $N(B)$ are the numbers of outcomes in $A \cap B$ and B, respectively. If we then divide the numerator and the denominator of this fraction by $N(S)$, the number of outcomes in the sample space, we have

$$P(A \mid B) = \frac{N(A \cap B)/N(S)}{N(B)/N(S)} = \frac{P(A \cap B)}{P(B)}.$$

We are thus led to the following definition.

DEFINITION 1.4-1

The **conditional probability** of an event A, given that event B has occurred, is defined by

$$P(A \mid B) = \frac{P(A \cap B)}{P(B)},$$

provided that $P(B) > 0$.

A formal use of the definition is given in the next example.

EXAMPLE 1.4-2 If $P(A) = 0.4$, $P(B) = 0.5$, and $P(A \cap B) = 0.3$, then $P(A \mid B) = 0.3/0.5 = 0.6$; $P(B \mid A) = P(A \cap B)/P(A) = 0.3/0.4 = 0.75$. ■

We can think of "given B" as specifying the new sample space for which, to determine $P(A \mid B)$, we now want to calculate the probability of that part of A which is contained in B. The next two examples illustrate this idea.

EXAMPLE 1.4-3 Suppose that $P(A) = 0.7$, $P(B) = 0.3$, and $P(A \cap B) = 0.2$. These probabilities are listed on the Venn diagram in Figure 1.4-1. Given that the outcome of the experiment belongs to B, what then is the probability of A? We are effectively restricting the sample space to B; of the probability $P(B) = 0.3$, 0.2 corresponds to $P(A \cap B)$ and hence to A. That is, 0.2/0.3 = 2/3 of the probability of B corresponds to A. Of course, by the formal definition, we also obtain

$$P(A \mid B) = \frac{P(A \cap B)}{P(B)} = \frac{0.2}{0.3} = \frac{2}{3}.$$ ■

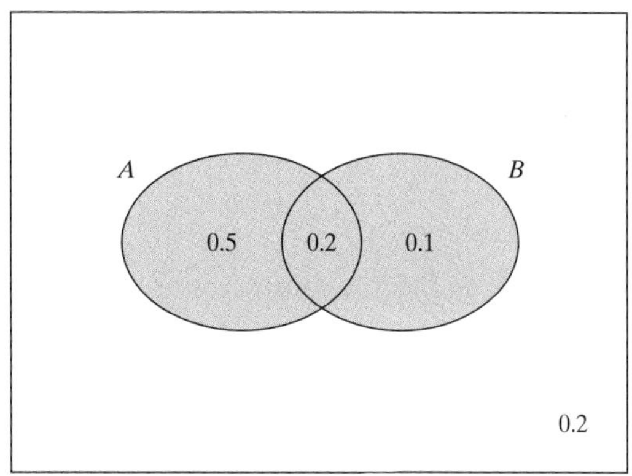

FIGURE 1.4-1: Conditional probability

EXAMPLE 1.4-4 A pair of four-sided dice is rolled and the sum is determined. Let A be the event that a sum of 3 is rolled, and let B be the event that a sum of 3 or a sum of 5 is rolled. In a sequence of rolls, the probability that a sum of 3 is rolled before a sum of 5 is rolled can be thought of as the conditional probability of a sum of 3 given that a sum of 3 or 5 has occurred; that is, the conditional probability of A given B is

$$P(A \mid B) = \frac{P(A \cap B)}{P(B)} = \frac{P(A)}{P(B)} = \frac{2/16}{6/16} = \frac{2}{6}.$$

Note that for this example, the only outcomes of interest are those having a sum of 3 or a sum of 5, and of these six equally likely outcomes, two have a sum of 3. (See Figure 1.4-2 and Exercise 1.4-13.) ■

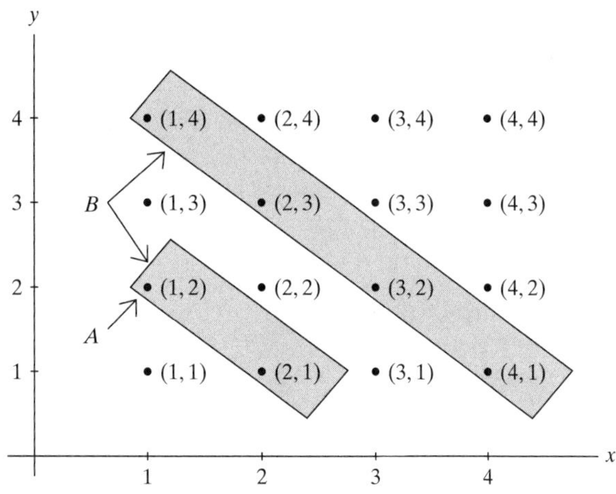

FIGURE 1.4-2: Dice example

It is interesting to note that conditional probability satisfies the axioms for a probability function, namely, with $P(B) > 0$,

(a) $P(A \mid B) \geq 0$.

(b) $P(B \mid B) = 1$.

(c) If $A_1, A_2, A_3, \ldots$ are mutually exclusive events, then

$$P(A_1 \cup A_2 \cup \cdots \cup A_k \mid B) = P(A_1 \mid B) + P(A_2 \mid B) + \cdots + P(A_k \mid B),$$

for each positive integer k, and

$$P(A_1 \cup A_2 \cup \cdots \mid B) = P(A_1 \mid B) + P(A_2 \mid B) + \cdots,$$

for an infinite, but countable, number of events.

Properties (a) and (b) are evident because

$$P(A \mid B) = \frac{P(A \cap B)}{P(B)} \geq 0,$$

since $P(A \cap B) \geq 0$, $P(B) > 0$, and

$$P(B \mid B) = \frac{P(B \cap B)}{P(B)} = \frac{P(B)}{P(B)} = 1.$$

Property (c) holds because, for the second part of (c),

$$\begin{aligned} P(A_1 \cup A_2 \cup \cdots \mid B) &= \frac{P[(A_1 \cup A_2 \cup \cdots) \cap B]}{P(B)} \\ &= \frac{P[(A_1 \cap B) \cup (A_2 \cap B) \cup \cdots]}{P(B)}. \end{aligned}$$

But $(A_1 \cap B), (A_2 \cap B), \ldots$ are also mutually exclusive events; so

$$\begin{aligned} P(A_1 \cup A_2 \cup \cdots \mid B) &= \frac{P(A_1 \cap B) + P(A_2 \cap B) + \cdots}{P(B)} \\ &= \frac{P(A_1 \cap B)}{P(B)} + \frac{P(A_2 \cap B)}{P(B)} + \cdots \\ &= P(A_1 \mid B) + P(A_2 \mid B) + \cdots. \end{aligned}$$

The first part of property (c) is proved in a similar manner.

Many times, the conditional probability of an event is clear because of the nature of an experiment. The next example illustrates this.

EXAMPLE 1.4-5 At a county fair carnival game there are 25 balloons on a board, of which 10 balloons are yellow, 8 are red, and 7 are green. A player throws darts at the balloons to win a prize and randomly hits one of them. Given that the first balloon hit is yellow, what is the probability that the next balloon hit is also yellow? Of the 24 remaining balloons, 9 are yellow, so a natural value to assign to this conditional probability is 9/24. ■

In Example 1.4-5, let A be the event that the first balloon hit is yellow, and let B be the event that the second balloon hit is yellow. Suppose that we are interested in the probability that both balloons hit are yellow. That is, we are interested in finding $P(A \cap B)$. We noted in that example that

$$P(B \mid A) = \frac{P(A \cap B)}{P(A)} = \frac{9}{24}.$$

Thus, multiplying through by $P(A)$, we have

$$P(A \cap B) = P(A)P(B \mid A) = P(A)\left(\frac{9}{24}\right), \tag{1.4-1}$$

or

$$P(A \cap B) = \left(\frac{10}{25}\right)\left(\frac{9}{24}\right).$$

That is, Equation 1.4-1 gives us a general rule for the probability of the intersection of two events once we know the conditional probability $P(B \mid A)$.

DEFINITION 1.4-2

The probability that two events, A and B, both occur is given by the **multiplication rule**,

$$P(A \cap B) = P(A)P(B \mid A)$$

or by

$$P(A \cap B) = P(B)P(A \mid B).$$

Sometimes, after considering the nature of the random experiment, one can make reasonable assumptions so that it is easier to assign $P(B)$ and $P(A \mid B)$ rather than $P(A \cap B)$. Then $P(A \cap B)$ can be computed with these assignments. This approach will be illustrated in Examples 1.4-6 and 1.4-7.

EXAMPLE 1.4-6

A bowl contains seven blue chips and three red chips. Two chips are to be drawn successively at random and without replacement. We want to compute the probability that the first draw results in a red chip (A) and the second draw results in a blue chip (B). It is reasonable to assign the following probabilities:

$$P(A) = \frac{3}{10} \text{ and } P(B \mid A) = \frac{7}{9}.$$

The probability of obtaining red on the first draw and blue on the second draw is

$$P(A \cap B) = \frac{3}{10} \cdot \frac{7}{9} = \frac{7}{30}.$$

■

Note that in many instances it is possible to compute a probability by two seemingly different methods. For instance, consider Example 1.4-6, but find the probability of drawing a red chip on each of the two draws. Following that example, it is

$$\frac{3}{10} \cdot \frac{2}{9} = \frac{1}{15}.$$

However, we can also find this probability by using combinations as follows:

$$\frac{\binom{3}{2}\binom{7}{0}}{\binom{10}{2}} = \frac{\dfrac{(3)(2)}{(1)(2)}}{\dfrac{(10)(9)}{(1)(2)}} = \frac{1}{15}.$$

Thus, we obtain the same answer, as we should, provided that our reasoning is consistent with the underlying assumptions.

EXAMPLE 1.4-7 From an ordinary deck of playing cards, cards are to be drawn successively at random and without replacement. The probability that the third spade appears on the sixth draw is computed as follows: Let A be the event of two spades in the first five cards drawn, and let B be the event of a spade on the sixth draw. Thus, the probability that we wish to compute is $P(A \cap B)$. It is reasonable to take

$$P(A) = \frac{\dbinom{13}{2}\dbinom{39}{3}}{\dbinom{52}{5}} = 0.274 \qquad \text{and} \qquad P(B\,|\,A) = \frac{11}{47} = 0.234.$$

The desired probability, $P(A \cap B)$, is the product of those numbers:

$$P(A \cap B) = (0.274)(0.234) = 0.064.$$ ■

EXAMPLE 1.4-8 Continuing with Example 1.4-4, in which a pair of four-sided dice is rolled, the probability of rolling a sum of 3 on the first roll and then, continuing the sequence of rolls, rolling a sum of 3 before rolling a sum of 5 is

$$\frac{2}{16} \cdot \frac{2}{6} = \frac{4}{96} = \frac{1}{24}.$$ ■

The multiplication rule can be extended to three or more events. In the case of three events, using the multiplication rule for two events, we have

$$\begin{aligned} P(A \cap B \cap C) &= P[(A \cap B) \cap C] \\ &= P(A \cap B)P(C\,|\,A \cap B). \end{aligned}$$

But

$$P(A \cap B) = P(A)P(B\,|\,A).$$

Hence,

$$P(A \cap B \cap C) = P(A)P(B\,|\,A)P(C\,|\,A \cap B).$$

This type of argument can be used to extend the multiplication rule to more than three events, and the general formula for k events can be officially proved by mathematical induction.

EXAMPLE 1.4-9 Four cards are to be dealt successively at random and without replacement from an ordinary deck of playing cards. The probability of receiving, in order, a spade, a heart, a diamond, and a club is

$$\frac{13}{52} \cdot \frac{13}{51} \cdot \frac{13}{50} \cdot \frac{13}{49},$$

a result that follows from the extension of the multiplication rule and reasonable assignments to the probabilities involved. ■

We close this section with a different type of example.

EXAMPLE 1.4-10 A grade school boy has five blue and four white marbles in his left pocket and four blue and five white marbles in his right pocket. If he transfers one marble at random from his left to his right pocket, what is the probability of his then drawing a blue marble from his right pocket? For notation, let BL, BR, and WL denote drawing blue from left pocket, blue from right pocket, and white from left pocket, respectively. Then

$$\begin{aligned} P(BR) &= P(BL \cap BR) + P(WL \cap BR) \\ &= P(BL)P(BR \mid BL) + P(WL)P(BR \mid WL) \\ &= \frac{5}{9} \cdot \frac{5}{10} + \frac{4}{9} \cdot \frac{4}{10} = \frac{41}{90} \end{aligned}$$

is the desired probability. ■

EXAMPLE 1.4-11 An insurance company sells a number of different policies, among which 60% are for autos, 40% are for homeowners, and 20% are for both types of policy. Let A_1 be people with only an auto policy, A_2 people with only a homeowner policy, A_3 people with both types of policy, and A_4 those with only other types of policies. If a person is selected at random from the policyholders, then $P(A_1) = 0.4$, $P(A_2) = 0.2$, $P(A_3) = 0.2$, and $P(A_4) = 0.2$, as these four events are mutually exclusive and exhaustive. Further, let B be the event that a policyholder will renew at least one of the auto or homeowner policies. Say from past experience that we can assign the conditional probabilities $P(B \mid A_1) = 0.6$, $P(B \mid A_2) = 0.7$, and $P(B \mid A_3) = 0.8$. Given that the person selected at random has an auto or homeowner policy, what is the conditional probability that the person will renew at least one of those policies? The desired probability is

$$\begin{aligned} P(B \mid A_1 \cup A_2 \cup A_3) &= \frac{P(A_1 \cap B) + P(A_2 \cap B) + P(A_3 \cap B)}{P(A_1) + P(A_2) + P(A_3)} \\ &= \frac{(0.4)(0.6) + (0.2)(0.7) + (0.2)(0.8)}{0.4 + 0.2 + 0.2} \\ &= \frac{0.54}{0.80} = \frac{27}{40} \\ &= 0.675. \end{aligned}$$

■

EXAMPLE 1.4-12 A device has two components, C_1 and C_2, but it will continue to operate with only one active component for a one-year period. The probability that each component will fail when both are in operation is 0.01 in that one-year period. However, when one component fails, the probability of the other failing is 0.03 in that period, due to added strain. Thus, the probability that the device fails in one year is

$$\begin{aligned} &P(C_1 \text{ fails})P(C_2 \text{ fails} \mid C_1 \text{ fails}) + P(C_2 \text{ fails})P(C_1 \text{ fails} \mid C_2 \text{ fails}) = \\ &\qquad (0.01)(0.03) + (0.01)(0.03) = 0.0006. \end{aligned}$$

■

EXERCISES

1.4-1. A common test for AIDS is called the ELISA (enzyme-linked immunosorbent assay) test. Among 1 million people who are given the ELISA test, we can expect results similar to those given in the following table:

	B_1: Carry AIDS Virus	B_2: Do Not Carry AIDS Virus	Totals
A_1: Test Positive	4,885	73,630	78,515
A_2: Test Negative	115	921,370	921,485
Totals	5,000	995,000	1,000,000

If one of these 1 million people is selected randomly, find the following probabilities: (a) $P(B_1)$, (b) $P(A_1)$, (c) $P(A_1 \mid B_2)$, (d) $P(B_1 \mid A_1)$. (e) In words, what do parts (c) and (d) say?

1.4-2. The following table classifies 1456 people by their gender and by whether or not they favor a gun law.

	Male (S_1)	Female (S_2)	Totals
Favor (A_1)	392	649	1041
Oppose (A_2)	241	174	415
Totals	633	823	1456

Compute the following probabilities if one of these 1456 persons is selected randomly: (a) $P(A_1)$, (b) $P(A_1 \mid S_1)$, (c) $P(A_1 \mid S_2)$. (d) Interpret your answers to parts (b) and (c).

1.4-3. Let A_1 and A_2 be the events that a person is left-eye dominant or right-eye dominant, respectively. When a person folds his or her hands, let B_1 and B_2 be the events that the left thumb and right thumb, respectively, are on top. A survey in one statistics class yielded the following table:

	B_1	B_2	Totals
A_1	5	7	12
A_2	14	9	23
Totals	19	16	35

If a student is selected randomly, find the following probabilities: (a) $P(A_1 \cap B_1)$, (b) $P(A_1 \cup B_1)$, (c) $P(A_1 \mid B_1)$, (d) $P(B_2 \mid A_2)$. (e) If the students had their hands folded and you hoped to select a right-eye-dominant student, would you select a "right thumb on top" or a "left thumb on top" student? Why?

1.4-4. Two cards are drawn successively and without replacement from an ordinary deck of playing cards. Compute the probability of drawing

(a) Two hearts.
(b) A heart on the first draw and a club on the second draw.
(c) A heart on the first draw and an ace on the second draw.

HINT: In part (c), note that a heart can be drawn by getting the ace of hearts or one of the other 12 hearts.

1.4-5. Suppose that $P(A) = 0.7$, $P(B) = 0.5$, and $P([A \cup B]') = 0.1$.

(a) Find $P(A \cap B)$.
(b) Calculate $P(A \mid B)$.
(c) Calculate $P(B \mid A)$.

1.4-6. A hand of 13 cards is to be dealt at random and without replacement from an ordinary deck of playing cards. Find the conditional probability that there are at least three kings in the hand, given that the hand contains at least two kings.

1.4-7. Suppose that the genes for eye color for a certain male fruit fly are (R, W) and the genes for eye color for the mating female fruit fly are (R, W), where R and W represent red and white, respectively. Their offspring receive one gene for eye color from each parent.

(a) Define the sample space of the genes for eye color for the offspring.
(b) Assume that each of the four possible outcomes has equal probability. If an offspring ends up with either two red genes or one red and one white gene for eye color, its eyes will look red. Given that an offspring's eyes look red, what is the conditional probability that it has two red genes for eye color?

1.4-8. A researcher finds that, of 982 men who died in 2002, 221 died from some heart disease. Also, of the 982 men, 334 had at least one parent who had some heart disease. Of the latter 334 men, 111 died from some heart disease. A man is selected from the group of 982. Given that neither of his parents had some heart disease, find the conditional probability that this man died of some heart disease.

1.4-9. An urn contains four colored balls: two orange and two blue. Two balls are selected at random without replacement, and you are told that at least one of them is orange. What is the probability that the other ball is also orange?

1.4-10. An urn contains 17 balls marked LOSE and 3 balls marked WIN. You and an opponent take turns selecting a single ball at random from the urn without replacement. The person who selects the third WIN ball wins the game. It does not matter who selected the first two WIN balls.

(a) If you draw first, find the probability that you win the game on your second draw.

(b) If you draw first, find the probability that your opponent wins the game on his second draw.

(c) If you draw first, what is the probability that you win? HINT: You could win on your second, third, fourth, . . . , or tenth draw, but not on your first.

(d) Would you prefer to draw first or second? Why?

1.4-11. In a string of 12 Christmas tree light bulbs, 3 are defective. The bulbs are selected at random and tested, one at a time, until the third defective bulb is found. Compute the probability that the third defective bulb is the

(a) Third bulb tested.

(b) Fifth bulb tested.

(c) Tenth bulb tested.

1.4-12. A small grocery store had 10 cartons of milk, 2 of which were sour. If you are going to buy the sixth carton of milk sold that day at random, compute the probability of selecting a carton of sour milk.

1.4-13. In the gambling game "craps," a pair of dice is rolled and the outcome of the experiment is the sum of the points on the up sides of the six-sided dice. The bettor wins on the first roll if the sum is 7 or 11. The bettor loses on the first roll if the sum is 2, 3, or 12. If the sum is 4, 5, 6, 8, 9, or 10, that number is called the bettor's "point." Once the point is established, the rule is as follows: If the bettor rolls a 7 before the point, the bettor loses; but if the point is rolled before a 7, the bettor wins.

(a) List the 36 outcomes in the sample space for the roll of a pair of dice. Assume that each of them has a probability of 1/36.

(b) Find the probability that the bettor wins on the first roll. That is, find the probability of rolling a 7 or 11, $P(7 \text{ or } 11)$.

(c) Given that 8 is the outcome on the first roll, find the probability that the bettor now rolls the point 8 before rolling a 7 and thus wins. Note that at this stage in the game the only outcomes of interest are 7 and 8. Thus, find $P(8 \mid 7 \text{ or } 8)$.

(d) The probability that a bettor rolls an 8 on the first roll and then wins is given by $P(8)P(8 \mid 7 \text{ or } 8)$. Show that this probability is (5/36)(5/11).

(e) Show that the total probability that a bettor wins in the game of craps is 0.49293. HINT: Note that the bettor can win in one of several mutually exclusive ways: by rolling a 7 or an 11 on the first roll or by establishing one of the points 4, 5, 6, 8, 9, or 10 on the first roll and then obtaining that point on successive rolls before a 7 comes up.

1.4-14. A single card is drawn at random from each of six well-shuffled decks of playing cards. Let A be the event that all six cards drawn are different.

(a) Find $P(A)$.

(b) Find the probability that at least two of the drawn cards match.

1.4-15. Consider the birthdays of the students in a class of size r. Assume that the year consists of 365 days.

(a) How many different ordered samples of birthdays are possible (r in sample) allowing repetitions (with replacement)?

(b) The same as part (a), except requiring that all the students have different birthdays (without replacement)?

(c) If we can assume that each ordered outcome in part (a) has the same probability, what is the probability that at least two students have the same birthday?

(d) For what value of r is the probability in part (c) about equal to 1/2? Is this number surprisingly small? HINT: Use a calculator or computer to find r.

1.4-16. You are a member of a class of 18 students. A bowl contains 18 chips: 1 blue and 17 red. Each student is to take 1 chip from the bowl without replacement. The student who draws the blue chip is guaranteed an A for the course.

(a) If you have a choice of drawing first, fifth, or last, which position would you choose? Justify your choice on the basis of probability.

(b) Suppose the bowl contains 2 blue and 16 red chips. What position would you now choose?

1.4-17. A drawer contains four black, six brown, and eight olive socks. Two socks are selected at random from the drawer.

(a) Compute the probability that both socks are the same color.

(b) Compute the probability that both socks are olive if it is known that they are the same color.

1.4-18. Bowl A contains three red and two white chips, and bowl B contains four red and three white chips. A chip is drawn at random from bowl A and transferred to bowl B. Compute the probability of then drawing a red chip from bowl B.

1.4-19. An urn contains four balls numbered 1 through 4. The balls are selected one at a time without replacement. A match occurs if ball numbered m is the mth ball selected. Let the event A_i denote a match on the ith draw, $i = 1, 2, 3, 4$.

(a) Show that $P(A_i) = \dfrac{3!}{4!}$.

(b) Show that $P(A_i \cap A_j) = \dfrac{2!}{4!}$.

(c) Show that $P(A_i \cap A_j \cap A_k) = \dfrac{1!}{4!}$.

(d) Show that the probability of at least one match is

$$P(A_1 \cup A_2 \cup A_3 \cup A_4) = 1 - \frac{1}{2!} + \frac{1}{3!} - \frac{1}{4!}.$$

(e) Extend this exercise so that there are n balls in the urn. Show that the probability of at least one match is

$$P(A_1 \cup A_2 \cup \cdots \cup A_n) = 1 - \frac{1}{2!} + \frac{1}{3!} - \frac{1}{4!} + \cdots + \frac{(-1)^{n+1}}{n!}$$

$$= 1 - \left(1 - \frac{1}{1!} + \frac{1}{2!} - \frac{1}{3!} + \cdots + \frac{(-1)^n}{n!}\right).$$

(f) What is the limit of this probability as n increases without bound?

1.4-20. Paper is often tested for "burst strength" and "tear strength." Say we classify these strengths as low, middle, and high. Then, after examining 100 pieces of paper, we find the following:

	Burst Strength		
Tear Strength	A_1 (low)	A_2 (middle)	A_3 (high)
B_1 (low)	7	11	13
B_2 (middle)	11	21	9
B_3 (high)	12	9	7

If we select one of the pieces at random, what are the probabilities that it has the following characteristics:

(a) A_1,

(b) $A_3 \cap B_2$,

(c) $A_2 \cup B_3$,

(d) A_1, given that it is B_2,

(e) B_1, given that it is A_3?

1.4-21. An urn contains eight red and seven blue balls. A second urn contains an unknown number of red balls and nine blue balls. A ball is drawn from each urn at random, and the probability of getting two balls of the same color is 151/300. How many red balls are in the second urn?

1.5 INDEPENDENT EVENTS

For certain pairs of events, the occurrence of one of them may or may not change the probability of the occurrence of the other. In the latter case, they are said to be **independent events**. However, before giving the formal definition of independence, let us consider an example.

EXAMPLE 1.5-1 Flip a coin twice and observe the sequence of heads and tails. The sample space is then

$$S = \{HH, HT, TH, TT\}.$$

It is reasonable to assign a probability of 1/4 to each of these four outcomes. Let

$$A = \{\text{heads on the first flip}\} = \{HH, HT\},$$
$$B = \{\text{tails on the second flip}\} = \{HT, TT\},$$
$$C = \{\text{tails on both flips}\} = \{TT\}.$$

Then $P(B) = 2/4 = 1/2$. Now, on the one hand, if we are given that C has occurred, then $P(B \mid C) = 1$, because $C \subset B$. That is, the knowledge of the occurrence of C has changed the probability of B. On the other hand, if we are given that A has occurred, then

$$P(B \mid A) = \frac{P(A \cap B)}{P(A)} = \frac{1/4}{2/4} = \frac{1}{2} = P(B).$$

So the occurrence of A has not changed the probability of B. Hence, the probability of B does not depend upon knowledge about event A, so we say that A and B are independent events. That is, events A and B are independent if the occurrence of one of them does not affect the probability of the occurrence of the other. A more mathematical way of saying this is

$$P(B \mid A) = P(B) \quad \text{or} \quad P(A \mid B) = P(A),$$

provided that $P(A) > 0$ or, in the latter case, $P(B) > 0$. With the first of these equalities and the multiplication rule (Definition 1.4-2), we have

$$P(A \cap B) = P(A)P(B \mid A) = P(A)P(B).$$

The second of these equalities, namely, $P(A \mid B) = P(A)$, gives us the same result

$$P(A \cap B) = P(B)P(A \mid B) = P(B)P(A).$$

■

This example motivates the following definition of independent events.

DEFINITION 1.5-1

Events A and B are **independent** if and only if $P(A \cap B) = P(A)P(B)$. Otherwise A and B are called **dependent** events.

Events that are independent are sometimes called **statistically independent**, **stochastically independent**, or **independent in a probabilistic sense**, but in most instances we use *independent* without a modifier if there is no possibility of misunderstanding. It is interesting to note that the definition always holds if $P(A) = 0$ or $P(B) = 0$, because then $P(A \cap B) = 0$, since $(A \cap B) \subset A$ and $(A \cap B) \subset B$. Thus, the left-hand and right-hand members of $P(A \cap B) = P(A)P(B)$ are both equal to zero and thus are equal to each other.

EXAMPLE 1.5-2

A red die and a white die are rolled. Let event $A = \{4 \text{ on the red die}\}$ and event $B = \{\text{sum of dice is odd}\}$. Of the 36 equally likely outcomes, 6 are favorable to A, 18 are favorable to B, and 3 are favorable to $A \cap B$. Thus,

$$P(A)P(B) = \frac{6}{36} \cdot \frac{18}{36} = \frac{3}{36} = P(A \cap B).$$

Hence, A and B are independent by Definition 1.5-1. ■

EXAMPLE 1.5-3

A red die and a white die are rolled. Let event $C = \{5 \text{ on red die}\}$ and event $D = \{\text{sum of dice is } 11\}$. Of the 36 equally likely outcomes, 6 are favorable to C, 2 are favorable to D, and 1 is favorable to $C \cap D$. Thus,

$$P(C)P(D) = \frac{6}{36} \cdot \frac{2}{36} = \frac{1}{108} \neq \frac{1}{36} = P(C \cap D).$$

Hence, C and D are dependent events by Definition 1.5-1. ■

THEOREM 1.5-1 If A and B are independent events, then the following pairs of events are also independent:

(a) A and B'.
(b) A' and B.
(c) A' and B'.

Proof. We know that conditional probability satisfies the axioms for a probability function. Hence, if $P(A) > 0$, then $P(B' \mid A) = 1 - P(B \mid A)$. Thus,

$$\begin{aligned} P(A \cap B') &= P(A)P(B' \mid A) = P(A)[1 - P(B \mid A)] \\ &= P(A)[1 - P(B)] \\ &= P(A)P(B'), \end{aligned}$$

since $P(B \mid A) = P(B)$ by hypothesis. Consequently, A and B' are independent events. The proofs of parts (b) and (c) are left as exercises. □

Before extending the definition of independent events to more than two events, we present the following example.

EXAMPLE 1.5-4 An urn contains four balls numbered 1, 2, 3, and 4. One ball is to be drawn at random from the urn. Let the events A, B, and C be defined by $A = \{1,2\}$, $B = \{1,3\}$, and $C = \{1,4\}$. Then $P(A) = P(B) = P(C) = 1/2$. Furthermore,

$$P(A \cap B) = \frac{1}{4} = P(A)P(B),$$

$$P(A \cap C) = \frac{1}{4} = P(A)P(C),$$

$$P(B \cap C) = \frac{1}{4} = P(B)P(C),$$

which implies that A, B, and C are independent in pairs (called **pairwise independence**). However, since $A \cap B \cap C = \{1\}$, we have

$$P(A \cap B \cap C) = \frac{1}{4} \neq \frac{1}{8} = P(A)P(B)P(C).$$

That is, something seems to be lacking for the complete independence of A, B, and C. ■

This example illustrates the reason for the second condition in the next definition.

DEFINITION 1.5-2

Events A, B, and C are **mutually independent** if and only if the following two conditions hold:

(a) A, B, and C are pairwise independent; that is,

$$P(A \cap B) = P(A)P(B), \qquad P(A \cap C) = P(A)P(C),$$

and

$$P(B \cap C) = P(B)P(C).$$

(b) $P(A \cap B \cap C) = P(A)P(B)P(C)$.

Definition 1.5-2 can be extended to the mutual independence of four or more events. In such an extension, each pair, triple, quartet, and so on, must satisfy this type of multiplication rule. If there is no possibility of misunderstanding, *independent* is often used without the modifier *mutually* when several events are considered.

EXAMPLE 1.5-5

A rocket has a built-in redundant system. In this system, if component K_1 fails, it is bypassed and component K_2 is used. If component K_2 fails, it is bypassed and component K_3 is used. (An example of a system with these kinds of components is a three-computer system.) Suppose that the probability of failure of any one component is 0.15, and assume that the failures of these components are mutually independent events. Let A_i denote the event that component K_i fails for $i = 1, 2, 3$. Because the system fails if K_1 fails and K_2 fails and K_3 fails, the probability that the system does not fail is given by

$$\begin{aligned} P[(A_1 \cap A_2 \cap A_3)'] &= 1 - P(A_1 \cap A_2 \cap A_3) \\ &= 1 - P(A_1)P(A_2)P(A_3) \\ &= 1 - (0.15)^3 \\ &= 0.9966. \end{aligned}$$

One way to increase the reliability of such a system is to add more components (realizing that this also adds weight and takes up space). For example, if a fourth component K_4 were added to this system, the probability that the system does not fail is

$$P[(A_1 \cap A_2 \cap A_3 \cap A_4)'] = 1 - (0.15)^4 = 0.9995. \qquad \blacksquare$$

If A, B, and C are mutually independent events, then the following events are also independent:

(a) A and $(B \cap C)$;
(b) A and $(B \cup C)$;
(c) A' and $(B \cap C')$.

In addition, A', B', and C' are mutually independent. (The proofs and illustrations of these results are left as exercises.)

Many experiments consist of a sequence of n trials that are mutually independent. If the outcomes of the trials, in fact, do not have anything to do with one another, then events, such that each is associated with a different trial, should be independent in the probability sense. That is, if the event A_i is associated with the ith trial, $i = 1, 2, \ldots, n$, then

$$P(A_1 \cap A_2 \cap \cdots \cap A_n) = P(A_1)P(A_2)\cdots P(A_n).$$

EXAMPLE 1.5-6 A fair six-sided die is rolled six independent times. Let A_i be the event that side i is observed on the ith roll, called a match on the ith trial, $i = 1, 2, \ldots, 6$. Thus, $P(A_i) = 1/6$ and $P(A_i') = 1 - 1/6 = 5/6$. If we let B denote the event that at least one match occurs, then B' is the event that no matches occur. Hence,

$$\begin{aligned} P(B) &= 1 - P(B') = 1 - P(A_1' \cap A_2' \cap \cdots \cap A_6') \\ &= 1 - \frac{5}{6}\cdot\frac{5}{6}\cdot\frac{5}{6}\cdot\frac{5}{6}\cdot\frac{5}{6}\cdot\frac{5}{6} = 1 - \left(\frac{5}{6}\right)^6 \end{aligned}$$

is the probability of B. ■

The sample space for an experiment of n trials is a set of n-tuples, where the ith component denotes the outcome on the ith trial. For example, if a six-sided die is rolled five times, then

$$S = \{(O_1, O_2, O_3, O_4, O_5) : O_i = 1,2,3,4,5, \text{ or } 6, \text{ for } i = 1,2,3,4,5\}.$$

That is, S is a set of five-tuples, where each component is one of the first six positive integers.

If a coin is tossed two times, then

$$S = \{(O_1, O_2) : O_i = H \text{ or } T, i = 1,2\}.$$

We often drop the commas and parentheses and let, for example, $(H, T) = HT$, as in Example 1.5-1.

EXAMPLE 1.5-7 The probability that a company's workforce has at least one accident during a certain month is $(0.01)k$, where k is the number of days in that month (say, February has 28 days). Assume that the numbers of accidents is independent from month to month. If the company's year starts with January, the probability that the first accident is in April is

$$\begin{aligned} &P(\text{none in Jan., none in Feb., none in March, at least one in April}) = \\ &(1 - 0.31)(1 - 0.28)(1 - 0.31)(0.30) = (0.69)(0.72)(0.69)(0.30) = 0.103. \end{aligned}$$ ■

EXAMPLE 1.5-8 Three inspectors look at a critical component of a product. Their probabilities of detecting a defect are different, namely, 0.99, 0.98, and 0.96, respectively. If we assume independence, then the probability of at least one detecting the defect is

$$1 - (0.01)(0.02)(0.04) = 0.999992.$$

The probability of *only* one finding the defect is

$$(0.99)(0.02)(0.04) + (0.01)(0.98)(0.04) + (0.01)(0.02)(0.96) = 0.001576.$$

As an exercise, compute the following probability exactly: (a) that two find the defect, (b) that three find the defect. ■

EXAMPLE 1.5-9 Suppose that on five consecutive days an "instant winner" lottery ticket is purchased and the probability of winning is 1/5 on each day. Assuming independent trials, we have

$$P(WWLLL) = \left(\frac{1}{5}\right)^2\left(\frac{4}{5}\right)^3,$$

$$P(LWLWL) = \frac{4}{5}\cdot\frac{1}{5}\cdot\frac{4}{5}\cdot\frac{1}{5}\cdot\frac{4}{5} = \left(\frac{1}{5}\right)^2\left(\frac{4}{5}\right)^3.$$

In general, the probability of purchasing two winning tickets and three losing tickets is

$$\binom{5}{2}\left(\frac{1}{5}\right)^2\left(\frac{4}{5}\right)^3 = \frac{5!}{2!3!}\left(\frac{1}{5}\right)^2\left(\frac{4}{5}\right)^3 = 0.2048,$$

because there are $\binom{5}{2}$ ways to select the positions (or the days) for the winning tickets and each of these $\binom{5}{2}$ ways has the probability $(1/5)^2(4/5)^3$. ■

EXERCISES

1.5-1. Let A and B be independent events with $P(A) = 0.7$ and $P(B) = 0.2$. Compute (a) $P(A \cap B)$, (b) $P(A \cup B)$, and (c) $P(A' \cup B')$.

1.5-2. Let $P(A) = 0.3$ and $P(B) = 0.6$.

(a) Find $P(A \cup B)$ when A and B are independent.

(b) Find $P(A \mid B)$ when A and B are mutually exclusive.

1.5-3. Let A and B be independent events with $P(A) = 1/4$ and $P(B) = 2/3$. Compute (a) $P(A \cap B)$, (b) $P(A \cap B')$, (c) $P(A' \cap B')$, (d) $P[(A \cup B)']$, and (e) $P(A' \cap B)$.

1.5-4. Prove parts (b) and (c) of Theorem 1.5-1.

1.5-5. If $P(A) = 0.8$, $P(B) = 0.5$, and $P(A \cup B) = 0.9$, are A and B independent events? Why or why not?

1.5-6. Show that if A, B, and C are mutually independent, then the following pairs of events are independent: A and $(B \cap C)$, A and $(B \cup C)$, A' and $(B \cap C')$. Show also that A', B' and C' are mutually independent.

1.5-7. Each of three football players will attempt to kick a field goal from the 25-yard line. Let A_i denote the event that the field goal is made by player i, $i = 1, 2, 3$. Assume that A_1, A_2, A_3 are mutually independent and that $P(A_1) = 0.5$, $P(A_2) = 0.7$, $P(A_3) = 0.6$.

(a) Compute the probability that exactly one player is successful.

(b) Compute the probability that exactly two players make a field goal (i.e., one misses).

1.5-8. Die A has orange on one face and blue on five faces, Die B has orange on two faces and blue on four faces, Die C has orange on three faces and blue on three faces. All are unbiased dice. If the three dice are rolled, find the probability that exactly two of the three dice come up orange.

1.5-9. Suppose that A, B, and C are mutually independent events and that $P(A) = 0.5$, $P(B) = 0.8$, and $P(C) = 0.9$. Find the probabilities that (a) all three events occur, (b) exactly two of the three events occur, and (c) none of the events occur.

1.5-10. Let D_1, D_2, D_3 be three four-sided dice whose sides have been labeled as follows:

$$D_1: 0\,3\,3\,3 \qquad D_2: 2\,2\,2\,5 \qquad D_3: 1\,1\,4\,6$$

The three dice are rolled at random. Let A, B, and C be the events that the outcome on die D_1 is larger than the outcome on D_2, the outcome on D_2 is larger than the outcome on D_3, and the outcome on D_3 is larger than the outcome on D_1, respectively. Show that (a) $P(A) = 9/16$, (b) $P(B) = 9/16$, and (c) $P(C) = 10/16$. Do you find it interesting that each of the probabilities that D_1 "beats" D_2, D_2 "beats" D_3, and D_3 "beats" D_1 is greater than 1/2? Thus, it is difficult to determine the "best" die.

1.5-11. Let A and B be two events.

(a) If the events A and B are mutually exclusive, are A and B always independent? If the answer is no, can they ever be independent? Explain.
(b) If $A \subset B$, can A and B ever be independent events? Explain.

1.5-12. Flip an unbiased coin five independent times. Compute the probability of

(a) $HHTHT$.
(b) $THHHT$.
(c) $HTHTH$.
(d) Three heads occurring in the five trials.

1.5-13. An urn contains two red balls and four white balls. Sample successively five times at random and with replacement, so that the trials are independent. Compute the probability of each of the two sequences $WWR\,WR$ and $R\,WWWR$.

1.5-14. In Example 1.5-5, suppose that the probability of failure of a component is $p = 0.4$. Find the probability that the system does not fail if the number of redundant components is

(a) 3.
(b) 8.

1.5-15. An urn contains 10 red and 10 white balls. The balls are drawn from the urn at random, one at a time. Find the probability that the fourth white ball is the sixth ball drawn if the sampling is done

(a) With replacement.
(b) Without replacement.
(c) In the World Series, the American League (red) and National League (white) teams play until one team wins four games. Do you think that the urn model presented in this exercise could be used to describe the probabilities of a 4-, 5-, 6-, or 7-game series? If your answer is yes, would you choose sampling with or without replacement in your model? (For your information, the numbers of 4-, 5-, 6-, and 7-game series, up to and including 2008, were 20, 23, 21, and 36, respectively. The World Series was canceled in 1994, and in 1903 and 1919–1921 winners had to take five out of nine games. Three of those series went eight games and one went seven.)

1.5-16. An urn contains five balls, one marked WIN and four marked LOSE. You and another player take turns selecting a ball at random from the urn, one at a time. The first person to select the WIN ball is the winner. If you draw first, find the probability that you will win if the sampling is done

(a) With replacement.
(b) Without replacement.

1.5-17. Each of the 12 students in a class is given a fair 12-sided die. In addition, each student is numbered from 1 to 12.

(a) If the students roll their dice, what is the probability that there is at least one "match" (e.g., student 4 rolls a 4)?
(b) If you are a member of this class, what is the probability that at least one of the other 11 students rolls the same number as you do?

1.5-18. An eight-team single-elimination tournament is set up as follows:

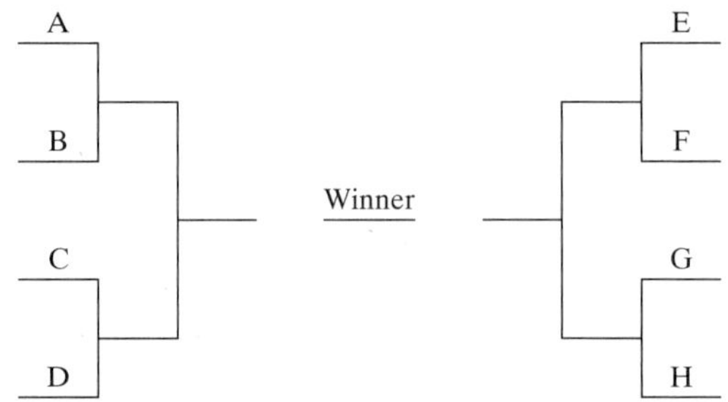

For example, eight students (called A–H) set up a tournament among themselves. The top-listed student in each bracket calls heads or tails when his or her opponent flips a coin. If the call is correct, the student moves on to the next bracket.

(a) How many coin flips are required to determine the tournament winner?
(b) What is the probability that you can predict all of the winners?
(c) In NCAA Division I basketball, after a "play-in" game between the 64th and 65th seeds, 64 teams participate in a single-elimination tournament to determine the national champion. Considering only the remaining 64 teams, how many games are required to determine the national champion?
(d) Assume that for any given game, either team has an equal chance of winning. (That is probably not true.) On page 43 of the March 22, 1999, issue, *Time*, claimed that the "mathematical odds of predicting all 63 NCAA games correctly is 1 in 75 million." Do you agree with this statement? If not, why not?

1.5-19. Extend Example 1.5-6 to an n-sided die. That is, suppose that a fair n-sided die is rolled n independent times. A match occurs if side i is observed on the ith trial, $i = 1, 2, \ldots, n$.

(a) Show that the probability of at least one match is

$$1 - \left(\frac{n-1}{n}\right)^n = 1 - \left(1 - \frac{1}{n}\right)^n.$$

(b) Find the limit of this probability as n increases without bound.

1.5-20. An urn contains n balls numbered from 1 through n. A sample of n balls is selected at random from the urn one at a time. A match occurs if ball i is selected on the ith draw.

(a) For $n = 1$ to 15, find the probability of at least one match if the sampling is done (i) with replacement (see Exercise 1.5-19), (ii) without replacement (see Exercise 1.4-19).

(b) How much does n affect these probabilities?

(c) How does sampling with and without replacement affect these probabilities?

(d) Illustrate these probabilities empirically, either performing the experiments physically or simulating them on a computer.

1.6 BAYES'S THEOREM

We begin this section by illustrating Bayes's theorem with an example.

EXAMPLE 1.6-1 Bowl B_1 contains two red and four white chips, bowl B_2 contains one red and two white chips, and bowl B_3 contains five red and four white chips. Say that the probabilities for selecting the bowls are not the same but are given by $P(B_1) = 1/3$, $P(B_2) = 1/6$, and $P(B_3) = 1/2$, where B_1, B_2, and B_3 are the events that bowls B_1, B_2, and B_3 are respectively chosen. The experiment consists of selecting a bowl with these probabilities and then drawing a chip at random from that bowl. Let us compute the probability of event R, drawing a red chip—say, $P(R)$. Note that $P(R)$ is dependent first of all on which bowl is selected and then on the probability of drawing a red chip from the selected bowl. That is, the event R is the union of the mutually exclusive events $B_1 \cap R$, $B_2 \cap R$, and $B_3 \cap R$. Thus,

$$\begin{aligned} P(R) &= P(B_1 \cap R) + P(B_2 \cap R) + P(B_3 \cap R) \\ &= P(B_1)P(R \mid B_1) + P(B_2)P(R \mid B_2) + P(B_3)P(R \mid B_3) \\ &= \frac{1}{3}\cdot\frac{2}{6} + \frac{1}{6}\cdot\frac{1}{3} + \frac{1}{2}\cdot\frac{5}{9} = \frac{4}{9}. \end{aligned}$$

Suppose now that the outcome of the experiment is a red chip, but we do not know from which bowl it was drawn. Accordingly, we compute the conditional probability that the chip was drawn from bowl B_1, namely, $P(B_1 \mid R)$. From the definition of conditional probability and the preceding result, we have

$$\begin{aligned} P(B_1 \mid R) &= \frac{P(B_1 \cap R)}{P(R)} \\ &= \frac{P(B_1)P(R \mid B_1)}{P(B_1)P(R \mid B_1) + P(B_2)P(R \mid B_2) + P(B_3)P(R \mid B_3)} \\ &= \frac{(1/3)(2/6)}{(1/3)(2/6) + (1/6)(1/3) + (1/2)(5/9)} = \frac{2}{8}. \end{aligned}$$

Similarly,

$$P(B_2 \mid R) = \frac{P(B_2 \cap R)}{P(R)} = \frac{(1/6)(1/3)}{4/9} = \frac{1}{8}$$

and

$$P(B_3 \mid R) = \frac{P(B_3 \cap R)}{P(R)} = \frac{(1/2)(5/9)}{4/9} = \frac{5}{8}.$$

Note that the conditional probabilities $P(B_1 \mid R)$, $P(B_2 \mid R)$, and $P(B_3 \mid R)$ have changed from the original probabilities $P(B_1)$, $P(B_2)$, and $P(B_3)$ in a way that agrees with your intuition. Once the red chip has been observed, the probability concerning B_3 seems more favorable than originally because B_3 has a larger percentage of red chips than do B_1 and B_2. The conditional probabilities of B_1 and B_2 decrease from their original ones once the red chip is observed. Frequently, the original probabilities are called *prior probabilities* and the conditional probabilities are the *posterior probabilities*. ■

We generalize the result of Example 1.6-1. Let $B_1, B_2, \ldots, B_m$ constitute a *partition* of the sample space S. That is,

$$S = B_1 \cup B_2 \cup \cdots \cup B_m \text{ and } B_i \cap B_j = \emptyset, i \neq j.$$

Of course, the events $B_1, B_2, \ldots, B_m$ are mutually exclusive and exhaustive (since the union of the disjoint sets equals the sample space S). Furthermore, suppose the **prior probability** of the event B_i is positive; that is, $P(B_i) > 0, i = 1, \ldots, m$. If A is an event, then A is the union of m mutually exclusive events, namely,

$$A = (B_1 \cap A) \cup (B_2 \cap A) \cup \cdots \cup (B_m \cap A).$$

Thus,

$$\begin{aligned} P(A) &= \sum_{i=1}^{m} P(B_i \cap A) \\ &= \sum_{i=1}^{m} P(B_i)P(A \mid B_i). \end{aligned} \tag{1.6-1}$$

If $P(A) > 0$, then

$$P(B_k \mid A) = \frac{P(B_k \cap A)}{P(A)}, \qquad k = 1, 2, \ldots, m. \tag{1.6-2}$$

Using Equation 1.6-1 and replacing $P(A)$ in Equation 1.6-2, we have **Bayes's theorem**:

$$P(B_k \mid A) = \frac{P(B_k)P(A \mid B_k)}{\sum_{i=1}^{m} P(B_i)P(A \mid B_i)}, \qquad k = 1, 2, \ldots, m.$$

The conditional probability $P(B_k \mid A)$ is often called the **posterior probability** of B_k. The next example illustrates one application of Bayes's theorem.

EXAMPLE 1.6-2 In a certain factory, machines I, II, and III are all producing springs of the same length. Of their production, machines I, II, and III, respectively produce 2%, 1%, and 3% defective springs. Of the total production of springs in the factory, machine I produces 35%, machine II produces 25%, and machine III produces 40%. If one spring is selected at random from the total springs produced in a day, the probability that it is defective, in an obvious notation, equals

$$P(D) = P(I)P(D \mid I) + P(II)P(D \mid II) + P(III)P(D \mid III)$$
$$= \left(\frac{35}{100}\right)\left(\frac{2}{100}\right) + \left(\frac{25}{100}\right)\left(\frac{1}{100}\right) + \left(\frac{40}{100}\right)\left(\frac{3}{100}\right) = \frac{215}{10{,}000}.$$

If the selected spring is defective, the conditional probability that it was produced by machine III is, by Bayes's formula,

$$P(III \mid D) = \frac{P(III)P(D \mid III)}{P(D)} = \frac{(40/100)(3/100)}{215/10{,}000} = \frac{120}{215}.$$

Note how the posterior probability of III increased from the prior probability of III after the defective spring was observed, because III produces a larger percentage of defectives than do I and II. ■

EXAMPLE 1.6-3 A Pap smear is a screening procedure used to detect cervical cancer. For women with this cancer, there are about 16% *false negatives*; that is,

$$P(T^- = \text{test negative} \mid C = \text{cancer}) = 0.16.$$

Thus,

$$P(T^+ = \text{test positive} \mid C = \text{cancer}) = 0.84.$$

For women without cancer, there are about 19% *false positives*; that is,

$$P(T^+ \mid C' = \text{not cancer}) = 0.19.$$

Hence,

$$P(T^- \mid C' = \text{not cancer}) = 0.81.$$

In the United States, there are about 8 women in 100,000 who have this cancer; that is,

$$P(C) = 0.00008; \text{ so } P(C') = 0.99992.$$

By Bayes's theorem,

$$P(C \mid T^+) = \frac{P(C \text{ and } T^+)}{P(T^+)}$$
$$= \frac{(0.00008)(0.84)}{(0.00008)(0.84) + (0.99992)(0.19)}$$
$$= \frac{672}{672 + 1{,}899{,}848} = 0.000354.$$

What this means is that for every million positive Pap smears, only 354 represent true cases of cervical cancer. This low ratio makes one question the value of the procedure. The reason that it is ineffective is that the percentage of women having that cancer is so small and the error rates of the procedure—namely, 0.16 and 0.19—are so high. (See Yobs, A .R., Swanson, R. A., and Lamotte, L. C. "Laboratory Reliability of the Papanicolaou Smear." *Obstetrics and Gynecology*, Volume 65, February 1985, pp. 235–244.) ■

EXERCISES

1.6-1. Bowl B_1 contains two white chips, bowl B_2 contains two red chips, bowl B_3 contains two white and two red chips, and bowl B_4 contains three white chips and one red chip. The probabilities of selecting bowl B_1, B_2, B_3, or B_4 are 1/2, 1/4, 1/8, and 1/8, respectively. A bowl is selected using these probabilities and a chip is then drawn at random. Find

(a) $P(W)$, the probability of drawing a white chip.

(b) $P(B_1 \mid W)$, the conditional probability that bowl B_1 had been selected, given that a white chip was drawn.

1.6-2. Bean seeds from supplier A have an 85% germination rate and those from supplier B have a 75% germination rate. A seed-packaging company purchases 40% of its bean seeds from supplier A and 60% from supplier B and mixes these seeds together.

(a) Find the probability $P(G)$ that a seed selected at random from the mixed seeds will germinate.

(b) Given that a seed germinates, find the probability that the seed was purchased from supplier A.

1.6-3. A doctor is concerned about the relationship between blood pressure and irregular heartbeats. Among her patients, she classifies blood pressures as high, normal, or low and heartbeats as regular or irregular and finds that (a) 16% have high blood pressure; (b) 19% have low blood pressure; (c) 17% have an irregular heartbeat; (d) of those with an irregular heartbeat, 35% have high blood pressure; and (e) of those with normal blood pressure, 11% have an irregular heartbeat. What percentage of her patients have a regular heartbeat and low blood pressure?

1.6-4. Assume that an insurance company knows the following probabilities relating to automobile accidents:

Age of Driver	Probability of Accident	Fraction of Company's Insured Drivers
16–25	0.05	0.10
26–50	0.02	0.55
51–65	0.03	0.20
66–90	0.04	0.15

A randomly selected driver from the company's insured drivers has an accident. What is the conditional probability that the driver is in the 16–25 age group?

1.6-5. At a hospital's emergency room, patients are classified and 20% of them are critical, 30% are serious, and 50% are stable. Of the critical ones, 30% die; of the serious, 10% die; and of the stable, 1% die. Given that a patient dies, what is the conditional probability that the patient was classified as critical.

1.6-6. A life insurance company issues standard, preferred, and ultrapreferred policies. Of the company's policyholders of a certain age, 60% have standard policies and a probability of 0.01 of dying in the next year, 30% have preferred policies and a probability of 0.008 of dying in the next year, and 10% have ultrapreferred policies and a probability of 0.007 of dying in the next year. A policyholder of that age dies in the next year. What are the conditional probabilities of the deceased having had a standard, a preferred, and an ultrapreferred policy?

1.6-7. Among 60-year-old college professors, 90% are nonsmokers and 10% are smokers. The probability of a nonsmoker dying in the next year is 0.005 and the probability for smokers is 0.05. Given that one of this group of college professors dies in the next year, what is the conditional probability that the professor was a smoker?

1.6-8. A store sells four brands of DVD players. The least expensive brand, B_1, accounts for 40% of the sales. The other brands (in order of their price) have the following percentages of sales: B_2, 30%; B_3, 20%; and B_4, 10%. The respective probabilities of needing repair during warranty are 0.10 for B_1, 0.05 for B_2, 0.03 for B_3, and 0.02 for B_4. A randomly selected purchaser has a DVD player that needs repair under warranty. What are the four conditional probabilities of being brand B_i, $i = 1, 2, 3, 4$?

1.6-9. There is a new diagnostic test for a disease that occurs in about 0.05% of the population. The test is not perfect, but will detect a person with the disease 99% of the time. It will, however, say that a person without the disease has the disease about 3% of the time. A person is selected at random from the population, and the test indicates that this person has the disease. What are the conditional probabilities that

(a) the person has the disease?

(b) the person does not have the disease?

Discuss. HINT: Note that the fraction 0.0005 of diseased persons in the population is much smaller than the error probabilities of 0.01 and 0.03.

1.6-10. Suppose we want to investigate the percentage of abused children in a certain population. To do this, doctors examine some of these children taken at random from that population. However, doctors are not perfect: They sometimes classify an abused child (A) as one not abused (ND) or they classify a nonabused child (N) as one that is abused (AD). Suppose these error rates are $P(ND \mid A) = 0.08$ and $P(AD \mid N) = 0.05$, respectively; thus, $P(AD \mid A) = 0.92$ and $P(ND \mid N) = 0.95$ are the probabilities of the correct decisions. Let us pretend that only 2 percent of all children are abused; that is, $P(A) = 0.02$ and $P(N) = 0.98$.

(a) Select a child at random. What is the probability that the doctor classifies this child as abused. That is, compute

$$P(AD) = P(A)P(AD \mid A) + P(N)P(AD \mid N).$$

(b) Given that the child is classified by the doctor as abused, compute $P(N \mid AD)$ and $P(A \mid AD)$.

(c) Also, compute $P(N \mid ND)$ and $P(A \mid ND)$.

(d) Are the probabilities in (b) and (c) alarming? This happens because the error rates of 0.08 and 0.05 are high relative to the fraction 0.02 of abused children in the population.

1.6-11. At the beginning of a certain study of a group of persons, 15% were classified as heavy smokers, 30% as light smokers, and 55% as nonsmokers. In the five-year study, it was determined that the death rates of the heavy and light smokers were five and three times that of the nonsmokers, respectively. A randomly selected participant died over the five-year period; calculate the probability that the participant was a nonsmoker.

1.6-12. A test indicates the presence of a particular disease 90% of the time when the disease is present and the presence of the disease 2% of the time when the disease is not present. If 0.5% of the population has the disease, calculate the conditional probability that a person selected at random has the disease if the test indicates the presence of the disease.

1.6-13. A hospital receives two-fifths of its flu vaccine from Company A and the remainder from Company B. Each shipment contains a large number of vials of vaccine. From Company A, 3% of the vials are ineffective; from Company B, 2% are ineffective. A hospital tests $n = 25$ randomly selected vials from one shipment and finds that 2 are ineffective. What is the conditional probability that this shipment came from Company A?

1.6-14. Two processes of a company produce rolls of materials: The rolls of Process I are 3% defective and the rolls of Process II are 1% defective. Process I produces 60% of the company's output, Process II 40%. A roll is selected at random from the total output. Given that this roll is defective, what is the conditional probability that it is from Process I?

1.6-15. A chemist wishes to detect an impurity in a certain compound that she is making. There is a test that detects an impurity with probability 0.90; however, this test indicates that an impurity is there when it is not about 5% of the time. The chemist produces compounds with the impurity about 20% of the time; that is, 80% do not have the impurity. A compound is selected at random from the chemist's output. The test indicates that an impurity is present. What is the conditional probability that the compound actually has an impurity?

HISTORICAL COMMENTS Most probabilists would say that the mathematics of probability began when, in 1654, Chevalier de Méré, a French nobleman who liked to gamble, challenged Blaise Pascal to explain a puzzle and a problem created from his observations concerning rolls of dice. Of course, there was gambling well before this, and actually, almost 200 years before this challenge, a Franciscan monk, Luca Paccioli, proposed the same puzzle. Here it is:

> A and B are playing a fair game of balla. They agree to continue until one has six rounds. However, the game actually stops when A has won five and B three. How should the stakes be divided?

And over 100 years before de Méré's challenge, a 16th-century doctor, Girolamo Cardano, who was also a gambler, had figured out the answers to many dice problems, but not the one that de Méré proposed. Chevalier de Méré had observed this: If a single die is tossed 4 times, the probability of obtaining at least one six was slightly greater than 1/2. However, keeping the same proportions, if a pair of dice is tossed 24 times, the probability of obtaining at least one double-six seemed to be slightly less than 1/2; at least de Méré was losing money betting on it. This is when he approached Blaise Pascal with the challenge. Not wanting to work on the problems alone, Pascal formed a partnership with Pierre de Fermat, a brilliant young mathematician. It was this 1654 correspondence between Pascal and Fermat that started the theory of probability.

Today an average student in probability could solve both problems easily. For the puzzle, note that B could win with six rounds only by winning the next three rounds, which has probability of $(1/2)^3 = 1/8$ because it was a fair game of balla. Thus, A's probability of winning six rounds is $1 - 1/8 = 7/8$, and stakes should be divided seven units to one. For the dice problem, the probability of at least one six in four rolls of a die is

$$1 - \left(\frac{5}{6}\right)^4 \approx 0.518,$$

while the probability of rolling at least one double-six in 24 rolls of a pair of dice is

$$1 - \left(\frac{35}{36}\right)^{24} \approx 0.491.$$

It seems amazing to us that de Méré could have observed enough trials of those events to detect the slight difference in those probabilities. However, he won betting on the first but lost by betting on the second.

Incidentally, the solution to the balla puzzle led to a generalization—namely, the binomial distribution—and to the famous Pascal triangle. Of course, Fermat was the great mathematician associated with "Fermat's last theorem."

The Reverend Thomas Bayes, who was born in 1701, was a Nonconformist (a Protestant who rejected most of the rituals of the Church of England). While he published nothing in mathematics when he was alive, two works were published after his death, one of which contained the essence of Bayes's theorem and a very original way of using data to modify prior probabilities to create posterior probabilities. It has had such an influence on modern statistics that many modern statisticians are associated with the Neo-Bayesian movement and we devote Chapter 9 to some of these methods.

Discrete Distributions

CHAPTER 2

2.1 RANDOM VARIABLES OF THE DISCRETE TYPE
2.2 MATHEMATICAL EXPECTATION
2.3 THE MEAN, VARIANCE, AND STANDARD DEVIATION
2.4 BERNOULLI TRIALS AND THE BINOMIAL DISTRIBUTION
2.5 THE MOMENT-GENERATING FUNCTION
2.6 THE POISSON DISTRIBUTION

2.1 RANDOM VARIABLES OF THE DISCRETE TYPE

An outcome space S may be difficult to describe if the elements of S are not numbers. We shall now discuss how we can use a rule by which each outcome of a random experiment, an element s of S, may be associated with a real number x. We begin the discussion with an example.

EXAMPLE 2.1-1 A rat is selected at random from a cage and its sex is determined. The set of possible outcomes is female and male. Thus, the outcome space is $S = \{\text{female, male}\} = \{\text{F, M}\}$. Let X be a function defined on S such that $X(\text{F}) = 0$ and $X(\text{M}) = 1$. X is then a real-valued function that has the outcome space S as its domain and the set of real numbers $\{x : x = 0, 1\}$ as its range. We call X a random variable, and in this example, the space associated with X is $\{x : x = 0, 1\}$. ■

We now formulate the definition of a random variable.

DEFINITION 2.1-1 Given a random experiment with an outcome space S, a function X that assigns one and only one real number $X(s) = x$ to each element s in S is called a **random variable**. The **space** of X is the set of real numbers $\{x : X(s) = x, s \in S\}$, where $s \in S$ means that the element s belongs to the set S.

REMARK As we give examples of random variables and their probability distributions, the reader will soon recognize that, when observing a random experiment, the experimenter must take some type of measurement (or measurements). This measurement can be thought of as the outcome of a random variable. We would simply like to know the probability of a measurement ending in A, a subset of the space of X. If this is known for all subsets A, then we know the probability distribution of the random variable. Obviously, in practice, we do not very often know this distribution exactly. Hence, statisticians make conjectures about these distributions; that is, we construct probabilistic models for random variables. The ability of a statistician to model a real situation appropriately is a valuable trait. In this chapter, we introduce some probability models in which the spaces of the random variables consist of sets of integers. ■

It may be that the set S has elements that are themselves real numbers. In such an instance, we could write $X(s) = s$, so that X is the identity function and the space of X is also S. This situation is illustrated in Example 2.1-2.

EXAMPLE 2.1-2 Let the random experiment be the cast of a die. Then the outcome space associated with this experiment is $S = \{1, 2, 3, 4, 5, 6\}$, with the elements of S indicating the number of spots on the side facing up. For each $s \in S$, let $X(s) = s$. The space of the random variable X is then $\{1, 2, 3, 4, 5, 6\}$.

If we associate a probability of 1/6 with each outcome, then, for example, $P(X = 5) = 1/6$, $P(2 \le X \le 5) = 4/6$, and $P(X \le 2) = 2/6$ seem to be reasonable assignments, where, in this example, $\{2 \le X \le 5\}$ means $\{X = 2, 3, 4, \text{ or } 5\}$ and $\{X \le 2\}$ means $\{X = 1 \text{ or } 2\}$. ■

The student will no doubt recognize two major difficulties here:

1. In many practical situations, the probabilities assigned to the events are unknown.
2. Since there are many ways of defining a function X on S, which function do we want to use?

As a matter of fact, the solutions to these problems in particular cases are major concerns in applied statistics. In considering (2), statisticians try to determine what *measurement* (or measurements) should be taken on an outcome; that is, how best do we "mathematize" the outcome? These measurement problems are most difficult and can be answered only by getting involved in a practical project. For (1), we often need to estimate these probabilities or percentages through repeated observations (called sampling). For example, what percentage of newborn girls in the University of Iowa Hospital weigh less than 7 pounds? Here a newborn baby girl is the outcome, and we have measured her one way (by weight), but obviously there are many other ways of measuring her. If we let X be the weight in pounds, we are interested in the probability $P(X < 7)$, and we can estimate this probability only by repeated observations. One obvious way of estimating it is by the use of the relative frequency of $\{X < 7\}$ after a number of observations. If it is reasonable to make additional assumptions, we will study other ways of estimating that probability. It is this latter aspect with which mathematical statistics is concerned. That is, if we assume certain models, we find that the theory of statistics can explain how best to draw conclusions or make predictions.

In many instances, it is clear exactly what function X the experimenter wants to define on the outcome space. For example, the caster in the dice game called craps is concerned about the sum of the spots (say X) that are facing upwards on the pair of dice. Hence, we go directly to the space of X, which we shall denote by the same letter S. After all, in the dice game, the caster is directly concerned only with the probabilities associated with X. Thus, for convenience, in many instances the reader can think of the space of X as being the outcome space.

Let X denote a random variable with space S. Suppose that we know how the probability is distributed over the various subsets A of S; that is, we can compute $P(X \in A)$. In this sense, we speak of the distribution of the random variable X, meaning, of course, the distribution of probability associated with the space S of X.

Let X denote a random variable with one-dimensional space S, a subset of the real numbers. Suppose that the space S contains a countable number of points; that is, either S contains a finite number of points, or the points of S can be put into a one-to-one correspondence with the positive integers. Such a set S is called a set of discrete points or simply a discrete outcome space. Furthermore, the random variable X is called a random variable of the **discrete type**, and X is said to have a distribution of the discrete type.

For a random variable X of the discrete type, the probability $P(X = x)$ is frequently denoted by $f(x)$, and this function $f(x)$ is called the **probability mass function**. Note that some authors refer to $f(x)$ as the probability function, the frequency function, or the probability density function. In the discrete case, we shall use "probability mass function," and it is hereafter abbreviated p.m.f.

Let $f(x)$ be the p.m.f. of the random variable X of the discrete type, and let S be the space of X. Since $f(x) = P(X = x)$ for $x \in S$, $f(x)$ must be nonnegative for $x \in S$, and we want all these probabilities to add to 1 because each $P(X = x)$ represents the fraction of times x can be expected to occur. Moreover, to determine the probability associated with the event $A \in S$, we would sum the probabilities of the x values in A. This idea leads us to the following definition.

DEFINITION 2.1-2

The **probability mass function** (p.m.f.) $f(x)$ of a discrete random variable X is a function that satisfies the following properties:

(a) $f(x) > 0, \quad x \in S;$

(b) $\sum_{x \in S} f(x) = 1;$

(c) $P(X \in A) = \sum_{x \in A} f(x), \quad$ where $A \subset S$.

Of course, we usually let $f(x) = 0$ when $x \notin S$; thus, the domain of $f(x)$ is the set of real numbers. When we define the p.m.f. $f(x)$ and do not say "zero elsewhere," we tacitly mean that $f(x)$ has been defined at all x's in the space S and it is assumed that $f(x) = 0$ elsewhere; that is, $f(x) = 0$ when $x \notin S$. Since the probability $P(X = x) = f(x) > 0$ when $x \in S$, and since S contains all the probabilities associated with X, we sometimes refer to S as the **support** of X as well as the space of X.

When a p.m.f. is constant on the space or support, we say that the distribution is **uniform** over that space. As an illustration, in Example 2.1-2 X has a discrete uniform distribution on $S = \{1, 2, 3, 4, 5, 6\}$ and its p.m.f. is

$$f(x) = \frac{1}{6}, \qquad x = 1, 2, 3, 4, 5, 6.$$

We can generalize this result by letting X have a discrete uniform distribution over the first m positive integers, so that its p.m.f. is

$$f(x) = \frac{1}{m}, \qquad x = 1, 2, 3, \cdots, m.$$

We now give an example in which X does not have a uniform distribution.

EXAMPLE 2.1-3 Roll a four-sided die twice, and let X equal the larger of the two outcomes if they are different and the common value if they are the same. The outcome space for this experiment is $S_0 = \{(d_1, d_2) : d_1 = 1, 2, 3, 4; d_2 = 1, 2, 3, 4\}$, where we assume that each of these 16 points has probability 1/16. Then $P(X = 1) = P[(1, 1)] = 1/16$, $P(X = 2) = P[\{(1, 2), (2, 1), (2, 2)\}] = 3/16$, and similarly $P(X = 3) = 5/16$ and $P(X = 4) = 7/16$. That is, the p.m.f. of X can be written simply as

$$f(x) = P(X = x) = \frac{2x - 1}{16}, \qquad x = 1, 2, 3, 4. \tag{2.1-1}$$

We could add that $f(x) = 0$ elsewhere; but if we do not, the reader should take $f(x)$ to equal zero when $x \notin S = \{1, 2, 3, 4\}$. ■

A better understanding of a particular probability distribution can often be obtained with a graph that depicts the p.m.f. of X. Note that the graph of the p.m.f. when $f(x) > 0$ would be simply the set of points $\{[x, f(x)] : x \in S\}$, where S is the space of X. Two types of graphs can be used to give a better visual appreciation of the p.m.f.: a bar graph and a probability histogram. A **bar graph** of the p.m.f. $f(x)$ of the random variable X is a graph having a vertical line segment drawn from $(x, 0)$ to $[x, f(x)]$ at each x in S, the space of X. If X can assume only integer values, a **probability histogram** of the p.m.f. $f(x)$ is a graphical representation that has a rectangle of height $f(x)$ and a base of length 1, centered at x for each $x \in S$, the space of X. Thus, the area of each rectangle is equal to the respective probability $f(x)$, and the total area of a probability histogram is 1.

Figure 2.1-1 displays a bar graph and a probability histogram for the p.m.f. $f(x)$ defined in Equation 2.1-1.

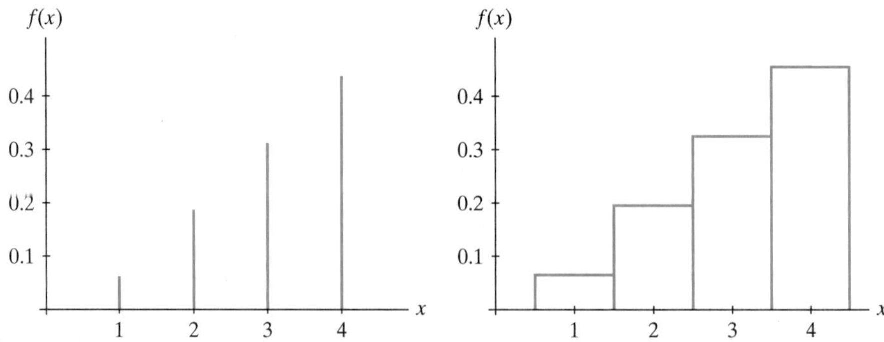

FIGURE 2.1-1: Bar graph and probability histogram

Our next probability model uses the material in Section 1.3 on methods of enumeration. Consider a collection of $N = N_1 + N_2$ similar objects, N_1 of them belonging to one of two dichotomous classes (red chips, say) and N_2 of them belonging to the second class (blue chips, say). A collection of n objects is selected from these

N objects at random and without replacement. Find the probability that exactly x (where the nonnegative integer x satisfies $x \le n, x \le N_1$, and $n - x \le N_2$) of these n objects are red (i.e., x belong to the first class and $n - x$ belong to the second). Of course, we can select x red chips in any one of $\binom{N_1}{x}$ ways and $n - x$ blue chips in any one of $\binom{N_2}{n-x}$ ways. By the multiplication principle, the product $\binom{N_1}{x}\binom{N_2}{n-x}$ equals the number of ways the joint operation can be performed. If we assume that each of the $\binom{N}{n}$ ways of selecting n objects from $N = N_1 + N_2$ objects has the same probability, it follows that the probability of selecting exactly x red chips is

$$f(x) = P(X = x) = \frac{\binom{N_1}{x}\binom{N_2}{n-x}}{\binom{N}{n}},$$

where the space S is the collection of nonnegative integers x that satisfies the inequalities $x \le n, x \le N_1$, and $n - x \le N_2$. We say that the random variable X has a **hypergeometric distribution**.

EXAMPLE 2.1-4 Some examples of hypergeometric probability histograms are given in Figure 2.1-2. The values of N_1, N_2, and n are given with each figure. ■

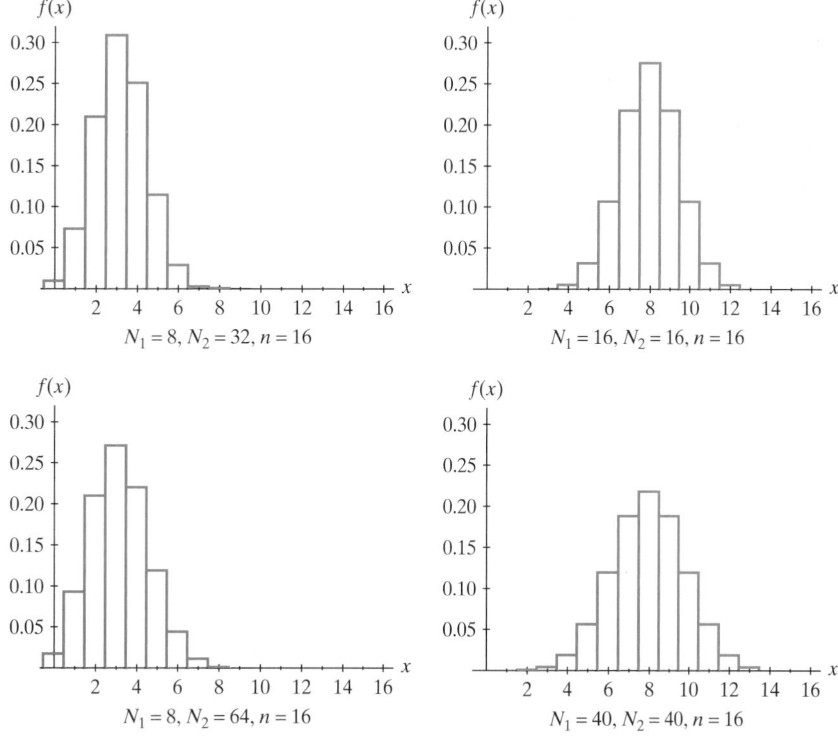

FIGURE 2.1-2: Hypergeometric probability histograms

EXAMPLE 2.1-5 In a small pond there are 50 fish, 10 of which have been tagged. If a fisherman's catch consists of 7 fish selected at random and without replacement, and X denotes the number of tagged fish, the probability that exactly 2 tagged fish are caught is

$$P(X = 2) = \frac{\binom{10}{2}\binom{40}{5}}{\binom{50}{7}} = \frac{(45)(658{,}008)}{99{,}884{,}400} = \frac{246{,}753}{832{,}370} \approx 0.2964. \quad \blacksquare$$

EXAMPLE 2.1-6 A lot (collection) consisting of 100 fuses is inspected by the following procedure: Five fuses are chosen at random and tested; if all 5 blow at the correct amperage, the lot is accepted. Suppose that the lot contains 20 defective fuses. If X is a random variable equal to the number of defective fuses in the sample of 5, the probability of accepting the lot is

$$P(X = 0) = \frac{\binom{20}{0}\binom{80}{5}}{\binom{100}{5}} = \frac{19{,}513}{61{,}110} \approx 0.3193.$$

More generally, the p.m.f. of X is

$$f(x) = P(X = x) = \frac{\binom{20}{x}\binom{80}{5-x}}{\binom{100}{5}}, \qquad x = 0, 1, 2, 3, 4, 5. \quad \blacksquare$$

EXAMPLE 2.1-7 A supplier ships parts to another company in lots (collections) of 25, some of which could be defective. The receiving company has an *acceptance sampling plan* which states that $n = 5$ parts are to be taken at random and without replacement from each lot. If there are zero defectives among those 5 parts, the entire lot is accepted; otherwise, the lot is rejected. That is, if one or more defectives are found among the 5 in the sample, the lot is rejected. If X is the number of defectives among the 5 sampled parts, X must have a hypergeometric distribution. But here we do not know the values of N_1, the number of defectives in the lot, and N_2, the number of good parts in the lot; we know only that $N_1 + N_2 = 25$. Clearly, we want the probability of accepting the lot—namely, $P(X = 0)$—to be large if N_1 is very small. This probability is usually called the *operating characteristic curve* when treated as a function of N_1, or equivalently, the fraction defective, $p = N_1/25$, in the lot. That is, the operating characteristic curve is

$$\text{OC}(p) = P(X = 0) = \frac{\binom{N_1}{0}\binom{25 - N_1}{5}}{\binom{25}{5}},$$

where $p = N_1/25$. Letting $N_1 = 0, 1, 2, \ldots$ so that $p = 0.00, 0.04, 0.08, \ldots$, we use Table I in the appendix to find that

$$\text{OC}(0.00) = \frac{\binom{0}{0}\binom{25}{5}}{\binom{25}{5}} = 1.00,$$

$$\text{OC}(0.04) = \frac{\binom{1}{0}\binom{24}{5}}{\binom{25}{5}} = 0.800,$$

$$\text{OC}(0.08) = \frac{\binom{2}{0}\binom{23}{5}}{\binom{25}{5}} = 0.633,$$

$$\text{OC}(0.12) = \frac{\binom{3}{0}\binom{22}{5}}{\binom{25}{5}} = 0.496,$$

$$\text{OC}(0.16) = \frac{\binom{4}{0}\binom{21}{5}}{\binom{25}{5}} = 0.383,$$

and so on. Upon observing these probabilities, the company might find this acceptance sampling plan unsatisfactory because, possibly, with $N_1 = (25)(0.04) = 1$, $\text{OC}(0.04) = P(X = 0) = 0.8$ is too low and, with $N_1 = (25)(0.16) = 4$, $\text{OC}(0.16) = P(X = 0) = 0.383$ is too high. If this is so, the plan must be changed. In industrial practice, usually lot sizes are much larger than 25, sometimes running into the thousands, and the sample sizes might be in the hundreds rather than $n = 5$. We kept the numbers small here so that we could use Table I, but we illustrate what is actually done in practice with those larger values in Section 2.6 on the Poisson distribution. (See Example 2.6-8.) ■

In Section 1.2, we discussed the relationship between the probability $P(A)$ of an event A and the relative frequency $\mathcal{N}(A)/n$ of occurrences of event A in n repetitions of an experiment. We shall now extend those ideas.

Suppose that a random experiment is repeated n independent times. Let $A = \{X = x\}$, the event that x is the outcome of the experiment. Then we would expect the relative frequency $\mathcal{N}(A)/n$ to be close to $f(x)$. The next example illustrates this property.

EXAMPLE 2.1-8 A tetrahedron (four-sided die with outcomes 1, 2, 3, and 4) is rolled twice. Let X equal the sum of the two outcomes. Then the possible values of X are 2, 3, 4, 5, 6, 7, and 8. The following argument suggests that the p.m.f. of X is given by

TABLE 2.1-1: Sum of Two Tetrahedral Dice

x	Number of Observations of x	Relative Frequency of x	Probability of $\{X = x\}$, $f(x)$
2	71	0.071	0.0625
3	124	0.124	0.1250
4	194	0.194	0.1875
5	258	0.258	0.2500
6	177	0.177	0.1875
7	122	0.122	0.1250
8	54	0.054	0.0625

$f(x) = (4 - |x - 5|)/16$, for $x = 2, 3, 4, 5, 6, 7, 8$ (i.e., $f(2) = 1/16$, $f(3) = 2/16$, $f(4) = 3/16$, $f(5) = 4/16$, $f(6) = 3/16$, $f(7) = 2/16$, and $f(8) = 1/16$): Intuitively, these probabilities seem correct if we think of the 16 points (result on first roll, result on second roll) and assume that each has probability 1/16. Then note that $X = 2$ only for the point (1, 1), $X = 3$ for the two points (2, 1) and (1, 2), and so on. This experiment was simulated 1000 times on a computer. Table 2.1-1 lists the results and compares the relative frequencies with the corresponding probabilities.

A graph can be used to display the results shown in Table 2.1-1. The probability histogram of the p.m.f. $f(x)$ of X is given in Figure 2.1-3. It is superimposed over the shaded histogram that represents the observed relative frequencies of the corresponding x values. The shaded histogram is the relative frequency histogram. For random experiments of the discrete type, this relative frequency histogram of a set of data gives an estimate of the probability histogram of the associated random variable when the latter is unknown. (Estimation is considered in detail later in the book.) ■

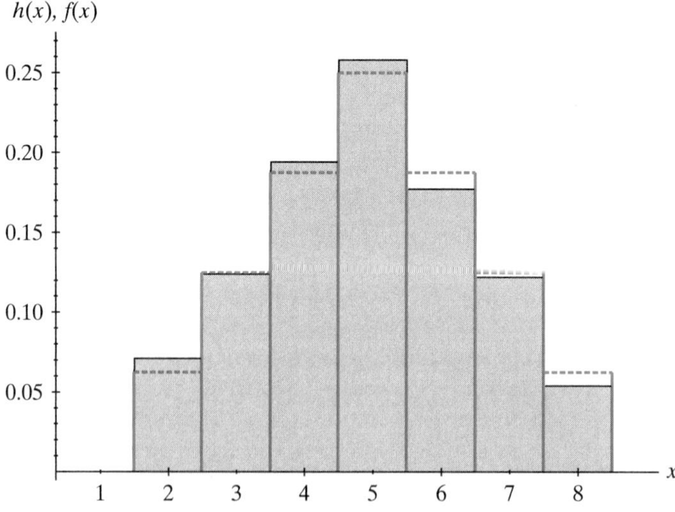

FIGURE 2.1-3: Sum of two tetrahedral dice

EXERCISES

2.1-1. Let the p.m.f. of X be defined by $f(x) = x/9$, $x = 2, 3, 4$.

(a) Draw a bar graph for this p.m.f.

(b) Draw a probability histogram for this p.m.f.

2.1-2. Let a chip be taken at random from a bowl that contains six white chips, three red chips, and one blue chip. Let the random variable $X = 1$ if the outcome is a white chip, let $X = 5$ if the outcome is a red chip, and let $X = 10$ if the outcome is a blue chip.

(a) Find the p.m.f. of X.

(b) Graph the p.m.f. as a bar graph.

2.1-3. For each of the following, determine the constant c so that $f(x)$ satisfies the conditions of being a p.m.f. for a random variable X, and then depict each p.m.f. as a bar graph:

(a) $f(x) = x/c, \quad x = 1, 2, 3, 4.$

(b) $f(x) = cx, \quad x = 1, 2, 3, \ldots, 10.$

(c) $f(x) = c(1/4)^x, \quad x = 1, 2, 3, \ldots.$

(d) $f(x) = c(x + 1)^2, \quad x = 0, 1, 2, 3.$

(e) $f(x) = x/c, \quad x = 1, 2, 3, \ldots, n.$

(f) $f(x) = \dfrac{c}{(x + 1)(x + 2)}, \quad x = 0, 1, 2, 3, \ldots.$

2.1-4. The state of Michigan generates a three-digit number at random six days a week for its daily lottery. The numbers are generated one digit at a time. Consider the following set of 50 three-digit numbers as 150 one-digit integers that were generated at random:

169	938	506	757	594	656	444	809	321	545
732	146	713	448	861	612	881	782	209	752
571	701	852	924	766	633	696	023	601	789
137	098	534	826	642	750	827	689	979	000
933	451	945	464	876	866	236	617	418	988

Let X denote the outcome when a single digit is generated.

(a) With true random numbers, what is the p.m.f. of X? Draw the probability histogram.

(b) For the 150 observations, determine the relative frequencies of 0, 1, 2, 3, 4, 5, 6, 7, 8, and 9, respectively.

(c) Draw the relative frequency histogram of the observations on the same graph paper as that of the probability histogram. Use a colored or dashed line for the relative frequency histogram.

2.1-5. The p.m.f. of X is $f(x) = (5 - x)/10$, $x = 1, 2, 3, 4$.

(a) Graph the p.m.f. as a bar graph.

(b) Use the following independent observations of X, simulated on a computer, to construct a table like Table 2.1-1:

3	1	2	2	3	2	2	2	1	3	3	2	3	2	4	4	2	1	1	3
3	1	2	2	1	1	4	2	3	1	1	1	2	1	3	1	1	3	3	1
1	1	1	1	1	4	1	3	1	2	4	1	1	2	3	4	3	1	4	2
2	1	3	2	1	4	1	1	1	2	1	3	4	3	2	1	4	4	1	3
2	2	2	1	2	3	1	1	4	2	1	4	2	1	2	3	1	4	2	3

(c) Construct a probability histogram and a relative frequency histogram like Figure 2.1-3.

2.1-6. Let a random experiment be the casting of a pair of unbiased dice, each having six faces, and let the random variable X denote the sum of the dice.

(a) With reasonable assumptions, determine the p.m.f. $f(x)$ of X. HINT: Picture the sample space consisting of the 36 points (result on first die, result on second die), and assume that each has probability 1/36. Find the probability of each possible outcome of X, namely, $x = 2, 3, 4, \ldots, 12$.

(b) Draw a bar graph for $f(x)$.

2.1-7. Let a random experiment be the casting of a pair of unbiased six-sided dice, and let X equal the smaller of the outcomes if they are different and the common value if they are equal.

(a) With reasonable assumptions, find the p.m.f. of X.

(b) Draw a probability histogram of the p.m.f. of X.

(c) Let Y equal the range of the two outcomes (i.e., the absolute value of the difference of the largest and the smallest outcomes). Determine the p.m.f. $g(y)$ of Y for $y = 0, 1, 2, 3, 4, 5$.

(d) Draw a probability histogram for $g(y)$.

2.1-8. An unbiased four-sided die X has two faces numbered 0 and two faces numbered 2. An unbiased four-sided die Y has its faces numbered 0, 1, 4, and 5. The two dice are rolled. Let $W = X + Y$.

(a) Determine the p.m.f. of W.

(b) Draw a probability histogram of the p.m.f. of W.

2.1-9. Let the p.m.f. of X be defined by $f(x) = (1 + |x - 3|)/11$, $x = 1, 2, 3, 4, 5$. Graph the p.m.f. of X as a bar graph.

2.1-10. Suppose there are 3 defective items in a lot (collection) of 50 items. A sample of size 10 is taken at random and without replacement. Let X denote the number of defective items in the sample. Find the probability that the sample contains

(a) Exactly one defective item.

(b) At most one defective item.

2.1-11. In a lot (collection) of 100 light bulbs, there are 5 bad bulbs. An inspector inspects 10 bulbs selected at random. Find the probability of finding at least one defective bulb. HINT: First compute the probability of finding no defectives in the sample.

2.1-12. A lot (collection) of $N_1 + N_2 = 25$ items is accepted if the number of defectives, X, among $n = 5$ items taken at random and without replacement from the lot is less than or equal to 1. The operating characteristic curve is defined as the probability of accepting the lot, namely,

$$\text{OC}(p) = P(X \le 1) = P(X = 0) + P(X = 1),$$

where $p = N_1/25$. Determine the probabilities OC(0.04), OC(0.08), OC(0.12), and OC(0.16) (and compare them with those in Example 2.1-7).

2.1-13. Let X be the number of accidents per week in a factory. Let the p.m.f. of X be

$$f(x) = \frac{1}{(x + 1)(x + 2)}, \qquad x = 0, 1, 2, \cdots.$$

Find the conditional probability of $X \ge 4$, given that $X \ge 1$.
HINT: Write $f(x) = 1/(x + 1) - 1/(x + 2)$.

2.1-14. Often in buying a product at a supermarket, there is a concern about the item being underweight. Suppose there are 20 "one-pound" packages of frozen ground turkey on display and 3 of them are underweight. A consumer group buys 5 of the 20 packages at random. What is the probability of at least 1 of the 5 being underweight?

2.1-15. A professor gave her students six essay questions, from which she will select three for a test. A student has time to study for only three of these questions. What is the probability that, of the questions studied,

(a) at least one is selected for the test?

(b) all three are selected?

(c) exactly two are selected?

2.1-16. An urn contains 20 chips, 10 marked H and 10 marked C. Randomly select chips, one at a time, without replacement. After 10 chips have been selected, let X equal the difference between the numbers of H and C chips that have been selected.

(a) Define the p.m.f. of X.

(b) What value of X is most likely? That is, what is the mode of X?

REMARK Hope College (H chips) and Calvin College (C chips) began playing basketball in 1920–21. After 166 games, each team had won 83. The 20 chips correspond to the first 20 games only, and assume that Hope and Calvin were tied after 20 games in order to keep the numbers reasonable. ■

2.1-17. Five cards are selected at random without replacement from a standard, thoroughly shuffled 52-card deck of playing cards. Let X equal the number of face cards (kings, queens, jacks) in the hand. Forty observations of X yielded the following data:

2	1	2	1	0	0	1	0	1	1	0	2	0	2	3	0	1	1	0	3
1	2	0	2	0	2	0	1	0	1	1	2	1	0	1	1	2	1	1	0

(a) Argue that the p.m.f. of X is

$$f(x) = \frac{\binom{12}{x}\binom{40}{5 - x}}{\binom{52}{5}}, \qquad x = 0, 1, 2, 3, 4, 5$$

and thus, that $f(0) = 2109/8330, f(1) = 703/1666, f(2) = 209/833, f(3) = 55/833, f(4) = 165/21{,}658$, and $f(5) = 33/108{,}290$.

(b) Draw a probability histogram for this distribution.

(c) Determine the relative frequencies of 0, 1, 2, 3, and superimpose the relative frequency histogram on your probability histogram.

2.1-18. (Michigan Mathematics Prize Competition, 1992, Part II) From the set $\{1, 2, 3, \ldots, n\}$, k distinct integers are selected at random and arranged in numerical order (from lowest to highest). Let $P(i, r, k, n)$ denote the probability that integer i is in position r. For example, observe that $P(1, 2, k, n) = 0$, as it is impossible for the number 1 to be in the second position after ordering.

(a) Compute $P(2, 1, 6, 10)$.

(b) Find a general formula for $P(i, r, k, n)$.

2.1-19. A bag contains 144 ping-pong balls. More than half of the balls are painted orange and the rest are painted blue. Two balls are simultaneously drawn at random. The probability of drawing two balls of the same color is the same as the probability of drawing two balls of different colors. How many orange balls are in the bag?

2.2 MATHEMATICAL EXPECTATION

An extremely important concept in summarizing important characteristics of distributions of probability is that of mathematical expectation, which we introduce with an example.

EXAMPLE 2.2-1 An enterprising young man who needs a little extra money devises a game of chance in which some of his friends might wish to participate. The game that he proposes is to let the participant cast an unbiased die and then receive a payment according to the following schedule: If the event $A = \{1, 2, 3\}$ occurs, he receives 1¢; if $B = \{4, 5\}$ occurs, he receives 5¢; and if $C = \{6\}$ occurs, he receives 35¢. The probabilities of the respective events are assumed to be 3/6, 2/6, and 1/6, since the die is unbiased. The problem that now faces the young man is the determination of the amount that should be charged for the opportunity of playing the game. He reasons, correctly, that if the game is played a large number of times, about 3/6 of the trials will require a payment of 1¢, about 2/6 of them will require one of 5¢, and about 1/6 of them will require one of 35¢. Thus, the approximate average payment is

$$(1)\left(\frac{3}{6}\right) + (5)\left(\frac{2}{6}\right) + (35)\left(\frac{1}{6}\right) = 8.$$

That is, he expects to pay 8¢ "on the average." Note that he never pays exactly 8¢; the payment is either 1¢, 5¢, or 35¢. However, the "weighted average" of 1, 5, and 35, in which the weights are the respective probabilities 3/6, 2/6, and 1/6, equals 8. Such a weighted average is called the mathematical expectation of payment. Thus, if the young man decides to charge 10¢ per play, he would make 2¢ per play "on the average." Since the most that a player would lose at the charge of 10¢ per play is 9¢, the young man might find that several players are attracted by the possible gain of 25¢. ■

A more mathematical way of formulating the preceding example would be to let X be the random variable defined by the outcome of the cast of the die. Thus, the p.m.f. of X is the uniform one given by

$$f(x) = \frac{1}{6}, \qquad x = 1, 2, 3, 4, 5, 6.$$

In terms of the observed value x, the payment is given by the function

$$u(x) = \begin{cases} 1, & x = 1, 2, 3, \\ 5, & x = 4, 5, \\ 35, & x = 6. \end{cases}$$

The mathematical expectation of payment is then equal to

$$\begin{aligned}\sum_{x=1}^{6} u(x)f(x) &= (1)\left(\frac{1}{6}\right) + (1)\left(\frac{1}{6}\right) + (1)\left(\frac{1}{6}\right) + (5)\left(\frac{1}{6}\right) + (5)\left(\frac{1}{6}\right) + (35)\left(\frac{1}{6}\right) \\ &= (1)\left(\frac{3}{6}\right) + (5)\left(\frac{2}{6}\right) + (35)\left(\frac{1}{6}\right) \\ &= 8.\end{aligned}$$

This discussion suggests the more general definition of mathematical expectation of a function of X.

DEFINITION 2.2-1 If $f(x)$ is the p.m.f. of the random variable X of the discrete type with space S, and if the summation

$$\sum_{x \in S} u(x)f(x), \qquad \text{which is sometimes written} \qquad \sum_{S} u(x)f(x),$$

exists, then the sum is called the **mathematical expectation** or the **expected value** of the function $u(X)$, and it is denoted by $E[u(X)]$. That is,

$$E[u(X)] = \sum_{x \in S} u(x)f(x).$$

We can think of the expected value $E[u(X)]$ as a weighted mean of $u(x)$, $x \in S$, where the weights are the probabilities $f(x) = P(X = x)$, $x \in S$.

REMARK The usual definition of mathematical expectation of $u(X)$ requires that the sum converge absolutely—that is, that

$$\sum_{x \in S} |u(x)|\,f(x)$$

converge and be finite. However, in this book, each $u(x)$ is such that the convergence is absolute, and we do not burden the student with this additional requirement. Moreover, sometimes $E[u(X)]$ is called, more simply, the expectation of $u(X)$. ■

There is another important observation that must be made about the consistency of Definition 2.1-1. Certainly, this function $u(X)$ of the random variable X is itself a random variable—say, Y. Suppose that we find the p.m.f. of Y to be $g(y)$ on the support S_1. Then $E(Y)$ is given by the summation

$$\sum_{y \in S_1} y\,g(y).$$

In general, it is true that

$$\sum_{x\in S} u(x)f(x) = \sum_{y\in S_1} y g(y).$$

That is, the same expectation is obtained by either formula. We do not prove this general result, but only illustrate it in the next example.

EXAMPLE 2.2-2 Let the random variable X have the p.m.f.

$$f(x) = \frac{1}{3}, \qquad x \in S,$$

where $S = \{-1, 0, 1\}$. Let $u(X) = X^2$. Then

$$\sum_{x\in S} x^2 f(x) = (-1)^2\left(\frac{1}{3}\right) + (0)^2\left(\frac{1}{3}\right) + (1)^2\left(\frac{1}{3}\right) = \frac{2}{3}.$$

However, the support of the random variable $Y = X^2$ is $S_1 = \{0, 1\}$ and

$$P(Y = 0) = P(X = 0) = \frac{1}{3},$$

$$P(Y = 1) = P(X = -1) + P(X = 1) = \frac{1}{3} + \frac{1}{3} = \frac{2}{3}.$$

That is,

$$g(y) = \begin{cases} \dfrac{1}{3}, & y = 0, \\ \dfrac{2}{3}, & y = 1; \end{cases}$$

and $S_1 = \{0, 1\}$. Hence,

$$\sum_{y\in S_1} y g(y) = (0)\left(\frac{1}{3}\right) + (1)\left(\frac{2}{3}\right) = \frac{2}{3},$$

which illustrates the preceding observation. ■

Before presenting additional examples, we list some useful facts about mathematical expectation in the following theorem.

THEOREM 2.2-1 When it exists, the mathematical expectation E satisfies the following properties:

(a) If c is a constant, then $E(c) = c$.

(b) If c is a constant and u is a function, then

$$E[cu(X)] = cE[u(X)].$$

(c) If c_1 and c_2 are constants and u_1 and u_2 are functions, then

$$E[c_1u_1(X) + c_2u_2(X)] = c_1E[u_1(X)] + c_2E[u_2(X)].$$

Proof. First, for the proof of (a), we have

$$E(c) = \sum_{x\in S} cf(x) = c\sum_{x\in S} f(x) = c$$

because

$$\sum_{x\in S} f(x) = 1.$$

Next, to prove (b), we see that

$$\begin{aligned} E[c\,u(X)] &= \sum_{x\in S} c\,u(x)f(x) \\ &= c\sum_{x\in S} u(x)f(x) \\ &= c\,E[u(X)]. \end{aligned}$$

Finally, the proof of (c) is given by

$$\begin{aligned} E[c_1u_1(X) + c_2u_2(X)] &= \sum_{x\in S} [c_1u_1(x) + c_2u_2(x)]f(x) \\ &= \sum_{x\in S} c_1u_1(x)f(x) + \sum_{x\in S} c_2u_2(x)f(x). \end{aligned}$$

By applying (b), we obtain

$$E[c_1u_1(X) + c_2u_2(X)] = c_1E[u_1(X)] + c_2E[u_2(X)]. \qquad \square$$

Property (c) can be extended to more than two terms by mathematical induction; that is, we have

$$(c)' \quad E\left[\sum_{i=1}^{k} c_i\,u_i(X)\right] = \sum_{i=1}^{k} c_i\,E[u_i(X)].$$

Because of property $(c)'$, the mathematical expectation E is often called a **linear** or **distributive** operator.

EXAMPLE 2.2-3 Let X have the p.m.f.

$$f(x) = \frac{x}{10}, \qquad x = 1, 2, 3, 4.$$

Then

$$\begin{aligned} E(X) &= \sum_{x=1}^{4} x\left(\frac{x}{10}\right) \\ &= (1)\left(\frac{1}{10}\right) + (2)\left(\frac{2}{10}\right) + (3)\left(\frac{3}{10}\right) + (4)\left(\frac{4}{10}\right) = 3, \\ E(X^2) &= \sum_{x=1}^{4} x^2\left(\frac{x}{10}\right) \\ &= (1)^2\left(\frac{1}{10}\right) + (2)^2\left(\frac{2}{10}\right) + (3)^2\left(\frac{3}{10}\right) + (4)^2\left(\frac{4}{10}\right) = 10, \end{aligned}$$

and

$$E[X(5 - X)] = 5E(X) - E(X^2) = (5)(3) - 10 = 5. \qquad \blacksquare$$

EXAMPLE 2.2-4 Let $u(x) = (x - b)^2$, where b is not a function of X, and suppose $E[(X - b)^2]$ exists. To find that value of b for which $E[(X - b)^2]$ is a minimum, we write

$$\begin{aligned} g(b) = E[(X - b)^2] &= E[X^2 - 2bX + b^2] \\ &= E(X^2) - 2bE(X) + b^2 \end{aligned}$$

because $E(b^2) = b^2$. To find the minimum, we differentiate $g(b)$ with respect to b, set $g'(b) = 0$, and solve for b as follows:

$$\begin{aligned} g'(b) &= -2E(X) + 2b = 0, \\ b &= E(X). \end{aligned}$$

Since $g''(b) = 2 > 0$, $E(X)$ is the value of b that minimizes $E[(X - b)^2]$. ■

EXAMPLE 2.2-5 Let X have a hypergeometric distribution in which n objects are selected from $N = N_1 + N_2$ objects as described in Section 2.1. Then

$$E(X) = \sum_{x \in S} x \frac{\binom{N_1}{x}\binom{N_2}{n - x}}{\binom{N}{n}}.$$

Since the first term of this summation equals zero when $x = 0$, and since

$$\binom{N}{n} = \left(\frac{N}{n}\right)\binom{N - 1}{n - 1},$$

we can write

$$E(X) = \sum_{0<x \in S} x \frac{N_1!}{x!(N_1 - x)!} \frac{\binom{N_2}{n - x}}{\left(\frac{N}{n}\right)\binom{N - 1}{n - 1}}.$$

Of course, $x/x! = 1/(x - 1)!$ when $x \neq 0$; thus,

$$\begin{aligned} E(X) &= \left(\frac{n}{N}\right) \sum_{0<x \in S} \frac{(N_1)(N_1 - 1)!}{(x - 1)!(N_1 - x)!} \frac{\binom{N_2}{n - x}}{\binom{N - 1}{n - 1}} \\ &= n\left(\frac{N_1}{N}\right) \sum_{0<x \in S} \frac{\binom{N_1 - 1}{x - 1}\binom{N_2}{n - 1 - (x - 1)}}{\binom{N - 1}{n - 1}}. \end{aligned}$$

However, when $x > 0$, the summand of this last expression represents the probability of obtaining, say, $x - 1$ red chips if $n - 1$ chips are selected from $N_1 - 1$ red chips and N_2 blue chips. Since the summation is over all possible values of $x - 1$, it must sum to 1, as it is the sum of all possible probabilities of $x - 1$. Thus,

$$E(X) = n\left(\frac{N_1}{N}\right),$$

which is a result that agrees with our intuition: We expect the number X of red chips to equal the product of the number n of selections and the fraction N_1/N of red chips in the original collection. ■

EXERCISES

2.2-1. Find $E(X)$ for each of the distributions given in Exercise 2.1-3.

HINT: Part (c). Note that the difference $E(X) - (1/4)E(X)$ is equal to the sum of a geometric series.

2.2-2. Let the random variable X have the p.m.f.

$$f(x) = \frac{(|x| + 1)^2}{9}, \qquad x = -1, 0, 1.$$

Compute $E(X)$, $E(X^2)$, and $E(3X^2 - 2X + 4)$.

2.2-3. In a particular lottery, 3 million tickets are sold each week for 50¢ apiece. Out of the 3 million tickets, 12,006 are drawn at random and without replacement and awarded prizes: twelve thousand \$25 prizes, four \$10,000 prizes, one \$50,000 prize, and one \$200,000 prize. If you purchased a single ticket each week, what is the expected value of this game to you?

2.2-4. In a state lottery, a three-digit integer is selected at random. A player bets \$1 on a particular number, and if that number is selected, the payoff is \$500 minus the \$1 paid for the ticket. Let X equal the payoff to the bettor, namely, −\$1 or \$499, and find $E(X)$.

2.2-5. Let the random variable X be the number of days that a certain patient needs to be in the hospital. Suppose X has the p.m.f.

$$f(x) = \frac{5 - x}{10}, \qquad x = 1, 2, 3, 4.$$

If the patient is to receive \$200 from an insurance company for each of the first two days in the hospital and \$100 for each day after the first two days, what is the expected payment for the hospitalization?

2.2-6. An insurance company sells an automobile policy with a deductible of one unit. Let X be the amount of the loss having p.m.f.

$$f(x) = \begin{cases} 0.9, & x = 0, \\ \dfrac{c}{x}, & x = 1, 2, 3, 4, 5, 6, \end{cases}$$

where c is a constant. Determine c and the expected value of the amount the insurance company must pay.

2.2-7. In the gambling game chuck-a-luck, for a \$1 bet it is possible to win \$1, \$2, or \$3 with respective probabilities 75/216, 15/216, and 1/216. One dollar is lost with probability 125/216. Let X equal the payoff for this game and find $E(X)$. Note that when a bet is won, the \$1 that was bet, in addition to the \$1, \$2, or \$3 that is won, is returned to the bettor.

2.2-8. Let the p.m.f. of X be defined by $f(x) = 6/(\pi^2 x^2)$, $x = 1, 2, 3, \ldots$. Show that $E(X)$ does not exist in this case. (Can you show that $f(x)$ is a p.m.f.?)

2.2-9. Let us select at random a number from the first n positive integers. If the payment is equal to the reciprocal of the number, find an expression for the expected payment. Evaluate this number when $n = 5$. Approximate this number when $n = 100$, or find the exact value using the computer. HINT: For the approximation, use a modification of the integral test for testing the convergence of a series.

2.2-10. Let X be a random variable with support $\{1, 2, 3, 5, 15, 25, 50\}$, each point of which has the same probability 1/7. Argue that $c = 5$ is the value that minimizes $h(c) = E(|X - c|)$. Compare c with the value of b that minimizes $g(b) = E[(X - b)^2]$.

2.2-11. A roulette wheel used in a U. S. casino has 38 slots, of which 18 are red, 18 are black, and 2 are green. A roulette wheel used in a French casino has 37 slots, of which 18 are red, 18 are black, and 1 is green. A ball is rolled around the wheel and ends up in one of the slots with equal probability. Suppose that a player bets on red. If a \$1 bet is placed, the player wins \$1 if the ball ends up in a red slot. (The player's \$1 bet is returned.) If the ball ends up in a black or green slot, the player loses \$1. Find the expected value of this game to the player in

(a) The United States.

(b) France.

2.2-12. In the casino game called **high–low**, there are three possible bets. Assume that \$1 is the size of the bet. A pair of fair six-sided dice is rolled and their sum is calculated. If you bet **low**, you win \$1 if the sum of the dice is $\{2, 3, 4, 5, 6\}$. If you bet

high, you win \$1 if the sum of the dice is $\{8, 9, 10, 11, 12\}$. If you bet on $\{7\}$, you win \$4 if a sum of 7 is rolled. Otherwise you lose on each of the three bets. In all three cases, your original dollar is returned if you win. Find the expected value of the game to the bettor for each of these three bets.

2.2-13. In the gambling game craps (see Exercise 1.4-13), the player wins \$1 with probability 0.49293 and loses \$1 with probability 0.50707 for each \$1 bet. What is the expected value of the game to the player?

2.2-14. Suppose that a school has 20 classes: 16 with 25 students in each, three with 100 students in each, and one with 300 students, for a total of 1000 students.

(a) What is the average class size?

(b) Select a student randomly out of the 1000 students. Let the random variable X equal the size of the class to which this student belongs, and define the p.m.f. of X.

(c) Find $E(X)$, the expected value of X. Does this answer surprise you?

2.3 THE MEAN, VARIANCE, AND STANDARD DEVIATION

Let us consider an example in which $x \in \{1,2,3\}$ and the p.m.f. is given by $f(1) = 3/6$, $f(2) = 2/6$, $f(3) = 1/6$. That is, the probability that the random variable X equals 1, denoted by $P(X = 1)$, is $f(1) = 3/6$. Likewise, $P(X = 2) = f(2) = 2/6$ and $P(X = 3) = f(3) = 1/6$. Of course, $f(x) > 0$ when $x \in S$, and it is always the case that

$$\sum_{x \in S} f(x) = f(1) + f(2) + f(3) = 1.$$

We can think of the points 1, 2, 3 having respective weights (probabilities) 3/6, 2/6, 1/6, and their weighted mean (weighted average) is

$$1 \cdot \frac{3}{6} + 2 \cdot \frac{2}{6} + 3 \cdot \frac{1}{6} = \frac{10}{6},$$

which, in this illustration, does not equal one of the x values in S. As a matter of fact, it is two-thirds of the way between $x = 1$ and $x = 2$. We denote this weighted average or mean by the Greek letter μ (mu). In our example,

$$\mu = \sum_{x \in S} xf(x) = \frac{10}{6}.$$

In general, suppose the random variable X has the space $S = \{u_1, u_2, \ldots, u_k\}$ and these points have respective probabilities $P(X = u_i) = f(u_i) > 0$, where $f(x)$ is the p.m.f. Of course,

$$\sum_{x \in S} f(x) = 1$$

and the **mean** of the random variable X (or of its distribution) is

$$\mu = \sum_{x \in S} xf(x) = u_1 f(u_1) + u_2 f(u_2) + \cdots + u_k f(u_k).$$

That is, in the notation of Section 2.2, $\mu = E(X)$.

Now, u_i is the distance of that ith point from the origin. In mechanics, the product of a distance and its weight is called a moment, so $u_i f(u_i)$ is a moment having a moment arm of length u_i. The sum of such products would be the moment of the system of distances and weights. Actually, it is called the first moment about the origin, since the distances are simply to the first power and the lengths of the arms (distances) are measured from the origin. However, if we compute the first moment about the mean μ, then, since here a moment arm equals $(x - \mu)$, we have

$$\sum_{x \in S} (x - \mu) f(x) = E[(X - \mu)] = E(X) - \mu$$
$$= \mu - \mu = 0.$$

That is, that first moment about μ is equal to zero. In mechanics μ is called the centroid. The last equation implies that if a fulcrum is placed at the centroid μ, then the system of weights would balance, as the sum of the positive moments (when $x > \mu$) about μ equals the sum of the negative moments (when $x < \mu$). In our first illustration, $\mu = 10/6$ is the centroid, so the negative moment

$$\left(1 - \frac{10}{6}\right) \cdot \frac{3}{6} = -\frac{12}{36}$$

equals the sum of the two positive moments

$$\left(2 - \frac{10}{6}\right) \cdot \frac{2}{6} + \left(3 - \frac{10}{6}\right) \cdot \frac{1}{6} = \frac{12}{36}.$$

Since $\mu = E(X)$, it follows from Example 2.2-4 that $b = \mu$ minimizes $E[(X - b)^2]$. Also, Example 2.2-5 shows that

$$\mu = n\left(\frac{N_1}{N}\right)$$

is the mean of the hypergeometric distribution.

Statisticians often find it valuable to compute the second moment about the mean μ. It is called the second moment because the distances are raised to the second power and is equal to

$$\sum_{x \in S} (x - \mu)^2 f(x) = (u_1 - \mu)^2 f(u_1) + (u_2 - \mu)^2 f(u_2) + \cdots + (u_k - \mu)^2 f(u_k).$$

This weighted mean of the squares of those distances is called the **variance** of the random variable X (or of its distribution). The positive square root of the variance is called the **standard deviation** of X and is denoted by the Greek letter σ (sigma). Thus, the variance is σ^2, sometimes denoted by $\text{Var}(X)$. That is, $\sigma^2 = E[(X - \mu)]^2 = \text{Var}(X)$. In our first illustration, since $\mu = 10/6$, the variance equals

$$\sigma^2 = \text{Var}(X) = \left(1 - \frac{10}{6}\right)^2 \cdot \frac{3}{6} + \left(2 - \frac{10}{6}\right)^2 \cdot \frac{2}{6} + \left(3 - \frac{10}{6}\right)^2 \cdot \frac{1}{6} = \frac{120}{216}.$$

Hence, the standard deviation is

$$\sigma = \sqrt{\sigma^2} = \sqrt{\frac{120}{216}} = 0.745.$$

It is worth noting that the variance can be computed in another way, because

$$\begin{aligned} \sigma^2 &= E[(X - \mu)^2] = E[X^2 - 2\mu X + \mu^2] \\ &= E(X^2) - 2\mu E(X) + \mu^2 \\ &= E(X^2) - \mu^2. \end{aligned}$$

That is, the variance σ^2 equals the difference of the second moment about the origin and the square of the mean. For our first illustration,

$$\sigma^2 = \sum_{x=1}^{3} x^2 f(x) - \mu^2$$
$$= 1^2\left(\frac{3}{6}\right) + 2^2\left(\frac{2}{6}\right) + 3^2\left(\frac{1}{6}\right) - \left(\frac{10}{6}\right)^2 = \frac{20}{6} - \frac{100}{36} = \frac{120}{216},$$

which agrees with our previous computation.

EXAMPLE 2.3-1 Let X equal the number of spots on the side facing upwards after a six-sided die (one of a pair of dice) is cast at random. If everything is fair about this experiment, a reasonable probability model is given by the p.m.f.

$$f(x) = P(X = x) = \frac{1}{6}, \qquad x = 1, 2, 3, 4, 5, 6.$$

The mean of X is

$$\mu = E(X) = \sum_{x=1}^{6} x\left(\frac{1}{6}\right) = \frac{1 + 2 + 3 + 4 + 5 + 6}{6} = \frac{7}{2}.$$

The second moment about the origin is

$$E(X^2) = \sum_{x=1}^{6} x^2\left(\frac{1}{6}\right) = \frac{1^2 + 2^2 + 3^2 + 4^2 + 5^2 + 6^2}{6} = \frac{91}{6}.$$

Thus, the variance equals

$$\sigma^2 = \frac{91}{6} - \left(\frac{7}{2}\right)^2 = \frac{182 - 147}{12} = \frac{35}{12}.$$

The standard deviation is $\sigma = \sqrt{35/12} = 1.708$. ■

EXAMPLE 2.3-2 Let the p.m.f. of X be defined by $f(x) = x/6, x = 1, 2, 3$. The mean of X is

$$\mu = E(X) = 1\left(\frac{1}{6}\right) + 2\left(\frac{2}{6}\right) + 3\left(\frac{3}{6}\right) = \frac{7}{3}.$$

To find the variance and standard deviation of X, we first find

$$E(X^2) = 1^2\left(\frac{1}{6}\right) + 2^2\left(\frac{2}{6}\right) + 3^2\left(\frac{3}{6}\right) = \frac{36}{6} = 6.$$

Thus, the variance of X is

$$\sigma^2 = E(X^2) - \mu^2 = 6 - \left(\frac{7}{3}\right)^2 = \frac{5}{9}$$

and the standard deviation of X is

$$\sigma = \sqrt{5/9} = 0.745.$$

■

Although most students understand that $\mu = E(X)$ is, in some sense, a measure of the middle of the distribution of X, it is difficult to get much of a feeling for the variance and the standard deviation. The next example illustrates that the standard deviation is a measure of the dispersion, or spread, of the points belonging to the space S.

EXAMPLE 2.3-3 Let X have the p.m.f. $f(x) = 1/3, x = -1, 0, 1$. Here the mean is

$$\mu = \sum_{x=-1}^{1} xf(x) = (-1)\left(\frac{1}{3}\right) + (0)\left(\frac{1}{3}\right) + (1)\left(\frac{1}{3}\right) = 0.$$

Accordingly, the variance, denoted by σ_X^2, is

$$\begin{aligned}\sigma_X^2 &= E[(X - 0)^2] \\ &= \sum_{x=-1}^{1} x^2 f(x) \\ &= (-1)^2\left(\frac{1}{3}\right) + (0)^2\left(\frac{1}{3}\right) + (1)^2\left(\frac{1}{3}\right) \\ &= \frac{2}{3},\end{aligned}$$

so the standard deviation is $\sigma_X = \sqrt{2/3}$. Next, let another random variable Y have the p.m.f. $g(y) = 1/3, y = -2, 0, 2$. Its mean is also zero, and it is easy to show that $\text{Var}(Y) = 8/3$, so the standard deviation of Y is $\sigma_Y = 2\sqrt{2/3}$. Here the standard deviation of Y is twice that of the standard deviation of X, reflecting the fact that the probability of Y is spread out twice as much as that of X. ■

EXAMPLE 2.3-4 The mean of X, which has a uniform distribution on the first m positive integers, is given by

$$\begin{aligned}\mu = E(X) &= \sum_{x=1}^{m} x\left(\frac{1}{m}\right) = \frac{1}{m}\sum_{x=1}^{m} x \\ &= \left(\frac{1}{m}\right)\frac{m(m+1)}{2} = \frac{m+1}{2}.\end{aligned}$$

To find the variance of X, we first find

$$\begin{aligned}E(X^2) &= \sum_{x=1}^{m} x^2\left(\frac{1}{m}\right) = \frac{1}{m}\sum_{x=1}^{m} x^2 \\ &= \left(\frac{1}{m}\right)\frac{m(m+1)(2m+1)}{6} = \frac{(m+1)(2m+1)}{6}.\end{aligned}$$

Thus, the variance of X is

$$\begin{aligned}\sigma^2 = \text{Var}(X) &= \text{E}[(X - \mu)^2] \\ &= E(X^2) - \mu^2 = \frac{(m+1)(2m+1)}{6} - \left(\frac{m+1}{2}\right)^2 \\ &= \frac{m^2 - 1}{12}.\end{aligned}$$

For example, we find that if X equals the outcome when rolling a fair six-sided die, the p.m.f. of X is

$$f(x) = \frac{1}{6}, \qquad x = 1, 2, 3, 4, 5, 6;$$

the respective mean and variance of X are

$$\mu = \frac{6+1}{2} = 3.5 \qquad \text{and} \qquad \sigma^2 = \frac{6^2-1}{12} = \frac{35}{12},$$

which agrees with calculations of Example 2.3-1. ■

Now let X be a random variable with mean μ_X and variance σ_X^2. Of course, $Y = aX + b$, where a and b are constants, is a random variable, too. The mean of Y is

$$\mu_Y = E(Y) = E(aX + b) = aE(X) + b = a\mu_X + b.$$

Moreover, the variance of Y is

$$\sigma_Y^2 = E[(Y - \mu_Y)^2] = E[(aX + b - a\mu_X - b)^2] = E[a^2(X - \mu_X)^2] = a^2\sigma_X^2.$$

Thus, $\sigma_Y = |a|\sigma_X$. To illustrate, note in Example 2.3-3 that the relationship between the two distributions could be explained by $Y = 2X$, so that $\sigma_Y^2 = 4\sigma_X^2$ and consequently $\sigma_Y = 2\sigma_X$, which we had observed there. In addition, we see that adding or subtracting a constant from X does not change the variance. In our example, $\text{Var}(X - 1) = \text{Var}(X)$, because $a = 1$ and $b = -1$.

Let r be a positive integer. If

$$E(X^r) = \sum_{x \in S} x^r f(x)$$

is finite, it is called the rth **moment** of the distribution about the origin. In addition, the expectation

$$E[(X - b)^r] = \sum_{x \in S} (x - b)^r f(x)$$

is called the rth moment of the distribution about b.

For a given positive integer r,

$$E[(X)_r] = E[X(X - 1)(X - 2)\cdots(X - r + 1)]$$

is called the rth **factorial moment**. We note that the second factorial moment is equal to the difference of the second and first moments:

$$E[X(X - 1)] = E(X^2) - E(X).$$

There is another formula that can be used to compute the variance. This formula uses the second factorial moment and sometimes simplifies the calculations. First find the values of $E(X)$ and $E[X(X - 1)]$. Then

$$\sigma^2 = E[X(X - 1)] + E(X) - [E(X)]^2,$$

since, by the distributive property of E, this becomes

$$\sigma^2 = E(X^2) - E(X) + E(X) - [E(X)]^2 = E(X^2) - \mu^2.$$

EXAMPLE 2.3-5 In Example 2.2-5 concerning the hypergeometric distribution, we found that the mean of that distribution is

$$\mu = E(X) = n\left(\frac{N_1}{N}\right) = np,$$

where $p = N_1/N$, the fraction of red chips in the N chips. In Exercise 2.3-17, it is determined that

$$E[X(X-1)] = \frac{(n)(n-1)(N_1)(N_1-1)}{N(N-1)}.$$

Thus, the variance of X is $E[X(X-1)] + E(X) - [E(X)]^2$, namely,

$$\sigma^2 = \frac{n(n-1)(N_1)(N_1-1)}{N(N-1)} + \frac{nN_1}{N} - \left(\frac{nN_1}{N}\right)^2.$$

After some straightforward algebra, we find that

$$\sigma^2 = n\left(\frac{N_1}{N}\right)\left(\frac{N_2}{N}\right)\left(\frac{N-n}{N-1}\right) = np(1-p)\left(\frac{N-n}{N-1}\right).$$ ■

Suppose that we now consider the situation in which we actually perform a certain random experiment n times, obtaining n observed values of the random variable—say, $x_1, x_2, \cdots, x_n$. Often the collection is referred to as a **sample**. It is possible that some of these values might be the same, but we do not worry about this at this time. We artificially create a probability distribution by placing the weight $1/n$ on each of these x values. Note that these weights are positive and sum to 1, so we have a distribution we call the **empirical distribution**, since it is determined by the data $x_1, x_2, \cdots, x_n$. The mean of the empirical distribution is

$$\sum_{i=1}^{n} x_i\left(\frac{1}{n}\right) = \frac{1}{n}\sum_{i=1}^{n} x_i,$$

which is the arithmetic mean of the observations $x_1, x_2, \cdots, x_n$. We denote this mean by $\overline{x}$ and call it the **sample mean** (or mean of the sample $x_1, x_2, \cdots, x_n$). That is, the sample mean is

$$\overline{x} = \frac{1}{n}\sum_{i=1}^{n} x_i,$$

which is, in some sense, an estimate of μ if the latter is unknown.

Likewise, the **variance of the empirical distribution** is

$$v = \sum_{i=1}^{n}(x_i - \overline{x})^2\left(\frac{1}{n}\right) = \frac{1}{n}\sum_{i=1}^{n}(x_i - \overline{x})^2,$$

which can be written as

$$v = \sum_{i=1}^{n} x_i^2\left(\frac{1}{n}\right) - \overline{x}^2 = \frac{1}{n}\sum_{i=1}^{n} x_i^2 - \overline{x}^2,$$

that is, the second moment about the origin, minus the square of the mean. However, v is not called the sample variance, but

$$s^2 = \left[\frac{n}{n-1}\right]v = \frac{1}{n-1}\sum_{i=1}^{n}(x_i - \bar{x})^2$$

is, because we will see later that, in some sense, s^2 is a better estimate of an unknown σ^2 than is v. Thus, the **sample variance** is

$$s^2 = \frac{1}{n-1}\sum_{i=1}^{n}(x_i - \bar{x})^2.$$

REMARK It is easy to expand the sum of squares; we have

$$\sum_{i=1}^{n}(x_i - \bar{x})^2 = \sum_{i=1}^{n}x_i^2 - \frac{(\sum_{i=1}^{n}x_i)^2}{n}.$$

Many find that the right-hand expression makes the computation easier than first taking the n differences, $x_i - \bar{x}$, $i = 1, 2, \ldots, n$; squaring them; and then summing. There is another advantage when $\bar{x}$ has many digits to the right of the decimal point. If that is the case, then $x_i - \bar{x}$ must be rounded off, and that creates an error in the sum of squares. In the easier form, that rounding off is not necessary until the computation is completed. Of course, if you are using a statistical calculator or statistics package on the computer, all of these computations are done for you. ■

The **sample standard deviation**, $s = \sqrt{s^2} \geq 0$, is a measure of how dispersed the data are from the sample mean. At this stage of your study of statistics, it is difficult to get a good understanding or meaning of the standard deviation s, but you can roughly think of it as the average distance of the values $x_1, x_2, \ldots, x_n$ from the mean $\bar{x}$. This is not true exactly, for, in general,

$$s > \frac{1}{n}\sum_{i=1}^{n}|x_i - \bar{x}|,$$

but it is fair to say that s is somewhat larger, yet of the same magnitude, as the average of the distances of $x_1, x_2, \cdots, x_n$ from $\bar{x}$.

EXAMPLE 2.3-6 Rolling a fair six-sided die five times could result in the following sample of $n = 5$ observations:

$$x_1 = 3,\ x_2 = 1,\ x_3 = 2,\ x_4 = 6,\ x_5 = 3.$$

In this case,

$$\bar{x} = \frac{3 + 1 + 2 + 6 + 3}{5} = 3$$

and

$$s^2 = \frac{(3-3)^2 + (1-3)^2 + (2-3)^2 + (6-3)^2 + (3-3)^2}{4} = \frac{14}{4} = 3.5.$$

It follows that $s = \sqrt{14/4} = 1.87$. We had noted that s can roughly be thought of as the average distance that the x-values are away from the sample mean $\overline{x}$. In this example, the distances from $\overline{x} = 3$ are 0, 2, 1, 3, 0, with an average of 1.2, which is less than $s = 1.87$. In general, s will be somewhat larger than this average distance. ■

There is an alternative way of computing s^2, because $s^2 = [n/(n-1)]v$ and

$$v = \frac{1}{n}\sum_{i=1}^{n}(x_i - \overline{x})^2 = \frac{1}{n}\sum_{i=1}^{n}x_i^2 - \overline{x}^2.$$

It follows that

$$s^2 = \frac{\sum_{i=1}^{n}x_i^2 - n\overline{x}^2}{n-1} = \frac{\sum_{i=1}^{n}x_i^2 - \frac{1}{n}\left(\sum_{i=1}^{n}x_i\right)^2}{n-1}.$$

COMPUTATIONAL COMMENTS **(CAS)** When it comes to computing probabilities, means, and variances in the discrete case, we need to evaluate summations and could use a computer algebra system (CAS) such as *Maple* or *Mathematica*. The same statement could be made about the continuous case in Chapter 3, with integrals replacing summations.

For example, let us consider the hypergeometric distribution:

```
> f:=binomial(N[1],x)*binomial(N[2],n-x)/binomial(N[1]+N[2],n);
```

$$f := \frac{\text{binomial}(N_1, x)\,\text{binomial}(N_2, n-x)}{\text{binomial}(N_1 + N_2, n)}$$

```
> simplify(sum(f, x = 0 .. N[1]));
```

$$1$$

```
> mu := simplify(sum(x*f, x = 0 .. N[1]));
```

$$\mu := \frac{N_1\, n}{N_1 + N_2}$$

```
> var := simplify(sum(x^2*f, x = 0 .. N[1]) - mu^2);
```

$$var := -\frac{N_2 N_1 (n - N_1 - N_2)\, n}{(N_1 + N_2)^2 (N_1 - 1 + N_2)}$$

```
> N[1] := 20: N[2] := 30: n := 10:
> mu := sum(x*f, x = 0 .. N[1]);
```

$$\mu := 4$$

```
> var := sum((x - mu)^2*f, x = 0 .. N[1]);
```

$$var := \frac{96}{49}$$

```
> sum(f, x = 3 .. 6);
```

$$\frac{8469282699}{10272278170}$$

```
> evalf(%);
```

$$0.8244794931$$

Maple does not always write the output in the standard way, so we note that usually we write

$$\mu = n\left(\frac{N_1}{N}\right) = np$$

and

$$\sigma^2 = n\left(\frac{N_1}{N}\right)\left(\frac{N_2}{N}\right)\left(\frac{N-n}{N-1}\right) = np(1-p)\left(\frac{N-n}{N-1}\right).$$

The last two commands in the *Maple* output give the values of $P(3 \le X \le 6)$, as a fraction and as a decimal. It is also possible to find these probabilities with the use of a program like Minitab—or some calculators can even do this. You are encouraged to use whatever computing facilities are available to you.

REMARK Note that we have introduced two types of means and standard deviations. The first pair is associated with the probability distribution and is denoted by the Greek symbols (μ, σ). The second pair is associated with data and is denoted by the Roman letters $(\overline{x}, s)$. ■

EXERCISES

2.3-1. Find the mean and variance for the following discrete distributions:

(a) $f(x) = \dfrac{1}{5}, \quad x = 5, 10, 15, 20, 25.$

(b) $f(x) = 1, \quad x = 5.$

(c) $f(x) = \dfrac{4-x}{6}, \quad x = 1, 2, 3.$

2.3-2. For each of the following distributions, find $\mu = E(X)$, $E[X(X-1)]$, and $\sigma^2 = E[X(X-1)] + E(X) - \mu^2$:

(a) $f(x) = \dfrac{3!}{x!(3-x)!}\left(\dfrac{1}{4}\right)^x\left(\dfrac{3}{4}\right)^{3-x}$,
$x = 0, 1, 2, 3.$

(b) $f(x) = \dfrac{4!}{x!(4-x)!}\left(\dfrac{1}{2}\right)^4$,
$x = 0, 1, 2, 3, 4.$

2.3-3. Given $E(X+4) = 10$ and $E[(X+4)^2] = 116$, determine (a) $\text{Var}(X+4)$, (b) μ, and (c) σ^2.

2.3-4. Let μ and σ^2 denote the mean and variance of the random variable X. Determine $E[(X-\mu)/\sigma]$ and $E\{[(X-\mu)/\sigma]^2\}$.

2.3-5. Consider an experiment that consists of selecting a card at random from an ordinary deck of cards. Let the random variable X equal the value of the selected card, where Ace = 1, Jack = 11, Queen = 12, and King = 13. Thus, the space of X is $S = \{1, 2, 3, \cdots, 13\}$. If the experiment is performed in an unbiased manner, assign probabilities to these 13 outcomes and compute the mean μ of this probability distribution.

2.3-6. Place eight chips in a bowl: Three have the number 1 on them, two have the number 2, and three have the number 3. Say each chip has a probability of 1/8 of being drawn at random. Let the random variable X equal the number on the chip that is selected, so that the space of X is $S = \{1, 2, 3\}$. Make reasonable probability assignments to each of these three outcomes, and compute the mean μ and the variance σ^2 of this probability distribution.

2.3-7. A fair coin is flipped successively at random until the first head is observed. Let the random variable X denote the number of flips of the coin that are required. Then the space of X is $S = \{x : x = 1, 2, 3, 4, \ldots\}$. Later we learn that, under certain conditions, we can assign probabilities to these outcomes in S with the function $f(x) = (1/2)^x, x = 1, 2, 3, 4, \cdots$. Compute the mean μ. HINT: Write out the series for μ, and then construct the series for $(1/2)\mu$ and take the difference. An alternative method would be to compare the series for μ with that of the negative binomial $(1-z)^{-2}$, with $z = 1/2$.

2.3-8. Let X equal the number of calls per hour received by 911 between midnight and noon and reported in the *Holland Sentinel*. On October 29 and October 30, the following numbers of calls were reported:

Oct. 29:	0	1	1	1	0	1	2	1	4	1	2	3
Oct. 30:	0	3	0	1	0	1	1	2	3	0	2	2

(a) Find the sample mean.

(b) Find the sample variance.

2.3-9. Let X equal an integer selected at random from the first m positive integers, $\{1,2,\ldots,m\}$.

(a) Give the values of $E(X)$ and $\text{Var}(X)$.
(b) Find the value of m for which $E(X) = \text{Var}(X)$. (See Zerger in the references.)

2.3-10. Students in a statistics class were asked to report the number of pets in their family. The following data were collected:

3 3 2 4 4 4 3 2 3 2 2 3 4 2 2 3
2 3 4 4 2 3 2 3 3 2 4 3 3 3 2 2
2 2 1 4 4 2 3 3 1 2 2 2 2 3 1

(a) Find the frequencies of 1, 2, 3, 4.
(b) Calculate the sample mean and the sample standard deviation.
(c) Construct a histogram and locate the mean on the histogram.

2.3-11. Calculate the mean $\bar{x}$ and the variance s^2 of the samples given in

(a) Exercise 1.1-3,
(b) Exercise 1.1-4,
(c) Exercise 1.1-5,
(d) Exercise 1.1-7.

2.3-12. Referring to Exercise 1.1-6, compute the sample mean $\bar{x}$. Could a statistician tell that family about how many boxes of cereal they could expect to purchase to obtain all four prizes?

2.3-13. A measure of **skewness** is defined by

$$\frac{E[(X-\mu)^3]}{\{E[(X-\mu)^2]\}^{3/2}} = \frac{E[(X-\mu)^3]}{(\sigma^2)^{3/2}} = \frac{E[(X-\mu)^3]}{\sigma^3}.$$

When a distribution is symmetrical about the mean, the skewness is equal to zero. If the probability histogram has a longer "tail" to the right than to the left, the measure of skewness is positive, and we say that the distribution is skewed positively, or to the right. If the probability histogram has a longer tail to the left than to the right, the measure of skewness is negative, and we say that the distribution is skewed negatively, or to the left. If the p.m.f. of X is given by $f(x)$, (i) depict the p.m.f. as a probability histogram and find the values of (ii) the mean, (iii) the standard deviation, and (iv) the skewness.

(a)
$$f(x) = \begin{cases} \dfrac{2^{6-x}}{64}, & x = 1,2,3,4,5,6, \\ \dfrac{1}{64}, & x = 7. \end{cases}$$

(b)
$$f(x) = \begin{cases} \dfrac{1}{64}, & x = 1, \\ \dfrac{2^{x-2}}{64}, & x = 2,3,4,5,6,7. \end{cases}$$

2.3-14. In LOTTO 49, Michigan's lottery game, a player selects 6 integers out of the first 49 positive integers. The state then randomly selects 6 out of the first 49 positive integers. Cash prizes are given to a player who matches 4, 5, or 6 integers. Let X equal the number of integers selected by a player that match integers selected by the state.

(a) State the p.m.f. of X.
(b) Calculate the mean, variance, and standard deviation of X.
(c) What value of X is most likely to occur?
(d) On February 25, 1995, the jackpot was worth \$45 million. When the prize is this large, many bets are placed. Out of the 25 million bets that were placed, 3 people matched all six numbers, with each winning \$15 million (most of which was paid by losers during preceding games); 390 matched five numbers, to win \$2500 each and; 22,187 matched four numbers, to win \$100 each. Are these numbers of winners consistent with the probability model?
(e) A mathematics professor convinced some colleagues to pool their LOTTO bets, so that they were able to purchase 138 tickets together. They let the state computer randomly select the numbers on which they placed their bets. Among their 138 bets, 65 matched none of the winning LOTTO numbers, $\{3, 20, 33, 34, 43, 46\}$; 55 matched one, 16 matched two, and 2 matched three numbers. How do these results compare with what they could have expected?

2.3-15. Let X equal the larger outcome when a pair of four-sided dice is rolled. The p.m.f. of X is

$$f(x) = \frac{2x-1}{16}, \qquad x = 1,2,3,4.$$

(a) Find the mean, variance, and standard deviation of X.

(b) Calculate the sample mean, sample variance, and sample standard deviation of the following 100 simulated observations of X, and compare these answers with those found in part (a):

4	4	4	4	2	2	2	3	1	4	3	3	2	3	2	4	4	2	3	4
4	3	4	3	4	3	3	2	4	4	3	2	3	3	3	2	4	4	3	4
1	4	3	4	4	4	3	2	4	4	4	3	1	3	2	4	4	4	4	1
3	4	3	2	4	4	3	3	1	3	3	3	3	2	2	2	3	4	3	3
2	4	2	3	3	2	4	4	3	4	4	4	4	3	4	4	4	4	4	4

(c) Draw the graphs of the probability histogram and the relative frequency histogram on the same figure.

(d) Generate your own data, either rolling (four-sided or six-sided) dice or simulating this experiment on a computer.

2.3-16. A Bingo card has 25 squares with numbers on 24 of them, the center being a free square. The integers that are placed on the Bingo card are selected randomly and without replacement from 1 to 75, inclusive. When a game called "cover-up" is played, balls numbered from 1 to 75, inclusive, are selected randomly and without replacement until a player covers each of the numbers on a card. Let X equal the number of balls that must be drawn to cover all the numbers on a single card.

(a) Argue that the p.m.f. of X, for $x = 24, 25, \ldots, 75$, is

$$f(x) = \frac{\binom{24}{23}\binom{51}{x-24}}{\binom{75}{x-1}} \cdot \frac{1}{75-(x-1)} = \frac{\binom{51}{x-24}}{\binom{75}{x}} \cdot \frac{24}{x} = \frac{\binom{x}{24}}{\binom{75}{24}} \cdot \frac{24}{x}.$$

(b) What value of X is most likely to occur? In other words, what is the mode of this distribution?

(c) To show that the mean of X is $(24)(76)/25 = 72.96$, use the combinatorial identity

$$\binom{k+n+1}{k+1} = \sum_{x=k}^{n+k} \binom{x}{k}.$$

(d) Show that $E[X(X+1)] = \dfrac{24 \cdot 77 \cdot 76}{26} = 5401.8462$.

(e) Calculate $\text{Var}(X) = \text{E}[\text{X}(\text{X}+1)] - \text{E}[\text{X}] - [\text{E}(\text{X})]^2 = \dfrac{46{,}512}{8125} = 5.7246$ and $\sigma = 2.39$.

(f) The following 100 observations of X were simulated on the computer:

75	73	74	74	73	75	75	71	71	74	75	74	74	73	75
75	75	71	68	75	74	72	73	75	74	67	73	71	74	74
73	75	71	73	71	68	74	75	66	75	75	74	75	71	75
72	75	74	75	75	72	75	75	74	73	75	62	64	75	72
74	74	75	73	75	75	73	74	75	68	75	69	74	75	61
73	73	73	72	74	68	74	71	73	75	73	74	72	74	73
75	73	71	70	62	74	74	72	75	74					

Compare these data with the probability model. In particular, make the following comparisons: (i) $\bar{x}$ with μ, (ii) s^2 with σ^2, (iii) s with σ, (iv) $(1/100)\sum_{i=1}^{100} x_i(x_i+1)$ with $E[X(X+1)]$.

(g) Compare the probability histogram with the relative frequency histogram.

2.3-17. To find the variance of a hypergeometric random variable in Example 2.3-5, we used the fact that

$$E[X(X-1)] = \frac{N_1(N_1-1)(n)(n-1)}{N(N-1)}.$$

Prove this result by making the change of variables $k = x - 2$ and noting that

$$\binom{N}{n} = \frac{N(N-1)}{n(n-1)}\binom{N-2}{n-2}.$$

2.3-18. A deck of $n = 10$ cards is numbered from 1 to 10. The cards are shuffled and laid down from left to right, face up. Order each of the five successive pairs of cards. Each of these five pairs determines a random interval. Let X equal the number of these five random intervals that intersect each of the other four intervals. It can be shown that

$$P(X \geq k) = \frac{2^k}{\binom{2k+1}{k}}, \qquad k = 0, 1, 2, 3, 4, 5.$$

(a) Find the probability that at least one interval intersects all the other intervals. (You could also simulate this.)

(b) Prove that $\mu = E(X) = \sum_{k=1}^{5} P(X \geq k)$.

(c) Find the value of $\mu = E(X)$ with $n = 10$ cards.

(d) Let the number of cards increase without bound. Find the value of

$$\mu = \sum_{k=0}^{\infty} \frac{2^k}{\binom{2k+1}{k}}.$$

2.3-19. A warranty is written on a product worth \$10,000 so that the buyer is given \$8000 if it fails in the first year, \$6000 if it fails in the second, \$4000 if it fails in the third, \$2000 if it fails in the fourth, and zero after that. The probability of the product's failing in a year is 0.1; failures are independent of those of other years. What is the expected value of the warranty?

2.4 BERNOULLI TRIALS AND THE BINOMIAL DISTRIBUTION

The probability models for random experiments that will be described in this section occur frequently in applications.

A **Bernoulli experiment** is a random experiment, the outcome of which can be classified in one of two mutually exclusive and exhaustive ways—say, success or failure (e.g., female or male, life or death, nondefective or defective). A sequence of **Bernoulli trials** occurs when a Bernoulli experiment is performed several *independent* times so that the probability of success—say, p—remains the *same* from trial to trial. That is, in such a sequence we let p denote the probability of success on each trial. In addition, we shall frequently let $q = 1 - p$ denote the probability of failure; that is, we shall use q and $1 - p$ interchangeably.

EXAMPLE 2.4-1 Suppose that the probability of germination of a beet seed is 0.8 and the germination of a seed is called a success. If we plant 10 seeds and can assume that the germination of one seed is independent of the germination of another seed, this would correspond to 10 Bernoulli trials with $p = 0.8$. ■

EXAMPLE 2.4-2 In the Michigan daily lottery, the probability of winning when placing a six-way boxed bet is 0.006. A bet placed on each of 12 successive days would correspond to 12 Bernoulli trials with $p = 0.006$. ■

Let X be a random variable associated with a Bernoulli trial by defining it as follows:

$$X(\text{success}) = 1 \quad \text{and} \quad X(\text{failure}) = 0.$$

That is, the two outcomes, success and failure, are denoted by one and zero, respectively. The p.m.f. of X can be written as

$$f(x) = p^x(1 - p)^{1-x}, \qquad x = 0, 1,$$

and we say that X has a **Bernoulli distribution**. The expected value of X is

$$\mu = E(X) = \sum_{x=0}^{1} x p^x (1 - p)^{1-x} = (0)(1 - p) + (1)(p) = p,$$

and the variance of X is

$$\sigma^2 = \text{Var}(X) = \sum_{x=0}^{1}(x-p)^2p^x(1-p)^{1-x}$$
$$= (0-p)^2(1-p) + (1-p)^2p = p(1-p) = pq.$$

It follows that the standard deviation of X is

$$\sigma = \sqrt{p(1-p)} = \sqrt{pq}.$$

In a sequence of n Bernoulli trials, we shall let X_i denote the Bernoulli random variable associated with the ith trial. An observed sequence of n Bernoulli trials will then be an n-tuple of zeros and ones, and we often call this collection a **random sample** of size n from a Bernoulli distribution.

EXAMPLE 2.4-3 Out of millions of instant lottery tickets, suppose that 20% are winners. If five such tickets are purchased, then $(0,0,0,1,0)$ is a possible observed sequence in which the fourth ticket is a winner and the other four are losers. Assuming independence among winning and losing tickets, we observe that the probability of this outcome is

$$(0.8)(0.8)(0.8)(0.2)(0.8) = (0.2)(0.8)^4.$$

■

EXAMPLE 2.4-4 If five beet seeds are planted in a row, a possible observed sequence would be (1, 0, 1, 0, 1), in which the first, third, and fifth seeds germinated and the other two did not. If the probability of germination is $p = 0.8$, the probability of this outcome is, assuming independence,

$$(0.8)(0.2)(0.8)(0.2)(0.8) = (0.8)^3(0.2)^2.$$

■

In a sequence of Bernoulli trials, we are often interested in the total number of successes and not in the order of their occurrence. If we let the random variable X equal the number of observed successes in n Bernoulli trials, then the possible values of X are $0, 1, 2, \ldots, n$. If x successes occur, where $x = 0, 1, 2, \ldots, n$, then $n - x$ failures occur. The number of ways of selecting x positions for the x successes in the n trials is

$$\binom{n}{x} = \frac{n!}{x!(n-x)!}.$$

Since the trials are independent and since the probabilities of success and failure on each trial are, respectively, p and $q = 1 - p$, the probability of each of these ways is $p^x(1-p)^{n-x}$. Thus, $f(x)$, the p.m.f. of X, is the sum of the probabilities of the $\binom{n}{x}$ mutually exclusive events; that is,

$$f(x) = \binom{n}{x}p^x(1-p)^{n-x}, \qquad x = 0, 1, 2, \ldots, n.$$

These probabilities are called binomial probabilities, and the random variable X is said to have a **binomial distribution**.

Summarizing, a binomial experiment satisfies the following properties:

1. A Bernoulli (success–failure) experiment is performed n times.
2. The trials are independent.
3. The probability of success on each trial is a constant p; the probability of failure is $q = 1 - p$.
4. The random variable X equals the number of successes in the n trials.

A binomial distribution will be denoted by the symbol $b(n,p)$, and we say that the distribution of X is $b(n,p)$. The constants n and p are called the **parameters** of the binomial distribution; they correspond to the number n of independent trials and the probability p of success on each trial. Thus, if we say that the distribution of X is $b(12, 1/4)$, we mean that X is the number of successes in a random sample of size $n = 12$ from a Bernoulli distribution with $p = 1/4$.

EXAMPLE 2.4-5 In the instant lottery with 20% winning tickets, if X is equal to the number of winning tickets among $n = 8$ that are purchased, then the probability of purchasing two winning tickets is

$$f(2) = P(X = 2) = \binom{8}{2}(0.2)^2(0.8)^6 = 0.2936.$$

The distribution of the random variable X is $b(8, 0.2)$. ■

EXAMPLE 2.4-6 In order to obtain a better feeling for the effect of the parameters n and p on the distribution of probabilities, four probability histograms are displayed in Figure 2.4-1. ■

EXAMPLE 2.4-7 In Example 2.4-1, the number X of seeds that germinate in $n = 10$ independent trials is $b(10, 0.8)$; that is,

$$f(x) = \binom{10}{x}(0.8)^x(0.2)^{10-x}, \qquad x = 0, 1, 2, \ldots, 10.$$

In particular,

$$\begin{aligned} P(X \le 8) &= 1 - P(X = 9) - P(X = 10) \\ &= 1 - 10(0.8)^9(0.2) - (0.8)^{10} = 0.6242. \end{aligned}$$

Also, with a little more work, we could compute

$$P(X \le 6) = \sum_{x=0}^{6} \binom{10}{x}(0.8)^x(0.2)^{10-x}.$$ ■

Cumulative probabilities like those in the previous example are often of interest. We call the function defined by

$$F(x) = P(X \le x), \qquad -\infty < x < \infty,$$

the **cumulative distribution function** or, more simply, the **distribution function** of the random variable X. Values of the distribution function of a random variable X that is $b(n,p)$ are given in Table II in the appendix for selected values of n and p.

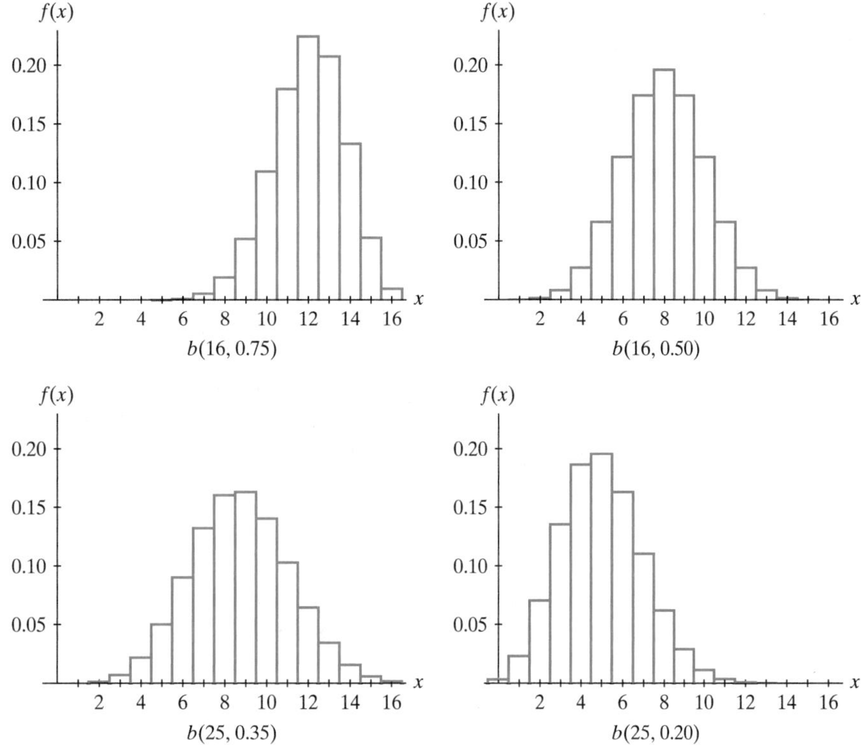

FIGURE 2.4-1: Binomial probability histograms

For the binomial distribution given in Example 2.4-7, namely, the $b(10, 0.8)$ distribution, the distribution function is defined by

$$F(x) = P(X \le x) = \sum_{y=0}^{\lfloor x \rfloor} \binom{10}{y} (0.8)^y (0.2)^{10-y},$$

where $\lfloor x \rfloor$ is the floor or greatest integer in x. A graph of this distribution function is shown in Figure 2.4-2 on the next page. Note that the jumps at the integers in this step function are equal to the probabilities associated with those respective integers.

EXAMPLE 2.4-8 Leghorn chickens are raised for laying eggs. Let $p = 0.5$ be the probability of a female chick hatching. Assuming independence, let X equal the number of female chicks out of 10 newly hatched chicks selected at random. Then the distribution of X is $b(10, 0.5)$. From Table II in the appendix, the probability of 5 or fewer female chicks is

$$P(X \le 5) = 0.6230.$$

The probability of exactly 6 female chicks is

$$\begin{aligned} P(X = 6) &= \binom{10}{6} \left(\frac{1}{2}\right)^6 \left(\frac{1}{2}\right)^4 \\ &= P(X \le 6) - P(X \le 5) \\ &= 0.8281 - 0.6230 = 0.2051, \end{aligned}$$

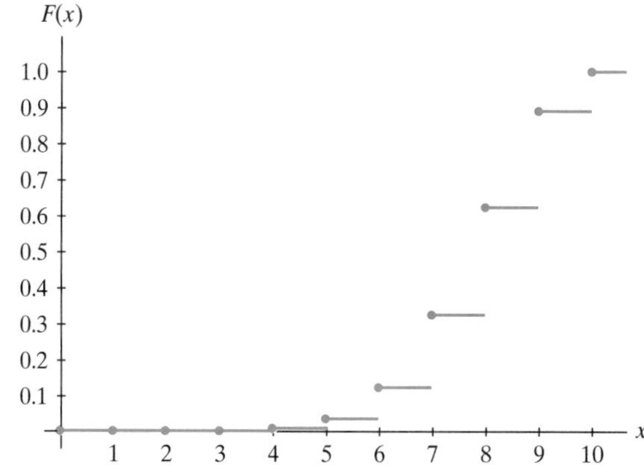

FIGURE 2.4-2: Distribution function for the $b(10, 0.8)$ distribution

since $P(X \le 6) = 0.8281$. The probability of at least 6 female chicks is

$$P(X \ge 6) = 1 - P(X \le 5) = 1 - 0.6230 = 0.3770.$$

COMPUTATIONAL COMMENTS Here is the Minitab solution for Example 2.4-8: To find the preceding probabilities, you use

Calc → Probability Distributions → Binomial

and input the necessary information, namely,

```
Cumulative Distribution Function
Binomial with n = 10 and p = 0.5
x P( X <= x )
5 0.623047

Probability Density Function
Binomial with n = 10 and p = 0.5
x P(X = x )
6 0.205078
```

Although probabilities for the binomial distribution $b(n,p)$ are given in Table II in the appendix for selected values of p that are less than or equal to 0.5, the next example demonstrates that this table can also be used for values of p that are greater than 0.5. In later sections we learn how to approximate certain binomial probabilities with those of other distributions. In addition, you may use your calculator and/or statistical package such as Minitab to find binomial probabilities.

EXAMPLE 2.4-9 Suppose that we are in one of those rare times when 65% of the American public approve of the way the President of the United States is handling his job. Take a random sample of $n = 8$ Americans and let Y equal the number who give approval. Then the distribution of Y is $b(8, 0.65)$. To find $P(Y \ge 6)$, note that

$$P(Y \ge 6) = P(8 - Y \le 8 - 6) = P(X \le 2),$$

where $X = 8 - Y$ counts the number who disapprove. Since $q = 1 - p = 0.35$ equals the probability of disapproval by each person selected, the distribution of X

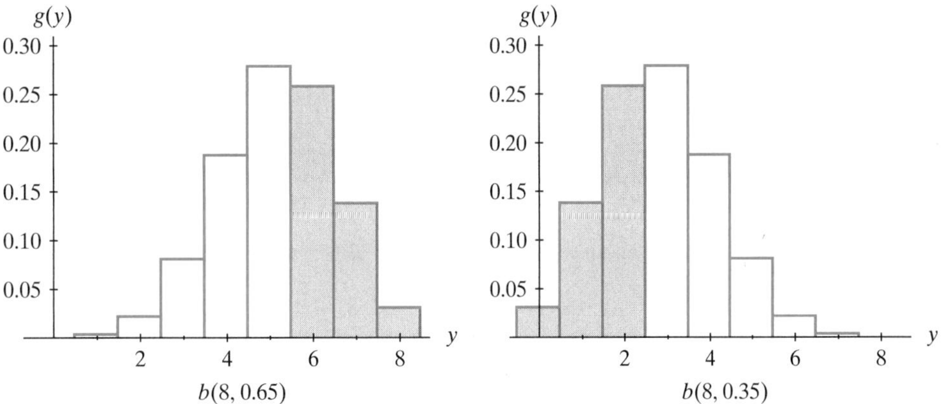

FIGURE 2.4-3: Presidential approval histogram

is $b(8, 0.35)$. (See Figure 2.4-3.) From Table II in the appendix, since $P(X \leq 2) = 0.4278$, it follows that $P(Y \geq 6) = 0.4278$.

Similarly,

$$\begin{aligned} P(Y \leq 5) &= P(8 - Y \geq 8 - 5) \\ &= P(X \geq 3) = 1 - P(X \leq 2) \\ &= 1 - 0.4278 = 0.5722 \end{aligned}$$

and

$$\begin{aligned} P(Y = 5) &= P(8 - Y = 8 - 5) \\ &= P(X = 3) = P(X \leq 3) - P(X \leq 2) \\ &= 0.7064 - 0.4278 = 0.2786. \end{aligned}$$

■

Recall that if n is a positive integer, then

$$(a + b)^n = \sum_{x=0}^{n} \binom{n}{x} b^x a^{n-x}.$$

Thus, if we use this binomial expansion with $b = p$ and $a = 1 - p$, then the sum of the binomial probabilities is

$$\sum_{x=0}^{n} \binom{n}{x} p^x (1 - p)^{n-x} = [(1 - p) + p]^n = 1,$$

a result that had to follow from the fact that $f(x)$ is a p.m.f.

We use the binomial expansion to find the mean and the variance of a binomial random variable X that is $b(n, p)$. The mean is given by

$$\begin{aligned} \mu = E(X) &= \sum_{x=0}^{n} x \frac{n!}{x!(n - x)!} p^x (1 - p)^{n-x} \\ &= \sum_{x=1}^{n} \frac{n!}{(x - 1)!(n - x)!} p^x (1 - p)^{n-x}. \end{aligned}$$

Let $k = x - 1$ or $x = k + 1$ in the latter sum. Then

$$\begin{aligned}\mu = E(X) &= \sum_{k=0}^{n-1} \frac{n!}{k!(n-k-1)!} p^{k+1}(1-p)^{n-k-1} \\ &= np \sum_{k=0}^{n-1} \frac{(n-1)!}{k!(n-1-k)!} p^k (1-p)^{n-1-k} \\ &= np(1-p+p)^{n-1} = np.\end{aligned}$$

To find the variance, we first find the value of $E[X(X-1)]$, the second factorial moment. Using the second factorial moment, we find that the variance of X is given by $\text{Var}(X) = E[X(X-1)] + E(X) - \mu^2$. Now,

$$\begin{aligned}E[X(X-1)] &= \sum_{x=0}^{n} x(x-1)\frac{n!}{x!(n-x)!} p^x (1-p)^{n-x} \\ &= \sum_{x=2}^{n} \frac{n!}{(x-2)!(n-x)!} p^x (1-p)^{n-x}.\end{aligned}$$

Letting $k = x - 2$ or $x = k + 2$, we obtain

$$\begin{aligned}E[X(X-1)] &= \sum_{k=0}^{n-2} \frac{n!}{k!(n-k-2)!} p^{k+2}(1-p)^{n-k-2} \\ &= n(n-1)p^2 \sum_{k=0}^{n-2} \frac{(n-2)!}{k!(n-2-k)!} p^k (1-p)^{n-2-k} \\ &= n(n-1)p^2(1-p+p)^{n-2} = n(n-1)p^2.\end{aligned}$$

Thus,

$$\begin{aligned}\sigma^2 = \text{Var}(X) &= E(X^2) - [E(X)]^2 = E[X(X-1)] + E(X) - [E(X)]^2 \\ &= n(n-1)p^2 + np - (np)^2 = np(1-p).\end{aligned}$$

Summarizing, if X is $b(n,p)$, then

$$\mu = np \qquad \text{and} \qquad \sigma^2 = np(1-p) = npq.$$

We find the mean and variance with the use of the moment-generating function in Example 2.5-3. (See page 91.)

Note that when p is the probability of success on each trial, the expected number of successes in n trials is np, a result that agrees with our intuition. Of course, the standard deviation is

$$\sigma = \sqrt{np(1-p)}.$$

EXAMPLE 2.4-10 Suppose that observation over a long period of time has disclosed that, on the average, 1 out of 10 items produced by a process is defective. Select 5 items independently from the production line and test them. Let X denote the number of defective items among the $n = 5$ items. Then X is $b(5, 0.1)$. Furthermore,

$$E(X) = 5(0.1) = 0.5, \ \text{Var}(X) = 5(0.1)(0.9) = 0.45.$$

For example, the probability of observing at most one defective item is

$$P(X \le 1) = \binom{5}{0}(0.1)^0(0.9)^5 + \binom{5}{1}(0.1)^1(0.9)^4 = 0.9185. \quad \blacksquare$$

The next example shows the relationship between the binomial probability model and a set of observed data. Replications of this example would of course yield different results, in which the fits could be better or worse than the given one.

EXAMPLE 2.4-11 Consider the simple experiment of flipping a fair coin five independent times. If X equals the number of heads observed, then X is $b(5, 0.5)$, $\mu = 2.5$, $\sigma^2 = 1.25$, and $\sigma = 1.118$. This experiment was simulated 100 times, yielding the following data:

2	3	2	4	1	2	1	1	4	2	4	2	0	4	4	2	4	4	3	4
2	2	4	4	1	1	3	3	1	4	2	3	1	2	4	1	2	5	3	2
4	3	2	2	2	3	5	2	0	3	2	1	3	4	2	2	4	0	2	1
3	3	2	3	2	1	3	2	2	2	1	1	3	3	1	1	4	2	1	5
3	2	3	0	3	5	3	2	4	3	3	5	2	3	3	1	3	2	1	1

For these data, $\bar{x} = 2.47$, $s^2 = 1.5243$, and $s = 1.235$. Figure 2.4-4 gives the probability histogram and the relative frequency histogram (shaded). ■

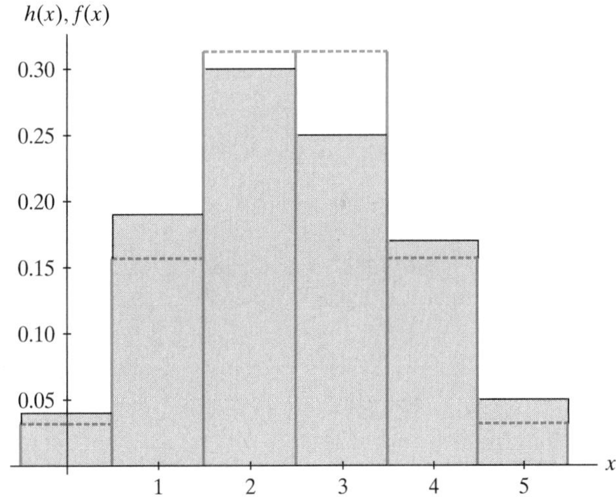

FIGURE 2.4-4: Number of heads when five coins are flipped

Suppose that an urn contains N_1 success balls and N_2 failure balls. Now, let $p = N_1/(N_1 + N_2)$, and let X equal the number of success balls in a random sample of size n that is taken from this urn. If the sampling is done one at a time with replacement, then the distribution of X is $b(n,p)$; if the sampling is done without replacement, then X has a hypergeometric distribution with p.m.f.

$$f(x) = \frac{\binom{N_1}{x}\binom{N_2}{n-x}}{\binom{N_1+N_2}{n}},$$

where x is a nonnegative integer such that $x \le n$, $x \le N_1$, and $n - x \le N_2$. When $N_1 + N_2$ is large and n is relatively small, it makes little difference if the sampling is done with or without replacement. In Figure 2.4-5, the probability histograms are compared for different combinations of n, N_1, and N_2. You are asked to compute some of these probabilities in Exercise 2.4-17.

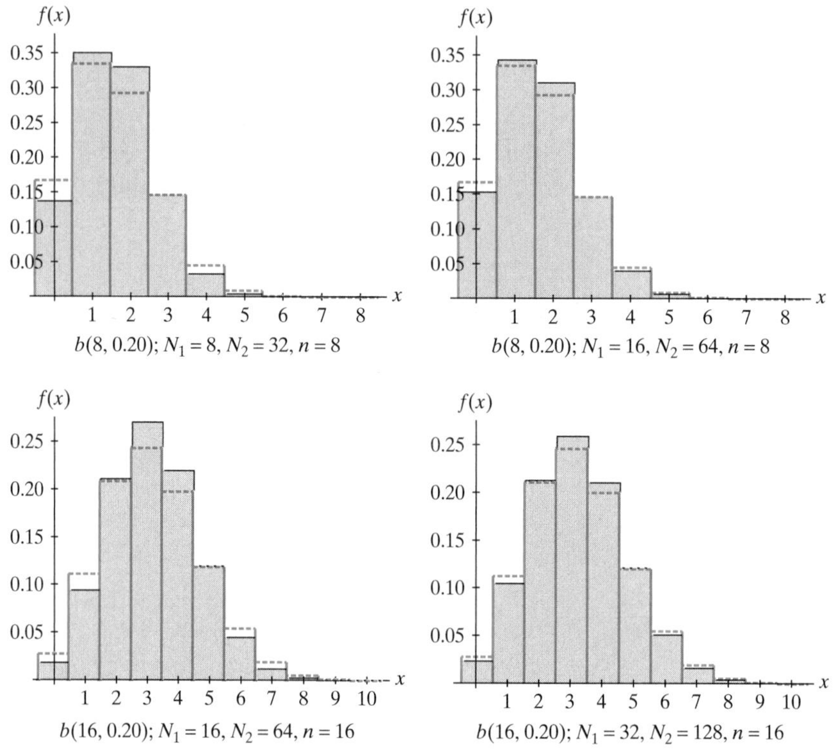

FIGURE 2.4-5: Binomial and hypergeometric (shaded) probability histograms

EXERCISES

2.4-1. An urn contains 7 red and 11 white balls. Draw one ball at random from the urn. Let $X = 1$ if a red ball is drawn, and let $X = 0$ if a white ball is drawn. Give the p.m.f., mean, and variance of X.

2.4-2. Suppose that in Exercise 2.4-1, $X = 1$ if a red ball is drawn and $X = -1$ if a white ball is drawn. Give the p.m.f., mean, and variance of X.

2.4-3. On a six-question multiple-choice test there are five possible answers for each question, of which one is correct (C) and four are incorrect (I). If a student guesses randomly and independently, find the probability of

(a) Being correct only on questions 1 and 4 (i.e., scoring C, I, I, C, I, I).

(b) Being correct on two questions.

2.4-4. Suppose that the percentage of college students who engaged in binge drinking, which is defined as having five drinks for male students and four drinks for female students at one "drinking occasion" during the previous two weeks, is approximately 40%. Let X equal the number of students in a random sample of size $n = 12$ who binge drink.

(a) Find the probability that X is at most 5.

(b) Find the probability that X is at least 6.

(c) Find the probability that X is equal to 7.

(d) Give the mean, variance, and standard deviation of X.

2.4-5. In a lab experiment involving inorganic syntheses of molecular precursors to organometallic ceramics, the final step of a five-step reaction involves the formation of a metal–metal bond. The probability of such a bond forming is $p = 0.20$. Let X equal the number of successful reactions out of $n = 25$ such experiments.

(a) Find the probability that X is at most 4.
(b) Find the probability that X is at least 5.
(c) Find the probability that X is equal to 6.
(d) Give the mean, variance, and standard deviation of X.

2.4-6. It is claimed that 15% of the ducks in a particular region have patent schistosome infection. Suppose that seven ducks are selected at random. Let X equal the number of ducks that are infected.

(a) Assuming independence, how is X distributed?
(b) Find (i) $P(X \geq 2)$, (ii) $P(X = 1)$, and (iii) $P(X \leq 3)$.

2.4-7. Suppose that 2000 points are selected independently and at random from the unit square $\{(x, y) : 0 \leq x < 1, 0 \leq y < 1\}$. Let W equal the number of points that fall into $A = \{(x, y) : x^2 + y^2 < 1\}$.

(a) How is W distributed?
(b) Give the mean, variance, and standard deviation of W.
(c) What is the expected value of $W/500$?
(d) Use the computer to select 2000 pairs of random numbers. Determine the value of W and use that value to find an estimate for π. (Of course, we know the real value of π, and more will be said about estimation later on in this text.)
(e) How could you extend part (d) to estimate the volume $V = (4/3)\pi$ of a ball of radius 1 in 3-space?
(f) How could you extend these techniques to estimate the "volume" of a ball of radius 1 in n-space?

2.4-8. It is believed that approximately 65% of Americans under the age of 65 have private health insurance. Suppose this is true, and let X equal the number of Americans under age 65 in a random sample of $n = 15$ with private health insurance.

(a) Find the probability that X is at least 10.
(b) Find the probability that X is at most 10.
(c) Find the probability that X is equal to 10.
(d) How is X distributed?
(e) Give the mean, variance, and standard deviation of X.

2.4-9. Suppose that the percentage of American drivers who are multitaskers (e.g., talk on cell phones, eat a snack, or text message at the same time they are driving) is approximately 80%. In a random sample of $n = 20$ drivers, let X equal the number of multitaskers.

(a) How is X distributed?
(b) Give the values of the mean, variance, and standard deviation of X.
(c) Find (i) $P(X = 15)$, (ii) $P(X > 15)$, and (iii) $P(X \leq 15)$.

2.4-10. A boiler has four relief valves. The probability that each opens properly is 0.99.

(a) Find the probability that at least one opens properly.
(b) Find the probability that all four open properly.

2.4-11. A random variable X has a binomial distribution with mean 6 and variance 3.6. Find $P(X = 4)$.

2.4-12. A certain type of mint has a label weight of 20.4 grams. Suppose that the probability is 0.90 that a mint weighs more than 20.7 grams. Let X equal the number of mints that weigh more than 20.7 grams in a sample of eight mints selected at random.

(a) How is X distributed if we assume independence?
(b) Find (i) $P(X = 8)$, (ii) $P(X \leq 6)$, and (iii) $P(X \geq 6)$.

2.4-13. It is given that the probability of germination of each beet seed is 0.8. Thus, if X denotes the number of seeds that germinate in a set of nine seeds, then X is $b(9, 0.8)$, provided that the assumption of independence is valid.

(a) Give the values of μ, σ^2, and σ.
(b) Draw the probability histogram for the p.m.f. of X.
(c) If 100 sets of nine beet seeds were planted, calculate $\bar{x}$, s^2, and s for the following 100 observations:

7	9	7	7	9	7	9	8	5	8	8	6	8	7	8	8	9	7	8	8
8	7	8	7	7	7	6	7	9	7	6	7	6	7	6	5	7	8	7	4
8	8	7	6	9	7	8	7	7	6	7	9	6	6	8	8	8	7	9	5
7	4	7	8	8	9	6	7	6	8	7	5	7	7	9	7	7	8	7	9
7	5	9	8	7	7	8	9	8	5	9	9	8	6	9	8	8	8	9	7

(d) Superimpose the relative frequency histogram of these observations on the graph of the probability histogram.

2.4-14. In the casino game chuck-a-luck, three unbiased six-sided dice are rolled. One possible bet is \$1 on fives, and the payoff is equal to \$1 for each five on that roll. In addition, the dollar bet is returned if at least one five is rolled. The dollar that was bet is lost only if no fives are rolled. Let X denote the payoff for this game. Then X can equal -1, 1, 2, or 3.

(a) Determine the p.m.f. $f(x)$.

(b) Calculate μ, σ^2, and σ.

(c) Depict the p.m.f. as a probability histogram.

(d) Calculate $\overline{x}$, s^2, and s, using the 100 following simulated observations of X:

$$
\begin{array}{rrrrrrrrrr}
-1 & 1 & -1 & -1 & 1 & -1 & -1 & -1 & -1 & 1 \\
-1 & 1 & -1 & 2 & 1 & -1 & -1 & -1 & 1 & -1 \\
1 & -1 & -1 & 1 & 1 & -1 & -1 & -1 & -1 & 1 \\
-1 & -1 & 2 & 1 & 1 & -1 & -1 & 1 & -1 & 1 \\
-1 & -1 & 1 & 2 & -1 & -1 & 1 & -1 & -1 & -1 \\
-1 & 1 & -1 & -1 & -1 & 1 & -1 & 1 & -1 & 2 \\
-1 & 1 & -1 & 1 & -1 & 2 & 1 & -1 & -1 & 1 \\
-1 & 1 & 1 & -1 & 1 & 1 & -1 & 3 & 1 & -1 \\
-1 & -1 & 1 & 1 & 1 & 1 & -1 & -1 & 2 & -1 \\
1 & -1 & 1 & -1 & 1 & 2 & -1 & 1 & 1 & -1
\end{array}
$$

(e) Superimpose the relative frequency histogram of these observations on the probability histogram.

2.4-15. It is claimed that for a particular lottery, 1/10 of the 50 million tickets will win a prize. What is the probability of winning at least one prize if you purchase (a) 10 tickets or (b) 15 tickets?

2.4-16. For the lottery described in Exercise 2.4-15, find the smallest number of tickets that must be purchased so that the probability of winning at least one prize is greater than (a) 0.50; (b) 0.95.

2.4-17. Construct a table that gives the probabilities for the $b(8, 0.2)$ distribution, the hypergeometric distribution with $N_1 = 8$, $N_2 = 32$, and $n = 8$, and the hypergeometric distribution with $N_1 = 16$, $N_2 = 64$, and $n = 8$. (See Figure 2.1-2.)

2.4-18. A hospital obtains 40% of its flu vaccine from Company A, 50% from Company B, and 10% from Company C. From past experience, it is known that 3% of the vials from A are ineffective, 2% from B are ineffective, and 5% from C are ineffective. The hospital tests five vials from each shipment. If at least one of the five is ineffective, find the conditional probability of that shipment's having come from C.

2.4-19. Many products can operate if, out of n parts, k of them are working. Say $n = 20$ and $k = 17$, $p = 0.05$ is the probability that a part fails, and assume independence. What is the probability that the product operates?

2.4-20. A company starts a fund of M dollars from which it pays \$1000 to each employee who achieves high performance during the year. The probability of each employee achieving this goal is 0.10 and is independent of the probabilities of the other employees doing so. If there are $n = 10$ employees, how much should M equal so that the fund has a probability of at least 99% of covering those payments?

2.4-21. A businessman has an important meeting to attend, but he is running a little late. He can take one route to work that has six stoplights or another, longer route that has two stoplights. He figures that if he stops at more than half of the lights on either route, he will be late for the meeting. Assume independence, and assume that the chance of stopping at each light is $p = 0.5$. Which route should he take?

2.4-22. In group testing for a certain disease, a blood sample was taken from each of n individuals and part of each sample was placed in a common pool. The latter was then tested. If the result was negative, there was no more testing and all n individuals were declared negative with one test. If, however, the combined result was found positive, all individuals were tested, requiring $n + 1$ tests. If $p = 0.05$ is the probability of a person's having the disease and $n = 5$, compute the expected number of tests needed, assuming independence.

2.4-23. Your stockbroker is free to take your calls about 60% of the time; otherwise he is talking to another client or is out of the office. You call him at five random times during a given month. (Assume independence.)

(a) What is the probability that he will take every one of the five calls?

(b) What is the probability that he will accept exactly three of your five calls?

(c) What is the probability that he will accept at least one of the calls?

2.5 THE MOMENT-GENERATING FUNCTION

The mean, variance, and standard deviation are important characteristics of a distribution. For some distributions—the binomial, for instance—it is fairly difficult to directly compute $E(X)$ and $E(X^2)$ to find the mean and the variance. In this section, we define a function of t that will help us generate the moments of a distribution. Thus, this function is called the moment-generating function. Although this generating characteristic is extremely important, there is a uniqueness property that is even more important. We first define the new function of t and then explain this uniqueness property before showing how it can be used to compute the moments of X.

DEFINITION 2.5-1

Let X be a random variable of the discrete type with p.m.f. $f(x)$ and space S. If there is a positive number h such that

$$E(e^{tX}) = \sum_{x \in S} e^{tx} f(x)$$

exists and is finite for $-h < t < h$, then the function of t defined by

$$M(t) = E(e^{tX})$$

is called the **moment-generating function of X** (or of the distribution of X). This function is often abbreviated as m.g.f.

First, it is evident that if we set $t = 0$, we have $M(0) = 1$. Moreover, if the space of S is $\{b_1, b_2, b_3, \ldots\}$, then the moment-generating function is given by the expansion

$$M(t) = e^{tb_1} f(b_1) + e^{tb_2} f(b_2) + e^{tb_3} f(b_3) + \cdots.$$

Thus, the coefficient of e^{tb_i} is the probability

$$f(b_i) = P(X = b_i).$$

Accordingly, if two random variables (or two distributions of probability) have the same moment-generating function, they must have the same distribution of probability. That is, if the two random variables had the two probability mass functions $f(x)$ and $g(y)$, as well as the same space $S = \{b_1, b_2, b_3, \ldots\}$, and if

$$e^{tb_1} f(b_1) + e^{tb_2} f(b_2) + \cdots = e^{tb_1} g(b_1) + e^{tb_2} g(b_2) + \cdots \qquad (2.5\text{-}1)$$

for all t, $-h < t < h$, then mathematical transform theory requires that

$$f(b_i) = g(b_i), \qquad i = 1, 2, 3, \cdots.$$

So we see that the moment-generating function uniquely determines the distribution of a random variable. In other words, if the m.g.f. exists, there is one and only one distribution of probability associated with that m.g.f.

REMARK From elementary algebra, we can get some understanding of why Equation 2.5-1 requires that $f(b_i) = g(b_i)$. In that equation, let $e^t = w$ and say the points in the support, namely, $b_1, b_2, \ldots, b_k$, are positive integers, the largest of which is m. Then Equation 2.5-1 provides the equality of two mth-degree polynomials in w for an uncountable number of values of w. A fundamental theorem of algebra requires that the corresponding coefficients of the two polynomials be equal; that is, $f(b_i) = g(b_i)$, $i = 1, 2, \ldots, k$. ■

EXAMPLE 2.5-1 If X has the m.g.f.

$$M(t) = e^t\left(\frac{3}{6}\right) + e^{2t}\left(\frac{2}{6}\right) + e^{3t}\left(\frac{1}{6}\right),$$

then the probabilities are

$$P(X = 1) = \frac{3}{6}, \qquad P(X = 2) = \frac{2}{6}, \qquad P(X = 3) = \frac{1}{6}.$$

We could write this, if we choose to do so, by saying that X has the p.m.f.

$$f(x) = \frac{4 - x}{6}, \qquad x = 1, 2, 3.$$ ■

EXAMPLE 2.5-2 Suppose the m.g.f. of X is

$$M(t) = \frac{e^t/2}{1 - e^t/2}, \qquad t < \ln 2.$$

Until we expand $M(t)$, we cannot detect the coefficients of $e^{b_i t}$. Recalling that

$$(1 - z)^{-1} = 1 + z + z^2 + z^3 + \cdots, \qquad -1 < z < 1,$$

we have

$$\begin{aligned}\frac{e^t}{2}\left(1 - \frac{e^t}{2}\right)^{-1} &= \frac{e^t}{2}\left(1 + \frac{e^t}{2} + \frac{e^{2t}}{2^2} + \frac{e^{3t}}{2^3} + \cdots\right)\\ &= \left(e^t\right)\left(\frac{1}{2}\right)^1 + \left(e^{2t}\right)\left(\frac{1}{2}\right)^2 + \left(e^{3t}\right)\left(\frac{1}{2}\right)^3 + \cdots\end{aligned}$$

when $e^t/2 < 1$ and thus $t < \ln 2$. That is,

$$P(X = x) = \left(\frac{1}{2}\right)^x$$

when x is a positive integer, or, equivalently, the p.m.f. of X is

$$f(x) = \left(\frac{1}{2}\right)^x, \qquad x = 1, 2, 3, \cdots.$$ ■

From the theory of Laplace transforms, it can be shown that the existence of $M(t)$, for $-h < t < h$, implies that derivatives of $M(t)$ of all orders exist at $t = 0$; moreover, it is permissible to interchange differentiation and summation as the series converges uniformly. Thus,

$$M'(t) = \sum_{x \in S} x e^{tx} f(x),$$

$$M''(t) = \sum_{x \in S} x^2 e^{tx} f(x),$$

and for each positive integer r,

$$M^{(r)}(t) = \sum_{x \in S} x^r e^{tx} f(x).$$

Setting $t = 0$, we see that

$$M'(0) = \sum_{x \in S} x f(x) = E(X),$$
$$M''(0) = \sum_{x \in S} x^2 f(x) = E(X^2),$$

and, in general,

$$M^{(r)}(0) = \sum_{x \in S} x^r f(x) = E(X^r).$$

In particular, if the moment-generating function exists, then

$$M'(0) = E(X) = \mu \quad \text{and} \quad M''(0) - [M'(0)]^2 = E(X^2) - [E(X)]^2 = \sigma^2.$$

The preceding argument shows that we can find the moments of X by differentiating $M(t)$. In using this technique, it must be emphasized that first we evaluate the summation representing $M(t)$ to obtain a closed-form solution and then we differentiate that solution to obtain the moments of X. The next example illustrates the use of the moment-generating function for finding the first and second moments and then the mean and variance of the important binomial distribution.

EXAMPLE 2.5-3 The p.m.f. of the binomial distribution is

$$f(x) = \binom{n}{x} p^x (1 - p)^{n-x}, \qquad x = 0, 1, 2, \ldots, n.$$

Thus, the m.g.f. is

$$\begin{aligned} M(t) = E(e^{tX}) &= \sum_{x=0}^{n} e^{tx} \binom{n}{x} p^x (1 - p)^{n-x} \\ &= \sum_{x=0}^{n} \binom{n}{x} (pe^t)^x (1 - p)^{n-x} \\ &= \left[(1 - p) + pe^t\right]^n, \qquad -\infty < t < \infty, \end{aligned}$$

from the expansion of $(a + b)^n$ with $a = 1 - p$ and $b = pe^t$. It is interesting to note that here and elsewhere the m.g.f. is usually rather easy to compute if the p.m.f. has a factor involving an exponential, like p^x in the binomial p.m.f.

The first two derivatives of $M(t)$ are

$$M'(t) = n[(1 - p) + pe^t]^{n-1}(pe^t)$$

and

$$M''(t) = n(n - 1)[(1 - p) + pe^t]^{n-2}(pe^t)^2 + n[(1 - p) + pe^t]^{n-1}(pe^t).$$

Thus,

$$\mu = E(X) = M'(0) = np$$

and

$$\sigma^2 = E(X^2) - [E(X)]^2 = M''(0) - [M'(0)]^2$$
$$= n(n-1)p^2 + np - (np)^2 = np(1-p),$$

as we showed in Section 2.4 using a longer derivation.

In the special case when $n = 1$, X has a Bernoulli distribution and

$$M(t) = (1-p) + pe^t$$

for all real values of t, $\mu = p$, and $\sigma^2 = p(1-p)$. ■

We turn now to the situation in which we observe a sequence of Bernoulli trials until exactly r successes occur, where r is a fixed positive integer. Let the random variable X denote the number of trials needed to observe the rth success. That is, X is the trial number on which the rth success is observed. By the multiplication rule of probabilities, the p.m.f. of X—say, $g(x)$—equals the product of the probability

$$\binom{x-1}{r-1}p^{r-1}(1-p)^{x-r} = \binom{x-1}{r-1}p^{r-1}q^{x-r}$$

of obtaining exactly $r - 1$ successes in the first $x - 1$ trials and the probability p of a success on the rth trial. Thus, the p.m.f. of X is

$$g(x) = \binom{x-1}{r-1}p^r(1-p)^{x-r} = \binom{x-1}{r-1}p^r q^{x-r}, \qquad x = r, r+1, \ldots.$$

We say that X has a **negative binomial distribution.**

REMARK The reason for calling this distribution the negative binomial distribution is as follows: Consider $h(w) = (1-w)^{-r}$, the binomial $(1-w)$ with the negative exponent $-r$. Using Maclaurin's series expansion (see Appendix D.4 on the CD-ROM), we have

$$(1-w)^{-r} = \sum_{k=0}^{\infty} \frac{h^{(k)}(0)}{k!}w^k = \sum_{k=0}^{\infty} \binom{r+k-1}{r-1}w^k, \qquad -1 < w < 1.$$

If we let $x = k + r$ in the summation, then $k = x - r$ and

$$(1-w)^{-r} = \sum_{x=r}^{\infty} \binom{r+x-r-1}{r-1}w^{x-r} = \sum_{x=r}^{\infty} \binom{x-1}{r-1}w^{x-r},$$

the summand of which is, except for the factor p^r, the negative binomial probability when $w = q$. In particular, the sum of the probabilities for the negative binomial distribution is 1 because

$$\sum_{x=r}^{\infty} g(x) = \sum_{x=r}^{\infty} \binom{x-1}{r-1}p^r q^{x-r} = p^r(1-q)^{-r} = 1.$$ ■

If $r = 1$ in the negative binomial distribution, we say that X has a **geometric distribution**, since the p.m.f. consists of terms of a geometric series, namely,

$$g(x) = p(1-p)^{x-1}, \qquad x = 1, 2, 3, \cdots.$$

Recall that for a geometric series (see Appendix D.4 on the CD-ROM for a review), the sum is given by

$$\sum_{k=0}^{\infty} ar^k = \sum_{k=1}^{\infty} ar^{k-1} = \frac{a}{1-r}$$

when $|r| < 1$. Thus, for the geometric distribution,

$$\sum_{x=1}^{\infty} g(x) = \sum_{x=1}^{\infty} (1-p)^{x-1}p = \frac{p}{1-(1-p)} = 1,$$

so that $g(x)$ does satisfy the properties of a p.m.f.

From the sum of a geometric series, we also note that when k is an integer,

$$P(X > k) = \sum_{x=k+1}^{\infty} (1-p)^{x-1}p = \frac{(1-p)^k p}{1-(1-p)} = (1-p)^k = q^k.$$

Thus, the value of the distribution function at a positive integer k is

$$P(X \le k) = \sum_{x=1}^{k} (1-p)^{x-1}p = 1 - P(X > k) = 1 - (1-p)^k = 1 - q^k.$$

EXAMPLE 2.5-4 Some biology students were checking eye color in a large number of fruit flies. For the individual fly, suppose that the probability of white eyes is 1/4 and the probability of red eyes is 3/4, and that we may treat these observations as having independent Bernoulli trials. The probability that at least four flies have to be checked for eye color to observe a white-eyed fly is given by

$$P(X \ge 4) = P(X > 3) = q^3 = \left(\frac{3}{4}\right)^3 = \frac{27}{64} = 0.4219.$$

The probability that at most four flies have to be checked for eye color to observe a white-eyed fly is given by

$$P(X \le 4) = 1 - q^4 = 1 - \left(\frac{3}{4}\right)^4 = \frac{175}{256} = 0.6836.$$

The probability that the first fly with white eyes is the fourth fly considered is

$$P(X = 4) = q^{4-1}p = \left(\frac{3}{4}\right)^3\left(\frac{1}{4}\right) = \frac{27}{256} = 0.1055.$$

It is also true that

$$\begin{aligned} P(X = 4) &= P(X \le 4) - P(X \le 3) \\ &= [1 - (3/4)^4] - [1 - (3/4)^3] \\ &= \left(\frac{3}{4}\right)^3\left(\frac{1}{4}\right). \end{aligned}$$

■

We now show that the mean and the variance of a negative binomial random variable X are, respectively,

$$\mu = E(X) = \frac{r}{p} \quad \text{and} \quad \sigma^2 = \frac{rq}{p^2} = \frac{r(1-p)}{p^2}.$$

In particular, if $r = 1$, so that X has a geometric distribution, then

$$\mu = \frac{1}{p} \quad \text{and} \quad \sigma^2 = \frac{q}{p^2} = \frac{1-p}{p^2}.$$

The mean $\mu = 1/p$ agrees with our intuition. Let's check: If $p = 1/6$, then we would expect, on the average, $1/(1/6) = 6$ trials before the first success.

To find these moments, we determine the m.g.f. of the negative binomial distribution. It is

$$\begin{aligned} M(t) &= \sum_{x=r}^{\infty} e^{tx}\binom{x-1}{r-1}p^r(1-p)^{x-r} \\ &= \left(pe^t\right)^r \sum_{x=r}^{\infty}\binom{x-1}{r-1}\left[(1-p)e^t\right]^{x-r} \\ &= \frac{(pe^t)^r}{[1-(1-p)e^t]^r}, \qquad \text{where } (1-p)e^t < 1 \end{aligned}$$

(or, equivalently, when $t < -\ln(1-p)$). Thus,

$$\begin{aligned} M'(t) &= (pe^t)^r(-r)[1-(1-p)e^t]^{-r-1}[-(1-p)e^t] + \\ &\qquad r(pe^t)^{r-1}(pe^t)[1-(1-p)e^t]^{-r} \\ &= r(pe^t)^r[1-(1-p)e^t]^{-r-1} \end{aligned}$$

and

$$\begin{aligned} M''(t) = r(pe^t)^r(-r-1)[1-(1-p)e^t]^{-r-2}[-(1-p)e^t] + \\ r^2(pe^t)^{r-1}(pe^t)[1-(1-p)e^t]^{-r-1}. \end{aligned}$$

Accordingly,

$$M'(0) = rp^rp^{-r-1} = rp^{-1}$$

and

$$\begin{aligned} M''(0) &= r(r+1)p^rp^{-r-2}(1-p) + r^2p^rp^{-r-1} \\ &= rp^{-2}[(1-p)(r+1) + rp] = rp^{-2}(r+1-p). \end{aligned}$$

Hence, we have

$$\mu = \frac{r}{p} \quad \text{and} \quad \sigma^2 = \frac{r(r+1-p)}{p^2} - \frac{r^2}{p^2} = \frac{r(1-p)}{p^2}.$$

Even these calculations are a little messy, so a somewhat easier way is given in Exercise 2.5-20.

EXAMPLE 2.5-5 Suppose that during practice a basketball player can make a free throw 80% of the time. Furthermore, assume that a sequence of free-throw shooting can be thought of as independent Bernoulli trials. Let X equal the minimum number of free throws that this player must attempt to make a total of 10 shots. The p.m.f. of X is

$$g(x) = \binom{x-1}{10-1}(0.80)^{10}(0.20)^{x-10}, \qquad x = 10, 11, 12, \ldots.$$

The mean, variance, and standard deviation of X are, respectively,

$$\mu = 10\left(\frac{1}{0.80}\right) = 12.5, \qquad \sigma^2 = \frac{10(0.20)}{0.80^2} = 3.125, \qquad \text{and} \qquad \sigma = 1.768.$$

And we have, for example,

$$P(X = 12) = g(12) = \binom{11}{9}(0.80)^{10}(0.20)^2 = 0.2362. \qquad \blacksquare$$

EXAMPLE 2.5-6 To consider the effect of p and r on the negative binomial distribution, Figure 2.5-1 gives the probability histograms for four combinations of p and r. Note that since $r = 1$ in the first of these, it represents a geometric p.m.f. $\blacksquare$

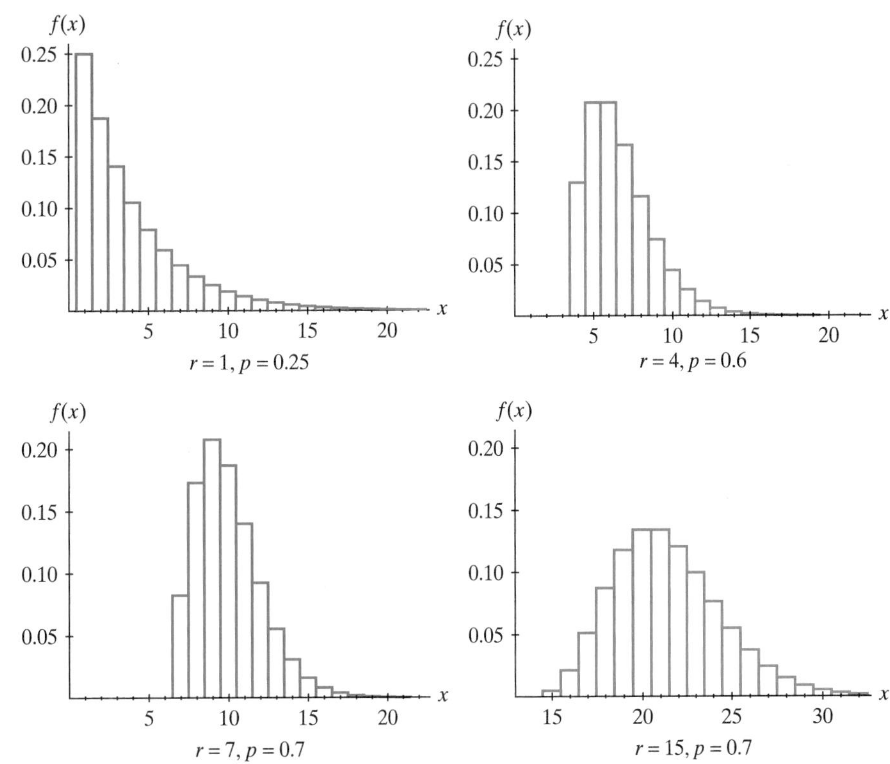

FIGURE 2.5-1: Negative binomial probability histograms

When the moment-generating function exists, derivatives of all orders exist at $t = 0$. Thus, it is possible to represent $M(t)$ as a Maclaurin series, namely,

$$M(t) = M(0) + M'(0)\left(\frac{t}{1!}\right) + M''(0)\left(\frac{t^2}{2!}\right) + M'''(0)\left(\frac{t^3}{3!}\right) + \cdots.$$

If the Maclaurin series expansion of $M(t)$ exists and the moments are given, we can frequently sum the Maclaurin series to obtain the closed form of $M(t)$. This approach is illustrated in the next example.

EXAMPLE 2.5-7 Let the moments of X be defined by

$$E(X^r) = 0.8, \qquad r = 1, 2, 3, \ldots.$$

The moment-generating function of X is then

$$\begin{aligned} M(t) &= M(0) + \sum_{r=1}^{\infty} 0.8\left(\frac{t^r}{r!}\right) = 1 + 0.8\sum_{r=1}^{\infty}\frac{t^r}{r!} \\ &= 0.2 + 0.8\sum_{r=0}^{\infty}\frac{t^r}{r!} = 0.2e^{0t} + 0.8e^{1t}. \end{aligned}$$

Thus,

$$P(X = 0) = 0.2 \qquad \text{and} \qquad P(X = 1) = 0.8. \qquad \blacksquare$$

COMPUTATIONAL COMMENTS **(CAS)** We now illustrate how *Maple* can be used to find the moment-generating function for the negative binomial distribution. It is then used to find the mean and the variance. Here is the *Maple* code:

```
> f := binomial(x - 1, r - 1)*p^r*(1 - p)^(x - r);
```

$$f := \text{binomial}(x - 1, r - 1)\,p^r\,(1 - p)^{(x-r)}$$

```
> mu := sum(x*f, x = r .. infinity);
```

$$\mu := \frac{r}{p}$$

```
> var := sum((x - mu)^2*f, x = r .. infinity);
```

$$var := -\frac{r(-1 + p)}{p^2}$$

```
> M := sum(exp(t*x)*f, x = r .. infinity);
```

$$M := \frac{e^{(tr)}\,p^r}{(1 - e^t + e^t\,p)^r}$$

```
> Mprime := diff(M, t):
> Mdoubleprime := diff(Mprime, t):
> mu := subs(t = 0, Mprime):
> mu := factor(%);
```

$$\mu := \frac{r}{p}$$

```
> var := subs(t = 0, Mdoubleprime) - mu^2:
> var := factor(%);
```

$$var := -\frac{r(-1 + p)}{p^2}$$

Note that although the result for the variance is correct, we would probably write it as

$$\sigma^2 = \frac{r(1 - p)}{p^2}.$$

EXERCISES

2.5-1. Define the p.m.f. and give the values of μ, σ^2, and σ when the moment-generating function of X is defined by

(a) $M(t) = 1/3 + (2/3)e^t$.
(b) $M(t) = (0.25 + 0.75e^t)^{12}$.

2.5-2. (i) Give the name of the distribution of X (if it has a name), (ii) find the values of μ and σ^2, and (iii) calculate $P(1 \le X \le 2)$ when the moment-generating function of X is given by

(a) $M(t) = (0.3 + 0.7e^t)^5$.
(b) $M(t) = \dfrac{0.3e^t}{1 - 0.7e^t}, \qquad t < -\ln(0.7)$.
(c) $M(t) = 0.45 + 0.55e^t$.
(d) $M(t) = 0.3e^t + 0.4e^{2t} + 0.2e^{3t} + 0.1e^{4t}$.
(e) $M(t) = (0.6e^t)^2(1 - 0.4e^t)^{-2}, \qquad t < -\ln(0.4)$.
(f) $M(t) = \sum_{x=1}^{10} (0.1)e^{tx}$.

2.5-3. If the moment-generating function of X is

$$M(t) = \frac{2}{5}e^t + \frac{1}{5}e^{2t} + \frac{2}{5}e^{3t},$$

find the mean, variance, and p.m.f. of X.

2.5-4. Let X equal the number of people selected at random that you must ask in order to find someone with the same birthday as yours. Assume that each day of the year is equally likely, and ignore February 29.

(a) What is the p.m.f. of X?
(b) Give the values of the mean, variance, and standard deviation of X.
(c) Find $P(X > 400)$ and $P(X < 300)$.

2.5-5. For each question on a multiple-choice test, there are five possible answers, of which exactly one is correct. If a student selects answers at random, give the probability that the first question answered correctly is question 4.

2.5-6. The probability that a machine produces a defective item is 0.01. Each item is checked as it is produced. Assume that these are independent trials, and compute the probability that at least 100 items must be checked to find one that is defective.

2.5-7. Apples are packaged automatically in 3-pound bags. Suppose that 4% of the time the bag of apples weighs less than 3 pounds. If you select bags randomly and weigh them in order to discover one underweight bag of apples, find the probability that the number of bags that must be selected is

(a) At least 20.
(b) At most 20.
(c) Exactly 20.

2.5-8. Show that 63/512 is the probability that the fifth head is observed on the tenth independent flip of an unbiased coin.

2.5-9. An excellent free-throw shooter attempts several free throws until she misses.

(a) If $p = 0.9$ is her probability of making a free throw, what is the probability of having the first miss on the 13th attempt or later?
(b) If she continues shooting until she misses three, what is the probability that the third miss occurs on the 30th attempt?

2.5-10. Suppose that a basketball player different from the one in Example 2.5-5 can make a free throw 60% of the time. Let X equal the minimum number of free throws that this player must attempt to make a total of 10 shots.

(a) Give the mean, variance, and standard deviation of X.
(b) Find $P(X = 16)$.

2.5-11. Let X equal the number of flips of a fair coin that are required to observe the same face on consecutive flips.

(a) Find the p.m.f. of X. HINT: Draw a tree diagram.
(b) Find the moment-generating function of X.
(c) Use the m.g.f. to find the values of (i) the mean and (ii) the variance of X.
(d) Find the values of (i) $P(X \le 3)$, (ii) $P(X \ge 5)$, and (iii) $P(X = 3)$.
(e) Simulate this experiment to confirm you answers to parts (c) and (d).

2.5-12. Let X have a geometric distribution. Show that

$$P(X > k + j \mid X > k) = P(X > j),$$

where k and j are nonnegative integers. NOTE: We sometimes say that in this situation there has been loss of memory.

2.5-13. Let X equal the number of flips of a fair coin that are required to observe heads–tails on consecutive flips.

(a) Find the p.m.f. of X. HINT: Draw a tree diagram.
(b) Show that the m.g.f. of X is $M(t) = e^{2t}/(e^t - 2)^2$.

(c) Use the m.g.f. to find the values of (i) the mean and (ii) the variance of X.

(d) Find the values of (i) $P(X \leq 3)$, (ii) $P(X \geq 5)$, and (iii) $P(X = 3)$.

(e) Simulate this experiment to confirm you answers to parts (c) and (d).

2.5-14. Let X equal the number of flips of a fair coin that are required to observe heads on consecutive flips. Let f_n equal the nth Fibonacci number, where $f_1 = 1$, $f_2 = 1$, and $f_n = f_{n-1} + f_{n-2}$, $n = 3, 4, 5, \ldots$.

(a) Show that the p.m.f. of X is

$$f(x) = \frac{f_{x-1}}{2^x}, \qquad x = 2, 3, 4, \ldots .$$

HINT: Draw a tree diagram.

(b) Use the fact that

$$f_x = \frac{1}{\sqrt{5}}\left[\left(\frac{1+\sqrt{5}}{2}\right)^x - \left(\frac{1-\sqrt{5}}{2}\right)^x\right]$$

to show that $\sum_{x=2}^{\infty} f(x) = 1$.

(c) Show that $\mu = E(X) = 6$.

(d) Show that $E[X(X-1)] = 52$, so that the variance of X is $\sigma^2 = 22$.

(e) Find the values of (i) $P(X \leq 3)$, (ii) $P(X \geq 5)$, and (iii) $P(X = 3)$.

(f) Simulate this experiment to confirm your answers to parts (c), (d), and (e). Either write a computer program or physically toss a coin to support the answers.

2.5-15. One of four different prizes was randomly put into each box of a cereal. If a family decided to buy this cereal until it obtained at least one of each of the four different prizes, what is the expected number of boxes of cereal that must be purchased?

2.5-16. Suppose an airport metal detector catches a person with metal 99% of the time. That is, it misses detecting a person with metal 1% of the time. Assume independence of people carrying metal. What is the probability that the first person missed (not detected) is among the first 50 persons scanned?

2.5-17. In 2006, Red Rose tea randomly began placing 1 of 10 English porcelain miniature animals in a 100-bag box of the tea, selecting from 10 "Pet Shop Friends."

(a) On the average, how many boxes of tea must be purchased by a customer to obtain a complete collection consisting of 10 different animals?

(b) If the customer uses one tea bag per day, how long can a customer expect to take, on the average, to obtain a complete collection?

(c) From 2002 to 2006, the figurines were part of the Noah's Ark Animal Series, which contains 15 pieces. Assume again that these figurines were selected randomly. How many boxes of tea would have had to be purchased, on the average, to obtain the complete collection?

2.5-18. If $E(X^r) = 5^r, r = 1, 2, 3, \ldots$, find the moment-generating function $M(t)$ of X and the p.m.f. of X.

2.5-19. Let the moment-generating function $M(t)$ of X exist for $-h < t < h$. Consider the function $R(t) = \ln M(t)$. The first two derivatives of $R(t)$ are, respectively,

$$R'(t) = \frac{M'(t)}{M(t)} \qquad \text{and}$$

$$R''(t) = \frac{M(t)M''(t) - [M'(t)]^2}{[M(t)]^2}.$$

Setting $t = 0$, show that

(a) $\mu = R'(0)$.

(b) $\sigma^2 = R''(0)$.

2.5-20. Use the result of Exercise 2.5-19 to find the mean and variance of the

(a) Bernoulli distribution.

(b) Binomial distribution.

(c) Geometric distribution.

(d) Negative binomial distribution.

2.5-21. Given a random permutation of the integers in the set $\{1, 2, 3, 4, 5\}$, let X equal the number of integers that are in their natural position. The moment-generating function of X is

$$M(t) = \frac{44}{120} + \frac{45}{120}e^t + \frac{20}{120}e^{2t} + \frac{10}{120}e^{3t} + \frac{1}{120}e^{5t}.$$

(a) Find the mean and variance of X.

(b) Find the probability that at least one integer is in its natural position.

(c) Draw a graph of the probability histogram of the p.m.f. of X.

2.5-22. The probability that a company's workforce has no accidents in a given month is 0.7. The numbers of accidents from month to month are independent. What is the probability that the third month in a year is the first month that at least one accident occurs?

2.6 THE POISSON DISTRIBUTION

Some experiments result in counting the number of times particular events occur at given times or with given physical objects. For example, we could count the number of phone calls arriving at a switchboard between 9 and 10 A.M., the number of flaws in 100 feet of wire, the number of customers that arrive at a ticket window between 12 noon and 2 P.M., or the number of defects in a 100-foot roll of aluminum screen that is 2 feet wide. Each count can be looked upon as a random variable associated with an approximate Poisson process, provided that the conditions in the following definition are satisfied.

DEFINITION 2.6-1

Let the number of changes that occur in a given continuous interval be counted. Then we have an **approximate Poisson process** with parameter $\lambda > 0$ if the following conditions are satisfied:

(a) The numbers of changes occurring in nonoverlapping intervals are independent.

(b) The probability of exactly one change occurring in a sufficiently short interval of length h is approximately λh.

(c) The probability of two or more changes occurring in a sufficiently short interval is essentially zero.

Suppose that an experiment satisfies the preceding three conditions of an approximate Poisson process. Let X denote the number of changes in an interval of length 1 (where "length 1" represents one unit of the quantity under consideration). We would like to find an approximation for $P(X = x)$, where x is a nonnegative integer. To achieve this, we partition the unit interval into n subintervals of equal length $1/n$. If n is sufficiently large (i.e., much larger than x), we shall approximate the probability that x changes occur in this unit interval by finding the probability that one change occurs in each of exactly x of these n subintervals. The probability of one change occurring in any one subinterval of length $1/n$ is approximately $\lambda(1/n)$, by condition (b). The probability of two or more changes in any one subinterval is essentially zero, by condition (c). So, for each subinterval, exactly one change occurs with a probability of approximately $\lambda(1/n)$. Consider the occurrence or nonoccurrence of a change in each subinterval as a Bernoulli trial. By condition (a), we have a sequence of n Bernoulli trials with probability p approximately equal to $\lambda(1/n)$. Thus, an approximation for $P(X = x)$ is given by the binomial probability

$$\frac{n!}{x!\,(n-x)!}\left(\frac{\lambda}{n}\right)^x\left(1-\frac{\lambda}{n}\right)^{n-x}.$$

If n increases without bound, then

$$\lim_{n\to\infty}\frac{n!}{x!\,(n-x)!}\left(\frac{\lambda}{n}\right)^x\left(1-\frac{\lambda}{n}\right)^{n-x}$$

$$= \lim_{n\to\infty}\frac{n(n-1)\cdots(n-x+1)}{n^x}\,\frac{\lambda^x}{x!}\left(1-\frac{\lambda}{n}\right)^n\left(1-\frac{\lambda}{n}\right)^{-x}.$$

Now, for fixed x, we have (see Appendix D.3 on the CD-ROM)

$$\lim_{n\to\infty} \frac{n(n-1)\cdots(n-x+1)}{n^x} = \lim_{n\to\infty}\left[(1)\left(1-\frac{1}{n}\right)\cdots\left(1-\frac{x-1}{n}\right)\right] = 1,$$

$$\lim_{n\to\infty}\left(1-\frac{\lambda}{n}\right)^n = e^{-\lambda},$$

$$\lim_{n\to\infty}\left(1-\frac{\lambda}{n}\right)^{-x} = 1.$$

Thus,

$$\lim_{n\to\infty} \frac{n!}{x!\,(n-x)!}\left(\frac{\lambda}{n}\right)^x\left(1-\frac{\lambda}{n}\right)^{n-x} = \frac{\lambda^x e^{-\lambda}}{x!} = P(X=x).$$

The distribution of probability associated with this process has a special name. We say that the random variable X has a **Poisson distribution** if its p.m.f. is of the form

$$f(x) = \frac{\lambda^x e^{-\lambda}}{x!}, \qquad x = 0, 1, 2, \ldots,$$

where $\lambda > 0$.

It is easy to see that $f(x)$ has the properties of a p.m.f. because, clearly, $f(x) \ge 0$ and, from the Maclaurin series expansion of e^λ (see Appendix D.4 on the CD-ROM), we have

$$\sum_{x=0}^{\infty} \frac{\lambda^x e^{-\lambda}}{x!} = e^{-\lambda}\sum_{x=0}^{\infty}\frac{\lambda^x}{x!} = e^{-\lambda}e^{\lambda} = 1.$$

To discover the exact role of the parameter $\lambda > 0$, let us find some of the characteristics of the Poisson distribution.

The moment-generating function of X is

$$M(t) = E(e^{tX}) = \sum_{x=0}^{\infty} e^{tx}\frac{\lambda^x e^{-\lambda}}{x!} = e^{-\lambda}\sum_{x=0}^{\infty}\frac{(\lambda e^t)^x}{x!}.$$

From the series representation of the exponential function, we have

$$M(t) = e^{-\lambda}e^{\lambda e^t} = e^{\lambda(e^t-1)}$$

for all real values of t. Now,

$$M'(t) = \lambda e^t e^{\lambda(e^t-1)}$$

and

$$M''(t) = (\lambda e^t)^2 e^{\lambda(e^t-1)} + \lambda e^t e^{\lambda(e^t-1)}.$$

The values of the mean and variance of X are, respectively,

$$\mu = M'(0) = \lambda$$

and

$$\sigma^2 = M''(0) - [M'(0)]^2 = (\lambda^2 + \lambda) - \lambda^2 = \lambda.$$

That is, for the Poisson distribution, $\mu = \sigma^2 = \lambda$.

REMARKS It is also possible to find the mean and the variance for the Poisson distribution directly, without using the moment-generating function. The mean for the Poisson distribution is given by

$$E(X) = \sum_{x=0}^{\infty} x \frac{\lambda^x e^{-\lambda}}{x!} = e^{-\lambda} \sum_{x=1}^{\infty} \frac{\lambda^x}{(x-1)!}$$

because $(0)f(0) = 0$ and $x/x! = 1/(x-1)!$ when $x > 0$. If we let $k = x - 1$, then

$$E(X) = e^{-\lambda} \sum_{k=0}^{\infty} \frac{\lambda^{k+1}}{k!} = \lambda e^{-\lambda} \sum_{k=0}^{\infty} \frac{\lambda^k}{k!}$$
$$= \lambda e^{-\lambda} e^{\lambda} = \lambda.$$

To find the variance, we first determine the second factorial moment $E[X(X-1)]$. We have

$$E[X(X-1)] = \sum_{x=0}^{\infty} x(x-1) \frac{\lambda^x e^{-\lambda}}{x!} = e^{-\lambda} \sum_{x=2}^{\infty} \frac{\lambda^x}{(x-2)!}$$

because $(0)(0-1)f(0) = 0$, $(1)(1-1)f(1) = 0$, and $x(x-1)/x! = 1/(x-2)!$ when $x > 1$. If we let $k = x - 2$, then

$$E[X(X-1)] = e^{-\lambda} \sum_{k=0}^{\infty} \frac{\lambda^{k+2}}{k!} = \lambda^2 e^{-\lambda} \sum_{k=0}^{\infty} \frac{\lambda^k}{k!}$$
$$= \lambda^2 e^{-\lambda} e^{\lambda} = \lambda^2.$$

Thus,

$$\text{Var}(X) = E(X^2) - [E(X)]^2 = E[X(X-1)] + E(X) - [E(X)]^2$$
$$= \lambda^2 + \lambda - \lambda^2 = \lambda.$$

We again see that, for the Poisson distribution, $\mu = \sigma^2 = \lambda$. ■

Table III in the appendix gives values of the distribution function of a Poisson random variable for selected values of λ. This table is illustrated in the next example.

EXAMPLE 2.6-1 Let X have a Poisson distribution with a mean of $\lambda = 5$. Then, using Table III in the appendix, we obtain

$$P(X \le 6) = \sum_{x=0}^{6} \frac{5^x e^{-5}}{x!} = 0.762,$$

$$P(X > 5) = 1 - P(X \le 5) = 1 - 0.616 = 0.384,$$

and

$$P(X = 6) = P(X \le 6) - P(X \le 5) = 0.762 - 0.616 = 0.146.$$ ■

EXAMPLE 2.6-2 To see the effect of λ on the p.m.f. $f(x)$ of X, Figure 2.6-1 shows the probability histograms of $f(x)$ for four different values of λ. ■

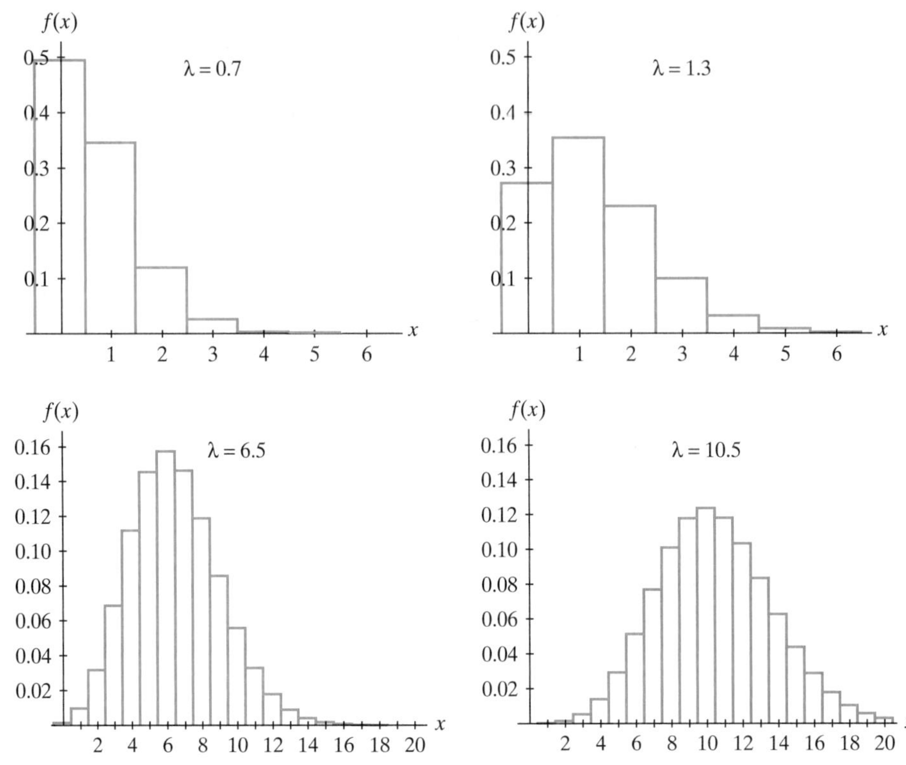

FIGURE 2.6-1: Poisson probability histograms

EXAMPLE 2.6-3 Let X denote the number of alpha particles emitted by barium-133 in one-tenth of a second and counted by a Geiger counter. One hundred observations of X produced the data in Table 2.6-1. For these data, $\bar{x} = 559/100 = 5.59$ and $s^2 = 3{,}619/99 - (559)^2/9900 = 4.992$. Thus, clearly, the sample mean and sample variance are fairly close to each other. In Figure 2.6-2, the probability histogram for a

TABLE 2.6-1: Barium 133

Outcome (x)	Frequency (f)	fx	fx^2
1	1	1	1
2	4	8	16
3	13	39	117
4	19	76	304
5	16	80	400
6	15	90	540
7	9	63	441
8	12	96	768
9	7	63	567
10	2	20	200
11	1	11	121
12	1	12	144
	100	559	3619

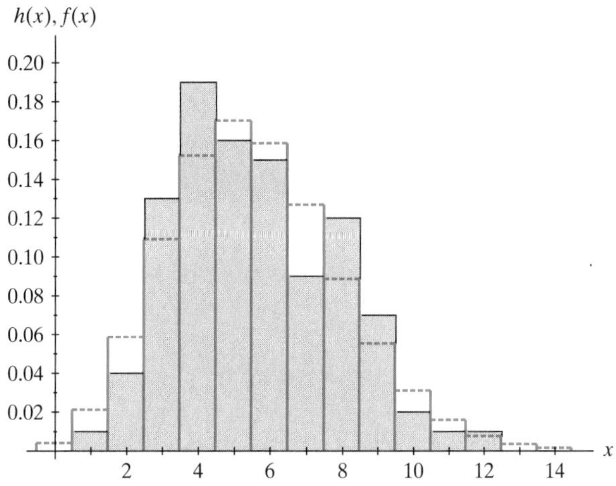

FIGURE 2.6-2: Barium histograms

Poisson distribution with $\lambda = 5.59$ is drawn. The relative frequency histogram of the data is shaded. Accordingly, it looks as if the Poisson distribution provides a fairly reasonable probability model for this random variable X. (Later in the text, formal tests of the goodness of fit of various models are given.) ■

If events in a Poisson process occur at a mean rate of λ per unit, then the expected number of occurrences in an interval of length t is λt. For example, if phone calls arrive at a switchboard following a Poisson process at a mean rate of three per minute, then the expected number of phone calls in a 5-minute period is $(3)(5) = 15$. Or if calls arrive at a mean rate of 22 in a 5-minute period, then the expected number of calls per minute is $\lambda = 22(1/5) = 4.4$. Moreover, the number of occurrences—say, X—in the interval of length t has the Poisson p.m.f.

$$f(x) = \frac{(\lambda t)^x e^{-\lambda t}}{x!}, \qquad x = 0, 1, 2, \ldots.$$

This equation follows if we treat the interval of length t as if it were the "unit interval" with mean λt instead of λ.

EXAMPLE 2.6-4 A USB flash drive is sometimes used to back up computer files. However, in the past, a less reliable backup system that was used was a computer tape, and flaws occurred on these tapes. In a particular situation, flaws (bad records) on a used computer tape occurred on the average of one flaw per 1200 feet. If one assumes a Poisson distribution, what is the distribution of X, the number of flaws in a 4800-foot roll? The expected number of flaws in $4800 = 4(1200)$ feet is 4; that is, $E(X) = 4$. Thus, the p.m.f. of X is

$$f(x) = \frac{4^x e^{-4}}{x!}, \qquad x = 0, 1, 2, \ldots,$$

and, in particular,

$$P(X = 0) = \frac{4^0 e^{-4}}{0!} = e^{-4} = 0.018,$$
$$P(X \le 4) = 0.629,$$

by Table III in the appendix. ■

EXAMPLE 2.6-5 Telephone calls enter a college switchboard on the average of two every 3 minutes. If one assumes an approximate Poisson process, what is the probability of five or more calls arriving in a 9-minute period? Let X denote the number of calls in a 9-minute period. We see that $E(X) = 6$; that is, on the average, six calls will arrive during a 9-minute period. Thus,

$$P(X \geq 5) = 1 - P(X \leq 4) = 1 - \sum_{x=0}^{4} \frac{6^x e^{-6}}{x!}$$
$$= 1 - 0.285 = 0.715,$$

by Table III in the appendix. ■

Not only is the Poisson distribution important in its own right, but it can also be used to approximate probabilities for a binomial distribution. Earlier we saw that if X has a Poisson distribution with parameter λ, then, with n large,

$$P(X = x) \approx \binom{n}{x}\left(\frac{\lambda}{n}\right)^x\left(1 - \frac{\lambda}{n}\right)^{n-x},$$

where $p = \lambda/n$, so that $\lambda = np$ in the above binomial probability. That is, if X has the binomial distribution $b(n, p)$ with large n and small p, then

$$\frac{(np)^x e^{-np}}{x!} \approx \binom{n}{x} p^x (1 - p)^{n-x}.$$

This approximation is reasonably good if n is large. But since λ was a fixed constant in that earlier argument, p should be small, because $np = \lambda$. In particular, the approximation is quite accurate if $n \geq 20$ and $p \leq 0.05$ or if $n \geq 100$ and $p \leq 0.10$, but it is not bad in other situations violating these bounds somewhat, such as $n = 50$ and $p = 0.12$.

EXAMPLE 2.6-6 A manufacturer of Christmas tree light bulbs knows that 2% of its bulbs are defective. Assuming independence, we have a binomial distribution with parameters $p = 0.02$ and $n = 100$. To approximate the probability that a box of 100 of these bulbs contains at most three defective bulbs, we use the Poisson distribution with $\lambda = 100(0.02) = 2$, which gives

$$\sum_{x=0}^{3} \frac{2^x e^{-2}}{x!} = 0.857,$$

from Table III in the appendix. Using the binomial distribution, we obtain, after some tedious calculations,

$$\sum_{x=0}^{3} \binom{100}{x} (0.02)^x (0.98)^{100-x} = 0.859.$$

Hence, in this case, the Poisson approximation is extremely close to the true value, but much easier to find. ■

REMARK With the availability of statistical computer packages and statistical calculators, it is often very easy to find binomial probabilities. So do not use the Poisson approximation if you are able to find the probability exactly. ■

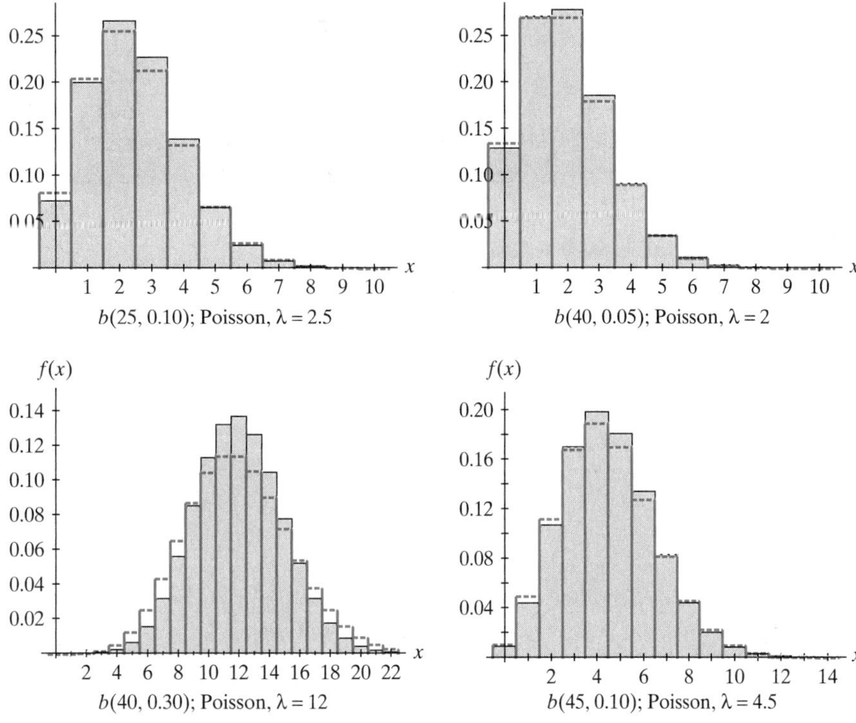

FIGURE 2.6-3: Binomial (shaded) and Poisson probability histograms

EXAMPLE 2.6-7 In Figure 2.6-3, Poisson probability histograms have been superimposed on shaded binomial probability histograms so that we can see whether or not these are close to each other. If the distribution of X is $b(n, p)$, the approximating Poisson distribution has a mean of $\lambda = np$. Note that the approximation is not good when p is large (e.g., $p = 0.30$). ■

EXAMPLE 2.6-8 A lot (collection) of 1000 parts is shipped to a company. A sampling plan dictates that $n = 100$ parts are to be taken at random and without replacement and the lot accepted if no more than 2 of these 100 parts are defective. Here Ac = 2 is usually called the **acceptance number**. The operating characteristic curve

$$\mathrm{OC}(p) = P(X \le 2),$$

where p is the fraction defective in the lot, is really the sum of the three hypergeometric probabilities

$$P(X = x) = \frac{\dbinom{N_1}{x}\dbinom{1000 - N_1}{100 - x}}{\dbinom{1000}{100}}, \qquad x = 0, 1, 2,$$

where $N_1 = (1000)(p)$. However, we have seen that the hypergeometric distribution can be approximated by the binomial distribution, which in turn can be approximated by the Poisson distribution, when n is large and p is small. This is exactly our situation, since $n = 100$ and since we are interested in values of p in the range from 0.00 to 0.10. Thus,

$$\text{OC}(p) = P(X \le 2) \approx \sum_{x=0}^{2} \frac{(100p)^x e^{-100p}}{x!}.$$

Using Table III in the appendix, we find that some approximate values of the operating characteristic curve are $\text{OC}(0.01) = 0.920$, $\text{OC}(0.02) = 0.677$, $\text{OC}(0.03) = 0.423$, $\text{OC}(0.05) = 0.125$, and $\text{OC}(0.10) = 0.003$, and this curve is plotted in Figure 2.6-4. If this is not a satisfactory operating characteristic curve for the type of parts involved, the sample size n and the acceptance number Ac must be changed. ■

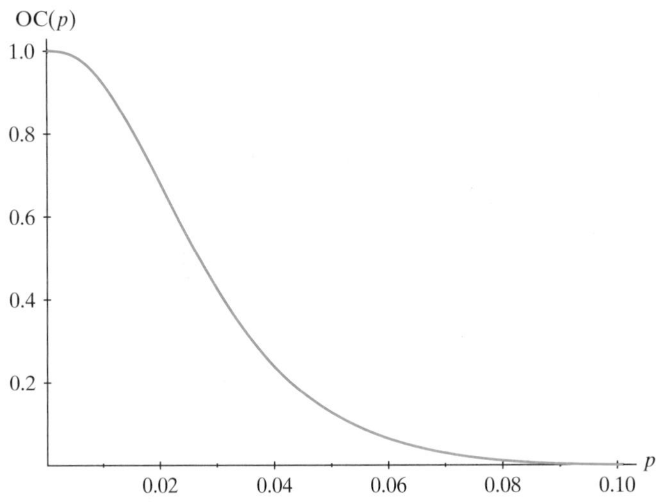

FIGURE 2.6-4: Operating characteristic curve

EXERCISES

2.6-1. Let X have a Poisson distribution with a mean of 4. Find

(a) $P(2 \le X \le 5)$.

(b) $P(X \ge 3)$.

(c) $P(X \le 3)$.

2.6-2. Let X have a Poisson distribution with a variance of 3. Find $P(X = 2)$.

2.6-3. Customers arrive at a travel agency at a mean rate of 11 per hour. Assuming that the number of arrivals per hour has a Poisson distribution, give the probability that more than 10 customers arrive in a given hour.

2.6-4. If X has a Poisson distribution such that $3P(X = 1) = P(X = 2)$, find $P(X = 4)$.

2.6-5. Flaws in a certain type of drapery material appear on the average of one in 150 square feet. If we assume a Poisson distribution, find the probability of at most one flaw appearing in 225 square feet.

2.6-6. A certain type of aluminum screen that is 2 feet wide has, on the average, one flaw in a 100-foot roll. Find the probability that a 50-foot roll has no flaws.

2.6-7. With probability 0.001, a prize of \$499 is won in the Michigan Daily Lottery when a \$1 straight bet is placed. Let Y equal the number of \$499 prizes won by a gambler after placing n straight bets. Note that Y is $b(n, 0.001)$. After placing $n = 2000$ \$1 bets, the gambler is behind if $\{Y \le 4\}$. Use the Poisson distribution to approximate $P(Y \le 4)$ when $n = 2000$.

2.6-8. Suppose that the probability of suffering a side effect from a certain flu vaccine is 0.005. If 1000 persons are inoculated, find the approximate probability that

(a) At most 1 person suffers.

(b) 4, 5, or 6 persons suffer.

2.6-9. A store selling newspapers orders only $n = 4$ of a certain newspaper because the manager does not get many calls for that publication. If the number of requests per day follows a Poisson distribution with mean 3,

(a) What is the expected value of the number sold?

(b) How many should the manager order so that the chance of running out is less than 0.05?

2.6-10. The mean of a Poisson random variable X is $\mu = 9$. Compute

$$P(\mu - 2\sigma < X < \mu + 2\sigma).$$

2.6-11. A Geiger counter was set up in the physics laboratory to record the number of alpha particle emissions of carbon-14 in 0.5 second. Following are 50 observations:

4	6	6	12	11	11	10	5	10	7
9	6	9	11	9	6	4	9	11	8
10	11	7	4	5	8	6	5	8	7
6	3	4	6	4	12	7	14	5	9
7	10	9	6	6	12	10	7	12	13

(a) Calculate the sample mean $\bar{x}$ and sample variance s^2 for these data. Are these two measurements close to each other?

(b) On the same graph, depict the probability histogram for a Poisson distribution with $\lambda = 8$ (we use 8 only because it is the closest value of λ to $\bar{x}$ in Table III in the appendix), with the relative frequency histogram of the data superimposed.

2.6-12. For determining the half-lives of radioactive isotopes, it is important to know what the background radiation is for a given detector over a certain period. A γ-ray detection experiment over 300 one-second intervals yielded the following data:

0	2	4	6	6	1	7	4	6	1	1	2	3	6	4	2	7	4	4	2
2	5	4	4	4	1	2	4	3	2	2	5	0	3	1	1	0	0	5	2
7	1	3	3	3	2	3	1	4	1	3	5	3	5	1	3	3	0	3	2
6	1	1	4	6	3	6	4	4	2	2	4	3	3	6	1	6	2	5	0
6	3	4	3	1	1	4	6	1	5	1	1	4	1	4	1	1	1	3	3
4	3	3	2	5	2	1	3	5	3	2	7	0	4	2	3	3	5	6	1
4	2	6	4	2	0	4	4	7	3	5	2	2	3	1	3	1	3	6	5
4	8	2	2	4	2	2	1	4	7	5	2	1	1	4	1	4	3	6	2
1	1	2	2	2	2	3	5	4	3	2	2	3	3	2	4	4	3	2	2
3	6	1	1	3	3	2	1	4	5	5	1	2	3	3	1	3	7	2	5
4	2	0	6	2	3	2	3	0	4	4	5	2	5	3	0	4	6	2	2
2	2	2	5	2	2	3	4	2	3	7	1	1	7	1	3	6	0	5	3
0	0	3	3	0	2	4	3	1	2	3	3	3	4	3	2	2	7	5	3
5	1	1	2	2	6	1	3	1	4	4	2	3	4	5	1	3	4	3	1
0	3	7	4	0	5	2	5	4	4	2	2	3	2	4	6	5	5	3	4

Do these look like observations of a Poisson random variable with mean $\lambda = 3$? To help answer this question, do the following:

(a) Find the frequencies of $0, 1, 2, \ldots, 8$.

(b) Calculate the sample mean and sample variance. Are they approximately equal to each other?

(c) Construct a probability histogram with $\lambda = 3$ and a relative frequency histogram on the same graph.

(d) What is your conclusion? (Later in this book we consider tests of hypotheses, which help give a statistical answer.)

2.6-13. Let X equal the number of telephone calls per hour that are received by 911 between midnight and noon and that are reported in the *Holland Sentinel*. On October 29 and October 30, the following numbers of calls were reported:

Oct. 29:	0	1	1	1	0	1	2	1	4	1	2	3
Oct. 30:	0	3	0	1	0	1	1	2	3	0	2	2

(a) Calculate the sample mean and sample variance for these data. Are they approximately equal to each other? (See Exercise 2.3-8.)

(b) Assume that $\lambda = 1.3$, so that Table III in the appendix can be used. Draw a probability histogram for the Poisson distribution and a relative frequency histogram of the data on the same graph.

(c) On the basis of these limited data, does it look like the Poisson distribution with $\lambda = 1.3$ could be a reasonable probability model?

2.6-14. Let X equal the number of green peanut M&M's in packages of size 22. Forty-five observations of X yielded the following frequencies for the possible outcomes of X:

Outcome (x):	0	1	2	3	4	5	6	7	8	9
Frequency:	0	2	4	5	7	9	8	5	3	2

(a) Use these data to construct a relative frequency histogram and superimpose over it a Poisson probability histogram with a mean of $\lambda = 5$.

(b) Do these data appear to be observations of a Poisson random variable?

2.6-15. A student trainer worked in the training room in the physical education building. The number of students coming in to be taped or for treatment of other injuries was recorded each half hour, yielding the following data:

3	3	2	0	4	5	6	4	4	3	2	1	2	3	0
5	5	3	2	3	5	4	1	2	0	3	2	4	2	6

(a) Find the sample mean, $\overline{x}$.

(b) Find the sample variance, s^2.

(c) Find the sample standard deviation, s.

(d) Draw a relative frequency histogram of these data with an appropriate Poisson probability histogram superimposed.

2.6-16. A lot (collection) of 10,000 items is accepted if a sample of $n = 400$ has no more than $\text{Ac} = 3$ defective items. Determine the approximate values of OC(0.002), OC(0.004), OC(0.006), OC(0.01), and OC(0.02), and plot the operating characteristic curve.

2.6-17. Consider a lot (collection) of 5000 items. Design a sampling plan (i.e., find n and Ac) such that $\text{OC}(0.02) = 0.95$ and $\text{OC}(0.08) = 0.10$, approximately.

HINT: Start with $n = 50$ and $\text{Ac} = 2$ and modify as necessary, noting that increasing n creates a steeper OC curve.

2.6-18. A baseball team loses \$10,000 for each consecutive day it rains. Say X, the number of consecutive days it rains at the beginning of the season, has a Poisson distribution with mean 0.2. What is the expected loss before the opening game?

2.6-19. An airline always overbooks if possible. A particular plane has 95 seats on a flight in which a ticket sells for \$300. The airline sells 100 such tickets for this flight.

(a) If the probability of an individual not showing up is 0.05, assuming independence, what is the probability that the airline can accommodate all the passengers who do show up?

(b) If the airline must return the \$300 price plus a penalty of \$400 to each passenger that cannot get on the flight, what is the expected payout (penalty plus ticket refund) that the airline will pay?

2.6-20. Assume that a policyholder is four times more likely to file exactly two claims as to file exactly three claims. Assume also that the number X of claims of this policyholder is Poisson. Determine the expectation $E(X^2)$.

2.6-21. In the decade of the 1980s, the number X of cases of diphtheria reported each year in the United States followed a Poisson distribution with mean 2.5. What is the probability that

(a) No cases were reported in a given year?

(b) Exactly three cases were reported?

(c) At least three cases were reported?

(d) At most three cases were reported?

2.6-22. For determining half-lives of radioactive isotopes, it is important to know what the background radiation is for a given detector over a certain period. A γ-ray detection experiment over 98 ten-second intervals (observations of a random variable X) yielded the following data:

58	50	57	58	64	63	54	64	59	41	43	56	60	50
46	59	54	60	59	60	67	52	65	63	55	61	68	58
63	36	42	54	58	54	40	60	64	56	61	51	48	50
60	42	62	67	58	49	66	58	57	59	52	54	53	53
57	43	73	65	45	43	57	55	73	62	68	55	51	55
53	68	58	53	51	73	44	50	53	62	58	47	63	59
59	56	60	59	50	52	62	51	66	51	56	53	59	57

(a) Find the sample mean.

(b) Find the sample variance.

HISTORICAL COMMENTS The next major items advanced in probability theory were by the Bernoullis, a remarkable Swiss family of mathematicians of the late 1600s to the late 1700s. There were eight mathematicians among them, but we shall mention just three of them: Jacob, Nicolaus II, and Daniel. While writing *Ars Conjectandi*

(*The Art of Conjecture*), Jacob died in 1705, and a nephew, Nicolaus II, edited the work for publication. However, it was Jacob who discovered the important law of large numbers, which is included in our Section 10.5.

Another nephew of Jacob, Daniel, noted in his St. Petersburg paper that "expected values are computed by multiplying each possible gain by the number of ways in which it can occur and then dividing the sum of these products by the total number of cases." His cousin, Nicolaus II, then proposed the so-called St. Petersburg paradox: Peter continues to toss a coin until a head first appears—say, on the xth trial—and he then pays Paul 2^{x-1} units (originally ducats, but for convenience we use dollars). With each additional throw, the number of dollars has doubled. How much should another person pay Paul to take his place in this game? Clearly,

$$E(2^{X-1}) = \sum_{x=1}^{\infty} (2^{x-1})\left(\frac{1}{2^x}\right) = \sum_{x=1}^{\infty} \frac{1}{2} = \infty.$$

However, if we consider this as a practical problem, would someone be willing to give Paul \$1000 to take his place even though there is this unlimited expected value? We doubt it and Daniel doubted it, and it made him think about the utility of money. For example, to most of us, \$3 million is not worth three times \$1 million. To convince you of that, suppose you had exactly \$1 million and a very rich man offers to bet you \$2 million against your \$1 million on the flip of a coin. You will have zero or \$3 million after the flip, so your expected value is

$$(\$0)\left(\frac{1}{2}\right) + (\$3{,}000{,}000)\left(\frac{1}{2}\right) = \$1{,}500{,}000,$$

much more than your \$1 million. Seemingly, then, this is a great bet and one that Bill Gates might take. However, remember you have \$1 million for certain and you could have zero with probability 1/2. None of us with limited resources should consider taking that bet, because the utility of that extra money to us is not worth the utility of the first \$1 million. Now, each of us has our own utility function. Two dollars is worth twice as much as one dollar for practically all of us. But is \$200,000 worth twice as much as \$100,000? It depends upon your situation; so while the utility function is a straight line for the first several dollars, it still increases, but begins to bend downward someplace as the amount of money increases. This occurs at different spots for all of us. Bob Hogg, one of the authors of this text, would bet \$1000 against \$2000 on a flip of the coin anytime, but probably not \$100,000 against \$200,000, so Hogg's utility function has started to bend downward someplace between \$1000 and \$100,000. Daniel Bernoulli made this observation, and it is extremely useful in all kinds of businesses.

As an illustration, in insurance, most of us know that the premium we pay for all types of insurance is greater than what the company expects to pay us; that is how they make money. Seemingly, insurance is a bad bet, but it really isn't always. It is true that we should self-insure less expensive items—those whose value is on that straight part of the utility function. We have even heard the "rule" that you not insure anything worth less than two month's salary; this is a fairly good guide, but each of us has our own utility function and must make that decision. Hogg can afford losses in the \$5000 to \$10,000 range (not that he likes them, of course), but he does not want to pay losses of \$100,000 or more. So his utility function for negative values of the argument follows that straight line for relatively small negative amounts, but again bends down for large negative amounts. If you insure expensive items, you will discover that the expected utility in absolute value will now exceed the premium. This is why most people insure their life, their home, and their car (particularly on the liability side). They should not, however, insure their golf clubs, eyeglasses, furs, or jewelry (unless the latter two items are extremely valuable).

Continuous Distributions

CHAPTER 3

3.1 CONTINUOUS-TYPE DATA
3.2 EXPLORATORY DATA ANALYSIS
3.3 RANDOM VARIABLES OF THE CONTINUOUS TYPE
3.4 THE UNIFORM AND EXPONENTIAL DISTRIBUTIONS
3.5 THE GAMMA AND CHI-SQUARE DISTRIBUTIONS
3.6 THE NORMAL DISTRIBUTION
3.7 ADDITIONAL MODELS

3.1 CONTINUOUS-TYPE DATA

In Chapter 2 we considered probability distributions of random variables whose space S contains a countable number of outcomes: either a finite number of outcomes or outcomes that can be put into a one-to-one correspondence with the positive integers. Such a random variable is said to be of the **discrete type**, and its distribution of probabilities is of the discrete type.

Many experiments or observations of random phenomena do not have integers as outcomes, but instead are measurements selected from an interval of numbers. For example, you could find the length of time that it takes when waiting in line to buy frozen yogurt. Or the weight of a "1-pound" package of hot dogs could be any number between 0.94 pound and 1.25 pounds. The weight of a miniature Baby Ruth candy bar could be any number between 20 and 27 grams. Even though such times and weights could be selected from an interval of values, times and weights are generally rounded off so that the data often look like discrete data. If, conceptually, the measurements could come from an interval of possible outcomes, we call them data from a continuous-type population or, more simply, **continuous-type data**.

Given a set of continuous-type data, we shall group the data into classes and then construct a histogram of the grouped data. This will help us better visualize the data. The following guidelines and terminology will be used to group continuous-type data into classes of equal length (these guidelines can also be used for sets of discrete data that have a large range):

1. Determine the largest (maximum) and smallest (minimum) observations. The **range** is the difference R = maximum − minimum.

2. In general, select from $k = 5$ to $k = 20$ classes, which are usually nonoverlapping intervals of equal length. These classes should cover the interval from the minimum to the maximum.
3. Each interval begins and ends halfway between two possible values of the measurements, which have been rounded off to a given number of decimal places.
4. The first interval should begin about as much below the smallest value as the last interval ends above the largest.
5. The intervals are called **class intervals** and the boundaries are called **class boundaries** or **cutpoints**. We shall denote these k class intervals by

$$(c_0, c_1), (c_1, c_2), \ldots, (c_{k-1}, c_k).$$

6. The **class limits** are the smallest and the largest possible observed (recorded) values in a class.
7. The **class mark** is the midpoint of a class.

A frequency table is constructed that lists the class intervals, the class limits, a tabulation of the measurements in the various classes, the frequency f_i of each class, and the class marks. A column is sometimes used to construct a relative frequency (density) histogram. With class intervals of equal length, a frequency histogram is constructed by drawing, for each class, a rectangle having as its base the class interval and a height equal to the frequency of the class. For the relative frequency histogram, each rectangle has an **area** equal to the relative frequency f_i/n of the observations for the class. That is, the function defined by

$$h(x) = \frac{f_i}{(n)(c_i - c_{i-1})}, \qquad \text{for } c_{i-1} < x \le c_i, \quad i = 1, 2, \ldots, k,$$

is called a **relative frequency histogram** or **density histogram**, where f_i is the frequency of the ith class and n is the total number of observations. Clearly, if the class intervals are of equal length, the relative frequency histogram, $h(x)$, is proportional to the **frequency histogram** f_i, for $c_{i-1} < x \le c_i, i = 1, 2, \ldots, k$. The frequency histogram should be used only in those situations in which the class intervals are of equal length.

EXAMPLE 3.1-1 The weights in grams of 40 miniature Baby Ruth candy bars, with the weights ordered, are given in Table 3.1-1.

TABLE 3.1-1: Candy Bar Weights

20.5	20.7	20.8	21.0	21.0	21.4	21.5	22.0	22.1	22.5
22.6	22.6	22.7	22.7	22.9	22.9	23.1	23.3	23.4	23.5
23.6	23.6	23.6	23.9	24.1	24.3	24.5	24.5	24.8	24.8
24.9	24.9	25.1	25.1	25.2	25.6	25.8	25.9	26.1	26.7

We shall group these data and then construct a histogram to visualize the distribution of weights. The range of the data is $R = 26.7 - 20.5 = 6.2$. The interval $(20.5, 26.7)$ could be covered with $k = 8$ classes of width 0.8 or with $k = 9$ classes of width 0.7. (There are other possibilities.) We shall use $k = 7$ classes of width 0.9. The first class interval will be $(20.45, 21.35)$ and the last class interval will be $(25.85, 26.75)$. The data are grouped in Table 3.1-2.

TABLE 3.1-2: Frequency Table of Candy Bar Weights

Class Interval	Class Limits	Tabulation	Frequency (f_i)	$h(x)$	Class Marks
(20.45, 21.35)	20.5–21.3	𝍸	5	5/36	20.9
(21.35, 22.25)	21.4–22.2	||||	4	4/36	21.8
(22.25, 23.15)	22.3–23.1	𝍸 |||	8	8/36	22.7
(23.15, 24.05)	23.2–24.0	𝍸 ||	7	7/36	23.6
(24.05, 24.95)	24.1–24.9	𝍸 |||	8	8/36	24.5
(24.95, 25.85)	25.0–25.8	𝍸	5	5/36	25.4
(25.85, 26.75)	25.9–26.7	|||	3	3/36	26.3

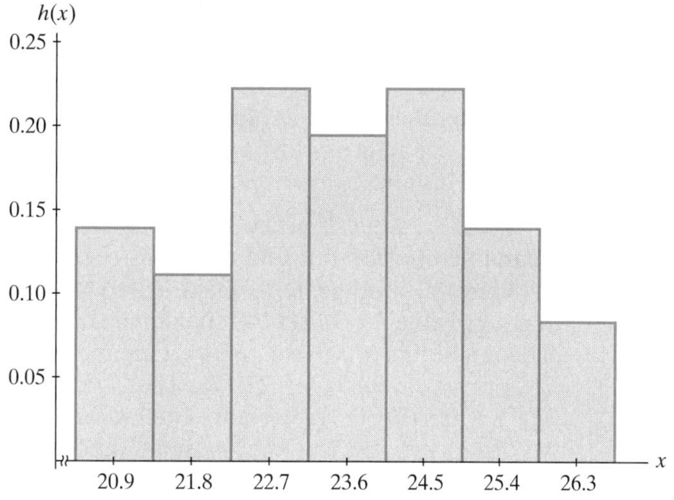

FIGURE 3.1-1: Relative frequency histogram of weights of candy bars

A relative frequency histogram of these data is given in Figure 3.1-1. Note that the total area of this histogram is equal to 1. We could also construct a frequency histogram in which the heights of the rectangles would be equal to the frequencies of the classes. The shape of the two histograms is the same. Later we will see the reason for preferring the relative frequency histogram. In particular, we will be superimposing on the relative frequency histogram the graph of a continuous function, called a probability density function, that corresponds to a probability model. ■

Given a set of measurements, the sample mean is the center of the data such that the deviations from that center sum to zero; that is, $\sum_{i=1}^{n}(x_i - \overline{x}) = 0$. The sample standard deviation gives a measure of how spread out the data are from the sample mean. If the histogram is "mound shaped" or "bell shaped," the following empirical rule gives rough approximations to the percentages of the data that fall between certain points.

Empirical Rule: Let $x_1, x_2, \ldots, x_n$ have a sample mean $\overline{x}$ and sample standard deviation s. If the histogram of these data is "bell shaped," then

- approximately 68% of the data are in the interval $(\overline{x} - s, \overline{x} + s)$.
- approximately 95% of the data are in the interval $(\overline{x} - 2s, \overline{x} + 2s)$.
- approximately 99.7% of the data are in the interval $(\overline{x} - 3s, \overline{x} + 3s)$.

For the data in Example 3.1-1, the sample mean is $\bar{x} = 23.505$ and the standard deviation is $s = 1.641$. The number of weights that fall within one standard deviation of the mean, $(23.505 - 1.641, 23.505 + 1.641)$, is 27, or 67.5%. For these particular weights, 100% fall within two standard deviations of $\bar{x}$. Thus, the histogram is missing part of the "bell" in the tails in order for the empirical rule to hold. The theory needed to explain why this approximation does or does not work is considered in Section 3.6.

When you draw a histogram, it is useful to indicate the location of $\bar{x}$, as well as that of the points $\bar{x} \pm s$ and $\bar{x} \pm 2s$.

There is a refinement of the relative frequency histogram that can be made when the class intervals are of equal length. The **relative frequency polygon** smooths out the corresponding histogram somewhat. To form such a polygon, mark the midpoints at the top of each "bar" of the histogram. Connect adjacent midpoints with straight-line segments. On each of the two end bars, draw a line segment from the top middle mark through the middle point of the outer vertical line of the bar. Of course, if the area underneath the tops of the relative frequency histogram is equal to 1, which it should be, then the area underneath the relative frequency polygon is also equal to 1, because the areas lost and gained cancel out by a consideration of congruent triangles. This idea is made clear in the next example.

EXAMPLE 3.1-2 A manufacturer of fluoride toothpaste regularly measures the concentration of fluoride in the toothpaste to make sure that it is within the specification of 0.85 to 1.10 mg/g. Table 3.1-3 lists 100 such measurements.

The minimum of these measurements is 0.85 and the maximum is 1.06. The range is $1.06 - 0.85 = 0.21$. We shall use $k = 8$ classes of length 0.03. Note that $8(0.03) = 0.24 > 0.21$. We start at 0.835 and end at 1.075. These boundaries are the same distance below the minimum and above the maximum. In Table 3.1-4, we also give the values of the heights of each rectangle in the relative frequency histogram, so that the total area of the histogram is 1. These heights are given by the formula

$$h(x) = \frac{f_i}{(0.03)(100)} = \frac{f_i}{3}.$$

The plots of the relative frequency histogram and polygon are given in Figure 3.1-2.

If you are using a computer program to analyze a set of data, it is very easy to find the sample mean, the sample variance, and the sample standard deviation. However, if you have only grouped data or if you are not using a computer, you can obtain close approximations of these values by computing the mean $\bar{u}$ and variance s_u^2 of the

TABLE 3.1-3: Concentrations of Fluoride in mg/g in Toothpaste

0.98	0.92	0.89	0.90	0.94	0.99	0.86	0.85	1.06	1.01
1.03	0.85	0.95	0.90	1.03	0.87	1.02	0.88	0.92	0.88
0.88	0.90	0.98	0.96	0.98	0.93	0.98	0.92	1.00	0.95
0.88	0.90	1.01	0.98	0.85	0.91	0.95	1.01	0.88	0.89
0.99	0.95	0.90	0.88	0.92	0.89	0.90	0.95	0.93	0.96
0.93	0.91	0.92	0.86	0.87	0.91	0.89	0.93	0.93	0.95
0.92	0.88	0.87	0.98	0.98	0.91	0.93	1.00	0.90	0.93
0.89	0.97	0.98	0.91	0.88	0.89	1.00	0.93	0.92	0.97
0.97	0.91	0.85	0.92	0.87	0.86	0.91	0.92	0.95	0.97
0.88	1.05	0.91	0.89	0.92	0.94	0.90	1.00	0.90	0.93

TABLE 3.1-4: Frequency Table of Fluoride Concentrations

Class Interval	Class Mark (u_i)	Tabulation	Frequency (f_i)	$h(x) = f_i/3$
(0.835, 0.865)	0.85	~~IIII~~ II	7	7/3
(0.865, 0.895)	0.88	~~IIII~~ ~~IIII~~ ~~IIII~~ ~~IIII~~	20	20/3
(0.895, 0.925)	0.91	~~IIII~~ ~~IIII~~ ~~IIII~~ ~~IIII~~ ~~IIII~~ II	27	27/3
(0.925, 0.955)	0.94	~~IIII~~ ~~IIII~~ ~~IIII~~ III	18	18/3
(0.955, 0.985)	0.97	~~IIII~~ ~~IIII~~ IIII	14	14/3
(0.985, 1.015)	1.00	~~IIII~~ IIII	9	9/3
(1.015, 1.045)	1.03	III	3	3/3
(1.045, 1.075)	1.06	II	2	2/3

grouped data, using the class marks weighted with their respective frequencies. We have

$$\begin{aligned}\overline{u} &= \frac{1}{n}\sum_{i=1}^{k} f_i u_i \\ &= \frac{1}{100}\sum_{i=1}^{8} f_i u_i = \frac{92.83}{100} = 0.9283,\end{aligned}$$

$$\begin{aligned}s_u^2 &= \frac{1}{n-1}\sum_{i=1}^{k} f_i(u_i - \overline{u})^2 = \frac{\displaystyle\sum_{i=1}^{k} f_i u_i^2 - \frac{1}{n}\left(\sum_{i=1}^{k} f_i u_i\right)^2}{n-1} \\ &= \frac{0.237411}{99} = 0.002398.\end{aligned}$$

Thus,

$$s_u = \sqrt{0.002398} = 0.04897.$$

These results compare rather favorably with $\overline{x} = 0.9293$ and $s_x = 0.04895$ of the original data. ■

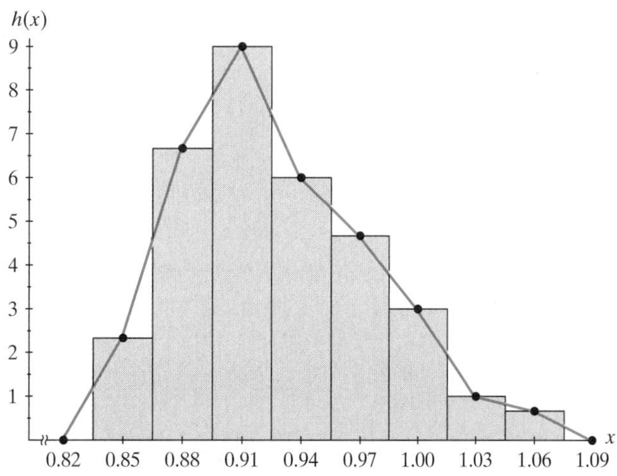

FIGURE 3.1-2: Concentrations of fluoride in toothpaste

In some situations, it is not necessarily desirable to use class intervals of equal widths in the construction of the frequency distribution and histogram. This is particularly true if the data are skewed with a very long tail. We now present an illustration in which it seems desirable to use class intervals of unequal lengths; thus, we cannot use the relative frequency polygon.

EXAMPLE 3.1-3 The following 40 losses, due to wind-related catastrophes, were recorded to the nearest \$1 million (these data include only losses of \$2 million or more; for convenience, they have been ordered and recorded in millions):

2	2	2	2	2	2	2	2	2	2
2	2	3	3	3	3	4	4	4	5
5	5	5	6	6	6	6	8	8	9
15	17	22	23	24	24	25	27	32	43

The selection of class boundaries is more subjective in this case. It makes sense to let $c_0 = 1.5$ and $c_1 = 2.5$ because only values of \$2 million or more are recorded and there are 12 observations equal to 2. We could then let $c_2 = 6.5$, $c_3 = 29.5$, and $c_4 = 49.5$, yielding the following relative frequency histogram:

$$h(x) = \begin{cases} \dfrac{12}{40}, & 1.5 < x \le 2.5, \\ \dfrac{15}{(40)(4)}, & 2.5 < x \le 6.5, \\ \dfrac{11}{(40)(23)}, & 6.5 < x \le 29.5, \\ \dfrac{2}{(40)(20)}, & 29.5 < x \le 49.5. \end{cases}$$

This histogram is displayed in Figure 3.1-3. It takes some experience before a person can display a relative frequency histogram that is most meaningful.

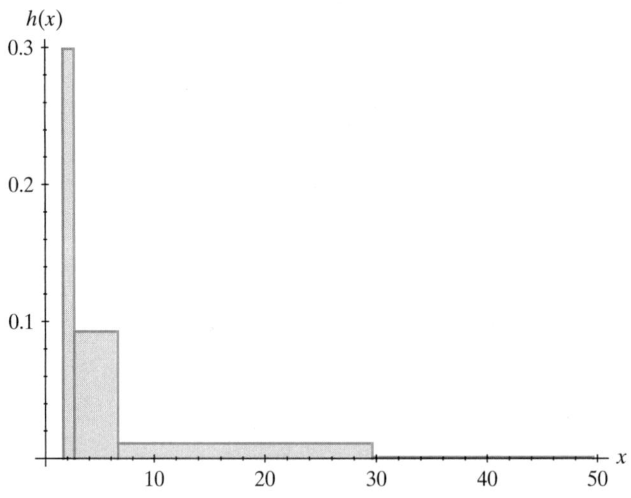

FIGURE 3.1-3: Relative frequency histogram of losses

The areas of the four rectangles—0.300, 0.375, 0.275, and 0.050—are the respective relative frequencies. It is important to note in the case of unequal lengths among class intervals that the *areas*, not the heights, of the rectangles are proportional to the frequencies. In particular, the first and second classes have frequencies $f_1 = 12$ and $f_2 = 15$, yet the height of the first is greater than the height of the second, while here $f_1 < f_2$. If we have equal lengths among the class intervals, then the heights are proportional to the frequencies. ■

For continuous-type data, the interval with the largest class height is called the **modal class** and the respective class mark is called the **mode**. Hence, in the last example, $x = 2$ is the mode and $(1.5, 2.5)$ the modal class.

EXERCISES

3.1-1. One characteristic of a car's storage console that is checked by the manufacturer is the time in seconds that it takes for the lower storage compartment door to open completely. A random sample of size $n = 5$ yielded the following times:

1.1 0.9 1.4 1.1 1.0

(a) Find the sample mean, $\bar{x}$.

(b) Find the sample variance, s^2.

(c) Find the sample standard deviation, s.

3.1-2. A leakage test was conducted to determine the effectiveness of a seal designed to keep the inside of a plug airtight. An air needle was inserted into the plug, which was then placed underwater. Next, the pressure was increased until leakage was observed. The magnitude of this pressure in psi was recorded for 10 trials:

3.1 3.5 3.3 3.7 4.5 4.2 2.8 3.9 3.5 3.3

Find the sample mean and sample standard deviation for these 10 measurements.

3.1-3. Before Halloween two bags of miniature Clark bars were purchased and each bar was weighed (in grams). There were 19 bars in the first bag and 23 in the second bag, yielding the following weights:

19.8	20.3	20.2	19.6	20.0	19.4	15.4	19.9	20.5	20.5	19.8
15.5	21.8	20.0	15.4	20.6	15.7	20.4	21.3	16.7	15.6	14.2
15.9	16.8	15.2	15.0	16.0	16.4	15.4	16.0	16.1	17.0	16.0
15.1	14.1	15.8	15.7	16.6	15.2	15.5	14.9	15.3		

(a) Using 13.95–14.95, 14.95–15.95, and so on as class boundaries, group these weights and construct a histogram.

(b) Calculate the values of the sample mean and sample standard deviation.

(c) Locate $\bar{x}$, $\bar{x} \pm s_x$, $\bar{x} \pm 2s_x$ on your histogram.

(d) Give an interpretation of your output.

3.1-4. When a customer purchases a laptop computer, one characteristic of interest is the weight of the laptop. Here are the weights of 100 laptop computers:

9.38	5.20	5.38	6.80	7.97	2.20	6.80	7.10	4.60	6.51
6.50	5.33	8.10	4.90	7.07	6.17	7.70	6.28	6.60	3.90
5.11	5.40	4.90	5.20	2.69	7.97	6.20	5.33	7.97	5.58
5.20	5.21	5.33	5.20	5.90	6.50	5.73	4.60	5.60	5.54
5.38	6.50	5.20	3.13	5.12	4.90	6.27	6.50	7.85	5.20
4.77	4.85	5.20	7.90	9.00	5.20	7.90	6.06	5.73	6.50
5.50	7.85	5.60	3.90	3.90	6.20	4.90	3.57	3.90	4.20
8.20	7.90	5.33	4.77	3.90	4.60	3.50	5.20	9.40	4.30
7.60	8.60	9.38	6.00	3.72	2.69	6.60	6.10	9.50	4.90
3.50	10.10	5.33	6.40	6.50	5.96	4.00	7.90	2.69	4.40

(a) Calculate the sample mean and sample standard deviation.

(b) Use the numbers $1.995, 2.995, \ldots, 10.995$ as cutpoints to construct a histogram of the weights.

3.1-5. During the course of an internship at a company that manufactures diesel engine fuel injector pumps, a student had to measure the category of the plungers that force the fuel out of the pumps. This category is based on a relative scale, measuring the difference in diameter (in microns or micrometers) of a plunger from that of an absolute minimum acceptable diameter. For 96 plungers randomly taken from the production line, the data are as follows:

17.1	19.3	18.0	19.4	16.5	14.4	15.8	16.6	18.5	14.9
14.8	16.3	20.8	17.8	14.8	15.6	16.7	16.1	17.1	16.5
18.8	19.3	18.1	16.1	18.0	17.2	16.8	17.3	14.4	14.1
16.9	17.6	15.5	17.8	17.2	17.4	18.1	18.4	17.8	16.7
17.2	13.7	18.0	15.6	17.8	17.0	17.7	11.9	15.9	17.8
15.5	14.6	15.6	15.1	15.4	16.1	16.6	17.1	19.1	15.0
17.6	19.7	17.1	13.6	15.6	16.3	14.8	17.4	14.8	14.9
14.1	17.8	19.8	18.9	15.6	16.1	15.9	15.7	22.1	16.1
18.9	21.5	17.4	12.3	20.2	14.9	17.1	15.0	14.4	14.7
15.9	19.0	16.6	15.3	17.7	15.8				

(a) Calculate the sample mean and the sample standard deviation of these measurements.

(b) Use the cutpoints $10.95, 11.95, \ldots, 22.95$ to construct a histogram of the data.

3.1-6. Decks have become very popular items for American homeowners. Lumberyards sell many styles of decks during the summer months, but they all use the same type of nail. The question that always arises is how many nails to buy. If 800 nails are needed, how many grams of nails should be purchased? The following weights (in grams) of 50 nails should help to answer the question:

9.42	8.69	8.93	8.27	8.82	8.66	8.90	8.31	9.15	9.63
9.41	8.56	8.82	8.58	8.43	8.05	8.56	8.55	8.88	8.73
8.29	8.79	8.51	8.85	9.34	9.21	8.38	8.51	8.41	8.98
8.58	9.21	8.27	8.76	9.26	8.59	8.36	8.71	8.51	8.88
9.20	8.24	8.57	8.85	8.69	8.85	9.08	9.40	9.25	8.79

(a) Using (7.995, 8.245), (8.245, 8.495), and so on as class intervals, group these data into seven classes.

(b) Construct a histogram of the data.

(c) Calculate the sample mean and sample standard deviation.

(d) How many grams of nails would you recommend?

3.1-7. In the casino game roulette, if a player bets \$1 on red, the probability of winning \$1 is 18/38 and the probability of losing \$1 is 20/38. Let X equal the number of successive \$1 bets that a player makes before losing \$5. One hundred observations of X were simulated on a computer, yielding the following data:

23	127	877	65	101	45	61	95	21	43
53	49	89	9	75	93	71	39	25	91
15	131	63	63	41	7	37	13	19	413
65	43	35	23	135	703	83	7	17	65
49	177	61	21	9	27	507	7	5	87
13	213	85	83	75	95	247	1815	7	13
71	67	19	615	11	15	7	131	47	25
25	5	471	11	5	13	75	19	307	33
57	65	9	57	35	19	9	33	11	51
27	9	19	63	109	515	443	11	63	9

(a) Find the sample mean and sample standard deviation of these data.

(b) Construct a relative frequency histogram of the data, using about 10 classes. The classes do not need to be of the same length.

(c) Locate $\bar{x}$, $\bar{x} \pm s$, $\bar{x} \pm 2s$, $\bar{x} \pm 3s$ on your histogram .

(d) In your opinion, does the median or sample mean give a better measure of the center of these data?

3.1-8. Ledolter and Hogg (see references) report that a manufacturer of metal alloys is concerned about customer complaints regarding the lack of uniformity in the melting points of one of the firm's alloy filaments. Fifty filaments are selected and their melting points determined. The following results were obtained:

320	326	325	318	322	320	329	317	316	331
320	320	317	329	316	308	321	319	322	335
318	313	327	314	329	323	327	323	324	314
308	305	328	330	322	310	324	314	312	318
313	320	324	311	317	325	328	319	310	324

(a) Construct a frequency distribution, and display the histogram, of the data.

(b) Calculate the sample mean and sample standard deviation.

(c) Locate $\bar{x}$, $\bar{x} \pm s$ on your histogram. How many observations lie within one standard deviation of the mean? How many lie within two standard deviations of the mean?

3.1-9. Ledolter and Hogg (see references) report 64 observations that are a sample of daily weekday afternoon (3 to 7 P.M.) lead concentrations (in micrograms per cubic meter, μg/m^3). The following data were recorded at an air-monitoring station near the San Diego Freeway in Los Angeles during the fall of 1976:

6.7	5.4	5.2	6.0	8.7	6.0	6.4	8.3	5.3	5.9	7.6
5.0	6.9	6.8	4.9	6.3	5.0	6.0	7.2	8.0	8.1	7.2
10.9	9.2	8.6	6.2	6.1	6.5	7.8	6.2	8.5	6.4	8.1
2.1	6.1	6.5	7.9	14.1	9.5	10.6	8.4	8.3	5.9	6.0
6.4	3.9	9.9	7.6	6.8	8.6	8.5	11.2	7.0	7.1	6.0
9.0	10.1	8.0	6.8	7.3	9.7	9.3	3.2	6.4		

(a) Construct a frequency distribution of the data and display the results in the form of a histogram. Is this distribution symmetric?

(b) Calculate the sample mean and sample standard deviation.

(c) Locate $\bar{x}, \bar{x} \pm s$ on your histogram. How many observations lie within one standard deviation of the mean? How many lie within two standard deviations of the mean?

3.1-10. An insurance company experienced the following mobile home losses in 10,000's of dollars for 50 catastrophic events:

1	2	2	3	3	4	4	5	5	5
5	6	7	7	9	9	9	10	11	12
22	24	28	29	31	33	36	38	38	38
39	41	48	49	53	55	74	82	117	134
192	207	224	225	236	280	301	308	351	527

(a) Using class boundaries 0.5, 5.5, 17.5, 38.5, 163.5, and 549.5, group these data into five classes.

(b) Construct a relative frequency histogram of the data.

(c) Describe the distribution of losses.

3.1-11. Old Faithful is a geyser in Yellowstone National Park. Tourists always want to know when the next eruption will occur, so data have been collected to help make those predictions. In the data set on the next page, observations were made on several consecutive days, and the data recorded give the starting time of the eruption (STE); the duration of the eruption, in seconds (DIS); the predicted time until the next eruption, in minutes (PTM); the actual time until the next eruption, in minutes (ATM); and the duration of the eruption, in minutes (DIM).

(a) Construct a histogram of the durations of the eruptions, in seconds. Use 10 to 12 classes.

(b) Calculate the sample mean and locate it on your histogram. Does it give a good measure of the average length of an eruption? Why or why not?

(c) Construct a histogram of the lengths of the times between eruptions. Use 10 to 12 classes.

(d) Calculate the sample mean and locate it on your histogram. Does it give a good measure of the average length of the times between eruptions?

STE	DIS	PTM	ATM	DIM	STE	DIS	PTM	ATM	DIM
706	150	65	72	2.500	1411	110	55	65	1.833
818	268	89	88	4.467	616	289	89	97	4.817
946	140	65	62	2.333	753	114	58	52	1.900
1048	300	95	87	5.000	845	271	89	94	4.517
1215	101	55	57	1.683	1019	120	58	60	2.000
1312	270	89	94	4.500	1119	279	89	84	4.650
651	270	89	91	4.500	1253	109	55	63	1.817
822	125	59	51	2.083	1356	295	95	91	4.917
913	262	89	98	4.367	608	240	85	83	4.000
1051	95	55	59	1.583	731	259	86	84	4.317
1150	270	89	93	4.500	855	128	60	71	2.133
637	273	89	86	4.550	1006	287	92	83	4.783
803	104	55	70	1.733	1129	253	65	70	4.217
913	129	62	63	2.150	1239	284	89	81	4.733
1016	264	89	91	4.400	608	120	58	60	2.000
1147	239	82	82	3.983	708	283	92	91	4.717
1309	106	55	58	1.767	839	115	58	51	1.917
716	259	85	97	4.317	930	254	85	85	4.233
853	115	55	59	1.917	1055	94	55	55	1.567
952	275	89	90	4.583	1150	274	89	98	4.567
1122	110	55	58	1.833	1328	128	64	49	2.133
1220	286	92	98	4.767	557	270	93	85	4.500
735	115	55	55	1.917	722	103	58	65	1.717
830	266	89	107	4.433	827	287	89	102	4.783
1017	105	55	61	1.750	1009	111	55	56	1.850
1118	275	89	82	4.583	1105	275	89	86	4.583
1240	226	79	91	3.767	1231	104	55	62	1.733

3.1-12. A small part for an automobile rearview mirror was produced on two different punch presses. In order to describe the distribution of the weights of those parts, a random sample was selected, and each piece was weighed in grams, resulting in the following data set:

3.968	3.534	4.032	3.912	3.572	4.014	3.682	3.608
3.669	3.705	4.023	3.588	3.945	3.871	3.744	3.711
3.645	3.977	3.888	3.948	3.551	3.796	3.657	3.667
3.799	4.010	3.704	3.642	3.681	3.554	4.025	4.079
3.621	3.575	3.714	4.017	4.082	3.660	3.692	3.905
3.977	3.961	3.948	3.994	3.958	3.860	3.965	3.592
3.681	3.861	3.662	3.995	4.010	3.999	3.993	4.004
3.700	4.008	3.627	3.970	3.647	3.847	3.628	3.646
3.674	3.601	4.029	3.603	3.619	4.009	4.015	3.615
3.672	3.898	3.959	3.607	3.707	3.978	3.656	4.027
3.645	3.643	3.898	3.635	3.865	3.631	3.929	3.635
3.511	3.539	3.830	3.925	3.971	3.646	3.669	3.931
4.028	3.665	3.681	3.984	3.664	3.893	3.606	3.699
3.997	3.936	3.976	3.627	3.536	3.695	3.981	3.587
3.680	3.888	3.921	3.953	3.847	3.645	4.042	3.692
3.910	3.672	3.957	3.961	3.950	3.904	3.928	3.984
3.721	3.927	3.621	4.038	4.047	3.627	3.774	3.983
3.658	4.034	3.778					

(a) Using about 10 (say, 8 to 12) classes, construct a frequency distribution of the data.
(b) Draw a histogram of the data.
(c) Describe the shape of the distribution represented by the histogram.

3.2 EXPLORATORY DATA ANALYSIS

To explore the other characteristics of an unknown distribution, we need to take a sample of n observations, $x_1, x_2, \ldots, x_n$, from that distribution and often need to order them from the smallest to the largest. One convenient way of doing this is to use a stem-and-leaf display, a method that was started by John W. Tukey. (For more details, see the books by Tukey (1977) and Velleman and Hoaglin (1981).)

Possibly the easiest way to begin is with an example to which all of us can relate. Say we have the following 50 test scores on a statistics examination:

93	77	67	72	52	83	66	84	59	63
75	97	84	73	81	42	61	51	91	87
34	54	71	47	79	70	65	57	90	83
58	69	82	76	71	60	38	81	74	69
68	76	85	58	45	73	75	42	93	65

We can do much the same thing as a frequency table and histogram can, but keep the original values, through a **stem-and-leaf display**. For this particular data set, we could use the following procedure: The first number in the set, 93, is recorded by treating the 9 (in the tens place) as the stem and the 3 (in the units place) as the corresponding leaf. Note that this leaf of 3 is the first digit after the stem of 9 in Table 3.2-1. The second number, 77, is then given by the leaf of 7 after the stem of 7; the third number, 67, by the leaf of 7 after the stem of 6; the fourth number, 72, as the leaf of 2 after the stem of 7 (note that this is the second leaf on the 7 stem); and so on. Table 3.2-1 is an example of a stem-and-leaf display. If the leaves are carefully aligned vertically, this table has the same effect as a histogram, but the original numbers are not lost.

TABLE 3.2-1: Stem-and-Leaf Display of Scores from 50 Statistics Examinations

Stems	Leaves	Frequency	Depths
3	4 8	2	2
4	2 7 5 2	4	6
5	2 9 1 4 7 8 8	7	13
6	7 6 3 1 5 9 0 9 8 5	10	23
7	7 2 5 3 1 9 0 6 1 4 6 3 5	13	(13)
8	3 4 4 1 7 3 2 1 5	9	14
9	3 7 1 0 3	5	5

An additional new term in these stem-and-leaf displays is **depths**. In the "depths" column, the frequencies are added together (accumulated) from the low end and the high end until the row is reached that contains the middle value in the ordered display. Later we call that middle value the median of the sample, and the frequency of that row is simply placed in parentheses. That is, the frequency of the row containing this median is not included in the sum from either the low end or the high end.

It is useful to modify the stem-and-leaf display by ordering the leaves in each row from smallest to largest. The resulting stem-and-leaf diagram is called an **ordered stem-and-leaf display**. Table 3.2-2 uses the data from Table 3.2-1 to produce an ordered stem-and-leaf display.

There is another modification that can also be helpful. Suppose that we want two rows of leaves with each original stem. We can do this by recording leaves 0, 1, 2, 3, and 4 with a stem adjoined with an asterisk ($*$) and leaves 5, 6, 7, 8, and 9 with a stem

TABLE 3.2-2: Ordered Stem-and-Leaf Display of Statistics Examinations

Stems	Leaves	Frequency	Depths
3	4 8	2	2
4	2 2 5 7	4	6
5	1 2 4 7 8 8 9	7	13
6	0 1 3 5 5 6 7 8 9 9	10	23
7	0 1 1 2 3 3 4 5 5 6 6 7 9	13	(13)
8	1 1 2 3 3 4 4 5 7	9	14
9	0 1 3 3 7	5	5

adjoined with a dot (•). Of course, in our example, by going from 7 original classes to 14 classes, we lose a certain amount of smoothness with this particular data set, as illustrated in Table 3.2-3, which is also ordered.

TABLE 3.2-3: Ordered Stem-and-Leaf Display of Statistics Examinations

Stems	Leaves	Frequency	Depths
3∗	4	1	1
3•	8	1	2
4∗	2 2	2	4
4•	5 7	2	6
5∗	1 2 4	3	9
5•	7 8 8 9	4	13
6∗	0 1 3	3	16
6•	5 5 6 7 8 9 9	7	23
7∗	0 1 1 2 3 3 4	7	(7)
7•	5 5 6 6 7 9	6	20
8∗	1 1 2 3 3 4 4	7	14
8•	5 7	2	7
9∗	0 1 3 3	4	5
9•	7	1	1

Tukey suggested another modification, which is used in the next example.

EXAMPLE 3.2-1 The following numbers represent ACT composite scores for 60 entering freshmen at a certain college:

26	19	22	28	31	29	25	23	20	33	23	26
30	27	26	29	20	23	18	24	29	27	32	24
25	26	22	29	21	24	20	28	23	26	30	19
27	21	32	28	29	23	25	21	28	22	25	24
19	24	35	26	25	20	31	27	23	26	30	29

An ordered stem-and-leaf display of these scores is given in Table 3.2-4, where leaves are recorded as zeros and ones with a stem adjoined with an asterisk (∗), twos and threes with a stem adjoined with t, fours and fives with a stem adjoined with f, sixes and sevens with a stem adjoined with s, and eights and nines with a stem adjoined with a dot (•). ■

TABLE 3.2-4: Ordered Stem-and-Leaf Display of 60 ACT Scores

Stems	Leaves	Frequency	Depths
1•	8 9 9 9	4	4
2*	0 0 0 0 1 1 1	7	11
2t	2 2 2 3 3 3 3 3 3	9	20
2f	4 4 4 4 4 5 5 5 5 5	10	30
2s	6 6 6 6 6 6 6 7 7 7 7	11	30
2•	8 8 8 8 9 9 9 9 9 9	10	19
3*	0 0 0 1 1	5	9
3t	2 2 3	3	4
3f	5	1	1

There is a reason for constructing ordered stem-and-leaf diagrams. For a sample of n observations, $x_1, x_2, \ldots, x_n$, when the observations are ordered from small to large, the resulting ordered data are called the **order statistics** of the sample. Statisticians have found that order statistics and certain of their functions are extremely valuable. It is very easy to determine the values of the sample, in order, from an ordered stem-and-leaf display. As an illustration, consider the values in Table 3.2-2 or Table 3.2-3. The order statistics of the 50 test scores are given in Table 3.2-5.

TABLE 3.2-5: Order Statistics of 50 Exam Scores

34	38	42	42	45	47	51	52	54	57
58	58	59	60	61	63	65	65	66	67
68	69	69	70	71	71	72	73	73	74
75	75	76	76	77	79	81	81	82	83
83	84	84	85	87	90	91	93	93	97

Sometimes we give ranks to these order statistics and use the rank as the subscript on y. The first order statistic $y_1 = 34$ has rank 1; the second order statistic $y_2 = 38$ has rank 2; the third order statistic $y_3 = 42$ has rank 3; the fourth order statistic $y_4 = 42$ has rank 4, ... ; and the 50th order statistic $y_{50} = 97$ has rank 50. It is also about as easy to determine these values from the ordered stem-and-leaf display. We see that $y_1 \le y_2 \le \cdots \le y_{50}$.

From either these order statistics or the corresponding ordered stem-and-leaf display, it is rather easy to find the **sample percentiles**. If $0 < p < 1$, then the $(100p)$th sample percentile has *approximately* np sample observations less than it and also $n(1 - p)$ sample observations greater than it. One way of achieving this is to take the $(100p)$th sample percentile as the $(n + 1)p$th order statistic, provided that $(n + 1)p$ is an integer. If $(n + 1)p$ is not an integer but is equal to r plus some proper fraction—say, a/b—use a weighted average of the rth and the $(r + 1)$st order statistics. That is, define the $(100p)$th sample percentile as

$$\widetilde{\pi}_p = y_r + (a/b)(y_{r+1} - y_r) = (1 - a/b)y_r + (a/b)y_{r+1}.$$

This formula is simply a linear interpolation between y_r and y_{r+1}. (If $p < 1/(n + 1)$ or $p > n/(n + 1)$, that sample percentile is not defined.)

As an illustration, consider the 50 ordered test scores. With $p = 1/2$, we find the 50th percentile by averaging the 25th and 26th order statistics, since

$(n + 1)p = (51)(1/2) = 25.5$. Thus, the 50th percentile is

$$\widetilde{\pi}_{0.50} = (1/2)y_{25} + (1/2)y_{26} = (71 + 71)/2 = 71.$$

With $p = 1/4$, we have $(n + 1)p = (51)(1/4) = 12.75$, and the 25th sample percentile is then

$$\widetilde{\pi}_{0.25} = (1 - 0.75)y_{12} + (0.75)y_{13} = (0.25)(58) + (0.75)(59) = 58.75.$$

With $p = 3/4$, so that $(n + 1)p = (51)(3/4) = 38.25$, the 75th sample percentile is

$$\widetilde{\pi}_{0.75} = (1 - 0.25)y_{38} + (0.25)y_{39} = (0.75)(81) + (0.25)(82) = 81.25.$$

Note that *approximately* 50%, 25%, and 75% of the sample observations are less than 71, 58.75, and 81.25, respectively.

Special names are given to certain percentiles. The 50th percentile is the **median** of the sample. The 25th, 50th, and 75th percentiles are, respectively, the **first, second**, and **third quartiles** of the sample. For notation, we let $\widetilde{q}_1 = \widetilde{\pi}_{0.25}$, $\widetilde{q}_2 = \widetilde{m} = \widetilde{\pi}_{0.50}$, and $\widetilde{q}_3 = \widetilde{\pi}_{0.75}$. The 10th, 20th, . . . , and 90th percentiles are the **deciles** of the sample, so note that the 50th percentile is also the median, the second quartile, and the fifth decile. With the set of 50 test scores, since $(51)(2/10) = 10.2$ and $(51)(9/10) = 45.9$, the second and ninth deciles are, respectively,

$$\widetilde{\pi}_{0.20} = (0.8)y_{10} + (0.2)y_{11} = (0.8)(57) + (0.2)(58) = 57.2$$

and

$$\widetilde{\pi}_{0.90} = (0.1)y_{45} + (0.9)y_{46} = (0.1)(87) + (0.9)(90) = 89.7.$$

The second decile is commonly called the 20th percentile, and the ninth decile is the 90th percentile.

EXAMPLE 3.2-2 We illustrate the preceding ideas with the data given in Table 3.1-3. For convenience, we use 0.02 as the length of a class interval. The ordered stem-and-leaf display is given in Table 3.2-6.

TABLE 3.2-6: Ordered Stem-and-Leaf Diagram of Fluoride Concentrations

Stems	Leaves	Frequency	Depths
0.8*f*	5 5 5 5	4	4
0.8*s*	6 6 6 7 7 7 7	7	11
0.8•	8 8 8 8 8 8 8 8 8 8 9 9 9 9 9 9	16	27
0.9∗	0 0 0 0 0 0 0 0 0 0 1 1 1 1 1 1 1	17	44
0.9*t*	2 2 2 2 2 2 2 2 2 2 3 3 3 3 3 3 3 3 3	19	(19)
0.9*f*	4 4 5 5 5 5 5 5 5	9	37
0.9*s*	6 6 7 7 7 7	6	28
0.9•	8 8 8 8 8 8 8 8 9 9	10	22
1.0∗	0 0 0 0 1 1 1	7	12
1.0*t*	2 3 3	3	5
1.0*f*	5	1	2
1.0*s*	6	1	1

This ordered stem-and-leaf diagram is useful for finding sample percentiles of the data. ■

We now find some of the sample percentiles associated with the fluoride data. Since $n = 100$, $(n+1)(0.25) = 25.25$, $(n+1)(0.50) = 50.5$, and $(n+1)(0.75) = 75.75$, so that the 25th, 50th, and 75th percentiles are, respectively,

$$\begin{aligned}
\widetilde{\pi}_{0.25} &= (0.75)y_{25} + (0.25)y_{26} = (0.75)(0.89) + (0.25)(0.89) = 0.89,\\
\widetilde{\pi}_{0.50} &= (0.50)y_{50} + (0.50)y_{51} = (0.50)(0.92) + (0.50)(0.92) = 0.92,\\
\widetilde{\pi}_{0.75} &= (0.25)y_{75} + (0.75)y_{76} = (0.25)(0.97) + (0.75)(0.97) = 0.97,
\end{aligned}$$

These three percentiles are often called the **first quartile**, the **median** or **second quartile**, and the **third quartile**, respectively. Along with the smallest (the **minimum**) and largest (the **maximum**) values, they give the **five-number summary** of a set of data. Furthermore, the difference between the third and first quartiles is called the **interquartile range, IQR**. Here, it is equal to

$$\widetilde{q}_3 - \widetilde{q}_1 = \widetilde{\pi}_{0.75} - \widetilde{\pi}_{0.25} = 0.97 - 0.89 = 0.08.$$

One graphical means for displaying the five-number summary of a set of data is called a **box-and-whisker diagram**. To construct a horizontal box-and-whisker diagram, or, more simply, a **box plot**, draw a horizontal axis that is scaled to the data. Above the axis, draw a rectangular box with the left and right sides drawn at $\widetilde{q}_1$ and $\widetilde{q}_3$ and with a vertical line segment drawn at the median, $\widetilde{q}_2 = \widetilde{m}$. A left whisker is drawn as a horizontal line segment from the minimum to the midpoint of the left side of the box, and a right whisker is drawn as a horizontal line segment from the midpoint of the right side of the box to the maximum. Note that the length of the box is equal to the IQR. The left and right whiskers represent the first and fourth quarters of the data, while the two middle quarters of the data are represented, respectively, by the two sections of the box, one to the left and one to the right of the median line.

EXAMPLE 3.2-3 Using the fluoride data shown in Table 3.2-6, we found that the five-number summary is given by

$$y_1 = 0.85,\ \widetilde{q}_1 = 0.89,\ \widetilde{q}_2 = \widetilde{m} = 0.92,\ \widetilde{q}_3 = 0.97,\ y_{100} = 1.06.$$

The box plot of these data is given in Figure 3.2-1. The fact that the long whisker is to the right and the right half of the box is larger than the left half of the box leads us to say that these data are slightly *skewed to the right*. Note that this skewness can also be seen in the histogram and in the stem-and-leaf diagram. ■

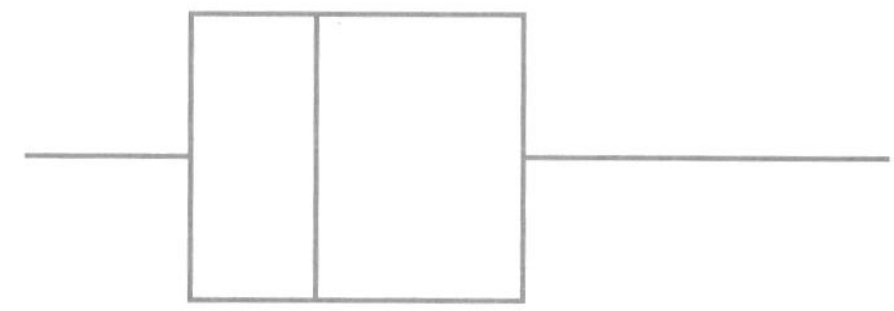

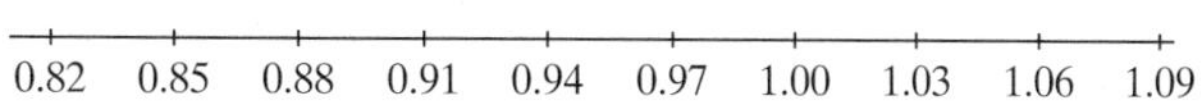

FIGURE 3.2-1: Box plot of fluoride concentrations

The next example illustrates how the box plot depicts data that are *skewed to the left*.

EXAMPLE 3.2-4 The following data give the ordered weights (in grams) of 39 gold coins that were produced during the reign of Verica, a pre-Roman British king:

4.90	5.06	5.07	5.08	5.15	5.17	5.18	5.19	5.24	5.25
5.25	5.25	5.25	5.27	5.27	5.27	5.27	5.28	5.28	5.28
5.29	5.30	5.30	5.30	5.30	5.31	5.31	5.31	5.31	5.31
5.32	5.32	5.33	5.34	5.35	5.35	5.35	5.36	5.37	

For these data, the minimum is 4.90 and the maximum 5.37. Since

$$(39+1)(1/4) = 10, \qquad (39+1)(2/4) = 20, \qquad (39+1)(3/4) = 30,$$

we have

$$\begin{aligned} \widetilde{q}_1 &= y_{10} = 5.25, \\ \widetilde{m} &= y_{20} = 5.28, \\ \widetilde{q}_3 &= y_{30} = 5.31. \end{aligned}$$

Thus the five-number summary is given by

$$y_1 = 4.90, \ \widetilde{q}_1 = 5.25, \ \widetilde{q}_2 = \widetilde{m} = 5.28, \ \widetilde{q}_3 = 5.31, \ y_{39} = 5.37.$$

The box plot associated with the given data is shown in Figure 3.2-2. Note that the box plot indicates that the data are skewed to the left. ■

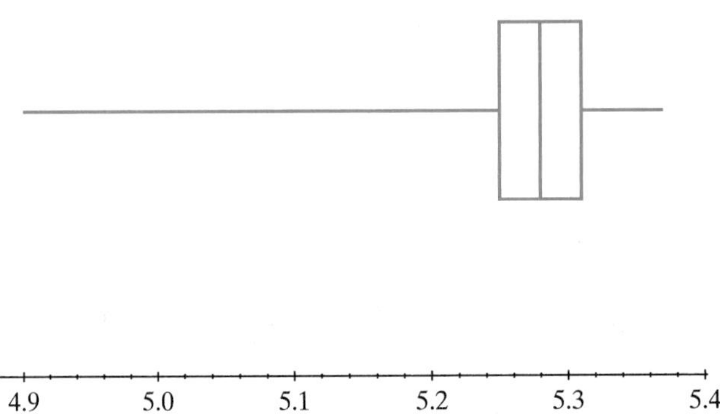

FIGURE 3.2-2: Box plot for weights of 39 gold coins

Sometimes we are interested in picking out observations that seem to be much larger or much smaller than most of the other observations. That is, we are looking for outliers. Tukey suggested a method for defining outliers that is resistant to the effect of one or two extreme values and makes use of the IQR. In a box-and-whisker diagram, construct **inner fences** to the left and right of the box at a distance of 1.5 times the IQR. **Outer fences** are constructed in the same way at a distance of 3 times the IQR. Observations that lie between the inner and outer fences are called **suspected outliers**. Observations that lie beyond the outer fences are called **outliers**. The observations beyond the inner fences are denoted with a circle (•), and the whiskers are drawn only to the extreme values within or on the inner fences. When you are analyzing a set of data, suspected outliers deserve a closer look and outliers should be looked at very carefully. It does not follow that suspected outliers should be removed from the data, unless some error (such as a recording error) has been made. Moreover, it is sometimes important to determine the cause of extreme values, because outliers can often provide useful insights into the situation under consideration (such as a better way of doing things).

EXAMPLE 3.2-5 Continuing with Example 3.2-4, we find that the interquartile range is IQR $= 5.31 - 5.25 = 0.06$. Thus, the inner fences would be constructed at a distance of $1.5(0.06) = 0.09$ to the left and right of the box, and the outer fences would be constructed at a distance of $3(0.06) = 0.18$ to the left and right of the box. Figure 3.2-3 shows a box plot with the fences. Of course, since the maximum is 0.06 greater than $\widetilde{q}_3$, there are no fences to the right. From this box plot, we see that there are three suspected outliers and two outliers. (You may speculate as to why there are outliers with these data and why they fall to the left—that is, they are lighter than expected.) Note that many computer programs use an asterisk to plot outliers and suspected outliers, and do not print fences. ■

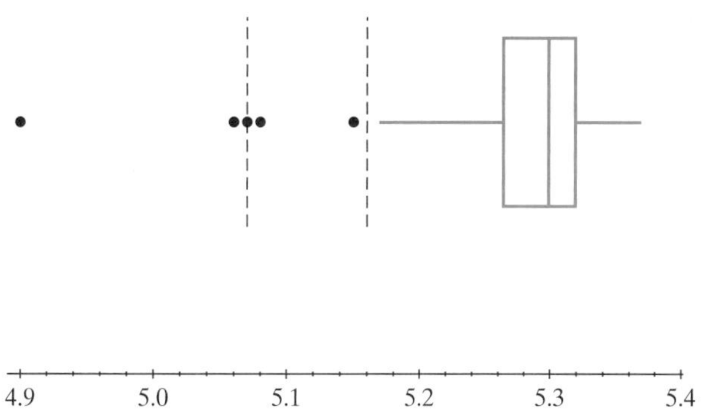

FIGURE 3.2-3: Box plot for weights of 39 gold coins with fences and outliers

Some functions of two or more order statistics are quite important in modern statistics. We mention and illustrate two more, along with the range and the IQR, using the 100 fluoride concentrations shown in Table 3.2-6.

(a) **Midrange** = average of the extremes

$$= \frac{y_1 + y_n}{2} = \frac{0.85 + 1.06}{2} = 0.955,$$

(b) **Trimean** $= \dfrac{\text{(1st quartile)} + 2\text{(2nd quartile)} + \text{(3rd quartile)}}{4}$

$$= \frac{\widetilde{q}_1 + 2\widetilde{q}_2 + \widetilde{q}_3}{4} = \frac{0.89 + 2(0.92) + 0.97}{4} = 0.925,$$

(c) **Range** = difference of the extremes

$$= y_n - y_1 = 1.06 - 0.85 = 0.21,$$

(d) **Interquartile range** = difference of third and first quartiles

$$= \widetilde{q}_3 - \widetilde{q}_1 = 0.97 - 0.89 = 0.08.$$

Thus, we see that the mean, the median, the midrange, and the trimean are measures of the middle of the sample. In some sense, the standard deviation, the range, and the interquartile range provide measures of spread of the sample.

EXERCISES

3.2-1. In Exercise 3.1-5, measurements for 96 plungers are given. Use those measurements to

(a) Construct a stem-and-leaf diagram using integer stems.
(b) Find the five-number summary of the data.
(c) Construct a box-and-whisker diagram. Are there any outliers?

3.2-2. Exercise 3.1-4 gives the weights of 100 laptop computers. Use those weights to

(a) Construct a stem-and-leaf diagram using integer stems.
(b) Find the five-number summary of the weights and construct a box-and-whisker diagram.

3.2-3. When you purchase "1-pound bags" of carrots, you can either buy "baby" carrots or regular carrots. We shall compare the weights of 75 bags of each of these types of carrots. The following table gives the weights of the bags of baby carrots:

1.03	1.03	1.06	1.02	1.03	1.03	1.03	1.02	1.03	1.03
1.06	1.04	1.05	1.03	1.04	1.03	1.05	1.06	1.04	1.04
1.03	1.04	1.04	1.06	1.03	1.04	1.05	1.04	1.04	1.02
1.03	1.05	1.05	1.03	1.04	1.03	1.04	1.04	1.03	1.04
1.03	1.04	1.04	1.04	1.05	1.04	1.04	1.03	1.03	1.05
1.04	1.04	1.05	1.04	1.03	1.03	1.05	1.03	1.04	1.05
1.04	1.04	1.04	1.05	1.03	1.04	1.04	1.04	1.04	1.03
1.05	1.05	1.05	1.03	1.04					

This table gives the weights of the regular-sized carrots:

1.29	1.10	1.28	1.29	1.23	1.20	1.31	1.25	1.13	1.26
1.19	1.33	1.24	1.20	1.26	1.24	1.11	1.14	1.15	1.15
1.19	1.26	1.14	1.20	1.20	1.20	1.24	1.25	1.28	1.24
1.26	1.20	1.30	1.23	1.26	1.16	1.34	1.10	1.22	1.27
1.21	1.09	1.23	1.03	1.32	1.21	1.23	1.34	1.19	1.18
1.20	1.20	1.13	1.43	1.19	1.05	1.16	1.19	1.07	1.21
1.36	1.21	1.00	1.23	1.22	1.13	1.24	1.10	1.18	1.26
1.12	1.10	1.19	1.10	1.24					

(a) Calculate the five-number summary of each set of weights.
(b) On the same graph, construct box plots for each set of weights.
(c) If the carrots are the same price per package, which is the better buy? Which type of carrots would you select?

3.2-4. In the Fifth Third River Bank Run (a 25K race), the times are listed separately for males and females and also by age group. The following table gives the race times, in order in minutes, for 125 50–54 year-old male runners:

96.35	98.40	100.43	101.38	101.48	101.63	103.18	103.97	104.47
105.03	105.23	106.00	106.23	108.82	109.47	109.53	109.70	110.82
110.90	111.80	111.90	112.28	112.55	112.80	112.90	112.92	113.15
113.17	113.25	113.72	114.50	114.60	115.47	115.65	115.73	116.18
116.57	116.93	117.75	118.17	118.18	118.20	118.47	118.50	118.73
119.17	119.45	119.88	120.28	120.32	121.20	122.25	122.28	122.77
122.95	122.98	123.77	124.07	124.10	124.82	124.92	125.23	125.25
125.27	126.15	126.20	126.48	126.72	127.35	127.42	127.95	128.03
128.38	129.22	129.35	129.65	130.02	130.12	130.48	130.57	131.12
131.37	131.97	132.45	132.85	132.97	133.85	134.07	134.67	134.88
135.08	135.68	136.45	136.85	136.87	136.88	137.15	137.22	137.52
137.80	138.02	138.22	138.73	139.57	139.85	140.05	140.08	141.33
142.47	143.13	143.77	144.17	144.58	145.67	147.08	148.20	151.30
151.65	152.00	156.22	160.72	161.20	162.48	166.70	169.90	

The following table gives the race times, in order in minutes, for 76 50–54 year-old female runners:

118.05	180.45	123.80	125.23	125.27	125.90	126.90	128.37	129.30
130.08	131.43	131.72	132.17	133.00	133.25	133.42	133.43	133.50
134.25	136.98	137.10	137.28	138.52	139.80	140.87	142.85	143.75
145.05	145.07	145.48	146.55	146.67	148.07	148.75	148.93	149.77
150.10	150.22	150.62	150.82	150.85	151.10	151.43	152.25	152.60
152.90	155.55	157.02	159.58	159.70	159.80	159.92	159.97	161.33
162.17	163.60	165.45	166.23	168.10	168.60	169.17	169.93	170.88
171.20	173.23	174.22	178.57	178.83	183.08	186.07	186.48	189.77
192.52	197.88	199.80	203.92					

(a) Group each set of data using class boundaries 94.95, 99.95, 104.95, ..., 169.95 for the men and 109.95, 119.95, ..., 209.95 for the women.
(b) Draw histograms of each set of grouped data.
(c) Construct a back-to-back stem-and-leaf display. Place the stems 9•, 10∗, 10•,... down the center, place leaves for the male times to the left, and place leaves for the female times to the right. (See Table 8.5-3 on page 449 for an example.)
(d) Find the five-number summaries of each set of data and draw box-and-whisker diagrams on the same figure.
(e) Use your graphical results to interpret what you see.

3.2-5. In Example 1.1-7, the sample space for underwater weights was given. Here are underwater weights for 82 male students:

3.7	3.6	4.0	4.3	3.8	3.4	4.1	4.0	3.7	3.4	3.5	3.8	3.7	4.9
3.5	3.8	3.3	4.8	3.4	4.6	3.5	5.3	4.4	4.2	2.5	3.1	5.2	3.8
3.3	3.4	4.1	4.6	4.0	1.4	4.3	3.8	4.7	4.4	5.0	3.2	3.1	4.2
4.9	4.5	3.8	4.2	2.7	3.8	3.8	2.0	3.4	4.9	3.3	4.3	5.6	3.2
4.7	4.5	5.2	5.0	5.0	4.0	3.8	5.3	4.5	3.8	3.8	3.4	3.6	3.3
4.2	5.1	4.0	4.7	6.5	4.4	3.6	4.7	4.5	2.3	4.0	3.7		

Here are underwater weights for 100 female students:

2.0	2.0	2.1	1.6	1.9	2.0	2.0	1.3	1.3	1.2	2.3	1.9
2.1	1.2	2.0	1.6	1.1	2.2	2.2	1.4	1.7	2.4	1.8	1.7
2.0	2.1	1.6	1.7	1.8	0.7	1.9	1.7	1.7	1.1	2.0	2.3
0.5	1.3	2.7	1.8	2.0	1.7	1.2	0.7	1.1	1.1	1.7	1.7
1.2	1.2	0.7	2.3	1.7	2.4	1.0	2.4	1.4	1.9	2.5	2.2
2.1	1.4	2.4	1.8	2.5	1.3	0.5	1.7	1.9	1.8	1.3	2.0
2.2	1.7	2.0	2.5	1.2	1.4	1.4	1.2	2.2	2.0	1.8	1.4
1.9	1.4	1.3	2.5	1.2	1.5	0.8	2.0	2.2	1.8	2.0	1.6
1.5	1.6	1.5	2.6								

(a) Group each set of data into classes with a class width of 0.5 kilograms and in which the class marks are $0.5, 1.0, 1.5, \ldots$.
(b) Draw histograms of the grouped data.
(c) Construct box-and-whisker diagrams of the data and draw them on the same graph. Describe what this graph shows.

3.2-6. An insurance company experienced the following mobile home losses in 10,000's of dollars for 50 catastrophic events:

1	2	2	3	3	4	4	5	5	5
5	6	7	7	9	9	9	10	11	12
22	24	28	29	31	33	36	38	38	38
39	41	48	49	53	55	74	82	117	134
192	207	224	225	236	280	301	308	351	527

(a) Find the five-number summary of the data and draw a box-and-whisker diagram.
(b) Calculate the IQR and the locations of the inner and outer fences.

(c) Draw a box plot that shows the fences, suspected outliers, and outliers.
(d) Describe the distribution of losses. (See Exercise 3.1-10.)

3.2-7. In Exercise 3.1-7, data are given for the number of \$1 bets a player can make in roulette before losing \$5. Use those data to respond to the following:

(a) Determine the order statistics.
(b) Find the five-number summary of the data.
(c) Draw a box-and-whisker diagram.
(d) Find the locations of the inner and outer fences, and draw a box plot that shows the fences, the suspected outliers, and the outliers.
(e) In your opinion, does the median or sample mean give a better measure of the center of the data?

3.2-8. In the casino game roulette, if a player bets \$1 on red (or on black or on odd or on even), the probability of winning \$1 is 18/38 and the probability of losing \$1 is 20/38. Suppose that a player begins with \$5 and makes successive \$1 bets. Let Y equal the player's maximum capital before losing the \$5. One hundred observations of Y were simulated on a computer, yielding the following data:

25	9	5	5	5	9	6	5	15	45
55	6	5	6	24	21	16	5	8	7
7	5	5	35	13	9	5	18	6	10
19	16	21	8	13	5	9	10	10	6
23	8	5	10	15	7	5	5	24	9
11	34	12	11	17	11	16	5	15	5
12	6	5	5	7	6	17	20	7	8
8	6	10	11	6	7	5	12	11	18
6	21	6	5	24	7	16	21	23	15
11	8	6	8	14	11	6	9	6	10

(a) Construct an ordered stem-and-leaf display.
(b) Find the five-number summary of the data and draw a box-and-whisker diagram.
(c) Calculate the IQR and the locations of the inner and outer fences.
(d) Draw a box plot that shows the fences, suspected outliers, and outliers.
(e) Find the 90th percentile.

3.2-9. Let X denote the concentration of calcium carbonate ($CaCO_3$) in milligrams per liter. Following are 20 observations of X:

130.8	129.9	131.5	131.2	129.5
132.7	131.5	127.8	133.7	132.2
134.8	131.7	133.9	129.8	131.4
128.8	132.7	132.8	131.4	131.3

(a) Construct an ordered stem-and-leaf display, using stems of 127, 128, ..., 134.
(b) Find the midrange, range, interquartile range, median, sample mean, and sample variance.
(c) Draw a box-and-whisker diagram.

3.2-10. The weights (in grams) of 25 indicator housings used on gauges are as follows:

102.0	106.3	106.6	108.8	107.7
106.1	105.9	106.7	106.8	110.2
101.7	106.6	106.3	110.2	109.9
102.0	105.8	109.1	106.7	107.3
102.0	106.8	110.0	107.9	109.3

(a) Construct an ordered stem-and-leaf display, using integers as the stems and tenths as the leaves.
(b) Find the five-number summary of the data and draw a box plot.
(c) Are there any suspected outliers? Are there any outliers?

3.2-11. In Exercise 3.1-8, the melting points of a firms's alloy filaments are given for a sample of 50 filaments.

(a) Construct a stem-and-leaf diagram of those melting points, using $30f, 30s, \ldots, 33f$ as stems.
(b) Find the five-number summary for these melting points.
(c) Construct a box-and-whisker diagram.
(d) Describe the symmetry of the data.

3.2-12. In Exercise 3.1-9, lead concentrations near the San Diego Freeway in 1976 are given. During the fall of 1977, the weekday afternoon lead concentrations (in $\mu g/m^3$) at the measurement station near the San Diego Freeway in Los Angeles were as follows:

9.5	10.7	8.3	9.8	9.1	9.4	9.6	11.9	9.5	12.6	10.5
8.9	11.4	12.0	12.4	9.9	10.9	12.3	11.0	9.2	9.3	9.3
10.5	9.4	9.4	8.2	10.4	9.3	8.7	9.8	9.1	2.9	9.8
5.7	8.2	8.1	8.8	9.7	8.1	8.8	10.3	8.6	10.2	9.4
14.8	9.9	9.3	8.2	9.9	11.6	8.7	5.0	9.9	6.3	6.5
10.2	8.8	8.0	8.7	8.9	6.8	6.6	7.3	16.7		

(a) Construct a frequency distribution and display the results in the form of a histogram. Is this distribution symmetric?
(b) Calculate the sample mean and sample standard deviation.
(c) Locate $\bar{x}$, $\bar{x} \pm s$ on your histogram. How many observations lie within one standard deviation of the mean? How many lie within two standard deviations of the mean?
(d) Using the data from Exercise 3.1-9 and the data from this exercise, construct a back-to-back stem-and-leaf diagram with integer stems in the center and the leaves for 1976 going to the left and those for 1977 going to the right.
(e) Construct box-and-whisker displays of both sets of data on the same graph.
(f) Use your numerical and graphical results to interpret what you see.

REMARK In the spring of 1977, a new traffic lane was added to the freeway. This lane reduced traffic congestion but increased traffic speed. ■

3.3 RANDOM VARIABLES OF THE CONTINUOUS TYPE

The relative frequency (or density) histogram $h(x)$ associated with n observations of a random variable of the continuous type is a nonnegative function defined so that the total area between its graph and the x-axis equals 1. This statement is also true of the function created by the relative frequency polygon. In addition, $h(x)$ is constructed so that the integral

$$\int_a^b h(x)\,dx$$

is approximately equal to the relative frequency of the interval $\{x: a < x < b\}$ and hence can be thought of as an estimate of the probability that the random variable X falls into the interval (a, b). This probability is often written $P(a < X < b)$.

Let us now consider what happens to the function $h(x)$ in the limit, or what happens to the relative frequency polygon as n increases without bound and as the lengths of the class intervals decrease to zero. It is to be hoped that $h(x)$ and the relative frequency polygon will become closer and closer to some function—say, $f(x)$—that gives the true probabilities, such as $P(a < X < b)$, through the integral

$$P(a < X < b) = \int_a^b f(x)\,dx.$$

That is, $f(x)$ should be a nonnegative function such that the total area between its graph and the x-axis equals 1. Moreover, the probability $P(a < X < b)$ is the area bounded by the graph of $f(x)$, the x-axis, and the lines $x = a$ and $x = b$. Thus, we say that the **probability density function (p.d.f.)** of a random variable X of the **continuous type**, with space S that is an interval or union of intervals, is an integrable function $f(x)$ satisfying the following conditions:

(a) $f(x) > 0, \qquad x \in S.$
(b) $\int_S f(x)\,dx = 1.$
(c) If $(a, b) \subseteq S$, then the probability of the event $\{a < X < b\}$ is

$$P(a < X < b) = \int_a^b f(x)\,dx.$$

The corresponding distribution of probability is said to be of the continuous type.

EXAMPLE 3.3-1 Let the random variable X be the lengths of time **in minutes** between calls to 911 in a small city that were reported in the newspaper on February 26 and 27. Suppose that a reasonable probability model for X is given by the p.d.f.

$$f(x) = \frac{1}{20}\,e^{-x/20}, \qquad 0 \le x < \infty.$$

Note that $S = \{x: 0 \le x < \infty\}$ and $f(x) > 0$ for $x \in S$. Also,

$$\begin{aligned}\int_S f(x)\,dx &= \int_0^{\infty} \frac{1}{20}\,e^{-x/20}\,dx \\ &= \lim_{b\to\infty}\left[-e^{-x/20}\right]_0^b \\ &= 1 - \lim_{b\to\infty} e^{-b/20} = 1.\end{aligned}$$

The probability that the time between calls is greater than 20 minutes is

$$P(X > 20) = \int_{20}^{\infty} \frac{1}{20}\,e^{-x/20}\,dx = e^{-1} = 0.368.$$

The p.d.f. and the probability of interest are depicted in Figure 3.3-1. ■

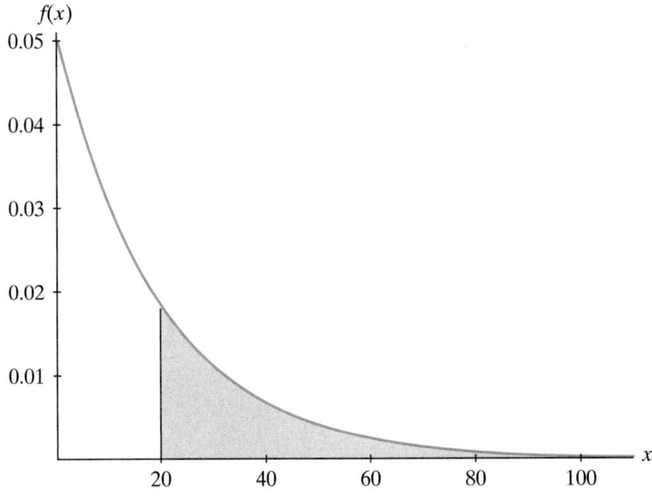

FIGURE 3.3-1: Times between calls to 911

So that we can avoid repeated references to the space (or support) S of the random variable X, we shall adopt the same convention when describing probability density functions of the continuous type as we did in the discrete case. We extend the definition of the p.d.f. $f(x)$ to the entire set of real numbers by letting it equal zero when $x \notin S$. For example,

$$f(x) = \begin{cases} \dfrac{1}{20}\,e^{-x/20}, & 0 \le x < \infty, \\ 0, & \text{elsewhere,} \end{cases}$$

has the properties of a p.d.f. of a continuous-type random variable X having support $\{x: 0 \le x < \infty\}$. It will always be understood that $f(x) = 0$ when $x \notin S$, even when this is not explicitly written out.

The **distribution function** of a random variable X of the continuous type, defined in terms of the p.d.f. of X, is given by

$$F(x) = P(X \le x) = \int_{-\infty}^{x} f(t)\,dt, \qquad -\infty < x < \infty.$$

Here, again, $F(x)$ accumulates (or, more simply, cumulates) all of the probability less than or equal to x. (This function is sometimes called a **cumulative distribution function** or c.d.f.) From the fundamental theorem of calculus, we have, for x values for which the derivative $F'(x)$ exists, $F'(x) = f(x)$.

EXAMPLE 3.3-2 Continuing with Example 3.3-1, we note that if the p.d.f. of X is

$$f(x) = \begin{cases} 0, & -\infty < x < 0, \\ \dfrac{1}{20}e^{-x/20}, & 0 \le x < \infty, \end{cases}$$

then, for $x < 0$, the distribution function of X is $F(x) = 0$ and for $x \ge 0$,

$$\begin{aligned} F(x) &= \int_{-\infty}^{x} f(t)\,dt = \int_{0}^{x} \frac{1}{20}e^{-t/20}\,dt \\ &= \Big[-e^{-t/20}\Big]_0^x = 1 - e^{-x/20}. \end{aligned}$$

Note also that

$$F'(x) = \begin{cases} 0, & -\infty < x < 0, \\ \dfrac{1}{20}e^{-x/20}, & 0 < x < \infty. \end{cases}$$

Furthermore, $F'(0)$ does not exist. (Sketch a graph of $y = F(x)$ to see why this is true.) ■

Since there are no steps or jumps in $F(x)$, a distribution function of the continuous type, it must be true that

$$P(X = b) = 0$$

for all real values of b. This agrees with the fact that the integral $\int_b^b f(x)\,dx$ is taken to be zero in calculus. In general,

$$P(a \le X \le b) = P(a < X < b) = P(a \le X < b) = P(a < X \le b) = F(b) - F(a),$$

provided that X is a random variable of the continuous type. Moreover, we can change the definition of a p.d.f. of a random variable of the continuous type at a finite (actually, countable) number of points without altering the distribution of probability. For example,

$$f(x) = \begin{cases} 0, & -\infty < x < 0, \\ \dfrac{1}{20}e^{-x/20}, & 0 \le x < \infty, \end{cases}$$

and

$$f(x) = \begin{cases} 0, & -\infty < x \le 0, \\ \dfrac{1}{20}e^{-x/20}, & 0 < x < \infty, \end{cases}$$

are equivalent in the computation of probabilities involving this random variable.

EXAMPLE 3.3-3 The following table lists 105 observations of X, the times between calls to 911:

30	17	65	8	38	35	4	19	7	14	12	4	5	4	2
7	5	12	50	33	10	15	2	10	1	5	30	41	21	31
1	18	12	5	24	7	6	31	1	3	2	22	1	30	2
1	3	12	12	9	28	6	50	63	5	17	11	23	2	46
90	13	21	55	43	5	19	47	24	4	6	27	4	6	37
16	41	68	9	5	28	42	3	42	8	52	2	11	41	4
35	21	3	17	10	16	1	68	105	45	23	5	10	12	17

To help determine visually whether the exponential model in Example 3.3-1 is perhaps appropriate for this situation, we shall look at two graphs. First, we have constructed a relative frequency histogram, $h(x)$, of these data in Figure 3.3-2(a), with $f(x) = (1/20)e^{-x/20}$ superimposed. Second, we have also constructed the empirical distribution function of these data in Figure 3.3-2(b), with the theoretical distribution function superimposed. Note that $F_n(x)$, the **empirical distribution function**, is a step function with a step of size $1/n$ at each observation of X. If k observations are equal, the step at that value is k/n. Later in the text we give statistical tests to help us decide whether this probability model provides a good fit for these data. ■

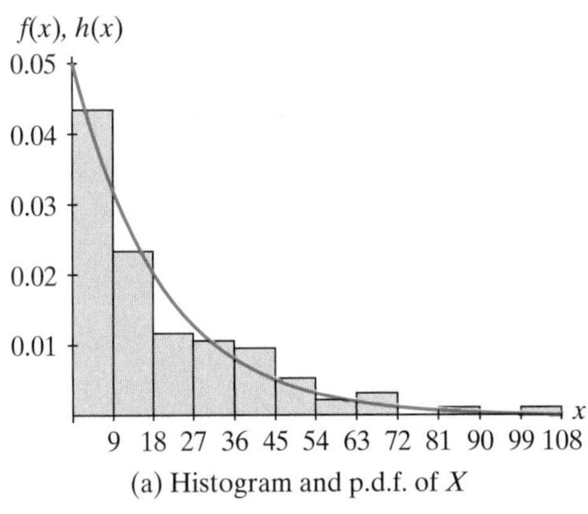

(a) Histogram and p.d.f. of X

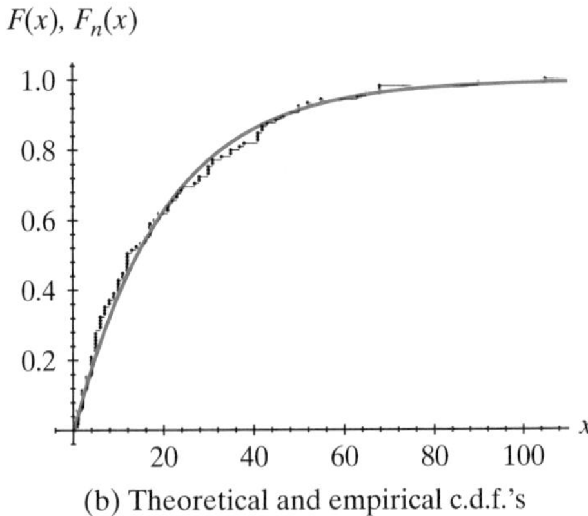

(b) Theoretical and empirical c.d.f.'s

FIGURE 3.3-2: Times between calls to 911

EXAMPLE 3.3-4 Let Y be a continuous random variable with p.d.f. $g(y) = 2y$, $0 < y < 1$. The distribution function of Y is defined by

$$G(y) = \begin{cases} 0, & y < 0, \\ \displaystyle\int_0^y 2t\,dt = y^2, & 0 \le y < 1, \\ 1, & 1 \le y. \end{cases}$$

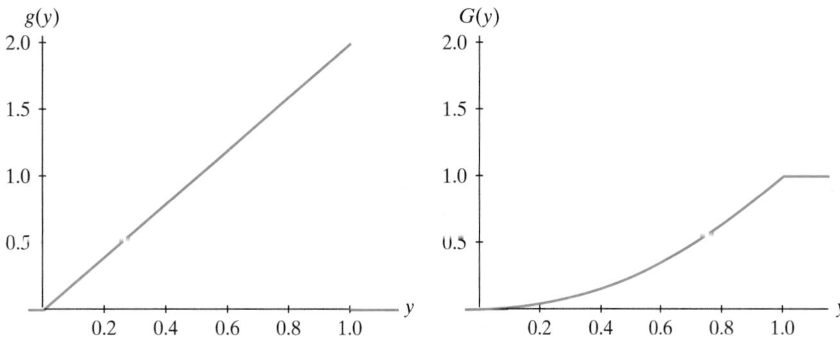

FIGURE 3.3-3: Continuous distribution p.d.f. and c.d.f.

Figure 3.3-3 gives the graph of the p.d.f. $g(y)$ and the graph of the distribution function $G(y)$. For examples of computations of probabilities, consider

$$P\left(\frac{1}{2} < Y \leq \frac{3}{4}\right) = G\left(\frac{3}{4}\right) - G\left(\frac{1}{2}\right) = \left(\frac{3}{4}\right)^2 - \left(\frac{1}{2}\right)^2 = \frac{5}{16}$$

and

$$P\left(\frac{1}{4} \leq Y < 2\right) = G(2) - G\left(\frac{1}{4}\right) = 1 - \left(\frac{1}{4}\right)^2 = \frac{15}{16}. \quad ■$$

Recall that the p.m.f. $f(x)$ of a random variable of the discrete type is bounded by 1 because $f(x)$ gives a probability, namely,

$$f(x) = P(X = x).$$

For random variables of the continuous type, the p.d.f. does not have to be bounded. [See Exercises 3.3-2(c) and 3.3-3(c).] The restriction is that *the area between the p.d.f. and the x-axis must equal 1*. Furthermore, the p.d.f. of a random variable X of the continuous type does not need to be a continuous function. For example, the function

$$f(x) = \begin{cases} \dfrac{1}{2}, & 0 < x < 1 \quad \text{or} \quad 2 < x < 3, \\ 0, & \text{elsewhere,} \end{cases}$$

enjoys the properties of a p.d.f. of a distribution of the continuous type and yet has discontinuities at $x = 0, 1, 2,$ and 3. However, the distribution function associated with a distribution of the continuous type is always a continuous function.

For continuous-type random variables, the definitions associated with mathematical expectation are the same as those in the discrete case, except that integrals replace summations. As an illustration, let X be a continuous random variable with a p.d.f. $f(x)$. Then the **expected value of** X, or the **mean of** X, is

$$\mu = E(X) = \int_{-\infty}^{\infty} xf(x)\,dx,$$

the **variance of** X is

$$\sigma^2 = \text{Var}(X) = E[(X - \mu)^2] = \int_{-\infty}^{\infty} (x - \mu)^2 f(x)\,dx,$$

the **standard deviation of** X is

$$\sigma = \sqrt{\text{Var}(X)},$$

and the **moment-generating function**, if it exists, is

$$M(t) = \int_{-\infty}^{\infty} e^{tx} f(x)\,dx, \qquad -h < t < h.$$

Moreover, important results such as $\sigma^2 = E(X^2) - \mu^2$, $\mu = M'(0)$, and $\sigma^2 = M''(0) - [M'(0)]^2$ are still valid. Again, it is important to note that the moment-generating function, if it is finite for $-h < t < h$ for some $h > 0$, completely determines the distribution.

REMARK In both the discrete and continuous cases, note that if the rth moment, $E(X^r)$, exists and is finite, then the same is true of all lower order moments, $E(X^k)$, $k = 1, 2, \ldots, r - 1$. However, the converse is not true; for example, the first moment can exist and be finite, but the second moment is not necessarily finite. (See Exercise 3.3-9.) Moreover, if $E(e^{tX})$ exists and is finite for $-h < t < h$, then all moments exist and are finite, but the converse is not necessarily true. ■

EXAMPLE 3.3-5 For the random variable Y in Example 3.3-4,

$$\mu = E(Y) = \int_0^1 y\,(2y)\,dy = \left[\left(\frac{2}{3}\right)y^3\right]_0^1 = \frac{2}{3}$$

and

$$\begin{aligned}\sigma^2 = \text{Var}(Y) &= E(Y^2) - \mu^2 \\ &= \int_0^1 y^2(2y)\,dy - \left(\frac{2}{3}\right)^2 = \left[\left(\frac{1}{2}\right)y^4\right]_0^1 - \frac{4}{9} = \frac{1}{18},\end{aligned}$$

are the mean and variance, respectively, of Y. ■

EXAMPLE 3.3-6 Let X have the p.d.f.

$$f(x) = \begin{cases} xe^{-x}, & 0 \le x < \infty, \\ 0, & \text{elsewhere.} \end{cases}$$

Then

$$\begin{aligned}M(t) &= \int_0^{\infty} e^{tx} xe^{-x}\,dx = \lim_{b\to\infty} \int_0^b xe^{-(1-t)x}\,dx \\ &= \lim_{b\to\infty}\left[-\frac{xe^{-(1-t)x}}{1-t} - \frac{e^{-(1-t)x}}{(1-t)^2}\right]_0^b \\ &= \lim_{b\to\infty}\left[-\frac{be^{-(1-t)b}}{1-t} - \frac{e^{-(1-t)b}}{(1-t)^2}\right] + \frac{1}{(1-t)^2} \\ &= \frac{1}{(1-t)^2},\end{aligned}$$

provided that $t < 1$. Note that $M(0) = 1$, which is true for every moment-generating function. Now,

$$M'(t) = \frac{2}{(1 - t)^3} \quad \text{and} \quad M''(t) = \frac{6}{(1 - t)^4}.$$

Thus,

$$\mu = M'(0) = 2$$

and

$$\sigma^2 = M''(0) - [M'(0)]^2 = 6 - 2^2 = 2.$$ ■

The **(100*p*)th percentile** is a number π_p such that the area under $f(x)$ to the left of π_p is p. That is,

$$p = \int_{-\infty}^{\pi_p} f(x)\,dx = F(\pi_p).$$

The 50th percentile is called the **median**. We let $m = \pi_{0.50}$. The 25th and 75th percentiles are called the **first** and **third quartiles**, respectively, and are denoted by $q_1 = \pi_{0.25}$ and $q_3 = \pi_{0.75}$. Of course, the median $m = \pi_{0.50} = q_2$ is also called the second quartile.

The $(100p)$th percentile of a distribution is often called the quantile of order p. So if $y_1 \le y_2 \le \cdots \le y_n$ are the order statistics associated with the sample $x_1, x_2, \ldots, x_n$, then y_r is called the **quantile of order $r/(n + 1)$** as well as the **$100r/(n + 1)$th percentile**. Also, the percentile π_p of a theoretical distribution is the quantile of order p. Now, suppose the theoretical distribution is a good model for the observations. Then if we plot (y_r, π_p), where $p = r/(n + 1)$, for several values of r (possibly even for all r values, $r = 1, 2, \ldots, n$), we would expect these points (y_r, π_p) to lie close to a line through the origin with slope equal to 1 because $y_r \approx \pi_p$. If they are not close to that line, then we would doubt that the theoretical distribution is a good model for the observations. The plot of (y_r, π_p) for several values of r is called the **quantile–quantile plot** or, more simply, the ***q*–*q* plot**. (See Figure 3.6-3 on page 165 for an example.)

EXAMPLE 3.3-7 The time X in months until failure of a certain product has the p.d.f. (of the Weibull type)

$$f(x) = \frac{3x^2}{4^3} e^{-(x/4)^3}, \qquad 0 < x < \infty.$$

Its distribution function is

$$F(x) = 1 - e^{-(x/4)^3}, \qquad 0 \le x < \infty.$$

For example, the 30th percentile, $\pi_{0.3}$, is given by

$$F(\pi_{0.3}) = 0.3$$

or, equivalently,

$$\begin{aligned} 1 - e^{-(\pi_{0.3}/4)^3} &= 0.3 \\ \ln(0.7) &= -(\pi_{0.3}/4)^3 \\ \pi_{0.3} &= -4\sqrt[3]{\ln(0.7)} = 2.84. \end{aligned}$$

Likewise, $\pi_{0.9}$ is found by

$$F(\pi_{0.9}) = 0.9;$$

so

$$\pi_{0.9} - -4\sqrt[3]{\ln(0.1)} = 5.28.$$

Thus,

$$P(2.84 < X < 5.28) = 0.6.$$

The 30th and 90th percentiles are shown in Figure 3.3-4. ■

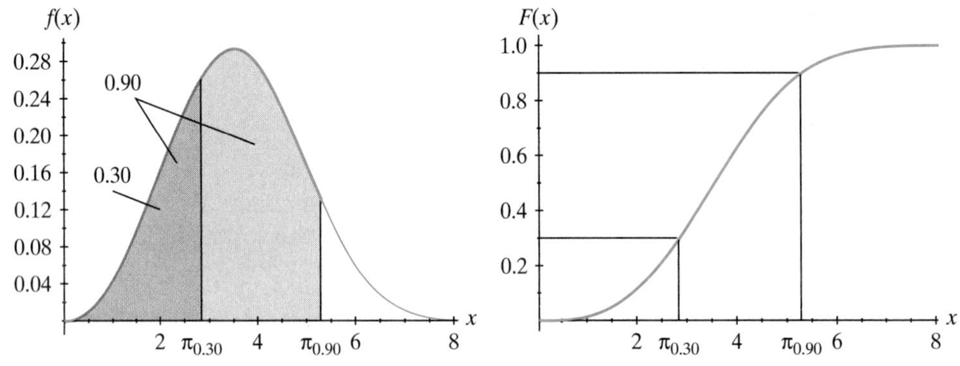

FIGURE 3.3-4: Illustration of percentiles $\pi_{0.30}$ and $\pi_{0.90}$

We conclude this section with an example that reviews its important ideas.

EXAMPLE 3.3-8 Let X have the p.d.f.

$$f(x) = e^{-x-1}, \qquad -1 < x < \infty.$$

Then

$$P(1 \le X) = \int_1^\infty e^{-x-1}dx = e^{-1}\left[-e^{-x}\right]_1^\infty = e^{-2} = 0.135.$$

Also,

$$\begin{aligned} M(t) = E(e^{tX}) &= \int_{-1}^\infty e^{tx}e^{-x-1}dx \\ &= e^{-1}\left[\frac{-e^{-(1-t)x}}{1 \quad t}\right]_{-1}^\infty \\ &= e^{-t}(1-t)^{-1}, \qquad t < 1. \end{aligned}$$

Thus, since

$$M'(t) = (e^{-t})(1-t)^{-2} - e^{-t}(1-t)^{-1}$$

and

$$M''(t) = (e^{-t})(2)(1-t)^{-3} - 2e^{-t}(1-t)^{-2} + e^{-t}(1-t)^{-1},$$

we have

$$\mu = M'(0) = 0 \qquad \text{and} \qquad \sigma^2 = M''(0) - [M'(0)]^2 = 1.$$

The distribution function is

$$F(x) = \int_{-1}^{x} e^{-w-1}dw = e^{-1}\left[-e^{-w}\right]_{-1}^{x}$$
$$= e^{-1}\left[e^{1} - e^{-x}\right] = 1 - e^{-x-1}, \qquad -1 < x < \infty,$$

and zero for $x \le -1$.

As an illustration, the median, $\pi_{0.5}$, is found by solving

$$F(\pi_{0.5}) = 0.5,$$

which is equivalent to

$$-\pi_{0.5} - 1 = \ln(0.5);$$

so

$$\pi_{0.5} = \ln 2 - 1 = -0.307.$$

■

EXERCISES

3.3-1. Let the random variable X have the p.d.f. $f(x) = 2(1 - x), 0 \le x \le 1$, zero elsewhere.

(a) Sketch the graph of this p.d.f.
(b) Determine and sketch the graph of the distribution function of X.
(c) Find (i) $P(0 \le X \le 1/2)$, (ii) $P(1/4 \le X \le 3/4)$, (iii) $P(X = 3/4)$, and (iv) $P(X \ge 3/4)$.

3.3-2. For each of the following functions, (i) find the constant c so that $f(x)$ is a p.d.f. of a random variable X, (ii) find the distribution function, $F(x) = P(X \le x)$, and (iii) sketch graphs of the p.d.f. $f(x)$ and the distribution function $F(x)$:

(a) $f(x) = x^3/4, \quad 0 < x < c;$
(b) $f(x) = (3/16)x^2, \quad -c < x < c;$
(c) $f(x) = c/\sqrt{x}, \quad 0 < x < 1$. Is this p.d.f. bounded?

3.3-3. For each of the following functions, (i) find the constant c so that $f(x)$ is a p.d.f. of a random variable X, (ii) find the distribution function, $F(x) = P(X \le x)$, and (iii) sketch graphs of the p.d.f. $f(x)$ and the distribution function $F(x)$:

(a) $f(x) = 4x^c, \quad 0 \le x \le 1,$
(b) $f(x) = c\sqrt{x}, \quad 0 \le x \le 4,$
(c) $f(x) = c/x^{3/4}, \quad 0 < x < 1.$

3.3-4. For each of the distributions in Exercise 3.3-2, find μ, σ^2, and σ.

3.3-5. For each of the distributions in Exercise 3.3-3, find μ, σ^2, and σ.

3.3-6. Let $f(x) = (1/2)x^2e^{-x}, 0 < x < \infty$, be the p.d.f. of X.

(a) Find the m.g.f. $M(t)$.
(b) Find the values of μ and σ^2.

3.3-7. Let $f(x) = (1/2)\sin x, 0 \le x \le \pi$, be the p.d.f. of X.

(a) Find μ and σ^2.
(b) Sketch the graph of the p.d.f. of X.
(c) Determine and sketch the graph of the distribution function of X.

3.3-8. The p.d.f. of X is $f(x) = c/x^2, 1 < x < \infty$.

(a) Calculate the value of c so that $f(x)$ is a p.d.f.
(b) Show that $E(X)$ is not finite.

3.3-9. The p.d.f. of Y is $g(y) = d/y^3, 1 < y < \infty$.

(a) Calculate the value of d so that $g(y)$ is a p.d.f.
(b) Find $E(Y)$.
(c) Show that $\mathrm{Var}(Y)$ is not finite.

3.3-10. Sketch the graphs of the following probability density functions, and find and sketch the graphs of the distribution functions associated with these distributions (note carefully the relationship between the shape of the graph of the p.d.f. and the concavity of the graph of the distribution function):

(a) $f(x) = \left(\dfrac{3}{2}\right)x^2, \quad -1 < x < 1.$

(b) $f(x) = \dfrac{1}{2}, \quad -1 < x < 1.$

(c) $f(x) = \begin{cases} x + 1, & -1 < x < 0, \\ 1 - x, & 0 \le x < 1. \end{cases}$

3.3-11. Find the mean and variance for each of the distributions in Exercise 3.3-10.

3.3-12. Let $R(t) = \ln M(t)$, where $M(t)$ is the moment-generating function of a random variable. Show that

(a) $\mu = R'(0)$.

(b) $\sigma^2 = R''(0)$.

3.3-13. If $M(t) = e^{-t}(1 - t)^{-1}$, $t < 1$, use $R(t) = \ln M(t)$ and the result in Exercise 3.3-12 to find (a) μ and (b) σ^2.

3.3-14. Find the moment-generating function $M(t)$ of the distribution with p.d.f. $f(x) = (1/10)e^{-x/10}$, $0 < x < \infty$. Use $M(t)$ or $R(t) = \ln M(t)$ to determine the mean μ and the variance σ^2.

3.3-15. The logistic distribution is associated with the distribution function $F(x) = (1 + e^{-x})^{-1}$, $-\infty < x < \infty$. Find the p.d.f. of the logistic distribution and show that its graph is symmetric about $x = 0$.

3.3-16. Let $f(x) = 1/2$, $0 < x < 1$ or $2 < x < 3$, zero elsewhere, be the p.d.f. of X.

(a) Sketch the graph of this p.d.f.

(b) Define the distribution function of X and sketch its graph.

(c) Find $q_1 = \pi_{0.25}$.

(d) Find $m = \pi_{0.50}$. Is it unique?

(e) Find $q_3 = \pi_{0.75}$.

3.3-17. The life X (in years) of a voltage regulator of a car has the p.d.f.

$$f(x) = \frac{3x^2}{7^3} e^{-(x/7)^3}, \qquad 0 < x < \infty.$$

(a) What is the probability that this regulator will last at least 7 years?

(b) Given that it has lasted at least 7 years, what is the conditional probability that it will last at least another 3.5 years?

3.3-18. Let $f(x) = (x + 1)/2$, $-1 < x < 1$. Find (a) $\pi_{0.64}$, (b) $q_1 = \pi_{0.25}$, and (c) $\pi_{0.81}$.

3.3-19. Let the random variable X_n have the p.d.f. $f(x_n) = n$, $0 < x_n < 1/n$.

(a) Define the distribution function of X_n—say, $F_n(x_n)$.

(b) Graph the p.d.f. and the distribution function for $n = 1, 5$, and 10.

3.3-20. It is interesting to note that back in 1940 if a person in the United States was selected at random, then his or her age X had a distribution that was almost given by the p.d.f. of the form

$$f(x) = \begin{cases} c, & 0 < x < 35, \\ c\left[1 + \dfrac{3}{140}(35 - x)\right], & 35 \le x \le 81\frac{2}{3}. \end{cases}$$

(a) Find c so that $f(x)$ is a p.d.f.

(b) In 1940, about what percentage of the U.S. population was older than 65?

(c) What was the median age then?

3.3-21. The lifetime X (in years) of a machine has a p.d.f.

$$f(x) = \frac{2x}{\theta^2} e^{-(x/\theta)^2}, \qquad 0 < x < \infty.$$

If $P(X > 5) = 0.01$, determine θ.

3.3-22. The weekly demand X for propane gas (in thousands of gallons) has the p.d.f.

$$f(x) = 4x^3 e^{-x^4}, \qquad 0 < x < \infty.$$

If the stockpile consists of two thousand gallons at the beginning of each week (and nothing extra is received during the week), what is the probability of not being able to meet the demand during a given week?

3.3-23. An insurance agent receives a bonus if the loss ratio L on his business is less than 0.5, where L is the total losses (say, X) divided by the total premiums (say, T). The bonus equals $(0.5 - L)(T/30)$ if $L < 0.5$ and equals zero otherwise. If X (in \$100,000) has the p.d.f.

$$f(x) = \frac{3}{x^4}, \qquad x > 1,$$

and if T (in \$100,000) equals 3, determine the expected value of the bonus.

3.3-24. The p.d.f. of time X to failure of an electronic component is

$$f(x) = \frac{2x}{1000^2} e^{-(x/1000)^2}, \qquad 0 < x < \infty.$$

(a) Compute $P(X > 2000)$.

(b) Determine the 75th percentile, $\pi_{0.75}$, of the distribution.

(c) Find the 10th and 60th percentiles, $\pi_{0.10}$ and $\pi_{0.60}$

3.3-25. The total amount of medical claims (in \$100,000) of the employees of a company has the p.d.f. $f(x) = 30x(1 - x)^4$, $0 < x < 1$. Find

(a) the mean and the standard deviation of the total in dollars,

(b) the probability that the total exceeds \$20,000.

3.3-26. Nicol (see references) lets the p.d.f. of X be defined by

$$f(x) = \begin{cases} x, & 0 \le x \le 1, \\ c/x^3, & 1 \le x < \infty, \\ 0, & \text{elsewhere.} \end{cases}$$

Find

(a) the value of c so that $f(x)$ is a p.d.f.
(b) the mean of X (if it exists).
(c) the variance of X (if it exists).
(d) $P(1/2 \le X \le 2)$.

3.4 THE UNIFORM AND EXPONENTIAL DISTRIBUTIONS

Let the random variable X denote the outcome when a point is selected at random from an interval $[a, b]$, $-\infty < a < b < \infty$. If the experiment is performed in a fair manner, it is reasonable to assume that the probability that the point is selected from the interval $[a, x]$, $a \le x < b$, is $(x - a)/(b - a)$. That is, the probability is proportional to the length of the interval, so the distribution function of X is

$$F(x) = \begin{cases} 0, & x < a, \\ \dfrac{x - a}{b - a}, & a \le x < b, \\ 1, & b \le x. \end{cases}$$

Because X is a continuous-type random variable, $F'(x)$ is equal to the p.d.f. of X whenever $F'(x)$ exists; thus, when $a < x < b$, we have $f(x) = F'(x) = 1/(b - a)$.

The random variable X has a **uniform distribution** if its p.d.f. is equal to a constant on its support. In particular, if the support is the interval $[a, b]$, then

$$f(x) = \frac{1}{b - a}, \qquad a \le x \le b.$$

Moreover, we shall say that X is $U(a, b)$. This distribution is also referred to as **rectangular**, because the graph of $f(x)$ suggests that name. Figure 3.4-1 shows the graph of $f(x)$ and the distribution function $F(x)$ when $a = 0.30$ and $b = 1.55$. Note that we could have taken $f(a) = 0$ or $f(b) = 0$ without altering the probabilities, since this is a continuous-type distribution. We shall do so in some cases.

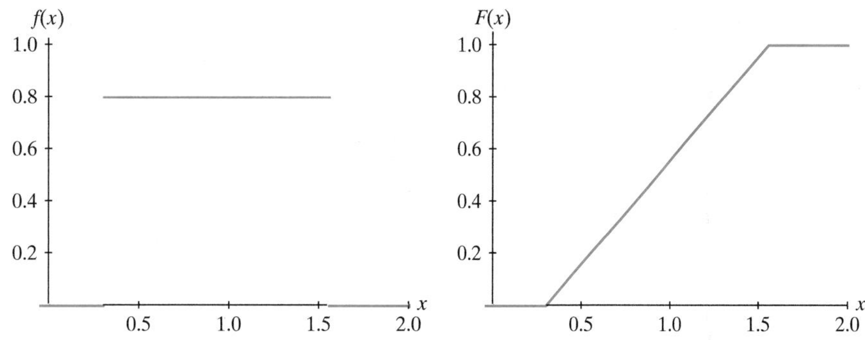

FIGURE 3.4-1: Uniform p.d.f. and distribution function

The mean, variance, and moment-generating function of X are not difficult to calculate. (See Exercise 3.4.) They are, respectively,

$$\mu = \frac{a + b}{2}, \qquad \sigma^2 = \frac{(b - a)^2}{12},$$

$$M(t) = \begin{cases} \dfrac{e^{tb} - e^{ta}}{t(b - a)}, & t \neq 0, \\ 1, & t = 0. \end{cases}$$

An important uniform distribution is that for which $a = 0$ and $b = 1$, namely, $U(0,1)$. If X is $U(0,1)$, approximate values of X can be simulated on most computers with the use of a random-number generator. In fact, it should be called a **pseudo-random number generator** because the programs that produce the random numbers are usually such that if the starting number (the seed number) is known, all subsequent numbers in the sequence may be determined by simple arithmetical operations. Yet, despite their deterministic origin, these computer-produced numbers do behave as if they were truly randomly generated, and we shall not encumber our terminology by adding *pseudo*. (Examples of computer-produced random numbers are given in the appendix in Table IX. Place a decimal point in front of each of the four-digit entries so that each is a number between 0 and 1.)

EXAMPLE 3.4-1 Let X have the p.d.f.

$$f(x) = \frac{1}{100}, \qquad 0 < x < 100,$$

so that X is $U(0,100)$. The mean and the variance are, respectively,

$$\mu = \frac{0 + 100}{2} = 50 \qquad \text{and} \qquad \sigma^2 = \frac{(100 - 0)^2}{12} = \frac{10{,}000}{12}.$$

The standard deviation is $\sigma = 100/\sqrt{12}$, which is 100 times that of the $U(0,1)$ distribution. This agrees with our intuition, since the standard deviation is a measure of spread and $U(0,100)$ is clearly spread out 100 times more than $U(0,1)$. ■

We turn now to a continuous distribution that is related to the Poisson distribution. When previously observing a process of the (approximate) Poisson type, we counted the number of changes occurring in a given interval. This number was a discrete-type random variable with a Poisson distribution. But not only is the number of changes a random variable; the waiting times between successive changes are also random variables. However, the latter are of the continuous type, since each of them can assume any positive value. In particular, let W denote the waiting time until the first change occurs during the observation of a Poisson process in which the mean number of changes in the unit interval is λ. Then W is a continuous-type random variable, and we proceed to find its distribution function.

Because this waiting time is nonnegative, the distribution function $F(w) = 0$, $w < 0$. For $w \geq 0$,

$$\begin{aligned} F(w) &= P(W \leq w) = 1 - P(W > w) \\ &= 1 - P(\text{no changes in } [0, w]) \\ &= 1 - e^{-\lambda w}, \end{aligned}$$

since we previously discovered that $e^{-\lambda w}$ equals the probability of no changes in an interval of length w. That is, if the mean number of changes per unit interval is λ, then the mean number of changes in an interval of length w is proportional to w, and hence is given by λw. Thus, when $w > 0$, the p.d.f. of W is

$$F'(w) = f(w) = \lambda e^{-\lambda w}.$$

We often let $\lambda = 1/\theta$ and say that the random variable X has an **exponential distribution** if its p.d.f. is defined by

$$f(x) = \frac{1}{\theta}e^{-x/\theta}, \qquad 0 \le x < \infty,$$

where the parameter $\theta > 0$. Accordingly, the waiting time W until the first change in a Poisson process has an exponential distribution with $\theta = 1/\lambda$. To determine the exact meaning of the parameter θ, we first find the moment-generating function of X. It is

$$M(t) = \int_0^\infty e^{tx}\left(\frac{1}{\theta}\right)e^{-x/\theta}\,dx = \lim_{b\to\infty}\int_0^b \left(\frac{1}{\theta}\right)e^{-(1-\theta t)x/\theta}\,dx$$

$$= \lim_{b\to\infty}\left[-\frac{e^{-(1-\theta t)x/\theta}}{1-\theta t}\right]_0^b = \frac{1}{1-\theta t}, \qquad t < \frac{1}{\theta}.$$

Thus,

$$M'(t) = \frac{\theta}{(1-\theta t)^2}$$

and

$$M''(t) = \frac{2\theta^2}{(1-\theta t)^3}.$$

Hence, for an exponential distribution, we have

$$\mu = M'(0) = \theta \qquad \text{and} \qquad \sigma^2 = M''(0) - [M'(0)]^2 = \theta^2.$$

So if λ is the mean number of changes in the unit interval, then $\theta = 1/\lambda$ is the mean waiting time for the first change. In particular, suppose that $\lambda = 7$ is the mean number of changes per minute; then the mean waiting time for the first change is 1/7 of a minute, a result that agrees with our intuition.

EXAMPLE 3.4-2 Let X have an exponential distribution with a mean of $\theta = 20$. Then the p.d.f. of X is that of Example 3.3-1, namely,

$$f(x) = \frac{1}{20}e^{-x/20}, \qquad 0 \le x < \infty.$$

(See Figure 3.3-1 for the graph of this p.d.f.) The probability that X is less than 18 is

$$P(X < 18) = \int_0^{18} \frac{1}{20}e^{-x/20}\,dx = 1 - e^{-18/20} = 0.593. \qquad \blacksquare$$

Let X have an exponential distribution with mean $\mu = \theta$. Then the distribution function of X is

$$F(x) = \begin{cases} 0, & -\infty < x < 0, \\ 1 - e^{-x/\theta}, & 0 \le x < \infty. \end{cases}$$

The p.d.f. and distribution function are graphed in Figure 3.4-2 for $\theta = 5$. The median, m, is found by solving $F(m) = 0.5$. That is,

$$1 - e^{-m/\theta} = 0.5.$$

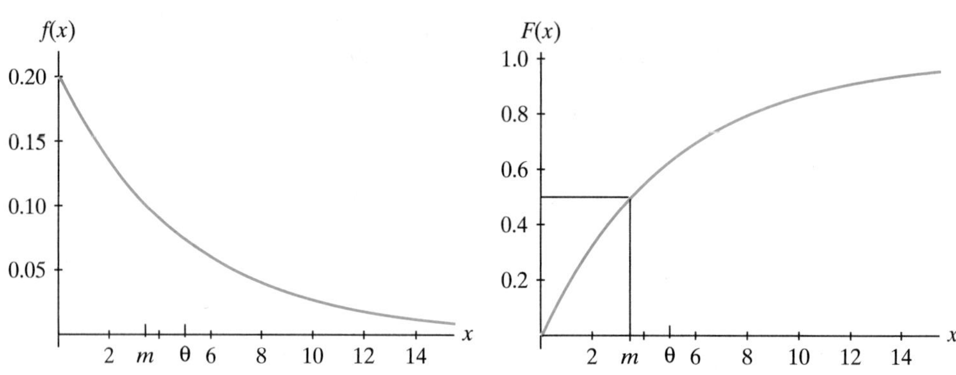

FIGURE 3.4-2: Exponential p.d.f. and distribution function

Thus,

$$m = -\theta \ln(0.5) = \theta \ln(2).$$

So with $\theta = 5$, the median is $m = -5\ln(0.5) = 3.466$. Both the median and the mean $\theta = 5$ are indicated on the graphs.

It is useful to note that for an exponential random variable, X, we have

$$\begin{aligned} P(X > x) &= 1 - F(x) = 1 - (1 - e^{-x/\theta}) \\ &= e^{-x/\theta} \qquad \text{when } x > 0. \end{aligned}$$

EXAMPLE 3.4-3 Customers arrive in a certain shop according to an approximate Poisson process at a mean rate of 20 per hour. What is the probability that the shopkeeper will have to wait more than 5 minutes for the arrival of the first customer? Let X denote the waiting time in minutes until the first customer arrives, and note that $\lambda = 1/3$ is the expected number of arrivals per minute. Thus,

$$\theta = \frac{1}{\lambda} = 3$$

and

$$f(x) = \frac{1}{3} e^{-(1/3)x}, \qquad 0 \le x < \infty.$$

Hence,

$$P(X > 5) = \int_5^\infty \frac{1}{3} e^{-(1/3)x}\, dx = e^{-5/3} = 0.1889.$$

The median time until the first arrival is

$$m = -3\ln(0.5) = 2.0794.$$

■

EXAMPLE 3.4-4 Suppose that a certain type of electronic component has an exponential distribution with a mean life of 500 hours. If X denotes the life of this component (or the time to failure of this component), then

$$P(X > x) = \int_x^\infty \frac{1}{500} e^{-t/500}\, dt = e^{-x/500}.$$

If the component has been in operation for 300 hours, the conditional probability that it will last for another 600 hours is

$$P(X > 900 \mid X > 300) = \frac{P(X > 900)}{P(X > 300)} = \frac{e^{-900/500}}{e^{-300/500}} = e^{-6/5}.$$

It is important to note that this conditional probability is exactly equal to $P(X > 600) = e^{-6/5}$. That is, the probability that the component will last an additional 600 hours, given that it has operated for 300 hours, is the same as the probability that it will last 600 hours when first put into operation. Thus, for such components, an old component is as good as a new one, and we say that the failure rate is constant. Certainly, with a constant failure rate, there is no advantage in replacing components that are operating satisfactorily. Obviously, however, this is not true in practice, because most components would have an increasing failure rate with time; hence, the exponential distribution is probably not the best model for the probability distribution of such a life. ■

REMARK In Exercise 3.4-11, the result of Example 3.4-4 is generalized; that is, if the component has an exponential distribution, then the probability that it will last a time of at least $x + y$ units, given that it has lasted at least x units, is exactly the same as the probability that it will last at least y units when first put into operation. In effect, this statement says that the exponential distribution has a "forgetfulness" (or "no memory") property. It is also interesting to observe that, for continuous random variables whose support is $(0, \infty)$, the exponential distribution is the only distribution with this forgetfulness property. Recall, however, that when we considered distributions of the discrete type, we noted that the geometric distribution has the property as well. (See Exercise 2.5-12.) ■

We often want to check whether the order statistics $y_1 \le y_2 \le \cdots \le y_n$ are those of a random sample from some exponential distribution with mean θ. If we knew θ (say, $\theta = \theta_0$), we could construct the q–q plot (y_r, π_p), where $p = r/(n + 1)$ and

$$F(\pi_p) = 1 - e^{-\pi_p/\theta_0} = p$$

or, equivalently,

$$\pi_p = -\theta_0 \ln(1 - p).$$

If θ_0 is the correct value of θ and if the exponential distribution is a suitable model, then (y_r, π_p), $r = 1, 2, \ldots, n$, would lie close to a straight line through the origin with slope 1. However, we do not know θ. Fortunately, there is a way out of our dilemma: Simply plot (y_r, π_p), with $\theta = 1$; that is, $\pi_p = -\ln(1 - p)$. If these points (y_r, π_p) fall close to a straight line through the origin, then the exponential model is appropriate. Moreover, the slope of the line—say, s_0—provides an estimate of θ through $s_0 = 1/\theta$. That is, with $\theta = 1/s_0$, the points $[y_r, \pi_p = -\theta \ln(1 - p)]$ lie close to a straight line through the origin with slope 1.

COMPUTATIONAL COMMENTS Minitab can be used to find the values of π_p. For example, if $\theta = 1$ and $n = 9$, label two columns p and π_p. Then use

Calc → Make Patterned Data → Simple Set of Numbers

to fill the p column with $0.1, 0.2, \ldots, 0.9$. Next, use the commands

Calc → Probability Distributions → Exponential

to find the values of π_p. Use `Inverse cumulative probability` with input column p and to fill the column π_p with 0.10536, 0.22314, ..., 2.30249.

EXERCISES

3.4-1. Show that the mean, variance, and moment-generating function of the uniform distribution are as given in this section.

3.4-2. Let $f(x) = 1/2$, $-1 \le x \le 1$, be the p.d.f. of X. Graph the p.d.f. and distribution function, and record the mean and variance of X.

3.4-3. Customers arrive randomly at a bank teller's window. Given that one customer arrived during a particular 10-minute period, let X equal the time within the 10 minutes that the customer arrived. If X is $U(0, 10)$, find

(a) the p.d.f. of X,
(b) $P(X \ge 8)$,
(c) $P(2 \le X < 8)$,
(d) $E(X)$, and
(e) $\text{Var}(X)$.

3.4-4. If the moment-generating function of X is

$$M(t) = \frac{e^{5t} - e^{4t}}{t}, \; t \neq 0, \quad \text{and} \quad M(0) = 1,$$

find (a) $E(X)$, (b) $\text{Var}(X)$, and (c) $P(4.2 < X \le 4.7)$.

3.4-5. Let Y have a uniform distribution $U(0, 1)$, and let

$$W = a + (b - a)Y, \qquad a < b.$$

(a) Find the distribution function of W.
HINT: Find $P[a + (b - a)Y \le w]$.
(b) How is W distributed?

3.4-6. Let X have an exponential distribution with a mean of $\theta = 20$.

(a) Compute $P(10 < X < 30)$.
(b) Compute $P(X > 30)$.
(c) Compute $P(X > 40 \mid X > 10)$.
(d) What are the variance and the moment-generating function of X?
(e) The following ordered data were simulated from an exponential distribution with $\theta = 20$:

0.45	0.65	0.66	0.70	0.94	1.05	1.17	1.28	1.32	1.35
1.45	1.52	1.59	1.76	1.92	2.05	2.75	2.88	3.48	3.63
4.01	4.37	4.54	4.84	5.39	5.53	5.95	6.26	6.44	6.79
6.85	7.45	7.51	7.75	8.23	8.41	9.42	9.45	9.57	9.72
9.85	9.97	10.26	10.27	10.34	11.05	11.37	11.42	11.45	11.78
12.26	12.90	13.09	13.19	13.45	16.29	16.55	17.07	17.18	17.32
19.40	19.49	20.04	20.95	21.11	21.13	21.37	22.49	23.34	23.88
25.06	25.41	27.86	27.91	28.32	28.60	29.41	30.84	31.74	33.64
35.42	35.60	36.26	37.06	37.98	39.49	40.13	41.34	44.13	45.11
46.10	47.67	47.68	54.36	55.98	62.81	72.92	76.08	92.16	120.54

Compare the relative frequencies of the appropriate events in the data with the respective probabilities in parts (a), (b), and (c).

3.4-7. The *Holland Sentinel* reported the following numbers of calls per hour received by 911 between noon, February 26, and all day February 27.

3	0	3	4	9	1	6	2	2	5	7	6	4	2	2	4	1	0
3	1	3	3	4	2	1	3	3	2	3	2	5	2	1	0	2	4

The *Sentinel* also reported the following lengths of time per minute between calls:

30	17	65	8	38	35	4	19	7	14	12	4	5	4	2
7	5	12	50	33	10	15	2	10	1	5	30	41	21	31
1	18	12	5	24	7	6	31	1	3	2	22	1	30	2
1	3	12	12	9	28	6	50	63	5	17	11	23	2	46
90	13	21	55	43	5	19	47	24	4	6	27	4	6	37
16	41	68	9	5	28	42	3	42	8	52	2	11	41	4
35	21	3	17	10	16	1	68	105	45	23	5	10	12	17

(a) Show graphically that the numbers of calls per hour have an approximate Poisson distribution with a mean of $\lambda = 3$.

(b) Show that the sample mean and the sample standard deviation of the times between calls are both approximately equal to 20.

(c) If X is an exponential random variable with mean $\theta = 20$, compare the probability $P(X > 15)$ with the proportion of times that are greater than 15.

(d) Compare $P(X > 45.5 \mid X > 30.5)$ with the proportion of observations that satisfy this condition.

3.4-8. Telephone calls enter a college switchboard according to a Poisson process on the average of two every 3 minutes. Let X denote the waiting time until the first call that arrives after 10 A.M.

(a) What is the p.d.f. of X?

(b) Find $P(X > 2)$.

3.4-9. What are the p.d.f., the mean, and the variance of X if the moment-generating function of X is given by the following?

(a) $M(t) = \dfrac{1}{1 - 3t}, \quad t < 1/3.$

(b) $M(t) = \dfrac{3}{3 - t}, \quad t < 3.$

3.4-10. A biologist is studying the life cycle of the avian schistosome that causes swimmers itch. His study uses Menganser ducks for the adult parasites and aquatic snails as intermediate hosts for the larval stages. The life history is cyclic. (For more information, see http://swimmersitch.org/.) As a part of this study, the biologist and his students used snails from a natural population to measure the distances that snails travel. The conjecture is that snails that had a patent infection would not travel as far as those without such an infection.

Here are the measurements in cm that snails traveled per day. There are 39 in the control group and 31 in the infected group.

Distances for Infected Snail Group (ordered):

263	238	226	220	170	155	139	123	119	107	107	97	90
90	90	79	75	74	71	66	60	55	47	47	47	45
43	41	40	39	38	38	35	32	32	28	19	10	10

Distances for Control Snail Group (ordered):

314	300	274	246	190	186	185	182	180	141	132
129	110	100	95	95	93	83	55	52	50	48
48	44	40	32	30	25	24	18	7		

(a) Find the sample means and sample standard deviations for the two groups of snails.

(b) Make box plots of the two groups of snails on the same graph.

(c) Construct two q–q plots (y_r, π_p), where $p = r/(n+1)$ and $\pi_p = -\ln(1-p)$. That is, because we do not know the values of θ, use $\theta = 1$ in constructing the q–q plot.

(d) Do the data appear to be exponentially distributed?

(e) What are your conclusions about the snails?

3.4-11. Let X have an exponential distribution with mean $\theta > 0$. Show that

$$P(X > x + y \mid X > x) = P(X > y).$$

3.4-12. Let $F(x)$ be the distribution function of the continuous-type random variable X, and assume that $F(x) = 0$ for $x \le 0$ and $0 < F(x) < 1$ for $0 < x$. Prove that if

$$P(X > x + y \mid X > x) = P(X > y),$$

then

$$F(x) = 1 - e^{-\lambda x}, \qquad 0 < x.$$

HINT: Show that $g(x) = 1 - F(x)$ satisfies the functional equation

$$g(x + y) = g(x)g(y),$$

which implies that $g(x) = a^{cx}$.

3.4-13. Let X equal the number of bad records in each 100 feet of a used computer tape. Assume that X has a Poisson distribution with mean 2.5. Let W equal the number of feet before the first bad record is found.

(a) Give the mean number of flaws per foot.

(b) How is W distributed?

(c) Give the mean and variance of W.

(d) Find (i) $P(W \leq 20)$, (ii) $P(W > 40)$, and (iii) $P(W > 60 \mid W > 20)$.

3.4-14. The initial value of an appliance is \$700 and its value in the future is given by

$$v(t) = 100\,(2^{3-t} - 1), \qquad 0 \leq t \leq 3,$$

where t is time in years. Thus, after the first 3 years the appliance is worth nothing as far as the warranty is concerned. If it fails in the first three years, the warranty pays $v(t)$. Compute the expected value of the payment on the warranty if T has an exponential distribution with mean five.

3.4-15. Let X equal the time (in minutes) between calls that are made over the public safety radio. On four different days (February 14, 21, and 28, and March 6) and during a period of one hour on each day, the following observations of X were made:

5	7	8	20	17	2	24	8	8	6	4
3	42	10	18	5	7	8	4	5	10	

If calls arrive randomly in accordance with an approximate Poisson process, then the distribution of X should be approximately exponential.

(a) Calculate the values of the sample mean and sample standard deviation. Are they close to each other in value?

(b) Construct a q–q plot of the ordered observations versus the respective quartiles of the exponential distribution with a mean of $\theta = 1$. If this plot is approximately linear, the exponential model is supported. Since the mean of these data is not close to 1, the line plotted will not have slope 1, but a linear fit will still indicate an exponential model. What is your conclusion?

3.4-16. A grocery store has n watermelons to sell and makes \$1.00 on each sale. Say the number of consumers of these watermelons is a random variable with a distribution that can be approximated by

$$f(x) = \frac{1}{200}, \qquad 0 < x < 200,$$

a p.d.f. of the continuous type. If the grocer does not have enough watermelons to sell to all consumers, she figures that she loses \$5.00 in goodwill from each unhappy customer. But if she has surplus watermelons, she loses 50 cents on each extra watermelon. What should n be to maximize profit? HINT: If $X \leq n$, then her profit is $(1.00)X + (-0.50)(n - X)$; but if $X > n$, her profit is $(1.00)n + (-5.00)(X - n)$. Find the expected value of profit as a function of n, and then select n to maximize that function.

3.4-17. There are times when a shifted exponential model is appropriate. That is, let the p.d.f. of X be

$$f(x) = \frac{1}{\theta}e^{-(x-\delta)/\theta}, \qquad \delta < x < \infty.$$

(a) Define the distribution function of X.

(b) Calculate the mean and variance of X.

3.4-18. A certain type of aluminum screen 2 feet in width has, on the average, three flaws in a 100-foot roll.

(a) What is the probability that the first 40 feet in a roll contain no flaws?

(b) What assumption did you make to solve part (a)?

3.4-19. Let X have an exponential distribution with mean θ.

(a) Find the first quartile, q_1.

(b) How far is the first quartile below the mean?

(c) Find the third quartile, q_3.

(d) How far is the third quartile above the mean?

3.4-20. Let X have a logistic distribution with p.d.f.

$$f(x) = \frac{e^{-x}}{(1 + e^{-x})^2}, \qquad -\infty < x < \infty.$$

Show that

$$Y = \frac{1}{1 + e^{-X}}$$

has a $U(0,1)$ distribution.
HINT: Find $G(y) = P(Y \leq y) = P\left(\frac{1}{1 + e^{-X}} \leq y\right)$ when $0 < y < 1$.

3.4-21. Suppose that the length of life of a human female, X, is modeled by the exponential p.d.f.

$$f(x) = \frac{1}{80}e^{-x/80}, \qquad 0 < x < \infty.$$

(a) Compute the probability $P(X > 10)$ and also compute the conditional probability $P(X > 90 \mid X > 80)$. Note that the answers are the same, indicating that if length of life has an exponential distribution, then those following it would have a "mathematical fountain of youth." Unfortunately, this is **not** a good model of length of life.

(b) Possibly a more realistic model for length of life is the distribution function

$$F(x) = 1 - \exp[-(a/b)(e^{bx} - 1)], \quad 0 < x < \infty, \text{ where } a > 0, b > 0.$$

Find and graph $f(x) = F'(x)$

(c) With $a = 0.000025$ and $b = 0.1$, determine the percentile of $x = 70$.

3.4-22. Let the random variable X be equal to the number of days that it takes a high-risk driver to have an accident. Assume that X has an exponential distribution. If $P(X < 50) = 0.25$, compute $P(X > 100 \mid X > 50)$.

3.4-23. A loss (in \$100,000) due to fire in a building has a p.d.f. $f(x) = (1/6)e^{-x/6}$, $0 < x < \infty$. Given that the loss is greater than 5, find the probability that it is greater than 8.

3.5 THE GAMMA AND CHI-SQUARE DISTRIBUTIONS

In the (approximate) Poisson process with mean λ, we have seen that the waiting time until the first change has an exponential distribution. We now let W denote the waiting time until the αth change occurs and find the distribution of W.

The distribution function of W when $w \geq 0$ is given by

$$\begin{aligned} F(w) &= P(W \leq w) = 1 - P(W > w) \\ &= 1 - P(\text{fewer than } \alpha \text{ changes occur in } [0, w]) \\ &= 1 - \sum_{k=0}^{\alpha-1} \frac{(\lambda w)^k e^{-\lambda w}}{k!}, \end{aligned} \tag{3.5-1}$$

since the number of changes in the interval $[0, w]$ has a Poisson distribution with mean λw. Because W is a continuous-type random variable, $F'(w)$, if it exists, is equal to the p.d.f. of W. Also, provided that $w > 0$, we have

$$\begin{aligned} F'(w) &= \lambda e^{-\lambda w} - e^{-\lambda w} \sum_{k=1}^{\alpha-1} \left[\frac{k(\lambda w)^{k-1}\lambda}{k!} - \frac{(\lambda w)^k \lambda}{k!} \right] \\ &= \lambda e^{-\lambda w} - e^{-\lambda w} \left[\lambda - \frac{\lambda(\lambda w)^{\alpha-1}}{(\alpha - 1)!} \right] \\ &= \frac{\lambda(\lambda w)^{\alpha-1}}{(\alpha - 1)!} e^{-\lambda w}. \end{aligned}$$

If $w < 0$, then $F(w) = 0$ and $F'(w) = 0$. A p.d.f. of this form is said to be one of the gamma type, and the random variable W is said to have a **gamma distribution**.

Before determining the characteristics of the gamma distribution, let us consider the gamma function for which the distribution is named. The **gamma function** is defined by

$$\Gamma(t) = \int_0^\infty y^{t-1} e^{-y}\, dy, \qquad 0 < t.$$

This integral is positive for $0 < t$ because the integrand is positive. Values of it are often given in a table of integrals. If $t > 1$, integration of the gamma function of t by parts yields

$$\begin{aligned} \Gamma(t) &= \left[-y^{t-1} e^{-y} \right]_0^\infty + \int_0^\infty (t - 1) y^{t-2} e^{-y}\, dy \\ &= (t - 1) \int_0^\infty y^{t-2} e^{-y}\, dy = (t - 1)\Gamma(t - 1). \end{aligned}$$

For example, $\Gamma(6) = 5\Gamma(5)$ and $\Gamma(3) = 2\Gamma(2) = (2)(1)\Gamma(1)$. Whenever $t = n$, a positive integer, we have, by repeated application of $\Gamma(t) = (t - 1)\Gamma(t - 1)$,

$$\Gamma(n) = (n - 1)\Gamma(n - 1) = (n - 1)(n - 2) \cdots (2)(1)\Gamma(1).$$

However,

$$\Gamma(1) = \int_0^\infty e^{-y}\,dy = 1.$$

Thus, when n is a positive integer, we have

$$\Gamma(n) = (n - 1)!.$$

For this reason, the gamma function is called the generalized factorial. (Incidentally, $\Gamma(1)$ corresponds to $0!$, and we have noted that $\Gamma(1) = 1$, which is consistent with earlier discussions.)

Let us now formally define the p.d.f. of the gamma distribution and find its characteristics. The random variable X has a **gamma distribution** if its p.d.f. is defined by

$$f(x) = \frac{1}{\Gamma(\alpha)\theta^\alpha} x^{\alpha-1} e^{-x/\theta}, \qquad 0 \le x < \infty.$$

Hence, W, the waiting time until the αth change in a Poisson process, has a gamma distribution with parameters α and $\theta = 1/\lambda$. To see that $f(x)$ actually has the properties of a p.d.f., note that $f(x) \ge 0$ and

$$\int_{-\infty}^{\infty} f(x)\,dx = \int_0^\infty \frac{x^{\alpha-1}e^{-x/\theta}}{\Gamma(\alpha)\theta^\alpha}\,dx,$$

which, by the change of variables $y = x/\theta$, equals

$$\int_0^\infty \frac{(\theta y)^{\alpha-1}e^{-y}}{\Gamma(\alpha)\theta^\alpha}\theta\,dy = \frac{1}{\Gamma(\alpha)}\int_0^\infty y^{\alpha-1}e^{-y}\,dy = \frac{\Gamma(\alpha)}{\Gamma(\alpha)} = 1.$$

The moment-generating function of X is (Exercise 3.5-3)

$$M(t) = \frac{1}{(1 - \theta t)^\alpha}, \qquad t < 1/\theta.$$

The mean and variance are (Exercise 3.5-4)

$$\mu = \alpha\theta \qquad \text{and} \qquad \sigma^2 = \alpha\theta^2.$$

EXAMPLE 3.5-1 Suppose the number of customers per hour arriving at a shop follows a Poisson process with mean 30. That is, if a minute is our unit, then $\lambda = 1/2$. What is the probability that the shopkeeper will wait more than 5 minutes before both of the first two customers arrive? If X denotes the waiting time in minutes until the second customer arrives, then X has a gamma distribution with $\alpha = 2$, $\theta = 1/\lambda = 2$. Hence,

$$\begin{aligned} P(X > 5) &= \int_5^\infty \frac{x^{2-1}e^{-x/2}}{\Gamma(2)2^2}\,dx = \int_5^\infty \frac{xe^{-x/2}}{4}\,dx \\ &= \frac{1}{4}\Big[(-2)xe^{-x/2} - 4e^{-x/2}\Big]_5^\infty \\ &= \frac{7}{2}e^{-5/2} = 0.287. \end{aligned}$$

We could also have used Equation 3.5-1 with $\lambda = 1/\theta$ because α is an integer. From that equation, we have

$$P(X > x) = \sum_{k=0}^{\alpha-1} \frac{(x/\theta)^k e^{-x/\theta}}{k!}.$$

Thus, with $x = 5$, $\alpha = 2$, and $\theta = 2$, this is equal to

$$\begin{aligned} P(X > 5) &= \sum_{k=0}^{2-1} \frac{(5/2)^k e^{-5/2}}{k!} \\ &= e^{-5/2}\left(1 + \frac{5}{2}\right) = \left(\frac{7}{2}\right)e^{-5/2}. \end{aligned}$$

■

EXAMPLE 3.5-2 Telephone calls arrive at a switchboard at a mean rate of $\lambda = 2$ per minute according to a Poisson process. Let X denote the waiting time in minutes until the fifth call arrives. The p.d.f. of X, with $\alpha = 5$ and $\theta = 1/\lambda = 1/2$, is

$$f(x) = \frac{2^5 x^4}{4!} e^{-2x}, \qquad 0 \le x < \infty.$$

The mean and the variance of X are, respectively, $\mu = 5/2$ and $\sigma^2 = 5/4$. ■

In order to see the effect of the parameters on the shape of the p.d.f., several combinations of α and θ have been used for graphs that are displayed in Figure 3.5-1. Note that for a fixed θ, as α increases, the probability moves to the right. The same is true for increasing θ with fixed α. Since $\theta = 1/\lambda$, as θ increases, λ decreases. That is, if $\theta_2 > \theta_1$, then $\lambda_2 = 1/\theta_2 < \lambda_1 = 1/\theta_1$. So if the mean number of changes per unit decreases, the waiting time to observe α changes can be expected to increase.

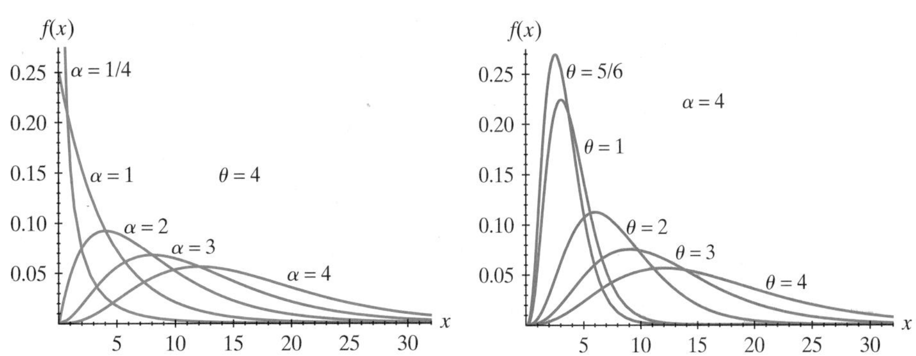

FIGURE 3.5-1: Gamma p.d.f.'s: $\theta = 4$, $\alpha = 1/4, 1, 2, 3, 4$; $\alpha = 4$, $\theta = 5/6, 1, 2, 3, 4$

We now consider a special case of the gamma distribution that plays an important role in statistics. Let X have a gamma distribution with $\theta = 2$ and $\alpha = r/2$, where r is a positive integer. The p.d.f. of X is

$$f(x) = \frac{1}{\Gamma(r/2)2^{r/2}} x^{r/2-1} e^{-x/2}, \qquad 0 \le x < \infty.$$

We say that X has a **chi-square distribution with r degrees of freedom**, which we abbreviate by saying that X is $\chi^2(r)$. The mean and the variance of this chi-square distribution are, respectively,

$$\mu = \alpha\theta = \left(\frac{r}{2}\right)2 = r \qquad \text{and} \qquad \sigma^2 = \alpha\theta^2 = \left(\frac{r}{2}\right)2^2 = 2r.$$

That is, the mean equals the number of degrees of freedom, and the variance equals twice the number of degrees of freedom. An explanation of "number of degrees of freedom" is given later. From the results concerning the more general gamma distribution, we see that its moment-generating function is

$$M(t) = (1 - 2t)^{-r/2}, \qquad t < \frac{1}{2}.$$

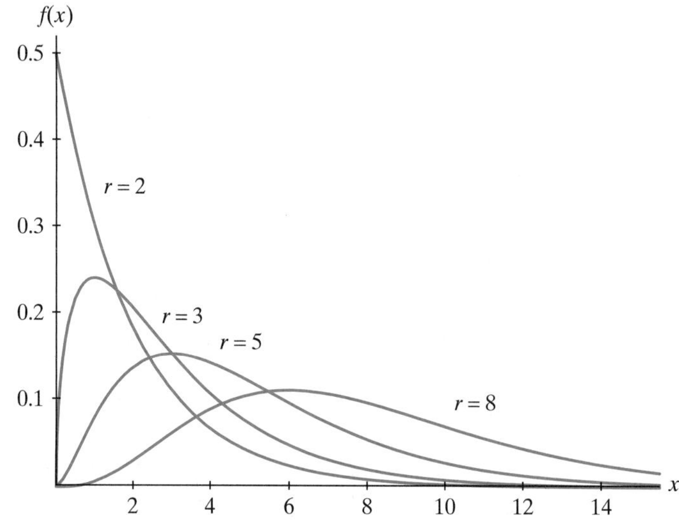

FIGURE 3.5-2: Chi-square p.d.f.'s with $r = 2, 3, 5, 8$

In Figure 3.5-2, the graphs of chi-square p.d.f.'s for $r = 2, 3, 5$, and 8 are given. Note the relationship between the mean μ $(= r)$ and the point at which the p.d.f. attains its maximum. (See Exercise 3.5-13.)

Because the chi-square distribution is so important in applications, tables have been prepared, giving the values of the distribution function

$$F(x) = \int_0^x \frac{1}{\Gamma(r/2)2^{r/2}} w^{r/2-1} e^{-w/2}\, dw$$

for selected values of r and x. (For an example, see Table IV in the appendix.)

EXAMPLE 3.5-3 Let X have a chi-square distribution with $r = 5$ degrees of freedom. Then, using Table IV in the appendix, we obtain

$$P(1.145 \le X \le 12.83) = F(12.83) - F(1.145) = 0.975 - 0.050 = 0.925$$

and

$$P(X > 15.09) = 1 - F(15.09) = 1 - 0.99 = 0.01.$$

■

EXAMPLE 3.5-4 If X is $\chi^2(7)$, then two constants, a and b, such that

$$P(a < X < b) = 0.95$$

are $a = 1.690$ and $b = 16.01$. Other constants a and b can be found, and we are restricted in our choices only by the limited table. ■

Probabilities like that of Example 3.5-4 are so important in statistical applications that we use special symbols for a and b. Let α be a positive probability (that is usually less than 0.5), and let X have a chi-square distribution with r degrees of freedom. Then $\chi^2_\alpha(r)$ is a number such that

$$P[X \geq \chi^2_\alpha(r)] = \alpha.$$

That is, $\chi^2_\alpha(r)$ is the $100(1 - \alpha)$th percentile (or upper 100αth percent point) of the chi-square distribution with r degrees of freedom. Then the 100αth percentile is the number $\chi^2_{1-\alpha}(r)$ such that

$$P[X \leq \chi^2_{1-\alpha}(r)] = \alpha.$$

That is, the probability to the right of $\chi^2_{1-\alpha}(r)$ is $1 - \alpha$. (See Figure 3.5-3.)

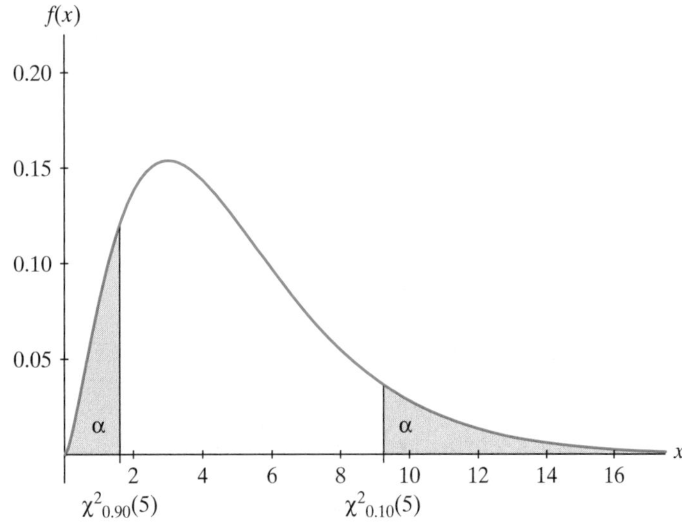

FIGURE 3.5-3: Chi-square tails, $r = 5, \alpha = 0.10$

EXAMPLE 3.5-5 Let X have a chi-square distribution with five degrees of freedom. Then, using Table IV in the appendix, we find that $\chi^2_{0.10}(5) = 9.236$ and $\chi^2_{0.90}(5) = 1.610$. These are the points that are indicated in Figure 3.5-3. ■

COMPUTATIONAL COMMENTS Some calculators and most statistical packages give values of the distribution functions and the inverse distribution functions for the gamma and chi-square distributions. For example, here is the Minitab solution for Example 3.5-1: To find the requested probability, select

Calc → Probability Distributions → Gamma

and select cumulative probability. Then input the values of the shape parameter $\alpha = 2$, the scale parameter $\theta = 2$, and the constant 5 to obtain

```
Cumulative Distribution Function
Gamma with shape = 2 and scale = 2
x    P( X <= x )
5      0.712703
```

Thus, $P(X > 5) = 1 - P(X \le 5) = 1 - 0.712703 = 0.287297$.

Using Minitab to find the values of $\chi^2_{0.10}(5)$ and $\chi^2_{0.90}(5)$ (see Example 3.5-5), select

Calc → Probability Distributions → Chi-Square

and then select inverse cumulative probability with 5 degrees of freedom. First input the value 0.10 and then repeat and input the value 0.90, to obtain

```
Inverse Cumulative Distribution Function
Chi-Square with 5 DF
P( X <= x )          x
        0.1    1.61031
        0.9    9.23636
```

Now see if you can find other values of a and b for Example 3.5-4.

EXAMPLE 3.5-6 If customers arrive at a shop on the average of 30 per hour in accordance with a Poisson process, what is the probability that the shopkeeper will have to wait longer than 9.390 minutes for the first nine customers to arrive? Note that the mean rate of arrivals per minute is $\lambda = 1/2$. Thus, $\theta = 2$ and $\alpha = r/2 = 9$. If X denotes the waiting time until the ninth arrival, then X is $\chi^2(18)$. Hence,

$$P(X > 9.390) = 1 - 0.05 = 0.95.$$

■

EXAMPLE 3.5-7 If X has an exponential distribution with a mean of 2, then the p.d.f. of X is

$$f(x) = \frac{1}{2}e^{-x/2} = \frac{x^{2/2-1}e^{-x/2}}{\Gamma(2/2)2^{2/2}}, \qquad 0 \le x < \infty.$$

That is, X is $\chi^2(2)$. As an illustration,

$$P(0.051 < X < 7.378) = 0.975 - 0.025 = 0.95.$$

■

COMPUTATIONAL COMMENTS A CAS can often be helpful in finding the mean, variance, and moment-generating function. We use *Maple* to illustrate this with the gamma distribution. In the *Maple* code that follows, we first must let *Maple* know the possible values of the parameters. Usually *Maple* denotes assumed variables with a tilde (~). The first line suppresses this symbol. The mean and variance are calculated by integration. Then the moment-generating function is calculated and is used to find the mean and the variance. Here is the *Maple* code:

```
> interface(showassumed=0);
> assume(alpha > 0): additionally(theta > 0):
```

```
> f := x^(alpha - 1)*exp(-x/theta)/GAMMA(alpha)/theta^alpha;
```

$$f := \frac{x^{(\alpha-1)}\, e^{(-\frac{x}{\theta})}}{\Gamma(\alpha)\,\theta^{\alpha}}$$

```
> mu := int(x*f, x = 0 .. infinity);
```

$$\mu := \theta\,\alpha$$

```
> var := factor(int((x - mu)^2*f, x = 0 .. infinity));
```

$$var := \theta^2\,\alpha$$

$$\sigma := \theta\,\sqrt{\alpha}$$

```
> M := int(exp(t*x)*f, x = 0 .. infinity);
```

$$M := (1 - t\theta)^{(-\alpha)}$$

```
> Mprime := diff(M, t);
```

$$Mprime := \frac{(1 - t\theta)^{(-\alpha)}\,\alpha\,\theta}{1 - t\theta}$$

```
> Mdoubleprime := diff(Mprime, t);
```

$$Mdoubleprime := \frac{(1 - t\theta)^{(-\alpha)}\,\alpha^2\,\theta^2}{(1 - t\theta)^2} + \frac{(1 - t\theta)^{(-\alpha)}\,\alpha\,\theta^2}{(1 - t\theta)^2}$$

```
> mu := subs(t = 0, Mprime);
```

$$\mu := \theta\,\alpha$$

```
> var := subs(t = 0, Mdoubleprime) - mu^2;
```

$$var := \theta^2\,\alpha$$

It is very easy to find probabilities for the gamma distribution for given values of the parameters.

EXERCISES

3.5-1. Telephone calls enter a college switchboard at a mean rate of two-thirds of a call per minute according to a Poisson process. Let X denote the waiting time until the tenth call arrives.

(a) What is the p.d.f. of X?

(b) What are the moment-generating function, mean, and variance of X?

3.5-2. If X has a gamma distribution with $\theta = 4$ and $\alpha = 2$, find $P(X < 5)$.

3.5-3. Find the moment-generating function for the gamma distribution with parameters α and θ.

HINT: In the integral representing $E(e^{tX})$, change variables by letting $y = (1 - \theta t)x/\theta$, where $1 - \theta t > 0$.

3.5-4. Use the moment-generating function of a gamma distribution to show that $E(X) = \alpha\theta$ and $\text{Var}(X) = \alpha\theta^2$.

3.5-5. If the moment-generating function of a random variable W is

$$M(t) = (1 - 7t)^{-20},$$

find the p.d.f., mean, and variance of W.

3.5-6. Let X denote the number of alpha particles emitted by barium-133 and observed by a Geiger counter in a fixed position. Assume that X has a Poisson distribution and $\lambda = 14.7$ is the mean number of counts per second. Let W denote the waiting time to observe 100 counts. Twenty-five independent observations of W are

6.9	7.3	6.7	6.4	6.3
5.9	7.0	7.1	6.5	7.6
7.2	7.1	6.1	7.3	7.6
7.6	6.7	6.3	5.7	6.7
7.5	5.3	5.4	7.4	6.9

(a) Give the p.d.f., mean, and variance of W.

(b) Calculate the sample mean and sample variance of the 25 observations of W.

(c) Use the relative frequency of event $\{W \le 6.6\}$ to approximate $P(W \le 6.6)$.

3.5-7. The waiting times in minutes until two calls to 911, as reported by the *Holland Sentinel* on November 13 between noon and midnight, were

20	28	81	4	9	41	9	11	10	24	20
44	18	30	16	53	15	38	50	84	44	69

Could these times represent a random sample from a gamma distribution with $\alpha = 2$ and $\theta = 120/7$?

(a) Compare the distribution and sample means.

(b) Compare the distribution and sample variances.

(c) Compare $P(X < 35)$ with the proportion of times that are less than 35.

(d) If possible, make some graphical comparisons. For example, if you have access to Minitab, construct a q–q plot for these data.

(e) What is your conclusion?

3.5-8. Let X equal the number of alpha particle emissions of carbon-14 that are counted by a Geiger counter each second. Assume that the distribution of X is Poisson with mean 16. Let W equal the time in seconds before the seventh count is made.

(a) Give the distribution of W.

(b) Find $P(W \le 0.5)$. HINT: Use Equation 3.5-1 with $\lambda w = 8$.

3.5-9. If X is $\chi^2(17)$, find

(a) $P(X < 7.564)$.

(b) $P(X > 27.59)$.

(c) $P(6.408 < X < 27.59)$.

(d) $\chi^2_{0.95}(17)$.

(e) $\chi^2_{0.025}(17)$.

3.5-10. If X is $\chi^2(12)$, find constants a and b such that

$$P(a < X < b) = 0.90 \text{ and } P(X < a) = 0.05.$$

3.5-11. If X is $\chi^2(23)$, find the following:

(a) $P(14.85 < X < 32.01)$.

(b) Constants a and b such that $P(a < X < b) = 0.95$ and $P(X < a) = 0.025$.

(c) The mean and variance of X.

(d) $\chi^2_{0.05}(23)$ and $\chi^2_{0.95}(23)$.

3.5-12. If the moment-generating function of X is $M(t) = (1 - 2t)^{-12}$, $t < 1/2$, find

(a) $E(X)$.

(b) $\text{Var}(X)$.

(c) $P(15.66 < X < 42.98)$.

3.5-13. Let the distribution of X be $\chi^2(r)$.

(a) Find the point at which the p.d.f. of X attains its maximum when $r \ge 2$. This is the mode of a $\chi^2(r)$ distribution.

(b) Find the points of inflection for the p.d.f. of X.

(c) Use the results of parts (a) and (b) to sketch the p.d.f. of X when $r = 4$ and when $r = 10$.

3.5-14. Cars arrive at a toll booth at a mean rate of five cars every 10 minutes according to a Poisson process. Find the probability that the toll collector will have to wait longer than 26.30 minutes before collecting the eighth toll.

3.5-15. If 15 observations are taken independently from a chi-square distribution with four degrees of freedom, find the probability that at most 3 of the 15 observations exceed 7.779.

3.5-16. If 10 observations are taken independently from a chi-square distribution with 19 degrees of freedom, find the probability that exactly 2 of the 10 sample items exceed 30.14.

3.5-17. In a medical experiment, a rat has been exposed to some radiation. The experimenters believe that the rat's survival time X (in weeks) has the p.d.f.

$$f(x) = \frac{3x^2}{120^3}\, e^{-(x/120)^3}, \qquad 0 < x < \infty.$$

(a) What is the probability that the rat survives at least 100 weeks?

(b) Find the expected value of the survival time. HINT: In the integral representing $E(X)$, let $y = (x/120)^3$ and get the answer in terms of a gamma function.

3.5-18. Say the serum cholesterol level (X) of U.S. males ages 25–34 follows a translated gamma distribution with p.d.f.

$$f(x) = \frac{x - 80}{50^2}\, e^{-(x - 80)/50}, \quad 80 < x < \infty.$$

(a) What are the mean and the variance of this distribution?

(b) What is the mode?

(c) What percentage have the model cholesterol level less than 200? HINT: Integrate by parts.

3.5-19. A bakery sells rolls in units of a dozen. The demand X (in 1000 units) for rolls has a gamma distribution with parameters $\alpha = 3, \theta = 0.5$. It costs 40 cents to make a unit that sells for \$1 on the first day when the rolls are fresh. Any leftover units are sold on the second day at 20 cents. How many units should be made to maximize the expected value of the profit?

3.6 THE NORMAL DISTRIBUTION

Sometimes certain measurements have (approximately) normal distributions. This assumption is sometimes applied too frequently, however; for example, it often bothers us when teachers "grade on the curve" because they believe that their students' grades are normally distributed and frequently they are not. Each student should be able to earn an A grade (or B or C or D) if he or she does the appropriate work; thus, grades should not depend upon what others do. Nevertheless, the normal distribution is extremely important and we must study its major characteristics.

In this section, we give the definition of the p.d.f. for the normal distribution, verify that it is a p.d.f., and then justify the use of μ and σ^2 in its formula. That is, we will show that μ and σ^2 are actually the mean and the variance of this distribution. Toward that end, the random variable X has a **normal distribution** if its p.d.f. is defined by

$$f(x) = \frac{1}{\sigma\sqrt{2\pi}} \exp\left[-\frac{(x-\mu)^2}{2\sigma^2}\right], \qquad -\infty < x < \infty,$$

where μ and σ are parameters satisfying $-\infty < \mu < \infty$ and $0 < \sigma < \infty$, and also where $\exp[v]$ means e^v. Briefly, we say that X is $N(\mu, \sigma^2)$.

Clearly, $f(x) > 0$. We now evaluate the integral

$$I = \int_{-\infty}^{\infty} \frac{1}{\sigma\sqrt{2\pi}} \exp\left[-\frac{(x-\mu)^2}{2\sigma^2}\right] dx$$

and show that it is equal to 1. In I, change the variables of integration by letting $z = (x - \mu)/\sigma$. Then

$$I = \int_{-\infty}^{\infty} \frac{1}{\sqrt{2\pi}} e^{-z^2/2}\, dz.$$

Since $I > 0$, it follows that if $I^2 = 1$, then $I = 1$. Now,

$$I^2 = \frac{1}{2\pi}\left[\int_{-\infty}^{\infty} e^{-x^2/2}\, dx\right]\left[\int_{-\infty}^{\infty} e^{-y^2/2}\, dy\right],$$

or, equivalently,

$$I^2 = \frac{1}{2\pi}\int_{-\infty}^{\infty}\int_{-\infty}^{\infty} \exp\left(-\frac{x^2+y^2}{2}\right) dx\, dy.$$

Letting $x = r\cos\theta$, $y = r\sin\theta$ (i.e., using polar coordinates), we have

$$\begin{aligned} I^2 &= \frac{1}{2\pi}\int_0^{2\pi}\int_0^{\infty} e^{-r^2/2} r\, dr\, d\theta \\ &= \frac{1}{2\pi}\int_0^{2\pi} d\theta = \frac{1}{2\pi} 2\pi = 1. \end{aligned}$$

Thus, $I = 1$, and we have shown that $f(x)$ has the properties of a p.d.f. The moment-generating function of X is

$$M(t) = \int_{-\infty}^{\infty} \frac{e^{tx}}{\sigma\sqrt{2\pi}} \exp\left[-\frac{(x-\mu)^2}{2\sigma^2}\right] dx$$

$$= \int_{-\infty}^{\infty} \frac{1}{\sigma\sqrt{2\pi}} \exp\left\{-\frac{1}{2\sigma^2}[x^2 - 2(\mu + \sigma^2 t)x + \mu^2]\right\} dx.$$

To evaluate this integral, we complete the square in the exponent:

$$x^2 - 2(\mu + \sigma^2 t)x + \mu^2 = [x - (\mu + \sigma^2 t)]^2 - 2\mu\sigma^2 t - \sigma^4 t^2.$$

Hence,

$$M(t) = \exp\left(\frac{2\mu\sigma^2 t + \sigma^4 t^2}{2\sigma^2}\right) \int_{-\infty}^{\infty} \frac{1}{\sigma\sqrt{2\pi}} \exp\left\{-\frac{1}{2\sigma^2}[x - (\mu + \sigma^2 t)]^2\right\} dx.$$

Note that the integrand in the last integral is like the p.d.f. of a normal distribution with μ replaced by $\mu + \sigma^2 t$. However, the normal p.d.f. integrates to 1 for all real μ—in particular, when μ is replaced by $\mu + \sigma^2 t$. Thus,

$$M(t) = \exp\left(\frac{2\mu\sigma^2 t + \sigma^4 t^2}{2\sigma^2}\right) = \exp\left(\mu t + \frac{\sigma^2 t^2}{2}\right).$$

Now,

$$M'(t) = (\mu + \sigma^2 t) \exp\left(\mu t + \frac{\sigma^2 t^2}{2}\right)$$

and

$$M''(t) = [(\mu + \sigma^2 t)^2 + \sigma^2] \exp\left(\mu t + \frac{\sigma^2 t^2}{2}\right).$$

Consequently,

$$E(X) = M'(0) = \mu,$$
$$\mathrm{Var}(X) = M''(0) - [M'(0)]^2 = \mu^2 + \sigma^2 - \mu^2 = \sigma^2.$$

That is, the parameters μ and σ^2 in the p.d.f. of X are the mean and the variance of X.

EXAMPLE 3.6-1 If the p.d.f. of X is

$$f(x) = \frac{1}{\sqrt{32\pi}} \exp\left[-\frac{(x+7)^2}{32}\right], \qquad -\infty < x < \infty,$$

then X is $N(-7, 16)$. That is, X has a normal distribution with a mean $\mu = -7$, a variance $\sigma^2 = 16$, and the moment-generating function

$$M(t) = \exp(-7t + 8t^2).$$ ■

EXAMPLE 3.6-2 If the moment-generating function of X is

$$M(t) = \exp(5t + 12t^2),$$

then X is $N(5, 24)$, and its p.d.f. is

$$f(x) = \frac{1}{\sqrt{48\pi}} \exp\left[-\frac{(x - 5)^2}{48} \right], \qquad \infty < x < \infty. \qquad ■$$

If Z is $N(0, 1)$, we shall say that Z has a **standard normal distribution**. Moreover, the distribution function of Z is

$$\Phi(z) = P(Z \le z) = \int_{-\infty}^{z} \frac{1}{\sqrt{2\pi}} e^{-w^2/2}\, dw.$$

It is not possible to evaluate this integral by finding an antiderivative that can be expressed as an elementary function. However, numerical approximations for integrals of this type have been tabulated and are given in Tables Va and Vb in the appendix. The bell-shaped curved in Figure 3.6-1 represents the graph of the p.d.f. of Z, and the shaded area equals $\Phi(z_0)$.

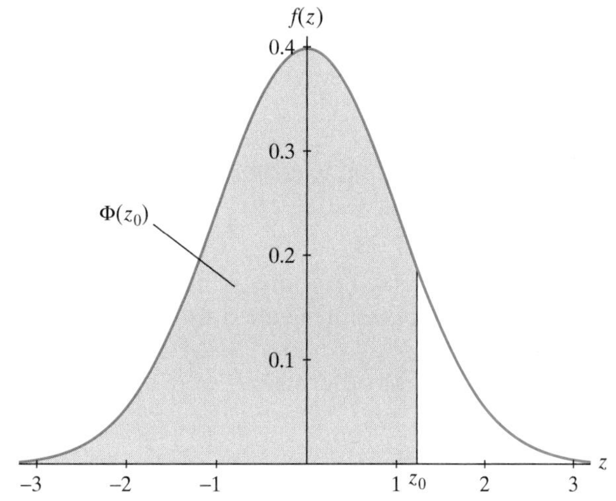

FIGURE 3.6-1: Standard normal p.d.f.

Values of $\Phi(z)$ for $z \ge 0$ are given in Table Va in the appendix. Because of the symmetry of the standard normal p.d.f., it is true that $\Phi(-z) = 1 - \Phi(z)$ for all real z. Thus, Table Va is enough. However, it is sometimes convenient to be able to read $\Phi(-z)$, for $z > 0$, directly from a table. This can be done by using values in Table Vb in the appendix, which lists right-tail probabilities. Again, because of the symmetry of the standard normal p.d.f., when $z > 0$, $\Phi(-z) = P(Z \le -z) = P(Z > z)$ can be read directly from Table Vb.

EXAMPLE 3.6-3 If Z is $N(0, 1)$, then, using Table Va in the appendix, we obtain

$$P(Z \le 1.24) = \Phi(1.24) = 0.8925,$$

$$P(1.24 \le Z \le 2.37) = \Phi(2.37) - \Phi(1.24) = 0.9911 - 0.8925 = 0.0986,$$
$$P(-2.37 \le Z \le -1.24) = P(1.24 \le Z \le 2.37) = 0.0986.$$

Now using Table Vb, we find that

$$P(Z > 1.24) = 0.1075,$$
$$P(Z \le -2.14) = P(Z \ge 2.14) = 0.0162,$$

and using both tables, we obtain

$$P(-2.14 \le Z \le 0.77) = P(Z \le 0.77) - P(Z \le -2.14)$$
$$= 0.7794 - 0.0162 = 0.7632.$$

■

There are times when we want to read the normal probability table in the opposite way, essentially finding the inverse of the standard normal distribution function. That is, given a probability p, we find a constant a so that $P(Z \le a) = p$. This situation is illustrated in the next example.

EXAMPLE 3.6-4 If the distribution of Z is $N(0,1)$, then, to find constants a and b such that

$$P(Z \le a) = 0.9147 \qquad \text{and} \qquad P(Z \ge b) = 0.0526,$$

we find the respective probabilities in Tables Va and Vb in the appendix and read off the corresponding values of z. From Table Va, we see that $a = 1.37$, and from Table Vb, we see that $b = 1.62$. ■

In statistical applications, we are often interested in finding a number z_α such that

$$P(Z \ge z_\alpha) = \alpha,$$

where Z is $N(0,1)$ and α is usually less than 0.5. That is, z_α is the $100(1 - \alpha)$th percentile (sometimes called the upper 100α percent point) for the standard normal distribution. (See Figure 3.6-2.) The value of z_α is given in Table Va for selected values of α. For other values of α, z_α can be found in Table Vb.

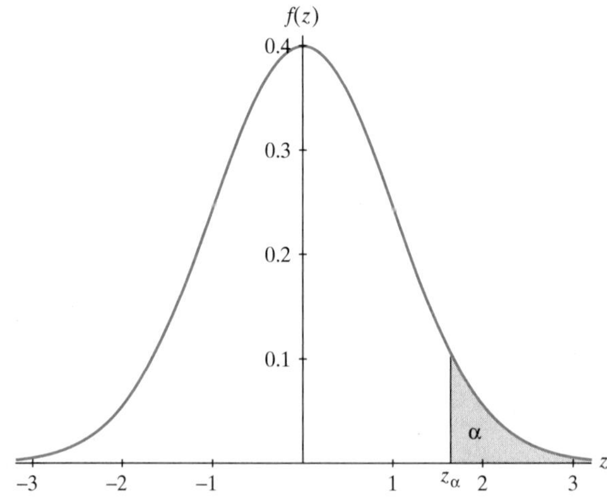

FIGURE 3.6-2: Upper 100α percent point, z_α

Because of the symmetry of the normal p.d.f.,

$$P(Z \leq -z_\alpha) = P(Z \geq z_\alpha) = \alpha.$$

Also, since the subscript of z_α is the right-tail probability,

$$z_{1-\alpha} = -z_\alpha.$$

For example,

$$z_{0.95} = z_{1-0.05} = -z_{0.05}.$$

EXAMPLE 3.6-5 To find $z_{0.0125}$, note that

$$P(Z \geq z_{0.0125}) = 0.0125.$$

Thus,

$$z_{0.0125} = 2.24,$$

from Table Vb in the appendix. Also,

$$z_{0.05} = 1.645 \qquad \text{and} \qquad z_{0.025} = 1.960,$$

from the last rows of Table Va. ■

REMARK Recall that the $(100p)$th percentile, π_p, for a random variable X is a number such that $P(X \leq \pi_p) = p$. If Z is $N(0,1)$, then since

$$P(Z \geq z_\alpha) = \alpha,$$

it follows that

$$P(Z < z_\alpha) = 1 - \alpha.$$

Thus, z_α is the $100(1 - \alpha)$th percentile for the standard normal distribution, $N(0,1)$. For example, $z_{0.05} = 1.645$ is the $100(1 - 0.05) = 95$th percentile and $z_{0.95} = -1.645$ is the $100(1 - 0.95) = 5$th percentile. ■

The next theorem shows that if X is $N(\mu, \sigma^2)$, then the random variable $(X - \mu)/\sigma$ is $N(0,1)$. Hence, Tables Va and Vb in the appendix can be used to find probabilities relating to X.

THEOREM 3.6-1 If X is $N(\mu, \sigma^2)$, then $Z = (X - \mu)/\sigma$ is $N(0,1)$.

Proof. The distribution function of Z is

$$P(Z \leq z) = P\left(\frac{X - \mu}{\sigma} \leq z\right) = P(X \leq z\sigma + \mu)$$

$$= \int_{-\infty}^{z\sigma+\mu} \frac{1}{\sigma\sqrt{2\pi}} \exp\left[-\frac{(x - \mu)^2}{2\sigma^2}\right] dx.$$

Now, in the integral representing $P(Z \leq z)$, we use the change of variable of integration given by $w = (x - \mu)/\sigma$ (i.e., $x = w\sigma + \mu$) to obtain

$$P(Z \leq z) = \int_{-\infty}^{z} \frac{1}{\sqrt{2\pi}} e^{-w^2/2}\, dw.$$

But this is the expression for $\Phi(z)$, the distribution function of a standardized normal random variable. Hence, Z is $N(0,1)$. □

REMARK Note that if $E(X) = \mu$ and $E[(X - \mu)^2] = \sigma^2$ exist and $Z = (X - \mu)/\sigma$, then

$$\mu_Z = E(Z) = E\left[\frac{X - \mu}{\sigma}\right] = \frac{E(X) - \mu}{\sigma} = 0$$

and

$$\sigma_Z^2 = E\left[\left(\frac{X - \mu}{\sigma}\right)^2\right] = \frac{E[(X - \mu)^2]}{\sigma^2} = \frac{\sigma^2}{\sigma^2} = 1.$$

That is, the mean and the variance of Z are 0 and 1, respectively, no matter what the distribution of X. The important aspect of the theorem is that if X is normally distributed, then Z is normally distributed—of course with zero mean and unit variance. ■

Theorem 3.6-1 can be used to find probabilities relating to X, which is $N(\mu, \sigma^2)$, as follows:

$$P(a \le X \le b) = P\left(\frac{a - \mu}{\sigma} \le \frac{X - \mu}{\sigma} \le \frac{b - \mu}{\sigma}\right) = \Phi\left(\frac{b - \mu}{\sigma}\right) - \Phi\left(\frac{a - \mu}{\sigma}\right),$$

since $(X - \mu)/\sigma$ is $N(0,1)$.

EXAMPLE 3.6-6 If X is $N(3,16)$, then

$$\begin{aligned} P(4 \le X \le 8) &= P\left(\frac{4 - 3}{4} \le \frac{X - 3}{4} \le \frac{8 - 3}{4}\right) \\ &= \Phi(1.25) - \Phi(0.25) = 0.8944 - 0.5987 = 0.2957, \\ P(0 \le X \le 5) &= P\left(\frac{0 - 3}{4} \le Z \le \frac{5 - 3}{4}\right) \\ &= \Phi(0.5) - \Phi(-0.75) = 0.6915 - 0.2266 = 0.4649, \end{aligned}$$

and

$$\begin{aligned} P(-2 \le X \le 1) &= P\left(\frac{-2 - 3}{4} \le Z \le \frac{1 - 3}{4}\right) \\ &= \Phi(-0.5) - \Phi(-1.25) = 0.3085 - 0.1056 = 0.2029. \end{aligned}$$ ■

EXAMPLE 3.6-7 If X is $N(25,36)$, we find a constant c such that

$$P(|X - 25| \le c) = 0.9544.$$

We want

$$P\left(\frac{-c}{6} \le \frac{X - 25}{6} \le \frac{c}{6}\right) = 0.9544.$$

Thus,

$$\Phi\left(\frac{c}{6}\right) - \left[1 - \Phi\left(\frac{c}{6}\right)\right] = 0.9544$$

and

$$\Phi\left(\frac{c}{6}\right) = 0.9772.$$

Hence, $c/6 = 2$ and $c = 12$. That is, the probability that X falls within two standard deviations of its mean is the same as the probability that the standard normal variable Z falls within two units (standard deviations) of zero. ■

In the next theorem, we give a relationship between the chi-square and normal distributions.

THEOREM 3.6-2 If the random variable X is $N(\mu, \sigma^2)$, $\sigma^2 > 0$, then the random variable $V = (X - \mu)^2/\sigma^2 = Z^2$ is $\chi^2(1)$.

Proof. Because $V = Z^2$, where $Z = (X - \mu)/\sigma$ is $N(0,1)$, the distribution function $G(v)$ of V is, for $v \ge 0$,

$$G(v) = P(Z^2 \le v) = P(-\sqrt{v} \le Z \le \sqrt{v}).$$

That is, with $v \ge 0$,

$$G(v) = \int_{-\sqrt{v}}^{\sqrt{v}} \frac{1}{\sqrt{2\pi}} e^{-z^2/2}\, dz = 2\int_0^{\sqrt{v}} \frac{1}{\sqrt{2\pi}} e^{-z^2/2}\, dz.$$

If we change the variable of integration by writing $z = \sqrt{y}$, then, since $D_y(z) = 1/(2\sqrt{y})$, we have

$$G(v) = \int_0^{v} \frac{1}{\sqrt{2\pi y}} e^{-y/2}\, dy, \qquad 0 \le v.$$

Of course, $G(v) = 0$ when $v < 0$. Hence, the p.d.f. $g(v) = G'(v)$ of the continuous-type random variable V is, by one form of the fundamental theorem of calculus,

$$g(v) = \frac{1}{\sqrt{\pi}\sqrt{2}} v^{1/2-1} e^{-v/2}, \qquad 0 < v < \infty.$$

Since $g(v)$ is a p.d.f., it must be true that

$$\int_0^{\infty} \frac{1}{\sqrt{\pi}\sqrt{2}} v^{1/2-1} e^{-v/2}\, dv = 1.$$

The change of variables $x = v/2$ yields

$$1 = \frac{1}{\sqrt{\pi}} \int_0^{\infty} x^{1/2-1} e^{-x}\, dx = \frac{1}{\sqrt{\pi}}\Gamma\left(\frac{1}{2}\right).$$

Hence, $\Gamma(1/2) = \sqrt{\pi}$, and it follows that V is $\chi^2(1)$. □

EXAMPLE 3.6-8 If Z is $N(0,1)$, then

$$P(|Z| < 1.96 = \sqrt{3.841}\,) = 0.95$$

and, of course,

$$P(Z^2 < 3.841) = 0.95$$

from the chi-square table with $r = 1$. ■

Given a set of observations of a random variable X, it is a challenge to determine the distribution of X. In particular, how can we decide whether or not X has an approximate normal distribution? If we have a large number of observations of X, a stem-and-leaf diagram or a histogram of the observations can often be helpful. (See Exercise 3.6-12 and 3.6-19, respectively.) For small samples, a q–q plot can be used to check on whether the sample arises from a normal distribution. For example, suppose the quantiles of a sample were plotted against the corresponding quantiles of a certain normal distribution and the pairs of points generated were on a straight line with slope 1 and intercept 0. Of course, we would then believe that we have an ideal sample from that normal distribution with that certain mean and standard deviation. Such a plot, however, requires that we know the mean and the standard deviation of this normal distribution, and we usually do not. However, since the quantile, q_p, of $N(\mu, \sigma^2)$ is related to the corresponding one, z_{1-p}, of $N(0,1)$ by $q_p = \mu + \sigma z_{1-p}$, we can always plot the quantiles of the sample against the corresponding ones of $N(0,1)$ and get the needed information. That is, if the sample quantiles are plotted as the x-coordinates of the pairs and the $N(0,1)$ quantiles as the y-coordinates, and if the graph is almost a straight line, then it is reasonable to assume that the sample arises from a normal distribution. Moreover, the reciprocal of the slope of that straight line is a good estimate of the standard deviation σ because $z_{1-p} = (q_p - \mu)/\sigma$.

EXAMPLE 3.6-9 In researching groundwater, it is often important to know the characteristics of the soil at a certain site. Many of these characteristics, such as porosity, are at least partially dependent upon the grain size. The diameter of individual grains of soil can be measured. Here are the diameters (in mm) of 30 randomly selected grains:

1.24	1.36	1.28	1.31	1.35	1.20	1.39	1.35	1.41	1.31
1.28	1.26	1.37	1.49	1.32	1.40	1.33	1.28	1.25	1.39
1.38	1.34	1.40	1.27	1.33	1.36	1.43	1.33	1.29	1.34

For these data, $\bar{x} = 1.33$ and $s^2 = 0.0040$. May we assume that these are observations of a random variable X that is $N(1.33, 0.0040)$? To help answer this question, we shall construct a q–q plot of the standard normal quantiles that correspond to $p = 1/31, 2/31, \ldots, 30/31$ versus the ordered observations. To find these quantiles, it is helpful to use the computer. Although we could utilize Minitab, we shall find the quantiles with *Maple* as follows:

k	Diameters in mm (x)	$p = k/31$	z_{1-p}	k	Diameters in mm (x)	$p = k/31$	z_{1-p}
1	1.20	0.0323	−1.85	16	1.34	0.5161	0.04
2	1.24	0.0645	−1.52	17	1.34	0.5484	0.12
3	1.25	0.0968	−1.30	18	1.35	0.5806	0.20
4	1.26	0.1290	−1.13	19	1.35	0.6129	0.29
5	1.27	0.1613	−0.99	20	1.36	0.6452	0.37
6	1.28	0.1935	−0.86	21	1.36	0.6774	0.46
7	1.28	0.2258	−0.75	22	1.37	0.7097	0.55

k	Diameters in mm (x)	$p = k/31$	z_{1-p}	k	Diameters in mm (x)	$p = k/31$	z_{1-p}
8	1.28	0.2581	−0.65	23	1.38	0.7419	0.65
9	1.29	0.2903	−0.55	24	1.39	0.7742	0.75
10	1.31	0.3226	−0.46	25	1.39	0.8065	0.86
11	1.31	0.3548	−0.37	26	1.40	0.8387	0.99
12	1.32	0.3871	0.29	27	1.40	0.8710	1.13
13	1.33	0.4194	−0.20	28	1.41	0.9032	1.30
14	1.33	0.4516	−0.12	29	1.43	0.9355	1.52
15	1.33	0.4839	−0.04	30	1.49	0.9677	1.85

A q–q plot of these data is shown in Figure 3.6-3. Note that the points do fall close to a straight line, so the normal probability model seems to be appropriate on the basis of these few data.

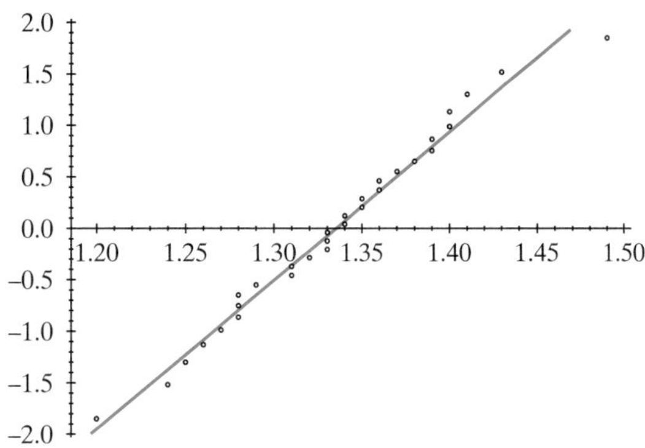

FIGURE 3.6-3: q–q, $N(0, 1)$ quantiles versus grain diameters

EXERCISES

3.6-1. If Z is $N(0, 1)$, find

(a) $P(0.53 < Z \le 2.06)$.
(b) $P(-0.79 \le Z < 1.52)$.
(c) $P(Z > -1.77)$. (d) $P(Z > 2.89)$.
(e) $P(|Z| < 1.96)$. (f) $P(|Z| < 1)$.
(g) $P(|Z| < 2)$. (h) $P(|Z| < 3)$.

3.6-2. If Z is $N(0, 1)$, find

(a) $P(0 \le Z \le 0.87)$.
(b) $P(-2.64 \le Z \le 0)$.
(c) $P(-2.13 \le Z \le -0.56)$. (d) $P(|Z| > 1.39)$.
(e) $P(Z < -1.62)$. (f) $P(|Z| > 1)$.
(g) $P(|Z| > 2)$. (h) $P(|Z| > 3)$.

3.6-3. Find the values of (a) $z_{0.01}$, (b) $-z_{0.005}$, (c) $z_{0.0475}$, and (d) $z_{0.985}$.

3.6-4. Find the values of (a) $z_{0.10}$, (b) $-z_{0.05}$, (c) $-z_{0.0485}$, and (d) $z_{0.9656}$.

3.6-5. If Z is $N(0, 1)$, find values of c such that

(a) $P(Z \ge c) = 0.025$. (b) $P(|Z| \le c) = 0.95$.
(c) $P(Z > c) = 0.05$. (d) $P(|Z| \le c) = 0.90$.

3.6-6. If the moment-generating function of X is $M(t) = \exp(166t + 200t^2)$, find

(a) The mean of X. (b) The variance of X.
(c) $P(170 < X < 200)$. (d) $P(148 \le X \le 172)$.

3.6-7. If X is normally distributed with a mean of 6 and a variance of 25, find

(a) $P(6 \le X \le 12)$. (b) $P(0 \le X \le 8)$.
(c) $P(-2 < X \le 0)$. (d) $P(X > 21)$.
(e) $P(|X - 6| < 5)$. (f) $P(|X - 6| < 10)$.
(g) $P(|X - 6| < 15)$. (h) $P(|X - 6| < 12.41)$.

3.6-8. Let the distribution of X be $N(\mu, \sigma^2)$ Show that the points of inflection of the graph of the p.d.f. of X occur at $x = \mu \pm \sigma$.

3.6-9. If X is $N(650, 625)$, find

(a) $P(600 \le X < 660)$.
(b) A constant $c > 0$ such that $P(|X - 650| \le c) = 0.9544$.

3.6-10. If X is $N(\mu, \sigma^2)$, show that $Y = aX + b$ is $N(a\mu + b, a^2\sigma^2)$, $a \ne 0$. HINT: Find the distribution function $P(Y \le y)$ of Y, and in the resulting integral, let $w = ax + b$ or, equivalently, $x = (w - b)/a$.

3.6-11. Find the distribution of $W = X^2$ when

(a) X is $N(0, 4)$,
(b) X is $N(0, \sigma^2)$.

3.6-12. A company manufactures windows that are inserted into an automobile. Each window has five studs for attaching it. A pullout test is used to determine the force required to pull a stud out of a window. (Note that this is an example of destructive testing.) Let X equal the force required for pulling studs out of position 4. Sixty observations of X were as follows:

159	150	147	160	155	142	143	151	154	133
151	146	140	146	137	148	154	157	142	153
135	144	135	165	118	158	126	147	123	140
125	151	153	158	144	163	150	150	137	164
137	156	139	134	171	144	160	147	155	175
162	160	149	149	158	152	165	131	150	120

(a) Construct an ordered stem-and-leaf diagram, using 11•, 12*, 12•, and so on as stems.
(b) Construct a q–q plot, using the ordered array and the corresponding quantiles of $N(0, 1)$. (You will probably want to use a statistical package on the computer to help you out.)
(c) Does it look like X has a normal distribution?

3.6-13. Some measurements (in mm) were made on specimens of the spider Sosippus floridanus, which is native to Florida. Here are the lengths of 9 female spiders and 9 male spiders.

Female spiders	11.06	13.87	12.93	15.08	17.82
	14.14	12.26	17.82	20.17	
Male spiders	12.26	11.66	12.53	13.00	11.79
	12.46	10.65	10.39	12.26	

(a) Construct a q–q plot, $N(0, 1)$ quantiles versus the ordered female spider lengths. Do they appear to be normally distributed?
(b) Construce a q–q plot, $N(0, 1)$ quantiles versus the ordered male spider lengths. Do they appear to be normally distributed?

3.6-14. A candy maker produces mints that have a label weight of 20.4 grams. Assume that the distribution of the weights of these mints is $N(21.37, 0.16)$.

(a) Let X denote the weight of a single mint selected at random from the production line. Find $P(X > 22.07)$.
(b) Suppose that 15 mints are selected independently and weighed. Let Y equal the number of these mints that weigh less than 20.857 grams. Find $P(Y \le 2)$.

3.6-15. A chemistry major weighed 19 plain M&M's (in grams) on a ±0.0001 scale. The ordered weights are as follows:

0.7938	0.8032	0.8089	0.8222	0.8268	0.8383	0.8442
0.8490	0.8528	0.8572	0.8674	0.8734	0.8786	
0.8850	0.8873	0.8920	0.9069	0.9150	0.9243	

(a) Construct a stem-and-leaf diagram using three-digit leaves, with stems 0.7•, 0.8∗, 0.8t, and so on.
(b) Construct a q-q plot of these data and the corresponding quantiles for the standard normal distribution, $N(0, 1)$.
(c) Do the data look like observations from a normal distribution? Why?

3.6-16. If the moment-generating function of X is $M(t) = e^{500t+5000t^2}$, find $P[27{,}060 \le (X - 500)^2 \le 50{,}240]$.

3.6-17. If X is $N(7, 4)$, find $P[15.364 \le (X - 7)^2 \le 20.096]$.

3.6-18. The strength X of a certain material is such that its distribution is found by $X = e^Y$, where Y is $N(10, 1)$. Find the distribution function and p.d.f. of X, and compute $P(10{,}000 < X < 20{,}000)$. NOTE: The random variable X is said to have a **lognormal distribution**.

3.6-19. A packaged product has a label weight of 450 grams. The company goal is to fill each package with at least 450 grams, but at most 458 grams. To check these goals, a random sample of 100 packages was selected and weighed, yielding the following weights, rounded to the nearest gram:

457 457 455 457 454 454 457 455 456 459
457 458 456 456 461 457 458 452 457 460
453 458 452 454 454 456 455 456 451 454
456 457 457 453 455 459 458 457 458 457
461 457 455 458 458 455 457 458 456 463
455 455 455 456 456 456 455 456 460 456
456 457 458 454 455 456 459 457 457 451
450 453 453 459 450 453 452 458 456 457
451 458 456 460 455 455 456 460 457 456
457 456 460 459 457 455 461 455 457 457

(a) Construct a frequency table and a corresponding relative frequency histogram.

(b) Do these data seem to come from a normal distribution with mean μ about equal to $\bar{x} = 456.2$ and variance about equal to $s^2 = 5.96$? Sketch the p.d.f. for the normal distribution $N(456.2, 5.96)$ on your histogram.

3.6-20. Nine measurements are taken on the strength of a certain metal. In order, they are 7.2, 8.9, 9.7, 10.5, 10.9, 11.7, 12.9, 13.9, 15.3, and these values correspond to the 10th, 20th, $\cdots$, 90th percentiles of this sample. Plot the measurements against the same percentiles of $N(0, 1)$. Does it seem reasonable that the underlying distribution of strengths could be normal?

3.6-21. The graphs of the moment-generating functions of three normal distributions—$N(0,1)$, $N(-1,1)$, and $N(2,1)$—are given in Figure 3.6-4(a). Identify them.

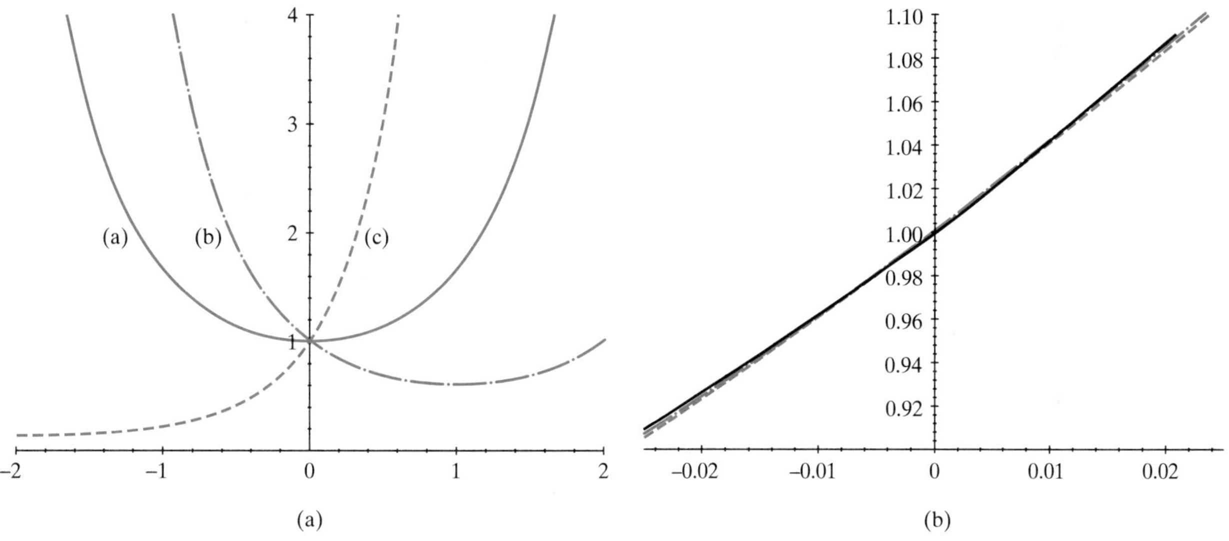

(a) (b)

FIGURE 3.6-4: Moment-generating functions

3.6-22. Figure 3.6-4(b) shows the graphs of the following three moment-generating functions:

$$g_1(t) = \frac{1}{1 - 4t}, \qquad t < 1/4,$$

$$g_2(t) = \frac{1}{(1 - 2t)^2}, \qquad t < 1/2,$$

$$g_3(t) = e^{4t + t^2/2}.$$

Why do these three graphs look so similar around $t = 0$?

3.6-23. The serum zinc level X in micrograms per deciliter for males between ages 15 and 17 has a distribution that is approximately normal with $\mu = 90$ and $\sigma = 15$. Compute the conditional probability $P(X > 120 \mid X > 105)$.

3.6-24. An interior automotive supplier places several electrical wires in a harness. A pull test measures the force required to pull spliced wires apart. A customer requires that each wire that is spliced into the harness withstand a pull force of 20 pounds. Let X equal the force required to pull the spliced wire apart. The following data give the values of a random sample of $n = 20$ observations of X:

28.8	24.4	30.1	25.6	26.4	23.9	22.1	22.5	27.6	28.1
20.8	27.7	24.4	25.1	24.6	26.3	28.2	22.2	26.3	24.4

(a) Construct a q–q plot, using the ordered array and the corresponding quantiles of $N(0, 1)$.

(b) Does it look like X has a normal distribution?

3.6-25. The "fill" problem is important in many industries, such as those making cereal, toothpaste, beer, and so on. If an industry claims that it is selling 12 ounces of its product in a container, it must have a mean greater than 12 ounces, or else the FDA will crack down, although the FDA will allow a very small percentage of the containers to have less than 12 ounces.

(a) If the content X of a container has a $N(12.1, \sigma^2)$ distribution, find σ so that $P(X < 12) = 0.01$.

(b) If $\sigma = 0.05$, find μ so that $P(X < 12) = 0.01$.

3.6-26. The ordered weights (in grams) of 24 bags of peanut M & M's, with a label weight of 49.2 g, are as follows:

52.3	53.6	54.0	54.1	54.4	54.5	54.7	55.2
55.4	55.4	55.5	55.7	55.9	56.1	56.5	56.5
57.0	57.0	57.3	57.3	57.3	57.8	59.6	59.7

(a) Calculate the sample mean and sample standard deviation of these weights.

(b) Construct a q–q plot, using the ordered weights and the percentiles of a standard normal distribution.

(c) Do these data look like they come from a normal distribution?

(d) Are the fill weights appropriate for this label weight?

3.6-27. Assume that the fill X of a filling machine for a beverage has a normal distribution with $\mu = 12.2$ and $\sigma = 0.1$, measured in fluid ounces.

(a) Compute $P(X < 12)$.

(b) In 50 independent such measurements, compute the probability that at least 1 is under 12 ounces.

3.7 ADDITIONAL MODELS

The binomial, Poisson, gamma, chi-square, and normal models are frequently used in statistics. However, many other interesting and very useful models can be found. We begin with a modification of one of the postulates of an approximate Poisson process as given in Section 2.6. In that definition, the numbers of changes occurring in nonoverlapping intervals are independent, and the probability of at least two changes in a sufficiently small interval is essentially zero. We continue to use these postulates, but now we say that the probability of exactly one change in a sufficiently short interval of length h is approximately λh, *where λ is a nonnegative function of the position of this interval.* To be explicit, say $p(x, w)$ is the probability of x changes in the interval $(0, w)$, $0 \le w$. Then the last postulate, in more formal terms, becomes

$$p(x + 1, w + h) - p(x, w) \approx \lambda(w)h,$$

where $\lambda(w)$ is a nonnegative function of w. This means that if we want the approximate probability of zero changes in the interval $(0, w + h)$, we could take, from the independence of the changes, the probability of zero changes in the interval $(0, w)$ times that of zero changes in the interval $(w, w + h)$. That is,

$$p(0, w + h) \approx p(0, w)[1 - \lambda(w)h],$$

because the probability of one or more changes in $(w, w + h)$ is about equal to $\lambda(w)h$. Equivalently,

$$\frac{p(0, w + h) - p(0, w)}{h} \approx -\lambda(w)p(0, w).$$

Taking limits as $h \to 0$, we have

$$D_w[p(0, w)] = -\lambda(w)p(0, w).$$

That is, the resulting differential equation is

$$\frac{D_w[p(0, w)]}{p(0, w)} = -\lambda(w);$$

thus,

$$\ln p(0, w) = -\int \lambda(w)\, dw + c_1.$$

Therefore,

$$p(0, w) = \exp\left[-\int \lambda(w)\, dw + c_1\right] = c_2 \exp\left[-\int \lambda(w)\, dw\right],$$

where $c_2 = e^{c_1}$. However, the boundary condition of the probability of zero changes in an interval of length zero must be 1; that is, $p(0,0) = 1$. So if we select

$$H(w) = \int \lambda(w)\, dw$$

to be such that $H(0) = 0$, then $c_2 = 1$. That is,

$$p(0, w) = e^{-H(w)},$$

where $H'(w) = \lambda(w)$ and $H(0) = 0$. Hence,

$$H(w) = \int_0^w \lambda(t)\, dt.$$

Suppose that we now let the continuous-type random variable W be the interval necessary to produce the first change. Then the distribution function of W is

$$G(w) = P(W \le w) = 1 - P(W > w), \qquad 0 \le w.$$

Because zero changes in the interval $(0, w)$ are the same as $W > w$, then

$$G(w) = 1 - p(0, w) = 1 - e^{-H(w)}, \qquad 0 \le w.$$

The p.d.f. of W is

$$g(w) = G'(w) = H'(w)e^{-H(w)} = \lambda(w) \exp\left[-\int_0^w \lambda(t)\, dt\right], \qquad 0 \le w.$$

From this formula, we see immediately that, in terms of $g(w)$ and $G(w)$,

$$\lambda(w) = \frac{g(w)}{1 - G(w)}.$$

In many applications of this result, W can be thought of as a random time interval. For example, if one change means "death" or "failure" of the item under consideration, then W is actually the length of life of the item. Usually $\lambda(w)$, which is commonly called the **failure rate** or **force of mortality**, is an increasing function of w. That is, the larger w (the older the item), the better is the chance of failure within a short interval of length h, namely, $\lambda(w)h$. As we review the exponential distribution of Section 3.4, we note that there $\lambda(w)$ is a constant; that is, the failure rate or force of mortality does not increase as the item gets older. If this were true in human populations, it would mean that a person 80 years old would have as much chance of living another year as would a person 20 years old (sort of a mathematical "fountain of youth"). However, a constant failure rate (force of mortality) is not the case in most human populations or in most populations of manufactured items. That is, the failure rate $\lambda(w)$ is usually an increasing function of w. We give two important examples of useful probabilistic models.

EXAMPLE 3.7-1 Let

$$H(w) = \left(\frac{w}{\beta}\right)^{\alpha}, \qquad 0 \le w,$$

so that the failure rate is

$$\lambda(w) = H'(w) = \frac{\alpha w^{\alpha-1}}{\beta^{\alpha}},$$

where $\alpha > 0, \beta > 0$. Then the p.d.f. of W is

$$g(w) = \frac{\alpha w^{\alpha-1}}{\beta^{\alpha}} \exp\left[-\left(\frac{w}{\beta}\right)^{\alpha}\right], \qquad 0 \le w.$$

Frequently, in engineering, this distribution, with appropriate values of α and β, is excellent for describing the life of a manufactured item. Often α is greater than 1 but less than 5. This p.d.f. is frequently called that of the **Weibull distribution** and, in model fitting, is a strong competitor of the gamma p.d.f.

The mean and variance of the Weibull distribution are

$$\mu = \beta\Gamma\left(1 + \frac{1}{\alpha}\right),$$

$$\sigma^2 = \beta^2\left[\Gamma\left(1 + \frac{2}{\alpha}\right) - \left\{\Gamma\left(1 + \frac{1}{\alpha}\right)\right\}^2\right].$$

Some graphs of Weibull p.d.f.s are shown in Figure 3.7-1. ■

EXAMPLE 3.7-2 People are often shocked to learn that human mortality increases almost exponentially once a person reaches 25 years of age. Depending on which mortality table is used, one finds that the increase is about 10% each year, which means that the rate of

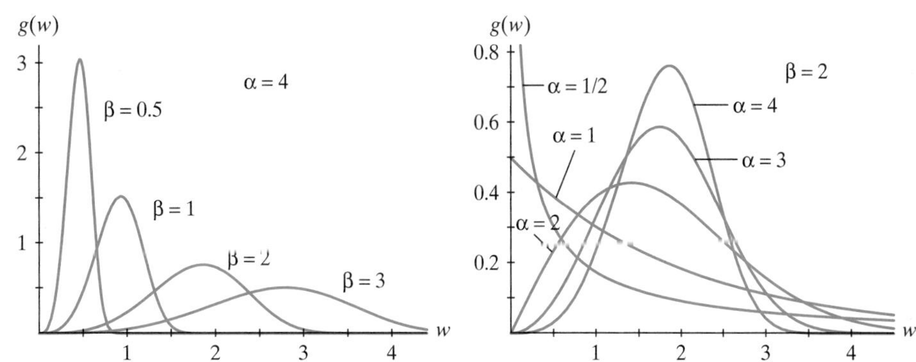

FIGURE 3.7-1: Weibull probability density functions

mortality will double about every 7 years. Although this fact can be shocking, we can be thankful that the force of mortality starts very low. The probability that a person in reasonably good health at age 63 dies within the next year is only about 1%. Now, assuming an exponential force of mortality, we have

$$\lambda(w) = H'(w) = ae^{bw}, \qquad a > 0,\ b > 0.$$

Thus,

$$H(w) = \int_0^w ae^{bt}\,dt = \frac{a}{b}e^{bw} - \frac{a}{b}.$$

Hence,

$$G(w) = 1 - \exp\left[-\frac{a}{b}e^{bw} + \frac{a}{b}\right], \qquad 0 \le w,$$

and

$$g(w) = ae^{bw}\exp\left[-\frac{a}{b}e^{bw} + \frac{a}{b}\right], \qquad 0 \le w,$$

are, respectively, the distribution function and the p.d.f. associated with the famous **Gompertz law** found in actuarial science. Some graphs of p.d.f.'s associated with the Gompertz law are shown in Figure 3.7-2. Note that the mode of the Gompertz distribution is $\ln(b/a)/b$. ■

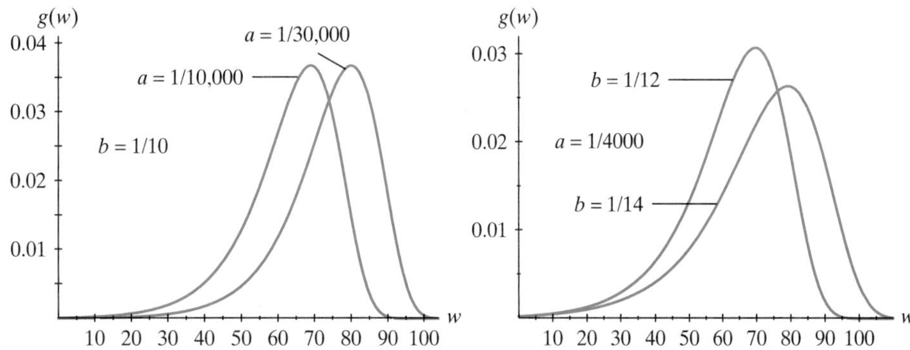

FIGURE 3.7-2: Gompertz law probability density functions

Both the gamma and Weibull distributions are skewed. In many studies (life testing, response times, incomes, etc.), these are valuable distributions for selecting a model.

Thus far we have considered random variables that are either discrete or continuous. In most applications these are the types that are encountered. However, on some occasions, combinations of the two types of random variables are found. That is, in some experiments, positive probability is assigned to each of certain points and also is spread over an interval of outcomes, each point of which has zero probability. An illustration will help clarify these remarks.

EXAMPLE 3.7-3 A bulb for a slide projector is tested by turning it on, letting it burn for 1 hour, and then turning it off. Let X equal the length of time that the bulb performs satisfactorily during this test. There is a positive probability that the bulb will burn out when it is turned on; hence,

$$0 < P(X = 0) < 1,$$

It could also burn out during the 1-hour period during which it is lit; thus,

$$P(0 < X < 1) > 0,$$

with $P(X = x) = 0$ when $x \in (0, 1)$. In addition, $P(X = 1) > 0$. The act of turning the bulb off after 1 hour so that the actual failure time beyond 1 hour is not observed is called censoring, a phenomenon that is considered later in this section. ■

The distribution function for a distribution of the **mixed type** will be a combination of those for the discrete and continuous types. That is, at each point of positive probability the distribution function will be discontinuous, so that the height of the step there equals the corresponding probability; at all other points the distribution function will be continuous.

EXAMPLE 3.7-4 Let X have a distribution function defined by

$$F(x) = \begin{cases} 0, & x < 0, \\ \dfrac{x^2}{4}, & 0 \le x < 1, \\ \dfrac{1}{2}, & 1 \le x < 2, \\ \dfrac{x}{3}, & 2 \le x < 3, \\ 1, & 3 \le x. \end{cases}$$

This distribution function is depicted in Figure 3.7-3 and can be used to compute probabilities. As an illustration, consider

$$P(0 < X < 1) = \frac{1}{4},$$

$$P(0 < X \le 1) = \frac{1}{2},$$

$$P(X = 1) = \frac{1}{4}.$$

■

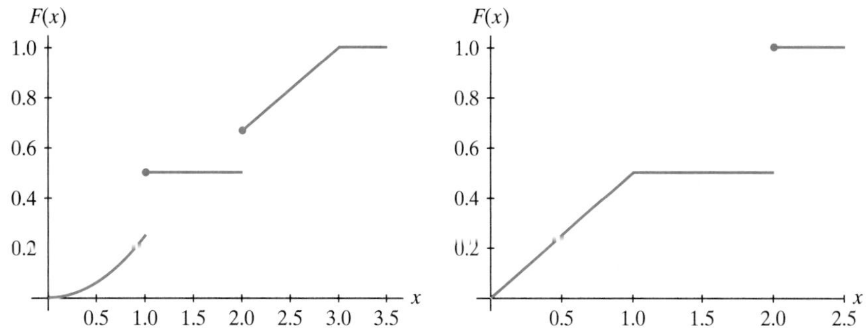

FIGURE 3.7-3: Mixed distribution functions

EXAMPLE 3.7-5 Consider the following game: An unbiased coin is tossed. If the outcome is heads, the player receives \$2. If the outcome is tails, the player spins a balanced spinner that has a scale from 0 to 1. The player then receives that fraction of a dollar associated with the point selected by the spinner. If X denotes the amount received, the space of X is $S = [0,1) \cup \{2\}$. The distribution function of X is defined by

$$F(x) = \begin{cases} 0, & x < 0, \\ \dfrac{x}{2}, & 0 \le x < 1, \\ \dfrac{1}{2}, & 1 \le x < 2, \\ 1, & 2 \le x. \end{cases}$$

The graph of the distribution function $F(x)$ is given in Figure 3.7-3. ■

Suppose that the random variable X has a distribution of the mixed type. To find the expectation of the function $u(X)$ of X, a combination of a sum and a Riemann integral is used, as shown in Example 3.7-6.

EXAMPLE 3.7-6 We shall find the mean and variance of the random variable given in Example 3.7-4. Note that there, $F'(x) = x/2$ when $0 < x < 1$ and $F'(x) = 1/3$ when $2 < x < 3$; also, $P(X = 1) = 1/4$ and $P(X = 2) = 1/6$. Accordingly, we have

$$\begin{aligned} \mu = E(X) &= \int_0^1 x\left(\frac{x}{2}\right)dx + 1\left(\frac{1}{4}\right) + 2\left(\frac{1}{6}\right) + \int_2^3 x\left(\frac{1}{3}\right)dx \\ &= \left[\frac{x^3}{6}\right]_0^1 + \frac{1}{4} + \frac{1}{3} + \left[\frac{x^2}{6}\right]_2^3 \\ &= \frac{19}{12} \end{aligned}$$

and

$$\begin{aligned} \sigma^2 &= E(X^2) - [E(X)]^2 \\ &= \int_0^1 x^2\left(\frac{x}{2}\right)dx + 1^2\left(\frac{1}{4}\right) + 2^2\left(\frac{1}{6}\right) + \int_2^3 x^2\left(\frac{1}{3}\right)dx - \left(\frac{19}{12}\right)^2 \\ &= \frac{31}{48}. \end{aligned}$$

■

Frequently, in life testing, we know that the length of life—say, X—exceeds the number b, but the exact value of X is unknown. This phenomenon is called **censoring**. It can happen, for instance, when a subject in a cancer study simply disappears; the investigator knows that the subject has lived a certain number of months, but the exact length of the subject's life is unknown. Or it might happen when an investigator does not have enough time to observe the moments of deaths of all the animals—say, rats—in some study. Censoring can also occur in the insurance industry, in the case of a loss with a limited-pay policy in which the top amount is exceeded but it is not known by how much.

EXAMPLE 3.7-7 Reinsurance companies are concerned with large losses because they might agree, for example, to cover losses due to wind damages that are between \$2 million and \$10 million. Say that X equals the size of a wind loss in millions of dollars, and suppose that X has the distribution function

$$F(x) = 1 - \left(\frac{10}{10 + x}\right)^3, \qquad 0 \le x < \infty.$$

If losses beyond \$10 million are reported only as 10, then $Y = X$, $X \le 10$, and $Y = 10$, $X > 10$, and the distribution function of this censored distribution is

$$G(y) = \begin{cases} 1 - \left(\dfrac{10}{10 + y}\right)^3, & 0 \le y < 10, \\ 1, & 10 \le y < \infty, \end{cases}$$

which has a jump of $[10/(10 + 10)]^3 = 1/8$ at $y = 10$. ■

EXAMPLE 3.7-8 A car worth 24 units (1 unit = \$1,000) is insured for a year with a one-unit deductible policy. The probability of no damage in a year is 0.95 and the probability of being totaled is 0.01. If the damage is partial, with probability 0.04, then this damage follows the p.d.f.

$$f(x) = \frac{25}{24}\,\frac{1}{(x + 1)^2}, \qquad 0 < x < 24.$$

In computing the expected payment, the insurance company recognizes that it will make zero payment if $X \le 1$, $24 - 1 = 23$ if the car is totaled, and $X - 1$ if $1 < X < 24$. Thus, the expected payment is

$$(0)(0.95) + (0)(0.04)\int_0^1 \frac{25}{24}\,\frac{1}{(x + 1)^2}\,dx + (23)(0.01) + (0.04)\int_1^{24} (x - 1)\frac{25}{24}\,\frac{1}{(x + 1)^2}\,dx.$$

That is, the answer is

$$0.23 + (0.04)(1.67) = 0.297,$$

because the last integral is equal to

$$\int_1^{24} (x + 1 - 2)\frac{25}{24}\frac{1}{(x + 1)^2}\,dx = (-2)\int_1^{24} \frac{25}{24}\frac{1}{(x + 1)^2}\,dx + \int_1^{24} \frac{25}{24}\frac{1}{(x + 1)}\,dx$$

$$= (-2)\left[\frac{25}{24}\frac{-1}{(x + 1)}\right]_1^{24} + \left[\frac{25}{24}\ln(x + 1)\right]_1^{24}$$

$$= 1.67.$$

■

EXERCISES

3.7-1. Let the life W (in years) of the usual family car have a Weibull distribution with $\alpha = 2$.

(a) Show that β must equal 10 for $P(W > 5) = e^{1/4} \approx 0.7788$.
HINT: $P(W > 5) = e^{-H(5)}$.

(b) Take a sample of size 8 from the uniform distribution $U(0, 1)$, and simulate eight values from the Weibull $(\alpha = 2, \beta = 10)$ distribution. HINT: You may use the random-number table. Also, recall that if U has that uniform distribution, then $F^{-1}(U)$ has a distribution with distribution function F.

3.7-2. Suppose that the length W of a human life does follow the Gompertz distribution with $\lambda(w) = a(1.1)^w = ae^{(\ln 1.1)w}$, $P(63 < W < 64) = 0.01$. Determine the constant a and then find $P(W \le 71 \mid 70 < W)$.

3.7-3. Let Y_1 be the smallest observation of three independent random variables W_1, W_2, W_3, each with a Weibull distribution with parameters α and β. Show that Y_1 has a Weibull distribution. What are the parameters of this latter distribution?
HINT:

$$G(y_1) = P(Y_1 \le y_1) = 1 - P(y_1 < W_i,\ i = 1, 2, 3) = 1 - [P(y_1 < W_1)]^3.$$

3.7-4. A frequent force of mortality used in actuarial science is $\lambda(w) = ae^{bw} + c$. Find the distribution function and p.d.f. associated with this **Makeham's law**.

3.7-5. From the graph of the first distribution function of X in Figure 3.7-4, determine the indicated probabilities:

(a) $P(X < 0)$. (b) $P(X < -1)$. (c) $P(X \le -1)$.

(d) $P(X < 1)$. (e) $P\left(-1 \le X < \frac{1}{2}\right)$. (f) $P(-1 < X \le 1)$.

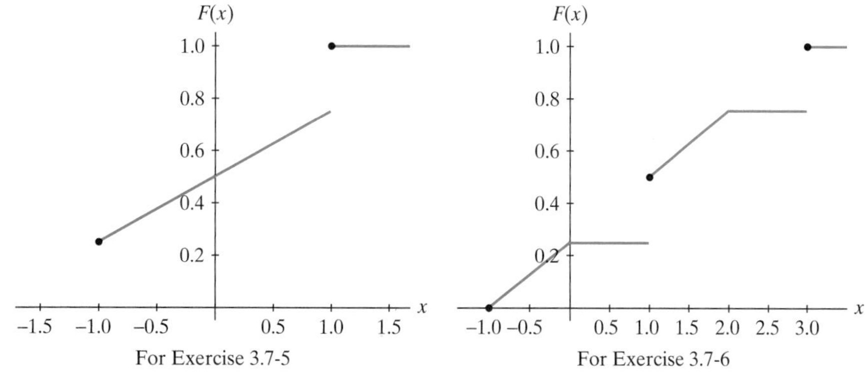

FIGURE 3.7-4: Mixed distribution functions

3.7-6. Determine the indicated probabilities from the graph of the second distribution function of X in Figure 3.7-4:

(a) $P\left(-\frac{1}{2} \le X \le \frac{1}{2}\right)$. (b) $P\left(\frac{1}{2} < X < 1\right)$. (c) $P\left(\frac{3}{4} < X < 2\right)$.

(d) $P(X > 1)$. (e) $P(2 < X < 3)$. (f) $P(2 < X \le 3)$.

3.7-7. Let X be a random variable of the mixed type having the distribution function

$$F(x) = \begin{cases} 0, & x < 0, \\ \dfrac{x^2}{4}, & 0 \le x < 1, \\ \dfrac{x+1}{4}, & 1 \le x < 2, \\ 1, & 2 \le x. \end{cases}$$

(a) Carefully sketch the graph of $F(x)$.
(b) Find the mean and the variance of X.
(c) Find $P(1/4 < X < 1)$, $P(X = 1)$, $P(X = 1/2)$, and $P(1/2 \le X < 2)$.

3.7-8. Find the mean and variance of X if the distribution function of X is

$$F(x) = \begin{cases} 0, & x < 0, \\ 1 - \left(\dfrac{2}{3}\right)e^{-x}, & 0 \le x, \end{cases}$$

3.7-9. Consider the following game: A fair die is rolled. If the outcome is even, the player receives a number of dollars equal to the outcome on the die. If the outcome is odd, a number is selected at random from the interval $(0, 1)$ with a balanced spinner, and the player receives that fraction of a dollar associated with the point selected.

(a) Define and sketch the distribution function of X, the amount received.
(b) Find the expected value of X.
(c) Simulate 10 plays of this game.
(d) Is the average of your 10 plays close to the expected value calculated in part (b)?

3.7-10. The weekly gravel demand X (in tons) follows the p.d.f.

$$f(x) = \left(\frac{1}{5}\right)e^{-x/5}, \qquad 0 < x < \infty.$$

However, the owner of the gravel pit can produce at most only 4 tons of gravel per week. Compute the expected value of the tons sold per week by the owner.

3.7-11. The lifetime X of a certain device has an exponential distribution with mean five years. However, the device is not observed on a continuous basis until after three years. Hence, we actually observe $Y = \max(X, 3)$. Compute $E(Y)$.

3.7-12. Let X have an exponential distribution with $\theta = 1$; that is, the p.d.f. of X is $f(x) = e^{-x}$, $0 < x < \infty$. Let T be defined by $T = \ln X$, so that the distribution function of T is

$$G(t) = P(\ln X \le t) = P(X \le e^t).$$

(a) Show that the p.d.f. of T is

$$g(t) = e^t e^{-e^t}, \qquad -\infty < x < \infty,$$

which is the p.d.f. of an extreme-value distribution.

(b) Let W be defined by $T = \alpha + \beta \ln W$, where $-\infty < \alpha < \infty$ and $\beta > 0$. Show that W has a Weibull distribution.

3.7-13. A loss X on a car has a mixed distribution with $p = 0.95$ on zero and $p = 0.05$ on an exponential distribution with mean of \$5000. If the loss X on a car is greater than the deductible of \$500, the difference $X - 500$ is paid to the owner of the car. Considering zero (if $X \le 500$) as a possible payment, determine the mean and the standard deviation of the payment.

3.7-14. A customer buys a \$1000 deductible policy on her \$31,000 car. The probability of having an accident in which the loss is greater than \$1000 is 0.03, and then that loss, as a fraction of the value of the car minus the deductible, has the p.d.f. $f(x) = 6(1 - x)^5$, $0 < x < 1$.

(a) What is the probability that the insurance company must pay the customer more than \$2000?
(b) What does the company expect to pay?

3.7-15. A certain machine has a life X that has an exponential distribution with mean 10. The warranty is such that 100% of the price is returned if the machine fails in the first year, 50% of the price is returned for a failure during the second year, and nothing is returned after that. If the machine cost \$2500, what are the expected value and the standard deviation of the return on the warranty?

3.7-16. A certain machine has a life X that has an exponential distribution with mean 10. The warranty is such that \$$m$ is returned if the machine fails in the first year, $(0.5)m$ of the price is returned for a failure during the second year, and nothing is returned after that. If the machine cost \$2500, find m so that the expected payment is \$200.

3.7-17. Some dental insurance policies cover the insurer only up to a certain amount, say, M. (This seems to us to be a dumb type of insurance policy because most people should want to protect themselves against large losses.) Say the dental expense X is a random variable with p.d.f. $f(x) = (0.001)e^{-x/1000}$, $0 < x < \infty$. Find M so that $P(X < M) = 0.08$.

3.7-18. The time X to failure of a machine has p.d.f. $f(x) = (x/4)^3 e^{-(x/4)^4}$, $0 < x < \infty$. Compute $P(X > 5 \mid X > 4)$.

3.7-19. Some banks now compound daily, but report only on a quarterly basis. It seems to us that it would be easier to compound every instant, for then a dollar invested at an annual rate of i for t years would be worth e^{ti}. (You might find it interesting to prove this statement by taking the limit of $(1 + i/n)^{nt}$ as $n \to \infty$.) If X is a random rate with p.d.f. $f(x) = ce^{-x}$, $0.04 < x < 0.08$, find the p.d.f. of the value of one dollar after three years invested at the rate of X.

3.7-20. Let X be the failure time (in months) of a certain insulating material. The distribution of X is modeled by the p.d.f.

$$f(x) = \frac{2x}{50^2}\, e^{-(x/50)^2}, \qquad 0 < x < \infty.$$

Find

(a) $P(40 < X < 60)$,
(b) $P(X > 80)$.

3.7-21. Sometimes the failure rate of an item is exponential, like $\lambda(x) = ae^{bx}$, where $a > 0$ and $b > 0$. The corresponding distribution function is

$$F(x) = 1 - \exp\left[-(a/b)(e^{bx} - 1)\right], \quad 0 < x < \infty,$$

and the p.d.f. is

$$f(x) = ae^{bx} \exp\left[-(a/b)(e^{bx} - 1)\right], \quad 0 < x < \infty.$$

Actuaries frequently use $f(x)$ as a good model for the length X of a life of a human. Find a and b so that $P(X < 70) = 0.4$ and $P(X < 78) = 0.6$. What is the mode of the resulting distribution? (See Figure 3.7-2.)

3.7-22. Let Y, with p.d.f. $f(y)$ and c.d.f. $F(y)$, be a random variable that represents the length of life (of a product, of a human, etc.). Given that the life exceeds some number x, the expected length of the remaining life is given by

$$e(x) = \frac{\int_x^\infty (y - x)f(y)\,dy}{1 - F(x)},$$

since $f(y)/[1 - F(x)]$ is the conditional p.d.f. of Y, when $Y > x$. The function $e(x)$ is called the **mean residual life**. For each of the following probability density functions, compute the mean residual life.

(a) $f(y) = \dfrac{1}{100}, \qquad 0 < y < 100,$
(b) $f(y) = \dfrac{50}{y^2}, \qquad 50 < y < \infty,$
(c) $f(y) = \dfrac{1}{75} e^{-y/75}, \qquad 0 < y < \infty.$

3.7-23. Suppose the birth weight (X) in grams of U.S. infants has an approximate Weibull model with p.d.f.

$$f(x) = \frac{3x^2}{3500^3}\, e^{-(x/3500)^3}, \qquad 0 < x < \infty.$$

Given that a birth weight is greater than 3000, what is the conditional probability that it exceeds 4000?

HISTORICAL COMMENTS In this chapter we studied several continuous distributions, including the very important normal distribution. Actually, the true importance of the normal distribution is given in Chapter 5, where we consider the central limit theorem and its generalizations. Together, that theorem and its generalizations imply that the sum of several random influences on some measurement suggests that the measurement has an approximate normal distribution. For example, in a study of the length of chicken eggs, different hens produce different eggs, the person measuring the eggs makes a difference, the way the egg is placed in a "holder" is a factor, the caliper used is important, and so on. Thus, the length of an egg might have an approximate normal distribution.

Sometimes instructors force grades to be normally distributed because they "grade on a (normal) curve." This is done too often, and it means that a certain percentage of the students should get A's, a certain percentage B's, etc. We believe that all students should be able to earn A's if they satisfy certain appropriate criteria. Thus, we think that it is wrong to restrict grades to a normal curve.

The normal distribution is symmetric, but many important distributions, like the gamma and Weibull, are skewed. We learned that the Weibull distribution has a failure rate equal to $\lambda(x) = \alpha x^{\alpha-1}/\beta^{\alpha}$, for $\alpha \geq 1$, and this distribution is appropriate for the length of the life of many manufactured products. It is interesting to note that if $\alpha = 1$, the failure rate is a constant, meaning that an old part is as good as a new one. If this were true for the lives of humans, an old man would have the same chance of living 50 more years as would a young man. That is, we would have a "mathematical fountain of youth." Unfortunately, as we learned in this chapter, the failure rate of humans is increasing with age and is close to being exponential (say, $\lambda(x) = ae^{bx}$, $a > 0$, $b > 0$), leading to the Gompertz distribution. As a matter of fact, most would find that force of mortality is such that it increases about 10 percent each year; so by the rule of 72, it would double about every $72/10 = 7.2$ years. (See Equation D.4-1 in Appendix D on the CD-ROM.) Fortunately, it is very small for persons in their twenties.

The reason we try to model any random phenomenon with a probability distribution is that if our model is reasonably good, we know the approximate percentages of being above or below certain marks. Having such information helps us make certain decisions—sometimes very important ones.

With these models, we learned how to simulate random variables having certain distributions. In many situations in practice, we cannot calculate exact solutions of equations that have numerous random variables. Thus, we simulate the random variables in question many times, leading to an approximate distribution of the random solution. "Monte Carlo" is a term often attached to such a simulation, and we believe that it was first used in a computer simulation of nuclear fission associated with the atom bomb in World War II. Of course, the name "Monte Carlo" was taken from that city, which is famous for gambling in its casinos.

Also in this chapter, we studied certain averages, including the mean of a distribution and a random sample. There is a story that statisticians tell about Ralph Sampson, who was an excellent basketball player at the University of Virginia in the early 1980s and later was drafted by the Houston Rockets. He supposedly majored in communication studies at Virginia, and it is reported that the department there said that the average starting salary of their majors was much higher than those in the sciences; that happened because of Sampson's high starting salary with the Rockets. If this story is true, it would have been much more appropriate to report the median starting salary of the communication majors and this median salary would have been much lower than the median starting salaries in the sciences.

The famous statistician John Tukey died a few years ago. Not only did he originate stem-and-leaf displays, but he also coined the terms "software" (as opposed to hardware) and "bit" (for binary digit). He rediscovered and made popular the fast Fourier transform. However, one of his notable quotes was "Far better an approximate answer to the right question, which is often vague, than the exact answer to the wrong question, which can always be made precise." We think that he was taking a crack at pure mathematicians, although Tukey was excellent in math, too.

We close these remarks with an observation about Sir Francis Galton, who everyone agrees was a great scientist. However, he contributed to statistics as well. One of his rules was "Whenever you can, count." Some might say that, on the basis of the data he collected, he was the first statistician, although that would be difficult to prove, as many before him collected lots of important data.

Bivariate Distributions

CHAPTER

4

4.1 DISTRIBUTIONS OF TWO RANDOM VARIABLES
4.2 THE CORRELATION COEFFICIENT
4.3 CONDITIONAL DISTRIBUTIONS
4.4 THE BIVARIATE NORMAL DISTRIBUTION

4.1 DISTRIBUTIONS OF TWO RANDOM VARIABLES

So far, we have taken only one measurement on a single item under observation. However, it is clear in many practical cases that it is possible, and often very desirable, to take more than one measurement of a random observation. Suppose, for example, that we are observing female college students to obtain information about some of their physical characteristics, such as height, x, and weight, y, because we are trying to determine a relationship between those two characteristics. For instance, there may be some pattern between height and weight that can be described by an appropriate curve $y = u(x)$. Certainly, not all the points observed will be on this curve, but we want to attempt to find the "best" curve to describe the relationship and then say something about the variation of the points around the curve.

Another example might concern high school rank—say, x—and the ACT (or SAT) score, say, y—of incoming college students. What is the relationship between these two characteristics? More importantly, how can we use those measurements to predict a third one, such as first-year college GPA—say, z—with a function $z = v(x, y)$? This is a very important problem for college admission offices, particularly when it comes to awarding an athletic scholarship, because the incoming student–athlete must satisfy certain conditions before receiving such an award.

REMARK We begin with bivariate distributions for the discrete case. The continuous case is essentially the same, but with integrals replacing summations. ■

DEFINITION 4.1-1 Let X and Y be two random variables defined on a discrete probability space. Let S denote the corresponding two-dimensional space of X and Y, the two random variables of the discrete type. The probability that $X = x$ and $Y = y$ is denoted by $f(x, y) = P(X = x, Y = y)$. The function $f(x, y)$ is called the **joint probability mass function** (joint p.m.f.) of X and Y and has the following properties:

(a) $0 \le f(x, y) \le 1$.

(b) $\displaystyle\sum_{(x,y)\in S}\sum f(x, y) = 1$.

(c) $P[(X, Y) \in A] = \displaystyle\sum_{(x,y)\in A}\sum f(x, y)$, where A is a subset of the space S.

The following example will make this definition more meaningful.

EXAMPLE 4.1-1 Roll a pair of unbiased dice. For each of the 36 sample points with probability 1/36, let X denote the smaller and Y the larger outcome on the dice. For example, if the outcome is $(3, 2)$, then the observed values are $X = 2$, $Y = 3$. The event $\{X = 2, Y = 3\}$ could occur in one of two ways—$(3, 2)$ or $(2, 3)$—so its probability is

$$\frac{1}{36} + \frac{1}{36} = \frac{2}{36}.$$

If the outcome is $(2, 2)$, then the observed values are $X = 2$, $Y = 2$. Since the event $\{X = 2, Y = 2\}$ can occur in only one way, $P(X = 2, Y = 2) = 1/36$. The joint p.m.f. of X and Y is given by the probabilities

$$f(x,y) = \begin{cases} \dfrac{1}{36}, & 1 \le x = y \le 6, \\[2ex] \dfrac{2}{36}, & 1 \le x < y \le 6, \end{cases}$$

when x and y are integers. Figure 4.1-1 depicts the probabilities of the various points of the space S. ■

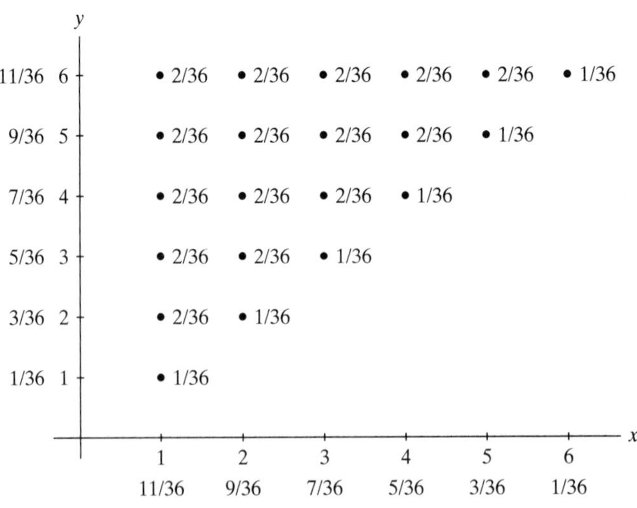

FIGURE 4.1-1: Discrete joint p.m.f.

Notice that certain numbers have been recorded in the bottom and left-hand margins of Figure 4.1-1. These numbers are the respective column and row totals of the probabilities. The column totals are the respective probabilities that X will assume the values in the x space $S_1 = \{1,2,3,4,5,6\}$, and the row totals are the respective probabilities that Y will assume the values in the y space $S_2 = \{1,2,3,4,5,6\}$. That is, the totals describe probability mass functions of X and Y, respectively. Since each collection of these probabilities is frequently recorded in the margins and satisfies the properties of a p.m.f. of one random variable, each is called a **marginal p.m.f.**

DEFINITION 4.1-2

Let X and Y have the joint probability mass function $f(x, y)$ with space S. The probability mass function of X alone, which is called the **marginal probability mass function of** X, is defined by

$$f_1(x) = \sum_y f(x, y) = P(X = x), \qquad x \in S_1,$$

where the summation is taken over all possible y values for each given x in the x space S_1. That is, the summation is over all (x, y) in S with a given x value. Similarly, the **marginal probability mass function of** Y is defined by

$$f_2(y) = \sum_x f(x, y) = P(Y = y), \qquad y \in S_2,$$

where the summation is taken over all possible x values for each given y in the y space S_2. The random variables X and Y are **independent** if and only if

$$P(X = x, Y = y) \equiv P(X = x)P(Y = y)$$

or, equivalently,

$$f(x,y) \equiv f_1(x)f_2(y), \qquad x \in S_1, \qquad y \in S_2;$$

otherwise X and Y are said to be **dependent**.

We note in Example 4.1-1 that X and Y are dependent because there are many x and y values for which $f(x,y) \neq f_1(x)f_2(y)$. For instance,

$$f_1(1)f_2(1) = \left(\frac{11}{36}\right)\left(\frac{1}{36}\right) \neq \frac{1}{36} = f(1, 1).$$

EXAMPLE 4.1-2

Let the joint p.m.f. of X and Y be defined by

$$f(x, y) = \frac{x + y}{21}, \qquad x = 1,2,3, \qquad y = 1,2.$$

Then

$$f_1(x) = \sum_y f(x, y) = \sum_{y=1}^{2} \frac{x + y}{21}$$

$$= \frac{x + 1}{21} + \frac{x + 2}{21} = \frac{2x + 3}{21}, \qquad x = 1,2,3,$$

and

$$f_2(y) = \sum_x f(x, y) = \sum_{x=1}^{3} \frac{x + y}{21} = \frac{6 + 3y}{21}, \qquad y = 1, 2.$$

Note that both $f_1(x)$ and $f_2(y)$ satisfy the properties of a probability mass function. Since $f(x,y) \not\equiv f_1(x)f_2(y)$, X and Y are dependent. ■

EXAMPLE 4.1-3 Let the joint p.m.f. of X and Y be

$$f(x,y) = \frac{xy^2}{30}, \qquad x = 1, 2, 3, \qquad y = 1, 2.$$

The marginal probability mass functions are

$$f_1(x) = \sum_{y=1}^{2} \frac{xy^2}{30} = \frac{x}{6}, \qquad x = 1, 2, 3,$$

and

$$f_2(y) = \sum_{x=1}^{3} \frac{xy^2}{30} = \frac{y^2}{5}, \qquad y = 1, 2.$$

Then $f(x,y) \equiv f_1(x)f_2(y)$ for $x = 1, 2, 3$ and $y = 1, 2$; thus, X and Y are independent. (See Figure 4.1-2.) ■

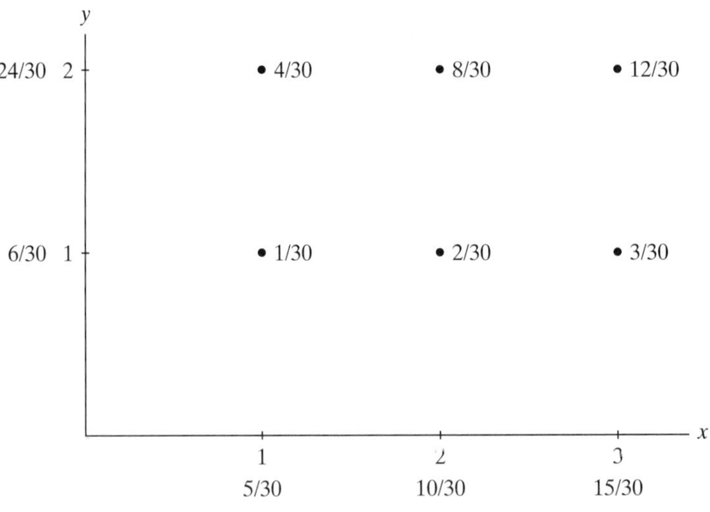

FIGURE 4.1-2: Joint p.m.f. $f(x,y) = \frac{xy^2}{30}$, $x = 1, 2, 3$; $y = 1, 2$

EXAMPLE 4.1-4 Let the joint p.m.f. of X and Y be

$$f(x, y) = \frac{xy^2}{13}, \qquad (x, y) = (1, 1), (1, 2), (2, 2).$$

Then the p.m.f. of X is

$$f_1(x) = \begin{cases} \dfrac{5}{13}, & x = 1, \\ \dfrac{8}{13}, & x = 2, \end{cases}$$

and that of Y is

$$f_2(y) = \begin{cases} \dfrac{1}{13}, & y = 1, \\ \dfrac{12}{13}, & y = 2. \end{cases}$$

X and Y are dependent because $f(x, y) \not\equiv f_1(x)f_2(y)$ for $x = 1, 2$ and $y = 1, 2$. ■

Note that in Example 4.1-4 the support S of X and Y is "triangular." Whenever the support S is not "rectangular," the random variables must be dependent, because S cannot then equal the product set $\{(x, y) : x \in S_1, y \in S_2\}$. That is, if we observe that the support S of X and Y is not a product set, then X and Y must be dependent. For example, in Example 4.1-4, X and Y are dependent because $S = \{(1, 1), (1, 2), (2, 2)\}$ is not a product set. On the other hand, if S equals the product set $\{(x, y): x \in S_1, y \in S_2\}$ and if the formula for $f(x, y)$ is the product of an expression in x alone and an expression in y alone, then X and Y are independent, as shown in Example 4.1-3. Example 4.1-2 illustrates the fact that the support can be rectangular but the formula for $f(x, y)$ is not such a product and thus X and Y are dependent.

It is possible to define a probability histogram for a joint p.m.f. just as we did for a p.m.f. for a single random variable. Suppose that X and Y have a joint p.m.f. $f(x, y)$ with space S, where S is a set of pairs of integers. At a point (x, y) in S, construct a "rectangular column" that is centered at (x, y) and has a one-unit-by-one-unit base and a height equal to $f(x, y)$. Note that $f(x, y)$ is equal to the "volume" of this rectangular column. Furthermore, the sum of the volumes of the rectangular columns in this probability histogram is equal to 1.

EXAMPLE 4.1-5 Let the joint p.m.f. of X and Y be

$$f(x,y) = \frac{xy^2}{30}, \qquad x = 1,2,3, \qquad y = 1,2.$$

The probability histogram is shown in Figure 4.1-3 on the next page. ■

Sometimes it is convenient to replace the symbols X and Y representing random variables by X_1 and X_2. This is particularly true in situations in which we have more than two random variables; so we use X and Y sometimes and then X_1 and X_2 at other times. The reader will see the advantage of the use of subscripts as we go further in the text.

Let X_1 and X_2 be random variables of the discrete type with the joint p.m.f. $f(x_1, x_2)$ on the space S. If $u(X_1, X_2)$ is a function of these two random variables, then

$$E[u(X_1, X_2)] = \sum\sum_{(x_1,x_2)\in S} u(x_1, x_2)f(x_1, x_2),$$

if it exists, is called the **mathematical expectation** (or **expected value**) of $u(X_1, X_2)$.

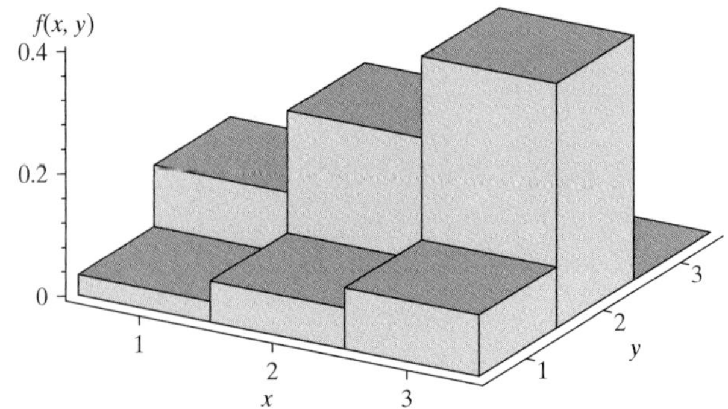

FIGURE 4.1-3: Joint p.m.f. $f(x,y) = \frac{xy^2}{30}$, $x = 1,2,3;\ y = 1,2$

REMARK The same remarks can be made here that were made in the univariate case, namely, that

$$\sum\sum_{(x_1,x_2)\in S} |u(x_1, x_2)| f(x_1, x_2)$$

must converge and be finite. Also, $Y = u(X_1, X_2)$ is a random variable—say, with p.m.f. $g(y)$ on space S_1—and it is true that

$$\sum\sum_{(x_1,x_2)\in S} u(x_1, x_2) f(x_1, x_2) = \sum_{y\in S_1} y g(y).$$

■

EXAMPLE 4.1-6 There are eight similar chips in a bowl: three marked (0, 0), two marked (1, 0), two marked (0, 1), and one marked (1, 1). A player selects a chip at random and is given the sum of the two coordinates in dollars. If X_1 and X_2 represent those two coordinates, respectively, their joint p.m.f. is

$$f(x_1, x_2) = \frac{3 - x_1 - x_2}{8}, \qquad x_1 = 0, 1 \qquad \text{and} \qquad x_2 = 0, 1.$$

Thus,

$$\begin{aligned} E(X_1 + X_2) &= \sum_{x_2=0}^{1} \sum_{x_1=0}^{1} (x_1 + x_2) \frac{3 - x_1 - x_2}{8} \\ &= (0)\left(\frac{3}{8}\right) + (1)\left(\frac{2}{8}\right) + (1)\left(\frac{2}{8}\right) + (2)\left(\frac{1}{8}\right) = \frac{3}{4}. \end{aligned}$$

That is, the expected payoff is 75¢. ■

The following mathematical expectations, if they exist, have special names:

(a) If $u_1(X_1, X_2) = X_i$, then

$$E[u_1(X_1, X_2)] = E(X_i) = \mu_i$$

is called the **mean** of X_i, $i = 1, 2$.

(b) If $u_2(X_1, X_2) = (X_i - \mu_i)^2$, then

$$E[u_2(X_1, X_2)] = E[(X_i - \mu_i)^2] = \sigma_i^2 = \mathrm{Var}(X_i)$$

is called the **variance** of X_i, $i = 1, 2$.

The mean μ_i and the variance σ_i^2 can be computed from the joint p.m.f. $f(x_1, x_2)$ or the marginal p.m.f. $f_i(x_i)$, $i = 1, 2$.

The idea of joint distributions of two random variables of the discrete type can be extended to that of two random variables of the continuous type. The definitions are really the same, except that integrals replace summations. The **joint probability density function** (joint p.d.f.) of two continuous-type random variables is an integrable function $f(x, y)$ with the following properties:

(a) $f(x, y) \geq 0$, where $f(x, y) = 0$ when (x, y) is not in the support (space) S of X and Y.

(b) $\int_{-\infty}^{\infty}\int_{-\infty}^{\infty} f(x, y)\,dx\,dy = 1$.

(c) $P[(X, Y) \in A] = \displaystyle\int\!\!\int_A f(x, y)\,dx\,dy$, where $\{(X, Y) \in A\}$ is an event defined in the plane.

Property (c) implies that $P[(X, Y) \in A]$ is the volume of the solid over the region A in the xy-plane and bounded by the surface $z = f(x, y)$.

EXAMPLE 4.1-7 Let X and Y have the joint p.d.f.

$$f(x, y) = \frac{3}{2}x^2(1 - |y|), \qquad -1 < x < 1, \qquad -1 < y < 1.$$

The graph of $z = f(x, y)$ is given in Figure 4.1-4. Let $A = \{(x, y) : 0 < x < 1, 0 < y < x\}$. Then the probability that (X, Y) falls into A is given by

$$\begin{aligned} P[(X, Y) \in A] &= \int_0^1 \int_0^x \frac{3}{2}x^2(1 - y)\,dy\,dx = \int_0^1 \frac{3}{2}x^2\left[y - \frac{y^2}{2}\right]_0^x dx \\ &= \int_0^1 \frac{3}{2}\left(x^3 - \frac{x^4}{2}\right) dx = \frac{3}{2}\left[\frac{x^4}{4} - \frac{x^5}{10}\right]_0^1 \\ &= \frac{9}{40}. \end{aligned}$$

■

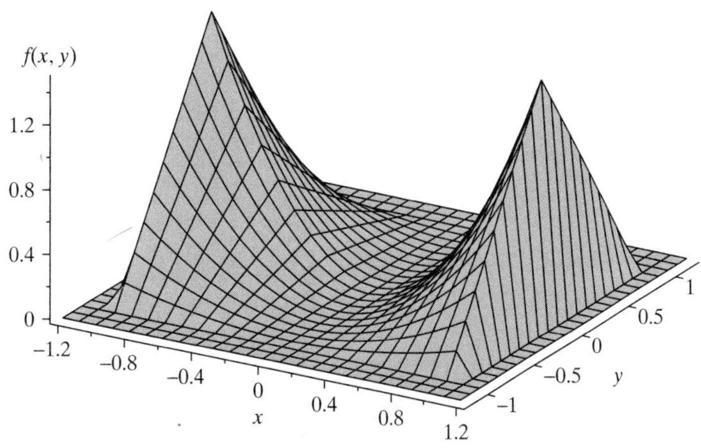

FIGURE 4.1-4: Joint p.d.f. $f(x, y) = \frac{3}{2}x^2(1 - |y|)$

The respective **marginal p.d.f.'s** of continuous-type random variables X and Y are given by

$$f_1(x) = \int_{-\infty}^{\infty} f(x,y)\,dy, \qquad x \in S_1,$$

and

$$f_2(y) = \int_{-\infty}^{\infty} f(x,y)\,dx, \qquad y \in S_2,$$

where S_1 and S_2 are the respective spaces of X and Y. The definitions associated with mathematical expectations in the continuous case are the same as those associated with the discrete case after replacing the summations with integrations.

For the random variables X and Y in Example 4.1-7, the marginal p.d.f.'s are

$$f_1(x) = \int_{-1}^{1} \frac{3}{2}x^2(1 - |y|)\,dy = \frac{3}{2}x^2, \qquad -1 < x < 1,$$

and

$$f_2(y) = \int_{-1}^{1} \frac{3}{2}x^2(1 - |y|)\,dx = 1 - |y|, \qquad -1 < y < 1.$$

EXAMPLE 4.1-8 Let X and Y have the joint p.d.f.

$$f(x,y) = 2, \qquad 0 \le x \le y \le 1.$$

Then $S = \{(x,y): 0 \le x \le y \le 1\}$ is the support; for example,

$$P\left(0 \le X \le \frac{1}{2}, 0 \le Y \le \frac{1}{2}\right) = P\left(0 \le X \le Y, 0 \le Y \le \frac{1}{2}\right)$$

$$= \int_0^{1/2}\int_0^{y} 2\,dx\,dy = \int_0^{1/2} 2y\,dy = \frac{1}{4}.$$

You should draw a figure to illustrate the set of points for which $f(x,y) > 0$ and then shade the region over which the integral is taken. The given probability is the volume above this shaded region under the surface $z = 2$. The marginal p.d.f.'s are given by

$$f_1(x) = \int_x^1 2\,dy = 2(1 - x), \qquad 0 \le x \le 1,$$

and

$$f_2(y) = \int_0^y 2\,dx = 2y, \qquad 0 \le y \le 1.$$

Three illustrations of expected values are

$$E(X) = \int_0^1\int_x^1 2x\,dy\,dx = \int_0^1 2x(1 - x)\,dx = \frac{1}{3},$$

$$E(Y) = \int_0^1\int_0^y 2y\,dx\,dy = \int_0^1 2y^2\,dy = \frac{2}{3},$$

and

$$E(Y^2) = \int_0^1 \int_0^y 2y^2\, dx\, dy = \int_0^1 2y^3\, dy = \frac{1}{2}.$$

From these calculations we see that $E(X)$, $E(Y)$, and $E(Y^2)$ could be calculated from the marginal p.d.f.'s instead of the joint one. ■

The definition of independent random variables of the continuous type carries over naturally from the discrete case. That is, X and Y are **independent** if and only if the joint p.d.f. factors into the product of their marginal p.d.f.'s; namely,

$$f(x, y) \equiv f_1(x) f_2(y), \qquad x \in S_1,\ y \in S_2.$$

Thus, the random variables X and Y in Example 4.1-7 are independent. In addition, the rules that allow us to easily determine dependent and independent random variables are valid here. So X and Y in Example 4.1-8 are dependent because the support S is not a product space, since it is bounded by the diagonal line $y = x$.

We give extensions of two important univariate distributions—the hypergeometric distribution and the binomial distribution—through examples.

EXAMPLE 4.1-9 Consider a population of 200 students who have just finished a first course in calculus. Of these 200, 40 have earned A's, 60 B's, and 100 C's, D's, or F's. A sample of size 25 is taken at random and without replacement from this population in a way that each possible sample has probability

$$\frac{1}{\binom{200}{25}}$$

of being selected. Within the sample of 25, let X_1 be the number of A students, X_2 the number of B students, and $25 - X_1 - X_2$ the number of other students. The space S of (X_l, X_2) is defined by the collection of nonnegative integers (x_1, x_2) such that $x_1 + x_2 \leq 25$. The joint p.m.f. of X_1, X_2 is

$$f(x_1, x_2) = \frac{\binom{40}{x_1}\binom{60}{x_2}\binom{100}{25 - x_1 - x_2}}{\binom{200}{25}},$$

for $(x_1, x_2) \in S$, where it is understood that $\binom{k}{j} = 0$ if $j > k$. Without actually summing, we know that the marginal p.m.f. of X_1 is

$$f_1(x_1) = \frac{\binom{40}{x_1}\binom{160}{25 - x_1}}{\binom{200}{25}}, \qquad x_1 = 0, 1, 2, \ldots, 25,$$

since X_1 alone has a hypergeometric distribution. Of course, the function $f_2(x_2)$ is a hypergeometric p.m.f. and

$$f(x_1, x_2) \not\equiv f_1(x_1) f_2(x_2),$$

so X_1 and X_2 are dependent. Note that the space S is not "rectangular," which implies that the random variables are dependent. ■

We now extend the binomial distribution to a trinomial distribution. Here we have three mutually exclusive and exhaustive ways for an experiment to terminate: perfect, "seconds," and defective. We repeat the experiment n independent times, and the probabilities $p_1, p_2, p_3 = 1 - p_1 - p_2$ of perfect, seconds, and defective, respectively, remain the same from trial to trial. In the n trials, let X_1 = number of perfect items, X_2 = number of seconds, and $X_3 = n - X_1 - X_2$ = number of defectives. If x_1 and x_2 are nonnegative integers such that $x_1 + x_2 \le n$, then the probability of having x_1 perfects, x_2 seconds, and $n - x_1 - x_2$ defectives, in that order, is

$$p_1^{x_1} p_2^{x_2} (1 - p_1 - p_2)^{n-x_1-x_2}.$$

However, if we want $P(X_1 = x_1, X_2 = x_2)$, then we must recognize that $X_1 = x_1, X_2 = x_2$ can be achieved in

$$\binom{n}{x_1, x_2, n - x_1 - x_2} = \frac{n!}{x_1!x_2!(n - x_1 - x_2)!}$$

different ways. Hence, the **trinomial** p.m.f. is

$$\begin{aligned} f(x_1, x_2) &= P(X_1 = x_1, X_2 = x_2) \\ &= \frac{n!}{x_1!x_2!(n - x_1 - x_2)!} p_1^{x_1} p_2^{x_2} (1 - p_1 - p_2)^{n-x_1-x_2}, \end{aligned}$$

where x_1 and x_2 are nonnegative integers such that $x_1 + x_2 \le n$. Without summing, we know that X_1 is $b(n, p_1)$ and X_2 is $b(n, p_2)$; thus, X_1 and X_2 are dependent, as the product of these marginal probability mass functions is not equal to $f(x_1, x_2)$.

EXAMPLE 4.1-10 In manufacturing a certain item, it is found that in normal production about 95% of the items are good ones, 4% are "seconds," and 1% are defective. A company has a program of quality control by statistical methods, and each hour an online inspector observes 20 items selected at random, counting the number X of seconds and the number Y of defectives. Suppose that the production is normal. Let us find the probability that, in this sample of size $n = 20$, at least two seconds or at least two defective items are discovered. If we let $A = \{(x,y) : x \ge 2 \text{ or } y \ge 2\}$, then

$$\begin{aligned} P(A) &= 1 - P(A') \\ &= 1 - P(X = 0 \text{ or } 1 \text{ and } Y = 0 \text{ or } 1) \\ &= 1 - \frac{20!}{0!0!20!}(0.04)^0(0.01)^0(0.95)^{20} - \frac{20!}{1!0!19!}(0.04)^1(0.01)^0(0.95)^{19} \\ &\quad - \frac{20!}{0!1!19!}(0.04)^0(0.01)^1(0.95)^{19} - \frac{20!}{1!1!18!}(0.04)^1(0.01)^1(0.95)^{18} \\ &= 0.204. \end{aligned}$$

■

EXAMPLE 4.1-11 Let X and Y have a trinomial distribution with parameters $p_1 = 1/5$, $p_2 = 2/5$, and $n = 5$. The probability histogram for the joint p.m.f. of X and Y is shown in Figure 4.1-5. ■

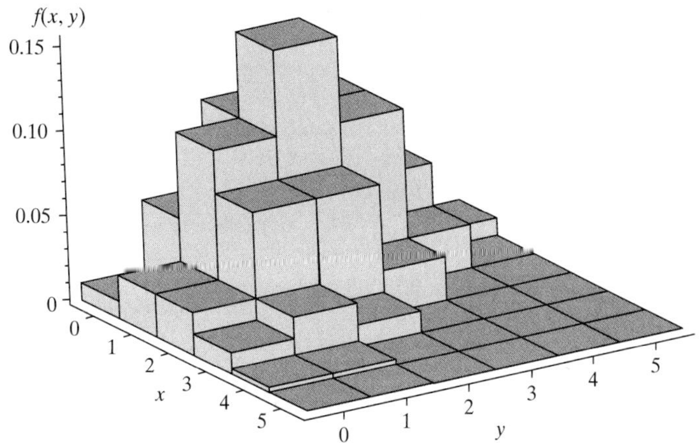

FIGURE 4.1-5: Trinomial distribution, $p_1 = 1/5$, $p_2 = 2/5$, and $n = 5$

EXERCISES

4.1-1. Let the joint p.m.f. of X and Y be defined by

$$f(x,y) = \frac{x+y}{32}, \qquad x = 1,2,\ y = 1,2,3,4.$$

(a) Find $f_1(x)$, the marginal p.m.f. of X.
(b) Find $f_2(y)$, the marginal p.m.f. of Y.
(c) Find $P(X > Y)$.
(d) Find $P(Y = 2X)$.
(e) Find $P(X + Y = 3)$.
(f) Find $P(X \leq 3 - Y)$.
(g) Are X and Y independent or dependent? Why or why not?

4.1-2. Roll a pair of four-sided dice, one red and one black, each of which has possible outcomes 1, 2, 3, 4 that have equal probabilities. Let X equal the outcome on the red die, and let Y equal the outcome on the black die.

(a) On graph paper, show the space of X and Y.
(b) Define the joint p.m.f. on the space (similar to Figure 4.1-1).
(c) Give the marginal p.m.f. of X in the margin.
(d) Give the marginal p.m.f. of Y in the margin.
(e) Are X and Y dependent or independent? Why or why not?

4.1-3. Roll a pair of four-sided dice, one red and one black. Let X equal the outcome on the red die and let Y equal the sum of the two dice.

(a) On graph paper, describe the space of X and Y.
(b) Define the joint p.m.f. on the space (similar to Figure 4.1-1).
(c) Give the marginal p.m.f. of X in the margin.
(d) Give the marginal p.m.f. of Y in the margin.
(e) Are X and Y dependent or independent? Why or why not?

4.1-4. Select an (even) integer randomly from the set $\{0, 2, 4, 6, 8\}$. Then select an integer randomly from the set $\{0, 1, 2, 3, 4\}$. Let X equal the integer that is selected from the first set and let Y equal the sum of the two integers.

(a) Show the joint p.m.f. of X and Y on the space of X and Y.
(b) Compute the marginal p.m.f.'s.
(c) Are X and Y independent? Why or why not?

4.1-5. A particle starts at (0,0) and moves in one-unit independent steps with equal probabilities of 1/4 in each of the four directions: north, south, east, and west. Let S equal the east–west position and T the north–south position after n steps.

(a) Define the joint p.m.f. of S and T with $n = 3$. On a two–dimensional graph, give the probabilities of the joint p.m.f. and the marginal p.m.f.'s (similar to Figure 4.1-1).
(b) Let $X = S + 3$ and let $Y = T + 3$. How are X and Y distributed?

4.1-6. The torque required to remove bolts in a steel plate is rated as very high, high, average, and low, and these occur about 30%, 40%, 20%, and 10% of the time, respectively. Suppose $n = 25$ bolts are rated; what is the probability of rating 7 very high, 8 high, 6 average, and 4 low? Assume independence of the 25 trials.

4.1-7. Two construction companies make bids of X and Y (in \$100,000's) on a remodeling project. The joint p.d.f. of X and Y is uniform on the space $2 < x < 2.5, 2 < y < 2.3$. If X and Y are within 0.1 of each other, the companies will be asked to rebid; otherwise the low bidder will be awarded the contract. What is the probability that they will be asked to rebid?

4.1-8. In a smoking survey among boys between the ages of 12 and 17, 78% prefer to date nonsmokers, 1% prefer to date smokers, and 21% don't care. Suppose seven such boys are selected randomly. Let X equal the number who prefer to date nonsmokers and Y equal the number who prefer to date smokers.

(a) Determine the joint p.m.f. of X and Y. Be sure to include the support of the p.m.f.

(b) Find the marginal p.m.f. of X. Again include the support.

4.1-9. A manufactured item is classified as good, a "second," or defective with probabilities 6/10, 3/10, and 1/10, respectively. Fifteen such items are selected at random from the production line. Let X denote the number of good items, Y the number of seconds, and $15 - X - Y$ the number of defective items.

(a) Give the joint p.m.f. of X and Y, $f(x, y)$.

(b) Sketch the set of points for which $f(x, y) > 0$. From the shape of this region, can X and Y be independent? Why or why not?

(c) Find $P(X = 10, Y = 4)$.

(d) Give the marginal p.m.f. of X.

(e) Find $P(X \le 11)$.

4.1-10. Let $f(x, y) = 3/2, x^2 \le y \le 1, 0 \le x \le 1$, be the joint p.d.f. of X and Y.

(a) Find $P(0 \le X \le 1/2)$.

(b) Find $P(1/2 \le Y \le 1)$.

(c) Find $P(1/2 \le X \le 1, 1/2 \le Y \le 1)$.

(d) Find $P(X \ge 1/2, Y \ge 1/2)$.

(e) Are X and Y independent? Why or why not?

4.1-11. Let $f(x, y) = 2e^{-x-y}, 0 \le x \le y < \infty$, be the joint p.d.f. of X and Y. Find $f_1(x)$ and $f_2(y)$, the marginal p.d.f.'s of X and Y, respectively. Are X and Y independent?

4.1-12. Let X and Y have the joint p.d.f. $f(x, y) = x + y$, $0 \le x \le 1, 0 \le y \le 1$.

(a) Find the marginal p.d.f.'s $f_1(x)$ and $f_2(y)$ and show that $f(x, y) \not\equiv f_1(x)f_2(y)$. Thus, X and Y are dependent.

(b) Compute (i) μ_X; (ii) μ_Y; (iii) σ_X^2; and (iv) σ_Y^2.

4.1-13. Let $f(x, y) = (3/16)xy^2, 0 \le x \le 2, 0 \le y \le 2$, be the joint p.d.f. of X and Y. Find $f_1(x)$ and $f_2(y)$, the marginal probability density functions. Are the two random variables independent? Why or why not?

4.1-14. Let T_1 and T_2 be random times for a company to complete two steps in a certain process. Say T_1 and T_2 are measured in days and they have the joint p.d.f. that is uniform over the space $1 < t_1 < 10$, $2 < t_2 < 6$, $t_1 + 2t_2 < 14$. What is $P(T_1 + T_2 > 10)$?

4.1-15. Let $f(x, y) = 4/3$, $0 < x < 1$, $x^3 < y < 1$, zero elsewhere.

(a) Sketch the region where $f(x, y) > 0$.

(b) Find $P(X > Y)$.

4.2 THE CORRELATION COEFFICIENT

In Section 4.1, we introduced the mathematical expectation of a function of two random variables—say, X_1, X_2. We gave the respective special names of mean and variance of X_i to

$$\mu_i = E(X_i) \qquad \text{and} \qquad \sigma_i^2 = E[(X_i - \mu_i)^2], \qquad i = 1, 2.$$

We introduce two more special names:

(a) If $u_3(X_1, X_2) = (X_1 - \mu_1)(X_2 - \mu_2)$, then

$$E[u_3(X_1, X_2)] = E[(X_1 - \mu_1)(X_2 - \mu_2)] = \sigma_{12} = \text{Cov}(X_1, X_2)$$

is called the **covariance** of X_1 and X_2.

(b) If the standard deviations σ_1 and σ_2 are positive, then

$$\rho = \frac{\text{Cov}(X_1, X_2)}{\sigma_1\sigma_2} = \frac{\sigma_{12}}{\sigma_1\sigma_2}$$

is called the **correlation coefficient** of X_1 and X_2.

It is convenient that the mean and the variance of X_1 can be computed from either the joint p.m.f. or the marginal p.m.f. of X_1. For example, in the discrete case,

$$\mu_1 = E(X_1) = \sum_{x_1}\sum_{x_2} x_1 f(x_1, x_2)$$

$$= \sum_{x_1} x_1\left[\sum_{x_2} f(x_1, x_2)\right] = \sum_{x_1} x_1 f_1(x_1).$$

However, to compute the covariance, we need the joint p.m.f.

Before considering the significance of the covariance and the correlation coefficient, let us note a few simple facts. First,

$$E[(X_1 - \mu_1)(X_2 - \mu_2)] = E(X_1X_2 - \mu_1X_2 - \mu_2X_1 + \mu_1\mu_2)$$
$$= E(X_1X_2) - \mu_1E(X_2) - \mu_2E(X_1) + \mu_1\mu_2,$$

because, even in the bivariate situation, E is still a linear or distributive operator. (See Exercise 4.2-4.) Thus,

$$\mathrm{Cov}(X_1, X_2) = E(X_1X_2) - \mu_1\mu_2 - \mu_2\mu_1 + \mu_1\mu_2 = E(X_1X_2) - \mu_1\mu_2.$$

Since $\rho = \mathrm{Cov}(X_1, X_2)/\sigma_1\sigma_2$, we also have

$$E(X_1X_2) = \mu_1\mu_2 + \rho\sigma_1\sigma_2.$$

That is, the expected value of the product of two random variables is equal to the product $\mu_1\mu_2$ of their expectations, plus their covariance $\rho\sigma_1\sigma_2$.

A simple example at this point would be helpful.

EXAMPLE 4.2-1 Let X_1 and X_2 have the joint p.m.f.

$$f(x_1, x_2) = \frac{x_1 + 2x_2}{18}, \qquad x_1 = 1, 2, \qquad x_2 = 1, 2.$$

The marginal probability mass functions are, respectively,

$$f_1(x_1) = \sum_{x_2=1}^{2} \frac{x_1 + 2x_2}{18} = \frac{2x_1 + 6}{18}, \qquad x_1 = 1, 2,$$

and

$$f_2(x_2) = \sum_{x_1=1}^{2} \frac{x_1 + 2x_2}{18} = \frac{3 + 4x_2}{18}, \qquad x_2 = 1, 2.$$

Since $f(x_1, x_2) \not\equiv f_1(x_1)f_2(x_2)$, X_1 and X_2 are dependent. The mean and the variance of X_1 are, respectively,

$$\mu_1 = \sum_{x_1=1}^{2} x_1 \frac{2x_1 + 6}{18} = (1)\left(\frac{8}{18}\right) + (2)\left(\frac{10}{18}\right) = \frac{14}{9}$$

and

$$\sigma_1^2 = \sum_{x_1=1}^{2} x_1^2 \frac{2x_1 + 6}{18} - \left(\frac{14}{9}\right)^2 = \frac{24}{9} - \frac{196}{81} = \frac{20}{81}.$$

The mean and the variance of X_2 are, respectively,

$$\mu_2 = \sum_{x_2=1}^{2} x_2 \frac{3 + 4x_2}{18} = (1)\left(\frac{7}{18}\right) + (2)\left(\frac{11}{18}\right) = \frac{29}{18}$$

and

$$\sigma_2^2 = \sum_{x_2=1}^{2} x_2^2 \frac{3 + 4x_2}{18} - \left(\frac{29}{18}\right)^2 = \frac{51}{18} - \frac{841}{324} = \frac{77}{324}.$$

The covariance of X_1 and X_2 is

$$\begin{aligned}
\text{Cov}(X_1, X_2) &= \sum_{x_2=1}^{2} \sum_{x_1=1}^{2} x_1 x_2 \frac{x_1 + 2x_2}{18} - \left(\frac{14}{9}\right)\left(\frac{29}{18}\right) \\
&= (1)(1)\left(\frac{3}{18}\right) + (2)(1)\left(\frac{4}{18}\right) + (1)(2)\left(\frac{5}{18}\right) \\
&\quad + (2)(2)\left(\frac{6}{18}\right) - \left(\frac{14}{19}\right)\left(\frac{29}{18}\right) \\
&= \frac{45}{18} - \frac{406}{162} = -\frac{1}{162}.
\end{aligned}$$

Hence, the correlation coefficient is

$$\rho = \frac{-1/162}{\sqrt{(20/81)(77/324)}} = \frac{-1}{\sqrt{1540}} = -0.025. \qquad \blacksquare$$

Insight into the correlation coefficient ρ of two discrete random variables X and Y may be gained by thoughtfully examining the definition of ρ, namely,

$$\rho = \frac{\displaystyle\sum_{x}\sum_{y} (x - \mu_X)(y - \mu_Y) f(x, y)}{\sigma_X \sigma_Y},$$

where μ_X, μ_Y, σ_X, and σ_Y denote the respective means and standard deviations. If positive probabilities are assigned to pairs (x, y) in which both x and y are either simultaneously above or simultaneously below their respective means, then the corresponding terms in the summation that defines ρ are positive because both factors $(x - \mu_X)$ and $(y - \mu_Y)$ will be positive or both will be negative. If, on the one hand, pairs (x, y), which yield large positive products $(x - \mu_X)(y - \mu_Y)$, contain most of the probability of the distribution, then the correlation coefficient will tend to be positive. If, on the other hand, the points (x, y), in which one component is below its mean and the other above its mean, have most of the probability, then the coefficient of correlation will tend to be negative because the products $(x - \mu_X)(y - \mu_Y)$ having higher probabilities are negative. (See Exercise 4.2-6.) This interpretation of the sign of the correlation coefficient will play an important role in subsequent work.

To gain additional insight into the meaning of the correlation coefficient ρ, consider the following problem: Think of the points (x, y) in the space S and their corresponding probabilities. Let us consider all possible lines in two-dimensional space, each with finite slope, that pass through the point associated with the means, namely, (μ_X, μ_Y). These lines are of the form $y - \mu_Y = b(x - \mu_X)$ or, equivalently,

$y = \mu_Y + b(x - \mu_X)$. For each point in S—say, (x_0, y_0), so that $f(x_0, y_0) > 0$—consider the vertical distance from that point to one of the aforesaid lines. Since y_0 is the height of the point above the x-axis and $\mu_Y + b(x_0 - \mu_X)$ is the height of the point on the line that is directly above or below the point (x_0, y_0), the absolute value of the difference of these two heights is the vertical distance from the point (x_0, y_0) to the line $y = \mu_Y + b(x - \mu_X)$. That is, the required distance is $|y_0 - \mu_Y - b(x_0 - \mu_X)|$. Let us now square this distance and take the weighted average of all such squares; in other words, let us consider the mathematical expectation

$$E\{[(Y - \mu_Y) - b(X - \mu_X)]^2\} = K(b).$$

The problem is to find that line (or that b) which minimizes this expectation of the square $\{Y - \mu_Y - b(X - \mu_X)\}^2$. This is an application of the principle of least squares, and the line is sometimes called the least squares regression line.

The solution of the problem is very easy, since

$$\begin{aligned} K(b) &= E\{(Y - \mu_Y)^2 - 2b(X - \mu_X)(Y - \mu_Y) + b^2(X - \mu_X)^2\} \\ &= \sigma_Y^2 - 2b\rho\sigma_X\sigma_Y + b^2\sigma_X^2, \end{aligned}$$

because E is a linear operator and $E[(X - \mu_X)(Y - \mu_Y)] = \rho\sigma_X\sigma_Y$. Accordingly, the derivative

$$K'(b) = -2\rho\sigma_X\sigma_Y + 2b\sigma_X^2$$

equals zero at $b = \rho\sigma_Y/\sigma_X$, and we see that $K(b)$ obtains its minimum for that b, since $K''(b) = 2\sigma_X^2 > 0$. Consequently, the **least squares regression line** (the line of the given form that is the best fit in the foregoing sense) is

$$y = \mu_Y + \rho\frac{\sigma_Y}{\sigma_X}(x - \mu_X).$$

Of course, if $\rho > 0$, the slope of the line is positive; but if $\rho < 0$, the slope is negative.

It is also instructive to note the value of the minimum of

$$K(b) = E\{[(Y - \mu_Y) - b(X - \mu_X)]^2\} = \sigma_Y^2 - 2b\rho\sigma_X\sigma_Y + b^2\sigma_X^2.$$

It is

$$\begin{aligned} K\left(\rho\frac{\sigma_Y}{\sigma_X}\right) &= \sigma_Y^2 - 2\rho\frac{\sigma_Y}{\sigma_X}\rho\sigma_X\sigma_Y + \left(\rho\frac{\sigma_Y}{\sigma_X}\right)^2\sigma_X^2 \\ &= \sigma_Y^2 - 2\rho^2\sigma_Y^2 + \rho^2\sigma_Y^2 = \sigma_Y^2(1 - \rho^2). \end{aligned}$$

Since $K(b)$ is the expected value of a square, it must be nonnegative for all b, and we see that $\sigma_Y^2(1 - \rho^2) \geq 0$; that is, $\rho^2 \leq 1$, and hence $-1 \leq \rho \leq 1$, which is an important property of the correlation coefficient ρ. On the one hand, if $\rho = 0$, then $K(\rho\sigma_Y/\sigma_X) = \sigma_Y^2$; on the other hand, if ρ is close to 1 or -1, then $K(\rho\sigma_Y/\sigma_X)$ is relatively small. That is, the vertical deviations of the points with positive probability from the line $y = \mu_Y + \rho(\sigma_Y/\sigma_X)(x - \mu_X)$ are small if ρ is close to 1 or -1 because $K(\rho\sigma_Y/\sigma_X)$ is the expectation of the square of those deviations. Thus, ρ measures, in this sense, the amount of *linearity* in the probability distribution. As a matter of fact, in the discrete case, all the points of positive probability lie on this straight line if and only if ρ is equal to 1 or -1.

REMARK More generally, we could have fitted the line $y = a + bx$ by the same application of the principle of least squares. We would then have proved that the "best" line actually passes through the point (μ_X, μ_Y). Recall that, in the preceding discussion, we assumed our line to be of that form. Students will find this derivation to be an interesting exercise using partial derivatives. (See Exercise 4.2-5.) ■

The next example illustrates a joint discrete distribution for which ρ is negative. In Figure 4.2-1, the line of best fit, or the least squares regression line, is also drawn.

EXAMPLE 4.2-2 Let X equal the number of ones and Y the number of twos and threes when a pair of fair four-sided dice is rolled. Then X and Y have a trinomial distribution with joint p.m.f.

$$f(x,y) = \frac{2!}{x!y!(2-x-y)!}\left(\frac{1}{4}\right)^x\left(\frac{2}{4}\right)^y\left(\frac{1}{4}\right)^{2-x-y}, \qquad 0 \le x + y \le 2,$$

where x and y are nonnegative integers. Since the marginal p.m.f. of X is $b(2, 1/4)$ and the marginal p.m.f. of Y is $b(2, 1/2)$, it follows that $\mu_X = 1/2$, $\text{Var}(X) = 6/16$, $\mu_Y = 1$, and $\text{Var}(Y) = 1/2$. Also, since $E(XY) = (1)(1)(4/16) = 4/16$, we have $\text{Cov}(X, Y) = 4/16 - (1/2)(1) = -4/16$; therefore, the correlation coefficient is $\rho = -1/\sqrt{3}$. Using these values for the parameters, we obtain the line of best fit, namely,

$$y = 1 + \left(-\frac{1}{\sqrt{3}}\right)\sqrt{\frac{1/2}{3/8}}\left(x - \frac{1}{2}\right) = -\frac{2}{3}x + \frac{4}{3}.$$

The joint p.m.f. is displayed in Figure 4.2-1 along with the line of best fit. ■

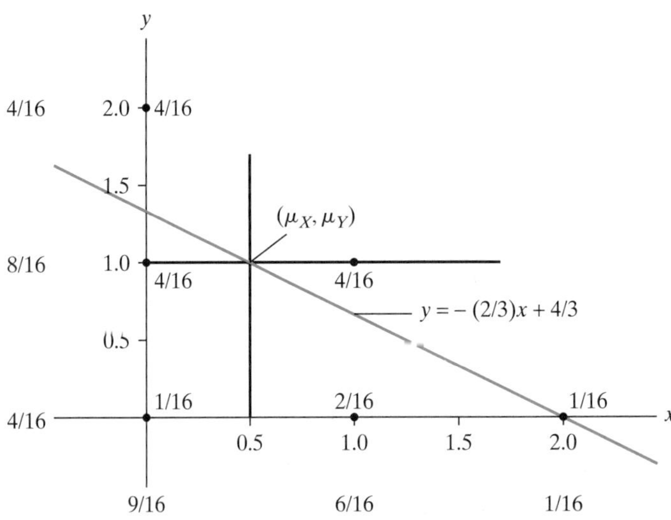

FIGURE 4.2-1: Trinomial distribution

Suppose that X and Y are independent, so that $f(x,y) \equiv f_1(x)f_2(y)$. Suppose also that we want to find the expected value of the product $u(X)v(Y)$. Subject to the existence of the expectations, we know that

$$\begin{aligned} E[u(X)v(Y)] &= \sum_{S_1}\sum_{S_2} u(x)v(y)f(x,y) \\ &= \sum_{S_1}\sum_{S_2} u(x)v(y)f_1(x)f_2(y) \\ &= \sum_{S_1} u(x)f_1(x)\sum_{S_2} v(y)f_2(y) \\ &= E[u(X)]E[v(Y)]. \end{aligned}$$

This formula can be used to show that the correlation coefficient of two independent variables is zero. For, in standard notation, we have

$$\begin{aligned} \text{Cov}(X, Y) &= E[(X - \mu_X)(Y - \mu_Y)] \\ &= E(X - \mu_X)E(Y - \mu_Y) = 0. \end{aligned}$$

The converse of this equation is not necessarily true, however: Zero correlation does not, in general, imply independence. It is most important to keep the relationship straight: Independence implies zero correlation, but zero correlation does not necessarily imply independence. We now illustrate the latter proposition.

EXAMPLE 4.2-3 Let X and Y have the joint p.m.f.

$$f(x,y) = \frac{1}{3}, \qquad (x,y) = (0,1),(1,0),(2,1).$$

Since the support is not "rectangular," X and Y must be dependent. The means of X and Y are $\mu_X = 1$ and $\mu_Y = 2/3$, respectively. Hence,

$$\begin{aligned} \text{Cov}(X, Y) &= E(XY) - \mu_X\mu_Y \\ &= (0)(1)\left(\frac{1}{3}\right) + (1)(0)\left(\frac{1}{3}\right) + (2)(1)\left(\frac{1}{3}\right) - (1)\left(\frac{2}{3}\right) = 0. \end{aligned}$$

That is, $\rho = 0$, but X and Y are dependent. ■

Although we have used discrete random variables to define the correlation coefficient and related concepts, these ideas carry over to the continuous case with the usual modifications—in particular, with integrals replacing summations. We illustrate the continuous relationships in Exercises 4.2-10, 4.2-11, and 4.2-12.

EXERCISES

4.2-1. Let the random variables X and Y have the joint p.m.f

$$f(x,y) = \frac{x + y}{32}, \qquad x = 1,2,\ y = 1,2,3,4.$$

Find the means μ_X and μ_Y, the variances σ_X^2 and σ_Y^2, and the correlation coefficient ρ. Are X and Y independent or dependent?

4.2-2. Let X and Y have the joint p.m.f. defined by $f(0,0) = f(1,2) = 0.2, f(0,1) = f(1,1) = 0.3$.

(a) Depict the points and corresponding probabilities on a graph.

(b) Give the marginal p.m.f.'s in the "margins."

(c) Compute $\mu_X, \mu_Y, \sigma_X^2, \sigma_Y^2$, $\text{Cov}(X, Y)$, and ρ.

(d) Find the equation of the least squares regression line and draw it on your graph. Does the line make sense to you intuitively?

4.2-3. Roll a fair four-sided die twice. Let X equal the outcome on the first roll and let Y equal the sum of the two rolls.

(a) Display the joint p.m.f. on a graph along with the marginal probabilities.

(b) Determine μ_X, μ_Y, σ_X^2, σ_Y^2, $\text{Cov}(X, Y)$, and ρ.

(c) Find the equation of the least squares regression line and draw it on your graph. Does the line make sense to you intuitively?

4.2-4. Show that, in the bivariate situation, E is a linear or distributive operator. That is, show that

$$E[a_1u_1(X_1, X_2) + a_2u_2(X_1, X_2)] = a_1E[u_1(X_1, X_2)] + a_2E[u_2(X_1, X_2)].$$

4.2-5. Let X and Y be random variables with respective means μ_X and μ_Y, respective variances σ_X^2 and σ_Y^2, and correlation coefficient ρ. Fit the line $y = a + bx$ by the method of least squares to the probability distribution by minimizing the expectation

$$K(a,b) = E[(Y - a - bX)^2]$$

with respect to a and b. HINT: Set $\partial K/\partial a = 0$ and $\partial K/\partial b = 0$, and solve simultaneously.

4.2-6. Let X and Y have a trinomial distribution with parameters $n = 3$, $p_1 = 1/6$, and $p_2 = 1/2$. Find

(a) $E(X)$.

(b) $E(Y)$.

(c) $\text{Var}(X)$.

(d) $\text{Var}(Y)$.

(e) $\text{Cov}(X, Y)$.

(f) ρ.

Note that $\rho = -\sqrt{p_1p_2/(1 - p_1)(1 - p_2)}$ in this case. (Indeed, the formula holds in general for the trinomial distribution; see Example 4.3-3.)

4.2-7. Let the joint p.m.f. of X and Y be

$$f(x,y) = 1/4,$$
$$(x,y) \in S = \{(0,0), (1,1), (1,-1), (2,0)\}.$$

(a) Are X and Y independent?

(b) Calculate $\text{Cov}(X, Y)$ and ρ.

This exercise also illustrates the fact that dependent random variables can have a correlation coefficient of zero.

4.2-8. The joint p.m.f. of X and Y is $f(x,y) = 1/6$, $0 \le x + y \le 2$, where x and y are nonnegative integers.

(a) Sketch the support of X and Y.

(b) Record the marginal p.m.f.'s $f_1(x)$ and $f_2(y)$ in the "margins."

(c) Compute $\text{Cov}(X, Y)$.

(d) Determine ρ, the correlation coefficient.

(e) Find the best-fitting line and draw it on your figure.

4.2-9. A certain raw material is classified as to moisture content X (in percent) and impurity Y (in percent). Let X and Y have the joint p.m.f. given by

	x			
y	1	2	3	4
2	0.10	0.20	0.30	0.05
1	0.05	0.05	0.15	0.10

(a) Find the marginal p.m.f.'s, the means, and the variances.

(b) Find the covariance and the correlation coefficient of X and Y.

(c) If additional heating is needed with high moisture content and additional filtering with high impurity such that the additional cost is given by the function $C = 2X + 10Y^2$ in dollars, find $E(C)$.

4.2-10. Let X and Y be random variables of the continuous type having the joint p.d.f.

$$f(x,y) = 2, \qquad 0 \le y \le x \le 1.$$

Draw a graph that illustrates the domain of this p.d.f.

(a) Find the marginal p.d.f.'s of X and Y.

(b) Compute μ_X, μ_Y, σ_X^2, σ_Y^2, $\text{Cov}(X, Y)$, and ρ.

(c) Determine the equation of the least squares regression line and draw it on your graph. Does the line make sense to you intuitively?

4.2-11. Let X and Y be random variables of the continuous type having the joint p.d.f.

$$f(x,y) = x + y, \qquad 0 < x < 1,\ 0 < y < 1.$$

Draw a graph that illustrates the domain of this p.d.f.

(a) Find the marginal p.d.f.'s of X and Y.

(b) Compute μ_X, μ_Y, σ_X^2, σ_Y^2, $\text{Cov}(X, Y)$, and ρ.

(c) Determine the equation of the least squares regression line and draw it on your graph. Does the line make sense to you intuitively?

4.2-12. Let X and Y be random variables of the continuous type having the joint p.d.f.

$$f(x,y) = 8xy, \qquad 0 \le x \le y \le 1.$$

Draw a graph that illustrates the domain of this p.d.f.

(a) Find the marginal p.d.f.'s of X and Y.
(b) Compute $\mu_X, \mu_Y, \sigma_X^2, \sigma_Y^2$, $\mathrm{Cov}(X, Y)$, and ρ.
(c) Determine the equation of the least squares regression line and draw it on your graph. Does the line make sense to you intuitively?

4.2-13. A car dealer sells X cars each day and always tries to sell an extended warranty on each of these cars. (In our opinion, most of these warranties are not good deals.) Let Y be the number of extended warranties sold; then $Y \le X$. The joint p.m.f. of X and Y is given by

$$f(x,y) = c(x + 1)(4 - x)(y + 1)(3 - y),$$

$$x = 0,1,2,3; \; y = 0,1,2 \text{ with } y \le x.$$

(a) Find the value of c.
(b) Sketch the support of X and Y.
(c) Record the marginal p.m.f.'s $f_1(x)$ and $f_2(y)$ in the "margins."
(d) Are X and Y independent?
(e) Compute μ_X and σ_X^2.
(f) Compute μ_Y and σ_Y^2.
(g) Compute $\mathrm{Cov}(X, Y)$.
(h) Determine ρ, the correlation coefficient.
(i) Find the best-fitting line and draw it on your figure.

4.3 CONDITIONAL DISTRIBUTIONS

Let X and Y have a joint discrete distribution with p.m.f. $f(x,y)$ on space S. Say the marginal probability mass functions are $f_1(x)$ and $f_2(y)$ with spaces S_1 and S_2, respectively. Let event $A = \{X = x\}$ and event $B = \{Y = y\}$, $(x,y) \in S$. Thus, $A \cap B = \{X = x, Y = y\}$. Because

$$P(A \cap B) = P(X = x, Y = y) = f(x,y)$$

and

$$P(B) = P(Y = y) = f_2(y) > 0 \qquad (\text{since } y \in S_2),$$

the conditional probability of event A given event B is

$$P(A \mid B) = \frac{P(A \cap B)}{P(B)} = \frac{f(x,y)}{f_2(y)}.$$

This formula leads to the following definition.

DEFINITION 4.3-1

The **conditional probability mass function of** X, given that $Y = y$, is defined by

$$g(x \mid y) = \frac{f(x,y)}{f_2(y)}, \qquad \text{provided that } f_2(y) > 0.$$

Similarly, the **conditional probability mass function of** Y, given that $X = x$, is defined by

$$h(y \mid x) = \frac{f(x,y)}{f_1(x)}, \qquad \text{provided that } f_1(x) > 0.$$

EXAMPLE 4.3-1 Let X and Y have the joint p.m.f.

$$f(x,y) = \frac{x + y}{21}, \qquad x = 1,2,3, \qquad y = 1,2.$$

In Example 4.1-2, we showed that

$$f_1(x) = \frac{2x + 3}{21}, \qquad x = 1,2,3,$$

and

$$f_2(y) = \frac{3y + 6}{21}, \qquad y = 1, 2.$$

Thus, the conditional p.m.f. of X, given that $Y = y$, is equal to

$$g(x \mid y) = \frac{(x + y)/21}{(3y + 6)/21} = \frac{x + y}{3y + 6}, \qquad x = 1, 2, 3, \text{ when } y = 1 \text{ or } 2.$$

For example,

$$P(X = 2 \mid Y = 2) = g(2 \mid 2) = \frac{4}{12} = \frac{1}{3}.$$

Similarly, the conditional p.m.f. of Y, given that $X = x$, is equal to

$$h(y \mid x) = \frac{x + y}{2x + 3}, \qquad y = 1, 2, \text{ when } x = 1, 2, \text{ or } 3.$$

The joint p.m.f. $f(x, y)$ is depicted in Figure 4.3-1(a) along with the marginal p.m.f.'s. Now, if $y = 2$, we would expect the outcomes of x—namely, 1, 2, and 3—to occur in the ratio 3:4:5. This is precisely what $g(x \mid y)$ does:

$$g(1 \mid 2) = \frac{1 + 2}{12}, \qquad g(2 \mid 2) = \frac{2 + 2}{12}, \qquad g(3 \mid 2) = \frac{3 + 2}{12}.$$

Figure 4.3-1(b) displays $g(x \mid 1)$ and $g(x \mid 2)$, while Figure 4.3-1(c) gives $h(y \mid 1)$, $h(y \mid 2)$, and $h(y \mid 3)$. Compare the probabilities in Figure 4.3-1(c) with those in Figure 4.3-1(a). They should agree with your intuition as well as with the formula for $h(y \mid x)$. ■

Note that $0 \le h(y \mid x)$. If we sum $h(y \mid x)$ over y for that fixed x, we obtain

$$\sum_y h(y \mid x) = \sum_y \frac{f(x, y)}{f_1(x)} = \frac{f_1(x)}{f_1(x)} = 1.$$

Thus, $h(y \mid x)$ satisfies the conditions of a probability mass function, and we can compute conditional probabilities such as

$$P(a < Y < b \mid X = x) = \sum_{\{y: a<y<b\}} h(y \mid x)$$

and conditional expectations such as

$$E[u(Y) \mid X = x] = \sum_y u(y) h(y \mid x)$$

in a manner similar to those associated with unconditional probabilities and expectations.

Two special conditional expectations are the **conditional mean** of Y, given that $X = x$, defined by

$$\mu_{Y|x} = E(Y \mid x) = \sum_y y\, h(y \mid x),$$

and the **conditional variance** of Y, given that $X = x$, defined by

$$\sigma^2_{Y|x} = E\{[Y - E(Y \mid x)]^2 \mid x\} = \sum_y [y - E(Y \mid x)]^2 h(y \mid x),$$

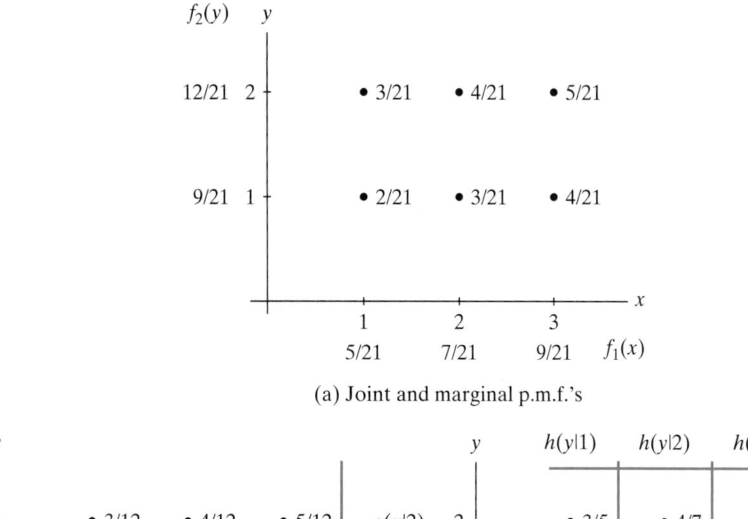

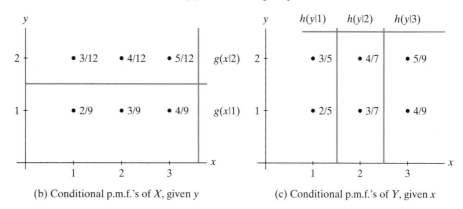

(a) Joint and marginal p.m.f.'s

(b) Conditional p.m.f.'s of X, given y

(c) Conditional p.m.f.'s of Y, given x

FIGURE 4.3-1: Joint, marginal, and conditional p.m.f.'s

which can be computed with

$$\sigma^2_{Y|x} = E(Y^2 \,|\, x) - [E(Y \,|\, x)]^2.$$

The conditional mean $\mu_{X|y}$ and the conditional variance $\sigma^2_{X|y}$ are given by similar expressions.

EXAMPLE 4.3-2 We use the background of Example 4.3-1 and compute $\mu_{Y|x}$ and $\sigma^2_{Y|x}$ when $x = 3$:

$$\mu_{Y|3} = E(Y \,|\, X = 3) = \sum_{y=1}^{2} y\, h(y \,|\, 3)$$

$$= \sum_{y=1}^{2} y\left(\frac{3 + y}{9}\right) = 1\left(\frac{4}{9}\right) + 2\left(\frac{5}{9}\right) = \frac{14}{9},$$

and

$$\sigma^2_{Y|3} = E\left[\left(Y - \frac{14}{9}\right)^2 \middle|\, X = 3\right] = \sum_{y=1}^{2}\left(y - \frac{14}{9}\right)^2\left(\frac{3 + y}{9}\right)$$

$$= \frac{25}{81}\left(\frac{4}{9}\right) + \frac{16}{81}\left(\frac{5}{9}\right) = \frac{20}{81}.$$

■

The conditional mean of X, given that $Y = y$, is a function of y alone; the conditional mean of Y, given that $X = x$, is a function of x alone. Suppose that the latter conditional mean is a linear function of x; that is, $E(Y\,|\,x) = a + bx$. Let us find the constants a and b in terms of characteristics μ_X, μ_Y, σ_X^2, σ_Y^2, and ρ. This development will shed additional light on the correlation coefficient ρ; accordingly, we assume that the respective standard deviations σ_X and σ_Y are both positive, so that the correlation coefficient will exist.

It is given that

$$\sum_y y\,h(y\,|\,x) = \sum_y y\,\frac{f(x,y)}{f_1(x)} = a + bx, \qquad \text{for } x \in S_1,$$

where S_1 is the space of X and S_2 is the space of Y. Hence,

$$\sum_y y f(x,y) = (a + bx)f_1(x), \qquad \text{for } x \in S_1, \tag{4.3-1}$$

and

$$\sum_{x\in S_1}\sum_y y f(x,y) = \sum_{x\in S_1}(a + bx)f_1(x).$$

That is, with μ_X and μ_Y representing the respective means, we have

$$\mu_Y = a + b\mu_X. \tag{4.3-2}$$

In addition, if we multiply both members of Equation 4.3-1 by x and sum the resulting product, we obtain

$$\sum_{x\in S_1}\sum_y xy f(x,y) = \sum_{x\in S_1}(ax + bx^2)f_1(x).$$

That is,

$$E(XY) = aE(X) + bE(X^2)$$

or, equivalently,

$$\mu_X\mu_Y + \rho\sigma_X\sigma_Y = a\mu_X + b(\mu_X^2 + \sigma_X^2). \tag{4.3-3}$$

The solution of Equations 4.3-2 and 4.3-3 is

$$a = \mu_Y - \rho\frac{\sigma_Y}{\sigma_X}\mu_X \qquad \text{and} \qquad b = \rho\frac{\sigma_Y}{\sigma_X},$$

which implies that if $E(Y\,|\,x)$ is linear, it is given by

$$E(Y\,|\,x) = \mu_Y + \rho\frac{\sigma_Y}{\sigma_X}(x - \mu_X).$$

So if the conditional mean of Y, given that $X = x$, is linear, it is exactly the same as the best-fitting line (least squares regression line) considered in Section 4.2.

By symmetry, if the conditional mean of X, given that $Y = y$, is linear, then

$$E(X\,|\,y) = \mu_X + \rho\frac{\sigma_X}{\sigma_Y}(y - \mu_Y).$$

We see that the point $[x = \mu_X, E(Y\,|\,x) = \mu_Y]$ satisfies the expression for $E(Y\,|\,x)$ and $[E(X\,|\,y) = \mu_X, y = \mu_Y]$ satisfies the expression for $E(X\,|\,y)$. That is, the point (μ_X, μ_Y) is on each of the two lines. In addition, we note that the product of the coefficient of x in $E(Y\,|\,x)$ and the coefficient of y in $E(X\,|\,y)$ equals ρ^2 and the ratio of these two coefficients equals σ_Y^2/σ_X^2. These observations sometimes prove useful in particular problems.

EXAMPLE 4.3-3 Let X and Y have the trinomial p.m.f. with parameters n, p_1, p_2, and $1 - p_1 - p_2 = p_3$. That is,

$$f(x,y) = \frac{n!}{x!\,y!\,(n - x - y)!}\,p_1^x p_2^y p_3^{n-x-y},$$

where x and y are nonnegative integers such that $x + y \le n$. From the development of the trinomial distribution, we note that X and Y have marginal binomial distributions $b(n, p_1)$ and $b(n, p_2)$, respectively. Thus,

$$h(y\,|\,x) = \frac{f(x,y)}{f_1(x)} = \frac{(n - x)!}{y!\,(n - x - y)!}\left(\frac{p_2}{1 - p_1}\right)^y\left(\frac{p_3}{1 - p_1}\right)^{n-x-y},$$

$$y = 0, 1, 2, \ldots, n - x.$$

That is, the conditional p.m.f. of Y, given that $X = x$, is binomial, or

$$b\left[n - x, \frac{p_2}{1 - p_1}\right],$$

and thus has conditional mean

$$E(Y\,|\,x) = (n - x)\frac{p_2}{1 - p_1}.$$

In a similar manner, we obtain

$$E(X\,|\,y) = (n - y)\frac{p_1}{1 - p_2}.$$

Since each of the conditional means is linear, the product of the respective coefficients of x and y is

$$\rho^2 = \left(\frac{-p_2}{1 - p_1}\right)\left(\frac{-p_1}{1 - p_2}\right) = \frac{p_1 p_2}{(1 - p_1)(1 - p_2)}.$$

However, ρ must be negative, because the coefficients of x and y are negative; thus,

$$\rho = -\sqrt{\frac{p_1 p_2}{(1 - p_1)(1 - p_2)}}.$$

■

In the next example we again look at conditional p.m.f.'s when X and Y have a trinomial distribution.

EXAMPLE 4.3-4 Let X and Y have a trinomial distribution with $p_1 = 1/3$, $p_2 = 1/3$, and $n = 5$. Using a result from the last example, we find that the conditional distribution of Y, given that $X = x$, is $b(5 - x, (1/3)/(1 - 1/3))$, or $b(5 - x, 1/2)$. The p.m.f.'s, $h(y\,|\,x)$ for $x = 0, 1, \ldots, 5$ are plotted in Figure 4.3-2(a) on the next page. Note that the orientation of the axes was selected so that the shapes of these p.m.f.'s can be

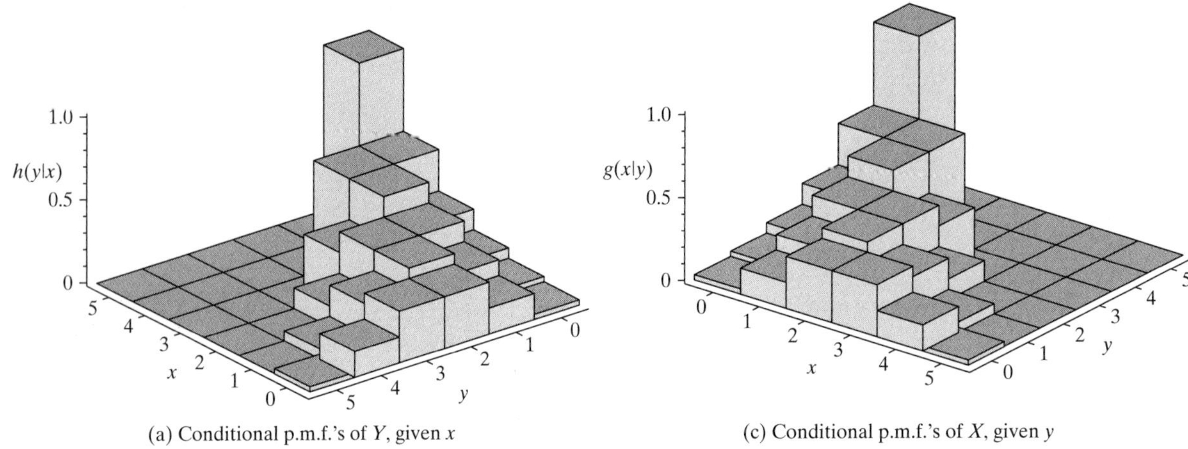

FIGURE 4.3-2: Conditional p.m.f.'s for the trinomial distribution

seen. Similarly, the conditional distribution of X, given that $Y = y$, is $b(n - y, 1/2)$. The p.m.f.'s, $g(x \mid y)$ for $y = 0, 1, \ldots, 5$ are shown in Figure 4.3-2(b). ■

Although we have used random variables of the discrete type to introduce the new definitions, they also hold for random variables of the continuous type. Let X and Y have a distribution of the continuous type with joint p.d.f. $f(x, y)$ and marginal p.d.f.'s $f_1(x)$ and $f_2(y)$, respectively. Then the conditional p.d.f., mean, and variance of Y, given that $X = x$, are, respectively,

$$h(y \mid x) = \frac{f(x, y)}{f_1(x)}, \qquad \text{provided that } f_1(x) > 0;$$

$$E(Y \mid x) = \int_{-\infty}^{\infty} y\, h(y \mid x)\, dy;$$

and

$$\begin{aligned} \text{Var}(Y \mid x) &= E\{[Y - E(Y \mid x)]^2 \mid x\} \\ &= \int_{-\infty}^{\infty} [y - E(Y \mid x)]^2\, h(y \mid x)\, dy \\ &= E[Y^2 \mid x] - [E(Y \mid x)]^2. \end{aligned}$$

Similar expressions are associated with the conditional distribution of X, given that $Y = y$.

EXAMPLE 4.3-5 Let X and Y be the random variables of Example 4.1-7. Thus,

$$\begin{aligned} f(x, y) &= 2, & 0 \le x \le y \le 1, \\ f_1(x) &= 2(1 - x), & 0 \le x \le 1, \\ f_2(y) &= 2y, & 0 \le y \le 1. \end{aligned}$$

Before we actually find the conditional p.d.f. of Y, given that $X = x$, we shall give an intuitive argument. The joint p.d.f. is constant over the triangular region bounded by $y = x$, $y = 1$, and $x = 0$. If the value of X is known (say, $X = x$), then the possible values of Y are between x and 1. Furthermore, we would expect Y to be uniformly distributed on the interval $[x, 1]$. That is, we would anticipate that $h(y \mid x) = 1/(1 - x), x \le y \le 1$.

More formally now, by definition, we have

$$h(y \mid x) = \frac{f(x,y)}{f_1(x)} = \frac{2}{2(1 - x)} = \frac{1}{1 - x}, \qquad x \le y \le 1, \qquad 0 \le x \le 1.$$

The conditional mean of Y, given that $X = x$, is

$$E(Y \mid x) = \int_x^1 y \frac{1}{1 - x}\, dy = \left[\frac{y^2}{2(1 - x)}\right]_x^1 = \frac{1 + x}{2}, \qquad 0 \le x \le 1.$$

Similarly, it can be shown that

$$E(X \mid y) = \frac{y}{2}, \qquad 0 \le y \le 1.$$

The conditional variance of Y, given that $X = x$, is

$$\begin{aligned} E\{[Y - E(Y \mid x)]^2 \mid x\} &= \int_x^1 \left(y - \frac{1 + x}{2}\right)^2 \frac{1}{1 - x}\, dy \\ &= \left[\frac{1}{3(1 - x)}\left(y - \frac{1 + x}{2}\right)^3\right]_x^1 \\ &= \frac{(1 - x)^2}{12}. \end{aligned}$$

Recall that if a random variable W is $U(a, b)$, then $E(W) = (a + b)/2$ and $\text{Var}(W) = (b - a)^2/12$. Since the conditional distribution of Y, given that $X = x$, is $U(x, 1)$, we could have inferred immediately that $E(Y \mid x) = (x + 1)/2$ and $\text{Var}(Y \mid x) = (1 - x)^2/12$.

An illustration of a computation of a conditional probability is

$$\begin{aligned} P\left(\frac{3}{4} \le Y \le \frac{7}{8} \,\middle|\, X = \frac{1}{4}\right) &= \int_{3/4}^{7/8} h\left(y \,\middle|\, \frac{1}{4}\right) dy \\ &= \int_{3/4}^{7/8} \frac{1}{3/4}\, dy = \frac{1}{6}. \end{aligned}$$

■

In general, if $E(Y \mid x)$ is linear, then

$$E(Y \mid x) = \mu_Y + \rho\left(\frac{\sigma_Y}{\sigma_X}\right)(x - \mu_X).$$

If $E(X \mid y)$ is linear, then

$$E(X \mid y) = \mu_X + \rho\left(\frac{\sigma_X}{\sigma_Y}\right)(y - \mu_Y).$$

Thus, in Example 4.3-5, the product of the coefficients of x in $E(Y \mid x)$ and y in $E(X \mid y)$ is $\rho^2 = 1/4$. It then follows that $\rho = 1/2$, since each coefficient is positive. Because the ratio of those coefficients is equal to $\sigma_Y^2/\sigma_X^2 = 1$, we have $\sigma_X^2 = \sigma_Y^2$.

STATISTICAL COMMENTS (**More on Simpson's Paradox**) Let us say that a small business employs 100 men and 100 women and the salary for each person is either \$20,000, \$30,000, or \$50,000. For the men, 20 make \$20,000, 20 make \$30,000, and 60 make \$50,000; the men's average is then

$$\frac{(20)(20{,}000) + (20)(30{,}000) + (60)(50{,}000)}{100} = \$40{,}000.$$

Among the women, 60 make \$20,000, 20 make \$30,000, and 20 make \$50,000; the women's average is then

$$\frac{(60)(20{,}000) + (20)(30{,}000) + (20)(50{,}000)}{100} = \$28{,}000.$$

This seems to be a fairly large gap in these two average salaries.

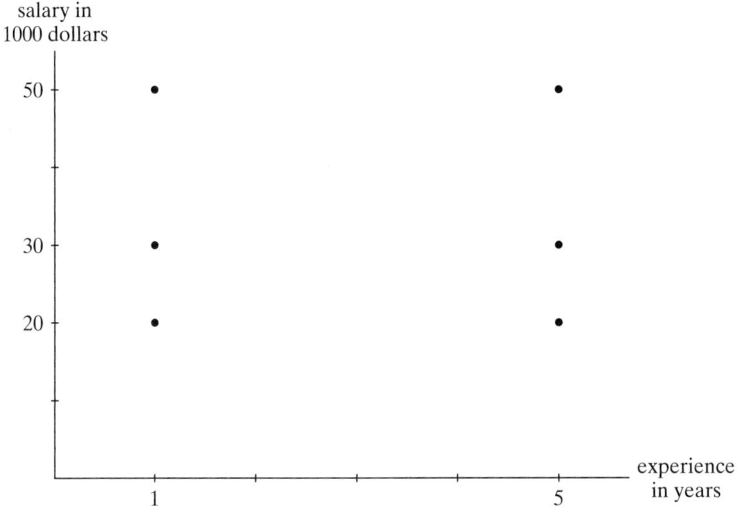

FIGURE 4.3-3: Salary versus experience

It turns out that there is another variable to consider, however, namely, experience. For simplicity, say each employee has either one year or five years of experience. Thus, we have, for the men (women), a bivariate distribution with space given by Figure 4.3-3. Now, on the one hand, we do not know the joint probabilities and hence cannot compute the conditional means, given one year and then five years of experience. On the other hand, we do have the data associated with these 100 men and 100 women and can therefore estimate the conditional means, namely, there are 20 men with one year of experience: 15 earn \$20,000 and 5 earn \$30,000, giving a mean of \$22,500. The other 80 men have five years of experience: 5 earn \$20,000, 15 earn \$30,000, and 60 earn \$50,000, for an average of \$44,375. As for the women, there are 80 with one year of experience: 60 earn \$20,000, 15 earn \$30,000, and 5 earn \$50,000, averaging \$23,750. Also, 20 women have five years of experience: 5 earn \$30,000 and 15 earn \$50,000, for an average of \$45,000. So while there is a large gap between the \$28,000 earned, on the average, by women and the \$40,000 earned by men, the women seem to have a slight advantage by a comparison of the conditional averages: \$23,750 to \$22,500, given one year of experience; and \$45,000 to \$44,375, given five years of experience. The preceding information is summarized in Table 4.3-1.

TABLE 4.3-1: Summary of Salaries

	Salary	Years of Experience: One year	Years of Experience: Five years	Total
Men	\$20,000	15	5	20
	\$30,000	5	15	20
	\$50,000	0	60	60
Average Salary		\$22,500	\$44,375	\$40,000
Women	\$20,000	60	0	60
	\$30,000	15	5	20
	\$50,000	5	15	20
Average Salary		\$23,750	\$45,000	\$28,000

This reversal is another illustration of Simpson's paradox. We are not arguing that there has not been discrimination in the pay for different genders, for there has certainly been a great deal of that in the past. Although we know in our business (academia) that most of this discrimination has been eliminated, we still insist that experience must be considered: not only years of teaching, but publications, professional field, activity in professional societies, service on committees, and so on. Clearly, we support the position that a woman and a man with the same credentials should receive the same rank and pay.

EXERCISES

4.3-1. Let X and Y have the joint p.m.f.

$$f(x,y) = \frac{x+y}{32}, \qquad x = 1,2, \qquad y = 1,2,3,4.$$

(a) Display the joint p.m.f. and the marginal p.m.f.'s on a graph like Figure 4.3-1(a).

(b) Find $g(x \mid y)$ and draw a figure like Figure 4.3-1(b), depicting the conditional p.m.f.'s for $y = 1,2,3$, and 4.

(c) Find $h(y \mid x)$ and draw a figure like Figure 4.3-1(c), depicting the conditional p.m.f.'s for $x = 1$ and 2.

(d) Find $P(1 \le Y \le 3 \mid X = 1), P(Y \le 2 \mid X = 2)$, and $P(X = 2 \mid Y = 3)$.

(e) Find $E(Y \mid X = 1)$ and $\text{Var}(Y \mid X = 1)$.

4.3-2. Let the joint p.m.f. $f(x,y)$ of X and Y be given by the following:

(x, y)	$f(x, y)$
(1, 1)	3/8
(2, 1)	1/8
(1, 2)	1/8
(2, 2)	3/8

Find the two conditional probability mass functions and the corresponding means and variances.

4.3-3. Let W equal the weight of laundry soap in a 1-kilogram box that is distributed in Southeast Asia. Suppose that $P(W < 1) = 0.02$ and $P(W > 1.072) = 0.08$. Call a box of soap light, good, or heavy, depending on whether $\{W < 1\}$, $\{1 \le W \le 1.072\}$, or $\{W > 1.072\}$, respectively. In $n = 50$ independent observations of these boxes, let X equal the number of light boxes and Y the number of good boxes.

(a) What is the joint p.m.f. of X and Y?

(b) Give the name of the distribution of Y along with the values of the parameters of this distribution.

(c) Given that $X = 3$, how is Y distributed conditionally?

(d) Determine $E(Y \mid X = 3)$.

(e) Find ρ, the correlation coefficient of X and Y.

4.3-4. The genes for eye color in a certain male fruit fly are (R, W). The genes for eye color in the mating female fruit fly are (R, W). Their offspring receive one gene for eye color from each parent. If an offspring ends up with either (R, R), (R, W), or

(W, R), its eyes will look red. Let X equal the number of offspring having red-eyes. Let Y equal the number of red eyed offspring having (R, W) or (W, R) genes.

(a) If the total number of offspring is $n = 400$, how is X distributed?
(b) Give the values of $E(X)$ and $\text{Var}(X)$.
(c) Given that $X = 300$, how is Y distributed?
(d) Give the values of $E(Y \mid X = 300)$ and $\text{Var}(Y \mid X = 300)$.

4.3-5. Let X and Y have a trinomial distribution with $n = 2$, $p_1 = 1/4$, and $p_2 = 1/2$.

(a) Give $E(Y \mid x)$.
(b) Compare your answer in part (a) with the equation of the line of best fit in Example 4.2-2. Are they the same? Why or why not?

4.3-6. An insurance company sells both homeowners insurance and automobile deductible insurance. Let X be the deductible on the homeowners insurance and Y the deductible on automobile insurance. Among those who take both types of insurance with this company, we find the following probabilities:

	x		
y	100	500	1000
1000	0.05	0.10	0.15
500	0.10	0.20	0.05
100	0.20	0.10	0.05

(a) Compute the following probabilities: $P(X = 500)$, $P(Y = 500)$, $P(Y = 500 \mid X = 500)$, $P(Y = 100 \mid X = 500)$.
(b) Compute the means μ_X, μ_Y, and the variances σ_X^2, σ_Y^2.
(c) Compute the conditional means $E(X \mid Y = 100)$, $E(Y \mid X = 500)$.
(d) Compute $\text{Cov}(X, Y)$.
(e) Compute the correlation coefficient $\rho = \text{Cov}(X, Y)/\sigma_X\sigma_Y$.

4.3-7. Using the joint p.m.f. from Exercise 4.2-3, find the value of $E(Y \mid x)$ for $x = 1, 2, 3, 4$. Do the points $[x, E(Y \mid x)]$ lie on the best-fitting line?

4.3-8. An unbiased six-sided die is cast 30 independent times. Let X be the number of ones and Y the number of twos.

(a) What is the joint p.m.f. of X and Y?
(b) Find the conditional p.m.f. of X, given $Y = y$.
(c) Compute $E(X^2 - 4XY + 3Y^2)$.

4.3-9. Let X and Y have a uniform distribution on the set of points with integer coordinates in $S = \{(x, y) : 0 \le x \le 7, x \le y \le x + 2\}$. That is, $f(x, y) = 1/24$, $(x, y) \in S$, and both x and y are integers. Find

(a) $f_1(x)$.
(b) $h(y \mid x)$.
(c) $E(Y \mid x)$.
(d) $\sigma_{Y|x}^2$.
(e) $f_2(y)$.

4.3-10. Let $f_1(x) = 1/10$, $x = 0, 1, 2, \ldots, 9$, and $h(y \mid x) = 1/(10 - x)$, $y = x, x + 1, \ldots, 9$. Find

(a) $f(x, y)$.
(b) $f_2(y)$.
(c) $E(Y \mid x)$.

4.3-11. An automobile repair shop makes an initial estimate X (in thousands of dollars) of the amount of money needed to fix a car after an accident. Say X has the p.d.f.

$$f(x) = 2e^{-2(x-0.2)}, \qquad 0.2 < x < \infty.$$

Given that $X = x$, the final payment Y has a uniform distribution between $x - 0.1$ and $x + 0.1$. What is the expected value of Y?

4.3-12. For the random variables defined in Example 4.3-5, calculate the correlation coefficient directly from the definition

$$\rho = \frac{\text{Cov}(X, Y)}{\sigma_X \sigma_Y}.$$

4.3-13. Let $f(x, y) = 1/40$, $0 \le x \le 10$, $10 - x \le y \le 14 - x$, be the joint p.d.f. of X and Y.

(a) Sketch the region for which $f(x, y) > 0$.
(b) Find $f_1(x)$, the marginal p.d.f. of X.
(c) Determine $h(y \mid x)$, the conditional p.d.f. of Y, given that $X = x$.
(d) Calculate $E(Y \mid x)$, the conditional mean of Y, given that $X = x$.

4.3-14. Let $f(x, y) = 1/8$, $0 \le y \le 4$, $y \le x \le y + 2$, be the joint p.d.f. of X and Y.

(a) Sketch the region for which $f(x, y) > 0$.
(b) Find $f_1(x)$, the marginal p.d.f. of X.
(c) Find $f_2(y)$, the marginal p.d.f. of Y.
(d) Determine $h(y \mid x)$, the conditional p.d.f. of Y, given that $X = x$.
(e) Determine $g(x \mid y)$, the conditional p.d.f. of X, given that $Y = y$.
(f) Compute $y = E(Y \mid x)$, the conditional mean of Y, given that $X = x$.

(g) Compute $x = E(X \mid y)$, the conditional mean of X, given that $Y = y$.

(h) Graph $y = E(Y \mid x)$ on your sketch in part (a). Is $y = E(Y \mid x)$ linear?

(i) Graph $x = E(X \mid y)$ on your sketch in part (a). Is $x = E(X \mid y)$ linear?

4.3-15. Let X have a uniform distribution $U(0, 2)$, and let the conditional distribution of Y, given that $X = x$, be $U(0, x^2)$.

(a) Determine $f(x, y)$, the joint p.d.f. of X and Y.

(b) Calculate $f_2(y)$, the marginal p.d.f. of Y.

(c) Compute $E(X \mid y)$, the conditional mean of X, given that $Y = y$.

(d) Find $E(Y \mid x)$, the conditional mean of Y, given that $X = x$.

4.3-16. Let X have a uniform distribution on the interval $(0, 1)$. Given that $X = x$, let Y have a uniform distribution on the interval $(0, x)$.

(a) Define the conditional p.d.f. of Y, given that $X = x$. Be sure to include the domain.

(b) Find $E(Y \mid x)$.

(c) Determine the joint p.d.f. of X and Y.

(d) Find the marginal p.d.f. of Y.

4.3-17. The marginal distribution of X is $U(0, 1)$. The conditional distribution of Y, given that $X = x$, is $U(0, e^x)$.

(a) Determine $h(y \mid x)$, the conditional p.d.f. of Y, given that $X = x$.

(b) Find $E(Y \mid x)$.

(c) Display the joint p.d.f. of X and Y. Sketch the region where $f(x, y) > 0$.

(d) Find $f_2(y)$, the marginal p.d.f. of Y.

4.3-18. Let X have a uniform distribution on the interval $(0, 1)$. Given that $X = x$, let Y have a uniform distribution on the interval $(0, x + 1)$.

(a) Find the joint p.d.f. of X and Y. Sketch the region where $f(x, y) > 0$.

(b) Find $E(Y \mid x)$, the conditional mean of Y, given that $X = x$. Draw this line on the region sketched in part (a).

(c) Find $f_2(y)$, the marginal p.d.f. of Y. Be sure to include the domain.

4.3-19. Let X and Y have the joint p.d.f. $f(x, y) = cx(1 - y)$, $0 < y < 1$ and $0 < x < 1 - y$.

(a) Determine c.

(b) Compute $P(Y < X \mid X \le 1/4)$.

4.3-20. Select x and y to create a triangle of perimeter 1 that has sides of lengths x, y, and $1 - x - y$. By Heron's formula, the area of such a triangle is

$$T = \frac{1}{4}\sqrt{(2x + 2y - 1)(1 - 2x)(1 - 2y)}.$$

If x and y are values of the jointly distributed random variables X and Y, then T is a random variable that can be thought of as the area of a "random triangle."

(a) Determine the possible values of (X, Y) and graph this region in the xy-plane. Call the region R.

(b) Select the random point (X, Y) uniformly from R. That is, the joint p.d.f. of (X, Y) is $f(x, y) = 1/A(R)$, where $A(R)$ is the area of R. Show that $E(T) = \pi/105$ and the variance of T is

$$E(T^2) - [E(T)]^2 = 1/960 - (\pi/105)^2.$$

Hint: Use Maple or some other computer algebra system.

(c) Find the marginal p.d.f. of X and the conditional p.d.f. of Y, given that $X = x$.

(d) Simulate 5000 pairs of observations of X and Y and then calculate the areas of the simulated triangles. Show that the sample mean and the sample variance of the areas of these 5000 triangles are close to the theoretical values.

(e) Now select (X, Y) as follows: The random variable X is selected randomly. That is, $f_1(x) = c$, where c is selected appropriately. Be sure to define the domain for this p.d.f. Given that $X = x$, Y is selected randomly (uniformly) from the appropriate interval. Define the joint p.d.f. of X and Y [the domain is R from part (a)], and again find $E(T)$ and the variance of T. Compare the theoretical and the sample values.

Remark This exercise is based on research at Hope College by students Andrea Douglass, Courtney Fitzgerald, and Scott Mihalik. (See references.) ■

4.4 THE BIVARIATE NORMAL DISTRIBUTION

Let X and Y be random variables with joint p.d.f. $f(x, y)$ of the continuous type. Many applications are concerned with the conditional distribution of one of the random variables—say, Y, given that $X = x$. For example, X and Y might be a student's grade point averages from high school and from the first year in college, respectively. Persons in the field of educational testing and measurement are extremely interested in the conditional distribution of Y, given that $X = x$, in such situations.

Suppose that we have an application in which we can make the following three assumptions about the conditional distribution of Y, given that $X = x$:

(a) It is normal for each real x.

(b) Its mean, $E(Y\,|\,x)$, is a linear function of x.

(c) Its variance is constant; that is, it does not depend upon the given value of x.

Of course, assumption (b), along with a result given in Section 4.3, implies that

$$E(Y\,|\,x) = \mu_Y + \rho\frac{\sigma_Y}{\sigma_X}(x - \mu_X).$$

Let us consider the implication of assumption (c). The conditional variance is given by

$$\sigma^2_{Y|x} = \int_{-\infty}^{\infty}\left[y - \mu_Y - \rho\frac{\sigma_Y}{\sigma_X}(x - \mu_X)\right]^2 h(y\,|\,x)\,dy,$$

where $h(y\,|\,x)$ is the conditional p.d.f. of Y given that $X = x$. Multiply each member of this equation by $f_1(x)$ and integrate on x. Since $\sigma^2_{Y|x}$ is a constant, the left-hand member is equal to $\sigma^2_{Y|x}$. Thus, we have

$$\sigma^2_{Y|x} = \int_{-\infty}^{\infty}\int_{-\infty}^{\infty}\left[y - \mu_Y - \rho\frac{\sigma_Y}{\sigma_X}(x - \mu_X)\right]^2 h(y\,|\,x)f_1(x)\,dy\,dx. \tag{4.4-1}$$

However, $h(y\,|\,x)f_1(x) = f(x, y)$; hence, the right-hand member is just an expectation and Equation 4.4-1 can be written as

$$\sigma^2_{Y|x} = E\left\{(Y - \mu_Y)^2 - 2\rho\frac{\sigma_Y}{\sigma_X}(X - \mu_X)(Y - \mu_Y) + \rho^2\frac{\sigma^2_Y}{\sigma^2_X}(X - \mu_X)^2\right\}.$$

But using the fact that the expectation E is a linear operator and recalling that $E[(X - \mu_X)(Y - \mu_Y)] = \rho\sigma_X\sigma_Y$, we have

$$\begin{aligned}\sigma^2_{Y|x} &= \sigma^2_Y - 2\rho\frac{\sigma_Y}{\sigma_X}\rho\sigma_X\sigma_Y + \rho^2\frac{\sigma^2_Y}{\sigma^2_X}\sigma^2_X \\ &= \sigma^2_Y - 2\rho^2\sigma^2_Y + \rho^2\sigma^2_Y = \sigma^2_Y(1 - \rho^2).\end{aligned}$$

That is, the conditional variance of Y, for each given x, is $\sigma^2_Y(1 - \rho^2)$. These facts about the conditional mean and variance, along with assumption (a), require that the conditional p.d.f. of Y, given that $X = x$, be

$$h(y\,|\,x) = \frac{1}{\sigma_Y\sqrt{2\pi}\sqrt{1 - \rho^2}}\exp\left[-\frac{[y - \mu_Y - \rho(\sigma_Y/\sigma_X)(x - \mu_X)]^2}{2\sigma^2_Y(1 - \rho^2)}\right],$$

$$-\infty < y < \infty, \text{ for every real } x.$$

Before we make any assumptions about the distribution of X, we give an example and a figure to illustrate the implications of our current assumptions.

EXAMPLE 4.4-1 Let $\mu_X = 10, \sigma_X^2 = 9, \mu_Y = 12, \sigma_Y^2 = 16$, and $\rho = 0.6$. We have seen that assumptions (a), (b), and (c) imply that the conditional distribution of Y, given that $X = x$, is

$$N\left[12 + (0.6)\left(\frac{4}{3}\right)(x - 10), 16(1 - 0.6^2)\right].$$

In Figure 4.4-1, the conditional mean line

$$E(Y\,|\,x) = 12 + (0.6)\left(\frac{4}{3}\right)(x - 10) = 0.8x + 4$$

has been graphed. For each of $x = 5, 10$, and 15, the conditional p.d.f. of Y, given that $X = x$, is displayed. ■

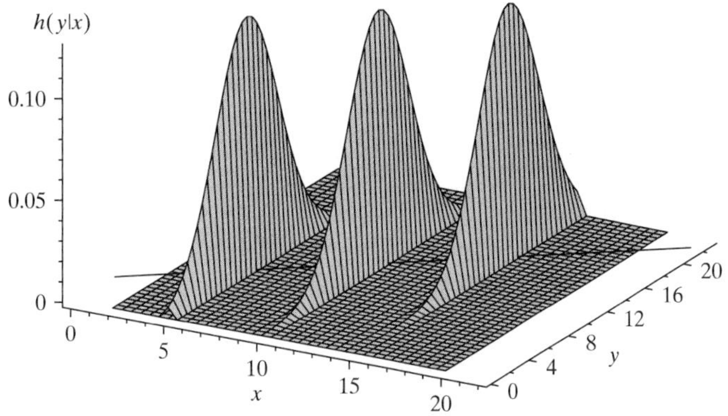

FIGURE 4.4-1: Conditional p.d.f. of Y, given that $x = 5, 10, 15$

Up to this point, nothing has been said about the distribution of X other than that it has mean μ_X and positive variance σ_X^2. Suppose, in addition, we assume that this distribution is also normal; that is, the marginal p.d.f. of X is

$$f_1(x) = \frac{1}{\sigma_X\sqrt{2\pi}}\exp\left[-\frac{(x - \mu_X)^2}{2\sigma_X^2}\right], \qquad -\infty < x < \infty.$$

Hence, the joint p.d.f. of X and Y is given by the product

$$f(x,y) = h(y\,|\,x)f_1(x) = \frac{1}{2\pi\sigma_X\sigma_Y\sqrt{1 - \rho^2}}\exp\left[-\frac{q(x,y)}{2}\right], \tag{4.4-2}$$

where it can be shown (see Exercise 4.4-2) that

$$q(x,y) = \frac{1}{1 - \rho^2}\left[\left(\frac{x - \mu_X}{\sigma_X}\right)^2 - 2\rho\left(\frac{x - \mu_X}{\sigma_X}\right)\left(\frac{y - \mu_Y}{\sigma_Y}\right) + \left(\frac{y - \mu_Y}{\sigma_Y}\right)^2\right].$$

A joint p.d.f. of this form is called a **bivariate normal p.d.f.**

EXAMPLE 4.4-2 Let us assume that in a certain population of college students, the respective grade point averages—say, X and Y—in high school and the first year in college have an approximate bivariate normal distribution with parameters $\mu_X = 2.9$, $\mu_Y = 2.4$, $\sigma_X = 0.4$, $\sigma_Y = 0.5$, and $\rho = 0.8$.

Then, for example,

$$\begin{aligned} P(2.1 < Y < 3.3) &= P\left(\frac{2.1 - 2.4}{0.5} < \frac{Y - 2.4}{0.5} < \frac{3.3 - 2.4}{0.5}\right) \\ &= \Phi(1.8) - \Phi(-0.6) = 0.6898. \end{aligned}$$

Since the conditional p.d.f. of Y, given that $X = 3.2$, is normal with mean

$$2.4 + (0.8)\left(\frac{0.5}{0.4}\right)(3.2 - 2.9) = 2.7$$

and standard deviation $(0.5)\sqrt{1 - 0.64} = 0.3$, we have

$$\begin{aligned} &P(2.1 < Y < 3.3 \mid X = 3.2) \\ &\quad = P\left(\frac{2.1 - 2.7}{0.3} < \frac{Y - 2.7}{0.3} < \frac{3.3 - 2.7}{0.3} \,\middle|\, X = 3.2\right) \\ &\quad = \Phi(2) - \Phi(-2) = 0.9544. \end{aligned}$$

From a practical point of view, however, the reader should be warned that the correlation coefficient of these grade point averages is, in many instances, much smaller than 0.8. ■

Since x and y enter the bivariate normal p.d.f. in a similar manner, the roles of X and Y could have been interchanged. That is, Y could have been assigned the marginal normal p.d.f. $N(\mu_Y, \sigma_Y^2)$, and the conditional p.d.f. of X, given that $Y = y$, would have then been normal, with mean $\mu_X + \rho(\sigma_X/\sigma_Y)(y - \mu_Y)$ and variance $\sigma_X^2(1 - \rho^2)$. Although this property is fairly obvious, we do want to make special note of it.

In order to have a better understanding of the geometry of the bivariate normal distribution, consider the graph of $z = f(x, y)$, where $f(x, y)$ is given by Equation 4.4-2. If we intersect this surface with planes parallel to the yz-plane (i.e., with $x = x_0$), we have

$$f(x_0, y) = f_1(x_0)h(y \mid x_0).$$

In this equation, $f_1(x_0)$ is a constant and $h(y \mid x_0)$ is a normal p.d.f. Thus, $z = f(x_0, y)$ is bell shaped; that is, has the shape of a normal p.d.f. However, note that it is not necessarily a p.d.f., because of the factor $f_1(x_0)$. Similarly, intersections of the surface $z = f(x, y)$ with planes $y = y_0$ parallel to the xz-plane will be bell shaped.

If

$$0 < z_0 < \frac{1}{2\pi\sigma_X\sigma_Y\sqrt{1 - \rho^2}},$$

then

$$0 < z_0 2\pi\sigma_X\sigma_Y\sqrt{1 - \rho^2} < 1.$$

If we intersect $z = f(x, y)$ with the plane $z = z_0$, which is parallel to the xy-plane, then we have

$$z_0 2\pi\sigma_X\sigma_Y\sqrt{1 - \rho^2} = \exp\left[\frac{-q(x, y)}{2}\right].$$

We show that these intersections are ellipses by taking the natural logarithm of each side to obtain

$$\left(\frac{x - \mu_X}{\sigma_X}\right)^2 - 2\rho\left(\frac{x - \mu_X}{\sigma_X}\right)\left(\frac{y - \mu_Y}{\sigma_Y}\right) + \left(\frac{y - \mu_Y}{\sigma_Y}\right)^2$$
$$= -2(1 - \rho^2)\ln(z_0 2\pi\sigma_X\sigma_Y\sqrt{1 - \rho^2}\,).$$

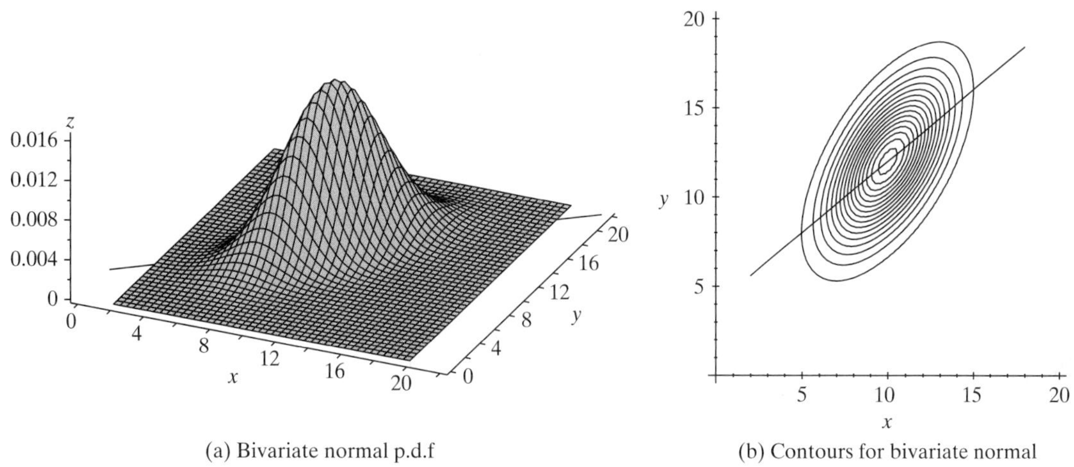

(a) Bivariate normal p.d.f

(b) Contours for bivariate normal

FIGURE 4.4-2: Bivariate normal, $\mu_X = 10$, $\sigma_X^2 = 9$, $\mu_Y = 12$, $\sigma_Y^2 = 16$, $\rho = 0.6$

EXAMPLE 4.4-3 With $\mu_X = 10$, $\sigma_X^2 = 9$, $\mu_Y = 12$, $\sigma_Y^2 = 16$, and $\rho = 0.6$, the bivariate normal p.d.f. has been graphed in Figure 4.4-2(a). For $\rho = 0.6$, level curves, or contours, are given in Figure 4.4-2(b). The conditional mean line,

$$E(Y \mid x) = 12 + (0.6)\left(\frac{4}{3}\right)(x - 10) = 0.8x + 4,$$

is also drawn on Figure 4.4-2(b). Note that this line intersects the level curves at points through which vertical tangents can be drawn to the ellipses. ■

We close this section by observing another important property of the correlation coefficient ρ if X and Y have a bivariate normal distribution. In Equation 4.4-2 of the product $h(y \mid x)f_1(x)$, let us consider the factor $h(y \mid x)$ if $\rho = 0$. We see that this product, which is the joint p.d.f. of X and Y, equals $f_1(x)f_2(y)$ because when $\rho = 0$, $h(y \mid x)$ is a normal p.d.f. with mean μ_Y and variance σ_Y^2. That is, if $\rho = 0$, then the joint p.d.f. factors into the product of the two marginal probability density functions and hence X and Y are independent random variables. Of course, if X and Y are *any* independent random variables (not necessarily normal), then ρ, if it exists, is always equal to zero. Hence, we have proved the following theorem.

THEOREM 4.4-1 If X and Y have a bivariate normal distribution with correlation coefficient ρ, then X and Y are independent if and only if $\rho = 0$.

Thus, in the bivariate normal case, $\rho = 0$ does imply independence of X and Y. Note that these characteristics of the bivariate normal distribution can be extended to the trivariate normal distribution or, more generally, the multivariate normal distribution. This is done in more advanced texts that assume some knowledge of matrices [e.g., Hogg, McKean, and Craig (2005)].

EXERCISES

4.4-1. Let X and Y have a bivariate normal distribution with parameters $\mu_X = -3$, $\mu_Y = 10$, $\sigma_X^2 = 25$, $\sigma_Y^2 = 9$, and $\rho = 3/5$. Compute

(a) $P(-5 < X < 5)$.
(b) $P(-5 < X < 5 \mid Y = 13)$.
(c) $P(7 < Y < 16)$.
(d) $P(7 < Y < 16 \mid X = 2)$.

4.4-2. Show that the expression in the exponent of Equation 4.4-2 is equal to the function $q(x, y)$ given in the text.

4.4-3. Let X and Y have a bivariate normal distribution with parameters $\mu_X = 2.8$, $\mu_Y = 110$, $\sigma_X^2 = 0.16$, $\sigma_Y^2 = 100$, and $\rho = 0.6$. Compute

(a) $P(106 < Y < 124)$.
(b) $P(106 < Y < 124 \mid X = 3.2)$.

4.4-4. Let X and Y have a bivariate normal distribution with $\mu_X = 70$, $\sigma_X^2 = 100$, $\mu_Y = 80$, $\sigma_Y^2 = 169$, and $\rho = 5/13$. Find

(a) $E(Y \mid X = 72)$.
(b) $\text{Var}(Y \mid X = 72)$.
(c) $P(Y \le 84 \mid X = 72)$.

4.4-5. Let X denote the height in centimeters and Y the weight in kilograms of male college students. Assume that X and Y have a bivariate normal distribution with parameters $\mu_X = 185$, $\sigma_X^2 = 100$, $\mu_Y = 84$, $\sigma_Y^2 = 64$, and $\rho = 3/5$.

(a) Determine the conditional distribution of Y, given that $X = 190$.
(b) Find $P(86.4 < Y < 95.36 \mid X = 190)$.

4.4-6. For a freshman taking introductory statistics and majoring in psychology, let X equal the student's ACT mathematics score and Y the student's ACT verbal score. Assume that X and Y have a bivariate normal distribution with $\mu_X = 22.7$, $\sigma_X^2 = 17.64$, $\mu_Y = 22.7$, $\sigma_Y^2 = 12.25$, and $\rho = 0.78$.

(a) Find $P(18.5 < Y < 25.5)$.
(b) Find $E(Y \mid x)$.
(c) Find $\text{Var}(Y \mid x)$.
(d) Find $P(18.5 < Y < 25.5 \mid X = 23)$.
(e) Find $P(18.5 < Y < 25.5 \mid X = 25)$.
(f) For $x = 21, 23$, and 25, draw a graph of $z = h(y \mid x)$ similar to Figure 4.4-1.

4.4-7. For a pair of gallinules, let X equal the weight in grams of the male and Y the weight in grams of the female. Assume that X and Y have a bivariate normal distribution with $\mu_X = 415$, $\sigma_X^2 = 611$, $\mu_Y = 347$, $\sigma_Y^2 = 689$, and $\rho = -0.25$. Find

(a) $P(309.2 < Y < 380.6)$.
(b) $E(Y \mid x)$.
(c) $\text{Var}(Y \mid x)$.
(d) $P(309.2 < Y < 380.6 \mid X = 385.1)$.

4.4-8. Let X and Y have a bivariate normal distribution with parameters $\mu_X = 10$, $\sigma_X^2 = 9$, $\mu_Y = 15$, $\sigma_Y^2 = 16$, and $\rho = 0$. Find

(a) $P(13.6 < Y < 17.2)$.
(b) $E(Y \mid x)$.
(c) $\text{Var}(Y \mid x)$.
(d) $P(13.6 < Y < 17.2 \mid X = 9.1)$.

4.4-9. Let X and Y have a bivariate normal distribution. Find two different lines, $a(x)$ and $b(x)$, parallel to and equidistant from $E(Y \mid x)$, such that

$$P[a(x) < Y < b(x) \mid X = x] = 0.9544$$

for all real x. Plot $a(x)$, $b(x)$, and $E(Y \mid x)$ when $\mu_X = 2$, $\mu_Y = -1$, $\sigma_X = 3$, $\sigma_Y = 5$, and $\rho = 3/5$.

4.4-10. In a college health fitness program, let X denote the weight in kilograms of a male freshman at the beginning of the program and Y denote his weight change during a semester. Assume that X and Y have a bivariate normal distribution with $\mu_X = 72.30$, $\sigma_X^2 = 110.25$, $\mu_Y = 2.80$, $\sigma_Y^2 = 2.89$, and $\rho = -0.57$. (The lighter students tend to gain weight, while the heavier students tend to lose weight.) Find

(a) $P(2.80 \le Y \le 5.35)$.
(b) $P(2.76 \le y \le 5.34 \mid X = 82.3)$.

4.4-11. For a female freshman in a health fitness program, let X equal her percentage of body fat at the beginning of the program and Y equal the change in her percentage of body fat measured at the end of the program. Assume that X and Y have a bivariate normal distribution with $\mu_X = 24.5$, $\sigma_X^2 = 4.8^2 = 23.04$, $\mu_Y = -0.2$, $\sigma_Y^2 = 3.0^2 = 9.0$, and $\rho = -0.32$. Find

(a) $P(1.3 \le Y \le 5.8)$.

(b) $\mu_{Y|x}$, the conditional mean of Y, given that $X = x$.

(c) $\sigma_{Y|x}^2$, the conditional variance of Y, given that $X = x$.

(d) $P(1.3 \le Y \le 5.8 \mid X = 18)$.

4.4-12. For a male freshman in a health fitness program, let X equal his percentage of body fat at the beginning of the program and Y equal the change in his percentage of body fat measured at the end of the program. Assume that X and Y have a bivariate normal distribution with $\mu_X = 15.00$, $\sigma_X^2 = 4.5^2$, $\mu_Y = -1.55$, $\sigma_Y^2 = 1.5^2$, and $\rho = -0.60$. Find

(a) $P(0.205 \le Y \le 0.805)$.

(b) $P(0.21 \le Y \le 0.81 \mid X = 20)$.

4.4-13. The concentration (X) and the viscosity (Y) of a chemical product have a bivariate normal distribution with parameters $\mu_X = 3, \mu_Y = 2$, $\sigma_X = 2, \sigma_Y = 1$, and $\rho = 0.6$.

(a) What is $P(X + Y \ge 4)$? HINT: Find the moment-generating function of $Z = X + Y$ and show that it has a normal distribution.

(b) Compute the conditional probability $P(X \ge 3.5 \mid Y = 2.5)$.

(c) Compute

$$P\left\{\left(\frac{1}{0.64}\right)\left[\left(\frac{X-3}{2}\right)^2 - (2)(0.6)\left(\frac{X-3}{2}\right)(Y-2) + (Y-2)^2\right] \ge 5.99\right\}.$$

HINT: Show that the moment-generating function of the second degree function $q(X, Y)$ in the probability statement is equal to $(1 - 2t)^{-1}$.

4.4-14. Suppose that in a certain population of cigarettes the tar (X) per cigarette in milligrams and the nicotine (Y) have a bivariate normal distribution with parameters $\mu_X = 14.1, \sigma_X = 2.5, \mu_Y = 1.3, \sigma_Y = 0.1$, and $\rho = 0.8$. Compute

(a) $P(Y > 1.4 \mid X = 15)$,

(b) $P(X > 15 \mid Y = 1.4)$.

4.4-15. An obstetrician does ultrasound examinations on her patients between their 16th and 25th weeks of pregnancy to check the growth of each fetus. Let X equal the widest diameter of the fetal head, and let Y equal the length of the femur, both measurements in mm. Assume that X and Y have a bivariate normal distribution with $\mu_X = 60.6$, $\sigma_X = 11.2$, $\mu_Y = 46.8$, $\sigma_Y = 8.4$, and $\rho = 0.94$.

(a) Find $P(40.5 < Y < 48.9)$.

(b) Find $P(40.5 < Y < 48.9 \mid X = 68.6)$.

HISTORICAL COMMENTS Now that we have studied conditional distributions, it might be appropriate to point out that there is a group of statisticians called Bayesians who believe in the following approach (it is considered again in Chapter 9): They treat the parameter θ (like μ, σ^2, α, and β in the various distributions) as a random variable with a p.m.f. (or p.d.f.), say, $g(\theta)$. Suppose another random variable X, given θ, has the p.m.f. (or p.d.f.) $f(x \mid \theta)$. Say the prior probabilities can be described by $g(\theta)$ so that the joint p.m.f. (or p.d.f.) is given by the sum (or integral)

$$h(x) = \sum_{\theta} g(\theta) f(x \mid \theta).$$

Thus, the conditional p.m.f. (or p.d.f.) of θ, given that $X = x$, is

$$k(\theta \mid x) = \frac{g(\theta) f(x \mid \theta)}{h(x)} = \frac{g(\theta) f(x \mid \theta)}{\sum_{\theta} g(\theta) f(x \mid \theta)}.$$

With a little thought you can recognize this formula as Bayes's theorem. Here the posterior probabilities, $k(\theta \mid x)$, of θ change from the prior probabilities given by $g(\theta)$, after X is observed to be x. Repeating the experiment n independent times (see Chapter 5), we obtain n values of x—say, $x_1, x_2, \ldots, x_n$. The Bayesians use the posterior distribution $k(\theta \mid x_1, x_2, \ldots, x_n)$ to make their inferences about the parameter θ because they then know the conditional probabilities of θ, given $x_1, x_2, \ldots, x_n$.

It is interesting to note that the Reverend Thomas Bayes, a minister who started this method of thinking, never published a mathematical article in his lifetime, and his famous paper was published about two years after his death. Clearly, he was not working for tenure at some university! More will be noted about Bayesian methods in Chapter 9.

CHAPTER 5

Distributions of Functions of Random Variables

5.1 FUNCTIONS OF ONE RANDOM VARIABLE
5.2 TRANSFORMATIONS OF TWO RANDOM VARIABLES
5.3 SEVERAL INDEPENDENT RANDOM VARIABLES
5.4 THE MOMENT-GENERATING FUNCTION TECHNIQUE
5.5 RANDOM FUNCTIONS ASSOCIATED WITH NORMAL DISTRIBUTIONS
5.6 THE CENTRAL LIMIT THEOREM
5.7 APPROXIMATIONS FOR DISCRETE DISTRIBUTIONS

5.1 FUNCTIONS OF ONE RANDOM VARIABLE

Let X be a random variable of the continuous type. If we consider a function of X—say, $Y = u(X)$—then Y must also be a random variable that has its own distribution. If we can find its distribution function, say,

$$G(y) = P(Y \le y) = P[u(X) \le y],$$

then its p.d.f. is given by $g(y) = G'(y)$. We now illustrate the **distribution function technique** by two examples.

EXAMPLE 5.1-1 Let X have a gamma distribution with p.d.f.

$$f(x) = \frac{1}{\Gamma(\alpha)\theta^{\alpha}} x^{\alpha-1}e^{-x/\theta}, \qquad 0 < x < \infty,$$

where $\alpha > 0$, $\theta > 0$. Let $Y = e^X$, so that the support of Y is $1 < y < \infty$. For each y in the support, the distribution function of Y is

$$G(y) = P(Y \le y) = P(e^X \le y) = P(X \le \ln y).$$

That is,

$$G(y) = \int_0^{\ln y} \frac{1}{\Gamma(\alpha)\theta^{\alpha}} x^{\alpha-1}e^{-x/\theta}dx$$

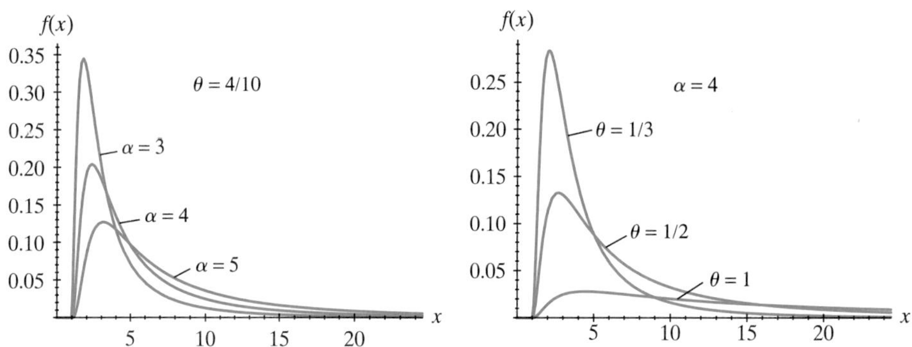

FIGURE 5.1-1: Loggamma probability density functions

and thus the p.d.f. $g(y) = G'(y)$ of Y is

$$g(y) = \frac{1}{\Gamma(\alpha)\theta^\alpha}(\ln y)^{\alpha-1}e^{-(\ln y)/\theta}\left(\frac{1}{y}\right), \qquad 1 < y < \infty.$$

Equivalently, we have

$$g(y) = \frac{1}{\Gamma(\alpha)\theta^\alpha}\frac{(\ln y)^{\alpha-1}}{y^{1+1/\theta}}, \qquad 1 < y < \infty,$$

which is called a **loggamma** p.d.f. (See Figure 5.1-1 for some graphs.) Note that $\alpha\theta$ and $\alpha\theta^2$ are the mean and the variance, not of Y, but of the original random variable $X = \ln Y$. For the loggamma distribution,

$$\mu = \frac{1}{(1-\theta)^\alpha}, \qquad \theta < 1,$$

$$\sigma^2 = \frac{1}{(1-2\theta)^\alpha} - \frac{1}{(1-\theta)^{2\alpha}}, \qquad \theta < \frac{1}{2}.$$ ■

There is another interesting distribution, this one involving a transformation of a uniform random variable.

EXAMPLE 5.1-2 A spinner is mounted at the point $(0, 1)$. Let w be the smallest angle between the y-axis and the spinner. (See Figure 5.1-2.) Assume that w is the value of a random variable W that has a uniform distribution on the interval $(-\pi/2, \pi/2)$. That is, W is $U(-\pi/2, \pi/2)$, and the distribution function of W is

$$P(W \le w) = F(w) = \begin{cases} 0, & -\infty < w < -\dfrac{\pi}{2}, \\ \left(w + \dfrac{\pi}{2}\right)\left(\dfrac{1}{\pi}\right), & -\dfrac{\pi}{2} \le w < \dfrac{\pi}{2}, \\ 1, & \dfrac{\pi}{2} \le w < \infty. \end{cases}$$

The relationship between x and w is given by $x = \tan w$; that is, x is the point on the x-axis which is the intersection of that axis and the linear extension of the spinner. To find the distribution of the random variable $X = \tan W$, we note that the distribution

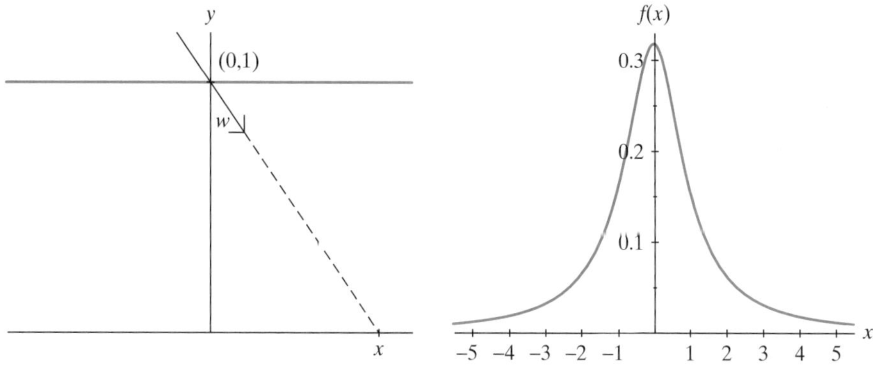

FIGURE 5.1-2: Spinner and Cauchy p.d.f.

function of X is given by

$$\begin{aligned} G(x) = P(X \le x) &= P(\tan W \le x) = P(W \le \arctan x) \\ = F(\arctan x) &= \left(\arctan x + \frac{\pi}{2}\right)\left(\frac{1}{\pi}\right), \qquad -\infty < x < \infty. \end{aligned}$$

The last equality follows because $-\pi/2 < w = \arctan x < \pi/2$. The p.d.f. of X is given by

$$g(x) = G'(x) = \frac{1}{\pi(1 + x^2)}, \qquad -\infty < x < \infty.$$

Figure 5.1-2 shows the graph of this **Cauchy p.d.f.** In Exercise 5.1-12, you will be asked to show that $E(X)$ does not exist because the tails of the Cauchy p.d.f. contain too much probability for this p.d.f. to "balance" at $x = 0$. ■

Thus far, the examples have illustrated the use of the distribution function technique. By making a simple observation, we can sometimes shortcut the distribution function technique by using what is frequently called the **change-of-variable technique.** Let X be a continuous-type random variable with p.d.f. $f(x)$ with support $c_1 < x < c_2$. We begin this discussion by taking $Y = u(X)$ as a continuous increasing function of X with inverse function $X = v(Y)$. Say the support of X, namely, $c_1 < x < c_2$, maps onto $d_1 = u(c_1) < y < d_2 = u(c_2)$, the support of Y. Then the distribution function of Y is

$$G(y) = P(Y \le y) = P[u(X) \le y] = P[X \le v(y)], \qquad d_1 < y < d_2,$$

since u and v are continuous increasing functions. Of course, $G(y) = 0,\ y \le d_1$, and $G(y) = 1,\ y \ge d_2$. Thus,

$$G(y) = \int_{c_1}^{v(y)} f(x)\,dx, \qquad d_1 < y < d_2.$$

Recall from calculus that the derivative, $G'(y) = g(y)$, of such an expression is given by

$$G'(y) = g(y) = f[v(y)][v'(y)], \qquad d_1 < y < d_2.$$

Of course, $G'(y) = g(y) = 0$ if $y < d_1$ or $y > d_2$. We may let $g(d_1) = g(d_2) = 0$.

To illustrate this change-of-variable technique, let us consider again Example 5.1-1 with $Y = e^X$, where X has p.d.f.

$$f(x) = \frac{1}{\Gamma(\alpha)\theta^\alpha} x^{\alpha-1} e^{-x/\theta}, \qquad 0 < x < \infty.$$

Here $c_1 = 0$ and $c_2 = \infty$; thus, $d_1 = 1$ and $d_2 = \infty$. Also, $X = \ln Y = v(Y)$. Since $v'(y) = 1/y$, the p.d.f. of Y is

$$g(y) = \frac{1}{\Gamma(\alpha)\theta^\alpha} (\ln y)^{\alpha-1} e^{-(\ln y)/\theta} \left(\frac{1}{y}\right), \qquad 1 < y < \infty,$$

which is the same result as obtained in that Example 5.1-1.

Suppose now the function $Y = u(X)$ and its inverse $X = v(Y)$ are continuous *decreasing* functions. Then the mapping of $c_1 < x < c_2$ is $d_1 = u(c_1) > y > d_2 = u(c_2)$.

Since u and v are decreasing functions, we have

$$G(y) = P(Y \le y) = P[u(X) \le y] = P[X \ge v(y)] = \int_{v(y)}^{c_2} f(x)\,dx, \qquad d_2 < y < d_1.$$

Accordingly, from calculus, we obtain

$$G'(y) = g(y) = f[v(y)][-v'(y)], \qquad d_2 < y < d_1,$$

and $G'(y) = g(y) = 0$ elsewhere. Note that in both the increasing and decreasing cases we could write

$$g(y) = f[v(y)]\,|v'(y)|, \qquad y \in S_y,$$

where S_y is the support of Y found by mapping the support of X (say, S_x) onto S_y. The absolute value $|v'(y)|$ assures that $g(y)$ is nonnegative.

EXAMPLE 5.1-3 Let X have the p.d.f.

$$f(x) = 3(1 - x)^2, \qquad 0 < x < 1.$$

Say $Y = (1 - X)^3 = u(X)$, a decreasing function of X. Thus, $X = 1 - Y^{1/3} = v(Y)$ and $0 < x < 1$ is mapped onto $0 < y < 1$. Since

$$v'(y) = -\frac{1}{3y^{2/3}},$$

we have

$$g(y) = 3[1 - (1 - y^{1/3})]^2 \left|\frac{-1}{3y^{2/3}}\right|, \qquad 0 < y < 1.$$

That is,

$$g(y) = 3y^{2/3}\left(\frac{1}{3y^{2/3}}\right) = 1, \qquad 0 < y < 1;$$

so $Y = (1 - X)^3$ has the uniform distribution $U(0,1)$. ■

As we have seen, it is sometimes easier to use the change-of-variable technique than the distribution function technique. However, there are many occasions on which the latter is more convenient to use. As a matter of fact, we had to use the distribution function in finding the gamma distribution from the Poisson process. (See Section 3.5.) We again use the distribution function technique to prove two theorems involving the uniform distribution.

THEOREM 5.1-1 Let Y have a distribution that is $U(0,1)$. Let $F(x)$ have the properties of a distribution function of the continuous type with $F(a) = 0$, $F(b) = 1$, and suppose that $F(x)$ is strictly increasing on the support $a < x < b$, where a and b could be $-\infty$ and ∞, respectively. Then the random variable X defined by $X = F^{-1}(Y)$ is a continuous-type random variable with distribution function $F(x)$.

Proof. The distribution function of X is

$$P(X \le x) = P[F^{-1}(Y) \le x], \qquad a < x < b.$$

Since $F(x)$ is strictly increasing, $\{F^{-1}(Y) \le x\}$ is equivalent to $\{Y \le F(x)\}$. It follows that

$$P(X \le x) = P[Y \le F(x)], \qquad a < x < b.$$

But Y is $U(0,1)$; so $P(Y \le y) = y$ for $0 < y < 1$, and accordingly,

$$P(X \le x) = P[Y \le F(x)] = F(x), \qquad 0 < F(x) < 1.$$

That is, the distribution function of X is $F(x)$. □

The next two examples illustrate how Theorem 5.1-1 can be used to simulate observations from a given distribution.

EXAMPLE 5.1-4 To see how we can simulate observations from an exponential distribution with a mean of $\theta = 10$, note that the distribution function of X is $F(x) = 1 - e^{-x/10}$ when $0 \le x < \infty$. Solving $y = F(x)$ for x yields $x = F^{-1}(y) = -10\ln(1 - y)$. So, given random numbers $y_1, y_2, \ldots, y_n$ from the $U(0,1)$ distribution, we would expect $x_i = -10\ln(1 - y_i)$, $i = 1, 2, \ldots, n$, to represent n observations of an exponential random variable X with mean $\theta = 10$. Table 5.1-1 gives the values of 15 random numbers, y_i, along with the values of $x_i = -10\ln(1 - y_i)$.

As a rough check on whether these 15 observations seem to come from an exponential distribution with mean 10, let us construct a q–q plot. We must order the 15 observations and plot them against the corresponding quantiles q_i of the exponential distribution with mean $\theta = 10$. The resulting quantiles are the solution of

$$F(q_i) = 1 - e^{-q_i/10} = \frac{i}{16}$$

or, equivalently,

$$q_i = -10\ln\left(1 - \frac{i}{16}\right).$$

The ordered x_i's and the respective quantiles, q_i, are given in Table 5.1-1.

Figure 5.1-3 shows the q–q plot for these data. The linearity of this plot confirms the possibility of the exponential distribution being the correct model. The sample

TABLE 5.1-1: Random Exponential Observations and Exponential Quantiles

y	$x = -10\ln(1 - y)$	Ordered x's	Quantiles
0.1514	1.6417	0.0431	0.6454
0.6697	11.0775	0.5414	1.3353
0.0527	0.5414	1.0569	2.0764
0.4749	6.4417	1.6417	2.8768
0.2900	3.4249	2.6840	3.7469
0.2354	2.6840	3.4249	4.7000
0.9662	33.8729	6.4417	5.7536
0.0043	0.0431	6.8736	6.9315
0.1003	1.0569	8.9526	8.2668
0.9192	25.1578	11.0775	9.8083
0.4971	6.8736	13.0674	11.6315
0.7293	13.0674	17.2878	13.8629
0.9118	24.2815	24.2815	16.7398
0.8225	17.2878	25.1578	20.7944
0.5915	8.9526	33.8729	27.7259

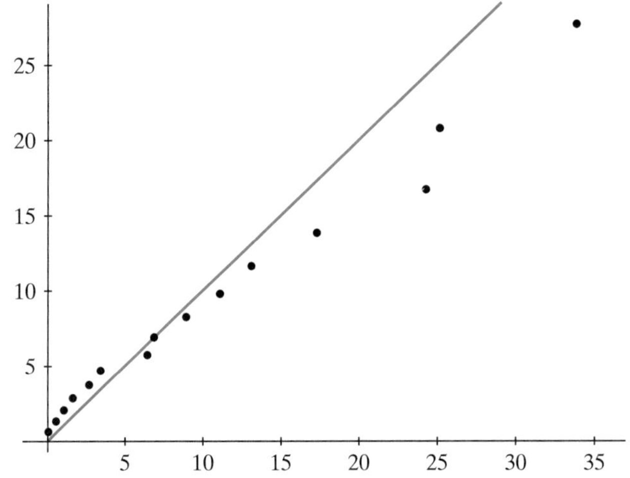

FIGURE 5.1-3: Exponential q–q plot

mean is $\bar{x} = 10.4270$ and the sample standard deviation is $s = 10.4311$, both of which are close to $\theta = 10$. We caution the reader that in other simulations the fit is sometimes better and sometimes not as good. ■

EXAMPLE 5.1-5 To help appreciate the large probability in the tails of the Cauchy distribution, it is useful to simulate some observations of a Cauchy random variable. We can begin with a random number, Y, that is an observation from the $U(0, 1)$ distribution. From the distribution function of X, namely, $G(x)$, which is that of the Cauchy distribution given in Example 5.1-2, we have

$$y = G(x) = \left(\arctan x + \frac{\pi}{2}\right)\left(\frac{1}{\pi}\right), \qquad -\infty < x < \infty,$$

or, equivalently,

$$x = \tan\left(\pi y - \frac{\pi}{2}\right). \tag{5.1-1}$$

The latter expression provides observations of X.

TABLE 5.1-2: Cauchy Observations

y	x	y	x
0.1514	−1.9415	0.2354	−1.0962
0.6697	0.5901	0.9662	9.3820
0.0527	−5.9847	0.0043	−74.0211
0.4749	−0.0790	0.1003	−3.0678
0.2900	−0.7757	0.9192	3.8545

In Table 5.1-2, the values of y are the first 10 random numbers in the last column of Table IX in the appendix. The corresponding values of x are given by Equation 5.1-1. Although most of these observations from the Cauchy distribution are relatively small in magnitude, we see that a very large value (in magnitude) occurs occasionally. Another way of looking at this situation is by considering sightings (or firing of a gun) from an observation tower, here with coordinates $(0, 1)$, at independent random angles, each with the uniform distribution $U(-\pi/2, \pi/2)$; the target points would then be at Cauchy observations. ■

The following probability integral transformation theorem is the converse of Theorem 5.1-1.

THEOREM 5.1-2 Let X have the distribution function $F(x)$ of the continuous type that is strictly increasing on the support $a < x < b$. Then the random variable Y, defined by $Y = F(X)$, has a distribution that is $U(0, 1)$.

Proof. Since $F(a) = 0$ and $F(b) = 1$, the distribution function of Y is

$$P(Y \le y) = P[F(X) \le y], \qquad 0 < y < 1.$$

However, $\{F(X) \le y\}$ is equivalent to $\{X \le F^{-1}(y)\}$; thus,

$$P(Y \le y) = P[X \le F^{-1}(y)], \qquad 0 < y < 1.$$

Since $P(X \le x) = F(x)$, we have

$$P(Y \le y) = P[X \le F^{-1}(y)] = F[F^{-1}(y)] = y, \qquad 0 < y < 1,$$

which is the distribution function of a $U(0, 1)$ random variable. □

REMARK Although, in our statements and proofs of Theorems 5.1-1 and 5.1-2, we required $F(x)$ to be strictly increasing, this restriction can be dropped and both theorems are still true. In our exposition, we did not want to bother students with certain difficulties that are experienced if $F(x)$ is not strictly increasing. ■

Another observation concerns the situation in which the transformation $Y = u(X)$ is not one-to-one, as it has been up to this point in this section. For example, let $Y = X^2$, where X is Cauchy. Here $-\infty < x < \infty$ maps onto $0 \le y < \infty$, so

$$G(y) = P(X^2 \le y) = P(-\sqrt{y} \le X \le \sqrt{y})$$
$$= \int_{-\sqrt{y}}^{\sqrt{y}} f(x)\,dx, \qquad 0 \le y < \infty,$$

where

$$f(x) = \frac{1}{\pi(1+x^2)}, \qquad -\infty < x < \infty.$$

Thus,

$$G'(y) = g(y) = f(\sqrt{y}\,)\left|\frac{1}{2\sqrt{y}}\right| + f(-\sqrt{y}\,)\left|\frac{-1}{2\sqrt{y}}\right|$$
$$= \frac{1}{\pi(1+y)\sqrt{y}}, \qquad 0 \le y < \infty.$$

That is, in this case of a two-to-one transformation, there is a need to sum two terms, each of which is similar to a counterpart term in the one-to-one case; but here $x_1 = \sqrt{y}$ and $x_2 = -\sqrt{y}$, $0 < y < \infty$, give the two inverse functions, respectively.

With careful thought, we can handle many situations that generalize this particular example.

EXAMPLE 5.1-6 Let X have the p.d.f.

$$f(x) = \frac{x^2}{3}, \qquad -1 < x < 2.$$

Then the random variable $Y = X^2$ will have the support $0 \le y < 4$. Now, on the one hand, for $0 < y < 1$, we obtain the two-to-one transformation represented by $x_1 = -\sqrt{y}$ for $-1 < x_1 < 0$ and by $x_2 = \sqrt{y}$ for $0 < x_2 < 1$. On the other hand, if $1 < y < 4$, the one-to-one transformation is represented by $x_2 = \sqrt{y}, 1 < x_2 < 2$. Since

$$\frac{dx_1}{dy} = \frac{-1}{2\sqrt{y}} \quad \text{and} \quad \frac{dx_2}{dy} = \frac{1}{2\sqrt{y}},$$

it follows that the p.d.f. of $Y = X^2$ is

$$g(y) = \begin{cases} \dfrac{(-\sqrt{y}\,)^2}{3}\left|\dfrac{-1}{2\sqrt{y}}\right| + \dfrac{(\sqrt{y}\,)^2}{3}\left|\dfrac{1}{2\sqrt{y}}\right| = \dfrac{\sqrt{y}}{3}, & 0 < y < 1, \\[2ex] \dfrac{(\sqrt{y}\,)^2}{3}\left|\dfrac{1}{2\sqrt{y}}\right| = \dfrac{\sqrt{y}}{6}, & 1 < y < 4. \end{cases}$$

Note that if $0 < y < 1$, the p.d.f. is the sum of two terms, but if $1 < y < 4$, then there is only one term. These different expressions in $g(y)$ correspond to the two types of transformations, namely, the two-to-one and the one-to-one transformations, respectively. ■

The change-of-variable technique can be used for a variable X of the discrete type, but there is one major difference: The p.m.f. $f(x) = P(X = x)$, $x \in S_X$, represents probability. Note that the support S_X consists of a countable number of points, say, $c_1, c_2, c_3, \ldots$. Let $Y = u(X)$ be a one-to-one transformation with inverse $X = v(Y)$. The function $y = u(x)$ maps S_X onto $d_1 = u(c_1)$, $d_2 = u(c_2)$, $d_3 = u(c_3), \ldots$, which we denote by S_Y. Hence, the p.m.f. of Y is

$$g(y) = P(Y = y) = P[u(X) = y] = P[X = v(y)], \qquad y \in S_Y.$$

Since $P(X = x) = f(x)$, we have $g(y) = f[v(y)]$, $y \in S_Y$. Note that, in this discrete case, the value of the derivative, namely, $|v'(y)|$, is not needed.

EXAMPLE 5.1-7 Let X have a Poisson distribution with $\lambda = 4$; thus, the p.m.f. is

$$f(x) = \frac{4^x e^{-4}}{x!}, \qquad x = 0, 1, 2, \ldots.$$

If $Y = \sqrt{X}$, then, since $X = Y^2$, we have

$$g(y) = \frac{4^{y^2} e^{-4}}{(y^2)!}, \qquad y = 0, 1, \sqrt{2}, \sqrt{3}, \ldots. \qquad ■$$

EXAMPLE 5.1-8 Let the distribution of X be binomial with parameters n and p. Since X has a discrete distribution, $Y = u(X)$ will also have a discrete distribution, with the same probabilities as those in the support of X. For example, with $n = 3$, $p = 1/4$, and $Y = X^2$, we have

$$g(y) = \binom{3}{\sqrt{y}} \left(\frac{1}{4}\right)^{\sqrt{y}} \left(\frac{3}{4}\right)^{3-\sqrt{y}}, \qquad y = 0, 1, 4, 9. \qquad ■$$

EXERCISES

5.1-1. Let X have the p.d.f. $f(x) = 4x^3$, $0 < x < 1$. Find the p.d.f. of $Y = X^2$.

5.1-2. Let X have the p.d.f. $f(x) = xe^{-x^2/2}$, $0 < x < \infty$. Find the p.d.f. of $Y = X^2$.

5.1-3. Let X have a gamma distribution with $\alpha = 3$ and $\theta = 2$. Determine the p.d.f. of $Y = \sqrt{X}$.

5.1-4. The p.d.f. of X is $f(x) = 2x$, $0 < x < 1$.

(a) Find the distribution function of X.

(b) Describe how an observation of X can be simulated.

(c) Simulate 10 observations of X.

(d) Use the ordered observations and the corresponding quantiles for the given distribution to construct a q–q plot.

5.1-5. The p.d.f. of X is $f(x) = \theta x^{\theta-1}$, $0 < x < 1$, $0 < \theta < \infty$. Let $Y = -2\theta \ln X$. How is Y distributed?

5.1-6. Let X have a **logistic distribution** with p.d.f.

$$f(x) = \frac{e^{-x}}{(1 + e^{-x})^2}, \qquad -\infty < x < \infty.$$

Show that

$$Y = \frac{1}{1 + e^{-X}}$$

has a $U(0, 1)$ distribution.

5.1-7. A sum of \$50,000 is invested at a rate R, selected from a uniform distribution on the interval (0.03, 0.07). Once R is selected, the sum is compounded instantaneously for a year, so that $X = 50000\,e^R$ dollars is the amount at the end of that year.

(a) Find the distribution function and p.d.f. of X.

(b) Verify that $X = 50000\,e^R$ is defined correctly if the compounding is done instantaneously. HINT: Divide the year into n equal parts, calculate the value of the amount at the end of each part, and then take the limit as $n \to \infty$.

5.1-8. The lifetime (in years) of a manufactured product is $Y = 5X^{0.7}$, where X has an exponential distribution with mean 1. Find the distribution function and p.d.f. of Y.

5.1-9. Statisticians frequently use the **extreme value distribution** given by the distribution function

$$F(x) = 1 - \exp\left[-e^{(x - \theta_1)/\theta_2}\right], \qquad -\infty < x < \infty.$$

A simple case is when $\theta_1 = 0$ and $\theta_2 = 1$, giving

$$F(x) = 1 - \exp\left[-e^{x}\right], \qquad -\infty < x < \infty.$$

Let $Y = e^X$ or $X = \ln Y$; then the support of Y is $0 < y < \infty$.

(a) Show that the distribution of Y is exponential when $\theta_1 = 0$ and $\theta_2 = 1$.

(b) Find the distribution function and the p.d.f. of Y when $\theta_1 \neq 0$ and $\theta_2 \neq 1$. What is this distribution?

(c) As suggested by its name, the extreme value distribution can be used to model the longest home run, the deepest mine, the greatest flood, and so on. Suppose the length X (in feet) of the maximum of someone's home runs was modeled by an extreme value distribution with $\theta_1 = 550$ and $\theta_2 = 25$. What is the probability that X exceeds 500 feet?

5.1-10. Let X have the uniform distribution $U(-1,3)$. Find the p.d.f. of $Y = X^2$.

5.1-11. Let X have a Cauchy distribution. Find

(a) $P(X > 1)$.

(b) $P(X > 5)$.

(c) $P(X > 10)$.

5.1-12. Let $f(x) = 1/[\pi(1 + x^2)]$, $-\infty < x < \infty$, be the p.d.f. of the Cauchy random variable X. Show that $E(X)$ does not exist.

5.1-13. If X is $N(\mu, \sigma^2)$, then $M(t) = E(e^{tX}) = \exp(\mu t + \sigma^2 t^2/2)$. We then say that $Y = e^X$ has a **lognormal distribution**.

(a) Show that the p.d.f. of Y is

$$g(y) = \frac{1}{y\sqrt{2\pi\sigma^2}} \exp[-(\ln y - \mu)^2/2\sigma^2], \qquad 0 < y < \infty.$$

(b) Using $M(t)$, find (i) $E(Y) = E(e^X) = M(1)$, (ii) $E(Y^2) = E(e^{2X}) = M(2)$, and (iii) $\text{Var}(Y)$.

5.1-14. Let X be $N(0,1)$. Find the p.d.f. of $Y = |X|$, a distribution that is often called the **half normal**. HINT: Here $y \in S_y = \{y : 0 < y < \infty\}$. Consider the two transformations $x_1 = -y, -\infty < x_1 < 0$, and $x_2 = y, 0 < y < \infty$.

5.1-15. Let $Y = X^2$.

(a) Find the p.d.f. of Y when the distribution of X is $N(0,1)$.

(b) Find the p.d.f. of Y when the p.d.f. of X is $f(x) = (3/2)x^2, \; -1 < x < 1$.

5.2 TRANSFORMATIONS OF TWO RANDOM VARIABLES

In Section 5.1, we considered the transformation of one random variable X with p.d.f. $f(x)$. In particular, in the continuous case, if $Y = u(X)$ was an increasing or decreasing function of X, with inverse $X = v(Y)$, then the p.d.f. of Y was

$$g(y) = |v'(y)| f[v(y)], \qquad c < y < d,$$

where the support $c < y < d$ corresponds to the support of X, say, $a < x < b$, through the transformation $x = v(y)$.

There is one note of warning here: If the function $Y = u(X)$ does not have a single-valued inverse, the determination of the distribution of Y will not be as simple. As a matter of fact, we did consider two examples in Section 5.1 in which there were two inverse functions, and we exercised special care in those examples. Here, we will not consider problems with many inverses; however, such a warning is nonetheless appropriate.

When two random variables are involved, many interesting problems can result. In the case of a single-valued inverse, the rule is about the same as that in the one-variable case, with the derivative being replaced by the Jacobian. That is, if X_1 and X_2 are two continuous-type random variables with joint p.d.f. $f(x_1, x_2)$, and if $Y_1 = u_1(X_1, X_2)$, $Y_2 = u_2(X_1, X_2)$ has the single-valued inverse $X_1 = v_1(Y_1, Y_2)$,

$X_2 = v_2(Y_1, Y_2)$, then the joint p.d.f. of Y_1 and Y_2 is

$$g(y_1, y_2) = |J| f[v_1(y_1, y_2), v_2(y_1, y_2)], \qquad (y_1, y_2) \in S_1,$$

where the Jacobian J is the determinant

$$J - \begin{vmatrix} \dfrac{\partial x_1}{\partial y_1} & \dfrac{\partial x_1}{\partial y_2} \\ \dfrac{\partial x_2}{\partial y_1} & \dfrac{\partial x_2}{\partial y_2} \end{vmatrix}.$$

Of course, we find the support S_1 of Y_1, Y_2 by considering the mapping of the support S of X_1, X_2 under the transformation $y_1 = u_1(x_1, x_2), y_2 = u_2(x_1, x_2)$. This method of finding the distribution of Y_1 and Y_2 is called the **change-of-variables technique**.

It is often the mapping of the support S of X_1, X_2 into that (say, S_1) of Y_1, Y_2 which causes the biggest challenge. That is, in most cases, it is easy to solve for x_1 and x_2 in terms of y_1 and y_2, say,

$$x_1 = v_1(y_1, y_2), \qquad x_2 = v_2(y_1, y_2),$$

and then to compute the Jacobian

$$J = \begin{vmatrix} \dfrac{\partial v_1(y_1, y_2)}{\partial y_1} & \dfrac{\partial v_1(y_1, y_2)}{\partial y_2} \\ \dfrac{\partial v_2(y_1, y_2)}{\partial y_1} & \dfrac{\partial v_2(y_1, y_2)}{\partial y_2} \end{vmatrix}.$$

However, the mapping of $(x_1, x_2) \in S$ into $(y_1, y_2) \in S_1$ can be more difficult. Let us consider two simple examples.

EXAMPLE 5.2-1 Let X_1, X_2 have the joint p.d.f.

$$f(x_1, x_2) = 2, \qquad 0 < x_1 < x_2 < 1.$$

Consider the transformation

$$Y_1 = \frac{X_1}{X_2}, \qquad Y_2 = X_2.$$

It is certainly easy enough to solve for x_1 and x_2, namely,

$$x_1 = y_1 y_2, \qquad x_2 = y_2$$

and compute

$$J = \begin{vmatrix} y_2 & y_1 \\ 0 & 1 \end{vmatrix} = y_2.$$

Let us now consider S, which is depicted in Figure 5.2-1(a). The boundaries of S are not part of the support, but let us see how they map. The points for which $x_1 = 0$, $0 < x_2 < 1$, map into $y_1 = 0$, $0 < y_2 < 1$; the points for which $x_2 = 1$, $0 \le x_1 < 1$ map into $y_2 = 1$, $0 \le y_1 < 1$; and $0 < x_1 = x_2 \le 1$ maps into $y_1 = 1$, $0 < y_2 \le 1$.

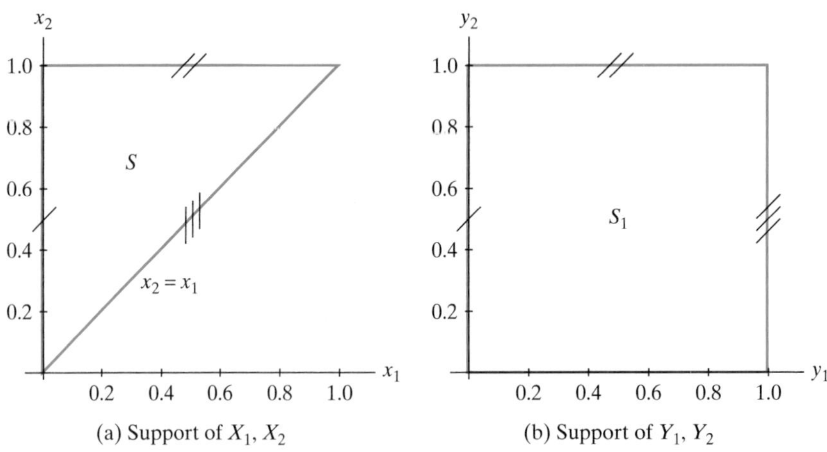

FIGURE 5.2-1: Mapping from x_1, x_2 to y_1, y_2

We depict these line segments in Figure 5.2-1(b) and mark them with the symbols corresponding to the line segments in Figure 5.2-1(a).

We note that the points for which $y_2 = 0$, $0 \le y_1 < 1$, all map into the single point $x_1 = 0$, $x_2 = 0$. That is, this is a many-to-one mapping, and yet we are restricting ourselves to one-to-one mappings. However, the boundaries are not part of our support! Thus, S_1 is as depicted in Figure 5.2-1(b), and, according to the rule, the joint p.d.f. of Y_1, Y_2 is

$$g(y_1, y_2) = |y_2| \cdot 2 = 2y_2, \qquad 0 < y_1 < 1,\ 0 < y_2 < 1.$$

It is interesting to note that the marginal probability density functions are

$$g_1(y_1) = \int_0^1 2y_2\,dy_2 = 1, \qquad 0 < y_1 < 1,$$

and

$$g_2(y_2) = \int_0^1 2y_2\,dy_1 = 2y_2, \qquad 0 < y_2 < 1.$$

Hence, $Y_1 = X_1/X_2$ and $Y_2 = X_2$ are independent. Even though the computation of Y_1 depends very much on the value of Y_2, still Y_1 and Y_2 are independent in the probability sense. ■

EXAMPLE 5.2-2 Let X_1 and X_2 be independent random variables, each with p.d.f.

$$f(x) = e^{-x}, \qquad 0 < x < \infty.$$

Hence, their joint p.d.f. is

$$f(x_1)f(x_2) = e^{-x_1-x_2}, \qquad 0 < x_1 < \infty,\ 0 < x_2 < \infty.$$

Let us consider

$$Y_1 = X_1 - X_2, \qquad Y_2 = X_1 + X_2.$$

Thus,

$$x_1 = \frac{y_1 + y_2}{2}, \qquad x_2 = \frac{y_2 - y_1}{2},$$

with

$$J = \begin{vmatrix} \frac{1}{2} & \frac{1}{2} \\ -\frac{1}{2} & \frac{1}{2} \end{vmatrix} = \frac{1}{2}.$$

The region S is depicted in Figure 5.2-2(a). The line segments on the boundary, namely, $x_1 = 0$, $0 < x_2 < \infty$, and $x_2 = 0$, $0 < x_1 < \infty$, map into the line segments $y_1 + y_2 = 0$, $y_2 > y_1$ and $y_1 = y_2$, $y_2 > -y_1$, respectively. These are shown in Figure 5.2-2(b) and the support of S_1 is depicted there. Since the region S_1 is not bounded by horizontal and vertical line segments, Y_1 and Y_2 are dependent.

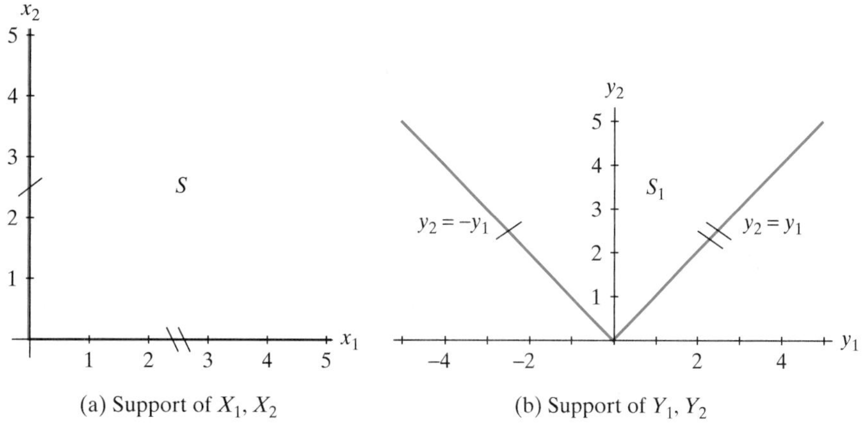

(a) Support of X_1, X_2 (b) Support of Y_1, Y_2

FIGURE 5.2-2: Mapping from x_1, x_2 to y_1, y_2

The joint p.d.f. of Y_1 and Y_2 is

$$g(y_1, y_2) = \frac{1}{2}e^{-y_2}, \qquad -y_2 < y_1 < y_2,\ 0 < y_2 < \infty.$$

The marginal p.d.f. of Y_2 is

$$g_2(y_2) = \int_{-y_2}^{y_2} \frac{1}{2}e^{-y_2}\,dy_1 = y_2 e^{-y_2}, \qquad 0 < y_2 < \infty.$$

That of Y_1 is

$$g_1(y_1) = \begin{cases} \displaystyle\int_{-y_1}^{\infty} \frac{1}{2}e^{-y_2}\,dy_2 = \frac{1}{2}e^{y_1}, & -\infty < y_1 < 0, \\ \displaystyle\int_{y_1}^{\infty} \frac{1}{2}e^{-y_2}\,dy_2 = \frac{1}{2}e^{-y_1}, & 0 < y_1 < \infty. \end{cases}$$

That is, the expression for $g_1(y_1)$ depends on the location of y_1, although this could be written as

$$g_1(y_1) = \frac{1}{2}e^{-|y_1|}, \qquad -\infty < y_1 < \infty,$$

which is called a **double exponential** p.d.f. ■

We now consider two examples that yield two important distributions. The second of these uses the distribution function technique rather than the change-of-variable method.

EXAMPLE 5.2-3 Let X_1 and X_2 have independent gamma distributions with parameters α, θ and β, θ, respectively. That is, the joint p.d.f. of X_1 and X_2 is

$$f(x_1, x_2) = \frac{1}{\Gamma(\alpha)\Gamma(\beta)\theta^{\alpha+\beta}} x_1^{\alpha-1} x_2^{\beta-1} \exp\left(-\frac{x_1 + x_2}{\theta}\right), \; 0 < x_1 < \infty, \; 0 < x_2 < \infty.$$

Consider

$$Y_1 = \frac{X_1}{X_1 + X_2}, \qquad Y_2 = X_1 + X_2,$$

or, equivalently,

$$X_1 = Y_1 Y_2, \qquad X_2 = Y_2 - Y_1 Y_2.$$

The Jacobian is

$$J = \begin{vmatrix} y_2 & y_1 \\ -y_2 & 1 - y_1 \end{vmatrix} = y_2(1 - y_1) + y_1 y_2 = y_2.$$

Thus, the joint p.d.f. $g(y_1, y_2)$ of Y_1 and Y_2 is

$$g(y_1, y_2) = |y_2| \frac{1}{\Gamma(\alpha)\Gamma(\beta)\theta^{\alpha+\beta}} (y_1 y_2)^{\alpha-1} (y_2 - y_1 y_2)^{\beta-1} e^{-y_2/\theta},$$

where the support is $0 < y_1 < 1, \; 0 < y_2 < \infty$, which is the mapping of $0 < x_i < \infty$, $i = 1, 2$. To see the shape of this joint p.d.f., $z = g(y_1, y_2)$ is graphed in Figure 5.2-3(a) with $\alpha = 4$, $\beta = 7$, and $\theta = 1$ and in Figure 5.2-3(b) with $\alpha = 8$, $\beta = 3$, and $\theta = 1$. To find the marginal p.d.f. of Y_1, we integrate this joint p.d.f. on y_2. We see that the marginal p.d.f. of Y_1 is

$$g_1(y_1) = \frac{y_1^{\alpha-1}(1 - y_1)^{\beta-1}}{\Gamma(\alpha)\Gamma(\beta)} \int_0^\infty \frac{y_2^{\alpha+\beta-1}}{\theta^{\alpha+\beta}} e^{-y_2/\theta} \, dy_2.$$

But the integral in this expression is that of a gamma p.d.f. with parameters $\alpha + \beta$ and θ, except for $\Gamma(\alpha + \beta)$ in the denominator; hence, the integral equals $\Gamma(\alpha + \beta)$, and we have

$$g_1(y_1) = \frac{\Gamma(\alpha + \beta)}{\Gamma(\alpha)\Gamma(\beta)} y_1^{\alpha-1}(1 - y_1)^{\beta-1}, \qquad 0 < y_1 < 1.$$

We say that Y_1 has a **beta p.d.f.** with parameters α and β. (See Figure 5.2-4.) Note the relationship between Figure 5.2-3 and Figure 5.2-4. ■

The next example illustrates the distribution function technique. You calculate the same results in Exercise 5.2-2, but using the change-of-variable technique.

EXAMPLE 5.2-4 We let

$$F = \frac{U/r_1}{V/r_2},$$

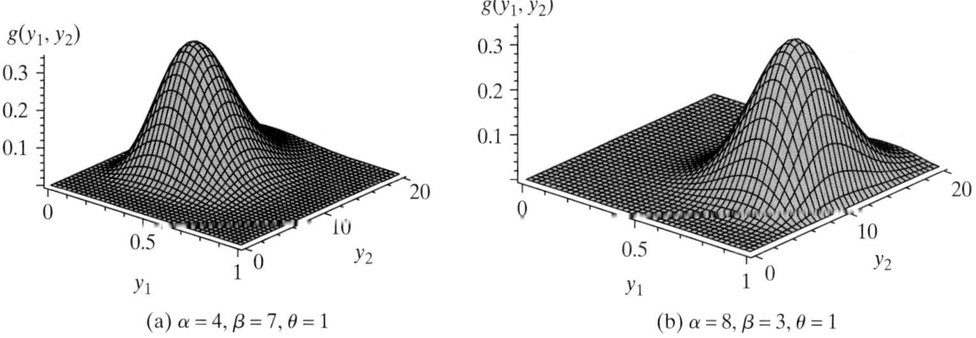

FIGURE 5.2-3: Joint p.d.f. of $z = g(y_1, y_2)$

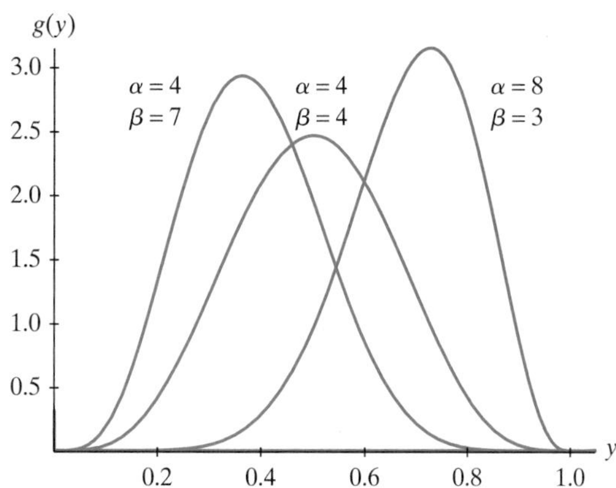

FIGURE 5.2-4: Beta distribution p.d.f.'s

where U and V are independent chi-square variables with r_1 and r_2 degrees of freedom, respectively. Thus, the joint p.d.f. of U and V is

$$g(u, v) = \frac{u^{r_1/2-1}e^{-u/2}}{\Gamma(r_1/2)2^{r_1/2}} \frac{v^{r_2/2-1}e^{-v/2}}{\Gamma(r_2/2)2^{r_2/2}}, \qquad 0 < u < \infty,\ 0 < v < \infty.$$

In this derivation, we let $W = F$ to avoid using f as a symbol for a variable. The distribution function $F(w) = P(W \le w)$ of W is

$$\begin{aligned} F(w) &= P\left(\frac{U/r_1}{V/r_2} \le w\right) = P\left(U \le \frac{r_1}{r_2}\, w\, V\right) \\ &= \int_0^{\infty} \int_0^{(r_1/r_2)wv} g(u, v)\, du\, dv. \end{aligned}$$

That is,

$$F(w) = \frac{1}{\Gamma(r_1/2)\Gamma(r_2/2)} \int_0^{\infty} \left[\int_0^{(r_1/r_2)wv} \frac{u^{r_1/2-1}e^{-u/2}}{2^{(r_1+r_2)/2}}\, du \right] v^{r_2/2-1}e^{-v/2}\, dv.$$

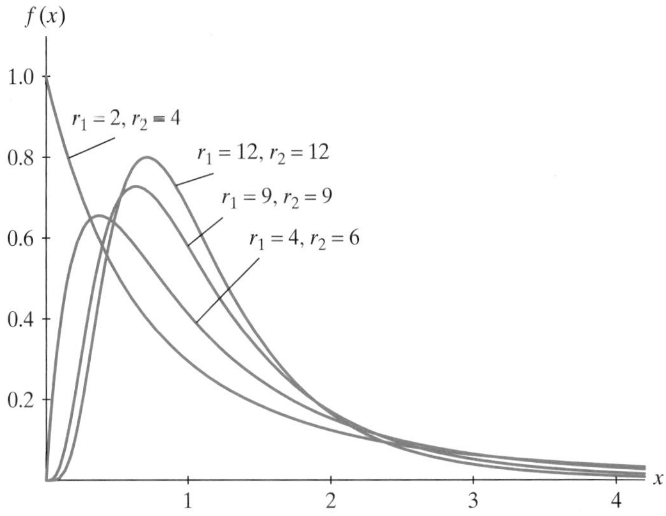

FIGURE 5.2-5: Graphs of F p.d.f.'s

The p.d.f. of W is the derivative of the distribution function; so, applying the fundamental theorem of calculus to the inner integral, we have

$$\begin{aligned} f(w) &= F'(w) \\ &= \frac{1}{\Gamma(r_1/2)\Gamma(r_2/2)} \int_0^\infty \frac{[(r_1/r_2)vw]^{r_1/2-1}}{2^{(r_1+r_2)/2}} e^{-(r_1/2r_2)(vw)} \left(\frac{r_1}{r_2}v\right) v^{r_2/2-1} e^{-v/2}\, dv \\ &= \frac{(r_1/r_2)^{r_1/2} w^{r_1/2-1}}{\Gamma(r_1/2)\Gamma(r_2/2)} \int_0^\infty \frac{v^{(r_1+r_2)/2-1}}{2^{(r_1+r_2)/2}} e^{-(v/2)[1+(r_1/r_2)w]}\, dv. \end{aligned}$$

In the integral, we make the change of variable

$$y = \left(1 + \frac{r_1}{r_2}w\right)v, \qquad \text{so that} \qquad \frac{dv}{dy} = \frac{1}{1 + (r_1/r_2)w}.$$

Thus, we have

$$\begin{aligned} f(w) &= \frac{(r_1/r_2)^{r_1/2}\Gamma[(r_1 + r_2)/2] w^{r_1/2-1}}{\Gamma(r_1/2)\Gamma(r_2/2)[1 + (r_1 w/r_2)]^{(r_1+r_2)/2}} \int_0^\infty \frac{y^{(r_1+r_2)/2-1} e^{-y/2}}{\Gamma[(r_1 + r_2)/2] 2^{(r_1+r_2)/2}}\, dy \\ &= \frac{(r_1/r_2)^{r_1/2}\Gamma[(r_1 + r_2)/2] w^{r_1/2-1}}{\Gamma(r_1/2)\Gamma(r_2/2)[1 + (r_1 w/r_2)]^{(r_1+r_2)/2}}, \end{aligned}$$

the p.d.f. of the $W = F$ **distribution** with r_1 and r_2 degrees of freedom. Note that the integral in this last expression for $f(w)$ is equal to 1 because the integrand is like a p.d.f. of a chi-square distribution with $r_1 + r_2$ degrees of freedom. Graphs of p.d.f.'s for the F distribution are given in Figure 5.2-5. ■

To find probabilities for an F random variable with r_1 (numerator) and r_2 (denominator) degrees of freedom, use either your calculator, a computer program, or Table VII in Appendix C. Table VII is limited, but is adequate for most of the applications in this text. For notation, if W has an F distribution with r_1 and r_2 degrees of freedom, we say that the distribution of W is $F(r_1, r_2)$. For a right-tail probability of α, we write

$$P[W \geq F_\alpha(r_1, r_2)] = \alpha.$$

For a left-tail probability of α, where α is generally small, we note that if the distribution of W is $F(r_1, r_2)$, then the distribution of $1/W$ is $F(r_2, r_1)$. Since

$$\alpha = P[W \leq F_{1-\alpha}(r_1, r_2)] = P[1/W \geq 1/F_{1-\alpha}(r_1, r_2)]$$

and

$$P[1/W \geq F_\alpha(r_2, r_1)] = \alpha,$$

it follows that

$$\frac{1}{F_{1-\alpha}(r_1, r_2)} = F_\alpha(r_2, r_1) \qquad \text{or} \qquad F_{1-\alpha}(r_1, r_2) = \frac{1}{F_\alpha(r_2, r_1)}.$$

EXAMPLE 5.2-5 Let the distribution of W be $F(4, 6)$. From Table VII, we see that

$$F_{0.05}(4, 6) = 4.53;$$

$$P(W \leq 9.15) = 0.99.$$

That is, $F_{0.01}(4, 6) = 9.15$. We also note that

$$F_{0.95}(4, 6) = \frac{1}{F_{0.05}(6, 4)} = \frac{1}{6.16} = 0.1623;$$

$$F_{0.99}(4, 6) = \frac{1}{F_{0.01}(6, 4)} = \frac{1}{15.21}.$$

It follows that

$$P(1/15.21 \leq W \leq 9.15) = 0.98;$$

$$P(1/6.16 \leq W \leq 4.53) = 0.90.$$

■

COMPUTATIONAL COMMENTS We illustrate the use of Minitab to find some of the solutions for Example 5.2-5. To find those probabilities, we use

Calc → Probability Distributions → F

and input the necessary information:

```
Inverse Cumulative Distribution Function
F distribution with 4 DF in numerator and 6 DF in denominator

P(X<=x)          x
   0.95    4.53368

P(X<=x)          x
   0.05   0.162255

Cumulative Distribution Function
F distribution with 4 DF in numerator and 6 DF in denominator
```

```
   x     P(X<=x)
9.15    0.990005
```

EXAMPLE 5.2-6 **(Box–Muller Transformation)** Consider the following transformation, where X_1 and X_2 are independent, each with the uniform distribution $U(0,1)$: Let

$$Z_1 = \sqrt{-2\ln X_1}\cos(2\pi X_2), \qquad Z_2 = \sqrt{-2\ln X_1}\sin(2\pi X_2)$$

or, equivalently,

$$X_1 = \exp\left(-\frac{Z_1^2 + Z_2^2}{2}\right) = e^{-q/2}, \qquad X_2 = \frac{1}{2\pi}\arctan\left(\frac{Z_2}{Z_1}\right),$$

which has Jacobian

$$J = \begin{vmatrix} -z_1 e^{-q/2} & -z_2 e^{-q/2} \\ \dfrac{-z_2}{2\pi(z_1^2 + z_2^2)} & \dfrac{z_1}{2\pi(z_1^2 + z_2^2)} \end{vmatrix} = \frac{-1}{2\pi}e^{-q/2}.$$

Since the joint p.d.f. of X_1 and X_2 is

$$f(x_1, x_2) = 1, \qquad 0 < x_1 < 1,\ 0 < x_2 < 1,$$

it follows that the joint p.d.f. of Z_1 and Z_2 is

$$\begin{aligned} g(z_1, z_2) &= \left|\frac{-1}{2\pi}e^{-q/2}\right|(1) \\ &= \frac{1}{2\pi}\exp\left(-\frac{z_1^2 + z_2^2}{2}\right), \qquad -\infty < z_1 < \infty, \quad -\infty < z_2 < \infty. \end{aligned}$$

Note that there is some difficulty with the definition of this transformation, particularly when $z_1 = 0$. However, these difficulties occur at events with probability zero and hence cause no problems. (See Exercise 5.2-17.) Summarizing, from two independent $U(0,1)$ random variables we have generated two independent $N(0,1)$ random variables through the **Box–Muller transformation.** ■

EXERCISES

5.2-1. Let X_1, X_2 denote two independent random variables, each with a $\chi^2(2)$ distribution. Find the joint p.d.f. of $Y_1 = X_1$ and $Y_2 = X_2 + X_1$. Note that the support of Y_1, Y_2 is $0 < y_1 < y_2 < \infty$. Also, find the marginal p.d.f. of each of Y_1 and Y_2. Are Y_1 and Y_2 independent?

5.2-2. Let X_1 and X_2 be independent chi-square random variables with r_1 and r_2 degrees of freedom, respectively. Let $Y_1 = (X_1/r_1)/(X_2/r_2)$ and $Y_2 = X_2$.

(a) Find the joint p.d.f. of Y_1 and Y_2.

(b) Determine the marginal p.d.f. of Y_1 and show that Y_1 has an F distribution. (This is another, but equivalent, way of finding the p.d.f. of F.)

5.2-3. Find the mean and the variance of an F random variable with r_1 and r_2 degrees of freedom by first finding $E(U)$, $E(1/V)$, $E(U^2)$, and $E(1/V^2)$.

5.2-4. Let the distribution of W be $F(9,24)$. Find the following:

(a) $F_{0.05}(9,24)$.

(b) $F_{0.95}(9,24)$.

(c) $P(0.277 \le W \le 2.70)$.

5.2-5. Let the distribution of W be $F(8,4)$. Find the following:

(a) $F_{0.01}(8,4)$.
(b) $F_{0.99}(8,4)$.
(c) $P(0.198 \le W \le 8.98)$.

5.2-6. Let X_1 and X_2 have independent gamma distributions with parameters α, θ and β, θ, respectively. Let $W = X_1/(X_1 + X_2)$. Use a method similar to that given in the derivation of the F distribution (Examples 5.2-4) to show that the p.d.f. of W is

$$g(w) = \frac{\Gamma(\alpha + \beta)}{\Gamma(\alpha)\Gamma(\beta)} w^{\alpha-1}(1 - w)^{\beta-1}, 0 < w < 1.$$

We say that W has a **beta distribution** with parameters α and β. (See Example 5.2-3.)

5.2-7. Let X_1 and X_2 be independent chi-square random variables with r_1 and r_2 degrees of freedom, respectively. Show that

(a) $U = X_1/(X_1 + X_2)$ has a beta distribution with $\alpha = r_1/2$ and $\beta = r_2/2$.
(b) $V = X_2/(X_1 + X_2)$ has a beta distribution with $\alpha = r_2/2$ and $\beta = r_1/2$.

5.2-8. Let X have a beta distribution with parameters α and β. (See Example 5.2-3.)

(a) Show that the mean and variance of X are, respectively,

$$\mu = \frac{\alpha}{\alpha + \beta}$$

and

$$\sigma^2 = \frac{\alpha\beta}{(\alpha + \beta + 1)(\alpha + \beta)^2}.$$

(b) Show that when $\alpha > 1$ and $\beta > 1$, the mode is at $x = (\alpha - 1)/(\alpha + \beta - 2)$.

5.2-9. Determine the constant c such that $f(x) = cx^3(1 - x)^6, 0 < x < 1$, is a p.d.f.

5.2-10. When α and β are integers and $0 < p < 1$, we have

$$\int_0^p \frac{\Gamma(\alpha + \beta)}{\Gamma(\alpha)\Gamma(\beta)} y^{\alpha-1}(1 - y)^{\beta-1}\, dy = \sum_{y=\alpha}^{n} \binom{n}{y} p^y (1 - p)^{n-y},$$

where $n = \alpha + \beta - 1$. Verify this formula when $\alpha = 4$ and $\beta = 3$. HINT: Integrate the left member by parts several times.

5.2-11. Evaluate

$$\int_0^{0.4} \frac{\Gamma(7)}{\Gamma(4)\Gamma(3)} y^3(1 - y)^2\, dy$$

(a) Using integration.
(b) Using the result of Exercise 5.2-10.

5.2-12. Let W_1, W_2 be independent, each with a Cauchy distribution. In this exercise, we find the p.d.f. of the sample mean, $(W_1 + W_2)/2$.

(a) Show that the p.d.f. of $X_1 = (1/2)W_1$ is

$$f(x) = \frac{2}{\pi(1 + 4x^2)}, \qquad -\infty < x < \infty.$$

(b) Let $Y_1 = X_1 + X_2 = \overline{W}$ and $Y_2 = X_1$, where $X_2 = (1/2)W_2$. Show that the joint p.d.f. of Y_1 and Y_2 is

$$g(y_1, y_2) = f(y_1 - y_2)f(y_2),$$
$$-\infty < y_1 < \infty, -\infty < y_2 < \infty.$$

(c) Show that the p.d.f. of $Y_1 = \overline{W}$ is given by the **convolution formula**,

$$g_1(y_1) = \int_{-\infty}^{\infty} f(y_1 - y_2)f(y_2)\, dy_2.$$

(d) Show that

$$g_1(y_1) = \frac{1}{\pi(1 + y_1^2)}, \qquad -\infty < y_1 < \infty.$$

That is, the p.d.f. of $\overline{W}$ is the same as that of an individual W.

5.2-13. Let X_1, X_2 be independent random variables representing lifetimes (in hours) of two key components of a device that fails when and only when both components fail. Say each X_i has an exponential distribution with mean 1000. Let $Y_1 = \min(X_1, X_2)$ and $Y_2 = \max(X_1, X_2)$, so that the space of Y_1, Y_2 is $0 < y_1 < y_2 < \infty$.

(a) Find $G(y_1, y_2) = P(Y_1 \le y_1, Y_2 \le y_2)$.
(b) Compute the probability that the device fails after 1200 hours; that is, compute $P(Y_2 > 1200)$.

5.2-14. A company provides earthquake insurance. The premium X is modeled by the p.d.f.

$$f(x) = \frac{x}{5^2} e^{-x/5}, \qquad 0 < x < \infty,$$

while the claims Y have the p.d.f.

$$g(y) = \frac{1}{5} e^{-y/5}, \qquad 0 < y < \infty.$$

If X and Y are independent, find the p.d.f. of $Z = X/Y$.

5.2-15. Let X be the fraction of a 24-hour period that a person is sleeping. We are trying to model the distribution of X with a beta p.d.f. Which of the following do you believe to be the best model for a person who sleeps for 8 hours, on the average: (1) $\alpha = 8, \beta = 16$, (2) $\alpha = 16, \beta = 32$, (3) $\alpha = 24, \beta = 48$? Why? Can you construct a better model?

5.2-16. Let X and Y be the fractions of a 24-hour period that a person spends sleeping and eating, respectively. We wish to model the distribution of X and Y by the joint p.d.f.

$$f(x, y) = \frac{\Gamma(\alpha + \beta + \gamma)}{\Gamma(\alpha)\Gamma(\beta)\Gamma(\gamma)} x^{\alpha-1}y^{\beta-1}(1 - x - y)^{\gamma-1}, \quad 0 < x, 0 < y, x + y < 1.$$

Select α, β, and γ so that this joint p.d.f. is a reasonable model for someone who sleeps for 8 hours and eats for 2 hours on the average.
HINT: X has a beta distribution with parameters $\alpha, \beta + \gamma$, and Y has a beta distribution with parameters $\beta, \alpha + \gamma$; thus, we want $\alpha/(\alpha + \beta + \gamma) = 1/3$ and $\beta/(\alpha + \beta + \gamma) = 1/12$. Now consider the standard deviations.

5.2-17. In Example 5.2-6, verify that the given transformation maps $\{(x_1,x_2) : 0 < x_1 < 1, 0 < x_2 < 1\}$ onto $\{(z_1, z_2) : -\infty < z_1 < \infty, -\infty < z_2 < \infty\}$, except for a set of points that has probability 0.
HINT: What is the image of vertical line segments? What is the image of horizontal line segments?

5.3 SEVERAL INDEPENDENT RANDOM VARIABLES

In Section 4.1, we introduced several distributions concerning two random variables. Each of these random variables could be thought of as a measurement in some random experiment. In this section, we consider the possibility of performing several random experiments or one random experiment several times in which each trial results in one measurement that can be considered a random variable. That is, we obtain one random variable from each experiment, and thus we obtain a collection of several random variables from the several experiments. Further, suppose that these experiments are performed in such a way that the events associated with any one of them are independent of the events associated with others, and hence the corresponding random variables are, in the probabilistic sense, independent.

Recall from Section 4.1 that if X_1 and X_2 are random variables of the discrete type with probability mass functions $f_1(x_1)$ and $f_2(x_2)$, respectively, and if

$$\begin{aligned} P(X_1 = x_1 \text{ and } X_2 = x_2) &= P(X_1 = x_1)\,P(X_2 = x_2) \\ &= f_1(x_1)f_2(x_2), \qquad x_1 \in S_1,\ x_2 \in S_2, \end{aligned}$$

then X_1 and X_2 are said to be independent and the joint p.m.f. is $f_1(x_1)f_2(x_2)$.

Sometimes the two random experiments are exactly the same. For example, we could cast the die twice, resulting first in X_1 and then in X_2. It is reasonable to say that the p.m.f. of X_1 is $f(x_1) = 1/6$, $x_1 = 1, 2, \ldots, 6$, and the p.m.f. of X_2 is $f(x_2) = 1/6$, $x_2 = 1, 2, \ldots, 6$. Assuming independence, which would be a fair way to perform the experiments, the joint p.m.f. is then

$$f(x_1)f(x_2) = \left(\frac{1}{6}\right)\left(\frac{1}{6}\right) = \frac{1}{36}, \qquad x_1 = 1, 2, \ldots, 6;\ x_2 = 1, 2, \ldots, 6.$$

In general, if the p.m.f. $f(x)$ of the independent random variables X_1 and X_2 is the same, then the joint p.m.f. is $f(x_1)f(x_2)$. Moreover, in this case, the collection of the two random variables X_1, X_2 is called a **random sample** of size $n = 2$ from a distribution with p.m.f. $f(x)$. Hence, in the two casts of the die, we say that we have a random sample of size $n = 2$ from the uniform distribution on the space $\{1, 2, 3, 4, 5, 6\}$.

EXAMPLE 5.3-1 Let X_1 and X_2 be two independent random variables resulting from two casts of an unbiased die. That is, X_1, X_2 is a random sample of size $n = 2$ from a distribution with p.m.f. $f(x) = 1/6$, $x = 1, 2, \ldots, 6$. We have

$$E(X_1) = E(X_2) = \sum_{x=1}^{6} xf(x) = 3.5,$$

where $f(x) = 1/6$, $x = 1, 2, \ldots, 6$. Moreover,

$$\text{Var}(X_1) = \text{Var}(X_2) = \sum_{x=1}^{6} (x - 3.5)^2 f(x) = \frac{35}{12}.$$

In addition, from independence,

$$E(X_1X_2) = E(X_1)E(X_2) = (3.5)(3.5) = 12.25$$

and

$$E[(X_1 - 3.5)(X_2 - 3.5)] = E(X_1 - 3.5)E(X_2 - 3.5) = 0.$$

If $Y = X_1 + X_2$, then

$$E(Y) = E(X_1) + E(X_2) = 3.5 + 3.5 = 7$$

and

$$\begin{aligned}
\text{Var}(Y) &= E[(X_1 + X_2 - 7)^2] = E\{[(X_1 - 3.5) + (X_2 - 3.5)]^2\} \\
&= E[(X_1 - 3.5)^2] + E[2(X_1 - 3.5)(X_2 - 3.5)] + E[(X_2 - 3.5)^2] \\
&= \text{Var}(X_1) + (2)(0) + \text{Var}(X_2) \\
&= (2)\left(\frac{35}{12}\right) = \frac{35}{6}.
\end{aligned}$$

■

In Example 5.3-1, we can find the p.m.f. $g(y)$ of $Y = X_1 + X_2$. Since the space of Y is $\{2, 3, 4, \ldots, 12\}$, we have, by a rather straightforward calculation,

$$g(2) = P(X_1 = 1, X_2 = 1) = f(1)f(1) = \left(\frac{1}{6}\right)\left(\frac{1}{6}\right) = \frac{1}{36},$$

$$g(3) = P(X_1 = 1, X_2 = 2 \text{ or } X_1 = 2, X_2 = 1) = \left(\frac{1}{6}\right)\left(\frac{1}{6}\right) + \left(\frac{1}{6}\right)\left(\frac{1}{6}\right) = \frac{2}{36},$$

$$g(4) = P(X_1 = 1, X_2 = 3 \text{ or } X_1 = 2, X_2 = 2 \text{ or } X_1 = 3, X_2 = 1) = \frac{3}{36},$$

and so on. This results in the p.m.f. given by

y	2	3	4	5	6	7	8	9	10	11	12
$g(y)$	$\frac{1}{36}$	$\frac{2}{36}$	$\frac{3}{36}$	$\frac{4}{36}$	$\frac{5}{36}$	$\frac{6}{36}$	$\frac{5}{36}$	$\frac{4}{36}$	$\frac{3}{36}$	$\frac{2}{36}$	$\frac{1}{36}$

With this p.m.f., it is simple to calculate

$$E(Y) = \sum_{y=2}^{12} y\,g(y) = 7$$

and

$$\text{Var}(Y) = \sum_{y=2}^{12} (y - 7)^2 g(y) = \frac{35}{6},$$

which agrees with the results of Example 5.3-1.

All of the definitions and results concerning two random variables of the discrete type can be carried over to two random variables of the continuous type. Moreover, the notions about two independent random variables can be extended to n independent random variables, which can be thought of as measurements on the outcomes of n random experiments. That is, if $X_1, X_2, \ldots, X_n$ are **independent**, then the joint p.d.f. is the product of the respective p.d.f.'s, namely, $f_1(x_1)f_2(x_2)\cdots f_n(x_n)$.

If all n of the distributions are the same, then the collection of n independent and identically distributed random variables, $X_1, X_2, \ldots, X_n$, is said to be a **random sample of size n from that common distribution**. If $f(x)$ is the common p.m.f. or p.d.f. of these n random variables, then the joint p.m.f. or p.d.f. is $f(x_1)f(x_2)\cdots f(x_n)$.

EXAMPLE 5.3-2 Let X_1, X_2, X_3 be a random sample from a distribution with p.d.f.

$$f(x) = e^{-x}, \qquad 0 < x < \infty.$$

The joint p.d.f. of these three random variables is

$$(e^{-x_1})(e^{-x_2})(e^{-x_3}) = e^{-x_1-x_2-x_3}, \qquad 0 < x_i < \infty,\ i = 1,2,3.$$

The probability

$$\begin{aligned} P(0 < X_1 < 1, 2 < X_2 < 4, 3 < X_3 < 7) &= \left(\int_0^1 e^{-x_1}\,dx_1\right)\left(\int_2^4 e^{-x_2}\,dx_2\right)\left(\int_3^7 e^{-x_3}\,dx_3\right) \\ &= (1 - e^{-1})(e^{-2} - e^{-4})(e^{-3} - e^{-7}), \end{aligned}$$

because of the independence of X_1, X_2, X_3. ■

EXAMPLE 5.3-3 An electronic device runs until one of its three components fails. The lifetimes (in weeks), X_1, X_2, X_3, of these components are independent, and each has the Weibull p.d.f.

$$f(x) = \frac{2x}{25} e^{-(x/5)^2}, \qquad 0 < x < \infty.$$

The probability that the device stops running in the first three weeks is equal to

$$\begin{aligned} 1 - P(X_1 > 3, X_2 > 3, X_3 > 3) &= 1 - P(X_1 > 3)P(X_2 > 3)P(X_3 > 3) \\ &= 1 - \left(\int_3^\infty f(x)dx\right)^3 \\ &= 1 - \left(\left[-e^{-(x/5)^2}\right]_3^\infty\right)^3 \\ &= 1 - \left[e^{-(3/5)^2}\right]^3 = 0.660. \end{aligned}$$

■

The special result following Example 5.3-1 (see also Exercise 5.3-5) with a linear function of two random variables extends to more general functions of several random variables. We accept the following theorem without proof. (See Hogg, McKean, and Craig, 2005.)

THEOREM 5.3-1 Let $X_1, X_2, \ldots, X_n$ be n independent random variables that have the joint p.m.f. $f_1(x_1)f_2(x_2)\cdots f_n(x_n)$. Let the random variable $Y = u(X_1, X_2, \ldots, X_n)$ have the p.m.f. $g(y)$. Then, in the discrete case,

$$E(Y) = \sum_y y g(y) = \sum_{x_1}\sum_{x_2}\cdots\sum_{x_n} u(x_1, x_2, \ldots, x_n) f_1(x_1)f_2(x_2)\cdots f_n(x_n),$$

provided that these summations exist. For random variables of the continuous type, obvious changes are made; in particular, integrals replace the summations.

The next theorem proves that the expected value of the product of functions of n independent random variables is the product of their expected values.

THEOREM 5.3-2 Say $X_1, X_2, \ldots, X_n$ are independent random variables and the random variable $Y = u_1(X_1)\,u_2(X_2)\cdots u_n(X_n)$. If $E[u_i(X_i)]$, $i = 1, 2, \ldots, n$, exist, then

$$E(Y) = E[u_1(X_1)\,u_2(X_2)\cdots u_n(X_n)] = E[u_1(X_1)]E[u_2(X_2)]\cdots E[u_n(X_n)].$$

Proof. In the discrete case, we have

$$\begin{aligned} &E[u_1(X_1)u_2(X_2)\cdots u_n(X_n)] \\ &\quad= \sum_{x_1}\sum_{x_2}\cdots\sum_{x_n} u_1(x_1)\,u_2(x_2)\cdots u_n(x_n)f_1(x_1)f_2(x_2)\cdots f_n(x_n) \\ &\quad= \sum_{x_1} u_1(x_1)f_1(x_1)\sum_{x_2} u_2(x_2)f_2(x_2)\cdots\sum_{x_n} u_n(x_n)f_n(x_n) \\ &\quad= E[u_1(X_1)]E[u_2(x_2)]\cdots E[u_n(X_n)]. \end{aligned}$$

In the proof of the continuous case, obvious changes are made; in particular, integrals replace summations. □

REMARK Sometimes students recognize that $X^2 = (X)(X)$ and thus believe that $E(X^2)$ is equal to $[E(X)][E(X)] = [E(X)]^2$ because Theorem 5.3-2 states that the expected value of the product is the product of the expected values. However, note the hypothesis of independence in the theorem, and certainly X is not independent of itself. Incidentally, if $E(X^2)$ did equal $[E(X)]^2$, then the variance of X, or

$$\sigma^2 = E(X^2) - [E(X)]^2,$$

would always equal zero. This happens only in the case of degenerate (one-point) distributions. ■

We now prove an important theorem about the mean and the variance of a linear combination of random variables.

THEOREM 5.3-3 If $X_1, X_2, \ldots, X_n$ are n independent random variables with respective means $\mu_1, \mu_2, \ldots, \mu_n$ and variances $\sigma_1^2, \sigma_2^2, \ldots, \sigma_n^2$, then the mean and the variance of $Y = \sum_{i=1}^{n} a_i X_i$, where $a_1, a_2, \ldots, a_n$ are real constants, are, respectively,

$$\mu_Y = \sum_{i=1}^{n} a_i \mu_i \quad \text{and} \quad \sigma_Y^2 = \sum_{i=1}^{n} a_i^2 \sigma_i^2.$$

Proof. We have

$$\mu_Y = E(Y) = E\left(\sum_{i=1}^{n} a_i X_i\right) = \sum_{i=1}^{n} a_i E(X_i) = \sum_{i=1}^{n} a_i \mu_i,$$

because the expected value of the sum is the sum of the expected values (i.e., E is a linear operator). Also,

$$\sigma_Y^2 = E[(Y - \mu_Y)^2] = E\left[\left(\sum_{i=1}^{n} a_i X_i - \sum_{i=1}^{n} a_i \mu_i\right)^2\right]$$

$$= E\left\{\left[\sum_{i=1}^{n} a_i (X_i - \mu_i)\right]^2\right\} = E\left[\sum_{i=1}^{n}\sum_{j=1}^{n} a_i a_j (X_i - \mu_i)(X_j - \mu_j)\right].$$

Again using the fact that E is a linear operator, we obtain

$$\sigma_Y^2 = \sum_{i=1}^{n}\sum_{j=1}^{n} a_i a_j \, E[(X_i - \mu_i)(X_j - \mu_j)].$$

However, if $i \neq j$, then from the independence of X_i and X_j, we have

$$E[(X_i - \mu_i)(X_j - \mu_j)] = E(X_i - \mu_i)E(X_j - \mu_j) = (\mu_i - \mu_i)(\mu_j - \mu_j) = 0.$$

Thus, the variance can be written as

$$\sigma_Y^2 = \sum_{i=1}^{n} a_i^2 E[(X_i - \mu_i)^2] = \sum_{i=1}^{n} a_i^2 \sigma_i^2. \qquad \square$$

REMARK Although Theorem 5.3-3 gives the mean and the variance of a linear function of independent random variables, the proof can easily be modified to the case in which X_i and X_j are correlated. Then

$$E[(X_i - \mu_i)(X_j - \mu_j)] = \rho_{ij}\sigma_i\sigma_j,$$

instead of zero, where ρ_{ij} is the correlation coefficient of X_i and X_j. Thus,

$$\sigma_Y^2 = \sum_{i=1}^{n} a_i^2 \sigma_i^2 + 2\sum_{i<j}\sum a_i a_j \rho_{ij} \sigma_i \sigma_j,$$

where the factor 2 appears because the sum is over $i < j$ and

$$a_i a_j \rho_{ij} \sigma_i \sigma_j = a_j a_i \rho_{ji} \sigma_j \sigma_i.$$

The mean of Y is still the same in both cases, namely,

$$\mu_Y = \sum_{i=1}^{n} a_i \mu_i.$$ ■

We give two illustrations of the theorem.

EXAMPLE 5.3-4 Let the independent random variables X_1 and X_2 have respective means $\mu_1 = -4$ and $\mu_2 = 3$ and variances $\sigma_1^2 = 4$ and $\sigma_2^2 = 9$. Then the mean and the variance of $Y = 3X_1 - 2X_2$ are, respectively,

$$\mu_Y = (3)(-4) + (-2)(3) = -18$$

and

$$\sigma_Y^2 = (3)^2(4) + (-2)^2(9) = 72.$$ ■

EXAMPLE 5.3-5 Let X_1, X_2 be a random sample from a distribution with mean μ and variance σ^2. Let $Y = X_1 - X_2$; then

$$\mu_Y = \mu - \mu = 0$$

and

$$\sigma_Y^2 = (1)^2\sigma^2 + (-1)^2\sigma^2 = 2\sigma^2.$$ ■

Now consider the **mean of a random sample**, $X_1, X_2, \ldots, X_n$, from a distribution with mean μ and variance σ^2, namely,

$$\overline{X} = \frac{X_1 + X_2 + \cdots + X_n}{n},$$

which is a linear function with each $a_i = 1/n$. Then

$$\mu_{\overline{X}} = \sum_{i=1}^{n} \left(\frac{1}{n}\right)\mu = \mu \qquad \text{and} \qquad \sigma_{\overline{X}}^2 = \sum_{i=1}^{n} \left(\frac{1}{n}\right)^2 \sigma^2 = \frac{\sigma^2}{n}.$$

That is, the mean of $\overline{X}$ is that of the distribution from which the sample arose, but the variance of $\overline{X}$ is that of the underlying distribution divided by n. Any function of the sample observations, $X_1, X_2, \ldots, X_n$, is called a **statistic,** so here $\overline{X}$ is a statistic and also an **estimator** of the distribution mean μ.

EXERCISES

5.3-1. Let X_1 and X_2 be independent Poisson random variables with respective means $\lambda_1 = 2$ and $\lambda_2 = 3$. Find

(a) $P(X_1 = 3, X_2 = 5)$.
(b) $P(X_1 + X_2 = 1)$.

HINT: Note that this event can occur if and only if $\{X_1 = 1, X_2 = 0\}$ or $\{X_1 = 0, X_2 = 1\}$.

5.3-2. Let X_1 and X_2 be independent random variables with respective binomial distributions $b(3, 1/2)$ and $b(5, 1/2)$. Determine

(a) $P(X_1 = 2, X_2 = 4)$.
(b) $P(X_1 + X_2 = 7)$.

5.3-3. Let X_1 and X_2 be independent random variables with probability density functions

$f_1(x_1) = 2x_1$, $0 < x_1 < 1$, and $f_2(x_2) = 4x_2^3$, $0 < x_2 < 1$, respectively. Compute

(a) $P(0.5 < X_1 < 1 \text{ and } 0.4 < X_2 < 0.8)$.
(b) $E(X_1^2 X_2^3)$.

5.3-4. Let X_1 and X_2 be a random sample of size $n = 2$ from the exponential distribution with p.d.f. $f(x) = 2e^{-2x}$, $0 < x < \infty$. Find

(a) $P(0.5 < X_1 < 1.0, 0.7 < X_2 < 1.2)$.
(b) $E[X_1(X_2 - 0.5)^2]$.

5.3-5. Let X_1 and X_2 be observations of a random sample of size $n = 2$ from a distribution with p.m.f. $f(x) = x/6$, $x = 1, 2, 3$. Then find the p.m.f. of $Y = X_1 + X_2$. Determine the mean and the variance of the sum in two ways.

5.3-6. Let X_1 and X_2 be a random sample of size $n = 2$ from a distribution with p.d.f. $f(x) = 6x(1 - x)$, $0 < x < 1$. Find the mean and the variance of $Y = X_1 + X_2$.

5.3-7. The distributions of incomes in two cities follow the two Pareto-type p.d.f.'s

$$f(x) = \frac{2}{x^3}, \qquad 1 < x < \infty,$$

and

$$g(y) = \frac{3}{y^4}, \qquad 1 < y < \infty,$$

respectively. Here one unit represents \$20,000. One person with income is selected at random from each city. Let X and Y be their respective incomes. Compute $P(X < Y)$.

5.3-8. Suppose two independent claims are made on two insured homes, where each claim has p.d.f.

$$f(x) = \frac{4}{x^5}, \qquad 1 < x < \infty,$$

in which the unit is \$1000. Find the expected value of the larger claim.

HINT: If X_1 and X_2 are the two independent claims and $Y = \max(X_1, X_2)$, then

$$G(y) = P(Y \le y) = P(X_1 \le y)P(X_2 \le y) = [P(X \le y)]^2.$$

Find $g(y) = G'(y)$ and $E(Y)$.

5.3-9. Let X_1, X_2 be a random sample of size $n = 2$ from a distribution with p.d.f. $f(x) = 3x^2$, $0 < x < 1$. Determine

(a) $P(\max X_i < 3/4) = P(X_1 < 3/4, X_2 < 3/4)$.
(b) The mean and the variance of $Y = X_1 + X_2$.

5.3-10. Let X_1, X_2, X_3 denote a random sample of size $n = 3$ from a distribution with the geometric p.m.f.

$$f(x) = \left(\frac{3}{4}\right)\left(\frac{1}{4}\right)^{x-1}, \qquad x = 1, 2, 3, \ldots.$$

(a) Compute $P(X_1 = 1, X_2 = 3, X_3 = 1)$.
(b) Determine $P(X_1 + X_2 + X_3 = 5)$.
(c) If Y equals the maximum of X_1, X_2, X_3, find

$$P(Y \le 2) = P(X_1 \le 2)P(X_2 \le 2)P(X_3 \le 2).$$

5.3-11. Let X_1, X_2, X_3 be three independent random variables with binomial distributions $b(4, 1/2)$, $b(6, 1/3)$, and $b(12, 1/6)$, respectively. Find

(a) $P(X_1 = 2, X_2 = 2, X_3 = 5)$.
(b) $E(X_1 X_2 X_3)$.
(c) The mean and the variance of $Y = X_1 + X_2 + X_3$.

5.3-12. Let X_1, X_2, X_3 be a random sample of size $n = 3$ from the exponential distribution with p.d.f. $f(x) = e^{-x}$, $0 < x < \infty$. Find

$$P(1 < \min X_i) = P(1 < X_1, 1 < X_2, 1 < X_3).$$

5.3-13. Flip $n = 8$ fair coins and remove all that came up heads. Flip the remaining coins (that came up tails) and remove the heads again. Continue flipping the remaining coins until each has come up heads. We shall find the p.m.f. of Y, the number of trials needed. Let X_i equal the number of flips required to observe heads on coin i, $i = 1, 2, \ldots, 8$. Then $Y = \max(X_1, X_2, \ldots, X_8)$.

(a) Show that $P(Y \le y) = [1 - (1/2)^y]^8$.
(b) Show that $P(Y = y) = [1 - (1/2)^y]^8 - [1 - (1/2)^{y-1}]^8$, $y = 1, 2, \ldots$.
(c) Use a computer algebra system such as *Maple* or *Mathematica* to show that $E(Y) = 13{,}315{,}424/3{,}011{,}805 = 4.421$.
(d) What happens to the expected value of Y as the number of coins is doubled?

5.3-14. Construct a sequence of squares with one vertex at the origin and having lengths $1 - 1/2^x$, $x = 1, 2, \ldots$. Select a point randomly from the unit square with one vertex at the origin and sides of length 1. Let the random variable X equal x if the point is in the region between the squares with sides of lengths $1 - 1/2^x$ and $1 - 1/2^{x-1}$, $x = 1, 2, 3, \ldots$.

(a) Draw a figure illustrating this exercise.

(b) Show that

$$\begin{aligned} f(x) &= P(X = x) \\ &= \left(1 - \frac{1}{2^x}\right)^2 - \left(1 - \frac{1}{2^{x-1}}\right)^2 \\ &= \frac{2^{x+1} - 3}{2^{2x}}, x = 1, 2, 3, \ldots. \end{aligned}$$

(c) Show that $f(x)$ is a p.m.f. (See Equation D.4-1 on the CD-ROM.)

(d) Find the mean of X. (See Equation D.4-2 on the CD-ROM.)

(e) Find the variance of X. (See Equation D.4-3 on the CD-ROM.)

(f) Use simulation to confirm your answers.

5.3-15. Construct a sequence of cubes with one vertex at the origin and having lengths $1/2^x$, $x = 1, 2, \ldots$. Select a point randomly from the unit cube with one vertex at the origin and sides of length 1. Let the random variable X equal x if the point is in the region between the cubes with sides of lengths $1 - 1/2^x$ and $1 - 1/2^{x-1}$, $x = 1, 2, 3, \ldots$.

Another way to state this problem is as follows: A 3-tuple (u_1, u_2, u_3) of random numbers u_1, u_2, and u_3 is selected from the unit cube. The random variable X is defined as follows:

If $u_1 \le 1 - 1/2$, $u_2 \le 1 - 1/2$, and $u_3 \le 1 - 1/2$, then $X = 1$;

else if $u_1 \le 1 - 1/2^2$, $u_2 \le 1 - 1/2^2$, and $u_3 \le 1 - 1/2^2$, then $X = 2$;

else if $u_1 \le 1 - 1/2^3$, $u_2 \le 1 - 1/2^3$, and $u_3 \le 1 - 1/2^3$, then $X = 3$; and so forth.

(a) Find the p.m.f. of X.

(b) Verify that what you found in part (a) is a p.m.f., and find its mean and variance. HINT: Use a CAS.

(c) Use simulation to compare the theoretical and empirical characteristics.

(d) Extend this problem to higher dimensions.

(e) How is the answer to this exercise related to the answer to Exercise 5.3-13?

5.3-16. Let X_1, X_2, X_3 be independent random variables that represent lifetimes (in hours) of three key components of a device. Say their respective distributions are exponential with means 1000, 1500, and 2000. Let Y be the minimum of X_1, X_2, X_3 and compute $P(Y > 1000)$.

5.3-17. A device contains three components, each of which has a lifetime in hours with the p.d.f.

$$f(x) = \frac{2x}{10^2}\, e^{-(x/10)^2}, \qquad 0 < x < \infty.$$

The device fails with the failure of one of the components. Assuming independent lifetimes, what is the probability that the device fails in the first hour of its operation?

5.3-18. Three drugs are being tested for use as the treatment of a certain disease. Let p_1, p_2, and p_3 represent the probabilities of success for the respective drugs. As three patients come in, each is given one of the drugs in a random order. After $n = 10$ "triples" and assuming independence, compute the probability that the maximum number of successes with one of the drugs exceeds eight if in fact $p_1 = p_2 = p_3 = 0.7$.

5.3-19. Three components are placed in series. The time in hours to failure of each has the p.d.f.

$$f(x) = \frac{x}{500^2}\, e^{-x/500}, \qquad 0 < x < \infty.$$

Since they are in series, we are concerned about the minimum time Y to failure of the three. Assuming independence, find the c.d.f. and the p.d.f. of Y and compute $P(Y \le 300)$. HINT: $G(y) = P(Y \le y) = 1 - P(Y > y) = 1 - P(\text{all three} > y)$.

5.3-20. Each of eight bearings in a bearing assembly has a diameter (in millimeters) that has the p.d.f.

$$f(x) = 10x^9, \qquad 0 < x < 1.$$

Assuming independence, find the distribution function and the p.d.f. of the maximum diameter (say, Y) of the eight bearings and compute $P(0.9999 < Y < 1)$.

5.3-21. In considering medical insurance for a certain operation, let X equal the amount (in dollars) paid for the doctor and let Y equal the amount paid to the hospital. In the past, the variances have been $\text{Var}(X) = 8100$, $\text{Var}(Y) = 10{,}000$, and $\text{Var}(X + Y) = 20{,}000$. Due to increased expenses, it was decided to increase the doctor's fee by \$500 and increase the hospital charge Y by 8 percent. Calculate the variance of $X + 500 + (1.08)Y$, the new total claim.

5.3-22. The lifetime in months of a certain part has a gamma distribution with $\alpha = \theta = 2$. A company buys three such parts and uses one until it fails, replacing it with a second part. When the latter fails, it is replaced by the third part. What are the mean and the variance of the total lifetime associated with this situation?

5.3-23. Two components operate in parallel in a device, so the device fails when and only when both components fail. The lifetimes, X_1 and X_2, of the respective components are independent and identically distributed with a gamma distribution, $\alpha = 1, \theta = 2$. The cost of operating the device is $Z = 2Y_1 + Y_2$, where $Y_1 = \min(X_1, X_2)$ and $Y_2 = \max(X_1, X_2)$. Compute $E(Z)$.

5.4 THE MOMENT-GENERATING FUNCTION TECHNIQUE

To illustrate the moment-generating function technique, we begin with a simple example.

EXAMPLE 5.4-1 Let X_1 and X_2 be independent random variables with uniform distributions on $\{1, 2, 3, 4\}$. Let $Y = X_1 + X_2$. For example, Y could equal the sum when two four-sided dice are rolled. The moment-generating function of Y is

$$M_Y(t) = E(e^{tY}) = E[e^{t(X_1+X_2)}] = E(e^{tX_1}e^{tX_2}).$$

The independence of X_1 and X_2 implies that

$$M_Y(t) = E(e^{tX_1})E(e^{tX_2}).$$

In this example, X_1 and X_2 have the same p.m.f., namely,

$$f(x) = \frac{1}{4}, \qquad x = 1,2,3,4,$$

and thus the same moment-generating function,

$$M_X(t) = \frac{1}{4}e^t + \frac{1}{4}e^{2t} + \frac{1}{4}e^{3t} + \frac{1}{4}e^{4t}.$$

It then follows that $M_Y(t) = [M_X(t)]^2$ equals

$$\frac{1}{16}e^{2t} + \frac{2}{16}e^{3t} + \frac{3}{16}e^{4t} + \frac{4}{16}e^{5t} + \frac{3}{16}e^{6t} + \frac{2}{16}e^{7t} + \frac{1}{16}e^{8t}.$$

Note that the coefficient of e^{bt} is equal to the probability $P(Y = b)$; for example, $4/16 = P(Y = 5)$. Thus, we can find the distribution of Y by determining its moment-generating function. ■

In some applications, it is sufficient to know the mean and variance of a linear combination of random variables, say, Y. However, it is often helpful to know exactly how Y is distributed. The next theorem can frequently be used to find the distribution of a linear combination of independent random variables.

THEOREM 5.4-1 If $X_1, X_2, \ldots, X_n$ are independent random variables with respective moment-generating functions $M_{X_i}(t)$, $i = 1,2,3,\ldots,n$, then the moment-generating function of $Y = \sum_{i=1}^{n} a_iX_i$ is

$$M_Y(t) = \prod_{i=1}^{n} M_{X_i}(a_it).$$

Proof. From Theorem 5.3-2, the moment-generating function of Y is given by

$$\begin{aligned} M_Y(t) &= E[e^{tY}] = E[e^{t(a_1X_1+a_2X_2+\cdots+a_nX_n)}] \\ &= E[e^{a_1tX_1}e^{a_2tX_2}\cdots e^{a_ntX_n}] \\ &= E[e^{a_1tX_1}]E[e^{a_2tX_2}]\cdots E[e^{a_ntX_n}]. \end{aligned}$$

However, since

$$E(e^{tX_i}) = M_{X_i}(t),$$

it follows that

$$E(e^{a_i t X_i}) = M_{X_i}(a_i t).$$

Thus, we have

$$M_Y(t) = M_{X_1}(a_1 t) M_{X_2}(a_2 t) \cdots M_{X_n}(a_n t) = \prod_{i=1}^{n} M_{X_i}(a_i t). \qquad \square$$

A corollary follows immediately, and it will be used in some important examples.

COROLLARY 5.4-1 If $X_1, X_2, \ldots, X_n$ are observations of a random sample from a distribution with moment-generating function $M(t)$, then

(a) the moment-generating function of $Y = \sum_{i=1}^{n} X_i$ is

$$M_Y(t) = \prod_{i=1}^{n} M(t) = [M(t)]^n;$$

(b) the moment-generating function of $\overline{X} = \sum_{i=1}^{n} (1/n) X_i$ is

$$M_{\overline{X}}(t) = \prod_{i=1}^{n} M\left(\frac{t}{n}\right) = \left[M\left(\frac{t}{n}\right)\right]^n.$$

Proof. For (a), let $a_i = 1$, $i = 1, 2, \ldots, n$, in Theorem 5.4-1. For (b), take $a_i = 1/n$, $i = 1, 2, \ldots, n$. $\square$

The next two examples and the exercises give some important applications of Theorem 5.4-1 and its corollary.

EXAMPLE 5.4-2 Let $X_1, X_2, \ldots, X_n$ denote the outcomes of n Bernoulli trials. The moment-generating function of X_i, $i = 1, 2, \ldots, n$, is

$$M(t) = q + pe^t.$$

If

$$Y = \sum_{i=1}^{n} X_i,$$

then

$$M_Y(t) = \prod_{i=1}^{n} (q + pe^t) = (q + pe^t)^n.$$

Thus, we again see that Y is $b(n, p)$. ■

EXAMPLE 5.4-3 Let X_1, X_2, X_3 be the observations of a random sample of size $n = 3$ from the exponential distribution having mean θ and, of course, moment-generating function

$M(t) = 1/(1 - \theta t), t < 1/\theta$. The moment-generating function of the random variable $Y = X_1 + X_2 + X_3$ is

$$M_Y(t) = [(1 - \theta t)^{-1}]^3 = (1 - \theta t)^{-3}, \qquad t < 1/\theta,$$

which is that of a gamma distribution with parameters $\alpha = 3$ and θ. Thus, Y has this distribution. On the other hand, the moment-generating function of $\overline{X}$ is

$$M_{\overline{X}}(t) = \left[\left(1 - \frac{\theta t}{3}\right)^{-1}\right]^3 = \left(1 - \frac{\theta t}{3}\right)^{-3}, \qquad t < 3/\theta.$$

Hence, the distribution of $\overline{X}$ is gamma with the parameters $\alpha = 3$ and $\theta/3$, respectively. ■

THEOREM 5.4-2 Let $X_1, X_2, \ldots, X_n$ be independent chi-square random variables with $r_1, r_2, \ldots, r_n$ degrees of freedom, respectively. Then the distribution of the random variable $Y = X_1 + X_2 + \cdots + X_n$ is $\chi^2(r_1+r_2+\cdots+r_n)$.

Proof. By Theorem 5.4-1 with each $a = 1$, the m.g.f. of Y is

$$\begin{aligned} M_Y(t) = \prod_{i=1}^{n} M_{X_i}(t) &= (1 - 2t)^{-r_1/2}(1 - 2t)^{-r_2/2}\cdots(1 - 2t)^{-r_n/2} \\ &= (1 - 2t)^{-\Sigma r_i/2}, \qquad \text{with } t < 1/2, \end{aligned}$$

which is the m.g.f. of a $\chi^2(r_1+r_2+\cdots+r_n)$ random variable. Thus, the distribution of Y is $\chi^2(r_1+r_2+\cdots+r_n)$. □

The next two corollaries combine and extend the results of Theorems 3.6-2 and 5.4-2 and give one interpretation of degrees of freedom.

COROLLARY 5.4-2 Let $Z_1, Z_2, \ldots, Z_n$ have standard normal distributions, $N(0,1)$. If these random variables are independent, then $W = Z_1^2 + Z_2^2 + \cdots + Z_n^2$ has a distribution that is $\chi^2(n)$.

Proof. By Theorem 3.6-2, Z_i^2 is $\chi^2(1)$ for $i = 1, 2, \ldots, n$. From Theorem 5.4-2, with $k = n$, $Y = W$, and $r_i = 1$, it follows that W is $\chi^2(n)$. □

COROLLARY 5.4-3 If $X_1, X_2, \ldots, X_n$ are independent and have normal distributions $N(\mu_i, \sigma_i^2)$, $i = 1, 2, \ldots, n$, respectively, then the distribution of

$$W = \sum_{i=1}^{n} \frac{(X_i - \mu_i)^2}{\sigma_i^2}$$

is $\chi^2(n)$.

Proof. This follows from Corollary 5.4-2, since $Z_i = (X_i - \mu_i)/\sigma_i$ is $N(0,1)$, $i = 1, 2, \ldots, n$. □

Note that the number of terms in the summation and the number of degrees of freedom are equal in Theorem 5.4-2 and the corollary.

EXERCISES

5.4-1. Let X_1, X_2, X_3 be a random sample of size 3 from the distribution with p.m.f. $f(x) = 1/4$, $x = 1, 2, 3, 4$. For example, observe three independent rolls of a fair four-sided die.

(a) Find the p.m.f. of $Y = X_1 + X_2 + X_3$.

(b) Sketch a bar graph of the p.m.f. of Y.

5.4-2. Let X_1 and X_2 have independent distributions $b(n_1, p)$ and $b(n_2, p)$. Find the moment-generating function of $Y = X_1 + X_2$. How is Y distributed?

5.4-3. Let X_1, X_2, X_3 be mutually independent random variables with Poisson distributions having means 2, 1, and 4, respectively.

(a) Find the moment-generating function of the sum $Y = X_1 + X_2 + X_3$.

(b) How is Y distributed?

(c) Compute $P(3 \le Y \le 9)$.

5.4-4. Generalize Exercise 5.4-3 by showing that the sum of n independent Poisson random variables with respective means $\mu_1, \mu_2, \ldots, \mu_n$ is Poisson with mean

$$\mu_1 + \mu_2 + \cdots + \mu_n.$$

5.4-5. Let $Z_1, Z_2, \ldots, Z_7$ be a random sample from the standard normal distribution $N(0, 1)$. Let $W = Z_1^2 + Z_2^2 + \cdots + Z_7^2$. Find $P(1.69 < W < 14.07)$.

5.4-6. Let X_1, X_2, X_3, X_4, X_5 be a random sample of size 5 from a geometric distribution with $p = 1/3$.

(a) Find the moment-generating function of $Y = X_1 + X_2 + X_3 + X_4 + X_5$.

(b) How is Y distributed?

5.4-7. Let X_1, X_2, X_3 denote a random sample of size 3 from a gamma distribution with $\alpha = 7$ and $\theta = 5$.

(a) Find the moment-generating function of $Y = X_1 + X_2 + X_3$.

(b) How is Y distributed?

5.4-8. Let $W = X_1 + X_2 + \cdots + X_h$, a sum of h mutually independent and identically distributed exponential random variables with mean θ. Show that W has a gamma distribution with mean $h\theta$.

5.4-9. Let X equal the outcome when a four-sided die is rolled. Let Y equal the outcome when a six-sided die is rolled. Let $W = X + Y$. Assume that X and Y are independent.

(a) Find the moment-generating function of W.

(b) Give the p.m.f. of W.

5.4-10. Let X equal the outcome when a fair four-sided die that has its faces numbered 0, 1, 2, and 3 is rolled. Let Y equal the outcome when a fair four-sided die that has its faces numbered 0, 4, 8, and 12 is rolled.

(a) Define the moment-generating function of X.

(b) Define the moment-generating function of Y.

(c) Let $W = X + Y$, the sum when the pair of dice is rolled. Find the moment-generating function of W.

(d) Give the p.m.f. of W; that is, determine $P(W = w)$, $w = 0, 1, \ldots, 15$, from the moment-generating function of W.

5.4-11. Let X and Y, with respective p.m.f.'s $f(x)$ and $g(y)$, be independent discrete random variables, each of whose support is a subset of the nonnegative integers $0, 1, 2, \ldots$. Show that the p.m.f. of $W = X + Y$ is given by the **convolution formula**

$$h(w) = \sum_{x=0}^{w} f(x)g(w - x), \qquad w = 0, 1, 2, \ldots.$$

HINT: Argue that $h(w) = P(W = w)$ is the probability of the $w + 1$ mutually exclusive events $(x, y = w - x)$, $x = 0, 1, \ldots, w$.

5.4-12. Let X and Y equal the outcomes when two fair six-sided dice are rolled. Let $W = X + Y$. Assuming independence, find the p.m.f. of W when

(a) The first die has three faces numbered 0 and three faces numbered 2, and the second die has its faces numbered 0, 1, 4, 5, 8, and 9.

(b) The faces on the first die are numbered 0, 1, 2, 3, 4, and 5, and the faces on the second die are numbered 0, 6, 12, 18, 24, and 30.

5.4-13. Let X and Y be the outcomes when a pair of fair eight-sided dice is rolled. Let $W = X + Y$. How should the faces of the dice be numbered so that W has a uniform distribution on $0, 1, \ldots, 15$?

5.4-14. Some states—for example, Texas and New York—have added a new extension to Daily 3 and Daily 4 games. The player selects a three-digit or a four-digit number. The player can bet on the sum of the digits selected in a game called Sum It Up. For the questions that follow, assume that the size of the bet is \$1. Recall that the state does not return this dollar. HINT: Use either Exercise 5.4-11 or the moment-generating function.

(a) In the three digit game, what is the expected value for the player if the prizes for sums of 0, 1, and 2 are \$500, \$166, and \$83, respectively?

(b) To be consistent, what prize should the state offer for a sum of 3?

(c) In the four-digit game, what is the expected value for the player if the prizes for sums of 0, 1, and 2 are \$5000, \$1250, and \$500, respectively?

(d) To be consistent, what prize should the state offer for a sum of 3?

5.4-15. Let $X_1, X_2, \ldots, X_8$ be a random sample from a distribution having p.m.f. $f(x) = (x + 1)/6$, $x = 0, 1, 2$.

(a) Use Exercise 5.4-11 to find the p.m.f. of $W_1 = X_1 + X_2$.

(b) What is the p.m.f. of $W_2 = X_3 + X_4$?

(b) Now find the p.m.f. of $W = W_1 + W_2 = X_1 + X_2 + X_3 + X_4$.

(c) Find the p.m.f. of $Y = X_1 + X_2 + \cdots + X_8$.

(d) Construct probability histograms for X_1, W_1, W, and Y. Are these histograms skewed or symmetric?

5.4-16. The number of accidents in a period of one week follows a Poisson distribution with mean 2. The numbers of accidents from week to week are independent. What is the probability of exactly seven accidents in a given three weeks. HINT: See Exercise 5.4-4.

5.4-17. Given a fair four-sided die, let Y equal the number of rolls needed to observe each face at least once.

(a) Argue that $Y = X_1 + X_2 + X_3 + X_4$, where X_i has a geometric distribution with $p_i = (5 - i)/4$, $i = 1, 2, 3, 4$, and X_1, X_2, X_3, X_4 are independent.

(b) Find the mean and variance of Y.

(c) Find $P(Y = y)$, $y = 4, 5, 6, 7$.

5.4-18. The number X of sick days taken during a year by an employee follows a Poisson distribution with mean 2. Let us observe four such employees. Assuming independence, compute the probability that their total number of sick days exceeds 10.

5.4-19. In a study concerning a new treatment of a certain disease, two groups of 25 participants in each were followed for five years. Those in one group took the old treatment and those in the other took the new treatment. The dropout rate for an individual was 50% in both groups over that 5-year period. Let X be the number that dropped out in the first group and Y the number in the second group. Assuming independence where needed, give the sum that equals the probability that $Y \geq X + 2$. HINT: What is the distribution of $Y - X + 25$?

5.4-20. The number of cracks on a highway averages 0.5 per mile and follows a Poisson distribution. Assuming independence (which may not be a good assumption; why?), what is the probability that, in a 40-mile stretch of that highway, there are fewer than 15 cracks?

5.4-21. Let X be the number of flaws on the outside of a new washing machine. Say $X_1, X_2, \ldots, X_{10}$ is a random sample of 10 such X values that has a Poisson distribution with mean 1.

(a) The manufacturer gives a discount to a buyer of any machine with two or more flaws. Among the 10 machines, what is the probability of giving at least three discounts?

(b) Among the 10 machines, what is the probability of fewer than 13 flaws?

5.4-22. The time X in minutes of a visit to a cardiovascular disease specialist by a patient is modeled by a gamma p.d.f. with $\alpha = 1.5$ and $\theta = 10$. Suppose that you are such a patient and have four patients ahead of you. Assuming independence, what integral gives the probability that you will wait more than 90 minutes?

5.4-23. A doorman at a hotel is trying to get three taxicabs for three different couples. The arrival of empty cabs has an exponential distribution with mean 2 minutes. Assuming independence, what is the probability that the doorman will get all three couples taken care of within 6 minutes?

5.5 RANDOM FUNCTIONS ASSOCIATED WITH NORMAL DISTRIBUTIONS

In statistical applications, it is often assumed that the population from which a sample is taken is normally distributed, $N(\mu, \sigma^2)$. There is then interest in estimating the parameters μ and σ^2 or in testing conjectures about these parameters. The usual statistics that are used in these activities are the sample mean $\overline{X}$ and the sample variance S^2; thus, we need to know something about the distribution of these statistics or functions of these statistics.

We now use the moment-generating function technique of Section 5.4 to prove a theorem that deals with linear functions of independent normally distributed random variables.

THEOREM 5.5-1 If $X_1, X_2, \ldots, X_n$ are n mutually independent normal variables with means $\mu_1, \mu_2, \ldots, \mu_n$ and variances $\sigma_1^2, \sigma_2^2, \ldots, \sigma_n^2$, respectively, then the linear function

$$Y = \sum_{i=1}^{n} c_i X_i$$

has the normal distribution

$$N\left(\sum_{i=1}^{n} c_i\mu_i, \sum_{i=1}^{n} c_i^2\sigma_i^2\right).$$

Proof. By Theorem 5.4-1, we have

$$M_Y(t) = \prod_{i=1}^{n} M_{X_i}(c_i t) = \prod_{i=1}^{n} \exp(\mu_i c_i t + \sigma_i^2 c_i^2 t^2/2)$$

because $M_{X_i}(t) = \exp(\mu_i t + \sigma_i^2 t^2/2)$, $i = 1, 2, \ldots, n$. Thus,

$$M_Y(t) = \exp\left[\left(\sum_{i=1}^{n} c_i\mu_i\right)t + \left(\sum_{i=1}^{n} c_i^2\sigma_i^2\right)\left(\frac{t^2}{2}\right)\right].$$

This is the moment-generating function of a distribution that is

$$N\left(\sum_{i=1}^{n} c_i\mu_i, \sum_{i=1}^{n} c_i^2\sigma_i^2\right).$$

Thus, Y has this normal distribution. □

From Theorem 5.5-1, we observe that the difference of two independent normally distributed random variables, say, $Y = X_1 - X_2$, has the normal distribution $N(\mu_1 - \mu_2, \sigma_1^2 + \sigma_2^2)$.

EXAMPLE 5.5-1 Let X_1 and X_2 equal the number of pounds of butterfat produced by two Holstein cows (one selected at random from those on the Koopman farm and one selected at random from those on the Vliestra farm, respectively) during the 305-day lactation period following the births of calves. Assume that the distribution of X_1 is $N(693.2, 22820)$ and the distribution of X_2 is $N(631.7, 19205)$. Moreover, let X_1 and X_2 be independent. We shall find $P(X_1 > X_2)$. That is, we shall find the probability that the butterfat produced by the Koopman farm cow exceeds that produced by the Vliestra farm cow. (Sketch p.d.f.'s on the same graph for these two normal distributions.) If we let $Y = X_1 - X_2$, then the distribution of Y is $N(693.2 - 631.7, 22820 + 19205)$. Thus,

$$\begin{aligned} P(X_1 > X_2) = P(Y > 0) &= P\left(\frac{Y - 61.5}{\sqrt{42025}} > \frac{0 - 61.5}{205}\right) \\ &= P(Z > -0.30) = 0.6179. \end{aligned}$$

■

COROLLARY 5.5-1 If $X_1, X_2, \ldots, X_n$ are observations of a random sample of size n from the normal distribution $N(\mu, \sigma^2)$, then the distribution of the sample mean $\overline{X} = (1/n)\sum_{i=1}^{n} X_i$ is $N(\mu, \sigma^2/n)$.

Proof. Let $c_i = 1/n$, $\mu_i = \mu$, and $\sigma_i^2 = \sigma^2$ in Theorem 5.5-1. □

Corollary 5.5-1 shows that if $X_1, X_2, \ldots, X_n$ is a random sample from the normal distribution, $N(\mu, \sigma^2)$, then the probability distribution of $\overline{X}$ is also normal with the same mean μ but a variance σ^2/n. This means that $\overline{X}$ has a greater probability of falling into an interval containing μ than does a single observation—say, X_1. For example, if $\mu = 50$, $\sigma^2 = 16$, and $n = 64$, then $P(49 < \overline{X} < 51) = 0.9544$, whereas $P(49 < X_1 < 51) = 0.1974$. This property is illustrated again in the next example.

EXAMPLE 5.5-2 Let $X_1, X_2, \ldots, X_n$ be a random sample from the $N(50, 16)$ distribution. We know that the distribution of $\overline{X}$ is $N(50, 16/n)$. To illustrate the effect of n, the graph of the p.d.f. of $\overline{X}$ is given in Figure 5.5-1 for $n = 1, 4, 16$, and 64. When $n = 64$, compare the areas that represent $P(49 < \overline{X} < 51)$ and $P(49 < X_1 < 51)$. ■

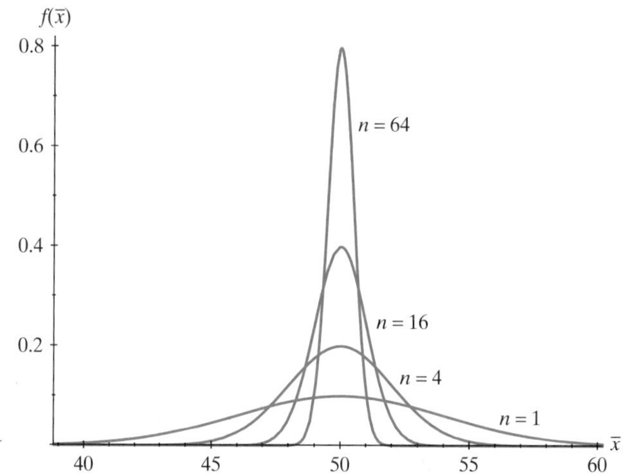

FIGURE 5.5-1: p.d.f.'s of means of samples from $N(50, 16)$

The next theorem gives an important result that will be used in statistical applications. In connection with those applications, we will use the sample variance s^2 to estimate the variance, σ^2, when sampling from the normal distribution, $N(\mu, \sigma^2)$. (More will be said about s^2 at the time of its use.)

THEOREM 5.5-2 Let $X_1, X_2, \ldots, X_n$ be observations of a random sample of size n from the normal distribution $N(\mu, \sigma^2)$. Then the sample mean,

$$\overline{X} = \frac{1}{n}\sum_{i=1}^{n} X_i,$$

and the sample variance,

$$S^2 = \frac{1}{n-1}\sum_{i=1}^{n}(X_i - \overline{X})^2,$$

are independent and

$$\frac{(n-1)S^2}{\sigma^2} = \frac{\sum_{i=1}^{n}(X_i - \overline{X})^2}{\sigma^2} \quad \text{is } \chi^2(n-1).$$

Proof. We are not prepared to prove the independence of $\overline{X}$ and S^2 at this time (see Section 10.1 for a proof), so we accept it without proof here. To prove the second part, note that

$$W = \sum_{i=1}^{n}\left(\frac{X_i - \mu}{\sigma}\right)^2 = \sum_{i=1}^{n}\left[\frac{(X_i - \overline{X}) + (\overline{X} - \mu)}{\sigma}\right]^2$$

$$= \sum_{i=1}^{n}\left(\frac{X_i - \overline{X}}{\sigma}\right)^2 + \frac{n(\overline{X} - \mu)^2}{\sigma^2} \qquad (5.5\text{-}1)$$

because the cross-product term is equal to

$$2\sum_{i=1}^{n}\frac{(\overline{X} - \mu)(X_i - \overline{X})}{\sigma^2} = \frac{2(\overline{X} - \mu)}{\sigma^2}\sum_{i=1}^{n}(X_i - \overline{X}) = 0.$$

But $Y_i = (X_i - \mu)/\sigma$, $i = 1, 2, \ldots n$, are standardized normal variables that are independent. Hence, $W = \sum_{i=1}^{n} Y_i^2$ is $\chi^2(n)$ by Corollary 5.4-3. Moreover, since $\overline{X}$ is $N(\mu, \sigma^2/n)$, it follows that

$$Z^2 = \left(\frac{\overline{X} - \mu}{\sigma/\sqrt{n}}\right)^2 = \frac{n(\overline{X} - \mu)^2}{\sigma^2}$$

is $\chi^2(1)$ by Theorem 3.6-2. In this notation, Equation 5.5-1 becomes

$$W = \frac{(n-1)S^2}{\sigma^2} + Z^2.$$

However, from the fact that $\overline{X}$ and S^2 are independent, it follows that Z^2 and S^2 are also independent. In the moment-generating function of W, this independence permits us to write

$$E[e^{tW}] = E[e^{t\{(n-1)S^2/\sigma^2 + Z^2\}}] = E[e^{t(n-1)S^2/\sigma^2} e^{tZ^2}]$$
$$= E[e^{t(n-1)S^2/\sigma^2}]E[e^{tZ^2}].$$

Since W and Z^2 have chi-square distributions, we can substitute their moment-generating functions to obtain

$$(1 - 2t)^{-n/2} = E[e^{t(n-1)S^2/\sigma^2}](1 - 2t)^{-1/2}.$$

Equivalently, we have

$$E[e^{t(n-1)S^2/\sigma^2}] = (1 - 2t)^{-(n-1)/2}, \qquad t < \frac{1}{2}.$$

This, of course, is the moment-generating function of a $\chi^2(n-1)$ variable; accordingly, $(n-1)S^2/\sigma^2$ has that distribution. □

Combining the results of Corollary 5.4-3 and Theorem 5.5-2, we see that when sampling is from a normal distribution,

$$U = \sum_{i=1}^{n} \frac{(X_i - \mu)^2}{\sigma^2}$$

is $\chi^2(n)$ and

$$W = \sum_{i=1}^{n} \frac{(X_i - \overline{X})^2}{\sigma^2}$$

is $\chi^2(n-1)$. That is, when the population mean, μ, in $\sum_{i=1}^{n}(X_i - \mu)^2$ is replaced by the sample mean, $\overline{X}$, one degree of freedom is lost. There are more general situations in which a degree of freedom is lost for each parameter estimated in certain chi-square random variables.

EXAMPLE 5.5-3 Let X_1, X_2, X_3, X_4 be a random sample of size 4 from the normal distribution, $N(76.4, 383)$. Then

$$U = \sum_{i=1}^{4} \frac{(X_i - 76.4)^2}{383} \quad \text{is} \quad \chi^2(4),$$

$$W = \sum_{i=1}^{4} \frac{(X_i - \overline{X})^2}{383} \quad \text{is} \quad \chi^2(3),$$

and, for examples,

$$P(0.711 \le U \le 7.779) = 0.90 - 0.05 = 0.85,$$
$$P(0.352 \le W \le 6.251) = 0.90 - 0.05 = 0.85.$$ ■

In later sections, we shall illustrate the importance of the chi-square distribution in applications.

We now prove a theorem that is the basis for some of the most important inferences in statistics.

THEOREM 5.5-3 **(Student's t distribution)** Let

$$T = \frac{Z}{\sqrt{U/r}},$$

where Z is a random variable that is $N(0,1)$, U is a random variable that is $\chi^2(r)$, and Z and U are independent. Then T has a t distribution with p.d.f.

$$f(t) = \frac{\Gamma((r+1)/2)}{\sqrt{\pi r}\,\Gamma(r/2)} \frac{1}{(1 + t^2/r)^{(r+1)/2}}, \qquad -\infty < t < \infty.$$

Proof. The joint p.d.f. of Z and U is

$$g(z,u) = \frac{1}{\sqrt{2\pi}} e^{-z^2/2} \frac{1}{\Gamma(r/2)2^{r/2}} u^{r/2-1} e^{-u/2}, \qquad -\infty < z < \infty,\ 0 < u < \infty.$$

The distribution function $F(t) = P(T \le t)$ of T is given by

$$\begin{aligned} F(t) &= P(Z/\sqrt{U/r} \le t) \\ &= P(Z \le \sqrt{U/r}\,t) \\ &= \int_0^\infty \int_{-\infty}^{\sqrt{(u/r)}\,t} g(z,u)\,dz\,du. \end{aligned}$$

That is,

$$F(t) = \frac{1}{\sqrt{\pi}\,\Gamma(r/2)} \int_0^\infty \left[\int_{-\infty}^{\sqrt{(u/r)}\,t} \frac{e^{-z^2/2}}{2^{(r+1)/2}}\,dz \right] u^{r/2-1} e^{-u/2}\,du.$$

The p.d.f. of T is the derivative of the distribution function; so, applying the fundamental theorem of calculus to the inner integral, we find that

$$\begin{aligned} f(t) = F'(t) &= \frac{1}{\sqrt{\pi}\,\Gamma(r/2)} \int_0^\infty \frac{e^{-(u/2)(t^2/r)}}{2^{(r+1)/2}} \sqrt{\frac{u}{r}}\, u^{r/2-1} e^{-u/2}\,du \\ &= \frac{1}{\sqrt{\pi r}\,\Gamma(r/2)} \int_0^\infty \frac{u^{(r+1)/2-1}}{2^{(r+1)/2}} e^{-(u/2)(1+t^2/r)}\,du. \end{aligned}$$

In the integral, make the change of variables

$$y = (1 + t^2/r)u, \qquad \text{so that} \qquad \frac{du}{dy} = \frac{1}{1 + t^2/r}.$$

Thus,

$$f(t) = \frac{\Gamma((r+1)/2)}{\sqrt{\pi r}\,\Gamma(r/2)} \left[\frac{1}{(1 + t^2/r)^{(r+1)/2}} \right] \int_0^\infty \frac{y^{(r+1)/2-1}}{\Gamma((r+1)/2)\,2^{(r+1)/2}} e^{-y/2}\,dy.$$

The integral in this last expression for $f(t)$ is equal to 1 because the integrand is like the p.d.f. of a chi-square distribution with $r + 1$ degrees of freedom. Hence, the p.d.f. is

$$f(t) = \frac{\Gamma((r+1)/2)}{\sqrt{\pi r}\,\Gamma(r/2)} \frac{1}{(1 + t^2/r)^{(r+1)/2}}, \qquad -\infty < t < \infty. \qquad \square$$

Graphs of the p.d.f. of T when $r = 1, 3$, and 7, along with the $N(0,1)$ p.d.f., are given in Figure 5.5-2(a) on page 252. In this figure, we see that the tails of the t distribution are heavier than those of a normal one; that is, there is more extreme probability in the t distribution than in the standardized normal one.

To find probabilities for a t random variable with r degrees of freedom, use either your calculator, a computer program, or Table VI in Appendix B. If T has a t distribution with r degrees of freedom, we say that the distribution of T is $t(r)$. Furthermore, right-tail probabilities of size α are denoted by $t_\alpha(r)$. [See Figure 5.5-2(b).]

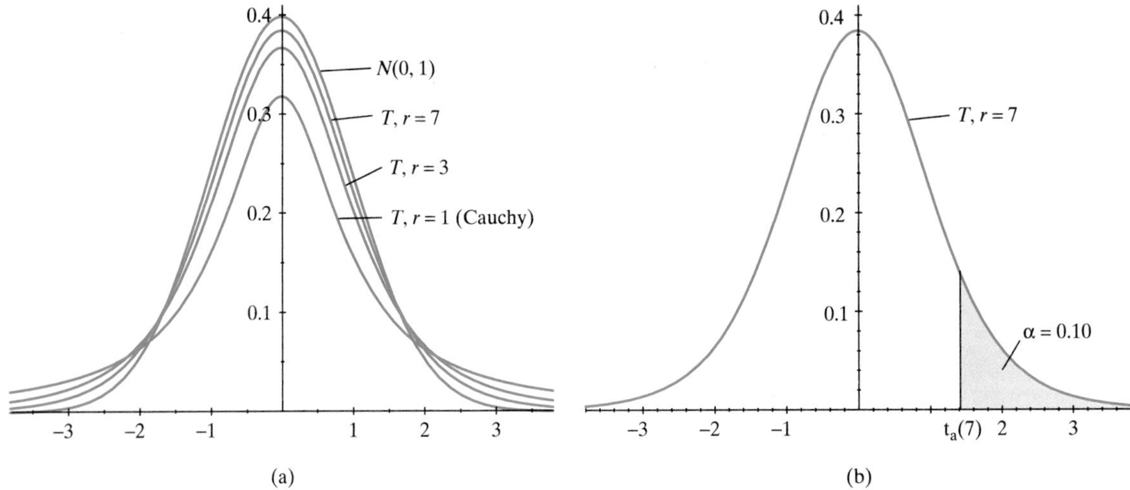

FIGURE 5.5-2: *t* distribution p.d.f.'s and right-tail probability

EXAMPLE 5.5-4 Let the distribution of T be $t(11)$. Then

$$t_{0.05}(11) = 1.796 \qquad \text{and} \qquad -\,t_{0.05}(11) = -1.796.$$

Thus,

$$P(-1.796 \le T \le 1.796) = 0.90.$$

We can also find values of the distribution function such as

$$P(T \le 2.201) = 0.975 \qquad \text{and} \qquad P(T \le -1.363) = 0.10.$$

■

COMPUTATIONAL COMMENTS We illustrate the use of Minitab to find the solutions for Example 5.5-4. To find those probabilities, we use

Calc → Probability Distributions → t

and input the necessary information:

```
Inverse Cumulative Distribution Function
Student's t distribution with 11 DF

P(X<=x)        x
   0.95  1.79588

P(X<=x)        x
   0.05 -1.79588

Cumulative Distribution Function
Student's t distribution with 11 DF

      x  P(X<=x)
  2.201  0.975001

      x  P(X<=x)
 -1.363  0.100066
```

We can use the results of Corollary 5.5-1 and Theorems 5.5-2 and 5.5-3 to construct an important T random variable. Given a random sample $X_1, X_2, \ldots, X_n$ from a normal distribution, $N(\mu, \sigma^2)$, let

$$Z = \frac{\overline{X} - \mu}{\sigma/\sqrt{n}} \quad \text{and} \quad U = \frac{(n-1)S^2}{\sigma^2}.$$

Then the distribution of Z is $N(0,1)$ by Corollary 5.5-1. Theorem 5.5-2 tells us that the distribution of U is $\chi^2(n-1)$ and that Z and U are independent. Thus,

$$T = \frac{\dfrac{\overline{X} - \mu}{\sigma/\sqrt{n}}}{\sqrt{\dfrac{(n-1)S^2}{\sigma^2}\Big/(n-1)}} = \frac{\overline{X} - \mu}{S/\sqrt{n}} \tag{5.5-2}$$

has a Student's t distribution (see subsequent remark) with $r = n - 1$ degrees of freedom by Theorem 5.5-3. We use this T in Section 6.2 to construct confidence intervals for an unknown mean μ of a normal distribution. (See also Exercise 5.5-20.)

REMARK The foregoing distribution was first discovered by W. S. Gosset when he was working for an Irish brewery. Because Gosset published under the pseudonym Student, this distribution is sometimes known as Student's t distribution. Actually, Gosset was, in a sense, lucky to find the distribution of the T given in Equation 5.5-2. The distribution of $\overline{X}$ was well known; but to determine the distribution of U, he found the first four moments of U and guessed that the distribution was in the Pearson family and that led to the $\chi^2(n-1)$ distribution. While he proved that $\overline{X}$ and U were uncorrelated, he guessed that they were independent. He then went on to find the distribution of T of Equation 5.5-2. So two educated guesses were needed in this process. Later Fisher gave the real proof, but he also gave credit to Gosset for all of his insight into the problem. This discovery was a giant leap in statistical theory. ■

EXERCISES

5.5-1. Let $X_1, X_2, \ldots, X_{16}$ be a random sample from a normal distribution $N(77, 25)$. Compute

(a) $P(77 < \overline{X} < 79.5)$. (b) $P(74.2 < \overline{X} < 78.4)$.

5.5-2. Let X be $N(50, 36)$. Using the same set of axes, sketch the graphs of the probability density functions of

(a) X.

(b) $\overline{X}$, the mean of a random sample of size 9 from this distribution.

(c) $\overline{X}$, the mean of a random sample of size 36 from this distribution.

5.5-3. Let X equal the widest diameter (in millimeters) of the fetal head measured between the 16th and 25th weeks of pregnancy. Assume that the distribution of X is $N(46.58, 40.96)$. Let $\overline{X}$ be the sample mean of a random sample of $n = 16$ observations of X.

(a) Give the values of $E(\overline{X})$ and $\text{Var}(\overline{X})$.

(b) Find $P(44.42 \le \overline{X} \le 48.98)$.

5.5-4. Let X equal the weight of the soap in a "6-pound" box. Assume that the distribution of X is $N(6.05, 0.0004)$.

(a) Find $P(X < 6.0171)$.

(b) If nine boxes of soap are selected at random from the production line, find the probability that at most two boxes weigh less than 6.0171 pounds each. HINT: Let Y equal the number of boxes that weigh less than 6.0171 pounds.

(c) Let $\overline{X}$ be the sample mean of the nine boxes. Find $P(\overline{X} \le 6.035)$.

5.5-5. If $X_1, X_2, \ldots, X_{16}$ is a random sample of size $n = 16$ from the normal distribution $N(50, 100)$, determine

(a) $P\left(796.2 \le \sum_{i=1}^{16}(X_i - 50)^2 \le 2630\right)$.

(b) $P\left(726.1 \le \sum_{i=1}^{16}(X_i - \overline{X})^2 \le 2500\right)$.

5.5-6. At a heat-treating company, iron castings and steel forgings are heat treated to achieve desired mechanical properties and machinability. One steel forging is annealed to soften the part for each machining. Two lots of this part, made of 1020 steel, are heat treated in two different furnaces. The specification for this part is 36-66 on the Rockwell G scale. Let X_1 and X_2 equal the respective hardness measurements for parts selected randomly from furnaces 1 and 2. Assume that the distributions of X_1 and X_2 are $N(47.88, 2.19)$ and $N(43.04, 14.89)$, respectively.

(a) Sketch the p.d.f.'s of X_1 and X_2 on the same graph.

(b) Compute $P(X_1 > X_2)$, assuming independence of X_1 and X_2.

5.5-7. Let X equal the weight (in grams) of a nail of the type that is used for making decks. Assume that the distribution of X is $N(8.78, 0.16)$. Let $\overline{X}$ be the mean of a random sample of the weights of $n = 9$ nails.

(a) Sketch, on the same set of axes, the graphs of the p.d.f.'s of X and of $\overline{X}$.

(b) Let S^2 be the sample variance of the nine weights. Find constants a and b so that $P(a \le S^2 \le b) = 0.90$.

HINT: $P(a \le S^2 \le b)$ is equivalent to $P(8a/0.16 \le 8S^2/0.16 \le 8b/0.16)$, and $8S^2/0.16$ is $\chi^2(8)$. Find $8a/0.16$ and $8b/0.16$ from Table IV in Appendix B.

5.5-8. Suppose that the distribution of the weight of a prepackaged "1-pound bag" of carrots is $N(1.18, 0.07^2)$ and the distribution of the weight of a prepackaged "3-pound bag" of carrots is $N(3.22, 0.09^2)$. Selecting bags at random, find the probability that the sum of three 1-pound bags exceeds the weight of one 3-pound bag.

HINT: First determine the distribution of Y, the sum of the three, and then compute $P(Y > W)$, where W is the weight of the 3-pound bag.

5.5-9. Let X equal the force required to pull a stud out of a window that is to be inserted into an automobile. Assume that the distribution of X is $N(147.8, 12.3^2)$.

(a) Find $P(X < 163.3)$.

(b) If $\overline{X}$ is the mean and S^2 is the variance of a random sample of size $n = 25$ from this distribution of X, determine $P(\overline{X} \le 150.9)$.

(c) Find constants a and b so that $P(a \le S^2 \le b) = 0.90$. (See the hint in Exercise 5.5-7.)

5.5-10. Let X denote the wing length in millimeters of a male gallinule and Y the wing length in millimeters of a female gallinule. Assume that X is $N(184.09, 39.37)$ and Y is $N(171.93, 50.88)$ and that X and Y are independent. If a male and a female gallinule are captured, what is the probability that X is greater than Y?

5.5-11. Suppose that the length of life in hours (say, X) of a light bulb manufactured by company A is $N(800, 14400)$ and the length of life in hours (say, Y) of a light bulb manufactured by company B is $N(850, 2500)$. One bulb is selected from each company and is burned until "death."

(a) Find the probability that the length of life of the bulb from company A exceeds the length of life of the bulb from company B by at least 15 hours.

(b) Find the probability that at least one of the bulbs "lives" for at least 920 hours.

5.5-12. Let X and Y equal the number of miles per gallon achieved by compact cars and midsized cars, respectively, as reported in fuel economy ratings. Assume that $\mu_X = 24.5$, $\sigma_X = 3.8$, $\mu_Y = 21.3$, and $\sigma_Y = 2.7$. Let $\overline{X}$ and $\overline{Y}$ be the sample means of independent random samples of eight observations of X and Y, respectively.

(a) What are the values of the means and variances of $\overline{X}$ and $\overline{Y}$?

(b) Assuming that $\overline{X}$ and $\overline{Y}$ are each (approximately) normally distributed, how is $\overline{X} - \overline{Y}$ distributed?

(c) Find the (approximate) probability $P(\overline{X} > \overline{Y})$.

5.5-13. Let X equal the weight of a fat-free Fig Newton cookie. Assume that the distribution of X is $N(14.22, 0.0854)$. These cookies are sold in packages that have a label weight of 340 grams. The number of cookies in a package is usually 24, 25, or 26. Assuming that a package is filled with a random sample of cookies, how many cookies should be put into a package to be quite certain (say, with a probability of at least 0.95) that the total weight of the cookies exceeds 340 grams? (Keep in mind that extra cookies in a package decrease profit.)

5.5-14. A consumer buys n light bulbs, each of which has a lifetime that has a mean of 800 hours, a standard deviation of 100 hours, and a normal distribution. A light bulb is replaced by another as soon as it burns out. Assuming independence of the lifetimes, find the smallest n so that the succession of light bulbs produces light for at least 10,000 hours with a probability of 0.90.

5.5-15. A marketing research firm suggests to a company that two possible competing products can generate incomes X and Y (in millions) that are $N(3, 1)$ and $N(3.5, 4)$, respectively. Clearly, $P(X < Y) > 1/2$. However, the company would prefer the one with the smaller variance if in fact $P(X > 2) > P(Y > 2)$. Which product does the company select?

5.5-16. Let the independent random variables X_1 and X_2 be $N(0,1)$ and $\chi^2(r)$, respectively. Let $Y_1 = X_1/\sqrt{X_2/r}$ and $Y_2 = X_2$.

(a) Find the joint p.d.f. of Y_1 and Y_2.

(b) Determine the marginal p.d.f. of Y_1 and show that Y_1 has a t distribution. (This is another, equivalent, way of finding the p.d.f. of T.)

5.5-17. Let T have a t distribution with r degrees of freedom. Show that $E(T) = 0$, $r \ge 2$, and $\text{Var}(T) = r/(r-2)$, provided that $r \ge 3$, by first finding $E(Z)$, $E(1/\sqrt{U})$, $E(Z^2)$, and $E(1/U)$.

5.5-18. Let the distribution of T be $t(23)$. Find

(a) $t_{0.05}(23)$.

(b) $t_{0.90}(23)$.

(c) $P(-2.069 \le T \le 2.500)$.

5.5-19. Let the distribution of T be $t(17)$. Find

(a) $t_{0.01}(17)$.

(b) $t_{0.95}(17)$.

(c) $P(-1.740 \le T \le 1.740)$.

5.5-20. Let $n = 9$ in the T statistic defined in Equation 5.5-2.

(a) Find $t_{0.025}$ so that $P(-t_{0.025} \le T \le t_{0.025}) = 0.95$.

(b) Solve the inequality $[-t_{0.025} \le T \le t_{0.025}]$ so that μ is in the middle.

5.5-21. Let Z_1, Z_2, and Z_3 have independent standard normal distributions, $N(0,1)$.

(a) Find the distribution of

$$W = \frac{Z_1}{\sqrt{(Z_2^2 + Z_3^2)/2}}.$$

(b) Show that

$$V = \frac{Z_1}{\sqrt{(Z_1^2 + Z_2^2)/2}}$$

has p.d.f. $f(v) = 1/(\pi\sqrt{2 - v^2})$, $-\sqrt{2} < v < \sqrt{2}$.

(c) Find the mean of V.

(d) Find the standard deviation of V.

(e) Why are the distributions of W and V so different?

5.6 THE CENTRAL LIMIT THEOREM

In Section 5.4, we found that the mean $\overline{X}$ of a random sample of size n from a distribution with mean μ and variance $\sigma^2 > 0$ is a random variable with the properties that

$$E(\overline{X}) = \mu \qquad \text{and} \qquad \text{Var}(\overline{X}) = \frac{\sigma^2}{n}.$$

As n increases, the variance of $\overline{X}$ decreases. Consequently, the distribution of $\overline{X}$ clearly depends on n, and we see that we are dealing with sequences of distributions.

In Theorem 5.5-1, we considered the p.d.f. of $\overline{X}$ when sampling is from the normal distribution $N(\mu, \sigma^2)$. We showed that the distribution of $\overline{X}$ is $N(\mu, \sigma^2/n)$, and in Figure 5.5-1, by graphing the p.d.f.'s for several values of n, we illustrated the property that as n increases, the probability becomes concentrated in a small interval centered at μ. That is, as n increases, $\overline{X}$ tends to converge to μ, or $(\overline{X} - \mu)$ tends to converge to 0 in a probability sense.

In general, if we let

$$W = \frac{\sqrt{n}}{\sigma}(\overline{X} - \mu) = \frac{\overline{X} - \mu}{\sigma/\sqrt{n}} = \frac{Y - n\mu}{\sqrt{n}\,\sigma},$$

where Y is the sum of a random sample of size n from some distribution with mean μ and variance σ^2, then, for each positive integer n,

$$E(W) = E\left[\frac{\overline{X} - \mu}{\sigma/\sqrt{n}}\right] = \frac{E(\overline{X}) - \mu}{\sigma/\sqrt{n}} = \frac{\mu - \mu}{\sigma/\sqrt{n}} = 0$$

and

$$\text{Var}(W) = E(W^2) = E\left[\frac{(\overline{X} - \mu)^2}{\sigma^2/n}\right] = \frac{E[(\overline{X} - \mu)^2]}{\sigma^2/n} = \frac{\sigma^2/n}{\sigma^2/n} = 1.$$

Thus, while $\overline{X} - \mu$ tends to "degenerate" to zero, the factor $\sqrt{n}/\sigma$ in $\sqrt{n}(\overline{X} - \mu)/\sigma$ "spreads out" the probability enough to prevent this degeneration. What, then, is the distribution of W as n increases? One observation that might shed some light on the answer to this question can be made immediately. If the sample arises from a normal distribution, then, from Theorem 5.5-1, we know that $\overline{X}$ is $N(\mu, \sigma^2/n)$, and hence W is $N(0,1)$ for each positive n. Thus, in the limit, the distribution of W must be $N(0,1)$. So if the solution of the question does not depend on the underlying distribution (i.e., it is unique), the answer must be $N(0,1)$. As we will see, that is exactly the case, and this result is so important that it is called the central limit theorem, the proof of which is given in Section 10.6.

THEOREM 5.6-1 **(Central Limit Theorem)** If $\overline{X}$ is the mean of a random sample $X_1, X_2, \ldots, X_n$ of size n from a distribution with a finite mean μ and a finite positive variance σ^2, then the distribution of

$$W = \frac{\overline{X} - \mu}{\sigma/\sqrt{n}} = \frac{\sum_{i=1}^{n} X_i - n\mu}{\sqrt{n}\,\sigma}$$

is $N(0,1)$ in the limit as $n \to \infty$.

When n is "sufficiently large," a practical use of the central limit theorem is approximating the distribution function of W, namely,

$$P(W \le w) \approx \int_{-\infty}^{w} \frac{1}{\sqrt{2\pi}} e^{-z^2/2}\, dz = \Phi(w).$$

We present some illustrations of this application, discuss the notion of "sufficiently large," and try to give an intuitive feeling for the central limit theorem.

EXAMPLE 5.6-1 Let $\overline{X}$ be the mean of a random sample of $n = 25$ currents (in milliamperes) in a strip of wire in which each measurement has a mean of 15 and a variance of 4. Then $\overline{X}$ has an approximate $N(15, 4/25)$ distribution. As an illustration,

$$P(14.4 < \overline{X} < 15.6) = P\left(\frac{14.5 - 15}{0.4} < \frac{\overline{X} - 15}{0.4} < \frac{15.6 - 15}{0.4}\right)$$
$$\approx \Phi(1.5) - \Phi(-1.5) = 0.9332 - 0.0668 = 0.8664. \blacksquare$$

EXAMPLE 5.6-2 Let $X_1, X_2, \ldots, X_{20}$ denote a random sample of size 20 from the uniform distribution $U(0,1)$. Here $E(X_i) = 1/2$ and $\text{Var}(X_i) = 1/12$, for $i = 1,2,\ldots,20$. If $Y = X_1 + X_2 + \cdots + X_{20}$, then

$$P(Y \le 9.1) = P\left(\frac{Y - 20(1/2)}{\sqrt{20/12}} \le \frac{9.1 - 10}{\sqrt{20/12}}\right) = P(W \le -0.697)$$
$$\approx \Phi(-0.697)$$
$$= 0.2423.$$

Also,

$$P(8.5 \le Y \le 11.7) = P\left(\frac{8.5 - 10}{\sqrt{5/3}} \le \frac{Y - 10}{\sqrt{5/3}} \le \frac{11.7 - 10}{\sqrt{5/3}}\right)$$
$$= P(-1.162 \le W \le 1.317)$$
$$\approx \Phi(1.317) - \Phi(-1.162)$$
$$= 0.9061 - 0.1226 = 0.7835.$$

■

EXAMPLE 5.6-3 Let $\overline{X}$ denote the mean of a random sample of size 25 from the distribution whose p.d.f. is $f(x) = x^3/4, 0 < x < 2$. It is easy to show that $\mu = 8/5 = 1.6$ and $\sigma^2 = 8/75$. Thus,

$$P(1.5 \le \overline{X} \le 1.65) = P\left(\frac{1.5 - 1.6}{\sqrt{8/75}/\sqrt{25}} \le \frac{\overline{X} - 1.6}{\sqrt{8/75}/\sqrt{25}} \le \frac{1.65 - 1.6}{\sqrt{8/75}/\sqrt{25}}\right)$$
$$= P(-1.531 \le W \le 0.765)$$
$$\approx \Phi(0.765) - \Phi(-1.531)$$
$$= 0.7779 - 0.0629 = 0.7150.$$

■

These examples show how the central limit theorem can be used for approximating certain probabilities concerning the mean $\overline{X}$ or the sum $Y = \sum_{i=1}^{n} X_i$ of a random sample. That is, $\overline{X}$ is approximately $N(\mu, \sigma^2/n)$, and Y is approximately $N(n\mu, n\sigma^2)$, when n is "sufficiently large," where μ and σ^2 are, respectively, the mean and the variance of the underlying distribution from which the sample arose. Generally, if n is greater than 25 or 30, these approximations will be good. However, if the underlying distribution is symmetric, unimodal, and of the continuous type, a value of n as small as 4 or 5 can yield an adequate approximation. Moreover, if the original distribution is approximately normal, $\overline{X}$ would have a distribution very close to normal when n equals 2 or 3. In fact, we know that if the sample is taken from $N(\mu, \sigma^2)$, $\overline{X}$ is exactly $N(\mu, \sigma^2/n)$ for every $n = 1,2,3,\ldots$.

The examples that follow will help to illustrate the previous remarks and will give the reader a better intuitive feeling about the central limit theorem. In particular, we shall see how the size of n affects the distribution of $\overline{X}$ and $Y = \sum_{i=1}^{n} X_i$ for samples from several underlying distributions.

EXAMPLE 5.6-4 Let X_1, X_2, X_3, X_4 be a random sample of size 4 from the uniform distribution $U(0,1)$ with p.d.f. $f(x) = 1, 0 < x < 1$. Then $\mu = 1/2$ and $\sigma^2 = 1/12$. We shall compare the graph of the p.d.f. of

$$Y = \sum_{i=1}^{n} X_i$$

with the graph of the $N[n(1/2), n(1/12)]$ p.d.f. for $n = 2$ and 4, respectively.

By methods given in Section 5.2, we can determine that the p.d.f. of $Y = X_1 + X_2$ is

$$g(y) = \begin{cases} y, & 0 < y \le 1, \\ 2 - y, & 1 < y < 2. \end{cases}$$

This is the triangular p.d.f. that is graphed in Figure 5.6-1(a). In this figure, the $N[2(1/2), 2(1/12)]$ p.d.f. is also graphed.

Moreover, the p.d.f. of $Y = X_1 + X_2 + X_3 + X_4$ is

$$g(y) = \begin{cases} \dfrac{y^3}{6}, & 0 \le y < 1, \\ \dfrac{-3y^3 + 12y^2 - 12y + 4}{6}, & 1 \le y < 2, \\ \dfrac{3y^3 - 24y^2 + 60y - 44}{6}, & 2 \le y < 3, \\ \dfrac{-y^3 + 12y^2 - 48y + 64}{6}, & 3 \le y \le 4. \end{cases}$$

This p.d.f. is graphed in Figure 5.6-1(b) along with the $N[4(1/2), 4(1/12)]$ p.d.f. If we are interested in finding $P(1.7 \le Y \le 3.2)$, we can do so by evaluating

$$\int_{1.7}^{3.2} g(y)\, dy,$$

which is tedious. (See Exercise 5.6-10.) It is much easier to use a normal approximation, which results in a number close to the exact value. ■

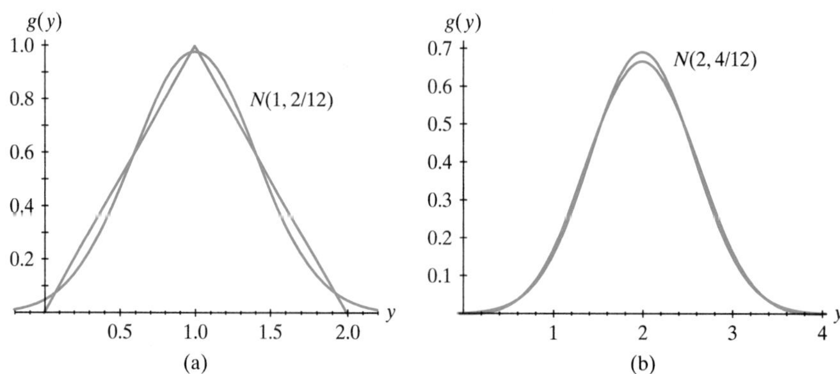

FIGURE 5.6-1: p.d.f.'s of sums of uniform random variables

In Example 5.6-4 and Exercise 5.6-10, we show that even for a small value of n, such as $n = 4$, the sum of the sample items has an approximate normal distribution. The next example illustrates that, for some underlying distributions (particularly skewed ones), n must be quite large in order for us to obtain a satisfactory approximation. To keep the scale on the horizontal axis the same for each value of n, we will use the following result: Let $f(x)$ and $F(x)$ respectively be the p.d.f. and distribution function of a random variable, X, of the continuous type having mean μ and variance σ^2. Let $W = (X - \mu)/\sigma$. The distribution function of W is given by

$$\begin{aligned} G(w) = P(W \le w) &= P\left(\frac{X - \mu}{\sigma} \le w\right) \\ = P(X \le \sigma w + \mu) &= F(\sigma w + \mu). \end{aligned}$$

Thus, the p.d.f. of W is given by

$$g(w) = F'(\sigma w + \mu) = \sigma f(\sigma w + \mu).$$

EXAMPLE 5.6-5 Let $X_1, X_2, \ldots, X_n$ be a random sample of size n from a chi-square distribution with one degree of freedom. If

$$Y = \sum_{i=1}^{n} X_i,$$

then Y is $\chi^2(n)$, and it follows that $E(Y) = n$ and $\operatorname{Var}(Y) = 2n$. Let

$$W = \frac{Y - n}{\sqrt{2n}}.$$

The p.d.f. of W is given by

$$g(w) = \sqrt{2n}\,\frac{(\sqrt{2n}\,w + n)^{n/2-1}}{\Gamma\left(\frac{n}{2}\right)2^{n/2}}\,e^{-(\sqrt{2n}\,w+n)/2}, \qquad -n/\sqrt{2n} < w < \infty.$$

Note that $w > -n/\sqrt{2n}$ corresponds to $y > 0$. In Figures 5.6-2, the graph of the p.d.f. of W is given along with the $N(0,1)$ p.d.f. for $n = 20$ and $n = 100$. ■

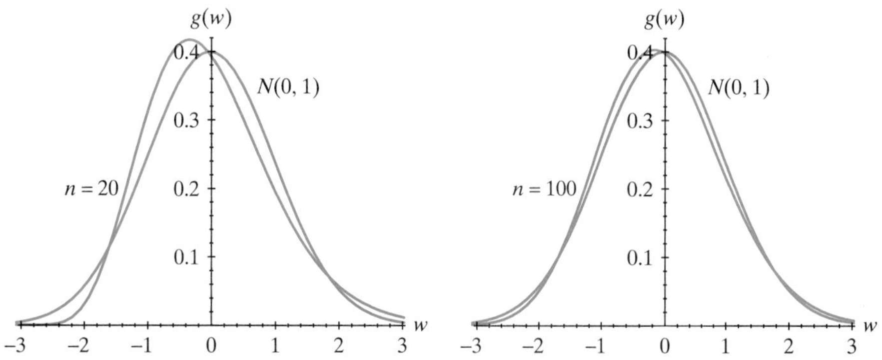

FIGURE 5.6-2: p.d.f.'s of sums of chi-square random variables

In order to gain an intuitive idea about how the sample size n affects the distribution of $W = (\overline{X} - \mu)/(\sigma/\sqrt{n})$, it is helpful to simulate values of W on a computer using different values of n and different underlying distributions. The next example illustrates this simulation.

REMARK Recall that we simulate observations from a distribution of X having a continuous-type distribution function $F(x)$ as follows: Suppose $F(a) = 0$, $F(b) = 1$, and $F(x)$ is strictly increasing for $a < x < b$. Let $Y = F(x)$ and let the distribution of Y be $U(0, 1)$. If y is an observed value of Y, then $x = F^{-1}(y)$ is an observed value of X. (See Section 5.1.) Thus, if y is the value of a computer-generated random number, then $x = F^{-1}(y)$ is the simulated value of X. ■

EXAMPLE 5.6-6 It is often difficult to find the exact distribution of the random variable $W = (\overline{X} - \mu)/(\sigma/\sqrt{n})$, unless you use a computer algebra system such as *Maple*. In this example, we give some empirical evidence about the distribution of W by simulating random samples on the computer. We also superimpose the theoretical p.d.f. of W, which we found by using *Maple*. Let $X_1, X_2, \ldots, X_n$ denote a random sample of size n from the distribution with p.d.f. $f(x)$, distribution function $F(x)$, mean μ, and variance σ^2. We simulated 1000 random samples of size $n = 2$ and $n = 7$ from each of two distributions. We then computed the value of W for each sample, thus obtaining 1000 observed values of W. Next, we constructed a histogram of these 1000 values by using 21 intervals of equal length. A relative frequency histogram of the observations of W, the p.d.f. for the standard normal distribution, and the theoretical p.d.f. of W are given in Figures 5.6-3 and 5.6-4.

(a) In Figure 5.6-3, $f(x) = (x + 1)/2$ and $F(x) = (x + 1)^2/4$ for $-1 < x < 1$; $\mu = 1/3$, $\sigma^2 = 2/9$; and $n = 2$ and 7. This underlying distribution is skewed to the left.

(b) In Figure 5.6-4, $f(x) = (3/2)x^2$ and $F(x) = (x^3 + 1)/2$ for $-1 < x < 1$; $\mu = 0$, $\sigma^2 = 3/5$; and $n = 2$ and 7. (Sketch the graph of $y = f(x)$. Give an argument as to why the histogram for $n = 2$ looks the way it does.) This underlying distribution is U shaped; thus, W does not follow a normal distribution with small n. ■

Note that these examples have not *proved* anything. They are presented to give *evidence* of the truth of the central limit theorem, and they do give a nice feeling for what is happening.

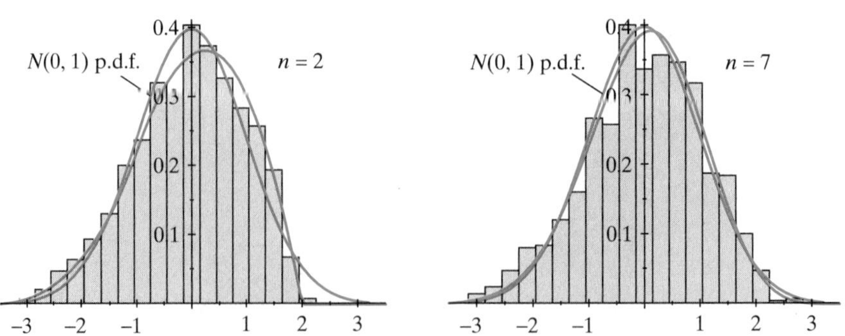

FIGURE 5.6-3: p.d.f.'s of $(\overline{X} - \mu)/(\sigma/\sqrt{n})$, underlying distribution triangular

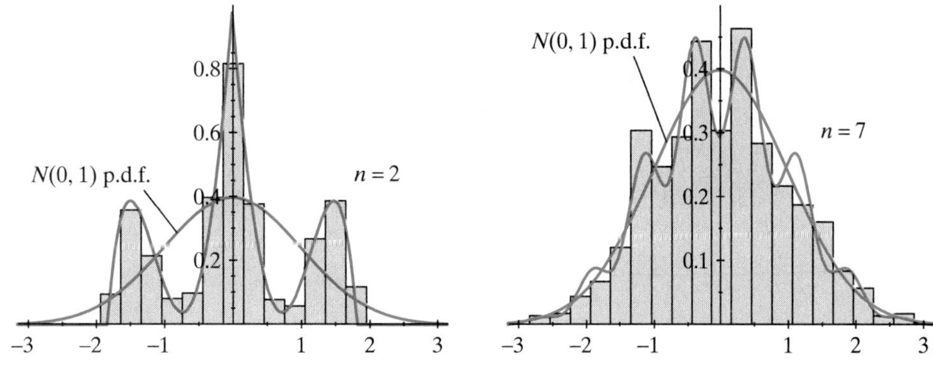

FIGURE 5.6-4: p.d.f.'s of $(\overline{X} - \mu)/(\sigma/\sqrt{n})$, underlying distribution U shaped

So far, all the illustrations have concerned distributions of the continuous type. However, the hypotheses for the central limit theorem do not require the distribution to be continuous. We shall consider applications of the central limit theorem for discrete-type distributions in the next section.

EXERCISES

5.6-1. Let $\overline{X}$ be the mean of a random sample of size 12 from the uniform distribution on the interval $(0, 1)$. Approximate $P(1/2 \le \overline{X} \le 2/3)$.

5.6-2. Let $Y = X_1 + X_2 + \cdots + X_{15}$ be the sum of a random sample of size 15 from the distribution whose p.d.f. is $f(x) = (3/2)x^2$, $-1 < x < 1$. Using the p.d.f. of Y, we find that $P(-0.3 \le Y \le 1.5) = 0.22788$. Use the central limit theorem to approximate this probability.

5.6-3. Let $\overline{X}$ be the mean of a random sample of size 36 from an exponential distribution with mean 3. Approximate $P(2.5 \le \overline{X} \le 4)$.

5.6-4. Approximate $P(39.75 \le \overline{X} \le 41.25)$, where $\overline{X}$ is the mean of a random sample of size 32 from a distribution with mean $\mu = 40$ and variance $\sigma^2 = 8$.

5.6-5. Let $X_1, X_2, \ldots, X_{18}$ be a random sample of size 18 from a chi-square distribution with $r = 1$. Recall that $\mu = 1$ and $\sigma^2 = 2$.

(a) How is $Y = \sum_{i=1}^{18} X_i$ distributed?

(b) Using the result of part (a), we see from Table IV in the appendix that

$$P(Y \le 9.390) = 0.05$$

and

$$P(Y \le 34.80) = 0.99.$$

Compare these two probabilities with the approximations found with the use of the central limit theorem.

5.6-6. A random sample of size $n = 18$ is taken from the distribution with p.d.f. $f(x) = 1 - x/2$, $0 \le x \le 2$.

(a) Find μ and σ^2. (b) Find, approximately, $P(2/3 \le \overline{X} \le 5/6)$.

5.6-7. Let X equal the maximal oxygen intake of a human on a treadmill, where the measurements are in milliliters of oxygen per minute per kilogram of weight. Assume that, for a particular population, the mean of X is $\mu = 54.030$ and the standard deviation is $\sigma = 5.8$. Let $\overline{X}$ be the sample mean of a random sample of size $n = 47$. Find $P(52.761 \le \overline{X} \le 54.453)$, approximately.

5.6-8. Let X equal the weight in grams of a miniature candy bar. Assume that $\mu = E(X) = 24.43$ and $\sigma^2 = \mathrm{Var}(X) = 2.20$. Let $\overline{X}$ be the sample mean of a random sample of $n = 30$ candy bars. Find

(a) $E(\overline{X})$. (b) $\mathrm{Var}(\overline{X})$. (c) $P(24.17 \le \overline{X} \le 24.82)$, approximately.

5.6-9. Let X equal the birth weight in grams of a baby born in the Sudan. Assume that $E(X) = 3320$ and $\mathrm{Var}(X) = 660^2$. Let $\overline{X}$ be the sample mean of a random sample of size $n = 225$. Find $P(3233.76 \le \overline{X} \le 3406.24)$, approximately.

5.6-10. In Example 5.6-4, with $n = 4$, compute $P(1.7 \le Y \le 3.2)$ and compare your answer with the normal approximation of this probability.

5.6-11. Five measurements in "ohms per square unit of area" of the electronic conductive coating (which allows light to pass through it) on a thin, clear piece of glass were made, and the average was calculated. This procedure was repeated 150 times, yielding the following averages:

83.86	75.86	79.65	90.57	95.37	97.97	77.00	80.80	83.53	83.17
80.20	81.42	89.14	88.68	85.15	90.11	89.03	85.00	82.57	79.46
81.20	82.80	81.28	74.64	69.85	75.60	76.60	78.30	88.51	86.32
84.03	95.27	90.05	77.50	75.14	81.33	86.12	78.30	80.30	84.96
79.30	88.96	82.76	83.13	79.60	86.20	85.16	87.86	91.00	91.10
84.04	92.10	79.20	83.76	87.87	86.71	81.89	85.72	75.84	74.27
93.08	81.75	75.66	75.35	76.55	84.86	90.68	91.02	90.97	98.30
91.84	97.41	73.60	90.65	80.20	74.75	90.35	79.66	86.88	83.00
86.24	80.50	74.25	91.20	70.16	78.40	85.60	80.82	75.95	80.75
81.86	82.18	82.98	84.00	76.85	85.00	79.50	86.56	83.30	72.40
79.20	86.20	82.36	84.08	86.11	88.25	88.93	93.12	78.30	77.24
82.52	81.37	83.72	86.90	84.37	92.60	95.01	78.95	81.40	88.40
76.10	85.33	82.95	80.20	88.21	83.49	81.00	82.72	81.12	83.62
91.18	85.90	79.01	77.56	81.13	80.60	81.65	70.70	69.36	79.09
71.35	67.20	67.43	69.95	66.76	76.35	69.45	80.13	84.26	88.13

(a) Using 10 intervals of equal length, and using (66.495, 69.695) for the first class interval, construct a frequency table for these 150 observations. Which is the modal class?

(b) Construct a relative frequency histogram for the grouped data.

(c) Using the sample mean 82.661 and the sample variance 42.2279 of these 150 values as the distribution mean and variance, superimpose a normal p.d.f. on the histogram you constructed in part (b). Do these 150 means of five measurements seem to be normally distributed?

5.6-12. A church has pledges (in dollars) with a mean of 2000 and a standard deviation of 500. A random sample of size $n = 25$ is taken from all of this church's pledges, and the sample mean $\overline{X}$ is considered. Approximate $P(\overline{X} > 2050)$.

5.6-13. A company has a one-year group life policy that divides its employees into two classes as follows:

Class	Probability of Death	Benefit	Number in Class
A	0.01	\$20,000	1000
B	0.03	\$10,000	500

The insurance company wants to collect a premium that equals the 90th percentile of the distribution of the total claims. What should that premium be?

5.6-14. Let X and Y equal the respective numbers of hours a randomly selected child watches movies or cartoons on TV during a certain month. From experience, it is known that $E(X) = 30$, $E(Y) = 50$, $\text{Var}(X) = 52$, $\text{Var}(Y) = 64$, and $\text{Cov}(X, Y) = 14$. Twenty-five children are selected at random. Let Z equal the total number of hours these 25 children watch TV movies or cartoons in the next month. Approximate $P(1970 < Z < 2090)$. HINT: Use the remark after Theorem 5.3-3.

5.6-15. The tensile strength X of paper, in pounds per square inch, has $\mu = 30$ and $\sigma = 3$. A random sample of size $n = 100$ is taken from the distribution of tensile strengths. Compute the probability that the sample mean $\overline{X}$ is greater than 29.5 pounds per square inch.

5.6-16. At certain times during the year, a bus company runs a special van holding 10 passengers from Iowa City to Chicago. After the opening of sales of the tickets, the time (in minutes) between sales of tickets for the trip has a gamma distribution with $\alpha = 3$ and $\theta = 2$.

(a) Assuming independence, record an integral that gives the probability of being sold out within one hour.

(b) Approximate the answer in part (a).

5.6-17. Let X_1, X_2, X_3, X_4 represent the random times in days needed to complete four steps of a project. These times are independent and have gamma distributions with common $\theta = 2$ and $\alpha_1 = 3$, $\alpha_2 = 2$, $\alpha_3 = 5$, $\alpha_4 = 3$, respectively. One step must be completed before the next can be started. Let Y equal the total time needed to complete the project.

(a) Find an integral that represents $P(Y \le 25)$.

(b) Using a normal distribution, approximate the answer to part (a). Is this approach justified?

5.6-18. Suppose that the sick leave taken by the typical worker per year has $\mu = 10$, $\sigma = 2$, measured in days. A firm has $n = 20$ employees. Assuming independence, how many sick days should the firm budget if the financial officer wants the probability of exceeding the number of days budgeted to be less than 20%?

5.7 APPROXIMATIONS FOR DISCRETE DISTRIBUTIONS

In this section, we illustrate how the normal distribution can be used to approximate probabilities for certain discrete-type distributions. One of the more important discrete distributions is the binomial distribution. To see how the central limit theorem can be applied, recall that a binomial random variable can be described as the sum of Bernoulli random variables. That is, let $X_1, X_2, \ldots, X_n$ be a random sample from a Bernoulli distribution with mean $\mu = p$ and variance $\sigma^2 = p(1-p)$, where $0 < p < 1$. Then $Y = \sum_{i=1}^{n} X_i$ is $b(n, p)$. The central limit theorem states that the distribution of

$$W = \frac{Y - np}{\sqrt{np(1-p)}} = \frac{\overline{X} - p}{\sqrt{p(1-p)/n}}$$

is $N(0, 1)$ in the limit as $n \to \infty$. Thus, if n is "sufficiently large," the distribution of Y is approximately $N[np, np(1-p)]$, and probabilities for the binomial distribution $b(n, p)$ can be approximated with this normal distribution. A rule often stated is that n is sufficiently large if $np \ge 5$ and $n(1-p) \ge 5$. This rule can be used as a rough guide, although as p deviates more and more from 0.5, we need larger and larger sample sizes because the underlying Bernoulli distribution becomes more skewed.

Note that we shall be approximating probabilities for a discrete distribution with probabilities for a continuous distribution. Let us discuss a reasonable procedure in this situation. If V is $N(\mu, \sigma^2)$, then $P(a < V < b)$ is equivalent to the area bounded by the p.d.f. of V, the v-axis, $v = a$, and $v = b$. Now recall that, for a Y that is $b(n, p)$, the probability histogram for Y was defined as follows: For each y such that $k - 1/2 < y = k < k + 1/2$, let

$$f(k) = \frac{n!}{k!(n-k)!} p^k (1-p)^{n-k}, \qquad k = 0, 1, 2, \ldots, n.$$

Then $P(Y = k)$ can be represented by the area of the rectangle with a height of $P(Y = k)$ and a base of length 1 centered at k. Figure 5.7-1 on the next page shows the graph of the probability histogram for the binomial distribution $b(4, 1/4)$. In using the normal distribution to approximate probabilities for the binomial distribution, areas under the p.d.f. for the normal distribution will be used to approximate areas of rectangles in the probability histogram for the binomial distribution.

EXAMPLE 5.7-1 Let the distribution of Y be $b(10, 1/2)$. Then, by the central limit theorem, $P(a < Y < b)$ can be approximated with the use of the normal distribution with mean $10(1/2) = 5$ and variance $10(1/2)(1/2) = 5/2$. Figure 5.7-2(a) on the next page shows the graph of the probability histogram for $b(10, 1/2)$ and the graph of the p.d.f. of the normal distribution $N(5, 5/2)$. Note that the area of the rectangle whose base is

$$\left(k - \frac{1}{2}, k + \frac{1}{2}\right)$$

and the area under the normal curve between $k - 1/2$ and $k + 1/2$ are approximately equal for each integer k. ■

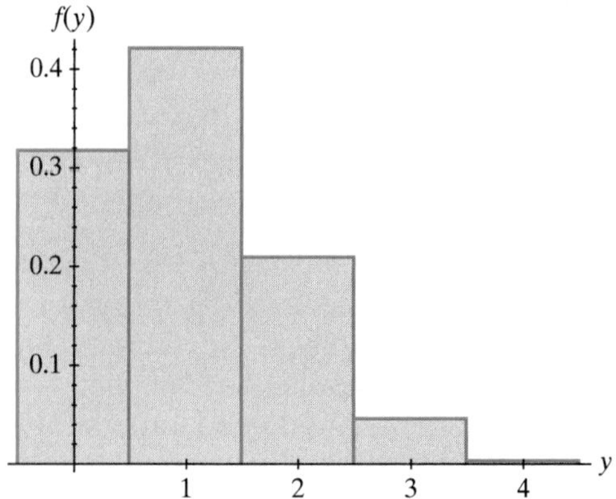

FIGURE 5.7-1: Probability histogram for $b(4, 1/4)$

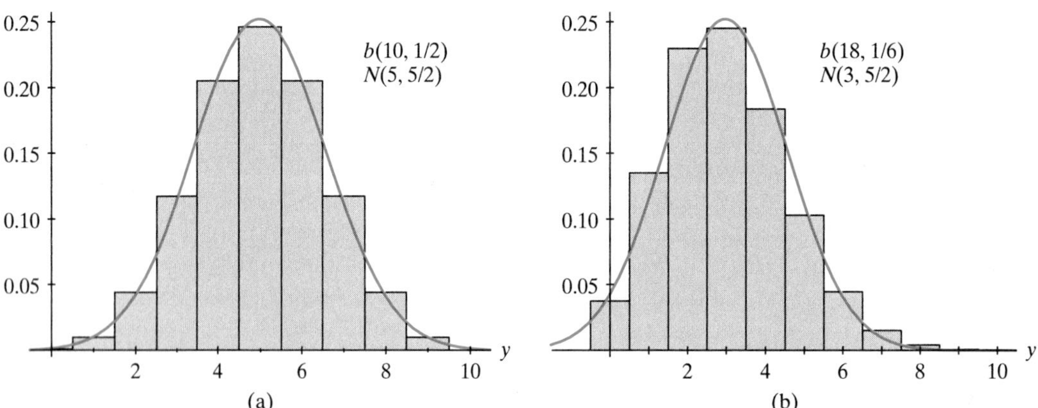

FIGURE 5.7-2: Normal approximation for the binomial distribution

EXAMPLE 5.7-2 Let Y be $b(18, 1/6)$. Because $np = 18(1/6) = 3 < 5$, the normal approximation is not as good here. Figure 5.7-2(b) illustrates this by depicting the skewed probability histogram for $b(18, 1/6)$ and the symmetric p.d.f. of the normal distribution $N(3, 5/2)$. ■

EXAMPLE 5.7-3 Let Y have the binomial distribution of Example 5.7-1 and Figure 5.7-2(a), namely, $b(10, 1/2)$. Then

$$P(3 \le Y < 6) = P(2.5 \le Y \le 5.5),$$

because $P(Y = 6)$ is not in the desired answer. But the latter equals

$$P\left(\frac{2.5 - 5}{\sqrt{10/4}} \le \frac{Y - 5}{\sqrt{10/4}} \le \frac{5.5 - 5}{\sqrt{10/4}}\right) \approx \Phi(0.316) - \Phi(-1.581)$$

$$= 0.6240 - 0.0570 = 0.5670.$$

Using Table II in the appendix, we find that $P(3 \le Y < 6) = 0.5683$. ■

EXAMPLE 5.7-4 Let Y be $b(36, 1/2)$. Then, since

$$\mu = (36)(1/2) = 18 \quad \text{and} \quad \sigma^2 = (36)(1/2)(1/2) = 9,$$

it follows that

$$\begin{aligned} P(12 < Y \leq 18) &= P(12.5 \leq Y \leq 18.5) \\ &= P\left(\frac{12.5 - 18}{\sqrt{9}} \leq \frac{Y - 18}{\sqrt{9}} \leq \frac{18.5 - 18}{\sqrt{9}}\right) \\ &\approx \Phi(0.167) - \Phi(-1.833) \\ &= 0.5329. \end{aligned}$$

Note that 12 was increased to 12.5 because $P(Y = 12)$ is not included in the desired probability. Using the binomial formula, we find that

$$P(12 < Y \leq 18) = P(13 \leq Y \leq 18) = 0.5334.$$

(You may verify this answer with your calculator or Minitab.) Also,

$$\begin{aligned} P(Y = 20) &= P(19.5 \leq Y \leq 20.5) \\ &= P\left(\frac{19.5 - 18}{\sqrt{9}} \leq \frac{Y - 18}{\sqrt{9}} \leq \frac{20.5 - 18}{\sqrt{9}}\right) \\ &\approx \Phi(0.833) - \Phi(0.5) \\ &= 0.1060. \end{aligned}$$

Using the binomial formula, we have $P(Y = 20) = 0.1063$. So, in this situation, the approximations are extremely good. ■

Note that, in general, if Y is $b(n, p)$, n is large, and $k = 0, 1, \ldots, n$, then

$$P(Y \leq k) \approx \Phi\left(\frac{k + 1/2 - np}{\sqrt{npq}}\right)$$

and

$$P(Y < k) \approx \Phi\left(\frac{k - 1/2 - np}{\sqrt{npq}}\right),$$

because in the first case k is included and in the second it is not.

We now show how the Poisson distribution with large enough mean can be approximated with the use of a normal distribution.

EXAMPLE 5.7-5 A random variable having a Poisson distribution with mean 20 can be thought of as the sum Y of the observations of a random sample of size 20 from a Poisson distribution with mean 1. Thus,

$$W = \frac{Y - 20}{\sqrt{20}}$$

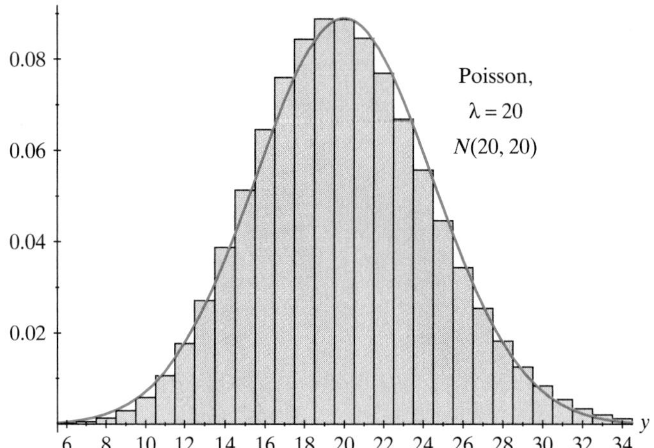

FIGURE 5.7-3: Normal approximation of Poisson, $\lambda = 20$

has a distribution that is approximately $N(0,1)$, and the distribution of Y is approximately $N(20,20)$. (See Figure 5.7-3.) For example,

$$\begin{aligned} P(16 < Y \le 21) &= P(16.5 \le Y \le 21.5) \\ &= P\left(\frac{16.5 - 20}{\sqrt{20}} \le \frac{Y - 20}{\sqrt{20}} \le \frac{21.5 - 20}{\sqrt{20}}\right) \\ &\approx \Phi(0.335) - \Phi(-0.783) \\ &= 0.4142. \end{aligned}$$

Note that 16 is increased to 16.5 because $Y = 16$ is not included in the event $\{16 < Y \le 21\}$. The answer obtained with the Poisson formula is 0.4226. ■

In general, if Y has a Poisson distribution with mean λ, then the distribution of

$$W = \frac{Y - \lambda}{\sqrt{\lambda}}$$

is approximately $N(0,1)$ when λ is sufficiently large.

REMARK If you have a statistical calculator or a statistics computer package, use it to compute discrete probabilities. However, it is important to learn how to apply the central limit theorem. ■

EXERCISES

5.7-1. Let the distribution of Y be $b(25, 1/2)$. Find the given probabilities in two ways: exactly, using Table II in the appendix; and approximately, using the central limit theorem. Compare the two results in each of the three cases.

(a) $P(10 < Y \le 12)$. (b) $P(12 \le Y < 15)$. (c) $P(Y = 12)$.

5.7-2. Suppose that among gifted seventh-graders who score very high on a mathematics exam, approximately 20% are left handed or ambidextrous. Let X equal the number of left-handed or ambidextrous students among a random sample of $n = 25$ gifted seventh-graders. Find $P(2 < X < 9)$

(a) Using Table II in the appendix.

(b) Approximately, using the central limit theorem.

Remark Since X has a skewed distribution, the approximation is not as good as that for the symmetrical distribution where $p = 0.50$, even though $np = 5$. ■

5.7-3. A public opinion poll in Southern California was conducted to determine whether southern Californians are prepared for the "big earthquake" that experts predict will devastate the region sometime in the next 50 years. It was learned that "60% have not secured objects in their homes that might fall and cause injury and damage during a temblor." In a random sample of $n = 864$ southern Californians, let X equal the number who "have not secured objects in their homes." Find $P(496 \le X \le 548)$, approximately.

5.7-4. Let X equal the number out of $n = 48$ mature aster seeds that will germinate when $p = 0.75$ is the probability that a particular seed germinates. Approximate $P(35 \le X \le 40)$.

5.7-5. Let p equal the proportion of all college students who would say yes to the question, "Would you drink from the same glass as your friend if you suspected that this friend were an AIDS virus carrier?" Assume that $p = 0.10$. Let X equal the number of students out of a random sample of size $n = 100$ who would say yes to the question. Approximate $P(X \le 11)$.

Remark The value used for p was based on a poll conducted in a class at San Diego State University. It would be interesting for you to conduct a survey at your college to estimate the value of p. ■

5.7-6. In adults, the pneumococcus bacterium causes 70% of pneumonia cases. In a random sample of $n = 84$ adults who have pneumonia, let X equal the number whose pneumonia was caused by the pneumococcus bacterium. Use the normal distribution to find $P(X \le 52)$, approximately.

5.7-7. Let $X_1, X_2, \ldots, X_{48}$ be a random sample of size 48 from the distribution with p.d.f. $f(x) = 1/x^2$, $1 < x < \infty$. Approximate the probability that at most 10 of these random variables have values greater than 4. HINT: Let the ith trial be a success if $X_i > 4$, $i = 1, 2, \ldots, 48$, and let Y equal the number of successes.

5.7-8. A candy maker produces mints that have a label weight of 20.4 grams. Assume that the distribution of the weights of these mints is $N(21.37, 0.16)$.

(a) Let X denote the weight of a single mint selected at random from the production line. Find $P(X < 20.857)$.

(b) During a particular shift, 100 mints are selected at random and weighed. Let Y equal the number of these mints that weigh less than 20.857 grams. Approximate $P(Y \le 5)$.

(c) Let $\overline{X}$ equal the sample mean of the 100 mints selected and weighed on a particular shift. Find $P(21.31 \le \overline{X} \le 21.39)$.

5.7-9. Let X equal the number of alpha particles emitted by barium-133 per second and counted by a Geiger counter. Assume that X has a Poisson distribution with $\lambda = 49$. Approximate $P(45 < X < 60)$.

5.7-10. Let X equal the number of alpha particles counted by a Geiger counter during 30 seconds. Assume that the distribution of X is Poisson with a mean of 4829. Determine (approximately) $P(4776 \le X \le 4857)$.

5.7-11. Let $X_1, X_2, \ldots, X_{30}$ be a random sample of size 30 from a Poisson distribution with a mean of 2/3. Approximate

(a) $P\left(15 < \sum_{i=1}^{30} X_i \le 22\right)$.

(b) $P\left(21 \le \sum_{i=1}^{30} X_i < 27\right)$.

5.7-12. In the casino game roulette, the probability of winning with a bet on red is $p = 18/38$. Let Y equal the number of winning bets out of 1000 independent bets that are placed. Find $P(Y > 500)$, approximately.

5.7-13. About 60% of all Americans have a sedentary lifestyle. Select $n = 96$ Americans at random. (Assume independence.) What is the probability that between 50 and 60, inclusive, do not exercise regularly?

5.7-14. If X is $b(100, 0.1)$, find the approximate value of $P(12 \le X \le 14)$, using

(a) The normal approximation.

(b) The Poisson approximation.

(c) The binomial.

5.7-15. Let $X_1, X_2, \ldots, X_{36}$ be a random sample of size 36 from the geometric distribution with p.m.f. $f(x) = (1/4)^{x-1}(3/4)$, $x = 1, 2, 3, \ldots$. Approximate

(a) $P\left(46 \le \sum_{i=1}^{36} X_i \le 49\right)$.

(b) $P(1.25 \le \overline{X} \le 1.50)$.

HINT: Observe that the distribution of the sum is of the discrete type.

5.7-16. A die is rolled 24 independent times. Let Y be the sum of the 24 resulting values. Recalling that Y is a random variable of the discrete type, approximate

(a) $P(Y \geq 86)$. (b) $P(Y < 86)$.
(c) $P(70 < Y \leq 86)$.

5.7-17. In the United States, the probability that a child dies in his or her first year of life is about $p = 0.01$. (It is actually slightly less than this.) Consider a group of 5000 such infants. What is the probability that between 45 and 53, inclusive, die in the first year of life?

5.7-18. Let Y equal the sum of $n = 100$ Bernoulli trials. That is, Y is $b(100, p)$. For each of (i) $p = 0.1$, (ii) $p = 0.5$, and (iii) $p = 0.8$,

(a) Draw the approximating normal p.d.f.'s, all on the same graph.

(b) Find $P(\,|\,Y/100 - p\,| \leq 0.015)$, approximately.

5.7-19. The number of trees in one acre has a Poisson distribution with mean 60. Assuming independence, compute $P(5950 \leq X \leq 6100)$, approximately, where X is the number of trees in 100 acres.

5.7-20. Assume that the background noise X of a digital signal has a normal distribution with $\mu = 0$ volts and $\sigma = 0.5$ volt. If we observe $n = 100$ independent measurements of this noise, what is the probability that at least 7 of them exceed 0.98 in absolute value?

(a) Use the Poisson distribution to approximate this probability.

(b) Use the normal distribution to approximate this probability.

(c) Use the binomial distribution to find the exact probability.

5.7-21. The number X of flaws on a certain tape of length 1 yard follows a Poisson distribution with mean 0.3. We examine $n = 100$ such tapes and count the total number Y of flaws.

(a) Assuming independence, what is the distribution of Y?

(b) Approximate $P(Y \leq 25)$.

5.7-22. One of the lottery games that New York State offers is called Quick Draw. In the 4-spot game, the player selects 4 numbers from 1 to 80, inclusive. Every 4 minutes, the Lottery's computer randomly selects 20 numbers from 1 to 80, inclusive. The prize is determined by the number of matches between the player's 4 numbers and the 20 that the computer selected. For a \$1 bet, the prizes are \$1 for two matches, \$5 for three matches, and \$55 for four matches. But the \$1 bet is not returned to the player. During a November promotion in 1997, the State doubled the prizes every Wednesday afternoon.

(a) Calculate the expected value of the regular game and of the double-payoff game.

(b) Calculate the standard deviation for the regular game and for the double-payoff game.

(c) Suppose that you are willing to "invest" \$2000 in 2000 independent bets. Let Y equal the sum of your "winnings." Estimate $P(Y > 0)$ for the regular game and for the promotion game.

(d) If possible, simulate your answers to this question.

HISTORICAL COMMENTS In this chapter, we have discussed the t and F distributions, among many other important ones. However, we should make a few comments about both of them. We mentioned that W. S. Gosset published his work on the t-distribution under the pseudonym "A Student" because Guinness did not want other breweries to know that they were using statistical methods. We have also heard the story that Gosset did not want Guinness to know that he was spending all his extra time on statistics; so he used "A Student," and it has become Student's t ever since. Whichever account is true, Gosset, in a sense, was lucky to discover the t-distribution, because, as mentioned in an earlier remark, he made two educated guesses, one of which involved the Pearson family of distributions. Incidentally, Karl Pearson, another famous statistician, had proposed this family a few years earlier. A few years later, the great statistician Sir Ronald A. Fisher (possibly the greatest statistician) actually proved that T had the t-distribution that Gosset had discovered. Concerning the F distribution, Fisher had worked with a function of what is now called F. It was George Snedecor of Iowa State University who put it in its present form and called it F (probably to honor Fisher), and Snedecor's was a much more useful form, as we will see later. We should also note that Fisher had been knighted, but so were two other statisticians: Sir Maurice G. Kendall and Sir David R. Cox. (The latter is still alive.) Their knighthood at least proves that the monarch of England appreciated some statistical efforts.

Another important person in the history of probability and statistics is Abraham de Moivre, who was born in France in 1667, but, as a Protestant, he did not fare very well in that Catholic country. As a matter of fact, he was imprisoned for about two years for his beliefs. After his release, he went to England, but led a gloomy life there, as he could not find an academic position. So de Moivre supported himself by tutoring or consulting with gamblers or insurance brokers. After publishing *The Doctrine of Chance*, he turned to a project that Nicolaus Bernoulli had suggested to him. Using the fact that Y is $b(n, p)$, he discovered that the relative frequency of successes, namely, Y/n, which Jacob Bernoulli had proved converged in probability to p, had an interesting approximating distribution itself. De Moivre had discovered the well-known bell-shaped curve called the normal distribution, and a special case of the central limit theorem. Although de Moivre did not have computers in his day, we show that if X is $b(100, 1/2)$, then $X/100$ has the p.m.f. displayed in Figure 5.7-4.

This distribution allowed de Moivre to determine a measure of spread, which we now call a standard deviation. Also, he could determine the approximate probability of Y/n falling into given intervals containing p. De Moivre was truly impressed with the orderliness of these random relative frequencies, which he attributed to the plan of the Almighty. Despite his great works, Abraham de Moivre died as a bitter and antisocial man, blind and in poverty, at the age of 87.

Two additional persons whom we would like to mention in the history of probability are Carl Friedrich Gauss and Marquis Pierre Simon de Laplace. Gauss was 29 years junior to Laplace, and Gauss was so secretive about his work that it is difficult to tell who discovered the central limit theorem first. The theorem was a generalization of de Moivre's result. In de Moivre's case, he was sampling from a Bernoulli distribution where $X_i = 1$ or 0 on the ith trial. Then

$$\frac{Y}{n} = \sum_{i=1}^{n} \frac{X_i}{n} = \overline{X},$$

the relative frequency of success, has that approximate normal distribution of de Moivre's. Laplace and Gauss were sampling from any distribution, provided that the second moment existed, and they found that the sample mean $\overline{X}$ had an approximate normal distribution. Seemingly, the central limit theorem was published in 1809 by

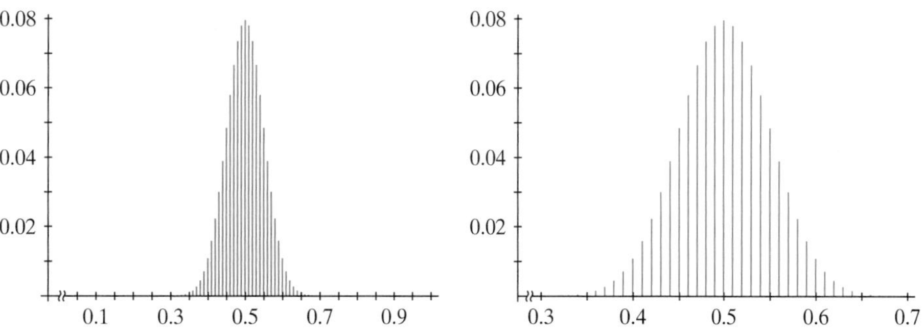

FIGURE 5.7-4: Bar graphs for the distribution of $X/100$

Laplace, just before Gauss's *Theoria Motus* in 1810. For some reason, the normal distribution is often referred to as the Gaussian distribution; people seem to forget about Laplace's contribution and (worse than that) de Moivre's original work 83 years earlier. Since then, there have been many more generalizations of the central limit theorem; in particular, most estimators of parameters in the regular case have approximate normal distributions. (See Section 10.7.)

There are many good histories of probability and statistics. However, the two that we find particularly interesting are Peter L. Bernstein's *Against the Gods: The Remarkable Story of Risk* (New York: John Wiley & Sons, Inc., 1996) and Stephen M. Stigler's *The History of Statistics: The Measurement of Uncertainty Before 1900* (Cambridge, MA: Harvard University Press, 1986).

STATISTICAL COMMENTS **(Simulation: Central Limit Theorem)** As we think about what de Moivre, Laplace, and Gauss discovered in their times, we see that it was truly amazing. Of course, de Moivre could compute the probabilities associated with various binomial distributions and see how they "piled up" in that bell shape, and he came up with the normal formula. Now, Laplace and Gauss had an even tougher task, as they could not easily find the probabilities associated with the sample mean $\overline{X}$, even with simple underlying distributions. As an illustration, suppose the random sample $X_1, X_2, \ldots, X_n$ arises from a uniform distribution on the space $[0, 1)$. It is extremely difficult to compute probabilities about $\overline{X}$ unless n is very small, such as $n = 2$ or $n = 3$. Today, of course, we can use a CAS to simulate the distribution of $\overline{X}$ for any sample size and get fairly accurate estimates of the probabilities associated with $\overline{X}$. We did this 10,000 times for $n = 6$, which resulted in Figure 5.7-5. In this chapter, we learned that $\overline{X}$ has an approximate normal distribution with mean 1/2 and variance 1/72. We could then superimpose this normal p.d.f. on the graph of the histogram for comparison. (Rather than superimposing the normal p.d.f., we used the actual p.d.f. $\overline{X}$ that is shown in the display that follows.) From the histogram, we see the bell-shaped curve resulting from this simulation. None of these three outstanding mathematicians had the advantage of the computer. Today, a researcher with a new idea about a probability distribution can check it easily with a simulation to see if the idea is worth devoting more time to it.

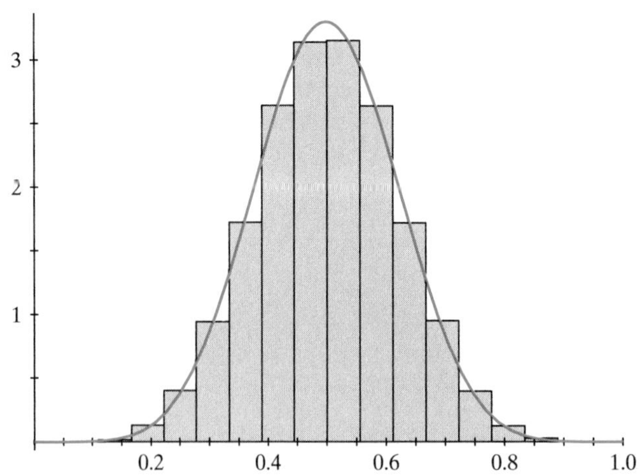

FIGURE 5.7-5: Simulation of 10,000 $\overline{x}$'s for samples of size 6 from $U(0, 1)$

The simulated $\bar{x}$'s were grouped into 18 classes with equal lengths of 1/18. The frequencies of the 18 classes are

0, 1, 9, 72, 223, 524, 957, 1467, 1744, 1751, 1464, 954, 528, 220, 69, 15, 2, 0.

Using these data, we can estimate certain probabilities—for example,

$$P\left(\frac{1}{6} \le \overline{X} \le \frac{2}{6}\right) \approx \frac{72 + 223 + 524}{10{,}000} = 0.0819$$

and

$$P\left(\frac{11}{18} \le \overline{X} \le 1\right) \approx \frac{954 + 528 + 220 + 69 + 15 + 2 + 0}{10{,}000} = 0.1788.$$

With a CAS, it is sometimes possible to find p.d.f.'s that involve rather complex calculations. For example, *Maple* was used to find the actual p.d.f. of $\overline{X}$ for this example. It is this p.d.f. that is superimposed on the histogram. Letting $u = \bar{x}$, we find that the p.d.f. is given by

$$g(u) = \begin{cases} 6\left(\dfrac{324u^5}{5}\right), & 0 < u < 1/6, \\ 6\left(\dfrac{1}{20} - 324u^5 + 324u^4 - 108u^3 + 18u^2 - \dfrac{3u}{2}\right), & 1/6 \le u < 2/6, \\ 6\left(-\dfrac{79}{20} + \dfrac{117u}{2} + 648u^5 - 1296u^4 + 972u^3 - 342u^2\right), & 2/6 \le u < 3/6, \\ 6\left(\dfrac{731}{20} - \dfrac{693u}{2} - 648u^5 + 1944u^4 - 2268u^3\right), & 3/6 \le u < 4/6, \\ 6\left(-\dfrac{1829}{20} + \dfrac{1227u}{2} - 1602u^2 + 2052u^3 \right. & \\ \qquad\qquad\qquad\qquad \left. + 324u^5 - 1296u^4\right), & 4/6 \le u < 5/6, \\ 6\left(\dfrac{324}{5} - 324u + 648u^2 - 648u^3 + 324u^4 - \dfrac{324u^5}{5}\right), & 5/6 \le u < 1. \end{cases}$$

We can also calculate

$$\int_{1/6}^{2/6} g(u)\,du = \frac{19}{240} = 0.0792$$

and

$$\int_{11/18}^{1} g(u)\,du = \frac{5{,}818}{32{,}805} = 0.17735.$$

Although these integrations are not difficult, they are tedious to do by hand.

Estimation

CHAPTER

6

6.1 POINT ESTIMATION
6.2 CONFIDENCE INTERVALS FOR MEANS
6.3 CONFIDENCE INTERVALS FOR THE DIFFERENCE OF TWO MEANS
6.4 CONFIDENCE INTERVALS FOR VARIANCES
6.5 CONFIDENCE INTERVALS FOR PROPORTIONS
6.6 SAMPLE SIZE
6.7 A SIMPLE REGRESSION PROBLEM
6.8 MORE REGRESSION

6.1 POINT ESTIMATION

In earlier chapters, we alluded to estimating characteristics of the distribution from the corresponding ones of the sample, hoping that the latter would be reasonably close to the former. For example, the sample mean $\overline{x}$ can be thought of as an estimate of the distribution mean μ, and the sample variance s^2 can be used as an estimate of the distribution variance σ^2. Even the relative frequency histogram associated with a sample can be taken as an estimate of the p.d.f. of the underlying distribution. But how good are these estimates? What makes an estimate good? Can we say anything about the closeness of an estimate to an unknown parameter?

In this section, we consider random variables for which the functional form of the p.m.f. or p.d.f. is known, but the distribution depends on an unknown parameter (say, θ) that may have any value in a set (say, Ω) called the **parameter space**. For example, perhaps it is known that $f(x;\theta) = (1/\theta)e^{-x/\theta}$, $0 < x < \infty$, and that $\theta \in \Omega = \{\theta : 0 < \theta < \infty\}$. In certain instances, it might be necessary for the experimenter to select precisely one member of the family $\{f(x,\theta), \theta \in \Omega\}$ as the most likely p.d.f. of the random variable. That is, the experimenter needs a point estimate of the parameter θ, namely, the value of the parameter that corresponds to the selected p.d.f.

In estimation, we take a random sample from the distribution to elicit some information about the unknown parameter θ. That is, we repeat the experiment n independent times, observe the sample, $X_1, X_2, \ldots, X_n$, and try to estimate the value of θ by using the observations $x_1, x_2, \ldots, x_n$. The function of $X_1, X_2, \ldots, X_n$ used to estimate θ—say, the statistic $u(X_1, X_2, \ldots, X_n)$—is called an **estimator** of θ. We want it to be such that the computed **estimate** $u(x_1, x_2, \ldots, x_n)$ is usually close to θ. Since we are estimating one member of $\theta \in \Omega$, such an estimator is often called a **point estimator**.

The following example should help motivate one principle that is often used in finding point estimates: Suppose that X is $b(1, p)$, so that the p.m.f. of X is

$$f(x; p) = p^x(1 - p)^{1-x}, \qquad x = 0, 1, \qquad 0 \le p \le 1.$$

We note that $p \in \Omega = \{p : 0 \le p \le 1\}$, where Ω represents the parameter space—that is, the space of all possible values of the parameter p. Given a random sample $X_1, X_2, \ldots, X_n$, the problem is to find an estimator $u(X_1, X_2, \ldots, X_n)$ such that $u(x_1, x_2, \ldots, x_n)$ is a good point estimate of p, where $x_1, x_2, \ldots, x_n$ are the observed values of the random sample. Now, the probability that $X_1, X_2, \ldots, X_n$ takes these particular values is (with Σx_i denoting $\Sigma_{i=1}^n x_i$)

$$P(X_1 = x_1, \ldots, X_n = x_n) = \prod_{i=1}^{n} p^{x_i}(1 - p)^{1-x_i} = p^{\Sigma x_i}(1 - p)^{n-\Sigma x_i},$$

which is the joint p.m.f. of $X_1, X_2, \ldots, X_n$ evaluated at the observed values. One reasonable way to proceed toward finding a good estimate of p is to regard this probability (or joint p.m.f.) as a function of p and find the value of p that maximizes it. That is, we find the p value most likely to have produced these sample values. The joint p.m.f., when regarded as a function of p, is frequently called the **likelihood function**. Thus, here the likelihood function is

$$\begin{aligned} L(p) &= L(p; x_1, x_2, \ldots, x_n) \\ &= f(x_1; p)f(x_2; p)\cdots f(x_n; p) \\ &= p^{\Sigma x_i}(1 - p)^{n-\Sigma x_i}, \qquad 0 \le p \le 1. \end{aligned}$$

To find the value of p that maximizes $L(p)$, we first take its derivative when $0 < p < 1$:

$$L'(p) = (\Sigma x_i)p^{\Sigma x_i - 1}(1 - p)^{n-\Sigma x_i} - (n - \Sigma x_i)p^{\Sigma x_i}(1 - p)^{n-\Sigma x_i - 1}.$$

Setting this first derivative equal to zero gives us, with the restriction that $0 < p < 1$,

$$p^{\Sigma x_i}(1 - p)^{n-\Sigma x_i}\left[\frac{\Sigma x_i}{p} - \frac{n - \Sigma x_i}{1 - p}\right] = 0.$$

Since $0 < p < 1$, the preceding equation equals zero when

$$\frac{\Sigma x_i}{p} - \frac{n - \Sigma x_i}{1 - p} = 0. \tag{6.1-1}$$

Multiplying each member of Equation 6.1-1 by $p(1 - p)$ and simplifying, we obtain

$$\sum_{i=1}^{n} x_i - np = 0$$

or, equivalently,

$$p = \frac{\Sigma_{i=1}^n x_i}{n} = \overline{x}.$$

It can be shown that $L''(\overline{x}) < 0$, so that $L(\overline{x})$ is a maximum. The corresponding statistic, namely, $(\Sigma_{i=1}^n X_i)/n = \overline{X}$, is called the **maximum likelihood estimator** and is denoted by $\widehat{p}$; that is,

$$\widehat{p} = \frac{1}{n}\sum_{i=1}^{n} X_i = \overline{X}.$$

When finding a maximum likelihood estimator, it is often easier to find the value of the parameter that maximizes the natural logarithm of the likelihood function rather than the value of the parameter that maximizes the likelihood function itself. Because the natural logarithm function is an increasing function, the solutions will be the same. To see this, note that for $0 < p < 1$, the example we have been considering gives us

$$\ln L(p) = \left(\sum_{i=1}^{n} x_i\right)\ln p + \left(n - \sum_{i=1}^{n} x_i\right)\ln(1 - p).$$

To find the maximum, we set the first derivative equal to zero to obtain

$$\frac{d\,[\ln L(p)]}{dp} = \left(\sum_{i=1}^{n} x_i\right)\left(\frac{1}{p}\right) + \left(n - \sum_{i=1}^{n} x_i\right)\left(\frac{-1}{1 - p}\right) = 0,$$

which is the same as Equation 6.1-1. Thus, the solution is $p = \overline{x}$ and the maximum likelihood estimator for p is $\widehat{p} = \overline{X}$.

Motivated by the preceding example, we present the formal definition of maximum likelihood estimators (this definition is used in both the discrete and continuous cases):

Let $X_1, X_2, \ldots, X_n$ be a random sample from a distribution that depends on one or more unknown parameters $\theta_1, \theta_2, \ldots, \theta_m$ with p.m.f. or p.d.f. denoted by $f(x; \theta_1, \theta_2, \ldots, \theta_m)$. Suppose that $(\theta_1, \theta_2, \ldots, \theta_m)$ is restricted to a given parameter space Ω. Then the joint p.m.f. or p.d.f. of $X_1, X_2, \ldots, X_n$, namely,

$$L(\theta_1, \theta_2, \ldots, \theta_m) = f(x_1; \theta_1, \ldots, \theta_m)f(x_2; \theta_1, \ldots, \theta_m) \cdots f(x_n; \theta_1, \ldots, \theta_m), \qquad (\theta_1, \theta_2, \ldots, \theta_m) \in \Omega,$$

when regarded as a function of $\theta_1, \theta_2, \ldots, \theta_m$, is called the **likelihood function**. Say

$$[u_1(x_1, \ldots, x_n), u_2(x_1, \ldots, x_n), \ldots, u_m(x_1, \ldots, x_n)]$$

is that m-tuple in Ω that maximizes $L(\theta_1, \theta_2, \ldots, \theta_m)$. Then

$$\begin{aligned}
\widehat{\theta_1} &= u_1(X_1, \ldots, X_n),\\
\widehat{\theta_2} &= u_2(X_1, \ldots, X_n),\\
&\ \ \vdots\\
\widehat{\theta_m} &= u_m(X_1, \ldots, X_n)
\end{aligned}$$

are **maximum likelihood estimators** of $\theta_1, \theta_2, \ldots, \theta_m$, respectively; and the corresponding observed values of these statistics, namely,

$$u_1(x_1, \ldots, x_n),\ u_2(x_1, \ldots, x_n), \ldots, u_m(x_1, \ldots, x_n),$$

are called **maximum likelihood estimates**. In many practical cases, these estimators (and estimates) are unique.

For many applications, there is just one unknown parameter. In these cases, the likelihood function is given by

$$L(\theta) = \prod_{i=1}^{n} f(x_i; \theta).$$

Some additional examples will help clarify these definitions.

EXAMPLE 6.1-1 Let $X_1, X_2, \ldots, X_n$ be a random sample from the exponential distribution with p.d.f.

$$f(x; \theta) = \frac{1}{\theta} e^{-x/\theta}, \qquad 0 < x < \infty, \qquad \theta \in \Omega = \{\theta : 0 < \theta < \infty\}.$$

The likelihood function is given by

$$\begin{aligned} L(\theta) &= L(\theta; x_1, x_2, \ldots, x_n) \\ &= \left(\frac{1}{\theta} e^{-x_1/\theta}\right)\left(\frac{1}{\theta} e^{-x_2/\theta}\right)\cdots\left(\frac{1}{\theta} e^{-x_n/\theta}\right) \\ &= \frac{1}{\theta^n} \exp\left(\frac{-\sum_{i=1}^{n} x_i}{\theta}\right), \qquad 0 < \theta < \infty. \end{aligned}$$

The natural logarithm of $L(\theta)$ is

$$\ln L(\theta) = -(n)\ln(\theta) - \frac{1}{\theta}\sum_{i=1}^{n} x_i, \qquad 0 < \theta < \infty.$$

Thus,

$$\frac{d\,[\ln L(\theta)]}{d\theta} = \frac{-n}{\theta} + \frac{\sum_{i=1}^{n} x_i}{\theta^2} = 0.$$

The solution of this equation for θ is

$$\theta = \frac{1}{n}\sum_{i=1}^{n} x_i = \overline{x}.$$

Note that

$$\frac{d\,[\ln L(\theta)]}{d\theta} = \frac{1}{\theta}\left(-n + \frac{n\overline{x}}{\theta}\right) \begin{cases} > 0, & \theta < \overline{x}, \\ = 0, & \theta = \overline{x}, \\ < 0, & \theta > \overline{x}. \end{cases}$$

Hence, $\ln L(\theta)$ does have a maximum at $\overline{x}$, and it follows that the maximum likelihood estimator for θ is

$$\widehat{\theta} = \overline{X} = \frac{1}{n}\sum_{i=1}^{n} X_i.$$

■

EXAMPLE 6.1-2 Let $X_1, X_2, \ldots, X_n$ be a random sample from the geometric distribution with p.m.f. $f(x; p) = (1-p)^{x-1}p$, $x = 1, 2, 3, \ldots$. The likelihood function is given by

$$\begin{aligned} L(p) &= (1-p)^{x_1-1}p(1-p)^{x_2-1}p\cdots(1-p)^{x_n-1}p \\ &= p^n(1-p)^{\sum x_i - n}, \qquad 0 \le p \le 1. \end{aligned}$$

The natural logarithm of $L(p)$ is

$$\ln L(p) = n \ln p + \left(\sum_{i=1}^{n} x_i - n \right) \ln(1 - p), \qquad 0 < p < 1.$$

Thus, restricting p to $0 < p < 1$, so as to be able to take the derivative, we have

$$\frac{d \ln L(p)}{dp} = \frac{n}{p} - \frac{\sum_{i=1}^{n} x_i - n}{1 - p} = 0.$$

Solving for p, we obtain

$$p = \frac{n}{\sum_{i=1}^{n} x_i} = \frac{1}{\bar{x}},$$

and this solution provides a maximum. So the maximum likelihood estimator of p is

$$\widehat{p} = \frac{n}{\sum_{i=1}^{n} X_i} = \frac{1}{\overline{X}}.$$

This estimator agrees with our intuition because, in n observations of a geometric random variable, there are n successes in the $\sum_{i=1}^{n} x_i$ trials. Thus, the estimate of p is the number of successes divided by the total number of trials. ■

In the following important example, we find the maximum likelihood estimators of the parameters associated with the normal distribution.

EXAMPLE 6.1-3 Let $X_1, X_2, \ldots, X_n$ be a random sample from $N(\theta_1, \theta_2)$, where

$$\Omega = \{(\theta_1, \theta_2) : -\infty < \theta_1 < \infty, 0 < \theta_2 < \infty\}.$$

That is, here we let $\theta_1 = \mu$ and $\theta_2 = \sigma^2$. Then

$$L(\theta_1, \theta_2) = \prod_{i=1}^{n} \frac{1}{\sqrt{2\pi\theta_2}} \exp\left[-\frac{(x_i - \theta_1)^2}{2\theta_2} \right]$$

or, equivalently,

$$L(\theta_1, \theta_2) = \left(\frac{1}{\sqrt{2\pi\theta_2}} \right)^n \exp\left[\frac{-\sum_{i=1}^{n} (x_i - \theta_1)^2}{2\theta_2} \right], \qquad (\theta_1, \theta_2) \in \Omega.$$

The natural logarithm of the likelihood function is

$$\ln L(\theta_1, \theta_2) = -\frac{n}{2} \ln(2\pi\theta_2) - \frac{\sum_{i=1}^{n} (x_i - \theta_1)^2}{2\theta_2}.$$

The partial derivatives with respect to θ_1 and θ_2 are

$$\frac{\partial (\ln L)}{\partial \theta_1} = \frac{1}{\theta_2} \sum_{i=1}^{n} (x_i - \theta_1)$$

and

$$\frac{\partial (\ln L)}{\partial \theta_2} = \frac{-n}{2\theta_2} + \frac{1}{2\theta_2^2}\sum_{i=1}^{n}(x_i - \theta_1)^2.$$

The equation $\partial(\ln L)/\partial\theta_1 = 0$ has the solution $\theta_1 = \overline{x}$. Setting $\partial(\ln L)/\partial\theta_2 = 0$ and replacing θ_1 by $\overline{x}$ yields

$$\theta_2 = \frac{1}{n}\sum_{i=1}^{n}(x_i - \overline{x})^2.$$

By considering the usual condition on the second partial derivatives, we see that these solutions do provide a maximum. Thus, the maximum likelihood estimators of $\mu = \theta_1$ and $\sigma^2 = \theta_2$ are

$$\widehat{\theta_1} = \overline{X} \qquad \text{and} \qquad \widehat{\theta_2} = \frac{1}{n}\sum_{i=1}^{n}(X_i - \overline{X})^2 = V.$$ ■

It is interesting to note that in our first illustration, where $\widehat{p} = \overline{X}$, and in Example 6.1-1, where $\widehat{\theta} = \overline{X}$, the expected value of the estimator is equal to the corresponding parameter. This observation leads to the following definition.

DEFINITION 6.1-1 If $E[u(X_1, X_2, \ldots, X_n)] = \theta$, then the statistic $u(X_1, X_2, \ldots X_n)$ is called an **unbiased estimator** of θ. Otherwise, it is said to be **biased**.

EXAMPLE 6.1-4 We have shown that when sampling from $N(\theta_1 = \mu, \theta_2 = \sigma^2)$, one finds that the maximum likelihood estimators of μ and σ^2 are

$$\widehat{\theta_1} = \widehat{\mu} = \overline{X} \qquad \text{and} \qquad \widehat{\theta_2} = \widehat{\sigma^2} = \frac{(n-1)S^2}{n}.$$

Recalling that the distribution of $\overline{X}$ is $N(\mu, \sigma^2/n)$, we see that $E(\overline{X}) = \mu$; thus, $\overline{X}$ is an unbiased estimator of μ.

In Theorem 5.5-2, we showed that the distribution of $(n-1)S^2/\sigma^2$ is $\chi^2(n-1)$. Hence,

$$E(S^2) = E\left[\frac{\sigma^2}{n-1}\,\frac{(n-1)S^2}{\sigma^2}\right] = \frac{\sigma^2}{n-1}(n-1) = \sigma^2.$$

That is, the sample variance

$$S^2 = \frac{1}{n-1}\sum_{i=1}^{n}(X_i - \overline{X})^2$$

is an unbiased estimator of σ^2. Consequently, since

$$E(\widehat{\theta_2}) = \frac{n-1}{n}E(S^2) = \frac{n-1}{n}\sigma^2,$$

$\widehat{\theta_2}$ is a biased estimator of $\theta_2 = \sigma^2$. ■

Sometimes it is impossible to find maximum likelihood estimators in a convenient closed form, and numerical methods must be used to maximize the likelihood function. For example, suppose that $X_1, X_2, \ldots, X_n$ is a random sample from a gamma distribution with parameters $\alpha = \theta_1$ and $\beta = \theta_2$, where $\theta_1 > 0$, $\theta_2 > 0$. It is difficult to maximize

$$L(\theta_1, \theta_2; x_1, \ldots, x_n) = \left[\frac{1}{\Gamma(\theta_1)\theta_2^{\theta_1}}\right]^n (x_1 x_2 \cdots x_n)^{\theta_1 - 1} \exp\left(-\sum_{i=1}^{n} x_i/\theta_2\right)$$

with respect to θ_1 and θ_2, owing to the presence of the gamma function $\Gamma(\theta_1)$. Thus, numerical methods must be used to maximize L once $x_1, x_2, \ldots, x_n$ are observed.

There are other ways, however, to easily obtain point estimates of θ_1 and θ_2. One of the early methods was to simply equate the first sample moment to the first theoretical moment. Next, if needed, the two second moments are equated, then the third moments, and so on, until we have enough equations to solve for the parameters. As an illustration, in the gamma distribution situation, let us simply equate the first two moments of the distribution to the corresponding moments of the empirical distribution. This seems like a reasonable way in which to find estimators, since the empirical distribution converges in some sense to the probability distribution, and hence corresponding moments should be about equal. In this situation, we have

$$\theta_1\theta_2 = \overline{X}, \qquad \theta_1\theta_2^2 = V,$$

the solutions of which are

$$\widetilde{\theta_1} = \frac{\overline{X}^2}{V} \quad \text{and} \quad \widetilde{\theta_2} = \frac{V}{\overline{X}}.$$

We say that these latter two statistics, $\widetilde{\theta_1}$ and $\widetilde{\theta_2}$, are respective estimators of θ_1 and θ_2 found by the **method of moments.**

To generalize this discussion, let $X_1, X_2, \ldots, X_n$ be a random sample of size n from a distribution with p.d.f. $f(x; \theta_1, \theta_2, \ldots, \theta_r)$, $(\theta_1, \ldots, \theta_r) \in \Omega$. The expectation $E(X^k)$ is frequently called the kth moment of the distribution, $k = 1, 2, 3, \ldots$. The sum $M_k = \sum_{i=1}^{n} X_i^k/n$ is the kth moment of the sample, $k = 1, 2, 3, \ldots$. The method of moments can be described as follows: Equate $E(X^k)$ to M_k, beginning with $k = 1$ and continuing until there are enough equations to provide unique solutions for $\theta_1, \theta_2, \ldots, \theta_r$—say, $h_i(M_1, M_2, \ldots)$, $i = 1, 2, \ldots, r$, respectively. Note that this could be done in an equivalent manner by equating $\mu = E(X)$ to $\overline{X}$ and $E[(X - \mu)^k]$ to $\sum_{i=1}^{n}(X_i - \overline{X})^k/n$, $k = 2, 3$, and so on, until unique solutions for $\theta_1, \theta_2, \ldots, \theta_r$ are obtained. This alternative procedure was used in the preceding illustration. In most practical cases, the estimator $\widetilde{\theta_i} = h_i(M_1, M_2, \ldots)$ of θ_i, found by the method of moments, is an estimator of θ_i that in some sense gets close to that parameter when n is large, $i = 1, 2, \ldots, r$.

The next two examples—the first for a one-parameter family and the second for a two-parameter family—illustrate the method-of-moments technique for finding estimators.

EXAMPLE 6.1-5 Let $X_1, X_2, \ldots, X_n$, be a random sample of size n from the distribution with p.d.f. $f(x; \theta) = \theta x^{\theta - 1}$, $0 < x < 1$, $0 < \theta < \infty$. Sketch the graphs of this p.d.f. for $\theta = 1/4$, 1, and 4. Note that sets of observations for these three values of θ would look very different. How do we estimate the value of θ? The mean of this distribution is given by

$$E(X) = \int_0^1 x\,\theta x^{\theta-1}\,dx = \frac{\theta}{\theta+1}.$$

We shall set the distribution mean equal to the sample mean and solve for θ. We have

$$\bar{x} = \frac{\theta}{\theta+1}.$$

Solving for θ, we obtain the method-of-moments estimator,

$$\tilde{\theta} = \frac{\overline{X}}{1-\overline{X}}.$$

Thus, an estimate of θ by the method of moments is $\bar{x}/(1-\bar{x})$. ■

Recall that in the method of moments, if two parameters have to be estimated, the first two sample moments are set equal to the first two distribution moments that are given in terms of the unknown parameters. These two equations are then solved simultaneously for the unknown parameters.

EXAMPLE 6.1-6 Let the distribution of X be $N(\mu, \sigma^2)$. Then

$$E(X) = \mu \qquad \text{and} \qquad E(X^2) = \sigma^2 + \mu^2.$$

For a random sample of size n, the first two moments are given by

$$m_1 = \frac{1}{n}\sum_{i=1}^{n} x_i \qquad \text{and} \qquad m_2 = \frac{1}{n}\sum_{i=1}^{n} x_i^2.$$

We set $m_1 = E(X)$ and $m_2 = E(X^2)$ and solve for μ and σ^2. That is,

$$\frac{1}{n}\sum_{i=1}^{n} x_i = \mu \qquad \text{and} \qquad \frac{1}{n}\sum_{i=1}^{n} x_i^2 = \sigma^2 + \mu^2.$$

The first equation yields $\bar{x}$ as the estimate of μ. Replacing μ^2 with $\bar{x}^2$ in the second equation and solving for σ^2, we obtain

$$\frac{1}{n}\sum_{i=1}^{n} x_i^2 - \bar{x}^2 = \sum_{i=1}^{n} \frac{(x_i - \bar{x})^2}{n} = v$$

as the solution of σ^2. Thus, the method-of-moments estimators for μ and σ^2 are $\tilde{\mu} = \overline{X}$ and $\widetilde{\sigma^2} = V$, which are the same as the maximum likelihood estimators. Of course, $\tilde{\mu} = \overline{X}$ is unbiased whereas $\widetilde{\sigma^2} = V$ is biased. ■

In Example 6.1-4, we showed that $\overline{X}$ and S^2 are unbiased estimators of μ and σ^2, respectively, when one is sampling from a normal distribution. This is also true when one is sampling from any distribution with a finite variance σ^2. That is, $E(\overline{X}) = \mu$ and $E(S^2) = \sigma^2$, provided that the sample arises from a distribution with variance $\sigma^2 < \infty$. (See Exercise 6.1-13.) Although S^2 is an unbiased estimator of σ^2, S is a biased estimator of σ. In Exercise 6.1-14, you are asked to show that, when one is sampling from a normal distribution, cS is an unbiased estimator of σ, where

$$c = \frac{\sqrt{n-1}\,\Gamma\left(\frac{n-1}{2}\right)}{\sqrt{2}\,\Gamma\left(\frac{n}{2}\right)}.$$

EXERCISES

6.1-1. Let $X_1, X_2, \ldots, X_n$ be a random sample from $N(\mu, \sigma^2)$, where the mean $\theta = \mu$ is such that $-\infty < \theta < \infty$ and σ^2 is a known positive number. Show that the maximum likelihood estimator for θ is $\widehat{\theta} = \overline{X}$.

6.1-2. A random sample $X_1, X_2, \ldots, X_n$ of size n is taken from $N(\mu, \sigma^2)$, where the variance $\theta = \sigma^2$ is such that $0 < \theta < \infty$ and μ is a known real number. Show that the maximum likelihood estimator for θ is $\widehat{\theta} = (1/n)\sum_{i=1}^{n}(X_i - \mu)^2$ and that this estimator is an unbiased estimator of θ.

6.1-3. A random sample $X_1, X_2, \ldots, X_n$ of size n is taken from a Poisson distribution with a mean of λ, $0 < \lambda < \infty$.

(a) Show that the maximum likelihood estimator for λ is $\widehat{\lambda} = \overline{X}$.

(b) Let X equal the number of flaws per 100 feet of a used computer tape. Assume that X has a Poisson distribution with a mean of λ. If 40 observations of X yielded 5 zeros, 7 ones, 12 twos, 9 threes, 5 fours, 1 five, and 1 six, find the maximum likelihood estimate of λ.

6.1-4. For determining half-lives of radioactive isotopes, it is important to know what the background radiation is in a given detector over a specific period. The following data were taken in a γ-ray detection experiment over 98 ten-second intervals:

58	50	57	58	64	63	54	64	59	41	43	56	60	50
46	59	54	60	59	60	67	52	65	63	55	61	68	58
63	36	42	54	58	54	40	60	64	56	61	51	48	50
60	42	62	67	58	49	66	58	57	59	52	54	53	53
57	43	73	65	45	43	57	55	73	62	68	55	51	55
53	68	58	53	51	73	44	50	53	62	58	47	63	59
59	56	60	59	50	52	62	51	66	51	56	53	59	57

Assume that these data are observations of a Poisson random variable with mean λ.

(a) Find the values of $\overline{x}$ and s^2 if you did not do this in Exercise 2.6-22.

(b) What is the value of the maximum likelihood estimator of λ?

(c) Is S^2 an unbiased estimator of λ?

(d) Which of $\overline{x}$ and s^2 would you recommend for estimating λ? Why? You could compare the variance of $\overline{X}$ with the variance of S^2, which is

$$\text{Var}(S^2) = \frac{\lambda(2\lambda n + n - 1)}{n(n-1)}.$$

6.1-5. Let $X_1, X_2, \ldots, X_n$ be a random sample from distributions with the given probability density functions. In each case, find the maximum likelihood estimator $\widehat{\theta}$.

(a) $f(x; \theta) = (1/\theta^2)\,x\,e^{-x/\theta}$, $0 < x < \infty$, $0 < \theta < \infty$.

(b) $f(x; \theta) = (1/2\theta^3)\,x^2\,e^{-x/\theta}$, $0 < x < \infty$, $0 < \theta < \infty$.

(c) $f(x; \theta) = (1/2)\,e^{-|x-\theta|}$, $-\infty < x < \infty$, $-\infty < \theta < \infty$.

HINT: Finding θ involves minimizing $\sum |x_i - \theta|$, which is a difficult problem. When $n = 5$, do it for $x_1 = 6.1, x_2 = -1.1, x_3 = 3.2, x_4 = 0.7$, and $x_5 = 1.7$, and you will see the answer. (See also Exercise 2.2-10.)

6.1-6. Find the maximum likelihood estimates for $\theta_1 = \mu$ and $\theta_2 = \sigma^2$ if a random sample of size 15 from $N(\mu, \sigma^2)$ yielded the following values:

31.5	36.9	33.8	30.1	33.9
35.2	29.6	34.4	30.5	34.2
31.6	36.7	35.8	34.5	32.7

6.1-7. Let $f(x;\theta) = \theta x^{\theta-1},\ 0 < x < 1,\ \theta \in \Omega = \{\theta: 0 < \theta < \infty\}$. Let $X_1, X_2, \ldots, X_n$ denote a random sample of size n from this distribution.

(a) Sketch the p.d.f. of X for (i) $\theta = 1/2$, (ii) $\theta = 1$, and (iii) $\theta = 2$.

(b) Show that $\widehat{\theta} = -n/\ln\left(\prod_{i=1}^{n} X_i\right)$ is the maximum likelihood estimator of θ.

(c) For each of the following three sets of 10 observations from the given distribution, calculate the values of the maximum likelihood estimate and the method-of-moments estimate of θ:

(i)	0.0256	0.3051	0.0278	0.8971	0.0739
	0.3191	0.7379	0.3671	0.9763	0.0102
(ii)	0.9960	0.3125	0.4374	0.7464	0.8278
	0.9518	0.9924	0.7112	0.2228	0.8609
(iii)	0.4698	0.3675	0.5991	0.9513	0.6049
	0.9917	0.1551	0.0710	0.2110	0.2154

6.1-8. Let $f(x;\theta) = (1/\theta)x^{(1-\theta)/\theta},\ 0 < x < 1,\ 0 < \theta < \infty$.

(a) Show that the maximum likelihood estimator of θ is $\widehat{\theta} = -(1/n)\sum_{i=1}^{n} \ln X_i$.

(b) Show that $E(\widehat{\theta}) = \theta$ and thus that $\widehat{\theta}$ is an unbiased estimator of θ.

6.1-9. Let $X_1, X_2, \ldots, X_n$ be a random sample of size n from the exponential distribution whose p.d.f. is $f(x;\theta) = (1/\theta)e^{-x/\theta}$, $0 < x < \infty$, $0 < \theta < \infty$.

(a) Show that $\overline{X}$ is an unbiased estimator of θ.

(b) Show that the variance of $\overline{X}$ is θ^2/n.

(c) What is a good estimate of θ if a random sample of size 5 yielded the sample values 3.5, 8.1, 0.9, 4.4, and 0.5?

6.1-10. Let $X_1, X_2, \ldots, X_n$ be a random sample of size n from a geometric distribution for which p is the probability of success.

(a) Use the method of moments to find a point estimate for p.

(b) Explain intuitively why your estimate makes good sense.

(c) Use the following data to give a point estimate of p:

3	34	7	4	19	2	1	19	43	2
22	4	19	11	7	1	2	21	15	16

6.1-11. Out of 50,000,000 instant-winner lottery tickets, the proportion of winning tickets is p. Each day, for 20 consecutive days, a bettor purchased tickets, one at a time, until a winning ticket was purchased. The numbers of tickets that were purchased each day to obtain the winning ticket were

1	26	19	6	6	1	2	3	1	23
19	3	6	8	4	1	18	34	1	8

By making reasonable assumptions, find the maximum likelihood estimate of p on the basis of these data.

6.1-12. Let $X_1, X_2, \ldots, X_n$ be a random sample from $b(1, p)$ (i.e., n Bernoulli trials). Thus,

$$Y = \sum_{i=1}^{n} X_i \text{ is } b(n, p).$$

(a) Show that $\overline{X} = Y/n$ is an unbiased estimator of p.

(b) Show that $\text{Var}(\overline{X}) = p(1 - p)/n$.

(c) Show that $E[\overline{X}(1 - \overline{X})/n] = (n - 1)[p(1 - p)/n^2]$.

(d) Find the value of c so that $c\overline{X}(1 - \overline{X})$ is an unbiased estimator of $\text{Var}(\overline{X}) = p(1 - p)/n$.

6.1-13. Let $X_1, X_2, \ldots, X_n$ be a random sample from a distribution having finite variance σ^2. Show that

$$S^2 = \sum_{i=1}^{n} \frac{(X_i - \overline{X})^2}{n - 1}$$

is an unbiased estimator of σ^2. HINT: Write

$$S^2 = \frac{1}{n - 1}\left(\sum_{i=1}^{n} X_i^2 - n\overline{X}^2\right)$$

and compute $E(S^2)$.

6.1-14. Let $X_1, X_2, \ldots, X_n$ be a random sample of size n from a normal distribution.

(a) Show that an unbiased estimator of σ is cS, where

$$c = \frac{\sqrt{n - 1}\,\Gamma\left(\frac{n - 1}{2}\right)}{\sqrt{2}\,\Gamma\left(\frac{n}{2}\right)}.$$

HINT: Recall that the distribution of $(n - 1)S^2/\sigma^2$ is $\chi^2(n - 1)$.

(b) Find the value of c when $n = 5$; when $n = 6$.

(c) Graph c as a function of n. What is the limit of c as n increases without bound?

6.1-15. Let $X_1, X_2, \ldots, X_n$ be a random sample from a uniform distribution on the interval $(\theta - 1, \theta + 1)$.

(a) Find the method-of-moments estimator of θ.

(b) Is your estimator in part (a) an unbiased estimator of θ?

(c) Given the following $n = 5$ observations of X, give a point estimate of θ:

6.61 7.70 6.98 8.36 7.26

(d) The method-of-moments estimator actually has greater variance than the estimator $[\min(X_i) + \max(X_i)]/2$, which is a maximum likelihood estimator of θ. Compute the value of the latter estimator for the $n = 5$ observations in (c).

6.1-16. Given the following 25 observations from a gamma distribution with mean $\mu = \alpha\theta$ and variance $\sigma^2 = \alpha\theta^2$, use the method-of-moments estimators to find point estimates of α and θ:

6.9 7.3 6.7 6.4 6.3 5.9 7.0 7.1 6.5 7.6 7.2 7.1 6.1
7.3 7.6 7.6 6.7 6.3 5.7 6.7 7.5 5.3 5.4 7.4 6.9

6.1-17. Let X equal the number of telephone calls per five minutes that are received at Great Lakes Pizza Co. in the evening. Assume that the distribution of X is Poisson with mean λ.

(a) Given n observations of X, find the method-of-moments estimate of λ.

(b) Give a point estimate of λ, using the following 12 observations of X:

1 2 1 1 2 4 0 1 0 1 1 0

(c) Compare the values of $\overline{x}$ and s^2. Does the information yielded by the comparison of $\overline{x}$ and s^2 support the assumption that X has a Poisson distribution?

6.1-18. An urn contains 64 balls, of which N_1 are orange and N_2 are blue. A random sample of $n = 8$ balls is selected from the urn without replacement, and X is equal to the number of orange balls in the sample. This experiment was repeated 30 times (the 8 balls being returned to the urn before each repetition), yielding the following data:

3 0 0 1 1 1 1 3 1 1 2 0 1 3 1
0 1 0 2 1 1 2 3 2 2 4 3 1 1 2

Using these data, guess the value of N_1 and give a reason for your guess.

6.1-19. A Geiger counter was set up in the physics laboratory to record the number of alpha particle emissions of carbon-14 in half a second. Ten observations yielded the following data:

4 6 9 6 10 11 6 3 7 10

Give the value of an unbiased estimate of λ, the mean number of counts per half second, assuming that these data are observations of a Poisson random variable.

6.1-20. Let the p.d.f. of X be defined by

$$f(x) = \begin{cases} \left(\dfrac{4}{\theta^2}\right)x, & 0 < x \le \dfrac{\theta}{2}, \\ -\left(\dfrac{4}{\theta^2}\right)x + \dfrac{4}{\theta}, & \dfrac{\theta}{2} < x \le \theta, \\ 0, & \text{elsewhere}, \end{cases}$$

where $\theta \in \Omega = \{\theta : 0 < \theta \le 2\}$.

(a) Sketch the graph of this p.d.f. when $\theta = 1/2$, $\theta = 1$, and $\theta = 2$.

(b) Find an estimator of θ by the method of moments.

(c) For the following observations of X, give a point estimate of θ:

0.3206 0.2408 0.2577 0.3557 0.4188
0.5601 0.0240 0.5422 0.4532 0.5592

6.2 CONFIDENCE INTERVALS FOR MEANS

Given a random sample $X_1, X_2, \ldots, X_n$ from a normal distribution $N(\mu, \sigma^2)$, we shall now consider the closeness of $\overline{X}$, the unbiased estimator of μ, to the unknown mean μ. To do this, we use the error structure (distribution) of $\overline{X}$, namely, that $\overline{X}$ is $N(\mu, \sigma^2/n)$ (see Corollary 5.5-1), to construct what is called a confidence interval for the unknown parameter μ when the variance σ^2 is known. For the probability $1 - \alpha$, we can find a number $z_{\alpha/2}$ from Table V in the appendix such that

$$P\left(-z_{\alpha/2} \le \frac{\overline{X} - \mu}{\sigma/\sqrt{n}} \le z_{\alpha/2}\right) = 1 - \alpha.$$

For example, if $1 - \alpha = 0.95$, then $z_{\alpha/2} = z_{0.025} = 1.96$, and if $1 - \alpha = 0.90$, then $z_{\alpha/2} = z_{0.05} = 1.645$. Now, recalling that $\sigma > 0$, we see that the following inequalities are equivalent:

$$-z_{\alpha/2} \le \frac{\overline{X} - \mu}{\sigma/\sqrt{n}} \le z_{\alpha/2},$$

$$-z_{\alpha/2}\left(\frac{\sigma}{\sqrt{n}}\right) \le \overline{X} - \mu \le z_{\alpha/2}\left(\frac{\sigma}{\sqrt{n}}\right),$$

$$-\overline{X} - z_{\alpha/2}\left(\frac{\sigma}{\sqrt{n}}\right) \le -\mu \le -\overline{X} + z_{\alpha/2}\left(\frac{\sigma}{\sqrt{n}}\right),$$

$$\overline{X} + z_{\alpha/2}\left(\frac{\sigma}{\sqrt{n}}\right) \ge \mu \ge \overline{X} - z_{\alpha/2}\left(\frac{\sigma}{\sqrt{n}}\right).$$

Thus, since the probability of the first of these is $1 - \alpha$, the probability of the last must also be $1 - \alpha$, because the latter is true if and only if the former is true. That is, we have

$$P\left[\overline{X} - z_{\alpha/2}\left(\frac{\sigma}{\sqrt{n}}\right) \le \mu \le \overline{X} + z_{\alpha/2}\left(\frac{\sigma}{\sqrt{n}}\right)\right] = 1 - \alpha.$$

So the probability that the random interval

$$\left[\overline{X} - z_{\alpha/2}\left(\frac{\sigma}{\sqrt{n}}\right), \overline{X} + z_{\alpha/2}\left(\frac{\sigma}{\sqrt{n}}\right)\right]$$

includes the unknown mean μ is $1 - \alpha$.

Once the sample is observed and the sample mean computed to equal $\overline{x}$, the interval $[\overline{x} - z_{\alpha/2}(\sigma/\sqrt{n}\,), \overline{x} + z_{\alpha/2}(\sigma/\sqrt{n}\,)]$ becomes known. Since the probability that the random interval covers μ before the sample is drawn is equal to $1 - \alpha$, we now call the computed interval, $\overline{x} \pm z_{\alpha/2}(\sigma/\sqrt{n}\,)$ (for brevity), a $100(1 - \alpha)\%$ **confidence interval** for the unknown mean μ. For example, $\overline{x} \pm 1.96(\sigma/\sqrt{n}\,)$ is a 95% confidence interval for μ. The number $100(1 - \alpha)\%$, or equivalently, $1 - \alpha$, is called the **confidence coefficient**.

We see that the confidence interval for μ is centered at the point estimate $\overline{x}$ and is completed by subtracting and adding the quantity $z_{\alpha/2}(\sigma/\sqrt{n}\,)$. Note that as n increases, $z_{\alpha/2}(\sigma/\sqrt{n}\,)$ decreases, resulting in a shorter confidence interval with the same confidence coefficient $1 - \alpha$. A shorter confidence interval indicates that we have more credence in $\overline{x}$ as an estimate of μ. Statisticians who are not restricted by time, money, effort, or the availability of observations can obviously make the confidence interval as short as they like by increasing the sample size n. For a fixed sample size n, the length of the confidence interval can also be shortened by decreasing the confidence coefficient $1 - \alpha$. But if this is done, we achieve a shorter confidence interval at the expense of losing some confidence.

EXAMPLE 6.2-1 Let X equal the length of life of a 60-watt light bulb marketed by a certain manufacturer. Assume that the distribution of X is $N(\mu, 1296)$. If a random sample of $n = 27$ bulbs is tested until they burn out, yielding a sample mean of $\overline{x} = 1478$ hours, then a 95% confidence interval for μ is

$$\left[\,\overline{x} - z_{0.025}\left(\frac{\sigma}{\sqrt{n}}\right),\ \overline{x} + z_{0.025}\left(\frac{\sigma}{\sqrt{n}}\right)\right]$$

$$= \left[1478 - 1.96\left(\frac{36}{\sqrt{27}}\right),\ 1478 + 1.96\left(\frac{36}{\sqrt{27}}\right)\right]$$

$$= [1478 - 13.58,\ 1478 + 13.58]$$

$$= [1464.42,\ 1491.58].$$

■

The next example will help to give a better intuitive feeling for the interpretation of a confidence interval.

EXAMPLE 6.2-2 Let $\overline{x}$ be the observed sample mean of five observations of a random sample from the normal distribution $N(\mu, 16)$. A 90% confidence interval for the unknown mean μ is

$$\left[\,\overline{x} - 1.645\sqrt{\frac{16}{5}},\ \overline{x} + 1.645\sqrt{\frac{16}{5}}\,\right].$$

For a particular sample, this interval either does or does not contain the mean μ. However, if many such intervals were calculated, about 90% of them should contain the mean μ. Fifty random samples of size 5 from the normal distribution $N(50, 16)$ were simulated on a computer. A 90% confidence interval was calculated for each random sample, as if the mean were unknown. Figure 6.2-1(a) depicts each of these 50 intervals as a line segment. Note that 45 (or 90%) of them contain the mean, $\mu = 50$. In other simulations of 50 confidence intervals, the number of 90% confidence intervals containing the mean could be larger or smaller. [In fact, if W is a random variable that counts the number of 90% confidence intervals containing the mean, then the distribution of W is $b(50, 0.90)$.] ■

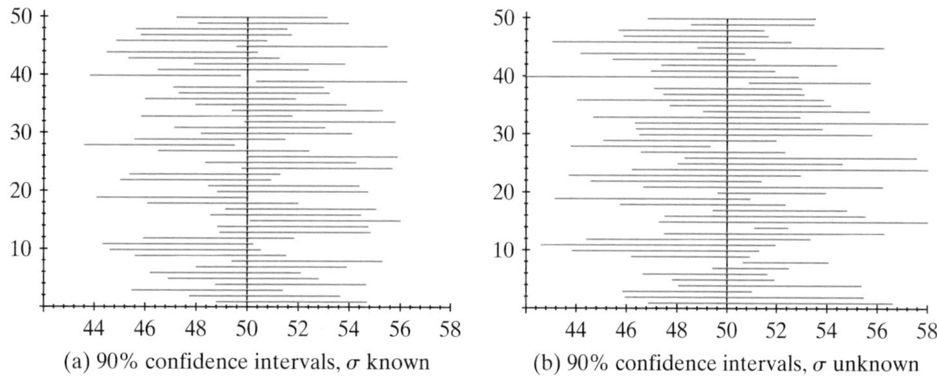

FIGURE 6.2-1: Confidence intervals using z and t

If we cannot assume that the distribution from which the sample arose is normal, we can still obtain an approximate confidence interval for μ. By the central limit theorem, provided that n is large enough, the ratio $(\overline{X} - \mu)/(\sigma/\sqrt{n})$ has the approximate normal distribution $N(0, 1)$ when the underlying distribution is not normal. In this case,

$$P\left(-z_{\alpha/2} \le \frac{\overline{X} - \mu}{\sigma/\sqrt{n}} \le z_{\alpha/2}\right) \approx 1 - \alpha,$$

and

$$\left[\overline{x} - z_{\alpha/2}\left(\frac{\sigma}{\sqrt{n}}\right), \overline{x} + z_{\alpha/2}\left(\frac{\sigma}{\sqrt{n}}\right)\right]$$

is an approximate $100(1 - \alpha)\%$ confidence interval for μ.

The closeness of the approximate probability $1 - \alpha$ to the exact probability depends on both the underlying distribution and the sample size. When the underlying distribution is unimodal (has only one mode) and continuous, the approximation is usually quite good even for small n, such as $n = 5$. As the underlying distribution becomes "less normal" (i.e., badly skewed or discrete), a larger sample size might be required to keep a reasonably accurate approximation. But, in almost all cases, an n of at least 30 is usually adequate.

EXAMPLE 6.2-3 Let X equal the amount of orange juice (in grams per day) consumed by an American. Suppose it is known that the standard deviation of X is $\sigma = 96$. To estimate the mean μ of X, an orange growers' association took a random sample of $n = 576$ Americans and found that they consumed, on the average, $\overline{x} = 133$ grams of orange juice per day. Thus, an approximate 90% confidence interval for μ is

$$133 \pm 1.645\left(\frac{96}{\sqrt{576}}\right), \qquad \text{or} \qquad [133 - 6.58, 133 + 6.58] = [126.42, 139.58]. \ ■$$

If σ^2 is unknown and the sample size n is 30 or greater, we shall use the fact that the ratio $(\overline{X} - \mu)/(S/\sqrt{n})$ has an approximate normal distribution $N(0, 1)$. This statement is true whether or not the underlying distribution is normal. However, if the underlying distribution is badly skewed or contaminated with occasional outliers, most statisticians would prefer to have a larger sample size—say, 50 or more—and even that might not produce good results. After this next example, we consider what to do when n is small.

EXAMPLE 6.2-4 Lake Macatawa, an inlet lake on the east side of Lake Michigan, is divided into an east basin and a west basin. To measure the effect on the lake of salting city streets in the winter, students took 32 samples of water from the west basin and measured the amount of sodium in parts per million in order to make a statistical inference about the unknown mean μ. They obtained the following data:

13.0	18.5	16.4	14.8	19.4	17.3	23.2	24.9
20.8	19.3	18.8	23.1	15.2	19.9	19.1	18.1
25.1	16.8	20.4	17.4	25.2	23.1	15.3	19.4
16.0	21.7	15.2	21.3	21.5	16.8	15.6	17.6

For these data, $\bar{x} = 19.07$ and $s^2 = 10.60$. Thus, an approximate 95% confidence interval for μ is

$$\bar{x} \pm 1.96\left(\frac{s}{\sqrt{n}}\right), \quad \text{or} \quad 19.07 \pm 1.96\sqrt{\frac{10.60}{32}}, \quad \text{or} \quad [17.94, 20.20]. \ ■$$

So we have found a confidence interval for the mean μ of a normal distribution, assuming that the value of the standard deviation σ is known or assuming that σ is unknown but the sample size is large. However, in many applications, the sample sizes are small and we do not know the value of the standard deviation, although in some cases we might have a very good idea about its value. For example, a manufacturer of light bulbs probably has a good notion from past experience of the value of the standard deviation of the length of life of different types of light bulbs. But certainly, most of the time, the investigator will not have any more idea about the standard deviation than about the mean—and frequently less. Let us consider how to proceed under these circumstances.

If the random sample arises from a normal distribution, we use the fact that

$$T = \frac{\overline{X} - \mu}{S/\sqrt{n}}$$

has a t distribution with $r = n - 1$ degrees of freedom (see Corollary 5.5-1, Theorem 5.5-2, and Equation 5.5-2), where S^2 is the usual unbiased estimator of σ^2. Select $t_{\alpha/2}(n-1)$ so that $P[T \ge t_{\alpha/2}(n-1)] = \alpha/2$. (See Figure 5.5-2(b) and Table VI in the appendix.) Then

$$\begin{aligned}
1 - \alpha &= P\left[-t_{\alpha/2}(n-1) \le \frac{\overline{X} - \mu}{S/\sqrt{n}} \le t_{\alpha/2}(n-1)\right] \\
&= P\left[-t_{\alpha/2}(n-1)\left(\frac{S}{\sqrt{n}}\right) \le \overline{X} - \mu \le t_{\alpha/2}(n-1)\left(\frac{S}{\sqrt{n}}\right)\right] \\
&= P\left[-\overline{X} - t_{\alpha/2}(n-1)\left(\frac{S}{\sqrt{n}}\right) \le -\mu \le -\overline{X} + t_{\alpha/2}(n-1)\left(\frac{S}{\sqrt{n}}\right)\right] \\
&= P\left[\overline{X} - t_{\alpha/2}(n-1)\left(\frac{S}{\sqrt{n}}\right) \le \mu \le \overline{X} + t_{\alpha/2}(n-1)\left(\frac{S}{\sqrt{n}}\right)\right].
\end{aligned}$$

Thus, the observations of a random sample provide $\bar{x}$ and s^2, and

$$\left[\bar{x} - t_{\alpha/2}(n-1)\left(\frac{s}{\sqrt{n}}\right), \bar{x} + t_{\alpha/2}(n-1)\left(\frac{s}{\sqrt{n}}\right)\right]$$

is a $100(1 - \alpha)\%$ confidence interval for μ.

EXAMPLE 6.2-5 Let X equal the amount of butterfat in pounds produced by a typical cow during a 305-day milk production period between her first and second calves. Assume that the distribution of X is $N(\mu, \sigma^2)$. To estimate μ, a farmer measured the butterfat production for $n = 20$ cows and obtained the following data:

481	537	513	583	453	510	570	500	457	555
618	327	350	643	499	421	505	637	599	392

For these data, $\overline{x} = 507.50$ and $s = 89.75$. Thus, a point estimate of μ is $\overline{x} = 507.50$. Since $t_{0.05}(19) = 1.729$, a 90% confidence interval for μ is

$$507.50 \pm 1.729\left(\frac{89.75}{\sqrt{20}}\right)$$

$$507.50 \pm 34.70, \qquad \text{or equivalently,} \qquad [472.80, 542.20].$$

Let T have a t distribution with $n - 1$ degrees of freedom. Then $t_{\alpha/2}(n-1) > z_{\alpha/2}$. Consequently, we would expect the interval $\overline{x} \pm z_{\alpha/2}(\sigma/\sqrt{n}\,)$ to be shorter than the interval $\overline{x} \pm t_{\alpha/2}(n - 1)(s/\sqrt{n}\,)$. After all, we have more information, namely, the value of σ, in constructing the first interval. However, the length of the second interval is very much dependent on the value of s. If the observed s is smaller than σ, a shorter confidence interval could result by the second procedure. But on the average, $\overline{x} \pm z_{\alpha/2}(\sigma/\sqrt{n}\,)$ is the shorter of the two confidence intervals (Exercise 6.2-16).

EXAMPLE 6.2-6 In Example 6.2-2, 50 confidence intervals were simulated for the mean of a normal distribution, assuming that the variance was known. For those same data, since $t_{0.05}(4) = 2.132$, $\overline{x} \pm 2.132(s/\sqrt{5}\,)$ was used to calculate a 90% confidence interval for μ. For those particular 50 intervals, 46 contained the mean $\mu = 50$. These 50 intervals are depicted in Figure 6.2-1(b). Note the different lengths of the intervals. Some are longer and some are shorter than the corresponding z intervals. The average length of the 50 t intervals is 7.137, which is quite close to the expected length of such an interval: 7.169. (See Exercise 6.2-16.) The length of the intervals that use z and $\sigma = 4$ is 5.885.

If we are not able to assume that the underlying distribution is normal, but μ and σ are both unknown, approximate confidence intervals for μ can still be constructed with the formula

$$T = \frac{\overline{X} - \mu}{S/\sqrt{n}},$$

which now only has an approximate t distribution. Generally, this approximation is quite good (i.e., it is robust) for many nonnormal distributions; in particular, it works well if the underlying distribution is symmetric, unimodal, and of the continuous type. However, if the distribution is highly skewed, there is great danger in using that approximation. In such a situation, it would be safer to use certain nonparametric methods for finding a confidence interval for the median of the distribution, one of which is given in Section 8.4.

There is one other aspect of confidence intervals that should be mentioned. So far, we have created only what are called **two-sided confidence intervals** for the mean μ. Sometimes, however, we might want only a lower (or upper) bound on μ. We proceed as follows.

Say $\overline{X}$ is the mean of a random sample of size n from the normal distribution $N(\mu, \sigma^2)$, where, for the moment, assume that σ^2 is known. Then

$$P\left(\frac{\overline{X} - \mu}{\sigma/\sqrt{n}} \le z_\alpha\right) = 1 - \alpha,$$

or equivalently,

$$P\left[\overline{X} - z_\alpha\left(\frac{\sigma}{\sqrt{n}}\right) \le \mu\right] = 1 - \alpha.$$

Once $\overline{X}$ is observed to be equal to $\overline{x}$, it follows that $[\overline{x} - z_\alpha(\sigma/\sqrt{n}\,), \infty)$ is a $100(1 - \alpha)\%$ **one-sided confidence interval** for μ. That is, with the confidence coefficient $1 - \alpha$, $\overline{x} - z_\alpha(\sigma/\sqrt{n}\,)$ is a lower bound for μ. Similarly, $(-\infty, \overline{x} + z_\alpha(\sigma/\sqrt{n}\,)]$ is a one-sided confidence interval for μ and $\overline{x} + z_\alpha(\sigma/\sqrt{n}\,)$ provides an upper bound for μ with confidence coefficient $1 - \alpha$.

When σ is unknown, we would use $T = (\overline{X} - \mu)/(S/\sqrt{n}\,)$ to find the corresponding lower or upper bounds for μ, namely, $\overline{x} - t_\alpha(n - 1)(s/\sqrt{n}\,)$ and $\overline{x} + t_\alpha(n - 1)(s/\sqrt{n}\,)$.

EXERCISES

6.2-1. A random sample of size 16 from the normal distribution $N(\mu, 25)$ yielded $\overline{x} = 73.8$. Find a 95% confidence interval for μ.

6.2-2. A random sample of size 8 from $N(\mu, 72)$ yielded $\overline{x} = 85$. Find the following confidence intervals for μ:

(a) 99%. (b) 95%. (c) 90%. (d) 80%.

6.2-3. To determine the effect of 100% nitrate on the growth of pea plants, several specimens were planted and then watered with 100% nitrate every day. At the end of two weeks, the plants were measured. Here are data on seven of them:

17.5 14.5 15.2 14.0 17.3 18.0 13.8

Assume that these data are observations from a normal distribution $N(\mu, \sigma^2)$.

(a) Find the value of a point estimate of μ.

(b) Find the value of a point estimate of σ.

(c) Give the endpoints for a 90% confidence interval for μ.

6.2-4. Let X equal the weight in grams of a "52-gram" snack pack of candies. Assume that the distribution of X is $N(\mu, 4)$. A random sample of $n = 10$ observations of X yielded the following data:

55.95	56.54	57.58	55.13	57.48
56.06	59.93	58.30	52.57	58.46

(a) Give a point estimate for μ.

(b) Find the endpoints for a 95% confidence interval for μ.

(c) On the basis of these very limited data, what is the probability that an individual snack pack selected at random is filled with less than 52 grams of candy?

6.2-5. As a clue to the amount of organic waste in Lake Macatawa (see Example 6.2-4), a count was made of the number of bacteria colonies in 100 milliliters of water. The number of colonies, in hundreds, for $n = 30$ samples of water from the east basin yielded

93	140	8	120	3	120	33	70	91	61
7	100	19	98	110	23	14	94	57	9
66	53	28	76	58	9	73	49	37	92

Find an approximate 90% confidence interval for the mean number (say, μ_E) of colonies in 100 milliliters of water in the east basin.

6.2-6. To determine whether the bacteria count was lower in the west basin of Lake Macatawa than in the east basin, $n = 37$ samples of water were taken from the west basin and the number of bacteria colonies in 100 milliliters of water was counted. The sample characteristics were $\overline{x} = 11.95$ and $s = 11.80$, measured in hundreds of colonies. Find the approximate 95% confidence interval for the mean number of colonies (say, μ_W) in 100 milliliters of water in the west basin.

6.2-7. Thirteen tons of cheese including "22-pound" wheels (label weight), is stored in some old gypsum mines. A random sample of $n = 9$ of these wheels yielded the following weights in pounds:

21.50 18.95 18.55 19.40 19.15
22.35 22.90 22.20 23.10

Assuming that the distribution of the weights of the wheels of cheese is $N(\mu, \sigma^2)$, find a 95% confidence interval for μ.

6.2-8. Assume that the yield per acre for a particular variety of soybeans is $N(\mu, \sigma^2)$. For a random sample of $n = 5$ plots, the yields in bushels per acre were 37.4, 48.8, 46.9, 55.0, and 44.0.

(a) Give a point estimate for μ.
(b) Find a 90% confidence interval for μ.

6.2-9. The grip strengths of 32 Hope College coeds were measured at the beginning of a health fitness program. The following data were obtained:

43 43 49 55 45 33 56 43 45 40 42 53 50 39 43 33
47 35 21 35 37 30 36 44 37 35 29 39 49 27 24 29

(a) Find the sample mean and the sample standard deviation for these grip strengths.
(b) Construct a (an approximate) 95% confidence interval for the mean, μ.

6.2-10. During the Friday night shift, $n = 28$ mints were selected at random from a production line and weighed. They had an average weight of $\bar{x} = 21.45$ grams and $s = 0.31$ grams. Give the lower endpoint of a 90% one-sided confidence interval for μ, the mean weight of all the mints.

6.2-11. In Exercise 3.1-5, 96 fuel injector pumps were selected randomly from the production line. Plungers force the fuel out of the pumps. The differences in diameter of the plungers from that of an absolute minimum were measured in microns. Use those data for this question.

(a) Give the value of a point estimate of μ.
(b) Determine point estimates of σ^2 and σ.
(c) Find a 90% confidence interval for μ.

6.2-12. A leakage test was conducted to determine the effectiveness of a seal designed to keep the inside of a plug airtight. An air needle was inserted into the plug, and the plug and needle were placed under water. The pressure was then increased until leakage was observed. Let X equal the pressure in pounds per square inch. Assume that the distribution of X is $N(\mu, \sigma^2)$. The following $n = 10$ observations of X were obtained:

3.1 3.3 4.5 2.8 3.5 3.5 3.7 4.2 3.9 3.3

Use the observations to

(a) Find a point estimate of μ.
(b) Find a point estimate of σ.
(c) Find a 95% one-sided confidence interval for μ that provides an upper bound for μ.

6.2-13. In groundwater research, it is often important to know the characteristics of the soil at a certain site. For example, let X equal the diameter of an individual grain of soil, and assume that the distribution of X is $N(\mu, \sigma^2)$. (See Example 3.6-9, where this assumption is discussed.) We again give the diameters of $n = 30$ individual grains:

1.24 1.36 1.28 1.31 1.35 1.20 1.39 1.35 1.41 1.31
1.28 1.26 1.37 1.49 1.32 1.40 1.33 1.28 1.25 1.39
1.38 1.34 1.40 1.27 1.33 1.36 1.43 1.33 1.29 1.34

Find a 90% confidence interval for μ.

6.2-14. In nuclear physics, detectors are often used to measure the energy of a particle. To calibrate a detector, particles of known energy are directed into it. The values of signals from 15 different detectors, for the same energy, are

260 216 259 206 265 284 291 229
232 250 225 242 240 252 236

(a) Find a 95% confidence interval for μ, assuming that these are observations from a $N(\mu, \sigma^2)$ distribution.
(b) Construct a box-and whisker diagram of the data.
(c) Are these detectors doing a good job or a poor job of putting out the same signal for the same input energy?

6.2-15. Students took $n = 35$ samples of water from the east basin of Lake Macatawa (see Example 6.2-4) and measured the amount of sodium in parts per million. For their data, they calculated $\bar{x} = 24.11$ and $s^2 = 24.44$. Find an approximate

90% confidence interval for μ, the mean of the amount of sodium in parts per million.

6.2-16. Let $X_1, X_2, \ldots, X_n$ be a random sample of size n from the normal distribution $N(\mu, \sigma^2)$. Calculate the expected length of a 95% confidence interval for μ, assuming that $n = 5$ and the variance is

(a) known,

(b) unknown.

HINT: To find $E(S)$, first determine $E[\sqrt{(n-1)S^2/\sigma^2}]$, recalling that $(n-1)S^2/\sigma^2$ is $\chi^2(n-1)$. (See also Exercise 6.1-14.)

6.2-17. Let X equal the weight (in pounds) of a "12-ounce" can of buttermilk biscuits. Assume that the distribution of X is $N(\mu, \sigma^2)$. Use the following 18 net weights to find a 95% one-sided confidence interval for μ that provides a lower bound for μ:

0.75 0.78 0.77 0.75 0.77 0.76 0.78 0.76 0.78
0.78 0.75 0.74 0.78 0.75 0.74 0.79 0.75 0.77

6.2-18. A manufacturer of soap powder packages the soap in "6-pound" boxes. To check the filling machine, a sample of $n = 1219$ boxes was weighed. Assuming that $\bar{x} = 6.05$ pounds and $s = 0.02$ pounds, give the endpoints for a 99% confidence interval for μ, the mean weight of the boxes of soap filled by this machine.

6.2-19. A study was conducted to measure (1) the amount of cervical spine movement induced by different methods of gaining access to the mouth and nose to begin resuscitation of a football player who is wearing a helmet and (2) the time it takes to complete each method. One method involves using a manual screwdriver to remove the side clips holding the face mask in place and then flipping the mask up. Twelve measured times in seconds for the manual screwdriver are

33.8 31.6 28.5 29.9 29.8 26.0 35.7 27.2 29.1 32.1 26.1 24.1

Assume that these are independent observations of a normally distributed random variable that is $N(\mu, \sigma^2)$.

(a) Find point estimates of μ and σ.

(b) Find a 95% one-sided confidence interval for μ that provides an upper bound for μ.

(c) Does the assumption of normality seem to be justified? Why?

6.2-20. Let X equal the weight of an unbreaded \$2.00 fish fry at a local restaurant in East Greenbush, New York. Assume that the distribution of X is $N(\mu, \sigma^2)$. A random sample of $n = 24$ weights (in ounces) was

4.4	3.8	5.1	4.6	4.5	4.5	4.8	4.1
3.9	4.2	4.4	4.9	5.0	4.3	4.4	3.6
5.2	4.8	4.4	4.6	4.6	5.0	4.0	4.5

(a) Find point estimates of μ, σ^2, and σ.

(b) Find a 95% one-sided confidence interval for μ that gives a lower bound for μ.

(c) Does the assumption that these weights are normal seem to be justified? Why?

6.2-21. An automotive supplier of interior parts places several electrical wires in a harness. A pull test measures the force required to pull spliced wires apart. A customer requires that each wire spliced into the harness must withstand a pull force of 20 pounds. Let X equal the force required to pull 20 gauge wires apart. Assume that the distribution of X is $N(\mu, \sigma^2)$. The following data give 20 observations of X:

28.8 24.4 30.1 25.6 26.4 23.9 22.1 22.5 27.6 28.1
20.8 27.7 24.4 25.1 24.6 26.3 28.2 22.2 26.3 24.4

(a) Find point estimates for μ and σ.

(b) Find a 99% one-sided confidence interval for μ that provides a lower bound for μ.

6.2-22. The weights of 100 laptop computers are given in Exercise 3.1-4. Use those 100 weights as a random sample of weights from the population of this type of computer.

(a) Find point estimates for the mean and standard deviation of laptop computer weights.

(b) Find an approximate 95% confidence interval for the mean weight of a laptop computer.

6.3 CONFIDENCE INTERVALS FOR THE DIFFERENCE OF TWO MEANS

Suppose that we are interested in comparing the means of two normal distributions. Let $X_1, X_2, \ldots, X_n$ and $Y_1, Y_2, \ldots, Y_m$ be, respectively, two independent random samples of sizes n and m from the two normal distributions $N(\mu_X, \sigma_X^2)$ and $N(\mu_Y, \sigma_Y^2)$.

Suppose, for now, that σ_X^2 and σ_Y^2 are known. The random samples are independent; thus, the respective sample means $\overline{X}$ and $\overline{Y}$ are also independent and have distributions $N(\mu_X, \sigma_X^2/n)$ and $N(\mu_Y, \sigma_Y^2/m)$. Consequently, the distribution of $W = \overline{X} - \overline{Y}$ is $N(\mu_X - \mu_Y, \sigma_X^2/n + \sigma_Y^2/m)$ and

$$P\left(-z_{\alpha/2} \le \frac{(\overline{X} - \overline{Y}) - (\mu_X - \mu_Y)}{\sqrt{\sigma_X^2/n + \sigma_Y^2/m}} \le z_{\alpha/2}\right) = 1 - \alpha,$$

which can be rewritten as

$$P[(\overline{X} - \overline{Y}) - z_{\alpha/2}\sigma_W \le \mu_X - \mu_Y \le (\overline{X} - \overline{Y}) + z_{\alpha/2}\sigma_W] = 1 - \alpha,$$

where $\sigma_W = \sqrt{\sigma_X^2/n + \sigma_Y^2/m}$ is the standard deviation of $\overline{X} - \overline{Y}$. Once the experiments have been performed and the means $\overline{x}$ and $\overline{y}$ computed, the interval

$$[\overline{x} - \overline{y} - z_{\alpha/2}\sigma_W, \overline{x} - \overline{y} + z_{\alpha/2}\sigma_W]$$

or, equivalently, $\overline{x} - \overline{y} \pm z_{\alpha/2}\sigma_W$ provides a $100(1 - \alpha)\%$ confidence interval for $\mu_X - \mu_Y$. Note that this interval is centered at the point estimate $\overline{x} - \overline{y}$ of $\mu_X - \mu_Y$ and is completed by subtracting and adding the product of $z_{\alpha/2}$ and the standard deviation of the point estimator.

EXAMPLE 6.3-1 In the preceding discussion, let $n = 15, m = 8, \overline{x} = 70.1, \overline{y} = 75.3, \sigma_X^2 = 60, \sigma_Y^2 = 40$, and $1 - \alpha = 0.90$. Thus, $1 - \alpha/2 = 0.95 = \Phi(1.645)$. Hence,

$$1.645\sigma_W = 1.645\sqrt{\frac{60}{15} + \frac{40}{8}} = 4.935,$$

and, since $\overline{x} - \overline{y} = -5.2$, it follows that

$$[-5.2 - 4.935, -5.2 + 4.935] = [-10.135, -0.265]$$

is a 90% confidence interval for $\mu_X - \mu_Y$. Because the confidence interval does not include zero, we suspect that μ_Y is greater than μ_X. ■

If the sample sizes are large and σ_X and σ_Y are unknown, we can replace σ_X^2 and σ_Y^2 with s_x^2 and s_y^2, where s_x^2 and s_y^2 are the values of the respective unbiased estimates of the variances. This means that

$$\overline{x} - \overline{y} \pm z_{\alpha/2}\sqrt{\frac{s_x^2}{n} + \frac{s_y^2}{m}}$$

serves as an approximate $100(1 - \alpha)\%$ confidence interval for $\mu_X - \mu_Y$.

Now consider the problem of constructing confidence intervals for the difference of the means of two normal distributions when the variances are unknown but the sample sizes are small. Let $X_1, X_2, \ldots, X_n$ and $Y_1, Y_2, \ldots, Y_m$ be two independent random samples from the distributions $N(\mu_X, \sigma_X^2)$ and $N(\mu_Y, \sigma_Y^2)$, respectively. If the sample sizes are not large (say, considerably smaller than 30), this problem can be a difficult one. However, even in these cases, if we can assume common, but unknown, variances (say, $\sigma_X^2 = \sigma_Y^2 = \sigma^2$), there is a way out of our difficulty.

We know that

$$Z = \frac{\overline{X} - \overline{Y} - (\mu_X - \mu_Y)}{\sqrt{\sigma^2/n + \sigma^2/m}}$$

is $N(0,1)$. Moreover, since the random samples are independent,

$$U = \frac{(n-1)S_X^2}{\sigma^2} + \frac{(m-1)S_Y^2}{\sigma^2}$$

is the sum of two independent chi-square random variables; thus, the distribution of U is $\chi^2(n+m-2)$. In addition, the independence of the sample means and sample variances implies that Z and U are independent. According to the definition of a T random variable,

$$T = \frac{Z}{\sqrt{U/(n+m-2)}}$$

has a t distribution with $n + m - 2$ degrees of freedom. That is,

$$T = \frac{\dfrac{\overline{X} - \overline{Y} - (\mu_X - \mu_Y)}{\sqrt{\sigma^2/n + \sigma^2/m}}}{\sqrt{\left[\dfrac{(n-1)S_X^2}{\sigma^2} + \dfrac{(m-1)S_Y^2}{\sigma^2}\right]\Big/(n+m-2)}}$$

$$= \frac{\overline{X} - \overline{Y} - (\mu_X - \mu_Y)}{\sqrt{\left[\dfrac{(n-1)S_X^2 + (m-1)S_Y^2}{n+m-2}\right]\left[\dfrac{1}{n} + \dfrac{1}{m}\right]}}$$

has a t distribution with $r = n + m - 2$ degrees of freedom. Thus, with $t_0 = t_{\alpha/2}(n+m-2)$, we have

$$P(-t_0 \le T \le t_0) = 1 - \alpha.$$

Solving the inequalities for $\mu_X - \mu_Y$ yields

$$P\left(\overline{X} - \overline{Y} - t_0 S_P\sqrt{\frac{1}{n} + \frac{1}{m}} \le \mu_X - \mu_Y \le \overline{X} - \overline{Y} + t_0 S_P\sqrt{\frac{1}{n} + \frac{1}{m}}\right),$$

where the pooled estimator of the common standard deviation is

$$S_P = \sqrt{\frac{(n-1)S_X^2 + (m-1)S_Y^2}{n+m-2}}.$$

If $\overline{x}$, $\overline{y}$, and s_p are the observed values of $\overline{X}$, $\overline{Y}$, and S_P, then

$$\left[\overline{x} - \overline{y} - t_0 s_p\sqrt{\frac{1}{n} + \frac{1}{m}},\ \overline{x} - \overline{y} + t_0 s_p\sqrt{\frac{1}{n} + \frac{1}{m}}\right]$$

is a $100(1-\alpha)\%$ confidence interval for $\mu_X - \mu_Y$.

EXAMPLE 6.3-2 Suppose that scores on a standardized test in mathematics taken by students from large and small high schools are $N(\mu_X, \sigma^2)$ and $N(\mu_Y, \sigma^2)$, respectively, where σ^2 is unknown. If a random sample of $n = 9$ students from large high schools yielded $\bar{x} = 81.31$, $s_x^2 = 60.76$, and a random sample of $m = 15$ students from small high schools yielded $\bar{y} = 78.61$, $s_y^2 = 48.24$, then the endpoints for a 95% confidence interval for $\mu_X - \mu_Y$ are given by

$$81.31 - 78.61 \pm 2.074\sqrt{\frac{8(60.76) + 14(48.24)}{22}}\sqrt{\frac{1}{9} + \frac{1}{15}}$$

because $t_{0.025}(22) = 2.074$. The 95% confidence interval is $[-3.65, 9.05]$. ■

REMARK The assumption of equal variances, namely, $\sigma_X^2 = \sigma_Y^2$, can be modified somewhat so that we are still able to find a confidence interval for $\mu_X - \mu_Y$. That is, if we know the ratio σ_X^2/σ_Y^2 of the variances, we can still make this type of statistical inference by using a random variable with a t distribution. (See Exercise 6.3-10.) However, if we do not know the ratio of the variances and yet suspect that the unknown σ_X^2 and σ_Y^2 differ by a great deal, what do we do? It is safest to return to

$$\frac{\overline{X} - \overline{Y} - (\mu_X - \mu_Y)}{\sqrt{\sigma_X^2/n + \sigma_Y^2/m}}$$

for the inference about $\mu_X - \mu_Y$ but replacing σ_X^2 and σ_Y^2 by their respective estimators S_X^2 and S_Y^2. That is, consider

$$W = \frac{\overline{X} - \overline{Y} - (\mu_X - \mu_Y)}{\sqrt{S_X^2/n + S_Y^2/m}}.$$

What is the distribution of W? As before, we note that if n and m are large enough and the underlying distributions are close to normal (or at least not badly skewed), then W has an approximate normal distribution and a confidence interval for $\mu_X - \mu_Y$ can be found by considering

$$P(-z_{\alpha/2} \le W \le z_{\alpha/2}) \approx 1 - \alpha.$$

However, for smaller n and m, Welch has proposed a Student's t distribution as the approximating one for W. Welch's proposal was later modified by Aspin. [See A. A. Aspin, "Tables for Use in Comparisons Whose Accuracy Involves Two Variances, Separately Estimated," *Biometrika*, **36** (1949), pp. 290–296, with an appendix by B. L. Welch in which he makes the suggestion used here.] The approximating Student's t distribution has r degrees of freedom, where

$$\frac{1}{r} = \frac{c^2}{n-1} + \frac{(1-c)^2}{m-1} \quad \text{and} \quad c = \frac{s_x^2/n}{s_x^2/n + s_y^2/m}.$$

An equivalent formula for r is

$$r = \frac{\left(\dfrac{s_x^2}{n} + \dfrac{s_y^2}{m}\right)^2}{\dfrac{1}{n-1}\left(\dfrac{s_x^2}{n}\right)^2 + \dfrac{1}{m-1}\left(\dfrac{s_y^2}{m}\right)^2}. \tag{6.3-1}$$

In particular, the assignment of r by this rule provides protection in the case in which the smaller sample size is associated with the larger variance by greatly reducing the number of degrees of freedom from the usual $n + m - 2$. Of course, this reduction increases the value of $t_{\alpha/2}$. If r is not an integer, then use the greatest integer in r; that is, $\lfloor r \rfloor$, the "floor," or greatest integer in r, is the number of degrees of freedom associated with the approximating Student's t distribution. An approximate $100(1 - \alpha)$ percent confidence interval for $\mu_X - \mu_Y$ is given by

$$\bar{x} - \bar{y} \pm t_{\alpha/2}(r)\sqrt{\frac{s_x^2}{n} + \frac{s_y^2}{m}}.$$

It is interesting to consider the two-sample T in more detail. It is

$$T = \frac{\overline{X} - \overline{Y} - (\mu_X - \mu_Y)}{\sqrt{\dfrac{(n-1)S_X^2 + (m-1)S_Y^2}{n+m-2}\left(\dfrac{1}{n} + \dfrac{1}{m}\right)}} \tag{6.3-2}$$

$$= \frac{\overline{X} - \overline{Y} - (\mu_X - \mu_Y)}{\sqrt{\left[\dfrac{(n-1)S_X^2}{nm} + \dfrac{(m-1)S_Y^2}{nm}\right]\left[\dfrac{n+m}{n+m-2}\right]}}.$$

Now, since $(n - 1)/n \approx 1$, $(m - 1)/m \approx 1$, and $(n + m)/(n + m - 2) \approx 1$, we have

$$T \approx \frac{\overline{X} - \overline{Y} - (\mu_X - \mu_Y)}{\sqrt{\dfrac{S_X^2}{m} + \dfrac{S_Y^2}{n}}}.$$

We note that, in this form, each variance is divided by the wrong sample size! That is, if the sample sizes are large or the variances known, we would like

$$\sqrt{\frac{S_X^2}{n} + \frac{S_Y^2}{m}} \quad \text{or} \quad \sqrt{\frac{\sigma_X^2}{n} + \frac{\sigma_Y^2}{m}}$$

in the denominator; so T seems to change the sample sizes. Thus, using this T is particularly bad when the sample sizes and the variances are unequal; hence, caution must be taken in using that T to construct a confidence interval for $\mu_X - \mu_Y$. That is, if $n < m$ and $\sigma_X^2 < \sigma_Y^2$, then T does not have a distribution which is close to that of a Student t-distribution with $n + m - 2$ degrees of freedom: Instead, its spread is much less than the Student t's, as the term s_y^2/n in the denominator is much larger than it should be. By contrast, if $m < n$ and $\sigma_X^2 < \sigma_Y^2$, then $s_x^2/m + s_y^2/n$ is generally smaller than it should be and the distribution of T is spread out more than that of the Student t.

There is a way out of this difficulty, however: When the underlying distributions are close to normal, but the sample sizes and the variances are seemingly much different, we suggest the use of

$$W = \frac{\overline{X} - \overline{Y} - (\mu_X - \mu_Y)}{\sqrt{\dfrac{S_X^2}{n} + \dfrac{S_Y^2}{m}}}, \tag{6.3-3}$$

where Welch proved that W has an approximate t distribution with $\lfloor r \rfloor$ degrees of freedom, with the number of degrees of freedom given by Equation 6.3-1. ■

EXAMPLE 6.3-3 To help understand the preceding remarks, a simulation was done with *Maple*. In order to obtain a q–q plot of the quantiles of a t distribution, a CAS or some type of computer program is very important because of the challenge in finding these quantiles.

Maple was used to simulate $N = 500$ observations of T (Equation 6.3-2) and $N = 500$ observations of W (Equation 6.3-3). In Figure 6.3-1, $n = 6$, $m = 18$, the X

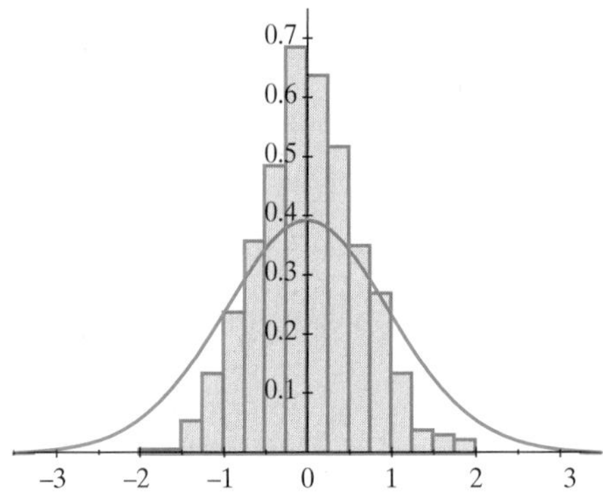

T Observations, $T(22)$ p.d.f. Superimposed

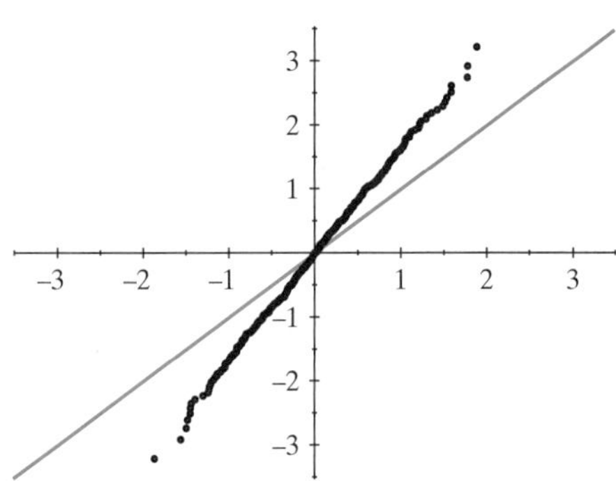

$T(22)$ Quantiles versus T Order Statistics

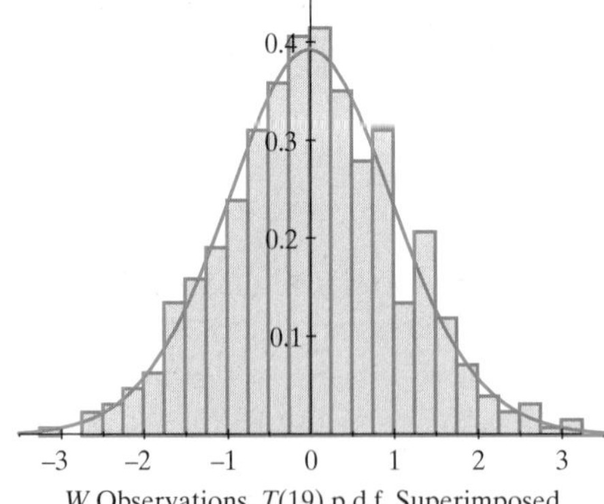

W Observations, $T(19)$ p.d.f. Superimposed

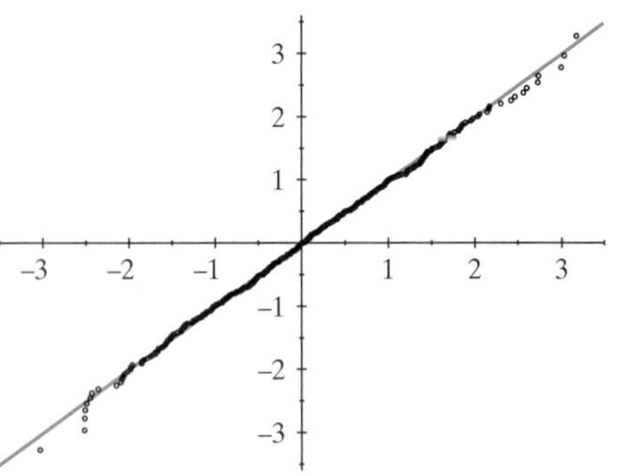

$T(19)$ Quantiles versus W Order Statistics

FIGURE 6.3-1: Observations of T and of W, $n = 6$, $m = 18$, $\sigma_X^2 = 1$, $\sigma_Y^2 = 36$

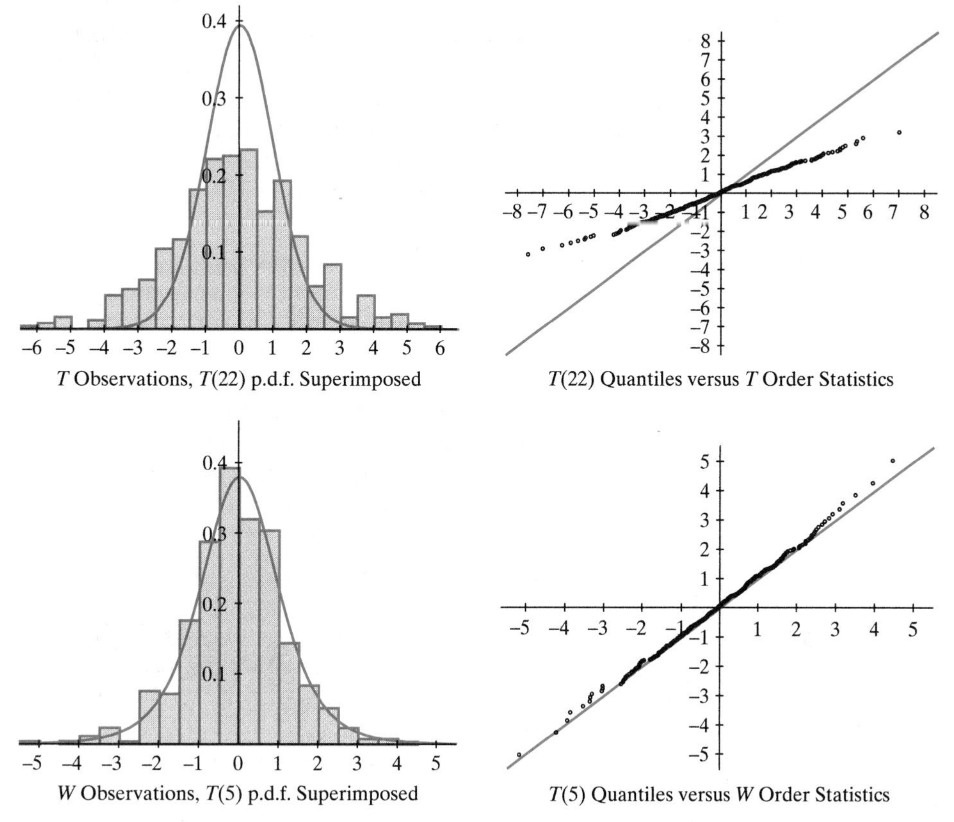

FIGURE 6.3-2: Observations of T and of W, $n = 18$, $m = 6$, $\sigma_X^2 = 1$, $\sigma_Y^2 = 36$

observations were generated from the $N(0, 1)$ distribution, and the Y observations were generated from the $N(0, 36)$ distribution. For the value of r for Welch's approximate t distribution, we used the distribution variances rather than the sample variances so that we could use the same r for each of the 500 values of W.

For the simulation results shown in Figure 6.3-2, $n = 18, m = 6$, the X observations were generated from the $N(0, 1)$ distribution, and the Y observations were generated from the $N(0, 36)$ distribution. In both cases, Welch's W with a corrected number of r degrees of freedom is much better than the usual T when the variances and sample sizes are unequal, as they are in these examples. ■

In some applications, two measurements—say, X and Y—are taken on the same subject. In these cases, X and Y are dependent random variables. Many times these are "before" and "after" measurements, such as weight before and after participating in a diet-and-exercise program. To compare the means of X and Y, it is not permissible to use the t statistics and confidence intervals that we just developed, because in that situation X and Y are independent. Instead, we proceed as follows.

Let $(X_1, Y_1), (X_2, Y_2), \ldots, (X_n, Y_n)$ be n pairs of dependent measurements. Let $D_i = X_i - Y_i$, $i = 1, 2, \ldots, n$. Suppose that $D_1, D_2, \ldots, D_n$ can be thought of as a random sample from $N(\mu_D, \sigma_D^2)$, where μ_D and σ_D are the mean and standard deviation of each difference. To form a confidence interval for $\mu_X - \mu_Y$, use

$$T = \frac{\overline{D} - \mu_D}{S_D/\sqrt{n}},$$

where $\overline{D}$ and S_D are, respectively, the sample mean and sample standard deviation of the n differences. Thus, T is a t statistic with $n - 1$ degrees of freedom. The endpoints for a $100(1 - \alpha)\%$ confidence interval for $\mu_D = \mu_X - \mu_Y$ are then

$$\overline{d} \pm t_{\alpha/2}(n-1)\frac{s_d}{\sqrt{n}},$$

where $\overline{d}$ and s_d are the observed mean and standard deviation of the sample of the D values. Of course, this is like the confidence interval for a single mean, presented in the last section.

EXAMPLE 6.3-4 An experiment was conducted to compare people's reaction times to a red light versus a green light. When signaled with either the red or the green light, the subject was asked to hit a switch to turn off the light. When the switch was hit, a clock was turned off and the reaction time in seconds was recorded. The following results give the reaction times for eight subjects:

Subject	Red (X)	Green (Y)	$D = X - Y$
1	0.30	0.43	−0.13
2	0.23	0.32	−0.09
3	0.41	0.58	−0.17
4	0.53	0.46	0.07
5	0.24	0.27	−0.03
6	0.36	0.41	−0.05
7	0.38	0.38	0.00
8	0.51	0.61	−0.10

For these data, $\overline{d} = -0.0625$ and $s_d = 0.0765$. To form a 95% confidence interval for $\mu_D = \mu_X - \mu_Y$, we find, from Table VI in the appendix, that $t_{0.025}(7) = 2.365$. Thus, the endpoints for the confidence interval are

$$-0.0625 \pm 2.365\,\frac{0.0765}{\sqrt{8}}, \qquad \text{or} \qquad [-0.1265, 0.0015].$$

In this very limited data set, zero is included in the confidence interval, but is close to the endpoint 0.0015. We suspect that if more data were taken, zero might not be included in the confidence interval. If that actually were to happen, it would seem that people react faster to a red light. ■

Of course, we can find one-sided confidence intervals for the difference of the means, $\mu_X - \mu_Y$. Suppose we believe that we have changed some characteristic of the X distribution and created a Y distribution such that we think that $\mu_X > \mu_Y$. Let us find a one-sided 95% confidence interval that is a lower bound for $\mu_X - \mu_Y$. Say this lower bound is greater than zero. Then we would feel 95% confident that the mean μ_X is larger than the mean μ_Y. That is, the change that was made seemed to decrease the mean; this would be good in some cases, such as golf or racing. In other cases, in which we hope the change would be such that $\mu_X < \mu_Y$, we would find a one-sided confidence interval which is an upper bound for $\mu_X - \mu_Y$, and we would hope that it would be less than zero. These ideas are illustrated in Exercises 6.3-5, 6.3-12, and 6.3-13.

EXERCISES

6.3-1. The length of life of brand X light bulbs is assumed to be $N(\mu_X, 784)$. The length of life of brand Y light bulbs is assumed to be $N(\mu_Y, 627)$ and independent of X. If a random sample of $n = 56$ brand X light bulbs yielded a mean of $\bar{x} = 937.4$ hours and a random sample of size $m = 57$ brand Y light bulbs yielded a mean of $\bar{y} = 988.9$ hours, find a 90% confidence interval for $\mu_X - \mu_Y$.

6.3-2. Let $X_1, X_2, \ldots, X_5$ be a random sample of SAT mathematics scores, assumed to be $N(\mu_X, \sigma^2)$, and let $Y_1, Y_2, \ldots, Y_8$ be an independent random sample of SAT verbal scores, assumed to be $N(\mu_Y, \sigma^2)$. If the following data are observed, find a 90% confidence interval for $\mu_X - \mu_Y$:

$$x_1 = 644 \quad x_2 = 493 \quad x_3 = 532 \quad x_4 = 462 \quad x_5 = 565$$
$$y_1 = 623 \quad y_2 = 472 \quad y_3 = 492 \quad y_4 = 661 \quad y_5 = 540$$
$$y_6 = 502 \quad y_7 = 549 \quad y_8 = 518$$

6.3-3. Independent random samples of the heights of adult males living in two countries yielded the following results: $n = 12$, $\bar{x} = 65.7$ inches, $s_x = 4$ inches; and $m = 15$, $\bar{y} = 68.2$ inches, $s_y = 3$ inches. Find an approximate 98% confidence interval for the difference $\mu_X - \mu_Y$ of the means of the populations of heights. Assume that $\sigma_X^2 = \sigma_Y^2$.

6.3-4. [*Medicine and Science in Sports and Exercise* (January 1990)] Let X and Y equal, respectively, the blood volumes in milliliters for a male who is a paraplegic and participates in vigorous physical activities and for a male who is able bodied and participates in everyday, ordinary activities. Assume that X is $N(\mu_X, \sigma_X^2)$ and Y is $N(\mu_Y, \sigma_Y^2)$. Following are $n = 7$ observations of X:

1612	1352	1456	1222	1560	1456	1924

Following are $m = 10$ observations of Y:

1082	1300	1092	1040	910
1248	1092	1040	1092	1288

Use the observations of X and Y to

(a) Give a point estimate for $\mu_X - \mu_Y$.

(b) Find a 95% confidence interval for $\mu_X - \mu_Y$. Since the variances σ_X^2 and σ_Y^2 might not be equal, use Welch's T.

6.3-5. A biologist who studies spiders was interested in comparing the lengths of female and male green lynx spiders. Assume that the length X of the male spider is approximately $N(\mu_X, \sigma_X^2)$ and the length Y of the female spider is approximately $N(\mu_Y, \sigma_Y^2)$. Following are $n = 30$ observations of X:

5.20	4.70	5.75	7.50	6.45	6.55
4.70	4.80	5.95	5.20	6.35	6.95
5.70	6.20	5.40	6.20	5.85	6.80
5.65	5.50	5.65	5.85	5.75	6.35
5.75	5.95	5.90	7.00	6.10	5.80

Following are $m = 30$ observations of Y:

8.25	9.95	5.90	7.05	8.45	7.55
9.80	10.80	6.60	7.55	8.10	9.10
6.10	9.30	8.75	7.00	7.80	8.00
9.00	6.30	8.35	8.70	8.00	7.50
9.50	8.30	7.05	8.30	7.95	9.60

The units of measurement for both sets of observations are millimeters. Find an approximate one-sided 95% confidence interval that is an upper bound for $\mu_X - \mu_Y$.

6.3-6. Consider the butterfat production (in pounds) of a cow during a 305-day milk production period following the birth of a calf. Let X and Y equal the butterfat production for such cows on a farm in Wisconsin and a farm in Michigan. Twelve observations of X are

649	657	714	877	975	468
567	849	721	791	874	405

Sixteen observations of Y are

699	891	632	815	589	764	524	727
597	868	652	978	479	733	549	790

(a) Assuming that X is $N(\mu_X, \sigma^2)$ and Y is $N(\mu_Y, \sigma^2)$, find a 95% confidence interval for $\mu_X - \mu_Y$.

(b) Construct box-and-whisker diagrams for these two sets of data on the same graph.

(c) Does there seem to be a significant difference in butterfat production for cows on these two farms?

6.3-7. An automotive supplier is considering changing its electrical wire harness to save money. The idea is to replace a current 20-gauge wire with a 22-gauge wire. Since not all wires in the harness can be changed, the new wire must work with the current wire splice process. To determine whether the new wire is compatible, random samples were selected and measured with with a pull test. A pull test measures the force required to pull the spliced wires apart. The minimum pull force required by the customer is 20 pounds. Twenty observations of the forces needed for the current wire are

28.8 24.4 30.1 25.6 26.4 23.9 22.1 22.5 27.6 28.1
20.8 27.7 24.4 25.1 24.6 26.3 28.2 22.2 26.3 24.4

Twenty observations of the forces needed for the new wire are

14.1 12.2 14.0 14.6 8.5 12.6 13.7 14.8 14.1 13.2
12.1 11.4 10.1 14.2 13.6 13.1 11.9 14.8 11.1 13.5

(a) Does the current wire meet the customer's specifications?
(b) Find a 90% confidence interval for the difference of the means for these two sets of wire.
(c) Construct box-and-whisker diagrams of the two sets of data on the same figure.
(d) What is your recommendation for this company?

6.3-8. A test was conducted to determine whether a wedge on the end of a plug fitting designed to hold a seal onto the plug was doing its job. The data taken were in the form of measurements of the force required to remove a seal from the plug with the wedge in place (say, X) and the force required without the plug (say, Y). Assume that the distributions of X and Y are $N(\mu_X, \sigma^2)$ and $N(\mu_Y, \sigma^2)$, respectively. Ten independent observations of X are

3.26 2.26 2.62 2.62 2.36 3.00 2.62 2.40 2.30 2.40

Ten independent observations of Y are

1.80 1.46 1.54 1.42 1.32 1.56 1.36 1.64 2.00 1.54

(a) Find a 95% confidence interval for $\mu_X - \mu_Y$.
(b) Construct box-and-whisker diagrams of these data on the same figure.
(c) Is the wedge necessary?

6.3-9. Students are weighed (in kilograms) at the beginning and the end of a semester-long health-fitness program. Let the random variable D equal the weight change for a student (post-program weight minus pre-program weight). Assume that the distribution of D is $N(\mu_D, \sigma_D^2)$. A random sample of $n = 12$ female students yielded the following observations of D:

2.0 −0.5 1.4 −2.2 0.3 −0.8
3.7 −0.1 0.6 0.2 0.9 −0.1

(a) Give a point estimate of μ_D.
(b) Find a 95% confidence interval for μ_D.

6.3-10. Let $\overline{X}$, $\overline{Y}$, S_X^2, and S_Y^2 be the respective sample means and unbiased estimates of the variances obtained from independent samples of sizes n and m from the normal distributions $N(\mu_X, \sigma_X^2)$ and $N(\mu_Y, \sigma_Y^2)$, where μ_X, μ_Y, σ_X^2, and σ_Y^2 are unknown. If $\sigma_X^2/\sigma_Y^2 = d$, a known constant,

(a) Argue that $\dfrac{(\overline{X} - \overline{Y}) - (\mu_X - \mu_Y)}{\sqrt{d\sigma_Y^2/n + \sigma_Y^2/m}}$ is $N(0,1)$.
(b) Argue that $\dfrac{(n-1)S_X^2}{d\sigma_Y^2} + \dfrac{(m-1)S_Y^2}{\sigma_Y^2}$ is $\chi^2(n+m-2)$.
(c) Argue that the two random variables in (a) and (b) are independent.
(d) With these results, construct a random variable (not depending upon σ_Y^2) that has a t distribution and that can be used to construct a confidence interval for $\mu_X - \mu_Y$.

6.3-11. Students in a semester-long health-fitness program have their percentage of body fat measured at the beginning of the semester and at the end of the semester. The following measurements give these percentages for 10 men and for 10 women:

Males		Females	
Pre-program %	Post-program %	Pre-program %	Post-program %
11.10	9.97	22.90	22.89
19.50	15.80	31.60	33.47
14.00	13.02	27.70	25.75
8.30	9.28	21.70	19.80
12.40	11.51	19.36	18.00

Males		Females	
Pre-program %	Post-program %	Pre-program %	Post-program %
7.89	7.40	25.03	22.33
12.10	10.70	26.90	25.26
8.30	10.40	25.75	24.90
12.31	11.40	23.63	21.80
10.00	11.95	25.06	24.28

(a) Find a 90% confidence interval for the mean of the difference in the percentages for the males.
(b) Find a 90% confidence interval for the mean of the difference in the percentages for the females.
(c) On the basis of these data, have these percentages decreased?
(d) If possible, check whether each set of differences comes from a normal distribution.

6.3-12. Twenty-four 9th- and 10th-grade high school girls were put on an ultraheavy rope-jumping program. The following data give the time difference for each girl ("before program time" minus "after program time") for the 40-yard dash:

0.28	0.01	0.13	0.33	−0.03	0.07	−0.18	−0.14
−0.33	0.01	0.22	0.29	−0.08	0.23	0.08	0.04
−0.30	−0.08	0.09	0.70	0.33	−0.34	0.50	0.06

(a) Give a point estimate of μ_D, the mean of the difference in race times.
(b) Find a one-sided 95% confidence interval that is a lower bound for μ_D.
(c) Does it look like the rope-jumping program was effective?

6.3-13. The Biomechanics Lab at Hope College tested healthy old women and healthy young women to discover whether or not lower extremity response time to a stimulus is a function of age. Let X and Y respectively equal the independent response times for these two groups when taking steps in the anterior direction. Find a one-sided 95% confidence interval that is a lower bound for $\mu_X - \mu_Y$ if $n = 60$ observations of X yielded $\bar{x} = 671$ and $s_x = 129$ while $m = 60$ observations of Y yielded $\bar{y} = 480$ and $s_y = 93$.

6.3-14. Let X and Y equal the hardness of the hot and cold water, respectively, in a campus building. Hardness is measured in terms of the calcium ion concentration (in ppm). The following data were collected ($n = 12$ observations of X and $m = 10$ observations of Y):

X: 133.5 137.2 136.3 133.3 137.5 135.4
138.4 137.1 136.5 139.4 137.9 136.8

Y: 134.0 134.7 136.0 132.7 134.6 135.2
135.9 135.6 135.8 134.2

(a) Calculate the sample means and the sample variances of these data.
(b) Construct a 95% confidence interval for $\mu_X - \mu_Y$, assuming that the distributions of X and Y are $N(\mu_X, \sigma_X^2)$ and $N(\mu_Y, \sigma_Y^2)$, respectively.
(c) Construct box plots of the two sets of data on the same graph.
(d) Do the means seem to be equal or different?

6.3-15. Ledolter and Hogg (see references) report that two rubber compounds were tested for tensile strength. Rectangular materials were prepared and pulled in a longitudinal direction. A sample of 14 specimens, 7 from compound A and 7 from compound B, was prepared, but it was later found that two B specimens were defective and they had to be removed from the test. The tensile strength (in units of 100 pounds per square inch) of the remaining specimens are as follows:

A: 32 30 33 32 29 34 32
B: 33 35 36 37 35

Calculate a 95 percent confidence interval for the difference of the mean tensile strengths of the two rubber compounds. State your assumptions.

6.3-16. Ledolter and Hogg (see references) report that two different fabrics—say, X and Y—are compared on a Martindale wear tester that can compare two materials in a single run. The weights losses (in milligrams) from seven runs are as follows:

X: 36 26 31 38 28 37 22
Y: 39 27 35 42 31 39 21

Analyze these data by constructing a 90% confidence interval for the difference of the means. State your assumptions.

6.4 CONFIDENCE INTERVALS FOR VARIANCES

In this section, we find confidence intervals for the variance of a normal distribution and for the ratio of the variances of two normal distributions. The confidence interval for the variance σ^2 is based on the sample variance

$$S^2 = \frac{1}{n-1}\sum_{i=1}^{n}(X_i - \overline{X})^2.$$

We use the fact that the distribution of $(n-1)S^2/\sigma^2$ is $\chi^2(n-1)$ to find a confidence interval for σ^2. We select constants a and b from Table IV in the appendix with $n - 1$ degrees of freedom such that

$$P\left(a \le \frac{(n-1)S^2}{\sigma^2} \le b\right) = 1 - \alpha.$$

One way to do this is by selecting a and b so that $a = \chi^2_{1-\alpha/2}(n-1)$ and $b = \chi^2_{\alpha/2}(n-1)$. That is, we select a and b so that the probabilities in the two tails are equal. Then, solving the inequalities, we have

$$\begin{aligned} 1 - \alpha &= P\left(\frac{a}{(n-1)S^2} \le \frac{1}{\sigma^2} \le \frac{b}{(n-1)S^2}\right) \\ &= P\left(\frac{(n-1)S^2}{b} \le \sigma^2 \le \frac{(n-1)S^2}{a}\right). \end{aligned}$$

Thus, the probability that the random interval $[(n-1)S^2/b, (n-1)S^2/a]$ contains the unknown σ^2 is $1 - \alpha$. Once the values of $X_1, X_2, \ldots, X_n$ are observed to be $x_1, x_2, \ldots, x_n$ and s^2 is computed, the interval $[(n-1)s^2/b, (n-1)s^2/a]$ is a $100(1-\alpha)\%$ confidence interval for σ^2. It follows that a $100(1-\alpha)\%$ confidence interval for σ, the standard deviation, is given by

$$\left[\sqrt{\frac{(n-1)s^2}{b}}, \sqrt{\frac{(n-1)s^2}{a}}\right] = \left[\sqrt{\frac{n-1}{b}}\,s, \sqrt{\frac{n-1}{a}}\,s\right].$$

EXAMPLE 6.4-1 Assume that the time in days required for maturation of seeds of a species of Guardiola, a flowering plant found in Mexico, is $N(\mu, \sigma^2)$. A random sample of $n = 13$ seeds, both parents having narrow leaves, yielded $\overline{x} = 18.97$ days and

$$12s^2 = \sum_{i=1}^{13}(x_i - \overline{x})^2 = 128.41.$$

A 90% confidence interval for σ^2 is

$$\left[\frac{128.41}{21.03}, \frac{128.41}{5.226}\right] = [6.11, 24.57]$$

because $5.226 = \chi^2_{0.95}(12)$ and $21.03 = \chi^2_{0.05}(12)$, from Table IV in the appendix. The corresponding 90% confidence interval for σ is

$$[\sqrt{6.11}, \sqrt{24.57}] = [2.47, 4.96].$$

■

Although a and b are generally selected so that the probabilities in the two tails are equal, the resulting $100(1 - \alpha)\%$ confidence interval is not the shortest that can be formed with the available data. Table X in the appendix gives solutions for a and b that yield confidence intervals of minimum length for the standard deviation. (See Exercise 6.4-16.)

EXAMPLE 6.4-2 Using the data in Example 6.4-1, we find that a 90% confidence interval for σ of minimum length is

$$\left[\sqrt{\frac{128.41}{24.202}}, \sqrt{\frac{128.41}{5.940}}\right] = [2.30, 4.65]$$

(since $a = 5.940$ and $b = 24.202$ from Table X). The length of this interval is 2.35, whereas the length of the interval given in Example 6.4-1 is 2.49. To see why this new interval is shorter, carefully sketch a graph of the $\chi^2(12)$ p.d.f. and compare $\chi^2_{0.95}(12)$ with a and $\chi^2_{0.05}(12)$ with b on the graph. ■

There are occasions when it is of interest to compare the variances of two normal distributions. We do this by finding a confidence interval for σ_X^2/σ_Y^2, using the ratio of S_X^2/σ_X^2 to S_Y^2/σ_Y^2, where S_X^2 and S_Y^2 are the two sample variances based on two independent samples of sizes n and m from $N(\mu_X, \sigma_X^2)$ and $N(\mu_Y, \sigma_Y^2)$, respectively. However, the reciprocal of that ratio can be rewritten as follows:

$$\frac{\dfrac{S_Y^2}{\sigma_Y^2}}{\dfrac{S_X^2}{\sigma_X^2}} = \frac{\left[\dfrac{(m - 1)S_Y^2}{\sigma_Y^2}\right]\Big/(m - 1)}{\left[\dfrac{(n - 1)S_X^2}{\sigma_X^2}\right]\Big/(n - 1)}.$$

Since $(m - 1)S_Y^2/\sigma_Y^2$ and $(n - 1)S_X^2/\sigma_X^2$ are independent chi-square variables with $(m - 1)$ and $(n - 1)$ degrees of freedom, respectively, we know from Example 5.2-4 that the distribution of this ratio is $F(m - 1, n - 1)$. That is,

$$F = \frac{\dfrac{(m - 1)S_Y^2}{\sigma_Y^2(m - 1)}}{\dfrac{(n - 1)S_X^2}{\sigma_X^2(n - 1)}} = \frac{\dfrac{S_Y^2}{\sigma_Y^2}}{\dfrac{S_X^2}{\sigma_X^2}}$$

has an F distribution with $r_1 = m - 1$ and $r_2 = n - 1$ degrees of freedom. This is the ratio that we want to use to find a confidence interval for σ_X^2/σ_Y^2.

To form the desired confidence interval, we select constants c and d from Table VII in the appendix so that

$$1 - \alpha = P\left(c \le \frac{S_Y^2/\sigma_Y^2}{S_X^2/\sigma_X^2} \le d\right)$$

$$= P\left(c\,\frac{S_X^2}{S_Y^2} \le \frac{\sigma_X^2}{\sigma_Y^2} \le d\,\frac{S_X^2}{S_Y^2}\right).$$

Because of the limitations of Table VII, we generally let $c = F_{1-\alpha/2}(m-1, n-1) = 1/F_{\alpha/2}(n-1, m-1)$ and $d = F_{\alpha/2}(m-1, n-1)$. If s_x^2 and s_y^2 are the observed values of S_X^2 and S_Y^2, respectively, then

$$\left[\frac{1}{F_{\alpha/2}(n-1, m-1)}\frac{s_x^2}{s_y^2}, F_{\alpha/2}(m-1, n-1)\frac{s_x^2}{s_y^2}\right]$$

is a $100(1-\alpha)\%$ confidence interval for σ_X^2/σ_Y^2. By taking square roots of both endpoints, we would obtain a $100(1-\alpha)\%$ confidence interval for σ_X/σ_Y.

EXAMPLE 6.4-3 In Example 6.4-1, denote σ^2 by σ_X^2. In that example, $(n-1)s_x^2 = 12s^2 = 128.41$. Assume that the time in days required for the maturation of seeds of a species of Guardiola, both parents having broad leaves, is $N(\mu_Y, \sigma_Y^2)$. A random sample of size $m = 9$ seeds yielded $\bar{y} = 23.20$ and

$$8s_y^2 = \sum_{i=1}^{8}(y_i - \bar{y})^2 = 36.72.$$

A 98% confidence interval for σ_X^2/σ_Y^2 is given by

$$\left[\left(\frac{1}{5.67}\right)\frac{(128.41)/12}{(36.72)/8}, (4.50)\frac{(128.41)/12}{(36.72)/8}\right] = [0.41, 10.49]$$

because $F_{0.01}(12, 8) = 5.67$ and $F_{0.01}(8, 12) = 4.50$. It follows that a 98% confidence interval for σ_X/σ_Y is

$$[\sqrt{0.41}, \sqrt{10.49}] = [0.64, 3.24].$$

■

Although we are able to formally find a confidence interval for the ratio of two distribution variances or standard deviations, we should point out that these intervals are generally not too useful because they are often very wide. Moreover, they are not very robust. That is, the confidence coefficients are not very accurate if we deviate much from underlying normal distributions, because, in those instances, the distribution of $(n-1)S^2/\sigma^2$ could deviate greatly from $\chi^2(n-1)$. This same statement is not true for confidence intervals for μ or $\mu_X - \mu_Y$ based upon the sample means, because the sample means have approximate normal distributions. Hence, the confidence coefficients are reasonably accurate in the situations associated with means. Having said that, we do warn the reader that in cases which are highly skewed or have very heavy tails, there are better ways of finding confidence intervals for the "middles" than using the sample means. We consider a few of these later in the text.

EXERCISES

6.4-1. Let X equal the length (in centimeters) of a certain species of fish caught in the springtime. A random sample of $n = 13$ observations of X is

13.1	5.1	18.0	8.7	16.5	9.8	6.8
12.0	17.8	25.4	19.2	15.8	23.0	

(a) Give a point estimate of the standard deviation σ of this species of fish.

(b) Find a 95% confidence interval for σ.

6.4-2. A random sample of $n = 9$ wheels of cheese yielded the following weights in pounds, assumed to be $N(\mu, \sigma^2)$:

21.50	18.95	18.55	19.40	19.15
22.35	22.90	22.20	23.10	

(a) Give a point estimate of σ.
(b) Find a 95% confidence interval for σ.
(c) Find a 90% confidence interval for σ.

6.4-3. A student who works in a blood lab tested 25 men for cholesterol levels and found the following values:

164	272	261	248	235	192	203	278	268
230	242	305	286	310	345	289	326	
335	297	328	400	228	194	338	252	

Assume that these values represent observations of a random sample taken from $N(\mu, \sigma^2)$.

(a) Calculate the sample mean and sample variance for these data.
(b) Find a 90% confidence interval for σ^2.
(c) Find a 90% confidence interval for σ.
(d) Find a 90% confidence interval for σ that has minimum length.
(e) Does the assumption of normality seem to be valid?

6.4-4. The data in Exercise 6.2-12 that give results of a leakage test are repeated here:

3.1	3.3	4.5	2.8	3.5	3.5	3.7	4.2	3.9	3.3

Use these data to find a 95% confidence interval for

(a) σ^2.
(b) σ.
(c) σ having minimum length.

6.4-5. Let $X_1, X_2, X_3, \ldots, X_n$ be a random sample from $N(\mu, \sigma^2)$ with known mean μ. Describe how you would construct a confidence interval for the unknown variance σ^2.

HINT: Use the fact that $\sum_{i=1}^{n}(X_i - \mu)^2/\sigma^2$ is $\chi^2(n)$.

6.4-6. Let $X_1, X_2, \ldots, X_n$ be a random sample of size n from an exponential distribution with unknown mean of $\mu = \theta$.

(a) Show that the distribution of the random variable $W = (2/\theta)\sum_{i=1}^{n} X_i$ is $\chi^2(2n)$.
HINT: Find the moment-generating function of W.
(b) Use W to construct a $100(1 - \alpha)\%$ confidence interval for θ.
(c) If $n = 7$ and $\bar{x} = 93.6$, give the endpoints for a 90% confidence interval for the mean θ.

6.4-7. Let X equal the time in seconds between phone calls at Great Lakes Pizza Company. Sixteen observations of X are

82	42	185	66	384	27	334	545
650	127	35	45	285	133	120	471

(a) Assuming that X has an exponential distribution with mean θ, use Exercise 6.4-6 to construct a 95% confidence interval for θ.
(b) Calculate the values of $\bar{x}$ and s. Do they support the assumption that X has an exponential distribution?
(c) Construct a q–q plot or a box-and-whiskers display to confirm or deny the assumption that X has an exponential distribution.

6.4-8. In Exercise 3.4-10, data are given for the distances that two sets of snails move. Assume that those distances are observations of an exponential random variable.

(a) Use Exercise 6.4-6 to construct a 95% confidence interval for the mean distance traveled by the infected snails. HINT: Either estimate the chi-square values or use a computer program such as Minitab.
(b) Use Exercise 6.4-6 to construct a 95% confidence interval for the mean distance traveled by the control snails. HINT: Either estimate the chi-square values or use a computer program such as Minitab.

6.4-9. Let $X_1, X_2, \ldots, X_n$ be a random sample of size n from an exponential distribution. If n is sufficiently large, the distribution of

$$Z = \frac{\overline{X} - \theta}{\theta/\sqrt{n}}$$

is approximately $N(0,1)$. Thus,

$$P(-z_{\alpha/2} \le Z \le z_{\alpha/2}) \approx 1 - \alpha.$$

(a) Show that a solution of the inequality yields

$$\bar{x} \pm z_{\alpha/2}(\theta/\sqrt{n})$$

as endpoints for an approximate $1 - \alpha$ confidence interval for θ.
(b) Since θ is unknown, what are two possible statistics that could be used to estimate θ in this confidence interval?
(c) Show that an exact solution of the inequality for θ yields

$$\left[\frac{\bar{x}}{1 + z_{\alpha/2}/\sqrt{n}}, \frac{\bar{x}}{1 - z_{\alpha/2}/\sqrt{n}}\right]$$

as endpoints.

(d) Using the data in Exercise 6.4-7, compare the 95% confidence interval in that exercise with the approximate 95% confidence intervals in this exercise. Which of these intervals would you recommend and why?

6.4-10. Let X and Y equal the weights of a phosphorus-free laundry detergent in a "6-pound" box and a "12-pound" box, respectively. Assume that the distributions of X and Y are $N(\mu_X, \sigma_X^2)$ and $N(\mu_Y, \sigma_Y^2)$, respectively. A random sample of $n = 10$ observations of X yielded a sample mean of $\bar{x} = 6.10$ pounds with a sample variance of $s_x^2 = 0.0040$, while an independent random sample of $m = 9$ observations of Y yielded a sample mean of $\bar{y} = 12.10$ pounds with a sample variance of $s_y^2 = 0.0076$.

(a) Give a point estimate of σ_X^2/σ_Y^2.

(b) Find a 95% confidence interval for σ_X^2/σ_Y^2.

6.4-11. Let X and Y equal the number of milligrams of tar in filtered and unfiltered cigarettes, respectively. Assume that the distributions of X and Y are $N(\mu_X, \sigma_X^2)$ and $N(\mu_Y, \sigma_Y^2)$, respectively. A random sample of $n = 9$ observations of X was

0.9 1.1 0.1 0.7 0.3 0.9 0.8 1.0 0.4

and an independent random sample of $m = 11$ observations of Y was

1.5 0.9 1.6 0.5 1.4 1.9 1.0 1.2 1.3 1.6 2.1

(a) Give a point estimate of σ_X^2/σ_Y^2.

(b) Find a one-sided 95% confidence interval that is an upper bound for σ_X^2/σ_Y^2. Does this confidence interval include the number 1?

6.4-12. A candy maker produces mints that have a label weight of 20.4 grams. For quality assurance, $n = 16$ mints were selected at random from the Wednesday morning shift, resulting in the statistics $\bar{x} = 21.95$ grams and $s_x = 0.197$. On Wednesday afternoon $m = 13$ mints were selected at random, giving $\bar{y} = 21.88$ grams and $s_y = 0.318$. Find a 90% confidence interval for σ_X/σ_Y, the ratio of the standard deviations of the mints produced by the morning and by the afternoon shifts, respectively.

6.4-13. Let X and Y equal the concentration in parts per billion of chromium in the blood for healthy persons and for persons with a suspected disease, respectively. Assume that the distributions of X and Y are $N(\mu_X, \sigma_X^2)$ and $N(\mu_Y, \sigma_Y^2)$, respectively. Following are $n = 8$ observations of X:

15 23 12 18 9 28 11 10

Following are $m = 10$ observations of Y:

25 20 35 15 40 16 10 22 18 32

Use these observations of X and Y to

(a) Give a point estimate of σ_X^2/σ_Y^2.

(b) Find a one-sided 95% confidence interval that is an upper bound for σ_X^2/σ_Y^2.

6.4-14. Some nurses were interested in the effect of prenatal care on the birth weight of babies. Mothers were divided into two groups, and their babies' weights were compared. The birth weight, in ounces, of babies of mothers who had received five or fewer prenatal visits were

49	108	110	82	93	114	134
114	96	52	101	114	120	116

and the birth weights of babies of mothers who had received six or more prenatal visits were

133	108	93	119	119	98	106
87	153	116	129	97	110	131

Assuming that these are independent observations of X and Y that are $N(\mu_X, \sigma_X^2)$ and $N(\mu_Y, \sigma_Y^2)$, respectively, find a 95% confidence interval for

(a) σ_X^2/σ_Y^2.

(b) σ_X/σ_Y.

6.4-15. Using a random sample of size n from the normal distribution $N(\mu, \sigma^2)$, find the $100(1 - \alpha)\%$ confidence interval for μ of minimum length based on the statistic $T = (\overline{X} - \mu)/(S/\sqrt{n})$, where $\overline{X}$ and S^2 are the unbiased estimators of μ and σ^2, respectively.

HINT: (i) Show that

$$\begin{aligned}1 - \alpha &= P(a \le T \le b)\\ &= P[\overline{X} - b(S/\sqrt{n}\,) \le \mu \le \overline{X} - a(S/\sqrt{n}\,)]\end{aligned}$$

and (ii) the length of the resulting confidence interval is $L = (s/\sqrt{n}\,)(b - a)$. (iii) Minimize L subject to the condition $\int_a^b g(t)\,dt = 1 - \alpha$, where $g(t)$ is the p.d.f. of a t random variable with $r = n - 1$ degrees of freedom.

6.4-16. Let $X_1, X_2, \ldots, X_n$ be a random sample of size n from a normal distribution $N(\mu, \sigma^2)$. Select a and b so that

$$P\left(a \le \frac{(n-1)S^2}{\sigma^2} \le b\right) = 1 - \alpha.$$

So a $100(1 - \alpha)\%$ confidence interval for σ is $[\sqrt{(n-1)/b}\,s, \sqrt{(n-1)/a}\,s]$. Find values of a

and b that minimize the length of this confidence interval. That is, minimize

$$k = s\sqrt{n-1}\left(\frac{1}{\sqrt{a}} - \frac{1}{\sqrt{b}}\right)$$

under the restriction

$$G(b) - G(a) = \int_a^b g(u)\,du = 1 - \alpha,$$

where $G(u)$ and $g(u)$ are, respectively, the distribution function and p.d.f. of a $\chi^2(n-1)$ distribution. HINT: Due to the restriction, b is a function of a. In particular, by taking derivatives of the restricting equation with respect to a, show that $\dfrac{db}{da} = \dfrac{g(a)}{g(b)}$. Determine $\dfrac{dk}{da}$. By setting $\dfrac{dk}{da} = 0$, show that a and b must satisfy

$$a^{n/2}e^{-a/2} - b^{n/2}e^{-b/2} = 0.$$

This condition, along with the restriction, was used to calculate the values in Table X in the appendix.

6.4-17. In Section 6.3, confidence intervals were found for the difference of the means for two normal distributions. It was sometimes assumed that the variances were equal. Find point estimates and 90% confidence intervals for the ratios of the variances for the data in

(a) Exercise 6.3-14.
(b) Exercise 6.3-15.
(c) Exercise 6.3-16.

6.4-18. Find a 95% confidence interval for the ratio of the variances in

(a) Exercise 6.3-6,
(b) Exercise 6.3-7,
(c) Exercise 6.3-8.

6.4-19. Measurements in millimeters were made on a species of spider named *Sosippus floridanus* that are native to Florida. Nine female spiders and nine male spiders were used. The lengths of the female spiders are

11.06 13.87 12.93 15.08 17.82 14.14 12.26 17.82 20.17

The lengths of the male spiders are

12.26 11.66 12.53 13.00 11.79 12.46 10.65 10.39 12.26

Assume that these lengths are $N(\mu_X, \sigma_X^2)$ and $N(\mu_Y, \sigma_Y^2)$, respectively.

(a) Find point estimates for the sample variances for the female and the male spiders.
(b) Find a 95% confidence interval for the ratio of the variances.
(c) Is the assumption of normality valid? Why or why not?

6.5 CONFIDENCE INTERVALS FOR PROPORTIONS

We have suggested that the histogram is a good description of how the observations of a random sample are distributed. We might naturally inquire about the accuracy of those relative frequencies (or percentages) associated with the various classes. To illustrate, in Example 3.1-1 concerning the weights of $n = 40$ candy bars, we found that the relative frequency of the class interval (22.25, 23.15) was $8/40 = 0.20$, or 20%. If we think of this collection of 40 weights as a random sample observed from a larger population of candy bar weights, how close is 20% to the true percentage (or 0.20 to the true proportion) of weights in that class interval for the entire population of weights for this type of candy bar?

In considering this problem, we generalize it somewhat by treating the class interval (22.25, 23.15) as "success." That is, there is some true probability of success, p—namely, the proportion of the population in that interval. Let Y equal the frequency of measurements in the interval out of the n observations, so that (under the assumptions of independence and constant probability p) Y has the binomial distribution $b(n, p)$. Thus, the problem is to determine the accuracy of the relative frequency Y/n as an estimator of p. We solve this problem by finding, for the unknown p, a confidence interval based on Y/n.

In general, when observing n Bernoulli trials with probability p of success on each trial, we shall find a confidence interval for p based on Y/n, where Y is the number of successes and Y/n is an unbiased point estimator for p.

In Section 5.7, we noted that

$$\frac{Y - np}{\sqrt{np(1 - p)}} = \frac{(Y/n) - p}{\sqrt{p(1 - p)/n}}$$

has an approximate normal distribution $N(0,1)$, provided that n is large enough. This means that, for a given probability $1 - \alpha$, we can find a $z_{\alpha/2}$ in Table V in the appendix such that

$$P\left[-z_{\alpha/2} \le \frac{(Y/n) - p}{\sqrt{p(1 - p)/n}} \le z_{\alpha/2}\right] \approx 1 - \alpha. \tag{6.5-1}$$

If we proceed as we did when we found a confidence interval for μ in Section 6.2, we would obtain

$$P\left[\frac{Y}{n} - z_{\alpha/2}\sqrt{\frac{p(1 - p)}{n}} \le p \le \frac{Y}{n} + z_{\alpha/2}\sqrt{\frac{p(1 - p)}{n}}\right] \approx 1 - \alpha.$$

Unfortunately, the unknown parameter p appears in the endpoints of this inequality. There are two ways out of this dilemma. First, we could make an additional approximation, namely, replacing p with Y/n in $p(1 - p)/n$ in the endpoints. That is, if n is large enough, it is still true that

$$P\left[\frac{Y}{n} - z_{\alpha/2}\sqrt{\frac{(Y/n)(1 - Y/n)}{n}} \le p \le \frac{Y}{n} + z_{\alpha/2}\sqrt{\frac{(Y/n)(1 - Y/n)}{n}}\right] \approx 1 - \alpha.$$

Thus, for large n, if the observed Y equals y, then the interval

$$\left[\frac{y}{n} - z_{\alpha/2}\sqrt{\frac{(y/n)(1 - y/n)}{n}}, \frac{y}{n} + z_{\alpha/2}\sqrt{\frac{(y/n)(1 - y/n)}{n}}\right]$$

serves as an approximate $100(1 - \alpha)\%$ confidence interval for p. Frequently, this interval is written as

$$\frac{y}{n} \pm z_{\alpha/2}\sqrt{\frac{(y/n)(1 - y/n)}{n}} \tag{6.5-2}$$

for brevity. This formulation clearly notes, as does $\bar{x} \pm z_{\alpha/2}(\sigma/\sqrt{n})$ in Section 6.2, the reliability of the estimate y/n, namely, that we are $100(1 - \alpha)\%$ confident that p is within $z_{\alpha/2}\sqrt{(y/n)(1 - y/n)/n}$ of $\widehat{p} = y/n$.

A second way to solve for p in the inequality in Equation 6.5-1 is to note that

$$\frac{|Y/n - p|}{\sqrt{p(1 - p)/n}} \le z_{\alpha/2}$$

is equivalent to

$$H(p) = \left(\frac{Y}{n} - p\right)^2 - \frac{z_{\alpha/2}^2 p(1-p)}{n} \le 0. \tag{6.5-3}$$

But $H(p)$ is a quadratic expression in p. Thus, we can find those values of p for which $H(p) \le 0$ by finding the two zeros of $H(p)$. Letting $\widehat{p} = Y/n$ and $z_0 = z_{\alpha/2}$ in Equation 6.5-3, we have

$$H(p) = \left(1 + \frac{z_0^2}{n}\right)p^2 - \left(2\widehat{p} + \frac{z_0^2}{n}\right)p + \widehat{p}^{\,2}.$$

By the quadratic formula, the zeros of $H(p)$ are, after simplification,

$$\frac{\widehat{p} + z_0^2/(2n) \pm z_0\sqrt{\widehat{p}\,(1-\widehat{p}\,)/n + z_0^2/(4n^2)}}{1 + z_0^2/n}, \tag{6.5-4}$$

and these zeros give the endpoints for an approximate $100(1-\alpha)\%$ confidence interval for p. If n is large, $z_0^2/(2n)$, $z_0^2/(4n^2)$, and z_0^2/n are small. Thus, the confidence intervals given by Equation 6.5-2 and Equation 6.5-4 are approximately equal when n is large.

EXAMPLE 6.5-1 Let us return to the example of the histogram of the candy bar weights, Example 3.1-1, with $n = 40$ and $y/n = 8/40 = 0.2$. If $1 - \alpha = 0.90$, so that $z_{\alpha/2} = 1.645$, then, using Equation 6.5-2, we find that the endpoints

$$0.2 \pm 1.645\sqrt{\frac{(0.2)(0.8)}{40}}$$

serve as an approximate 90% confidence interval for the true fraction p. That is, [0.096, 0.304], which is the same as [9.6%, 30.4%], is an approximate 90% confidence interval for the percentage of weights of the entire population in the interval (22.25, 23.15). If we had used the endpoints given by Equation 6.5-4, the confidence interval would be [0.117, 0.321]. Because of the small sample size, there is a difference in the lengths of these intervals. If the sample size had been $n = 400$, the two 90% confidence intervals would have been [0.167, 0.233] and [0.169, 0.235], respectively, which differ very little. ■

EXAMPLE 6.5-2 In a certain political campaign, one candidate has a poll taken at random among the voting population. The results are that $y = 185$ out of $n = 351$ voters favor this candidate. Even though $y/n = 185/351 = 0.527$, should the candidate feel very confident of winning? From Equation 6.5-2, an approximate 95% confidence interval for the fraction p of the voting population who favor the candidate is

$$0.527 \pm 1.96\sqrt{\frac{(0.527)(0.473)}{351}}$$

or, equivalently, [0.475, 0.579]. Thus, there is a good possibility that p is less than 50%, and the candidate should certainly take this possibility into account in campaigning. ■

One-sided confidence intervals are sometimes appropriate for p. For example, we may be interested in an upper bound on the proportion of defectives in manufacturing some item. Or we may be interested in a lower bound on the proportion of voters who favor a particular candidate. The one-sided confidence interval for p given by

$$\left[0, \frac{y}{n} + z_\alpha\sqrt{\frac{y/n(1 - y/n)}{n}}\right]$$

provides an upper bound for p, while

$$\left[\frac{y}{n} - z_\alpha\sqrt{\frac{y/n(1 - y/n)}{n}}, 1\right]$$

provides a lower bound for p.

REMARK Sometimes the confidence intervals suggested here are not very close to having the stated confidence coefficient. This is particularly true if n is small or if one of Y or $n - Y$ is close to zero. It is obvious that something is wrong if $Y = 0$ or $n - Y = 0$, because the radical is then equal to zero.

It has been suggested (see, for example, Agresti and Coull) that we use $\widetilde{p} = (Y + 2)/(n + 4)$ as an estimator for p in those cases because the results are usually much better. It is true that $\widetilde{p}$ is a biased estimator of p, but we will see later that it is a certain kind of Bayes shrinkage estimator. In those cases in which n is small or Y or $n - Y$ is close to zero,

$$\widetilde{p} \pm z_{\alpha/2}\sqrt{\widetilde{p}(1 - \widetilde{p})/n} \tag{6.5-5}$$

provides a much better $100(1 - \alpha)\%$ confidence interval for p. A similar statement can be made about one-sided confidence intervals.

Look again at Equation 6.5-4. If we form a 95% confidence interval using this equation, we find that $z_0 = 1.96 \approx 2$. Thus, a 95% confidence interval is centered approximately at

$$\frac{\widehat{p} + z_0^2/(2n)}{1 + z_0^2/n} = \frac{y + z_0^2/2}{n + z_0^2} \approx \frac{y + 2}{n + 4}.$$

This result is consistent with Equation 6.5-5 for 95% confidence intervals. ■

EXAMPLE 6.5-3 Returning to the data in Example 6.5-1, and using Equation 6.5-5, we have $\widetilde{p} = (8 + 2)/(40 + 4) = 0.227$. Thus, a 90% confidence interval is

$$0.227 \pm 1.645\sqrt{\frac{(0.227)(0.773)}{40}},$$

or [0.118, 0.336]. If it had been true that $y = 80$ and $n = 400$, the confidence interval given by Equation 6.5-5 would have been [0.170, 0.236]. ■

Frequently, there are two (or more) possible independent ways of performing an experiment; suppose these have probabilities of success p_1 and p_2, respectively. Let

n_1 and n_2 be the number of independent trials associated with these two methods, and let us say that they result in Y_1 and Y_2 successes, respectively. In order to make a statistical inference about the difference $p_1 - p_2$, we proceed as follows.

Since the independent random variables Y_1/n_1 and Y_2/n_2 have respective means p_1 and p_2 and variances $p_1(1 - p_1)/n_1$ and $p_2(1 - p_2)/n_2$, we know from Section 5.4 that the difference $Y_1/n_1 - Y_2/n_2$ must have mean $p_1 - p_2$ and variance

$$\frac{p_1(1 - p_1)}{n_1} + \frac{p_2(1 - p_2)}{n_2}.$$

(Recall that the variances are added to get the variance of a difference of two independent random variables.) Moreover, the fact that Y_1/n_1 and Y_2/n_2 have approximate normal distributions would suggest that the difference

$$\frac{Y_1}{n_1} - \frac{Y_2}{n_2}$$

would have an approximate normal distribution with the above mean and variance. (See Theorem 5.5-1.) That is,

$$\frac{(Y_1/n_1) - (Y_2/n_2) - (p_1 - p_2)}{\sqrt{p_1(1 - p_1)/n_1 + p_2(1 - p_2)/n_2}}$$

has an approximate normal distribution $N(0,1)$. If we now replace p_1 and p_2 in the denominator of this ratio by Y_1/n_1 and Y_2/n_2, respectively, it is still true for large enough n_1 and n_2 that the new ratio will be approximately $N(0,1)$. Thus, for a given $1 - \alpha$, we can find $z_{\alpha/2}$ from Table V in the appendix, so that

$$P\left[-z_{\alpha/2} \le \frac{(Y_1/n_1) - (Y_2/n_2) - (p_1 - p_2)}{\sqrt{(Y_1/n_1)(1 - Y_1/n_1)/n_1 + (Y_2/n_2)(1 - Y_2/n_2)/n_2}} \le z_{\alpha/2}\right] \approx 1 - \alpha.$$

Once Y_1 and Y_2 are observed to be y_1 and y_2, respectively, this approximation can be solved to obtain an approximate $100(1 - \alpha)\%$ confidence interval

$$\frac{y_1}{n_1} - \frac{y_2}{n_2} \pm z_{\alpha/2}\sqrt{\frac{(y_1/n_1)(1 - y_1/n_1)}{n_1} + \frac{(y_2/n_2)(1 - y_2/n_2)}{n_2}}$$

for the unknown difference $p_1 - p_2$. Note again how this form indicates the reliability of the estimate $y_1/n_1 - y_2/n_2$ of the difference $p_1 - p_2$.

EXAMPLE 6.5-4 Two detergents were tested for their ability to remove stains of a certain type. An inspector judged the first one to be successful on 63 out of 91 independent trials and the second one to be successful on 42 out of 79 independent trials. The respective relative frequencies of success are 0.692 and 0.532. An approximate 90% confidence interval for the difference $p_1 - p_2$ of the two detergents is

$$0.692 - 0.532 \pm 1.645\sqrt{\frac{(0.692)(0.308)}{91} + \frac{(0.532)(0.468)}{79}}$$

or, equivalently, [0.038, 0.282]. Accordingly, since this interval does not include zero, it seems that the first detergent is definitely better than the second one for removing the type of stains in question. ■

EXERCISES

6.5-1. A machine shop manufactures toggle levers. A lever is flawed if a standard nut cannot be screwed onto the threads. Let p equal the proportion of flawed toggle levers that the shop manufactures. If there were 24 flawed levers out of a sample of 642 that were selected randomly from the production line,

(a) Give a point estimate of p.
(b) Use Equation 6.5-2 to find an approximate 95% confidence interval for p.
(c) Use Equation 6.5-4 to find an approximate 95% confidence interval for p.
(d) Use Equation 6.5-5 to find an approximate 95% confidence interval for p.
(e) Find a one-sided 95% confidence interval for p that provides an upper bound for p.

6.5-2. Let p equal the proportion of letters mailed in the Netherlands that are delivered the next day. Suppose that $y = 142$ out of a random sample of $n = 200$ letters were delivered the day after they were mailed.

(a) Give a point estimate of p.
(b) Use Equation 6.5-2 to find an approximate 90% confidence interval for p.
(c) Use Equation 6.5-4 to find an approximate 90% confidence interval for p.
(d) Use Equation 6.5-5 to find an approximate 90% confidence interval for p.
(e) Find a one-sided 90% confidence interval for p that provides a lower bound for p.

6.5-3. Let p equal the proportion of adult Americans who favor a law requiring a teenager to have her parents' consent before having an abortion. In a survey of 1000 adult Americans (conducted by *Time*/CNN and reported in *Time* on July 9, 1990), 690 said they favored such a law.

(a) Give a point estimate of p.
(b) Find an approximate 95% confidence interval for p.

6.5-4. Let p equal the proportion of Americans who favor the death penalty. If a random sample of $n = 1234$ Americans yielded $y = 864$ who favored the death penalty, find an approximate 95% confidence interval for p.

6.5-5. Let p equal the proportion of triathletes who suffered a training-related overuse injury during the past year. Out of 330 triathletes who responded to a survey, 167 indicated that they had suffered such an injury during the past year.

(a) Use these data to give a point estimate of p.
(b) Use these data to find an approximate 90% confidence interval for p.
(c) Do you think that the 330 triathletes who responded to the survey may be considered a random sample from the population of triathletes?

6.5-6. Let p equal the proportion of Americans who select jogging as one of their recreational activities. If 1497 out of a random sample of 5757 selected jogging, find an approximate 98% confidence interval for p.

6.5-7. In order to estimate the proportion, p, of a large class of college freshmen that had high school GPAs from 3.2 to 3.6, inclusive, a sample of $n = 50$ students was taken. It was found that $y = 9$ students fell into this interval.

(a) Give a point estimate of p.
(b) Use Equation 6.5-2 to find an approximate 95% confidence interval for p.
(c) Use Equation 6.5-4 to find an approximate 95% confidence interval for p.
(d) Use Equation 6.5-5 to find an approximate 95% confidence interval for p.

6.5-8. A proportion, p, that many public opinion polls estimate is the number of Americans who would say yes to the question, "If something were to happen to the President of the United States, do you think that the Vice President would be qualified to take over as President?" In one such random sample of 1022 adults, 388 said yes.

(a) On the basis of the given data, find a point estimate of p.
(b) Find an approximate 90% confidence interval for p.
(c) Give updated answers to this question if new poll results are available.

6.5-9. To obtain an estimate of the proportion, p, of New York City residents who feel that the quality of life in New York City has become worse in the past few years, a telephone poll by *Time*/CNN on August 2–5, 1990, revealed that 686 out of 1009 residents said that life has become worse.

(a) Give a point estimate of p.
(b) Find an approximate 98% confidence interval for p.

6.5-10. The January 17, 1994, issue of *Time* magazine reported that 58% of adult Americans said yes to the question "If you or your spouse were pregnant, would you want the unborn child tested for genetic defects?" These results were based on a telephone poll of 500 adult Americans. Let p equal the proportion of all adult Americans who would say yes to this question.

(a) Give the endpoints for a 90% confidence interval for p.

(b) The poll takers claimed that their sampling error was 4.5%. What is their confidence coefficient?

6.5-11. The January 29, 1996, issue of *Time* magazine reported that 48% of adult Americans "like the principle of a flat tax." It further claimed that this estimate had a sampling error of $\pm 3\%$. Let p equal the proportion of all adult Americans who like the principle of a flat tax.

(a) Give the endpoints for a 95% confidence interval for p, given that the sample size was $n = 800$.

(b) Given that the reported sampling error was $\pm 3\%$ with $n = 800$, what is *Time*'s confidence coefficient?

6.5-12. The March 29, 1993, issue of *Time* magazine reported the proportions of adult Americans who favor "stricter gun-control laws." A telephone poll of 800 adult Americans, of whom 374 were gun owners and 426 did not own guns, showed that 206 gun owners and 338 non–gun owners favored stricter gun-control laws. Let p_1 and p_2 be the respective proportions of gun owners and non–gun owners who favor stricter gun-control laws.

(a) Give point estimates of p_1 and p_2.

(b) Find a 95% confidence interval for $p_1 - p_2$.

6.5-13. In developing countries in Africa and the Americas, let p_1 and p_2 be the respective proportions of women with nutritional anemia. Find an approximate 90% confidence interval for $p_1 - p_2$, given that a random sample of $n_1 = 2100$ African women yielded $y_1 = 840$ with nutritional anemia and a random sample of $n_2 = 1900$ women from the Americas yielded $y_2 = 323$ women with nutritional anemia.

6.5-14. A candy manufacturer selects mints at random from the production line and weighs them. For one week, the day shift weighed $n_1 = 194$ mints and the night shift weighed $n_2 = 162$ mints. The numbers of these mints that weighed at most 21 grams was $y_1 = 28$ for the day shift and $y_2 = 11$ for the night shift. Let p_1 and p_2 denote the proportions of mints that weigh at most 21 grams for the day and night shifts, respectively.

(a) Give a point estimate of p_1.

(b) Give the endpoints for a 95% confidence interval for p_1.

(c) Give a point estimate of $p_1 - p_2$.

(d) Find a one-sided 95% confidence interval that gives a lower bound for $p_1 - p_2$.

6.5-15. Consider the following two groups of women; Group 1 consists of women who spend less than \$500 annually on clothes; group 2 comprises women who spend over \$1000 annually on clothes. Let p_1 and p_2 equal the proportions of women in these two groups, respectively, who believe that clothes are too expensive. If 1009 out of a random sample of 1230 women from group 1 and 207 out of a random sample 340 from group 2 believe that clothes are too expensive,

(a) Give a point estimate of $p_1 - p_2$.

(b) Find an approximate 95% confidence interval for $p_1 - p_2$.

6.5-16. For developing countries in Asia (excluding China) and Africa, let p_1 and p_2 be the respective proportions of preschool children with chronic malnutrition (stunting). If respective random samples of $n_1 = 1300$ and $n_2 = 1100$ yielded $y_1 = 520$ and $y_2 = 385$ children with chronic malnutrition, find an approximate 95% confidence interval for $p_1 - p_2$.

6.5-17. The following question was asked in a *Newsweek* poll: "Would you prefer to live in a neighborhood with mostly whites, with mostly blacks, or in a neighborhood mixed half and half?" Let p_1 and p_2 equal the proportion of black and white adult respondents, respectively, who prefer "half and half." If 207 out of 305 black adults and 291 out of 632 white adults prefer "half and half,"

(a) Give a point estimate of $p_1 - p_2$.

(b) Find an approximate one-sided 90% confidence interval that gives a lower bound for $p_1 - p_2$.

6.5-18. An environmental survey contained a question asking what respondents thought was the major cause of air pollution in this country, giving the choices "automobiles," "factories," and "incinerators." Two versions of the test, A and B, were used. Let p_A and p_B be the respective proportions of people using forms A and B who select "factories." If 170 out of 460 people who used version A chose "factories" and 141 out of 440 people who used version B chose "factories,"

(a) Find a 95% confidence interval for $p_A - p_B$.

(b) Do the versions seem to be consistent concerning this answer? Why or why not?

6.5-19. Let p_1 equal the proportion of 30-year-old men in the United States who weigh over 200 pounds, and let p_2 be the proportion of 30-year-old men in Vietnam who weigh over 200 pounds. Suppose that in a random sample of 766 Americans who were asked if they weighed more than 200 pounds, 586 responded yes, and in a random sample of 725 Vietnamese who were asked the same question, 357 responded yes.

(a) Give a point estimate for $p_1 - p_2$.

(b) Give the endpoints for a 95% confidence interval for $p_1 - p_2$.

6.6 SAMPLE SIZE

In statistical consulting, the first question frequently asked is "How large should the sample size be to estimate a mean?" In order to convince the inquirer that the answer will depend on the variation associated with the random variable under observation, the statistician could correctly respond, "Only one observation is needed, provided that the standard deviation of the distribution is zero." That is, if σ equals zero, then the value of that one observation would necessarily equal the unknown mean of the distribution. This, of course, is an extreme case and one that is not met in practice; however, it should help convince people that the smaller the variance, the smaller is the sample size needed to achieve a given degree of accuracy. This assertion will become clearer as we consider several examples. Let us begin with a problem that involves a statistical inference about the unknown mean of a distribution.

EXAMPLE 6.6-1 A mathematics department wishes to evaluate a new method of teaching calculus with a computer. At the end of the course, the evaluation will be made on the basis of scores of the participating students on a standard test. There is particular interest in estimating μ, the mean score for students taking the course. Thus, there is a desire to determine the number of students, n, who are to be selected at random from a larger group of students to take the course. Since new computing equipment must be purchased, the department cannot afford to let all of the school's students take calculus the new way. In addition, some of the staff question the value of this approach and hence do not want to expose every student to this new procedure. So, let us find the sample size n such that we are fairly confident that $\overline{x} \pm 1$ contains the unknown test mean μ. From past experience, it is believed that the standard deviation associated with this type of test is about 15. (The mean is also known when students take the standard calculus course.) Accordingly, using the fact that the sample mean of the test scores, $\overline{X}$, is approximately $N(\mu, \sigma^2/n)$, we see that the interval given by $\overline{x} \pm 1.96(15/\sqrt{n}\,)$ will serve as an approximate 95% confidence interval for μ. That is, we want

$$1.96\left(\frac{15}{\sqrt{n}}\right) = 1$$

or, equivalently,

$$\sqrt{n} = 29.4 \qquad \text{and thus} \qquad n \approx 864.36,$$

or $n = 865$ because n must be an integer. ■

It is quite likely that, in the preceding example, it had not been anticipated that as many as 865 students would be needed in this study. If that is the case, the statistician must discuss with those involved in the experiment whether or not the accuracy and the confidence level could be relaxed some. For example, rather than requiring $\overline{x} \pm 1$ to be a 95% confidence interval for μ, possibly $\overline{x} \pm 2$ would be a satisfactory 80%

one. If this modification is acceptable, we now have

$$1.282\left(\frac{15}{\sqrt{n}}\right) = 2$$

or, equivalently,

$$\sqrt{n} = 9.615 \qquad \text{so that} \qquad n \approx 92.4.$$

Since n must be an integer, we would probably use 93 in practice. Most likely, the persons involved in the project would find that a more reasonable sample size. Of course, any sample size greater than 93 could be used. Then either the length of the confidence interval could be decreased from $\bar{x} \pm 2$, or the confidence coefficient could be increased from 80%, or a combination of both approaches could be taken. Also, since there might be some question as to whether the standard deviation σ actually equals 15, the sample standard deviation s would no doubt be used in the construction of the interval. For instance, suppose that the sample characteristics observed are

$$n = 145, \qquad \bar{x} = 77.2, \qquad s = 13.2;$$

then

$$\bar{x} \pm \frac{1.282s}{\sqrt{n}}, \qquad \text{or} \qquad 77.2 \pm 1.41,$$

provides an approximate 80% confidence interval for μ.

In general, if we want the $100(1 - \alpha)\%$ confidence interval for μ, $\bar{x} \pm z_{\alpha/2}(\sigma/\sqrt{n}\,)$, to be no longer than that given by $\bar{x} \pm \varepsilon$, then the sample size n is the solution of

$$\varepsilon = \frac{z_{\alpha/2}\sigma}{\sqrt{n}}, \qquad \text{where} \qquad \Phi(z_{\alpha/2}) = 1 - \frac{\alpha}{2}.$$

That is,

$$n = \frac{z_{\alpha/2}^2\sigma^2}{\varepsilon^2}, \tag{6.6-1}$$

where it is assumed that σ^2 is known. We sometimes call $\varepsilon = z_{\alpha/2}(\sigma/\sqrt{n}\,)$ the **maximum error of the estimate**. If the experimenter has no idea about the value of σ^2, it may be necessary to first take a preliminary sample to estimate σ^2.

The type of statistic we see most often in newspapers and magazines is an estimate of a proportion p. We might, for example, want to know the percentage of the labor force that is unemployed or the percentage of voters favoring a certain candidate. Sometimes, extremely important decisions are made on the basis of these estimates. If this is the case, we would most certainly desire short confidence intervals for p with large confidence coefficients. We recognize that these conditions will require a large sample size. If, to the contrary, the fraction p being estimated is not too important, an estimate associated with a longer confidence interval with a smaller confidence coefficient is satisfactory, and in that case a smaller sample size can be used.

EXAMPLE 6.6-2 Suppose we know that the unemployment rate has been about 8% (0.08). However, we wish to update our estimate in order to make an important decision about the national economic policy. Accordingly, let us say we wish to be 99% confident that the new estimate of p is within 0.001 of the true p. If we assume Bernoulli trials (an assumption that might be questioned), the relative frequency y/n, based upon a large sample size n, provides the approximate 99% confidence interval:

$$\frac{y}{n} \pm 2.576\sqrt{\frac{(y/n)(1 - y/n)}{n}}.$$

Although we do not know y/n exactly before sampling, since y/n will be near 0.08 we do know that

$$2.576\sqrt{\frac{(y/n)(1 - y/n)}{n}} \approx 2.576\sqrt{\frac{(0.08)(0.92)}{n}},$$

and we want this number to equal 0.001. That is,

$$2.576\sqrt{\frac{(0.08)(0.92)}{n}} = 0.001$$

or, equivalently,

$$\sqrt{n} = 2576\sqrt{0.0736}, \qquad \text{and then} \qquad n \approx 488{,}394.$$

That is, under our assumptions, such a sample size is needed in order to achieve the reliability and the accuracy desired. Because n is so large, we would probably be willing to increase the error, say, to 0.01, and perhaps reduce the confidence level to 98%. In that case,

$$\sqrt{n} = (2.326/0.01)\sqrt{0.0736} \qquad \text{and} \qquad n \approx 3{,}982,$$

which is a more reasonable sample size. ■

From the preceding example, we hope that the student will recognize how important it is to know the sample size (or the length of the confidence interval and the confidence coefficient) before he or she can place much weight on a statement such as "Fifty-one percent of the voters seem to favor candidate A, 46% favor candidate B, and 3% are undecided." Is this statement based on a sample of 100 or 2000 or 10,000 voters? If we assume Bernoulli trials, the approximate 95% confidence intervals for the fraction of voters favoring candidate A in these cases are, respectively, [0.41, 0.61], [0.49, 0.53], and [0.50, 0.52]. Quite obviously, the first interval, with $n = 100$, does not assure candidate A of the support of at least half the voters, whereas the interval with $n = 10{,}000$ is more convincing.

In general, to find the required sample size to estimate p, recall that the point estimate of p is $\widehat{p} = y/n$ and an approximate $1 - \alpha$ confidence interval for p is

$$\widehat{p} \pm z_{\alpha/2}\sqrt{\frac{\widehat{p}(1 - \widehat{p})}{n}}.$$

Suppose we want an estimate of p that is within ε of the unknown p with $100(1 - \alpha)\%$ confidence, where $\varepsilon = z_{\alpha/2}\sqrt{\widehat{p}(1 - \widehat{p})/n}$ is the **maximum error of the point estimate** $\widehat{p} = y/n$. Since $\widehat{p}$ is unknown before the experiment is run, we cannot use the value of $\widehat{p}$ in our determination of n. However, if it is known that p is about equal to p^*, the necessary sample size n is the solution of

$$\varepsilon = \frac{z_{\alpha/2}\sqrt{p^*(1 - p^*)}}{\sqrt{n}}.$$

That is,

$$n = \frac{z_{\alpha/2}^2 p^*(1 - p^*)}{\varepsilon^2}. \tag{6.6-2}$$

Often, however, we do not have a strong prior idea about p, as we did in Example 6.6-2 about the rate of unemployment. It is interesting to observe that no matter what value p takes between 0 and 1, it is always true that $p^*(1 - p^*) \le 1/4$. Hence,

$$n = \frac{z_{\alpha/2}^2 p^*(1 - p^*)}{\varepsilon^2} \le \frac{z_{\alpha/2}^2}{4\varepsilon^2}.$$

Thus, if we want the $100(1 - \alpha)\%$ confidence interval for p to be no longer than $y/n \pm \varepsilon$, a solution for n that provides this protection is

$$n = \frac{z_{\alpha/2}^2}{4\varepsilon^2}. \tag{6.6-3}$$

REMARK Up to this point in the text, we have used the "hat" ($\widehat{\ }$) notation to indicate an estimator, as in $\widehat{p} = Y/n$ and $\widehat{\mu} = \overline{X}$. Note, however, that in the previous discussion we used $\widehat{p} = y/n$, an estimate of p. Occasionally, statisticians find it convenient to use the "hat" notation for an estimate as well as an estimator. It is usually clear from the context which is being used. ■

EXAMPLE 6.6-3 A possible gubernatorial candidate wants to assess initial support among the voters before making an announcement about her candidacy. If the fraction p of voters who are favorable, without any advance publicity, is around 0.15, the candidate will enter the race. From a poll of n voters selected at random, the candidate would like the estimate y/n to be within 0.03 of p. That is, the decision will be based on a 95% confidence interval of the form $y/n \pm 0.03$. Since the candidate has no idea about the magnitude of p, a consulting statistician formulates the equation

$$n = \frac{(1.96)^2}{4(0.03)^2} = 1067.11.$$

Thus, the sample size should be around 1068 to achieve the desired reliability and accuracy. Suppose that 1068 voters around the state were selected at random and interviewed and $y = 214$ express support for the candidate. Then $\widehat{p} = 214/1068 = 0.20$ is a point estimate of p, and an approximate 95% confidence interval for p is

$$0.20 \pm 1.96\sqrt{(0.20)(0.80)/n}, \qquad \text{or} \qquad 0.20 \pm 0.024.$$

That is, we are 95% confident that p belongs to the interval [0.176, 0.224]. On the basis of this sample, the candidate decided to run for office. Note that, for a confidence coefficient of 95%, we found a sample size so that the maximum error of the estimate would be 0.03. From the data that were collected, the maximum error of the estimate is only 0.024. We ended up with a smaller error because we found the sample size assuming that $p = 0.50$ while, in fact, p is closer to 0.20. ■

Suppose that you want to estimate the proportion p of a student body that favors a new policy. How large should the sample be? If p is close to 1/2 and you want to be 95% confident that the maximum error of the estimate is $\varepsilon = 0.02$, then

$$n = \frac{(1.96)^2}{4(0.02)^2} = 2401.$$

Such a sample size makes sense at a large university. However, if you are a student at a small college, the entire enrollment could be less than 2401. Thus, we now give a procedure that can be used to determine the sample size when the population is small relative to the desired sample size.

Let N equal the size of a population, and assume that N_1 individuals in the population have a certain characteristic C (e.g., favor a new policy). Let $p = N_1/N$, the proportion with this characteristic. Then $1 - p = 1 - N_1/N$. If we take a sample of size n without replacement, then X, the number of observations with the characteristic C, has a hypergeometric distribution. The mean and variance of X are, respectively,

$$\mu = n\left(\frac{N_1}{N}\right) = np$$

and

$$\sigma^2 = n\left(\frac{N_1}{N}\right)\left(1 - \frac{N_1}{N}\right)\left(\frac{N - n}{N - 1}\right) = np(1 - p)\left(\frac{N - n}{N - 1}\right).$$

The mean and variance of X/n are, respectively,

$$E\left(\frac{X}{n}\right) = \frac{\mu}{n} = p$$

and

$$\operatorname{Var}\left(\frac{X}{n}\right) = \frac{\sigma^2}{n^2} = \frac{p(1 - p)}{n}\left(\frac{N - n}{N - 1}\right).$$

To find an approximate confidence interval for p, we can use the normal approximation:

$$P\left[-z_{\alpha/2} \le \frac{(X/n) - p}{\sqrt{\dfrac{p(1 - p)}{n}\left(\dfrac{N - n}{N - 1}\right)}} \le z_{\alpha/2}\right] \approx 1 - \alpha.$$

Thus, $1 - \alpha \approx$

$$P\left[\frac{X}{n} - z_{\alpha/2}\sqrt{\frac{p(1 - p)}{n}\left(\frac{N - n}{N - 1}\right)} \le p \le \frac{X}{n} + z_{\alpha/2}\sqrt{\frac{p(1 - p)}{n}\left(\frac{N - n}{N - 1}\right)}\right].$$

Replacing p under the radical with $\widehat{p} = x/n$, we find that an approximate $1 - \alpha$ confidence interval for p is

$$\widehat{p} \pm z_{\alpha/2}\sqrt{\frac{\widehat{p}(1 - \widehat{p})}{n}\left(\frac{N - n}{N - 1}\right)}.$$

This is similar to the confidence interval for p when the distribution of X is $b(n, p)$. If N is large relative to n, then

$$\frac{N - n}{N - 1} = \frac{1 - n/N}{1 - 1/N} \approx 1,$$

so in this case the two intervals are essentially equal.

Suppose now that we are interested in determining the sample size n that is required to have $1 - \alpha$ confidence that the maximum error of the estimate of p is ε. We let

$$\varepsilon = z_{\alpha/2}\sqrt{\frac{p(1 - p)}{n}\left(\frac{N - n}{N - 1}\right)}$$

and solve for n. After some simplification, we obtain

$$\begin{aligned} n &= \frac{Nz_{\alpha/2}^2 p(1 - p)}{(N - 1)\varepsilon^2 + z_{\alpha/2}^2 p(1 - p)} \\ &= \frac{z_{\alpha/2}^2 p(1 - p)/\varepsilon^2}{\dfrac{N - 1}{N} + \dfrac{z_{\alpha/2}^2 p(1 - p)/\varepsilon^2}{N}}. \end{aligned}$$

If we let

$$m = \frac{z_{\alpha/2}^2 p^*(1 - p^*)}{\varepsilon^2},$$

which is the n value given by Equation 6.6-2, then we choose

$$n = \frac{m}{1 + \dfrac{m - 1}{N}}$$

for our sample size n.

If we know nothing about p, we set $p^* = 1/2$ to determine m. For example, if the size of the student body is $N = 4000$ and $1 - \alpha = 0.95$, $\varepsilon = 0.02$, and we let $p^* = 1/2$, then $m = 2401$ and

$$n = \frac{2401}{1 + 2400/4000} = 1501,$$

rounded up to the nearest integer. Thus, we would sample approximately 37.5% of the student body.

EXAMPLE 6.6-4 Suppose that a college of $N = 3000$ students is interested in assessing student support for a new form for teacher evaluation. To estimate the proportion p in favor of the new form, how large a sample is required so that the maximum error of the estimate of p is $\varepsilon = 0.03$ with 95% confidence? If we assume that p is completely unknown, we use $p^* = 1/2$ to obtain

$$m = \frac{(1.96)^2}{4(0.03)^2} = 1068,$$

rounded up to the nearest integer. Thus, the desired sample size is

$$n = \frac{1068}{1 + 1067/3000} = 788,$$

rounded up to the nearest integer. ■

EXERCISES

6.6-1. Let X equal the tarsus length for a male grackle. Assume that the distribution of X is $N(\mu, 4.84)$. Find the sample size n that is needed so that we are 95% confident that the maximum error of the estimate of μ is 0.4.

6.6-2. Let X equal the excess weight of soap in a "1000-gram" bottle. Assume that the distribution of X is $N(\mu, 169)$. What sample size is required so that we have 95% confidence that the maximum error of the estimate of μ is 1.5?

6.6-3. A company packages powdered soap in "6-pound" boxes. The sample mean and standard deviation of the soap in these boxes are currently 6.09 pounds and 0.02 pound, respectively. If the mean fill can be lowered by 0.01 pound, \$14,000 would be saved per year. Adjustments were made in the filling equipment, but it can be assumed that the standard deviation remains unchanged.

(a) How large a sample is needed so that the maximum error of the estimate of the new μ is $\varepsilon = 0.001$ with 90% confidence?

(b) A random sample of size $n = 1219$ yielded $\bar{x} = 6.048$ and $s = 0.022$. Calculate a 90% confidence interval for μ.

(c) Estimate the savings per year with these new adjustments.

(d) Estimate the proportion of boxes that will now weigh less than 6 pounds.

6.6-4. Measurements of the length in centimeters of $n = 29$ fish (species nezumia) yielded an average length of $\bar{x} = 16.82$ and $s^2 = 34.9$. Determine the size of a new sample so that $\bar{x} \pm 0.5$ is an approximate 95% confidence interval for μ.

6.6-5. A quality engineer wanted to be 98% confident that the maximum error of the estimate of the mean strength, μ, of the left hinge on a vanity cover molded by a machine is 0.25. A preliminary sample of size $n = 32$ parts yielded a sample mean of $\bar{x} = 35.68$ and a standard deviation of $s = 1.723$.

(a) How large a sample is required?

(b) Does this seem to be a reasonable sample size? (Note that destructive testing is needed to obtain the data.)

6.6-6. A manufacturer sells a light bulb that has a mean life of 1450 hours with a standard deviation of 33.7 hours. A new manufacturing process is being tested, and there is interest in knowing the mean life μ of the new bulbs. How large a sample is required so that $\bar{x} \pm 5$ is a 95% confidence interval for μ? You may assume that the change in the standard deviation is minimal.

6.6-7. For a public opinion poll for a close presidential election, let p denote the proportion of voters who favor candidate A. How large a sample should be taken if we want the maximum error of the estimate of p to be equal to

(a) 0.03 with 95% confidence?

(b) 0.02 with 95% confidence?

(c) 0.03 with 90% confidence?

6.6-8. Let p equal the proportion of all college and university students who would say yes to the question, "Would you drink from the same glass as your friend if you suspected that this friend were an AIDS virus carrier?" Find the sample size required to be 95% confident that the maximum error of the estimate of p is 0.025. (For your information, it was reported in *Sociology and Social Research* **72**, 2 [January 1988] that 30 out of 375 San Diego State University students answered yes to this question.)

6.6-9. A die has been loaded to change the probability of rolling a 6. In order to estimate p, the new probability of rolling a 6, how many times must the die be rolled so that we are 99% confident that the maximum error of the estimate of p is $\varepsilon = 0.02$?

6.6-10. Some college professors and students examined 137 Canadian geese for patent schistosome in the year they hatched. Of these 137 birds, 54 were infected. The professors and students were interested in estimating p, the proportion of infected birds of this type. For future studies, determine the sample size n so that the estimate of p is within $\varepsilon = 0.04$ of the unknown p with 90% confidence.

6.6-11. According to the Department of Health Care of the Elderly at Sherwood Hospital, Nottingham, England, only 25% of the patients who were using canes had canes of the correct length. Suppose that you were interested in estimating the proportion p of Americans who used canes of the correct length. How large a sample is required so that, with 95% confidence, the maximum error of the estimate of p is 0.04?

6.6-12. A seed distributor claims that 80% of its beet seeds will germinate. How many seeds must be tested for germination in order to estimate p, the true proportion that will germinate, so that the maximum error of the estimate is $\varepsilon = 0.03$ with 90% confidence?

6.6-13. Some dentists were interested in studying the fusion of embryonic rat palates by a standard transplantation technique. When no treatment is used, the probability of fusion equals approximately 0.89. The dentists would like to estimate p, the probability of fusion, when vitamin A is lacking.

(a) How large a sample n of rat embryos is needed for $y/n \pm 0.10$ to be a 95% confidence interval for p?

(b) If $y = 44$ out of $n = 60$ palates showed fusion, give a 95% confidence interval for p.

6.6-14. Let p equal the proportion of New York City residents who feel that the quality of life in New York City has become worse in the past few years. To update the estimate given in Exercise 6.5-9, how large a sample is required to be 98% confident that the maximum error of the estimate of p is 0.025?

6.6-15. Let p equal the proportion of triathletes who suffered a training-related overuse injury during the past year. (See Exercise 6.5-5.) How large a sample would be required to estimate p so that the maximum error of the estimate of p is 0.04 with 95% confidence?

6.6-16. Let p equal the proportion of college students who favor a new policy for alcohol consumption on campus. How large a sample is required to estimate p so that the maximum error of the estimate of p is 0.04 with 95% confidence when the size of the student body is

(a) $N = 1500$?

(b) $N = 15{,}000$?

(c) $N = 25{,}000$?

6.6-17. Out of 1000 welds that have been made on a tower, it is suspected that 15% are defective. To estimate p, the proportion of defective welds, how many welds must be inspected to have approximately 95% confidence that the maximum error of the estimate of p is 0.04?

6.6-18. If Y_1/n and Y_2/n are the respective independent relative frequencies of success associated with the two binomial distributions $b(n, p_1)$ and $b(n, p_2)$, compute n such that the approximate probability that the random interval $Y_1/n - Y_2/n \pm 0.05$ covers $p_1 - p_2$ is at least 0.80. HINT: Take $p_1^* = p_2^* = 1/2$ to provide an upper bound for n.

6.6-19. If $\overline{X}$ and $\overline{Y}$ are the respective means of two independent random samples of the same size n, find n if we want $\overline{x} - \overline{y} \pm 4$ to be a 90% confidence interval for $\mu_X - \mu_Y$ if the standard deviations are known to be $\sigma_X = 15$ and $\sigma_Y = 25$.

6.7 A SIMPLE REGRESSION PROBLEM

There is often interest in the relation between two variables—for example, a student's scholastic aptitude test score in mathematics and this same student's grade in calculus. Frequently, one of these variables, say, x, is known in advance of the other, so there is interest in predicting a future random variable Y. Since Y is a random variable, we cannot predict its future observed value $Y = y$ with certainty. Let us first concentrate on the problem of estimating the mean of Y—that is, $E(Y)$. Now, $E(Y)$ is usually a function of x. For example, in our illustration with the calculus grade, say, Y, we would expect $E(Y)$ to increase with increasing mathematics aptitude score x. Sometimes $E(Y) = \mu(x)$ is assumed to be of a given form, such as linear, quadratic, or exponential; that is, $\mu(x)$ could be assumed to be equal to $\alpha + \beta x$, $\alpha + \beta x + \gamma x^2$, or $\alpha e^{\beta x}$. To estimate $E(Y) = \mu(x)$, or, equivalently, the parameters α, β, and γ, we observe the random variable Y for each of n different values of x—say, $x_1, x_2, \ldots, x_n$. Once the n independent experiments have been performed, we have n pairs of known numbers $(x_1, y_1), (x_2, y_2), \ldots, (x_n, y_n)$. These pairs are then used to estimate the mean $E(Y)$. Problems like this are often classified under **regression** because $E(Y) = \mu(x)$ is frequently called a regression curve.

REMARK A model for the mean that is of the form $\alpha + \beta x + \gamma x^2$ is called a linear model because it is linear in the parameters, α, β, and γ. Thus, $\alpha e^{\beta x}$ is not a linear model, because it is not linear in α and β. ■

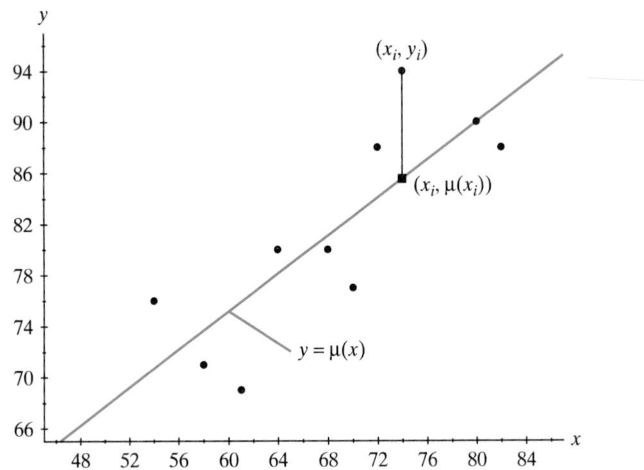

FIGURE 6.7-1: Scatter plot and least squares regression line

Let us begin with the case in which $E(Y) = \mu(x)$ is a linear function. The data points are $(x_1, y_1), (x_2, y_2), \ldots, (x_n, y_n)$, so the first problem is that of fitting a straight line to the set of data. (See Figure 6.7-1.) In addition to assuming that the mean of Y is a linear function, we assume that, for a particular value of x, the value of Y will differ from its mean by a random amount ε. We further assume that the distribution of ε is $N(0, \sigma^2)$. So we have, for our linear model,

$$Y_i = \alpha_1 + \beta x_i + \varepsilon_i,$$

where ε_i, for $i = 1, 2, \ldots, n$, are independent and $N(0, \sigma^2)$.

We shall now find point estimates for α_1, β, and σ^2. For convenience, we let $\alpha_1 = \alpha - \beta\bar{x}$, so that

$$Y_i = \alpha + \beta(x_i - \bar{x}) + \varepsilon_i, \text{ where } \bar{x} = \frac{1}{n}\sum_{i=1}^{n} x_i.$$

Then Y_i is equal to a constant, $\alpha + \beta(x_i - \bar{x})$, plus a normal random variable ε_i. Hence, $Y_1, Y_2, \ldots, Y_n$ are mutually independent normal variables with respective means $\alpha + \beta(x_i - \bar{x})$, $i = 1, 2, \ldots, n$, and unknown variance σ^2. Their joint p.d.f. is therefore the product of the individual probability density functions; that is, the likelihood function equals

$$\begin{aligned} L(\alpha, \beta, \sigma^2) &= \prod_{i=1}^{n} \frac{1}{\sqrt{2\pi\sigma^2}} \exp\left\{-\frac{[y_i - \alpha - \beta(x_i - \bar{x})]^2}{2\sigma^2}\right\} \\ &= \left(\frac{1}{2\pi\sigma^2}\right)^{n/2} \exp\left\{-\frac{\sum_{i=1}^{n}[y_i - \alpha - \beta(x_i - \bar{x})]^2}{2\sigma^2}\right\}. \end{aligned}$$

To maximize $L(\alpha, \beta, \sigma^2)$ or, equivalently, to minimize

$$-\ln L(\alpha, \beta, \sigma^2) = \frac{n}{2}\ln(2\pi\sigma^2) + \frac{\sum_{i=1}^{n}[y_i - \alpha - \beta(x_i - \bar{x})]^2}{2\sigma^2},$$

we must select α and β to minimize

$$H(\alpha, \beta) = \sum_{i=1}^{n}[y_i - \alpha - \beta(x_i - \bar{x})]^2.$$

Since $|y_i - \alpha - \beta(x_i - \bar{x})| = |y_i - \mu(x_i)|$ is the vertical distance from the point (x_i, y_i) to the line $y = \mu(x)$, we note that $H(\alpha, \beta)$ represents the sum of the squares of those distances. Thus, selecting α and β so that the sum of the squares is minimized means that we are fitting the straight line to the data by the **method of least squares**.

To minimize $H(\alpha, \beta)$, we find the two first partial derivatives

$$\frac{\partial H(\alpha, \beta)}{\partial \alpha} = 2\sum_{i=1}^{n}[y_i - \alpha - \beta(x_i - \bar{x})](-1)$$

and

$$\frac{\partial H(\alpha, \beta)}{\partial \beta} = 2\sum_{i=1}^{n}[y_i - \alpha - \beta(x_i - \bar{x})][-(x_i - \bar{x})].$$

Setting $\partial H(\alpha, \beta)/\partial \alpha = 0$, we obtain

$$\sum_{i=1}^{n} y_i - n\alpha - \beta\sum_{i=1}^{n}(x_i - \bar{x}) = 0.$$

Since

$$\sum_{i=1}^{n}(x_i - \bar{x}) = 0,$$

we have

$$\sum_{i=1}^{n} y_i - n\alpha = 0;$$

thus,

$$\widehat{\alpha} = \overline{Y}.$$

With α replaced by $\bar{y}$, the equation $\partial H(\alpha, \beta)/\partial \beta = 0$ yields,

$$\sum_{i=1}^{n}(y_i - \bar{y})(x_i - \bar{x}) - \beta\sum_{i=1}^{n}(x_i - \bar{x})^2 = 0$$

or, equivalently,

$$\widehat{\beta} = \frac{\sum_{i=1}^{n}(Y_i - \overline{Y})(x_i - \bar{x})}{\sum_{i=1}^{n}(x_i - \bar{x})^2} = \frac{\sum_{i=1}^{n} Y_i(x_i - \bar{x})}{\sum_{i=1}^{n}(x_i - \bar{x})^2}.$$

Hence, to find the mean line of best fit, $\mu(x) = \alpha + \beta(x_i - \bar{x})$, we use

$$\widehat{\alpha} = \bar{y} \tag{6.7-1}$$

and

$$\widehat{\beta} = \frac{\sum_{i=1}^{n} y_i(x_i - \bar{x})}{\sum_{i=1}^{n}(x_i - \bar{x})^2} = \frac{\sum_{i=1}^{n} x_i y_i - \left(\frac{1}{n}\right)\left(\sum_{i=1}^{n} x_i\right)\left(\sum_{i=1}^{n} y_i\right)}{\sum_{i=1}^{n} x_i^2 - \left(\frac{1}{n}\right)\left(\sum_{i=1}^{n} x_i\right)^2}. \tag{6.7-2}$$

To find the maximum likelihood estimator of σ^2, consider the partial derivative

$$\frac{\partial[-\ln L(\alpha, \beta, \sigma^2)]}{\partial(\sigma^2)} = \frac{n}{2\sigma^2} - \frac{\sum_{i=1}^{n}[y_i - \alpha - \beta(x_i - \bar{x})]^2}{2(\sigma^2)^2}.$$

Setting this equal to zero and replacing α and β by their solutions $\widehat{\alpha}$ and $\widehat{\beta}$, we obtain

$$\widehat{\sigma^2} = \frac{1}{n}\sum_{i=1}^{n}[Y_i - \widehat{\alpha} - \widehat{\beta}(x_i - \bar{x})]^2. \tag{6.7-3}$$

A formula that is useful in calculating $n\widehat{\sigma^2}$ is

$$n\widehat{\sigma^2} = \sum_{i=1}^{n} y_i^2 - \frac{1}{n}\left(\sum_{i=1}^{n} y_i\right)^2 - \widehat{\beta}\sum_{i=1}^{n} x_i y_i + \widehat{\beta}\left(\frac{1}{n}\right)\left(\sum_{i=1}^{n} x_i\right)\left(\sum_{i=1}^{n} y_i\right). \tag{6.7-4}$$

Note that the summand in Equation 6.7-3 for $\widehat{\sigma^2}$ is the square of the difference between the value of Y_i and the predicted mean of Y_i. Let $\widehat{Y_i} = \widehat{\alpha} + \widehat{\beta}(x_i - \bar{x})$, the predicted mean value of Y_i. The difference

$$Y_i - \widehat{Y_i} = Y_i - \widehat{\alpha} - \widehat{\beta}(x_i - \bar{x})$$

is called the ith **residual**, $i = 1, 2, \ldots, n$. The maximum likelihood estimate of σ^2 is then the sum of the squares of the residuals divided by n. It should always be true that the sum of the residuals is equal to zero. However, in practice, due to rounding off, the sum of the observed residuals, $y_i - \widehat{y_i}$, sometimes differs slightly from zero. A graph of the residuals plotted as a scatter plot of the points x_i, $y_i - \widehat{y_i}$, $i = 1, 2, \ldots, n$, can show whether or not linear regression provides the best fit.

EXAMPLE 6.7-1 The data plotted in Figure 6.7-1 are 10 pairs of test scores of 10 students in a psychology class, x being the score on a preliminary test and y the score on the final examination. The values of x and y are shown in Table 6.7-1. The sums that are needed to calculate estimates of the parameters are also given. Of course, the estimates of α and β have to be found before the residuals can be calculated.

Thus, $\widehat{\alpha} = 813/10 = 81.3$, and

$$\widehat{\beta} = \frac{56{,}089 - (683)(813)/10}{47{,}405 - (683)(683)/10} = \frac{561.1}{756.1} = 0.742.$$

TABLE 6.7-1: Calculations for Test Score Data

x	y	x^2	xy	y^2	$\widehat{y}$	$y - \widehat{y}$	$(y - \widehat{y})^2$
70	77	4,900	5,390	5,929	82.561566	−5.561566	30.931016
74	94	5,476	6,956	8,836	85.529956	8.470044	71.741645
72	88	5,184	6,336	7,744	84.045761	3.954239	15.636006
68	80	4,624	5,440	6,400	81.077371	−1.077371	1.160728
58	71	3,364	4,118	5,041	73.656395	−2.656395	7.056434
54	76	2,916	4,104	5,776	70.688004	5.311996	28.217302
82	88	6,724	7,216	7,744	91.466737	−3.466737	12.018265
64	80	4,096	5,120	6,400	78.108980	1.891020	3.575957
80	90	6,400	7,200	8,100	89.982542	0.017458	0.000305
61	69	3,721	4,209	4,761	75.882687	−6.882687	47.371380
683	813	47,405	56,089	66,731		0.000001	217.709038

Since $\overline{x} = 683/10 = 68.3$, the least squares regression line is

$$\widehat{y} = 81.3 + (0.742)(x - 68.3).$$

The maximum likelihood estimate of σ^2 is

$$\widehat{\sigma^2} = \frac{217.709038}{10} = 21.7709.$$

A plot of the residuals for these data is shown in Figure 6.7-2. ■

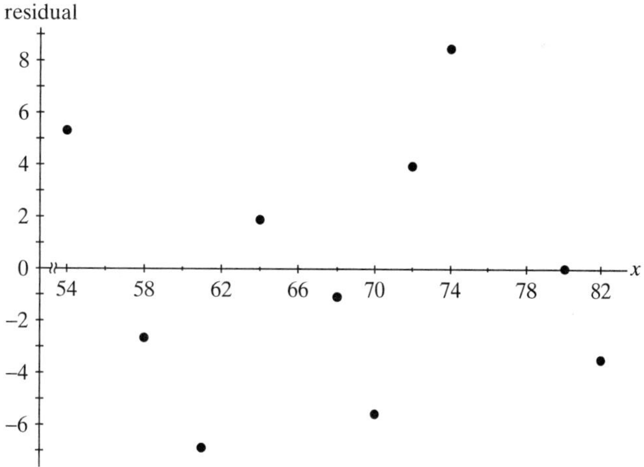

FIGURE 6.7-2: Residuals plot for data in Table 6.7-1

We shall now consider the problem of finding the distributions of $\widehat{\alpha}$, $\widehat{\beta}$, and $\widehat{\sigma^2}$ (or distributions of functions of these estimators). We would like to be able to say something about the error of the estimates to find confidence intervals for the parameters.

The preceding discussion treated $x_1, x_2, \ldots, x_n$ as constants. Of course, many times they can be set by the experimenter; for example, an experimental chemist might produce a compound at many different temperatures. But these numbers might instead be observations on an earlier random variable, such as an SAT score or a preliminary test grade (as in Example 6.7-1), but we consider the problem on the condition that the x values are given in either case. Thus, in finding the distributions of $\widehat{\alpha}$, $\widehat{\beta}$, and $\widehat{\sigma^2}$, the only random variables are $Y_1, Y_2, \ldots, Y_n$.

Since $\widehat{\alpha}$ is a linear function of independent and normally distributed random variables, $\widehat{\alpha}$ has a normal distribution with mean

$$E(\widehat{\alpha}) = E\left(\frac{1}{n}\sum_{i=1}^{n} Y_i\right) = \frac{1}{n}\sum_{i=1}^{n} E(Y_i)$$

$$= \frac{1}{n}\sum_{i=1}^{n} [\alpha + \beta(x_i - \overline{x})] = \alpha$$

and variance

$$\mathrm{Var}(\widehat{\alpha}) = \sum_{i=1}^{n}\left(\frac{1}{n}\right)^2 \mathrm{Var}(Y_i) = \frac{\sigma^2}{n}.$$

The estimator $\widehat{\beta}$ is also a linear function of $Y_1, Y_2, \ldots, Y_n$ and hence has a normal distribution with mean

$$E(\widehat{\beta}) = \frac{\sum_{i=1}^{n} (x_i - \overline{x})E(Y_i)}{\sum_{i=1}^{n} (x_i - \overline{x})^2}$$

$$= \frac{\sum_{i=1}^{n} (x_i - \overline{x})[\alpha + \beta(x_i - \overline{x})]}{\sum_{i=1}^{n} (x_i - \overline{x})^2}$$

$$= \frac{\alpha\sum_{i=1}^{n} (x_i - \overline{x}) + \beta\sum_{i=1}^{n} (x_i - \overline{x})^2}{\sum_{i=1}^{n} (x_i - \overline{x})^2} = \beta$$

and variance

$$\mathrm{Var}(\widehat{\beta}) = \sum_{i=1}^{n}\left[\frac{x_i - \overline{x}}{\sum_{j=1}^{n} (x_j - \overline{x})^2}\right]^2 \mathrm{Var}(Y_i)$$

$$= \frac{\sum_{i=1}^{n} (x_i - \overline{x})^2}{\left[\sum_{i=1}^{n} (x_i - \overline{x})^2\right]^2}\sigma^2 = \frac{\sigma^2}{\sum_{i=1}^{n} (x_i - \overline{x})^2}.$$

It can be shown (Exercise 6.7-6) that

$$\sum_{i=1}^{n}[Y_i - \alpha - \beta(x_i - \bar{x})]^2 = \sum_{i=1}^{n}\{(\widehat{\alpha} - \alpha) + (\widehat{\beta} - \beta)(x_i - \bar{x}) + [Y_i - \widehat{\alpha} - \widehat{\beta}(x_i - \bar{x})]\}^2$$
$$= n(\widehat{\alpha} - \alpha)^2 + (\widehat{\beta} - \beta)^2\sum_{i=1}^{n}(x_i - \bar{x})^2 + \sum_{i=1}^{n}[Y_i - \widehat{\alpha} - \widehat{\beta}(x_i - \bar{x})]^2. \qquad (6.7\text{-}5)$$

From the fact that Y_i, $\widehat{\alpha}$, and $\widehat{\beta}$ have normal distributions, it follows that each of

$$\frac{[Y_i - \alpha - \beta(x_i - \bar{x})]^2}{\sigma^2}, \qquad \frac{(\widehat{\alpha} - \alpha)^2}{\left[\dfrac{\sigma^2}{n}\right]}, \qquad \text{and} \qquad \frac{(\widehat{\beta} - \beta)^2}{\left[\dfrac{\sigma^2}{\sum_{i=1}^{n}(x_i - \bar{x})^2}\right]}$$

has a chi-square distribution with one degree of freedom. Since $Y_1, Y_2, \ldots, Y_n$ are mutually independent,

$$\frac{\sum_{i=1}^{n}[Y_i - \alpha - \beta(x_i - \bar{x})]^2}{\sigma^2}$$

is $\chi^2(n)$. That is, the left-hand member of Equation 6.7-5 divided by σ^2 is $\chi^2(n)$ and is equal to the sum of two $\chi^2(1)$ variables and

$$\frac{\sum_{i=1}^{n}[Y_i - \widehat{\alpha} - \widehat{\beta}(x_i - \bar{x})]^2}{\sigma^2} = \frac{n\widehat{\sigma^2}}{\sigma^2} \geq 0.$$

Thus, we might guess that $n\widehat{\sigma^2}/\sigma^2$ is $\chi^2(n - 2)$. This is true, and moreover, $\widehat{\alpha}$, $\widehat{\beta}$, and $\widehat{\sigma^2}$ are mutually independent. [For a proof, see Hogg, McKean, and Craig, *Introduction to Mathematical Statistics*, 6th ed. (Upper Saddle River, NJ: Prentice Hall, 2005).]

Suppose now that we are interested in forming a confidence interval for β, the slope of the line. We can use the fact that

$$T_1 = \frac{\sqrt{\sum_{i=1}^{n}(x_i - \bar{x})^2}\left(\dfrac{\widehat{\beta} - \beta}{\sigma}\right)}{\sqrt{\dfrac{n\widehat{\sigma^2}}{\sigma^2(n - 2)}}} = \frac{\widehat{\beta} - \beta}{\sqrt{\dfrac{n\widehat{\sigma^2}}{(n - 2)\sum_{i=1}^{n}(x_i - \bar{x})^2}}}$$

has a t distribution with $n - 2$ degrees of freedom. Therefore,

$$P\left[-t_{\gamma/2}(n-2) \le \frac{\widehat{\beta} - \beta}{\sqrt{\dfrac{n\widehat{\sigma^2}}{(n-2)\sum_{i=1}^{n}(x_i - \overline{x})^2}}} \le t_{\gamma/2}(n-2)\right] = 1 - \gamma,$$

and it follows that

$$\left[\widehat{\beta} - t_{\gamma/2}(n-2)\sqrt{\frac{n\widehat{\sigma^2}}{(n-2)\sum_{i=1}^{n}(x_i - \overline{x})^2}},\right.$$
$$\left.\widehat{\beta} + t_{\gamma/2}(n-2)\sqrt{\frac{n\widehat{\sigma^2}}{(n-2)\sum_{i=1}^{n}(x_i - \overline{x})^2}}\right]$$

is a $100(1 - \gamma)\%$ confidence interval for β.

Similarly,

$$T_2 = \frac{\dfrac{\sqrt{n}(\widehat{\alpha} - \alpha)}{\sigma}}{\sqrt{\dfrac{n\widehat{\sigma^2}}{\sigma^2(n-2)}}} = \frac{\widehat{\alpha} - \alpha}{\sqrt{\dfrac{\widehat{\sigma^2}}{n-2}}}$$

has a t distribution with $n - 2$ degrees of freedom. Thus, T_2 can be used to make inferences about α. (See Exercise 6.7-7.) The fact that $n\widehat{\sigma^2}/\sigma^2$ has a chi-square distribution with $n - 2$ degrees of freedom can be used to make inferences about the variance σ^2. (See Exercise 6.7-8.)

STATISTICAL COMMENTS We now give an illustration (see Ledolter and Hogg in the references) using data from the *Challenger* explosion on January 28, 1986. The *Challenger* space shuttle was launched from Cape Kennedy in Florida on a very cold January morning. Meteorologists had forecasted temperatures (as of January 27) in the range of 26°–29° Fahrenheit. The night before the launch there was much debate among engineers and NASA officials whether a launch under such low-temperature conditions would be advisable. Several engineers advised against a launch because they thought that O-ring failures were related to temperature. Data on O-ring failures experienced in previous launches were available and were studied the night before the launch. There were seven previous incidents of known distressed O-rings. Figure 6.7-3(a) displays this information; it is a simple scatter plot of the number of distressed rings per launch against temperature at launch.

From this plot alone, there does not seem to be a strong relationship between the number of O-ring failures and temperature. On the basis of this information, along with many other technical and political considerations, it was decided to launch the *Challenger* space shuttle. As you all know, the launch resulted in disaster: the loss of seven lives and billions of dollars, and a serious setback to the space program.

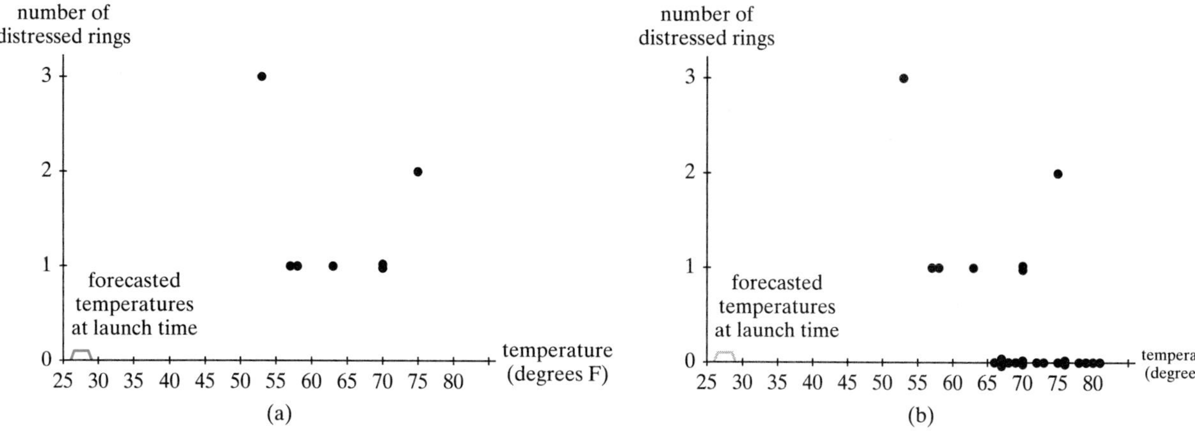

FIGURE 6.7-3: Number of distressed rings per launch versus temperature

One may argue that engineers looked at the scatter plot of the number of failures against temperature, but could not see a relationship. However, this argument misses the fact that engineers did not display *all the data that were relevant to the question*. They looked only at instances in which there were failures; they ignored the cases where there were no failures. In fact, there were 17 previous launches in which no failures occurred. A scatter plot of the number of distressed O-rings per launch against temperature using data from all previous shuttle launches is given in Figure 6.7-3(b).

It is difficult to look at these data and not see a relationship between failures and temperature. Moreover, one recognizes that an extrapolation is required and that an inference about the number of failures outside the observed range of temperature is needed. The actual temperature at launch was 31°F, while the lowest temperature recorded at a previous launch was 53°F. It is always very dangerous to extrapolate inferences to a region for which one does not have data. If NASA officials had looked at this plot, certainly the launch would have been delayed. This example shows why it is important to have statistically minded engineers involved in important decisions.

These comments raise two interesting points: (1) It is important to produce a scatter plot of one variable against another. (2) It is also important to plot *relevant data*. Yes, it is true that some data were used in making the decision to launch the *Challenger*. But not all the relevant data were utilized. To make good decisions, it takes knowledge of statistics as well as subject knowledge, common sense, and an ability to question the relevance of information.

EXERCISES

Remark In many of these exercises, to find the confidence intervals, we need the distributional assumptions made in this section. ■

6.7-1. The midterm and final exam scores of 10 students in a statistics course are tabulated as shown.

(a) Calculate the least squares regression line for these data.

(b) Plot the points and the least squares regression line on the same graph.

(c) Find the value of $\widehat{\sigma^2}$.

Midterm	Final	Midterm	Final
70	87	67	73
74	79	70	83
80	88	64	79
84	98	74	91
80	96	82	94

6.7-2. The final grade in a calculus course was predicted on the basis of the student's high school grade point average in mathematics, Scholastic Aptitude Test (SAT) score in mathematics, and score on a mathematics entrance examination. The predicted grades x and the earned grades y for 10 students are given (2.0 represents a C, 2.3 a C+, 2.7 a B−, etc.).

(a) Calculate the least squares regression line for these data.

(b) Plot the points and the least squares regression line on the same graph.

(c) Find the value of $\widehat{\sigma^2}$.

x	y	x	y
2.0	1.3	2.7	3.0
3.3	3.3	4.0	4.0
3.7	3.3	3.7	3.0
2.0	2.0	3.0	2.7
2.3	1.7	2.3	3.0

6.7-3. The following table from Ledolter and Hogg (see references) gives the attendance at a racetrack (x) and the amount that was bet (y) on $n = 10$ randomly selected days:

Attendance, x (in hundreds)	Amount Bet, y (in millions of dollars)
117	2.07
128	2.80
122	3.14
119	2.26
131	3.40
135	3.89
125	2.93
120	2.66
130	3.30
127	3.54

(a) Make a scatter plot of y against x.

(b) Fit a simple linear regression model to the data and calculate the least squares regression line.

(c) Make a scatter plot of the residuals.

6.7-4. Chemists often use ion-sensitive electrodes (ISEs) to measure the ion concentration of aqueous solutions. These devices measure the migration of ionic charge and give a reading in millivolts (mV). A standard curve is produced by measuring known concentrations (in ppm) and fitting a line to the millivolt data. The following table gives the concentrations in ppm and the voltage in mV at a calcium ISE:

ppm	mV	ppm	mV
0	1.72	100	2.91
0	1.68	100	3.00
0	1.74	100	2.89
50	2.04	150	4.47
50	2.11	150	4.51
50	2.17	150	4.43
75	2.40	200	6.67
75	2.32	200	6.66
75	2.33	200	6.57

(a) Calculate the least squares regression line for mV versus ppm.

(b) Plot the points and the least squares regression line on the same graph.

(c) Calculate and plot the residuals. Does linear regression seem to be appropriate? (See Exercise 6.8-15.)

6.7-5. A student who considered himself to be a "car guy" was interested in how the horsepower and weight of a car affected the time that it takes the car to go from 0 to 60 mph. The following table gives, for each of 14 cars, the horsepower, the time in seconds to go from 0 to 60 mph, and the weight in pounds:

Horse Power	0–60	Weight	Horse Power	0–60	Weight
230	8.1	3516	282	6.2	3627
225	7.8	3690	300	6.4	3892
375	4.7	2976	220	7.7	3377
322	6.6	4215	250	7.0	3625
190	8.4	3761	315	5.3	3230
150	8.4	2940	200	6.2	2657
178	7.2	2818	300	5.5	3518

(a) Calculate the least squares regression line for "0–60" versus horsepower.

(b) Plot the points and the least squares regression line on the same graph.

(c) Calculate the least squares regression line for "0–60" versus weight.

(d) Plot the points and the least squares regression line on the same graph.

(e) Which of the two variables, horsepower or weight, has the most effect on the "0–60" time?

6.7-6. Show that

$$\sum_{i=1}^{n}[Y_i - \alpha - \beta(x_i - \bar{x})]^2$$
$$= n(\widehat{\alpha} - \alpha)^2 + (\widehat{\beta} - \beta)^2 \sum_{i=1}^{n}(x_i - \bar{x})^2$$
$$+ \sum_{i=1}^{n}[Y_i - \widehat{\alpha} - \widehat{\beta}(x_i - \bar{x})]^2.$$

6.7-7. Show that the endpoints for a $100(1 - \gamma)\%$ confidence interval for α are

$$\widehat{\alpha} \pm t_{\gamma/2}(n-2)\sqrt{\frac{\widehat{\sigma^2}}{n-2}}.$$

6.7-8. Show that a $100(1 - \gamma)\%$ confidence interval for σ^2 is

$$\left[\frac{n\widehat{\sigma^2}}{\chi^2_{\gamma/2}(n-2)}, \frac{n\widehat{\sigma^2}}{\chi^2_{1-\gamma/2}(n-2)}\right].$$

6.7-9. Find 95% confidence intervals for α, β, and σ^2 for the data in Exercise 6.7-1.

6.7-10. Find 95% confidence intervals for α, β, and σ^2 for the data in Exercise 6.7-2.

6.7-11. In a "48.1-gram" package of candies, let x equal the number of pieces of candy and let y equal the total weight of the candies. For each of five different values of x, four observations of y are given.

x	y	x	y
54	48.8	56	50.8
54	49.4	56	50.9
54	49.2	57	50.7
54	50.4	57	51.6
55	49.5	57	51.3
55	49.0	57	50.8
55	50.2	58	52.1
55	48.9	58	51.3
56	49.9	58	51.4
56	50.1	58	52.0

(a) Calculate the least squares regression line for these data.

(b) Plot the points and the least squares regression line on the same graph.

(c) Find the value of $\widehat{\sigma^2}$.

(d) Find a 95% confidence interval for β under the usual assumptions.

6.7-12. The Federal Trade Commission measured the number of milligrams of tar and carbon monoxide (CO) per cigarette for all domestic cigarettes. Let x and y equal the measurements of tar and CO, respectively, for 100-millimeter filtered and mentholated cigarettes. A sample of 12 brands yielded the following data:

Brand	x	y	Brand	x	y
Capri	9	6	Now	3	4
Carlton	4	6	Salem	17	18
Kent	14	14	Triumph	6	8
Kool Milds	12	12	True	7	8
Marlboro Lights	10	12	Vantage	8	13
Merit Ultras	5	7	Virginia Slims	15	13

(a) Calculate the least squares regression line for these data.

(b) Plot the points and the least squares regression line on the same graph.

(c) Find point estimates for α, β, and σ^2.

(d) Find 95% confidence intervals for α, β, and σ^2 under the usual assumptions.

6.7-13. Let x and y equal the lengths in inches of a foot and a hand, respectively. The following measurements were made on 15 women:

x	y	x	y	x	y
9.00	6.50	10.00	7.00	9.25	7.00
8.50	6.25	9.50	6.50	10.00	7.50
9.25	7.25	9.00	7.00	10.00	7.25
9.75	7.00	9.25	7.00	9.75	7.25
9.00	6.75	9.50	7.00	9.50	7.25

(a) Calculate the least squares regression line for these data.

(b) Plot the points and the least squares regression line on the same graph.

(c) Find point estimates for α, β, and σ^2.

(d) Find 95% confidence intervals for α, β, and σ^2 under the usual assumptions.

6.7-14. Let x and y equal the ACT scores in social science and natural science, respectively, for a student who is applying for admission to a small liberal arts college. A sample of $n = 15$ such students yielded the following data:

x	y	x	y	x	y
32	28	30	27	26	32
23	25	17	23	16	22
23	24	20	30	21	28
23	32	17	18	24	31
26	31	18	18	30	26

(a) Calculate the least squares regression line for these data.
(b) Plot the points and the least squares regression line on the same graph.
(c) Find point estimates for α, β, and σ^2.
(d) Find 95% confidence intervals for α, β, and σ^2 under the usual assumptions.

6.7-15. The data in the following table, part of a set of data collected by Ledolter and Hogg (see references), provide the number of miles per gallon (mpg) for city and highway driving of 2007 midsize-model cars, as well as the curb weight of the cars:

Type	mpg City	mpg Hwy	Curb Weight
Ford Fusion V6 SE	20	28	3230
Chevrolet Sebring Sedan Base	24	32	3287
Toyota Camry Solara SE	24	34	3240
Honda Accord Sedan	20	29	3344
Audi A6 3.2	21	29	3825
BMW 5-series 525i Sedan	20	29	3450
Chrysler PT Cruiser Base	22	29	3076
Mercedes E-Class E350 Sedan	19	26	3740
Volkswagen Passat Sedan 2.0T	23	32	3305
Nissan Altima 2.5	26	35	3055
Kia Optima LX	24	34	3142

(a) Find the least squares regression line for highway mpg (y) and city mpg (x).
(b) Plot the points and the least squares regression line on the same graph.
(c) Find 95% confidence intervals for α, β, and σ^2.

6.7-16. Some measurements in millimeters were made on a species of spider named *Sosippus floridanus* that are native to Florida. Ten female spiders and 10 male spiders were used. The total lengths and the lengths of their front and their back legs are as follows:

Female body lengths	Female front legs	Female back legs	Male body lengths	Male front legs	Male back legs
11.06	15.03	19.29	12.26	20.22	25.54
13.87	17.96	22.74	11.66	18.62	23.94
12.93	17.56	21.28	12.53	18.62	23.94
15.08	21.22	25.54	13.00	19.95	25.80
17.82	22.61	28.86	11.79	19.15	25.40
14.14	20.08	25.14	12.46	19.02	25.27
12.26	16.49	20.22	10.65	17.29	22.21
17.82	18.75	24.61	10.39	17.02	21.81
20.17	23.01	28.46	12.26	18.49	23.41
16.88	22.48	28.60	14.07	22.61	28.86

Calculate the least squares regression line, and plot the points and the least squares regression line on the same graph, for

(a) Female body lengths and the lengths of their front legs.
(b) The lengths of the front and back legs of the female spiders.
(c) Male body lengths and the lengths of their back legs.
(d) The lengths of the front and back legs of the male spiders.

6.7-17. Using an Instron 4204, rectangular strips of Plexiglas® were stretched to failure in a tensile test. The following data give the change in length, in millimeters (mm), before breaking (x) and the cross-sectional area in square millimeters (mm^2) (y):

(5.28, 52.36) (5.40, 52.58) (4.65, 51.07) (4.76, 52.28) (5.55, 53.02)
(5.73, 52.10) (5.84, 52.61) (4.97, 52.21) (5.50, 52.39) (6.24, 53.77)

(a) Find the equation of the least squares regression line.
(b) Plot the points and the line on the same graph.
(c) Interpret your output.

6.7-18. The "Golden Ratio" is $\phi = (1 + \sqrt{5})/2$. John Putz, a mathematician who is interested in music, analyzed Mozart's sonata movements, which are divided into two distinct sections, both of which are repeated in performance (see references). The length of the "Exposition" in measures is represented by a, and the length of the "Development and Recapitulation" is represented by b. Putz's conjecture was that Mozart divided his movements near to the golden ratio. That is, Putz was interested in studying whether a scatter plot of $a + b$ against b not only would be linear, but also would actually fall along the line $y = \phi x$. Here are the data in tabular form, in which the first column identifies the piece and movement by the Köchel cataloging system:

Köchel	a	b	$a + b$	Köchel	a	b	$a + b$
279, I	38	62	100	279, II	28	46	74
279, III	56	102	158	280, I	56	88	144
280, II	24	36	60	280, III	77	113	190
281, I	40	69	109	281, II	46	60	106
282, I	15	18	33	282, III	39	63	102
283, I	53	67	120	283, II	14	23	37
283, III	102	171	273	284, I	51	76	127
309, I	58	97	155	311, I	39	73	112
310, I	49	84	133	330, I	58	92	150
330, III	68	103	171	332, I	93	136	229
332, III	90	150	245	333, I	63	102	165
333, II	31	50	81	457, I	74	93	167
533, I	102	137	239	533, II	46	76	122
545, I	28	45	73	547a, I	78	118	196
570, I	79	130	209				

(a) Make a scatter plot of the points $a + b$ against the points b. Is this plot linear?
(b) Find the equation of the least squares regression line. Superimpose it on the scatter plot.
(c) On the scatter plot, superimpose the line $y = \phi x$. Compare this line with the least squares regression line (graphically if you wish).
(d) Find the sample mean of the points $(a + b)/b$. Is the mean close to ϕ?

6.8 MORE REGRESSION

In this section, we use the notation and assumptions of Section 6.7. We have noted that $\widehat{Y} = \widehat{\alpha} + \widehat{\beta}(x - \overline{x})$ is a point estimate for the mean of Y for some given x, or we could think of this as a prediction of the value of Y for this given x. But how close is $\widehat{Y}$ to the mean of Y or to Y itself? We shall now find a confidence interval for $\alpha + \beta(x - \overline{x})$ and a prediction interval for Y, given a particular value of x.

To find a confidence interval for

$$E(Y) = \mu(x) = \alpha + \beta(x - \overline{x}),$$

let

$$\widehat{Y} = \widehat{\alpha} + \widehat{\beta}(x - \overline{x}).$$

Recall that $\widehat{Y}$ is a linear combination of normally and independently distributed random variables $\widehat{\alpha}$ and $\widehat{\beta}$, so $\widehat{Y}$ has a normal distribution. Furthermore,

$$\begin{aligned} E(\widehat{Y}) &= E[\widehat{\alpha} + \widehat{\beta}(x - \overline{x})] \\ &= \alpha + \beta(x - \overline{x}) \end{aligned}$$

and

$$\begin{aligned} \mathrm{Var}(\widehat{Y}) &= \mathrm{Var}[\widehat{\alpha} + \widehat{\beta}(x - \overline{x})] \\ &= \frac{\sigma^2}{n} + \frac{\sigma^2}{\sum_{i=1}^n (x_i - \overline{x})^2}(x - \overline{x})^2 \\ &= \sigma^2\left[\frac{1}{n} + \frac{(x - \overline{x})^2}{\sum_{i=1}^n (x_i - \overline{x})^2}\right]. \end{aligned}$$

Recall that the distribution of $n\widehat{\sigma^2}/\sigma^2$ is $\chi^2(n-2)$. Since $\widehat{\alpha}$ and $\widehat{\beta}$ are independent of $\widehat{\sigma^2}$, we can form the t statistic

$$T = \frac{\dfrac{\widehat{\alpha} + \widehat{\beta}(x - \overline{x}) - [\alpha + \beta(x - \overline{x})]}{\sigma\sqrt{\dfrac{1}{n} + \dfrac{(x - \overline{x})^2}{\sum_{i=1}^n (x_i - \overline{x})^2}}}}{\sqrt{\dfrac{n\widehat{\sigma^2}}{(n-2)\sigma^2}}},$$

which has a t distribution with $r = n - 2$ degrees of freedom. Next, we select $t_{\gamma/2}(n-2)$ from Table VI in the appendix so that

$$P[-t_{\gamma/2}(n-2) \le T \le t_{\gamma/2}(n-2)] = 1 - \gamma.$$

This becomes

$$P[\widehat{\alpha} + \widehat{\beta}(x - \overline{x}) - ct_{\gamma/2}(n-2) \le \alpha + \beta(x - \overline{x}) \le \widehat{\alpha} + \widehat{\beta}(x - \overline{x}) + ct_{\gamma/2}(n-2)] = 1 - \gamma,$$

where

$$c = \sqrt{\frac{n\widehat{\sigma^2}}{n-2}}\sqrt{\frac{1}{n} + \frac{(x - \overline{x})^2}{\sum_{i=1}^n (x_i - \overline{x})^2}}.$$

Thus, the endpoints for a $100(1-\gamma)\%$ confidence interval for $\mu(x) = \alpha + \beta(x - \overline{x})$ are

$$\widehat{\alpha} + \widehat{\beta}(x - \overline{x}) \pm ct_{\gamma/2}(n-2).$$

Note that the width of this interval depends on the particular value of x, because c depends on x. (See Example 6.8-1.)

We have used $(x_1, y_1), (x_2, y_2), \ldots, (x_n, y_n)$ to estimate α and β. Suppose that we are given a value of x, say, x_{n+1}. A point estimate of the corresponding value of Y is

$$\widehat{y}_{n+1} = \widehat{\alpha} + \widehat{\beta}(x_{n+1} - \overline{x}).$$

However, $\widehat{y}_{n+1}$ is just one possible value of the random variable

$$Y_{n+1} = \alpha + \beta(x_{n+1} - \bar{x}) + \varepsilon_{n+1}.$$

What can we say about possible values for Y_{n+1}? We shall now obtain a **prediction interval** for Y_{n+1} when $x = x_{n+1}$ that is similar to the confidence interval for the mean of Y when $x = x_{n+1}$.

We have

$$Y_{n+1} = \alpha + \beta(x_{n+1} - \bar{x}) + \varepsilon_{n+1},$$

where ε_{n+1} is $N(0,\sigma^2)$ and $\bar{x} = (1/n)\sum_{i=1}^{n} x_i$. Now,

$$W = Y_{n+1} - \widehat{\alpha} - \widehat{\beta}(x_{n+1} - \bar{x})$$

is a linear combination of normally and independently distributed random variables, so W has a normal distribution. The mean of W is

$$\begin{aligned} E(W) &= E[Y_{n+1} - \widehat{\alpha} - \widehat{\beta}(x_{n+1} - \bar{x})] \\ &= \alpha + \beta(x_{n+1} - \bar{x}) - \alpha - \beta(x_{n+1} - \bar{x}) = 0. \end{aligned}$$

Since Y_{n+1}, $\widehat{\alpha}$ and $\widehat{\beta}$ are independent, the variance of W is

$$\begin{aligned} \operatorname{Var}(W) &= \sigma^2 + \frac{\sigma^2}{n} + \frac{\sigma^2}{\sum_{i=1}^{n}(x_i - \bar{x})^2}(x_{n+1} - \bar{x})^2 \\ &= \sigma^2\left[1 + \frac{1}{n} + \frac{(x_{n+1} - \bar{x})^2}{\sum_{i=1}^{n}(x_i - \bar{x})^2}\right]. \end{aligned}$$

Recall that $n\widehat{\sigma^2}/[(n-2)\sigma^2]$ is $\chi^2(n-2)$. Since Y_{n+1}, $\widehat{\alpha}$, and $\widehat{\beta}$ are independent of $\widehat{\sigma^2}$, we can form the t statistic

$$T = \frac{\dfrac{Y_{n+1} - \widehat{\alpha} - \widehat{\beta}(x_{n+1} - \bar{x})}{\sigma\sqrt{1 + \dfrac{1}{n} + \dfrac{(x_{n+1} - \bar{x})^2}{\sum_{i=1}^{n}(x_i - \bar{x})^2}}}}{\sqrt{\dfrac{n\widehat{\sigma^2}}{(n-2)\sigma^2}}}$$

which has a t distribution with $r = n - 2$ degrees of freedom. Now we select a constant $t_{\gamma/2}(n-2)$ from Table VI in the appendix so that

$$P[-t_{\gamma/2}(n-2) \le T \le t_{\gamma/2}(n-2)] = 1 - \gamma.$$

Solving this inequality for Y_{n+1}, we have

$$P[\widehat{\alpha} + \widehat{\beta}(x_{n+1} - \bar{x}) - d\,t_{\gamma/2}(n-2) \le Y_{n+1} \le \widehat{\alpha} + \widehat{\beta}(x_{n+1} - \bar{x}) + d\,t_{\gamma/2}(n-2)] = 1 - \gamma,$$

where

$$d = \sqrt{\frac{n\widehat{\sigma^2}}{n-2}}\sqrt{1 + \frac{1}{n} + \frac{(x_{n+1} - \bar{x})^2}{\sum_{i=1}^{n}(x_i - \bar{x})^2}}.$$

Thus, the endpoints for a $100(1-\gamma)\%$ prediction interval for Y_{n+1} are

$$\widehat{\alpha} + \widehat{\beta}(x_{n+1} - \bar{x}) \pm d t_{\gamma/2}(n-2).$$

We shall now use the data in Example 6.7-1 to illustrate a 95% confidence interval for $\mu(x)$ and a 95% prediction interval for Y for a given value of x. To find such intervals, we use Equations 6.7-1, 6.7-2, and 6.7-4.

EXAMPLE 6.8-1 To find a 95% confidence interval for $\mu(x)$ using the data in Example 6.7-1, note that we have already found that $\bar{x} = 68.3$, $\widehat{\alpha} = 81.3$, $\widehat{\beta} = 561.1/756.1 = 0.7421$, and $\widehat{\sigma^2} = 21.7709$. We also need

$$\sum_{i=1}^{n}(x_i - \bar{x})^2 = \sum_{i=1}^{n} x_i^2 - \left(\frac{1}{n}\right)\left(\sum_{i=1}^{n} x_i\right)^2$$
$$= 47{,}405 - \frac{683^2}{10} = 756.1.$$

For 95% confidence, $t_{0.025}(8) = 2.306$. When $x = 60$, the endpoints for a 95% confidence interval for $\mu(60)$ are

$$81.3 + 0.7421(60 - 68.3) \pm \left[\sqrt{\frac{10(21.7709)}{8}}\sqrt{\frac{1}{10} + \frac{(60-68.3)^2}{756.1}}\right](2.306),$$

or

$$75.1406 \pm 5.2589.$$

Similarly, when $x = 70$, the endpoints for a 95% confidence interval for $\mu(70)$ are

$$82.5616 \pm 3.8761.$$

Note that the lengths of these intervals depend on the particular value of x. A 95% confidence band for $\mu(x)$ is graphed in Figure 6.8-1(a) along with the scatter diagram and $\widehat{y} = \widehat{\alpha} + \widehat{\beta}(x - \bar{x})$.

The endpoints for a 95% prediction interval for Y when $x = 60$ are

$$81.3 + 0.7421(60 - 68.3) \pm \left[\sqrt{\frac{10(21.7709)}{8}}\sqrt{1.1 + \frac{(60-68.3)^2}{756.1}}\right](2.306),$$

or

$$75.1406 \pm 13.1289.$$

Note that this interval is much wider than the confidence interval for $\mu(60)$. In Figure 6.8-1(b), the 95% prediction band for Y is graphed along with the scatter diagram and the least squares regression line. ■

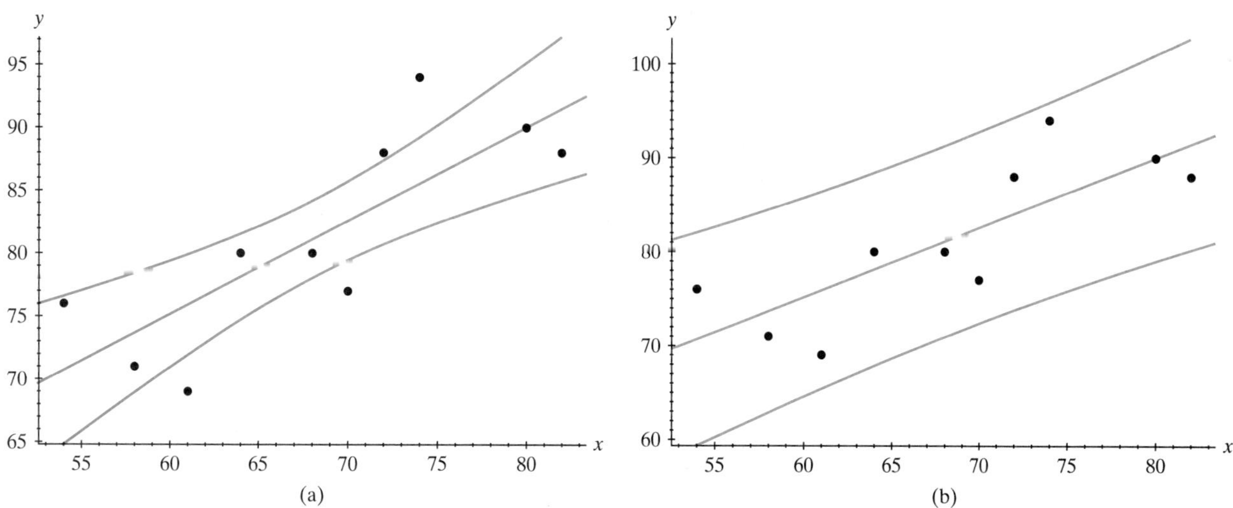

FIGURE 6.8-1: A 95% (a) confidence band for $\mu(x)$ and (b) prediction band for Y

We now generalize the simple regression model to the **multiple regression** case. Suppose we observe several x values—say $x_1, x_2, \ldots, x_k$—along with the y value. For example, suppose that x_1 equals the student's ACT composite score, x_2 equals the student's high school class rank, and y equals the student's first-year GPA in college. We want to estimate a regression function $E(Y) = \mu(x_1, x_2, \ldots, x_k)$ from some observed data. If

$$\mu(x_1, x_2, \ldots, x_k) = \beta_1 x_1 + \beta_2 x_2 + \cdots + \beta_k x_k,$$

then we say that we have a **linear model** because this expression is linear in the coefficients $\beta_1, \beta_2, \ldots, \beta_k$.

To illustrate, note that the model in Section 6.7 is linear in $\alpha = \beta_1$ and $\beta = \beta_2$, with $x_1 = 1$ and $x_2 = x$, giving the mean $\alpha + \beta x$. (For convenience, there the mean of the x values was subtracted from x.) Suppose, however, that we had wished to use the cubic function $\beta_1 + \beta_2 x + \beta_3 x^2 + \beta_4 x^3$ as the mean. This cubic expression still provides a linear model (i.e., linear in the β-values), and we would take $x_1 = 1$, $x_2 = x$, $x_3 = x^2$, and $x_4 = x^3$.

Say our n observation points are

$$(x_{1j}, x_{2j}, \ldots, x_{kj}, y_j), \qquad j = 1, 2, \ldots, n.$$

To fit the linear model $\beta_1 x_1 + \beta_2 x_2 + \cdots + \beta_k x_k$ by the method of least squares, we minimize

$$G = \sum_{j=1}^{n} (y_j - \beta_1 x_{1j} - \beta_2 x_{2j} - \cdots - \beta_k x_{kj})^2.$$

If we equate the k first partial derivatives

$$\frac{\partial G}{\partial \beta_i} = \sum_{j=1}^{n} (-2)(y_j - \beta_1 x_{1j} - \beta_2 x_{2j} - \cdots - \beta_k x_{kj})(x_{ij}), \qquad i = 1, 2, \ldots, k,$$

to zero, we obtain the k **normal equations**

$$
\begin{array}{llllll}
\beta_1 \sum_{j=1}^{n} x_{1j}^2 & + \beta_2 \sum_{j=1}^{n} x_{1j}x_{2j} & + & \cdots & + \beta_k \sum_{j=1}^{n} x_{1j}x_{kj} & = \sum_{j=1}^{n} x_{1j}y_j, \\
\beta_1 \sum_{j=1}^{n} x_{2j}x_{1j} & + \beta_2 \sum_{j=1}^{n} x_{2j}^2 & + & \cdots & + \beta_k \sum_{j=1}^{n} x_{2j}x_{kj} & = \sum_{j=1}^{n} x_{2j}y_j, \\
\vdots & \vdots & & \ddots & \vdots & \vdots \\
\beta_1 \sum_{j=1}^{n} x_{kj}x_{1j} & + \beta_2 \sum_{j=1}^{n} x_{kj}x_{2j} & + & \cdots & + \beta_k \sum_{j=1}^{n} x_{kj}^2 & = \sum_{j=1}^{n} x_{kj}y_j.
\end{array}
$$

The solution of the preceding k equations provides the least squares estimates of $\beta_1, \beta_2, \ldots, \beta_k$. These estimates are also maximum likelihood estimates of $\beta_1, \beta_2, \ldots, \beta_k$, provided that the random variables $Y_1, Y_2, \ldots, Y_n$ are mutually independent and Y_j is $N(\beta_1 x_{1j} + \beta_2 x_{2j} + \cdots + \beta_k x_{kj}, \sigma^2)$, $j = 1, 2, \ldots, n$.

By the method of least squares, we fit $y = \beta_1 x_1 + \beta_2 x_2 + \beta_3 x_3$ to the five observed points (x_1, x_2, x_3, y):

$$(1,1,0,4),\ (1,0,1,3),\ (1,2,3,2),\ (1,3,0,6),\ (1,0,0,1).$$

Note that $x_1 = 1$ in each point, so we are really fitting $y = \beta_1 + \beta_2 x_2 + \beta_3 x_3$. Since

$$
\begin{array}{llll}
\sum_{j=1}^{5} x_{1j}^2 = 5, & \sum_{j=1}^{5} x_{1j}x_{2j} = 6, & \sum_{j=1}^{5} x_{1j}x_{3j} = 4, & \sum_{j=1}^{5} x_{1j}y_j = 16, \\
\sum_{j=1}^{5} x_{2j}x_{1j} = 6, & \sum_{j=1}^{5} x_{2j}^2 = 14, & \sum_{j=1}^{5} x_{2j}x_{3j} = 6, & \sum_{j=1}^{5} x_{2j}y_j = 26, \\
\sum_{j=1}^{5} x_{3j}x_{1j} = 4, & \sum_{j=1}^{5} x_{3j}x_{2j} = 6, & \sum_{j=1}^{5} x_{3j}^2 = 10, & \sum_{j=1}^{5} x_{3j}y_j = 9,
\end{array}
$$

the normal equations are

$$
\begin{aligned}
5\beta_1 + 6\beta_2 + 4\beta_3 &= 16, \\
6\beta_1 + 14\beta_2 + 6\beta_3 &= 26, \\
4\beta_1 + 6\beta_2 + 10\beta_3 &= 9.
\end{aligned}
$$

Solving these three linear equations in three unknowns, we obtain

$$\widehat{\beta}_1 = \frac{274}{112}, \qquad \widehat{\beta}_2 = \frac{127}{112}, \qquad \widehat{\beta}_3 = -\frac{85}{112}.$$

Thus, the least squares fit is

$$y = \frac{274x_1 + 127x_2 - 85x_3}{112}.$$

If x_1 always equals 1, then the equation reads

$$y = \frac{274 + 127x_2 - 85x_3}{112}.$$

It is interesting to observe that the usual two-sample problem is actually a linear model. Let $\beta_1 = \mu_1$ and $\beta_2 = \mu_2$, and consider n pairs of (x_1, x_2) that equal $(1, 0)$ and m pairs that equal $(0, 1)$. This would require each of the first n variables $Y_1, Y_2, \ldots, Y_n$ to have the mean

$$\beta_1 \cdot 1 + \beta_2 \cdot 0 = \beta_1 = \mu_1$$

and the next m variables $Y_{n+1}, Y_{n+2}, \ldots, Y_{n+m}$ to have the mean

$$\beta_1 \cdot 0 + \beta_2 \cdot 1 = \beta_2 = \mu_2.$$

This is the background of the two-sample problem, but with the usual $X_1, X_2, \ldots, X_n$ and $Y_1, Y_2, \ldots, Y_m$ replaced by $Y_1, Y_2, \ldots, Y_n$ and $Y_{n+1}, Y_{n+2}, \ldots, Y_{n+m}$, respectively.

EXERCISES

6.8-1. For the data given in Exercise 6.7-1, with the usual assumptions,

(a) Find a 95% confidence interval for $\mu(x)$ when $x = 68, 75$, and 82.

(b) Find a 95% prediction interval for Y when $x = 68, 75$, and 82.

6.8-2. For the data given in Exercise 6.7-2, with the usual assumptions,

(a) Find a 95% confidence interval for $\mu(x)$ when $x = 2, 3$, and 4.

(b) Find a 95% prediction interval for Y when $x = 2, 3$, and 4.

6.8-3. For the data given in Exercise 6.7-3, with the usual assumptions,

(a) Find a 95% confidence interval for $\mu(x)$ when $x = 120, 125$, and 130.

(b) Find a 95% prediction interval for Y when $x = 120, 125$, and 130.

6.8-4. For the candy data given in Exercise 6.7-11, with the usual assumptions,

(a) Find a 90% confidence interval for $\mu(x)$ when $x = 54, 56$, and 58.

(b) Determine a 90% prediction interval for Y when $x = 54, 56$, and 58.

6.8-5. For the cigarette data in Exercise 6.7-12, with the usual assumptions,

(a) Find a 95% confidence interval for $\mu(x)$ when $x = 5, 10$, and 15.

(b) Determine a 95% prediction interval for Y when $x = 5, 10$, and 15.

6.8-6. A computer center recorded the number of programs it maintained during each of 10 consecutive years.

(a) Calculate the least squares regression line for the data shown.

(b) Plot the points and the line on the same graph.

(c) Find a 95% prediction interval for the number of programs in year 11 under the usual assumptions.

Year	Number of Programs
1	430
2	480
3	565
4	790
5	885
6	960
7	1200
8	1380
9	1530
10	1591

6.8-7. For the ACT scores in Exercise 6.7-14, with the usual assumptions,

(a) Find a 95% confidence interval for $\mu(x)$ when $x = 17, 20, 23, 26$, and 29.

(b) Determine a 90% prediction interval for Y when $x = 17, 20, 23, 26$, and 29.

6.8-8. By the method of least squares, fit the regression plane $y = \beta_1 + \beta_2 x_1 + \beta_3 x_2$ to the following 12 observations of (x_1, x_2, y): (1, 1, 6), (0, 2, 3), (3, 0, 10), $(-2, 0, -4)$, $(-1, 2, 0)$, (0, 0, 1), (2, 1, 8), $(-1, -1, -2)$, $(0, -3, -3)$, (2, 1, 5), (1, 1, 1), $(-1, 0, -2)$.

6.8-9. By the method of least squares, fit the cubic equation $y = \beta_1 + \beta_2 x + \beta_3 x^2 + \beta_4 x^3$ to the following 10 observed data points (x, y): (0, 1), $(-1, -3)$, (0, 3), (1, 3), $(-1, -1)$, (2, 10), (0, 0), $(-2, -9)$, $(-1, -2)$, (2, 8).

6.8-10. The data that follow give the times of 22 male swimmers who entered the 50-yard freestyle race in the conference championship meet. For these data, x is the swimmer's best time for the season and y is the swimmer's time in the meet.

x	y	x	y	x	y	x	y
24.97	23.98	24.76	23.63	23.80	23.61	22.84	23.58
24.07	23.57	22.98	23.17	22.93	22.83	23.41	22.75
22.10	22.74	23.08	22.70	23.59	22.62	23.80	22.53
22.38	22.39	22.91	22.34	22.08	21.95	22.46	21.73
21.34	21.68	22.76	21.66	21.82	21.68	21.80	21.58
22.26	21.57	21.36	21.35				

(a) Graph the points and the regression line for the data.
(b) Calculate and plot the residuals. Does linear regression seem to be appropriate?
(c) Find a 90% confidence band for the regression line. Make usual assumptions.
(d) Find a 90% prediction band for these data. Make usual assumptions.
(e) Find 95% confidence intervals for α, β, and σ^2. Make usual assumptions.

6.8-11. Explain why the model $\mu(x) = \beta_1 e^{\beta_2 x}$ is not a linear model. Would the logarithm, $\ln \mu(x)$, be a linear model?

6.8-12. We would like to fit the quadratic curve $y = \beta_1 + \beta_2 x + \beta_3 x^2$ to a set of points $(x_1, y_1), (x_2, y_2), \ldots, (x_n, y_n)$ by the method of least squares. To do this, let

$$h(\beta_1, \beta_2, \beta_3) = \sum_{i=1}^{n} (y_i - \beta_1 - \beta_2 x_i - \beta_3 x_i^2)^2.$$

(a) By setting the three first partial derivatives of h with respect to β_1, β_2, and β_3 equal to 0, show that β_1, β_2, and β_3 satisfy the following set of equations (called normal equations), all of which are sums going from 1 to n:

$$\begin{aligned}
\beta_1 n + \beta_2 \sum x_i + \beta_3 \sum x_i^2 &= \sum y_i; \\
\beta_1 \sum x_i + \beta_2 \sum x_i^2 + \beta_3 \sum x_i^3 &= \sum x_i y_i; \\
\beta_1 \sum x_i^2 + \beta_2 \sum x_i^3 + \beta_3 \sum x_i^4 &= \sum x_i^2 y_i.
\end{aligned}$$

(b) For the data

(6.91, 17.52)	(4.32, 22.69)	(2.38, 17.61)	(7.98, 14.29)
(8.26, 10.77)	(2.00, 12.87)	(3.10, 18.63)	(7.69, 16.77)
(2.21, 14.97)	(3.42, 19.16)	(8.18, 11.15)	(5.39, 22.41)
(1.19, 7.50)	(3.21, 19.06)	(5.47, 23.89)	(7.35, 16.63)
(2.32, 15.09)	(7.54, 14.75)	(1.27, 10.75)	(7.33,17.42)
(8.41, 9.40)	(8.72, 9.83)	(6.09, 22.33)	(5.30, 21.37)
(7.30, 17.36)			

$n = 25$, $\sum x_i = 133.34$, $\sum x_i^2 = 867.75$, $\sum x_i^3 = 6197.21$, $\sum x_i^4 = 46{,}318.88$, $\sum y_i = 404.22$, $\sum x_i y_i = 2138.38$, and $\sum x_i^2 y_i = 13{,}380.30$. Show that $a = -1.88$, $b = 9.86$, and $c = -0.995$.

(c) Plot the points and the linear regression line for these data.
(d) Calculate and plot the residuals. Does linear regression seem to be appropriate?
(e) Show that the least squares quadratic regression line is $\hat{y} = -1.88 + 9.86x - 0.995x^2$.
(f) Plot the points and this least squares quadratic regression curve on the same graph.
(g) Plot the residuals for quadratic regression and compare this plot with that in part (d).

6.8-13. (The information presented in this exercise comes from the Westview Blueberry Farm and National Oceanic and Atmospheric Administration Reports [NOAA].) For the following paired data, (x, y), x gives the

Holland, Michigan, rainfall for June and y gives the blueberry production in thousands of pounds from the Westview Blueberry Farm:

$$\begin{array}{llll} (4.11, 56.2) & (5.49, 45.3) & (5.35, 31.0) & (6.53, 30.1) \\ (5.18, 40.0) & (4.89, 38.5) & (2.09, 50.0) & (1.40, 45.8) \\ (4.52, 45.9) & (1.11, 32.4) & (0.60, 18.2) & (3.80, 56.1) \end{array}$$

The data are from 1971 to 1989 for those years in which the last frost occurred May 10 or earlier.

(a) Find the correlation coefficient for these data.
(b) Find the least squares regression line.
(c) Make a scatter plot of the data with the least squares regression line on the plot.
(d) Calculate and plot the residuals. Does linear regression seem to be appropriate?
(e) Find the least squares quadratic regression curve.
(f) Calculate and plot the residuals. Does quadratic regression seem to be appropriate?
(g) Give a short interpretation of your results.

6.8-14. The March 13, 1994, issue of *Parade* stated, "Heart surgeries, including bypass and angioplasty, totaled 196,000 in 1980 and reached 839,000 in 1991." (*Source*: National Hospital Discharge Survey, 1991.) The data for the years 1980 to 1991 in thousands are

$$\begin{array}{llllll} (1980, 196) & (1981, 217) & (1982, 243) & (1983, 275) & (1984, 314) & (1985, 379) \\ (1986, 490) & (1987, 588) & (1988, 674) & (1989, 719) & (1990, 781) & (1991, 839) \end{array}$$

(a) Make a scatter plot (here a time sequence) of the data with the least squares regression line superimposed.
(b) If possible, find a polynomial that provides a better fit of these data. Construct a scatter plot of the data with this polynomial superimposed.
(c) Calculate and plot the residuals for the polynomial that you select.

6.8-15. If, in Exercise 6.7-4, a linear regression fit does not seem appropriate, fit the quadratic curve $\beta_1 + \beta_2 x + \beta_3 x^2$ to the data. Does this curve seem to provide a better fit?

HISTORICAL COMMENTS When a statistician thinks of estimation, he or she recalls R. A. Fisher's contributions to many aspects of the subject: maximum likelihood estimation, efficiency (Section 10.7), and sufficiency (Section 10.1). Of course, many more statisticians have contributed to that discipline since the 1920s. It would be an interesting exercise for the reader to go through the tables of contents of the *Journal of the American Statistical Association*, the *Annals of Statistics*, and related journals to observe how many articles are about estimation. Often our friends ask, "What is there left to do in mathematics?" University libraries are full of expanding journals of new mathematics, including statistics.

The other topic, among many important ones, in this chapter is regression, a technique that leads to a mathematical model of the result of some process in terms of some associated (explanatory) variables. We create such models to give us some idea of the value of a response variable if we know the values of certain explanatory variables. If we have an idea of the form of the equation relating these variables, then we can "fit" this model to the data; that is, we can determine approximate values for the unknown constants in the model from the data. Now, no model is exactly correct; but, as the well-known statistician George Box observed, "Some are useful." That is, while models may be wrong and we should check them as best we can, they may be good enough approximations to shed some light on the issues of interest.

Once satisfactory models are found, they may be used

1. to determine the effect of each explanatory variable (some may have very little effect and can be dropped),

2. to estimate the response variable for given values of important explanatory variables,
3. to predict the future, such as upcoming sales (although this sometimes should be done with great care),
4. to often substitute a cheaper explanatory variable for an expensive one that is difficult to obtain [such as chemical oxygen demand (COD) for biological oxygen demand (BOD)].

Finally, we must observe (and we will give a heuristic proof of it in Chapter 10) that most maximum likelihood estimators have approximate normal distributions. (See Section 10.7.) These estimators are of what is called the *regular cases*—in particular, those cases in which the parameters are not in the endpoints of the support of X. Abraham de Moivre proved this theorem for $\widehat{p}$ of the binomial distribution, and Laplace and Gauss did for $\overline{X}$ in a number of other distributions. This is the real reason the normal distribution is so important: Most estimators of parameters have approximate normal distributions, allowing us to construct confidence intervals and perform tests with such estimates.

Tests of Statistical Hypotheses

CHAPTER 7

7.1 TESTS ABOUT PROPORTIONS
7.2 TESTS ABOUT ONE MEAN
7.3 TESTS OF THE EQUALITY OF TWO MEANS
7.4 TESTS FOR VARIANCES
7.5 ONE-FACTOR ANALYSIS OF VARIANCE
7.6 TWO-FACTOR ANALYSIS OF VARIANCE
7.7 TESTS CONCERNING REGRESSION AND CORRELATION

7.1 TESTS ABOUT PROPORTIONS

A first major area of statistical inference, namely, estimation of parameters, was introduced in Chapter 6. Here we consider a second major area: **tests of statistical hypotheses**. This very important topic is introduced through an illustration.

Suppose a manufacturer of a certain printed circuit observes that about $p = 0.06$ of the circuits fail. An engineer and statistician working together suggest some changes that might improve the design of the product. To test this new procedure, it was agreed that $n = 200$ circuits would be produced by the proposed method and then checked. Let Y equal the number of these 200 circuits that fail. Clearly, if the number of failures, Y, is such that $Y/200$ is about equal to 0.06, then it seems that the new procedure has not resulted in an improvement. Also, on the one hand, if Y is small, so that $Y/200$ is about 0.02 or 0.03, we might believe that the new method is better than the old. On the other hand, if $Y/200$ is 0.09 or 0.10, the proposed method has perhaps caused a greater proportion of failures.

What we need to establish is a formal rule that tells us when to accept the new procedure as an improvement. In addition, we must know the consequences of this rule. As an example of such a rule, we could accept the new procedure as an improvement if $Y \le 7$ or $Y/n \le 0.035$. We do note, however, that the probability of failure could still be about $p = 0.06$ even with the new procedure, and yet we could observe 7 or fewer failures in $n = 200$ trials. That is, we would erroneously accept the new method as being an improvement when, in fact, it was not. This decision is a mistake we call a **Type I error**. By contrast, the new procedure might actually improve the product so that p is much smaller, say, $p = 0.03$, and yet we could observe $y = 9$ failures, so that $y/200 = 0.045$. Thus, we would, again erroneously, not accept the new method as resulting in an improvement when in fact it had. This decision is a mistake we call a **Type II error**. We must study the probabilities of these two types of errors to understand fully the consequences of our rule.

Let us begin by modeling the situation. If we believe that these trials, conducted under the new procedure, are independent, and that each trial has about the same probability of failure, then Y is binomial $b(200, p)$. We wish to make a statistical inference about p using the unbiased estimator $\widehat{p} = Y/200$. Of course, we could construct a one-sided confidence interval—say, one that has 95% confidence of providing an upper bound for p—and obtain

$$\left[0,\ \widehat{p} + 1.645\sqrt{\frac{\widehat{p}\,(1 - \widehat{p}\,)}{200}}\,\right].$$

This inference is appropriate and many statisticians simply make it. If the limits of this confidence interval contain 0.06, they would not say that the new procedure is necessarily better, at least until more data are taken. If, however, the upper limit of the confidence interval is less than 0.06, then those same statisticians would feel 95% confident that the true p is now less than 0.06. Hence, they would support the fact that the new procedure has improved the manufacturing of the printed circuits in question.

While this use of confidence intervals is highly appropriate, and later we indicate the relationship of confidence intervals to tests of hypotheses, every student of statistics should also have some understanding of the basic concepts in the latter area. Here, in our illustration, we are testing whether the probability of failure has or has not decreased from 0.06 when the new manufacturing procedure is used. The *no-change* hypothesis, H_0: $p = 0.06$, is called the **null hypothesis**. Since H_0: $p = 0.06$ completely specifies the distribution, it is called a **simple hypothesis**; thus, H_0: $p = 0.06$ is a **simple null hypothesis**. The *research worker's* (here the engineer's or the statistician's) hypothesis H_1: $p < 0.06$ is called the **alternative hypothesis**. Since H_1: $p < 0.06$ does not completely specify the distribution, it is a **composite hypothesis**, because it is composed of many simple hypotheses. Our rule of rejecting H_0 and accepting H_1 if $Y \le 7$, and otherwise accepting H_0, is called a **test of a statistical hypothesis**. We now see that the two types of errors can be recorded as follows:

Type I error: Rejecting H_0 and accepting H_1 when H_0 is true;

Type II error: Failing to reject H_0 when H_1 is true (i.e., when H_0 is false).

Since, in our illustration, we make a Type I error if $Y \le 7$ when in fact $p = 0.06$, we can calculate the probability of this error. We denote that probability by α and call it the **significance level of the test.** Under our assumptions, it is

$$\alpha = P(Y \le 7;\ p = 0.06) = \sum_{y=0}^{7} \binom{200}{y} (0.06)^y (0.94)^{200-y}.$$

Since n is rather large and p is small, these binomial probabilities can be approximated very well by Poisson probabilities with $\lambda = 200(0.06) = 12$. That is, from the Poisson table, the probability of a Type I error is

$$\alpha \approx \sum_{y=0}^{7} \frac{12^y e^{-12}}{y!} = 0.090.$$

Thus, the approximate significance level of this test is $\alpha = 0.090$. (Using the binomial distribution, we find that the exact value of α is 0.0829, which you can easily verify with Minitab.)

This value of α is reasonably small. However, what about the probability of a Type II error in case p has been improved to, say, 0.03? This error occurs if $Y > 7$ when in fact $p = 0.03$; hence, its probability, denoted by β, is

$$\beta = P(Y > 7;\ p = 0.03) = \sum_{y=8}^{200} \binom{200}{y} (0.03)^y (0.97)^{200-y}.$$

Again we use the Poisson approximation, here with $\lambda = 200(0.03) = 6$, to obtain

$$\beta \approx 1 - \sum_{y=0}^{7} \frac{6^y e^{-6}}{y!} = 1 - 0.744 = 0.256.$$

(The binomial distribution tells us that the exact probability is 0.2539, so the approximation is very good.) The engineer and the statistician who created the new procedure probably are not too pleased with this answer. That is, they might note that if their new procedure of manufacturing circuits has actually decreased the probability of failure to 0.03 from 0.06 (*a big improvement*), there is still a good chance, 0.256, that $H_0: p = 0.06$ is accepted and their improvement rejected. Thus, in their eyes, this test of $H_0: p = 0.06$ against $H_1: p = 0.03$ is unsatisfactory. In Section 10.2, more will be said about modifying tests so that satisfactory values of the probabilities of the two types of errors, namely, α and β, can be obtained; however, to decrease both of them, we need larger sample sizes.

Without worrying more about the probability of the Type II error here, we present a frequently used procedure for testing $H_0: p = p_0$, where p_0 is some specified probability of success. This test is based upon the fact that the number of successes Y in n independent Bernoulli trials is such that Y/n has an approximate normal distribution $N[p_0, p_0(1 - p_0)/n]$, provided that $H_0: p = p_0$ is true and n is large. Suppose the alternative hypothesis is $H_1: p > p_0$; that is, it has been hypothesized by a research worker that something has been done to increase the probability of success. Consider the test of $H_0: p = p_0$ against $H_1: p > p_0$ that rejects H_0 and accepts H_1 if and only if

$$Z = \frac{Y/n - p_0}{\sqrt{p_0(1 - p_0)/n}} \geq z_\alpha.$$

That is, if Y/n exceeds p_0 by z_α standard deviations of Y/n, we reject H_0 and accept the hypothesis $H_1: p > p_0$. Since, under H_0, Z is approximately $N(0,1)$, the approximate probability of this occurring when $H_0: p = p_0$ is true is α. So the significance level of this test is approximately α.

If the alternative is $H_1: p < p_0$ instead of $H_1: p > p_0$, then the appropriate α-level test is given by $Z \leq -z_\alpha$. Hence, if Y/n is smaller than p_0 by z_α standard deviations of Y/n, we accept $H_1: p < p_0$.

EXAMPLE 7.1-1 It was claimed that many commercially manufactured dice are not fair because the "spots" are really indentations, so that, for example, the 6-side is lighter than the 1-side. Let p equal the probability of rolling a 6 with one of these dice. To test $H_0: p = 1/6$ against the alternative hypothesis $H_1: p > 1/6$, several such dice will be rolled to yield a total of $n = 8000$ observations. Let Y equal the number of times that

6 resulted in the 8000 trials. The test statistic is

$$Z = \frac{Y/n - 1/6}{\sqrt{(1/6)(5/6)/n}} = \frac{Y/8000 - 1/6}{\sqrt{(1/6)(5/6)/8000}}.$$

If we use a significance level of $\alpha = 0.05$, the critical region is

$$z \geq z_{0.05} = 1.645.$$

The results of the experiment yielded $y = 1389$, so the calculated value of the test statistic is

$$z = \frac{1389/8000 - 1/6}{\sqrt{(1/6)(5/6)/8000}} = 1.670.$$

Since

$$z = 1.670 > 1.645,$$

the null hypothesis is rejected, and the experimental results indicate that these dice favor a 6 more than a fair die would. (You could perform your own experiment to check out other dice; see also Exercise 7.1-6.) ■

Tests of $H_0\colon p = p_0$ against $H_1\colon p < p_0$ or $H_0\colon p = p_0$ against $H_1\colon p > p_0$ are called **one-sided** tests because the alternative hypotheses are **one sided**. There are times when **two-sided** alternatives and tests are appropriate, as in $H_1\colon p \neq p_0$. For example, suppose that the pass rate in the usual beginning statistics course is p_0. There has been an intervention (say, some new teaching method) and it is not known whether the pass rate will increase, decrease, or stay about the same. Thus, we test the null (no-change) hypothesis $H_0\colon p = p_0$ against the two-sided alternative $H_1\colon p \neq p_0$. A test with the approximate significance level α for doing this is to reject $H_0\colon p = p_0$ if

$$|Z| = \frac{|Y/n - p_0|}{\sqrt{p_0(1 - p_0)/n}} \geq z_{\alpha/2},$$

since, under H_0, $P(|Z| \geq z_{\alpha/2}) \approx \alpha$. These tests of approximate significance level α are summarized in Table 7.1-1. The rejection region for H_0 is often called the **critical region** of the test, and we use that terminology in the table.

TABLE 7.1-1: Tests of Hypotheses for One Proportion

H_0	H_1	Critical Region
$p = p_0$	$p > p_0$	$z = \dfrac{y/n - p_0}{\sqrt{p_0(1 - p_0)/n}} \geq z_\alpha$
$p = p_0$	$p < p_0$	$z = \dfrac{y/n - p_0}{\sqrt{p_0(1 - p_0)/n}} \leq -z_\alpha$
$p = p_0$	$p \neq p_0$	$\|z\| = \dfrac{\|y/n - p_0\|}{\sqrt{p_0(1 - p_0)/n}} \geq z_{\alpha/2}$

For a number of years, there has been another value associated with a statistical test, and most statistical computer programs automatically print this value out; it is called the **probability value** or, for brevity, ***p*-value**. The p-value associated with a test is the probability, under the null hypothesis H_0, that the test statistic (a random variable) is equal to or exceeds the observed value (a constant) of the test statistic in the direction of the alternative hypothesis. Rather than select the critical region ahead of time, the p-value of a test can be reported and the reader then makes a decision.

In Example 7.1-1, the value of the test statistic was $z = 1.67$. Because the alternative hypothesis was $H_1: p > 1/6$, the p-value is

$$P(Z \geq 1.67) = 0.0475.$$

Note that this p-value is less than $\alpha = 0.05$, which would lead to the rejection of H_0 at an $\alpha = 0.05$ significance level. If the alternative hypothesis were two sided, $H_1: p \neq 1/6$, then the p-value would be $P(|Z| \geq 1.67) = 0.095$ and would not lead to the rejection of H_0 at $\alpha = 0.05$.

Often there is interest in tests about p_1 and p_2, the probabilities of success for two different distributions or the proportions of two different populations having a certain characteristic. For example, if p_1 and p_2 denote the respective proportions of homeowners and renters who vote in favor of a proposal to reduce property taxes, a politician might be interested in testing $H_0: p_1 = p_2$ against the one-sided alternative hypothesis $H_1: p_1 > p_2$.

Let Y_1 and Y_2 represent, respectively, the numbers of observed successes in n_1 and n_2 independent trials with probabilities of success p_1 and p_2. Recall that the distribution of $\widehat{p_1} = Y_1/n_1$ is approximately $N[p_1, p_1(1 - p_1)/n_1]$ and the distribution of $\widehat{p_2} = Y_2/n_2$ is approximately $N[p_2, p_2(1 - p_2)/n_2]$. So the distribution of $\widehat{p_1} - \widehat{p_2} = Y_1/n_1 - Y_2/n_2$ is approximately $N[p_1 - p_2, p_1(1 - p_1)/n_1 + p_2(1 - p_2)/n_2]$. It follows that the distribution of

$$Z = \frac{Y_1/n_1 - Y_2/n_2 - (p_1 - p_2)}{\sqrt{p_1(1 - p_1)/n_1 + p_2(1 - p_2)/n_2}} \tag{7.1-1}$$

is approximately $N(0,1)$. To test H_0: $p_1 - p_2 = 0$ or, equivalently, H_0: $p_1 = p_2$, let $p = p_1 = p_2$ be the common value under H_0. We shall estimate p with $\widehat{p} = (Y_1 + Y_2)/(n_1 + n_2)$. Replacing p_1 and p_2 in the denominator of Equation 7.1-1 with this estimate, we obtain the test statistic

$$Z = \frac{\widehat{p_1} - \widehat{p_2} - 0}{\sqrt{\widehat{p}\,(1 - \widehat{p}\,)(1/n_1 + 1/n_2)}},$$

which has an approximate $N(0,1)$ distribution when the null hypothesis is true.

The three possible alternative hypotheses and their critical regions are summarized in Table 7.1-2.

TABLE 7.1-2: Tests of Hypotheses for Two Proportions

H_0	H_1	Critical Region
$p_1 = p_2$	$p_1 > p_2$	$z = \dfrac{\widehat{p_1} - \widehat{p_2}}{\sqrt{\widehat{p}\,(1 - \widehat{p}\,)(1/n_1 + 1/n_2)}} \geq z_\alpha$
$p_1 = p_2$	$p_1 < p_2$	$z = \dfrac{\widehat{p_1} - \widehat{p_2}}{\sqrt{\widehat{p}\,(1 - \widehat{p}\,)(1/n_1 + 1/n_2)}} \leq -z_\alpha$
$p_1 = p_2$	$p_1 \neq p_2$	$\lvert z \rvert = \dfrac{\lvert \widehat{p_1} - \widehat{p_2} \rvert}{\sqrt{\widehat{p}\,(1 - \widehat{p}\,)(1/n_1 + 1/n_2)}} \geq z_{\alpha/2}$

REMARKS In testing both $H_0: p = p_0$ and $H_0: p_1 = p_2$, statisticians sometimes use different denominators for z. For tests of single proportions, $\sqrt{p_0(1 - p_0)/n}$ can be replaced by $\sqrt{(y/n)(1 - y/n)/n}$, and for tests of the equality of two proportions, the following denominator can be used:

$$\sqrt{\frac{\widehat{p_1}(1 - \widehat{p_1})}{n_1} + \frac{\widehat{p_2}(1 - \widehat{p_2})}{n_2}}.$$

We do not have a strong preference one way or the other, since the two methods provide about the same numerical result. The substitutions do provide better estimates of the standard deviations of the numerators when the null hypotheses are clearly false. There is some advantage to this result if the null hypothesis is likely to be false. In addition, the substitutions tie together the use of confidence intervals and tests of hypotheses. For example, if the null hypothesis is $H_0: p = p_0$, then the alternative hypothesis $H_1: p < p_0$ is accepted if

$$z = \frac{\widehat{p} - p_0}{\sqrt{\dfrac{\widehat{p}(1 - \widehat{p})}{n}}} \le -z_\alpha.$$

This formula is equivalent to the statement that

$$p_0 \notin \left[0, \widehat{p} + z_\alpha\sqrt{\frac{\widehat{p}(1 - \widehat{p})}{n}}\right),$$

where the latter is a one-sided confidence interval providing an upper bound for p. Or if the alternative hypothesis is $H_1: p \ne p_0$, then H_0 is rejected if

$$\frac{|\widehat{p} - p_0|}{\sqrt{\dfrac{\widehat{p}(1 - \widehat{p})}{n}}} \ge z_{\alpha/2}.$$

This inequality is equivalent to

$$p_0 \notin \left(\widehat{p} - z_{\alpha/2}\sqrt{\frac{\widehat{p}(1 - \widehat{p})}{n}}, \widehat{p} + z_{\alpha/2}\sqrt{\frac{\widehat{p}(1 - \widehat{p})}{n}}\right),$$

where the latter is a confidence interval for p. However, using the forms given in Tables 7.1-1 and 7.1-2, we do get better approximations to α-level significance tests. Thus, there are trade-offs, and it is difficult to say that one is better than the other. Fortunately, the numerical answers are about the same.

In the second situation in which the estimates of p_1 and p_2 are the observed $\widehat{p_1} = y_1/n_1$ and $\widehat{p_2} = y_2/n_2$, we have, with large values of n_1 and n_2, an approximate 95% confidence interval for $p_1 - p_2$ given by

$$\frac{y_1}{n_1} - \frac{y_2}{n_2} \pm 1.96\sqrt{\frac{(y_1/n_1)(1 - y_1/n_1)}{n_1} + \frac{(y_2/n_2)(1 - y_2/n_2)}{n_2}}.$$

If $p_1 - p_2 = 0$ is not in this interval, we reject $H_0: p_1 - p_2 = 0$ at the $\alpha = 0.05$ significance level. This is equivalent to saying that we reject $H_0: p_1 - p_2 = 0$ if

$$\frac{\left|\dfrac{y_1}{n_1} - \dfrac{y_2}{n_2}\right|}{\sqrt{\dfrac{(y_1/n_1)(1 - y_1/n_1)}{n_1} + \dfrac{(y_2/n_2)(1 - y_2/n_2)}{n_2}}} \geq 1.96.$$

In general, if the estimator $\widehat{\theta}$ (often, the maximum likelihood) of θ has an approximate (sometimes exact) normal distribution $N(\theta, \sigma^2_{\widehat{\theta}})$, then $H_0: \theta = \theta_0$ is rejected in favor of $H_1: \theta \neq \theta_0$ at the α significance level if

$$\theta_0 \notin (\widehat{\theta} - z_{\alpha/2}\sigma_{\widehat{\theta}}, \widehat{\theta} + z_{\alpha/2}\sigma_{\widehat{\theta}})$$

or, equivalently,

$$\frac{|\widehat{\theta} - \theta_0|}{\sigma_{\widehat{\theta}}} \geq z_{\alpha/2}.$$

Note that $\sigma_{\widehat{\theta}}$ often depends upon some unknown parameter that must be estimated and substituted in $\sigma_{\widehat{\theta}}$ to obtain $\widehat{\sigma_{\widehat{\theta}}}$. Sometimes $\sigma_{\widehat{\theta}}$ or its estimate is called the **standard error** of $\widehat{\theta}$. This was the case in our last illustration when, with $\theta = p_1 - p_2$ and $\widehat{\theta} = \widehat{p_1} - \widehat{p_2}$, we substituted y_1/n_1 for p_1 and y_2/n_2 for p_2 in

$$\sqrt{\frac{p_1(1 - p_1)}{n_1} + \frac{p_2(1 - p_2)}{n_2}}$$

to obtain the standard error of $\widehat{p_1} - \widehat{p_2} = \widehat{\theta}$. ■

EXERCISES

7.1-1. Bowl A contains 100 red balls and 200 white balls; bowl B contains 200 red balls and 100 white balls. Let p denote the probability of drawing a red ball from a bowl, but say p is unknown, since it is unknown whether bowl A or bowl B is being used. We shall test the simple null hypothesis H_0: $p = 1/3$ against the simple alternative hypothesis H_1: $p = 2/3$. Draw three balls at random, one at a time and with replacement, from the selected bowl. Let X equal the number of red balls drawn. Then let the critical region be $C = \{x : x = 2, 3\}$. What are the values of α and β, the probabilities of Type I and Type II errors, respectively?

7.1-2. A bowl contains two red balls, two white balls, and a fifth ball that is either red or white. Let p denote the probability of drawing a red ball from the bowl. We shall test the simple null hypothesis H_0: $p = 3/5$ against the simple alternative hypothesis H_1: $p = 2/5$. Draw four balls at random from the bowl, one at a time and with replacement. Let X equal the number of red balls drawn.

(a) Define a critical region C for this test in terms of X.

(b) For the critical region C defined in part (a), find the values of α and β.

7.1-3. Let Y be $b(100, p)$. To test H_0: $p = 0.08$ against H_1: $p < 0.08$, we reject H_0 and accept H_1 if and only if $Y \leq 6$.

(a) Determine the significance level α of the test.

(b) Find the probability of the Type II error if in fact $p = 0.04$.

7.1-4. Let p denote the probability that, for a particular tennis player, the first serve is good. Since $p = 0.40$, this player decided to take lessons in order to increase p. When the lessons are completed, the hypothesis $H_0: p = 0.40$ will be tested against $H_1: p > 0.40$ on the basis of $n = 25$ trials. Let y equal the number of first serves that are good, and let the critical region be defined by $C = \{y: y \geq 13\}$.

(a) Determine $\alpha = P(Y \geq 13; p = 0.40)$. Use Table II in the appendix.

(b) Find $\beta = P(Y < 13)$ when $p = 0.60$; that is, $\beta = P(Y \leq 12; p = 0.60)$. Use Table II.

7.1-5. Let Y be $b(192, p)$. We reject $H_0: p = 0.75$ and accept $H_1: p > 0.75$ if and only if $Y \geq 152$. Use the normal approximation to determine

(a) $\alpha = P(Y \geq 152; p = 0.75)$.

(b) $\beta = P(Y < 152)$ when $p = 0.80$.

7.1-6. To determine whether the 1-side on a commercially manufactured die is heavy and the 6-side is light (see Example 7.1-1), some students kept track of the number of observed "ones" in $n = 8000$ rolls of the dice. Let p equal the probability of rolling a one with such a die. We shall test the null hypothesis $H_0: p = 1/6$ against the alternative hypothesis $H_1: p < 1/6$.

(a) Define the test statistic and an $\alpha = 0.05$ critical region.

(b) If $y = 1265$ ones were observed in 8000 rolls, calculate the value of the test statistic and state your conclusion.

(c) Is 1/6 in the 95% one-sided confidence interval providing an upper bound for p?

7.1-7. If a newborn baby has a birth weight that is less than 2500 grams (5.5 pounds), we say that the baby has a low birth weight. The proportion of babies with a low birth weight is an indicator of lack of nutrition for the mothers. For the United States, approximately 7% of babies have a low birth weight. Let p equal the proportion of babies born in the Sudan who weigh less than 2500 grams. We shall test the null hypothesis H_0: $p = 0.07$ against the alternative hypothesis H_1: $p > 0.07$. In a random sample of $n = 209$ babies, $y = 23$ weighed less than 2500 grams.

(a) What is your conclusion at a significance level of $\alpha = 0.05$?

(b) What is your conclusion at a significance level of $\alpha = 0.01$?

(c) Find the p-value for this test.

7.1-8. It was claimed that 75% of all dentists recommend a certain brand of gum for their gum-chewing patients. A consumer group doubted this claim and decided to test H_0: $p = 0.75$ against the alternative hypothesis H_1: $p < 0.75$, where p is the proportion of dentists who recommend that brand of gum. A survey of 390 dentists found that 273 recommended the given brand of gum.

(a) Which hypothesis would you accept if the significance level is $\alpha = 0.05$?

(b) Which hypothesis would you accept if the significance level is $\alpha = 0.01$?

(c) Find the p-value for this test.

7.1-9. It was claimed that the proportion of Americans who select jogging as one of their recreational activities is $p = 0.25$. A shoe manufacturer thought that p was larger than 0.25 and decided to test the null hypothesis H_0: $p = 0.25$ against the alternative hypothesis H_1: $p > 0.25$. Out of a random sample of $n = 5757$, $y = 1497$ selected jogging.

(a) What is your conclusion at a significance level of $\alpha = 0.05$?

(b) What is your conclusion at a significance level of $\alpha = 0.025$?

(c) Find the p-value for this test.

7.1-10. Let p equal the proportion of drivers who use a seat belt in a state that does not have a mandatory seat belt law. It was claimed that $p = 0.14$. An advertising campaign was conducted to increase this proportion. Two months after the campaign, $y = 104$ out of a random sample of $n = 590$ drivers were wearing their seat belts. Was the campaign successful?

(a) Define the null and alternative hypotheses.

(b) Define a critical region with an $\alpha = 0.01$ significance level.

(c) What is your conclusion?

7.1-11. The management of the Tigers baseball team decided to sell only low-alcohol beer in their ballpark to help combat rowdy fan conduct. They claimed that more than 40% of the fans would approve of this decision. Let p equal the proportion of Tiger fans on opening day who approved of the decision. We shall test the null hypothesis H_0: $p = 0.40$ against the alternative hypothesis $H_1: p > 0.40$.

(a) Define a critical region that has an $\alpha = 0.05$ significance level.

(b) If, out of a random sample of $n = 1278$ fans, $y = 550$ said that they approved of the new policy, what is your conclusion?

7.1-12. Because of tourism in the State, it was proposed that public schools in Michigan begin after

Labor Day. To determine whether support for this change was greater than 65%, a public poll was taken. Let p equal the proportion of Michigan adults who favor a post–Labor Day start. We shall test $H_0: p = 0.65$ against $H_1: p > 0.65$.

(a) Define a test statistic and an $\alpha = 0.025$ critical region.

(b) Given that 414 out of a sample of 600 favor a post–Labor Day start, calculate the value of the test statistic.

(c) Find the p-value and state your conclusion.

(d) Find a 95% one-sided confidence interval that gives a lower bound for p.

7.1-13. Let p equal the proportion of women who agree that "men are basically selfish and self-centered." Suppose that in the past it was believed that $p = 0.40$. It is now claimed that p has increased.

(a) Define the null and alternative hypotheses, a test statistic, and a critical region that has an approximate $\alpha = 0.01$ significance level. Sketch a standard normal p.d.f. and illustrate this critical region.

(b) The *Detroit Free Press* (April 26, 1990) reported that $y = 1260$ out of a random sample of $n = 3000$ women agree with the aforesaid statement about men. What is the conclusion of your test? Locate the calculated value of your test statistic on the p.d.f. in part (a).

7.1-14. A physician at a local hospital wrote, "In medicine we are now asked to perform quality assurance studies by various regulatory governmental or quasi-governmental agencies." He continued, "Dr. X was notified that for a particular procedure, his complication rate of 20% last year ($n = 20$) was unacceptable for continued privileges. So he took a one month remedial course for improving his technique. His complication rate is now 15% ($n = 15$). Has he really improved?" (You may assume that some rounding off was done in the letter and that the 15% is really 2/15.)

7.1-15. According to a population census in 1986, the percentage of males who are 18 or 19 years old and are married was 3.7%. We shall test whether this percentage increased from 1986 to 1988.

(a) Define the null and alternative hypotheses.

(b) Define a critical region that has an approximate significance level of $\alpha = 0.01$. Sketch a standard normal p.d.f. to illustrate this critical region.

(c) If $y = 20$ out of a random sample of $n = 300$ males, each 18 or 19 years old, were married (*U.S. Bureau of the Census, Statistical Abstract of the United States: 1988*), what is your conclusion? Show the calculated value of the test statistic on your figure in part (b).

7.1-16. Let p equal the proportion of yellow candies in a package of mixed colors. It is claimed that $p = 0.20$.

(a) Define a test statistic and critical region with a significance level of $\alpha = 0.05$ for testing $H_0: p = 0.20$ against a two-sided alternative hypothesis.

(b) To perform the test, each of 20 students counted the number of yellow candies, y, and the total number of candies, n, in a 48.1-gram package, yielding the following ratios, y/n: 8/56, 13/55, 12/58, 13/56, 14/57, 5/54, 14/56, 15/57, 11/54, 13/55, 10/57, 8/59, 10/54, 11/55, 12/56, 11/57, 6/54, 7/58, 12/58, 14/58. If each individual tests $H_0: p = 0.20$, what proportion of the students rejected the null hypothesis?

(c) If we may assume that the null hypothesis is true, what proportion of the students would you have expected to reject the null hypothesis?

(d) For each of the 20 ratios in part (b), a 95% confidence interval for p can be calculated. What proportion of these 95% confidence intervals contain $p = 0.20$?

(e) If the 20 results are pooled so that $\sum_{i=1}^{20} y_i$ equals the number of yellow candies and $\sum_{i=1}^{20} n_i$ equals the total sample size, do we reject $H_0: p = 0.20$?

7.1-17. A machine shop that manufactures toggle levers has both a day and a night shift. A toggle lever is defective if a standard nut cannot be screwed onto the threads. Let p_1 and p_2 be the proportion of defective levers among those manufactured by the day and night shifts, respectively. We shall test the null hypothesis, $H_0: p_1 = p_2$, against a two-sided alternative hypothesis based on two random samples, each of 1000 levers taken from the production of the respective shifts.

(a) Define the test statistic and a critical region that has an $\alpha = 0.05$ significance level. Sketch a standard normal p.d.f. illustrating this critical region.

(b) If $y_1 = 37$ and $y_2 = 53$ defectives were observed for the day and night shifts, respectively, calculate the value of the test statistic. Locate the calculated test statistic on your figure in part (a) and state your conclusion.

7.1-18. The April 18, 1994, issue of *Time* magazine reported the results of a telephone poll of 800 adult Americans, 605 of them nonsmokers, who were asked the following question: "Should the federal tax on cigarettes be raised by $1.25 to pay for health care reform?" Let p_1 and p_2 equal the proportions of nonsmokers and smokers, respectively, who would say yes to this question. Given that $y_1 = 351$ nonsmokers and $y_2 = 41$ smokers said yes,

(a) With $\alpha = 0.05$, test $H_0: p_1 = p_2$ against $H_1: p_1 \neq p_2$.

(b) Find a 95% confidence interval for $p_1 - p_2$. Is your interval in agreement with the conclusion of part (a)?

(c) Find a 95% confidence interval for p, the proportion of adult Americans who would say yes.

7.1-19. Let p_m and p_f be the respective proportions of male and female white-crowned sparrows that return to their hatching site. Give the endpoints for a 95% confidence interval for $p_m - p_f$ if 124 out of 894 males and 70 out of 700 females returned. (*The Condor*, 1992, pp. 117–133.) Does your result agree with the conclusion of a test of $H_0: p_1 = p_2$ against $H_1: p_1 \neq p_2$ with $\alpha = 0.05$?

7.1-20. For developing countries in Africa and the Americas, let p_1 and p_2 be the respective proportions of babies with a low birth weight (below 2500 grams). We shall test H_0: $p_1 = p_2$ against the alternative hypothesis $H_1: p_1 > p_2$.

(a) Define a critical region that has an $\alpha = 0.05$ significance level.

(b) If respective random samples of sizes $n_1 = 900$ and $n_2 = 700$ yielded $y_1 = 135$ and $y_2 = 77$ babies with a low birth weight, what is your conclusion?

(c) What would your decision be with a significance level of $\alpha = 0.01$?

(d) What is the p-value of your test?

7.1-21. The following text was shown to a large class of students for 30 seconds, and they were told to report the number of F's that they found:

FINISHED FILES ARE THE RESULT OF YEARS OF SCIENTIFIC STUDY COMBINED WITH THE EXPERIENCE OF MANY YEARS.

Let p equal the proportion of students who find six F's. We shall test the null hypothesis $H_0: p = 0.5$ against the alternative hypothesis $H_1: p < 0.5$.

(a) Given a sample size of $n = 200$, define a critical region with an approximate significance level of $\alpha = 0.05$.

(b) If $y = 88$ students reported that they found six F's, what is your conclusion?

(c) What is the p-value of this test?

(d) Test this hypothesis or a modification of it with a class of students.

7.1-22. Each of six students has a deck of cards and selects a card randomly from his or her deck.

(a) Show that the probability of at least one match is equal to 0.259.

(b) Now let each of the students randomly select an integer from 1–52, inclusive. Let p equal the probability of at least one match. Test the null hypothesis H_0: $p = 0.259$ against an appropriate alternative hypothesis. Give a reason for your alternative.

(c) Perform this experiment a large number of times. What is your conclusion?

7.1-23. In a certain industry, about 15 percent of the workers showed some signs of ill effects due to radiation. After the management claimed that improvements had been made, 140 workers were tested and 19 experienced some ill effects due to radiation. Does this result support the management's claim? Use $\alpha = 0.05$.

7.1-24. Let p be the fraction of engineers who do not understand certain basic statistical concepts. Unfortunately, in the past, this number has been high, about $p = 0.73$. A new program to improve the knowledge of statistical methods has been implemented, and it is expected that under this program p would decrease from the aforesaid 0.73 value. To test $H_0: p = 0.73$ against $H_1: p < 0.73$, 300 engineers in the new program were tested and 204 (i.e., 68%) did not comprehend certain basic statistical concepts. Compute the p-value to determine whether this result indicates progress. That is, can we reject H_0 is favor of H_1? Use $\alpha = 0.05$.

7.1-25. A certain washing machine manufacturer claims that the fraction p_1 of its washing machines that need repairs in the first five years of operation is less than the fraction p_2 of another brand's. To test this claim, we observe $n_1 = n_2 = 200$ machines of each brand. We find that $y_1 = 21$ and $y_2 = 37$ machines need repairs. Do these data support the manufacturer's claim? Use $\alpha = 0.05$.

7.2 TESTS ABOUT ONE MEAN

Many applications assume that we are sampling from a normal distribution. We begin this section with such an application, for which we also assume that the variance is known.

EXAMPLE 7.2-1 Let X equal the breaking strength of a steel bar. If the bar is manufactured by process I, X is $N(50, 36)$. It is hoped that if process II (a new process) is used, X will be $N(55, 36)$. Given a large number of steel bars manufactured by process II, how could we test whether the increase in the mean breaking strength was realized?

In answering this question, we review some of the terminology that was introduced in Section 7.1, because we find that is helpful to most readers. So in this problem, we are assuming that X is $N(\mu, 36)$ and μ is equal to 50 or 55. We want to test the **simple null hypothesis** H_0: $\mu = 50$ against the **simple alternative hypothesis** H_1: $\mu = 55$. Note that each of these hypotheses completely specifies the distribution of X. That is, H_0 states that X is $N(50, 36)$ and H_1 states that X is $N(55, 36)$. (If the alternative hypothesis had been H_1: $\mu > 50$, it would be a **composite hypothesis**, because it is composed of all normal distributions with $\sigma^2 = 36$ and means greater than 50.) In order to test which of the two hypotheses, H_0 or H_1, is true, we shall set up a rule based on the breaking strengths $x_1, x_2, \ldots, x_n$ of n bars (the observed values of a random sample of size n from this new normal distribution). The rule leads to a decision to accept or reject H_0; hence, it is necessary to partition the sample space into two parts—say, C and C'—so that if $(x_1, x_2, \ldots, x_n) \in C$, H_0 is rejected, and if $(x_1, x_2, \ldots, x_n) \in C'$, H_0 is accepted (not rejected). The rejection region C for H_0 is called the **critical region** for the test. Often, the partitioning of the sample space is specified in terms of the values of a statistic called the **test statistic**. In this example, we could let $\overline{X}$ be the test statistic and, say, take $C = \{(x_1, x_2, \ldots, x_n) : \overline{x} \ge 53\}$. We could then define the critical region as those values of the test statistic for which H_0 is rejected. That is, the given critical region is equivalent to defining $C = \{\overline{x} : \overline{x} \ge 53\}$ in the $\overline{x}$ space. If $(x_1, x_2, \ldots, x_n) \in C$ when H_0 is true, H_0 would be rejected when it is true, a **Type I error**. If $(x_1, x_2, \ldots, x_n) \in C'$ when H_1 is true, H_0 would be accepted (i.e., not rejected) when in fact H_1 is true, a **Type II error**. Recall that the probability of a Type I error is called the **significance level** of the test and is denoted by α. That is, $\alpha = P[(X_1, X_2, \ldots, X_n) \in C; H_0]$ is the probability that $(X_1, X_2, \ldots, X_n)$ falls into C when H_0 is true. The probability of a Type II error is denoted by β; that is, $\beta = P[(X_1, X_2, \ldots, X_n) \in C'; H_1]$ is the probability of accepting (failing to reject) H_0 when it is false. As an illustration, suppose $n = 16$ bars were tested and $C = \{\overline{x} : \overline{x} \ge 53\}$. Then $\overline{X}$ is $N(50, 36/16)$ when H_0 is true and is $N(55, 36/16)$ when H_1 is true. Thus,

$$\begin{aligned}\alpha = P(\overline{X} \ge 53; H_0) &= P\left(\frac{\overline{X} - 50}{6/4} \ge \frac{53 - 50}{6/4}; H_0\right)\\ &= 1 - \Phi(2) = 0.0228\end{aligned}$$

and

$$\begin{aligned}\beta = P(\overline{X} < 53; H_1) &= P\left(\frac{\overline{X} - 55}{6/4} < \frac{53 - 55}{6/4}; H_1\right)\\ &= \Phi\left(-\frac{4}{3}\right) = 1 - 0.9087 = 0.0913.\end{aligned}$$

Figure 7.2-1 shows the graphs of the probability density functions of $\overline{X}$ when H_0 and H_1, respectively, are true. Note that a decrease in the size of α leads to an increase in the size of β, and vice versa. Both α and β can be decreased if the sample size n is increased. ■

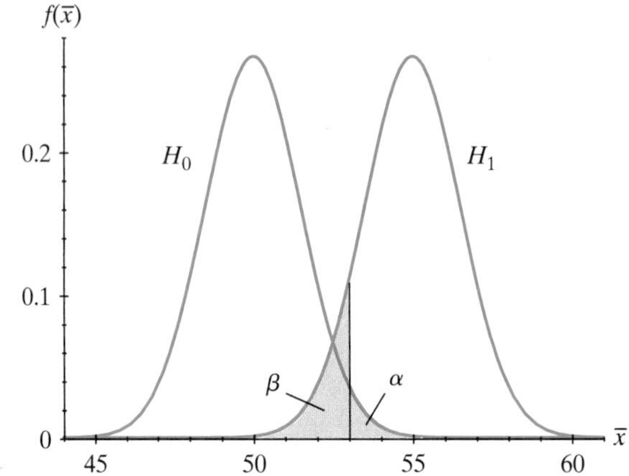

FIGURE 7.2-1: p.d.f. of $\overline{X}$ under H_0 and H_1

The definition of *p-value* is given in Section 7.1. We now give an example of a p-value obtained in testing a hypothesis about a mean.

EXAMPLE 7.2-2 Assume that the underlying distribution is normal with unknown mean μ but known variance $\sigma^2 = 100$. Say we are testing H_0: $\mu = 60$ against H_1: $\mu > 60$ with a sample mean $\overline{X}$ based on $n = 52$ observations. Suppose that we obtain the observed sample mean of $\overline{x} = 62.75$. If we compute the probability of obtaining an $\overline{X}$ of that value of 62.75 or greater when $\mu = 60$, then we obtain the p-value associated with $\overline{x} = 62.75$. That is,

$$\begin{aligned} p\text{-value} &= P(\overline{X} \ge 62.75;\ \mu = 60) \\ &= P\left(\frac{\overline{X} - 60}{10/\sqrt{52}} \ge \frac{62.75 - 60}{10/\sqrt{52}};\ \mu = 60\right) \\ &= 1 - \Phi\left(\frac{62.75 - 60}{10/\sqrt{52}}\right) = 1 - \Phi(1.983) = 0.0237. \end{aligned}$$

If this p-value is small, we tend to reject the hypothesis H_0: $\mu = 60$. For example, rejecting H_0: $\mu = 60$ if the p-value is less than or equal to $\alpha = 0.05$ is exactly the same as rejecting H_0 if

$$\overline{x} \ge 60 + (1.645)\left(\frac{10}{\sqrt{52}}\right) = 62.718.$$

Here

$$p\text{-value} = 0.0237 < \alpha = 0.05 \quad \text{and} \quad \overline{x} = 62.75 > 62.718.$$

To help the reader keep the definition of **p-value** in mind, we note that it can be thought of as that **tail-end probability**, under H_0, of the distribution of the statistic (here $\overline{X}$), beyond the observed value of the statistic. (See Figure 7.2-2 for the p-value associated with $\overline{x} = 62.75$.)

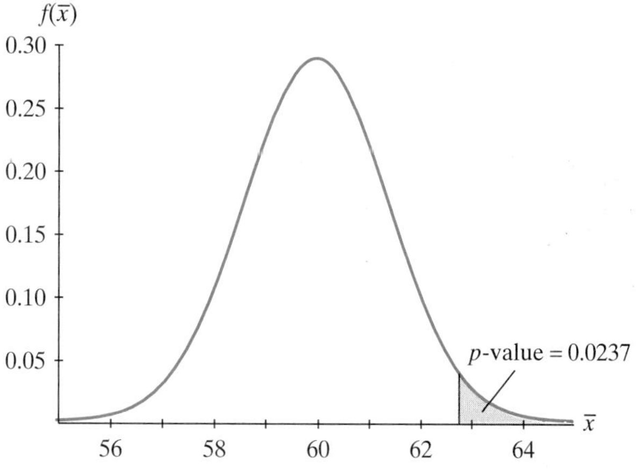

FIGURE 7.2-2: Illustration of p-value

If the alternative were the two-sided $H_1\colon \mu \neq 60$, then the p-value would have been double 0.0237; that is, then the p-value $= 2(0.0237) = 0.0474$ because we include both tails. ■

When we sample from a normal distribution, the null hypothesis is generally of the form $H_0\colon \mu = \mu_0$. There are essentially three possibilities for the alternative hypothesis: (i) that μ has increased, or $H_1\colon \mu > \mu_0$; (ii) that μ has decreased, or $H_1\colon \mu < \mu_0$; and (iii) that μ has changed, but it is not known whether it has increased or decreased, which leads to the two-sided alternative hypothesis, or $H_1\colon \mu \neq \mu_0$.

To test $H_0\colon \mu = \mu_0$ against one of these three alternative hypotheses, a random sample is taken from the distribution and an observed sample mean, $\overline{x}$, that is close to μ_0 supports H_0. The closeness of $\overline{x}$ to μ_0 is measured in terms of standard deviations of $\overline{X}$, $\sigma/\sqrt{n}$, when σ is known, a measure that is sometimes called the **standard error of the mean**. Thus, the test statistic could be defined by

$$Z = \frac{\overline{X} - \mu_0}{\sqrt{\sigma^2/n}} = \frac{\overline{X} - \mu_0}{\sigma/\sqrt{n}}, \tag{7.2-1}$$

and the critical regions, at a significance level α, for the three respective alternative hypotheses would be (i) $z \geq z_\alpha$, (ii) $z \leq -z_\alpha$, and (iii) $|z| \geq z_{\alpha/2}$. In terms of $\overline{x}$ these three critical regions become (i) $\overline{x} \geq \mu_0 + z_\alpha(\sigma/\sqrt{n}\,)$, (ii) $\overline{x} \leq \mu_0 - z_\alpha(\sigma/\sqrt{n}\,)$, and (iii) $|\overline{x} - \mu_0| \geq z_{\alpha/2}(\sigma/\sqrt{n}\,)$.

The three tests and critical regions are summarized in Table 7.2-1 on the next page. The underlying assumption is that the distribution is $N(\mu, \sigma^2)$ and σ^2 is known.

It is usually the case that the variance σ^2 is not known. Accordingly, we now take a more realistic position and assume that the variance is unknown. Suppose our null hypothesis is $H_0\colon \mu = \mu_0$ and the two-sided alternative hypothesis is $H_1\colon \mu \neq \mu_0$. Recall from Section 6.2, that, for a random sample $X_1, X_2, \ldots, X_n$ taken from a normal distribution $N(\mu, \sigma^2)$, a confidence interval for μ is based on

$$T = \frac{\overline{X} - \mu}{\sqrt{S^2/n}} = \frac{\overline{X} - \mu}{S/\sqrt{n}}.$$

TABLE 7.2-1: Tests of Hypotheses About One Mean, Variance Known

H_0	H_1	Critical Region
$\mu = \mu_0$	$\mu > \mu_0$	$z \ge z_\alpha$ or $\bar{x} \ge \mu_0 + z_\alpha \sigma/\sqrt{n}$
$\mu = \mu_0$	$\mu < \mu_0$	$z \le -z_\alpha$ or $\bar{x} \le \mu_0 - z_\alpha \sigma/\sqrt{n}$
$\mu = \mu_0$	$\mu \ne \mu_0$	$\lvert z\rvert \ge z_{\alpha/2}$ or $\lvert\bar{x} - \mu_0\rvert \ge z_{\alpha/2}\sigma/\sqrt{n}$

This suggests that T might be a good statistic to use for the test of H_0: $\mu = \mu_0$ with μ replaced by μ_0. In addition, it is the natural statistic to use if we replace σ^2/n by its unbiased estimator S^2/n in $(\overline{X} - \mu_0)/\sqrt{\sigma^2/n}$ in Equation 7.2-1. If $\mu = \mu_0$, we know that T has a t distribution with $n - 1$ degrees of freedom. Thus, with $\mu = \mu_0$,

$$P[\,|T| \ge t_{\alpha/2}(n-1)] = P\left[\frac{|\overline{X} - \mu_0|}{S/\sqrt{n}} \ge t_{\alpha/2}(n-1)\right] = \alpha.$$

Accordingly, if $\bar{x}$ and s are, respectively, the sample mean and sample standard deviation, then the rule that rejects H_0: $\mu = \mu_0$ and accepts H_1: $\mu \ne \mu_0$ if and only if

$$|t| = \frac{|\bar{x} - \mu_0|}{s/\sqrt{n}} \ge t_{\alpha/2}(n-1)$$

provides a test of this hypothesis with significance level α. Note that this rule is equivalent to rejecting H_0: $\mu = \mu_0$ if μ_0 is not in the open $100(1 - \alpha)\%$ confidence interval

$$(\bar{x} - t_{\alpha/2}(n-1)(s/\sqrt{n}\,), \bar{x} + t_{\alpha/2}(n-1)(s/\sqrt{n}\,)).$$

Table 7.2-2 summarizes tests of hypotheses for a single mean, along with the three possible alternative hypotheses, when the underlying distribution is $N(\mu, \sigma^2)$, σ^2 is unknown, $t = (\bar{x} - \mu_0)/(s/\sqrt{n}\,)$, and $n \le 30$. If $n > 30$, we use Table 7.2-1 for approximate tests, with σ replaced by s.

TABLE 7.2-2: Tests of Hypotheses for One Mean, Variance Unknown

H_0	H_1	Critical Region
$\mu = \mu_0$	$\mu > \mu_0$	$t \ge t_\alpha(n-1)$ or $\bar{x} \ge \mu_0 + t_\alpha(n-1)s/\sqrt{n}$
$\mu = \mu_0$	$\mu < \mu_0$	$t \le -t_\alpha(n-1)$ or $\bar{x} \le \mu_0 - t_\alpha(n-1)s/\sqrt{n}$
$\mu = \mu_0$	$\mu \ne \mu_0$	$\lvert t\rvert \ge t_{\alpha/2}(n-1)$ or $\lvert\bar{x} - \mu_0\rvert \ge t_{\alpha/2}(n-1)s/\sqrt{n}$

EXAMPLE 7.2-3 Let X (in millimeters) equal the growth in 15 days of a tumor induced in a mouse. Assume that the distribution of X is $N(\mu, \sigma^2)$. We shall test the null hypothesis H_0: $\mu = \mu_0 = 4.0$ millimeters against the two-sided alternative hypothesis H_1: $\mu \ne 4.0$. If we use $n = 9$ observations and a significance level of $\alpha = 0.10$, the critical region is

$$|t| = \frac{|\bar{x} - 4.0|}{s/\sqrt{9}} \ge t_{\alpha/2}(8) = 1.860.$$

If we are given that $n = 9, \overline{x} = 4.3$, and $s = 1.2$, we see that

$$t = \frac{4.3 - 4.0}{1.2/\sqrt{9}} = \frac{0.3}{0.4} = 0.75.$$

Thus,

$$|t| = |0.75| < 1.860,$$

and we accept (do not reject) H_0: $\mu = 4.0$ at the $\alpha = 10\%$ significance level. (See Figure 7.2-3.) The p-value is

$$p\text{-value} = P(|T| \ge 0.75) = 2P(T \ge 0.75).$$

With our t tables with eight degrees of freedom, we cannot find this p-value exactly. It is about 0.50, because

$$P(|T| \ge 0.706) = 2P(T \ge 0.706) = 0.50.$$

Minitab gives a p-value of 0.4747. (See Figure 7.2-3.) ■

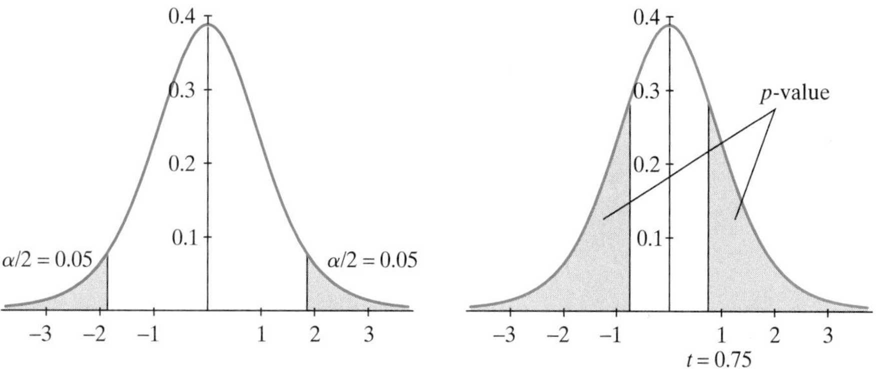

FIGURE 7.2-3: Test about mean of tumor growths

REMARK In discussing the test of a statistical hypothesis, the word *accept* H_0 might better be replaced by *do not reject* H_0. That is, if, in Example 7.2-3, $\overline{x}$ is close enough to 4.0 so that we accept $\mu = 4.0$, we do not want that acceptance to imply that μ is actually equal to 4.0. We want to say that the data do not deviate enough from $\mu = 4.0$ for us to reject that hypothesis; that is, we do not reject $\mu = 4.0$ with these observed data. With this understanding, we sometimes use *accept*, and sometimes *fail to reject* or *do not reject*, the null hypothesis. ■

The next example illustrates the use of the t statistic with a one-sided alternative hypothesis.

EXAMPLE 7.2-4 In attempting to control the strength of the wastes discharged into a nearby river, a paper firm has taken a number of measures. Members of the firm believe that they have reduced the oxygen-consuming power of their wastes from a previous mean μ of 500 (measured in parts per million of permanganate). They plan to test

H_0: $\mu = 500$ against H_1: $\mu < 500$, using readings taken on $n = 25$ consecutive days. If these 25 values can be treated as a random sample, then the critical region, for a significance level of $\alpha = 0.01$, is

$$t = \frac{\overline{x} - 500}{s/\sqrt{25}} \le -t_{0.01}(24) = -2.492.$$

The observed values of the sample mean and sample standard deviation were $\overline{x} = 308.8$ and $s = 115.15$. Since

$$t = \frac{308.8 - 500}{115.15/\sqrt{25}} = -8.30 < -2.492,$$

we clearly reject the null hypothesis and accept H_1: $\mu < 500$. Note, however, that although an improvement has been made, there still might exist the question of whether the improvement is adequate. The one-sided 99% confidence interval for μ, namely,

$$[0, 308.8 + 2.492(115.25/\sqrt{25}\,)] = [0, 366.191],$$

provides an upper bound for μ and may help the company answer this question. ■

Oftentimes, there is interest in comparing the means of two different distributions or populations. We must consider two situations: that in which X and Y are dependent and that in which X and Y are independent. We consider the independent case in the next section.

If X and Y are dependent, let $W = X - Y$, and the hypothesis that $\mu_X = \mu_Y$ would be replaced with the hypothesis H_0: $\mu_W = 0$. For example, suppose that X and Y equal the resting pulse rate for a person before and after taking an eight-week program in aerobic dance. We would be interested in testing H_0: $\mu_W = 0$ (no change) against H_1: $\mu_W > 0$ (the aerobic dance program decreased the resting pulse rate). Because X and Y are measurements on the same person, X and Y are clearly dependent. If we can assume that the distribution of W is (approximately) $N(\mu_W, \sigma^2)$, then we can choose to use the appropriate t-test for a single mean from Table 7.2-2. This is often called a **paired *t* test.**

EXAMPLE 7.2-5 Twenty-four girls in the 9th and 10th grades were put on an ultraheavy rope-jumping program. Someone thought that such a program would increase their speed in the 40-yard dash. Let W equal the difference in time to run the 40-yard dash—the "before-program time" minus the "after-program time." Assume that the distribution of W is approximately $N(\mu_W, \sigma_W^2)$. We shall test the null hypothesis H_0: $\mu_W = 0$ against the alternative hypothesis H_1: $\mu_W > 0$. The test statistic and the critical region that has an $\alpha = 0.05$ significance level are given by

$$t = \frac{\overline{w} - 0}{s_W/\sqrt{24}} \ge t_{0.05}(23) = 1.714.$$

The following data give the difference in time that it took each girl to run the 40-yard dash, with positive numbers indicating a faster time after the program:

0.28	0.01	0.13	0.33	−0.03	0.07	−0.18	−0.14
−0.33	0.01	0.22	0.29	−0.08	0.23	0.08	0.04
−0.30	−0.08	0.09	0.70	0.33	−0.34	0.50	0.06

For these data, $\overline{w} = 0.079$ and $s_w = 0.255$. Thus, the observed value of the test statistic is

$$t = \frac{0.079 - 0}{0.255/\sqrt{24}} = 1.518.$$

Since $1.518 < 1.714$, the null hypothesis is not rejected. Note, however, that $t_{0.10}(23) = 1.319$ and $t = 1.518 > 1.319$. Hence, the null hypothesis would be rejected at an $\alpha = 0.10$ significance level. Another way of saying this is that

$$0.05 < p\text{-value} < 0.10.$$

It would be instructive for you to draw a figure illustrating this double inequality. ■

There are two ways of viewing a statistical test. One of these is through the p-value of the test; this approach is becoming more popular and is included in most computer printouts, so we mention it again. After observing the test statistic, we can say that the p-value is the probability, under the hypothesis H_0, of the test statistic being as extreme (in the direction of rejection of H_0) as the observed one. That is, the p-value is the tail-end probability. As an illustration, say a golfer averages about 90, with a standard deviation of 3, and she takes some lessons to improve. To test her possible improvement, namely, H_0: $\mu = 90$, against H_1: $\mu < 90$, she plays $n = 16$ rounds of golf. Assume a normal distribution with $\sigma = 3$. If the golfer averaged $\overline{x} = 87.94$, then

$$p\text{-value} = P(\overline{X} \le 87.94) = P\left(\frac{\overline{X} - 90}{3/4} \le \frac{87.94 - 90}{3/4}\right) = 0.0027.$$

The fact that the p-value is less than 0.05 is equivalent to the fact that $\overline{x} < 88.77$, because $P(\overline{X} \le 88.77;\ \mu = 90) = 0.05$. Since $\overline{x} = 87.94$ is an observed value of a random variable, namely, $\overline{X}$, it follows that the p-value, a function of $\overline{x}$, is also an observed value of a random variable. That is, before the random experiment is performed, the probability that the p-value is less than α is equal to α when the null hypothesis is true. Many statisticians believe that the observed p-value provides an understandable measure of the truth of H_0: The smaller the p-value, the less they believe in H_0.

Three additional examples of the p-value are given in Examples 7.2-3, 7.2-4, and 7.2-5. In two-sided tests for means and proportions, the p-value is the probability of the extreme values in both directions. With the mouse data (Example 7.2-3), the p-value is

$$p\text{-value} = P(|T| \ge 0.75).$$

In Table VI in the appendix, we see that if T has a t distribution with eight degrees of freedom, then $P(T \ge 0.706) = 0.25$. Thus, $P(|T| \ge 0.706) = 0.50$ and the p-value will be a little smaller than 0.50. In fact, $P(|T| \ge 0.75) = 0.4747$ (a probability that was found with Minitab), which is not less than $\alpha = 0.10$; hence, we do not reject H_0 at that significance level. In the example concerned with waste (Example 7.2-4), the p-value is essentially zero, since $P(Z \le -8.30) \approx 0$, where Z is a standardized normal variable. Consequently, we reject H_0.

The other way of looking at tests of hypotheses is through the consideration of confidence intervals, particularly for two-sided alternatives and the corresponding tests. For example, with the mouse data (Example 7.2-3), a 90% confidence interval for the unknown mean is

$$4.3 \pm (1.86)(1.2)/\sqrt{9}, \qquad \text{or} \qquad [3.56, 5.04],$$

since $t_{0.05}(8) = 1.86$. Note that this confidence interval covers the hypothesized value $\mu = 4.0$ and we do not reject H_0: $\mu = 4.0$. If the confidence interval did not cover $\mu = 4.0$, then we would have rejected H_0: $\mu = 4.0$. Many statisticians believe that estimation is much more important than tests of hypotheses and accordingly approach statistical tests through confidence intervals. For one-sided tests, we use one-sided confidence intervals.

EXERCISES

7.2-1. Assume that IQ scores for a certain population are approximately $N(\mu, 100)$. To test H_0: $\mu = 110$ against the one-sided alternative hypothesis H_1: $\mu > 110$, we take a random sample of size $n = 16$ from this population and observe $\overline{x} = 113.5$.

(a) Do we accept or reject H_0 at the 5% significance level?

(b) Do we accept or reject H_0 at the 10% significance level?

(c) What is the p-value of this test?

7.2-2. Assume that the weight of cereal in a "12.6-ounce box" is $N(\mu, 0.2^2)$. The Food and Drug Association (FDA) allows only a small percentage of boxes to contain less than 12.6 ounces. We shall test the null hypothesis H_0: $\mu = 13$ against the alternative hypothesis H_1: $\mu < 13$.

(a) Use a random sample of $n = 25$ to define the test statistic and the critical region that has a significance level of $\alpha = 0.025$.

(b) If $\overline{x} = 12.9$, what is your conclusion?

(c) What is the p-value of this test?

7.2-3. Let X equal the Brinell hardness measurement of ductile iron subcritically annealed. Assume that the distribution of X is $N(\mu, 100)$. We shall test the null hypothesis H_0: $\mu = 170$ against the alternative hypothesis H_1: $\mu > 170$, using $n = 25$ observations of X.

(a) Define the test statistic and a critical region that has a significance level of $\alpha = 0.05$. Sketch a figure showing this critical region.

(b) A random sample of $n = 25$ observations of X yielded the following measurements:

170 167 174 179 179 156 163 156 187
156 183 179 174 179 170 156 187
179 183 174 187 167 159 170 179

Calculate the value of the test statistic and state your conclusion clearly.

(c) Give the approximate p-value of this test.

7.2-4. Let X equal the thickness of spearmint gum manufactured for vending machines. Assume that the distribution of X is $N(\mu, \sigma^2)$. The target thickness is 7.5 hundredths of an inch. We shall test the null hypothesis H_0: $\mu = 7.5$ against a two-sided alternative hypothesis, using 10 observations.

(a) Define the test statistic and critical region for an $\alpha = 0.05$ significance level. Sketch a figure illustrating this critical region.

(b) Calculate the value of the test statistic and state your decision clearly, using the following $n = 10$ thicknesses in hundredths of an inch for pieces of gum that were selected randomly from the production line:

7.65 7.60 7.65 7.70 7.55
7.55 7.40 7.40 7.50 7.50

(c) Is $\mu = 7.50$ contained in a 95% confidence interval for μ?

7.2-5. The mean birth weight in the United States is $\mu = 3315$ grams, with a standard deviation of $\sigma = 575$. Let X equal the birth weight in grams in Jerusalem. Assume that the distribution of X is $N(\mu, \sigma^2)$. We shall test the null hypothesis H_0: $\mu = 3315$ against the alternative hypothesis H_1: $\mu < 3315$, using a random sample of size $n = 30$.

(a) Define a critical region that has a significance level of $\alpha = 0.05$.

(b) If the random sample of $n = 30$ yielded $\overline{x} = 3189$ and $s = 488$, what would be your conclusion?

(c) What is the approximate p-value of your test?

7.2-6. Let X equal the forced vital capacity (FVC) in liters for a female college student. (The FVC is the amount of air that a student can force out of her lungs.) Assume that the distribution of X is approximately $N(\mu, \sigma^2)$. Suppose it is known that $\mu = 3.4$ liters. A volleyball coach claims that the FVC of volleyball players is greater than 3.4. She plans to test her claim with a random sample of size $n = 9$.

(a) Define the null hypothesis.

(b) Define the alternative (coach's) hypothesis.

(c) Define the test statistic.

(d) Define a critical region for which $\alpha = 0.05$. Draw a figure illustrating your critical region.

(e) Calculate the value of the test statistic given that the random sample yielded the following FVC's:

3.4 3.6 3.8 3.3 3.4 3.5 3.7 3.6 3.7

(f) What is your conclusion?

(g) What is the approximate p value of this test?

7.2-7. Vitamin B_6 is one of the vitamins in a multiple vitamin pill manufactured by a pharmaceutical company. The pills are produced with a mean of 50 milligrams of vitamin B_6 per pill. The company believes that there is a deterioration of 1 milligram per month, so that after 3 months it expects that $\mu = 47$. A consumer group suspects that $\mu < 47$ after 3 months.

(a) Define a critical region to test H_0: $\mu = 47$ against H_1: $\mu < 47$ at an $\alpha = 0.05$ significance level based on a random sample of size $n = 20$.

(b) If the 20 pills yielded a mean of $\bar{x} = 46.94$ with a standard deviation of $s = 0.15$, what is your conclusion?

(c) What is the approximate p-value of this test?

7.2-8. Assume that the birth weight in grams of a baby born in the United States is $N(3315, 525^2)$ for boys and girls combined. Let X equal the weight of a baby girl who is born at home in Ottawa County, and assume that the distribution of X is $N(\mu_X, \sigma_X^2)$.

(a) Using 11 observations of X, give the test statistic and the critical region for testing H_0: $\mu_X = 3315$ against the alternative hypothesis H_1: $\mu_X > 3315$ (home-born babies are heavier) if $\alpha = 0.01$.

(b) Calculate the value of the test statistic and state your conclusion, using the following weights:

3119 2657 3459 3629 3345 3629
3515 3856 3629 3345 3062

(c) What is the approximate p-value of the test?

7.2-9. Let Y equal the weight in grams of a baby boy who is born at home in Ottawa County, and assume that the distribution of Y is $N(\mu_Y, \sigma_Y^2)$. Use the weights:

4082 3686 4111 3686 3175 4139
3686 3430 3289 3657 4082

to answer the questions in Exercise 7.2-8.

7.2-10. A company that manufactures brackets for an automaker regularly selects brackets from the production line and performs a torque test. The goal is for mean torque to equal 125. Let X equal the torque and assume that X is $N(\mu, \sigma^2)$. We shall use a sample of size $n = 15$ to test H_0: $\mu = 125$ against a two-sided alternative hypothesis.

(a) Give the test statistic and a critical region with significance level $\alpha = 0.05$. Sketch a figure illustrating the critical region.

(b) Use the following observations to calculate the value of the test statistic and state your conclusion:

128 149 136 114 126 142 124 136
122 118 122 129 118 122 129

7.2-11. The ornamental ground cover *Vinca minor* is spreading rapidly through the Hope College Biology Field Station because it can outcompete the small, native woody vegetation. In an attempt to discover whether *Vinca minor* utilized natural chemical weapons to inhibit the growth of the native vegetation, Hope biology students conducted an experiment in which they treated 33 sunflower seedlings with extracts taken from *Vinca minor* roots for several weeks and then measured the heights of the seedlings. Let X equal the height of one of these seedlings and assume that the distribution of X is $N(\mu, \sigma^2)$. The observed growths (in cm) were

11.5 11.8 15.7 16.1 14.1 10.5 15.2 19.0 12.8 12.4 19.2
13.5 16.5 13.5 14.4 16.7 10.9 13.0 15.1 17.1 13.3 12.4
8.5 14.3 12.9 11.1 15.0 13.3 15.8 13.5 9.3 12.2 10.3

The students also planted some control sunflower seedlings that had a mean height of 15.7 cm. We shall test the null hypothesis H_0: $\mu = 15.7$ against the alternative hypothesis H_1: $\mu < 15.7$.

(a) Calculate the value of the test statistic and give limits for the p-value of this test.

(b) What is your conclusion?

(c) Find an approximate 98% one-sided confidence interval that gives an upper bound for μ.

7.2-12. In a mechanical testing lab, Plexiglass® strips are stretched to failure. Let X equal the change in length in mm before breaking. Assume that the distribution of X is $N(\mu, \sigma^2)$. We shall test the null hypothesis H_0: $\mu = 5.70$ against the alternative hypothesis H_1: $\mu > 5.70$, using $n = 8$ observations of X.

(a) Define the test statistic and a critical region that has a significance level of $\alpha = 0.05$. Sketch a figure showing this critical region.

(b) A random sample of eight observations of X yielded the following data:

5.71 5.80 6.03 5.87 6.22 5.92 5.57 5.83

Calculate the value of the test statistic and state your conclusion clearly.

(c) Give the approximate value of or bounds for the p-value of this test.

7.2-13. A vendor of milk products produces and sells low-fat dry milk to a company that uses it to produce baby formula. In order to determine the fat content of the milk, both the company and the vendor take an observation from each lot and test it for fat content in percent. Ten sets of paired test results are as follows:

Lot Number	Company Test Results (X)	Vendor Test Results (Y)
1	0.50	0.79
2	0.58	0.71
3	0.90	0.82
4	1.17	0.82
5	1.14	0.73
6	1.25	0.77
7	0.75	0.72
8	1.22	0.79
9	0.74	0.72
10	0.80	0.91

Let μ_D denote the mean of the difference $X - Y$. Test H_0: $\mu_D = 0$ against H_1: $\mu_D > 0$, using a paired t test with the differences. Let $\alpha = 0.05$.

7.2-14. To test whether a golf ball of brand A can be hit a greater distance off the tee than a golf ball of brand B, each of 17 golfers hit a ball of each brand, 8 hitting ball A before ball B and 9 hitting ball B before ball A. The results are as follows:

Golfer	Distance for Ball A	Distance for Ball B	Golfer	Distance for Ball A	Distance for Ball B
1	265	252	10	274	260
2	272	276	11	274	267
3	246	243	12	269	267
4	260	246	13	244	251
5	274	275	14	212	222
6	263	246	15	235	235
7	255	244	16	254	255
8	258	245	17	224	231
9	276	259			

Assume that the differences of the paired A distance and B distance are approximately normally distributed, and test the null hypothesis H_0: $\mu_D = 0$ against the alternative hypothesis H_1: $\mu_D > 0$, using a paired t test with the 17 differences. Let $\alpha = 0.05$.

7.2-15. The following data give the times of 22 male swimmers who entered the 50 yard freestyle race in the Conference Championship Meet (for these data, x is the swimmer's best time for the season and y is the swimmer's time in the meet).

(24.97, 23.98) (24.76, 23.63) (23.80, 23.61) (22.84, 23.58) (24.07, 23.57)
(22.93, 22.83) (23.41, 22.75) (22.10, 22.74) (23.08, 22.70) (23.59, 22.62)
(22.38, 22.39) (22.91, 22.34) (22.08, 21.95) (22.46, 21.73) (21.34, 21.68)
(22.76, 21.66) (21.82, 21.68) (21.80, 21.58) (22.26, 21.57) (21.36, 21.35)
(22.98, 23.17) (23.80, 22.53)

Let $d = x - y$, a swimmer's best time minus the swimmer's meet time. Assume that the distribution of D is $N(\mu_D, \sigma_D^2)$. Test the null hypothesis H_0: $\mu_D = 0$ against the alternative hypothesis H_1: $\mu_D > 0$. You may select the significance level. Interpret your conclusion.

7.2-16. A company that manufactures motors receives reels of 10,000 terminals per reel. Before using a reel of terminals, 20 terminals are randomly selected to be tested. The test is the amount of pressure needed to pull the terminal apart from its mate. This amount of pressure should continue to increase from test to test as the terminal is "roughed up." (Since this kind of testing is destructive testing, a terminal that is tested cannot be used in a motor.) Let W equal the difference of the pressures: "test No. 1 pressure" minus "test No. 2 pressure." Assume that the distribution of W is $N(\mu_W, \sigma_W^2)$. We shall test the null hypothesis H_0: $\mu_W = 0$ against the alternative hypothesis H_1: $\mu_W < 0$, using 20 pairs of observations.

(a) Give the test statistic and a critical region that has a significance level of $\alpha = 0.05$. Sketch a figure illustrating this critical region.

(b) Use the following data to calculate the value of the test statistic, and state your conclusion clearly:

Terminal	Test 1	Test 2	Terminal	Test 1	Test 2
1	2.5	3.8	11	7.3	8.2
2	4.0	3.9	12	7.2	6.6
3	5.2	4.7	13	5.9	6.8
4	4.9	6.0	14	7.5	6.6
5	5.2	5.7	15	7.1	7.5
6	6.0	5.7	16	7.2	7.5
7	5.2	5.0	17	6.1	7.3
8	6.6	6.2	18	6.3	7.1
9	6.7	7.3	19	6.5	7.2
10	6.6	6.5	20	6.5	6.7

(c) What would the conclusion be if $\alpha = 0.01$?

(d) What is the approximate p-value of this test?

7.3 TESTS OF THE EQUALITY OF TWO MEANS

Let independent random variables X and Y have normal distributions $N(\mu_X, \sigma_X^2)$ and $N(\mu_Y, \sigma_Y^2)$, respectively. There are times when we are interested in testing whether the distributions of X and Y are the same. So if the assumption of normality is valid, we would be interested in testing whether the two means are equal. (A test for the equality of the two variances is given in the next section.)

When X and Y are independent and normally distributed, we can test hypotheses about their means with the same t statistic that we used to construct a confidence interval for $\mu_X - \mu_Y$ in Section 6.3. Recall that the t statistic used to construct the confidence interval assumed that the variances of X and Y were equal. (That is why we shall consider a test for the equality of two variances in the next section.)

We begin with an example and then give a table that lists some hypotheses and critical regions. A botanist is interested in comparing the growth response of dwarf pea stems against two different levels of the hormone indoleacetic acid (IAA). Using 16-day-old pea plants, the botanist obtains 5-millimeter sections and floats these sections on solutions with different hormone concentrations to observe the effect of the hormone on the growth of the pea stem. Let X and Y denote, respectively, the independent growths that can be attributed to the hormone during the first 26 hours after sectioning for $(0.5)(10)^{-4}$ and 10^{-4} levels of concentration of IAA. The botanist would like to test the null hypothesis H_0: $\mu_X - \mu_Y = 0$ against the alternative hypothesis H_1: $\mu_X - \mu_Y < 0$. If we can assume that X and Y are independent and normally distributed with a common variance, and if we assume respective random samples of sizes n and m, then we can find a test based on the statistic

$$T = \frac{\overline{X} - \overline{Y}}{\sqrt{\{[(n-1)S_X^2 + (m-1)S_Y^2]/(n+m-2)\}(1/n + 1/m)}} = \frac{\overline{X} - \overline{Y}}{S_P\sqrt{1/n + 1/m}}, \tag{7.3-1}$$

where

$$S_P = \sqrt{\frac{(n-1)S_X^2 + (m-1)S_Y^2}{n+m-2}}. \tag{7.3-2}$$

Now, T has a t distribution with $r = n + m - 2$ degrees of freedom when H_0 is true and the variances are (approximately) equal. Thus, the hypothesis H_0 will be rejected in favor of H_1 if the observed value of T is less than $-t_\alpha(n + m - 2)$.

EXAMPLE 7.3-1 In the preceding discussion, the botanist measured the growths of pea stem segments, in millimeters, for $n = 11$ observations of X:

0.8 1.8 1.0 0.1 0.9 1.7 1.0 1.4 0.9 1.2 0.5

She did the same with $m = 13$ observations of Y:

1.0 0.8 1.6 2.6 1.3 1.1 2.4
1.8 2.5 1.4 1.9 2.0 1.2

For these data, $\overline{x} = 1.03$, $s_x^2 = 0.24$, $\overline{y} = 1.66$, and $s_y^2 = 0.35$. The critical region for testing H_0: $\mu_X - \mu_Y = 0$ against H_1: $\mu_X - \mu_Y < 0$ is $t \le -t_{0.05}(22) = -1.717$, where t is the two-sample t found in Equation 7.3-1. Since

$$t = \frac{1.03 - 1.66}{\sqrt{\{[10(0.24) + 12(0.35)]/(11 + 13 - 2)\}(1/11 + 1/13)}} = -2.81 < -1.717,$$

H_0 is clearly rejected at an $\alpha = 0.05$ significance level. Notice that the approximate p-value of this test is 0.005, because $-t_{0.005}(22) = -2.819$. (See Figure 7.3-1.) Notice also that the sample variances do not differ too much; thus, most statisticians would use this two-sample t test.

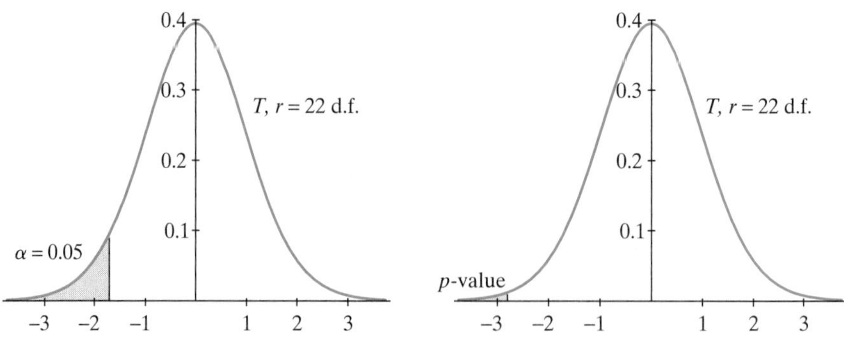

FIGURE 7.3-1: Critical region and p-value for pea stem growths

It is instructive to construct box-and-whisker diagrams to gain a visual comparison of the two samples. For these two sets of data, the five-number summaries (minimum, three quartiles, maximum) are

$$0.1 \quad 0.8 \quad 1.0 \quad 1.4 \quad 1.8$$

for the X sample and

$$0.8 \quad 1.15 \quad 1.6 \quad 2.2 \quad 2.6$$

for the Y sample. The two box plots are shown in Figure 7.3-2. ■

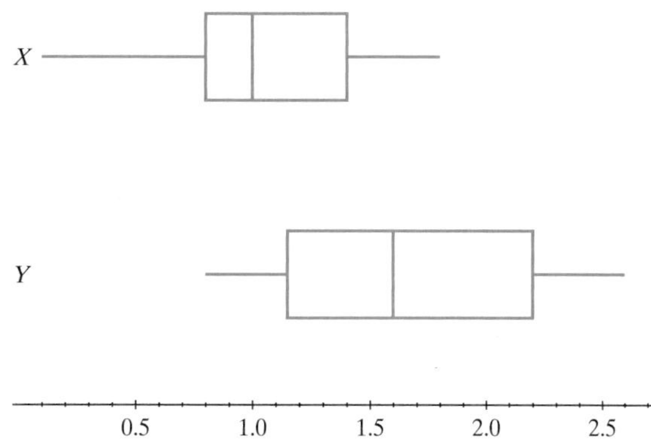

FIGURE 7.3-2: Box plots for pea stem growths

Assuming independent random samples of sizes n and m, let $\overline{x}$, $\overline{y}$, and s_p^2 represent the observed unbiased estimates of the respective parameters μ_X, μ_Y, and $\sigma_X^2 = \sigma_Y^2$ of two normal distributions with a common variance. Then α-level tests of certain hypotheses are given in Table 7.3-1 when $\sigma_X^2 = \sigma_Y^2$. If the common-variance assumption is violated, but not too badly, the test is satisfactory, but the significance levels are only approximate. The t statistic and s_p are given in Equations 7.3-1 and 7.3-2, respectively.

TABLE 7.3-1: Tests of Hypotheses for Equality of Two Means

H_0	H_1	Critical Region
$\mu_X = \mu_Y$	$\mu_X > \mu_Y$	$t \ge t_\alpha(n+m-2)$ or $\overline{x} - \overline{y} \ge t_\alpha(n+m-2)s_p\sqrt{1/n + 1/m}$
$\mu_X = \mu_Y$	$\mu_X < \mu_Y$	$t \le -t_\alpha(n+m-2)$ or $\overline{x} - \overline{y} \le -t_\alpha(n+m-2)s_p\sqrt{1/n + 1/m}$
$\mu_X = \mu_Y$	$\mu_X \ne \mu_Y$	$\lvert t\rvert \ge t_{\alpha/2}(n+m-2)$ or $\lvert\overline{x} - \overline{y}\rvert \ge t_{\alpha/2}(n+m-2)s_p\sqrt{1/n + 1/m}$

REMARK Again to emphasize the relationship between confidence intervals and tests of hypotheses, we note that each of the tests in Table 7.3-1 has a corresponding confidence interval. For example, the first one-sided test is equivalent to saying that we reject H_0: $\mu_X - \mu_Y = 0$ if zero is not in the one-sided confidence interval with lower bound

$$\overline{x} - \overline{y} - t_\alpha(n+m-2)s_p\sqrt{1/n + 1/m}.$$ ■

EXAMPLE 7.3-2 A product is packaged by a machine with 24 filler heads numbered 1 to 24, with the odd numbered heads on one side of the machine and the even on the other side. Let X and Y equal the fill weights in grams when a package is filled by an odd-numbered head and an even-numbered head, respectively. Assume that the distributions of X and Y are $N(\mu_X, \sigma^2)$ and $N(\mu_Y, \sigma^2)$, respectively, and that X and Y are independent. We would like to test the null hypothesis H_0: $\mu_X - \mu_Y = 0$ against the alternative hypothesis H_1: $\mu_X - \mu_Y \neq 0$. To perform the test, after the machine has been set up and is running, we shall select one package at random from each filler head and weigh it. The test statistic is that given by Equation 7.3-1 with $n = m = 12$. At an $\alpha = 0.10$ significance level, the critical region is $|t| \geq t_{0.05}(22) = 1.717$.

For the $n = 12$ observations of X, namely,

$$\begin{array}{cccccc} 1071 & 1076 & 1070 & 1083 & 1082 & 1067 \\ 1078 & 1080 & 1075 & 1084 & 1075 & 1080 \end{array}$$

$\bar{x} = 1076.75$ and $s_x^2 = 29.30$. For the $m = 12$ observations of Y, namely,

$$\begin{array}{cccccc} 1074 & 1069 & 1075 & 1067 & 1068 & 1079 \\ 1082 & 1064 & 1070 & 1073 & 1072 & 1075 \end{array}$$

$\bar{y} = 1072.33$ and $s_y^2 = 26.24$. The calculated value of the test statistic is

$$t = \frac{1076.75 - 1072.33}{\sqrt{\dfrac{11(29.30) + 11(26.24)}{22}\left(\dfrac{1}{12} + \dfrac{1}{12}\right)}} = 2.05.$$

Since

$$|t| = |2.05| = 2.05 > 1.717,$$

the null hypothesis is rejected at an $\alpha = 0.10$ significance level. Note, however, that

$$|t| = 2.05 < 2.074 = t_{0.025}(22),$$

so that the null hypothesis would not be rejected at an $\alpha = 0.05$ significance level. That is, the p-value is between 0.05 and 0.10.

Again, it is instructive to construct box plots on the same graph for these two sets of data. The box plots in Figure 7.3-3 were constructed with the use of the five-number summary for the observations of X (1067, 1072, 1077, 1081.5, and 1084) and the five-number summary for the observations of Y (1064, 1068.25, 1072.5, 1075, and 1082). It looks like additional sampling would be advisable to test that the filler heads on the two sides of the machine are filling in a similar manner. If not, some corrective action needs to be taken. ■

We would like to give two modifications of tests about two means. If we are able to assume that we know the variances of X and Y, then the appropriate test statistic to use for testing H_0: $\mu_X = \mu_Y$ is

$$Z = \frac{\overline{X} - \overline{Y}}{\sqrt{\dfrac{\sigma_X^2}{n} + \dfrac{\sigma_Y^2}{m}}}, \tag{7.3-3}$$

which has a standard normal distribution when the null hypothesis is true and, of course, when the populations are normally distributed. If the variances are unknown

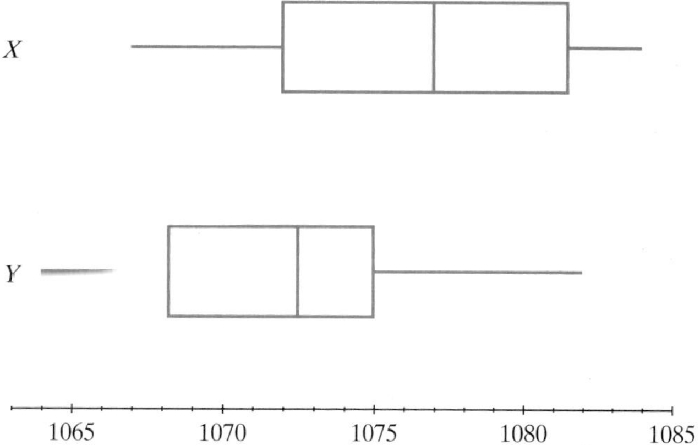

FIGURE 7.3-3: Box plots for fill weights

and the sample sizes are large, replace σ_X^2 with S_X^2 and σ_Y^2 with S_Y^2 in Equation 7.3-3. The resulting statistic will have an approximate $N(0,1)$ distribution.

EXAMPLE 7.3-3 The target thickness for Fruit Flavored Gum and for Fruit Flavored Bubble Gum is 6.7 hundredths of an inch. Let the independent random variables X and Y equal the respective thicknesses of these gums in hundredths of an inch, and assume that their distributions are $N(\mu_X, \sigma_X^2)$ and $N(\mu_Y, \sigma_Y^2)$, respectively. Because bubble gum has more elasticity than regular gum, it seems as if it would be harder to roll it out to the correct thickness. Thus, we shall test the null hypothesis H_0: $\mu_X = \mu_Y$ against the alternative hypothesis H_1: $\mu_X < \mu_Y$, using samples of sizes $n = 50$ and $m = 40$.

Because the variances are unknown and the sample sizes are large, the test statistic that is used is

$$Z = \frac{\overline{X} - \overline{Y}}{\sqrt{\dfrac{S_X^2}{50} + \dfrac{S_Y^2}{40}}}.$$

At an approximate significance level of $\alpha = 0.01$, the critical region is

$$z \le -z_{0.01} = -2.326.$$

The observed values of X were

6.85	6.60	6.70	6.75	6.75	6.90	6.85	6.90	6.70	6.85
6.60	6.70	6.75	6.70	6.70	6.70	6.55	6.60	6.95	6.95
6.80	6.80	6.70	6.75	6.60	6.70	6.65	6.55	6.55	6.60
6.60	6.70	6.80	6.75	6.60	6.75	6.50	6.75	6.70	6.65
6.70	6.70	6.55	6.65	6.60	6.65	6.60	6.65	6.80	6.60

for which $\overline{x} = 6.701$ and $s_x = 0.108$. The observed values of Y were

7.10	7.05	6.70	6.75	6.90	6.90	6.65	6.60	6.55	6.55
6.85	6.90	6.60	6.85	6.95	7.10	6.95	6.90	7.15	7.05
6.70	6.90	6.85	6.95	7.05	6.75	6.90	6.80	6.70	6.75
6.90	6.90	6.70	6.70	6.90	6.90	6.70	6.70	6.90	6.95

for which $\overline{y} = 6.841$ and $s_y = 0.155$. Since the calculated value of the test statistic is

$$z = \frac{6.701 - 6.841}{\sqrt{0.108^2/50 + 0.155^2/40}} = -4.848 < -2.326,$$

the null hypothesis is clearly rejected.

The box-and-whisker diagrams in Figure 7.3-4 were constructed with the use of the five-number summary of the observations of X (6.50, 6.60, 6.70, 6.75, and 6.95) and the five-number summary of the observations of Y (6.55, 6.70, 6.90, 6.94, and 7.15). This graphical display also confirms our conclusion. ■

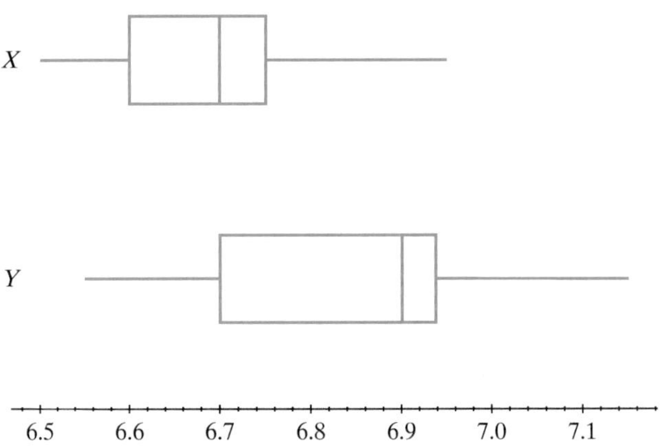

FIGURE 7.3-4: Box plots for gum thicknesses

REMARKS To have satisfactory tests, our assumptions must be satisfied reasonably well. As long as the underlying distributions are not highly skewed, the normal assumptions are not too critical, as $\overline{X}$ and $\overline{Y}$ have approximate normal distributions by the central limit theorem. As distributions become nonnormal and highly skewed, the sample mean and sample variance become more dependent, and that causes problems in using the Student's t as an approximating distribution for T. In these cases, some of the nonparametric methods described later could be used.

When the distributions are close to normal, but the variances seem to differ by a great deal, the t statistic should again be avoided, particularly if the sample sizes are also different. In that case, use Z or the modification produced by substituting the sample variances for the distribution variances. In the latter situation, if n and m are large enough, there is no problem. With small n and m, most statisticians would use Welch's suggestion (or other modifications of it); that is, they would use an approximating Student's t distribution with r degrees of freedom, where r is given by Equation 6.3-1. We actually give a test for the equality of variances that could be employed to decide whether to use T or a modification of Z. However, most statisticians do not place much confidence in this test of $\sigma_X^2 = \sigma_Y^2$ and would use a modification of Z (possibly Welch's) if they suspected that the variances differed greatly. ■

EXERCISES

(In some of the exercises that follow, we must make assumptions such as the existence of normal distributions with equal variances.)

7.3-1. The botanist in Example 7.3-1 is really interested in testing for synergistic interaction. That is, given the two hormones gibberellin (GA_3) and indoleacetic acid (IAA), let X_1 and X_2 equal the growth responses (in millimeters) of dwarf pea stem segments to GA_3 and IAA, respectively and separately. Also, let $X = X_1 + X_2$ and let Y equal the growth response when both hormones are present. Assuming that X is $N(\mu_X, \sigma^2)$ and Y is $N(\mu_Y, \sigma^2)$, the botanist is interested in testing the hypothesis H_0: $\mu_X = \mu_Y$ against the alternative hypothesis of synergistic interaction H_1: $\mu_X < \mu_Y$.

(a) Using $n = m = 10$ observations of X and Y, define the test statistic and the critical region. Sketch a figure of the t p.d.f. and show the critical region on your figure. Let $\alpha = 0.05$.

(b) Given $n = 10$ observations of X, namely,

2.1 2.6 2.6 3.4 2.1 1.7 2.6 2.6 2.2 1.2

and $m = 10$ observations of Y, namely,

3.5 3.9 3.0 2.3 2.1 3.1 3.6 1.8 2.9 3.3

calculate the value of the test statistic and state your conclusion. Locate the test statistic on your figure.

(c) Construct two box plots on the same figure. Does this confirm your conclusion?

7.3-2. Let X and Y denote the weights in grams of male and female gallinules, respectively. Assume that X is $N(\mu_X, \sigma_X^2)$ and Y is $N(\mu_Y, \sigma_Y^2)$.

(a) Given $n = 16$ observations of X and $m = 13$ observations of Y, define a test statistic and a critical region for testing the null hypothesis H_0: $\mu_X = \mu_Y$ against the one-sided alternative hypothesis H_1: $\mu_X > \mu_Y$. Let $\alpha = 0.01$. (Assume that the variances are equal.)

(b) Given that $\bar{x} = 415.16$, $s_x^2 = 1356.75$, $\bar{y} = 347.40$, and $s_y^2 = 692.21$, calculate the value of the test statistic and state your conclusion.

(c) Although we assumed that $\sigma_X^2 = \sigma_Y^2$, let us say we suspect that that equality is not valid. Thus, use the test proposed by Welch.

7.3-3. Let X equal the weight in grams of a Low Fat Strawberry Kudo and Y the weight of a Low Fat Blueberry Kudo. Assume that the distributions of X and Y are $N(\mu_X, \sigma_X^2)$ and $N(\mu_Y, \sigma_Y^2)$, respectively. Let

21.7 21.0 21.2 20.7 20.4 21.9 20.2 21.6 20.6

be $n = 9$ observations of X, and let

21.5 20.5 20.3 21.6 21.7 21.3 23.0 21.3 18.9 20.0 20.4 20.8 20.3

be $m = 13$ observations of Y. Use these observations to answer the following questions:

(a) Test the null hypothesis H_0: $\mu_X = \mu_Y$ against a two-sided alternative hypothesis. You may select the significance level. Assume that the variances are equal.

(b) Construct and interpret box-and-whisker diagrams to support your conclusions.

7.3-4. Among the data collected for the World Health Organization air quality monitoring project is a measure of suspended particles, in μg/m^3. Let X and Y equal the concentration of suspended particles in μg/m^3 in the city centers (commercial districts) of Melbourne and Houston, respectively. Using $n = 13$ observations of X and $m = 16$ observations of Y, we shall test H_0: $\mu_X = \mu_Y$ against H_1: $\mu_X < \mu_Y$.

(a) Define the test statistic and critical region, assuming that the variances are equal. Let $\alpha = 0.05$.

(b) If $\bar{x} = 72.9$, $s_x = 25.6$, $\bar{y} = 81.7$, and $s_y = 28.3$, calculate the value of the test statistic and state your conclusion.

(c) Give limits for the p-value of this test.

7.3-5. Some nurses in county public health conducted a survey of women who had received inadequate prenatal care. They used information from birth certificates to select mothers for the survey. The mothers selected were divided into two groups: 14 mothers who said they had five or fewer prenatal visits and 14 mothers who said they had six or more prenatal visits. Let X and Y equal the respective birth weights of the babies from these two sets of mothers, and assume that the distribution of X is $N(\mu_X, \sigma^2)$ and the distribution of Y is $N(\mu_Y, \sigma^2)$,

(a) Define the test statistic and critical region for testing H_0: $\mu_X - \mu_Y = 0$ against H_1: $\mu_X - \mu_Y < 0$. Let $\alpha = 0.05$.

(b) Given that the observations of X were

49	108	110	82	93	114	134
114	96	52	101	114	120	116

and the observations of Y were

133	108	93	119	119	98	106
131	87	153	116	129	97	110

calculate the value of the test statistic and state your conclusion.

(c) Approximate the p-value.

(d) Construct box plots on the same figure for these two sets of data. Do the box plots support your conclusion?

7.3-6. Let X and Y equal the forces required to pull stud No. 3 and stud No. 4 out of a window that has been manufactured for an automobile. Assume that the distributions of X and Y are $N(\mu_X, \sigma_X^2)$ and $N(\mu_Y, \sigma_Y^2)$, respectively.

(a) If $m = n = 10$ observations are selected randomly, define a test statistic and a critical region for testing H_0: $\mu_X - \mu_Y = 0$ against a two-sided alternative hypothesis. Let $\alpha = 0.05$. Assume that the variances are equal.

(b) Given $n = 10$ observations of X, namely,

111 120 139 136 138 149 143 145 111 123

and $m = 10$ observations of Y, namely,

152 155 133 134 119 155 142 146 157 149

calculate the value of the test statistic and state your conclusion clearly.

(c) What is the approximate p-value of this test?

(d) Construct box plots on the same figure for these two sets of data. Do the box plots confirm your decision in part (b)?

7.3-7. Let X and Y equal the number of milligrams of tar in filtered and nonfiltered cigarettes, respectively. Assume that the distributions of X and Y are $N(\mu_X, \sigma_X^2)$ and $N(\mu_Y, \sigma_Y^2)$, respectively. We shall test the null hypothesis H_0: $\mu_X - \mu_Y = 0$ against the alternative hypothesis H_1: $\mu_X - \mu_Y < 0$, using random samples of sizes $n = 9$ and $m = 11$ observations of X and Y, respectively.

(a) Define the test statistic and a critical region that has an $\alpha = 0.01$ significance level. Sketch a figure illustrating this critical region.

(b) Given $n = 9$ observations of X, namely,

0.9 1.1 0.1 0.7 0.4 0.9 0.8 1.0 0.4

and $m = 11$ observations of Y, namely,

1.5 0.9 1.6 0.5 1.4 1.9 1.0 1.2 1.3 1.6 2.1

calculate the value of the test statistic and state your conclusion clearly. Locate the value of the test statistic on your figure.

7.3-8. In Exercise 6.3-4, we let X and Y equal the blood volumes in milliliters for males who are paraplegics participating in vigorous physical activities and males who are able bodied participating in everyday activities. We assumed that X was $N(\mu_X, \sigma_X^2)$ and Y was $N(\mu_Y, \sigma_Y^2)$. Using $n = 7$ observations of X, namely,

1612 1352 1456 1222 1560 1456 1924

and $m = 10$ observations of Y, namely,

1082	1300	1092	1040	910
1248	1092	1040	1092	1288

you were asked to find a 95% confidence interval for $\mu_X - \mu_Y$.

(a) Test the hypothesis that the means are equal against a two-sided alternative hypothesis. Let $\alpha = 0.05$.

(b) Did 0 belong to the 95% confidence interval in Exercise 6.3-4? Did you reject the null hypothesis in the current exercise? Are your answers to these questions compatible?

7.3-9. An office furniture manufacturer installed a new adhesive application process. To compare the new process with the old process, random samples were selected from the two processes and "pull tests" were performed to determine the number of pounds of pressure that were required to pull apart the glued parts. (This kind of test is an example of destructive testing.) Let X and Y denote the pounds of pressure needed for the new and old processes, respectively,

(a) On the basis of $n = m = 24$ observations, define the test statistic and the critical region for testing H_0: $\mu_X - \mu_Y = 0$ against H_1: $\mu_X - \mu_Y > 0$. Let $\alpha = 0.05$. State your assumptions.

(b) Let the following be $n = 24$ observations of X:

1250	1210	990	1310	1320	1200	1290	1360
1120	1360	1310	1110	1320	980	950	1430
960	1050	1310	1240	1420	1170	1470	1060

Let the following be $m = 24$ observations of Y:

1180 1360 1310 1190 920 1060 1440 1010
1310 980 1310 1030 960 800 1280 1080
930 1050 1010 1310 940 860 1450 1070

Use these observations of X and Y to calculate the value of the test statistic and state your conclusion clearly.

(c) What is the approximate p-value of this test?

(d) Construct two box plots on the same graph. Do the box plots support your conclusion?

7.3-10. Let X and Y denote the tarsus lengths of male and female grackles, respectively. Assume that X is $N(\mu_X, \sigma_X^2)$ and Y is $N(\mu_Y, \sigma_Y^2)$. Given that $n = 25$, $\bar{x} = 33.80$, $s_x^2 = 4.88$, $m = 29$, $\bar{y} = 31.66$, and $s_y^2 = 5.81$, test the null hypothesis $H_0: \mu_X = \mu_Y$ against $H_1: \mu_X > \mu_Y$ with $\alpha = 0.01$.

7.3-11. Weight checks are done on the scales for an automatic bagger for water softener pellets. Each bagger has two scales (say, south and north) that operate alternately to fill 80-lb bags of pellets. Let X and Y equal the weights of the bags of pellets from these two scales. Assume that the distributions of X and Y are $N(\mu_X, \sigma^2)$ and $N(\mu_Y, \sigma^2)$, respectively. Ten bags were selected randomly from each scale and weighed by hand on a scale with a "high" degree of accuracy, yielding the following weights:

X:	80.51	80.46	80.75	80.50	80.36
	80.32	80.36	80.78	80.26	80.34
Y:	80.51	80.28	80.40	80.35	80.38
	80.28	80.27	80.16	80.59	80.56

(a) Test $H_0: \mu_X = \mu_Y$ against $H_1: \mu_X \neq \mu_Y$. Assume that $\sigma_X^2 = \sigma_Y^2$. Give limits for the p-value of the test and state your conclusion.

(b) Draw box-and-whisker diagrams on the same graph. Does this figure confirm your answer?

7.3-12. Two different saws are used to cut columns for a gazebo that has a diameter of 16 feet. Suspecting that one saw is cutting columns shorter than the other saw, the company is interested in comparing the two saws. Let the lengths of the columns cut by the two saws be observations of random variables X and Y that are $N(\mu_X, \sigma_X^2)$ and $N(\mu_Y, \sigma_Y^2)$, respectively. We shall use the following observations of X and Y:

X: 8.02 8.10 8.04 8.04 8.00 8.11 8.07 8.02 8.04
Y: 8.04 8.04 8.10 8.06 8.08 8.10 8.07 8.08 8.06

(a) Test $H_0: \mu_X = \mu_Y$ against $H_1: \mu_X < \mu_Y$. Assume that $\sigma_X^2 = \sigma_Y^2$. Give limits for the p-value of the test and state your conclusion.

(b) Draw box-and-whisker diagrams on the same graph. Does this figure confirm your answer?

7.3-13. When a stream is turbid, it is not completely clear due to suspended solids in the water. The higher the turbidity, the less clear is the water. A stream was studied on 26 days, half during dry weather (say, observations of X) and the other half immediately after a significant rainfall (say, observations of Y). Assume that the distributions of X and Y are $N(\mu_X, \sigma^2)$ and $N(\mu_Y, \sigma^2)$, respectively. The following turbidities were recorded in units of NTUs (nephelometric turbidity units):

X:	2.9	14.9	1.0	12.6	9.4	7.6	3.6
	3.1	2.7	4.8	3.4	7.1	7.2	
Y:	7.8	4.2	2.4	12.9	17.3	10.4	5.9
	4.9	5.1	8.4	10.8	23.4	9.7	

(a) Test the null hypothesis $H_0: \mu_X = \mu_Y$ against $H_1: \mu_X < \mu_Y$. Give limits for the p-value and state your conclusion.

(b) Draw box-and-whisker diagrams on the same graph. Does this figure confirm your answer?

7.3-14. Plants convert carbon dioxide (CO_2) in the atmosphere, along with water and energy from sunlight, into the energy they need for growth and reproduction. Experiments were performed under normal atmospheric air conditions and in air with enriched CO_2 concentrations to determine the effect on plant growth. The plants were given the same amount of water and light for a four-week period. The following table gives the plant growths in grams:

Normal Air	4.67	4.21	2.18	3.91	4.09	5.24	2.94	4.71
	4.04	5.79	3.80	4.38				
Enriched Air	5.04	4.52	6.18	7.01	4.36	1.81	6.22	5.70

On the basis of these data, determine whether CO_2-enriched atmosphere increases plant growth.

7.3-15. Let X equal the fill weight in April and Y the fill weight in June for an 8-pound box of bleach. We shall test the null hypothesis H_0: $\mu_X - \mu_Y = 0$ against the alternative hypothesis H_1: $\mu_X - \mu_Y > 0$ given that $n = 90$ observations of X yielded $\bar{x} = 8.10$ and $s_x = 0.117$ and

$m = 110$ observations of Y yielded $\bar{x} = 8.07$ and $s_y = 0.054$.

(a) What is your conclusion if $\alpha = 0.05$?
HINT: Do the variances seem to be equal?

(b) What is the approximate p-value of this test?

7.3-16. Let X and Y denote the respective lengths of male and female green lynx spiders. Assume that the distributions of X and Y are $N(\mu_X, \sigma_X^2)$ and $N(\mu_Y, \sigma_Y^2)$, respectively. In Example 7.4-2, we will show that $\sigma_Y^2 > \sigma_X^2$. Thus, use the modification of Z to test the hypothesis H_0: $\mu_X - \mu_Y = 0$ against the alternative hypothesis H_1: $\mu_X - \mu_Y < 0$.

(a) Define the test statistic and a critical region that has a significance level of $\alpha = 0.025$.

(b) Using the data given in Exercise 6.3-5 (see also Example 7.4-2), calculate the value of the test statistic and state your conclusion.

(c) Draw two box-and-whisker diagrams on the same figure. Does your figure confirm both the conclusion of this exercise and that of Example 7.4-2?

7.3-17. Some measurements in mm were made on a species of spiders named *Sosippus floridanus* that are native to Florida. (See Exercise 6.7-16.) There are 10 female spiders and 10 male spiders. The total lengths and the lengths of their front and their back legs are repeated here:

Female body lengths	Female front legs	Female back legs	Male body lengths	Male front legs	Male back legs
11.06	15.03	19.29	12.26	20.22	25.54
13.87	17.96	22.74	11.66	18.62	23.94
12.93	17.56	21.28	12.53	18.62	23.94
15.08	21.22	25.54	13.00	19.95	25.80
17.82	22.61	28.86	11.79	19.15	25.40
14.14	20.08	25.14	12.46	19.02	25.27
12.26	16.49	20.22	10.65	17.29	22.21
17.82	18.75	24.61	10.39	17.02	21.81
20.17	23.01	28.46	12.26	18.49	23.41
16.88	22.48	28.59	14.07	22.61	28.86

In this exercise, we shall compare the sizes of the female and male spiders. For each of these questions, construct box plots on the same graph to confirm your answers. Do not assume that the variances are equal.

(a) Test the null hypothesis that the lengths of female and male spiders are equal against the alternative hypothesis that female spiders are longer.

(b) Test the null hypothesis that the lengths of the front legs of the female and male spiders are equal against a two-sided alternative.

(c) Test the null hypothesis that the lengths of the back legs of the female and male spiders are equal against a two-sided alternative.

7.3-18. An ecology laboratory studied tree dispersion patterns for the sugar maple, whose seeds are dispersed by the wind, and the American beech, whose seeds are dispersed by mammals. In a plot of area 50 m by 50 m, they measured distances between like trees, yielding the following distances in meters for 19 American beech trees and 19 sugar maple trees:

American beech:	5.00	5.00	6.50	4.25	4.25	8.80	6.50
	7.15	6.15	2.70	2.70	11.40	9.70	
	6.10	9.35	2.85	4.50	4.50	6.50	
sugar maple:	6.00	4.00	6.00	6.45	5.00	5.00	5.50
	2.35	2.35	3.90	3.90	5.35	3.15	
	2.10	4.80	3.10	5.15	3.10	6.25	

(a) Test the null hypothesis that the means are equal against the one-sided alternative that the mean for the distances between beech trees is greater than that between maple trees.

(b) Construct two box plots to confirm your answer.

7.3-19. Students looked at the effect of a certain fertilizer on plant growth. The students tested this fertilizer on one group of plants (Group A) and did not give fertilizer to a second group (Group B). The growths of the plants, in mm, over six weeks were as follows:

Group A:	55	61	33	57	17	46	50	42	71	51	63
Group B:	31	27	12	44	9	25	34	53	33	21	32

(a) Test the null hypothesis that the mean growths are equal against the alternative that the fertilizer enhanced growth. Assume that the variances are equal.

(b) Construct box plots of the two sets of growths on the same graph. Does this confirm your answer to part (a)?

7.3-20. Ledolter and Hogg (see references) report that a new emergency procedure was developed to reduce the time that is required to fix a certain manufacturing problem. Past data under the old system were available ($n = 25$). The staff was trained under the new procedure, and the response times for the next 15 occurrences of this manufacturing problem were recorded. The data are as follows:

Old Procedure:	4.3	6.5	4.6	4.3	6.4	4.8	5.1	6.8	4.9
	4.5	5.1	7.3	3.3	5.0	4.6	7.0	5.1	3.8
	5.2	4.1	5.7	4.6	5.9	3.1	6.2		
New Procedure:	6.2	4.0	3.3	4.5	2.3	3.0	3.2	6.0	3.7
	4.5	5.3	4.0	5.4	4.3	3.8			

(a) Test the null hypothesis that the mean response times are equal against a one-sided alternative that the mean for the new procedure is less than that for the old procedure. You may assume that the variances are equal.

(b) Construct box plots on the same graph.

(c) What is your conclusion?

7.4 TESTS FOR VARIANCES

Tests for a single variance and for equality of two variances are given in this section. An example follows a brief discussion, and then formal rules are given for tests for a single variance.

A psychology professor claims that the variance of IQ scores for college students is equal to $\sigma^2 = 100$. To test this claim, it is decided to test the hypothesis H_0: $\sigma^2 = 100$ against a two-sided alternative hypothesis H_1: $\sigma^2 \neq 100$. A random sample of n students will be selected, and the test will be based on the observed unbiased estimate s^2 of the variance σ^2 of their IQ scores. The hypothesis H_0 will be rejected if s^2 differs "too much" from $\sigma^2 = 100$. That is, H_0 will be rejected if $s^2 \le c_1$ or $s^2 \ge c_2$ for some constants $c_1 < 100$ and $c_2 > 100$. Generally, c_1 and c_2 are selected so that

$$P(S^2 \le c_1) = \alpha/2 \qquad \text{and} \qquad P(S^2 \ge c_2) = \alpha/2.$$

If we may assume that IQ scores are normally distributed, then the distribution of $(n-1)S^2/100$ is $\chi^2(n-1)$ when H_0 is true. Thus, the chi-square probability table can be used to give us

$$P\left[\frac{(n-1)S^2}{100} \le \frac{(n-1)c_1}{100}\right] = \alpha/2 \;\; \text{and} \;\; P\left[\frac{(n-1)S^2}{100} \ge \frac{(n-1)c_2}{100}\right] = \alpha/2.$$

Accordingly,

$$\frac{(n-1)c_1}{100} = \chi^2_{1-\alpha/2}(n-1) \qquad \text{and} \qquad \frac{(n-1)c_2}{100} = \chi^2_{\alpha/2}(n-1).$$

Hence,

$$c_1 = [100/(n-1)]\chi^2_{1-\alpha/2}(n-1) \quad \text{and} \quad c_2 = [100/(n-1)]\chi^2_{\alpha/2}(n-1).$$

Actually, it is easier to base this test on the value of the chi-square statistic

$$\chi^2 = \frac{(n-1)S^2}{100}.$$

We would reject the null hypothesis if

$$\chi^2 \le \chi^2_{1-\alpha/2}(n-1) \quad \text{or} \quad \chi^2 \ge \chi^2_{\alpha/2}(n-1).$$

EXAMPLE 7.4-1 Suppose that, in the preceding discussion, $n = 23$ and $\alpha = 0.05$. To test $H_0\colon \sigma^2 = 100$ against $H_1\colon \sigma^2 \ne 100$, we let $\chi^2 = (n-1)S^2/\sigma_0^2 = 22S^2/100$. Because

$$\chi^2_{0.975}(22) = 10.98 \quad \text{and} \quad \chi^2_{0.025}(22) = 36.78,$$

H_0 will be rejected if

$$\chi^2 = \frac{22s^2}{100} \le 10.98 \quad \text{or} \quad \chi^2 = \frac{22s^2}{100} \ge 36.78$$

or, equivalently, if

$$s^2 \le c_1 = \frac{100(10.98)}{22} = 49.91 \quad \text{or} \quad s^2 \ge c_2 = \frac{100(36.78)}{22} = 167.18.$$

(Exercise 7.4-6 gives some insight into why these critical values are so far apart.) Given that the observed value of the sample variance was $s^2 = 147.82$, the hypothesis $H_0\colon \sigma^2 = 100$ was not rejected. Note that the 95% confidence interval for σ^2, namely,

$$\left[\frac{(22)(147.82)}{36.78}, \frac{(22)(147.82)}{10.98}\right] = [88.42, 296.18],$$

contains $\sigma^2 = 100$. Also, the observed value of the chi-square test statistic is

$$\chi^2 = \frac{22(147.82)}{100} = 32.52.$$

Because

$$10.98 < 32.52 < 36.78,$$

we would again accept H_0, as expected. (See Figure 7.4-1.)

If $H_1\colon \sigma^2 > 100$ had been the alternative hypothesis, $H_0\colon \sigma^2 = 100$ would have been rejected if

$$\chi^2 = \frac{22s^2}{100} \ge \chi^2_{0.05}(22) = 33.92$$

or, equivalently,

$$s^2 \ge \frac{100\chi^2_{0.05}(22)}{22} = \frac{(100)(33.92)}{22} = 154.18.$$

Because

$$\chi^2 = 32.52 < 33.92 \quad \text{and} \quad s^2 = 147.82 < 154.18,$$

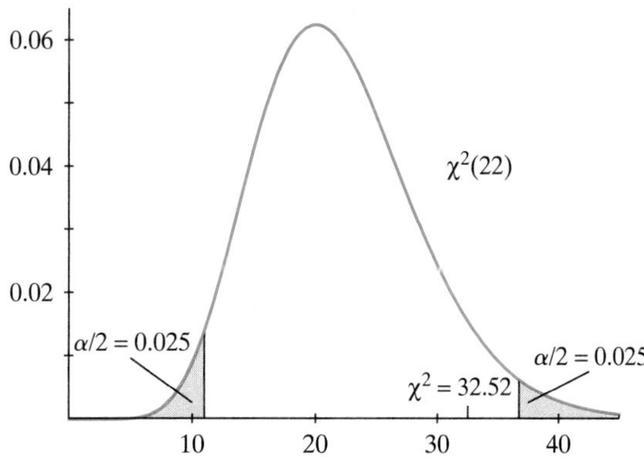

FIGURE 7.4-1: Test about the variance of IQ scores

H_0 would not be rejected in favor of this one-sided alternative hypothesis for $\alpha = 0.05$, although we suspect a slightly larger data set might lead to rejection. ■

TABLE 7.4-1: Tests About the Variance

H_0	H_1	Critical Region
$\sigma^2 = \sigma_0^2$	$\sigma^2 > \sigma_0^2$	$s^2 \ge \dfrac{\sigma_0^2\chi_\alpha^2(n-1)}{n-1}$ or $\chi^2 \ge \chi_\alpha^2(n-1)$
$\sigma^2 = \sigma_0^2$	$\sigma^2 < \sigma_0^2$	$s^2 \le \dfrac{\sigma_0^2\chi_{1-\alpha}^2(n-1)}{n-1}$ or $\chi^2 \le \chi_{1-\alpha}^2(n-1)$
$\sigma^2 = \sigma_0^2$	$\sigma^2 \ne \sigma_0^2$	$s^2 \le \dfrac{\sigma_0^2\chi_{1-\alpha/2}^2(n-1)}{n-1}$ or $s^2 \ge \dfrac{\sigma_0^2\chi_{\alpha/2}^2(n-1)}{n-1}$ or $\chi^2 \le \chi_{1-\alpha/2}^2(n-1)$ or $\chi^2 \ge \chi_{\alpha/2}^2(n-1)$

With normal distributions, Table 7.4-1 summarizes tests of hypotheses for a single variance. The critical region is given in terms of the sample variance. The critical region is also given in terms of the chi-square test statistic

$$\chi^2 = \frac{(n-1)s^2}{\sigma_0^2}.$$

We discussed the p-value for tests about proportions and means. We can also find p-values for tests about a variance. In Example 7.4-1, with the one-sided alternative $H_1\colon \sigma^2 > 100$, the p-value is

$$p\text{-value} = P(W \ge 32.52),$$

where $W = 22S^2/100$ has a chi-square distribution with 22 degrees of freedom when H_0 is true. From Table IV in the appendix, we see that

$$P(W \ge 30.81) = 0.10 \qquad \text{and} \qquad P(W \ge 33.92) = 0.05.$$

Thus,

$$0.05 < p\text{-value} = P(W \ge 32.52) < 0.10,$$

and the null hypothesis would not be rejected at an $\alpha = 0.05$ significance level. To find the p-value for a two-sided alternative for tests about the variance, double the tail probability beyond the chi-square test statistic if the sample variance is larger than σ_0^2, or double the tail probability below the chi-square test statistic if the sample variance is below σ_0^2. So, in Example 7.4-1, since $s^2 = 147.82 > 100$, the p-value equals $2[P(W \geq 32.52)]$ and it follows that

$$0.10 < p\text{-value} < 0.20.$$

We now give a test for the equality of two variances when sampling occurs from normal populations. Let the independent random variables X and Y have respective distributions that are $N(\mu_X, \sigma_X^2)$ and $N(\mu_Y, \sigma_Y^2)$. To test the null hypothesis H_0: $\sigma_X^2/\sigma_Y^2 = 1$ (or, equivalently, $\sigma_X^2 = \sigma_Y^2$), take random samples of n observations of X and m observations of Y. Recall that $(n-1)S_X^2/\sigma_X^2$ and $(m-1)S_Y^2/\sigma_Y^2$ have independent chi-square distributions $\chi^2(n-1)$ and $\chi^2(m-1)$, respectively. Thus, when H_0 is true,

$$F = \frac{\dfrac{(n-1)S_X^2}{\sigma_X^2(n-1)}}{\dfrac{(m-1)S_Y^2}{\sigma_Y^2(m-1)}} = \frac{S_X^2}{S_Y^2}$$

has an F distribution with $r_1 = n - 1$ and $r_2 = m - 1$ degrees of freedom. This F statistic is our test statistic. When H_0 is true, we would expect the observed value of F to be close to 1.

With normal distributions, three possible alternative hypotheses, along with critical regions of size α, are summarized in Table 7.4-2. Recall that $1/F$, the reciprocal of F, has an F distribution with $m - 1$ and $n - 1$ degrees of freedom so all critical regions may be written in terms of right-tail rejection regions and the critical values can be selected easily from Table VII in the appendix.

TABLE 7.4-2: Tests of Hypotheses of the Equality of Variances

H_0	H_1	Critical Region
$\sigma_X^2 = \sigma_Y^2$	$\sigma_X^2 > \sigma_Y^2$	$\dfrac{s_x^2}{s_y^2} \geq F_\alpha(n-1, m-1)$
$\sigma_Y^2 = \sigma_Y^2$	$\sigma_X^2 < \sigma_Y^2$	$\dfrac{s_y^2}{s_x^2} \geq F_\alpha(m-1, n-1)$
$\sigma_X^2 = \sigma_Y^2$	$\sigma_X^2 \neq \sigma_Y^2$	$\dfrac{s_x^2}{s_y^2} \geq F_{\alpha/2}(n-1, m-1)$ or $\dfrac{s_y^2}{s_x^2} \geq F_{\alpha/2}(m-1, n-1)$

EXAMPLE 7.4-2 A biologist who studies spiders believes that not only do female green lynx spiders tend to be longer than their male counterparts, but also the lengths of the female spiders seem to vary more than those of the male spiders. We shall test whether this

latter belief is true. Suppose that the distribution of the length X of male spiders is $N(\mu_X, \sigma_X^2)$, the distribution of the length Y of female spiders is $N(\mu_Y, \sigma_Y^2)$, and X and Y are independent. We shall test H_0: $\sigma_X^2/\sigma_Y^2 = 1$ (i.e., $\sigma_X^2 = \sigma_Y^2$) against the alternative hypothesis H_1: $\sigma_X^2/\sigma_Y^2 < 1$ (i.e., $\sigma_X^2 < \sigma_Y^2$). If we use $n = 30$ and $m = 30$ observations of X and Y, respectively, then a critical region that has a significance level of $\alpha = 0.01$ is

$$\frac{s_y^2}{s_x^2} \geq F_{0.01}(29, 29) \approx 2.42,$$

by interpolation from Table VII in the appendix (or 2.4234 with Minitab). In Exercise 6.3-5, $n = 30$ observations of X yielded $\overline{x} = 5.917$ and $s_x^2 = 0.4399$, while $m = 30$ observations of Y yielded $\overline{y} = 8.153$ and $s_y^2 = 1.4100$. Since

$$\frac{s_y^2}{s_x^2} = \frac{1.4100}{0.4399} = 3.2053 > 2.42,$$

the null hypothesis is rejected in favor of the biologist's belief. Using Minitab, we find that the p-value is equal to 0.0012, as illustrated in Figure 7.4-2. (See Exercise 7.3-16.) ■

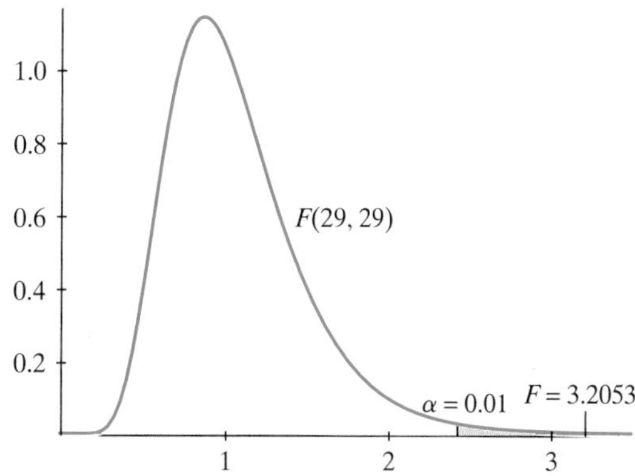

FIGURE 7.4-2: Test of variances for green lynx spiders

In Example 7.3-1, we used a t statistic for testing the equality of means which assumed that the variances were equal. In the next example, we shall test whether that assumption is valid.

EXAMPLE 7.4-3 For Example 7.3-1, given $n = 11$ observations of X and $m = 13$ observations of Y, where X is $N(\mu_X, \sigma_X^2)$ and Y is $N(\mu_Y, \sigma_Y^2)$, we shall test the null hypothesis H_0: $\sigma_X^2/\sigma_Y^2 = 1$ against a two-sided alternative hypothesis. At an $\alpha = 0.05$ significance level, H_0 is rejected if

$$s_x^2/s_y^2 \geq F_{0.025}(10, 12) = 3.37$$

or

$$s_y^2/s_x^2 \geq F_{0.025}(12, 10) = 3.62.$$

Using the data in Example 7.3-1, we obtain

$$s_x^2/s_y^2 = 0.24/0.35 = 0.686 \qquad \text{and} \qquad s_y^2/s_x^2 = 1.458,$$

so we do not reject H_0. Thus, the assumption of equal variances for the t statistic that was used in Example 7.3-1 seems to be valid. (See Figure 7.4-3, noting that $F_{0.975}(10, 12) = 1/F_{0.025}(12, 10) = 1/3.62 = 0.276$.) ■

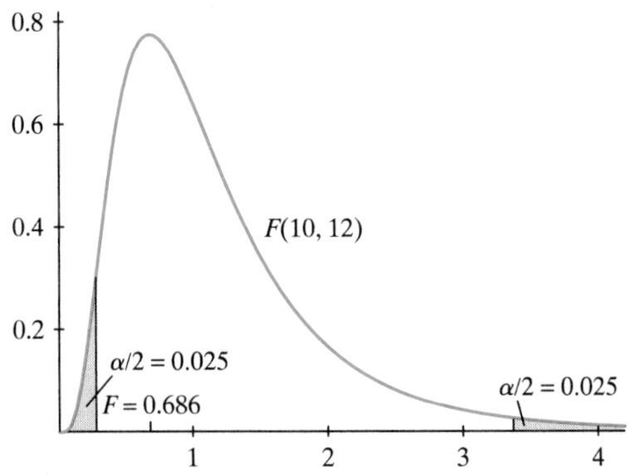

FIGURE 7.4-3: Test of variances for pea stem growths

EXERCISES

(In some of the exercises that follow, we must make assumptions such as the existence of normal distributions with the usual notation.)

7.4-1. Assume that the birth weight in grams of a baby born in the United States is $N(3315, 525^2)$ for boys and girls combined. Let X equal the weight of a baby girl who is born at home in Ottawa County, and assume that the distribution of X is $N(\mu_X, \sigma_X^2)$.

(a) Using 11 observations of X, give the test statistic and the critical region for testing H_0: $\sigma_X^2 = 525^2$ against the alternative hypothesis H_1: $\sigma_X^2 < 525^2$ (less variation of weights of home-born babies) if $\alpha = 0.05$.

(b) Calculate the value of the test statistic and state your conclusion, using the following weights:

3119 2657 3459 3629 3345 3629
3515 3856 3629 3345 3062

(c) What is the approximate p-value of the test?

7.4-2. Let Y equal the weight in grams of a baby boy who is born at home in Ottawa County, and assume that the distribution of Y is $N(\mu_Y, \sigma_Y^2)$. The following weights are for 11 boys:

4082 3686 4111 3686 3175 4139
3686 3430 3289 3657 4082

(a) Test H_0: $\sigma_Y^2 = 525^2$ against the alternative hypothesis H_1: $\sigma_Y^2 < 525^2$. Use $\alpha = 0.05$.

(b) Test the equality of the variances of the weights of girls (Exercise 7.4) and the weights of boys against a two-sided alternative.

(c) Test the equality of the means of the weights of girls and boys born at home in Ottawa County against a two-sided alternative.

7.4-3. Let X equal the number of pounds of butterfat produced by a Holstein cow during the 305-day milking period following the birth of a calf. We shall test the null hypothesis H_0: $\sigma^2 = 140^2$ against the alternative hypothesis H_1: $\sigma^2 > 140^2$.

(a) Give the test statistic and a critical region that has a significance level of $\alpha = 0.05$, assuming that there are $n = 25$ observations.

(b) Calculate the value of the test statistic and state your conclusion, using the following 25 observations of X:

425 710 661 664 732 714 934 761 744
653 725 657 421 573 535 602 537 405
874 791 721 849 567 468 975

7.4-4. In May, the fill weights of 6-pound boxes of laundry soap had a mean of 6.13 pounds with a standard deviation of 0.095. The goal was to decrease the standard deviation. The company decided to adjust the filling machines and then test $H_0\colon \sigma = 0.095$ against $H_1\colon \sigma < 0.095$. In June, a random sample of size $n = 20$ yielded $\overline{x} = 6.10$ and $s = 0.065$.

(a) At an $\alpha = 0.05$ significance level, was the company successful?

(b) What is the approximate p-value of your test?

7.4-5. The mean birth weight in the United States is $\mu = 3315$ grams, with a standard deviation of $\sigma = 575$. Let X equal the birth weight in Rwanda. Assume that the distribution of X is $N(\mu, \sigma^2)$. We shall test the hypothesis $H_0\colon \sigma = 575$ against the alternative hypothesis $H_1\colon \sigma < 575$ at an $\alpha = 0.10$ significance level.

(a) What is your decision if a random sample of size $n = 81$ yielded $\overline{x} = 2819$ and $s = 496$?

(b) What is the approximate p-value of this test?

7.4-6. Let $X_1, X_2, \ldots, X_{23}$ be a random sample from a normal distribution that has variance $\sigma^2 = 100$. Let $S^2 = (1/22)\sum_{i=1}^{23}(X_i - \overline{X})^2$ be the sample variance. Of course, $22S^2/100$ is $\chi^2(22)$. Show that $\text{Var}(S^2) = 10{,}000/11$. Thus, the standard deviation of S^2 is 30.15, and this helps explain the critical region $s^2 \le 49.91$ or $s^2 \ge 167.18$ in Example 7.4-1.

7.4-7. Let $X_1, X_2, \ldots, X_{19}$ be a random sample of size $n = 19$ from the normal distribution $N(\mu, \sigma^2)$.

(a) Find a critical region, C, of size $\alpha = 0.05$ for testing $H_0\colon \sigma^2 = 30$ against $H_1\colon \sigma^2 = 80$.

(b) Find the approximate value of β, the probability of a Type II error, for the critical region C of part (a).

7.4-8. Let X and Y equal the times in days required for maturation of Guardiola seeds from narrow-leaved and broad-leaved parents, respectively. Assume that X is $N(\mu_X, \sigma_X^2)$ and Y is $N(\mu_Y, \sigma_Y^2)$ and that X and Y are independent. Test the hypothesis $H_0\colon \sigma_X^2/\sigma_Y^2 = 1$ against the alternative hypothesis $H_1\colon \sigma_X^2/\sigma_Y^2 > 1$ if a sample size $n = 13$ yielded $\overline{x} = 18.97$, $s_x^2 = 9.88$ and a sample of size $m = 9$ yielded $\overline{y} = 23.20$, $s_y^2 = 4.08$. Let $\alpha = 0.05$.

7.4-9. To measure air pollution in a home, let X and Y equal the amount of suspended particulate matter (in μg/m^3) measured during a 24-hour period in a home in which there is no smoker and a home in which there is a smoker, respectively. We shall test the null hypothesis $H_0\colon \sigma_X^2/\sigma_Y^2 = 1$ against the one-sided alternative hypothesis $H_1\colon \sigma_X^2/\sigma_Y^2 > 1$. If a random sample of size $n = 9$ yielded $\overline{x} = 93$ and $s_x = 12.9$ while a random sample of size $m = 11$ yielded $\overline{y} = 132$ and $s_y = 7.1$, define a critical region and give your conclusion if $\alpha = 0.05$. Now test $H_0\colon \mu_X = \mu_Y$ against $H_1\colon \mu_X < \mu_Y$ if $\alpha = 0.05$.

7.4-10. A random sample of $n = 7$ brand X light bulbs yielded $\overline{x} = 891$ hours and $s_x^2 = 9201$. A random sample of $m = 10$ brand Y light bulbs yielded $\overline{y} = 592$ hours and $s_y^2 = 4856$. Use these data to test $H_0\colon \sigma_X^2/\sigma_Y^2 = 1$ against $H_1\colon \sigma_X^2/\sigma_Y^2 > 1$. Let $\alpha = 0.05$ and state your assumptions.

7.4-11. In Section 7.3 for tests of the equality of two means, the assumption was often made that the variances were equal. In this exercise, we shall test $H_0\colon \sigma_X^2/\sigma_Y^2 = 1$ against the alternative hypothesis $H_1\colon \sigma_X^2/\sigma_Y^2 \neq 1$. Perform this test at the $\alpha = 0.05$ significance level for the following exercises:

(a) Exercise 7.3-3.

(b) Exercise 7.3-4.

(c) Exercise 7.3-5.

(d) Exercise 7.3-6.

(e) Exercise 7.3-8.

(f) Exercise 7.3-10.

(g) Exercise 7.3-11.

7.5 ONE-FACTOR ANALYSIS OF VARIANCE

Frequently, experimenters want to compare more than two treatments: yields of several different corn hybrids, results due to three or more teaching techniques, or miles per gallon obtained from many different types of compact cars. Sometimes the different treatment distributions of the resulting observations are due to changing the level of a certain factor (e.g., different doses of a given drug). Thus, the consideration of the equality of the different means of the various distributions comes under the analysis of a **one-factor experiment**.

In Section 7.3, we discussed how to compare the means of two normal distributions. More generally, let us now consider m normal distributions with unknown means

$\mu_1, \mu_2, \ldots, \mu_m$ and an unknown, but common, variance σ^2. One inference that we wish to consider is a test of the equality of the m means, namely, H_0: $\mu_1 = \mu_2 = \cdots = \mu_m = \mu$, with μ unspecified, against all possible alternative hypotheses H_1. In order to test this hypothesis, we shall take independent random samples from these distributions. Let $X_{i1}, X_{i2}, \ldots, X_{in_i}$ represent a random sample of size n_i from the normal distribution $N(\mu_i, \sigma^2)$, $i = 1, 2, \ldots, m$. In Table 7.5-1, we have indicated these random samples along with the row means (sample means), where, with $n = n_1 + n_2 + \cdots + n_m$,

$$\overline{X}_{\cdot\cdot} = \frac{1}{n}\sum_{i=1}^{m}\sum_{j=1}^{n_i} X_{ij} \quad \text{and} \quad \overline{X}_{i\cdot} = \frac{1}{n_i}\sum_{j=1}^{n_i} X_{ij}, \qquad i = 1, 2, \ldots, m.$$

TABLE 7.5-1: One-factor Random Samples

					Means
X_1:	X_{11}	X_{12}	$\cdots$	X_{1n_1}	$\overline{X}_{1\cdot}$
X_2:	X_{21}	X_{22}	$\cdots$	X_{2n_2}	$\overline{X}_{2\cdot}$
$\vdots$	$\vdots$	$\vdots$	$\vdots$	$\vdots$	$\vdots$
X_m:	X_{m1}	X_{m2}	$\cdots$	X_{mn_m}	$\overline{X}_{m\cdot}$
Grand Mean:					$\overline{X}_{\cdot\cdot}$

The dot in the notation for the means, $\overline{X}_{\cdot\cdot}$ and $\overline{X}_{i\cdot}$, indicates the index over which the average is taken. Here $\overline{X}_{\cdot\cdot}$ is an average taken over both indices, while $\overline{X}_{i\cdot}$ is taken over just the index j.

To determine a critical region for a test of H_0, we shall first partition the sum of squares associated with the variance of the combined samples into two parts. This sum of squares is given by

$$\begin{aligned}
\text{SS(TO)} &= \sum_{i=1}^{m}\sum_{j=1}^{n_i}(X_{ij} - \overline{X}_{\cdot\cdot})^2 \\
&= \sum_{i=1}^{m}\sum_{j=1}^{n_i}(X_{ij} - \overline{X}_{i\cdot} + \overline{X}_{i\cdot} - \overline{X}_{\cdot\cdot})^2 \\
&= \sum_{i=1}^{m}\sum_{j=1}^{n_i}(X_{ij} - \overline{X}_{i\cdot})^2 + \sum_{i=1}^{m}\sum_{j=1}^{n_i}(\overline{X}_{i\cdot} - \overline{X}_{\cdot\cdot})^2 \\
&\quad + 2\sum_{i=1}^{m}\sum_{j=1}^{n_i}(X_{ij} - \overline{X}_{i\cdot})(\overline{X}_{i\cdot} - \overline{X}_{\cdot\cdot}).
\end{aligned}$$

The last term of the right-hand member of this identity may be written as

$$2\sum_{i=1}^{m}\left[(\overline{X}_{i\cdot} - \overline{X}_{\cdot\cdot})\sum_{j=1}^{n_i}(X_{ij} - \overline{X}_{i\cdot})\right] = 2\sum_{i=1}^{m}(\overline{X}_{i\cdot} - \overline{X}_{\cdot\cdot})(n_i\overline{X}_{i\cdot} - n_i\overline{X}_{i\cdot}) = 0,$$

and the preceding term may be written as

$$\sum_{i=1}^{m}\sum_{j=1}^{n_i}(\overline{X}_{i\cdot} - \overline{X}_{\cdot\cdot})^2 = \sum_{i=1}^{m} n_i(\overline{X}_{i\cdot} - \overline{X}_{\cdot\cdot})^2.$$

Thus,

$$\text{SS(TO)} = \sum_{i=1}^{m}\sum_{j=1}^{n_i}(X_{ij} - \overline{X}_{i\cdot})^2 + \sum_{i=1}^{m} n_i(\overline{X}_{i\cdot} - \overline{X}_{\cdot\cdot})^2.$$

For notation, let

$\text{SS(TO)} = \sum_{i=1}^{m}\sum_{j=1}^{n_i}(X_{ij} - \overline{X}_{\cdot\cdot})^2$, the total sum of squares;

$\text{SS(E)} = \sum_{i=1}^{m}\sum_{j=1}^{n_i}(X_{ij} - \overline{X}_{i\cdot})^2$, the sum of squares within treatments, groups, or classes, often called the error sum of squares;

$\text{SS(T)} = \sum_{i=1}^{m} n_i(\overline{X}_{i\cdot} - \overline{X}_{\cdot\cdot})^2$, the sum of squares among the different treatments, groups, or classes, often called the between-treatment sum of squares.

Hence,

$$\text{SS(TO)} = \text{SS(E)} + \text{SS(T)}.$$

When H_0 is true, we may regard X_{ij}, $i = 1,2,\ldots,m$, $j = 1,2,\ldots,n_i$, as a random sample of size $n = n_1 + n_2 + \cdots + n_m$ from the normal distribution $N(\mu, \sigma^2)$. Then $\text{SS(TO)}/(n - 1)$ is an unbiased estimator of σ^2 because $\text{SS(TO)}/\sigma^2$ is $\chi^2(n-1)$, so that $E[\text{SS(TO)}/\sigma^2] = n - 1$ and $E[\text{SS(TO)}/(n - 1)] = \sigma^2$. An unbiased estimator of σ^2 based only on the sample from the ith distribution is

$$W_i = \frac{\sum_{j=1}^{n_i}(X_{ij} - \overline{X}_{i\cdot})^2}{n_i - 1} \qquad \text{for } i = 1,2,\ldots,m,$$

because $(n_i - 1)W_i/\sigma^2$ is $\chi^2(n_i - 1)$. Thus,

$$E\left[\frac{(n_i - 1)W_i}{\sigma^2}\right] = n_i - 1,$$

and so

$$E(W_i) = \sigma^2, \qquad i = 1,2,\ldots,m.$$

It follows that the sum of m of these independent chi-square random variables, namely,

$$\sum_{i=1}^{m}\frac{(n_i - 1)W_i}{\sigma^2} = \frac{\text{SS(E)}}{\sigma^2},$$

is also chi-square with $(n_1 - 1) + (n_2 - 1) + \cdots + (n_m - 1) = n - m$ degrees of freedom. Hence, $\text{SS(E)}/(n - m)$ is an unbiased estimator of σ^2. We now have

$$\frac{\text{SS(TO)}}{\sigma^2} = \frac{\text{SS(E)}}{\sigma^2} + \frac{\text{SS(T)}}{\sigma^2},$$

where

$$\frac{SS(TO)}{\sigma^2} \text{ is } \chi^2(n-1) \quad \text{and} \quad \frac{SS(E)}{\sigma^2} \text{ is } \chi^2(n-m).$$

Because $SS(T) \geq 0$, there is a theorem (see subsequent remark) which states that SS(E) and SS(T) are independent and the distribution of $SS(T)/\sigma^2$ is $\chi^2(m-1)$.

REMARK The sums of squares, SS(T), SS(E), and SS(TO), are examples of **quadratic forms** in the variables X_{ij}, $i = 1, 2, \ldots, m$, $j = 1, 2, \ldots, n_i$. That is, each term in these sums of squares is of second degree in X_{ij}. Furthermore, the coefficients of the variables are real numbers, so these sums of squares are called **real quadratic forms**. The next theorem, stated without proof, is used in this chapter. [For a proof, see Hogg, McKean, and Craig, *Introduction to Mathematical Statistics*, 6th ed. (Upper Saddle River: Prentice Hall, 2005).] ■

THEOREM 7.5-1 Let $Q = Q_1 + Q_2 + \cdots + Q_k$, where $Q, Q_1, \ldots, Q_k$ are $k + 1$ real quadratic forms in n mutually independent random variables normally distributed with the same variance σ^2. Let $Q/\sigma^2, Q_1/\sigma^2, \ldots, Q_{k-1}/\sigma^2$ have chi-square distributions with $r, r_1, \ldots, r_{k-1}$ degrees of freedom, respectively. If Q_k is nonnegative, then

(a) $Q_1, \ldots, Q_k$ are mutually independent, and hence,

(b) Q_k/σ^2 has a chi-square distribution with $r - (r_1 + \cdots + r_{k-1}) = r_k$ degrees of freedom.

Since, under H_0, $SS(T)/\sigma^2$ is $\chi^2(m-1)$, we have $E[SS(T)/\sigma^2] = m - 1$ and it follows that $E[SS(T)/(m-1)] = \sigma^2$. Now, the estimator of σ^2, namely, $SS(E)/(n-m)$, which is based on SS(E), is always unbiased, whether H_0 is true or false. However, if the means $\mu_1, \mu_2, \ldots, \mu_m$ are not equal, the expected value of the estimator that is based on SS(T) will be greater than σ^2. To make this last statement clear, we have

$$\begin{aligned} E[SS(T)] &= E\left[\sum_{i=1}^{m} n_i(\overline{X}_{i\cdot} - \overline{X}_{\cdot\cdot})^2\right] = E\left[\sum_{i=1}^{m} n_i\overline{X}_{i\cdot}^2 - n\overline{X}_{\cdot\cdot}^2\right] \\ &= \sum_{i=1}^{m} n_i\{\mathrm{Var}(\overline{X}_{i\cdot}) + [E(\overline{X}_{i\cdot})]^2\} - n\{\mathrm{Var}(\overline{X}_{\cdot\cdot}) + [E(\overline{X}_{\cdot\cdot})]^2\} \\ &= \sum_{i=1}^{m} n_i\left\{\frac{\sigma^2}{n_i} + \mu_i^2\right\} - n\left\{\frac{\sigma^2}{n} + \overline{\mu}^2\right\} \\ &= (m-1)\sigma^2 + \sum_{i=1}^{m} n_i(\mu_i - \overline{\mu})^2, \end{aligned}$$

where $\overline{\mu} = (1/n)\sum_{i=1}^{m} n_i\mu_i$. If $\mu_1 = \mu_2 = \cdots = \mu_m = \mu$, then

$$E\left(\frac{SS(T)}{m-1}\right) = \sigma^2.$$

If the means are not all equal, then

$$E\left[\frac{SS(T)}{m-1}\right] = \sigma^2 + \sum_{i=1}^{m} n_i \frac{(\mu_i - \overline{\mu})^2}{m-1} > \sigma^2.$$

Exercise 7.5-4 also illustrates the fact that the estimator using SS(T) is usually greater than that using SS(E) when H_0 is false.

We can base our test of H_0 on the ratio of $SS(T)/(m-1)$ and $SS(E)/(n-m)$, both of which are unbiased estimators of σ^2, provided that H_0: $\mu_1 = \mu_2 = \cdots = \mu_m$ is true, so that, under H_0, the ratio would assume values near 1. However, in the case that the means $\mu_1, \mu_2, \ldots, \mu_m$ begin to differ, this ratio tends to become large, since $E[SS(T)/(m-1)]$ gets larger. Under H_0, the ratio

$$\frac{SS(T)/(m-1)}{SS(E)/(n-m)} = \frac{[SS(T)/\sigma^2]/(m-1)}{[SS(E)/\sigma^2]/(n-m)} = F$$

has an F distribution with $m-1$ and $n-m$ degrees of freedom because $SS(T)/\sigma^2$ and $SS(E)/\sigma^2$ are independent chi-square variables. We would reject H_0 if the observed value of F is too large, because this would indicate that we have a relatively large SS(T), suggesting that the means are unequal. Thus, the critical region is of the form $F \ge F_\alpha(m-1, n-m)$.

The information used for tests of the equality of several means is often summarized in an **analysis-of-variance table**, or **ANOVA** table, like that given in Table 7.5-2, where the mean square (MS) is the sum of squares (SS) divided by its degrees of freedom.

TABLE 7.5-2: Analysis-of-Variance Table

Source	Sum of Squares (SS)	Degrees of Freedom	Mean Square (MS)	F Ratio
Treatment	SS(T)	$m-1$	$MS(T) = \dfrac{SS(T)}{m-1}$	$\dfrac{MS(T)}{MS(E)}$
Error	SS(E)	$n-m$	$MS(E) = \dfrac{SS(E)}{n-m}$	
Total	SS(TO)	$n-1$		

EXAMPLE 7.5-1 Let X_1, X_2, X_3, X_4 be independent random variables that have normal distributions $N(\mu_i, \sigma^2)$, $i = 1, 2, 3, 4$. We shall test

$$H_0\colon \mu_1 = \mu_2 = \mu_3 = \mu_4 = \mu$$

against all alternatives on the basis of a random sample of size $n_i = 3$ from each of the four distributions. A critical region of size $\alpha = 0.05$ is given by

$$F = \frac{SS(T)/(4-1)}{SS(E)/(12-4)} \ge 4.07 = F_{0.05}(3, 8).$$

The observed data are shown in Table 7.5-3. (Clearly, these data are not observations from normal distributions; they were selected to illustrate the calculations.)

TABLE 7.5-3: Illustrative Data

	Observations			$\overline{X}_{i\cdot}$
X_1:	13	8	9	10
X_2:	15	11	13	13
X_3:	8	12	7	9
X_4:	11	15	10	12
$\overline{X}_{\cdot\cdot}$				11

For the given data, the calculated SS(TO), SS(E), and SS(T) are

$$\begin{aligned} SS(TO) &= (13-11)^2+(8-11)^2+\cdots+(15-11)^2+(10-11)^2=80; \\ SS(E) &= (13-10)^2+(8-10)^2+\cdots+(15-12)^2+(10-12)^2=50; \\ SS(T) &= 3[(10-11)^2+(13-11)^2+(9-11)^2+(12-11)^2]=30. \end{aligned}$$

Note that since SS(TO) = SS(E) + SS(T), only two of the three values need to be calculated directly from the data. Here the computed value of F is

$$\frac{30/3}{50/8} = 1.6 < 4.07,$$

and H_0 is not rejected. The p-value is the probability, under H_0, of obtaining an F that is at least as large as this computed value of F. It is often given by computer programs.

The information for this example is summarized in Table 7.5-4. Again we note that (here and elsewhere) the F statistic is the ratio of two appropriate mean squares. ■

TABLE 7.5-4: ANOVA Table for Illustrative Data

Source	Sum of Squares (SS)	Degrees of Freedom	Mean Square (MS)	F Ratio	p-value
Treatment	30	3	30/3	1.6	0.264
Error	50	8	50/8		
Total	80	11			

Formulas that sometimes simplify the calculations of SS(TO), SS(T), and SS(E) (and also reduce roundoff errors created by subtracting the averages from the observations) are

$$SS(TO) = \sum_{i=1}^{m}\sum_{j=1}^{n_i} X_{ij}^2 - \frac{1}{n}\left[\sum_{i=1}^{m}\sum_{j=1}^{n_i} X_{ij}\right]^2,$$

$$SS(T) = \sum_{i=1}^{m}\frac{1}{n_i}\left[\sum_{j=1}^{n_i} X_{ij}\right]^2 - \frac{1}{n}\left[\sum_{i=1}^{m}\sum_{j=1}^{n_i} X_{ij}\right]^2,$$

and

$$SS(E) = SS(TO) - SS(T).$$

It is interesting to note that in these formulas each square is divided by the number of observations in the sum being squared: X_{ij}^2 by 1, $(\sum_{j=1}^{n_i} X_{ij})^2$ by n_i, and $(\sum_{i=1}^{m} \sum_{j=1}^{n_i} X_{ij})^2$ by n. The preceding formulas are used in Example 7.5-2. Although they are useful, you are encouraged to use appropriate statistical packages on a computer to aid you with these calculations.

If the sample sizes are all at least equal to 7, insight can be gained by plotting box-and-whisker diagrams on the same figure, for each of the samples. This technique is also illustrated in Example 7.5-2.

EXAMPLE 7.5-2 A window that is manufactured for an automobile has five studs for attaching it. A company that manufactures these windows performs "pullout tests" to determine the force needed to pull a stud out of the window. Let X_i, $i = 1, 2, 3, 4, 5$, equal the force required at position i, and assume that the distribution of X_i is $N(\mu_i, \sigma^2)$. We shall test the null hypothesis H_0: $\mu_1 = \mu_2 = \mu_3 = \mu_4 = \mu_5$, using seven independent observations at each position. At an $\alpha = 0.01$ significance level, H_0 is rejected if the computed

$$F = \frac{SS(T)/(5 - 1)}{SS(E)/(35 - 5)} \ge 4.02 = F_{0.01}(4, 30).$$

TABLE 7.5-5: Pullout Test Data

	Observations							$\sum_{j=1}^{7} x_{ij}$	$\sum_{j=1}^{7} x_{ij}^2$
X_1:	92	90	87	105	86	83	102	645	59,847
X_2:	100	108	98	110	114	97	94	721	74,609
X_3:	143	149	138	136	139	120	145	970	134,936
X_4:	147	144	160	149	152	131	134	1017	148,367
X_5:	142	155	119	134	133	146	152	981	138,415
Totals								4334	556,174

The observed data, along with certain sums are given in Table 7.5-5. For these data,

$$\begin{aligned} SS(TO) &= 556{,}174 - \frac{1}{35}(4334)^2 = 19{,}500.97, \\ SS(T) &= \frac{1}{7}(645^2 + 721^2 + 970^2 + 1017^2 + 981^2) \\ &\quad - \frac{1}{35}(4334)^2 = 16{,}672.11, \\ SS(E) &= 19{,}500.97 - 16{,}672.11 = 2828.86. \end{aligned}$$

Since the computed F is

$$F = \frac{16{,}672.11/4}{2828.86/30} = 44.20,$$

the null hypothesis is clearly rejected. This information obtained from the equations is summarized in Table 7.5-6.

TABLE 7.5-6: ANOVA Table for Pullout Tests

Source	Sum of Squares (SS)	Degrees of Freedom	Mean Square (MS)	F
Treatment	16,672.11	4	4,168.03	44.20
Error	2,828.86	30	94.30	
Total	19,500.97	34		

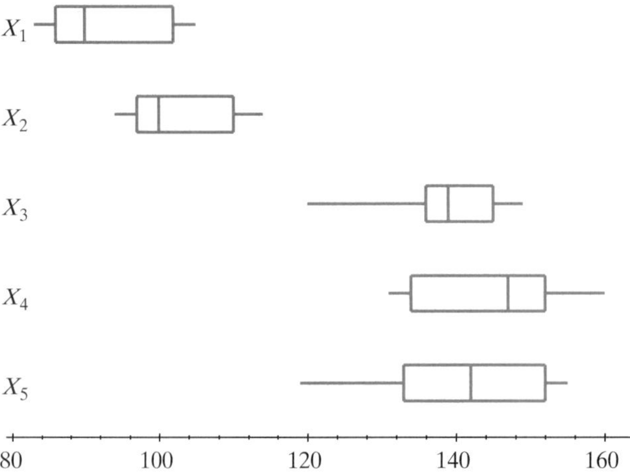

FIGURE 7.5-1: Box plots for pullout tests

But why is H_0 rejected? The box-and-whisker diagrams shown in Figure 7.5-1 help to answer this question. It looks like the forces required to pull out studs in positions 1 and 2 are similar, and those in positions 3, 4, and 5 are quite similar, but different from, positions 1 and 2. (See Exercise 7.5-12.) An examination of the window would confirm that this is the case. ■

As with the two-sample t test, the F test works quite well even if the underlying distributions are nonnormal, unless they are highly skewed or the variances are quite different. In these latter cases, we might need to transform the observations to make the data more symmetric with about the same variances or to use certain nonparametric methods that are beyond the scope of this text.

EXERCISES

(In some of the exercises that follow, we must make assumptions, such as normal distributions with equal variances.)

7.5-1. Let μ_1, μ_2, μ_3 be, respectively, the means of three normal distributions with a common, but unknown, variance σ^2. In order to test, at the $\alpha = 0.05$ significance level, the hypothesis $H_0: \mu_1 = \mu_2 = \mu_3$ against all possible alternative hypotheses, we take a random sample of size 4 from each of these distributions. Determine whether we accept or reject H_0 if the observed values from the three distributions are, respectively, as follows:

X_1:	5	9	6	8
X_2:	11	13	10	12
X_3:	10	6	9	9

7.5-2. Let μ_i be the average yield in bushels per acre of variety i of corn, $i = 1, 2, 3, 4$. In order to test the hypothesis H_0: $\mu_1 = \mu_2 = \mu_3 = \mu_4$ at the 5% significance level, four test plots for each of the four varieties of corn are planted. Determine whether we accept or reject H_0 if the yield in bushels per acre of the four varieties of corn are, respectively, as follows:

X_1:	68.82	76.99	74.30	78.73
X_2:	86.84	75.69	77.87	76.18
X_3:	90.16	78.84	80.65	83.58
X_4:	61.58	73.51	74.57	70.75

7.5-3. Four groups of three pigs each were fed individually four different feeds for a specified length of time to test the hypothesis H_0: $\mu_1 = \mu_2 = \mu_3 = \mu_4$, where μ_i, $i = 1, 2, 3, 4$, is the mean weight gain for each of the feeds. Determine whether the null hypothesis is accepted or rejected at a 5% significance level if the observed weight gains are, respectively, as follows:

X_1:	194.11	182.80	187.43
X_2:	216.06	203.50	216.88
X_3:	178.10	189.20	181.33
X_4:	197.11	202.68	209.18

7.5-4. For the following set of data, show that the computed $\text{SS(E)}/(n - m) = 1$ and $\text{SS(T)}/(m - 1) = 75$ (this suggests that the unbiased estimate of σ^2 based on SS(T) is usually greater than σ^2 when the true means are unequal):

X_1:	4	5	6
X_2:	9	10	11
X_3:	14	15	16

7.5-5. The female cuckoo lays her eggs in other birds' nests. The "foster parents" are usually deceived, probably because of the similarity in sizes of their own eggs and cuckoo eggs. Latter (see references) investigated this possible explanation and measured the lengths of cuckoo eggs (in millimeters) that were found in the nests of three species. Following are his results:

Hedge sparrow:	22.0	23.9	20.9	23.8	25.0
	24.0	21.7	23.8	22.8	23.1
	23.1	23.5	23.0	23.0	
Robin:	21.8	23.0	23.3	22.4	23.0
	23.0	23.0	22.4	23.9	22.3
	22.0	22.6	22.0	22.1	21.1
	23.0				
Wren:	19.8	22.1	21.5	20.9	22.0
	21.0	22.3	21.0	20.3	20.9
	22.0	20.0	20.8	21.2	21.0

(a) Construct an ANOVA table to test the equality of the three means.
(b) For each set of data, construct box-and-whisker diagrams on the same figure.
(c) Interpret your results.

7.5-6. Ledolter and Hogg (see references) report that a civil engineer wishes to compare the strengths of three different types of beams, one (A) made of steel and two (B and C) made of different and more expensive alloys. A certain deflection (in units of 0.001 inch) was measured for each beam when submitted to a given force; thus, a small deflection would indicate a beam of great strength. The order statistics for the three samples, of respective sizes $n_1 = 8$, $n_2 = 6$, and $n_3 = 6$, are as follows:

A:	79	82	83	84	85	86	86	87
B:	74	75	76	77	78	82		
C:	77	78	79	79	79	82		

(a) Use these data, $\alpha = 0.05$, and the F test to test the equality of the three means.
(b) For each set of data, construct box-and-whisker diagrams on the same figure and give an interpretation of your diagrams.

7.5-7. Montgomery (see references) examines the strengths of a synthetic fiber that may be affected by the percentage of cotton in the fiber. Five levels of this percentage are considered, with five observations taken at each level.

Percentage of Cotton	Tensile Strength in Pounds per Square Inch				
15	7	7	15	11	9
20	12	17	12	18	18
25	14	18	18	19	19
30	19	25	22	19	23
35	7	10	11	15	11

Use the F test, with $\alpha = 0.05$, to see if there are differences in the breaking strengths due to the percentages of cotton used.

7.5-8. Let X_1, X_2, X_3, X_4 equal the cholesterol level of a woman under the age of 50, a man under 50, a woman 50 or older, and a man 50 or older, respectively. Assume that the distribution of X_i is $N(\mu_i, \sigma^2)$, $i = 1,2,3,4$. We shall test the null hypothesis H_0: $\mu_1 = \mu_2 = \mu_3 = \mu_4$, using seven observations of each X_i.

(a) Give a critical region for an $\alpha = 0.05$ significance level.

(b) Construct an ANOVA table and state your conclusion, using the following data:

X_1:	221	213	202	183	185	197	162
X_2:	271	192	189	209	227	236	142
X_3:	262	193	224	201	161	178	265
X_4:	192	253	248	278	232	267	289

(c) Give bounds on the p-value for this test.

(d) For each set of data, construct box-and-whisker diagrams on the same figure and give an interpretation of your diagram.

7.5-9. Let X_i, $i = 1,2,3,4$, equal the distance that a golf ball travels when hit from a tee, where i denotes the index of the ith manufacturer. Assume that the distribution of X_i is $N(\mu_i, \sigma^2)$, $i = 1,2,3,4$ when a ball is hit by a certain golfer. We shall test the null hypothesis H_0: $\mu_1 = \mu_2 = \mu_3 = \mu_4$, using three observations of each random variable.

(a) Give a critical region for an $\alpha = 0.05$ significance level.

(b) Construct an ANOVA table and state your conclusion, using the following data:

X_1:	240	221	265
X_2:	286	256	272
X_3:	259	245	232
X_4:	239	215	223

(c) What would your conclusion be if $\alpha = 0.025$?

(d) What is the approximate p-value of this test?

7.5-10. Different sizes of nails are packaged in "1-pound" boxes. Let X_i equal the weight of a box with nail size $(4i)C$, $i = 1,2,3,4,5$, where $4C, 8C, 12C, 16C$, and $20C$ are the sizes of the sinkers from smallest to largest. Assume that the distribution of X_i is $N(\mu_i, \sigma^2)$. To test the null hypothesis that the mean weights of "1-pound" boxes are all equal for different sizes of nails, we shall use random samples of size 7, weighing the nails to the nearest hundredth of a pound.

(a) Give a critical region for an $\alpha = 0.05$ significance level.

(b) Construct an ANOVA table and state your conclusion, using the following data:

X_1:	1.03	1.04	1.07	1.03	1.08	1.06	1.07
X_2:	1.03	1.10	1.08	1.05	1.06	1.06	1.05
X_3:	1.03	1.08	1.06	1.02	1.04	1.04	1.07
X_4:	1.10	1.10	1.09	1.09	1.06	1.05	1.08
X_5:	1.04	1.06	1.07	1.06	1.05	1.07	1.05

(c) For each set of data, construct box-and-whisker diagrams on the same figure and give an interpretation of your diagrams.

7.5-11. The driver of a diesel-powered automobile decided to test the quality of three types of diesel fuel sold in the area. The test is to be based on miles per gallon (mpg). Make the usual assumptions, take $\alpha = 0.05$, and use the following data to test the null hypothesis that the three means are equal:

Brand A:	38.7	39.2	40.1	38.9	
Brand B:	41.9	42.3	41.3		
Brand C:	40.8	41.2	39.5	38.9	40.3

7.5-12. From the box-and-whisker diagrams in Figure 7.5-1, it looks like the means of X_1 and X_2 could be equal and also that the means of X_3, X_4, and X_5 could be equal but different from the first two.

(a) Using the data in Example 7.5-2, as well as a t test and an F test, test H_0: $\mu_1 = \mu_2$ against a two-sided alternative hypothesis. Let $\alpha = 0.05$. Do the F and t tests give the same result?

(b) Using the data in Example 7.5-2, test H_0: $\mu_3 = \mu_4 = \mu_5$. Let $\alpha = 0.05$.

7.5-13. For an aerosol product, there are three weights: the tare weight (container weight), the concentrate weight, and the propellant weight. Let X_1, X_2, X_3 denote the propellant weights on three different days. Assume that each of these independent random variables has a normal distribution with common variance and respective means μ_1, μ_2, and μ_3. We shall test the null hypothesis H_0: $\mu_1 = \mu_2 = \mu_3$, using nine observations of each of the random variables.

(a) Give a critical region for an $\alpha = 0.01$ significance level.

(b) Construct an ANOVA table and state your conclusion, using the following data:

X_1: 43.06 43.32 42.63 42.86 43.05
42.87 42.94 42.80 42.36

X_2: 42.33 42.81 42.13 42.41 42.39
42.10 42.42 41.42 42.52

X_3: 42.83 42.57 42.96 43.16 42.25
42.24 42.20 41.97 42.61

(c) For each set of data, construct box-and-whisker diagrams on the same figure and give an interpretation of your diagrams.

7.5-14. A particular process puts a coating on a piece of glass so that it is sensitive to touch. Randomly throughout the day, pieces of glass are selected from the production line and the resistance is measured at 12 different locations on the glass. On each of three different days, December 6, December 7, and December 22, the following data give the means of the 12 measurements on each of 11 pieces of glass:

December 6:	175.05	177.44	181.94	176.51	182.12	164.34
	163.20	168.12	171.26	171.92	167.87	
December 7:	175.93	176.62	171.39	173.90	178.34	172.90
	174.67	174.27	177.16	184.13	167.21	
December 22:	167.27	161.48	161.86	173.83	170.75	172.90
	173.27	170.82	170.93	173.89	177.68	

(a) Use these data to test whether the means on all three days are equal.

(b) Use box-and-whisker diagrams to confirm your answer.

7.5-15. Ledolter and Hogg (see references) report that an operator of a feedlot wants to compare the effectiveness of three different cattle feed supplements. He selects a random sample of 15 one-year old heifers from his lot of over 1000 and divides them into three groups at random. Each group gets a different feed supplement. Upon noting that one heifer in group A was lost due to an accident, the operator records the gains in weight over a 6-month period as follows:

Group A:	500	650	530	680	
Group B:	700	620	780	830	860
Group C:	500	520	400	580	410

(a) Test whether there are differences in the mean weight gains due to the three different feed supplements.

(b) Do box plots of the data confirm your answer in part (a)?

7.5-16. Ledolter and Hogg (see references) report the comparison of three workers with different experience who manufacture brake wheels for a magnetic brake. Worker A has four years of experience, worker B has seven years, and worker C has one year. The company is concerned about the product's quality, which is measured by the difference between the specified diameter and the actual diameter of the brake wheel. On a given day, the supervisor selects nine brake wheels at random from the output of each worker. The following data give the differences between specified and actual diameters in hundredths of an inch:

Worker A:	2.0	3.0	2.3	3.5	3.0	2.0	4.0	4.5	3.0
Worker B:	1.5	3.0	4.5	3.0	3.0	2.0	2.5	1.0	2.0
Worker C:	2.5	3.0	2.0	2.5	1.5	2.5	2.5	3.0	3.5

(a) Test whether there are statistically significant differences in the quality among the three different workers.

(b) Do box plots of the data confirm your answer in part (a)?

7.6 TWO-FACTOR ANALYSIS OF VARIANCE

The test of the equality of several means, considered in Section 7.5, is an example of a statistical inference method called the analysis of variance (ANOVA). This method derives its name from the fact that the quadratic form SS(TO) $= (n - 1)S^2$—the total sum of squares about the combined sample mean—is decomposed into its components and analyzed. In this section, other problems in the analysis of variance will be investigated; here we restrict our considerations to the two-factor case, but the reader can see how it can be extended to three-factor and other cases.

Consider a situation in which it is desirable to investigate the effects of two factors that influence an outcome of an experiment. For example, a teaching method (lecture, discussion, computer assisted, television, etc.) and the size of a class might influence a student's score on a standard test; or the type of car and the grade of gasoline used might change the number of miles per gallon. In this latter example, if the number of miles per gallon is not affected by the grade of gasoline, we would no doubt use the least expensive grade.

The first analysis-of-variance model that we discuss is referred to as a **two-way classification with one observation per cell**. Assume that there are two factors (attributes), one of which has a levels and the other b levels. There are thus $n = ab$ possible combinations, each of which determines a cell. Let us think of these cells as being arranged in a rows and b columns. Here we take one observation per cell, and we denote the observation in the ith row and jth column by X_{ij}. Assume further that X_{ij} is $N(\mu_{ij}, \sigma^2)$, $i = 1, 2, \ldots, a$, and $j = 1, 2, \ldots, b$; and the $n = ab$ random variables are independent. [The assumptions of normality and homogeneous (same) variances can be somewhat relaxed in applications, with little change in the significance levels of the resulting tests.] We shall assume that the means μ_{ij} are composed of a row effect, a column effect, and an overall effect in some additive way, namely, $\mu_{ij} = \mu + \alpha_i + \beta_j$, where $\sum_{i=1}^{a} \alpha_i = 0$ and $\sum_{j=1}^{b} \beta_j = 0$. The parameter α_i represents the ith row effect, and the parameter β_j represents the jth column effect.

REMARK There is no loss in generality in assuming that

$$\sum_{i=1}^{a} \alpha_i = \sum_{j=1}^{b} \beta_j = 0.$$

To see this, let $\mu_{ij} = \mu' + \alpha_i' + \beta_j'$. Write

$$\overline{\alpha}' = \left(\frac{1}{a}\right)\sum_{i=1}^{a} \alpha_i' \text{ and } \overline{\beta}' = \left(\frac{1}{b}\right)\sum_{j=1}^{b} \beta_j'.$$

We have

$$\mu_{ij} = (\mu' + \overline{\alpha}' + \overline{\beta}') + (\alpha_i' - \overline{\alpha}') + (\beta_j' - \overline{\beta}') = \mu + \alpha_i + \beta_j,$$

where $\sum_{i=1}^{a} \alpha_i = 0$ and $\sum_{j=1}^{b} \beta_j = 0$. The reader is asked to find μ, α_i, and β_j for one display of μ_{ij} in Exercise 7.6-2. ■

To test the hypothesis that there is no row effect, we would test $H_A\colon \alpha_1 = \alpha_2 = \cdots = \alpha_a = 0$, since $\sum_{i=1}^{a} \alpha_i = 0$. Similarly, to test that there is no column effect, we would test $H_B\colon \beta_1 = \beta_2 = \cdots = \beta_b = 0$, since $\sum_{j=1}^{b} \beta_j = 0$. To test these hypotheses, we shall again partition the total sum of squares into several components. Letting

$$\overline{X}_{i\cdot} = \frac{1}{b}\sum_{j=1}^{b} X_{ij},\ \overline{X}_{\cdot j} = \frac{1}{a}\sum_{i=1}^{a} X_{ij},\ \overline{X}_{\cdot\cdot} = \frac{1}{ab}\sum_{i=1}^{a}\sum_{j=1}^{b} X_{ij},$$

we have

$$\begin{aligned}
\text{SS(TO)} &= \sum_{i=1}^{a}\sum_{j=1}^{b}(X_{ij} - \overline{X}_{\cdot\cdot})^2 \\
&= \sum_{i=1}^{a}\sum_{j=1}^{b}[(\overline{X}_{i\cdot} - \overline{X}_{\cdot\cdot}) + (\overline{X}_{\cdot j} - \overline{X}_{\cdot\cdot}) + (X_{ij} - \overline{X}_{i\cdot} - \overline{X}_{\cdot j} + \overline{X}_{\cdot\cdot})]^2 \\
&= b\sum_{i=1}^{a}(\overline{X}_{i\cdot} - \overline{X}_{\cdot\cdot})^2 + a\sum_{j=1}^{b}(\overline{X}_{\cdot j} - \overline{X}_{\cdot\cdot})^2 \\
&\quad + \sum_{i=1}^{a}\sum_{j=1}^{b}(X_{ij} - \overline{X}_{i\cdot} - \overline{X}_{\cdot j} + \overline{X}_{\cdot\cdot})^2 \\
&= \text{SS(A)} + \text{SS(B)} + \text{SS(E)},
\end{aligned}$$

where SS(A) is the sum of squares among levels of factor A, or among rows; SS(B) is the sum of squares among levels of factor B, or among columns; and SS(E) is the error or residual sum of squares. In Exercise 7.6-4, the reader is asked to show that the three cross-product terms in the square of the trinomial sum to zero. The distribution of the error sum of squares does not depend on the mean μ_{ij}, provided that the additive model is correct. Hence, its distribution is the same whether H_A or H_B is true or not, and thus SS(E) acts as a "measuring stick," as did SS(E) in Section 7.5. This can be seen more clearly by writing

$$\begin{aligned}
\text{SS(E)} &= \sum_{i=1}^{a}\sum_{j=1}^{b}(X_{ij} - \overline{X}_{i\cdot} - \overline{X}_{\cdot j} + \overline{X}_{\cdot\cdot})^2 \\
&= \sum_{i=1}^{a}\sum_{j=1}^{b}[X_{ij} - (\overline{X}_{i\cdot} - \overline{X}_{\cdot\cdot}) - (\overline{X}_{\cdot j} - \overline{X}_{\cdot\cdot}) - \overline{X}_{\cdot\cdot}]^2
\end{aligned}$$

and noting the similarity of the summand in the right-hand member to

$$X_{ij} - \mu_{ij} = X_{ij} - \alpha_i - \beta_j - \mu.$$

We now show that $\text{SS(A)}/\sigma^2$, $\text{SS(B)}/\sigma^2$, and $\text{SS(E)}/\sigma^2$ are independent chi-square variables, provided that both H_A and H_B are true—that is, when all the means μ_{ij} have a common value μ. To do this, we first note that $\text{SS(TO)}/\sigma^2$ is $\chi^2(ab-1)$. In addition, from Section 7.5, we see that expressions such as $\text{SS(A)}/\sigma^2$ and $\text{SS(B)}/\sigma^2$ are chi-square variables, namely, $\chi^2(a-1)$ and $\chi^2(b-1)$, by replacing the n_i of Section 7.5 by a and b, respectively. Obviously, $\text{SS(E)} \ge 0$, and hence by Theorem 7.5-1, $\text{SS(A)}/\sigma^2$, $\text{SS(B)}/\sigma^2$, and $\text{SS(E)}/\sigma^2$ are independent chi-square variables with $a - 1, b - 1$, and $ab - 1 - (a - 1) - (b - 1) = (a - 1)(b - 1)$ degrees of freedom, respectively.

To test the hypothesis $H_A\colon \alpha_1 = \alpha_2 = \cdots = \alpha_a = 0$, we shall use the row sum of squares SS(A) and the residual sum of squares SS(E). When H_A is true, $\text{SS(A)}/\sigma^2$ and $\text{SS(E)}/\sigma^2$ are independent chi-square variables with $a - 1$ and $(a - 1)(b - 1)$ degrees of freedom, respectively. Thus, $\text{SS(A)}/(a - 1)$ and $\text{SS(E)}/[(a - 1)(b - 1)]$ are both unbiased estimators of σ^2 when H_A is true. However, $E[\text{SS(A)}/(a-1)] > \sigma^2$ when H_A is not true, and hence we would reject H_A when

$$F_A = \frac{\text{SS(A)}/[\sigma^2(a - 1)]}{\text{SS(E)}/[\sigma^2(a - 1)(b - 1)]} = \frac{\text{SS(A)}/(a - 1)}{\text{SS(E)}/[(a - 1)(b - 1)]}$$

is "too large." Since F_A has an F distribution with $a - 1$ and $(a - 1)(b - 1)$ degrees of freedom when H_A is true, H_A is rejected if the observed value of $F_A \geq F_\alpha[a - 1, (a - 1)(b - 1)]$.

Similarly, the test of the hypothesis H_B: $\beta_1 = \beta_2 = \cdots = \beta_b = 0$ against all alternatives can be based on

$$F_B = \frac{\text{SS(B)}/[\sigma^2(b - 1)]}{\text{SS(E)}/[\sigma^2(a - 1)(b - 1)]} = \frac{\text{SS(B)}/(b - 1)}{\text{SS(E)}/[(a - 1)(b - 1)]},$$

which has an F distribution with $b - 1$ and $(a - 1)(b - 1)$ degrees of freedom, provided that H_B is true.

Table 7.6-1 is the ANOVA table that summarizes the information needed for these tests of hypotheses. The formulas for F_A and F_B show that each of them is a ratio of two mean squares.

TABLE 7.6-1: Two-Way ANOVA Table, One Observation per Cell

Source	Sum of Squares (SS)	Degrees of Freedom	Mean Square (MS)	F
Factor A (row)	SS(A)	$a - 1$	$\text{MS(A)} = \dfrac{\text{SS(A)}}{a - 1}$	$\dfrac{\text{MS(A)}}{\text{MS(E)}}$
Factor B (column)	SS(B)	$b - 1$	$\text{MS(B)} = \dfrac{\text{SS(B)}}{b - 1}$	$\dfrac{\text{MS(B)}}{\text{MS(E)}}$
Error	SS(E)	$(a - 1)(b - 1)$	$\text{MS(E)} = \dfrac{\text{SS(E)}}{(a - 1)(b - 1)}$	
Total	SS(TO)	$ab - 1$		

EXAMPLE 7.6-1 Each of three cars is driven with each of four different brands of gasoline. The number of miles per gallon driven for each of the $ab = (3)(4) = 12$ different combinations is recorded in Table 7.6-2.

TABLE 7.6-2: Gas Mileage Data

	Gasoline				
Car	1	2	3	4	$\overline{X}_{i\cdot}$
1	26	28	31	31	29
2	24	25	28	27	26
3	25	25	28	26	26
$\overline{X}_{\cdot j}$	25	26	29	28	27

We would like to test whether we can expect the same mileage for each of these four brands of gasoline. In our notation, we test the hypothesis

$$H_B: \beta_1 = \beta_2 = \beta_3 = \beta_4 = 0$$

against all alternatives. At a 1% significance level, we shall reject H_B if the computed F, namely,

$$\frac{SS(B)/(4-1)}{SS(E)/[(3-1)(4-1)]} \geq 9.78 = F_{0.01}(3,6).$$

We have

$$SS(B) = 3[(25-27)^2 + (26-27)^2 + (29-27)^2 + (28-27)^2] = 30;$$

$$SS(E) = (26-29-25+27)^2 + (24-26-25+27)^2 + \cdots + (26-26-28+27)^2 = 4.$$

Hence, the computed F is

$$\frac{30/3}{4/6} = 15 > 9.78,$$

and the hypothesis H_B is rejected. That is, the gasolines seem to give different performances (at least with these three cars).

The information for this example is summarized in Table 7.6-3. ■

TABLE 7.6-3: ANOVA Table for Gas Mileage Data

Source	Sum of Squares (SS)	Degrees of Freedom	Mean Square (MS)	F	p-value
Row (A)	24	2	12	18	0.003
Column (B)	30	3	10	15	0.003
Error	4	6	2/3		
Total	58	11			

In a two-way classification problem, particular combinations of the two factors might interact differently from what is expected from the additive model. For instance, in Example 7.6-1 gasoline 3 seemed to be the best gasoline and car 1 the best car; however, it sometimes happens that the two best do not "mix" well and the joint performance is poor. That is, there might be a strange interaction between this combination of car and gasoline, and accordingly, the joint performance is not as good as expected. Sometimes it happens that we get good results from a combination of some of the poorer levels of each factor. This phenomenon is called interaction, and it frequently occurs in practice (e.g., in chemistry). In order to test for possible interaction, we shall consider a two-way classification problem in which $c > 1$ independent observations per cell are taken.

Assume that X_{ijk}, $i = 1,2,\ldots,a$; $j = 1,2,\ldots,b$; and $k = 1,2,\ldots,c$, are $n = abc$ random variables that are mutually independent and have normal distributions with a common, but unknown, variance σ^2. The mean of each X_{ijk}, $k = 1,2,\ldots,c$, is $\mu_{ij} = \mu + \alpha_i + \beta_j + \gamma_{ij}$, where $\sum_{i=1}^{a} \alpha_i = 0$, $\sum_{j=1}^{b} \beta_j = 0$, $\sum_{i=1}^{a} \gamma_{ij} = 0$, and $\sum_{j=1}^{b} \gamma_{ij} = 0$. The parameter γ_{ij} is called the **interaction** associated with cell (i,j). That is, the interaction between the ith level of one classification and the jth level of the other classification is γ_{ij}. In Exercise 7.6-6, the reader is asked to determine μ, α_i, β_j, and γ_{ij} for some given μ_{ij}.

To test the hypotheses that (a) the row effects are equal to zero, (b) the column effects are equal to zero, and (c) there is no interaction, we shall again partition the total sum of squares into several components. Letting

$$\begin{aligned}
\overline{X}_{ij\cdot} &= \frac{1}{c}\sum_{k=1}^{c} X_{ijk},\\
\overline{X}_{i\cdot\cdot} &= \frac{1}{bc}\sum_{j=1}^{b}\sum_{k=1}^{c} X_{ijk},\\
\overline{X}_{\cdot j\cdot} &= \frac{1}{ac}\sum_{i=1}^{a}\sum_{k=1}^{c} X_{ijk},\\
\overline{X}_{\cdots} &= \frac{1}{abc}\sum_{i=1}^{a}\sum_{j=1}^{b}\sum_{k=1}^{c} X_{ijk},
\end{aligned}$$

we have

$$\begin{aligned}
SS(TO) &= \sum_{i=1}^{a}\sum_{j=1}^{b}\sum_{k=1}^{c}(X_{ijk} - \overline{X}_{\cdots})^2\\
&= bc\sum_{i=1}^{a}(\overline{X}_{i\cdot\cdot} - \overline{X}_{\cdots})^2 + ac\sum_{j=1}^{b}(\overline{X}_{\cdot j\cdot} - \overline{X}_{\cdots})^2\\
&\quad + c\sum_{i=1}^{a}\sum_{j=1}^{b}(\overline{X}_{ij\cdot} - \overline{X}_{i\cdot\cdot} - \overline{X}_{\cdot j\cdot} + \overline{X}_{\cdots})^2 + \sum_{i=1}^{a}\sum_{j=1}^{b}\sum_{k=1}^{c}(X_{ijk} - \overline{X}_{ij\cdot})^2\\
&= SS(A) + SS(B) + SS(AB) + SS(E),
\end{aligned}$$

where SS(A) is the row sum of squares, or the sum of squares among levels of factor A; SS(B) is the column sum of squares, or the sum of squares among levels of factor B; SS(AB) is the interaction sum of squares; and SS(E) is the error sum of squares. Again, we can show that the cross-product terms sum to zero.

To consider the joint distribution of SS(A), SS(B), SS(AB), and SS(E), let us assume that all the means equal the same value μ. Of course, we know that $SS(TO)/\sigma^2$ is $\chi^2(abc - 1)$. Also, by letting the n_i of Section 7.5 equal bc and ac, respectively, we know that $SS(A)/\sigma^2$ and $SS(B)/\sigma^2$ are $\chi^2(a - 1)$ and $\chi^2(b - 1)$. Moreover,

$$\frac{\displaystyle\sum_{k=1}^{c}(X_{ijk} - \overline{X}_{ij\cdot})^2}{\sigma^2}$$

is $\chi^2(c - 1)$; hence, $SS(E)/\sigma^2$ is the sum of ab independent chi-square variables such as this and thus is $\chi^2[ab(c - 1)]$. Of course, $SS(AB) \ge 0$; so, according to Theorem 7.5-1, $SS(A)/\sigma^2$, $SS(B)/\sigma^2$, $SS(AB)/\sigma^2$, and $SS(E)/\sigma^2$ are mutually independent chi-square variables with $a - 1, b - 1, (a - 1)(b - 1)$, and $ab(c - 1)$ degrees of freedom, respectively.

To test the hypotheses concerning row, column, and interaction effects, we form F statistics in which the numerators are affected by deviations from the respective hypotheses whereas the denominator is a function of SS(E), whose distribution depends only on the value of σ^2 and not on the values of the cell means. Hence, SS(E) acts as our measuring stick here.

The statistic for testing the hypothesis

$$H_{AB}\colon \gamma_{ij} = 0,\ i = 1,2,\ldots,a,\ j = 1,2,\ldots,b,$$

against all alternatives is

$$F_{AB} = \frac{c\sum_{i=1}^{a}\sum_{j=1}^{b}(\overline{X}_{ij\cdot} - \overline{X}_{i\cdot\cdot} - \overline{X}_{\cdot j\cdot} + \overline{X}_{\cdots})^2/[\sigma^2(a-1)(b-1)]}{\sum_{i=1}^{a}\sum_{j=1}^{b}\sum_{k=1}^{c}(X_{ijk} - \overline{X}_{ij\cdot})^2/[\sigma^2 ab(c-1)]} = \frac{\text{SS(AB)}/[(a-1)(b-1)]}{\text{SS(E)}/[ab(c-1)]},$$

which has an F distribution with $(a - 1)(b - 1)$ and $ab(c - 1)$ degrees of freedom when H_{AB} is true. If the computed $F_{AB} \ge F_\alpha[(a-1)(b-1), ab(c-1)]$, we reject H_{AB} and say that there is a difference among the means, since there seems to be interaction. Most statisticians do *not* proceed to test row and column effects if H_{AB} is rejected.

The statistic for testing the hypothesis

$$H_A\colon \alpha_1 = \alpha_2 = \cdots = \alpha_a = 0$$

against all alternatives is

$$F_A = \frac{bc\sum_{i=1}^{a}(\overline{X}_{i\cdot\cdot} - \overline{X}_{\cdots})^2/[\sigma^2(a-1)]}{\sum_{i=1}^{a}\sum_{j=1}^{b}\sum_{k=1}^{c}(X_{ijk} - \overline{X}_{ij\cdot})^2/[\sigma^2 ab(c-1)]} = \frac{\text{SS(A)}/(a-1)}{\text{SS(E)}/[ab(c-1)]},$$

which has an F distribution with $a - 1$ and $ab(c - 1)$ degrees of freedom when H_A is true. The statistic for testing the hypothesis

$$H_B\colon \beta_1 = \beta_2 = \cdots = \beta_b = 0$$

against all alternatives is

$$F_B = \frac{ac\sum_{j=1}^{b}(\overline{X}_{\cdot j\cdot} - \overline{X}_{\cdots})^2/[\sigma^2(b-1)]}{\sum_{i=1}^{a}\sum_{j=1}^{b}\sum_{k=1}^{c}(X_{ijk} - \overline{X}_{ij\cdot})^2/[\sigma^2 ab(c-1)]} = \frac{\text{SS(B)}/(b-1)}{\text{SS(E)}/[ab(c-1)]},$$

which has an F distribution with $b - 1$ and $ab(c - 1)$ degrees of freedom when H_B is true. Each of these hypotheses is rejected if the observed value of F is greater than a given constant that is selected to yield the desired significance level.

On the next page, Table 7.6-4 gives the ANOVA table that summarizes the information needed for these tests of hypotheses.

EXAMPLE 7.6-2 Consider the following experiment: One hundred eight people were randomly divided into six groups with 18 people in each group. Each person was given sets of three

TABLE 7.6-4: Two-Way ANOVA Table, c Observations per Cell

Source	Sum of Squares (SS)	Degrees of Freedom	Mean Square (MS)	F
Factor A (row)	SS(A)	$a-1$	$\text{MS(A)} = \dfrac{\text{SS(A)}}{a-1}$	$\dfrac{\text{MS(A)}}{\text{MS(E)}}$
Factor B (column)	SS(B)	$b-1$	$\text{MS(B)} = \dfrac{\text{SS(B)}}{b-1}$	$\dfrac{\text{MS(B)}}{\text{MS(E)}}$
Factor AB (interaction)	SS(AB)	$(a-1)(b-1)$	$\text{MS(AB)} = \dfrac{\text{SS(AB)}}{(a-1)(b-1)}$	$\dfrac{\text{MS(AB)}}{\text{MS(E)}}$
Error	SS(E)	$ab(c-1)$	$\text{MS(E)} = \dfrac{\text{SS(E)}}{ab(c-1)}$	
Total	SS(TO)	$abc-1$		

numbers to add. The three numbers were either in a "down array" or an "across array," representing the two levels of factor A. The levels of factor B are determined by the number of digits in the numbers to be added: one-digit, two-digit, or three-digit numbers. Table 7.6-5 illustrates this experiment with a sample problem for each cell; note, however, that an individual person works problems only of one of these types. Each person was placed in one of the six groups and was told to work as many problems as possible in 90 seconds. The measurement that was recorded was the average number of problems worked correctly in two trials.

TABLE 7.6-5: Illustration of Arrays for Numbers of Digits

Type of Array	Number of Digits 1	2	3
Down	5	25	259
	3	69	567
	8	37	130
Across	5 + 3 + 8 =	25 + 69 + 37 =	259 + 567 + 130 =

Whenever this many subjects are used, a computer becomes an invaluable tool. A computer program provided the summary shown in Table 7.6-6 of the sample means of the rows, the columns, and the six cells. Each cell mean is the average for 18 people.

Simply considering these means, we can see clearly that there is a column effect: It is not surprising that it is easier to add one-digit than three-digit numbers.

The most interesting feature of these results is that they show the possibility of interaction. The largest cell mean occurs for those adding one-digit numbers in an across array. Note, however, that for two- and three-digit numbers, the down arrays have larger means than the across arrays.

The computer provided the ANOVA table given in Table 7.6-7. The number of degrees of freedom for SS(E) is not in our F table in the appendix. However, the

TABLE 7.6-6: Cell, Row, and Column Means for Adding Numbers

	Number of Digits			
Type of Array	1	2	3	Row Means
Down	23.806	10.694	6.278	13.593
Across	26.056	6.750	3.944	12.250
Column means	24.931	8.722	5.111	

TABLE 7.6-7: ANOVA Table for Adding Numbers

Source	Sum of Squares	Degrees of Freedom	Mean Square	F	p-value
Factor A (array)	48.678	1	48.669	2.885	0.0925
Factor B (number of digits)	8022.73	2	4011.363	237.778	<0.0001
Interaction	185.92	2	92.961	5.510	0.0053
Error	1720.76	102	16.870		
Total	9978.08	107			

right-most column, obtained from the computer printout, provides the p-value of each test, namely, the probability of obtaining an F as large as or larger than the calculated F ratio. Note, for example, that, to test for interaction, $F = 5.51$ and the p-value is 0.006. Thus, the hypothesis of no interaction would be rejected at the $\alpha = 0.05$ or $\alpha = 0.01$ significance level, but it would not be rejected with $\alpha = 0.001$. ■

EXERCISES

(In some of the exercises that follow, we must make assumptions, such as normal distributions with equal variances.)

7.6-1. For the data given in Example 7.6-1, test the hypothesis H_A: $\alpha_1 = \alpha_2 = \alpha_3 = 0$ against all alternatives at the 5% significance level.

7.6-2. With $a = 3$ and $b = 4$, find μ, α_i, and β_j if μ_{ij}, $i = 1, 2, 3$ and $j = 1, 2, 3, 4$, are given by

$$\begin{array}{cccc} 6 & 3 & 7 & 8 \\ 10 & 7 & 11 & 12 \\ 8 & 5 & 9 & 10 \end{array}$$

Note that in an "additive" model such as this one, one row (column) can be determined by adding a constant value to each of the elements of another row (column).

7.6-3. We wish to compare compressive strengths of concrete corresponding to $a = 3$ different drying methods (treatments). Concrete is mixed in batches that are just large enough to produce three cylinders. Although care is taken to achieve uniformity, we expect some variability among the $b = 5$ batches used to obtain the following compressive strengths (there is little reason to suspect interaction; hence, only one observation is taken in each cell):

	Batch				
Treatment	B_1	B_2	B_3	B_4	B_5
A_1	52	47	44	51	42
A_2	60	55	49	52	43
A_3	56	48	45	44	38

(a) Use the 5% significance level and test $H_A: \alpha_1 = \alpha_2 = \alpha_3 = 0$ against all alternatives.

(b) Use the 5% significance level and test $H_B: \beta_1 = \beta_2 = \beta_3 = \beta_4 = \beta_5 = 0$ against all alternatives. (See Ledolter and Hogg in references.)

7.6-4. Show that the cross-product terms formed from $(\overline{X}_{i\cdot} - \overline{X}_{\cdot\cdot})$, $(\overline{X}_{\cdot j} - \overline{X}_{\cdot\cdot})$, and $(X_{ij} - \overline{X}_{i\cdot} - \overline{X}_{\cdot j} + \overline{X}_{\cdot\cdot})$ sum to zero, $i = 1,2,\ldots,a$ and $j = 1,2,\ldots,b$.

HINT: For example, write

$$\sum_{i=1}^{a}\sum_{j=1}^{b}(\overline{X}_{\cdot j} - \overline{X}_{\cdot\cdot})(X_{ij} - \overline{X}_{i\cdot} - \overline{X}_{\cdot j} + \overline{X}_{\cdot\cdot})$$
$$= \sum_{j=1}^{b}(\overline{X}_{\cdot j} - \overline{X}_{\cdot\cdot})\sum_{i=1}^{a}[(X_{ij} - \overline{X}_{\cdot j}) - (\overline{X}_{i\cdot} - \overline{X}_{\cdot\cdot})]$$

and sum each term in the inner summation, as grouped here, to get zero.

7.6-5. A psychology student was interested in testing how food consumption by rats would be affected by a particular drug. She used two levels of one attribute, namely, drug and placebo, and four levels of a second attribute, namely, male (M), castrated (C), female (F), and ovariectomized (O). For each cell, she observed five rats. The amount of food consumed in grams per 24 hours is listed in the following table:

	M	C	F	O
Drug	22.56	16.54	18.58	18.20
	25.02	24.64	15.44	14.56
	23.66	24.62	16.12	15.54
	17.22	19.06	16.88	16.82
	22.58	20.12	17.58	14.56
Placebo	25.64	22.50	17.82	19.74
	28.84	24.48	15.76	17.48
	26.00	25.52	12.96	16.46
	26.02	24.76	15.00	16.44
	23.24	20.62	19.54	15.70

(a) Use the 5% significance level and test $H_{AB}: \gamma_{ij} = 0, i = 1,2, j = 1,2,3,4$.

(b) Use the 5% significance level and test $H_A: \alpha_1 = \alpha_2 = 0$.

(c) Use the 5% significance level and test $H_B: \beta_1 = \beta_2 = \beta_3 = \beta_4 = 0$.

(d) How could you modify this model so that there are three attributes of classification, each with two levels?

7.6-6. With $a = 3$ and $b = 4$, find μ, α_i, β_j, and γ_{ij} if μ_{ij}, $i = 1,2,3$ and $j = 1,2,3,4$ are given by

6	7	7	12
10	3	11	8
8	5	9	10

Note the difference between the layout here and that in Exercise 7.6-2. Does the interaction help explain the difference?

7.6-7. In order to test whether four brands of gasoline give equal performance in terms of mileage, each of three cars was driven with each of the four brands of gasoline. Then each of the (3)(4) = 12 possible combinations was repeated four times. The number of miles per gallon for each of the four repetitions in each cell is recorded in the following table:

	Brand of Gasoline							
Car	1		2		3		4	
1	31.0	24.9	26.3	30.0	25.8	29.4	27.8	27.3
	26.2	28.8	25.2	31.6	24.5	24.8	28.2	30.4
2	30.6	29.5	25.5	26.8	26.6	23.7	28.1	27.1
	30.8	28.9	27.4	29.4	28.2	26.1	31.5	29.1
3	24.2	23.1	27.4	28.1	25.2	26.7	26.3	26.4
	26.8	27.4	26.4	26.9	27.7	28.1	27.9	28.8

Test the hypotheses H_{AB}: no interaction, H_A: no row effect, and H_B: no column effect, each at the 5% significance level.

7.6-8. The data in the following table could represent the outcomes of some experiment, but in actuality they were generated on a computer:

	B_1	B_2
A_1	14.552	13.980
	17.024	5.777
	10.132	7.638
	16.979	12.089
A_2	11.378	20.825
	12.578	17.333
	17.709	20.329
	11.037	25.277
A_3	12.345	22.223
	11.044	21.844
	9.458	16.176
	16.156	17.946

Recall that $\mu_{ij} = \mu + \alpha_i + \beta_j + \gamma_{ij}$ is the mean of cell (i,j), and in the simulation, we took $\mu = 15$,

$\alpha_1 = -3, \alpha_2 = 2, \alpha_3 = 1, \beta_1 = -1.5, \beta_2 = 1.5, \gamma_{11} = 4, \gamma_{12} = -4, \gamma_{21} = -2, \gamma_{22} = 2, \gamma_{31} = -2, \gamma_{32} = 2$, and $\sigma^2 = 9$. Use the data and the two-factor analysis-of-variance model with four repetitions per cell to test the hypotheses H_{AB}: no interaction, H_A: no row effect, and H_B: no column effect, each at the $\alpha = 0.05$ significance level.

7.6-9. Ledolter and Hogg (see references) report on an engineer in a textile mill who studies the effects of temperature and time on the brightness of a synthetic fabric in a process involving dye. (Brightness is measured on a 50-point scale.) Three observations were taken at each combination of temperature and time:

	Temperature		
Time (cycles)	350°F	375°F	400°F
40	38, 32, 30	37, 35, 40	36, 39, 43
50	40, 45, 36	39, 42, 46	39, 48, 47

Construct the ANOVA table, and conduct tests for the interaction first and then, if appropriate, the main effects. Use $\alpha = 0.05$ for each test.

7.6-10. There is another way of looking at Exercise 7.5-8, namely, as a two-factor analysis-of-variance problem with the levels of gender being female and male, the levels of age being less than 50 and at least 50, and the measurement for each subject being their cholesterol level. The data would then be set up as follows:

	Age	
Gender	<50	≥50
Female	221	262
	213	193
	202	224
	183	201
	185	161
	197	178
	162	265
Male	271	192
	192	253
	189	248
	209	278
	227	232
	236	267
	142	289

(a) Test H_{AB}: $\gamma_{ij} = 0$, $i = 1,2$; $j = 1,2$ (no interaction).

(b) Test H_A: $\alpha_1 = \alpha_2 = 0$ (no row effect).

(c) Test H_B: $\beta_1 = \beta_2 = 0$ (no column effect).

Use a 5% significance level for each test.

7.6-11. Ledolter and Hogg (see references) report that volunteers who had a smoking history classified as heavy, moderate, and nonsmoker were accepted until nine men were in each category. Three men in each category were randomly assigned to each of the following three stress tests: bicycle ergometer, treadmill, and step tests. The time until maximum oxygen uptake was recorded in minutes as follows:

	Test		
Smoking History	Bicycle	Treadmill	Step Test
Nonsmoker	12.8, 13.5, 11.2	16.2, 18.1, 17.8	22.6, 19.3, 18.9
Moderate	10.9, 11.1, 9.8	15.5, 13.8, 16.2	20.1, 21.0, 15.9
Heavy	8.7, 9.2, 7.5	14.7, 13.2, 8.1	16.2, 16.1, 17.8

(a) Analyze the results of this experiment. Obtain the ANOVA table and test for main effects and interactions.

(b) Use box plots to compare the data graphically.

7.7 TESTS CONCERNING REGRESSION AND CORRELATION

In Section 6.7, we considered the estimation of the parameters of a very simple regression curve, namely, a straight line. We can use confidence intervals for the parameters to test hypotheses about them. For example, with the same model as that in Section 6.7, we could test the hypothesis H_0: $\beta = \beta_0$ by using a t random variable that was used for a confidence interval with β replaced by β_0, namely,

$$T_1 = \frac{\widehat{\beta} - \beta_0}{\sqrt{\dfrac{n\widehat{\sigma^2}}{(n-2)\sum_{i=1}^{n}(x_i - \overline{x})^2}}}.$$

The null hypothesis, along with three possible alternative hypotheses, is given in Table 7.7-1; these tests are equivalent to stating that we reject H_0 if β_0 is not in certain confidence intervals. For example, the first test is equivalent to rejecting H_0 if β_0 is not in the one-sided confidence interval with lower bound

$$\widehat{\beta} - t_\alpha(n-2)\sqrt{\frac{n\widehat{\sigma^2}}{(n-2)\sum_{i=1}^{n}(x_i - \overline{x})^2}}.$$

Often we let $\beta_0 = 0$ and test the hypothesis H_0: $\beta = 0$. That is, we test the null hypothesis that the slope is equal to zero.

TABLE 7.7-1: Tests About the Slope of the Regression Line

H_0	H_1	Critical Region
$\beta = \beta_0$	$\beta > \beta_0$	$t_1 \ge t_\alpha(n-2)$
$\beta = \beta_0$	$\beta < \beta_0$	$t_1 \le -t_\alpha(n-2)$
$\beta = \beta_0$	$\beta \ne \beta_0$	$\lvert t_1\rvert \ge t_{\alpha/2}(n-2)$

EXAMPLE 7.7-1 Let x equal a student's preliminary test score in a psychology course and y equal the same student's score on the final examination. With $n = 10$ students, we shall test H_0: $\beta = 0$ against H_1: $\beta \ne 0$. At the 0.01 significance level, the critical region is $\lvert t_1\rvert \ge t_{0.005}(8) = 3.355$. Using the data in Example 6.7-1, we find that the observed value of T_1 is

$$t_1 = \frac{0.742 - 0}{\sqrt{10(21.7709)/8(756.1)}} = \frac{0.742}{0.1897} = 3.911.$$

Thus, we reject H_0. ■

We consider tests about the correlation coefficient ρ of a bivariate normal distribution. Let X and Y have a bivariate normal distribution. We know that if the correlation coefficient ρ is zero, then X and Y are independent random variables. Furthermore, the value of ρ gives a measure of the linear relationship between X and Y. We now give methods for using the sample correlation coefficient to test the hypothesis H_0: $\rho = 0$ and also to form a confidence interval for ρ.

Let $(X_1, Y_1), (X_2, Y_2), \ldots, (X_n, Y_n)$ denote a random sample from a bivariate normal distribution with parameters μ_X, μ_Y, σ_X^2, σ_Y^2, and ρ. That is, the n pairs of (X, Y) are independent, and each pair has the same bivariate normal distribution.

The **sample correlation coefficient** is

$$R = \frac{\dfrac{1}{n-1}\sum_{i=1}^{n}(X_i - \overline{X})(Y_i - \overline{Y})}{\sqrt{\dfrac{1}{n-1}\sum_{i=1}^{n}(X_i - \overline{X})^2}\sqrt{\dfrac{1}{n-1}\sum_{i=1}^{n}(Y_i - \overline{Y})^2}} = \frac{S_{XY}}{S_X S_Y}.$$

We note that

$$R\frac{S_Y}{S_X} = \frac{S_{XY}}{S_X^2} = \frac{\dfrac{1}{n-1}\sum_{i=1}^{n}(X_i - \overline{X})(Y_i - \overline{Y})}{\dfrac{1}{n-1}\sum_{i=1}^{n}(X_i - \overline{X})^2}$$

is exactly the solution that we obtained for $\widehat{\beta}$ in Section 6.7 when the X values were fixed at $X_1 = x_1, X_2 = x_2, \ldots, X_n = x_n$. Let us consider these values fixed temporarily so that we are considering conditional distributions, given $X_1 = x_1, \ldots, X_n = x_n$. Moreover, if H_0: $\rho = 0$ is true, then the distributions of $Y_1, Y_2, \ldots, Y_n$ are independent of $x_1, x_2, \ldots, x_n$ and thus $\beta = \rho\sigma_Y/\sigma_X = 0$. Under these conditions. the conditional distribution of

$$\widehat{\beta} = \frac{\sum_{i=1}^{n}(x_i - \overline{x})(Y_i - \overline{Y})}{\sum_{i=1}^{n}(x_i - \overline{x})^2}$$

is $N[0, \sigma_Y^2/(n-1)s_x^2]$ when $s_x^2 > 0$. Moreover, recall from Section 6.7 that the conditional distribution of

$$\frac{\sum_{i=1}^{n}[Y_i - \overline{Y} - (S_{xY}/s_x^2)(x_i - \overline{x})]^2}{\sigma_Y^2} = \frac{(n-1)S_Y^2(1-R^2)}{\sigma_Y^2},$$

given that $X_1 = x_1, \ldots, X_n = x_n$, is $\chi^2(n-2)$ and is independent of $\widehat{\beta}$. (See Exercise 7.7-8.) Thus, when $\rho = 0$, the conditional distribution of

$$T = \frac{(RS_Y/s_X)/(\sigma_Y/\sqrt{n-1}\,s_X)}{\sqrt{[(n-1)S_Y^2(1-R^2)/\sigma_Y^2][1/(n-2)]}} = \frac{R\sqrt{n-2}}{\sqrt{1-R^2}}$$

is t with $n-2$ degrees of freedom. However, since the conditional distribution of T given that $X_1 = x_1, \ldots, X_n = x_n$, does not depend on $x_1, x_2, \ldots, x_n$, the unconditional distribution of T must be t with $n-2$ degrees of freedom, and T and $(X_1, X_2, \ldots, X_n)$ are independent when $\rho = 0$.

REMARK It is interesting to note that in the discussion about the distribution of T, nothing was said about the distribution of $X_1, X_2, \ldots, X_n$. This means that if X and Y are independent and Y has a normal distribution, then T has a t distribution whatever the distribution of X. Obviously, the roles of X and Y can be reversed in all of this development. In particular, if X and Y are independent, then T and $Y_1, Y_2, \ldots, Y_n$ are also independent. ■

Now T can be used to test $H_0: \rho = 0$. If the alternative hypothesis is $H_1: \rho > 0$, we would use the critical region defined by the observed $T \geq t_\alpha(n - 2)$, since large T implies large R. Obvious modifications would be made for the alternative hypotheses $H_1: \rho < 0$ and $H_1: \rho \neq 0$, the latter leading to a two-sided test.

Using the p.d.f. $h(t)$ of T, we can find the distribution function and p.d.f. of R when $-1 < r < 1$, provided that $\rho = 0$:

$$G(r) = P(R \leq r) = P\left(T \leq \frac{r\sqrt{n - 2}}{\sqrt{1 - r^2}}\right)$$

$$= \int_{-\infty}^{r\sqrt{n-2}/\sqrt{1-r^2}} h(t)\,dt$$

$$= \int_{-\infty}^{r\sqrt{n-2}/\sqrt{1-r^2}} \frac{\Gamma[(n - 1)/2]}{\Gamma(1/2)\,\Gamma[(n - 2)/2]} \frac{1}{\sqrt{n - 2}}\left(1 + \frac{t^2}{n - 2}\right)^{-(n-1)/2} dt.$$

The derivative of $G(r)$, with respect to r, is (see Appendix D.4)

$$g(r) = h\left(\frac{r\sqrt{n - 2}}{\sqrt{1 - r^2}}\right)\frac{d(r\sqrt{n - 2}/\sqrt{1 - r^2})}{dr},$$

which equals

$$g(r) = \frac{\Gamma[(n - 1)/2]}{\Gamma(1/2)\,\Gamma[(n - 2)/2]}(1 - r^2)^{(n-4)/2}, \qquad -1 < r < 1.$$

Thus, to test the hypothesis $H_0: \rho = 0$ against the alternative hypothesis $H_1: \rho \neq 0$ at a significance level α, select either a constant $r_{\alpha/2}(n - 2)$ or a constant $t_{\alpha/2}(n - 2)$ so that

$$\alpha = P(\,|R|\, \geq r_{\alpha/2}(n - 2); H_0) = P(\,|T|\, \geq t_{\alpha/2}(n - 2); H_0),$$

depending on the availability of R or T tables.

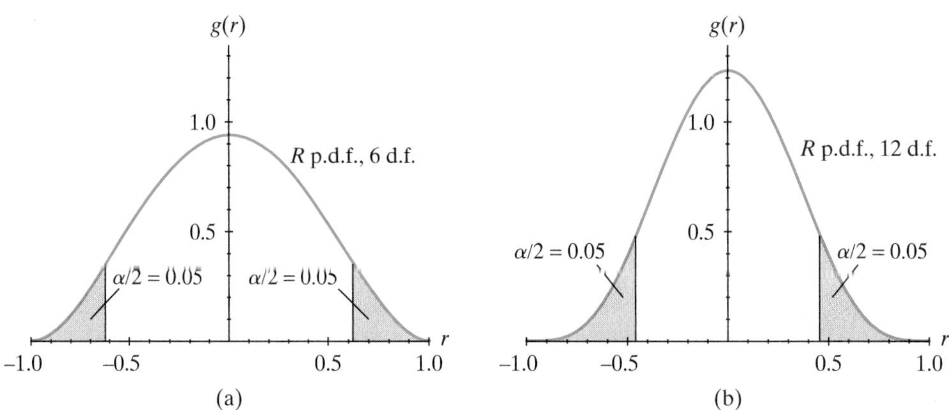

FIGURE 7.7-1: R p.d.f.'s when $n = 8$ and $n = 14$

It is interesting to graph the p.d.f. of R. Note in particular that if $n = 4$, $g(r) = 1/2$, $-1 < r < 1$, and if $n = 6$, $g(r) = (3/4)(1 - r^2)$, $-1 < r < 1$. The graphs of the p.d.f. of R when $n = 8$ and when $n = 14$ are given in Figure 7.7-1. Recall that this is the p.d.f. of R when $\rho = 0$. As n increases, R is more likely to equal values close to 0.

Table XI in the appendix lists selected values of the distribution function of R when $\rho = 0$. For example, if $n = 8$, then the number of degrees of freedom is 6 and $P(R \le 0.7887) = 0.99$. Also, if $\alpha = 0.10$, then $r_{\alpha/2}(6) = r_{0.05}(6) = 0.6215$. [See Figure 7.7-1(a).]

It is also possible to obtain an approximate test of size α by using the fact that

$$W = \frac{1}{2}\ln\frac{1 + R}{1 - R}$$

has an approximate normal distribution with mean $(1/2)\ln[(1 + \rho)/(1 - \rho)]$ and variance $1/(n - 3)$. We accept this statement without proof. (See Exercise 7.7-10.) Thus, a test of H_0: $\rho = \rho_0$ can be based on the statistic

$$Z = \frac{\dfrac{1}{2}\ln\dfrac{1 + R}{1 - R} - \dfrac{1}{2}\ln\dfrac{1 + \rho_0}{1 - \rho_0}}{\sqrt{\dfrac{1}{n - 3}}},$$

which has a distribution that is approximately $N(0, 1)$.

EXAMPLE 7.7-2 We would like to test the hypothesis H_0: $\rho = 0$ against H_1: $\rho \ne 0$ at an $\alpha = 0.05$ significance level. A random sample of size 18 from a bivariate normal distribution yielded a sample correlation coefficient of $r = 0.35$. From Table XI in the appendix, since $0.35 < 0.4683$, H_0 is accepted (not rejected) at an $\alpha = 0.05$ significance level. Using the t distribution, we would reject H_0 if $|t| \ge 2.120 = t_{0.025}(16)$. Since

$$t = \frac{0.35\sqrt{16}}{\sqrt{1 - (0.35)^2}} = 1.495,$$

H_0 is not rejected. If we had used the normal approximation for Z, H_0 would be rejected if $|z| \ge 1.96$. Because

$$z = \frac{(1/2)\ln[(1 + 0.35)/(1 - 0.35)] - 0}{\sqrt{1/(18 - 3)}} = 1.415,$$

H_0 is not rejected. ■

To develop an approximate $100(1 - \alpha)\%$ confidence interval for ρ, we use the normal approximation for the distribution of Z. Thus, we select a constant $c = z_{\alpha/2}$ from Table V in the appendix so that

$$P\left(-c \le \frac{(1/2)\ln[(1 + R)/(1 - R)] - (1/2)\ln[(1 + \rho)/(1 - \rho)]}{\sqrt{1/(n - 3)}} \le c\right) \approx 1 - \alpha.$$

After several algebraic manipulations, this formula becomes

$$P\left(\frac{1 + R - (1 - R)\exp(2c/\sqrt{n - 3})}{1 + R + (1 - R)\exp(2c/\sqrt{n - 3})} \le \rho \le \frac{1 + R - (1 - R)\exp(-2c/\sqrt{n - 3})}{1 + R + (1 - R)\exp(-2c/\sqrt{n - 3})}\right) \approx 1 - \alpha.$$

EXAMPLE 7.7-3 Suppose that a random sample of size 12 from a bivariate normal distribution yielded a correlation coefficient of $r = 0.6$. An approximate 95% confidence interval for ρ would be

$$\left[\frac{1 + 0.6 - (1 - 0.6)\exp\left(\dfrac{2(1.96)}{3}\right)}{1 + 0.6 + (1 - 0.6)\exp\left(\dfrac{2(1.96)}{3}\right)}, \frac{1 + 0.6 - (1 - 0.6)\exp\left(\dfrac{-2(1.96)}{3}\right)}{1 + 0.6 + (1 - 0.6)\exp\left(\dfrac{-2(1.96)}{3}\right)}\right]$$

$$= [0.040, 0.873].$$

If the sample size had been $n = 39$ and $r = 0.6$, the approximate 95% confidence interval would have been $[0.351, 0.770]$. ■

EXERCISES

(In some of the exercises that follow, we must make assumptions of normal distributions with the usual notation.)

7.7-1. For the data given in Exercise 6.7-1, use a t test to test $H_0\colon \beta = 0$ against $H_1\colon \beta > 0$ at the $\alpha = 0.025$ significance level.

7.7-2. For the data given in Exercise 6.7-2, use a t test to test $H_0\colon \beta = 0$ against $H_1\colon \beta > 0$ at the $\alpha = 0.025$ significance level.

7.7-3. For the data given in Exercise 6.7-3, use a t test to test $H_0\colon \beta = 0$ against $H_1\colon \beta > 0$ at the $\alpha = 0.01$ significance level.

7.7-4. For the candy data given in Exercise 6.7-11, test $H_0\colon \beta = 0$ against $H_1\colon \beta > 0$ at an $\alpha = 0.01$ significance level.

7.7-5. A random sample of size $n = 27$ from a bivariate normal distribution yielded a sample correlation coefficient of $r = -0.45$. Would the hypothesis $H_0\colon \rho = 0$ be rejected in favor of $H_1\colon \rho \neq 0$ at an $\alpha = 0.05$ significance level?

7.7-6. In bowling, it is often possible to score well in the first game and then bowl poorly in the second game, or vice versa. The following six pairs of numbers give the scores of the first and second games bowled by the same person on six consecutive Tuesday evenings:

Game 1:	170	190	200	183	187	178
Game 2:	197	178	150	176	205	153

Assume a bivariate normal distribution, and use these scores to test the hypothesis $H_0\colon \rho = 0$ against $H_1\colon \rho \neq 0$ at $\alpha = 0.10$.

7.7-7. A random sample of size 28 from a bivariate normal distribution yielded a sample correlation coefficient of $r = 0.65$. Find an approximate 90% confidence interval for ρ.

7.7-8. By squaring the binomial expression $[(Y_i - \overline{Y}) - (S_{xY}/s_x^2)(x_i - \overline{x})]$, show that

$$\sum_{i=1}^n [(Y_i - \overline{Y}) - (S_{xY}/s_x^2)(x_i - \overline{x})]^2$$
$$= \sum_{i=1}^n (Y_i - \overline{Y})^2 - 2\left(\frac{S_{xY}}{s_x^2}\right)\sum_{i=1}^n (x_i - \overline{x})$$
$$(Y_i - \overline{Y}) + \frac{S_{xY}^2}{s_x^4}\sum_{i=1}^n (x_i - \overline{x})^2$$

equals $(n - 1)S_Y^2(1 - R^2)$, where $X_1 = x_1$, $X_2 = x_2, \ldots, X_n = x_n$.

HINT: Replace $S_{xY} = \sum_{i=1}^n (x_i - \overline{x})(Y_i - \overline{Y})/(n - 1)$ by Rs_xS_Y.

7.7-9. To help determine whether gallinules selected their mate on the basis of weight, 14 pairs of gallinules were captured and weighed. Test the null hypothesis $H_0\colon \rho = 0$ against a two-sided alternative at an $\alpha = 0.01$ significance level. Given that the male and female weights for the $n = 14$ pairs of birds yielded a sample correlation coefficient of $r = -0.252$, would H_0 be rejected?

7.7-10. In sampling from a bivariate normal distribution, it is true that the correlation coefficient R has an approximate normal distribution $N[\rho, (1 - \rho^2)^2/n]$ if the sample size n is large. Since, for large n, R is close to ρ, use two terms of the Taylor's expansion of $u(R)$ about ρ and determine that function $u(R)$ such that it has a variance which is (essentially) free of p. (The solution of this exercise explains why the transformation $(1/2)\ln[(1 + R)/(1 - R)]$ was suggested.)

7.7-11. Show that when $\rho = 0$,

(a) the points of inflection for the graph of the p.d.f. of R are at $r = \pm 1/\sqrt{n - 5}$ for $n \geq 7$;

(b) $E(R) = 0$;

(c) $\text{Var}(R) = 1/(n - 1), n \geq 3$.
HINT: Note that $E(R^2) = E[1 - (1 - R^2)]$.

7.7-12. In a college health fitness program, let X equal the weight in kilograms of a female freshman at the beginning of the program and let Y equal her change in weight during the semester. We shall use the following data for $n = 16$ observations of (x, y) to test the null hypothesis H_0: $\rho = 0$ against a two-sided alternative hypothesis:

(61.4, −3.2) (62.9, 1.4) (58.7, 1.3) (49.3, 0.6)
(71.3, 0.2) (81.5, −2.2) (60.8, 0.9) (50.2, 0.2)
(60.3, 2.0) (54.6, 0.3) (51.1, 3.7) (53.3, 0.2)
(81.0, −0.5) (67.6, −0.8) (71.4, −0.1) (72.1, −0.1)

(a) What is the conclusion if $\alpha = 0.10$?
(b) What is the conclusion if $\alpha = 0.05$?

7.7-13. Let X and Y have a bivariate normal distribution with correlation coefficient ρ. To test H_0: $\rho = 0$ against H_1: $\rho \neq 0$, a random sample of n pairs of observations is selected. Suppose that the sample correlation coefficient is $r = 0.68$. Using a significance level of $\alpha = 0.05$, find the smallest value of the sample size n so that H_0 is rejected.

7.7-14. In Exercise 6.7-5, data are given for horsepower, the time it takes a car to go from 0 to 60, and the weight in pounds of a car, for 14 cars. Those data are repeated here:

Horsepower	0–60	Weight	Horsepower	0–60	Weight
230	8.1	3516	282	6.2	3627
225	7.8	3690	300	6.4	3892
375	4.7	2976	220	7.7	3377
322	6.6	4215	250	7.0	3625
190	8.4	3761	315	5.3	3230
150	8.4	2940	200	6.2	2657
178	7.2	2818	300	5.5	3518

(a) Let ρ be the correlation coefficient of horsepower and weight. Test H_0: $\rho = 0$ against H_1: $\rho \neq 0$.
(b) Let ρ be the correlation coefficient of horsepower and "0–60." Test H_0: $\rho = 0$ against H_1: $\rho < 0$.
(c) Let ρ be the correlation coefficient of weight and "0–60." Test H_0: $\rho = 0$ against H_1: $\rho \neq 0$.

7.7-15. The data in the following table, collected by Ledolter and Hogg (see references), for 2007 midsize model cars, provide the number of miles per gallon (MPG) for city and highway driving, as well as the curb weight of the cars:

Type	MPG City	MPG Hwy	Curb Weight
Ford Fusion V6 SE	20	28	3230
Chevrolet Sebring Sedan Base	24	32	3287
Toyota Camry Solara SE	24	34	3240
Honda Accord Sedan	20	29	3344
Audi A6 3.2	21	29	3825
BMW 5-series 525i Sedan	20	29	3450
Chrysler PT Cruiser Base	22	29	3076
Mercedes E-Class E350 Sedan	19	26	3740
Volkswagen Passat Sedan 2.0T	23	32	3305
Nissan Altima 2.5	26	35	3055
Kia Optima LX	24	34	3142

(a) Construct a scatter plot of city MPG against curb weight and find the least squares regression line.
(b) Let ρ be the correlation coefficient, and test the null hypothesis H_0: $\rho = 0$ against the alternative hypothesis H_1: $\rho < 0$. Give limits for the p-value of your test.
(c) Repeat parts (a) and (b) for highway MPG against curb weight.
(d) Construct a scatter plot of city MPG against highway MPG. What is the correlation coefficient of these two variables?

HISTORICAL COMMENTS Most of the tests presented in this section result from the use of methods found in the theories of Neyman and Pearson (Egon, who is Karl's son). J. Neyman and E. Pearson formed a team, particularly in the 1920s and 1930s, which produced theoretical results that were important contributions to the area of testing statistical hypotheses. These results will be studied in Sections 10.1–10.3.

The other important item in this section is the analysis of variance (ANOVA). This is just the beginning of what is called the design of experiments, developed by R. A. Fisher. In our simple cases in this section, he shows how to test for the best levels of factors in the one-factor and two-factor cases. We study a few important generalizations in Section 11.3. The design of experiments was a huge contribution by Fisher.

Nonparametric Methods

CHAPTER 8

8.1 CHI-SQUARE GOODNESS-OF-FIT TESTS
8.2 CONTINGENCY TABLES
8.3 ORDER STATISTICS
8.4 DISTRIBUTION-FREE CONFIDENCE INTERVALS FOR PERCENTILES
8.5 THE WILCOXON TESTS
8.6 RUN TEST AND TEST FOR RANDOMNESS
8.7 KOLMOGOROV–SMIRNOV GOODNESS-OF-FIT TEST
8.8 RESAMPLING METHODS

8.1 CHI-SQUARE GOODNESS-OF-FIT TESTS

We now consider applications of the very important chi-square statistic, first proposed by Karl Pearson in 1900. As the reader will see, it is a very adaptable test statistic and can be used for many different types of tests. In particular, one application allows us to test the appropriateness of different probabilistic models and, in this sense, is a competitor of the Kolmogorov–Smirnov test (Section 8.7).

So that the reader can get some idea as to why Pearson first proposed his chi-square statistic, we begin with the binomial case. That is, let Y_1 be $b(n, p_1)$, where $0 < p_1 < 1$. According to the central limit theorem,

$$Z = \frac{Y_1 - np_1}{\sqrt{np_1(1 - p_1)}}$$

has a distribution that is approximately $N(0, 1)$ for large n, particularly when $np_1 \ge 5$ and $n(1 - p_1) \ge 5$. Thus, it is not surprising that $Q_1 = Z^2$ is approximately $\chi^2(1)$. If we let $Y_2 = n - Y_1$ and $p_2 = 1 - p_1$, we see that Q_1 may be written as

$$Q_1 = \frac{(Y_1 - np_1)^2}{np_1(1 - p_1)} = \frac{(Y_1 - np_1)^2}{np_1} + \frac{(Y_1 - np_1)^2}{n(1 - p_1)}.$$

Since

$$(Y_1 - np_1)^2 = (n - Y_1 - n[1 - p_1])^2 = (Y_2 - np_2)^2,$$

we have

$$Q_1 = \frac{(Y_1 - np_1)^2}{np_1} + \frac{(Y_2 - np_2)^2}{np_2}.$$

Let us now carefully consider each term in this last expression for Q_1. Of course, Y_1 is the number of "successes," and np_1 is the expected number of "successes"; that is, $E(Y_1) = np_1$. Likewise, Y_2 and np_2 are, respectively, the number and the expected number of "failures." So each numerator consists of the square of the difference of an observed number and an expected number. Note that Q_1 can be written as

$$Q_1 = \sum_{i=1}^{2} \frac{(Y_i - np_i)^2}{np_i}, \tag{8.1-1}$$

and we have seen intuitively that it has an approximate chi-square distribution with one degree of freedom. In a sense, Q_1 measure the "closeness" of the observed numbers to the corresponding expected numbers. For example, if the observed values of Y_1 and Y_2 equal their expected values, then the computed Q_1 is equal to $q_1 = 0$; but if they differ much from them, then the computed $Q_1 = q_1$ is relatively large.

To generalize, we let an experiment have k (instead of only two) mutually exclusive and exhaustive outcomes, say, $A_1, A_2, \ldots, A_k$. Let $p_i = P(A_i)$ and thus $\sum_{i=1}^{k} p_i = 1$. The experiment is repeated n independent times, and we let Y_i represent the number of times the experiment results in A_i, $i = 1, 2, \ldots, k$. This joint distribution of $Y_1, Y_2, \ldots, Y_{k-1}$ is a straightforward generalization of the binomial distribution, as follows.

In considering the joint p.m.f., we see that

$$f(y_1, y_2, \ldots, y_{k-1}) = P(Y_1 = y_1, Y_2 = y_2, \ldots, Y_{k-1} = y_{k-1}),$$

where $y_1, y_2, \ldots, y_{k-1}$ are nonnegative integers such that $y_1 + y_2 + \cdots + y_{k-1} \le n$. Note that we do not need to consider Y_k, since, once the other $k - 1$ random variables are observed to equal $y_1, y_2, \ldots, y_{k-1}$, respectively, we know that

$$Y_k = n - y_1 - y_2 - \cdots - y_{k-1} = y_k, \text{ say.}$$

From the independence of the trials, the probability of each particular arrangement of y_1 A_1s, y_2 A_2s, $\ldots, y_k$ A_ks is

$$p_1^{y_1} p_2^{y_2} \cdots p_k^{y_k}.$$

The number of such arrangements is the multinomial coefficient

$$\binom{n}{y_1, y_2, \ldots, y_k} = \frac{n!}{y_1!\, y_2! \cdots y_k!}.$$

Hence, the product of these two expressions gives the joint p.m.f. of $Y_1, Y_2, \ldots, Y_{k-1}$:

$$f(y_1, y_2, \ldots, y_{k-1}) = \frac{n!}{y_1!\, y_2! \cdots y_k!} p_1^{y_1} p_2^{y_2} \cdots p_k^{y_k}.$$

(Recall that $y_k = n - y_1 - y_2 - \cdots - y_{k-1}$.)

Pearson then constructed an expression similar to Q_1 (Equation 8.1-1), which involves Y_1 and $Y_2 = n - Y_1$, that we denote by Q_{k-1}, which involves $Y_1, Y_2, \ldots, Y_{k-1}$, and $Y_k = n - Y_1 - Y_2 - \cdots - Y_{k-1}$, namely,

$$Q_{k-1} = \sum_{i=1}^{k} \frac{(Y_i - np_i)^2}{np_i}.$$

He argued that Q_{k-1} has an approximate chi-square distribution with $k - 1$ degrees of freedom in much the same way we argued that Q_1 is approximately $\chi^2(1)$. We accept Pearson's conclusion, as the proof is beyond the level of this text.

Some writers suggest that n should be large enough so that $np_i \geq 5, i = 1, 2, \ldots, k$, to be certain that the approximating distribution is adequate. This is probably good advice for the beginner to follow, although we have seen the approximation work very well when $np_i \geq 1, i = 1, 2, \ldots, k$. The important thing to guard against is allowing some particular np_i to become so small that the corresponding term in Q_{k-1}, namely, $(Y_i - np_i)^2/np_i$, tends to dominate the others because of its small denominator. In any case, it is important to realize that Q_{k-1} has only an approximate chi-square distribution.

We shall now show how we can use the fact that Q_{k-1} is approximately $\chi^2(k-1)$ to test hypotheses about probabilities of various outcomes. Let an experiment have k mutually exclusive and exhaustive outcomes, $A_1, A_2, \ldots, A_k$. We would like to test whether $p_i = P(A_i)$ is equal to a known number $p_{i0}, i = 1, 2, \ldots, k$. That is, we shall test the hypothesis

$$H_0\colon\ p_i = p_{i0}, \qquad i = 1, 2, \ldots, k.$$

In order to test such a hypothesis, we shall take a sample of size n; that is, we repeat the experiment n independent times. We tend to favor H_0 if the observed number of times that A_i occurred, say, y_i, and the number of times A_i was expected to occur if H_0 were true, namely, np_{i0}, are approximately equal. That is, if

$$q_{k-1} = \sum_{i=1}^{k} \frac{(y_i - np_{i0})^2}{np_{i0}}$$

is "small," we tend to favor H_0. Since the distribution of Q_{k-1} is approximately $\chi^2(k-1)$, we shall reject H_0 if $q_{k-1} \geq \chi^2_\alpha(k-1)$, where α is the desired significance level of the test.

EXAMPLE 8.1-1 If persons are asked to record a string of random digits, such as

$$3\ 7\ 2\ 4\ 1\ 9\ 7\ 2\ 1\ 5\ 0\ 8 \ldots,$$

we usually find that they are reluctant to record the same or even the two closest numbers in adjacent positions. And yet, in true random-digit generation, the probability of the next digit being the same as the preceding one is $p_{10} = 1/10$, the probability of the next being only one away from the preceding (assuming that 0 is one away from 9) is $p_{20} = 2/10$, and the probability of all other possibilities is $p_{30} = 7/10$. We shall test one person's concept of a random sequence by asking her to record a string of 51 digits that seems to represent a random-digit generation. Thus, we shall test

$$H_0\colon\ p_1 = p_{10} = \frac{1}{10}, \quad p_2 = p_{20} = \frac{2}{10}, \quad p_3 = p_{30} = \frac{7}{10}.$$

The critical region for an $\alpha = 0.05$ significance level is $q_2 \geq \chi^2_{0.05}(2) = 5.991$. The sequence of digits was as follows:

5	8	3	1	9	4	6	7	9	2	6	3	0
8	7	5	1	3	6	2	1	9	5	4	8	0
3	7	1	4	6	0	4	3	8	2	7	3	9
8	5	6	1	8	7	0	3	5	2	5	2	

We went through this listing and observed how many times the next digit was the same as or was one away from the preceding one:

	Frequency	Expected Number
Same	0	$50(1/10) = 5$
One away	8	$50(2/10) = 10$
Other	42	$50(7/10) = 35$
Total	50	50

The computed chi-square statistic is

$$\frac{(0-5)^2}{5} + \frac{(8-10)^2}{10} + \frac{(42-35)^2}{35} = 6.8 > 5.991 = \chi^2_{0.05}(2).$$

Thus, we would say that this string of 51 digits does not seem to be random. ■

One major disadvantage in the use of the chi-square test is that it is a many-sided test. That is, the alternative hypothesis is very general, and it would be difficult to restrict alternatives to situations such as H_1: $p_1 > p_{10}$, $p_2 > p_{20}$, $p_3 < p_{30}$ (with $k = 3$). As a matter of fact, some statisticians would probably test H_0 against this particular alternative H_1 by using a linear function of Y_1, Y_2, and Y_3. However, that sort of discussion is beyond the scope of the book because it involves knowing more about the distributions of linear functions of the dependent random variables Y_1, Y_2, and Y_3. In any case, the student who truly recognizes that this chi-square statistic tests H_0: $p_i = p_{i0}$, $i = 1, 2, \ldots, k$, against all alternatives can usually appreciate the fact that it is more difficult to reject H_0 at a given significance level α when the chi-square statistic is used than it would be if some appropriate "one-sided" test statistic were available.

Many experiments yield a set of data, say, $x_1, x_2, \ldots, x_n$, and the experimenter is often interested in determining whether these data can be treated as the observed values of a random sample $X_1, X_2, \ldots, X_n$ from a given distribution. That is, would this proposed distribution be a reasonable probabilistic model for these sample items? To see how the chi-square test can help us answer questions of this sort, consider a very simple example.

EXAMPLE 8.1-2 Let X denote the number of heads that occur when four coins are tossed at random. Under the assumption that the four coins are independent and the probability of heads on each coin is 1/2, X is $b(4, 1/2)$. One hundred repetitions of this experiment resulted in 0, 1, 2, 3, and 4 heads being observed on 7, 18, 40, 31, and 4 trials, respectively. Do these results support the assumptions? That is, is $b(4, 1/2)$ a reasonable model for the distribution of X? To answer this, we begin by letting $A_1 = \{0\}, A_2 = \{1\}, A_3 = \{2\}, A_4 = \{3\}$, and $A_5 = \{4\}$. If $p_{i0} = P(X \in A_i)$ when X is $b(4, 1/2)$, then

$$p_{10} = p_{50} = \binom{4}{0}\left(\frac{1}{2}\right)^4 = \frac{1}{16} = 0.0625,$$

$$p_{20} = p_{40} = \binom{4}{1}\left(\frac{1}{2}\right)^4 = \frac{4}{16} = 0.25,$$

$$p_{30} = \binom{4}{2}\left(\frac{1}{2}\right)^4 = \frac{6}{16} = 0.375.$$

At an approximate $\alpha = 0.05$ significance level, the null hypothesis

$$H_0\colon\ p_i = p_{i0}, \qquad i = 1, 2, \ldots, 5,$$

is rejected if the observed value of Q_4 is greater than $\chi^2_{0.05}(4) = 9.488$. If we use the 100 repetitions of this experiment that resulted in the observed values $y_1 = 7$, $y_2 = 18$, $y_3 = 40$, $y_4 = 31$, and $y_5 = 4$, of $Y_1, Y_2, \ldots, Y_5$, respectively, then the computed value of Q_4 is

$$\begin{aligned} q_4 &= \frac{(7-6.25)^2}{6.25} + \frac{(18-25)^2}{25} + \frac{(40-37.5)^2}{37.5} + \frac{(31-25)^2}{25} + \frac{(4-6.25)^2}{6.25} \\ &= 4.47. \end{aligned}$$

Since $4.47 < 9.488$, the hypothesis is not rejected. That is, the data support the hypothesis that $b(4, 1/2)$ is a reasonable probabilistic model for X. Recall that the mean of a chi-square random variable is its number of degrees of freedom. In this example, the mean is 4 and the observed value of Q_4 is 4.47, just a little greater than the mean. ■

Thus far, all the hypotheses H_0 tested with the chi-square statistic Q_{k-1} have been simple ones (i.e., completely specified—namely, in $H_0\colon p_i = p_{i0}, i = 1, 2, \ldots, k$, each p_{i0} has been known). This is not always the case, and it frequently happens that $p_{10}, p_{20}, \ldots, p_{k0}$ are functions of one or more unknown parameters. For example, suppose that the hypothesized model for X in Example 8.1-2 was H_0: X is $b(4, p)$, $0 < p < 1$. Then

$$p_{i0} = P(X \in A_i) = \frac{4!}{(i-1)!(5-i)!}p^{i-1}(1-p)^{5-i}, \qquad i = 1, 2, \ldots, 5,$$

which is a function of the unknown parameter p. Of course, if $H_0\colon p_i = p_{i0}$, $i = 1, 2, \ldots, 5$, is true, then, for large n,

$$Q_4 = \sum_{i=1}^{5} \frac{(Y_i - np_{i0})^2}{np_{i0}}$$

still has an approximate chi-square distribution with four degrees of freedom. The difficulty is that when $Y_1, Y_2, \ldots, Y_5$ are observed to be equal to $y_1, y_2, \ldots, y_5$, Q_4 cannot be computed, since $p_{10}, p_{20}, \ldots, p_{50}$ (and hence Q_4) are functions of the unknown parameter p.

One way out of the difficulty would be to estimate p from the data and then carry out the computations with the use of this estimate. It is interesting to note the following: Say the estimation of p is carried out by minimizing Q_4 with respect to p, yielding $\widetilde{p}$. This $\widetilde{p}$ is sometimes called a **minimum chi-square estimator** of p. If, then, this $\widetilde{p}$ is used in Q_4, the statistic Q_4 still has an approximate chi-square distribution, but with only $4 - 1 = 3$ degrees of freedom. That is, the number of degrees of freedom of the approximating chi-square distribution is reduced by one for each parameter estimated by the minimum chi-square technique. We accept this result without proof (as it is a rather difficult one). Although we have considered it when p_{i0}, $i = 1, 2, \ldots, k$, is a function of only one parameter, it holds when there is more than one unknown parameter, say, d. Hence, in a more general situation, the test would be completed by computing Q_{k-1}, using Y_i and the estimated p_{i0}, $i = 1, 2, \ldots, k$, to obtain q_{k-1} (i.e., q_{k-1} is the minimized chi-square). This value q_{k-1} would then be compared with a critical value $\chi^2_\alpha(k - 1 - d)$. In our special case, the computed (minimized) chi-square q_4 would be compared with $\chi^2_\alpha(3)$.

There is still one trouble with all of this: It is usually very difficult to find minimum chi-square estimators. Hence, most statisticians usually use some reasonable method of estimating the parameters. (Maximum likelihood is satisfactory.) They then compute q_{k-1}, recognizing that it is somewhat larger than the minimized chi-square, and compare it with $\chi^2_\alpha(k - 1 - d)$. Note that this approach provides a slightly larger probability of rejecting H_0 than would the scheme in which the minimized chi-square were used because the computed q_{k-1} is larger than the minimum q_{k-1}.

EXAMPLE 8.1-3 Let X denote the number of alpha particles emitted by barium-133 in one-tenth of a second. The following 50 observations of X were taken with a Geiger counter in a fixed position:

7	4	3	6	4	4	5	3	5	3
5	5	3	2	5	4	3	3	7	6
6	4	3	11	9	6	7	4	5	4
7	3	2	8	6	7	4	1	9	8
4	8	9	3	9	7	7	9	3	10

The experimenter is interested in determining whether X has a Poisson distribution. To test H_0: X is Poisson, we first estimate the mean of X—say, λ—with the sample mean, $\overline{x} = 5.4$, of these 50 observations. We then partition the set of outcomes for this experiment into the sets $A_1 = \{0, 1, 2, 3\}, A_2 = \{4\}, A_3 = \{5\}, A_4 = \{6\}, A_5 = \{7\}$, and $A_6 = \{8, 9, 10, \ldots\}$. (Note that we combined $\{0, 1, 2, 3\}$ into one set A_1 and $\{8, 9, 10, \ldots\}$ into another A_6 so that the expected number of outcomes for each set would be at least five when H_0 is true.) In Table 8.1-1, the data are grouped and the estimated probabilities specified by the hypothesis that X has a Poisson distribution with an estimated $\widehat{\lambda} = \overline{x} = 5.4$ are given. Since one parameter was estimated, Q_{6-1} has an approximate chi-square distribution with $r = 6 - 1 - 1 = 4$ degrees of freedom. Also, since

$$q_5 = \frac{[13 - 50(0.213)]^2}{50(0.213)} + \cdots + \frac{[10 - 50(0.178)]^2}{50(0.178)}$$

$$= 2.763 < 9.488 = \chi^2_{0.05}(4),$$

H_0 is not rejected at the 5% significance level. That is, with only these data, we are quite willing to accept the model that X has a Poisson distribution. ■

TABLE 8.1-1: Grouped Geiger Counter Data

	Outcome					
	A_1	A_2	A_3	A_4	A_5	A_6
Frequency	13	9	6	5	7	10
Probability	0.213	0.160	0.173	0.156	0.120	0.178
Expected ($50p_i$)	10.65	8.00	8.65	7.80	6.00	8.90

Let us now consider the problem of testing a model for the distribution of a random variable W of the continuous type. That is, if $F(w)$ is the distribution function of W, we wish to test

$$H_0\colon\ F(w) = F_0(w),$$

where $F_0(w)$ is some known distribution function of the continuous type. In Section 8.7, we will use a Kolmogorov–Smirnov test for H_0. Also, recall that we have considered problems of this type in which we used q–q plots. In order to use the chi-square statistic, we must partition the set of possible values of W into k sets. One way this can be done is as follows: Partition the interval $[0, 1]$ into k sets with the points $b_0, b_1, b_2, \ldots, b_k$, where

$$0 = b_0 < b_1 < b_2 < \cdots < b_k = 1.$$

Let $a_i = F_0^{-1}(b_i)$, $i = 1, 2, \ldots, k - 1$; $A_1 = (-\infty, a_1]$, $A_i = (a_{i-1}, a_i]$ for $i = 2, 3, \ldots, k - 1$, and $A_k = (a_{k-1}, \infty)$; and $p_i = P(W \in A_i)$, $i = 1, 2, \ldots, k$. Let Y_i denote the number of times the observed value of W belongs to A_i, $i = 1, 2, \ldots, k$, in n independent repetitions of the experiment. Then $Y_1, Y_2, \ldots, Y_k$ have a multinomial distribution with parameters $n, p_1, p_2, \ldots, p_{k-1}$. Also, let $p_{i0} = P(W \in A_i)$ when the distribution function of W is $F_0(w)$. The hypothesis that we actually test is a modification of H_0, namely,

$$H_0'\colon\ p_i = p_{i0}, \qquad i = 1, 2, \ldots, k.$$

This hypothesis is rejected if the observed value of the chi-square statistic

$$Q_{k-1} = \sum_{i=1}^{k} \frac{(Y_i - np_{i0})^2}{np_{i0}}$$

is at least as great as $\chi^2_\alpha(k - 1)$. If the hypothesis $H_0'\colon p_i = p_{i0}$, $i = 1, 2, \ldots, k$, is not rejected, we do not reject the hypothesis $H_0\colon F(w) = F_0(w)$.

EXAMPLE 8.1-4 Example 3.3-3 gives 105 observations of the times between calls to 911. Also given is a histogram of these data, with the exponential p.d.f. with $\theta = 20$ superimposed. We shall now use a chi-square goodness-of-fit test to see whether or not this is an appropriate model for the data. That is, if X is equal to the time between calls to 911, we shall test the null hypothesis that the distribution of X is exponential with a mean of $\theta = 20$. Table 8.1-2 groups the data into nine classes and gives the probabilities and expected values of these classes. Using the frequencies and expected values, the chi-square goodness-of-fit statistic is

$$q_8 = \frac{(41 - 38.0520)^2}{38.0520} + \frac{(22 - 24.2655)^2}{24.2655} + \cdots + \frac{(2 - 2.8665)^2}{2.8665} = 4.6861.$$

TABLE 8.1-2: Summary of Times between Calls to 911

Class	Frequency	Probability	Expected
$A_1 = [0, 9]$	41	0.3624	38.0520
$A_2 = (9, 18]$	22	0.2311	24.2655
$A_3 = (18, 27]$	11	0.1473	15.4665
$A_4 = (27, 36]$	10	0.0939	9.8595
$A_5 = (36, 45]$	9	0.0599	6.2895
$A_6 = (45, 54]$	5	0.0382	4.0110
$A_7 = (54, 63]$	2	0.0244	2.5620
$A_8 = (63, 72]$	3	0.0155	1.6275
$A_9 = (72, \infty)$	2	0.0273	2.8665

The p-value associated with this test is 0.7905, which means that it is an extremely good fit.

Note that we assumed that we knew $\theta = 20$. We could also have run this test letting $\theta = \overline{x}$, remembering that we then lose one degree of freedom. For this example, the outcome would be about the same. ■

It is also true, in dealing with models of random variables of the continuous type, that we must frequently estimate unknown parameters. For example, let H_0 be that W is $N(\mu, \sigma^2)$, where μ and σ^2 are unknown. With a random sample $W_1, W_2, \ldots, W_n$, we first can estimate μ and σ^2, possibly with $\overline{w}$ and s_w^2. We partition the space $\{w: -\infty < w < \infty\}$ into k mutually disjoint sets $A_1, A_2, \ldots, A_k$. We then use the estimates of μ and σ^2—say, $\overline{w}$ and $s^2 = s_w^2$, respectively, to estimate

$$p_{i0} = \int_{A_i} \frac{1}{s\sqrt{2\pi}} \exp\left[-\frac{(w - \overline{w})^2}{2s^2}\right] dw,$$

$i = 1, 2, \ldots, k$. Using the observed frequencies $y_1, y_2, \ldots, y_k$ of $A_1, A_2, \ldots, A_k$, respectively, from the observed random sample $w_1, w_2, \ldots, w_n$, and $\widehat{p}_{10}, \widehat{p}_{20}, \ldots, \widehat{p}_{k0}$ estimated with $\overline{w}$ and $s^2 = s_w^2$, we compare the computed

$$q_{k-1} = \sum_{i=1}^{k} \frac{(y_i - n\widehat{p}_{i0})^2}{n\widehat{p}_{i0}}$$

with $\chi^2_\alpha(k - 1 - 2)$. This value q_{k-1} will again be somewhat larger than that which would be found using minimum chi-square estimation, and certain caution should be observed. Several exercises illustrate the procedure, in which one or more parameters must be estimated. Finally, note that the methods given in this section frequently are classified under the more general title of goodness-of-fit tests. In particular, then, the tests in this section would be **chi-square goodness-of-fit tests**.

EXERCISES

8.1-1. A 1-pound bag of candy-coated chocolate-covered peanuts contained 224 pieces of candy, each colored brown, orange, green, or yellow. Test the null hypothesis that the machine filling these bags treats the four colors of candy equally likely; that is, test

$$H_0\colon\ p_B = p_O = p_G = p_Y = \frac{1}{4}.$$

The observed values were 42 brown, 64 orange, 53 green, and 65 yellow candies. You may select the significance level or give an approximate p-value.

8.1-2. A particular brand of candy-coated chocolate comes in five different colors that we shall denote as $A_1 = \{\text{brown}\}$, $A_2 = \{\text{yellow}\}$, $A_3 = \{\text{orange}\}$, $A_4 = \{\text{green}\}$, and $A_5 = \{\text{coffee}\}$. Let p_i equal the probability that the color of a piece of candy selected at random belongs to A_i, $i = 1, 2, \ldots, 5$. Test the null hypothesis

$$H_0\colon\ p_1 = 0.4,\ p_2 = 0.2,\ p_3 = 0.2,\\ p_4 = 0.1,\ p_5 = 0.1,$$

using a random sample of $n = 580$ pieces of candy whose colors yielded the respective frequencies 224, 119, 130, 48, and 59. You may select the significance level or give an approximate p-value.

8.1-3. In the Michigan Daily Lottery, each weekday a three-digit integer is generated one digit at a time. Let p_i denote the probability of generating digit i, $i = 0, 1, \ldots, 9$. Let $\alpha = 0.05$, and use the following 50 digits to test $H_0\colon p_0 = p_1 = \cdots = p_9 = 1/10$:

1	6	9	9	3	8	5	0	6	7
4	7	5	9	4	6	5	6	4	4
4	8	0	9	3	2	1	5	4	5
7	3	2	1	4	6	7	1	3	4
4	8	8	6	1	6	1	2	8	8

8.1-4. In a biology laboratory, students use corn to test the Mendelian theory of inheritance. The theory claims that frequencies of the four categories "smooth and yellow," "wrinkled and yellow," "smooth and purple," and "wrinkled and purple" will occur in the ratio 9:3:3:1. If a student counted 124, 30, 43, and 11, respectively, for these four categories, would these data support the Mendelian theory? Let $\alpha = 0.05$.

8.1-5. Let X equal the number of female children in a three-child family. We shall use a chi-square goodness-of-fit statistic to test the null hypothesis that the distribution of X is $b(3, 0.5)$.

(a) Define the test statistic and critical region, using an $\alpha = 0.05$ significance level.

(b) Among students who were taking statistics, 52 came from families with three children. For these families, $x = 0, 1, 2$, and 3 for 5, 17, 24, and 6 families, respectively. Calculate the value of the test statistic and state your conclusion, considering how the sample was selected.

8.1-6. It has been claimed that, for a penny minted in 1999 or earlier, the probability of observing heads upon spinning the penny is $p = 0.30$. Three students got together, and they would each spin a penny and record the number X of heads out of the three spins. They repeated this experiment $n = 200$ times, observing 0, 1, 2, and 3 heads 57, 95, 38, and 10 times, respectively. Use these data to test the hypotheses that X is $b(3, 0.30)$. Give limits for the p-value of this test. In addition, out of the 600 spins, calculate the number of heads occurring and then a 95% confidence interval for p.

8.1-7. In Example 2.6-3, it is claimed that X has a Poisson distribution, and 100 observations of X are given in Table 2.6-1. Use a chi-square goodness-of-fit statistic to test whether this claim is true. Since $\bar{x} = 5.59$, let the estimate of λ be 5.6 so that you can use the Poisson probability table in the appendix. Let $A_1 = \{x \le 1\}$ and $A_{11} = \{x \ge 11\}$. Use an $\alpha = 0.05$ significance level.

8.1-8. In Exercise 2.6-12, we are asked whether the data look like observations of a Poisson random variable with mean $\lambda = 3$. Use $\alpha = 0.05$ and a chi-square goodness-of-fit test to answer this question.

8.1-9. While testing a used tape for bad records, a computer operator counted the number of flaws per 100 feet of tape. Let X equal this random variable. Test the null hypothesis that X has a Poisson distribution with a mean of $\lambda = 2.4$, given that 40 observations of X yielded 5 zeros, 7 ones, 12 twos, 9 threes, 5 fours, 1 five, and 1 six. Let $\alpha = 0.05$.

HINT: Combine the last two sets into one; that is, the last set would be all x values ≥ 5.

8.1-10. Let X equal the distance between bad records on a used computer tape. Letting $\alpha = 0.05$ and taking $\bar{x} = 42.2$ as an estimate of θ, use the following 90 observations of X and 10 classes of equal probability to test the hypothesis that the distribution of X is exponential:

30	79	38	47	22	52	36	36	7	57
3	22	30	14	8	32	15	21	12	12
6	67	6	7	35	78	28	74	5	9
37	1	3	3	44	160	50	27	61	15
39	44	130	18	6	1	32	116	23	12
58	101	68	53	58	21	21	7	79	41
80	33	71	81	17	10	13	49	21	56
107	21	17	64	14	36	26	1	54	207
64	238	25	51	82	8	2	3	43	87

8.1-11. A sample of 100 2.2K-ohm resistors was tested, yielding the following measurements:

2.17	2.18	2.17	2.19	2.23	2.18	2.16	2.23	2.29	2.20
2.24	2.13	2.18	2.22	2.21	2.22	2.23	2.18	2.23	2.25
2.24	2.20	2.21	2.20	2.25	2.15	2.20	2.25	2.16	2.19
2.20	2.18	2.18	2.19	2.22	2.19	2.20	2.19	2.22	2.21
2.22	2.18	2.18	2.28	2.19	2.23	2.21	2.19	2.21	2.21
2.19	2.18	2.21	2.17	2.20	2.18	2.18	2.21	2.22	2.18
2.22	2.23	2.19	2.23	2.18	2.19	2.18	2.21	2.18	2.15
2.20	2.23	2.20	2.20	2.23	2.20	2.19	2.22	2.17	2.20
2.20	2.17	2.19	2.19	2.25	2.19	2.19	2.20	2.20	2.19
2.21	2.14	2.24	2.21	2.19	2.23	2.18	2.22	2.23	2.19

(a) Group these data into nine classes of equal length, with the class boundaries for the first class being 2.125–2.145.

(b) Use a chi-square goodness-of-fit statistic to test whether the data constitute observations of a normally distributed random variable, after grouping the first two classes and the last two classes to avoid small expected numbers. Estimate μ and σ with the mean and standard deviation, respectively, of the grouped data. Let $\alpha = 0.05$.

8.1-12. Let X equal the amount of butterfat (in pounds) produced by 90 cows during a 305-day milk production period following the birth of their first calf. Test the hypothesis that the distribution of X is $N(\mu, \sigma^2)$, using $k = 10$ classes of equal probability. You may take $\bar{x} = 511.633$ and $s_x = 87.576$ as estimates of μ and σ, respectively. The data are as follows:

486	537	513	583	453	510	570	500	458	555
618	327	350	643	500	497	421	505	637	599
392	574	492	635	460	696	593	422	499	524
539	339	472	427	532	470	417	437	388	481
537	489	418	434	466	464	544	475	608	444
573	611	586	613	645	540	494	532	691	478
513	583	457	612	628	516	452	501	453	643
541	439	627	619	617	394	607	502	395	470
531	526	496	561	491	380	345	274	672	509

8.1-13. A rare type of heredity change causes the bacterium *E. coli* to become resistant to the drug streptomycin. This type of change, called *mutation*, can be detected by plating many bacteria on petri dishes containing an antibiotic medium. Any colonies that grow on this medium result from a single mutant cell. A sample of $n = 150$ petri dishes of streptomycin agar were each plated with 10^6 bacteria, and the numbers of colonies were counted on each dish. The observed results were that 92 dishes had 0 colonies, 46 had 1, 8 had 2, 3 had 3, and 1 dish had 4 colonies. Let X equal the number of colonies per dish. Test the hypothesis that X has a Poisson distribution. Use $\bar{x} = 0.5$ as an estimate of λ. Let $\alpha = 0.01$.

8.1-14. In Exercise 3.4-10, data are given for the distances that snails travel. These distances are repeated here for your convenience:

Distances for Infected Snail Group (ordered):

263	238	226	220	170	155	139	123	119	107	107	97	90
90	90	79	75	74	71	66	60	55	47	47	47	45
43	41	40	39	38	38	35	32	32	28	19	10	10

Distances for Control Snail Group (ordered):

314	300	274	246	190	186	185	182	180	141	132
129	110	100	95	95	93	83	55	52	50	48
48	44	40	32	30	25	24	18	7		

(a) For the control snail group, test the hypothesis that the distances come from an exponential distribution. Use $\bar{x}$ as an estimate of θ. Group the data into 5 or 10 classes, with equal probabilities for each class. Thus, the expected values will be either 6.2 or 3.1, respectively.

(b) For the infected snail group, test the hypothesis that the distances come from a gamma distribution with $\alpha = 2$ and $\theta = 42$. Use 10 classes with equal probabilities so that the expected value of each class is 3.9. Use Minitab or some other computer program to calculate the boundaries of the classes.

8.1-15. In Exercise 3.1-8, data are given for the melting points for 50 metal alloy filaments. Here the data are repeated:

320	326	325	318	322	320	329	317	316	331
320	320	317	329	316	308	321	319	322	335
318	313	327	314	329	323	327	323	324	314
308	305	328	330	322	310	324	314	312	318
313	320	324	311	317	325	328	319	310	324

Test the hypothesis that these are observations of a normally distributed random variable. Note that you must estimate two parameters: μ and σ.

8.1-16. In Exercise 3.1-4, the weights of 100 laptop computers are given. Use 10 classes of equal probability to test the hypothesis that these weights come from a normal distribution. Note that you must estimate two parameters. Let $\alpha = 0.05$.

8.2 CONTINGENCY TABLES

In this section, we demonstrate the flexibility of the chi-square test. We first look at a method for testing whether two or more multinomial distributions are equal, sometimes called a *test for homogeneity*. Then we consider a *test for independence of attributes of classification*. Both of these lead to a similar test statistic.

Suppose that each of two independent experiments can end in one of the k mutually exclusive and exhaustive events $A_1, A_2, \ldots, A_k$. Let

$$p_{ij} = P(A_i), \qquad i = 1, 2, \ldots, k, \qquad j = 1, 2.$$

That is, $p_{11}, p_{21}, \ldots, p_{k1}$ are the probabilities of the events in the first experiment, and $p_{12}, p_{22}, \ldots, p_{k2}$ are those associated with the second experiment. Let the experiments be repeated n_1 and n_2 independent times, respectively. Also, let $Y_{11}, Y_{21}, \ldots, Y_{k1}$ be the frequencies of $A_1, A_2, \ldots, A_k$ associated with the n_1 independent trials of the first experiment. Similarly, let $Y_{12}, Y_{22}, \ldots, Y_{k2}$ be the respective frequencies associated with the n_2 trials of the second experiment. Of course, $\sum_{i=1}^{k} Y_{ij} = n_j$, $j = 1, 2$. From the sampling distribution theory corresponding to the basic chi-square test, we know that each of

$$\sum_{i=1}^{k} \frac{(Y_{ij} - n_j p_{ij})^2}{n_j p_{ij}}, \qquad j = 1, 2,$$

has an approximate chi-square distribution with $k - 1$ degrees of freedom. Since the two experiments are independent (and thus the two chi-square statistics are independent), the sum

$$\sum_{j=1}^{2} \sum_{i=1}^{k} \frac{(Y_{ij} - n_j p_{ij})^2}{n_j p_{ij}}$$

is approximately chi-square with $k - 1 + k - 1 = 2k - 2$ degrees of freedom.

Usually the p_{ij}, $i = 1, 2, \ldots, k$, $j = 1, 2$, are unknown, and frequently we wish to test the hypothesis

$$H_0\colon p_{11} = p_{12},\ p_{21} = p_{22},\ \ldots,\ p_{k1} = p_{k2};$$

that is, H_0 is the hypothesis that the corresponding probabilities associated with the two independent experiments are equal. Under H_0, we can estimate the unknown

$$p_{i1} = p_{i2}, \qquad i = 1, 2, \ldots, k,$$

by using the relative frequency $(Y_{i1} + Y_{i2})/(n_1 + n_2)$, $i = 1, 2, \ldots, k$. That is, if H_0 is true, we can say that the two experiments are actually parts of a larger one in which $Y_{i1} + Y_{i2}$ is the frequency of the event A_i, $i = 1, 2, \ldots, k$. Note that we have to estimate only the $k - 1$ probabilities $p_{i1} = p_{i2}$, using

$$\frac{Y_{i1} + Y_{i2}}{n_1 + n_2}, \qquad i = 1, 2, \ldots, k - 1,$$

since the sum of the k probabilities must equal 1. That is, the estimator of $p_{k1} = p_{k2}$ is

$$1 - \frac{Y_{11} + Y_{12}}{n_1 + n_2} - \cdots - \frac{Y_{k-1,1} + Y_{k-1,2}}{n_1 + n_2} = \frac{Y_{k1} + Y_{k2}}{n_1 + n_2}.$$

Substituting these estimators, we find that

$$Q = \sum_{j=1}^{2} \sum_{i=1}^{k} \frac{[Y_{ij} - n_j(Y_{i1} + Y_{i2})/(n_1 + n_2)]^2}{n_j(Y_{i1} + Y_{i2})/(n_1 + n_2)}$$

has an approximate chi-square distribution with $2k - 2 - (k - 1) = k - 1$ degrees of freedom. Here $k - 1$ is subtracted from $2k - 2$, because that is the number of estimated parameters. The critical region for testing H_0 is of the form

$$q \ge \chi^2_\alpha(k - 1).$$

EXAMPLE 8.2-1 To test two methods of instruction, 50 students are selected at random from each of two groups. At the end of the instruction period, each student is assigned a grade (A, B, C, D, or F) by an evaluating team. The data are recorded as follows:

	Grade					
	A	B	C	D	F	Totals
Group I	8	13	16	10	3	50
Group II	4	9	14	16	7	50

Accordingly, if the hypothesis H_0 that the corresponding probabilities are equal is true, then the respective estimates of the probabilities are

$$\frac{8 + 4}{100} = 0.12,\ 0.22,\ 0.30,\ 0.26,\ \frac{3 + 7}{100} = 0.10.$$

Thus, the estimates of $n_1 p_{i1} = n_2 p_{i2}$ are 6, 11, 15, 13, and 5, respectively. Hence, the computed value of Q is

$$q = \frac{(8 - 6)^2}{6} + \frac{(13 - 11)^2}{11} + \frac{(16 - 15)^2}{15} + \frac{(10 - 13)^2}{13} + \frac{(3 - 5)^2}{5}$$
$$+ \frac{(4 - 6)^2}{6} + \frac{(9 - 11)^2}{11} + \frac{(14 - 15)^2}{15} + \frac{(16 - 13)^2}{13} + \frac{(7 - 5)^2}{5}$$
$$= \frac{4}{6} + \frac{4}{11} + \frac{1}{15} + \frac{9}{13} + \frac{4}{5} + \frac{4}{6} + \frac{4}{11} + \frac{1}{15} + \frac{9}{13} + \frac{4}{5} = 5.18.$$

Now, under H_0, Q has an approximate chi-square distribution with $k - 1 = 4$ degrees of freedom, so the $\alpha = 0.05$ critical region is $q \geq 9.488 = \chi^2_{0.05}(4)$. Here $q = 5.18 < 9.488$, and hence H_0 is not rejected at the 5% significance level. Furthermore, the p-value for $q = 5.18$ is 0.268, which is greater than most significance levels. Thus, with these data, we cannot say that there is a difference between the two methods of instruction. ■

It is fairly obvious how this procedure can be extended to testing the equality of h independent multinomial distributions. That is, let

$$p_{ij} = P(A_i), \qquad i = 1, 2, \ldots, k, \qquad j = 1, 2, \ldots, h,$$

and test

$$H_0\colon\ p_{i1} = p_{i2} = \cdots = p_{ih} = p_i, \qquad i = 1, 2, \ldots, k.$$

Repeat the jth experiment n_j independent times, and let $Y_{1j}, Y_{2j}, \ldots, Y_{kj}$ denote the frequencies of the respective events $A_1, A_2, \ldots, A_k$. Now,

$$Q = \sum_{j=1}^{h} \sum_{i=1}^{k} \frac{(Y_{ij} - n_j p_{ij})^2}{n_j p_{ij}}$$

has an approximate chi-square distribution with $h(k - 1)$ degrees of freedom. Under H_0, we must estimate $k - 1$ probabilities, using

$$\widehat{p}_i = \frac{\sum_{j=1}^{h} Y_{ij}}{\sum_{j=1}^{h} n_j}, \qquad i = 1, 2, \ldots, k - 1,$$

because the estimate of p_k follows from $\widehat{p}_k = 1 - \widehat{p}_1 - \widehat{p}_2 - \cdots - \widehat{p}_{k-1}$. We use these estimates to obtain

$$Q = \sum_{j=1}^{h} \sum_{i=1}^{k} \frac{(Y_{ij} - n_j \widehat{p}_i)^2}{n_j \widehat{p}_i},$$

which has an approximate chi-square distribution, with its degrees of freedom given by $h(k - 1) - (k - 1) = (h - 1)(k - 1)$.

Let us see how we can use the preceding procedures to test the equality of two or more independent distributions that are not necessarily multinomial. Suppose first that we are given random variables U and V with distribution functions $F(u)$ and $G(v)$, respectively. It is sometimes of interest to test the hypothesis H_0: $F(x) = G(x)$ for all x. Previously, we considered tests of $\mu_U = \mu_V$, $\sigma^2_U = \sigma^2_V$. In Section 8.5, we will look at the two-sample Wilcoxon test. Now we shall assume only that the distributions are independent and of the continuous type.

We are interested in testing the hypothesis H_0: $F(x) = G(x)$ for all x. This hypothesis will be replaced by another one. Partition the real line into k mutually disjoint sets $A_1, A_2, \ldots, A_k$. Let

$$p_{i1} = P(U \in A_i), \qquad i = 1, 2, \ldots, k,$$

and

$$p_{i2} = P(V \in A_i), \qquad i = 1, 2, \ldots, k.$$

We observe that if $F(x) = G(x)$ for all x, then $p_{i1} = p_{i2}$, $i = 1, 2, \ldots, k$. We replace the hypothesis H_0: $F(x) = G(x)$ with the less restrictive hypothesis H_0': $p_{i1} = p_{i2}$, $i = 1, 2, \ldots, k$. That is, we are now essentially interested in testing the equality of two multinomial distributions.

Let n_1 and n_2 denote the number of independent observations of U and V, respectively. For $i = 1, 2, \ldots, k$, let Y_{ij} denote the number of these observations of U and V, $j = 1, 2$, respectively, that fall into a set A_i. At this point, we proceed to make the test of H_0' as described earlier. Of course, if H_0' is rejected at the (approximate) significance level α, then H_0 is rejected with the same probability. However, if H_0' is true, H_0 is not necessarily true. Thus, if H_0' is accepted, it is probably better to say that we do not reject H_0 than to say that H_0 is accepted.

In applications, the question of how to select $A_1, A_2, \ldots, A_k$ is frequently raised. Obviously, there is no single choice for k or for the dividing marks of the partition. But it is interesting to observe that the combined sample can be used in this selection without upsetting the approximate distribution of Q. For example, suppose that $n_1 = n_2 = 20$. Then we could easily select the dividing marks of the partition so that $k = 4$ and one-fourth of the combined sample falls into each of the four sets.

EXAMPLE 8.2-2 Select, at random, 20 cars of each of two comparable major-brand models. All 40 cars are submitted to accelerated life testing; that is, they are driven many miles over very poor roads in a short time, and their failure times (in weeks) are recorded as follows:

Brand U:	25	31	20	42	39	19	35	36	44	26
	38	31	29	41	43	36	28	31	25	38
Brand V:	28	17	33	25	31	21	16	19	31	27
	23	19	25	22	29	32	24	20	34	26

If we use 23.5, 28.5, and 34.5 as dividing marks, we note that exactly one-fourth of the 40 cars fall into each of the resulting four sets. Thus, the data can be summarized as follows:

	A_1	A_2	A_3	A_4	Totals
Brand U	2	4	4	10	20
Brand V	8	6	6	0	20

The estimate of each p_i is $10/40 = 1/4$, which, multiplied by $n_j = 20$, gives 5. Hence, the computed Q is

$$\begin{aligned} q &= \frac{(2-5)^2}{5} + \frac{(4-5)^2}{5} + \frac{(4-5)^2}{5} + \frac{(10-5)^2}{5} + \frac{(8-5)^2}{5} \\ &\quad + \frac{(6-5)^2}{5} + \frac{(6-5)^2}{5} + \frac{(0-5)^2}{5} \\ &= \frac{72}{5} = 14.4 > 7.815 = \chi^2_{0.05}(3). \end{aligned}$$

Also, the p-value is 0.0028. Thus, it seems that the two brands of cars have different distributions for the length of life under accelerated life testing. Brand U seems better than brand V. ■

Again, it should be clear how this approach can be extended to more than two distributions, and this extension will be illustrated in the exercises.

Now let us suppose that a random experiment results in an outcome that can be classified by two different attributes, such as height and weight. Assume that the first attribute is assigned to one and only one of k mutually exclusive and exhaustive events—say, $A_1, A_2, \ldots, A_k$—and the second attribute falls into one and only one of h mutually exclusive and exhaustive events—say, $B_1, B_2, \ldots, B_h$. Let the probability of $A_i \cap B_j$ be defined by

$$p_{ij} = P(A_i \cap B_j), \qquad i = 1, 2, \ldots, k, \qquad j = 1, 2, \ldots, h.$$

The random experiment is to be repeated n independent times, and Y_{ij} will denote the frequency of the event $A_i \cap B_j$. Since there are kh such events as $A_i \cap B_j$, the random variable

$$Q_{kh-1} = \sum_{j=1}^{h} \sum_{i=1}^{k} \frac{(Y_{ij} - np_{ij})^2}{np_{ij}}$$

has an approximate chi-square distribution with $kh - 1$ degrees of freedom, provided that n is large.

Suppose that we wish to test the hypothesis of the independence of the A and B attributes, namely,

$$H_0\colon P(A_i \cap B_j) = P(A_i)P(B_j), \qquad i = 1, 2, \ldots, k, \qquad j = 1, 2, \ldots, h.$$

Let us denote $P(A_i)$ by $p_{i\cdot}$ and $P(B_j)$ by $p_{\cdot j}$; that is,

$$p_{i\cdot} = \sum_{j=1}^{h} p_{ij} = P(A_i) \qquad \text{and} \qquad p_{\cdot j} = \sum_{i=1}^{k} p_{ij} = P(B_j).$$

Of course,

$$1 = \sum_{j=1}^{h} \sum_{i=1}^{k} p_{ij} = \sum_{j=1}^{h} p_{\cdot j} = \sum_{i=1}^{k} p_{i\cdot}.$$

Then the hypothesis can be formulated as

$$H_0\colon p_{ij} = p_{i\cdot}p_{\cdot j}, \qquad i = 1, 2, \ldots, k, \qquad j = 1, 2, \ldots, h.$$

To test H_0, we can use Q_{kh-1} with p_{ij} replaced by $p_{i\cdot}p_{\cdot j}$. But if $p_{i\cdot}$, $i = 1, 2, \ldots, k$, and $p_{\cdot j}$, $j = 1, 2, \ldots, h$, are unknown, as they usually are in applications, we cannot compute Q_{kh-1} once the frequencies are observed. In such a case, we estimate these unknown parameters by

$$\widehat{p}_{i\cdot} = \frac{y_{i\cdot}}{n}, \qquad \text{where } y_{i\cdot} = \sum_{j=1}^{h} y_{ij}$$

is the observed frequency of A_i, $i = 1, 2, \ldots, k$; and

$$\widehat{p}_{\cdot j} = \frac{y_{\cdot j}}{n}, \qquad \text{where } y_{\cdot j} = \sum_{i=1}^{k} y_{ij}$$

is the observed frequency of B_j, $j = 1, 2, \ldots, h$. Since $\sum_{i=1}^{k} p_{i\cdot} = \sum_{j=1}^{h} p_{\cdot j} = 1$, we actually estimate only $k - 1 + h - 1 = k + h - 2$ parameters. So if these estimates are used in Q_{kh-1}, with $p_{ij} = p_{i\cdot}p_{\cdot j}$, then, according to the rule stated earlier, the random variable

$$Q = \sum_{j=1}^{h}\sum_{i=1}^{k} \frac{[Y_{ij} - n(Y_{i\cdot}/n)(Y_{\cdot j}/n)]^2}{n(Y_{i\cdot}/n)(Y_{\cdot j}/n)}$$

has an approximate chi-square distribution with $kh - 1 - (k + h - 2) = (k - 1)(h - 1)$ degrees of freedom, provided that H_0 is true. The hypothesis H_0 is rejected if the computed value of this statistic exceeds $\chi^2_\alpha[(k - 1)(h - 1)]$.

EXAMPLE 8.2-3 The 400 undergraduate students in a random sample at the University of Iowa were classified according to the college in which the students were enrolled and according to their gender. The results are recorded in Table 8.2-1, called a $k \times h$ **contingency table**, where, in this case, $k = 2$ and $h = 5$. (Do not be concerned about the numbers in parentheses at this point.) Incidentally, these data do actually reflect the composition of the undergraduate colleges at Iowa, but they were modified a little to make the computations easier in this example.

We desire to test the null hypothesis H_0: $p_{ij} = p_{i\cdot}p_{\cdot j}$, $i = 1,2$ and $j = 1,2,3,4,5$, that the college in which a student enrolls is independent of the gender of that student. Under H_0, estimates of the probabilities are

$$\widehat{p}_{1\cdot} = \frac{190}{400} = 0.475 \qquad \text{and} \qquad \widehat{p}_{2\cdot} = \frac{210}{400} = 0.525$$

and

$$\widehat{p}_{\cdot 1} = \frac{35}{400} = 0.0875,\ \widehat{p}_{\cdot 2} = 0.05,\ \widehat{p}_{\cdot 3} = 0.8,\ \widehat{p}_{\cdot 4} = 0.0375,\ \widehat{p}_{\cdot 5} = 0.025.$$

The expected numbers $n(y_{i\cdot}/n)(y_{\cdot j}/n)$ are computed as follows:

$$400(0.475)(0.0875) = 16.625,$$
$$400(0.525)(0.0875) = 18.375,$$
$$400(0.475)(0.05) = 9.5,$$

and so on. These are the values recorded in parentheses in Table 8.2-1. The computed chi-square statistic is

$$\begin{aligned} q &= \frac{(21 - 16.625)^2}{16.625} + \frac{(14 - 18.375)^2}{18.375} + \cdots + \frac{(4 - 5.25)^2}{5.25} \\ &= 1.15 + 1.04 + 4.45 + 4.02 + 0.32 + 0.29 + 3.69 \\ &\quad + 3.34 + 0.33 + 0.30 = 18.93. \end{aligned}$$

TABLE 8.2-1: Undergraduates at the University of Iowa

	College					
Gender	Business	Engineering	Liberal Arts	Nursing	Pharmacy	Totals
Male	21 (16.625)	16 (9.5)	145 (152)	2 (7.125)	6 (4.75)	190
Female	14 (18.375)	4 (10.5)	175 (168)	13 (7.875)	4 (5.25)	210
Totals	35	20	320	15	10	400

Since the number of degrees of freedom equals $(k - 1)(h - 1) = 4$, this $q = 18.93 > 13.28 = \chi^2_{0.01}(4)$, and we reject H_0 at the $\alpha = 0.01$ significance level. Moreover, since the first two terms of q come from the business college, the next two from engineering, and so on, it is clear that the enrollments in engineering and nursing are more highly dependent on gender than in the other colleges, because they have contributed the most to the value of the chi-square statistic. It is also interesting to note that one expected number is less than 5, namely 4.75. However, as the associated term in q does not contribute an unusual amount to the chi-square value, it does not concern us. ■

It is fairly obvious how to extend the preceding testing procedure to more than two attributes. For example, if the third attribute falls into one and only one of m mutually exclusive and exhaustive events—say, $C_1, C_2, \ldots, C_m$—then we test the independence of the three attributes by using

$$Q = \sum_{r=1}^{m}\sum_{j=1}^{h}\sum_{i=1}^{k} \frac{[Y_{ijr} - n(Y_{i\cdot\cdot}/n)(Y_{\cdot j\cdot}/n)(Y_{\cdot\cdot r}/n)]^2}{n(Y_{i\cdot\cdot}/n)(Y_{\cdot j\cdot}/n)(Y_{\cdot\cdot r}/n)},$$

where Y_{ijr}, $Y_{i\cdot\cdot}$, $Y_{\cdot j\cdot}$, and $Y_{\cdot\cdot r}$ are the respective observed frequencies of the events $A_i \cap B_j \cap C_r$, A_i, B_j, and C_r in n independent trials of the experiment. If n is large and if the three attributes are independent, then Q has an approximate chi-square distribution with $khm - 1 - (k - 1) - (h - 1) - (m - 1) = khm - k - h - m + 2$ degrees of freedom.

Rather than explore this extension further, it is more instructive to note some interesting uses of contingency tables.

EXAMPLE 8.2-4 Say we observed 30 values $x_1, x_2, \ldots, x_{30}$ that are claimed to be the values of a random sample. That is, the corresponding random variables $X_1, X_2, \ldots, X_{30}$ were supposed to be mutually independent and each of these random variables is supposed to have the same distribution. Say, however, by looking at the 30 values, we detect an upward trend which indicates that there might have been some dependence and/or the random variables did not actually have the same distribution. One simple way to test whether they could be thought of as being observed values of a random sample is the following: Mark each x high (H) or low (L), depending on whether it is above or below the sample median. Then divide the x values into three groups: $x_1, \ldots, x_{10}$; $x_{11}, \ldots, x_{20}$; and $x_{21}, \ldots, x_{30}$. Certainly, if the observations are those of a random sample, we would expect five H's and five L's in each group. That is, the attribute classified as H or L should be independent of the group number. The summary of these data provides a 3×2 contingency table. For example, say the 30 values are

5.6	8.2	7.8	4.8	5.5	8.1	6.7	7.7	9.3	6.9
8.2	10.1	7.5	6.9	11.1	9.2	8.7	10.3	10.7	10.0
9.2	11.6	10.3	11.7	9.9	10.6	10.0	11.4	10.9	11.1

The median can be taken to be the average of the two middle observations in magnitude, namely, 9.2 and 9.3. Marking each item H or L after comparing it with this median, we obtain the following 3×2 contingency table:

Group	L	H	Totals
1	9	1	10
2	5	5	10
3	1	9	10
Totals	15	15	30

Here each $n(y_{i\cdot}/n)(y_{\cdot j}/n) = 30(10/30)(15/30) = 5$, so that the computed value of Q is

$$q = \frac{(9-5)^2}{5} + \frac{(1-5)^2}{5} + \frac{(5-5)^2}{5} + \frac{(5-5)^2}{5} + \frac{(1-5)^2}{5} + \frac{(9-5)^2}{5}$$
$$= 12.8 > 5.991 = \chi^2_{0.05}(2),$$

since in this instance $(k-1)(h-1) = 2$ degrees of freedom. (The p-value is 0.0017.) Hence, we reject the conjecture that these 30 values could be the observations of a random sample. Obviously, modifications could be made to this scheme: dividing the sample into more (or fewer) than three groups and rating items differently, such as low (L), middle (M), and high (H). ■

It cannot be emphasized enough that the chi-square statistic can be used fairly effectively in almost any situation in which there should be independence. For example, suppose that we have a group of workers who have essentially the same qualifications (training, experience, etc.). Many believe that the salary and gender of the workers should be independent attributes, yet there have been several claims in special cases that there is a dependence—or discrimination—in attributes associated with such a problem.

EXAMPLE 8.2-5 Two groups of workers have the same qualifications for a particular type of work. Their experience in salaries is summarized by the following 2×5 contingency table, in which the upper bound of each salary range is not included in that listing:

	Salary (Thousands of Dollars)					
Group	27–29	29–31	31–33	33–35	35 and over	Totals
1	6	11	16	14	13	60
2	5	9	8	6	2	30
Totals	11	20	24	20	15	90

To test whether the group assignment and the salaries seem to be independent with these data at the $\alpha = 0.05$ significance level, we compute

$$q = \frac{[6 - 90(60/90)(11/90)]^2}{90(60/90)(11/90)} + \cdots + \frac{[2 - 90(30/90)(15/90)]^2}{90(30/90)(15/90)}$$
$$= 4.752 < 9.488 = \chi^2_{0.05}(4).$$

Also, the p-value is 0.313. Hence, with these limited data, group assignment and salaries seem to be independent. ■

Before turning to the exercises, note that we could have thought of the last two examples in this section as testing the equality of two or more multinomial distributions. In Example 8.2-4 the three groups define three binomial distributions, and in Example 8.2-5 the two groups define two multinomial distributions. What would have happened if we had used the computations outlined earlier in the section? It is interesting to note that we obtain exactly the same value of chi-square and in each case the number of degrees of freedom is equal to $(k-1)(h-1)$. Hence, it makes no difference whether we think of it as a test of independence or a test of the equality of several multinomial distributions. Our advice is to use the terminology that seems most natural for the particular situation.

EXERCISES

8.2-1. We wish to see if two groups of nurses distribute their time in six different categories about the same way. That is, the hypothesis under consideration is $H_0\colon p_{i1} = p_{i2}, i = 1, 2, \ldots, 6$. To test this hypothesis, nurses are observed at random throughout several days, each observation resulting in a mark in one of the six categories. A summary of the results is given by the following frequency table:

	Category						
	1	2	3	4	5	6	Totals
Group I	95	36	71	21	45	32	300
Group II	53	26	43	18	32	28	200

Use a chi-square test with $\alpha = 0.05$.

8.2-2. Suppose that a third group of nurses was observed along with groups I and II of Exercise 8.2-1, resulting in the respective frequencies 130, 75, 136, 33, 61, and 65. Test $H_0\colon p_{i1} = p_{i2} = p_{i3}, i = 1, 2, \ldots, 6$, at the $\alpha = 0.025$ significance level.

8.2-3. Each of two comparable classes of 15 students responded to two different methods of instructions, giving the following scores on a standardized test:

Class U:	91	42	39	62	55	82	67	44
	51	77	61	52	76	41	59	
Class V:	80	71	55	67	61	93	49	78
	57	88	79	81	63	51	75	

Use a chi-square test with $\alpha = 0.05$ to test the equality of the distributions of test scores by dividing the combined sample into three equal parts (low, middle, high).

8.2-4. Suppose that a third class (W) of 15 students was observed along with classes U and V of Exercise 8.2-3, resulting in scores of

91	73	67	83	59	98	87	69
78	80	65	94	82	74	85	

Again, use a chi-square test with $\alpha = 0.05$ to test the equality of the three distributions by dividing the combined sample into three equal parts.

8.2-5. In the following contingency table, 1015 individuals are classified by gender and by whether they favor, oppose, or have no opinion on a complete ban on smoking in public places:

	Smoking in Public Places			
Gender	Favor	Oppose	No Opinion	Totals
Male	262	231	10	503
Female	302	205	5	512
Totals	564	436	15	1015

Test the null hypothesis that gender and opinion on smoking in public places are independent. Give the approximate p-value of this test.

8.2-6. A random survey of 100 students asked each student to select the most preferred form of recreational activity from five choices. Following are the results of the survey:

	Recreational Choice					
Gender	Basketball	Baseball Softball	Swimming	Jogging Running	Tennis	Totals
Male	21	5	9	12	13	60
Female	9	3	1	15	12	40
Totals	30	8	10	27	25	100

Test whether the choice is independent of the gender of the respondent. Approximate the p-value of the test. Would we reject the null hypothesis at $\alpha = 0.05$?

8.2-7. One hundred students in a random sample were classified as follows by gender and by the kind of instrument (including voice) that they played:

	Instrument					
Gender	Piano	Woodwind	Brass	String	Vocal	Totals
Male	4	11	15	6	9	45
Female	7	18	6	6	18	55
Totals	11	29	21	12	27	100

Test whether the selection of instrument is independent of the gender of the respondent. Approximate the p-value of this test.

8.2-8. A student who uses a certain college's recreational facilities was interested in whether there is a difference between the facilities used by men and those used by women. Use $\alpha = 0.05$ and the following data to test the null hypothesis that facility and gender are independent attributes:

	Facility		
Gender	Racquetball Court	Track	Totals
Male	51	30	81
Female	43	48	91
Totals	94	78	172

8.2-9. A survey of high school girls classified them by two attributes: whether or not they participated in sports and whether or not they had one or more older brothers. Use the following data to test the null hypothesis that these two attributes of classification are independent:

	Participated in Sports		
Older Brother(s)	Yes	No	Totals
Yes	12	8	20
No	13	27	40
Totals	25	35	60

Approximate the p-value of this test. Do we reject the null hypothesis if $\alpha = 0.05$?

8.2-10. A random sample of 50 women who were tested for cholesterol was classified according to age and cholesterol level and grouped into the following contingency table.

	Cholesterol Level			
Age	< 180	180–210	> 210	Totals
< 50	5	11	9	25
≥ 50	4	3	18	25
Totals	9	14	27	50

Test the null hypothesis H_0: Age and cholesterol level are independent attributes of classification. What is your conclusion if $\alpha = 0.01$?

8.2-11. Although high school grades and testing scores, such as SAT or ACT, can be used to predict first-year college grade point average (GPA), many educators claim that a more important factor influencing GPA is the living conditions of students. In particular, it is claimed that the roommate of the student will have a great influence on his or her grades. To test this hypothesis, suppose we selected at random 200 students and classified each according to the following two attributes:

(a) Ranking of the student's roommate on a scale from 1 to 5, with 1 denoting a person who was difficult to live with and discouraged scholarship, and 5 signifying a person who was congenial and encouraged scholarship.

(b) The student's first-year GPA.

Say this classification gives the following 5 × 4 contingency table:

	Grade-Point Average				
Rank of Roommate	Under 2.00	2.00–2.69	2.70–3.19	3.20–4.00	Totals
1	8	9	10	4	31
2	5	11	15	11	42
3	6	7	20	14	47
4	3	5	22	23	53
5	1	3	11	12	27
Totals	23	35	78	64	200

Compute the chi-square statistic used to test the independence of the two attributes, and compare it with the critical value associated with $\alpha = 0.05$.

8.2-12. (*How Americans Watch TV: A Nation of Grazers.*) A random sample of 395 people were classified by their age and by whether or not they change channels during programs when watching television. Use the following data to test the null hypothesis H_0: Changing channels and age are independent attributes:

	Age				
Change?	18–24	25–34	35–49	50–64	Totals
Yes	60	54	46	41	201
No	40	44	53	57	194
Totals	100	98	99	98	395

(a) Give a significance level α for which H_0 is rejected.

(b) Give a value of the significance level α for which H_0 is not rejected.

8.2-13. A study was conducted to determine the media credibility for reporting news. Those surveyed were asked to give their age, gender, education, and the most credible medium. The results of the survey are as follows:

	Most Credible Medium			
Age	Newspaper	Television	Radio	Totals
Under 35	30	68	10	108
35–54	61	79	20	160
Over 54	98	43	21	162
Totals	189	190	51	430

	Most Credible Medium			
Gender	Newspaper	Television	Radio	Totals
Male	92	108	19	219
Female	97	81	32	210
Totals	189	189	51	429

	Most Credible Medium			
Education	Newspaper	Television	Radio	Totals
Grade School	45	22	6	73
High School	94	115	30	239
College	49	52	13	114
Totals	188	189	49	426

(a) Test whether media credibility and age are independent.

(b) Test whether media credibility and gender are independent.

(c) Test whether media credibility and education are independent.

(d) Give the approximate p-value for each test.

8.2-14. In a psychology experiment, 140 students were divided into majors emphasizing left-hemisphere brain skills (e.g., philosophy, physics, and mathematics) and majors emphasizing right-hemisphere skills (e.g., art, music, theater, and dance). They were also classified into one of three groups on the basis of hand posture (right noninverted, left inverted, and left noninverted). The data are as follows:

	LH	RH
RN	89	29
LI	5	4
LN	5	8

Do these data show sufficient evidence to reject the claim that the choice of college major is independent of hand posture? Let $\alpha = 0.025$.

8.2-15. Ledolter and Hogg (see references) report the starting salaries of $n = 200$ engineers classified as being in the lower 25% (A_1), second 25% (A_2), third 25% (A_3), and upper 25% (A_4) of their class. In addition, these 200 engineers were classified according to the color of their eyes. Here are the summarized results:

	Salary				
Eyes	A_1	A_2	A_3	A_4	Totals
Blue	22	17	21	20	80
Brown	14	20	20	16	70
Other	14	13	9	14	50
Totals	50	50	50	50	200

Are color of eyes and starting salary independent attributes. Use $\alpha = 0.05$.

8.2-16. In the Michigan Daily Lottery, one three-digit integer is generated six days a week. Twenty weeks of lottery numbers have been classified as follows by the day of the week and the magnitude of the number:

	Magnitude of Number		
Days	000–499	500–999	Totals
Monday and Tuesday	22	18	40
Wednesday and Thursday	19	21	40
Friday and Saturday	13	27	40
Totals	54	66	120

Test whether these attributes of classification are independent at the 10% significance level.

8.3 ORDER STATISTICS

Order statistics are the observations of the random sample, arranged, or ordered, in magnitude from the smallest to the largest. In recent years, the importance of order statistics has increased owing to the more frequent use of nonparametric inferences and robust procedures. However, order statistics have always been prominent because, among other things, they are needed to determine rather simple statistics, such as the sample median, the sample range, and the empirical distribution function. Recall that in Section 3.2 we discussed observed order statistics in connection with descriptive and exploratory statistical methods. We will consider certain interesting aspects about their distributions in this section.

In most of our discussions about order statistics, we will assume that the n independent observations come from a continuous-type distribution. This means, among other things, that the probability of any two observations being equal is zero. That is, the probability is 1 that the observations can be ordered from smallest to largest without having two equal values. Of course, in practice, we do frequently observe *ties*; but if the probability of a tie is small, the distribution theory that follows will hold approximately. Thus, in the discussion here, we are assuming that the probability of a tie is zero.

EXAMPLE 8.3-1 The values $x_1 = 0.62$, $x_2 = 0.98$, $x_3 = 0.31$, $x_4 = 0.81$, and $x_5 = 0.53$ are the $n = 5$ observed values of five independent trials of an experiment with p.d.f. $f(x) = 2x$, $0 < x < 1$. The observed order statistics are

$$y_1 = 0.31 < y_2 = 0.53 < y_3 = 0.62 < y_4 = 0.81 < y_5 = 0.98.$$

Recall that the middle observation in the ordered arrangement, here $y_3 = 0.62$, is called the *sample median* and the difference of the largest and the smallest, here

$$y_5 - y_1 = 0.98 - 0.31 = 0.67,$$

is called the *sample range*. ■

If $X_1, X_2, \ldots, X_n$ are observations of a random sample of size n from a continuous-type distribution, we let the random variables

$$Y_1 < Y_2 < \cdots < Y_n$$

denote the order statistics of that sample. That is,

$$\begin{aligned} Y_1 &= \text{smallest of } X_1, X_2, \ldots, X_n, \\ Y_2 &= \text{second smallest of } X_1, X_2, \ldots, X_n, \\ &\vdots \\ Y_n &= \text{largest of } X_1, X_2, \ldots, X_n. \end{aligned}$$

There is a very simple procedure for determining the distribution function of the rth order statistic, Y_r. This procedure depends on the binomial distribution and is illustrated in Example 8.3-2.

EXAMPLE 8.3-2 Let $Y_1 < Y_2 < Y_3 < Y_4 < Y_5$ be the order statistics associated with n independent observations X_1, X_2, X_3, X_4, X_5, each from the distribution with p.d.f. $f(x) = 2x$, $0 < x < 1$. Consider $P(Y_4 < 1/2)$. For the event $\{Y_4 < 1/2\}$ to occur, at least four of the random variables X_1, X_2, X_3, X_4, X_5 must be less than $1/2$, because Y_4 is the fourth smallest among the five observations. Thus, if the event $\{X_i < 1/2\}$, $i = 1, 2, \ldots, 5$, is called "success," we must have at least four successes in the five mutually independent trials, each of which has probability of success

$$P\left(X_i \le \frac{1}{2}\right) = \int_0^{1/2} 2x\,dx = \left(\frac{1}{2}\right)^2 = \frac{1}{4}.$$

Hence,

$$P\left(Y_4 \le \frac{1}{2}\right) = \binom{5}{4}\left(\frac{1}{4}\right)^4\left(\frac{3}{4}\right) + \left(\frac{1}{4}\right)^5 = 0.0156.$$

In general, if $0 < y < 1$, then the distribution function of Y_4 is

$$G(y) = P(Y_4 < y) = \binom{5}{4}(y^2)^4(1 - y^2) + (y^2)^5,$$

since this represents the probability of at least four "successes" in five independent trials, each of which has probability of success

$$P(X_i < y) = \int_0^y 2x\,dx = y^2.$$

For $0 < y < 1$, the p.d.f. of Y_4 is therefore

$$g(y) = G'(y) = \binom{5}{4}4(y^2)^3(2y)(1 - y^2) + \binom{5}{4}(y^2)^4(-2y) + 5(y^2)^4(2y)$$
$$= \frac{5!}{3!\,1!}(y^2)^3(1 - y^2)(2y), \qquad 0 < y < 1.$$

Note that in this example the distribution function of each X is $F(x) = x^2$ when $0 < x < 1$. Thus,

$$g(y) = \frac{5!}{3!\,1!}[F(y)]^3[1 - F(y)]f(y), \qquad 0 < y < 1. \qquad \blacksquare$$

The preceding example should make the following generalization easier to read: Let $Y_1 < Y_2 < \cdots < Y_n$ be the order statistics of n independent observations from a distribution of the continuous type with distribution function $F(x)$ and p.d.f. $F'(x) = f(x)$, where $0 < F(x) < 1$ for $a < x < b$ and $F(a) = 0$, $F(b) = 1$. (It is possible that $a = -\infty$ and/or $b = +\infty$.) The event that the rth order statistic Y_r is at most y, $\{Y_r \le y\}$, can occur if and only if at least r of the n observations are less than or equal to y. That is, here the probability of "success" on each trial is $F(y)$, and we must have at least r successes. Thus,

$$G_r(y) = P(Y_r \le y) = \sum_{k=r}^{n}\binom{n}{k}[F(y)]^k[1 - F(y)]^{n-k}.$$

Rewriting this slightly, we have

$$G_r(y) = \sum_{k=r}^{n-1}\binom{n}{k}[F(y)]^k[1 - F(y)]^{n-k} + [F(y)]^n.$$

Hence, the p.d.f. of Y_r is

$$\begin{aligned} g_r(y) = G_r'(y) = {} & \sum_{k=r}^{n-1}\binom{n}{k}(k)[F(y)]^{k-1}f(y)[1 - F(y)]^{n-k} \\ & + \sum_{k=r}^{n-1}\binom{n}{k}[F(y)]^k(n - k)[1 - F(y)]^{n-k-1}[-f(y)] \\ & + n[F(y)]^{n-1}f(y). \end{aligned} \qquad (8.3\text{-}1)$$

However, since

$$\binom{n}{k}k = \frac{n!}{(k - 1)!\,(n - k)!} \quad \text{and} \quad \binom{n}{k}(n - k) = \frac{n!}{k!\,(n - k - 1)!},$$

it follows that the p.d.f. of Y_r is

$$g_r(y) = \frac{n!}{(r - 1)!\,(n - r)!}[F(y)]^{r-1}[1 - F(y)]^{n-r}f(y), \qquad a < y < b,$$

which is the first term of the first summation in $g_r(y) = G_r'(y)$, Equation 8.3-1. The remaining terms in $g_r(y) = G_r'(y)$ sum to zero because the second term of the first summation (when $k = r + 1$) equals the negative of the first term in the second summation (when $k = r$), and so on. Finally, the last term of the second summation equals the negative of $n[F(y)]^{n-1}f(y)$. To see this clearly, the student is urged to write out a number of terms in these summations. (See Exercise 8.3-4.)

It is worth noting that the p.d.f. of the smallest order statistic is

$$g_1(y) = n[1 - F(y)]^{n-1}f(y), \qquad a < y < b,$$

and the p.d.f. of the largest order statistic is

$$g_n(y) = n[F(y)]^{n-1}f(y), \qquad a < y < b.$$

REMARK There is one quite satisfactory way to construct heuristically the expression for the p.d.f. of Y_r. To do this, we must recall the multinomial probability and then consider the probability element $g_r(y)(\Delta y)$ of Y_r. If the length Δy is *very* small, $g_r(y)(\Delta y)$ represents approximately the probability

$$P(y < Y_r \le y + \Delta y).$$

Thus, we want the probability, $g_r(y)(\Delta y)$, that $(r - 1)$ items fall less than y, that $(n - r)$ items are greater than $y + \Delta y$, and that one item falls between y and $y + \Delta y$. Recall that the probabilities on a single trial are

$$\begin{aligned} P(X \le y) &= F(y), \\ P(X > y + \Delta y) &= 1 - F(y + \Delta y) \approx 1 - F(y), \\ P(y < X \le y + \Delta y) &\approx f(y)(\Delta y). \end{aligned}$$

Thus, the multinomial probability is approximately

$$g_r(y)(\Delta y) = \frac{n!}{(r - 1)!\,1!\,(n - r)!}[F(y)]^{r-1}[1 - F(y)]^{n-r}[f(y)(\Delta y)].$$

If we divide both sides by the length Δy, the formula for $g_r(y)$ results. ■

EXAMPLE 8.3-3 Returning to Example 8.3-2, we shall now graph the p.d.f.s of the order statistics $Y_1 < Y_2 < Y_3 < Y_4 < Y_5$ when sampling from a distribution with p.d.f. $f(x) = 2x$, $0 < x < 1$. These graphs are given in Figure 8.3-1 on the next page. The respective p.d.f.'s and their means are as follows:

$$\begin{aligned} g_1(y) &= 10y(1 - y^2)^4; & \mu_1 &= \frac{256}{693}, \\ g_2(y) &= 40y^3(1 - y^2)^3; & \mu_2 &= \frac{128}{231}, \\ g_3(y) &= 60y^5(1 - y^2)^2; & \mu_3 &= \frac{160}{231}, \\ g_4(y) &= 40y^7(1 - y^2); & \mu_4 &= \frac{80}{99}, \\ g_5(y) &= 10y^9; & \mu_5 &= \frac{10}{11}. \end{aligned}$$

■

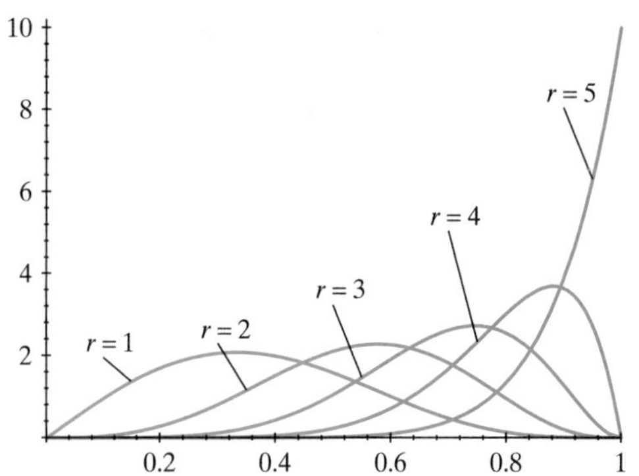

FIGURE 8.3-1: p.d.f.'s of order statistics, $f(x) = 2x, 0 < x < 1$

EXAMPLE 8.3-4 Let $Y_1 < Y_2 < Y_3 < Y_4$ be the order statistics of a random sample X_1, X_2, X_3, X_4 from a uniform distribution with p.d.f. $f(x; \theta) = 1/\theta$, $0 < x \le \theta$. The likelihood function is

$$f(x; \theta) = \left(\frac{1}{\theta}\right)^4, \qquad 0 < x_i \le \theta, \; i = 1, 2, 3, 4,$$

and equals zero if $\theta < x_i$. To maximize $L(\theta)$, we must make θ as small as possible; hence,

$$\widehat{\theta} = \max(X_i) = Y_4$$

because θ cannot be less than any X_i. Since $F(x; \theta) = x/\theta$, $0 < x \le \theta$, the p.d.f. of Y_4 is

$$g_4(y_4) = \frac{4!}{3!1!}\left(\frac{y_4}{\theta}\right)^3\left(\frac{1}{\theta}\right) = 4\frac{y_4^3}{\theta^4}, \qquad 0 < y_4 \le \theta.$$

Accordingly,

$$E(Y_4) = \int_0^\theta y_4 \cdot 4\frac{y_4^3}{\theta^4}\, dy_4 = \frac{4}{5}\theta$$

and Y_4 is a biased estimator of θ. However, $5Y_4/4$ is unbiased. So, since, with $0 < c < 1$, we have

$$\int_{c\theta}^{\theta} 4\, y_4^3/\theta^4\, dy_4 = 1 - c^4,$$

it follows that

$$1 - c^4 = P(c\theta < Y_4 < \theta) = P(Y_4 < \theta < Y_4/c).$$

Then, with an observed Y_4 of y_4, the interval from y_4 to y_4/c would be a $100(1 - c^4)$ percent confidence interval for θ. Say $c = (0.05)^{1/4} = 0.47$; then the interval from y_4 to $2.11y_4$ is a 95% confidence interval for θ. ■

Recall that in Theorem 5.1-2 we proved that if X has a distribution function $F(x)$ of the continuous type, then $F(X)$ has a uniform distribution on the interval from 0 to 1. If $Y_1 < Y_2 < \cdots < Y_n$ are the order statistics of n independent observations $X_1, X_2, \ldots, X_n$, then

$$F(Y_1) < F(Y_2) < \cdots < F(Y_n),$$

because F is a nondecreasing function and the probability of an equality is again zero. Note that this ordering could be looked upon as an ordering of the mutually independent random variables $F(X_1), F(X_2), \ldots, F(X_n)$, each of which is $U(0,1)$. That is,

$$W_1 = F(Y_1) < W_2 = F(Y_2) < \cdots < W_n = F(Y_n)$$

can be thought of as the order statistics of n independent observations from that uniform distribution. Since the distribution function of $U(0,1)$ is $G(w) = w$, $0 < w < 1$, the p.d.f. of the rth order statistic, $W_r = F(Y_r)$, is

$$h_r(w) = \frac{n!}{(r-1)!\,(n-r)!} w^{r-1}(1-w)^{n-r}, \qquad 0 < w < 1.$$

Of course, the mean, $E(W_r) = E[F(Y_r)]$ of $W_r = F(Y_r)$, is given by the integral

$$E(W_r) = \int_0^1 w \frac{n!}{(r-1)!\,(n-r)!} w^{r-1}(1-w)^{n-r}\,dw.$$

This integral can be evaluated by integrating by parts several times, but it is easier to obtain the answer if we rewrite the integration as follows:

$$E(W_r) = \left(\frac{r}{n+1}\right)\int_0^1 \frac{(n+1)!}{r!\,(n-r)!} w^r(1-w)^{n-r}\,dw.$$

The integrand in this last expression can be thought of as the p.d.f. of the $(r+1)$st order statistic of $n+1$ independent observations from a $U(0,1)$ distribution. This is a beta p.d.f. with $\alpha = r+1$ and $\beta = n-r+1$; hence, the integral must equal 1, and it follows that

$$E(W_r) = \frac{r}{n+1}, \qquad r = 1, 2, \ldots, n.$$

There is an extremely interesting interpretation of $W_r = F(Y_r)$. Note that $F(Y_r)$ is the cumulated probability up to and including Y_r or, equivalently, the area under $f(x) = F'(x)$ but less than Y_r. Consequently, $F(Y_r)$ can be treated as a random area. Since $F(Y_{r-1})$ is also a random area, $F(Y_r) - F(Y_{r-1})$ is the random area under $f(x)$ between Y_{r-1} and Y_r. The expected value of the random area between any two adjacent order statistics is then

$$\begin{aligned} E[F(Y_r) - F(Y_{r-1})] &= E[F(Y_r)] - E[F(Y_{r-1})] \\ &= \frac{r}{n+1} - \frac{r-1}{n+1} = \frac{1}{n+1}. \end{aligned}$$

Also, it is easy to show (see Exercise 8.3-6) that

$$E[F(Y_1)] = \frac{1}{n+1} \quad \text{and} \quad E[1 - F(Y_n)] = \frac{1}{n+1}.$$

That is, the order statistics $Y_1 < Y_2 < \cdots < Y_n$ partition the support of X into $n+1$ parts and thus create $n+1$ areas under $f(x)$ and above the x-axis. On the average, each of the $n+1$ areas equals $1/(n+1)$.

If we recall that the $(100p)$th percentile π_p is such that the area under $f(x)$ to the left of π_p is p, then the preceding discussion suggests that we let Y_r be an estimator of π_p, where $p = r/(n+1)$. For this reason, we define the **(100*p*)th percentile of the sample** as Y_r, where $r = (n+1)p$. In case $(n+1)p$ is not an integer, we use a weighted average (or an average) of the two adjacent order statistics Y_r and Y_{r+1}, where r is the greatest integer $\lfloor (n+1)p \rfloor$ in $(n+1)p$. In particular, the sample median is

$$\widetilde{m} = \begin{cases} Y_{(n+1)/2}, & \text{when } n \text{ is odd,} \\ \dfrac{Y_{n/2} + Y_{(n/2)+1}}{2}, & \text{when } n \text{ is even.} \end{cases}$$

EXAMPLE 8.3-5 Let X equal the weight of soap in a "1000-gram" bottle. A random sample of $n = 12$ observations of X yielded the following weights, which have been ordered:

1013	1019	1021	1024	1026	1028
1033	1035	1039	1040	1043	1047

Since $n = 12$ is even, the sample median is

$$\widetilde{m} = \frac{y_6 + y_7}{2} = \frac{1028 + 1033}{2} = 1030.5.$$

The location of the 25th percentile (or first quartile) is

$$(n+1)(0.25) = (12+1)(0.25) = 3.25.$$

Thus, using a weighted average, we find that the first quartile is

$$\begin{aligned} \widetilde{q}_1 = y_3 + (0.25)(y_4 - y_3) &= (0.75)y_3 + (0.25)y_4 \\ &= (0.75)(1021) + (0.25)(1024) = 1021.75. \end{aligned}$$

Similarly, the 75th percentile (or third quartile) is

$$\begin{aligned} \widetilde{q}_3 = y_9 + (0.75)(y_{10} - y_9) &= (0.25)y_9 + (0.75)y_{10} \\ &= (0.25)(1039) + (0.75)(1040) = 1039.75, \end{aligned}$$

because $(12+1)(0.75) = 9.75$. Since $(12+1)(0.60) = 7.8$, the 60th percentile is

$$\widetilde{\pi}_{0.60} = (0.2)y_7 + (0.8)y_8 = (0.2)(1033) + (0.8)(1035) = 1034.6.$$ ■

EXERCISES

8.3-1. Some biology students were interested in analyzing the amount of time that bees spend gathering nectar in flower patches. Thirty-nine bees visited a high-density flower patch and spent the following times (in seconds) gathering nectar:

235	210	95	146	195	840	185	610	680	990
146	404	119	47	9	4	10	169	270	95
329	151	211	127	154	35	225	140	158	116
46	113	149	420	120	45	10	18	105	

(a) Find the order statistics.

(b) Find the median and 80th percentile of the sample.

(c) Determine the first and third quartiles (i.e., 25th and 75th percentiles) of the sample.

8.3-2. Let X equal the forced vital capacity (the volume of air a person can expel from his or her lungs) of a male freshman. Seventeen observations of X, which have been ordered, are

3.7	3.8	4.0	4.3	4.7	4.8	4.9	5.0	
5.2	5.4	5.6	5.6	5.6	5.7	6.2	6.8	7.6

(a) Find the median, the first quartile, and the third quartile.

(b) Find the 35th and 65th percentiles.

8.3-3. Let $Y_1 < Y_2 < Y_3 < Y_4 < Y_5$ be the order statistics of five independent observations from an exponential distribution that has a mean of $\theta = 3$.

(a) Find the p.d.f. of the sample median Y_3.

(b) Compute the probability that Y_4 is less than 5.

(c) Determine $P(1 < Y_1)$.

8.3-4. In the expression for $g_r(y) = G'_r(y)$ in Equation 8.3-1, let $n = 6$, and $r = 3$, and write out the summations, showing that the "telescoping" suggested in the text is achieved.

8.3-5. Let $Y_1 < Y_2 < \cdots < Y_8$ be the order statistics of eight independent observations from a continuous-type distribution with 70th percentile $\pi_{0.7} = 27.3$.

(a) Determine $P(Y_7 < 27.3)$.

(b) Find $P(Y_5 < 27.3 < Y_8)$.

8.3-6. Let $W_1 < W_2 < \cdots < W_n$ be the order statistics of n independent observations from a $U(0,1)$ distribution.

(a) Find the p.d.f. of W_1 and that of W_n.

(b) Use the results of (a) to verify that $E(W_1) = 1/(n+1)$ and $E(W_n) = n/(n+1)$.

(c) Show that the p.d.f. of W_r is beta.

8.3-7. Let $Y_1 < Y_2 < \cdots < Y_{19}$ be the order statistics of $n = 19$ independent observations from the exponential distribution with mean θ.

(a) What is the p.d.f. of Y_1?

(b) Using integration, find the value of $E[F(Y_1)]$, where F is the distribution function of the exponential distribution.

8.3-8. Let $W_1 < W_2 < \cdots < W_n$ be the order statistics of n independent observations from a $U(0,1)$ distribution.

(a) Show that $E(W_r^2) = \dfrac{r(r+1)}{(n+1)(n+2)}$, using a technique similar to that used in determining that $E(W_r) = r/(n+1)$.

(b) Find the variance of W_r.

8.3-9. Let $X_1, X_2, \ldots, X_{10}$ be a random sample of size $n = 10$ from a distribution with p.d.f. $f(x;\theta) = e^{-(x-\theta)}$, $\theta \le x < \infty$.

(a) Show that $Y_1 = \min(X_i)$ is the maximum likelihood estimator of θ.

(b) Find the p.d.f. of Y_1 and show that $E(Y_1) = \theta + 1/10$, so that $Y_1 - 1/10$ is an unbiased estimator of θ.

(c) Compute $P(\theta \le Y_1 \le \theta + c)$ and use the result to construct a 95% confidence interval for θ.

8.3-10. Let $Y_1 < Y_2 < \cdots < Y_n$ be the order statistics of a random sample of size n from an exponential distribution with mean θ. Let $1 < m < n$. Then

$$W = \left[\frac{2}{\theta}\right]\left[\sum_{i=1}^{m} Y_i + (n-m)Y_m\right]$$

has a chi-square distribution with $2m$ degrees of freedom. (This statistic could be used in a life-testing experiment in which only the first m "deaths" are observed.)

(a) Use W to construct a $100(1-\alpha)\%$ confidence interval for θ.

(b) The following observed order statistics were simulated from an exponential distribution with $\theta = 10$:

0.043 2.836 4.962 5.297 6.730 7.338 8.888 13.259 20.558 36.852

Use the first (i) four, (ii) five, (iii) six, and (iv) seven order statistics to construct 90% confidence intervals for θ. Describe these intervals.

REMARK It is possible to simulate only the first m out of n order statistics. [See Karian and Tanis (Questions and Comments 10.1-2) or Lurie and Hartley in the references.] ■

8.3-11. Let $Y_1 < Y_2 < \cdots < Y_n$ be the order statistics of a random sample of size n from a distribution with p.d.f. $f(x) = e^{-x}, 0 < x < \infty$.

(a) Find the p.d.f. of Y_r.

(b) Determine the p.d.f. of $U = e^{-Y_r}$.

8.3-12. Use the heuristic argument to show that the joint p.d.f. of the two order statistics $Y_i < Y_j$ is

$$g(y_i, y_j) = \frac{n!}{(i-1)!(j-i-1)!(n-j)!} \times [F(y_i)]^{i-1}[F(y_j) - F(y_i)]^{j-i-1} \times [1 - F(y_j)]^{n-j} f(y_i) f(y_j),$$
$$-\infty < y_i < y_j < \infty.$$

8.3-13. Use the result of Exercise 8.3-12.

(a) Find the joint p.d.f. of Y_1 and Y_n, the first and the nth order statistics of a random sample of size n from the $U(0,1)$ distribution.

(b) Find the joint and the marginal p.d.f.s of $W_1 = Y_1/Y_n$ and $W_2 = Y_n$.

(c) Are W_1 and W_2 independent?

(d) Use simulation to confirm your theoretical results.

8.3-14. Let $Y_1 < Y_2 < Y_3$ be the order statistics of a random sample X_1, X_2, X_3 of size 3 from the uniform distribution $U(\theta - 1/2, \theta + 1/2)$. That is, $Y_1 = \min\{X_1, X_2, X_3\}$, $Y_2 = \text{median}\{X_1, X_2, X_3\}$, and $Y_3 = \max\{X_1, X_2, X_3\}$. Three possible estimators of θ are the sample mean,

$$W_1 = \overline{X} = \frac{1}{3}\sum_{i=1}^{3} X_i,$$

the sample median, $W_2 = Y_2$, and the midrange, $W_3 = (Y_1 + Y_3)/2$.

(a) Simulate 100 samples of size 3 from $U(\theta - 1/2, \theta + 1/2)$ for a particular value of θ—for example, $\theta = 1/2$. For each sample, calculate the values of W_1, W_2, and W_3.

(b) Compare the values of the sample means and sample variances of the 100 observations of each of W_1, W_2, and W_3. Which of these statistics seems to be the best estimator of θ?

(c) Verify that $E(W_1) = E(W_2) = E(W_3) = 1/2$ and that $\text{Var}(W_1) = 1/36$, $\text{Var}(W_2) = 1/20$, and $\text{Var}(W_3) = 1/40$ when $\theta = 1/2$.

8.4 DISTRIBUTION-FREE CONFIDENCE INTERVALS FOR PERCENTILES

In Section 8.3, we defined sample percentiles in terms of order statistics and noted that sample percentiles can be used to estimate corresponding distribution percentiles. In this section, we use order statistics to construct confidence intervals for unknown distribution percentiles. Since little is assumed about the underlying distribution (except that it is of the continuous type) in the construction of these confidence intervals, they are often called **distribution-free confidence intervals**.

If $Y_1 < Y_2 < Y_3 < Y_4 < Y_5$ are the order statistics of a random sample of size $n = 5$ from a continuous-type distribution, then the sample median Y_3 could be thought of as an estimator of the distribution median $\pi_{0.5}$. We shall let $m = \pi_{0.5}$. We could simply use the sample median Y_3 as an estimator of the distribution median m. However, we are certain that all of us recognize that, with only a sample of size 5, we would be quite lucky if the observed $Y_3 = y_3$ were very close to m. Thus, we now describe how a confidence interval can be constructed for m.

Instead of simply using Y_3 as an estimator of m, let us also compute the probability that the random interval (Y_1, Y_5) includes m. That is, let us determine $P(Y_1 < m < Y_5)$. Doing this is easy if we say that we have success if an individual observation—say, X—is less than m; then the probability of success on one of the independent trials is $P(X < m) = 0.5$. In order for the first order statistic Y_1 to be less than m and the last order statistic Y_5 to be greater than m, we must have at least one success, but not five successes. That is,

$$\begin{aligned} P(Y_1 < m < Y_5) &= \sum_{k=1}^{4} \binom{5}{k} \left(\frac{1}{2}\right)^k \left(\frac{1}{2}\right)^{5-k} \\ &= 1 - \left(\frac{1}{2}\right)^5 - \left(\frac{1}{2}\right)^5 = \frac{15}{16}. \end{aligned}$$

So the probability that the random interval (Y_1, Y_5) includes m is $15/16 \approx 0.94$. Suppose now that this random sample is actually taken and the order statistics are observed to equal $y_1 < y_2 < y_3 < y_4 < y_5$, respectively. Then (y_1, y_5) is a 94% confidence interval for m.

It is interesting to note what happens as the sample size increases. Let $Y_1 < Y_2 < \cdots < Y_n$ be the order statistics of a random sample of size n from a distribution of the continuous type. Then $P(Y_1 < m < Y_n)$ is the probability that there is at least one "success" but not n successes, where the probability of success on each trial is

$P(X < m) = 0.5$. Consequently,

$$P(Y_1 < m < Y_n) = \sum_{k=1}^{n-1} \binom{n}{k} \left(\frac{1}{2}\right)^k \left(\frac{1}{2}\right)^{n-k}$$
$$= 1 - \left(\frac{1}{2}\right)^n - \left(\frac{1}{2}\right)^n = 1 - \left(\frac{1}{2}\right)^{n-1}.$$

This probability increases as n increases, so that the corresponding confidence interval (y_1, y_n) would have the very large confidence coefficient $1 - (1/2)^{n-1}$. Unfortunately, the interval (y_1, y_n) tends to get wider as n increases; thus, we are not "pinning down" m very well. However, if we used the interval (y_2, y_{n-1}) or (y_3, y_{n-2}), we would obtain shorter intervals, but also smaller confidence coefficients. Let us investigate this possibility further.

With the order statistics $Y_1 < Y_2 < \cdots < Y_n$ associated with a random sample of size n from a continuous-type distribution, consider $P(Y_i < m < Y_j)$, where $i < j$. For example, we might want

$$P(Y_2 < m < Y_{n-1}) \quad \text{or} \quad P(Y_3 < m < Y_{n-2}).$$

On each of the n independent trials, we say that we have success if that X is less than m; thus, the probability of success on each trial is $P(X < m) = 0.5$. Consequently, to have the ith order statistic Y_i less than m and the jth order statistic greater than m, we must have at least i successes, but fewer than j successes (or else $Y_j < m$). That is,

$$P(Y_i < m < Y_j) = \sum_{k=i}^{j-1} \binom{n}{k} \left(\frac{1}{2}\right)^k \left(\frac{1}{2}\right)^{n-k} = 1 - \alpha.$$

For particular values of n, i, and j, this probability—say, $1 - \alpha$—which is the sum of probabilities from a binomial distribution, can be calculated directly or approximated by an area under the normal p.d.f., provided that n is large enough. The observed interval (y_i, y_j) could then serve as a $100(1 - a)\%$ confidence interval for the unknown distribution median.

EXAMPLE 8.4-1 The lengths in centimeters of $n = 9$ fish of a particular species (*nezumia*) captured off the New England coast were 32.5, 27.6, 29.3, 30.1, 15.5, 21.7, 22.8, 21.2, and 19.0. Thus, the observed order statistics are

$$15.5 < 19.0 < 21.2 < 21.7 < 22.8 < 27.6 < 29.3 < 30.1 < 32.5.$$

Before the sample is drawn, we know that

$$P(Y_2 < m < Y_8) = \sum_{k=2}^{7} \binom{9}{k} \left(\frac{1}{2}\right)^k \left(\frac{1}{2}\right)^{9-k}$$
$$= 0.9805 - 0.0195 = 0.9610,$$

from Table II in the appendix. Thus, the confidence interval $(y_2 = 19.0, y_8 = 30.1)$ for m, the median of the lengths of all fish of this species, has a 96.1% confidence coefficient. ■

So that the student need not compute many of these probabilities, Table 8.4-1 on the next page lists the necessary information for constructing confidence intervals

TABLE 8.4-1: Information for Confidence Intervals for m

n	$(i, n+1-i)$	$P(Y_i < m < Y_{n+1-i})$	n	$(i, n+1-i)$	$P(Y_i < m < Y_{n+1-i})$
5	(1,5)	0.9376	13	(3,11)	0.9776
6	(1,6)	0.9688	14	(4,11)	0.9426
7	(1,7)	0.9844	15	(4,12)	0.9648
8	(2,7)	0.9296	16	(5,12)	0.9232
9	(2,8)	0.9610	17	(5,13)	0.9510
10	(2,9)	0.9786	18	(5,14)	0.9692
11	(3,9)	0.9346	19	(6,14)	0.9364
12	(3,10)	0.9614	20	(6,15)	0.9586

of the form (y_i, y_{n+1-i}) for the unknown m for sample sizes $n = 5, 6, \cdots, 20$. The subscript i is selected so that the confidence coefficient $P(Y_i < m < Y_{n+1-i})$ is greater than 90% and as close to 95% as possible.

For sample sizes larger than 20, we approximate those binomial probabilities with areas under the normal curve. To illustrate how good these approximations are, we compute the probability corresponding to $n = 16$ in Table 8.4-1. Here, using Table II, we have

$$\begin{aligned} 1 - \alpha = P(Y_5 < m < Y_{12}) &= \sum_{k=5}^{11} \binom{16}{k} \left(\frac{1}{2}\right)^k \left(\frac{1}{2}\right)^{16-k} \\ &= P(W = 5, 6, \ldots, 11) \\ &= 0.9616 - 0.0384 = 0.9232, \end{aligned}$$

where W is $b(16, 1/2)$. The normal approximation gives

$$1 - \alpha = P(4.5 < W < 11.5) = P\left(\frac{4.5 - 8}{2} < \frac{W - 8}{2} < \frac{11.5 - 8}{2}\right),$$

because W has mean $np = 8$ and variance $np(1 - p) = 4$. The standardized variable $Z = (W - 8)/2$ has an approximate normal distribution. Thus,

$$\begin{aligned} 1 - \alpha \approx \Phi\left(\frac{3.5}{2}\right) - \Phi\left(\frac{-3.5}{2}\right) &= \Phi(1.75) - \Phi(-1.75) \\ &= 0.9599 - 0.0401 = 0.9198. \end{aligned}$$

This value compares very favorably with the probability 0.9232 recorded in Table 8.4-1. (Note that Minitab or some other computer program can also be used.)

The argument used to find a confidence interval for the median m of a distribution of the continuous type can be applied to any percentile π_p. In this case, we say that we have success on a single trial if that X is less than π_p. Thus, the probability of success on each of the independent trials is $P(X < \pi_p) = p$. Accordingly, with $i < j$, $1 - \alpha = P(Y_i < \pi_p < Y_j)$ is the probability that we have at least i successes, but fewer than j successes. Hence,

$$1 - \alpha = P(Y_i < \pi_p < Y_j) = \sum_{k=i}^{j-1} \binom{n}{k} p^k (1 - p)^{n-k}.$$

Once the sample is observed and the order statistics determined, the known interval (y_i, y_j) could serve as a $100(1 - \alpha)\%$ confidence interval for the unknown distribution percentile π_p.

EXAMPLE 8.4-2 Let the following numbers represent the order statistics of the $n = 27$ observations obtained in a random sample from a certain population of incomes (measured in hundreds of dollars):

261	280	292	305	329	364
269	283	293	313	341	391
271	284	296	321	343	417
274	286	300	322	356	476
279	287	304			

Say we are interested in estimating the 25th percentile, $\pi_{0.25}$, of the population. Since $(n + 1)p = 28(1/4) = 7$, the seventh order statistic, namely, $y_7 = 283$, would be a point estimate of $\pi_{0.25}$. To find a confidence interval for $\pi_{0.25}$, let us move down and up a few order statistics from y_7—say, to y_4 and y_{10}. What is the confidence coefficient associated with the interval (y_4, y_{10})? Before the sample was drawn, we had

$$1 - \alpha = P(Y_4 < \pi_{0.25} < Y_{10}) = \sum_{k=4}^{9} \binom{27}{k} (0.25)^k (0.75)^{27-k} = 0.8201,$$

from Minitab. For the normal approximation, we use W, which is $b(27, 1/4)$ with mean $27/4 = 6.75$ and variance $81/16$. Hence,

$$\begin{aligned} 1 - \alpha = P(4 \le W \le 9) &= P(3.5 < W < 9.5) \\ &\approx \Phi\left(\frac{9.5 - 6.75}{9/4}\right) - \Phi\left(\frac{3.5 - 6.75}{9/4}\right) \\ &= \Phi\left(\frac{11}{9}\right) - \Phi\left(-\frac{13}{9}\right) = 0.8149. \end{aligned}$$

Thus, $(y_4 = 274, y_{10} = 287)$ is an 82.01% (or approximate 81.49%) confidence interval for $\pi_{0.25}$. Note that we could choose other intervals, such as $(y_3 = 271, y_{11} = 292)$, and these would have different confidence coefficients. The persons involved in the study must select the desired confidence coefficient, and then the appropriate order statistics are taken, usually quite symmetrically about the $(n + 1)p$th order statistic. ■

When the number of observations is large, it is important to be able to determine the order statistics rather easily. As illustrated in the next example, a stem-and-leaf diagram, as introduced in Section 3.2, can be helpful in determining the needed order statistics.

EXAMPLE 8.4-3 The measurements of butterfat produced by $n = 90$ cows during a 305-day milk production period following their first calf are summarized in Table 8.4-2, in which each leaf consists of two digits. From this display, it is quite easy to see that $y_8 = 392$. It takes a little more work to show that $y_{38} = 494$ and $y_{53} = 526$ creates an interval

TABLE 8.4-2: Ordered Stem-and-Leaf Diagram of Butterfat Production

Stems	Leaves	Depths
2s	74	1
2•		1
3*		1
3t	27 39	3
3f	45 50	5
3s		5
3•	80 88 92 94 95	10
4*	17 18	12
4t	21 22 27 34 37 39	18
4f	44 52 53 53 57 58	24
4s	60 64 66 70 70 72 75 78	32
4•	81 86 89 91 92 94 96 97 99	41
5*	00 00 01 02 05 09 10 13 13 16	(10)
5t	24 26 31 32 32 37 37 39	39
5f	40 41 44 55	31
5s	61 70 73 74	27
5•	83 83 86 93 99	23
6*	07 08 11 12 13 17 18 19	18
6t	27 28 35 37	10
6f	43 43 45	6
6s	72	3
6•	91 96	2

$(494, 526)$ which serves as a confidence interval for the unknown median m of all butterfat production for the given breed of cows. Its confidence coefficient is

$$P(Y_{38} < m < Y_{53}) = \sum_{k=38}^{52} \binom{90}{k} \left(\frac{1}{2}\right)^k \left(\frac{1}{2}\right)^{90-k}$$

$$\approx \Phi\left(\frac{52.5 - 45}{\sqrt{22.5}}\right) - \Phi\left(\frac{37.5 - 45}{\sqrt{22.5}}\right)$$

$$= \Phi(1.58) - \Phi(-1.58) = 0.8858.$$

Similarly, $(y_{17} = 437,\ y_{29} = 470)$ is a confidence interval for the first quartile, $\pi_{0.25}$, with confidence coefficient

$$P(Y_{17} < \pi_{0.25} < Y_{29}) \approx \Phi\left(\frac{28.5 - 22.5}{\sqrt{16.875}}\right) - \Phi\left(\frac{16.5 - 22.5}{\sqrt{16.875}}\right)$$

$$= \Phi(1.46) - \Phi(-1.46) = 0.8558.$$

Minitab gives the exact confidence coefficients of 0.8867 and 0.8569, respectively. ■

It is interesting to compare the length of a confidence interval for the mean μ obtained with $\bar{x} \pm t_{\alpha/2}(n-1)(s/\sqrt{n})$ against the length of a $100(1-\alpha)\%$ confidence interval for the median m obtained with the distribution-free techniques of this section. Usually, if the sample arises from a distribution that does not deviate too much from the normal, the confidence interval based upon $\bar{x}$ is much shorter. After all, we assume much more when we create that confidence interval. With the distribution-free method, all we assume is that the distribution is of the continuous type. So if the distribution is highly skewed or heavy tailed so that outliers could exist, a distribution-free technique is safer and much more robust. Moreover, the distribution-free technique provides a way to get confidence intervals for various percentiles, and investigators are often interested in such intervals.

EXERCISES

8.4-1. Let $Y_1 < Y_2 < Y_3 < Y_4 < Y_5 < Y_6$ be the order statistics of a random sample of size $n = 6$ from a distribution of the continuous type having $(100p)$th percentile π_p. Compute

(a) $P(Y_2 < \pi_{0.5} < Y_5)$.
(b) $P(Y_1 < \pi_{0.25} < Y_4)$.
(c) $P(Y_4 < \pi_{0.9} < Y_6)$.

8.4-2. For $n = 12$ year-2007 model sedans whose horsepower is between 290 and 390, the following measurements give the time in seconds for the car to go from 0 to 60 mph:

6.0 6.3 5.0 6.0 5.7 5.9 6.8 5.5 5.4 4.8 5.4 5.8

(a) Find a 96.14% confidence interval for the median, m.
(b) The interval (y_1, y_7) could serve as a confidence interval for $\pi_{0.3}$. Find it and give its confidence coefficient.

8.4-3. A sample of $n = 9$ electrochromic mirrors was used to measure the following low-end reflectivity percentages:

7.12 7.22 6.78 6.31 5.99 6.58 7.80 7.40 7.05

(a) Find the endpoints for an approximate 95% confidence interval for the median, m.
(b) The interval (y_3, y_7) could serve as a confidence interval for m. Find it and give its confidence coefficient.

8.4-4. Let m denote the median weight of "80-pound" bags of water softener pellets. Use the following random sample of $n = 14$ weights to find an approximate 95% confidence interval for m:

80.51 80.28 80.40 80.35 80.38 80.28 80.27
80.16 80.59 80.56 80.32 80.27 80.53 80.32

(a) Find a 94.26% confidence interval for m.
(b) The interval (y_6, y_{12}) could serve as a confidence interval for $\pi_{0.6}$. What is its confidence coefficient?

8.4-5. Use the following weights of an observed random sample of $n = 11$ pieces of candy to find an approximate 95% confidence interval for the median weight, m:

2.76 2.96 2.67 2.97 2.77 2.72
2.74 2.84 2.61 2.82 2.72

Also, give the exact confidence coefficient.

8.4-6. A company manufactures mints that have a label weight of 20.4 grams. The company regularly samples from the production line and weighs the selected mints. During two mornings of production it sampled 81 mints, obtaining the following weights:

21.8 21.7 21.7 21.6 21.3 21.6 21.5 21.3 21.2
21.0 21.6 21.6 21.6 21.5 21.4 21.8 21.7 21.6
21.6 21.3 21.9 21.9 21.6 21.0 20.7 21.8 21.7
21.7 21.4 20.9 22.0 21.3 21.2 21.0 21.0 21.9
21.7 21.5 21.5 21.1 21.3 21.3 21.2 21.0 20.8
21.6 21.6 21.5 21.5 21.2 21.5 21.4 21.4 21.3
21.2 21.8 21.7 21.7 21.6 20.5 21.8 21.7 21.5
21.4 21.4 21.9 21.8 21.7 21.4 21.3 20.9 21.9
20.7 21.1 20.8 20.6 20.6 22.0 22.0 21.7 21.6

(a) Construct an ordered stem-and-leaf display using stems of $20f$, $20s$, $20\bullet$, $21*$, ..., $22*$.
(b) Find (i) the three quartiles, (ii) the 60th percentile, and (iii) the 15th percentile.
(c) Find approximate 95% confidence intervals for (i) $\pi_{0.25}$, (ii) $m = \pi_{0.5}$, and (iii) $\pi_{0.75}$.

8.4-7. A biologist who studies spiders selected a random sample of 20 male green lynx spiders (a spider that does not weave a web, but chases and leaps on its prey) and measured the lengths (in millimeters) of one of the front legs of the 20 spiders. Use the following measurements to construct a confidence interval for m that has a confidence coefficient about equal to 0.95:

15.10 13.55 15.75 20.00 15.45
13.60 16.45 14.05 16.95 19.05
16.40 17.05 15.25 16.65 16.25
17.75 15.40 16.80 17.55 19.05

8.4-8. The biologist of Exercise 8.4-7 also selected a random sample of 20 female green lynx spiders and measured the length (again in millimeters) of one of their front legs. Use the following data to construct a confidence interval for m that has a confidence coefficient about equal to 0.95:

15.85	18.00	11.45	15.60	16.10
18.80	12.85	15.15	13.30	16.65
16.25	16.15	15.25	12.10	16.20
14.80	14.60	17.05	14.15	15.85

8.4-9. Here are the weights (in grams) of 25 indicator housings used on gauges (see Exercise 3.2-10):

102.0	106.3	106.6	108.8	107.7
106.1	105.9	106.7	106.8	110.2
101.7	106.6	106.3	110.2	109.9
102.0	105.8	109.1	106.7	107.3
102.0	106.8	110.0	107.9	109.3

(a) List the observations in order of magnitude.

(b) Give point estimates of $\pi_{0.25}$, m, and $\pi_{0.75}$.

(c) Find the following confidence intervals and, from Table II in the appendix, state the associated confidence coefficient:

(i) (y_3, y_{10}), a confidence interval for $\pi_{0.25}$.

(ii) (y_9, y_{17}), a confidence interval for the median m.

(iii) (y_{16}, y_{23}), a confidence interval for $\pi_{0.75}$.

(d) Use $\bar{x} \pm t_{\alpha/2}(24)(s/\sqrt{25}\,)$ to find a confidence interval for μ, whose confidence coefficient corresponds to that of (d), part (ii). Compare these two confidence intervals of the middles.

8.4-10. Let X equal the weight in grams of a miniature candy bar. A random sample of candy bar weights yielded the following observations of X:

22.4	23.7	22.4	23.6	24.0	24.5	23.4	23.9
22.8	22.5	23.4	23.0	22.8	22.6	24.0	23.3

(a) Give a point estimate of the median $m = \pi_{0.50}$.

(b) Find a confidence interval for m with confidence level between 90% and 95%. Give the value of the exact confidence coefficient.

8.4-11. Let X equal the amount of fluoride in a certain brand of toothpaste. The specifications are 0.85–1.10 mg/g. Table 3.1-3 lists 100 such measurements.

(a) Give a point estimate of the median $m = \pi_{0.50}$.

(b) Find an approximate 95% confidence interval for the median m. If possible, use a computer to find the exact confidence level.

(c) Give a point estimate for the first quartile.

(d) Find an approximate 95% confidence interval for the first quartile and, if possible, give the exact confidence coefficient.

(e) Give a point estimate for the third quartile.

(f) Find an approximate 95% confidence interval for the third quartile and, if possible, give the exact confidence coefficient.

8.4-12. When placed in solutions of varying ionic strength, paramecia grow blisters in order to counteract the flow of water. The following 60 measurements in microns are blister lengths:

7.42	5.73	3.80	5.20	11.66	8.51	6.31	8.49
10.31	6.92	7.36	5.92	6.74	8.93	9.61	11.38
12.78	11.43	6.57	13.50	10.58	8.03	10.07	8.71
10.09	11.16	7.22	10.10	6.32	10.30	10.75	11.51
11.55	11.41	9.40	4.74	6.52	12.10	6.01	5.73
7.57	7.80	6.84	6.95	8.93	8.92	5.51	6.71
10.40	13.44	9.33	8.57	7.08	8.11	13.34	6.58
8.82	7.70	12.22	7.46				

(a) Construct an ordered stem-and-leaf diagram.

(b) Give a point estimate of the median $m = \pi_{0.50}$.

(c) Find an approximate 95% confidence interval for m.

(d) Give a point estimate for the 40th percentile, $\pi_{0.40}$.

(e) Find an approximate 90% confidence interval for $\pi_{0.40}$.

8.4-13. Using the weights of Verica's 39 gold coins given in Example 3.2-4, find approximate 95% confidence intervals for $\pi_{0.25}$, $\pi_{0.5}$, and $\pi_{0.75}$.

8.4-14. Let $Y_1 < Y_2 < \cdots < Y_8$ be the order statistics of eight independent observations from a continuous-type distribution with 70th percentile $\pi_{0.7} = 27.3$.

(a) Determine $P(Y_7 < 27.3)$.

(b) Find $P(Y_5 < 27.3 < Y_8)$.

8.4-15. Let X equal the weight in grams of peanuts in a "14-gram" snack package. The order statistics of a sample of size $n = 16$ are

13.9	14.4	14.6	14.7	14.7	15.2	15.2	15.2
15.3	15.4	15.4	15.5	15.6	15.6	15.9	16.4

(a) Find the 30th percentile of this sample.

(b) Find $P(Y_2 < \pi_{0.30} < Y_8)$, where Y_2 and Y_8 are the respective second- and eighth-order statistics of 16 independent observations.

8.5 THE WILCOXON TESTS

As mentioned earlier in the text, at times it is clear that the normal assumptions are not met and that other procedures, sometimes referred to as **nonparametric** or **distribution-free** methods, should be considered. For example, suppose some hypothesis, say, H_0: $m = m_0$, against H_1: $m \neq m_0$, is made about the unknown median, m, of a continuous-type distribution. From the data, we could construct a $100(1 - \alpha)$ percent confidence interval for m, and if m_0 is not in that interval, we would reject H_0 at the α significance level.

Now let X be a continuous-type random variable and let m denote the median of X. To test the hypothesis H_0: $m = m_0$ against an appropriate alternative hypothesis, we could also use a **sign test**. That is, if $X_1, X_2, \ldots, X_n$ denote the observations of a random sample from this distribution, and if we let Y equal the number of negative differences among $X_1 - m_0, X_2 - m_0, \ldots, X_n - m_0$, then Y has the binomial distribution $b(n, 1/2)$ under H_0 and is the test statistic for the sign test. If Y is too large or too small, we reject H_0: $m = m_0$.

EXAMPLE 8.5-1 Let X denote the length of time in seconds between two calls entering a college switchboard. Let m be the unique median of this continuous-type distribution. We test the null hypothesis H_0: $m = 6.2$ against the alternative hypothesis H_1: $m < 6.2$. Table II in the appendix tells us that if Y is the number of lengths of time in a random sample of size 20 that are less than 6.2, then the critical region $C = \{y : y \geq 14\}$ has a significance level of $\alpha = 0.0577$. A random sample of size 20 yielded the following data:

6.8	5.7	6.9	5.3	4.1	9.8	1.7	7.0
2.1	19.0	18.9	16.9	10.4	44.1	2.9	2.4
4.8	18.9	4.8	7.9				

Since $y = 9$, the null hypothesis is not rejected. ■

The sign test can also be used to test the hypothesis that two dependent continuous-type random variables X and Y are such that $p = P(X > Y) = 1/2$. To test the hypothesis H_0: $p = 1/2$ against an appropriate alternative hypothesis, consider the independent pairs $(X_1, Y_1), (X_2, Y_2), \ldots, (X_n, Y_n)$. Let W denote the number of pairs for which $X_i - Y_i > 0$. When H_0 is true, W is $b(n, 1/2)$, and the test can be based upon the statistic W. For example, say X is the length of the right foot of a person and Y the length of the corresponding left foot. Thus, there is a natural pairing, and here H_0: $p = P(X > Y) = 1/2$ suggests that either foot of a particular individual is equally likely to be longer.

One major objection to the sign test is that it does not take into account the magnitude of the differences $X_1 - m_0, \ldots, X_n - m_0$. We now discuss a **test of Wilcoxon** that does take into account the magnitude of the differences $|X_i - m_0|$, $i = 1, 2, \ldots, n$. However, in addition to assuming that the random variable X is of the continuous type, we must also assume that the p.d.f. of X is symmetric about the median in order to find the distribution of this new statistic. Because of the continuity assumption, we assume, in the discussion which follows, that no two observations are equal and that no observation is equal to the median.

We are interested in testing the hypothesis H_0: $m = m_0$, where m_0 is some given constant. With our random sample $X_1, X_2, \ldots, X_n$, we rank the absolute values $|X_1 - m_0|, |X_2 - m_0|, \ldots, |X_n - m_0|$ in ascending order according to magnitude.

That is, for $i = 1, 2, \ldots, n$, we let R_i denote the rank of $|X_i - m_0|$ among $|X_1 - m_0|, |X_2 - m_0|, \ldots, |X_n - m_0|$. Note that $R_1, R_2, \ldots, R_n$ is a permutation of the first n positive integers, $1, 2, \ldots, n$. Now, with each R_i, we associate the sign of the difference $X_i - m_0$; that is, if $X_i - m_0 > 0$, we use R_i, but if $X_i - m_0 < 0$, we use $-R_i$. The Wilcoxon statistic W is the sum of these n signed ranks.

EXAMPLE 8.5-2 Suppose the lengths of $n = 10$ sunfish are

$$x_i\colon\ 5.0\ 3.9\ 5.2\ 5.5\ 2.8\ 6.1\ 6.4\ 2.6\ 1.7\ 4.3$$

We shall test $H_0\colon m = 3.7$ against the alternative hypothesis $H_1\colon m > 3.7$. Thus, we have

$x_i - m_0$:	1.3,	0.2,	1.5,	1.8,	−0.9,	2.4,	2.7,	−1.1,	−2.0,	0.6
$\lvert x_i - m_0\rvert$:	1.3,	0.2,	1.5,	1.8,	0.9,	2.4,	2.7,	1.1,	2.0,	0.6
Ranks:	5,	1,	6,	7,	3,	9,	10,	4,	8,	2
Signed Ranks:	5,	1,	6,	7,	−3,	9,	10,	−4,	−8,	2

Therefore, the Wilcoxon statistic is equal to

$$W = 5 + 1 + 6 + 7 - 3 + 9 + 10 - 4 - 8 + 2 = 25.$$

Incidentally, the positive answer seems reasonable because the number of the 10 lengths that are less than 3.7 is 3, which is the statistic used in the sign test. ■

If the hypothesis $H_0\colon m = m_0$ is true, about one-half of the differences would be negative and thus about one-half of the signs would be negative. Hence, it seems that the hypothesis $H_0\colon m = m_0$ is supported if the observed value of W is close to zero. If the alternative hypothesis is $H_1\colon m > m_0$, we would reject H_0 if the observed $W = w$ is too large, since, in this case, the larger deviations $|X_i - m_0|$ would usually be associated with observations for which $x_i - m_0 > 0$. That is, the critical region would be of the form $\{w\colon\ w \ge c_1\}$. If the alternative hypothesis is $H_1\colon m < m_0$, the critical region would be of the form $\{w\colon\ w \le c_2\}$. Of course, the critical region would be of the form $\{w\colon\ w \le c_3 \text{ or } w \ge c_4\}$ for a two-sided alternative hypothesis $H_1\colon m \ne m_0$. In order to find the values of c_1, c_2, c_3, and c_4 that yield desired significance levels, it is necessary to determine the distribution of W under H_0. Accordingly, we consider certain characteristics of this distribution.

When $H_0\colon m = m_0$ is true,

$$P(X_i < m_0) = P(X_i > m_0) = \frac{1}{2}, \qquad i = 1, 2, \ldots, n.$$

Hence, the probability is $1/2$ that a negative sign is associated with the rank R_i of $|X_i - m_0|$. Moreover, the assignments of these n signs are independent because $X_1, X_2, \ldots, X_n$ are mutually independent. In addition, W is a sum that contains the integers $1, 2, \ldots, n$, each with a positive or negative sign. Since the underlying distribution is symmetric, it seems intuitively obvious that W has the same distribution as the random variable

$$V = \sum_{i=1}^{n} V_i,$$

where $V_1, V_2, \ldots, V_n$ are independent and

$$P(V_i = i) = P(V_i = -i) = \frac{1}{2}, \qquad i = 1, 2, \ldots, n.$$

That is, V is a sum that contains the integers $1, 2, \dots, n$, and these integers receive their algebraic signs by independent assignments.

Since W and V have the same distribution, their means and variances are equal, and we can easily find those of V. Now, the mean of V_i is

$$E(V_i) = -i\left(\frac{1}{2}\right) + i\left(\frac{1}{2}\right) = 0;$$

thus,

$$E(W) = E(V) = \sum_{i=1}^{n} E(V_i) = 0.$$

The variance of V_i is

$$\text{Var}(V_i) = E(V_i^2) = (-i)^2\left(\frac{1}{2}\right) + (i)^2\left(\frac{1}{2}\right) = i^2.$$

Hence,

$$\text{Var}(W) = \text{Var}(V) = \sum_{i=1}^{n} \text{Var}(V_i) = \sum_{i=1}^{n} i^2 = \frac{n(n+1)(2n+1)}{6}.$$

We shall not try to find the distribution of W in general, since that p.m.f. does not have a convenient expression. However, we demonstrate how we could find the distribution of W (or V) with enough patience and computer support. Recall that the moment-generating function of V_i is

$$M_i(t) = e^{t(-i)}\left(\frac{1}{2}\right) + e^{t(+i)}\left(\frac{1}{2}\right) = \frac{e^{-it} + e^{it}}{2}, \qquad i = 1, 2, \dots, n.$$

Let $n = 2$; then the moment-generating function of $V_1 + V_2$ is

$$M(t) = E[e^{t(V_1+V_2)}].$$

From the independence of V_1 and V_2, we obtain

$$\begin{aligned} M(t) &= E(e^{tV_1})E(e^{tV_2}) \\ &= \left(\frac{e^{-t} + e^{t}}{2}\right)\left(\frac{e^{-2t} + e^{2t}}{2}\right) \\ &= \frac{e^{-3t} + e^{-t} + e^{t} + e^{3t}}{4}. \end{aligned}$$

This means that each of the points $-3, -1, 1, 3$ in the support of $V_1 + V_2$ has probability $1/4$.

Next let $n = 3$; then the moment-generating function of $V_1 + V_2 + V_3$ is

$$\begin{aligned} M(t) &= E[e^{t(V_1+V_2+V_3)}] \\ &= E[e^{t(V_1+V_2)}]E(e^{tV_3}) \\ &= \left(\frac{e^{-3t} + e^{-t} + e^{t} + e^{3t}}{4}\right)\left(\frac{e^{-3t} + e^{3t}}{2}\right) \\ &= \frac{e^{-6t} + e^{-4t} + e^{-2t} + 2e^{0} + e^{-2t} + e^{-4t} + e^{-6t}}{8}. \end{aligned}$$

Thus, the points $-6, -4, -2, 0, 2, 4$, and 6 in the support of $V_1 + V_2 + V_3$ have the respective probabilities $1/8, 1/8, 1/8, 2/8, 1/8, 1/8$, and $1/8$. Obviously, this procedure can be continued for $n = 4, 5, 6, \ldots$, but it is rather tedious. Fortunately, however, even though $V_1, V_2, \ldots, V_n$ are not identically distributed random variables, the sum V of them still has an approximate normal distribution. To obtain this normal approximation for V (or W), a more general form of the central limit theorem, due to Liapounov, can be used which allows us to say that the standardized random variable

$$Z = \frac{W - 0}{\sqrt{n(n + 1)(2n + 1)/6}}$$

is approximately $N(0,1)$ when H_0 is true. We accept this theorem without proof; therefore we can use this normal distribution to approximate probabilities such as $P(W \geq c; H_0) \approx P(Z \geq z_\alpha; H_0)$ when the sample size n is sufficiently large. The next example illustrates this approximation.

EXAMPLE 8.5-3 The moment-generating function of W or of V is given by

$$M(t) = \prod_{i=1}^{n} \frac{e^{-it} + e^{it}}{2}.$$

Using a computer algebra system (CAS) such as *Maple*, we can expand $M(t)$ and find the coefficients of e^{kt}, which is equal to $P(W = k)$. In Figure 8.5-1, we have drawn a probability histogram for the distribution of W along with the approximating $N[0, n(n + 1)(2n + 1)/6]$ p.d.f. for $n = 4$ (a poor approximation) and for $n = 10$. It is important to note that the widths of the rectangles in the probability histogram are equal to 2, so the "half-unit correction for continuity" now becomes a unit correction. ■

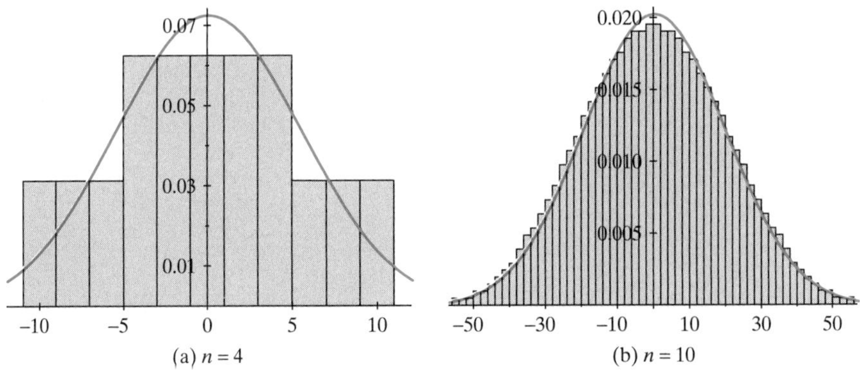

FIGURE 8.5-1: The Wilcoxon distribution

EXAMPLE 8.5-4 Let m be the median of a symmetric distribution of the continuous type. To test the hypothesis H_0: $m = 160$ against the alternative hypothesis H_1: $m > 160$, we take a random sample of size $n = 16$. For an approximate significance level of $\alpha = 0.05$, H_0 is rejected if the computed $W = w$ is such that

$$z = \frac{w}{\sqrt{16(17)(33)/6}} \geq 1.645,$$

TABLE 8.5-1: Ordered Absolute Differences from 160

0.1	$\underline{0.3}$	0.5	$\underline{1.2}$	$\underline{1.7}$	2.7	$\underline{3.4}$	5.2
1	2	3	4	5	6	7	8
$\underline{7.9}$	9.8	$\underline{12.2}$	12.4	14.5	16.9	17.8	24.4
9	10	11	12	13	14	15	16

or

$$w \geq 1.645\sqrt{\frac{16(17)(33)}{6}} = 63.626.$$

Say the observed values of a random sample are 176.9, 158.3, 152.1, 158.8, 172.4, 169.8, 159.7, 162.7, 156.6, 174.5, 184.4, 165.2, 147.8, 177.8, 160.1, and 160.5. In Table 8.5-1, the magnitudes of the differences $|x_i - 160|$ have been ordered and ranked. Those differences $x_i - 160$ which were negative have been underlined, and the ranks are under the ordered values. For this set of data,

$$w = 1 - 2 + 3 - 4 - 5 + 6 + \cdots + 16 = 60.$$

Since $60 < 63.626$, H_0 is not rejected at the 0.05 significance level. It is interesting to note that H_0 would have been rejected at $\alpha = 0.10$, since, with a unit correction made for continuity, the approximate p-value is,

$$\begin{aligned} p\text{-value} &= P(W \geq 60) \\ &= P\left(\frac{W - 0}{\sqrt{(16)(17)(33)/6}} \geq \frac{59 - 0}{\sqrt{(16)(17)(33)/6}}\right) \\ &\approx P(Z \geq 1.525) = 0.0636. \end{aligned}$$

(*Maple* produces a p-value equal to $4{,}251/65{,}536 = 0.0649$.) Such a p-value would indicate that the data are too few to reject H_0, but if the pattern continues, we shall most certainly reject H_0 with a larger sample size. ■

Although theoretically we could ignore the possibilities that $x_i = m_0$ for some i and that $|x_i - m_0| = |x_j - m_0|$ for some $i \neq j$, these situations do occur in applications. Usually, in practice, if $x_i = m_0$ for some i, that observation is deleted and the test is performed with a reduced sample size. If the absolute values of the differences from m_0 of two or more observations are equal, each observation is assigned the average of the corresponding ranks. The change this causes in the distribution of W is not very great; thus, we continue using the same normal approximation.

We now give an example that has some tied observations. This example also illustrates that the Wilcoxon rank sum test can be used to test hypotheses about the median of paired data.

EXAMPLE 8.5-5 We consider some paired data for percentage of body fat measured at the beginning and the end of a semester. Let m equal the median of the differences, $x - y$. We shall use the Wilcoxon statistic to test the null hypothesis H_0: $m = 0$ against the alternative hypothesis H_1: $m > 0$ with the differences given shortly. Since there are

$n = 25$ nonzero differences, we reject H_0 if

$$z = \frac{w - 0}{\sqrt{(25)(26)(51)/6}} \geq 1.645$$

or, equivalently, if

$$w \geq 1.645\sqrt{\frac{(25)(26)(51)}{6}} = 122.27$$

at an approximate $\alpha = 0.05$ significance level. The 26 differences are

1.8	−3.1	0.1	1.1	0.6	−5.1	9.2	0.2	0.4
0.0	1.9	−0.4	−1.5	1.4	−1.0	2.2	0.8	−0.4
2.0	−5.8	−3.4	−2.3	3.0	2.7	0.2	3.2	

Table 8.5-2 lists the ordered nonzero absolute values, with those that were originally negative underlined. The rank is under each observation. Note that in the case of ties, the average of the ranks of the tied measurements is given.

TABLE 8.5-2: Ordered Absolute Values, Changes in Percentage of Body Fat

0.1	0.2	0.2	0.4	$\underline{0.4}$	$\underline{0.4}$	0.6	0.8	$\underline{1.0}$	1.1	1.4	$\underline{1.5}$	1.8
1	2.5	2.5	5	5	5	7	8	9	10	11	12	13
1.9	2.0	2.2	$\underline{2.3}$	2.7	3.0	$\underline{3.1}$	3.2	$\underline{3.4}$	$\underline{5.1}$	$\underline{5.8}$	9.2	
14	15	16	17	18	19	20	21	22	23	24	25	

The value of the Wilcoxon statistic is

$$w = 1 + 2.5 + 2.5 + 5 - 5 - 5 + \cdots + 25 = 51.$$

Since $51 < 122.27$, we fail to reject the null hypothesis. The approximate p-value of this test is

$$\begin{aligned} p\text{-value} &= P(W \geq 51) = P(W \geq 50) \\ &\approx P\left(Z \geq \frac{50 - 0}{\sqrt{(25)(26)(51)/6}}\right) = P(Z \geq 0.673) = 0.2505. \end{aligned}$$

■

Another method due to Wilcoxon for testing the equality of two distributions of the continuous type uses the magnitudes of the observations. For this test, it is assumed that the respective distribution functions F and G have similar shapes. To proceed with the test, place the combined sample of $X_1, X_2, \ldots, X_{n_1}$ and $Y_1, Y_2, \ldots, Y_{n_2}$ in increasing order of magnitude. Assign the ranks $1, 2, 3, \ldots, n_1 + n_2$ to the ordered values. In the case of ties, assign the average of the ranks associated with the tied values. Let W equal the sum of the ranks of $Y_1, Y_2, \ldots, Y_{n_2}$. If the distribution of Y is shifted to the right of that of X, the values of Y would tend to be larger than the values of X and W would usually be larger than expected when $F(z) = G(z)$. If m_X and m_Y are the respective medians, the critical region for testing $H_0\colon m_X = m_Y$ against $H_1\colon m_X < m_Y$ would be of the form $w \geq c$. Similarly, if the alternative hypothesis is $m_X > m_Y$, the critical region would be of the form $w \leq c$.

We shall not derive the distribution of W. However, if n_1 and n_2 are both greater than 7, a normal approximation can be used. With $F(z) = G(z)$, the mean and variance of W are

$$\mu_W = \frac{n_2(n_1 + n_2 + 1)}{2}$$

and

$$\text{Var}(W) = \frac{n_1 n_2(n_1 + n_2 + 1)}{12},$$

and the statistic

$$Z = \frac{W - n_2(n_1 + n_2 + 1)/2}{\sqrt{n_1 n_2(n_1 + n_2 + 1)/12}}$$

is approximately $N(0,1)$.

EXAMPLE 8.5-6 The weights of of the contents of $n_1 = 8$ and $n_2 = 8$ tins of cinnamon packaged by companies A and B, respectively, selected at random, yielded the following observations of X and Y:

X: 117.1 121.3 127.8 121.9 117.4 124.5 119.5 115.1,

Y: 123.5 125.3 126.5 127.9 122.1 125.6 129.8 117.2.

The critical region for testing H_0: $m_X = m_Y$ against H_1: $m_X < m_Y$ is of the form $w \geq c$. Since $n_1 = n_2 = 8$, at an approximate $\alpha = 0.05$ significance level H_0 is rejected if

$$z = \frac{w - 8(8 + 8 + 1)/2}{\sqrt{[(8)(8)(8 + 8 + 1)]/12}} \geq 1.645,$$

or

$$w \geq 1.645\sqrt{\frac{(8)(8)(17)}{12}} + 4(17) = 83.66.$$

To calculate the value of W, it is sometimes helpful to construct a **back-to-back stem-and-leaf display**. In such a display, the stems are put in the center and the leaves go to the left and the right. (See Table 8.5-3.)

TABLE 8.5-3: Back-to-Back Stem-and-Leaf Diagram of Weights of Cinnamon

X leaves		Stems	Y leaves	
	51	11f		
74	71	11s	72	
	95	11•		
19	13	12∗		
		12t	21	35
	45	12f	53	56
	78	12s	65	79
		12•	98	

Multiply numbers by 10^{-1}

TABLE 8.5-4: Combined Ordered Samples

115.1	117.1	<u>117.2</u>	117.4	119.5	121.3	121.9	<u>122.1</u>
1	2	3	4	5	6	7	8
<u>123.5</u>	124.5	<u>125.3</u>	<u>125.6</u>	<u>126.5</u>	127.8	<u>127.9</u>	<u>129.8</u>
9	10	11	12	13	14	15	16

Reading from this two-sided stem-and-leaf display, we show the combined sample in Table 8.5-4, with the Company B (Y) weights underlined. The ranks are given beneath the values.

From Table 8.5-4, the computed W is

$$w = 3 + 8 + 9 + 11 + 12 + 13 + 15 + 16 = 87 > 83.66.$$

Thus, H_0 is rejected. Finally, making a half-unit correction for continuity, we see that the p-value of this test is

$$\begin{aligned} p\text{-value} &= P(W \geq 87) \\ &= P\left(\frac{W - 68}{\sqrt{90.667}} \geq \frac{86.5 - 68}{\sqrt{90.667}}\right) \\ &\approx P(Z \geq 1.943) = 0.0260. \end{aligned}$$

■

REMARKS Shortly after Wilcoxon proposed his two-sample test, Mann and Whitney suggested a test based on the estimate of the probability $P(X < Y)$. In this test, they let U equal the number of times that $X_i < Y_j$, $i = 1, 2, \ldots, n_1$ and $j = 1, 2, \ldots, n_2$. Using the data in Example 8.5-6, we find that the computed U is $u = 51$ among all $n_1 n_2 = (8)(8) = 64$ pairs of (X, Y). Thus, the estimate of $P(X < Y)$ is $51/64$ or, in general, $u/n_1 n_2$. At the time of the Mann–Whitney suggestion, it was noted that U was just a linear function of Wilcoxon's W and hence really provided the same test. That relationship is

$$U = W - \frac{n_2(n_2 + 1)}{2},$$

which in our special case is

$$51 = 87 - \frac{8(9)}{2} = 87 - 36.$$

Thus, we often read about the test of Mann, Whitney, and Wilcoxon. From this observation, this test could be thought of as one testing H_0: $P(X < Y) = 1/2$ against the alternative H_1: $P(X < Y) > 1/2$ with critical region of the form $w \geq c$.

Note that the two-sample Wilcoxon test is much less sensitive to extreme values than is the Student's t test based on $\overline{X} - \overline{Y}$. Therefore, if there is considerable skewness or contamination, these proposed distribution-free tests are much safer. In particular, that of Wilcoxon is quite good and does not lose too much in case the distributions are close to normal ones. It is important to note that the one-sample Wilcoxon test requires symmetry of the underlying distribution, but the two-sample Wilcoxon test does not and thus can be used for skewed distributions.

From theoretical developments beyond the scope of this text, the two Wilcoxon tests are strong competitors of the usual one- and two-sample tests based upon normal assumptions, so the Wilcoxon tests should be considered if those assumptions are questioned.

Computer programs, including Minitab, will calculate the value of the Wilcoxon or Mann–Whitney statistic. However, it is instructive to do these tests by hand so that you can see what is being calculated! ■

EXERCISES

8.5-1. It is claimed that the median weight m of certain loads of candy is 40,000 pounds.

(a) Use the following 13 observations and the Wilcoxon statistic to test the null hypothesis H_0: $m = 40{,}000$ against the one-sided alternative hypothesis H_1: $m < 40{,}000$ at an approximate significance level of $\alpha = 0.05$:

41,195	39,485	41,229	36,840	38,050	40,890	38,345
34,930	39,245	31,031	40,780	38,050	30,906	

(b) What is the approximate p-value of this test?

(c) Use the sign test to test the same hypothesis.

(d) Calculate the p-value from the sign test and compare it with the p-value obtained from the Wilcoxon test.

8.5-2. A course in economics was taught to two groups of students, one in a classroom situation and the other by TV. There were 24 students in each group. The students were first paired according to cumulative grade point averages and background in economics, and then assigned to the courses by a flip of a coin. (The procedure was repeated 24 times.) At the end of the course each class was given the same final examination. Use the Wilcoxon test to test the hypothesis that the two methods of teaching are equally effective against a two-sided alternative. The differences in the final scores for each pair of students were as follows (the TV student's score was subtracted from the corresponding classroom student's score):

14	−4	−6	−2	−1	18
6	12	8	−4	13	7
2	6	21	7	−2	11
−3	−14	−2	17	−4	−5

8.5-3. Let X equal the weight (in grams) of a Hershey's grape-flavored Jolly Rancher. Denote the median of X by m. We shall test H_0: $m = 5.900$ against H_1: $m > 5.900$. A random sample of size $n = 25$ yielded the following ordered data:

5.625	5.665	5.697	5.837	5.863	5.870	5.878	5.884	5.908
5.967	6.019	6.020	6.029	6.032	6.037	6.045	6.049	
6.050	6.079	6.116	6.159	6.186	6.199	6.307	6.387	

(a) Use the sign test to test the hypothesis.

(b) Use the Wilcoxon test statistic to test the hypothesis.

(c) Use a t test to test the hypothesis.

(d) Write a short comparison of the three tests.

8.5-4. The outcomes on $n = 10$ simulations of a Cauchy random variable were −1.9415, 0.5901, −5.9848, −0.0790, −0.7757, −1.0962, 9.3820, −74.0216, −3.0678, and 3.8545. For the Cauchy distribution, the mean does not exist, but for this one, the median is believed to equal zero. Use the Wilcoxon test and these data to test H_0: $m = 0$ against the alternative hypothesis H_1: $m \neq 0$. Let $\alpha \approx 0.05$.

8.5-5. Let x equal a student's GPA in the fall semester and y the same student's GPA in the spring semester. Let m equal the median of the differences, $x - y$. We shall test the null hypothesis H_0: $m = 0$ against an appropriate alternative hypothesis that you select on the basis of your past experience. Use a Wilcoxon test and the following 15 observations of paired data to test H_0:

x	y	x	y
2.88	3.22	3.98	3.76
3.67	3.49	4.00	3.96
2.76	2.54	3.39	3.52
2.34	2.17	2.59	2.36
2.46	2.53	2.78	2.62
3.20	2.98	2.85	3.06
3.17	2.98	3.25	3.16
2.90	2.84		

8.5-6. Let m equal the median of the posttest grip strengths in the right arms of male freshmen in a study of health dynamics. We shall use observations on $n = 15$ such students to test the null hypothesis H_0: $m = 50$ against the alternative hypothesis H_1: $m > 50$.

(a) Using the Wilcoxon statistic, define a critical region that has an approximate significance level of $\alpha = 0.05$.

(b) Given the observed values

58.0 52.5 46.0 57.5 52.0 45.5 65.5 71.0
57.0 54.0 48.0 58.0 35.5 44.0 53.0,

what is your conclusion?

(c) What is the p-value of this test?

8.5-7. Let X equal the weight in pounds of a "1-pound" bag of carrots. Let m equal the median weight of a population of these bags. Test the null hypothesis H_0: $m = 1.14$ against the alternative hypothesis H_1: $m > 1.14$.

(a) With a sample of size $n = 14$, use the Wilcoxon statistic to define a critical region. Use $\alpha \approx 0.10$.

(b) What would be your conclusion if the observed weights were

1.12 1.13 1.19 1.25 1.06 1.31 1.12
1.23 1.29 1.17 1.20 1.11 1.18 1.23

(c) What is the p-value of your test?

8.5-8. A pharmaceutical company is interested in testing the effect of humidity on the weight of pills that are sold in aluminum packaging. Let X and Y denote the respective weights of pills and their packaging, when the packaging is good and when it is defective, after the pill has spent 1 week in a chamber containing 100% humidity and heated to 30°C.

(a) Use the Wilcoxon test to test H_0: $m_X = m_Y$ against H_0: $m_X - m_Y < 0$ on the following random samples of $n_1 = 12$ observations of X and $n_2 = 12$ observations of Y:

X:	0.7565	0.7720	0.7776	0.7750	0.7494	0.7615
	0.7741	0.7701	0.7712	0.7719	0.7546	0.7719
Y:	0.7870	0.7750	0.7720	0.7876	0.7795	0.7972
	0.7815	0.7811	0.7731	0.7613	0.7816	0.7851

What is the p-value?

(b) Construct and interpret a q–q plot of these data. HINT: This is a q–q plot of the empirical distribution of X against that of Y.

8.5-9. Let us compare the failure times of a certain type of light bulb produced by two different manufacturers, X and Y, by testing 10 bulbs selected at random from each of the outputs. The data, in hundreds of hours used before failure, are

X: 5.6 4.6 6.8 4.9 6.1 5.3 4.5 5.8 5.4 4.7
Y: 7.2 8.1 5.1 7.3 6.9 7.8 5.9 6.7 6.5 7.1

(a) Use the Wilcoxon test to test the equality of medians of the failure times at the approximate 5% significance level. What is the p-value?

(b) Construct and interpret a q–q plot of these data. HINT: This is a q–q plot of the empirical distribution of X against that of Y.

8.5-10. Let X and Y denote the heights of blue spruce trees, measured in centimeters, growing in two large fields. We shall compare these heights by measuring 12 trees selected at random from each of the fields. Take $\alpha \approx 0.05$, and use the statistic W—the sum of the ranks of the observations of Y in the combined sample—to test the hypothesis H_0: $m_X = m_Y$ against the alternative hypothesis H_1: $m_X < m_Y$ on the basis of the following $n_1 = 12$ observations of X and $n_2 = 12$ observations of Y:

X:	90.4	77.2	75.9	83.2	84.0	90.2
	87.6	67.4	77.6	69.3	83.3	72.7
Y:	92.7	78.9	82.5	88.6	95.0	94.4
	73.1	88.3	90.4	86.5	84.7	87.5

8.5-11. Let X and Y equal the sizes of grocery orders from, respectively, a south-side and a north-side food store of the same chain. We shall test the null hypothesis H_0: $m_X = m_Y$ against a two-sided alternative, using the following ordered observations:

X:	5.13	8.22	11.81	13.77	15.36
	23.71	31.39	34.65	40.17	75.58
Y:	4.42	6.47	7.12	10.50	12.12
	12.57	21.29	33.14	62.84	72.05

(a) Use the Wilcoxon test when $\alpha = 0.05$. What is the p-value of this two-sided test?

(b) Construct a q–q plot and interpret it. HINT: This is a q–q plot of the empirical distribution of X against that of Y.

8.5-12. A charter bus line has 48-passenger and 38-passenger buses. Let m_{48} and m_{38} denote the median number of miles traveled per day by the respective buses. With $\alpha = 0.05$, use the Wilcoxon statistic to test H_0: $m_{48} = m_{38}$ against the one-sided alternative H_1: $m_{48} > m_{38}$. Use the following data, which give the numbers of miles traveled per day for respective random samples of sizes 9 and 11:

48-passenger buses:	331	308	300	414	253	
	323	452	396	104		
38-passenger buses:	248	393	260	355	279	184
	386	450	432	196	197	

8.5-13. A company manufactures and packages soap powder in 6-pound boxes. The quality assurance department was interested in comparing the fill weights of packages from the East and West lines. Taking random samples from the two lines, the department obtained the following weights:

East line (X):	6.06	6.04	6.11	6.06	6.06
	6.07	6.06	6.08	6.05	6.09
West line (Y):	6.08	6.03	6.04	6.07	6.11
	6.08	6.08	6.10	6.06	6.04

(a) Let m_X and m_Y denote the median weights for the East and West lines, respectively. Test H_0: $m_X = m_Y$ against a two-sided alternative hypothesis, using the Wilcoxon test with $\alpha \approx 0.05$. Find the p-value of this two-sided test.

(b) Construct and interpret a q–q plot of these data.

8.5-14. In Exercise 7.3-19, data are given that show the effect of a certain fertilizer on plant growth. The growths of the plants in mm over six weeks are repeated here, where Group A received fertilizer and Group B did not:

Group A:	55	61	33	57	17	46	50	42	71	51	63
Group B:	31	27	12	44	9	25	34	53	33	21	32

We shall test the hypothesis that fertilizer enhanced the growth of the plants.

(a) Construct a back-to-back stem-and-leaf display in which the stems are put down the center of the diagram and the Group A leaves go to the left while the Group B leaves go to the right.

(b) Calculate the value of the Wilcoxon statistic and give your conclusion.

(c) How does this result compare with that using the t test in Exercise 7.3-19?

8.5-15. With $\alpha = 0.05$, use the Wilcoxon statistic to test H_0: $m_X = m_Y$ against a two-sided alternative. Use the following observations of X and Y, which have been ordered for your convenience:

X:	−2.3864	−2.2171	−1.9148	−1.9097	−1.4883
	−1.2007	−1.1077	−0.3601	0.4325	1.0598
	1.3035	1.5241	1.7133	1.7656	2.4912
Y:	−1.7613	−0.9391	−0.7437	−0.5530	−0.2469
	0.0647	0.2031	0.3219	0.3579	0.6431
	0.6557	0.6724	0.6762	0.9041	1.3571

8.5-16. Data were collected during a step-direction experiment in the biomechanics laboratory of Hope College. The goal of the study is to establish differences in stepping responses between healthy young and healthy older adults. In one part of the experiment, the subjects are told in what direction they should take a step. Then, when given a signal, the subject takes a step in that direction, and the time it takes for them to lift their foot to take the step is measured. The direction is repeated a few times throughout the testing, and for each subject, a mean of all the "liftoff" times in a certain direction is calculated. The mean liftoff times (in thousandths of a second) for the anterior direction, ordered for your convenience, are as follows:

Young Subjects

397 433 450 468 485 488 498 504 561 565 569 576 577 579 581 586 696

Older Subjects

463 538 549 573 588 590 594 626 627 653 674 728 818 835 863 888 936

(a) Construct a back-to-back stem-and-leaf display. Use stems 3•, 4∗, ..., 9∗.
(b) Use the Wilcoxon statistic to test the null hypothesis that the response times are equal against the alternative that the times for the young subjects are less than that for the older subjects.
(c) What outcome does a t test give?

8.5-17. Some measurements in mm were made on a species of spiders named *Sosippus floridanus* that are native to Florida. (See Exercises 6.7-16 and 7.3-17.) There are 10 female spiders and 10 male spiders. The body lengths and the lengths of their front and their back legs are repeated here:

Female body lengths	Female front legs	Female back legs	Male body lengths	Male front legs	Male back legs
11.06	15.03	19.29	12.26	21.22	25.54
13.87	17.96	22.74	11.66	18.62	23.94
12.93	17.56	21.28	12.53	18.62	23.94
15.08	21.22	25.54	13.00	19.95	25.80
17.82	22.61	28.86	11.79	19.15	25.40
14.14	20.08	25.14	12.46	19.02	25.27
12.26	16.49	20.22	10.65	17.29	22.21
17.82	18.75	24.61	10.39	17.02	21.81
20.17	23.01	28.46	12.26	18.49	23.41
16.88	22.48	28.59	14.07	22.61	28.86

In this exercise, we shall use the Wilcoxon statistic to compare the sizes of the female and male spiders. For each of the following instructions, construct back-to-back stem-and-leaf displays:

(a) Test the null hypothesis that the lengths of female and male spiders are equal against the alternative hypothesis that female spiders are longer.
(b) Test the null hypothesis that the lengths of the front legs of the female and male spiders are equal against a two-sided alternative.
(c) Test the null hypothesis that the lengths of the back legs of the female and male spiders are equal against a two-sided alternative.

8.5-18. In Exercise 7.3-14, growth data are given for plants in normal air and for plants in CO_2-enriched air. Those data are repeated here:

Normal Air (X)	4.67	4.21	2.18	3.91	4.09	5.24	2.94	4.71
	4.04	5.79	3.80	4.38				
Enriched Air (Y)	5.04	4.52	6.18	7.01	4.36	1.81	6.22	5.70

In this exercise, we shall test test the null hypothesis that the medians are equal, namely, H_0: $m_X = m_Y$, against the alternative hypothesis H_1: $m_X < m_Y$. You may select the significance level. However, give the approximate p-value or state clearly why you arrived at a particular conclusion, for each of the tests. Show your work.

(a) What is your conclusion from the Wilcoxon test?
(b) What was your conclusion from the t test in Exercise 7.3-14?
(c) Write a comparison of these two tests.

8.5-19. In Exercise 7.3-20, we noted that Ledolter and Hogg reported the times needed for an old procedure and for a new procedure. The data are repeated here:

Old Procedure:	4.3	6.5	4.6	4.3	6.4	4.8	5.1	6.8	4.9
	4.5	5.1	7.3	3.3	5.0	4.6	7.0	5.1	3.8
	5.2	4.1	5.7	4.6	5.9	3.1	6.2		
New Procedure:	6.2	4.0	3.3	4.5	2.3	3.0	3.2	6.0	3.7
	4.5	5.3	4.0	5.4	4.3	3.8			

(a) Construct a back-to-back stem-and-leaf display.

(b) Use the Wilcoxon test to test the null hypothesis that the median response times are equal against a one-sided alternative that the median for the new procedure is less than that for the old procedure. Let $\alpha = 0.01$.

(c) What is the approximate p-value of your test?

(d) What was your conclusion from the t test in Exercise 7.3-20?

(e) How do the two tests compare?

8.6 RUN TEST AND TEST FOR RANDOMNESS

Under the assumption that the random variables X and Y are of the continuous type and have distribution functions $F(x)$ and $G(y)$, respectively, we describe another test of the hypothesis H_0: $F(z) = G(z)$. This new test can also be used to test for randomness. In either application, we need the concept of runs, which we now define.

Suppose that we have n_1 observations of the random variable X and n_2 observations of the random variable Y. The combination of two sets of independent observations into one collection of $n_1 + n_2$ observations, placed in ascending order of magnitude, might yield an ordered arrangement

$$\underline{y\ y\ y}\ \underline{x\ x}\ \underline{y}\ \underline{x}\ \underline{y}\ \underline{x\ x}\ \underline{y\ y},$$

where x denotes an observation of X and y an observation of Y. We have underlined groups of successive values of X and Y. Each underlined group is called a **run**. Thus, we have a run of three values of Y, followed by a run of two values of X, followed by a run of one value of Y, and so on. In this example, there are seven runs.

We give two more examples to show what might be indicated by the number of runs. If the five x's and seven y's had the ordering

$$\underline{x\ x\ x\ x}\ \underline{y}\ \underline{x}\ \underline{y\ y\ y\ y\ y\ y},$$

we might suspect that $F(z) \geq G(z)$. Note that there are four runs in this ordering. By contrast, the ordered arrangement

$$\underline{y\ y\ y}\ \underline{x\ x}\ \underline{y}\ \underline{x\ x\ x}\ \underline{y\ y\ y}$$

might suggest that the medians of the two distributions are equal, but that the spread of the Y distribution is greater than the spread of the X distribution—for example, that $\sigma_Y > \sigma_X$. All three examples suggest that the hypothesis $F(z) = G(z)$ should be rejected if the number of runs is too small, where a small number of runs could be caused by differences in the location or in the spread of the two distributions.

Let the random variable R equal the number of runs in the combined ordered sample of n_1 observations of X and n_2 observations of Y. We shall find the distribution of R when $F(z) = G(z)$ and then describe a test of the hypothesis H_0: $F(z) = G(z)$.

Under H_0, all permutations of the n_1 observations of X and n_2 observations of Y have equal probabilities. We can select the n_1 positions for the n_1 values of X in

$$\binom{n_1 + n_2}{n_1}$$

ways, the probability of each arrangement being

$$\frac{1}{\binom{n_1 + n_2}{n_1}}.$$

To find $P(R = r)$, we must determine the number of permutations that yield r runs.

First suppose that $r = 2k$, where k is a positive integer. In this case, the n_1 ordered values of X and the n_2 ordered values of Y must each be separated into k runs. We can form k runs of the n_1 values of X by inserting $k - 1$ dividers into the $n_1 - 1$ spaces between the values of X, with no more than one divider per space. This can be done in

$$\binom{n_1 - 1}{k - 1}$$

ways. (See Exercise 8.6-4.) Similarly, k runs of the n_2 values of Y can be formed in

$$\binom{n_2 - 1}{k - 1}$$

ways. These two sets of runs can be placed together to form $r = 2k$ runs, of which

$$\binom{n_1 - 1}{k - 1}\binom{n_2 - 1}{k - 1}$$

begin with a run of x's and

$$\binom{n_2 - 1}{k - 1}\binom{n_1 - 1}{k - 1}$$

begin with a run of y's. Thus,

$$P(R = 2k) = \frac{2\binom{n_1 - 1}{k - 1}\binom{n_2 - 1}{k - 1}}{\binom{n_1 + n_2}{n_2}}, \tag{8.6-1}$$

where $2k$ is an element of the space of R.

When $r = 2k + 1$, it is possible to have $k + 1$ runs of the ordered values of X and k runs of the ordered values of Y or k runs of Xs and $k + 1$ runs of Ys. We can form $k + 1$ runs of the n_1 values of X by inserting k dividers into the $n_1 - 1$ spaces between the values of X, with no more than one divider per space, in

$$\binom{n_1 - 1}{k}$$

ways. Similarly, k runs of n_2 values of Y can be done in

$$\binom{n_2 - 1}{k - 1}$$

ways. These two sets of runs can be placed together to form $2k + 1$ runs in

$$\binom{n_1 - 1}{k}\binom{n_2 - 1}{k - 1}$$

ways. In addition, $k + 1$ runs of the n_2 values of Y and k runs of the n_1 values of X can be placed together to form

$$\binom{n_2 - 1}{k}\binom{n_1 - 1}{k - 1}$$

sets of $2k + 1$ runs. Hence,

$$P(R = 2k + 1) = \frac{\binom{n_1 - 1}{k}\binom{n_2 - 1}{k - 1} + \binom{n_1 - 1}{k - 1}\binom{n_2 - 1}{k}}{\binom{n_1 + n_2}{n_2}}, \tag{8.6-2}$$

for $2k + 1$ in the space of R.

A test based on the number of runs can be used to test the hypothesis H_0: $F(z) = G(z)$. The hypothesis is rejected if the observed number of runs r is too small. That is, the critical region is of the form $r \le c$, where the constant c is determined by using the p.d.f. of R to yield the desired significance level. The **run test** is sensitive to both differences in location and differences in spread of the two distributions.

EXAMPLE 8.6-1 Let X and Y equal the percentages of body fat for freshman women and men, respectively, with distribution functions $F(x)$ and $G(y)$. We shall use the run test to test the hypothesis H_0: $F(z) = G(z)$ against the alternative hypothesis H_1: $F(z) < G(z)$. (That is, the alternative hypothesis is that the X distribution is to the right of the Y distribution.) Ten observations of both X and Y that have been ordered are

X:	16.6	16.7	18.5	19.2	21.5
	22.4	22.6	23.2	24.2	26.3
Y:	9.4	9.7	11.3	11.8	13.3
	15.6	16.1	16.5	18.2	21.7

The critical region is of the form $r \le c$. To determine the value of c, we use Formulas 8.6-1 and 8.6-2 with $n_1 = n_2 = 10$. Table I in the appendix is very useful for evaluating these probabilities. We have

$$P(R = 2) = \frac{2}{184{,}756}; \quad P(R = 3) = \frac{18}{184{,}756};$$

$$P(R = 4) = \frac{162}{184{,}756}; \quad P(R = 5) = \frac{648}{184{,}756};$$

$$P(R = 6) = \frac{2592}{184{,}756}; \quad P(R = 7) = \frac{6048}{184{,}756}.$$

The sum of these six probabilities is $9470/184{,}756 = 0.051$, so we can take for our critical region $C = \{r\colon\ r \le 7\}$ with a significance level of $\alpha = 0.051$. To determine the number of runs, we order the combined samples and underline adjacent x and y values:

9.4 9.7 11.3 11.8 13.3 15.6 16.1 16.5 16.6 16.7
18.2 18.5 19.2 21.5 21.7 22.4 22.6 23.2 24.2 26.3

We see that the number of runs is $r = 6$, so we reject the null hypothesis. Note that the p-value of this test is

$$p\text{-value} = P(R \le 6) = \frac{3422}{184{,}756} = 0.0185.$$

■

When n_1 and n_2 are large (say, each is at least equal to 10), R can be approximated with a normally distributed random variable. That is, it can be shown that

$$\mu_R = E(R) = \frac{2n_1n_2}{n_1 + n_2} + 1,$$

$$\text{Var}(R) = \frac{(\mu_R - 1)(\mu_R - 2)}{n_1 + n_2 - 1} = \frac{2n_1n_2(2n_1n_2 - n_1 - n_2)}{(n_1 + n_2)^2(n_1 + n_2 - 1)},$$

and

$$Z = \frac{R - \mu_R}{\sqrt{\text{Var}(R)}}$$

is approximately $N(0, 1)$. The critical region for testing the null hypothesis H_0: $F(z) = G(z)$ is of the form $z \le -z_\alpha$, where α is the desired significance level.

EXAMPLE 8.6-2 We use the normal approximation to calculate the significance level and the p-value for Example 8.6-1. With $n_1 = n_2 = 10$,

$$\mu_R = \frac{2(10)(10)}{10 + 10} + 1 = 11; \qquad \sigma_R^2 = \frac{(11 - 1)(11 - 2)}{19} = \frac{90}{19}.$$

With the critical region $C = \{r\colon\ r \le 7\}$, the approximate significance level, with a half-unit correction for continuity, is

$$\begin{aligned}\alpha = P(R \le 7) &= P\left(\frac{R - 11}{\sqrt{90/19}} \le \frac{7.5 - 11}{\sqrt{90/19}}\right)\\ &\approx P(Z \le -1.608) = 0.0539.\end{aligned}$$

Note that this value compares very favorably with $\alpha = 0.051$ given in Example 8.6-1. Since $r = 6$, the approximate p-value, under the assumption of a normal approximation, is

$$\begin{aligned}p\text{-value} &= P(R \le 6)\\ &\approx P\left(Z \le \frac{6.5 - 11}{\sqrt{90/19}}\right) = P(Z \le -2.068) = 0.0193,\end{aligned}$$

which is close to the p-value given in Example 8.6-1. ■

Applications of the run test include tests for randomness. Analyses of runs can also be useful in quality-control studies. To illustrate these applications, let $x_1, x_2, \ldots, x_k$ be the observed values of a random variable X, where the subscripts now designate the order in which the outcomes were observed and the observations are not arranged in order of magnitude. In a quality-control situation, the observations may be made systematically—for example, every hour. Assume that k is even. The median divides the k numbers into a lower and an upper half. Replace each observation by L if it falls below the median and by U if it falls above the median. Then, on the one hand, a sequence such as

U U U L U L L L

might suggest a trend toward decreasing values of X. If the existence of a trend is the alternative hypothesis to randomness, the critical region would be of the form $r \le c$.

On the other hand, if we have a sequence such as

$$\text{U L U L U L U L U L},$$

we would suspect a cyclic effect and would reject the hypothesis of randomness if r were too large. To test for both trend and cyclic effects, the critical region for testing the hypothesis of randomness is of the form $r \le c_1$ or $r \ge c_2$.

If the sample size k is odd, the number of observations in the "upper half" and "lower half" will differ by one. In this case, we will always put the extra observation in the upper group and, of course, $n_2 = n_1 + 1$. If the median is equal to a value that is tied with other values, we will again put the tied values in the upper group and then perform the test in which n_1 and n_2 are not equal to each other.

EXAMPLE 8.6-3 We shall use a sample of size $k = 14$ to test for both trend and cyclic effects. To determine the critical region for rejecting the hypothesis of randomness, we use the p.m.f. of R with $n_1 = n_2 = 7$. Since

$$\begin{aligned} P(R = 2) = P(R = 14) &= \frac{2}{3432}, \\ P(R = 3) = P(R = 13) &= \frac{12}{3432}, \\ P(R = 4) = P(R = 12) &= \frac{72}{3432}, \end{aligned}$$

the critical region $\{r\colon\ r \le 4 \text{ or } r \ge 12\}$ would yield a test at a significance level of $\alpha = 172/3432 = 0.05$. The 14 observations are

81.4	76.3	85.6	76.4	88.4	80.2	85.6
84.6	78.3	82.8	88.1	85.4	87.7	86.6

The median of these outcomes is $(84.6 + 85.4)/2 = 85.0$. Replacing each outcome with L if it falls below 85.0 and U if it falls above 85.0 yields the sequence

$$\underline{\text{L L}}\ \underline{\text{U}}\ \underline{\text{L}}\ \underline{\text{U}}\ \underline{\text{L}}\ \underline{\text{U}}\ \underline{\text{L L L}}\ \underline{\text{U U U U}}.$$

Since $r = 8$, the hypothesis of randomness is not rejected. ■

EXERCISES

8.6-1. Let the total lengths of the male and female trident lynx spiders be denoted by X and Y, respectively, with corresponding distribution functions $F(x)$ and $G(y)$. Measurement of the lengths, in millimeters, of eight male and eight female spiders yielded the following observations of X and Y:

X:	5.40	5.55	6.00	5.00	5.70	5.20	5.45	4.95
Y:	6.20	6.25	5.75	5.85	6.55	6.05	5.50	6.65

(a) Use these data to test the hypothesis $H_0\colon F(z) = G(z)$ against the alternative $H_1\colon F(z) > G(z)$. Let $\alpha \approx 0.10$, and use a run test.

(b) Use the two-sample Wilcoxon test to test $H_0\colon m_X = m_Y$ against the alternative $H_1\colon m_X < m_Y$ with $\alpha \approx 0.10$.

8.6-2. Let X and Y denote the times in hours per week that students in two different schools watch television. Let $F(x)$ and $G(y)$ denote the respective distribution functions. To test the hypothesis $H_0\colon F(z) = G(z)$, a random sample of eight students was selected from each school. Use the following observations to test this hypothesis:

X:	16.75	19.25	22.00	20.50	22.50	15.50	17.25	20.75
Y:	24.75	21.50	19.75	17.50	22.75	23.50	13.00	19.00

8.6-3. A parade consists of six bands and 12 floats. How many different parade lineups are possible if the parade begins and ends with a band and there is at least 1 float between each pair of bands?

8.6-4. List the $\binom{5}{3} = 10$ ways in which three dividers can be inserted between six given values of x, with no more than one divider per space.

8.6-5. Given the observations of X and Y listed in Exercise 8.5-15, use the run test to test $H_0: F(z) = G(z)$.

(a) Show that if $C = \{r: r \le 11\}$, then the significance level is $\alpha \approx 0.0473$.

(b) Calculate the value of r and state your conclusion.

(c) What is the p-value of this test?

8.6-6. Let $\alpha \approx 0.05$, and use the run test to test $H_0: F(z) = G(z)$ on the following observations of X and Y, which have been ordered for your convenience:

X:	−2.0482	−1.5748	−0.8797	−0.7170	−0.4907
	−0.2051	0.1651	0.2893	0.3186	0.3550
	0.4056	0.6975	0.7113	0.7377	1.7356
Y:	−1.2311	−1.0228	−0.8836	−0.6684	−0.6157
	−0.5755	−0.1019	−0.0297	0.3781	0.7400
	0.8479	1.0901	1.1397	1.1748	1.2921

NOTE: These data were simulated on a computer, using the standard normal distribution for X and a $U(-1.5, 1.5)$ for Y.

8.6-7. Use the following sample of size $k = 14$ to test the hypothesis of randomness against the alternative hypothesis of a trend effect at an $\alpha = 0.025$ significance level:

12.4	14.2	11.7	14.0	12.7	15.7	12.8
14.1	17.9	18.4	17.5	20.2	20.8	20.3

8.6-8. Use the following sample of size $k = 16$ to test the hypothesis of randomness against the alternative hypothesis of a cyclic effect:

12.4	31.8	22.2	24.5	17.9	24.6	15.7	27.3
22.7	26.0	14.5	22.0	21.8	31.9	11.5	28.3

What is your conclusion if
(a) $\alpha = 0.0317$?
(b) $\alpha = 0.10$?

8.6-9. A manufacturer of powdered soap checks the weights of soap in the company's 6-pound boxes periodically throughout the day. At each of 22 times, four boxes are selected at random, and the average of the weights of the soap in the boxes is recorded. Use the following 22 average weights to test the hypothesis of randomness against the alternative hypothesis of a trend at an approximate significance level of $\alpha = 0.025$:

6.050	6.038	6.003	6.015	6.025	6.063	6.033	6.010
5.995	6.020	6.060	6.060	6.065	6.050	6.043	6.040
6.045	6.065	6.055	6.060	6.060	6.070		

8.6-10. Each hour, a manufacturer of mints selects four mints at random from the production line and finds the average weight in grams. For 1 week, the following average weights were observed:

21.2	21.7	21.3	21.4	21.8	21.9	21.6	21.7	21.3	21.9
21.3	22.0	21.3	21.5	21.6	21.3	21.6	21.9	21.3	21.6
21.9	22.0	21.9	21.4	21.4	21.3	21.7	21.6	21.5	21.7
21.3	21.7	21.0	21.3	21.3	21.6	20.9	21.4		

Use these weights to test the hypothesis of randomness against the alternative hypothesis of a cyclic effect.

8.6-11. It is claimed that X is $U(0, 1)$. A random sample of 14 observations of X yielded the following data:

0.15	0.67	0.05	0.47	0.29	0.23	0.10
0.01	0.96	0.92	0.51	0.73	0.91	0.82

(a) Test $H_0: m = 0.5$ against the two-sided alternative hypothesis $H_1: m \ne 0.5$, using the sign test with significance level $\alpha = 0.0574$.

(b) Use a run test with the preceding observations of X to test for both trend and cyclic effects at the approximate significance level $\alpha = 0.05$.

8.6-12. On an introductory statistics test, 27 form A and 29 form B tests were used. The order in which the tests were returned is as follows:

A B B A B A B A A B B A B B
A B B A A A B A B A A A B B
B A B A B A B A A A B A B B
A B A A B A B B A B A B B B

(a) Use a run test to test the null hypothesis that this is a random sequence against the alternative hypothesis that there is a cyclic effect. Use the normal approximation and an $\alpha = 0.01$ significance level.

(a) On the basis of your conclusion, what advice would you give to the professor who gave this test?

8.6-13. In Exercise 11.1-4, the U.S. birthrates are given for 1960–2002. In order, they are

23.7	23.3	22.4	21.7	21.1	19.4	18.4	17.8	17.6
17.9	18.4	17.2	15.6	14.8	14.8	14.6	14.6	15.1
15.0	15.6	15.9	15.8	15.9	15.5	15.5	15.8	15.6
15.7	15.9	16.3	16.7	16.2	15.8	15.4	15.0	14.6
14.4	14.2	14.3	14.2	14.4	14.1	13.9		

Use the run test to test whether this is a random sequence against the alternative that there is a trend effect. Give the p-value of your test.

8.6-14. A window is manufactured that will be inserted into a car. To attach the window, five studs are located in the frame in locations A, B, C, D, and E. Periodically, a window is selected randomly from the production line and a standard "stud pull-out test" is performed that measures the force required to pull a stud out of the window. For each window, the tests are always performed in the order A, B, C, D, and E. Seventy observations that resulted from 14 windows were

140	159	138	102	84	126	147	126	103	92
149	155	135	120	94	149	143	109	101	86
144	154	120	105	97	149	151	140	103	99
157	140	120	96	87	146	137	120	93	89
149	154	139	100	84	148	142	130	98	81
112	135	109	84	87	112	135	109	84	87
126	118	135	90	77	125	126	131	78	75

For these data, the median is equal to 120. Use the run test to test whether this is a random sequence against the alternative hypothesis of a cyclic effect. Give the approximate p-value of the test. Interpret your conclusion. (See Exercise 11.1-6.)

8.6-15. In Exercises 7.3-19 and 8.5-14, the effect of a certain fertilizer was tested. For those data, calculate the number of runs and compare this number with the expected number of runs. Does the run test detect any fertilizer effect?

8.6-16. In Exercise 8.5-16, reaction times are given for young and older subjects. Use the run test to test whether the reaction times are equal or whether the young react more quickly. Compare the p-value for this test with the result for the Wilcoxon test.

8.6-17. In Exercise 8.5-17, several measurements are given for spiders. Does the run test detect any differences between females and males for either body lengths or leg lengths?

8.6-18. In Exercise 8.5-18, plants growths are compared for normal and enriched air. Compare the number of runs with the mean number of runs. Would the run test detect any difference?

8.6-19. In Exercises 7.3-20 and 8.5-19, data are given comparing an old and a new procedure. How does the result of the run test compare with the tests performed in those exercises?

8.7 KOLMOGOROV–SMIRNOV GOODNESS-OF-FIT TEST

In this section, we discuss a test that considers the goodness of fit between a hypothesized distribution function and an empirical distribution function. The empirical distribution function is given here in terms of its order statistics. Let $y_1 < y_2 < \cdots < y_n$ be the observed values of the order statistics of a random sample $x_1, x_2, \ldots, x_n$ of size n. When no two observations are equal, the empirical distribution function is defined by

$$F_n(x) = \begin{cases} 0, & x < y_1, \\ k/n, & y_k \le x < y_{k+1}, \qquad k = 1, 2, \ldots, n-1, \\ 1, & y_n \le x. \end{cases}$$

In this case, the empirical distribution function has a jump of magnitude $1/n$ occurring at each observation. If n_k observations are equal to x_k, a jump of magnitude n_k/n

occurs at x_k. In any case, $F_n(x)$ is simply the fraction of sample observations that are less than or equal to x.

Suppose that a random sample of size n is taken from a distribution of the continuous type that has the distribution function $F(x)$. How can we measure the"closeness" of $F(x)$ and the empirical distribution function $F_n(x)$? How does the sample size affect this closeness? We give some theoretical results to help answer these questions and then give a test for goodness of fit.

Let $X_1, X_2, \ldots, X_n$ denote a random sample of size n from a distribution of the continuous type with the distribution function $F(x)$. Consider a fixed value of x. Then $W = F_n(x)$, the value of the empirical distribution function at x, can be thought of as a random variable that takes on the values $0, 1/n, 2/n, \ldots, 1$. Now, $nW = k$ if, and only if, exactly k observations are less than or equal to x (say, success) and $n - k$ observations are greater than x. The probability that an observation is less than or equal to x is given by $F(x)$. That is, the probability of success is $F(x)$. Because of the independence of the random variables $X_1, X_2, \ldots, X_n$, the probability of k successes is given by the binomial distribution, namely,

$$
\begin{aligned}
P(nW = k) &= P\left(W = \frac{k}{n}\right) \\
&= \binom{n}{k}[F(x)]^k[1 - F(x)]^{n-k}, \qquad k = 0, 1, 2, \ldots, n.
\end{aligned}
$$

Since nW has a binomial distribution with $p = F(x)$, the mean and variance of nW are, respectively, given by

$$E(nW) = nF(x) \qquad \text{and} \qquad \text{Var}(nW) = n[F(x)][1 - F(x)].$$

Hence, the mean and the variance of $W = F_n(x)$ are

$$E[F_n(x)] = E(W) = F(x)$$

and

$$\text{Var}[F_n(x)] = \text{Var}(W) = \frac{F(x)[1 - F(x)]}{n}.$$

Since the variance of $F_n(x)$ approaches zero as n becomes large, $F_n(x)$ and its mean $F(x)$ tend to be closer with large n. As a matter of fact, there is a theorem by Glivenko, the proof of which is beyond the level of this book, which states that, with probability 1, $F_n(x)$ converges to $F(x)$ uniformly in x as $n \to \infty$.

Because of the convergence of the empirical distribution function to the theoretical distribution function, it makes sense to construct a goodness-of-fit test based on the closeness of the empirical and a hypothesized distribution function, say, $F_n(x)$ and $F_0(x)$, respectively. We shall use the Kolmogorov–Smirnov statistic defined by

$$D_n = \sup_x[\,|F_n(x) - F_0(x)|\,].$$

That is, D_n is the least upper bound of all pointwise differences $|F_n(x) - F_0(x)|$.

The exact distribution of the statistic D_n can be derived. We shall not do so, but we give some values of the distribution function of D_n, namely, $P(D_n \le d)$, in Table VIII in the appendix, that will be used for goodness-of-fit tests. We also point out that the distribution of D_n does not depend on the particular function $F_0(x)$ of the continuous type. [This is essentially due to the fact that $Y = F_0(X)$ has a uniform distribution $U(0, 1)$.] Thus, D_n can be thought of as a distribution-free statistic.

We are interested in using the Kolmogorov–Smirnov statistic D_n to test the hypothesis H_0: $F(x) = F_0(x)$ against all alternatives H_1: $F(x) \neq F_0(x)$, where $F_0(x)$ is some specified distribution function. Intuitively, we accept H_0 if the empirical distribution function $F_n(x)$ is sufficiently close to $F_0(x)$—that is, if the value of D_n is sufficiently small. The hypothesis H_0 is rejected if the observed value of D_n is greater than the critical value selected from Table VIII in the appendix, where this critical value depends upon the desired significance level and sample size.

We illustrate the use of the Kolmogorov–Smirnov statistic by two examples.

EXAMPLE 8.7-1 We shall test the hypothesis H_0: $F(x) = F_0(x)$ against H_1: $F(x) \neq F_0(x)$, where

$$F_0(x) = \begin{cases} 0, & x < 0, \\ x, & 0 \le x < 1, \\ 1, & 1 \le x. \end{cases}$$

That is, the null hypothesis is that X is $U(0,1)$. If the test is based on a sample of size $n = 10$ and if $\alpha = 0.10$, then the critical region is $C = \{d_{10}\colon d_{10} \ge 0.37\}$, where d_{10} is the observed value of the Kolmogorov–Smirnov statistic D_{10}. Suppose that the observed values of the random sample are 0.62, 0.36, 0.23, 0.76, 0.65, 0.09, 0.55, 0.26, 0.38, and 0.24. In Figure 8.7-1, we have plotted the empirical and hypothesized distribution functions for $0 \le x \le 1$. We see that $d_{10} = F_{10}(0.65) - F_0(0.65) = 0.25$; hence, H_0 is not rejected. Note that the more carefully you plot the empirical and theoretical distribution functions, the more you can minimize the number of points at which you should calculate the possible value of the Kolmogorov–Smirnov goodness-of-fit statistic. ■

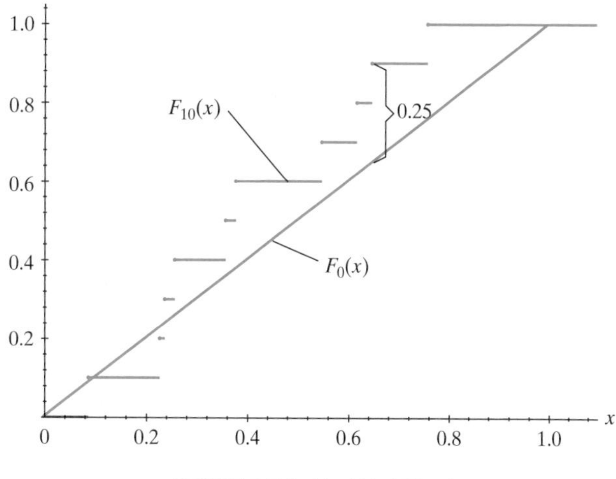

FIGURE 8.7-1: H_0: X is $U(0,1)$

REMARK If you have a computer program such as Minitab available, you can have it plot the empirical and theoretical distribution functions for you. Minitab will also give the value of the Kolmogorov–Smirnov goodness-of-fit statistic when you are testing for normality. ■

EXAMPLE 8.7-2 For a Poisson process with a mean rate of arrivals $\lambda = 1/\theta$, the random variable W, which denotes the waiting time until the αth arrival, has a gamma distribution. The p.d.f. of W is

$$f(w) = \frac{w^{\alpha-1}e^{-w/\theta}}{\Gamma(\alpha)\theta^{\alpha}}, \qquad 0 \le w < \infty.$$

A Geiger counter was set up to record the waiting time W in seconds required to observe $\alpha = 100$ alpha particle emissions of barium 133. It is claimed that the number of counts per second has a Poisson distribution with $\lambda = 14.7$ and hence, that $\theta = 0.068$. We shall test the hypothesis

$$H_0\colon\ F(w) = \int_{-\infty}^{w} f(t)\,dt,$$

where $f(t)$ is the gamma p.d.f. with $\theta = 0.068$ and $\alpha = 100$. On the basis of 25 observations, H_0 is rejected if $d_{25} \ge 0.24$ for $\alpha = 0.10$. The empirical and theoretical distribution functions are depicted in Figure 8.7-2 for 25 observations. For these data (Exercise 3.5-6), $d_{25} = 0.123$ and hence H_0 is not rejected. ■

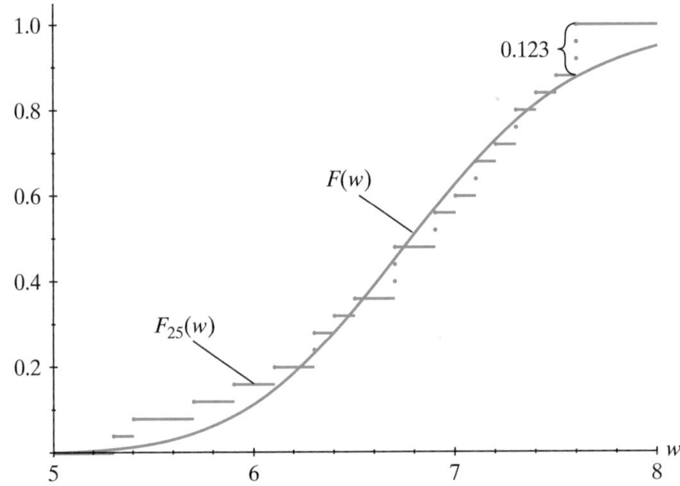

FIGURE 8.7-2: H_0: X has a gamma distribution

Note that we have been assuming that $F(x)$ is a continuous function. That is, we have considered only random variables of the continuous type. This procedure may also be applied in the discrete case; however, the true significance level will then be at most α. That is, the resulting test will be conservative.

Another application of the Kolmogorov–Smirnov statistic is in forming a confidence band for an unknown distribution function $F(x)$. To form a confidence band based on a sample of size n, select a number d such that

$$P(D_n \ge d) = \alpha.$$

Then

$$\begin{aligned} 1 - \alpha &= P[\sup_x |F_n(x) - F(x)| \le d] \\ &= P[\,|F_n(x) - F(x)\,| \le d \text{ for all } x] \\ &= P[F_n(x) - d \le F(x) \le F_n(x) + d \text{ for all } x]. \end{aligned}$$

Let

$$F_L(x) = \begin{cases} 0, & F_n(x) - d \le 0, \\ F_n(x) - d, & F_n(x) - d > 0, \end{cases}$$

and

$$F_U(x) = \begin{cases} F_n(x) + d, & F_n(x) + d < 1, \\ 1, & F_n(x) + d \ge 0. \end{cases}$$

The two-step functions $F_L(x)$ and $F_U(x)$ yield a $100(1 - \alpha)\%$ confidence band for the unknown distribution function $F(x)$.

EXAMPLE 8.7-3 A random sample of size $n = 15$ from an unknown distribution yielded the sample values 3.88, 3.97, 4.03, 2.49, 3.18, 3.08, 2.91, 3.43, 2.41, 1.57, 3.78, 3.25, 1.29, 2.57, and 3.40. Now,

$$P(D_{15} \ge 0.30) = 0.10.$$

A 90% confidence band for the unknown distribution function $F(x)$ is depicted in Figure 8.7-3. ■

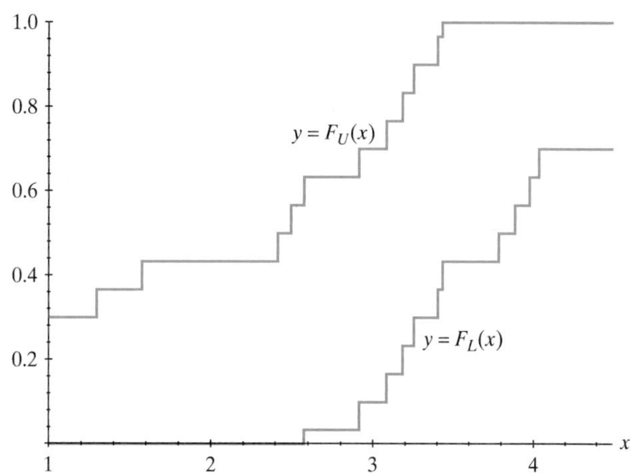

FIGURE 8.7-3: A 90% confidence band for an unknown distribution function

EXERCISES

8.7-1. Five ordered observations of X are 0.40, 0.51, 0.53, 0.62, 0.74. Use the Kolmogorov–Smirnov statistic to test the hypothesis that X is $U(0,1)$. Let $\alpha = 0.20$.

8.7-2. Select 10 sets of 10 random numbers from Table IX in the appendix. For each set of 10 random numbers, calculate the value of the Kolmogorov–Smirnov statistic d_{10} with $F_0(x) = x$, $0 \le x \le 1$. Is it true that about 20% of the observations of D_{10} are greater than 0.32? (Compare your results with those of other students, provided that they selected different random numbers.)

8.7-3. A doctor of obstetrics used an ultrasound examination between the 16th and 25th weeks of a patient's pregnancy to measure the widest diameter of the fetal head, in millimeters. Let X equal this diameter. Use the following 10 observations of X to test the hypothesis that the distribution of X is $N(60, 100)$:

56 65 47 57 62 48 68 75 79 49

8.7-4. In Exercise 8.5-4, the outcomes of 10 simulations of a Cauchy random variable are given.

(a) Sketch the empirical distribution function and superimpose the Cauchy distribution function.

(b) Use the Kolmogorov–Smirnov statistic to test whether the 10 observations represent a random sample from a Cauchy distribution. Let $\alpha = 0.10$.

8.7-5. In Exercise 3.6-9, diameters (in mm) of 30 individual grains of soil were given as follows:

1.24 1.36 1.28 1.31 1.35 1.20 1.39 1.35 1.41 1.31
1.28 1.26 1.37 1.49 1.32 1.40 1.33 1.28 1.25 1.39
1.38 1.34 1.40 1.27 1.33 1.36 1.43 1.33 1.29 1.34

(a) Calculate the sample mean and the sample variance for these data.

(b) Use a Kolmogorov–Smirnov goodness-of-fit statistic to test the null hypothesis that these data are observations of a normally distributed random variable.

8.7-6. Use the following 15 observations of X to construct a 90% confidence band for the unknown distribution function $F(x)$:

20.2 85.4 59.9 72.7 88.0 33.7 87.1 99.5 93.8
18.4 60.6 98.9 90.9 86.9 74.2

8.7-7. While testing a computer tape for bad records, the computer operator counted the number of flaws per 100 feet. Let X equal this number, and test, at a significance level of $\alpha \approx 0.10$, the hypothesis that the distribution of X is Poisson with a mean of $\lambda = 2.4$, using the following 40 observations of X:

x	Frequency
0	5
1	7
2	12
3	9
4	5
5	1
6	1
	40

8.7-8. The computer operator in Exercise 8.7-7 also measured the distances between flaws. These distances, reported in Exercise 8.1-10, in which a chi-square goodness-of-fit test was used, are repeated here:

30	79	38	47	22	52	36	36	7	57
3	22	30	14	8	32	15	21	12	12
6	67	6	7	35	78	28	74	5	9
37	1	3	3	44	160	50	27	61	15
39	44	130	18	6	1	32	116	23	12
58	101	68	53	58	21	21	7	79	41
80	33	71	81	17	10	13	49	21	56
107	21	17	64	14	36	26	1	54	207
64	238	25	51	82	8	2	3	43	87

Now use a Kolmogorov–Smirnov goodness-of-fit statistic to test the null hypothesis that we are observing observations of an exponential random variable. Are your conclusions consistent with each other?

8.7-9. In Exercise 8.6-14, 70 observations of a random variable X are listed that give the force required to pull a stud out of a window.

(a) Test the null hypothesis that the distribution of X is $N(117.5, 252)$. Use the Kolmogorov–Smirnov statistic with a significance level of $\alpha = 0.20$. What is your conclusion?

(b) Carefully analyzing the graphs of the empirical and theoretical distribution functions or by constructing a histogram, do you agree with the conclusion in part (a)? Why or why not?

(c) Construct and interpret a q–q plot for these data.

8.7-10. Let X equal the number of chocolate chips in a chocolate-chip cookie. Let $\alpha \approx 0.10$, and use the Kolmogorov–Smirnov goodness-of-fit statistic and the following data to test the hypothesis that the distribution of X is Poisson with a mean of $\lambda = 5.6$:

x	Frequency
0	0
1	0
2	2
3	8
4	7
5	13
6	13
7	10
8	4
9	4
10	1
	62

8.7-11. In Example 3.3-3, 105 times between calls to 911 are listed. Also given is a graph of the empirical distribution function with an exponential distribution function superimposed. Does this graph and the Kolmogorov–Smirnov goodness-of-fit statistic support the suggestion that the 105 times are observations of an exponential random variable? Why?

8.7-12. In Exercise 8.4-15, the weights in grams of "14-gram" snack packages of peanuts were given as follows:

13.9 14.4 14.6 14.7 14.7 15.2 15.2 15.2
15.3 15.4 15.4 15.5 15.6 15.6 15.9 16.4

Test the null hypothesis that these weights are observations of a normally distributed random variable with mean $\mu = 15.3$ and standard deviation $\sigma = 0.6$. Use a 10% significance level.

8.7-13. The March 29, 1992, issue of *Parade Magazine* reported the results of a study by Runzheimer International that gathered data from around the world on the cost in U.S. dollars per gallon for the least expensive gasoline available. The study compared each cost in December 1990 (before the Gulf War) with the cost in December 1991. Let X equal the difference—the 1991 cost minus the 1990 cost. Assume that the following $n = 18$ differences represent a random sample of observations of X:

−0.28	−0.40	0.06	0.04	−0.29	0.38
−0.08	−0.02	−0.22	−0.28	0.11	0.44
−0.17	−0.39	−0.36	−0.18	−0.39	−0.31

Test whether the times are observations of a shifted (two-parameter) exponential distribution. Estimate δ and θ with their unbiased estimators. That is, let y_1 equal the minimum value of the X observations. Then unbiased estimates of θ and δ are

$$\widehat{\theta} = [n/(n-1)][\overline{x} - y_1] \quad \text{and} \quad \widehat{\delta} = y_1 - \widehat{\theta}/n.$$

8.8 RESAMPLING METHODS

Sampling and resampling methods have become more useful in recent years due to the power of computers. These methods are even used in introductory courses to convince students that statistics have distributions—that is, that statistics are random variables with distributions. At this stage in the book, the reader should be convinced that this is true, although we did use some sampling in Section 5.6 to help sell the idea that the sample mean has an approximate normal distribution.

Resampling methods, however, are used for more than showing that statistics have certain distributions. Rather, they are needed in finding approximate distributions of certain statistics that are used to make statistical inferences. We already know a great deal about the distribution of $\overline{X}$, and resampling methods are not needed for $\overline{X}$. In particular, $\overline{X}$ has an approximate normal distribution with mean μ and standard deviation $\sigma/\sqrt{n}$. Of course, if the latter is unknown, we can estimate it by $s/\sqrt{n}$ and note that $(\overline{X} - \mu)/(s/\sqrt{n})$ has an approximate $N(0,1)$ distribution, provided that the sample size is large enough and the underlying distribution is not too badly skewed with a long, heavy tail.

We know something about the distribution of S^2 *if the random sample arises from a normal distribution* or one fairly close to it. However, the statistic S^2 is not very robust, in that its distribution changes a great deal as the underlying distribution changes. It is not like $\overline{X}$, which always has an approximate normal distribution, provided that the mean μ and variance σ^2 of the underlying distribution exist. So what do we do about distributions of statistics like the sample variance S^2, whose distribution depends so much on having a given underlying distribution? We use resampling methods that essentially substitute computation for theory. We need to have some idea about the distributions of these various estimators to find confidence intervals for the corresponding parameters.

Let us now explain resampling. Suppose that we need to find the distribution of some statistic, such as S^2, but we do not believe that we are sampling from a normal distribution. We observe the values of $X_1, X_2, \ldots, X_n$ to be $x_1, x_2, \ldots, x_n$. Actually, if we know nothing about the underlying distribution, then the empirical distribution found by placing the weight $1/n$ on each x_i is the best estimate of that distribution. Therefore, to get some idea about the distribution of S^2, let us take a random sample of size n from this empirical distribution; then we are sampling from the n values with replacement. We compute S^2 for that sample; say it is s_1^2. We then do it again, getting s_2^2. And again, we compute s_3^2. We continue to do this a large number of times, say, N, where N might be 1000, 2000, or even 10,000. Once we have these

N values of S^2, we can construct a histogram, a stem-and-leaf display, or a q–q plot—anything to help us get some information about the distribution of S^2 when the sample arises from this empirical distribution, which is an estimate of the real underlying distribution. Clearly, we must use the computer for all of this sampling. We illustrate the resampling procedure by using, not S^2, but a statistic called the *trimmed mean*.

Although we usually do not know the underlying distribution, we state that, in this illustration, it is of the Cauchy type, because there are certain basic ideas we want to review or introduce for the first time. The p.d.f. of the Cauchy is

$$f(x) = \frac{1}{\pi(1 + x^2)}, \qquad -\infty < x < \infty.$$

The distribution function is

$$F(x) = \int_{-\infty}^{x} \frac{1}{\pi(1 + w^2)}\, dw = \frac{1}{\pi}\arctan x + \frac{1}{2}, \qquad -\infty < x < \infty.$$

If we want to generate some X values that have this distribution, we let Y have the uniform distribution $U(0,1)$ and define X by

$$Y = F(X) = \frac{1}{\pi}\arctan X + \frac{1}{2}$$

or, equivalently,

$$X = \tan\left[\pi\left(Y - \frac{1}{2}\right)\right].$$

We can generate 40 values of Y on the computer and then calculate the 40 values of X. Let us now add $\theta = 5$ to each X value to create a sample from a Cauchy distribution with a median of 5. That is, we have a random sample of 40 W values, where $W = X + 5$. We will consider some statistics used to estimate the median, θ, of this distribution. Of course, usually the value of the median is unknown, but here we know that it is equal to $\theta = 5$, and our statistics are estimates of this known number. These 40 values of W are as follows, after ordering:

−7.34	−5.92	−2.98	0.19	0.77	0.95	2.86	3.17	3.76	4.20
4.20	4.27	4.31	4.42	4.60	4.73	4.84	4.87	4.90	4.96
4.98	5.00	5.09	5.09	5.14	5.22	5.23	5.42	5.50	5.83
5.94	5.95	6.00	6.01	6.24	6.82	9.62	10.03	18.27	93.62

It is interesting to observe that many of these 40 values are between 3 and 7 and hence, are close to $\theta = 5$; it is almost as if they had arisen from a normal distribution with mean $\mu = 5$ and $\sigma^2 = 1$. But then we note the outliers; these very large or small values occur because of the heavy and long tails of the Cauchy distribution and suggest that the sample mean $\overline{X}$ is not a very good estimator of the middle. And it is not in this sample because $\overline{x} = 6.67$. In a more theoretical course, it can be shown that, due to the fact that the mean μ and the variance σ^2 do not exist for a Cauchy distribution, $\overline{X}$ is not any better than a single observation X_i in estimating the median θ. The sample median $\widetilde{m}$ is a much better estimate of θ, as it is not influenced by the outliers. Here the median equals 4.97, which is fairly close to 5. Actually, the maximum likelihood estimator found by maximizing

$$L(\theta) = \prod_{i=1}^{40} \frac{1}{\pi[1 + (x_i - \theta)^2]}$$

is extremely good, but requires difficult numerical methods to compute. Then advanced theory shows that, in the case of a Cauchy distribution, a **trimmed mean**, found by ordering the sample, discarding the smallest and largest $3/8 = 37.5\%$ of the sample, and averaging the middle 25%, is almost as good as the maximum likelihood estimator, but is much easier to compute. This trimmed mean is usually denoted by $\overline{X}_{0.375}$; we use $\overline{X}_t$ for brevity, and here $\overline{x}_t = 4.96$. For this sample, it is not quite as good as the median; but, for most samples, it is better. Trimmed means are often very useful and many times are used with a smaller trimming percentage. For example, in sporting events such as skating and diving, often the smallest and largest of the judges' scores are discarded.

For this Cauchy example, let us resample from the empirical distribution created by placing the "probability" 1/40 on each of our 40 observations. With each of these samples, we find our trimmed mean $\overline{X}_t$. That is, we order the observations of each resample and average the middle 25% of the order statistics—namely, the middle 10 order statistics. We do this $N = 1000$ times, thus obtaining $N = 1000$ values of $\overline{X}_t$. These values are summarized with the histogram in Figure 8.8-1(a).

From this resampling procedure, which is called **bootstrapping**, we have some idea about the distribution if the sample arises from the empirical distribution and, hopefully, from the underlying distribution, which is approximated by the empirical distribution. While the distribution of the sample mean $\overline{X}$ is not normal if the sample arises from a Cauchy-type distribution, the approximate distribution of $\overline{X}_t$ is normal. From the histogram of trimmed mean values in Figure 8.8-1(a), that looks to be the case. This observation is supported by the q–q plot in Figure 8.8-1(b) of the quantiles of a standard normal distribution versus those of the 1000 $\overline{x}_t$ values: The plot is very close to being a straight line.

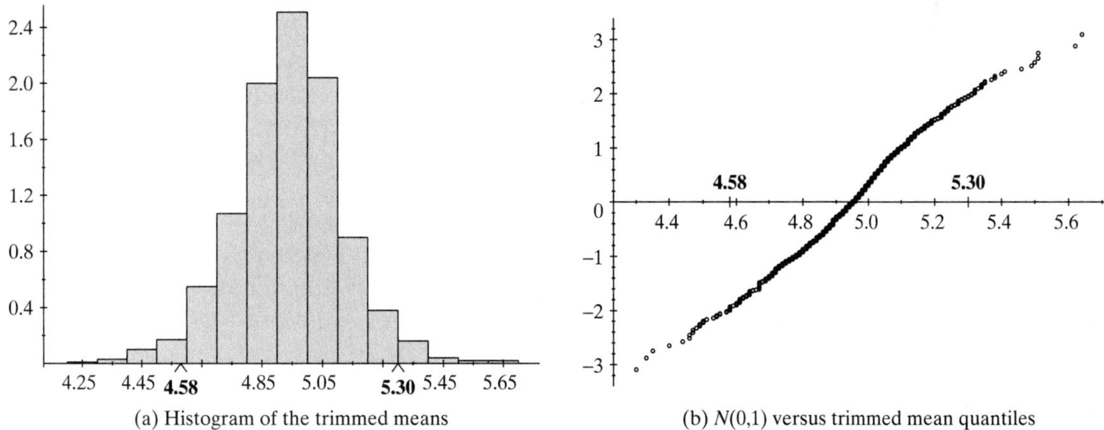

(a) Histogram of the trimmed means

(b) $N(0,1)$ versus trimmed mean quantiles

FIGURE 8.8-1: $N = 1000$ observations of trimmed means

How do we find a confidence interval for θ? Recall that the middle of the distribution of $\overline{X}_t - \theta$ is zero. So a guess at θ would be the amount needed to move the histogram of $\overline{X}_t$ values over so that zero is more or less in the middle of the translated histogram. We recognize that this histogram was generated from the original sample $X_1, X_2, \ldots, X_{40}$ and thus is really only an estimate of the distribution of $\overline{X}_t$.

We could get a point estimate of θ by moving it over until its median (or mean) is at zero. Clearly, however, some error is incurred in doing so—and we really want some bounds for θ as given by a confidence interval.

To find that confidence interval, let us proceed as follows: In the $N = 1000$ resampled values of $\overline{X}_t$, we find two points—say, c and d—such that about 25 values are less than c and about 25 are greater than d. That is, c and d are about on the respective 2.5th and 97.5th percentiles of the empirical distribution of these $N = 1000$ resampled $\overline{X}_t$ values. Thus, θ should be big enough so that over 2.5 percent of the $\overline{X}_t$ values are less than c and small enough so that over 2.5 percent of the $\overline{X}_t$ values are greater than d. This requires that $c < \theta$ and $\theta < d$; thus, $[c, d]$ serves as an approximate 95% confidence interval for θ as found by the **percentile method**. With our bootstrapped distribution of $N = 1000$ $\overline{X}_t$ values, this 95% confidence interval for θ runs from 4.58 to 5.30, and these two points are marked on the histogram and the q–q plot. Clearly, we could change this percentage to other values, such as 90%.

This percentile method, associated with the bootstrap method, is a nonparametric procedure, as we make no assumptions about the underlying distribution. It is interesting to compare the answer it produces with that obtained by using the order statistics $Y_1 < Y_2 < \cdots < Y_{40}$. If the sample arises from a continuous-type distribution, then, with the use of a calculator or computer, we have, when θ is the median,

$$P(Y_{14} < \theta < Y_{27}) = \sum_{k=14}^{26} \binom{40}{k}\left(\frac{1}{2}\right)^{40} = 0.9615.$$

(See Section 8.4.) Since, in our illustration, $Y_{14} = 4.42$ and $Y_{27} = 5.23$, the interval $[4.42, 5.23]$ is an approximate 96% confidence interval for θ. Of course, $\theta = 5$ is included in each of the two confidence intervals. In this case, the bootstrap confidence interval is a little more symmetric about $\theta = 5$ and somewhat shorter, but it did require much more work.

We have now illustrated bootstrapping, which allows us to substitute computation for theory to make statistical inferences about characteristics of the underlying distribution. This method is becoming more important as we encounter complicated data sets that clearly do not satisfy certain underlying assumptions. For example, consider the distribution of $T = (\overline{X} - \mu)/(S/\sqrt{n})$ when the random sample arises from an exponential distribution that has p.d.f. $f(x) = e^{-x}$, $0 < x < \infty$, with mean $\mu = 1$. First we will *not* use resampling, but we will simulate the distribution of T when the sample size $n = 16$ by taking $N = 1000$ random samples from this known exponential distribution. Here

$$F(x) = \int_0^x e^{-w}\,dw = 1 - e^{-x}, \qquad 0 < x < \infty.$$

So $Y = F(X)$ means

$$X = -\ln(1 - Y)$$

and X has that given exponential distribution with $\mu = 1$, provided that Y has the uniform distribution $U(0,1)$. With the computer, we select $n = 16$ values of Y, determine the corresponding $n = 16$ values of X, and, finally, compute the value of $T = (\overline{X} - 1)/(S/\sqrt{16})$—say, T_1. We repeat this process over and over again, obtaining not only T_1, but also the values of $T_2, T_3, \ldots, T_{1000}$. We have done this and display the histogram of the 1000 T values in Figure 8.8-2(a). Moreover the q–q plot with quantiles of $N(0, 1)$ on the y-axis is displayed in Figure 8.8-2(b). Both the histogram and the q–q plot show that the distribution of T in this case is skewed to the left.

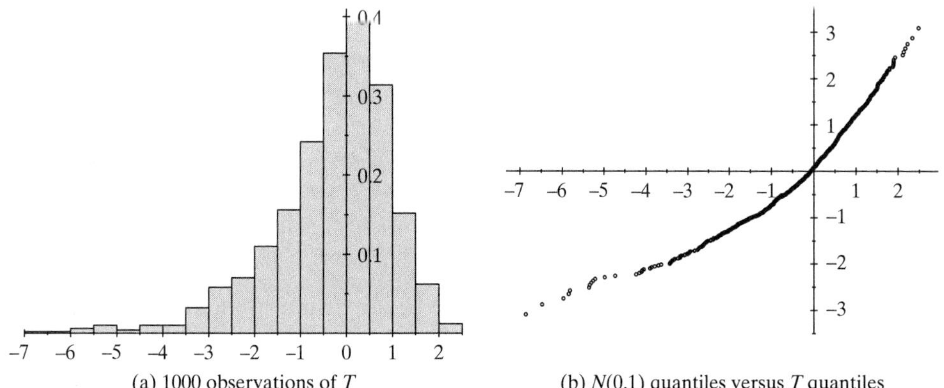

FIGURE 8.8-2: T observations from an exponential distribution

In the preceding illustration, we knew the underlying distribution. Let us now sample from the exponential distribution with mean $\mu = 1$, but add a value θ to each X. Thus, we will try to estimate the new mean $\theta + 1$. The authors know the value of θ, but the readers do not at this time. The observed 16 values of this random sample are

11.9776	9.3889	9.9798	13.4676	9.2895	10.1242	9.5798	9.3148
9.0605	9.1680	11.0394	9.1083	10.3720	9.0523	13.2969	10.5852

At this point we are trying to find a confidence interval for $\mu = \theta + 1$, and we pretend that we do not know that the underlying distribution is exponential. Actually, this is the case in practice: We do not know the underlying distribution. So we use the empirical distribution as the best guess of the underlying distribution; it is found by placing the weight 1/16 on each of the observations. The mean of this empirical distribution is $\overline{x} = 10.3003$. Therefore, we obtain some idea about the distribution of T by now simulating

$$T = \frac{\overline{X} - 10.3003}{S/\sqrt{16}}$$

with $N = 1000$ random samples from the empirical distribution.

We obtain $t_1, t_2, \ldots, t_{1000}$, and these values are used to construct a histogram, shown in Figure 8.8-3(a), and a q–q plot, illustrated in Figure 8.8-3(b). These two figures look somewhat like those in Figure 8.8-2. Moreover, the 0.025th and 0.975th quantiles of the 1000 t-values are $c = -3.1384$ and $d = 1.8167$, respectively.

Now we have some idea about the 2.5th and 97.5th percentiles of the T distribution. Hence, as a very rough approximation, we can write

$$P\left(-3.1384 \leq \frac{\overline{X} - \mu}{S/\sqrt{16}} \leq 1.8167\right) \approx 0.95.$$

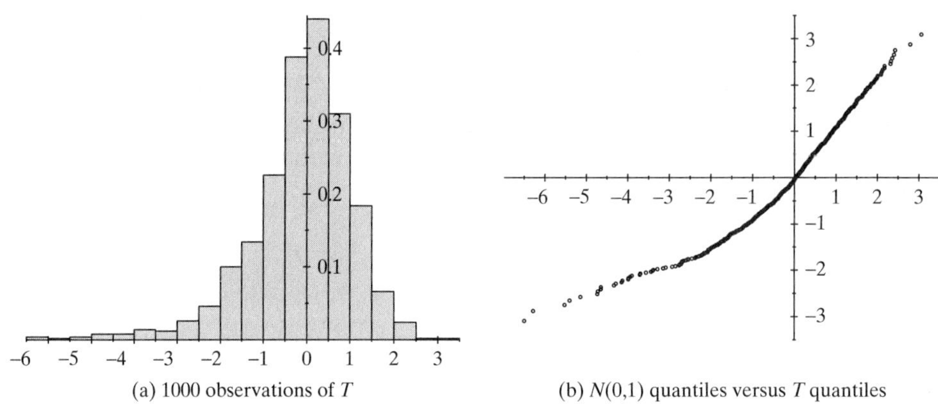

(a) 1000 observations of T

(b) $N(0,1)$ quantiles versus T quantiles

FIGURE 8.8-3: *T* observations from an empirical distribution

This formula leads to the rough approximate 95 percent confidence interval

$$[\bar{x} - 1.8167s/\sqrt{16}, \bar{x} - (-3.1384)s/\sqrt{16}]$$

once the $\bar{x}$ and s of the *original* sample are substituted. With $\bar{x} = 10.3003$ and $s = 1.4544$, we have

$$[10.3003 - 1.8167(1.4544)/4, 10.3003 + 3.1384(1.4544)/4] = [9.6397, 11.4414]$$

as a 95% approximate confidence interval for $\mu = \theta + 1$. Note that, because we added $\theta = 9$ to each x-value, the interval does cover $\theta + 1 = 10$.

It is easy to see how this procedure gets its name, because it is like "pulling yourself up by your own bootstraps," with the empirical distribution acting as the bootstraps.

EXERCISES

8.8-1. If time and computing facilities are available, consider the following 40 losses, due to wind-related catastrophes, that were recorded to the nearest \$1 million (these data include only those losses of \$2 million or more, and, for convenience, they have been ordered and recorded in millions of dollars):

2	2	2	2	2	2	2	2	2	2
2	2	3	3	3	3	4	4	4	5
5	5	5	6	6	6	6	8	8	9
15	17	22	23	24	24	25	27	32	43

To illustrate bootstrapping, take resamples of size $n = 40$ as many as $N = 100$ times, computing $T = (\bar{X} - 5)/(S/\sqrt{40})$ each time. Here the value 5 is the median of the original sample. Construct a histogram of the bootstrapped values of T.

8.8-2. Consider the following 16 observed values, rounded to the nearest tenth, from the exponential distribution that was given in this section:

12.0	9.4	10.0	13.5	9.3	10.1	9.6	9.3
9.1	9.2	11.0	9.1	10.4	9.1	13.3	10.6

(a) Take resamples of size $n = 16$ from these observations about $N = 200$ times, and compute s^2 each time. Construct a histogram of these 200 bootstrapped values of S^2.

(b) Simulate $N = 200$ random samples of size $n = 16$ from an exponential distribution with θ equal to the mean of the data in part (a) minus 9. For each sample, calculate the value of s^2. Construct a histogram of these 200 values of S^2.

(c) Construct a q–q plot of the two sets of sample variances and compare these two empirical distributions of S^2.

8.8-3. Let $X_1, X_2, \ldots, X_{21}$ and $Y_1, Y_2, \ldots, X_{21}$ be random samples of sizes $n = 21$ and $m = 21$ from independent $N(0,1)$ distributions. Then $F = S_X^2/S_Y^2$ has an F distribution with 20 and 20 degrees of freedom.

(a) Illustrate this situation empirically by simulating 100 observations of F.
(i) Plot a relative frequency histogram with the $F(20,20)$ p.d.f. superimposed.
(ii) Construct a q–q plot of the quantiles of $F(20,20)$ versus the order statistics of your simulated data. Is the plot linear?

(b) Consider the following 21 observations of the $N(0,1)$ random variable X:

0.1616	−0.8593	0.3105	0.3932	−0.2357	0.9697	1.3633
−0.4166	0.7540	−1.0570	−0.1287	−0.6172	0.3208	0.9637
0.2494	−1.1907	−2.4699	−0.1931	1.2274	−1.2826	−1.1532

Consider also the following 21 observations of the $N(0,1)$ random variable Y:

0.4419	−0.2313	0.9233	−0.1203	1.7659	−0.2022	0.9036
−0.4996	−0.8778	−0.8574	2.7574	1.1033	0.7066	1.3595
−0.0056	−0.5545	−0.1491	−0.9774	−0.0868	1.7462	−0.2636

Sampling with replacement, resample with a sample of size 21 from each of these sets of observations. Calculate the value of $w = s_x^2/s_y^2$. Repeat in order to simulate 100 observations of W from these two empirical distributions. Use the same graphical comparisons that you used in part (a) to see if the 100 observations represent observations from an approximate $F(20,20)$ distribution.

(c) Consider the following 21 observations of the exponential random variable X with mean 1:

0.6958	1.6394	0.2464	1.5827	0.0201	0.4544	0.8427
0.6385	0.1307	1.0223	1.3423	1.6653	0.0081	5.2150
0.5453	0.08440	1.2346	0.5721	1.5167	0.4843	0.9145

Consider also the following 21 observations of the exponential random variable Y with mean 1:

1.1921	0.3708	0.0874	0.5696	0.1192	0.0164	1.6482
0.2453	0.4522	3.2312	1.4745	0.8870	2.8097	0.8533
0.1466	0.9494	0.0485	4.4379	1.1244	0.2624	1.3655

Sampling with replacement, resample with a sample of size 21 from each of these sets of observations. Calculate the value of $w = s_x^2/s_y^2$. Repeat in order to simulate 100 observations of W from these two empirical distributions. Use the same graphical comparisons that you used in part (a) to see if the 100 observations represent observations from an approximate $F(20,20)$ distribution.

8.8-4. The following 54 pairs of data give, for Old Faithful geyser, the duration in minutes of an eruption and the time in minutes until the next eruption:

(2.500, 72)	(4.467, 88)	(2.333, 62)	(5.000, 87)	(1.683, 57)	(4.500, 94)
(4.500, 91)	(2.083, 51)	(4.367, 98)	(1.583, 59)	(4.500, 93)	(4.550, 86)
(1.733, 70)	(2.150, 63)	(4.400, 91)	(3.983, 82)	(1.767, 58)	(4.317, 97)
(1.917, 59)	(4.583, 90)	(1.833, 58)	(4.767, 98)	(1.917, 55)	(4.433, 107)
(1.750, 61)	(4.583, 82)	(3.767, 91)	(1.833, 65)	(4.817, 97)	(1.900, 52)
(4.517, 94)	(2.000, 60)	(4.650, 84)	(1.817, 63)	(4.917, 91)	(4.000, 83)
(4.317, 84)	(2.133, 71)	(4.783, 83)	(4.217, 70)	(4.733, 81)	(2.000, 60)
(4.717, 91)	(1.917, 51)	(4.233, 85)	(1.567, 55)	(4.567, 98)	(2.133, 49)
(4.500, 85)	(1.717, 65)	(4.783, 102)	(1.850, 56)	(4.583, 86)	(1.733, 62)

(a) Calculate the correlation coefficient, and construct a scatterplot, of these data.

(b) To estimate the distribution of the correlation coefficient, R, resample 500 samples of size 54 from the empirical distribution, and for each sample, calculate the value of R.

(c) Construct a histogram of these 500 observations of R.

(d) Simulate 500 samples of size 54 from a bivariate normal distribution with correlation coefficient equal to the correlation coefficient of the geyser data. For each sample of 54, calculate the correlation coefficient.

(e) Construct a histogram of the 500 observations of the correlation coefficient.

(f) Construct a q–q plot of the 500 observations of R from the bivariate normal distribution of part (d) versus the 500 observations in part (b). Do the two distributions of R appear to be about equal?

8.8-5. Consider the following 12 pairs of data, which are values of a random sample of size 12 from a bivariate normal distribution with correlation coefficient $\rho = -0.8$:

$$\begin{array}{cccc} (-0.8118, 0.5205) & (-1.7527, 1.2374) & (-0.0639, 1.1181) & (-0.5526, 0.7047) \\ (-0.6387, -0.3772) & (0.1743, 0.2298) & (1.7126, -2.2842) & (0.3114, 0.0846) \\ (-0.6270, 1.0964) & (0.5996, -1.1564) & (-0.9370, 0.6896) & (0.6739, -0.0470) \end{array}$$

(a) To estimate the distribution of the correlation coefficient, R, resample 500 samples of size 12 from the empirical distribution, and for each sample, calculate the value of R.
(b) Construct a histogram of these 500 observations of R.
(c) Simulate 500 samples of size 12 from a bivariate normal distribution with correlation coefficient equal to the correlation coefficient of the given data. For each sample of 12, calculate the correlation coefficient.
(d) Construct a histogram of the 500 observations of the correlation coefficient given in part (c).
(e) Construct a q–q plot of the 500 observations of R from the bivariate normal distribution of part (c) versus the 500 observations found in part (a). Do the two distributions of R appear to be about equal?

8.8-6. Consider the following 20 pairs of data, which are paired data from two exponential distributions, each having a mean of 5:

$$\begin{array}{cccc} (5.4341, 8.4902) & (33.2097, 4.7063) & (0.4034, 1.8961) & (1.4137, 0.2996) \\ (17.9365, 3.1350) & (4.4867, 6.2089) & (11.5107, 10.9784) & (8.2473, 19.6554) \\ (1.9995, 3.6339) & (1.8965, 1.7850) & (1.7116, 1.1545) & (4.4594, 1.2344) \\ (0.4036, 0.7260) & (3.0578, 19.0489) & (21.4049, 4.6495) & (3.8845, 13.7945) \\ (5.9536, 9.2438) & (11.3942, 1.7863) & (5.4813, 4.3356) & (7.0590, 1.15834) \end{array}$$

(a) Calculate the correlation coefficient, and construct a scatterplot, of these data.
(b) To estimate the distribution of the correlation coefficient, R, resample 500 samples of size 20 from the empirical distribution, and for each sample, calculate the value of R.
(c) Construct a histogram of these 500 observations of R.
(d) Simulate 500 samples of size 20 from a bivariate normal distribution with correlation coefficient 0. For each sample of 20, calculate the correlation coefficient.
(e) Construct a histogram of the 500 observations of the correlation coefficient.
(f) Construct a q–q plot of the 500 observations of R from the bivariate normal distribution of part (d) versus the 500 observations in part (b). Do the two distributions of R appear to be about equal?

8.8-7. Consider the following 20 pairs of data, which are paired data from two Cauchy distributions:

$$\begin{array}{cccc} (-6.0141, 3.1634) & (-1.0420, 16.6134) & (0.0894, 0.1775) & (-4.0680, -0.4082) \\ (2.4561, -3.0045) & (-3.7596, -1.0007) & (0.1678, -1.1852) & (-0.5504, -0.9796) \\ (1.4399, -0.1211) & (-0.2510, -0.7397) & (-5.3430, 0.4839) & (-0.8826, -2.9297) \\ (1.4219, 1.7424) & (-5.7973, 0.1788) & (1.0064, -0.2806) & (-2.1313, -0.5802) \\ (5.8900, 0.8383) & (-2.2183, -0.4968) & (1.1598, 1.2758) & (-1.0269, -15.7753) \end{array}$$

(a) To estimate the distribution of the correlation coefficient, R, resample 500 samples of size 20 from the empirical distribution, and for each sample, calculate the value of R.
(b) Construct a histogram of these 500 observations of R.
(c) Simulate 500 samples of size 20 from a bivariate normal distribution with correlation coefficient 0. For each sample of 20, calculate the correlation coefficient.
(d) Construct a histogram of the 500 observations of the correlation coefficient.
(e) Construct a q–q plot of the 500 observations of R from the bivariate normal distribution of part (c) versus the 500 observations found in part (a). Do the two distributions of R appear to be about equal?

HISTORICAL COMMENTS From the 1940s to well into the 1960s, most statisticians thought that nonparametric methods referred to distribution-free inferences. For example, under the null hypothesis, the one-sample Wilcoxon test does not depend upon the underlying distribution as long as it is symmetric and of the continuous type. Also, the two-sample Wilcoxon test of $F(x) = G(x)$ does not depend upon the distributions $F(x) = G(x)$ as long as they are of the continuous type. In later years, the term *nonparametric methods* came to mean something that is possibly broader than distribution-free methods, such as the bootstrap technique.

The name *bootstrap* and the resulting technique were first used by Brad Efron of Stanford University. Efron knew that the expression "to pull oneself up by his or her own bootstraps" seems to come from *The Surprising Adventures of Baron Munchausen* by Rudolph Erich Raspe. The Baron had fallen from the sky and found himself in a hole 9 fathoms deep and had no idea how to get out. He comments as follows: "Looking down I observed that I had on a pair of boots with exceptionally sturdy straps. Grasping them firmly, I pulled with all my might. Soon I had hoisted myself to the top and stepped out on terra firma without further ado."

Of course, in statistical *bootstrapping*, statisticians pull themselves up by their bootstraps (the empirical distributions) by recognizing that the empirical distribution is the best estimate of the underlying distribution without a lot of other assumptions. So they use the empirical distribution as if it is the underlying distribution to find approximate distributions of statistics of interest.

Chi-square tests were the invention of Karl Pearson, except that he had it wrong in the case in which parameters are estimated. When R. A. Fisher was a brash young man, he told his senior Pearson that he should reduce the number of degrees of freedom of the chi-square distribution by 1 for every parameter that was estimated. Pearson never believed this (of course, Fisher was correct), and, as editor of the very prestigious journal *Biometrika*, Pearson blocked Fisher in his later professional life from publishing in that journal. Fisher was disappointed, and the two men battled during their lifetimes; however, later Fisher saw this conflict to be to his advantage, as it made him consider applied journals in which to publish, and thus he became a better, more well rounded scientist.

CHAPTER 9

Bayesian Methods

9.1 SUBJECTIVE PROBABILITY
9.2 BAYESIAN ESTIMATION
9.3 MORE BAYESIAN CONCEPTS

9.1 SUBJECTIVE PROBABILITY

Subjective probability is the foundation for Bayesian methods. Thus, we devote this short section to understanding how a Bayesian would assign probabilities to certain events. In a thorough study of Bayesian methods, there would be greater discussion about how a Bayesian would assess the prior probabilities.

Consider an event A, and let us say that we believe that $P(A) = 2/5$. This means that the odds *against* the event A are

$$O(A) = \frac{1 - P(A)}{P(A)} = \frac{1 - 2/5}{2/5} = \frac{3}{2},$$

or 3 to 2. Likewise the odds *for* A are

$$\frac{P(A)}{1 - P(A)} = \frac{2/5}{1 - 2/5} = \frac{2}{3},$$

or 2 to 3. Moreover, if a person really believes that $P(A) = 2/5$ and is willing to bet, he or she would take either side of this bet:

1. Win 3 dollars if A occurs and lose 2 dollars if A does not occur or
2. Win 2 dollars if A does not occur and lose 3 dollars if A does occur.

If this is not the case, then that person should review his or her subjective probability $P(A)$.

Another way of thinking about this subjective probability, $P(A)$, is to say that it is equal to the amount you are willing to pay to receive \$1 [the bet of $P(A)$ plus the winnings of $\{1 - P(A)\}$] if A actually occurs. That is, you lose $P(A)$ if A does not occur, and you win $1 - P(A)$ if A occurs. So if you believe that $P(A) = 2/5$, you would be willing to pay 2/5 of a dollar to play "a game" in which you win 3/5 (plus your bet of 2/5) if A occurs. Note that $(2/5)/(3/5) = 2/3$, or 2 to 3, are the odds in favor of A. Or $(3/5)/(2/5) = 3/2$, or 3 to 2, are the odds against A. Again, you must be willing to take either side of the bet.

This is really much like two children dividing a candy bar as equally as possible: One divides it, and the other gets to choose which of the two parts seems most desirable—that is, the larger. Accordingly, the child dividing the candy bar tries extremely hard to cut it as equally as possible. Clearly, this is exactly what the person selecting the subjective probability does, as he or she must be willing to take either side of the bet with the odds established.

Now, every person has his or her own personal probability of almost any statement A, which could be something like "There must be some type of life on the planet Mars." Since we often think of A as something on which we might bet, let us consider the statement A that Iowa will beat Michigan in their football game this year. A man who studies the strengths of those two teams might offer the subjective probability $P(A) = 1/3$, or odds against Iowa of

$$O(A) = \frac{1 - 1/3}{1/3} = 2 = \frac{2}{1},$$

(i.e., 2 to 1) and be willing to take either side of the bet. Suppose his opponent in this gamble is a strong Michigan fan who he thinks might accept 3 to 1 odds. Then he might offer those odds to that individual, hoping that she will bet on Michigan. In that case, he would have quite a satisfactory bet: He wins three units if Iowa wins and loses one unit if Michigan wins. Does he dare do that if he really believes that $P(A) = 1/3$? His opponent also knows a lot about these two teams and actually thinks that $P(A) = 1/3$ is about right; so she takes the 3 to 1 bet, but chooses Iowa, as she likes those 3 to 1 odds even though she is a Michigan fan. So the first person has a bad bet according to his subjective probability $P(A) = 1/3$.

Recall, however, that each person has his or her own subjective probability and that the Michigan fan might really believe that $P(A) = 1/5$, or odds of $(1 - 1/5)/(1/5)$—that is, 4 to 1 against Iowa. Thus, she would be glad to bet three units to one unit; that is, she would be happy to give three units if Iowa wins and accept one unit if Michigan wins. In this case, each player would have a satisfactory bet, consistent with their subjective probabilities. We are certain that this is why bookmakers (bookies) tend to stay in business and often make a great deal of money. They offer odds, and others think that they are wrong and thus bet. Later we shall point out how bookies (and racetracks, casinos, and even state lotteries) can "cover themselves." Accordingly, it is a good rule, in our opinion, never to bet against people who are professional gamblers. How can casinos afford to have such fancy buildings? The persons who bet against them pay for those nice facilities. (Incidentally, we have no objection to, say, a friendly poker game in which none of the participants could "be hurt" by the stakes involved. Even one of the authors has participated in friendly games and wagers; still, the reader must be warned about playing against statisticians, as well as professional gamblers.)

Let us now explain how a racetrack can always make money; of course, the owners have certain fixed costs that must be covered, so they obviously must make some money. To keep it simple, suppose there are only three horses, A, B, and C, and we will worry only about bets to "win," not "place" or "show." The following table shows the amount of money bet on each horse to win and the "subjective probability" determined by all the bettors:

Horse	Amount	Probability
A	\$50,000	0.50
B	\$40,000	0.40
C	\$10,000	0.10
Total	\$100,000	1.00

In a sense, these are not really subjective probabilities as we have been describing them, but some sort of degrees of belief in the various horses as determined by all the bettors.

If we used those probabilities and the associated odds to determine fair payoffs (track bets are made in \$2 units), a \$2 bet on A would yield \$4 if A wins: the \$2 bet plus \$2 more. A \$2 bet on B would yield \$5 if B wins: Recall that the odds are $(1 - 0.4)/0.4 = 1.5$ against B, so the track puts up \$3 against the bettor's \$2. Finally, a \$2 bet on C would yield \$20 if C wins: the \$2 bet plus \$18 more, as the odds are $(1 - 0.1)/0.1 = 9$ to 1 against C.

If the track would make these payoffs, what would be the total payoff in case A wins, in case B wins, and in case C wins? There are 25,000 \$2 bets in that \$50,000 bet on A; so if A wins, then

$$25{,}000 \times \$4 = \$100{,}000$$

would be the total payoff. There are 20,000 \$2 bets in that \$40,000 bet on B; so if B wins, then

$$20{,}000 \times \$5 = \$100{,}000$$

would be the total payoff. Similarly, for C winning, the total payoff is

$$5000 \times \$20 = \$100{,}000.$$

That is, with these probabilities, the track would pay off as much as the total amount bet. The track could never stay in business in that situation, so it must take something off the top, and this is now explained.

A typical percentage of the track's take is 17%, so we will use that figure. In our example, this amounts to \$17,000, and thus there is only \$83,000 to distribute. Accordingly, the payoffs are adjusted by the factor $83/100 = 0.83$. That is, instead of payoffs of \$4, \$5, and \$20, they are, respectively,

$$\begin{aligned} 4(0.83) &= 3.32, \\ 5(0.83) &= 4.15, \\ 20(0.83) &= 16.60, \end{aligned}$$

and the three possible total payoffs are, respectively,

$$\begin{aligned} 25{,}000(3.32) &= 83{,}000, \\ 20{,}000(4.15) &= 83{,}000, \\ 5000(16.60) &= 83{,}000. \end{aligned}$$

Hence, this track is always assured of making the money necessary to cover all expenses, provided that it has enough bettors.

Other gambling establishments cover themselves by having the probabilities slightly favor the "house." Sometimes the take is nothing like 17%, but the probabilities of the bettor winning are slightly under 0.50. For example, in American roulette, the probability of winning by betting on red is $18/38 = 0.474$, because 18 out of the 38 equally likely places favor red. Actually, the game that provides a probability closest to one-half is "craps," if you bet on the caster. There, the probability of the caster winning is 0.493, which is extremely close to 0.5. Sometimes the side bets in craps are not so favorable; be careful making those. With such slim odds favoring the house, how does a casino make money? Mainly because it has lots of bettors. And, of course, some games (e.g., the slots) are not quite as favorable as roulette or craps. (As a side note, we mention that, in state lotteries, the expected payoff for a $1 bet is usually about 45 or 50 cents; so these are bad bets, although states claim they do good things with their winnings.)

In addition to the preceding, many bookies have two sets of odds, such as 2 to 1 if you bet on Iowa and 3 to 1 if you bet on Michigan. That is, on the one hand, they will pay $3 ($2 + 1 = 3$) for a $1 bet on Iowa if Iowa wins, while on the other hand, they will pay $4 ($1 + 3 = 4$) for a $3 bet on Michigan if Michigan wins. Clearly, if they can get the right number of bettors on each side, they have created a position such that they cannot lose. Suppose 10,000 people bet on Iowa (you might not need 10,000 people, as some will bet more than the minimum) and 7500 bet on Michigan. Then the bookies take in

$$(10{,}000)(\$1) + (7500)(\$3) = \$32{,}500.$$

If Iowa wins, they pay off $2 + 1 = 3$ for each $1 bet, or a total of

$$(10{,}000)(\$3) = \$30{,}000.$$

If Michigan wins, they pay off $1 + 3 = 4$ for each $3 bet, or a total of

$$(7500)(\$4) = \$30{,}000.$$

In either case, they make money, namely,

$$\$32{,}500 - \$30{,}000 = \$2500.$$

Clearly, they must balance the bettors or change the odds (which they do) to have a sure win. That is, just like the racetrack, they change the odds, depending upon the amount of money bet on each side. So if the bookies can get enough bettors, they can make lots of money, and they generally do! Hence, do not bet against professional gamblers unless you achieve a certain amount of enjoyment from betting; but, even then, make certain that the stakes are such that you can afford possible losses. [For a further discussion of betting, see Berry (1996).]

Now, not all betting is bad. For example, most people are betting when they buy insurance. The insurance companies do exactly the same thing that casinos do, as they know the probabilities and the corresponding premiums favor them somewhat. Is this bad? Certainly not, and one of the authors is associated with a Department of Statistics and Actuarial Science, has helped teach many actuaries over the years, and even has a daughter who is an actuary. However, to understand the value of buying insurance, the reader must understand the utility of money.

Most of us would say that $4 are worth twice as much as $2. Also, $100 are worth 20 times as much as $5. But to most individuals, is $2,000,000 worth twice as much as \$1,000,000? For very rich people, it is. However, suppose a person has retired and has exactly \$1,000,000. A very rich person offers that person the following bet: Toss a coin fairly, and if a head occurs, the rich person gives the retiree \$2,000,000; but if a tail results, the retiree gives the rich person \$1,000,000. That is, the retiree gains \$2,000,000 with probability 0.5 and loses \$1,000,000 with probability 0.5. The expected gain is

$$(\$2{,}000{,}000)(0.5) + (-\$1{,}000{,}000)(0.5) = \$500{,}000.$$

Seemingly, this is a great bet, but any reasonable person with only \$1,000,000 would turn it down because that first \$1,000,000 is worth a lot more than the second \$1,000,000 or a third \$1,000,000. Clearly, with the bet described, he could have zero or \$3,000,000, each with probability 0.5, but the retiree would rather have \$1,000,000 with certainty. While the utility function $u(x)$ of money for this individual is just about $u(x) = x$ for relatively small values of x, it starts to bend downward for larger values of x. Where this bending occurs is also subjective; Bill Gates would immediately accept the proposed bet, because his utility function is $u(x) = x$ into the millions, but Bob Hogg would not take the bet, because his utility function bends downward long before \$1,000,000.

So why do we buy insurance? To keep it simple, suppose a man wishes to buy term life insurance valued at \$100,000 for one year, possibly to protect a young family—say, a wife and two children—in case he dies. Say his probability of dying in that year is 0.002. What is a fair premium for this insurance if it will cost the company \$100,000 with probability 0.002 and zero with probability 0.998? The answer is

$$(\$100{,}000)(0.002) + (\$0)(0.998) = \$200.$$

However, the company asks for a loading factor of, say, 15%, or \$30. Thus, the charge is \$230, which seemingly is not a fair bet. However, if the insured does die, the widow with two children have nothing without the insurance and \$100,000 with the insurance. Under those circumstances, most men would buy the insurance because the value of the policy is worth much more than the \$230 premium in their minds, and hence the bet is more than fair to them *personally*. Note, then, that insurance companies, like casinos, have nice facilities, but we believe in that type of betting.

So it is smart to insure valuable items, such as one's life, liability associated with car accidents, home, and so on. Things of smaller value should not be insured; that is, you carry your own insurance. The cutoff value differs with each individual, although we find that the rule of not insuring anything with a value under one or two months' salary is a good one; most of our utility functions are $u(x) = x$ in that range, and there is no sense paying a "load." Bill Gates does not need to insure for collision on a new car valued at \$40,000 (he carries liability, however, as most states require it); Bob Hogg does. However, once the value of the car drops to under \$10,000, even Bob Hogg drops the collision insurance. But note that these are personal decisions that depend upon the subjective probabilities and a person's utility of money.

Let us now say that the reader is willing to accept the subjective probability $P(A)$ as the fair price for event A, given that you will receive one unit [win $1 - P(A)$] in case A occurs and, of course, lose $P(A)$ if it does not occur. Then it turns out that all rules (definitions and theorems) in Section 1.2 follow for subjective probabilities. We do not give proofs of them all, but only one of them, leaving some of the others as exercises. The following proof was given to us in a personal communication from George Woodworth of the University of Iowa.

THEOREM 9.1-1 If A_1 and A_2 are mutually exclusive, then

$$P(A_1 \cup A_2) = P(A_1) + P(A_2).$$

Proof. Suppose a person thinks that a fair price for A_1 is $p_1 = P(A_1)$ and a fair price for A_2 is $p_2 = P(A_2)$. However, that person believes that the fair price for $A_1 \cup A_2$ is p_3, which differs from $p_1 + p_2$. Say $p_3 < p_1 + p_2$, and let the difference be $d = (p_1 + p_2) - p_3$. A gambler offers the person the price $p_3 + d/4$ for $A_1 \cup A_2$. The person takes the offer because it is better than p_3. The gambler sells A_1 at a discount price of $p_1 - d/4$ and sells A_2 at a discount price of $p_2 - d/4$ to the person. Being a rational person, and given the prices p_1, p_2, and p_3, the person believes that all three of these deals are satisfactory. However, the person received $p_3 + d/4$ and paid $p_1 + p_2 - d/2$. Thus, before any bets are paid off, the person has

$$p_3 + \frac{d}{4} - \left(p_1 + p_2 - \frac{d}{2}\right) = p_3 - p_1 - p_2 + \frac{3d}{4} = -\frac{d}{4}.$$

That is, the person is down $d/4$ before any bets are settled. Now,

1. Suppose A_1 happens: The gambler has $A_1 \cup A_2$ and the person has A_1; so they exchange units and the person is still down $d/4$. The same thing occurs if A_2 happens.
2. Suppose neither A_1 nor A_2 happens; then the gambler and that person receive zero, and the person is still down $d/4$.
3. Of course, A_1 and A_2 cannot occur together, since they are mutually exclusive.

Thus, we see that it is bad for the person to assign

$$p_3 = P(A_1 \cup A_2) < p_1 + p_2 = P(A_1) + P(A_2),$$

because the gambler can put the person in a position to lose $(p_1 + p_2 - p_3)/4$ no matter what happens. This kind of bet is sometimes referred to as a *Dutch book*.

The argument when $p_3 > p_1 + p_2$ is similar and also can lead to a Dutch book; it is left as an exercise. Hence, p_3 must equal $p_1 + p_2$ to avoid a Dutch book; that is, $P(A_1 \cup A_2) = P(A_1) + P(A_2)$. □

EXERCISES

9.1-1. Think of some event A (it could or could not be a sporting outcome) that might or might not happen on your college campus. Get several students to assign their personal probabilities to A. If they differ and the students are not opposed to betting, could you find any friendly (small-stakes) bets among them? For example, if two students, S_1 and S_2, assigned $P_1(A) = 0.5$ and $P_2(A) = 0.3$, respectively, they might agree that their odds of $(1 - 0.4)/0.4 = 1.5$ to 1 would be reasonable as they are between odds associated with their respective probabilities. That is, S_1 would place one unit on A to 1.5 units on A' by S_2. According to their subjective probabilities, this would be a satisfactory bet for both.

9.1-2. As in Exercise 9.1-1, consider some event A around your campus. Let one student, S_1, determine $P_1(A)$, the subjective probability of A. Then, on the basis of $P_1(A)$, let a second student, S_2, take either side of a friendly bet established by these odds. Try this several times, with students exchanging roles.

9.1-3. In American roulette, suppose that 3800 consecutive \$5 bets were placed on red. Show that the casino's expected gain is \$1000. Determine the standard deviation associated with the casino's gain.

9.1-4. On a certain fight involving boxer A and boxer B, A is the favorite over B. A bookie finds that \$30,000 is bet on A and only \$5000 is bet on B. Determine two sets of odds, one for those betting on A and one for those betting on B.

HINT: Note that the bets suggest a "subjective probability" of $5000/35{,}000 = 1/7$ for B, or odds of 6 to 1 against B. Find odds on either side of the 6 to 1 for the two possible odds. Make certain that your choice (it is not unique) will be such that the bookie always makes money.

9.1-5. The following amounts are bet on horses A, B, C, D, and E to win:

Horse	Amount
A	\$600,000
B	\$200,000
C	\$100,000
D	\$75,000
E	\$25,000
Total	\$1,000,000

Suppose the track wants to take 20% off the top, or \$200,000. Determine the payoff for winning with a \$2 bet on each of the five horses.

9.1-6. In the proof of Theorem 9.1-1, we considered the case in which $p_3 < p_1 + p_2$. Now say the person believes that $p_3 > p_1 + p_2$. Create a Dutch book for him.

HINT: Let $d = p_3 - (p_1 + p_2)$. The gambler buys A_1 from the person at a premium price of $p_1 + d/4$ and A_2 for $p_2 + d/4$. Then the gambler sells $A_1 \cup A_2$ to the person at a discount of $p_3 - d/4$. All those deals are good for the person, who believes that p_1, p_2, and p_3 are correct, with $p_3 > p_1 + p_2$. Show that the person has a Dutch book.

9.1-7. Show that $P(S) = 1$.

HINT: Suppose a person thinks $P(S) = p \neq 1$. Consider two cases: $p > 1$ and $p < 1$. In the first case, say $d = p - 1$ and the gambler sells the person S at a discount price $1 + d/2$. Of course, S happens and the gambler pays the person one unit, but the person is down $1 + d/2 - 1 = d/2$, so he has a Dutch book. Do the other case.

9.1-8. Show that $P(A') = 1 - P(A)$.

HINT: Note that $A' \cup A = S$, and use the result of Theorem 9.1-1 and Exercise 9.1-7.

9.2 BAYESIAN ESTIMATION

We now describe another approach to estimation that is used by a group of statisticians who call themselves Bayesians. To understand their approach fully would require more text than we can allocate to this topic, but let us begin this brief introduction by considering a simple application of the theorem of the Reverend Thomas Bayes. (See Section 1.6.)

EXAMPLE 9.2-1 Suppose we know that we are going to select an observation from a Poisson distribution with mean λ equal to 2 or 4. Moreover, prior to performing the experiment, we believe that $\lambda = 2$ has about four times as much chance of being the parameter as does $\lambda = 4$; that is, the prior probabilities are $P(\lambda = 2) = 0.8$ and $P(\lambda = 4) = 0.2$. The experiment is now performed and we observe that $x = 6$. At this point, our intuition tells us that $\lambda = 2$ seems less likely than before, as the observation $x = 6$ is much more probable with $\lambda = 4$ than with $\lambda = 2$, because, in an obvious notation,

$$P(X = 6 \mid \lambda = 2) = 0.995 - 0.983 = 0.012$$

and

$$P(X = 6 \mid \lambda = 4) = 0.889 - 0.785 = 0.104,$$

from Table III in the appendix. Our intuition can be supported by computing the conditional probability of $\lambda = 2$, given that $X = 6$:

$$
\begin{aligned}
P(\lambda = 2 \mid X = 6) &= \frac{P(\lambda = 2, X = 6)}{P(X = 6)} \\
&= \frac{P(\lambda = 2)P(X = 6 \mid \lambda = 2)}{P(\lambda = 2)P(X = 6 \mid \lambda = 2) + P(\lambda = 4)P(X = 6 \mid \lambda = 4)} \\
&= \frac{(0.8)(0.012)}{(0.8)(0.012) + (0.2)(0.104)} = 0.316.
\end{aligned}
$$

This conditional probability is called the posterior probability of $\lambda = 2$, given the single data point (here, $x = 6$). In a similar fashion, the posterior probability of $\lambda = 4$ is found to be 0.684. Thus, we see that the probability of $\lambda = 2$ has decreased from 0.8 (the prior probability) to 0.316 (the posterior probability) with the observation of $x = 6$. ■

In a more practical application, the parameter, say, θ can take many more than two values as in Example 9.2-1. Somehow Bayesians must assign prior probabilities to this total parameter space through a prior p.d.f. $h(\theta)$. They have developed procedures for assessing these prior probabilities, and we simply cannot do justice to these methods here. Somehow $h(\theta)$ reflects the prior weights that the Bayesian wants to assign to the various possible values of θ. In some instances, if $h(\theta)$ is a constant and thus θ has the uniform prior distribution, we say that the Bayesian has a *noninformative* prior. If, in fact, some knowledge of θ exists in advance of experimentation, noninformative priors should be avoided if at all possible.

Also, in more practical examples, we usually take several observations, not just one. That is, we take a random sample, and there is frequently a good statistic, say, Y, for the parameter θ. Suppose we are considering a continuous case and the p.d.f. of Y, say, $g(y; \theta)$, can be thought of as the conditional p.d.f. of Y, given θ. [Henceforth in this section, we write $g(y; \theta) = g(y \mid \theta)$.] Thus, we can treat

$$g(y \mid \theta)h(\theta) = k(y, \theta)$$

as the joint p.d.f. of the statistic Y and the parameter. Of course, the marginal p.d.f. of Y is

$$k_1(y) = \int_{-\infty}^{\infty} h(\theta)g(y \mid \theta)\, d\theta.$$

Consequently,

$$\frac{k(y, \theta)}{k_1(y)} = \frac{g(y \mid \theta)h(\theta)}{k_1(y)} = k(\theta \mid y)$$

would serve as the conditional p.d.f. of the parameter, given that $Y = y$. This formula is essentially Bayes's theorem, and $k(\theta \mid y)$ is called the *posterior p.d.f. of θ*, given that $Y = y$.

Bayesians believe that everything which needs to be known about the parameter is summarized in this posterior p.d.f. $k(\theta \mid y)$. Suppose, for example, that they were pressed into making a point estimate of the parameter θ. They would note that they would be guessing the value of a random variable, here θ, given its p.d.f. $k(\theta \mid y)$. There are many ways that this could be done: The mean, the median, or the mode of that distribution would be reasonable guesses. However, in the final analysis, the best guess would clearly depend upon the penalties for various errors created by incorrect guesses. For instance, if we were penalized by taking the square of the error between the guess, say, $w(y)$, and the real value of the parameter θ, clearly we would use the conditional mean

$$w(y) = \int_{-\infty}^{\infty} \theta k(\theta \mid y)\, d\theta$$

as our Bayes estimate of θ. The reason is that, in general, if Z is a random variable, then the function of b, $E[(Z - b)^2]$, is minimized by $b = E(Z)$. (See Example 2.2-4.) Likewise, if the penalty (loss) function is the absolute value of the error, $|\theta - w(y)|$, then we use the median of the distribution, because with any random variable Z, $E[\,|Z - b|\,]$ is minimized when b equals the median of the distribution of Z. (See Exercise 2.2-10.)

EXAMPLE 9.2-2 Suppose that Y has a binomial distribution with parameters n and $p = \theta$. Then the p.m.f. of Y, given θ, is

$$g(y \mid \theta) = \binom{n}{y} \theta^y (1 - \theta)^{n-y}, \qquad y = 0, 1, 2, \ldots, n.$$

Let us take the prior p.d.f. of the parameter to be the beta p.d.f:

$$h(\theta) = \frac{\Gamma(\alpha + \beta)}{\Gamma(\alpha)\Gamma(\beta)} \theta^{\alpha-1}(1 - \theta)^{\beta-1}, \qquad 0 < \theta < 1.$$

Such a prior p.d.f. provides a Bayesian a great deal of flexibility through the selection of the parameters α and β. Thus, the joint probabilities can be described by a product of a binomial p.m.f. with parameters n and θ and this beta p.d.f., namely,

$$k(y, \theta) = \binom{n}{y} \frac{\Gamma(\alpha + \beta)}{\Gamma(\alpha)\Gamma(\beta)} \theta^{y+\alpha-1}(1 - \theta)^{n-y+\beta-1},$$

on the support given by $y = 0, 1, 2, \ldots, n$ and $0 < \theta < 1$. We find

$$\begin{aligned} k_1(y) &= \int_0^1 k(y, \theta)\, d\theta \\ &= \binom{n}{y} \frac{\Gamma(\alpha + \beta)}{\Gamma(\alpha)\Gamma(\beta)} \frac{\Gamma(\alpha + y)\Gamma(n + \beta - y)}{\Gamma(n + \alpha + \beta)} \end{aligned}$$

on the support $y = 0, 1, 2, \ldots, n$ by comparing the integral with one involving a beta p.d.f. with parameters $y + \alpha$ and $n - y + \beta$. Therefore,

$$\begin{aligned} k(\theta \mid y) &= \frac{k(y, \theta)}{k_1(y)} \\ &= \frac{\Gamma(n + \alpha + \beta)}{\Gamma(\alpha + y)\Gamma(n + \beta - y)} \theta^{y+\alpha-1}(1 - \theta)^{n-y+\beta-1}, \qquad 0 < \theta < 1, \end{aligned}$$

which is a beta p.d.f. with parameters $y + \alpha$ and $n - y + \beta$. With the square error loss function, we must minimize, with respect to $w(y)$, the integral

$$\int_0^1 [\theta - w(y)]^2 k(\theta \mid y)\, d\theta$$

to obtain the Bayes solution. But, as noted earlier, if Z is a random variable with a second moment, then $E[(Z - b)^2]$ is minimized by $b = E(Z)$. In the preceding integration, θ is like the Z with p.d.f. $k(\theta \mid y)$, and $w(y)$ is like the b, so the minimization is accomplished by taking

$$w(y) = E(\theta \mid y) = \frac{\alpha + y}{\alpha + \beta + n},$$

which is the mean of the beta distribution with parameters $y + \alpha$ and $n - y + \beta$. (See Exercise 5.2-8.) It is instructive to note that this Bayes solution can be written as

$$w(y) = \left(\frac{n}{\alpha + \beta + n}\right)\left(\frac{y}{n}\right) + \left(\frac{\alpha + \beta}{\alpha + \beta + n}\right)\left(\frac{\alpha}{\alpha + \beta}\right),$$

which is a weighted average of the maximum likelihood estimate y/n of θ and the mean $\alpha/(\alpha + \beta)$ of the prior p.d.f. of the parameter. Moreover, the respective weights are $n/(\alpha + \beta + n)$ and $(\alpha + \beta)/(\alpha + \beta + n)$. Thus, we see that α and β should be selected so that not only is $\alpha/(\alpha + \beta)$ the desired prior mean, but also the sum $\alpha + \beta$ plays a role corresponding to a sample size. That is, if we want our prior opinion to have as much weight as a sample size of 20, we would take $\alpha + \beta = 20$. So if our prior mean is 3/4, we select $\alpha = 15$ and $\beta = 5$. That is, the prior p.d.f. of θ is beta(15, 5). If we observe $n = 40$ and $y = 28$, then the posterior p.d.f. is beta($28 + 15 = 43$, $12 + 5 = 17$). The prior and posterior p.d.f.'s are shown in Figure 9.2-1. ■

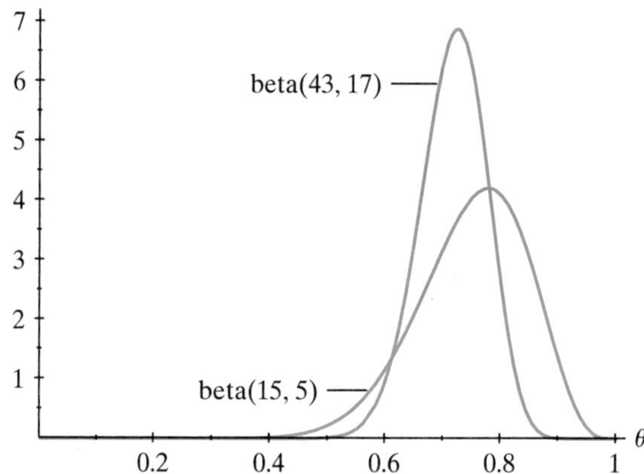

FIGURE 9.2-1: Beta prior and posterior p.d.f.'s

In Example 9.2-2, it is quite convenient to note that it is not really necessary to determine $k_1(y)$ to find $k(\theta \mid y)$. If we divide $k(y, \theta)$ by $k_1(y)$, we get the product of a factor that depends on y but does *not* depend on θ—say, $c(y)$—and we have

$$\theta^{y+\alpha-1}(1 - \theta)^{n-y+\beta-1}.$$

That is,

$$k(\theta \mid y) = c(y)\,\theta^{y+\alpha-1}(1 - \theta)^{n-y+\beta-1}, \qquad 0 < \theta < 1.$$

However, $c(y)$ must be that "constant" needed to make $k(\theta \mid y)$ a p.d.f., namely,

$$c(y) = \frac{\Gamma(n + \alpha + \beta)}{\Gamma(y + \alpha)\Gamma(n - y + \beta)}.$$

Accordingly, Bayesians frequently write that $k(\theta \mid y)$ is proportional to $k(y, \theta) = g(y \mid \theta)h(\theta)$; that is,

$$k(\theta \mid y) \propto g(y \mid \theta)\, h(\theta).$$

Then, to actually form the p.d.f. $k(\theta \mid y)$, they simply find a "constant" (which is, of course, actually some function of y) such that the expression integrates to 1.

EXAMPLE 9.2-3 Suppose that $Y = \overline{X}$ is the mean of a random sample of size n that arises from the normal distribution $N(\theta, \sigma^2)$, where σ^2 is known. Then $g(y \mid \theta)$ is $N(\theta, \sigma^2/n)$. Suppose further that we are able to assign prior weights to θ through a prior p.d.f. $h(\theta)$ that is $N(\theta_0, \sigma_0^2)$. Then we have

$$k(\theta \mid y) \propto \frac{1}{\sqrt{2\pi}\,(\sigma/\sqrt{n})} \frac{1}{\sqrt{2\pi}\sigma_0} \exp\left[-\frac{(y - \theta)^2}{2(\sigma^2/n)} - \frac{(\theta - \theta_0)^2}{2\sigma_0^2}\right].$$

If we eliminate all constant factors (including factors involving y only), then

$$k(\theta \mid y) \propto \exp\left[-\frac{(\sigma_0^2 + \sigma^2/n)\theta^2 - 2(y\sigma_0^2 + \theta_0\sigma^2/n)\theta}{2(\sigma^2/n)\sigma_0^2}\right].$$

This expression can be simplified by completing the square, to read (after eliminating factors not involving θ)

$$k(\theta \mid y) \propto \exp\left\{-\frac{[\theta - (y\sigma_0^2 + \theta_0\sigma^2/n)/(\sigma_0^2 + \sigma^2/n)]^2}{[2(\sigma^2/n)\sigma_0^2]/[\sigma_0^2 + (\sigma^2/n)]}\right\}.$$

That is, the posterior p.d.f. of the parameter is obviously normal with mean

$$\frac{y\sigma_0^2 + \theta_0\sigma^2/n}{\sigma_0^2 + \sigma^2/n} = \left(\frac{\sigma_0^2}{\sigma_0^2 + \sigma^2/n}\right)y + \left(\frac{\sigma^2/n}{\sigma_0^2 + \sigma^2/n}\right)\theta_0$$

and variance $(\sigma^2/n)\sigma_0^2/(\sigma_0^2 + \sigma^2/n)$. If the square error loss function is used, then this posterior mean is the Bayes solution. Again, note that it is a weighted average of the maximum likelihood estimate $y = \overline{x}$ and the prior mean θ_0. The Bayes solution $w(y)$ will always be a value between the prior judgment and the usual estimate. Note also, here and in Example 9.2-2, that the Bayes solution gets closer to the maximum likelihood estimate as n increases. Thus, the Bayesian procedures permit the decision maker to enter his or her prior opinions into the solution in a very formal way so that the influence of those prior notions will be less and less as n increases. ■

In Bayesian statistics, all the information is contained in the posterior p.d.f. $k(\theta \mid y)$. In Examples 9.2-2 and 9.2-3, we found Bayesian point estimates with the use of the squared error loss function. Note that if the loss function is the absolute value of the error, $|w(y) - \theta|$, then the Bayes solution would be the median of the posterior distribution of the parameter, which is given by $k(\theta \mid y)$. Hence, the Bayes solution changes—as it should—with different loss functions.

Finally, if an interval estimate of θ is desired, we would find two functions of y—say, $u(y)$ and $v(y)$—such that

$$\int_{u(y)}^{v(y)} k(\theta \mid y)\, d\theta = 1 - \alpha,$$

where α is small—say, $\alpha = 0.05$. Then the observed interval from $u(y)$ to $v(y)$ would serve as an interval estimate for the parameter in the sense that the posterior probability of the parameter's being in that interval is $1 - \alpha$. In Example 9.2-3, where the posterior p.d.f. of the parameter was normal, the interval

$$\frac{y\sigma_0^2 + \theta_0\sigma^2/n}{\sigma_0^2 + \sigma^2/n} \pm 1.96\sqrt{\frac{(\sigma^2/n)\sigma_0^2}{\sigma_0^2 + \sigma^2/n}}$$

serves as an interval estimate for θ with posterior probability of 0.95.

In closing this short section on Bayesian estimation, note that we could have begun with the sample observations $X_1, X_2, \ldots, X_n$, rather than some statistic Y. Then, in our discussion, we would replace $g(y \mid \theta)$ by the likelihood function

$$L(\theta) = f(x_1 \mid \theta)f(x_2 \mid \theta) \cdots f(x_n \mid \theta),$$

which is the joint p.d.f. of $X_1, X_2, \ldots, X_n$, given θ. Thus, we find that

$$k(\theta \mid x_1, x_2, \ldots, x_n) \propto h(\theta)f(x_1 \mid \theta)f(x_2 \mid \theta) \cdots f(x_n \mid \theta) = h(\theta)L(\theta).$$

Now, $k(\theta \mid x_1, x_2, \ldots, x_n)$ contains all the information about θ, given the data. Thus, depending on the loss function, we would choose our Bayesian estimate of θ as some characteristic of this posterior distribution, such as the mean or the median. It is interesting to observe that if the loss function is zero for some small neighborhood about the true parameter θ and is some large positive constant otherwise, then the Bayesian estimate, $w(x_1, x_2, \ldots, x_n)$, is essentially the mode of this conditional p.d.f., $k(\theta \mid x_1, x_2, \ldots, x_n)$. The reason for this is that we want to take the estimate so that it has as much posterior probability as possible in a small neighborhood around it. Finally, note that if $h(\theta)$ is a constant (a noninformative prior), then this Bayesian estimate using the mode is exactly the same as the maximum likelihood estimate. More generally, if $h(\theta)$ is not a constant, then the Bayesian estimate using the mode can be thought of as a weighted maximum likelihood estimate in which the weights reflect prior opinion about θ. That is, that value of θ which maximizes $h(\theta)L(\theta)$ is the mode of the posterior distribution of the parameter given the data and can be used as the Bayesian estimate associated with the appropriate loss function.

EXAMPLE 9.2-4 Let us consider again Example 9.2-2, but now say that $X_1, X_2, \ldots, X_n$ is a random sample from the Bernoulli distribution with p.m.f.

$$f(x \mid \theta) = \theta^x(1 - \theta)^{1-x}, \qquad x = 0, 1.$$

With the same prior p.d.f. of θ, the joint distribution of $X_1, X_2, \ldots, X_n$ and θ is given by

$$\frac{\Gamma(\alpha + \beta)}{\Gamma(\alpha)\Gamma(\beta)}\theta^{\alpha-1}(1 - \theta)^{\beta-1}\theta^{\sum_{i=1}^n x_i}(1 - \theta)^{n-\sum_{i=1}^n x_i}, \qquad 0 < \theta < 1, \; x_i = 0, 1.$$

Of course, the posterior p.d.f. of θ, given that $X_1 = x_1, X_2 = x_2, \ldots, X_n = x_n$ is such that

$$k(\theta \mid x_1, x_2, \ldots, x_n) \propto \theta^{\sum_{i=1}^n x_i + \alpha - 1}(1 - \theta)^{n-\sum_{i=1}^n x_i + \beta - 1}, \qquad 0 < \theta < 1,$$

which is beta with $\alpha^* = \sum x_i + \alpha$, $\beta^* = n - \sum x_i + \beta$. The conditional mean of θ is

$$\frac{\sum_{i=1}^{n} x_i + \alpha}{n + \alpha + \beta} = \left(\frac{n}{n + \alpha + \beta}\right)\left(\frac{\sum_{i=1}^{n} x_i}{n}\right) + \left(\frac{\alpha + \beta}{n + \alpha + \beta}\right)\left(\frac{\alpha}{\alpha + \beta}\right),$$

which, with $y = \sum x_i$, is exactly the same result as that of Example 9.2-2. ■

REMARK In Section 6.5, there was a remark about improving the confidence intervals for probability $p = \theta$ if Y is $b(n,p)$. There it was suggested that we should use $\widetilde{p} = (Y + 2)/(n + 4)$ instead of $\widehat{p} = Y/n$. Note that $\widetilde{p}$ is the Bayes estimator when the prior p.d.f. is beta with $\alpha = \beta = 2$. Since it brings the estimator Y/n closer to the prior mean $\alpha/(\alpha + \beta)$—here, 1/2—$\widetilde{p}$ is often called a *shrinkage estimator*. To get an interval estimate for p, the Bayesian takes the posterior p.d.f. $k(p \mid y)$, which is beta, and finds $u(y)$ and $v(y)$ so that

$$\int_{u(y)}^{v(y)} k(p \mid y)dp = 1 - \alpha.$$

Beta tables or the computer are needed to do this, but it would be an interesting project to compare such intervals for various values of n, p, and y with those found by

$$\widetilde{p} \pm z_{\alpha/2}\sqrt{\widetilde{p}(1 - \widetilde{p})/n}.$$

■

EXERCISES

9.2-1. Let Y be the sum of the observations of a random sample from a Poisson distribution with mean θ. Let the prior p.d.f. of θ be gamma with parameters α and β.

(a) Find the posterior p.d.f. of θ, given that $Y = y$.

(b) If the loss function is $[w(y) - \theta]^2$, find the Bayesian point estimate $w(y)$.

(c) Show that the $w(y)$ found in part (b) is a weighted average of the maximum likelihood estimate y/n and the prior mean $\alpha\beta$, with respective weights of $n/(n + 1/\beta)$ and $(1/\beta)/(n + 1/\beta)$.

9.2-2. Let $X_1, X_2, \ldots, X_n$ be a random sample from a gamma distribution with known α and with $\theta = 1/\tau$. Say τ has a prior p.d.f. that is gamma with parameters α_0 and θ_0, so that the prior mean is $\alpha_0\theta_0$.

(a) Find the posterior p.d.f. of τ, given that $X_1 = x_1, X_2 = x_2, \ldots, X_n = x_n$.

(b) Find the mean of the posterior distribution found in part (a), and write it as a function of the sample mean $\overline{X}$ and $\alpha_0\theta_0$.

(c) Explain how you would find a 95% interval estimate of τ if $n = 10$, $\alpha = 3$, $\alpha_0 = 10$, and $\theta_0 = 2$.

9.2-3. In Example 9.2-2, take $n = 30$, $\alpha = 15$, and $\beta = 5$.

(a) Using the squared error loss, compute the expected loss (risk function) associated with the Bayes solution $w(Y)$.

(b) The risk function associated with the usual estimator Y/n is, of course, $\theta(1 - \theta)/30$. Find those values of θ for which the risk function in part (a) is less than $\theta(1 - \theta)/30$. In particular, if the prior mean $\alpha/(\alpha + \beta) = 3/4$ is a reasonable guess, then the risk function in part (a) is the better of the two (i.e., is smaller in a neighborhood of $\theta = 3/4$) for what values of θ?

9.2-4. Consider a random sample $X_1, X_2, \ldots, X_n$ from a distribution with p.d.f.

$$f(x \mid \theta) = 3\theta x^2 e^{-\theta x^3}, \qquad 0 < x < \infty.$$

Let θ have a prior p.d.f. that is gamma with $\alpha = 4$ and the usual $\theta = 1/4$. Find the conditional mean of θ, given that $X_1 = x_1, X_2 = x_2, \ldots, X_n = x_n$.

9.2-5. In Example 9.2-3, suppose the loss function $|\theta - w(Y)|$ is used. What is the Bayesian estimator $w(Y)$?

9.2-6. Let Y be the largest order statistic of a random sample of size n from a distribution with p.d.f.

$f(x \mid \theta) = 1/\theta$, $0 < x < \theta$. Say θ has the prior p.d.f.

$$h(\theta) = \beta\alpha^\beta/\theta^{\beta+1}, \qquad \alpha < \theta < \infty,$$

where $\alpha > 0$, $\beta > 0$.

(a) If $w(Y)$ is the Bayesian estimator of θ and $[\theta - w(Y)]^2$ is the loss function, find $w(Y)$.

(b) If $n = 4$, $\alpha = 1$, and $\beta = 2$, find the Bayesian estimator $w(Y)$ if the loss function is $|\theta - w(Y)|$.

9.2-7. Refer to Example 9.2-3. Suppose we select $\sigma_0^2 = d\sigma^2$, where σ^2 is known in that example. What value do we assign to d so that the variance of the posterior p.d.f. of the parameter is two-thirds of the variance of $Y = \overline{X}$, namely, σ^2/n?

9.3 MORE BAYESIAN CONCEPTS

Let $X_1, X_2, \ldots, X_n$ be a random sample from a distribution with p.d.f. (p.m.f.) $f(x \mid \theta)$, and let $h(\theta)$ be the prior p.d.f. Then the distribution associated with the marginal p.d.f. of $X_1, X_2, \ldots, X_n$, namely,

$$k_1(x_1, x_2, \ldots, x_n) = \int_{-\infty}^{\infty} f(x_1 \mid \theta) f(x_2 \mid \theta) \cdots f(x_n \mid \theta) h(\theta)\, d\theta,$$

is called the **predictive distribution** because it provides the best description of the probabilities on $X_1, X_2, \ldots, X_n$. Often this creates some interesting distributions. For example, suppose there is only one X with the normal p.d.f.

$$f(x \mid \theta) = \frac{\sqrt{\theta}}{\sqrt{2\pi}} e^{-(\theta x^2)/2}, \qquad -\infty < x < \infty.$$

Here, $\theta = 1/\sigma^2$, the inverse of the variance, is called the **precision** of X. Say this precision has the gamma p.d.f.

$$h(\theta) = \frac{1}{\Gamma(\alpha)\beta^\alpha}\theta^{\alpha-1}e^{-\theta/\beta}, \qquad 0 < \theta < \infty.$$

Then the predictive p.d.f. is

$$\begin{aligned} k_1(x) &= \int_0^{\infty} \frac{\theta^{\alpha+1/2-1}e^{-(x^2/2+1/\beta)\theta}}{\Gamma(\alpha)\beta^\alpha\sqrt{2\pi}}\, d\theta \\ &= \frac{\Gamma(\alpha + 1/2)}{\Gamma(\alpha)\beta^\alpha\sqrt{2\pi}} \frac{1}{(1/\beta + x^2/2)^{\alpha+1/2}}, \qquad -\infty < x < \infty. \end{aligned}$$

Note that if $\alpha = r/2$ and $\beta = 2/r$, where r is a positive integer, then

$$k_1(x) \propto \frac{1}{(1 + x^2/r)^{(r+1)/2}}, \qquad -\infty < x < \infty,$$

which is a t p.d.f. with r degrees of freedom. So if the inverse of the variance—or precision θ—of a normal distribution varies as a gamma random variable, a generalization of a t distribution has been created that has heavier tails than the normal distribution. This **mixture** of normals (different from a mixed distribution) is attained by weighing with the gamma distribution in a process often called **compounding**.

Another illustration of compounding is given in the next example.

EXAMPLE 9.3-1 Suppose X has a gamma distribution with the two parameters k and θ^{-1}. (That is, the usual α is replaced by k and θ by its reciprocal.) Say $h(\theta)$ is gamma with parameters

α and β, so that

$$
\begin{aligned}
k_1(x) &= \int_0^\infty \frac{\theta^k x^{k-1} e^{-\theta x}}{\Gamma(k)} \frac{1}{\Gamma(\alpha)\beta^\alpha} \theta^{\alpha-1} e^{-\theta/\beta}\, d\theta \\
&= \int_0^\infty \frac{x^{k-1} \theta^{k+\alpha-1} e^{-\theta(x+1/\beta)}}{\Gamma(k)\Gamma(\alpha)\beta^\alpha}\, d\theta \\
&= \frac{\Gamma(k + \alpha) x^{k-1}}{\Gamma(k)\Gamma(\alpha)\beta^\alpha} \frac{1}{(x + 1/\beta)^{k+\alpha}} \\
&= \frac{\Gamma(k + x)\beta^k x^{k-1}}{\Gamma(k)\Gamma(\alpha)(1 + \beta x)^{k+\alpha}}, \qquad 0 < x < \infty.
\end{aligned}
$$

Of course, this is a generalization of the F distribution, which we obtain by letting $\alpha = r_2/2$, $k = r_1/2$, and $\beta = r_1/r_2$. ■

Note how well the prior $h(\theta)$ "fits" with $f(x \mid \theta)$ or $f(x_1 \mid \theta)f(x_2 \mid \theta) \cdots f(x_n \mid \theta)$ in all of our examples, and the posterior distribution is of exactly the same form as the prior. In Example 9.2-2, both the prior and the posterior were beta. In Example 9.2-3, both the prior and posterior were normal. In Example 9.3-1, both the prior and the posterior (if we had found it) were gamma. When this type of pairing occurs, we say that the class of prior p.d.f.'s (p.m.f.'s) is a **conjugate family of priors**. Obviously, this makes the mathematics easier, and usually the parameters in the prior distribution give us enough flexibility to obtain good fits.

EXAMPLE 9.3-2 (Berry, 1996) This example deals with *predictive probabilities*, and it concerns the breakage of glass panels in high-rise buildings. One such case involved 39 panels, and of the 39 panels that broke, it was known that 3 broke due to nickel sulfide (NiS) stones found in them. Loss of evidence prevented the causes of breakage of the other 36 panels from being known. So the court wanted to know whether the manufacturer of the panels or the builder was at fault for the breakage of these 36 panels.

From expert testimony, it was thought that usually about 5% breakage is caused by NiS stones. That is, if this value of p is selected from a beta distribution, we have

$$\frac{\alpha}{\alpha + \beta} = 0.05. \tag{9.3-1}$$

Moreover, the expert thought that if two panels from the same lot break and one breakage was caused by NiS stones, then, due to the pervasive nature of the manufacturing process, the probability of the second panel's breaking due to NiS stones increases to about 95%. Thus, the posterior estimate of p (see Example 9.2-2) with one "success" after one trial is

$$\frac{\alpha + 1}{\alpha + \beta + 1} = 0.95. \tag{9.3-2}$$

Solving Equations 9.3-1 and 9.3-2 for α and β, we obtain

$$\alpha = \frac{1}{360} \quad \text{and} \quad \beta = \frac{19}{360}.$$

Now updating the posterior probability with 3 "successes" out of 3 trials, we obtain the posterior estimate of p:

$$\frac{\alpha + 3}{\alpha + \beta + 3} = \frac{1/360 + 3}{20/360 + 3} = \frac{1081}{1100} = 0.983.$$

Of course, the court that heard the case wanted to know the expert's opinion about the probability that all of the remaining 36 panels broke because of NiS stones. Using updated probabilities after the third break, then the fourth, and so on, we obtain the product

$$\left(\frac{1/360 + 3}{20/360 + 3}\right)\left(\frac{1/360 + 4}{20/360 + 4}\right)\left(\frac{1/360 + 5}{20/360 + 5}\right)\cdots\left(\frac{1/360 + 38}{20/360 + 38}\right) = 0.8664.$$

That is, the expert held that the probability that all 36 breakages were caused by NiS stones was about 87%, which is the needed value in the court's decision. ■

We now look at a situation in which we have two unknown parameters; we will use, for convenience, what is called a **noninformative prior**, which usually puts uniform distributions on the parameters. Let us begin with a random sample $X_1, X_2, \ldots, X_n$ from the normal distribution $N(\theta_1, \theta_2)$, and suppose we have little prior knowledge about θ_1 and θ_2. We then use the noninformative prior that θ_1 and $\ln \theta_2$ are uniform and independent; that is,

$$h_1(\theta_1)h_2(\theta_2) \propto \frac{1}{\theta_2}, \qquad -\infty < \theta_1 < \infty,\ 0 < \theta_2 < \infty.$$

Of course, we immediately note that we cannot find a constant c such that c/θ_2 is a joint p.d.f. on that support. That is, this noninformative prior p.d.f. is not a p.d.f. at all; hence, it is called an **improper** prior. However, we use it anyway, because it will be satisfactory when multiplied by the joint p.d.f. of $X_1, X_2, \ldots, X_n$. We have the product

$$\left(\frac{1}{\theta_2}\right)\left(\frac{1}{\sqrt{2\pi\theta_2}}\right)^n \exp\left[-\sum_{i=1}^{n}\frac{(x_i - \theta_1)^2}{2\theta_2}\right].$$

Thus,

$$k_{12}(\theta_1, \theta_2 \,|\, x_1, x_2, \ldots, x_n) \propto \left(\frac{1}{\theta_2}\right)^{\frac{n}{2}+1} \exp\left[-\frac{1}{2}\left\{(n - 1)s^2 + n(\overline{x} - \theta_1)^2\right\}/\theta_2\right]$$

since $\sum_{i=1}^{n}(x_i - \theta_1)^2 = (n - 1)s^2 + n(\overline{x} - \theta_1)^2 = D$. It then follows that

$$k_1(\theta_1 \,|\, x_1, x_2, \ldots, x_n) \propto \int_0^\infty k_{12}(\theta_1, \theta_2 \,|\, x_1, x_2, \ldots, x_n)\, d\theta_2.$$

Changing variables by letting $z = 1/\theta_2$, we obtain

$$k_1(\theta_1 \,|\, x_1, x_2, \ldots, x_n) \propto \int_0^\infty \frac{z^{n/2+1}}{z^2} e^{(-1/2)Dz}\, dz$$

$$\propto D^{-n/2} = \left[(n - 1)s^2 + n(\overline{x} - \theta_1)^2\right]^{-n/2}.$$

To get this p.d.f. in a more familiar form, let $t = (\theta_1 - \bar{x})/(s/\sqrt{n}\,)$, with Jacobian $s/\sqrt{n}$, to yield

$$k(t \mid x_1, x_2, \ldots, x_n) \propto \frac{1}{[1 + t^2/(n - 1)]^{[(n-1)+1]/2}}, \qquad -\infty < t < \infty.$$

That is, the conditional p.d.f. of t, given $x_1, x_2, \ldots, x_n$, is Student's t with $n - 1$ degrees of freedom. Thus, a $(1 - \alpha)$ probability interval for θ_1 is given by

$$-t_{\alpha/2}(n - 1) < \frac{\theta_1 - \bar{x}}{s/\sqrt{n}} < t_{\alpha/2}(n - 1),$$

or

$$\bar{x} - t_{\alpha/2}(n - 1)\, s/\sqrt{n} < \theta_1 < \bar{x} + t_{\alpha/2}(n - 1)\, s/\sqrt{n},$$

which is the same as the standard $100(1 - \alpha)\%$ confidence interval for θ_1.

The reason we get the same answer in this case is that we use a noninformative prior. Bayesians do not like to use a noninformative prior if they really know something about the parameters. For example, say they believe that the precision $1/\theta_2$ has a gamma distribution with parameters α and β instead of the noninformative prior. Then finding the conditional p.d.f. of θ_1 becomes a much more difficult integration. However, it can be done, but we leave it to a more advanced course. (See Hogg, McKean, and Craig, 2005.)

EXAMPLE 9.3-3 (Johnson and Albert, 1999) The data in this example, a sample of $n = 13$ measurements of the National Oceanographic and Atmospheric Administration (NOAA)/Environmental Protection Agency (EPA) ultraviolet (UV) index taken in Los Angeles, were collected from archival data of every Sunday in October during the years 1995–1997 in a database maintained by NOAA. The 13 UV readings are

$$7,\ 6,\ 5,\ 5,\ 3,\ 6,\ 5,\ 5,\ 3,\ 5,\ 5,\ 4,\ 4,$$

and, although they are integer values, we assume that they are taken from a $N(\mu, \sigma^2)$ distribution.

The Bayesian analysis, using a noninformative prior in the preceding discussion, implies that, with $\mu = \theta_1$,

$$\frac{\mu - 4.846}{0.317}, \qquad \text{where} \qquad \bar{x} = 4.846 \qquad \text{and} \qquad \frac{s}{\sqrt{n}} = 0.317,$$

has a posterior t distribution with $n - 1 = 12$ degrees of freedom. For example, a posterior 95% probability interval for μ is

$$(4.846 - [t_{0.025}(12)][0.317],\ 4.846 + [t_{0.025}(12)][0.317]) = (4.155,\ 5.537). \quad ■$$

EXAMPLE 9.3-4 Tsutakawa et. al. (1985) discuss the rates of death from stomach cancer in males aged 45–61 in the 20 largest cities in Missouri. Suppose p_i, $i = 1, 2, \ldots, 20$, are 20 respective probabilities of death due to stomach cancer. On one model, we can assume that $p_1, p_2, \ldots, p_{20}$ are taken independently from a beta distribution with parameters α and β. If y_i is the number of "successes" out of n_i observations in city i, then the posterior mean of p_i is

$$\widehat{p_i}\left(\frac{n_i}{n_i + \alpha + \beta}\right) + \left(\frac{\alpha}{\alpha + \beta}\right)\left(\frac{\alpha + \beta}{n_i + \alpha + \beta}\right), \quad i = 1, 2, \ldots, 20,$$

where $\widehat{p_i} = y_i/n_i$. Of course, the parameters α and β are unknown, but we have assumed that $p_1, p_2, \ldots, p_{20}$ arose from a similar distribution for these cities in Missouri; that is, we assume that our prior knowledge concerning the proportions is *exchangeable.* So it would be reasonable to estimate $\alpha/(\alpha + \beta)$, the prior mean of a proportion, with the formula

$$\bar{y} = \frac{y_1 + y_2 + \cdots + y_{20}}{n_1 + n_2 + \cdots + n_{20}} = \frac{71}{71{,}478} = 0.000993,$$

for the data given in Table 9.3-1. Thus, the posterior estimate of p_i is found by *shrinking* $\widehat{p_i}$ towards the pooled estimate of the mean $\alpha/(\alpha + \beta)$—namely, $\bar{y}$. That is, the posterior estimate is

$$\widehat{p_i}\left(\frac{n_i}{n_i + \alpha + \beta}\right) + \bar{y}\left(\frac{\alpha + \beta}{n_i + \alpha + \beta}\right).$$

The only question remaining is how much weight should be given to the prior, represented by $\alpha + \beta$, relative to $n_1, n_2, \ldots, n_{20}$. Considering the sizes of the samples from the various cities, we selected $\alpha + \beta = 3000$ (which means that the prior is worth about a sample of 3000), which resulted in the posterior probabilities given in Table 9.3-1. Note how this type of shrinkage tends to pull the posterior estimates much closer to the average, particularly those associated with small sample sizes. Baseball fans might try this type of shrinkage in predicting some of the final batting averages of the better batters about a quarter of the way through the season. ■

TABLE 9.3-1: Cancer Mortality Rates

y_i	n_i	$\widehat{p_i}$	posterior estimate	y_i	n_i	$\widehat{p_i}$	posterior estimate
0	1083	0	0.00073	0	855	0	0.00077
2	3461	0.00058	0.00077	0	657	0	0.00081
1	1208	0.00083	0.00095	1	1025	0.00098	0.00099
0	527	0	0.00084	2	1668	0.00120	0.00107
1	583	0.00172	0.00111	3	582	0.00515	0.00167
0	917	0	0.00076	1	857	0.00117	0.00103
1	680	0.00147	0.00108	1	917	0.00109	0.00102
54	53637	0.00101	0.00101	0	874	0	0.00077
0	395	0	0.00088	1	581	0.00172	0.00111
3	588	0.00510	0.00167	0	383	0	0.00088

It is clear that difficult integration caused Bayesians great problems until very recent times, in which advances in computer methods "solved" many of these problems. As a simple illustration, suppose the p.d.f. of a good statistic Y is $f(y\,|\,\theta)$ and the prior p.d.f. $h(\theta)$ is such that

$$k(\theta \mid y) = \frac{f(y \mid \theta)\, h(\theta)}{\int_{-\infty}^{\infty} f(y \mid \theta)\, h(\theta)\, d\theta}$$

is not a nice p.d.f. with which to deal. In particular, say that we have a squared error loss and we wish to determine $E(\theta \mid y)$, namely,

$$\delta(y) = \frac{\int_{-\infty}^{\infty} \theta f(y \mid \theta)\, h(\theta)\, d\theta}{\int_{-\infty}^{\infty} f(y \mid \theta)\, h(\theta)\, d\theta},$$

but cannot do it easily. Let $f(y \mid \theta) = w(\theta)$. Then we wish to evaluate the ratio

$$\frac{E[\theta\, w(\theta)]}{E[w(\theta)]},$$

where y is given and the expected values are taken with respect to θ. To do so, we simply generate a number of θ values, say, $\theta_1, \theta_2, \ldots, \theta_m$ (where m is large), from the distribution given by $h(\theta)$. Then we estimate the numerator and denominator of the desired ratio by

$$\sum_{i=1}^{m} \frac{\theta_i\, w(\theta_i)}{m} \qquad \text{and} \qquad \sum_{i=1}^{m} \frac{w(\theta_i)}{m},$$

respectively, to obtain

$$\tau = \frac{\sum_{i=1}^{m} \theta_i\, w(\theta_i)/m}{\sum_{i=1}^{m} w(\theta_i)/m}.$$

In addition to this simple Monte Carlo procedure, there are additional ones that are extremely useful in Bayesian inferences. Two of these are the *Gibbs sampler* and the *Markov chain Monte Carlo (MCMC)*. The latter is used in *hierarchical Bayes models* in which the prior has another parameter that has its own prior. That is, we have

$$f(y \mid \theta), \qquad h(\theta \mid \tau), \qquad \text{and} \qquad g(\tau).$$

Hence,

$$k(\theta, \tau \mid y) = \frac{f(y \mid \theta)\, h(\theta \mid \tau)\, g(\tau)}{\int_{-\infty}^{\infty}\int_{-\infty}^{\infty} f(y \mid \theta)\, h(\theta \mid \tau)\, g(\tau)\, d\theta\, d\tau}$$

and

$$k_1(\theta \mid y) = \int_{-\infty}^{\infty} k(\theta, \tau \mid y)\, d\tau.$$

Thus, a Bayes estimator, for a squared error loss, is

$$\int_{-\infty}^{\infty} \theta\, k_1(\theta \mid y)\, d\theta.$$

Using the Gibbs sampler, we can generate a stream of values $(\theta_1, \tau_1), (\theta_2, \tau_2), \ldots$ that allows us to estimate $k(\theta, \tau \mid y)$ and $\int_{-\infty}^{\infty} \theta\, k_1(\theta \mid y)\, d\theta$. These procedures are the MCMC procedures. (For additional references, see Hogg, McKean, and Craig, 2005.)

EXERCISES

9.3-1. Let X have a Poisson distribution with parameter θ. Let θ be $\Gamma(\alpha, \beta)$. Show that the marginal p.m.f. of X (the compound distribution) is

$$k_1(x) = \frac{\Gamma(\alpha + x)\beta^x}{\Gamma(\alpha)x!(1 + \beta)^{\alpha+x}}, \quad x = 0, 1, 2, 3, \ldots,$$

which is a generalization of the negative binomial distribution.

9.3-2. Suppose X is $b(n, \theta)$ and θ is beta(α, β). Show that the marginal p.d.f. of X (the compound distribution) is

$$k_1(x) = \frac{n!\,\Gamma(\alpha + \beta)\Gamma(x + \alpha)\Gamma(n - x + \beta)}{x!\,(n - x)!\,\Gamma(\alpha)\Gamma(\beta)\Gamma(n + \alpha + \beta)}, \quad x = 0, 1, 2, \ldots, n.$$

9.3-3. Let X have the geometric p.m.f. $\theta(1 - \theta)^{x-1}$, $x = 1, 2, 3, \ldots$, where θ is beta with parameters α and β. Show that the compound p.m.f. is

$$\frac{\Gamma(\alpha + \beta)\Gamma(\alpha + 1)\Gamma(\beta + x - 1)}{\Gamma(\alpha)\Gamma(\beta)\Gamma(\alpha + \beta + x)}, \quad x = 1, 2, 3, \ldots.$$

With $\alpha = 1$, this is one form of **Zipf's law**,

$$\frac{\beta}{(\beta + x)(\beta + x - 1)}, \quad x = 1, 2, 3, \ldots.$$

9.3-4. Let X have the p.d.f.

$$f(x\,|\,\theta) = \theta\tau x^{\tau-1}e^{-\theta x^{\tau}}, \quad 0 < x < \infty,$$

where the distribution of θ is $\Gamma(\alpha, \beta)$. Find the compound distribution of X, which is called the **Burr distribution**.

9.3-5. Let $X_1, X_2, \ldots, X_n$ be a random sample from a gamma distribution with $\alpha = 1, \theta$. Let $h(\theta) \propto 1/\theta$, $0 < \theta < \infty$, be an improper noninformative prior.

(a) Find the posterior p.d.f. of θ.

(b) Change variables by letting $z = 1/\theta$, and show that the posterior distribution of Z is $\Gamma(n, 1/y)$, where $y = \sum_{i=1}^{n} x_i$.

(c) Use $2yz$ to obtain a $(1 - \alpha)$ probability interval for z and, of course, for θ.

9.3-6. Let X_1, X_2 be a random sample from the Cauchy distribution with p.d.f.

$$f(x\,|\,\theta_1, \theta_2) = \frac{1}{\pi}\frac{\theta_2}{\theta_2^2 + (x - \theta_1)^2}, \quad -\infty < x < \infty,\ -\infty < \theta_1 < \infty,\ 0 < \theta_2 < \infty.$$

Consider the noninformative prior $h(\theta_1, \theta_2) \propto 1$ on that support. Obtain the posterior p.d.f. (except for constants) of θ_1, θ_2 if $x_1 = 3$ and $x_2 = 7$. For estimates, find θ_1, θ_2 that maximizes this posterior p.d.f.; that is, find the mode of that posterior. (This might require some reasonable "trial and error" or an advanced method of maximizing a function of two variables.)

HISTORICAL COMMENTS The Neo-Bayesian movement in America really started with J. Savage in the 1950s. Initially, Bayesians were limited in their work because it was extremely difficult to compute certain distributions, such as the conditional one, $k(\theta\,|\,x_1, x_2, \ldots, x_n)$. However, towards the end of the 1970s, computers were becoming more useful and thus computing was much easier. In particular, the Bayesians developed Gibbs sampling and Markov chain Monte Carlo (MCMC). It is our opinion that the Bayesians will continue to expand and Bayes's methods will be a major approach to statistical inferences, possibly even dominating professional applications. This is difficult for two fairly classical statisticians (as we are) to admit, but, in all fairness, we cannot ignore the strong trend toward Bayesian methods.

Some Theory

CHAPTER 10

10.1 SUFFICIENT STATISTICS
10.2 POWER OF A STATISTICAL TEST
10.3 BEST CRITICAL REGIONS
10.4 LIKELIHOOD RATIO TESTS
10.5 CHEBYSHEV'S INEQUALITY AND CONVERGENCE IN PROBABILITY
10.6 LIMITING MOMENT-GENERATING FUNCTIONS
10.7 ASYMPTOTIC DISTRIBUTIONS OF MAXIMUM LIKELIHOOD ESTIMATORS

10.1 SUFFICIENT STATISTICS

We first define a sufficient statistic $Y = u(X_1, X_2, \ldots, X_n)$ for a parameter, using a statement that, in most books, is given as a necessary and sufficient condition for sufficiency, namely, the well-known Fisher–Neyman factorization theorem. We do this because we find that readers at the introductory level can apply such a definition easily. However, using this definition, we shall note, by examples, its implications, one of which is also sometimes used as the definition of sufficiency. The understanding of Example 10.1-3 is most important in an appreciation of the value of sufficient statistics.

DEFINITION 10.1-1

(Factorization Theorem) Let $X_1, X_2, \ldots, X_n$ denote random variables with joint p.d.f. or p.m.f. $f(x_1, x_2, \ldots, x_n; \theta)$, which depends on the parameter θ. The statistic $Y = u(X_1, X_2, \ldots, X_n)$ is sufficient for θ if and only if

$$f(x_1, x_2, \ldots, x_n; \theta) = \phi[u(x_1, x_2, \ldots, x_n); \theta]h(x_1, x_2, \ldots, x_n),$$

where ϕ depends on $x_1, x_2, \ldots, x_n$ only through $u(x_1, \ldots, x_n)$ and $h(x_1, \ldots, x_n)$ does not depend on θ.

Let us consider several important examples and consequences of this definition. We first note, however, that in all instances in this book the random variables $X_1, X_2, \ldots, X_n$ will be of a random sample, and hence their joint p.d.f. or p.m.f. will be of the form

$$f(x_1; \theta)f(x_2; \theta)\cdots f(x_n; \theta).$$

EXAMPLE 10.1-1 Let $X_1, X_2, \ldots, X_n$ denote a random sample from a Poisson distribution with parameter $\lambda > 0$. Then

$$f(x_1; \lambda)f(x_2; \lambda)\cdots f(x_n; \lambda) = \frac{\lambda^{\Sigma x_i} e^{-n\lambda}}{x_1!x_2!\cdots x_n!} = (\lambda^{n\bar{x}}e^{-n\lambda})\left(\frac{1}{x_1!x_2!\cdots x_n!}\right),$$

where $\bar{x} = (1/n)\sum_{i=1}^{n} x_i$. Thus, from the factorization theorem (Definition 10.1-1), it is clear that the sample mean $\overline{X}$ is a sufficient statistic for λ. It can easily be shown that the maximum likelihood estimator for λ is also $\overline{X}$, so here the maximum likelihood estimator is a function of the sufficient statistic. ■

In Example 10.1-1, if we replace $n\bar{x}$ by $\sum_{i=1}^{n} x_i$, it is quite obvious that the sum $\sum_{i=1}^{n} X_i$ is also a sufficient statistic for λ. This certainly agrees with our intuition, because if we know one of the statistics $\overline{X}$ and $\sum_{i=1}^{n} X_i$, we can easily find the other. If we generalize this idea, we see that if Y is sufficient for a parameter θ, then every single-valued function of Y not involving θ, but with a single-valued inverse, is also a sufficient statistic for θ. Again, the reason is that knowing either Y or that function of Y, we know the other. More formally, if $W = v(Y) = v[u(X_1, X_2, \ldots, X_n)]$ is that function and $Y = v^{-1}(W)$ is the single-valued inverse, then the factorization theorem can be written as

$$f(x_1, x_2, \ldots, x_n; \theta) = \phi[v^{-1}\{v[u(x_1, x_2, \ldots, x_n)]\}; \theta]\, h(x_1, x_2, \ldots, x_n).$$

The first factor of the righthand member of this equation depends on $x_1, x_2, \ldots, x_n$ through $v[u(x_1, x_2, \ldots, x_n)]$, so $W = v[u(X_1, X_2, \ldots, X_n)]$ is a sufficient statistic for θ. We illustrate this fact and the factorization theorem with an underlying distribution of the continuous type.

EXAMPLE 10.1-2 Let $X_1, X_2, \ldots, X_n$ be a random sample from $N(\mu, 1)$, $-\infty < \mu < \infty$. The joint p.d.f. of these random variables is

$$\begin{aligned}
&\frac{1}{(2\pi)^{n/2}} \exp\left[-\frac{1}{2}\sum_{i=1}^{n}(x_i - \mu)^2\right] \\
&\qquad = \frac{1}{(2\pi)^{n/2}} \exp\left[-\frac{1}{2}\sum_{i=1}^{n}[(x_i - \bar{x}) + (\bar{x} - \mu)]^2\right] \\
&\qquad = \left\{\exp\left[-\frac{n}{2}(\bar{x} - \mu)^2\right]\right\}\left\{\frac{1}{(2\pi)^{n/2}} \exp\left[-\frac{1}{2}\sum_{i=1}^{n}(x_i - \bar{x})^2\right]\right\}.
\end{aligned}$$

From the factorization theorem, we see that $\overline{X}$ is sufficient for μ. Now, $\overline{X}^3$ is also sufficient for μ, because knowing $\overline{X}^3$ is equivalent to having knowledge of the value of $\overline{X}$. However, $\overline{X}^2$ does not have this property, and it is not sufficient for μ. ■

One extremely important consequence of the sufficiency of a statistic Y is that the conditional probability of any given event A in the support of $X_1, X_2, \ldots, X_n$, given that $Y = y$, does not depend on θ. This consequence is sometimes used as the definition of sufficiency and is illustrated in the next example.

EXAMPLE 10.1-3 Let $X_1, X_2, \ldots, X_n$ be a random sample from a distribution with p.m.f.

$$f(x; p) = p^x(1 - p)^{1-x}, \qquad x = 0, 1,$$

where the parameter p is between 0 and 1. We know that

$$Y = X_1 + X_2 + \cdots + X_n$$

is $b(n, p)$ and Y is sufficient for p because the joint p.m.f. of $X_1, X_2, \ldots, X_n$ is

$$p^{x_1}(1 - p)^{1-x_1} \cdots p^{x_n}(1 - p)^{1-x_n} = [p^{\Sigma x_i}(1 - p)^{n-\Sigma x_i}](1),$$

where $\phi(y; p) = p^y(1 - p)^{n-y}$ and $h(x_1, x_2, \ldots, x_n) = 1$. What, then, is the conditional probability $P(X_1 = x_1, \ldots, X_n = x_n \mid Y = y)$, where $y = 0, 1, \ldots, n - 1$, or n? Unless the sum of the nonnegative integers $x_1, x_2, \ldots, x_n$ equals y, this conditional probability is obviously equal to zero, which does not depend on p. Hence, it is interesting to consider the solution only when $y = x_1 + \cdots + x_n$. From the definition of conditional probability, we have

$$\begin{aligned} P(X_1 = x_1, \ldots, X_n = x_n \mid Y = y) &= \frac{P(X_1 = x_1, \ldots, X_n = x_n)}{P(Y = y)} \\ &= \frac{p^{x_1}(1 - p)^{1-x_1} \cdots p^{x_n}(1 - p)^{1-x_n}}{\binom{n}{y} p^y(1 - p)^{n-y}} \\ &= \frac{1}{\binom{n}{y}}, \end{aligned}$$

where $y = x_1 + \cdots + x_n$. Since y equals the number of ones in the collection $x_1, x_2, \ldots, x_n$, this answer is only the probability of selecting a particular arrangement, namely, $x_1, x_2, \ldots, x_n$, of y ones and $n - y$ zeros, and does not depend on the parameter p. That is, given that the sufficient statistic $Y = y$, the conditional probability of $X_1 = x_1, X_2 = x_2, \ldots, X_n = x_n$ does not depend on the parameter p. ■

It is interesting to observe that the underlying p.d.f. or p.m.f. in Examples 10.1-1, 10.1-2, and 10.1-3 can be written in the exponential form

$$f(x; \theta) = \exp[K(x)p(\theta) + S(x) + q(\theta)],$$

where the support is free of θ. That is, we have, respectively,

$$\frac{e^{-\lambda}\lambda^x}{x!} = \exp\{x \ln \lambda - \ln x! - \lambda\}, \qquad x = 0, 1, 2, \ldots,$$

$$\frac{1}{\sqrt{2\pi}} e^{-(x-\mu)^2/2} = \exp\left\{x\mu - \frac{x^2}{2} - \frac{\mu^2}{2} - \frac{1}{2}\ln(2\pi)\right\}, \qquad -\infty < x < \infty,$$

and

$$p^x(1 - p)^{1-x} = \exp\left\{x \ln\left(\frac{p}{1 - p}\right) + \ln(1 - p)\right\}, \qquad x = 0, 1.$$

In each of these examples, the sum $\sum_{i=1}^{n} X_i$ of the observations of the random sample was a sufficient statistic for the parameter. This idea is generalized by Theorem 10.1-1.

THEOREM 10.1-1 Let $X_1, X_2, \ldots, X_n$ be a random sample from a distribution with a p.d.f. or p.m.f. of the exponential form

$$f(x;\theta) = \exp[K(x)p(\theta) + S(x) + q(\theta)]$$

on a support free of θ. Then the statistic $\sum_{i=1}^{n} K(X_i)$ is sufficient for θ.

Proof. The joint p.d.f. (p.m.f.) of $X_1, X_2, \ldots, X_n$ is

$$\begin{aligned}&\exp\left[p(\theta)\sum_{i=1}^{n} K(x_i) + \sum_{i=1}^{n} S(x_i) + nq(\theta)\right] \\ &\quad = \left\{\exp\left[p(\theta)\sum_{i=1}^{n} K(x_i) + nq(\theta)\right]\right\}\left\{\exp\left[\sum_{i=1}^{n} S(x_i)\right]\right\}.\end{aligned}$$

In accordance with the factorization theorem, the statistic $\sum_{i=1}^{n} K(X_i)$ is sufficient for θ. □

In many cases, Theorem 10.1-1 permits the student to find a sufficient statistic for a parameter with very little effort, as shown in the next example.

EXAMPLE 10.1-4 Let $X_1, X_2, \ldots, X_n$ be a random sample from an exponential distribution with p.d.f.

$$f(x;\theta) = \frac{1}{\theta}e^{-x/\theta} = \exp\left[x\left(-\frac{1}{\theta}\right) - \ln\theta\right], \qquad 0 < x < \infty,$$

provided that $0 < \theta < \infty$. Here, $K(x) = x$. Thus, $\sum_{i=1}^{n} X_i$ is sufficient for θ; of course, $\overline{X} = \sum_{i=1}^{n} X_i/n$ is also sufficient. ■

Note that if there is a sufficient statistic for the parameter under consideration and if the maximum likelihood estimator of this parameter is unique, then the maximum likelihood estimator is a function of the sufficient statistic. To see this heuristically, consider the following: If a sufficient statistic exists, then the likelihood function is

$$L(\theta) = f(x_1, x_2, \ldots, x_n; \theta) = \phi[u(x_1, x_2, \ldots, x_n); \theta]\, h(x_1, x_2, \ldots, x_n).$$

Since $h(x_1, x_2, \ldots, x_n)$ does not depend on θ, we maximize $L(\theta)$ by maximizing $\phi[u(x_1, x_2, \ldots, x_n); \theta]$. But ϕ is a function of $x_1, x_2, \ldots, x_n$ only through the statistic $u(x_1, x_2, \ldots, x_n)$. Thus, if there is a unique value of θ that maximizes ϕ, then it must be a function of $u(x_1, x_2, \ldots, x_n)$. That is, $\widehat{\theta}$ is a function of the sufficient statistic $u(X_1, X_2, \ldots, X_n)$. This fact was alluded to in Example 10.1-1, but it could be checked with the use of other examples and exercises.

In many cases, we have two (or more) parameters—say, θ_1 and θ_2. All of the preceding concepts can be extended to these situations. For example, Definition 10.1-1 (the factorization theorem) becomes the following in the case of two parameters: If

$$f(x_1, \ldots, x_n; \theta_1, \theta_2) = \phi[u_1(x_1, \ldots, x_n), u_2(x_1, \ldots, x_n); \theta_1, \theta_2]h(x_1, \ldots, x_n),$$

where ϕ depends on $x_1, x_2, \ldots, x_n$ only through $u_1(x_1, \ldots, x_n)$, $u_2(x_1, \ldots, x_n)$, and $h(x_1, x_2, \ldots, x_n)$ does not depend upon θ_1 or θ_2, then $Y_1 = u_1(X_1, X_2, \ldots, X_n)$ and $Y_2 = u_2(X_1, X_2, \ldots, X_n)$ are **joint sufficient statistics** for θ_1 and θ_2.

EXAMPLE 10.1-5 Let $X_1, X_2, \ldots, X_n$ denote a random sample from a normal distribution $N(\theta_1, \theta_2)$. That is, $\theta_1 = \mu$ and $\theta_2 = \sigma^2$. Then

$$\prod_{i=1}^{n} f(x_i; \theta_1, \theta_2) = \left(\frac{1}{\sqrt{2\pi\theta_2}}\right)^n \exp\left[-\sum_{i=1}^{n}(x_i - \theta_1)^2 \bigg/ 2\theta_2\right]$$

$$= \exp\left[\left(-\frac{1}{2\theta_2}\right)\sum_{i=1}^{n} x_i^2 + \left(\frac{\theta_1}{\theta_2}\right)\sum_{i=1}^{n} x_i - \frac{n\theta_1^2}{2\theta_2} - n\ln\sqrt{2\pi\theta_2}\right] \cdot (1).$$

Thus,

$$Y_1 = \sum_{i=1}^{n} X_i^2 \quad \text{and} \quad Y_2 = \sum_{i=1}^{n} X_i$$

are joint sufficient statistics for θ_1 and θ_2. Of course, the single-valued functions of Y_1 and Y_2, namely,

$$\overline{X} = \frac{Y_2}{n} \quad \text{and} \quad S^2 = \frac{Y_1 - Y_2^2/n}{n - 1},$$

are also joint sufficient statistics for θ_1 and θ_2. ■

Actually, we can see from Definition 10.1-1 and Example 10.1-5 that if we can write the p.d.f. in the exponential form, it is easy to find the joint sufficient statistics. In that example,

$$f(x; \theta_1, \theta_2) = \exp\left(\frac{-1}{2\theta_2}x^2 + \frac{\theta_1}{\theta_2}x - \frac{\theta_1^2}{2\theta_2} - \ln\sqrt{2\pi\theta_2}\right);$$

so

$$Y_1 = \sum_{i=1}^{n} X_i^2 \quad \text{and} \quad Y_2 = \sum_{i=1}^{n} X_i$$

are joint sufficient statistics for θ_1 and θ_2. A much more complicated illustration is given if we take a random sample $(X_1, Y_1), (X_2, Y_2), \ldots, (X_n, Y_n)$ from a bivariate normal distribution with parameters $\theta_1 = \mu_X, \theta_2 = \mu_Y, \theta_3 = \sigma_X^2, \theta_4 = \sigma_Y^2$, and $\theta_5 = \rho$. In Exercise 10.1-3, we write the bivariate normal p.d.f. $f(x, y; \theta_1, \theta_2, \theta_3, \theta_4, \theta_5)$ in exponential form and see that $Z_1 = \sum_{i=1}^{n} X_i^2$, $Z_2 = \sum_{i=1}^{n} Y_i^2$, $Z_3 = \sum_{i=1}^{n} X_iY_i$, $Z_4 = \sum_{i=1}^{n} X_i$, and $Z_5 = \sum_{i=1}^{n} Y_i$ are joint sufficient statistics for $\theta_1, \theta_2, \theta_3, \theta_4$, and θ_5. Of course, the single-valued functions

$$\overline{X} = \frac{Z_4}{n}, \quad \overline{Y} = \frac{Z_5}{n}, \quad S_X^2 = \frac{Z_1 - Z_4^2/n}{n - 1},$$

$$S_Y^2 = \frac{Z_2 - Z_5^2/n}{n - 1}, \quad R = \frac{(Z_3 - Z_4Z_5/n)/(n - 1)}{S_XS_Y},$$

are also joint sufficient statistics for those parameters.

The important point to stress for cases in which sufficient statistics exist is that once the sufficient statistics are given, there is no additional information about the parameters left in the remaining (conditional) distribution. That is, all statistical inferences should be based upon the sufficient statistics. To help convince the reader of this in point estimation, we state and prove the well-known **Rao–Blackwell theorem**.

THEOREM 10.1-2 Let $X_1, X_2, \ldots, X_n$ be a random sample from a distribution with p.d.f. or p.m.f. $f(x; \theta)$, $\theta \in \Omega$. Let $Y_1 = u_1(X_1, X_2, \ldots, X_n)$ be a sufficient statistic for θ, and let $Y_2 = u_2(X_1, X_2, \ldots, X_n)$ be an unbiased estimator of θ, where Y_2 is not a function of Y_1 alone. Then $E(Y_2 \mid y_1) = u(y_1)$ defines a statistic $u(Y_1)$, a function of the sufficient statistic Y_1, which is an unbiased estimator of θ, and its variance is less than that of Y_2.

Proof. Let $g(y_1, y_2; \theta)$ be the joint p.d.f. or p.m.f. of Y_1 and Y_2. Let $g_1(y_1; \theta)$ be the marginal of Y_1; thus,

$$\frac{g(y_1, y_2; \theta)}{g_1(y_1; \theta)} = h(y_2 \mid y_1)$$

is the conditional p.d.f. or p.m.f. of Y_2, given that $Y_1 = y_1$. This equation does not depend upon θ, since Y_1 is a sufficient statistic for θ. Of course, in the continuous case,

$$u(y_1) = \int_{y_2} y_2 h(y_2 \mid y_1)\, dy_2 = \int_{y_2} y_2 \frac{g(y_1, y_2; \theta)}{g_1(y_1; \theta)}\, dy_2$$

and

$$\begin{aligned} E[u(Y_1)] &= \int_{y_1} \left(\int_{y_2} y_2 \frac{g(y_1, y_2; \theta)}{g_1(y_1; \theta)}\, dy_2 \right) g_1(y_1; \theta)\, dy_1 \\ &= \int_{y_1} \int_{y_2} y_2\, g(y_1, y_2; \theta)\, dy_2\, dy_1 = \theta, \end{aligned}$$

because Y_2 is an unbiased estimator of θ. Thus, $u(Y_1)$ is also an unbiased estimator of θ.

Now, consider

$$\begin{aligned} \text{Var}(Y_2) = E[(Y_2 - \theta)^2] &= E[\{Y_2 - u(Y_1) + u(Y_1) - \theta\}^2] \\ &= E[\{Y_2 - u(Y_1)\}^2] + E[\{u(Y_1) - \theta\}^2] \\ &\quad + 2E[\{Y_2 - u(Y_1)\}\{u(Y_1) - \theta\}]. \end{aligned}$$

But the latter expectation is equal to

$$\int_{y_1} [u(y_1) - \theta] \left\{ \int_{y_2} [y_2 - u(y_1)] h(y_2 \mid y_1)\, dy_2 \right\} g(y_1; \theta)\, dy_1 = 0,$$

because $u(y_1)$ is the mean $E(Y_2 \mid y_1)$ of Y_2 in the conditional distribution given by $h(y_2 \mid y_1)$. Thus,

$$\text{Var}(Y_2) = E[\{Y_2 - u(Y_1)\}^2] + \text{Var}[u(Y_1)].$$

However, $E[\{(Y_2 - u(Y_1)\}^2 \geq 0$, as it is the expected value of a positive expression. Therefore,

$$\text{Var}(Y_2) \geq \text{Var}[u(Y_1)]. \qquad \square$$

The importance of this theorem is that it shows that for every other unbiased estimator of θ, we can always find an unbiased estimator based on the sufficient statistic which has a smaller variance than the first unbiased estimator. Hence, in that sense, the one based upon the sufficient statistic is better than the first one. More important, we might as well begin our search for an unbiased estimator with the smallest variance by considering only those unbiased estimators based upon the sufficient statistics. Moreover, in an advanced course we show that if the underlying distribution is described by a p.d.f. or p.m.f. of the exponential form, then, if an unbiased estimator exists, there is only one function of the sufficient statistic that is unbiased. That is, that unbiased estimator is unique. (See Hogg, McKean, and Craig, 2005.)

There is one other useful result involving a sufficient statistic Y for a parameter θ, particularly with a p.d.f. of the exponential form. It is that if another statistic Z has a distribution that is free of θ, then Y and Z are independent. This is the reason $Z = (n - 1)S^2$ is independent of $Y = \overline{X}$ when the sample arises from a distribution that is $N(\theta, \sigma^2)$. The sample mean is the sufficient statistic for θ, and

$$Z = (n - 1)S^2 = \sum_{i=1}^{n}(X_i - \overline{X})^2$$

has a distribution that is free of θ. To see this, we note that the m.g.f. of Z, namely, $E(e^{tZ})$, is

$$\int_{-\infty}^{\infty}\int_{-\infty}^{\infty}\cdots\int_{-\infty}^{\infty}\exp\left[t\sum_{i=1}^{n}(x_i - \overline{x})^2\right]\left(\frac{1}{\sqrt{2\pi}\sigma}\right)^n \exp\left[-\frac{\Sigma(x_i - \theta)^2}{2\sigma^2}\right]dx_1 dx_2 \ldots dx_n.$$

Changing variables by letting $x_i - \theta = w_i$, $i = 1, 2, \ldots, n$, the preceding expression becomes

$$\int_{-\infty}^{\infty}\int_{-\infty}^{\infty}\cdots\int_{-\infty}^{\infty}\exp\left[t\sum_{i=1}^{n}(w_i - \overline{w})^2\right]\left(\frac{1}{\sqrt{2\pi}\sigma}\right)^n \exp\left[-\frac{\Sigma w_i^2}{2\sigma^2}\right]dw_1 dw_2 \ldots dw_n,$$

which is free of θ.

An outline of the proof of this result is given by noting that

$$\int_y [h(z\,|\,y) - g_2(z)]g_1(y;\theta)\,dy = g_2(z) - g_2(z) = 0$$

for all $\theta \in \Omega$. However, because $h(z\,|\,y)$ is free of θ due to the hypothesis of sufficiency, $h(z\,|\,y) - g_2(z)$ is free of θ, since Z has a distribution that is free of θ. Because $N(\theta, \sigma^2)$ is of the exponential form, and thus $Y = \overline{X}$ has a p.d.f. $g_1(y\,|\,\theta)$ that is called a **complete kernel**, $h(z\,|\,y) - g_2(z)$ must be equal to zero. That is,

$$h(z\,|\,y) = g_2(z),$$

which means that Z and Y are independent. This proves the independence of $\overline{X}$ and S^2, which was stated in Theorem 5.5-2.

EXAMPLE 10.1-6 Let $X_1, X_2, \ldots, X_n$ be a random sample from a gamma distribution with α (given) and $\theta > 0$. Now, $Y = \sum_{i=1}^n X_i$ is a sufficient statistic for θ, since the gamma p.d.f. is of the exponential form. Clearly, then,

$$Z = \frac{\sum_{i=1}^n a_i X_i}{\sum_{i=1}^n X_i},$$

where not all constants $a_1, a_2, \ldots, a_n$ are equal, has a distribution that is free of the spread parameter θ because the moment-generating function of Z, namely,

$$E(e^{tZ}) = \int_0^\infty \int_0^\infty \cdots \int_0^\infty \frac{e^{t\Sigma a_i X_i/\Sigma X_i}}{[\Gamma(\alpha)]^n \theta^{n\alpha}} (x_1 x_2 \cdots x_n)^{\alpha-1} e^{-\Sigma x_i/\theta} dx_1 dx_2 \ldots dx_n,$$

does not depend upon θ, as is seen by the transformation $w_i = x_i/\theta$, $i = 1, 2, \ldots, n$. So Y and Z are independent statistics. ■

This special case of the independence of Y and Z concerning one sufficient statistic Y and one parameter θ was first observed by Hogg (1953) and then generalized to several sufficient statistics for more than one parameter by Basu (1955) and is usually called **Basu's theorem**.

Due to these results, sufficient statistics are extremely important and future estimation problems are based upon them when they exist.

EXERCISES

10.1-1. Let $X_1, X_2, \ldots, X_n$ be a random sample from $N(0, \sigma^2)$.

(a) Find a sufficient statistic Y for σ^2.

(b) Show that the maximum likelihood estimator for σ^2 is a function of Y.

(c) Is the maximum likelihood estimator for σ^2 unbiased?

10.1-2. Let $X_1, X_2, \ldots, X_n$ be a random sample from a Poisson distribution with mean $\lambda > 0$. Find the conditional probability $P(X_1 = x_1, \ldots, X_n = x_n | Y = y)$, where $Y = X_1 + \cdots + X_n$ and the nonnegative integers $x_1, x_2, \ldots, x_n$ sum to y. Note that this probability does not depend on λ.

10.1-3. Write the bivariate normal p.d.f. $f(x, y; \theta_1, \theta_2, \theta_3, \theta_4, \theta_5)$ in exponential form, and show that $Z_1 = \sum_{i=1}^n X_i^2$, $Z_2 = \sum_{i=1}^n Y_i^2$, $Z_3 = \sum_{i=1}^n X_i Y_i$, $Z_4 = \sum_{i=1}^n X_i$, and $Z_5 = \sum_{i=1}^n Y_i$ are joint sufficient statistics for $\theta_1, \theta_2, \theta_3, \theta_4$, and θ_5.

10.1-4. Let $X_1, X_2, \ldots, X_n$ be a random sample from a distribution with p.d.f. $f(x; \theta) = \theta x^{\theta-1}$, $0 < x < 1$, where $0 < \theta$.

(a) Find the sufficient statistic Y for θ.

(b) Show that the maximum likelihood estimator $\widehat{\theta}$ is a function of Y.

(c) Argue that $\widehat{\theta}$ is also sufficient for θ.

10.1-5. Let $X_1, X_2, \ldots, X_n$ be a random sample from a gamma distribution with $\alpha = 1$ and $1/\theta > 0$. Show that $Y = \sum_{i=1}^n X_i$ is a sufficient statistic, Y has a gamma distribution with parameters n and $1/\theta$, and $(n-1)/Y$ is an unbiased estimator of θ.

10.1-6. Let $X_1, X_2, \ldots, X_n$ be a random sample from a gamma distribution with known parameter α and unknown parameter $\theta > 0$.

(a) Show that $Y = \sum_{i=1}^n X_i$ is a sufficient statistic for θ.

(b) Show that the maximum likelihood estimator of θ is a function of the sufficient statistic and is an unbiased estimator of θ.

10.1-7. Let $X_1, X_2, \ldots, X_n$ be a random sample from the distribution with p.m.f. $f(x; p) = p(1-p)^{x-1}$, $x = 1, 2, 3, \ldots$, where $0 < p < 1$.

(a) Show that $Y = \sum_{i=1}^n X_i$ is a sufficient statistic for p.

(b) Find a function of $Y = \sum_{i=1}^n X_i$ that is an unbiased estimator of $\theta = 1/p$.

10.1-8. Let $X_1, X_2, \ldots, X_n$ be a random sample from $N(0, \theta)$, where $\sigma^2 = \theta > 0$ is unknown. Argue that the sufficient statistic $Y = \sum_{i=1}^n X_i^2$ for θ and $Z = \sum_{i=1}^n a_i X_i / \sum_{i=1}^n X_i$ are independent.

HINT: Let $x_i = \theta w_i$, $i = 1, 2, \ldots, n$, in the multivariate integral representing $E[e^{tZ}]$.

10.1-9. Let $X_1, X_2, \ldots, X_n$ be a random sample from $N(\theta_1, \theta_2)$. Show that the sufficient statistics $Y_1 = \overline{X}$ and $Y_2 = S^2$ are independent of the statistic

$$Z = \sum_{i=1}^{n-1} \frac{(X_{i+1} - X_i)^2}{S^2}$$

because Z has a distribution that is free of θ_1 and θ_2.

HINT: Let $w_i = (x_i - \theta_1)/\sqrt{\theta_2}$, $i = 1, 2, \ldots, n$, in the multivariate integral representing $E[e^{tZ}]$.

10.2 POWER OF A STATISTICAL TEST

In Chapter 7, we gave several tests of fairly common statistical hypotheses in such a way that we described the significance level α and the p-values of each. Of course, those tests were based on good (sufficient) statistics of the parameters, when the latter exist. In this section, we consider the probability of making the other type of error: accepting the null hypothesis H_0 when the alternative hypothesis H_1 is true. This consideration leads to ways to find most powerful tests of the null hypothesis H_0 against the alternative hypothesis H_1.

The first example introduces a new concept using a test about p, the probability of success. The sample size is kept small so that Table II in the appendix can be used to find probabilities. The application is one that you can actually perform.

EXAMPLE 10.2-1 Assume that when given a name tag, a person puts it on either the right or left side. Let p equal the probability that the name tag is placed on the right side. We shall test the null hypothesis H_0: $p = 1/2$ against the composite alternative hypothesis H_1: $p < 1/2$. (Included with the null hypothesis are those values of p which are greater than 1/2; that is, we could think of H_0 as H_0: $p \ge 1/2$.) We shall give name tags to a random sample of $n = 20$ people, denoting the placements of their name tags with Bernoulli random variables, $X_1, X_2, \ldots, X_{20}$, where $X_i = 1$ if a person places the name tag on the right and $X_i = 0$ if a person places the name tag on the left. For our test statistic, we can then use $Y = \sum_{i=1}^{20} X_i$, which has the binomial distribution $b(20, p)$. Say the critical region is defined by $C = \{y : y \le 6\}$ or, equivalently, by $\{(x_1, x_2, \ldots, x_{20}) : \sum_{i=1}^{20} x_i \le 6\}$. Since Y is $b(20, 1/2)$ if $p = 1/2$, the significance level of the corresponding test is

$$\alpha = P\left(Y \le 6;\ p = \frac{1}{2}\right) = \sum_{y=0}^{6} \binom{20}{y} \left(\frac{1}{2}\right)^{20} = 0.0577,$$

from Table II in the appendix. Of course, the probability β of a Type II error has different values, with different values of p selected from the composite alternative hypothesis H_1: $p < 1/2$. For example, with $p = 1/4$,

$$\beta = P\left(7 \le Y \le 20;\ p = \frac{1}{4}\right) = \sum_{y=7}^{20} \binom{20}{y} \left(\frac{1}{4}\right)^{y} \left(\frac{3}{4}\right)^{20-y} = 0.2142,$$

whereas with $p = 1/10$,

$$\beta = P\left(7 \le Y \le 20;\ p = \frac{1}{10}\right) = \sum_{y=7}^{20} \binom{20}{y} \left(\frac{1}{10}\right)^{y} \left(\frac{9}{10}\right)^{20-y} = 0.0024.$$

Instead of considering the probability β of accepting H_0 when H_1 is true, we could compute the probability K of rejecting H_0 when H_1 is true. After all, β and $K = 1 - \beta$ provide the same information. Since K is a function of p, we denote this explicitly by writing $K(p)$. The probability

$$K(p) = \sum_{y=0}^{6} \binom{20}{y} p^y (1 - p)^{20-y}, \qquad 0 < p \le \frac{1}{2},$$

is called the **power function of the test**. Thus, $\alpha = K(1/2) = 0.0577$, $1 - K(1/4) = 0.2142$, and $1 - K(1/10) = 0.0024$. The value of the power function at a specified p is called the **power** of the test at that point. For instance, $K(1/4) = 0.7858$ and $K(1/10) = 0.9976$ are the powers at $p = 1/4$ and $p = 1/10$, respectively. An acceptable power function is a power function that assumes small values when H_0 is true and larger values when p differs much from $p = 1/2$. (See Figure 10.2-1 for a graph of this power function.) ■

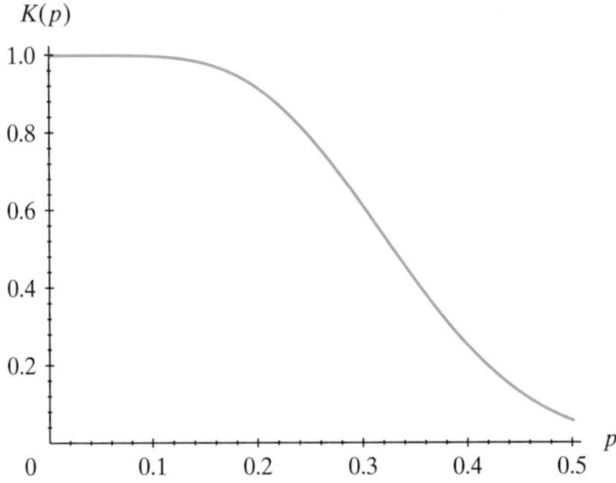

FIGURE 10.2-1: Power function $K(p) = P(Y \le 6; p)$, where Y is $b(20, p)$

In Example 10.2-1, we introduced the new concept of the power function of a test. We now show how the sample size can be selected so as to create a test with appropriate power.

EXAMPLE 10.2-2 Let $X_1, X_2, \ldots, X_n$ be a random sample of size n from the normal distribution $N(\mu, 100)$, which we can suppose is a possible distribution of scores of students in a statistics course that uses a new method of teaching (e.g., computer-related materials). We wish to decide between H_0: $\mu = 60$ (the *no-change* hypothesis because, let us say, this was the mean by the previous method of teaching) and the research worker's hypothesis H_1: $\mu > 60$. Let us consider a sample of size $n = 25$. Of course, the sample mean $\overline{X}$ is the maximum likelihood estimator of μ; thus, it seems reasonable to base our decision on this statistic. Initially, we use the rule to reject H_0 and accept H_1 if and only if $\overline{x} \ge 62$. What are the consequences of this test? These are summarized in the power function of the test.

We first find the probability of rejecting H_0: $\mu = 60$ for various values of $\mu \ge 60$. The probability of rejecting H_0 is given by

$$K(\mu) = P(\overline{X} \ge 62; \mu),$$

because this test calls for the rejection of H_0: $\mu = 60$ when $\overline{x} \ge 62$. When the new process has the general mean μ, $\overline{X}$ has the normal distribution $N(\mu, 100/25 = 4)$.

Accordingly,

$$K(\mu) = P\left(\frac{\overline{X} - \mu}{2} \geq \frac{62 - \mu}{2};\ \mu\right)$$

$$= 1 - \Phi\left(\frac{62 - \mu}{2}\right), \qquad 60 \leq \mu,$$

is the probability of rejecting H_0: $\mu = 60$ by using this particular test. Several values of $K(\mu)$ are given in Table 10.2-1. Figure 10.2-2 depicts the graph of the function $K(\mu)$.

TABLE 10.2-1: Values of the Power Function

μ	$K(\mu)$
60	0.1587
61	0.3085
62	0.5000
63	0.6915
64	0.8413
65	0.9332
66	0.9772

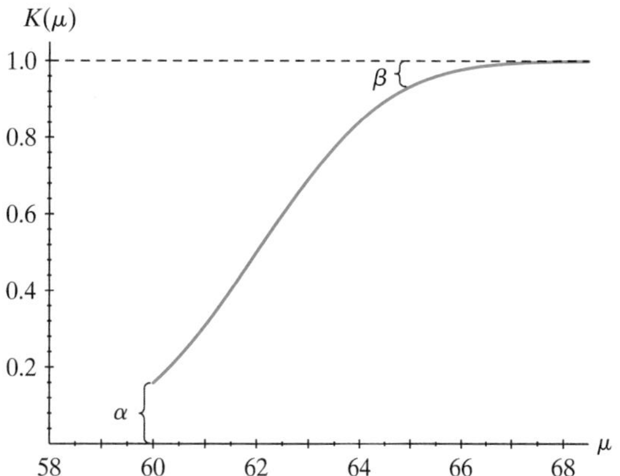

FIGURE 10.2-2: Power function $K(\mu) = 1 - \Phi([62 - \mu]/2)$

The probability $K(\mu)$ of rejecting H_0: $\mu = 60$ is called the *power function* of the test. At the value μ_1 of the parameter, $K(\mu_1)$ is the power at μ_1. The power at $\mu = 60$ is $K(60) = 0.1587$, and this is the probability of rejecting H_0: $\mu = 60$ when H_0 is true. That is, $K(60) = 0.1587 = \alpha$ is the probability of a Type I error and is called the *significance level* of the test.

The power at $\mu = 65$ is $K(65) = 0.9332$, and this is the probability of making the correct decision (namely, rejecting H_0: $\mu = 60$ when $\mu = 65$). Hence, we are pleased that here it is large. When $\mu = 65$, $1 - K(65) = 0.0668$ is the probability of not rejecting H_0: $\mu = 60$ when $\mu = 65$; that is, it is the probability of a Type II error and is denoted by $\beta = 0.0668$. These α and β values are displayed in Figure 10.2-2. Clearly, the probability $\beta = 1 - K(\mu_1)$ of a Type II error depends on which value—say,

μ_1, is taken in the alternative hypothesis H_1: $\mu > 60$. Thus, while $\beta = 0.0668$ when $\mu = 65$, β is equal to $1 - K(63) = 0.3085$ when $\mu = 63$.

Frequently, statisticians like to have the significance level α smaller than 0.1587—say, around 0.05 or less—because it is a probability of an error, namely, a Type I error. Thus, if we would like $\alpha = 0.05$, then, with $n = 25$, we can no longer use the critical region $\overline{x} \geq 62$; rather, we use $\overline{x} \geq c$, where c is selected such that

$$K(60) = P(\overline{X} \geq c;\ \mu = 60) = 0.05.$$

However, when $\mu = 60$, $\overline{X}$ is $N(60, 4)$, and it follows that

$$\begin{aligned} K(60) &= P\left(\frac{\overline{X} - 60}{2} \geq \frac{c - 60}{2};\ \mu = 60\right) \\ &= 1 - \Phi\left(\frac{c - 60}{2}\right) = 0.05. \end{aligned}$$

From Table Va in the appendix, we have

$$\frac{c - 60}{2} = 1.645 = z_{0.05} \qquad \text{and} \qquad c = 60 + 3.29 = 63.29.$$

Although this change reduces α from 0.1587 to 0.05, it increases β at $\mu = 65$ from 0.0668 to

$$\begin{aligned} \beta &= 1 - P(\overline{X} \geq 63.29;\ \mu = 65) \\ &= 1 - P\left(\frac{\overline{X} - 65}{2} \geq \frac{63.29 - 65}{2};\ \mu = 65\right) \\ &= \Phi(-0.855) = 0.1963. \end{aligned}$$

In general, without changing the sample size or the type of test of the hypothesis, a decrease in α causes an increase in β, and a decrease in β causes an increase in α. *Both probabilities α and β of the two types of errors can be decreased only by increasing the sample size or, in some way, constructing a better test of the hypothesis.*

For example, if $n = 100$ and we desire a test with significance level $\alpha = 0.05$, then, since $\overline{X}$ is $N(\mu,\ 100/100 = 1)$,

$$\alpha = P(\overline{X} \geq c;\ \mu = 60) = 0.05$$

means that

$$P\left(\frac{\overline{X} - 60}{1} \geq \frac{c - 60}{1};\ \mu = 60\right) = 0.05$$

and $c - 60 = 1.645$. Thus, $c = 61.645$. The power function is

$$\begin{aligned} K(\mu) &= P(\overline{X} \geq 61.645;\ \mu) \\ &= P\left(\frac{\overline{X} - \mu}{1} \geq \frac{61.645 - \mu}{1};\ \mu\right) = 1 - \Phi(61.645 - \mu). \end{aligned}$$

In particular, this means that at $\mu = 65$,

$$\beta = 1 - K(\mu) = \Phi(61.645 - 65) = \Phi(-3.355) \approx 0;$$

so, with $n = 100$, both α and β have decreased from their respective original values of 0.1587 and 0.0668 when $n = 25$.

Rather than guess at the value of n, an ideal power function determines the sample size. Let us use a critical region of the form $\bar{x} \ge c$. Further, suppose that we want $\alpha = 0.025$ and, when $\mu = 65$, $\beta = 0.05$. Thus, since $\overline{X}$ is $N(\mu, 100/n)$, it follows that

$$0.025 = P(\overline{X} \ge c;\ \mu = 60) = 1 - \Phi\left(\frac{c - 60}{10/\sqrt{n}}\right)$$

and

$$0.05 = 1 - P(\overline{X} \ge c;\ \mu = 65) = \Phi\left(\frac{c - 65}{10/\sqrt{n}}\right).$$

That is,

$$\frac{c - 60}{10/\sqrt{n}} = 1.96 \qquad \text{and} \qquad \frac{c - 65}{10/\sqrt{n}} = -1.645.$$

Solving these equations simultaneously for c and $10/\sqrt{n}$, we obtain

$$c = 60 + 1.96\,\frac{5}{3.605} = 62.718;$$

$$\frac{10}{\sqrt{n}} = \frac{5}{3.605}.$$

Hence,

$$\sqrt{n} = 7.21 \qquad \text{and} \qquad n = 51.98.$$

Since n must be an integer, we would use $n = 52$ and obtain $\alpha \approx 0.025$ and $\beta \approx 0.05$. ■

The next example is an extension of Example 10.2-1.

EXAMPLE 10.2-3 To test $H_0\colon p = 1/2$ against $H_1\colon p < 1/2$, we take a random sample of Bernoulli trials, $X_1, X_2, \ldots, X_n$, and use for our test statistic $Y = \sum_{i=1}^{n} X_i$, which has a binomial distribution $b(n, p)$. Let the critical region be defined by $C = \{y\colon y \le c\}$. The power function for this test is defined by $K(p) = P(Y \le c;\ p)$. We shall find the values of n and c so that $K(1/2) \approx 0.05$ and $K(1/4) \approx 0.90$. That is, we would like the significance level to be $\alpha = K(1/2) = 0.05$ and the power at $p = 1/4$ to equal 0.90. We proceed as follows: Since

$$0.05 = P\left(Y \le c;\ p = \frac{1}{2}\right) = P\left(\frac{Y - n/2}{\sqrt{n(1/2)(1/2)}} \le \frac{c - n/2}{\sqrt{n(1/2)(1/2)}}\right),$$

it follows that

$$(c - n/2)/\sqrt{n/4} \approx -1.645;$$

and since

$$0.90 = P\left(Y \le c;\ p = \frac{1}{4}\right) = P\left(\frac{Y - n/4}{\sqrt{n(1/4)(3/4)}} \le \frac{c - n/4}{\sqrt{n(1/4)(3/4)}}\right),$$

it follows that

$$(c - n/4)/\sqrt{3n/16} \approx 1.282.$$

Therefore,

$$\frac{n}{4} \approx 1.645\sqrt{\frac{n}{4}} + 1.282\sqrt{\frac{3n}{16}} \qquad \text{and} \qquad \sqrt{n} \approx 4(1.378) = 5.512.$$

Thus, n is about equal to 31, and from either of the first two approximate equalities, we find that c is about equal to 10.9. Using $n = 31$ and $c = 10.9$ means that $K(1/2) = 0.05$ and $K(1/4) = 0.90$ are only approximate. In fact, since Y must be an integer, we could let $c = 10.5$. Then, with $n = 31$,

$$\alpha = K\left(\frac{1}{2}\right) = P\left(Y \le 10.5;\ p = \frac{1}{2}\right) \approx 0.0362;$$

$$K\left(\frac{1}{4}\right) = P\left(Y \le 10.5;\ p = \frac{1}{4}\right) \approx 0.8729.$$

Or we could let $c = 11.5$ and $n = 31$, in which case

$$\alpha = K\left(\frac{1}{2}\right) = P\left(Y \le 11.5;\ p = \frac{1}{2}\right) \approx 0.0558;$$

$$K\left(\frac{1}{4}\right) = P\left(Y \le 11.5;\ p = \frac{1}{4}\right) \approx 0.9235. \quad \blacksquare$$

EXERCISES

10.2-1. A certain size of bag is designed to hold 25 pounds of potatoes. A farmer fills such bags in the field. Assume that the weight X of potatoes in a bag is $N(\mu, 9)$. We shall test the null hypothesis H_0: $\mu = 25$ against the alternative hypothesis H_1: $\mu < 25$. Let X_1, X_2, X_3, X_4 be a random sample of size 4 from this distribution, and let the critical region C for this test be defined by $\bar{x} \le 22.5$, where $\bar{x}$ is the observed value of $\overline{X}$.

(a) What is the power function $K(\mu)$ of this test? In particular, what is the significance level $\alpha = K(25)$ for your test?

(b) If the random sample of four bags of potatoes yielded the values $x_1 = 21.24$, $x_2 = 24.81$, $x_3 = 23.62$, and $x_4 = 26.82$, would your test lead you to accept or reject H_0?

(c) What is the p-value associated with $\bar{x}$ in part (b)?

10.2-2. Let X equal the number of milliliters in a bottle that has a label volume of 350 milliliters. Assume that the distribution of X is $N(\mu, 4)$. To test the null hypothesis H_0: $\mu = 355$ against the alternative hypothesis H_1: $\mu < 355$, let the critical region be defined by $C = \{\bar{x} : \bar{x} \le 354.05\}$, where $\bar{x}$ is the sample mean of the contents of a random sample of $n = 12$ bottles.

(a) Find the power function $K(\mu)$ for this test.

(b) What is the (approximate) significance level of the test?

(c) Find the values of $K(354.05)$ and $K(353.1)$, and sketch the graph of the power function.

(d) Use the following 12 observations to state your conclusion from this test:

350	353	354	356	353	352
354	355	357	353	354	355

(e) What is the approximate p-value of the test?

10.2-3. Assume that SAT mathematics scores of students who attend small liberal arts colleges are $N(\mu, 8100)$. We shall test H_0: $\mu = 530$ against the alternative hypothesis H_1: $\mu < 530$. Given a random sample of size $n = 36$ SAT mathematics scores, let the critical region be defined by $C = \{\bar{x} : \bar{x} \le 510.77\}$, where $\bar{x}$ is the observed mean of the sample.

(a) Find the power function, $K(\mu)$, for this test.

(b) What is the value of the significance level of the test?

(c) What is the value of $K(510.77)$?

(d) Sketch the graph of the power function.

(e) What is the p-value associated with (i) $\bar{x} = 507.35$; (ii) $\bar{x} = 497.45$?

10.2-4. Let X be $N(\mu, 100)$. To test H_0: $\mu = 80$ against H_1: $\mu > 80$, let the critical region be defined by $C = \{(x_1, x_2, \ldots, x_{25}) : \bar{x} \geq 83\}$, where $\bar{x}$ is the sample mean of a random sample of size $n = 25$ from this distribution.

(a) What is the power function $K(\mu)$ for this test?

(b) What is the significance level of the test?

(c) What are the values of $K(80)$, $K(83)$, and $K(86)$?

(d) Sketch the graph of the power function.

(e) What is the p-value corresponding to $\bar{x} = 83.41$?

10.2-5. Let X equal the yield of alfalfa in tons per acre per year. Assume that X is $N(1.5, 0.09)$. It is hoped that a new fertilizer will increase the average yield. We shall test the null hypothesis H_0: $\mu = 1.5$ against the alternative hypothesis H_1: $\mu > 1.5$. Assume that the variance continues to equal $\sigma^2 = 0.09$ with the new fertilizer. Using $\overline{X}$, the mean of a random sample of size n, as the test statistic, reject H_0 if $\bar{x} \geq c$. Find n and c so that the power function $K(\mu) = P(\overline{X} \geq c : \mu)$ is such that $\alpha = K(1.5) = 0.05$ and $K(1.7) = 0.95$.

10.2-6. Let X equal the number of pounds of butterfat produced by a Holstein cow during the 305-day milking period following the birth of a calf. Assume that the distribution of X is $N(\mu, 140^2)$. To test the null hypothesis H_0: $\mu = 715$ against the alternative hypothesis H_1: $\mu < 715$, let the critical region be defined by $C = \{\bar{x} : \bar{x} \leq 668.94\}$, where $\bar{x}$ is the sample mean of $n = 25$ butterfat weights from 25 cows selected at random.

(a) Find the power function $K(\mu)$ for this test.

(b) What is the significance level of the test?

(c) What are the values of $K(668.94)$ and $K(622.88)$?

(d) Sketch a graph of the power function.

(e) What conclusion do you draw from the following 25 observations of X?

425 710 661 664 732 714 934 761 744
653 725 657 421 573 535 602 537 405
874 791 721 849 567 468 975

(f) What is the approximate p-value of the test?

10.2-7. In Exercise 10.2-6, let $C = \{\bar{x} : \bar{x} \leq c\}$ be the critical region. Find values for n and c so that the significance level of this test is $\alpha = 0.05$ and the power at $\mu = 650$ is 0.90.

10.2-8. Let X have a Bernoulli distribution with p.m.f.

$$f(x; p) = p^x(1 - p)^{1-x}, \quad x = 0, 1, \quad 0 \leq p \leq 1.$$

We would like to test the null hypothesis H_0: $p \leq 0.4$ against the alternative hypothesis H_1: $p > 0.4$. For the test statistic, use $Y = \sum_{i=1}^{n} X_i$, where $X_1, X_2, \ldots, X_n$ is a random sample of size n from this Bernoulli distribution. Let the critical region be of the form $C = \{y : y \geq c\}$.

(a) Let $n = 100$. On the same set of axes, sketch the graphs of the power functions corresponding to the three critical regions, $C_1 = \{y : y \geq 40\}$, $C_2 = \{y : y \geq 50\}$, and $C_3 = \{y : y \geq 60\}$. Use the normal approximation to compute the probabilities.

(b) Let $C = \{y : y \geq 0.45n\}$. On the same set of axes, sketch the graphs of the power functions corresponding to the three samples of sizes 10, 100, and 1000.

10.2-9. Let p denote the probability that, for a particular tennis player, the first serve is good. Since $p = 0.40$, this player decided to take lessons in order to increase p. When the lessons are completed, the hypothesis H_0: $p = 0.40$ will be tested against H_1: $p > 0.40$ on the basis of $n = 25$ trials. Let y equal the number of first serves that are good, and let the critical region be defined by $C = \{y : y \geq 14\}$.

(a) Find the power function $K(p)$ for this test.

(b) What is the value of the significance level, $\alpha = K(0.40)$? Use Table II in the appendix.

(c) Evaluate $K(p)$ at $p = 0.45, 0.50, 0.60, 0.70, 0.80$, and 0.90. Use Table II.

(d) Sketch the graph of the power function.

(e) If $y = 15$ following the lessons, would H_0 be rejected?

(f) What is the p-value associated with $y = 15$?

10.2-10. Let $X_1, X_2, \ldots, X_8$ be a random sample of size $n = 8$ from a Poisson distribution with mean λ. Reject the simple null hypothesis H_0: $\lambda = 0.5$, and accept H_1: $\lambda > 0.5$, if the observed sum $\sum_{i=1}^{8} x_i \geq 8$.

(a) Compute the significance level α of the test.

(b) Find the power function $K(\lambda)$ of the test as a sum of Poisson probabilities.

(c) Using Table III in the appendix, determine $K(0.75)$, $K(1)$, and $K(1.25)$.

10.2-11. Let p equal the fraction defective of a certain manufactured item. To test H_0: $p = 1/26$ against

H_1: $p > 1/26$, we inspect n items selected at random and let Y be the number of defective items in this sample. We reject H_0 if the observed $y \ge c$. Find n and c so that $\alpha = K(1/26) \approx 0.05$ and $K(1/10) \approx 0.90$, where $K(p) = P(Y \ge c; p)$.

HINT: Use either the normal or Poisson approximation to help solve this exercise.

10.2-12. Let X_1, X_2, X_3 be a random sample of size $n = 3$ from an exponential distribution with mean $\theta > 0$. Reject the simple null hypothesis H_0: $\theta = 2$, and accept the composite alternative hypothesis H_1: $\theta < 2$, if the observed sum $\sum_{i=1}^{3} x_i \le 2$.

(a) What is the power function $K(\theta)$, written as an integral?

(b) Using integration by parts, define the power function as a summation.

(c) With the help of Table III in the appendix, determine $\alpha = K(2)$, $K(1)$, $K(1/2)$, and $K(1/4)$.

10.3 BEST CRITICAL REGIONS

In this section, we consider the properties a satisfactory test (or critical region) should possess. To introduce our investigation, we begin with a nonstatistical example.

EXAMPLE 10.3-1 Say that you have α dollars with which to buy books. Further, suppose that you are not interested in the books themselves, but only in filling as much of your bookshelves as possible. How do you decide which books to buy? Does the following approach seem reasonable? First of all, take all the available free books. Then start choosing those books for which the cost of filling an inch of bookshelf is smallest. That is, choose those books for which the ratio c/w is a minimum, where w is the width of the book in inches and c is the cost of the book. Continue choosing books this way until you have spent the α dollars. ■

To see how Example 10.3-1 provides the background for selecting a good critical region of size α, let us consider a test of the simple hypothesis H_0: $\theta = \theta_0$ against a simple alternative hypothesis H_1: $\theta = \theta_1$. In this discussion, we assume that the random variables $X_1, X_2, \ldots, X_n$ under consideration have a joint p.m.f. of the discrete type, which we here denote by $L(\theta; x_1, x_2, \ldots, x_n)$. That is,

$$P(X_1 = x_1, X_2 = x_2, \ldots, X_n = x_n) = L(\theta; x_1, x_2, \ldots, x_n).$$

A critical region C of size α is a set of points $(x_1, x_2, \ldots, x_n)$ with probability α when $\theta = \theta_0$. For a good test, this set C of points should have a large probability when $\theta = \theta_1$, because, under H_1: $\theta = \theta_1$, we wish to reject H_0: $\theta = \theta_0$. Accordingly, the first point we would place in the critical region C is the one with the smallest ratio

$$\frac{L(\theta_0; x_1, x_2, \ldots, x_n)}{L(\theta_1; x_1, x_2, \ldots, x_n)}.$$

That is, the "cost" in terms of probability under H_0: $\theta = \theta_0$ is small compared with the probability that we can "buy" if $\theta = \theta_1$. The next point to add to C would be the one with the next-smallest ratio. We would continue to add points to C in this manner until the probability of C, under H_0: $\theta = \theta_0$, equals α. In this way, for the given significance level α, we have achieved the region C with the largest probability when H_1: $\theta = \theta_1$ is true. We now formalize this discussion by defining a best critical region and proving the well-known Neyman–Pearson lemma.

DEFINITION 10.3-1 Consider the test of the simple null hypothesis H_0: $\theta = \theta_0$ against the simple alternative hypothesis H_1: $\theta = \theta_1$. Let C be a critical region of size α; that is,

$\alpha = P(C; \theta_0)$. Then C is a **best critical region of size** α if, for every other critical region D of size $\alpha = P(D; \theta_0)$, we have

$$P(C; \theta_1) \geq P(D; \theta_1).$$

That is, when $H_1: \theta = \theta_1$ is true, the probability of rejecting $H_0: \theta = \theta_0$ with the use of the critical region C is at least as great as the corresponding probability with the use of any other critical region D of size α.

Thus, a best critical region of size α is the critical region that has the greatest power among all critical regions of size α. The Neyman–Pearson lemma gives sufficient conditions for a best critical region of size α.

THEOREM 10.3-1 **(Neyman–Pearson Lemma)** Let $X_1, X_2, \ldots, X_n$ be a random sample of size n from a distribution with p.d.f. or p.m.f. $f(x; \theta)$, where θ_0 and θ_1 are two possible values of θ. Denote the joint p.d.f. or p.m.f. of $X_1, X_2, \ldots, X_n$ by the likelihood function

$$L(\theta) = L(\theta; x_1, x_2, \ldots, x_n) = f(x_1; \theta)f(x_2; \theta)\cdots f(x_n; \theta).$$

If there exist a positive constant k and a subset C of the sample space such that

(a) $P[(X_1, X_2, \ldots, X_n) \in C; \theta_0] = \alpha$,

(b) $\dfrac{L(\theta_0)}{L(\theta_1)} \leq k$ for $(x_1, x_2, \ldots, x_n) \in C$, and

(c) $\dfrac{L(\theta_0)}{L(\theta_1)} \geq k$ for $(x_1, x_2, \ldots, x_n) \in C'$,

then C is a best critical region of size α for testing the simple null hypothesis $H_0: \theta = \theta_0$ against the simple alternative hypothesis $H_1: \theta = \theta_1$.

Proof. We prove the theorem when the random variables are of the continuous type; for discrete-type random variables, replace the integral signs by summation signs. To simplify the exposition, we shall use the following notation:

$$\int_B L(\theta) = \int \underset{B}{\cdots} \int L(\theta; x_1, x_2, \ldots, x_n)\, dx_1\, dx_2 \cdots dx_n.$$

Assume that there exists another critical region of size α—say, D—such that, in this new notation,

$$\alpha = \int_C L(\theta_0) = \int_D L(\theta_0).$$

Then we have

$$\begin{aligned} 0 &= \int_C L(\theta_0) - \int_D L(\theta_0) \\ &= \int_{C \cap D'} L(\theta_0) + \int_{C \cap D} L(\theta_0) - \int_{C \cap D} L(\theta_0) - \int_{C' \cap D} L(\theta_0). \end{aligned}$$

Hence,

$$0 = \int_{C\cap D'} L(\theta_0) - \int_{C'\cap D} L(\theta_0).$$

By hypothesis (b), $kL(\theta_1) \geq L(\theta_0)$ at each point in C and therefore in $C \cap D'$; thus,

$$k\int_{C\cap D'} L(\theta_1) \geq \int_{C\cap D'} L(\theta_0).$$

By hypothesis (c), $kL(\theta_1) \leq L(\theta_0)$ at each point in C' and therefore in $C' \cap D$; thus, we obtain

$$k\int_{C'\cap D} L(\theta_1) \leq \int_{C'\cap D} L(\theta_0).$$

Consequently,

$$0 = \int_{C\cap D'} L(\theta_0) - \int_{C'\cap D} L(\theta_0) \leq (k)\left\{\int_{C\cap D'} L(\theta_1) - \int_{C'\cap D} L(\theta_1)\right\}.$$

That is,

$$0 \leq (k)\left\{\int_{C\cap D'} L(\theta_1) + \int_{C\cap D} L(\theta_1) - \int_{C\cap D} L(\theta_1) - \int_{C'\cap D} L(\theta_1)\right\}$$

or, equivalently,

$$0 \leq (k)\left\{\int_{C} L(\theta_1) - \int_{D} L(\theta_1)\right\}.$$

Thus,

$$\int_{C} L(\theta_1) \geq \int_{D} L(\theta_1);$$

that is, $P(C;\theta_1) \geq P(D;\theta_1)$. Since that is true for every critical region D of size α, C is a best critical region of size α. □

For a realistic application of the Neyman–Pearson lemma, consider the next example, in which the test is based on a random sample from a normal distribution.

EXAMPLE 10.3-2 Let $X_1, X_2, \ldots, X_n$ be a random sample from the normal distribution $N(\mu, 36)$. We shall find the best critical region for testing the simple hypothesis $H_0\colon \mu = 50$ against the simple alternative hypothesis $H_1\colon \mu = 55$. Using the ratio of the likelihood functions, namely, $L(50)/L(55)$, we shall find those points in the sample space for which this ratio is less than or equal to some constant k. That is, we shall solve the following inequality:

$$\frac{L(50)}{L(55)} = \frac{(72\pi)^{-n/2} \exp\left[-\left(\frac{1}{72}\right)\sum_{i=1}^{n}(x_i - 50)^2\right]}{(72\pi)^{-n/2} \exp\left[-\left(\frac{1}{72}\right)\sum_{i=1}^{n}(x_i - 55)^2\right]}$$

$$= \exp\left[-\left(\frac{1}{72}\right)\left(10\sum_{i=1}^{n} x_i + n50^2 - n55^2\right)\right] \le k.$$

If we take the natural logarithm of each member of the inequality, we find that

$$-10\sum_{i=1}^{n} x_i - n50^2 + n55^2 \le (72)\ln k.$$

Thus,

$$\frac{1}{n}\sum_{i=1}^{n} x_i \ge -\frac{1}{10n}[n50^2 - n55^2 + (72)\ln k]$$

or, equivalently,

$$\overline{x} \ge c,$$

where $c = -(1/10n)[n50^2 - n55^2 + (72)\ln k]$. Hence, $L(50)/L(55) \le k$ is equivalent to $\overline{x} \ge c$. According to the Neyman–Pearson lemma, a best critical region is

$$C = \{(x_1, x_2, \ldots, x_n) : \overline{x} \ge c\},$$

where c is selected so that the size of the critical region is α. Say $n = 16$ and $c = 53$. Then, since $\overline{X}$ is $N(50, 36/16)$ under H_0, we have

$$\alpha = P(\overline{X} \ge 53;\ \mu = 50)$$
$$= P\left(\frac{\overline{X} - 50}{6/4} \ge \frac{3}{6/4};\ \mu = 50\right) = 1 - \Phi(2) = 0.0228.$$

■

This last example illustrates what is often true, namely, that the inequality

$$L(\theta_0)/L(\theta_1) \le k$$

can be expressed in terms of a function $u(x_1, x_2, \ldots, x_n)$, say,

$$u(x_1, \ldots, x_n) \le c_1$$

or

$$u(x_1, \ldots, x_n) \ge c_2,$$

where c_1 or c_2 is selected so that the size of the critical region is α. Thus, the test can be based on the statistic $u(x_1, \ldots, x_n)$. As an example, if we want α to be a given value—say, 0.05—we could then choose our c_1 or c_2. In Example 10.3-2, with

$\alpha = 0.05$, we want

$$0.05 = P(\overline{X} \geq c;\ \mu = 50)$$

$$= P\left(\frac{\overline{X} - 50}{6/4} \geq \frac{c - 50}{6/4};\ \mu = 50\right) = 1 - \Phi\left(\frac{c - 50}{6/4}\right).$$

Hence, it must be true that $(c - 50)/(3/2) = 1.645$, or, equivalently,

$$c = 50 + \frac{3}{2}(1.645) \approx 52.47.$$

EXAMPLE 10.3-3 Let $X_1, X_2, \ldots, X_n$ denote a random sample of size n from a Poisson distribution with mean λ. A best critical region for testing $H_0\colon \lambda = 2$ against $H_1\colon \lambda = 5$ is given by

$$\frac{L(2)}{L(5)} = \frac{2^{\Sigma x_i} e^{-2n}}{x_1!x_2!\cdots x_n!} \frac{x_1!x_2!\cdots x_n!}{5^{\Sigma x_i} e^{-5n}} \leq k.$$

This inequality can be written as

$$\left(\frac{2}{5}\right)^{\Sigma x_i} e^{3n} \leq k, \qquad \text{or} \qquad (\Sigma x_i) \ln\left(\frac{2}{5}\right) + 3n \leq \ln k.$$

Since $\ln(2/5) < 0$, the latter inequality is the same as

$$\sum_{i=1}^{n} x_i \geq \frac{\ln k - 3n}{\ln(2/5)} = c.$$

If $n = 4$ and $c = 13$, then

$$\alpha = P\left(\sum_{i=1}^{4} X_i \geq 13;\ \lambda = 2\right) = 1 - 0.936 = 0.064,$$

from Table III in the appendix, since $\sum_{i=1}^{4} X_i$ has a Poisson distribution with mean 8 when $\lambda = 2$. ■

When $H_0\colon \theta = \theta_0$ and $H_1\colon \theta = \theta_1$ are both simple hypotheses, a critical region of size α is a best critical region if the probability of rejecting H_0 when H_1 is true is a maximum compared with all other critical regions of size α. The test using the best critical region is called a **most powerful test**, because it has the greatest value of the power function at $\theta = \theta_1$ compared with that of other tests with significance level α. If H_1 is a composite hypothesis, the power of a test depends on each simple alternative in H_1.

DEFINITION 10.3-2 A test defined by a critical region C of size α is a **uniformly most powerful test** if it is a most powerful test against each simple alternative in H_1. The critical region C is called a **uniformly most powerful critical region of size** α.

Let us consider again Example 10.3-2 when the alternative hypothesis is composite.

EXAMPLE 10.3-4 Let $X_1, \ldots, X_n$ be a random sample from $N(\mu, 36)$. We have seen that, in testing $H_0\colon \mu = 50$ against $H_1\colon \mu = 55$, a best critical region C is defined by

$C = \{(x_1, x_2, \ldots, x_n) : \overline{x} \geq c\}$, where c is selected so that the significance level is α. Now consider testing H_0: $\mu = 50$ against the one-sided composite alternative hypothesis H_1: $\mu > 50$. For each simple hypothesis in H_1—say, $\mu = \mu_1$—the quotient of the likelihood functions is

$$\frac{L(50)}{L(\mu_1)} = \frac{(72\pi)^{-n/2} \exp\left[-\left(\frac{1}{72}\right)\sum_{i=1}^{n}(x_i - 50)^2\right]}{(72\pi)^{-n/2} \exp\left[-\left(\frac{1}{72}\right)\sum_{i=1}^{n}(x_i - \mu_1)^2\right]}$$

$$= \exp\left[-\frac{1}{72}\left\{2(\mu_1 - 50)\sum_{i=1}^{n} x_i + n(50^2 - \mu_1^2)\right\}\right].$$

Now, $L(50)/L(\mu_1) \leq k$ if and only if

$$\overline{x} \geq \frac{(-72)\ln(k)}{2n(\mu_1 - 50)} + \frac{50 + \mu_1}{2} = c.$$

Thus, the best critical region of size α for testing H_0: $\mu = 50$ against H_1: $\mu = \mu_1$, where $\mu_1 > 50$, is given by $C = \{(x_1, x_2, \ldots, x_n): \overline{x} \geq c\}$, where c is selected such that $P(\overline{X} \geq c;\ H_0:\ \mu = 50) = \alpha$. Note that the same value of c can be used for each $\mu_1 > 50$, but (of course) k does not remain the same. Since the critical region C defines a test that is most powerful against each simple alternative $\mu_1 > 50$, this is a uniformly most powerful test, and C is a uniformly most powerful critical region of size α. Again, if $\alpha = 0.05$, then $c \approx 52.47$. ■

EXAMPLE 10.3-5 Let Y have the binomial distribution $b(n, p)$. To find a uniformly most powerful test of the simple null hypothesis H_0: $p = p_0$ against the one-sided alternative hypothesis H_1: $p > p_0$, consider, with $p_1 > p_0$,

$$\frac{L(p_0)}{L(p_1)} = \frac{\binom{n}{y} p_0^y (1 - p_0)^{n-y}}{\binom{n}{y} p_1^y (1 - p_1)^{n-y}} \leq k.$$

This is equivalent to

$$\left[\frac{p_0(1 - p_1)}{p_1(1 - p_0)}\right]^y \left[\frac{1 - p_0}{1 - p_1}\right]^n \leq k$$

and

$$y \ln\left[\frac{p_0(1 - p_1)}{p_1(1 - p_0)}\right] \leq \ln k - n \ln\left[\frac{1 - p_0}{1 - p_1}\right].$$

Since $p_0 < p_1$, we have $p_0(1 - p_1) < p_1(1 - p_0)$, and it follows that $\ln[p_0(1 - p_1)/p_1(1 - p_0)] < 0$. Thus,

$$\frac{y}{n} \geq \frac{\ln k - n \ln[(1 - p_0)/(1 - p_1)]}{n \ln[p_0(1 - p_1)/p_1(1 - p_0)]} = c$$

for each $p_1 > p_0$.

It is interesting to note that if the alternative hypothesis is the one-sided $H_1: p < p_0$, then a uniformly most powerful test is of the form $(y/n) \le c$. Thus, the tests of $H_0: p = p_0$ against the one-sided alternatives given in Table 7.1-1 are uniformly most powerful. ■

Exercise 10.3-5 will demonstrate that uniformly most powerful tests do not always exist; in particular, they usually do not exist when the composite alternative hypothesis is two sided.

REMARK We close this section with one easy, but important, observation: If a sufficient statistic $Y = u(X_1, X_2, \ldots, X_n)$ exists for θ, then, by the factorization theorem,

$$\frac{L(\theta_0)}{L(\theta_1)} = \frac{\phi[u(x_1, x_2, \ldots, x_n); \theta_0]\, h(x_1, x_2, \ldots, x_n)}{\phi[u(x_1, x_2, \ldots, x_n); \theta_1]\, h(x_1, x_2, \ldots, x_n)} = \frac{\phi[u(x_1, x_2, \ldots, x_n); \theta_0)}{\phi[u(x_1, x_2, \ldots, x_n); \theta_1]}.$$

Thus, $L(\theta_0)/L(\theta_1) \le k$ provides a critical region that is a function of the observations $x_1, x_2, \ldots x_n$ only through the observed value of the sufficient statistic $y = u(x_1, x_2, \ldots, x_n)$. Hence, best critical and uniformly most powerful critical regions are based upon sufficient statistics when they exist. ■

EXERCISES

10.3-1. Let $X_1, X_2, \ldots, X_n$ be a random sample from a normal distribution $N(\mu, 64)$.

(a) Show that $C = \{(x_1, x_2, \ldots, x_n): \bar{x} \le c\}$ is a best critical region for testing $H_0: \mu = 80$ against $H_1: \mu = 76$.
(b) Find n and c so that $\alpha \approx 0.05$ and $\beta \approx 0.05$.

10.3-2. Let $X_1, X_2, \ldots, X_n$ be a random sample from $N(0, \sigma^2)$.

(a) Show that a best critical region for testing $H_0: \sigma^2 = 4$ against $H_1: \sigma^2 = 16$ is given by $C = \{(x_1, x_2, \ldots, x_n): \sum_{i=1}^n x_i^2 \ge c\}$.
(b) If $n = 15$, find the value of c so that $\alpha = 0.05$. HINT: Recall that $\sum_{i=1}^n X_i^2/\sigma^2$ is $\chi^2(n)$.
(c) If $n = 15$ and c is the value found in part (b), find the approximate value of $\beta = P(\sum_{i=1}^n X_i^2 < c;\ \sigma^2 = 16)$.

10.3-3. Let X have an exponential distribution with a mean of θ; that is, the p.d.f. of X is $f(x; \theta) = (1/\theta)e^{-x/\theta}, 0 < x < \infty$. Let $X_1, X_2, \ldots, X_n$ be a random sample from this distribution.

(a) Show that a best critical region for testing $H_0: \theta = 3$ against $H_1: \theta = 5$ can be based on the statistic $\sum_{i=1}^n X_i$.
(b) If $n = 12$, use the fact that $(2/\theta)\sum_{i=1}^{12} X_i$ is $\chi^2(24)$ to find a best critical region of size $\alpha = 0.10$.
(c) If $n = 12$, find a best critical region of size $\alpha = 0.10$ for testing $H_0: \theta = 3$ against $H_1: \theta = 7$.
(d) If $H_1: \theta > 3$, is the common region found in parts (b) and (c) a uniformly most powerful critical region of size $\alpha = 0.10$?

10.3-4. Let $X_1, X_2, \ldots, X_n$ be a random sample of Bernoulli trials $b(1, p)$.

(a) Show that a best critical region for testing $H_0: p = 0.9$ against $H_1: p = 0.8$ can be based on the statistic $Y = \sum_{i=1}^n X_i$, which is $b(n,p)$.
(b) If $C = \{(x_1, x_2, \ldots, x_n): \sum_{i=1}^n x_i \le (0.85)n\}$ and $Y = \sum_{i=1}^n X_i$, find the value of n such that $\alpha = P[\,Y \le n(0.85);\ p = 0.9] \approx 0.10$. HINT: Use the normal approximation for the binomial distribution.
(c) What is the approximate value of $\beta = P[\,Y > n(0.85);\ p = 0.8]$ for the test given in part (b)?
(d) Is the test of part (b) a uniformly most powerful test when the alternative hypothesis is $H_1: p < 0.9$?

10.3-5. Let $X_1, X_2, \ldots, X_n$ be a random sample from the normal distribution $N(\mu, 36)$.

(a) Show that a uniformly most powerful critical region for testing H_0: $\mu = 50$ against H_1: $\mu < 50$ is given by $C_2 = \{\overline{x}: \overline{x} \le c\}$.

(b) With this result and that of Example 10.3-4, argue that a uniformly most powerful test for testing H_0: $\mu = 50$ against H_1: $\mu \ne 50$ does not exist.

10.3-6. Let $X_1, X_2, \ldots, X_n$ be a random sample from the normal distribution $N(\mu, 9)$. To test the hypothesis H_0: $\mu = 80$ against H_1: $\mu \ne 80$, consider the following three critical regions: $C_1 = \{\overline{x}: \overline{x} \ge c_1\}$, $C_2 = \{\overline{x}: \overline{x} \le c_2\}$, and $C_3 = \{\overline{x}: |\overline{x} - 80| \ge c_3\}$.

(a) If $n = 16$, find the values of c_1, c_2, c_3 such that the size of each critical region is 0.05. That is, find c_1, c_2, c_3 such that

$$\begin{aligned} 0.05 &= P(\overline{X} \in C_1;\ \mu = 80) \\ &= P(\overline{X} \in C_2;\ \mu = 80) \\ &= P(\overline{X} \in C_3;\ \mu = 80). \end{aligned}$$

(b) On the same graph paper, sketch the power functions for these three critical regions.

10.3-7. Let $X_1, X_2, \ldots, X_{10}$ be a random sample of size 10 from a Poisson distribution with mean μ.

(a) Show that a uniformly most powerful critical region for testing H_0: $\mu = 0.5$ against H_1: $\mu > 0.5$ can be defined with the use of the statistic $\sum_{i=1}^{10} X_i$.

(b) What is a uniformly most powerful critical region of size $\alpha = 0.068$? Recall that $\sum_{i=1}^{10} X_i$ has a Poisson distribution with mean 10μ.

(c) Sketch the power function of this test.

10.4 LIKELIHOOD RATIO TESTS

In this section, we consider a general test-construction method that is applicable when both the null and alternative hypotheses—say, H_0 and H_1—are composite. We continue to assume that the functional form of the p.d.f. is known, but that it depends on an unknown parameter or unknown parameters. That is, we assume that the p.d.f. of X is $f(x;\ \theta)$, where θ represents one or more unknown parameters. We let Ω denote the total parameter space—that is, the set of all possible values of the parameter θ given by either H_0 or H_1. These hypotheses will be stated as

$$H_0: \theta \in \omega, \qquad H_1: \theta \in \omega',$$

where ω is a subset of Ω and ω' is the complement of ω with respect to Ω. The test will be constructed with the use of a ratio of likelihood functions that have been maximized in ω and Ω, respectively. In a sense, this is a natural generalization of the ratio appearing in the Neyman–Pearson lemma when the two hypotheses were simple.

DEFINITION 10.4-1 The **likelihood ratio** is the quotient

$$\lambda = \frac{L(\widehat{\omega})}{L(\widehat{\Omega})},$$

where $L(\widehat{\omega})$ is the maximum of the likelihood function with respect to θ when $\theta \in \omega$ and $L(\widehat{\Omega})$ is the maximum of the likelihood function with respect to θ when $\theta \in \Omega$.

Because λ is the quotient of nonnegative functions, $\lambda \ge 0$. In addition, since $\omega \subset \Omega$, it follows that $L(\widehat{\omega}) \le L(\widehat{\Omega})$ and hence $\lambda \le 1$. Thus, $0 \le \lambda \le 1$. If the maximum of L in ω is much smaller than that in Ω, it would seem that the data $x_1, x_2, \ldots, x_n$ do not support the hypothesis H_0: $\theta \in \omega$. That is, a small value of the ratio $\lambda = L(\widehat{\omega})/L(\widehat{\Omega})$ would lead to the rejection of H_0. In contrast, a value of the ratio λ that is close to 1 would support the null hypothesis H_0. This reasoning leads us to the next definition.

DEFINITION 10.4-2

To test $H_0: \theta \in \omega$ against $H_1: \theta \in \omega'$, the **critical region for the likelihood ratio test** is the set of points in the sample space for which

$$\lambda = \frac{L(\widehat{\omega})}{L(\widehat{\Omega})} \le k,$$

where $0 < k < 1$ and k is selected so that the test has a desired significance level α.

The next example illustrates these definitions.

EXAMPLE 10.4-1

Assume that the weight X in ounces of a "10-pound" bag of sugar is $N(\mu, 5)$. We shall test the hypothesis $H_0: \mu = 162$ against the alternative hypothesis $H_1: \mu \neq 162$. Thus, $\Omega = \{\mu: -\infty < \mu < \infty\}$ and $\omega = \{162\}$. To find the likelihood ratio, we need $L(\widehat{\omega})$ and $L(\widehat{\Omega})$. When H_0 is true, μ can take on only one value, namely, $\mu = 162$. Hence, $L(\widehat{\omega}) = L(162)$. To find $L(\widehat{\Omega})$, we must find the value of μ that maximizes $L(\mu)$. Recall that $\widehat{\mu} = \overline{x}$ is the maximum likelihood estimate of μ. Then $L(\widehat{\Omega}) = L(\overline{x})$, and the likelihood ratio $\lambda = L(\widehat{\omega})/L(\widehat{\Omega})$ is given by

$$\lambda = \frac{(10\pi)^{-n/2}\exp\left[-\left(\frac{1}{10}\right)\sum_{i=1}^{n}(x_i - 162)^2\right]}{(10\pi)^{-n/2}\exp\left[-\left(\frac{1}{10}\right)\sum_{i=1}^{n}(x_i - \overline{x})^2\right]}$$

$$= \frac{\exp\left[-\left(\frac{1}{10}\right)\sum_{i=1}^{n}(x_i - \overline{x})^2 - \left(\frac{n}{10}\right)(\overline{x} - 162)^2\right]}{\exp\left[-\left(\frac{1}{10}\right)\sum_{i=1}^{n}(x_i - \overline{x})^2\right]}$$

$$= \exp\left[-\frac{n}{10}(\overline{x} - 162)^2\right].$$

On the one hand, a value of $\overline{x}$ close to 162 would tend to support H_0, and in that case λ is close to 1. On the other hand, an $\overline{x}$ that differs from 162 by too much would tend to support H_1. (See Figure 10.4-1 for the graph of this likelihood ratio when $n = 5$.)

A critical region for a likelihood ratio test is given by $\lambda \le k$, where k is selected so that the significance level of the test is α. Using this criterion and simplifying the inequality as we do when we use the Neyman–Pearson lemma, we find that $\lambda \le k$ is equivalent to each of the following inequalities:

$$-\left(\frac{n}{10}\right)(\overline{x} - 162)^2 \le \ln k,$$

$$(\overline{x} - 162)^2 \ge -\left(\frac{10}{n}\right)\ln k,$$

$$\frac{|\overline{x} - 162|}{\sigma/\sqrt{n}} \ge \frac{\sqrt{-(10/n)\ln k}}{\sigma/\sqrt{n}} = c.$$

Since $Z = (\overline{X} - 162)/(\sigma/\sqrt{n})$ is $N(0,1)$ when H_0: $\mu = 162$ is true, let $c = z_{\alpha/2}$. Thus, the critical region is

$$C = \left\{\overline{x}: \frac{|\overline{x} - 162|}{\sigma/\sqrt{n}} \geq z_{\alpha/2}\right\}.$$

To illustrate, if $\alpha = 0.05$, then $z_{0.025} = 1.96$. ■

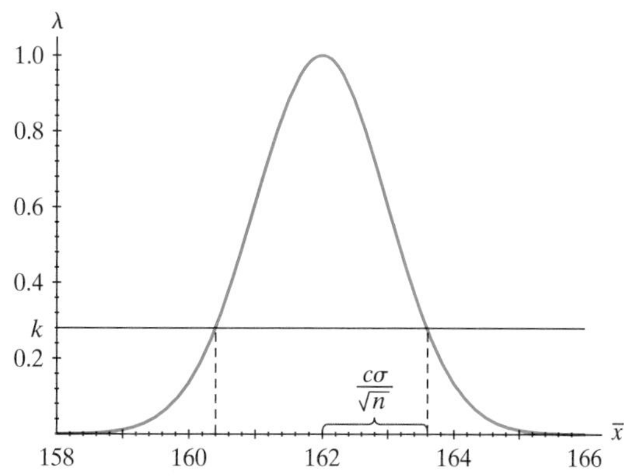

FIGURE 10.4-1: The likelihood ratio for testing $H_0: \mu = 162$

As illustrated in Example 10.4-1, the inequality $\lambda \leq k$ can often be expressed in terms of a statistic whose distribution is known. Also, note that although the likelihood ratio test is an intuitive test, it leads to the same critical region as that given by the Neyman–Pearson lemma when H_0 and H_1 are both simple hypotheses.

Suppose now that the random sample $X_1, X_2, \ldots, X_n$ arises from the normal population $N(\mu, \sigma^2)$. where both μ and σ^2 are unknown. Let us consider the likelihood ratio test of the null hypothesis H_0: $\mu = \mu_0$ against the two-sided alternative hypothesis H_1: $\mu \neq \mu_0$. For this test,

$$\omega = \{(\mu, \sigma^2): \mu = \mu_0,\ 0 < \sigma^2 < \infty\}$$

and

$$\Omega = \{(\mu, \sigma^2): -\infty < \mu < \infty,\ 0 < \sigma^2 < \infty\}.$$

If $(\mu, \sigma^2) \in \Omega$, then the observed maximum likelihood estimates are $\widehat{\mu} = \overline{x}$ and $\widehat{\sigma^2} = (1/n)\sum_{i=1}^{n}(x_i - \overline{x})^2$. Thus,

$$L(\widehat{\Omega}) = \left[\frac{1}{2\pi\left(\dfrac{1}{n}\right)\displaystyle\sum_{i=1}^{n}(x_i - \overline{x})^2}\right]^{n/2} \exp\left[-\frac{\displaystyle\sum_{i=1}^{n}(x_i - \overline{x})^2}{\left(\dfrac{2}{n}\right)\displaystyle\sum_{i=1}^{n}(x_i - \overline{x})^2}\right]$$

$$= \left[\frac{ne^{-1}}{2\pi\displaystyle\sum_{i=1}^{n}(x_i - \overline{x})^2}\right]^{n/2}.$$

Similarly, if $(\mu, \sigma^2) \in \omega$, then the observed maximum likelihood estimates are $\widehat{\mu} = \mu_0$ and $\widehat{\sigma^2} = (1/n)\sum_{i=1}^{n}(x_i - \mu_0)^2$. Hence,

$$L(\widehat{\omega}) = \left[\frac{1}{2\pi\left(\frac{1}{n}\right)\sum_{i=1}^{n}(x_i - \mu_0)^2}\right]^{n/2} \exp\left[-\frac{\sum_{i=1}^{n}(x_i - \mu_0)^2}{\left(\frac{2}{n}\right)\sum_{i=1}^{n}(x_i - \mu_0)^2}\right]$$

$$= \left[\frac{ne^{-1}}{2\pi\sum_{i=1}^{n}(x_i - \mu_0)^2}\right]^{n/2}.$$

The likelihood ratio $\lambda = L(\widehat{\omega})/L(\widehat{\Omega})$ for this test is

$$\lambda = \frac{\left[\dfrac{ne^{-1}}{2\pi\sum_{i=1}^{n}(x_i - \mu_0)^2}\right]^{n/2}}{\left[\dfrac{ne^{-1}}{2\pi\sum_{i=1}^{n}(x_i - \overline{x})^2}\right]^{n/2}} = \left[\frac{\sum_{i=1}^{n}(x_i - \overline{x})^2}{\sum_{i=1}^{n}(x_i - \mu_0)^2}\right]^{n/2}.$$

However, note that

$$\sum_{i=1}^{n}(x_i - \mu_0)^2 = \sum_{i=1}^{n}(x_i - \overline{x} + \overline{x} - \mu_0)^2$$
$$= \sum_{i=1}^{n}(x_i - \overline{x})^2 + n(\overline{x} - \mu_0)^2.$$

If this substitution is made in the denominator of λ, we have

$$\lambda = \left[\frac{\sum_{i=1}^{n}(x_i - \overline{x})^2}{\sum_{i=1}^{n}(x_i - \overline{x})^2 + n(\overline{x} - \mu_0)^2}\right]^{n/2}$$

$$= \left[\frac{1}{1 + \dfrac{n(\overline{x} - \mu_0)^2}{\sum_{i=1}^{n}(x_i - \overline{x})^2}}\right]^{n/2}.$$

Note that λ is close to 1 when $\overline{x}$ is close to μ_0 and λ is small when $\overline{x}$ and μ_0 differ by a great deal. The likelihood ratio test, given by the inequality $\lambda \le k$, is the same as

$$\frac{1}{1 + \dfrac{n(\overline{x} - \mu_0)^2}{\sum_{i=1}^{n}(x_i - \overline{x})^2}} \le k^{2/n}$$

or, equivalently,

$$\frac{n(\overline{x} - \mu_0)^2}{\dfrac{\sum_{i=1}^{n}(x_i - \overline{x})^2}{n - 1}} \ge (n - 1)(k^{-2/n} - 1).$$

When H_0 is true, $\sqrt{n}(\overline{X} - \mu_0)/\sigma$ is $N(0,1)$ and $\sum_{i=1}^{n}(X_i - \overline{X})^2/\sigma^2$ has an independent chi-square distribution $\chi^2(n - 1)$. Hence, under H_0,

$$T = \frac{\sqrt{n}(\overline{X} - \mu_0)/\sigma}{\sqrt{\sum_{i=1}^{n}(X_i - \overline{X})^2/[\sigma^2(n - 1)]}} = \frac{\sqrt{n}(\overline{X} - \mu_0)}{\sqrt{\sum_{i=1}^{n}(X_i - \overline{X})^2/(n - 1)}} = \frac{\overline{X} - \mu_0}{S/\sqrt{n}}$$

has a t distribution with $r = n - 1$ degrees of freedom. In accordance with the likelihood ratio test criterion, H_0 is rejected if the observed

$$T^2 \ge (n - 1)(k^{-2/n} - 1).$$

That is, we reject H_0: $\mu = \mu_0$ and accept H_1: $\mu \ne \mu_0$ if the observed $|T| \ge t_{\alpha/2}(n-1)$.

Note that this test is exactly the same as that listed in Table 7.2-2 for testing H_0: $\mu = \mu_0$ against H_1: $\mu \ne \mu_0$. That is, the test listed there is a likelihood ratio test. As a matter of fact, all six of the tests given in Tables 7.2-2 and 7.3-1 are likelihood ratio tests. Thus, the examples and exercises associated with those tables are illustrations of the use of such tests.

The final development of this section concerns a test about the variance of a normal population. Let $X_1, X_2, \ldots, X_n$ be a random sample from $N(\mu, \sigma^2)$, where μ and σ^2 are unknown. We wish to test H_0: $\sigma^2 = \sigma_0^2$ against H_1: $\sigma^2 \ne \sigma_0^2$. For this purpose, we have

$$\omega = \{(\mu, \sigma^2): -\infty < \mu < \infty, \sigma^2 = \sigma_0^2\}$$

and

$$\Omega = \{(\mu, \sigma^2): -\infty < \mu < \infty, 0 < \sigma^2 < \infty\}.$$

As in the test concerning the mean, we obtain

$$L(\widehat{\Omega}) = \left[\frac{ne^{-1}}{2\pi \sum_{i=1}^{n}(x_i - \overline{x})^2}\right]^{n/2}.$$

If $(\mu, \sigma^2) \in \omega$, then $\widehat{\mu} = \overline{x}$ and $\widehat{\sigma^2} = \sigma_0^2$; thus,

$$L(\widehat{\omega}) = \left(\frac{1}{2\pi\sigma_0^2}\right)^{n/2} \exp\left[-\frac{\sum_{i=1}^{n}(x_i - \overline{x})^2}{2\sigma_0^2}\right].$$

Accordingly, the likelihood ratio test $\lambda = L(\widehat{\omega})/L(\widehat{\Omega})$ is

$$\lambda = \left(\frac{w}{n}\right)^{n/2} \exp\left(-\frac{w}{2} + \frac{n}{2}\right) \le k,$$

where $w = \sum_{i=1}^{n}(x_i - \overline{x})^2/\sigma_0^2$. Solving this inequality for w, we obtain a solution of the form $w \le c_1$ or $w \ge c_2$, where the constants c_1 and c_2 are appropriate functions of the constants k and n so as to achieve the desired significance level α. Since $W = \sum_{i=1}^{n}(X_i - \overline{X})^2/\sigma_0^2$ is $\chi^2(n-1)$ if H_0: $\sigma^2 = \sigma_0^2$ is true, most statisticians modify this test slightly by taking $c_1 = \chi^2_{1-\alpha/2}(n-1)$ and $c_2 = \chi^2_{\alpha/2}(n-1)$. That is, this test and the others listed in Table 7.4-1 are either likelihood ratio tests or slight modifications of likelihood ratio tests. As a matter of fact, most tests involving normal assumptions are likelihood ratio tests or modifications of them; included are tests involving regression and analysis of variance.

REMARK Note that likelihood ratio tests are based on sufficient statistics when they exist, as was also true of best critical and uniformly most powerful critical regions. ■

EXERCISES

10.4-1. In Example 10.4-1, suppose that $n = 20$ and $\overline{x} = 161.1$.

(a) Is H_0 accepted if $\alpha = 0.10$?
(b) Is H_0 accepted if $\alpha = 0.05$?
(c) What is the p-value of this test?

10.4-2. Assume that the weight X in ounces of a "10-ounce" box of cornflakes is $N(\mu, 0.03)$. Let $X_1, X_2, \ldots, X_n$ be a random sample from this distribution.

(a) To test the hypothesis H_0: $\mu \ge 10.35$ against the alternative hypothesis H_1: $\mu < 10.35$, what is the critical region of size $\alpha = 0.05$ specified by the likelihood ratio test criterion?
HINT: Note that if $\mu \ge 10.35$ and $\overline{x} < 10.35$, then $\widehat{\mu} = 10.35$.
(b) If a random sample of n = 50 boxes yielded a sample mean of $\overline{x} = 10.31$, is H_0 rejected?
HINT: Find the critical value z_α when H_0 is true by taking $\mu = 10.35$, which is the extreme value in $\mu \ge 10.35$.
(c) What is the p-value of this test?

10.4-3. Let $X_1, X_2, \ldots, X_n$ be a random sample from the normal distribution $N(\mu, 100)$.

(a) To test H_0: $\mu = 230$ against H_1: $\mu > 230$, what is the critical region specified by the likelihood ratio test criterion?
(b) Is this test uniformly most powerful?
(c) If a random sample of $n = 16$ yielded $\overline{x} = 232.6$, is H_0 accepted at a significance level of $\alpha = 0.10$?
(d) What is the p-value of this test?

10.4-4. Let $X_1, X_2, \ldots, X_n$ be a random sample from the normal distribution $N(\mu, 225)$.

(a) To test H_0: $\mu = 59$ against H_1: $\mu \ne 59$, what is the critical region of size $\alpha = 0.05$ specified by the likelihood ratio test criterion?
(b) If a sample of size $n = 100$ yielded $\overline{x} = 56.13$, is H_0 accepted?
(c) What is the p-value of this test? Note that H_1 is a two-sided alternative.

10.4-5. It is desired to test the hypothesis H_0: $\mu = 30$ against the alternative hypothesis H_1: $\mu \ne 30$, where μ is the mean of a normal distribution and σ^2 is unknown. If a random sample of size $n = 9$ has $\bar{x} = 32.8$ and $s = 4$, is H_0 accepted at an $\alpha = 0.05$ significance level? What is the approximate p-value of this test?

10.4-6. To test H_0: $\mu = 335$ against H_1: $\mu < 335$ under normal assumptions, a random sample of size 17 yielded $\bar{x} = 324.8$ and $s = 40$. Is H_0 accepted at an $\alpha = 0.10$ significance level?

10.4-7. Let X have a normal distribution in which μ and σ^2 are both unknown. It is desired to test H_0: $\mu = 1.80$ against H_1: $\mu > 1.80$ at an $\alpha = 0.10$ significance level. If a random sample of size $n = 121$ yielded $\bar{x} = 1.84$ and $s = 0.20$, is H_0 accepted or rejected? What is the p-value of this test?

10.4-8. Let $X_1, X_2, \ldots, X_n$ be a random sample from an exponential distribution with mean θ. Show that the likelihood ratio test of H_0: $\theta = \theta_0$ against H_1: $\theta \neq \theta_0$ has a critical region of the form $\sum_{i=1}^n x_i \leq c_1$ or $\sum_{i=1}^n x_i \geq c_2$. How would you modify this test so that chi-square tables can be used easily?

10.4-9. Let independent random samples of sizes n and m be taken respectively from two normal distributions with unknown means μ_X and μ_Y and unknown variances σ_X^2 and σ_Y^2.

(a) Show that when $\sigma_X^2 = \sigma_Y^2$, the likelihood ratio for testing H_0: $\mu_X = \mu_Y$ against H_1: $\mu_X \neq \mu_Y$ is a function of the usual two-sample t statistic.

(b) Show that the likelihood ratio for testing H_0: $\sigma_X^2 = \sigma_Y^2$ against H_1: $\sigma_X^2 \neq \sigma_Y^2$ is a function of the usual two-sample F statistic.

The tests described in parts (a) and (b) are listed in Tables 7.3-1 and 7.4-2, respectively, with the second modified slightly.

10.5 CHEBYSHEV'S INEQUALITY AND CONVERGENCE IN PROBABILITY

In this section, we use Chebyshev's inequality to show, in another sense, that the sample mean, $\bar{x}$, is a good statistic to use to estimate a population mean μ; the relative frequency of success in n Bernoulli trials, y/n, is a good statistic for estimating p; and the empirical distribution function $F_n(x)$ can be used to estimate the theoretical distribution function $F(x)$. We examine the effect of the sample size n on these estimates.

We begin by showing that Chebyshev's inequality gives added significance to the standard deviation in terms of bounding certain probabilities. The inequality is valid for *all* distributions for which the standard deviation exists. The proof is given for the discrete case, but it holds for the continuous case with integrals replacing summations.

THEOREM 10.5-1

(Chebyshev's Inequality) If the random variable X has a mean μ and variance σ^2, then, for every $k \geq 1$,

$$P(|X - \mu| \geq k\sigma) \leq \frac{1}{k^2}.$$

Proof. Let $f(x)$ denote the p.m.f. of X. Then

$$\sigma^2 = E[(X - \mu)^2] = \sum_{x \in S} (x - \mu)^2 f(x)$$

$$= \sum_{x \in A} (x - \mu)^2 f(x) + \sum_{x \in A'} (x - \mu)^2 f(x), \qquad (10.5\text{-}1)$$

where

$$A = \{x \colon |x - \mu| \geq k\sigma\}.$$

The second term in the right-hand member of Equation 10.5-1 is the sum of nonnegative numbers and thus is greater than or equal to zero. Hence,

$$\sigma^2 \geq \sum_{x \in A} (x - \mu)^2 f(x).$$

However, in A, $|x - \mu| \ge k\sigma$; so

$$\sigma^2 \ge \sum_{x \in A} (k\sigma)^2 f(x) = k^2\sigma^2 \sum_{x \in A} f(x).$$

But the latter summation equals $P(X \subset A)$; thus,

$$\sigma^2 \ge k^2\sigma^2 P(X \in A) = k^2\sigma^2 P(|X - \mu| \ge k\sigma).$$

That is,

$$P(|X - \mu| \ge k\sigma) \le \frac{1}{k^2}. \quad \square$$

COROLLARY 10.5-1 If $\varepsilon = k\sigma$, then

$$P(|X - \mu| \ge \varepsilon) \le \frac{\sigma^2}{\varepsilon^2}.$$

In words, Chebyshev's inequality states that the probability that X differs from its mean by at least k standard deviations is less than or equal to $1/k^2$. It follows that the probability that X differs from its mean by less than k standard deviations is at least $1 - 1/k^2$. That is,

$$P(|X - \mu| < k\sigma) \ge 1 - \frac{1}{k^2}.$$

From the corollary, it also follows that

$$P(|X - \mu| < \varepsilon) \ge 1 - \frac{\sigma^2}{\varepsilon^2}.$$

Thus, Chebyshev's inequality can be used as a bound for certain probabilities. However, in many instances, the bound is not very close to the true probability.

EXAMPLE 10.5-1 If it is known that X has a mean of 25 and a variance of 16, then, since $\sigma = 4$, a lower bound for $P(17 < X < 33)$ is given by

$$\begin{aligned} P(17 < X < 33) &= P(|X - 25| < 8) \\ &= P(|X - 25| < 2\sigma) \ge 1 - \frac{1}{4} = 0.75 \end{aligned}$$

and an upper bound for $P(|X - 25| \ge 12)$ is found to be

$$P(|X - 25| \ge 12) = P(|X - \mu| \ge 3\sigma) \le \frac{1}{9}. \quad \blacksquare$$

Note that the results of the last example hold for any distribution with mean 25 and standard deviation 4. But, even stronger, the probability that any random variable X differs from its mean by 3 or more standard deviations is at most 1/9, which may be seen by letting $k = 3$ in the theorem. Also, the probability that any random variable X differs from its mean by less than 2 standard deviations is at least 3/4, which may be seen by letting $k = 2$.

The following consideration partially indicates the value of Chebyshev's inequality in theoretical discussions: If Y is the number of successes in n Bernoulli trials with probability p of success on each trial, then Y is $b(n, p)$. Furthermore, Y/n gives the relative frequency of success, and when p is unknown, Y/n can be used as an estimate of its mean p. To gain some insight into the closeness of Y/n to p, we shall use Chebyshev's inequality. With $\varepsilon > 0$, we note from Corollary 10.5-1 that, since $\text{Var}(Y/n) = pq/n$, it follows that

$$P\left(\left|\frac{Y}{n} - p\right| \geq \varepsilon\right) \leq \frac{pq/n}{\varepsilon^2}$$

or, equivalently,

$$P\left(\left|\frac{Y}{n} - p\right| < \varepsilon\right) \geq 1 - \frac{pq}{n\varepsilon^2}. \tag{10.5-2}$$

On the one hand, when p is completely unknown, we can use the fact that $pq = p(1 - p)$ is a maximum when $p = 1/2$ in order to find a lower bound for the probability in Equation 10.5-2. That is,

$$1 - \frac{pq}{n\varepsilon^2} \geq 1 - \frac{(1/2)(1/2)}{n\varepsilon^2}.$$

For example, if $\varepsilon = 0.05$ and $n = 400$, then

$$P\left(\left|\frac{Y}{400} - p\right| < 0.05\right) \geq 1 - \frac{(1/2)(1/2)}{400(0.0025)} = 0.75.$$

On the other hand, if it is known that p is close to 1/10, we would have

$$P\left(\left|\frac{Y}{400} - p\right| < 0.05\right) \geq 1 - \frac{(0.1)(0.9)}{400(0.0025)} = 0.91.$$

Note that Chebyshev's inequality is applicable to all distributions with a finite variance, and thus the bound is not always a tight one; that is, the bound is not necessarily close to the true probability.

In general, however, it should be noted that, with fixed $\varepsilon > 0$ and $0 < p < 1$, we have

$$\lim_{n\to\infty} P\left(\left|\frac{Y}{400} - p\right| < \varepsilon\right) \geq \lim_{n\to\infty}\left(1 - \frac{pq}{n\varepsilon^2}\right) = 1.$$

But since the probability of every event is less than or equal to 1, it must be that

$$\lim_{n\to\infty} P\left(\left|\frac{Y}{400} - p\right| < \varepsilon\right) = 1.$$

That is, the probability that the relative frequency Y/n is within ε of p is close to 1 when n is large enough. This is one form of the **law of large numbers**, and we say that Y/n **converges in probability** to p.

This theoretical result has something to contribute to our understanding of the properties of the **empirical distribution function**, $F_n(x)$. For a fixed x, $F_n(x)$ is the proportion of sample observations that are less than or equal to x. That is, if "success" is an observed X being less than or equal to the fixed x, then $F_n(x)$ is the relative frequency of success. The *law of large numbers* states that $F_n(x)$ converges, in that probabilistic sense, to the true probability $P(X \le x)$ of success, namely, $p = F(x)$. Thus, $F_n(x)$ does approach $F(x)$ in this sense and hence provides an estimate of the distribution function. (We used this idea of the empirical distribution approximating the theoretical distribution function in Section 8.7.)

A more general form of the law of large numbers is found by considering the mean $\overline{X}$ of a random sample from a distribution with mean μ and variance σ^2. This form of the law is more general because the relative frequency Y/n can be thought of as $\overline{X}$ when the sample arises from a Bernoulli distribution. To derive it, we note that

$$E(\overline{X}) = \mu \qquad \text{and} \qquad \text{Var}(\overline{X}) = \frac{\sigma^2}{n}.$$

Thus, from Corollary 10.5-1, for every $\varepsilon > 0$, we have

$$P[|\overline{X} - \mu| \ge \varepsilon] \le \frac{\sigma^2/n}{\varepsilon^2} = \frac{\sigma^2}{n\varepsilon^2}.$$

Since probability is nonnegative, it follows that

$$\lim_{n\to\infty} P(|\overline{X} - \mu| \ge \varepsilon) \le \lim_{n\to\infty} \frac{\sigma^2}{\varepsilon^2 n} = 0,$$

which implies that

$$\lim_{n\to\infty} P(|\overline{X} - \mu| \ge \varepsilon) = 0,$$

or, equivalently,

$$\lim_{n\to\infty} P(|\overline{X} - \mu| < \varepsilon) = 1.$$

The preceding discussion shows that the probability associated with the distribution of $\overline{X}$ becomes concentrated in an arbitrarily small interval centered at μ as n increases. This is a more general form of the law of large numbers, and we say that $\overline{X}$ *converges in probability* to μ.

Although Chebyshev's inequality is quite useful in theoretical discussions, it also shows that in a collection of numbers—say, $x_1, x_2, \ldots, x_n$—a certain proportion of them must be within $k\sqrt{v}$ of $\overline{x}$, where $\overline{x}$ and v are the respective mean and variance of the empirical distribution defined by the numbers. That is,

$$\overline{x} = \frac{1}{n}\sum_{i=1}^{n} x_i \qquad \text{and} \qquad v = \frac{1}{n}\sum_{i-1}^{n} (x_i - \overline{x})^2.$$

To show this, think of the empirical distribution as defining the probability distribution; thus, $\overline{x}$ and v are, respectively, the mean and the variance of this distribution. Hence, for every $k \ge 1$, we have

$$\frac{\mathcal{N}\{x_i\colon |x_i - \overline{x}| \ge k\sqrt{v}\}}{n} \le \frac{1}{k^2}$$

or, equivalently,

$$\frac{\mathcal{N}\{x_i\colon |x_i - \overline{x}| < k\sqrt{v}\}}{n} \ge 1 - \frac{1}{k^2}.$$

In words, the second inequality says, "The proportion of the numbers $x_1, x_2, \ldots, x_n$ that lie within $k\sqrt{v}$ of the mean $\bar{x}$ is at least $1 - 1/k^2$."

EXERCISES

10.5-1. If X is a random variable with mean 33 and variance 16, use Chebyshev's inequality to find

(a) A lower bound for $P(23 < X < 43)$.
(b) An upper bound for $P(|X - 33| \geq 14)$.

10.5-2. If $E(X) = 17$ and $E(X^2) = 298$, use Chebyshev's inequality to determine

(a) A lower bound for $P(10 < X < 24)$.
(b) An upper bound for $P(|X - 17| \geq 16)$.

10.5-3. Let X denote the outcome when a fair die is rolled. Then $\mu = 7/2$ and $\sigma^2 = 35/12$. Note that the maximum deviation of X from μ equals 5/2. Express this deviation in terms of number of standard deviations; that is, find k, where $k\sigma = 5/2$. Determine a lower bound for $P(|X - 3.5| < 2.5)$.

10.5-4. If Y is $b(n, 0.5)$, give a lower bound for $P(|Y/n - 0.5| < 0.08)$ when

(a) $n = 100$.
(b) $n = 500$.
(c) $n = 1000$.

10.5-5. If Y is $b(n, 0.25)$, give a lower bound for $P(|Y/n - 0.25| < 0.05)$ when

(a) $n = 100$.
(b) $n = 500$.
(c) $n = 1000$.

10.5-6. Let $\overline{X}$ be the mean of a random sample of size $n = 15$ from a distribution with mean $\mu = 80$ and variance $\sigma^2 = 60$. Use Chebyshev's inequality to find a lower bound for $P(75 < \overline{X} < 85)$.

10.5-7. The characteristics of the empirical distribution of test scores of 900 students are $\bar{x} = 83$ and $v = 36$, respectively. At least how many students received test scores between 71 and 95?

10.5-8. Suppose that W is a random variable with mean $\mu = 0$ and variance $\sigma^2 = 1$. Then, for $k \geq 1$, Chebyshev's inequality becomes

$$P(|W| < k) \geq 1 - \frac{1}{k^2}.$$

Suppose further that W is a continuous random variable with a symmetric p.d.f. $f(w)$ and distribution function $F(w)$. Finally, suppose that there exists a continuous and symmetric random variable, W, such that **equality** holds in "Chebyshev's inequality." That is, suppose that

$$P(|W - 0| < k) = 1 - \frac{1}{k^2}.$$

Then the distribution function satisfies

$$F(w) - F(-w) = 1 - \frac{1}{w^2}, \qquad w \geq 1.$$

Also, the symmetry assumption implies that

$$F(-w) = 1 - F(w).$$

(a) Show that the p.d.f. of W is

$$f(w) = \begin{cases} \dfrac{1}{|w|^3}, & |w| > 1, \\ 0, & |w| \leq 1. \end{cases}$$

(b) Find the mean and the variance of W and interpret your results.
(c) Graph the distribution function of W.

10.6 LIMITING MOMENT-GENERATING FUNCTIONS

We would like to begin this section by showing that the binomial distribution can be approximated by the Poisson distribution when n is sufficiently large and p is fairly small. Of course, we proved this in Section 2.6 by showing that, under these conditions, the binomial p.m.f. is close to that of the Poisson. Here, however, we show that the binomial moment-generating function is close to that of the Poisson distribution. We do so by taking the limit of a moment-generating function.

Consider the moment-generating function of Y, which is $b(n,p)$. We shall take the limit of this function as $n \to \infty$ such that $np = \lambda$ is a constant; thus, $p \to 0$. The moment-generating function of Y is

$$M(t) = (1 - p + pe^t)^n.$$

Because $p = \lambda/n$, we have

$$M(t) = \left[1 - \frac{\lambda}{n} + \frac{\lambda}{n}e^t\right]^n$$

$$= \left[1 + \frac{\lambda(e^t - 1)}{n}\right]^n.$$

Since

$$\lim_{n\to\infty}\left(1 + \frac{b}{n}\right)^n = e^b,$$

we have

$$\lim_{n\to\infty} M(t) = e^{\lambda(e^t-1)},$$

which exists for all real t. But this is the moment-generating function of a Poisson random variable with mean λ. Hence, this Poisson distribution seems like a reasonable approximation to the binomial distribution when n is large and p is small. That approximation is usually found to be fairly successful if $n \geq 20$ and $p \leq 0.05$ and is found to be very successful if $n \geq 100$ and $p \leq 0.10$, but it is not bad if these bounds are violated somewhat. That is, the approximation could be used in other situations, too; we only want to stress that it becomes better with larger n and smaller p.

The preceding result illustrates the theorem we now state without proof.

THEOREM 10.6-1 If a sequence of moment-generating functions approaches a certain m.g.f., say, $M(t)$, then the limit of the corresponding distributions must be the distribution corresponding to $M(t)$.

REMARK This theorem certainly appeals to one's intuition! In a more advanced course, the theorem is proven, and there the existence of the moment-generating function is not even needed, for we would use the characteristic function $\phi(t) = E(e^{itX})$ instead. ■

The next example illustrates graphically the convergence of the binomial moment-generating functions to that of a Poisson distribution.

EXAMPLE 10.6-1 Consider the moment-generating function for the Poisson distribution with $\lambda = 5$ and those for three binomial distributions for which $np = 5$, namely, $b(50, 1/10)$, $b(100, 1/20)$, and $b(200, 1/40)$. These four moment-generating functions are, respectively,

$$M(t) = e^{5(e^t-1)},$$

$$M(t) = (0.9 + 0.1e^t)^{50},$$

$$M(t) = (0.95 + 0.05e^t)^{100},$$

$$M(t) = (0.975 + 0.025e^t)^{200}.$$

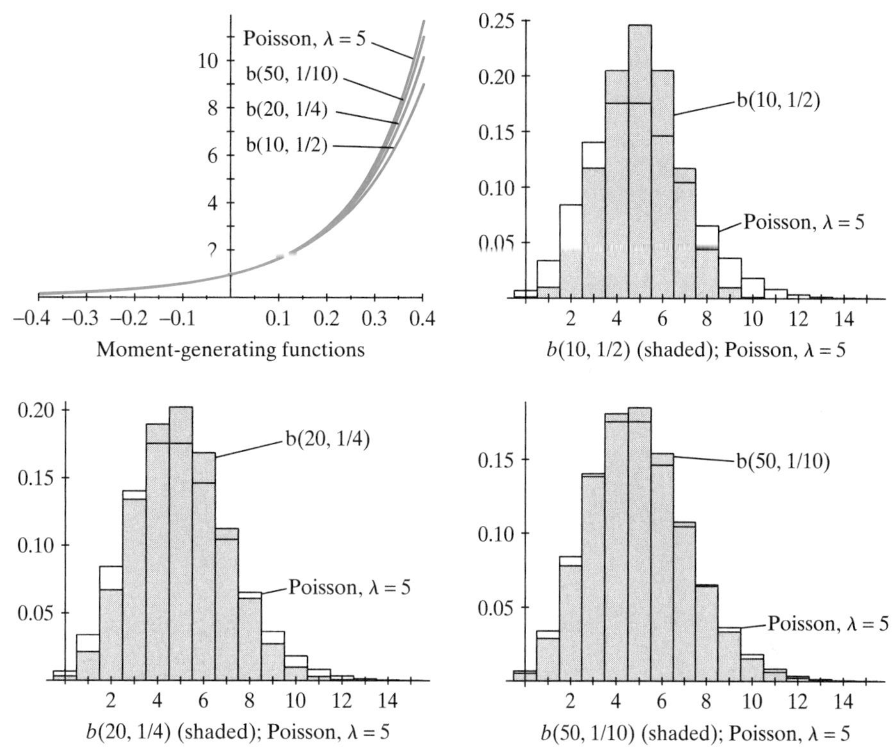

FIGURE 10.6-1: Poisson approximation to the binomial distribution

The graphs of the moment-generating functions with $n = 10, 20$, and 50 are shown in Figure 10.6-1. Although the proof and the figure show the convergence of the binomial moment-generating functions to that of the Poisson distribution, the last three graphs in Figure 10.6-1 show more clearly how the Poisson distribution can be used to approximate binomial probabilities with large n and small p. ■

The next example gives a numerical approximation.

EXAMPLE 10.6-2 Let Y be $b(50, 1/25)$. Then

$$P(Y \le 1) = \left(\frac{24}{25}\right)^{50} + 50\left(\frac{1}{25}\right)\left(\frac{24}{25}\right)^{49} = 0.400.$$

Since $\lambda = np = 2$, the Poisson approximation is

$$P(Y \le 1) \approx 0.406,$$

from Table III in the appendix. ■

Theorem 10.6-1 is used to prove the central limit theorem. To help in understanding this proof, let us first consider a different problem: that of the limiting distribution of the mean $\overline{X}$ of a random sample $X_1, X_2, \ldots, X_n$ from a distribution with mean μ. If the distribution has moment-generating function $M(t)$, then the moment-generating function of $\overline{X}$ is $[M(t/n)]^n$. But, by Taylor's expansion, there exists a number t_1

between 0 and t/n such that

$$M\left(\frac{t}{n}\right) = M(0) + M'(t_1)\frac{t}{n}$$
$$= 1 + \frac{\mu t}{n} + \frac{[M'(t_1) - M'(0)]t}{n},$$

because $M(0) = 1$ and $M'(0) = \mu$. Since $M'(t)$ is continuous at $t = 0$ and since $t_1 \to 0$ as $n \to \infty$, it follows that

$$\lim_{n\to\infty} [M'(t_1) - M'(0)] = 0.$$

Thus, using a result from advanced calculus, we obtain

$$\lim_{n\to\infty}\left[M\left(\frac{t}{n}\right)\right]^n = \lim_{n\to\infty}\left\{1 + \frac{\mu t}{n} + \frac{[M'(t_1) - M'(0)]t}{n}\right\}^n$$
$$= e^{\mu t}$$

for all real t. But this limit is the moment-generating function of a degenerate distribution with all of the probability on μ. Accordingly, $\overline{X}$ has this limiting distribution, indicating that $\overline{X}$ converges to μ in a certain sense. This is one form of the law of large numbers.

We have seen that, in some probability sense, $\overline{X}$ converges to μ in the limit, or, equivalently, $\overline{X} - \mu$ converges to zero. Let us multiply the difference $\overline{X} - \mu$ by some function of n so that the result will not converge to zero. In our search for such a function, it is natural to consider

$$W = \frac{\overline{X} - \mu}{\sigma/\sqrt{n}} = \frac{\sqrt{n}(\overline{X} - \mu)}{\sigma} = \frac{Y - n\mu}{\sqrt{n}\,\sigma},$$

where Y is the sum of the observations of the random sample. The reason for this is that, by the remark after the proof of Theorem 3.6-1, W is a standardized random variable. That is, W has mean 0 and variance 1 for each positive integer n. We are now ready to prove the central limit theorem, which is stated in Section 5.6.

Proof. (of the Central Limit Theorem):
We first consider

$$E[\exp(tW)] = E\left\{\exp\left[\left(\frac{t}{\sqrt{n}\sigma}\right)\left(\sum_{i=1}^{n} X_i - n\mu\right)\right]\right\}$$
$$= E\left\{\exp\left[\left(\frac{t}{\sqrt{n}}\right)\left(\frac{X_1 - \mu}{\sigma}\right)\right]\cdots\exp\left[\left(\frac{t}{\sqrt{n}}\right)\left(\frac{X_n - \mu}{\sigma}\right)\right]\right\}$$
$$= E\left\{\exp\left[\left(\frac{t}{\sqrt{n}}\right)\left(\frac{X_1 - \mu}{\sigma}\right)\right]\right\}\cdots E\left\{\exp\left[\left(\frac{t}{\sqrt{n}}\right)\left(\frac{X_n - \mu}{\sigma}\right)\right]\right\},$$

which follows from the independence of $X_1, X_2, \ldots, X_n$. Then

$$E[\exp(tW)] = \left[m\left(\frac{t}{\sqrt{n}}\right)\right]^n, \qquad -h < \frac{t}{\sqrt{n}} < h,$$

where

$$m(t) = E\left\{\exp\left[t\left(\frac{X_i - \mu}{\sigma}\right)\right]\right\}, \qquad -h < t < h,$$

is the common moment-generating function of each

$$Y_i = \frac{X_i - \mu}{\sigma}, \qquad i = 1, 2, \ldots, n.$$

Since $E(Y_i) = 0$ and $E(Y_i^2) = 1$, it must be that

$$m(0) = 1, \qquad m'(0) = E\left(\frac{X_i - \mu}{\sigma}\right) = 0, \qquad m''(0) = E\left[\left(\frac{X_i - \mu}{\sigma}\right)^2\right] = 1.$$

Hence, using Taylor's formula with a remainder, we know that there exists a number t_1 between 0 and t such that

$$m(t) = m(0) + m'(0)t + \frac{m''(t_1)t^2}{2} = 1 + \frac{m''(t_1)t^2}{2}.$$

Adding and subtracting $t^2/2$, we have

$$m(t) = 1 + \frac{t^2}{2} + \frac{[m''(t_1) - 1]t^2}{2}.$$

Using this expression of $m(t)$ in $E[\exp(tW)]$, we can represent the moment-generating function of W by

$$E[\exp(tW)] = \left\{1 + \frac{1}{2}\left(\frac{t}{\sqrt{n}}\right)^2 + \frac{1}{2}[m''(t_1) - 1]\left(\frac{t}{\sqrt{n}}\right)^2\right\}^n$$

$$= \left\{1 + \frac{t^2}{2n} + \frac{[m''(t_1) - 1]t^2}{2n}\right\}^n, \qquad -\sqrt{n}\,h < t < \sqrt{n}\,h,$$

where now t_1 is between 0 and $t/\sqrt{n}$. Since $m''(t)$ is continuous at $t = 0$ and $t_1 \to 0$ as $n \to \infty$, we have

$$\lim_{n\to\infty} [m''(t_1) - 1] = 1 - 1 = 0.$$

Thus, using a result from advanced calculus, we obtain

$$\lim_{n\to\infty} E[\exp(tW)] = \lim_{n\to\infty}\left\{1 + \frac{t^2}{2n} + \frac{[m''(t_1) - 1]t^2}{2n}\right\}^n$$

$$= \lim_{n\to\infty}\left\{1 + \frac{t^2}{2n}\right\}^n = e^{t^2/2}$$

for all real t. We know that $e^{t^2/2}$ is the m.g.f. of the standard normal distribution, $N(0,1)$. It then follows that the limiting distribution of

$$W = \frac{\overline{X} - \mu}{\sigma/\sqrt{n}} = \frac{\sum_{i=1}^{n} X_i - n\mu}{\sqrt{n}\,\sigma}$$

is $N(0,1)$. This completes the proof of the central limit theorem. □

Examples of the use of the central limit theorem as an approximating distribution were given in Sections 5.6 and 5.7.

To help appreciate the proof of the central limit theorem, the next example graphically illustrates the convergence of the moment-generating functions for two distributions.

EXAMPLE 10.6-3 Let $X_1, X_2, \ldots, X_n$ be a random sample of size n from an exponential distribution with $\theta = 2$. The moment-generating function of $(\overline{X} - \theta)/(\theta/\sqrt{n})$ is

$$M_n(t) = \frac{e^{-t\sqrt{n}}}{(1 - t/\sqrt{n})^n}.$$

The central limit theorem says that, as n increases, this moment-generating function approaches that of the standard normal distribution, namely,

$$M(t) = e^{t^2/2}.$$

The moment-generating functions for $M(t)$ and $M_n(t), n = 5, 15, 50$, are shown in Figure 10.6-2(a). [See also Figure 5.6-2, in which samples were taken from a $\chi^2(1)$ distribution, and recall that the exponential distribution with $\theta = 2$ is $\chi^2(2)$.]

In Example 5.6-6, a U-shaped distribution was considered for which the p.d.f. is $f(x) = (3/2)x^2$, $-1 < x < 1$. For this distribution, $\mu = 0$ and $\sigma^2 = 3/5$. Its moment-generating function, for $t \neq 0$, is

$$M(t) = \left(\frac{3}{2}\right)\frac{e^t t^2 - 2e^t t + 2e^t - e^{-t}t^2 - 2e^{-t}t - 2e^{-t}}{t^3}.$$

Of course, $M(0) = 1$. The moment-generating function of

$$W_n = \frac{\overline{X} - 0}{\sqrt{3/(5n)}}$$

is

$$E[e^{tW_n}] = \left\{E\left[\exp\left(\sqrt{\frac{5}{3n}}\,t\right)\right]\right\}^n = \left[M\left(\sqrt{\frac{5}{3n}}\,t\right)\right]^n.$$

The graphs of these moment-generating functions when $n = 2, 5, 10$ and the graph of the moment-generating function for the standard normal distribution are shown in Figure 10.6-2(b). Note how much more quickly these moment-generating functions converge compared with those for the exponential distribution. ■

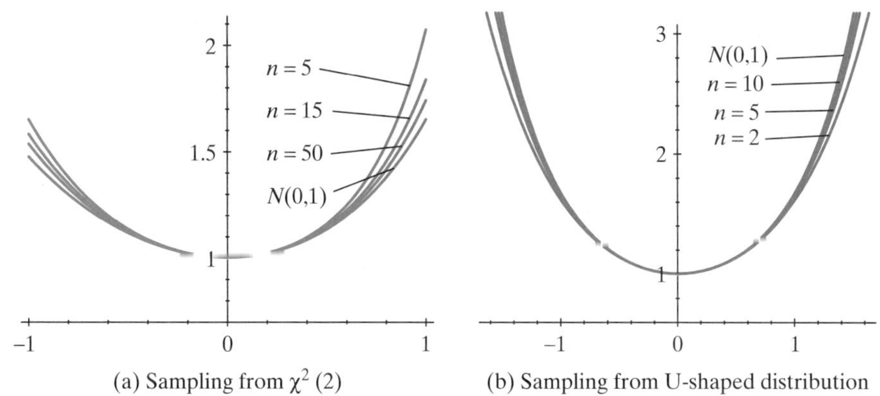

(a) Sampling from χ^2 (2) (b) Sampling from U-shaped distribution

FIGURE 10.6-2: Convergence of moment-generating functions

EXERCISES

10.6-1. Let Y be the number of defectives in a box of 50 articles taken from the output of a machine. Each article is defective with probability 0.01. Find the probability that $Y = 0, 1, 2,$ or 3.

(a) By using the binomial distribution.

(b) By using the Poisson approximation.

10.6-2. The probability that a certain type of inoculation takes effect is 0.995. Use the Poisson distribution to approximate the probability that at most 2 out of 400 people given the inoculation find that it has not taken effect.

HINT: Let $p = 1 - 0.995 = 0.005$.

10.6-3. Let S^2 be the sample variance of a random sample of size n from $N(\mu, \sigma)$. Show that the limit, as $n \to \infty$, of the moment-generating function of S^2 is $e^{\sigma^2 t}$. Thus, in the limit, the distribution of S^2 is degenerate with probability 1 at σ^2.

10.6-4. Let Y be $\chi^2(n)$. Use the central limit theorem to demonstrate that $W = (Y - n)/\sqrt{2n}$ has a limiting distribution function that is $N(0, 1)$.

HINT: Think of Y as being the sum of a random sample from a certain distribution.

10.6-5. Let Y have a Poisson distribution with mean $3n$. Use the central limit theorem to show that $W = (Y - 3n)/\sqrt{3n}$ has a limiting distribution that is $N(0, 1)$.

10.7 ASYMPTOTIC DISTRIBUTIONS OF MAXIMUM LIKELIHOOD ESTIMATORS

Let us consider a distribution of the continuous type with p.d.f. $f(x; \theta)$ such that the parameter θ is not involved in the support of the distribution. Moreover, we want $f(x; \theta)$ to possess a number of mathematical properties that we do not list here. However, in particular, we want to be able to find the maximum likelihood estimator $\widehat{\theta}$ by solving

$$\frac{\partial[\ln L(\theta)]}{\partial\theta} = 0,$$

where here we use a partial-derivative sign because $L(\theta)$ involves $x_1, x_2, \ldots, x_n$, too. That is,

$$\frac{\partial[\ln L(\widehat{\theta})]}{\partial\theta} = 0,$$

where now, with $\widehat{\theta}$ in this expression, $L(\widehat{\theta}) = f(X_1; \widehat{\theta})f(X_2; \widehat{\theta})\cdots f(X_n; \widehat{\theta})$. We can approximate the left-hand member of this latter equation by a linear function found from the first two terms of a Taylor's series expanded about θ, namely,

$$\frac{\partial[\ln L(\theta)]}{\partial\theta} + (\widehat{\theta} - \theta)\frac{\partial^2[\ln L(\theta)]}{\partial\theta^2} \approx 0,$$

when $L(\theta) = f(X_1;\theta)f(X_2;\theta)\cdots f(X_n;\theta)$.

Obviously, this approximation is good enough only if $\widehat{\theta}$ is close to θ, and an adequate mathematical proof involves those conditions, which we have not given here. (See Hogg, McKean, and Craig, 2005.) But a heuristic argument can be made by solving for $\widehat{\theta} - \theta$ to obtain

$$\widehat{\theta} - \theta = \frac{\dfrac{\partial[\ln L(\theta)]}{\partial\theta}}{-\dfrac{\partial^2[\ln L(\theta)]}{\partial\theta^2}}. \tag{10.7-1}$$

Recall that

$$\ln L(\theta) = \ln f(X_1;\theta) + \ln f(X_2;\theta) + \cdots + \ln f(X_n;\theta)$$

and

$$\frac{\partial \ln L(\theta)}{\partial\theta} = \sum_{i=1}^{n} \frac{\partial[\ln f(X_i;\theta)]}{\partial\theta}, \tag{10.7-2}$$

which is the numerator in Equation 10.7-1. However, Equation 10.7-2 gives the sum of the n independent and identically distributed random variables

$$Y_i = \frac{\partial[\ln f(X_i;\theta)]}{\partial\theta}, \qquad i = 1,2,\ldots,n,$$

and thus, by the central limit theorem, has an approximate normal distribution with mean (in the continuous case) equal to

$$\begin{aligned}
\int_{-\infty}^{\infty} \frac{\partial[\ln f(x;\theta)]}{\partial\theta} f(x;\theta)\,dx &= \int_{-\infty}^{\infty} \frac{\partial[f(x;\theta)]}{\partial\theta}\frac{f(x;\theta)}{f(x;\theta)}\,dx \\
&= \int_{-\infty}^{\infty} \frac{\partial[f(x;\theta)]}{\partial\theta}\,dx \\
&= \frac{\partial}{\partial\theta}\left[\int_{-\infty}^{\infty} f(x;\theta)\,dx\right] \\
&= \frac{\partial}{\partial\theta}[1] \\
&= 0.
\end{aligned}$$

Clearly, we need a certain mathematical condition that makes it permissible to interchange the operations of integration and differentiation in those last steps. Of course, the integral of $f(x;\theta)$ is equal to 1 because it is a p.d.f.

Since we now know that the mean of each Y is

$$\int_{-\infty}^{\infty} \frac{\partial[\ln f(x;\theta)]}{\partial\theta} f(x;\theta)\,dx = 0,$$

let us take derivatives of each member of this equation with respect to θ, obtaining

$$\int_{-\infty}^{\infty} \left\{ \frac{\partial^2[\ln f(x;\theta)]}{\partial\theta^2} f(x;\theta) + \frac{\partial[\ln f(x;\theta)]}{\partial\theta} \frac{\partial[f(x;\theta)]}{\partial\theta} \right\} dx = 0.$$

However,

$$\frac{\partial[f(x;\theta)]}{\partial\theta} = \frac{\partial[\ln f(x;\theta)]}{\partial\theta} f(x;\theta);$$

so

$$\int_{-\infty}^{\infty} \left\{ \frac{\partial[\ln f(x;\theta)]}{\partial\theta} \right\}^2 f(x;\theta)\, dx = -\int_{-\infty}^{\infty} \frac{\partial^2[\ln f(x;\theta)]}{\partial\theta^2} f(x;\theta)\, dx.$$

Since $E(Y) = 0$, this last expression provides the variance of $Y = \partial[\ln f(X;\theta)]/\partial\theta$. Then the variance of the sum in Equation 10.7-2 is n times this value, namely,

$$-nE\left\{ \frac{\partial^2[\ln f(X;\theta)]}{\partial\theta^2} \right\}.$$

Let us rewrite Equation 10.7-1 as

$$\frac{\sqrt{n}(\widehat{\theta} - \theta)}{\dfrac{1}{\sqrt{-E\{\partial^2[\ln f(X;\theta)]/\partial\theta^2\}}}} = \frac{\dfrac{\partial[\ln L(\theta)]/\partial\theta}{\sqrt{-nE\{\partial^2[\ln f(X;\theta)]/\partial\theta^2\}}}}{\dfrac{-\dfrac{1}{n}\dfrac{\partial^2[\ln L(\theta)]}{\partial\theta^2}}{E\{-\partial^2[\ln f(X;\theta)]/\partial\theta^2\}}}. \qquad (10.7\text{-}3)$$

The numerator of the right-hand member of Equation 10.7-3 has an approximate $N(0,1)$ distribution, and the aforementioned unstated mathematical conditions require, in some sense, that

$$-\frac{1}{n}\frac{\partial^2[\ln L(\theta)]}{\partial\theta^2} \quad \text{converge to} \quad E\{-\partial^2[\ln f(X;\theta)]/\partial\theta^2\}.$$

Accordingly, the ratios given in Equation 10.7-3 must be approximately $N(0,1)$. That is, $\widehat{\theta}$ has an approximate normal distribution with mean θ and standard deviation

$$\frac{1}{\sqrt{-nE\{\partial^2[\ln f(X;\theta)]/\partial\theta^2\}}}.$$

EXAMPLE 10.7-1 (continuation of Example 6.1-1). With the underlying exponential p.d.f.

$$f(x;\theta) = \frac{1}{\theta}e^{-x/\theta}, \qquad 0 < x < \infty, \qquad \theta \in \Omega = \{\theta : 0 < \theta < \infty\},$$

$\overline{X}$ is the maximum likelihood estimator. Since

$$\ln f(x;\theta) = -\ln\theta - \frac{x}{\theta}$$

and

$$\frac{\partial[\ln f(x;\theta)]}{\partial\theta} = -\frac{1}{\theta} + \frac{x}{\theta^2} \quad \text{and} \quad \frac{\partial^2[\ln f(x;\theta)]}{\partial\theta} = \frac{1}{\theta^2} - \frac{2x}{\theta^3},$$

we have

$$-E\left[\frac{1}{\theta^2} - \frac{2X}{\theta^3}\right] = -\frac{1}{\theta^2} + \frac{2\theta}{\theta^3} = \frac{1}{\theta^2},$$

because $E(X) = \theta$. That is, $\overline{X}$ has an approximate normal distribution with mean θ and standard deviation $\theta/\sqrt{n}$. Thus, the random interval $\overline{X} \pm 1.96(\theta/\sqrt{n}\,)$ has an approximate probability of 0.95 that it covers θ. Substituting the observed $\overline{x}$ for θ, as well as for $\overline{X}$, we say that $\overline{x} \pm 1.96\overline{x}/\sqrt{n}$ is an approximate 95% confidence interval for θ. ■

While the development of the preceding result used a continuous-type distribution, the result holds for the discrete type also, as long as the support does not involve the parameter. This is illustrated in the next example.

EXAMPLE 10.7-2 (continuation of Exercise 6.1-3). If the random sample arises from a Poisson distribution with p.m.f.

$$f(x;\lambda) = \frac{\lambda^x e^{-\lambda}}{x!}, \qquad x = 0, 1, 2, \ldots; \qquad \lambda \in \Omega = \{\lambda : 0 < \lambda < \infty\},$$

then the maximum likelihood estimator for λ is $\widehat{\lambda} = \overline{X}$. Now,

$$\ln f(x;\lambda) = x \ln \lambda - \lambda - \ln x!.$$

Also,

$$\frac{\partial[\ln f(x;\lambda)]}{\partial\lambda} = \frac{x}{\lambda} - 1 \quad \text{and} \quad \frac{\partial^2[\ln f(x;\lambda)]}{\partial\lambda^2} = -\frac{x}{\lambda^2}.$$

Thus,

$$-E\left(-\frac{X}{\lambda^2}\right) = \frac{\lambda}{\lambda^2} = \frac{1}{\lambda},$$

and $\widehat{\lambda} = \overline{X}$ has an approximate normal distribution with mean λ and standard deviation $\sqrt{\lambda/n}$. Finally, $\overline{x} \pm 1.645\sqrt{\overline{x}/n}$ serves as an approximate 90% confidence interval for λ. With the data in Exercise 6.1-3, $\overline{x} = 2.225$ and it follows that this interval ranges from 1.887 to 2.563. ■

It is interesting that there is another theorem which is somewhat related to the preceding result in that the variance of $\widehat{\theta}$ serves as a lower bound for the variance of every unbiased estimator of θ. Thus, we know that if a certain unbiased estimator has a variance equal to that lower bound, we cannot find a better one, and hence that estimator is the best in the sense of being the minimum-variance unbiased estimator. So, in the limit, the maximum likelihood estimator is this type of best estimator.

We describe this **Rao–Cramér inequality** here without proof. Let $X_1, X_2, \ldots, X_n$ be a random sample from a distribution of the continuous type with p.d.f. $f(x;\theta)$, $\theta \in \Omega = \{\theta : c < \theta < d\}$, where the support of X does not depend upon θ, so that we can differentiate, with respect to θ, under integral signs like that in the following integral:

$$\int_{-\infty}^{\infty} f(x;\theta)\,dx = 1.$$

If $Y = u(X_1, X_2, \ldots, X_n)$ is an unbiased estimator of θ, then

$$\begin{aligned}\mathrm{Var}(Y) &\ge \frac{1}{n\int_{-\infty}^{\infty}\{[\partial \ln f(x;\theta)/\partial\theta]\}^2 f(x;\theta)\,dx}\\ &= \frac{-1}{n\int_{-\infty}^{\infty}[\partial^2 \ln f(x;\theta)/\partial\theta^2]\, f(x;\theta)\,dx}.\end{aligned}$$

Note that the integrals in the denominators are, respectively, the expectations

$$E\left\{\left[\frac{\partial \ln f(X;\theta)}{\partial\theta}\right]^2\right\} \quad \text{and} \quad E\left[\frac{\partial^2 \ln f(X;\theta)}{\partial\theta^2}\right];$$

sometimes one is easier to compute than the other. Note also that although the Rao–Cramér lower bound has been stated only for a continuous-type distribution, it is also true for a discrete-type distribution, with summations replacing integrals.

We have computed this lower bound for each of two distributions: exponential and Poisson. Those respective lower bounds were θ^2/n and λ/n. (See Examples 10.7-1 and 10.7-2.) Since, in each case, the variance of $\overline{X}$ equals the lower bound, then $\overline{X}$ is the minimum-variance unbiased estimator.

Let us consider another example.

EXAMPLE 10.7-3 (continuation of Exercise 6.1-7). Let the p.d.f. of X be given by

$$f(x;\theta) = \theta x^{\theta-1}, \qquad 0 < x < 1, \qquad \theta \in \Omega = \{\theta : 0 < \theta < \infty\}.$$

We then have

$$\ln f(x;\theta) = \ln\theta + (\theta - 1)\ln x,$$

$$\frac{\partial \ln f(x;\theta)}{\partial\theta} = \frac{1}{\theta} + \ln x,$$

and

$$\frac{\partial^2 \ln f(x;\theta)}{\partial\theta^2} = -\frac{1}{\theta^2}.$$

Since $E(-1/\theta^2) = -1/\theta^2$, the lower bound of the variance of every unbiased estimator of θ is θ^2/n. Moreover, the maximum likelihood estimator $\widehat{\theta} = -n/\ln\prod_{i=1}^{n} X_i$ has an approximate normal distribution with mean θ and variance θ^2/n. Thus, in a limiting sense, $\widehat{\theta}$ is the minimum variance unbiased estimator of θ. ■

To measure the value of estimators, their variances are compared with the Rao–Cramér lower bound. The ratio of the Rao–Cramér lower bound to the actual variance of any unbiased estimator is called the **efficiency** of that estimator. An estimator with an efficiency of, say, 50%, means that $1/0.5 = 2$ times as many sample observations are needed to do as well in estimation as can be done with the minimum-variance unbiased estimator (the 100% efficient estimator).

EXERCISES

10.7-1. Let $X_1, X_2, \ldots, X_n$ be a random sample from $N(\theta, \sigma^2)$, where σ^2 is known.

(a) Show that $Y = (X_1 + X_2)/2$ is an unbiased estimator of θ.

(b) Find the Rao–Cramér lower bound for the variance of an unbiased estimator of θ for a general n.

(c) What is the efficiency of Y in part (a)?

10.7-2. Let $X_1, X_2, \ldots, X_n$ denote a random sample from $b(1,p)$. We know that $\overline{X}$ is an unbiased estimator of p and that $\text{Var}(\overline{X}) = p(1-p)/n$. (See Exercise 6.1-12.)

(a) Find the Rao–Cramér lower bound for the variance of every unbiased estimator of p.

(b) What is the efficiency of $\overline{X}$ as an estimator of p?

10.7-3. (Continuation of Exercise 6.1-2.) In sampling from a normal distribution with known mean μ, $\widehat{\theta} = \sum_{i=1}^{n}(X_i - \mu)^2/n$ is the maximum likelihood estimator of $\theta = \sigma^2$.

(a) Determine the Rao–Cramér lower bound.

(b) What is the approximate distribution of $\widehat{\theta}$?

(c) What is the exact distribution of $n\widehat{\theta}/\theta$, where $\theta = \sigma^2$?

10.7-4. Find the Rao–Cramér lower bound, and thus the asymptotic variance of the maximum likelihood estimator $\widehat{\theta}$, if the random sample $X_1, X_2, \ldots, X_n$ is taken from each of the distributions having the following p.d.f.'s:

(a) $f(x;\theta) = (1/\theta^2)\,x\,e^{-x/\theta}$,
$0 < x < \infty, \quad 0 < \theta < \infty.$

(b) $f(x;\theta) = (1/2\theta^3)\,x^2\,e^{-x/\theta}$,
$0 < x < \infty, \quad 0 < \theta < \infty.$

(c) $f(x;\theta) = (1/\theta)\,x^{(1-\theta)/\theta}$,
$0 < x < 1, \quad 0 < \theta < \infty.$

HISTORICAL COMMENTS This chapter on theory briefly explains the best tests of statistical hypotheses, the importance of the use of sufficient statistics in estimation and testing, and certain limiting distributions, including the proof of the central limit theorem. We mention again some of the statistical giants who contributed to these theories: R. A. Fisher, J. Neyman, and E. Pearson. Of course, we cannot forget those early pioneers associated with the central limit theorem: de Moivre, Laplace, and Gauss. Many fine statisticians have worked on generalizations and extensions of their results since the 1930s.

Quality Improvement through Statistical Methods

CHAPTER 11

11.1 TIME SEQUENCES
11.2 STATISTICAL QUALITY CONTROL
11.3 GENERAL FACTORIAL AND 2^k FACTORIAL DESIGNS
11.4 UNDERSTANDING VARIATION

11.1 TIME SEQUENCES

Thus far, we have treated $x_1, x_2, \ldots, x_n$ as if they were observations from some random experiment. That is, each one of these observations has the same distribution with mean μ and variance σ^2, and we therefore might use $\bar{x}$ and s^2 as respective estimates of μ and σ^2. In practice, however, we often find that $x_1, x_2, \ldots, x_n$ are observed in *time sequence*, and that there is frequently a change in the distribution as we continue to observe the x values. Consequently, we do not in fact want to use $\bar{x}$ and s^2 as estimates of those characteristics. To see what is actually going on in these cases, we should plot the data in the order collected. In a **time sequence**, observations are recorded in the order in which they were collected as ordered pairs, where the usual x-coordinate denotes the time t (in order of collection, which could be days, weeks, years, etc.) and the usual y-coordinate records the observation x. When measurements are taken sequentially and plotted in this time sequence, it turns out that trends, cycles, or major changes in processes (like government interventions) are often observed. As an illustration, consider the three time sequences in Figures 11.1-1(a), 11.1-1(b), and 11.1-1(c).

Figure 11.1-1(a) might be a record of a company's sales for the last 12 years. Despite occasional drops in sales from one year to the next, there has been an upward trend. Suppose, however, that only the last two points had been recorded for the stockholders. Since sales went down during that time, the stockholders might believe that there are some difficulties and that changes should be made. If they look at the entire sequence, however, they clearly see the long-term improvement, and only variability about that upward trend accounts for the last drop. If, by contrast, several successive drops were to appear, then some action might be needed.

The points in Figure 11.1-1(b) might also represent sales, but now plotted by quarters. Clearly, in this business, there is a cyclic effect, with increases from the first to second quarters and from the second to the third, but decreases from the third to

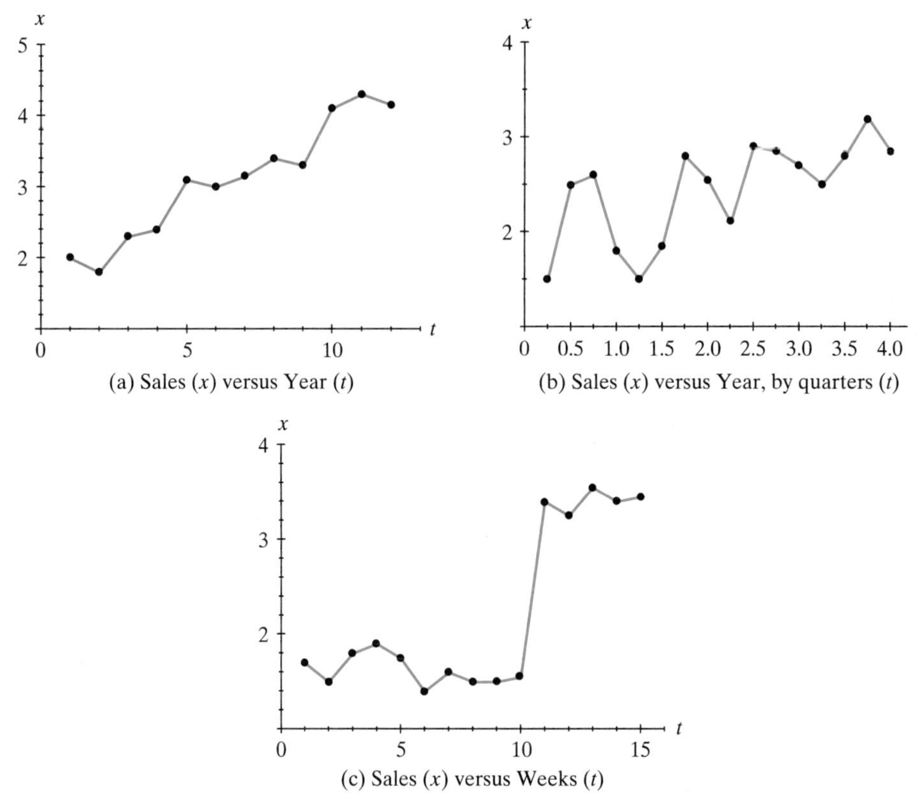

(a) Sales (x) versus Year (t)
(b) Sales (x) versus Year, by quarters (t)
(c) Sales (x) versus Weeks (t)

FIGURE 11.1-1: Sales of company over time

the fourth and the fourth to the first quarter of the next year. Again we note that there seems to be an overall upward trend.

Figure 11.1-1(c) could be the plot of some measure of success (possibly sales) of the company. Clearly, something happened after the tenth week. Perhaps management did not like the past level of performance and instituted a new program (possibly one based on statistical quality control). Alternatively, there might have been some outside intervention (like war) that increased the sales of this particular product.

We have listed three possible scenarios associated with the three time sequences shown. There are others, but in any case, we clearly see that plotting the points in a time sequence often helps explore the variability of the outcomes associated with a particular system. That is, time is frequently an important factor in dealing with variability, possibly when purchasing stock. The following example is a simple one based on one student's experience.

EXAMPLE 11.1-1 A student monitored some stock that she purchased in March for \$5 per share. She recorded the value of a share every two weeks, yielding the following paired data, (t, x), with t equal to the time in weeks after the purchase and x the value of a share at that time:

$$\begin{array}{ccccc} (0, 5.00) & (2, 5.00) & (4, 5.25) & (6, 5.25) & (8, 5.50) \\ (10, 5.50) & (12, 5.25) & (14, 5.75) & (16, 6.25) & (18, 6.50) \\ (20, 6.25) & (22, 7.25) & (24, 7.50) & & \end{array}$$

A time sequence of these data is shown in Figure 11.1-2. ■

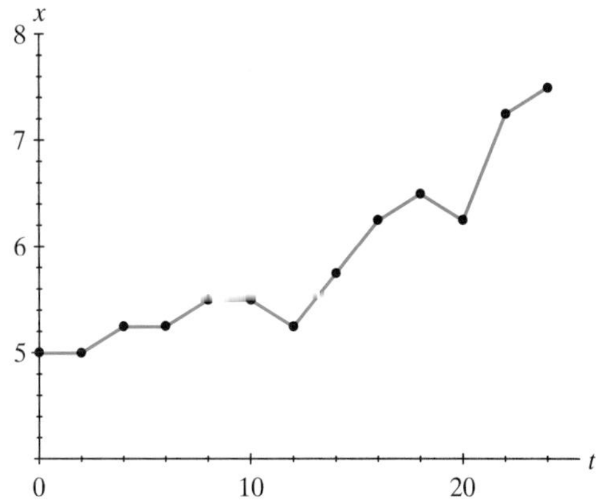

FIGURE 11.1-2: Value of a share of stock plotted biweekly

Sometimes, however, time is not an important factor in the response variable, and yet time-sequence plots still help us understand the concept of variation. Suppose that a process or an individual performs at some average level, sometimes doing better and sometimes doing worse than that average. For example, suppose a certain worker's output is plotted by the month, as in Figure 11.1-3.

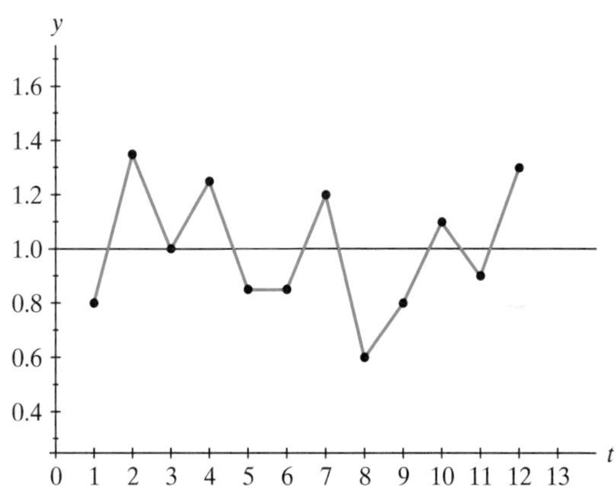

FIGURE 11.1-3: Average output of worker (y) versus month (t)

Let us say that the manager of the company decides to do the following: On good months (like the second month), the worker is given a "pat on the back" (maybe a bonus or even being named "worker of the month"). What happens? Usually the performance goes down the next month. Recall that the worker is averaging below the performance of her high month; that is, she was performing above average when she was made worker of the month. So there is a tendency to do worse the month following a very good performance. (Statisticians sometimes call this "regression toward the mean.")

This phenomenon explains what is often called the "sophomore jinx" in sports. A player might have an unusually good first year, actually one far above his average. So he tends to do worse the next year. Fans will say it's the sophomore jinx; he probably got overconfident and didn't work as hard. Although there might be some truth to this, it could also be that he worked just as hard as before, but still went down because his first year was over his average. So, often the "rookie of the year" will do worse the second year because not many players win that award with an average year. That is, he was performing far above his average when he won the award.

As regards the worker described by Figure 11.1-3, on bad months (such as the eighth month) the manager could call in the worker and have a serious talk with her or, in some way, penalize her. What happens? Usually, she does better the next month (again regression toward the mean). So the boss gets the idea that it is better to get tough because the workers seem to do better after these little talks. Of course, like the "pat on the back" technique, this strategy does not really work, because the workers keep varying about their average. They usually do better after a very poor performance and worse after an excellent performance.

If the manager does not like the average level of performance, then he or she must do something to change the system. Most of the time, individual workers can do very little to change the system; major decisions regarding improvements must be made by the manager or even in the boardroom. After these decisions, the workers must be given "road maps" directing them to use the improvements. Most workers (as well as students) want to do better and would like to take pride in their performance. Managers (as well as teachers) should provide workers (students) the opportunity to improve their self-esteem.

The next example could help some of you analyze performances in events that are repeated over time.

EXAMPLE 11.1-2 Consider the following 20 quiz scores of a student in a two-semester calculus course (each quiz was graded on a 20-point scale, and the quizzes are given in the order in which they were taken):

18	20	16	12	15	15	10	13	14	9
12	10	8	11	12	11	10	11	8	6

We could calculate the average of all 20 quiz scores, which is 12.05. We could calculate the average of the first 10 and the second 10. A graphic display of what has happened to this student over the course of the two semesters is shown in Figure 11.1-4. Clearly, the student was not making a great effort throughout the year in this calculus class. If interested, students can correct trends like this, but they must make changes in their behavior to do so. By continuing the past pattern, nothing will change and the downward trend will persist. What improvements could be made to change this trend? Each student must answer this in his or her own way. ■

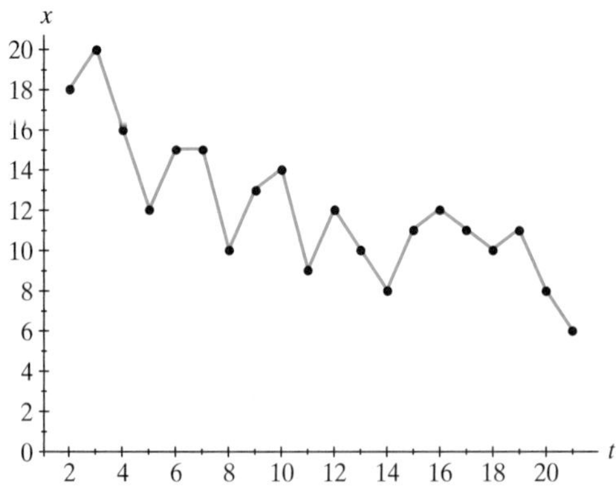

FIGURE 11.1-4: Calculus scores over time

The next example illustrates how, in a production process, tracking something over time can be beneficial.

EXAMPLE 11.1-3 Containers of a prewash concentrate are selected regularly from the production line, and the concentrate is weighed. The target weight is 330.5–336.5 grams. We now construct a time-sequence plot (see Figure 11.1-5) for the following 60 weights that were observed in order from left to right, line by line:

337.9	338.1	337.7	338.3	337.3	338.1	337.3	338.0	337.9	338.9
337.6	338.2	338.1	338.6	338.0	338.4	334.4	334.3	334.5	333.9
335.1	334.0	335.6	334.1	335.0	334.8	335.2	335.2	335.2	334.0
334.5	334.6	335.4	335.9	335.6	335.8	334.5	335.4	335.0	335.5
335.1	335.0	334.1	334.6	334.4	334.7	333.8	335.0	334.0	334.3
334.0	333.7	334.7	333.5	334.8	333.9	335.7	335.1	335.1	334.6

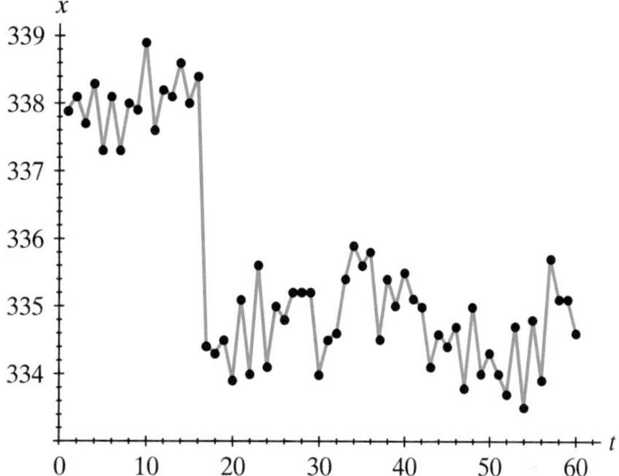

FIGURE 11.1-5: Prewash concentrate fill weights

It is pretty clear that during the beginning of production the fill weights were slightly above the target weight. This is good news for the customer, as long as the containers do not overflow. However, if the trend had continued, the company would have lost money. After adjustments were made, the process seemed to come under control, with the weights reflecting the normal variability for such a process. ■

EXERCISES

11.1-1. The following data give the percentage of solids in a product:

69.8	71.3	65.6	66.3	70.1	71.9	69.6	71.9	71.1	71.7
71.9	69.8	66.8	68.3	64.4	64.2	65.1	63.7	66.2	61.9
66.1	62.9	66.9	67.3	63.3	63.4	67.2	67.4	65.5	66.2
67.5	67.3	66.9	66.5	65.5	63.9	64.6	62.3	66.2	67.2
66.0	69.8	69.7	71.0	69.8	66.0	70.3	65.5	67.0	66.8
67.6	68.6	66.5	66.2	70.4	68.1	64.3	65.2	68.0	65.1

The specifications call for the percentage to be between 60.0% and 72.0%. The data were observed in order from left to right, line by line.

(a) Construct a time sequence of these percentages.
(b) Interpret your output.

11.1-2. Twenty-four "3-pound" bags of apples were filled and weighed automatically by scale number 5. The weights are as follows, in the time order shown:

3.26	3.62	3.39	3.12	3.53	3.30	3.10	3.26
3.19	3.22	3.14	3.39	3.31	3.21	3.49	3.41
3.02	3.17	3.20	3.12	3.42	3.36	3.21	3.26

(a) Construct and interpret a time sequence of these weights.
(b) Compare scale number 5 with scale number 6 in the next exercise.

11.1-3. Twenty-four "3-pound" bags of apples were filled and weighed automatically by scale number 6. The weights are as follows, in the time order shown:

3.22	2.97	3.00	3.08	3.04	3.09	3.04	3.21
3.00	3.05	3.11	3.00	3.10	3.13	3.08	3.22
3.12	3.04	3.03	3.02	3.10	3.09	3.18	3.00

(a) Construct and interpret a time sequence of these weights.
(b) Compare scale number 6 with scale number 5 in the last exercise.

11.1-4. The year, x, and the birthrate, y (number of births per 1000 population) for 1960–2002 are as follows:

(1960, 23.7) (1961, 23.3) (1962, 22.4) (1963, 21.7)
(1964, 21.1) (1965, 19.4) (1966, 18.4) (1967, 17.8)
(1968, 17.6) (1969, 17.9) (1970, 18.4) (1971, 17.2)
(1972, 15.6) (1973, 14.8) (1974, 14.8) (1975, 14.6)
(1976, 14.6) (1977, 15.1) (1978, 15.0) (1979, 15.6)
(1980, 15.9) (1981, 15.8) (1982, 15.9) (1983, 15.5)
(1984, 15.5) (1985, 15.8) (1986, 15.6) (1987, 15.7)
(1988, 15.9) (1989, 16.3) (1990, 16.7) (1991, 16.2)
(1992, 15.8) (1993, 15.4) (1994, 15.0) (1995, 14.6)
(1996, 14.4) (1997, 14.2) (1998, 14.3) (1999, 14.2)
(2000, 14.4) (2001, 14.1) (2002, 13.9)

(a) Construct a time sequence of these birthrates.
(b) Interpret your output.

11.1-5. Dish drop viscosity has a specification of 120–230 cps (centipoise). One hundred observations were selected and measured, yielding the following viscosities (read across, line by line, in the time order shown):

158	147	158	159	169	151	166	151	143	169
153	174	151	164	185	168	140	180	176	154
160	187	145	164	158	169	153	149	144	157
156	183	157	140	162	158	160	180	154	160
164	168	154	158	164	159	153	170	158	170
150	161	169	166	154	157	138	155	134	165
161	172	156	145	153	143	152	152	156	163
179	157	135	172	143	154	165	145	152	145
171	189	144	154	147	187	147	159	167	151
153	168	148	188	152	165	155	140	157	176

(a) Construct a time sequence of the viscosities.
(b) If there seems to be no significant time factor, construct a histogram of the viscosities.
(c) Use the two graphs to interpret these measurements.

11.1-6. A manufacturer of car windows has studs in the windows for attaching them to the car. A standard "stud pullout test" measures the force required to pull each of the five studs out of a window. Because of the shape of the window, the two studs on one side are attached in one way and the three studs on the other side in a different way. The target mean is 123. Seventy observations, going around each of 14 windows in a clockwise direction, were as follows:

140	159	138	102	84	126	147	126	103	92
149	155	135	120	94	149	143	109	101	86
144	154	120	105	97	149	151	140	103	99
157	140	120	96	87	146	137	120	93	89
149	154	139	100	84	148	142	130	98	81
112	135	109	84	87	112	135	109	84	87
118	135	90	77	125	126	131	78	75	126

(a) Construct a time sequence of these forces.
(b) Construct a histogram of the forces.
(c) Give an interpretation.

11.1-7. The amount of fluoride in a certain brand of toothpaste has a specification of 0.85–1.10 mg/g. One hundred tubes of toothpaste were selected randomly from the production line, and the amounts of fluoride were measured, yielding the following data:

0.98	0.92	0.89	0.90	0.94	0.99	0.86	0.85	1.06	1.01
1.03	0.85	0.95	0.90	1.03	0.87	1.02	0.88	0.92	0.88
0.88	0.90	0.98	0.96	0.98	0.93	0.98	0.92	1.00	0.95
0.88	0.90	1.01	0.98	0.85	0.91	0.95	1.01	0.88	0.89
0.99	0.95	0.90	0.88	0.92	0.89	0.90	0.95	0.93	0.96
0.93	0.91	0.92	0.86	0.87	0.91	0.89	0.93	0.93	0.95
0.92	0.88	0.87	0.98	0.98	0.91	0.93	1.00	0.90	0.93
0.89	0.97	0.98	0.91	0.88	0.89	1.00	0.93	0.92	0.97
0.97	0.91	0.85	0.92	0.87	0.86	0.91	0.92	0.95	0.97
0.88	1.05	0.91	0.89	0.92	0.94	0.90	1.00	0.90	0.93

(a) Construct a time sequence of these measurements.

(b) Construct a histogram of the measurements.

(c) Construct a box-plot of the measurements.

11.1-8. Use the data in Exercise 3.1-11 for this exercise.

(a) Construct and interpret a time sequence of the durations of eruptions of Old Faithful geyser. Note the starting times in making your interpretation.

(b) Construct and interpret a time sequence of the times between eruptions of Old Faithful geyser. Note the starting times in making your interpretation.

11.1-9. Ledolter and Hogg (see references) report the following $n = 52$ weekly sales of thermostat replacement parts (read across):

206	245	185	169	162	177	207	216	193	230	212	192	162
189	244	209	207	211	210	173	194	234	156	206	188	162
172	210	205	244	218	182	206	211	273	248	262	258	233
255	303	282	291	280	255	312	296	307	281	308	280	345

(a) Construct a time sequence for these data and discuss your findings.

(b) What do you think will happen in the next month?

(c) What do you think will happen in the next two months?

11.2 STATISTICAL QUALITY CONTROL

Statistical methods can be used in many scientific fields, such as medical research, engineering, chemistry, and psychology. Often, it is necessary to compare two ways of doing something—say, the old way and a possible new way. We collect data on each way, quite possibly in a laboratory situation, and try to decide whether the new way is actually better than the old. Needless to say, it would be terrible to change to the new way at great expense, only to find out that it is really not any better than the old. That is, suppose the lab results indicate, by some statistical method, that the new is seemingly better than the old. Can we actually extrapolate those outcomes in the lab to the situations in the real world? Clearly, statisticians cannot make these decisions, but they should be made by some professional who knows both statistics and the specialty in question very well. The statistical analysis might provide helpful guidelines, but we still need the expert to make the final decision.

However, even before investigating possible changes in any process, it is extremely important to determine exactly what the process in question is doing at the present time. Often, people in charge of an organization do not understand the capabilities of many of its processes. Simply measuring what is going on frequently leads to improvements. In many cases measurement is easy, such as determining the diameter of a bolt, but sometimes it is extremely difficult, as in evaluating good teaching or many other service activities. But if at all possible, we encourage those involved to begin to "listen" to their processes; that is, they should measure what is going on in their organization. These measurements alone often are the beginning of desirable improvements. While most of our remarks in this chapter concern measurements made in manufacturing, service industries frequently find them just as useful.

At one time, some manufacturing plants would make parts to be used in the construction of some piece of equipment. Say a particular line in the plant, making a certain part, might produce several hundreds of them each day. These items would then be sent on to an inspection cage, where they would be checked for goodness, often several days or even weeks later. Occasionally, the inspectors would discover many defectives among the items made, say, two weeks ago. There was little that could be done at that point except scrap or rework the defective parts, both expensive outcomes.

In the 1920s, W. A. Shewhart, who was working for AT&T Bell Labs, recognized that this was an undesirable situation and suggested that, with some suitable frequency, a sample of these parts should be taken as they were being made. If the sample indicated that the items were satisfactory, the manufacturing process would continue. But if the sampled parts were not satisfactory, corrections should be made then so that things became satisfactory. This idea led to what are commonly called *Shewhart control charts*—the basis of what was called *statistical quality control* in those early days; today it is often referred to as *statistical process control.*

Shewhart control charts consist of calculated values of a statistic, say, $\overline{x}$, plotted in sequence. That is, in making products, every so often (each hour, each day, or each week, depending upon how many items are being produced) a sample of size n of them is taken, and they are measured, resulting in the observations $x_1, x_2, \ldots, x_n$. The average $\overline{x}$ and the standard deviation s are computed. This is done k times, and the k values of $\overline{x}$ and s are averaged, resulting in $\overline{\overline{x}}$ and $\overline{s}$, respectively; usually, k is equal to some number between 10 and 30.

The central limit theorem states that if the true mean μ and standard deviation σ of the process were known, then almost all of the $\overline{x}$ values would plot between $\mu - 3\sigma/\sqrt{n}$ and $\mu + 3\sigma/\sqrt{n}$, unless the system has actually changed. However, suppose we know neither μ nor σ, and thus μ is estimated by $\overline{\overline{x}}$ and $3\sigma/\sqrt{n}$ by $A_3\overline{s}$, where $\overline{\overline{x}}$ and $\overline{s}$ are the respective means of the k observations of $\overline{x}$ and s, and where A_3 is a factor depending upon n that can be found in books on statistical quality control. A few values of A_3 (and some other constants that will be used later) are given in Table 11.2-1 for typical values of n.

The estimates of $\mu \pm 3\sigma/\sqrt{n}$ are called the *upper control limit* (UCL), $\overline{\overline{x}} + A_3\overline{s}$, and the *lower control limit* (LCL), $\overline{\overline{x}} - A_3\overline{s}$, and $\overline{\overline{x}}$ provides the estimate of the centerline. A typical plot is given in Figure 11.2-1. Here, in the 13th sampling period, $\overline{x}$ is outside the control limits, indicating that the process has changed and that some investigation and action are needed to correct this change, which seems like an upward shift in the process.

Note that there is a control chart for the s values, too. From sampling distribution theory, values of B_3 and B_4 have been determined and are given in Table 11.2-1, so we know that almost all the s values should be between $B_3\overline{s}$ and $B_4\overline{s}$ if there is no

TABLE 11.2-1: Some Constants Used with Control Charts

n	A_3	B_3	B_4	A_2	D_3	D_4
4	1.63	0	2.27	0.73	0	2.28
5	1.43	0	2.09	0.58	0	2.11
6	1.29	0.03	1.97	0.48	0	2.00
8	1.10	0.185	1.815	0.37	0.14	1.86
10	0.98	0.28	1.72	0.31	0.22	1.78
20	0.68	0.51	1.49	0.18	0.41	1.59

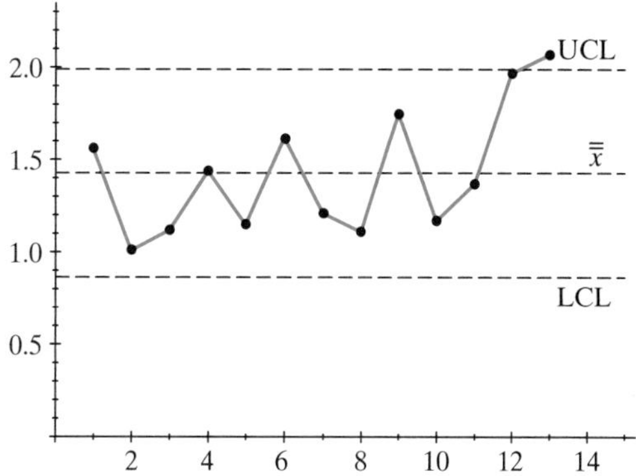

FIGURE 11.2-1: Typical control chart

change in the underlying distribution. So again, if an individual s value is outside these control limits, some action should be taken, as it seems as if there has been a change in the variation of the underlying distribution.

Often, when these charts are first constructed after $k = 10$ to 30 sampling periods, many points fall outside the control limits. A team consisting of workers, the manager of the process, the supervisor, an engineer, and even a statistician should try to find the reasons that this has occurred, and the situation should be corrected. After this is done and the points plot within the control limits, the process is "in statistical control." However, being in statistical control is not a guarantee of satisfaction with the products. Since $A_3\bar{s}$ is an estimate of $3\sigma/\sqrt{n}$, it follows that $\sqrt{n}A_3\bar{s}$ is an estimate of 3σ, and with an underlying distribution close to a normal one, almost all items would be between $\bar{\bar{x}} \pm \sqrt{n}A_3\bar{s}$. If these limits are too wide, then corrections must be made again.

If the variation is under control (i.e., if $\bar{x}$ and s are within their control limits), we say that the variations seen in $\bar{x}$ and s are due to common causes. If products made under such a system with these existing common causes are satisfactory, then production continues. If either $\bar{x}$ or s, however, is outside the control limits, that is an indication that some special causes are at work, and they must be corrected. That is, a team should investigate the problem and some action should be taken.

EXAMPLE 11.2-1 A company produces a storage console. Twice a day, nine critical characteristics are tested on five consoles that are selected randomly from the production line. One of these characteristics is the time it takes the lower storage component door to open completely. Table 11.2-2 lists the opening times in seconds for the consoles that were

TABLE 11.2-2: Console Opening Times

Group	x_1	x_2	x_3	x_4	x_5	$\overline{x}$	s	R
1	1.2	1.8	1.7	1.3	1.4	1.480	0.259	0.60
2	1.5	1.2	1.0	1.0	1.8	1.300	0.346	0.80
3	0.9	1.6	1.0	1.0	1.0	1.100	0.283	0.70
4	1.3	0.9	0.9	1.2	1.0	1.060	0.182	0.40
5	0.7	0.8	0.9	0.6	0.8	0.760	0.114	0.30
6	1.2	0.9	1.1	1.0	1.0	1.040	0.104	0.30
7	1.1	0.9	1.1	1.0	1.4	1.100	0.187	0.50
8	1.4	0.9	0.9	1.1	1.0	1.060	0.207	0.50
9	1.3	1.4	1.1	1.5	1.6	1.380	0.192	0.50
10	1.6	1.5	1.4	1.3	1.5	1.460	0.114	0.30
						$\overline{\overline{x}} = 1.174$	$\overline{s} = 0.200$	$\overline{R} = 0.49$

tested during one week. Also included in the table are the sample means, the sample standard deviations, and the ranges.

The upper control limit (UCL) and the lower control limit (LCL) for $\overline{x}$ are found using A_3 in Table 11.2-1 with $n = 5$ as follows:

$$\text{UCL} = \overline{\overline{x}} + A_3\overline{s} = 1.174 + 1.43(0.20) = 1.460$$

and

$$\text{LCL} = \overline{\overline{x}} - A_3\overline{s} = 1.174 - 1.43(0.20) = 0.888.$$

These control limits and the sample means are plotted on the $\overline{x}$ chart in Figure 11.2-2. There should be some concern about the fifth sampling period; thus, there should be an investigation to determine why that particular $\overline{x}$ is below the LCL.

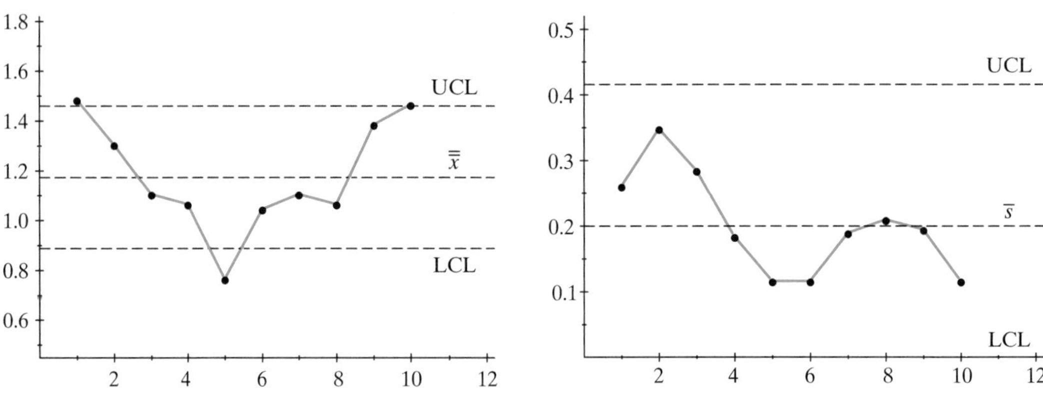

FIGURE 11.2-2: The $\overline{x}$ chart and s chart

The UCL and LCL for s are found using B_3 and B_4 in Table 11.2-1 with $n = 5$ as follows:

$$\text{UCL} = B_4\overline{s} = 2.09(0.200) = 0.418$$

and

$$\text{LCL} = B_3\overline{s} = 0(0.200) = 0.$$

These control limits and the sample standard deviations are plotted on the s chart in Figure 11.2-2.

Almost all of the observations should lie between $\overline{\overline{x}} \pm \sqrt{n}\,A_3\overline{s}$, namely,

$$1.174 + \sqrt{5}\,(1.43)(0.20) = 1.814$$

and

$$1.174 - \sqrt{5}\,(1.43)(0.20) = 0.535.$$

This situation is illustrated in Figure 11.2-3, in which all 50 observations do fall within these control limits. ■

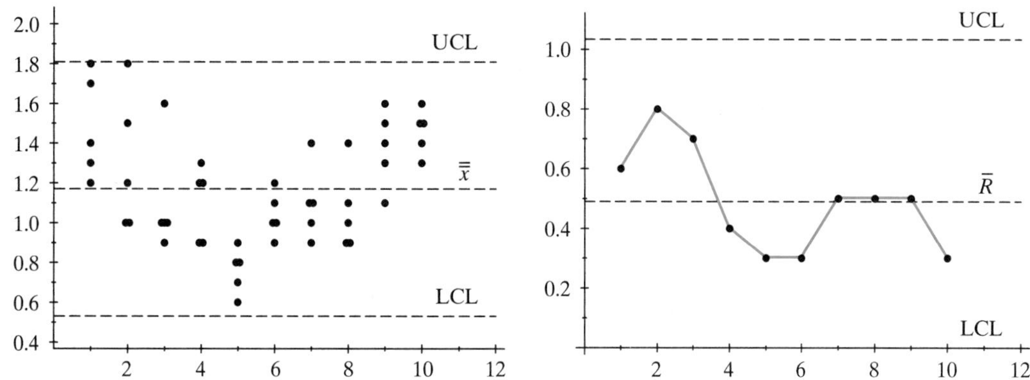

FIGURE 11.2-3: Plot of 50 console opening times and R chart

In most books on statistical quality control, there is an alternative way of constructing the limits on an $\overline{x}$ chart. For each sample, we compute the range, R, which is the absolute value of the difference of the extremes of the sample. This computation is much easier than that for calculating s. After k samples are taken, we compute the average of these R values, obtaining $\overline{R}$ as well as $\overline{\overline{x}}$. The statistic $A_2\,\overline{R}$ serves as an estimate of $3\sigma/\sqrt{n}$, where A_2 is found in Table 11.2-1. Thus, the estimates of $\mu \pm 3\sigma/\sqrt{n}$, namely, $\overline{\overline{x}} \pm A_2\,\overline{R}$, can be used as the UCL and LCL of an $\overline{x}$ chart.

In addition, $\sqrt{n}A_2\,\overline{R}$ is an estimate of 3σ; so, with an underlying distribution that is close to a normal one, we find that almost all observations are within the limits $\overline{\overline{x}} \pm \sqrt{n}A_2\,\overline{R}$.

Moreover, an R chart can be constructed with centerline $\overline{R}$ and control limits equal to $D_3\overline{R}$ and $D_4\overline{R}$, where D_3 and D_4 are given in Table 11.2-1 and were determined so that almost all R values should be between the control limits if there is no change in the underlying distribution. Thus, a value of R falling outside those limits would indicate a change in the spread of the underlying distribution, and some corrective action should be considered.

The use of R, rather than s, is illustrated in the next example.

EXAMPLE 11.2-2 Using the data in Example 11.2-1, we compute UCL and LCL for an $\overline{x}$ chart. We use $\overline{\overline{x}} \pm A_2\,\overline{R}$ as follows:

$$\text{UCL} = \overline{\overline{x}} + A_2\,\overline{R} = 1.174 + 0.58(0.49) = 1.458$$

and

$$\text{LCL} = \overline{\overline{x}} - A_2\,\overline{R} = 1.174 - 0.58(0.49) = 0.890.$$

Note that these values are very close to the limits that we found for the $\bar{x}$ chart in Figure 11.2-2 using $\bar{\bar{x}} \pm A_3\bar{s}$. In addition, almost all of the observations should lie within the limits $\bar{\bar{x}} + \sqrt{n}A_2\bar{R}$, which are

$$\text{UCL} = 1.174 + \sqrt{5}(0.58)(0.49) = 1.809$$

and

$$\text{LCL} = 1.174 - \sqrt{5}(0.58)(0.49) = 0.539.$$

Note that these are almost the same as the limits found in Example 11.2-1 and plotted in Figure 11.2-3.

An R chart can be constructed with centerline $\bar{R} = 0.49$ and control limits given by

$$\text{UCL} = D_4\bar{R} = 2.11(0.49) = 1.034$$

and

$$\text{LCL} = D_3\bar{R} = 0(0.49) = 0.$$

Figure 11.2-3 illustrates this control chart for the range, and we see that its pattern is similar to that of the s chart in Figure 11.2-2. ■

There are two other Shewhart control charts: the p and c charts. The central limit theorem, which provided a justification for the three-sigma limits in the $\bar{x}$ chart, also justifies the control limits in the p chart. Suppose the number of defectives among n items that are selected randomly—say, D—has a binomial distribution $b(n,p)$. Then the limits $p \pm 3\sqrt{p(1-p)/n}$ should include almost all of the D/n values. However, p must be approximated by observing k values of D—say, $D_1, D_2, \ldots, D_k$—and computing what is called $\bar{p}$ in the statistical quality control literature, namely,

$$\bar{p} = \frac{D_1 + D_2 + \cdots + D_k}{kn}.$$

Thus, the LCL and UCL for the fraction defective, D/n, are respectively given by

$$\text{LCL} = \bar{p} - 3\sqrt{\bar{p}(1-\bar{p})/n}$$

and

$$\text{UCL} = \bar{p} + 3\sqrt{\bar{p}(1-\bar{p})/n}.$$

If the process is in control, almost all D/n values are between LCL and UCL. Still, this may not be satisfactory and improvements might be needed to decrease $\bar{p}$. If it is satisfactory, however, let the process continue under these common causes of variation until a point, D/n, outside the control limits would indicate that some special cause has changed the variation. (Incidentally, if D/n is below the LCL, this might very well indicate that some type of change for the better has been made, and we want to find out why. In general, outlying statistics can often suggest that good (as well as bad) breakthroughs have been made.)

The next example gives the results of a simple experiment that you can easily duplicate.

EXAMPLE 11.2-3 Let D_i equal the number of yellow candies in a 1.69-ounce bag. Because the number of pieces of candy varies slightly from bag to bag, we shall use an average value for n when we construct the control limits. Table 11.2-3 lists, for 20 packages, the number

TABLE 11.2-3: Data on Yellow Candies

Package	n_i	D_i	D_i/n_i	Package	n_i	D_i	D_i/n_i
1	56	8	0.14	11	57	10	0.18
2	55	13	0.24	12	59	8	0.14
3	58	12	0.21	13	54	10	0.19
4	56	13	0.23	14	55	11	0.20
5	57	14	0.25	15	56	12	0.21
6	54	5	0.09	16	57	11	0.19
7	56	14	0.25	17	54	6	0.11
8	57	15	0.26	18	58	7	0.12
9	54	11	0.20	19	58	12	0.21
10	55	13	0.24	20	58	14	0.24

of pieces of candy in the package, the number of yellow ones, and the proportion of yellow ones.

For these data,

$$\sum_{i=1}^{20} n_i = 1124 \qquad \text{and} \qquad \sum_{i=1}^{20} D_i = 219.$$

It follows that

$$\overline{p} = \frac{219}{1124} = 0.195 \qquad \text{and} \qquad \overline{n} = \frac{1124}{20} \approx 56.$$

Thus, the LCL and UCL are respectively given by

$$\text{LCL} = \overline{p} - 3\sqrt{\overline{p}(1-\overline{p})/56} = 0.195 - 3\sqrt{0.195(0.805)/56} = 0.036$$

and

$$\text{UCL} = \overline{p} + 3\sqrt{\overline{p}(1-\overline{p})/56} = 0.195 + 3\sqrt{0.195(0.805)/56} = 0.354.$$

The control chart for p is depicted in Figure 11.2-4 on the next page. (For your information the "true" value for p is 0.20.) ■

Consider the following explanation of the c chart: Suppose the number of flaws, say, C, on some product has a Poisson distribution with parameter λ. If λ is sufficiently large, as in Example 5.7-5, we consider approximating the discrete Poisson distribution with the continuous $N(\lambda, \lambda)$ distribution. Thus, the interval from $\lambda - 3\sqrt{\lambda}$ to $\lambda + 3\sqrt{\lambda}$ contains virtually all of the C values. Since λ is unknown, however, it must be approximated by $\overline{c}$, the average of the k values, $c_1, c_2, \ldots, c_k$. Hence, the two control limits for C are computed as

$$\text{LCL} = \overline{c} - 3\sqrt{\overline{c}} \qquad \text{and} \qquad \text{UCL} = \overline{c} + 3\sqrt{\overline{c}}.$$

The remarks made about the $\overline{x}$ and $\overline{p}$ charts apply to the c chart as well, but we must remember that each c value is the number of flaws on one manufactured item, not an average $\overline{x}$ or a fraction defective D/n.

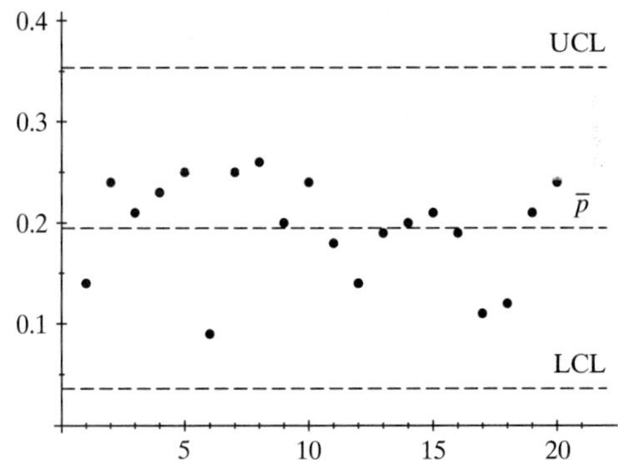

FIGURE 11.2-4: The p chart

STATISTICAL COMMENTS As with control charts, in observing time-sequence plots, do not read too much into a short sequence of points. For example, after a pep talk by the coach of a women's golf team, three successive decreasing scores (remember, in golf, the lower the score, the better it is) might indicate that the coach had some influence. But even if the process has not changed, the probability of three decreasing scores (ruling out ties) is 1/6, since there are $3! = 6$ equally likely ways of arranging three points. Often, businesspeople are worse offenders because they might think that two increasing sales points indicate improvement. We know that with no change in the system, the probability of that is 1/2. Now, maybe 4 points that successively increase after an intervention would be cause for claiming improvement, because the probability of such an event is $1/4! = 1/24$ if no change has actually been made. This probability is small enough to justify a celebration.

EXERCISES

11.2-1. It is important to control the viscosity of liquid dishwasher soap so that it flows out of the container but does not run out too rapidly. Thus, samples are taken randomly throughout the day and the viscosity is measured. Use the following 20 sets of five observations for this exercise:

Observations					$\bar{x}$	s	R
158	147	158	159	169	158.20	7.79	22
151	166	151	143	169	156.00	11.05	26
153	174	151	164	185	165.40	14.33	34
168	140	180	176	154	163.60	16.52	40
160	187	145	164	158	162.80	15.29	42
169	153	149	144	157	154.40	9.48	25
156	183	157	140	162	159.60	15.47	43
158	160	180	154	160	162.40	10.14	26
164	168	154	158	164	161.60	5.55	14
159	153	170	158	170	162.00	7.65	17
150	161	169	166	154	160.00	7.97	19
157	138	155	134	165	149.80	13.22	31
161	172	156	145	153	157.40	10.01	27

Observations					$\bar{x}$	s	R
143	152	152	156	163	153.20	7.26	20
179	157	135	172	143	157.20	18.63	44
154	165	145	152	145	152.20	8.23	20
171	189	144	154	147	161.00	18.83	45
187	147	159	167	151	162.20	15.85	40
153	168	148	188	152	161.80	16.50	40
165	155	140	157	176	158.60	13.28	36

(a) Calculate the values of $\bar{\bar{x}}$, $\bar{s}$, and $\overline{R}$.
(b) Use the values of A_3 and $\bar{s}$ to construct an $\bar{x}$ chart.
(c) Construct an s chart.
(d) Use the values of A_2 and $\overline{R}$ to construct an $\bar{x}$ chart.
(e) Construct an R chart.
(f) Do the charts indicate that viscosity is in statistical control?

11.2-2. It is necessary to control the percentage of solids in a product, so samples are taken randomly throughout the day and the percentage of solids is measured. Use the following 20 sets of five observations for this exercise:

Observations					$\bar{x}$	s	R
69.8	71.3	65.6	66.3	70.1	68.62	2.51	5.7
71.9	69.6	71.9	71.1	71.7	71.24	0.97	2.3
71.9	69.8	66.8	68.3	64.4	68.24	2.86	7.5
64.2	65.1	63.7	66.2	61.9	64.22	1.61	4.3
66.1	62.9	66.9	67.3	63.3	65.30	2.06	4.4
63.4	67.2	67.4	65.5	66.2	65.94	1.61	4.0
67.5	67.3	66.9	66.5	65.5	66.74	0.79	2.0
63.9	64.6	62.3	66.2	67.2	64.84	1.92	4.9
66.0	69.8	69.7	71.0	69.8	69.26	1.90	5.0
66.0	70.3	65.5	67.0	66.8	67.12	1.88	4.8
67.6	68.6	66.5	66.2	70.4	67.86	1.71	4.2
68.1	64.3	65.2	68.0	65.1	66.14	1.78	3.8
64.5	66.6	65.2	69.3	62.0	65.52	2.69	7.3
67.1	68.3	64.0	64.9	68.2	66.50	1.96	4.3
67.1	63.8	71.4	67.5	63.7	66.70	3.17	7.7
60.7	63.5	62.9	67.0	69.6	64.74	3.53	8.9
71.0	68.6	68.1	67.4	71.7	69.36	1.88	4.3
69.5	61.5	63.7	66.3	68.6	65.92	3.34	8.0
66.7	75.2	79.0	75.3	79.2	75.08	5.07	12.5
77.3	67.2	69.3	67.9	65.6	69.46	4.58	11.7

(a) Calculate the values of $\bar{\bar{x}}$, $\bar{s}$, and $\overline{R}$.
(b) Use the values of A_3 and $\bar{s}$ to construct an $\bar{x}$ chart.
(c) Construct an s chart.
(d) Use the values of A_2 and $\overline{R}$ to construct an $\bar{x}$ chart.
(e) Construct an R chart.
(f) Do the charts indicate that the percentage of solids in this product is in statistical control?

11.2-3. It is important to control the net weight of a packaged item; thus, items are selected randomly throughout the day from the production line and their weights are recorded. Use the following 20 sets of five weights (in grams) for this exercise (note that a weight recorded here is the actual weight minus 330):

Observations					$\bar{x}$	s	R
7.97	8.10	7.73	8.26	7.30	7.872	0.3740	0.96
8.11	7.26	7.99	7.88	8.88	8.024	0.5800	1.62
7.60	8.23	8.07	8.51	8.05	8.092	0.3309	0.91
8.44	4.35	4.33	4.48	3.89	5.098	1.8815	4.55
5.11	4.05	5.62	4.13	5.01	4.784	0.6750	1.57
4.79	5.25	5.19	5.23	3.97	4.886	0.5458	1.28
4.47	4.58	5.35	5.86	5.61	5.174	0.6205	1.39
5.82	4.51	5.38	5.01	5.54	5.252	0.5077	1.31
5.06	4.98	4.13	4.58	4.35	4.620	0.3993	0.93
4.74	3.77	5.05	4.03	4.29	4.376	0.5199	1.28
4.05	3.71	4.73	3.51	4.76	4.152	0.5748	1.25
3.94	5.72	5.07	5.09	4.61	4.886	0.6599	1.78
4.63	3.79	4.69	5.13	4.66	4.580	0.4867	1.34
4.30	4.07	4.39	4.63	4.47	4.372	0.2079	0.56
4.05	4.14	4.01	3.95	4.05	4.040	0.0693	0.19
4.20	4.50	5.32	4.42	5.24	4.736	0.5094	1.12
4.54	5.23	4.32	4.66	3.86	4.522	0.4999	1.37
5.02	4.10	5.08	4.94	5.18	4.864	0.4360	1.08
4.80	4.73	4.82	4.69	4.27	4.662	0.2253	0.55
4.55	4.76	4.45	4.85	4.02	4.526	0.3249	0.83

(a) Calculate the values of $\bar{\bar{x}}$, $\bar{s}$, and $\overline{R}$.
(b) Use the values of A_3 and $\bar{s}$ to construct an $\bar{x}$ chart.
(c) Construct an s chart.
(d) Use the values of A_2 and $\overline{R}$ to construct an $\bar{x}$ chart.
(e) Construct an R chart.
(f) Do the charts indicate that these fill weights are in statistical control?

11.2-4. The following data give fill weights (in grams) of "4-ounce bags" of candy as packed by a vertical form, fill, and seal machine:

118.8	116.6	116.2	113.8	116.9	118.1	116.2	115.6	113.5	119.2
115.2	117.0	113.6	115.1	113.5	117.0	113.6	115.5	113.5	117.0
119.0	117.5	119.2	118.1	121.2	117.2	113.5	119.7	118.4	116.6
119.0	113.6	118.8	118.1	117.7	116.0	117.1	119.1	116.8	118.7
115.9	116.8	118.7	115.9	116.8	117.2	115.5	120.0	117.6	117.8
117.0	116.2	119.9	118.9	118.2	118.8	118.9	116.5	116.8	116.6
119.3	116.2	116.4	114.5	114.8	121.1	118.3	113.6	116.7	118.0
118.3	117.3	115.2	114.6	114.2	117.2	115.8	113.6	121.6	120.8
117.2	117.0	115.4	118.2	119.4	117.5	113.5	119.1	116.3	118.1
119.7	118.5	119.6	119.2	116.7	117.3	115.6	115.0	117.5	114.1
118.4	118.3	117.4	117.2	116.3	116.5	116.7	117.8	118.8	118.0
115.4	113.5	118.2	116.5	117.4	113.6	113.5	119.0	116.7	117.0
117.5	117.9	117.2	118.7	117.6	118.2	120.5	116.4	114.9	116.8

116.7	116.5	117.8	116.4	116.9	118.4	116.8	120.8	118.2	119.3
118.9	118.0	120.1	114.9	119.5	119.0	115.5	115.8	115.8	115.4
120.8	118.3	115.9	117.7	114.8	116.6	118.1	114.0	113.4	113.4
116.0	121.8	119.3	117.7	118.3	118.4	116.8	118.0	117.8	116.1
119.1	115.9	118.8	117.9	118.5					

(a) Taking the data in consecutive sets of five (row by row; 118.8, 116.6, 116.2, 113.8, 116.9 is the first set), construct $\bar{x}$, R and $\bar{x}$, s charts.

(b) Describe what these charts show. Is the machine performing satisfactorily?

11.2-5. To give some indication of how the values in Table 11.2-1 are calculated, values of A_3 are found in this exercise. Let $X_1, X_2, \ldots, X_n$ be a random sample of size n from the normal distribution $N(\mu, \sigma^2)$. Let S^2 equal the sample variance of this random sample.

(a) Use the fact that $Y = (n-1)S^2/\sigma^2$ has a distribution that is $\chi^2(n-1)$ to show that $E[S^2] = \sigma^2$.

(b) Using the $\chi^2(n-1)$ p.d.f., find the value of $E(\sqrt{Y})$.

(c) Show that

$$E\left[\frac{\sqrt{n-1}\,\Gamma\left(\frac{n-1}{2}\right)}{\sqrt{2}\,\Gamma\left(\frac{n}{2}\right)}\,S\right] = \sigma.$$

(d) Verify that

$$\frac{3}{\sqrt{n}}\left[\frac{\sqrt{n-1}\,\Gamma\left(\frac{n-1}{2}\right)}{\sqrt{2}\,\Gamma\left(\frac{n}{2}\right)}\right] = A_3,$$

found in Table 11.2-1 for $n = 5$ and $n = 6$. Thus, $A_3\bar{s}$ approximates $3\sigma/\sqrt{n}$.

11.2-6. A company has been producing bolts that are about $\bar{p} = 0.02$ defective, and this is satisfactory. To monitor the quality of the process, 100 bolts are selected at random each hour and the number of defective bolts counted. With $\bar{p} = 0.02$, compute the UCL and LCL of the $\bar{p}$ chart. Then suppose that, over the next 24 hours, the following numbers of defective bolts are observed:

4 1 1 0 5 2 1 3 4 3 1 0
0 4 1 1 6 2 0 0 2 8 7 5

Would any action have been required during this time?

11.2-7. In the past, $n = 50$ fuses are tested each hour and $\bar{p} = 0.03$ have been found defective. Calculate the UCL and LCL. After a production error, say the true p shifts to $p = 0.05$.

(a) What is the probability that the next observation exceeds the UCL?

(b) What is the probability that at least one of the next five observations exceeds the UCL? HINT: Assume independence and compute the probability that none of the next five observations exceeds the UCL.

11.2-8. In a woolen mill, 100-yard pieces are inspected. In the last 20 observations, the following numbers of flaws were found:

2 4 0 1 0 3 4 1 1 2 4 0 0 1 0 3 2 3 5 0

(a) Compute the control limits of the c chart and draw this control chart.

(b) Is the process in statistical control?

11.2-9. Suppose we find that the number of blemishes in 50-foot tin strips averages about $\bar{c} = 1.4$. Calculate the control limits. Say the process has gone out of control and this average has increased to 3.

(a) What is the probability that the next observation will exceed the UCL?

(b) What is the probability that at least 1 of the next 10 observations will exceed the UCL?

11.2-10. Snee (see references) has measured the thickness of the "ears" of paint cans. (The "ear" of a paint can is the tab that secures the lid of the can.) At periodic intervals, samples of five paint cans are taken from a hopper that collects the production from two machines, and the thickness of each ear is measured. The results (in inches × 1000) of 30 such samples are as follows:

Observations	$\bar{x}$	s	R
29 36 39 34 34	34.4	3.64692	10
29 29 28 32 31	29.8	1.64317	4
34 34 39 38 37	36.4	2.30217	5
35 37 33 38 41	36.8	3.03315	8
30 29 31 38 29	31.4	3.78153	9

Observations	$\bar{x}$	s	R
34 31 37 39 36	35.4	3.04959	8
30 35 33 40 36	34.8	3.70135	10
28 28 31 34 30	30.2	2.48998	6
32 36 38 38 35	35.8	2.48998	6
35 30 37 35 31	33.6	2.96648	7
35 30 35 38 35	34.6	2.88097	8
38 34 35 35 31	34.6	2.50998	7
34 35 33 30 34	33.2	1.92354	5
40 35 34 33 35	35.4	2.70185	7
34 35 38 35 30	34.4	2.88097	8
35 30 35 29 37	33.2	3.49285	8
40 31 38 35 31	35.0	4.06202	9
35 36 30 33 32	33.2	2.38747	6
35 34 35 30 36	34.0	2.34521	6
35 35 31 38 36	35.0	2.54951	7
32 36 36 32 36	34.4	2.19089	4
36 37 32 34 34	34.6	1.94936	5
29 34 33 37 35	33.6	2.96648	8
36 36 35 37 37	36.2	0.83666	2
36 30 35 33 31	33.0	2.54951	6
35 30 29 38 35	33.4	3.78153	9
35 36 30 34 36	34.2	2.48998	6
35 30 36 29 35	33.0	3.24037	7
38 36 35 31 31	34.2	3.11448	7
30 34 40 28 30	32.4	4.77493	12

(a) Calculate the values of $\bar{\bar{x}}$, $\bar{s}$, and $\overline{R}$.
(b) Use the values of A_3 and $\bar{s}$ to construct an $\bar{x}$ chart.
(c) Construct an s chart.
(d) Use the values of A_2 and $\overline{R}$ to construct an $\bar{x}$ chart.
(e) Construct an R chart.
(f) Do the charts indicate that these fill weights are in statistical control?

11.2-11. Ledolter and Hogg (see references) report that, in the production of stainless steel pipes, the number of defects per 100 feet should be controlled. From 15 randomly selected pipes of length 100 feet, the following data on the number of defects were observed:

6 10 8 1 7 9 7 4 5 10 3 4 9 8 5

(a) Compute the control limits of the c chart and draw this control chart.
(b) Is the process in statistical control?

11.3 GENERAL FACTORIAL AND 2^k FACTORIAL DESIGNS

In Section 7.6, we studied two-factor experiments in which the A factor is performed at a levels and the B factor has b levels. Without replications, we need ab level combinations, and with c replications with each of these combinations, we need a total of abc experiments.

Let us consider a situation with three factors—say, A, B, and C, with a, b, and c levels, respectively. Here there are a total of abc level combinations, and if, at each of these combinations, we have d replications, there is a need for $abcd$ experiments. Once these experiments are run, in some random order, and the data collected, there are computer programs available to calculate the entries in the ANOVA table, as in Table 11.3-1.

The main effects (A, B, and C) and the two-factor interactions (AB, AC, and BC) have the same interpretations as in the two-factor ANOVA. The three-factor interaction represents that part of the model for the means μ_{ijh}; $i = 1,2,\ldots,a$; $j = 1,2,\ldots,b$; $h = 1,2,\ldots,c$ that cannot be explained by a model including only the main effects and two-factor interactions. In particular, if, for each fixed h, the "plane" created by μ_{ijh} is "parallel" to the "plane" created by every other fixed h, then the three-factor interaction is equal to zero. Usually, higher order interactions tend to be small.

TABLE 11.3-1: ANOVA Table

Source	SS	d.f.	MS	F
A	SS(A)	$a - 1$	MS(A)	MS(A)/MS(E)
B	SS(B)	$b - 1$	MS(B)	MS(B)/MS(E)
C	SS(C)	$c - 1$	MS(C)	MS(C)/MS(E)
AB	SS(AB)	$(a - 1)(b - 1)$	MS(AB)	MS(AB)/MS(E)
AC	SS(AC)	$(a - 1)(c - 1)$	MS(AC)	MS(AC)/MS(E)
BC	SS(BC)	$(b - 1)(c - 1)$	MS(BC)	MS(BC)/MS(E)
ABC	SS(ABC)	$(a - 1)(b - 1)(c - 1)$	MS(ABC)	MS(ABC)/MS(E)
Error	SS(E)	$abc(d - 1)$	MS(E)	
Total	SS(TO)	$abcd - 1$		

In the testing sequence, we test the three-factor interaction first by checking to see whether or not

$$\text{MS(ABC)}/\text{MS(E)} \geq F_\alpha[(a - 1)(b - 1)(c - 1), abc(d - 1)].$$

If this inequality holds, the ABC interaction is significant at the α level. We would then not continue testing the two-factor interactions and the main effects with those F values, but analyze the data otherwise. For example, for each fixed h, we could look at a two-factor ANOVA for factors A and B. Of course, if the inequality does not hold, we next check the two-factor interactions with the appropriate F values. If these are not significant, we check the main effects, A, B, and C.

Factorial analyses with three or more factors require many experiments, particularly if each factor has several levels. Often, in the health, social, and physical sciences experimenters want to consider several factors (maybe as many as 10, 20, or even hundreds), and they cannot afford to run that many experiments. This is particularly true with preliminary or screening investigations, in which they want to detect the factors that seem most important. In these cases, they often consider factorial experiments such that each of k factors is run at just two levels, frequently without replication. We consider only this situation, although the reader should recognize that it has many variations. In particular, there are methods for investigating only *fractions of these* 2^k *designs*. The reader interested in more information should refer to a good book on the design of experiments, such as that by Box, Hunter, and Hunter (see references). Many statisticians in industry believe that these statistical methods are the most useful in improving product and process designs. Hence, this is clearly an extremely important topic, as many industries are greatly concerned about the quality of their products.

In factorial experiments in which each of the k factors is considered at only two levels, those levels are selected at some reasonable low and high values. That is, with the help of someone in the field, the typical range of each factor is considered. For instance, if we are considering baking temperatures in the range from 300° to 375°, a representative low is selected—say, 320°—and a representative high is selected—say, 355°. There is no formula for these selections, and someone familiar with the experiment would help make them. Often, it happens that only two different types of a material (e.g., fabric) are considered, and one is called low and the other high.

Thus, we select a low and a high for each factor and code them as -1 and $+1$ or, more simply, $-$ and $+$, respectively. We give three 2^k designs, for $k = 2, 3,$ and 4, in standard order in Tables 11.3-2, 11.3-3, and 11.3-4, respectively. From these three

TABLE 11.3-2: 2^2 Design

Run	2^2 Design A	B	Observation
1	−	−	X_1
2	+	−	X_2
3	−	+	X_3
4	+	+	X_4

TABLE 11.3-3: 2^3 Design

Run	2^3 Design A	B	C	Observation
1	−	−	−	X_1
2	+	−	−	X_2
3	−	+	−	X_3
4	+	+	−	X_4
5	−	−	+	X_5
6	+	−	+	X_6
7	−	+	+	X_7
8	+	+	+	X_8

tables, we can easily note what is meant by standard order. The A column starts with a minus sign and then the sign alternates. The B column begins with two minus signs and then the signs alternate in blocks of two. The C column has 4 minus signs and then 4 plus signs and so on. The D column starts with 8 minus signs and then 8 plus signs. It is easy to extend this idea to 2^k designs, where $k \geq 5$. To illustrate, under the E column in a 2^5 design, we have 16 minus signs followed by 16 plus signs, which together account for the 32 experiments.

To be absolutely certain what these runs mean, consider run number 12 in Table 11.3-4: A is set at its high level, B at its high, C at its low, and D at its high level. The value X_{12} is the random observation resulting from this one combination of these four settings. It must be emphasized that the runs are not necessarily performed in the order $1, 2, 3, \ldots, 2^k$; in fact, they should be performed in a random order if at all possible. That is, in a 2^3 design, we might perform the experiment in the order 3, 2, 8, 6, 5, 1, 4, 7 if this, in fact, was a random selection of a permutation of the first eight positive integers.

Once all 2^k experiments have been run, it is possible to consider the total sum of squares

$$\sum_{i=1}^{2^k} (X_i - \overline{X})^2$$

and decompose it very easily into $2^k - 1$ parts, which represent the respective measurements (estimators) of the k main effects, $\binom{k}{2}$ two-factor interactions, $\binom{k}{3}$ three-factor interactions, and so on, until we have the one k-factor interaction. We

TABLE 11.3-4: 2^4 Design

	2^4 Design				
Run	A	B	C	D	Observation
1	−	−	−	−	X_1
2	+	−	−	−	X_2
3	−	+	−	−	X_3
4	+	+	−	−	X_4
5	−	−	+	−	X_5
6	+	−	+	−	X_6
7	−	+	+	−	X_7
8	+	+	+	−	X_8
9	−	−	−	+	X_9
10	+	−	−	+	X_{10}
11	−	+	−	+	X_{11}
12	+	+	−	+	X_{12}
13	−	−	+	+	X_{13}
14	+	−	+	+	X_{14}
15	−	+	+	+	X_{15}
16	+	+	+	+	X_{16}

TABLE 11.3-5: 2^3 Design Decomposition

	2^3 Design							
Run	A	B	C	AB	AC	BC	ABC	Observation
1	−	−	−	+	+	+	−	X_1
2	+	−	−	−	−	+	+	X_2
3	−	+	−	−	+	−	+	X_3
4	+	+	−	+	−	−	−	X_4
5	−	−	+	+	−	−	+	X_5
6	+	−	+	−	+	−	−	X_6
7	−	+	+	−	−	+	−	X_7
8	+	+	+	+	+	+	+	X_8

illustrate this decomposition with the 2^3 design in Table 11.3-5. Note that column AB is found by formally multiplying the elements of column A by the corresponding ones in B. Likewise, AC is found by multiplying the elements of column A by the corresponding ones in column C, and so on, until column ABC is the product of the corresponding elements of columns A, B, and C. Next, we construct seven linear forms, using these seven columns of signs with the corresponding observations. The resulting measures (estimates) of the main effects (A, B, C), the two-factor interactions (AB, AC, BC), and the three-factor interaction (ABC) are then found by dividing the linear forms by $2^k = 2^3 = 8$. (Some statisticians divide by $2^{k-1} = 2^{3-1} = 4$.) These measures are denoted by

$$
\begin{aligned}
[\mathrm{A}] &= (-X_1 + X_2 - X_3 + X_4 - X_5 + X_6 - X_7 + X_8)/8,\\
[\mathrm{B}] &= (-X_1 - X_2 + X_3 + X_4 - X_5 - X_6 + X_7 + X_8)/8,\\
[\mathrm{C}] &= (-X_1 - X_2 - X_3 - X_4 + X_5 + X_6 + X_7 + X_8)/8,\\
[\mathrm{AB}] &= (+X_1 - X_2 - X_3 + X_4 + X_5 - X_6 - X_7 + X_8)/8,\\
[\mathrm{AC}] &= (+X_1 - X_2 + X_3 - X_4 - X_5 + X_6 - X_7 + X_8)/8,\\
[\mathrm{BC}] &= (+X_1 + X_2 - X_3 - X_4 - X_5 - X_6 + X_7 + X_8)/8,\\
[\mathrm{ABC}] &= (-X_1 + X_2 + X_3 - X_4 + X_5 - X_6 - X_7 + X_8)/8.
\end{aligned}
$$

With assumptions of normality, mutual independence, and common variance σ^2, under the overall null hypothesis of the equality of all the means, each of these measures has a normal distribution with mean zero and variance $\sigma^2/8$ (in general, $\sigma^2/2^k$). This implies that the square of each measure divided by $\sigma^2/8$ is $\chi^2(1)$. Moreover, it can be shown (see Exercise 11.3-2) that

$$
\begin{aligned}
&\sum_{i=1}^{8} (X_i - \overline{X})^2\\
&\quad = 8([\mathrm{A}]^2 + [\mathrm{B}]^2 + [\mathrm{C}]^2 + [\mathrm{AB}]^2 + [\mathrm{AC}]^2 + [\mathrm{BC}]^2 + [\mathrm{ABC}]^2).
\end{aligned}
$$

So, by Theorem 7.5-1, the terms on the right-hand side, divided by σ^2, are mutually independent random variables, each being $\chi^2(1)$. While it requires a little more theory, it follows that the linear forms [A], [B], [C], [AB], [AC], [BC], and [ABC] are mutually independent $N(0, \sigma^2/8)$ random variables.

Since we have assumed that we have not run any replications, how can we obtain an estimate of σ^2 to see if any of the main effects or interactions are significant? To help us, we fall back on the use of a q–q plot because, under the overall null hypothesis, those seven measures are mutually independently, normally distributed variables with the same mean and variance. Thus, a q–q plot of the normal percentiles against the corresponding ordered values of the measures should be about on a straight line if, in fact, the null hypothesis is true. If one of these points is "out of line," we might believe that the overall null hypothesis is not true and that the effect associated with the factor represented by that point is significant. It is possible that two or three points might be out of line; then all corresponding effects (main or interaction) should be investigated. Clearly, this is not a formal test, but it has been extremely successful in practice.

As an illustration, we use the data from an experiment designed to evaluate the effects of laundering on a certain fire-retardant treatment for fabrics. These data, somewhat modified, were taken from *Experimental Statistics, National Bureau of Standards Handbook 91*, by Mary G. Natrella (Washington, DC: U.S. Government Printing Office, 1963). Factor A is the type of fabric (sateen or monk's cloth), factor B corresponds to two different fire-retardant treatments, and factor C describes the laundering conditions (no laundering, after one laundering). The observations are inches burned, measured on a standard-size fabric after a flame test. They are as follows, in standard order:

$$
\begin{aligned}
x_1 &= 41.0, & x_2 &= 30.5, & x_3 &= 47.5, & x_4 &= 27.0,\\
x_5 &= 39.5, & x_6 &= 26.5, & x_7 &= 48.0, & x_8 &= 27.5.
\end{aligned}
$$

Thus, the measures of the effects are

$$
\begin{aligned}
[A] &= (-41.0 + 30.5 - 47.5 + 27.0 - 39.5 + 26.5 - 48.0 + 27.5)/8 = -8.06,\\
[B] &= (-41.0 - 30.5 + 47.5 + 27.0 - 39.5 - 26.5 + 48.0 + 27.5)/8 = 1.56,\\
[C] &= (-41.0 - 30.5 - 47.5 - 27.0 + 39.5 + 26.5 + 48.0 + 27.5)/8 = 0.56,\\
[AB] &= (+41.0 - 30.5 - 47.5 + 27.0 + 39.5 - 26.5 - 48.0 + 27.5)/8 = -2.19,\\
[AC] &= (+41.0 - 30.5 + 47.5 - 27.0 - 39.5 + 26.5 - 48.0 + 27.5)/8 = -0.31,\\
[BC] &= (+41.0 + 30.5 - 47.5 - 27.0 - 39.5 - 26.5 + 48.0 + 27.5)/8 = 0.81,\\
[ABC] &= (-41.0 + 30.5 + 47.5 - 27.0 + 39.5 - 26.5 - 48.0 + 27.5)/8 = 0.31.
\end{aligned}
$$

In Table 11.3-6, we order these seven measures, determine their percentiles, and find the corresponding percentiles of the standard normal distribution.

TABLE 11.3-6: Seven Measures Ordered

Identity of Effect	Ordered Effect	Percentile	Percentile from $N(0,1)$
[A]	−8.06	12.5	−1.15
[AB]	−2.19	25.0	−0.67
[AC]	−0.31	37.5	−0.32
[ABC]	0.31	50.0	0.00
[C]	0.56	62.5	0.32
[BC]	0.81	75.0	0.67
[B]	1.56	87.5	1.15

The q–q plot is given in Figure 11.3-1. Each point has been identified with its effect. A straight line fits six of those points reasonably well, but the point associated with [A] = −8.06 is far from this straight line. Hence, the main effect of factor A (the type of fabric) seems to be significant. It is interesting to note that the laundering factor, C, does not seem to be a significant factor.

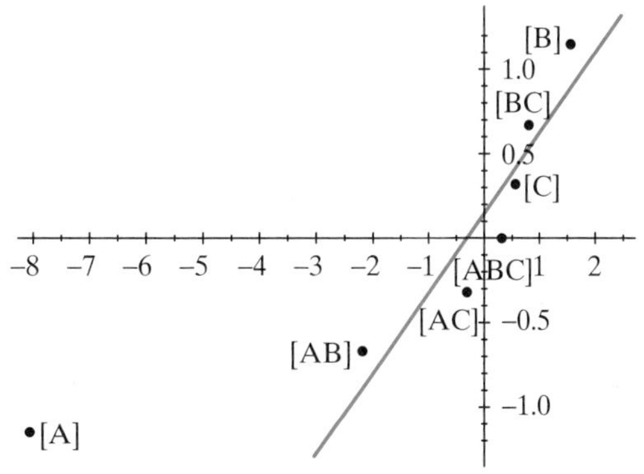

FIGURE 11.3-1: A q–q plot of normal percentiles versus estimated effects

EXERCISES

11.3-1. Write out a 2^2 design, displaying the A, B, and AB columns for the four runs.

(a) If X_1, X_2, X_3, and X_4 are the four observations for the respective runs in standard order, write out the three linear forms, [A], [B], and [AB], that measure the two main effects and the interaction. These linear forms should include the divisor $2^2 = 4$.

(b) Show that $\sum_{i=1}^{4}(X_i - \overline{X})^2 = 4([A]^2 + [B]^2 + [AB]^2)$.

(c) Under the null hypothesis that all the means are equal and with the usual assumptions (normality, mutual independence, and common variance), what can you say about the distributions of the expressions in (b) after each is divided by σ^2?

11.3-2. Show that, in a 2^3 design,

$$\sum_{i=1}^{8}(X_i - \overline{X})^2 = 8([A]^2 + [B]^2 + [C]^2 + [AB]^2 + [AC]^2 + [BC]^2 + [ABC]^2).$$

HINT: Since both the right and the left members of this equation are symmetric in the variables $X_1, X_2, \ldots, X_8$, it is necessary to show only that the corresponding coefficients of X_1X_i, $i = 1, 2, \ldots, 8$, are the same in each member of the equation. Of course, recall that $\overline{X} = (X_1 + X_2 + \cdots + X_8)/8$.

11.3-3. Show that the unbiased estimator of the variance σ^2 from a sample of size $n = 2$ is one-half of the square of the difference of the two observations. Thus, show that, if a 2^k design is replicated, say, with X_{i1} and X_{i2}, $i = 1, 2, \ldots, 2^k$, then the estimate of the common σ^2 is

$$\frac{1}{2^{k+1}}\sum_{i=1}^{2^k}(X_{i1} - X_{i2})^2 = \text{MS(E)}.$$

Under the usual assumptions, this equation implies that each of $2^k[A]^2/\text{MS(E)}$, $2^k[B]^2/\text{MS(E)}$, $2^k[AB]^2/\text{MS(E)}$, and so on has an $F(1, 2^k)$ distribution under the null hypothesis. This approach, of course, would provide tests for the significance of the various effects, including interactions.

11.3-4. Ledolter and Hogg (see references) note that percent yields from a certain chemical reaction for changing temperature (factor A), reaction time (factor B), and concentration (factor C) are $x_1 = 79.7$, $x_2 = 74.3$, $x_3 = 76.7$, $x_4 = 70.0$, $x_5 = 84.0$, $x_6 = 81.3$, $x_7 = 87.3$, and $x_8 = 73.7$, in standard order with a 2^3 design.

(a) Estimate the main effects, the three two-factor interactions, and the three-factor interaction.

(b) Construct an appropriate q–q plot to see if any of these effects seem to be significantly larger than the others.

11.3-5. Box, Hunter, and Hunter (see references) studied the effects of catalyst charge (10 pounds $= -1$, 20 pounds $= +1$), temperature ($220°\text{C} = -1$, $240°\text{C} = +1$), pressure (50 psi $= -1$, 80 psi $= +1$), and concentration ($10\% = -1$, $12\% = +1$) on percent conversion (X) of a certain chemical. The results of a 2^4 design, in standard order, are

$$\begin{array}{llllll} x_1 = 71, & x_2 = 61, & x_3 = 90, & x_4 = 82, & x_5 = 68, & x_6 = 61, \\ x_7 = 87, & x_8 = 80, & x_9 = 61, & x_{10} = 50, & x_{11} = 89, & \\ x_{12} = 83, & x_{13} = 59, & x_{14} = 51, & x_{15} = 85, & x_{16} = 78. & \end{array}$$

(a) Estimate the main effects and the two-, three-, and four-factor interactions.

(b) Construct an appropriate q–q plot and assess the significance of the various effects.

11.4 UNDERSTANDING VARIATION

Really understanding variation, which is the key element of probability and statistics, is extremely important in so many phases of life. Yet, as frequently happens in studying a textbook like this, we are so involved in the mathematics of probability, distributions, sampling distributions, and even descriptive statistics that we miss the real meanings of some of these concepts, particularly as far as the role they play in day-to-day activities.

To illustrate, variability explains what is commonly called the "sophomore jinx": Some freshmen (rookies) have great first years (above their averages), and then most of them do worse the second year. The same explanation can be applied to movies that have sequels; often the original was outstanding, but even with the same cast and same director, the sequel is usually worse than the original. This phenomenon is sometimes called *regression to the mean*.

We also note that, on the one hand, workers who do very well (above their averages) and who thus might be given some reward usually do worse during the next work period. On the other hand, those who have bad periods (below average) and are reprimanded frequently do better the next. Yet it is wrong to think that a policy of reprimand is better than that of a pat on the back. Both situations can be explained by understanding the worker's pattern of variation. If the employer really wants to improve the outcome of the process, he or she must consider ways of improving the *level* (average). The workers can sometimes make small adjustments, but they need road maps to make the major ones. Thus, it is really the responsibility of management to improve the process substantially. That is, management must realize that working harder with techniques that have failed will not improve the situation much. Changes must be made, and often data and the resulting statistical analysis can suggest changes for the better.

It is disturbing to see the following situation: Suppose that the manager has created a team (say, of 10) of outstanding workers, and it is time to give raises. The workers are ranked from 1 to 10. It is always true that 10 workers, no matter how good or how bad, will get the ranks $1, 2, 3, \ldots, 10$. Then say they get raises according to their ranks, which might have been determined simply by a random process for this particular period. That is, in the next period, their ranks might be entirely different. How does the small raise make the one with lowest rank feel if, in fact, all 10 are members of an outstanding team and there might be little or no difference among the persons ranked 1 and 10? Not good, and he or she is less likely to help the ones with higher ranks in a future period. That is, such a strategy does not promote teamwork. As a matter of fact, there is always this danger in any kind of reward, such as the "worker of the month." Others are not likely to help that person the next month, because they want to be the worker of the month and receive the corresponding bonus.

A better way of rewarding a good team would be to give them essentially the same raises. Clearly, a good manager will continuously monitor the team's performance and supply appropriate feedback to the workers. Of course, if one worker is consistently on the high side, then he or she should be considered for promotion or a substantial raise. By contrast, if a worker is on the low end most of the time, some help for this worker is in order: maybe additional training or even a transfer to a different department to which the worker's talents are more suitable. It is important not to demean the worker, because each of us needs to take pride in our accomplishments. If at all possible, firing the worker should be avoided, possibly by finding him or her some other suitable job in the company.

In one state, legislators appropriated enough money for 2% raises at a state university one year. The administrators thought that that percentage was not adequate, so they had the "brilliant" idea to give one-third of the faculty 6% raises and zero to the other two-thirds. Thus, in a department of 18, 6 received raises and 12 did not. Who ranked those 18? Was there much difference between the 6th and 7th? Or between the 5th and 10th for that matter? So the person who received a raise could have people close to him or her in the ranking who got nothing. The administrators' idea created a terrible morale problem. It certainly would have been better to give every faculty member an approximate 2% raise and blame it on the legislators. Of course, we must recognize differences among people, and accordingly, they must be treated differently, but certainly not on the basis of mere chance variation.

Many of the ideas in this area are those of W. Edwards Deming, an esteemed statistician who went to Japan after World War II and taught the Japanese how to make quality products. For his work there, he was awarded the Emperor's Medal, and the Japanese established the Deming Prize to be awarded each year to the company or individual contributing the most to quality improvement. One of the things Deming stressed was the need for "profound knowledge," and a major item in that concept is understanding variation and statistical theory.

In making quality products, you want to reduce variation as much as possible and move levels closer to their targets. Deming believed that barriers between departments, between management and workers, and among workers must be broken down to improve communication and the ability to work as a team. The lines of communication, all the way from suppliers to customers, must be open to help reduce variation and improve products and services. For example, he argued that a company should not buy only on price tag, but should have a few reliable suppliers (and possibly only one) for a single part because that will reduce variation. That is, many different suppliers would obviously increase variation. Moreover, he argued that you should become partners—friends if you like—with your suppliers. You learn to trust each other; that way, you can use methods like "just in time," in which your inventory can be kept reasonably small, to keep costs down.

If each of us thinks about these ideas, we might become obsessed by understanding variation, and that might make a big difference in our everyday lives. For example, once we have selected good suppliers, we continue to go to the same barber, the same service station, the same clothier, the same bank, and on and on. We like to buy items, even if a little more expensive, from places that will give us good service if something goes wrong. If this does not happen, then, of course, we must consider changing suppliers.

Clearly, listening to the customer can help improve the quality of our products and services. We can then meet—or even exceed—the expectations of our customers. We should continually try to improve by reducing variation and moving the process to a better level. Although the customer—as well as the supplier—must be part of the total team, more often management must continue to look for better ways to do things, ways that the customer never would have imagined. For example, in the early days of automobiles, not many owners would have thought of driving on pneumatic tires. Harvey Firestone did and, in this way, exceeded the expectations of those early customers.

Deming also preached constancy of purpose. If management's ideas tend to change too much, employees really do not know what to do and cannot do their best. That is, they get mixed up, thereby increasing variation. It is better for them to receive a constant signal from their employer—a signal that changes only if research dictates ways of improving.

More training and education for everyone associated with a company also decreases variation, by teaching how to make the product more uniform. Workers must know that they do not have to be afraid to make suggestions to improve the process. Often, being on a team will make it easier for workers to speak up without fear of reprisal.

Many of us remember playing a game called "telephone": One whispers a message to the next person, who whispers the message to the next, and so on. The message at the end is compared with the original message, and it is usually much different from the original. This is like trying to hit a target (say, at zero) with a random variable X_1 and then, starting with X_1 as the center and adding on another error X_2, and so on, creating the sum of the errors, $X_1 + X_2 + \cdots + X_n$, which has an ever-increasing variance with independent errors. Deming would say, "We are off to the Milky Way."

Yet we actually do this in business and industry by letting worker train worker. Once errors are introduced, they will stay there, and others will add on and on. Incidentally, we might say the same thing about too many layers of management. To decrease variation, wouldn't it be better to have a master instructor train each worker or have fewer layers of management?

Deming also noted that requiring quotas does not help the quality of a product or service. A manager or worker who has a quota of 100 items per day will often ship out 90 good and 10 bad items just to make the quota. Clearly, it would reduce variation and satisfy the customer better if only the 90 good ones were shipped.

All this discussion leads to the point that a final inspection of products often does not really improve quality. With such a procedure, you can only eliminate the bad items and send on the good ones. *Improvements* in the design of the products and manufacturing processes are needed. If these are done well, often with the help of statistical methods, that final inspection can be eliminated. That is, improvements should be made continuously in the manufacturing process, rather than trying to correct things at a final inspection by weeding out the bad items.

Once you recognize that there is variation in almost every process, you begin to think like a statistician. Often, you want to reduce that variation and center the variation that remains at the right level, because then "the doors will fit better." But while we want to reduce undesirable variation, we do not want to reduce *all* variation: Most of us do not want to eat, say, Chinese food every night, even though we enjoy it from time to time. A certain amount of variation is "the spice of life."

This desire to understand variation is the key to statistical thinking. As a matter of fact, many interested in quality improvement believe that statistical thinking recognizes that variation is present in everything we do. To provide better products and services we must strive to reduce undesirable variation as much as possible. They become obsessed with determining whether the variation is due to special or common causes and then correcting or controlling them, as the case may be.

In a sense, statistical thinking can affect everything about us, including our relationships with others. All of us have our "ups and downs," and we must seriously think about how to deal with others, recognizing this variation.

It was not until the 1980s that Americans paid much attention to Deming's ideas. At that time Deming started to give short courses on his quality philosophy, the highlight of which was his famous "red beads" experiment. He brought out a box with over 1000 beads, about 20 percent of which were red (defective), and a paddle that held exactly 50 beads. His audience did not know the exact proportion of defectives. He selected about six "willing workers" from the audience who had to dip the paddle into the box and remove a set of beads. Deming gave detailed instructions on how to do this, emphasizing the "correct" way to scooping with just the right amount of "shaking" and the appropriate "angle" of the paddle. Two inspectors would count the number of defectives (i.e., the number of reds) and report the results to a secretary. The first worker, say, Mike, happened to have 9 defectives. "We can do better than that," Deming would declare, and he advised a little more shaking before drawing out the paddle. The next worker, Joe, had 13 defectives. Deming would "give him hell" because, in his words, the paddle came out at the wrong angle. This would continue until Mary ended up with 6 defectives. "That's more like it," Deming would praise, and, pointing to the next worker, he would say, "Tim, you saw how she did this." Tim might end up with 12 defectives and would get the question, "Didn't you learn anything from Mary?" Occasionally, someone would get 16 defectives and be fired, although Deming was known to encourage managers to retrain, not fire, those who needed help. This process would continue for well over an hour, with Deming playing the role of the tough boss encouraging the participants to "work harder and reduce the number of defects."

The "red beads" experiment was a good and also very entertaining illustration, and it communicated a very important point. Members of the audience, as well as the willing participants, knew that the only way to reduce the number of defectives, on average, was to improve the process, and this meant removing a number of red beads from the box. It is the managers and the engineers who can facilitate improvements, usually by redesigning and changing the underlying processes. Workers cannot make major improvements to the system just by trying harder; if the system is bad, such good efforts will not help. Workers may have good ideas for improvements, but it is the "owner" of the process (the one responsible for the process and in charge of changes) who can affect improvements. Deming also realized that many valuable suggestions will not come to the surface if people are afraid to speak up and question the status quo. "Driving out fear" was another principle that Deming communicated to his audience.

It is the authors' opinion that quality improvement must begin with the individual who should create a personal vision, goals, and principles by which to live. Hopefully, one of those individuals is the chief of the organization, for then things go much smoother. Bob Galvin, who was the CEO of Motorola during the 1980s, believes that "quality improvement is a daily, personal, priority obligation," and his company made great improvements in the quality of its products during that period. Much of this progress was due to understanding variation and statistical methods. Even Motorola's program was called Six Sigma, in which *sigma* referred to the standard deviation, a name that is a delight to a statistician.

Although three-sigma limits have proved to be an effective guide, many companies are now considering six-sigma limits. The Six Sigma program has its statistical underpinnings in the following idea: There are specifications in manufacturing items that are usually set by the engineers—or possibly by customers. These specifications are usually given in terms of a target value and upper and lower specification limits—USL and LSL, respectively. The mean μ of the values resulting from the process is, hopefully, close to the target value. The "specs" are 6σ away from the target, where, as mentioned, σ is the standard deviation associated with the process. However, the mean μ is often dynamic, and Six Sigma companies try to keep it at least 4.5σ from the closest spec. If the values of the items are distributed normally and the nearest spec is 4.5σ from μ, there are only 3.4 defectives per million. This is the very worthwhile goal of the Six Sigma companies, and they use many of Deming's ideas, some of which are outlined earlier, in their attempts to achieve that goal.

While an understanding of quality improvement ideas and basic statistical methods, such as those in this chapter, is extremely important to the Six Sigma programs, possibly the major factor is the attitude of the CEOs and other important administrators. There were many total quality management programs in the 1980s, but they were not as successful as Six Sigma, for now each CEO is demanding "Show me the money!" That is, companies hire a Six Sigma expert to come in for four one-week periods, about one month apart, for a fee of about $15,000 per person. If the company has 20 participants, this cost is $300,000 plus the four weeks of time "lost" to the work process by each trainee. That is a great deal of money. However, each of these individuals (sometimes a pair) has a project associated with some process that has not been very efficient. They work on these projects, using statistical methods, during the "off weeks" and report to the Six Sigma expert during the training weeks to get advice. Often, these projects, if successful, will save millions of dollars for a company, so the expenses are well worth the benefits. As a matter of fact, if a participant's project saves the company at least \$1 million (possibly the required amount differs from company to company), then the participant earns a "six-sigma Black Belt." So the CEO does see the money saved, and thus the bottom line looks extremely good to him or her.

Each of us should use as much statistical thinking as we know to help us build trust with the persons with whom we deal directly or indirectly. Let us not do what those administrators of that university did when they did not understand the variability associated with ranking people. That action destroyed any trust that was there and created a mean-spirited competition among the members of that faculty. Why should anyone help others when their gain only hurts that individual? While statistical thinking cannot solve all problems, it most certainly can help in many situations. We hope you use what statistics you know to benefit you the rest of your life.

There is a huge demand for statistical scientists in many fields to make sense out of the increasing volumes of data that scientists discover every day. Statistics is needed to turn quality data into useful information upon which decisions can be made. The striking thing about any data set is that there is variation: simply put, not all of the data points lie within a pattern. It is the statistician's job to find that pattern and describe the variation about it. Done properly, this clearly helps the decision maker significantly.

One observation about variation should be noted before any major adjustments or decisions are made. Frequently, persons in charge jump at conclusions too quickly; that is, major decisions are often made after too few observations. For example, we know that if X_1, X_2, and X_3 are independent and identically distributed continuous-type observations, then

$$P(X_1 < X_2 < X_3) = \frac{1}{3!} = \frac{1}{6}.$$

Yet if this event occurred and these observations were taken on, say, sales and plotted in time sequence, the fact that the three points plotted were "going up" might suggest to management that "the company is on a roll." In some cases, only two increasing points might cause such a reaction. If there is no change in the system, two or three increasing points have respective probabilities of 1/2 and 1/6, and those probabilities do not warrant that sort of reaction. If, however, we observe four or five such points, with respective probabilities of 1/24 and 1/120, then an appropriate reaction is in order.

An interesting question to ask is why statisticians treat $1/20 = 0.05$ as the value at which the probability of an event is considered small and often suggests some type of action. Possibly it was because Ronald A. Fisher suggested that 1 out of 20 seemed small enough. Obviously, the value of 0.05 is not written in stone, but statisticians seem to look for differences of two or three standard deviations as a guide for action. Since many estimators have approximate normal distributions, such differences do have small probabilities.

For instance, suppose a candidate believes that he or she has at least 50% of the votes. Yet, in a poll of $n = 400$, only 160 favor that candidate; thus, the standardized value

$$\frac{160 - 400(1/2)}{\sqrt{400(1/2)(1/2)}} = -4$$

suggests that the candidate does not in fact have 50% of the votes. Depending upon the financial situation, the candidate must change his or her approach or possibly even consider dropping from the race. However, we note that this simple statistical analysis can be a guide in the decision process.

Although the reader has now studied enough statistics to appreciate the importance of understanding variation, there are many more useful statistical techniques to be studied if the reader is so inclined. For example, there are courses in regression and time series in which we learn how to predict future observations. Or a study of the design of experiments can help an investigator select the most efficient levels of the various factors. After all, if we have 10 factors and run each even at only two levels, we have created $2^{10} = 1024$ runs. Can we perform just a fraction of these runs without losing too much information? Additional study of multivariate analysis can lead to interesting problems in classification. Say a doctor takes several measurements on a patient and then classifies the patient's condition as one of many possible diseases. There are errors of misclassification, and statisticians can help reduce the probabilities of those errors. Doctors—and statisticians—can make mistakes, and second or third opinions should be requested if there is some doubt.

The computer has opened the door to a wide variety of new statistical techniques, and researchers, computer scientists, and statisticians are working together to reduce huge amounts of data into nuggets of quality information on the basis of which important decisions can be made. Statistics is an exciting field that finds many useful applications in the social, health, and physical sciences. The authors have found statistics to be a great profession; we hope a few of you find it that way, too. In any case, we hope that statistical thinking will make you more aware of the need of understanding variation, which can be a great influence on your daily life.

HISTORICAL COMMENTS Quality improvement made a substantial change in manufacturing beginning in the 1920s, with Walter A. Shewart's control charts. In fairness, it should be noted that the British started a similar program about the same time. Statistical quality control, as described in Section 11.2, really had a huge influence during World War II, with many universities giving short courses in the subject. These courses continued after the war, but the development of the importance of total quality improvement lagged behind. W. Edwards Deming complained that the Japanese used his quality ideas beginning in the 1950s, but Americans did not adopt them until 1980. That year NBC televised a program entitled "If Japan can, why can't we?" and Deming was the "star" of that broadcast. He related that the next day his phone "started ringing off the hook." Various companies requested that he spend one day with them to get them started on the right path. According to Deming, they all wanted "instant pudding," and he noted that he had asked the Japanese to give him five years to make the improvements he pioneered. Actually, using his philosophy, many of these companies did achieve substantial results in quality sooner than that. However it was after the NBC program that Deming started his famous four-day courses, and he taught his last one in December of 1993, about 10 days before his death at the age of 93.

Many of these quality efforts in the 1970s and 1980s used the name "Total Quality Management" or, later, "Continuous Process Improvements." However, it was Motorola's Six Sigma program, which started in the late 1980s and has continued for over 20 years since then, that has had the biggest impact. In addition to Motorola, GE and Allied, as well as a number of smaller companies, have used this system. In our opinion, Six Sigma is leading development in the quality improvement effort.

References

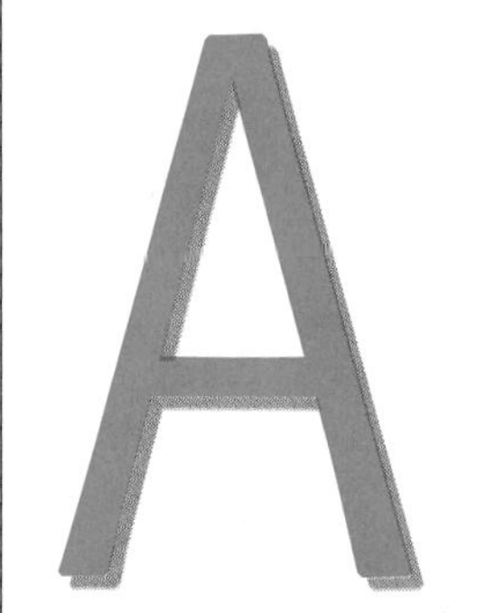

Aspin, A. A., "Tables for Use in Comparisons Whose Accuracy Involves Two Variances, Separately Estimated," *Biometrika*, **36** (1949), pp. 290–296.

Agaresti, A., and B.A. Coull, "Approximate is Better than 'Exact' for Interval Estimation of Binomial Proportions," *Amer. Statist.*, **52**, 2(1998), pp. 119–126.

Barnett, A., "How Numbers Can Trick You," *Technology Review*, 1994.

Basu, D., "On Statistics Independent of a Complete Sufficient Statistic," *Sankhya*, 15, 377 (1955).

Bernstein, P. L., *Against the Gods: The Remarkable Story of Risk*. New York: John Wiley & Sons, Inc., 1996.

Berry, D. A., *Statistics: A Bayesian Perspective*. Belmont, CA: Duxbury Press, An Imprint of Wadsworth Publishing Co., 1996.

Box, George E. P., J. Stuart Hunter, and William G. Hunter, *Statistics for Experimenters: Design, Innovation, and Discovery*, 2d ed., New York: John Wiley & Sons, Inc., 2005.

Box, G. E. P., and M. E. Muller, "A Note on the Generation of Random Normal Deviates," *Ann. Math. Statist.*, **29** (1958), p. 610.

Crisman, R., "Shortest Confidence Interval for the Standard Deviation of a Normal Distribution," *J. Undergrad. Math.*, **7**, 2 (1975), p. 57.

Douglas, Andrea, Courtney Fitzgerald, and Scott Mihalik, "Expected Areas of Randomly Generated Triangles of Fixed Perimeter," *The ΠME Journal*, Vol. 11, Num. 7, Fall, 2002, pp. 365–371.

Guenther, William C., "Shortest Confidence Intervals," *Amer. Statist.*, **23**, 1(1969), p. 22.

Hogg, R. V., "Testing the Equality of Means of Rectangular Populations," *Ann. Math. Statist.*, **24** (1953), p. 691.

Hogg, R. V., J. W. McKean, and A. T. Craig, *Introduction to Mathematical Statistics*, 6th ed. Upper Saddle River, NJ: Prentice Hall, 2005.

Hogg, R. V., and A. T. Craig, "On the Decomposition of Certain Chi-Square Variables," *Ann. Math. Statist.*, **29** (1958), p. 608.

Johnson, V. E., and J. H. Albert, *Ordinal Data Modeling*, New York: Springer-Verlag, 1999.

Karian, Z. A., and E. A. Tanis, *Probability & Statistics: Explorations with MAPLE*, 2d ed. Upper Saddle River, NJ: Prentice Hall, 1999.

Keating, Jerome P., and David W. Scott, "Ask Dr. STATS," *Stats, The Magazine for Students of Statistics*, **25**, Spring, 1999, pp. 16–22.

Kinney, J., "Mathematica As an Aid in Teaching Probability and Statistics," *Proceedings of the Statistical Computing Section*, (1998), American Statistical Association, pp. 25–32.

Latter, O. H., "The Cuckoo's Egg," *Biometrika*, 1: pp. 164–176, 1901.

Ledolter, J., and R. V. Hogg, *Applied Statistics for Engineers and Scientists*, 3d ed. Upper Saddle River, NJ: Prentice Hall, 2010.

Lurie, D., and H. O. Hartley, "Machine-Generation of Order Statistics for Monte Carlo Computations," *The American Statistician*, February, 1972, pp. 26–27.

Montgomery, D. C., *Design and Analysis of Experiments*, 2d ed. New York: John Wiley & Sons, Inc., 1984.

Natrella, M. G., *Experimental Statistics, National Bureau of Standards Handbook 91*. Washington, DC: U.S. Government Printing Office, 1963.

Nicol, Sherrie J., "Who's Picking Up the Pieces?" *Primus*, Volume IV, Number 2, June 1994, pp. 182–184.

Pearson, K., "On the Criterion That a Given System of Deviations from the Probable in the Case of a Correlated System of Variables Is Such That It Can Be Reasonably Supposed to Have Arisen from Random Sampling," *Phil. Mag.*, Series 5, **50** (1900), p. 157.

Putz, John, "The Golden Section and the Piano Sonatas of Mozart," *Mathematics Magazine*, Volume 68, No. 4, October, 1995, pp. 275–282.

Quain, J. R., "Going Mainstream," *PC Magazine*, February, 1994.

Rafter, J. A., M. L. Abell, and J. P. Braselton, *Statistics with Maple*. Amsterdam and Boston: Academic Press, An imprint of Elsevier Science (USA), 2003.

Raspe, Rudolph Erich, *The Surprising Adventures of Baron Munchausen*, IndyPublish.com, 2001.

Snee, R. D., "Graphical Analysis of Process Variation Studies," *Journal of Quality Technology* 15: April 1983, pp. 76–88.

Snee, R. D., L. B. Hare, and J. R. Trout, *Experiments in Industry*, Milwaukee: American Society of Quality Control, 1985.

Stigler, S. M., *The History of Statistics: The Measurement of Uncertainty Before 1900*. Cambridge, MA: Harvard University Press, 1986.

Tanis, E. A., "Maple Integrated Into the Instruction of Probability and Statistics," *Proceedings of the Statistical Computing Section* (1998), American Statistical Association, pp. 19–24.

Tanis, E. A., and R. V. Hogg, *A Brief Course in Mathematical Statistics*. Upper Saddle River, NJ: Prentice Hall, 2008.

Tate, R. F., and G. W. Klett, "Optimum Confidence Intervals for the Variance of a Normal Distribution," *J. Am. Statist. Assoc.*, **54** (1959), p. 674.

Tsutakawa, R. K., G. L. Shoop, and C. J. Marienfeld, "Empirical Bayes estimation of cancer mortality rates," *Statistics in Medicine*, **4** (1985), pp. 201–212.

Tukey, John W., *Exploratory Data Analysis*. Reading, MA: Addison-Wesley Publishing Company, 1977.

Velleman, P. F., and D. C. Hoaglin, *Applications, Basics, and Computing of Exploratory Data Analysis*, Boston: Duxbury Press, 1981.

Wilcoxon, F., "Individual Comparisons by Ranking Methods," *Biometrics Bull.*, **1** (1945), p. 80.

Zerger, Monte, "Mean Meets Variance," *Primus*, Volume IV, Number 2, June 1994, pp. 106–108.

APPENDIX B

Tables

Table I	Binomial Coefficients	574
Table II	The Binomial Distribution	575–579
Table III	The Poisson Distribution	580–582
Table IV	The Chi-Square Distribution	583
Table Va	The Standard Normal Distribution Function	584
Table Vb	The Standard Normal Right-Tail Probabilities	585
Table VI	The t Distribution	586
Table VII	The F Distribution	587–591
Table VIII	Kolmogrov–Smirnov Acceptance Limits	592
Table IX	Random Numbers on the Interval $(0, 1)$	593
Table X	Divisors for the Confidence Interval for σ of Minimum Length	594
Table XI	Distribution Function of the Correlation Coefficient R, $\rho = 0$	595
Table XII	Discrete Distributions	596
Table XIII	Continuous Distributions	597
Table XIV	Confidence Intervals and Tests of Hypotheses	598–599

TABLE I: Binomial Coefficients

$$\binom{n}{r} = \frac{n!}{r!(n-r)!} = \binom{n}{n-r}$$

n	$\binom{n}{0}$	$\binom{n}{1}$	$\binom{n}{2}$	$\binom{n}{3}$	$\binom{n}{4}$	$\binom{n}{5}$	$\binom{n}{6}$	$\binom{n}{7}$	$\binom{n}{8}$	$\binom{n}{9}$	$\binom{n}{10}$	$\binom{n}{11}$	$\binom{n}{12}$	$\binom{n}{13}$
0	1													
1	1	1												
2	1	2	1											
3	1	3	3	1										
4	1	4	6	4	1									
5	1	5	10	10	5	1								
6	1	6	15	20	15	6	1							
7	1	7	21	35	35	21	7	1						
8	1	8	28	56	70	56	28	8	1					
9	1	9	36	84	126	126	84	36	9	1				
10	1	10	45	120	210	252	210	120	45	10	1			
11	1	11	55	165	330	462	462	330	165	55	11	1		
12	1	12	66	220	495	792	924	792	495	220	66	12	1	
13	1	13	78	286	715	1,287	1,716	1,716	1,287	715	286	78	13	1
14	1	14	91	364	1,001	2,002	3,003	3,432	3,003	2,002	1,001	364	91	14
15	1	15	105	455	1,365	3,003	5,005	6,435	6,435	5,005	3,003	1,365	455	105
16	1	16	120	560	1,820	4,368	8,008	11,440	12,870	11,440	8,008	4,368	1,820	560
17	1	17	136	680	2,380	6,188	12,376	19,448	24,310	24,310	19,448	12,376	6,188	2,380
18	1	18	153	816	3,060	8,568	18,564	31,824	43,758	48,620	43,758	31,824	18,564	8,568
19	1	19	171	969	3,876	11,628	27,132	50,388	75,582	92,378	92,378	75,582	50,388	27,132
20	1	20	190	1,140	4,845	15,504	38,760	77,520	125,970	167,960	184,756	167,960	125,970	77,520
21	1	21	210	1,330	5,985	20,349	54,264	116,280	203,490	293,930	352,716	352,716	293,930	203,490
22	1	22	231	1,540	7,315	26,334	74,613	170,544	319,770	497,420	646,646	705,432	646,646	497,420
23	1	23	253	1,771	8,855	33,649	100,947	245,157	490,314	817,190	1,144,066	1,352,078	1,352,078	1,144,066
24	1	24	276	2,024	10,626	42,504	134,596	346,104	735,471	1,307,504	1,961,256	2,496,144	2,704,156	2,496,144
25	1	25	300	2,300	12,650	53,130	177,100	480,700	1,081,575	2,042,975	3,268,760	4,457,400	5,200,300	5,200,300
26	1	26	325	2,600	14,950	65,780	230,230	657,800	1,562,275	3,124,550	5,311,735	7,726,160	9,657,700	10,400,600

For $r > 13$ you may use the identity $\binom{n}{r} = \binom{n}{n-r}$.

TABLE II: The Binomial Distribution

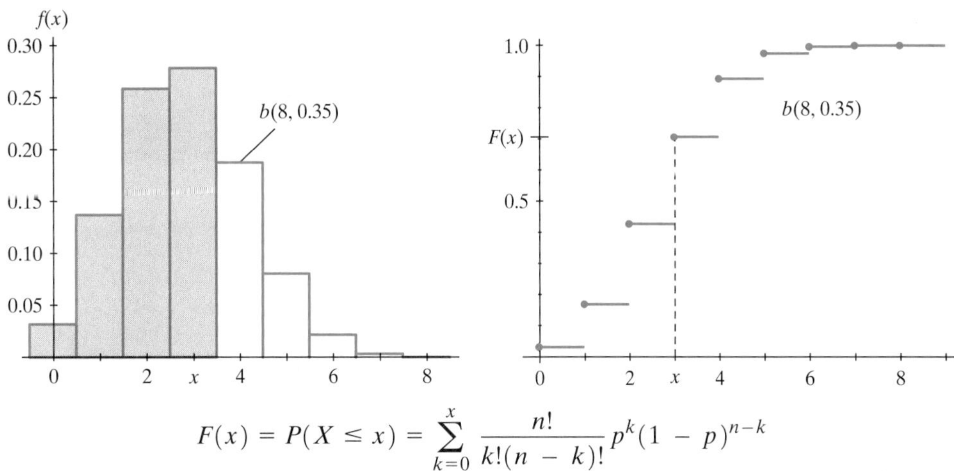

$$F(x) = P(X \le x) = \sum_{k=0}^{x} \frac{n!}{k!(n-k)!} p^k (1-p)^{n-k}$$

n	x	p = 0.05	0.10	0.15	0.20	0.25	0.30	0.35	0.40	0.45	0.50
2	0	0.9025	0.8100	0.7225	0.6400	0.5625	0.4900	0.4225	0.3600	0.3025	0.2500
	1	0.9975	0.9900	0.9775	0.9600	0.9375	0.9100	0.8775	0.8400	0.7975	0.7500
	2	1.0000	1.0000	1.0000	1.0000	1.0000	1.0000	1.0000	1.0000	1.0000	1.0000
3	0	0.8574	0.7290	0.6141	0.5120	0.4219	0.3430	0.2746	0.2160	0.1664	0.1250
	1	0.9928	0.9720	0.9392	0.8960	0.8438	0.7840	0.7182	0.6480	0.5748	0.5000
	2	0.9999	0.9990	0.9966	0.9920	0.9844	0.9730	0.9571	0.9360	0.9089	0.8750
	3	1.0000	1.0000	1.0000	1.0000	1.0000	1.0000	1.0000	1.0000	1.0000	1.0000
4	0	0.8145	0.6561	0.5220	0.4096	0.3164	0.2401	0.1785	0.1296	0.0915	0.0625
	1	0.9860	0.9477	0.8905	0.8192	0.7383	0.6517	0.5630	0.4752	0.3910	0.3125
	2	0.9995	0.9963	0.9880	0.9728	0.9492	0.9163	0.8735	0.8208	0.7585	0.6875
	3	1.0000	0.9999	0.9995	0.9984	0.9961	0.9919	0.9850	0.9744	0.9590	0.9375
	4	1.0000	1.0000	1.0000	1.0000	1.0000	1.0000	1.0000	1.0000	1.0000	1.0000
5	0	0.7738	0.5905	0.4437	0.3277	0.2373	0.1681	0.1160	0.0778	0.0503	0.0312
	1	0.9774	0.9185	0.8352	0.7373	0.6328	0.5282	0.4284	0.3370	0.2562	0.1875
	2	0.9988	0.9914	0.9734	0.9421	0.8965	0.8369	0.7648	0.6826	0.5931	0.5000
	3	1.0000	0.9995	0.9978	0.9933	0.9844	0.9692	0.9460	0.9130	0.8688	0.8125
	4	1.0000	1.0000	0.9999	0.9997	0.9990	0.9976	0.9947	0.9898	0.9815	0.9688
	5	1.0000	1.0000	1.0000	1.0000	1.0000	1.0000	1.0000	1.0000	1.0000	1.0000
6	0	0.7351	0.5314	0.3771	0.2621	0.1780	0.1176	0.0754	0.0467	0.0277	0.0156
	1	0.9672	0.8857	0.7765	0.6553	0.5339	0.4202	0.3191	0.2333	0.1636	0.1094
	2	0.9978	0.9842	0.9527	0.9011	0.8306	0.7443	0.6471	0.5443	0.4415	0.3438
	3	0.9999	0.9987	0.9941	0.9830	0.9624	0.9295	0.8826	0.8208	0.7447	0.6562
	4	1.0000	0.9999	0.9996	0.9984	0.9954	0.9891	0.9777	0.9590	0.9308	0.8906
	5	1.0000	1.0000	1.0000	0.9999	0.9998	0.9993	0.9982	0.9959	0.9917	0.9844
	6	1.0000	1.0000	1.0000	1.0000	1.0000	1.0000	1.0000	1.0000	1.0000	1.0000
7	0	0.6983	0.4783	0.3206	0.2097	0.1335	0.0824	0.0490	0.0280	0.0152	0.0078
	1	0.9556	0.8503	0.7166	0.5767	0.4449	0.3294	0.2338	0.1586	0.1024	0.0625
	2	0.9962	0.9743	0.9262	0.8520	0.7564	0.6471	0.5323	0.4199	0.3164	0.2266
	3	0.9998	0.9973	0.9879	0.9667	0.9294	0.8740	0.8002	0.7102	0.6083	0.5000
	4	1.0000	0.9998	0.9988	0.9953	0.9871	0.9712	0.9444	0.9037	0.8471	0.7734
	5	1.0000	1.0000	0.9999	0.9996	0.9987	0.9962	0.9910	0.9812	0.9643	0.9375

TABLE II: *continued*

n	x	p = 0.05	0.10	0.15	0.20	0.25	0.30	0.35	0.40	0.45	0.50
	6	1.0000	1.0000	1.0000	1.0000	0.9999	0.9998	0.9994	0.9984	0.9963	0.9922
	7	1.0000	1.0000	1.0000	1.0000	1.0000	1.0000	1.0000	1.0000	1.0000	1.0000
8	0	0.6634	0.4305	0.2725	0.1678	0.1001	0.0576	0.0319	0.0168	0.0084	0.0039
	1	0.9428	0.8131	0.6572	0.5033	0.3671	0.2553	0.1691	0.1064	0.0632	0.0352
	2	0.9942	0.9619	0.8948	0.7969	0.6785	0.5518	0.4278	0.3154	0.2201	0.1445
	3	0.9996	0.9950	0.9786	0.9437	0.8862	0.8059	0.7064	0.5941	0.4770	0.3633
	4	1.0000	0.9996	0.9971	0.9896	0.9727	0.9420	0.8939	0.8263	0.7396	0.6367
	5	1.0000	1.0000	0.9998	0.9988	0.9958	0.9887	0.9747	0.9502	0.9115	0.8555
	6	1.0000	1.0000	1.0000	0.9999	0.9996	0.9987	0.9964	0.9915	0.9819	0.9648
	7	1.0000	1.0000	1.0000	1.0000	1.0000	0.9999	0.9998	0.9993	0.9983	0.9961
	8	1.0000	1.0000	1.0000	1.0000	1.0000	1.0000	1.0000	1.0000	1.0000	1.0000
9	0	0.6302	0.3874	0.2316	0.1342	0.0751	0.0404	0.0207	0.0101	0.0046	0.0020
	1	0.9288	0.7748	0.5995	0.4362	0.3003	0.1960	0.1211	0.0705	0.0385	0.0195
	2	0.9916	0.9470	0.8591	0.7382	0.6007	0.4628	0.3373	0.2318	0.1495	0.0898
	3	0.9994	0.9917	0.9661	0.9144	0.8343	0.7297	0.6089	0.4826	0.3614	0.2539
	4	1.0000	0.9991	0.9944	0.9804	0.9511	0.9012	0.8283	0.7334	0.6214	0.5000
	5	1.0000	0.9999	0.9994	0.9969	0.9900	0.9747	0.9464	0.9006	0.8342	0.7461
	6	1.0000	1.0000	1.0000	0.9997	0.9987	0.9957	0.9888	0.9750	0.9502	0.9102
	7	1.0000	1.0000	1.0000	1.0000	0.9999	0.9996	0.9986	0.9962	0.9909	0.9805
	8	1.0000	1.0000	1.0000	1.0000	1.0000	1.0000	0.9999	0.9997	0.9992	0.9980
	9	1.0000	1.0000	1.0000	1.0000	1.0000	1.0000	1.0000	1.0000	1.0000	1.0000
10	0	0.5987	0.3487	0.1969	0.1074	0.0563	0.0282	0.0135	0.0060	0.0025	0.0010
	1	0.9139	0.7361	0.5443	0.3758	0.2440	0.1493	0.0860	0.0464	0.0233	0.0107
	2	0.9885	0.9298	0.8202	0.6778	0.5256	0.3828	0.2616	0.1673	0.0996	0.0547
	3	0.9990	0.9872	0.9500	0.8791	0.7759	0.6496	0.5138	0.3823	0.2660	0.1719
	4	0.9999	0.9984	0.9901	0.9672	0.9219	0.8497	0.7515	0.6331	0.5044	0.3770
	5	1.0000	0.9999	0.9986	0.9936	0.9803	0.9527	0.9051	0.8338	0.7384	0.6230
	6	1.0000	1.0000	0.9999	0.9991	0.9965	0.9894	0.9740	0.9452	0.8980	0.8281
	7	1.0000	1.0000	1.0000	0.9999	0.9996	0.9984	0.9952	0.9877	0.9726	0.9453
	8	1.0000	1.0000	1.0000	1.0000	1.0000	0.9999	0.9995	0.9983	0.9955	0.9893
	9	1.0000	1.0000	1.0000	1.0000	1.0000	1.0000	1.0000	0.9999	0.9997	0.9990
	10	1.0000	1.0000	1.0000	1.0000	1.0000	1.0000	1.0000	1.0000	1.0000	1.0000
11	0	0.5688	0.3138	0.1673	0.0859	0.0422	0.0198	0.0088	0.0036	0.0014	0.0005
	1	0.8981	0.6974	0.4922	0.3221	0.1971	0.1130	0.0606	0.0302	0.0139	0.0059
	2	0.9848	0.9104	0.7788	0.6174	0.4552	0.3127	0.2001	0.1189	0.0652	0.0327
	3	0.9984	0.9815	0.9306	0.8389	0.7133	0.5696	0,4256	0.2963	0.1911	0.1133
	4	0.9999	0.9972	0.9841	0.9496	0.8854	0.7897	0.6683	0.5328	0.3971	0.2744
	5	1.0000	0.9997	0.9973	0.9883	0.9657	0.9218	0.8513	0.7535	0.6331	0.5000
	6	1.0000	1.0000	0.9997	0.9980	0.9924	0.9784	0.9499	0.9006	0.8262	0.7256
	7	1.0000	1.0000	1.0000	0.9998	0.9988	0.9957	0.9878	0.9707	0.9390	0.8867
	8	1.0000	1.0000	1.0000	1.0000	0.9999	0.9994	0.9980	0.9941	0.9852	0.9673
	9	1.0000	1.0000	1.0000	1.0000	1.0000	1.0000	0.9998	0.9993	0.9978	0.9941

TABLE II: *continued*

n	x	p 0.05	0.10	0.15	0.20	0.25	0.30	0.35	0.40	0.45	0.50
	10	1.0000	1.0000	1.0000	1.0000	1.0000	1.0000	1.0000	1.0000	0.9998	0.9995
	11	1.0000	1.0000	1.0000	1.0000	1.0000	1.0000	1.0000	1.0000	1.0000	1.0000
12	0	0.5404	0.2824	0.1422	0.0687	0.0317	0.0138	0.0057	0.0022	0.0008	0.0002
	1	0.8816	0.6590	0.4435	0.2749	0.1584	0.0850	0.0424	0.0196	0.0083	0.0032
	2	0.9804	0.8891	0.7358	0.5583	0.3907	0.2528	0.1513	0.0834	0.0421	0.0193
	3	0.9978	0.9744	0.9078	0.7946	0.6488	0.4925	0.3467	0.2253	0.1345	0.0730
	4	0.9998	0.9957	0.9761	0.9274	0.8424	0.7237	0.5833	0.4382	0.3044	0.1938
	5	1.0000	0.9995	0.9954	0.9806	0.9456	0.8822	0.7873	0.6652	0.5269	0.3872
	6	1.0000	0.9999	0.9993	0.9961	0.9857	0.9614	0.9154	0.8418	0.7393	0.6128
	7	1.0000	1.0000	0.9999	0.9994	0.9972	0.9905	0.9745	0.9427	0.8883	0.8062
	8	1.0000	1.0000	1.0000	0.9999	0.9996	0.9983	0.9944	0.9847	0.9644	0.9270
	9	1.0000	1.0000	1.0000	1.0000	1.0000	0.9998	0.9992	0.9972	0.9921	0.9807
	10	1.0000	1.0000	1.0000	1.0000	1.0000	1.0000	0.9999	0.9997	0.9989	0.9968
	11	1.0000	1.0000	1.0000	1.0000	1.0000	1.0000	1.0000	1.0000	0.9999	0.9998
	12	1.0000	1.0000	1.0000	1.0000	1.0000	1.0000	1.0000	1.0000	1.0000	1.0000
13	0	0.5133	0.2542	0.1209	0.0550	0.0238	0.0097	0.0037	0.0013	0.0004	0.0001
	1	0.8646	0.6213	0.3983	0.2336	0.1267	0.0637	0.0296	0.0126	0.0049	0.0017
	2	0.9755	0.8661	0.6920	0.5017	0.3326	0.2025	0.1132	0.0579	0.0269	0.0112
	3	0.9969	0.9658	0.8820	0.7473	0.5843	0.4206	0.2783	0.1686	0.0929	0.0461
	4	0.9997	0.9935	0.9658	0.9009	0.7940	0.6543	0.5005	0.3530	0.2279	0.1334
	5	1.0000	0.9991	0.9924	0.9700	0.9198	0.8346	0.7159	0.5744	0.4268	0.2905
	6	1.0000	0.9999	0.9987	0.9930	0.9757	0.9376	0.8705	0.7712	0.6437	0.5000
	7	1.0000	1.0000	0.9998	0.9988	0.9944	0.9818	0.9538	0.9023	0.8212	0.7095
	8	1.0000	1.0000	1.0000	0.9998	0.9990	0.9960	0.9874	0.9679	0.9302	0.8666
	9	1.0000	1.0000	1.0000	1.0000	0.9999	0.9993	0.9975	0.9922	0.9797	0.9539
	10	1.0000	1.0000	1.0000	1.0000	1.0000	0.9999	0.9997	0.9987	0.9959	0.9888
	11	1.0000	1.0000	1.0000	1.0000	1.0000	1.0000	1.0000	0.9999	0.9995	0.9983
	12	1.0000	1.0000	1.0000	1.0000	1.0000	1.0000	1.0000	1.0000	1.0000	0.9999
	13	1.0000	1.0000	1.0000	1.0000	1.0000	1.0000	1.0000	1.0000	1.0000	1.0000
14	0	0.4877	0.2288	0.1028	0.0440	0.0178	0.0068	0.0024	0.0008	0.0002	0.0001
	1	0.8470	0.5846	0.3567	0.1979	0.1010	0.0475	0.0205	0.0081	0.0029	0.0009
	2	0.9699	0.8416	0.6479	0.4481	0.2811	0.1608	0.0839	0.0398	0.0170	0.0065
	3	0.9958	0.9559	0.8535	0.6982	0.5213	0.3552	0.2205	0.1243	0.0632	0.0287
	4	0.9996	0.9908	0.9533	0.8702	0.7415	0.5842	0.4227	0.2793	0.1672	0.0898
	5	1.0000	0.9985	0.9885	0.9561	0.8883	0.7805	0.6405	0.4859	0.3373	0.2120
	6	1.0000	0.9998	0.9978	0.9884	0.9617	0.9067	0.8164	0.6925	0.5461	0.3953
	7	1.0000	1.0000	0.9997	0.9976	0.9897	0.9685	0.9247	0.8499	0.7414	0.6047
	8	1.0000	1.0000	1.0000	0.9996	0.9978	0.9917	0.9757	0.9417	0.8811	0.7880
	9	1.0000	1.0000	1.0000	1.0000	0.9997	0.9983	0.9940	0.9825	0.9574	0.9102
	10	1.0000	1.0000	1.0000	1.0000	1.0000	0.9998	0.9989	0.9961	0.9886	0.9713

TABLE II: *continued*

n	x	p 0.05	0.10	0.15	0.20	0.25	0.30	0.35	0.40	0.45	0.50
	11	1.0000	1.0000	1.0000	1.0000	1.0000	1.0000	0.9999	0.9994	0.9978	0.9935
	12	1.0000	1.0000	1.0000	1.0000	1.0000	1.0000	1.0000	0.9999	0.9997	0.9991
	13	1.0000	1.0000	1.0000	1.0000	1.0000	1.0000	1.0000	1.0000	1.0000	0.9999
	14	1.0000	1.0000	1.0000	1.0000	1.0000	1.0000	1.0000	1.0000	1.0000	1.0000
15	0	0.4633	0.2059	0.0874	0.0352	0.0134	0.0047	0.0016	0.0005	0.0001	0.0000
	1	0.8290	0.5490	0.3186	0.1671	0.0802	0.0353	0.0142	0.0052	0.0017	0.0005
	2	0.9638	0.8159	0.6042	0.3980	0.2361	0.1268	0.0617	0.0271	0.0107	0.0037
	3	0.9945	0.9444	0.8227	0.6482	0.4613	0.2969	0.1727	0.0905	0.0424	0.0176
	4	0.9994	0.9873	0.9383	0.8358	0.6865	0.5155	0.3519	0.2173	0.1204	0.0592
	5	0.9999	0.9978	0.9832	0.9389	0.8516	0.7216	0.5643	0.4032	0.2608	0.1509
	6	1.0000	0.9997	0.9964	0.9819	0.9434	0.8689	0.7548	0.6098	0.4522	0.3036
	7	1.0000	1.0000	0.9994	0.9958	0.9827	0.9500	0.8868	0.7869	0.6535	0.5000
	8	1.0000	1.0000	0.9999	0.9992	0.9958	0.9848	0.9578	0.9050	0.8182	0.6964
	9	1.0000	1.0000	1.0000	0.9999	0.9992	0.9963	0.9876	0.9662	0.9231	0.8491
	10	1.0000	1.0000	1.0000	1.0000	0.9999	0.9993	0.9972	0.9907	0.9745	0.9408
	11	1.0000	1.0000	1.0000	1.0000	1.0000	0.9999	0.9995	0.9981	0.9937	0.9824
	12	1.0000	1.0000	1.0000	1.0000	1.0000	1.0000	0.9999	0.9987	0.9989	0.9963
	13	1.0000	1.0000	1.0000	1.0000	1.0000	1.0000	1.0000	1.0000	0.9999	0.9995
	14	1.0000	1.0000	1.0000	1.0000	1.0000	1.0000	1.0000	1.0000	1.0000	1.0000
	15	1.0000	1.0000	1.0000	1.0000	1.0000	1.0000	1.0000	1.0000	1.0000	1.0000
16	0	0.4401	0.1853	0.0743	0.0281	0.0100	0.0033	0.0010	0.0003	0.0001	0.0000
	1	0.8108	0.5147	0.2839	0.1407	0.0635	0.0261	0.0098	0.0033	0.0010	0.0003
	2	0.9571	0.7892	0.5614	0.3518	0.1971	0.0994	0.0451	0.0183	0.0066	0.0021
	3	0.9930	0.9316	0.7899	0.5981	0.4050	0.2459	0.1339	0,0651	0.0281	0.0106
	4	0.9991	0.9830	0.9209	0.7982	0.6302	0.4499	0.2892	0.1666	0.0853	0.0384
	5	0.9999	0.9967	0.9765	0.9183	0.8103	0.6598	0.4900	0.3288	0.1976	0.1051
	6	1.0000	0.9995	0.9944	0.9733	0.9204	0.8247	0.6881	0.5272	0.3660	0.2272
	7	1.0000	0.9999	0.9989	0.9930	0.9729	0.9256	0.8406	0.7161	0.5629	0.4018
	8	1.0000	1.0000	0.9998	0.9985	0.9925	0.9743	0.9329	0.8577	0.7441	0.5982
	9	1.0000	1.0000	1.0000	0.9998	0.9984	0.9929	0.9771	0.9417	0.8759	0.7728
	10	1.0000	1.0000	1.0000	1.0000	0.9997	0.9984	0.9938	0.9809	0.9514	0.8949
	11	1.0000	1.0000	1.0000	1.0000	1.0000	0.9997	0.9987	0.9951	0.9851	0.9616
	12	1.0000	1.0000	1.0000	1.0000	1.0000	1.0000	0.9998	0.9991	0.9965	0.9894
	13	1.0000	1.0000	1.0000	1.0000	1.0000	1.0000	1.0000	0.9999	0.9994	0.9979
	14	1.0000	1.0000	1.0000	1.0000	1.0000	1.0000	1.0000	1.0000	0.9999	0.9997
	15	1.0000	1.0000	1.0000	1.0000	1.0000	1.0000	1.0000	1.0000	1.0000	1.0000
	16	1.0000	1.0000	1.0000	1.0000	1.0000	1.0000	1.0000	1.0000	1.0000	1.0000
20	0	0.3585	0.1216	0.0388	0.0115	0.0032	0.0008	0.0002	0.0000	0.0000	0.0000
	1	0.7358	0.3917	0.1756	0.0692	0.0243	0.0076	0.0021	0,0005	0.0001	0.0000
	2	0.9245	0.6769	0.4049	0.2061	0.0913	0.0355	0.0121	0.0036	0.0009	0.0002
	3	0.9841	0.8670	0.6477	0.4114	0.2252	0.1071	0.0444	0.0160	0.0049	0.0013
	4	0.9974	0.9568	0.8298	0.6296	0.4148	0.2375	0.1182	0.0510	0.0189	0.0059

TABLE II: *continued*

n	x	p = 0.05	0.10	0.15	0.20	0.25	0.30	0.35	0.40	0.45	0.50
	5	0.9997	0.9887	0.9327	0.8042	0.6172	0.4164	0.2454	0.1256	0.0553	0.0207
	6	1.0000	0.9976	0.9781	0.9133	0.7858	0.6080	0.4166	0.2500	0.1299	0.0577
	7	1.0000	0.9996	0.9941	0.9679	0.8982	0.7723	0.6010	0.4159	0.2520	0.1316
	8	1.0000	0.9999	0,9987	0.9900	0.9591	0.8867	0.7624	0.5956	0.4143	0.2517
	9	1.0000	1.0000	0.9998	0.9974	0.9861	0.9520	0.8782	0.7553	0.5914	0.4119
	10	1.0000	1.0000	1.0000	0.9994	0.9961	0.9829	0.9468	0.8725	0.7507	0.5881
	11	1.0000	1.0000	1.0000	0.9999	0.9991	0.9949	0.9804	0.9435	0.8692	0.7483
	12	1.0000	1.0000	1.0000	1.0000	0.9998	0.9987	0.9940	0.9790	0.9420	0.8684
	13	1.0000	1.0000	1.0000	1.0000	1.0000	0.9997	0.9985	0.9935	0.9786	0.9423
	14	1.0000	1.0000	1.0000	1.0000	1.0000	1.0000	0.9997	0.9984	0.9936	0.9793
	15	1.0000	1.0000	1.0000	1.0000	1.0000	1.0000	1.0000	0.9997	0.9985	0.9941
	16	1.0000	1.0000	1.0000	1.0000	1.0000	1.0000	1.0000	1.0000	0.9997	0.9987
	17	1.0000	1.0000	1.0000	1.0000	1.0000	1.0000	1.0000	1.0000	1.0000	0.9998
	18	1.0000	1.0000	1.0000	1.0000	1.0000	1.0000	1.0000	1.0000	1.0000	1.0000
	19	1.0000	1.0000	1.0000	1.0000	1.0000	1.0000	1.0000	1.0000	1.0000	1.0000
	20	1.0000	1.0000	1.0000	1.0000	1.0000	1.0000	1.0000	1.0000	1.0000	1.0000
25	0	0.2774	0.0718	0.0172	0.0038	0.0008	0.0001	0.0000	0.0000	0.0000	0.0000
	1	0.6424	0.2712	0.0931	0.0274	0.0070	0.0016	0.0003	0.0001	0.0000	0.0000
	2	0.8729	0.5371	0.2537	0.0982	0.0321	0.0090	0.0021	0,0004	0.0001	0.0000
	3	0.9659	0.7636	0.4711	0.2340	0.0962	0.0332	0.0097	0.0024	0.0005	0.0001
	4	0.9928	0.9020	0.6821	0.4207	0.2137	0.0905	0.0320	0.0095	0.0023	0.0005
	5	0.9988	0.9666	0.8385	0.6167	0.3783	0.1935	0.0826	0.0294	0.0086	0.0020
	6	0.9998	0.9905	0.9305	0.7800	0.5611	0.3407	0.1734	0.0736	0.0258	0.0073
	7	1.0000	0.9977	0.9745	0.8909	0.7265	0.5118	0.3061	0.1536	0.0639	0.0216
	8	1.0000	0.9995	0.9920	0.9532	0.8506	0.6769	0.4668	0.2735	0.1340	0.0539
	9	1.0000	0.9999	0.9979	0.9827	0.9287	0.8106	0.6303	0.4246	0.2424	0.1148
	10	1.0000	1.0000	0.9995	0.9944	0.9703	0.9022	0.7712	0.5858	0.3843	0.2122
	11	1.0000	1.0000	0.9999	0.9985	0.9893	0.9558	0.8746	0.7323	0.5426	0.3450
	12	1.0000	1.0000	1.0000	0.9996	0.9966	0.9825	0.9396	0.8462	0.6937	0.5000
	13	1.0000	1.0000	1.0000	0.9999	0.9991	0.9940	0.9745	0.9222	0.8173	0.6550
	14	1.0000	1.0000	1,0000	1.0000	0.9998	0.9982	0.9907	0.9656	0.9040	0.7878
	15	1.0000	1.0000	1.0000	1.0000	1.0000	0.9995	0.9971	0.9868	0.9560	0.8852
	16	1.0000	1.0000	1.0000	1.0000	1.0000	0.9999	0.9992	0.9957	0.9826	0.9461
	17	1.0000	1.0000	1.0000	1.0000	1.0000	1.0000	0.9998	0.9988	0.9942	0.9784
	18	1.0000	1.0000	1.0000	1.0000	1.0000	1.0000	1.0000	0.9997	0.9984	0.9927
	19	1.0000	1.0000	1.0000	1.0000	1.0000	1.0000	1.0000	0.9999	0.9996	0.9980
	20	1.0000	1.0000	1.0000	1.0000	1.0000	1.0000	1.0000	1.0000	0.9999	0.9995
	21	1.0000	1.0000	1.0000	1.0000	1.0000	1.0000	1.0000	1.0000	1.0000	0.9999
	22	1.0000	1.0000	1.0000	1.0000	1.0000	1.0000	1.0000	1.0000	1.0000	1.0000
	23	1.0000	1.0000	1.0000	1.0000	1.0000	1.0000	1.0000	1.0000	1.0000	1.0000
	24	1.0000	1.0000	1.0000	1.0000	1.0000	1.0000	1.0000	1.0000	1.0000	1.0000
	25	1.0000	1.0000	1.0000	1.0000	1.0000	1.0000	1.0000	1.0000	1.0000	1.0000

TABLE III: The Poisson Distribution

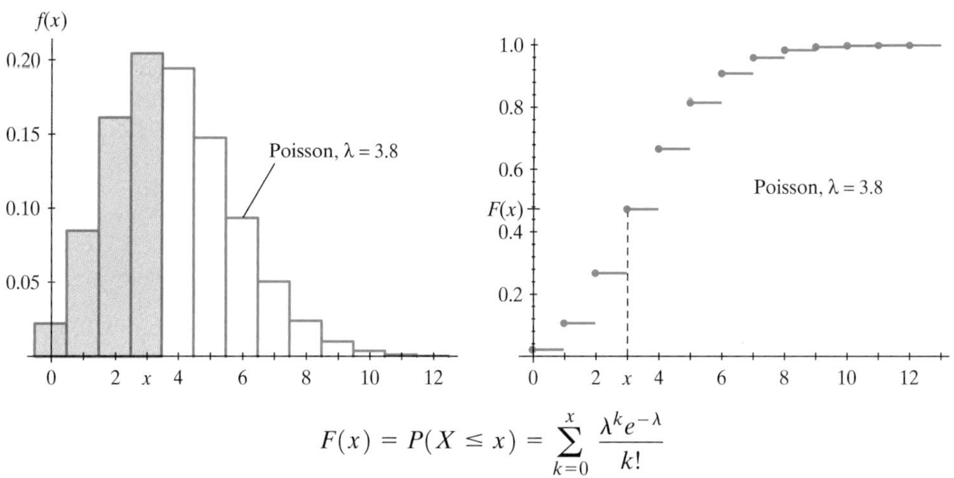

$$F(x) = P(X \le x) = \sum_{k=0}^{x} \frac{\lambda^k e^{-\lambda}}{k!}$$

	$\lambda = E(X)$									
x	0.1	0.2	0.3	0.4	0.5	0.6	0.7	0.8	0.9	1.0
0	0.905	0.819	0.741	0.670	0.607	0.549	0.497	0.449	0.407	0.368
1	0.995	0.982	0.963	0.938	0.910	0.878	0.844	0.809	0.772	0.736
2	1.000	0.999	0.996	0.992	0.986	0.977	0.966	0.953	0.937	0.920
3	1.000	1.000	1.000	0.999	0.998	0.997	0.994	0.991	0.987	0.981
4	1.000	1.000	1.000	1.000	1.000	1.000	0.999	0.999	0.998	0.996
5	1.000	1.000	1.000	1.000	1.000	1.000	1.000	1.000	1.000	0.999
6	1.000	1.000	1.000	1.000	1.000	1.000	1.000	1.000	1.000	1.000
x	1.1	1.2	1.3	1.4	1.5	1.6	1.7	1.8	1.9	2.0
0	0.333	0.301	0.273	0.247	0.223	0.202	0.183	0.165	0.150	0.135
1	0.699	0.663	0.627	0.592	0.558	0.525	0.493	0.463	0.434	0.406
2	0.900	0.879	0.857	0.833	0.809	0.783	0.757	0.731	0.704	0.677
3	0.974	0.966	0.957	0.946	0.934	0.921	0.907	0.891	0.875	0.857
4	0.995	0.992	0.989	0.986	0.981	0.976	0.970	0.964	0.956	0.947
5	0.999	0.998	0.998	0.997	0.996	0.994	0.992	0.990	0.987	0.983
6	1.000	1.000	1.000	0.999	0.999	0.999	0.998	0.997	0.997	0.995
7	1.000	1.000	1.000	1.000	1.000	1.000	1.000	0.999	0.999	0.999
8	1.000	1.000	1.000	1.000	1.000	1.000	1.000	1.000	1.000	1.000
x	2.2	2.4	2.6	2.8	3.0	3.2	3.4	3.6	3.8	4.0
0	0.111	0.091	0.074	0.061	0.050	0.041	0.033	0.027	0.022	0.018
1	0.355	0.308	0.267	0.231	0.199	0.171	0.147	0.126	0.107	0.092
2	0.623	0.570	0.518	0.469	0.423	0.380	0.340	0.303	0.269	0.238
3	0.819	0.779	0.736	0.692	0.647	0.603	0.558	0.515	0.473	0.433
4	0.928	0.904	0.877	0.848	0.815	0.781	0.744	0.706	0.668	0.629
5	0.975	0.964	0.951	0.935	0.916	0.895	0.871	0.844	0.816	0.785
6	0.993	0.988	0.983	0.976	0.966	0.955	0.942	0.927	0.909	0.889
7	0.998	0.997	0.995	0.992	0.988	0.983	0.977	0.969	0.960	0.949
8	1.000	0.999	0.999	0.998	0.996	0.994	0.992	0.988	0.984	0.979
9	1.000	1.000	1.000	0.999	0.999	0.998	0.997	0.996	0.994	0.992
10	1.000	1.000	1.000	1.000	1.000	1.000	0.999	0.999	0.998	0.997
11	1.000	1.000	1.000	1.000	1.000	1.000	1.000	1.000	0.999	0.999
12	1.000	1.000	1.000	1.000	1.000	1.000	1.000	1.000	1.000	1.000

TABLE III: *continued*

x	4.2	4.4	4.6	4.8	5.0	5.2	5.4	5.6	5.8	6.0
0	0.015	0.012	0.010	0.008	0.007	0.006	0.005	0.004	0.003	0.002
1	0.078	0.066	0.056	0.048	0.040	0.034	0.029	0.024	0.021	0.017
2	0.210	0.185	0.163	0.143	0.125	0.109	0.095	0.082	0.072	0.062
3	0.395	0.359	0.326	0.294	0.265	0.238	0.213	0.191	0.170	0.151
4	0.590	0.551	0.513	0.476	0.440	0.406	0.373	0.342	0.313	0.285
5	0.753	0.720	0.686	0.651	0.616	0.581	0.546	0.512	0.478	0.446
6	0.867	0.844	0.818	0.791	0.762	0.732	0.702	0.670	0.638	0.606
7	0.936	0.921	0.905	0.887	0.867	0.845	0.822	0.797	0.771	0.744
8	0.972	0.964	0.955	0.944	0.932	0.918	0.903	0.886	0.867	0.847
9	0.989	0.985	0.980	0.975	0.968	0.960	0.951	0.941	0.929	0.916
10	0.996	0.994	0.992	0.990	0.986	0.982	0.977	0.972	0.965	0.957
11	0.999	0.998	0.997	0.996	0.995	0.993	0.990	0.988	0.984	0.980
12	1.000	0.999	0.999	0.999	0.998	0.997	0.996	0.995	0.993	0.991
13	1.000	1.000	1.000	1.000	0.999	0.999	0.999	0.998	0.997	0.996
14	1.000	1.000	1.000	1.000	1.000	1.000	0.999	0.999	0.999	0.999
15	1.000	1.000	1.000	1.000	1.000	1.000	1.000	1.000	1.000	0.999
16	1.000	1.000	1.000	1.000	1.000	1.000	1.000	1.000	1.000	1.000

x	6.5	7.0	7.5	8.0	8.5	9.0	9.5	10.0	10.5	11.0
0	0.002	0.001	0.001	0.000	0.000	0.000	0.000	0.000	0.000	0.000
1	0.011	0.007	0.005	0.003	0.002	0.001	0.001	0.000	0.000	0.000
2	0.043	0.030	0.020	0.014	0.009	0.006	0.004	0.003	0.002	0.001
3	0.112	0.082	0.059	0.042	0.030	0.021	0.015	0.010	0.007	0.005
4	0.224	0.173	0.132	0.100	0.074	0.055	0.040	0.029	0.021	0.015
5	0.369	0.301	0.241	0.191	0.150	0.116	0.089	0.067	0.050	0.038
6	0.527	0.450	0.378	0.313	0.256	0.207	0.165	0.130	0.102	0.079
7	0.673	0.599	0.525	0.453	0.386	0.324	0.269	0.220	0.179	0.143
8	0.792	0.729	0.662	0.593	0.523	0.456	0.392	0.333	0.279	0.232
9	0.877	0.830	0.776	0.717	0.653	0.587	0.522	0.458	0.397	0.341
10	0.933	0.901	0.862	0.816	0.763	0.706	0.645	0.583	0.521	0.460
11	0.966	0.947	0.921	0.888	0.849	0.803	0.752	0.697	0.639	0.579
12	0.984	0.973	0.957	0.936	0.909	0.876	0.836	0.792	0.742	0.689
13	0.993	0.987	0.978	0.966	0.949	0.926	0.898	0.864	0.825	0.781
14	0.997	0.994	0.990	0.983	0.973	0.959	0.940	0.917	0.888	0.854
15	0.999	0.998	0.995	0.992	0.986	0.978	0.967	0.951	0.932	0.907
16	1.000	0.999	0.998	0.996	0.993	0.989	0.982	0.973	0.960	0.944
17	1.000	1.000	0.999	0.998	0.997	0.995	0.991	0.986	0.978	0.968
18	1.000	1.000	1.000	0.999	0.999	0.998	0.096	0.993	0.988	0.982
19	1.000	1.000	1.000	1.000	0.999	0.999	0.998	0.997	0.994	0.991
20	1.000	1.000	1.000	1.000	1.000	1.000	0.999	0.998	0.997	0.995
21	1.000	1.000	1.000	1.000	1.000	1.000	1.000	0.999	0.999	0.998
22	1.000	1.000	1.000	1.000	1.000	1.000	1.000	1.000	0.999	0.999
23	1.000	1.000	1.000	1.000	1.000	1.000	1.000	1.000	1.000	1.000

TABLE III: *continued*

x	11.5	12.0	12.5	13.0	13.5	14.0	14.5	15.0	15.5	16.0
0	0.000	0.000	0.000	0.000	0.000	0.000	0.000	0.000	0.000	0.000
1	0.000	0.000	0.000	0.000	0.000	0.000	0.000	0.000	0.000	0.000
2	0.001	0.001	0.000	0.000	0.000	0.000	0.000	0.000	0.000	0.000
3	0.003	0.002	0.002	0.001	0.001	0.000	0.000	0.000	0.000	0.000
4	0.011	0.008	0.005	0.004	0.003	0.002	0.001	0.001	0.001	0.000
5	0.028	0.020	0.015	0.011	0.008	0.006	0.004	0.003	0.002	0.001
6	0.060	0.046	0.035	0.026	0.019	0.014	0.010	0.008	0.006	0.004
7	0.114	0.090	0.070	0.054	0.041	0.032	0.024	0.018	0.013	0.010
8	0.191	0.155	0.125	0.100	0.079	0.062	0.048	0.037	0.029	0.022
9	0.289	0.242	0.201	0.166	0.135	0.109	0.088	0.070	0.055	0.043
10	0.402	0.347	0.297	0.252	0.211	0.176	0.145	0.118	0.096	0.077
11	0.520	0.462	0.406	0.353	0.304	0.260	0.220	0.185	0.154	0.127
12	0.633	0.576	0.519	0.463	0.409	0.358	0.311	0.268	0.228	0.193
13	0.733	0.682	0.629	0.573	0.518	0.464	0.413	0.363	0.317	0.275
14	0.815	0.772	0.725	0.675	0.623	0.570	0.518	0.466	0.415	0.368
15	0.878	0.844	0.806	0.764	0.718	0.669	0.619	0.568	0.517	0.467
16	0.924	0.899	0.869	0.835	0.798	0.756	0.711	0.664	0.615	0.566
17	0.954	0.937	0.916	0.890	0.861	0.827	0.790	0.749	0.705	0.659
18	0.974	0.963	0.948	0.930	0.908	0.883	0.853	0.819	0.782	0.742
19	0.986	0.979	0.969	0.957	0.942	0.923	0.901	0.875	0.846	0.812
20	0.992	0.988	0.983	0.975	0.965	0.952	0.936	0.917	0.894	0.868
21	0.996	0.994	0.991	0.986	0.980	0.971	0.960	0.947	0.930	0.911
22	0.999	0.997	0.995	0.992	0.989	0.983	0.976	0.967	0.956	0.942
23	0.999	0.999	0.998	0.996	0.994	0.991	0.986	0.981	0.973	0.963
24	1.000	0.999	0.999	0.998	0.997	0.995	0.992	0.989	0.984	0.978
25	1.000	1.000	0.999	0.999	0.998	0.997	0.996	0.994	0.991	0.987
26	1.000	1.000	1.000	1.000	0.999	0.999	0.998	0.997	0.995	0.993
27	1.000	1.000	1.000	1.000	1.000	0.999	0.999	0.998	0.997	0.996
28	1.000	1.000	1.000	1.000	1.000	1.000	0.999	0.999	0.999	0.998
29	1.000	1.000	1.000	1.000	1.000	1.000	1.000	1.000	0.999	0.999
30	1.000	1.000	1.000	1.000	1.000	1.000	1.000	1.000	1.000	0.999
31	1.000	1.000	1.000	1.000	1.000	1.000	1.000	1.000	1.000	1.000
32	1.000	1.000	1.000	1.000	1.000	1.000	1.000	1.000	1.000	1.000
33	1.000	1.000	1.000	1.000	1.000	1.000	1.000	1.000	1.000	1.000
34	1.000	1.000	1.000	1.000	1.000	1.000	1.000	1.000	1.000	1.000
35	1.000	1.000	1.000	1.000	1.000	1.000	1.000	1.000	1.000	1.000

TABLE IV: The Chi-Square Distribution

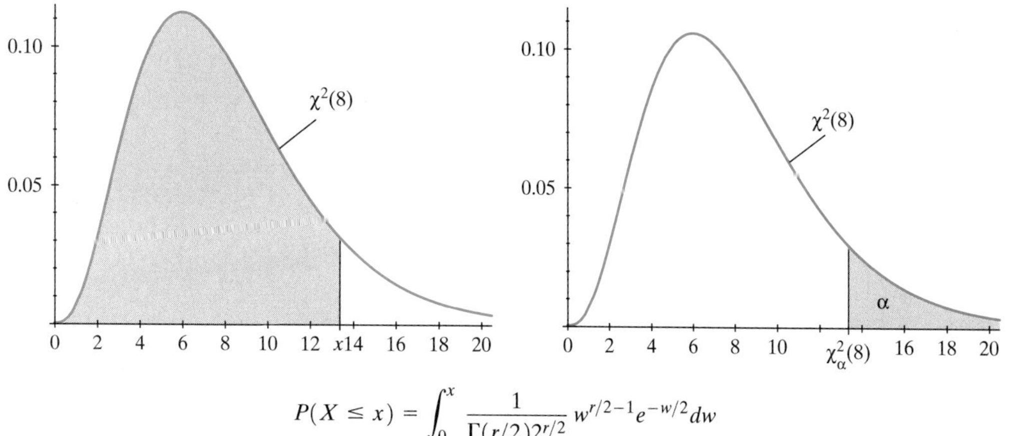

$$P(X \le x) = \int_0^x \frac{1}{\Gamma(r/2)2^{r/2}} w^{r/2-1} e^{-w/2} dw$$

	$P(X \le x)$							
	0.010	0.025	0.050	0.100	0.900	0.950	0.975	0.990
r	$\chi^2_{0.99}(r)$	$\chi^2_{0.975}(r)$	$\chi^2_{0.95}(r)$	$\chi^2_{0.90}(r)$	$\chi^2_{0.10}(r)$	$\chi^2_{0.05}(r)$	$\chi^2_{0.025}(r)$	$\chi^2_{0.01}(r)$
1	0.000	0.001	0.004	0.016	2.706	3.841	5.024	6.635
2	0.020	0.051	0.103	0.211	4.605	5.991	7.378	9.210
3	0.115	0.216	0.352	0.584	6.251	7.815	9.348	11.34
4	0.297	0.484	0.711	1.064	7.779	9.488	11.14	13.28
5	0.554	0.831	1.145	1.610	9.236	11.07	12.83	15.09
6	0.872	1.237	1.635	2.204	10.64	12.59	14.45	16.81
7	1.239	1.690	2.167	2.833	12.02	14.07	16.01	18.48
8	1.646	2.180	2.733	3.490	13.36	15.51	17.54	20.09
9	2.088	2.700	3.325	4.168	14.68	16.92	19.02	21.67
10	2.558	3.247	3.940	4.865	15.99	18.31	20.48	23.21
11	3.053	3.816	4.575	5.578	17.28	19.68	21.92	24.72
12	3.571	4.404	5.226	6.304	18.55	21.03	23.34	26.22
13	4.107	5.009	5.892	7.042	19.81	22.36	24.74	27.69
14	4.660	5.629	6.571	7.790	21.06	23.68	26.12	29.14
15	5.229	6.262	7.261	8.547	22.31	25.00	27.49	30.58
16	5.812	6.908	7.962	9.312	23.54	26.30	28.84	32.00
17	6.408	7.564	8.672	10.08	24.77	27.59	30.19	33.41
18	7.015	8.231	9.390	10.86	25.99	28.87	31.53	34.80
19	7.633	8.907	10.12	11.65	27.20	30.14	32.85	36.19
20	8.260	9.591	10.85	12.44	28.41	31.41	34.17	37.57
21	8.897	10.28	11.59	13.24	29.62	32.67	35.48	38.93
22	9.542	10.98	12.34	14.04	30.81	33.92	36.78	40.29
23	10.20	11.69	13.09	14.85	32.01	35.17	38.08	41.64
24	10.86	12.40	13.85	15.66	33.20	36.42	39.36	42.98
25	11.52	13.12	14.61	16.47	34.38	37.65	40.65	44.31
26	12.20	13.84	15.38	17.29	35.56	38.88	41.92	45.64
27	12.88	14.57	16.15	18.11	36.74	40.11	43.19	46.96
28	13.56	15.31	16.93	18.94	37.92	41.34	44.46	48.28
29	14.26	16.05	17.71	19.77	39.09	42.56	45.72	49.59
30	14.95	16.79	18.49	20.60	40.26	43.77	46.98	50.89
40	22.16	24.43	26.51	29.05	51.80	55.76	59.34	63.69
50	29.71	32.36	34.76	37.69	63.17	67.50	71.42	76.15
60	37.48	40.48	43.19	46.46	74.40	79.08	83.30	88.38
70	45.44	48.76	51.74	55.33	85.53	90.53	95.02	100.4
80	53.34	57.15	60.39	64.28	96.58	101.9	106.6	112.3

This table is abridged and adapted from Table III in *Biometrika Tables for Statisticians*, edited by E.S.Pearson and H.O.Hartley.

TABLE Va: The Normal Distribution

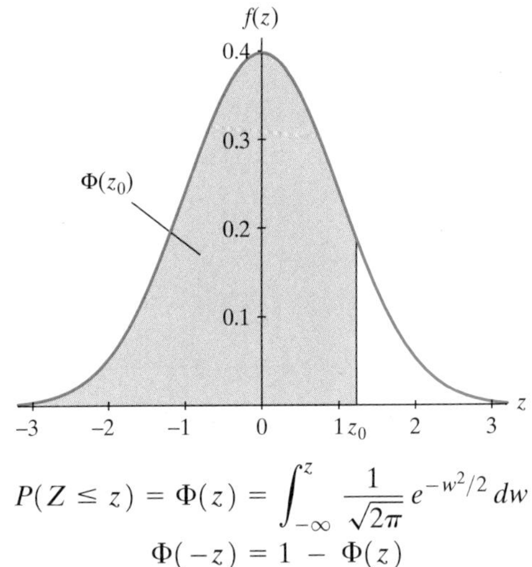

$$P(Z \le z) = \Phi(z) = \int_{-\infty}^{z} \frac{1}{\sqrt{2\pi}} e^{-w^2/2}\, dw$$

$$\Phi(-z) = 1 - \Phi(z)$$

z	0.00	0.01	0.02	0.03	0.04	0.05	0.06	0.07	0.08	0.09
0.0	0.5000	0.5040	0.5080	0.5120	0.5160	0.5199	0.5239	0.5279	0.5319	0.5359
0.1	0.5398	0.5438	0.5478	0.5517	0.5557	0.5596	0.5636	0.5675	0.5714	0.5753
0.2	0.5793	0.5832	0.5871	0.5910	0.5948	0.5987	0.6026	0.6064	0.6103	0.6141
0.3	0.6179	0.6217	0.6255	0.6293	0.6331	0.6368	0.6406	0.6443	0.6480	0.6517
0.4	0.6554	0.6591	0.6628	0.6664	0.6700	0.6736	0.6772	0.6808	0.6844	0.6879
0.5	0.6915	0.6950	0.6985	0.7019	0.7054	0.7088	0.7123	0.7157	0.7190	0.7224
0.6	0.7257	0.7291	0.7324	0.7357	0.7389	0.7422	0.7454	0.7486	0.7517	0.7549
0.7	0.7580	0.7611	0.7642	0.7673	0.7703	0.7734	0.7764	0.7794	0.7823	0.7852
0.8	0.7881	0.7910	0.7939	0.7967	0.7995	0.8023	0.8051	0.8078	0.8106	0.8133
0.9	0.8159	0.8186	0.8212	0.8238	0.8264	0.8289	0.8315	0.8340	0.8365	0.8389
1.0	0.8413	0.8438	0.8461	0.8485	0.8508	0.8531	0.8554	0.8577	0.8599	0.8621
1.1	0.8643	0.8665	0.8686	0.8708	0.8729	0.8749	0.8770	0.8790	0.8810	0.8830
1.2	0.8849	0.8869	0.8888	0.8907	0.8925	0.8944	0.8962	0.8980	0.8997	0.9015
1.3	0.9032	0.9049	0.9066	0.9082	0.9099	0.9115	0.9131	0.9147	0.9162	0.9177
1.4	0.9192	0.9207	0.9222	0.9236	0.9251	0.9265	0.9279	0.9292	0.9306	0.9319
1.5	0.9332	0.9345	0.9357	0.9370	0.9382	0.9394	0.9406	0.9418	0.9429	0.9441
1.6	0.9452	0.9463	0.9474	0.9484	0.9495	0.9505	0.9515	0.9525	0.9535	0.9545
1.7	0.9554	0.9564	0.9573	0.9582	0.9591	0.9599	0.9608	0.9616	0.9625	0.9633
1.8	0.9641	0.9649	0.9656	0.9664	0.9671	0.9678	0.9686	0.9693	0.9699	0.9706
1.9	0.9713	0.9719	0.9726	0.9732	0.9738	0.9744	0.9750	0.9756	0.9761	0.9767
2.0	0.9772	0.9778	0.9783	0.9788	0.9793	0.9798	0.9803	0.9808	0.9812	0.9817
2.1	0.9821	0.9826	0.9830	0.9834	0.9838	0.9842	0.9846	0.9850	0.9854	0.9857
2.2	0.9861	0.9864	0.9868	0.9871	0.9875	0.9878	0.9881	0.9884	0.9887	0.9890
2.3	0.9893	0.9896	0.9898	0.9901	0.9904	0.9906	0.9909	0.9911	0.9913	0.9916
2.4	0.9918	0.9920	0.9922	0.9925	0.9927	0.9929	0.9931	0.9932	0.9934	0.9936
2.5	0.9938	0.9940	0.9941	0.9943	0.9945	0.9946	0.9948	0.9949	0.9951	0.9952
2.6	0.9953	0.9955	0.9956	0.9957	0.9959	0.9960	0.9961	0.9962	0.9963	0.9964
2.7	0.9965	0.9966	0.9967	0.9968	0.9969	0.9970	0.9971	0.9972	0.9973	0.9974
2.8	0.9974	0.9975	0.9976	0.9977	0.9977	0.9978	0.9979	0.9979	0.9980	0.9981
2.9	0.9981	0.9982	0.9982	0.9983	0.9984	0.9984	0.9985	0.9985	0.9986	0.9986
3.0	0.9987	0.9987	0.9987	0.9988	0.9988	0.9989	0.9989	0.9989	0.9990	0.9990

α	0.400	0.300	0.200	0.100	0.050	0.025	0.020	0.010	0.005	0.001
z_α	0.253	0.524	0.842	1.282	1.645	1.960	2.054	2.326	2.576	3.090
$z_{\alpha/2}$	0.842	1.036	1.282	1.645	1.960	2.240	2.326	2.576	2.807	3.291

TABLE Vb: The Normal Distribution

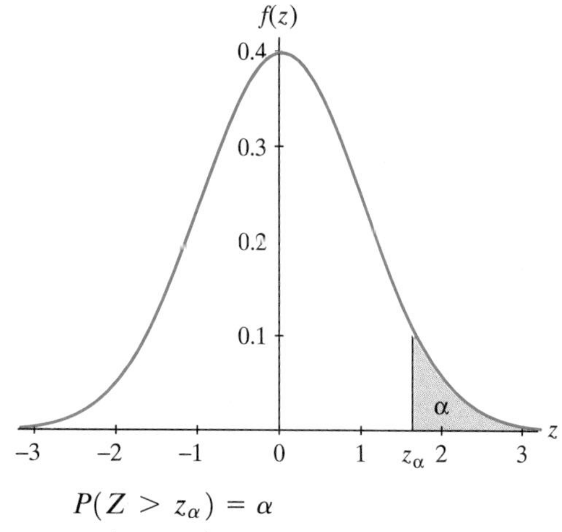

$P(Z > z_\alpha) = \alpha$

$P(Z > z) = 1 - \Phi(z) = \Phi(-z)$

z_α	0.00	0.01	0.02	0.03	0.04	0.05	0.06	0.07	0.08	0.09
0.0	0.5000	0.4960	0.4920	0.4880	0.4840	0.4801	0.4761	0.4721	0.4681	0.4641
0.1	0.4602	0.4562	0.4522	0.4483	0.4443	0.4404	0.4364	0.4325	0.4286	0.4247
0.2	0.4207	0.4168	0.4129	0.4090	0.4052	0.4013	0.3974	0.3936	0.3897	0.3859
0.3	0.3821	0.3783	0.3745	0.3707	0.3669	0.3632	0.3594	0.3557	0.3520	0.3483
0.4	0.3446	0.3409	0.3372	0.3336	0.3300	0.3264	0.3228	0.3192	0.3156	0.3121
0.5	0.3085	0.3050	0.3015	0.2981	0.2946	0.2912	0.2877	0.2843	0.2810	0.2776
0.6	0.2743	0.2709	0.2676	0.2643	0.2611	0.2578	0.2546	0.2514	0.2483	0.2451
0.7	0.2420	0.2389	0.2358	0.2327	0.2296	0.2266	0.2236	0.2206	0.2177	0.2148
0.8	0.2119	0.2090	0.2061	0.2033	0.2005	0.1977	0.1949	0.1922	0.1894	0.1867
0.9	0.1841	0.1814	0.1788	0.1762	0.1736	0.1711	0.1685	0.1660	0.1635	0.1611
1.0	0.1587	0.1562	0.1539	0.1515	0.1492	0.1469	0.1446	0.1423	0.1401	0.1379
1.1	0.1357	0.1335	0.1314	0.1292	0.1271	0.1251	0.1230	0.1210	0.1190	0.1170
1.2	0.1151	0.1131	0.1112	0.1093	0.1075	0.1056	0.1038	0.1020	0.1003	0.0985
1.3	0.0968	0.0951	0.0934	0.0918	0.0901	0.0885	0.0869	0.0853	0.0838	0.0823
1.4	0.0808	0.0793	0.0778	0.0764	0.0749	0.0735	0.0721	0.0708	0.0694	0.0681
1.5	0.0668	0.0655	0.0643	0.0630	0.0618	0.0606	0.0594	0.0582	0.0571	0.0559
1.6	0.0548	0.0537	0.0526	0.0516	0.0505	0.0495	0.0485	0.0475	0.0465	0.0455
1.7	0.0446	0.0436	0.0427	0.0418	0.0409	0.0401	0.0392	0.0384	0.0375	0.0367
1.8	0.0359	0.0351	0.0344	0.0336	0.0329	0.0322	0.0314	0.0307	0.0301	0.0294
1.9	0.0287	0.0281	0.0274	0.0268	0.0262	0.0256	0.0250	0.0244	0.0239	0.0233
2.0	0.0228	0.0222	0.0217	0.0212	0.0207	0.0202	0.0197	0.0192	0.0188	0.0183
2.1	0.0179	0.0174	0.0170	0.0166	0.0162	0.0158	0.0154	0.0150	0.0146	0.0143
2.2	0.0139	0.0136	0.0132	0.0129	0.0125	0.0122	0.0119	0.0116	0.0113	0.0110
2.3	0.0107	0.0104	0.0102	0.0099	0.0096	0.0094	0.0091	0.0089	0.0087	0.0084
2.4	0.0082	0.0080	0.0078	0.0075	0.0073	0.0071	0.0069	0.0068	0.0066	0.0064
2.5	0.0062	0.0060	0.0059	0.0057	0.0055	0.0054	0.0052	0.0051	0.0049	0.0048
2.6	0.0047	0.0045	0.0044	0.0043	0.0041	0.0040	0.0039	0.0038	0.0037	0.0036
2.7	0.0035	0.0034	0.0033	0.0032	0.0031	0.0030	0.0029	0.0028	0.0027	0.0026
2.8	0.0026	0.0025	0.0024	0.0023	0.0023	0.0022	0.0021	0.0021	0.0020	0.0019
2.9	0.0019	0.0018	0.0018	0.0017	0.0016	0.0016	0.0015	0.0015	0.0014	0.0014
3.0	0.0013	0.0013	0.0013	0.0012	0.0012	0.0011	0.0011	0.0011	0.0010	0.0010
3.1	0.0010	0.0009	0.0009	0.0009	0.0008	0.0008	0.0008	0.0008	0.0007	0.0007
3.2	0.0007	0.0007	0.0006	0.0006	0.0006	0.0006	0.0006	0.0005	0.0005	0.0005
3.3	0.0005	0.0005	0.0005	0.0004	0.0004	0.0004	0.0004	0.0004	0.0004	0.0003
3.4	0.0003	0.0003	0.0003	0.0003	0.0003	0.0003	0.0003	0.0003	0.0003	0.0002

TABLE VI: The *t* Distribution

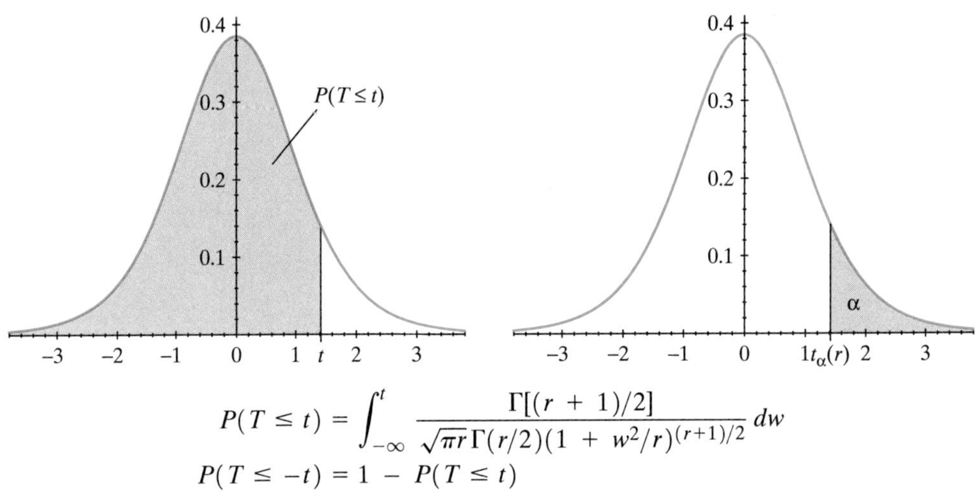

$$P(T \le t) = \int_{-\infty}^{t} \frac{\Gamma[(r+1)/2]}{\sqrt{\pi r}\,\Gamma(r/2)(1 + w^2/r)^{(r+1)/2}}\,dw$$

$$P(T \le -t) = 1 - P(T \le t)$$

	$P(T \le t)$						
	0.60	0.75	0.90	0.95	0.975	0.99	0.995
r	$t_{0.40}(r)$	$t_{0.25}(r)$	$t_{0.10}(r)$	$t_{0.05}(r)$	$t_{0.025}(r)$	$t_{0.01}(r)$	$t_{0.005}(r)$
1	0.325	1.000	3.078	6.314	12.706	31.821	63.657
2	0.289	0.816	1.886	2.920	4.303	6.965	9.925
3	0.277	0.765	1.638	2.353	3.182	4.541	5.841
4	0.271	0.741	1.533	2.132	2.776	3.747	4.604
5	0.267	0.727	1.476	2.015	2.571	3.365	4.032
6	0.265	0.718	1.440	1.943	2.447	3.143	3.707
7	0.263	0.711	1.415	1.895	2.365	2.998	3.499
8	0.262	0.706	1.397	1.860	2.306	2.896	3.355
9	0.261	0.703	1.383	1.833	2.262	2.821	3.250
10	0.260	0.700	1.372	1.812	2.228	2.764	3.169
11	0.260	0.697	1.363	1.796	2.201	2.718	3.106
12	0.259	0.695	1.356	1.782	2.179	2.681	3.055
13	0.259	0.694	1.350	1.771	2.160	2.650	3.012
14	0.258	0.692	1.345	1.761	2.145	2.624	2.997
15	0.258	0.691	1.341	1.753	2.131	2.602	2.947
16	0.258	0.690	1.337	1.746	2.120	2.583	2.921
17	0.257	0.689	1.333	1.740	2.110	2.567	2.898
18	0.257	0.688	1.330	1.734	2.101	2.552	2.878
19	0.257	0.688	1.328	1.729	2.093	2.539	2.861
20	0.257	0.687	1.325	1.725	2.086	2.528	2.845
21	0.257	0.686	1.323	1.721	2.080	2.518	2.831
22	0.256	0.686	1.321	1.717	2.074	2.508	2.819
23	0.256	0.685	1.319	1.714	2.069	2.500	2.807
24	0.256	0.685	1.318	1.711	2.064	2.492	2.797
25	0.256	0.684	1.316	1.708	2.060	2.485	2.787
26	0.256	0.684	1.315	1.706	2.056	2.479	2.779
27	0.256	0.684	1.314	1.703	2.052	2.473	2.771
28	0.256	0.683	1.313	1.701	2.048	2.467	2.763
29	0.256	0.683	1.311	1.699	2.045	2.462	2.756
30	0.256	0.683	1.310	1.697	2.042	2.457	2.750
∞	0.253	0.674	1.282	1.645	1.960	2.326	2.576

This table is taken from Table III of Fisher and Yates: *Statistical Tables for Biological, Agricultrual, and Medical Research*, published by Longman Group Ltd., London (previously published by Oliver and Boyd, Edinburgh).

TABLE VII: The F Distribution

$$P(F \le f) = \int_0^f \frac{\Gamma[(r_1 + r_2)/2](r_1/r_2)^{r_1/2} w^{r_1/2-1}}{\Gamma(r_1/2)\Gamma(r_2/2)(1 + r_1 w/r_2)^{(r_1+r_2)/2}}\, dw$$

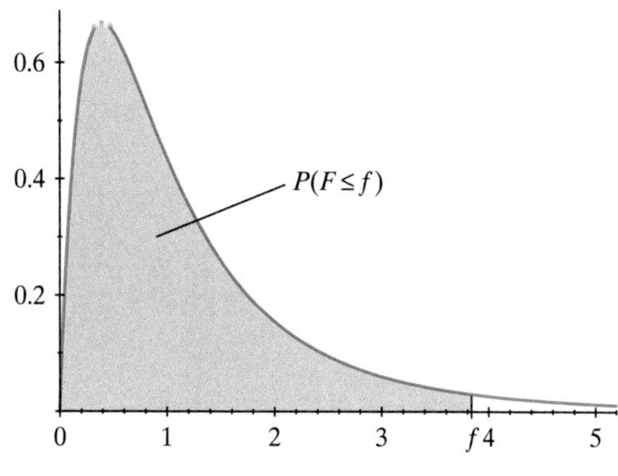

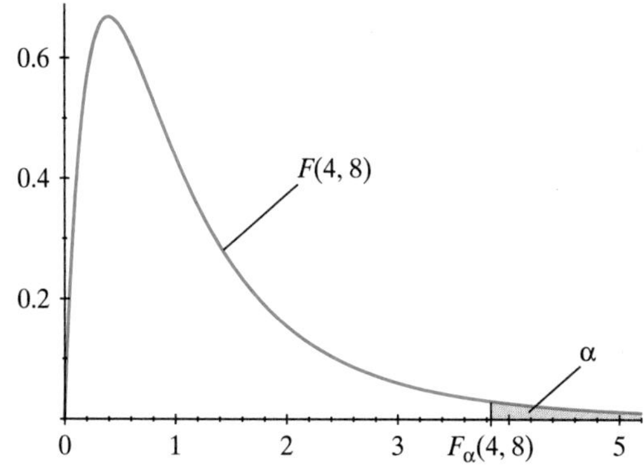

TABLE VII: *continued*

$$P(F \le f) = \int_0^f \frac{\Gamma[(r_1 + r_2)/2](r_1/r_2)^{r_1/2} w^{r_1/2-1}}{\Gamma(r_1/2)\Gamma(r_2/2)(1 + r_1 w/r_2)^{(r_1+r_2)/2}}\, dw$$

		Den. d.f.	Numerator Degrees of Freedom, r_1									
α	$P(F \le f)$	r_2	1	2	3	4	5	6	7	8	9	10
0.05	0.95	1	161.4	199.5	215.7	224.6	230.2	234.0	236.8	238.9	240.5	241.9
0.025	0.975		647.79	799.50	864.16	899.58	921.85	937.11	948.22	956.66	963.28	968.63
0.01	0.99		4052	4999.5	5403	5625	5764	5859	5928	5981	6022	6056
0.05	0.95	2	18.51	19.00	19.16	19.25	19.30	19.33	19.35	19.37	19.38	19.40
0.025	0.975		38.51	39.00	39.17	39.25	39.30	39.33	39.36	39.37	39.39	39.40
0.01	0.99		98.50	99.00	99.17	99.25	99.30	99.33	99.36	99.37	99.39	99.40
0.05	0.95	3	10.13	9.55	9.28	9.12	9.01	8.94	8.89	8.85	8.81	8.79
0.025	0.975		17.44	16.04	15.44	15.10	14.88	14.73	14.62	14.54	14.47	14.42
0.01	0.99		34.12	30.82	29.46	28.71	28.24	27.91	27.67	27.49	27.35	27.23
0.05	0.95	4	7.71	6.94	6.59	6.39	6.26	6.16	6.09	6.04	6.00	5.96
0.025	0.975		12.22	10.65	9.98	9.60	9.36	9.20	9.07	8.98	8.90	8.84
0.01	0.99		21.20	18.00	16.69	15.98	15.52	15.21	14.98	14.80	14.66	14.55
0.05	0.95	5	6.61	5.79	5.41	5.19	5.05	4.95	4.88	4.82	4.77	4.74
0.025	0.975		10.01	8.43	7.76	7.39	7.15	6.98	6.85	6.76	6.68	6.62
0.01	0.99		16.26	13.27	12.06	11.39	10.97	10.67	10.46	10.29	10.16	10.05
0.05	0.95	6	5.99	5.14	4.76	4.53	4.39	4.28	4.21	4.15	4.10	4.06
0.025	0.975		8.81	7.26	6.60	6.23	5.99	5.82	5.70	5.60	5.52	5.46
0.01	0.99		13.75	10.92	9.78	9.15	8.75	8.47	8.26	8.10	7.98	7.87
0.05	0.95	7	5.59	4.74	4.35	4.12	3.97	3.87	3.79	3.73	3.68	3.64
0.025	0.975		8.07	6.54	5.89	5.52	5.29	5.12	4.99	4.90	4.82	4.76
0.01	0.99		12.25	9.55	8.45	7.85	7.46	7.19	6.99	6.84	6.72	6.62
0.05	0.95	8	5.32	4.46	4.07	3.84	3.69	3.58	3.50	3.44	3.39	3.35
0.025	0.975		7.57	6.06	5.42	5.05	4.82	4.65	4.53	4.43	4.36	4.30
0.01	0.99		11.26	8.65	7.59	7.01	6.63	6.37	6.18	6.03	5.91	5.81
0.05	0.95	9	5.12	4.26	3.86	3.63	3.48	3.37	3.29	3.23	3.18	3.14
0.025	0.975		7.21	5.71	5.08	4.72	4.48	4.32	4.20	4.10	4.03	3.96
0.01	0.99		10.56	8.02	6.99	6.42	6.06	5.80	5.61	5.47	5.35	5.26
0.05	0.95	10	4.96	4.10	3.71	3.48	3.33	3.22	3.14	3.07	3.02	2.98
0.025	0.975		6.94	5.46	4.83	4.47	4.24	4.07	3.95	3.85	3.78	3.72
0.01	0.99		10.04	7.56	6.55	5.99	5.64	5.39	5.20	5.06	4.94	4.85

TABLE VII: *continued*

$$P(F \le f) = \int_0^f \frac{\Gamma[(r_1 + r_2)/2](r_1/r_2)^{r_1/2} w^{r_1/2-1}}{\Gamma(r_1/2)\Gamma(r_2/2)(1 + r_1 w/r_2)^{(r_1+r_2)/2}}\, dw$$

		Den. d.f.	Numerator Degrees of Freedom, r_1									
α	$P(F \le f)$	r_2	1	2	3	4	5	6	7	8	9	10
0.05	0.95	12	4.75	3.89	3.49	3.26	3.11	3.00	2.91	2.85	2.80	2.75
0.025	0.975		6.55	5.10	4.47	4.12	3.89	3.73	3.61	3.51	3.44	3.37
0.01	0.99		9.33	6.93	5.95	5.41	5.06	4.82	4.64	4.50	4.39	4.30
0.05	0.95	15	4.54	3.68	3.29	3.06	2.90	2.79	2.71	2.64	2.59	2.54
0.025	0.975		6.20	4.77	4.15	3.80	3.58	3.41	3.29	3.20	3.12	3.06
0.01	0.99		8.68	6.36	5.42	4.89	4.56	4.32	4.14	4.00	3.89	3.80
0.05	0.95	20	4.35	3.49	3.10	2.87	2.71	2.60	2.51	2.45	2.39	2.35
0.025	0.975		5.87	4.46	3.86	3.51	3.29	3.13	3.01	2.91	2.84	2.77
0.01	0.99		8.10	5.85	4.94	4.43	4.10	3.87	3.70	3.56	3.46	3.37
0.05	0.95	24	4.26	3.40	3.01	2.78	2.62	2.51	2.42	2.36	2.30	2.25
0.025	0.975		5.72	4.32	3.72	3.38	3.15	2.99	2.87	2.78	2.70	2.64
0.01	0.99		7.82	5.61	4.72	4.22	3.90	3.67	3.50	3.36	3.26	3.17
0.05	0.95	30	4.17	3.32	2.92	2.69	2.53	2.42	2.33	2.27	2.21	2.16
0.025	0.975		5.57	4.18	3.59	3.25	3.03	2.87	2.75	2.65	2.57	2.51
0.01	0.99		7.56	5.39	4.51	4.02	3.70	3.47	3.30	3.17	3.07	2.98
0.05	0.95	40	4.08	3.23	2.84	2.61	2.45	2.34	2.25	2.18	2.12	2.08
0.025	0.975		5.42	4.05	3.46	3.13	2.90	2.74	2.62	2.53	2.45	2.39
0.01	0.99		7.31	5.18	4.31	3.83	3.51	3.29	3.12	2.99	2.89	2.80
0.05	0.95	60	4.00	3.15	2.76	2.53	2.37	2.25	2.17	2.10	2.04	1.99
0.025	0.975		5.29	3.93	3.34	3.01	2.79	2.63	2.51	2.41	2.33	2.27
0.01	0.99		7.08	4.98	4.13	3.65	3.34	3.12	2.95	2.82	2.72	2.63
0.05	0.95	120	3.92	3.07	2.68	2.45	2.29	2.17	2.09	2.02	1.96	1.91
0.025	0.975		5.15	3.80	3.23	2.89	2.67	2.52	2.39	2.30	2.22	2.16
0.01	0.99		6.85	4.79	3.95	3.48	3.17	2.96	2.79	2.66	2.56	2.47
0.05	0.95	∞	3.84	3.00	2.60	2.37	2.21	2.10	2.01	1.94	1.88	1.83
0.025	0.975		5.02	3.69	3.12	2.79	2.57	2.41	2.29	2.19	2.11	2.05
0.01	0.99		6.63	4.61	3.78	3.32	3.02	2.80	2.64	2.51	2.41	2.32

TABLE VII: *continued*

$$P(F \le f) = \int_0^f \frac{\Gamma[(r_1 + r_2)/2](r_1/r_2)^{r_1/2} w^{r_1/2-1}}{\Gamma(r_1/2)\Gamma(r_2/2)(1 + r_1 w/r_2)^{(r_1+r_2)/2}}\, dw$$

		Den. d.f.	Numerator Degrees of Freedom, r_1								
α	$P(F \le f)$	r_2	12	15	20	24	30	40	60	120	∞
0.05	0.95	1	243.9	245.9	248.0	249.1	250.1	251.1	252.2	253.3	254.3
0.025	0.975		976.71	984.87	993.10	997.25	1001.4	1005.6	1009.8	1014.0	1018.3
0.01	0.99		6106	6157	6209	6235	6261	6287	6313	6339	6366
0.05	0.95	2	19.41	19.43	19.45	19.45	19.46	19.47	19.48	19.49	19.50
0.025	0.975		39.42	39.43	39.45	39.46	39.47	39.47	39.48	39.49	39.50
0.01	0.99		99.42	99.43	99.45	99.46	99.47	99.47	99.48	99.49	99.50
0.05	0.95	3	8.74	8.70	8.66	8.64	8.62	8.59	8.57	8.55	8.53
0.025	0.975		14.34	14.25	14.17	14.12	14.08	14.04	13.99	13.95	13.90
0.01	0.99		27.05	26.87	26.69	26.60	26.50	26.41	26.32	26.22	26.13
0.05	0.95	4	5.91	5.86	5.80	5.77	5.75	5.72	5.69	5.66	5.63
0.025	0.975		8.75	8.66	8.56	8.51	8.46	8.41	8.36	8.31	8.26
0.01	0.99		14.37	14.20	14.02	13.93	13.84	13.75	13.65	13.56	13.46
0.05	0.95	5	4.68	4.62	4.56	4.53	4.50	4.46	4.43	4.40	4.36
0.025	0.975		6.52	6.43	6.33	6.28	6.23	6.18	6.12	6.07	6.02
0.01	0.99		9.89	9.72	9.55	9.47	9.38	9.29	9.20	9.11	9.02
0.05	0.95	6	4.00	3.94	3.87	3.84	3.81	3.77	3.74	3.70	3.67
0.025	0.975		5.37	5.27	5.17	5.12	5.07	5.01	4.96	4.90	4.85
0.01	0.99		7.72	7.56	7.40	7.31	7.23	7.14	7.06	6.97	6.88
0.05	0.95	7	3.57	3.51	3.41	3.41	3.38	3.34	3.30	3.27	3.23
0.025	0.975		4.67	4.57	4.47	4.42	4.36	4.31	4.25	4.20	4.14
0.01	0.99		6.47	6.31	6.16	6.07	5.99	5.91	5.82	5.74	5.65
0.05	0.95	8	3.28	3.22	3.15	3.12	3.08	3.04	3.01	2.97	2.93
0.025	0.975		4.20	4.10	4.00	3.95	3.89	3.84	3.78	3.73	3.67
0.01	0.99		5.67	5.52	5.36	5.28	5.20	5.12	5.03	4.95	4.86
0.05	0.95	9	3.07	3.01	2.94	2.90	2.86	2.83	2.79	2.75	2.71
0.025	0.975		3.87	3.77	3.67	3.61	3.56	3.51	3.45	3.39	3.33
0.01	0.99		5.11	4.96	4.81	4.73	4.65	4.57	4.48	4.40	4.31

TABLE VII: *continued*

$$P(F \le f) = \int_0^f \frac{\Gamma[(r_1 + r_2)/2](r_1/r_2)^{r_1/2} w^{r_1/2-1}}{\Gamma(r_1/2)\Gamma(r_2/2)(1 + r_1 w/r_2)^{(r_1+r_2)/2}}\, dw$$

		Den. d.f.	Numerator Degrees of Freedom, r_1								
α	$P(F \le f)$	r_2	12	15	20	24	30	40	60	120	∞
0.05	0.95	10	2.91	2.85	2.77	2.74	2.70	2.66	2.62	2.58	2.54
0.025	0.975		3.62	3.52	3.42	3.37	3.31	3.26	3.20	3.14	3.08
0.01	0.99		4.71	4.56	4.41	4.33	4.25	4.17	4.08	4.00	3.91
0.05	0.95	12	2.69	2.62	2.54	2.51	2.47	2.43	2.38	2.34	2.30
0.025	0.975		3.28	3.18	3.07	3.02	2.96	2.91	2.85	2.79	2.72
0.01	0.99		4.16	4.01	3.86	3.78	3.70	3.62	3.54	3.45	3.36
0.05	0.95	15	2.48	2.40	2.33	2.29	2.25	2.20	2.16	2.11	2.07
0.025	0.975		2.96	2.86	2.76	2.70	2.64	2.59	2.52	2.46	2.40
0.01	0.99		3.67	3.52	3.37	3.29	3.21	3.13	3.05	2.96	2.87
0.05	0.95	20	2.28	2.20	2.12	2.08	2.04	1.99	1.95	1.90	1.84
0.025	0.975		2.68	2.57	2.46	2.41	2.35	2.29	2.22	2.16	2.09
0.01	0.99		3.23	3.09	2.94	2.86	2.78	2.69	2.61	2.52	2.42
0.05	0.95	24	2.18	2.11	2.03	1.98	1.94	1.89	1.84	1.79	1.73
0.025	0.975		2.54	2.44	2.33	2.27	2.21	2.15	2.08	2.01	1.94
0.01	0.99		3.03	2.89	2.74	2.66	2.58	2.49	2.40	2.31	2.21
0.05	0.95	30	2.09	2.01	1.93	1.89	1.84	1.79	1.74	1.68	1.62
0.025	0.975		2.41	2.31	2.20	2.14	2.07	2.01	1.94	1.87	1.79
0.01	0.99		2.84	2.70	2.55	2.47	2.39	2.30	2.21	2.11	2.01
0.05	0.95	40	2.00	1.92	1.84	1.79	1.74	1.69	1.64	1.58	1.51
0.025	0.975		2.29	2.18	2.07	2.01	1.94	1.88	1.80	1.72	1.64
0.01	0.99		2.66	2.52	2.37	2.29	2.20	2.11	2.02	1.92	1.80
0.05	0.95	60	1.92	1.84	1.75	1.70	1.65	1.59	1.53	1.47	1.39
0.025	0.975		2.17	2.06	1.94	1.88	1.82	1.74	1.67	1.58	1.48
0.01	0.99		2.50	2.35	2.20	2.12	2.03	1.94	1.84	1.73	1.60
0.05	0.95	120	1.83	1.75	1.66	1.61	1.55	1.50	1.43	1.35	1.25
0.025	0.975		2.05	1.95	1.82	1.76	1.69	1.61	1.53	1.43	1.31
0.01	0.99		2.34	2.19	2.03	1.95	1.86	1.76	1.66	1.53	1.38
0.05	0.95	∞	1.75	1.67	1.57	1.52	1.46	1.39	1.32	1.22	1.00
0.025	0.975		1.94	1.83	1.71	1.64	1.57	1.48	1.39	1.27	1.00
0.01	0.99		2.18	2.04	1.88	1.79	1.70	1.59	1.47	1.32	1.00

TABLE VIII: Kolmogorov-Smirnov Acceptance Limits

$$D_n = \sup_x[\,|F_n(x) - F_0(x)|\,]$$

$$\alpha = 1 - P(D_n \leq d)$$

	α			
n	0.20	0.10	0.05	0.01
1	0.90	0.95	0.98	0.99
2	0.68	0.78	0.84	0.93
3	0.56	0.64	0.71	0.83
4	0.49	0.56	0.62	0.73
5	0.45	0.51	0.56	0.67
6	0.41	0.47	0.52	0.62
7	0.38	0.44	0.49	0.58
8	0.36	0.41	0.46	0.54
9	0.34	0.39	0.43	0.51
10	0.32	0.37	0.41	0.49
11	0.31	0.35	0.39	0.47
12	0.30	0.34	0.38	0.45
13	0.28	0.32	0.36	0.43
14	0.27	0.31	0.35	0.42
15	0.27	0.30	0.34	0.40
16	0.26	0.30	0.33	0.39
17	0.25	0.29	0.32	0.38
18	0.24	0.28	0.31	0.37
19	0.24	0.27	0.30	0.36
20	0.23	0.26	0.29	0.35
25	0.21	0.24	0.26	0.32
30	0.19	0.22	0.24	0.29
35	0.18	0.21	0.23	0.27
40	0.17	0.19	0.21	0.25
45	0.16	0.18	0.20	0.24
Large n	$\frac{1.07}{\sqrt{n}}$	$\frac{1.22}{\sqrt{n}}$	$\frac{1.36}{\sqrt{n}}$	$\frac{1.63}{\sqrt{n}}$

TABLE IX: Random Numbers on the Interval (0, 1)

3407	1440	6960	8675	5649	5793	1514
5044	9859	4658	7779	7986	0520	6697
0045	4999	4930	7408	7551	3124	0527
7536	1448	7843	4801	3147	3071	4749
7653	4231	1233	4409	0609	6448	2900
6157	1144	4779	0951	3757	9562	2354
6593	8668	4871	0946	3133	3941	9662
3187	7434	0315	4418	1569	1101	0043
4780	1071	6814	2733	7968	8541	1003
9414	6170	2581	1398	2429	4763	9192
1948	2360	7244	9682	5418	0596	4971
1843	0914	9705	7861	6861	7865	7293
4944	8903	0460	0188	0530	7790	9118
3882	3195	8287	3298	9532	9066	8225
6596	9009	2055	4081	4842	7852	5915
4793	2503	2906	6807	2028	1075	7175
2112	0232	5334	1443	7306	6418	9639
0743	1083	8071	9779	5973	1141	4393
8856	5352	3384	8891	9189	1680	3192
8027	4975	2346	5786	0693	5615	2047
3134	1688	4071	3766	0570	2142	3492
0633	9002	1305	2256	5956	9256	8979
8771	6069	1598	4275	6017	5946	8189
2672	1304	2186	8279	2430	4896	3698
3136	1916	8886	8617	9312	5070	2720
6490	7491	6562	5355	3794	3555	7510
8628	0501	4618	3364	6709	1289	0543
9270	0504	5018	7013	4423	2147	4089
5723	3807	4997	4699	2231	3193	8130
6228	8874	7271	2621	5746	6333	0345
7645	3379	8376	3030	0351	8290	3640
6842	5836	6203	6171	2698	4086	5469
6126	7792	9337	7773	7286	4236	1788
4956	0215	3468	8038	6144	9753	3131
1327	4736	6229	8965	7215	6458	3937
9188	1516	5279	5433	2254	5768	8718
0271	9627	9442	9217	4656	7603	8826
2127	1847	1331	5122	8332	8195	3322
2102	9201	2911	7318	7670	6079	2676
1706	6011	5280	5552	5180	4630	4747
7501	7635	2301	0889	6955	8113	4364
5705	1900	7144	8707	9065	8163	9846
3234	2599	3295	9160	8441	0085	9317
5641	4935	7971	8917	1978	5649	5799
2127	1868	3664	9376	1984	6315	8396

TABLE X: Divisors for the Confidence Interval for σ of Minimum Length

Let $X_1, X_2, \ldots, X_n$ be a random sample of size n from $N(\mu, \sigma^2)$; let $\overline{x} = (1/n)\sum_{i=1}^{n} x_i$ and $s^2 = (1/[n - 1])\sum_{i=1}^{n}(x_i - \overline{x})^2$. A $(100\gamma)\%$ confidence interval for σ which has minimum length is given by $[\sqrt{(n - 1)s^2/b}, \sqrt{(n - 1)s^2/a}]$. In the table, a is the upper number, b the lower number; $r = n - 1$, the number of degrees of freedom; and $\gamma = 1 - \alpha$, the confidence level.

	$\gamma = 1 - \alpha$				$\gamma = 1 - \alpha$		
r	0.90	0.95	0.99	r	0.90	0.95	0.99
2	0.206 12.521	0.101 15.111	0.020 20.865	16	8.774 29.233	7.604 32.072	5.649 38.097
3	0.565 13.153	0.345 15.589	0.114 20.973	17	9.505 30.480	8.282 33.362	6.226 39.469
4	1.020 14.18	0.692 16.573	0.294 21.838	18	10.242 31.721	8.969 34.647	6.814 40.835
5	1.535 15.350	1.109 17.743	0.546 22.985	19	10.986 32.959	9.663 35.927	7.413 42.195
6	2.093 16.581	1.578 18.996	0.837 24.262	20	11.736 34.192	10.365 37.202	8.021 43.550
7	2.683 17.839	2.085 20.286	1.214 25.602	21	12.492 35.420	11.073 38.472	8.638 44.899
8	3.298 19.110	2.623 21.595	1.611 26.975	22	13.253 36.646	11.788 39.738	9.264 46.243
9	3.934 20.385	3.187 22.912	2.039 28.364	23	14.019 37.867	12.509 41.000	9.898 47.586
10	4.588 21.660	3.773 24.230	2.496 29.760	24	14.790 39.084	13.236 42.257	10.539 48.914
11	5.257 22.933	4.377 25.547	2.976 31.158	25	15.565 40.299	13.968 43.510	11.186 50.243
12	5.940 24.202	4.997 26.862	3.477 32.554	26	16.344 41.509	14.704 44.760	11.841 51.566
13	6.634 25.467	5.631 28.172	3.997 33.947	27	17.127 42.717	15.446 46.006	12.501 52.886
14	7.338 26.727	6.278 29.477	4.533 35.336	28	17.914 43.922	16.192 47.248	13.168 54.200
15	8.052 27.982	6.936 30.777	5.084 36.719	29	18.705 45.123	16.942 48.487	13.840 55.511

TABLE XI: Distribution Function of the Correlation Coefficient R, $\rho = 0$

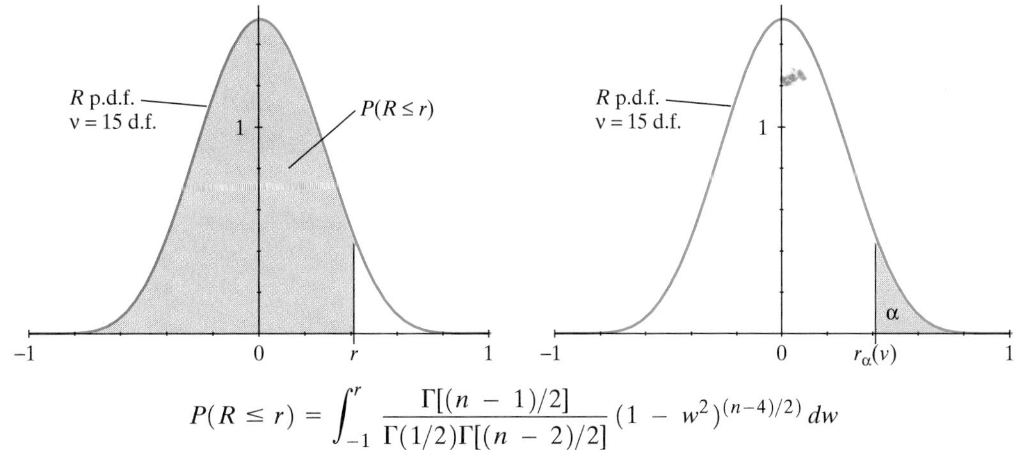

$$P(R \le r) = \int_{-1}^{r} \frac{\Gamma[(n-1)/2]}{\Gamma(1/2)\Gamma[(n-2)/2]} (1 - w^2)^{(n-4)/2}\, dw$$

$\nu = n - 2$ degrees of freedom	$P(R \le r)$			
	0.95	0.975	0.99	0.995
	$r_{0.05}(\nu)$	$r_{0.025}(\nu)$	$r_{0.01}(\nu)$	$r_{0.005}(\nu)$
1	0.9877	0.9969	0.9995	0.9999
2	0.9000	0.9500	0.9800	0.9900
3	0.8053	0.8783	0.9343	0.9587
4	0.7292	0.8113	0.8822	0.9172
5	0.6694	0.7544	0.8329	0.8745
6	0.6215	0.7067	0.7887	0.8343
7	0.5822	0.6664	0.7497	0.7977
8	0.5493	0.6319	0.7154	0.7646
9	0.5214	0.6020	0.6850	0.7348
10	0.4972	0.5759	0.6581	0.7079
11	0.4761	0.5529	0.6338	0.6835
12	0.4575	0.5323	0.6120	0.6613
13	0.4408	0.5139	0.5922	0.6411
14	0.4258	0.4973	0.5742	0.6226
15	0.4123	0.4821	0.5577	0.6054
16	0.4000	0.4683	0.5425	0.5897
17	0.3887	0.4555	0.5285	0.5750
18	0.3783	0.4437	0.5154	0.5614
19	0.3687	0.4328	0.5033	0.5487
20	0.3597	0.4226	0.4920	0.5367
25	0.3232	0.3808	0.4450	0.4869
30	0.2959	0.3494	0.4092	0.4487
35	0.2746	0.3246	0.3809	0.4182
40	0.2572	0.3044	0.3578	0.3931
45	0.2428	0.2875	0.3383	0.3721
50	0.2306	0.2732	0.3218	0.3541
60	0.2108	0.2500	0.2948	0.3248
70	0.1954	0.2318	0.2736	0.3017
80	0.1829	0.2172	0.2565	0.2829
90	0.1725	0.2049	0.2422	0.2673
100	0.1638	0.1946	0.2300	0.2540

TABLE XII: Discrete Distributions

Probability Distribution and Parameter Values	Probability Mass Function	Moment-Generating Function	Mean $E(X)$	Variance $\text{Var}(X)$	Examples
Bernoulli $0 < p < 1$ $q = 1 - p$	$p^x q^{1-x},\ x = 0, 1$	$q + pe^t$	p	pq	Experiment with two possible outcomes—say, success and failure; $p = P(\text{success})$
Binomial $n = 1, 2, 3, \ldots$ $0 < p < 1$	$\binom{n}{x} p^x q^{n-x}$, $x = 0, 1, \ldots, n$	$(q + pe^t)^n$	np	npq	Number of successes in a sequence of n Bernoulli trials; $p = P(\text{success})$
Geometric $0 < p < 1$ $q = 1 - p$	$q^{x-1}p$, $x = 1, 2, \ldots$	$\dfrac{pe^t}{1 - qe^t}$	$\dfrac{1}{p}$	$\dfrac{q}{p^2}$	The number of trials taken to obtain the first success in a sequence of Bernoulli trials
Hypergeometric $x \le n, x \le N_1$ $n - x \le N_2$ $N = N_1 + N_2$ $N_1 > 0,\ N_2 > 0$	$\dfrac{\binom{N_1}{x}\binom{N_2}{n - x}}{\binom{N}{n}}$		$n\left(\dfrac{N_1}{N}\right)$	$n\left(\dfrac{N_1}{N}\right)\left(\dfrac{N_2}{N}\right)\left(\dfrac{N - n}{N - 1}\right)$	Selecting r objects at random without replacement from a set composed of two types of objects
Negative Binomial $r = 1, 2, 3, \ldots$ $0 < p < 1$	$\binom{x - 1}{r - 1} p^r q^{x-r}$, $x = r, r + 1, \ldots$	$\dfrac{(pe^t)^r}{(1 - qe^t)^r}$	$\dfrac{r}{p}$	$\dfrac{rq}{p^2}$	The number of trials taken to obtain the rth success in a sequence of Bernoulli trials
Poisson $0 < \lambda$	$\dfrac{\lambda^x e^{-\lambda}}{x!}$, $x = 0, 1, \ldots$	$e^{\lambda(e^t - 1)}$	λ	λ	Number of events occurring in a unit interval, where events are occurring randomly at a mean rate of λ per unit interval
Uniform $m > 0$	$\dfrac{1}{m},\ x = 1, 2, \ldots, m$		$\dfrac{m + 1}{2}$	$\dfrac{m^2 - 1}{12}$	Select an integer randomly from $1, 2, \ldots, m$

TABLE XIII: Continuous Distributions

Probability Distribution and Parameter Values	Probability Density Function	Moment-Generating Function	Mean $E(X)$	Variance $\mathrm{Var}(X)$	Examples
Beta $0 < \alpha$ $0 < \beta$	$\dfrac{\Gamma(\alpha + \beta)}{\Gamma(\alpha)\Gamma(\beta)} x^{\alpha-1}(1 - x)^{\beta-1}$, $0 < x < 1$		$\dfrac{\alpha}{\alpha + \beta}$	$\dfrac{\alpha\beta}{(\alpha + \beta + 1)(\alpha + \beta)^2}$	$X = X_1/(X_1 + X_2)$, where X_1 and X_2 have independent gamma distributions with same θ
Chi-square $r = 1, 2, \ldots$	$\dfrac{x^{r/2-1}e^{-x/2}}{\Gamma(r/2)2^{r/2}}$, $0 < x < \infty$	$\dfrac{1}{(1 - 2t)^{r/2}},\ t < \dfrac{1}{2}$	r	$2r$	Gamma distribution, $\theta = 2$, $\alpha = r/2$; sum of squares of r independent $N(0, 1)$ random variables
Exponential $0 < \theta$	$\dfrac{1}{\theta} e^{-x/\theta},\ 0 \le x < \infty$	$\dfrac{1}{1 - \theta t},\ t < \dfrac{1}{\theta}$	θ	θ^2	Waiting time to first arrival when observing a Poisson process with a mean rate of arrivals equal to $\lambda = 1/\theta$
Gamma $0 < \alpha$ $0 < \theta$	$\dfrac{x^{\alpha-1}e^{-x/\theta}}{\Gamma(\alpha)\theta^{\alpha}}$, $0 < x < \infty$	$\dfrac{1}{(1 - \theta t)^{\alpha}},\ t < \dfrac{1}{\theta}$	$\alpha\theta$	$\alpha\theta^2$	Waiting time to αth arrival when observing a Poisson process with a mean rate of arrivals equal to $\lambda = 1/\theta$
Normal $-\infty < \mu < \infty$ $0 < \sigma$	$\dfrac{e^{-(x-\mu)^2/2\sigma^2}}{\sigma\sqrt{2\pi}}$, $-\infty < x < \infty$	$e^{\mu t + \sigma^2 t^2/2}$	μ	σ^2	Errors in measurements; heights of children; breaking strengths of materials
Uniform $-\infty < a < b < \infty$	$\dfrac{1}{b - a},\ a \le x \le b$	$\dfrac{e^{tb} - e^{ta}}{t(b - a)},\ t \ne 0$ $1,\ t = 0$	$\dfrac{a + b}{2}$	$\dfrac{(b - a)^2}{12}$	Select a point at random from the interval $[a, b]$

TABLE XIV: Tests and Confidence Intervals

Distribution	θ: The parameter of interest	W: The variable used to test $H_0: \theta = \theta_0$	Two-sided $1 - \alpha$ Confidence Interval for θ	Comments
$N(\mu, \sigma^2)$ or n large σ^2 known	μ	$\dfrac{\overline{X} - \theta_0}{\sigma/\sqrt{n}}$	$\overline{x} \pm z_{\alpha/2}\dfrac{\sigma}{\sqrt{n}}$	W is $N(0,1)$; $P(W \ge z_{\alpha/2}) = \alpha/2$
$N(\mu, \sigma^2)$ σ^2 unknown	μ	$\dfrac{\overline{X} - \theta_0}{S/\sqrt{n}}$	$\overline{x} \pm t_{\alpha/2}(n-1)\dfrac{s}{\sqrt{n}}$	W has a t distribution with $n - 1$ degrees of freedom; $P[W \ge t_{\alpha/2}(n-1)] = \alpha/2$
Any distribution with known variance, σ^2	μ	$\dfrac{\overline{X} - \theta_0}{\sigma/\sqrt{n}}$	$\overline{x} \pm z_{\alpha/2}\dfrac{\sigma}{\sqrt{n}}$	W has an approximate $N(0,1)$ distribution for n sufficiently large
$N(\mu_X, \sigma_X^2)$ $N(\mu_Y, \sigma_Y^2)$ σ_X^2, σ_Y^2 known	$\mu_X - \mu_Y$	$\dfrac{\overline{X} - \overline{Y} - \theta_0}{\sqrt{\dfrac{\sigma_X^2}{n} + \dfrac{\sigma_Y^2}{m}}}$	$\overline{x} - \overline{y} \pm z_{\alpha/2}\sqrt{\dfrac{\sigma_X^2}{n} + \dfrac{\sigma_Y^2}{m}}$	W is $N(0,1)$
$N(\mu_X, \sigma_X^2)$ $N(\mu_Y, \sigma_Y^2)$ σ_X^2, σ_Y^2 unknown	$\mu_X - \mu_Y$	$\dfrac{\overline{X} - \overline{Y} - \theta_0}{\sqrt{\dfrac{S_X^2}{n} + \dfrac{S_Y^2}{m}}}$	$\overline{x} - \overline{y} \pm z_{\alpha/2}\sqrt{\dfrac{s_x^2}{n} + \dfrac{s_y^2}{m}}$	W is approximately $N(0,1)$ if sample sizes are large
$N(\mu_X, \sigma_X^2)$ $N(\mu_Y, \sigma_Y^2)$ $\sigma_X^2 = \sigma_Y^2$, unknown	$\mu_X - \mu_Y$	$\dfrac{\overline{X} - \overline{Y} - \theta_0}{\sqrt{\dfrac{(n-1)S_X^2 + (m-1)S_Y^2}{n+m-2}\left(\dfrac{1}{n} + \dfrac{1}{m}\right)}}$	$\overline{x} - \overline{y} \pm t_{\alpha/2}(n+m-2)s_P\sqrt{\dfrac{1}{n} + \dfrac{1}{m}}$ $s_P = \sqrt{\dfrac{(n-1)s_x^2 + (m-1)s_y^2}{n+m-2}}$	W has a t distribution with $r = n + m - 2$ degrees of freedom
$D = X - Y$ is $N(\mu_X - \mu_Y, \sigma_D^2)$ X and Y dependent	$\mu_X - \mu_Y$	$\dfrac{\overline{D} - \theta_0}{S_D/\sqrt{n}}$	$\overline{d} \pm t_{\alpha/2}(n-1)\dfrac{s_d}{\sqrt{n}}$	W has a t distribution with $n - 1$ degrees of freedom

TABLE XIV: *continued*

Distribution	θ: The parameter of interest	W: The variable used to test $H_0: \theta = \theta_0$	Two-sided $1 - \alpha$ Confidence Interval for θ	Comments
$N(\mu, \sigma^2)$ μ unknown	σ^2	$\frac{(n-1)S^2}{\theta_0}$	$\frac{(n-1)s^2}{\chi^2_{\alpha/2}(n-1)}, \frac{(n-1)s^2}{\chi^2_{1-\alpha/2}(n-1)}$	W is $\chi^2(n-1)$, $P[W \le \chi^2_{1-\alpha/2}(n-1)] = \alpha/2$, $P[W \ge \chi^2_{\alpha/2}(n-1)] = \alpha/2$
$N(\mu, \sigma^2)$ μ unknown	σ	$\frac{(n-1)S^2}{\theta_0^2}$	$\sqrt{\frac{(n-1)s^2}{b}}, \sqrt{\frac{(n-1)s^2}{a}}$	W is $\chi^2(n-1)$. Select a and b from Table X in the appendix for interval of minimum length
$N(\mu_X, \sigma_X^2)$ $N(\mu_Y, \sigma_Y^2)$ μ_X, μ_Y unknown	$\frac{\sigma_X^2}{\sigma_Y^2}$	$\frac{S_Y^2}{S_X^2}\theta_0$	$\frac{s_x^2/s_y^2}{F_{\alpha/2}(n-1, m-1)}, F_{\alpha/2}(m-1, n-1)\frac{s_x^2}{s_y^2}$	W has an F distribution with $m-1$ and $n-1$ degrees of freedom
$b(n, p)$	p	$\frac{\frac{Y}{n} - \theta_0}{\sqrt{\left(\frac{Y}{n}\right)\left(1 - \frac{Y}{n}\right)/n}}$	$\frac{y}{n} \pm z_{\alpha/2}\sqrt{\left(\frac{y}{n}\right)\left(1 - \frac{y}{n}\right)/n}$	W is approximately $N(0,1)$ for n sufficiently large
$b(n_1, p_1)$ $b(n_2, p_2)$	$p_1 - p_2$	$\frac{\frac{Y_1}{n_1} - \frac{Y_2}{n_2} - \theta_0}{\sqrt{\left(\frac{Y_1 + Y_2}{n_1 + n_2}\right)\left(1 - \frac{Y_1 + Y_2}{n_1 + n_2}\right)\left(\frac{1}{n_1} + \frac{1}{n_2}\right)}}$	$\frac{y_1}{n_1} - \frac{y_2}{n_2} \pm$ $z_{\alpha/2}\sqrt{\frac{y_1}{n_1}\left(1 - \frac{y_1}{n_1}\right)/n_1 + \frac{y_2}{n_2}\left(1 - \frac{y_2}{n_2}\right)/n_2}$	W is approximately $N(0,1)$ when n_1 and n_2 are sufficiently large

APPENDIX

Answers to Selected Odd-Numbered Exercises

Chapter 1

1.1-1 **(a)** $S = \{1, 2, 3, \ldots, 36\}$;
(b) $S = \{w\colon\ 19 \le w \le 23\}$, where w is the weight in grams;
(c) $S = \{HHH, HHT, HTH, THH, HTT, THT, TTH, TTT\}$.

1.1-3 **(a)** $f(x) = 1/10, \quad x = 0, 1, 2, \ldots, 9$;
(b) The respective frequencies are 21, 15, 16, 13, 6, 15, 13, 17, 17, 17;
(d) The respective frequencies are 8, 13, 15, 10, 12, 10, 4, 9, 15, 0;

1.1-5 **(a)**

Clutch size:	4	5	6	7	8	9	10
Frequency:	4	5	6	4	6	7	1

(c) No.

1.1-7 **(a)** Number: 0 1 2 3 4 5
(b) Frequency: 4 16 27 35 14 4

1.1-11 **(a)** $0.261, 0.196$;
(b) $0.327, 0.315$;
(c) $0.270, 0.273$;
(d) Example of Simpson's paradox.

1.1-13 **(a)** $0.889 > 0.856, 0.948 > 0.921, 0.914 > 0.855, 0.831 > 0.713, 0.858 > 0.767$;
(b) $0.867 < 0.891$;
(c) Example of Simpson's paradox.

1.2-1 0.68.

1.2-3 **(a)** 12/52; **(b)** 2/52; **(c)** 16/52; **(d)** 1; **(e)** 0.

1.2-5 27/64.

1.2-7 **(a)** (i) 4/8, (ii) 2/8, (iii) 3/8, (iv) 4/8;
(b) (i) 1/8, (ii) 0, (iii) 2/8;
(c) (i) 5/8, (ii) 5/8, (iii) 5/8.

1.2-9 0.63.

1.2-11 **(a)** $3(1/3) - 3(1/3)^2 + (1/3)^3$;
(b) $P(A_1 \cup A_2 \cup A_3) = 1 - [1 - 3(1/3) + 3(1/3)^2 - (1/3)^3] = 1 - (1 - 1/3)^3$.

1.2-13 **(a)** $1 - (1/2)^{10}$; **(b)** $1 - (1/2)^{20}$;
(c) $1 - (1/2)^{20}$; **(d)** $1 - (1/2)^{10}$;
(e) $(1/2)^{10} - (1/2)^{20}$; **(f)** $(1/2)^{20}$.

1.2-15 **(a)** $S = \{00, 0, 1, 2, 3, \ldots, 36\}$;
(b) $P(A) = 2/38$;
(c) $P(B) = 4/38$;
(d) $P(D) = 18/38$.

1.2-17 2/3.

1.3-1 4096.

1.3-3 **(a)** 6,760,000; **(b)** 17,576,000.

1.3-5 **(a)** 24; **(b)** 256.

1.3-7 **(a)** 0.0024; **(b)** 0.0012; **(c)** 0.0006; **(d)** 0.0004.

1.3-9 **(a)** 60; **(b)** 125.

1.3-11 **(a)** 2; **(b)** 8; **(c)** 20; **(d)** 40.

1.3-13 **(a)** 96; **(b)** 393,216; **(c)** 2,973,696.

1.3-15 **(a)** 362,880; **(b)** 84; **(c)** 512.

1.3-17 **(a)** 0.00024; **(b)** 0.00144; **(c)** 0.02113;
(d) 0.04754; **(e)** 0.42257.

1.3-19 14,702,688.

1.3-21 **(a)** 560; **(b)** 3,688.

1.4-1 **(a)** 5000/1,000,000; **(b)** 78,515/1,000,000;
(b) 73,630/995,000; **(d)** 4,885/78,515.

1.4-3 **(a)** 5/35; **(b)** 26/35; **(c)** 5/19; **(d)** 9/23; **(e)** left.

1.4-5 **(a)** 3/10; **(b)** 3/5; **(c)** 3/7.

1.4-7 **(a)** $S = \{(\text{R}, \text{R}), (\text{R}, \text{W}), (\text{W}, \text{R}), (\text{W}, \text{W})\}$; **(b)** 1/3.

1.4-9 1/5.

1.4-11 **(a)** 1/220; **(b)** 3/110; **(c)** 9/55.

1.4-13 **(a)** 8/36; **(c)** 5/11;
(b) $8/36 + 2[(5/36)(5/11) + (4/36)(4/10) + (3/36)(3/9)] = 0.49293$.

1.4-15 **(a)** 365^r; **(b)** ${}_{365}P_r$; **(c)** $1 - {}_{365}P_r/365^r$; **(d)** 23.

1.4-17 **(a)** 49/153; **(b)** 4/7.

1.4-19 **(f)** $1 - 1/e$.

1.4-21 11.

1.5-1 **(a)** 0.14; **(b)** 0.76; **(c)** 0.86.

1.5-3 **(a)** 1/6; **(b)** 1/12; **(c)** 1/4; **(d)** 1/4; **(e)** 1/2.

1.5-5 Yes; $0.9 = 0.8 + 0.5 - (0.8)(0.5)$.

1.5-7 **(a)** 0.29; **(b)** 0.44.

1.5-9 **(a)** 0.36; **(b)** 0.49; **(c)** 0.01.

1.5-11 **(a)** No.
(b) Only if $P(A) = 0$ or $P(B) = 1$.

1.5-13 $(2/3)^3(1/3)^2$; $(2/3)^3(1/3)^2$.

1.5-15 **(a)** $10(1/2)^6$;
(b) $[(120)(45)/15{,}504][7/15]$;
(c) Neither model is very good.

1.5-17 **(a)** $1 - (11/12)^{12}$; **(b)** $1 - (11/12)^{11}$.

1.5-19 **(b)** $1 - 1/e$.

1.6-1 **(a)** 21/32; **(b)** 16/21.

1.6-3 0.151.

1.6-5 60/95 = 0.632.

1.6-7 50/95 = 0.526.

1.6-9 **(a)** 495/30,480 = 0.016; **(b)** 29,985/30,480 = 0.984.

1.6-11 1/4.

1.6-13 0.54229.

1.6-15 0.8182.

Chapter 2

2.1-3 10; **(b)** 1/55; **(c)** 3; **(d)** 1/30; **(e)** $n(n + 1)/2$; **(f)** 1.

2.1-5 **(b)**

x	Frequency	Relative Frequency	$f(x)$
1	38	0.38	0.40
2	27	0.27	0.30
3	21	0.21	0.20
4	14	0.14	0.10

2.1-7 **(a)** $f(x) = \dfrac{13 - 2x}{36}$, $x = 1, 2, 3, 4, 5, 6$;
(b) $g(0) = \dfrac{6}{36}$, $g(y) = \dfrac{12 - 2y}{36}$, $y = 1, 2, 3, 4, 5$.

2.1-11 0.416.

2.1-13 2/5.

2.1-15 **(a)** 19/20; **(b)** 1/20; **(c)** 9/20.

2.1-17 **(c)**

x	Frequency	Relative Frequency	$f(x)$
0	13	0.325	0.253
1	16	0.400	0.422
2	9	0.225	0.251
3	2	0.050	0.066
4	0	0.000	0.008

2.1-19 78.

2.2-1 **(a)** 3; **(b)** 7; **(c)** 4/3; **(d)** 7/3; **(e)** $(2n + 1)/3$; **(f)** does not exist.

2.2-3 $-91/300$ or -30.33 cents.

2.2-5 \$360.

2.2-7 $E(X) = -17/216 = -0.0787$.

2.2-9 $E(X) = \sum_{x=1}^{n} \frac{1}{x}\left(\frac{1}{n}\right)$; $\dfrac{137}{300} = 0.4567$;

$$\frac{1}{100}\left[\frac{\ln(101) + 1 + \ln(100)}{2}\right] = 0.05110$$

≈ 0.05187.

2.2-11 **(a)** $-1/19$; **(b)** $-1/37$.

2.2-13 $-\$0.01414$.

2.3-1 **(a)** 15; 50; **(b)** 5; 0; **(c)** 5/3; 5/9.

2.3-3 **(a)** 16; **(b)** 6; **(c)** 16.

2.3-5 7.

2.3-7 2.

2.3-9 **(a)** $\mu = (m + 1)/2$; $\sigma^2 = (m^2 - 1)/12$;
(b) $m = 7$.

2.3-11 **(a)** 4.473; 9.607; 3.937; 6.964;
(b) 938/117; 8,657/3,393;
(c) 226/33; 215/66;
(d) 251/100; 403/300.

2.3-13 **(a)** (ii) 127/64; (iii) $\sqrt{7359}/64$; (iv) 1.6635;
(b) (ii) 385/64; (iii) $\sqrt{7359}/64$; (iv) -1.6635.

2.3-15 **(a)** $25/8 = 3.125$, $55/64 = 0.8594$, $\sqrt{55}/8 = 0.9270$;
(b) $79/25 = 3.16$, $662/825 = 0.8024$, $\sqrt{21{,}846}/165 = 0.8958$.

2.3-19 \$1809.80.

2.4-1 $f(x) = (7/18)^x(11/18)^{1-x}$, $x = 0, 1$;
$\mu = 7/18$; $\sigma^2 = 77/324$.

2.4-3 **(a)** $(1/5)^2(4/5)^4 = 0.0164$;
(b) $\dfrac{6!}{2!4!}(1/5)^2(4/5)^4 = 0.2458$.

2.4-5 **(a)** 0.4207; **(b)** 0.5793; **(c)** 0.1633; **(d)** $\mu = 5$, $\sigma^2 = 4$, $\sigma = 2$.

2.4-7 **(a)** $b(2000, \pi/4)$; **(b)** 1570.796, 337.096, 18.360; **(c)** π; **(f)** $V_n = \pi^{n/2}/\Gamma(n/2 + 1)$ is the volume of a ball of radius 1 in n-space.

2.4-9 **(a)** $b(20, 0.80)$; **(b)** $\mu = 16, \sigma^2 = 3.2, \sigma = 1.789$; **(c)** (i) 0.1746, (ii) 0.6296, (iii) 0.3704.

2.4-11 0.1268.

2.4-13 **(a)** $\mu = 7.2, \sigma^2 = 1.44, \sigma = 1.2$; **(c)** $\bar{x} = 7.32, s^2 = 1.4117, s = 1.1882$.

2.4-15 **(a)** 0.6513; **(b)** 0.7941.

2.4-17

x	$b(8, 0.2)$	$N_1 = 8$, $N_2 = 32$	$N_1 = 16$, $N_2 = 64$
0	0.1678	0.1368	0.1527
1	0.3355	0.3501	0.3429
2	0.2936	0.3299	0.3104
3	0.1468	0.1466	0.1473
4	0.0459	0.0327	0.0399
5	0.0092	0.0036	0.0063
6	0.0011	0.0002	0.0006
7	0.0001	0.0000	0.0000
8	0.0000	0.0000	0.0000

2.4-19 0.9841.

2.4-21 Take longer route.

2.4-23 **(a)** 0.0778; **(b)** 0.3456; **(c)** 0.9898.

2.5-1 **(a)** $b(1, 2/3)$; **(b)** $b(12, 0.75)$.

2.5-3 $\mu = 2, \sigma^2 = 4/5$,

$$f(x) = \begin{cases} 2/5, & x = 1, \\ 1/5, & x = 2, \\ 2/5, & x = 3. \end{cases}$$

2.5-5 $(4/5)^3(1/5)$.

2.5-7 **(a)** 0.4604; **(b)** 0.5580; **(c)** 0.0184.

2.5-9 **(a)** $0.9^{12} = 0.2824$; **(b)** 0.0236.

2.5-11 **(a)** $f(x) = (1/2)^{x-1}, x = 2, 3, 4, \ldots$; **(b)** $M(t) = e^{2t}/(2 - e^t),\ t < \ln 2$; **(c)** $\mu = 3, \sigma^2 = 2, \sigma = 1.414$; **(d)** (i) 3/4, (ii) 1/8, (iii) 1/4.

2.5-13 **(a)** $f(x) = (x - 1)/2^x,\ x = 2, 3, \ldots$; **(c)** $\mu = 4, \sigma^2 = 4, \sigma = 2$; **(d)** (i) 1/2, (ii) 5/16, (iii) 1/4.

2.5-15 25/3.

2.5-17 **(a)** 29.29; **(b)** about 8 years; **(c)** 49.77.

2.5-21 **(a)** $\mu = 1, \sigma^2 = 1$; **(b)** 19/30.

2.6-1 **(a)** 0.693; **(b)** 0.762; **(c)** 0.433.

2.6-3 0.540.

2.6-5 0.558.

2.6-7 0.947.

2.6-9 **(a)** 2.681; **(b)** $n = 6$.

2.6-11 **(a)** $\bar{x} = 7.94, s^2 = 7.73$, yes.

2.6-13 **(a)** $\bar{x} = 4/3 = 1.333,\ s^2 = 88/69 = 1.275$, yes; **(c)** yes.

2.6-15 **(a)** 2.967; **(b)** 2.792; **(c)** 1.671.

2.6-17 If $n = 80$, $Ac = 3$, $Oc(0.02) \approx 0.92$, $Oc(0.08) \approx 0.12$.

2.6-19 **(a)** 0.564 using binomial, 0.560 using Poisson approximation **(b)** \$598.56 using binomial, \$613.90 using Poisson approximation.

2.6-21 Using Minitab, **(a)** 0.0821; **(b)** 0.2138; **(c)** 0.4562; **(d)** 0.7576.

Chapter 3

3.1-1 **(a)** $\bar{x} = 1.1$; **(b)** $s^2 = 0.0350$; **(c)** $s = 0.1871$.

3.1-3 **(a)** Frequencies: [3, 15, 8, 1, 0, 5, 8, 2]; **(b)** $\bar{x} = 17.30$; $s_x = 2.34$.

3.1-5 **(a)** $\bar{x} = 16.706, s = 1.852$; **(b)** Frequencies: [1, 1, 2, 14, 18, 16, 23, 10, 7, 2, 1, 1].

3.1-7 **(a)** $\bar{x} = 112.12$; $s = 231.3576$; **(d)** Half of the observations are less than 48.

3.1-9 **(b)** $\bar{x} = 7.275, s = 1.967$.

3.1-11 **(a)** With class boundaries 90.5, 108.5, 126.5, ..., 306.5:
Frequencies: [8, 11, 4, 1, 0, 0, 0, 1, 2, 12, 12, 3]; **(b)** $\bar{x} = 201$; **(c)** With class boundaries 47.5, 52.5, ..., 107.5:
Frequencies: [4, 4, 9, 4, 4, 0, 3, 9, 7, 5, 4, 1]; **(d)** $\bar{x} = 76.35$.

3.2-1 **(a)**

Stems	Leaves	Frequency	Depths
11	9	1	1
12	3	1	2
13	6 7	2	4
14	1 1 4 4 4 6 7 8 8 8 8 9 9 9	14	18
15	0 0 1 3 4 5 5 6 6 6 6 6 7 8 8 9 9 9	18	36
16	1 1 1 1 1 3 3 5 5 6 6 6 7 7 8 9	16	(16)
17	0 1 1 1 1 1 2 2 2 3 4 4 4 6 6 7 7 8 8 8 8 8 8	23	44
18	0 0 0 1 1 4 5 8 9 9	10	21
19	0 1 3 3 4 7 8	7	11
20	2 8	2	4
21	5	1	1
22	1	1	1

(Multiply numbers by 10^{-1}.)

(b) 11.9, 15.5, 16.65, 17.8, 22.1; **(c)** There are three suspected outliers.

3.2-3 **(a)** Baby carrots: 1.02, 1.03, 1.04, 1.04, 1.06; **(b)** Regular-size carrots: 1.00, 1.15, 1.21, 1.26, 1.43; **(c)** Regular-size packages tend to be heavier.

3.2-5 **(a)** Frequencies for males: [1, 1, 3, 4, 20, 23, 16, 10, 3, 0, 1],
Frequencies for females: [5, 14, 32, 36, 13],
(c) Five-number summary for males: 1.4, 3.5, 4.0, 4.525, 6.5;
Five-number summary for females: 0.5, 1.325, 1.7, 2.0, 2.7.

3.2-7 **(b)** Five-number summary: 5, 35/2, 48, 173/2, 1,815; **(d)** Inner fence at 190, outer fence at 293.5; **(e)** The mean is greatly influenced by outliers.

3.2-9 **(a)**

Stems	Leaves	Frequency	Depths
127	8	1	1
128	8	1	2
129	5 8 9	3	5
130	8	1	6
131	2 3 4 4 5 5 7	7	(7)
132	2 7 7 8	4	7
133	7 9	2	3
134	8	1	1

(Multiply numbers by 10^{-1}.)

(b) 131.3, 7.0, 2.575, 131.45, 131.47, 3.034.
(c) Five-number summary: 127.8, 130.125, 131.45, 132.70, 134.8.

3.2-11 **(a)**

Stems	Leaves	Frequency	Depths
30*f*	5	1	1
30*s*		0	1
30•	8 8	2	3
31∗	0 0 1	3	6
31*t*	2 3 3	3	9
31*f*	4 4 4	3	12
31*s*	6 6 7 7 7	5	17
31•	8 8 8 9 9	5	22
32∗	0 0 0 0 0 1	6	(6)
32*t*	2 2 2 3 3	5	22
32*f*	4 4 4 4 5 5	6	17
32*s*	6 7 7	3	11
32•	8 8 9 9 9	5	8
33∗	0 1	2	3
33*t*		0	1
33*f*	5	1	1

(b) Five-number summary: 305, 315.5, 320, 325, 335;

3.3-1 **(b)**

$$F(x) = \begin{cases} 0, & x < 0, \\ x(2 - x), & 0 \le x < 1, \\ 1, & 1 \le x. \end{cases}$$

(c) (i) 3/4, (ii) 1/2, (iii) 0, (iv) 1/16.

3.3-3 **(a)** (i) 3; (ii) $F(x) = x^4$, $0 \le x \le 1$;
(b) (i) 3/16; (ii) $F(x) = (1/8)x^{3/2}$, $0 \le x \le 4$;
(c) (i) 1/4; (ii) $F(x) = x^{1/4}$, $0 \le x \le 1$.

3.3-5 **(a)** 4/5, 2/75, $\sqrt{6}/15$;
(b) 12/5, 192/175; $8\sqrt{21}/35$;
(c) 1/5, 16/225, 4/15.

3.3-7 **(a)** $\pi/2, (\pi^2 - 8)/4$;
(c) $F(x) = (1 - \cos x)/2,\ 0 \le x \le \pi$.

3.3-9 **(a)** d = 2; **(b)** $E(Y) = 2$; **(c)** $E(Y^2)$ is unbounded.

3.3-11 **(a)** $\mu = 0, \sigma^2 = 3/5$;
(b) $\mu = 0, \sigma^2 = 1/3$;
(c) $\mu = 0, \sigma^2 = 1/6$.

3.3-13 **(a)** $\mu = 0$; **(b)** $\sigma^2 = 1$.

3.3-15 $$f(x) = \frac{e^{-x}}{(1 + e^{-x})^2} = \frac{e^{-x}}{(1 + e^{-x})^2}\frac{e^{2x}}{e^{2x}} = \frac{e^x}{(e^x + 1)^2} = f(-x).$$

3.3-17 **(a)** $1/e$; **(b)** $1/e^{19/8}$.

3.3-19 **(a)** $F_n(x) = nx,\ 0 \le x \le 1/n$.

3.3-21 $\theta = 2.33$.

3.3-23 $740.74.

3.3-25 **(a)** μ = $28,571.43, σ = $15,971.91; **(b)** 0.6554.

3.4-3 **(a)** $f(x) = 1/10,\ 0 < x < 10$; **(b)** 0.2; **(c)** 0.6;
(b) $\mu = 5$; (e) $\sigma^2 = 25/3$.

3.4-5 **(a)** $G(w) = (w - a)/(b - a),\ a \le w \le b$;
(b) $U(a, b)$.

3.4-7 **(b)** $\overline{x} = 20.486, s^2 = 20.344$;
(c) $0.472 \approx 0.467$;
(d) $0.472 \approx 0.462 = 12/26$.

3.4-9 **(a)** $f(x) = (1/3)e^{-x/3},\ 0 < x < \infty$; 3; 9;
(b) $f(x) = 3e^{-3x},\ 0 < x < \infty$; 1/3; 1/9.

3.4-11 $$P(X > x + y \mid X > x) = \frac{P(X > x + y)}{P(X > x)} = \frac{e^{-(x+y)/\theta}}{e^{-x/\theta}} = P(X > y).$$

3.4-13 **(a)** $\lambda = 0.025$;
(b) exponential distribution, $\theta = 40$;
(c) $\mu = 40, \sigma^2 = 1600$; **(d)** (i) $1 - e^{-1/2}$, (ii) e^{-1}, (iii) e^{-1}.

3.4-15 **(a)** 10.524; 9.320; yes.

3.4-17 **(a)** $F(x) = 1 - e^{-(x-\delta)/\theta},\ \delta \le x < \infty$;
(b) $\theta + \delta;\ \theta^2$.

3.4-19 **(a)** $-\theta \ln 0.75 = 0.2877\,\theta$;
(b) $(\ln 0.75 + 1)\theta = 0.7123\,\theta$;
(c) $-\theta \ln 0.25 = 1.3863\,\theta$;
(d) $(-\ln 0.25 - 1)\theta = 0.3863\,\theta$.

3.4-21 **(a)** $e^{-1/8}$;
(b) $f(x) = ae^{bx}\exp[-(a/b)(e^{bx}-1)], 0 < x < \infty$;
(c) 0.24.

3.4-23 $e^{-1/2}$.

3.5-1 **(a)** $f(x) = \dfrac{1}{\Gamma(10)(3/2)^{10}} x^9 e^{-2x/3}$, $0 \le x < \infty$;
(b) $M(t) = (1 - 3t/2)^{-10}$, $t < 2/3$; $\mu = 15$; $\sigma^2 = 45/2$.

3.5-5 $f(x) = \dfrac{1}{\Gamma(20)7^{20}} x^{19} e^{-x/7}$, $0 \le x < \infty$; $\mu = 140$; $\sigma^2 = 980$.

3.5-7 **(a)** $\mu = 240/7 = 34.286, \overline{x} = 32.636$;
(b) $\sigma^2 = 28{,}800/49 = 587.755, s^2 = 548.338$;
(c) $0.605 \approx 0.591 = 13/22$.

3.5-9 **(a)** 0.025; **(b)** 0.05; **(c)** 0.94; **(d)** 8.672; **(e)** 30.19.

3.5-11 **(a)** 0.80; **(b)** $a = 11.69, b = 38.08$;
(c) $\mu = 23, \sigma^2 = 46$; **(d)** 35.17, 13.09.

3.5-13 **(a)** $r - 2$; **(b)** $x = r - 2 \pm \sqrt{2r - 4}, r \ge 4$.

3.5-15 0.9444.

3.5-17 **(a)** $e^{-(125/216)}$; **(b)** $120 * \Gamma(4/3) = 107.1575$.

3.5-19 1.96 yields an expected profit of \$660.99.

3.6-1 **(a)** 0.2784; **(b)** 0.7209; **(c)** 0.9616; **(d)** 0.0019;
(e) 0.9500; **(f)** 0.6826; **(g)** 0.9544; **(h)** 0.9974.

3.6-3 **(a)** 2.326; **(b)** −2.576; **(c)** 1.67; **(d)** −2.17.

3.6-5 **(a)** 1.96; **(b)** 1.96; **(c)** 1.645; **(d)** 1.645.

3.6-7 **(a)** 0.3849; **(b)** 0.5403; **(c)** 0.0603; **(d)** 0.0013;
(e) 0.6826; **(f)** 0.9544; **(g)** 0.9974; **(h)** 0.99.

3.6-9 **(a)** 0.6326; **(b)** 50.

3.6-11 **(a)** Gamma ($\alpha = 1/2, \theta = 8$); **(b)** Gamma ($\alpha = 1/2, \theta = 2\sigma^2$).

3.6-13 Both could be normal because of the linearity of the q–q plots.

3.6-15 **(a)**

Stems	Leaves	Frequency	Depths
7•	938	1	1
8∗	032 089	2	3
8t	222 268 383	3	6
8f	442 490 528 572	4	(4)
8s	674 734 786	3	9
8•	850 873 920	3	6
9∗	069 150	2	3
9t	243	1	1

(Multiply numbers by 10^{-4}.)

(b) Normal quantiles: −1.645, −1.282, −1.036, −0.842, −0.674, −0.524, −0.385, −0.253, −0.126, 0, 0.126, 0.253, 0.385, 0.524, 0.674, 0.842, 1.036, 1.282, 1.645.

(c) Yes, because of the linearity of the q–q plot.

3.6-17 0.025.

3.6-19 **(a)** The frequencies of 450, 451, 452, and so on are 2, 3, 3, 5, 6, 15, 19, 22, 11, 5, 5, 3, 0, 1; **(b)** yes.

3.6-21 **(a)** $N(0,1)$; **(b)** $N(-1,1)$; **(c)** $N(2,1)$.

3.6-23 0.1437.

3.6-25 **(a)** $\sigma = 0.043$; **(b)** $\mu = 12.116$.

3.6-27 **(a)** 0.0228; **(b)** 0.6844.

3.7-1 **(a)** $e^{-(5/10)^2} = e^{-1/4} = 0.7788$.

3.7-3 Weibull with parameters α and $\beta/3^{1/\alpha}$.

3.7-5 **(a)** 0.5; **(b)** 0; **(c)** 0.25; **(d)** 0.75; **(e)** 0.625; **(f)** 0.75.

3.7-7 **(b)** $\mu = 31/24, \sigma^2 = 167/567$;
(c) 15/64; 1/4; 0; 11/16.

3.7-9 **(a)**

$$F(x) = \begin{cases} 0, & x < 0, \\ x/2, & 0 \le x < 1, \\ 1/2, & 1 \le x < 2, \\ 4/6, & 2 \le x < 4, \\ 5/6, & 4 \le x < 6, \\ 1, & 6 \le x. \end{cases}$$

(b) \$2.25.

3.7-11 $3 + 5e^{-3/5} = 5.744$.

3.7-13 226.21, 1,486.92.

3.7-15 $\mu = 345.54, \sigma = 780.97$.

3.7-17 $M = 83.38$.

3.7-19 $g(y) = \dfrac{c}{3y}\exp(-(1/3)\ln y)$, $e^{0.12} < y < e^{0.24}$; $c = 1/0.0376730928$.

3.7-21 $a = 0.00023 \approx 1/4000, b = 0.07270 \approx 1/14$, mode $= 79.155$.

3.7-23 0.4219.

Chapter 4

4.1-1 **(a)** $f_1(x) = (2x + 5)/16, x = 1, 2$;
(b) $f_2(y) = (2y + 3)/32, y = 1, 2, 3, 4$;
(c) 3/32; **(d)** 9/32; **(e)** 3/16; **(f)** 1/4; **(g)** dependent.

4.1-3 **(b)** $f(x,y) = 1/16$, $x = 1, 2, 3, 4$; $y = x + 1, x + 2, x + 3, x + 4$;
(c) $f_1(x) = 1/4, x = 1, 2, 3, 4$;
(d) $f_2(y) = (4 - |y - 5|)/16, y = 2, 3, 4, 5, 6, 7, 8$;
(e) dependent because the space is not rectangular.

4.1-5 **(b)** $b(6, 1/2), b(6, 1/2)$.

4.1-7 11/30.

4.1-9 **(a)** $f(x,y) = \dfrac{15!}{x!\,y!\,(15 - x - y)!} \times \left(\dfrac{6}{10}\right)^x \left(\dfrac{3}{10}\right)^y \left(\dfrac{1}{10}\right)^{15-x-y}$, $0 \le x + y \le 15$;
(b) no, because the space is not rectangular;
(c) 0.0735;
(d) X is $b(15, 0.6)$;
(e) 0.9095.

4.1-11 $f_1(x) = 2e^{-2x}$, $0 < x < \infty$;
$f_2(y) = 2e^{-y}(1 - e^{-y})$, $0 < y < \infty$; no.

4.1-13 $f_1(x) = x/2,\ 0 \le x \le 2; f_2(y) = 3y^2/8,\ 0 \le y \le 2$; yes.

4.1-15 **(b)** 1/3.

4.2-1 $\mu_X = 25/16;\ \mu_Y = 45/16;\ \sigma_X^2 = 63/256$; $\sigma_Y^2 = 295/256$; $\text{Cov}(X, Y) = -5/256$; $\rho = -\sqrt{2{,}065}/1{,}239 = -0.0367$; dependent.

4.2-3 **(a)** $f(x,y) = 1/16,\ x = 1,2,3,4;\ y = x + 1, x + 2, x + 3, x + 4$; $f_1(x) = 1/4,\ x = 1,2,3,4$; $f_2(y) = (4 - |y - 5|)/16,\ y = 2,3,\ldots,8$; **(b)** $\mu_X = 5/2;\ \mu_Y = 5;\ \sigma_X^2 = 5/4;\ \sigma_Y^2 = 5/2$; $\text{Cov}(X, Y) = 5/4; \rho = \sqrt{2}/2$; **(c)** $y = x + 5/2$.

4.2-5 $a = \mu_Y - \mu_X b,\ b = \text{Cov}(X, Y)/\sigma_X^2$.

4.2-7 **(a)** No; **(b)** $\text{Cov}(X, Y) = 0,\ \rho = 0$.

4.2-9 **(a)** $f_1(1) = 0.15,\ f_1(2) = 0.25,\ f_1(3) = 0.45,\ f_1(4) = 0.15;\ f_2(1) = 0.35,\ f_2(2) = 0.65$; $\mu_X = 2.60;\ \mu_Y = 1.65;\ \sigma_X^2 = 0.8400$; $\sigma_Y^2 = 0.2275$; **(b)** $\text{Cov}(X, Y) = -0.0900;\ \rho = -0.2059$; **(c)** $E(C) = 34.70$.

4.2-11 **(a)** $f_1(x) = x + 1/2,\ 0 < x < 1$, $f_2(y) = y + 1/2,\ 0 < y < 1$; **(b)** $\mu_X = 7/12;\ \mu_Y = 7/12;\ \sigma_X^2 = 11/144$; $\sigma_Y^2 = 11/144$; $\text{Cov}(X, Y) = -1/144$; $\rho = -1/11$; **(c)** $y = 7/11 - x/11$.

4.2-13 **(a)** $c = 1/154$; **(c)** $f_1(0) = 6/77, f_1(1) = 21/77$, $f_1(2) = 30/77, f_1(3) = 20/77$; $f_2(0) = 30/77, f_2(1) = 32/77,\ f_2(2) = 15/77$; **(d)** no; **(e)** $\mu_X = 141/77, \sigma_X^2 = 4836/5929$; **(f)** $\mu_Y = 62/77, \sigma_Y^2 = 3240/5929$; **(g)** $\text{Cov(X,Y)} = 1422/5929$; **(h)** $\rho = 79\sqrt{12090}/24180$; **(i)** $y = 215/806 + 237/806x$.

4.3-1 **(d)** 9/14, 7/18, 5/9; **(e)** 20/7, 55/49.

4.3-3 **(a)** $f(x,y) = \dfrac{50!}{x!\,y!\,(50 - x - y)!} \times (0.02)^x(0.90)^y(0.08)^{50-x-y},\ 0 \le x + y \le 50$; **(b)** Y is $b(50, 0.90)$; **(c)** $b(47, 0.90/0.98)$; **(d)** 2115/49; (e) $\rho = -3/7$.

4.3-5 **(a)** $E(Y\,|\,x) = 2(2/3) - (2/3)x,\ x = 1,2$; **(b)** yes.

4.3-7 $E(Y\,|\,x) = x + 5/2,\ x = 1,2,3,4$; yes.

4.3-9 **(a)** $f_1(x) = 1/8,\ x = 0,1,\ldots,7$; **(b)** $h(y\,|\,x) = 1/3,\ y = x, x + 1, x + 2$, for $x = 0,1,\ldots,7$; **(c)** $E(Y\,|\,x) = x + 1,\ x + 0,1,\ldots,7$; **(d)** $\sigma_Y^2 = 2/3$; **(e)**

$$f_2(y) = \begin{cases} 1/24, & y = 0,9, \\ 2/24, & y = 1,8, \\ 3/24, & y - 2,3,4,5,6,7. \end{cases}$$

4.3-11 $E(Y) = x$ and $E(X) = 0.700$; thus \$700.

4.3-13 **(b)** $f_1(x) = 1/10,\ 0 \le x \le 10$; **(c)** $h(y\,|\,x) = 1/4,\ 10 - x \le y \le 14 - x$ for $0 \le x \le 10$; **(d)** $E(Y\,|\,x) = 12 - x$.

4.3-15 **(a)** $f(x,y) = 1/(2x^2),\ 0 < x < 2,\ 0 < y < x^2$; **(b)** $f_2(y) = (2 - \sqrt{y})/(4\sqrt{y}),\ 0 < y < 4$; **(c)** $E(X\,|\,y) = [2\sqrt{y}\ln(2/\sqrt{y})]/[2 - \sqrt{y}]$; **(d)** $E(Y\,|\,x) = x^2/2$.

4.3-17 **(a)** $h(y\,|\,x) = e^{-x},\ 0 < y < e^x$ for $0 < x < 1$; **(b)** $E(Y\,|\,x) = e^x/2,\ 0 < x < 1$; **(c)** $f(x,y) = e^{-x},\ 0 < x < 1,\ 0 < y < e^x$; **(d)**

$$f_2(y) = \begin{cases} 1 - 1/e, & 0 < y < 1, \\ 1/y - 1/e, & 1 \le y < e. \end{cases}$$

4.3-19 **(a)** $c = 8$; **(b)** 29/93.

4.4-1 **(a)** 0.6006; **(b)** 0.7888; **(c)** 0.8185; **(d)** 0.9371.

4.4-3 **(a)** 0.5746; **(b)** 0.7357.

4.4-5 **(a)** $N(86.4, 40.96)$; **(b)** 0.4192.

4.4-7 **(a)** 0.8248; **(b)** $E(Y\,|\,x) = 457.1735 - 0.2655x$; **(c)** $\text{Var}(Y\,|\,x) = 645.9375$; **(d)** 0.8079.

4.4-9 $a(x) = x - 11,\ b(x) = x + 5$.

4.4-11 **(a)** 0.2857; **(b)** $\mu_{Y|z} = -0.2x + 4.7$; **(c)** $\sigma_{Y|z}^2 = 8.0784$; **(d)** 0.4230.

4.4-13 **(a)** $X + Y$ is $N(5, 7.4)$, 0.6434; **(b)** 0.5249; **(c)** 0.05.

4.4-15 **(a)** 0.3721; **(b)** 0.1084.

Chapter 5

5.1-1 $g(y) = 2y,\ 0 < y < 1$.

5.1-3 $g(y) = (1/8)y^5e^{-y^2/2},\ 0 < y < \infty$.

5.1-5 $M(t) = (1 - 2t)^{-1},\ t < 1/2$; exponential distribution with $\theta = 2$.

5.1-7 **(a)** $F(r) = (x - 0.03)/0.04,\ 0.03 < r < 0.07$; $f(r) = 1/0.04,\ 0.03 < r < 0.07$; **(b)** The interest for each of n equal parts is R/n. The amount at the end of the year is $50{,}000(1 + R/n)^n$; the limit as $n \to \infty$ is $50{,}000\,e^R$.

5.1-9 **(a)** Exponential; **(b)** in the *Solutions Manual*; **(c)** $\exp(-e^{-2}) = 0.873$.

5.1-11 **(a)** $\dfrac{1}{2} - \dfrac{\arctan 1}{\pi} = 0.25$;

(b) $\dfrac{1}{2} - \dfrac{\arctan 5}{\pi} = 0.0628$;

(c) $\dfrac{1}{2} - \dfrac{\arctan 10}{\pi} = 0.0317$.

5.1-13 **(b)** (i) $\exp(\mu + \sigma^2/2)$, (ii) $\exp(2\mu + 2\sigma^2)$, (iii) $\exp(2\mu + 2\sigma^2) - \exp(2\mu + \sigma^2)$.

5.1-15 **(a)** $g(y) = \dfrac{1}{\sqrt{2\pi y}} \exp(-y/2), \qquad 0 < y < \infty$;

(b) $g(y) = \dfrac{3}{2}\sqrt{y}, \qquad 0 < y < 1$.

5.2-1 $g(y_1, y_2) = (1/4)e^{-y_2/2}$, $0 < y_1 < y_2 < \infty$;
$g_1(y_1) = (1/2)e^{-y_1/2}$, $0 < y_1 < \infty$;
$g_2(y_2) = (y_2/4)e^{-y_2/2}$, $0 < y_2 < \infty$; no.

5.2-3 $\mu = \dfrac{r_2}{r_2 - 2}$, $r_2 > 2$;

$\sigma^2 = \dfrac{2r_2^2(r_1 + r_2 - 2)}{r_1(r_2 - 2)^2(r_2 - 4)}$, $r_2 > 4$.

5.2-5 **(a)** 14.80; **(b)** 1/7.01 = 0.1427; **(c)** 0.95.

5.2-9 840.

5.2-11 **(a)** 0.1792; **(b)** 0.1792.

5.2-13 **(a)**

$$\begin{aligned} G(y_1, y_2) &= \int_0^{y_1} \int_u^{y_2} 2(1/1000^2) \\ &\qquad \times \exp[-(u + v)/1000]\, dv\, du \\ &= 2\exp[-(y_1 + y_2)/1000] \\ &\qquad - \exp[-y_1/500] \\ &\qquad - 2\exp[-y_2/1000] \\ &\qquad + 1, \quad 0 < y_1 < y_2 < \infty; \end{aligned}$$

(b) $2e^{-6/5} - e^{-12/5} \approx 0.5117$.

5.2-15 Each has mean 1/3 (8 hours). The respective standard deviations are 0.0943, 0.0673, and 0.0552. In case (3), the probability that a person sleeps between 7 and 9 hours is 0.546 and between 6 and 10 hours is 0.869. If we let $\alpha = 48$ and $\beta = 96$, then $\sigma = 0.0391$ and the probability that a person sleeps between 7 and 9 hours is 0.7116.

5.3-1 **(a)** 0.0182; **(b)** 0.0337.

5.3-3 **(a)** 36/125; **(b)** 2/7.

5.3-5

$$g(y) = \begin{cases} 1/36, & y = 2, \\ 4/36, & y = 3, \\ 10/36, & y = 4, \\ 12/36, & y = 5, \\ 9/36, & y = 6; \end{cases}$$

$\mu = 14/3, \sigma^2 = 10/9$.

5.3-7 2/5.

5.3-9 **(a)** 729/4096; **(b)** $\mu = 3/2$; $\sigma^2 = 3/40$.

5.3-11 **(a)** 0.0035; **(b)** 8; **(c)** $\mu_Y = 8, \sigma_Y^2 = 4$.

5.3-13 **(c)** Using *Maple*, we obtain μ = 13,315,424/3,011,805 = 4.4211.

(d) $E(Y) = 5.377$ with 16 coins, $E(Y) = 6.355$ with 32 coins.

5.3-15 **(a)** $f(x) = [1 - (1/2)^x]^3 - [1 - (1/2)^{x-1}]^3$, $x = 1, 2, \ldots$.

(b) $\mu = 22/7 = 3.1429$, $\sigma^2 = 430/147 \approx 2.9252$;

(e) Like flipping a number of coins equal to the dimension.

5.3-17 $1 - e^{-3/100} \approx 0.03$.

5.3-19 $G(y) = 1 - ([y/500]e^{-y/500} + e^{-y/500})^3$, $0 < y < \infty$; $P(Y < 300) = 1 - ([8/5]e^{-3/5})^3 \approx 0.323$.

5.3-21 21,816.

5.3-23 5.

5.4-1 **(a)**

$$g(y) = \begin{cases} 1/64, & y = 3, 12, \\ 3/64, & y = 4, 11, \\ 6/64, & y = 5, 10, \\ 10/64, & y = 6, 9, \\ 12/64, & y = 7, 8. \end{cases}$$

5.4-3 **(a)** $M(t) = e^{7(e^t - 1)}$; **(b)** Poisson, $\lambda = 7$; **(c)** 0.800.

5.4-5 0.925.

5.4-7 **(a)** $M(t) = 1/(1 - 5t)^{21}$, $t < 1/5$;

(b) gamma distribution, $\alpha = 21, \theta = 5$.

5.4-9 **(a)** $(1/24)(e^{2t} + 2e^{3t} + 3e^{4t} + 4e^{5t} + 4e^{6t} + 4e^{7t} + 3e^{8t} + 2e^{9t} + e^{10t})$;

(b)

$$g(w) = \begin{cases} 1/24, & w = 2, 10, \\ 2/24, & w = 3, 9, \\ 3/24, & w = 4, 8, \\ 4/24, & w = 5, 6, 7. \end{cases}$$

5.4-13 First die has 0 on four faces and 2 on four faces; second die has faces numbered 0, 1, 4, 5, 8, 8, 12, 13.

5.4-15 **(a)**

$$h_1(w_1) = \begin{cases} 1/36, & w_1 = 0, \\ 4/36, & w_1 = 1, \\ 10/36, & w_1 = 2, \\ 12/36, & w_1 = 3, \\ 9/36, & w_1 = 4. \end{cases}$$

(b) $h_2(w) = h_1(w)$;

(c)

$$h(w) = \begin{cases} 1/1296, & w = 0 \\ 8/1296, & w = 1, \\ 36/1296, & w = 2, \\ 104/1296, & w = 3, \\ 214/1296, & w = 4, \\ 312/1296, & w = 5, \\ 324/1296, & w = 6, \\ 216/1296, & w = 7, \\ 81/1296, & w = 8. \end{cases}$$

(d) With denominators equal to $6^8 = 1{,}679{,}616$, the respective numerators of $0, 1, \ldots, 16$ are 1, 16, 136, 784, 3,388, 11,536, 31,864, 72, 592, 137,638, 217,776, 286,776, 311,472, 274, 428, 190,512, 99,144, 34,992, 6,561.

(e) They are becoming more symmetric as n increases.

5.4-17 **(b)** $\mu_Y = 25/3, \sigma_Y^2 = 130/9$;

(c)

$$P(Y = y) = \begin{cases} 96/1024, & y = 4, \\ 144/1024, & y = 5, \\ 150/1024, & y = 6, \\ 135/1024, & y = 7. \end{cases}$$

5.4-19 $Y - X + 25$ is $b(50, 1/2)$;

$$P(Y - X \geq 2) = \sum_{k=27}^{50} \binom{50}{k} \left(\frac{1}{2}\right)^{50} = 0.3359.$$

5.4-21 **(a)** $\displaystyle\sum_{k=3}^{10} \binom{10}{k} (1 - 2/e)^k (2/e)^{10-k} = 0.5167$;

(b) 0.792.

5.4-23 $1 - 17/2e^3 = 0.5678$.

5.5-1 **(a)** 0.4772; **(b)** 0.8561.

5.5-3 **(a)** 46.58, 2.56; **(b)** 0.8447.

5.5-5 **(a)** 0.90; **(b)** 0.90.

5.5-7 **(b)** 0.05466; 0.3102.

5.5-9 **(a)** 0.8962; **(b)** 0.8962; **(c)** 87.31; 229.58.

5.5-11 **(a)** 0.3085; **(b)** 0.2267.

5.5-13 25.

5.5-15 $0.8413 > 0.7734$, select X.

5.5-17 $E(Z) = 0$; $E(1/\sqrt{U}) = \Gamma[(r - 1)/2]/\{\Gamma[r/2]\sqrt{2}\}$; $E(Z^2) = 1$; $E(1/U) = 1/(r - 2)$.

5.5-19 **(a)** 2.567; **(b)** -1.740; **(c)** 0.90.

5.5-21 **(a)** $t(2)$; **(c)** $\mu_V = 0$; **(d)** $\sigma_V = 1$;

(e) In part b, numerator and denominator are not independent.

5.6-1 0.4772.

5.6-3 0.8185.

5.6-5 **(a)** $\chi^2(18)$; **(b)** 0.0756, 0.9974.

5.6-7 0.6247.

5.6-9 0.95.

5.6-11 **(a)** The frequencies are 5, 6, 12, 18, 31, 31, 20, 17, 6, 4; the fifth and sixth classes; **(c)** yes.

5.6-13 $444,338.13.

5.6-15 0.9522.

5.6-17 **(a)** $\displaystyle\int_0^{25} \frac{1}{\Gamma(13)2^{13}} y^{13-1} e^{-y/2}\, dy = 0.4810$ (using *Maple*);

(b) 0.4449 using normal approximation.

5.7-1 **(a)** 0.2878, 0.2881; **(b)** 0.4428, 0.4435; **(c)** 0.1550, 0.1554.

5.7-3 0.9258 using normal approximation, 0.9258 using binomial.

5.7-5 0.6915 using normal approximation, 0.7030 using binomial.

5.7-7 0.3085.

5.7-9 0.6247 using normal approximation, 0.6148 using Poisson.

5.7-11 **(a)** 0.5548; **(b)** 0.3823.

5.7-13 0.6813 using normal approximation, 0.6788 using binomial.

5.7-15 **(a)** 0.3802; **(b)** 0.7571.

5.7-17 0.4734 using normal approximation; 0.4749 using Poisson approximation with $\lambda = 50$; 0.4769 using $b(5000, 0.01)$.

5.7-19 0.6455 using normal approximation, 0.6449 using Poisson.

5.7-21 **(a)** 0.8289 using normal approximation, 0.8294 using Poisson.

(b) 0.0261 using tables in book, 0.0218 using *Maple*.

Chapter 6

6.1-3 **(b)** $\bar{x} = 89/40 = 2.225$.

6.1-5 **(a)** $\widehat{\theta} = \overline{X}/2$; **(b)** $\widehat{\theta} = \overline{X}/3$; **(c)** $\widehat{\theta}$ equals the sample median

6.1-7 **(c)** (i) $\widehat{\theta} = 0.5493$, $\widetilde{\theta} = 0.5975$,
(ii) $\widehat{\theta} = 2.2101$, $\widetilde{\theta} = 2.4004$,
(iii) $\widehat{\theta} = 0.9588$, $\widetilde{\theta} = 0.8646$.

6.1-9 **(c)** $\bar{x} = 3.48$.

6.1-11 $1/9.5 = 20/190 = 0.1053$.

6.1-15 **(a)** $\widetilde{\theta} = \overline{X}$; **(b)** yes; **(c)** 7.382; **(d)** 7.485.

6.1-17 **(a)** $\widetilde{\lambda} = \overline{X}$;

(b) $\bar{x} = 1.17$;

(c) $s^2 = 1.24$, yes.

6.1-19 7.2.

6.2-1 [71.35, 76.25].

6.2-3 **(a)** $\bar{x} = 15.757$, **(b)** $s = 1.792$, **(c)** [14.441, 17.073].

6.2-5 [48.467, 72.266] or [48.076, 72.657].

6.2-7 [19.47, 22.33].

6.2-9 **(a)** $\bar{x} = 633/16 = 39.5625$, $s = 8.7949$;

(b) [36.39, 42.73] using t, [36.52, 42.61] using normal approximation.

6.2-11 **(a)** $\bar{x} = 16.706$;

(b) $s^2 = 3.4315$, $s = 1.852$;

(c) [16.392, 17.020] with $t_{0.05}(95) = 1.661$, [16.395, 17.017] using normal approximation.

6.2-13 $\bar{x} = 1.3347$, $s = 0.0630$, $[1.3151, 1.3542]$.

6.2-15 $[22.74, 25.48]$.

6.2-17 $[0.757, \infty)$.

6.2-19 **(a)** 29.49, 3.41; **(b)** $[0, 31.259]$;
(c) yes, because of the linearity of the q–q plot of the data and the corresponding normal quantiles.

6.2-21 **(a)** $\bar{x} = 25.475$, $s = 2.4935$; **(b)** $[24.059, \infty)$.

6.3-1 $[-59.725, -43.275]$.

6.3-3 $[-5.845, 0.845]$.

6.3-5 $(-\infty, -1.828]$.

6.3-7 **(a)** Yes; **(b)** $[11.5, 13.7]$; **(d)** do not change.

6.3-9 **(a)** $\bar{d} = 0.450$; **(b)** $[-0.494, 1.394]$.

6.3-11 **(a)** $[-0.556, 1.450]$;
(b) $[0.367, 1.863]$;
(c) no for men, yes for women.

6.3-13 $[157.227, \infty)$.

6.3-15 $[-5.599, -1.373]$ assuming equal variances, otherwise $[-5.577, -1.394]$.

6.4-1 **(a)** $s = 6.144$; **(b)** $[4.406, 10.142]$ or $[4.107, 9.521]$.

6.4-3 **(a)** $\bar{x} = 273.04, s^2 = 3,155.54$;
(b) $[2,079.43, 5,468.08]$;
(c) $[45.60, 73.95]$; **(d)** $[44.02, 71.56]$; **(e)** yes.

6.4-5 $\left[\dfrac{\sum_{i=1}^{n}(X_i - \mu)^2}{\chi^2_{\alpha/2}(n)}, \dfrac{\sum_{i=1}^{n}(X_i - \mu)^2}{\chi^2_{1-\alpha/2}(n)}\right]$.

6.4-7 **(a)** $[142.72, 386.10]$; **(b)** $\bar{x} = 220.69$, $s = 200.27$, yes.

6.4-9 **(b)** $\bar{x}$ or s; **(d)** $[148.11, 432.72]$ is an approximate 95% confidence interval.

6.4-11 **(a)** 0.5688; **(b)** $[0, 1.905]$, yes.

6.4-13 **(a)** 0.4987; **(b)** $[0, 1.835]$.

6.4-15 $g(a) = g(b)$ and $a = -b$; so $a = -t_{\alpha/2}(n-1) = -b$.

6.4-17 **(a)** $[0.97, 8.72]$; **(b)** $[0.214, 5.980]$; **(c)** $[0.155, 2.833]$.

6.4-19 **(a)** 8.9963, 0.7616; **(b)** $[2.67, 52.33]$;
(c) both could be normal because of the linearity of the q–q plots.

6.5-1 **(a)** 0.0374; **(b)** $[0.0227, 0.0521]$; **(c)** $[0.0252, 0.0550]$; **(d)** $[0.0250, 0.0555]$; **(e)** $[0, 0.0497]$.

6.5-3 **(a)** 0.6900; **(b)** $[0.6613, 0.7187]$ or $[0.6607, 0.7179]$ or $[0.6606, 0.7179]$.

6.5-5 **(a)** 0.5061; **(b)** $[0.4608, 0.5513]$ or $[0.4609, 0.5511]$ or $[0.4607, 0.5513]$; **(c)** not necessarily.

6.5-7 **(a)** 0.1800; **(b)** $[0.0735, 0.2865]$; **(c)** $[0.0977, 0.3080]$; **(d)** $[0.0921, 0.3153]$.

6.5-9 **(a)** 0.6799; **(b)** $[0.6457, 0.7140]$ or $[0.6448, 0.7130]$ or $[0.6450, 0.7134]$.

6.5-11 **(a)** $[0.445, 0.515]$; **(b)** 91.04%.

6.5-13 $[0.207, 0.253]$.

6.5-15 **(a)** 0.2115; **(b)** $[0.1554, 0.2676]$.

6.5-17 **(a)** 0.2182; **(b)** $[0.1756, 1]$.

6.5-19 **(a)** 0.2726; **(b)** $[0.2254, 0.3198]$.

6.6-1 117.

6.6-3 **(a)** 1083; **(b)** $[6.047, 6.049]$; **(c)** \$58,800; **(d)** 0.0145.

6.6-5 **(a)** 257; **(b)** yes.

6.6-7 **(a)** 1068; **(b)** 2401; **(c)** 752.

6.6-9 2305.

6.6-11 451.

6.6-13 **(a)** 38; **(b)** $[0.621, 0.845]$.

6.6-15 601.

6.6-17 235.

6.6-19 144.

6.7-1 **(a)** $\widehat{y} = 86.8 + (842/829)(x - 74.5)$;
(c) $\widehat{\sigma^2} = 17.9998$.

6.7-3 **(b)** $\widehat{y} = -7.877 + 0.0868x$.

6.7-5 **(a)** $\widehat{y} = 10.6 - 0.015x$;
(c) $\widehat{y} = 5.47 + 0.0004x$;
(e) horsepower.

6.7-7 Solve for α: $-t_{\alpha/2}(n-2) \le \dfrac{\widehat{\alpha} - \alpha}{\sqrt{\widehat{\sigma^2}/(n-2)}} \le t_{\alpha/2}(n-2)$.

6.7-9 $[83.341, 90.259]$, $[0.478, 1.553]$, $[10.265, 82.578]$.

6.7-11 **(a)** $\widehat{y} = 15.695 + 0.620x$;
(c) $\widehat{\sigma^2} = 0.2595$;
(d) $[0.4416, 0.7984]$.

6.7-13 **(a)** $\widehat{y} = 1.896 + 0.538x$;
(c) $\widehat{\alpha} = 6.9667$, $\widehat{\beta} = 0.5385$, $\widehat{\sigma^2} = 0.0549$;
(d) $[6.8263, 7.1070]$, $[0.2081, 0.8688]$, $[0.0333, 0.1643]$.

6.7-15 **(a)** $\widehat{y} = 3.575 + 1.225x$;
(c) $[29.987, 31.285]$, $[0.923, 1.527]$, $[0.428, 3.018]$.

6.7-17 **(a)** $\widehat{y} = 46.59 + 1.085x$.

6.8-1 **(a)** $[75.283, 85.113]$, $[83.838, 90.777]$, $[89.107, 99.728]$;
(b) $[68.206, 92.190]$, $[75.833, 98.783]$, $[82.258, 106.577]$.

6.8-3 **(a)** $[2.246, 2.821]$, $[2.761, 3.174]$, $[3.133, 3.669]$;
(b) $[1.821, 3.246]$, $[2.284, 3.651]$, $[2.696, 4.106]$.

6.8-5 **(a)** $[4.897, 8.444]$, $[9.464, 12.068]$, $[12.718, 17.004]$;
(b) $[1.899, 11.442]$, $[6.149, 15.383]$, $[9.940, 19.782]$.

6.8-7 **(a)** $[19.669, 26.856]$, $[22.122, 27.441]$, $[24.048, 28.551]$, $[25.191, 30.445]$, $[25.791, 32.882]$;

(b) $[15.530, 30.996]$, $[17.306, 32.256]$, $[18.915, 33.684]$, $[20.351, 35.285]$, $[21.618, 37.055]$.

6.8-9 $\widehat{y} = 1.1037 + 2.0327x - 0.2974x^2 + 0.6204x^3$.

6.8-13 **(a)** $r = 0.143$;
(b) $\widehat{y} = 37.68 + 0.83x$;
(d) no;
(e) $\widehat{y} = 12.845 + 22.566x - 3.218x^2$;
(f) yes.

6.8-15 $\widehat{y} = 1.735042 - 0.000377x + 0.000124x^2$, yes.

Chapter 7

7.1-1 $\alpha = 7/27$; $\beta = 7/27$.

7.1-3 **(a)** 0.3032 using $b(100, 0.08)$, 0.313 using Poisson approximation, 0.2902 using normal approximation;
(b) 0.1064 using $b(100, 0.04)$, 0.111 using Poisson approximation, 0.1010 using normal approximation.

7.1-5 **(a)** $\alpha = 0.1056$; **(b)** $\beta = 0.3524$.

7.1-7 **(a)** $z = 2.269 > 1.645$, reject H_0;
(b) $z = 2.269 < 2.326$, do not reject H_0;
(c) p-value $= 0.0116$.

7.1-9 **(a)** $z = 1.758 > 1.645$, reject H_0;
(b) $z = 1.758 < 1.96$, do not reject H_0;
(c) p-value $= 0.0394$.

7.1-11 **(a)** $z = \dfrac{y/n - 0.40}{\sqrt{(0.40)(0.60)/n}} \ge 1.645$;
(b) $z = 2.215 > 1.645$, reject H_0.

7.1-13 **(a)** $H_0: p = 0.40$, $H_1: p > 0.40$, $z \ge 2.326$;
(b) $2.236 < 2.326$, do not reject H_0.

7.1-15 **(a)** $H_0: p = 0.037$, $H_1: p > 0.037$;
(b) $z \ge 2.326$;
(c) $z = 2.722 > 2.326$, reject H_0.

7.1-17 **(a)** $|z| \ge 1.960$;
(b) $1.726 < 1.960$, do not reject H_0.

7.1-19 $[0.007, 0.071]$, yes.

7.1-21 **(a)** $z = (\widehat{p} - 0.5)/\sqrt{(0.5)(0.5)/200} \le -1.645$, reject H_0;
(b) $z = -1.697$; **(c)** p-value $= 0.045$.

7.1-23 $z = -0.473$, p-value $= 0.318$, does not support management's claim.

7.1-25 $z = -2.272$, p-value $= 0.012$, supports the manufacturer's claim.

7.2-1 **(a)** $1.4 < 1.645$, do not reject H_0;
(b) $1.4 > 1.282$, reject H_0.
(c) p-value $= 0.0808$.

7.2-3 **(a)** $z = (\overline{x} - 170)/2$, $z \ge 1.645$;
(b) $1.260 < 1.645$, do not reject H_0;
(c) 0.1038.

7.2-5 **(a)** $t = (\overline{x} - 3{,}315)/(s/\sqrt{30}) \le -1.699$;
(b) $-1.414 > -1.699$, do not reject H_0;
(c) $0.05 < p$-value < 0.10 or p-value ≈ 0.08.

7.2-7 **(a)** $t = (\overline{x} - 47)/(s/\sqrt{20}) \le -1.729$;
(b) $-1.789 < -1.729$, reject H_0;
(c) $0.025 < p$-value < 0.05, p-value ≈ 0.045.

7.2-9 **(a)** $t \ge 2.764$;
(b) $4.028 > 2.764$, reject H_0;
(c) p-value < 0.005.

7.2-11 **(a)** -4.60, p-value < 0.0001;
(b) clearly reject H_0;
(c) $[0, 14.573]$.

7.2-13 $1.477 < 1.833$, do not reject H_0.

7.2-15 $\overline{d} = 0.357$, $s_d = 0.561$, $t = 2.985$, p-value < 0.005.

7.3-1 **(a)** $t \le -1.734$; **(b)** $t = -2.221 < -1.734$, reject H_0.

7.3-3 **(a)** $|t| = 0.374 < 2.086$, do not reject H_0 at $\alpha = 0.05$.

7.3-5 **(a)** $t < -1.706$; **(b)** $-1.714 < -1.706$, reject H_0;
(c) $0.025 < p$-value < 0.05.

7.3-7 **(a)** $t < -2.552$; **(b)** $t = -3.638 < -2.552$, reject H_0.

7.3-9 **(a)** $z > 1.645$; **(b)** $1.957 > 1.645$, reject H_0;
(c) p-value $= 0.0252$.

7.3-11 **(a)** $t = 1.20$, $0.20 < p$-value < 0.50, p-value $= 0.246$, do not reject H_0.

7.3-13 **(a)** $t = -1.67$, $0.05 < p$-value < 0.10, p-value $= 0.054$, fail to reject H_0.

7.3-15 **(a)** $z = 2.245 > 1.645$, reject H_0; **(b)** p-value $= 0.0124$.

7.3-17 **(a)** $r = 11$, $t = 3.177$, p-value < 0.005, reject H_0;
(b) $r = 14$, $t = 0.320$, p-value $= 0.754$, do not reject H_0;
(c) $r = 14$, $t = -0.112$, p-value $= 0.913$, do not reject H_0.

7.3-19 **(a)** $t = 3.440$, p-value < 0.005, reject H_0.

7.4-1 **(a)** $\chi^2 = \dfrac{10s^2}{525^2} \le 3.940$; **(b)** $4.104 > 3.940$, do not reject H_0; **(c)** $0.05 < p$-value < 0.10, p-value $= 0.057$ using Minitab.

7.4-3 **(a)** $\chi^2 = 24s^2/140^2$, $\chi^2 \ge 36.42$;
(b) $29.18 < 36.42$, do not reject H_0.

7.4-5 **(a)** $59.53 < 64.28$, reject H_0;
(b) $0.025 < p$-value < 0.05, p-value $= 0.042$ using Minitab.

7.4-7 **(a)** $\chi^2 \geq 28.87$ or $s^2 \geq 48.117$;
(b) $\beta \approx 0.10$.

7.4-9 $F = 3.30 > 3.07$, reject $\sigma_X^2 = \sigma_Y^2$;
Welch's test: $t = -8.119 < -t_{0.05}(12) = -1.782$.

7.4-11 **(a)** $2.759 < 4.20$, do not reject H_0 at $\alpha = 0.05$;
(b) $s_x^2/s_y^2 = 0.818 < 2.96$, $s_y^2/s_x^2 = 1.222 < 3.18$; do not reject H_0;
(c) $1.836 < 3.28$, do not reject H_0;
(d) $1.318 < 4.03$, $0.759 < 4.03$, do not reject H_0;
(e) $3.247 < 4.32$, $0.308 < 5.52$, do not reject H_0;
(f) $0.84 < F_{0.025}(24, 28)$, $1.19 < F_{0.025}(28, 24)$, do not reject H_0;
(g) $1.624 < 4.03$, do not reject H_0.

7.5-1 $7.875 > 4.26$, reject H_0.

7.5-3 $13.773 > 4.07$, reject H_0.

7.5-5 **(a)**

Source	SS	DF	MS	F	p-value
Treatment	31.112	2	15.556	22.33	0.000
Error	29.261	42	0.697		
Total	60.372	44			

(c) the respective means are 23.114, 22,556, and 21.120, with the eggs of the shortest lengths in the nests of the smallest bird.

7.5-7 $14.757 > 2.87$, reject H_0.

7.5-9 **(a)** $F \geq 4.07$;
(b) $4.106 > 4.07$, reject H_0;
(c) $4.106 < 5.42$, do not reject H_0;
(d) $0.025 < p\text{-value} < 0.05$, $p\text{-value} \approx 0.05$.

7.5-11 $10.224 > 4.26$, reject H_0.

7.5-13 **(a)** $F \geq 5.61$;
(b) $6.337 > 5.61$, reject H_0.

7.5-15 **(a)** $F = 12.47$, there seems to be a difference in feed supplements;
(b) yes, supplement B looks best and supplement C the poorest.

7.6-1 $18.00 > 5.14$, reject H_A.

7.6-3 **(a)** $7.624 > 4.46$, reject H_A;
(b) $15.538 > 3.84$, reject H_B.

7.6-5 **(a)** $1.723 < 2.90$, accept H_{AB};
(b) $5.533 > 4.15$, reject H_A;
(c) $28.645 > 2.90$, reject H_B.

7.6-7 **(a)** $1.727 < 2.37$, accept H_{AB};
(b) $2.238 < 3.27$, do not reject H_A;
(c) $2.063 < 2.87$, do not reject H_B.

7.6-9 **(a)** $0.111 < 3.89$, accept H_{AB};
(b) $9.692 > 4.75$, reject H_A;
(c) $2.606 < 3.89$, do not reject H_B.

7.6-11 **(a)**

Source	SS	DF	MS	F	p-value
Smoking History	84.899	2	42.449	12.90	0.000
Test	298.072	2	149.036	45.28	0.000
Interaction	2.815	4	0.704	0.21	0.927
Error	59.247	18	3.291		
Total	445.032	26			

7.7-1 $4.359 > 2.306$, reject H_0.

7.7-3 $5.373 > 2.896$, reject H_0.

7.7-5 $-0.45 < -0.3808$, reject H_0.

7.7-7 $[0.419, 0.802]$.

7.7-9 $|r| = 0.252 < 0.6613$, do not reject H_0.

7.7-13 $n = 9$.
(a) $\widehat{y} = 42.02 - 0.0060x$;
(b) $r = -0.656$, $0.01 < p\text{-value} < 0.025$, $p\text{-value} = 0.014$;
(c) $\widehat{y} = 55.67 - 0.0075x$, $r = -0.639$, $0.01 < p\text{-value} < 0.025$, $p\text{-value} = 0.017$;
(d) $r = 0.951$.

Chapter 8

8.1-1 $6.25 < 7.815$, do not reject if $\alpha = 0.05$; $p\text{-value} \approx 0.10$.

8.1-3 $7.60 < 16.92$, do not reject H_0.

8.1-5 **(a)** $q_3 \geq 7.815$;
(b) $q_3 = 1.744 < 7.815$; do not reject H_0.

8.1-7 $6.113 < 16.92$, do not reject H_0.

8.1-9 $2.010 < 11.07 = \chi^2_{0.05}(5)$, do not reject null hypothesis.

8.1-11 **(a)** Frequencies are 2, 4, 21, 33, 20, 14, 4, 1, 1;
(b) $q = 4.653 < 9.488$, do not reject H_0.

8.1-13 Grouping last two classes: $2.75 < 9.210$, not grouping: $3.46 < 11.34$; in either case, do not reject H_0.

8.1-15 $\bar{x} = 320.10$, $s^2 = 45.56$; using class boundaries $303.5, 307.5, \ldots, 335.5$, $q = 3.21 < 11.07 = \chi^2_{0.05}(5)$, do not reject.

8.2-1 $3.23 < 11.07$, do not reject H_0.

8.2-3 $2.40 < 5.991$, do not reject H_0.

8.2-5 $5.975 < \chi^2_{0.05}(2) = 5.991$, do not reject the null hypothesis; however, $p\text{-value} \approx 0.05$.

8.2-7 $8.449 < \chi^2_{0.05}(4) = 9.488$, do not reject the null hypothesis; $0.05 < p\text{-value} < 0.10$; $p\text{-value} = 0.076$.

8.2-9 $4.149 > \chi^2_{0.05}(1) = 3.841$, reject the null hypothesis; $0.025 < p$-value < 0.05; p-value ≈ 0.042.

8.2-11 $23.78 > 21.03$, reject hypothesis of independence.

8.2-13 **(a)** $39.591 > 9.488$, reject hypothesis of independence;
(b) $7.117 > 5.991$, reject hypothesis of independence;
(c) $11.398 > 9.488$, reject hypothesis of independence.
(d) 0, 0.03, 0.02.

8.2-15 $3.603 < 12.59$, do not reject hypothesis of independent attributes.

8.3-1 **(b)** $\widetilde{m} = 146, \widetilde{\pi}_{0.80} = 270$;
(c) $\widetilde{q}_1 = 95, \widetilde{q}_3 = 225$.

8.3-3 **(a)** $g_3(y) = 10(1 - e^{-y/3})^2 e^{-y}, 0 < y < \infty$;
(b) $5(1 - e^{-5/3})^4 e^{-5/3} + (1 - e^{-5/3})^5 = 0.7599$;
(c) $e^{-5/3} = 0.1889$.

8.3-5 **(a)** 0.2553; **(b)** 0.7483.

8.3-7 **(a)** $g_1(y) = 19(e^{-y/\theta})^{18} \frac{1}{\theta} e^{-y/\theta}, 0 < y < \infty$;
(b) 1/20.

8.3-9 **(a)** $L(\theta) = \exp[-\Sigma_{i=1}^{10}(x_i - \theta)]$ is a maximum when θ is as large as possible. Thus, $\widehat{\theta} = Y_1$.
(b) $g_1(y_1) = 10e^{-10(y_1-\theta)}, \ \theta \le y_1 < \infty$.
(c) $[y_1 - (1/10)\ln(20), y_1]$.

8.3-11 **(a)** $g_r(y) = \dfrac{n!}{(r-1)!(n-r)!}(1 - e^{-y})^{r-1} \times (e^{-y})^{n-r} e^{-y}, \ 0 < y < \infty$;
(b) a beta p.d.f. with $\alpha = n - r + 1, \beta = r$.

8.3-13 **(a)** $g(y_1, y_n) = \dfrac{n!}{(n-2)!}(y_n - y_1)^{(n-2)}, \ 0 < y_1 < y_n < 1$;
(b) $h(w_1, w_2) = n(n-1)w_2^{n-1}(1 - w_1)^{n-2}, \ 0 < w_1 < 1, 0 < w_2 < 1$;
$h_1(w_1) = (n-1)(1 - w_1)^{n-2}, 0 < w_1 < 1$;
$h_2(w_2) = n w_2^{n-1}, 0 < w_2 < 1$;
(c) yes.

8.4-1 **(a)** 0.7812; **(b)** 0.7844; **(c)** 0.4528.

8.4-3 **(a)** (6.31, 7.40); **(b)** (6.58, 7.22), 0.8204.

8.4-5 (2.72, 2.84), 93.46%.

8.4-7 (15.40, 17.05).

8.4-9 **(a)**

Stems	Leaves	Frequency	Depths
101	7	1	1
102	0 0 0	3	4
103		0	4
104		0	4
105	8 9	2	6
106	1 3 3 6 6 7 7 8 8	9	(9)
107	3 7 9	3	10
108	8	1	7
109	1 3 9	3	6
110	0 2 2	3	3

(b) $\widetilde{\pi}_{0.25} = 106.0, \widetilde{m} = 106.7, \widetilde{\pi}_{0.75} = 108.95$;
(c) (i) (102.0, 106.6), 89.66%; (ii) (106.3, 107.7), 89.22%; (iii) (107.3, 110.0), 89.66%.
(d) [106.3, 107.7], 89.22%; [105.87, 107.63], 90%.

8.4-11 **(a)** $\widetilde{\pi}_{0.50} = \widetilde{m} = 0.92$;
(b) $(y_{41}, y_{60}) = (0.92, 0.93)$; 0.9426 using normal approximation, 0.9431 using binomial;
(c) $\widetilde{\pi}_{0.25} = 0.89$;
(d) $(y_{17}, y_{34}) = (0.88, 0.90)$; 0.9504 using normal approximation, 0.9513 using binomial;
(e) $\widetilde{\pi}_{0.75} = 0.97$;
(f) $(y_{67}, y_{84}) = (0.95, 0.98)$; 0.9504 using normal approximation, 0.9513 using binomial.

8.4-13 $y_4 = 5.08 < \pi_{0.25} < y_{15} = 5.27$, $y_{14} = 5.27 < \pi_{0.5} < y_{26} = 5.31$, $y_{24} = 5.30 < \pi_{0.75} < y_{35} = 5.35$.

8.4-15 **(a)** 14.75; **(b)** 0.8995.

8.5-1 **(a)** $-55 < -47.08$, reject H_0; **(b)** 0.0296;
(c) $9 < 10$, do not reject H_0; **(d)** p-value $= 0.1334$.

8.5-3 **(a)** $y = 17$, p-value $= 0.0539$;
(b) $w = 171$, p-value $= 0.0111$;
(c) $t = 2.608$, p-value $= 0.0077$.

8.5-5 $w = 54$, $z = 1.533$, p-value $= 0.0661$, do not reject H_0.

8.5-7 **(a)** Let Y equal the number of weights less that 1.14 pounds. Then $C = \{y: \ y \le 4\}, \alpha = 0.0898$.
(b) $y = 5$, fail to reject H_0;
(c) p-value $= 0.2120$;
(d) $z = 2.072 > 1.282$, p-value $= 0.0207$, reject H_0.

8.5-9 **(a)** $w = 145 > 126$ or $z = 3.024 > 1.645$, reject H_0; p-value ≈ 0.0014.

8.5-11 **(a)** $C = \{w\colon w \le 79 \text{ or } w \ge 131\}, \alpha \approx 0.0539$, $w = 95$, do not reject H_0.

8.5-13 **(a)** $C = \{w\colon w \le 79 \text{ or } w \ge 131\}, \alpha \approx 0.0539$, $w = 107.5$, p-value $= 0.8798$, do not reject H_0.

8.5-15 $C = \{w\colon w \le 184 \text{ or } w \ge 280\}, \alpha \approx 0.0489$, $w = 241$, do not reject H_0.

8.5-17 **(a)** $w = 71$, reject H_0, p-value $= 0.0057$;
(b) $w = 101$, do not reject H_0, p-value $= 0.7913$;
(c) $w = 108$, do not reject H_0, p-value $= 0.8501$.

8.5-19 **(b)** $w = 223.5 < 224.25$, reject H_0;
(c) p-value ≈ 0.01;
(d) reject H_0;
(e) the p-values are approximately equal.

8.6-1 **(a)** $C = \{r\colon r \le 6\}, \alpha = 43/429, r = 6$, reject H_0;
(b) $w = 95$, p-value ≈ 0.0027, clearly reject H_0.

8.6-3 $(6!)(12!)\binom{11}{4} = 113{,}810{,}780{,}160{,}000$.

8.6-5 **(b)** $r = 11$, reject H_0; **(c)** p-value $= 0.0457$.

8.6-7 $r = 4$, p-value $= 43/1{,}716 = 0.025$, reject the hypothesis of randomness. There appears to be a trend effect.

8.6-9 $r = 7$, p-value $= 1{,}331/58{,}786 = 0.0226$, reject the hypothesis of randomness.

8.6-11 **(a)** $C = \{y\colon\ y \le 3 \text{ or } y \ge 11\}$, $y = 7$, do not reject H_0;
(b) $C = \{r\colon\ r \le 4 \text{ or } r \ge 12\}$, $\alpha = 43/858 = 0.05$, $r = 4$, reject the hypothesis of randomness. There appears to be a trend effect.

8.6-13 $C = \{r\colon\ r \le 10\}, \alpha = 919/22{,}287 = 0.041, r = 6$, p-value $= 1{,}133/1{,}002{,}915 = 0.0011$, reject H_0.

8.6-15 The number of runs, 10, is within one standard deviation of $\mu = 12$.

8.6-17 No, because the numbers of runs are close to the mean, 10.

8.6-19 Do not reject the null hypothesis at $\alpha = 0.10$.

8.7-1 $d_5 = 0.40 < 0.45$, do not reject H_0.

8.7-3 $d_{10} = 0.1643$ at $x = 49$, do not reject H_0.

8.7-5 **(a)** $\overline{x} = 1.3347, s^2 = 0.00397$;
(b) $d_{30} = 0.0738$ at $x = 1.28$, do not reject H_0.

8.7-7 $d_{40} = 0.04559$, do not reject H_0.

8.7-9 **(a)** $d_{70} = 0.1295 > 1.07/\sqrt{70} = 0.1279$, reject H_0;
(b) yes, the histogram is bimodal.

8.7-11 $d_{105} = 0.07$ at $x = 6$; fit is very good.

8.7-13 $\widehat{\theta} = 0.28588$, $\widehat{\delta} = -0.41588$, $d_{18} = 0.0873$ at $x = -0.31$.

Chapter 9

9.1-3 $3800(10/38) = 1000$; 307.79.

9.1-5 2.67, 8, 16, 21.33, 64.

9.2-1 **(a)** $k(\theta \,|\, y) \propto \theta^{\alpha+y-1}e^{-\theta(n+1/\beta)}$.
Thus, the posterior p.d.f. of θ is gamma with parameters $\alpha + y$ and $1/(n + 1/\beta)$.
(b) $w(y) = E(\theta \,|\, y) = (\alpha + y)/(n + 1/\beta)$.
(c) $w(y) = \left(\dfrac{y}{n}\right)\left(\dfrac{n}{n + 1/\beta}\right) + (\alpha\beta)\left(\dfrac{1/\beta}{n + 1/\beta}\right)$.

9.2-3 **(a)** $E[\{w(Y) - \theta\}^2] = \{E[w(Y) - \theta]\}^2 + \mathrm{Var}[w(Y)] = (74\theta^2 - 114\theta + 45)/500$;
(b) $\theta = 0.569$ to $\theta = 0.872$.

9.2-5 The median (or mean), because the posterior p.d.f. is symmetric.

9.2-7 $d = 2/n$.

9.3-5 **(c)** $2yz$ is $\chi^2(2n)$; $\left(\dfrac{2y}{\chi^2_{\alpha/2}(2n)}, \dfrac{2y}{\chi^2_{1-\alpha/2}(2n)}\right)$.

Chapter 10

10.1-1 **(a)** $\sum_{i=1}^{n} X_i^2$; **(b)** $\widehat{\sigma^2} = \left(\dfrac{1}{n}\right)\sum_{i=1}^{n} X_i^2$; **(c)** yes.

10.1-7 **(a)** $f(x;p) = \exp\{x\ln(1 - p) + \ln[p/(1 - p)]\}$; $K(x) = x$; $\sum_{i=1}^{n} X_i$ is sufficient.
(b) $\overline{X}$.

10.2-1 **(a)** $K(\mu) = \Phi\left(\dfrac{22.5 - \mu}{3/2}\right)$; $\alpha = 0.0478$;
(b) $\overline{x} = 24.1225 > 22.5$, do not reject H_0;
(c) 0.2793.

10.2-3 **(a)** $K(\mu) = \Phi\left(\dfrac{510.77 - \mu}{15}\right)$;
(b) $\alpha = 0.10$;
(c) 0.5000;
(e) (i) 0.0655, (ii) 0.0150.

10.2-5 $n = 25, c = 1.6$.

10.2-7 $n = 40, c = 678.38$.

10.2-9 **(a)** $K(p) = \sum_{y=14}^{25}\binom{25}{y}p^y(1 - p)^{25-y}$, $0.40 \le p \le 1.0$;
(b) $\alpha = 0.0778$;
(c) 0.1827, 0.3450, 0.7323, 0.9558, 0.9985, 1.0000;
(e) yes;
(f) 0.0344.

10.2-11 With $n = 130, c = 8.5, \alpha \approx 0.055, \beta \approx 0.094$.

10.3-1 **(a)** $\dfrac{L(80)}{L(76)} = \exp\left[\dfrac{6}{128}\sum_{i=1}^{n} x_i - \dfrac{624n}{128}\right] \le k$ or $\overline{x} \le c$;
(b) $n = 43, c = 78$.

10.3-3 **(a)** $\dfrac{L(3)}{L(5)} \le k$ if and only if $\sum_{i=1}^{n} x_i \ge (-15/2)[\ln(k) - \ln(5/3)^n] = c$;
(b) $\overline{x} \ge 4.15$;
(c) $\overline{x} \ge 4.15$;
(d) yes.

10.3-5 **(a)** $\dfrac{L(50)}{L(\mu_1)} \le k$ if and only if $\overline{x} \le \dfrac{(-72)\ln(k)}{2n(\mu_1 - 50)} + \dfrac{50 + \mu_1}{2} = c$.

10.3-7 **(a)** $\dfrac{L(0.5)}{L(\mu)} \le k$ if and only if $\sum_{i=1}^{n} x_i \ge \dfrac{\ln(k) + n(0.05 - \mu)}{\ln(0.5/\mu)} = c$;
(b) $\sum_{i=1}^{10} x_i \ge 9$.

10.4-1 **(a)** $|-1.80| > 1.645$, reject H_0;
(b) $|-1.80| < 1.96$, do not reject H_0;
(c) p-value $= 0.0718$.

10.4 3 **(a)** $\bar{x} \ge 230 + 10z_\alpha/\sqrt{n}$ or $\dfrac{\bar{x} - 230}{10/\sqrt{n}} \ge z_\alpha$;
(b) yes; **(c)** $1.04 < 1.282$, do not reject H_0;
(d) p-value $= 0.1492$.

10.4-5 **(a)** $|2.10| < 2.306$, do not reject H_0; $0.05 < p\text{-value} < 0.10$.

10.4-7 $2.20 > 1.282$, reject H_0; p-value $= 0.0139$.

10.5-1 **(a)** 0.84; **(b)** 0.082.

10.5-3 $k = 1.464$; 8/15.

10.5-5 **(a)** 0.25; **(b)** 0.85; **(c)** 0.925.

10.5-7 675.

10.6-1 **(a)** 0.9984; **(b)** 0.998.

10.6-3 $M(t) = \left[1 - \dfrac{2t\sigma^2}{n-1}\right]^{-(n-1)/2} \to e^{\sigma^2 t}$.

10.7-1 **(b)** σ^2/n; **(c)** $2/n$.

10.7-3 **(a)** $2\theta^2/n$; **(b)** $N(\theta, 2\theta^2/n)$; **(c)** $\chi^2(n)$.

Chapter 11

11.1-9 **(a)** There is a quadratic trend upwards.

11.2-1 **(a)** 158.97, 12.1525, 30.55; **(f)** yes.

11.2-3 **(a)** 5.176(335.176), 0.5214, 1.294; **(f)** no.

11.2-5 **(b)** $E(\sqrt{Y}) = \dfrac{\sqrt{2}\,\Gamma\left(\frac{n}{2}\right)}{\Gamma\left(\frac{n-1}{2}\right)}$;

(c) $S = \dfrac{\sigma\sqrt{Y}}{\sqrt{n-1}}$ so

$$E(S) = \frac{\sqrt{2}\,\Gamma\left(\frac{n}{2}\right)}{\sqrt{n-1}\,\Gamma\left(\frac{n-1}{2}\right)}\sigma.$$

11.2-7 LCL $= 0$, UCL $= 0.1024$;
(a) 0.0378; **(b)** 0.1752.

11.2-9 LCL $= 0$, UCL $= 4.9496$;
(a) 0.185; **(b)** 0.871.

11.2-11 (a) LCL $= 0$, UCL $= 13.99$; (b) yes.

11.3-1

2^2 Design

Run	A	B	AB	Observations
1	−	−	+	X_1
2	+	−	−	X_2
3	−	+	−	X_3
4	+	+	+	X_4

(a) $[A] = (-X_1 + X_2 - X_3 + X_4)/4$,
$[B] = (-X_1 - X_2 + X_3 + X_4)/4$,
$[AB] = (X_1 - X_2 - X_3 + X_4)/4$.

(b) It is sufficient to compare the coefficients on both sides of the equations of X_1^2, X_1X_2, X_1X_3, and X_1X_4, which are $3/4, -1/2, -1/2$, and $-1/2$, respectively.

(c) Each is $\chi^2(1)$.

11.3-3 [A] is $N(0, \sigma^2/2)$ so $E[(X_2 - X_1)^2/4] = \sigma^2/2$ or $E[(X_2 - X_1)^2/2] = \sigma^2$.

11.3-5 **(a)** $[A] = -4$, $[B] = 12$, $[C] = -1.125$, $[D] = -2.75$, $[AB] = 0.5$, $[AC] = 0.375$, $[AD] = 0$, $[BC] = -0.625$, $[BD] = 2.25$, $[CD] = -0.125$, $[ABC] = -0.375$, $[ABD] = 0.25$, $[ACD] = -0.125$, $[BCD] = -0.375$, $[ABCD] = -0.125$.

(b) There is clearly a temperature (B) effect. There is also a catalyst charge (A) effect and probably a concentration (D) and a temperature–concentration (BD) effect.

Index

A

Acceptance number, 105
Acceptance sampling plan, 56, 105
Additive model, 391
Algebra of sets, 12, D1
Alternative hypothesis, 344
Analysis-of-variance table, 383
ANOVA table, 383, 392, 395
Approximate chi-square distribution, 409
Assignment of probability, 18, 477
Associative laws, D3
Asymptotic distributions, 535

B

Bar graph, 54
Basu's theorem, 504
Bayes's formula, 46
Bayes's theorem, 45, 46
Bayes, Thomas, 50, 214, 483
Bayesian estimation, 483
Bayesian methods, 477
Bernoulli
  distribution, 78, 596
  experiment, 78
  trials, 78
Bernoulli distribution, 92
Bernoulli, Daniel, 108
Bernoulli, Jacob, 108
Bernoulli, Nicolaus II, 108
Bernstein, Peter L., 270
Best critical region, 513
Best fitting line, 193
Beta distribution, 228, 233, 493, 597
Biased estimator, 278
Binomial coefficients, 24, 574
Binomial distribution, 79, 91, 263, 429, 529, 596
Birthday problem, 37
Bivariate normal distribution, 209
Bootstrapping, 469
Box plot, 125
Box, George, 341
Box-and-whisker diagram, 125, 385
Box–Muller transformation, 232
Burr distribution, 496

C

c chart, 553
c.d.f., 133
Cardano, Girolamo, 49
CAS, 74, 96, 154, 271, 446
Cauchy distribution, 217, 468
Censoring, 174
Central limit theorem, 256, 263, 269, 270, 532
Cervical cancer, 47
Challenger space shuttle, 328
Change-of-variable technique, 217
Change-of-variables technique, 225
Characteristic function, 530
Chebyshev's inequality, 525
Chi-square distribution, 151, 163, 244, 382, 391, 597
Chi-square goodness-of-fit tests, 407, 414
Chi-square random variables, 381
Class boundaries, 112
Class intervals, 112
Class limits, 112

Any entries referring to D1-D17 are found in Appendix D on the CD-ROM

Class marks, 112
Column effects, 394
Combination, 23
Commutative laws, D3
Complement of A, 12
Complement of a set, D2
Composite hypothesis, 344, 353
Compounding, 490
Conditional mean, 198, 202
Conditional p.d.f., 202
Conditional p.m.f., 197
Conditional probability, 30
Conditional variance, 198, 202
Confidence band, 464
Confidence band for $\mu(x)$, 336
Confidence coefficient, 284
Confidence interval, 283
Confidence intervals
  difference of means, 291, 598
  distribution-free, 436
  for means, 284, 287, 291, 598
  for percentiles, 436
  for proportions, 307, 599
  for regression, 325
  for ρ, 403
  for σ_X/σ_Y, 304
  for standard deviations, 302, 599
  for variances, 302, 599
  of minimum length, 303, 306
  one-sided, 289, 310
  ratio of variances, 303, 599
  two-sided, 288
Conjugate family of priors, 491
Contingency table, 422
Continuous outcome space, 111
Continuous-type data, 111
Continuous-type random variables, 131
Contours for bivariate normal distribution, 211
Control charts
  for flaws, 553
  for p, 552
  for the mean, 551
  for the range, 551
  for the standard deviation, 551
Converges in probability, 527
Convolution formula, 233, 245
Correlation analysis, 399
Correlation coefficient, 190
  distribution, 402
  of sample, 401
Counting data, 4
Covariance, 190
Cox, Sir David R., 269
Craps, 37
Critical region, 346, 353, 520
Cumulative distribution function, 80, 133
Cutpoints, 112

D

Daily lottery, 9
Data
  continuous-type, 111
  counting, 4
  discrete, 4
  relevant, 329
de Fermat, Pierre, 50
de Laplace, Marquis Pierre Simon, 269
de Méré, Chevalier, 49
de Moivre, Abraham, 269, 342, 540
De Morgan's laws, D3
Deciles, 124
Degrees of freedom, 151, 245, 250, 383
Deming, W. Edwards, 566
Density histogram, 5, 112
Dependent random variables, 181
Depths, 121
Discrete data, 4
Discrete outcome space, 53
Discrete-type random variables, 111
Distinguishable permutations, 25
Distribution
  Bernoulli, 78, 92, 596
  beta, 228, 233, 493, 597
  binomial, 79, 91, 263, 429, 529, 596
  bivariate normal, 209
  Burr, 496
  Cauchy, 217, 468
  chi-square, 151, 163, 244, 382, 391, 597
  discrete uniform, 53, 596
  double exponential, 227
  empirical, 72, 134
  exponential, 143, 597
  extreme value, 176, 224
  F, 230, 383, 391, 491
  gamma, 149, 150, 463, 490, 597

geometric, 92, 596, D11
Gompertz, 171
half normal, 224
hypergeometric, 55, 596, D4
limiting, 530
loggamma, 216
logistic, 140, 223
lognormal, 166, 224
Makeham, 175
mixed type, 172
multinomial, 408, 417
multivariate hypergeometric, 187
negative binomial, 92, 596, D10
normal, 157, 246, 256, 269, 597
of *R*, 402
of linear combination, 238
of runs, 455
of sample mean, 248
of the random variable, 4
Pareto, 240
Poisson, 100, 529, 596
rectangular, 141
shifted exponential, 148, 467
standard normal, 159
Student's *t*, 250, 255, 493
sum of chi-square variables, 244
t, 490
trinomial, 188, 196, 201
uniform, 53, 141, 596, 597
Weibull, 137, 170, 177
Wilcoxon, 446
Zipf's law, 496
Distribution function, 80, 133
Distribution function technique, 215
Distribution mean, 75
Distribution standard deviation, 75
Distribution-free confidence intervals, 436
Distribution-free tests, 443
Distributive laws, D3
Distributive operator, 64
Double exponential distribution, 227
Double integral, 16
Dutch book, 482

E

Efficiency, 539
Efron, Brad, 475
Element, D1
ELISA, 36
Empirical distribution, 72, 134
Empirical distribution function, 134, 527
Empty set, 12, D2
Equally likely outcomes, 17
Error sum of squares, 381
Estimate(s), 4, 8, 273
Estimator, 239, 273
biased, 278
efficiency of, 539
maximum likelihood, 275
method of moments, 279
minimum chi-square, 412
minimum variance unbiased, 539
point, 274
sufficient, 497
unbiased, 278
Event, D1
Event(s), 11
dependent, 39
exhaustive, 12
has occurred, 11
independent, 38, 39
mutually exclusive, 12
statistically independent, 39
Exchangeable, 494
Exhaustive events, 12
Expected value, 62, 183, 238
Expected value of *X*, 135
Exploratory data analysis, 121
Exponential distribution, 143, 597
Exponential form, 499
Extreme value distribution, 176, 224

F

F distribution, 230, 383, 391, 491
Factorial designs, 558
Factorial moment, 71, 84
Factorization theorem, 497
Factors, 558
Failure rate, 170
Fences
inner, 126
outer, 126
Fill problem, 168
First quartile, 124, 125, 137
Fisher, Sir Ronald A., 268, 341, 406, 540, 569

Any entries referring to D1-D17 are found in Appendix D on the CD-ROM

Fisher–Neyman factorization theorem, 497
Five-number summary, 125
Force of mortality, 170
Frequency, 4
Frequency histogram, 5, 112
Frequency table, 4

G

Galton, Sir Francis, 178
Galvin, Bob, 568
Gamma distribution, 149, 150, 463, 490, 597
Gamma function, 149
Gauss, Carl Friedrich, 269, 540
Geometric distribution, 92, 596, D11
Gibbs sampler, 495
Gompertz law, 171
Goodness-of-fit, 461
Gosset, William Sealy, 268

H

Half normal distribution, 224
Hierarchical Bayes models, 495
Histogram, 4, 5
  density, 5, 112
  frequency, 5, 112
  probability, 6, 54
  relative frequency, 5, 112
History, 49, 108, 177, 213, 268, 341, 406, 474, 496, 540, 570
Hypergeometric distribution, 55, 596, D4
Hypotheses, 343

I

Improper prior, 492
Independent, 236
Independent events, 38
Independent random variables, 181, 187
Independent trials, 41
Infinite series, D8
Inner fences, 126
Integration, D12
Interaction, 393
Interquartile range, 125, 127
Intersection of A and B, 12
Intersection of sets, D2
IQR, 125

J

Jacobian, 224, 493, D17
Joint probability density function, 185
Joint probability mass function, 180
Joint sufficient statistics, 501

K

Kendall, Sir Maurice G., 269
Kolmogorov–Smirnov test, 461

L

Laplace, Pierre, 540
Law of large numbers, 109, 527
Least squares, 196
Least squares regression line, 193
Level curves for bivariate normal distribution, 211
L'Hôpital's rule, D8
Liapounov, 446
Likelihood function, 274, 275
Likelihood ratio, 519
Limiting distribution, 530
Limiting moment-generating functions, 530
Limits, D7
Line of best fit, 193
Linear model, 337
Linear operator, 64
Logarithmic series, D11
Loggamma distribution, 216
Logistic distribution, 140, 223
Lognormal distribution, 166, 224
Lower control limit (LCL), 548

M

Maclaurin series, D9
Maclaurin's series, 92, 95
Makeham's law, 175
Mann–Whitney–Wilcoxon test, 450
Mann–Whitney test, 450
Maple, 74, 96, 154, 164, 271, 446
Mapping, 225
Marginal probability density function, 186
Marginal probability mass function, 181
Markov chain Monte Carlo (MCMC), 495
Mathematica, 74
Mathematical expectation, 62, 183, 237
Maximum, 125

Any entries referring to D1-D17 are found in Appendix D on the CD-ROM

Maximum error of the estimate, 315, 316
Maximum likelihood estimates, 275
Maximum likelihood estimator, 275
Mean, 135
  of a random sample, 239
  of distribution, 67, 75
  of empirical distribution, 72
  of linear combination, 237
  of sample, 72, 75
  of X, 67, 135, 184
  trimmed, 469
Mean square, 383
Median, 124, 125, 137
Median test, 443
Method of least squares, 193, 196, 323, 337
Method of moments estimator, 279
Methods of enumeration, 20
Midrange, 127
Minimum, 125
Minimum chi-square estimator, 412
Minimum-variance unbiased estimator, 539
Minitab, 82, 145, 153, 154, 164
Mixed-type distribution, 172
Mixture of normals, 490
Modal class, 117
Mode, 5, 7, 117
Moment, 67, 71
  second factorial, 71, 101
Moment-generating function, 89, 136
Monte Carlo procedure, 495
Most powerful test, 516
Multinomial coefficients, 26, 408
Multinomial distribution, 408, 417
Multiple regression, 337
Multiplication principle, 20
Multiplication rule, 33
Multivariate calculus, D14
Multivariate hypergeometric distribution, 187
Mutually exclusive, D2
Mutually exclusive events, 12
Mutually independent, 41

N

Negative binomial distribution, 92, 596, D10
Neyman, Jerzy, 406, 540
Neyman–Pearson lemma, 513
Noninformative prior, 484, 492
Nonparametric methods, 443
Normal distribution, 157, 246, 256, 269, 597
Normal equations, 338
Null hypothesis, 344
Null set, 12, D2

O

Odds against, 477
Odds for, 477
Old Faithful geyser, 119, 547
One-factor analysis of variance, 379
One-factor experiment, 379
One-sided test, 346
Operating characteristic curve, 56, 105
Order statistics, 123, 428
Ordered sample, 22
Ordered stem-and-leaf display, 121, 124
Outcome space, 3, 11, 51
Outer fences, 126
Outliers, 126

P

p chart, 552
p-value, 346, 354
p.d.f., 131
p.m.f., 6
Paccioli, Luca, 49
Paired t test, 358
Pairwise independent events, 41
Pap smear, 47
Parameter space, 273
Parameters, 80
Pareto distribution, 240
Partition, 46
Pascal's equation, 28
Pascal's triangle, 28
Pascal, Blaise, 49, 50
Pearson, Egon, 406, 540
Pearson, Karl, 268, 407, 475
Penalty (loss) function, 485
Percentile, 123, 137
  of the distribution, 433
  of the sample, 125, 433
Percentile method, 470
Permutation, 21
Point estimator, 274
Poisson distribution, 100, 529, 596
Poisson process, 99

Any entries referring to D1-D17 are found in Appendix D on the CD-ROM

Poker, 28
Population, 4
Posterior p.d.f., 484
Posterior probability, 46, 484
Power function, 506
Power of a test, 506
Precision, 490
Prediction band for Y, 336
Prediction interval, 335
Predictive distribution, 490
Predictive probabilities, 491
Prior and posterior p.d.f.s, 486
Prior probability, 46, 484
Probability, 4, 11, 14
  posterior, 46
  prior, 46
Probability density function, 131
Probability histogram, 6, 54
Probability mass function, 6, 53
Probability of event A, 13
Probability value, 346
Pseudorandom numbers, 142

Q

Quadratic forms, 382
Quantile, 137
q–q plot, 137, 164
Quantile–quantile plot, 137, 164
Quantiles, 219
Quartiles, 124, 125, 137

R

R chart, 551
Random experiments, 3
Random interval, 78, 284
Random numbers, 142
Random sample, 79, 234, 236
Random variable, 51, 131
  of the continuous type, 131
  of the discrete type, 53, 111
Random variables, 4
Range, 111, 127
Rao–Blackwell theorem, 502
Rao–Cramér inequality, 538
Rao–Cramér lower bound, 539
Raspe, Rudolph Erich, 475
Ratio test, D9
Real quadratic forms, 382
Rectangular distribution, 141
Regression, 322
Regression to the mean, 565
Relative frequency, 4, 12
Relative frequency histogram, 5, 112
Relative frequency polygon, 114
Relevant data, 329
Resampling, 467
Residual, 324
Right-tail probability, 161
Row effects, 394
Rule of 72, D12
Run, 455
Run test, 457
Runs distribution, 455

S

s chart, 551
Sample, 4, 72
Sample correlation coefficient, 401
Sample mean, 72, 75
Sample mean distribution, 248
Sample median, 429
Sample percentiles, 123, 125
Sample range, 429
Sample size, 314
  to estimate μ, 315
  to estimate p, 317, 319
Sample space, 3, D1
Sample standard deviation, 73, 75
Sample variance, 72
Sampling
  with replacement, 22
  without replacement, 22
Sampson, Ralph, 178
Savage, Leonard J., 496
Scatter plot, 322
Second factorial moment, 101
Second quartile, 124, 125, 137
Set function, 14
Shewhart control charts, 548
Shewhart, W. A., 548, 570
Shifted exponential distribution, 148, 467
Shortest confidence interval for σ, 303
Shrinkage estimator, 489
Shrinking, 494
Sign test, 443

Any entries referring to D1-D17 are found in Appendix D on the CD-ROM

Significance level, 344, 353
Simple alternative hypothesis, 353
Simple hypothesis, 344
Simple null hypothesis, 344, 353
Simpson's paradox, 8, 204
Simulate, 13
Simulation, 219, 220, 259
Six Sigma program, 568
Skewed, 126
Skewness, 76
Snedecor, George, 268
Space S, 3
Space of X, 51
St. Petersburg paradox, 109
Standard deviation, 136
  of X, 68, 136
  of distribution, 68, 75
  of empirical distribution, 73
  of sample, 73, 75
Standard error, 349
Standard error of the mean, 355
Standard normal distribution, 159
Statistic, 8, 239
Statistical hypotheses, 343
Statistical inference, 4, 8
Statistical process control, 548
Statistical quality control, 548
Statistical thinking, 567
Statistically independent events, 39
Stem-and-leaf display, 121, 449
  back-to-back, 449
Stigler, Stephen M., 270
Stochastically independent, 39
Student's t distribution, 250, 493
Subjective probability, 477
Subset, 12, D1
Sufficient statistic, 497
Sum of squares between treatments, 381
Sum of squares within treatments, 381
Support, 53
Suspected outliers, 126

T

t distribution, 250, 255, 490
Tail-end probability, 354
Taylor series, D8
Test for homogeneity, 417
Test of a statistical hypothesis, 344
Test statistics, 353
Testing probability models, 412, 461
Tests of statistical hypotheses, 343
  critical region, 346
  for correlation coefficient, 400
  for difference of means, 365
  for equality of multinomial distributions, 417
  for homogeneity, 417
  for means, 380, 392
  for medians, 443
  for one mean, 355, 356
  for one proportion, 346
  for one variance, 375
  for randomness, 458
  for slope of the regression line, 400
  for two proportions, 348
  for variances, 376
  one-sided, 346
  paired t-test, 358
  run test, 457
  sign test, 443
  two-sided, 346
  Wilcoxon test, 443, 448
Third quartile, 124, 125, 137
Time sequence, 541
Total sum of squares, 381
Transformation of random variables, 224
Tree diagram, 20
Trimean, 127
Trimmed mean, 469
Trinomial distribution, 188, 196, 201
Tukey, John W., 121, 126, 178
Two factor ANOVA, 389
Two-sided test, 346
Type I error, 343, 344, 353
Type II error, 344, 353

U

Unbiased estimator, 278
Uniform distribution, 53, 141, 596, 597
Uniformly most powerful critical region, 516
Uniformly most powerful test, 516
Union of A and B, 12
Union of sets, D2
Universal set, 11, D1
Upper 100α percent point, 160
Upper control limit (UCL), 548
Utility, 480

Any entries referring to D1-D17 are found in Appendix D on the CD-ROM

V

Variance, 135
  of distribution, 68
  of empirical distribution, 72
  of sample, 72
  of *X*, 68, 135, 184
Venn diagram, D3
Venn diagrams, 12
Verica, 126, 442

W

Waiting time, 142, 149
Weibull distribution, 137, 170, 177
Welch's modified *T*, 294, 296, 368
Welch, B. L., 296
Wilcoxon test, 443, 448
Woodworth, George, 481
World Series, 28, 44

X

$\bar{x}$ chart, 551

Y

Zipf's law, 496

Any entries referring to D1-D17 are found in Appendix D on the CD-ROM